教育部人文社会科学研究规划基金项目(15YJAZH005)"近百年中国文献西译书目研究"

A Bibliography of Western Translation of Chinese Works

新编中国文献西译书目

(1900-2017)

陈剑光　毛一国　编著

ZHEJIANG UNIVERSITY PRESS
浙江大学出版社

图书在版编目(CIP)数据

新编中国文献西译书目:1900—2017 / 陈剑光,毛
一国编著. —杭州:浙江大学出版社,2019.9
ISBN 978-7-308-19609-3

Ⅰ.①新…　Ⅱ.①陈…②毛…　Ⅲ.①译本—图书目
录—中国—1900—2017　Ⅳ.①Z839.1

中国版本图书馆 CIP 数据核字(2019)第 212565 号

新编中国文献西译书目(1900—2017)

陈剑光　毛一国　编著

责任编辑　石国华
责任校对　郑成业　董齐琪　陆雅娟
封面设计　周　灵
出版发行　浙江大学出版社
　　　　　(杭州市天目山路 148 号　邮政编码 310007)
　　　　　(网址:http://www.zjupress.com)
排　　版　杭州星云光电图文制作有限公司
印　　刷　浙江印刷集团有限公司
开　　本　889mm×1194mm　1/16
印　　张　52.75
字　　数　2300 千
版 印 次　2019 年 9 月第 1 版　2019 年 9 月第 1 次印刷
书　　号　ISBN 978-7-308-19609-3
定　　价　398.00 元(含光盘)

浙江大学出版社市场运营中心联系方式:(0571) 88925591;http://zjdxcbs.tmall.com

内容简介

本书汇编了 1900 年以来国内外公开出版的以英文、法文、德文和西班牙文四种语言翻译的中国历代文献,反映了百余年来西文对中国人文社会科学领域文献的翻译情况。所收书目信息来自国内外出版的纸质目录和 OCLC 的 WorldCat 数据库等。四个语种的翻译书目按照《中国图书馆图书分类法》(第五版)依次分为 A、B、C、D、E、F、G、H、I、J、K、N、Z 共 13 个大类,每个大类之下又分若干小类,便于使用者按学科查检,附赠的光盘可用于全文检索。本书对于翻译、出版、对外传播、比较文学等众多学科研究具有重要的参考作用。

前　言

中国文献西译源于 400 多年前的明末，当时的西方来华传教士已经用拉丁文部分翻译了四书五经等儒家典籍。1814 年，法国法兰西学院正式设立"汉满鞑靼语言文学讲席"，这标志着欧洲的汉学（Sinology）研究已从传教士为主的业余阶段上升到了专业层次。中国传统经典著作被欧洲的汉学家不断翻译成各种欧洲文字，对当时的法国启蒙运动产生了影响。西方学者研究中国思想文化主要通过阅读文献的办法，而阅读中国文献的方式只有三种：一是直接阅读，能者不多；二是通过他人以西方文字所写的游记报告等；三是借助于译著。在以上三种途径中，阅读翻译文献是西方人士认识和研究中国的最重要的方式。

海外对中国文献的翻译有几种形式，特别是对中国古典文学的翻译一般可以分为"学者型翻译"和"文学性翻译"两种。前者以康达维（David R. Knechtges）《文选》的翻译文本作为例子，这类译文总是伴随着详尽的笺注与考证，广泛参考和征引其他学者的研究成果，翻译成为一种严肃的学术活动。西方汉学研究的一般流程是：当选定一个研究题目后，确定关于此题目的"首要文献"以及其他相关文献，并进行认真解读（close reading）和研究。研究者首先要将所选的"首要文献"以西文译出，并注入相关的训诂考证资料，写成"译注本"（annotated translation, translation with annotations），这些考证注释文字往往又是所译"首要文献"的几倍。附有详细注释的翻译称为笺注性翻译，是学者研究的重要成果，它会出现在博士论文、研究论文或专著之内，有的也成为单独出版发行的一部译著。海外汉学研究之所以形成这一独特的研究方式，是因为海外学界的研究语言不是汉语，故译文成为必需，况且，重视文本研究是海外汉学（中国学）一贯的指导思想。后者以欣顿（David Hinton）对中国古典诗歌的通俗性翻译为例，译者少了一些羁绊，更加注重文本的可阅读性和接受度。此外，还有一些翻译介乎两者之间，既注重准确性，又注重可读性。

西方最乐于翻译的文献是最能反映中国文化精华的思想、文学和历史三大类著作。本书收录的译著以人文社会科学为主，兼收中国译者和域外译者的译著。本书收集的译著，以英、法、德、西四种文字为限，英、法、德三种文字的译著也是所有中国文献西译中数量最多的。除了欧美西方国家，日本是域外翻译和研究中国文化的另一个中心，反映日译中国文献的书目已有《日本译中国书综合目录（1660—1978）》（实藤惠秀监修、小川博合编，香港中文大学出版社，1981 年）。1949 年中华人民共和国成立以来，以外文出版社为主的对外宣传出版文献也是本书的重要组成部分，但自 20 世纪 80 年代后期以来，能够反映我国出版书目的《全国总书目》和《中国国家书目》都已无法完整收录全国出版物的情况，因此，本书目也不可避免地存在无法完整体现所有中国文献外译情况的缺憾。对于海外出版的翻译著作，主要根据 OCLC 数据库的信息下载整理，该数据库的英文书目记录最为规范和齐全。相比之下，OCLC 记录法文、德文和西班牙文的书目数据不够全面。尽管如此，本书目仍是目前所见收录最多的中国文献西译书目，篇幅大大超过了我国台湾地区历史学家王尔敏（1927—）先生编写的《中国文献西译书目》（1975 年由台北商务印书馆出版），可为研究者提供各学科或领域里最基本的文献信息。

中国文献的外译是传播中华文化的主要方式，有着"润物细无声"的作用，借用日本诺贝尔文学奖获得者大江健三郎的话或许可以说明中国文化的魅力和影响："很小的时候，我就从母亲那里接受中国文学的影响。可以说，我的血管里流淌着中国文学的血液，我的身上有着中国文学的遗传因子。没有鲁迅和郁达夫等中国作家及其文学作品的存在，就不会有诺贝尔文学奖获得者大江健三郎的存在。"（《鲁迅域外百年传播史》，王家平著，北京大学出版社，2019 年第 381 页）。中国文献西译书目的整理和编制是一项非常重要的学术研究基础工作，我们坚信数年来艰辛的付出定能得到同行和行家的反响！

本书为教育部人文社会科学研究规划基金项目"近百年中国文献西译书目研究"（编号：15YJAZH005）研究成果。陈剑光负责全书统筹和规划，完成英文（除 J、K、N 类）、西班牙文书目的整理和编纂；费群蝶负责法文书目的整理和编纂；赵珉负责德文书目的整理和编纂（其中冯晞整理了约 300 条书目）；毛一国负责书目资料的国内外搜集以及最后的格式统一和校核，并完成英文 J、K、N 类的整理和编纂。由于时间紧迫，书中难免有谬误之处，恳请读者批评指正。

凡　例

一、收录说明

1.本书所收的西文文献是指以英文、法文、德文和西班牙文四种语言翻译且公开出版的图书,主要是指汉籍外译本,以单行本为主,无论其出版地。

2.本书力求收录1900年以来中国对外翻译的出版图书,域外国家出版的涉及中国文献的翻译著作也竭力搜集,以各种书目和数据库所揭示为主。法文、德文的部分国外出版文献酌情回溯到更早的年代。

3.本书所收文献的类型为公开出版的图书,酌情收录少于48页以下的小册子。发表在期刊上的论文原则上不予收录,虽然中国文献的西译还大量见之于西方的汉学刊物,如《通报》等。

4.儿童文学读物,以文本图书为主,页数在48页以上酌情收录。

5.本书收录的图书主要限于人文社会科学,自然和工程类图书没有收录,但尽量收录了1900年之前的涉及天文、算学、医学、农学等方面的古籍外译版本。

二、不予收录说明

1.以外国语撰写的著作,不予收录。

2.电子图书、影像作品不予收录。

3.儿童连环画册不予收录。

4.博士论文所含的译文,因博士论文为非公开出版物,不予收录。

5.双语教材主要为学习汉语而编写出版,原则上不予收录。

6.季度、年度等连续出版物(年度报告、年鉴等)不予收录。

7.期刊论文、会议论文不予收录。

8.图片为主的图书,如摄影集、画册等一般不予收录。

9.外文撰写的某地的旅游指南、投资招商指南不在收录之列。

10.盲文等不予收录。

三、编排说明

1.本书对每种译著的书目编制,参照国际标准书目著录(ISBD)规则中关于普通图书的编制方法,以卡片形式反映每种书的主要信息:

书名/著者;译者.版本.出版地:出版社,出版年.页数;尺寸.国际标准书号(ISBN).(丛书名)

内容注释。

《中文书名》(或主题);原著者(生卒年);译者(生卒年)。

(1)其他各种版本信息:以上书目信息包含了十几项信息,每种译著因具体情况略有差别,有的译著还会因多次出版,其不同版本的信息也会详细列出,但若是同一版本的不同印刷年,一般只罗列其最早的版本印刷年,其余印刷年一般省略不标。凡有确切中文题名的以方括号注释,无确切中文题名的以主题或内容标注,少数不宜翻译的题名则不予翻译。

(2)由于西方国家图书编目规则并不完全统一,即使采用相同编目规则,又因编目员对规则理解的差异,图书编目数据可能会有多个不同版本。本书的编目数据绝大多数直接从OCLC的WorldCat数据库导出,遵从以前的编目规则,对格式、拼写和符号尽量不加改动。

(3)为了ISBN格式一致,本书统一略去图书代码"978",在OCLC的WorldCat数据库存使用ISBN号来检索图书时,无法查到,可在本书的ISBN号前加"978"再检索。

2.同一著者的图书,一般按出版年代的先后编排;同一时代的不同著者,按著者的出生年先后编排。

3.由于本书收录内容和篇幅较大,不再编写著者索引和题名索引,本书提供的光盘可为使用者提供著者、题名、ISBN等检索。

目 录

第二编　中国文献法译书目

第一编 中国文献英译书目

A 类 毛泽东著作及相关文献

A1 领导人著作合集

1. How the Eight Army fights in North China/Chu Teh; Peng Teh-huei. Chungking: New China Information Committee[u. a.],1938. 33 p.
《八路军在华北战场作战》,朱德,彭德怀.

2. Complete and consolidate the victory. Peking: Foreign Languages Press, 1950. 48 pages;19cm. (New China library series; no. 1)
《巩固胜利》,毛泽东,周恩来等.

3. 700 millions for peace and democracy. Peking: Foreign Languages Press,1950. 82 pages: illustrations;19cm.
Contents: Stalin, friend of the Chinese people/Mao Tse-tung—The Soviet Army, the most powerful defender of world peace/Chu Teh—Inviolable Sino-Soviet friendship/Liu Shaochi—The difference between Soviet and American foreign policies/Soong Ching Ling—Chinese and Soviet people are confident of safeguarding world peace/Kuo Mo-jo—Stalin and the Chinese Revolution/Chen Po-ta—New era of Sino-Soviet friendship and cooperation (NCNA editorial).
《七亿人民拥护和平》,毛泽东,朱德等.

4. China wins economic battles. Peking: Foreign Languages Press,1950. iii, 58 pages;19cm.
Contents: Fight for a fundamental turn for the better in the financial and economic situation, by Mao Tse-tung. —The financial and food situation, by Chen Yun. —The economic situation and problems concerning readjustment of industry, commerce and taxation, by Chen Yun. —Appendix: Decisions on the unification of the financial and economic work of the state.
《经济战线上的胜利》,毛泽东,陈云等.

5. Lessons of the Chinese Revolution/Mao Tse-tung & Liu Shao-chi. Bombay: J. Bhatt for People's Pub. House, 1950. 31 pages;21cm.
Contents: Introducing The Communist, by Mao Tse-Tung. —On the Party's mass line, by Liu Shao-chi. —An armed people opposes armed counter-revolution, a reply to a reader, from the editor of the Peking People's Daily, published on June 16,1950.
中国革命的经验. 毛泽东,刘少奇著.

6. Significance of agrarian reforms in China/by Mao Tse-tung & Liu Shao-chi. [Bombay], [Printed at New Age Printing Press for People's Pub. House],1950. 40 pages.
中国的土地改革. 毛泽东,刘少奇著.

7. China fights for peace. Peking: Foreign Languages Press, 1950. iv, 64 pages: illustrations, portraits;19cm.
Contents: Broaden the peace movement. —China signs for peace, by Soong Ching Ling. —Mankind demands peace, by Kuo Mo-jo. —A call to action against the U. S. aggressors, by Kuo Mo-jo. —Report to the Stockholm Conference, by Emi Siao. —The movement in China in defense of peace, by Liu Ning-yi. Short items from the peace front. —Appendices: Declaration of the defense of world peace. China supports the Stockholm decisions. An answer to President Truman. Joint appeal to trade unionists, women, youth, and students.
《中国为和平而斗争》,宋庆龄,郭沫若等.

8. The first year of victory. Peking: Foreign Languages Press,1950. 95 pages: folded color map;21cm.
《胜利第一年》,周恩来,陈云等.

9. China's revolutionary wars. Peking: Foreign Languages Press,1951. 47 pages: illustrations;21cm.
《中国的革命战争》,朱德,聂荣臻,萧华著.

10. New China's economic achievements: 1949—1952/China Committee for the Promotion of International Trade. Peking: China Committee for the Promotion of International Trade, 1952. 285 p. :ill. ; 21cm.
《新中国三年来的经济成就》,毛泽东,刘少奇等著.

11. Dr. Sun Yat-sen:commemorative articles and speeches/by Mao Tse-tung, Soong Ching Ling, Chou En-lai. Peking: Foreign Languages Press, 1957. 86[1] s. : ill. ; 23cm.
《孙中山纪念文集》,毛泽东,宋庆龄,周恩来等.

12. Mao Tse-tung and Lin Piao: post-revolutionary writings/edited by K. Fan. Garden City, N. Y.: Anchor Books, 1972. xxiv, 536 pages;18cm.
Notes: Collected here are all the major published writings and statements of Mao Tse-tung and of his former heir designate, Lin Piao, since the founding of the People's Republic in 1949. All the items included here are authorized versions published either in pamphlet form or in official newspapers and magazines by the Foreign Languages Press, in Peking.

收录毛泽东和林彪 1949 年以后的文章,来自外文出版社所出的小册子及官方报刊.

13. Jiang Zemin and Li Peng on Taiwan question. Beijing：China Intercontinental Press，1996. 77 pages：illustrations（some color）；18cm. ISBN：7801131355，7801131355，7801131584，7801131584

Contents：Continue to promote the reunification of China/by Jiang Zemin—Reunification of the motherland，a common wish of all Chinese people/by Li Peng—Questions and answers of the Taiwan issue

《江泽民、李鹏谈台湾问题》,江泽民,李鹏;国务院台湾事务办公室编写.五洲传播出版社.

14. China's policy on Taiwan：selected English, Chinese documents/Deng Xiaoping, Jiang Zemin, Hu Jintao and others；edited by Luc Guo.［Beijing］：ICP，2011. 124 pages；22cm. ISBN：1461183631，1461183634

中国的台湾政策.收录邓小平、江泽民、胡锦涛等领导人的讲话.五洲传播出版社.

A2 毛泽东著作与研究

1. Red China；being the report on the progress and achievements of the Chinese soviet republic, delivered by the president，Mao Tse-tung，at the second Chinese national soviet congress, at Juikin, Kiangsi, January 22，1934. London，M. Lawrence，Limited，1934. 34 pages：illustrations（map）；22cm.

红色中国报告.毛泽东 1934 年在瑞金中华苏维埃第二次全国代表大会上所做的报告.

2. China：the march toward unity, by Mao Tse-tung［and others］. New York：Workers Library Publishers，［1937］. 125 p. ；21cm.

Contents：Jack, I. A united national anti-Japanese front in China.—Central Committee of the Communist Party of China. Open letter addressed to the Kuomintang. —Snow，E. Interviews with Mao Tse-tung, Communist leader.—Members of the All-China National Salvation Union. A number of essential conditions and minimum demands for united resistance to foreign aggression.—Mao，T. To Messrs. Chang lai-chi, Tao Heng-chi, Chow Tao-fen and Shen Chun-ju, members of the All-China National Salvation Union.—Dimitroff，C. The fifteenth anniversary of the Communist Party of China.—Ming, W. Fifteen years of struggle for the independence and freedom of the Chinese people. —The Communist position on the Sian incidents：three documents of the Central Committee of the Communist Party of China.

中国走向统一.毛泽东等著.汇集毛泽东多篇文章.

(1) New York：AMS Press，1978. 125 p. ；23cm. ISBN：0404144756，0404144753

3. On practice：written in 1937, this critical essay attacked misconceptions about the role of theory and practice prevalent at the time among certain circles of the Chinese Communist Party. New York：International Publishers，1937. 16 pages

《实践论》

(1) New York：International Publishers，1950. 16 pages；21cm.

(2) New York：International Publishers，1960. 16 pages

4. On practice：on the relation between knowledge and practice-between knowing and doing. Peking，1951. 23 pages：illustrations；19cm.

《实践论》

(1) 2nd ed. Peking：Foreign Languages Press，1953. 26 pages

(2) Rev. translation. Peking：Foreign Languages Press，1958. 21 pages；19cm.

(3) 3rd ed. Peking：Foreign Languages Press，1960. 23 pages；19cm.

(4) 4th ed. ，rev. trans. Peking：Foreign Languages Press，1964. 21 pages，［1］leaf of plates：portraits；19cm.

(5) 5th ed. Peking：Foreign Languages Press，1965. 20 pages；18cm.

(6) 1st pocket ed. Peking：Foreign Languages Press，1965. 29 pages；15cm.

(7) 6th ed. Peking：Foreign Languages Press，1966. 21，［1］pages；19cm.

(8) Pocket ed. Peking：Foreign Languages Press，1967. 29 pages；15cm.

(9) 1st pocket ed. Peking：Foreign Languages Press，1968. 29 pages；21cm.

5. Concerning practice：on the connection between cognition and practice, the connection between knowledge and deeds. ［Bombay］，［People's Pub. House］，1951. 15 pages；18cm.

《实践论》

6. The new stage：report to the sixth enlarged plenum of the Central Committee of the Communist Party of China（October 12，1938）. Chongqing-Hong Kong：New China Information Committee，1938. 76 p.

《新阶段:在中国共产党中央委员会第六次扩大会议上的报告》

7. The Chinese revolution and the communist party of China/by Mao Tze-dong. New York：Distributed by the Committee for a Democratic Far Eastern Policy，1940. 20 pages；29cm.

Contents：pt. 1. The Chinese society.—pt. 2. The Chinese revolution.

《中国革命和中国共产党》

(1) New York, Distributed by the Committee for a Democratic Far Eastern Policy，1950. 20 pages；29cm.

8. Chinese Revolution and the Communist Party of China. ［Bombay］People's Pub. House，1950. 30 pages；22cm.

《中国革命和中国共产党》

9. The Chinese revolution and the Chinese Communist Party. Peking：Foreign Languages Press, 1954. 56 pages：illustrations；19cm.

《中国革命和中国共产党》

　　(1)［Rev.］. Peking：Foreign Languages Press, 1959. 43 pages：illustrations；19cm.

　　(2)3rd ed. Peking：Foreign Languages Press；［Chicago］：［Distributors, China Books & Periodicals］, 1960. 50 pages；19cm.

　　(3)4th ed. Peking：Foreign Languages Press, Beijing：Wai wen chu ban she, 1965. 46,［1］ pages；19cm.

　　(4)Peking：Foreign Languages Press, 1967. 46 pages；19cm.

　　(5)4th ed. Peking：Foreign Languages Press, 1968. 46,［1］ pages；19cm.

10. China's new democracy. New York：New Century Publishers, 1941. 72 pages；20cm.

　　Notes："The text of this pamphlet originally appeared in the January 15, 1941, issue of the magazine Chinese culture, under the title 'The politics and culture of new democracy.'"—Title page verso.

　　中国的新民主主义. Browder, Earl(1891—1973)导言.

　　(1)China's new democracy/with an introduction by Earl Browder. New York：Worker's Library Publishers, 1944. 72 pages：portraits；20cm.

　　(2)［Bombay］,［People's Pub. House］, 1944. 47,［1］ pages；19cm.

　　(3)Sydney：Current Book Distributors, 1945. 63 pages

　　(4)New York：New Century Publishers, 1945. 72 pages：portraits；20cm.

　　(5)4th ed. Bombay：People's Pub. House, 1950. 42 pages；21cm.

　　(6)New York：New Century, 1967. 72 pages：portraits；20cm.

11. New life in new China/by Mao Tsê-tung and others. ［1st Indian ed.］. Calcutta：Purabi Publishers, 1943. 163 pages；19cm.

　　新中国的新生活. 毛泽东等著.

12. Aspects of China's anti-Japanese struggle. Bombay：People's Pub. House, 1943. 80 pages；22cm.

　　中国的抗日战争.

　　(1)Bombay：People's Pub. House, 1948. 80 pages

　　(2)Bombay：People's Pub. House, 1976. 80 pages；20cm.

　　(3)Ann Arbor, Mich.：University Microfilms International, 1985. 80 pages

13. Abundant clothing, sufficient food.［Yenan］：［publisher not identified］, 1944. 33 pages；22cm.

　　Contents：(1)Organize for production! /Mao Tse-tung—On cooperatives/Mao Tse-tung—Declaration of the Labor Heroes Conference of the Shensi-Kansu-Nighsia border region—Sketches of labor heroes in Shen-Kan-Ning border region. How Chao Tsan-kui became respected by everyone. (2)Liu Kwei-ying, the spinner-heroine. (3)Liu Chian-chang—how he operates the most successful cooperative in the border region. (4)The story of Wu Man-yu.

《丰衣足食》

14. China's strategy for victory/by Mao Zedong. 1st Indian ed. Bombay：People's Pub. House, 1945. xxix, 116 pages；18cm.

　　毛泽东关于中国获得胜利的战略问题.

15. On coalition government/by Mao Tze-tung.［Place of publication not identified］：China News Agency, 1945. 2,149 pages (on double leaves)；18cm.

《论联合政府》

16. On coalition government：report to the 7th Congress of the Chinese Communist Party at Yenan/by Mao Tze-dong. Chefoo, China：Culture Supply Co., 1946. 96 pages；19cm.

《论联合政府》

17. On coalition government. Peking：Foreign Languages Press, 1955. 118 pages：illustrations；19cm.

《论联合政府》

　　(1)［2nd ed.］. Peking：Foreign Languages Press, 1960. 110 pages；19cm.

　　(2)3rd ed (2nd rev. trans.). Peking：Foreign Languages Press, 1965. 97 pages；19cm.

　　(3)3rd ed. Peking：Foreign Languages Press, 1967. 97 pages；19cm.

18. Our task in 1945. Np, New China News Agency, 1945. 20 pages.

《我们的任务》

19. Turning point in China/by Mao Tse-tung. New York：New Century Publishers, 1948. 24 pages；19cm.

　　Notes："Report... on the 'present situation and our tasks' to the Central Committee of the Communist Party of China, December 25, 1947...The text... is from New China News Agency, Hongkong."

《当前的形势和我们的任务》

20. The fight for a new China/by Mao Zedong. New York：New Century Publishers, 1945. 80 pages；20cm.

　　Notes："Delivered... to the Seventh National Congress of the Chinese Communist Party［April 24, 1945］."

　　为新中国而战：在中国共产党第七次全国代表大会上的讲话.

21. The way out of China's civil war：a report on coalition government delivered to the 7th National Congress of the Chinese Communist Party/by Mao Zedong. Bombay：People's Pub. House, 1946. iv, 84 pages；19cm.

　　毛泽东在"中国共产党第七届中央委员会"会议上做的关于联合政府的报告.

22. Report by Mao Tze-tung to the Central Committee of the Chinese Communist Party, December 25, 1947 (broadcast from North Shensi on January 1, 1948). New York：[publisher not identified], 1948. 12 leaves; 29cm.

毛泽东在 1947 年 12 月 25 日中央扩大会议(十二月会议)上的报告.

23. Unbreakable China. Singapore：Low Phay Hock, 1949. 141 pages：illustrations; 26cm.

Contents：Coalition government (1945) by Mao Tse-tung [a report made to the 7th National Congress of the Chinese Communist Party, on April 24th 1945]—Eight years of war with Japan (1937—1944) by Hsia Zoh-tsung.

《坚强的中国》,夏淑贞. 收录毛泽东在"中国共产党第七届中央委员会"会议上做的关于联合政府的报告.

24. New democracy：basis of social, political & economic structure of new China/Shanghai, China：Chinese-American Pub. Co., 1949. 83 pages; 19cm.

《新民主主义论》

25. On new democracy. Peking：Foreign Languages Press, 1954. 84 pages; 19cm.

Notes："Present English translation of On new democracy has been made from the Chinese text given in the second edition of the Selected works of Mao Tse-tung, volume II... published in 1952."

《新民主主义论》

   (1) 2nd ed. Peking：Foreign Languages Press, 1960. 78 pages：portraits; 20cm.

   (2) [3rd ed.]. Peking：Foreign Languages Press, 1964. 66 pages：portraits; 19cm.

   (3) [4th ed. (2nd rev. translation)]. Peking：Foreign Languages Press, 1966. 71, [1] pages; 19cm.

   (4) 4th ed. Peking：Foreign Languages Press, 1967. 71 pages：portrait

26. On new democracy. Honolulu, Hawaii：University Press of the Pacific, [2003]. ISBN：1410205643, 1410205649

《新民主主义论》

27. The dictatorship of the people's democracy/by Mao Tze-tung. New York：Committee for a Democratic Far Eastern Policy, 1949. 9 pages; 28cm.

《论人民民主专政》

28. On people's democratic dictatorship; and, speech at the preparatory meeting of the new PCC/Mao Tze-tung. Peiping：English Language Service, New China News Agency, 1949. [4], 25 pages：portraits; 19cm.

《论人民民主专政》

   (1) On people's democratic dictatorship/Mao Tse-tung; together with his two speeches delivered at the preparatory committee meeting and the first plenary session of the Chinese People's Political Consultative Conference. 3rd ed. Peking：Foreign Languages Press, 1950. 45 pages：portraits; 19cm.

   (2) [4th ed.]. Peking：Foreign Languages Press, 1951. 45 pages：portrait.

   (3) 5th ed. Peking：Foreign Languages Press, 1952. 40 pages：portraits; 19cm.

   (4) [6th ed.]. Peking：Foreign Languages Press, 1953. 22 pages；18cm.

   (5) On people's democratic dictatorship：written in commemoration of the 28th anniversary of the Chinese Communist Party, July 1, 1949/Mao Zedong. 7th ed. Peking：Foreign Languages Press, 1959. 19 pages; 19cm.

   (6) On the people's democratic dictatorship. [8th ed.]. Peking：Foreign Languages Press, 1961. 19 pages：18cm.

   (7) 1st pocket ed. Peking：Foreign Languages Press, 1963. 28 pages

   (8) 9th ed. Peking：Foreign Languages Press, 1965. 20 pages; 19cm.

   (9) 9th ed. Peking：Foreign Languages Press, 1967. 20 pages; 19cm.

29. On people's democratic rule/Mao-Tse-tung. New York：New Century Publishers, 1950. 24 pages; 20cm. (Marxist pamphlets; no. 5)

《论人民民主专政》

30. The dictatorship of people's democracy; article written for the 28th anniversary (July 1, 1949) of the Communist Party of China. Bombay：People's Pub. House, 1950. 13 pages; 23cm.

《论人民民主专政》

31. The dictatorship of the people's democracy/by Mao Tse-tung; edited by Tien-yi Li. New Haven, Conn.：Institute of Far Eastern Languages, Yale University, 1951. (Mirror series. C; 5)

《论人民民主专政》,Mao, Zedong, 1893—1976. Li, Tien-yi, ; 1915—; editor.

   (1) [3rd ed.]. New Haven：Institute of Far Eastern Languages, Yale University, 1955. 13, 21 pages; 24cm.

   (2) [Rev. ed.]. New Haven, Conn.：Far Eastern Publication, Yale University, 1965. 16 pages; 23cm.

   (3) New Haven：Yale University, 1965. xvii, [34] pages; 24cm.

   (4) [3rd rev. ed.]. New Haven, CT：Far Eastern publications, Yale University, 1968. xvii, [15], 16 p. ; 24cm. (Mirror series. C; no. 5)

   (5) New Haven, CT：Far Eastern publications, Yale University, 1973. xvii, 16, 16 p. ; 24cm. (Mirror series. C; no. 5)

32. Problems of art and literature. New York：International Publishers [1950]. 48 p. ; 20cm.

Notes：Addresses given on May 2 and 23, 1942, in

Yonan, at the "conference on the problems of art and literature as related to the struggle for liberation in China."

《论文学与艺术》

(1)2nd ed. 〔Bombay〕, 〔Published by J. Bhatt for People's Pub. House〕, 1951. 40 pages；18cm.

(2)Bombay, People's Pub. House, 1952. 44 pages；18cm.

33. Mao Tse-tung on art and literature. 2nd ed. Peking：Foreign Languages Press, 1960. 145 pages, 1 leaf of plates：portraits；19cm.

Notes：Translated from the Chinese text published December 1958. Subsequent edition has title：Mao Tse-tung on literature and art.

《毛泽东论文学与艺术》

(1)Mao Tse-tung on literature and art. 3rd ed. Peking：Foreign Languages Press,1967. 161 pages：portraits；19cm.

(2)3rd ed. , 2nd rev. translation. Peking：Foreign Languages Press,1977. 161 pages：portraits；19cm.

34. Mao Zedong：on art and literature. Calcutta：National Book Agency,1967. 127 pages；19cm.

《毛泽东论文学与艺术》

35. Mao Tse-tung on literature and art. Honolulu, Hi. ：University Press of the Pacific, 2001. 161 pages；21cm. ISBN：089875206X, 0898752069

《毛泽东论文学与艺术》

36. Oppose Liberalism in the Party. New York：Jefferson School of Social Science, 1950. 1 volume

《反对自由主义》

37. Combat liberalism/Mao Zedong. Peking：Foreign Languages Press,1954. 6 pages；19cm.

《反对自由主义》

(1)Peking：Foreign Languages Press,1956. 6 pages；19cm.

(2)2nd ed. Peking：Foreign Languages Press,1960. 5 pages；19cm.

(3)〔3rd ed. , 2nd rev. trans.〕. Peking：Foreign Languages Press,1965. 3 pages；19cm.

(4)4th ed. Peking：Foreign Languages Press,1967. 3 pages；19cm.

38. Three important writings of Mao Tse-tung. Bombay, People's Pub. House, 1950. 86 pages

毛泽东3篇重要著作.

39. Maoism：a sourcebook；selections from the Writings of Mao Tse-tung/Introduced and edited by H. Arthur Steiner. 〔Los Angeles〕 University of California at Los Angeles, 1952. vi, 142 pages；28cm.

毛泽东文选. Steiner, H. Arthur(1905—1991)编.

40. Mao Tse-tung：an anthology of his writings/Edited with an introd. by Anne Fremantle. 〔New York〕 New

American Library, 1962. 300 pages；18cm.

Contents：Analysis of the classes in Chinese society (March 1926)—The struggle in the Chingkang Mountains (November 25，1928)—Strategic problems in China's Revolutionary War (December 1936)—Strategic problems in the anti-Japanese Guerrilla War (May 1938)—On the protracted war (May 1938)—On coalition government (April 24, 1945)—Talk with the American correspondent Anna Louise Strong (August 1946)—Proclamation of the Chinese People's Liberation Army (April 25, 1949)—On the people's democratic dictatorship (June 30, 1949)—Combat liberalism (September 7, 1937)—On practice (July 1937)—On contradiction (August 1937)—Talks at the Yenan Forum on Art and Literature (May 23，1942)—On the correct handling of contradictions among the people (July 1，1957).

毛泽东文选. Fremantle, Anne 编.

(1)New York：Mentor Books, 1963. 300 p.

(2)Updated and expanded. New York：New American Library, 1971. 319 pages；18cm.

Notes：with additional writings of Chiang Ching and Lin Piao

(3)Updated and expanded/to include a special selection of the poems of Mao. New York：New American Library, 1972. 320 pages；18cm.

(4)Mattituck, N. Y. ：Americon House, 1972. 320 pages；23cm. ISBN：0848812093, 0848812096

41. Selected readings from the works of Mao Tse-tung. Peking：Foreign Languages Press, 1967. 406 pages：portraits；23cm.

《毛泽东著作选读》

(1)Peking：Foreign Languages Press, 1967. 504 pages：portraits；19cm.

(2)Peking：Foreign Languages Press, 1971. 504 pages：portraits；19cm.

42. A definitive translation of Mao Tsê-tung on literature and art；the cultural revolution in context. Edited by Thomas N. White. 〔Washington〕：Alwhite Publications, 1967. vi, 43 p. ；22cm.

Contents：The compass for the great proletarian cultural revolution：note on the reprinting of Talks at the Yenan forum on literature and art, by the Hung-ch'i editorial board. —Talks at the Yenan forum on literature and art, May 1942. —Ten poems. —"An army of one million crosses the great river"：upon reading one of the newly published poems of Chairman Mao, by Kuo Mo-jo.

毛泽东文选,White, Thomas N. 编译.

43. The wisdom of Mao Tse-tung. New York：Philosophical Library；〔distributed by Book Sales〕, 1968. 114 pages；19cm.

Contents：On practice. July 1937. Notes. —On contradiction. Aug. 1937. Notes. —On new democracy. Jan. 1940. Notes. Notes："A selection［of the author's works］from an English translation of the second Chinese edition of The selected works of Mao Tse-tung, published by the People's Publishing House, Peking, April 1960."

《毛泽东选集》选译，包括《实践论》《矛盾论》和《论新民主主义》。

44. On revolution and war/edited with an introd. and notes by M. Rejai. Garden City, N. Y.：Doubleday, 1969. xix, 355 pages；22cm.

毛泽东文选. Rejai, M. (Mostafa)编.

(1)Anchor books ed. Garden City, N. Y.：Doubleday, 1969. xxii, 452 pages；19cm.

(2)Garden City, N. Y.：Anchor Books, 1970. xxii, 452 pages；18cm.

(3)Gloucester, Mass.：Peter Smith, 1976. xxii, 452 pages；21cm.

(4)Gloucester, Mass.：Peter Smith, 1983. xxii, 452 pages；21cm. ISBN：084465275X, 0844652757

45. Selections from Chairman Mao. ［Washington］Joint Publications Research Service, 1970. 2 volumes in 1. 29cm. (Translations on Communist China；no. 90,109)

毛泽东文选.

46. Talks and writings of Chairman Mao. Arlington, Va.：Joint Publications Research Service, 1970. (Translations on Communist China；128)

毛泽东文选.

47. Collected writings of Mao Tse-tung/Mao Tse-tung；ed. by Minoru Takeuchi. Tokyo：Hokubô Sha, 1970—1972. 10 vol.；21cm.

Contents：v. 1,Mars 1917—Avril 1927. v. 2,Mai 1927—Août 1931. v. 3, Septembre 1931—Août 1933. v. 4, Septembre 1933—Octobre 1935. v. 5, Novembre 1935—Mai 1938. v. 6, Mai 1938—Août 1939. v. 7, Septembre 1939—Juin 1941. v. 8, Juillet 1941—Décembre 1942. v. 9, Janvier 1943—Décembre 1945. v. 10, Janvier 1946—Octobre 1949

毛泽东文选. 10 卷. Takeuchi, Minoru 编.

48. What Peking keeps silent about：what Mao said earlier but contradicts today. New Dehli：People's Pub. House,1972. 38 pages；22cm.

Notes："The present collection contains excerpts from articles and speeches by Mao Tse-tung written or delivered at different periods."

毛泽东文选.

(1)Moscow：Novosti Press Agency Pub. House, 1972. 47 pages；17cm.

49. Mao Tse-tung unrehearsed：talks and letters, 1956—71/edited and introduced by Stuart Schram；translated ［from the Chinese］by John Chinnery and Tieyun.

Harmondsworth：Penguin，1974. 352 pages；18cm. ISBN：014021786X, 0140217865. (Pelican books)

毛泽东文选. Schram, Stuart R. (Stuart Reynolds, 1924—2012)编.

50. Miscellany of Mao Tse-tung thought（1949—1968）.［Arlington, Va.］Joint Publications Research Service, 1974. 2 volumes (a-f, 498 pages)27cm.

毛泽东文选.

51. Chairman Mao talks to the people：talks and letters 1956—1971/edited with an introd. by Stuart Schram；translated by John Chinnery and Tieyun. New York：Pantheon Books. A division of Random House, 1974. 352 p. ISBN：0394486889, 0394486888, 0394706412, 0394706412. (The Pantheon Asia Library)

Schram, Stuart R. (Stuart Reynolds, 1924—2012)编；Chinnery, John 译. 收录 1956—1971 年间毛泽东的谈话与书信.

52. Unselected works of Mao Tse-tung, 1957. Kowloon, Hong Kong：Union Research Institute, 1976. viii, 482 pages：illustrations；23cm.

毛泽东文选. 英汉对照.

53. Maoism as it really is：pronouncements of Mao Zedong, some already known to the public and others hitherto not published in the Chinese press：a collection/［translated from the Russian by Cynthia Carlile；editor, O. E. Vladimirov；compiled and prefaced by M. I. Altaisky；comments by V. S. Kulikov］. Moscow：Progress, 1981. 282 pages；20cm.

毛泽东文选. 译自俄语.

54. The writings of Mao Zedong,1949—1976/edited by Michael Y. M. Kau, John K. Leung. Armonk, N. Y.：M. E. Sharpe, 1986—1992. volumes 1—2；24cm. ISBN：0873323912, 0873323918, 0873323920, 0873323925

毛泽东言论集，1949—1976. Kau, Michael Y. M. (1934—)和 Leung, John K. 合编.

55. The secret speeches of Chairman Mao：from the hundred flowers to the great leap forward/edited by Roderick MacFarquhar, Timothy Cheek, Eugene Wu；with contributions by Merle Goldman and Benjamin I. Schwartz. Cambridge, Mass.：Council on East Asian Studies/Harvard University：Distributed by Harvard University Press, 1989. xxiii, 561 pages；23cm. ISBN：067479673X, 0674796737. (Harvard contemporary China series；6)

毛泽东讲话.

56. Mao's road to power：revolutionary writings 1912—1949/Stuart R. Schram, editor. Armonk, N. Y.：M. E. Sharpe, 1992—. 8 volumes：maps；24cm. ISBN：1563240491, 1563240492, 1563244306, 1563244308, 156324439X, 1563244391, 0765603497, 0765603494, 076560793X, 0765607935, 0765607948, 0765607942, 0765643353, 0765643359, 1563244575, 1563244578,

1563248917, 1563248913

Contents：v. 1. The pre-Marxist period，1912—1920. —v. 2. National revolution and social revolution，December 1920—June 1927. —v. 3. From the Jinggangshan to the establishment of the Jiangxi Soviets，July 1927—December 1930. —v. 4. The rise and fall of the Chinese Soviet Republic，1931—1934. —v. 5. Toward the second united front，January 1935—July 1937—v. 6. The new stage，August 1937—1938—v. 7. New democracy，1939—1941—v. 8. From rectification to coalition government，1942—July 1945.

毛泽东文选. Schram，Stuart R. (Stuart Reynolds，1924—2012)编. 8 卷.

57. Selected readings from the works of Mao Tsetung/［Mao Tse-tung］. Honolulu，Hawaii：University Press of the Pacific，2001. 504 pages：portraits；19cm. ISBN：0898754917, 0898754919

毛泽东文选.

58. The wisdom of Mao/Mao Tse-tung. New York：Citadel Press/Kensington Pub. Corp.，2002. x，230 pages；22cm. ISBN：0806523735, 0806523736. (Philosophical library；Wisdom library)

Notes："The selections in this volume have been taken from The selected works of Mao Tse-tung or Selected readings from the works of Mao Tse-tung（both，Peking：Foreign Languages Press，1967 and 1971 respectively)... the poems are from Mao Tsetung：poems（Peking：Foreign Languages Press，1976）"—Editor's note.

毛泽东文选.

59. Selected readings from the works of Mao Tse-tung. 1st Indian ed. Lucknow：Rahul Foundation，2002. 504 pages；18cm. ISBN：8187728140, 8187728146

毛泽东文选.

60. Selected articles of Mao Tse-tung. Delhi：New Vistas Publications，2003. 369 p. ISBN：8188293199, 8188293193

毛泽东文选

61. Collected writings of Chairman Mao/by Mao Zedong；［edited by Shawn Conners；translation by Foreign Languages Press，Peking］.［El Paso］：El Paso Norte Press，Special Edition Books，2009. 3 volumes；22cm. ISBN：1934255254,1934255254,1934255261,1934255262, 1934255247,1934255246

Contents：v. 1. Politics and tactics. —v. 2. Guerrilla warfare—v. 3. On policy, practice and contradiction.

毛泽东文选. Conners，Shawn 编.

62. Selected works of Mao Zedong.［Canada］：Marx-Engels-Lenin Institute,2014. 269 pages；23cm. ISBN：1312143081, 1312143088

Contents：Analysis of the classes in Chinese society—Report on an investigation of the peasant movement in Hunan—Be concerned with the well-being of the masses，

pay attention to methods of work—On guerrilla warfare—On practice—On contradiction—Combat liberalism—On protracted war.

毛泽东文选.

63. On contradiction. Peking：Foreign Languages Press，1952. 71 pages：illustrations；19cm.

《矛盾论》

（1）Peking：Foreign Languages Press，1953. 65 pages：illustrations

（2）3rd ed. Peking：Foreign Languages Press，1956. 65 pages；19cm.

（3）Peking：Foreign Languages Press，1958. 54 pages：19cm.

（4）［3rd ed.］. Peking：Foreign Languages Press，1960. 61 pages：portraits；19cm.

（5）4th ed. Peking：Foreign Languages Press，1964. 56 pages：portraits；19cm.

（6）［5th ed.］. Peking：Foreign Languages Press，1965. 56 pages

（7）5th ed. Peking：Foreign Languages Press，1967. 56，［1］pages；19cm.

（8）1st pocket ed. Peking：Foreign Languages Press，1967. 79，［1］pages；15cm.

64. On contradiction/Mao Tse-tung. New York：International Publishers,1953. 61 pages；21cm.

《矛盾论》

（1）3rd. ed. New York：Internat. Publ.，1956. 65 p.：Ill.

（2）New York：International Publishers，1963. 61 p.

65. Mao Zedong's On contradiction：an annotated translation of the pre-liberation text/translated，annotated and introduced by Nick Knight. Nathan，Australia：Griffith University，1981. 53 pages；30cm. ISBN：0868571296, 0868571294,(Griffith Asian papers；3)

翻译了毛泽东的《矛盾论》. Knight，Nick 译注.

66. On practice. On contradiction. On the correct handling of contradictions among the people. Calcutta，National Book Agency,1967. 161 pages；18cm.

《实践论·矛盾论·关于正确处理人民内部矛盾的问题》

67. Four essays on China & world communism. New York：Lancer Books,1972. 136 pages；18cm. (A Lancer contempora book)

Contents：On practice. —On contradiction. —On the correct handling of contraditions among the people. —Where do correct ideas come from?

《实践论》《矛盾论》《关于正确处理人民内部矛盾的问题》和《人的正确思想是从哪里来的?》4 篇.

68. On practice and contradiction/Tse-tung Mao；introduction［and commentary］by Slavoj Žižek. London：Verso,2007. 199 pages；20cm. ISBN：1844675876,1844675874. (Revolutions)

1. A single spark can start a prairie fire—2. Oppose book

worship—3. On practice：on the relation between knowledge and practice，between knowing and doing—4. On contradiction—5. Combat liberalism—6. The Chinese people cannot be cowed by the atom bomb—7. US imperialism is a paper tiger—8. Concerning Stalin's economic problems of socialism in the USSR—9. Critique of Stalin's economic problems of socialism in the USSR—10. On the correct handling of contradictions among the people—11. Where do correct ideas come from? —12. Talk on questions of philosophy.

《实践论》与《矛盾论》，Žižek，Slavoj 评.

69. Introductory remarks to "The Communist". Peking：Foreign Languages Press, 1953. 23 pages；19cm.

《"共产党人"发刊词》

(1)Introducing The Communist/Mao Tse-tung. ［2nd ed. , rev. translation］. Peking：Foreign Languages Press, 1966. 19 pages；18cm.

(2)Introducing The Communist/Mao Tse-tung. 2nd ed. Peking：Foreign Languages Press, 1968. 19 pages；19cm.

70. Report of an investigation into the peasant movement in Hunan. Peking：Foreign Languages Press, 1953. 64 pages；portraits；19cm.

《湖南农民运动考察报告》

(1)［2nd ed. ］. Peking：Foreign Languages Press, 1965. 51 pages：portraits；19cm.

(2)Report on an investigation of the peasant movement in Hunan/Mao Tse-tung. 2nd ed. Peking：Foreign Languages Press, 1967. 51 pages；19cm.

71. Why can China's red political power exist? Peking：Foreign Languages Press, 1953. 17 pages；19cm.

《中国的红色政权为什么能够存在?》

(1)Peking：Foreign Languages Pr. , 1963. 18 pages

(2)［2nd ed. ］. Peking：Foreign Languages Press, 1965. 14 pages

(3)Peking：Foreign Languages Press, 1967. 14 pages；19cm.

72. On the rectification of incorrect ideas in the Party. Peking：Foreign Languages Press, 1953. 19 pages；19cm.

《关于纠正党内的错误思想》

(1)On correcting mistaken ideas in the party/Mao Zedong. 2nd ed. , rev. translation. Peking：Foreign Languages Press, 1965. 15 pages；19cm.

(2)On correcting mistaken ideas in the party/Mao Tse-tung. 3rd ed. Peking：Foreign Languages Press, 1966. 15 pages；19cm.

73. A single spark can start a prairie fire. Peking：Foreign Languages Press, 1953. 22 pages；19cm.

《星星之火,可以燎原》

(1)1st pocket ed. Peking：Foreign Languages Press, 1963. 23, ［1］ pages；15cm.

(2)［2nd ed. ］. Peking：Foreign Languages Press, 1965. 16 pages；19cm.

(3)［3rd ed. ］. Peking：Foreign languages Press, 1966. 17 pages；18cm.

74. A single spark can start a prairie fire/Mao Tse-tung. Ann Arbor, Mich. ：U. M. I. , 1994. 22 leaves；19cm.

《星星之火,可以燎原》

75. Mind the living conditions of the masses and attend to the methods of work. Peking：Foreign Languages Press, 1953. 10 pages；19cm.

《关心群众生活,注意工作方法》

(1)Be concerned with the well-being of the masses：pay attention to methods of work/Mao Zedong. 2nd ed. (rev. translation). Peking：Foreign Languages Press, 1965. 7 pages；19cm.

(2)Be concerned with the well-being of the masses：pay attention to methods of work/Mao Zedong. 3rd ed. Peking：Foreign Languages Press, 1966. 7 pages；19cm.

76. On the tactics of fighting Japanese imperialism. Peking：Foreign Languages Press, 1953. 47 pages；19cm.

《论反对日本帝国主义的策略》

(1)2nd ed. Peking：Foreign Languages Press, 1960. 40 pages, ［1］ leaf of plates：portraits；19cm.

(2)On tactics against Japanese imperialism/Mao Tse-tung. 3rd ed. Peking：Foreign Languages Press, 1965. 52 pages：illustrations；19cm.

(3)4th ed. Peking：Foreign Languages Press, 1966. 36 pages；19cm.

(4)first pocket edition, second printing. Peking：Foreign Languages Press, 1968. 52 pages

77. Strategic problems of China's revolutionary war. ［1st Indian ed. ］. Bombay：People's Pub. House, 1951. 82 pages：maps；18cm.

《中国革命战争的战略问题》

78. Strategic problems of China's revolutionary war. Peking：Foreign Languages Press, 1954. 132 pages：illustrations；19cm.

《中国革命战争的战略问题》

(1)Problems of strategy in China's revolutionary war/Mao Zedong. 1st pocket ed. Peking：Foreign Languages Press, 1963. 150 pages；15cm.

(2)［2nd ed. ］. Peking：Foreign Languages Press, 1965. 108 pages；19cm.

(3)Peking：Foreign Languages Pr. , 1967. 152 pages

(4)Peking：Foreign Languages Press, 1968. 107 pages

79. The policies, measures and perspectives of combating Japanese invasion/Mao Tse-tung. Peking：Foreign Languages Press, 1954. 14 pages；19cm.

《反对日本进攻的方针、办法和前途》

(1)Two policies and programmes to combat Japanese

invasion and two perspectives/Mao Zedong. 2nd ed. Peking：Foreign Languages Press, 1960. 12 pages；19cm.

(2)Policies, measures and perspectives for resisting the Japanese invasion/Mao Zedong. 3rd ed. 2nd rev. translation. Peking：Foreign languages Press, 1966. [1],11 pages；19cm.

(3)The policies, measures and perspectives of combating Japanese invasion/Mao Tse-tung. pocket ed. Peking：Foreign Languages Press, 1969

(4)Policies, measures and perspectives for resisting the Japanese invasion/Mao Zedong. pocket edition. Peking：Foreign Languages Press, 1969. 15 pages；15cm.

80. On the protracted war. Peking：Foreign Languages Press, 1954. 140 pages：illustrations；19cm.

《论持久战》

(1)[2nd ed.]. Peking：Foreign Languages Press, 1960. 131 pages

(2)On protracted war/Mao Tse-tung. 1st pocket ed. Peking：Foreign Languages Press, 1963. 163 pages；15cm.

(3)[3rd rev. ed.]. Peking：Foreign Languages Press, 1966. 115 pages；19cm.

(4)On protracted war/Mao Tse-Tung. [3rd ed.]. Peking：Foreign Languages Press, 1967. 115 pages；19cm.

81. Strategic problems in the anti-Japanese guerrilla war/Mao Tse-tung. Peking：Foreign Languages Press, 1954. 65 pages：portraits；19cm.

《抗日游击战争的战略问题》

(1)2nd ed. Peking：Foreign Languages Press, 1960. 59 pages；19cm.

(2)Problems of strategy in guerrilla war against Japan. pocket ed. Peking：Foreign Languages Pr. , 1963. 70 pages

(3)Problems of strategy in guerrilla war against Japan. [3rd ed.]. Peking：Foreign Languages Press, 1965. 51 pages frontispiece 19cm.

(4)Problems of strategy in guerrilla war against Japan. 4th ed. Peking：Foreign Languages Press, 1966. 51 pages；19cm.

(5)Problems of strategy in guerrilla war against Japan. Peking：Foreign Languages P. , 1968. 51 pages；19cm.

82. The question of independence and autonomy within the united front. Peking：Foreign Languages Press, 1954. 9 pages；11cm.

《统一战线中的独立自主问题》

(1)The question of independence within the united front/Mao Zedong. 2nd ed. Peking：Foreign Languages

Press, 1960. 6 pages；19cm.

(2)3rd ed. (2nd rev. tr). Peking：Foreign Languages Pr. , 1966. 7 pages

(3)3rd ed. Peking：Foreign Languages Press, 1968. 5 pages；19cm.

83. Problems of war and strategy/Mao Zedong. Peking：Foreign Languages Press, 1954. 30 pages；19cm.

《战争和战略问题》

(1)2nd ed. Peking：Foreign Languages Press, 1960. 26 pages；19cm.

(2)pocket ed. Peking：Foreign Languages Press, 1963. 150 pages；15cm.

(3)3rd ed. Peking：Foreign Languages Press, 1965. 26 pages；19cm.

(4)4th ed. Peking：Foreign Languages Press, 1966. 26 pages；19cm.

(5)Peking：Foreign Languages Press, 1968. 107 pages

84. Mao Tse-tung on war. Dehra Dun：English Book Depot, 1966. 199, xxxii pages；22cm.

毛泽东论战争.

85. Chairman Mao Tse-tung on people's war. Colombo：Praja Prakasakayo, 1967. 39 pages

《毛主席论人民战争》

86. The art of war/by Mao Tse-tung. Special edition. El Paso, Tx. ：El Paso Norte Press, 2005. 315 pages；22cm. ISBN：097607267X, 0976072676

Contents：Part 1. Problems of strategy in China's Revolutionary War—Part 2. Problems of strategy in Guerilla War against Japan—Part 3. On protracted war—Part 4. Problems of war

毛泽东论军事.

(1) Special edition. El Paso, Texas：El Paso Norte Press, 2011. 315 pages；22cm.

87. Mao on warfare：On guerilla warfare, On protracted war, and other military writings/Mao Zedong. New York：CN Times Books, Inc. , 2013. xiv, 258 pages；23cm. ISBN：1627740081, 1627740082

Contents：Introduction/by Arthur Waldron—Problems of strategy in China's Revolutionary War, December 1936—Problems of war and strategy, November 6,1938—On guerilla warfare—On protracted war—Concentrate a superior force to destroy the enemy forces one by one, September 16, 1946—The concept of operations for the northwestern war theater, April 15,1947—Strategy for the second year of the war of liberation, September 1,1947—The concept of operations for the Liaohsi-Shenyang campaign.

毛泽东论战争. 包括《游击战》《持久战》和其他军事篇章.

88. On guerrilla warfare/Translated and with an introd. by Samuel B. Griffith. New York：Praeger, 1961. 114 pages；

21cm. (Praeger publications in Russian history and world communism; no. 99;.Books that matter)

《游击战》,Griffith, Samuel B. 译.

(1)Urbana：University of Illinois, 1961. 114 pages；tables

(2)New York：Praeger, 1962. 114 p.

(3)New York：Praeger, 1966. 114 pages；21cm. (Praeger publications in Russian history and world communism；no. 99)

(4)New York：Praeger, 1967. 114 pages；21cm.

(5)New York：Praeger, 1970. 114 pages；21cm.

(6)Garden City, N. Y.：Anchor Press, 1978. viii, 101 pages；22cm. ISBN：0385129025, 0385129022

(7)Baltimore, Md.：Nautical & Aviation Pub. Co. of America,1992. 160 pages；23cm. ISBN：1877853100, 1877853104

(8)Mao Tse-tung on guerrilla warfare/［translated, with an introduction by Samuel B. Griffith II］. ［Washington, DC］：U. S. Marine Corps,1989. 114 pages：illustrations；20cm.

(9)Baltimore, Md.：Nautical & Aviation Pub. Co. of America,1991. 168 pages；26cm. ISBN：1877853100, 1877853104

(10)Collector's ed. Norwalk, Conn.：Easton Press, 1996. 160 pages；23cm.

(11)Urbana：University of Illinois Press, 2000. 114 pages；21cm. ISBN：0252068920, 0252068928

(12)Mineola, NY：Dover Publications, 2005. 114 pages；22cm. ISBN：0486443760, 0486443768, 0486119571, 0486119572

(13)［Thousand Oaks, Calif.］：BN Publishing, 2007. 122 p.；22cm. ISBN：9563100131, 9563100136

89. Guerrilla warfare/by Mao Tse-tung and by Che Guevara；with a foreword by Captain B. H. Liddell Hart. London：Cassell, 1962. xvi, 162 pages：illustrations；23cm.

Notes：Translation of original Chinese and original Spanish pamphlets.

收录毛泽东的《游击战》.

(1)3rd ed. London：Cassell, 1963. xvi, 162；23cm.

(2)4th ed. London：Cassell, 1964. 164 pages；22cm.

(3)5th ed. London：Cassell, 1965. xvi, 162 pages. ISBN：0304931950, 0304931958

(4)［5th ed.］. London：Cassell, 1969. xvi, 162 pages；23cm.

90. On guerilla warfare/by Mao Tse-tung. New York：Classic House Books, 2009. 57 pages；22cm. ISBN：1442166714, 1442166711

Contents：What is guerrilla warfare? —The relation of guerrilla hostilities to regular operations—Guerrilla warfare in history—Can victory be attained by guerrilla operations? —Organization for guerrilla warfare—The political problems of guerrilla warfare—The strategy of guerrilla resistance against Japan.

《游击战》

91. The red book of guerrilla warfare/by Mao Zedong；［edited by Shawn Connors］. El Paso, Tex.：El Paso Norte Press, Special Edition Books, 2010. 122 pages；22cm. ISBN：1934255270, 1934255278

《游击战》. Connors, Shawn 编.

92. Questions of tactics in the present anti-Japanese united front；On policy/Mao Zedong. Peking：Foreign Languages Press, 1954. 38 pages；19cm.

Notes："The present English translation... has been made from the Chinese text given in the second edition of the Selected works of Mao Tse-tung, volume II... 1952."

《目前抗日统一战线中的策略问题·论政策》

(1)Tactics in the anti-Japanese united front/Mao Zedong. 2nd ed. Peking：Foreign Languages Press, 1960. 15 pages；19cm.

(2)Current problems of tactics in the anti-Japanese united front/Mao Zedong. 3rd ed. Peking：Foreign Languages Press, 1966. 13 pages；19cm.

(3)Current problems of tactics in the anti-Japanese united front/Mao Zedong. 3rd ed. Peking：Foreign Languages Press, 1967. 13 pages；19cm.

(4)Current problems of tactics in the anti-Japanese united front/Mao Zedong. 3rd ed. Peking：Foreign Languages Press, 1968. 13 pages；19cm.

93. Preface and postscript to "Rural survey"/Mao Zedong. Peking：Foreign Languages Press, 1955. 8 pages；18cm.

《"农村调查"序言和跋》

(1)2nd ed. Peking：Foreign Languages Press, 1960. 8 pages；18cm.

(2)Third edition, revised translation. Peking：Foreign Languages Press, 1962. 7 pages,［1］leaf of plates：portraits；19cm.

94. Reform our study. Peking：Foreign Languages Press, 1955. 13 pages

《改造我们的学习》

(1)Peking：Foreign Languages Press, 1959. 13 pages；19cm.

(2)2nd ed. Peking：Foreign Languages Press, 1960. 12 pages；19cm.

(3)［3rd ed.］. Peking：Foreign Languages Press,1962. 10 pages；19cm.

(4)［4th ed.］. Peking：Foreign Languages Press,1965. 10 pages；18cm.

95. Rectify the party's style in work/Mao Zedong. Peking：Foreign Languages Press,1955. 29 pages；19cm.

《整顿党的作风》

(1)2nd ed. Peking：Foreign Languages Press，1960. 27 pages；19cm.

(2)[3rd ed.]. Peking：Foreign Languages Press，1962. 23 pages；19cm.

(3)Rectify the party's style of work/Mao Zedong. 4th ed. Peking：Foreign Languages Press，1965. 23，[1] pages；19cm.

(4)4th ed. Peking：Foreign Languages Press，1967. 23 pages；19cm.

96. Oppose the party "eight-legged essay"/Mao Zedong. Peking：Foreign Languages Press，1955. 27 pages；19cm.

《反对党八股》

(1)2nd ed. Peking：Foreign Languages Press，1960. 24 pages；19cm.

(2)Oppose stereotyped party writing/Mao Zedong. 3rd ed. ，rev. Peking：Foreign Languages Press，1962. 22 pages；19cm.

(3)Oppose stereotyped party writing/Mao Zedong. 4th ed. Peking：Foreign Languages Press，1965. 23 pages；19cm.

97. Economic and financial problems during the anti-Japanese war, and other articles. Peking：Foreign Languages Press，1955. 64 pages：illustrations；19cm.

《抗日时期的经济问题和财政问题及其他论文》

98. On methods of leadership/Mao Zedong. Peking：Foreign Languages Press，1955. 10 pages；18cm.

《关于领导方法的若干问题》

(1)2nd ed. Peking：Foreign Languages Press，1960. 8 pages；18cm.

(2)Some questions concerning methods of leadership. [3rd ed.]. Peking：Foreign Languages Press，1962. 7 pages：portraits；19cm.

(3)Some questions concerning methods of leadership. 4th ed. ，3rd rev. trans. Peking：Foreign Languages，1965. 7 pages；19cm.

(4)Some questions concerning methods of leadership. [4th ed. ，rev. translation]. Peking：Foreign Languages Press，1967. 7 pages

99. Our study and the current situation. Appendix：Resolution on some questions in the history of our Party. Peking：Foreign Languages Press，1955.116 pages

《学习和时局》，附录：关于若干历史问题的决议.

(1)[2nd ed.]. Peking：Foreign Languages Press，1960. 104 pages：portraits；20cm.

(2)3rd ed. ，rev. trans. Peking：Foreign Languages Press，1962. 90 pages，[1] leaf of plates：portraits；19cm.

(3)[4th ed.]. Peking：Foreign Languages Press，1966. 93 pages：illustrations；19cm.

(4)Peking：Foreign Languages Press，1967. 21 pages；19cm.

100. Analysis of the classes in Chinese society. Peking：Foreign Languages Press，1956. 17 pages

《中国社会各阶级的分析》

(1)[2nd ed.]. Peking：Foreign Languages Press，1960. 14 pages；19cm.

(2)3rd ed. (rev. translation). Peking：Foreign Languages Press，1962. 12 pages：portraits；19cm.

(3)Fourth edition. Peking：Foreign Languages Press，1965. [13] pages；18cm.

(4)Peking：Foreign Languages Press，1965. 17 unnumbered pages；15cm.

(5)4th ed. Peking：Foreign Languages Press，1967. 12 pages：portraits；19cm.

(6)4th ed. Peking：Foreign Languages Press，1968. 12 pages；18cm.

101. Analysis of the classes in Chinese society/Mao Tse-tung；edited by Gregor Benton. [Amsterdam]：University of Amsterdam，Dept. of South and Southeast Asian Studies，1985. 16 pages；30cm. (Amsterdam Asia studies，；no. 53)

《中国社会各阶级的分析》，Benton，Gregor 编.

102. The tasks of the Chinese Communist Party in the period of resistance to Japan/Mao Zedong. Peking：Foreign Languages Press，1956. 44 pages；19cm.

《中国共产党在抗日时期的任务》

(1)2nd ed. Peking：Foreign Languages Press，1960. 30 pages，[1] leaf of plates：portraits；19cm.

(2)3rd ed. ，2nd rev. trans. Peking：Foreign Languages Press，1965. 33 pages；19cm.

(3)3rd ed. ，2nd rev. translation. Peking：Foreign Languages Press，1967. 33 pages；19cm.

103. The situation and tasks in the anti-Japanese war after the fall of Shanghai and Taiyuan/Mao Zedong. Peking：Foreign Languages Press，1956. 23 pages；19cm.

《上海太原失陷以后抗日战争的形势和任务》

(1)2nd ed. Peking：Foreign Languages Press，1960. 21 pages；19cm.

(2)3rd ed. ，2nd rev. trans. Peking：Foreign Languages Press，1966. 19，[1] pages；19cm.

104. The role of the Chinese Communist Party in the national war. Peking：Foreign Languages Press，1956. 33 pages；19cm.

《中国共产党在民族战争中的地位》

(1)[2nd ed.]. Peking：Foreign Languages Press，1960. 26 pages；119cm.

(2)3rd ed. Peking：Foreign Languages Press，1966. 24 pages；18cm.

(3)3rd ed. Peking：Foreign Languages Press，1967. 24 pages

105. Talks at the Yenan forum on art and literature. Peking：Foreign Languages Press，1956. 51 pages：illustrations；19cm.

《在延安文艺座谈会上的讲话》，毛泽东(1893—1976).

(1)［2nd ed.］. Peking：Foreign Languages Press，1960. 47 p. ；19cm.

(2)3rd ed. (rev. translation). Peking：Foreign Languages Press，1962. 42 pages：illustrations；19cm.

(3)［Fourth edition (Third revised translation)］，Peking：Foreign Languages Press，1965. 42 pages：portraits；19cm.

(4)［4th ed.］. Peking：Foreign Languages Press，1967. 42 pages；19cm.

(5)［1st pocket ed.］. Peking：Foreign Languages Press，1967. 79 pages：portraits；14cm.

(6)［2nd ed.］. Peking：Foreign Languages Press，1967. 80 pages：illustrations

(7)北京：商务印书馆，1972. 100 pages；19cm. 汉英对照

106. Mao Zedong's "Talks at the Yan'an conference on literature and art"：a translation of the 1943 text with commentary/by Bonnie S. McDougall. Ann Arbor：Center for Chinese Studies；University of Michigan，1980. ix，112 pages；23cm. ISBN：0892640391，0892640393. (Michigan papers in Chinese studies；no. 39)

《在延安文艺座谈会上的讲话》，McDougall, Bonnie S. (1941—)译.

(1)Ann Arbor：Center for Chinese University of Michigan，1992. ix，112 pages；23cm. ISBN：0892640391，0892640393

107. Five documents on literature and art/Mao Tse-tung. Peking：Foreign Languages Press，1967. 10 pages；20cm.

《毛主席关于文学艺术的五个文件》

108. The question of agricultural co-operation. Peking：Foreign Languages Press，1956. 39 pages；19cm.

《关于农业合作化问题》

(1)2nd ed. (rev. translation). Peking：Foreign Languages Press，1962. 33 p.

(2)3rd edition. (2nd revised translation). Peking：Foreign Languages Press，1966. 35 pages；19cm.

(3)On the question of agricultural co-operation. 3rd ed. (2nd printing). Peking：Foreign languages Press，1967. 35 p. ；19cm.

109. On the correct handling of contradictions among the people：this is the text of a speech made on February 27，1957，at the Eleventh Session (enlarged) of the Supreme State Conference/by Mao Tse-tung. ［Rev. ed.］. Peking：Foreign Languages Press，1957. 69 pages

《关于正确处理人民内部矛盾的问题》

Notes："Text of a speech made on February 27，1957 at the eleventh session (enlarged)—of the Supreme State Conference."

(1)Peking：Foreign Languages Press，1959. 69 pages；

19cm.

(2)Peking：Foreign Languages Press，1960. 69 pages；19cm.

(3)6th ed. Peking：Foreign Languages Press，1964. 54 pages：portrait.

(4)［7th ed. (Rev. translation)］. Peking：Foreign Languages Press，1966. 54 pages；19cm.

(5)1st pocket ed. Peking：Foreign Languages Press，1966. 76 pages；15cm.

(6)Rev. English translation. Peking：Foreign Languages Press，1967. 32 pages；25cm.

110. On the correct handling of contradictions among the people/Mao Zedong. New York：New Century Publishers，1957. 32 pages；20cm.

《关于正确处理人民内部矛盾的问题》

111. On the question of the correct handling of contradictions among the people：a report by Mao Tse-tung；as reprinted in "Pravda" on June 19，1957. Ottawa：Press Office of the U. S. S. R. Embassy，1957. 65 pages

《关于正确处理人民内部矛盾的问题》

112. On the correct handling of contradictions among the people. Text of a speech made on February 27，1957，at the Eleventh Session (enlarged) of the Supreme State Conference. ［London］：Communist Party，1957. 14 pages；portraits；28cm.

《关于正确处理人民内部矛盾的问题》

113. Let a hundred flowers bloom：the complete text of "On the correct handling of contradictions among the people"/by Mao Zedong；with notes and an introduction by G. F. Hudson. New York：New leader，1957. 58 pages；22cm.

《关于正确处理人民内部矛盾的问题》

114. Comrade Mao Tsê-tung on "imperialism and all reactionaries are paper tigers"/Renmin Ribao Editorial Department. Peking：Foreign Languages Press，1958. 31 pages；19cm.

《毛泽东同志论帝国主义和一切反动派都是纸老虎》

(1)Enl. ed. Peking：Foreign Languages Press，1958. 123 pages；19cm.

Notes：Contains Comrade Mao Tse-tung on "Imperialism and all reactionaries are paper tigers" together with related documents，editorials，and commentaries.

(2)3rd ed. (2nd rev. translation). Peking：Foreign Languages Press，1958. 32 pages；19cm.

(3)［Peking］：［Guozi Shudian］，1959. 15 pages；25cm.

(4)Rev. trans. Peking：Foreign Languages Press，1961. 31 pages；19cm.

(5)1st pocket ed.，rev. translation. Peking：Foreign Languages Press，1963. 41 pages；15cm.

(6)［3rd ed.］. Peking：Foreign Languages Press，1966. 31 pages；19cm.

115. Nineteen poems. With notes by Chou Chen-fu and an

appreciation by Tsang Keh-chia. Peking：Foreign Languages Press，1958. 62 p. illus. 19cm.

Notes："Andrew Boyd... translated the first eighteen poems... The rest of the book has been translated by Mrs. Gladys Yang."

《毛泽东诗词十九首》，毛泽东；周振甫注释；臧克家讲解.

116. Poems. Peking：Foreign Languages Press，1959. 38 pages：portrait，facsimiles；19cm.

Notes：Translation of Mao zhu xi shi ci san shi qi shou. / "Mr. Andrew Boyd... translated the first eighteen poems... the last one has been translated by Mrs. Gladys Yang."

《毛泽东诗词》，译自《毛泽东诗词三十七首》.

117. Mao and the Chinese revolution. With thirty-seven poems by Mao Tse-tung translated from the Chinese by Michael Bullock and Jerome Ch'ên. London，New York：Oxford University Press，1965. ix，419 p. maps，port. 23cm.

毛泽东与中国革命：毛泽东 37 首诗词英译. Bullock，Michael 和 Ch'ên，Jerome(1919—)合译.

(1) London，New York：Oxford University Press，1966. ix，419 pages：maps，portrait 23cm.

(2)[New ed.]. New York：Oxford University Press，1967. xi，419 pages：maps，portraits；21cm.

(3) London；New York：Oxford University Press，1970. xi，419 pages：maps，portraits；21cm.

(4) London，New York：Oxford University Press，1972. ix，419 pages：illustrations；23cm.

(5) New York：Oxford University Press，1976. xi，419 pages：maps，portraits；21cm.

118. Poems of Mao Tse-tung/translated and annotated by Wong Man. Hong Kong：Eastern Horizon Press，1966. xiv，95 pages：folded facsimiles (6 pages)，portraits；23cm.

毛泽东诗词. Huang，Wen 译. 中英对照.

(1) Hong Kong：Eastern Horizon Press，1972. 95 pages；23cm.

119. Ten more poems of Mao Tse-tung. Hong Kong，Eastern Horizon Press，1967. iv，33 p. fold. facsim.，port. 23cm.

毛泽东诗词又 10 首. 英汉对照.

120. Poems of Mao Tse-tung. Translation，introd.，and notes by Hua-ling Nieh Engle and Paul Engle. New York：Simon and Schuster［1972］. 160 p.；22cm. ISBN：0671214020，0671214029

毛泽东诗词英译. 聂华苓(Nie，Hualing，1925—)，保罗(Engle，Paul，1908—1991)译注.

(1) Poetry of Mao Tse-tung/translation，introd. and notes by Hua-ling Nieh Engle and Paul Engle. London：Wildwood House，1972. 115 pages；22cm. ISBN：0704500418，0704500419

(2) The poetry of Mao Tse-tung/translation［from the Chinese］，introduction，and notes by Hua-ling Nieh Engle and Paul Engle；with illustrations by Cheng Kar-chun. London：Wildwood House，1973. 115 p. ：ill.；23cm. ISBN：070450118X，0704501188

121. The poems of Mao Tse-tung. Translation，introd.，notes by Willis Barnstone in collaboration with Ko Ching-po. New York：Harper & Row［1972］. viii，149 p. port. 22cm. ISBN：0060102195，0060102197

《毛主席诗词三十七首》，Barnstone，Willis(1927—)，Ko，Ching-po 译注.

(1) New York：Bantam Books，1972. 164 pages：portraits；22cm.

(2) London：Barrie and Jenkins，1972. ix，149 pages：1 illustration，facsimiles；21cm. ISBN：021466824X，0214668241

(3) The poems of Mao Zedong/translations，introduction，and notes by Willis Barnstone. Berkeley：University of California Press，[2008]. 151 p. ：ill.；21cm. ISBN：0520256651，0520256654，0520261624，0520261623

122. Ten poems and lyrics/by Mao Tse-tung；translation and woodcuts by Wang Hui-ming. Amherst：University of Massachusetts Press，1975. 71 p. ：ill.；24cm. ISBN：0870231782，0870231780，0870231820，0870231827

《毛主席诗词手稿十首》，Wang，Hui-ming 英译. 中英对照.

(1) London：J. Cape，1976. 71 pages：illustrations；24cm. ISBN：0224012428，0224012423

123. Mao Zedong poems/translated by Zhao Zhentao. Changsha，Hunan，China：Hunan People's Pub. House，1980. v，117 p. ，[2] leaves of plates (1 folded)：ill. ，port. ；21cm.

《毛泽东诗词》，赵甄陶(Zhao，Zhentao)译.

(1) 长沙：湖南师范大学出版社. 1992. v，169 pages，[2] leaves of plates：illustrations，portraits；21cm. ISBN：781031131X，7810311311

124. 毛主席诗词英译：四十首/黄龙译. ［China］：［publisher not identified］，1980. 5，117 pages：illustrations；19cm.

Notes：东北师大学报增刊

英语题名：An English version of chairman Mao's poems：forty pieces/translated by Huang Long

125. Reverberations：a new translation of complete poems of Mao Tse-tung/with notes by Nancy T. Lin = Mao Zedong shi ci/Lin Tongduan yi chu. Hongkong：Joint Pub. Co. ，1980. 124 p. ；22cm. ISBN：9620400461，9620400469，962040047X，9620400476

毛泽东诗词全译. 林同瑞(Lin，Nancy T. ，1922—)译. 英汉对照.

126. Poems/Mao Zedong；transl. and annot. by Ronald Harry Bathgate. Eindhoven：Ronald Harry Bathgate，

1983. x, 279, 94 blz. ; 30cm.

毛主席诗词. Bathgate, Ronald Harry 译注.

127. Snow glistens on the Great Wall: a new translation of the complete collection of Mao Tse-tung's poetry with notes & historical commentary/by Ma Wen-yee.［Santa Barbara, Calif.］: Santa Barbara Press, 1986. 193 p. , ［16］p. of plates: ill. ; 22cm. ISBN: 0915520788, 0915520796

毛泽东诗词全译与注评. Ma, Wen-yee(1939—)译.

128. Mao Zedong shi ci/Chao Heng-yüan, Paul Woods pien i. Tianjin Shi: Tianjin ren min chu ban she, 1993. 151 p. ; 19cm. ISBN: 7201014765

《毛泽东诗词》, 赵恒元, Paul Woods 编译. 天津人民出版社.

129. Poems of Mao Zedong: with rhymed versions and annotations/translated and annotated by Guy Zhengkun. Beijing: Peking University Press, 1993. 308 pages; 20cm.

《毛泽东诗词: 汉英对照韵译》; 辜正坤译注. 北京大学出版社.

(1)2nd ed. Beijing: Beijing da xue chu ban she, 2010. 11, 305 p. : ill. ; 24cm. ISBN: 7301171240, 7301171242

130. Poems of Mao Tsetung/translation by Kim Unsong ＝［Mao Tse-tung shih tz'u/Chin Yün-sung Ch'ao Ying i］. San Bruno, CA: One Mind Press, c1994. 102 p. : ill. ; 22cm. ISBN: 0942049055, 0942049053

毛泽东诗词. Kim, Unsong 译. 中英对照.

131. Mao Zedong selected poems/poems by Chairman Mao; translated by Haiying Zhang. 3rd ed.［Westcliff on Sea］: Little Bird Publishing, 2006. 28 pages; 21cm. ISBN: 0955167225, 0955167221

毛泽东诗词选译. Zhang, Haiying(1972—)译. 英汉对照, 收录毛泽东诗词 20 首.

132. Poems of Mao Zedong/translated by Li Zhengshuan; notes in English by Li Zhengshuan; notes in Chinese by Liu Sen and Ren Min; introduction about Mao Zedong by Sun Yan and Li Zhengshuan. Toronto, Ontario, Canada: UCANDU Learning Centres, 2011. 109 pages: illustrations (some colour); 29cm. ISBN: 1894534888, 1894534883

毛泽东诗词, Li, Zhengshuan(1956—)译. 英汉对照.

133. Illustrated poems of Mao Zedong ＝ Jing xuan Mao Zedong shi ci yu shi yi hua/Xu Yuanchong yi shi. Beijing: Wu zhou chuan bo chu ban she, 2006. 147 p. : col. ill. ; 23cm. ISBN: 7508508475, 7508508474

《精选毛泽东诗词与诗意画》; 许渊冲(1921—)英译. 英汉对照.

134. The orientation of the youth movement/Mao Zedong. Peking: Foreign Languages Press, 1960. 14 pages; 19cm.

《青年运动的方向》

(1)［2nd ed. (Rev. translation)］. Peking: Foreign Languages Press, 1965. 15 pages

(2)2nd ed. Peking: Foreign Languages Press, 1967. 15 pages

135. New-democratic constitutionalism. Peking: Foreign Languages Press, 1960. 15 pages; 19cm.

《新民主主义的宪政》

(1)［2nd ed.］. Peking: Foreign Languages Press, 1966. 13 pages; 20cm.

(2)Peking: Foreign Languages Press, 1967. 13 pages

136. Chairman Mao Tse-tung's important talks with guests from Asia, Africa and Latin America.［2nd ed.］. Peking: Foreign Languages Press;［Chicago］:［Distributors, China Books & Periodicals］, 1960. 9 pages; 19cm.

《毛泽东主席同亚洲、非洲、拉丁美洲人士的几次重要谈话》

(1)pocket edition. Peking: Foreign Languages Press, 1963. 12 pages; 15cm.

(2)［4th ed.］. Peking: Foreign Languages Press, 1964. 8 pages; 19cm.

(3)3rd ed. Peking: Foreign Languages Pr. , 1965. 9 pages; 19cm.

(4)2nd pocket ed. Peking: Foreign Languages Press, 1966. 12 pages

137. Struggle to mobilize all forces in winning victory in the armed resistance. Peking: Foreign Languages Pr. , 1960. 10 pages; 19cm.

《为动员一切力量争取抗战胜利而斗争》

(1)For the mobilization of all the nation's forces for victory in the war of resistance/Mao Tse-Tung. 2nd ed. (rev. translation). Peking: Foreign Languages Press, 1966. 9 pages; 19cm.

(2)2nd ed. Peking: Foreign Languages Press, 1967. 9 pages; 19cm.

138. On policy/Mao Zedong. 2nd ed. Peking: Foreign Languages Press, 1960. 13 pages; 19cm.

《论政策》, 1954 年第一版.

(1)［3rd ed. , 2nd rev. trans.］. Peking: Foreign Languages Press, 1966. 13 pages

139. Economic and financial problems during the anti-Japanese war/Mao Zedong. 2nd ed. Peking: Foreign Languages Press, 1960. 7,［1］pages; 19cm.

《抗日时期的经济问题和财政问题》

(1)Economic and financial problems in the anti-Japanese war: (December 1942)/Mao Tsetung. 1st pocket ed. Peking: Foreign Languages Press, 1969. 12 pages; 13cm.

140. Speech before the Assembly of the Shensi-Kansu-Ningsia border region/Mao Zedong. Peking: Foreign Languages Press, 1960. 5 pages; 19cm.

《在陕甘宁边区参议会的演说》

(1)Peking: Foreign Languages Press, 1965. 5 pages;

19cm.

    (2)2nd ed. (rev. translation). Peking：Foreign Languages Press,1967. 5 pages；19cm.

141. Struggle to mobilize all forces in winning victory in the armed resistance. Peking：Foreign Languages Pr., 1960. 10 S. 8.

《为动员一切力量争取抗战胜利而斗争》

    (1)For the mobilization of all the nation's forces for victory in the war of resistance/Mao Tse-tung. 2nd ed. (rev. translation). Peking：Foreign Languages Press, 1966. 9 pages；19cm.

    (2)2nd ed. Peking：Foreign Languages Press, 1967. 9 pages；19cm.

142. On the Chungking negotiations/Mao Tse-tung. Peking：Foreign Languages Press, 1961. 22 pages：portraits；19cm.

Notes：Translated from the Chinese text given in the 1st ed. of the Selected Works of Mao Tse-tung, vol. IV, published by the People's Publishing House, 1960.

《关于重庆谈判》

    (1)pocket ed. Peking：Foreign Languages Pr. , 1963. 32 pages

    (2)2nd ed. Peking：Foreign Languages Press, 1967. 23 pages；19cm.

143. Talk with the American correspondent Anna Louise Strong/Mao Tse-tung. Peking：Foreign Languages Press, 1961. 27 pages；19cm.

《和美国记者安娜·路易斯·斯特朗的谈话》

    (1)pocket ed. Peking：Foreign Languages Pr. , 1963. 9 pages

    (2)Peking：Foreign Languages Press, 1967. 7 pages：portraits；19cm.

    (3)Peking, Foreign Languages, 1968. 9 pages；15cm.

144. The present situation and our tasks/Mao Tse-tung. Peking：Foreign Languages Press, 1961. 30 pages；18cm.

《目前形势和我们的任务》

    (1)[1st pocket ed.]. Peking：Foreign Languages Press, 1963. 44 pages

    (2)Peking：Foreign Languages Press, 1967. 31 pages；19cm.

    (3)Peking：Foreign Languages Pr. , 1969. 46 pages

145. Carry the revolution through to the end/Mao Zedong. Peking：Foreign Languages Press, 1961. 16 pages：portraits；18cm.

Notes："new year message for 1949 written by Comrade Mao Tseê-tung on December 30, 1948, for the Hsinhua News Agency."

《将革命进行到底》

    (1)1st pocket ed. Peking：Foreign Languages Press, 1963. 24 pages；18cm.

    (2)Peking：Foreign Languages Press, 1967. 16 pages；15cm.

146. On the U. S. white paper：[Five articles, commentaries written for the Hsinhua News Agency on the U. S. State Department's white paper and Dean Achieson's letter of transmittal, originally pub. 1949]/Mao Zedong. Peking：Foreign Languages Press, 1961. 47 pages；19cm.

《评白皮书》

    (1)pocket ed. Peking：Foreign Languages Press, 1963. 66 pages；13cm.

    (2)2nd ed. Peking：Foreign Languages Press, 1967. 48 pages；19cm.

    (3)1st pocket ed. Peking：Foreign Languages Press, 1967. 67 pages；15cm.

147. The situation and our policy after the victory in the war of resistance against Japan. Peking：Foreign Languages Press, 1961. 20 pages,[1] leaf of plates：portraits；20cm.

《抗日战争胜利后的时局和我们的方针》

    (1)pocket ed. Peking：Foreign Languages Pr. , 1963. 29 pages

    (2)Peking：Foreign Languages Press, 1967. 29 pages

148. On some important problems of the Party's present policy/Mao Zedong. Peking：Foreign Languages Press, 1961. 10 pages：portraits；18cm.

《关于目前党的政策中的几个重要问题》

    (1)pocket ed. Peking：Foreign Languages Press, 1964. 14 pages；15cm.

    (2)1st pocket ed. Peking：Foreign Languages Press, 1967. 14 pages

149. Report to the Second Plenary Session of the Seventh Central Committee of the Communist Party of China/Mao Zedong. Peking：Foreign Languages Press, 1961. 22 pages,[1] leaf of plates：portraits；19cm.

《在中国共产党第七届中央委员会第二次全体会议上的报告》

    (1)pocket ed. Peking：Foreign Languages Press, 1964. 32 pages；15cm.

    (2)2nd ed. Peking：Foreign Languages Pr. , 1967. 33 p.

    (3)Peking：Foreign Languages Press, 1968. 31 pages；19cm.

    (4)3rd ed. Peking：Foreign Languages Press, 1973. 24 pages；19cm.

150. Mao Tse-tung's oral report to the seventh congress of the CCP：summary notes/Steven I. Levine. Santa Monica, Calif. : Rand Corp. , 1977. 32 pages；28cm. (The Rand paper series; P-6007)

Notes：Text translated from P. P. Vladimirov's Russian transcription of the Chinese speech, published in his Osobyǐ raǐon Kitaǐ raǐā/ Cover title.

毛泽东在"中国共产党第七届中央委员会"会议上的口头报告. Levine, Steven I. Vladimirov, P. P. (Petr Parfenovich, 1905—1953)的从中文译成俄文,本文从俄文转译成英文.

151. Speech at a conference of cadres in the Shansi-Suiyuan Liberated Area. Peking：Foreign Languages Pr., 1961. 17 pages；19cm.

《在晋绥干部会议上的讲话》

(1)Peking：Foreign Languages Pr., 1967. 17 pages；19cm.

(2)pocket edition. Foreign Languages Pr., 1969. 32 pages；13cm.

152. On strengthening the party committee system/Mao Zedong. Peking：Foreign Languages Press, 1961. 9 pages；19cm.

《关于健全党委制》

(1)Peking：Foreign Languages Press, 1967. 9 pages

153. U. S. imperialism must fail：Cuba must win!. Peking：Workers' Pub. House, 1961. 1 volume

工人出版社.

154. The political thought of Mao Tse-tung/[sel., annot., transl. from the Chinese and introd. by] Stuart R. Schram. Stuart R. Schram. London：Pall Mall Press, 1963. ix, 319 pages；22cm.

Notes：Chapters 1－5 translated from the Chinese by S. M. Long；chapters 6－10 translated by S. B. Schram. Includes bibliographical references (pages 307－319).

毛泽东的政治思想. Schram, Stuart R. 编译.

(1)New York；Washington；London：F. A. Praeger, 1965. 319 p.

(2)Rev. and enlarged ed. New York [etc.]：Praeger, 1969. 479 p. ISBN：0275670732, 0275670733

(3)Enlarged and revised edition. Harmondsworth, Middlesex [etc.]：Penguin Books, 1969. 479 p.；18cm. ISBN：014021013X, 0140210132. (Pelican books；A 1013)

(4)Rev. and enl. ed. New York：Praeger, 1971. 479 pages；21cm.

(5)Rev. and enl. ed. New York：Praeger, 1976. 479 pages. (Praeger University series；；U-548)

155. Selected military writings of Mao Tse-tung. Peking：Foreign Languages Press, 1963. 408 pages；portraits；23cm.

《毛泽东军事文选》

(1)2nd ed. Peking, China：Foreign Languages Press, 1966. 410 pages；portraits；23cm.

(2)［2nd ed.］. Peking：Foreign Languages Press, 1967. 410 pages；portraits；23cm.

(3)Peking：Foreign Languages Press, 1968. 410

pages；portraits；17cm.

(4)[2nd pocket ed.]. Peking：Foreign Languages Press, 1972. 410 pages；portraits；17cm.

156. Chairman Mao Tsê-tung on people's war. Peking：Foreign Languages Press, 1967. 44 pages；portraits；14cm.

《毛主席论人民战争》

(1)Vest-pocket ed. Peking：Foreign Languages Press, 1967. 52 pages；portraits；12cm.

157. Statement opposing aggression against southern Viet Nam and slaughter of its people by the U. S. -Ngo Dinh Diem clique/Mao Zedong. Peking：Foreign Languages Press, 1963. 32 pages；18cm.

《反对美国——吴庭艳集团侵略越南南方和屠杀越南南方人民的声明》

158. Statement calling on the people of the world to unite to oppose racial discrimination by U. S. imperialism；and support the American Negroes in their struggle against racial discrimination/Mao Tse-tung. Peking：Foreign Languages Press, 1964. 91 pages；illustrations；19cm.

《呼吁世界人民联合起来反对美国帝国主义的种族歧视、支持美国黑人反对种族歧视的斗争的声明》

159. Statement expressing the Chinese people's firm support for the Panamanian people's just, patriotic struggle, Jan. 12, 1964/Mao Tse-tung. Peking：Foreign Languages Press, 1964. 26 pages；19cm.

《毛泽东主席谈话——中国人民坚决支持巴拿马人民的正义斗争》

160. Statements by Mao Zedong：calling on the people of the world to unite to oppose the aggressive and bellicose policies of U. S. imperialism and defend world peace (August 1963—January 1964). Peking：Foreign Languages Press, 1964. 15 pages；19cm.

《毛泽东主席声明、谈话集——全世界人民联合起来,反对美帝国主义的侵略政策和战争政策,保卫世界和平》

161. Four essays on philosophy/Mao Tse-tung. Peking：Foreign Languages Press, 1964. 135 pages, 1 leaf of plates：portrait.

Contents：On practice—On contradiction—On the correct handling of contradictions among the people—Where do correct ideas come from?

《毛泽东的四篇哲学论文》

(1)Peking：Foreign Languages Press, 1966. 135 pages,[1] leaf of plates：portraits；19cm.

(2)2nd ed. Peking：Foreign Languages Press, 1968. 135 pages：portraits；21cm.

162. We must learn to do economic work/Mao Zedong. Peking：Foreign Languages Press, 1965. 9 pages；19cm.

《必须学会做经济工作》

(1)Peking：Foreign Languages Press, 1967. 9 pages

163. Mao Tsetung thought on financial and monetary front. New York：Maud Russell,1969. 16 pages
　　毛泽东关于财经的思想.

164. Get organized! /Mao Tse-tung. Peking：Foreign Languages Press,1965. 11 pages；19cm.
　　《组织起来!》
　　(1)Peking：Foreign Languages Pr. , 1967. 11 pages
　　(2)Peking：Foreign Languages Press, 1968. 11 pages；19cm.

165. The foolish old man who removed the mountains. 1st pocket ed. Peking：Foreign Languages Press, 1965. 5 pages；15cm.
　　《愚公移山》
　　(1)愚公移山/毛泽东著. 北京：商务印书馆, 1965. 16 pages；19cm.
　　英汉对照.
　　(2)[2nd pocket ed.]. Peking：Foreign Languages Press, 1966. 5 pages；15cm.

166. Quotations from chairman Mao Tse-tung. [2nd ed.]. Peking：Foreign Languages Press, 1966. 311 pages；portraits；14cm.
　　《毛主席语录》
　　(1) Quotations from Chairman Mao Tsetung. [2nd ed.]. Peking：Foreign Languages Press, 1967. iii, 311 pages：portraits；14cm.
　　(2)Beijing：Dong fang hong chu ban she, 1967. xv, 589 pages；14cm.
　　(3)1st vest-pocket ed. Peking：Foreign Languages Press, 1968. 311 pages：portraits；10cm.
　　(4)[2nd ed.]. Peking：Foreign Languages Press, 1969. iii, 311 pages：facsimile, portraits；10cm.
　　(5)Peking：Foreign Languages Press, 1972. 311 pages：portraits；13cm. ISBN：083512388X, 0835123884
　　(6) Peking：Foreign Languages Press, 1974. 311 pages：portraits；14cm.
　　(7)[2nd ed.]. Peking：Foreign Languages Press, 1976. iii, 311 pages：portraits；14cm.

167. Quotations from Chairman Mao Tse-tung/edited and with an introductory essay by Stuart R. Schram；introduction by A. Doak Barnett. New ed. New York：Bantam Books, 1966. xxx, 182 pages；18cm.
　　《毛主席语录》
　　(1) Quotations from Chairman Mao Tse-tung/Edited and with an introductory essay and notes by Stuart R. Schram. Foreword by A. Doak Barnett. New York：Praeger, 1967. xxxiv, 182 pages facsimile 22cm.
　　(2)Quotations from Chairman Mao Tse-tung/Introduction by A. Doak Barnett. New York：Bantam Books, 1967. vi, 179 p. facsim. 18cm. (A Bantam extra, PZ3608)
　　(3)Mao Tsê-tung's quotations：the Red Guard's handbook/Zedong Mao. Introd. Stewart Fraser. [Nashville International Center, George Peabody College for Teachers], 1967. xiv, 311 p port 20cm. (Research monographs in international and comparative education)
　　(4)Quotations from Chairman Mao Tse-tung/edited and with an introductory essay by Stuart R. Schram；introd. by A. Doak Barnett. New amplified ed. Toronto；New York：Bantam Books, 1967. xxx, 182 pages；18cm. ISBN：0553100599, 0553100594. (Bantam political science；Q6956)
　　(5)Quotations from Chairman Mao Tse-tung. New York：Bantam Books, 1967. 311 pages；14cm.
　　(6)2nd ed. Detroit：Blake Industries, 1967. iii, 311 pages：portraits；14cm.
　　(7)London：Corgi Books, 1967. 179 pages；17cm.
　　(8) Quotations from Chairman Mao Tse-tung/Edited and with an introductory essay and notes by Stuart R. Schram. Foreword by A. Doak Barnett. New York：Praeger, 1968. xxxiv, 182 pages facsimile 22cm.
　　(9) Quotations from Chairman Mao Tse-tung. Glendale, Calif.：Voice of Americanism, 1969. iv, 96 pages；19cm.
　　(10)[2nd ed.]. New York[Universal-Award House], 1971. 185 pages；18cm. (Award books)
　　(11)New amplified ed. New York：Bantam Books, 1972. xxx, 182 pages：facsimile；19cm.
　　(12)[San Francisco, CA]：[China Books], 1990. 311 pages：portraits；14cm. ISBN：083512388X, 0835123884
　　(13)Collector's ed. Norwalk, Conn.：Easton Press, 1996. xvi, 252 pages：portraits；18cm.
　　(14)Honolulu, Hawaii：University Press of the Pacific, 2005. [viii], 311 pages：portraits；21cm. ISBN：1410224880,1410224880
　　(15)Collector's ed. Dubuque, Iowa：Synergy International of The Americas, 2006. 206 pages；23cm. ISBN：1934568354, 193456835X
　　(16)Miami：BN Publishing, 2007. 111 p. ISBN：097931190X, 0979311901
　　(17)Quotations from Chairman Mao Tse-tung/ foreword by Lin Piao. [Thousand Oaks, CA]：BN Publishing, 2007. 111 pages；25cm. ISBN：0979311901, 097931190X
　　(18)2nd ed. La Vergne, Tenn.：Distributed by Lightning Source, 2009. 311 p.；22cm. ISBN：1409724759, 1409724751
　　(19) Memphis, Tenn.：General Books, 2011. 47

pages；25cm. ISBN：1232461487，1232461482

(20) Quotations from Mao Zedong/Mao Zedong. New York：CN Times Books，2013. vii，237 pages；20cm. ISBN：1627740074，1627740074

168. Supplement to quotations from Chairman Mao Tse-tung/with an introd. by C. P. Fitzgerald. Melbourne：P. Flesch，1969. vii，114 pages，[2] leaves of plates：illustrations；13cm.

《毛主席语录》补编. Fitzgerald, C. P. (Charles Patrick, 1902—1992)编.

169. Annotated quotations from Chairman Mao/(by) John DeFrancis. New Haven；London：Yale University Press, 1975. xi，314 pages；26cm. ISBN：0300017499，0300017496，0300018703，0300018707

Notes：Text in parallel Chinese and Pinyin romanization, introduction and notes in English

《毛主席语录》，DeFrancis, John(1911—2009)编.

170. Quotations from Chairman Mao Tse-tung/Mao Zedong. [United States]：Zhingoora Books，2012. 187 pages，23cm. ，ISBN：1480078543，1480078549

《毛主席语录》

171. Oppose book worship/Mao Tse-tung. Peking：Foreign Languages Press，1966. 17 pages；15cm.

《反对本本主义》

(1)Peking：Foreign Languages Press，1968. 17 pages；15cm.

172. To be attacked by the enemy is not a bad thing but a good thing：on the third anniversary of the founding of the Chinese people's Anti-Japanese Military and Political College，May 26，1939. 1st pocket ed. Peking：Foreign Languages Press，1966. 4 pages；15cm.

《被敌人反对是好事而不是坏事》

(1)[2nd ed.]. Peking：Foreign Languages，1967. 4 pages

173. Serve the people/Mao Tse-tung. Peking：Foreign Languages Press，1966. 7 pages；15cm.

Contains two articles：In memory of Norman Bethune, and Serve the people.

《为人民服务》

(1)Peking：Foreign Languages Press，1967. 7 pages；15cm.

174. Speech at the Chinese Communist Party's National Conference on Propaganda Work：March 12，1957. Peking：Foreign Languages Press；U. S. distributors：China Books & Periodicals, San Francisco，1966. 29 pages；15cm.

《在中国共产党全国宣传工作会议上的讲话》

(1)Peking：Foreign Languages Press，1967. 20 pages；19cm.

(2)Peking：Foreign Languages Press，1968. 30 unnumbered pages；15cm.

175. Where do correct ideas come from? May 1963/Mao Tse-tung. 2nd Pocket ed. Peking：Foreign Languages Press，1966. 3 pages；15cm.

《人的正确思想是从哪里来的?》

176. People of the world，unite and defeat the U. S. aggressors and all their lackeys：statements supporting the American Negroes and the peoples of Southern Vietnam，Panama，Japan，the Congo (L.)，and the Dominican Republic in their just struggle against U. S. imperialism/Mao Zedong. Second (enlarged) edition. Peking：Foreign Languages Press，1966. 16 pages；19cm.

《全世界人民团结起来打败美国侵略者及其一切走狗：关于支持美国黑人、越南南方人民、巴拿马人民、日本人民、刚果(利)人民和多米尼加人民反对美帝国主义的正义斗争的声明和谈话》

(1)[2nd enl. ed.]. Peking：Foreign Languages Press，1967. 16 pages；19cm.

177. People of the world，unite and defeat the U. S. aggressors and all their running dogs，(May 20，1970)/Mao Tsetung. Hong Kong：Life Reader Sinzh Joint Pub. Co. ，1970. 5 pages；13cm.

《全世界人民团结起来打败美国侵略者及其一切走狗》

178. Selected works. London：Lawrence & Wishart，1954—1956. 4 volumes：illustrations；23cm.

Notes："Based on the Chinese edition in four volumes. "

《毛泽东选集》，4 卷.

179. Selected works. New York：International Publishers，1954—1956. 4 volumes 23cm.

Contents：v. 1. 1926—1936. —v. 2. 1937—1938. —v. 3. 1939—1941. —v. 4. 1941—1945.

《毛泽东选集》，4 卷.

180. Selected works of Mao Tse-tung. New York：International Publishers，1954—1962. 5 volumes；22cm.

Contents：v. 1. 1926—1936—v. 2. 1937—1938—v. 3. 1939—1941—v. 4. 1941—1945—v. 5. 1945—1949.

《毛泽东选集》，5 卷.

(1)Mao Tse-tung；selected works，1926—1949. N. Y；International，1954. 5 volumes frontispiece 21cm.

181. Selected works of Mao Tse-tung/Mao Tse-tung. Bombay：People's Pub. House，1956. [4 volumes]；22cm.

《毛泽东选集》，4 卷.

182. Chinese Communist revolutionary strategy，1945—1949；extracts from volume 4 of Mao Tse-tung's Selected works/by S. M. Chiu. [Princeton，N. J.] Center of International Studies，Woodrow Wilson School of Public and International Affairs，Princeton University，1961. 40 pages；28cm. (Princeton University，Center of International Studies. Research monograph；no. 13)

中国共产主义革命的战略：《毛泽东选集》第 4 卷选译.

Chao, Shan-ming 编.

(1) [Ann Arbor], [University Microfilms], 1973. 49 pages; 28cm. (Woodrow Wilson School of Public and International Affairs. Center of International Studies. Research monograph; no. 13)

183. Selected works. Peking：Foreign Languages Press, 1961—1965. 4 volumes portrait 23cm.

Contents：v. 1. The first revolutionary civil war period. The second revolutionary civil war period.—v. 2—3. The period of the war of resistance against Japan.— v. 4. The third revolutionary civil war period.

《毛泽东选集》，4 卷.

(1) Selected works of Mao Tse-tung. Peking：Foreign Languages Press, 1967. 4 volumes; 22cm.

184. Selected works of Mao Zedong. Peking：Foreign Languages Press, 1967—1975. 5 volumes; 22cm.

Contents：v. 1. 1926—1937—v. 2. 1937—1941—v. 3. 1941—1945.—v. 4. 1945—1949.—v. 5. 1949—1957.

Notes：Vols. 1 — 3 are a translation of the second Chinese edition (Peking：People's Publishing House, April, 1960)—Vol. 4—5 are a translation of the first Chinese edition.

《毛泽东选集》，5 卷.

(1) Peking：Foreign Languages Press，1975—1977. 5 volumes; 23cm.

185. Selected works of Mao Tse-tung. Oxford; New York：Distributed throughout the world by Pergamon Press, 1967—1977. 5 volumes; portraits; 23cm. ISBN：0080222625, 0080222622, 0080229824, 0080229829

Contents：v. 1. The first revolutionary Civil War period.—v. 2—3. The period of the war of resistance against Japan.—v. 4. The third revolutionary civil war period.—v. 5. The period of the socialist revolution and socialist construction.

Notes："Translation of the second Chinese edition"— Title page verso.

《毛泽东选集》，5 卷.

186. Selected works of Mao Tse-tung：[translated from the Chinese]/abridged by Bruno Shaw. [Abridged ed.]New York; London：Harper and Row, 1970. xiv, 434 pages, 1 portraits; 21cm. ISBN: 0060901780, 0060901783. (Harper colophon books; CN 178)

Notes：Originally published in 4 v. , Peking：Foreign Languages P. , 1961—65.

《毛泽东选集》，Shaw, Bruno 编.

(1) [Mass.], [Gloucester], [P. Smith], 1976. xiv, 434 pages：portraits; 21cm. (Harper colophon books, CN 178)

187. Selected works of Mao Tse-tung. Honolulu, Hi.：University Press of the Pacific, 2001. 4 v. ; 24cm. ISBN：0898752345(v. 1), 0898752342(v. 1)

毛泽东选集. 4 卷.

188. On new democracy；Talks at the Yenan forum on literature and art；On the correct handling of contradictions among the people；Speech at the Chinese Communist Party's National Conference on Propaganda Work. Pocket edition. Peking：Foreign Languages Press, 1967. 263 pages：illustrations; 14cm.

《新民主主义论，在延安文艺座谈会上的讲话，关于正确处理人民内部矛盾的问题，在中国共产党全国宣传工作会议上的讲话》

(1) Peking：Foreign Languages Press, 1967. 189 pages：portraits; 19cm.

189. Serve the people；In memory of Norman Bethune；The foolish old man who removed the mountains/Mao Zedong. Peking：Foreign Languages Press, 1967. 11 pages；19cm.

《为人民服务，纪念白求恩，愚公移山》

(1) 1st pocket ed. Peking：Foreign Languages Press, 1967. 15 pages; 15cm.

(2) Serve the people, in memory of Norman Bethune, the foolish old man who removed the mountains/ Mao Tse-tung. Beijing：Commercial Press, 1972. 29 pages; 19cm.

(3) Peking：Foreign Languages Press, 1978. 11 pages; 19cm.

190. Why is it that red political power can exist in China？：the struggle in the Chingkang Mountains. On correcting mistaken ideas in the party. A single spark can start a prairie fire/Mao Zedong. Peking：Foreign Languages Press, 1968. 132 pages：portraits; 15cm.

《中国的红色政权为什么能够存在？井冈山的斗争；关于纠正党内的错误思想；星星之火，可以燎原》

191. Five articles/by Chairman Mao Tse-tung. Peking：Foreign Languages Press, 1968. 59 pages：portraits; 11cm.

《毛主席的五篇著作》

(1) 2nd vest-pocket ed. Peking：Foreign Languages Press, 1972. 59 pages：portraits; 11cm.

(2) Peking：Foreign Languages Press, 1976. 59 pages, 1 leaf of plates：portraits; 10cm.

(3) Peking：Foreign Languages Press, 1982. 27 pages, [2] pages of plates：portraits; 19cm.

192. The struggle in the Chingkang Mountains/Mao Tse-tung. Peking：Foreign Languages Press, 1968. 62 pages; 13cm.

《井冈山的斗争》

(1) Peking：Foreign Languages, 1968, 45 pages; 19cm.

193. Win the masses in their millions for the anti-Japanese national united front：May 7, 1937/Mao Tse-tung. Pocket ed. Peking：Foreign Languages Press, 1968. 18 pages; 15cm.

《为争取千百万群众进入抗日民族统一战线而斗争》

(1)Peking：Foreign Languages Press，1968. 13 pages；19cm.

194. Urgent tasks following the establishment of Kuomintang-Communist co-operation, Sept. 29, 1937. [1st Pocket ed.]. Peking：Foreign Languages Press，1968. 20 pages；15cm.

《国共合作成立后的迫切任务》

(1)Peking：Foreign Languages Press，1968. 15 pages；19cm.

195. Interview with the British journalist James Bertram (October 25，1937)/Mao Zedong. Peking：Foreign Languages Press，1968. 18 pages；19cm.

《和英国记者贝特兰的谈话》

(1)1st pocket ed. Peking：Foreign Languages Press，1968. 26 pages；15cm.

196. The May 4th movement：May 1939/Mao Tsetung. 1st pocket ed. Peking：Foreign Languages Press，1968. 7 pages；13cm.

《五四运动》

(1)Peking：Foreign Languages Press，1969. 7 pages；13cm.

197. Recruit large numbers of intellectuals/Mao Zedong. Peking：Foreign Languages Press，1968. 5 pages；15cm.

Notes："This was a decision drafted by Comrade Mao Tse-tung on December 1，1939 for the Central Committee of the Chinese Communist Party. "

《大量吸收知识分子》

198. On the question of political power in the anti-Japanese base areas/Mao Tse-tung. Peking：Foreign Languages Press，1968. 5 pages；15cm.

Notes："This inner-Party directive was issued by Comrade Mao Tse-tung on March 6，1940 on behalf of the Central Committee of the Communist Party of China. "

《抗日根据地的政权问题》

199. Freely expand the anti-Japanese forces and resist the onslaughts of the anti-communist die-hards/Mao Tse-tung. Peking：Foreign Languages Press，1968. 11 pages；15cm.

《放手发展抗日力量，抵抗反共顽固派的进攻》

200. A most important policy/Mao Tse-tung. Peking：Foreign Languages Press，1968. 6 pages；15cm.

Notes："This editorial was written by Comrade Mao Tse-tung on September 7，1942 for the Liberation Daily, Yenan. "

《一个极其重要的政策》

201. The turning point in World War II/Mao Zedong. 1st pocket ed. Peking：Foreign Languages Press，1968. 9 pages；15cm.

《第二次世界大战的转折点》

202. Spread the campaigns to reduce rent, increase production and "support the government and cherish the people" in the base areas/Mao Zedong. Peking：Foreign Languages Press，1968. 9 pages；15cm.

Notes："This inner-Party directive was written by Comrade Mao Tse-tung on October 1，1943 on behalf of the Central Committee of the Communist Party of China. "

《开展根据地的减租、生产和拥政爱民运动》

203. The united front in cultural work/Mao Tse-tung. Peking：Foreign Languages Press，1968. 4 pages；15cm.

《文化工作中的统一战线》

204. On production by the army for its own support and on the importance of the great movements for rectification and for production/Mao Tse-tung. Peking：Foreign Languages Press，1968. 8 pages；15cm.

Notes："This was an editorial written by Comrade Mao Tse-tung on April 27，1945 for the Liberation Daily, Yenan. "

《论军队生产自给，兼论整风和生产两大运动的重要性》

205. Concentrate a superior force to destroy the enemy forces one by one/Mao Tse-tung. Peking：Foreign Languages Press，1968. 8 pages；15cm.

Notes："This inner-Party directive was drafted by Comrade Mao Tse-tung on September 16，1946 for the Revolutionary Military Commission of the Central Committee of the Communist Party of China. "

《集中优势兵力，各个歼灭敌人》

206. Greet the new high tide of the Chinese revolution/Mao Zedong. First pocket edition. Peking：Foreign Languages Press，1968. 17 pages；15cm.

Notes："This inner-Party directive was drafted by comrade Mao Tse-tung on February 1，1947 for the Central Committee of the Communist Party of China. "

《迎接中国革命的新高潮》

207. Manifesto of the Chinese People's Liberation Army/Mao Tse-tung. Peking：Foreign Languages Press，1968. 14 pages；15cm.

Notes："This political manifesto was drafted by Comrade Mao Tse-tung in October 1947 for the General Headquarters of the Chinese People's Liberation Army. "

《中国人民解放军宣言》

208. On the policy concerning industry and commerce/Mao Zedong. Peking：Foreign Languages Press，1968. 4 pages；15cm.

《关于工商业政策》

209. On the great victory in the Northwest and on the new type of ideological education movement in the liberation army/Mao Tse-tung. Peking：Foreign Languages Press，1968. 11 pages；15cm.

《评西北大捷兼论解放军的新式整风运动》

210. A talk to the editorial staff of the Shansi-suiyuan Daily：(April 2，1948)/Mao Zedong. Peking：Foreign Languages Press，1968. 9 pages；15cm.

《对晋绥日报编辑人员的谈话》

211. On the September meeting：circular of the Central Committee of the Communist Party of China/Mao Tse-tung. Peking：Foreign Languages Press，1968. 15 pages；15cm.

Notes：This inner-Party circular was drafted by Comrade Mao Tse-tung on October 10, 1948 for the Central Committee of the Communist Party of China.

《中共中央关于九月会议的通知》

212. Revolutionary forces of the world unite, fight against imperialist aggression! /Mao Zedong. Peking：Foreign Languages Press，1968. 6 pages；15cm.

Notes："This article was written by Comrade Mao Tse-tung in November 1948 in commemoration of the thirty-first anniversary of the October Revolution..."

《全世界革命力量团结起来，反对帝国主义的侵略》

213. Address to the preparatory committee of the new political consultative conference：June 15, 1949/Mao Tse-tung. Peking：Foreign Languages Press，1968. 7 pages；15cm.

《在新政治协商会议筹备会上的讲话》

214. Statement by Comrade Mao Tse-tung, Chairman of the Central Committee of the Communist Party of China, in support of the Afro-American struggle against violent repression：(April 16，1968). Peking：Foreign Languages Press，1968. 4 pages；13cm.

《中国共产党中央委员会主席毛泽东同志支持美国黑人抗暴斗争的声明》

215. How to differentiate the classes in the rural areas：(October 1933)/Mao Tsetung. Peking：Foreign Languages Press，1969. 5 pages；13cm.

《怎样分析农村阶级》

216. Oppose capitulationist activity：(June 30，1939)/Mao Tsetung. Peking：Foreign Languages Press，1969. 12 pages；15cm.

《反对投降活动》

217. The reactionaries must be punished：(August 1，1939)/Mao Tsetung. 1st pocket ed. Peking：Foreign Languages Press，1969. 10 pages；13cm.

《必须制裁反动派》

218. Interview with a New China Daily correspondent on the new international situation/Mao Tsetung. Peking：Foreign Languages Press，1969. 15 pages；13cm.

Notes："The present English translation... has been made from the Chinese text given in the... first edition... of the Selected Works of Mao Tsetung, volume II... 1952."

《关于国际新形势：对新华日报记者的谈话》

219. Overcome the danger of capitulation and strive for a turn for the better：(January 28，1940)/Mao Tsetung. 1st pocket ed. Peking：Foreign Languages Press，1969. 7 pages；13cm.

《克服投降危险，力争时局好转》

220. On the reissue of the three main rules of discipline and the eight points for attention：instruction of the general head quarters of the Chinese People's Liberation Army：October 10，1947/Mao Tsetung. 1st pocket ed. Peking：Foreign Languages Press，1969. 3 pages；13cm.

《中国人民解放军总部关于重新颁布三大纪律八项注意的训令》

(1)中国人民解放军总部关于重新颁布三大纪律八项注意的训令：汉英对照. 北京：商务印书馆，新华书店北京发行所发行，1972. 7 pages；19cm.

221. On the question of the national bourgeoisie and the enlightened gentry：（March 1，1948)/Mao Tsetung. 1st pocket ed. Peking：Foreign Languages Press，1969. 9 pages；13cm.

《关于民族资产阶级和开明绅士问题》

222. The concept of operations for the Liaohsi-Shenyang campaign：(September and October 1948)/Mao Tsetung. First pocket edition. Peking：Foreign Languages Press，1969. 13 pages；13cm.

《关于辽沈战役的作战方针》

223. The concept of operations for the Huaihai campaign：(October 11，1948)/Mao Tsetung. Peking：Foreign Languages Press，1969. 7 pages；13cm.

《关于淮海战役的作战方针》

224. The concept of operations for the Peiping-Tientsin campaign：(December 11，1948)/Mao Tsetung. First pocket edition. Peking：Foreign Languages Press，1969. 10 pages；13cm.

《关于平津战役的作战方针》

225. Collection of statements/by Mao Zedong. Hong Kong, American Consulate General, 1969. 52 leaves 29cm. (Current background；no. 892)

毛泽东声明集.

226. People of Asia, unite and drive the U. S. aggressors out of Asia!：[quotation from Chairman Mao Tsetung]. Peking：Foreign Languages Press，1970. 120 pages，[7] pages of plates：illustrations, portraits；19cm.

《亚洲人民团结起来，把美国侵略者从亚洲赶出去!》，《人民日报》、《红旗》杂志、《解放军报》社论.

227. Six essays on military affairs. Peking：Foreign Languages Press，1971. 393 pages：portraits；16cm.

Contents：Problems of strategy in China's revolutionary war. —Problems of strategy in guerrilla war against Japan. —On protracted war. —Problems of war and strategy. —Concentrate a superior force to destroy the enemy forces one by one. —The present situation and our tasks.

《毛主席的六篇军事著作》

(1)［New ed.］. Beijing：Foreign Languages Press，1972. 393 p.

228. Mao Tse-tung on education/［editor, Peter J. Seybolt］. White Plains, N. Y.：International Arts and Sciences Press, 1974. 101 pages；23cm.（Chinese education, winter 1973—74；v. 6, no. 4）

毛泽东论教育.

229. Five essays on philosophy/Mao Tsetung. Peking：Foreign Languages Press，1977. 156 pages；19cm.

Contents：On practice. —On contradiction. —On the correct handling of contradictions among the people. —Speech at the Chinese Communist Party's National Conference on Propaganda Works. —Where do correct ideas come from?

《毛主席的五篇哲学著作》

230. On the ten major relationships/Mao Tsetung. Peking：Foreign Languages Press，1977. 32 pages；19cm.

《论十大关系》

231. Mao on Stalin：the economics and politics of socialism. Edinburgh：Proletarian Pub. for Communist Formation，1977.［3］,45 pages；21cm. ISBN：0950397210,0950397214

Notes："With a critical introduction by Communist Formation"—Page 4 of cover. / "These texts by Mao Tse-tung were originally translated into English by a United States Government agency, and published by the US Government, along with other texts, in 1974"—Introduction.

毛泽东论斯大林.

232. A critique of Soviet economics/by Mao Tsetung；translated by Moss Roberts；annotated by Richard Levy；with an introd. by James Peck. New York：Monthly Review Press，1977. 157 pages；21cm. ISBN：0853454124, 0853454120

苏联经济批判.

233. The Theory of the Three Worlds. New York：Books New China，1977. 1 volume

三个世界理论.

234. Mao Tsetung on democratic centralism. Porirua［N. Z.］：Struggle Publications，1978. 20 unnumbered pages；29cm.（Struggle；no. 13）

Notes：Talk at an enlarged working conference convened by the Central Committee of the Communist Party of China, January 30,1962, from Peking review, no. 27

论民主集中制.

235. Talk at an enlarged working conference convened by the Central Committee of the Communist Party of China：January 30，1962/Mao Tsetung. Peking：Foreign Languages Press，1978. 35 pages；19cm.

《在扩大的中央工作会议上的讲话》

236. Report from Xunwu/Mao Zedong；translated, and with an introduction and notes by Roger R. Thompson. Stanford, Calif. ：Stanford University Press, 1990. ix, 278 pages,［12］pages of plates；illustrations；23cm. ISBN：0804716781, 0804716789, 0804721823, 0804721820

《寻乌调查》,Thompson, Roger R. 译.

237. Mao Zedong on dialectical materialism：writings on philosophy, 1937/edited by Nick Knight. Armonk, N. Y. ：M. E. Sharpe, 1990. 295 p. ；24cm. ISBN：0873326822,0873326827.（Chinese studies on China）

Contents：Introduction：Soviet Marxism and the development of Mao Zedong's philosophical thought/Nick Knight—Lecture notes on dialectical materialism/Mao Zedong—On practice/Mao Zedong—The law of the unity of contradictions［on contradiction］/Mao Zedong—Extracts from Ai Siqi's Philosophy and life/Mao Zedong—Philosophical annotations and marginalia/Mao Zedong—On Mao, philosophy and ideology/compiled by Nick Knight and Jeff Russell.

毛泽东论辩证唯物主义. Knight, Nick(1947—)编译.

238. A study of physical culture/Mao Zedong. Beijing：People's Sports Publishing House, 1996. 92 pages；22cm. ISBN：7500913117,7500913115

《体育之研究》

239. Mao Zedong on diplomacy/compiled by the Ministry of Foreign Affairs of the People's Republic of China and the Party Literature Research Center under the Central Committee of the Communist Party of China. Beijing：Foreign Languages Press, 1998. viii, 498 p. ；21cm. ISBN：7119011413,7119011417

《毛泽东外交文选》,外交部,中共中央文献研究室.

A3　毛泽东研究相关著作

1. The early revolutionary activities of comrade Mao Tse-tung/by Li Jui；translated by Anthony W. Sariti；edited by James C. Hsiung；introd. by Stuart R. Schram. White Plains, N. Y. ：M. E. Sharpe, c1977. xliii, 355 p. ；24cm. ISBN：0873320700.（China book project）

《毛泽东同志的初期革命活动》,李锐(1917—)；Sariti, Anthony W. 译.

2. Chairman Mao's theory of the differentiation of the three worlds is a major contribution to Marxism-Leninism：People's Daily, November 1，1977/Editorial Dept. of Renmin Ribao. Peking：Foreign Languages Press, 1977. 79 p. ；19cm.

《毛主席关于三个世界划分的理论是对马克思列宁主义的重大贡献》,《人民日报》社.

3. Put Mao Tse-tung's thought in command of everything：new year editorial for 1969/by Renmin Ribao（People's

Daily)，Hongqi（Red Flag）and Jiefangjun Bao（Liberation Army Daily）. Peking：Foreign Languages P. ，1969. 20 pages；13cm.

《用毛泽东思想统帅一切》，1969 年《人民日报》、《红旗》杂志、《解放军报》元旦社论.

4. Mao Tse-tung；his childhood and youth/by Emi Siao. Bombay：People's Pub. House，1953. 76 p. ：illus. ；19cm.

《毛泽东同志的青少年时代》，萧三著.

5. Mao Tse-tung on the Chinese Revolution，etc. Peking：Foreign Languages Press，1953. 86 pages

《毛泽东论中国革命》，陈伯达.

(1) Mao Tse-tung on the Chinese revolution. Second edition，revised translation. Peking：Foreign Languages Press，1963. 73 pages；19cm.

6. Notes on Mao Tse-tung's "Talk with the American correspondent Anna Louise Strong". Peking：Foreign Languages Press，1968. 29 pages；15cm.

《学习〈和美国记者安娜·路易斯·斯特朗的谈话〉》

7. Notes on Mao Tse-tung's "Report on an investigation of the peasant movement in Hunan"/editorial board of Jiefangjun Bao. Peking：Foreign Languages Press，1968. 33 pages；15cm.

《学习〈湖南农民运动考察报告〉》

8. In his mind，a million bold warriors：reminiscences of the life of Chairman Mao Tsetung during the northern Shensi campaign. Peking：Foreign Languages Press，1972. 81 pages：illustrations；19cm.

《胸中自有雄兵百万：记毛主席在陕北战争中》，阎长林著.

9. Mao Tse-tung's thought is the invincible weapon. Peking：Foreign Languages Press，1968. 79 p. ；18cm.

《毛泽东思想是百战百胜的武器》

10. Put Mao Tse-tung's thought in command of everything. Peking：Foreign Languages Press，1969. 19 pages：portraits；13cm.

《用毛泽东思想统帅一切》

11. The Whole country should become a great school of Mao Tse-tung's thought：in commemoration of the 39th anniversary of the founding of the Chinese People's Liberation Army. Peking：Foreign Languages Press，1966. 18 pages；19cm.

《全国都应该成为毛泽东思想的大学校》

12. Chairman Mao's theory of the differentiation of the three worlds is a major contribution to Marxism-Leninism/editorial Dept. of Renmin Ribao（People's daily）. Peking：Foreign Languages Press，1977. [1]，79 pages；19cm.

《毛泽东关于三个世界划分的理论是对马克思列宁主义的重大贡献》

13. Continue the revolution under the dictatorship of the proletariat to the end：a study of volume V of the Selected works of Mao Tsetung/Hua Kuo-feng. Peking：Foreign Languages Press，1977. 39 pages；19cm.

《把无产阶级专政下的继续革命进行到底：学习〈毛泽东选集〉第五卷》，华国锋著.

14. Eternal glory to the great leader and teacher Chairman Mao Tsetung. Peking：Foreign Languages Press，1976. 40 p. ，[1] leaf of plates. ：portr. ；23cm.

《伟大的领袖和导师毛泽东永垂不朽》

15. Mao Zedong：biography，assessment，reminiscences/compiled by Zhong Wenxian. Beijing：Foreign Languages Press；Distributed by China International Book Trading Corp. ，1986. ii，238 pages，[37] pages of plates：illustrations（some color）；23cm. ISBN：083511886X，0835118866

《关于毛泽东：传略·评价·回忆》，钟宪文编.

16. Mao Zedong：man，not god/by Quan Yanchi；[translated by Wang Wenjiong；English text edited by Gale Hadfield]. Beijing：Foreign Languages Press；Distributed by China International Book Trading Corp. ，1992. 213 pages，[4] pages of plates：illustrations；21cm. ISBN：0835127893，0835127899，0835127907，0835127905，7119014447，7119014449，7119014455，7119014456

《走向神坛的毛泽东》，权延赤.

17. The autobiography of Mao Tse-tung/[dictated to Edgar Snow；annotated by Tang Szu-chen]. [dictated to Edgar Snow，annotated by Tang Szu-chen]. [2nd rev. ed.]. Hong Kong，Truth Book Co. ，1949. 51 pages；20cm.

毛泽东自传. 斯诺（Snow，Edgar，1905—1972）记录.

B 类　哲学、宗教

B1　中国哲学

B11　哲学史

1. A history of Chinese philosophy；the period of the philosophers（from the beginnings to circa 100 B. C. ）by Fung Yu-lan. Translated by Derk Bodde，with introd. ，notes，bibliography and index. Peiping，H. Vetch，1937. 455 p. fold. map. 28cm.

《中国哲学史》，冯友兰（1895—1990）著；卜德（Bodde，Derk，1909—2003）（美国汉学家）译.

(1) 2nd. ed. Princeton：Princeton Univ. Press，1973. XXXIV，455 Seiten：Karten. ISBN：0691071144，0691071145

2. The spirit of Chinese philosophy. tr. by E. R. Hughes. London：K. Paul，Trench，Trubner [1947]. xiv，224 p. 21cm.

《新原道：中国哲学之精神》，冯友兰（1895—1990）；休士（Hughes，E. R. 〈Ernest Richard〉，1883—1956）（美国学者）译.

(1) London：Routledge and Kegan Paul，1962. XIV，224 p. ；in-8

(2)Westport, Conn. : Greenwood Press, 1970. XIV, 224 Seiten

(3)London and New York：Routledge,2005. xiv,224 pages；24cm. ISBN：0415361494,0415361491. (China, history, philosophy, economics；5)

3. A history of Chinese philosophy/by Fung Yu-lan；translated by Derk Bodde, with introd. , notes, bibliography and index. Princeton：Princeton University Press，1952—1953. 2 v. fold. map, diagrs. 25cm.

Contents：1. The period of the philosophers from the beginnings to circe 100 B. C. —2. The period of classical learning from the second century B. C. to the twentieth century A. D.

《中国哲学史》，冯友兰（1895—1990）著；卜德（Bodde, Derk, 1909—2003）（美国汉学家）译.

(1)Princeton：Princeton University Press, 1969. 2 volumes：folded map, diagrams；25cm.

(2)Princeton：Princeton University Press, 1983. 2 v. : ill, map；23cm. ISBN：0691020213, 0691071144. (Princeton paperbacks)

(3)Delhi, India：Motilal Banarsidass Publishers, Private Ltd. , 1994. 2 volumes：map, diagrams；23cm. ISBN：8120811615, 8120811614

4. 英汉中国哲学简史 /冯友兰著；赵复三译. 南京：江苏文艺出版社，2012. 687 pages；illustrations；21cm. ISBN：7539946788, 7539946784

英文题名：Short history of Chinese philosophy

(1)中国哲学简史/冯友兰著；赵复三译. 北京：外语教学与研究出版社，2015. 660 页；23cm. ISBN：7513561280.（"博雅双语名家名作"系列）

英文题名：A short history of Chinese philosophy. 英汉对照.

5. Selected philosophical writings of Feng Yu-lan/Feng Yu-lan. Beijing：Foreign Languages Press, 1991. 673 p. ；21cm. ISBN：7119010638, 7119010632, 711901062X, 7119010625, 0835122697, 0835127468

《冯友兰哲学文集》，冯友兰著.

6. A new treatise on the methodology of metaphysics/Fung Yu-lan；translated by Chester C. I. Wang. Beijing：Foreign Languages Press, 1997. 127 pages；21cm. ISBN：7119019475, 7119019473

《中国哲学与形而上学方法新论：新知言》，冯友兰著.

7. The hall of three pines：an account of my life/Feng Youlan；translated by Denis C. Mair. Honolulu：University of Hawaii Press, c2000. xii, 409 p. ；24cm. ISBN：0824814282, 082482220X. (SHAPS library of translations)

《三松堂自序》，冯友兰（1895—1990）；丹尼斯·马尔（Mair, Denis C. ）译.

8. A short history of Chinese philosophy/Hou Wai-lu in collaboration with Chang Chi-Chih, Li Hsueh-Chin；translated by Wang Cheng-Chung. Peking：Foreign Languages Press, 1959. 178 p. ；19cm. (China knowledge series [5])

《中国哲学史略》，侯外庐主编；张岂之等编写；王正中译.

(1)Honolulu, Hawaii：University Press of the Pacific, 2002. 177 p. ISBN：1410200248, 1410200242

9. An outline history of Chinese philosophy/[edited] by Xiao Jiefu, Li Jinquan. Beijing：Foreign Languages Press, 2008. 2 volumes (x, 977 pages)；24cm. ISBN：7119027197, 7119027190. (China studies)

《中国哲学史》，萧萐父，李锦全著.

10. Chinese philosophy：Chinese political philosophy, metaphysics, epistemology and comparative philosophy/Wen Haiming；translated by Wen Haiming. Beijing：China Intercontinental Press, 2010. 152 pages：illustrations (some color), portraits；23cm. ISBN：7508513195, 7508513193. (Cultural China series)

《中国哲学思想》，温海明著. 五洲传播出版社.

11. An intellectual history of China/He Zhaowu [and others]；revised and translated by He Zhaowu. Beijing：Foreign Languages Press, 1991. v, 620 pages；22cm. ISBN：7119000039, 7119000039, 0835118800, 0835118804, 7119000063, 7119000060, 0835118819, 0835118811, 0835123006, 0835123006. (China knowledge series)

《中国思想发展史》，何兆武等著.

(1)Beijing：Foreign Languages Press, 2008. 620 pages；24cm. ISBN：7119052953, 7119052950. （China studies)

12. Chinese philosophy in classical times, edited and translated by E. R. Hughes. London：J. M. Dent & Sons Ltd. ；New York：E. P. Dutton & Co. Inc. [1942]. xiii, [1], 336 p. , 1 l. 18cm. (Everyman's library, Philosophy. [No. 973])

《中国古典哲学》，休士（Hughes, E. R. 〈Ernest Richard〉, 1883—1956）（美国学者）编译.

(1)London：Dent；New York：Dutton [1954]. xiv, 336 p. 19cm. (Everyman's library, 973. Philosophy)

13. Key concepts in Chinese philosophy/Zhang Dainian；translated and edited by Edmund Ryden. Beijing：Foreign Languages Press, 2002. xivi, 532 pages；24cm. ISBN：7119031910, 7119031910. （The culture & civilization of China)

《中国古典哲学概念范畴要论》，张岱年著；赖登译.

14. A critical history of classical Chinese philosophy/by He Zhaowu & Peng Gang. Beijing：New World Press, 2009. 309 pages；illustrations；24cm. ISBN：7510405372, 7510405378

《中国古代哲学批评史》，何兆武，彭刚著. 新世界出版社.

15. Order in early Chinese excavated texts：natural, supernatural, and legal approaches/by Zhongjiang Wang；translated by Misha Tadd. New York：Palgrave

Macmillan，2015. 241pages；23cm. ISBN：1137546968，1137546964

《宇宙、秩序、信仰》，王中江；Tadd，Misha 译. 中国古代哲学研究.

16. Three major struggles on China's philosophical front，1949—1964. Peking：Foreign Languages Press，1973. 66 pages；19cm.

Contents：Three major struggles on China's philosophical front.—The theory of "Synthesized economic base" must be thoroughly criticized.—Momentous struggle on the question of identity between thinking and being.—The theory of "Combine two into one" is a reactionary philosophy for restoring capitalism.

《中国哲学战线上的三次斗争：1949—1964 年》

17. 诸子百家/王佳编著. 合肥：黄山书社，2016. 137 页：彩图，地图；23cm. ISBN：7546141787.（印象中国）

英文题名：The hundred schools of thought. 英汉对照.

18. Tai Chên's inquiry into goodness；a translation of the Yuan Shan，with an introductory essay. Honolulu：East-West Center Press，1971. xi，176 pages facsimiles 23cm. ISBN：0824800931，0824800932

Notes：Originally published in 1969 under title：Tai Chen's Yuan Shan

《戴震〈原善〉研究》，戴震（1724—1777）；成中英（1935—）. 初版于 1969 年. 英汉文本.

19. Intellectual trends in the Chi'ng period（Chi'ng-tai hsüeh-shu kai-lun）translated with introd. and notes by Immanuel C. Y. Hsüh. Foreword by Benjamin I. Schwartz. Cambridge：Harvard University Press，1959. xxii，147，lii p. 24cm.（Harvard East Asian studies，2）

《清代学术概论》，梁启超；徐中约（C. Y. Hsu，1923—2005）译.

20. Philosophy is no mystery：peasants put their study to work. Peking：Foreign Languages Press，1972. 74 pages：illustrations；20cm.

《哲学的解放》

21. 人心三百态：英汉对照/李义堂著；何友编译. 北京：北京工艺美术出版社，2007. 2 册：21cm. ISBN：7805266312，780526631X.（图说心气）

英文题名：Three hundred moods of human beings annotated with dicta & paintings. 本书总结了生活中人心和人气的各种状态，以优美的线描图，配以富有哲理的名言警句，是一本适合广大读者的休闲读物.

22. The Chinese dream：real-life stories of the young in contemporary China/by An Dun. Beijing：New World Press，2008. 3，243 pages：illustrations；24cm. ISBN：7802285644，780228564X

《一百个中国人的梦：中国青年生活实录》，安顿著. 新世界出版社. 介绍人生观的青年读物，通过介绍 11 个年龄在 16～40 岁的中国青年的人生成长和梦想的实现，告诉读者正确的人生观、哲学观.

B2　中国历代哲学著作与研究

注：以下出版的英译中国古代经典著作，少数标注了中文题名的以实际名称注明，其余无中文题名的统一冠以相应的题名，如《易经》《论语》《孙子兵法》等.

B21　总　论

1. Three Chinese philosophers，or，The door to all spirituality：studies from the Yellow Emperor，Lao Tze，and the poet，Shao Yung in English and Chinese for students studying English/translated by A. J. Brace. ［Chengtu，West China］：［publisher not identified］，1932. 188 pages；22cm.

Brace，A. J. 译，包括对《道德经》和邵雍（1011—1077 年）作品的选译. 英汉对照.

2. A source book in Chinese philosophy. Princeton，N. J.：Princeton University Press，1963. xxv，856 p.；25cm.

《中国哲学文献选编》，陈荣捷（Chan，Wing-tsit，1901—1994）（美国华裔学者）编译.

（1）Princeton，N. J.：Princeton University Press，1969. xxv，856 pages；21cm. ISBN：0691019649，0691019642

（2）Princeton，N. J.：Princeton University Press，1973. xxv，856 pages；21cm. ISBN：0691019649，0691019642，0691071373，0691071374

3. Selected essays on the study of philosophy by workers，peasants and soldiers. Peking：Foreign Languages Press，1971. 83 pages；19cm.

《工农兵学哲学文选》

4. 汉英对照中国哲学名著选读/石峻主编. 北京：中国人民大学出版社，2009. 397 页；21cm. ISBN：7300104164，7300104169

英文题名：Selected readings from Chinese philosophers：with annotations and English translation.

B22　先秦哲学

B221　诸子前哲学

B221.1　周易

1. I ching ＝ Yijing：the book of change/translated with an introduction and commentary by John Minford. New York：Viking，2014. lxv，855 pages；25cm. ISBN：0670024698，0670024694

《易经》，闵福德（Minford，John.，1946—）（英国汉学家）译.

（1）Penguin Classics deluxe edition. New York：Penguin Books，2015. lxv，855 pages：illustrations；20cm. ISBN：0143106929，0143106920，0670024694，0670024698

2. I ching mandalas：a program of study for the Book of changes/translated and edited by Thomas Cleary. Boston：Shambhala；［New York］：distributed in the U. S. by Random House，1989. viii，113 p.；23cm. ISBN：

0877734186，0877734185.（Shambhala dragon editions）
《易经》，Cleary，Thomas F.（1949—）（美国翻译家）编译.
是一部通俗读物.

3. I Ching: The book of change/a complete & unabridged translation by Thomas Cleary. Boston, Mass.：Shambhala Publications, 1992. xx, 169 p.；12cm. ISBN：0877736618, 0877736615. (Shambhala pocket classics)
《易经》，Cleary，Thomas F.（1949—）（美国翻译家）编译.
是一部通俗读物.

(1) 1st mass market ed. Boston, Mass.；London：Shambhala, 2006. xvi, 118 pages：illustrations；18cm. ISBN：1590304037, 1590304039

4. I Ching = The classic of changes/translated with an introduction and commentary by Edward L. Shaughnessy. New York：Ballantine Books, 1997. x, 349 p.；25cm. ISBN：0345362438. (Classics of ancient China)
《易经》，夏含夷（Shaughnessy，Edward L.，1952—）（美国汉学家）译. 根据马王堆《易经》抄本翻译.

(1) 1st trade paperback ed. New York：Ballantine Books, 1998. x, 348 p.；21cm. ISBN：0345421124, 0345421128. (Classics of ancient China)

5. I Ching：the book of change/translated by David Hinton. New York：Farrar, Straus and Giroux, 2015. 1 volume.；24cm. ISBN：0374220907, 1466848528
《易经》，戴维·欣顿（Hinton，David，1954—）（美国汉学家）译.

6. I ching；Book of changes/translated by James Legge. 2nd ed. New York：Dover Publications [1963]. xxi, 448 p. 22cm. (The Sacred books of the East, v. 16)
Notes："Except for the new material added by the editors, the text... is that published in a second edition of 1899... as volume XVI of The sacred books of the East and also designated as part II of the The texts of Confucicianism."
《易经》，理雅各（Legge，James，1815—1897）（英国汉学家）译. 翟楚（Ch'u Chai，1906—1986），翟文伯（Winberg Chai）合编. 首版于 1899 年.

(1) Edited with introd. and study guide by Ch'u Chai with Winberg Chai. New Hyde Park, N. Y.，University Books [c1964]. ci, 448 p. illus.；25cm.

(2) Edited and with an introd. by Raymond Van Over. Based on the translation by James Legge. New York：New American Library [1971]. 444 p. illus.；18cm. (A Mentor book)

(3) New York：Causeway Books, c1973. 444 p.，[3] leaves of plates：ill.；25cm. ISBN：0883560003, 0883560006

(4) Secaucus, N. J.：Citadel Press, 1975. xxix, 448 pages：illustrations；23cm. ISBN：0806504587, 0806504582

(5) Singapore：Graham Brash, 1990. 448 pages：illustrations；22cm. ISBN：9971492008, 9971492007

(6) New York：Gramercy Books, 1996. xxv, 448 p.：ill.；24cm. ISBN：0517149907, 0517149904

(7) [Place of publication not identified]：Kessinger Pub.，2003. 448 pages；illustrations；28cm. ISBN：076617672X, 0766176720

(8) Radford, VA：Wilder Publications, 2007. 363 pages：illustrations；23cm. ISBN：1604590364, 160459036X

(9) [California]：CreateSpace, 2008. 240 pages：illustrations；26cm. ISBN：1438259635, 1438259638

(10) I Ching：the book of changes；bold-faced answers to eternal questions of life, love, and career/translated and with the original introduction by James Legge；edited by Laura Ross. New York：Sterling，[2011]. 528 pages；16cm. ISBN 1402786495

7. Yi jing：the Chinese book of changes/arranged from the work of James Legge by Clae Waltham. New York：Ace Pub. Corp.，1969. 349 pages；18cm. (Ace book)
《易经》，理雅各（Legge，James，1815—1897）（英国汉学家）译；Waltham，Clae 编.

8. I ching for the millions/Edward Albertson. Los Angeles, Sherbourne Press, 1969. 188 pages；22cm. (For the millions series, FM 29)
《易经》，Albertson，Edward 译.

9. Yijing, shamanic oracle of China：a new Book of change/translated with commentary by Richard Bertschinger. London；Philadelphia：Singing Dragon, 2012. 335 pages：illustrations；26cm. ISBN：1848190832, 1848190832
《易经》，Bertschinger，Richard 译.

10. Yi jing：the Book of Change/A new translation of the ancient Chinese text with detailed instructions for its practical use in divination, by John Blofeld. London：George Allen & Unwin, 1965. 228 pages：illustrations；23cm.
《易经》，普乐道（Blofeld，John，1913—1987）（英国汉学家）译.

(1) New York：Dutton [1966, c1965]. 228 p. 23cm.

(2) New York：E. P. Dutton, 1968. 228 pages：illustrations；18cm. ISBN：0525472126, 0525472124. (A Dutton Paperback)

(3) 2nd ed. London：Allen & Unwin, 1968. 228 pages：illustrations；22cm. ISBN：0041810015, 0041810011

(4) 2nd ed. London：Mandala Books, 1978. 228 p. ISBN：004181021X, 0041810219

(5) London：Mandala, 1984. 228 pages：illustrations；20cm. ISBN：0041810260, 0041810264, 004181021X, 0041810219

(6) London：Unwin Paperbacks, 1989. 228 pages；20cm. ISBN：0041810260, 0041810264

(7) New York：Arkana, 1991. 228 pages：illustrations；20cm. ISBN：0140193359, 0140193350

(8) New York：Penguin Compass, 2002. 228 pages：

illustrations；20cm. ISBN：0140193359, 0140193350

11. The I ching; or, Book of changes. The Richard Wilhelm translation/rendered into English by Cary F. Baynes. Foreword by C. G. Jung. ［New York］：Pantheon Books ［1950］. 2 v. 24cm. (Bollingen series，19)

《易经》，卫礼贤（Richard Wilhelm，1873—1930）（德国汉学家）德译；贝恩斯（Baynes，Cary F.）（英国翻译家）英译.

(1) 2nd ed. ［New York］：Pantheon Books ［1961，c1950］. xlii，395，376 p.；24cm. (Bollingen series，19)

(2) Pref. to the 3rd ed. by Hellmut Wilhelm. ［3rd ed.］. ［Princeton，N. J.］：Princeton University Press ［1967］. lxii，740 p.；21cm. (Bollingen series，19)

(3) ［London］，Routledge & K. Paul，1968. 2 v. 23cm.

(4) preface to the third edition by Hellmut Wilhelm. 3rd ed. London：Routledge & K. Paul，1968. lxii，740 p. fold. plate. 21cm. ISBN：071001581X

(5) 3rd ed. Princeton，N. J.：Princeton University Press，1977. lxii，740 pages；21cm. ISBN：069109750X, 0691097503. (Bollingen series；19)

(6) London；New York：Arkana，1989. ixii，740 pages：illustrations；20cm. ISBN：0140194088, 0140194081, 0140192077, 0140192070

(7) London：Penguin，1997. lxii，739 pages；20cm. ISBN：0140192077, 0140192070

(8) ［3rd ed.］. ［Princeton，N. J.］：Princeton University Press，1997. lxii，740 pages；21cm. (Bollingen series；19)

12. The Pocket I ching：the Richard Wilhelm translation/rendered into English by Cary F. Baynes；edited and simplified by W. S. Boardman. London：Arkana，1984. xiii，130 pages；20cm. ISBN：1850630003, 1850630005

《易经》，卫礼贤（Wilhelm，Richard，1873—1930）德译；Boardman，W. S. 英译.

(1) London；New York：Arkana，1987. xiii，130 pages；20cm. ISBN：014019049X, 0140190496

13. Yi Jing/translated by Richard Wilhelm. Rochester：Grange，2001. 128 pages：illustrations；21cm. ISBN：1840134747, 1840134742

《易经》，卫礼贤（Richard Wilhelm，1873—1930）（德国汉学家）译.

14. Creative energy；being an introduction to the study of the Yih king, or Book of changes, with translations from the original text, by I. Mears, and L. E. Mears. London：J. Murray，［1931］. xxiii，239，［1］ p. diagrs. 19cm.

Notes："The first portion of the text of the Yih king—a literal translation of the fifty-seven paragraphs (in nine groups) relative to K'ien, with explanatory notes appended to each of the groups"；p. 126—226.

《易经》（选译），Mears，I. 和 Mears，L. E. 合译.

15. The I ching, or, Book of changes：a guide to life's turning points/Brian Browne Walker. New York：St. Martin's Press，1992. ix，133 p. ：ill. ；22cm. ISBN：031207798X

《易经》，Walker，Brian Browne 译.

16. The text of Yi king（and its appendixes）Chinese original，with English translation by Z. D. Sung. Shanghai：China Modern Education Co. ，1935. xvi，369，ii pages：diagrams；19cm.

《易经》，沈仲涛译. 英汉对照.

(1) New York：Paragon Book Reprint Corp. ，1969. xvi，369，ii p. illus. 20cm.

(2) Taipei：Cheng Wen Pub. Co. ，1971. xvi，369，ii pages；20cm.

(3) Táiběi：Wén Huá TúShū Gōng Sī，1973. xvi，369 pages：illustrations；20cm.

(4) 台北：文化图书公司，1980. xvi，369 pages：illustrations；20cm.

(5) 台北：文化图书公司，［1994］. 12，369 pages，ii. ；22cm.

17. I Ching, the oracle/［edited and translated by］Kerson Huang. Singapore：World Scientific，1984. ［5］，180 pages：illustrations；24cm. ISBN：9971966247, 9971966249, 9971966255, 9971966256

Notes：Text of Yi jing in Chinese, parallel English translation

《易经》，Huang，Kerson（1928—）译. 中英对照.

(1) I ching/by Kerson Huang and Rosemary Huang. New York：Workman Pub. ，1987. 207 pages：illustrations；23cm. ISBN：0894803190, 0894803192

(2) Revised edition. Hackensack，NJ：World Century；Singapore：World Scientific，2014. xiv，192 pages：illustrations；24cm. ISBN：9814522600, 9814522601, 9814522627, 9814522625

18. The complete I ching：the definitive translation/by the Taoist Master Alfred Huang. Rochester，Vt. ：Inner Traditions，1998. xxxiii，539 pages：illustrations；24cm. ISBN：0892816562, 0892816569

《易经》，Huang，Alfred 译.

(1) Rochester，Vt. ：Inner Traditions，2004. xxvi，539 pages：illustrations；24cm. ISBN：0892811455, 0892811458, 0892816562, 0892816569

19. Tai Chi, a way of centering and I ching；a book of oracle imagery/in a new translation by Gia-fu Feng and Jerome Kirk. Photos. by Hugh L. Wilkerson. With forewords by Alan W. Watts and Laura Huxley. ［New York］：Macmillan，1970. 155 pages：illustrations；29cm. ISBN：0020761309, 0020761303. (Collier books)

《易经》，Feng，Gia-fu 和 Kirk，Jerome 合译.

20. The laws of change：I ching and the philosophy of life/Jack M. Balkin. New York：Schocken Books，2002. xiii，655

pages：illustrations；25cm. ISBN：080524199X，0805241990
Balkin, J. M. 著. 包括对《易经》的翻译.

21. I ching：the classic Chinese oracle of change：the first complete translation with concordance ＝［Chou i］/ translated by Rudolf Ritsema and Stephen Karcher. Shaftesbury, Dorset；Rockport, Mass. ：Element，1994. 816 pages：illustrations；24cm. ISBN：1852305363， 1852305369，1852306696，1852306694
《易经》，Ritsema, Rudolf 和 Karcher, Stephen L. 合译.
(1) New York：Barnes & Noble，1995. 816 pages；24cm. ISBN：156619945X，1566199452

22. Yi jing/translated by Wu Jing-Nuan. Washington, D. C. ：Taoist Center；Honolulu, Hawaii：Distributed by University of Hawaii Press，1991. 297 pages：illustrations；24cm. ISBN：0824813626，0824813628. (Asian spirituality, Taoist studies series)
《易经》，Wu, Jing-Nuan(1933—)译.

23. How to consult the I ching, the oracle of change/Alfred Douglas；illustrated by David Sheridan. New York：G. P. Putnam's Sons，1971. 251 pages：illustrations；22cm. ISBN：0575005998，0575005990
Notes：British ed. published under title：The oracle of change. Includes English translation of the I ching.
Douglas, Alfred 著,包括对《易经》的翻译.
(1)New York, N. Y. ：Berkely Pub. Co. ，1971. 251 pages：illustrations；20cm. ISBN：425034704
(2)Markham, Ont. ：Penguin Books，1972. 238 p.

24. Embracing change：postmodern interpretations of the I ching from a Christian perspective/Jung Young Lee. Scranton：University of Scranton Press，1994. 251 pages：illustrations；24cm. ISBN：0940866234，0940866232
《易经》，Lee, Jung Young 译.

25. The book of changes (Zhouyi)：a Bronze Age document/ translated with introduction and notes by Richard Rutt. Richmond, Surrey：Curzon，1996. xii, 497 pages：illustrations, map；24cm. ISBN：0700704671，0700704675. (Durham East-Asia series；no. 1；)
《易经》，Rutt, Richard 译注.
(1) Richmond, Surrey：Curzon，2002. xii, 497 pages：illustrations, map；23cm. ISBN：070071491X，0700714919, 0700704671, 0700704675. (Durham East-Asia series；no. 1)

26. Unearthing the changes：recently discovered manuscripts of the Yi Jing (I Ching) and related texts/Edward L. Shaughnessy. New York：Columbia University Press，2014. xxii, 335 pages：illustrations；27cm. ISBN：0231161848, 0231161840, 0231533306, 0231533300. (Translations from the Asian classics)
《易经》，Shaughnessy, Edward L. (1952—)译. 译自阜阳汉简《周易》.

27. The original I ching：an authentic translation of The book of changes/Margaret J. Pearson. North Clarendon, VT：Tuttle Pub. ，2011. 256 pages；21cm. ISBN：0804841818, 0804841810
《易经》，Pearson, Margaret 译.

28. The essentials of the yi jing：translated, annotated, and with an introduction and notes/Chung Wu. St. Paul, Minn. ：Paragon House，2003. lxix, 566 pages：illustrations；24cm. ISBN：1557788278, 1557788276
《易经》，Wu, Chung(1919—)译.
(1)The essentials of the Yi Jing (I Ching)/Chung Wu. New York：Paragon House；Northam：Roundhouse, 2004. 640 pages：illustrations；23cm. ISBN：1557788278, 1557788276

29. I Ching：the shamanic oracle of change/translated by Martin Palmer and Jay Ramsay with Zhao Xiaomin；calligraphy by Kwok Man Ho. London；San Francisco：Thorsons，1995. 261 pages：illustrations, map；24cm. ISBN：1855384167, 1855384163. (Classics of Chinese wisdom)
《易经》，Palmer, Martin, Ramsay, Jay, Zhao, Xiaomin 合译.

30. I ching；the book of changes/translated by Frank J. MacHovec with illus. by Marian Morton. Mount Vernon, N. Y. , Peter Pauper Press，1971. 63 pages：color illustrations；19cm.
《易经》，MacHovec, Frank J. 译.

31. Understanding the I ching/Cyrille Javary；translated by Kirk McElhearn. Boston：Shambhala，1997. xv, 134 pages：illustrations；19cm. ISBN：1570622272,1570622274
Javary, Cyrille 著，McElhearn, Kirk 英译,包括《易经》的翻译.

32. Total I Ching：myths for change/Stephen Karcher. London：Piatkus，2009. 451 pages：illustrations；20cm. ISBN：0749939809, 074993980X
Notes："First published in Great Britain in 2003 by Time Warner Books"—Title page verso
《易经》，Karcher, Stephen L. 译.
(1)London：Piatkus，2013. xii,451 pages：illustrations；20. ISBN：0749939809, 074993980X

33. Chou Yi：the oracle of encompassing versatility/ translated from the Chinese and edited by Rudolf Ritsema and Stephen L. Karcher. Ascona：Eranos Foundation,1999. 3 vol. ISBN：395200541X,3952005415, 3952005428, 3952005422, 3952005436, 3952005439
《易经》，Ritsema, Rudolf 和 Karcher, Stephen L. 合译.

34. Rediscovering the I ching/Gregory Whincup. New York：St. Martin's Griffin，1996. viii, 237 pages；24cm. ISBN：0312141319, 0312141318
《易经》，Whincup, Gregory 译.

35. I ching coin prediction/Liu Da. New York：Harper &

Row，1975. xiii，170 pages；21cm. ISBN：0060616649，0060616656

Notes：Includes an English translation of the text of the I ching.

Liu Da 著，包括对《易经》的英译.

(1)London：Routledge and Kegan Paul，1975. xiii，170 pages：illustrations；23cm. ISBN：071008188X，0710081889，0710081936，0710081933

36. I ching clarified：a practical guide/by Mondo Secter. Boston：Charles E. Tuttle Co.，1993. xxvii，172 pages：illustrations；22cm. ISBN：0804818029，0804818025. (Tuttle library of enlightenment)

Secter，Mondo(1941—)著，对《易经》作了选译.

37. Divination，order，and the Zhouyi/Richard Gotshalk. Lanham：University Press of America，1999. x，418 pages：illustrations；24cm. ISBN：0761813152，0761813156

《易经》，Gotshalk，Richard 译.

38. The Book of change：how to understand and use the I ching/Neil Powell. London：Orbis，1979. 89 pages：illustrations；30cm. ISBN：085613063X，0856130632

Powell，Neil(1928—2014)著，对《易经》作了选译.

(1)London：Macdonald & Co.，1988. 89 pages：illustrations，some color；30cm. ISBN：0748102043，0748102044

39. An exposition of the I-ching，or Book of changes/by Wei Tat. Taipei，Taiwan：Institute of Cultural Studies，1970. xliii，565 pages：illustrations (1 folded)；26cm.

《易经》，韦达(Wei，Tat)译.

(1)Rev. ed. Hong Kong：Pr. by Dai Nippon Printing Co.，1977. xliii，597 pages：illustrations，1 folded leaf of plates，1 color portraits；27cm.

40. The fortune teller's I ching/Kwok Man Ho，Martin Palmer，and Joanne O'Brien. New York：Ballantine Books，1987. 232 pages：illustrations；23cm. ISBN：0345345398，0345345394

《易经》，Kwok，Man-Ho（1943—），Palmer，Martin，O'Brien，Joanne(1959—)合译，中英对照.

(1)Hertfordshire［England］：Wordsworth，1993. 232 pages：illustrations；23cm. ISBN：1853269964，1853269967

41. The I Ching or book of changes：a guide to life's turning points/Brian Browne. Walker. London：Piatkus，1993. ix，133 pages. ISBN：0749912650，0749912659

《易经》，Walker，Brian Browne 译.

42. The illustrated book of changes/Li Yan yi hui. Beijing：Foreign Languages Press，1997. vi，456 pages：illustrations；20cm. ISBN：7119019910，7119019918，7119019902，7119019901

《易经画传》，李燕(1943—)译绘.

43. The book of changes and the unchanging truth＝Tian di bu yi zhi jing/by Ni，Hua Ching. Malibu，Calif.：Shrine

of the Eternal Breath of Tao；Los Angeles，CA：College of Tao and Traditional Chinese Healing，1983. vi，732 pages，［1］leaf of plates：illustrations；24cm. ISBN：068684582X，0686845829

《天地不易之经》，Ni，Hua Ching 译.

(1)2nd ed. Malibu，Calif.：Shrine of the Eternal Breath of Tao；Los Angeles：College of Tao and Traditional Chinese Healing，1990. v，669 pages：illustrations；25cm. ISBN：0937064297，0937064290

(2)Revised edition. Santa Monica，CA：Tao of Wellness，Sevenstar Communications，1994. v，671，［22］pages：illustrations；24cm. ISBN：0937064815，0937064818

(3)2nd ed. Santa Monica，Calif.：Sevenstar Communications，1997. v，671，［22］pages：illustrations；24cm. ISBN：0937064815，0937064818

44. The Yi jing/interpreted by Wu Wei. Los Angeles，Calif.：Power Press，1995. xxiii，274 pages；19cm. ISBN：0943015073，0943015071

《易经》，Wu Wei 译.

45. The original I Ching oracle：the pure and complete texts with concordance/translated under the auspices of the Eranos Foundation by Rudolf Ritsema and Shantena Augusto Sabbadini. London：Watkins；New York：Distributed in the USA and Canada by Sterling Pub. Co.，2007. ISBN：1905857050，1905857055

《易经》，Ritsema，Rudolf 和 Sabbadini，Shantena Augusto 合译.

46. The Yi jing：text and annotated translation/modern Chinese translation by Liu Dajun and Lin Zhongjun；English translation by Fu Youde；revision by Frank Lauran. Jinan，China：Shandong Friendship Pub. House，1995. 2，141 pages；21cm. ISBN：7805516960，7805516967

《易经》，Liu Dajun，Lin Zhongjun 中文注释；Fu Youde 英译；Lauran，Frank 校对. 济南：山东友谊出版社.

47. I ching. Book of change. A new simplified version in verse，combining the original text and commentaries into one easily consulted decision for divination/by Chin Lee and Kay Wong. Tujunga，Calif.：K. King Co.，1971. iii，97 pages：illustrations；22cm.

《易经》，Lee，Chin(1923—)和 Wong，Kay(1918—)著. 含对《易经》的英译.

48. The I ching/A new translation of the book of changes by the master therion Aleister Crowley；edited for Level Press by Shepard. San Francisco：Level Press，1974. 92 unnumbered pages：illustrations，diags.，charts；22cm.

《易经》，Crowley，Aleister(1875—1947)译.

49. The Zhou book of change/translated into modern Chinese by Fu Huisheng；translated into English by Fu Huisheng. 济南：山东友谊出版社，2000. 3，3，14，27，

409 pages；21cm. ISBN：7806422919，7806422915. (儒学经典译丛＝Translations of Confucian classics)

《周易》，傅惠生(1955—)今译与英译. 英汉对照.

50. 周易/张善文今译；傅惠生英译. Changsha：Hunan ren min chu ban she，2008. 2 volumes；24cm. ISBN：7543853300，7543853302. (大中华文库＝Library of Chinese classics)

英文题名：Zhou book of change

51. The astrology of I Ching/translated from the "Ho map lo map rational number" manuscript by W. K. Chu；edited and commentaries added by W. A. Sherrill. New York：Arkana/Penguin Books，1993. ix，451 pages：illustrations；20cm. ISBN：0140194398，0140194395

《河洛理数》，Chu, Wen-kuang(1934—1986)译；Sherrill, W. A. (Wallace Andrew)编注.

52. I Ching：the book of change/a translation by John Blofeld；foreword by Lama Anagarika Govinda. London：Unwin Paperbacks，1986. 227 pages；21cm. ISBN：0041810260，0041810264

《易经》，Blofeld, John 译.

53. Book of changes, with Biblical references/compiled and translated by Samuel Yang. Adelphi, Md. ：Advanced Technology and Research，1973. 136 pages；21cm.

《易经》，Yang, Samuel 编译.

54. Language of the lines：the I Ching Oracle/Nigel Richmond. London：Wildwood House，1977. [5]，178 pages：illustrations；21cm. ISBN：0704502992，0704502994，0704502984，0704502987

《易经》，Richmond, Nigel 译.

(1)2nd ed. [Stroud]：N. Richmond，1985. 166 pages：illustrations 1 color；30cm.

55. I ching/Chris Marshall. Chippendale, N. S. W. ：Pan Macmillan，1994. 160 pages：illustrations, samples；28cm. ISBN：0732908051，0732908058

《易经》，Marshall, Chris 译.

56. Book chameleon：a new version in verse/by C. F. Russell. [Place of publication not identified]：C. F. Russell，1940. 66 pages：illustrations；16cm.

《易经》(选译)，Russell, C. F. (Charles Frank, 1882—)著译.

(1)2nd ed. Los Angeles：C. F. Russell，1967. xx，163 pages；22cm.

57. I ching：the Book of changes：an authentic Taoist translation/by John Bright-Fey. [Birmingham, Ala.]：Sweetwater Press，2006. 159 pages：illustrations；18cm. ISBN：1581735420，1581735421

《易经》(选译)，Bright-Fey, J. (John)译.

58. Yi jing：the book of changes/a new translation by Asa Bonnershaw. Santa Barbara：Bandanna Books，1986. 106 pages；93 mm. ISBN：0942208005，0942208009. (Little humanist classics；1)

《易经》，Bonnershaw, Asa 译.

59. The illuminated I Ching/by Flora Beresford. Hornsby, N. S. W. ：R. Hutchison Publishing，2013. 268 pages：colour illustrations, portraits；25cm. ISBN：0975817735

《易经》，Beresford, Flora(1915—1984)译.

60. Book of change/executive editor, Joyce Du. Vancouver：Chiao Liu Pub. (Canada) Inc. ，2008. [32], 731 pages：illustrations；21cm. ISBN：0978275396，097827539X. (中华文化智慧系列＝Wisdom of Chinese culture series；no. 2)

《易经》，Du, Joyce 主编.

61. I ching：a new translation/[translated and annotated by] Titus Yu, Douglas Flemons. [British Columbia]：Simon Fraser University, Department of Interdisciplinary Studies，1983. 225 pages：illustrations；28cm.

《易经》，Flemons, Douglas G. 和 Yu, Titus 合译.

62. The sun, the moon, and the trigrams/Yang Zhouming；translated with an introduction by Marion Yang. Alhambra, CA：Marion Yang，1998. 145 pages：illustrations；20cm. ISBN：096634071X，0966340716

《易经》，Yang, Zhouming(1943—)著；Yang, Marion 译.

63. A translation of the Confucian [I ching]；or, the Classic of change/with notes and appendix by the Rev. Canon McClatchie. Shanghai：American Presbyterian Mission Press，1906. x，xvii，455 pages：illustrations；20cm.

《易经》，McClatchie, Thos. (Thomas, —1886)译. 英汉对照. 首版于1876年.

(1)Taipei：Ch'eng Wen Pub. Co，1973. x，xvii，455 pages：diagrams；20cm.

64. The basic Yi jing, oracle of change/Dany Chin & Budhy Chen. Amsterdam：Olive Press，2008. xl，427 pages：illustrations；22cm. ISBN：9077787186，9077787182

《易经》，Chin, Dany 和 Chen, Budhy 著.

65. The man of many qualities：a legacy of the I ching/R. G. H. Siu. Cambridge, Mass. ：MIT Press，1968. xv，463 pages；21cm. ISBN：0262190478，0262190473，0262690306，0262690300

Notes：Includes an English translation of the text of the I ching.

Siu, R. G. H. (Ralph Gun Hoy, 1917—)著，包括对《易经》的翻译.

66. Portable dragon：the western man's guide to the I ching/by R. G. H. Siu. Cambridge, Mass. ：M. I. T. Press，1968. xv，463 pages；21cm. ISBN：026219047，026269030，0026219047，0026690030

Notes：Originally published under the title：The man of many qualities：a legacy of the I ching. /Includes an English translation of the text of the I ching

《易经》，Siu, R. G. H. (Ralph Gun Hoy, 1917—)著，包括对《易经》的翻译.

67. I-Ching/written by Jayme F. Simmons；illustrated by

Bob Burns; edited by Ken White. [Place of publication not identified]: Dynamic Design, 1972. 64 pages: illustrations; 22cm. +3 hexogram coins.

《易经》, Simmons, Jayme F. 译.

68. The book of changes = Yi Jing, word by word. volume one/translation and commentary by Bradford Hatcher. Nucla, Colo.: Hermetica. info., 2009. 578 pages; 23cm. ISBN: 0982419113, 0982419112

Notes: Two literal English translations: one simple, one complex, the Chinese test and a Pinyin transcription.

《易经》, Hatcher, Bradford 译.

69. 中英对照易经话解/张成秋著. 新竹市: [Selbstverlag], 2009. 351 p. ISBN: 95741675204

英文题名: An exposition of "Book of changes" in Chinese and English compare

70. Changing: Zhouyi: the heart of the Yijing: a translation and commentary/by Liu Ming. Oakland, CA: Da Yuan Circle, 2005. vi, 169 p.: ill.; 24cm. ISBN: 0976751208, 0976751205

《易》, Liu, Ming 译注.

71. 易经新译/罗志野译; 王贤才审校. 青岛: 青岛出版社, 1995. 5, 8, 6, 258 pages; 21cm.

英汉对照.

72. 英译易经 = Book of change/汪榕培, 任秀桦. 上海: 上海外语教育出版社, 1993. iii, 131 pages; 21cm. ISBN: 7810098322, 7810098328

(1)上海: 上海外语教育出版社, 2007. 131 页; 24cm. ISBN: 7544604635, 7544604632. (外教社中国文化汉外对照丛书. 外教社中国文化汉外对照丛书)

73. The illustrated Book of changes/written and illustrated by Zhou Chuncai; translated by Paul White; [edited by Li Shujuan]. Beijing, China: New World Press, 2010. 263 pages: illustrations; 24cm. ISBN: 1592650934, 1592650937, 7510408472, 7510408474. (The illustrated Chinese classics series)

《易经图典》, 周春才著绘. 新世界出版社.

74. 易经新注: 中英双语本 = Yijing or book of changes: a new translation with annotations/邵乃读译; Carl Waluconis 校译. Beijing: Zhong yi chu ban she, 2017. xviii, 364 pages: illustrations; 21cm. ISBN: 7500150695, 7500150695

75. Yi jing numerology: based on Shao Yung's classic Plum blossom numerology/Yong Shao; Da Liu. London: Routledge & Kegan Paul, 1979. xiii, 145 pages: illustrations. ISBN: 0710004087, 0710004086

《梅花易数》, 邵雍 (1011—1077 年) 著; Liu Da 译.

76. I ching, the tao of organization/Cheng Yi; translated by Thomas Cleary. Boston: Shambhala; [New York]: Distributed in the U. S. by Random House, 1988. xviii, 234 p.; 23cm. ISBN: 0877734194. (Shambhala dragon editions)

《易传》, 程颐 (1033—1107); Cleary, Thomas F.

(1949—) (美国翻译家) 译.

77. The Tao of organization: the I ching for group dynamics/Cheng Yi; translated by Thomas Cleary. Boston: Shambhala, 1995. xviii, 234 p.: ill.; 23cm. ISBN: 1570620865, 1570620867

《易传》, 程颐 (1033—1107); Cleary, Thomas F. (1949—) (美国翻译家) 译.

78. I ching: the book of change/Cheng Yi; translated by Thomas Cleary. 1st Shambhala library ed. Boston: Shambhala: Distributed in the United States by Random House, 2003. xiii, 403 p. ill.; 18cm. ISBN: 1590300157, 1590300152. (Shambhala library)

《易传》, 程颐 (1033—1107); Cleary, Thomas F. (1949—) (美国翻译家) 译.

79. The classic of changes: a new translation of the I Ching as interpreted by Wang Bi/translated by Richard John Lynn. New York: Columbia University Press, c1994. 602 p.; 24cm. ISBN: 0231082940. (Translations from the Asian classics)

《易经注》, 王弼 (226—249); 林理璋 (Lynn, Richard John) (美国汉学家) 译.

(1)New York; Chichester: Columbia University Press, 2004. 602 pages; 22cm. ISBN: 0231082959, 0231082952. (Translations from the Asian classics)

80. The Buddhist I ching/Chih-hsu Ou-i; translated by Thomas Cleary. Boston: Shambhala; [New York]: Distributed in the U. S. by Random House, 1987. xxi, 236 p.: ill.; 23cm. ISBN: 0877734089, 0877734086

《周易禅解》, 智旭 (公元 1559—1655); Cleary, Thomas F., (1949—) (美国翻译家) 译.

(1)The Buddhist I jing/Zhixu Ouyi; translated by Thomas Cleary. Boston: Shambhala, 2001. xxi, 236 pages: illustrations; 23cm. ISBN: 0877734089, 0877734086. (Shambhala dragon editions)

81. The Taoist I ching/translated by Thomas Cleary.. Boston: Shambhala, 1986. 338 p.; 23cm. ISBN: 087773352X, 0877733522, 0394743873, 0394743875

《周易阐真》, 刘一明 (1734—1821); Cleary, Thomas F. (1949—) (美国翻译家) 译.

(1)Kuala Lumpur, Malaysia: Eastern Dragon Books, 1991. 338 pages; 23cm. ISBN: 9839629964, 9839629965

(2)Boston: Shambhala, 2005. 338 p.; 23cm. ISBN: 1590302605, 1590302606, 087773352X, 0877733522, 0394743873, 0394743875. (Shambhala classics)

82. The book of changes and statistics/Hou Wenxi. Beijing, People's Republic of China: International Academic Publishers, 1993. viii, 128 pages: illustrations; 19cm. ISBN: 7800032284

《易经与统计学手册》. 万国学术出版社.

B222 儒家

B222.1 四书五经

1. The Chinese classics：with a translation, critical and exegetical notes, prolegomena and copious indexes, by James Legge. 2nd ed., rev. Oxford, Clarendon Press, 1893—95. 5 v. in 8. fold. maps. 26cm.

《中国经典》，理雅各（Legge, James, 1815—1897)（英国汉学家）编译. 共 5 卷，第一卷，《论语，大学，中庸》(Confucian analects, the Great learning, and the Doctrine of the mean)，第二卷，《孟子》(The works of Mencius)，第三卷，《尚书》(The Shoo king, or the Book of historical documents)，第四卷，《诗经》(The She king, or the Book of poetry)，第五卷，《春秋左传》(The Ch'un ts'ew, with the Tso chuen). 初版于 1861—72 年，由伦敦的 Trübner 出版。

(1)2nd ed., rev. Oxford：Clarendon Press, 1939. 5 volumes in 8.：folded maps；27cm.

(2)Hong Kong, Hong Kong University Press, 1960. 5 v. port., fold. col. maps. 28cm. 中英对照.

(3)2nd ed. rev. Taipei：Wen Shi Zhe Chubanshe,1972. 5 tomes en 4 v.

(4)Hong Kong, Hong Kong University Press ［1970, c1960］.5 v. fold. col. maps, port. 28cm. 中英对照本

(5)Taibei Shi：Nan tian shu ju, 1991. 5 volumes in 4：illustrations, color map, portraits；24cm. ISBN：9576380383, 9576380389, 9576380391, 9576380396, 9576380405, 9576380402, 9576380413, 9576380419, 9576380421, 9576380426

2. The four books：The great learning, The doctrine of the mear ［i. e. mean］ Confucian Analects ［and］ The works of Mencius/by James Legge. Hong Kong：The International Publication Society, 1900. 1 v. (various pagings)

《四书：〈论语〉、〈大学〉、〈中庸〉、〈孟子〉》，理雅各（Legge, James, 1815—1897)（英国汉学家）译.

(1)Hong Kong, International Publication Society, ［1953］. 22, 43, 184, 351 p. 19cm.

(2)Hong Kong, International Publication Society, ［1955］.21, 43, 184, 351 p. 19cm.

(3)Hong Kong：Hop Kuen Book Co., 1961. 351 pages；19cm.

(4)Hong Kong, International Publication Society, ［1962］.22, 43, 184, 351 p. 19cm.

(5)Tai-pei：Wen-hsing, 1966. volumes in 1：portraits；25cm.

(6)［Hong Kong］：Kwong Ming Book Store Hong Kong, 1971. ［2], 21, ［1], 43, ［1], 160, 351, ［1] pages；19cm.

(7)［South Carolina］：Nabu Press, 2010. 600 pages；25cm. ISBN：1172037124, 1172037124

3. The philosophy of Confucius/in the translation of James Legge；with illus. by Jeanyee Wong. Mount Vernon, N. Y.：Peter Pauper Press，1900. 220 pages：illustrations；26cm.

Contents：An introduction to Confucius. —Confucian analects. —The great learning. —The doctrine of the mean.

儒家哲学. 理雅各（Legge, James, 1815—1897)（英国汉学家）译；Wong, Jeanyee 插图. 包括《论语》《大学》和《中庸》.

(1)Mount Vernon, N. Y.：Peter Pauper Press, 1946. 215 pages；21cm.

(2)Mount Vernon, New York：Peter Pauper Press, 1953. 220 pages：illustrations；25cm.

(3)New York：Crescent Books, 1970. 220 pages：illustrations；24cm.

(4)New York：Crescent Books, 1974. 220 pages：illustrations；24cm. ISBN：0517138972, 0517138977

4. Hua-Ying Zhushuji Shujing hebian＝The annals of the bamboo books, the Shoo king/edited and translated by James Legge. ［Shanghai］：Shanghai shu ju, 1904. 2 volumes in 1：illustrations；21cm. ；21cm.

《华英竹书记，书经合编》，理雅各（Legge, James, 1815—1897)（英国汉学家）译. 中英对照.

5. The Four books：Confucian analects, the great learning, the doctrine of the mean, and the works of Mencius/with English translation and notes by James Legge. Shanghai, China：Chinese Book Co., 1923. 1014 pages；19cm.

《四书：〈论语〉、〈大学〉、〈中庸〉、〈孟子〉》，理雅各（Legge, James, 1815—1897)（英国汉学家）译. 中英对照.

(1)Shanghai, China：Chinese Book Co., 1930. 1014 pages；21cm.

(2)Shanghai, China, The Chinese Book Company ［1933]. 1014 p. ；19cm.

(3)［Shanghai］：The Commercial Press, ［1945]. 1014 p. ；19cm.

(4)New York：Paragon Book Reprint Corp., c1966. 1014 p. ；23cm.

(5)Taibei Shi：Wen xing shu dian, 1966. 2 volumes in 1：portraits；25cm.

(6)Tai-pei：Wen hua tu shu kung shih, 1968. 1014 pages；20cm.

(7)Hong Kong：Wei Tung Book Store, 1970. 22, 43, 184, 351 pages；21cm.

(8)［Taipei, Taiwan］：［Chengwen Pub. Co.], 1971. xv, 503, viii, 587 pages；24cm.

(9)Taichung：I Shih Pub. Ser, 1971. xv, 587 pages；25cm.

(10)New York, Dover Publications ［1971]. viii, 503 p. ；22cm. ISBN：0486227464, 0486227467

(11)Taipei：Southern Materials Center, 1972. xv, 587 pages：portraits；24cm. (The Chinese classics)

6. 注 释 校 正 华 英 四 书/translated by James Legge. [Shanghai]：商务印书馆，[1948]. 376 pages；20cm.

目次：论语 ＝ Confucian analects—大学 ＝ The great learning—中庸＝The doctrine of the mean—孟子

理雅各(Legge，James，1815—1897)(英国汉学家)译.

7. The Sacred books of China：The texts of Confucianism. translated by James Legge. Delhi, Motilal Banarsidass, [1966]. v. illus. 23cm. (Sacred books of the East series；v. 3，16，27－28，39－40). (UNESCO collection of representative works. Indian series)

Notes："First published... 1879；reprinted... 1966."

《中国圣书：〈书经〉、〈诗经〉、〈孝经〉、〈易经〉、〈礼记〉》，理雅各(Legge，James，1815—1897)(英国汉学家)译.

(1)New Delhi：Atlantic Publishers & Distributors, 1990. 6 volumes：illustrations；22cm. (The Sacred books of the East；v. 3，16，27－28，39－40)

8. Confucius and the Chinese classics；or，Readings in Chinese literature/edited and comp. by A. W. Loomis. Ann Arbor, Mich.：University Microfilms International, 1977. xiii，[15]-432 pages；18cm.

Contents：Selections from Legge's translation of the Four books, and from various other sources.

理雅各(Legge，James，1815—1897)(英国汉学家)译；Loomis，A. W. (Augustus Ward，1816—1891)编. 包括《论语》和《孟子》的翻译.

9. The Shu King；The religious portion of the Shih King；The Hsiao King/translated by James Legge. Delhi；Varanasi；Patma：Motilal Banarsidass, 1978. xxx，492 p.，1 c. di tav. ripieg.；22cm.

《书经》《诗经》《孝经》，理雅各(Legge，James，1815—1897)(英国汉学家)译.

10. The Chinese classics. Volume 1/by James Legge. Safety Harbor, Fla.：Simon Publications：Distributed by Ingram Book Co.，2001. xv，503 pages；22cm. ISBN：1931313903，1931313902

Contents：The Prolegomena. I. Confucian analects—II. The Great learning—III. The doctrine of the mean.

Notes：Originally published：Hong Kong, China：The Author, 1861

理雅各(Legge，James，1815—1897)(英国汉学家)译. 包括《论语》《大学》《中庸》的英译. 中英对照.

11. Essential writings of Confucianism：the Analects of Confucius and the Mencius/by Kung Fu Tzu and Men-Ke. St. Petersburg, Fla.：Red and Black Publishers, [2008]. 116 p.；23cm. ISBN：1934941515

Partial reprint；originally published under title：Chinese classics. Oxford；Clarendon Press, 1893—1995.

《论语·孟子》(节译)，理雅各(Legge，James，1815—1897)(英国汉学家)译.

12. The analects of Confucius；A selection of the sayings of Muncius；The way and its power of Laozi/English

translation by James Legge. East Bridgewater, MA：Signature Press Editions, 2008. xii，196 pages；23cm. ISBN：1572152885，1572152885

理雅各(Legge，James，1815—1897)(英国汉学家)译. 包括《论语》《孟子》《道德经》.

13. Collected works of Confucius and Mencius/Confucius & Mencius with their students；translated by Arthur Waley & James Legge. Expanded edition. Beijing；Washington：Intercultural Press, 2013. 386 s. ISBN：1492346449，1492346446

韦利(Waley，Arthur，1889—1966)(英国汉学家)，理雅各(Legge，James，1815—1897)(英国汉学家)译. 包括对孔子、孟子著作的翻译.

14. The four books, or, The Chinese classics in English/compiled from the best previous works [by L. Y. T.]. [Rev. ed.]. Shanghai：China Book Co.，1927. 619 pages；20cm.

Contents；The great learning—The doctrine of the mean—Confucian analects—The works of Mencius.

《四书》，林语堂(1895—1976)编译. 包括《大学》《中庸》《论语》《孟子》的英译. 英汉对照.

15. Literary Chinese by the inductive method/prepared by Herrlee Glessner Creel, editor, Chang Tsung-Ch'ien [and] Richard C. Rudolph. Chicago, University of Chicago Press，1938—1952. 3 volumes；25cm.

Contents：v. 1. The Hsiao ching. —v. 2. Selections from the Lun yü. —v. 3. The Mencius, books 1—3.

Creel，Herrlee Glessner(1905—1994)编. 包括《孝经》《论语》和《孟子》的选译.

(1)Chicago, University of Chicago Press，1952—1960. 3 volumes

(2)Rev. and enl. ed. Chicago, Univ. of Chicago Press, 1960—1967. 3 volumes 25cm.

16. Three ways of thought in ancient China, by Arthur Waley. London, G. Allen & Unwin Ltd. [1939]. 275，[1] p. 20cm.

Notes："This book consists chiefly of extracts from Chuang tzu, Mencius and Han fei tzu."—Pref.

韦利(Waley，Arthur，1889—1966)(英国汉学家)译. 内容译自《庄子》(《南华经》)、《孟子》和《韩非子》.

(1)Garden City，N. Y.，Doubleday，1956. 216 p. 18cm. (Doubleday anchor books，A75)

(2)Stanford，Calif.：Stanford University Press，1982. xi，216 p.；22cm. ISBN：0804711690

17. The great learning & The mean-in-action；newly translated from the Chinese, with an introductory essay on the history of Chinese philosophy, by E. R. Hughes. London, J. M. Dent and Sons, Ltd. [1942]. xii，176 p. 19cm.

《大学》与《中庸》，休士(Hughes，E. R. 〈Ernest Richard〉，1883—1956)(美国学者)译.

(1) New York：E. P. Dutton and Company，Inc.，

1943. xi p., 2 l. 176 p. 20cm.

(2)1st AMS ed. New York: AMS Press, 1979, xi, 176 p.; 18cm. ISBN: 0404144888

(3)Ann Arbor, Mich.: UMI, 2006. xi, 176 pages; 20cm.

18. Confucius: the Unwobbling pivot & the Great digest/ translated by Ezra Pound; with notes and commentary on the text and the ideograms; together with Ciu [i. e. Chu] Hsi's "Preface" to the Chung yung and Tseng's commentary on the Testament. [Murray, Utah: s. n., 1947]. 52 p.; 24cm. (Pharos; no. 4)

《中庸》与《大学》,庞德(Pound, Ezra, 1885—1972)(美国诗人)译.

(1)[Norfolk, Conn.]: Pharos, 1947. 52 pages; 24cm. (Pharos; no. 4)

(2)Bombay: Published for Kavitabhavan by Orient Longmans, 1949. [4] leaves, 44 pages; 22cm.

(3)Washington: Square Dollar series, 1951. 96 pages; 21cm. (Square dollar series; 1)

19. Confucius: the Great digest, the Unwobbling pivot, and the Analects/translation & commentary by Ezra Pound; stone text from rubbings supplied by William Hawley; a note on the stone editions by Achilles Fang. New York: New Directions, 1951. 187 pages: illustrations; 25cm. (New Directions book)

Contents:The great digest—The unwobbling pivot—The analects

《大学》《中庸》与《论语》,庞德(Pound, Ezra, 1885—1972)(美国诗人)译;方志彤(Fang, Achilles)(美国华裔学者)注.

(1)London, Peter Owen, 1968. 187 pages; 22cm.

(2)New York: [New Directions Pub. Corp.], 1969. 288 pages; 21cm. ISBN: 0811201544, 0811201546. (A New Directions book; 285)

20. The four books: Confucian classics/translated from the Chinese texts, rectified and edited with an introduction by Cheng Lin. Shanghai: World Publishers, 1948. xxxvi, 487 pages; 19cm. (Ancient Chinese classics series)

Contents: The analects of Confucius.—The ideal of learning.—The doctrine of harmony.—The discourses of Mencius.

《英译四书》,郑麟译.

(1)The four books: Confucian classics/translated from the Chinese texts, rectified and edited with an introduction by Cheng Lin. [台北]:[publisher not identified],[1987]. xxxvi, 487, 20, 16 pages; 19cm. (Ancient Chinese classics series＝古籍新编;中华全书荟要)

21. The gospel of China, Adyar, Madras, Theosophical Pub. House, 1949. lxxi, 180 p. port. 18cm. (World gospel series, 2.)

《四书》,Pauthier, G. (Guillaume, 1801—1873), Greenlees, Duncan 编译.

22. Basic writings of Mo Tzu, Hsu'n Tzu, and Han Fei Tzu, translated by Burton Watson. New York: Columbia University Press, 1964. 140, 177, 135 p. 21cm. ISBN: 0231025157, 0231025157. (Records of civilization, sources and studies, no. 74.). (UNESCO collection of representative works. Chinese series)

《墨子、荀子、韩非子》,华兹生(Watson, Burton, 1925—)(美国翻译家)译.

(1)New York: Columbia University Press, 1967. 140, 177, 135 pages. (Records of civilization, sources and studies, no. 74.). (UNESCO collection of representative works. Chinese series)

23. The sacred books of Confucius, and other Confucian classics. Edited and translated by Ch'u Chai and Winberg Chai. Introd. by Ch'u Chai. New Hyde Park, N. Y., University Books [1965]. 384 p. 24cm.

Contents: Confucius.—Mencius.—Hsühn tzu—Ta hsüeh (The great learning)—Chung yung (The doctrine of the mean)—Hsiao ching (The classic of filial piety)—Li chi (The book of rites)—Tung Chung-shu.

《儒家经典》,翟楚(Ch'u Chai, 1906—1986),翟文伯(Winberg Chai)编译.包括《论语》《孟子》《荀子》《大学》《中庸》《孝经》《礼记》.

24. The humanist way in ancient China; essential works of Confucianism. Edited and translated by Ch'u Chai and Winberg Chai. New York: Bantam Books [1965]. 373 p. 18cm.

Contents: Introduction: Confucianism as humanism. Confucianism as a religion. The spirit of Confucianism.—Confucius.—Mencius.—Hsühn Tzu.—Ta hsüeh (The great learning)—Chung yung (The doctrine of the mean)—Hsiao ching (The classic of filial piety)—Li chi (The book of rites)—Tung chung-shu.

翟楚(Ch'u Chai, 1906—1986),翟文伯(Winberg Chai)编译.包括对《论语》《孟子》《荀子》《书经》《中庸》《孝经》《礼记》的翻译.

25. The wisdom of China; the sayings of Confucius, Mencius, Lao Tzu, Chuang Tzu and Lieh Tzu/With illus. by Maggie Jarvis. Mount Vernon., N. Y.: Peter Pauper Press, [c1965]. 62 p.: illus.; 19cm.

《中国的智慧:孔子、孟子、老子、庄子、列子语录》,Maggie Jarvis 插图.

26. The extensive learning and the practice of impartiality and harmony in life/translation from Chinese into English with annotations by Joseph H. C. Sung. 台北市,1966. 129 pages; 21cm.

《大学与中庸》,宋选铨译.

27. The heart of Confucius; interpretations of Genuine living

and Great wisdom/[by] Archie J. Bahm. With a foreword by Thome' H. Fang. New York: Walker/Weatherhill, 1969. 159 pages: illustrations; 20cm.

《中庸》与《大学》, Bahm, Archie J. 英译.

(1) 1st Perennial Library ed. New York: Perennial Library, 1971. 159 pages: illustrations; 19cm. ISBN: 0060802030, 0060802035

(2) New York: Harper & Row, 1971. 159 pages: illustrations; 18cm. (Perennial library; P203)

(3) Carbondale: Southern Illinois University Press, 1977. 159 pages: illustrations; 20cm. ISBN: 0809308282, 0809308286. (Arcturus paperbacks; 138)

(4) Berkeley, Calif.: Asian Humanities Press, 1992. 159 pages: illustrations; 21cm. ISBN: 0875730213, 0875730219

(5) Fremont, Calif.: Jain Pub., 1998. 158 pages: illustrations; 21cm. ISBN: 0875730213

28. The Chinese classical work commonly called the Four books (1828). Translated and illustrated with notes by David Collie. A facsimile reproduction with an introd. by William Bysshe Stein. Gainesville, Fla., Scholars' Facsimiles & Reprints, 1970. xvii, 341 p. 23cm. ISBN: 0820110795

《四书》, Collie, David(? —1828)译. 初版于1828年.

29. The Confucian vision/edited, with an introd. and new translations, by William McNaughton. Ann Arbor: University of Michigan Press, 1974. viii, 164 p.; 20cm. ISBN: 0472086200, 0472061941. (Ann Arbor paperbacks; AA 194)

McNaughton, William(1933—)译注, 包括对《论语》在内的儒家学术的翻译.

30. Wisdom of the Daoist masters: the works of Lao zi (Lao tzu), lie zi (lieh tzu), Zhuang zi (chuang tzu)/rendered into English by Derek Bryce from the French of Leon Wieger. Llanerch: Llanerch Enterprises, 1984. x, 302 pages; 21cm.

Wieger, Le'on(1856—1933)法译, Bryce, Derek 从法译版转译成英语. 包括《道德经》《列子》《南华经》的翻译.

31. Three smaller wisdom books: Lao Zi's Dao de jing, the Great learning (Da xue), and the Doctrine of the mean (Zhong yong)/translated with introductions and commentaries by Patrick Edwin Moran. Lanham: University Press of America, 1993. xi, 298 pages; 23cm. ISBN: 0819192147, 0819192141, 0819192155, 0819192158

Moran, Patrick Edwin 译. 包括对《道德经》《大学》《中庸》的英译.

32. Ethics: the classic readings/edited by David E. Cooper; advisory editors, Robert L. Arrington, James Rachels. Oxford; Malden, MA: Blackwell Publishers, 1998. vii,

287 pages. ISBN: 0631206329, 0631206323, 0631206329, 0631206323, 0631206337, 0631206330. (Philosophy, the classic readings)

Contents: 1. Gorgias, 482 — 4, 488 — 500/Plato—2. Nicomachean Ethics, Book I/Aristotle—3. 'Letter to Menoeceus' and 'Leading Doctrines'/Epicurus—4. 'Human Nature is Good'/Mencius—'Man's Nature is Evil'/Hsun Tzu—5. The Book of Chuang Tzu, chapters 9, 13—14

Cooper, David Edward 编, 包括孟子的《性本善》, 荀子的《性本恶》以及庄子的第9,13,14篇.

33. Sources of the Confucian tradition: the five classics and the four books/written by Li Sijing; translated by Lao Guangxu and Ding Jun; version revised by An Zengcai. Jinan, Shandong: Shandong Friendship Press, 1998. 2, 111 pages; 27cm. ISBN: 7806421122 7806421123

《五经四书说略》, 李思敬著. 山东友谊出版社出版.

34. The way: according to Lao Tzu, Chuang Tzu, and Seng Tsan/Rendered and illustrated by Gerald Schoenewolf. Fremont, Calif.: Jain Pub., 2000. 143 pages: illustrations; 22cm. ISBN: 0875730820, 0875730825

Schoenewolf, Gerald 编译. 选译了《道德经》《南华经》和僧璨(公元510—606年)的《信心铭》.

35. Readings in classical Chinese philosophy/edited by Philip J. Ivanhoe and Bryan W. Van Norden. New York: Seven Bridges Press, 2000. xviii, 362 pages: illustrations, 1 map; 23cm. ISBN: 1889119091, 1889119090

Contents: Comparative Romanization Table—; Map of China during the Spring and Autumn Period—; Ch. 1.; Kongzi (Confucius) "The Analects"—; Introduction /; Edward Gilman Slingerland—; Ch. 2.; Mozi—; Introduction / Philip J. Ivanhoe—; Ch. 3.; Mengzi (Mencius)—; Introduction / Bryan W. Van Norden—; Ch. 4.; Laozi ("The Daodejing")—; Introduction / Philip J. Ivanhoe—; Ch. 5.; Zhuangzi—; Introduction / Paul Kjellberg—; Ch. 6.; Xunzi—; Introduction / Eric L. Hutton—; Ch. 7.; Han Feizi—; Introduction / Joel Sahleen.

Ivanhoe, P. J., Van Norden 和 Bryan W. (Bryan William)编, 包括《论语》《孟子》《墨子》《道德经》《南华经》《荀子》《韩非子》等篇章.

(1) Indianapolis: Hackett, 2003. xviii, 362 pages: illustrations, 1 map; 23cm. ISBN: 087220703X, 0872207035, 0872207048, 0872207042

(2) 2nd ed. Indianapolis: Hackett Pub., 2005. xviii, 394 pages; 23cm. ISBN: 0872207811, 0872207813, 0872207803, 0872207806

36. 儒家名言: 英汉对照/齐鲁书社编. 济南: 齐鲁书社, 2005. 100页; 22×6cm. ISBN: 7533315472, 7533315474

37. 国学365: 汉英对照/罗安宪主编. 北京: 同心出版社, 2006. 164页; 24cm. ISBN: 7807163577, 7807163572.

（中国人民大学孔子研究院文库·推广系列丛书）
选取国学经典中具有代表性的《论语》《孟子》《大学》《中庸》《周易》《荀子》《老子》《庄子》《孙子兵法》《墨子》《韩非子》等加以编校整理，并将其翻译成现代汉语和英语.

38. The anti-war stance of Lao-Tzu, Mo-tzu, & Mencius: ancient Chinese philosophy revisited/interpreted & translated by Tan Boon Tee. Bedfordshire, England: Authors Online Ltd. , 2006. 86 pages; 21cm. ISBN: 0755210379, 0755210374

Tee, Tan Boon 译. 包括对《道德经》《墨子》《孟子》的选译.

39. Tao, the way: the sayings of Lao Tzu, Chuang Tzu and Lieh Tzu/translated by Lionel Giles and Herbert A. Giles. El Paso, Tex. : El Paso Norte Press, 2007. vi, 200 pages; 22cm. ISBN: 1934255130, 1934255131

翟林奈(Giles, Lionel, 1875—1958)(英国汉学家),翟理斯(Giles, Herbert Allen, 1845—1935)(英国汉学家)合译. 包括对《道德经》《南华经》《列子》的选译.

40. Eastern wisdom: five paths to enlightenment/Edmond Holmes; S. N. Dasgupta. Radford, VA : Wilder Publications, 2008. 247 pages; 24cm. ISBN: 1604593040, 1604593044

Contents: Creed of Buddha/by Edmond Holmes—Sayings of Lao Tzu/by Lao Tzu; translated by Lionel Giles—Hindu mysticism/by S. N. Dasgupta—Great learning/by Confucius; translated by James Legge

Holmes, Edmond(1850—1936) 和 Dasgupta, S. N. 合译. 包括对《老子》《大学》的翻译.

41. The second book of the Tao: compiled and adapted from the Chuang-tzu and the Chung yung, with commentaries/Stephen Mitchell. New York: Penguin Press, 2009. xvi, 202 p. ; 25cm. ISBN: 1594202032, 1594202036

Mitchell, Stephen(1943—)著, 包括《中庸》(节译)和《南华经》(节译).

(1)New York: Penguin Books, 2010. xvi, 202 pages; 22cm. ISBN: 0143116707, 0143116703

42. The way of the world: readings in Chinese philosophy/translated and edited by Thomas Cleary. Boston: Shambhala, 2009. 120 pages; 23cm. ISBN: 1590307380, 1590307380

Contents: Inner work/from Guanzi—Mental arts I/from Guanzi—Mental arts II/from Guanzi—Purifying the mind/from Guanzi—Interpreting Lao/Han Fei—Taking lessons from Lao/Han Fei—The fisherman and the woodcutter/Shao Yong—The man of Deer Gate: a letter from retirement/Pi Rixiu—Huang Shi's silk text/Zhang Shangying—Wenshi's classic on reality/Officer Xi.

中国典籍, 包括管子、韩非子等著作. Cleary, Thomas F. (1949—)(美国翻译家)译.

43. 中国经典/中华宗教文化交流协会编. 北京:宗教文化出版社,2011.445 页;24cm. ISBN: 7802544123,7802544122

注:本书为三种最重要的中国经典《道德经》《论语》《坛经》的汉文、英文读本.

44. Daxue and Zhongyong/translated and annotated by Ian Johnson and Wang Ping. Bilingual ed. Hong Kong: Chinese University of Hong Kong, 2012. vi, 567 p. ; 24cm. ISBN: 9629964457, 9629964450

《大学》与《中庸》,Johnston, Ian 和 Ping, Wang 合译. 英汉对照.

45. The four Chinese classics: Tao Te Ching, Chuang Tzu, Analects, Mencius/David Hinton. Berkeley, CA: Counterpoint, 2013. 575 pages: illustrations; 24cm. ISBN: 1619022273; 1619022270

《道德经》《南华经》《论语》《孟子》,戴维·欣顿(Hinton, David, 1954—)(美国汉学家)译.

46. The Art of War and Other Classics of Eastern Thought. New York: Barnes & Noble, 2013. xiii, 746 pages; 24cm. ISBN: 1435146211, 1435146212

Contents: The art of war/Sun Tzu; translated with selected commentary by Lionel Giles—The Tao Te Ching/Lao-Tzu; translated by James Legge—The writings of Confucius—The works of Mencius/translated by James Legge.

《〈孙子兵法〉与其他东方经典》,翟林奈(Giles, Lionel, 1875—1958)(英国汉学家),理雅各(Legge, James, 1815—1897)(英国汉学家)译. 包括《孙子兵法》《道德经》《论语》《孟子》.

47. Three confucian classics: the Gu Hongming translations of higher education: a new translation; The conduct of life, or the universal order of Confucius; The discourses and sayings of Confucius (the analects)/Zeng Ziyu, Kong Ji Zisi, Confucius; [translated by Gu Hongming]. New York: CN Times Books, 2013. xvii, 228 pages; 21cm. ISBN: 1627740104,1627740104

Contents: Higher education: a new translation/Zeng Ziyu—The conduct of life, or the universal order of Confucius/Kong Ji Zisi—The discourses and sayings of Confucius (the analects)/Confucius

《大学》《中庸》《论语》,辜鸿铭(1857—1928)译.

48. Four testaments: Tao Te Ching, Analects, Dhammapada, Bhagavad Gita: sacred scriptures of Taoism, Confucianism, Buddhism, and Hinduism/edited by Brian Arthur Brown; foreword by Francis X. Clooney, SJ. Lanham, Maryland: Rowman & Littlefield Publishers, 2016. ISBN: 1442265776, 1442265779

Brown, Brian A. (1942—)编. 包括《道德经》《论语》的英译.

49. 《诗经》《论语》《孟子》英译/罗志野译. 南京:东南大学出版社,2017.271 页;26cm. ISBN: 7564153977. (中华经典英译丛书)

50. 《易经》《尚书》英译/罗志野译. 南京:东南大学出版社,2017.238 页;26cm. ISBN: 7564153953. (中华经典英译

丛书)

英文题名：Book of change：ancient China's natural philosophy. Book of history, or fragments of ancient Chinese history

51. 大学 中庸/辜鸿铭注译. 武汉：崇文书局，2017. 255 页；20cm. ISBN：7540343637. (民国双语译丛)

52. The Confucian way：a new and systematic study of the "Four books"/by Li Fu Chen；translated from the Chinese by Shih Shun Liu. [Taipei]：Commercial Press, 1972. xxvi, 614 p.；24cm.

《四书道贯》，陈立夫(1900—)；刘师舜译.

(1) foreword by Joseph Needham. London；New York：KPI；New York：USA：Distributed by Routledge & Kegan Paul, 1986. xxv, 614 p.；24cm. ISBN：0710301715

(2) foreword by Joseph Needham. London；New York：KPI；New York：USA：Distributed by Routledge & Kegan Paul, 1987, xxv, 614 p.；20cm. ISBN：0710301715. (KPI paperbacks)

B222.2　大学

1. Higher education/a new translation by Ku Hung-Ming. Shanghai：Shanghai Mercury, 1915. 17 pages；19cm.

《大学》，曾子(前 505—前 436)；Ku, Hung-ming 译.

2. The great learning/[ed.] by Cheung-ja; tr. into English and Korean vernacular by J. S. Gale. Seoul：Christian Literature Society of Korea, 1924. 20, 11 pages；21cm. Notes：Parallel text in Chinese and Korean, with English translation.

《大学》，曾子(前 505—前 436)；Gale, James Scarth (1863—1937)译.

3. Ta hio, the great learning, newly rendered into the American language, by Ezra Pound. Seattle, University of Washington book store, 1928. 35 p. 19cm. (University of Washington chapbooks, no. 14)

《大学》，庞德(Pound, Ezra, 1885—1972)(美国诗人)译.

(1) London：S. Nott, 1936. 32 pages；21cm. (Ideogramic series；II)

(2) Norfolk, Conn.：New Directions, 1938. 2 preliminary leaves, [7]-32 pages；22cm.

(3) Norfolk, Conn., New Directions, 1939. 30 pages；22cm. (New Directions pamphlets；no. 4)

(4) [Folcroft, Pa.] Folcroft Press, 1970. 35 pages；22cm. (University of Washington chapbooks；no. 14)

(5) Seattle：University of Washington Book Store, 1970. 35 pages；19cm. (University of Washington chapbooks；no. 14)

(6) Folcroft, Pa.：Folcroft Library Editions, 1975. 35 p.；24cm. (University of Washington chapbooks；no. 14). ISBN：0841467056, 0841467057

(7) Norwood, Pa.：Norwood Editions, 1977 [c1928]. 35 p.；22cm. (University of Washington chapbooks；no. 14.). ISBN：0848220994

(8) [Whitefish, Mont.]：Kessinger, 2000. 30 pages；23cm. ISBN：1432577840, 1432577841. (Kessinger Publishing's rare reprints)

4. 《大学》精华版：汉英对照/傅云龙，蔡希勤编注. 北京：华语教学出版社，2006. 100 页；21cm. ISBN：7802002176, 7802002173. (中国圣人文化丛书)

5. Chu Hsi and the Ta-hsueh：neo-Confucian reflection on the Confucian canon/Daniel K. Gardner. Cambridge, Mass.：Council on East Asian Studies, Harvard University：Distributed by Harvard University Press, 1986. vii, 181 p.；24cm. ISBN：0674130650. (Harvard East Asian monographs；118)

《朱熹与大学：宋儒对儒家经典的反思》，伽德纳(Gardner, Daniel K., 1950—)(美国汉学家)著，翻译了朱熹(1130—1200)对《大学》的注释.

B222.3　中庸

1. The conduct of life, or, The universal order of Confucius：a translation of one of the four Confucian books hitherto known as The doctrine of the mean/translation of the Zhong yong, which is attributed to Kong Ji (Zisi). London：John Murray, 1906. 60 pages；17cm. (Wisdom of the East)

《中庸》，辜鸿铭(1857—1928)译.

(1) London, J. Murray, 1908. 60 p. 17cm. (The wisdom of the East series)

(2) New York：E. P. Dutton, 1909. 60 pages；19cm. (Wisdom of the East)

(3) New York：E. P. Dutton, 1910. 60 pages；19cm. (Wisdom of the East)

(4) London：Murray, 1912. 60 pages；17cm. (The Wisdom of the East series)

(5) London, J. Murray, 1920. 60 pages；17cm. (The Wisdom of the East series)

(6) London, J. Murray [1928]. 60 p. 17cm. (The wisdom of the East series)

(7) Taipei, 1956. 60 p. 19cm. (Wisdom of the East)

(8) 台北：先知出版社，1976. 56 pages；22cm.

2. The Chung-yung；or, The centre, the common, London, New York [etc.] Longmans, Green and Co. Ltd., 1927. 2 p. l., vii-xxvii, 24 p. 23cm.

《中庸》，Lyall, Leonard A. (Leonard Arthur, 1867—)译.

3. Zhong yong＝The practice of impartiality and harmony in life/written in Chinese by Kung Chi, grandson of Confucius, translated from Chinese into English with annotations by Joseph H. C. Sung. [台北]：大中华图书公司，1965. 67 pages；21cm.

《中庸》，宋选铨英译.

4. The doctrine of the mean/translated into modern Chinese by Xu Chao, translated into English by He Baihua；edited

by the Editorial Department of the Complete Works of Confucian Culture. Jinan Shi：Shandong you yi shu she，1992. 77 p.；20cm. ISBN：7805513295.（Translations of Confucian classics＝儒学经典译丛）

《中庸》，今译者，徐超(1945—)；英译者，何百华；《孔子文化大全》编辑部编.

5. The doctrine of the mean.［Kila，Mont.］：Kessinger Pub.，2004. 18 pages；24cm. ISBN：141916001X，1419160011.（Kessinger Publishing's rare reprints）

《中庸》

6. 《中庸》精华版：汉英对照/傅云龙，蔡希勤编注. 北京：华语教学出版社，2006. 134 页；21cm. ISBN：7802002168，7802002166.（中国圣人文化丛书）

B222.4 礼记

1. Li chi：book of rites. An encyclopedia of ancient ceremonial usages，religious creeds，and social institutions. Translated by James Legge. Edited with an introd. and study guide by Ch'u Chai and Winberg Chai. New Hyde Park，N. Y.，University Books［1967］. 2 v. illus. 24cm.

"Except for the new material added by the editors，the text of this edition is that published by Oxford University press in 1885 as volumes xxvii and xxviii of The sacred books of the East and also designated as parts III and IV of The text of Confucianism."

《礼记》，理雅各(Legge，James，1815—1897)(英国汉学家)译. 翟楚(Ch'u Chai，1906 — 1986)，翟文伯(Winberg Chai)合编.

(1)［Whitefish，Mont.］：Kessinger Publishing，2003. 2 volumes：illustrations；28cm. ISBN：0766139183，0766139182，0766139190，0766139190

(2) The li ki/translated by James Legge.［Whitefish，Mont.］：Kessinger Pub.，2004. 720 pages；28cm. ISBN：141916922X，1419169229

(3)［Charleston，S. C.］：Forgotten Books，2008. 2 volumes：illustrations；23cm. ISBN：1605064048，1605064041，1605064055，160506405X

2. 《礼记》名言：汉英对照/齐鲁书社编；孙昌坤译；王铭基绘. 济南：齐鲁书社，2006. 100 页；23cm. ISBN：7533317181，7533317188.（儒家名典箴言录）

B222.5 书经

1. Ancient China，the Shoo-king，or，The historical classic：being the most ancient authentic record of the annals of the Chinese empire/illustrated by later commentators. Translated by W. H. Medhurst. Shanghae，Printed at the Mission Press，1846. xvi，413 pages：illustrations，double plates，double maps；23cm.

《书经》，Medhurst，Walter Henry(1796—1857)译.

2. The Shu king；or，The Chinese historical classic，being an authentic record of the religion，philosophy，customs and government of the Chinese from the earliest times/translated from the ancient text，with a commentary，by

Walter Gorn Old，M. R. A. S. London And Benares，Theosophical Pub. Society；New York：John Lane，1904. 306 pages：illustrations；20cm.

《书经》，Sepharial(1864—1929)编译.

3. Extracts from Shu Ch'ing：historical classic of China，which is commonly regarded as one of the classics of Confucius/translated by W. Gorn Old；and with introductory note by W. Loftus Hare. London：C. W. Daniel，1906. 35 pages；15cm.（The oriental classics；no. 1）

《书经》(选译)，Sepharial(1864—1929)译；Hare，William Loftus(1868—1943)作序.

4. The classics of Confucius. Book of history (Shu King)/rendered and compiled by W. Gorn Old. London，J. Murray，1906. 67 pages；17cm.（The wisdom of the East series）

《书经》，Sepharial(1864—1929)编译.

(1) New York，E. P. Dutton，1908. 67 pages；17cm.（The wisdom of the East series）

(2) New York：Dutton，1909. 67 pages；17cm.（The wisdom of the East series）

(3) New York：Dutton，1911. 67 pages；17cm.（The wisdom of the East series）

(4) London，J. Murray，1918. 67 pages；17cm.（The wisdom of the East series）

(5) London：John Murray，2007. 67 pages；17cm.（Wisdom of the East series）

(6)［S. l.］：Nabu Press，2010. ISBN：1176580329，1176580329

5. The book of documents［i. e.］the Shu king. A word-for-word translation of all authentic chapters/by Bernhard Karlgren. Göteborg，Elanders Boktryckeri Aktiebolag，1950. 81 pages

《书经》，高本汉(Karlgren，Bernhard，1889—1978)译.

6. Shu ching：book of history. A modernized edition of the translations of James Legge.［Edited by］Clae Waltham. Chicago，H. Regnery Co.［1971］. xvii，277 p. map.；21cm.

《书经》，理雅各(Legge，James，1815—1897)(英国汉学家)译；Waltham，Clae编.

7. The shifting center：the original "Great plan" and later readings/Michael Nylan. Sankt Augustin：Institut Monumenta Serica；Nettetal：Steyler Verlag，1992. 211 p.：ill.；24cm. ISBN：3805002939.（Monumenta serica monograph series，0179－261X；24)

Nylan，Michael 著，含有《书经·洪范》的翻译.

8. The most venerable book (Shang shu)/Confucius；translated by Martin Palmer. London：Penguin Classics，2014. 190 pages；20cm. ISBN：0141197463，0141197463.（Penguin classics）

《书经》，Palmer，Martin 译.

9. The English and Chinese Shu-king and the Annals of the Bamboo books/Confucius; compiler. Shanghai：Shanghai Book Co., 1905. 700 pages；20cm.

《书经》与《竹书纪年》. 英汉对照.

B222.6　孝经

1. The book of filial duty/translated from the Chinese of the Hsiao ching by Ivan Che'n; with the twenty-four examples from the Chinese. London：J. Murray, 1908. 60 p.；17cm. Wisdom of the East series (London, England)

《孝经及二十四孝故事》,Che'n, Ivan 译.

2. The Hsiao ching＝孝经/translated by Mary Lelia Makra; edited by Paul K. T. Sih. New York：St. John's University Press,c1961. xiv, 67 p.；24cm. (Asian Institute translations; no. 2)

《孝经》,Makra, Mary Lelia 译.

3. The classic of filial piety/translated into modern Chinese by Fu Genqing, translated into English by Liu Ruixiang and Lin Zhihe; edited by the Editorial Department of the Complete Works of Confucian Culture. Jinan Shi：Shandong you yi shu she, 1993. 125 p.；20cm. ISBN：7805513279. (Translations of Confucian classics＝儒学经典译丛)

《孝经》,今译者,傅根清;英译者,刘瑞祥,林之鹤;《孔子文化大全》编辑部编. 英汉对照.

4. The Chinese classic of family reverence：a philosophical translation of the Xiaojing/Henry Rosemont, Jr. and Roger T. Ames. Honolulu：University of Hawaii Press,c2009. xv, 132 p.；23cm. ISBN：0824832841,0824832841, 0824833480, 0824833481

《孝经》,罗思文（Rosemont, Henry, 1934—）,安乐哲（Ames, Roger T.,1947—）（美国汉学家）合译.

5. The classic of filial respect/translated by students from the Developing Virtue Secondary School, Ukiah, California. Published in association with the Dharma Realm Buddhist University and Dharma Realm Buddhist Association. Burlingame, CA：Buddhist Text Translation Society, 2009. 80 pages：illustrations（some color）; 26cm. ISBN：9867328441, 9867328442

《孝经》. 中英对照.

B222.7　孔子（约公元前 551—前 479）

1. The discourses and sayings of Confucius. Shanghai［etc.］ Kelly and Walsh, limited, 1898. x p.，1 l.，182 p.，1 l.; 25cm.

《论语》,辜鸿铭(1857—1928)译.

   (1)The discourses and sayings of Confucius：a new special translation, illustrated with quotations from Goethe and other writers/Confucius; Hongming Gu. Taipei, Taiwan：Prophet Press, 1976. 182 pages; 22cm.

2. English translation of The Analects/Confucius.; translation by Ku Hung-ming. Rev. ed. Taipei, Republic of China：Taipei City Government, 1984. 114 pages English text,［unpaged in English］Chinese text；22cm.

《论语》,辜鸿铭(1857—1928)译.

3. 论语/辜鸿铭注译. 武汉：崇文书局,2017. 2 册（793 页）; 19cm. ISBN：7540343644, 7540343648. （民国双语译丛） 英文题名：The discourses and sayings of confucius

4. Considerations from Confucius/Confucius; R. Dimsdale Stocker. London：Siegle, Hill, 1909. 95 pages；10cm. (Langham booklets)

《论语》（节译）,Stocker, R. Dimsdale(〈Richard Dimsdale〉, 1877—1935)译.

5. The analects of Confucius, by William Edward Soothill. Yokohama, the author; Agent in U. S. A., The F. H. Revell Company, 1910. 1 p. l., v p., 1 l., 1028 p., 1 l. front（port.）fold. map.；20cm.

《论语》,苏慧廉（Soothill, William Edward, 1861—1935）（英国传教士）译. 中英对照.

   (1)2nd ed. New York：Paragon Book Reprint Corp., 1968. v, 1028 p. port. 23cm.

6. The Analects; or, The conversations of Confucius with his disciples and certain others, as translated into English by William Edward Soothill... Edited by his daughter, Lady Hosie. London, Oxford University Press, H. Milford, 1937. lx, 254 p., 1 l. front.；16cm. (The world's classics, CDXLII)

《论语》,苏慧廉（Soothill, William Edward, 1861—1935）（英国传教士）译;Hosie, Lady(1885—)编.

   (1) London, New York［etc.］H. Milford, Oxford University Press［1941］.

7. The Analects/Confucius;［translation from the Chinese by William Edward Soothill］. New York：Dover Publications,1995. xii,128 p.；22cm. ISBN：0486284840. (Dover thrift editions)

《论语》,苏慧廉（Soothill, William Edward, 1861—1935）（英国传教士）译.

8. "Rongo"：(Confucian analects) in English, Japanese and Chinese/Confucius; James Legge; Masataro Yamano. ［3rd ed.］Tokyo：M. Yamano, 1913. [8, 2]-302, [1], 38 pages, 1 leaf：frontispiece；15cm.

《论语》,理雅各（Legge, James, 1815—1897）（英国汉学家）译;Yamano, Masataro 编. 英、汉、日三种文字对照.

9. Confucian analects; a selection from the philosophy and reflective writings of Confucius on harmony and equilibrium in living. Printed for the entertainment of the friends of Dr. C. C. Burlin. New York and Hartford, 1939. 201 p.；23×13cm.

《论语》,理雅各（Legge, James, 1815—1897）（英国汉学家）译;Burlingame, C. Charles (Clarence Charles, 1885—1950)编. 中英文本.

10. Confucian analects/Legge, James. 台北：世纪书局,民 74［1985］. 240 面；19cm. (中国文化基本丛书)

《英译论语》,李芝(Legge, James)英译.

11. Confucius: the wisdom/watercolors by Claudia Karabaic Sargent; selected and edited by Peg Streep, from the translation by James Legge. Boston: Bulfinch Press, c1995. 96 p.: col. ill.; 19cm. ISBN: 0821221612

《论语》,理雅各(Legge, James, 1815—1897)(英国汉学家)译;Streep, Peg. Legge, James(1815—1897)选编.

12. The analects of Confucius: discourses and dialogues of K'ung Fû-Tsze/compiled by his disciples; interpreted and illustrated by Holly Harlayne Roberts. [United States]: Anjeli Press, c2007. xiv, 314 p.: ill.; 24cm. ISBN: 0975484486

Based upon the 1893 translation of James Legge.

《论语》,理雅各(Legge, James, 1815—1897)(英国汉学家)译;Roberts, Holly(1945—)插图. 中英文本.

13. 论语:中英文对照/孔祥林今译;理雅各(James Legge)英译. 北京:外文出版社,2009. 323 页;24cm. ISBN: 7119044569, 7119044567

14. Confucius, the analects: the path of the sage: selections annotated & explained/annotation by Rodney L. Taylor; translation by James Legge; revised by Rodney L. Taylor. Quality pbk. ed. Woodstock, Vt.: SkyLight Paths Pub., 2011. xxxiii, 143 p.; 22cm. ISBN: 1594733062, 1594733066. (SkyLight illuminations series)

《论语》(选译),Taylor, Rodney Leon(1944—)注;理雅各(Legge, James, 1815—1897)(英国汉学家)译.

15. Digest of the Analects. Milan [P. Vera, 1937]. [20] p., 1 l. 10×8cm.

《论语》,庞德(Pound, Ezra, 1885—1972)(美国诗人)译.

16. Confucian analects/[translated by Ezra Pound]. New York: Kasper & Horton: Gotham Book Mart [distributor], 1951. 98 p.; 23cm. (Square MYM series)

《论语》,庞德(Pound, Ezra, 1885—1972)(美国诗人)译.

(1)New York, N. Y.: Kasper & Horton: Gotham Book Mart [distributor], 1951, c1950. 98 p.; 23cm. (Square dollar series)

(2)London, P. Owen [1956]. 135 p. 23cm.

17. The sayings of Confucius: a new translation of the greater part of the Confucian analects/with introduction and notes by Lionel Giles. London: J. Murray, [1927]. 132 p.; 17cm. (Wisdom of the Eastseries)

《论语》,翟林奈(Giles, Lionel, 1875—1958)(英国汉学家)译.

(1)Boston: Charles E. Tuttle, 1993, c1992. 132 p.; 18cm. ISBN: 0804818479. (Wisdom of the East series)

18. The analects of Confucius/translated from the Chinese, with an introduction and notes, by Lionel Giles. Shanghai: Printed for the members of the Limited Editions Club by the Commercial Press, 1933. 114 p.: ill.; 28cm.

《论语》,翟林奈(Giles, Lionel, 1875—1958)(英国汉学家)译.

(1)New York: Limited Editions Club, 1970 (Los Angeles: Plantin Press). xxvii, 131 p., [24] leaves of plates: col. ill.; 29cm. illustrated with paintings by Tseng Yu-ho.

(2)Illustrated with paintings by Tseng Yu-ho. [Los Angeles]: Printed at the Plantin Press for the members of the Limited Editions Club, New York: 1976. xxvii, 131 p.: 12 col. plates.; 27cm.

19. The Analects of Confucius; translated and annotated by Arthur Waley. London, G. Allen & Unwin Ltd. [1938]. 4 p. l., [11]-268 p., 1 l. 22cm.

《论语》,韦利(Waley, Arthur, 1889—1966)(英国汉学家)译.

(1)Limited ed. Franklin Center, Pa.: Franklin Library, 1980. . 221 p.: ill.; 22cm.

(2)1st Vintage Books ed. New York: Vintage Books, 1989. 257 p.; 21cm. ISBN: 0679722963

(3)New York: Knopf, 2000. xxxi, 257 p.; 21cm. ISBN: 0375412042(Everyman's library; 184).

20. Confucianism: the Analects of Confucius/trans. by Arthur Waley; ed. by Jaroslave Pelikan. Quality pbk. Book Club ed. New York: Quality Paperback Book Club, 1992. xvi, 262 pages; 22cm.

《论语》,韦利(Waley, Arthur, 1889—1966)(英国汉学家)译;Pelikan, Jaroslav(1923—2006)编.

21. Lun yu = The analects/[translated into English by Arthur Waley; translated into modern Chinese by Yang Bojun]. Hunan: Hunan Pub. House, 1999. 344 pages; 24cm. ISBN: 7543820889, 7543820883. (Library of Chinese classics)

《论语》,韦利(Waley, Arthur, 1889—1966)(英国汉学家)英译;杨伯峻中译. 英汉对照.

22. Sacred writings: in two volumes; with introductions and notes. Registered ed. New York: Collier, 1938. 2 volumes (1007 pages): illustrations. (The Harvard classics; v. 44—45)

《论语》选译,译者不详.

(1)New York: Collier, 1961. 2 volumes (1007 pages): illustrations; 22cm. (Harvard classics; v. 44—45)

23. The sayings of Confucius/decorated by Paul McPharlin. [Mount Vernon, N. Y.]: Peter Pauper Press, [1939]. 85 p.: ill.; 19cm.

《论语》(选译),McPharlin, Paul(1903—1948)译.

24. The sayings of Confucius/Confucius; Leonard A. Lyall. London, Longmans, Green, 1939. 117 pages; 24cm.

《论语》(选译),Lyall, Leonard A. (Leonard Arthur,

1867—)译.

25. Confucius：bold-faced thoughts on loyalty，leadership，and teamwork/translated by LeonardA. Lyall；edited by Laura Ross. New ed. New York：Sterling Innovation，c2010. 288 p.；16cm. ISBN：1402774652，1402774656

《论语》(节译)，Lyall，Leonard A.（Leonard Arthur，1867—)译；Ross，Laura(1956—)编.

26. Selections from the Lun Yü/H. G. Creel；Zhang Zongqian.；Richard C Rudolph. Chicago：University of Chicago Press，1939. 252 p.；25cm.

《论语》(选译)，Creel，H. G.（Herrlee Glessner，1905—1994)，Zhang Zongqian 和 Rudolph，Richard C. 合编.

27. Selections from the Confucian texts/by A. L. Sadler. Glebe：Australasian Medical Pub. Co.，1942. 45，iv pages；15cm.

《论语》(选译)，Sadler，A. L.（Arthur Lindsay，1882—)译.英汉对照.

28. The best of Confucius，translated from the Chinese by James R. Ware. Garden City，N. Y.，Halcyon House[1950]. 192 p. illus. 20cm.

《论语》，魏鲁男（Ware，James R.，1901—)（美国汉学家)译.

29. The sayings of Confucius：a new translation/James Roland Ware. New York：New American Library of World Literature，1955. [128] pages；18cm.（Mentor religious classic)

Notes：Cover title：The sayings of Confucius：the teachings of China's greatest sage. / Includes index.

《论语》，魏鲁男（Ware，James R.，1901—)（美国汉学家)译.

(1) The sayings of Confucius：Lun yu：a new translation/James Roland Ware；Chao Shih，editor. Taibei：Wen zhi chu ban she，1969. 2，212 pages；19cm.

(2)4th ed. Taipei：Confucius，1973. 212 pages；19cm.

30. Sacred writings：with introductions and notes/[Charles William Eliot]. Registered ed. New York：P. F. Collier and Son，1963. 2 volumes（1007 pages)：illustrations；22cm.（The Harvard classics；044；The Harvard classics；045)

Notes：Reprints. Originally published：New York：P. F. Collier & Son，© 1910. / "The Harvard classics edited by Charles W. Eliot."

查尔斯·威廉·艾略特（Charles William Eliot，1834—1926)著.包括《论语》的选译.

(1) Sacred writings/Charles William Eliot.[Whitefish，CT]：Kessinger Pub.，2004，1910. 2 volumes：illustrations；23cm. ISBN：0766181979，0766181977.（The Harvard classics；v. 44—45；Kessinger Publishing's rare reprints)

31. Confucian memorabilia/selected and arranged with

commentary by Y. Ogaeri. 东京：原书房，昭和 39 [1964]. 223 pages

《论语》(选译)，鱼返善雄(1910—1966)编.文本为英文和日文对照.

32. Han Ying Lun yu/Confucius；Kanshō Mori. Wakayama-ken Kōyasan：Mori Kanshō，1967. 127 pages；26cm.

《汉英论语》(《论语》选译)，森宽绍(1899—)编.中英文本，日语解释.

33. The wisdom of Confucius. New York：Philosophical Library；[distributed by Book Sales，Inc.]，1968. 128 pages；19cm.

Notes：Translation of Lun yu. / "The present selection is taken from The Confucian analects，translated by William Jennings... [published in] 1895."

《论语》(选译)，威廉·詹宁斯(Jennings，William，1847—1927)（英国汉学家)译.

(1)The wisdom of Confucius/[translated into English by William Jennings]；with critical and biographical sketches by Epiphanius Wilson. Art-type ed. New York：Avenel Books：Distributed by Crown Publishers，1982，c1900. xii，236 p.；21cm. ISBN：0517381060.（World's popular classics)

(2)New York：Wings Books；Avenel，N. J.：Distributed by Random House Value Pub.，1995. xii，236 p.；19cm. ISBN：0517122979

(3)Carol Publishing Group ed. Secaucus，NJ：Carol Pub. Group，1996. xii，197 p.；19cm. ISBN：0806517026

(4)Ithaca，N. Y.：Cornell University Library，2010. xi，236 p.；18cm.（Cornell University Library digital collections)

34. The Confucian analects＝[Lun yü]：a translation，with annotations and an introduction/Confucius.；William Jennings. Ann Arbor，Mich.：University Microfilms International，1980. 224 pages：illustrations；19cm.（Sir John Lubbock's hundred books；93)

Notes：Includes index. / Photocopy of original published：London：G. Routledge，1895.（Sir John Lubbock's hundred books；93).

《论语》，威廉·詹宁斯(Jennings，William，1847—1927)（英国汉学家)译.

35. The sayings of Confucius/Confucius.；Shih-wei Ch'ien.[Hong Kong]：[Chih wen ch'u pan she]，1973. 211 pages；19cm.

Notes：English and Chinese on opposite pages. / With parallel title in Chinese characters. / Translation of selections from：Lun yu.

《论语》，Ch'ien，Shih-wei 编.

36. The sayings of Confucius：a new translation of the Analects based closely on the meaning and frequency of the Chinese characters/by Lawrence Faucett. San Diego，

Calif. ：Faucett, 1978. iv, 50 p. ；28cm.

《论语》,Faucett,Lawrence 译.

37. The analects （Lun yü）/Confucius; translated with an introd. by D. C. Lau. Harmondsworth; New York：Penguin Books, 1979. 249 p. ；19cm. ISBN：0140443487, 0140443486. (Penguin classics)

《论语》,刘殿爵(Lau, D. C. 〈Dim Cheuk〉,1921—2010)(中国香港学者)译.

    (1)New York：Dorset Press, 1979. 249 pages; 19cm. ISBN：0880291028, 0880291026

    (2)Hong Kong：Chinese University Press, 1983. xlix, 284 pages; 24cm. ISBN：9622012922, 9622012929

    (3)New York：Dorset Press, 1986. 249 pages; 19cm. ISBN：0880291028, 0880291026

    (4)2nd ed. Hong Kong：Chinese University Press, 1992. liii, 288 p. ；23cm. ISBN：9622015271, 9622015272, 9622019803, 9622019805. 中英对照.

    (5)London：Folio Society, 2008. xii, 248 pages, [9] pages of plates：color illustrations；28cm.

38. Confucius says/edited and translated from classical Chinese into modern Chinese by Keong Tow Yung; English translation by D. C. Lau. Singapore：Federal Publications,1981. vii,68 pages;20cm. ISBN：9971431351, 9971431358

Notes：English text based on D. C. Lau's Confucius：the analects, published by Penguin Books, 1979.

《子曰》,刘殿爵(Lau, D. C. 〈Dim Cheuk〉, 1921—2010)(中国香港学者)英译；Yung, Keong Tow 中文今译. 中英对照.

    (1)Confucius says＝Zi yue/Confucius; D C Lau; Keong Tow Yung. 2nd ed. Singapore：Federal Publications, 1995. 82 pages；20cm. ISBN：9810123035, 9810123031

39. The first ten books /translated by D. C. Lau. London：Penguin Books,2005. 58 pages;18cm. ISBN：0141023805, 0141023809. (Great ideas)

《论语》1—10 篇. 刘殿爵(Lau, D. C. 〈Dim Cheuk〉, 1921—2010)(中国香港学者)译.

40. Lun yu：bai hua Zhong wen Ying wen shuang yi ben＝Confucius, the analects：Chinese - English edition/jin yi Yang Bojun; Ying yi Liu Dianjue. Taibei Shi：Lian jing chu ban shi ye gu fen you xian gong si, 2009. iii, 299 p. ；21cm. ISBN：9570834130,9570834137

《论语：白话中文英文双译本》,今译杨伯峻；英译刘殿爵. 英汉对照. 本书附带"重新认识孔子"/杨照. 由台北市联经出版事业股份有限公司出版.

41. 论语选萃/(春秋)孔丘著；D.C.劳英译；付雅丽白话文翻译注释. 北京：中国对外翻译出版有限公司,2010. 159页；18cm. ISBN：7500125228. (企鹅口袋书系列. 伟大的思想)

英文题名：The first ten books. D.C.劳英即刘殿爵(D.

C. Lau,1921—2010)

    (1)北京：中国对外翻译出版有限公司,2012. 197 页；22cm. ISBN：7500128809. (企鹅人文经典系列；第 1 辑)

42. The sayings of Confucius. Singapore：G. Brash, 1983. v, 70 pages：illustrations；19cm. ISBN：9971947226, 9971947224

《论语》(节译)

43. The sayings of Confucius. 1st American ed. Torrance, Ca：Heian International, 1983. v, 70 pages：illustrations；19cm. ISBN：0893468959, 0893468958

《论语》(选译)

44. The Confucian analects：a new translation of the corrected text/Confucius; Shih-chuan Chen. Taipei：Li Ming Cultural Enterprise, 1986. xi, 304 pages；21cm. (Confucius & Mencius Society book series)

《论语》,Zhen,Shizhuan 译.

45. Collected sayings of Confucius and his students/Confucius; William Dolby. Edinburgh：W. Dolby, 1987. 99 pages；30cm.

《论语》(选译),Dolby, William 编译.

    (1) Carreg, 2004. 192 pages；illustrations；21cm. (Chinese culture series；6). 中英对照.

46. Lun yü/Confucius; Wei-ling Cheung. ［Hongkong］：[Confucius Pub. Co.], 1987. [269] pages；28cm.

Notes：Cover title. / Text in classical Chinese, vernacular Chinese, English, Spanish and Portuguese. / President of the Confucius Hall of Hong Kong and Founding Director of Confucius Publishing Co. Ltd.：William Cheung. / Added title：Wan shih szŭ piao ＝Confucius—the grand master of all ages ＝Confucio—maestro de la sabiduri'a ＝Confu'cio—mestre da sabedoria.

《论语》,Cheung, Wei-ling 编. 包括《论语》的中文与英语、西班牙语、葡萄牙语的对照.

47. The Confucian bible. Book 1, Analects：the non-theocentric code for concerned humans ＝［Lun yü］. English and modern Chinese versions/authored, compiled and edited by John B. Khu... ［et al.］. Metro Manila：Granhill Corp. , c1991. 384 p. ；24cm. ISBN：9719125209

《论语英译今译》,丘文明(Khu, John B.)译. 英汉对照.

    (1)北京：世界知识出版社, 1997. 10, 2, 407 pages：facsimile；21cm. ISBN：7501205418, 7501205417

48. The analects of Confucius/translated into modern Chinese by Bao Shixiang, translated into English by Lao An; edited by the Editorial Department of the Complete Works of Confucian Culture. Jinan Shi：Shandong you yi shu she, 1992. 369 p. ；20cm. ISBN：7805513260, 7805513263. (Translations of Confucian classics ＝儒学经典译丛)

《论语》,今译者,鲍时祥;英译者,老安;《孔子文化大全》编辑部编.

49. The analects/Confucius; translated with an introduction and notes by Raymond Dawson. Oxford; New York: Oxford University Press, 1993. xxxiv, 110 p.; 19cm. ISBN: 0192830910. (The world's classics)

《论语》,Dawson, Raymond Stanley 译.

(1) The analects/Confucius; Raymond Stanley Dawson. Oxford; New York: Oxford University Press, 2000. xxxiv, 110 pages; 20cm. ISBN: 0192839209, 0192839206. (Oxford world's classics)

(2) Oxford; New York: Oxford University Press, 2008. xxxiv, 110 pages; 20cm. ISBN: 0199540617, 0199540616

50. Lun yu = Analects of Confucius/Confucius; Xiqin Cai; Bo Lai; Yuhe Xia. Beijing, China: Sinolingua, 1994. 7, 385 pages, [4] pages of plates: color illustrations; 21cm. ISBN: 7800524078, 7800524073

《论语》,中文译注蔡希勤;英文翻译赖波,夏玉和. 华语教学出版社(中国圣人文化丛书)

(1)《论语》精华版:汉英对照/蔡希勤编注;赖波,夏玉和英译. 北京:华语教学出版社,2006. 234 页;21cm. ISBN: 7802002180, 7802002184. (中国圣人文化丛书)

51. The Analects of Confucius/Confucius; Kuan-chieh Hsin. Beijing: Sinolingua, 1994. 385 pages.

Notes: Translation of: Lun yü, into modern Chinese and into English

《论语》,Xin Guanjie 译.

52. The Confucian bible. Book 1, Analects = Lun yu Ying yi jin yi/John B. Khu. Beijing: Shi jie zhi shi chu ban she, 1996. 10, 2, 407 pages; 21cm. ISBN: 7501206821, 7501206827

《论语英译今译》. 世界知识出版社. 英汉对照.

53. The Analects of Confucius/translation and notes by Simon Leys. 1st ed. New York: W. W. Norton, c1997. xxxii, 224 p.; 21cm. ISBN: 0393040194

《论语》,Simon Leys(1935—2014)(澳大利亚籍比利时汉学家)译.

(1) 1st Replica books ed. Bridgewater, N. J.: Replica Books, 1998. pages cm. ISBN: 0735100276, 0735100275

54. The Analects: the Simon Leys Translation, Interpretations/Confucius; edited by Michael Nylan, University of California at Berkeley. First edition. New York: W. W. Norton & Company, [2014]. lxxv, 314 pages: illustrations; 22cm. ISBN: 0393911954

《论语》,Simon Leys(1935—2014)(澳大利亚籍比利时汉学家)译.

55. The Analects of Confucius = Lun yu/a literal translation with an introduction and notes by Chichung Huang.

New York: Oxford University Press, 1997. viii, 216 p.: ill., map; 22cm. ISBN: 0195061578, 0195112768

《论语》,黄治中(Huang, Chichung)(美国华裔学者)译注. 该书编有"术语"、"中国历史年代表"、"孔子生平"和"索引"等附录.

56. The Analects/Confucius; translated by David Hinton. Washington, D. C.: Counterpoint, c1998. xxxv, 252 p.: map; 21cm. ISBN: 1887178635

《论语》,戴维·欣顿(Hinton, David, 1954—)(美国汉学家)选译.

(1) Berkeley: Counterpoint, 2014. 167 pages: map; 23cm. ISBN: 1619024441, 1619024446

57. The analects of Confucius: a philosophical translation/Roger T. Ames, Henry Rosemont, Jr. New York: Ballantine Pub. Group, 1998. xv, 327 p.: ill.; 22cm. ISBN: 0345401549. (Classics of ancient China)

《论语》,安乐哲(Ames, Roger T., 1947—)(美国汉学家),罗思文(Rosemont, Henry, 1934—)合译.

(1) 1st trade pbk. ed. New York: Ballantine Books, 1999. xv, 326 p.: ill.; 21cm. ISBN: 0345434072. (Classics of ancient China)

Notes: "A new translation based on the Dingzhou fragments and other recent archaeological finds"—Cover. 根据定县出土的《论语》翻译.

58. The analects of Confucius (unabridged)/translated with references by Jack J. Cai, associate translator Emma Yu. Madison, WI: Americd-rom Publ. Co., c1998. 313 p.; 23cm. ISBN: 1580755011, 1580755003

《论语》,Cai, Jack J. 和 Yu, Emma 英译. 英汉对照.

59. The original analects: sayings of Confucius and his successors: a new translation and commentary/by Ernest Bruce Brooks; A Taeko Brooks. New York: Columbia University Press, 1998. x, 342 pages: illustrations; 24cm. ISBN: 0231104308, 0231104302. (Translations from the Asian classics)

《论语辨》,白牧之(Brooks, E. Bruce,〈Ernest Bruce〉,1936—),白妙子(Brooks, A. Taeko)著,是对《论语》的译注.

60. The Lun yü in English = Lun yü dalam Bahasa Melayu in Chinese and Tamil. Singapore: Confucius Publishing Co., 1998. 1 volume (unpaged); 28cm. ISBN: 9627050091, 9627050094

Contents: Lun yu—Bai hua Lun yu—The Lun yü in English—Lun yü dalam Bahasa Melayu—[The Lun yü in Tamil].

Notes: "Based on 'The Lun yü in Chinese, English, Spanish and Portuguese' published in 1985."

包括"白话论语"、"英译论语"和"马来语论语".

61. The Lun Yü in Chinese English Italiano Deutsch/Confucius; William Cheung. Richmond BC, Canada: Confucius Publishing Co. LTD, 1999. ISBN:

9627050164，9627050162
Notes：Based on "The Lun Yü in Chinese，English，Spanish and Portugese" published in 1985.
《论语》，Cheung，William 英译.

62. The analects of Confucius：a new-millennium translation/translated and annotated by David H. Li. Bethesda, Md. ：Premier Pub. ，c1999. 286 p. ：ill. ；23cm. ISBN：0963785281
《论语》，Li，David H. (1928—)译注. 英汉对照.

63. The Lun Yü in English/Confucius. Richmond BC. ，Canada：Confucius Publishing Company，Ltd. ，1999. approximately 300 pages：illustrations；28cm. ISBN：96270501210
Notes：Text in Chinese，English，Russian，Dutch
《白话论语》.

64. The Analects of Confucius/Confucius；translated by Li Tianchen；revised by John Kirkley；[calligraph by Kong Decheng]. [Taipei，Taiwan]：Zhonghua Book Co. ，2000s. 2 volumes：illustrations；29cm. ISBN：7101035868，7101035865
《论语》，Li Tianchen 译；Kirkley，John 校. 中英对照.

65. Confucius said/Confucius；by Tom Te-Wu Ma. [Bloomington，Ind.]：1st Books Library，2001. xvi，92 pages；21cm. ISBN：0759650772，0759650770
《论语》(选译)，Ma，Tom 译.

66. Confucius said：excerpts from Confucian analects/Confucius. ；J. L. Lu. [Bloomington，Ind.]：1st Books，2001. vi，226 pages；21cm. ISBN：0759618224；0759618220
《论语》(选译)，Lu，J. L. 译.

67. Confucius analects：with selection from traditional commentaries/translated by Edward Slingerland. Indianapolis，IN：Hackett Pub. Co. ，c2003. xxix，279 p. ；23cm. ISBN：087220636X，0872206366，0872206351，0872206359
《论语》，Slingerland，Edward G. (Edward Gilman)译注.

68. The essential analects：selected passages with traditional commentary/Edward Gilman Slingerland. Indianapolis Hackett Pub. Co. ，2006. xxvi，164 p 22cm. ISBN：0872207722，0872207730，0872207738，0872207721.
《论语》(选译)，Slingerland，Edward Gilman 译.

69. 孔子语录：英汉双语版/李军峰白话整理；管晓霞英文翻译. 2 版. 济南：山东友谊出版社，2011. 159 页；18cm. ISBN：7807378464，7807378468
本书为"中国先贤语录口袋书"的其中一册.

70. The Analects/Confucius. Fairfiled，IA：1st World Library Literary Society，2004. 154 pages；22cm. ISBN：1595404228，1595404220. (Classic literature)
《论语》

71. 论语百则＝One hundred quotations from the analects/冯大建编注；王健，李盈，谢琰翻译. 天津市：南开大学出版社，2004. 243 pages；21cm. ISBN：7310020286，7310020287
中英对照选编读本.

72. 论语今译：汉英对照/(春秋)孔丘著；杨伯峻，吴树平译；潘富恩，温少霞英译. 济南：齐鲁书社，2005. 2 册；29cm. ISBN：7533315481，7533315480
(1)济南：齐鲁书社，2009. 232 页；25cm. ISBN：7533321628，7533321626. (齐鲁文化经典文库)

73. Lun yu of Confucius/Confucius. ；translated by Tze Yau Pang. Shenyang：Volumes Pub. Co. ，2005. 3，240 pages；25cm. ISBN：7806017542；7806017548
Notes："First published in the United States of America by Voyage Publishing"—Title page verso.
《论语》，彭子游译. 英汉对照. 万卷出版公司.

74. The Analects of Confucius/Confucius. Stilwell，KS：Digireads. com Pub. ，2005. 94 pages；21cm. ISBN：1420926378，1420926373
《论语》

75. 论语精译：汉英对照/(春秋)孔丘著；洪青皎译. 哈尔滨：黑龙江教育出版社，2006. 290 页；20cm. ISBN：7531646374 7531646372

76. 《论语》名言：汉英对照/齐鲁书社编选；李慧今译；刘立壹英译；王铭基绘. 济南：齐鲁书社，2006. 100 页；23cm. ISBN：7533316649，7533316648. (儒家名典箴言录)

77. The analects/Confucius. Place of publication not identified：Filiquarian Pub. ，2006. 137 pages；23cm. ISBN：1599869748，1599869742
《论语》

78. The analects of Confucius/translated by Burton Watson. New York：Columbia University Press，c2007. 162 p. ；22cm. ISBN：0231141642. (Translations from the Asian classics)
《论语》，华兹生(Watson，Burton，1925—)(美国翻译家)译.

79. Confucius for today：a century of Chinese proverbs/Gerd de Ley；David Potter. London：Robert Hale，2008. 127 pages；21cm. ISBN：0709085508，0709085508
Ley，Gerd de(1944—)和 Potter，David(1940—)著. 包括对《论语》的选译.

80. The mankind bible：do unto others as you would have others do unto you/Compiled by George K. F. Wang. Savannah，GA：Continental Shelf Pub. ，2010. xxi，191 p. ；18cm. ISBN：0982258354
《论语》，Wang，George K. F. (1927—)译.

81. The Analects /Confucius；introduction and notes by John Baldock. New York：Chartwell Books，2010. 128 pages：color illustrations；19cm. ISBN：0785826132，0785826130
《论语》，Baldock，John 译.

82. The Analects/Confucius. Abridged ed. London：Arcturus，2010. 128 pages；18cm. ISBN：1848374843，

1848374844

《论语》(节译)

83. Confucius's analects：an advanced reader of Chinese language and culture/Confucius；Chen，Zu-yan. Washington，D. C.：Georgetown University Press，2010. xix，290 pages：illustrations；26cm. ISBN：1589016354，1589016351

《读论语学中文》，Chen，Zu-yan 译. 中英对照.

84. Confucius：eternal sage/edited by Zu-yan Chen. San Francisco，CA：Long River Press，2013. ISBN：1592651597，1592651593

《论语》，Chen，Zu-yan 译.

85. Getting to know Confucius：a new translation of the Analects/translated by Lin Wusun. Beijing：Foreign Languages Press，2010. v，359 pages：illustrations；21cm. ISBN：7119061658，7119061658

《论语新译》，林戊荪(Lin，Wusun)译. 中英对照.

86. The definitive Confucius：a new translation of the analects/translated from the Chinese by Wusun Lin. San Francisco：Long River Press，2012. 164 p. ISBN：1592651276

《论语》，林戊荪(Lin，Wusun)译.

87. 论语注释·今译·英译：普及读本/王福林注译. 南京：东南大学出版社，2011. 284 页；24cm. ISBN：7564124922，756412492X

88. 漫画《论语》：全译本/于健主编. 北京：北京语言大学出版社，2011. 281 页；19×21cm. ISBN：7561930137（v. 1)，7561930135（v. 1)，7561930465（v. 2)，7561930461（v. 2).(中国国学经典学习丛书)

英文题名：The analects of Confucius with illustrations：a complete translated version

89. 论语新译/梁亚东今译；梁治平英译. 长春：吉林大学出版社，2011. 220 页；21cm. ISBN：7560174495，7560174493

90. 论语：中·英文对照版/刘示范主编. 济南：山东教育出版社，2011. 2 册(388 页)；29cm. ISBN：7532867935，7532867936

91. The analects/Confucius.［United States］：Simon ＆ Brown，2012. 136 pages；23cm. ISBN：1613822463，1613822464

《论语》. 译自中文.

92. Thus spoke the master/translated by Xu Yuanchong＝Lun yu/Xu Yuanchong yi；［Yang Bojun Zhong wen yi zhu］. Beijing：China Intercontinental Press；Zhonghua Book Company，2012. 8，442 p.；22cm. ISBN：7508521994，7508521992.(Classical Chinese poetry and prose＝许译中国经典诗文集)

Notes："Project for translation and publication of Chinese cultural works＝中国文化著作翻译出版工程项目."

《论语》，许渊冲(1921—)译；杨伯峻(1909—1992)中文译注.

93. 论语：精选/丁往道译. 北京：中国对外翻译出版有限公司，2012.12，227 页；23cm. ISBN：7500134473.(双语名著无障碍阅读丛书)

英文题名：The analects of confucius：selections

94. "Lun yu" zui xin Ying wen quan yi quan zhu ben＝A new annotated English version of the analects of confucius/Wu Guozhen jin yi，Ying yi ji Ying zhu；Yan xiuhong，Luo Shiping Zhong Ying wen jiao yue. Fuzhou：Fujian jiao yu chu ban she，2012. 562 pages. ；24cm. ISBN：7533457532，7533457536

《论语》最新英文全译全注本，吴国珍今译、英译及英注；严修鸿，骆世平中英文校阅. 福建教育出版社.

95. The new analects：Confucius reconstructed：a modern reader/compiled by Qian Ning；translated by Tony Blishen.［New York］：Better Link Press，2014. 278 pages；20cm. ISBN：1602201460，1602201463.

《论语》，Ning，Qian，编；Blishen，Tony 译.

96. The analects＝Lunyu/Confucius；translated with an introduction and commentary by Annping Chin. New York：Penguin Books，2014. xxx，399 pages；20cm. ISBN：0143106852. (Penguin classics)

《论语》，Chin，Ann-ping(1950—)译.

97. The Jesuit reading of Confucius：the first complete translation of the Lunyu (1687) published in the West/by Thierry Meynard，SJ. Leiden；Boston：Brill，［2015］. ix，675 pages：illustrations；25cm. ISBN：9004289772. (Jesuit studies，2214－3289；volume 3)

Notes：Includes bibliographical references（pages 635－640)，appendix，vocabulary，and index. Chinese text with the Latin translation of the Lunyu and its commentaries，and their rendition in modern English，with notes.

Meynard，Thierry 著. 包括《论语》的拉丁文译本和英文译本.

98. Discussions/conversations or，The analects (Lun-yu)：translation，commentary，interpretation/Confucius；David R Schiller. 2nd edition，revised and updated. Charlton，MA：Saga Virtual Publishers，2015. 2 volumes；23cm. ISBN：0981748313，0981748317

Contents：Volume 1. Books 1－11－Volume II. Books 12－20.

《论语》(选译)，Schiller，David R. 译.

99. The wisdom of Confucius/edited and translated with notes by Lin Yutang. London，H. Hamilton［1938］. xvii，290 p. illus. (map) 17cm. (The Modern library of the world's best books)

《孔子的智慧》，林语堂(1895—1976)编译. 其中第三章由辜鸿铭(1857—1928)译.

(1)New York：Modern Library，1938. xvii，290 pages：illustrations (map)；17cm. (The Modern library of the world's best books)

（2）New York：The Modern Library [1943]. xvii，[1]，265，[1] p. illus.（incl. map）col. plates. 19cm.（Illustrated modern library）

（3）New York：Random House, 1943. xvii, 265 p.：ill.（some col.）map；19cm.

（4）London：M. Joseph, 1958. 237 pages；22cm.

（5）New York：Modern Library, 1966. 290 pages：map；19cm.

（6）New York：Modern Library, 1994. xvii, 290 pages, map；20cm. ISBN：0679601236, 0679601234

（7）Mumbai：Wilco Pub. House, 2005. 233 pages；19cm. ISBN：8182520371, 8182520370.（Classic Library）

（8）Beijing：Foreign Language Teaching and Research Press, 2009. xii, 231 pages；illustrations；22cm. ISBN：7560086330, 7560086330.（English works of Lin Yutang＝林语堂英文作品集）

100. 孔子名言录：汉英对照/国际语言研究与发展中心编. 北京：高等教育出版社,2006. 31 页；26cm. ISBN：7040203294,7040203295

101. Confucius says/Cai Xiqin. Beijing：Sinolingua Press, 2006. iv, 201 p.：ill.；22cm. ISBN：7802002111, 7802002117.（Wise men talking series）
《孔子说：汉英对照》,蔡希勤编注；赖波, 夏玉和, 郁苓英译. 华语教学出版社（中国圣人文化丛书. 老人家说系列）

102. 孔子：汉英对照/（满）闫东主编. 北京：新世界出版社, 2018. 17,211 页；21cm. ISBN：7510464430

103. The essential Confucius：the heart of Confucius' teachings in authentic I ching order：a compendium of ethical wisdom/translated and presented by Thomas Cleary. San Francisco：Harper San Francisco, c1992. xii, 179 p.；22cm. ISBN：0062501577, 0062501578, 006250178X, 0062501783
《论语》,程颐（1033—1107）；Cleary, Thomas F.（1949—）（美国翻译家）译.
（1）San Francisco：Castle Books,1992. xii, 179 pages；22cm. ISBN：0785809031, 0785809036
（2）San Francisco：HarperSanFrancisco, 1993. xii, 179 pages；21cm. ISBN：0062502158, 0062502155

104. Zhu Xi's Reading of the Analects：canon, commentary, and the classical tradition /Daniel K Gardner. New York：Columbia University Press,2003. x, 226 pages；24cm. ISBN：0231128649；0231128643；0231128657；0231128650
伽德纳（Gardner, Daniel K., 1950—）（美国汉学家）著. 包括朱熹（1130—1200）《论语集注》的英译.

105. Confucius from the heart/Dan Yu；Esther Tyldesley. 2009 1st Atria books hardcover ed. New York：Atria Books,2009. ix, 182 pages；illustrations（some color）；23cm. ISBN：1416596561；1416596707；1416596569

《于丹〈论语〉心得》,于丹（1965—）著；Tyldesley, Esther 译.
（1）Sydney：Pan Macmillan, 2009. 1 v. ISBN：0330425353,0330425358
（2）北京：中华书局, 2009.［187］pages,［7］pages of plates：illustrations（some color）；20cm. ISBN：7101067194, 7101067190

106. A life of confucius/Chang Chi-yun；translated by Shih Chao-yin. Taipei：China Culture Pub. Foundation, c1954. 113 p.；22cm.
《孔子传》,张其昀（1900 年—1985）著；时昭瀛译.
（1）Rev. ed. Taipei：Hwakang Press, China Academy, c1975. 235 p.：ill., geneal. tables；22cm.
Notes：Includes an English adaptation of the author's Life of Confucius in Chinese, and 7 other articles.

107. The story of Confucius/written by Luo Chengjie；translation supervisor, Alatan；translators, Li Yonggui, Wang Xin, Pang Lixia. Beijing：Foreign Languages Press, 2004. 266 pages：illustrations；18cm. ISBN：711903071X, 7119030715
《孔子的故事》,骆承烈著. 孔子生平事迹.

108. 孔子说：汉英对照/马德五编著；潘智勇绘. 上海：上海世界图书出版公司, 2004. 6, 290 pages：illustrations；19cm. ISBN：7506262347, 7506262347
本书收有〈如何做一个仁者〉,〈如何从政〉,〈孔子,一位伟大的教师〉,〈孔子,一位伟大的平民〉四章内容,并以美国口语为特点进行英译.

109. 《论语》的公理化诠释/甘筱青等著；桑龙扬等译. 北京：外语教学与研究出版社,2014. 17, 337 页；24cm. ISBN：7513543866
英文题名：The analects of confucius：an axiomatic interpretation. 中英文对照.《论语》研究.

110. Confucius：a philosopher for the ages/by Xu Yuanxiang.［Beijing］：China Intercontinental Press, 2007. 109 pages：color illustrations；21cm. ISBN：7508510372, 7508510378.（Ancient sages of China）
《一代宗师：孔子：英文》,徐远翔著；汉佳, 王国振译. 五洲传播出版社. 孔子思想评论.

111. 孔子和他的主张/张红主编. 天津：天津教育出版社, 2009. 48 页；26cm. ISBN：7530956472, 7530956477
中英对照.

112. Confucius：collection of critical biographies of Chinese thinkers/author Zhou Qun；translator David B. Honey. Nanjing：Nanjing University Press, 2010. 5, 3, 169 p.：ill.；24cm. ISBN：7305066115, 7305066117.（Collection of critical biographies of Chinese thinkers）
《孔子》,周群著. 南京大学出版社（中国思想家评传简明读本）. 介绍了中国伟大思想家孔子的平生经历,阐述了孔子的宗教观、道德哲学、教育思想、德治思想和文艺观,深刻分析了孔子对后世的文化影响.

113. Confucius/written and edited by Kong Xianglin. Beijing：Foreign Languages Press, 2010. 258 pages：color illustrations； 24cm. ISBN：7119060040, 711906004X

《孔子》,孔祥林编著.介绍了孔子的生平事迹及思想.

114. 孔子智慧故事＝Wisdom of Confucius/中文作者 厉琳,英文作者束慧娟,英文审订汪榕培. 上海：上海外语教育出版社, 2010. ［10］, 227 pages：illustrations； 21cm. ISBN：7544618205, 754461820X. (诸子百家智慧故事＝Wisdom of ancient Chinese sages)

B222.8　孔子家语

1. K'ung tsǔ chia yü. The school sayings of Confucius/introduction, translation of sections 1－10 with critical notes by R. P. Kramers. Leiden, E. J. Brill, 1950. xii, 406 p. port. 26cm. (Sinica Leidensia, v. 7.)

《孔子家语》,王肃（195—256）；Kramers, Robert Paul 编译.

B222.9　孔丛子

1. K'ung-Ts'ung-Tzu：the K'ung family masters' anthology：a study and translation of chapters 1－10, 12－14/Yoav Ariel. Princeton, N. J.：Princeton University Press, c1989. xi, 220 p.：ill.； 25cm. ISBN：0691067708. (Princeton library of Asian translations)

《孔丛子》,孔鲋（约前 264 年—前 208 年）；Ariel, Yoav (1946—)译.

B222.10　孟子(约公元前 372—前 289)

1. The mind of Mencius; or, Political economy founded upon moral philosophy. A systematic digest of the doctrines of the Chinese philosopher Mencius, B. C. 325. The original text classified and translated with notes and explanations, by the Rev. E. Faber. Translated from the German, and revised, by the Rev. Arthur B. Hutchinson. 2nd rev. ed. Tokyo, Nippon seikokwai shuppan kwaisha; Yokohama ［etc.］ Kelly & Walsh limited, 1897. xvi, 316, ［2］ p. 22cm.

Translation of Eine staatslehre auf ethischer grundlage; oder Lehrbegriff des chinesischen philosophen Mencius.

《孟子思想》,Ernst Faber 译成德语；Hutchinson, Arthur B. 转译成英语. 初版于 1882 年.

(1)［Whitefish, MT］：Kessinger Pub., 2003. xvi, 291 pages； 28cm. ISBN：0766177173, 0766177178. (Kessinger Publishing's rare reprints)

2. Mencius, translated by Leonard A. Lyall. London, New York ［etc.］ Longmans, Green and Co., 1932. xxviii, 277 p. ill. 24cm.

《孟子》,Lyall, Leonard A. （Leonard Arthur, 1867—）译.

3. Mencius on the mind; experiments in multiple definition, by I. A. Richards. New York：Harcourt, Brace and Company; London, K. Paul, Trench, Trubner & Co.,

Ltd., 1932. xv, ［1］, 131, 44 p. front. （port.）； 22cm. (International library of psychology, philosophy, and scientific method)

"Appendix. Passages of psychology from Mencius ［in Chinese, Chinese transliterated, and English］"： 44 p. at end.

Richards, I. A. （Ivor Armstrong, 1893—1979）著,附录孟子关于心理方面论述段落的英译.

(1)London, Routledge & K. Paul, 1964. 131, 44 pages：illustrations； 22cm. （International library of psychology, philosophy, and scientific method)

(2)Hyperion reprint ed. Westport, CT：Hyperion Press, 1983. xv, 131, 44 p.； 22cm. ISBN：0830500154. (International library of psychology, philosophy, and scientific method)

(3)Richmond, Surrey：Curzon, 1997. xv, 131, 44 pages：1 portraits； 23cm. ISBN：0700704345, 0700704347

(4)I. A. Richards； ed. by John Constable； with corrections to the Chinese appendices by Ming Xie. London：Routledge, 2001. xxxvi, 170 p.：ill.； 23cm. ISBN：0415217369, 0415217361

4. The book of Mencius (abridged)/Mencius; Lionel Giles. London, J. Murray, 1942. 128 pages； 17cm. （The wisdom of the East series)

《孟子》(节译),翟林奈(Giles, Lionel, 1875—1958)(英国汉学家)译.

(1)London, J. Murray, 1949. 128 pages； 17cm. （The wisdom of the East series)

(2)Westport, Conn.：Greenwood Press, 1983. 128 p.； 22cm. ISBN：0313239665, 0313239663

(3)Boston：Charles E. Tuttle, 1993, c1992. 128 p.； 18cm. ISBN：0804818444, 0804818445. (Wisdom of the East series)

5. The sayings of Mencius＝［Meng-Tzu］/Mencius; a new translation by James R. Ware. ［Taipei］：Confucius Pub. Co., 1959. 247 pages：map； 19cm.

《孟子语录》《孟子》,魏鲁男(Ware, James R, 1901—)(美国汉学家)译.英汉对照.

(1)New York：American Library of World Literature, Inc., 1960. 173 pages； 18cm. (A mentor classic)

(2)Taipei：Confucius, 1970. 247 pages； 19cm.

(3)4th ed. Taipei：Confucius Pub., 1973. 247 pages. 中英对照.

(4)The sayings of Mencius/a new translation by James R. Ware； ［editor, Shi Chao］. 台北：文致出版社, 1984. 246 pages：map； 19cm. 中英对照.

6. Mencius：a new translation arranged and annotated for the general reader, by W. A. C. H. Dobson. ［Toronto］ University of Toronto Press ［c1963］. xviii, 215 p. 24cm. (UNESCO collection of representative works：Chinese

series)

《孟子》,Dobson,W. A. C. H. 编译.

(1)London：Oxford University Press, 1963. xviii, 215 pages；24cm.（UNESCO collection of representative works. Chinese series)

(2)Toronto：University of Toronto Press, 1966. xviii, 215 pages；23cm.

(3)Toronto：Toronto University Press, 1967. pages xviii, 215. 23cm.（UNESCO collection of representative works. Chinese series. Canadian University paperbooks. no. 52)

(4)［Toronto］：University of Toronto Press, 1974,（c）1963. xviii, 215 pages；24cm. ISBN：0802060579, 0802060570.（UNESCO collection of representative works. Chinese series)

(5)Toronto；Buffalo：University of Toronto Press, 1981. xviii, 215 pages. ISBN：0802060579.（UNESCO collection of representative works. Chinese series)

7. Mang tzu. A translation by D. M. Gordon. Firenze, Tip. STIAV, 1964. 1 v. 17cm.

《孟子》,Gordon,David M.（David McCall）译. 翻译了《孟子》第一篇《梁惠王》.

8. The works of Mencius. Translated, and with critical and exegetical notes, prolegomena, and copious indexes by James Legge. New York：Dover Publications ［1970］. viii, 587 p.；22cm. ISBN：0486225909, 0486225906

"An unabridged and unaltered republication of the second revised edition as published by the Clarendon Press, Oxford, in 1895 as volume II in 'The Chinese classics' series."

《孟子》,理雅各（Legge,James, 1815—1897）（英国汉学家）译. 中英文本.

(1)Taipei：Chin Shan, 1970. viii, 587 pages；22cm.

(2)New York：Dover Publications, 1990. viii, 587 pages；22cm. ISBN：0486263754, 0486263755

9. Mencius/translated by James Legge. Charleston, NC：Bibliobazaar, 2008. 202 pages；24cm.（Chinese Classics；v. 2)

《孟子》,理雅各（Legge,James, 1815—1897）（英国汉学家）译.

10. 孟子：中国儒家经典/理雅各（Legge,James）译. 沈阳：辽宁人民出版社,2017. 17, 13, 1169 页；18cm. ISBN：7205089733

英文题名：Works of Mencius：the Chinese classic

11. Mencius, translated ［from the Chinese］ with an introduction by D. C. Lau. Harmondsworth, Penguin, 1970. 280 p. 19cm.（Penguin classics).

《孟子》,刘殿爵（Lau,D. C.〈Dim Cheuk〉,1921—2010）（中国香港学者）译.

(1)［Bilingual ed.］ Hong Kong：Chinese University Press,1984. 2 volumes（xl, 384 pages）；24cm. ISBN：9622013015, 9622013018, 9622013139, 9622013131.（Chinese classics, Chinese-English series)

(2)Rev. ed. Hong Kong：Chinese University Press, 2003. xlviii, 429 pages；22cm. ISBN：9622018513, 9622018518

(3)Revised ed. New York Penguin Books, 2003. 246 pages；20cm. ISBN：0140442286, 0140442281.（Penguin classics)

(4)Mencius/Mencius；Lau, D. C.；（Dim Cheuk）. Rev. ed. London：Penguin, 2004. xlviii, 246 pages；20cm. ISBN：014044971X, 0140449716.（Penguin classics)

12. Mencius says/Mencius. ；selected with an introduction by Martin Lu；English translation by D. C. Lau. Singapore：Federal Publications, 1983. ISBN：9971431483, 9971431488

Notes："English text based on D. C. Lau's Mencius, first published 1970"—Title page verso.

《孟子》,刘殿爵（Lau,D. C.〈Dim Cheuk〉,1921—2010）（中国香港学者）译.

(1)English/Chinese ed. Singapore：Federal Publications, 1995. xii, 84 pages；19cm. ISBN：9810123027, 9810123024

13. Mengzi = The sayings of Mencius. Gang chu ban. Xianggang Jiulong：Zhi wen chu ban she, 1973. 245 p. ；19cm.

《英译孟子》,史俊超校编. 英汉文本. 志文出版社.

14. Mencius/translated by David Hinton. Washington, D. C. ：Counterpoint, c1998. xxiv, 288 p. ：map；21cm. ISBN：1887178627, 1887178624

《孟子》,戴维·欣顿（Hinton,David,1954—）（美国汉学家）译.

(1)Washington, D. C. ：Counterpoint, 1999. xxiv, 288 pages：map；21cm. ISBN：1582430209, 1582430201

(2)Berkeley, CA：Counterpoint, 2015. 203 pages：illustrations；23cm. ISBN：1619025554, 1619025558

15. Mencius/translated into English by Zhao Zhentao, Zhang Wenting, Zhou Dingzhi；translated into modern Chinese by Yang Bojun. Changsha：Hunan ren min chu ban she；Beijing：Wai wen chu ban she, 1999. 354 p. ；24cm. ISBN：7543820854, 7543820852.（Library of Chinese classics)

《孟子》,赵甄陶,张文庭,周定之英译. 湖南人民出版社.

16. Mengzi shuo = Mencius says// Xiqin Cai；Zuokang He；Ling Yu；Shiji Li. 北京：华语教学出版社, 2006. iv, 15, 201 pages：illustrations；22cm. ISBN：7802002125, 7802002128.（中国圣人文化丛书老人家说系列丛书 = Wise men talking series)

《孟子说》,蔡希勤编注;责任编辑韩晖;翻译何祚康,郁苓;绘图李士伋.中英对照.

(1)Petaling Jaya: ZI Publications, 2009. iv, 201 p. : ill. ; 21cm. ISBN: 9675215001, 9675215003, 9834352189, 9834352182.(Wise men talking series＝老人家说系列丛书)

17.《孟子》精华版:汉英对照/蔡希勤编注.北京:华语教学出版社,2006. 246 页;21cm. ISBN: 7802002192, 7802002197.(中国圣人文化丛书)

英文题名:A selected collection of Mencius

18. 孟子语录:汉英对照/金沛霖主编;金沛霖,李亚斯编译.北京:中国文联出版社,2006. 236 页;21cm. ISBN: 750595220X, 7505952201

英文题名:The quotation by Mencius

19.《孟子》名言:汉英对照/齐鲁书社;李慧英译;王铭基绘.济南:齐鲁书社,2006. 100 页;23cm. ISBN: 7533317173, 7533317171.(儒家名典箴言录)

英文题名:Aphorisms From MENGZI

20. A basic Mencius: the wisdom and advice of China's second sage/compiled by Kuijie Zhou. South San Francisco, CA: Long River Press, 2006. viii, 146 p. : ill. ; 18cm. ISBN:1592650465, 1592650460

《孟子》,Zhou, Kuijie 译.

21. Mengzi: with selections from traditional commentaries/translated, with introduction and notes, by Bryan W. Van Norden. Indianapolis: Hackett Pub. Co. , 2008. liv, 207 p. ; 22cm. ISBN: 0872209138, 087220913X, 0872209145, 0872209148

《孟子》,万百安(Van Norden, Bryan W.〈Bryan William〉)(美国汉学家)译.

22. The essential Mengzi: selected passages with traditional commentary/translated, with introduction and notes, by Bryan W. Van Norden. [Abridged ed.]. Indianapolis, Ind. : Hackett Pub. Co. , 2009. xlix, 142 p. ; 22cm. ISBN: 0872209862, 0872209865, 0872209855, 0872209857, 1603841412, 1603841415, 1603841405, 1603841407

《孟子》,万百安(Van Norden, Bryan W.〈Bryan William〉)(美国汉学家)译.

23. Mencius/translated by Irene Bloom; edited and with an introduction by Philip J. Ivanhoe. New York: Columbia University Press, c2009. xxii, 178 p. ; 22cm. ISBN: 0231122047, 0231122047, 0231520584, 0231520581, 0231122054, 0231122055. (Translations from the Asian classics)

《孟子》,Bloom, Irene 译.

24. 孟子＝Mencius. [Vancouver]:交流出版社(Canada),2009. 333 pages;21cm. ISBN: 0981181622, 0981181627.(中华文化智能系列. 第 2 辑)

中英对照.

25. Mencius/ Mencius. New York: New York: Classic

Books International, 2010. 176 pages; 22cm. ISBN: 1452808093, 1452808090

《孟子》

26. Mencius/translated by Irene Bloom; edited and with an introduction by Philip J. Ivanhoe. New York; Chichester: Columbia University Press, 2011. 1 volume. ISBN: 0231122054, 0231122055.(Translations from the Asian classics)

《孟子》,Bloom, Irene 译.

27. 孟子今译/孙芝斋编注.杭州:浙江大学出版社,2011. 355 页;24cm. ISBN: 7308085571, 7308085570.(经典重温)

28. 孟子语录:英汉双语版/颜建真白话整理;管晓霞英文翻译.济南:山东友谊出版社,2011. 195 页;18cm. ISBN:7807378457, 780737845X

以原文、白话、英文三种形式对孟子的精华思想加以解释与翻译.

29. 孟子名言录/编注蔡希勤;英译何祚康,郁苓;绘图李士伋.北京:华语教学出版社,2002. 262 页:图;19cm. ISBN:7800528065.(中国圣人文化丛书)

30. Tai Chen on Mencius: explorations in words and meaning＝[Dai Zhen, Mengzi zi yi shu zheng]/a translation of the Meng Tzu tzu-i shu-cheng, with a critical introduction, by Ann-ping Chin and Mansfield Freeman. New Haven: Yale University Press, c1990. xi, 222 p. ; 25cm. ISBN:0300046545, 0300046540

《孟子字义疏证》,戴震(1724—1777)著;Chin, Ann-ping (1950—)和 Freeman, Mansfield 合译.

31. The life of Mencius/by qu Chunli; [translated by Zhang Zengzhi]. Beijing, China: Foreign Languages Press, 1998. 544 pages: illustrations;22cm. ISBN: 7119014609, 7119014609

《孟子传》,曲春礼著;张增秩译.

32. The story of Mencius/written by Cao Raode [i. e. Yaode] and Cao Xiaomei; translated by Xu Rong [and others]. Beijing: Foreign Languages Press, 2001. ISBN: 7119028545, 7119028545

《孟子的故事》,曹尧德、曹笑梅著.

33. 孟子圣迹图:汉英对照/刘仲本,朱庆安主编;邵泽水撰文;董振中绘.北京:中国旅游出版社,2006. 151 页;28×29cm. ISBN:7503229535, 7503229534

本书以国画配文字的形式反映孟子生平.

34. Mencius: a benevolent saint for the ages/by Xu Yuanxiang & Zhang Bing. [Beijing]: China Intercontinental Press, 2007. 81 pages: color illustrations;21cm. ISBN:7508510399, 7508510392.(Ancient sages of China)

《亚圣:孟子:英文》,徐远翔、张兵著;汉佳,王国振译.五洲传播出版社.孟子思想评论.

35. Mencius/Xu Xingwu; transl. David B. Honey. Nanjing: Nanjing University Press, 2010. 251 p: ill; 24cm.

ISBN：7305075834，7305075833，7305075834.（Collection of critical biographies of Chinese thinkers；9）

《孟子》，徐兴无著.南京大学出版社.全面讲述孟子的生平经历和思想内核，中英文对照.

36. 孟子智慧故事＝Wisdom of Mencius/中文作者王小曼，英文作者王晓伟，英文审订汪榕培.上海：上海外语教育出版社，2011. 338 pages：illustrations；21cm. ISBN：7544618175，754461817X.（诸子百家智慧故事＝Wisdom of ancient Chinese sages）

37. 孟子的故事/编注蔡希勤；英译郁苓英；绘图李士仮. 北京：华语教学出版社，2002. 238 页；图；19cm. ISBN：7800528332.（中国圣人文化丛书）

B222.11　荀子（约公元前 313—前 238）

1. The works of Hsühntze/translated from the Chinese, with notes, by Homer H. Dubs. London, A. Probsthain, 1928. 336 p.；20cm.

《荀子》，德效骞（Dubs, Homer H., 1892—1969）（美国历史学家）译.

(1) Taipei, Chengwen Pub. Co., 1966. 336 pages；20cm.

(2) New York：Paragon Book Gallery, 1966. 336 pages；20cm.（Probsthain's Oriental series；；v. 16）

(3) 台北市：文致出版社，[1972].2 volumes（[10]，[3]，553 pages）；19cm.

(4) Taipei：Ch'eng-Wen, 1973. 336 pages；20cm.（Probsthain's oriented series；v. 16）

(5) New York：Paragon Book Gallery, 1973. 336 pages

(6) New York：AMS Press, 1977. 336 p.；18cm. ISBN：0404147544

(7) 台北：文致出版社，[1977].553 pages；19cm.

(8) 台北：文致出版社，[1983].553 pages；19cm.

2. Hsühn Tzu：basic writings. Translated by Burton Watson. New York：Columbia University Press, 1963. vi, 177 p. 21cm. ISBN：0231086075, 0231086073, 0231106890, 0231106894.（UNESCO collection of representative works. Chinese series）

《荀子》（选译），华兹生（Watson, Burton, 1925—）（美国翻译家）译.

(1) New York：Columbia University Press, 1969. vi, 177 pages；21cm.（UNESCO collection of representative works：Chinese series）

(2) Xunzi：basic writings/translated by Burton Watson. New York：Columbia University Press, c2003. x, 190 p.；21cm. ISBN：0231129653, 0231129657.（Translations from the Asian classics）

3. Xunzi：a translation and study of the complete works/John Knoblock. Stanford, Calif.：Stanford University Press, c1988—c1994. 3 v.；24cm. ISBN：0804714517, 0804714518, 0804717710, 0804717717, 0804722986, 0804722988

Contents：v. 1. Books 1－6 v. 2. Books7－16 v. 3.

Books 17－32.

《荀子》，Knoblock, John（美国汉学家）译.

4. Nature and heaven in the Xunzi：a study of the Tian lun/by Edward J. Machle. Albany：State University of New York Press, 1993. xiii, 224 pages；24cm. ISBN：0791415538, 0791415535, 0791415546, 0791415542.（SUNY series in Chinese philosophy and culture）

Machle, Edward J.（1918—）著.包括对《荀子》的翻译.

5. Rituals of the way：the philosophy of Xunzi/Paul Rakita Goldin. Chicago, Ill.：Open Court, c1999. xvi, 182 p.；23cm. ISBN：0812694007

Goldin, Paul Rakita（1972—）著.含有《荀子》的节译.

6. 《荀子》名言：汉英对照/齐鲁书社编选；李晓亮今译；朱新林英译；王铭基绘. 济南：齐鲁书社，2006. 100 页；23cm. ISBN：7533316630, 7533316631.（儒家名典箴言录）

英文题名：Aphorisms from Xunzi

7. 荀子语录：英汉双语版/颜建真白话整理；王滢，管晓霞英文翻译. 济南：山东友谊出版社，2011. 195 页；18cm. ISBN：7807378433, 7807378433

8. Xunzi：the complete text/translated and with an introduction by Eric L. Hutton. Princeton：Princeton University Press, [2014]. xxx, 397 pages；25cm. ISBN：0691161044, 0691161046

《荀子》，Hutton, Eric L. 译.

(1) Princeton：Princeton University Press, 2016. xxx, 397 pages.；25cm. ISBN：0691169314, 0691169316

9. 荀子选译＝Xunzi（selections）/原著（战国）荀况；选释郭玉贤；翻译吴思远；v 绘图关瑞琳，尹红，杨阳. 桂林：广西师范大学出版社，2017. 21, 155 页：彩图；22cm. ISBN：7549594900.（东方智慧丛书）

10. 荀子智慧故事＝Wisdom of Xunzi/中文作者王学松刘炳瑞，英文作者潘智丹，英文审订汪榕培. 上海：上海外语教育出版社，2010. 10, 241 pages：illustrations；2010. ISBN：7544616867, 754461686X.（诸子百家智慧故事＝Wisdom of ancient Chinese sages）

B223　道家

B223.1　道家总类

1. The wisdom of Laotse/translated, edited and with an introduction and notes by Lin Yutang. New York：Modern Library, 1948. xx, 326 pages；19cm.（Modern library of the world's best books；262）

《道家智慧》，林语堂（1895—1976）译，包括《南华经》（节译）和《道德经》.

(1) London：M. Joseph, 1958. 303 pages；23cm.

(2) Westport, Conn.：Greenwood Press, 1979, c1948. xx, 326 p.；23cm. ISBN：0313211647, 0313211645

(3) New York：Modern Library, 1983, c1976. 325 p.；19cm. ISBN：0394604768, 0394604763

(4) The wisdom of Laotse/Laozi zhu；Lin Yutang Ying yi；Li Ming bian jiao. Taibei Xian Xindian Shi：Zheng

zhong shu ju gu fen you xian gong si, 2009. 2 v. (xiii, 1038 p.); 22cm. ISBN: 9570918441 (v. 1), 9570918446 (v. 1), 9570918458 (v. 2), 9570918454 (v. 2). (华语经典)

黎明编校. 台湾正中书局股份有限公司出版.

(5) Beijing: Foreign Language Teaching and Research Press, 2012. xl, 270 pages, 16 unnumbered pages of plates: illustrations, portraits; 21cm. ISBN: 7560081403 7560081401. (English works of Lin Yutang＝林语堂英文作品集)

中文书名《老子的智慧》

2. Complete works of Lao Tzu: Tao the ching & Hua hu ching/translation & elucidation by Ni Hua-Ching. Malibu, Calif.: Shrine of the Eternal Breath of Tao, 1979. ix, 219 pages: illustrations; 22cm.

《老子全书》, Ni, Hua Ching 译. 包括《道德经》和《庄子》.

(1) Santa Monica: Seven Star Communications, 1995. 233 pages: illustrations; 22cm. ISBN: 0937064009, 0937064009

Cleary, Thomas F. (1949—)（美国翻译家）译, 包括《道德经》《太乙金华宗旨》的翻译.

3. The spirit of Tao/translated & edited by Thomas Cleary. Boston: Shambhala; [New York]: distributed in the United States by Randon House, 1993. 198 p.; 12cm. ISBN: 0877738777, 0877738770. (Shambhala pocket classics)

《道家思想》, Cleary, Thomas F. (1949—)（美国翻译家）编译.

(1) Shambhala Centaur eds. Boston: Shambhala; [New York]: distributed in the United States by Randon House, 1998. v, 161 p.; 19cm. ISBN: 1570623708, 1570623707. (Shambhala pocket classics)

(2) The Taoism reader/translated and edited by Thomas Cleary. Boston: Shambhala; [New York]: Distributed by Random House, 2011. 183 pages; 18cm. ISBN: 1590309506, 1590309502

4. Wandering on the way: early Taoist tales and parables of Chuang Tzu/translated with an introduction and commentary by Victor H Mair. New York: Bantam Books, 1994. liv, 402 p.: ill., map; 21cm. ISBN: 0553374060, 0553374063

《漫游: 早期的道家故事和庄周的寓言》, 梅维恒(Mair, Victor H., 1943—)（美国翻译家）编译.

(1) Honolulu: University of Hawaii Press, 1998. liv, 402 p.: ill., map; 21cm. ISBN: 082482038X, 0824820381

5. Early Daoist scriptures/Stephen R. Bokenkamp; with a contribution by Peter Nickerson. Berkeley: University of California Press, c1997. xviii, 502 p.: ill.; 23cm. ISBN: 0520203224. (Taoist classics; 1)

Translation of several Chinese religious texts with extensive analysis, commentary, and notes

《道家早期文典》, Bokenkamp, Stephen R. (1949—), 倪克生(Nickerson, Peter S.)（美国汉学家）编译. 收录了《大冢颂章》的翻译.

6. Five lost classics: Tao, Huanglao, and Yin-yang in Han China/translated, with an introduction, and commentary by Robin D. S. Yates. New York: Ballantine Books, 1997. x, 301 pages; 25cm. ISBN: 0345365380, 0345365385. (Classics of ancient China)

Contents: The Discovery of Mawangdui—The Historical Background to the Silk Manuscripts—HuangLao Daoism and Yin-Yang Thought—The Myth of the Yellow Emperor and the Origins of HuangLao Daoism—The Organization and Philosophy of the Silk Manuscripts—The Canon: Law (Jing Fa)—The Canon (Jing)—Designations (Cheng)—Dao the origen (Dao Yuan)—The nine rulers (Yi Yin Jiu Zhu).

马王堆黄老五经英译本, Yates, Robin D. S. (1948—) 译著.

7. Thunder in the sky: on the acquisition and exercise of power/translated by Thomas Cleary; foreword by Chin-Ning Chu. Boston: Shambhala, 1993. xv, 161 pages; 19cm. ISBN: 087773951X, 0877739517

Cleary, Thomas F. (1949—)（美国翻译家）译. 对《鬼谷子》和《洞灵真经》的翻译.

(1) Boston: Shambhala: Distributed in the United States by Random House, 1994. xv, 161 pages; 19cm. ISBN: 157062027X, 1570620270

8. Taoist miscellany/compiled by Yuan Guang; translated by Cheng Yu. Beijing: Foreign Languages Press, 1999. vi, 268 pages: illustrations; 19cm. ISBN: 711902163X, 7119021638

《中国道家故事选》, 元光编.

9. The Taoist classics: the collected translations of Thomas Cleary. Boston: Shambhala: Distributed in the United States by Random House, 2003. 4 volumes: illustrations; 23cm. ISBN: 1570624852, 1570624858, 1570624860, 1570624865, 1570624879, 1570624872, 1570624887, 1570624889, 1570629056, 1570629051, 1570629064, 1570629072, 1570629075, 1570629080, 1570629082, 1570629068

Contents: v. 1. Tao te ching. Chuang-tzu. Wen-tzu. The book of leadership & strategy. Sex, health, and long life—v. 2. Understanding reality. The inner teaching of Taoism. The book of balance and harmony. Practical Taoism—v. 3. Vitality, energy, spirit. The secret of the golden flower. Immortal sister. Awakening to the Tao—v. 4. The Taoist I Ching, I Ching mandalas.

Cleary, Thomas F. (1949—)（美国翻译家）译, 包括《道德经》《太乙金华宗旨》的翻译.

10. Essential writings of Taoism: the Tao te ching and the Chuang tzu/Lao Tzu and Chuang Tzu; translated by James Legge. St Petersburg, Fla.: Red and Black Publishers, 2008. 237 p.; 22cm. ISBN: 1934941126, 1934941123

《道德经·南华经》，理雅各（Legge，James，1815—1897)(英国汉学家)译.

11. The sacred books of China: The texts of Tâoism. Oxford, The Clarendon Press, 1891.
Contents: v. 1. The Tao te ching of Lao tzu. The writings of Chuang tzu（Books I-XVII).—v. 2. The writings of Chang tzu（Books XVIII-XXXIII). The T'ai Shang tractate of actions and their retributions. Appendices I-VIII).

《中国圣书:〈道德经〉与〈南华经〉》，理雅各（Legge，James，1815—1897)(英国汉学家)译.

　(1)London: Oxford University Press: Humphrey Milford, 1927. 2 volumes; 23cm. (The Sacred books of the East; v. 39—40)

　(2)London: Oxford University Press, 1927. 2 volumes in 1 (xxii, 396, viii, 340 pages); 23cm. (The sacred books of the East; v. 39—40)

　(3)New York: Dover Publications [1962]. 2 v. 22cm. (The sacred books of the East, v. 39—40)

　(4)Delhi, Motilal Banarsidass [1966]. 2 v. 23cm. (Sacred books of the East (Delhi); v. 39—40)

　(5)London: Oxford University Press, 1927. 2 volumes in 1; 23cm. (The Sacred books of the East; v. 39—40)

　(6)The Tao te Ching; the writings of Chuang-tzu; the Thai-Shang: tractate of actions and their retributions/translated by James Legge. New York: Paragon Book Gallery, 1952. 790 pages. (The sacred books of the East; 39—40)

　(7)New York: Julian Press, 1959. 790 pages; 24cm.

　(8) The texts of Taoism: in two parts/translated by James Legge. New York: Dover, 1962. 2 volumes; 21cm.

　(9)The Tao têching: the writings of Chuang-tzŭ; the Thâi-shan tractate of actions and their retributions/translated by James Legge. [Taipei]: [Book World Co.], 1963. 790 pages; 27cm.

　(10)Dao de jing & the writings of Zhuangzi/translated [into English] by James Legge. 台北:文星书店，1963. [47]-790 pages; 27cm. 中文题名《道德经及庄子全集》

　(11) Delhi, Motilal Banarsidass, 1966. 2 volumes; 23cm. (The sacred books of the East; v. 39—40)

　(12)Taipei: Ch'eng-wen, 1969. [1] leaf, [4, 48]-790 pages; 21cm.

　(13)New York: Gordon Press, 1976. 2 volumes; 24cm.

（Sacred books of the East; v. 39,40)

　(14)The Tao te ching [and] the writings of Chuang-tzu: the Thai-shan tractate of actions and their retributions/translated by James Legge. 台北: 成文出版社，1976. 790 p.; 27cm. 中文题名《道德经及庄子全集》

　(15)Thornhill, Dumfriesshire, Scotland: Tynron Press, 1989. 2 volumes in 1

　(16)Delhi: Motilal Banarsidass, [1993]. 23cm. ISBN: 8120801407, 8120801400. (Sacred books of the East; v. 39, 40)

　(17)Delhi: Motilal Banarsidass, 1994. 6 volumes: illustrations. ISBN: 8120801040, 8120801042, 8120801172,8120801172,8120801288,8120801288, 8120801296,8120801295,8120801407,8120801400, 8120801415,8120801417

　(18)The texts of Taoism/translated by James Legge. Singapore: Graham Brash, [2001]. xxii, 336 p.; 22cm. ISBN: 9971492083, 9971492083

　(19)[Whitefish, MT]: Kessinger. Pub., 2006. 790 pages; 24cm. ISBN: 1428622187, 1428622180

　(20)The texts of Taoism /translated by James Legge; introduction by D. T. Suzuki. [Whitefish, MT]: Kessinger Publishing,2010. 790 pages;27cm. ISBN: 1161607048, 1161607048. (Kessinger Publishing's legacy reprints)

12. Rediscovering the roots of Chinese thought: Laozi's philosophy/Guying Chen; [translated by Paul D'Ambrosio]. St. Petersburg, FL: Three Pines Press, 2015. 139 pages; 23cm. ISBN:1931483612,1931483612. (Contemporary Chinese scholarship in daoist studies)

《老庄新论》，陈鼓应，D'Ambrosio，Paul 译.

B223.2　老子(约公元前571—前471)

1. Lao-Tze's Tao-teh-king: Chinese-English, with introduction, transliteration, and notes by Dr. Paul Carus. Chicago, The Open Court Publishing Company; London, K. Paul, Trench, Truebner & co., 1898. xxxiii p., 2 l., [3]-345 p. 1 illus.,pl., diagrs.; 21cm.

《道德经》，保罗·卡卢斯（Paul Carus，1852—1919)(美国学者)编译.

2. The canon of reason and virtue (Lao-Tze's Tao teh king)/translated from the Chinese, by Dr. Paul Carus. Chicago, The Open court Pub. Co.; London, K. Paul, Trench, Trübner & Co., 1903. iv pages, 1 leaf, [95]—138 pages: frontispiece;20cm. (Religion of science library, no.55)

《道德经》(选译)，保罗·卡卢斯（Paul Carus，1852—1919)(美国学者)译.

　(1)Chicago: The Open Court Publishing Co., 1909. 24 preliminary leaves, [95]—138 pages: frontispiece; 16cm.

(2) The canon of reason and virtue... being Lao-tze's Tao teh king; Chinese and English by Paul Carus. Chicago: The Open court publishing co., 1913. 2 p. l., [3]-209 p. front., illus. 16cm. 英汉对照.

(3) Chicago, Open court Pub. Co., 1927. 209 pages frontispiece, illustrations 16cm.

(4) La Salle, Ill.: Open Court Pub. Co., 1945. 209 pages, [1] leaf of plates: illustrations; 16cm. 英汉对照.

(5) La Salle, Ill.: Open Court Pub. Co., 1954. 209 pages: portraits; 16cm.

(6) La Salle, Illinois: The Open Court Publishing Company, 1964. 209 pages, 1 unnumbered leaf of plates: illustrations; 16cm. 英汉对照.

(7) Translated by D. T. Suzuki & Paul Carus. La Salle, Ill., Open Court [1974, c1927] 209 p. illus. 21cm. ISBN: 0875480640, 0875480640 英汉对照. 铃木大拙 (Suzuki, Daisetz Teitaro, 1870—1966), 保罗·卡卢斯 (Paul Carus, 1852—1919) 合译.

3. The teachings of Lao-Tzu: the Tao te ching/translated by Paul Carus. Rev. ed. London: Rider, 1999. 144 pages: illustrations (some color); 20cm. ISBN: 0712608990, 0712608992

Notes: Originally published: The canon of reason and virtue. Chicago: Open Court, 1903. / Includes bibliographical references (page 144).

《道德经》, 保罗·卡卢斯 (Paul Carus, 1852—1919)(美国学者)译.

(1) New York: Thomas Dunne Books, 2000. 144 pages: illustrations (some color); 20cm. ISBN: 0312261098, 0312261092

4. The light of China, the Tâo Teh King of Lâo Tsze, 604—504 B. C.; an accurate metrical rendering, translated directly from the Chinese text, and critically compared with the standard translations... with preface, analytical index, and full list of important words and their radical significations by I. W. Heysinger. Philadelphia, Research Pub. Co., [c1903]. 165 p.; 19cm.

《道德经》, Heysinger, Isaac W. (Isaac Winter, 1842—)译.

(1) [Philadelphia]: [Research Pub. Co.], 1992. 165 pages; 20cm.

(2) [Place of publication not identified]: Solar Energy, 1999. 165 pages; 21cm.

5. The Tao Teh King: a short study in comparative religion/translated by C. Spurgeon Medhurst. Chicago: Theosophical Book Concern, 1905. xix, 134 pages; 24cm.

《道德经》, Medhurst, C. Spurgeon 译.

(1) The Tao-teh-king; sayings of Lao-tzu. Translated with commentary by C. Spurgeon Medhurst. [Rev. Quest book ed.] Wheaton, Ill., Theosophical Pub.

House [1972]. 165 p. 21cm. ISBN: 0835604306, 0835604307. (A Quest book)

6. The simple way/a new translation of the Tao-teh-king with introduction and commentary by Walter Gorn Old. Popular ed. London: Philip Wellby, 1905. ix, 186, [72] pages; 19cm.

《道德经》, Sepharial (1864—1929) 译; Old, Walter Gorn 评注.

(1) The simple way: a new translation of the Tao-teh-king/Laotze (the 'Old boy'); with introduction and commentary by Walter Gorn Old. 3rd ed. London: W. Rider & Son, 1913. xi, 186 pages; 20cm.

(2) 6th ed. London, Rider, 1929. xi, 186 pages; 19cm. (The book of the simple way)

(3) The book of the simple way of Laotze/Sepharial; with introduction and commentary by Walter Gorn Old. [Chestnut Hill, Mass.]: Elibron Classics, 2007. ix, 186 pages; 21cm. ISBN: 140214136X, 1402141362.

7. The sayings of Lao Tzü; translated from the Chinese, with an introduction, by Lionel Giles... 2nd impression. London, J. Murray, 1906. 3 p. l., 9—53, [1] p.; 17cm. (Wisdom of the East series)

《老子语录》(《道德经》), 翟林奈 (Giles, Lionel, 1875—1958)(英国汉学家)译.

(1) London, J. Murray, 1911. 2 p. l., [7]-53, [1] p.; 17cm.

(2) London, J. Murray [1926]. 2 p. l., [7]-53, [1] p.; 17cm. (Wisdom of the East)

(3) London: John Murray, 1959. 60 pages. (The Wisdom of the East)

8. Studies in Chinese religion/by E. H. Parker... Fourteen illustrations. London, Chapman and Hall, Ltd., 1910. xi, 308 p. incl. front. plates, ports.; 23cm.

Notes: "Original studies from which a summary was made and a popular work published, in 1905, called China and religion. "—Pref.

"The Tao-têh king, or 'Providential grace' classic": p. 96—131.

Parker, Edward Harper (1849—1926) 著, 包括对《道德经》的翻译.

9. Tao Teh King/a tentative translation from the Chinese by Isabella Mears. Glasgow (Scotland): William McLellan & Co., 1916. 105 pages; 19cm.

《道德经》, Mears, Isabella 译.

(1) 2nd ed. London: Theosophical Pub. House, 1922. 111 pages; 19cm.

(2) London, Wheaton, Ill., Theosophical Publishing, 1971. [4], 105 p.; 19cm. ISBN: 0722903006, 0722903001

(3) Mamaroneck, N. Y.: Aeon Pub. Co., 2000. 117 p.; 24cm. ISBN: 1893766152, 1893766150

10. Laotzu's tao and wu wei; translation by Dwight Goddard. Wu wei, an interpretation by Henri Borel, translated by M. E. Reynolds. New York：Brentano's, 1919. 116 pages；19cm.

《道德经》,德怀特·戈达德(Goddard, Dwight, 1861—1939)(美国传教士), Borel, Henri (1869—1933), Reynolds, M. E. Mabel Edith(1871—)译.

(1) New York：Brentano's ［c1919］. 2 p. l. , 116 p. ; 19cm.

(2) 2nd ed. rev. and enl. A new translation by Bhikshu Wai-Tao and Dwight Goddard. Interpretive essays by Henry Borel. Outline of Taoist philosophy and religion, by Dr. Kiang Kang-Hu. Santa Barbara, Calif. , D. Goddard, 1935. 2 p. l. , 7 — 149 p. ; 19cm.

(3) 2nd ed. , rev. and enl. Thetford, Vt. , D. Goddard, 1939. 139 p. ; 19cm.

(4) ［Whitefish, MT］：Kessinger Pub. , 2003. 116 pages；28cm. ISBN：0766138526, 0766138520. (Kessinger Publishing's rare reprints)

(5) Laotzu's Tao and Wu Wei/a new translation by Wai-Tao and Dwight Goddard; interpretive essays by Henri Borel; outline of Taoist philosophy and religion by Kiang Kang-hu. 2nd ed. Charleston, SC：BiblioBazaar, 2008. 107 pages；21cm. ISBN：1434698106, 1434698100

(6) Radford, Va.：Wilder Pub. , 2008. 1 volume (various pagings)；23cm. ISBN: 1604593952, 1604593954

11. Tao Te Ching：the book of the way/translated by Dwight Goddard; rev. and ed. by Sam Torode. ［Nashville, Tenn.］：Sam Torode Book Arts, 2009. 81 pages；21cm. ISBN：1449552701, 1449552706. (Ancient renewal)

《道德经》,德怀特·戈达德(Goddard, Dwight, 1861—1939)(美国传教士)译；Torode, Sam 编.

12. Tao te ching：six complete translations/translations by Dwight Goddard and Henri Borel, Aleister Crowley, Lionel Giles, Walter Gorn-Old, Isabella Mears, and James Legge. Radford, VA：A & D Pub. ：Db Wilder Publications, 2008. 1 volume (unpaged)；24cm. ISBN：1604593946, 1604593945

《道德经》的 6 个翻译版本,德怀特·戈达德(Goddard, Dwight, 1861—1939)(美国传教士), Borel, Henri (1869—1933),Crowley, Aleister(1875—1947),翟林奈(Giles, Lionel, 1875—1958)(英国汉学家),Sepharial (1864—1929),Mears, Isabella,理雅各(Legge, James, 1815—1897)(英国汉学家)译.

13. Lao-Tze's Tao-te-king. With comments by Dr. John Gustav Weiss. ［Place of publication not identified］, 1923. 104 p.

《道德经》,Weiss, John Gustav 译注.

14. Tao... a rendering into English verse of the Tao teh ching of Lao Tsze (B. C. 604)/translation ［from the Chinese］ by Charles Henry Mackintosh. Chicago：The Theosophical Press ［1926］. 79 p. ；16cm.

《道德经》,Mackintosh, Charles Henry(1885—1947)译.

(1) Wheaton, Illinois：Theosophical Press, 1945. 4 preliminary leaves, ［7］-79 pages；16cm.

(2) Wheaton, Ill. ：Theosophical Pub. House, 1968. 79 pages；16cm.

(3) Wheaton；London：Theosophical Pub. , 1971. 79 pages；15cm. ISBN：0835604268, 0835604260. (A Quest miniature)

15. The teaching of the Old Boy/Tom MacInnes. London & Toronto, J. M. Dent, 1927. 227 pages；20cm.

《道德经》,MacInnes, Tom(1867—1951)译.

16. Laotse (Tao the king)/translated from the Chinese by Shuten Inouye, with critical and exegetical notes, comparing various renderings in Chinese, Japanese and English, including new English versions by the translator. Tokyo：Daitokaku, 1928. 3 preliminary leaves, 58, 9, 745 pages；20cm.

《道德经》,Inoue, Tetsujirō(1856—1944)译.

17. The way and its power; a study of the Tao tê ching and its place in Chinese thought. London, G. Allen & Unwin, Ltd. [1934]. 4 p l. , 11—262 p. , 1 l. ；21cm.

韦利(Waley, Arthur, 1889—1966)(英国汉学家)著. 书中含有著者对《道德经》的英译.

(1) Boston, Houghton Mifflin, 1935. 262 pages；21cm.

(2) New York, Grove Press ［1958］. 262 p. ；21cm. (UNESCO collection of representative works. Chinese series)

(3) London：Unwin Paperbacks, 1968. 5 — 260 pages；20cm. (A Mandala Book)

(4) New York：Grove Weidenfeld, 1990. 262 pages；21cm. (Evergreen book). (UNESCO collection of representative works. Chinese series)

(5) London；New York：Routledge, 2005. 262 pages；24cm. ISBN：0415361818, 0415361811. (China, history, philosophy, economics；37)

(6) Lao Tzu tao te ching：the way and its power and its place in Chinese thought/by Arthur Waley；with an introductory essay by Frances Wood. London：Folio Society, 2010. xxiii, 235 pages, ［8］ plates, ［2］ doubled folded plates：color illustrations；28cm.

18. 老子＝Lao zi/韦利英译；陈鼓应今译；傅惠生校注. 长沙市：湖南出版社, 1994. 6, 4, 18, 249 pages；21cm. ISBN：7543807939, 7543807938. (汉英对照中国古典名著丛书＝Chinese-English bilingual series of Chinese classics)

(1) 长沙：湖南人民出版社；北京：外文出版社,1999.

67，293 pages：illustrations；24cm. ISBN：7543820897，
7543820890.（大中华文库 ＝ Library of Chinese
classics）

英汉对照

（2）海口：南海出版公司，2013. 336 p.；21cm. ISBN：
7544265455，7544265454.（中华古典文化精粹中英
文对照）

19. Tao te ching/translated with notes by Arthur Waley；with
an introduction by Robert Wilkinson. Ware, Hertfordshire：
Wordsworth Editions, 1997. xix, 89 pages；20cm. ISBN：
1853264717，1853264719.（Wordsworth Classics of World
Literature）

《道德经》，韦利（Waley, Arthur, 1889—1966）（英国汉
学家）译；Wilkinson, Robert 导读.

20. Tao te ching/［translated by］Arthur Waley. Beijing：
Foreign Language Teaching and Research Press；Ware,
Hertfordshire：Wordsworth Editions, 1997. 171 pages；
21cm. ISBN：7560013725，7560013724.（Wordsworth
Classics of World Literature）

《道德经》，韦利（Waley, Arthur, 1889—1966）（英国汉
学家）译. 英汉对照.

21. Tao teh ching/Lao tsu. Transl. and annotated by Hu
Tse Ling. Chengtu：Canadian Mission Press, 1936. IV,
11, 128 p.

《道德经》，胡子霖译.

22. Tao teh king（The way of peace）of Lao-Tzu, 600 B. C.
Palo Alto, Calif. , The School of simplicity, c1936. vii,
55 p.；15cm.

《道德经》（选译），Kitselman, Alva LaSalle（1914—）译.

23. Dao de jing：a new translation/translated from the
Chinese by Ch'u, Ta-Kao. London：Buddhist Lodge,
1937. 94 pages；19cm.

《新定章句老子道德经》，初大告（Ch'u, Ta-kao）译.

（1）2nd ed. London：Buddhist Lodge, 1939. 94 pages；
19cm.

（2）3rd ed. London：Buddhist Lodge, 1942. 94 pages；
19cm.

（3）［London］：Buddhist Society London, 1945. 94
pages；19cm.

（4）London, Buddhist Society, 1948. 94 pages；19cm.

（5）5th ed. London：Published for the Buddhist Society
by Allen & Unwin, 1959. 95 pages

（6）London：Unwin Books, 1972. 96 pages；19cm.
ISBN：004299005X, 0042990057

（7）New York：Weiser, 1973. 95 pages；21cm. ISBN：
0877281459, 0877281450

（8）New ed. London：Unwin Paperbacks, 1976. 96
pages；20cm. ISBN：0042990076, 0042990071

（9）Tao tê ching/translated from the Chinese by Ch'u,
Ta-Kao；illustrated by Willow Winston. London；
Boston：Unwin Paperbacks, 1982. 126 pages；

illustrations；20cm. ISBN：0042990114, 0042990118.
（Mandala books）

（10）London；Boston：Mandala, 1985. 126 pages：illustrations；
20cm. ISBN：0042990122, 0042990125.（Unwin
paperbacks）

24. Lao tze's Tao the king：the Bible of Taoism/English
version by Sum Nung Au-Young；with an introduction
by Merton S. Yewdale. New York：March & Greenwood,
1938. 123 pages；24cm.

《道德经》，Ou-yang, Hsin-nung 译.

25. The Tao te ching of Lao Tzu/translated by Wing-tsit
Chan. Honolulu：Oriental Institute, University of Hawai,
1939. 81 pages；22cm.

《道德经》，陈荣捷（Chan, Wing-tsit, 1901—1994）（美国
华裔学者）译.

26. The way of Lao Tzu（Tao-tê ching）Translated with
introductory essays, comments, and notes by Wing-tsit
Chan. Indianapolis, Bobbs-Merrill［c1963］. viii, 285 p.
21cm. ISBN：0672601729, 0672601729.（Library of
liberal arts；LLA139）

《道德经》，陈荣捷（Chan, Wing-tsit, 1901—1994）（美国
华裔学者）译.

（1）Upper Saddle River, N. J.：Prentice-Hall, 1963.
viii, 285 pages；21cm. ISBN：0023207000, 0023207006.
（Library of liberal arts；139）

（2）New York：Macmillan, 1981. viii, 285 pages；
21cm.（Library of liberal arts；139）

27. The simple way of Lao Tsze/an analysis of the Tao-Têh
canon with comments by the editors of the Shrine of
Wisdom. 2nd ed. London, Shrine of Wisdom, 1941. 55
pages frontispiece, illustrations 22cm.

《道德经》，Shrine of Wisdom 出版社（英国）编辑部
编译.

（1）4th ed. Fintry, Surrey：Shrine of Wisdom, 1974. 55
pages；23cm.

28. The way of life according to Laotzu：an American
version/by Witter Bynner. New York：John Day Co. ,
c1944. 76 p.；18cm.

《道德经》，陶白友（Bynner, Witter, 1881—1968）（美国诗
人）译.

（1）［London］Editions Poetry London［1946］. 74 p.
19cm.

（2）New York, Capricorn Books, 1962. 76 pages：
illustrations；（including frontispiece）19cm.

（3）New York：Capricorn, 1972. 76 pages；18cm.

（4）London：Lyrebird Press Ltd. , 1972. 99 p. ，［8］
leaves of plates：ill. ；22cm. ISBN：0856290017,
0856290015.（Editions poetry London；2）插图版

（5）New York：Putnam, 1980. 76 pages：illustrations；
18cm. ISBN：0399502416, 0399502415

29. The way of acceptance, a new version of Lao Tse's Tao

tê ching. London：A. Dakers，[1946]. 95 p. 19cm.

《道德经》，Ould，Hermon(1886—1951)译.

30. The great Sinderesis：being a translation of Tao te ching/attributed by tradition to Li Erh（Lao-tze）；[translated by Orde Poynton]. Adelaide：Hassell Press，1949. 85 p.；19cm.

《道德经》，Poynton，Orde 译.

31. Truth and nature：popularly known as Daw-Der-Jing/appended with Chinese texts and the oldest commentaries；edited & translated with an introduction by Cheng Lin. [Shanghai]：World Book Co.，1949. xii，71，148 pages；19cm.（Ancient Chinese classics series）

《道德经》，郑麟(1901—)译. 英汉文本.

(1)Taipei：World Book Co.，1953. 40，34 p.（Ancient Chinese classics series）

(2)Truth and nature/[translated by Cheng Lin；with an introductory essay in Chinese by Yang Chia-Lo]. [Hong Kong]：[publisher not identified]，1967. 143 pages；18cm.

(3)Taipei：World Book Company，1969.（Sino-International library series；Ancient Chinese classics series）

(4)Tai bei：Shi jie shu ju，1992. 24，40，34，10 pages；22cm.（Zhongguo guo ji cong shu）

32. Selections from the Upanishads and the Tao te king/[Translations by Charles Johnston.] Los Angeles：Cunningham Press，1951. 142 pages；14cm.

Johnston，Charles 译. 选译了《道德经》.

33. The Tao Teh King：Lao Tse's book of the way and of righteousness/translated with an interpretation by Charles Johnston. [United States]：Kshetra Books，2014. v，137 pages；23cm. ISBN：1484869161，1484869168

《道德经》，Johnston，Charles(1867—1931)译.

34. Tao te ching, the Book of the way and its virtue. London：J. Murray，[1954]. vi，172 p. facsim. 18cm.（Wisdom of the East series.）

《道德经》，戴闻达(Duyvendak，J. J. L. 〈Jan Julius Lodewijk〉，1889—)（荷兰汉学家）译.

(1)Boston：C. E. Tuttle Co.，1992. 172 p.；17cm. ISBN：0804818134，0804818131.（Wisdom of the East series）

(2)London：John Murray，1992. 172 pages；17cm. ISBN：0719551935，0719551932.（Wisdom of the East series）

35. Ho-shang-kung's commentary on Lao-tse/[translated and annotated by] Eduard Erkes. Ascona，Switzerland：Artibus Asiae，1950（1958 printing）. 135 p.；32cm.（Artibus Asiae.）

《老子河上公注》，Erkes，Eduard 译.

36. The way of life/a new translation of the Tao Tê Ching by R. B. Blakney. New York：New American Library，

1955. 134 pages；18cm.

《道德经》，Blakney，R. B.（Raymond Bernard）译.

(1)[Taiwan] Confucius Pub. House，1970. 18，163 pages；19cm.

(2)[T'ai-pei]：Wen chih chu pan she，1970. 163 pages

(3)The way of life：a new translation of the Tao te ching/by R. B. Blakney. New York：Penguin，1983. 134 pages；18cm. ISBN：0451626745，0451626745，0451625633，0451625632

(4)New York，N. Y.：New American Library，2001. 134 pages；18cm. ISBN：0451527941，0451527943

37. The parting of the way：Lao Tzu and the Taoist movement. Boston：Beacon Press [1957]. 204 p. illus. 22cm.

《道德经》，霍姆斯 · 维尔奇(Welch，Holmes)译.

38. Tao teh king, interpreted as nature and intelligence, by Archie J. Bahm. New York：F. Ungar Pub. Co.，[1958]. 126 p. 20cm.

《道德经》，Bahm，Archie J. 译.

(1)2nd ed. Albuquerque：World Books，c1986（1992 reprinting）. 129 p.；18cm. ISBN：0911714200，0911714203

(2)New York：Continuum，1988. 126 pages；18cm. ISBN：0804463875，0804463874

(3)Fremont，Calif.：Jain Pub. Co.，c1996. 129 p.；22cm. ISBN：087573040X，0875730400

39. The Lao tze/Translated into English by Hsu Chao. [Taipei]，1960. 41，27 pages

《道德经》，徐照译.

40. Tao teh ching/translated by John C. H. Wu. New York：St. John's University Press，1961. xiv，115 p. 24cm.（Asian institute translations，no. 1）

《道德经》，吴经熊(Wu，Jingxiong，1899—1986)译；Sih，Paul K. T.（Paul Kwang Tsien，1910—)编. 英汉对照.

(1)Boston：Shambhala；[New York]：Distributed in the United States by Random House，1989. xiv，165 p.；23cm. ISBN：0877733880，0877733881.（Asian institute translations；no. 1.）

(2)Boston：Shambhala，1990. 115 pages；12cm. 115 pages；12cm. ISBN：0877735425，0877735427.（Shambhala pocket classics）

(3)New York：Barnes & Noble，1997. x，165 pages；24cm. ISBN：0760706166，0760706169

(4)Boston：Shambhala：[New York]：Random House，2003. xiv，181 p.：ill.；18cm. ISBN：1570629617，1570629617.（Shambhala library）

41. The book of Tao/translation by Frank J. MacHovec；illustrated by Jeff Hill. Mount Vernon，N. Y.：Peter Pauper Press，1962. 63 pages：illustrations（chiefly color）；19cm. ISBN：0880885084，0880885089

《道德经》，MacHovec，Frank J. 译.

42. Tao te ching. Translated with an introd. by D. C. Lau. ［Baltimore］：Penguin Books，［1963］. 191 p. 18cm. (The Penguin classics，L131)

《道德经》，刘殿爵（Lau, D. C.〈Dim Cheuk〉，1921—2010）（中国香港学者）译.

(1) Baltimore, Md. ：Penguin, 1968. 191 p. ；18cm.

(2) ［Baltimore］Penguin Books, 1970. 191 pages；18cm. (The Penguin classics；L131)

(3) Middlesex：Penguin Books, 1971. ［192］pages；18cm. (Penguin classics)

(4) Baltimore, Penguin Books, 1972. 191 pages；18cm. (The Penguin classics；L131)

(5) Harmondsworth；New York：Penguin Books，1978. 191 pages；19cm. ISBN：014044131X, 0140441314. (Penguin classics；L131)

(6) Hong Kong：Chinese University Press, 1982. 325 pages；24cm. ISBN：9622012523, 9622012523. (Chinese classics) 本版为中英对照.

(7) Rev. ed. Hong Kong：Chinese University Press, c1989. xl, 325 p. ；24cm. ISBN：9622014674, 9622014671. (Chinese classics). 本版为中英对照.

(8) Hong Kong：Chinese University Press, 2001. xl, 325 pages；22cm. ISBN：9622019927, 9622019928. (Chinese classics) 本版为中英对照.

(9) London：Penguin, 2003. xlv, 131 pages；20cm. (Penguin classics)

(10) London；New York：Penguin Books, 2009. 85 pages；18cm. ISBN：0141399300, 0141399309, 0141043685, 0141043687. (Penguin books—great ideas)

(11) Revised edition. Hong Kong, China：The Chinese University Press, 2012. xl, 325 pages；22cm. ISBN：9622019927, 9622019928. (Chinese classics)

(12) 道德经/（春秋）老子著；刘殿爵英译；章婉凝白话文翻译、注释. 北京：中国对外翻译出版有限公司，2012. 164 页；18cm. ISBN：7500133216

43. Wisdom of Dao/recompiled, annotated and translated by Tang Zi-chang. San Rafael, Calif. ：T. C. Press, 1969. 244，42，2，2 pages：illustrations, portraits (1 color)；25cm.

《老子重编》，唐子长编译. 英汉文本.

44. The philosophy of Taoism/［edited and translated by］T. H. Yu. San Francisco：Falcon Publishers, 1970. x, 66 leaves：illustrations；23cm.

《道德经》，Yu, Tinn-hugh(1887—)译.

(1) Hong Kong：World Wide Publications, 1989. x, 66 pages：illustrations；23cm.

45. Tao te ching/Lao Tsu；a new translation by Gia-fu Feng and Jane English. New York：Vintage Books, 1972. 1 volume（unpaged）：illustrations；28cm. ISBN：039471833X, 0394718330

《道德经》，Feng, Gia-fu 和 English, Jane(1942—)合译.

(1) New York：Knopf, 1972. 1 v. （unpaged）illus. 29cm. ISBN：0394480848, 0394480848

(2) London：Wildwood House, 1973. approximately 170 pages： illustrations. ISBN： 0704500043, 0704500044, 0704500078, 0704500075

(3) Taipei：Caves Books, 1982. 1 volume （unpaged）：illustrations；27cm.

(4) Vintage books ed. New York：Vintage Books, 1989. xxxiii, 107 pages；21cm. ISBN：0679724346, 0679724346

(5) 25th anniversary ed. New York：Vintage Books, 1997. 1 volume （unpaged）：illustrations；28cm. ISBN：0679776192, 0679776192

(6) 3rd Vintage books ed. New York：Vintage Books, 2011. 1 volume （unpaged）：illustrations；28cm. ISBN：0307949301, 0307949303

46. The great art of Laotse：a new English version ［translated from the Chinese］/by A. R. Home. Exeter, Newbard, 1972. ［6］, 81 pages；16cm. ISBN：0950262803, 0950262802

《道德经》，Home, A. R. 译.

47. The sayings of Lao Tzu/［edited by Shih Chun-ch'ao］. Hong Kong：［Chih wen ch'u pan she］, 1973. 163 pages；19cm.

《道德经》，Chih, Chun-ch'ao 译. 英汉对照.

48. Tao, a new way of thinking：a translation of the Tao te ching, with an introduction and commentaries/Chang Chung-yuan. New York：Harper & Row, 1975. xxx, 223 pages；21cm. ISBN：0060903562, 0060903565. (Harper colophon books, CN 356)

《道德经》，Zhang, Zhongyuan 译.

(1) Taiwan：Caves Books Co. , 1975. xxx, 223 pages；21cm.

(2) Taibei Shi：Dun huang shu ju, 1977. xxx, 223 pages；21cm.

(3) New York：Harper & Row, 1977. xxx, 206 pages；18cm. ISBN：0060804130, 0060804138. (Perennial library；P413)

(4) Philadelphia：Jessica Kingsley Publishers, ［2014］. ISBN：1848192010, 1848192010, 0857011537, 0857011534

49. Dao- teh-jing：Laotse's book of life/introduction and commentary by K. O. Schmidt；translated by Le'one Muller. Lakemont, Ga. ：CSA Press, 1975. 261 pages；23cm. ISBN：0877071489, 0877071488

《道德经》，Schmidt, K. O. (Karl Otto, 1904—)导读和评论；Muller, Le'one 译.

50. Taoist texts：ethical, political, and speculative/［compiled and translated］by Frederic Henry Balfour. New York：Gordon Press, 1975. vi, 118 p. ：ill. ；24cm.

ISBN：0879681918

《道德经》，Balfour，Frederic Henry 译.

51. A reconstructed Lao Tzu with English translation/ compiled by Yen Ling-feng；translated by Chu Ping-yi；edited by Ho Kuang-mo. Taipei：Ch'eng Wen，1976. i，152 pages；22cm.

Notes：Translation of Lao-tzu chang chü hsin pien. / Added title in Chinese：Chung Ying tui chao Lao-tzu chang chü hsin pien. /Chinese and English on opposite pages.

《中英对照老子章句新编》，严灵峰（Yan，Lingfeng，1904—）译.

52. The Tao teh king：liber CLVII：a new translation/by Ko Yuen. Kings Beach, Calif.：Thelema Publications，c1976.［104］p.；23cm. ISBN：0913576069，0913576069

《道德经》，Crowley，Aleister（1875—1947）译.

53. Aleister Crowley's Tao Teh King［translated from the Chinese］：Liber CLVII/edited and introduced by Stephen Skinner. London：Askin Publishers，1976.［5］，116 p.：facsims；22cm. ISBN：0950387649，0950387642，0877282811，0877282815

《道德经》，Crowley，Aleister（1875—1947）和 Skinner，Stephen（1948—）合译.

　　（1）Tao te ching：liber CLXV11/translated，and introduced with a commentary by Aleister Crowley. York Beach，ME：Samuel Weiser，1995. xvi，112 pages：illustrations；23cm. ISBN：0877288461，0877288466.（Equinox；v. 3，no. 8）

54. Lao Tzu：text，notes，and comments/by Ch'en Kuying；translated and adapted by Rhett Y. W. Young，Roger T. Ames. San Francisco：Chinese Materials Center，1977. viii，341 p.；22cm.（Occasional series /Chinese Materials and Research Aids Service Center；no. 27.）

《老子今注今译及评介》，陈鼓应著；Young，Rhett Y. W.，安乐哲（Ames，Roger T.，1947—）（美国汉学家）合译.中英对照.

　　（1）［San Francisco］：Chinese Materials Center，1981. viii，341 pages；22cm. ISBN：0896446565，0896446564.（Occasional series/Chinese Materials and Research Aids Service Center；no. 27）

55. A translation of Lao Tzu's Tao te ching and Wang Pi's commentary/by Paul J. Lin. Ann Arbor：Center for Chinese Studies, University of Michigan，1977. xxvii，198 p.；23cm. ISBN：0892640308，0892640300.（Michigan papers in Chinese studies；no. 30）

Lin，Paul J. 著.包括对《道德经》的英译，以及王弼（226—249）对《道德经》的评论的英译.

56. The way of Tao：discourses on Lao Tse's Tao-Te-King/ Bhagwan Shree Rajneesh；translator Dolli Didi. Delhi：Motifal Banarsidass，1978. 574 pages；22cm.

包括对《道德经》的英译.

57. Tao the ching：classic of the way and its nature/translated by John R. Leebrick. Urbana，IL：Afterimage Book Publishers，1980. 64 pages；21cm. ISBN：0934862044，0934862042

《道德经》，Leebrick，John R. 译.

58. The way to life：at the heart of the Tao te ching/ Benjamin Hoff. New York：Weatherhill，1981. 86 pages：color illustrations；16 × 24cm. ISBN：0834801566，0834801561

Notes：Selections adapted from various English translations of the Dao de jing.

Hoff，Benjamin（1946—）著.包括对《道德经》的选译.

59. The tao：the sacred way/edited by Tolbert McCarroll. New York：Crossroad，1982. viii pages，167 leaves；21cm. ISBN：0824504607，0824504601

《道德经》，McCarroll，Tolbert 译.

60. Tao：the way of the ways/translation，and with a commentary，by Herrymon Maurer. New York：Schocken Books，1982. 108 pages；22cm.

《道德经》，Maurer，Herrymon（1914—1998）译.

　　（1）The way of the ways＝Tao teh ching/translated and with a commentary by Herrymon Maurer. New York：Schocken Books，1985. 108 pages；22cm. ISBN：0805239855，0805239850

　　（2）Aldershot，Hants，England：Wildwood House，1986. 108 pages；22cm. ISBN：0704505274，0704505278

61. The guiding light of Lao Tzu：a new translation and commentary on the Tao the ching/by Henry Wei. Wheaton，Ill.：Theosophical Pub. House，1982. xi，234 pages：illustrations；21cm. ISBN：0835605620，0835605625，0835605582 0835605588

《道德经》，Wei，Henry（1909—）译.

62. Tao te ching. London；Santa Barbara：Concord Grove Press，1983.［iv］，72 pages；23cm. ISBN：0886950074，0886950071.（Sacred texts）

《道德经》

63. The Sayings of Laozi：a new translation of the Dao de jing/by R. B. Blakney［and Lin Youdang；bian jiao zhe，Shi Chao］. 7 版. 台北：文致出版社，［1983］. 266 pages；19cm.

Notwes："The wisdom of Laotse, tr. by Lin Yutang"：p. 167－266. / English and Chinese（in classic and modern versions）.

《道德经》，Blakney，R. B.（Raymond Bernard），林语堂（1895—1976）译；时超（Shih，Ch'ao）编校.

　　（1）8 版.［台北］：文致出版社，［1992］. 266 pages；19cm. ISBN：9579689008，9579689007

64. Tao tê ching/translated with an introduction by R. B. Blakney with a new afterword by Richard John Lynn. New York：Signet Classics，2007. 170 pages；18cm.

ISBN：0451530403，0451530400

Notes：Previously published as "The way of life", in 1955 by Mentor, an imprint of New American Library, a division of Penguin Putnam Inc.

《道德经》，Blakney，R. B. (Raymond Bernard)译.

65. Dao de jing/translation and commentary by Richard Wilhelm；translated into English by H. G. Ostwald. London；New York：Arkana/Penguin，1985. viii，144，[1] pages：illustrations；20cm. ISBN：0140190600，0140190601

《道德经》，卫礼贤(Wilhelm，Richard，1873—1930)(德国汉学家)德译；Ostwald，H. G.英译自德语版.

(1)Arkana，1985. viii，144 pages. ISBN：1850630119 1850630111

66. The Tao of power：a translation of the Tao te ching by Lao Tzu/by R. L. Wing. Garden City，N. Y.：Doubleday，1986. 23，81 [i. e. 162] p.：ill.；28cm. ISBN：0385196377，0385196376

《道德经》，Wing，R. L.译. 中英文本.

(1)Wellingborough：Aquarian，1986. [192] pages：illustrations；28cm. ISBN：0850305333，0850305330

(2)London：Thorsons，1997. 23，81，[81] pages：illustrations；24cm. ISBN：0722534914，0722534915

67. Lao Tzu's Tao-te ching/by Kim Unsong. Seoul，Korea：One Mind Press，1986. 258 pages；20cm. ISBN：0942049039，0942049039

《道德经》，Kim，Unsong 译.

68. Tao the chin：the Taoist's new library/translated by Shi Fu Hwang. Austin，Tex.：Taoism Publisher，1987. 92 pages；21cm. ISBN：0962963221

《道德经》，Shi，Fu Hwang 译.

(1)Austin，Tex.：Taoism Publisher，1991. 92 pages；21cm. ISBN：0962963321，0962963322. (Taoism classics)

69. Tao te ching/translated by Jonathan Star. Princeton，NJ：Theone Press，1988. 81，[14] pages；22cm.

《道德经》，Star，Jonathan 译.

70. Tao te ching：the definitive edition/translation and commentary by Jonathan Star. New York：Jeremy P Tarcher/Putnam，2001. 349 p.；23cm. ISBN：1585420999，1585420995

《道德经》，Star，Jonathan 译.

(1)New York：Jeremy P Tarcher/Penguin，2003. 349 pages；23cm. ISBN：158542269X，1585422692

(2)New York：Jeremy P. Tarcher/Penguin，2008. xvi，103 pages；18cm. ISBN：1585426188，1585426180

71. Tao te ching：a new English version/with foreword and notes by Stephen Mitchell. New York：Harper & Row，1988. x,108 pages；22cm. ISBN：0060160012，0060160012，0060161698，0060161699

《道德经》，Mitchell，Stephen(1943—)译.

(1)New York：HarperCollins，1988. xi，121 pages；17cm. ISBN：0060171545，0060171544

(2)London：Macmillan，1988. x，111 pages；23cm. ISBN：0333512758，0333512753

(3)Kyle Cathie，1990. x，108 pages. ISBN：1856260100，1856260107

(4)New York：HarperPerennial，1991. x，111 pages；19cm. ISBN：0060916087，0060916084，0060160012，0060160012

(5)New York，NY：HarperPerennial，1992. xii，128 pages；13cm. ISBN：0060812451，0060812454

(6)Norwalk，Conn.：Easton Press，1995. xvi，108 pages；22cm.

(7)London：Kyle Cathie，1996. x，108 pages；20cm. ISBN：1856262340，1856262347

(8)London：Kyle Cathie，1998. 108 pages；20cm. ISBN：1856262871，1856262873

(9)London：Frances Lincoln，1999. unnumbered pages：color illustrations；22cm. ISBN：0711212783，0711212787

(10)Tao te ching/Stephen Mitchell. New York：Harper Collins，2000. 113 pages；21cm. ISBN：0060955430，0060955434，0060916087，0060916084，0060160012，0060160012. (Perennial classics)

(11)Tao te ching journal/with extracts from Stephen Mitchell's translation. London：Frances Lincoln，2000. 117 pages：color illustrations；21cm. ISBN：0711214379，0711214378

(12)New York：Perennial Classics，2000. x，113 pages；21cm. ISBN：0060955430，0060955434

(13)Tao te ching (book of the way)/translated by Stephen Mitchell. New ed. London：Kyle Cathie，2000. ISBN：1856263967，1856263962

(14)1st Harper Perennial Modern Classics ed. New York：HarperCollins，2006. x，113 pages. ISBN：0061142662，0061142666

(15)London：Frances Lincoln Limited，2009. 1 volume (unpaged)：color illustrations；22cm. ISBN：0711229648，0711229643

(16)Tao te ching：[the book of the way]/translated by Stephen Mitchell. 1st Asian ed. Singapore：Words & Visuals Press，2011. x，108 pages；20cm. ISBN：9810879822，9810879822

(17)London：Frances Lincoln Limited，2013. 1 volume (unpaged)：color illustrations；22cm.

72. The Tao te ching：a new translation with commentary/Ellen M. Chen. New York：Paragon House，1989. xi，274 pages；24cm. ISBN：1557782385，1557782380，1557780838，1557780836. (A New ERA book)

《道德经》，Chen，Ellen M. (1933—)译.

73. The book of Lao Tzu，the tao te ching/by Yi Wu. San

Francisco, CA：Great Learning Pub. Co.，1989. xxxv，287 pages；28cm.

《道德经》，Wu，Yi(1939—)译. 英汉对照.

74. Te-tao ching；a new translation based on the recently discovered Ma-wang-tui texts/translated，with an introduction and commentary by Robert G. Henricks. New York：Ballantine Books，1989. xxxi，282 pages；21cm. ISBN：0345370996，0345370990，0345347900，0345347909.（Classics of ancient China）

《道德经》，韩禄伯(Henricks，Robert G.，1943—)(美国汉学家)译. 根据马王堆发现的版本译出. 英汉对照.

(1)London：Bodley Head，1990. xxxi，282 pages；24cm. ISBN：0370314069，0370314068

(2)London：Rider，1991. xxxi，282 pages；23cm. ISBN：0712646450，0712646451

(3)New York：Modern Library，1993. xxxviii，293 p.；20cm. ISBN：0679600604，0679600602

75. Lao Tzu's Tao Te Ching：a translation of the startling new documents found at Guodian/Robert G. Henricks. New York：Columbia University Press，c2000. x，241 p.；24cm. ISBN：0231118163，0231118163.（Translations from the Asian classics）

《道德经》，韩禄伯(Henricks，Robert G.，1943—)(美国汉学家)译. 根据郭店发现之版本译出.

(1)New York；Chichester：Columbia University Press，2005. x，241 pages：illustrations；22cm. x，241 pages：illustrations；22cm. ISBN：0231118171，0231118170.（Translations from the Asian classics）

76. Tao te ching：the classic book of integrity and the way/Lao Tzu；translated，annotated，and with an afterword by Victor H. Mair；woodcuts by Dan Heitkamp. New York：Bantam Books，1990. xvi，168 p.：ill.；22cm. ISBN：0553070053，0553070057，055334935X，0553349351

An entirely new translation based on the recently discovered Ma-wang-tui manuscripts

《道德经：关于诚实处世的经典》，梅维恒(Mair，Victor H.，1943—)(美国翻译家)译注. 据马王堆发现之版本而译.

(1)New York：Book-of-the-Month Club，1997. xvi，168 pages：illustrations；22cm.

(2)New York：Quality Paperback Book Club，1998. xxii，168 pages：illustrations；22cm. ISBN：0965064750，0965064751.（Mystical classics of the world）

77. Dao de jing：the old sage's classic of the way of virtue/translation，with introduction and commentary，by Patrick Michael Byrne. Santa Fe，N. M.：Sun Books，1991. 162 pages；21cm. ISBN：0895401601，0895401606

《道德经》，Byrne，Patrick Michael 译.

(1) The way of virtue/translation and commentary by Patrick M. Byrne. Garden City Park，NY：Square

One Publishers，2002. x，113 pages；22cm. ISBN：0757000290，0757000294

78. Laotse：Ying Yi Lao-tzu/translated by Wang Rongpei and William Puffenberger. Liaoning，China：Liaoning University Press，1991. ii，181 pages；22cm. ISBN：7561013701，7561013700

《英译老子》，Wang，Rougpei 和 Puffenberger，William 合译. 英汉文本.

79. Tao te ching：about the way of nature and its powers/a translation with commentary by Thomas H. Miles. Garden City Park，NY：Avery Pub. Group，1992. xvii，152 pages：illustrations；23cm. ISBN：0895295067，0895295064

《道德经》，Miles，Thomas H. 译.

80. Daodejing：with summaries of the writings of Huai-nantzu，Kuan-yin-tzu and Tung-ku-ching/translated from the Chinese L. Wieger. New ed. Llanerch，1992. 112 pages. ISBN：0947992863，0947992866.（Taoist masters series）

《道德经》，Wieger，Le'on(1856—1933)译.

81. Tao-te-ching/a new translation by Derek Bryce &. Le'on Wieger. York Beach，Me.：Samuel Weiser，1999. xi，108 pages：illustrations；21cm. ISBN：1578631238 1578631230

《道德经》，Bryce，Derek 和 Wieger，Le'on(1856—1933)合译.

(1)New York：Gramercy Books，2005. xi，108 pages：illustrations；22cm. ISBN：0517225344，0517225349

82. The tao of the Tao te ching：a translation and commentary/Michael LaFargue. Albany，N. Y.：State University of New York Press，c1992. xvi，270 p.；23cm. ISBN：0791409864，0791409862.（SUNY series in Chinese philosophy and culture）

《道德经》，LaFargue，Michael(美国汉学家)译.

83. Tao te ching/Lao-tzu；introduced by Burton Watson；translated，with translater's preface，glossary，&. pronunciation guide，by Stephen Addiss &. Stanley Lombardo；ink paintings by Stanley Addiss. Indianapolis：Hackett Pub. Co.，c1993. xx，106 p.；22cm. ISBN：087220233X，0872202337，0872202321，0872202320

《道德经》，华兹生(Watson，Burton，1925—)(美国翻译家)，Addiss，Stephen(1935—)，Lombardo，Stanley(1943—)译.

(1)1st Shambhala ed. Boston：Shambhala；Distributed in the U. S. by Random House，2007. xxx，122 pages：illustrations；21cm. ISBN：1590305461，1590305469

84. Tao te ching：a new translation/by Man-Ho Kwok，Martin Palmer，Jay Ramsay；calligraphy by Kwok-lap Chan. Shaftesbury，Dorset；Rockport，Mass.：Element，1993. 189 pages：color illustrations；28cm. ISBN：

1852303220，1852303228，1862042713，1862042711.
(Sacred arts)

《道德经》，Kwok，Man-Ho(1943—)等合译.

(1) New York：Barnes & Noble, 1994. 189 pages：illustrations（some color）；29cm. ISBN：1566196175, 1566196178

(2) Shaftesbury, Dorset；Rockport, Mass.：Element, 1994. 201 pages；24cm. ISBN：1852304847, 1852304843. (Element classic editions)

(3) Rockport, Mass.：Element, 1996. 133 pages；23cm. ISBN：1852309164, 1852309169

(4) Rockport, Mass.：Element, 1997. 133 pages；23cm. ISBN：1852309164, 1852309169. (Element classics of world spirituality)

(5) London：Vega, 2002. 189 pages，［1］pages of plates：illustrations（chiefly color）；28cm. ISBN：1843336278, 1843336273

85. Another way：the tao of Lao Tzu/English version by Gerald Kaminski. Belmont, CA：Cove View Press, 1993. 82，［1］pages；15×20cm. ISBN：0931896150, 0931896156

《道德经》，Kaminski, Gerald 译.

86. Tao te ching. New York：Knopf,1994. xxxv,126 pages；21cm. ISBN：0679433163, 0679433163. Everyman's library (Alfred A. Knopf, Inc.)

《道德经》

87. Tao te ching：the book of the way and its power/a new translation by John R. Mabry；illustrations by Jim Hardesty. Berkeley, CA：Apocryphile Press, 1994. ix, 87 pages：illustrations；22cm. ISBN：0974762334, 0974762333

Notes："Originally published in God as nature sees God."

《道德经》，Mabry, John R. 译.

88. The little book of the Tao te ching/translated by John R. Mabry. Shaftesbury, Dorset：Element, 1995. 48 pages：color illustrations；13cm. ISBN：1852307072,1852307073

《道德经》，Mabry, John R. 译.

89. Tao te ching：an illustrated journey/Lao Tzu；edited by Peg Streep from the translation by James Legge；watercolors by Claudia Karabaic Sargent. Boston：Little, Brown, c1994. 81 p.：col. ill.；18cm. ISBN：0821220756, 0821220757

《道德经》，理雅各（Legge, James, 1815—1897）（英国汉学家）译；Streep, Peg 编.

90. Tao te ching/by Lao tzu；translation and commentary by James Legge. Dover ed.，unabridged. Mineola, N. Y.：Dover Publications, 1997. 78 p.；21cm. ISBN：0486297926, 0486297927. (Dover thrift editions)

《道德经》，理雅各（Legge, James, 1815—1897）（英国汉学家）译.

(1) Rockville, MD：Arc Manor, 2008. 105 pages；23cm. ISBN：1604500998, 1604500999

(2) translated by James Legge；foreword by Livia Kohn. New York：Fall River Press, c2008. 1 v. (unpaged)：col. ill.；21×28cm. ISBN：1435107434, 1435107438

(3) Radford, VA：Wilder Publications, 2008. 1 volume (unpaged)；23cm.

(4) New York：Wellfleet Press, 2015. 1 volume (unpaged)：illustrations（some color）；16×21cm. ISBN：157715116X, 1577151166

91. A companion to Lao Tzu's Tao Te Ching/R. D. Hermann. Harrogate：D. M. Hermann, 1999. 1 volume（various pagings）；30cm. ISBN：0953596001, 0953596003

Notes：Includes Chinese text and English translation. Translation by James Legge.

Hermann, R. 著. 包括理雅各（Legge, James, 1815—1897）（英国汉学家）翻译的《道德经》.

92. Tao the ching/translated by James Legge；graphics by Greg C. Grace. Stepney, South Australia：Axiom, 2001. 81 pages；21cm. ISBN：1864761385, 1864761382

《道德经》，理雅各（Legge, James, 1815—1897）（英国汉学家）译；Grace, Greg C. 插图.

(1) ［Rockville, Md.］：BN Publishing, 2007. 60 pages；21cm. ISBN：9562910286, 9562910288

(2) ［Gloucester, UK］：Dodo Press, 2007. 51 pages；21cm. ISBN：1406509981, 1406509984

(3) Charleston, SC：BiblioBazaar, 2008. 89 pages；21cm. ISBN：0559118988, 0559118982

(4) Toronto：Prohyptikon Publishing Inc.，2009. x, 88 pages；21cm. ISBN：0981224497, 0981224490. (Prohyptikon value classics)

(5) ［Place of publication not identified］：Simon & Brown, 2012. 90 pages；23cm. ISBN：1613822425, 1613822421

93. The path of virtue：the illustrated Tao te ching/Lao Tzu；translated from the Chinese by James Legge；with illustrations from the Cleveland Museum of Art. New York：Abrams, 2009. 1 v. (unpaged)：col. ill.；11×17cm. ISBN：0810984097,0810984091

《道德经》，理雅各（Legge, James, 1815—1897）（英国汉学家）译. 插图版.

94. The book of Lao Zi. Beijing：Foreign Languages Press；Distributed by China International Book Trading Corp.，1993. 103 p.；23cm. ISBN：7119015710, 7119015712

"This English translation, by He Guanghu, Gao Shining, Song Liao and Xu Junyao, is based on Ren Jiyu's Book of Lao Zi—a modern Chinese translation, published by the Shanghai Chinese Classics Publishing House in 1985"—T. p. verso.

《道家经典：老子》,任继愈新译；He, Guanghu 等英译.

95. Tao Te Ching：backward down the path/Jerry O. Dalton. Atlanta, Ga.：Humanics Trade Paperback, 1993. xi,170 pages：illustrations；24cm. ISBN：0893342238, 0893342234

《道德经》,Dalton, Jerry O. 译.

(1)New York：Avon Books, 1994. xvi, 174 pages：illustrations；18cm. ISBN：0380725606 0380725601

96. Lao zi：the book of Tao and Teh/translated by Gu Zhengkun. Beijing：Peking University Press, 1995. 320 pages；19cm. ISBN：7301028156, 7301028155. (Chinese-English classics series＝汉英对照古代著名丛书)

《老子道德经》,辜正坤译. 中英文本.

97. Lao-ce Tao te king in seven languages. Budapest：Farkas, 1995. 81 leaves；35cm. ISBN：9637310037, 9637310034

《老子道德经》,7 种语言.

98. The Tao te ching of Lao Tzu：a new translation/by Brian Browne Walker. New York：St. Martin's Press, 1995. 81 p.；22cm. ISBN：0312131909, 0312131906

《道德经》,Walker, Brian Browne 译.

(1)1st St. Martin's Griffin ed. New York：St. Martin's Griffin, 1996. 81 pages；21cm. ISBN：0312147449, 0312147440

99. Tao te ching/a new version by Timothy Freke. London：Piatkus, 1995. 128 pages；22cm. ISBN：0749914688, 0749914684. (Chinese popular classics)

《道德经》,Freke, Timothy(1959—)译.

(1)Lao Tzu's Tao te ching：a new version/by Timothy Freke；editor, Martin Palmer. New ed. London：Piatkus, 1999. 128 pages：illustrations；22cm. ISBN：0749919663, 0749919665. (Chinese popular classics)

100. The Tao te ching/foreword by Ann-ping Chin. Collector's edition. Norwalk, Connecticut：Easton Press, 1996. xvi pages, 81 leaves, 25 unnumbered pages：color illustration；24cm.

《道德经》,Chin, Ann-ping(1950—)译.

101. The way of life：a new translation＝Tao tê ching/by Gary N. Arnold. Metairie, LA：Windhorse Corp., 1996.176 pages：color illustrations；22cm. ＋2 audiocassettes (analog). ISBN：1578670012, 1578670017

《道德经》,Arnold, Gary N. (1954—)译.

102. Tao now：a new rendition of "The way of virtue" by the Master Lao-Tzu/rendered by Richard Shining Thunder Francis. Worthville, KY：Love Ministries, Inc., 1997. 47 pages：1 illustration；22cm.

《道德经》,Francis, Richard Shining Thunder 译.

103. The creative Tao/Pamela Metz. Atlanta, GA：Humanics Trade, 1997. x, 166 pages；23cm. ISBN：0893342556 0893342555

《道德经》,Metz, Pamela 译. 英汉文本.

104. Tao te ching：a book about the way and the power of the way/new English version by Ursula K. Le Guin with the collaboration of J. P. Seaton. Boston：Shambhala, 1997. 125 p.；23cm. ISBN：1570623333, 1570623332, 1570623953, 1570623950

《道德经》,Le Guin, Ursula K. (1929—)和 Seaton, Jerome P. 合译.

(1) Boston, Mass.：Shambhala, 2009. xi, 144 pages；17cm. ＋2 audio disc. ISBN：1590307441, 1590307445

105. The gate of all marvelous things：a guide to reading the Tao te ching/translated by Gregory C. Richter. South San Francisco, Calif.：Red Mansions Pub.；San Franscisco, CA：Distributed by China Books and Periodicals, Inc., 1998. ix, 153 pages；28cm. ISBN：1891688006, 1891688003

《道德经》,Richter, Gregory C. 译. 英汉对照.

106. The book of the way and virtue/translation and commentary by Yeshe Palden. Santa Cruz, CA：Seven Hawk Pub., 1998. 119 pages：illustrations；21cm.

《道德经》,Palden, Yeshe 译.

107. Lao Zi zhi Dao de Jing＝Lao Tzu's Dao de jing：word for word/[translated] by Bradford Hatcher. [Ridgway, Colo.]：Bradford Hatcher, 1998. 231 pages [on 118]；28cm.

Notes："Two literal English translations：one basic, one advanced, and a Pinyin transcription. "

《道德经》,Hatcher, Bradford 译.

108. The great way of all beings/Paul Ferrini. Greenfield, MA：Heartways Press, 1999. 314 pages：illustrations；22cm. ISBN：1879159465, 1879159464

Notes："The great way of all beings：renderings of Lao Tzu is composed of two different versions of Lao Tzu's masterful scripture Tao Te Ching. Part one, River of light, is an intuitive, spontaneous rendering of the material that captures the spirit of the Tao Te Ching, but does not presume to be a close translation. Part two is a more conservative translation of the Tao Te Ching. "

《道德经》,Ferrini, Paul 译.

109. Of nourishment and grace, stillness, and compassion：an interpretation of the Tao Teh Ching, a collection of ancient Tao wisdom/said to be recorded by one Lao Tzu about 525 bc；[translation by Louisa Milne]. 2nd ed. Wimborne, Dorset：Gaunts, 1999. 96 pages；21cm. ISBN：1901166007, 1901166002

《道德经》,Milne, Louisa 译.

110. Tao te ching/Lao Tzu；translated by David Hinton. Washington, D. C.：Counterpoint, c2000. xxix, 97 p.；21cm. ISBN：1582430470, 1582430478

《道德经》,戴维・欣顿(Hinton, David,1954—)(美国

汉学家)译.

　　(1)Washington, D. C.：Counterpoint, 2002. xxix, 97 pages：illustrations；21cm. ISBN：1582431825, 1582431826

　　(2)Berkeley, CA：Counterpoint, 2015. 126 pages：illustrations；23cm. ISBN：1619025566, 1619025561

111. Lao-tzǔ：the way and its virtue＝Rōshi. 东京：庆应义塾大学出版会, 2001. 199 pages；24cm. ISBN：4766408594, 4766408591. (The Izutsu Library series on Oriental philosophy；1)

　　《老子》,井筒俊彦(1914—)译. 中英文本.

112. Dao de jing：a new-millennium translation/translated and annotated with appendices on comparison with The analects by Confucius and with The art of war by Sun Tzu, by David H. Li. Bethesda, Md.：Premier Pub., c2001. 264 p.；23cm. ISBN：0971169004, 0971169005

　　《道德经》,Li, David H. (1928—)译. 英汉对照.

113. The Daodejing of Laozi/translation and commentary by Philip J. Ivanhoe. New York：Seven Bridges Press, 2001. xxxii, 125 pages；20cm. ISBN：1889119709, 1889119700, 1889119822, 1889119823

　　《道德经》,Ivanhoe, P. J. 译.

　　(1)New York：Seven Bridges Press, 2002. 125 S：ill. ISBN：1889119822, 1889119823

　　(2)Indianapolis, IN：Hackett Pub. Co., 2003. xxxii, 125 pages；20cm. ISBN：0872207013, 0872207011, 0872207021, 0872207028

114. Dao de jing：the book of the way/translation and commentary by Moss Roberts. Berkeley：University of California Press, c2001. ix, 226 p.；23cm. ISBN：0520205553, 0520205550

　　《道德经》,罗慕士(Roberts, Moss, 1937—)译注.

　　(1)Berkeley；London：University of California Press, 2004. ix, 226 pages. ISBN：0520242211, 0520242210. (A Philip E. Lilienthal book in Asian studies)

115. The illustrated Tao Te Ching：a new translation and commentary/by Stephen Hodge. Hauppauge, NY：Barron's, 2002. 176 pages：color illustrations, map；26cm. ISBN：0764121685, 0764121685

　　《道德经》,Hodge, Stephen(1947—)译.

　　(1)Old Alresford：Godsfield, 2002. 176 pages：color illustrations, map；26cm. ISBN：1841811513, 1841811512

116. Tao te ching：the cornerstone of Chinese culture/newly translated by Chou-Wing Chohan, Abe Bellenteen and Rosemary Brant. Israel：Astrolog Pub. House, 2002. 158 pages；21cm. ISBN：9654941562, 9654941563

　　《道德经》,Chohan, Chou-Wing, Bellenteen, Abe, Brant, Rosemary 合译.

117. Reading Lao Tzu：a companion to the Tao te ching with a new translation/Ha Poong Kim. ［Philadelphia］：Xlibris, 2002. 197 pages；22cm. ISBN：140108317X, 1401083175, 1401083161, 1401083168

　　《道德经》,Kim, Ha Poong(1928—)译.

118. The Way/a new translation by Liu Qixuan. Warrensburg, Mo.：Mid-America Press, 2002. xiii, 38 pages；23cm. ISBN：0910479216, 0910479219

　　《道德经》,Liu, Qixuan 译.

119. Tao te ching：a new translation ＆ commentary/translated by Ralph Alan Dale；photographs by John Cleare. London：Watkins, 2002. xxviii, 284 pages：illustrations；28cm. ISBN：1842930567, 1842930564

　　《道德经》,Dale, Ralph Alan 译. 附有中文《道德经》.

　　(1)New York：Barnes ＆ Noble Books, 2002. xxviii, 284 pages：illustrations；28cm. ISBN：0760749982, 0760749981

　　(2)London：Watkins, 2005. 222 pages；16cm. ISBN：1842930966, 1842930960. (Sacred texts)

　　(3)London：Sacred Wisdom, 2006. 222 pages；16cm. ISBN：1842931237, 1842931233

120. The wisdom of Lao Zi：Dao de jing/translated by Han Hiong Tan. Queensland, Australia：H. H. Tan (Medical) P/L, 2003. 303 pages；21cm. ISBN：0958006725, 0958006729

　　《道德经》,Tan, Han Hiong 译. 英汉对照.

121. The art of peace：a new reading of the philosophical poem Tao Te Ching/［translated by］John Patterson. Wellington, N. Z.：Steele Roberts, 2003. x, 81 pages；19cm.

　　《和法》,Patterson, John(1941—)译.《道德经》英译.

　　(1)Wellington, N. Z.：Steele Roberts, 2007. x, ［81］ p.；19cm. ISBN：1877338977, 1877338974

122. Lao Tzu's Tao te ching/［translated by H. H. Lui］. Cloud Hands ed. ［Chicago, Ill.］：Cloud Hands, Inc., 2003. 81 pages；23cm. ISBN：0974201316, 0974201313

　　《道德经》,Lui, Hubert H. 译.

123. Dao de jing：making this life significant：a philosophical translation/Roger T. Ames and David L. Hall. New York：Ballantine Books, 2003. xiii, 241 p.；25cm. ISBN：0345444159, 0345444158

　　《道德经》,安乐哲(Ames, Roger T., 1947—)(美国汉学家),郝大维(Hall, David L.)合译. 基于郭店发现的《道德经》版本而译出.

　　(1)New York：Ballantine Books, 2004. xiii, 241 pages；21cm. ISBN：0345444191, 0345444196

124. Tao te jing in plain English/translation and commentary by Thomas Z. Zhang and Jackie X. Zhang. ［U. S.］：AuthorHouse, 2004. xii, 90 pages；23cm. ISBN：1418429716, 1418429713

　　《道德经》,Zhang, Thomas Z. 和 Zhang, Jackie X. 合

译.

125. Your Dao de Jing（Tao te ching）/Nina Correa. ［Place of publication not identified］：N. Correa, 2004. v, 745 pages；28cm.

Correa, Nina 著，包括对《道德经》的翻译.

126. Tao te ching/a version in English by Curt Dornberg. Tucson, Ariz.：Deer's Run Press, 2004. 4 volumes；15cm.

《道德经》，Dornberg, Curt 译.

127. The Tao of an Indian：a native inspirational translation of the Tao "The Book of changes"/by Red Hawk. U. S.：MC Printing, 2005. 108 pages；22cm. ISBN：1576361691, 1576361696

《道德经》，Hawk, Red 译.

128. Tao te ching：the book about the power of the word and its world/translation from classical Chinese and introduction by Daniel Deleanu. London；New York：Buxton University Press, 2005. 71 pages；23cm.

《道德经》，Deleanu, Daniel(1972—)译.

129. Tao te ching/with an introduction and notes by Yi-Ping Ong；translated by Charles Muller；George Stade, consulting editorial director. New York：Barnes & Noble Classics, 2005. xxxi, 175 pages；21cm. ISBN：1593082568, 1593082567

《道德经》，Yi-Ping, Ong 导读；Muller, Charles 译.

130. Revealing the Tao te ching：in-depth commentaries on an ancient classic/translation and commentary by Hu Xuezhi；edited by Jesse Lee Parker. Los Angeles, CA：Ageless Classics Press, 2005. 239 p.：ill.；23cm. ISBN：1887575189, 1887575188

《道德经》，Hu, Xuezhi 译评；Parker, Jesse Lee 编.

131. Tao te ching/Lao Tzu；translated from the Chinese by Sam Hamill；calligraphy by Kaz Tanahashi. Boston：Shambhala, 2005. xvii, 119；21cm. ISBN：1590300114, 1590300114, 159030246X, 1590302460

《道德经》，Hamill, Sam(美国诗人)译.

(1) 1st pbk. ed. Boston：Shambhala, 2007. xvii, 119 p.：ill.；20cm. ISBN：1590303870, 1590303873

132. Tao te ching：a new version for all seekers/Guy Leekley. The Woodlands, TX：Anusara, 2004. 81 pages；23cm. ISBN：0965776859, 0965776851

《道德经》，Leekley, Guy 译.

(1) The Woodlands, TX：Anusara Press TM, 2008. 81 pages；23cm. ISBN：0979150949, 0979150944

133. Tao te ching：a literal translation with an introduction, notes, and commentary/Chichung Huang. Fremont, Calif.：Asian Humanities Press, 2003. xii, 200 p.：ill.；22cm. ISBN：0895818531, 0895818539, 0895818523, 0895818522

《道德经》，黄治中（Huang, Chichung）（美国华裔学者）译.

134. Tao teh ching/Lao Tzu；translated by John C. H. Wu. Boston：Shambhala；［New York］：Random House, 2003. xiv, 181 p.：ill.；18cm. ISBN：1570629617, 1570629617. (Shambhala library)

Originally published：New York：St. John's University Press, 1961.

《道德经》，Wu, John C. H. 英译. 初版于 1961 年. 英汉文本.

135. A Chinese reading of the Daodejing：Wang Bi's commentary on the Laozi with critical text and translation/Rudolf G. Wagner. Albany：State University of New York Press, 2003. viii, 531 p.；23cm. ISBN：079145181X, 0791451816, 0791451828, 0791451823. (SUNY series in Chinese philosophy and culture)

Wagner, Rudolf G. 著. 包括《道德经》和王弼（226—249）对《道德经》的评论的英译.

136. Tao te ching：an authentic taoist translation＝Lao-tzu/by John Bright-Fey. ［Birmingham, Ala.］：Sweetwater Press, 2004. 144 pages：illustrations；18cm. ISBN：158173333X, 1581733334

《道德经》，Bright-Fey, J. (John)译.

137. The book of balance：Lao Tzu's Tao Teh Ching, a new translation/by Yasuhiko Genku Kimura. New York：Paraview Special Editions, 2004. 109 pages；23cm. ISBN：1931044905, 1931044902

《道德经》，Kimura, Yasuhiko Genku 译.

138. Tao te ching：a literal translation＝Dao de jing Lao Zi：bi de lan zhi yi/［translated by］Peter Land. Kaikohe, N. Z.：Landseer Press, 2005. 81 pages；23cm. ISBN：1411645462, 1411645464

《道德经》，Land, Peter(1927—)译.

139. Daode jing/translated by Thomas Meyer. Chicago, Ill.：Flood Editions, 2005. 111 pages；20cm. ISBN：0974690279, 0974690278

《道德经》，Meyer, Thomas(1947—)译.

140. The Tao te ching：a contemporary translation/by Joseph B. Lumpkin. Blountsville, AL：Fifth Estate, 2005. xii, 168 pages：illustrations；23cm. ISBN：0976823314, 0976823315

《道德经》，Lumpkin, Joseph(1955—)译.

141. Tao te ching：the art and the journey/translated and illustrated by Holly Roberts. ［Little Silver, N. J.］：Anjeli Press, 2005. x, 163, ［2］ pages：illustrations；24cm. ISBN：0975484419, 0975484418

《道德经》，Roberts, Holly(1945—)译. 英汉对照.

142. Lao Tzu：Tao Te Ching：a new version, with introduction, notes, glossary and index/Keith Seddon. ［Place of publication not identified］：Lulu, 2006. 136 pages：illustrations；23cm. ISBN：1847282637, 1847282636

《道德经》，Seddon，Keith(1956—)译注.

143. 老子说：图文本：汉英对照/顾丹柯译；赵兵绘. 上海：上海世界图书出版公司，2006. 173 页；18×21cm. ISBN：750628054X，7506280549

144. 老子说：汉英对照/蔡希勤编注. 北京：华语教学出版社，2006. 201 页；21cm. ISBN：780200215X，7802002159.(中国圣人文化丛书. 老人家说系列)

英文题名：Laozi says

145. Thoughts on becoming a sage：interpretations of Lao Tzu's Tao Te Ching：the guidebook to leading a virtuous life/Dan C. DeCarlo；[translated by Binhe Gu]. [Beijing]：Ctcp，2006. 212 pages：illustrations；21cm. ISBN：750011639X，7500116394

《成圣之思辩：〈道德经〉解读》，德卡罗(Carlo，Dan C.)著；古滨河译. 包括对《道德经》的英汉对照翻译. 中国对外翻译出版公司.

146. Tao te ching：annotated & explained/translation and annotation by Derek Lin；foreword by Lama Surya Das. Woodstock，Vt.：SkyLight Paths Pub.，c2006. xxxi，169 p.；22cm. ISBN：1594732043，1594732041.(Skylight Illuminations series)

《道德经》，Lin，Derek(1964—)译.

147. Daodejing（Laozi）：a complete translation and commentary/by Hans-Georg Moeller. Chicago，Ill.：Open Court，2007. xvi，213 p.：ill.；23cm. ISBN：0812696257，0812696255

《道德经》，Moeller，Hans-Georg(1964—)译.

148. Lao Zi's Dao de jing/translated by Dr. Lin Yutang. [Beijing]：Foreign Languages Press，2007. 2 volumes of folded silk leaves；28cm. + 1 box and 1 pair of gloves. ISBN：7119051390 7119051393

《道德经》，林语堂(1895—1976)译. 英汉文本.

149. The classic of way and her power，a miscellany：a translation and study of the Dao-de jing，offering a proposal as to its order and composition/Richard Gotshalk. Lanham，MD：University Press of America，2007. xiv，247 pages；23cm. ISBN：0761838295，0761838296

Gotshalk，Richard 著，包括对《道德经》的翻译.

150. Daodejing：study aids with annotations on the complete Chinese text and concordance listings/Muhammad Wolfgang G A Schmidt. Berlin：Viademica-Verl.，2007. iv，143 pages；30cm. ISBN：3937494579，393749457X

《道德经》，Schmidt，Muhammad Wolfgang G. A. 译. 英汉文本.

151. Tao te ching/translated and interpreted by David Burke. Moorooka，Qld.：Boolarong Press for David Burke，2007. ISBN：1921054099，1921054093

《道德经》，Burke，David(David Justin，1958—)译.

152. Lao Tzu：the eternal Tao te ching/by Xu Yuanxiang &

Yin Yongjian. [Beijing]：China Intercontinental Press，2007. 81 pages：color illustrations；21cm. ISBN：7508510385，7508510380.(Ancient sages of China)

《千年道德经：老子》，徐远翔，印永健[著]；汉佳，王国振译.

153. 老子名言精选 ＝Quotations from Laozi/汪榕培，潘智丹，冯秋香编译. 上海：上海外语教育出版社，2008. 159 p.：ill.；19cm. + 1CD. ISBN：7544609852，7544609855

154. Dao de jing/translated with a thematic reading guide by Wang Keping. Beijing：Foreign Languages Press，2008. 159 pages：illustrations；21cm. ISBN：7119034454，7119034456

《道德经》，王柯平(1955—)译.

155. The classic of the Dao：a new investigation/by Wang Keping. Beijing：Foreign Languages Press，1998. iv，322 pages；21cm. ISBN：7119022296，7119022291

《道德经》，王柯平(1955—)译. 英汉文本.

(1) Beijing：Foreign Languages Press，2010. iv，322 pages；24cm. ISBN：7119065397，7119065394

156. The tao te ching："my words are easy to understand"/by Lao-Tzu；and interpretation by Gordon J. Van de Water. Diamond Bar，Calif.：Featherwood Press，2008. 1 volume；22cm.

《道德经》，Water，Gordon J. van de 译.

(1) The tao te ching（dao de jing）：a plain English version："life's little instruction book"/an interpretation by Gordon J. Van de Water. Diamond Bar，Calif.：Featherwood Press，2011. 125 pages；22cm. ISBN：1456814090，1456814095，1456814083，145681408，7 1456814106，1456814109

157. Daodejing/translated with notes by Edmund Ryden；with an introduction by Benjamin Penny. Oxford；New York：Oxford University Press，2008. xxxvi，187 pages；20cm. ISBN：0199208555，0199208557.(Oxford world's classic)

《道德经》，Ryden，Edmund 译；Penny，Benjamin 作序.

158. Daodejing：a literal-critical translation/Joseph Hsu. Lanham，Md.：University Press of America，2008. xvii，159 pages；23cm. ISBN：0761841520，0761841524

《道德经》，Hsu，Joseph 译.

159. Tao te ching：on the art of harmony：the new illustrated edition of the Chinese philosophical masterpiece/translated by Chad Hansen. London：Duncan Baird Publishers，2009. 272 pages：color illustrations；24cm. ISBN：1844838509，1844838501，1844838271，1844838277

《道德经》，Hansen，Chad(1942—)译.

(1)2011 ed. New York：Metro Books，2011. 272 pages：color illustrations；24cm. ISBN：1435132948，1435132947

160. Tao te ching/translated by John H. McDonald; introduction by John Baldock. New York：Chartwell Books, 2009. 126 pages：illustrations；19cm. ISBN：0785825166, 0785825169

《道德经》，McDonald, John H. 译.

(1) Illustrated ed. New York：Chartwell Books; London：Arcturus Pub. Ltd., 2010. 128 pages：color illustrations；25cm. ISBN：0785826880, 0785826882

161. Tao Te Ching：a new interpretive translation/written by Lao-tzu, interpretive translation by Robert Brooks. Canada：IC Gtesting, 2010. 81 pages；23cm. ISBN：1453707661, 1453707662

《道德经》，Brooks, Robert 译.

162. Lao Zi：Dao de jing：with interpretations of classic scholars/translated by Wenliang Tao. Baltimore：Baltimore Press, 2010. 218 pages；21cm. ISBN：0982524602, 0982524609, 0982524619, 0982524617

《老子：道德经》，陶文亮(1953—)译.

163. Tao te ching：teachings from silence/translation and annotation by Herbert B. Fox. Jacksonville, FL：A. Raposa, Inc., 2010. xx, 81 pages；21cm. ISBN：0615408750, 0615408753

《道德经》，Fox, Herbert B. 译.

164. Lao Tzu and anthroposophy：a translation of the Tao te ching with commentary and a Lao Tzu document "The great one excretes water"/[edited by] Kwan-Yuk Claire Sit. Great Barrington, MA：Lindisfarne Books, 2010. xv, 189 pages：illustrations；23cm. ISBN：1584200871, 1584200871

《道德经》，Sit, Kwan-Yuk C. 译.

(1) Rev. second edition. Great Barrington, MA：Lindisfarne Books, 2012. xv, 189 pages；23cm. ISBN：1584201267, 1584201266

165. The illustrated book of the Laozi/written and illustrated by Chuncai Zhou; translated by Paul White; edited by Li Shujuan. San Francisco：Long River Press, 2010. 226 pages. ISBN：1592650910, 1592650910. (The illustrated Chinese classics series)

《老子图典》，Zhou, Chuncai 编写和绘画；White, Paul 英译；Li, Shujuan 编.

166. Tao Te Ching：Zen teachings on the Taoist classic/Lao-tzu and Takuan Sōhō; translated from Chinese and Japanese by Thomas Cleary. Boston：Shambhala, 2010. x, 192 pages；22cm. ISBN：1590308967, 1590308964

《道德经》，Takuan Sōhō(1573—1645)日语注释；Cleary, Thomas F.(1949—)英译.

167. Tao te ching：an all-new translation/translated by William Scott Wilson. Tokyo；New York：Kodansha International, 2010. 255 pages：illustrations；20cm.

ISBN：4770030917, 4770030916

《道德经》，Wilson, William Scott(1944—)译.

(1) Boston & London：Shambhala, 2012. xlvi, 209 pages；20cm. ISBN：1590309919, 159030991X

(2) Boston：Shambhala, 2013. xlvi, 209 pages：illustrations；19cm. ISBN：1611800777, 1611800773

168. Dao de jing awaking：uncover a forgotten non-violent pro-democracy campaign of 25 centuries ago fighting poverty and fighting for human-right and equality among people/explained and translated by Henry Tso. Hong Kong：Wuming Press, 2010. vi, 178 pages；21cm.

《道德经》，Tso, Henry(1955—)译. 英汉文本.

169. Laozi's Daodejing：from philosophical and hermeneutical perspectives：the English and Chinese translations based on Laozi's original Daoism/Chen Lee Sun. Bloomington, IN：iUniverse, 2011. lxxix, 324 p.；23cm. ISBN：1462067237, 1462067239

《老子的道德经：中英白话句解与老学简介》，陈丽生编译.

170. Lǎo zǐ raǐ- Dào dé jǐ raǐng：a classic on the way of the eternal principle and its virtues/by Joseph McHugh. [Place of publication not identified]：Lulu.com, 2011. 456 pages：illustrations；28cm.

《道德经》，McHugh, Joseph 译. 中英文本.

171. 老子语录：英汉双语版/李军峰白话整理；管晓霞英文翻译. 2 版. 济南：山东友谊出版社,2011. 143 页；18cm. ISBN：7807378440, 7807378441

本书为"中国先贤语录口袋书"的其中一册.

172. Laws divine and human/translated by Xu Yuanchong. Singapore：World Culture Books, 2011. 310 pages；22cm. ISBN：9810705732, 9810705735. (Classical Chinese poetry and prose＝许译中国经典诗文集)

《道德经》，[老子著]；许渊冲(1921—)译；[辛战军中文译注]. 英汉对照.

(1) Beijing：Wu zhou chuan bo chu ban she：Zhonghua shu ju, 2012. 10, 310 pages；22cm. ISBN：7508522001, 7508522005. (Classical Chinese poetry and prose＝许译中国经典诗文集)

173. 道德经与神仙画：汉英对照/五洲传播出版社编；许渊冲，曾传辉译. 北京：五洲传播出版社, 2006. 185 页；23cm. ISBN：7508508467, 7508508467. (中国传统文化精粹书系)

174. The complete Tao te ching with the Four canons of the Yellow Emperor/translation and commentary by Jean Levi; English translation by Jody Gladding. Rochester, Vt.：Inner Traditions, 2011. 184 pages；22cm. ISBN：1594773594, 1594773599

Notes：Translation of：Le Lao-tseu suivi des Quatre Canons de l'empereur Jaune.

《道德经》，Levi, Jean 法译；Gladding, Jody(1955—)转

译成英文.

175. The secret Tao：uncovering the hidden history and meaning of Lao Tzu：with an updated translation of the Tao te ching/D. W. Kreger. Palmdale, CA：Windham Everitt Pub. Co., 2011. xii, 308 pages：illustrations；22cm. ISBN：0983309901, 0983309906

《道德经》, Kreger, D. W. 译.

176. Tao teh ching：the book of tao/translated with a retroduction by T. Givó. Durango, Colorado：White Cloud Publishing, 2012. iii, 158 pages；21cm. ISBN：0985018917, 0985018917

《道德经》, Givó, Talmy(1936—)译.

177. The old master：a syncretic reading of the Laozi from the Mawangdui text A onward/Hongkyung Kim. Albany：State University of New York Press, 2012. vii, 310 pages；24cm. ISBN：1438440118, 1438440111. (SUNY series in Chinese philosophy and culture)

《道德经》, Kim, Hongkyung(1959—)译. 中英文本.

178. Tao te ching：the ancient classic/Lao Tzu；with an introduction by Tom Butler-Bowdon. Chichester, West Sussex, United Kingdom：Capstone, 2012. xxvi, 167 pages；21cm. ISBN：0857083111, 0857083112

《道德经》, Butler-Bowdon, Tom 译.

179. Thus spoke Laozi：Dao de jing, a new translation with commentaries/Charles Q. Wu. Beijing：Foreign Language Teaching and Research Press, 2013. xiv, 189 pages；23cm. ISBN：7513536387, 7513536384

《道德经》, Wu, Charles 译评. 中英文本.

(1) Honolulu：University of Hawaii Press, 2016. pages cm. ISBN：0824856403, 0824856406, 0824856410, 0824856414

180. The Tao te ching：the way of goodness/a new translation by Aaron Brachfeld. Agate, Colorado：Coastalfields Press of the Meadowlark Herald, 2013. 1 volume (unpaged)；22cm. ISBN：1483953359, 1483953351

《道德经》, Brachfeld, Aaron 译.

181. Lao Zi：Dao de jing：(Chinese - English)/Harold B. Stromeyer. Meiringen：[Selbstverl.], 2014. 454 p.：Ill. ISBN：3033042018, 3033042015

《道德经》, Stromeyer, Harold 译. 英汉文本.

182. Dáodé jīng ＝ tao te ching：the way to goodness and power/translator, James Trapp. New York：Chartwell Books, 2015. 96 pages：portraits；27cm. ISBN：0785833196, 0785833192

《道德经》, Trapp, James 译. 英汉对照.

183. The wisdom and peace of the teaching of the Tao Te Ching：a modern, practical guide, plain and simple/[translated and intepreted] by Matthew S. Barnes. [North Charleston, S. C.]：CreateSpace, 2015. 134 pages；23cm. ISBN：1507632635, 1507632630

《道德经》, Barnes, Matthew S. 译.

184. 老子选译/选释张葆全；翻译李芝燊；绘图关瑞琳, 尹红, 刘荣. 桂林：广西师范大学出版, 2017. [32], 313 页：彩图；22cm. ISBN：7559800268. (东方智慧丛书)

英文题名：A selected translation of Laozi's philosophy.

本书精选《老子》中最具代表性的 100 句（章）, 精确释析, 精心翻译, 英汉对照.

185. Commentary on the Lao Tzu/by Wang Pi；translated by Ariane Rump in collaboration with Wing-tsit Chan. [Honolulu]：University of Hawaii Press, 1979. xxxvii, 219 p.；23cm. ISBN：0824806778, 0824806774. (Monograph of the Society for Asian and Comparative Philosophy；no. 6)

《道德经注》, 王弼(226—249)著；Ariane Rump, 陈荣捷 (Chan, Wing-tsit, 1901—1994)(美国华裔学者)合译.

186. The classic of the way and virtue：a new translation of the Tao-te ching of Laozi as interpreted by Wang Bi/translated by Richard John Lynn. New York：Columbia University Press, c1999. 244 p.；24cm. ISBN：0231105800, 0231105804. (Translations from the Asian classics)

《道德经注》, 王弼（226—249 年）；林理璋（Lynn, Richard John）(美国汉学家)译.

187. The classic of the Dao：a new investigation/by Wang Keping. Beijing：Foreign Languages Press, 1998. iv, 322 pages；21cm. ISBN：7119022296, 7119022291

《老子思想新释》, 王柯平著. 英汉对照.

188. 老子的智慧/林语堂编译. 北京：外语教学与研究出版社, 2009. 40 页, 270 页；21cm. ISBN：7560081403, 7560081401

英文题名：The wisdom of Laotse

189. The story of Lao Zi/written by Chen Jian；translated by Fang Zhiyun, Tan Manni. Beijing：Foreign Languages Press, 2001. 241 pages：illustrations；19cm. ISBN：7119028537, 7119028538

《老子的故事》, 陈健著.

190. Laozi/author Gao Huaping；translator Wang Rongpei, Cao Ying, Wang Shanjiang. Nanjing：Nanjing University Press, 2010. 1 vol. (5－3－157 p.)：ill., couv. ill.；25cm. ISBN：7305066078, 7305066079. (Collection of critical biographies of Chinese thinkers)

《老子》, 著者高华平；译者汪榕培, 曹盈, 王善江. 南京大出版社. 老子评传.

191. 老子智慧故事 ＝ Wisdom of Laozi/中文作者 张利满, 英文作者李简, 英文审订汪榕培. 上海：上海外语教育出版社, 2010. 12, 215 pages：illustrations；21cm. ISBN：7544618243, 7544618242. (诸子百家智慧故事 ＝ Wisdom of ancient Chinese sages)

B223.3　列子（约公元前 450—约前 375）

1. Yang Chu's garden of pleasure/tr. from the Chinese by

Professor Anton Forke with an introduction by Hugh Cranmer-Byng. New York：Dutton，1912. 64 pages；17cm. (The wisdom of the East series)

Forke，Alfred(1867—1944)译. 对《列子》中的杨朱(约公元前450—约公元前370)的言论作了翻译.

(1) London：John Murray，Hazell，Watson & Viney，1936. 64 pages；17cm. (The wisdom of the East series)

(2) Yang Chu's garden of pleasure/edited by Rosemary Brant. Hod Hasharon，Israel：Astrolog Pub. House，2005. 93 pages；21cm. ISBN：9654942062，9654942065

2. Taoist teachings from the book of Lieh Tzŭ；tr. from the Chinese，with introduction and notes，by Lionel Giles. London，J. Murray，1912. 121，[1] p.；17cm. (The wisdom of the East series)

《列子》，翟林奈(Giles，Lionel，1875—1958)(英国汉学家)译.

(1) London：J. Murray，1925. 121 pages；17cm. (Wisdom of the East series)

(2) London：J. Murray，1939. 121 pages；17cm. (The wisdom of the East series)

(3) 2nd ed. London：J. Murray，1947. 121 pages；17cm. (The wisdom of the East series)

(4) Taoist teachings/Translated from the Book of Lieh-Tzŭ，with introd. and notes，by Lionel Giles. [2nd ed.]. London，J. Murray，1959. 112 pages；20cm. (The wisdom of the East)

(5) Ann Arbor：University Microfilms International，1983. 121 leaves. (Wisdom of the East)

(6) London：J. Murray，1987. 121 pages；17cm. (The Wisdom of the East series)

(7) [United States]：Kessinger Pub.，[2000—2004]. 112 pages；24cm. ISBN：0766186970，0766186972

(8) Charleston，S. C.：BiblioBzaar，2009. 120 pages；21cm. ISBN：0559270451，0559270453. (BiblioBazaar Reproduction series)

3. The book of Lieh-tzŭ. London，Murray [1961，c1960]. xi，183 p.；20cm. (Wisdom of the East series，W-58)

《列子》，葛瑞汉(Graham，A. C.〈Angus Charles〉，1919—1991)(英国汉学家)译.

(1) Book of Lieh-tzu：a classic of the Tao/translated by A. C. Graham. London，Murray [1961，c1960]. xi，183 p.；20cm. (Wisdom of the East series，W-58.)

(2) London：J. Murray，1973. xi，183 pages；20cm. ISBN：0719529581，0719529580. (The Wisdom of the East)

(3) Columbia University Press Morningside ed. New York：Columbia University Press，1990. xix，192 p.；22cm. ISBN：0231072368，0231072366，0231072376，0231072373. (Translations from the Oriental classics)

4. Ch'ung-hu-ch'en-ching，or，The treatise of the transcendent master of the void/translated by Le'on Wieger；English edition by Derek Bryce. Felinfach：Llanerch Publishers，1992. 120 pages；21cm. ISBN：0947992936，0947992934. (he Taoist masters)

《列子》，Wieger，Le'on(1856—1933)法译；Bryce，Derek 英译自法文版.

5. Lieh-tzu：a Taoist guide to practical living/Eva Wong. Boston，Mass.：Shambhala，1995. x，246 p.；22cm. ISBN：1570621535，1570621536，1570628998，1570628993. (Shambhala dragon editions)

《列子》，Wong，Eva(1951—)译.

(1) Boston，Mass.；London：Shambhala，2002. 272 pages；23cm. ISBN：1570628998，1570628993

6. 列子：汉英对照/(战国)列子著；李建国今译；梁晓鹏英译. 北京：中华书局，2005. 227 页；24cm. ISBN：7101042732，7101042733. (大中华文库)

B223.4　庄子(约公元前369—前275)

1. Chuang-tzu：Taoist philosopher and Chinese mystics/translated from the Chinese by Herbert A. Giles. 2nd rev. ed. London：G. Allen & Unwin，1926. 335 pages. Notes：Originally published 1889. / Translation of：Nan-Hua ching.

《庄子》，翟理斯(Giles，Herbert Allen，1845—1935)(英国汉学家)译.

(1) 2nd ed. London：Allen & Unwin，1951. 335 pages；22cm.

(2) 2nd rev. ed. London：Allen & Unwin，1961. 335 pages；22cm.

(3) London；Boston：Unwin Paperbacks，1980. 335 pages；20cm. ISBN：0042990092，0042990095

(4) 2nd ed. London：Routledge，2005. 320 pages；25cm. ISBN：0415361508，0415361507

2. Chuang Tzŭ，mystic，moralist，and social reformer，translated from the Chinese by Herbert A. Giles. 2nd ed.，rev. London，B. Quaritch，1926. xxviii，466 p.；23cm. Notes：First published in 1889.

《庄子》，翟理斯(Giles，Herbert Allen，1845—1935)(英国汉学家)译.

(1) 2nd ed. rev. [Taipei]，[Cheng Wen Pub. Co.]，1969. xxviii，466 pages；20cm.

(2) 2nd ed. rev. [New York：AMS Press，1974]. xxviii，466 p.；23cm. ISBN：0404569153，0404569150

(3) [Place of publication not identified]：Kessinger Publishing，2000s. xxviii，466 pages；24cm. ISBN：0548123942，0548123942

(4) [Brighton，MA]：Adamant Media，2005. xxviii，467 pages；21cm. ISBN：1402152159，1402152153，1402104308，1402104305. (Elibron classics)

3. Musings of a Chinese mystic；selections from the

philosophy of Chuang Tzǔ；with an introduction by Lionel Giles. London，J. Murray，1906. 112 pages；17cm.

《庄子》（选译），翟理斯（Giles，Herbert Allen，1845—1935）（英国汉学家）译；翟林奈（Giles，Lionel，1875—1958）（英国汉学家）作序.

(1) London：J. Murray，1911. 8，11—112 p. ；17cm. (Wisdom of the East series)

(2) London：J. Murray，1920. 112 pages；17cm. (Wisdom of the East series)

(3) London：J. Murray［1927］. 112 p. ；17cm. (Wisdom of the East series)

(4) London：J. Murray，1947. 112 p. ；17cm. (The Wisdom of the East series)

(5) London：John Murray，1955. 112 pages；17cm. (Wisdom of the East series)

(6) San Francisco：Chinese Materials Center，1977. 112 p. ；20cm. (Wisdom of the East series)

(7) Teachings and sayings of Chuang Tzǔ. Mineola, N. Y. ：Dover Publications，2001. viii, 68 pages；22cm. ISBN：0486419460，0486419466

(8) Stilwell，KS：Digireads. com Pub. ，2007. 112 pages；21cm. ISBN：1420928440，1420928449

4. Chuang Tzǔ；a new selected translation with an exposition of the philosophy of Kuo Hsiang/by Youlan Fung. Shanghai，China，The Commercial Press，Limited，1931. vi pages，1 leaf，164 pages；19cm.

《庄子：据郭象〈庄子注〉选译》，冯友兰（1895—1990）著. 中文书名"道家经典庄子".

(1) Shanghai：Commercial Press，1933. vi，164 pages；19cm.

(2) 2nd ed. New York：Paragon Book Reprint Corp. ，1964. vi，164 pages；20cm. (Paragon reprint oriental series)

(3) New York：Gordon Press，1975. vi，164 p. ；24cm. ISBN：087968187X，0879681876

(4) Beijing：Foreign Languages Press，1989（1994 printing）. 150 p. ；23cm. ISBN：083511970X，0835119702，7119001043，7119001043

(5) Beijing：Wai yu jiao xue yu yan jiu chu ban she，2012. xxvi，217 pages；22cm. ISBN：7513525053，7513525056

(6) Heidelberg：Springer，2016. ISBN：3662480743，3662480748. (China academic library)

5. Chuangtse/translated by Lin Yutang. Taipei：World Book Co. ，1957. 81 pages；21cm. (English translations of the Chinese classics＝英译汉学名著丛刊)

《庄子》，林语堂（1895—1976）译.

6. The sayings of Chuang Chou. A new translation by James R. Ware.［New York］New American Library，［1963］. 240 p. map. 18cm. (A Mentor classic).

《庄子语录》（《庄子》），魏鲁男（Ware，James R. 1901—）（美国汉学家）译. 英汉对照.

(1) 台北，文致出版社，［1974］. 438 pages；map 20cm.

(2) 台北：文致出版社，［1983］. 436 pages；map；19cm.

7. Basic writings/translated by Burton Watson. New York：Columbia University Press，1964. vi，148 pages；21cm. ISBN：0231086067，0231086066. (UNESCO collection of representative works. Chinese series)

《庄子》（节译），华兹生（Watson，Burton，1925—）（美国翻译家）译.

(1) New York：Columbia University Press，1994. ［xi］，159 pages. (Translations from the Asian classics)

(2) New York：Columbia University Press，c1996. ix，159 p. ；20cm. ISBN：0231105959，0231105958，0231086067，0231086066. (Translations from the Asian classics)

(3) New York：Columbia University Press，c2003. ix，163 p. ；21cm. ISBN：0231129599，0231129596. (Translations from the Asian classics)

8. The complete works of Chuang Tzu/Translated by Burton Watson. New York：Columbia University Press，1968. 397 p. ；21cm. ISBN：0231031475，0231031479. (UNESCO collection of representative works. Chinese series). (Records of civilization，sources and studies；no. 80)

《庄子》，华兹生（Watson，Burton，1925—）（美国翻译家）译.

(1) New York；London：Columbia University Press，1970. X，397 p. ；21cm.

(2) New York：Columbia University Press，2013. xxxi，327 pages；24cm. ISBN：0231164740，0231164742，0231164757，0231164750. (Translations from the Asian classics)

9. The way of Chuang-Tzǔ/ by Thomas Merton.［New York］：New Directions，1965. 159 pages：illustrations；21cm. ISBN：0811201031，0811201032

Notes：Free renderings of selections from the works of Zhuangzi，taken from various translations.

Merton，Thomas(1915—1968)著，包括《庄子》的翻译.

(1) New York：New Directions，1969. 159 pages：illustrations；21cm. (ND paperbook 276)

(2) London：Unwin Books，1970. 159 pages：illustrations；19cm. ISBN：0042990041，0042990040

(3) Tunbridge Wells，Kent，U. K. ：Burns & Oates，1994. 159 p. ：ill. ；22cm.

(4) Boston；London：Shambhala，1992. XIX，240 p；12cm. ISBN：0877736766，0877736769. (Shambhala pocket classics)

10. The book of Chuang Tzu/translated by Martin Palmer；with Elizabeth Breuilly，Chang wai Ming and Jay Ramsay. London：Arkana，1966. xxx，320 pages：

illustrations.

《庄子》,彭马田(Palmer,Martin)(英国汉学家)等译.

(1) London；New York：Arkana,1996. xxx,320 p.：ill.；20cm. ISBN：0140194886,0140194883

(2) London：Penguin,2006. xxx,320 pages；20cm. ISBN：014045537X,0140455373.(Penguin classics)

11. Chuang tzu：genius of the absurd/arranged from the work of James Legge by Clae Waltham. New York：Ace Books,1971. 398 pages；18cm.

《庄子》,理雅各(Legge,James,1815—1897)(英国汉学家)译；Waltham,Clae 编.

(1) Felinfach：Llanerch Publishers,1994. 229 pages；21cm. ISBN：1897853955.(The Taoist masters)

12. 庄子＝The sayings of Chuang Chou/庄子. 史俊超(1934). 香港九龙：志文出版社,1973. [2],435 pages；19cm.

13. Inner chapters/Chuang Tsu；a new translation [from the Chinese] by Gia-fu Feng and Jane English；[photography by Jane English；calligraphy by Gia-fu Feng]. London：Wildwood House,1974. [7],161 p.：ill.；28cm. ISBN：0704501015,0704501010

《庄子·内篇》,Feng,Gia-fu 和 English,Jane 合译. 中英文本.

(1) Chuang tsu：inner chapters. A new translation by Gia-fu Feng and Jane English. Photography by Jane English. Calligraphy by Gia-fu Feng. New York：Vintage Books [1974]. vii,161 p. illus.；28cm. ISBN：0394719905,0394719900

(2) New York：Knopf；[distributed by Random House] 1974. vii,161 p. illus.；29cm. ISBN：0394487613,0394487618

(3) Taipei：Caves Books,1981. vii,161 p.：illus.；28cm. ISBN：0394719905,0394719900

(4) 4th ed. Portland,Ore.：Amber Lotus,2008. xi,164 pages：illustrations；28cm. ISBN：1602371170,1602371172,0394719905,0394719900

(5) Updated edition. Australia：Hay House,2014. 1 volume：illustrations；23cm. ISBN：1401946593,1401946593

14. Chuang-tzǔ：the seven inner chapters and other writings from the book Chuang-tzǔ/translated by A. C. Graham. London；Boston：Allen & Unwin,1981. viii,293 p.：23cm. ISBN：0042990106,0042990101

《庄子》(选译),葛瑞汉(Graham,A. C.〈Angus Charles〉,1919—1991)(英国汉学家)译. 另有配套的学习辅导书.

(1) The inner chapters/[translated by] A. C. Graham. London：Unwin Paperbacks,1986. viii,293 pages；20cm. ISBN：0042990130,0042990132.(Mandala books)

(2) London：Unwin Paperbacks,1989. viii,293 pages；23cm. ISBN：0042990132,0042990130

(3) Indianapolis：Hackett Pub. Co.,2001. viii,293 p.：23cm. ISBN：0872205819,0872205819,0872205827,0872205826

15. A companion to Angus C. Graham's Chuang Tzu：the inner chapters/Harold D. Roth. Honolulu：University of Hawaii Press,c2003. x,243 p.；23cm. ISBN：082482634,0824826437.(Monograph of the Society for Asian and Comparative Philosophy；no. 20)

Roth,Harold David 著. 包括葛瑞汉(Graham,A. C.〈Angus Charles〉,1919—1991)(英国汉学家)对《庄子·内篇》的英译文本.

16. Attaining unlimited life：the teachings of Chuang Tzu/by Ni Hua-Ching. Los Angeles：Shrine of the Eternal Breath of Tao,College of Tao and Traditional Chinese Healing,c1989. xi,467 p.；21cm. ISBN：0937064181,0937064184,0937064238,0937064238.(The wisdom of three masters；v. 1)

《庄子》,Ni,Hua Ching 译.

17. The butterfly as companion：meditations on the first three chapters of the Chuang Tzu/Kuang-ming Wu. Albany,N. Y.：State University of New York Press,c1990. xiv,509 p.；24cm. ISBN：0887066852,0887066856,0887066860,0887066863.(SUNY series in religion and philosophy)

Wu,Kuang-ming 著,包括对《庄子》前三篇的翻译.

18. 庄子＝Zhuang zi/汪榕培,任秀桦英译；秦旭卿,孙雍长今译. 长沙市：湖南人民出版社,1997. [3],3,62,742 pages；21cm. ISBN：7543815699,7543815698

中英对照.

(1) 长沙：湖南人民出版社,1999. 2 volumes (78,630 pages)；24cm. ISBN：7543820870,7543820876.(大中华文库＝Library of Chinese classics)

19. 庄子名言精选/敖雪岗编；汪榕培译. 上海：上海外语教育出版社,2008. 129 页：图；19cm. ＋1 光盘. ISBN：7544609876,7544609871

英文题名：Quotations from zhuangzi.

20. Nan-hua-ch'en ching or The treatise of the transcendent master from Nan-Hua/Chuang-Tzu. Lampeter：Llanerch,1992. 137 pages. ISBN：0947992871,0947992873

《南华经》,Bryce,Derek 和 Wieger,Le'on(1856—1933)合译.

21. Dreams of a butterfly/translation from the ancient Chinese and calligraphy by Bun-Ching Lam；design and illustration by Gunnar A. Kaldewey. [Poestenkill,N. Y.]：[Kaldewey Press],1995. 1 volume (unpaged)：illustrations (some color)；31×31cm.(Edition Gunnar A. Kaldewey；v. 24)

《庄子》，Kaldewey, Gunnar A.（1946—）译. 中英文本.

22. I and Tao: Martin Buber's encounter with Chuang Tzu/ Jonathan R. Herman. Albany: State University of New York Press, c1996. xiii, 278 p.；24cm. ISBN: 0791429237, 0791429235, 0791429245, 0791429242. Content: Includes a translation into English of Martin Buber's German translation of selections from the Nanhua jing of Zhuangzi
Herman, Jonathan R.（1957—）著，包括由作者从 Buber, Martin（1878—1965）所译的《庄子》德语版转译 的英语版文本.

23. Chuang Tzu. The inner chapters/Chuang-Tzu; translated by David Hinton. Washington, D. C.：Counterpoint: Distributed by Publishers Group West, c1997. xix, 118 p.：ill.；20cm. ISBN: 1887178341, 1887178341, 1887178791, 1887178792
《庄子·内篇》，戴维·欣顿（Hinton, David, 1954—）（美 国汉学家）译.
　(1)Berkely, California：Counterpoint, 2014. 85 pages：illustrations；23cm. ISBN: 1619024434, 1619024438

24. The essential Chuang Tzu/translated from the Chinese by Sam Hamill and J. P. Seaton. Boston: Shambhala Publications,1998. xx,170 p.；24cm. ISBN:1570623368, 1570623363
《庄子》，Hamill, Sam（美国诗人）译.
　(1)Boston；London：Shambhala, 1999. xx, 170 pages；23cm. ISBN: 1570624577, 1570624575

25. Chuang-Zue Lan Hou Cheng: in Chinese/English spoken languages/translated/commented by Yang Ju-chou. Tong su Zhong Ying wen ben. Taibei Shi: Lao Zhuang xue shu ji jin hui, Minguo 89［2000］. ［5］, 339, ［1］ p.：ill., music；21cm.
《庄子南华经:通俗中英文本》,杨汝舟(1925—)译注. 台 北市老庄学术基金会.

26. Village philosopher: the stories of Zhuangzi（Chuang Tzu)/Zhuangzi; translated and commentary by River Soul. Lismore, N. S. W.：C. Tricker, 2006. 1 volume. ISBN: 0646458817, 0646458816
《庄子》，Soul, River（1972—）译.

27. 庄子说:汉英对照/蔡希勤编注. 北京:华语教学出版社, 2006. 201 页；21cm. ISBN: 7802002133, 7802002135. (中国圣人文化丛书. 老人家说系列)

28. Zhuangzi/ Hyun Höchsmann, Yang Guorong. New York: Pearson Longman, 2007. xix, 342 pages；21cm. ISBN: 0321273567, 0321273567. (The Longman library of primary sources in philosophy)
《庄子》，Höchsmann, Hyun 和 Yang, Guorong（1957—）合译.

29. The wisdom of Zhuang Zi on Daoism/translated with annotations and commentaries by Chung Wu. New York: Peter Lang, c2008. vi, 452 p.；24cm. ISBN: 1433100789, 1433100789. (American university studies. series V, Philosophy, 0739－6392；v. 201)
《庄子》，Wu, Chung 译.

30. Zhuang zi/［executive editor, Joyce Du］. Vancouver: Chiao Liu Pub.（Canada), 2008. 529 pages：illustrations；21cm. (Wisdom of chinese culture series. First series；no. 3)
《庄子》，Du, Joyce 译. 英汉对照.

31. Zhuangzi: the essential writings with selections from traditional commentaries/translated, with introduction and notes, by Brook Ziporyn. Indianapolis: Hackett Pub. Co., c2009. xviii, 238 p.；22cm. ISBN: 0872209114, 0872209113, 0872209121, 0872209121
《庄子》（节译），Ziporyn, Brook（1964—）译注.

32. The inner chapters: the classic Taoist text: a new translation of the Chuang Tzu with commentary/Solala Towler. London: Watkins Publishing；New York: Distributed in the USA and Canada by Sterling Publishing, 2010. 170 pages：illustrations；28cm. ISBN：1906787998, 1906787999
《庄子·内篇》，Towler, Solala 译.
　(1)New ed. London：Watkins, 2011. 1 volume：illustrations；19cm. ISBN: 1780280202, 1780280203

33. The tao of nature/Chuang Tzu. London: Penguin, 2010. ISBN: 0141192741, 0141192747. (Penguin great ideas)
《庄子》

34. 庄子语录:英汉双语版/菅咏梅白话整理;管晓霞英文翻 译. 济南:山东友谊出版社,2011. 166 页；18cm. ISBN: 7807378617, 7807378611

35. Chuang-tzu: the Tao of perfect happiness: selections annotated & explained/translated & annotated by Livia Kohn. Quality paperback ed. Woodstock, Vt.: SkyLight Paths Pub., 2011. xvi, 210 p.：ill.；22cm. ISBN: 1594732966, 1594732965
《庄子》（节译），孔丽维（Kohn, Livia, 1956—）（美国汉 学家）译注.

36. Zhuang Zi /［Zhuang Zi］. San Francisco: China Books, 2014. 201 pages：maps and illustrations；17cm. ISBN: 0835102315, 0835102319. (Essential Chinese wisdom)
《庄子》. 中英对照.

37. 道法自然:英汉双语/庄子著;（英）马丁·帕尔默,（英） 伊丽莎白·布罗伊利,（英）杰伊·拉姆齐英译;（英）马 丁·帕尔默编选;王相峰汉译. 北京:中国对外翻译出版 有限公司,2014. 255 页；18cm. ISBN: 7500138846. (企鹅 口袋书系列. 伟大的思想)
英文题名:Tao of nature

38. The story of Zhuang Zi/written by Zhang Fuxin; translated by Zhang Tingquan. Beijing: Foreign Languages Press, 2002. 214 pages：illustrations；19cm.

ISBN:7119030701,7119030708
《庄子的故事》,张福信著.

39. 庄子/包兆会著;米歇尔(Thomas Mitchell)译.南京:南京大学出版社,2010.205 页;24cm. ISBN:7305071775,7305071773

40. 庄子智慧故事＝Wisdom of Zhuangzi/ 中文作者陶黎铭,英文作者顾薇,英文审订汪榕培.上海:上海外语教育出版社,2011.10,256 pages:illustrations;21cm. ISBN:7544620048,7544620042.(诸子百家智慧故事＝Wisdom of ancient Chinese sages)

41. Zhuangzi:thinking through the inner chapters/Bo Wang;[translated by Livia Kohn]. St. Petersburg, FL:Three Pines Press,2014. x, 221 p.;23cm. ISBN:1931483605.(Contemporary Chinese Scholarship in Daoist Studies)
《庄子哲学》,王博(1967—)著;孔丽维(Kohn, Livia,1956—)(美国汉学家)译.

B224 墨子(约公元前 480—前 420)

1. The social teachings of Meh Tse/[translated by L. Tomkinson]. Tokyo, Asiatic Society of Japan, 1927. 1 preliminary leaf,184 pages;22cm.(Transactions of the Asiatic Society of Japan, 2nd ser.;vol. 4)
《墨子》,Tomkinson, L. 译.

2. The ethical and political works of Motse, translated from the original Chinese text by Yi-Pao Mei. London, A. Probsthain, 1929. xiv, 275 p.;20cm.(Probsthain's Oriental series, vol. XIX)
《墨子》,梅贻宝(1900—)(美国华裔学者)译.
(1)Westport, Conn.:Hyperion Press[1973]. xiv, 275 p.;23cm. ISBN:0883550857
(2)台北:文致出版社,[1976]. 519 pages;19cm.
(3)台北:文致出版社,1983. 519 pages;19cm.

3. Mo Tzu;basic writings. Translated by Burton Watson. New York:Columbia University Press,1963. vi, 140 p.;21cm. ISBN:0231086083, 0231086080.(UNESCO collection of representative works. Chinese series)
《墨子》(选译),华兹生(Watson, Burton,1925—)(美国翻译家)译.
(1)New York:Columbia University Press,2003. 156 p.;21cm. ISBN:0231130015, 0231130011.(Translations from the Asian classics)

4. Later Mohist logic, ethics, and science/A. C. Graham. Hong Kong:Chinese University Press, Chinese University of Hong Kong;London:School of Oriental and African Studies, University of London, 1978. xv, 590 p.:ill.;23cm. ISBN:962201142X
Notes:Includes an annotated Chinese text and an English translation of Mozi
葛瑞汉(Graham, A. C.〈Angus Charles〉,1919—1991)(英国汉学家)著.含有对《墨子》的英译.

5. 墨子/周才珠,齐瑞端今译;汪榕培,王宏英译.长沙市:湖南人民出版社,2006. 2 volumes(59, 611 pages):illustrations;24cm. ISBN:7543840294, 7543840294.(大中华文库＝Library of Chinese classics)

6. The complete works of Motzu in English/translated by Cyrus Lee.[Beijing]:Commercial Press, 2009. 3, 5, 464 pages;24cm. ISBN:7100064903, 7100064902
《英译墨子全书》,李绍昆(美籍华裔学者)译注.商务印书馆.

7. The Mozi:a complete translation/translated and annotated by Ian Johnston. New York:Columbia University Press, c2010. lxxxv, 944 p.;24cm. ISBN:0231152402, 023115240X.(Translations from the Asian classics)
《墨子全译》,Johnston, Ian(1939—)译.中英文本.
(1)Hong Kong:Chinese University Press, 2010. lxxxv, 944 pages;24cm. ISBN:9629962708, 9629962705

8. The book of Master Mo/Mo Zi;translated and edited with notes by Ian Johnston. London;New York:Penguin Books, 2013. xliii, 452 pages;20cm. ISBN:0141392103, 014139210X,0141392118,0141392110.(Penguin classics)
《墨子》,Johnston, Ian(1939—)译.

9. Mozi/Zheng Jiewen, Zhang Qian;translator David B. Honey. Nanjing:Nanjing University Press, 2010. 1 vol. (189. p.);24cm. ISBN:7305079702, 7305079707. (Collection of Critical biographies of chinese thinkers)
《墨子》,郑杰文,张倩著.英汉对照.

10. 英译墨经＝The Mohist canons/汪榕培,王宏译.上海:上海外语教育出版社,2011. 139 pages;24cm. ISBN:7544619448, 7544619443.(外教社中国文化汉外对照丛书＝SFLEP bilingual Chinese Culture series)

11. Mozi:a study and translation of the ethical and political writings/John Knoblock and Jeffrey Riegel. Berkeley, CA:Institute of East Asian Studies, University of California, Berkeley,[2013]. xvii, 501 pages;23cm. ISBN:1557291039.(China research monograph;68)
《墨子》(选译),Knoblock, John(美国汉学家),王国安(Riegel, Jeffrey K.,1945—)(美国汉学家)合译.

12. The moral philosophy of Mo-tze, Taipei, Taiwan, China Printing[c1965]. 407 p. 22cm.
《墨子伦理哲学》,周幼伟(Tseu, Augustinus A.)译.

13. 墨子智慧故事＝Wisdom of Mozi/中文作者杨蓉蓉,英文作者王宏赵峥,英文审订汪榕培.上海:上海外语教育出版社,2010. 236 pages:illustrations;21cm. ISBN:7544615570, 754461557X.(诸子百家智慧故事＝Wisdom of ancient Chinese sages)

B225 名家

B225.1 公孙龙(约公元前 320—前 250)

1. Works;with a translation from the parallel Chinese

original text, critical and exegetical notes, punctuation and literal translation, the Chinese commentary, prolegomena, and index, by Max Perleberg. Hongkong, 1952. xxiii, 160 p. 27cm.

《公孙龙子》，Perleberg，Max(1900—)编译. 中英文本.

(1)Westport, Conn., Hyperion Press〔1973〕. xxi, 160 p. 24cm. ISBN：08835507761322.

B226 法家

B226.1 管子(约公元前723—前645)

1. Economic thought in ancient China; economic selections from the Kuan-tzŭ, 300 B. C., with modern commentaries by Huang Han and Fan Ping-t'ung. All three translated by T'an Po-fu and Wen Kung-wen (Adam K. W. Wen) the translation directed and the work edited by Lewis A. Maverick, Carbondale, Ill., 1947—1950. Manuscript to be presented for publication 1950. 586 p.

《管子》，Huang，Han，Fan，Bingtong，Maverick，Lewis A. (Lewis Adams，1891—)译评.

(1)〔Carbondale, Ill.〕1954. x,470p. 24cm.

2. Economic dialogues in ancient China; selections from the Kuan-tzŭ, a book written probably three centuries before Christ. Translators：T'an Po-fu and Wen Kung-wen (Adam K. W. Wen) Expert critic：Hsiao Kung-chüan. The enterprise directed, the book edited and published by Lewis Maverick. 〔Carbondale, Ill.〕1954. x, 470p. 24cm.

《管子》，檀伯孚(T'an Po-fu)，温孔文(Wen Kung-wen (Adam K. W. Wen)译；萧公权(Hsiao Kung-chüan)评.

3. Kuan-tzu：a repository of early Chinese thought/a translation and study of twelve chapters by W. Allyn Rickett; foreword by Derk Bodde. Hong Kong：Hong Kong University Press, 1965—. volumes：illustrations; 25cm.

《管子》(选译)，李可(Rickett, W. Allyn, 1921—)(美国汉学家)译.

(1) Hong Kong：Hong Kong University Press, 1996. volumes；illustrations；25cm.

4. Guanzi：political, economic, and philosophical essays from early China：a study and translation＝〔Guanzi〕/by W. Allyn Rickett. Princeton, N. J.：Princeton University Press, c1985—c1998. 2 v.；25cm. ISBN：0691066051, 0691066059, 0691048169, 0691048161, 0887273246, 0887273247. (Princeton library of Asian translations)
Contents：v. 1. Chapters I, 1-XI, 34, and XX, 64—XXI, 65—66-v. 2. Chapters XII, 35—XXIV, 86.

《管子》，李可(Rickett, W. Allyn, 1921—)(美国汉学家)译注.

(1)Rev. ed. Boston, MA：Cheng & Tsui Company, 2001— v.〈1〉；ill.；23cm. ISBN：0887273246, 0887273247

5. The means to win：strategies for success in business and politics/by Kuan Tzu; commentary by William Bodri. Fremont, Calif.：Jain Pub., c2000. ix, 172 p.；22cm. ISBN：0875730833

Bodri, William 译评.

6. Guanzi/ translated into English and modern Chinese by Zhai Jiangyue. Guilin：Guangxi shi fan da xue chu ban she, 2005. 4 v. (16, 20, 1691 p.)；24cm. ISBN：7563353461. (Library of Chinese classics＝大中华文库)

《管子》，翟江月今译、英译.

7. 管子语录：英汉双语版/周振雯白话整理；王滢，管晓霞英文翻译. 济南：山东友谊出版社，2011. 192 页；18cm. ISBN：7807378426，7807378425

B226.2 商鞅(约公元前395—前338)

1. The book of Lord Shang; a classic of the Chinese school of law; translated from the Chinese with introduction and notes by Dr. J. J. L. Duyvendak. London, A. Probsthain, 1928. xiv p., 1 l., 346 p. 20cm. (Probstain's oriental series, vol. XVII)

《商君书》，戴闻达 Duyvendak, J. J. L.〈Jan Julius Lodewijk〉，1889—)(荷兰汉学家)译.

(1)University of Chicago Press〔1963〕. 346 p.；20cm. (UNESCO collection of representative works：Chinese series)

2. The book of lord Shang/〔transl. from the Chinese〕into English by J. J. L. Duyvendak; trans. into modern Chinese by Gao Heng. Beijing：Commercial Press, 2006. 357 p.；24cm. ISBN：7100048796, 7100048798. (Library of Chinese classics)

《商君书：汉英对照》，(荷)戴闻达(Duyvendak, J. J. L.)英译；高亨今译.

3. Sun Tzu：The art of war；The book of Lord Shang/with a commentary by Tao Hanzhang;〔Shang Yang〕；translated by Yuan Shibing; introduction by Robert Wilkinson；translated by J. J. L. Duyvendak; introduction by Robert Wilkinson. Ware, Herts.：Wordsworth Editions Ltd., 1998. 243 pages；20cm. ISBN：1853267791 1853267796. (Wordsworth classics of world literature)

《孙子兵法．商君书》，陶汉章；Yuan, Shibing 译.

B226.3 慎到(慎子，约公元前390—前315)

1. Fragments from an early Chinese political theorist：a philosophical analysis and translation of the Shenzi/Eirik Lang Harris. New York：Columbia University Press, 2016. ISBN：0231177665. (Translations from the Asian classics)

Harris, Eirik Lang 著. 包括对慎到(约公元前390—前315)所著《慎子》的节译.

B226.4 韩非子(约公元前280—前233)

1. The complete works of HanFeiTzǔ. London：A. Probsthain, 1939. 2 v.；20cm. (Probsthain's oriental

series；vol. XXV)

Contents：v. 1. A classic of Chinese legalism—v. 2. A classic of Chinese political science.

《韩非子全集》，廖文奎(Liao, W. K, 1905—)译.

(1) London：Probsthain，1959. 2 volumes；20cm. (Probsthain's oriental series；v. 25—26)

2. Han Fei Tzu：basic writings/translated by Burton Watson. New York：Columbia University Press, 1964. vi，134 p. 21cm. ISBN：0231086091，0231086097. (UNESCO collection of representative works. Chinese series)

《韩非》(选译)，华兹生(Watson, Burton, 1925—)(美国翻译家)译.

(1) New York：Columbia University Press，1967. vi, 134 p. ；20cm. (UNESCO collection of representative works. Chinese series)

(2) New York：Columbia University Press，1970. vi，134 pages；21cm. (UNESCO collection of representative works. Chinese series)

(3) New York：Columbia University Press，c2003. x, 148 p. ；21cm. ISBN：0231129696，0231129695. (Translations from the Asian classics)

3. 韩非子语录：英汉双语版/文慧白话整理；王滢，管晓霞英文翻译. 济南：山东友谊出版社，2011. 159 页；18cm. ISBN：7807378419，7807378417

4. 韩非子智慧故事＝Wisdom of Han Feizi/中文作者姚萱，英文作者潘智丹，英文审订汪榕培. 上海：上海外语教育出版社，2010. 294 pages：illustrations；21cm. ISBN：7544619417，7544619419. (诸子百家智慧故事＝Wisdom of ancient Chinese sages)

B227 纵横家

1. The book of vertical alliances：horizontal dissensions (Principles & practices of lobbying from ancient China)/ original written by Gui Gu Zi；[English edition translated and interpreted by Soo Chi-Yin John]. Hong Kong：Red Publish，2005. volumes：illustrations；19cm. ISBN：9628870742，9628870745

《纵横经》，鬼谷子(公元前 400—公元前 320 年)；苏子贤译. 英汉对照.

2. Guiguzi, China's first treatise on rhetoric：a critical translation and commentary/translated by Hui Wu；edited by Hui Wu and C. Jan Swearingen. Carbondale：Southern Illinois University Press，2016. ISBN：0809335268，0809335263，0809335275 (e-book). (Landmarks in rhetoric and public address)

《鬼谷子》，鬼谷子(公元前 400—公元前 320 年)；Wu, Hui(1953—)译.

B228 杂家

B228.1 吕不韦(公元前 292—前 235)

1. The annals of Lü Buwei＝[Lü shi chun qiu]：a complete translation and study/by John Knoblock and Jeffrey Riegel. Stanford, Calif. ：Stanford University Press, 2000. xxii, 847 p. ；24cm. ISBN：0804733546，0804733540

《吕氏春秋》，Knoblock，John(美国汉学家)，王国安(Riegel, Jeffrey K.，1945—)(美国汉学家)合译.

2. Lü's commentaries of history/Lü Buwei；translated by Tang Bowen. Beijing：Foreign Languages Press, 2010. v，367 pages；23cm. ISBN：7119060088，7119060082. (Chinese classics＝中国经典)

《吕氏春秋》，汤博文(Tang, Bowen)译.

(1) San Francisco, CA：Long River Press, 2012. v, 367 pages；23cm. ISBN：1592651337，159265133X

3. Lü's commentaries of history/Lü Buwei；translated by Tang Bowen. Beijing：Foreign Languages Press, 2010. v，367 pages；23cm. ISBN：7119060088，7119060082. (Chinese classics)

《吕氏春秋》

4. Lü's commentaries of history/Lü Buwei；translated by Tang Bowen. Beijing：Foreign Languages Press, 2010. v，367 pages；23cm. ISBN：7119060088，7119060082. (Chinese classics)

《吕氏春秋》. 外文出版社(中国经典)

5. 吕氏春秋故事：英文＝ Selections from Lu's commentaries of history/(战国)吕不韦著；王国振译. 北京：五洲传播出版社，2017. 286 页；22cm. ISBN：7508530529. (中国经典名著故事)

B23 汉代哲学

B231 淮南子(刘安，公元前 179—前 122)

1. The Tao of politics：lessons of the masters of Huainan：translations from the Taoist classics Huainanzi/by Thomas Cleary. Boston：Shambhala；[New York]：Distributed in the U. S. and Canada by Random House, 1990. x, 101 p. ；23cm. ISBN：0877735867，0877735861. (Shambhala dragon editions)

《淮南子》(节译)，Cleary, Thomas F. (1949—)(美国翻译家)编译.

2. The book of leadership and strategy：lessons of the Chinese masters/translations from the Taoist classic Huainanzi by Thomas Cleary. Boston：Shambhala：[New York]：Distributed in the United States by Random House，1992. x, 121 p. ；22cm. ISBN：0877736677，0877736677

《淮南子》(节译)，Cleary, Thomas F. (1949—)(美国翻译家)编译.

(1) Boston：Shambhala；[New York]：Distributed in the United States by Random House, 1996. xiv, 209 pages；12cm. ISBN：1570622205，1570622205. (Shambala pocket classics)

3. Yuan Dao：tracing Dao to its source/translated by D. C.

Lau and Roger T. Ames; with an introduction by Roger T. Ames. New York: Ballantine Books, 1998. vii, 149 p.; 21cm. ISBN: 0345425685, 0345425683. (Classics of ancient China)

《淮南子·原道训》，刘殿爵（Lau, D. C.〈Dim Cheuk〉，1921—2010)（中国香港学者），安乐哲（Ames, Roger T., 1947—)（美国汉学家）合译.

4. The Huainanzi: a guide to the theory and practice of government in early Han China/Liu An, King of Huainan; translated and edited by John S. Major... [et al.], with additional contributions by Michael Puett and Judson Murray. New York: Columbia University Press, c2010. xi, 988 p.: ill., maps; 25cm. ISBN: 0231142045, 0231142048, 0231520850, 0231520859. (Translations from the Asian classics)

《淮南子》，Major, John S. (美国汉学家)译.

5. The essential Huainanzi/Liu An, King of Huainan; translated, edited, and selected by John S. Major ... [et al.]. New York: Columbia University Press, c2012. xiii, 254 p.; 24cm. ISBN: 0231159807, 0231159803, 0231159814, 0231159811, 0231501453, 0231501455. (Translations from the Asian classics)

《淮南子》(选译)，Major, John S. (美国汉学家)译.

6. Tao, the great luminant; essays from Huai nan tzu. With introductory articles, notes, analyses, by Evan Morgan. Foreword by J. C. Ferguson. London, K. Paul, Trench, Trubner & co. [1935] xlv, 287 p. illus.; 23cm.

《淮南子》，Morgan, Evan（1860—1941）译；Ferguson, John C. (John Calvin, 1866—1945)作序.

   (1)New York: Paragon Book Reprint Corp., 1969. xlv, 287 p. illus.; 23cm.

   (2)台北：成文，1974. xlv, 287 pages; illustrations; 23cm.

7. The Dao of the Military: Liu An's Art of War/Translated, with an Introduction, by Andrew Seth Meyer. New York: Columbia University Press, [2012]. xiii, 157 pages; 22cm. ISBN: 0231153324, 0231153325, 0231153331, 0231153333, 0231526881, 0231526883. (Translations from the Asian Classics)

   Translation previously published in: The Huainanzi. New York: Columbia University Press, 2010.

《淮南子·兵略训》，Meyer, Andrew Seth 译评.

8. Heaven and earth in early Han thought: chapters three, four and five of the Huainanzi/John S. Major; with an appendix by Christopher Cullen. Albany: State University of New York Press, 1993. xvi, 388 p.: ill.; 24cm. ISBN: 0791415856, 0791415856, 0791415864, 0791415863. (SUNY series in Chinese philosophy and culture)

   Contents: 1. Preliminary Considerations—2. A General Introduction to Early Han Cosmology—3. Huainanzi Chapter 3: Tianwenxun: The Treatise on the Patterns of Heaven: Translation and Commentary—4. Huainanzi Chapter 4: Dixingxun: The Treatise on Topography: Translation and Commentary—5. Huainanzi Chapter 5: Shicixun: The Treatise on the Seasonal Rules: Translation and Commentary

Major, John S. 著，包括对《淮南子》第三卷《天文训》、第四卷《墬形训》和第五卷《时则训》的译注.

9. Huai-nan tzu: philosophical synthesis in early Han thought: the idea of resonance (感应) with a translation and analysis of chapter six/Charles Le Blanc. [Hong Kong]: Hong Kong University Press, 1985. xiv, 253 pages: illustrations; 25cm. ISBN: 9622091792, 9622091795, 9622091695, 9622091696

Le Blanc, Charles 著. 是对《淮南子·览冥训》的翻译.

10. Tao, the great luminant; essays from Huai nan tzu/with introductory articles, notes, analyses, by Evan Morgan. Foreword by J. C. Ferguson. New York: Paragon Book Reprint Corp., 1969. xlv, 287 pages: illustrations; 23cm. Notes: Reprint of 1935 ed. / A translation by E. Morgan of 8 of Huai-nan tzu's 21 essays found in Liu Wen-tien's Chinese ed. of the author's works published by the Commercial Press, Shanghai.

《淮南子》(选译)，Morgan, Evan(1860—)著.

11. Being Taoist: wisdom for living a balanced life/edited and translated by Eva Wong. Boston: Shambhala, 2015. vi, 193 pages; 23cm. ISBN: 1611802412, 1611802415

《淮南子》(选译)，Wong, Eva(1951—)编译.

12. Philosophy of peace in Han China: a study of the Huainanzi ch. 15, on military strategy/Edmund Ryden. Taipei: Taipei Ricci Institute, 1998. 130 pages; 22cm. ISBN: 957918559X, 9579185592. (Variétés sinologiques; 88)

Ryden, Edmund 译，翻译了《淮南子·兵略训》.

13. Jing shen: a translation of Huainanzi chapter 7/Michelle Bromley, Deena Freeman, Alan Hext, Sandra Hill; under the aegis of Elisabeth Rochat de la Vallée. [Place of publication not identified]: Monkey Press, 2010. xii, 124 pages; 20cm. ISBN: 1872468105, 1872468101

Bromley, Michelle 等译，翻译了《淮南子·精神训》.

14. The Huai-nan-tzŭ, Book eleven: behavior, culture and the cosmos/transl. and notes by Benjamin E. Wallacker. New Haven, Conn., 1962. (American oriental series; 48)

Wallacker, Benjamin E. 译. 翻译了《淮南子·齐俗训》.

15. 淮南子/翟江月今译；牟爱鹏英译. 桂林：广西师范大学出版社，2010. 3册（16页，50页，1603页）；24cm. ISBN: 7563393060, 7563393064. (大中华文库：汉英对照)

B232 董仲舒(公元前179—前104)

1. Luxuriant gems of the spring and autumn; attributed to

Dong Zhongshu; edited and translated by Sarah A. Queen and John S. Major. New York: Columbia University Press, [2016]. xii,681 pages;24cm. ISBN: 0231169325. (Translations from the Asian classics)

《春秋繁露》，桂思卓（Queen, Sarah A.〈Sarah Ann〉），Major, John S.（美国汉学家）编译.

B233 《太玄经》(扬雄，公元前53—公元18)

1. The T'ai hsüan ching: the hidden classic/by Derek Walters. Wellingborough, Northamptonshire: Aquarian Press, 1983. 224 pages: illustrations; 22cm. ISBN: 0850303117, 0850303117

   Walters, Derek(1936—)著. 翻译了（汉）扬雄（公元前53年—公元18年）的《太玄经》.

   (1) The alternative I Ching/by Derek Walters. Wellingborough: Aquarian, 1987. 224 pages: illustrations, facsimiles, portraits; 22cm. ISBN: 0850306590, 0850306590

2. The canon of supreme mystery=[Tai xuan jing]/by Yang Hsiung; a translation with commentary of the T'ai hsüan ching by Michael Nylan. Albany: State University of New York Press, 1993. xiv, 680 pages: illustrations; 24cm. ISBN: 0791413950, 0791413951, 0791413969, 0791413968. (SUNY series in Chinese philosophy and culture)

   《太玄经》，Nylan, Michael 译.

3. The elemental changes: the ancient Chinese companion to the I ching/the Tai hsüan ching of Master Yang Hsiung; text and commentaries; translated by Michael Nylan. Albany, N. Y.: State University of New York Press, 1994. viii, 391 pages: illustrations; 23cm. ISBN: 0791416283, 0791416280. (SUNY series in Chinese philosophy and culture)

   《太玄经》，Nylan, Michael 译.

B234 王充(27—约97)

1. Lun-heng/ translated from the Chinese and annotated by Alfred Forke. Leipzig [etc.] 1907—11. 2 v. 25cm.
   Contents: pt. I. Philosophical essays of Wang Ch'ung.—pt. II. Miscellaneous essays on Wang Ch'ung.

   《论衡》，佛尔克（Forke, Alfred, 1867—1944）（德国汉学家）编译.

   (1) 2nd ed. New York: Paragon Book Gallery, 1962. 2 volumes; 24cm.

2. Spontaneity & the pattern of things: the Zìrán and Wùshi of Wáng Chōng's Lùn héng/by M. Henri Day. Stockholm: Föreningen för orientaliska studier, 1972. 37 pages; 30cm. (Skrifter utgivna av Föreningen för orientaliska studier; 6)

   Day, M. Henri 著,包括对王充(27—97)《论衡》的选译.

B235 王符(约85—163)

1. Wang Fu and the comments of a recluse/by Margaret J. Pearson. Tempe, Ariz.: Center for Asian Studies, Arizona State University, 1989. xiii, 195 p.; 23cm. ISBN: 093925221X. (Monograph series (Arizona State University. Center for Asian Studies); no. 24)

   Pearson, Margaret 著,包含了汉代王符（约公元85年—约公元163年）《潜夫论》的英译.

2. The art of the Han essay: Wang Fu's Ch'ien-fu lun/by Anne Behnke Kinney. Tempe, Ariz.: Center for Asian Studies, Arizona State University, 1990. 154 p.; 23cm. ISBN: 0939252236. (Monograph series (Arizona State University. Center for Asian Studies); no. 26.)

   《汉代散文艺术：王符的〈潜夫论〉》，肯尼（Kinney, Anne Behnke）（美国汉学家），包含了汉代王符（约公元85年—约公元163年）《潜夫论》的英译.

B236 荀悦(148—209)

1. Hsühn Yüeh and the mind of late Han China: a translation of the Shen-chien with introd. and annotations/Ch'i-yün Ch'en. Princeton, N. J.: Princeton University Press, c1980. ix, 225 p.; 23cm. (Princeton library of Asian translations)

   《申鉴》，陈启云（Chi-yun Chen）（美国华裔汉学家）译注.

B24 晋代哲学

B241 傅玄(217—278)

1. The Fu-tzu: a post-Han Confucian text/by Jordan D. Paper. Leiden; New York: E. J. Brill, 1987. viii, 108 p.; 24cm. ISBN: 9004080996. (T'oung pao. Monographie, 0169—832X; 13)

   《〈傅子〉:后汉儒家读本》，Paper, Jordan D.;含有对傅玄(217—278年)的《傅子》一书的英译.该书为著者博士论文.

B242 葛洪(284—364)

1. Alchemy, medicine, religion in the China of A. D. 320: The Nei p'ien of Ko Hung (Pao-p'u tzu)/translated by James R. Ware. Cambridge, Mass., M. I. T. Press, 1967. xiv, 388 pages; 24cm.

   《公元320年中国的炼丹术、医学和宗教：葛洪的〈抱朴子·内篇〉》，魏鲁男（Ware, James R., 1901—）（美国汉学家）编译.

   (1) New York: Dover Publications, 1981. xiv, 388 p.; 21cm. ISBN: 0486240886, 0486240886

2. The master who embraces simplicity: a study of the philosopher Ko Hung, A. D. 283—343/by Jay Sailey. San Francisco: Chinese Materials Center, 1978. xxvi, 658 pages; 22cm. ISBN: 0896445224, 0896445222. (Asian library series; no. 9)
   Notes: Includes annotated translations of 21 chapters of the Baopuziwai pian.

   Sailey, Jay 著,包括对《抱朴子·外篇》的翻译.

B25　宋代哲学

B251　朱熹(1130—1200)

1. Confucian cosmogony: a translation of section forty-nine of the complete works of the philosopher Choo-Foo-Tze/ with explanatory notes by the Rev. Thos. M'Clatchie. Shanghai: American Presbyterian Mission Press, 1874. xviii, 161 pages: illustrations; 22cm.

   《朱子全书》(选译),McClatchie, Thos. (—1886)译,英汉对照.选译第 29 节.

2. The philosophy of human nature, by Chu Hsi, translated from the Chinese, with notes, by J. Percy Bruce. London, Probsthain, 1922. xvi, 444 p.; 20cm.

   Notes: "The work here translated forms a part of the imperial edition of Chu Hsis? complete works... published in... 1713... The title of the present work, which is complete in itself, is Hsing li."—Pref.

   Bruce, J. Percy (Joseph Percy,1861—)译.翻译了朱熹的全集的部分内容.

3. Reflections on things at hand; the Neo-Confucian anthology. Compiled by Chu Hsi and Lü Tsu-ch'ien. Translated, with notes, by Wing-tsit Chan. New York: Columbia University Press, 1967. xli, 441 p. port. 23cm. (UNESCO collection of representative works: Chinese series). (Records of civilization: sources and studies, no. 75)

   《近思录》,朱熹(1130—1200),吕祖谦(1137—1181)合编;陈荣捷(Chan, Wing-tsit, 1901—1994)(美国华裔学者)译注.

B252　陈淳(1159—1223)

1. Neo-Confucian terms explained: the Pei-hsi tzu-i/by Ch'en Ch'un; translated, edited, and with an introduction by Wing-tsit Chan. New York: Columbia University Press, 1986. xiii,277 p.;24cm. ISBN:0231063849,0231063845. (Neo-Confucian studies)

   《北溪字义》,陈荣捷(Chan, Wing-tsit, 1901—1994)(美国华裔学者)译注.南宋哲学著作.

B26　明代哲学

1. Readings from the Lu-Wang school of Neo-Confucianism/ translated, with introductions and notes, by Philip J. Ivanhoe. Indianapolis: Hackett Pub. Co., c2009. xi, 197 p.; 22cm. ISBN:0872209602, 0872209601, 0872209619, 087220961X

   《新儒家陆(九渊)王(阳明)学派选读》,Ivanhoe, P. J. 译,含有陆(九渊)王(阳明)诗文和《六祖大师法宝坛经》的选译.

B261　罗钦顺(1465—1547)

1. Knowledge painfully acquired: the K'un chih chi/by Lo Ch'in-shun; translated, edited, and with an introduction by Irene Bloom. New York: Columbia University Press, 1987. ix, 226 pages; 24cm. ISBN: 023106408X, 0231064088. (Neo-Confucian studies)

   《困知记》,Bloom, Irene 编译.

   (1)New York: Columbia University Press, 1995. ix, 226 p.; 23cm. ISBN: 0231064098, 0231064095, 023106408X, 0231064088

B262　王阳明(1472—1529)

1. The philosophy of Wang Yang-ming, translated from the Chinese by Frederick Goodrich Henke... introduction by James H. Tufts. London, Chicago, The Open Court Publishing Co., 1916. xvii, 512 p. illus.; 24cm.

   《传习录》,Henke, Frederick Goodrich(1876—)译.

   (1) 2nd ed. New York: Paragon Book Reprint Corp., 1964. xvii, 512 p. ports.; 23cm. (Paragon reprint Oriental series, 25)

2. Instructions for practical living and other Neo-Confucian writing/by Wang Yang-ming; translated, with notes, by Wing-tsit Chan. New York: Columbia University Press, 1963. xii, 358 p. port. 24cm. ISBN: 0231024843, 0231024846. (Records of civilization: sources and studies; no. 68). (UNESCO collection of representative works. Chinese series)

   《传习录》,陈荣捷(Chan, Wing-tsit, 1901—1994)(美国华裔学者)译注.

   (1) New York: Columbia University Press, 1985. 358 pages: portrait. ISBN: 0231060394, 0231060394. (Records of civilisation: sources and studies; no 68)

3. The philosophical letters of Wang Yang-ming. Translated and annotated by Julia Ching. Canberra, Australian National University Press, 1972. xxiii, 142 p.; 24cm. ISBN: 0708101275. (Asian publications series, no. 1)

   王阳明哲学书信,Ching, Julia 译注.

   (1)Columbia, University of South Carolina Press [1973, c1972]. xxiii, 142 p. front.; 25cm. ISBN: 0872492656. (Asian publication series, no. 1)

4. To acquire wisdom: the way of Wang Yang-ming/Julia Ching. New York: Columbia University Press, 1976. xxvi, 373 p.: ill.; 24cm. ISBN: 0231039387. (Studies in oriental culture; no. 11). (Oriental monograph series; no. 16)

   Notes: Includes selected essays and poems by Wang Yang-ming in English translation

   王阳明著作选,Ching, Julia 译.

B263　黄宗羲(1610—1695)

1. Waiting for the dawn: a plan for the Prince/Wm. Theodore de Bary. New York: Columbia University Press, c1993. xiv, 340 p.; 24cm. ISBN:0231080964

   《明夷待访录》,狄百瑞(De Bary, William Theodore,

1919—)(美国汉学家)译.

B27 清代哲学

B271 颜元(1635—1704)

1. Preservation of learning＝［Cun xue bian］：with an introduction on his life and thought／Yen Yüan；translated by Mansfield Freeman. Los Angeles：Monumenta Serica at the University of California, 1972. v, 215 p. ；27cm. (Monumenta serica monograph；16)
《存学编》,Freeman, Mansfield 译.

B272 康有为(1858—1927)

1. Da t'ung shu, the one-world philosophy of K'ang Yu-wei. London, Allen & Unwin［1958］. 300 p. ；23cm.
《大同书》,Laurence G. Thompson 译.

B3 伦理学

1. Family instructions for the Yen clan. Yen-shih chia-hsün. An annotated translation［from the Chinese］with introduction by Teng Ssu-yü. Leiden, E. J. Brill, 1968［1969］. xxxiv, 250 p. ；25cm. (T'oung pao. Monographie；4)
《颜氏家训》,(南北朝)颜之推(531 年—591 年);邓嗣禹(Teng, Ssu-yü, 1906—1988)(美国华裔学者)等译注.

2. Admonitions for the Yan Clan：a Chinese classic on household management：Chinese-English/written by YanZhitui；translated by Zong Fuchang. 北京：外文出版社, 2004. 29, 422 pages：facsimile；24cm. ISBN：7119033247, 7119033242. (Library of Chinese classics)
《颜氏家训》,(南北朝)颜之推(531—591)著;宗福常译.

3. Back to beginnings：reflections on the Tao/Huanchu Daoren；translated by Thomas Cleary. Boston：Shambhala：Distributed in the United States by Random House, 1990. vi, 143 pages：illustrations；13cm. ISBN：0877735778, 0877735779
《菜根谭》,洪应明(字自诚,生卒不祥,1596 年还在世);Cleary, Thomas F. (1949—)(美国翻译家)译.
   (1) Unabridged. Boston：Shambhala；［New York］：Distributed in the United States by Random House, 1994. vi, 138 p. ；12cm. ISBN：1570620156, 1570620157. (Shambhala pocket classics)
   (2) Boston：Shambhala；［New York］：Distributed in the U. S. by Random House, 1998. vi, 143 pages；13cm. ISBN：1570623775, 1570623776. (Shambhala pocket classics)

4. Vegetable roots discourse：wisdom from Ming China on life and living：Caigentan/by Hong Zicheng；translated by Robert Aitken with Daniel W. Y. Kwok. Emeryville, Calif. ：Shoemaker & Hoard；［Berkeley, Calif.］：Distributed by Publishers Group West, c2006. xiii, 224 p. ；19cm. ISBN：1593760914
《菜根谭》,洪应明(字自诚,生卒不祥,1596 年还在世);

Aitken, Robert(1917—2010),郭颖颐(Kwok, D. W. Y. 〈Danny Wynn Ye〉, 1932—)(美国汉学家)合译.

5. Family and property in Sung China：Yu'an Ts'ai's precepts for social life/translated, with annotations and introduction by Patricia Buckley Ebrey. Princeton, N. J. ：Princeton University Press, c1984. x, 367 p. ；23cm. ISBN：0691054266. (Princeton library of Asian translations)
《袁氏世范》,袁采(？—1195);伊佩霞(Ebrey, Patricia Buckley, 1947—)(美国汉学家)译. 家庭道德.

6. Chinese values：traditional culture and contemporary values. Beijing：Foreign Languages Press, 2016. xi, 192 pages. ；23cm. ISBN：7119100654
《中国价值观：中国传统文化与中国当代价值》,曹雅欣著.

B4 中国宗教

B41 概况

1. Religions and religious life in China/author Sang Li；translator Li Zhurun. Beijing：China Intercontinental Press, 2004. 154 p. ：col. ill. ；21cm. ISBN：7508504968, 7508504964. (China basics series)
《中国宗教》,桑吉著;李竹润译. 五洲传播出版社(中国基本情况丛书/郭长建主编)

2. China's ethnic groups and religions/Zheng Qian；translated by Hou Xiaocui, Rong Xueqin and Huang Ying. ［Beijing］：China intercontinental Press, 2010. 183 pages：color illustrations；23cm. ISBN：7508516851, 7508516850
《中国民族与宗教》,吴伟主编. 五洲传播出版社. 介绍当代中国的民族、宗教基本情况,以及五大宗教在中国的发展情况和中国政府的宗教政策.

3. The Taoist tradition in Chinese thought/by Yao-yü Wu；translated by Laurence G. Thompson；edited by Gary Seaman. Los Angeles, CA：Ethnographics Press, Center for Visual Anthropology, University of Southern California, c1991. xiii, 315 p. ：ill. ；22cm. ISBN：1878986031
"A translation of part 1 of San chiao li ts'e, a history and comparative study of literati, Taoist and Buddhist thought in China. "
《三教蠡测》(第一部分),吴耀玉(1915—1991);汤普森(Thompson, Laurence G.)(美国汉学家)译,Seaman, Gary(1942—)编.

4. The literati tradition in Chinese thought/by Yao-Yü Wu；translated by Laurence G. Thompson；edited by Gary Seaman. Los Angeles, CA：Ethnographics Press, Center for Visual Anthropology, University of Southern California, c1995. xxi, 539 p. ；ill. ；22cm. ISBN：

1878986066

"Part 2 of San chiao li ts'e, a history and comparative study of literati, Taoist, and Buddhist thought in China."

《三教蠡测》(第二部分),吴耀玉(1915—1991);汤普森(Thompson, Laurence G.)(美国汉学家)译,Seaman, Gary(1942—)编.

5. The Buddhist tradition on Chinese thought/by Yao-yü Wu; translated by Laurence G. Thompson; edited by Gary Seaman. Los Angeles, CA: Ethnographics Press, c1996. xvi, 273 p.; 21cm. ISBN: 1878986085, 1878986082

Notes: "A translation of part 3 of San chiao li ts'e, a history and comparative study of literati, Taoist and Buddhist thought in China."

《三教蠡测》(第三部分),吴耀玉(1915—1991);汤普森(Thompson, Laurence G.)(美国汉学家)译,Seaman, Gary(1942—)编.

6. Chinese religious traditions collated/by Yao-yü Wu; translated by Laurence G. Thompson; edited by Gary Seaman. Los Angeles: Ethnographics Press, Center for Visual Anthropology, University of Southern California, c1997. xvi, 264 p.; 22cm. ISBN: 1878986112

Notes: "Part 4 of San chiao li ts'e, a history and comparative study of literati, Taoist, and Buddhist thought in China."

《三教蠡测》(第四部分),吴耀玉(1915—1991);汤普森(Thompson, Laurence G.)(美国汉学家)译,Seaman, Gary(1942—)编.

7. Marxism and religion/edited by Lü Daji and Gong Xuezeng; translated by Chi Zhen. Boston: Brill, [2014]. xiv, 421 pages: illustrations; 24cm. ISBN: 9004174566, 9047428021, 9004174566, 9004174567. (Religious studies in contemporary China collection; volume 4)

《马克思主义与宗教》,吕大吉,龚学增主编;池桢(Chi Zhen,1975—)译.该书是一本论文集,收录多位学者的14篇论文.

8. Treatise on Buddhism and Taoism; an English translation of the original Chinese text of Wei-shu CXIV and the Japanese annotation of Tsukamoto Zenryü, by Leon Hurvitz. [Kyoto] Jimbunkagaku Kenkyusho, Kyoto University, 1956. 25—103 p. 38cm.

《魏书·释老志》(《魏书》第114卷),魏收(506—572);Hurvitz, Leon 译.有关佛教和道教的内容.

9. The great Asian religions: an anthology/compiled by Wing-tsit Chan [and three others]. New York: Macmillan, 1969. xvii, 412 pages; 24cm. ISBN: 0023206802, 0023206801

Contents: Part one: Religions of India. Part two: Religions of China. Part three: Religions of Japan

陈荣捷(Chan, Wing-tsit, 1901—1994)(美国华裔学者)

选编.第二部分收录中国宗教的文献.

10. The origin of Chinese deities/Cheng Manchao. Beijing: Foreign Languages Press: Distributed by China International Book Trading Corp., 1995. 241 pages: illustrations (some color); 19cm. ISBN: 7119000306, 7119000305

《中国诸神由来》,程曼超编著.

11. China's famous Buddhist temples, Taoist shrines, mosques and churches/written by Yu Guiyuan; translated by Zhang Huizhen, Li Tao and Yang Liehuan. Jinan, China: Shandong Friendship Press, 1998. 76 pages; 27cm. ISBN: 7805519897, 7805519890

《中国的著名寺庙、宫观与教堂》,余桂元著;张会珍等译.山东友谊出版社.

B42　佛教

B421　概括

1. Buddhism in China. Peking: Chinese Buddhist Association, 1957. 55 pages: illustrations; 19cm.

《中国的佛教》,赵朴初著.

2. Tibetan Buddhism/Ou Shengming. Beijing: China International Press, 1996. 43 pages: color illustrations; 19cm. ISBN: 7801131541, 7801131546. (Tibet series)

《藏传佛教》,欧声明著.五洲传播出版社.

3. Guide to Chinese Buddhism/written by Zheng Lixin; translated by Ling Yuan; English text edited by Sara Grimes. Beijing: Foreign Languages Press, 2004. iv, 216 pages, [8] pages of plates: illustrations (chiefly color); 21cm. ISBN: 7119033344, 7119033341.

《中国旅游:佛教》,郑立新著.本书对中国佛教的历史和宗派、佛事活动、佛教组织和佛教事业都做了简要介绍.

4. Buddhism in China/written by Ling Haicheng; translated by Jin Shaoqing. Beijing: China Intercontinental Press, 2004. 268 p.: ill.; 22cm. ISBN: 7508505352, 7508505350. (China Religious Culture series)

Contents: (1) Buddhism and Contemporary China; (2) Buddhist Association of China; (3) Contemporary Buddhist Figures; (4) Buddhism Ceremonies; (5) Buddhism education; (6) Buddhist culture; (7) Buddhist Caves; (8) Buddhist Architecture; (9) Buddhist Music; (10) Buddhist publications; (11) Buddhist Dances; (12) Buddhist Paintings; (13) Charity; (14) Friend ship ites with Hong Kong, Macao and Taiwan Buddhist circles; (15) Fereign exchanges.

《中国佛教》,凌海成著.五洲传播出版社(中国宗教基本情况丛书).介绍中国佛教的源头与传入,中国佛教的派系以及中国当代佛教发展的概况.

5. Buddhism in China/written by Ling Haicheng; translated by Liu Jun and Xie Tao. Beijing: Wu zhou chuan bo chu ban she, 2005. 158 pages: illustrations; 22cm. ISBN:

7508508408, 7508508405

《中国佛教:英文》,凌海诚编著;刘浚,谢涛译. 五洲传播出版社.

6. Buddhism: rituals and monastic life/written by Zheng Lixin; translated by Ling Yuan. Beijing: Foreign Languages Press, 2007. 267 pages, [6] pages of plates: illustrations; 21cm. ISBN: 7119044903, 7119044907. (China tour guide)

《中国佛教:英文》,郑立新著.

7. Basic Buddhism: exploring Buddhism and Zen/by Huai-Chin Nan. Beijing: Dong fang chu ban she, 2008. 383 pages; 23cm. ISBN: 7506033312, 7506033313. (Tai Hu da xue tang)

《中国佛教发展史略述》,南怀瑾著. 东方出版社.

8. 佛教常识答问/赵朴初著;赵桐译. 北京:外语教学与研究出版社,2012. xi, 272 页;23cm. ISBN: 7513524926. ("博雅双语名家名作"系列)

英文题名: Essentials of buddhism: questions and answers. 英汉对照.

9. Buddhism/edited by Lou Yulie; translated by Pei-Ying Lin. Boston: Brill, 2015. ISBN: 9004174511. (Religious studies in contemporary China collection; volume 5)

《佛教》,楼宇烈编;Lin, Pei-Ying 译.

10. The Buddha scroll/Ding Guanpeng; introduced by Thomas Cleary. Boston: Shambhala; [New York]: Distributed in the U. S. by Random House, 1999. 1 volume (unpaged): color illustrations; 20cm. ISBN: 1570625131, 781570625138

《法界源流图》,(清)丁观鹏;Cleary, Thomas F. (1949—)译.

B422 佛教史地

1. Travels of Fah-Hian and Sung-Yun, Buddhist pilgrims, from China to India (400 A. D. and 518 A. D.). London, Trübner, 1869. lxxiii, 208 p. fold. map.;19cm.

《佛国记》,法显(约 337 年—422 年);比尔(Beal, Samuel, 1825—1889)(英国汉学家)译.

(1) 2nd ed. London: Susil Gupta, 1964. lxxiii, 208, [2] p.;22cm.

(2) 2nd ed. New York: Kelley, 1969. lxxiii, 208, [2] pages;22cm. (Reprints of economic classics)

(3) New Delhi: Asian Education Services, 1993. lxxiii, 208 pages: folded map; 19cm. ISBN: 8120608240, 8120608245

(4) Reprint pbk. ed. New Delhi: Rupa & Co., 2003. lxxiii, 208 pages: map; 18cm. ISBN: 8129102064, 8129102065

(5) New Delhi: Low Price Publications, 2005. lxxiii, 208 pages: map; 19cm. ISBN: 8175363827, 8175363823

2. A record of Buddhistic kingdoms, being an account by the Chinese monk Fâ-Hien of his travels in India and Ceylon (A. D. 399—414) in search of the Buddhist books of discipline. Oxford, Clarendon Press, 1886. xv, 123, 45 p. plates, map. 23cm.

《佛国记》,理雅各(Legge, James, 1815—1897)(英国汉学家)译.

(1) New York: Paragon Book Reprint Corp.: Dover, 1965. ix, 123, 47 p.: ill., map.; 23cm.

(2) Islamabad, Pakistan: Lok Virsa, [1984]. xi, 123 p., [9] p. of plates: ill., map; 22cm.

(3) New York: Dover Publications, [1991]. i, 123, 45 p.: ill., map; 21cm.

(4) New York: Cosimo Classics, c2005. 1 v. (various pagings): ill., map; 21cm. ISBN: 1596055723

3. The travels of Fa-hsien (399—414 A. D.), or Record of the Buddhistic kingdoms, retranslated by H. A. Giles. Cambridge [Eng.] University Press, 1923. xvi, 96 p. front. 18cm.

《佛国记》,法显(约 337 年—422 年);翟理斯(Giles, Herbert Allen, 1845—1935)(英国汉学家)译.

首版于 1877 年,题名为"Record of the Buddhistic kingdoms".

(1) London: Routledge & Paul, 1956. xx, 96 p.: ill., map.; 17cm.

(2) Westport, Conn.: Greenwood Press, 1981. xx, 96 p.: folded map; 23cm. ISBN: 0313232407

4. A record of the Buddhist countries/by Fa-hsien; [translated from the Chinese by Li Yung-hsi]. Peking: Chinese Buddhist Association, c1957. 93, [1] p.: 1 fold. map; 19cm.

《佛国记》,法显(约 337 年—422 年);李永熙译.

5. A record of Buddhist monasteries in Lo-yang/by Yang Hsü'an-chih; translated by Yi-t'ung Wang. Princeton, N. J.: Princeton University Press, c1984. xxii, 310 p.: ill.; 25cm. ISBN: 0691054037. (Princeton Library of Asian translations)

《洛阳珈蓝记》,杨炫之(生卒不详,北魏人);Wang, Yi-t'ung(1914—)译.

6. Buddhist monastic traditions of Southern Asia: a record of the inner law sent home from the south seas/by S'ramana Yijing; translated from the Chinese (Taishō volume 54, number 2125) by Li Rongxi. Berkeley, Calif.: Numata Center for Buddhist Translation and Research, 2000. xi, 198 p.; 25cm. ISBN: 1886439095. (BDK English Tripitaka; 93—1)

《南海寄归内法传》,义净(635—713);Li, Jung-hsi 译.

7. A record of the Buddhist religion as practised in India and the Malay archipelago (A. D. 671—695) by I-Tsing. Translated by J. Takakusu, with a letter from the Right Hon. Professor F. Max Müller. Oxford, Clarendon Press, 1896. lxiv, 240 p. front. (fold. map) diagrs.;

23cm.

《南海寄归内法传》，义净（635—713）；Takakusu, Junjirō（1866—1945）译.

(1) Delhi, Munshirma Manoharlal［1966］. lxiv, 240 p. fold. map. ; 22cm.

(2) Oxford：Clarendon Press,［Taipei］：Cheng Wen Pub. Co. , 1970. lxiv, 240 pages：folded map；20cm.

(3) 2nd Indian ed. New Delhi：Munshiram Manoharlal, 1982. lxiv, 240 pages：1 folded map；22cm.

(4) New Delhi：Asian Educational Services, 2005. lxiv, 240 pages；25cm. ISBN：8120616227, 8120616226

8. Si-yu-ki. Buddhist records of the Western World. London, Trübner, 1884. 2 v. fold. map. ; 22cm.

《大唐西域记》，玄奘（约596—664）述，辩机（620—648）撰文；比尔（Beal, Samuel, 1825—1889）（英国汉学家）译.

(1) Boston, J. R. Osgood, 1885. 2 v. fold. map. ; 21cm.

(2) London, K. Paul, Trench, Trübner &. Co. , 1906. 2 volumes map；22cm. (Trübner's oriental series)

(3) Popular ed. London, K. Paul, Trench, Trübner, 1914. 2 volumes in 1 folded map；22cm. (Trübner's original series)

(4) Popular edition. London：Kegan Paul, Trench &. Co. , 1920. 369 pages；24cm. (Trubner's oriental series)

(5) Si-yu-ki. Buddhist records of the Western World. Chinese accounts of India. /translated from the Chinese of Hiuen Tsiang, by Samuel Beal.［New ed.］. Calcutta, Susil Gupta, 1957—1958. 4 volumes；23cm.

(6) Popular ed. London, D. Paul, Trench, Trübner. New York：Paragon Book Reprint Corp. , 1968. 2 v. in 1. map；23cm.

(7) Delhi, Oriental Books Reprint Corp. ;［exclusively distributed by Munshiram Manoharlal, 1969］. 2 v. in 1. fold. map；22cm. (Trübner's oriental series)

(8)［New ed.］Calcutta, Susil Gupta［1957—58］. 4 v. ; 23cm.

(9) Popular ed. San Francisco：Chinese Materials Center, 1976. 2 volumes in 1：folded map；21cm. (Chinese Materials Center. Reprint series; no. 40)

(10) Delhi：Bharatiya, c1980. 4 v. ; 23cm.

(11) Delhi, India：Motilal Banarsidass, 1981. 2 volumes in 1；22cm. ISBN：0895811316, 0895811318

(12) 2nd ed. New Delhi：Oriental Books Reprint Corp. : Exclusively distributed by Munshiram Manoharlal, 1983. 2 volumes in 1. : folded map；22cm.

(13) Delhi：Motilal Banarsidass, 1994. 2 volumes in 1. ; 23cm. ISBN：8120811070, 8120811072

(14) Dehli：Low Price Publications, 1995. cviii, 242, vii, 369 pages：folded map；19cm. ISBN：8185557578, 8185557571

(15) London：Routledge, c2000. 2 v. ; 22cm. ISBN：0415231884, 0415231886, 041524286X, 0415242868, 0415244692, 0415244695, 0415244706, 0415244701. (Buddhism; v. II). (Trubner's oriental series)

(16) New Delhi：Asian Educational Services, 2003. 2 volumes：1 folded map；23cm. ISBN：8120613929, 8120613928, 8120613937, 8120613935

(17) London：Trubner, 2003. 478 pages：map；24cm. ISBN：1844530167, 1844530168. （Trübner's oriental series)

(18) New Delhi：Munshiram Manoharlal Publishers, 2004. cviii, 369 pages：1 folded map；23cm. ISBN：8121507417, 8121507413

(19) Lexington, KY：Adamant Media Corporation, 2005. 2 volumes；21cm. ISBN：1402167584, 140216758X, 1402167591, 1402167598. (Elibron classics)

(20) Delhi：Low Price Publications, 2008. 478 pages；18cm. ISBN：8175364370, 8175364378

(21)［United States］：Kessinger Publishing, 2013. 2 volumes in 1；23cm. ISBN：1417922260, 1417922265

9. On Yuan Chwang's travels in India, 629—645 A. D/by Thomas Watters; ed. , after his death by T. W. Rhys Davids and S. W. Bushell; with two maps and an itinerary by Vincent A. Smith. London, Royal Asiatic Society, 1904—1905. 2 volumes 2 folded maps；22cm. (Oriental Translation Fund. New ser. ; 14—15)

《大唐西域记》，Watters, Thomas（1840—1901）；Davids, T. W. Rhys（Thomas William Rhys, 1843—1922）和 Bushell, Stephen W.（Stephen Wootton, 1844—1908）编.

(1) Leipzig：C. G. Röeder, 1923. 2 volumes：2 folded maps；22cm. （New series/Oriental Translation Fund; xiv-xv)

(2) Peking, 1941. 2 volumes maps 24cm. (Oriental Translation Fund. New series, 14—15)

(3) 1st Indian ed. Delhi, Munshi Ram Manohar Lal, 1961. 2 volumes in 1. illustrations, folded maps；23cm.

(4) New York：AMS Press, 1971. 2 volumes 2 folded maps；23cm. ISBN：0404068790, 0404068790, 0404068804, 0404068806. （Oriental Translation Fund. New series, 14—15)

(5) 2nd Indian ed. Delhi, Munshiram Manoharlal, 1973. 2 volumes in 1, 22cm.

(6) San Francisco：Chinese Materials Center, 1975. 2 volumes：2 folded maps；20cm. (Oriental Translation Fund. New series, 14—15)

(7) New Delhi：Asian Educational Services, 1988. 2 volumes：maps；22cm. ISBN：812060296X, 8120602960, 8120602978, 8120602977

（8）New Delhi：Munshiram Manoharlal, 1996. 2 dl. in 1 bd. (XVII, 401 p.；357 p.，2 vouwbl. pl.)：krt.；23cm. ISBN：8121503361, 8121503365

（9）New Delhi：Munshiram Manoharlal Publishers, 2000. XVII,357 p.；22cm. ISBN：8121503361,8121503365

（10）Delhi：Low Price Publications；New Delhi：Distributed by D. K. Publishers Distributors, 2004. xiii, 401, 357 pages：2 folded maps；23cm. ISBN：8175363444, 8175363441

（11）［S. l.］：Nabu Press，［2010］. ISBN：117650942X, 1176509429

（12）［S. l.］：Primary Sources, Historic，［2011］. ISBN：1241112428, 1241112424

（13）Memphis：General Books, 2012. 134 pages；25cm. ISBN：1152199910, 1152199919

（14）［Place of publication not identified］：Hardpress Ltd, 2013. ISBN：1314614746, 1314614749

10. The great Tang dynasty record of the western regions/translated by the Tripitaka-Master Xuanzang under Imperial Order；composed by S'ramana Bianji；translated into English by Li Rongxi. Berkeley, Calif.：Numata Center for Buddhist Translation & Research, 1996. xiii, 425 p.；25cm. ISBN：1886439028. (BDK English Tripitaka；79)
Notes："Taishō, volume 51, number 2087."
《大唐西域记》，玄奘（约 596—664）述，辩机（620—648）撰文；Li, Jung-his 译.

11. India in China：the gift of Buddha/authored and translated from the Chinese by Samuel Beal. New Delhi：Lotus Press Publishers & Distributors，［2012］. 335 pages：illustrations；23cm. ISBN：8183822916, 8183822916. (India bookvarsity；Lotus choices)
印度在中国：佛陀的礼物. 比尔（Beal, Samuel，1825—1889）（英国汉学家）英译，翻译了玄奘游历印度的资料.

12. 玄奘西天取经/常征著；李莉，王文亮翻译. 北京：五洲传播出版社，2010. 175 页；23cm. ISBN：7508517407, 7508517407. (中外文化交流故事丛书)

13. Diary；the record of a pilgrimage to China in search of the law；translated from the Chinese by Edwin O. Reischauer. New York：Ronald Press Co. ［1955］. xvi, 454 p. col. port.，maps (on lining papers) 25cm.
《入唐求法巡礼行记》，（日）圆仁（794—864）著；赖世和（Reischauer, Edwin O.〈Edwin Oldfather〉，1910—1990）（美国日本史专家）译.

14. The biographical scripture of King As'oka/translated from the Chinese of Samghapāla, Taishō, vol. 50, number 2043）by Li Rongxi. Berkeley, Calif.：Numata Center for Buddhist Translation and Research, 1993. xii, 203 p.；24cm. ISBN：0962561843. (BDK English Tripitaka；76—II)

阿育王传稿. 译自中文《大正藏》第 50 卷.

15. 佛陀和他的十大弟子＝The Buddha and His Ten Principal Disciples：英汉对照/明旸长老著；本性法师译. 厦门：厦门大学出版社，2007. 245 页；23cm. ISBN：7561528235, 756152823X
书名原文：The Buddha and his ten principal Disciples. 本书系佛陀及其十大弟子传略中英文对照读本.

16. Lives of great monks and nuns. Berkeley, Calif.：Numata Center for Buddhist Translation and Research, c2002. 245 p.；25cm. ISBN：1886439141. (BDK English Tripitaka；76—III—VII)
Contents：The life of As'vaghosha Bodhisattva/translated from the Chinese of Kumārajīva by Li Rongxi—The life of Nāgārjīva Bodhisattva/translated from the Chinese of Kumārajīva by Li Rongxi—Biography of Dharma Master Vasubandhu/translated from the Chinese of Paramārtha by Albert A. Dalia—Biographies of Budhist nuns/translated from the Chinese of Baochang by Li Rongxi—The journey of the eminent monk Faxian/translated from the Chinese of Faxian by Li Rongxi
高僧名尼传.（日本）沼田佛教翻译与研究中心编.

17. Biographies of Buddhist nuns：Pao-chang's Pi-chiu-ni-chuan/translated by Li Jung-hsi. Osaka：Tohokai, c1981. 144 p.：ill.；19cm.
《比丘尼传》，宝唱（约 465—）撰；李荣熙（Li, Jung-his）译.

18. Lives of the nuns：biographies of Chinese Buddhist nuns from the fourth to sixth centuries：a translation of the Pi-ch'iu-ni chuan/compiled by Shih Pao-ch'ang；translated by Kathryn Ann Tsai. Honolulu：University of Hawaii Press, c1994. xi, 188 p.：map；23cm. ISBN：0824815416
《比丘尼传：四至六世纪中国佛教比丘尼传》，宝唱（约 465—）撰；蔡安妮（Tsai, Kathryn Ann）（美国汉学家）译.

19. Chinese monks in India：biography of eminent monks who went to the western world in search of the law during the great T'ang dynasty/by I-ching；translated［and edited］by Latika Lahiri. Delhi：Motilal Banarsidass, 1986. xxvii, 160 p.；23cm. ISBN：8120800621. (Buddhist traditions；v. 3)
《大唐西域求法高僧传》，义净（635—713）；Lahiri, Latika(1923—)译. 英汉文本.

20. The life of Hiuen-Tsiang, by the shaman Hwui Li. With an introd. containing an account of the works of I-tsing, by Samuel Beal. With a pref. by L. Cranmer-Byng. New ed. London, K. Paul, Trench, Trübner, 1911. xlvii, 218 p. 22cm. (Trübner's oriental series)
《大唐大慈恩寺三藏法师传》，慧立（唐代人，生卒不祥），彦悰（活动时间公元 7 世纪）；比尔（Beal，Samuel，1825—1889）（英国汉学家）译.

(1) Popular ed. London：K. Paul, Trench, Trübner, 1914. xlvii, 218 pages；24cm. (Trübner's Oriental series)

(2) Westport, Conn.：Hyperion Press [1973]. xlvii, 218 p. 23cm. ISBN：0883550741

(3) Delhi, India：Academica Asiatica, 1973. xlvii, 317 pages；maps；22cm.

(4) San Francisco：Chinese Materials Center, 1974. xlvii, 218 pages；20cm. (Reprint series (Chinese Materials Center)；no. 2)

(5) Popular ed. San Francisco：Chinese Materials Center, 1976. xlvii, 218 pages；20cm.

(6) Ann Arbor, Mich.：University Microfilms International, 1978. xlvii, 218 pages；19cm.

(7) Ann Arbor, Mich.：University Microfilms International, 1978. xlvii, 218 pages；19cm.

(8) New ed. London：K. Paul, Trench, Trubner, Tylers Green：University microfilms, 1979. 218 pages；20cm.

(9) Delhi, India：Gian Pub. House, 1986. xlvii, 218 pages；23cm.

(10) New Delhi：Asian Educational Services, 1998. xlvii, 218 p.；23cm. ISBN：8120612787, 8120612785

(11) London：Routledge, 2000. xvii, 218 pages；23cm. ISBN：0415244684, 0415244688, 041524286X, 0415242868. (Trubner's oriental series. Buddhism；1)

(12) New ed. Delhi：Low Price Press；Distributed by D. K. Publishers, New Delhi, 2001. xlvii, 218 pages；23cm. ISBN：8175362480, 8175362482)

(13) London；Portland：Trubner, 2003. xlvii, 218 p.；24cm. ISBN：1844530132, 1844530137. (Trübner's oriental series)

(14) New Delhi：Munshiram Manoharlal Publishers, 2003. xvii, 218 pages；24cm. ISBN：8121503329, 8121503327

(15) New Delhi：Rupa Publications, 2013. 185 pages；20cm. ISBN：8129120311, 8129120313. (Rupa antiquities)

21. A biography of the Tripitaka master of the great Ci'en Monastery of the great Tang dynasty/translated from the Chinese of S'ramana Huili and Shi Yancong；by Li Rongxi. Berkeley, Calif.：Numata Center for Buddhist Translation and Research, 1995. xii, 385 p.；25cm. ISBN：1886439001. (BDK English Tripitaka；77)

《大唐大慈恩寺三藏法师传》，慧立（唐代人，生卒不详），彦悰（活动时间公元 7 世纪）；Li, Jung-his 译.

22. A chronicle of Buddhism in China, 581—960 A. D：

translations from Monk Chih-p'an's Fo-tsu t'ung-chi/Ed., transl., and annot. with an introd. by Jan Yün-hua. Santiniketan Visva-Bharati, 1966. vi, 189, iii p；25cm. (Visva-Bharati research publications)

《佛祖统纪》（选译），（宋）志磐撰. 选译了该书第 39－42 卷.

23. The biographies of the Dalai Lamas/by Ya Hanzhang；translated by Wang Wenjiong. Beijing：Foreign Languages Press：Distributed by China International Book Trading Corp. , 1991. vii, 442 pages：illustrations (some color)；21cm. ISBN：7119012673, 7119012674, 0835122662, 0835122665

《达赖喇嘛传》，牙含章编著.

24. The 14th Dalai Lama/Siren & Gewang. Beijing, China：China Intercontinental Press, 1997. 75 pages；21cm. ISBN：7801132998, 7801132994.

《十四世达赖喇嘛》，司仁，格旺著，五洲传播出版社.

25. Biographies of the Tibetan spiritual leaders Panchen Erdenis/by Ya Hanzhang；translated by Chen Guansheng and Li Peizhu. Beijing：Foreign Languages Press, 1994. 415 pages；20cm. ISBN：7119016881, 7119016887

《班禅额尔德尼传》，牙含章著.

26. The reincarnation of the Panchen Lama：facts about the identification, confirmation and enthronement of the eleventh Panchen Erdeni/compiled by Shanzhou. [Beijing]：China Intercontinental Press, 1996. 83 pages, 1 folded leaf：color illustrations；21cm. ISBN：7801131088, 7801131089

《班禅转世：第十一班禅额尔德尼寻访、认定、坐床纪实》，金晖主编，杉舟编著，五洲传播出版社.

27. T he 11th Panchen, Erdeni Qoigyi Gyaibo/[by Li Chunsheng；translated by Wang Yanjuan]. Beijing：Zhongguo Zang xue chu ban she：China Pictorial Pub. House, 2005. [4] pages of leaves, 109 pages：chiefly color illustrations；29cm. ISBN：7800249600, 7800249603

《第十一世班禅额尔德尼·确吉杰布：英文》，李春生著. 中国画报出版社.

28. Empty cloud：the autobiography of the Chinese Zen master Hsu Yun/transl. by Upasaka Lu K'uan Yu (Charles Luk). [Rochester]：Empty Cloud Press, 1974. 120 p：Ill.

虚云禅师（1840—1959）传记. 陆宽昱（1898—1979）译.

29. In search of the Dharma：memoirs of a modern Chinese Buddhist pilgrim/Chen-Hua；edited with an introduction by Chün-fang Yü and translated by Denis C. Mair. Albany, N. Y.：State University of New York Press, c1992. xvii, 292 p.：ill., maps；24cm. ISBN：0791408450, 0791408469. (SUNY series in Buddhist

studies)

《参学琐谈》,真华长老(Zhenhua,1921—)著;丹尼斯·马尔(Mair,Denis C.)译. 僧人回忆录.

B422.1 佛教组织及寺庙

1. The visit of the Teshoo lama to Peking/Ch'ien Lung's inscription; translated by Ernest Ludwig. Peking：Tientsin Press, c1904. 88 p.；19cm.
Notes：With Chinese text and translation of the "Inscription on the stone tablet in the eastern pavilion of the western Yellow Temple." The inscription refers to the visit of the third Tashi lama to Peking toward the end of the eighteenth century.
《乾隆题西黄寺碑文》,乾隆(1711—1799)；Ludwig, Ernest(1876—)译.

2. 资寿寺/侯廷亮主编. 太原：山西人民出版社,2004. 124页；19cm. ISBN：7806367438；
Notes：本书以中英文对照的形式,介绍了创建于唐代,曾以元代壁画,明代彩塑艺术闻名遐迩的位于山西省中部灵石县的资寿寺.

3. The temples of Beijing/planned by Xiao Xiaoming. Beijing：Foreign Languages Press, 2006. [8] leaves of plates, 112 pages：illustrations, maps；23cm. ISBN：7119043883, 7119043889
《北京寺庙道观：英文》,廖频,吴文撰;何炳富等摄. 外文出版社(漫游北京).
为2008年奥运会而编写的漫游北京系列丛书之一,古都北京历史悠久,存留许多著名的寺庙、道观、清真寺等.

4. 承德普宁寺/赵纯洁[等]主编;中国承德市民族宗教事务局,荷兰莱顿大学合著. 北京：中国旅游出版社,2009. 320页；30cm. ISBN：7503238887, 7503238888

5. Buddhist monastery south of the Yangtze/written by Wang Yuan; translated by Helen Yuan; English-edited by Tony Wai. Shanghai：Shanghai Jiao Tong University Press, 2010. 2, 241 pages：illustrations；24cm. ISBN：7313063465, 7313063466. (Architectural culture south of the Yangtze)
《江南禅寺》,王媛著. 上海交通大学出版社(江南建筑文化丛书). 介绍禅寺的历史与现状.

B423 经及其释

1. A catena of Buddhist scriptures from the Chinese. By Samuel Beal. London, Trübner, 1871. xiii, 436 p.；23cm.
中国佛经翻译. 比尔(Beal, Samuel, 1825—1889)(英国汉学家)译.
(1) Taipei：Cheng Wen Pub. Co., 1970. xii, 436 pages；22cm.
(2) Ann Arbor, Mich.：[University Microfilms International], 1980. xiii, 436 pages；21cm.
(3) 2nd ed. Delhi：Sri Satguru Publications, 1989. [x], 436 pages；23cm. ISBN：8170301831, 8170301837

2. The threefold lotus sutra/translated by Bunnō Katō, Yoshiroō Tamura, and Kōjirō Miyasaka; with revisions by W. E. Soothill, Wilhelm Schiffer, and Pier P. Del Campana. 1st ed. New York：Weatherhill, 1975. xviii, 383 p.；23cm. ISBN：0834801051, 083480106X
《法华三部经》,Bunnō Katō, Yoshiroō Tamura, Kōjirō Miyasaka 合译. 包括三部佛经：
(1) Sutra of innumerable meanings/translated by Yoshiro Tamura; with revisions by Wilhelm Schiffer, Pier P. Del Campana.《无量义经》,Yoshiro Tamura 译.
(2) Sutra of the lotus flower of the wonderful law/translated by Bunno Kato; with revisions by W. E. Soothill, Wilhelm Schiffer, Yoshiro Tamura.《妙法莲华经》,Bunno Kato 译.
(3) Sutra of meditation on the Bodhisattva universal virtue/translated by Kojiro Miyasaka; with revisions by Pier P. Del Campana.《佛说观普贤菩萨行法经》,Katō, Bunnō 等译;苏慧廉(Soothill, William Edward, 1861—1935)(英国传教士)校.
① Tokoyo：Kosei Pub. Co.；New York：Weatherhill, 1987. xviii, 383 pages；23cm. ISBN：4333002087, 4333002085

3. 金刚般若波罗密经. 般若波罗密多心经 /陆宽昱译. Hongkong：香港佛经流通处, 1976. 1, 23, 2, 2 pages；19cm.
Notes：中英文合订本

4. The Sutra of Queen S'rīmālā of the Lion's Roar/translated from the Chinese (Taishō volume 12, number 353) by Diana Y. Paul. The Vimalakīrti Sutra/translated from the Chinese (Taishō volume 14, number 475) by John R. McRae. Berkeley, Calif.：Numata Center for Buddhist Translation and Research, 2004. xi, 229 p.；25cm. ISBN：1886439311. (BDK English Tripitaka；20—I, 26—I)
Tripitaka. Sūtrapitaka. S'rīmālādevīsimˌhanāda. English. Paul, Diana Y. McRae, John R., 1947—
《胜鬘狮子吼一乘大方便方广经》,Diana Y. Paul 译自《大正藏》12卷.《维摩诘所说经》,John R. McRae 译自《大正藏》14卷.

5. Tiantai Lotus texts. Berkeley, California：Bukkyō Dendō Kyōkai America, Inc., 2013. xi, 251 pages；25cm. ISBN：1886439450, 1886439451. (BDK English Tripitaka series)
Contents：The infinite meanings Sutra (Taishō volume 9, number 276)；The Sutra expounded by the Buddha on practice of the way through contemplation of the Bodhisattva all-embracing goodness (Taishō volume 9, number 277)/translated by Tsugunari Kubo and Joseph M. Logan—The commentary on the Lotus Sutra (Taishō volume 26, number 1519)/translated by Terry Abbott—A guide to the Tiantai fourfold teachings (Taishō volume 46, number 1931)/translated by Masao Ichishima and

David W. Chappell.

《天台莲花教典》，包括：1.《无量义经》，译自《大正藏》9卷；2.《佛说观普贤菩萨行法经》，Tsugunari Kubo and Joseph M. Logan 译自《大正藏》9卷；3.《妙法莲华经忧波提舍》，Terry Abbott 译自《大正藏》26卷.

6. The new testament of higher Buddhism/by Timothy Richard. Edinburgh：T. & T. Clark, 1910. viii, 275 pages；22cm.

　　Contents：General introduction—Introduction to the Awakening of faith—Translation of the Awakening of faith—Translator's introduction to the Lotus scripture—Translation of the essence of the Lotus scripture—Translation of the Great physician's twelve desires—The creed of half Asia.

　　Notes：includes English translation of a Chinese text.

　　Richard, Timothy(1845—1919)译. 包括《大乘起信论》《妙法莲华经》的英译.

　　(1)[S. l.]：Nabu Press, [2010]. ISBN：1172367841, 1172367849

　　(2)[S. l.]：Hardpress Publishing, [2012]. ISBN：140779518X, 1407795188

　　(3)[Place of publication not identified]：Book On Demand Ltd, 2013. ISBN：5518552092, 5518552098

7. Early Buddhist scriptures. London, K. Paul, Trench, Trubner & Co., Ltd., 1935. xxv, 232 p.；23cm.

　　《大藏经》（选译），Thomas, E. J. (Edward Joseph, 1869—1958)编译.

8. Apocryphal Scriptures. Berkeley, Calif.：Numata Center for Buddhist Translation and Research, 2005. xii, 161 p.；25cm. ISBN：188643929X. (BDK English Tripitaka；25-I, 25-V, 25-VI, 29-I, 104-VI)

　　Contents：The Bequeathed teaching sutra/translated from the Chinese by J. C. Cleary—The Ullambana sutra/translated from Chinese by Bandō Shōjun—The Sutra of forty-two sections/translated from the Chinese by Hen-ching Shih—The Sutra of perfect enlightenment/translated from the Chinese by Peter N. Gregory—The Sutra on the profundity of filial love/translated from the Chinese by Arai Keiyo.

　　《大藏经》（选译）；Cleary, J. C. (Jonathan Christopher)译.

9. Myoho-renge-kyo：the sutra of the Lotus flower of the wonderful law/transl. [from the Chinese] by Bunno Kato；rev. by W. E. Soothill [and] Wilhelm Schiffer. Tokyo：Kosei, 1971. 440p.

　　《妙法莲华经》

10. The lotus of the wonderful law；or, The lotus gospel, Saddharma pundarīka sūtra, Miao-fa lien hua ching, by W. E. Soothill. Oxford, The Clarendon Press, 1930. xi, 275, [1] p. col. front., 13 pl.；23cm.

《妙法莲华经》，苏慧廉（Soothill, William Edward, 1861—1935)（英国传教士）译.

　　(1)London：Curzon Press；Totowa, N. J.：Rowman and Littlefield, 1975. xi, 275 p., [12] leaves of plates：ill.；23cm. ISBN：0874716063

　　(2)San Francisco：Chinese Materials Center, 1977. 275 p., [14] leaves of plates：ill.；22cm. (Reprint series - Chinese Materials Center；no. 61)

　　(3)Pbk. ed. London：Curzon Press；Atlantic Highlands, NJ：Humanities Press International, 1987. xi, 275 p., [12] leaves of plates：ill.；21cm. ISBN：0391034650

11. Myōhō-Renge-Kyō；the Sutra of the lotus flower of the wonderful law. Translated by Bunnō Katō. Rev. by W. E. Soothill [and] Wilhelm Schiffer. Tokyo, 1971. xii, 440 p.；21cm.

　　《妙法莲华经》，Katō, Bunnō 译，苏慧廉（Soothill, William Edward, 1861—1935)（英国传教士）校.

12. The Sutra of the lotus Flower of the wonderful law/translated from Kumārajīva's version of the Saddharmapundarīka-sūtra by Senchu Murano. Tokyo：Nichiren Shu Headquarters, c1974. xiv, 371 p.；25cm.

　　《妙法莲华经》，Murano, Senchü. 译. 译自中文.

13. Scripture of the lotus blossom of the fine dharma/translated from the Chinese of Kumarajiva by Leon Hurvitz. New York：Columbia University Press, 1976. xxviii, 421 p.；24cm. ISBN：0231037899. 0231039204. (Buddhist studies and translations.). (Translations from the Asian classics). (Records of civilization, sources and studies；no. 94.)

　　《妙法莲华经》，Hurvitz, Leon(1923—)译.

　　(1)New York：Columbia University Press, [1982] c1976. xxviii, 421 p.；23cm. ISBN：0231039204. (IASWR series). (Buddhist studies and translations.). (Translations from the Asian classics). (Records of civilization, sources and studies；no. 94.)

　　(2)New York：Columbia University Press, 1989. xxviii, 421 pages；24cm. ISBN：0231037899, 0231037891, 0231039204, 0231039208

　　(3)Hong Kong：H. K. Buddhist Book Distributor, 1995. 1 volume (various pagings)：illustrations；23cm. ISBN：0231039204, 0231039208

　　(4)Rev. ed. New York：Columbia University Press, c2009. xxviii, 384 p.；23cm. ISBN：0231148948, 0231148941, 0231148955, 023114895X. (Translations from the Asian classics)

14. The wonderful Dharma lotus flower sutra：translated into Chinese by Tripitaka Master Kumarajiva of Yao Chin/with the commentary of Tripitaka Master Hua；translated by the Buddhist Text Translation Society；[edited by Kuo-lin Lethcoe]. San Francisco：Buddhist

Text Translation Society, 1976—. 10 volumes；22cm. ISBN：0917512162 0917512162

《妙法莲华经》

15. The wonderful Dharma Lotus Flower Sūtra 5. Chapter 4：Belief and understanding/transl. into English by the Buddhist Text Translation Society. With the commentary of Tripitaka Master Hua. San Francisco Sino-American Buddhist Assoc.，1979. XV, S. 859—1034, IX S. ISBN：0917512642 0917512643

《妙法莲华经》，第4章.

16. The Lotus Sutra/translated by Burton Watson. New York：Columbia University Press, 1993. xxix, 359 p.；23cm. ISBN：023108160X.（Translations from the Asian classics）

Translated from：Miao fa lian hua jing, which was translated from Sanskrit into Chinese by Kumarajiva

《妙法莲华经》，华兹生（Watson, Burton, 1925—）（美国汉学家）译.

17. The essential Lotus：selections from the Lotus Sutra/translated by Burton Watson. New York：Columbia University Press, c2002. xxxvii, 163 p.；23cm. ISBN：0231125070.（Translations from the Asian classics）

《妙法莲华经》（选译），华兹生（Watson, Burton, 1925—）（美国汉学家）译.

18. The Lotus Sutra/translated from the Chinese of Kumārajīva（Taishō, Volume 9, Number 262）by Kubo Tsugunari and Yuyama Akira. Berkeley, Calif.：Numata Center for Buddhist Translation and Research，1993. xii, 363 p.；25cm. ISBN：0962561800.（BDK English Tripit̠aka；13—1）

《妙法莲华经》，Kubo, Tsugunari（1936—），Yuyama, Akira 合译.

(1) Rev. 2nd ed. Berkeley, Calif.：Numata Center for Buddhist Translation and Research，2007. xvi, 362 p.；25cm. ISBN：1886439399.（BDK English Tripit̠aka series；13—I）

19. The Lotus sutra：a contemporary translation of a Buddhist classic/translation and introduction by Gene Reeves. Boston：Wisdom Publications, c2008. xi, 489 p.；23cm. ISBN：0861715713, 0861715718

《妙法莲华经》，Reeves, Gene 译.

20. The wonderful Dharma lotus flower sutra/a simple explamation by Hsuan Hua；English translation by the Buddhist Text Translation Society. 2nd English ed. Burlingame, Calif.：The Society；［Talmage, Calif.］：Dharma Realm Buddhist University, 2001—. volumes ⟨1—⟩：color illustrations；22cm. ISBN：0881394335, 0881394337

《妙法莲华经》，宣化（1908—1995）解释；Buddhist Text Translation Society 译.

21. The essentials of the Dharma blossom sutra ［by］ Tripitaka Master Tu Lun ［i. e. Hsühan-hua］. Translated by Bhikshu Heng Ch'ien. San Francisco, Buddhist Text Translation Society；distributed in the United States by the Sino-American Buddhist Association, 1974—. v. illus.；22cm.

The text of the sutra is a translation of Kumarajiva's version entitled Miao fa lien hua ching

《〈妙法莲华经〉之基础》，宣化（1908—1995）著；Heng Ch'ien, Bhikshu 译.

22. Tao-sheng's commentary on the Lotus Sūtra：a study and translation/Young-ho Kim. Albany：State University of New York Press, c1990. xix, 374 p.；24cm. ISBN：0791402274,0791402282.（SUNY series in Buddhist studies）

《法华经疏》，竺道生（？—434 年）；Kim, Young-ho（1941—）译.

(1) Delhi, India：Sri Satguru Publications：［Distributed by］Indian Books Centre,1992. xix,374 pages；24cm. ISBN：8170303060, 8170303060.（Bibliotheca Indo-Buddhica series；no. 101）

23. Entry into the realm of reality. The guide/Li Tongxuan；translated by Thomas Cleary. Boston：Shambhala；［New York］：Distributed in the U. S. by Random House, 1989. 85 p.；23cm. ISBN：0877734771, 0877734772

《华严经合论》，李通玄（635—730）著，Cleary, Thomas F.（1949—）（美国翻译家）译.

24. The heart sutra：the womb of Buddhas/translation and commentary by Red Pine. Washington, DC：Shoemaker & Hoard, c2004. 201 p.；19cm. ISBN：1593760094

《般若波罗蜜多心经》，赤松（Red Pine, 1943—，真名，Bill Porter）（美国翻译家、诗人）译.

25. The sutra of contemplation on the Buddha of immeasurable life as expounded by S'ākyamuni Buddha＝Fo-shuo-Kuan-wu-liang-shou-ching/translated and annotated by the Ryūkoku University Translation Center，under the direction of Meiji Yamada. Kyoto, Japan：Ryukoku University, 1984. xl, 169 pages, ［2］ leaves of plates：illustrations；26cm.

《佛说观无量寿经》，英汉对照

26. The dawn of Chinese pure land Buddhist doctrine：Ching-ying Hui-yuan's Commentary on the Visualization sutra/Kenneth K. Tanaka. Albany：State University of New York Press, c1990. xxiv, 304 p.；24cm. ISBN：0791402975, 0791402983.（SUNY series in Buddhist studies）

《观无量寿经义疏》，慧远（523—592 年）；Tanaka, Kenneth Kenichi 译.

(1) Delhi：Sri Satguru Publications, 1995. xxiv, 304 pages；23cm. ISBN：8170304466, 8170304463.

(Bibliotheca Indo-Buddhica series; no. 154)

27. Visions of Sukhāvatī: Shan-tao's commentary on the Kuan Wu-liang shou-fo ching/Julian F. Pas. Albany: State University of New York Press, c1995. xviii, 452 p.; ill.; 24cm. ISBN: 0791425193, 0791425207. (SUNY series in Buddhist studies)
善导大师对《观无量寿经》评论。Pas, Julian F. 著. 研究了善导大师(613年—681年)对佛经《观无量寿经》的评论以及《观无量寿经》的英译.

28. The Vimalakirti Sutra/translated by Burton Watson from the Chinese version by Kumarajiva. New York: Columbia University Press, c1997. xi, 168 p.; 23cm. ISBN: 0231106564. (Translations from the Asian classics)
《维摩诘经》,华兹生(Watson, Burton, 1925—)(美国翻译家)译. 译自中文.

29. The Vimalakīrti nirdes'a sūtra: (Weimojie suo shuo jing)/translated by Lu K'uan Yü (Charles Luk). Berkeley: Shambala, 1972. xviii, 157 pages; 23cm. ISBN: 0877730350, 0877730354. (The clear light series)
《维摩诘所说经》,陆宽昱(1898—1979)译.

30. Ordinary enlightenment: a translation of the Vimalakirti Nirdesa Sutra/Charles Luk. Boston, Mass.; London: Shambhala, 2003. 192 pages; 22cm. ISBN: 1570629714, 1570629716
《维摩诘经》,陆宽昱(1898—1979)译.

31. Expository commentary on the Vimalakirti sutra: (Taishō volume 56, number 2186)/translated from the Chinese by Jamie Hubbard. Berkeley: Bukkyō Dendō Kyōkai America, Inc., 2012. xvii, 284 pages; 25cm. ISBN: 1886439443, 1886439443. (BDK English Tripitaka series)
《〈维摩诘所说经〉评释》(《大正藏》第56册,N2186).

32. The Lankavatara sutra: a Mahayana text, translated for the first time from the original Sanskirt by Daisetz Teitaro Suzuki. London, G. Routledge and Sons, Ltd., 1932. xlix, 300 p. front., fold. plates. 23cm. (Eastern Buddhist library)
《楞伽阿跋多罗宝经》(楞伽经),铃木大拙(Suzuki, Daisetz Teitaro, 1870—1966)译.
   (1) 1st Ind. ed. Delhi: Motilal Banarsidass Publishers, 1999. li, 300 p.; 23cm. ISBN: 8120816552. (Buddhist tradition series; v. 40)

33. The Lankavatara sutra: an epitomized version/translated by D. T. Suzuki; compiled and edited by Dwight Goddard; foreword by John Daido Loori. Rhineback, N. Y.: Monkfish Book Pub. Co., c2003. xxii, 125 p.; 21cm. ISBN: 0972635742. (Provenance editions; v. 1)
《楞伽阿跋多罗宝经》(楞伽经),铃木大拙(Suzuki, Daisetz Teitaro, 1870—1966)译;德怀特·戈达德

(Goddard, Dwight, 1861—1939)(美国传教士)编.

34. The Lankavatara sutra: a Zen text/translation and commentary by Red Pine. Berkeley: Counterpoint, [2012]. 303 pages; 24cm. ISBN: 1582437910
Translated from the Chinese translation of the Sanskrit original
《楞伽阿跋多罗宝经》(楞伽经),赤松(Red Pine, 1943—,真名,Bill Porter)(美国翻译家、诗人)译.

35. The Avalokitesvara Maha-bodhisattva = All Encompassing Door Sutra (Kuan-yin Sutra): the way of pra[c]tice/editor and approved by Thích Hải-Quang; translated by Chon Hoan (William B. Nguyen). Tucson, Ariz.: Dharma Flower Publication, 1999. xix, 96 p.: ill.; 21cm.
Notes: Translated from the Vietnamese translation of the Chinese translation of the Sanskrit original.
《观世音菩萨普门品》(《观音经》),转译自越南语.

36. The universal gate: a commentary on Avalokitesvara's Universal gate sutra/Venerable Master Hsing Yun. Los Angeles, CA: Buddha's Light Pub., 2011. x, 235 p.; 22cm. ISBN: 1932293487
"Translated by Robert Smitheram." Translated from the Chinese translation of the Sanskrit original.
《观世音菩萨普门品讲话》,星云大师著;Smitheram, Robert 译. 含《妙法莲华经》的选作.

37. The threefold lotus sutra/translated by Bunnō Katō, Yoshiroō Tamura, and Kōjirō Miyasaka; with revisions by W. E. Soothill, Wilhelm Schiffer, and Pier P. Del Campana. New York: Weatherhill, 1975. xviii, 383 p.; 23cm. ISBN: 834801051, 083480106X
《观普贤菩萨行法经》,Katō, Bunnō, 等译;苏慧廉(Soothill, William Edward, 1861—1935)(英国传教士)校.

38. The scripture on the ten kings and the making of purgatory in medieval Chinese Buddhism/Stephen F. Teiser. Honolulu, HI: University of Hawaii Press, c1994 xxiii, 340 p.: ill.; 25cm. ISBN: 0824815874. (Kuroda Institute studies in East Asian Buddhism; 9)
太史文(Teiser, Stephen F.),包括对《十王经》的英译.

39. Bodhisattvas of the forest and the formation of the Mahāyāna: a study and translation of the Rāstrapālapariprcchaā-sūtra/Daniel Boucher. Honolulu: University of Hawaii Press, c2008. xxiii, 287 p.; 24cm. ISBN: 0824828813. (Studies in the Buddhist traditions)
鲍彻(Boucher, Daniel)(美国汉学家).包括对西晋竺法护译的《德光太子经》的英译.

40. Sutra of the medicine Buddha: with an introduction, comments, and prayers by Venerable Master Hsing Yun. Hacienda Heights, CA: Buddha's Light Pub., c2002. 176 p.; 23cm. ISBN: 097156129X
《药师经及其修持法门》,星云大师(1927—). 英汉

对照.

(1) Los Angeles, CA: Buddha's Light Pub., 2005. 186 p.; 22cm. ISBN: 193229306X

41. The Pratyutpanna Samadhi Sutra/translated by Lokaksema; translated from the Chinese (Tashō volume 13, number 418) by Paul Harrison. The Surangama Samadhi Sutra translated by Kumārajīva; translated from the Chinese (Taishō volume 15, number 642) by John McRae. Berkeley, CA: Numata Center, 1997. xvi, 116, 94 p.; 25cm. ISBN: 1886439060. (BDK English Tripitaka; 25—II, III)

《佛说般舟三昧经》，译自《大正藏》第 13 卷.

42. The sutra on the concentration of sitting meditation/translated from the Chinese of Kumārajīva by Nobuyoshi Yamabe and Fumihiko Sueki. Berkeley, CA: Numata Center for Buddhist Translation and Research, 2009. xix, 122 p.; 25cm. ISBN: 1886439344, 1886439346. (BDK English Tripitaka series. First series) Notes: "Taishō volume 15, number 614."

《坐禅三昧经》，鸠摩罗什（Kumārajīva，—412?）；Yamabe, Nobuyoshi(1960—), Sueki, Fumihiko 合译自汉语.

43. Texts from the Buddhist canon, commonly known as Dhammapada, with accompanying narratives/Translated from the Chinese by Samuel Beal. Boston, Houghton, Osgood, 1878. viii, 176 pages; 22cm. (The English and foreign philosophical library; v. 12)

《法句譬喻经》，Beal, Samuel（1825—1889）（英国汉学家）译.

(1) London: K. Paul, Trench, Trübner & Co., 1902. 1 vol. (VIII-211 p.); 16cm.

(2) Dhammapada: with accompanying narratives/tr. from the Chinese by Samuel Beal. 2nd ed. Calcutta: Susil Gupta (India) Ltd., 1952. 104 pages; 19cm.

(3) Dhammapada with accompanying narratives/translated from the Chinese by Samuel Beal. 3rd ed. Varanasi, Indological Book House, 1971. 104 pages; 23cm.

(4) San Francisco: Chinese Materials Center, 1977. viii, 176 pages; 22cm. (Reprint series; no. 58)

(5) 3rd ed. Varanasi: Indological Book House, 1991. 104 pages; 23cm.

(6) London: Routledge, 2000. viii, 176 pages; 23cm. ISBN: 0415244714, 0415244718, 041524286X, 0415242868, 0415231884, 0415231886. (Trübner's oriental series; 019; Buddhism; 4)

(7) [Place of publication not identified]: Routledge, 2013. ISBN: 0415865603, 0415865609

(8) [Place of publication not identified]: Hardpress Ltd., 2013. ISBN: 1313602299, 1313602297

44. The scriptural text: verses of the doctrine, with parables/translated from the Chinese of Fa-li and Fa-chü (Taishō Volume 4, Number 211) by Charles Willemen. Berkeley, Calif.: Numata Center for Buddhist Translation and Research, 1999. xi, 238 p.; 25cm. ISBN: 1886439087. (BDK English Tripitaka; 10—II)

《法句譬喻经》，Willemen, Charles 译.

45. The storehouse of Sundry valuables/translated from the Chinese of Kikkāya and Liu Hsiao-piao (compiled by T'an-yao; Taishō Volume 4, Number 203) by Charles Willemen. Berkeley, CA: Numata Center for Buddhist Translation & Research, 1994. xix, 275 p.; 24cm. ISBN: 0962561835. (BDK English Tripitaka; 10—I)

《杂宝藏经》，吉迦夜（Kikkāya，活动时间公元 5 世纪），刘孝标(462—521)译：昙曜（活动时间公元 5 世纪）编；Willemen, Charles 英译.

46. The three Pure Land sutras/by Hisao Inagaki in collaboration with Harold Stewart. Berkeley, CA: Numata Center for Buddhist Translation and Research, 1995. 173 p.; 25cm. ISBN: 188643901X. (BDK English Tripitaka; 12—II, III, IV) Notes: Translated from Chinese translation of the Sanskrit original.

《净土三经》，Inagaki, Hisao(1929—)与 Stewart, Harold 合译.

47. The Scripture on the Explication of Underlying Meaning/translated from the Chinese of Hsühan-tsang (Taishō vol. 16, no. 676) by John P. Keenan. Berkeley, Calif.: Numata Center for Buddhist Translation and Research, 2000. xii, 126 p.; 25cm. ISBN: 1886439109. (BDK English Tripitaka; 25—IV)

《解深密经》（玄奘译），Keenan, John P. 英译自《大正藏》16 卷.

48. Two esoteric sutras/[translated] by Rolf W. Giebel. Berkeley, Calif.: Numata Center for Buddhist Translation and Research, 2001. xi, 346 p.; 25cm. ISBN: 188643915X. (BDK English Tripitáka; 29—II, 30—II) Notes: "Translated from the Chinese (Taishō volume 18, numbers 865, 893)."

《两部密教经典》，Giebel, Rolf W. 译自《大正藏》18 卷.

49. The interpretation of the Buddha land/by Bandhuprabha; translated from the Chinese of Hsühan-tsang (Taishō volume 26, number 1530) by John P. Keenan. Berkeley, Calif.: Numata Center for Buddhist Translation and Research, 2002. xv, 266 p.; 25cm. ISBN: 0962561827. (BDK English Tripitaka; 46—II)

《佛地经论》，Keenan, John P. 译自《大正藏》26 卷.

50. The Vairocanābhisam bodhi Sutra/[translated] by Rolf W. Giebel. Berkeley, Calif.: Numata Center for Buddhist Translation and Research, 2005. xix, 320 p.;

24cm. ISBN：1886439320. (BDK English Tripitaka；30
—I)

Notes："Translated from the Chinese (Taishō volume 18,
number 848)."

《大毗卢遮那成佛神变加持经》，Giebel, Rolf W. 译自
《大正藏》18 卷.

51. Prince Shōtoku's commentary on the S'rīmālā Sutra
(Taishō volume 56，number 2185)/translated from the
Chinese by Mark W. Dennis. Berkeley：Bukkyō Dendō
Kyōkai America, Inc.，2011. xxi, 176 pages；25cm.
ISBN：1886439436 （hbk.），1886439435 （hbk.），
1886439245 (hbk.)，1886439249 (hbk.). (BDK English
Tripitaka series)

《胜鬘经义疏》，Dennis, Mark W. 译自中文《大正藏》56
卷.

52. The Madhyama āgama （middle-length discourses）.
Volume 1 Taishō volume 2，number 26/Marcus
Bingenheimer，editor-in-chief；Bhikko Anālayo and
Roderick S. Bucknell, co-editors. Berkeley：California：
Bukkyo Dendo Kyokai America, Inc.，2013. xxviii, 599
pages；25cm. ISBN：1886439478, 1886439474. （BDK
English Tripitaka series）

Notes：Translation of the Zhong ahan jing. Cf. page xv.

《中阿含经》.

53. The Nirvana Sutra：(Mahāparinirvān a-sūtra)/translated
from the Chinese by Mark L. Blum. Berkeley, CA：
Bukkyo Dendo Kyokai America, Inc.，2013. volumes；
24cm. ISBN：1886439467. （BDK English Tripitaka
series）

Notes："Taishō volume 12，number 374."

《涅槃经》，Blum, Mark L. 译自《大正藏》12 卷.

54. Land of bliss：the paradise of the Buddha of measureless
light：Sanskrit and Chinese versions of the Sukhāvatīvyūha
sutras/introductions and English translations by Luis O.
Gómez. Honolulu：University of Hawaii Press, c1996. xvi,
356 p. ：ill. ；24cm. ISBN：0824816943, 0824817605

《极乐世界：无量光佛国》，Gómez, Luis O. 英译并导言.

55. The Diamond sutra：a buddhist scripture：a new
translation from the Chinese text of Kumarajiva/by
Bhikshu Waidao and Dwight Goddard. Santa Barbara,
Calif. ：Dwight Goddard, 1935. 32 pages；19cm.

《金刚经》，Wai-tao, Bhikshu 和 Goddard, Dwight
(1861—1939)译自中文.

(1)［U. S. ］：Theosophy Weekly, 1973. vi, 24 pages；
22cm.

56. The jewel of transcendental wisdom：（Jin Gang Jing）/
translated from the Chinese by A. F. Price；with a foreword
by Dr. W. Y. Evans Wentz. London：Buddhist Society,
1947. 71 pages；19cm.

《金刚经》，Price, A. F. 译.

(1)The diamond sutra, or The jewel of transcendental
wisdom/translated from the Chinese by A. F. Price,
with a foreword by W. Y. Evans-Wentz. ［2nd ed. ］.
London，Buddhist Society, 1955. 74 pages；19cm.

57. The diamond sutra：how to practice undiscriminating
thoughts in an uncertain and changing world/translated
by Wayne H. Huang. Hacienda Heights, Calif. ：CUBT
Publishing, 1993. 130 p. ；18cm.

《金刚经》，Huang, Wayne H. 译.

58. The Diamond Sutra：the perfection of wisdom/text and
commentaries translated from Sanskrit and Chinese by
Red Pine. Washington, D. C. ：Counterpoint, 2001. 471
p. ；22cm. ISBN：1582430594

《蒙藏梵汉和合璧金刚般若波罗蜜经》，赤松（Red Pine,
1943—，真名，Bill Porter)(美国翻译家、诗人)译.

59. The diamond sutra ＝ Chin-kang-ching ＝ or，Prajna-
paramita/translated from the Chinese with an
introduction and notes by William Gemmell. Berwick,
Me. ：Ibis Press, 2003. xxxii, 117 p. ，［1］leaf of plates：
ill. ；18cm. ISBN：0892540753

Reprint. Originally published：London：Kegan Paul,
Trench, Trübner & Co.，1912.

《金刚经》，Gemmell, William 译自中文. 初版于 1912
年.

60. Diamond Sutra explained/Master Nan Huai-Chin；
translated by Hue En (Pia Giammasi). Florham Park,
N. J. ：Prim Primodia, c2004. xi, 324 p. ：ill. ；23cm.
ISBN：0971656126

《金刚经释义》，南怀瑾著；Hue En 译.

61. The Sutra of Maitreya's attaining Buddahood/［translated
and distributed by Buddhist Church of Diamond
Springs］. Diamond Springs, CA：Buddhist Bliss Culture
Center, c1996. 62, 48 p. ；21cm. ISBN：1886925003

《佛说弥勒大成佛经》，中英文对照.

62. The romantic legend of Sakya Buddha：from the Chinese-
Sanscrit. By Samuel Beal. London, Trübner & Co.，
1875. xii, 395 p. ；20cm.

《佛本行集经》，比尔（Beal, Samuel, 1825—1889）（英国
汉学家）英译.

(1)Delhi：Motilal Banarsidass, 1985. xii, 395 p. ；19cm.
ISBN：0895818205, 0895818201

(2)The romantic legend of S'ākya Buddha：a translation
of the Chinese version of the Abhiniskramanasūtra/
Samuel Beal. ［Montana］：Kessinger Pub.，2006.
xii, 395 pages；28cm.

63. The two Buddhist books in Mahayana. ［Hong Kong,
printed by Rumford Printing Press, 1936］. 5 p. l.，
［5］—145，［1］p. pl. ；20cm.

净土宗经典. 吕碧城（Lü, Pi-ch'êng）编译.

(1)2nd ed. Penang, Malaya, Siak Kong Ghee；1960.

118 p. illus. , ports. ; 19cm.

64. Arthapada Sutra, spoken by the Buddha; translated by the Upāsaka Che-Kien under the Wu dynasty (222—280 A. D.) By P. V. Bapat. Santiniketan, Visva-Bharati, 1951—. pts. 〈1—2 (in 1 v.)〉

《佛说菩萨本业经》，Bapat，P. V. 译.

65. The S'ūraṅgama Sūtra（Leng Yen Ching）/Chinese rendering by Master Paramiti of Central North India at Chih Chih Monastery, Canton, China, A. D. 705; commentary（abridged）by Ch'an Master Han Shan (1546—1623); translated by Upsāsaka Lu K'uan Yü (Charles Luk). London, Rider, 1966. xxiii, 262 pages; 22cm. ISBN: 0090759710, 0090759712

《楞严经》，Pramiti；憨山（1546—1623）评析；陆宽昱（1898—1979）译.

(1) London：Rider, 1969. XXII, 262 p. ISBN：0090759710, 0090759712
(2) London：Rider, 1973. xxiii, 262 pages; 22cm. ISBN：0090759710, 0090759712
(3) Bombay：B. I. Publications, 1978. xxii, 262 pages; 21cm.
(4) New Delhi：Munshiram Manoharlal Publishers, 2001. xxii, 262 pages; 22cm. ISBN：8121510023, 8121510028
(5) New Delhi：Munshiram Manoharlal Publishers, 2002. 1 vol.（XXII-262 p.）; 23cm. ISBN：8121510023 (rel), 8121510028 (rel)
(6)〔Taipei, Taiwan〕,〔Corporate Body of the Buddha Education Foundation〕,2005. xiv, 351 pages; 24cm.

66. The Shurangama sutra：sutra text and supplements/with commentary by Hsuan Hua; English translation by the Buddhist Text Translation Society. Burlingame, CA. ： Buddhist Text Translation Society, 2003. pages cm. ISBN：088139940X 0881399400

《楞严经》释义与补充. 宣化（1908—1995）；加州佛典翻译协会（Buddhist Text Translation Society）译.

67. The Shurangama sutra with commentary/by Hsuan Hua; English translation by the Buddhist Text Translation Society. Burlingame, CA：Buddhist Text Translation Society, 2003. 9 volumes; illustrations; 23cm. ISBN：0881399418, 0881399417, 0881399426, 0881399424, 0881399434, 0881399431, 0881399442, 0881399448, 0881399450, 0881399455, 0881399469, 0881399462, 0881399477, 0881399479, 0881399485, 0881399486, 088139940X, 0881399400, 0881399493, 0881399493

《楞严经》释义，宣化（1908—1995）；加州佛典翻译协会（Buddhist Text Translation Society）译.

68. The S'ūraṅgama sūtra：a new translation/with excerpts from the commentary by the venerable master Hsühan Hua. Ukiah, Calif. ：Buddhist Text Translation Society,

2009. lii, 492 pages, 〔4〕pages of plates：color illustrations；24cm. ISBN: 0881399622 0881399620

《楞严经》，宣化（1908—1995）；加州佛典翻译协会（Buddhist Text Translation Society）译.

69. Buddhabhāsita-amitāyuh-sūtra：(the smaller Sukhāvatī-vyūha)/translated from the Chinese version of Kumārajīva by Nishu Utsuki. Kyoto, Japan：Educational Department of the West Hongwanji, 1929. vii, 43 pages；23cm.

《英译阿弥陀经》，Kumārajīva（—412?）；宇津木二秀（Utsuki, Nishū）译. 初版于 1924 年.

(1) 3rd ed. Kyoto, Publication Bureau of Buddhist Books, 1941. 33 pages；19cm.

70. Shih shan yeh tao ching = Buddhabhasita Dasabhadra Karmamarga sutra：sutra spoken by Buddha on the way of ten meritorious deeds/translated by Wong Mow-Lam from the Chinese version of Sikshananda-Nanjio's catalogue no. 1100. Shanghai：Buddhist Book Store, 1933. 23 〔i. e. 46〕pages；19cm.

Notes：Text in English and Chinese, originally translated from Sanskirt. / Opposite pages bear duplicate numbering.

《十善业道经》，实叉难陀（652—710）中译；Wong Mow-Lam 译自上海佛学书局 1933 年版本.

71. The two Buddhist books in Mahayana/translated, compiled and edited by Upasika Chihmann (Miss P. C. Lee of China). Hong Kong：Buddhist Lecture Hall, 1900. 149, 124, 50 pages：plates；19cm.

Contents：Avatamsaka sūtra, chap. 39, the vows of Samantabhadra. —Synopsis of the Aparimitāyur sūtra. —Part of the Amitāyur-dhyāna sūtra, 14th—16th meditations. —The (smaller) Sukhāvatī-vyūha sūtra

《净土四经》，吕碧城（1883—1943）编译.

(1)〔Shanghai〕, 1937. 142 pages；19cm.
(2)〔Hong Kong〕〔printed by Rumford printing Press〕, 1938. 142 pages plates；19cm.
(3) Hong Kong：Commercial Press, 1960. 118 pages：illustrations, portraits；19cm.
(4) 3rd ed. Oxford：Printed by Kemp Hall Press, 1960. 149 pages：illustrations；20cm.

72. The Sutra of the lord of healing = Bhaishajyaguru vaiduryaprabha tathagata/〔ed. by Zhou Sujia；tr. by Walter Liebenthal〕. Peiping：Society of Chinese Buddhists：Sales agent, the French Bookstore, 1936. xii, 32 pages, 〔1〕leaf of plates：folded illustrations；23cm. (Buddhist scriptures series；no. 1)

Notes：Based on the Chinese translation of Xuanzang.

《药师如来本愿经》，周叔迦博士（1899—1970 年）编；Liebenthal, Walter 译.

73. A treasury of Mahāyāna Sūtras：selections from the

Mahāratnakūṭa Sūtra (Da bao ji jing)/transl. from the Chinese by The Buddhist Association of the United States; Garma C. C. Chang, general ed. University Park; London: The Pennsylvania State University Press, 1983. XV, 496 p.; 24cm. ISBN: 0271003413, 0271003412. (IASWR series)

《大乘佛典宝库》(大乘佛经选译：《大宝积经》)，美国佛教联合会编译自中文.

(1) Delhi: Motilal Banarsidass Publishers, Private Ltd., 1991. xv, 496 pages; 24cm. ISBN: 812080936X, 8120809369

(2) Delhi: Motilal Banarsidass, 2002. 496 p.; 23cm. ISBN: 812080953X, 8120809536

74. The Mahayana Mahaparinirvana-sutra; a complete translation from the classical Chinese language in 3 volumes/Annotated and with full glossary, index, and concordance by Kosho Yamamoto. [Ube, Japan] Karinbunko, 1973—1975. 3 volumes music; 27cm. (The Karin Buddhological series; no. 5)

《大般涅盘经》，Yamamoto, Kōshō 注.

(1) The Mahayana Mahaparinirvana sutra. Vol. 4/translated from the classical Chinese and Japanese by Kosho Yamamoto; copy-edited and revised by Tony Page. London: Nirvana, 1999. ISBN: 1903036038, 1903036037

(2) The Mahayana Mahaparinirvana sutra. Vol. 5/translated from the classical Chinese and Japanese by Kosho Yamamoto; copy-edited and revised by Tony Page. London: Nirvana, 1999. ISBN: 1903036046, 1903036044

(3) The Mahayana Mahaparinirvana sutra. Vol. 6/translated from the classical Chinese and Japanese by Kosho Yamamoto; copy-edited and revised by Tony Page. London: Nirvana, 1999. ISBN: 1903036054, 1903036051

75. Mahāvairocana-sūtra: translated into English from Ta-p'i lu che na ch'eng-fo shen-pien chia-ch'ih ching, the Chinese version of S'ubhākarasimha and I-hsing, A. D. 725/by Chikyo Yamamoto; [preface by Lokesh Chandra]. New Delhi: International Academy of Indian Culture and Aditya Prakashan, 1990. xi, 210, v pages; 28cm. ISBN: 8185179468, 8185179469. (Sata-pitaka series; 359)

《大毗卢遮那成佛神变加持经》，Yamamoto, Chikyō 译.

(1) New Delhi: International Academy of Indian Culture and Aditya Prakashan, 2009. xi, 210, v pages. ISBN: 8185179468, 8185179469, 8177420937, 8177420933. (Sata-pitaka series; v. 359)

76. The flower ornament scripture: a translation of the Avatamsaka sutra/translated from the Chinese by Thomas Cleary. Boulder: Shambhala Publications; [New York]: Distributed in the U. S. by Random House, 1984—1987. 3 volumes; 24cm. ISBN: 0877737673, 0877737674, 0394536908, 0394536903, 0394552521, 0394552520, 0877732990, 087773299X

《华严经》，Cleary, Thomas F. (1949—)译.

(1) Boston: Shambhala, 1993. vi, 1643 pages; 24cm. ISBN: 0877739404, 0877739401

77. Flower adornment sutra: chapter 39, entering the Dharma realm/translated into Chinese by T'ang Dynasty Tripitaka Master Shikshananda of Khotan; with the commentary of Tripitaka Master Hua; translated into English by Dharma Realm Buddhist University International Institute for the Translation of Buddhist Texts. Talmage, Calif.: Buddhist Text Translation Society, 1980—. volumes ⟨1—8⟩: illustrations; 22cm. ISBN: 0917512685, 0917512681, 0917512707, 0917512704, 0917512731, 0917512735, 0917512766, 0917512766, 0917512812, 0917512810, 0917512480, 0917512483, 088139050X, 0881390506, 0881390550, 0881390551

《华严经》卷 39 "入法界品"，唐（于阗）三藏法师实叉难陀译自梵文，法界佛教大学国际研究所(Dharma Realm Buddhist University International Institute)英译.

78. The great means expansive Buddha flower adornment sutra: chapter 17, merit & virtue from first bringing forth the mind/commentary by Tripitaka Master Hsuan Hua; translated into English by Dharma Realm Buddhist University, Buddhist Text Translation Society. Talmage, Calif.: Dharma Realm Buddhist University, Buddhist Text Translation Society, 1983. 177 pages: illustrations, portraits; 22cm. ISBN: 0917512839, 0917512834

《华严经》，宣化(1908—1995)释义；加州佛典翻译协会(Buddhist Text Translation Society)译.

79. Flower adornment dharmas: Conduct and vows of universal worthy, Flower adornment repentance, Flower adornment preface/translation by the Buddhist Text Translation Society. Burlingame, Calif.: Dharma Realm Buddhist University: Dharma Realm Buddhist Association, 1999. 169 pages: illustrations; 27cm. ISBN: 0881390313, 0881390315

《华严经普贤行愿品》，加州佛典翻译协会(Buddhist Text Translation Society)译.

80. Sutra of the merit and virtue of the past vows of Medicine Master Vaidurya Light Tathagata/English translation by the Buddhist Text Translation Society. Burlingame, Calif.: Buddhist Text Translation Society: Dhama Realm Buddhist University: Dharma Realm Buddhist Association, 1997. viii, 221 pages: color

illustrations；21cm. ISBN：0881393061，0881393064

《药师琉璃光如来本愿功德经浅释》，宣化（1908—1995）释义；加州佛典翻译协会（Buddhist Text Translation Society)译.

81. Sutra of the past vows of Earth Store Bodhisattva/English translation by the Buddhist Text Translation Society. 2nd ed. Burlingame, Calif.：The Society, Dharma Realm Buddhist University, Dharma Realm Buddhist Association, 2003. ix,127 pages：illustrations；22cm. ISBN：0881393126, 0881393125

《地藏菩萨本愿经》，加州佛典翻译协会（Buddhist Text Translation Society)译.

(1) Third edition. Burlingame, California, U. S. A.：Buddhist Text Translation Society, 2014. 131 pages；22cm. ISBN：1601030474, 1601030479

82. The great means expansive Buddha flower adornment sutra：chapter 40, universal worthy's conduct and vows/commentary by Tripitaka Master Hsuan Hua; translated into English by Dharma Realm Buddhist University, Buddhist Text Translation Society. Talmage, Calif.：Dharma Realm Buddhist University, Buddhist Text Translation Society, 1982. xxv, 279 pages：illustrations, portraits；22cm. ISBN：0917512847, 0917512841

《大方广佛华严经·卷40》，宣化（1908—1995）释义；加州佛典翻译协会（Buddhist Text Translation Society)译

83. The great means expansive Buddha flower adornment sutra：chapter 24, praises in the Tushita Heaven Palace/commentary by Tripitaka Master Hsühan Hua; translated into English by Dharma Realm Buddhist University, Buddhist Text Translation Society. Talmage, Calif.：Dharma Realm Buddhist University, Buddhist Text Translation Society, 1982. 123, ［3］ pages： illustrations, portraits； 22cm. ISBN： 0917512391, 0917512391

《大方广佛华严经·卷24》，宣化（1908—1995）释义；加州佛典翻译协会（Buddhist Text Translation Society)译.

84. Medicine master sūtra：a translation of the sutra of the merit and virtue of the past vows of Medicine Master Vaidūrya Light Tathagata（Taisho 450）with commentary by the venerable Master Hsuan Hua/English translation by the Buddhist Text Translation Society, Dharma Realm Buddhist University, Dharma Realm Buddhist Association. Second edition. Ukiah, CA：Buddhist Text Translation Society, 2016. ISBN：1601030597, 1601030592

《药师琉璃光如来本愿功德经浅释》，宣化（1908—1995）释义；加州佛典翻译协会（Buddhist Text Translation Society)译.

85. Sutra of the foremost Shurangama at the great Buddha's summit concerning the Tathagata's secret cause of cultivation.../［comment. by Tripitaka master Hsühan Hua; transl. from the Chinese by the Buddhist Text Translation Society］. San Francisco：Sino-American Buddhist Association, 1977—1981. 6 vol.：ill.；22cm.

《大佛顶首楞严经》，宣化（1908—1995）释义；加州佛典翻译协会（Buddhist Text Translation Society)译.

86. The great means expansive Buddha flower adornment sūtra/preface by T'ang dynasty national master Ch'ing Liang；comment. by Tripitaka master Hsuan Hua; transl. into Chinese by T'ang dynasty tripitaka master Shikshananda of Khotan；trans. by the Buddhist Text Translation Society. Talmage：Dharma Realm Buddhist University Buddhist Text Translation Society, 1978—. ill.；23cm.

Contents：

［Vol. 1］：［Verse preface/by Ch'ing Liang］.—1979.—XXIV, 135 p. 0917512170

［Vol. 2］：Prologue：first door.—1981.—242 p. 0917512669

［Vol. 3］：Prologue：second door, part one.—1981.—XIII, 257 p. 0917512731

［Vol. 4］：Prologue：second door, part two.—1982.—219 p. 0917512987

［Vol. 5］：Prologue：seconfd door, part three.—1983.—142 p. 0881390097

Chapter 5, vol. 1：Flower store sea of worlds.—1983.—194 p. 0917512545

Chapter 9：Light enlightenment.—1983.—196 p. 0881390054

Chapter 11：Pure conduct.—1982.—249 p. 0917512375

Chapter 15：The ten dwelling.—1981.—XI, 178 p. 0917512774

Chapter 16：Brahma conduct.—1981.—56 p. 0917512804

Chapter 17：Merit and virtue from first bringing forth the mind.—1982.—XIV, 177 p. 0917512839

Chapter 22：The ten inexhaustible treasuries.—1982.—158 p. 0917512383

Chapter 24：Praises in the Tushita heaven palace.—1982.—123 p. 0917512391

Chapter 26, part 1：The ten grounds：the first ground.—1982.—0917512871

Chapter 26, part 2：The ten grounds：the second, third, fourth ground.—1981.—188 p. 091751274X

Chapter 36：Universal worthy's conduct.—1983.—78 p. 0881390119

Chapter 39：Entering the dharma realm.—1980—1982.—6 vol.

Chapter 40：Universal worthy's conduct and vows.—1982.—XXIV, 279 p. 0917512847

《大方广佛华严经》，宣化（1908—1995）释义；加州佛典翻译协会（Buddhist Text Translation Society）译.

87. Sutra on the Buddha's bequeathed teaching＝Foě yi' jiào jīng/translation into Chinese by Tripitaka Master Kumarajiva of Yao Qin Dynasty（ca. A. D. 400）. Provisional translation into English by The Buddhist Text Translation Society（1999）—page 1B.；Parallel text in Chinese and English. Berkeley, Calif. ：Berkeley Buddhist Monastery, 1999. 33A, 33B pages：illustrations（black and white, and colour）；22cm.

《佛遗教经》，鸠摩罗什（Kumārajīva, —412?）译；加州佛典翻译协会（Buddhist Text Translation Society）译.

B424 律及其释

1. Shan-Chien-P'i-P'o-Sha：a chinese version by Saṅghabhadra of Samantapāsādikā/ Buddhaghosa. Commentary on Pali Vinaya, transl. into Engl. for the first time. By P. V. Bapat in collab. with A. Hirakawa. Poona（India）：Bhandarkar Oriental Research Institute, 1970. LXIII, 588 p.（Bhandakar oriental series；10）

《善见毗婆沙律》（又名《一切善见律》），觉音（Buddhaghosa）释；Bapat, P. V. 和 Hirakawa, A. 英译.

2. Monastic discipline for the Buddhist nuns：an English translation of the Chinese text of the Mahāsāmghika-Bhiksuni-Vinaya/by Akira Hirakawa. Patna：Kashi Prasad Jayaswal Research Institute, 1982. xvi, 434 pages；25cm.（Tibetan Sanskrit works series；no. 21）

《尼众戒律》，Hirakawa, Akira（1915—2002）译自中文.

3. The Buddha speaks the Brahma net sutra：the ten major and forty-eight minor bodhisattva precepts/translated into Chinese by Yao Ch'in dynasty triptaka master Kumarajiva；with the commentary of Elder Master Hui Seng. Talmadge, Ca. ：Buddhist Text Translation Society, 1981—1982. 2 volumes（various pagings）：illustrations；22cm. ISBN：0917512790, 0917512797, 091751288X, 0917512889

《佛说梵网经讲录》，Kumārajīva（—412?）；慧僧释义；加州佛典翻译协会（Buddhist Text Translation Society）译.

4. The Sutra on Upāsaka Precepts/translated from the Chinese of Dharmaraksa（Taishō, Volume 24, Number 1488）by Bhiksunī SHIH Heng-Ching. Berkeley, Calif. ：Numata Center for Buddhist Translation & Research, 1994. 225 p. ；25cm. ISBN：0962561851.（BDK English Tripitaka；45—II）

《优婆塞戒经》，释恒清（SHIH Heng-Ching）译自《大正藏》24 卷.

5. The origins of Buddhist monastic codes in China：an annotated translation and study of the Chanyuan qinggui/Yifa. Honolulu：University of Hawaii Press, c2002. xxx, 352 p. ：ill. ；24cm. ISBN：0824824946

《中国佛教寺院戒律之起源：〈禅苑清规〉之译注与研究》，依法（Yifa）译.

6. The Baizhang Zen monastic regulations：Taishō volume 48, number 2025/translated from the Chinese by Shohei Ichimura. Berkeley, Calif. ：Numata Center for Buddhist Translation and Research, 2006. xix, 447 p. ；25cm. ISBN：1886439257.（BDK English Tripitaka series；74—IV）

《敕修百丈清规》，Ichimura, Shohei（1929—）译.

7. The Brahma net sutra：bodhisattva precepts handbook/translated into English be the Buddhist Text Translation Society. Oakland, CA：OpenDust, Inc. , 2009. 197 pages；25cm. ISBN：1602360105, 1602360103

《梵网经菩萨戒本》，加州佛典翻译协会（Buddhist Text Translation Society）译. 英汉对照.

B425 论及其释

1. The awakening of faith in the Mahayana doctrine：the new Buddhism/Translated into Chinese by Paramartha. Translated into English in 1894 by Timothy Richard. Shanghai, Christian Literature Society, 1907. 45［48］pages frontispiece；21cm.

《大乘起信论》，古印度马鸣著；Paramartha 汉译；Richard, Timothy（1845—1919）英译. 英汉对照.

(1) 2nd ed. Shanghai：Kelly and Walsh, 1918. 45,［48］pages：illustrations；20cm.

(2) 2nd ed. Delhi：Sri Satguru, 2008. 45,［48］pages：illustrations；23cm. ISBN：8170308836, 8170308836

2. The new testament of higher Buddhism, by Timothy Richard. Edinburgh, T. & T. Clark, 1910. viii, 275,［1］p. 22cm.

《大乘起信论》，法藏（643—712）；Richard, Timothy（1845—1919）译.

3. The awakening of faith/attributed to As'vaghosha；transl. , with commentary by Yoshito S. Hakeda. New York；London：Columbia University Press, 1967. XI, 128 p. ；21cm. ISBN：023108336X（paperbound）, 0231083362（paperbound）, 0231030258（clothbound）, 0231030250（clothbound）

《大乘起信论》，古印度马鸣著；Hakeda, Yoshito S. 译.

(1) New York；London：Columbia University Press, 1974. xi, 128 pages；21cm. ISBN：023108336X, 0231083362.（Program of translations from the oriental classics Columbia College）

(2) New York；London：Columbia University Press, 1977. xi, 128 pages；21cm.

(3) 台北：新文丰出版公司，［1993］. xi, 128 p. ；24cm.

(4) Berkeley, Calif. ：Numata Center for Buddhist Translation and Research, 2005. xxxiv, 114 pages；25cm. ISBN：1886439338, 1886439337.（BDK English Tripitáka；63—IV. ）

(5) New York：Columbia University Press, c2006. xii,

117 p.： ill.； 24cm. ISBN： 0231131569, 0231131577. (Translations from the Asian classics)

4. Açvaghosha's discourse on the awakening of faith in the Mahāyāna/translated for the first time from the Chinese version by Teitaro Suzuki. San Francisco：Chinese Materials Center, 1976. xiv, 160 p.； 22cm. (Chinese Materials Center. Reprint series-Chinese Materials Center； no. 46.)

Note：Reprint of the 1900 ed. published by the Open Court Pub. Co., Chicago.

《大乘起信论》,铃木大拙(Suzuki, Daisetz Teitaro,1870—1966)译自中文版. 初版于 1900 年.

(1)［San Francisco］: Chinese Materials Center, 1983. xiv, 160 pages； 20cm. ISBN： 0896444759, 0896444751

(2) Taipei：SMC Pub. Co, 1990. xiv, 100 p.； 21cm. ISBN：9579482187, 9579482189

(3) Fremont, Calif.： Asian Humanities Press, ［2001］. 160 p.： ill.； 22cm. ISBN：0895819392

(4) Dover ed. Mineola, N. Y.： Dover Publications, 2003. xiv, 160 p.； 22cm. ISBN： 048643141X

（5）Charleston, SC： BiblioLife, 2008. 160 pages： illustrations； 22cm. ISBN： 0559617485, 0559617488

5. An English translation of Fa-Tsang's commentary on the awakening of faith/translated by Dirck Vorenkamp. Lewiston, N. Y.： Edwin Mellen Press, c2004. iv, 450 p.； 24cm. ISBN： 0773463739. (Studies in Asian thought and religion； v. 28)

《大乘起信论》,法藏(643—712)；Vorenkamp,Dirck 译.

6. Wei shih er shih lun… or, The treatise in twenty stanzas on representation-only, by Vasubandhu… Translated from the Chinese version of Hsühan Tsang, Tripit‚aka master of the T'ang dynasty, by Clarence H. Hamilton New Haven, Conn., American Oriental Society, 1938. 3 p. l., 82 p. 26cm. (American oriental series, v. 13)

Notes："Hsühan Tsang's Wei-shih-er-shih-lun is the Chinese version of… the… Sanskrit… Vijñaptimātratāsiddhi; Vims'atikā."—Introd

《唯识二十论》,世亲(Vasubandhu)原著；玄奘(约 596—664 年)译；Clarence Herbert(1886—)英译.

7. Dharmapalas's Yogācāra critique of Bhavāviveka's Mādhyamika explanation of emptiness：the tenth chapter of Ta-ch'eng Kuang pai-lun shih, commenting on Āryadeva's Catuhs' ataka chapter sixteen/John P. Keenan. Lewiston, N. Y.： Edwin Mellen Press, c1997. 153 p.； 24cm. ISBN：0773486151,0889460507. (Studies in Asian thought and religion； v. 20)

Keenan, John P. 著. 包括对《大乘广百论释论》第十卷的英译. 英汉对照.

8. Three texts on Consciousness Only：Demonstration of Consciousness Only/by Hsühan-tsang. The thirty verses on Consciousness Only/by Vasubandhu. The treatise in twenty verses on Consciousness Only/by Vasubandhu； translated from the Chinese of Hsühan-tsang by Francis H. Cook. Berkeley, Calif.： Numata Center for Buddhist Translation and Research, 1999. xi, 452 p.； 25cm. ISBN： 1886439044. (BDK English Tripitaka； 60－I, II, III)

Notes：Taishō vol. 31, nos. 1585, 1586, 1590.

《唯识三论》,Francis H. Cook 译自中文三颂本.

9. The treatise on the elucidation of the knowable/translated from the Chinese by Charles Willemen. The cycle of the formation of the schismatic doctrines/translated from the Chinese by Tsukamoto Keishō. Berkeley, CA： Numata Center for Buddhist Translation and Research, 2004. xi, 171 p.； 25cm. ISBN： 1886439303. （BDK English Tripitaka； 61－VI, 76－I)

Notes："Taishō volume 32, number 1645... Taishō volume 49, number 2031."

《彰所知论》,Willemen, Charles 译自《大正藏》32 卷.

10. Mahāyānavims' aka of Nāgārjuna： reconstructed Sanskrit text, the Tibetan and the Chinese versions, with an English translation/edited by Vidhushekhara Bhattacharya. Calcutta： Visva-Bharati Book-Shop, 1931. 44 p.； 25cm. (Visva-Bharati studies； no. 1)

《大乘唯识论》,真谛原译；Bhattacharya, Vidhushekhara 英译.

11. Coming to terms with Chinese Buddhism：a reading of the treasure store treatise/Robert H. Sharf. Honolulu： University of Hawaii Press, c2002. xiii, 400 p.； 24cm. ISBN：0824824431. (Studies in East Asian Buddhism； 14)

Introduction：Prolegomenon to the Study of Medieval Chinese Buddhist Literature—The Historical and Cosmological Background—1. The Date and Provenance of the Treasure Store Treatise—2. Chinese Buddhism and the Cosmology of Sympathetic Resonance— Annotated Translation of the Treasure Store Treatise Introduction to the Translation—The Treasure Store Treatise/Chapter One The Broad Illumination of Emptiness and Being—The Treasure Store Treatise/ Chapter Two The Essential Purity of Transcendence and Subtlety—The Treasure Store Treatise/Chapter Three The Empty Mystery of the Point of Genesis—Appendix 1：On Esoteric Buddhism in China—Appendix 2： Scriptural Quotations in the Treasure Store Treatise.

Sharf, Robert H. 著. 对佛教汉籍经典《宝藏论》进行了英译和注解. 该书也有中文译本.

12. Ch'eng Wei-shih Lun： the doctrine of mere-consciousness/［Dharmapāla；Translated into Chinese］ by Hsühan Tsang；Translated from the Chinese text by

Wei Tat. Hong Kong：Ch'eng Wei-Shih Lun Publication Committee，1973. cxxxix，818 pages：illustrations；27cm.

Contents：Vasuhandhu. Original thirty stanzas，in Sanskrit. —The thirty stanzas in Swami Chinmayananda's hand-writing（Sanskrit）. —The thirty stanzas in Chinese and English.

《成唯识论》，玄奘. 中英对照.

13. Nāgārjuna's twelve gate treatise/transl. ［from the Chinese］，with introductory essays，comments and notes by Hsueh-li Cheng. Dordrecht，Holland；Boston：D. Reidel Pub. Co.，1982. xv，151 pages；23cm. ISBN：9027713804，9027713803.（Studies of classical India；v. 5）

《十二门论》，Hsueh-li Cheng 译自中文.

14. The Vigrahavyavartani Sastra：Gatha part/transl. from the chinese text of Prajnaruchi & Vimoksasena by Chou Hsiang-Kuang. Calcutta ［u. a.］ Overseas Buddhist Chinese in India & Malaya，1962. II，13，9 S Ill.

《回净论》

15. Philosophy of mind in sixth-century China：Paramārtha's "evolution of consciousness"/Diana Y. Paul. Stanford，Calif.：Stanford University Press，1984. vi，266 pages；illustrations；23cm. ISBN：0804711879，0804711876

《中国六世纪的心识哲学：真谛的〈转识论〉》，Paul，Diana Y. 著. 翻译了真谛（Paramārtha，；499—569）的《转识论》.

B426 教义理论

1. Pre-Diṅnāga Buddhist texts on logic from Chinese sources，Baroda，Oriental institute，1929. ［373］ p.；25cm.

佛家逻辑. 图齐（Tucci，Giuseppe，1894—1984）（意大利藏学家）译. 译自中文、藏文.

（1）2nd ed. Madras：Vesta Publications，1981. xxx，40，32，77，89，91 p.；23cm.

2. The summary of the great vehicle/by Bodhisattva Asaṅga；translated from the Chinese of Paramārtha（Taishō，volume 31，number 1593）by John P. Keenan. Berkley，Calif.：Numata Center for Buddhist Translation and Research，1992. xii，147 p.；25cm. ISBN：096256186X.（BDK English Tripitaka；46—III）

《大乘佛教概要》，无著菩萨著；Keenan，John P. 译自《大正藏》.

3. The Vais'esika philosophy according to the Das'apa-dārthas'āstra/Chinese text with introd.，translation，and notes，by H. Ui，ed. by F. W. Thomas. London，Royal Asiatic Society，1917. xii，265 pages；23cm.（Oriental translation fund ［London］ Publications，new ser.，v. 24）

《胜论派哲学：据〈胜宗十句义论〉》. H. Ui 译；

Thomas，Frederick William（1867—1956）编. 中英文本.

（1）2nd ed. Varanasi：Chowkhamba Sanskrit series Office，1962. xii，265 pages；23cm.（Chowkhamba Sanskrit studies；v. 22）

（2）San Francisco：Chinese Materials Center，1977. xii，265 pages；22cm.（Reprint series - Chinese Materials Center；64）

（3）［Whitefish，MT］：Kessinger Legacy Reprints，2010. xii，265 pages；24cm.（Oriental Translation Fund；new ser.，v. 24）

4. The book of Chao：a translation from the original Chinese with introduction，notes and appendices/by W. Liebenthal. Peking：Catholic University of Peking，1948. 195 p.（Monumenta Serica Monograph series；13）

《肇论》，僧肇（384—414）；Liebenthal，Walter 译.

（1）Chao Lun/the treatises of Seng-Chao；a translation ［from the Chinese］ with introduction，notes and appendices，by Walter Liebenthal. 2nd rev. ed. Hong Kong：Hong Kong U. P；London：［Distributed by］ Oxford U. P，1968. xli，153 pages；24cm.

5. Entry into the inconceivable：an introduction to Hua-yen Buddhism/Thomas Cleary. Honolulu：University of Hawaii Press，1983. 222 pages；22cm. ISBN：082480824X，0824808242

Contents：Translations. Cessation and contemplation in the five teachings of the Hua-yen/by Tu Shun；Mirror of the mysteries of the universe of the Hua-yen/by Tu Shun and Cheng-kuan；Ten mysterious gates of the unitary vehicle of the Hua-yen/by Chih-yen；Cultivation of contemplation of the inner meaning of the Hua-yen：the ending of delusion and return to the source/by Fa-tsang.

华严佛学. Cleary，Thomas F.（1949—）（美国翻译家）译.

（1）Pbk. ed. Honolulu：University of Hawaii Press，1994. 222 pages；21cm. ISBN：0824816978，0824816971

（2）Delhi，India：Sri Satguru Pub.，1996. 222 pages；22cm. ISBN：8170305055，8170305057

6. Inquiry into the origin of humanity：an annotated translation of Tsung-mi's Yüan jen lun with a modern commentary/Peter N. Gregory. Honolulu：University of Hawaii Press，c1995. xv，264 p.；25cm. ISBN：0824817281，0824817648.（Classics in East Asian Buddhism）

《探究人类起源：对宗密〈猿人论〉的现代评论与注释》，宗密（780—841）著；Peter N.（1945—）（美国汉学家）译注.

7. How master Mou removes our doubts：a reader-response study and translation of the Mou-tzu Li-huo lun/John P. Keenan. Albany：State University of New York Press，

c1994. x, 229 p. ; 24cm. ISBN：0791422038,0791422046. (SUNY series in Buddhist studies)

《〈牟子理惑论〉译读》，Keenan，John P. 著，对佛教论书《牟子理惑论》作了翻译。

8. A study of the Twenty-two dialogues on Mahāyāna Buddhism/W. Pachow. Taipei, Taiwan：[publisher not identified]，1979. [2] leaves, pages [15]-64, [35]—110, 127—131: facsimile; 26cm. (Chinese culture; v. 20, no. 1;)

Notes：Reprinted from The Chinese culture, a quarterly review, v. 20, no. 1, March 1979 and v. 20, no. 2, June 1979. / Includes the author's translation of the Twenty-two dialogues by T'an-k'uang and the critically edited original text in Chinese (Ta-ch'êng êrh-shih êrh wên).

《大乘二十二问》，Pachow，W.（1918—）著译. 英汉对照。

(1)增修版. 台北：东初出版社;(1993). 9, 312 pages: illustrations; 21cm. ISBN：9576330408, 9576330407.（东初智慧海丛书；24）

9. Transcending the world ＝ [Chu chen]/translated by Buddhist Text Translation Society. Burlingame, Calif.：Buddhist Text Translation Society, 2004. 93 pages: color illustrations; 14 × 15cm. ISBN：0881398659 0881398656. (Pearls of wisdom by the Venerable Master Hua＝[Xuan Hua shang ren yi li ming zhu]；2)

《出尘》,宣化(1908—1995)译. 英汉对照。

10. 无杂相/一诚禅师著. 北京：宗教文化出版社,2009. 170页;21cm. ISBN：7802541085

本书为已经出版的《无杂相》一书的节选及中英对照版本,主要内容是一诚老和尚日常生活起居中的言行开示.（禅宗通俗读物）

11. 中国禅/刘涛编著. 合肥：黄山书社,2013. 146页;彩图;21cm. ISBN：7546135823.（中国红）

英文题名：Chinese zen Buddhism

12. 中国禅宗公案精选:中英双语/(宋) 无门慧开… [等]著;张优译. 郑州：郑州大学出版社,2017. 380页:图;24cm. ISBN：7564536497.（卓越学术文库）

B427　仪轨修炼

1. Guide to Buddhahood: being a standard manual of Chinese Buddhism/translated by Timothy Richard. Shanghai：Christian Literature Society, 1907. xxiii, 108 pages, [1] leaf of plates: illustrations; 22cm.

《选佛谱》,（明）释智旭（1599—1655）撰;Richard, Timothy(1845—1919)译.

(1)Delhi：Sri Satguru Pub.，2008. 1 vol. (XXIII—108 p.): couv. ill. en coul.; 22cm. ISBN：8170308720 (rel), 8170308720 (rel)

(2)Cosmo ed. New Delhi：India Cosmo Publications, 2014. xxv, 105 pages; 26cm. ISBN：8130717326, 8130717328

2. Buddhist practice of concentration. Santa Barbara, Calif.，D. Goddard, 1934. vii, 59 p. 21cm.

《修习止观坐禅法要》,智顗(538—597);德怀特·戈达德（Goddard，Dwight，1861—1939)（美国传教士)英译。

3. An outline of principal methods of meditation/translated from the Chinese by Sujitkumar Mukhopadhaya. Pondicherry：Sri Aurobindo Ashram Press, 1972. 55 p.; 19cm.

《坐禅的基本法则》,Mukhopadhyaya，Sujitkumar 译自中文。

4. Minding mind：a course in basic meditation/translated and explained by Thomas Cleary. Boston, Mass.：Shambhala；[New York:]：Distributed in the United States by Random House, 1995. xiv, 129 pages; 19cm. ISBN：1570620040，1570620041

Contents：Treatise on the supreme vehicle/Chan master Hongren—Models for sitting meditation/Chan master Cijiao of Changlu—Guidelines for sitting meditation/Chan master Foxin Bencai—A generally recommended mode of sitting meditation/Zen master Dogen—Secrets of cultivating the mind/Son master Chinul—Absorptionin the treasury of light/Zen master Ejo—An elementary talk on Zen/Man-an.

有关坐禅文献的翻译. Cleary，Thomas F. (1949—)（美国翻译家)译。

(1)Boston, Mass.：Shambhala, 2009. xiv, 129 pages; 19cm. ISBN：1590306857, 1590306856

5. The Chinese Hevajratantra：the scriptural text of the Ritual of the Great King of the Teaching, the Adamantine One with Great Compassion and Knowledge of the Void/Charles Willemen. Leuven, België：Peeters, 1983. 208 pages：illustrations； 26cm. ISBN：280170220X, 2801702208. (Orientalia Gandensia；8)

《喜金刚本续》(拟似),Willemen，Charles 译. 英汉对照。

(1)Delhi：Motilal·Banarsidass Publishers, 2004. 208 pages; 23cm. ISBN：8120819454, 8120819450. (Buddhist tradition series；50)

6. A few good men：the Bodhisattva path according to the Inquiry of Ugra（Ugraparipṛcchā)/study and translation by Jan Nattier. Honolulu：University of Hawaii Press, 2003. xvi, 383 p.; 24cm. ISBN：0824826078. (Studies in the Buddhist traditions)

好人寥寥. 那体慧(Nattier，Jan, 1949—)（美国汉学家)译。

7. The dharani sutra：the sutra of the vast, great, perfect, full, unimpeded great compassion heart dharani of the thousand-handed, thousand-eyed Bodhisattva who regards the world's sounds/with the commentary of Hsüan Hua; [translated for the first time from the Chinese by the

Buddhist Text Translation Society; primary translation Bhikshuni Heng Yin]. San Francisco: The Society, 1976. 399 pages, ［3］ leaves of plates: illustrations; 22cm. ISBN: 0917512138, 0917512131

《千手千眼观世音菩萨广大圆满无碍大悲心陀罗尼经》，宣化（1908—1995）释义；加州佛典翻译协会（Buddhist Text Translation Society）译。

8. Kindness: a vegetarian poetry anthology/published and translated by Buddhist Text Translation Society. Burlingame, CA: Buddhist Text Translation Society, 2006. pages cm. ISBN: 0881398717, 0881398713
Buddhist Text Translation Society. (Chinese poetry—Translations into English.)

《善行：素食诗集》，加州佛典翻译协会（Buddhist Text Translation Society）译。

B428　佛教艺文

注：佛教诗合集入此，僧人的作品分散在诗歌类中。

1. The Fo-sho-hing-tsan-king, a life of Buddha, by Asvaghosa, Bodhisattva; translated from Sanskrit into Chinese by Dharmaraksha, A. D. 420, and from Chinese into English by Samuel Beal. Oxford, The Clarendon Press, 1883. xxxvii, 380 p. 23cm. (The Sacred books of the East, v. 19)

《佛所行赞经》（又名，佛本行经，佛本行赞），古印度马鸣；昙无谶（南北朝）译成中文；比尔（Beal, Samuel, 1825—1889)(英国汉学家）译成英语。

(1)New York: Scribner, 1900. xxxvii, 380 pages; 23cm. (Sacred books of the East; v. 19)

(2)Taipei, Taiwan: World Buddhist Scriptures House, 1956. 163, ［58］ pages; 21cm. (Chinese English Buddhist scriptures series)

(3)Delhi: Motilal Banarsidass, 1964. xxxvii, 380 pages; 23cm. ISBN: 0895815230, 0895815231, 8120801202, 8120801202. (UNESCO collection of representative works: Indian series; The Sacred books of the East; v. 19)

(4)The Fo-sho-hing-tsan-king; a life of Buddha. Delhi: Mōtilāl Barnarsidass ［1966］. 380 p.; 23cm. (Sacred books of the East, v. 19)

(5)Dehli: Banarsidass, 1968. xxxvii, 380 pages; 23cm. (The Sacred books of the East; v. 19)

(6)Delhi: Motilal Banarsidass, 1975. xxxvii, 380 pages; 23cm. (The Sacred books of the East...; vol. XIX). (UNESCO collection of representative works: Indian series)

(7)Delhi: Motilal Banarsidass, 1984. xxxvii, 380 pages; 23cm. ISBN: 0895815230, 0895815231. (The Sacred books of the East; 19)

(8)Oxford: Clarendon Press, 1987. xxxvii, 380 pages; 23cm. (The Sacred books of the East; v. 19)

(9)Delhi: Motilal Banarsidass, 1990. xxxvii, 380 p.: il.; 22cm. ISBN: 8120801016, 8120801011, 8120801202, 8120801202. (The Sacred books of the East; v. 19. Unesco collection of representative works. Indian series)

(10)Delhi: Low Price Publications, 1996. xxxv, 380 pages; 23cm. (The Sacred books of the East; v. 19)

(11)Delhi: Motilal Banarsidass, 1998. xxxvii, 380 pages; 23cm. ISBN: 8120801202, 8120801202. (Sacred books of the East; v. 19;)

(12)London: RoutledgeCurzon, 2001. xxxvii, 380 pages; 23cm. ISBN: 0700715363, 0700715367. (The Sacred books of the East; v. 19)

(13)Delhi, India: Sri Satguru, 2002. xxxvii, 380 pages; 21cm. ISBN: 8170307422, 8170307426. (Bibliotheca Indo-Buddhica series; no. 223)

(14)San Diego, Calif.: The Book Tree, 2003. 163 pages: illustrations; 23cm. ISBN: 1585092339, 1585092338

(15)Delhi: K. N. Book House, 2010. iv, 132 pages: illustrations; 29cm. ISBN: 8190672428, 8190672429

(16)Delhi: Divine Books, 2011. xxxvii, 380 pages; 23cm. ISBN: 9381218143, 9381218145. (Divine Buddhist texts and studies series; no. 3)

2. Selections from Buddha/by Max Müller. Boston: Cupples, Upham & Co., 1886. 52 pages; 21cm.
Notes: "The following extracts are taken from one of the books of the East, known as the 'Life of Buddha' by Asvaghosa Bodhisattva, translated from the Chinese into English by Samuel Beal, edited by the oriental scholar, F. Max Müller."—Page ［3］.

《佛所行赞》（选译），马鸣菩萨（As'vaghosha）从梵文译成汉语；比尔（Beal, Samuel, 1825—1889)(英国汉学家）从汉语译成英语；Müller, F. Max(Friedrich Max, 1823—1900)编。

(1)New York: The Metaphysical Publishing Co., 1905. 52 p..

(2)New York: Theosophical Pub. Co., 1910. 52 pages; 21cm.

3. Buddhacarita: in praise of Buddha's acts: (Taishō volume 4, number 192)/translated from the Chinese by Charles Willemen. Berkeley, Calif.: Numata Center for Buddhist Translation and Research, 2009. xvii, 254 p.; 25cm. ISBN: 1886439429. (BDK English Tripitaka series)
Buddhacarita. English. As'vaghosa. Willemen, Charles.

《佛所行赞》，Willemen, Charles 译自《大正藏》4 卷.

4. Suh-ki-li-lih-kiu: the suhrillekha or 'friendly letter' addressed to King Sadvaha/written by Lung Shu (Nâgârjuna); translated from the Chinese edition of I-Tsing by Samuel Beal. London: Luzac'; Shanghai: Kelly

& Walsh, 1892. 51, xiii pages；23cm.

Notes：Text in English and Chinese, notes in English

《龙树菩萨劝诫王颂》，义净（635—713）；比尔（Beal, Samuel,1825—1889）（英国汉学家）译.

5. Sakyamuni's one hundred fables＝Bai yü jing/translated and annotated by Tetcheng Liao. New York：R. Liao, 1981. 119 pages；19cm.

Notes：Selections in English from the Chinese version of S'atāvadāna

《百喻经》，古天竺僧伽斯那撰；Liao, Dezhen 译. 英汉对照.

6. A garland for the fool：the scripture of one hundred parables ＝ Bai yu jing/composed by Venerable Sanghasena；translated from the Chinese into English by Li Rongxi. Taipei：Fokuang Cultural Enterprise, 1997. viii, 176 p.；21cm. ISBN：9575437217, 9575437213. (Buddhist scripture；A002)

《百喻经》，古天竺僧伽斯那撰；李荣熙（Li, Rongxi）译.

7. Chi hua mun stories/interpreted & written by Ven. Shih Shen Kai； English translation by Shih Ta-Lien. Singapore：Jen Chen Buddhist Book Publisher, 1992—. volumes〈1〉：illustrations；19cm. ISBN：9810016514, 9810016517

《痴花鬘故事》，圣开法师述作；释大莲英译.

8. The Satapañcāsatka of Mātrceta, Sanskrit text, Tibetan translation & commentary, and Chinese translation/ edited by D. R. Shackleton Bailey. With an introd., English translation and notes. Cambridge［England］ University Press, 1951. xi, 237 pages facsimiles 25cm.

Notes：Includes Nandipriya's commentary, Dignāga's commentary, entitled Mis'rakastotra, both translated into Tibetan, and the Chinese version by I-ching, entitled I pai wu shih tsan sung

《一百五十赞佛颂》，Shackleton Bailey, D. R.（1917—）译.

(1)Cambridge：University Press, 1980. xi, 237 pages：facsimiles

(2)Ann Arboer, Michigan：UMI, 1999. xi, 237 pages：facsimiles；25cm.

(3)Cambridge：University Press, 2009. xi, 237 pages：illustrations；25cm.

9. Signs from the unseen realm：Buddhist miracle tales from early medieval China/a translation and study by Robert Ford Campany. Honolulu：University of Hawaii Press, c2012. xix, 300 p.：map；24cm. ISBN：0824836023, 0824836022. (Classics in East Asian Buddhism)

《冥祥记》，王琰（南朝梁，活动时间约 5 世纪）；康儒博 (Campany, Robert Ford, 1959—)（美国汉学家）著译. 收录中国中世纪初期的佛教圣徒的传记.

10. The real Tripitaka, and other pieces. London, Allen and Unwin［1952］. 291 p.；22cm.

Contents：Includes eight stories from the Chinese, two from the Japanese and three original stories.

韦利(Waley, Arthur, 1889—1966)（英国汉学家）编译，翻译了包括玄奘在内的关于中国佛教的八个故事.

(1)London；New York：Routledge, 2005. 291 pages；24cm. ISBN：0415361788；0415361781. （China, history，philosophy，economics；34)

11. 佛经故事/张庆年编选、英译；齐沣白话文翻译. 北京：中国对外翻译出版公司, 2007. 380 页；21cm. ISBN：7500118183. （中译经典文库·中华传统文化精粹）

英文题名：Buddhist Parables

12. After many autumns：a collection of Chinese Buddhist literature/edited by John Gill and Susan Tidwell；translated by John Balcom. Los Angeles, CA：Buddha's Light Pub., c2011. xxvii, 383 p.：ill.；21cm. ISBN：1932293494

《中国佛教文学集》，Gill, John（John B., 1985—）, Tidwell, Susan 选编；陶忘机(Balcom, John)（美国汉学家）译.

13. Chinese Buddhist verse/translated by Richard Robinson. London, J. Murray, 1954. 85 pages. (The Wisdom of the East series)

佛教诗. Robinson, Richard H.（1926—）译.

(1)Westport, Conn.：Greenwood Press, 1980. xxiv, 85 pages；23cm. ISBN：0313221685, 0313221682. (Wisdom of the East series)

14. Where the world does not follow：Buddhist China in picture and poem/translated and edited by Mike O'Connor；photographs by Steven R. Johnson；foreword by William Neill. Boston：Wisdom Publications, 2002. 143 pages：illustrations；26cm. ISBN：0861713095, 0861713097

中国佛教诗. Johnson, Steven R. 和 O'Connor, Mike 合译. 英汉对照.

15. Daughters of emptiness：poems of Chinese Buddhist nuns/Beata Grant. Boston：Wisdom Publications, 2003. x, 192 pages：illustrations；23cm. ISBN：0861713621, 0861713622

中国女尼诗. Grant, Beata(1954—)译.

16. Zen poems of China and Japan；the crane's bill. Translated by Lucien Stryk and Takashi Ikemoto, with the assistance of Taigan Takayama. Garden City, N. Y., Anchor Press, 1973. li, 143 p. illus.；19cm. ISBN：0385046243, 0385046244

Stryk, Lucien, Ikemoto, Takashi（1906—）和 Takayama, Taigan 合译. 包括对中国禅诗的英译.

(1)The Crane's bill：Zen poems of China and Japan/ translated by Lucien Stryk and Takashi Ikemoto with the assistance of Taigan Takayama；［drawings by

Raymond Davidson]. 1st Black Cat ed. New York：Grove Press：Distributed by Random House, 1981, c1973. li, 143 p.：ill.；19cm. ISBN：0394179129, 0802143466

(2)1st Evergreen ed. New York：Grove Press, 1987. xlix, 143 p.；21cm. ISBN：0802130194. (An Evergreen book)

17. A drifting boat：an anthology of Chinese Zen poetry/edited by Jerome P. Seaton & Dennis Maloney；translated by Tony Barnstone... [et al.]. Fredonia, NY：White Pine Press, c1994. 200 p.；22cm. ISBN：1877727377

《中国禅诗集》,托尼·巴恩斯通（Barnstone, Tony, 1961—）（美国诗人）译.

18. Zen poems/selected amd edited by Peter Harris. New York：Alfred A. Knopf, 1999. 256 p.；17cm. ISBN：0375405526, 0375405525

《禅诗》,Harris, Peter(1947—)选译.

19. The poetry of Zen/edited and translated by Sam Hamill and J. P. Seaton. Boston：Shambhala：distributed in the U. S. by Random House, 2004. vii, 194 p.；18cm. ISBN：1570628637, 1570628634

《禅诗》,Hamill, Sam（美国诗人）,Seaton, Jerome P. 编译,是中国和日本的禅诗的选译.

20. Clouds thick, whereabouts unknown：poems by Zen monks of China/[translated by] Charles Egan；illustrations by Charles Chu. New York：Columbia University Press, c2010. xviii, 306 p.,［16］p. of plates：ill.；24cm. ISBN：0231150385, 0231150385, 0231150392, 0231150393, 0231520980, 0231520980. (Translations from the Asian classics)

禅诗. Egan, Charles 译.中英文本.

B429　世界各地宗派

1. Sacred books of the East, with critical and biographical sketches/by Epiphanius Wilson. Rev. ed. New York：Colonial Press, 1900. v, 457 pages；2 portrait (including frontispiece) plates, facsimiles 24cm. (The World's great classics)

Contents：Vedic hymns, translation by F. M. Müller.—Selections from the Zend-Avesta, translation by J. Darmesteter.—The Dhammapada, translation by F. M. Müller.—The Upanishads, translation by F. M. Müller.—Selections from the Koran, translation by George Sale.—Life of Buddha, by Asvaghosha Bodhisattva, tr. from Sanscrit into Chinese by Dharmaraksha, A. D. 420；from Chinese into English by Samuel Beal.

比尔（Beal, Samuel, 1825—1889）（英国汉学家）英译, Wilson, Epiphanius(1845—1916)编. 包括对汉籍《佛所行赞》一书的英译.

(1)Limited éd. de luxe. London, New York［etc.］The Colonial Press［1902］. 2 p. l. , v p. , 1 l. , 457 p. col. front. , plates, facsim.；24cm. (Literature of the Orient. Byzantine edition)

(2)Rev. ed. New York：Willey Book Co. , 1945. v, 457 p. plates.；24cm.

(3)Albuquerque：Sun Pub. , 1981. 457 p. ISBN：0895400995, 0895400994

(4)Rev. ed. New Delhi：Asian Educational Services, 1987. v,457 pages;23cm. (World's greatest literature)

2. The Vais'esika philosophy according to the Das'apadārtha-S'āstra：Chinese text with introduction, translation, and notes/by H. Ui. London：Royal Asiatic Soc. , 1917. XII, 265 p. (Oriental translation fund；new ser. vol. 24)

Notes：Composed probably by Maticandra and translated from Sanskrit into Chinese by Hsühan-tsang in 648 A. D.

胜论派哲学. Ui, Hakuju 著译.英汉对照.

(1)2nd ed. Varanasi：Chowkhamba Sanskrit Series Office, 1962. xii, 265 pages；23cm. (Chowkhamba Sanskrit studies；v. 22)

(2)San Francisco：Chinese Materials Center, 1977. xii, 265 pages；22cm. (Reprint series - Chinese Materials Center；64)

(3)［Whitefish, MT］：Kessinger Legacy Reprints, 2010. xii, 265 pages；24cm. (Oriental Translation Fund；new ser. , v. 24)

3. Senchaku hongan nembutsu shū：a collection of passages on the nembutsu chosen in the original vow/compiled by Genkū (Hōnen)；translated into English by Morris J. Augustine and Kondō Tesshō. Berkeley, Calif. : Numata Center, 1997. xii, 170 p.；25cm. ISBN：1886439052. (BDK English Tripitaka；104－II)

Notes：Translation of Taishō volume 83, number 2608.

《本愿念佛集》,Genkū（Hōnen）编,Augustine, Morris J. 和 Kondō, Tesshō(1923—)合译.

B430　中国佛教宗派

1. Popular Buddhism in China, with translations of ten Buddhist poems, thirty-two Buddhist proverbs, Hsühan ts'ang's Essence of the wisdom sutra, and Kumarajiva's Diamond sutra. Introd. by Johannes Rahder.［Shanghai］Commercial Press, 1939. 52,22 p. plates. ;19cm.

Notes：Xuanzang's Essence of the wisdom sutra is a translation of the smaller Prajñāpāramitā, Kumārajiva's Diamond sutra a translation of the Vajracchedikā

《中国的民众佛教》.上海商务印书馆.

2. The Nyāyamukha of Dignāga：the oldest Buddhist text on logic, after Chinese and Tibetan materials/by Giuseppi Tucci. San Francisco：Chinese Materials Center, 1976. 72 p. ;24cm. (Chinese Materials Center. Reprint series - Chinese Materials Center；no. 51). (Materialien zur

kunde des Buddhismus；heft 15)

Note：Reprint of the 1930 ed. published by O. Harrassowitz, Heidelberg, which was issued as heft 15 of Materialien zur kunde des Buddhismus.

图齐(Tucci, Giuseppe,1894—1984)(意大利藏学家)译.

3. Zen essence：the science of freedom/translated & edited by Thomas Cleary. Boston, Mass.：Shambhala；［New York］：Distributed in the United States by Random House, 1989. xviii,116 pages；23cm. ISBN：0877734984, 0877734987. (Shambhala dragon editions)

Notes：Translation of an anthology of the teachings drawn from the records of the great Chinese Zen masters from the Tang and Sung dynasties.

《禅宗基础》,Cleary, Thomas F. (1949—)(美国翻译家)编译.

(1)Boston, Mass.：Shambhala；［New York］：Distributed in the U. S. by Random House, 1995. xvi, 162 p.；12cm. ISBN：1570620970, 1570620973. (Shambhala pocket classics)

(2)Boston, Mass.：Shambhala, 2000. xviii, 116 pages；23cm. ISBN：1570625883, 1570625886. (Shambhala dragon editions)

4. Zen lessons：the art of leadership/translated by Thomas Cleary. Boston：Shambhala；［New York］：Distributed in the U. S. by Random House, 1989. xxii, 138 pages；22cm. ISBN：0877734461, 0877734468, 1570628831, 1570628832

《禅林宝训》,Cleary, Thomas F. ,(1949—)(美国翻译家)译.

(1)Boston：Shambhala Publications；［New YorK］：Distributed in the U. S. by Random House, 1993. 261 p.；12cm. ISBN：0877738939. (Shambhala pocket classics)

(2)New York：Barnes & Noble Books, 1998. 138 pages；22cm. ISBN：0760707707, 0760707708

(3)Boston, Mass.：Shambhala；Enfield：Publishers Group UK［distributor］, 2007. xviii, 171 pages；18cm. ISBN：1590305072, 1590305078

5. The five houses of Zen/［translated by］Thomas Cleary. Boston：Shambhala, 1997. xvii, 167 pages；23cm. ISBN：1570622922, 1570622922. (Shambhala dragon editions)

禅学. Cleary, Thomas F. (1949—)(美国翻译家)译.

6. Teachings of Zen/compiled and translated by Thomas Cleary. Boston：Shambhala；［New York］：Distributed in the U. S. by Random House, 1998. xviii, 199 pages；19cm. ISBN：1570623384, 1570623387

禅学. Cleary, Thomas F. (1949—)(美国翻译家)编译.

(1)Rev. and exp. ed. New York：Barnes & Noble Books, 2000. xviii, 199 pages；19cm. ISBN：

0760720509, 0760720509

7. Zen and the art of insight/selected and translated by Thomas Cleary. Boston：Shambhala；New York：Distributed in the United States by Random House, 1999. xiii, 159 pages；23cm. ISBN：1570625166, 1570625169. (Shambhala dragon editions)

禅学选译. Cleary, Thomas F. (1949—)(美国翻译家)译.

8. Classics of Buddhism and Zen：the collected translations of Thomas Cleary. Boston：Shambhala, 2001—2002. 5 volumes；24cm. ISBN：1570628319, 1570628313, 1570628327, 1570628320, 1570628335, 1570628337, 1570628343, 1570628344

Contents：v. 1. Zen lessons. Zen essence. The five houses of Zen. Minding mind. Instant Zen—v. 2. Teachings of Zen. Zen reader, Zen letters. Shōbōgenzō：Zen essays/by Dōgen. The ecstasy of enlightenment—v. 3. The Sutra of Hui-neng. Dream conversations. Kensho：the heart of Zen. Rational Zen. Zen and the art of insight—v. 4. Transmission of light. Unlocking the Zen Koan. The original face. Timeless spring. Zen antics. Record of things heard. Sleepless nights—v. 5. The Dhammapada. The Buddhist I Ching. Stopping and seeing. Entry into the inconceivable. Buddhist Yoga.

佛教和禅学经典著作选译. Cleary, Thomas F. (1949—)(美国翻译家)翻译.

(1)Boston：Shambhala, 2005. 5 volumes；23cm. ISBN：1590302184, 1590302187, 1590302192, 1590302194, 1590302206, 1590302200, 1590302214, 1590302217, 1590302222, 1590302224

9. Zen flesh, zen bones：a collection of Zen and pre-Zen writings/compiled by Paul Reps and Nyogen Senzaki. 1st Shambhala ed. Boston：Shambhala；［New York］：Distributed in the United States by Random House, 1994. xi, 285 p.：ill.；12cm. ISBN：1570620636. (Shambhala pocket classics)

《禅心佛骨》,Reps, Paul(1895—1990),Senzaki, Nyogen. 编译. 禅宗文献翻译.

10. The roaring stream：a new Zen reader/edited by Nelson Foster and Jack Shoemaker；foreword by Robert Aitken. Hopewell, N. J. ：The Ecco Press, c1996. xx, 374 p. ；25cm. ISBN：0880013443, 088001511X

怒吼的小溪：一个新的禅宗读者. Foster, Nelson (1951—),Shoemaker, Jack(1946—)编译.

11. 禅宗语录：英汉对照/江蓝生编选；黎翠珍,张佩瑶英译. 北京：中国对外翻译出版公司,2008. 380 页；21cm. ISBN：7500118275. (中译经典文库•中华传统文化精粹)

英文题名：Excerpts from Zen Buddhist Texts

12. 禅/刘涛编著. 合肥：黄山书社,2016. 146 页：图；23cm.

ISBN：7546152813.（印象中国）

英文题名：Chinese Zen Buddhism.英汉对照.

13. Tibetan Zen：discovering a lost tradition/Sam van Schaik. Boston：Snow Lion，2015. 224 pages；23cm. ISBN：1559394468

Notes：This book translates the key texts of Tibetan Zen preserved in Dunhuang. The book is divided into ten sections, each containing a translation of a Zen text illuminating a different aspect of the tradition, with brief introductions discussing the roles of ritual, debate, lineage, and meditation in the early Zen tradition. Van Schaik not only presents the texts but also explains how they were embedded in actual practices by those who used them

《西藏禅宗》,翻译了敦煌石窟中保藏的西藏禅宗文献.

14. The central philosophy of Tibet：a study and translation of Jey Tsong Khapa's Essence of true eloquence/translated with an introduction by Robert A. F. Thurman；［with a foreword by the Dalai Lama］. Princeton, N. J.：Princeton University Press, 1991. xviii, 442 p., ［12］ p. of plates：ill.；24cm. ISBN：0691020671. (Princeton library of Asian translations)

《西藏的中心哲学:宗喀巴辩才本质研究》,Thurman, Robert A. F.英译并导言.

15. Tsong Khapa's speech of gold in The essence of true eloquence：reason and enlightenment in the central philosophy of Tibet/translated with an introduction by Robert A. F. Thurman. Princeton, N. J.：Princeton University Press, c1984. xviii, 442 p., ［12］ leaves of plates：ill.；25cm. ISBN：069107285X. (Princeton library of Asian translations)

《宗喀巴辩才无碍的讲演》,Thurman, Robert A. F.英译.

16. Tibetan Buddhism/text by Zhang Xiaoming；［translator, Su Faxiang, Losai, Zhang Haiyang］. Beijing：China Pictorial Pub. House, 2004. 147 pages：chiefly color illustrations；29cm. ISBN：7800248216, 7800248214.

《藏传佛教》,张晓明著;张海洋译.中国画报出版社.本书反映藏传佛教的发展源流;五大教派的形成与演变;活佛转世制度;僧侣与佛学教育;现状与发展等内容.

17. The system of the Dalai Lama reincarnation/Chen Qingying. Beijing：China Intercontinental Press, 2005. 140 p.：ill.；21cm. ISBN：7508507452, 7508507453

《达赖喇嘛转世:英文》,陈庆英著;王国振译.五洲传播出版社.介绍藏传佛教与活佛转世制度、达赖喇嘛转世概况以及形定的历史定制.

18. 现代经文/英文/龙安志著.北京:五洲传播出版社,2006.164 页;14×25cm. ISBN：7508509390

本书是作者在游历西藏及青海、云南等藏区时编写的,

汇集了作者对藏族文化及藏传佛教的理解.喇嘛教研究.

19. The great calming and contemplation：a study and annotated translation of the first chapter of Chih-i's Mo-ho chih-kuan/Neal Donner and Daniel B. Stevenson. Honolulu：University of Hawaii Press, c1993. xx, 385 p.；24cm. ISBN：0824815149. (Classics in East Asian Buddhism)

《摩诃止观》（节译）,智顗（538—597）;Donner, Neal Arvid., Stevenson, Daniel B. (1952—)译注.

20. Sutra spoken by the sixth patriarch, Wei Lang, on the high seat of the gem of law (message from the East). ［Shanghai, Yu Ching Press, pref. 1930］. 76 p.；27cm.

《六祖坛经》,惠能（638—713）;黄茂林译.

21. The sutra of Wei Lang (or Hui Neng) translated from the Chinese by Wong Mou-lam. New ed. by Christmas Humphreys. London, Pub. for the Buddist Society by Luzac, 1944. 128 p.；17cm.

《六祖坛经》（选译）,惠能（638—713）;Wong, Mou-lam 译.

（1）Westport, Conn., Hyperion Press ［1973］. 128 p. 22cm. ISBN：0883550733

22. The commentary of Formless Gatha/by Yung Hsi；translated by Chou Hsiang-Kuang. Kuala Lumpur, Malaya：Published for Yuan Yin Buddhist Institute；Allahabad, India：Indo-Chinese Literature Publications, 1956. 92 pages：facsimile, portraits；18cm.

融熙法师（1888—1959）著;周祥光译.是对《六祖坛经》的讲解.

23. Ch'an and Zen teaching/edited, translated and explained by Lu K'uan Yü (Charles Luk). London：Rider & Co., 1961—c1962. 3 v.：ill.；22cm. ISBN：0091052319 (v. 1)

Contents：1. Master Hsu Yun's discourses and Dharma words. Stories of six Ch'an masters. The diamond cutter of doubts. A straight talk on the Heart sūtra—ser. 2. The forty transmission Gāthās. The stories of the founders of the five Ch'an sects. —ser. 3. The altar sūtra of the sixth patriarch. Yung Chia's song of enlightenment. The sūtra of complete enlightenment.

陆宽昱(Lu, K'uan Yü, 1898—)译. 关于《六祖坛经》的释义.

（1）［1st American ed.］. Berkeley ［Calif.］ Shambala Publications, 1970— ［c1960］. v. 22cm. ISBN：0877730091. (The Clear light series)

（2）London：Century, ⟨1987— ⟩. v. ⟨2 ⟩：ill.；22cm. ISBN：0712617167. (A Rider book). (Century paperbacks)

（3）York Beach, Me.：Samuel Weiser, Inc., 1993. 3 v.：ill.；21cm. ISBN：0877287953 (v. 1), 087728797X

(v. 2),0877287988 (v. 3)

24. The Platform Scripture. New York：St. John's University Press，1963. ix, 193 p.；24cm.（Asian Institute translations；no. 3）
《六祖坛经》,惠能(638—713);陈荣捷(Chan, Wing-tsit, 1901—1994)(美国华裔学者)译.

25. The sutra of the sixth patriarch on the pristine orthodox dharma. Translated from the Chinese by Paul F. Fung [and] George D. Fung. San Francisco, Buddha's Universal Church [1964]. 187 p.；23cm.
《六祖坛经》(选译),惠能(638—713);Fung, Paul F. 和 Fung, George D. 合译.
(1)San Francisco：Buddha's Universal Church, 1969. 4 p. l.，187 p.；23cm.
(2)San Francisc：Buddha's Universal Church, 1980. 189 pages；23cm.
(3)London：Watkins, 2002. 192 pages；22cm. ISBN：1842930435 1842930434

26. The platform sutra of the sixth patriarch：the text of the Tun-huang manuscript/with translation, intro.，and notes, by Philip B. Yampolsky. New York：Columbia University Press, 1967. xii, 216 [30] p.；24cm.
《六祖坛经》,惠能(638—713);Yampolsky, Philip B.(Philip Boas, 1920—1996)(美国学者)译注. 根据敦煌写本为主要资料而译.
(1)New York：Columbia University Press, c2012. xvi, 220 p.；24cm. ISBN：0231159562, 0231159579. 中英文对照.

27. The Diamond sutra and the Sutra of Hui Neng. Translated by A. F. Price and Wong Mou-lam. With forewords by W. Y. Evans-Wentz, J. Miller, and C. Humphreys. Berkeley, Calif.，Shambala Publications, 1969. 74, 114 p.；20cm. ISBN：0877730059, 0877730057.（The Clear light series）
《六祖坛经》,惠能(638—713);Price, A. F.，Wong, Mou-lam 译.
(1)Berkeley, Calif. : Shambala Publications, 1973. 74, 114 pages；20cm.（Clear light series）
(2)Boston：Shambhala, 1985. 114 p. ISBN：0877730059, 0877730057, 0394730194, 0394730196
(3)Boston：Shambhala, 1990. 168 p.；23cm. ISBN：0877730059, 0877730057, 0394730194, 0394730196.（Shambhala dragon editions）
(4)Boston：Shambhala, 2005. vi, 166 p. 23cm. ISBN：1590301374, 1590301371.（Shambhala classics）

28. The Sixth Patriarch's Dharma jewel platform sutra, with the commentary of Tripitaka Master Hua [translated from the Chinese by the Buddhist Text Translation Society]. 2nd ed. San Francisco：Sino-American Buddhist Association, 1977. xxviii, 344 p.，[1] leaf of plates：ill.；22cm. ISBN：0917512197, 0917512193
《六祖坛经》(选译),惠能(638—713);宣化(1908—1995)释义;加州佛典翻译协会(Buddhist Text Translation Society)译.
(1)Burlingame, CA：Buddhist Text Translation Society, c2002. xxxv, 445 p. : ill.；22cm. ISBN：0881393169, 0881393163
(2)Fourth edition. Ukiah, CA：Buddhist Text Translation Society, 2014. lxxvii, 226 pages：illustrations, maps；24cm. ISBN：1601030702, 1601030703

29. The Sutra of Hui-neng, grand master of Zen：with Hui-neng's commentary on the Diamond Sutra/translated from the Chinese by Thomas Cleary. Boston：Shambhala；[New York]：Distributed in the U. S. by Random House, 1998. vi, 161 p.；23cm. ISBN：1570623481, 1570623486.（Shambhala dragon editions）
《六祖坛经》(选译),惠能(638—713);Cleary, Thomas F.(1949—)(美国翻译家)译.

30. The Platform sutra of the Sixth Patriarch/translated from the Chinese of Tsung-pao（Taishō volume 48, number 2008）by John R. McRae. Berkeley, Calif. : Numata Center for Buddhist Translation and Research, 2000. xii, 169 p.；24cm. ISBN：1886439133.（BDK English Tripit̩aka；73—II）
《六祖坛经》,惠能(638—713);McRae, John R.(1947—)译.

31. Master of Zen：extraordinary teachings from Hui Neng's Altar sutra/translated and adapted by Tze-si Huang; illustrated by Demi. Bloomington, IN：World Wisdom, Inc.，[2012]. 171 pages：illustrations；23cm. ISBN：1936597185
《六祖坛经》,惠能(638—713);Huang, Tze-si(1938—)编译;Demi 绘图.

32. Readings of the Platform sūtra/edited by Morten Schlütter & Stephen F. Teiser. New York：Columbia University Press, c2012. ix, 220 p.；22cm. ISBN：0231158206, 0231158213, 0231500555.（Columbia readings of buddhist literature）
《六祖坛经》(选译),惠能(638—713);Schlütter, Morten.，Teiser, Stephen F. 译.

33. Buddhism and Zen. Philosophical Library [1953]. 91 p.
《证道歌》,玄觉(665—713);Senzaki, Nyogen 编译.

34. Song of enlightenment/by Great Master Yung Chia of the T'ang dynasty; commentary by Tripitaka Master Hua; translated into English by Dharma Realm Buddhist University, International Institute for the Translation of Buddhist Texts. Talmadge：Buddhist Text Translation Society, 1983. 84 pages：illustrations, portraits；22cm. ISBN：0881391002

《证道歌》，永嘉玄觉禅师（？—713）；宣化（1908—1995）释义．英汉对照．

   （1）Talmage, Calif.：City of Ten Thousand Buddhas, 1983. 84 pages；22cm. ISBN：088139100X, 0881391008

35. The recorded sayings of Ma-tsu/translated from the Dutch by Julian F. Pas；introduced, translated into Dutch and annotated by Bavo Lievens；with a preface and commentaries by Nan Huai-chin. Lewiston, N. Y.：E. Mellen Press, c1987. 140 p.；24cm. ISBN：0889460582. (Studies in Asian thought and religion；v. 6)

《马祖道一禅师语录》，马祖（709—788）；Lievens, Bavo 译成荷兰语，Pas, Julian F. 转译成英语．

36. The teachings of Master Wuzhu：Zen and religion of no-religion/Wendi L. Adamek. New York：Columbia University Press, c2011. x, 208 p.；21cm. ISBN：0231150224,0231150231. (Translations from the Asian classics). (Translations from the Oriental classics)

Adamek, Wendi Leigh 著．包括对唐代无住禅师（713—774年）《历代法宝记》的翻译．

37. Sayings and doings of Pai-chang/Ch'an Master of Great Wisdom [i. e. Huai-hai]；translated from the Chinese by Thomas F. Cleary. Los Angeles：Center Publications, 1978. 131 pages；21cm. ISBN：0916820106 0916820107. (Zen writings series)

百丈怀海禅师（约公元720年—814年）学说．Cleary, Thomas F. (1949—)（美国翻译家）译．

38. The record of Tung-shan/translated by William F. Powell. Honolulu：University of Hawaii Press, c1986. x, 99 p.：map；23cm. ISBN：0824810708

《洞山悟本禅师语录》，良价（悟本禅师，807—869）；鲍畏廉（1940—）（美国学者）译．

39. The Zen teachings of Master Lin-chi：a translation of the Lin-chi lu/by Burton Watson. Boston：Shambhala；[New York]：distributed in the United States by Random House, c1993. xxx, 140 p.；23cm. ISBN：0877738912. (Shambhala dragon editions)

《临济录》，义玄（？—867）；华兹生（Watson, Burton, 1925—)（美国翻译家）译．

40. The Huang Po doctrine of universal mind：being the teaching of dhyana master Hsi Yun/as recorded by P'ei Hsiu, a noted scholar of the T'ang dynasty；translated by Chu Ch'an. London：Buddhist Society, 1947. iv, 52 pages；22cm.

《黄檗传心法要》，黄檗希运禅师（？—850）；裴休（791—864）集录；Blofeld, John Eaton Calthorpe(1913—)译．

   （1）London：Buddhist Society, 1957. ii, 106 leaves；22cm.

   （2）The Zen teaching of Huang Po on the transmission of mind：being the teaching of the Zen Master Huang Po as recorded by the scholar P'ei Hsiu of the T'ang dynasty/Rendered into English by John Blofeld (Chu Ch'an). London：Rider & Co. , 1958. 135 pages；22cm.

41. The Zen teaching of Huang Po on the transmission of mind/translated by John Blofeld. First Shambhala Edition. Boston：Shambhala, 1994. 263 p.；12cm. ISBN：0877739692. (Shambhala pocket classics)

《黄檗禅师传心法要》，普乐道（Blofeld, John, 1913—1987)（英国汉学家）译，包含对黄檗禅师（？—855）的《黄檗禅师诗》和《传心法要》的翻译．

42. Zongmi on Chan/Jeffrey Lyle Broughton. New York：Columbia University, c2009. xv, 348 p. , [1] leaf of plates：ill. ；24cm. ISBN：0231143929, 0231143923. (Translations from the Asian classics.)

Contents：Biographical sketch of Guifeng Zongmi：an erudite Chan monk—Zongmi's four works on Chan—Influence of the Chan prolegomenon and Chan letter in Song China, the Kingdom of Xixia, Koryo Korea, and Kamakura-Muromachi Japan—Guifeng Chan：an assessment—Translation of the Chan letter—Translation of the Chan prolegomenon—Translation of the Chan notes

《宗密论禅》，Broughton, Jeffrey L. (1944—)著，翻译了大量宗密（780—841)著述．

43. The Huang Po doctrine of universal mind, being the teaching of dhyana master Hsi Yun as recorded by P'ei Hsiu. London, Budahist Society, 1947. iv, 52 p. 19cm.

《传心法要》，裴休居士（791—864)编；普乐道（Blofeld, John,1913—1987)（英国汉学家）译．

44. The path to sudden attainment：a treatise of the Ch'an (Zen) school of Chinese Buddhism/translated by John Blofeld. London：Buddhist Society, 1948. 51 p.；19cm.

Notes：Originally planned as an Appendix to Mr. Blofeld's work：The Jewel in the lotus. / Chinese title：Dunwu Ru Dao Yaomen Lun.

《顿悟入道要门论》，大珠慧海神禅师（唐代高僧，生卒年代不详）；Blofeld, John Eaton Calthorpe(1913—)译．

45. The Zen teaching of Hui Hai on sudden illumination：being the teaching of the Zen Master Hui Hai, known as the Great Pearl. London, Rider [1962]. 160 p. ；19cm.

"A complete translation of the Dun wu ru dao yao men lun and of the previously unpublished Tsung Ching Record"

《顿悟入道要门论》，大珠慧海禅师（唐代高僧，生卒年代不详）；普乐道（Blofeld, John, 1913—1987)（英国汉学家）译．

   （1）London：Rider, 1969. 160 p. ；20cm.

46. Original teachings of Ch'an Buddhism：selected from the

transmission of the lamp/translated, with introductions, by Chang Chung-yuan. New York：Pantheon Books, 1969. xvi, 333 pages；25cm.

《景德传灯录》,道原(宋代人,1004 年撰写该书);Chang, Chung-Yuan(1907—)译.

(1) New York：Pantheon Books, 1993. XVI, 333 p.； 21cm. ISBN：9579561672, 9579561679

(2) Pantheon paperback ed. New York：Pantheon Books, 1994. xvi, 333 pages；21cm. ISBN：0679758240, 0679758242

47. The transmission of the lamp：early masters/compiled by Tao Yuan；translated by Sohaku Ogata. Wolfeboro, N. H. ：Longwood Academic, 1990. xxiv, 401 pages； 22cm. ISBN：0893415626, 0893415624, 0893415650, 0893415655

《景德传灯录》,道原(宋代人,1004 年撰写该书); Ogata, Sōhaku(1901—1973)译.

48. Zen letters：teachings of Yuanwu/translated and edited by J. C. Cleary and Thomas Cleary. Boston：Shambhala；[New York]：Distributed in the U. S. by Random House, 1994. ix, 107 pages；22cm. ISBN：0877739315, 0877739319

圜悟克勤(1063—1135)学说. Cleary, J. C. (Jonathan Christopher)；Cleary, Thomas F. (1949—)合译.

49. The blue cliff record/translated from the Chinese Pi yen lu by Thomas and J. C. Cleary；foreword by Taizan Maezumi Roshi. Boulder, Colo. ：Shambhala；[New York]：distributed by Random House, 1977. 3 v. (xxv, 656 p.)；22cm. ISBN：0877730946 (v. 1)：

《碧岩录》,圆悟克勤(1063—1135);Cleary, Thomas F. (1949—)译.

(1) Boulder, Colo. ：Prajñā Press, 1978. 3 volumes in 1. (xxv, 656 pages)；23cm. ISBN：0877737061, 0877737063

(2) Boston, Mass. ：Shambhala Publications；[New York]：Distributed by Random House, 1992. . xxxiv, 648 p. ； 23cm. ISBN：0877736227, 0877736226

(3) Berkeley, Calif. ：Numata Center for Buddhist Translation and Research, 1998. xv, 453 p. ；24cm. ISBN：0962561886, 0962561887. (BDK English Tripitaka；75)

(4) Boston：Shambhala, 2005. 648 p. ；22cm. ISBN：159030232X, 1590302323

50. Instant Zen：waking up in the present/translated by Thomas Cleary. Berkeley, CA：North Atlantic Books, 1994. xix, 137 pages；23cm. ISBN：1556431937, 1556431937

Notes："This book contains translations of general lectures on Zen by Foyan (1067—1120)"—Page xviii.

佛眼清远禅师(1067—1120)学说. Cleary, Thomas F.

(1949—)(美国翻译家)译.

51. The ox and his herdsman；a Chinese Zen text；with commentary and pointers by Master D. R. Otsu and Japanese illustrations of the fifteenth century. Translated from the Tsujimura-Buchner version by M. H. Trevor. [Tokyo] Hokuseido Press [1969]. vi, 96 p. illus. 19cm.

Translation of Shih niu t'u.

《十牛图》,廓庵禅师(生活时间约 12 世纪);Trevor, M. H. 译;Otsu, D. R. 绘.

52. Book of serenity/translated and introduced by Thomas Cleary；foreword by Robert Aitken. Hudson, NY：Lindisfarne Press, 1990. xlii, 463 pages；23cm. ISBN：094026224X, 0940262249, 0940262258, 0940262256.

《从容录》,行秀禅师(1166—1246);Cleary, Thomas F. (1949—)(美国翻译家)译.

(1) Boston：Shambhala；[New York]：Distributed in the U. S. by Random House, 1998. xl, 463 pages； 24cm. ISBN：1570623813, 1570623813

(2) Boston, Mass. ：Shambhala, 2005. xl, 463 pages； 24cm. ISBN：1590302494, 1590302491

53. The gateless gate；translated from the Chinese by Nyogen Senzaki and Saladin Reps. Los Angeles, J. Murray, 1934. 1 p. l. , 5—70 p. ；21cm.

《无门关》,慧开(1183—1260);Senzaki, Nyogen, Reps, Paul(1895—1990)合译.

54. The gateless gate：a collection of Zen koan/by Mumon；translated by Nyogen Senzaki and Paul Reps. St Petersburg, Fla. ：Red and Black Publishers, 2008. 105 p. ：ill. ；23cm. ISBN：1934941188

Note："This translation first published 1934"—T. P. verso.

《无门关》,慧开(1183—1260);Senzaki, Nyogen 和 Reps, Paul(1895—1990)合译.

55. Zen comments on the Mumonkan. Translated into English by Sumiko Kudo. New York：Harper & Row [1974]. xvi, 361 p. illus. ；24cm. ISBN：006067279X

《无门关》,慧开(1183—1260);Shibayama, Zenkei (1894—1974)译.

56. Gateless gate/newly translated with commentary by Zen master Kōun Yamada. Los Angeles：Center Publications, 1979. xliv, 283 p. , [5] leaves of plates；23cm. ISBN：0916820149,0916820084. (Zen writings series；v. 7)

《无门关》,慧开(1183—1260);Yamada, Kōun(1907—1989)译.

(1) 2nd ed. Tucson：University of Arizona Press, c1990. xxv, 280 p. ；25cm. ISBN：0816512094,0816512167

(2) 1st Wisdom ed. Boston, Mass. ：Wisdom Publications, c2004. ix, 301 p. ；23cm. ISBN：0861713826

57. No barrier：unlocking the Zen koan：a new translation of

the Zen classic Wumenguan（Mumonkan）/translated from the Chinese and commentary by Thomas Cleary. New York：Bantam Books，1993. xxiii，213 p.；21cm. ISBN：055337138X,0553371383,0553082477, 0553082470

《无门关》，慧开（1183—1260）；Cleary，Thomas F. (1949—）译.

58. Unlocking the Zen koan：a new translation of the Zen classic Wumenguan/translated from the Chinese with commentary by Thomas Cleary. Berkeley，Calif.：North Atlantic Books，c1997. xxv，213 p.；21cm. ISBN：155643247X, 1556432477

《无门关》，慧开（1183—1260）；Cleary，Thomas F. (1949—）译.

59. Passing through the gateless barrier：kōan practice for real life/Guo Gu. First US edition. Boulder，Colorado：Shambhala，2016. ix，427 pages；23cm. ISBN：1611802818, 1611802814

《无门关》，慧开（1183—1260）；Guo gu(1968—）编译.

60. Two Zen classics：Mumonkan and Hekiganroku/translated with commentaries by Katsuki Sekida；edited and introduced by A. V. Grimstone. -I，II，III. New York：Weatherhill，1977. 413 p.；24cm. ISBN：0834801310, 0834801302

《两部禅经：〈无门关〉和〈碧岩录〉》，慧开（1183—1260）；圜悟克勤(1063—1135)；Sekida，Katsuki 译.

(1) Two Zen classics：the Gateless gate and the Blue cliff records/translated with commentaries by Katsuki Sekida；edited and introduced by A. V. Grimstone. 1st Shambhala ed. Boston，Mass.：Shambhala：Distributed by Random House，2005. 413 pages；23cm. ISBN：1590302826, 1590302828

61. Koans：the lessons of Zen/edited by Manuela Dunn Mascetti；introduction by T. H. Barrett. New York：Hyperion，c1996. 56 p.：col. ill.；16cm. ISBN：0786862521

《无门关》和《碧岩录》(选译)，慧开(1183—1260)；圜悟克勤(1063—1135)；Dunn-Mascetti，Manuela 编译.

62. Zen for the West. For the Buddhist Society of London. New York：Dial Press，1959. 182 p. illus.；22cm.

Notes：Appendices（ p.［79］-［176］）：1. A new translation of the Mu mon kwan.—2. A Zen interpretation of the Tao tê ching.—3. List of Chinese characters with Japanese and Chinese transliterations and dates of people，places，and technical terms in Zen for the West and in the Mu mon kwan.

对《无门关》和《道德经》作的英译。Ogata，Sōhaku (1901—1973)译.

(1) Westport，Conn.，Greenwood Press［1973，c1959］. 182 p. illus.；22cm. ISBN：0837165830,0837165837

63. Three Chan classics：The recorded sayings of Linji.

Wumen's gate. The faith-mind maxim. Berkeley，Calif.：Numata Center for Buddhist Translation and Research，1999. xi，136 p.；25cm. ISBN：1886439079.（BDK English Tripitaka；74—I，II，III)

《三个禅学经典：〈临济录〉，〈无门关〉，〈信心铭〉》，包括义玄(? —867)的《临济录》，慧开(1183—1260)的《无门关》和僧璨(? —606)的《信心铭》的翻译.

64. Zen texts. Berkeley，Calif.：Numata Center for Buddhist Translation and Research，2005. xii，328 p.；25cm. ISBN：1886439281.（BDK English Tripit,aka；73—III，98—VIII，98—IX，104—I)

Contents：Essentials of the transmission of mind (Taishō volume 48，number 2012—A）/translated from the Chinese by John R. McRae—A treatise on letting Zen flourish to protect the state (Taishō volume 80，number 2543)/translated from the Japanese by Gishin Tokiwa—A universal recommendation for true zazen（Taishō volume 82，number 2580)/translated from the Japanese by Osamu Yoshida—Advice on the practice of zazen (Taishō volume 82，number 2586)/Steven Heine.

《禅宗典籍》，包括：《黄檗山断际禅师传心法要》，McRae，John R. (1947—)译自《大正藏》48 卷；《兴禅护国论》，Gishin Tokiwa 译自日文；《普劝坐禅仪》，Osamu Yoshida 译自日文.

65. A dialogue on the contemplation-extinguished：a translation based on Professor Seizan Yanagida's modern Japanese translation and consultations with Professor Yoshitaka Iriya/translated by Gishin Tokiwa. ［Kyoto］：Institute for Zen Studies，1973. 39，135 pages：facsimiles；26cm.

《绝观论》，常盘义伸(Tokiwa，Gishin)译. 敦煌写本翻译. 中、英、日三语对照.

66. An exhortation to resolve upon Bodhi/with commentary by Venerable Master Hsuan Hua；English translation by the Buddhist Text Translation Society. Burlingame，Calif.：Buddhist Text Translation Society，Dharma Realm Buddhist University，Dharma Realm Buddhist Association，2003. viii，92 pages：illustrations；21cm. ISBN：0881394246,0881394245,0881393126,0881393125

《劝发菩提心文》，省庵大师(1686—1734)；宣化(1908—1995)释义.

B43 道教

1. Taoism as an indigenous Chinese religion/written by Liu Feng；translated by Lao An［and others］；version revised by An Zengcai. Jinan，China：Shandong Friendship Press，1998. 427 pages；20cm. ISBN：780551934X, 7805519340

《中国道教》，刘锋原著；老安等译. 山东友谊出版社.

2. Taoism/by the Taoist Association of China. Beijing：

Foreign Languages Press, 2002. 105 pages：color illustrations, color map；17×19cm. (Culture of China) Taoism/by the Taoist Association of China. Beijing：Foreign Languages Press, 2002. 105 pages：color illustrations, color map；17×19cm. (Culture of China)

《中国道教》,中国道教协会主编.

3. Daoism in China/written by Wang Yi'e；translated by Zeng Chuanhui；edited by Adam Chanzit. Beijing：China Intercontinental Press, 2004. 9, 209 pages：illustrations；22cm. ISBN：7508505980,7508505985. (China Religious Culture series)

《中国道教》,王宜峨著；曾传辉译(中国宗教基本情况丛书).介绍中国道教的历史渊源、各道教宗派、道教圣地、主经籍及当代中国道教的状况.

4. Taoism in China/written by Wang Yi'e, translated by Shao Da. Beijing：China Intercontinental Press, 2005. 125 pages：color illustrations；21cm. ISBN：7508508386, 7508508382

《中国道教：英文》,王宜娥编著；邵达译.五洲传播出版社.中国道教史.

5. 中国旅游.道教：英文/尹志华编著.北京：外文出版社, 2005.177 页；21cm. ISBN：7119034537

本书重点介绍了道教的名山宫观,并简要介绍了道教的一些基本知识.

6. History of Chinese Taoism/written by Li Yangzheng；compiled and translated by Yan Zhonghu. Beijing：Foreign Languages Press,2009. 340 pages；24cm. ISBN：7119020150,7119020153

《中国道教史》,李养正著.

7. 道教/刘涛编著.合肥：黄山书社,2016.170 页；图；23cm. ISBN：7546152837.(印象中国)

英文题名：Taoism. 英汉对照.

8. Understanding reality：a Taoist alchemical classic/by Chang Po-tuan；with a concise commentary by Liu I-ming；translated from the Chinese by Thomas Cleary. Honolulu：University of Hawaii Press,1987. xiv,203 pages；22cm. ISBN：0824811399, 0824811396, 08248110381, 0824811037

《悟真篇》,张伯端(约公元 983 年—1082 年)；刘一明(公元 1734—1821)评注；Cleary, Thomas F. (1949—)(美国翻译家)译.

9. A mission to heaven：a great Chinese epic and allegory/by Qiu Chang Chun；translated by Timothy Richard. Shanghai：Christian Literature Society's Depot, 1913. xxxix,362,vii pages；[30] leaves of plates：illustrations；23cm.

《长春真人西游记》,丘长春(1148 年—1227 年)；Richard, Timothy(1845—1919)译.

(1)Shanghai：[s. n.], 1940. 1 vol. (XXXIX-362 — VI p.)：ill.；21cm.

10. The book of balance and harmony/translated and with an introduction by Thomas Cleary. San Francisco：North Point Press,1989. xxxii,153 p.；23cm. ISBN：0865473633, 0865473638

《中和集》,李道纯(1219—1296)著；Cleary, Thomas F. (1949—)(美国翻译家)译.

(1)Rider, 1990. xxxii, 153 pages. ISBN：0712635211, 0712635219

(2)The book of balance and harmony：a Taoist handbook/translated by Thomas Cleary. Boston：Shambhala, 2003. xxx, 135 pages；23cm. ISBN：1590300777, 1590300770

B431　道教人物

1. Seven Taoist masters：a folk novel of China/translated by Eva Wong. Boston：Shambhala；[New York]：Distributed in the United States by Random House, 1990. xxiii, 178 pages：illustrations；22cm. ISBN：0877735441, 0877735441

《七真传》,Wong, Eva(1951—)译.

(1)Boston, Mass.；London：Shambhala, 2004. 176 pages：illustrations；23cm. ISBN：1590301765, 1590301760. (Shambhala classics)

2. Opening the Dragon Gate：the making of a modern Taoist wizard/Chen Kaiguo and Zheng Shunchao；translated from the original Chinese by Thomas Cleary. Boston：Charles E. Tuttle, 1996. 282 p.；23cm. ISBN：0804830983, 80804830980, 0804831858, 0804831857

《大道行：访孤独居士王力平先生》,陈开国,郑顺潮(1966—)著；Cleary, Thomas F. (1949—)(美国翻译家)译.

(1)Boston, MA：Charles E. Tuttle, 1998. 282 pages；23cm. ISBN：0804831858, 0804831857

3. Tales of immortals/compiled by Yuan Yang. Beijing：Foreign Languages Press, 2000. 291 pages：illustrations；18cm. ISBN：7119021427, 7119021423

《中国神仙家故事选》,元央编.

B44　伊斯兰教

1. Islam in China/written by Mi Shoujiang & You Jia；translated by Min Chang. Beijing：China Intercontinental Press, 2004. 205 pages：illustrations；22cm. ISBN：7508505336, 7508505336. (China Religious Culture series)

《中国伊斯兰教》,米寿江,尤佳著.五洲传播出版社(中国宗教基本情况丛书).介绍伊斯兰教在中国的传播和发展,中国伊斯兰教的民族化进程以及现代伊斯兰教在中国的概况.

2. The Arabian prophet：a life of Mohammed from Chinese and Arabic sources. Shanghai [Printed by the Commercial Press, limited] 1921. 313 p.

《天方至圣实录》,刘智(1669—1764 年)；Mason, Isaac

译.

3. Chinese gleams of Sufi light：Wang Tai-yü's great learning of the pure and real and Liu Chih's Displaying the concealment of the real realm；with a new translation of Jāmi's Lawa'ih from the Persian by William C. Chittick/Sachiko Murata；with a foreword by Tu Weiming. Albany, NY：State University of New York Press，c2000. xiv，264 p.；24cm. ISBN：0791446379，0791446387

Murata, Sachiko（1943—）著. 翻译了清朝王岱舆（约1584—?）的《清真大学》和刘智（1662—1730）的《真境昭微》

4. The sage learning of Liu Zhi：Islamic thought in Confucian terms/Sachiko Murata, William C. Chittick, and Tu Weiming；with a foreword by Seyyed Hossein Nasr. Cambridge, Mass.：Published by the Harvard University Asia Center for the Harvard-Yenching Institute：Distributed by Harvard University Press，2009. xxiii，678 p.：ill.；24cm. ISBN：0674033252，0674033256.（Harvard-Yenching Institute monographs series；65）

Murata, Sachiko（1943—），Chittick, William C. 和 Tu, Weiming（1940—）著. 包含对清朝刘智的《天方性理》的翻译. 该书为中国伊斯兰教的哲学著作.

B45 基督教

1. Catholic church in China/written by Yan Kejia；translated by Chen Shujie. Beijing：China Intercontinental Press，2004. 3，166 p.：ill.；22cm. ISBN：7508505999，7508505992.（China Religious Culture series）

《中国天主教》，晏可佳著；陈书杰译. 五洲传播出版社（中国宗教基本情况丛书）. 介绍清明两朝天主教传入中国的情况，鸦片战争后的中国天主教以及改革开放后的天主教.

2. Catholic church in China/written by Zhou Tailiang and Li Hui；translated by Zhou Tailiang. Beijing：Wu zhou chuan bo chu ban she，2005. 132 pages：chiefly illustrations；22cm. ISBN：7508508394，7508508399

《中国天主教：英文》，周太良编著；陈书杰译. 五洲传播出版社.

3. Christianity in China/[Luo Weihong；translated by] Zhu Chengming.[China]：China Intercontinental Press，2005. 156 pages：illustrations；21cm. ISBN：7508505344，7508505343

Contents：Early missionary activities in China—Climax of missionary activities and revitalization of the Christian Churches in the early 20th century—The independence movement and localization movement of the Christian churches in China—Three-self patriotic movement of Chinese churches—Chinese churches during the period of reform and opening up to the outside world.

《中国基督教》，罗伟虹著. 五洲传播出版社（中国宗教基本情况丛书）. 介绍基督教早期传入中国的情况，基督教在中国的自立运动和本色化运动、爱国运动以及改革开放时期的基督教.

4. Christianity in China/written by Mei Kangjun；translated by Zhu Chengming. Beijing：China Intercontinental Press，2005. 120 pages：color illustrations；22cm. ISBN：7508508416，7508508412

中国基督教：英文/梅康钧编著；朱承铭译. 五洲传播出版社. 中国基督教史.

5. Christianity/edited by Zhuo Xinping；translated by Chi Zhen and Caroline Mason. Leiden；Boston：Brill，2013. xxxi，422 pages；24cm. ISBN：9004174528，9004174524.（Religious studies in contemporary China collection；volume 3）

《基督教》，卓新平（1955—）；Mason, C.（Caroline）译.

6. The Nestorian monument；an ancient record of Christianity in China. Chicago, The Open Court Publishing Company，1909. 42 p. front.，illus. 24cm.

《大秦景教流行中国碑》，景净；伟烈亚力（Wylie, A.（Alexander），1815—1887）（英国传教士）译.

7. The Nestorian monument in China, by P. Y. Saeki... with an introductory note by Lord William Gascoyne-Cecil and a preface by the Rev. Professor A. H. Sayce. London, Society for Promoting Christian Knowledge，1916. x，1 l.，342 p. front.，plates. 23cm.

《大秦景教流行中国碑》，景净；佐伯好郎（Saeki, Yoshiroō，1871—1965）译，初版于1911年.

8. The luminous religion：a study of Nestorian Christianity in China, with a translation of the inscription upon the Nestorian tablet/by Mrs. C. E. Couling. London：The Carey Press，1925. 63，[1] p.：ill.；19cm.

Note：The Nestorian tablet. The inscriptions translated by Professor Saeki, Tokyo—P. 49—63.

《大秦景教流行中国碑》，Couling, C. E.（Charlotte Eliza，1860—）著；碑文由 Saeki, P. Yoshio（1881—）翻译.

9. The Nestorian tablet at Sianfu：a new English translation of the inscription and a history of the stone/by Ignatius Ying-ki（Ying Ch'ien-li）and Barry O'Toole. Peking, China：Peking Leader Press，1929. 18 p.，[1] leaf of plates：ill.；23cm.（Peking Leader reprints；no. 47）

《大秦景教流行中国碑》，景净；Ying, Ch'ien-li 和 O'Toole, George Barry（1886—1944）合译.

10. The Nestorian monument of Hsî-an Fû in Shen-hsî, China, relating to the diffusion of Christianity in China in the seventh and eighth centuries；with the Chinese text of the inscription, a translation, and notes, and a lecture on the monument with a sketch of subsequent Christian missions in China and their present state, by

James Legge. London, Trübner, 1888. New York：
Reprinted by Paragon Book Reprint Corp. , 1966. iv, 65
p. illus. 23cm.

《大秦景教流行中国碑》，景净；理雅各(Legge，James，
1815—1897)(英国汉学家)译.

11. The church of the T'ang dynasty/John Foster. London,
Society for Promoting Christian Knowledge, 1939. xvi,
168 pages folded map, folded table,19cm.

关于景教的资料翻译.John Foster 译.译自《唐书》.

(1) New York：Macmillan. 1939. xvi, 168 pages folded
map, folded table 19cm.

12. A study of the history of Nestorian Christianity in China
and its literature in Chinese：together with a new English
translation of the Dunhuang Nestorian documents/Li
Tang. Frankfurt am Main；New York：P. Lang, 2002.
230 p. ；21cm. ISBN：0820459704. (European university
studies. series XXVII, Asian and African studies；vol.
87 = Europäische Hochschulschriften. Reihe XXVII,
Asiatische und afrikanische Studien；Bd. 87)

对敦煌的景教文献进行了翻译.

(1) 2nd rev. ed. Frankfurt am Main；New York：Peter
Lang, c2004. 230 p. ；21cm. ISBN：3631522746,
082046578X. (European university studies. series
XXVII, Asian and African studies, 0721－3581；vol.
87＝Europäische Hochschulschriften. Reihe XXVII,
Asiatische und afrikanische Studien；Bd. 87)

13. Paradise in war, by Esther Woo... translated by Eleanor
J. Woo. New York：Island Press Cooperative, Inc.
[1947]. 1 p. l. , viii, 117 p. front. , plates, ports. ；
21cm.

中国基督教传教活动.Esther Woo；伍苏群(Woo，
Eleanor J.)译.

B451　传教士

1. Chinese Christians speak out：addresses and sermons/by
K. H. Ting and other church leaders. Beijing, China：
New World Press：Distributed by China International
Book Trading Corp. (Guoji Shudian), 1984. 140 pages, [4]
pages of plates：illustrations；19cm. (China spotlight series)

《中国基督教人士言论集》，丁光训等著.新世界出版社.

2. Kouduo richao：Li Jiubiao's Diary of oral admonitions：a
late Ming Christian journal/translated, with introduction
and notes by Erik Zürcher. Sankt Augustin：Institut
Monumenta Serica；Brescia：Fondazione Civiltà
Bresciana, 2007. 2 v. （862 p.）：ill. , maps；24cm.
ISBN：3805005432, 3805005431. (Monumenta serica
monograph series, 0179－261X；56/1－2)

《口铎日抄》，李九标(? —1647)；许理和(Erik Zürcher,
1928—2008)译.

3. An illustrated life of Christ presented to the Chinese
emperor：the history of Jincheng shuxiang (1640)/

Nicolas Standaert. Sankt Augustin：Institut Monumenta
Serica, 2007. 333 p. ：ill. （some col. ）；24cm. ISBN：
3805005487, 3805005482. (Monumenta serica monograph
series；59. 0179－261X)

"Part II contains the reproduction of the Chinese text and
illustrations, the reproduction of the identified original
European sources and a translation of the Chinese text"—
pref.

《基督教徒在中国皇帝前的生活纪实:〈进呈书像〉》，
Standaert，N. 著,含有对汤若望(Schall von Bell，Johann
Adam，1592—1666)《进呈书像》的翻译.

4. 穿儒服的传教士/朱菁编著；Andrea Lee 翻译.北京：五洲
传播出版社,2010. 155 页；23cm. ISBN：7508517186,
7508517180. (中外文化交流故事丛书)

英文题名：Missionary in Confucian garb.

B46　其他宗教

1. Totemism in Chinese minority ethnic groups/by He
Xingliang. [Beijing]：China Intercontinental Press, 2006.
128 pages：color illustrations；23cm. ISBN：7508510097,
7508510095. (Ethnic cultures of China)

《中国少数民族图腾崇拜:英文》，何星亮编著；王国振等
译.五洲传播出版社(中国民族多元文化丛书)

2. Popular religion and Shamanism/edited by Xisha Ma and
Huiying Meng；translated by Zhen Chi and Thomas David
DuBois. Boston：Brill, 2011. vi, 499 p. ；25cm. ISBN：
9004174559, 9004174559. （ Religious studies in
contemporary China collection；v. 1)

《原始宗教与萨满教》，Ma，Xisha 和 Meng，Huiying 主编；
池桢（Chi Zhen，1975—）和 DuBois，Thomas David
（1969—）合译.

B47　占卜、风水

1. The great prophecies of China/by Li Chunfeng and Yuan
Tienkang；translated and annotated by Charles L. Lee
[pseud.]New York：Franklin Co. [1950]. 64 p. ；23cm.

《推背图》，李淳风，袁天罡；Lee，Charles L. (1914—)译.

2. A translation of the ancient Chinese：the book of burial
(Zang Shu) by Guo Pu（276—324)/translated with an
introduction by Juwen Zhang. Lewiston, N. Y：Edwin
Mellen Press, 2004. xii, 230 p. ISBN：0773463526,
0773463523. (Chinese studies；vol. 34)

《葬书》，郭璞(276 年—324 年).

3. 风水趣谈/完颜绍元；姚振军译. 王卉译.上海：上海外语
教育出版社,2010. 408 页；23cm. ISBN：7544616379,
7544616371. (外教社汉英双语中国民俗文化丛书)

英文题名：At peace with nature traditional customs of
Chinese Feng-shui.

C类 社会科学总论

C1 社会科学理论

1. The fighting task confronting workers in philosophy and the social sciences：speech at the fourth enlarged session of the Committee of the Department of Philosophy and Social Science of the Chinese Academy of Sciences held on October 26, 1963/Chou Yang. Peking：Foreign Languages Press, 1963. 67 pages；19cm.

《哲学社会科学工作者的战斗任务：一九六三年十月二十六日在中国科学院哲学社会科学部委员会第四次扩大会议上的讲话》，周扬.

C2 社会科学文集

1. 梦溪笔谈/沈括（1031—1095）著；胡道静（1913—2003）今译，金良年（1951—）今译，胡小静今译；王宏，赵峥英译.成都：四川人民出版社，2008. 2册（41页，1065页）；24cm. ISBN：7220077418，7220077416.（大中华文库：汉英对照）

英文题名：Brush talks from dream brook. 本书载有609篇文章，分为17门类. 涉及典章制度、财政、军事、外交、历史、考古、文学、艺术以及科学技术等广阔的领域，是一部百科全书式的著作.

2. Chen Han-seng's writings, 1919—1949/edited by Xin-Yu Li. Beijing：Commercial Press International, 1996. viii, 618 pages：illustrations；21cm. ISBN：7801030885, 7801030887

《陈翰笙文集：1919—1949》，李新玉主编；陈翰笙著.商务印书馆国际有限公司.

C3 统计资料汇编

1. China compendium of statistics 1949—2008. Beijing：China Statistics Publishing, 2010. ISBN：7503758945, 7503758942

《新中国六十年统计资料汇编》，国家统计局国民经济综合统计司编.中国统计出版社.

2. Ten great years：statistics of the economic and cultural achievements of the People's Republic of China. Peking：Foreign Languages Press, 1960. 223 pages：illustrations；21cm.

《伟大的十年：中华人民共和国经济和文化建设成就的统计》，国家统计局编.

3. A survey of income and household conditions in China/compiled by State Statistical Bureau, People's Republic of China. Beijing：New World Press：China Statistical Information and Consultancy Service Centre, 1985. viii, 303 pages；27cm.

《中国城镇居民家庭基本调查资料》，国家统计局，新世界出版社.

C4 社会学与人类学

1. A history of Chinese sociology（newly-compiled）/authors：Zheng Hang-sheng；Li Ying-sheng. Translator：Zhang Chun. Beijing：China Renmin University Press, 2003. 544 p.；23cm. ISBN：7300046592, 7300046594.（Textbook series for 21st century）

《中国社会学史新编》，郑杭生，李迎生著.中国人民大学出版社.

2. 20世纪中国的社会学本土化/郑杭生，王万俊著；陆益龙译.北京：中国人民大学出版社，2009. 330页；23cm. ISBN：7300105321, 7300105327

英文题名：Indigenization of Chinese sociology in the 20th century.

3. Toward a people's anthropology/Fei Hsiao Tung. Beijing：New World Press, 1981. VI—121 p.；21cm.（China studies series）

《迈向人民的人类学》，费孝通著.

4. The study of human abilities；the Jen wu chih of Liu Shao, with an introductory study by J. K. Shryock. New Haven, Conn., American Oriental Society, 1937. x, 168 p.；26cm.（American oriental series, v. 11）

《人类能力研究：刘劭的〈人物志〉》，施莱奥克（Shryock, John Knight, 1890—）（美国学者）.收录对刘劭（生卒年不详，活动时间在公元3世纪）的《人物志》的英译.

  （1）New Haven, American Oriental Society；reprinted［by］Kraus Reprint Corp., New York：1966. x, 168 p.；24cm.（American oriental series, v. 11）

C5 婚姻与家庭

1. Love in China/Chen Xiao；translated by Shan Juan & Yuan Kang. Beijing：China Intercontinental Press, 2006. 127 pages：color illustrations；21cm. ISBN：7508509341, 750850934X.（Fashion China＝时尚中国）

《爱与家庭：英文》，陈潇著；袁康译.五洲传播出版社.本书反映了当代中国人的婚恋，家庭中出现的一些新现象和新观念.

2. The marriage customs among China's ethnic minority groups/by Jia Zhongyi. Beijing：China Intercontinental Press, 2006. 136 pages：color illustrations；23cm. ISBN：7508510033, 7508510038.（Ethnic cultures of China）

《中国少数民族婚俗：英文》，贾仲谊编著；王国振等译.五洲传播出版社（中国民族多元文化丛书）

3. Sex histories：China's first modern treatise on sex education by Dr. Chang Ching-Sheng. Translated by Howard S. Levy. Yokohama, 1967. 117 p. 26cm.

《性史》，张竞生（1888—1970）著；Levy, Howard S.（Howard Seymour, 1923—）译.

C6 人口学

1. China's population situation and policies/Wu Cangping & Mu Guangzong；translated by Zhang Tingquan. Beijing：Foreign Languages Press，2004. 154 p.：il.；23cm. ISBN：7119033263，7119033266.（Focus on China series）
《中国人口的现状与对策》，邬沧萍，穆光宗著；章挺权译. 外文出版社（聚焦中国丛书）

2. China's population and development/authors Tian Xueyuan and Zhou Liping；translator Chen Gengtao. Beijing：China Intercontinental Press，2004. 135 pages：color illustrations；22cm. ISBN：7508504410，7508504414.（China basics series）
《中国人口》，田雪原，周丽苹著；陈耕涛译. 五洲传播出版社.

3. 2010 年第六次全国人口普查主要数据/国务院第六次全国人口普查办公室，国家统计局人口和就业统计司编. 北京：中国统计出版社，2011. 70 页；30cm. ISBN：7503762608，7503762604
英文题名：Major figures on 2010 population census of China.

4. China's population：problems and prospects/by Liu Zheng，Song Jian，and others. Beijing，China：New World Press：Distributed by Guoji Shudian（China Publications Centre），1981. vi, 180 pages；21cm.（China studies series）
《中国人口问题与展望》，刘铮等著.

5. China population series：Inner Mongolia volume/Wenlin Xu, Qin Si. Beijing：Financial & Economic Pub. House，1990. 297 p. ISBN：7500510993，7500510994
《中国人口丛书：内蒙古分册》，中国财政经济出版社.

6. China population series：Shaanxi volume /Chuzhu Zhu，Yongxi Yuan. Beijing：Financial & Economic Pub. House，1990. 318 p. ISBN：7500512052
《中国人口丛书：陕西分册》，中国财政经济出版社.

7. 中国齐鲁人口：汉英对照/山东省人口和计划生育委员会编. 北京：中国人口出版社，2004. 47 页；26cm. ISBN：7802020131
英文题名：Shandong population of China. 本书中英文介绍了山东省计划生育工作的状况、成绩及经验.

8. 七彩云南：人口与数字：汉英对照/云南省人民政府 1‰人口抽样调查领导小组办公室编. 昆明：云南民族出版社，2006. 96 页；29cm. ISBN：7536734859，7536734852
英文题名：Paradisiacal Yunnan：population and data. 本书为云南省 2005 年人口抽样调查主要数据集.

9. A study of China's population/Li Chengrui. Beijing：Foreign Languages Press，1992. iv, 275 pages；19cm. ISBN：0835122654，0835122658，7119013262，7119013268
《中国人口问题的研究》，李成瑞著.

10. Ma Yinchu's collected papers on population. Zhejiang：Zhejiang People's Publishing House，1997. 186 pages：illustrations；21cm. ISBN：7213016261，7213016264
《马寅初人口文集》，马寅初著，浙江人民出版社.

11. General report of China's changing population and its development/editor-in-chief，Wu Cangping.［Beijing]：Higher Education Press，1997. v, 121 pages；23cm. ISBN：7040061643，7040061642
《转变中的中国人口与发展总报告》，高等教育出版社.

C7 中国各民族

1. Policy towards nationalities of the People's Republic of China. Peking：Foreign Languages Press，1953. 70 pages；19cm.
《中华人民共和国的民族政策》

2. China, land of many nationalities/Wang Sjoe-tang. Pekin：Foreign Languages Press，1955. 63 pages：illustrations；19cm.
《中国：一个多民族的国家》，王树棠著.

3. The national question and class struggle/Liu Chun. Peking：Foreign Languages Press，1966. 27 pages；19cm.
《民族问题和阶级斗争》，刘春著.

4. Ethnic groups in China/author Wang Can；translator Wang Pingxing. Beijing：China Intercontinental Press，2004. 170 pages：color illustrations；22cm. ISBN：7508504909，7508504902.（China basics series）
《中国民族》，王灿著；王平兴译. 五洲传播出版社（中国基本情况丛书/郭长建主编）

5. Regional autonomy for ethnic minorities in China. Beijing：New Star Publishers，2005. 49 pages；26cm. ISBN：7801486919，7801486912
《中国的民族区域自治：英文》，中华人民共和国国务院新闻办公室发布. 新星出版社.

6. Ethnic minorities of China/Xu Ying & Wang Baoqin；translation by Li Guoqing. Beijing：China Intercontinental Press，2007. 133 pages：color illustrations，color maps；25cm. ISBN：7508511009，750851100X.（Journey into China）
《民族之旅：英文》，徐英，王宝琴编著；李国庆译. 五洲传播出版社（中国之旅丛书/郭长建，李向平主编）. 本书选取了代表中国不同地区的 20 个民族，展现各自的物质文化和精神文化的精华，从中可以感受到真实的民族生活、浓郁的民族风情、神秘多彩的民族文化.

7. China's ethnic policy and common prosperity and development of all ethnic groups（September 2009）；Regional autonomy for ethnic minorities in China（February 2005）；National minorities policy and its practice in China（September 1999）. Beijing：Foreign Languages Press，2009. 153 pages：illustrations；21cm. ISBN：7119060798，7119060791.（White papers of The

Information Office of The State Council of the People's Republic of China＝中国国务院新闻办公室白皮书）

《中国的民族政策与各民族共同繁荣发展,中国的民族区域自治,中国的少数民族政策及其实践》,中华人民共和国国务院新闻办公室[编].

8. 中国的民族政策与各民族共同繁荣发展/中华人民共和国国务院新闻办公室[编].北京:外文出版社,2009. 62页;21cm. ISBN:7119060545,7119060538

9. 走近56个民族/线云强主编.北京:民族出版社,2009. 427页;28×32cm. ISBN:7105100033,7105100036
本书稿为汉文、英文双语,以图文并茂的形式向读者简明扼要地介绍了我国56个民族的基本情况.

10. 中国的各个民族:英汉对照/方华文编著;于应机,李其金译.合肥:安徽科学技术出版社,2010. 474页;25cm. ISBN:7533745165, 7533745167
英文题名:Nationalities in China.

11. The ethnic groups of China/by Wu Shimin. Beijing: Foreign Languages Press, 2011. 178 pages; color illustrations; 21×22cm. ISBN:7119068725, 7119068725
《东方中华》,吴仕民著.

12. Western and central Asians in China under the Mongols: their transformation into Chinese＝［Yuan xi yu ren Hua hua kao］/by Ch'en Yüan; translated and annotated by Ch'ien Hsing-hai and L. Carrington Goodrich. Los Angeles: Monumenta Serica at the University of California, 1966. iv, 328 p.; 27cm. (Monumenta serica monograph; 15)
《元西域人华化考》,陈垣(1880—1971);Ch'ien, Hsing-hai.,博路特（又名,傅路德,Goodrich, L. Carrington〈Luther Carrington〉,1894—）(美国汉学家)译.从文学、儒学、佛老、美术、礼俗等各个方面考察了元代进入中原的西域人(色目人)逐渐为中原文化所同化的情况.
(1)Nettetal: Steyler Verlag, 1989. 328 p.; 24cm. (Monumenta serica monograph series, 0179－261X; 15)

13. United and equal: the progress of China's minority nationalities/by Yin Ming. Peking: Foreign Languages Press, 1977. 109 pages, ［23］ leaves of plates: illustrations; 19cm.
《中国少数民族在前进》,尹明著.

14. Questions and answers about China's minority nationalities/compiled by the National Minorities Questions Editorial Panel; consisting of Ma Yin (chief compiler) and Ma Xifu ［and others］. Beijing, China: New World Press: Distributed by China International Book Trading Corp. (Guoji Shudian), 1985. 203 pages; 21cm. ISBN:0835115305, 0835115308
《中国少数民族问题回答》,中国少数民族问题编写组编写.新世界出版社.

15. China's minority nationalities/edited by Ma Yin. Beijing:

Foreign Languages Press, 1989. v, 450 pages, ［49］ pages of plates: illustrations (some color), map; 21cm. ISBN:0835119521,0835119528,7119000012,7119000015
《中国少数民族》,马寅主编.

16. The Oroqens: China's nomadic hunters/Qiu Pu; translated by Wang Huimin. Beijing: Foreign Languages Press: Distributed by China Publications Centre (Guoji Shudian), 1983. 125 pages, ［17］ pages of plates: illustrations (some color), map;26cm. ISBN:0835111512, 0835111515
《游猎社会的鄂伦春人》

17. Where the Dai people live/edited by An Chunyang and Liu Bohua; photographed by Liu Bohua ［and others］. Beijing: Foreign Languages Press, 1985. 117 pages: color illustrations; 26cm. ISBN: 0835111873, 0835111874. (China's nationalities series)
《在傣族聚居的土地上》

18. 羌族文化/陈蜀玉主编.成都:西南交通大学出版社,2008. 390页;24cm. ISBN:7811049862, 7811049864
外文题名:Culture of Qiang＝Culture de Qiang.本书为中英法三种文字对照版本,旨在用三种文字向海内外介绍羌族.

19. 文明交汇中的民族:中国回族/马庆生,马玉祥编著;黄树桦,王池英英文翻译.北京:外文出版社有限责任公司,2016.320页;图,照片,地图;24cm. ISBN:7119102122
英文题名:Hui of China an ethnic group at the intersection of civilizations.

20. 柯尔克孜族 英汉对照/王建新,王铁男编著.民族出版社,2018. 80页;26cm. ISBN:7105152667

D 类　政治、法律

D1　中国政治

D11　概况

1. Handbook on People's China. Peking: Foreign Languages Press, 1957. 235 pages; 3 color illustrations (1 mounted) tables; 19cm.
Notes: "Chinese national anthem (The march of the volunteers), words by Tian Han, music by Nie Er" (unacc. melody): fold. leaf inserted
《人民中国手册》

2. China: a general survey/Qi Wen. Beijing: Foreign Languages Press, 1979. 252 p., ［33］ leaves of plates (1 fold.): ill., krt.; 19cm.
《中国概貌》,齐雯编.
(1)Beijing: Foreign Languages Press, 1982. 251 p.: ill.
(2)3rd ed., rev. Beijing: Foreign Languages Press, 1984. 216 pages: illustrations, maps, tables

(3)China: a general survey/Qi Wen; English text edited by Jianguang Wang. Beijing: Foreign Languages Press, 1989. 262 pages: illustrations; 22cm. SBN: 0835121607, 0835121606, 7119010174, 7119010175

3. Politics/ compiled by the China Handbook Editorial Committee; translated by Huang Zengming and Zhou Ji. Beijing: Foreign Languages Press: Distributed by China International Book Trading Corp., 1985. 209 pages, [8] pages of plates: illustrations, portraits; 19cm. ISBN: 0835109860, 0835109864. (China handbook series)
《政治》,《中国手册》编辑委员会编.

4. China for peace. Beijing: New World Press: Distributed by China International Book Trading Corp., 1985. 145 pages, [4] leaves of plates: illustrations; 19cm.
Contents: "excepts of talks and articles by some of China's government and party leaders..."
《中国与和平》.新世界出版社.

5. Land and resources/edited and published by Foreign Languages Press. Beijing, China: Foreign Languages Press, 1987. 30 pages: color illustrations; 18cm. (China—facts & figures)
《国土与资源》,外文出版社编.

6. Multi-party co-operation in China. Beijing: New Star Publishers, 1990. 49 pages; 19cm. ISBN: 7800851788, 7800851780. (China, issues and ideas; 1)
《中国的多党合作》,北京周报编.新星出版社.

7. Survival and development: a study of China's long-term development/the National Conditions Investigation Group under the Chinese Academy of Sciences. Beijing; N. Y.: Science Press, 1992. xvii, 188 pages: illustrations; 25cm. ISBN: 7030028538, 7030028532
《生存与发展》.科学出版社.

8. China handbook/compiled by Qin Shi. Beijing: New Star, 1993. 199 pages, [1] folded leaf of plates: illustrations (some color), color map; 21cm. ISBN: 7800859207, 7800859205
《中国》,秦石编.新星出版社.

9. China in diagrams/compiled by the State Council Information Office; [translators: Wang Guozhen, Tian Jian]. Beijing: China Intercontinental Press, 2003. 200 pages: color illustrations, color maps; 24cm. ISBN: 7508503376, 7508503370
《图说中国》,新华社新闻信息中心,五洲传播出版社编.
(1)China in diagrams/[compiled by Jing Xiaomin; translator, Wang Guozhen]. Beijing: China Intercontinental Press, 2011. 200 pages: color illustrations, color maps, music; 24cm. ISBN: 7508521268, 7508521269

10. A passage to China: aspects of culture, education, business, tourism and more/chief editors, Ning Aihua, Li Zhonghua. Qingdao: China Ocean University Press, 2004. 283 pages: illustrations, maps; 23cm. ISBN: 7810676350, 7810676359
《走近中国》,宁爱花,李忠华主编.中国海洋大学出版社.本书从文化、教育、经济、旅游的多个视角,介绍了中华民族辉煌的文明史,蓬勃发展的今天及美好的未来,有利于外国读者全面了解中国,从而拓宽中外交流.

11. 论中国和平崛起发展新道路:汉英对照/郑必坚著.北京:中共中央党校出版社,2005. 174 页;23cm. ISBN: 7503533471

12. Building of political democracy in China. Beijing: New Star Publishers, 2005. 83 pages; 26cm. ISBN: 7801488377, 7801488374,7801488385,7801488381
《中国的民主政治建设:英文》,中华人民共和国国务院新闻办公室发布.新星出版社.

13. Consultative democracy in China/[李君如著;外文出版社英文编译部译]. Beijing: Foreign Languages Press, 2014. 29 p.: ill.; 21cm. ISBN: 7119091747. (China in focus＝中国进行时)
《协商民主在中国》.

14. 中国地方可持续发展规划指南＝Planning Guide on the Local Sustainable Development in China:汉英对照/科学技术部农村与社会发展司,中国 21 世纪议程中心,中国科学院地理科学与资源研究所编著.北京:社会科学文献出版社,2006. 294 页;24cm. ISBN: 7802300711, 7802300712.(国家可持续发展实验区系列丛书)
英文题名: The planning guide on local sustainable development in China.

15. 中国梦:英文/李君如著;丛国玲,欧阳伟平译.北京:外文出版社,2006. 115 页:照片;21cm. ISBN: 7119044620, 7119044621.(中国的和平发展系列)
英文题名:The China dream.

16. 中国概况/孙岩,崔艳鲲编著.北京:海洋出版社,2000. 212 pages: illustrations; 19cm. ISBN: 7502751017, 7502751012
Notes: 正文为英文.

17. 中国概况＝The outline of China:英文/孙岩,熊瑛,高侠等编著.北京:海洋出版社,2007. 21cm. ISBN: 7502768669, 7502768661
书名原文:The outline of China. 介绍中国的基本情况.

18. Understanding China: Introduction to China's history, society and culture/Jin Bo; [Wang Guozhen, Li Ping, translators]. Beijing: China Intercontinental Press, 2008. [6], 260 pages: color illustrations, color maps; 24cm. ISBN: 7508512143, 7508512146
《阅读中国:历史、社会和文化》,金帛编著.五洲传播出版社.

19. Start point: thirty years of reform in China/Chin Fulin. Beijing: Foreign Languages Press, 2008. ii, 240 p.; 23cm. ISBN: 7119051819, 7119051814
《起点:中国改革步入三十年》,迟福林著.总结了前三十年的改革情况,并对中国今后的改革之路做出了展望.

20. China's path：the scientific outlook on development/Tian Yingkui. Beijing：Foreign Languages Press, 2008. 167 pages；23cm. ISBN：7119054131, 7119054139

《中国道路：从科学发展观解读中国发展》,田应奎著.

21. Key words for better understanding China/compiled by Guo Yakun, Tian Jie, Ma Yanrong；translated by Li Yang〔and others〕. Beijing：Foreign Languages Press, 2008. viii, 238 pages：illustrations；23cm. ISBN：7119053479, 7119053477. (Focus on China series)

《关键词读中国》,夏和文编. 精选了反映现代中国的200多个关键词,内容涉及政治、经济、社会、文化、科技、环保、体育各个领域,每个关键词都是一条翔实可靠的信息.

22. Growing with China：MNC executives talk about China/compiled by Zhu Ling. Beijing：New World Press, 2009. 288 pages：illustrations (chiefly color), color portraits；24cm. ISBN：7802289925, 7802289920

《赢之道：跨国公司高管谈改革开放》,朱灵主编. 新世界出版社.

23. 突围：国门初开的岁月 The birth of China's opening-up policy/李岚清著. 北京：外语教学与研究出版社,2009. 453 页；24cm. ISBN：7560084336, 7560084338

英文题名：Breaking through：the birth of China's opening-up policy. 作者以自己的所知、所为、所见为素材,回顾了对外开放初期的有关重大事件,再现了中国对外开放的伟大探索和实践.

24. China's political system/Yin Zhongqing；translated by Wang Pingxing. 〔Beijing〕：China Intercontinental Press, 2010. 180 pages：color illustrations；23cm. ISBN：7508513003,7508513002

《中国政治制度》,吴伟主编. 尹中卿著. 五洲传播出版社.

25. Big power's responsibility：China's perspective/Jin Canrong；trans. Tu Xiliang. Beijing：China Renmin University Press, 2011. 13, 2, 255 pages：color illustrations；24cm. ISBN：7300131580, 7300131581

《大国的责任》,金灿荣著. 中国人民大学出版社.

26. China's peaceful development/Information Office of the State Council, the People's Republic of China. Beijing：Foreign languages press, 2011. 37 pages：illustrations；27cm. ISBN：7119072388, 7119072382, 7119072395, 7119072390

《中国的和平发展》,中华人民共和国国务院新闻办公室〔发布〕.

27. The choice of China：peaceful development and construction of a harmonious world/Li Jingzhi, Pu Ping；transl. by Xu Ying, Gu Hua, Wang Jinhe. Beijing：China Renmin University Press, 2012. 212 p.：ill.；25cm. ISBN：7300152974, 730015297X

《中国的抉择：和平发展与构建和谐世界》,李景治 (1943—),蒲傅(Pu, Ping)；徐莹(Xu, Ying)等译.

28. 中国梦,什么梦？/李君如著；王之光,樊凡翻译. 北京：外文出版社,2014. 152 页；24cm. ISBN：7119093222

英文题名：In pursuit of the Chinese dream

29. The China dream：great power thinking & strategic posture in the post-American era/Liu Mingfu；foreword by Liu Yazhou. New York：CN Times Books, 2015. ii, 272 pages；24cm. ISBN：1627741408, 1627741402

Notes："First published in Beijing in 2010；now available in English"—Back of dust jacket cover

《中国梦：后美国时代的大国思维与战略定位》,刘明福 (1951—).

30. 中国改革开放进行时/章百家著；闫威,毛琦英文翻译. 北京：外文出版社, 2015. 221 页：图；25cm. ISBN：7119093482

英文题名：China's ongoing reform and opening up

31. Paper tiger：inside the real China/Xu Zhiyuan；translated from the Chinese by Michelle Deeter and Nicky Harman. London：Head of Zeus, 2015. xi, 305 pages；24cm. ISBN：1781859780, 1781859787, 1781859797, 1781859795

Contents：The face of China—Things seen and things thought—Earthquakes and grand occasions—Fear and fearlessness—Anger and absurdity.

纸老虎：真实的中国. 许知远(1976—)；Deeter, Michelle 和 Harman, Nicky 合译. 收录了许知远自 2007 年在境外媒体上所设专栏的英译合辑.

32. 中国走社会主义道路为什么成功：英文版 /戴木才著；贺龙平译. 北京：五洲传播出版社, 2016. 246 页；24cm. ISBN：7508533278

英文题名：Why has China achieved success by taking the socialist road

33. 改革方法论/艾丰著,谭振学英译. 济南：山东大学出版社；2004. 304 页；20cm. ISBN：7560728049

英文题名：Methodology for Reform. 中英文对照.

D12　中国政治思想史

1. A history of Chinese political thought/by Kung-chuan Hsiao；translated by F. W. Mote. Princeton, N. J.：Princeton University Press, c1979 — v. 〈1 — 〉；25cm. ISBN：0691031169, 0691100616. (Princeton library of Asian translations)

《中国政治思想史》,萧公权(1897—1981 年)；牟复礼 (Frederick W. Mote,1922—2005)(美国汉学家)译.

2. Traditional government in imperial China：a critical analysis/by Ch'ien Mu；translated by Chün-tu Hsüeh and George O. Totten, with Wallace Johnson... 〔et al.〕. Hong Kong：Chinese University Press；New York：St.

Martin's Press, c1982. xxii, 159 p. ; 24cm. ISBN：
0312812329

Translation of：Zhongguo li dai zheng zhi de shi. Rev.
ed. , 1955

《中国历代政治得失》，钱穆（1895—1990）；Hsüheh, Chün-
tu, 陶慕廉（Totten, George O. 〈George Oakley〉，
1922—)合译.

3. Chinese bureaucracy & government administration；
   selected essays/translated by Joseph Jiang. Check-edited
   by T. W. Kwok. [Honolulu]: East-West Center, 1966.
   90 leaves; 28cm. (East-West Center, Honolulu, Institute
   of Advanced Projects. Occasional papers of research
   translations. Translation series；no. 14)

   Contents： The mo liao system in the Ch'ing
   administration, by Ch'üan Tseng-yu. —Patterns of change
   in Chinese officialism, by T'ao Yuan-chen. —The rise of
   Confucianists and the formation of the bureaucracy in Han
   times, by Sa Meng-wu. —The social and economic bases
   of Chinese bureaucracy, by Wang Ya-nan. —
   Characteristics of Chinese bureaucracy, by Chang Chin-
   chien.

   Jiang, Binglun 译；郭德华（Kwok, Tak-Wa, 1901—)编.
   翻译了中国官僚制与政府管理的 5 篇文章，包括中国的
   幕僚制度、官制变化、汉朝儒家的推崇、中国官僚政治的
   社会和经济基础、官僚政治的特点等.

4. China's only hope. New York: Chicago [etc.] Fleming
   H. Revell Company, 1900. 2 p. l., 151 p. front.
   (port.); 20cm.

   《劝学篇》，张之洞（1837—1909）；Woodbridge, Samuel
   Isett(1856—)译.

   (1)Edinburgh and London, Oliphant, Anderson &
      Ferrier, 1901. 2 p. l., 151 p. front. (port.) 20cm.

   (2)China's only hope: an appeal by her greatest viceroy/
      Chang Chih-tung; with the sanction of the present
      emperor, Kwang Sü; translated from the Chinese ed.
      by Samuel I. Woodbridge; introd. by Griffith John.
      Westport, Conn. : Hyperion Press, 1975. 151 p.
      port. ; 23cm. ISBN: 0883551640

5. History of Chinese political thought during the early Tsin
   period. Translated by L. T. Chen. New York: Harcourt,
   Brace & Company; London, K. Paul, Trench, Trubner
   & Co. Ltd. , 1930. viii, 210 p. 2 port. (incl. front.)
   diagr. ; 23cm.

   《先秦政治思想史》，梁启超（1873—1929）；陈立庭（L. T.
   Chen）译.

   (1)New York: AMS Press, [1969]. viii, 210 p. ports. ;
      23cm.

6. The political thoughts of China before Ch'in/the original
   author Liang-Jen-Kung; and its being render ed into
   English by Prof. Hsu-Chao. [Taipei]: Ho-Ping

Typewriting Co, 1965. 299, 4, 12 pages; 26cm.

《先秦政治思想史》，梁启超（1873—1929）；徐照译.

7. The political history of China, 1840—1928. Translated
   and edited by Ssu-yu Teng and Jeremy Ingalls. Princeton,
   N. J. , D. Van Nostrand Co. [1956]. 545 p. illus. ;
   24cm.

   《中国近百年政治史》，李剑农（1880—1963）著；邓嗣禹
   （Teng, Ssu-yü, 1906—1988）（美国华裔学者），Ingalls,
   Jeremy(1911—2000)译.

   (1)Stanford, Calif. , Stanford University Press [1967,
      c1956]. xii, 545 p. maps. ; 22cm.

8. China after the war/by Hsu Shih-chang, translated by the
   Bureau of Economic Information. Peking, China, c1920.
   164 p. ; 24cm.

   《欧战后之中国》，徐世昌（1855—1939）著.

D121　孙中山（1866—1925）

1. San min chu i. The three principles of the people, by Dr.
   Sun Yat-sen. Translated into English by Frank W.
   Price... edited by L. T. Chen... Shanghai, China, China
   Committee, Institute of Pacific Relations, 1927. xvii p. ,
   2 l. , [3]-514 p. incl. front. (port.) diagrs. 22cm.
   (International understanding series)

   《三民主义》，Price, Frank W. （Frank Wilson, 1895—
   1974)译；陈立廷（Chen, L. T.）编.

   (1)Chungking, Ministry of Information of the Republic of
      China, 1943. xvii p. , 2 l. , [3]-514 p. incl. front.
      (port.) diagrs. 21cm.

   (2)New York: Da Capo Press, 1975. xvii, 514 p. :
      port. ; 22cm. ISBN: 0306706989. (China in the 20th
      century). (International understanding series)

2. The triple demism of Sun Yat-sen, translated from the
   Chinese, annotated and appraised by Paschal M. d'Elia,
   S. J. with introduction and index. English ed. Wuchang,
   The Franciscan Press, 1931. 747 p. incl. front. (port.)
   illus. (1 col.) diagrs. (1 fold.) 23cm.

   Translation of San min zhu yi, from the French ed.
   published in 1929 under title: Le triple de'misme.

   《三民主义》，DÉlia, Paschal M. 译. 从法文版转译来.

   (1)[New York: AMS Press, 1974]. xxxvii, 747 p.
      illus. ; 23cm. ISBN: 0404569293

3. San min chu i; The three principles of the people.
   [Calcutta] Calcutta Office, Chinese Ministry of
   Information, 1942 [i. e. 1944]. xvii, 317 p. port. ;
   22cm.

   《三民主义》

4. The three principles of the people=San min chu i/by Sun
   Yat-sen; [translated into English by Frank W. Price;
   abridged and edited by the Commission for the
   Compilation of the History of the Kuomintang]; with two

supplementary chapters by Chiang Kai-shek. Taipei：China Pub. Co.，[197—?]. vi, ix, 329 p.；21cm.

《三民主义》（删编），Price，Price，Frank W.（Frank Wilson，1895—1974）译；蒋介石（1887—1975）补（2 章）.

(1) 2nd ed. Taipei, Taiwan, Republic of China：China Cultural Service, 1981. xiv, 141 p.，[1] p. of plates：col. ill.；22cm.

(2) Taipei, Taiwan, Republic of China：China Pub. Co.，[1989]. ix, 329 p.；21cm.

(3) [Taipei, Taiwan]：China Cultural Service, 2003. 2，14，366 p.；19cm. +1 CD-ROM (4 3/4 in.)

5. The cult of Dr. Sun；Sun Wen hsueh shu... by Dr. Sun Yat-sen；the translation by Wei Yung. Shanghai, The Independent Weekly, 1931. 1 p. l, ii p.，1 l.，230, xx p.；19cm.

《孙文学说》，韦荣（Wei，Yong）译.

6. Sun Yat-sen, his political and social ideals；a source book, compiled, translated and annotated by Leonard Shihlien Hsüh. Los Angeles, University of Southern California Press［c1933］. xxiii, 505p. incl. front. (port.) diagrs.；24cm.

《孙中山的政治与社会理想》，许仕廉（Hsüh，Leonard Shih-lien，1901—）编译.

7. The teachings of Sun Yat-sen；selections from his writings, compiled and introduced by Professor N. Gangulee... Foreword by His Excellency Dr. V. K. Wellington Koo... London, The Sylvan Press［1945］. 2 p. l.，ix-xi, 132 p.，1 l. incl. front. (port.) 1 illus.，diagr. 19cm.

《孙文学说》，Gangulee，Nagendranath（1889—），Koo，V. K. Wellington（1888—1985）编译.

8. Fundamentals of national reconstruction, by Sun Yat-sen. Chungking, China, Chinese Ministry of Information［1945］. iv, p.，1 l.，96,［1］p. incl. facsim.，diagrs.，front. (port.)；22cm.

"This English edition is based largely on one of the four volumes of Dr. Sun's works collected under the name of The bequeathed teachings of the Tsungli."—Translator's preface.

《建国大纲》，Toong，Z. B. 译.

(1) [Taipei] China Cutural Service［1953］. vii, 266 p. port.，diagrs.，facsim；22cm.

9. The principle of democracy. ［With Chinese text］Translated into English by Frank W. Price；abridged and edited by the Commission for the Compilation of the History of the Kuomintang. Taipei, Chinese Cultural Service［pref. 1953］142 p.；22cm.

《民权主义》

(1) Westport, Conn.，Greenwood Press［1970］. xxv, 142 p.；23cm. ISBN：0837131472

10. The principle of livelihood. ［With Chinese text］Translated into English by Frank W. Price；abridged and edited by the Commission for the Compilation of the History of the Kuomintang. Taipei, China Cultural Service［pref. 1953］. 89 p.；22cm.

《民生主义》

11. The principle of nationalism. ［With Chinese text］Translated into English by Frank W. Price, abridged and edited by the Commission for the Compilation of the History of the Kuomintang. Taipei, Chinese Cultural Service［pref. 1953］. 69 p.；22cm.

《民族主义》

12. Prescriptions for saving China：selected writings of Sun Yat-sen/edited, with an introduction and notes by Julie Lee Wei, Ramon H. Myers, Donald G. Gillin；translated by Julie Lee Wei, E-su Zen, Linda Chao. Stanford, Calif.：Hoover Institution Press, c1994. xlv, 328 p.：ill.；24cm. ISBN：0817992812, 0817992820.（Studies in economic, social, and political change, the Republic of China）

《孙文选集》，Wei，Julie Lee（1935—），Myers，Ramon Hawley（1929—），Gillin，Donald G. 译注.

D122　邹容（1885—1905）

1. The revolutionary army：a Chinese nationalist tract of 1903/Introduction and translation［from the Chinese］with notes by John Lust. The Hague；Paris：Mouton, 1968. 256 pages；22cm.（Mate'riaux pour l'étude de l'extrême-orient moderne et contemporain, textes；6）

《革命军》，Lust，John 译.

D123　蒋介石（1887—1975）

1. Outline of the New life movement/by Chiang Kai-shek；translated by Madame Chiang Kai-shek. Nanchang, Kiangsi, China, Association for the Promotion of the New Life Movement，1930. 14 pages color plates 22cm.

《新生活运动》，宋美龄（1897—2003）译.

2. Resisting external aggression and regenerating the Chinese nation. Hankow, China, China Information Committee, 1938. 54 p.；26cm.

抗日和民族自救.

3. A philosophy of action；or, What I mean by action, by Generalissimo Chiang Kai-shek；translated into English with a foreword and notes in the nature of a discursive commentary. Chungking, China, The China Information Committee, 1940. 28 p. 25cm.

《行的哲学》

4. China fights on：war messages of Chiang Kai-shek/translated by Frank Wilson Price. Chungking [etc.] The China Publishing Company，[1941]. 365 pages；22cm.

中国的抗日战争. Price，Francis Wilson（1895—）译.

5. The new life movement in China. 〔Calcutta〕Calcutta Office, Chinese Ministry of Information，1942. 19 p. port. 19cm.

《新生活运动》,宋美龄(Chiang, May-ling Soong, 1897—2003)译.

6. All we are and all we have; speeches and messages since Pearl harbor 〔by〕Generalissimo Chiang Kai-shek, December 9，1941—November 17，1942. New York：Chinese News Service〔1942〕. 3 p. l.，61 p. illus. (port.)；23cm.

蒋介石在 1941 年 12 月 9 日至 1942 年 11 月 17 日间的讲话.

(1)New York：The John Day Company, 〔1943〕.

7. Resistance and reconstruction; messages during China's six years of war, 1937—1943, by Generalissimo Chiang Kai-shek. New York：London, Harper & Brothers 〔1943〕. xxiv, 322 p. ；23cm.

Contents：I. China resists Japan（1937—1938）—II. China fights on（1938—1940）—III. China fights and builds（1940—1941）—IV. China fights on with allies（1941—1943）.

蒋介石在 1937—1943 年抗战期间的信息. Lutley, Albert French, Price, Frank W.（Frank Wilson, 1895—1974），Ma, Pin-ho 合译.

(1)Freeport, N. Y.，Books for Libraries Press〔1970, c1943〕. xxiv, 322 p. ；23cm. ISBN：0836915976. (Essay index reprint series)

8. Before final victory, speeches by Generalissimo Chiang Kai-shek, 1943—1944. New York：Chinese News Service〔1944〕. 80 p. ；22cm.

蒋介石 1943—1944 年间的讲话.

9. Generalissimo Chiang Kai-shek's war speeches. Chungking, China, The Chinese Ministry of Information 〔1944〕. 2 p. l.，129 p. port. ；22cm.

《战时蒋委员长言论集》,中国国民党中央执行委员会宣传部编.

10. The voice of China; speeches of Generalissimo and Madame Chiang Kai-shek between December 7，1941, and October 10，1943, including some recent messages to British leaders and the British people. London, New York 〔etc.〕Published on behalf of the London office, Chinese Ministry of Information by Hutchinson & Co. Ltd. 〔1944〕. 112 p. incl. front. ；19cm.

蒋介石与宋美龄在 1941 年 12 月至 1943 年 10 月的一些言论.

11. The collected wartime messages of Generalissimo Chiang Kai-shek, 1937—1945, compiled by Chinese Ministry of Information. New York：The John Day Company 〔1946〕. 2 v. ports.，facsims. ；23cm.

Contents：v. 1, 1937—1940. Prologue. China resists Japan. China fights on. China fights and builds. v. 2, 1940—1945. China fights and builds（continued）China fights on with allies. China fights on to victory. Epilogue.

《战时蒋委员长言论集》,高克毅(Kao, George, 1912—2008)译. 中国国民党宣传部编.

(1)New York：Kraus Reprint, 1969. 2 volumes in 1. （xxx，888 pages）illustrations, facsimiles, portraits；24cm.

12. China's destiny, New York：The Macmillan Company, 1947. xi, 260 p. ；21cm.

《中国之命运》,王宠惠(Wang, Chung-hui, 1882—1958)译.

(1)China's destiny/by Chiang Kai-shek; translation by Wang Chung-hui; with an introd. by Lin Yutang. New York：Da Capo Press, 1976, c1947. xi, 260 p. ；23cm. ISBN：0306708213

(2)Westport, Conn. ：Greenwood Press, 1985, c1947. xi, 260 p. ；23cm. ISBN：0313246769

13. The destiny of China. 〔Singapore，194—〕. 141 p. ；18cm.

《中国之命运》,蒋介石.

14. China's destiny & Chinese economic theory, by Chiang Kai-shek, with notes and commentary by Philip Jaffe. New York：Roy Publishers〔1947〕. 347 p. ；22cm.

Contents：The secret of China's destiny/by Philip Jaffe—China's destiny/by Chiang Kai-shek—Chinese economic theory/by Chiang Kai-shek—Commentary on China's destiny and Chinese economic theory/by Philip Jaffe.

中国之命运与中国经济理论. Jaffe, Philip J.（Philip Jacob, 1895—1980)译.

(1)New York：Roy Publishers, 1976. 347 p.

(2)Folkestone：Global Oriental, 2008. ISBN：1905246816, 1905246811

(3)Leiden；Boston：Global Oriental, 2013. 347 pages；25cm. ISBN：1905246816. (Global Oriental classic reprints；no. 12)

15. Chapters on national fecundity, social welfare, education, and health and happiness/written by Chiang Kai-shek, as supplements to Dr. Sun Yat-sen's Lectures on the principle of people's livelihood. Rendered into English by Durham S. F. Chen. Taipei, Taiwan：China Cultural Service, 〔1952〕. 107 p. ；22cm.

《民生主义育乐两篇补述》,陈石孚(Chen, Durham S. F.)译.

16. On nature and recreation, being texts to continue and complete the late Dr. Sun Yat-Sen's discourse on the principle of people's livelihood. Translated by Beauson Tseng. Taipei, Commercial Press 〔1968〕. 117 p. ；

22cm.

《民生主义育乐两篇补述》，曾约农(Tseng,Beauson)译.

17. Soviet Russia in China：a summing-up at seventy, by Chiang Chung-cheng（Chiang Kai-shek）. New York：Farrar, Straus and Cudahy ［1957］. 392 p. ；22cm.

《苏俄在中国》，蒋介石.

(1) Rev. , enl. ed. , with maps. New York：Farrar, Straus and Cudahy ［1958］. 432 p. illus. ；22cm.

(2) Rev. , abridged ed. New York：Farrar, Straus and Giroux ［1965］. xiv, 218 p. col. fold. maps. ；22cm.

(3) Rev. , enlarged ed. Taipei：China Pub. Comp. , c1969. xv, 432 p. , ［2］ leaves of plates：col. fold. maps. ；22cm.

18. Aphorisms of President Chiang Kai-shek. ［Taipei］：Govt. Information Office, Republic of China, 1974. x, 145 p. ；24cm.

蒋介石语录.

D13　中国共产党

1. Thirty years of the Communist Party of China/by Hu Ch'iau-mu. Peking：Foreign Languages Press, 1951. 99 pages；22cm.

《中国共产党的三十年》，胡乔木.

(1) Peking：Foreign Languages Press, 1952. 93 pages；21cm.

(2) Peking：Foreign Languages Press, 1954. 99 pages；22cm.

(3) 4th ed. Peking：Foreign Languages Press, 1959. 113 pages；19cm.

2. Thirty years of the Communist Party of China, an outline history. London, Lawrence & Wishart, 1951. 95 pages：illustrations；19cm.

《中国共产党的三十年》，胡乔木.

(1) Westport, Conn. , Hyperion Press, 1973. 95 pages；23cm. ISBN：0883550717, 0883550717

3. The Communist Party, leader of the Chinese revolution. Peking：Foreign Languages Press, 1951. 41 pages：illustrations；21cm.

Contents：Address on the 30th anniversary of the Communist Party of China, by Liu Shao-chi. —World significance of the Chinese Revolution, by Lu Ting-yi. —Communist Party of China and People's Democratic United Front, by Li Wei-han. —Close contact with masses is glorious tradition of our party, by Teng Hsiao-ping.

《共产党：中国革命的领导者》，刘少奇（1898—1969）；陆定一（1906—1996）等.

4. The constitution of the Communist Party of China：report on the revision of the constitution of the Communist Party of China/［by］ Teng Hsiao-ping. Peking：Foreign Languages Press, 1956. 109 pages；21cm.

《中国共产党章程：关于修改党的章程的报告》

5. The constitution of the Communist Party of China：adopted by the ninth National Congress of the Communist Party of China on April 14, 1969. Peking：Foreign Languages Press, 1969. 38 pages；11cm.

Contents：Ch. 1. General programme—ch. 2. Membership—Ch. 3. Organizational principle of the party—ch. 4. Central organizations of the party—ch. 5. Party organization in the localities and the army units—ch. 6. Primary organizations of the party.

《中国共产党章程》

6. The communist party of China：its organizations and their functions/Zhang Rongchen. Beijing：China Intercontinental Press,2007. 102 pages：illustrations；21cm. ISBN：7508511320, 7508511328

《中国共产党组织与机制：英文》，张荣臣编著；王平兴译. 五洲传播出版社.

7. 中国共产党与中国社会的发展进步：英文/章百家编著. 北京：五洲传播出版社,2007. 21cm. ISBN：7508511894, 7508511891

英文题名：Communist Party of China and China's social development.

8. Why and how the CPC works in China/edited by Xie Chuntao；［translated by Li Yi, Zhang Ruiqing and Zhou Gang. ］. Beijing：New World Press, 2011. iv, 225 pages，［20］ pages of plates：illustrations；24cm. ISBN：7510418822, 7510418828

《历史的轨迹：中国共产党为什么能?》，谢春涛主编. 新世界出版社. 围绕国内外读者关注的十三个重大问题，从历史的角度做了深入的思考和准确的解读.

9. What do you know about the Communist Party of China/Li Junru. Beijing：Foreign Languages Press, 2011. 191 pages：illustrations（some color）；23cm. ISBN：7119070179, 7119070177

《你了解中国共产党吗?》，李君如著.

10. 中国共产党如何治党? / 谢春涛主编；王君翻译. 北京：新世界出版社,2017. ISBN：7510463303

英文题名：Governing the party：how the CPC works. 本书介绍中国共产党在不同时期，特别是改革开放以及十八大、十八届三中全会以来的治党努力及成效.

11. Training successors for the revolution is the party's strategic task. Peking：Foreign Languages Press, 1965. 58 pages；19cm.

《培养革命接班人是党的一项战略任务》

12. Absorb proletarian fresh blood：an important question in party consolidation. Peking：Foreign Languages Press, 1968. 26 pages；13cm.

《吸收无产阶级的新鲜血液》

13. Regulations on the work of selecting and appointing leading party and government cadres/Zhong Xin, editor. Beijing：Foreign Languages Press, 2002. 60 pages; 21cm. ISBN：7119031562, 7119031569
《党政干部选拔任用工作条例》,钟欣编.

14. Address at the meeting in celebration of the 40th anniversary of the founding of the Communist Party of China. Peking：Foreign Languages Press, 1961. 36 pages; 21cm.
《在庆祝中国共产党成立四十周年大会上的讲话》,刘少奇.

15. Long live the Communist Party of China：in commemoration of the 48th anniversary of the founding of the Communist Party of China/［Mao Tse-tung］. Peking：Foreign Languages Press, 1969. 17 pages；illustrations, portraits; 13cm.
《中国共产党万岁：纪念中国共产党诞生四十八周年》,《人民日报》、《红旗》杂志、《解放军报》社论.

16. Commemorate the 50th anniversary of the Communist Party of China/by the editorial departments of Renmin Ribao (People's daily), Hongqi (Red flag) and Jiefangjun Bao (Liberation Army daily). Peking：Foreign Languages Press, 1971. 51 pages：portraits; 19cm.
《纪念中国共产党五十周年》,《人民日报》、《红旗》杂志、《解放军报》编辑部.

17. A concise history of the communist party of China：seventy years of the CPC/Hu Sheng (chief editor)；Party History Research Centre of the CPC Central Committee；translated by Central Translation Bureau Beijing Review. Beijing, China：Foreign Languages Press, 1994. ii, 873 pages; 20cm. ISBN：7119016016, 7119016016, 7119016695, 7119016696
《中国共产党简明历史：中国共产党的七十年》,胡绳主编；中共中央党史研究室著.

18. Speech at the rally in celebration of the 80th anniversary of the founding of the Communist Party of China：(July 1, 2001)/Jiang Zemin. Beijing, China：New Star Publishers, 2001. 52 pages；21cm. ISBN：7801483855, 7801483850
《在庆祝中国共产党成立八十周年大会上的讲话》,江泽民.

19. Resolution on CPC history (1949—1981). Beijing, China：Foreign Languages Press, 1981. 126 pages；19cm. (Chinese documents)
《关于建国以来党的若干历史问题的决议》

20. Resolution on CPC history (1949—1981). Beijing：Contemporary World Pub., 1996. pages；19cm. ISBN：7801150090, 7801150097. (Chinese documents)
《关于建国以来党的若干历史问题的决议：1949—

1981》,齐聚译. 当代世界出版社.

21. Mao's China；party reform documents, 1942—1944. Translation and introd. by Boyd Compton. Seattle, University of Washington Press, 1952. lii, 278 p. map.；21cm. (University of Washington publications on Asia)
Contents：Report of the Propaganda Bureau of the Central Committee on the Cheng Feng movement. — Reform in learning, the party, and literature, by Mao Tse-tung. —In opposition to party formalism, by Mao Tse-tung. —Second preface to "Village investigations," by Mao Tse-tung. —The reconstruction of our studies, by Mao Tse-tung. —Central Committee resolution on investigation and research. —Resolution of the Central Committee of the Chinese Communist Party on the Yenan Cadre School. —Resolution of the Central Committee of the Chinese Communist Party on the education of cadres in service. —How to be a Communist Party member, by Ch'en Yün. —Training of the Communist Party member, by Liu Shao-ch'i. —Central Committee resolution on strengthening the party spirit. —Central Committee resolution on the unification of leadership in the anti-Japanese war bases. — Resolution of the Central Committee of the Chinese Communist Party on methods of leadership. —In opposition to liberalism, by Mao Tse-tung. —On the intra-party struggle, by Liu Shao-ch'i. —In opposition to several incorrect tendencies within the party, by Mao Tse-tung. —Address to the Shen-Kan-Ning Border Region Assembly, by Mao Tse-tung. —Propaganda guide. —Liquidation of Menshevik though in the part, by Liu Shao-sh'i. —The Bolshevization of the party, by J. Stalin. —Remolding the party's style of work and improving its state of organization.
Compton, Boyd 编译,汇集中国共产党 1942—1944 年的改革文件.
(1)Washington University Press, 1966. 278 pages：illustrations；21cm.

22. Documents of the National Conference of the Communist Party of China, March 1955. Peking：Foreign Languages Press, 1955. 1 volume
《中国共产党全国代表大会文件集》

23. The political report of the Central Committee of the Communist Party of China to the Eighth National Congress of the party, delivered on September 15, 1956/［by］Liu Shao-chi. Peking：Foreign Languages Press, 1956. 100 pages；21cm.
《中国共产党中央委员会向第八次全国代表大会的政治报告》,刘少奇.

24. Eighth National Congress of the Communist Party of

China. Peking: Foreign Languages Press, 1956. 3 v.; 21cm.

Contents: v. 1. Documents. —v. 2. Speeches. —v. 3. Greetings from fraternal parties.

《中国共产党第八次全国代表大会文件集》,共三卷.

(1)Beijing: Foreign Languages Press, 1981. 3 volumes; 19cm.

25. Second session of the Eight National Congress of the Communist Party of China. Peking: Foreign Languages Press, 1958. 93 pages; 21cm.

《中国共产党第八届全国代表大会第二次会议文件》

26. Sixth plenary session of the Eight Central committee of the Comunist Party of China. Peking: Foreign Languages Press, 1958. 51 p.; 19cm.

《中国共产党第八届中央委员会第六次全体会议文件》

27. Eighth plenary session of the Eighth Central Committee of the Communist Party of China: documents. Peking: Foreign Languages Press, 1959. 26 pages; 19cm.

《中国共产党第八届中央委员会第八次全体会议文件》

28. Communique of the eleventh plenary session of the Eighth Central Committee of the Communist Party of China: adopted on August 12, 1966. Peking: Foreign Languages Press, 1966. 9 pages; 21cm.

《中国共产党第八届中央委员会第十一次全体会议公报》

29. Communique of the enlarged twelfth plenary session of the Eighth Central Committee of the Communist Party of China (Adopted on October 31, 1968). Peking: Foreign Languages Press, 1968. 19 pages: portraits; 13cm.

《中国共产党第八届扩大的第十二次中央委员会全会公报》

30. The Ninth National Congress of the Communist Party of China (documents). Peking: Foreign Languages Press, 1969. 175 pages: illustrations, portraits; 14cm.

《中国共产党第九次全国代表大会文件汇编》

31. Press communiques of the Secretariat of the Presidium of the Ninth National Congress of the Communist Party of China: April 1, 14 and 24, 1969; Press communique of the first plenary session of the Ninth Central Committee of the Communist Party of China: April 28, 1969. Peking: Foreign Languages Press, 1969. 45 pages: illustrations, portraits; 13cm.

《中国共产党第九次全国代表大会主席团秘书处新闻公告,中国共产党第九届中央委员会第一次全体会议新闻公告》

32. Report to the Ninth National Congress of the Communist Party of China: (delivered on April 1 and adopted on April 14, 1969)/Lin Piao. Peking: Foreign Languages Press, 1969. 105 pages; 13cm.

《在中国共产党第九次全国代表大会上的报告》,林彪.

33. China's great proletarian cultural revolution: Lin Piao's report to the Ninth National Congress of the Communist Party of China, April 1969. New York: M. Russell, 1969. 41 pages; 22cm. (Far East reporter)

《在中国共产党第九次全国代表大会上的报告》,林彪.

34. Polit Bureau statement on the Ninth National Congress of the Communist Party of China: with Lin Piao's report to the Ninth Congress, new constitution of the Communist Party of China/Communist Party of India (Marxist). Calcutta: Published by D. Chadha on behalf of the Communist Party of India (Marxist), 1969. 67 pages; 21cm.

Contents: I. Report to the Ninth Congress of the Communist Party of China (delivered on April 1 and adopted on April 14, 1969), by Lin Piao. —II. The constitution of the Communist Party of China (adopted by the Ninth National Congress of the Communist Party of China on April 14, 1969).

包括:1. 林彪所作的《在中国共产党第九次全国代表大会上的报告》2.《中国共产党章程》.

35. Communique of the second plenary session of the Ninth Central Committee of the Communist Party of China: September 6, 1970. Peking: Foreign Languages Press, 1970. 14 pages: portraits; 13cm.

《中国共产党第九届中央委员会第二次全体会议公报》

36. The Tenth National Congress of the Communist Party of China: documents. Peking: Foreign Languages Press, 1973. 98 pages, [15] leaves of plates: illustrations; 19cm.

《中国共产党第十次全国代表大会文件汇编》

37. The Eleventh National Congress of the Communist Party of China: documents. Peking: Foreign Languages Press, 1977. iii, 236 pages, [12] leaves of plates: illustrations; 19cm.

《中国共产党第十一次全国代表大会文件汇编》

38. The Twelfth National Congress of the CPC (September 1982). Beijing: Foreign Languages Press, 1982. 157 pages; 19cm. (Chinese documents)

《中国共产党在第十二次全国代表大会文献》

39. The Twelfth National Congress of the CPC: September 1982. Beijing: Foreign Languages Press, 1982. 157 p.; 19cm.

《中国共产党第十二次全国代表大会文献》,胡耀邦.

40. Uphold reform and strive for the realization of socialist modernization: documents of the CPC national conference (September 18 − 23, 1985)/Hu Yaobang. Beijing: Foreign Languages Pr., 1985. 140 p. ISBN: 0835115976. 0835115971

《坚持改革,为实现社会主义现代化而斗争:中国共产党全国代表会议文献》

41. Selected documents of the 15th CPC National Congress. Beijing: Xinxing Chubanshe, 1997. 154 p.；21cm. ISBN：7801029445, 7801029447

《中国共产党第十五次全国代表大会文献选编》，《中国共产党第十五次全国代表大会文献选编》编委会编，新星出版社.包括江泽民作的《高举邓小平理论伟大旗帜，把建设有中国特色社会主义事业全面推向二十一世纪》的报告，和《中国共产党章程修正案》.

42. Documents of the 16th National Congress of the Communist Party of China（2002）. Beijing, China：Foreign Languages Press, 2002. 246 pages，［4］pages of plates：color illustrations；23cm. ISBN：7119032267, 7119032269

《中国共产党第十六次全国代表大会文献》，钟欣编.

43. The election of delegates to th 16th National Congress of the Communist Party of China/Zhong Xin, editor. Beijing：New Star Publishers，2002. 8 pages：color illustrations；21cm. ISBN：7801485017, 7801485014

《中国共产党第十六次全国代表大会的选举》，钟欣编，新星出版社.

44. Documents of the 17th National Congress of the Communist Party of China（2007）. Beijing, China：Foreign Languages Press, 2007. 275 pages，［4］pages of plates：color illustrations, portraits；23cm. ISBN：7119051406, 7119051407

《中国共产党第十七次全国代表大会文献：英文》，外文出版社.

45. The National Congresses of the Communist Party of China/Zhong Xin, editor. Beijing：New Star Publishers，2002. 27 pages：color illustrations；21cm. ，ISBN：7801484991, 7801484994

《中国共产党历次全国代表大会简介》，钟欣编，新星出版社.

D131　政治领导人著作

朱德（1886—1976）

1. On the battlefronts of the liberated areas. Peking：Foreign Languages Press, 1952. 91 pages；19cm.

《论解放区战场》.

（1）2nd ed. Peking：Foreign Languages Press, 1955. 85 pages：portrait；19cm.

（2）［3rd ed.］. Peking：Foreign Languages Press, 1962. 79 pages：portraits；19cm.

2. Selected works of Zhu De/translated by the Bureau for the Compilation and Translation of Works of Marx, Engels, Lenin and Stalin under the Central Committee of the Communist Party of China. Beijing：Foreign Languages Press；Distributed by China International Book Trading Corp.（Guoji Shudian），1986. 450 pages：1 portraits；23cm. ISBN：0835115739, 0835115735, 0835115747,

0835115742

《朱德选集》，中央编译局译.

宋庆龄（1893—1981）

1. The struggle for new China/by Soong Ching Ling. Peking：Foreign Languages Press, 1952. 398 pages：20cm.

Notes："A collection... of the articles, speeches and statements... made between July 1927 and July 1952."

《为新中国奋斗》.

（1）Peking：Foreign Languages Press, 1953. xiv, 398 pages；19cm.

（2）Honolulu, Hawaii：University Press of the Pacific，2004. 398 pages；21cm. ISBN：1410215796, 1410215792

2. Good neighbours meet；Speeches in India, Burma and Pakistan, 1955—1956/［by］Soong Ching Ling. Peking：Foreign Languages Press, 1956. 85 pages：illustrations；19cm.

《宋庆龄在印度、缅甸、巴基斯坦演讲集》

3. A message from New China/Soong Ching Ling. Pekin：Foreign Languages Press, 1950. 16 pages；19cm.

Notes："Supplement to People's China."/ Full text of a recorded message by Soong Ching-ling（Mme. Sun Yat-sen），broadcast on Nov. 18, 1950.

中文题名未知.

（1）Pekin：Foreign Languages Press, 1952. 16 p.；18cm.

李维汉（1896—1984）

1. The struggle for proletarian leadership in the period of the new-democratic revolution in China. Peking：Foreign Languages Press, 1962. 106 pages；19cm.

《中国新民主主义革命时期争取无产阶级革命领导权的斗争》.

邓子恢（1896—1972）

1. The outstanding success of the agrarian reform movement in China/Deng Zehui. Peking：Foreign Languages Press, 1954. 20 pages；19cm.（China, a collection of pamphlets；no. 33）

《中国土地改革运动的伟大胜利》

刘少奇（1898—1969）

1. Quotations from President Liu Shao-Ch'i./With an introd. by C. P. FitzGerald. New York：Tokyo, Walker/Weatherhill, 1968. 223 pages：portraits；14cm.

《刘少奇语录》

（1）Melbourne：Paul Flesch & Co.，1968. 223 p.：portr.，talv.；14cm.

2. Collected works of Liu Shao-ch'i. Kowloon, Hong Kong，Union Research Institute, 1968—1969. 3 volumes；24cm.

Contents：［1］Before 1944.—［2］1945—1957.—［3］1958—1967.

刘少奇文选.

3. Selected works of Liu Shaoqi. Beijing: Foreign Languages Press, 1984. 2 volumes: portraits; 23cm. ISBN: 0080318037, 0080318035, 0080318029, 0080318028
《刘少奇选集》

4. Selected works of Liu Shaoqi, volume 1. Beijing: Foreign Languages Press: Distributed by China Publications Centre, 1984. 460 pages: portraits; 23cm. ISBN: 0835111806, 0835111805, 0835111814, 0835111812
《刘少奇选集》(上卷)

5. Selected works of Liu Shaoqi/[compiled by the Editorial Committee on Party Literature of the Central Committee of the Communist Party of China]. Beijing: Foreign Languages Press, 1990. 1 volumes; 21cm. ISBN: 7119012746, 7119012742
《刘少奇选集》(下卷)

6. Three essays on party-building/Liu Shaoqi. Beijing: Foreign Languages Press, 1980. ii, 300 pages, [1] leaf of plates: portraits; 19cm.
Contents: How to be a good Communist—On inner-party struggle—On the party.
收录刘少奇关于党的建设的三篇文章:《论共产党员的修养》《论党内斗争》《论党》.
(1) Beijing: Foreign Languages Press, 1982. 300 p.

7. Internationalism and nationalism/by Liu Shao-chi. Peking: Foreign Languages Press, 1949. [3], 54 p., [1] k. tabl. ; 18cm.
《论国际主义与民族主义》
(1)[2nd ed.]. Peking: Foreign Languages Press, 1951. 44 pages: illustrations; 19cm.
(2) 3rd ed. Peking: Foreign Languages Press, 1952. 44 pages: portraits; 19cm.
(3) 4th ed. Peking: Foreign Languages Press, 1954. 1 vol. (50 p.); 18cm.

8. How to be a good Communist. Peking: Foreign Languages Press, 1951. 122 pages: illustrations; 19cm.
《论共产党员的修养》
(1) 2nd rev. ed. Peking: Foreign Languages Press, 1952. 118 pages: illustrations; 19cm.
(2)[4th ed., rev.]. Peking: Foreign Languages Press, 1964. 94 pages: portraits; 20cm.
(3) 5th ed. Peking: Foreign Languages Press, 1965. 94 pages: portraits; 20cm.

9. How to be a good communist/by Liu Shao-Chi. New York: New Century Publishers, 1952. 64 pages; 20cm.
《论共产党员的修养》

10. How to be a good Communist. Calcutta: Nat. Book Agency, 1966. 99 p.
《论共产党员的修养》

11. How to be a good Communist: Lectures delivered at the Institute of Marxism-Leninism in Yenan, July 1939. Boulder, Colo. , Panther Publications, 1967. 94 pages; 19cm.
《论共产党员的修养》
(1)Boulder, Colorado, Paladin Press, 2005. 94 pages; 19cm. ISBN: 0873640799, 0873640794

12. On the party/Liu Shao-Chi. [2nd ed.]. Peking: Foreign Languages Press, 1950. 206 pages: portraits; 19cm.
《论党》
(1) 3rd ed. Peking: Foreign Languages Press, 1951. 190 pages: portraits; 19cm.
(2)[4th ed.]. Peking: Foreign Languages Press, 1952. 190 pages, [1] leaf of plates: portraits; 19cm.
(3)[5th ed.]. Peking: Foreign Languages Press, 1954. 188 pages: illustrations; 19cm.
(4)5th ed. Peking: Foreign Languages Press, 1982. 188 pages: portraits; 19cm.

13. On the party. Bombay, People's Pub. House, 1951. 114 pages; 22cm.
《论党》

14. On the party: extracts from a report to the 7th Congress of the Communist Party of China. [Brisbane]: Central Committee, Australian Communist Party, 1951. 47 pages: 1 portraits; 18cm.
《论党》(摘要):澳大利亚共产党中央委员会编.

15. On inner-party struggle: a lecture delivered on July 2, 1941 at the party school for Central China/by Liu Shao-chi. Peking: Foreign Languages Press, 1950. 92 pages, [1] leaf of plates: portraits; 19cm.
《论党内斗争》.
(1) Bombay, People's Pub. House, 1951. 92 pages; 19cm.
(2)Peking: Foreign Languages Press, 1951. 92 p.
(3)New York: New Century Publishers, 1952. 48 pages; 20cm.
(4)On inner-party struggle: a series of lectures delivered in July, 1941 at the Party School for Central China/by Liu Shao-chi. 3rd ed. Peking, China: Foreign Languages Press, 1952. 90 pages: portraits; 19cm.
(5)On inner-party struggle: a series of lectures delivered in July, 1941 at the Party School for Central China. Peking: Foreign Languages Press, 1962. 90 pages: portrait

16. Three essays on party-building/Liu Shaoqi. Beijing: Foreign Languages Press, 1980. ii, 300 pages, [1] leaf of plates: portraits; 19cm.
Contents: How to be a good Communist—On inner-party struggle—On the party.
《刘少奇同志关于党的建设的三篇著作》

17. The victory of Marxism-Leninism in China. Peking:

Foreign Languages Press，1959. 38 pages；19cm.

《马克思列宁主义在中国的胜利》

(1)Peking：Foreign Languages Press，1960. 38 pages；19cm.

18. Ten glorious years，1949—1959. Peking：Foreign Languages Press，1960. 367 p.

Notes：This edition contains 19 articles written by liu Shao-Chi.

《光辉的十年》，收录了刘少奇的19篇文章.

周恩来(1898—1976)

1. Quotations from Chou En-lai/With an introduction by C. P. Fitzgerald. Melbourne，Flesch，1969. vii，120 pages：illustrations，portraits；13cm. ISBN：0855650036，0855650032

周恩来语录.

2. Quotations from Premier Chou En-lai. New York：Crowell，1973. xiii，107 pages：illustrations；21cm. ISBN：0690664184，0690664188

周恩来语录.

3. Selected works of Zhou Enlai. Beijing：Foreign Languages Press：Distributed by Guoji Shudian，1981. 486 p.：portraits；23cm. ISBN：0080245501，0080245508，008024551X，0080245515

《周恩来选集》(上卷)

4. Selected works of Zhou Enlai. Beijing：Foreign Languages Press，1989. 556 p. ISBN：0835122522，0835122528，7119009486，7119009483，7119009494，7119009490

《周恩来选集》(下卷)

5. China's resistance，1937—1939/by Chou En-lai and others. Chung King：New China Information Committee，1940. 71 pages：portraits；18cm. (Bulletin... of the New China Information Committee；no. 12)

中国的抗日. 周恩来等.

6. Early writings of Zhou Enlai/edited by the Second Edit-Research Department of the Party Literature Research Office of the CPC Central Committee and Tianjin Nankai High School；translated by Tian Hualu. Beijing：New World Press，2015. xii，179 pages；25cm. ISBN：7510453427，7510453429，7510452161，7510452163

《周恩来青少年论说文集》，中央文献研究室第二编研部；天津南开中学合编；田华露英译.

7. On the long march as guard to Chou En-lai/by Wei Kuo-lu；[ill. by Shen Yao-yi]. Peking：Foreign Languages Press，1978. 104 pages，[5] leaves of plates (1 folded)：illustrations；19cm.

《随周恩来副主席长征》，魏国禄著；沈尧伊插图.

8. The early life of Zhou Enlai. Beijing：Foreign Languages Pr.，1980. 105 p.

《青少年时期的周恩来》，胡华著，陈小莹译.

9. We will always remember Premier Chou En-lai. Peking：

Foreign Languages Press，1977. 196 p. ：ill.

《怀念周恩来总理》，外文出版社编.

10. Zhou Enlai and the Xi'an incident：an eyewitness account：a turning point in Chinese history/Luo Ruiqing，Lü Zhengcao & Wang Bingnan. Beijing：Foreign Languages Press：Distributed by China Publications Centre (Guoji Shudian)，1983. 117，[8] pages of plates：illustrations，portraits；19cm. ISBN：0835110532，0835110532

《西安事变与周恩来同志》，罗瑞卿等著.

11. Zhou Enlai：a profile/Percy Jucheng Fang，Lucy Guinong J. Fang. Beijing：Foreign Languages Press：Distributed by China International Book Trading Corp.，1986. iii，238 pages，[1] leaf of plates：illustrations (some color)；23cm. ISBN：083511712X，0835117128

《周恩来传略》，方钜成，姜桂侬著.

陈云(1905—1995)

1. Selected works of Chen Yun，1926—1949/translated by the Bureau for the Compilation and Translation of Works of Marx，Engels，Lenin and Stalin under the Central Committee of the Communist Party of China. Beijing：Foreign Languages Press，1988. 297 pages：illustrations；23cm. ISBN：7119000667，7119000664，0835119653，0835119658，7119000675，7119000671，0835119661，0835119665

《陈云文选：1926—1949》.

2. Selected works of Chen Yun/translated by the Bureau for the Compilation and Translation of Works of Marx，Engels，Lenin and Stalin under the Central Committee of the Communist Party of China. Beijing：Foreign Languages Press，1997—1999. volumes；23cm. ISBN：7119016911（v. 2），7119016917（v. 2），7119016938（pbk. v. 2.），7119016931（pbk. v. 2.），7119017209（v. 3），7119017204（v. 3），7119007866（pbk. v. 3.），7119007861（pbk. v. 3.）

Contents：v. 2. 1949—1956—v. 3. 1956—1994

Notes：The present volume is a translation of the second Chinese edition of the Selected Works of Chen Yun... published in May 1995 by the People's Publishing House，Beijing

《陈云文选》(第二卷，第三卷).

罗瑞卿(1906—1978)

1. Commemorate the victory over German fascism! Carry the struggle against U. S. imperialism through to the end! / Luo Ruijing. Peking：Foreign Languages Press，1965. 29 pages；19cm.

《纪念战胜德国法西斯把反对美帝国主义的斗争进行到底》

2. The people defeated Japanese fascism and they can certainly defeat U. S. imperialism too：speech at the rally

of the people of all circles in Peking in celebration of the 20th anniversary of the victory of the War of Resistance against Japan/Lo Jui-Ching. Peking：Foreign Languages Press, 1965. 29 pages；19cm.

《人民战胜了日本法西斯，人民也一定能够战胜美帝国主义》

陆定一（1906—1996）

1. "Let flowers of many kinds blossom, diverse schools of thought contend!" A speech on the policy of the Communist Party of China on art, literature and science delivered on May 26,1956/[by] Lu Ting-yi. [Translation by Peng Fu-min and Yin Chia-chen]. Peking：Foreign Languages Press, 1957. 39 pages；19cm.

《百花齐放，百家争鸣》

(1) Peking：Foreign Languages Press, 1957. 39 p.；19cm.

(2) Peking：Foreign Languages Press, 1958. 36 pages；19cm.

(3) 3rd ed. Peking：Foreign Languages Press, 1964. 34 pages；19cm.

薄一波（1908—2007）

1. A memoir of some strategic policy decisions and major historical events/Bo Yibo. [Beijing]：Academy Press of the Central Committee of the Chinese Communist Party, 2007. 591 pages；28cm. ISBN：2923194738,292319473X

《若干重大决策与事件的回顾》

邓小平（1904—1997）著作与研究

1. Report on the rectification campaign, delivered at the third plenary session, enlarged, of the Eighth Central Committee of the Communist Party of China, on September 23, 1957. Peking：Foreign Languages Press, 1957. 58 pages；22cm.

Guan yu zheng feng yun dong de bao gao.

《关于整风运动的报告》

2. The great unity of the Chinese people and the great unity of the peoples of the world：written for Pravda of the Soviet Union in celebration of the tenth anniversary of the People's Republic of China/Teng Hsiao-ping. Peking：Foreign Languages Press, 1959. 16 pages；18cm.

《中国人民大团结和世界人民大团结》，邓小平.

3. Speeches and writings/Deng Xiaoping. Oxford [Oxfordshire]；New York：Pergamon, 1984. xii, 101 pages，[30] pages of plates：illustrations, portraits；26cm. ISBN：0080281656, 0080281650, 0080281664, 0080281667. (Leaders of the world)

邓小平文选.

(1) 2nd expanded ed. Oxford；New York：Pergamon Press, 1987. x, 114 pages，[36] pages of plates：illustrations (some color)；26cm. ISBN：0080348726, 0080348728

4. Selected works of Deng Xiaoping/translated by the Bureau for the Compilation and Translation of Works of Marx, Engels, Lenin, and Stalin under the Central Committee of the Communist Party of China. Beijing：Foreign Languages Press, 1984—1994. 3 volumes：portraits；22cm. ISBN：0835128865（v. 1, pbk.），780835128865（v. 1, pbk.），7119014579（v. 1, pbk.），7119014579（v. 1, pbk.），0835113051（v. 2, pbk.），0835113052（v. 2, pbk.），7119016903（v. 3, pbk.），7119016900（v. 3, pbk.），0835128857；0835128858；0835113027；0835113021；711901689X；7119016894

Contents：[v. 1.] 1938—1965—[v. 2.] 1975—1982—v. 3. 1982—1992.

《邓小平文选》，中共中央马克思恩格斯列宁斯大林著作编译局译.

(1) 2nd ed. Beijing：Foreign Languages Press, 1995—. 3 volumes：portraits；22cm. ISBN：7119014560, 7119014562, 7119014579, 7119014579, 7119001671, 7119001678, 7119006428, 7119006420, 7119016903, 7119016900

5. Selected works of Deng Xiaoping, 1938—1965/translated by the Bureau for the Compilation and Translation of Works of Marx, Engels, Lenin, and Stalin under the Central Committee of the Communist Party of China. Beijing：Foreign Languages Press, 1992. 342 pages；22cm. ISBN：7119014560, 7119014562, 7119014579, 7119014579, 0835128857, 0835128858, 0835128865, 0835128865

《邓小平文选：1938—1965》（第一卷），中共中央马克思恩格斯列宁斯大林著作编译局.

(1) 2nd. ed. Beijing：Foreign Languages Press, 1995. 373 p. ISBN：7119014560,7119014562,7119014579

6. Selected works of Deng Xiaoping, 1975—1982/translated by the Bureau for the Compilation and Translation of Works of Marx, Engels, Lening and Stalin under the Central Committee of the Communist Party of China. Beijing：Foreign Languages Press, 1984. 418 pages；22cm. ISBN：0835113051, 0835113052, 0835113027, 0835113021

《邓小平文选：1975—1982》（第二卷），中共中央马克思恩格斯列宁斯大林著作编译局.

(1) 2nd ed. Beijing：Foreign Languages Press, 1995. 434 pages；22cm. ISBN：7119001671, 7119001678, 7119006428, 7119006420, 7119016900, 7119016903

7. Selected works of Deng Xiaoping. Volume III, 1982—1992/translated by the Bureau for the Compilation and Translation of Works of Marx, Engels, Lenin and Stalin under the Central Committee of the Communist Party of China. Beijing：Foreign Languages Press, 1994. 400 pages；23cm. ISBN：7119016903, 7119016900,

711901689X，7119016894

《邓小平文选：1982—1992》（第三卷），中共中央马克思恩格斯列宁斯大林著作编译局.

8. Build socialism with Chinese characteristics/Deng Xiaoping；translated by the Bureau for the Compilation and Translation of Works of Marx, Engels, Lenin and Stalin Under the Central Committee of the Communist Party of China. Beijing：Foreign Languages Press, 1985. 73 pages；19cm. ISBN：0835115534, 0835115537

《建设有中国特色的社会主义》

9. Fundamental issues in present-day China/Deng Xiaoping；translated by the Bureau for the Compilation and Translation of Works of Marx, Engels, Lenin and Stalin under the Central Committee of the Communist Party. Beijing：Foreign Languages Press；Oxford；New York：Pergamon Press, 1987. 202 pages，[12] pages of plates：illustrations (some color)；20cm. ISBN：0080363636, 0080363639, 0835121062, 0835121064, 0835121038, 0835121033, 7119003445, 7119003443, 7119003453, 7119003450

《论当代中国基本问题》，中共中央马克思恩格斯列宁斯大林著作编译局译.

10. Deng Xiaoping on the question of Hong Kong/translated by the Bureau for the Compilation and Translation of Works of Marx, Engels, Lenin and Stalin under the Central Committee of the Communist Party of China. Beijing：Foreign Languages Press, 1993. 76 pages；23cm. ISBN：7119017241, 7119017242

《邓小平论香港问题》

(1) Hong Kong：New Horizon Press, 1993. 76 pages；22cm. ISBN：9627176273, 9627176275

11. Quotations from Deng Xiaoping/edited by Kui-Hung Nam；translated by Andy Ho On-tat［and others］. Hong Kong：Sub Culture Ltd.，, 1997. 136 pages：portraits；17cm. ISBN：96274200272

《邓小平语录》

(1) Deconstructing quotations from Deng Xiaoping/edited by Kui-Hung Nam；translated by Andy Ho On-tat. Hong Kong：Sub Culture Ltd.，1999. ［20］, 150 pages：illustrations, portraits；17cm. ISBN：96274200740

12. On reform/Deng Xiaoping. New York：CN Times Books, 2013. viii, 272 pages；24cm. ISBN：1627740098, 1627740090

论改革.

13. On Deng Xiaoping thought/Wu Jie. Beijing：Foreign Languages Press, 1996. 292 pages；21cm. ISBN：711901868X,7119018683

《邓小平思想论》，乌杰著.

14. Outline programme for studying comrade Deng

Xiaoping's theory of building socialism with Chinese characteristics. Beijing：Contemporary World Pub.，1997. 138 pages；21cm. ISBN：780115083X, 7801150837

《邓小平同志建设有中国特色社会主义理论学习纲要》，中共中央宣传部编；王毓琳等译. 当代世界出版社.

15. Deng Xiaoping and the cultural revolution：a daughter recalls the critical years/by Deng Rong；translated by Sidney Shapiro. Beijing：Foreign Languages Press, 2002. vii, 481 pages：illustrations；24cm. ISBN：711903040X, 7119030401

《邓小平文革岁月》，邓榕著.

16. My father Deng Xiaoping：the war years/Deng Rong. Beijing：Foreign Languages Press, 2008. 540 pages：illustrations；25cm. ISBN：7119044088, 7119044087

《我的父亲邓小平：战争年代》，邓榕著.

胡耀邦（1915—1989）

1. The radiance of the great truth of Marxism lights our way forward：report at the meeting in commemoration of the death of Karl Marx, March 13，1983/Hu Yaobang. Beijing：Foreign Languages Press：Distributed by China Publications Centre (Guoji Shudian), 1983. 47 pages；18cm. ISBN：0835111520, 0835111522

《马克思主义伟大真理的光芒照耀我们前进》

江泽民（1926—）

1. Jiang Zemin on the "Three represents"/Jiang Zemin. Beijing：Foreign Languages Press, 2002. 217. pages；23cm. ISBN：7119029185, 7119029184

《论"三个代表"》.

2. Research on energy issues in China/Jiang Zemin；translated by the Central Translation Bureau, Beijing；translators, Jia Yuling［and others］. Amsterdam；Boston：Elsevier/Academic Press, 2010. vi, 94 pages：illustrations；24cm. ISBN：0123786197, 0123786193

《中国能源问题研究》

3. On the development of China's information technology industry/Jiang Zemin. Amsterdam；Boston：Elsevier/Academic Press, 2010. xx, 316 pages：illustrations；24cm. ISBN：0123813695 0123813697

《论中国信息技术产业发展》

4. Selected works of Jiang Zemin/translated by the Bureau for the Compilation and Translation of Works of Marx, Engels, Lenin and Stalin under the Central Committee of the Communist Party of China. Beijing：Foreign Languages Press, 2010—2013. 3 volumes：1 plate；23cm. ISBN：7119060248, 7119060244, 7119073842, 7119073842, 7119079851, 7119079859, 7119060255, 7119060252

《江泽民文选》

朱镕基(1928—)

1. Zhu Rongji on the record/Zhu Rongji；translated by June Y. Mei；forewords by Henry A. Kissinger, Helmut Schmidt. Washington, D. C.：Brookings Institution Press,2013—2015. 2 volumes：illustrations；24cm. ISBN：0815725190, 0815725191, 0815725183, 0815725183, 0815725374,081572537X

   Contents：v. 1. The road to reform, 1991—1997—v. 2. The road to reform, 1998—2003.

   《朱镕基讲话实录》,(美)梅缵月(Mei，June Y.)译.

2. Zhu Rongji meets the press/Zhu Rongji；[translated by Lin Qiufeng]. Hong Kong：Oxford University Press, 2011. xvi, 474 pages；[16] pages of plates：illustrations (some color)；25cm. ISBN：0193966417, 0193966413

   《朱镕基答记者问》

   (1)Beijing：People's Publishing House, 2011. XVII, 474 p.；25cm. ISBN：7010103358, 7010103356

3. China and Asia in the new century/Zhu Rongji. Singapore：Institute of Southeast Asian Studies, 2000. 54 pages；25cm. ISBN：9812300902, 9812300904.

   (Singapore lecture)

   《迈向新世纪的中国与亚洲》.英汉对照.

胡锦涛(1942—)

1. Selected works of Hu Jintao：2001 - 2012/Hu Jintao；Luc Guo, general ed. [Lexington，KY]：Intercultural Publ. , 2012. VIII,169 p. ：Ill. ISBN：1475192789, 7801475192. (CCP leaders series)

   胡锦涛文选:2001—2012 年.

温家宝(1942—)

1. Meeting the challenges：a historical record of China's development/speeches by Wen Jiabao at World Economic Forum events. Hong Kong：Chinese University Press, 2014. xiv, 274 pages：illustrations；24cm. ISBN：9629966360, 9629966362

   《应对挑战》

2. Wen Jiabao on education. Singapore：Cengage Learning Asia Pte Ltd, 2015. xii, 562 pages：illustrations；25cm. ISBN：9814698061, 9814698067

   Notes："This book touches on various topics such as basic education, higher education, teachers' education and vocational education, and covers Wen Jiabao's representative thoughts on education from September 1995 to March 2013."—Page [4] of cover.

   温家宝论教育.

习近平(1953—)

1. The governance of China/Xi Jinping. Beijing：Foreign Languages Press, 2014. vi, 515 pages, 45 unnumbered pages of plates：illustrations (some color), portraits；24cm. ISBN：7119090232, 7119090238, 7119090573, 7119090577

《习近平谈治国理政》

2. The Chinese dream of the great rejuvenation of the Chinese nation/Xi Jinping；compiled by the Party Literature Research Office of the Central Committee of the Communist Party of China. Beijing：Foreign Languages Press, 2014. 99 pages；23cm. ISBN：7119086965, 7119086960

   《中华民族伟大复兴的中国梦》

3. How to deepen reform comprehensively/Xi Jinping；Chinese edition compiled by the Party Literature Research Office of the Central Committee of the Communist Party of China；translated by the Compilation and Translation Bureau of the Central Committee of the Communist Party of China. Beijing：Foreign Languages Press, 2014. 217 pages；23cm. ISBN：7119090887, 7119090887

   《全面深化改革》,习近平；中共中央文献研究室,中央编译局.

4. Forging a strong partnership to enhance prosperity of Asia/Xi Jinping. Singapore：ISEAS Yusof Ishak Institute, 2015. 35 pages；23cm. ISBN：9814695688, 9814695688. (Singapore lecture, ；36th)

   《深化合作伙伴关系共建亚洲美好家园》

5. Xi Jinping selected speeches to the United Nations：September 26-28, 2015. Beijing：Wai wen chu ban she, 2015. 28 pages；23cm. ISBN：7119097312, 7119097318

   《习近平 2015 年联合国讲话选编》

6. Building good conduct and political integrity and fighting corruption/Xi Jinping；compiled by the Central Commission for Discipline Inspection of the Communist Party of China, the Party Literature Research Office of the Central Committee of the Communist Party of China；translated by The Compilation and Translation Bureau of the Central Committee of the Communist Party of China. Beijing：Central Compilation & Translation Press, 2016. 192 pages；23cm. ISBN：7511732200, 7511732208

   《习近平关于党风廉政建设和反腐败斗争论述摘编》,习近平；中共中央纪律检查委员会,中共中央文献研究室,中央编译局.

7. Up and out of poverty：selected speeches in Fujian/by Xi Jinping. Beijing：Foreign Languages Press, 2016. 223 pages. ISBN：7119105567, 7119105566, 7119105550, 7119105558.

   《摆脱贫困》

8. 决胜全面建成小康社会,夺取新时代中国特色社会主义伟大胜利:英文/习近平著. 北京:外文出版社,2018. 87 页;23cm. ISBN:7119111964

D14　政策、政论

1. On the historical experience of the dictatorship of the proletariat. Peking：Foreign Languages Press, 1956. 20 pages；22cm.

Notes："... Written by the editorial department of the People's Daily on the basis of the discussion which took place at an enlarged meeting of the Political Bureau of the Central Committee of the Communist Party of China..."
《关于无产阶级专政的历史经验》,《人民日版》社论部.

2. More on the historical experience of the dictatorship of the proletariat：Prepared on the basis of a discussion at an enlarged meeting of the Political Bureau of the Central Committee of the Communist Party of China and was published in the People's Daily on December 29，1956. Hsiao Ping. Peking：Foreign Languages Press，1957. 43 pages
《再论无产阶级专政的历史经验》,人民日报编辑部编.

3. The historical experience of the dictatorship of the proletariat. Peking：Foreign Languages Press，1959. 64 p.；19cm.
Contents：On the historical experience of the dictatorship of the proletariat—More on the historical experience of the dictatorship of the proletariat.
《无产阶级专政的历史经验》,《人民日报》编辑部. 包括"论无产阶级"和"再论无产阶级专政"两篇文章.
(1)Peking：Foreign Languages Press，1964
(2) New York：AMS Press，[1979]. 64 p.；18cm. ISBN：0404144802

4. March ahead under the red flag of the party's general line and Mao Tse-tung's military thinking/Lin Piao. Peking：Foreign Languages Press，1959. 26 pages；19cm.
《高举党的总路线和毛泽东军事思想的红旗阔步前进》,林彪.
(1)Peking：Foreign Languages Press，1960. 26 pages；19cm.
(2)Hold high the red flag：the party's general line and Mao Tse-Tung's military thinking and march forward in mighty strides/Lin Piao. 2nd ed.；rev. translation. Peking：Foreign Languages Press，1961. 27 pages；19cm.

5. Raise high the red flag of the general line and continue to march forward/Li Fu-chun. Peking：Foreign Languages Press，1960. 40 pages；19cm.
《高举总路线的红旗继续前进》,李富春.

6. Advance along the road opened up by the October Socialist Revolution；in commemoration of the 50th anniversary of the great October Socialist revolution. Peking：Foreign Languages Press，1967. 27 pages；19cm.
《沿着十月社会主义革命开辟的道路前进:纪念伟大的十月社会主义革命五十周年》

7. Compass for the victory of the revolutionary people of all countries. Peking：Foreign Languages Press，1968. 12 pages，[2] leaves of plates (1 folded)：illustration，portraits；13cm.
《各国革命人民胜利的航向》

8. On the proletarian revolutionaries' struggle to seize power. Peking：Foreign Languages Press，1968. 31 pages；21cm.
《论无产阶级革命派的夺权斗争》

9. Forward along the high road of Mao Tse-tung's thought：in celebration of the 17th anniversary of the founding of the People's Republic of China. Peking：Foreign Languages Press，1967. 31 pages；portraits；21cm.
《在毛泽东思想的大道上奋勇前进:庆祝中华人民共和国成立十七周年》

10. Fight for the further consolidation of the dictatorship of the proletariat：in celebration of the 20th anniversary of the founding of the People's Republic of China. Peking：Foreign Languages Press，1969. 41 pages：illustrations；13cm.
《为进一步巩固无产阶级专政而斗争:庆祝中华人民共和国成立二十周年》

11. Continue the revolution，advance from victory to victory：In celebration of the 21st anniversary of the founding of the People's Republic of China. Peking：Foreign Languages Press，1970. 17 pages：illustrations；19cm.
《继续革命乘胜前进:庆祝中华人民共和国成立二十一周年》
(1) Hong Kong：Joint Pub. Co.，1970. 30 pages；13cm.

12. Advance victoriously along Chairman Mao's revolutionary line：1971 New Year's Day editorial/by Renmin Ribao, Hongqi, and Jiefangjun Bao. Peking：Foreign Languages Press，1971. 1 vol. (19 p.)；13cm.
《沿着毛主席革命路线胜利前进:〈人民日报〉、〈红旗〉杂志、〈解放军报〉一九七一年元旦社论》

13. Unite to win still greater victories：1972 New Year's Day editorial by Renmin Ribao（People's daily），Hongqi（Red flag），and Jiefangjun Bao（Liberation army daily）. Peking：Foreign Languages Press，1972. 13 pages；19cm.
《团结起来,争取更大的胜利:〈人民日报〉、〈红旗〉杂志、〈解放军报〉一九七二年元旦社论》

14. Strive for new victories：In celebration of the 23rd anniversary of the founding of the People's Republic of China（October 1，1972）/editorial by Renmin Ribao [and others]. Peking：Foreign Languages Press，1972. 11 pages；19cm.
《夺取新的胜利:庆祝中华人民共和国成立二十三周年》

15. Speech at the meeting in celebration of the 30th anniversary of the founding of the Peoples's Republic of China，September 29，1979/Ye Jianying. Beijing：Foreign Languages Press，1979. 76 pages；19cm.
《在庆祝中华人民共和国成立三十周年大会上的讲话》,叶剑英.

16. Speech at the meeting in celebration of the 40th

anniversary of the founding of the Peoples Republic of China/Jiang Zemin；comp. by Beijing Review. Beijing：New Star Publishers，1989. 33 p.

《在庆祝中华人民共和国成立四十周年大会上的讲话》，江泽民.

D15　建设成就

1. The first year of people's China. Bombay，People's Pub. House，1950. 39 pages

   《新中国的第一年》，周恩来.

2. A great decade/Chou En-lai. Peking：Foreign Languages Press，1959. 37 pages；19cm.

   《伟大的十年》，周恩来.

3. Socialist industrialization and agricultural collectivization in China. Peking：Foreign Languages Press，1964. 50 pages；19cm.

   《中国的社会主义工业化和农业集体化》，薄一波，廖鲁言著.

   (1)2nd ed. Peking：Foreign Languages Press，1965. 50 pages；19cm.

4. New China's first quarter-century. Peking：Foreign Languages Press，1975. 209 pages，[22] leaves of plates：illustrations (some color)；19cm.

   Contents：Forward along the great road of socialism. —A stable socialist economy. —Tapping mineral resources in a big way. —Producing machinery self-reliantly. —Why China builds small industrial enterprises. —Peking from consumer city to industrial centre. —Transformation and expansion of Shanghai's industry. —How China achieves self-sufficiency in grain. —Why China has no inflation. —Revolution in education. —New medical system. —Minority nationalities now and before. —Women in socialist new China. —Changes at the Anshan Iron and Steel Company. —Battle in the Taching new oil zone. —Trunk railway line in China's southwest. —A railway in rugged mountains. —A successful voyage. —How the Chinese people control their rivers. —A new dam across the Yellow River. —The Tachai road. —Three former grain-deficient provinces show surpluses. —Development in science and technology. —The "barefoot doctor" system grows in strength.

   《新的二十五年》

5. China's socialist modernization/edited by Yu Guangyuan. Beijing，China：Foreign Languages Press：Distributed by China Publications Centre，1984. 775 pages；21cm. ISBN：0835110117，0835110112

   《中国社会主义现代化建设》，于光远主编.

6. China emerging，1978—2008：how thinking about business changed/Wu Xiaobo；translated by Martha Avery. Beijing：China Intercontinental Press，2008. 195 pages：illustrations；24cm. ISBN：7508513638，7508513630

   《中国巨变：1978—2008》，吴晓波著. 五洲传播出版社. 全面回顾中国改革开放 30 年的发展历程，特别是经济持续高度发展带来的巨大社会变革.

7. China in diagrams 1978—2008/[edited by] Jin Quan. Beijing：China Intercontinental Press，2009. [12]，180 pages：color illustrations；24cm. ISBN：7508513829，7508513827

   《图说中国改革开放 30 年：1978—2008》，吴伟主编. 五洲传播出版社.

8. Looking back at 2009：a survey on the economic and social development in the regions inhabited by ethnic minority groups of China/by Qian Jiang. Beijing：China Intercontinental Pr.，2010. 72 pages：color illustrations；21cm. ISBN：7508518039，7508518039

   《回眸 2009：中国民族地区经济社会发展概况：英文版》，钱江编著. 五洲传播出版社.

D16　政府组织

1. Structure of the state/edited and published by Foreign Languages Press. Beijing：Foreign Languages Press，1987. 29 pages：illustrations (some color)；18cm. (China—facts & figures)

   《国家机构》，外文出版社编.

2. The Chinese People's Political Consultative Conference/by the General Affairs Office of the CPPCC National Committee. Beijing：Foreign Languages Press，2004. vi，186 pages；24cm. ISBN：7119033387，7119033389

   《中国全国政协》，中国全国政协办公厅编.

3. 中国政府机构名录：2004—2005 版：汉英对照/新华社《中国政府机构名录》编辑部编. 北京：中央文献出版社，2005. 6 册；29cm. ISBN：7507318737，7507318739

   英文题名：Directory of government organizations of the People's Republic of China. 本书收集了国务院、各部委、国务院直属机构(包括事业单位)及办事机构、部委所属司局以及司局所属的处(室)；国务院直属部分全国性公司、人民团体和事业单位等机构的名称、地址等情况及其主要职能.

D161　选举

1. Grassroots election in China/by Zhang Chunxia；[translated by Li Yang]. Beijing：New World Press，2008. 99 pages：color illustrations；19cm. ISBN：7802285033，7802285038. (Stories from China)

   《中国的基层选举》，张春侠编著. 新世界出版社.

D162　人权

1. China and human rights/compiled by Beijing Review. English ed. Beijing，China：New Star Publishers，1991. 67 pages；19cm. ISBN：7800852377，7800852374. (China，issues and ideas；3)

   《中国与人权》，北京周报社编. 新星出版社.

2. Fifty years of progress in China's human rights/Information Office of the State Council of the People's Republic of China. Beijing：New Star Publishers：Distributed by China International Book Trading Corp.，2000. 43 pages；19cm. ISBN：7801482689, 7801482686
《中国人权发展五十年》,中华人民共和国国务院新闻办公室发布.新星出版社.

3. 中国人权保障制度研究/孙平华著.北京：中国对外翻译出版公司，2011. 258 页；27cm. ISBN：7500132660, 7500132662.（中译法律文库,中国学人（英文）法学论著丛书）

4. In the shadow of the rising dragon：stories of repression in the new China/edited by Xu Youyu, Hua Ze；translated by Stacy Mosher. New York City：Palgrave Macmillan，2013. xx，236 pages；24cm. ISBN：1137278791,113727879X
《遭遇警察》,徐友渔,华泽合编.

5. Comparison of human rights in China with those in the United States. Beijing：China Intercontinental Press，1996. 44 pages；21cm. ISBN：7801131304, 7801131300 Contents：Comparison of human rights in China with those in the United States/R. Yanshi—Differing status of Chinese and American women/Y. Dong—Plight of US children/R. Yanshi.
《中美两国人权比较》,任言实等著.五洲传播出版社.

D163　全国人民代表大会

1. The electoral law for the All-China People's Congress and local People's Congresses of all levels, with an explanation/[by Teng Hsiao-ping]. Peking：Foreign Languages Press, 1953. 48 pages
《中华人民共和国全国人民代表大会和地方各级人民代表大会选举法》

2. Report on the work of the government, made at the first session of the First National People's Congress of the People's Republic of China, September 23，1954. Peking：Foreign Languages Press, 1954. 55 pages：illustrations；21cm.
《政府工作报告：1954 年 9 月 23 日在第一届全国人民代表大会第一次会议上》,周恩来.

3. Documents of the first session of the First National People's Congress of the People's Republic of China. Peking：Foreign Languages Press, 1955. 231 p.；22cm.
《中华人民共和国第一届全国人民代表大会第一次会议文件集》

4. New China advances to socialism：a selection of speeches delivered at the third session of the First National People's Congress. Peking：Foreign Languages Press,1956.199 p.
《新中国向社会主义跃进：第一次全国人民代表大会第三次会议发言选编》

5. Proposals of the Eighth National Congress of the Communist Party of China for the second five-year plan for development of national economy，1958—1962：Report on the proposals for the second five-year plan of development of the national economy/Chou En-lai. Peking：Foreign Languages Press，1956. 104 pages；20cm.
《中国共产党第八次全国代表大会关于发展国民经济的第二个五年计划(1958—1962)的建议·关于发展国民经济的第二个五年计划的建议的报告》,周恩来.
（1）Peking：Foreign Languages Press, 1969. 104 p；21cm.

6. Report on the work of the government：delivered at the first session of the Second National People's Congress on April 18, 1959/Chou En-lai. Peking：Foreign Languages Press, 1959. 71 pages；19cm.
《政府工作报告：1959 年 4 月 18 日在第二届全国人民代表大会第一次会议上》,周恩来.

7. National People's Congress of the People's Republic of China second session of Second National People's Congress of the People's Republic of China. (Documents). Beijing：Foreign Languages Pr.，1960. 188 p.
《中华人民共和国第二届全国人民代表大会第二次会议文件》.另一题名：Second session of the Second National People's Congress of the People's Republic of China (documents). Peking：Foreign Languages Press，1960. 187 pages；21cm.

8. Main documents of the first session of the Third National People's Congress of the People's Republic of China. Peking：Foreign Languages Press, 1965. 92 pages；19cm.
《中华人民共和国第三次全国人民代表大会第一次会议主要文件》

9. Documents of the first session of the Fourth National People's Congress of the People's Republic of China. Peking：Foreign Languages Press, 1975. 88 pages，[2] leaves of plates：illustrations；19cm.
《中华人民共和国第四届全国人民代表大会第一次会议文件》

10. Report on the work of the government：delivered on January 13，1975 at the first session of the Fourth National People's Congress of the People's Republic of China/Chou En-lai. Peking：Foreign Languages Press, 1975. 34 pages；21cm.
《中华人民共和国第四届全国人民代表大会第一次会议文件》

11. Documents of the first session of the Fifth National People's Congress of the People's Republic of China. Beijing：Foreign Languages Press, 1978. 2]，237 pages，[6] leaves of plates：illustrations；19cm.
《中华人民共和国第五届全国人民代表大会第一次会议文件》

12. First session of the Fifth National People's Congress. Beijing：Foreign Languages Press，1982. 214 p. (Chinese documents)

《中华人民共和国第五届全国人民代表大会第一次会议文件》，彭真，王炳乾，赵紫阳.

13. Main documents of the second session of the Fifth National People's Congress of the People's Republic of China. Beijing：Foreign Languages Press，1979. 249 pages；19cm.

《中华人民共和国第五届全国人民代表大会第二次会议主要文件》

14. Main documents of the third session of the fifth National People's Congress of the People's Republic of China. Beijing：Foreign Languages Press：Distributed by Guoji Shudian，1980. 245 pages；19cm.

《中华人民共和国第五届全国人民代表大会第三次会议主要文件》

15. Fifth session of the Fifth National People's Congress (main documents). Beijing：Foreign Languages Press：Distributed by China Publications Centre，1983. 214 pages；19cm.

《中华人民共和国第五届全国人民代表大会第五次会议主要文件》

16. The first session of the Sixth National People's Congress (Main documents). Beijing：Foreign Languages Press，1983. 146 p. ISBN：0835111849, 0835111843

《中华人民共和国第六届全国人民代表大会第一次会议主要文件》

17. The second session of the Sixth National People's Congress. Beijing：Foreign Languages Press，1984. 102 p. ISBN：0835113590, 0835113595

《中华人民共和国第六届全国人民代表大会第二次会议主要文件》

18. The third session of the Sixth National People's Congress (Main documents). Beijing：Foreign Languages Press，1985. 125 p. ISBN：0835115682,0835115681. (Chinese documents)

《中华人民共和国第六届全国人民代表大会第三次会议主要文件》，赵紫阳，宋平，王炳乾.

19. The fourth session of the sixth National People's Congress (Main documents). Beijing：Foreign Languages Press，1986. 197 p. ISBN：0835118541,0835118545

《中华人民共和国第六届全国人民代表大会第四次会议主要文件》，赵紫阳，宋平，王炳乾.

20. The fifth session of the Sixth National People's Congress (main documents). Beijing，China：Foreign Languages Press：Distributed by China International Trading Corp. (Guoji Shudian)，1987. 104 pages；19cm. （Chinese documents）

《中华人民共和国第六届全国人民代表大会第五次会议主要文件》

21. The first session of the Seventh National People's Congress of the People's Republic of China：(March 25-April 13，1988). Beijing：Foreign Languages Press，1988. 187 pages：illustrations (some color)；21cm. ISBN：0835122417,0835122412,0835122425,0835122429

《中华人民共和国第七届全国人民代表大会第一次会议主要文献》

22. The second session of the Seventh National People's Congress of the People's Republic of China：March 20-April 4，1989. Beijing：Foreign Languages Press，1989. 112 p.：couv. ill. ；21cm. ISBN：0835122719,0835122719, 7119010840,7119010847

《中华人民共和国第七届全国人民代表大会第二次会议主要文献》

23. The third session of the Seventh National People's Congress of the People's Republic of China：(March 20-April 4，1990). Beijing：Foreign Languages Press，1990. 188 pages；21cm. ISBN：0835124622, 0835124621, 0835124614, 0835124614, 7119013270, 7119013275, 7119013289,7119013282. (Chinese documents)

《中华人民共和国第七次全国人民代表大会第三次会议主要文献》

24. 1st session of the 9th NCP of China：main documents. Beijing，China：Foreign Languages Press：Distributed by China International Book Trading Corp. ，1998. 128 pages：color illustrations，color portraits；20cm. ISBN：7119021931, 7119021935

《中华人民共和国第九届全国人名代表大会第一次会议主要文件》

D164 中国人民政治协商会议

1. The important documents of the first plenary session of the Chinese People's Political Consultative Conference. Peking：Foreign Languages Press，1949. 44 p. ；19cm.

《中国人民政治协商会议第一届全体会议重要文件》

2. The common program and other documents of the first plenary session of the Chinese People's Political Consultative Conference. Peking：Foreign Languages Press，1950. 44 pages；19cm.

Contents：The common program of the Chinese People's Political Consultative Conference. —The organic law of the Chinese People's Consultative Conference. —The organic law of the Central People's Government of the People's Republic of China. —The declaration of the first plenary session of the Chinese People's Political Consultative Conference

中国人民政治协商会议第一届全体会议共同纲领和其他文件,包括《中国人民政治协商会议共同纲领》《中国人民政治协商会议组织法》《中华人民共和国中央人民政府组织法》和《中国人民政治协商会议第一届全体会议宣言》

3. New China forges ahead：important documents of the

third session of the First National Committee of the Chinese People's Political Consultative Conference. Peking：Foreign Languages Press, 1952. 78 p. ，[5] leaves of plates：port. ；21cm.

《新中国向前迈进：中国人民政治协商会议第一届会议第三次会议文件》，毛泽东，周恩来等著.

4. Political report；delivered at the second session of the Second National Committee of the Chinese People's Political Consultative Conference on January 30，1956. Peking：Foreign Languages Press, 1956. 47 pages；21cm.

《政治报告(1956年1月30日，在中国人民政治协商会议第二届全国委员会第二次全体会议上)》，周恩来.

D165　其他全国性会议

1. The National Conference of Outstanding Groups and Individuals in Socialist Construction in Industry, Communications and Transport, Capital Construction, Finance and Trade. Peking：Foreign Languages Press, 1960. [10], 144 p. ，[2] la'ms. dobles；18cm.

《全国社会主义建设先进集体和先进生产者代表大会》

2. The National Conference of Outstanding Groups and Individuals in Socialist Construction in Education, Culture, Health, Physical Culture, and Journalism：Important documents. Peking：Foreign Languages Press, 1960. 45 p. ；ill.

《全国教育和文化、卫生、体育、新闻方面社会主义建设先进单位和先进工作者代表大会重要文件》

3. Revolutionize our youth!：report on the work of the Chinese Communist League, delivered at its 9th congress, June 11, 1964/Hu Yao-pang. Peking：Foreign Languages Press, 1964. 51 p. ；19cm.

《为我国青年革命化而斗争：1964年6月11日在中国共产主义青年团第九次全国代表大会上的工作报告》，胡耀邦.

D17　国家行政管理

D171　反腐败与廉政建设

1. China's efforts to combat corruption and build a clean government/Information Office of the State Council, the People's Republic of China. Beijing：Foreign Languages Press, 2010. 44 pages；21cm. ISBN：7119068244；7119068245, 7119068244

《中国的反腐败和廉政政策》，中华人民共和国国务院新闻办公室[发布].

2. China's efforts to combat corruption and build a clean government/Information Office of the State Council, the People's Repulic of China. Beijing：Foreign Languages Press, 2011. 42 p. ；26cm. ISBN：7119068237, 7119068237

《中国的反腐败和廉政政策》，中华人民共和国国务院新闻办公室发布.

D172　慈善与公益活动

1. Philanthropy in China/Wang Gaoli；translated by Li Huailin. Beijing：China intercontinental Press, 2006. 127 pages：color illustrations；21cm. ISBN：7508509334, 7508509331. (Fashion China＝时尚中国)

《公益在行动：英文》，王高利著：李怀林译. 五洲传播出版社. 本书反映当代中国人对公益事业的日益关注与投入，如志愿者行动、慈善事业等.

2. 历史的铭刻：中国慈善飞跃印度洋：中英文对照/李玉林著：赵颖译. 北京：中国社会出版社, 2007. 303页：彩照；24cm. ISBN：7508716237, 750871623X

英文题名：The historical memories：China charity goes across the Indian Ocean

3. Volunteer campaigns in China/compiled by Zhang Chunxia；translated by He Xuewen；edited by Li Shujuan. Beijing, China：New World Press, 2009. 147 pages：color illustrations；19cm. ISBN：7802289949, 7802289947. (Stories of China)

《志愿者在行动》，张春侠著. 新世界出版社. 介绍了中国志愿者事业的兴起和发展.

D173　抗震救灾与危机管理

1. An ode to life：China's earthquake relief in 2008/edited by Xinhua News Agency. Beijing：Xinhua Pub. House, 2008. 269 pages：chiefly color illustrations；37cm. ISBN：7501184644, 750118464X

《生命壮歌》，新华通讯社编. 新华出版社. 本书全面记录汶川抗震救灾的历史进程.

2. Public crisis management in China/chief editors, Chen Fujin and Tang Tiehan. Beijing：Foreign Languages Press, 2008. 179 pages：illustrations；22cm. ISBN：7119049465, 7119049461. (Focus on China series)

《中国的公共危机管理》，陈福今，唐铁汉主编.

3. The national mourning：the first official mourning period in China to commemorate ordinary citizens/compiled by China Foundation for Human Rights Development；advisor：Yang Zhengquan；chief compiler：Lin Bocheng；executive chief compiler：Xia Xianhu. Beijing：China Translation & Publishing Corporation, 2008. 132 pages：illustrations；23cm. ISBN：7500119531, 7500119534

《哀悼日》，中国人权发展基金会编. 中国对外翻译出版公司. 抗震救灾.

4. China's actions for disaster prevention and reduction/Information Office of the State Council of the People's Republic of China. Beijing：Foreign Languages Press, 2009. 41 pages；21cm. ISBN：7119057002, 7119057006

《中国的减灾行动》，中华人民共和国国务院新闻办公室[发布].

5. 中国的减灾行动/中华人民共和国国务院新闻办公室[发布]. 北京：外文出版社, 2009. 36页；26cm. ISBN：7119056999

6. After the Tangshan earthquake: how the Chinese people overcame a major natural disaster. Peking: Foreign Languages Press, 1976. 79 p., [28] p. pl.: ill.; 19cm.

《一场大地震之后:中国人民战胜自然灾害的事迹》

D174 脱贫

1. 搬离贫困:英文/林良旗著;丁志涛译. 北京:外文出版社,2006. 109 页:照片;19cm. ISBN:7119044613, 7119044613. (国情故事)

英文题名:Rising out of poverty. 介绍了宁夏回族自治区移民扶贫计划,以及移民在搬迁地逐渐富裕起来的新生活.

2. International aid projects for poverty alleviation in China/Shen Honglei and Lei Xiangqing. Beijing: Foreign Languages Press, 2007. 89 pages: color illustrations; 21cm. ISBN: 7119046389, 7119046381. (China in peaceful development)

《国际扶贫援助项目在中国:英文》,申宏磊,雷向晴著. 介绍了中国的国际扶贫救援项目开展的具体情况,以及取得的成效.

3. The legend of a man and a poor village's road to riches/by Xiao Feng; [translated by Xie Shengzhe]. Beijing: New World Press, 2008. 81 pages: illustrations; 19cm. ISBN: 7802285736, 7802285739. (Stories of China)

《一个人和一个贫困村庄的致富传奇》,晓风编著. 新世界出版社. 介绍吉林甘南县兴十四村脱贫致富的经历.

4. 中国贫困山区生态补偿体制研究. 英文卷/吕星,何俊主编. 昆明:云南大学出版社,2009. 270 页;21cm. ISBN:7811125580, 7811125587

英文题名:Payment for environment services: China's experiences of rewarding upland poor.

D175 华侨工作

1. Forty-one red hearts are with Chairman Mao forever. Peking: Foreign Languages Press, 1967. 46 pages, [4] pages of plates: illustrations; 18cm.

《四十一颗红心向太阳》,新华社记者等撰写. 伟大的毛泽东思想鼓舞华侨青少年向印尼反动派进行英勇斗争的光辉事迹.

2. 心向统一:华侨华人反"独"促统活动纪实:汉英对照/王长鱼主编;中国和平统一促进会秘书处,北京世界知识音像电子出版社编. 北京:世界知识出版社,2006. 175 页:照片;28cm. +光盘 1 张. ISBN:7501226202, 7501226207

英文题名:Aspirations for reunification. 本书记录全球华侨华人反独促统活动. 包括华侨华人所举办的六次全球性反独促统大会,三次洲际性大会和四次论坛.

D176 反邪教

1. Li Hongzhi & his "falun gong": deceiving the public and ruining lives/Ji Shi. Beijing: New Star Publishers, 1999. 150 pages: illustrations (some color); 22cm. ISBN: 7801482387, 7801482389

《欺世害人的李洪志及其"法轮功"》,季石编. 新星出版社.

2. "Falun Gong" is a cult. Beijing: New Star Publishers, 1999. 1 volumes; 20cm. ISBN: 7801482514 (v. 1), 7801482530 (v. 2),7801482532 (v. 2), 7801482557 (v. 3), 7801482556 (v. 3), 7801482573 (v. 4), 7801482570 (v. 4), 780148259X (v. 5), 7801482594 (v. 5)

Contents: v. 1./compiled by Ji Shi-v. 2./compiled by Ji Shi-v. 3./compiled by Guo Xinzhao-v. 7./compiled by Wang Xue

《邪教"法轮功"》,1—5 卷,季石等编. 新星出版社.

3. 《邪教"法轮功"》(第 6 册),马江编. 新星出版社,2000. ISBN:7801483200

4. 《邪教"法轮功"》(第 7 册),王雪编. 新星出版社,2000. ISBN:7801483324

5. Combat evil cults safeguard human rights/compiled by the China Anti-Cult Association. Beijing: China Science & Technology Press, 2001. 43 pages: color illustrations; 21cm. ISBN: 7504630403, 7504630407

《反对邪教,保障人权》中国反邪教协会编. 中国科学技术出版社.

6. Handbook of Falun Gong issue/China association for cultic studies. Beijing: Popular Science Press, 2009. 272 pages; 20cm. ISBN: 7110071106, 7110071103

《"法轮功"问题简明手册:英文》,中国反邪教协会编著. 科学普及出版社.

7. Perspective on Falun Gong's mental control/editor-in-chief: Yijia, Wang Yusheng; deputy editor Zhang Tao, Li Anping Wu Lin. Beijing: Popular Science Press, 2010. 254 pages;24cm. ISBN: 7110072462,7110072460. (Study series on Falun Gong issue)

《"法轮功"精神控制透视》,一家,王渝生主编. 科学普及出版社.

D177 精神文明建设

1. The diary of Wang Chieh. Peking: Foreign Languages Press, 1967. 96 pages: portraits; 19cm.

《王杰日记》

2. Resolution of the Central Committee of the Communist Party of China on the guiding principles for building a socialist society with an advanced culture ideology. Beijing: Foreign Languages Press, 1986. 22 pages; 19cm. ISBN: 0835119548, 0835119542. (Chinese documents)

Notes: "Adopted at the sixth plenary session of the Twelfth Central Committee of the Communist Party of China on September 28, 1986."

《中共中央关于社会主义精神文明建设指导方针的决定》

3. 传统美德/刘涛编著. 合肥:黄山书社,2016. 130 页:彩图,肖像,摹真;23cm. ISBN:7546152820. (印象中国)

英文题名:Traditional virtues of China. 英汉对照.

D18 社会各阶层

D181 知识分子

1. Report on the question of intellectuals, delivered on

January 14，1956，at a meeting held under the auspices of the Central Committee of the Communist Party of China to discuss the question of intellectuals. Peking：Foreign Languages Press，1956. 44 pages；22cm.

《关于知识分子问题的报告》，周恩来.

2. On the re-education of intellectuals/by Renmin Ribao and Hongqi，commentators. Peking：Foreign Languages Press，1968. 11 pages；13cm.

《关于知识分子再教育问题》

D182　青年

1. China's youth march forward. Peking：Foreign Languages Press，1950. ii，70 pages：illustrations；19cm.

《中国青年在前进》

2. Young builders of China/［Edited by the Central Committee of the New Democratic Youth League of China］. Peking：Foreign Languages Press，1953. 75 pages：illustrations，portraits，map；21cm.

《中国青年建设者》，中华青年民主青年联合会编.

3. China's countryside：a vast school for her youth. Peking：Foreign Languages Press，1976. iv，110 pages：illustrations；19cm.

《农村也是大学》，晓兵编.

D183　妇女

1. Women in new China. Peking：Foreign Languages Press，1949. 55 pages：illustrations；19cm.

《新中国妇女》

(1)Peking：Foreign Languages Press，1950. 55 p.：ill.

2. China celebrates the 50th anniversary of March 8th. Peking：Foreign Languages Press，1960. v.（27 p.，［15］p. de pl.）：ill.；19cm.

《"三八"五十周年在中国》

3. Chinese women in the great leap forward. Peking：Foreign Languages Press，1960. 96 pages，illustrations；19cm.

《中国妇女在跃进》，马信德等著.

4. New women in New China. Peking：Foreign Languages Press，1972. 78 pages：illustrations；19cm.

《今日中国妇女》

5. Chinese women in the fight for socialism/compiled by Chi Pen. Peking：Foreign Languages Press，1977. 117 pages，［16］leaves of plates：illustrations；19cm.

《为社会主义而斗争的中国妇女》，季本编.

6. Women's status in contemporary China/edited by Sha Jicai & Liu Qiming. Beijing：Peking University Press，1995. viii，402 pages；21cm. ISBN：7301026552，7301026557

《当代中国妇女地位》. 北京大学出版社.

7. Women's education in China/editor in chief，Wei Yu；Chinese Education Association for International Exchange，China National Institute for Educational Research，Department of Planning and Construction of the State Education Commission. Beijing：Higher Education Press，1995. 400 pages：illustrations；23cm. ISBN：7040055384，7040055382

Notes："Translated into English by Beijing Foreign Studies University"—Title page verso.

《中国妇女教育》，韦钰主编. 高等教育出版社

8. Theory and practice of protection of women's rights and interests in contemporary China：investigation and study on the enforcement of UN convention on the elimination of all forms of discrimination against women in China/the Center for Women's Law Studies and Legal Services of Peking University；［chief editors，Yang Dawen，Guo Jianmei］. Beijing：Worker Press，2001. 734 pages：illustrations；21cm. ISBN：7500824955，7500824954

《当代中国妇女权益保障的理论与实践：〈消除对妇女一切形式歧视公约〉在中国执行情况的调查研究》，北京大学法学院妇女法律研究与服务中心编. 中国工人出版社.

9. Women of China/compiled by the All-China Women's Federation；［translators，Zhang Fengru，A Rong］. Beijing：China Intercontinental Press，2004. 116 pages：color illustrations；21cm. ISBN：7508504895，7508504896

《中国妇女》，中华全国妇女联合会编. 五洲传播出版社. 介绍中国妇女将近半个世纪的奋斗，现实的工作生活情况以及她们对中国社会主义建设事业的贡献.

10. Gender equality and women's development in China/Information Office of the State Council of the People's Republic of China. Beijing：New Star Publishers，2005. 37 pages；26cm. ISBN：7801488275，780148827X

《中国性别平等与妇女发展状况：英文》，中华人民共和国国务院新闻办公室发布. 新星出版社.

11. 中国性别平等与妇女发展状况：英文/中华人民共和国国务院新闻办公室发布. 北京：新星出版社，2005. 40 页；20cm. ISBN：7801488288，7801488282

英文题名：Gender equality and women's development in China.

12. 历史的印痕·最后的文面人：汉英对照/陈瑞金，罗金合撰文；杨发顺，罗金合摄影. 北京：中国旅游出版社，2006. 96 页；19×21cm. ISBN：7503228679，7503228674

英文题名：Imprints of history：the last face tattooed women. 本书主要介绍云南独龙族妇女文面的历史以及他们生活的场景.

13. Studies on contemporary Chinese women development/author Feng Yang；translators Lixiao Dong，Aidong Qin，Xiaoxia Li. Beijing：People's Publishing House，2009. 2，4，24，188 pages；21cm. ISBN：7010080604，7010080607

《当代中国女性发展研究》，杨凤著. 人民出版社.

D184　残疾人

1. Work programme for disabled persons during the period of

the 8th five-year national development plan：(1991—1995). Huaxia Publishing House，1992. [1 volume].
ISBN：7800534731，7800534737

《中国残疾人事业"八五"计划纲要：1991 年—1995 年》. 华夏出版社.

D19　工运与工会

1. The trade union law of the People's Republic of China，together with other relevant documents. Peking：Foreign Languages Press，1950. ii，38 p.；19cm.
《中华人民共和国工会法》
   (1)Rev. ed. Peking：Foreign Languages Press，1951. 38 p.；19cm.
   (2)3rd ed. Peking：Foreign Languages Press，1952. 38 p.；19cm.

2. The Trade union law of the People's Republic of China，with the constitution of the trade unions of the People's Republic of China. Peking：Foreign Languages Press，1955. 31 pages；19cm.
《中华人民共和国工会法》

3. Labour insurance in new China. Peking：Foreign Languages Press，1953. 32 p.；ill.；19cm.
《新中国劳动保险》

4. China's chemical workers/[edited by the Preparatory Committee of the Chemical Workers' Trade Union of China]. Peking：Foreign Languages Press，1953. 17 pages；19cm. (China，a collection of pamphlets；no. 31)
《中国化学工人》,中国化学工会筹备委员会编.

5. The Seventh All-China Congress of Trade Unions. Peking：Foreign Languages Press，1953. 141 pages：illustrations，portraits；21cm.
《中国工会第七次全国代表大会主要文件》,刘少奇,陈叔通等.

6. Eighth All-China Congress of the Trade Unions/Ed. by the All-China Federation of Trade Unions. Peking：Foreign Languages Press，1958. 124 p.：ill.
《中国工会第八次全国代表大会》,中华全国总工会编.

7. Chinese workers march towards socialism. Peking：Foreign Languages Press，1956. 93 p.：illus.；19cm.
《向社会主义迈进的中国工人》

8. Labour protection in new China/edited by Labour Protection Bureau，Ministry of Labour. Peking：Foreign Languages Press，1960. 94 p.：illus.；19cm.
《新中国的劳动保护》,劳动保护局著.

9. Trade unions in People's China. Peking：Foreign Languages Press，1956. 58 pages；19cm.
《中国工会概况手册》

10. Trade unions in China. Peking：Foreign Languages Press，1987. 22 pages：illustrations（some color）；18cm. (China：facts & figures)
《中国工会》

11. 上海市工会条例：汉英对照/上海市总工会编. 上海：上海教育出版社,2005. 87 页；21cm. ISBN：7544401219

12. China enters the machine age：a study of labor in Chinese war industry/by Kuo-heng Shih，with a supplementary chapter by Ju-K'ang T'ien；edited and translated by Hsiao-Tung Fei and Francis L. K. Hsu. Cambridge，Mass.：Harvard University Press，c1944. xxiv，206 p.：ill.；21cm.
《昆厂劳工》,史国衡著；费孝通,许烺光译. 民国时期工人运动.

13. History of the labor movement in China/by Ma Chao-chun；Translated by Peter Min Chi Liang. Taipei：China Cultural Service，c1955. 169 p.：ill.；22cm.
《中国劳工运动史》,马超俊(1886—)著；梁明致译.

D191　政治运动和事件

1. The great socialist cultural revolution in China. Peking：Foreign Languages Press，1966—1967. 7 volumes
《中国的社会主义文化大革命》,7 集.

2. The great proletarian cultural revolution in China. Peking：Foreign Languages Press，1966. 3 volumes；21cm.
《中国的无产阶级文化大革命》,3 集.

3. Circular of the Central Committee of the Chinese Communist Party，May 16，1966：A great historic document/by the editorial departments of Hongqi and Renmin Ribao. Peking：Foreign Languages Press，1967. 46 pages；21cm.
《通知·伟大的历史》

4. An epoch-making document：in commemoration of the second anniversary of the publication of the circular/editorial departments of Renmin Ribao，Hongqi and Jiefangjun Bao. Peking：Foreign Languages Press，1968. 14 pages；19cm.
《划时代的文献：纪念〈通知〉发表两周年》

5. Important documents on the great proletarian cultural revolution in China. Peking：Foreign Languages Press，1970. 323 pages：portraits；14cm.
《无产阶级文化大革命重要文件集》

6. Selected articles criticizing Lin Piao and Confucius. Peking：Foreign Languages Press，1974. 1 volumes；19cm.
《批林批孔文选（一）》

7. Selected articles criticizing Lin Piao and Confucius. 2. Peking：Foreign Languages Press，1975. 1 vol.（229 p.）；19cm.
《批林批孔文选（二）》

8. Workers，peasants and soldiers criticize Lin Piao and Confucius：a collection of articles. Peking：Foreign Languages Press，1976. 108 pages；19cm.
《工农兵批林批孔文集》

9. Great historic victory：in warm celebration of Chairman Hua Kuo-feng's becoming leader of the Communist Party of China，and of the crushing of the Wang-Chang-Chiang-Yao anti-party clique. Peking：Foreign Languages Press，1976. 44 p.，[2] bl. pl.：portr.；19cm.

《伟大的历史性胜利》

10. The struggle against the anti-party "Gang of Four" in China. Peking：Foreign Languages Press，1977. 91 pages；18cm.

《中国粉碎"四人帮"反党集团的斗争》

11. A great trial in Chinese history. Beijing，China：New World Press；Elmsford，N. Y.：Distribution by Pergamon Press the trial of the Lin Biao and Jiang Qing counter-revolutionary cliques，Nov. 1980—Jan. 1981. 234 pages，11 pages of plates：illustrations；21cm. ISBN：0080279198，0080279190，008027918X，0080279183

《历史的审判》.对林彪、"四人帮"集团的审判.

12. 56 days of turbulence：April 15 to June 9，1989/edited by People's China Press. Beijing：New Star Publishers，1989. 181 pages：maps；19cm. ISBN：7800851001，7800851001

《动荡的 56 天》，人民中国出版社编.

13. The June turbulence in Beijing/compiled by New Star Publishers. Beijing：New Star Publishers，1989. 48 pages

《北京的六月风波》

14. How Chinese view the riot in Beijing/compiled by New Star Publishers. Beijing：New Star Publishers，1989. 36 pages，[8] pages of plates：illustrations；19cm. ISBN：7800850005，7800850004

《中国人如何看北京的暴乱》.新星出版社.

D191.1 恐怖活动

1. Record of the terrorist activities of the "East Turkistan" forces. Beijing：Wu zhou chuan bo chu ban she，2002. 23 pages：color illustrations；28cm. ISBN：7508501063，7508501062

《"东突"势力恐怖活动录》，五洲传播出版社编.五洲传播出版社.

D192 社会生活

1. Life in modern China. Beijing，China：New World Press；Distributed by Guoji Shudian（China Publications Centre），1984. iii，90 pages；19cm. （China spotlight series）
Contents：Introduction—The people's livelihood—Employment and wage systems—Life cycle，customs and religion—Appendix. The Marriage Law of the People's Republic of China.

《中国人民的生活》.新世界出版社.

2. Life and lifestyles/compiled by the China Handbook Editorial Committee；translated by Chen Zhucai. Beijing：Foreign Languages Press；Distributed by China International Book Trading Corp.，1985. 261 pages，[16] pages of plates：illustrations；19cm. ISBN：0835113027，0835113021，0835109925，0835109925. （China handbook series）

《社会生活》，《中国手册》编辑委员会编.

3. Portraits of ordinary Chinese/edited by Liu Bingwen and Xiong Lei with in-house editor Tong Xiuying. Beijing，China：Foreign Languages Press，1990. 383 pages；18cm. ISBN：0835125610，0835125611，711901160X，7119011608

《形形色色的中国人》，刘炳文，熊蕾编.

4. Timeout in China/text by Wu Di；translated by Yan Xinjian. [Beijing]：China Intercontinental Press，2006. 123 pages：color illustrations；21cm. ISBN：7508509765，7508509761. （Fashion China＝时尚中国）

《休闲好时光：英文》，吴迪著；闫新建译.五洲传播出版社.本书是一本向国外读者全面介绍中国人时尚休闲观念、休闲方式、休闲潮流的书.

5. Shopping in China/text by Yan Hao；translated by Li Huailin ＆ W. Y. Kang. [Beijing]：China Intercontinental Press，2006. 127 pages：color illustrations；21cm. ISBN：7508509773，7508509778. （Fashion China＝时尚中国）

《消费新时代：英文》，闫浩著；李怀林等译.五洲传播出版社.本书向国外读者全面介绍中国人消费观念、消费方式最新变化，以客观的角度展现当代中国人在消费领域的动态.

6. Networks in China/Zhao Shijun；translated by Nie Peng ＆ Xu Weifeng. [Beijing]：China Intercontinental Press，2006. 127 pages：color illustrations；21cm. ISBN：7508509315，7508509310. （Fashion China＝时尚中国）

《网动中国：英文》，赵世俊著；聂蓬译.五洲传播出版社.本书反映信息社会数字化发展给中国人生活带来的变化，如网络、通信产品对人们工作、娱乐、人际交往等方面的深刻影响.

7. Every community is a family/Yang Jibin. Beijing：Foreign Languages Press，2007. 111 pages：color illustrations；19cm. ISBN：7119051154，7119051156. （Stories from China）

《社区如家：英文》，杨继斌编著；孙雷，雨秋译；彭玉珊等摄.（国情故事）.对中国城市社区的现状建设进行了详细的介绍.

8. Life begins at sixty/Liu Xuehong. Beijing：Foreign Languages Press，2007. 111 pages：color illustrations；19cm. ISBN：7119051383，7119051385. （国情故事）

《生活到老：英文》，刘学红编著；汪光强译.介绍了进入老龄化社会的中国老年人的生活.

9. Lifestyle in China/Gong Wen；translation by Li Ziliang，Zhao Feifei ＆ Li Zhaoguo. Beijing：China Intercontinental Press，

2007. 176 pages: color illustrations; 25cm. ISBN: 7508511023, 7508511026. (Journey into China)

《生活之旅：英文》，龚纹著；李子亮等译. 五洲传播出版社（中国之旅丛书/郭长建，李向平主编）

10. Cybercitizens and the internet in China/Dong Shaopeng and Han Hua; [translated by Han Hua]. Beijing: New World Press, 2008. 113 pages: color illustrations; 19cm. ISBN: 7802284999, 7802284996. (Stories of China)

《中国的互联网与网民》，董少鹏，韩桦著. 新世界出版社.

11. Chinese life bitter-sweet portraits: 1978—1990/Liu Bingwen, Xiong Lei. Beijing: Foreign Languages Press, 2008. 343 pages; 21cm. ISBN: 7119055558, 7119055550

《形形色色的中国人：1978—1989》，刘炳文，熊蕾主编. 讲述改革开放 30 年来各行各业普通中国人的寻常和不寻常的生活.

12. Chinese life: bitter-sweet portraits 1991—2008/Yu Yuanjiang. Beijing: Foreign Languages Press, 2008. 316 p.; 21cm. ISBN: 7119055565; 7119055569

《形形色色的中国人：1991—2008》，于元江主编. 讲述改革开放 30 年来各行各业普通中国人的寻常和不寻常的生活.

13. Chorus singing from the people/by Wang Yang, Ju Zi; translated by Shi Wei; photo provided by Qin Zhaonong... [et al.]. Beijing: New World Press, 2009. 98 pages: color illustrations; 19cm. ISBN: 7802289987, 780228998X. (Stories of China＝国情故事)

《来自百姓的歌声》，王洋，桔子著. 新世界出版社.

14. Chinese stuff/Bopuke Popcorn; transl. by Liu Jun. Beijing: China Intercontinental Press, 2008. 169 pages: color illustrations; 23cm. ISBN: 7508512808, 7508512804. (Essentially Chinese)

《中国东西》，波普客编著. 五洲传播出版社. 本书选取了有中国特色的 125 个日用品，从一个侧面反映了当下中国社会普通百姓的日常生活.

15. Eye on China: it's all in the bag/[edited by Li Tie]. Beijing: Foreign Languages Press, 2009. 155 pages: illustrations (some color); 22cm. ISBN: 7119055923, 7119055925

《挎包里的中国》，李铁主编.

16. Sixty years of life in Beijing 1949—2009: a collection of drawings from an ordinary Beijing resident/by Guan Geng; [English translation Wang Yongqiu; English text edited by Liang Liangxing, David A. Williams]. Beijing: Foreign Languages Press, 2009. 3, 207 pages: illustrations; 24cm. ISBN: 7119059679, 711905967X

《我这 60 年：一个北京平民的生活绘本》，关庚著.

17. Chinese house/Popcorn; translated by Liu Jun; zhuan wen Li Risong. Beijing: China Intercontinental Press, 2009. 171 pages: color illustrations; 23cm. ISBN: 7508515182, 7508515188. (Essentially Chinese)

《中国房子》，波普客著. 五洲传播出版社. 选取了 100 多所有中国特色的房子，从社会学角度展示了中国普通百姓的生活.

18. China's social development/Tang Jun [et al.]; translated by Pan Zhongming, Zhang Hongpeng, & Gao Jin'an. Beijing: China International Press, 2010. 140 p.: ill. (some col.); 23cm. ISBN: 7508513065, 7508513061

《中国社会》，吴伟主编. 五洲传播出版社. 选取当代中国社会的主要方面，诸如婚姻家庭、人口、就业、劳动力流动、社会保障、医疗等最能反映和揭示当代中国社会现状的问题.

D192.1　劳动就业与保障

1. China's employment/[editors, Deng Shulin and others]. Beijing, China: New Star Publishers, 1990. 40 pages: illustrations; 19cm. ISBN: 7800852016, 7800852015. (What's new in China; 45)

《中国的劳动就业》，今日中国杂志编辑，新星出版社.

2. Labor and social security in China/Information Office of the State Council of the People's Republic of China. Beijing: New Star Publishers, 2002. 37 pages; 26cm. ISBN: 7801484061, 7801484062

Contents: Foreword—I. Overall stability in employment situation—II. Formation of new labor relations—III. The establishment of a social security system—IV. Development in the early period of the 21st century.

《中国的劳动和社会保障状况》，中华人民共和国国务院新闻办公室分布，新星出版社.

3. China's employment situation and policies/Information Office of the State Council of the People's Republic of China. Beijing: New Star Publishers, 2004. 40 pages: illustrations; 21cm. ISBN: 7801486129, 7801486127

《中国的就业状况和政策》，中华人民共和国国务院新闻办公室发布. 新星出版社. 为国务院新闻办公室发表的白皮书.

4. China's employment situation and policies/Information Office of the State Council of the People's Republic of China. Beijing: New Star Publishers, 2004. 38 pages: illustrations; 26cm. ISBN: 7801486110, 7801486110

《中国的就业状况和政策》，中华人民共和国国务院新闻办公室发布. 新星出版社. 为国务院新闻办公室发表的白皮书.

5. China's social security and its policy/Information Office of the State Council of the People's Republic of China. Beijing: New Star Publishers, 2004. 37 pages; 21cm. ISBN: 7801486544, 7801486547

《中国的社会保障状况和政策》，中华人民共和国国务院新闻办公室发布. 新星出版社. 为国务院新闻办公室发表的白皮书.

6. China's social security and its policy/Information Office of the State Council of the People's Republic of China. Beijing: New Star Publishers, 2004. 35 pages; 26cm.

ISBN：7801486536，7801486530

《中国的社会保障状况和政策》，中华人民共和国国务院新闻办公室发布. 新星出版社.

7. China's social security system/chief editors, Gao Shangquan and Chi Fulin；written by Sun Xiuping. Beijing：Foreign Languages Press：Distributed by China International Book Trading Corp.，1996. 184 pages；21cm. ISBN：7119017330，7119017334.（Studies on the Chinese market economy series）

《中国的社会保障制度》，高尚全，迟福林主编.

8. China's social security system/chief editors Tian Chengping. Beijing：Foreign Languages Press，2008. 229 pages；21cm. ISBN：7119052991，7119052993.（Focus on China series）

《中国的社会保障制度》，田成平主编.

9. China's humanitarian relief operations/Li Jun；translated by Tang Haimin, Zhang Wei, Wang Biao. Beijing：China Intercontinental Press，2014. 209 pages：colour illustrations；23cm. ISBN：7508529387

《中国救援行动》，李军编著；唐海民等译.

D192.2 禁毒

1. Narcotics control in China/Information Office of the State Council of the People's Republic of China. Beijing, China：New Star Publishers，2000. 35 pages；21cm. ISBN：7801482832，7801482839

《中国的禁毒》，中华人民共和国国务院新闻办公室发布. 新星出版社.

2. China always says "no" to narcotics/［written and compiled by Ting Chang；English translator, Zhang Tingquan］. Beijing：Foreign Languages Press，2004. iv, 183 pages：illustrations；21cm. ISBN：7119033484，7119033488

《中国对毒品永远说"不"！》，廷长编. 简介中国百年禁毒史，详介改革开放以来中国政府禁毒的决心和近几年禁毒斗争的成果.

D192.3 社会问题与调查

1. Modernization in China：the effects on its people and economic development/Beijing Youth Daily ＆ Youth Humanities and Social Science Research Center of the Chinese Academy of Social Science；［translated by Liang Faming［and others］；english text edited by Foster Stockwell, Huang Youyi］. China：Foreign Languages Press，2004. 249 pages；23cm. ISBN：7119032976，7119032979

Contents：Economy—Population—Education—Quality of life—Social security—The concept of values and the state of mind—Science and technology—Environment and resources—The reunification of the country and unity of the nation—China and the world

《中国现代化：对中国百姓及经济发展的影响》，北京青年报社，中国社会科学院青年人文社会科学研究中心主编；

郝光锋等译.

2. 农民工反贫困：城市问题与政策导向：汉英对照/黄平，杜铭那克主编. 北京：社会科学文献出版社，2006. 284，276页；24cm. ISBN：7802303184，7802303188

英文题名：Urban poverty reduction among migrants：problems and policy orientation in China. 本书是联合国教科文组织与中国社科院历时近5年的"农民工反贫困"项目的研究成果.

D192.4 地方政治

D192.41 台湾

1. Important documents concerning the question of Taiwan. Peking：Foreign Languages Press，1955. 183 pages；19cm.

《台湾问题重要文件集》

2. Twenty-sixth anniversary of the "February 28" uprising of the people of Taiwan Province. Peking：Foreign Languages Press，1973. 23 pages：illustrations；19cm.

《纪年台湾省人民"二·二八"起义二十六周年》

3. Questions and answers concerning the Taiwan question and reunification of China/［Guo wu yuan Taiwan shi wu ban gong shi］.［Beijing］：China Intercontinental Press，1997. 113 pages：color illustrations；23cm. ISBN：7801133366，7801133366

《〈台湾问题与祖国统一〉问答》，国务院台湾事务办公室编. 五洲传播出版社.

4. The Chinese government's policy towards Taiwan/by TaiXuan.［Beijing］：China Intercontinental Press，2002. 110 pages：illustrations；18cm. ISBN：7508500873，7508500874

《台湾问题ABC》，陆闻编著. 五洲传播出版社.

D192.42 香港

1. Hong Kong - cross 1997/by Wang Qiaolong.［Beijing］：China Intercontinental Press，1997. 77 pages：color illustrations；19cm. ISBN：7801132815，7801132819.（Hong Kong series）

Contents：Foreword—The origin of the question of Hong Kong and the Chinese Government's position on it—Satisfactory solution to the question of Hong Kong—The Basic Law of the Hong Kong Special Administration Region—The Chinese Government strives to ensure the stable transition of Hong Kong—Even more beautiful future of Hong Kong.

《"九七"前后谈香港》，王巧珑著. 五洲传播出版社.

2. Hong Kong：China's special administrative region/by Wang Qiaolong.［Beijing］：China Intercontinental Press，1997. 69 pages：color illustrations；18cm. ISBN：7801132890，7801132895.（Hong Kong series）

Contents：Foreword—The legal status of the Hong Kong Special Administration Region—Relations between the Hong Kong Special Administration Region and the Central authorities—The political structure of the Hong Kong

Special Administration Region—Hong Kong's existing capitalist system to remain unchanged.

《香港：中国的特别行政区》，王巧珑著. 五洲传播出版社.

3. Origin and solution of the Hong Kong question/by Huang Fengwu. [China]：China Intercontinental Press，1997. 77 pages：color illustrations；18cm. ISBN：7801132491，7801132499.（Hongkong series）

《香港问题的由来及解决》，黄凤武著. 五洲传播出版社.

4. The basic law：a blue print for the Hong Kong SAR/by Ge Guangzhi, Kou Qi. [Beijing]：China Intercontinental Press，1997. 77 pages：color illustrations；19cm. ISBN：7801132572，7801132574.（Hong Kong series）

《香港特别行政区的蓝图：基本法》，葛广智，寇琪著. 五洲传播出版社.

5. Hong Kong economy：with backing of the Chinese mainland/by Cai Chimeng. [Beijing]：China Intercontinental Press，1997. 85 pages：color illustrations；18cm. ISBN：7801132653，7801132659.（Hong Kong series）

《背靠祖国的香港经济》，蔡赤萌著. 五洲传播出版社.

6. Who have created Hong Kong's prosperity/by Chen Duo, Lian Jintian. [Beijing]：China Intercontinental Press，1997. 77 pages：color illustrations；18cm. ISBN：7801132734，7801132734.（Hong Kong series）

《是谁创造了香港的繁荣》，陈多，连锦添著. 五洲传播出版社.

7. One country, two systems：an account of the drafting of the Hong Kong Basic Law/by Xiao Weiyun. Beijing：Peking University Press，2001. 529 pages；21cm. ISBN：7301048289，7301048283

《香港基本法与一国两制的伟大实践》，肖蔚云著；宋小庄等译. 北京大学出版社.

8. Lu Ping：the return of Hong Kong/narrated by Lu Ping, compiled by Qian Yijiao, translated by Betty Lew Ting. Shanghai：China Welfare Institute Publishing House，2009. 238 pages：illustrations；23cm. ISBN：7507215120，7507215121

《鲁平：口述香港回归》，鲁平口述. 中国福利会出版社. 由国务院港澳办前主任鲁平口述的关于香港回归的幕后故事.

D192.43　澳门

1. Macao 400 years/author, Fei Chengkang；English translator，Wang Yintong；English revisors，Sarah K. Schneewind, Fei Chengkang. Shanghai：Pub. House of Shanghai Academy of Social Sciences，1996. 360 pages；24cm. ISBN：7806182667，7806182666

《澳门 400 年》，费成康著；王寅通译. 上海社会科学院出版社.

2. The homecoming of Macao/by Wang Qiaolong. Beijing：China Intercontinental Press，1999. 87 pages：illustrations（some color）；18cm. ISBN：7801136128，7801136121

《归来，澳门》，王巧珑著. 五洲传播出版社.

3. The ABC of the basic law of the Macao Special Administrative Region/by Zhao Guoqiang. Beijing：China Intercontinental Press，1999. 271 pages：illustrations；19cm. ISBN：7801134915，7801134912

《澳门特别行政区基本法 ABC》，赵国强著. 五洲传播出版社.

D2　外交、国际关系

D21　概论

1. China's diplomacy/author Zhou Yinhuang；translator Wang Pingxing. Beijing：China Intercontinental Press，2004. 166 pages：illustrations（some color）；22cm. ISBN：7508506278，7508506272.（China basics series）

《中国外交》，周溢潢主编；王平兴译. 五洲传播出版社（中国基本情况丛书/郭长建主编）

2. China's diplomacy/Zhang Qingmin；translated by Zhang Qingmin. Beijing：China Intercontinental Press，2010. 160 pages；23cm. ISBN：7508513126，7508513126

《中国外交》，张清敏著. 五洲传播出版社.

3. China's foreign relations：a chronology of events （1949—1988）/compiled by Home News Library of the Xinhua News Agency. Beijing：Foreign Languages Press，1989. vi，618 pages；21cm. ISBN：0835122484，0835122481，711900798X，7119007984

《中华人民共和国对外关系大事记：1949—1988》，新华通讯社国内资料组编.

4. Contemporary diplomacy of China/by Wu Zhou. [Beijing, China]：China Intercontinental Press，2001. 81 pages：color illustrations；21cm. ISBN：7801139526，7801139528

《当代中国外交概况》，吴州编. 五洲传播出版社.

5. Contemporary China and its foreign policy /editor-in-chief，Yang Fuchang；deputy editors-in-chief，Qin Yaqing，Heng Xiaojun. Beijing：World Affairs Press，2003. 427 pages；22cm. ISBN：7501220492，7501220496

《当代中国与中国外交》，杨福昌主编. 世界知识出版社.

6. China's philosophy on foreign affairs in the 21st century/Liu Binjie. Beijing：Foreign Languages Press，2006. 111 pages：color illustrations；21cm. ISBN：7119044656，7119044651.（China in peaceful development）

《21 世纪中国对外交往的哲学：英文》，柳斌杰著；郝光锋译.（中国的和平发展系列）

7. Peace：the roots of the cultural tradition and values of the Chinese people/Wu Genyou. Beijing：Foreign Languages Press，2007. 200 pages：illustrations；24cm. ISBN：7119044934，7119044931.

《和平：中国人的文化根柢》，吴根友著；郝光锋等译.

8. Dialogue between nations：speeches by Zhao Qizheng. Beijing, China：Foreign Languages Press，2009. iii，238

pages：color illustrations；24cm. ISBN：7119059631，7119059637

《让世界对话：赵启正演讲录》，赵启正著. 收录 35 篇赵启正的演讲和访谈.

9. China's foreign aid/Information Office of the State Council of the People's Republic of China. Beijing：Foreign Languages Press, 2011. 47 p.；ill.；21cm. ISBN：7119069265，7119069268，7119069258，711906925X

《中国的对外援助》，中华人民共和国国务院新闻办公室［发布］.

10. Imperialism and Chinese politics/Hu Sheng. Peking：Foreign Languages Press, 1955. 308 pages；22cm.

《帝国主义与中国政治》，胡绳(1918—2000).

(1)Westport, Conn.：Hyperion Press, 1973. 308 pages；23cm. ISBN：0883550725, 0883550724

(2)［Arlington, Va.］：［University Publications of America, Inc.］, 1975. 308 pages；23cm. ISBN：0890930546, 0890930540. （Studies in Chinese government and law）

(3)6th ed. Beijing：Foreign Languages Press, 1978. 332 pages；19cm.

(4)Beijing：Foreign Languages Press：Distributed by Guoji Shudian, 1981. 332 pages；19cm.

(5)Beijing：Foreign Languages Press：Distributed by Guoji Shudian, 1985. 259 pages；21cm. ISBN：0835113116, 0835113113

11. On present international situation, China's foreign policy, and the liberation of Taiwan：delivered at the third session of the First National People's Congress, June 28, 1956/Chou En-lai. Peking：Foreign Languages Press, 1956. 31 pages；21cm.

《关于目前国际形势，我国外交政策和解放台湾问题》，周恩来.

12. On the current international situation. Peking：Foreign Languages Press, 1958. 73 pages；19cm.

《目前国际形势》

13. Smash the big U. S. -Soviet conspiracy! /by Observer of Renmin Ribao（People's Daily）. Peking：Foreign Languages Press, 1967. 12 pages；14cm.

《粉碎美苏的一个大阴谋》

14. Great strategic concept/Jen Ku-ping；Tung Ming. Peking：Foreign Languages Press, 1967. 50 pages；19cm.

《伟大的战略思想》

15. Statement of the Government of the People's Republic of China, October 7, 1969. Peking：Foreign Languages Press, 1973. 29 pages；19cm.

Contents：Statement of the government of the People's Republic of China.—Document of the Ministry of Foreign Affairs of the People's Republic of China.

《中华人民共和国政府声明：1969 年 10 月 7 日》

16. 中国特色大国外交与"一带一路"/吴建民著；陈枫英文

翻译. 北京：外文出版社有限责任公司，2016. 37 页；21cm. ISBN：7119103587

英文题名：Major-country diplomacy with Chinese characteristics and The Belt and Road Initiative

17. China's belt and road initiatives and its neighboring diplomacy/editor Zhang Jie；translator Xu Mengqi. Singapore：Social Sciences Academic Press China：World Scientific Publishing, 2017. XV, 298 p.；24cm. ISBN：9813140202, 9813140208

中国的"一带一路"构想与周边外交. Xu, Mengqi 译.

18. Texts of selected speeches and final communique of the Asian-African Conference, Bandung, Indonesia, April 18—24, 1955：with additional report on the Conference/by Premier Chou En-lai. ［New York］：［Far East Reporter］, 1955. 63 pages；18cm.

Contents：Introduction—Speech/by President Soekarno of the Republic of Indonesia—Speech/by Premier Chou En-lai, People's Republic of China—Supplementary Speech/by Premier Chou En-lai—Asian African Conference：Joint communique—Report on the Asian-African Conference/by Premier Chou En-lai in Peking on May 13, 1955.

收录周恩来在 1955 年印尼亚非会议上的几个讲话.

19. China and the Asian-African conference/Chou En-lai. Peking：Foreign Languages Press, 1955. 81 p.；ill.；18cm.

《中国与亚非会议》，周恩来.

(1)China and the Asian-African Conference：documents. Peking：Foreign Languages Press, 1979. 80 pages, ［4］leaves of plates：illustrations；19cm.

20. Afro-Asian solidarity against imperialism：a collection of documents, speeches and press interviews from the visits of Chinese leaders to thirteen African and Asian countries. Peking：Foreign Languages Press, 1964. viii, 439 pages；19cm.

《亚非人民反帝大团结万岁：中国领导人访问亚非十三国文件集》

21. Resolutely struggle against imperialism and neo-colonialism and for the economic emancipation of the Afro-Asian peoples. Peking：Foreign Languages Press, 1965. 34 pages

《坚决进行反对帝国主义和新殖民主义的斗争，实现亚非人民的经济解放》，南汉宸著.

22. 中国的亚太安全合作政策/中华人民共和国国务院新闻办公室［发布］. 北京：外文出版社有限责任公司，2017. 49 页；21cm. ISBN：7119105109

英文题名：China's policies on Asia-Pacific security cooperation

D22　国际关系

D221　国际共产主义运动

1. In refutation of modern revisionism. Peking：Foreign

languages Press，1958. 91 pages；19cm.

Notes：Articles which appeared in the Chinese press regarding Yugoslav politics

《现代修正主义必须批判》

(1) Peking：Foreign languages Press，1963. 91 pages；19cm.

2. Lenin on imperialism, the eve of the proletarian revolution：in commemoration of the 90th anniversary of the birth of Lenin，1870—1960. Peking：Foreign Languages Press，1960. 90 p. ；19cm.

《列宁论帝国主义是无产阶级社会主义革命的前夜：纪念列宁诞生九十周年(1870—1960)》，《人民日版》社编辑部编.

3. Lenin on war and peace：in commemoration of the 90th anniversary of birth of Lenin. Peking：Foreign Languages Press，1960. 68 p.

《列宁论战争与和平：纪念列宁诞生九十周年(1870—1960)》，人民日版社编辑部编.

4. Lenin on the revolutionary proletarian party of a new type. 〔2nd ed.〕. Peking：Foreign Languages Press，1960. 78 pages；19cm.

《列宁论新型的革命的无产阶级政党：纪念列宁诞生九十周年(1870—1960)》，人民日版社编辑部编.

5. Lenin on the struggle against revisionism. Peking：Foreign Languages Press，1960. 97 p.

《列宁论反对修正主义：纪念列宁诞生九十周年(1870—1960)》，人民日版社编辑部编.

6. Lenin on the national liberation movement：in commemoration of the 90th anniversary of the birth of Lenin. Peking：Foreign Languages Press，1960. 57 p.

《列宁论民族解放运动：纪念列宁诞生九十周年(1870—1960)》，人民日版社编辑部编.

7. Workers of all countries, unite, oppose our common enemy! Peking：Foreign Languages Press，1962. 26 p.；19cm.

《全世界无产者联合起来反对我们的共同敌人》，外文出版社，1962 年.

(1)Peking：Foreign Languages Press，1963. 393 pages；19cm.

8. Long live Leninism. 〔3rd ed.〕. Peking：Foreign Languages Press，1960. 106 pages：portraits；21cm.

Notes：Articles from various sources published in commemoration of the 90th anniversary of Lenin's birth.

《列宁主义万岁》

(1) 5th ed. rev. trans. Peking：Foreign Languages Press，1964. 124 pages：portraits；21cm.

9. The differences between Comrade Togliatti and us. Peking：Foreign Languages Press，1963. 47 p.

《陶里亚蒂同志同我们的分歧》

10. More on the differences between Comrade Togliatti and us, some important problems of Leninism in the

contemporary world/by the Editorial Department of Hongqi (Red Flag). Peking：Foreign Languages Press，1963. 198 pages；19cm.

《再论陶里亚蒂同志同我们的分歧：关于列宁主义在等待的若干重大问题》，《红旗》杂志编辑部.

11. Whence the differences? A reply to Thorez and other comrades/"Renmin Ribao" editorial. Peking：Foreign Languages Press，1963. 35 pages；19cm.

《分歧从何而来？答多列士等同志》

12. A comment on the statement of the Communist Party of the U. S. A. Peking：Foreign Languages Press，1963. 17 pages

《评美国共产党声明》

13. Raise higher the revolutionary banner of Marxism-Leninism. Peking：Foreign Languages Press，1963. 36 pages；19cm.

《更高地举起马克思列宁主义的革命旗帜》

14. The polemic on the general line of the international communist movement. Peking：Foreign Languages Press，1965. 585 p. ；21cm.

《关于国际共产主义运动总路线的建议》，《人民日报》社.

15. The polemic on the general line of the international communist movement. Peking：Foreign Languages Press，1965. 585 pages；21cm.

《关于国际共产主义运动总路线的论战》

16. A great victory for Leninism：in commemoration of the 95th anniversary of the birth of Lenin：Hongqi editorial, no. 4，1965. Peking：Foreign Languages Press，1965. 13 pages；19cm.

《列宁主义的伟大胜利：纪念列宁诞生九十五周年》

17. Lenin's fight against revisionism and opportunism/ compiled by Zheng Yanshi. Peking：Foreign Languages Press，1965. 275 pages；19cm.

《列宁反对修正主义、机会主义的斗争》，郑言实编.

18. A struggle between two lines over the question of how to deal with U. S. imperialism/Fan Hsiu-Chu. Peking：Foreign Languages Press，1965. 40 pages；19cm.

《在对待美帝国主义问题上两条路线的斗争》，范秀珠著.

19. Advance along the road opened up by the October Socialist Revolution：in commemoration of the 50th anniversary of the great October Socialist Revolution. Peking：Foreign Languages Press，1967. 27 pages；19cm.

《沿着十月社会主义革命开辟的道路前进：纪念伟大的十月社会主义革命五十周年》

20. Long live the victory of the dictatorship of the proletariat-in the commemoration of the centenary of the Paris Commune/by the Editorial Departments of Renmin Ribao (People's Daily)，Hongqi (Red Flag) and

Jiefangjun Bao (Liberation Army Daily). Peking: Foreign Languages Press, 1971. 32 pages; 19cm.

《无产阶级专政万岁：纪念巴黎公社一百周年》

D222 中国与联合国

1. 中国与联合国：纪念联合国成立六十周年：汉英对照/刘结一等主编.北京：世界知识出版社,2005. 221 页：彩页；29cm. ISBN：7501226342

   英文题名：1945—2005 China and the United Nations: in commemoration of the 60th anniversary of the founding of the United Nation.

2. China accuses! Speeches of the special representative of the Central People's Government of the People's Republic of China in the United Nations. Peking: Foreign Languages Press, 1951. x, 107 pages

   《中国控诉》,中华人民共和国中央人民政府特别代表在联合国的发言.伍修权.

3. Irresistible historical trend. Peking: Foreign Languages Press, 1971. 47 pages; 19cm.

   Contents：Statement of the Government of the People's Republic of China (Oct. 29, 1971)—Speech by Chiao Kuan-hua, chairman of the delegation of the People's Republic of China, at the plenary meeting of the 26th session of the U. N. General Assembly (Nov. 15, 1971)—Telegrams from Chi Peng-fei, Acting Minister of Foreign Affairs of the People's Republic of China, to U Thant, Secretary-General of the United Nations (Oct. 29 and Nov. 2, 1971)—Statement of Chiao Kuan-hua, chairman of the delegation of the People's Republic of China, at New York Airport (Nov. 11, 1971)—Irresistible historical trend (Renmin Ribao editorial, Oct. 28, 1971)—Draft resolution of Albania, Algeria, and other countries calling for the restoration of China's lawful rights in the U. N. and the expulsion of the Chiang gang adopted by an overwhelming majority at the U. N. General Assembly.—Text of the resolution of Albania, Algeria, and 21 other countries and the U. N. General Assembly voting results.—Taiwan has been China's sacred territory since ancient times.—U. S. imperialist "Independent Taiwan" plot is doomed to failure.—Japanese reactionaries' plot to create "an Independent Taiwan" will never succeed.

   《历史潮流,不可抗拒》

3. Speeches welcoming the delegation of the People's Republic of China by the U. N. General Assembly President and representatives of various countries, at the plenary meeting of the 26th session of the U. N. General Assembly (November 15, 1971). Peking: Foreign Languages Press, 1971. v, 158 pages; 19cm.

   《在联大第二十六届会议一九七一年十一月十五日全体会议上大会主席和各国代表欢迎中华人民共和国代表团

的讲话》

4. Speech by Chiao Kuan-hua, chairman of the delegation of the People's Republic of China, at the plenary meeting of the 27th session of the U. N. General Assembly (October 3, 1972). Peking: Foreign Languages Press, 1972. 24 pages; 19cm.

   《中华人民共和国代表团团长乔冠华在联合国大会第二十七届会议全体会议上的发言》

5. Speech by Chiao Kuan-hua, chairman of the delegation of the People's Republic of China, at the plenary meeting of the 28th session of the U. N. General Assembly, October 2, 1973. Peking: Foreign Languages Press, 1973. 26 pages; 19cm.

   《中华人民共和国代表团团长乔冠华在联合国大会第二十八届会议全体会议上的发言》

6. Speech by Chiao Kuan-hua, chairman of the delegation of the People's Republic of China, at the plenary meeting of the 29th Session of the U. N. General Assembly (October 2, 1974). Peking: Foreign Languages Press, 1974. 26 pages; 19cm.

   《中华人民共和国代表团团长在联合国大会第二十九届会议上的发言》,乔冠华.

7. Speech by chairman of the delegation of the People's Republic of China, Teng Hsiao-ping, at the special session of the U. N. General Assembly, April 10, 1974. Peking: Foreign Languages Press, 1974. 22 pages; 19cm.

   《中华人民共和国代表团团长邓小平在联大特别会议上的发言》

8. Speech by Chiao Kuan-hua, chairman of the Delegation of the People's Republic of China, at the plenary meeting of the 30th session of the U. N. General Assembly (September 26, 1975). Peking: Foreign Languages Press, 1975. 34 pages; 19cm.

   《中华人民共和国代表团团长在联合国大会第三十届会议全体会议上的发言》

9. The Chinese government will continue firmly to implement chairman Mao's revolutionary line and policies in foreign affairs: speech by Chiao Kuan-hua, chairman of the Chinese delegation, at the plenary meeting of the 31st session of the U. N. General Assembly, October 5, 1976. Peking: Foreign Languages Press, 1976. 15 pages; 19cm.

   《中国政府继续坚决执行毛主席的革命外交路线和政策：中国代表团团长在联合国大会第三十一届全体会议上的发言》.

10. Speech by Huang Hua, chairman of the Chinese Delegation, at a plenary meeting of the tenth special session of the United Nations General Assembly. Peking: Foreign Languages Press, 1978. 26 pages; 19cm;

《中国代表团团长黄华在联合国大会第十届特别会议全体会议上的发言》

11. Fighting for peace：narratives of Chinese forces on UN peacekeeping missions' frontlines/written by Yu Yin；translated by Liu Jun，Erik Nilsson and Xie Tao. Beijing：China Intercontinental Press，2011. 7，154 pages：illustrations；23cm. ISBN：7508520322，7508520327

《中国维和警察纪实》，余音［著］. 五洲传播出版社. 记述了中国维和警察在东帝汶、波黑、利比里亚以及海地执行联合国维和任务的故事.

D223　禁止核武器

1. People of the world unite for the complete，thorough，total and resolute prohibition and destruction of nuclear weapons. Peking：Foreign Languages Press，1963. 207 pages；21cm.

《全世界人民团结起来，全面、彻底、干净、坚决地禁止和销毁核武器》

2. Break the nuclear monopoly，eliminate nuclear weapons. Peking：Foreign Languages Press，1965. 28 pages；19cm.

《打破核垄断，消灭核武器》

3. People of the world，unite and struggle for the complete prohibition and thorough destruction of nuclear weapons！Peking：Foreign Languages Press，1971. 18 pages；19cm.

《全世界人民团结起来，为全面禁止和彻底销毁核武器而奋斗》

D23　中国外交

D231　中美关系

1. Oppose U. S. military provocations in the Taiwan Straits area：a selection of important documents. Peking：Foreign Languages Press，1958. viii，70 pages；15cm.

《反对美国在台湾海峡地区的军事挑衅》，中国人民外交学会编.

2. Oppose U. S. occupation of Taiwan and "two Chinas" plot：a selection of important documents/compiled by the Chinese People's Institute of Foreign Affairs. Peking：Foreign Languages Press，1958. 161 pages；19cm.

《反对美国霸占台湾、制造"两个中国"的阴谋》

3. Two tactics，one aim：an exposure of the peace tricks of U. S. imperialism/edited by the Chinese People's Institute of Foreign Affairs. Peking：Foreign Languages Press，1960. 145 pages；19cm.

《两套手法、一个目的：揭穿美帝国主义玩弄和平的阴谋》，中国人民外交学会编.

4. Drive U. S. imperialism out of Asia. Peking，Foreign Languages Press；Chicago，China Books & Periodicals [distributor]，1960. 47 pages：illustrations，portraits；19cm.

《把美帝国主义赶出亚洲！》

5. Oppose the new U. S. plots to create "two Chinas"：[a collection of relevant important documents，commentaries and some background materials which have appeared in the Chinese press since 1959]. Peking：Foreign Languages Press，1962. 107 pages；19cm.

《反对美国制造"两个中国"的新阴谋》

6. Oppose the outrageous persecution of the Communist Party of the U. S. A. by the U. S. reactionaries. Peking：Foreign Languages Press，1962. 42 pages；19cm.

《反对美国反动派迫害美国共产党的暴行》

7. The Kennedy administration unmasked. Peking：Foreign Languages Press，1962. 74 pages；19cm.

《肯尼迪政府的真面目》

8. U. S. aggression has no bounds and our counter to aggression has no bounds. Peking：Foreign Languages Press，1966. 29 pages；19cm.

《美国侵略没有界限，我们反侵略也没有界限》

9. Sino-U. S. joint communique（February 28，1972）. Peking：Foreign Languages Press，1972. 7 p.

《中美联合公报》（1972 年 2 月 28 日）

10. Speeches made by Chinese premier Zhao Ziyang during his visit to the United States of America. ［Washington］：Embassy of the People's Republic of China，1984. 64 pages；20cm.

赵紫阳总理访美期间讲话.

11. On the human rights of the United States and its human rights report. ［Beijing］：China Intercontinental Press，1997. 41 pages；21cm. ISBN：7801132203，7801132208 Contents：Look at the US human rights record/R. Yanshi—Another act of creating confrontation by using the pretext of human rights/Information Office of the State Council of P. R. C.

《评美国人权的人权报告》，国务院新闻办公室，任言实著，五洲传播出版社.

12. 全面推进21世纪中美建设性合作关系：胡锦涛主席对美国进行国事访问：汉英对照/钟建和编. 北京：世界知识出版社，3，152 pages，［13］pages of plates：彩照；26cm. ISBN：7501231294，750123129X

本书分三个部分：（1）胡锦涛主席访美期间的重要演讲和讲话；（2）新华社有关胡主席访美的报道；（3）附录部分收录了胡主席与布什总统在纽约、圣彼得堡、河内会晤的三篇报道及中美三个联合公报. 书中还附有胡主席访美期间的彩色照片 13 幅.

D232　中苏关系

1. The Sino-Soviet treaty and agreements：（signed in Moscow on February 14，1950）. Peking：Foreign Languages Press，1951. 25 pages，1 folded leaf of plates：portraits；19cm.

《中苏友好同盟互助条约》

2. Sino-Soviet alliance mighty bulwark of world peace. Peking：Foreign Languages Press, 1960. 1 vol (48 p.); 19cm.

《中苏同盟是世界和平的强大堡垒》

3. Support the just stand of the Soviet Union and oppose U. S. imperialism's wrecking of the four-power conference of government heads. Peking：Foreign Languages Press, 1960. 31 p.：Ill.

《支持苏联正义立场、反对美帝国主义破坏四国首脑会议》

4. Leninism and modern revisionism/Hongqi editorial. Peking：Foreign Languages Press, 1963. 20 pages; 19cm.

《列宁主义和现代修正主义》

5. Let us unite on the basis of the Moscow declaration and the Moscow statement. Peking：Foreign Languages Press, 1963. 34 pages; 19cm.

《在莫斯科宣言和莫斯科声明的基础上团结起来》

6. A proposal concerning the general line of the international Communist movement; the letter of the Central Committee of the Communist Party of China in reply to the letter of the Central Committee of the Communist Party of the Soviet Union of March 30, 1963. Peking：Foreign Languages Press, 1963. 114 pages; 19cm.

《关于国际共产主义运动总路线的建议：中国共产党中央委员会对苏联共产党中央委员会 1963 年 3 月 30 日来信的复信》

7. The origin and development of the differences between the leadership of the CPSU and ourselves：comment on the open letter of the Central Committee of the CPSU/by the Editorial Departments of Renmin Ribao（People's Daily）and Hongqi（Red Flag）. Peking：Foreign Languages Press, 1963. 101 pages; 15cm.

《苏共领导同我们分歧的由来和发展：评苏共中央的公开信》,《人民日报》编辑部,《红旗》杂志编辑部.

8. On the question of Stalin：comment on the open letter of the Central Committee of the CPSU (II)/by the editorial departments of Renmin Ribao（People's daily）and Hongqi（Red flag）. Peking：Foreign Languages Press, 1963. 23 pages; 19cm.

《关于斯大林问题：二评苏共中央的公开信》,《人民日报》编辑部,《红旗》杂志编辑部.

9. Is Yugoslavia a socialist country?：Comment on the open letter of the Central Committee of the CPSU (III)/By the editorial departments of Renmin Ribao（People's Daily）and Hongqi（Red Flag）. Peking：Foreign Languages Press, 1963. 47 pages; 19cm.

《南斯拉夫是社会主义国家吗?：三评苏共中央的公开信》,《人民日报》编辑部,《红旗》杂志编辑部.

10. Apologists of neo-colonialism：comment on the open letter of the Central Committee of the CPSU(IV)/by the editorial departments of Renmin Ribao（People's daily）and Hongqi（Red flag）. Peking：Foreign Languages Press, 1963. 36 pages; 19cm.

《新殖民主义的辩护士：四评苏共中央的公开信》,《人民日报》编辑部,《红旗》杂志编辑部.

11. Two different lines on the question of war and peace：comment on the open letter of the Central Committee of the CPSU (V)/by the editorial departments of Renmin ribao（People's daily）and Hongqi（Red flag）. Peking：Foreign Languages Press, 1963. 37 pages; 19cm.

《在战争与和平问题上的两条路线：五评苏共中央的公开信》,《人民日报》编辑部,《红旗》杂志编辑部.

12. Peaceful coexistence—two diametrically opposed policies：comment on the open letter of the Central Committee of the CPSU (VI)/by the editorial departments of Renmin Ribao（People's daily）and Hongqi（Red flag）. Peking：Foreign Languages Press, 1963. 47 pages; 19cm.

《两种根本对立的和平共处政策：六评苏共中央的公开信》,《人民日报》编辑部,《红旗》杂志编辑部.

13. The truth about how the leaders of the CPSU have allied themselves with India against China/by the Editorial Dept. of Renmin Ribao（People's Daily）. Peking：Foreign Languages Press, 1963. 49 pages; 19cm.

《苏共领导联印反华的真相》,《人民日报》编辑部.

14. The Struggle between two lines at the Moscow World Congress of Women. Peking：Foreign Languages Press, 1963. 60 pages; 19cm.

《在莫斯科世界妇女大会上两条路线的斗争》

15. Seven letters exchanged between the Central Committees of the Communist Party of China and the Communist Party of the Soviet Union. Peking：Foreign Languages Press, 1964. 75 pages; 19cm.

《中共中央和苏共中央来往的七封信》

16. Letter of the Central Committee of the Communist Party of China in reply to the letter of the Central Committee of the Communist Party of the Soviet Union dated June 15, 1964. Peking：Foreign Languages Press, 1964. 73 [1] pages; 15cm.

《中国共产党中央委员会对苏联共产党中央委员会一九六四年六月十五日来信的复信》

17. Letter of the Central Committee of the Communist Party of China in reply to the letter of the Central Committee of the Communist Party of the Soviet Union dated July 30, 1964. Peking：Foreign Languages Press, 1964. 14 pages; 19cm.

《中国共产党中央委员会对苏联共产党中央委员会一九六四年七月三十日来信的复信》

18. The leaders of the CPSU are the greatest splitters of our times：comment on the open letter of the Central

Committee of the CPSU （VII）/by the editorial departments of Renmin ribao（People's daily）and Hongqi（Red flag）. Peking：Foreign Languages Press，1964. 62 pages；19cm.

《苏联领导是当代最大的分裂主义者：七评苏共中央的公开信》，《人民日报》编辑部，《红旗》杂志编辑部.

19. The proletarian revolution and Khrushchov's revisionism：comment on the open letter of the Central Committee of the CPSU（VIII）/by the Editorial Dept. of Renmin Ribao（People's Daily）and Honggi（Red Flag）. Peking：Foreign Languages Press：Guozi Shudian [distributor]，1964. 66 pages；19cm.

《无产阶级革命和赫鲁晓夫修正主义：八评苏共中央的公开信》，《人民日报》编辑部，《红旗》杂志编辑部.

20. On Khrushchov's phoney communism and its historical lessons for the world：comment on the open letter of the Central Committee of the CPSU（IX）/by the editorial departments of Renmin Ribao（People's Daily）and Hongqi（Red Flag）. Peking：Foreign Languages Press，1964. 74 pages；19cm.

《关于赫鲁晓夫的假共产主义及其在世界历史上的教训：九评苏共中央的公开信》，《人民日报》编辑部，《红旗》杂志编辑部.

21. Why Khrushchov fell/editorial，Hongqi（Red Flag）. Peking：Foreign Languages Press，1964. 11 pages：19cm.

《赫鲁晓夫是怎样下台的》

22. Carry the struggle against Khrushchov revisionism through to the end：on the occasion of the second anniversary of the publication of "A proposal concerning the general line of the international Communist movement"/by the editorial departments of Renmin Ribao（People's daily）and Hongqi（Red flag）. Peking：Foreign Languages Press，1965. 16 pages；21cm.

《把反对赫鲁晓夫修正主义的斗争进行到底：纪念〈关于国际共产主义运动总路线的建议〉发表两周年，1965 年 6 月 14 日》，《人民日报》编辑部，《红旗》杂志编辑部.

23. Refutation of the new leaders of the CPSU on "united action"/by the editorial departments of Renmin Ribao（People's daily）and Hongqi（Red flag）. Peking：Foreign Languages Press，1965. 33 pages；21cm.

《驳苏共新领导的所谓"联合行动"：1965 年 11 月 11 日》，《人民日报》编辑部，《红旗》杂志编辑部.

24. The leaders of the CPSU are betrayers of the declaration and the statement/by the Editorial Department of Renmin Ribao（People's Daily）. Peking：Foreign Languages Press，1965. 8 pages；19cm.

《苏共领导是宣言和声明的背叛者：1965 年 12 月 30 日》，《人民日报》编辑部.

25. Letter of reply dated March 22，1966 of the Central Committee of the Communist Party of China to the Central Committee of the Communist Party of the Soviet Union. Peking：Foreign Languages Press，1966. 9 pages；14cm.

《中国共产党中央委员会一九六六年三月二十二日给苏联共产党中央委员会的复信》

26. China's great revolution and the Soviet Union's great tragedy/by Renmin Ribao（People's daily）observer. Peking：Foreign Languages Press，1967. 14 pages；14cm.

《中国大革命和苏联的大悲剧》

27. Total bankruptcy of Soviet modern revisionism. Peking：Foreign Languages Press，1968. 83 pages；13cm.

Notes：Includes two speeches by Chou En-lai

《苏联现代修正主义的总破产》，包括周恩来的两个讲话.

28. Ugly features of Soviet social-imperialism. Peking：Foreign Languages Press，1976. 88 pages；19cm.

《苏联社会帝国主义的丑恶面目》

29. The Soviet Union under the new tsars/Wei Chi. Peking：Foreign Languages Press，1978. ii，90 pages；19cm.

《新沙皇统治下的苏联》

30. Ghost of Confucius, fond dream of the new tsars. Peking：Foreign Languages Press，1974. 40 pages；19cm.

Contents：Ghost of Confucius, fond dream of the new tsars. —Expose the "Humanitarianism" hoax. —Soviet revisionist renegade clique and Confucius.

《孔老二的亡灵和新沙皇的迷梦》

31. Cheap propaganda. Peking：Foreign Languages Press，1974. 31 pages；19cm.

《廉价的宣传》

32. A comment on the March Moscow meeting/by the editorial departments of Renmin Ribao（People's daily）and Hongqi（Red flag）. Peking：Foreign Languages Press，1965. 23 pages；19cm.

《评莫斯科三月会议：1965 年 3 月 23 日》，《人民日报》编辑部，《红旗》杂志编辑部.

D233 中国与世界其他各国外交关系

1. Joint statement of Chairman Liu Shao-chi and President Ho Chi Minh. Peking：Foreign Languages Press，1963. 34 pages；19cm.

《刘少奇主席和胡志明主席联合声明》

2. Support the people of Viet Nam, defeat the U. S. aggressors. Peking：Foreign Languages Press，1965. 4 volumes；19cm.

《支援越南人民，打败美国侵略者》（第 1、2、3、4 辑）

3. Solemn pledge of the thirty million Vietnamese people. Peking：Foreign Languages Press，1965. 47 pages；19cm.

《三千万越南人民的庄严誓言》

4. Long live the great friendship and militant unity between the Chinese and Vietnamese peoples! Peking：Foreign Languages Press，1971. 77 pages：illustrations，portraits；20cm.

《中越两国人民的伟大友谊和战斗团结万岁!》

5. Resolutely back Vietnamese people in carrying war against U. S. aggression and for national salvation to complete victory. Peking：Foreign Languages Press，1971. 22 pages；19cm.

《坚决支持越南人民把抗美救国战争进行到彻底胜利》

6. Welcome the signing of the Paris agreement on Viet Nam. Peking：Foreign Languages Press，1973. 37 pages，[6] pages of plates：illustrations；19cm.

《欢迎越南协议的签订》

7. The Vietnamese people's great victory：warm congratulations to the South Vietnamese people on the liberation of Saigon and all South Viet Nam. Peking：Foreign Languages Press，1975. 52 pages，[1] leaf of plates：illustrations；19cm.

《越南人民的伟大胜利:热烈庆祝越南南方人民解放西贡和完全解放越南南方》

8. On Viet Nam's expulsion of Chinese residents. Peking：Foreign Languages Press，1978. 222 pages，[8] leaves of plates；19cm.

《关于越南驱赶华侨问题》

9. On the Vietnamese foreign ministry's white book concerning Viet Nam-China relations/by the People's Daily and Xinhua News Agency commentators. Beijing：Foreign Languages Press，1979. 38 pages；19cm.

《评越南外交部关于越中关系的白皮书》，人民日报评论员，新华社评论员.

10. Fighting Cambodia：reports of the Chinese journalists delegation to Cambodia. Peking：Foreign Languages Press，1975. 60 pages，[4] leaves of plates：illustrations；19cm.

《战斗的柬埔寨:中国新闻代表团访问柬埔寨通讯集》

11. Great victory of the Cambodian people：warmly congratulating the patriotic Cambodian armed forces and people on the liberation of Phnom Penh and all Cambodia. Peking：Foreign Languages Press，1975. 36 pages，[1] leaf of plates：illustrations；19cm.

《柬埔寨人民的伟大胜利:热烈庆祝柬埔寨爱国军民解放金边和解放全国》

12. A victory for the five principles of peaceful co-existence：important documents on the settlement of the Sino-Burmese boundary question through friendly negotiations and on the development of friendly relations between China and Burma/edited by the Chinese People's Institute of Foreign Affairs. Peking：Foreign Languages Press，1960. [6]，56，[1] p. 19cm.

《和平共处五大原则的胜利:中缅友好协商解决边界问题、发展友好关系的重要文件》，中国人民外交学会编.

13. New development in friendly relations between China and Nepal/Edited by the Chinese People's Institute of Foreign Affairs. Peking：Foreign Languages Press，1960. 92 pages：portraits；19cm.

《中尼友好关系的新发展》，中国人民外交学会编.

14. Documents on the sino-indian boundary question. Peking：Foreign Languages Press，1959. 101 pages

《中印边界问题文件集》

(1)Peking：Foreign Languages Press，1960. 144 p.

15. The Sino-Indian boundary question. (enl.) ed. Peking：Foreign Languages Press，1962. 133 p.

《中印边界问题》(1)

16. The Sino-Indian boundary question II. Peking：Foreign Languages Press，1965. 43 pages

《中印边界问题》(2)

17. A mirror for revisionists/"Renmin Ribao" editorial. Peking：Foreign Languages Press，1963. 11 pages：19cm.

《修正主义者的一面镜子》.中印边界问题.

18. Premier Chou En-lai's letter to the leaders of Asian and African countries on the Sino-Indian boundary question (November 15，1962). Peking：Foreign Languages Press，1973. 32 pages，[13] folded leaves of plates：13 maps；19cm.

《周恩来总理就中印边界问题致亚非拉国家领导人的信(1962 年 11 月 15 日)》

(1)Peking：Foreign Languages Press，1974. 34 pages：13 folded maps；19cm.

19. Oppose the revival of Japanese militarism：a selection of important documents and commentaries/edited by the Chinese People's Institute of Foreign Affairs. Peking：Foreign Languages Press，1960. 191 pages；19cm.

《反对日本军国主义的复活》，中国人民外交学会编.

20. Support the just struggle of the Japanese people against the Japan-U. S. treaty of military alliance. Peking：Foreign Languages Press，1960. 147 pages，[4] leaves of plates：illustrations；19cm.

《支持日本人民反对日美军事同盟条约的正义斗争》

21. Down with revived Japanese militarism. Peking：Foreign Languages Press，1971. 76 pages；19cm.

《打倒复活的日本军国主义》

22. A new page in the annals of Sino-Japanese relations. Peking：Foreign Languages Press，1972. 26 pages：illustrations；19cm.

《中日关系史上的新篇章》

23. A historic visit to Japan：speeches of Hu Yaobang, General Secretary to the Communist Party of China (November 23—30，1983). Beijing：Foreign Languages Press：Distributed by China International Book Trading Corp.，1983. 53 pages，[16] pages of plates：

illustrations；21cm. ISBN：083511306X，0835113069

《中日友好关系新发展：胡耀邦总书记访日言论集》

24. Support the just and patriotic struggle of the South Korean people. Peking：Foreign Languages Press，1960.，37 p.；18cm.

《支持南朝鲜人民的爱国正义斗争》

25. Joint statement of Chairman Liu Shao-chi and President Choi Yong Kun. Peking：Foreign Languages Press，1963. 16 pages；19cm.

《刘少奇主席和崔庸健委员长联合声明》

26. The heroic Korean people. Peking：Foreign Languages Press，1972. 72 pages：color illustrations；21cm. Contents：The flowering of China-Korea militant friendship. —Anti-imperialist fortress in the East. —Speeding along the road of socialist construction. —Vigorous growth of Korea's local industries. —Building a new socialist countryside. —The Korean People's Army marches forward courageously. —The valiant women of Korea. —Beautiful, heroic Pyongyang.

《英雄的朝鲜人民》

27. Chinese-Korean friendship, deep-rooted and flourishing：the Party and Government Delegation of the Democratic People's Republic of Korea visits China. Peking：Foreign Languages Press，1975. 67 pages，[6] leaves of plates：illustrations；19cm.

《中朝友谊根深叶茂：朝鲜党政代表团访问中国》

28. Certain international questions affecting Malaya. Peking：Foreign Languages Press，1963. 15 pages；19cm.

《与马来西亚有关的一些国际问题》

29. Malayan people's experience refutes revisionist fallacies：sixteenth anniversary of the Malayan people's armed struggle. Peking：Foreign Languages Press，1965. 15 pages；19cm.

《马来西亚人民的经历驳斥了修正主义者的谬论：纪念马来西亚人民武装斗争十六周年》

30. Speech at the Aliarcham Academy of Social Sciences in Indonesia，May 25，1965/Peng Chen. Peking：Foreign Languages Press，1965. 27 pages；21cm.

《在印度尼西亚阿里亚哈姆社会科学学院的讲话：1965年5月25日》，彭真.

31. Concerning the situation in Laos. Peking：Foreign Languages Press，1959. 84 pages；19cm. Notes：Includes "Foreign Ministry [People's Republic of China] statements on the Laotian situation... [and] editorials and commentaries on Laos from Renmin Ribao, in addition to news reports."

《关于老挝问题》

32. China's indisputable sovereignty over the Xisha and Nansha Islands：document of the Ministry of Foreign Affairs of the People's Republic of China. Beijing：Foreign Languages Press，1980. 31 pages，5 leaves of plates （some folded）：illustrations，maps；19cm.

《我国对西沙群岛和南沙群岛的主权无可争辩：中华人民共和国外交部文件（一九八〇年一月三十日）》

33. 中国坚持通过谈判解决中国与菲律宾在南海的有关争议/中华人民共和国国务院新闻办公室[发布].北京：外文出版社有限责任公司，2016. 56 页；21cm. ISBN：7119102948

英文题名：China adheres to the position of settling through negotiation the relevant disputes between China and the Philippines in the South China Sea

34. China supports the Arab people's struggle for national independence：a selection of important documents/compiled by the Chinese People's Institute of Foreign Affairs. Peking：Foreign Languages Press，1958. [7]，242 pages；19cm.

《支持阿拉伯人民争取民族独立的斗争》，中国人民外交学会编.

35. We are with you，Arab brothers！/[By] Mao Tun and others. Peking：Foreign Languages Press，1958. 84 pages：illustrations；19cm.

《支援持阿拉伯兄弟的呼声》，茅盾等.

36. Support the patriotic and just struggle of the Turkish people. Peking：Foreign Languages Press，1960. [8]，14 p.，[1] c. di tav. 19cm.

《支持土耳其人民的爱国正义斗争》

37. China and Africa/Yuan Wu；translated by Li Guoqing. [China]：China Intercontinental Press，2006. 116 pages：illustrations，maps；25cm. ISBN：7508509838，7508509839

《中国与非洲：英文》，袁武著；李国庆译.五洲传播出版社.

38. The Chinese people resolutely support the just struggle of the African people. Peking：Foreign Languages Press，1961. 139 pages plates，group portraits；19cm.

《中国人民坚决支持非洲人民的正义斗争》，中国非洲人民友好协会编.

39. In support of the people of the Congo （Leopoldville） against U. S. aggression. Peking：Foreign Languages Press，1965. 25 pages：illustrations；19cm.

《支持刚果（利奥波德维尔）人民反对美国侵略》

40. China and Albania，friends in a common struggle：a collection of speeches and documents from the visit of Chinese leaders to Albania. Peking：Foreign Languages Press，1964. 172 pages；19cm.

《中巴战斗友谊万岁：中国领导人访问阿尔巴尼亚文件集》

41. Support the Cuban and other Latin American people's just struggle against U. S. imperialism. Peking Foreign Languages Press，1961. 184 pages：illustrations；19cm.

《支持古巴和拉丁美洲各国人民反对美帝国主义的斗争》

42. Support the Dominican people's resistance to U. S. armed aggression. Peking：Foreign Languages Press, 1965. 33 pages，[4] leaves of plates：illustrations；19cm.

《支持多米尼加人民反对美国武装侵略》

43. Joint statement of the Communist Party of China and the Communist Party of New Zealand. Peking：Foreign Languages Press, 1963. 12 pages；19cm.

《中国共产党新西兰共产党联合声明》

44. For friendship and cooperation：speeches by General Secretary Hu Yaobang during his South Pacific tour. Beijing Foreign Languages Press, 1985. 73 p. ；19cm. ISBN：0835115879, 0835115872

《中国同南太平洋五国友好合作关系的新发展：胡耀邦总书记访问南太平洋五国言论集》

D3 中国法律

D31 古代法律及研究

1. Remnants of Ch'in law：an annotated translation of the Ch'in legal and administrative rules of the 3rd century B. C. ，discovered in Yün-meng Prefecture, Hu-pei Province, in 1975/by A. F. P. Hulsewé. Leiden：E. J. Brill, 1985. viii, 242 p. ；25cm. ISBN：9004071032. (Sinica Leidensia；vol. 17)

《秦律：睡虎地秦墓竹简注释》，何四维(Hulsewé, A. F. P. 〈Anthony Francois Paulus〉)译.

2. Remnants of Han law/Anthony Francois Paulus Hulsewe. Leiden：E. J. Brill, 1955. 455 p. ；25cm. (Sinica Leidensia；9)

Notes：v. 1. Introductory studies and an annotated translation of chapters 22 and 23 of the History of the former Han dynasty

翻译了《前汉书》的第22、23章中涉及汉朝的刑法和司法管理的内容.

3. The T'ang code /translated with an introd. by Wallace Johnson. Princeton, N. J. ：Princeton University Press, c1979—c1997. 2 v. ；24cm. ISBN：0691092397 (vol. 1), 0691025797 (vol. 2). (Studies in East Asian law). (Princeton library of Asian translations)

《唐律疏义》，Johnson, Wallace (Wallace Stephen, 1932—2007)译.

4. The law and the lore of China's criminal justice/by Sidney Shapiro. Beijing, China：New World Press：Distributed by China International Book Trading Corp. , 1990. 275 pages： illustrations；21cm. ISBN： 7800051293；7800051296

《中国古代刑法及案例故事》，是对宋慈(1186—1249)《洗冤集录》的选译.

5. Chinese legal tradition under the Mongols：the Code of 1291 as reconstructed/Paul Heng-chao Ch'en. Princeton, N. J. ：Princeton University Press, c1979. xix, 205 p. ；23cm. ISBN：0691092389. (Studies in East Asian law)

《元朝的中国法律：1291 年法典》，陈恒昭（Ch'en, Paul Heng-Chao, 1944—）（日本华裔学者）. 书中含有元朝的第一部成文法典《至元新格》的翻译.

6. The enlightened judgments：Ch'ing-ming chi：the Sung dynasty collection/translated by Brian E. McKnight and James T. C. Liu；annotated and introduced by Brian E. McKnight. Albany：State University of New York Press, 1999. xi, 567 p. ；24cm. ISBN：0791442438, 0791442446. (SUNY series in Chinese philosophy and culture)

《名公书判清明集》（节译），McKnight, Brian E. , Liu, James T. C. (1919—1993)译.

7. The case of the red pills：six sensational Ming and Qing Dynasty court cases/written by Liu Jianye；translated by Liu Jianwei. Beijing：Foreign Languages Press：Distributed by China International Book Trading, 2001. 300 pages：illustrations；18cm. ISBN：7119020501, 7119020501

《红丸迷案：中国明清奇案选》，刘建业.

D32 清代法律法规及研究

1. Cases from Hsing-an-Hui-lan：a conspectus of Chinese criminal law in the Ch'ing dynasty. Translated from the Chinese by Derk Bodde. With the editorial assistance of Clarence Morris. [n. p.] 1964. 210 l. ；29cm.

《刑案汇览》，（清）祝庆祺编纂；卜德（Bodde, Derk, 1909—2003)（美国汉学家）译.

2. Law in Imperial China：exemplified by 190 Ch'ing Dynasty cases, translated from the Hsing-an hui-lan. With historical, social, and juridical commentaries, by Derk Bodde and Clarence Morris. Cambridge, Mass. , Harvard University Press, 1967. xiii, 615 p. illus. ；24cm. (Harvard studies in East Asian law, 1)

《刑案汇览》，（清）祝庆祺编纂；卜德（Bodde, Derk, 1909—2003)（美国汉学家）译.

3. Chinese family and commercial law/by G. Jamieson. Shanghai, China：Kelly and Walsh, 1921. ii, 188 p. ；22cm.

Contents：Law of succession and inheritance—Marriage laws—Village organization—Land tenure and taxation—Commercial law—Criminal cases—Mixed court cases

Notes："The basis of the work is a translation of selected sections from the Ta Ching lu li or General code of laws of the Chinese Empire. "

《大清律例》选译，Jamieson, George(1843—1920)译.

(1) Hong Kong：Vetch and Lee, 1970. ii, 192 p. ；22cm.

4. Ta Tsing Leu Lee；being the fundamental laws, and a selection from the supplementary statutes, of the Penal code of China；originally printed and published in Pekin,

in various successive editions, under the sanction, and by the authority, of the several emperors of the Ta Tsing, or present dynasty. Translated from the Chinese; and accompanied with an appendix, consisting of authentic documents, and a few occasional notes, illustrative of the subject of the work; by Sir George Thomas Staunton, bart. Taipei, Ch'eng-wen Pub. Co., 1966. xxvi, (i. e. lxxvi), 581 p. facsim. ;22cm.

《大清律例》,小斯当东(Staunton, George Thomas, Sir, 1781—1859)(英国汉学家)译,初版于 1810 年.

(1)Taipei: Ch'eng-wen Pub. Co., c1966. xxvi, (i. e. lxxvi), 581 p. : ill., facsim. ; 22cm.

(2)Cambridge: Cambridge University Press, c2012. [4], xxvi [i. e. lxxvi], 581, [3] p., [1] leaf of plates: facsim. ; 31cm.

5. The great Qing code/translated by William C. Jones; with the assistance of Tianquan Cheng and Yongling Jiang. Oxford: Clarendon Press; New York: Oxford University Press, 1994. xxx, 441 p. ; 24cm. ISBN: 0198257945

《大清律例》,钟威廉(Jones, William C.)(美国法学家)译.

6. The Emperor Kuang Hsu's reform decrees, 1898. [Shanghai]: North China Herald Office, 1900. 61 pages; 23cm.

Notes: "Reprinted from the North-China daily news."

光绪皇帝改革法令.

7. Recent Chinese legislation relating to commercial, railway and mining enterprises/translated by E. T. Williams. Shanghai: Printed at the Shanghai Mercury, Limited, 1904. 100 p. ; 23cm.

清代有关商业、铁路和矿业的立法,Williams, E. T. 译.

(1)2nd ed. Shanghai: Shanghai Mercury, Ltd., 1905. 145 p. ; 20cm.

D33　中华民国时期法律

D331　法学理论、案例、法律汇编

1. On the reconstruction of the Chinese system of law/by Chu Cheng. Nanking, China: [s. n.], c1947. 32 p. ; 25cm.

《为什么要重建中国法系》,居正(Ju, Zheng, 1876—1951);张企泰译.

2. The Chinese Supreme Court decisions: first instalment translation relating to general principles of civil law and to commercial law/with prefaces by Yao Tseng; translated by F. T. Cheng. Peking: Supreme Court, 1920. ix, 36, 3, 39 pages;26cm.

《大理院判例要旨汇览》,大理院出版;郑天锡(Cheng, F. T.)译.

(1)Peking: Commission on Extra-territoriality, 1923. ix,

229 pages; 24cm.

(2)Arlington, Virginia: University Publications of America, 1974. ix, 229, [2] pages; 27cm. (China studies; Studies in Chinese government and law)

(3)Arlington, Va. : University Publications of America, 1976. ix, 229, [2] pages; 24cm. ISBN: 0890930651, 0890930656. (Studies in Chinese government and law)

(4)[Memphis, Tenn.]: General Books, 2010. 52 pages; 23cm. ISBN: 1152192126, 1152192124

(5)[S. l.]: Nabu Press, [2010]. ISBN: 1176383531, 1176383531

(6)[Sligo]: Hardpress Publishing, 2013. 1 vol. (pagination multiple); 23cm. ISBN: 1313452854, 1313452858. (Classic series)

3. Interpretations of the Supreme Court at Peking: years 1915 and 1916/translations, notes and introduction by M. H. van der Valk. Batavia: Sinological Institute, Faculty of Arts, University of Indonesia, 1949. 382 p. ; 25cm. (Sinica Indonesian; 1)

Notes: "The translations are based on the Chinese text as published in the private edition by... Guo Wei,... Da li yuan jie shi li quan wen, fourth edition, September 1931."—p. 6.

《大理院解释例全文》,郭卫;Valk, Marius Hendrikus van der 翻译.

(1)Taipei: Ch'eng-wen Publishing Company, 1968. 382 p. ; 25cm.

4. Regulations and tables relating to cases involving subjects of non-extraterritorial powers of the Republic of China. Peking: Translated and Pub. by the Commission on Extraterritoriality, c1925. 12, 64, 25 p. ; 25cm.

治外法权的规定. 中国治外法权委员会翻译并出版.

5. Judgments of the High Prize Court of the Republic of China: with an appendix containing Prize Court rules, detailed rules of the High Prize Court, regulations governing capture at sea, and regulations governing the safe-keeping of captured property in the naval warehouse/translated by F. T. Cheng for the High Prize Court. Peking: High Prize Court, 1919. 146 p. ; 25cm. (Legal classics library)

《中华民国高等捕获审检厅判决书汇编》

(1)Littleton, Colo. : F. B. Rothman, 1983. 146 pages; 24cm. ISBN: 0837704499, 0837704494

6. The Chinese Supreme Court decisions (relating to general principles of civil law, obligations, and commercial law)/translated by F. T. Cheng. Peking: The Commission on Extra-Territoriality, c1923. ix, 229 p. ; 25cm.

《中华民国最高法院法令》,郑天赐(Cheng, F. T.)(1884—)译.

(1)Taipei: Cheng wen Pub. Co., 1974. ix, 229, [2] pages; 27cm. (China studies; Studies in Chinese government and law)

7. Chinese laws: registration of companies regulations; insurance enterprise regulations; new draft patent law. New York: China-America Council of Commerce and Industry, 1943. 32 pages; 28cm. (Legal series; no. 2)
中华民国法律:公司注册法规、保险公司法规和专利法草案.

D332　国家法、宪法

1. Constitution of the Republic of China. [Peking, c1924]. 34, [16] p. ; 25cm.
《中华民国宪法》,中国治外法权委员会译.

2. Constitution and supplementary laws and documents of the Republic of China/tr. and pub. by the Commission on Extraterritoriality. Peking: Comm. on Extraterritoriality, 1924. 2 preliminary leaves, 198 pages, 1 leaf; 25cm.
《中华民国宪法》及补充法律文献,中国治外法权委员会翻译出版.
　(1) Arlington, VA: University Publications of America, 1976. 198 pages; 24cm. ISBN: 0890930597, 0890930595. (Studies in Chinese government and law; China studies)

3. First draft of the permanent constitution of China/drafted by John C. H. Wu; translated into English by Yui Ming. Shanghai: [China Press], 1933. 17 pages; illustrations; 22cm.
中国民国宪法草案.吴经熊(Wu, Jingxiong,1899—1986)起草;余铭(Yui, Ming)译.

4. The draft constitution of the Republic of China/by Sun Fo, translated by Albert T. Lu. Nanking: published by the Council of international affairs, 1936. 33 p. (Information bulletin; vol. I, no. 1)
中华民国宪法草案.Sun Fo;Liang, M. C. 译.

5. China's draft constitution, the full text of two important documents in the evolution of Chinese democracy: organic law of the National Government of the Republic of China. New York: Chinese News Service, 1945. 30 p. ; 22cm.
中华民国宪法草案.

6. China's constitutions: permanent and provisional/translated by the Ministry of Information. Chungking: Chinese Ministry of Information, 1945. 16 p. ; 21cm.
中华民国宪法:临时版本和批准版本.

7. The Constitution of the Republic of China/translated by by Hoh Chih-Hsiang. Rev. ed. Nanking, 1946. 37 pages; 18cm.
中华民国宪法.

8. The Constitution of the Republic of China. New York: Chinese News Service, [1947]. 25 p. ; 22cm.
中华民国宪法.

9. The Constitution of the Republic of China/English translation by Charles C. H. Wan. Nanking: Chinese Ministry of Information, 1947. 20 pages; 22cm.
中华民国宪法.

10. The Constitution of the Republic of China: adopted by the National assembly on Dec. 25 [1946], the 35th year of the Republic of China/translator, Hoh Chih-hsiang. [Shanghai, China], [The Commercial Press.], 1947. 2 preliminary leaves, [1], 36, 37 pages, 1 leaf; 18cm.
中华民国宪法.

11. Revised law of nationality; detailed rules for the application of revised law of nationality; rules for the application of laws (with Chinese text)/translated & published by the Comission on Extraterritoriality. Peking: Commission on Extraterritoriality, c1925. 21, 12 p. : ill. ; 24cm.
国籍法.中国治外法权委员会翻译并出版.

D333　行政法

1. The police offence law of the Republic of China/published by Ministry of Interior Peking; translated by Jermyn C. H. Lynn. Peking: Printed by the "Peking Gazette", c1917. 17, 24 p. ; 22cm.
中华民国警察法.Lynn, Jermyn C. H. 译.北平内政部出版.

2. Quarantine regulations of the Republic of China/translated by the National Quarantine Service. [1931]. 53 p.
中华民国检疫法.

D334　财政法

1. Chinese insurance law: Promulgated by the national government, Republic of China, 30th December, 1929/Tr. by Charles Kliene. Shanghai, Kelly and Walsh, 1929. 53 pages
中华民国保险法.英汉对照.

2. The Chinese insurance business act. Shanghai: The Mercury Press, c[1935]. 1 p. l. , 28 p. ; 24cm.
中国保险企业法.魏文瀚,张似旭合译.英汉对照.

3. The negotiable instrument law of the republic of China/translated by S. Francis Liu, Boyer P. H. Chu, and Lin-chong Chen. Shanghai, 1929. preliminary leaf, vii, [2], 40, 40 pages; 27cm.
《中华民国票据法》,Liu, S. Francis, Chu, Boyer P. H. , Chen, Lin-chong 译.英汉对照.

4. The Chinese law on negotiable instruments: promulgated by the National government of China on the thirtieth of October, 1929/translated into English by Hao-Hsuan Sun. Shanghai: Kelly and Walsh limited, c1930. viii, 78 p. ; 23cm.
中国票据法.孙浩煊译.

5. Revised temporary regulations with regard to trade and foreign exchange transactions: promulgated by the national government of the Republic of China, August,

1947；with notifications，full text of Finance Minister's and Central Bank Governor's statements，preamble and resolutions adopted by State Council，etc. Shanghai：China Daily Tribune Pub. Co.，1947. 20 p.；20cm.

修正进出口贸易暂行办法及管理外汇暂行办法：附申请手续及各种表式.

6. Direct tax；laws and regulations/translated into English by Sun Tsao-Hsuan. ［Chungking］Direct Tax Administration，Ministry of Finance，1943. 30 p.

中华民国所得税法.Sun，Tsao-Hsuan 译.

7. The banking law of China/english translation by Chaoyuen C. Chang. ［s. l.：s. n.］，1947. 35 p.；22cm.

中华民国银行法.Chang，Chaoyuen C. 译.

8. Code of customs regulations and procedure. 2nd ed.：rev. and enl. Shanghai：Statistical Department of the Inspectorate General of Customs，1935. xii，463 p.：ill.；25cm. (The Maritime Customs III. Miscellaneous series；no. 44)

中国海关规章和程序.海关总税务司，Wright，Stanley Fowler(1873—)译.第二版.

(1)3rd ed.：rev. and enl. Shanghai：Statistical Dept. of the Inspectorate General of Customs，1937. xiii，562 p.：ill.；25cm. (The Maritime Customs III. Miscellaneous series；no. 44)

9. Customs preventive law and rules of the Customs Penalty Board of Inquiry and Appeal. Shanghai，Statistical Dept. of the Inspectorate General of Customs，1935. 19，19 pages；17cm. (China. Statistical Department. Miscellaneous series；no. 48)

《海关关税法和关税处罚及上诉规定》，英汉对照.

(1) Customs preventive law and rules of the customs penalty board of inquiry and appeal. Published by order of the inspector General of Customs，Shanghai，1946. 1 preliminary leaf，19，19 pages，1 leaf 16cm. (Chinese Maritime Customs. III，Miscellaneous series，；no. 48)

D335 经济法

1. Code of maritime law，promulgated the 30th December，18th year（1929）：and enforced the 1st January，20th year（1931）of the republic：Chinese text with English translation/translated and edited by John McNeill and Wei Wen-Han. Shanghai：China Law Journal，c［1931］. ［4］，［1］，49 p.，［1］p.；21cm.

《海洋法》，McNeill，John，魏文瀚合译.英汉对照.

2. Code of maritime law，promulgated the 30th December，18th year（1929）：and enforced the 1st January，20th year（1931）of the republic：Chinese text with English translation/translated and edited by John McNeill and Wei Wen-Han. Shanghai，China：China Law Journal，

［1931］. ［4］，［1］，49 p.，［1］p.；21cm.

《中国海事法规》，McNeill，John，Wei，Wenhan 译.英汉对照.

3. Regulations for preventing collisions at sea：Became internationally operative in 1910. Shanghai，Statistical Dept. of the Inspectorate General of Customs，1912. 24，34 pages chart 16cm

Notes：The acceptance by China of the "Regulations for preventing collisions at sea," refers only to Chinese vessels of foreign type—Chinese vessels of native type do not come under their operation. —cf. Prefatory note.

国际海上避碰法规.英汉对照.

(1)Shanghai，Statistical Dept. of the Inspectorate General of Customs，1923. 24 ［37］ pages chart 17cm.

4. Translation of the chinese bankruptcy code of 1905/by Chang Nieh-Yün；with an editorial by J. H. Teesdale. Shanghai，American Presbyterian Mission Press，1907. 33 pages；21cm.

破产法.张云(Chang Nieh-Yün)译.英汉对照.

(1)Place of publication not identified]：Book on Demand Ltd，2013. ISBN：5518530862，5518530867

5. The bankruptcy law of the Republic of China：promulgated 1935/translated into English by Yukon Chang，B. SC. and Lily C. Yung，A. B.；introduction by the Hon. Foo Ping-Sheung. Shanghai ［etc.］：Kelly & Walsh，limited，c1936. xvii p.，1 l.，53 p.；26cm.

中国民国破产法.张舆公(Chang，Yukon)和 Yung，Lily C. 合译.

6. Commercial associations ordinance of the Chinese republic/translated and published by Ministry of Justice. ［Paris，Impr. de Vaugirard，1914］. 63 p.；23cm.

中华民国公司条例.司法部编译法律会译印.

7. The ordinance for the general regulation of traders of the Chinese Republic/tr. by the Law Codification Commission. Peking：Ministry of Justice，1914. 16 p.

中华民国商人通例.

(1)Peking：Ministry of Justice，1922. 16 pages；21cm.

8. Regulations relating to commerce. Peking：Commission on Extraterritoriality，1923. 126 pages；25cm.

Contents：I. Ordinance for the general regulations of traders. II. Commercial associations' ordinance. III. Regulations of the Arbitration Court of Commerce. IV. Detailed regulations relating to the administration of the Arbitration Court of Commerce. V. The law of chambers of commerce

商业法规汇编.

9. The modern commercial legislation of China/translated & compiled by Theodore Chen，B. A.，and Norwood F. Allman. Shanghai：［s. n.］，c1926. 152，86 p.；21cm.

中国商业法令.郑希陶译撰.

10. Company law/translated into English by H. K. Shih.

Shanghai： Published by the Bureau of Industrial and Commercial Information， Ministry of Industry，1929. 41 pages.

《公司法》，Shih，H. K. 译.

11. The company law of China： promulgated 12th April, 1946/English translation by Chao-yuen C. Chang; foreword by Sun Fo. 2nd ed.，rev. Shanghai：Kelly & Walsh，c1946. 103 p.；23cm.

《中国公司法》，张肇元(1892—)译.

(1) Rev. 1946.［New York：Chinese News Service］, c1946. 58 p.；22cm.

12. Chinese company law. rev. ed. Shanghai：Ao Sen Law Office，［c1946］. 82 p.；21cm.

中国公司法，修订版.

D336 土地法

1. The Chinese land law and the law governing the enforcement of the Chinese land law：(amended and promulgated on April 29，1946 by the National Government of the Republic of China)/Translated by the Land Division， Joint Commission on Rural Reconstruction. Taipei，1949. 37 p.；33×21cm.

中国土地法与实施细则. Joint Commission on Rural Reconstruction 翻译.

D337 劳动法

1. Three of the recent labour laws promulgated by the National government of the Republic of China. Nanking：Ministry of Industry，Commerce and Labor，1929. 24 pages；22cm.

Notes：Includes English translations of the Labor union law，the Factory law，and the Law on conciliation and arbitration of Labour disputes

中华民国政府批准的三个劳动法，包括工会法、工厂法、劳动调解和仲裁法.

2. China's national factory law：promulgated by the national government，Republic of China，Nanking，December 30, 1929/translation by N. F. Allman and Lowe Chuan-hua. Shanghai，China：China Weekly Review，［1930］. 11, ［10］ p.；21cm.

工厂法. Allman，Norwood F. (Norwood Francis,1893—1987)与 Lowe，Chuan-hua 合译.

3. China's labor laws，1929—1935：Chinese text with English translation/edited by Koo Ping Yuen. Shanghai：Commercial Press，1935. xiii，156，144 p.；19cm.

《中国劳工法规》，Gu，Bingyuan 编.

D338 刑法

1. The provisional criminal code of the Republic of China/translated by T. T. Yuen & Tachuen S. K. Loh. ［Peking］：Printed by the "Peking gazette"，c［1915］. ii, 101 p.；22cm.

中华民国刑法草案(1915). Yuen，T. T. Loh 和 Tachuen S. K. 合译.

(1)［Paris：Impr. de Vaugirard，c1915］. ii，102 p.； 26cm.

(2) The provisional criminal code of the Republic of China/translated by the Law Codification Commission. Peking，Ministry of Justice，c1919. 129 p.；21cm.

2. The criminal code of the Republic of China. 2nd rev. draft. Peking：Law Codification Commission，1919. 4, 122 p.；26cm.

中华民国刑法.

3. The provisional Criminal code of the Republic of China： embodying presidential mandates，the provisional criminal code amendment act，the revised draft of the law on offences relating to morphine，revised regulations governing military criminal cases，regulations governing naval criminal cases/published by the Commission on Extraterritoriality. Peking： Commission on Extraterritoriality，c1923. 190 p.；25cm.

中华民国刑法草案. 中国治外法权委员会译.

4. The criminal code of the Republic of China/translated into English by S. L. Burdett... in collaboration with Lone Liang＝Zhonghua min guo xing fa/Kadete，Liang Long tong yi.［Shanghai］：Shanghai lin shi fa yuan，［1928］. 103，103 p.；24cm.

《中华民国刑法》(1928 年)，Burdett，S. L.，梁龙合译. 中英文本.

5. The Chinese criminal code：(promulgated by the Chinese nationalist government)/translated by Yu Tinn-hugh. Shanghai，China：International Pub. Co.，c1928. 2 p. l.，［iii]-xii p.，1 l.，293 p.；20cm.

《中华民国刑法》，余天休译.

6. The Chinese criminal code and special criminal and administrative laws/translated and annotated by the Legal Department of the Shanghai Municipal Council.［2nd ed.］. Shanghai，China：Commercial Press，1935. 416 p. in various paginations；23cm.

《中华民国刑法》，上海公共租界工商局法律部译注. 英汉对照.

7. The criminal code of the Republic of China，embodying the law governing the application of the criminal code and the penal code of army，navy and air forces of the Republic of China. Translated into English by Chao-yuen C. Chang... foreword by the Hon. Sun Fo. Shanghai：Kelly & Walsh，c1935. 6 p. l.，184 p.；26cm.

Notes："The criminal code... promulgated January 1st in the 24th year of the Republic of China (1935). Becomes effective July 1st in the 24th year of the republic of China (1935).

《中华民国刑法》，张肇元（1892—）译.

8. The Criminal Code of the Republic of China/translated into English by Ching-Lin Hsia and Boyer P. H. Chu. Shanghai：Kelly & Walsh, 1936. xiii, 161 pages；26cm.
中华民国刑法. Xia, Jinlin（1896—）和 Chu, Boyer Pao-hsien 合译.

D339 民法

1. Draft Chinese Civil Code：presented by the Ministry of Justice to the chief executive of the Republic of China for promulgation on the 23rd day of the 11th month of the 14th year of the Republic（Nov. 23rd, 1925）/translated and published by the Commission on Extraterritoriality. Peking：Commission on Extraterritoriality in China, c1926. 1 v.；24cm.
《民律草案总则草编》，中国治外法权委员会译. 英汉对照.

2. The civil code of the Republic of China/translated into English by Ching-lin Hsia...［et al.］；introduction by Hon. Foo Ping-sheung. Shanghai：Kelly & Walsh, Limited, c1931. xxxii, 382 p.；26cm.
Content：book I. General principles—book II. Obligations—book III. Rights over things—book IV. Family—book V. Succession.
中华民国民法. 夏晋麟（1896—）译.
(1) Taipei：Mimeographed by the Law School of Soochow University（Taiwan School）, c［1953］. 154 l.；34cm.
(2) Arlington, Va.：University Publications of America, 1976. 2 volumes in 1；24cm. ISBN：0890930554, 0890930557.（Studies in Chinese government and law；China studies）

3. The principles of the law of succession in China：Chung kuo sze hsu fa/by Tsai Tsong Wong；adapted and translated into English by R. C. W. Sheng.［Shanghai, China］：［Comparative Law School of China］, 1922. 31 pages；23cm.
《中国继承法》，Wong, Tsai Tsong 著；Sheng, R. C. W. 译.
(1) Shanghai：Commercial Press, 1924. 31 pages；23cm.

4. Copyright law of China. Shanghai, c［1928］. 12 p.；23cm.
《中国版权法》，Allman, Norwood Francis（1893—）译.

5. Trade mark law and detailed regulations. Peking：Commission on Extraterritoriality, 1923. 33 p.；26cm.
商标法及其实施细则. 法权讨论委员会翻译.

6. The trade mark law and detailed regulations/translated and published by the Bureau of Trade Marks. Peking：The Bureau, 1924. 45 p.；23cm.
商标法与实施细则. 中国民国商标局翻译并出版.

7. Registration of trade marks：detailed regulations. Shanghai：British Chamber of Commerce, 1931. 7 pages；31cm.
《商标法施行细则》

8. Revised Chinese trade-mark law. regulations and classification of merchandise/translated by Norwood F. Allman. Shanghai：Allman & Co., 1936. 20 p.；23cm.
《中国商标法》，Allman, Norwood F.（Norwood Francis, 1893—1987）译. 中英对照.

9. Revised Chinese trade-mark law. regulations and classification of merchandise/translated by Norwood F. Allman. Shanghai：Allman & Co., 1936. 20 pages；23cm.
Notes：Includes Shang biao fa, Promulgated by the Chinese government on Nov. 23, 1935：39 articles（p. 1—6）；Shang biao fa shi xing xi ze, promulgated on Dec. 30, 1930 and revised on Sept. 3, 1932：40 articles（p. 6—20）.
Allman, Norwood F.（Norwood Francis, 1893—1987）译. 包括商标法和商标法施行细则修订版.

D339.1 诉讼法

1. The draft code of criminal procedure of China（1910）/translated by F. T. Cheng, for the Ministry of Justice. Peking：［s. n.］, c1919. 2, 141 p.；25cm.
《中国刑事诉讼法》（初稿），郑天赐（Cheng, F. T.）（1884—）译.

2. Regulations relating to criminal procedure of the Republic of China：promulgated on November 14, 1921；embodying presidential mandates, regulations relating on the enforcement of the regulations relating to criminal procedure, regulations relating to summary criminal procedure and provisional regulations relating to sentence by order/published by the Commission on Extraterritoriality. Peking：Commission on Extraterritoriality, 1923. 131, 4, 3, 4, ［2］ pages；25cm.
中华民国刑事诉讼法规.

3. The Code of criminal procedure of the Republic of China and the Court agreement relating to the Chinese courts in the international settlement of Shanghai, China/translated by the Legal Department of the Shanghai Municipal Council. Shanghai, China, Commercial Press, c1936. vii, 140, 140, 141—239 p., 1 l.；23cm.
Notes："Court agreement；agreement between His Majesty's government in the United kingdom and the Brazilian, Netherlands, Norwegian and United States governments and the Chinese government relating to the Chinese courts in the international settlement at Shanghai, with relative exchanges of notes and declaration"：p. 141—159.
中国民国刑事诉讼法，以及中华民国与英国、巴西、荷兰、挪威和美国关于在上海地方法院的国际诉讼处理的协议.上海工部局法律处译.英汉对照.

4. The Regulations relating to civil procedure of the Republic of China. Peking：Commission on Extraterritoriality, 1923. iii, 189 p.；25cm.（Commission on Extraterritoriality Pamphlets；1, pt. 4）
中华民国民事诉讼法规.

5. The Code of civil procedure of the Republic of China and the organic law of the judiciary/translated by Kwei Yu. Shanghai：Commercial Press, Ltd. , 1939. xii, 142 p.；22cm.
《中华民国民事诉讼法》

6. The Regulations of the arbitration court of the Chinese Republic/translated and published by Ministry of Justice. Peking：Ministry of Justice, ［c1913］. 9 p.；25cm.
中华民国商事公断处章程.

7. The law of compulsory execution of the Republic of China/translated from Chinese by N. M. Shoolingin. Tientsin, China：International Law Office, c1946. v, 26 p.；26cm.
中国民国强制执行法.

D339.2　司法制度

1. Regulations for the detention houses：promulgated on the 28th of January, the 2nd year ［1913］ of the Republic of China. ［Paris］, ［Imprimerie de Vaugirard］, 1914. ［1 volume］
中华民国监狱法规.

2. Rules for the government and administration of prisons in China/［translated by］ Ministry of Justice. ［Paris：Impr. de Vaugirard, 1915］. 24 p.；23cm.
中国监狱管理条文

3. The First Peking prison/translated by Chen Chi, Lin Shu Ming, Chow Tsuei Chi, Woo Tseng Yu. Peking, China：Pub. by the First Peking Prison, 1916. 2 v.：incl. forms. ；23cm.
Contents：v.1. Text (79 p.)—v.2. ill.
北平第一监狱.Chen, Chi 等译.

4. The law of the organization of the judiciary of the Chinese Republic/translated by the Law Codification Commission and published by the Ministry of Justice. ［Peking］：Peking Leader Press, ［1919］. 34 p.；22cm.
《中国民国司法组织法》

5. Laws, ordinances, regulations and rules relating to the judicial administration of the Republic of China/translated and published by the Commission on Extraterritoriality. Peking：Commission on Extraterritoriality, c1923. 4 leaves, 364 p.；25cm.
中华民国司法管理的法律、法规汇总.中国治外法权委员会翻译,初版于 1923 年.

（1）Reprint ed.　Taipei：Ch'eng Wen Publ. Co. , 1971. 364 pages；22cm.

（2）Arlington, Va.：University Publications of America, c1976. 364 p.；24cm. ISBN：0890930627, 0890930625.
（China studies；Studies in Chinese government law）

6. Interpretations of the Supreme Court at Peking, years 1915 and 1916：translations, notes and introduction/by M. H. van der Valk. Batavia：Sinological Institute, Faculty of Arts, University of Indonesia, ［1949］. 382 p. ；25cm. (Sinica Indonesiana；1.)
《大理院解释例全文》,Valk, Marius Hendrikus van der 译.中英文本.

7. Provisional regulations of the High Courts and their subordinate courts of the Chinese Republic/translated by the Law Codification Commission and published by the Ministry of Justice. Paris：Ministry of Justice, c［1915］. 24 p.；24cm.
《高等以下各级审判厅试办章程》,Law Codification Commission 译.
（1）［Peking］：Printed by the "Peking Leader" Press, c［191—?］

8. The Supreme Court regulations of China/translated by F. T. Cheng for the Supreme Court. Peking：Supreme Court, c1919.5 p. , 79 p.；26cm.
《大理院规程》,Chen, F. T. 译.

9. Provisional regulations of the High Courts and their subordinate courts of the Chinese Republic/Tr. by the Law Codification Commission and pub. by the Ministry of Justice. Peking, 1918. 24 pages
《高等以下各级审判厅试办章程》,司法部.

10. Tables of comparative statistics relating to civil and criminal cases in the Supreme Court from year I to year X of the Republic of China. Peking,1925. 25 p.；39cm.
中华民国大理院自民国第 1 年至 10 年的民事和刑事案件统计报表.大理院翻译并出版.

11. Tables of comparative statistics relating to civil and criminal cases in the Supreme Court from year I to year X of the Republic of China. Peking, c1925. 25 p.；39cm.
中华民国 1—10 年最高法院民事和刑事案件的统计.中国治外法权委员会翻译并出版.

D34　中华人民共和国法律法规

D341　法学理论、案例、法律汇编

1. China's legal system：a general survey/Du Xichuan, Zhang Lingyuan. Beijing, China：New World Press, 1990. 243 pages；21cm. ISBN：7800050874, 7800050879
《中国法律制度概述》,杜西川,张龄元著.新世界出版社.

2. The building of the legal system in China/New Star Publishers. Beijing：New Star Publishers, 2001. 61

pages：color illustrations；19cm．ISBN：7801484460，7801484468
《中国的法制建设》．新星出版社．

3. China：outlines of the legal system of the People's Republic of China/editor in chief Zhang Fusen；associate editor Hu Zejun．［Beijing］：Law Press China，2004．ii，iv，354 p．；23cm．ISBN：7503650052，7503650055
《中华人民共和国法律制度概览》，张福森主编．法律出版社．本书是有关中国法律制度的概括性介绍．

4. The rule of law in full swing in China/Hu Jinguang；［Wang Qin trans．］．Beijing：Foreign Languages Press，2009．123 pages：color illustrations；21cm．ISBN：7119061030，7119061038．（China in peaceful development）
《中国法治进行时》，胡锦光［著］．

5. China's laws/Pan Guoping & Ma Limin；translated by Chang Guojie．［Beijing］：China International Press，2010．173 pages：illustrations（chiefly color）；24cm．ISBN：7508517193，7508517199
《中国法律》，吴伟主编．五洲传播出版社．介绍中国法律制度建设和法治建设的各个方面情况．

6. 三个至上：寻找中国特色的司法体制改革之路：中英文双语版/徐振博著．北京：法律出版社，2010．402 页；23cm．ISBN：7511811943，7511811949
英文题名："The three supremacies"：finding a Chinese road to judicial reform．

7. The socialist system of laws with Chinese characteristics/Information Office of the State Council，the People's Republic of China．Beijing：Foreign Languages Press，2011．55 pages；26cm．ISBN：7119073040，7119073044，7119073064，7119073060
《中国特色社会主义法律体系》，中华人民共和国国务院新闻办公室［发布］．

8. 法治政府建设实施纲要 2015—2020 年：中英文对照/国务院法制办公室编．北京：中国法制出版社，2017．77 页；21cm．ISBN：7509383377

9. 敬海律师文集/王敬主编．大连：大连海事大学出版社，2009．522 页；23cm．ISBN：7563223770，7563223770
选取了 11 篇典型海事海商案例评析，中英文对照．

10. Fundamental laws of the Chinese Soviet Republic/with an introduction by Bela Kun．New York：International Publishers，1934．2 p. l.，87，［5］p．：ill．（map）diagrs．；19cm．
Contents：Preface by Bela Kun．—Constitution of the Chinese Soviet Republic—Agrarian legislation—Red army—Labour—Economics—Miscellaneous—Appendix．
收录中华苏维埃（1931—1937）共和国的法律，包括中华苏维埃宪法、土地法、婚姻法、劳动法、经济法和其他法规．

11. Fundamental legal documents of Communist China/edited by Albert P. Blaustein．South Hackensack，N. J.：Fred B. Rothman，1962．xxix，603 p．；23cm．
收录中华人民共和国的法律．

12. Selected legal documents of the People's Republic of China/edited by Joseph En-Pao Wang．Arlington，Va.：University Publications of America，1976—1979．2 volumes；24cm．ISBN：0890930678，0890930670，0890932417（v. 2），0890932414（v. 2）．（Studies in Chinese government and law；China studies）
Contents：Constitution of the People's Republic of China．—Documents of the first session of the Fourth National People's Congress of the People's Republic of China．—The Tenth National Congress of the Communist Party of China．—The electoral law of the People's Republic of China for the All-China People's Congress and local people's congresses of all levels．—Important labour laws and regulations of the People's Republic of China．—The marriage law of the People's Republic of China．—The agrarian reform law of the People's Republic of China，and other relevant documents．—Model regulations for an agricultural producers' co-operative．—Model regulations for advanced agricultural producers' co-operatives．
《中华人民共和国法律文选》，Wang，Joseph En-pao（1909—）编．

13. The laws of the People's Republic of China，1987—1989/compiled by the Legislative Affairs Commission of the Standing Committee of the National People's Congress of the People's Republic of China．Beijing：Science Press，1990．vi，361 p．；25cm．ISBN：7030019512，7030019516
《中华人民共和国法律汇编：1987—1989》．科学出版社．

15. The laws of the People's Republic of China 1993/compiled by the Legislative Affairs Commission of the Standing Committee of the National People's Congress of the People's Republic of China．Vol. 5．Beijing：Science Press，1995．vi，385 pages；25cm．ISBN：7030047079，7030047076
《中华人民共和国法律汇编 1993》．科学出版社．

16. The laws of the People's Republic of China 1994/compiled by the Legislative Affairs Commission of the Standing Committee of the National People's Congress of the People's Republic of China．Beijing：Science Press，1996．volumes［1－6］；25cm．ISBN：7030054466，7030054463
《中华人民共和国法律汇编 1994》．科学出版社．

17. The laws of the People's Republic of China，1996/compiled by the Legislative Affairs Commission of the Standing Committee of the National People's Congress of the People's Republic of China．Beijing：Publishing

House of Law, 1997. iv, 367 pages；25cm. ISBN：
7503622040, 7503622045

《中华人民共和国法律汇编1996》，全国人大法工委编.
法律出版社.

18. 中华人民共和国法律汇编：中英对照＝Laws of the
People's Republic of China：Chinese-English edition/全
国人大常委会法制工作委员会办公室编译. 北京：法律
出版社，1998. 2 volumes；25cm. ISBN：7503621273,
7503621277

目次：[1] 行政法(经济类)卷—[2] 民法，商法卷.

19. The laws of the People's Republic of China, 1999/
compiled by the Legislative Affairs Commission of the
Standing Committee of the National People's Congress of
the People's Republic of China. Beijing, China：Law Pr.
China，2000. 379 pages；26cm. ISBN：7503631856,
7503631856

《中华人民共和国法律汇编1999》，全国人大法工委编
译. 法律出版社.

20. The laws of the People's Republic of China 2000/
compiled by the Legislative Affairs Commission of the
Standing Committee of the National People's Congress of
the People's Republic of China. Beijing：Law Press，
2001. 294 pages；25cm. ISBN：7503635126,
7503635120

《中华人民共和国法律汇编2000》，全国人民代表大会常
务委员会法制工作委员会编译. 法律出版社.

21. The laws of the People's Republic of China 2001/
compiled by the Legislative Affairs Commission of the
Standing Committee of the National People's Congress of
the People's Republic of China. Beijing：Law Press，
2002. 391 pages；25cm. ISBN：7503639237,
7503639234

《中华人民共和国法律2001》，全国人大常委会法律工作
委员会. 法律出版社.

22. The laws of the People's Republic of China，2002/
compiled by the Legislative Affairs Commission of the
Standing Committee of the National People's Congress
of the People's Republic of China. Beijing：Law Press，
2002. v, 367 pages；26cm. ISBN：7503642920,
7503642920

《中华人民共和国法律2002》，全国人大法工委审定. 法
律出版社.

23. The laws of the People's Republic of China，2004/
compiled by the Legislative Affairs Commission of the
Standing Committee of the National People's Congress
of the People's Republic of China. Beijing：Law Press，
2005. v, 525 pages；26cm. ISBN：7503658258,
7503658259

《中华人民共和国法律：英文. 2004 年》，全国人大常委会
法制工作委员会编译. 法律出版社. 收录 2004 年颁布的

所有法律及法律性文件的英文版本.

24. 中华人民共和国法律＝The Laws of the People's
Republic of China：英文. 2005 年/全国人大法工委编译.
北京：法律出版社，2006. 293 页；25cm. ISBN：
7503666986, 7503666988

25. The laws of the People's Republic of China 2006/
compiled by the Legislative Affairs Commission of the
Standing Committee of the National People's Congress of
the People's Republic of China. Beijing：Law Press
China，2007. iv, 226 pages；26cm. ISBN：7503677205,
7503677201

《中华人民共和国法律：英文. 2006 年》，全国人大法工委
编译. 法律出版社. 本书收录 2006 年我国公布及修订的
法律及法律决定的英文官方译本.

26. The laws of the People's Republic of China, 2007/
compiled by the Legislative Affairs Commission of the
Standing Committee of the National People's Congress
of the People's Republic of China. Beijing：Law Press
China，2008. v, 495 pages；26cm. ISBN：7503689321,
7503689323

《中华人民共和国法律. 2007》，全国人大法工委编译. 法
律出版社. 收录 2007 年所有法律的英文译本.

27. The laws of the People's Republic of China，2008/
compiled by the Legislative Affairs Commission of the
Standing Committee of the National People's Congress
of the People's Republic of China. Beijing：Law Press，
2009. 180 pages；25cm. ISBN：7511800893,
7511800890

《中华人民共和国法律》，全国人大法工委编译. 法律出
版社. 本书是 2008 年我国全国人大及其常委会公布的
全部法律、法律性文件的官方英文译本.

28. The laws of the People's Republic of China 2009/
compiled by the Legislative Affairs Commission of the
Standing Committee of the National People's Congress of
the People's Republic of China. Beijing：Law Press，
2010. iv., 245 pages；26cm. ISBN：7511814036,
7511814034

《中华人民共和国法律》，全国人大法工委编译. 法律出
版社. 收录了 2009 年全国人民代表大会以及全国人民
代表大会常务委员会通过、由中华人民共和国国家主席
颁布的所有法律及法律性解释的官方英文译本.

29. 中华人民共和国常用法律法规全书：中英文版/国务院
法制办公室编. 北京：中国法制出版社，2011. 2 册(244
页,476 页)；25cm. ISBN：7509322314, 7509322316

本书选取了我国目前现行有效的常用法律及行政法规
文件 100 多件，以中、英双语对照的模式出版，英文版本
为全国人大常委会和国务院法制办公室翻译审定并对
外公布的官方译本.

30. 中华人民共和国涉外法规汇编. 2009/中华人民共和国
国务院法制办公室编. 北京：中国法制出版社，2011. 12

页,765 页;27cm. ISBN:7509329887,7509329884
本书收录了 2009 年颁布或修订的法律及行政法规中英文译本。

31. 中华人民共和国法律法规汇编/国务院法制办公室编. 国务院法制办公室编. 北京:中国法制出版社,2011—2012. 6 卷;26cm. ISBN:7509321508（v. 1）,7509321506（v.1）,7509321478（v. 2）,7509321476（v. 2）,7509331095（v. 3, 2 pts.）,7509331099（v.3,2 pts.）,7509331088（v.4,2 pts.）,7509331080（v.4,2 pts.）,7509321485（v. 5）,7509321484（v. 5）,7509321492（v.6）,7509321492（v.6）

目次:［v. 1］宪法卷＝Constitutional law—［v. 2］民商法卷＝Civil and commercial law—［v. 3, 2 pts.］行政法卷（I-II）＝Administrative law I-II—［v. 4, 2 pts.］经济法卷（I-II）＝Economic law I-II—［v. 5］社会法卷＝Social law—［v. 6］刑法,程序法卷＝Criminal law and procedure law.

英文题名:Laws and regulations of the People's Republic of China. 本汇编收集了现行有效的中华人民共和国法律法规中文本和英文译本. 英文译本由国务院法制办公室组织翻译和审定.

32. Compilation of laws and regulations concerning foreign investment in China/compiled by Information Office of the State Council of the People's Republic of China. ［Beijing］: China international Press, 1999. 261 pages; 21cm. ISBN: 7801136209, 7801136206

《外商在华投资法规和投资政策》,赵晓笛编. 五洲传播出版社.

33. Compilation of laws and regulations concerning foreign investment in China/compiled by Information Office of the State Council of the People's Republic of China. 2nd ed. ［Peking］: China international Press, 2001. 576 pages; 21cm. ISBN: 7801139305, 7801139306

《外商在华投资法规和投资政策》,中华人民共和国国务院新闻办公室选编. 2 版. 五洲传播出版社.

34. The tradition and modern transition of Chinese law/Jinfan Zhang; chief translator, Zhang Lixin; other translators, Yan Chen, Li Xing, Zhang Ye, Xu Hongfen. Third revision. Heidelberg: Springer, ［2014］. xvii, 710 pages; 25cm. ISBN: 3642232657, 3642232655

《中国法律的传统与近代转型》,张晋藩编著; Zhang Lixin 等译.

D342 国家法、宪法

1. Report on the draft constitution of the People's Republic of China. Constitution of the People's Republic of China. ［Adopted on September 20, 1954 by the First National People's Congress at its first session］. Peking: Foreign Languages Press, 1954. 101 pages: portraits; 22cm.

《关于中华人民共和国宪法草案的报告》,刘少奇.

(1) Peking: Foreign Languages Press, 1956. 101 pages: portrait.
(2) ［2nd ed.］. Peking: Foreign Languages Press, 1962. 93 pages: portraits; 22cm.

2. Constitution of the People's Republic of China: adopted on Sept. 20, 1954 by the First National People's Congress of the People's Republic of China, at its first session. Peking: Foreign Languages Press, 1954. 57 p.; 21cm.

《中华人民共和国宪法》(1954)
(1) Rev. translation. Peking: Foreign Languages Press, 1961. 42 p.; 21cm.
(2) Peking: Foreign Languages Press, 1975. 61 p.; 19cm.

3. The constitution of the People's Republic of China: adopted on March, 5, 1978 by the Fifth National People's Congress of the People's Republic of China at its first session. Peking: Foreign Languages Press, 1978. 41 p.; 22cm.

《中华人民共和国宪法》(1978)

4. Constitution of the People's Republic of China: adopted at the fifth session of the Fifth National People's Congress and promulgated for implementation by the proclamation of the National People's Congress on December 4, 1982. Beijing: Foreign Languages Press, 1987. 79 p.; 23cm.

《中华人民共和国宪法》(1982)
(1) Oxford ［Oxfordshire］; New York: Pergamon Press; Beijing: Foreign Languages Press, 1983. 93 p.; 20cm. ISBN: 008030818X, 0080308171
(2) 2nd ed. Beijung: Foreign Languages Press, 1990. 83 p.; 23cm. ISBN: 0835119823, 7119000446
(3) 3rd ed. Beijing: Foreign Languages Press, 1994. 96 p.; 19cm. ISBN: 7119016997, 7119016993
(4) 4th ed. Beijing: Foreign Languages Press, 1999. 138 p.; 23cm. ISBN: 7119023888

5. 中华人民共和国宪法＝Constitution of the People's Republic of China. 北京:中国法制出版社,2001. 121 pages; 21cm. ISBN: 7800838137, 7800838132

注:"1982 年 12 月 4 日第五届全国人民代表大会第五次会议通过 1982 年 12 月 4 日全国人民代表大会公告公布施行"

英汉对照.

6. 中华人民共和国宪法＝Constitution of the People's Republic of China. 北京:中国方正出版社,2004. 101 pages; 20cm. ＋ 1 CD-ROM（4 3/4 in.）. ISBN: 7801077474, 7801077479.（中英文对照法律法规系列）; 8)

7. Constitution of the People's Republic of China＝中华人民共和国宪法. 第 5 版. 北京:外文出版社,2004. 155 pages; 23cm. ISBN: 7119036823, 7119036823

本书包括 1982 年和 2004 年《宪法》及其各次的修正案.

8. China: Outlines of the Constitution of the People's

Republic of China/editor in chief：Zhang Fusen; associate editor：Hu Zejun. Beijing：Fa lü chu ban she, 2004. ii, iii, 187 pages; 23cm. ISBN：7503650036, 7503650031

《中华人民共和国宪法概要》，张福森主编.法律出版社.本书是对中国宪法的概要介绍.

9. 中华人民共和国宪法：汉英对照/全国人民代表大会常务委员会法制工作委员会编译.北京：人民出版社，2004. 213 页；20cm. ISBN：7010042861, 7010042862

英文题名：Constitution of the People's Republic of China. 本书由全国人大常委会法工委编译，中英文对照. 收有 1982 年五届人大通过的《宪法》文本，和 1993 年、1999 年、2004 年共四次的修正案和公告，以及为方便使用的《宪法》修正文本.

10. 宪法：汉英对照/中国法制出版社编.北京：中国法制出版社，2005. 241 页；20cm. ISBN：7801828445.（中英文对照法规系列）

英文题名 Constitutional law. 本书为关于宪法法律法规的中英文法律文本对照

11. 中华人民共和国国家赔偿法 ＝ Law of the People's Republic of China on state compensation. 北京：中国法制出版社，2001. 37 pages；20cm. ISBN：7800838137, 7800838132

英汉对照.

12. 中华人民共和国立法法 ＝ Legislation Law of the People's Republic of China. 北京：中国法制出版社，2002. 63 pages；21cm. ISBN：7800838137, 7800838132

英汉对照.

D343　行政法

1. China's administrative law＝Zhong guo xing zheng fa/Yan Tieyi［and others］. Dalian shi：Dalian Maritime University，2005. 2, iii, 226 pages；23cm. ISBN：7563217960, 7563217967

《中国行政法：英文》，阎铁毅等著.大连海事大学出版社.阐述了中国行政法的基本理论，内容主要包括：行政法基本原则；行政主体；行政行为；行政处罚；行政许可；行政复议；国家赔偿法及行政赔偿等.

2. 行政法：汉英对照/中国法制出版社编.北京：中国法制出版社，2005. 215 页；21cm. ISBN：7801828380.（中英文对照法规系列）

本书是关于行政法律法规的中英文法律文本对照.包括了中华人民共和国行政许可法，中华人民共和国行政处罚法，中华人民共和国行政复议法，中华人民共和国行政监察法等内容.英文题名 Administrative law.

3. 中华人民共和国文物保护法：汉英对照/国家文物局编.北京：文物出版社，2005. 128 页；20cm. ISBN：7501017425

英文题名：Law of the People's Republic of China on protection of cultural relics. 本书包括中华人民共和国文物保护法及中华人民共和国文物保护法实施条例.

4. 中华人民共和国教育法：Education Law of the People's Republic of China. 北京：中国法制出版社，2001. 49 pages；21cm. ISBN：7800838137, 7800838132

注："1995 年 3 月 18 日第八届全国人民代表大会第三次会议通过 1995 年 3 月 18 日中华人民共和国主席令第 45 号公布自 1995 年 9 月 1 日起施行"—Page 2

英汉对照.

5. 中华人民共和国义务教育法 ＝ Compulsory Education Law of the People's Republic of China. 中华人民共和国教育法 ＝ Education Law of the People's Republic of China. 中华人民共和国民办教育促进法 ＝ Law of the People's Republic of China on Promotion of Privately-run Schools. 北京：法律出版社，2004. 97 pages；21cm. ISBN：7503636599, 7503636592.（中英对照法律文本. 8 元系列. 2；3）

本书收录了义务教育法、教育法与民办教育促进法的中文本和英文本.

6. 中华人民共和国药品管理法·中华人民共和国药品管理法实施条例：汉英对照/国家食品药品监督管理局编译.北京：中国医药科技出版社，2003. 134 页；21cm. ISBN：7506727358, 7506727358

英文题名：Drug administration law of the People's Republic of China

7. 中华人民共和国中医药条例＝Regulations of the People's Republic of China on Traditional Chinese Medicine. 北京：中国法制出版社，2003. 33 pages；21cm. ISBN：7800838137, 7800838132

英汉对照

8. 宗教事务条例. 第 2 版. 北京：宗教文化出版社，2010. 61 页；21cm. ISBN：7802542341, 7802542340

英文题名：Regulations on religious affairs. 按照中华人民共和国国务院令第 426 号，《宗教事务条例》经 2004 年 7 月 7 日国务院第 57 次常务会议通过，自 2005 年 3 月 1 日起施行.

9. 中华人民共和国科学技术进步法 ＝ Law of the People's Republic of China on Progress of Science and Technology. 北京：中国法制出版社，2001. 45 pages；21cm. ISBN：7800838137, 7800838132

英汉对照

10. 突发公共卫生事件应急条例 ＝ Regulations on preparedness for and response to emergent public health hazards. 北京：中国法制出版社，2003. 45 pages；21cm. ISBN：7800838137, 7800838132

英汉对照

11. 中华人民共和国食品卫生法＝Food Hygiene Law of the People's Republic of China. 北京：中国法制出版社，2001. 47 pages；21cm. ISBN：7800838137, 7800838132

英汉对照

12. 中华人民共和国进出口商品检验法实施条例：汉英对照/国务院法制办公室编.北京：中国法制出版社，2006. 55 页；20cm. ISBN：7802263689, 7802263680

英文题名：Regulations on Implementation of the Law of the People's Republic of China on Import and Export Commodity Inspection. 本书为中华人民共和国进出口商品检验法实施条例的中英文对照版.

13. 进出口商品免验办法/国家质检总局法规司,国家质检总局标准法规中心编译. 北京:中国标准出版社,2010. 29页;21cm. ISBN:7506657006, 7506657007

14. 进出口商品复验办法/国家质检总局法规司,国家质检总局标准法规中心编译. 北京:中国标准出版社,2010. 23页;21cm. ISBN:7506657013
英文题名：Measures on exemption of import and export commodity inspection.

15. 进口商品残损检验鉴定管理办法/国家质检总局法规司,国家质检总局标准法规中心编译. 北京:中国标准出版社, 2010. 30页;21cm. ISBN:7506657020, 7506657023
英文题名：Administrative measures for inspection and survey of damage to import commodities.

16. 国境口岸突发公共卫生事件出入境检验检疫应急处理规定/国家质检总局法规司,国家质检总局标准法规中心编译. 北京:中国标准出版社,2010. 35页;21cm. ISBN:7506656962, 7506656965
英文题名：Provisions on entry-exit inspection and quarantine response toward public health emergencies at frontier ports.

17. 出境水果检验检疫监督管理办法/国家质检总局法规司,国家质检总局标准法规中心编译. 北京:中国标准出版社,2010. 42页;21cm. ISBN:7506656955, 7506656957
英文题名：Administrative measures of inspection, quarantine and supervision on exit fruits.

18. 口岸艾滋病防治管理办法/国家质检总局法规司,国家质检总局标准法规中心编译. 北京:中国标准出版社,2010. 24页;21cm. ISBN:7506656931, 7506656930
英文题名：Administrative measures for the prevention and treatment of port acquired immune deficiency syndrome.

19. 出入境口岸食品卫生监督管理规定/国家质检总局法规司,国家质检总局标准法规中心编译. 北京:中国标准出版社,2010. 37页;21cm. ISBN:7506656948, 7506656949
英文题名：Provisions on supervision and administration of food hygiene at entry-exit ports.

20. 进口涂料检验监督管理办法/国家质检总局法规司,国家质检总局标准法规中心编译. 北京:中国标准出版社,2010. 26页;21cm. ISBN:7506656993, 750665699X
英文题名：Administrative measures on inspection and supervision of imported coating.

21. 进口许可制度民用商品入境验证管理办法/国家质检总局法规司,国家质检总局标准法规中心编译. 北京:中国标准出版社,2010. 12页;21cm. ISBN:7506656986, 7506656981
英文题名：Administrative measures on entry verification of civil commodities subject to import licensing system.

22. 出入境人员携带物检疫管理办法/国家质检总局法规司,国家质检总局标准法规中心编译. 北京:中国标准出版社,2010. 34页;21cm. ISBN:7506656979, 7506656973
英文题名：Administrative measures on quarantine of articles carried by entry and exit passengers.

23. 出入境检验检疫报检员管理规定. 北京:中国标准出版社,2011. 25页;21cm. ISBN:7506662154, 7506662159
英文题名：Administrative stipulation on applicant for entry-exit inspection and quarantine.

24. 进出口玩具检验监督管理办法/国家质检总局法规司,国家质检总局标准法规中心编译. 北京:中国标准出版社,2011. 42页;21cm. ISBN:7506662147, 7506662140
英文题名：Measures for the inspection, supervision and administration of import and export toys.

25. 出入境检验检疫查封、扣押管理规定/国家质检总局法规司,国家质检总局标准法规中心编译. 北京:中国标准出版社,2011. 31页;21cm. ISBN:7506662130, 7506662132
英文题名：Administrative stipulation on seizure/detainment in entry-exit inspection and quarantine.

26. 出入境检验检疫代理报检管理规定. 北京:中国标准出版社,2011. 37页;21cm. ISBN:7506662123, 7506662124
英文题名：Administrative provisions on entry-exit inspection and quarantine application by agency.

27. 出入境快件检验检疫管理办法. 北京:中国标准出版社,2011. 27页;21cm. ISBN:7506662116, 7506662116
英文题名：Administrative measures on inspection and quarantine of entry-exit express consignments.

28. 进出口肉类产品检验检疫监督管理办法/国家质检总局法规司,国家质检总局标准法规中心编译. 北京:中国质检出版社:中国标准出版社,2011. 44页;21cm. ISBN:7506666053, 7506666057
英文题名：Administrative measures of inspection, quarantine and supervision on import and export meat products.

29. 进出口水产品检验检疫监督管理办法/国家质检总局法规司,国家质检总局标准法规中心编译. 北京:中国质检出版社:中国标准出版社,2011. 49页;21cm. ISBN:7506666060, 7506666065
英文题名：Administrative measures of inspection, quarantine and supervision on import and export aquatic products.

30. 出境水生动物检验检疫管理办法. 北京:中国质检出版社:中国标准出版社,2011. 54页;21cm. ISBN:7506664646, 750666464X
英文题名：Measures for supervision and administration of the inspection and quarantine of export-oriented aquatic animals.

31. 进出口饲料和饲料添加剂检验检疫监督管理办法. 北京:中国质检出版社:中国标准出版社,2011. 69页;21cm. ISBN:7506664608, 7506664607

英文题名：Administrative measures of inspection, quarantine and supervision on import and export feed and feed additives.

32. 出入境特殊物品卫生检疫管理规定.北京：中国质检出版社：中国标准出版社，2011. 30 页；21cm. ISBN：7506664615, 7506664615

英文题名：Administrative regulations for entry and exit quarantine of special goods.

33. 进境货物木质包装检疫监督管理办法.北京：中国质检出版社：中国标准出版社，2011. 23 页；21cm. ISBN：7506664592, 7506664593

英文题名：Measures for supervising and administering the quarantine of wooden packages of imported goods.

34. 进境动物隔离检疫场使用监督管理办法.北京：中国质检出版社：中国标准出版社，2011. 42 页；21cm. ISBN：7506664639, 7506664631

英文题名：Supervisory and administrative measures on inspection and quarantine of import solid wastes used as raw materials

35. 进口可用作原料的固体废物检验检疫监督管理办法.北京：中国标准出版社，2011. 52 页；21cm. ISBN：7506662178, 7506662175

英文题名：Supervisory and administrative measures on inspection and quarantine of import solid wastes used as raw materials

D344 财政法

1. Invest in China：a practical guide to tax law＝投资中国：税收法律实务指南/Liu Zuo 著；Liu Tieying 译. 北京：法律出版社，2006. 526 pages：illustrations；21cm. ISBN：7503661593, 7503661594
介绍中国税收法律制度及最新变革.

2. 中国金融财会法律法规：汉英对照/法律出版社法规中心编. 北京：法律出版社，2007. 572 页；21cm. ISBN：7503671463, 7503671467.（中国法律法规中英对照系列；6）
英文题名：Finance ＆ accounting laws and regulations of China. 本书收录金融财会方面的法律法规的中英文对照文本.

3. 中国最新税务合规指南：税收法律、法规及评注：2007 年：英文/刘佐，刘铁英编译. 北京：中国财政经济出版社，2007. 611 页；23cm. ISBN：7500596608, 750059660X
英文题名：2007 latest PRC tax compliance：laws, regulations ＆ commentaries.

4. 中华人民共和国基本税收法律法规手册：2009 汉英对照/中华人民共和国国务院法制办公室，中华人民共和国财政部编.北京：中国财政经济出版社，2009. 493 页；27cm. ISBN：7509517895, 7509517893
英文题名：Handbook of basic laws and regulations regarding taxation of the People's Republic of China. 收录截至 2009 年 4 月 1 日现行有效的基本税收法律、行政法规和必要的规章 50 篇.

5. 中华人民共和国企业所得税法，中华人民共和国个人所得税法/国务院法制办公室编. 北京：中国法制出版社，2009. 61 页；21cm. ISBN：7509311493, 7509311497

英文题名：Law of the People's Republic of China on Enterprise Income Tax；Individual income tax law of the People's Republic of China. 本书收录 2007 年公布的中华人民共和国企业所得税法和个人所得税法中英文本.

6. Customs laws ＆ regulations of the People's Republic of China/Victor F. S. Sit, editor. Hong Kong：Tai Dao Pub., c1984. v, 462 p.；27cm. ISBN：9627084069, 9627084068
《中国海关法规及税率》,Xue, Fengxuan 译. 中英文本.

7. The foreign-related tax laws and regulations of the People's Republic of China：authorized English texts of laws, regulations, rulings, and tax treaties/compiled and translated by the State Bureau and the Law Department of the Ministry of Finance of the People's Republic of China.［Amsterdam］：International Bureau of Fiscal Documentation, c1991—. 2 v. (loose-leaf)；23cm.
《中华人民共和国涉外税收法规》,财政部条法司编译.

8. 中华人民共和国进出口贸易管理措施海关报关手册：汉英对照.2005/中华人民共和国进出口贸易管理措施编委会编.北京：经济科学出版社，2005. 2, 1092 pages；29cm. ＋光盘 1 张. ISBN：7505846817, 7505846814
英文题名：Administrative measures regarding import ＆ export trade of the People's Republic of China：handbook of customs practices. 本书是根据国务院关税税则委员会 2005 年最新调整的进出口关税税率编写而成.

9. 中华人民共和国进出口贸易管理措施海关报关手册：汉英对照/《中华人民共和国进出口贸易管理措施》编委会编.北京：经济日报出版社，2006. 1128 页；29cm. ＋光盘 1 张. ISBN：7801805194, 7801805195
英文题名：Administrative measures regarding import ＆ export trade of the People's Republic of China handbook of customs practices.

10. 中华人民共和国注册会计师法＝Law of the People's Republic of China on certified public accountants. 北京：中国法制出版社，2001. 33 pages；21cm. ISBN：7800838137, 7800838132
英汉对照.

11. 中华人民共和国审计法＝Audit Law of the People's Republic of China. 北京：中国法制出版社，2001. 31 pages；21cm. ISBN：7800838137, 7800838132
英汉对照.

12. 中华人民共和国票据法＝Law of the People's Republic of China on negotiable instruments. 北京：中国方正出版社，2004. 51 pages；20cm. ＋1 CD-ROM (4 3/4 in.). ISBN：7801077482, 7801077486.（中英文对照法律法规系列；16）

D345 经济法

1. 经济法：汉英对照/中国法制出版社编.北京：中国法制出版社，2005. 308 页；21cm. ISBN：7801828399.（中英文对照法规系列）
本书收录了中华人民共和国税收征收管理法，政府采购法，中外合资经营企业法，外资企业法，反不正当竞争法，产品质量法等，本书是关于经济法律法规的中英文法律文本对照.

2. Comprehensive guide to Chinese business laws/Xie Zhao Hua Law Firm. Beijing：Pub. House of Law, 1995. 2, 12, 453 pages；21cm. ISBN：7503616148, 7503616143

《中国商事法律要览》，谢朝华律师事务所编. 法律出版社.

3. PRC laws for China traders [sic] & investors：practice & interpretation/editor, Thomas C. W. Chiu. North Point, Hong Kong：Institute of Contemporary Chinese Economic and Legal Studies, 1983. volumes〈1〉：illustrations；26cm. ISBN：9627105015.

中华人民共和国贸易与投资法. Chiu, C. W. (Chor-wing)编译.

4. China trade documents/[edited by]Thomas C. W. Chiu. Hong Kong：Tai Dao Pub. Ltd. ；Distributed by Ranges Publications, 1985. 415 pages：illustrations；27cm. ISBN：9627084132

中国贸易法规. Chiu, C. W. (Chor-wing)编译.
(1)2nd ed. , rev. Philadelphia：Taylor & Francis, 1988. xv, 427 pages：forms；27cm. ISBN：0800280016, 0800280017

5. 中华人民共和国对外贸易法＝Foreign Trade Law of the People's Republic of China. 北京：中国法制出版社，2001. 29 pages；21cm. ISBN：7800838137, 7800838132

注："1994年5月12日第八届全国人民代表大会常务委员会第七次会议通过1994年5月12日中华人民共和国主席令第22号公布1994年7月1日起施行"—Page 2. 英汉对照

6. 中华人民共和国对外贸易法/中华人民共和国商务部条法司编译. 北京：中国商务出版社，2004. 46 页：20cm. ISBN：7801812425

本书为新修订的对外贸易法，共11章70条.

7. 中华人民共和国对外贸易法＝Foreign trade law of the People's Republic of China＝La loi du commerce extérieur de la Republicque Populaire de Chine＝Aussenhandelsgesetz der Volksrepublik China＝中华人民共和国对外贸易法. 北京：中国法制出版社，2004. 2, 121 pages；20cm. ISBN：7801822706, 7801822703

中文、英、法、德、韩、日5种文字.

8. 中国对外贸易与经济合作法律法规：汉英对照/法律出版社法规中心编. 北京：法律出版社，2007. 621 页；21cm. ISBN：7503671425, 7503671424. （中国法律法规中英对照系列；5）

英文题名：Foreign trade & economy cooperation laws and regulations of China. 本书收录对外经济贸易与合作方面的法律法规的中英文对照本.

9. China laws for foreign business. Business regulations. Hong Kong：CCH Asia Pte Limited, 2009. 6 volumes in 11 (loose-leaf)：illustrations；24cm.

Notes：Includes text of documents in Chinese with English translation in parallel columns

中国对外经济贸易法规汇编. 英汉对照.

10. China laws for foreign business. Special zones & cities. Hong Kong：CCH Asia Pte Limited, 2009. 4 volumes (loose-leaf)：illustrations；25cm.

中国对外经济贸易法规汇编：特区和城市. 英汉对照.

11. 中国对外贸易与外商投资法律制度＝Logal System Foreign Trade and Investment in China：英文/孙南申，孙雯著. 北京：新星出版社，2007. 5, 236 pages；21cm. ISBN：7802252738, 7802252733

书名原文：Logal system foreign trade and investment in China.

12. 出口工业产品企业分类管理办法/国家质检总局法规司，国家质检总局标准法规中心编译. 北京：中国标准出版社，2011. 30 页；21cm. ISBN：7506662185, 7506662183

英文题名：Administrative measures on classification of industrial export products manufacturers.

13. 进出口商品数量重量检验鉴定管理办法. 北京：中国标准出版社，2011. 37 页；21cm. ISBN：7506662161, 7506662167

英文题名：Administrative measures on the quantity and/or weight inspection and survey of import and export commodities.

14. 中华人民共和国反不正当竞争法＝Law of the People's Republic of China Against Unfair Competition. 北京：中国法制出版社，2001. 25 pages；21cm. ISBN：7800838137, 7800838132

英汉对照.

15. 中华人民共和国反垄断法：中英文对照/国务院法制办公室编. 北京：中国法制出版社，2009 47 页；21cm. ISBN：7509311486, 7509311489

英文题名：Anti-monopoly law of the People's Republic of China.

16. 直销管理条例、禁止传销条例：汉英对照/国务院法制办公室编. 北京：中国法制出版社，2006. 71 页；20cm. ISBN：7802263670, 7802263673

英文题名：Regulations on administration of direct sales；Regulations on prohibition of chuanxiao. 本书是直销管理条例、禁止传销条例的中英文对照版本.

17. China's company law：the new legislation/with English translation and introduction by Guiguo Wang. Singapore：Butterworths Asia in co-operation with the Centre for Chinese and Comparative Law of the City Polytechnic of Hong Kong, 1994. vii, 98 p. ；25cm. ISBN：0409996769

《公司法》，Wang, Kuei-kuo 译. 中英文本.

18. 中国公司企业法律法规：汉英对照/法律出版社法规中心编. 北京：法律出版社，2007. 560 页；21cm. ISBN：7503671456, 7503671459. （中国法律法规中英对照系

列;4）

英文题名:Company & enterprise laws and regulations of China.本书收录公司与企业常用的法律法规中英文对照文本.

19. 中华人民共和国公司法解析/李桂平著.北京:中国时代经济出版社,2010. 250 页;24cm. ISBN:7511902696, 7511902693

英文题名:Analysis of company law of the People's Republic of China.

20. 外资并购法律实务指南:英文/黎作恒著.北京:法律出版社,2007. 334 页;21cm. ISBN:7503671173, 7503671173.（投资中国）

英文题名:Invest in China:a practical legal guide to mergers and acquisitions.

21. A guide to the latest foreign economic law and regulations of the People's Republic of China:Chinese and English version/zhu bian Hu Weibo. Beijing:Fa lü chu ban she, 1995. 1, 2208 p.;27cm. ISBN: 7503616385

《最新中国涉外经济法律实用全书》,胡微波主编.法律出版社.中英对照.

22. 中华人民共和国飞行基本规则:[英汉对照]/中国法制出版社编.北京:中国法制出版社,2002. 95 pages;20cm. ISBN:7800838137, 7800838132

英文题名:General Flight Rules of the People's Republic of China

23. 中华人民共和国广告法 = Advertisement Law of the People's Republic of China. 北京:中国法制出版社,2001. 35 pages;21cm. ISBN:7800838137, 7800838132

注:"1994 年 10 月 27 日第八届全国人民代表大会常务委员会第十次会议通过 1994 年 10 月 27 日中华人民共和国主席令第 34 号公布 1995 年 2 月 1 日起施行".英汉对照.

24. 企业国有资产监督管理暂行条例 = Interim regulations on supervision and management of state-owned assets of enterprises. 北京:中国法制出版社,2004. 28 pages;21cm. ISBN:7800838137, 7800838132
英汉对照.

25. 中华人民共和国政府采购法 = Government Procurement Law of the People's Republic of China;中华人民共和国招标投标法 = Tender Bidding Law of the People's Republic of China. 北京:中国法制出版社,2002. 107 pages;21cm. ISBN:7800838137, 7800838132
英汉对照.

26. 中华人民共和国拍卖法 = Auction law of the People's Republic of China. 北京:中国方正出版社,2004. 29 pages; 20cm. + 1 CD-ROM (4 3/4 in.). ISBN:7801077644,7801077646.（中英文对照法律法规系列;14）

27. 中华人民共和国招标投标法 = Law of the People's Republic of China on bid invitation and bidding. 北京:

中国方正出版社,2004. 41 pages;20cm. +1 CD-ROM (4 3/4 in.). ISBN:7801077504,7801077509.（中英文对照法律法规系列;13）

28. 中华人民共和国城市规划法、测绘法 = 中英对照法律文本系列/人大法工委法制工作委员会编.北京:法律出版社;2004.74 页;20cm. ISBN:7503636599.（中英对照法律文本系列）

本书收录了城市规划法、测绘法的中文本和英文本.

D346 土地法、房地产法

1. The agrarian reform law of the People's Republic of China:together with other relevant documents. Peking: Foreign Languages Press, 1950. 104 pages;19cm.
Contents:The agrarian reform law of the People's Republic of China—Decisions concerning the differentiation of class status in the countryside—General regulations governing the organisation of peasants' associations—On the agrarian reform law/by Liu Shao-chi.
《中华人民共和国土地改革法》及相关文件.
(1)2nd ed. Peking:Foreign Languages Press, 1951. 98 pages;19cm.
(2)The agrarian reform law of the People's Republic of China and other relevant documents. 3th ed. Peking: Foreign Languages Press, 1952. 85 pages;19cm.
(3)4th ed. Peking:Foreign Languages Press, 1953. 85 pages
(4)[4th ed. reprinted]. Peking:Foreign Languages Press, 1959. 2 preliminary leaves, 85 [1] pages; 19cm.

2. 中国建筑与房地产法律法规:英汉对照/法律出版社法规中心编. 北京:法律出版社,2007. 466 页;21cm. ISBN:7503671487, 7503671483.（中国法律法规中英对照系列;7）

英文题名:Construction & real estate laws and regulations of China.

D347 农业经济管理法

1. 中华人民共和国农业法 = Agriculture Law of the People's Republic of China. 北京:中国法制出版社,2001. 47 pages;21cm. ISBN:7800838137, 7800838132
英汉对照

D348 劳动法

1. Labour insurance regulations of the People's Republic of China. Peking:Foreign Languages Press, 1952. 42 pages;19cm.
Notes:"An explanatory report on the draft labour insurance regulations... by Li Li-san, Minister of Labour, on February 23, 1951":pages;27—42.
《中华人民共和国劳动保险条例》,李立三.
(1)2nd ed. Peking:Foreign Languages Press, 1953. 34 pages;19cm.

2. Labour laws and regulations of the People's Republic of

China. Peking：Foreign Languages Press，1956. 87 p.；19cm.

《重要劳动法令汇编》

3. Worker's insurance regulations of the People's Republic of China. New York：1958. 59 p.；29cm.

中华人民共和国劳动保险法令.

4. Important labour laws and regulations of the People's Republic of China. Enl. ed. Peking：Foreign Languages Press，1961. 82 p.；20cm.

《中华人民共和国重要劳动法令》，增订版.

5. Labour law of the People's Republic of China/translated by the Legislative Affairs Commission of the Standing Committee of the National People's Congress of the People's Republic of China. Beijing：Zhongguo lao dong she hui bao zhang chu ban she，2000. 51 pages；19cm. ISBN：7504516430，7504516435

《中华人民共和国劳动法》，法规编辑部编. 中国劳动社会保障出版社,英汉对照.

6. 中华人民共和国劳动法＝Labour Law of the People's Republic of China. 北京：中国法制出版社，2001. 57 pages；21cm. ISBN：7800838137，7800838132

英汉对照.

7. 中国行政与劳动法律法规:汉英对照/法律出版社法规中心编. 北京：法律出版社，2007. 638 页；21cm. ISBN：7503671470，7503671475.（中国法律法规中英对照系列；3）

英文题名：Administrative & labour laws and regulations of China. 本书是收录劳动法律法规的中英文对照本.

8. 中华人民共和国劳动合同法、中华人民共和国就业促进法、中华人民共和国劳动争议调解仲裁法:中英文对照/国务院法制办公室编. 北京：中国法制出版社，2009. 143 页；21cm. ISBN：7509311448，7509311446

英文题名：Labor contract law of the People's Republic of China；Law of the People's Republic of China on Promotion of employment；Law of the People's Republic of China on labour-dispute mediation and arbitration. 本书收录了劳动合同法、就业促进法、劳动争议调解仲裁法的中英文对照文本.

D349 自然资源与环境保护法

1. 中华人民共和国矿产资源法＝Mineral resources law of the People's Republic of China. 北京：地质出版社，1996. 41 p.；20cm. ISBN：7116022619，7116022614

中英文本.

2. 中华人民共和国电力法＝Electric power law of the People's Republic of China. 北京：中国法制出版社，2001. 53 pages；21cm. ISBN：7800838137，7800838132

英汉对照.

3. 中华人民共和国水土保持法＝Law of the People's Republic of China on water and soil conservation；中华人民共和国水污染防治法＝Law of the People's Republic of

China on prevention and control of water pollution；中华人民共和国水法＝Water law of the People's Republic of China. 北京：法律出版社，2004. 165 pages；20cm. ISBN：7503638885，7503638886.（中英对照法律文本. 15 元系列；2）

本书收录了我国水土保持法、水污染防治法、水法的中文和英文本.

4. 中华人民共和国森林法＝Forestry law of the People's Republic of China. 中华人民共和国渔业法＝Fisheries law of the People's Republic of China. 中华人民共和国草原法＝Grassland Law of the People's Republic of China. 北京：法律出版社，2004. 175 pages；21cm. ISBN：7503638885，7503638886.（中英对照法律文本. 15 元系列. 2；2）

本书收录了我国森林法、渔业法、与草原法的中文本和英文本.

5. 中华人民共和国固体废物污染环境防治法＝Law of the People's Republic of China on the prevention and control of environmental pollution by solid waste. 北京：中国法制出版社，2001. 57 pages；21cm. ISBN：7800838137，7800838132

英汉对照.

6. Environmental protection law of the People's Republic of China. Beijing：China Legal Publishing House，2001. 33 pages；21cm. ISBN：7800838132，7800838137

《中华人民共和国环境保护法》.英汉对照.

7. 中华人民共和国清洁生产促进法、环境影响评价法＝中英对照法律文本系列/全国人大法工委法制工作委员会编. 北京：法律出版社，2004. 63 页；20cm. ISBN：7503636599.（中英对照法律文本系列）

本书收录了清洁生产促进法、环境影响评价法的中文和英文对照本.

D350 传媒法、信息法

1. 中华人民共和国电信条例＝Regulation of the People's Republic of China on telecommunications. 北京：中国法制出版社，2002. 73 pages；21cm. ISBN：7800838137，7800838132

英汉对照

2. 中国广播影视法规汇编/中国国家广播电影电视总局法规司,中国国家广播电影电视总局国际合作司编译. 北京:法律出版社,2009. 544 页；25cm. ISBN：7503694592，7503694599

英文题名：China's laws & regulations on radio, film and television

D351 刑法

1. 中华人民共和国刑法. 北京：中国方正出版社，2004. 337 pages；20cm. ＋ 1 MP3（12cm.）. ISBN：780107744X，7801077448，7899969301，7899969304

Notes：1979 年7 月1 日第五届全国人民代表大会第二次会议通过，1997 年3 月14 日第八届全国人民代表大会第五次会议修订,自 1997 年 10 月 1 日起施行.

英文题名:Criminal Law of the People's Republic of China. 书中内容均配以英文对照.

2. The amended and annotated Criminal Code of the People's Republic of China with official interpretations/by Wei Luo. 2nd ed. Buffalo, N. Y.:William S. Hein & Co., 2012. xxv, 604 p.;23cm. ISBN:0837738192, 0837738199

《中华人民共和国刑法》(1997 年修订版),罗伟(Luo, Wei, 1957—)(美国华裔学者)译.

3. The evolution of criminal legislations of China/coauthored by Gao Mingxuan & Zhao Bingzhi. [Bejing]:Law Press China, 2007. 471, 166 p. ISBN:7503670008, 7503670002. (Series of Criminal Law of BNU;12)

《中国刑法立法之演进:汉英对照》,高铭暄,赵秉志著. 法律出版社(京师刑事法文库;12)

D352 民法

1. Basic problems in the civil law of the People's Republic of China:Communist China/by the Institute of Civil Law Central Political-Judicial Cadres' School. Washington, D. C.:U. S. Joint Publications Research Service, 1961. 358 p.;20cm.

Notes:Translation of Chung-hua jên min. Kung ho kuo min fa chi pên wên t'i

《中华人民共和国民法基本问题》,中央政法干部学校民法教研室.

2. Basic principles of civil law in China/edited by William C. Jones. Armonk, N. Y.:M. E. Sharpe, c1989. xviii, 378 p.;24cm. ISBN:0873325745. (Chinese studies on China)

《中华人民共和国民法通则选译》,钟威廉(Jones, William C.)(美国法学家)译.

3. 民事法:汉英对照/中国法制出版社编. 北京:中国法制出版社,2005. 294 页;21cm. ISBN:7801828437. (中英文对照法规系列)

本书是关于民事法律法规的中英文法律文本对照.

4. 中国民事法律法规:汉英对照/法律出版社法规中心编. 北京:法律出版社,2007. 711 页;21cm. ISBN:7503671449, 7503671440. (中国法律法规中英对照系列;2)

英文题名:Civil laws and regulations of China. 本书是收录常用的民事与诉讼法律法规的中英文对照本.

5. The draft civil code of the People's Republic of China:English translation/prepared by the Legislative Research Group of Chinese Academy of Social Sciences;[edited] by Liang Huixing;translated from the Chinese by Junwei Fu... [et al.]. Leiden;Boston:Martinus Nijhoff Publishers, 2010. xxvii, 550 p.;25cm. ISBN:9004190429, 9004179158

《中华人民共和国民法通则初稿》,梁彗星;Fu, Junwei

等译.

6. 中华人民共和国物权法. 北京:中国法制出版社,2009. 127 页;21cm. SBN 7509311455, 7509311454

英文题名:Property law of the People's Republic of China. 本书收录了 2007 年颁布的中华人民共和国物权法.

7. Copyright in China/Sangiang Qu. Beijing:Foreign Languages Press, 2002, v, 436 pages;20cm. ISBN:7119029312, 7119029313

《WTO 与中国知识产权》,曲三强著.

8. 知识产权法:汉英对照/中国法制出版社编. 北京:中国法制出版社,2005. 233 页;21cm. ISBN:7801828402. (中英文对照法规系列)

英文题名:Intellectual property law. 本书是关于知识产权法律法规的中英文法律文本对照.

9. New progress in China's protection of intellectual property rights. Beijing:New Star Publishers, 2005. 33 pages;26cm. ISBN:7801488180, 7801488183

《中国知识产权保护的新进展:英文》,中华人民共和国国务院新闻办公室发布. 新星出版社.

10. 中国知识产权保护的新进展:英文/中华人民共和国国务院新闻办公室发布. 北京:新星出版社,2005. 36 页;20cm. ISBN:7801488199

11. 中国保护知识产权法律指南:英文/中国国际贸促进委员会法律事务部编写. 北京:中国市场出版社,2006. 220 页;24cm. ISBN:7509201322

12. Intellectual property: the real story/Huang Wei. Beijing:Foreign Languages Press, 2007. 115 p.:ill.;19cm. ISBN:7119051475, 7119051474. (Stories from China)

《知识产权的故事:英文》,黄卫编著;闫威,曲磊译;黑龙江省知识产权局等摄. (国情故事)

13. China IP protection handbook/by the Editorial Committee of China IP Protection Handbook. Beijing:Intellectual Property Publishing House, 2008. xxiii, 400 pages:illustrations;23cm. ISBN:7802470033, 780247003X

《中国知识产权保护手册》,《中国知识产权保护手册》编委会编著. 知识产权出版社.

14. Gazette of State Intellectual Property Office of the People's Republic of China/edited by State Intellectual Property Office of the People's Republic of China. Beijing:Intellectual Property Press, 2011. 66 pages:forms;30cm. ISBN:7513005081, 7513005087

《中华人民共和国国家知识产权局公报》,国家知识产权局办公室编. 知识产权出版社.

15. 2009 年苏州市知识产权发展与保护状况/苏州市人民政府知识产权联席会议办公室编著. 苏州:苏州大学出版社,2010. 59 页;21cm. ISBN:7811375701, 7811375702

本书以中英文两种语言全面论述、介绍了苏州市 2009 年知识产权的发展与保护措施,为苏州地方经济发展提供了机制保障.

16. 中国知识产权典型案例：英汉双语/郑胜利，（意）玛丽娜·提莫泰欧，龚红兵主编. 北京：知识产权出版社，2011. 301 页；26cm. ISBN：7513007245，7513007241
英文题名：Leading court cases on Chinese intellectual property. 本书选取中国各级法院近年来的 26 个典型知识产权案例进行编译，提炼案情，总结裁判要点，并进行相关分析，全书分为两编，第一编由 15 个案例的中英编译稿组成，第二编的 11 个案例为英文编译稿，并将法院原文件作为附录.

17. 中华人民共和国商标法＝Trademark law of the People's Republic of China. 北京：中国方正出版社，2004. 43 pages；20cm. ＋ 1 CD-ROM（4 3/4 in.）. ISBN：7801077520，7801077523.（中英文对照法律法规系列；10）

18. 中华人民共和国专利法＝Patent law of the People's Republic of China. 北京：中国方正出版社，2004. 43 pages；20cm. ＋ 1 CD-ROM（4 3/4 in.）. ISBN：7801077512，7801077516.（中英文对照法律法规系列；12）

19. 中华人民共和国专利法，中华人民共和国专利法实施细则：中英文对照. 北京：知识产权出版社，2010. 200 页；21cm. ISBN：7802479739，7802479738
本书将 2008 年 12 月 27 日最新颁布的《中华人民共和国专利法》和 2010 年 1 月 9 日最新颁布的《中华人民共和国专利法实施细则》合订为一册，中英文对照.

20. 中华人民共和国著作权法＝Copyright law of the People's Republic of China. 北京：中国方正出版社，2004. 49 pages；20cm. ＋1 CD-ROM（4 3/4 in.）. ISBN：7801077490；7801077493.（中英文对照法律法规系列；11）

21. 中华人民共和国著作权法律法规选编/新闻出版总署（国家版权局）法规司编. 北京：商务印书馆，2010. 231 页；21cm. ISBN：7100071109，7100071100
本书选编我国改革开放以来所制定的有关著作权的法律法规，分法律、行政法规、司法解释、规章、规范性文件以及公告等. 中英文双语.

22. 中华人民共和国种子法＝Seed law of the People's Republic of China. 中华人民共和国农村土地承包法＝Law of the People's Republic of China on land contract in rural areas. 中华人民共和国农业法＝Agriculture Law of the People's Republic of China. 北京：法律出版社，2004. 173 pages；21cm. ISBN：7503638885，7503638886.（中英对照法律文本. 15 元系列. 2；1）
本书收录了我国种子法、农村土地承包法、农业法的中文本和英文本.

23. The contract law of the People's Republic of China：with English translation and introduction/by Wei Luo. Buffalo, N. Y.：W. S. Hein & Co.，1999. x，190 p.；23cm. ISBN：1575884909.（Chinese law series；v. 2）
《中华人民共和国合同法》，罗伟（Luo，Wei，1957—）（美

国华裔学者）译.

24. 中华人民共和国合同法. 北京：中国方正出版社，2004. 161 pages；20cm. ＋ 1 MP3（12cm.）. ISBN：7801077458，7801077455，7899969298，7899969298
Notes：1999 年 3 月 15 日第九届全国人民代表大会第二次会议通过，自 1999 年 10 月 1 日起施行.
英文题名：Contract law of the People's Republic of China

25. The marriage law of the People's Republic of China：together with other relevant articles. Peking：Foreign Languages Press，1950. 43 pages；19cm.
Contents：The marriage law of the People's Republic of China—A much needed marriage law/by Chang-Chih-jang—On marriage law of the People's Republic of China/by Teng Ying-chao
《中华人民共和国婚姻法》及相关文章.
　(1)3rd ed. Peking：Foreign Languages Press，1952. iv，41 pages；23cm.
　(2)4th ed. Peking：Foreign Languages Press，1953. 44 pages；19cm.
　(3)Peking：Foreign Languages Press，1959. 43 pages；19cm.

26. The marriage law of the People's Republic of China：adopted by the Central People's Government Council at its 7th meeting on April 13，1950. Promulgated on May 1，1950 by order of the Chairman of the Central People's Government on April 30，1950. Peking：Foreign Languages Press，1950. 10 p.；19cm.
《中华人民共和国婚姻法》
　(1)2nd ed. Peking：Foreign Languages Press，1965. 9 pages；19cm.
　(2)[3rd ed.]. Peking：Foreign Languages Press，1973. 9，[1] pages；19cm.
　(3)Peking：Foreign Languages Press，1977. 9 pages；19cm.

27. Marriage law of the People's Republic of China. China：China Legal Pub. House，2001. 31 pages；21cm. ISBN：7800838137，7800838132
《中华人民共和国婚姻法》，英汉对照.

D353　诉讼法

1. 中华人民共和国仲裁法＝Arbitration law of the People's Republic of China. 北京：中国法制出版社，2001. 47 pages；21cm. ISBN：7800838137，7800838132
英汉对照.

2. 中华人民共和国仲裁法＝Arbitration law of the People's Republic of China. 北京：中国方正出版社，2004. 37 pages；20cm. ＋ 1 CD-ROM（4 3/4 in.）. ISBN：7801077636，7801077639.（中英文对照法律法规系列；15）

3. 民事诉讼法与仲裁法：汉英对照/中国法制出版社编. 北京：中国法制出版社，2005. 207 页；21cm. ISBN：

7801828429.(中英文对照法规系列)

本书是关于民事诉讼与仲裁法律法规的中英文法律文本对照.

4. 中华人民共和国行政诉讼法＝Administrative procedure law of the People's Republic of China. 北京：中国方正出版社，2004. 43 pages；20cm.＋1 CD-ROM (4 3/4 in.). ISBN：7801077628, 7801077622. (中英文对照法律法规系列；9)

5. The civil procedure law and court rules of the People's Republic of China/by Wei Luo. Buffalo, N. Y.：W. S. Hein, 2006. viii, 419 p.；24cm. ISBN：083773410X. (Chinese law series；v. 10)

《中华人民共和国民事诉讼法及法庭规则》，罗伟(Luo, Wei, 1957—)(美国华裔学者)译.

6. 中华人民共和国民事诉讼法：中英文对照/国务院法制办公室编. 北京：中国法制出版社，2009. 179 页；21cm. ISBN：7509311479, 7509311470

英文题名：Civil procedure law of the People's Republic of China.本书收录 2007 年颁布的中华人民共和国民事诉讼法中英文本.

7. The criminal procedure law of the People's Republic of China/translated and edited with annotations by Joe Zhen-xiong Zhou；with foreword by Judge Li Chang Dao；and introduction by Richard H. Ward. Chicago, Ill.：Office of International Criminal Justice, c1998. iv, 185 p.；22cm. ISBN：0942511824, 0942511816

《中华人民共和国刑事诉讼法》(1996)，Zhou, Joe Zhen-xiong 编译，中英文本.

8. Criminal procedure law of the People's Republic of China/〔Translated by the Legislative Affairs Commission of the Standing Committee of the National People's Congress of the People's Republic of China〕. Beijing：Zhongguo jian cha chu ban she, 1998. 256 p.；22cm. ISBN：780086541X, 7800865411

《中华人民共和国刑事诉讼法》(1996)，全国人民代表大会常务委员会法制工作委员会译.中英文本.

9. The amended criminal procedure law and the criminal court rules of the People's Republic of China：with English translation, introduction, and annotation/by Wei Luo. Buffalo, N. Y.：W. S. Hein & Co., 2000. x, 397 p.；23cm. ISBN：1575884917, 1575884912. (Chinese law series；v. 3)

《中华人民共和国刑事诉讼法》(1996 年修订版)，罗伟(Luo, Wei, 1957—)(美国华裔学者)译.

10. 中国刑法与刑事诉讼法：汉英对照/法律出版社法规中心编. 北京：法律出版社，2007. 422 页；21cm. ISBN：7503671432, 7503671432. (中国法律法规中英文对照系列；1)

英文题名：Criminal laws & criminal procedure laws of China.

D354　司法制度

1. 中华人民共和国律师法＝Law of the People's Republic of China on lawyers. 北京：中国法制出版社，2001. 33 pages；20cm. ISBN：7800838137, 7800838132

英汉对照

2. 中国涉外律师：汉英对照/《中国涉外律师》编辑部编. 北京：法律出版社，2005. 276 页；29cm. ISBN：7503658649, 7503658648

英文题名：Chinese lawyers engaged in international practices.本书是介绍中国涉外律师的相关信息、联系方式的手册.

3. Preliminary study of China's juvenile delinquency/by Shao Daosheng. Beijing：Foreign Languages Press, 1992. v, 174 pages；19cm. ISBN：0835127966, 0835127967, 7119014005, 7119014005

《中国青少年犯罪初探》，邵道生编.

D355　地方法制

1. 海南省法规规章汇编：汉英对照/海南省法制办公室编. 海口：海南出版社，2005. 499 页；21cm. ISBN：7544314898, 7544314893

本书汇编了 1988 年建省以来海南省人民代表大会及其常务委员会制定的地方性法规 15 件、海南省人民政府制定的规章 7 件，共 22 件.按发布时间先后排列，法规在前，规章在后.

2. 2005 年广州市政府规章汇编：中英对照/广州市法制办公室编. 北京：新世界出版社，2007. 2 册；23cm. ISBN：7802281547, 7802281547. (广州市人民政府法制丛书)

英文题名：Compilation of government regulations of Guangzhou municipality ～2005.本书分 2 册，分别收录了广州市人民政府 2005 年的政府规章制度.

D356　国际法

1. 中华人民共和国引渡法＝Extradition Law of the People's Republic of China. 北京：中国法制出版社，2001. 45 pages；21cm. ISBN：7800838137, 7800838132

英汉对照.

E 类　军事

E1　军事史

1. The military establishment of the Yuan dynasty/by Ch'i-ch'ing Hsiao. Cambridge, Mass.：Council on East Asian Studies, Harvard University：distributed by Harvard University Press, 1978. vii, 314 p.：map；29cm. ISBN：0674574613. (Harvard East Asian monographs；77)

"Translations from the Ping-chih of the Yuan shih"：p. 65—124.

Hsiao, Ch'i-ch'ing 著.该书包括对宋濂(1310—1381)所撰的《元史·兵器》的翻译.

2. Weapons in ancient China/edited by Yang Hong. New York：Science Presse, 1992. vol. (III-298 p. -[16 p. de pl.]：nombreuses ill. ；27cm. ISBN：1880132036，1880132036，7030002237，7030002235.

《中国古代兵器》. 科学出版社.

E11 古代兵法、战法

1. Three military classics of China/[translated] by A. L. Sadler. Sydney：Australasian Medical Pub. Co. ，1944. 55，23 pages；22cm.

《三种中国兵书》，Sadler, A. L. （Arthur Lindsay，1882—）译. 包括对《吴子》《孙子兵法》《司马法》3 部兵书的翻译. 吴起（440—381 B. C. ），孙子（约公元前 545 年—约公元前 470 年），司马穰苴（春秋末期齐国人）.

2. The Chinese martial code/[translated and with commentary] by Arthur Lindsay Sadler；foreword and annotations by Edwin Lowe. Tokyo；Rutland, Vt. ：Tuttle Pub. ，2008. 190 p. ；21cm. ISBN：0804840040，0804840040

Contents：The art of war of Sun Tzu—The precepts of war by Sima Rangju—Wu Zi on the art of war.

《三种中国兵书》，Sadler, A. L. （Arthur Lindsay，1882—）和 Lowe, Edwin, 1972—）译注. 包括对《孙子兵法》《吴子》（吴起）和《司马法》三部兵法的翻译.

3. The art of the warrior：leadership and strategy from the Chinese military classics：with selections from the seven military classics of ancient China and Sun Pin's military methods/translated, compiled, and introduced by Ralph D. Sawyer, with the collaboration of Mei-chün Lee Sawyer. Boston：Shambhala, 1996. xiv, 304 p. ；23cm. ISBN：1570621632. (Shambhala dragon editions)

《武经七书》（选译），Sawyer, Ralph D. 和 Sawyer, Mei-chün. 合译. 由《孙子兵法》《吴子兵法》《六韬》《司马法》《三略》《尉缭子》《李卫公问对》七部著名兵书著名兵书汇编而成.

4. Wu zi, the methods of the Sima, Wei Liao zi/edited and translated into modern Chinese by Wang Shijin, Huang Pumin and Ren Li；translated into English by Pan Jiabin. Beijing：Jun shi ke xue chu ban she, 2004. 16，18，355 p. ；24cm. ISBN：7801377214，7801377210. (Library of Chinese classics＝大中华文库)

《吴子, 司马法, 尉缭子》，王式金, 黄朴民, 任力校释；潘嘉玢译. 军事科学出版社.

5. Military strategy classics of ancient China：the art of war, methods of war 36 stratagems ＆ selected teachings. [Place of publication not identified]：Special Edition Books, 2013. xvi, 412 pages；23cm. ISBN：1937021030，1937021033

Contents：Six secret teachings/Jiang Ziya—Art of war/Sun Tzu—Methods of war/Sima Rangju—Book of Wuzi/Wu Qi—Book of Wei Liaozi/Wei Liao—Three strategies of Huang Shigong—Thirty six stratagems—Questions and replies/Tang Taizong and Li Jing.

Conners, Shawn 编；Song, Chen 译. 包括《孙子兵法》《六韬》《武子》《尉缭子》的英译. 英汉对照.

6. The art of war：Sun Tzu, in plain English/D. E. Tarver. New York：Writers Club Press, 2002. xix, 157 pages；23cm. ISBN：0595224725，0595224722. （The warrior series；bk. 1)

Notes：The art of war/Sun Tzu—The art of warfare/Sun Pin.

Tarver, D. E. 译, 包括《孙子兵法》和《孙膑兵法》的英译.

7. Sun Zi：the art of war；Sun Bin：the art of war/chief editors, Wu Rusong, Wu Xianlin；editors, Zheng Tian, Zhang He；[translator, Lin Wusun]. Beijing：People's China Pub. House；San Francisco, CA：China Books ＆ Periodicals [distributor], 1995. 152，158 pages：map；20cm. ISBN：7800655105，7800655104

《孙子兵法・孙膑兵法》，吴如嵩（Wu, Rusong, ；1940—）；吴显林（Wu, Hsien-lin)校释；林戊荪（Lin, Wu-sun) 译. 英汉对照.

(1) 2nd ed. Beijing：People's China Pub. House, 1996. 152，158 pages

(2) Beijing：Foreign Languages Press；Changsha：Hunan People's Publishing House, 1999. 29，304 pages：illustrations；24cm. ISBN：7119024124，7119024127. (Library of Chinese classics＝大中华文库)

(3) The art of war；[and] Sun Bin：The art of war/edited and translated into modern Chinese by Wu Rusong and Wu Xianlin；translated into English by Lin Wusun. Beijing：Foreign Languages Press, 2000. 345 pages：portraits；13cm. ISBN：7119026917，7119026916，7119025244，7119025247. (经典的回声＝Echo of classics FLP 汉英对照经典读本. 古典精华；3)

(4) Sunzi：the art of war；Sun Bin：the art of war/translated by Lin Wusun. Beijing：Foreign Languages Press, 2007. 229 pages：illustrations；24cm. ISBN：7119034836，7119034839

8. 活用三十六计：汉英对照/千艺主编. 上海：上海大学出版社，2006. 562 页；21cm. ISBN：7810588893，7810588898

英文题名：Make flexible use of "thirty-six stratagems"

9. The wiles of war：36 military strategies from ancient China＝San shi liu ji li shi/Sun Wu zhu；Sun Haichen bian yi. Beijing：Foreign Languages Press, 2009. 379 pages：illustrations；20cm. ISBN：7119034829，7119034820

《三十六计历史》，孙海晨编译.

10. 三十六计：英汉双语版/于汝波, 吕雪主编. 2 版. 济南：山东友谊出版社，2011. 43 页；28cm. ISBN：7807378402，7807378409

英文题名：New translations the thirty-six stratagems

11. The political and military thought of Xin Qiji, 1140—1207, with a translation of his ten discussions（Meiqin shi lun）/Bai Yan. Lewiston, N. Y. ：Edwin Mellen Press, 2005. viii, 318 pages：illustrations；24cm. ISBN：0773462058, 0773462052.（Chinese studies；vol. 39）

Yan, Bai 著,包括对辛弃疾（1140—1207）的《美芹十论》的英译.

12. Mastering the art of war/Zhuge Liang & Liu Ji；translated and edited by Thomas Cleary. Boston：Shambhala, 1989. ix, 134 pages；23cm. ISBN：0877735131, 0877735137, 1570620814, 1570620812.（Shambhala dragon editions）

诸葛亮（181—234）与刘基（1311—1375）军事文献. Cleary, Thomas F.（1949—）（美国翻译家）译.

13. Guerrilla war：Mao Tse-tung, Che Guevara, Sun Tzu, Chuko Liang, edited and translated by William McNaughton. Oberlin, Ohio, Crane Press, 1970. 69 p. 21cm.

McNaughton, William（1933—）编. 对中国历史上游击战军事理论的编译.

14. Ways of warriors, codes of kings：lessons in leadership from the Chinese classics/translated by Thomas Cleary. Boston：Shambhala, 1999. xv, 109 pages；23cm. ISBN：1570624437, 1570624438

中国古代军事理论与领导学有关文献. Cleary, Thomas F.（1949—）（美国翻译家）译.

(1) Boston, MA：Shambhala, 2000. xv, 109 pages；22cm. ISBN：1570625697, 1570625695

15. 兵书/王慧编著. 合肥：黄山书社,2016. 144 页：彩图,肖像；23cm. ISBN：7546141626.（印象中国）

英文题名：Ancient books on the art of war. 英汉对照.

16. On the art of war/Sun Tzu；Mao Ze Dong；[translated by Samuel B. Griffith]. New York；Pennington, NJ：Collectors Reprints, 1996. xvi, 261 pages：illustrations, maps；24cm.（The great commanders）

Notes：Translation of：Sunzi bing fa, and, You ji zhan Griffith, Samuel B. 译,包括《孙子兵法》和毛泽东《论游击战》的翻译.

17. 孙子说：汉英对照/蔡希勤编注. 北京：华语教学出版社, 2006. 201 页；21cm. ISBN：7802002141, 7802002142.（中国圣人文化丛书. 老人家说系列）

英文题名：Sun zi says

18. 孙子智慧故事＝Wisdom of Sun Tzu/中文作者 张英, 英文作者 王善江, 英文审订 汪榕培. 上海：上海外语教育出版社, 2010. 10, 266 pages：illustrations；21cm. ISBN：7544616416, 754461641X.（诸子百家智慧故事 ＝Wisdom of ancient Chinese sages）

19. The wisdom of Sun Tzu/retold by Guo Wenping & Zhong Shaoyi；translated by Tiffany Gray. Beijing：China Intercontinental Press, 2010. [2], 128 pages：illustrations；21cm. ISBN：7508517544, 7508517547.（Chinese classics）

《孙子的智慧》,郭闻平,钟少异著；Gray, Tiffany 译.

20. 论孙子兵法/杜一平著；许迎军译. 北京：海潮出版社, 2010. 206 页；21cm. ISBN：7802138919, 7802138914

E111　孙子兵法

翟林奈（Giles, Lionel, 1875—1958）（英国汉学家）翻译版本.

1. Sun Tzǔ on the art of war, the oldest military treatise in the world, translated from the Chinese with introduction and critical notes, by Lionel Giles. London, Luzac & Co., 1910. liii, 204 p. ；25cm.

2. The art of war；the oldest military treatise in the world/translated from the Chinese by Lionel Giles；introduction and notes by Brigadier General Thomas R. Phillips. Harrisburg, Pa. , Military Service Pub. Co. , 1944. 90 pages；20cm.（Military classics）

《孙子兵法》,翟林奈（Giles, Lionel, 1875—1958）（英国汉学家）译.

(1) Harrisburg, Pa. ：Military Service Pub. Co. , （Telegraph Press）, 1949. 99 pages；20cm.

(2) Harrisburg：The Military Service Publishing Company, 1957. 99 s. ；20cm.

(3) [Harrisburg, Pa.]：[publisher not identified], 1963. 99 pages；20cm.（Military classics）

(4) The art of war/Sun Tzu；translated from the Chinese by Lionel Giles. [New ed.]. Mineola, N. Y. ：Dover；Newton Abbot：David & Charles, 2002. 99 s. ；22cm. ISBN：0486425576, 0486425573

3. The art of war：the oldest military treatise in the world/translated from the Chinese by Lionel Giles；notes by Liu Shi Siang. Taiwan, China：Civilian Pub. Service, 1953. 76 unnumbered pages；19cm.

4. 孙子兵法,中英对照本/陶希圣校订. 台北, 全民出版社, [1954]. [118] pages；20cm.

注：翟林奈（Giles, Lionel, 1875—1958）（英国汉学家）译.

5. Sun Tzu on the art of war：the oldest military treatise in the world/transl. from the Chinese with introd. and critical notes, by Lionel Giles. Taipei Ch'eng-Wen Publishing Company, 1971. liii, 204 p. , 22cm.

(1) [Place of publication not identified]：Chèng Wen Pub. Co. , 1978. liii, 204 pages；22cm.

6. The art of war：the oldest military treatise in the world/translated from the Chinese by Lionel Giles. 2nd ed. Taipei：Confucius Pub. Co. , 1972. 1 volume（various pagings）；19cm.

7. Sun Tzǔ on the art of war：the oldest military treatise in the world/translated from the Chinese with introduction

and critical notes by Lionel Giles. 〔Hong Kong〕: Hong Kong Book Co. , 1974. liii, 204 pages；23cm.

8. Sun Tzŭ on the art of war：the oldest military treatise in the world/translated from the Chinese with introduction and critical notes by Lionel Giles. 台北：敦煌书局, 〔1983〕. liii, 204 pages；23cm.

《孙子兵法》,翟林奈(Giles, Lionel, 1875—1958)(英国汉学家)译.

(1)台北：敦煌书局,〔1984〕. liii, 204 pages；23cm.

9. The art of war/Sun Tzu. San Francisco, CA: Chelonia Press, 1988. vi, 76 pages；19cm. ISBN：093894701X, 0938947011

10. Sun Tzŭ on the art of war：the oldest military treatise in the world/translated from the Chinese with introduction and critical notes by Lionel Giles. Singapore: Graham Brash (Pte) Ltd. , 1988. liii, 204 pages；21cm. ISBN：9971491079, 9971491079, 9971491915, 9971491918

11. The art of war/by Sun Tzu；〔translated by Lionel Giles；edited and〕 foreword by James Clavell. London: Hodder & Stoughton, 1995. 95 pages. ISBN：0340276044, 0340276045

12. The art of war：the oldest military treatise in the world/ Sun Tzu；translated from the Chinese by Lionel Giles. Gainesville, Fl. : InstaBook EBAM, 1998. 108 pages；21cm. ISBN：1891355937, 1891355936

13. Sun Tzŭ on the art of war：the oldest military treatise in the world/Sun-tzu；translated from the Chinese with introduction and critical notes by Lionel Giles. London；New York: Kegan Paul, 2002. liii, 204 pages；27cm. ISBN：0710307381, 0710307385. (The Kegan Paul China library)

14. The art of war/Sun Tzu；translated from the Chinese by Lionel Giles. Mineola, N. Y. : Dover Publications：〔Distributed by the Legacy Project〕, 2002. 90 pages；11 × 17cm. ISBN：0486428923, 0486428925. (Armed Services edition；LP-4)

15. Art of war/by Sun Tzu；translated by Lionel Giles；edited by Shawn Conners. Lg. print ed. 〔El Paso, Tex. 〕: El Paso Norte Press, 2003. 83 pages (large type)；23cm. ISBN：1934255179, 1934255173

16. The art of war/Sun Tzu；edited with an introduction by Dallas Galvin；translated from the Chinese by Lionel Giles, with his notes and commentaries from the Chinese Masters；George Stade consulting editorial director. New York: Barnes & Noble Classics, 2003. xxvi, 272 pages；22cm. ISBN：1593081723, 1593081720

17. The art of war/by Sun Tzu；translated by Lionel Giles. Philadelphia: Pavilion Press, 2004. 112 pages；22cm. ISBN： 1414503199, 1414503196, 1414503431, 1414503431

18. The art of war/by Sun Tzu；English translation 〔and commentary〕 by Lionel Giles. Special ed. El Paso, Tex. : El Paso Norte Press, 2005. 259 pages；22cm. ISBN：0976072696, 0976072690, 1934255122, 1934255124

19. Sun Tzu on the art of war：the oldest military treatise in the world/translated from the Chinese with critical notes by Lionel Giles. 〔England〕: Dodo Press, 2005. 151 pages；23cm. ISBN：1406500534, 1406500530

20. Sun Tzu on the art of war：the oldest military treatise in the world/Sun-tzu；translated from the Chinese with introduction and critical notes by Lionel Giles. McLean, VA: IndyPublish. com, 2005. 1 volumes；23cm. ISBN：1588276945, 1588276940, 1588276953, 1588276957

21. Sun Tzŭ on the art of war：the oldest military treatise in the world/Sun-tzu；translated from the Chinese by Lionel Giles. 〔Place of publication not identified〕: Sallie Stone through Lulu PR. , 2005. 142 pages；28cm. ISBN：1411649257, 1411649255

22. Sun Tzu on the art of war：the oldest military treatise in the world/translated from the Chinese by Lionel Giles. Elgin, IL: New Dawn Press, 2005. 95 pages；22cm. ISBN：1845575180, 1845575182

23. The art of war/Sun Tzu；translated from the Chinese by Lionel Giles. New York: Cosimo Classics, 2006. 47 pages；21cm. ISBN：1596054786, 1596054783

24. The art of war/Sun Tzu；translated by Lionel Giles. Lavergne, TN: PSI Books, 2006. 73 pages；23cm.

25. The art of war/Sun Tzu；translated by Lionel Giles. West Valley City, UT: Inkstone Books, 2006. 243 pages（large print）；23cm. ISBN：1600964796, 1600964794

26. Art of war/Sun Tzu；〔translated by Lionel Giles〕. EasyRead large edition. 〔Australia〕: Objective Systems Pty Ltd, 〔N. S. W. , Australia〕: ReadHowYouWant. com. , 2007. III, 73 pages (large print)；26cm. ISBN：1425060763, 1425060765

27. The art of war：the oldest military treatise in the world/ by Sun Tzu；translated from the Chinese by Lionel Giles；including original Chinese text. 〔Minooka, Ill. 〕: BN Publishing, 2007. 110 pages；23cm. ISBN：9562912518, 9562912515, 9568351957, 9568351953

28. The art of war：the oldest military treatise in the world/ by Sun Tzu；translated from the Chinese by Lionel Giles. 〔Minooka, Illinois〕: BN Publishing, 2007. 79 pages；22cm. ISBN：9568355847, 9568355845

29. Sun tz'u on the art of war：the oldest military treatise in the world/translated from the Chinese with introduction and critical notes by Lionel Giles. 〔Whitefish, MT〕: Kessinger Pub. , 2007. liii, 204 pages；23cm. ISBN：0548609323, 0548609322

30. The art of war/Sun Tzu；translated and annotated by Lionel Giles. 〔United States〕: Borders Classics, 2007.

165 pages；22cm. ISBN：1587264781, 1587264788

31. The art of war＝Sunzi bing fa/Sun Tzu；translated by Lionel Giles, introduction by Jon Babcock；illustrations by Derek Aylward. Berkeley, CA：Ulysses Press, 2007. 130 pages；illustrations；19cm. ISBN：1569756140,1569756147
英汉对照

32. The art of war/by Sun Tzu；translated and commented on by Lionel Giles. Radford, VA：Wilder Publications, 2007. 79 pages；23cm. ISBN：1934451540, 1934451541

33. The art of war/by Sun Tzu；［translated from Chinese by Lionel Giles］. ［Charleston, SC］：P & L Publications, 2007. 74 pages；19cm. ISBN：1452831084, 1452831084

34. Sun Tzu's the art of war/translated by Lionel Giles；with a new foreword by John Minford. Tokyo；Rutland, Vermont：Tuttle Publishing, 2008. lxvii, 188 pages；portraits；20cm. ISBN：0804839440, 0804839441. (Tuttle classics)
《孙子兵法》，翟林奈（Giles, Lionel, 1875—1958）（英国汉学家）译. 英汉对照.
(1) Sun Tzu's the art of war：bilingual Chinese and English text/with a new foreword by John Minford；translated by Lionel Giles. Tokyo：North Clarendon, VT Tuttle Publishing, 2016. lxvii, 188 pages；19cm. ISBN：0804848206, 0804848203

35. Sun Tzǔ on the art of war：the oldest military treatise in the world/translated from the Chinese with introduction and critical notes, by Lionel Giles. ［Whitefish, MT］：Kessinger Pub. , 2008. liii, 204 pages, 1 leaf；25cm. ISBN：0548923900, 0548923906. (Kessinger Publishing's rare reprints)

36. The art of war/translated from the Chinese by Lionel Giles. ［S. I.］：Best Success Books, 2008. 122 pages；portraits；20cm. ISBN：1442119451, 1442119454

37. The art of war/by Sun Tzu；translated and commented on by Lionel Giles. Radford, VA：Wilder Publications, 2008. 100 pages；23cm. ISBN：1604593547, 1604593549, 1604593556, 1604593555

38. The art of war/by Sun Tzu；translated by Lionel Giles. St. Petersburg, FL：Red and Black Publishers, 2008. 102 pages；illustrations；23cm. ISBN：1934941164, 1934941166

39. The art of war/by Sun Tzu；translator, Lionel Giles. ［Champaign, IL］：［Book Jungle］, 2008. 202 pages；24cm. ISBN：1605975054, 1605975052

40. The art of war/by Sun Tzu；translated and commented on by Lionel Giles. Radford, VA：Wilder Publications, 2008. 80 pages；23cm. ISBN：1604593539, 1604593532

41. Sun tzu's The art of war/by Sun Tzu. New York：Classic Books, 2009. 52 pages；22cm. ISBN：1449556761, 1449556760
Notes："Translated from the Chinese by Lionel Giles"—

Page ［1］.

42. Sun Tzu on the art of war/by Sun Tzu；translated from the Chinese by Lionel Giles, M. A. ［Scotts Valley, Calif.］：［CreateSpace］, 2009. 51 pages；23cm. ISBN：1449918750, 1449918751

43. Sun Tzu on the art of war：the oldest military treatise in the world/translated from the Chinese by Lionel Giles. WingSpan classics ed. Livermore, CA：WingSpan Press, 2009. 68 pages；21cm. ISBN：1595948171, 1595948175

44. The art of war/by Sun Tzu；translated by Lionel Giles；edited by Shawn Conners. Deluxe hardcover ed. El Paso, Texas：El Paso Norte Press, 2009. viii, 242 pages；23cm. ISBN：1934255162, 1934255165

45. Art of war/by Sun Tzu；translated by Lionel Giles. ［United States］：Nabla, 2009. 46 pages；23cm. ISBN：1936276011, 1936276011

46. The art of war＝Sunzi bing fa/by Sun Tzu；translated from the Chinese by Lionel Giles. Charleston, SC. ：BiblioBazaar, 2009. 54 pages；21cm. ISBN：0559121623, 0559121628, 0559121562, 0559121563
英汉对照.

47. The art of war：the oldest military treatise in the world/Sun Tzu；translated from the Chinese by Lionel Giles. ［Sioux Falls, S. D.］：EZReads, 2009. cii pages；24cm. ISBN：1615341191, 1615341196, 161534117X, 1615341177

48. Sun Tzu's the art of war/translated by Lionel Giles. Toronto：Prohyptikon Pub. , 2009. vii, 58 pages；21cm. ISBN：0981224407, 0981224404. (Prohyptikon value classics)

49. The art of war/Sun Tzu；［translation：Lionel Giles］. ［Seattle, WA］：Pacific Pub. Studio, 2010. 69 pages；22cm. ISBN：1453640951, 1453640959, 1451550559, 1451550553

50. The art of war/Sun Tzu；［translation：Lionel Giles］. ［Seattle, WA］：Pacific Pub. Studio, 2010. 77 pages；21cm. ISBN：1451563863, 1451563868

51. Sun Tzu on the art of war/by Sun Tzu；translated from the Chinese by Lionel Giles. ［Hollywood, FL］：Simon & Brown, 2010. 61 pages；23cm. ISBN：1936041381, 1936041383

52. Sun Tzǔ on the art of war/Sun-tzu；translated from the Chinese by Lionel Giles. Lexington, Ky. ：［publisher not identified］, 2010. 51 pages；23cm.

53. The art of war/Sun Tzu；translated from the Chinese with introduction and critical notes by Lionel Giles. New ed. New Delhi：Lexicon Books, 2010. 220 pages；18cm. ISBN：9380703066, 9380703060

54. The art of war：the oldest military treatise in the world/Sun Tzu；translated from the Chinese by Lionel Giles.

［Place of publication not identified］: Center Pillar Pub. ,
2010. 90 pages; 22cm. ISBN: 1452858180, 1452858187

55. Sun Tzu on the art of war: the oldest military treatise in
the world/translated from the Chinese by Lionel Giles,
M. A. ［South Carolina］: Craft Publishing, 2010. 42
pages; 22×14cm. ISBN: 1450592741, 1450592740

56. The art of war/by Sun Tzu. ［Hollywood, FL］: Simon
& Brown Publishers, 2010. 61 pages; 23cm. ISBN:
1936041053, 1936041057, 1936041756, 1936041758

57. The art of war/Sun Tzu; translated from the Chinese by
Lionel Giles. New York: Cosimo Classics, 2010. 47
pages; 21cm. ISBN: 1616404000, 1616404000

58. Art of war/Sun Tzu; ［translated by Lionel Giles］.
London: Arcturus, 2011. 126 pages: illustrations;
19cm. ISBN: 1841933580, 1841933589

59. The art of war/Sun Tzu; translator, Lionel Giles.
［Place of publication not identified］: Emereo, 2011. 68
pages; 25cm. ISBN: 1486143948, 1486143946,
1743337288, 1743337280

60. The art of war=［Sunzi bing fa］/Sun Tzu; translated by
Lionel Giles, Barton Williams, Sian Kim; edited by
Shawn Conners. Classic collector's ed. El Paso, Tex. :
El Paso Norte Press Special Edition Books, 2011. viii,
242 pages; 22cm. ISBN: 1934255155, 1934255157

61. Sun Tzu on the art of war: the oldest military treatise in
the world/translated from the Chinese, with introduction
and critical notes, by Lionel Giles. Franklin, Tenn. :
Dalmatian Press Classics, 2011. 226 pages; 21cm.
ISBN: 1403774644, 1403774641

62. Sun Tzu on the art of war: the oldest military treatise in
the world/ by translated from the original Chinese with
introduction and critical notes by Lionel Giles; additional
contributions and original content compiled by James
Garton. United States: The author, 2011. x, 209
pages; 23cm. ISBN: 1460969120, 146096912X

63. The illustrated art of war/Sun Tzu; ［translated from the
Chinese by Lionel Giles; introduction and notes by
Brigadier General Thomas R. Phillips］. Dover ed.
Mineola, N. Y. : Dover Pub. Co. , 2012. 256 pages:
illustrations; 14cm. ISBN: 0486482255, 0486482251

64. The art of war/Sun Tzŭ; translation and commentary by
Lionel Giles; introduction by Jan Willem Honig;
supplementary material by Ilmari Käihkö. New York:
Barnes & Noble, 2012. xxiii, 248 pages: illustrations;
22cm. ISBN: 1435136502, 1435136500. (Signature
edtions)

65. Sun Tzu's the art of war/［translated by Lionel Giles］;
edited & compiled by Anis Verma. Noida: Calvin Pub. ,
2012. 128 pages: illustrations; 23cm. ISBN:
8190570262

66. The art of war/Sun Tzu; translated from the Chinese by

Lionel Giles. Large print edition. ［Place of publication
not identified］: Denton & White, 2013. 107 pages
(large print); 23cm. ISBN: 1494408862, 1494408864

67. The art of war/Sun Tzu; translated by Lionel Giles.
［United States］: CreateSpace Independent Publishing,
2013. 64 pages; 21cm. ISBN: 1482686890,
1482686899. (Bridgeford classics)

68. The art of war: the oldest military treatise in the world/
translated from the Chinese with introduction and critical
notes by Lionel Giles; foreword by Don Mann with
Ralph Pezzulo. New York: Skyhorse Publishing, 2013.
lxi, 204 pages; 24cm. ISBN: 1620874028, 1620874024

69. The art of war/Sun Tzu; ［translated from the Chinese
by Lionel Giles］. Illustrated edition. New York: Fall
River Press, an imprint of Sterling Publishing, 2014.
272 pages: color illustrations; 20cm. ISBN:
1454911869, 1454911867

70. The art of war/Sun Tzu; translation and commentary by
Lionel Giles. San Diego, California: Canterbury
Classics, 2014. 224 pages; 20cm. ISBN: 1626860605,
1626860602. (Word cloud classics)

71. Art of war/Sun Tzu. ［Transl. by Lionel Giles］.
Leipzig, 2014. 255 p. ; 7cm. ISBN: 3861842835,
3861842831, 3861842842, 386184284X

72. The art of war/by Sun Tzu; translated from the Chinese
with introduction and critical notes by Lionel Giles.
Sweden: Chiron Academic Press, 2015. 106 pages;
23cm. ISBN: 9176371107, 9176371107

73. The art of war: the oldest military treatise in the world/
Sun Tzu; translated from the Chinese, with an
introduction and critical notes by Lionel Giles. ［Place of
publication not identified］: Escamilla Editions ［sic］,
2015. 191 pages: portraits; 23cm. ISBN: 1514864180,
1514864185

74. Sun Tzu on the art of war: the oldest military treatise in
the world/by Lionel Giles. ［Charleston, SC］: ［Create
Space］, 2015. 158 pages; 23cm. ISBN: 1519649294,
1519649290

75. Art of war/Sun Tzu; translated from the Chinese with
introduction and critical notes by Lionel Giles. ［Place of
publication not identified］: Erik Publishing House,
2016. 156 pages; 23cm. ISBN: 1532998300,
1532998309

76. Sun Tzu's the art of war/translated from the Chinese by
Lionel Giles, M. A. ［Place of publication not
identified］: ［Publisher not identified］, 2016. 23 pages;
23cm. ISBN: 1523893645, 1523893648

77. The art of war/by Sun Tzu; translated from the Chinese
by Lionel Giles. Sweden: Wisehouse Classics, 2016. 39
pages; 24cm. ISBN: 9176374548, 9176374542

78. The art of war/Sun Tzu; translation and commentary by

Lionel Giles. West Valley City, UT：Inkstone Books, a trademark of The Editorium, 2016. 195 pages；23cm. ISBN：1600967177，1600967175. （Classic Books Library)

79. The art of war/Sun Tzǔ；translated by Lionel Giles. North York, Ontario：Orissiah Publishing Inc. , 2016. ISBN：0994898951, 0994898959. (Orissiah classics)

80. The art of war：the oldest military treatise in the world/ Sun Tzu；translated from the Chinese, with an introduction and critical notes by Lionel Giles (M. A.). Delhi：Kalpaz, New Delhi；Distributed by Gyan Books Pvt. Ltd. , 2017. 160 pages；23cm. ISBN：9351286691, 935128669X

81. The art of war/Sun Tzuì；translation and commentary by Lionel Giles. New York：Race Point Publishing, 2017. 251 pages：illustration；20cm. ISBN：1631063294, 1631063299. (Knickerbocker classics)

82. The art of war：the ultimate book of ancient Chinese military strategy, leadership and politics/translated from the Chinese by Lionel Giles. ［Place of publication not identified］：［Publisher not identified］, 2016. 135 pages；24cm. ISBN：1519626295, 1519626290

83. Roots of strategy：a collection of military classics/Edited by Major Thomas R. Phillips. Harrisburg, Pa. , The Military Service Publishing Company, 1940. 448 pages. ISBN：0811722600, 0811722605

Notes：v. 1. The art of war/Sun Tzu. The military institutions of the Romans/Vegetius. My reveries on the art of war/Maurice de Saxe. The instruction of Frederick the Great for his generals. The military maxims of Napoleon v. 2. Battle studies/Ardant du Picq Principles of war/Carl von Clausewitz Art of war/Jomini v. 3. Von Leeb's defense. Freytag Loringhoven's. The power of personality in war. Erfurth's surprise.

收录翟林奈（Giles, Lionel, 1875—1958）（英国汉学家）英译的《孙子兵法》.

（1）Harrisburg, Pas. , Military Service Pub. Co. , 1941. 448 pages：illustrations

（2）London：John Lane, 1943. 242 pages：illustrations；22cm.

（3）Roots of strategy：The 5 greatest military classics of all time/edited by Thomas R. Phillips. Harrisburg, Pa. ：Stackpole Books, 1985. 448 pages：illustrations；21cm. ISBN：0811721949, 0811721943

84. The art of war/by Sun Tzu；［translated from the Chinese with introduction and critical notes by Lionel Giles］. The prince/by Nicolo Machiavelli；［translated by W. K. Marriott］；with a preface by Peter Spang Goodrich. Redding, Calif. ：CAT Pub. Co. , 1998. vi, 225 pages；23cm. ISBN：1562263838, 1562263836. (Management classics)

85. The prince & The art of war：the classic works of Niccolò Machiavelli and Sun Tzu/English translations by W. K. Marriott and Lionel Giles. Jupiter, FL：Limitless Press, 2008. 100 pages：portraits；24cm. ISBN：0978868178, 097886817X

86. Understanding Sun Tzu on the art of war：the oldest military treatise in the world/by Robert L. Cantrell. Arlington, VA：Center For Advantage, 2003. ii, 122 pages；23cm. ISBN：0972291407, 0972291408

Contents：Six principles of Sun Tzu—Observations of Sun Tzu's principles outside the military—The six Sun Tzu principles as one—Sun Tzu on the art of war/ translated by Lionel Giles；edited version by Robert Cantrell.

包括《孙子兵法》，翟林奈（Giles, Lionel, 1875—1958）（英国汉学家）译；Cantrell, Robert L. 编.

87. The art of war：the oldest military treatise in the world/ by Sun Tzu；translated by Lionel Giles. A book of five rings/by Miyamoto Musashi；translated by D. W.. Miami, Fla. ：BN Publishing, 2007. 69, 74 pages. ；21cm. ISBN：9562912507, 9562912501

包括由翟林奈（Giles, Lionel, 1875—1958）（英国汉学家）翻译的《孙子兵法》和日本 Musashi, Miyamoto（1584—1645)的《五轮书》的英译.

《孙子兵法》其他翻译版本

1. The Chinese military classic/［by］Sonshi. Translated by E. F. Calthrop. Tokyo, Sanseidō, 1905. 48, ［29］pages；20cm.

《孙子正文》，Calthrop, Everard Ferguson；（1876—1915）译. 中英对照.

2. The book of war, the military classic of the Far East/ translated from the Chinese by Captain E. F. Calthrop. London：John Murray, 1908. 132 pages

《孙子兵法》，Calthrop, Everard Ferguson 译.

3. The principles of war, by Sun Tzu；a new translation from a revised text. Ceylon：Royal Air Force, c1943. 1 p. l. , x, 77, ［1］p. ；14cm. (Classic of the military art)

《孙子兵法》，Machell-Cox, E. 译.

4. The art of war：military manual written cir. B. C. 510, the original Chinese text appended/translated, with an introduction, by Cheng Lin. Chungking：World Encyclopedia Institute, China Section, 1945. 1 preliminary leaf, v, ［3］, 59 pages；1 pages leaves, 6, 18 pages；21cm. (Ancient Chinese classics series)

《孙子兵法》，郑麟(1901—)译.

（1）［Shanghai］, ［Printed by the World Book Co. ］, 1946. iii, 29, ［20］pages；26cm.

（2）Taipei, Taiwan, China：World Book Co. , 1953. iii, 29, ［17］pages；22cm. （Sino-International Library series)

（3）香港：东亚书局，［1960］. 115 pages；19cm.

5. The art of war/advocated and written by Sun Zi; translated by Dai Mianleng. ［China］：［publisher not identified］，1954. 68 pages；19cm.

《孙子兵法》，Dai，Mianleng 译. 英汉对照.

6. The art of war. Translated and with an introd. by Samuel B. Griffith. With a foreword by B. H. Liddell Hart. Oxford，Clarendon Press，1963. xvi，197 pages：frontispiece，maps；23cm. （UNESCO collection of representative works. Chinese series）

《孙子兵法》，Griffith，Samuel B. （1906—1983）译.

（1）New York：Oxford University Press ［c1963］. xvi，197 p. ；illus. ，maps. ；22cm. ISBN：0195015401，0195015409

（2）Oxford ［England］：Clarendon Press，1965. xvi，197 pages：illustrations，maps；23cm. （UNESCO collection of representative works. Chinese series）

（3）London；New York：Oxford University Press，1971. xvi，197 pages，2 unnumbered pages of plates：maps；21cm. ISBN：0195014761，0195014766. （UNESCO collection of representative works. Chinese series；A Galaxy Book）

（4）New York：Oxford University Press，1972. 197 pages：illustrations，maps；22cm. （UNESCO collection of representative works. ）

（5）London，Oxford University Press，1973. xvii，197 pages

（6）New York：Oxford University Press，1975. 197 pages；22cm. （UNESCO collection of representative works. Chinese series）

（7）Cutchogue，NY：Buccaneer Books，1976. xvi，197 pages；23cm. ISBN：0899666604，0899666600

（8）London：Oxford University Press，1981. xvii，197 pages，［1］leaf of plates：illustrations；21cm. （UNESCO collection of representative works. Chinese series；A Galaxy Book）

（9）New York：Oxford University Press，1982. xvi，197 pages：illustrations，maps

（10）Collector's ed. Norwalk，Conn. ：Easton Press，1988. xvi，197 pages：maps；24cm.

（11）The illustrated art of war/the definitive English translation by Samuel B. Griffith. New York：Oxford University Press，2005. 272 pages：color illustrations，color maps；25cm. ISBN：019518999X. 0195189995

（12）The art of war/［translated by］Samuel B. Griffith. The new illustrated ed. London：Watkins；New York：Distributed in the USA and Canada by Sterling Pub. ，2005. 272 pages：color illustrations；24cm. ISBN：1780282992，1780282990

（13）New illustrated ed. London：Duncan Baird，2005. 272 pages：color illustrations，color maps；25cm. ISBN：1844831791，1844831795

（14）The art of war/Samuel B. Griffith. London：Duncan Baird，2005. 272 pages：illustrations（some color），photographs（some color）；24cm. ISBN：1844833603，1844833607

（15）The art of war：the new illustrated edition/translated and with an introduction by Samuel B. Griffith；with a foreword by B. H. Liddell Hart. Vancouver：Blue Heron Books，2006. ISBN：1897035357，1897035351

（16）New illustrated ed. London：Watkins，2011. 272 pages：color illustrations；24cm. ISBN：1907486999，1907486992

7. Principles of conflict, recompilation and new English translation with annotation on Sun Zi's Art of war/by Tang Zi-chang. San Rafael，Calif. ，T. C. Press，1969. 256 pages：illustrations，facsimiles，maps（1 folded），plates，portraits；25cm.

《孙子兵法》，唐子长译.

8. The art of war/by Sun tzŭ；edited and foreword by James Clavell. London：Hodder and Stoughton，1981. 95 pages；22cm. ISBN：0340276045，0340276044

《孙子兵法》，Clavell，James 编译

（1）New York：Dell Publishing，1983. 82 p. ；20cm.

（2）New York：Delacorte Press，1983. 82 pages；22cm. ISBN：0440002435，0385292163，0385292160，0440002437

（3）London：Hodder & Stoughton，1995. 95 pages；22cm. ISBN：0340276045，0340276044

（4）London：Hodder & Stoughton，1997. 96 pages；22cm. ISBN：0340276045，0340276044

（5）New ed. New York：Delta，1988. 82 pages；21cm. ISBN：044055005X，0440550051，0385299855，0385299850. （A Dell book）

（6）Rev. ed. London：Hodder and Stoughton，2006. 102 pages；22cm. ISBN：034093784X，0340937846. （A Mobius book）

9. The art of war：a treatise on Chinese military science compiled about 500 B. C. /A. and C. Chen. Singapore：Graham Brash，1982. 78 pages：illustrations；20cm. ISBN：9971947277，9971947279

《孙子兵法》，Chen，A. 和 Chen，C. 编译.

10. Sun-tzu ping fa＝The art of war/（Ying）Chia-erh-ssu ying i；Ch'eng Yü，Chang Ho-sheng chiao chu；Ch'eng Yü，Chang Ho-sheng chin i. Ch'ang-sha-shih：Hu-nan ch'u pan she，1983. ISBN：7543806630，7543806634

《孙子兵法》，张和生校注；程郁校注；贾尔斯英译.

11. Sun Tzu's art of war：the modern Chinese interpretation/Tao Hanzhang；translated by Yuan Shibing. New York：Sterling Pub. Co. ，1987. 128 pages：illustrations；26cm. ISBN：0806966386，0806966380

《孙子兵法》,陶汉章著;袁士槟译.

(1) New York：Sterling Pub. Co.，1990. 128 pages：
illustrations；26cm. ISBN：0806966394，0806966397

(2) Rev. ed. New York：Sterling Pub.，2000. 128 pages：
illustrations, maps；26cm. ISBN：0806927895,
0806927893

(3) New York：Main Street，2004. 176 pages；18cm.
ISBN：140271291X，1402712913

(4) New York：Sterling Innovation，2007. 223 pages；16
×12cm. ISBN：1402745524，1402745522

12. The art of strategy：a new translation of Sun Tzu's
classic, the art of war/R. L. Wing. New York：
Doubleday，1988. 163 pages；28cm. ISBN：
0385237847, 0385237840, 0850308518, 0850308518
《孙子兵法》,Wing, R. L. 译.

(1) London：Thorsons，1997. 163 pages；24cm. ISBN：
0722534884，0722534885

13. The art of war/Sun Tzu；translated by Thomas Cleary.
Boston：Shambhala；[New York]：Distributed in the
United States by Random House，1988. viii, 172 p.；
23cm. ISBN：0877734526，0877734529
《孙子兵法》,Cleary, Thomas F. (1949—)（美国翻译家）
译.

(1) Boston：Shambhala；[New York：]：Distributed in
the U. S. by Random House，1991. xiv, 114 p.；
12cm. ISBN：0877735379, 0877735373, 1570620296,
1570620294. (Shambhala pocket classics)

(2) Boston, Mass.；London：Shambhala，2005. 224
pages；18cm. ISBN：1590302257, 1590302255

(3) Boston, Mass.：Shambhala；Enfield：Publishers
Group UK [distributor]，2007. ISBN：1590304761,
1590304764

(4) Boston：Shambhala，2009. xiii, 221 p.：col. ill.；
17cm.＋2 sound discs（digital；4 3/4 in.）. ISBN：
1590307434, 1590307437

14. The illustrated art of war/Sun Tzu；translated by
Thomas Cleary. Boston：Shambhala；[New York：]：
Distributed in the U. S. by Random House，1998. 223
p.：ill.（some col.）；25cm. ISBN：1570624224,
1570624223
《孙子兵法》,Cleary, Thomas F. (1949—)（美国翻译家）
译.

15. The art of war：complete texts and commentaries/Sun
Tzu；translated by Thomas Cleary. Boston：Shambhala,
2003. vi, 457 p.：ill.；25cm. ISBN：1590300548,
1590300541
《孙子兵法》,Cleary, Thomas F. (1949—)（美国翻译家）
译.

16. The art of war：an illustrated edition/Sun Tzu；
translated by Thomas Cleary. 1st paperback ed.
Boston, MA：Shambhala Publications，2004. 223 p.：

ill.；24cm. ISBN：1590301854，1590301852
《孙子兵法》,Cleary, Thomas F. (1949—)（美国翻译
家）译.

17. Sun-Tzu, manual for war/translator ＆ editor, T. W.
Kuo. Chicago, Ill.：ATLI Press，1989. 170 pages；
21cm. ISBN：0910169020, 0910169028
《孙子兵法》,Kuo, T. W. 译.

18. Sunzi on the art of war and its general application to
business/[translated by] M. W. Luke Chan, Chen
Bingfu. Shanghai, China：Fudan University Press,
1989. 127 pages；19cm. ISBN：730900227X,
7309002270
《孙子兵法》,Chan, M. W. Luke 和 Chen, Bingfu 合译.

19. Sun Tzu's art of war/edited by Khoo Kheng-Hor；
translated by Hwang Zhongmei. Petaling Jaya, Selangor
Darul Ehsan, Malaysia：Pelanduk Publications，1992.
54 pages；22cm. ISBN：9679784045, 9679784046
《孙子兵法》,Khoo, Kheng-Hor 编；Hwang Chung-Mei
译.

20. Sun Zi's art of war：the world's greatest military works
in English ＆ Chinese/[edited ＆ translated by C. C.
Low ＆ Associates]. Singapore：Canfonian，1992. 144
pages；22cm. ISBN：9810032773, 9810032777.
(Chinese classical stories in English ＆ Chinese；3)
《孙子兵法》,C. C. Low 等译.

21. Sun tzu：the new translation/Sun-tzu；research and
reinterpretation by J. H. Huang. 1st Quill ed. New
York：Quill，1993. 299 pages：illustrations；23cm.
《孙子兵法》,Huang, J. H. 译.

(1) New York：Quill，1993. 299 pages：illustrations；
23cm. ISBN：0688124003, 0688124007

(2) The art of war/research and reinterpretation by J.
H. Huang. Fort Wayne, IN：Sweetwater Press,
2006. 96 pages：illustrations；19. ISBN：
1581737585, 1581737580

(3) New York：HarperPerenial，2008. 299 pages；
23cm. ISBN：0061351419, 0061351415

22. 汉英对照《孙子兵法》/潘嘉玢,刘瑞祥英译. [北京]：军
事科学出版社，1993. xxv, 125 pages；21cm. ISBN：
7800215121；7800215124.
英文题名：A Chinese-English bilingual reader the art of
war

23. Sun-tzu：the art of warfare：the first English translation
incorporating the recently discovered Yin-ch'üeh-shan
texts/translated, with an introduction and commentary,
by Roger T. Ames. New York：Ballantine Books，1993.
xiv, 321 p.：ill.；24cm. ISBN：034536239X,
0345362391. (Classics of ancient China)
《孙子兵法》,安乐哲（Ames, Roger T.，1947—）（美国
汉学家）合译. 根据最新发现的山东临沂银雀山版本
翻译.

24. The art of war/translated, with an introduction and commentary, by Roger T. Ames; preface by Rupert Smith. London: Folio Society, 2008. vi, 252 pages, [12] pages of plates: illustrations (chiefly color); 29cm.

《孙子兵法》,安乐哲(Ames, Roger T.,1947—)(美国汉学家)译.

25. 孙子兵法:中英文对照/李零今译;(美)安乐哲(Roger T. Ames)英译. 北京:中华书局,2012. 159 页;20cm. ISBN:7101088038

本书由《孙子兵法》原文、中文今译和英文翻译三部分构成,并且中译与今译两相对照,便于互相参考. 中文今译选用的是北京大学李零先生的译本,英文翻译选用的是美国夏威夷大学安乐哲(Roger Ames)的译本.

26. The art of war/translated by Roger T. Ames. Illustrated edition; First Frances Lincoln edition. London Frances Lincoln Limited Publishers, 2015. 93 pages: colour illustrations; 17cm. ISBN: 0711236509, 071123650X. (Traditional wisdom)

《孙子兵法》,安乐哲(Ames, Roger T.,1947—)(美国汉学家)译.

27. The art of war = [Sunzi bing fa]/Sun-tzu; translated, with introductions and commentary, by Ralph D. Sawyer; with the collaboration of Mei-Chün Lee Sawyer. Boulder, Colorado: Westview Press, 1994. 375 pages: illustrations; 21cm. ISBN: 0813319513, 081331951X, 1566192972, 1566192978, 1566192986, 566192989. (History and warfare)

《孙子兵法》,Sawyer, Ralph D. 译注.

(1) New York: Barnes & Noble Books, 1994. 375 pages: maps; 23cm. ISBN: 7566792976, 7566792970

(2) Taipei: SMC Publishing, 1996. 375 pages: illustrations; 22cm. ISBN: 9576383420, 9576383427

(3) NewYork: MetroBooks, 2001. 375 pages: illustrations; 22cm. ISBN: 1586635603, 1586635602

(4) Running Press miniature ed. Philadelphia, Pa.: Running Press, 2003. 127 pages; 9cm. ISBN: 0762415983, 0762415984, 0877734526, 0877734529

28. The complete art of war/translated, with historical introduction and commentary, by Ralph D. Sawyer; with the collaboration of Mei-chün Lee Sawyer. Boulder, Colo.: Westview Press, 1996. xv, 304 pages; 21cm. ISBN: 0813330858, 0813330853, 0813388880, 0813388885. (History and warfare)

《孙子兵法》,Sawyer, Ralph D. 译注.

29. The essential art of war = Sun-tzu ping-fa/translated, with historical introduction and commentaries, by Ralph D. Sawyer; with the collaboration of Mei-chün Lee Sawyer. New York: Basic Books, 2005. xlv, 137 pages; 20cm. ISBN: 0465072046, 0465072040

《孙子兵法》,Sawyer, Ralph D. 译注

30. Art of war/translated by Ralph D. Sawyer. Hoo: Grange, 2005. 128 pages; 21cm.

《孙子兵法》,Sawyer, Ralph D. 译.

31. Sun Zi: the art of war, with commentaries = Sunzi bing fa yu bing shu/annotated by Xie Guoliang; translated by Zhang Huimin. [Beijing]: Panda Books, 1995. 327 pages; 20cm. ISBN: 0835131769, 0835131766

《孙子兵法与兵书》,Hsieh, Kuo-liang 注; Chang, Hui-min 英译. 英汉对照.

32. 孙子兵法一百则:汉英对照 = Sun Tzu's the art of war: Chinese-English/罗志野译. 北京:中国对外翻译出版公司;香港:商务印书馆,1996. 8, 211 pages; 19cm. ISBN: 7500103239, 7500103233. (一百丛书)

33. The art of war: the definitive interpretation of Sun Tzu's classic book of strategy for the martial artist/Stephen F. Kaufman. Boston: C. E. Tuttle, 1996. xii, 109 pages; 22cm. ISBN: 0804830800, 0804830805

《孙子兵法》,Kaufman, Steve(1939—)译.

34. The art of war/by Sun Tzu; adapted and introduced by Stefan Rudnicki. West Hollywood, CA: Dove, 1996. 92 pages; 20cm. ISBN: 0787105619, 0787105617

《孙子兵法》,Rudnicki, Stefan(1945—)编译.

35. The essentials of war = [Sunzi bing fa]/transcription, translation by Prof. Zhong Qin. Beijing: New World Press, 1996. 140 pages; 18cm. ISBN: 7800053318, 7800053313

《孙子兵法》,Zhong, Qin 译.

36. Sun tzu: the art of war for managers: new translation with commentary: 50 rules for strategic thinking/Gerald A. Michaelson. Alcoa, Tenn.: Pressmark International, 1998. ix, 160 pages; 23cm. ISBN: 188399909X, 1883999094

Michaelson, Gerald A. 著,包括对《孙子兵法》的英译.

(1) Avon, Mass.: Adams Media Corp., 2001. xxi, 202 p.; 23cm. ISBN: 1580624596, 1580624596

(2) Sun Tzu: the art of war for managers: 50 strategic rules, updated for today's business/Gerald A. Michaelson and Steven W. Michaelson. 2nd ed. Avon, Mass.: Adams Media; Newton Abbot: David & Charles [distributor], 2010. xx, 204 pages; 21cm. ISBN: 1605500300, 1605500305

37. Sun Tzu: the art of war; The book of Lord Shang/with a commentary by Tao Hanzhang; [Shang Yang]; translated by Yuan Shibing; introduction by Robert Wilkinson; translated by J. J. L. Duyvendak; introduction by Robert Wilkinson. Ware, Herts.: Wordsworth Editions Ltd., 1998. 243 pages; 20cm. ISBN: 1853267791 1853267796. (Wordsworth classics of world literature)

《孙子兵法·商君书》,袁士槟翻译了陶汉章的《孙子兵法概论》.

38. The art of war：in Sun Tzu's own words/translation and foreword by Gary Gagliardi. Shoreline, WA：Clearbridge Pub.，1999. xi, 147 pages；22cm. ISBN：1929194005, 1929194001

《孙子兵法》，Gagliardi，Gary 译.

39. Amazing secrets of Sun Tzu's the art of war/by Sun Tzu & Gary Gagliardi. Seattle, WA：Clearbridge Pub.，2001. xv, 141 pages：illustrations；22cm. ISBN：1929194072, 1929194070

Notes：Contains the translated text of The art of war and a phrase by phrase commentary.

《孙子兵法》，Gagliardi，Gary 译.

40. The art of war：plus the ancient Chinese revealed/translation and foreword by Gary Gagliardi. Seattle, WA：Clearbridge Pub.，2002. xi, 159 pages；23cm. ISBN：1929194193.（Art of war plus. Mastering bing-fa series）

《孙子兵法》，Gagliardi，Gary 译.

（1）2nd ed. Seattle, WA：Clearbridge Pub.，2004. 159 pages；23cm. ISBN：1929194196.（Art of war plus. Mastering Sun Tzu series）

（2）Seattle, WA：Clearbridge Pub.，2007. 159 pages；23cm. ISBN：1929194421, 1929194420

41. Sun Tzu's The art of war：plus, the art of starting a business/by Gary Gagliardi. Shoreline, WA：Clearbridge Pub.，2002. xiii, 146 pages；22cm. ISBN：1929194153, 1929194155

Notes："This book includes both a complete translation of Sun Tzu's The art of war and a special version, The art of starting a business"—Page 4 of cover.

Gagliardi，Gary 译,包括对《孙子兵法》的翻译.

42. Sun Tzu's The art of war plus, the warrior class：306 lessons in strategy/by Gary Gagliardi. 2nd ed. Seattle, WA：Clearbridge Pub.，2003. 317 pages：illustrations；23cm. ISBN：1929194099; 1929194094.（The art of war plus. Mastering bing-fa series）

《孙子兵法》，Gagliardi，Gary 译.

（1）1st hardcover ed. Seattle, WA：Clearbridge Pub.，2004. 347 pages；24cm. ISBN：1929194307, 1929194308.（Art of war plus. Mastering strategy series）

43. Sun Tzu's the art of war：plus, the warrior's apprentice：your first guide to the magic of strategy/by Gary Gagliardi. Shoreline, WA：Clearbridge Pub.，2005. 189 pages：illustrations；23cm. ISBN：1929194323, 1929194322.（Art of war plus. Mastering strategy series）

《孙子兵法》（选译），Gagliardi，Gary 译.

44. The ancient bing-fa：martial arts strategy：the science of personal power＝［Sunzi bing fa］/by Sun Tzu & Gary Gagliardi. Seattle, WA：Clearbridge Pub./Science of Strategy Institute, 2006. 189 pages：illustrations；

24cm. ISBN：1929194382, 1929194384

Notes：Contains the translated text of "The art of war" and a phrase by phrase commentary.

《孙子兵法》，Gagliardi，Gary 译.

45. The book of war/Sunzi；Carl von Clausewitz；introduction by Ralph Peters. New York：Modern Library, 2000. xxiv, 984 pages；21cm. ISBN：0375754776, 0375754777

Contents：The art of war/Sun Tzu—On war/Carl von Clausewitz.

包括《孙子兵法》的英译.

46. The art of Leadership by Sun Tzu：a new millennium translation of Sun Tzu's art of war/translated and annotted, with cases by David H. Li. Bethesda, Md.：Premier Pub.，2000. 272 pages：illustrations；23cm. ISBN：096378529X, 0963785299

《孙子兵法》，Li，David H. 译注.

47. Sun Tzu and the art of modern warfare/Mark McNeilly. Oxford；New York：Oxford University Press，2001. xii, 304 pages：illustrations, maps；24cm. ISBN：0195133404, 0195133400

McNeilly，Mark 著,包括对《孙子兵法》的英译.

（1）New York：Oxford University Press，2015. x, 311 pages：illustrations, maps；24cm. ISBN：0199957859, 0199957851

48. The art of war：a new translation/translation, essays and commentary by the Denma Translation Group. Boston：Shambhala, 2001. xxii, 250 pages；24cm. ISBN：1570625522, 1570625527, 1570629048, 1570629044

《孙子兵法》，Denma Translation Group 译.

（1）Abridged ed. Boston：Shambhala, 2002. xxv, 292 p.；18cm. ISBN：1570629781, 1570629785.（Shambhala library）

（2）Boston, Mass.；London：Shambhala, 2002. 272 pages：illustrations, maps；23cm. ISBN：1570629048, 1570629044

（3）The art of war：the Denma translation/translation and essays by the Denma Translation Group. Boston：Shambhala, 2003. 165 pages；19cm. ISBN：1570625522, 1570625527, 1570629048, 1570629044, 1590300718, 1590300718

（4）The art of war：the Denma translation/translations and essays by the Denma Translation Group. Boston, Mass.：Shambhala, 2007. 165 pages；19cm. ISBN：1570629781, 1570629785

（5）Boston, Mass.：Shambhala, 2009. xxiii, 292 pages；17cm. ISBN：1590307281, 1590307283.（Shambhala classics）

49. The art of war/Sun-tzu（Sun-zi）；translated with an introduction and commentary by John Minford. New York：Viking, c2002. lvi, 325 p.；24cm. ISBN：

0670031569，0670031566，0143105756，0143105752

《孙子兵法》，闵福德（Minford，John，1946—）（英国汉学家）译.

(1) Deluxe ed. New York：Penguin，2003. lvi，325 pages；22cm. ISBN：0140439196，0140439199，0670031569，0670031566.（Penguin classics）

(2) London：Penguin，2005. lvi，325 pages；20cm. ISBN：0140439196，0140439199，0670031569，0670031566

(3) London：Penguin，2005. 100 pages；18cm. ISBN：0141023813，0141023816，0140439196，0140439199，0670031569，0670031566

(4) New York：Penguin Books，2006. 100 p.；18cm. ISBN：0143037528，0143037521.（Great ideas）

(5) London；New York：Penguin，2008. 100 pages；20cm. ISBN：0140455526，0140455523.（Penguin classics）

(6) New York：Penguin Books，2009. lvi，325 pages；20cm. ISBN：0143105756，0143105752

(7) Stepney，S. Australia：Axiom Pub.，2009. 128 pages；21cm. ISBN：0141045276，0141045272.（Popular Penguins）

(8) London：Penguin Classics，an imprint of Penguin Books，2014. lxxxv，448 pages；18cm. ISBN：0141395845，0141395842

50. Sun Zi's the art of war/translated by H. H. Tan. Aspley，Qld.：H H Tan Medical P/L，2002. 192 pages；21cm. ISBN：0958006709，0958006705

《孙子兵法》，Tan，Han Hiong 译.

51. The art of peace：balance over conflict in Sun-tzu's The art of war/translated and adapted by Philip Dunn. New York：Jeremy P. Tarcher/Putnam，2003. 192 pages；1 illustration；18cm. ISBN：1585422258，1585422258

《孙子兵法》，Dunn，Philip（1946—）译.

52. The art of war/Sun Tzu；translated by Wu Sun Lin. San Francisco，CA：Long River Press，2003. xiii，158 pages；illustrations；18cm. ISBN：1592650007，1592650002，1592650287，1592650286

《孙子兵法》，林戊荪译.

(1) The art of war/translated by Lin Wusun. San Francisco，CA：Long River Press，2013. xiii，158 pages；illustrations，maps；17cm. ISBN：1592651481，1592651488，1494417277，1494417278

53. Sun Zi art of war：an illustrated translation with Asian perspectives and insights/［translated by］Chow-Hou Wee. Singapore；New York：Pearson Prentice Hall，2003. xvi，438 pages；24cm. ISBN：013100137X，0131001374

《孙子兵法》，Wee，Chow Hou 译. 英汉对照.

54. The art of war：the cornstone［i. e. cornerstone］of Chinese strategy/newly translated by Chou-Wing Chohan and Abe Bellenteen；edited by Rosemary Brant. Israel：

Astrolog Pub. House，2003. 83 pages；22cm. ISBN：9654941791，9654941792

《孙子兵法》，Chohan，Chou-Wing 和 Bellenteen，Abe 合译；Brant，Rosemary 编.

55. The art of war：the complete text of Sun Tzu's classic compiled in this special edition with Frederick the Great's Instructions to his generals and Machiavelli's The prince，with an introduction by Marc A. Moore.［Place of publication not identified］：Sweetwater Press，2004. 383 pages；22cm. ISBN：1602613652，1602613656 Contents：Sun Tzu's Art of war—The Prince/Niccolo Machiavelli—Frederick the Great's Instructions to his general.

包括《孙子兵法》的翻译.

(1)［Place of publication not identified］：Sweetwater Press，2006. 383 pages；24cm. ISBN：1581735871，1581735871

(2)［Raleigh，N. C.］：Sweetwater Press，2007. 383 pages；22cm. ISBN：1581733208，1581733204

56. The art of war/Sun Tzu.［Place of publication not identified］：Filiquarian Pub. 2006. 68 pages；23cm. ISBN：1599869772，1599869773

《孙子兵法》

57. The art of war/Sun Tzu. Middlesex：Echo Library，2006. 112 pages；23cm. ISBN：1406831417，1406831412

《孙子兵法》，译者不详.

58. 孙子说：汉英对照/蔡希勤编注. 北京：华语教学出版社，2006. 201 页；21cm. ISBN：7802002141，7802002142.（中国圣人文化丛书. 老人家说系列）

英文题名：Sun zi says

59. 孙子兵法新译＝The art of war by Sun Zi. 加拿大：交流（加拿大）出版社，2007. 198 pages；illustrations；21cm. ISBN：0978275310，9780275314.（中华文化智慧系列＝Wisdom of Chinese culture series. 第一辑）

60. Sun Tzu：the ultimate master of war/by Xu Yuanxiang & Li Jing.［Beijing］：China Intercontinental Press，2007. 77 pages：color illustrations；21cm. ISBN：7508510408，7508510402.（Ancient sages of China）

《兵圣：孙子》，徐远翔，李京著；汉佳，王国振译.

61. 孙子兵法/罗志野编选、英译；王诒卿白话文翻译. 北京：中国对外翻译出版公司，2007. 263 页；21cm. ISBN：7500118121，7500118120.（中译经典文库·中华传统文化精粹）

英文题名：Sun Tzu's the Art of War

62. The art of war：Sun Zi's military methods/translated by Victor H. Mair. New York：Columbia University Press，2007. lii，189 pages：illustrations（some color）；22cm. ISBN：0231133821，0231133820，0231133838，0231133839，0231508537，0231508530.（Translations from the Asian classics）

《孙子兵法》，梅维恒（Mair，Victor H.，1943—）（美国

翻译家)编译.

63. Art of war & the prince/Sunzi；Niccolò Machiavelli. Radford, VA：Wilder Pub.，2008. 236 pages；21cm. ISBN：1604593617，160459361X

Contents：Sun Tzu's Art of war—The Prince/Niccolo Machiavelli

包括《孙子兵法》的翻译.

64. Classic works on the art of war/Sun Tzu, Niccolò Machiavelli, Carl von Clausewitz. Mineola, N. Y.：Dover；Newton Abbot：David & Charles [distributor]，2008. ISBN：0486467870, 0486467872

Contents：The art of war/Sun Tzu—The art of war/Niccolò Machiavelli—Principles of war/Carl von Clausewitz. Translated from the Chinese, German and Italian.

包括对《孙子兵法》的英译.

65. The complete art of war/Sun Tzu [and others]. Radford，VA：Wilder Publications, 2008. 742 pages；23cm. ISBN：1604593600, 1604593601

Contents：The art of war/by Sun Tzu—On war/by Carl von Clausewitz—The art of war/by Niccolò Machiavelli—The art of war/by Antoine-Henri Jomini.

包括对《孙子兵法》的英译.

66. The art of war：the complete and fully illustrated edition of Sun Tzu's philosophical masterpiece with four other classics in the ancient warrior tradition, foreword by Paul Couch. [Place of publication not identified]：Sweetwater Press, 2008. 584 pages；22cm.

Contents：Sun Tzu's Art of war—The Prince/Niccolo Machiavelli—Frederick the Great's Instructions to his general.

包括《孙子兵法》的翻译.

67. Sun Tzu's The art of war/compiled and translated by Luo Zhiye. Sydney：CPG International, 2008. 263 pages；illustrations；21cm. ISBN：0958000444, 0958000441

《孙子兵法》, 罗志野译.

68. The art of war：spirituality for conflict：annotated & explained/annotation by Thomas Huynh；translation by Thomas Huynh and the editors of Sonshi. com；foreword by Marc Benioff；preface by Thomas Cleary. Woodstock, Vt.：SkyLight Paths Pub.，c2008. xl, 210 p.；22cm. ISBN：1594732447, 1594732442. (Skylight Illuminations series)

《孙子兵法》, Huynh, Thomas 译.

69. The art of war：Sun Tzu, Barack Obama, and the modern moment/Brian Browne Walker. [Boulder, CO]：Brian Browne Walker, 2009. 79 pages；23cm. ISBN：0982599310, 0982599315

Notes："A new translation of the ancient classic."

《孙子兵法》, Walker, Brian Browne 译.

70. Sun Tzu's original art of war：Sun Tzu bing fa recovered from the latest archaeological discoveries/translation and commentary by Andrew W. Zieger. Vancouver, Canada：Colors Network Publishing, 2010. 209 pages；27cm. ISBN：0981313702, 0981313701

《孙子兵法》, Zieger, Andrew W. 译.

71. Sun Tzu's the art of war：the oldest military treatise in the world. [Place of publication not identified]：WaterMark, Inc.，2010. 358 pages；25cm. ISBN：1581738261, 1581738269

Contents：Sun Tzu's Art of war—The Prince/Niccolo Machiavelli—On war/General Claus von Clausewitz—Frederick the Great's Instructions to his generals

包括《孙子兵法》的英译.

72. The technology of war/a new translation by Colin I. Thorne. Los Angeles, Calif.：Colin I. Thorme, 2010. xxxiii, 154 pages；24cm. ISBN：1450707688, 1450707688

《孙子兵法》, Thorne, Colin I. 译.

73. The art of war/Sun Tzu；introduction by Nigel Cawthorne. London：Arcturus, 2010. 128 pages：illustrations；26cm. ISBN：1848582446, 1848582447

《孙子兵法》, Cawthorne, Nigel(1951—)译.

(1)New York：Chartwell, 2010. 128 pages：illustrations (chiefly color)；26cm. ISBN：0785826873, 0785826874

(2)London：Capella, 2012. 126 pages：illustrations；18cm. ISBN：1782120520, 1782120521

(3)London：Arcturus, 2014. 126 pages：illustrations；19cm. ISBN：1841933580, 1841933589, 1784042028, 1784042021

(4)London：Arcturus, 2015. 160 pages：color illustrations；24cm. ISBN：1784048174, 1784048178

74. The art of war：a new translation/Sun Tzu；[translator, James Trapp]. London：Amber Books, 2011. 96 pages；27cm. ISBN：1907446788, 1907446788

《孙子兵法》, Trapp, James 译. 英汉对照.

(1) New York：Chartwell Books, 2012. 96 pages；27cm. ISBN：0785829225, 0785829229

75. Master Sun's Art of war/Sun Tzu；translated, with introduction, by Philip J. Ivanhoe. Indianapolis：Hackett Pub. Co.，2011. xxx, 113 pages：illustrations；23cm. ISBN：1603844666, 160384466X, 1603844673, 1603844678

《孙子兵法》, Ivanhoe, P. J. 译.

76. The essential art of war collection：the most respected military strategy books ever written. Memphis, TN：Bottom of the Hill Publishing, 2012. 520 pages；23cm. ISBN：1612034393, 161203439X

包括《孙子兵法》的英译.

77. Sun-Tzu：the art of war/[translated by] Vinay B. Dalvi. New Delhi：Pentagon Press, 2012. 104 pages：color

illustrations；15cm. ISBN：8182746152，8182746159

《孙子兵法》，Dalvi, Vinay B.（1951—）译.

78. The art of war/Sun Tzu； translated by Jonathan Clements. London： Constable, 2012. 175 pages； 20cm. ISBN：1780330013，1780330014

《孙子兵法》，Clements, Jonathan（1971—）译.

　　(1) London： Collector's Library, 2014. 151 pages； 16cm. ISBN：1909621220，1909621226

79. Sun Tzu： the art of war through the ages/edited and introduced by Bob Carruthers. Barnsley： Pen & Sword Military, 2013. 176 pages： illustrations（black and white）； 24cm. ISBN： 1781592349， 1781592342. (Military history from primary sources)

《孙子兵法》，Carruthers, Bob 编译.

80. Art of war/Sun Tzu and Victoria Charles［compiler］. New York： Parkstone Press International, 2013. 255 pages： illustrations （ some color ）； 33cm. ISBN： 1844848126，1844848124

《孙子兵法》，Charles, Victoria 译.

81. Sunzi speaks： the art of war/adapted and illustrated by Tsai Chih Chung； translated by Brian Bruya. New York： Anchor Books, 1994. 140 pages： chiefly illustrations；21cm. ISBN：0385472587，0385472586

《兵学的先知》，蔡志忠（1948—）编；Bruya, Brian （1966—）英译. 英汉对照.

E112　孙膑兵法

1. The lost art of war/Sun Tzu II； translated with commentary by Thomas Cleary. ［San Francisco, Calif.］： HarperSanFrancisco, c1996. vi, 154 p.； 22cm. ISBN： 0062513613, 0062513618, 0062514059, 0062514059

《孙膑兵法》，Cleary, Thomas F.（1949—）（美国翻译家）译.

2. Sun Pin： the art of warfare/［translated］ by D. C. Lau & Roger T. Ames. New York： Ballantine Books, 1996. xiii, 352 p.： ［16 plates］, ill.； 25cm. ISBN：0345379918, 0345379917

《孙膑兵法》，刘殿爵（Lau, D. C.〈Dim Cheuk〉, 1921—2010）（中国香港学者），安乐哲（Ames, Roger T., 1947—）（美国汉学家）合译.

　　(1) Albany： State University of New York Press, c2003. xii, 253 p.； 23cm. ISBN：0791454959, 0791454954, 0791454967, 0791454961.（SUNY series in Chinese philosophy and culture）

E2　中国军事

1. China's national defense/author Peng Guangqian； translator Chen Ru. Beijing： China Intercontinental Press, 2004. 173 pages： illustrations， maps；22cm. ISBN：7508506200， 7508506203.（Chinese basics series）

《中国国防》，彭光谦著；陈茹译. 五洲传播出版社（中国基本情况丛书/郭长建主编）

2. China's national defense/Peng Guangqian, Zhao Zhiyin & Luo Yong； translated by Ma Chenguang & Yan Shuang. Beijing： China International Press, 2010. 154 pages： color illustrations， color maps；23cm. ISBN： 7508513102, 750851310X

《中国国防》，彭光谦、赵智印、罗永著. 五洲传播出版社.

3. China's endeavors for arms control, disarmament and non-proliferation. Beijing： Information Office of the State Council of the People's Republic of China, 2005. 49 p. ISBN：7801489209，7801489203，7801489197，7801489195

《中国的军控、裁军与防扩散势力：英文》，中华人民共和国国务院新闻办公室发布.

4. China's non-proliferation policy and measures/Information Office of the State Council of the People's Republic of China. Beijing： New Star Publishers, 2003. 24 pages； 26cm. ISBN：7801485653，7801485656

《中国的防扩散政策和措施》，中华人民共和国国务院新闻办公室发布. 新星出版社.

5. China's propositions and practice on disarmament issue. Beijing： Foreign Languages Press, 1987. 36 p.； 19cm.

《中国对裁军问题的主张及实践》

6. China and disarmament. Beijing： Foreign Languages Press, 1988. 64 p. ISBN：7119006711, 7119006710

《中国与裁军》

7. The Chinese People's Liberation Army. Peking： Foreign Languages Press, 1950. 62 p.： ill.

《中国人民解放军》

8. From Yenan to Peking： the Chinese People's War of Liberation： From Reconstruction to First Five-year Plan/ Liao Kai-lung. Peking： Foreign Languages Press, 1954. ［8］, 187 p.； maps；19cm.

《中国人民解放战争简史》，廖盖隆著.

9. Three years of the Chinese people's liberation war. Peking： Foreign Languages Press, 1949. 78 pages； 19cm.

Contents： The Chinese people's struggle for liberation—A general summary of the three years war of liberation of the Chinese people—PLA general headquarters sums up three year's war gains—Liberated areas occupy 30. 83% of China's land—The relative strength of PLA and KMT troops.

《中国人民解放战争三年战绩》

10. Eight years of the Chinese people's volunteers' resistance to American aggression and siding Korea. Peking： Foreign Languages Press, 1958. 112 pages；19cm.

《中国人民志愿军抗美援朝八年》

11. Democratic tradition of the Chinese People's Liberation Army. Peking： Foreign Languages Press, 1965. 38 pages；19cm.

《中国人民解放军的民主传统》，贺龙著.

12. The politics of the Chinese Red Army：a translation of the Bulletin of activities of the People's Liberation Army/edited by J. Chester Cheng, with the collaboration of Ch'ing-lien Han...［et al.］. Stanford, Calif.：Hoover Institution on War, Revolution, and Peace，1966. 776 p.；28cm.

Notes：Bulletin of activities of the people's Liberation Army.

《中国军队的政治》，Cheng，J. Chester(James Chester，1926—)编译，译自中国人民解放军的工作通讯.

13. The People's Army is invincible：in commemoration of the 42nd anniversary of the founding of the Chinese People's Liberation Army：editorial/by Renmin Ribao, Hongqi and Jiefangjun Bao. Peking：Foreign Languages Press，1969. 16 pages，1 leaf of plates：portraits；13cm.

《人民军队所向无敌》

14. Commemorate the 44th anniversary of the founding of the Chinese People's Liberation Army. Peking：Foreign Languages Press，1971. 30 pages；14cm.

《纪念中国人民解放军建军四十四周年》

15. Fifty years of the Chinese People's Liberation Army. Peking：Foreign Languages Press，1978. 175 pages；19cm.

《光辉的战斗历程：纪年中国人民解放军建军五十周年》

16. Great victory for the military line of chairman Mao Tsetung：a criticism of Lin Piao's bourgeois military line in the Liaoshi-Shenyang and Peiping-Tientsin campaigns/Chan Shih-pu. Peking：Foreign Languages Press，1976. 115 p.，2 vouwbl.：ill.，krt.；19cm.

《毛主席军事路线的伟大胜利：批判林彪在辽沈、平津两大战役中的资产阶级军事路线》，詹时圃著.

F 类　经济

F1　中国经济

F11　概论

1. A glance at China's economy/Cheng Shih. Peking：Foreign Languages Press，1974. 52 pages，［23］leaves of plates：illustrations；19cm.

《中国经济简况》，郑实著.

2. China's economy/authors Wang Mengkui and others；translator Liu Bingwen. Beijing：China Intercontinental Press，2004. 187 pages：color illustrations；22cm. ISBN：7508506340，7508506340. (China basics series)

《中国经济》，王梦奎等编著；刘炳文译. 五洲传播出版社 (中国基本情况丛书/郭长建主编).

(1)2nd ed. Beijing：China Intercontinental Press，2006. 185 pages：illustrations (some color)；21cm. ISBN：

7508509105，7508509102. (China basics series)

3. China's economy/Wu Li, Sui Fumin, Zheng Lei；translated by David Gu.［Beijing］：China Intercontinental Press，2010. 160 pages：illustrations (some color), color maps；23cm. ISBN：7508513041，7508513045

《中国经济》，武力，隋福民，郑磊著. 五洲传播出版社.

4. A social and economic atlas of western China/compiled by Jin Fengjun & Qian Jinkai；translated by Wang Pingxing. Beijing：China Intercontinental Press，2003. 94 pages：color illustrations，color maps；29cm. ISBN：7508503341，7508503349

《中国西部社会经济发展图册》，金凤君，钱金凯编著，五洲传播出版社.

5. 西部人民的生活＝Life in western China："中国西部省份社会与经济发展监测研究"数据报告：英文/中国科学技术促进发展研究中心社会发展研究部，挪威 Fafo 应用国际研究所编. 北京：中国统计出版社，2006. 589 页；30cm. ISBN：7503750251，7503750250

英文题名：Life in western China：tabulation report of monitoring social and economic development in western China. 本书为中国西部省份社会经济发展监测研究数据报告，是《西部人民的生活》的英文版.

6. The eventful years：memoirs of Chen Jinhua/Chen Jinhua. Beijing：Foreign Languages Press，2008. iv，546 pages：illustrations；23cm. ISBN：7119051918，7119051911

《亲历中国改革：陈锦华国事忆述》，陈锦华著. 回顾了自20世纪70年代以来党和政府实施的一系列有关中国经济发展、工业现代化的重大政策.

7. Seeking changes. The economic development in contemporary China/George J. Gilboy...［et al.］；［editor］Zhou Yanhui. Beijing：Central Compilation & Translation，2011. I，263 p.；24cm. ISBN：7511708151，7511708153

《当代中国经济发展》，周艳辉主编. 中央编译出版社.

8. The international development of China, by Sun Yat-sen, with 16 maps in the text and a folding map at end. New York：G. P. Putnam's Sons；London：Knickerbocker Press，1922. x，265 p.：17 maps (1 fold. in pocket) 21cm.

《实业计划》，孙中山(1866—1925).

(1)2nd ed. New York：London, G. P. Putnam's Sons，1929. xvi，265 p. pl.（2 plans) 17 maps (1 fold. in pocket) 21cm.

(2)London；New York［etc.］，Pub. on behalf of the London Office, Chinese ministry of information, by Hutchinson & Co.，［194—?］. 176 p.，pl.（2 plans) maps (1 fold.)，19cm.

(3)Chungking, Ministry of information of the republic of China. 1943. xiii，191 p. pl.（2 plans) maps (1 fold.) 21cm.

（4）2nd ed. New York：Da Capo Press，1975，c1922. xvi，265 p.：maps；22cm. ISBN：0306706970.（China in the 20th century）

（5）北京：外语教学与研究出版社，2011. xvii，318 页；图；23cm. ISBN：7513515405，7513528399.（"博雅双语名家名作"系列；第二辑）

9. China's post-war economic reconstruction/by Generalissimo Chiang Kai-shek and T. V. Soong... with English translation〔Shanghai〕International Publishers，1945. 1 preliminary leaf，16 pages；1 preliminary leaves，13 pages；18cm.

《中国经济建设方案》，蒋介石，宋子文.

（1）再版本. 上海：国际出版社，〔1946〕

10. The 1953 state budget of the People's Republic of China：a report/by Po I-Po.〔Peking〕：〔Foreign Languages Press〕，1953. 15 pages：illustrations；26cm.（People's China. 1953，6，Suppl.；〔2〕）

《关于 1953 年国家预算的报告》

11. Report on the first five-year plan for development of the national economy of the People's Republic of China in 1953—1957：delivered on July 5 and 6，1955 at the second session of the First National People's Congress. Peking：Foreign Languages Press，1955. 134 pages；22cm.

《中华人民共和国关于发展国民经济的第一个五年计划的报告》，李富春著.

12. Report on national economic development and fulfilment of the State plan in 1954. Peking：Foreign Languages Press，1956. 48 pages；21cm.

Notes："Issued by the State Statistical Bureau of the People's Republic of China."

《中华人民共和国统计局关于一九五四年度国民经济发展和国家计划执行结果的公报》

13. Report on fulfilment of the national economic plan of the People's Republic of China in 1955；with statistical summary/issued by the State Statistical Bureau of the People's Republic of China. Peking：Foreign Languages Press，1956. 57 pages；21cm.

《中华人民共和国国家统计局关于 1955 年度计划执行结果的公报》

14. First five-year plan for development of the national economy of the People's Republic of China in 1953—1957. Peking：Foreign Languages Press，1956. 231 pages；22cm.

《中华人民共和国发展国民经济的第一个五年计划（1953—1957）》

15. Decision of the Central Committee of the Communist Party of China of the transformation of caritalist industry and commerce. Peking：Foreign Languages Press，1956. 21 pages；21cm.

《中共中央关于资本主义工商业社会主义改造问题的决

议》

16. The socialist transformation of capitalist industry and commerce in China/Kuan Ta-tung. Peking：Foreign Languages Press，1960. 133 pages；20cm.

《中国资本主义工商业的社会主义改造》，管大同著.

17. Report on adjusting the major targets of the 1959 National economic plan and further developing the campaign for increasing production and practising economy/Chou En-lai. Peking：Foreign Languages Press，1959. 45 pages；19cm.

《关于调整一九五九年国民经济计划主要指标和进一步开展增产节约运动的报告》，周恩来.

18. Press communique on the growth of China's national economy in 1959. Peking：Foreign Languages Press，1960. 25 pages；19cm.

《关于一九五九年国民经济发展情况的新闻公报》

19. The second five-year plan fulfilled in two years；facts on the development of the national economy in 1959. Peking：Foreign Languages Press，1960. 1 volume （unpaged）illustrations（some color）19cm.（People's China in pictures）

《五年计划二年完成》

20. The socialist transformation of the national economy in China/Hsueh Mu-chiao，Su Hsing and Lin Tse-li. Peking：Foreign Languages Press，1960.〔4〕，287，〔1〕s.；18cm.（China knowledge series）

《中国国民经济的社会主义改造》，薛暮桥等著

21. China's economy and development principles：a report/by Zhao Ziyang. Beijing：Foreign Languages Press：Distributed by China Publications Centre（Cuoji Shudian），1982. 105 pages；19cm.

《中国经济形势和建设方针：国务院总理赵紫阳的报告》

22. The sixth five-year plan of the People's Republic of China for economic and social development，1981—1985. Beijing，China：Foreign Languages Press：Distributed by China Publications Centre，1984. 267 pages；19cm. ISBN：0835111601，0835111607

《中华人民共和国国民经济和社会发展第六个五年计划》

23. Decision of the Central Committee of the Communist Party of China on reform of the economic structure：adopted by the Twelfth Central Committee of the Communist Party of China at its third plenary session on October 20，1984. Beijing：Foreign Languages Press，1984. 38 pages；19cm. ISBN：0835114562，0835114561

《中共中央关于经济体制改革的决定》

24. Economy/compiled by the China Handbook Editorial Committee；translated by Hu Gengkang，Zhang Tingquan and Liu Bingwen. Beijing：Foreign Languages Press：Distributed by China Publications Centre，1984. 425 pages，〔24〕pages of plates：illustrations；19cm.

ISBN：0835109879. 0835109871. （China handbook series）

《经济》，《中国手册》，编辑委员会编.

25. Modern China's economy and management/edited by Ma Hong. Beijing：Foreign Languages Press, 1990. x, 486 pages; 22cm. ISBN：7119003704, 7119003702, 0835122255, 0835122252, 7119003712, 7119003719, 0835122263, 0835122269. （China knowledge series）

《现代中国经济与管理》，马洪主编.

26. 15 years of economic reform in China（1978—1993）/compiled by Beijing Review. Beijing：New Star Pub., 1994. 53 pages: illustrations（some color）; 20cm. ISBN：7800853853, 7800853852

《中国经济改革15年：1978—1993》，北京周报社编.

27. Report on China's national economic and social development for 1996/editor-in-chief, Chen Jinhua. Beijing：China Planning Press, 1996. 612 pages; 21cm. ISBN：7800584704, 7800584701

《1996年中国国民经济和社会发展报告》，陈锦华主编. 中国计划出版社.

28. The tenth five-year plan of China/New Star Publishers. Beijing：New Star Publishers, 2001. 95 pages: color illustrations; 19cm. ISBN：7801484568, 7801484567

《中国的"十五"计划》，王传民编. 新星出版社.

29. The twelfth five-year plan for national economic and social development of the People's Republic of China/translated by English Section of the Central Document Translation Department of the Central Compilation and Translation Bureau, Beijing, China. Beijing：Central Compilation & Translation Press, 2011. 1 vol.（V-293 p.）; ill.; 23cm. ISBN：7511709271, 7511709273

《中华人民共和国国民经济和社会发展第十二个五年规划纲要》，中国中央编译局中央文献翻译部编译. 中央编译出版社.

30. The development of China's nongovernmentally and privately operated economy/chief editors, Gao Shangquan and Chi Fulin; written by Zhu Huayou and Liu Chenghui. Beijing：Foreign Languages Press, 1996. 209 pages; 21cm. ISBN：7119017756, 7119017754. （Studies on the Chinese market economy series）

《中国民私营经济的发展》，高尚全，迟福林主编.

31. China：opening up and economic development/New Star Publishers. Beijing：New Star Publishers, 2001. 79 pages: color illustrations; 19cm. ISBN：7801484541, 7801484543

《中国：对外开放与经济发展》，吴乃陶编，新星出版社.

32. 用英语说中国. 经济 /田华实，徐静良主编. 上海：上海科学普及出版社，2009. 323 页; 24cm. ISBN：7542744197, 7542744194

英文题名：Talk about China in English. Economy

F12　经济理论与研究

1. Why China has no inflation/by Peng Kuang-hsi. Peking：Foreign Languages Press, 1976. 44 pages, [16] pages of plates: illustrations; 19cm.

《中国为什么没有通货膨胀》，彭光玺.

2. China's socialist economy/Xue Muqiao. Beijing：Foreign Languages Press：Distributed by Guoji Shudian（China Publications Centre）, 1981. xii, 316 pages; 21cm. （China knowledge series）

《中国社会主义经济问题研究》，薛暮桥著.

（1）2版. 北京：外文出版社，1986

3. China's search for economic growth：the Chinese economy since 1949：essays/by Xu Dixin, and others; translated by Andrew Watson. Beijing, China：New World Press：Distributed by China Publications Centre, 1982. vi, 217 pages; 22cm. （China studies series）

《中国对经济发展的探索：一九四九年以来的中国国民经济》，许涤新等著; 华安德译.

4. New strategy for China's economy/by Ma Hong; translated by Yang Lin. Beijing, China：New World Press：Distributed by China Publications Centre, 1983. 166 pages; 22cm. （China studies series）

《中国经济发展的新战略》，马洪著; 杨林译. 新世界出版社.

5. China's economy in 2000/compiled by Liu Guoguang... et al.; Chinese-English translation, Gao Guopei and others. Beijing, China：New World Press：Distributed by China International Book Trading Corp. （Guoji Shudian）, 1987. 546 pages; 22cm. ISBN：7800050432, 7800050435, 7800050351, 7800050350

《2000年的中国经济》，刘国光编著，新世界出版社.

6. China：changes in 40 years/compiled by Beijing Review. Beijing：New Star Publishers, 1989. 123 p., [80] p. of plates: ill., ports.; 19cm. ISBN：7800851397, 7800851391. （China in focus）

《中国：四十年的变化》，新星出版社. 1949—1989年经济.

7. China's economic policies, theories & reforms since 1949/author Xie Bai-san; translators Luo Han... [et al.]; revisors Yang Lie, Luo Han. Shanghai, P. R. China：Fudan University Press, c1991. 562 p.: ill.; 20cm. ISBN：7309007573

《1949年以来中国的经济政策：理论与改革》，谢百三著; 杨烈等译.

8. Theory and reality of transition to a market economy/chief editors, Gao Shangquan and Chi Fulin; written by Sun Xiuping, Zhu Huayou, and Yao Tiejun. Beijing：Foreign Languages Press, 1995. 358 pages; 21cm. ISBN：7119018167, 7119018164. （Studies on the Chinese market economy series）

Contents：Essential issues concerning China's transition to a market economy—Macro-control of the socialist market economy—Reform of the state-owned enterprises—Issues concerning the socialist market system and market mechanisms—Economic development and inflation—Develop the market economy while opening to the outside world.

《中国走向市场经济的理论与现实》，高尚全，迟福林主编.

9. Pressing tasks of China's economic transition/by Chi Fulin. Beijing：Foreign Languages Press，1996. 296 pages；21cm. ISBN：7119019678，7119019673.（Studies on the Chinese market economy series）

《中国经济转型的迫切任务》，迟福林著.

10. Several issues arising during the retracking of the Chinese economy/Chief editors, Gao Shangquan and Chi Fulin. Beijing：Foreign Languages Press，1997. 191 pages；21cm. ISBN：7119019767，7119019765.（Studies on the Chinese market economy series）

《中国经济转轨中若干改革问题研究》，迟福林著.

11. Rapid economic development in China and controlling inflation/chief editors，Gao Shangquan and Chi Fulin；written by Zhu Huayou. Beijing：Foreign Languages Press，1997. 269 pages；21cm. ISBN：711900025X，7119000251.（Studies on the Chinese market economy series）

《中国经济快速发展与抑制通货膨胀》，高尚全，迟福林主编.

12. China's economic reform at the turn of the century/organized and sponsored by China Institute for Reform and Development；chief editor, Chi Fulin. Beijing：Foreign Languages Press，2000. ii，448 pages；21cm. ISBN：7119026267，7119026268

《世纪之交：中国经济改革》，迟福林主编.

13. Reform determines future of China/Chi Fulin. Beijing：Foreign Languages Press，2000. viii，iii，421 pages；21cm. ISBN：7119027387，7119027388

《中国：改革决定未来》，迟福林著；黄友义等译.

14. China's economic transformation over 20 years/chief editor Wang Mengkui. Beijing：Foreign Languages Press，2000. 483 pages；21cm. ISBN：7119026100，7119026107

《中国经济转轨二十年》，王梦奎主编.

15. China 2010：charting the path to the future/editor-in-chief，Wang Mengkui. Beijing：Foreign Languages Press，2001. 360 pages；21cm. ISBN：7119027417，7119027418

《中国2010：目标、政策与前景》，王梦奎主编.

16. China's road to development in a global perspective/Yin Wenquan. Beijing：Foreign Languages Press，2007. 97 pages：color illustrations；22cm. ISBN：7119046600，

7119046608

《全球化视野下的中国发展之路：英文》，银温泉著；郭辉，梁发明等译.（中国的和平发展系列）

17. 制度适宜与经济发展：基于中国实践的发展经济学/李若谷. 北京：中国经济出版社，2008. 462 页；24cm. ISBN：7501788361

18. Study on the China model：analysis of economic development path of China/author：Jinquan Jiang；translators：Fen Li，Yanjun He. Beijing：People's Publishing House，2009. 1，3，4，5，695 pages；21cm. ISBN：7010081090，7010081093

《"中国模式"研究：英文版 中国经济发展道路解析》，江金权著. 人民出版社.

19. China's reform in the shadow of the global financial crisis/chief compiler，Chi Fulin. Beijing：Foreign Languages Press，2009. 203 pages：illustrations；23cm. ISBN：7119060262，7119060260

《中国信心：全球危机下的中国改革》，迟福林主编.

20. Chang of China's development models at the crossroads/chief editor：Chi Fulin；deputy chief editors：Fang Shuanxi & Kuang Xianming；translators：Ego & Zhang Tianxin. Beijing：China International Press，2010. 6，408 pages：illustrations；23cm. ISBN：7508519807，7508519809

《第二次转型》，迟福林主编. 五洲传播出版社.

21. The road to China's prosperity：in the next three decades/Chi Fulin；translated by Ego. Beijing：China International Prress，2010. 8，396 pages；23cm. ISBN：7508519845，7508519841

《第二次改革》，迟福林著. 五洲传播出版社.

22. 中国经济改革发展之路/厉以宁著；凌原译. 北京：外语教学与研究出版社，2010. xii，661 页：图；23cm. ISBN：7513503693.（"博雅双语名家名作"系列）

英文题名：Economic reform and development the Chinese way. 英汉对照.

22. Giving priority to enriching people：orientation of the second round of transition and reform/chief editor，Chi Fulin；deputy chief editors，Fang Shuanxi & Kuang Xianming；translator，Ego. Beijing：China Intercontinental Press，2011. 8，291 pages：illustrations；23cm. ISBN：7508521749，7508521749

《民富优先：二次转型与改革走向》，迟福林主编. 五洲传播出版社.

23. 非均衡的中国经济/厉以宁著；（美）陈菽浪译. 北京：外语教学与研究出版社，2013. xi，524 页；23cm. ISBN：7513537957.（"博雅双语名家名作"系列）

英文题名：Chinese economy in disequilibrium. 汉英对照.

24. A new development model and China's future/Deng Yingtao；Nicky Harman is the translator；Peter Nolan wrote the foreword；Phil Hand is the translator of the

afterword. London：Routledge, Taylor & Francis Group, 2014. xxxiii, 271 pages：illustrations；24cm. ISBN：0415610926, 0415610923. (Routledge studies on the Chinese economy；54)

《新发展方式与中国的未来》，邓英淘著；Harman, Nicky 译.

25. 超越市场与超越政府：论道德力量在经济中的作用/厉以宁著；苑爱玲译. 北京：外语教学与研究出版社，2015. xi, 487 页；23cm. ISBN：7513558440. ("博雅双语名家名作"系列)

英文题名：Beyond market and government：influence of moral factors on economy. 汉英对照.

26. Chinese economists on economic reform：collected works of Xue Muqiao/Xue Muqiao. Ed. by China Development Research Foundation. London：Routledge, 2011. XIII, 209 S.：Ill. ISBN：0203837245, 020383724X, 0415598217, 0415598214. (Routledge studies on the Chinese economy；41)

《薛暮桥改革论集》，薛暮桥；中国发展研究基金会.

27. Chinese economists on economic reform：collected works of Guo Shuqing/Guo Shujing；ed. by China Development Research Foundation. London：Routledge, 2011. xxxvi, 219 s. ISBN：0415582223, 0415582229. (Routledge studies on the Chinese economy；44)

《郭树清改革论集》，郭树清；中国发展研究基金会.

28. Chinese economists on economic reform：collected works of Ma Hong/Ma Hong；edited by China Development Research Foundation. London：Routledge, 2013. 199 pages；24cm. ISBN：0415857666, 041585766X. (Routledge studies on the Chinese economy；6)

《马洪改革论集》，马洪；中国发展研究基金会.

29. Chinese economists on economic reform. Collected works of Du Runsheng/Du Runsheng；edited by China Development Research Foundation. Abingdon, Oxon：Routledge, 2014. xix, 237 pages；24cm. ISBN：0415857673, 0415857678, 0203796802, 0203796801. (Routledge studies on the Chinese economy. Chinese economists on economic reform；4)

《杜润生改革论集》，杜润生；中国发展研究基金会.

30. Chinese economists on economic reform. Collected works of Yu Guangyuan/Yu Guangyuan；edited by China Development Research Foundation. London；New York：Routledge, Taylor & Francis Group, 2014. xxvi, 137 pages；25cm. ISBN：0415857550, 0415857554. (Routledge studies on the Chinese economy. Chinese economist on economic reform；8)

《于光远改革论集》，于光远(1915—2013)；中国发展研究基金会编.

31. Chinese economists on economic reform. Collected works of Lou Jiwei/Lou Jiwei；edited by China Development Research Foundation. London；New York：Routledge/ Taylor & Francis Group, 2014. xviii, 235 pages：illustrations；25cm. ISBN：0415857604, 0415857600, 0203797159, 0203797150. (Routledge studies on the Chinese economy. Chinese economists on economic reform；5)

《楼继伟改革论集》，楼继伟；中国发展研究基金会.

32. Chinese economists on economic reform. Collected works of Wang Mengkui/Wang Mengkui；edited by China Development Research Foundation. London；New York：Routledge, Taylor & Francis Group, 2014. xiv, 231 pages；24cm. (Routledge studies on the Chinese economy. Chinese economists on economic reform；7)

《王梦奎改革论集》，王梦奎；中国发展研究基金会.

33. Chinese economists on economic reform. Collected works of Chen Xiwen/Chen Xiwen；edited by China Development Research Foundation. London；NewYork：Routledge/Taylor & Francis Group, 2014. ISBN：0415857482, 0415857481. (Routledge studies on the Chinese economy. Chinese economists on economic reform；3)

《陈锡文改革论集》，陈锡文；中国发展研究基金会.

34. Chinese economists on economic reform. Collected works of Li Jiange/Li Jiange；edited by China Development Research Foundation. London；New York：Routledge, Taylor & Francis Group, 2017. xvii, 218 pages；24cm. ISBN：1138671263, 1138671266. (Routledge studies on the Chinese economy；10)

《李剑阁改革论集》，李剑阁；中国发展研究基金会.

35. Chinese economists on economic reform. Collected works of Zhou Xiaochuan/Zhou Xiaochuan；edited by China Development Research Foundation. London；New York：Routledge, Taylor & Francis Group, 2017. xiv, 220 pages；24cm. ISBN：1138669864, 1138669865. (Routledge studies on the Chinese economy；9)

《周小川改革论集》，周小川；中国发展研究基金会.

36. Guidelines for Hebei provincial-level budget management：a rev olution in budget management/editor-in-chief, Wang Jialin；vice editors-in-chief, Qi Shouyin, Gao Zhili. Beijing：China Financial & Economic Publishing House, 2002. 5, 432 pages；22cm. ISBN：7500562047, 7500562047

《河北预算管理制度体系：预算管理的革命》，王加林主编，中国财政经济出版社.

F13　经济史

1. Economic structure of the Yuan dynasty：translation of chapters 93 and 94 of the Yuan Shih/by Herbert Franz Schurmann. Cambridge：Harvard Univ. Press, c1951. xviii, 251 p.：bill., 3 maps；26cm. (Harvard-Yenching Institute Studies；v. 16)

元朝经济结构. Schurmann, Herbert Franz 译自宋濂

(1310—1381)的《元史》.
   (1)Taibei：Rainbom-Bridge Bookshop，1956. 251 p.；
      23cm.（Harvard-Yenching Institute studies；XVI）
   (2)Cambridge：Harvard Univ. Press，c1967. 249p.；
      25cm.（Harvard-Yenching Institute Studies；v. XVI）

2. The single-whip method of taxation in China/by Liang Fang-chung；translated from the Chinese by Wang Yü-ch'uan. Cambridge：Chinese Economic and Political Studies，Harvard University：distributed by Harvard University Press，c1956. 71 p.；28cm.
   《一条鞭法》，梁方仲(1908—1970)著；王毓铨译.
   (1) Cambridge，Mass.：East Asian Research Center，c1970. 71 p.；28cm.（Harvard East Asian monographs；1）

3. Chinese economic thought before the seventeenth century/Hu Jichuang；English text edited by Foster Stockwell, Zhao Shuhan. Beijing：Foreign Languages Press：Distributed by the China Publications Centre，1984. iv, 107 pages；19cm. ISBN：0835111563，0835111560
   《从世界范围考察十七世纪以前中国经济思想的光辉成就》，胡寄窗著.

4. A concise history of chinese economic thought/by Hu Jichuang. Peking：Foreign Languages Press，1988. iii, 572 p. 21cm. ISBN：0835117111，0835117111.（China knowledge series）
   《中国经济思想史简编》，胡寄窗著.
   (1)Beijing：Foreign Languages Press，2009. iii, 570 p.；23cm. ISBN：7119057552，7119057553.（China studies）

F14　地方经济

上海

1. Report on development of Pudong：1991—1994/edited by Pudong Academy of Development.［Shanghai］：Shanghai People's Pub. House，1995. 56 pages：illustrations；26cm. ISBN：7208020175，7208020177
   《浦东发展报告：1991—1994》，浦东改革与发展研究院编撰.上海人民出版社.

2. Shanghai basic facts：commerce/editors-in-chief：Cai Hongsheng, Fan Chuangshi. Beijing：China Intercontinental Pr.，1998. 56 pages：color illustrations；18cm. ISBN：7801133781，7801133786
   《上海商业概览》，上海市政府新闻办公室，上海市政府商业委员会编.五洲传播出版社.

3. Shanghai basic facts：foreign business and trade. Beijing：China Intercontinental Pr.，1998. 45 pages：color illustrations map；18cm. ISBN：7801133706，7801133700
   《上海对外经济概览》，上海市人民政府新闻办公室，上海市对外经济贸易委员会主编.五洲传播出版社.

4. 上海市国民经济和社会发展第十一个五年规划纲要 ＝ Outline of the eleventh five-year plan for national economic and social development in Shanghai：汉英对照.上海：上海人民出版社，2006. 295 页；26cm. ISBN：7208063583，7208063587
   英文题名：Outline of the eleventh five-year plan for national economic and social development in Shanghai：approved by the Fourth Session of the Twelfth Municipal People's Congress of Shanghai on January 20，2006
   本书是"十一五"期间上海市国民经济和社会发展的战略性、纲领性、综合性的总体规划.

5. 上海市国民经济和社会发展第十二个五年规划纲要：英文版/上海市人民政府制订.上海：上海人民出版社，2011. 171 页；21cm. ISBN：7208102750

北京

1. The outline of the eleventh five-year program for the national economic and social development in Beijing：approved by the Fourth Session of the Twelfth Beijing Municipal People's Congress on January 20th，2006. Beijing：China Population Publishing House，2006. 186 pages：map；21cm. ISBN：7802023300，7802023307
   《北京市国民经济和社会发展第十一个五年规划纲要：英文》，北京市发展和改革委员会编.中国人口出版社.

2. Stories of innovation：Zhongguancun Science Park/by Feng Yongfeng；translated by Ego. Beijing：China Intercontinental Press，2008. 152 pages：illustrations (some color)；19cm. ISBN：7508513508，7508513509，7508513492，7508513495.（Stories from China）
   《中关村的创新故事》，冯永锋著.五洲传播出版社.介绍中关村经济开发区从1980到2008年的发展历程.

F2　经济管理

F21　会计与审计

1. 企业会计准则 ＝ Accounting standard for business enterprises：汉英对照.基本准则/中华人民共和国财政部制定.北京：经济科学出版社，2006. 30 页；21cm. ISBN：7505854933，7505854932
   本书是中华人民共和国财政部2006年最新制定发布的《企业会计准则.基本准则》的中、英文详细内容.

2. China standards on auditing and quality control/developed by the Chinese Institute of Certified Public Accountants；approved by the Ministry of Finance，PRC. Beijing：Economic Science Press，2011. 269 p.；25cm. ISBN：7514107746，7514107746
   《中国注册会计师执业准则》，中国注册会计师协会编著.经济科学出版社.

3. Application materials of China standards on auditing and quality control 2010/The Chinese Institute of Certified Public Accountants. Beijing：Economic Science Press，2011. 438 p.：ill.；30cm. ISBN：7514107715，7514107711
   《中国注册会计师执业准则应用指南》，中国注册会计师协会编著.经济科学出版社.

4. China code of ethics for certified public accountants/The Chinese Institute of Certified Public Accountants. Beijing：China Financial & Economic Publishing House，2011. 4，164 p. ；25cm. ISBN：7509527108，7509527104

《中国注册会计师职业道德守则》,中国注册会计师协会编译.中国财政经济出版社.

5. Auditing in P. R. China/edited by Guo Zhenqian. Beijing：China Audit Press，1998. 531 pages；22cm. ISBN：7800646653，7800646652

《中国审计学》,郭振乾主编,中国审计出版社.

F22　劳动经济

1. China's human resources/Information Office of the State Council ［of］ the People's Republic of China. Beijing：Foreign Languages Press，2010. 41 pages：illustrations；21cm. ISBN：7119066677，7119066676

《中国的人力资源状况》,中华人民共和国国务院新闻办公室[发布].

2. 中国当代劳动关系研究：以广州企业工资集体协商与非公企业工会组建为例/谢建社等著；彭曦译. 北京：中国书籍出版社,2010. 324 页；24cm. ISBN：7506822688，7506822687

英文题名：Research on contemporary Chinese labour relations：based on collective wage negotiations of enterprises and the trade union establishment of non-public-owned enterprise in Guangzhou

F23　物流经济

1. China's expanding highway network. Beijing：New Star Publishers，1990. 26 pages：illustrations；19cm. ISBN：7800852830，7800852831

《公路通向四面八方》.新星出版社.

2. Inland navigation in China. Beijing：New Star Publishers，1990. 25 pages：illustrations；19cm. ISBN：7800852873，7800852879

《中国的内河航运》.新星出版社.

3. Maritime silk road/Li Qingxin；translated by William W. Wang. ［Beijing］：China Intercontinental Press，2006. 199 pages：illustrations（some color），maps（some color）；25cm. ISBN：7508509323，7508509327

《海上丝绸之路：英文》,李庆新编著；王晚成译. 五洲传播出版社(中外文化交流系列)

4. 古代交通/王亦儒编著. 合肥：黄山书社,2016. 140 页：彩图；23cm. ISBN：7546141633. (印象中国)

英文题名：Ancient transport. 英汉对照.

F24　投资与建设

1. Investing in China：questions and answers/Pan Zhihong and Pan Chi. Beijing Foreign Languages Press，1999. XII，395 p. ISBN：7119021001，7119021003

《中国投资问答》,潘志洪,潘驰编著.

2. Major investment areas in China/State Council Office for Economic Restructuring P. R. C. ，Department of Special Economic Zones. Beijing：China Intercontinental Press，1999. 51 pages：color illustrations，maps；29cm. ISBN：7801136217，7801136213

《中国对外开放的重点》,中华人民共和国国务院经济体制改革办公室经济特区和开放司编. 五洲传播出版社.

（1）2nd ed. ［Beijing］：China Intercontinental Press，2001. 59，［2］ pages：illustrations，map；29cm. ISBN：7801139224，7801139221

3. 20 questions on investing in China/compiled by the Ministry of Foreign Trade and Economic Cooperation and China Today Magazine. Beijing：New Star Publishers，2001. 79 pages：illustrations；21cm. ISBN：7801484304，7801484307

《来华投资二十问》,对外贸易经济合作部,《今日中国》编辑部编. 新星出版社.

4. 投资并购在中国：英文/肖金泉,张婷编著. 北京：外文出版社,2005. 247 页；22cm. ISBN：711903975X

本书针对国外企业、法律界等层面,介绍中国经济中大的投资环境、各行业准入制度,国外企业在中国投资的程序及涉外法律等.

5. 中国投资项目社会评价：变风险为机遇：汉英对照/中国国际工程咨询公司编著. 北京：中国计划出版社,2007. 1册（267,265 页）；26cm. ISBN：7801779489,7801779487. (中咨研究系列丛书)

英文题名：Social assessment manual for investment projects in China：Turning risks into opportunities.

6. Report on the multiple purpose plan for permanently controlling the Yellow River and exploiting its water resources：delivered on July 18，1955 at the Second Session of the First National People's Congress/by Teng Tse-Hui. Peking：Foreign Languages Press，1955. 48 pages：color map

《关于根治黄河水害和开发黄河水利的综合规划的报告》,邓子恢.

7. China's key construction projects/Li Ning. Beijing：Foreign Languages Press，2007. 111 pages：color illustrations；21cm. ISBN：7119051345，7119051342. (China's peaceful development series)

《国家重点建设工程：英文》,李宁著；金绍卿译. (和平发展的中国丛书).本书主要介绍了20世纪90年代开始中国陆续投资建设的重点工程,如三峡工程、西气东送、南水北调、青藏铁路等大型工程,讲述了工程的背景、进展以及带来的收益. (重大建设项目概况)

8. Changes in housing for 1. 3 billion people/Xue Kai；［translated by Wang Qin］. Beijing：Foreign Languages Press，2007. 115 pages：color illustrations；21cm. ISBN：7119051215，7119051210. （China's peaceful development series）

《13亿人的住房变迁：英文》,薛凯著；王琴译. (和平发展的中国丛书).

9. 长江三峡水利枢纽工程/孙荣刚著. 北京：五洲传播出版社,2008. 126 页；19cm. ISBN：7508514468

三峡工程简介.

10. The railroad to the top of the world：from dream to reality/by Lei Fengxing；translated by Zhu Jianting, Li Li & He Yunzhao. Beijing：China Intercontinental Press, 2008. 142 pages：color illustrations；19cm. ISBN：7508513522, 7508513525. (Stories from China)

《青藏铁路通到拉萨》,雷风行著. 五洲传播出版社. 讲述青藏铁路建设过程及其对西藏经济发展的意义.

11. Moving the flow：China reshapes its water supply/by Shui Qingshan；translated by Li Rong, Wang Li & Xiao Ying. Beijing：China Intercontinental Press, 2008. 162 pages：color illustrations；19cm. ISBN：7508513546, 7508513541. (Stories from China)

《水资源的南北大调配》,水青山著. 五洲传播出版社. 介绍南水北调工程的决策过程、东线和中线建设进度及沿线文物保护与考古发掘.

12. Shenzhou spacecraft and lunar exploration project：China's space exploration/by Wu Weiren；translated by Ma Chenguang, Yan Shuang & Zhang Hongpeng. Beijing：China Intercontinental Press, 2008. 113 pages：color illustrations；19cm. ISBN：7508513560, 7508513568. (Stories from China)

《神舟飞船和探月工程》,吴伟仁编著. 中国航天概况、神舟系列飞船与载人航天计划,探月工程及深空探测计划.

13. China's biggest natural gas pipeline：challenges and achievements/Liu Jing；translated by Wang Wenliang, Han Huizhi & Kang Jian. Beijing：China Intercontinental Press, 2008. 93 pages：color illustrations；19cm. ISBN：7508513461, 7508513460. (Stories from China)

《天然气输送的大动脉》,刘晶著. 五洲传播出版社. 介绍西气东输工程.

F25　房地产经济

1. Housing construction and reform/［English editor, He Zunlong］. ［Beijing, China］：New Star Publishers, 1990. 44 pages：illustrations；19cm. ISBN：7800851990, 7800851995. (What's new in China；43)

《住宅建设与改革》,今日中国杂志社编辑. 新星出版社.

2. Living in China/written by Xia Jun & Yin Shan；translated by Yu Fei & Quan Xiaoshu. ［Beijing］：China Intercontinental Press, 2007. 128 pages：color illustrations；22cm. ISBN：7508510828, 7508510828. (Fashion China)

《人居中国；英文》,夏骏,阴山撰文；喻菲,全晓书译. 五洲传播出版社.

3. 王健林与大连万达：汉英双语/周璇著；（英）Zuzana

Strakova 译. 北京：中译出版社,2018. 300 页；22cm. ISBN：7500155652. (中国著名企业家与企业丛书)

英文题名：Wang Jianlin & Dalian Wanda

F3　"三农"问题

1. How the tillers win back their land/Qian Xiao；illustrated with 11 drawings by Chiang Chao-ho and 22 photos. Peking：Foreign Languages Press, 1951. 148 pages：illustrations；21cm.

《土地回老家》,萧乾(1910—1999)著.

　　(1)Peking：Foreign Languages Press, 1954. 148 pages：illustrations；19cm.

2. Agriculture in new China. Peking：Foreign Languages Press, 1953. 51 pages：illustrations；21cm.

《新中国的农业》

3. Mutual aid and co-operation in China's agricultural production. Peking：Foreign Languages Press, 1953. 38 pages；19cm.

Contents：Decisions on mutual aid and co-operation in agricultural production adopted by the Central Committee of the Communist Party of China.—Basic tasks and policies in rural areas, by Teng Tse-hui.

《中国农业生产的互助合作》,邓子恢.

4. Co-operative farming in China：decisions on the development of agricultural producers' co-operatives/adopted by the Central Committee of the Communist Party of China. Peking：Foreign Languages Press, 1954. 34 p.；19cm.

《中共中央关于发展农业生产合作社的决议》

5. Decisions on agricultural cooperation：adopted at the 6th plenary session (enlarged) of the 7th Central Committee of the Communist Party of China, October 11, 1955. Peking：Foreign Languages Press, 1956. 55 p.

《中国共产党第七届中央委员会第六次全体会议(扩大)关于农业合作化问题的决议》

　　(1)Peking：Foreign Languages Press, 1967.

6. Model regulations for advanced agricultural producers' co-operatives, adopted on June 30, 1956, by the First National People's Congress of the People's Republic of China at its third session. Peking：Foreign Languages Press, 1956. 33 pages；21cm.

《高级农业生产合作社示范章程》

　　(1) 2nd ed. (rev. translation). Peking：Foreign Languages Press, 1976. 29 pages；21cm.

7. The draft programme for agricultural development in the People's Republic of China, 1956—1967. Peking：Foreign Languages Press, 1956. 43 pages；22cm.

Notes：The draft national programme for agricultural development, 1956—1967, submitted by the Political Bureau of the Central Committee of the Communist Party of China on January 23, 1956.—Some explanations on the draft national programme for agricultural development, 1956—1967, by Liao Lu-yen.

《1956 年到 1967 年全国农业发展纲要（草案）》

8. Not winter but spring, and other stories on mutual aid and co-operation in Chinese agriculture. Peking：Foreign Languages Press, 1956. 193 pages；19cm.

《不是冬天是春天》. 主题：农村的农业合作.

9. New earth：how the peasants in one chinese county solved the problem of poverty/by Jack Chen. Peking：New world Press, 1957. 255 p.：ill.；21cm.

《新地》，陈依范（Chen, Jack, 1908—1995）著. 主题：农村合作化.

10. Socialist upsurge in China's countryside. Peking：Foreign Languages Press, 1957. 504 pages；21cm.
Notes："Compiled by the General Office of the Central Committee of the Communist Party of China."

《中国农村的社会主义高潮》，中共中央办公厅编.

11. People's communes in China. Peking：Foreign Languages Press, 1958. 89 p.；19cm.
Notes："A collection of editorials and articles... published by the Renmin ribao（People's daily）and the Hongqi（Red flag）magazine."

《中国的人民公社》. 来自《人民日报》和《红旗》杂志的社论文章.

12. Agricultural co-operation in China. Peking：Foreign Languages Press, 1958. 69 pages；19cm.

《中国农业合作化的道路》，童大林著.

13. People's communes in China. Peking：Foreign Languages Press, 1958. [4], 89, [3] s.；18cm.

《中国人民公社化运动》

14. The whole party and the whole people go in for agriculture in a big way/Liao Lu-Yen. Peking：Foreign Languages Press, 1960. 19 p.

《全党全民动手大办农业》

15. The people's communes forge ahead：a basic summary of five years' experience in the rural people's communes of Kwangtung Province/Tao Chu. Peking：Foreign Languages Press, 1964. 36 pages；19cm.

《人民公社在前进》，陶铸著.

16. The struggle between the two roads in China's countryside/by the editorial departments of Renmin ribao, Hongqi, and Jiefangjun bao. Peking：Foreign Languages Press, 1968. 25 pages；21cm.

《中国农村两条道路的斗争》

17. Tachai：standard bearer in China's agriculture. Beijing：Foreign Languages Press, 1972. 29 pages, [6] leaves of plates：illustrations；19cm.
Contents：Tachai：standard bearer in agriculture/Xin Huawen—Learning from Tachai brings big changes/Zhao Fengnian.

《大寨：中国农业战线上的一面旗帜》

18. Serving the people with dialectics/essays on the study of philosophy by workers and peasants. Peking：Foreign Languages Press, 1972. 48 pages：illustrations；19cm.
Contents：Raising peanut yields—Applying philosophy in transport—Weather keepers for the revolution—Keeping vegetables fresh—Patients with broken backs walk again—Delivering dead letters

《打开了花生增产的秘密》

19. Inside a people's commune：report from Chiliying/by Chu Li, Tien Chieh-yun. Peking：Foreign Languages Press, 1974. 212 pages, [14] leaves of plates：illustrations；19cm.

《在七里营人民公社里》，朱力，田洁云著.
（1）Peking：Foreign Languages Press, 1975. 212 pages, [14] leaves of plates：illustrations, maps；19cm.

20. Let the whole party mobilize for a vast effort to develop agriculture and build Tachai-type counties throughout the country：summing-up report at the National Conference on Learning from Tachai in Agriculture（October 15, 1975）/Hua Kuo-feng. Peking：Foreign Languages Press, 1975. 72 pages；19cm.

《全党动员，大办农业，为普及大寨县而奋斗》，华国锋.

21. Sandstone Hollow：transformation of a mountain village/Tang Feng-chang；[photographs by Chih Yuan and Lan Hui]. Peking：Foreign Languages Press, 1975. 128 pages, [12] leaves of plates：illustrations；19cm.

《沙石峪》，唐凤章著. 主题：农业学大寨.

22. Report from Tungting：a people's commune on Taihu Lake/Wu Chou. Peking：Foreign Languages Press, 1975. 49 pages, [13] leaves of plates：illustrations；19cm.

《洞庭人民公社》，吴周著.

23. Tachai, the red banner/by Wen Yin；Liang Hua. Peking：Foreign Languages Pr., 1977. [22], 199 p.：ill.

《大寨红旗》，文荫，梁华.

24. Speech at the second National Conference on Learning from Tachai in Agriculture：December 25, 1976/Hua Kuo-Feng. Peking：Foreign Languages Press, 1977. 44 pages；19cm.

《中国共产党中央委员会主席华国锋同志在第二次全国农业学大寨会议上的讲话》

25. Thoroughly criticize the "Gang of Four" and bring about a new upsurge in the movement to build Tachai-type counties throughout the country：report at the Second National Conference on Learning from Tachai in Agriculture（December 20, 1976）/Chen Yung-Kuei. Peking：Foreign Languages Press, 1977. 47 pages；19cm.

《彻底批判"四人帮"掀起普及大寨县运动的新高潮：中共中央政治局委员、国务院副总理陈永贵在第二次全国

农业学大寨会议上的报告》

26. Socialist upsurge in China's countryside/edited by the General Office of the Central Committee of the Communist Party of China. Peking：Foreign Languages Press, 1978. v, 547 pages；19cm.

《中国农村的社会主义高潮》(选本)，中共中央办公厅编.

27. Economic changes in rural China/by Luo Hanxian; translated by Wang Huimin. Beijing, China New World Press, 1985. 217 pages, ［4］ pages of plates：illustrations（some color）；21cm. ISBN：0835115259, 0835115254. (China studies series)

《中国农村的经济变革》，罗涵先编著. 新世界出版社.

28. Smashing the communal pot：formulation ＆ development of China's rural responsibility system/by Wang Guichen, Zhou Qiren and others. Beijing, China：New World Press；Distributed by China International Book Trading Corp. , 1985. 200 pages；21cm. (China studies series)

《中国农业生产责任制的建立与发展》，王贵宸，周其仁著. 新世界出版社.

29. A glimpse of China's rural reform/Li Yaowu and Liu Changhe. Beijing：Foreign Languages Press, 1989. vi, 125 pages, ［20］ pages of plates：illustrations（some color）；19cm. ISBN：0835122476, 0835122474

《中国农村改革掠影》，李耀武，刘长贺编著.

30. Many people, little land：China's rural economic reform/Du Runsheng. Beijing, China：Foreign Languages Press：Distributed by China International Book Trading Corp. (Guoji Shudian), 1989. iii, 212 pages；19cm. ISBN：0835122182, 0835122184, 7119006401, 7119006406

《中国农村的经济改革》，杜润生著.

31. Agriculture in China, 1949—1989/edited by the Ministry of Agriculture, People's Republic of China. Beijing, China：Agricultural Pub. House, 1989. 152 pages：206 color illustrations；30cm. ISBN：7109013960, 7109013964

《中国农业四十年：1949—1989》，中华人民共和国农业部编. 农业出版社.

32. Agriculture action plan for China's Agenda 21/Ministry of Agriculture, People's Republic of China. Beijing：China Agriculture Press, 1999. 73 pages；29cm. ISBN：7109057844, 7109057845

《中国二十一世纪议程：农业行动计划》，中华人民共和国农业部. 中国农业出版社.

33. The development-oriented poverty reduction program for rural China/Information Office of the State Council of the People's Republic of China. Beijing：New Star, 2001. 42 pages；27cm. ISBN：7801483944, 7801483942

《中国农村的扶贫开发》，中华人民共和国国务院新闻办公室发布. 新星出版社.

34. Rural reform in China/Zhang Gensheng；translated by Zhang Bo. ［Shenzhen, China］：Hai tian chu ban she, 2001. ［10］, 663 pages；21cm. ISBN：7806544615, 7806544617

《中国农村改革决策纪实》，张根生编，海天出版社.

35. People and forests：Yunnan swidden agriculture in human-ecological perspective/written by Yin Shaoting；translated by Magnus Fiskesjo. ［Kunming］：Yunnan Education Publ. House, 2001. 560 pages：illustrations, maps；22cm. ISBN：7541519596, 7541519598. (Border cultures series)

《人与森林：生态人类学视野中的刀耕火种》，尹绍亭著；马思中译. 云南教育出版社.

36. People's Republic of China：a study on ways to support rural poverty reduction projects/Foreign Capital Project Management Centre of LGOP；Asian Development Bank. Beijing：China Agriculture Press, 2002. 485 pages：illustrations；27cm. ISBN：7109076903, 7109076907

《中国农村扶贫方式研究》，国务院扶贫办外资项目管理中心，亚洲开发银行编. 中国农业出版社.

37. Can China feed itself?：Chinese scholars on China's food issue/edited by Liu Shouying and Luo Dan. Beijing：Foreign Languages Press, 2004. iv, 218 pages：illustrations；23cm. ISBN：7119037471, 7119037479. (Focus on China series)

《中国不会饥饿世界》，刘守英，罗丹主编.（聚焦中国丛书）.

本书主编为国务院发展中心研究员，参与制定农业政策的学者，书中选用了11篇论文.

38. Clashes and balances：the transition of the economy and society in rural China/Rural Development Institute, Chinese Academy of Social Sciences. Beijing：Foreign Languages Press, 2006. 172 pages；23cm. ISBN：7119039067, 7119039060. (Focus on China series)

《冲突与平衡：中国农村的社会经济转型：英文》，中国社会科学院农村发展研究所著（聚焦中国）. 论述中国农村的经济发展.

39. Agriculture, rural areas and farmers in China/author Dang Guoying；translator Wang Pingxing. Beijing：China Intercontinental Press, 2006. 142 pages：illustrations（some color）；21cm. ISBN：7508509716, 7508509714. (China basics series)

《中国农业、农村、农民：英文》，党国英著；王平兴译. 五洲传播出版社（中国基本情况丛书/李向平主编）

40. Rural development and a harmonious society/Zhan Zhuangqing, Wang Tianyi, Wang Qiongjin. Beijing：Foreign Languages Press, 2007. 150 pages；23cm.

ISBN：7119045269，7119045261.（Focus on China＝和谐社会丛书）

《农村发展与和谐社会：英文》，詹庄卿等著.（"和谐社会"丛书/傅治平主编）.

41. 新型农村合作医疗制度研究：英文/王枝茂著.太原：山西经济出版社,2007. 20cm. ISBN：7806369296

英文题名：Research on the New Rural Cooperative Medical Insurance System. 本书对农村新型合作医疗制度作了系统的研究,并提出可行性建议.

42. The road to a new countryside/Wang Tai, Zhao Jingyu [i. e. ping], Li Haitao. Beijing：Foreign Languages Press，2007. 119 pages：color illustrations；21cm. ISBN：7119051338c 7119051334.（China's peaceful development series）

《新农村建设从这里起步：英文》，王太等著. 外文出版社（和平发展的中国丛书）

43. Countryside of China/Guo Huancheng, Ren Guozbu and Lü Mingwei；translation by Tong Xiaohua. Beijing：China Intercontinental Press，2007. 173 pages：color illustrations, color maps；25cm. ISBN：7508510965, 7508510968.（Journey into China）

《乡村之旅：英文》，郭焕成等著；童孝华译. 五洲传播出版社（中国之旅丛书/郭长建，李向平主编）. 本书选取三十多个村镇作为代表介绍中国乡村.

44. Beautiful villages of Beijing/text by Li Gang, Sun Keqin, et al.；photographs by Li Gang, Sun Keqin, Fang Xin, et al.；translated by Wang Yufan. Beijing：China Pictorial Pub. House, 2008. 111 pages：illustrations（some color）；22cm. ISBN：7802202146, 7802202140

《北京的美丽村庄》，李刚撰稿；王寓帆翻译. 中国画报出版社.

45. Abstract of the second national agricultural census in China/Office of the Leading Group of the State Council for the Second National Agricultural Census, National Bureau of Statistics of China. Beijing：Zhongguo tong ji chu ban she, 2010. 376 pages：illustrations；30cm. ISBN：7503759093, 7503759097

《中国第二次全国农业普查资料综合提要》，国务院第二次全国农业普查领导小组办公室，中华人民共和国国家统计局编. 中国统计出版社.

45. "省管县"财政改革与新农村建设问题研究/王德祥，李建军著. 武汉：武汉大学出版社,2010. 358 页；24cm. ISBN：7307078277

本书通过调查浙江、贵州、湖北等省的"省管县"财政改革与新农村建设情况,采用实证和规范的方法对相关问题作了理论研究并提出了政策建议.

46. Chinese three-dimensional rural issues concerning agriculture, countryside and farmers：traditional culture, institutional change and system reform/by Peng Liu.

Zhenzhou：Henan People's Publishing House, 2011. 3, 258 p. ：ill. ；21cm. ISBN：7215077232, 7215077233

《中国三农问题：传统文化制度变革与体制改革》，刘鹏著. 河南人民出版社.

47. New progress in development-oriented poverty reduction program for rural China/Information Office of the State Council, the People's Republic of China. Beijing：Foreign Languages Press，2011. 41 pages：illustrations；26cm. ISBN：7119073309, 7119073303, 7119073316, 7119073311

《中国农村扶贫开发的新进展》，中华人民共和国国务院新闻办公室［发布］.

48. Apiculture in China/editor-in-chief, Chen Yaochun；［chief writers, Wang Yijie and others］. Beijing：Agricultural Pub. House, 1993. 157 pages, ［21］ pages of plates：illustrations（some color）；29cm. ISBN：7109030865, 7109030862

《中国蜂业》. 农业出版社.

49. Agrarian China：selected source materials from Chinese authors/compiled and translated by the research staff of the Secretariat, Institute of Pacific Relations；with an introd. by R. H. Tawney. 1st AMS ed. New York：AMS Press, 1978. xviii, 258 p. ；23cm. ISBN：0404595324.（International research series）

中国农村与农业. 美国"太平洋关系研究所"研究人员编译. 初版于 1938 年.

50. Landlord and labor in late imperial China：case studies from Shandong/by Jing Su and Luo Lun；translated from the Chinese with an introd. by Endymion Wilkinson. Cambridge, Mass. ：Council on East Asian Studies, Harvard University：distributed by Harvard University Press, 1978. xiii, 310 p. ：maps；24cm. ISBN：0674508661.（Harvard East Asian monographs；80）

《清代山东经营地主底社会性质》，景苏，罗仑；Wilkinson，Endymion 译.

51. China along the Yellow River：reflections on rural society/Cao Jinqing；translated by Nicky Harman and Huang Ruhua. London；New York：RoutledgeCurzon, 2005. x, 254 pages：maps；24cm. ISBN：0415341132, 0415341134.（RoutledgeCurzon studies on the Chinese economy；12）

《黄河边的中国》，曹锦清.

52. 宗族政治的理想标本：新叶村/安旭著；徐成钢等译. 杭州：浙江大学出版社,2016. 262 页：图,照片；24cm. ISBN：7308151337

英文题名：Xinye Village：an ideal sample of clan politics

53. 乡土中国/费孝通著；（美）韩格理，王政译. 北京：外语教学与研究出版社,2012. 187 页；23cm. ISBN：7513521178.（"博雅双语名家名作"系列）

英文题名：From the soil：the foundations of Chinese

Society. 英汉对照.

F31　粮食经济

1. How China became self-sufficient in grain. Peking：Foreign Languages Press, 1977. 74 pages，[10] leaves of plates：illustrations；19cm.

《中国是怎样实现粮食自给的》

2. 中国粮食企业风采：英汉对照/国家粮食局编. 北京：经济管理出版社，2006. 102 页：照片；30cm. ISBN：7802075645，7802075641

英文题名：China food enterprises demeanour.

3. Food，population and employment in China/Zhang Guoqing. Beijing：Foreign Languages Press, 2006. 127 pages：color illustrations，charts；21cm. ISBN：7119044682，7119044680.（China in peaceful development）

《粮食、人口与就业：英文》，张国庆著；丛国玲，布布译.（中国的和平发展系列）

F32　林业经济

1. Participatory forestry in China/chief editor, Zhu Zhaohua；editor，Wu Jinghu...[et al.]；editorial board，Jiang Chunqian...[et al.]；International Farm Forestry Training Centre，the Chinese Academy of Forestry. Beijing，China：International Academic Publishers, 1997. xx，308 p.：ill.，map；26cm. ISBN：7800033929，7800033926

《中国的参与林业》，竺肇华编. 万国学术出版社.

2. Protecting China's ecological environment/by Gao Jixi；translated by Zhu Jianting，Li Rong & Wang Wenliang. Beijing：China Intercontinental Press，2008. 130 pages：color illustrations；19cm. ISBN：7508513751，7508513754.（Stories from China）

《保护生态环境行动》，高吉喜编著. 五洲传播出版社. 介绍中国改革开放以来，在退耕还林，退牧还草等方面取得的成就.

F4　工业经济

1. Building a new life：stories about China's construction. Peking Foreign Languages Press，1955. 163 pages：illustrations；19cm.

《我们在建设》，朱波、杨朔等著.

2. Builders of Anshan. Peking：Foreign Languages Press, 1956. 118 pages，[5] leaves of plates：illustrations；19cm.

《建设鞍山的人们》

3. 600 million build industry. Peking：Foreign Languages Press，1958. 148 pages：illustrations；18cm.

《全民办工业的高潮》

4. China will overtake Britain. Peking：Foreign Languages Press，1958. 65，[1] p. 19cm.

《赶上英国，赶超英国》，牛中黄著.

5. Grasp revolution，promote production and win new victories on the industrial front. Peking：Foreign Languages Press，1969. 15 pages；18cm.

《抓革命，促生产，夺取工业战线的新胜利》

6. The National Conference on Learning from Taching in Industry， selected documents. Peking：Foreign Languages Press，1977. 89 pages；19cm.

《中国工业学大庆会议文件选编》

7. Industrialization and economic reform in China/Wang Huijiong[and] Li Shantong. Beijing，China：New World Press：Distributed by China International Book Trading Corp.，1995. 186，[6] pages；21cm. ISBN：7800052605，7800052606

《中国的工业化和经济改革》，王慧炯，李善同著. 新世界出版社.

8. China's policy on mineral resources/Information Office of the State Council of the People's Republic of China. Beijing：New Star Publishers，2003. 35 pages；26cm. ISBN：7801485564，7801485564

《中国的矿产资源政策》，中华人民共和国国务院新闻办公室分布. 新星出版社.

9. 中国林纸联合面临的机遇和挑战：林纸一体化战略研究：汉英对照/张蕾等著. 北京：中国大地出版社，2006. 78 页；21cm. ISBN：7800978524

本书论述了我国造纸业的现状、存在的主要问题及加入WTO对我国造纸业的影响. 提出林纸联合是重塑我国造纸工业的金牌战略，并对林纸联合提出对策和建议.

10. The international competitiveness of Chinese industry/Jin Bei. Beijing：Foreign Languages Press，2007. 187 pages：illustrations；23cm. ISBN：7119040844，7119040847.（Focus on China series）

《中国工业的国际竞争力：英文》，金碚著；李洋等译.

11. 开启国有企业的金钥匙/范宪著. 上海：上海交通大学出版社，2008. 286 页；23cm. ISBN：7313050014，7313050011

英文题名：The golden dey to opening the door of Chinese enterprises.

12. Chinese enterprises in the 21st century/by Che Yuming，Han Jie and Zhao Xiaohui. Beijing：Foreign languages Press，2008. 131 pages：illustrations（some color）；21cm. ISBN：7119055381，7119055380

《走进 21 世纪的中国企业》，车玉明，韩洁，赵晓辉著. 梳理了中国改革开放三十年来中国企业的发展历史.

13. Dreams which have come true/by Xue Hong. Beijing：Foreign Languages Press，2008. 107 pages：coi. ill.；19cm. ISBN：7119055435，7119055437.（Stories of China）

《梦想成真》，雪虹著. 讲述了改革开放 30 年来中国企业家白手起家、艰苦创业的故事.

14. 中国上市公司治理发展报告：OECD-中国：公司治理共同评估项目自评估 OECD-China：corporate governance joint assessment programme self-assessment/中国证券监督管理委员会[编].北京：中国金融出版社,2011. 245页；27cm. ISBN：7504957986, 7504957984

15. The gold mining history of Zhaoyuan with a review of gold industry in the P. R. China/authors：Gong Runtan, Zhu Fengsan；editor-in-chief：Wei Youzhi. Beijing：China Ocean Press, 2004. 162, 35, 120 pages：illustrations, maps；29cm. ISBN：7502762360, 7502762361

《招远采金史及中国黄金工业回顾》,魏有志主编；宫润潭,朱奉三编著.海洋出版社.

16. 任正非与华为：汉英双语/李洪文著；（美）Justin Hebert,周丹译. 北京：中译出版社,2018. 319 页；22cm. ISBN：7500155560.（中国著名企业家与企业丛书）

17. 马化腾与腾讯：汉英双语/冷湖著；（澳）Declan Fry 译. 北京：中译出版社,2018. 339 页；22cm. ISBN：7500155607.（中国著名企业家与企业丛书）

英文题名：Ma Huateng & Tencent.

18. 董明珠与格力：汉英双语/郭宏文著；（美）Justin Hebert,周丹译. 北京：中译出版社,2018. 345 页；22cm. ISBN：7500155591.（中国著名企业家与企业丛书；第一辑）

英文题名：Dong Mingzhu & Gree.

F41 企业名录

1. Survey of the key & backbone enterprises in China's machine building industry/China Machinery & Electronics News Agency. English ed. Beijing：Pub. House of Ordnance Industry, 1989. 1104 pages；27cm. ISBN：7800381013, 7800381010

《中国机械工业骨干企业重点企业概况》,中国机械电子报社编.兵器工业出版社.

2. Enterprise groups (corporations) in China/"Enterprise Groups (Corporations) in China" Editing Committee；[chief editor, Wan Guangming]. Beijing：Economic Science Pub. House, 1991. 1 volumes：illustrations (some color)；27cm. ISBN：7505804189 (v. 2), 7505804180 (v. 2)

《中国企业集团（公司）》（第二卷）,《中国企业集团（公司）》编委会编.经济科学出版社.英汉对照.

3. China's 1000 industrial enterprises/compiled by China Statistical News of the State Statistical Bureau；consultee, Ma Hong [and others]. Beijing：China Statistical Pub. House, 1992. 694 pages；26cm. ISBN：7503707291, 7503707292

《中国 1000 家工业企业》,中国统计局编.中国统计出

版社.

4. China 3000 largest foreign-funded enterprises/compilers, Huang Zheng Shen, Xie Wenxia, Chen Xianjing；[translated by Zhou Bao]. Beijing：China Reform Publishing House, 1994. 28, 592, 41 pages；29cm. ISBN：7800723844, 7800723841

《中国 3000 家大型外资企业》,黄正身等编.改革出版社.

5. China enterprises/edited by Guangdong Research Institute of Foreign Economic & Trade Relations. ［Beijing］：China Foreign Economic Relations & Trade, 1999. 811 pages；30cm. ISBN：7800047768, 7800047763

《中国出口商品生产名册》,广东省对外经济贸易发展研究所编.中国对外经济贸易出版社.

F42 工业部门经济

1. Taching：red banner on China's industrial front. Beijing：Foreign Languages Press, 1972. 46 pages：illustrations；19cm.

《大庆——中国工业战线上的一面旗帜》

2. The Kailuan story：old mines into new/by the Kailuan Workers' Writing Group. Peking：Foreign Languages Press, 1977. 74 pages, ［17］ leaves of plates：illustrations；19cm.

《开滦新貌》,开滦工人写作组著.

3. 今日中国电力工业：汉英对照/叶荣泗主编；匡佩华等译. 北京：外文出版社, 2004. 511 页；29cm. ISBN：7119038117, 7119038117

英文题名：Chinese power industry today.

4. 中国电力监管机构能力建设研究报告：汉英对照/国家电力监管委员会,中华人民共和国财政部,世界银行编著. 北京：中国水利水电出版社,2007. 248 页；29cm. ISBN：7508443782, 7508443780

英文题名：Study of capacity building of the electricity regulatory agency (SERC), P. R. China.

5. China's energy issue/Zhou Dadi. Beijing：Foreign Languages Press, 2006. 117 pages：color illustrations, charts；21cm. ISBN：7119046187, 7119046181.（China in peaceful development）

《中国的能源问题：英文》,周大地著；章挺权译.（中国的和平发展系列）.本书重点介绍了中国当前存在的能源问题,并详细阐述了中国政府的能源政策,解决措施及取得的成效.最后对中国能源技术的发展进行了展望.

6. China's energy sector：a sustainable strategy/［Que Guanghui］. Beijing：Foreign Languages Press, 2007. 165 pages：illustrations (some color)；24cm. ISBN：7119051512, 7119051512.（Panoramic China）

《中国能源：可持续战略：英文》,阙光辉编著（全景中国）

7. Powering up the nation：China's West-to-East power

transmission project/written by Zhao Cheng, translated by Zhang Hongpeng, Yan Shuang. Beijing：China Intercontinental Press ［Wuzhou chuanbo chubanshe］, 2008. 102 p. ： ill. ； 19cm. ISBN：7508513485, 7508513487. (Guoqing gushi)

《优化电力资源的工程》, 赵承著. 五洲传播出版社. 展示了"西电东送"这一中国电力史上的大型工程.

F5　贸易经济

1. What China exports. Peking：Foreign Languages Press, 1954. 53 pages：illustrations.

《新中国外销物产》

2. More for the dinner table. Beijing：New Star Publishers, 1990. 31 pages. ISBN：7800853012, 7800853012

《为了丰富居民的菜篮子》. 新星出版社.

3. A grand market in China：retrospect and prospect/compiled by Sun Shangqing, Ren Xingzhou. Beijing, China：New World Press：Distributed by China International Book Trading Corp., 1997. 282 pages；21cm. ISBN：7800053334, 7800053337. (China market yearbook；1996)

《中国大市场：回顾与展望》, 孙尚清主编. 新世界出版社.

4. China's foreign trade and economic cooperation/by Wu Zhou & Xian Guoyi. ［Beijing］：China Intercontinental Press, 2001. 102 pages：illustrations (some color)；21cm. ISBN：7801139542, 7801139542

《中国对外经济贸易》, 吴州, 冼国义编. 五洲传播出版社.

5. China and APEC/New Star Publishers. Beijing：New Star Publishers, 2001. 43 pages：color illustrations；19cm. ISBN：7801484444, 7801484444

《中国与APEC》, 李荣霞编. 新星出版社.

6. China business/compiled by Ma Ke, Li Jun, etc；translated by Song Peiming and Zhu Youruo. Beijing：China Intercontinental Press, 2004. 454 pages：illustrations (some color)；24cm. ＋1 CD-ROM (4 3/4 in.). ISBN：7508504135, 7508504131

Contents of CD-ROM：Legal documents of China's WTO accession—Laws and regulations governing business relations with foreign countries—Business websites.

《中国商务》, 马可, 李俊主编；宋佩铭等译. 五洲传播出版社.

7. Shop signs of imperial China/［text by Wang Shucun；English translation by Li Xin；designed by Tang Shaowen］. Beijing：Foreign Languages Press, 2006. 1 vol. (159 p.)：ill. ；2006. ISBN：7119042106, 7119042107

《中国店铺招幌：英文》, 王树村编著. 李欣译.

8. 中国制造的故事：英文/林希鹤, 林良旗著. 丛国玲等译. 北京：外文出版社, 2006. 111 页：照片；19cm. ISBN：7119045016, 7119045016. (国情故事)

英文题名：Story of "made in China. 本书讲述中国制造的商品大量出口到世界各地的故事. (对外贸易)

9. Brand in China/written by Wang Yifan；translated by Pan Zhongming & Gao Jinan. Beijing：China Intercontinental Press, 2007. 145 pages：color illustrations；22cm. ISBN：7508510866, 7508510860. (Fashion China)

《品牌中国：英文》, 王逸凡撰文；潘忠明, 高进安译. 五洲传播出版社(时尚中国)

10. China-Africa economic and trade cooperation/Information Office of the State Council, the People's Republic of China. Beijing：Foreign Languages Press, 2010. 30 pages；21cm. ISBN：7119068169, 7119068164, 7119068152, 7119068156

《中国与非洲的经贸合作》, 国务院新闻办公室发布.

11. 商之江南/伊文著；李洁译. 上海：上海远东出版社, 2010. 165 页；21cm. ISBN：7547600474, 7547600476

英文题名：Commerce of Jiang Nan.

12. China's foreign trade/Information Office of the State Council, the People's Republic of China. Beijing：Foreign Languages Press, 2011. 39 pages；26cm. ISBN：7119074085, 7119074083, 7119074078, 7119074075

《中国的对外贸易》, 中华人民共和国国务院新闻办公室发布.

13. China sourcing：an emerging competitive edge in global sourcing/Yin Guopeng and Chen Jin. Beijing：Economy & Management Publishing House, 2011. 3, 8, 2, 5, 277 p. ：ill. ；26cm. ISBN：7509617281, 7509617286

《中国服务》, 殷国鹏等主编. 经济管理出版社. 本书从宏观层面和区域层面分别对中国服务外包进行了详细研究.

14. 马云与阿里巴巴：汉英双语/严岐成著；（英）Imogen Page-Jarrett 译. 北京：中译出版社, 2018. 299 页；23cm. ISBN：7500155614. (中国著名企业家与企业丛书)

英文题名：Jack Ma & Alibabazeng.

F51　旅游经济

1. The China guidebook for travelers with special interests/Xu Xingchen & Feng Yuqing. Beijing：Foreign Languages Press, 1992. 216 pages：illustrations, maps；18cm. ISBN：0835128482, 0835128483, 7119014870, 7119014876

《特种旅游》, 徐兴臣著.

2. China tourism：exploring a dreamland/author：Li Hairui；translator：Chen Gengtao. Beijing：China Intercontinental Press, 1998. 164 pages：color illustrations, maps；21cm. ISBN：7801133501, 7801133502. (China basics series)

《中国旅游》, 李海瑞著. 五洲传播出版社.

3. A comparative study of travel services management/written by Du Jiang, Dai Bin；translator-in-chief, Wang

Xiangning, translated by Zhang Xiaoge, Wang Xiangning, English language editor, （Amer.）W. Daniel Garst. Beijing：China Tourism Education，2010. ［12］，443 pages：illustrations；23cm. ISBN：7563718962，7563718966

《旅行社管理比较研究：英文版》，杜江，戴斌著. 旅游教育出版社.

4. Industrial reorganization & group management of state-owned hotels/written by Dai Bin；translator-in-chief, Wang Xiangning, translated by Zhang Wei, Kang Rui, Han Ge, English language editor, （Amer.）Sherry Ylder. Beijing：China Tourism Education，2010. 4，3，3，336 pages：illustrations；23cm. ISBN：7563718979，7563718974

《国有饭店产业重组与集团化管理》，戴斌著. 旅游教育出版社.

5. 丁莲芳：从历史深巷走向上海世博/郑天枝，曹勤主编. 杭州：浙江科学技术出版社，2010. 322 页；24cm. ISBN：7534138898，7534138892

本书分三章讲述世界名小吃，"中华老字号"丁莲芳的故事.

6. 中国国有饭店的转型与变革研究：英文版/戴斌著；王向宁总主译；束菊萍，徐明宇，摆志靖译. 北京：旅游教育出版社，2011. 397 页；23cm. ISBN：7563721726，756372172X

英文题名：Transformation and reformation of China's state-owned hotels.

7. 中国旅游景区管理模式研究：英文版/邹统钎著；王向宁总主译. 北京：旅游教育出版社，2011. 294 页；23cm. ISBN：7563722389，7563722386.（中国旅游学术推广文丛）

8. 中国金钥匙服务哲学/编著张斌，王伟；翻译：王国真. 北京：五洲传播出版社，2018. 205 页：图；24cm. ISBN：7508538662

英文题名：China's golden key service philosophy

F6 财经、税收

F61 中国财经

1. China's finance/by Xue Wei. ［Beijing］：China Intercontinental Press，2001. 47 pages：color illustrations；21cm. ISBN：7801139348，7801139344

《中国财政》，薛伟著. 五洲传播出版社.

2. 中国财政政策：理论与实践＝Financial policy in China：theory and practice：英文/金人庆著. 北京：中国财政经济出版社，2005. 175 页；24cm. ISBN：7500586620，7500586623

英文题名：Fiscal policy in China：theory and practice. 本书对中国财政政策的制定背景、主要措施及成效作了总结，并对今后财政政策制定作了前瞻.

3. China's public finance/chief editor, Lou Juwei. Beijing：Foreign Languages Press，2008. 170 pages；22cm. ISBN：7119049472，711904947X.（Focus on China series）

《中国公共财政》，楼继伟主编.

F62 中国税收

1. China's international tax administration：the achievement of China's international tax administration in the past two decades. Beijing：State Administration of Taxation China Pictorial Publishing House，1999. 251 pages：color，illustrations；37cm. ISBN：7800245241，7800245244

《走向辉煌：中国涉外税务巡礼，中国涉外税务 20 年回顾》，范巍主编. 中国画报出版社.

2. 中华人民共和国海关进出口税则：十位编码·监管条件·政策法规·出口退税·海关代征税一览表/《中华人民共和国海关进出口税则》编委会编. 北京：经济科学出版社，2005. 1511 页；29cm. ＋光盘 1 张. ISBN：7505846809 7505846807

英文题名：Customs import and export tariff of the People's Republic of China：decade coding of HS，customs control conditions，laws and regulations，export drawback，detailed customs duties levied on commission basis. 汉英对照.

3. 中华人民共和国海关进出口税则：十位编码·监管条件·政策法规·出口退税·海关代征税一览表：汉英对照/《中华人民共和国海关进出口税则》编委会编. 北京：经济日报出版社，2006. 1560 页；29cm. ＋光盘 1 张. ISBN：7801805208，7801805201

英文题名：Customs import and export tariff of the Peolple's Repubilc of China.

4. 中华人民共和国海关进出口税则：十位编码·监管条件·申报说明·出口退税·政策法规·海关代征税一览表：2007 年中英文对照版：汉英对照. 2007/中华人民共和国海关进出口税则编委会编. 北京：经济日报出版社，2007. 29cm. ＋光盘 1 张. ISBN：7801806307，7801806301

英文题名：Customs import and export tariff of the People's Republic of China：decade coding of HS，customs control conditions，declare explanation，regulations，export drawback，detailed customs duties levied on commission basis.

5. 中华人民共和国海关进出口税则＝Customs import and export tariff of the People's Republic of China/中华人民共和国海关进出口税则编委会编. 北京：经济日报出版社，2009. 1297 pages：illustrations，forms；30cm. ＋1 CD-ROM（sd.，color；4 3/4 in.）. ISBN：7801809629，7801809629

本书介绍有关中国海关进出口货物名称、编码、税率及有关规定，中英文对照.

6. 中华人民共和国进出口税则：法律文本 the legal texts/国务院关税税则委员会办公室，中华人民共和国财政部关税司编. 北京：中国财政经济出版社，2009. 1069 页；29cm. ISBN：7509519318，7509519318，7509519314

英文题名：Customs tariff of import and export of the People's Republic of China.

7. 中华人民共和国海关进出口税则：中英对照版/中华人民共和国海关进出口税则编委会编. 北京：经济日报出版社，2010. 1284 页；29cm. ISBN：7802571099，780257109X

英文题名：Customs import and export tariff of the People's Republic of China：decade coding of HS, customs control conditions，declare explanation，regulations，legal inspection，detailed customs duties levied on commission basis. 本书介绍2010 年中国海关发布的就出口税则、税率、优惠税率、监管条件、货物编码表及有关进出口规章制度. 全书配有英文翻译.

8. 中华人民共和国海关进出口税则及申报指南：中英文对照版/中华人民共和国海关进出口税则及申报指南编委会. 北京：中国商务出版社，2010. 1232 页；29cm. ISBN：7510301933，7510301939

英文题名：Import and export tariff of the People's Republic of China：a declaration guidebook.

9. 中华人民共和国海关进出口税则：十位编码·监管条件·申报目录·出口退税·政策法规·海关代征税一览表：2011 年中英文对照版/中华人民共和国海关进出口税则编委会编. 北京：经济日报出版社，2011. 1235 页；29cm. ISBN：7802572737，7802572738

英文题名：Customs import and export tariff of the People's Republic of China：decade coding of HS, customs control conditions，declare explanation，regulations，legal inspection，detailed customs duties levied on commission basis.

F7　金融与证券

1. China's renminbi：one of the few most stable currencies in the world. Peking：Foreign Languages Press，1969. 31 pages；19cm.

《中国人民币：世界上少有的最稳定的货币》

2. The banking system of China. Beijing：China planning Press，1993. 352 p. ISBN：7800583023，7800583025

《中国的金融机构及其主要经营》，中国银行北京国际金融研究所编. 中国计划出版社.

3. Reforming China's financial system/chief editors，Gao Shangquan and Chi Fulin；written by Zhu Huayou. Beijing：Foreign Languages Press，1996. 168 pages；21cm. ISBN：7119013416，7119013411. (Studies on the Chinese market economy series)

《中国金融体制改革》，高尚全，迟福林主编.

4. Questions & answers：China's financial market/by Xu Hongcai. Beijing：Foreign Languages Press，2000. xiv，279 pages；21cm. ISBN：7119022229，7119022222

《中国金融市场问答》，徐洪才编著.

5. China's financial industry/［by］Haoyi Cai；［translated by］Jinpu Jiao. Beijing：China International Press，2001. 59 pages：color illustrations，charts；21cm. ISBN：7801139321，7801139320

《中国金融》，焦瑾璞等著. 五洲传播出版社.

6. 中国金融体系：英汉对照/张健华主编. 北京：中国金融出版社，2010. 545 页；24cm. ISBN：7504955654，7504955655. (中国金融丛书)

英文题名：China financial system.

7. The Chinese securities market/chief editors，Gao Shangquan and Chi Fulin；written by Zhu Huayou. Beijing：Foreign Languages Press，1996. 210 pages；21cm. ISBN：7119014919，7119014913. (Studies on the Chinese market economy series)

《中国的证券市场》，高尚全，迟福林主编.

8. A history of the Bank of China，1912—1949：condensed edition/by the Editorial Committee on the History of the Bank of China. Beijing：Sinolingua，1999. 235 pages；21cm. ISBN：7800527506，7800527500

《中国银行行史：1912—1949》，中国银行行史编委会编. 华语教学出版社.

9. The banking industry in China/Chief editor Xiao Gang. Beijing：China Financial Publishing House，1999. illustrations (some color)，color portraits；29cm.

《中国银行业》，肖刚主编. 中国金融出版社.

10. Questions and answers concerning China's control of foreign exchange，foreign debts and guarantees/Zheng Shuangqing；［translated by Zhang Tingquan］. Beijing：Foreign Languages Press，2000. xxii，252 pages；20cm. ISBN：7119020765，7119020761

《中国外汇、外债、担保问题》，郑双庆编著.

11. A history of the Bank of China，1912—1949/by Editorial Committee on The History of the Bank of China. Beijing：Economic Science Press，2006. 18，240 pages；21cm. ISBN：7505859234，7505859234

《中国银行行史：英文》，《中国银行行史》编委会编著. 经济科学出版社.

12. 投资中国：银行业规则透视与实务指南 banking rules review and practice guides 中英文对照/陈胜，周辉著，法律翻译社译. 北京：中信出版社，2008. 711 页；23cm. ISBN：7508613222，7508613228

英文题名：Invest in China：banking rules review and practice guides.

13. 财政部代理发行 2009 年地方政府债券问题解答：汉英对照/中华人民共和国财政部预算司编. 北京：中国财政经济出版社，2009. 188 页，12 页，217 页；23cm. ISBN：7509513934，7509513936

英文题名：Questions and answers of 2009 sub-national government bonds issued by MOF on behalf of sub-national governments.

F8　保险业

1. 中国的保险业和保险监管：英汉对照/周道许主编. 北京：中国金融出版社，2010. 386 页；24cm. ISBN：7504954596，7504954594

英文题名：China's insurance and its regulation.

G类 文化、教育、体育

G1 中国文化概论

1. The wisdom of China and India. New York：Random House，[1942]. xiii, 1104 pages；24cm.

   Note：pt. 1. The wisdom of India. pt. 2. The wisdom of China

   《中国印度之智慧》，林语堂(1895—1976)编译. 包括对中国思想、历史、文学的翻译和介绍.

   (1)London，M. Joseph，1949. 516 pages；22cm.

   (2) New York：Modern Library，1955. 1104 pages；21cm.

   (3)New York：Modern Library，1968. xiii, 1104 pages；21cm.

   (4)New York：Random House，1978. xiii, 1103 pages；24cm.

2. The wisdom of China/edited by Lin Yutang. London：M. Joseph，1944. 516 pages；22cm.

   《中国的智慧》，林语堂(1895—1976)编译. 收录了中国哲学、文学和宗教等方面的代表作(或其中的章节)，包括《诗经》、《史记》、民间故事、诸子百家等，生动全面地介绍了中国的传统文化.

   (1)London：Michael Joseph，1948. 515 pages

   (2)[3rd ed.]. London：M. Joseph，1949. 516 pages；22cm.

   (3)London，M. Joseph Ltd. , 1954. 516 pages；22cm.

   (4)Bombay，India：Jaico，1955. 624 pages；19cm.

   (5)London：Michael Joseph，1956. 516 pages；22cm.

   (6)Foursquare ed. London：New English Library，1963. 590 pages；19cm.

   (7)Beijing：Foreign language Teaching and Research Press，2009. xxiv, 618 pages，[16] pages of plates：illustrations，portraits；21cm. ISBN：7560086446，7560086446. (English works of Lin Yutang＝林语堂英文作品集)

3. A harp with a thousand strings：a Chinese anthology in six parts/Comp. by Hsiao Ch'ien. London：Pilot Press，1944. XXIV, 536 S；23cm.

   萧乾(1910—1999)编. 主题：中国文化.

4. Culture and education in new China. Peking：Foreign Languages Press，1951. 82 pages：illustrations；19cm.

   Contents：Report on cultural and educational work，by Kuo Mo-Jo. —The policy of educational construction in present-day China，by Chien Chun-jui. —The press in new China，by Liu Tsun-chi. —The Chinese people's broadcasting system，by Mei Tso. —Publication works in new China，by Hu Yu-chih. —Science in new China，by Coching Chu. —The Chinese film industry，by Tsai Chu-sheng.

   《新中国文化与教育》，马叙伦、沈雁冰等.

(1)Beijing：Foreign Languages Press，1955. 82 p.

5. Culture，education and health in New China. Peking：Foreign Languages Press，1952. 40 pages；19cm.

   Contents：Successes of people's education，by Ma Hsu-lun. —New developments n culture and art，by Shen Yen-ping (Mao Tun). —Publishing serves the people，by Hu Yu-chih. —The people's health services，by Li Teh-chuan.

   《新中国文化、教育与保健》，马叙伦等.

6. Sources of Chinese tradition，compiled by Wm. Theodore de Bary，Wing-tsit Chan [and] Burton Watson. With contributions by Yi-pao Mei [and others]. New York：Columbia University Press，1960. xxiv, 976 p. illus. , maps. ；24cm. (Records of civilization：sources and studies，55. Introduction to Oriental civilizations). (Records of civilization，sources and studies；55). (Introduction to Oriental civilizations)

   De Bary，William Theodore(1919—)，陈荣捷等译. 主题：中华文明.

   (1)New York：Columbia University Press，1964. 2 v. ：il. ；22cm. ISBN：0231086024(v. 1)，0231086028(v. 1)，0231086032(v. 2)，0231086035(v.2)

   (2)New York：Columbia University Press，1966. xxiv, 976 pages：illustrations；24cm. (Record of civilization；sources and studies；55)

   (3)New York，Columbia University Press，1970. 2 volumes illustrations，maps；22cm. (Records of civilization；sources and studies；55. Introduction to oriental civilizations)

   (4)2nd ed. New York：Columbia University Press，1999—2000. 2 v. ：map；24cm. ISBN：0231109385 (v. 1)，0231109393 (v. 1：pbk.)，023111270X. (Introduction to Asian civilization)

7. A glance at China's culture/Zhai Bian. Peking：Foreign Languages Press，1975. 60 p.

   《中国文化简况》，翟边.

8. Culture/compiled by the China Handbook Editorial Committee；translated by Liang Liangxing and Zhu Peiyu. Beijing：Foreign Languages Press，141 pages，1982. [12] pages of leaves：illustrations；19cm. ISBN：0835109917，0835109918. (China handbook series)

   《文化事业》，《中国手册》编辑委员会编.

9. A history of Chinese culture/compiled by Guo Shangxing，Sheng Xingqing；revised by Qiu ke'an，Zhang Jin. [Kaifeng Shi]：Henan University Press，1993. xii, 559 pages；21cm. ISBN：7810189115，7810189118

   《中国文化史》，郭尚兴，盛兴庆编著. 河南大学出版社.

10. China's cultural heritage：rediscovering a past of 7,000 years/[editor-in-chief，Xiao Shiling]. Beijing，China：Morning Glory Publishers，1995. 286 pages：color

illustrations；35cm. ISBN：7505404083，7505404083

中国文化遗产. 萧师铃主编.

11. Cultural flow between China and outside world throughout history/Shen Fuwei. Beijing：Foreign Languages Press，1996. 416 pages，［16］pages of plates：illustrations（some color），color maps；21cm. ISBN：711900431X，7119004310

《中外文化因缘》，沈福伟著.

12. 中国那个地方＝China：a great country in the east/编写张英；英译傅勇. 北京：北京语言大学出版社，2002. 4 volumes：illustrations；19cm. ISBN：7561909330（set）；7561909331（set）

Contents：v. 1. 龙的故乡（Homeland of the dragon）—v. 2. 华夏春秋（Eminent figures in Chinese history）—v. 3. 九州名胜（Outstanding tourist spots in China）—v. 4. 中华物产（In search of Chinese treasures）.

英汉对照.

13. Highlights of China/edited by Weixin Sun［and others］. Shanghai：Shanghai yi wen chu ban she，2004. 314 pages；22cm. ISBN：7532734684，7532734689

《经典中国》，孙维新等编著. 上海译文出版社. 介绍中国传统文化的各个方面：历史、文学、艺术（书法、绘画等）、戏剧、旅游、饮食、体育（武术）、手工艺等.

14. The basics of traditional Chinese culture/compiled by Zhi Exiang. Beijing，China：Foreign Languages Press，2005. v，122 pages：illustrations；21cm. ISBN：7119039040，7119039046

《中国传统文化 ABC：英文》，支鄂湘主编. 本书以短文的形式向读者介绍了中国传统文化的方方面面，如中国的儒教、道教、服装、瓷器等.

15. 中国文化掠影/张蓓，韩江编著. 广州：华南理工大学出版社，2005.236 页；22cm. ISBN：756232204X

《中国文化掠影》（上、下），分 30 个单元，每个单元围绕一个主题，用英文从各个侧面系统、完整和客观地介绍了中国文化的方方面面.

16. Highlights of Chinese culture＝风采中国：中国文化概况/主编宋莉；副主编张瑾，贾雪睿；主审傅利，刘爱华；英文审校 Krista Stevenson，Mike Dicker. 哈尔滨：哈尔滨工业大学出版社，2005. iii，357 pages：illustrations，maps，portraits，facsimiles；23cm. ISBN：7560322042，7560322049

17. A reader on China/Shuyang Su；［edited and designed by the Editorial Committee of Cultural China series］. South San Francisco：Long River Press，2005. 247 pages：color illustrations；25cm. ISBN：1592650597，1592650590. （Cultural China）

《中国读本》，苏叔阳著. Chen，Zijian 译.

(1)New York：Better Link Press，2007. 247 pages：color illustrations；25cm. ISBN：1602201033，160220103X. （Cultural China）

(2)New York：Better Link Press，2006. 173 pages；

21cm. ISBN：1602209014，1602209015. （Chinese-English readers series＝《文化中国》汉英对照阅读系列）

18. China：insight traditions and culture/by Su Shuyang. Beijing，China：Dolphin Books，2010. 287 pages：illustrations（chiefly color），1 color map，color portraits，color facsimiles；25cm. ISBN：7801387967，7801387961

《中国读本》，苏叔阳. 青少年读本.

19. 四大发明：汉英对照/王毅编；柯文礼译. 北京：人民文学出版社，2006. 109 页；21cm. ISBN：7020048765，7020048762. （中国传统文化双语读本）

英文题名：Four great inventions. 本书介绍中国古代四大发明.

20. 中国文化导读：英汉对照/常宗林，李旭奎主编；杨恩华等编. 北京：清华大学出版社，2006.180 页；21cm. ISBN：7302126321. （高校英语选修课系列教材）

21. Culture is like water/Sun Jiazheng. Beijing：Foreign Languages Press，2006. iv，127 pages：color illustrations；21cm. ISBN：711904494X，7119044941. （China in peaceful development）

《文化如水：英文》，孙家正著；梁发明译. （中国的和平发展系列）.

22. 英释中国传统文化：英文/何其亮，张晔编著. 杭州：浙江大学出版社，2006. 193 页；23cm. ISBN：7308047997，7308047999. （现代传播. 国际传播/王文科，何其亮主编）

英文题名：A talk on traditional Chinese culture：the language perspective.

23. 中国文化掠影＝Glimpses of Chinese Culture：英文/丁往道著. 北京：外语教学与研究出版社，2006. 174 页：图；19cm. ISBN：7560061516

书名原文：Glimpses of Chinese culture. 对中国文化的几个主要方面的介绍.

24. 中国传统文化概论：英文/余惠芬主编；王东等编. 广州：暨南大学出版社，2007.［10］，358 p.；23cm. ISBN：7810799188，7810799185

英文题名：An introduction to Chinese culture.

25. Creativity in China/written by Wang Xian；translated by Song Peiming. Beijing：China Intercontinental Press，2007. 141 pages：color illustrations；22cm. ISBN：7508511368，7508511360. （Fashion China）

《创意中国：英文》，王弦撰文；宋佩铭译. 五洲传播出版社（时尚中国）. 本书对中国创意产业的发展现状进行全面介绍.

26. Colorful China/written by Liang Minling；translated by Liu Bingwen & Pan Zhongming. Beijing：China Intercontinental Press，2007. 148 pages：color illustrations；25cm. ISBN：7508510804，7508510801

《多彩中国：英文》，梁敏玲撰文；刘炳文，潘忠明译. 五洲传播出版社.

27. 中国文化导读/毛晓霞主编. 北京：中国农业科学技术出

版社，2008. 282 页；29cm. ISBN：7802335479

28. Things Chinese/authors，Du Feibao and Du Bai；translators，Li Nianpei，Ling Yuan and Cui Sigan. 3rd ed. ［i. e. 2nd and rev. ed.］. Beijing：China Travel & Tourism Press，2008. 10，323 pages：illustrations (chiefly color)；24cm. ISBN：7503235009，7503235004
《中国风物》，杜飞豹，杜白著. 中国旅游出版社. 本书分门别类介绍中国独有的传统文化之物.

29. 聚焦中国文化/贾荣香，夏岩，孙希磊著. 北京：石油工业出版社，2008. 255 页；26cm. ISBN：7502163365，7502163360

30. Traditional Chinese culture/edited by Zhang Qizhi. Beijing：Foreign Languages Press，2009. 331 pages；24cm. ISBN：7119057569，7119057561.（China studies）
《中国传统文化》，张岂之主编.

31. Value of traditional culture for the present era/by Zhang Xiping. Beijing：Foreign Languages Press，2009. 113 pages：color illustrations；21cm. ISBN：7119061122，7119061127.（China in peaceful development）
《传统文化的当代价值》，张西平［著］.

32. 中国文化概览：英汉对照/龙毛忠，贾爱兵，颜静兰主编. 上海：华东理工大学出版社，2009. 312 页；24cm. ISBN：7562825388，7562825386
英文题名：A bird's-eye view of Chinese culture.

33. 中国人的文化：中英对照/周济著. 上海：上海文化出版社，2009. 199 页；24cm. ISBN：7807404583，7807404582
英文题名：Tales of the Chinese culture.

34. Symbols of China/［edited by］Feng Jicai. London：Compendium，2009. 256 pages：illustrations（some color）；29cm. ISBN：1849120180，1849120188
Contents：Cultural icons—Natural wonders—Architectural heritage—Ceremonies and festivals—Daily life—Arts and crafts—Legend—Famous figures—Performing arts.
《符号中国》，冯骥才. 对中国辉煌文化进行系统全面、深入浅出的介绍和解读.

35. Chinese symbols/compiled by Wang Yang；translated by Transn. Beijing：New Star Press，2010. 241 pages：illustrations；23cm. ISBN：7802259034，7802259037
《中国元素》，王阳编著. 新星出版社.

36. China's culture/Shi Zhongwen & Chen Qiaosheng；translated by Wang Guozheng. ［Beijing］：China Intercontinental Press，2010. 170 pages：illustrations (some color)；23cm. ISBN：7508512983，7508512987
《中国文化》，史仲文，陈桥生著. 五洲传播出版社.

37. Introduction to Chinese culture/Chung Mou Si，Yun Cheng Si. Beijing：Peking University Press，2011. vi，203 pages：illustrations；23cm. ISBN：7301185285，7301185286
《中华文化精粹》，Chung Mou Si，Yun Cheng Si 编著. 北京大学出版社.

38. An outline of Chinese culture：English edition/Jun Yue Chang. Peking：Peking University Press，2011. 196 p.：ill. ISBN：7301193259，7301193254
《中国文化：英文版》，常俊跃主编. 北京大学出版社.

39. 走进中国文化：英文版/陈岩，王秀娟编著. 天津：南开大学出版社，2011. 226 页；21cm. ISBN：7310037421，7310037421

40. The history of Chinese civilization/general editors，Yuan Xingpei...［et al.］；English text edited by David R. Knechtges. Cambridge；New York：Cambridge University Press，2012. 4 v.：ill.（some col.）；24cm. ISBN：1107013094（set），1107013097（set）（The Cambridge China library）
《中国文明之光》，袁行霈主编；康达维（Knechtges，David R.），英文主编. 译自中文.

41. 石/姚琪编著. 合肥：黄山书社，2016. 160 页：图；23cm. ISBN：7546142227.（印象中国）
英文题名：Chinese stones. 英汉对照.

42. 木头里的东方：英文/石映照著；章挺权译. 北京：外文出版社，2006. 175 页：彩图；23cm. ISBN：7119044583，7119044583.（东西文丛）
英文题名：The story of wood.

43. 中国木文化/尚景编著. 合肥：黄山书社，2011. 168 页；21cm. ISBN：7546120331，7546120330.（中国红）
英文题名：Chinese wood culture. 英汉对照.
(1)木文化/尚景编著. 合肥：黄山书社，2016. 168 页：彩图；23cm. ISBN：7546141480.（印象中国）

44. 梅兰竹菊/王静编著. 合肥：黄山书社，2016. 156 页：图；23cm. ISBN：7546141701.（印象中国）
英文题名：Plum blossom，orchid，bamboo and chrysanthemum.

G11　地方文化

1. 闽文化＝Min culture/郑立宪主编；译著者何锦山，郑立宪，谢燕华. 厦门：厦门大学出版社，2004. 471 pages；21cm. ISBN：7561521790，7561521793
中英文对照.

G2　新闻

1. Carry the great revolution on the journalistic front through to the end：repudiating the counter-revolutionary revisionist line on journalism of China's Khrushchov/by the editorial departments of Renmin Ribao，Hongqi，and Jiefangjun Bao. Peking：Foreign Languages Press，1969. 63 pages；13cm.
《把新闻战线的大革命进行到底》

G3　出版

1. Story of the Chinese book/Kuo-chun Liu. Peking：Foreign Languages Press，1958. 87 pages：illustrations；

19cm.

《中国书的故事》，刘国钧著.

2. Reading in China/written by Yu Hui；translated by Ai Xianghua. Beijing：China Intercontinental Press，2007. 155 pages：color illustrations；22cm. ISBN：7508511382，7508511387. (Fashion China)

《书香飘飘：英文》，郁辉撰文；艾湘华译. 五洲传播出版社（时尚中国）.本书介绍中国图书出版、消费、图书阅读的现状.

3. From oracle bones to e-publications：three millennia of publishing in China/[Engl. ed.：Sue Duncan... Ed. -in-chief：Xiao Dongfa. Transl.：Yan Wei...]. Beijing：Foreign Languages Press，2009. 89 p.；ill.；22cm. ISBN：7119059648，7119059645

《从甲骨文到 E-publications：跨越三千年的中国出版》，肖东发主编.

4. Chinese publishing：homeland of printing/Yang Hu，Xiao Yang；translated by Zha Xiaoyun & Lei Jing. Beijing：China Intercontinental Press，2010. 205 pages：illustrations（some color），facsimiles；23cm. (Cultural China series)

《中国书业》，杨虎，肖阳著. 五洲传播出版社.介绍中国古代出版业的发展，印刷技术的发展及其在中国古代文化中的重要地位.

G4　文化机构

1. China's museums/Li Xianyao，Luo Zhewen；translated by Martha Avery. ［Beijing］：China Intercontinental Press，2004. 201 pages：color illustrations；24cm. ISBN：7508506030，7508506036. (Cultural China series)

《中国博物馆＝This is China》，黎先耀，罗哲文编著；罗哲文等摄；（美）艾梅霞（Avery，M.）译. 五洲传播出版社.介绍中国二千余博物馆中最有代表性的七十座.

(1) 2nd ed. Beijing：China Intercontinental Press，2010. 141 pages：color illustrations；23cm. ISBN：7508516998，7508516990，7508516936，7508516931. (Cultural China series)

(2) A China's museums/Li Xianyao，Luo Zhewen；［translated from the original Chinese by Martha Avery］. Updated ed. Cambridge，UK；New York：Cambridge University Press，2011. 211 p.：col. ill.；23cm. ISBN：0521186902，0521186900. (Introductions to Chinese culture)

2. 访问北京＝Visit Beijing/[马希桂，刘一达主编]. 北京：紫禁城出版社，2005. 243 pages. illustrations，maps；21cm. ISBN：7800474992；7800474996

《访问北京：汉英对照》，马希桂，刘一达主编；北京市博物馆学会. 紫禁城出版社（北京文化之旅.博物馆卷）.对北京地区107家博物馆、纪念馆的情况介绍.

3. 同兴公镖局：汉英对照/王夷典编著. 太原：山西经济出版社，2005. 102 页；照片；19cm. ISBN：7806368108

本书介绍了清末平遥唯一的最大的镖局的兴衰历史以及主要人物和逸闻趣事，同兴公镖局现为博物馆，是平遥旅游景点.

4. Private collections in Shanghai/[compiled] by Lan Xiang；[translator]，Qu Lei. Beijing：Foreign Languages Press，2007. 159 pages：color illustrations，maps；21cm. ISBN：7119043937，7119043935

《上海民间收藏：英文》，蓝翔编著；聂万翔摄；曲磊译.介绍上海50家民间收藏馆，藏品与中国传统文化、习俗等.

5. Museums in Beijing/[edited by Lan Peijin；text by Zi Hui；translated by Ji Hua，Gao Wenxing]. Beijing：Foreign Languages Press，2008. 167 pages：color illustrations；23cm. ISBN：7119043876，7119043870

《京城博物馆》，子慧撰.

6. China and world expo/compiled by Dou Ziwen. Beijing：China Intercontinental Press，2009. 138 pages：illustrations（some color），portraits；26cm. ISBN：7508517575，7508517571

《中国与世界博览会：英文版》，吴伟主编. 五洲传播出版社.介绍上海举办世界博览会的概况.

7. 尽善尽美：殿本精华/故宫博物院编. 北京：紫禁城出版社，2009. 111 页；29cm. ISBN：7800478666，7800478661

英文题名：Perfection：palace editions from the Hall of Martial Valor. 本书系统地阐述了武英殿修书处的产生及发展过程、殿本书版本特点、印刷技术及装帧艺术、故宫图书馆存藏状况等.

8. 嘉业藏书楼/浙江图书馆编著. 杭州：浙江人民美术出版社，2004. 101 页；26cm. ISBN：7534018773，7534018770

本书以图文并茂的形式，将嘉业藏书楼背景知识、历史资料、所藏文物、现状分门别类进行介绍并配以中英文对照.

9. 图书馆权力与道德：汉英对照/程焕文，张靖编译. 桂林：广西师范大学出版社，2007. 25cm. ISBN：7563368853，756336885X

英文题名：Rights and professional ethics of library

G41　收藏

1. Finding pleasure in planning for treasures/by Dong Shaopeng and Long Shu. Beijing，China：New World Press，2009. 129 pages：color illustrations；19cm. ISBN：7802289970，7802289971. (Stories from China)

《淘宝找乐》，董少鹏，龙树著. 新世界出版社.以马未都的收藏故事为主，介绍了中国人的收藏热和各色人物的淘宝趣闻故事，这些故事中表现中国普通百姓盛世收藏的心态.

G411　文具

1. Mi Fu on ink-stones，translated by R. H. van Gulik，with an introduction and notes. Peking，H. Vetch，1938. vii，70 p. illus. 25cm.

《砚史》，米芾（1051—1107）；高罗佩（Gulik，Robert Hans

van,1910—1967)(荷兰汉学家)译.

2. 紫方馆藏砚：汉英对照/李碧珊,许乐心编纂.北京：文物出版社,2006. 252 pages：彩照；29cm. ISBN：750102071X, 7501020713

英文题名：Inkstone collection of Zi Fang Guan. 本书收录紫方馆藏砚 230 方,从古至今应有尽有,可使读者从中领略砚文化的发展脉络.

3. Chinese seals/Niu Kecheng. Beijing：Foreign Languages Press,2008. 91 p.：ill.；24cm. ISBN：7119041971, 7119041975

《中国印》,牛克诚编著；章挺权译.

4. The history and art of Chinese seals/by Sun Weizu. Beijing：Foreign Languages Press,2010. 573 pages：color illustrations；26cm. ISBN：7119066035, 711906603X

《中国印章：历史与艺术》,孙慰祖著.

5. 笔墨纸砚/季孙歙编著.合肥：黄山书社,2016. 180 页：彩图；23cm. ISBN：7546141602.（印象中国）

英文题名：Writing brush, ink stick, paper and ink slab. 英汉对照.

6. 文房清供/茅翊编著.合肥：黄山书社,2016. 160 页：图；23cm. ISBN：7546142234.（印象中国）

英文题名：Stationery and bibelot in ancient studies.

G412 生活用具

1. Chinese chopsticks/by Lan Xiang；[translated by Chen Yin]. Beijing：Foreign Languages Press,2005. 101 pages：color illustrations；23cm. ISBN：7119038524, 7119038520

《中国筷子：英文》,蓝翔编著；陈林译.

2. Tea set research/translated by Li Zenglong, Ji Xuqiang, Yin Changzhi. Beijing：China Academy of Art Press, 2009. 233 pages,[28] pages of plates：illustrations, portraits；21cm. ISBN：7810838221, 7810838229

《茶具研究》,吴光荣著.中国美术学院出版社.

3. Chinese furniture：exploring China's furniture culture/ Zhang Xiaoming；translated by Kang Jian, Han Huizhi, & Wang Wenliang. Beijing：China Intercontinental Press,2009. 145 pages：illustrations（some color）；23cm. ISBN：7508513218, 7508513215.（Cultural China series）

《中国家具》,张晓明编著.五洲传播出版社.

4. Classic Chinese furniture：Ming and early Qing dynasties/ Wang Shixiang；translated by Sarah Handler and the author. 1st Hong Kong English ed. Hong Kong：Joint Pub. Co.（HK）,1986. 327 p.：ill.（some col.）；31cm. ISBN：9620404637

《明式家具珍赏》,王世襄（1914—2009）著；Handler, Sarah（美国汉学家）译.

5. 明清家具＝Furniture of the Ming and Qing dynasties/《北京文物鉴赏》编委会编. 北京：北京美术摄影出版社,

2005. 2 volumes：illustrations（chiefly color）；21cm. ISBN：7805012911（v. 1）, 7805012919（v. 1）, 7805013047（v. 2）, 7805013046（v. 2）.（北京文物鉴赏＝Appreciating Beijing cultural relics）

G5 预测学

1. Theory of forecasting/Weng Wen-Bo. Beijing, China：International Academic Publishers,1991. xii, 132 pages；21cm. ISBN：7800031268, 7800031267

《预测学》,翁文波.万国学术出版社.

2. Forecastology/original by Weng Wenbo；compiled by Lü Niudun, Zhang Qing. Beijing：Petroleum Industry Press, 1997. 233 pages：illustrations. ISBN：7502120645, 7502120641

《预测学》,翁文波原著；吕牛顿,张清编.石油工业出版社.

G6 教育

1. Education must be combined with productive labour. Peking：Foreign Languages Press,1958. 32 pages；19cm.

《教育必须与生产劳动相结合》,陆定一.

(1)2nd ed. Peking：Foreign Languages Press,1964. 31, [1] pages；19cm.

2. Take the road of the Shanghai Machine Tools Plant in training technicians from among the workers：two investigation reports on the revolution in education in colleges of science and engineering. Peking：Foreign Languages Press,1968. 56 pages；13cm.

《走上海机床厂从工人中培养技术人员的道路》

3. Strive to build a socialist university of science and engineering. Peking：Foreign Languages Press,1972. 69 pages：illustrations；19cm.

Contents：Workers' and People's Liberation Army Men's Mao Tsetung Thought Propaganda Team at Tsinghua University. Strive to build a socialist university of science and engineering.—Summary of the Forum on the Revolution in Education in Shanghai Colleges of Science and Engineering (p. 38—69).

《为创办社会主义理工大学而奋斗》

4. Decision of the Central Committee of the Communist Party of China on the reform of the educational structure：May 27, 1985. Beijing：Foreign Languages Press；Distributed by China International Book Trading Corp.（Guoji Shudian）,1985. 22 pages；19cm. ISBN：0835115887, 0835115889.（Chinese documents）

《中共中央关于教育体制改革的决定》

5. Chinese universities and colleges：a guide to institutions of higher education in China/Chinese Education Association for International Exchanges. Beijing：Higher Education Press,1989. 544 pages；26cm. ISBN：7040023865,

7040023862

《中国高等学校》，中国教育国际交流协会编.

(1) 2nd ed. Beijing：Higher Education Press，1994. 26，
760 pages：map；27cm. ISBN：7040050706，
7040050707

(2) 3rd ed. Beijing，China：Higher Education Press，971
pages：map；29cm. ＋1 computer optical disc. ISBN：
7040090465，7040090468

(3) 4th ed. Beijing，China：Higher Education Press，
2004. 1295 pages：map；29cm. ＋1 computer optical
disc (4 3/4 in.). ISBN：7040159309，7040159301

(4) 5th ed. Beijing：Higher Education Press，2008. 1703，
[130] pages：color illustrations；28cm. ＋1 CD-ROM
(4 3/4 in.). ISBN：7040229390，7894897663，
7040229394，7894897664

6. Directory of selected scientists of universities and colleges
in China/Dept. of Science and Technology，SEDC，Dept.
of Foreign Affairs，SEDC，Chinese National Commission
for UNESCO. Beijing：Science Press，1996. xiv，501
pages：portraits；25cm. ISBN：7030056167，7030056160

《中国高等学校名录》，科学出版社.

7. 中国大学指南/《中国大学指南》编委会编. 北京：外文出
版社；2004. 617 页；29cm. ISBN：7119036998

介绍国家教育部正式批准的 700 多所本科大学的基本情
况、学科情况、学术与研究状况等.

8. Chinese universities and colleges/China Education
Association for International Exchange. Beijing：Higher
Education Press，2008. 1703，[130] pages：color
illustrations；28cm. ＋1 CD-ROM (4 3/4 in.). ISBN：
7040229390，7894897663，7040229394

《中国高等学校大全》，中国教育国际交流协会编. 高等
教育出版社.

(1) Chinese universities and colleges/China Education
Association for International Exchange；Editorial
Board：Honorary Director：Zhang Xinsheng；
Consultants：Zhan Xinqin... [et al.]；Director：
Shao Wei；Seputy Directors：Yang Meng... [et
al.]；Members：Shen Xuesong... [et al.]；Editors：
Song Bicheng... [et al.]. Beijing：Higher Education
Press，2013. 24，1227 p.：ill.；28cm. ＋CD-ROM
(4 3/4 in.)

9. Directory of Chinese institutions of higher learning and
research institutes authorized to confer doctor's and
master's degrees/Office of the Academic Degrees，
Committee of the State Council，the People's Republic of
China. Beijing：Higher Education Press，1988. 3，8，804
pages；27cm. ISBN：7040002620，7040002621

《中华人民共和国授予博士和硕士学位的高等学校及科
研机构名册》，国务院学位委员会办公室编，高等教育出
版社.

10. Higher education research in China. Wu Han：Hua

Zhong University of Science and Technology Pr.，1997.
167 pages：illustrations；26cm. ISBN：7560917232，
7560917238

《高等教育研究在中国》，《高等教育研究在中国》编委会
编，华中理工大学出版社.

11. 古代教育/张光奇编著. 合肥：黄山书社，2016. 140 页：彩
图，肖像；23cm. ISBN：7546152851.（印象中国）

英文题名：Education in ancient China. 英汉对照.

12. 岳麓书院概览/唐子畏编. 长沙：湖南大学出版社，2004.
96 页；19cm. ISBN：781053730X

本书对岳麓书院历史沿革、建筑古迹、匾额、楹联、主要
碑刻以及书院园林景物作了较为全面的介绍.

13. 华西坝＝ Memory of West China Union University：英
文/吕重九主编；张丽萍等著；邓洪等译. 成都：四川大学
出版社，2006. 202 页：图；23cm. ISBN：7561434109，
7561434103

英文题名：Memory of West China Union University. 华
西协合大学校史.

14. Confucian temples south of the Yangtze/written by
Zhang Yaxiang；translated by Ding Yi；English-edited
by Kevin Budd. Shanghai：Shanghai Jiao Tong
University Press，2010. 2，3，278 p.：ill.，maps；
24cm. ISBN：7313063700，7313063709.（Architectural
culture south of Yangtze）

《江南文庙：英文版》，张亚祥著. 上海交通大学出版社.

15. 为了 13 亿人的教育：英文/李岚清著；外研社译. 北京：外
语教学与研究出版社，2004. 483 页；23cm. ISBN：
7560043704，7560043708

英文题名：Education for 1. 3 billion：former Chinese vice
premier Li Lanqing on 10 years of education reform and
development.

16. A history of Chinese educational thought/Guo Qijia；
[translated by Li Lei]. [Beijing]：Foreign Languages
Press，2006. 601 p.；21cm. ISBN：7119013866，
7119013862.（China knowledge series）

《中国教育思想史：英文》，郭齐家著.（中国知识丛书）.

(1) Beijing：Foreign Languages Press，2009. 601 pages；
24cm. ISBN：7119057521，7119057529.（China
studies）

17. 中国海员培训、考试和发证：汉英对照/中华人民共和国
海事局编. 大连：大连海事大学出版社，2006. 112 页；
29cm. ISBN：7563219714，7563219711

本书介绍中国海员考试、评估和发证，中国海员教育和
培训，海员教育、培训、考试、评估和发证的质量管理，国
际合作与交流等发展状况.

18. Studying in China/written by Yang Yang；translated by
Pan Zhongming. Beijing：China Intercontinental Press，
2007. 112 pages：color illustrations；22cm. ISBN：
7508510880，7508510887.（Fashion China）

《求学中国：英文》，杨阳撰文；潘忠明译. 五洲传播出版
社（时尚中国）. 本书介绍了外国留学生在中国学习、工

作和生活的方方面面.

19. China's science, technology, and education/compiled by Xi Qiaojuan, Zhang Aixiu; translated by Lei Jing. Beijing：China International Press, 2010. 146 pages：illustrations (some color)；23cm. ISBN：7508516875, 7508516877

《中国科技和教育》,席巧娟等著.五洲传播出版社.展示中华人民共和国成立 60 年来中国科技和教育事业取得的伟大成就.

20. Education and science/compiled by the China Handbook Editorial Committee；translated by Zhou Yicheng, Cai Guanping and Liu Huzhang. Beijing：Foreign Languages Press：Distributed by China Publications Centre, 1983. iv, 243 pages, ［16］ pages of plates：illustrations；19cm. ISBN：0835109887, 0835109888. (China handbook series)

《教育科学》,《中国手册》编辑委员会编.

21. Education in contemporary China/［compiled by Zhou Yuliang and others］. Changsha, Hunan Province, P. R. China：Hunan Education Pub. House, 1990. x, 813 pages；21cm. ISBN：7535511120, 7535511126

《当代中国教育》,周玉良主编.湖南教育出版社.

22. 为生活而教育/陶行知著；储朝晖编译.北京：外语教学与研究出版社,2012. 289 页；23cm. ISBN：7513526098. ("博雅双语名家名作"系列)

英文题名：Education for life. 英汉对照.

G7　体育

1. The conquest of Minya Konka/Shi Zhanchun；［translated by Huang Gaiping］. Peking：Foreign Languages Press, 1959. 53 pages：illustrations, map；19cm.

《征服贡嘎山记》,史占春著.黄开平译.

2. Sports and public health/compiled by the China Handbook Editorial Committee；translated by Wen Botang. Beijing：Foreign Languages Press：Distributed by China Publications Centre (Guoji Shudian), 1983. 176 pages, ［16］ pages of plates：illustrations；19cm. ISBN：0835109909, 0835109901. (China handbook series)

《体育卫生》,《中国手册》编辑委员会编.

3. Sports and games in ancient China. Beijing, China：New World Press：Distributed by China International Book Trading Corp., 1986. 136 pages, ［8］ leaves of plates：illustrations (some color)；19cm. ISBN：0835115348, 0835115346. (China spotlight series)

《体育史话》,新世界出版社.

4. Traditional sports and games of national minorities in China/Mu Fushan ［and others］；translated by Song Xianchun；co-translators Wu Guihong ［and］ Qi Zhikui. ［Beijing］：Tourism Education Press, 1990. 179 pages：color illustrations；19cm. ISBN：7563700536, 7563700530

《中国少数民族传统体育运动》,莫福山等编.宋献春译.旅游教育出版社.

5. China's sports：Honors and dreams. Beijing：Foreign Languages Press, 2008. 168 pages：color illustrations；24cm. ISBN：7119053905, 7119053906. (Panoramic China)

《中国体育：光荣与梦想》,张永恒编著.

G71　比赛项目

1. Regularized management of Special Olympics Games：practices of 2007 Special Olympics World Summer Games/Shanghai Academy of Quality Management. Beijing：Standards Press of China, 2008. , 12, 334 pages：illustrations (some color)；26cm. ISBN：7506649919, 7506649918

《特殊奥运会的规范管理：2007 年世界夏季特殊奥运会的实践》,上海质量管理科学研究院编著.中国标准出版社.

G72　群众运动

1. Fitness in China/Song Yiqi ＆ Wang Yi；translated by Wang Zhongji. ［Beijing］：China Intercontinental Press, 2006. 127 pages：color illustrations；21cm. ISBN：750850965X, 7508509655. (Fashion China＝时尚中国)

《运动无极限：英文》,宋懿芪,王弈著；王忠吉译.五洲传播出版社(时尚中国)

本书反映当代中国人的运动健身观念,以及传统与现代、时尚并存的多种运动健身方式.

G73　文体活动

1. Chinese chess：Xiangqi for beginners. Chengdu：Shu Rong Chess ＆ Bridge Press, 1993. 285 pages：illustrations；18cm.

《中国象棋入门》,刘国彬等编著.蜀蓉棋艺出版社.

2. Chinese chess for beginners/Alex Liu. Beijing：Foreign languages Press, 2005. 127 pages：illustrations；21 × 20cm. ＋1 Chinese chess set (1 game board, 32 chess pieces). ISBN：7119042084, 7119042084. (How to)

《怎样下中国象棋：英文》,刘晓峰著.

3. 棋艺/房明编著.合肥：黄山书社,2016. 132 页：彩图；23cm. ISBN：7546141510. (印象中国)

英文题名：Art of Chinese board games. 英汉对照.

4. 古代游戏/王慧编著.合肥：黄山书社,2016. 127 页：图；23cm. ISBN：7546141640. (印象中国)

英文题名：Chinese traditional games. 英汉对照.

G74　传统武术

G741　中国武术概论

1. Chinese martial arts. Beijing, China：Zhaohua Pub. House：Distributed by China Publications Centre, 1982.

36 pages：illustrations；21cm.

《中国武术》. 朝华出版社.

(1)2nd ed. Beijing：Zhaohua Pub. House：Distributor, China International Book Trading Corp., 1984. 36, [4] pages：illustrations (some color)；21cm.

(2)3rd ed. Beijing, China：Morning Glory Press：Distributor：China International Book Trade, 1987. 36 pages：color illustrations；21cm. ISBN：7505400568, 7505400566

2. Chinese martial arts：teach yourself. Beijing：Zhaohua Pub. House：Distributor, China Publications Centre, 1983. 94 pages：illustrations (some color)；21cm. ISBN：0887270034, 0887270031

《自学中国武术基本功》. 朝华出版社.

(1) 2nd ed. Beijing：Morning Glory Press, 1986. 94 pages：illustrations (some color)；21cm. ISBN：7505400584, 7505400580

3. Chinese Wushu/compiled and written by Cheng Chuanrui；translated and proofread by Pan Zhiwei. Beijing, China：Beijing Institute of Physical Education Press, 1990. 460 pages：illustrations；19cm. ISBN：7810033204, 7810033206

《中国武术》, 成传锐编著；潘志伟译. 北京体育学院出版社.

4. A guide to Chinese martial arts/by Li Tianji and Du Xilian. Beijing, China：Foreign Languages Press, 1991. 178 pages，[4] pages of plates：illustrations (some color)；19cm. ISBN：7119013939, 7119013930

《中国武术指南》, 李天骥(1914—)、杜希廉编著.

5. Essentials of Chinese Wushu/Wu Bin, Li Xingdong and Yu Gongbao. Beijing：Foreign Languages Press, 1992. 169 pages：illustrations；19cm. ISBN：083512830X, 0835128308, 7119014773, 7119014777. (Chinese Wushu series)

《中国武术概要》, 吴彬等编著.

6. 外国人学武术/韩凤芝, 姚希虹主编. 天津：天津科学技术出版社；2004. 243 页；20cm. ISBN：7530838946

介绍中国武术中太极拳、太极剑和长拳的入门技法、采用中英文对照方式, 便于中外武术爱好者学习、阅读.

7. 武术双语教程＝Bilingual teaching course for Wushu/王俊法编著. 青岛：中国海洋大学出版社, 2005. 4, 348 pages：illustrations；21cm. ISBN：7810677594, 7810677592. (中国文化双语书系)

介绍中国传统武术(太极拳、刀术、长拳等), 以及国际武术组织、武术竞赛的评分标准及武术竞赛中的礼仪.

8. 10-minute primer Chinese Wushu/Zhou, Qingjie. Beijing, China：Foreign Languages Press, 2009. 83 pages：color illustrations；22cm. ＋ 1 DVD. ISBN：7119054643, 7119054643

《十分钟学会中国武术》, 周庆杰主编.

9. Chinese kungfu：masters, schools and combats/Wang

Guangxi；translated by Han Huizhi, Wang Wenliang & Kang Jian. Beijing：China Intercontinental Press, 2010. 125 p.：ill. (some col.)；23cm. ISBN：7508513171, 7508513177. (Cultural China series)

《中国功夫》, 王广西编著. 五洲传播出版社.

10. 武术/蒋剑民, 黄一棉编著. 合肥：黄山书社, 2016. 178 页：彩图；23cm. ISBN：7546141541. (印象中国)

英文题名：Chinese martial arts. 英汉对照.

G742 太极拳

1. 《简化太极拳》/《中国体育》杂志社编辑, 1980. 英文题名：Simplitied "tiajiquan"/compiled by China Sports Editorial Board.

(1)2 版, 人民体育出版社, 1999. ISBN：7505916779

2. 《太极拳》. 北京：朝华出版社, 1983

3. Basics of taiji quan/Li Xingdong. Beijing, China：Foreign Languages Press：Distributed by China International Trading Corp., 1995. ISBN：711900171X, 7119001715. (Chinese Wushu series)

《太极拳初步》, 李兴东编著.

4. Tàijíquán/by Li Deyin；[translated by Yu Ling… et al.；edited by Sara Grimes]. Beijing：Foreign Language Teaching and Research Press, 2004. 402 p.，[6] leaves of plates：ill.；26cm. ISBN：7119037080, 7119037080

《太极拳》, 李德印著. 讲解了24式简化太极拳、81式传统太极拳、42式太极拳等竞赛套路.

5. The body parts of Taichi/James Wong. [Beijing]：[Beijing Sport University Press], 2005. 1 volume (various pagings)：color illustrations；21cm. ISBN：7811003066, 7811003062

《太极拳基本技术：英文》, 王伟光著. 北京体育大学出版社.

6. Taichi/[edited and translated] by Cai Jialing. Hangzhou, Zhejiang：China Academy of Art Press, 2008. 108 pages：illustrations；21cm. ISBN：7810837491, 7810837494

《太极拳》, 蔡嘉陵编译. 中国美术学院出版社.

7. 10-minute primer：tai ji quan/Qingjie Zhou. Beijing：Foreign Languages, 2009. 121 pages：color illustrations；23cm. ＋1 DVD (digital；4 3/4 in.). ISBN：7119054629, 7119054627, 1592650958, 1592650953

《十分钟学会太极拳》, 周庆杰编.

8. Simplified Taiji Quan/chielf editor：Yu Cuilan. Nanjing：Jiangsu Science and Technology Publishing House, 2009. 2, 6, 161 pages：color illustrations；24cm. ISBN：7534567636, 7534567637

《简化太极拳教程》, 于翠兰主编. 江苏科学技术出版社.

9. 学太极拳/张红主编. 天津：天津教育出版社, 2009. 38 页；26cm. ISBN：7530956472, 7530956477

10. A beginner's guide to taijiquan/Guan Yongnian. Beijing：Foreign Languages Press, 2010. 75 pages：illustrations；22cm. ＋ 1 videodisc (approximately 11 min.). ISBN：

7119060231, 7119060236

《简易太极拳养生法》,关永年著.

11. 中英日精解太极拳/包晓波,包延桥著.北京:群众出版社,2011. 216 页;26cm. ISBN:7501448753,7501448752

本书采用中文、英文、日文三种语言对二十四式太极拳进行了精辟解说.

12. 太极/胡秀娟,尹博编著.合肥:黄山书社,2011. 176 页;21cm. ISBN:7546120492, 7546120497. (中国红)

13. Taiji Qigong: twenty-eight steps/compiled by Li Ding & Bambang Sutomo; translated by Flingoh C. H. Oh. Beijing: Foreign Languages Press, 1988. 170 pages; illustrations;19cm.

《太极气功二十八式》,李丁,(印度尼西亚)陈中行编著;(马来西亚)胡泉和译.

14. Competition routines for four styles taijiquan/examined and approved by Chinese Wushu Association; translated by Xie Shoude. Beijing, China: People's Sports Pub. House of China: Distributed by China International Book Trading Corp. , 1991. 408 pages: illustrations;19cm. ISBN: 7500904355, 7500904359

《四式太极拳竞赛套路》,解守德译. 人民体育出版社.

15. Taiji quan: 48 forms/compiled by the Chinese Wushu Association. Beijing: Foreign Languages Press, 2001. 135 pages: illustrations;20cm. ISBN: 7119019643, 7119019642

《四十八式太极拳》,中国武术协会编.

16. 24 式太极拳呼吸配合法:汉英对照/毛景广编著;张学谦译.郑州:海燕出版社,2007. 3, 85 pages;28cm. ISBN:7535035561, 7535035566. (中国民间武术经典/毛景广主编)

英文题名:Breathing method of 24 form Taiji Quan.

17. 32 式太极拳呼吸配合法:汉英对照/毛景广编著;杨源译.郑州:海燕出版社,2007. 105 pages: illustrations;28cm. ISBN:7535035585, 7535035582. (中国民间武术经典/毛景广主编)

英文题名:Breathing method of 32 form Taiji Quan.

18. 42 式太极拳呼吸配合法:汉英对照/毛景广编著;郭勇译.郑州:海燕出版社,2007. 123 p.;28cm. ISBN:7535035608, 7535035604. (中国民间武术经典/毛景广主编)

英文题名:Breathing method of 42 form Taiji Quan.

19. 88 式太极拳呼吸配合法:汉英对照/毛景广编著;杨源,吴必强译.郑州:海燕出版社,2007. 7, 208 p.;28cm. ISBN:7535035639, 7535035639. (中国民间武术经典/毛景广主编)

英文题名:Breathing method of 88 form Taiji Quan.

20. 48 式太极拳呼吸配合法:汉英对照/毛景广编著;张大海,吴必强译.郑州:海燕出版社,2007. 147 pages;28cm. ISBN:7535035615, 7535035612. (中国民间武术经典/毛景广主编)

英文题名:Breathing method of 48 form Taiji Quan.

21. 太极拳进阶教程之 16 式太极剑呼吸配合法/李素玲主编/著.郑州:海燕出版社;河南电子音像出版社,2008. 45 页;28cm. ISBN:7535037800, 7535037801. (中国民间武术经典丛书)

英文题名:Breathing method of 16 form Taiji Sword.

22. 太极拳进阶教程之 16 式太极拳呼吸配合法/李素玲主编/著,赵蕊译.郑州:海燕出版社;河南电子音像出版社,2008. 65 页;28cm. ISBN:7535037817, 753503781X. (中国民间武术经典丛书)

23. Chen style Taijiquan/compiled by Zhaohua Publishing House. Hong Kong: Hai Feng Pub. Co.; Beijing, China: Zhaohua Pub. House, 1984. 227 pages: illustrations;22cm. ISBN: 9622380166, 9622380165

《陈式太极拳》. 朝华出版社.

24. Chen style Taijiquan, sword and broadsword/by Chen Zhenglei, translated by Zhang XinHu, Chen Bin, Xu Hailiang, and Gregory Bissell. Zhengzhou: Zhongzhou gu ji chu ban she, 2003. 368 pages: illustrations, portraits;21cm. ISBN: 7534823218, 7534823213

《陈氏太极拳剑刀》,陈正雷主编;张新虎等译. 中州古籍出版社.

25. 陈式太极拳老架二路:汉英对照/袁剑龙编著;吴必强译.郑州:海燕出版社,2007. 92 p.;28cm. ISBN:7535035646, 7535035647. (中国民间武术经典/毛景广主编)

英文题名:Old form's routine II of Chen-style Taiji Quan.

26. 陈式太极拳新架二路:汉英对照/袁剑龙编著;刘世翔,吴必强译.郑州:海燕出版社,2007. 6, 123 pages;28cm. ISBN:7535035653, 7535035655. (中国民间武术经典/毛景广主编)

英文题名:New form's routine II of Chen-Style Taiji Quan.

27. 56 式陈式太极拳:汉英对照/高秀明编著;赵艳霞译.郑州:海燕出版社,2007. 137 p.;28cm. ISBN:7535035622, 7535035620. (中国民间武术经典/毛景广主编)

英文题名:56 form Chen family Taiji Quan.

28. 陈式太极拳老架一路:汉英对照/毛景宇编著;何航宁译.郑州:海燕出版社,2007. 162 p.;28cm. ISBN:7535035554, 7535035558. (中国民间武术经典/毛景广主编)

英文题名:Old form's routine I of Chen-style Taiji Quan.

29. 陈式太极拳新架一路:汉英对照/毛景宇编著;赵艳霞译.郑州:海燕出版社,2007. 6, 164 pages;28cm. ISBN:7535035660, 7535035663. (中国民间武术经典/毛景广主编)

英文题名:New form's routine I of Chen-style Taiji Quan.

30. 26 式陈式太极拳:汉英对照/任天麟编著;赵艳霞译.郑

州：海燕出版社，2007．65 pages；28cm．ISBN：7535035578，7535035574．（中国民间武术经典/毛景广主编）

英文题名：26 form Chen Family Taiji Quan.

31. 38式陈式太极拳/李素玲主编．郑州：海燕出版社：河南电子音像出版社，2008．109 页；28cm．ISBN：7535037879，7535037879．（中国民间武术经典丛书）

英文题名：38 form Chen Family Taiji Quan.

32. 陈氏太极拳十九势/陈自强编著，郭勇[等]翻译．郑州：海燕出版社：河南电子音像出版社，2008．116 页；28cm．ISBN：7535037930，7535037933．（中国民间武术经典丛书）

33. 陈氏太极拳三十四式：中英文对照/刘云香著．太原：山西科学技术出版社，2011．286 页；21cm．ISBN：7537737203，7537737207．（国术丛书）

34. 陈氏太极拳七十四式：中英文对照/刘云香著．太原：山西科学技术出版社，2011．300 页；21cm．ISBN：7537737180，7537737185．（国术丛书）

35. 陈氏太极拳四十八式：中英文对照/刘云香著．太原：山西科学技术出版社，2011．224 页；21cm．ISBN：7537737197，7537737193．（国术丛书）

36. T'ai-chi touchstones：Yang family secret transmissions/compiled and translated by Douglas Wile. Brooklyn, N. Y.（622 Union St., Brooklyn 11215）：Sweet Ch'i Press, c1983. xii, 159 p.：ill., ports.；21cm.

《杨家太极拳秘诀》，Wile, Douglas（美国汉学家）编译．

37. Taiji Quan Yang style/Yu Gongbao. Beijing, China：Foreign Languages Press, 1996. 194 pages：illustrations；20cm. ISBN：7119018078, 7119018072.（Chinese Wushu series）

《太极拳：杨式》，余功保著．

38. Wu style taijiquan/Wang Peisheng & Zeng Weiqi; editor Zeng Weiqi and Yu Shenquan; traductor Zeng Weiqi and Li Jiaqiao; ubierta e ilustraciones Li Shiji. Beijing, China：Morning Glory：China International Book Trading Corporation, 1983. 234 p., [3] h. dela'ms.：il.；22cm. ISBN：750540427X, 7505404274

《吴氏太极拳》，王培生，曾维祺编著．朝华出版社．

G743　拳术

1. Chinese boxing and kungfu/written by Fan Tingqiang; translated by Yang Daping; illustrated by Li Zhaoqiu and Shi Lin. Jinan, China：Shandong Friendship Press, 1998. 122 pages：illustrations；27cm. ISBN：7805519870, 7805519876

《中国拳术与功夫》，樊廷强著；杨太平译．山东友谊出版社．

2. Basics of long-style boxing/Cheng Huikun. Beijing：Foreign Languages Press, 1996. 179 pages：illustrations；21cm. ISBN：7119015389, 7119015385.（Chinese Wushu series）

《长拳拳术入门》，程慧琨著．

3. Advanced routines of long-style boxing/by Cheng Huikun. Beijing：Foreign Languages Press, 1996. 190p.：illus.；21×14cm. ISBN：7119017918, 7119017914.（Chinese Wushu series）

《长拳拳术提高套路》，程慧琨著．

4. Mantis boxing/Zhang Yuping. Beijing：Foreign Languages Press：Distributed by China International Book Trading Corp., 1998. 182 pages；illustrations；21cm. ISBN：7119018035, 7119018034.（Chinese Wushu series）

《螳螂拳》，张玉萍著．

5. 大洪拳：汉英对照/释永信主编．郑州：河南人民出版社，2007. 4, 153 pages；21cm. ISBN：7215061637, 7215061639.（少林寺拳谱）

英文题名：Shaolin monastery's compendium of pugilism.

6. 鹰爪拳/李素玲 主编；凌长鸣著；赵蕊译．郑州：海燕出版社：河南电子音像出版社，2008．70；28cm．ISBN：7535037954，753503795X.（中国民间武术经典丛书）

英文题名：Eagle claw quan.

7. 翻子拳/李素玲主编．郑州：海燕出版社：河南电子音像出版社，2008．88 页；28cm．ISBN：7535038081，7535038085.（中国民间武术经典丛书）

英文题名：Fan zi quan.

8. 劈挂拳/李素玲主编．郑州：海燕出版社：河南电子音像出版社，2008．75 页；28cm．ISBN：7535038074，7535038077.（中国民间武术经典丛书）

英文题名：Pi gua quan.

9. 武松脱铐拳/李素玲主编．郑州：海燕出版社：河南电子音像出版社，2008．69 页；28cm．ISBN：7535038029，7535038026.（中国民间武术经典丛书）

10. 综合形意拳/李素玲主编，赵蕊译．郑州：海燕出版社：河南电子音像出版社，2008．64 页；28cm．ISBN：7535038012，7535038018.（中国民间武术经典丛书）

11. 游身八卦掌/李素玲主编．郑州：海燕出版社：河南电子音像出版社，2008．95 页；28cm．ISBN：7535037961，7535037968.（中国民间武术经典丛书）

12. 中国武术入门之初级长拳/李素玲，郭笑丹主编．郑州：海燕出版社：河南电子音像出版社，2008．54 页；28cm．ISBN：7535037855，7535037852.（中国民间武术经典丛书）

英文题名：The basic form of Chinese Wushu primary Chang quan.

13. 中国道家养生功夫之太乙五行拳/李素玲主编．郑州：海燕出版社：河南电子音像出版社，2008．80 页；28cm．ISBN：7535037992，7535037992.（中国民间武术经典丛书）

14. 卢氏心意六合拳入门：中英文对照/余江著．太原：山西科学技术出版社，2011．132 页；21cm．ISBN：7537735032，7537735034.（国术丛书）

15. 卢氏心意六合拳开拳：中英文对照/余江著．太原：山西科学技术出版社，2011．146 页；21cm．ISBN：

7537735025, 7537735026. (国术丛书)

G744 刀术

1. Basics of broadsword play/Dong Wenyu. Beijing, China: Foreign Languages Press, 1993. 138 pages: illustrations; 19cm. ISBN: 0835128490, 0835128490, 7119015028, 7119015026. (Chinese Wushu series)

《刀术入门》,董文玉著.

2. 《中国单刀:从基本技术到表演套路的教学全书》,谢志奎编著.北京:外文出版社,1990. ISBN:7119008307

3. 29式陈式太极剑:汉英对照/任天麟编著;吴必强译.郑州:海燕出版社,2007. 4, 68 p.; 28cm. ISBN: 7535035424, 7535035426. (中国民间武术经典/毛景广主编)

英文题名:29 form Chen family Taiji sword.

4. 42式太极剑呼吸配合法:汉英对照/毛景广编著;张学谦译.郑州:海燕出版社,2007. 5, 81 p.: ill.; 28cm. ISBN: 7535035592, 7535035590. (中国民间武术经典/毛景广主编)

英文题名:Breathing method of 42 form Taiji sword.

5. 双手剑/李素玲主编.郑州:海燕出版社:河南电子音像出版社, 2008. 58 页; 28cm. ISBN: 7535038036, 7535038034. (中国民间武术经典丛书)

6. 中国武术入门之初级剑术/李素玲,郭笑丹主编.郑州:海燕出版社:河南电子出版社 2008. 46 页; 28cm. ISBN: 7535037862, 7535037860. (中国民间武术经典丛书)

英文题名:The basic form of Chinese Wushu primary sword play.

7. 中国武术入门之初级刀术/李素玲,郭笑丹主编.郑州:海燕出版社:河南电子音像出版社,2008. 52 页; 28cm. ISBN:7535037824, 7535037828. (中国民间武术经典丛书)

英文题名:The basic form of Chinese Wushu primary broadsword play.

8. 苗刀/李素玲主编.郑州:海燕出版社:河南电子音像出版社,2008. 42 页; 28cm. ISBN: 7535038067, 7535038069. (中国民间武术经典丛书)

G745 器械

1. 中国武术入门之初级棍术/李素玲,郭笑丹主编.郑州:海燕出版社:河南电子音像出版社,2008. 62 页; 28cm. ISBN:7535038098, 7535038093. (中国民间武术经典丛书

英文题名:The basic form of Chinese Wushu primary cudgel play.

2. 双节棍/李素玲主编.郑州:海燕出版社:河南电子音像出版社, 2008. 43 页; 28cm. ISBN: 7535038005, 753503800X. (中国民间武术经典丛书)

英文题名:Two-segmented cudgel.

3. 陈氏太极齐眉棍/陈自强编著,郭勇[等]翻译.郑州:海燕出版社:河南电子音像出版社,2008. 92 页; 28cm. ISBN: 77535037947, 7535037941. (中国民间武术经典丛书)

4. Basics of spear play/Qiu Pixiang. Beijing: Foreign Languages Press,1999. 207 pages: illustrations;21cm. ISBN: 7119013920, 7119013923. (Chinese Wushu series)

《枪术入门》,邱丕相著.

5. 中国武术入门之初级枪术/李素玲,郭笑丹主编.郑州:海燕出版社:河南电子音像出版社,2008. 66 页; 28cm. ISBN:7535037848, 7535037844. (中国民间武术经典丛书)

英文题名:The basic form of Chinese Wushu primary spear play.

6. 陈氏太极二十四枪/陈自强编著,郭勇翻译.郑州:海燕出版社:河南电子音像出版社,2008. 113 页; 28cm. ISBN: 7535037886, 7535037887. (中国民间武术经典丛书)

7. 陈氏太极梢杆/陈自强编著,郭勇[等]翻译.郑州:海燕出版社:河南电子音像出版社,2008. 92 页; 28cm. ISBN: 7535037893, 7535037895. (中国民间武术经典丛书)

8. 醉剑/李素玲主编.郑州:海燕出版社:河南电子音像出版社,2008. 88 页; 28cm. ISBN: 7535037978, 7535037976. (中国民间武术经典丛书)

英文题名:Drunk sword.

9. 护手双钩/李素玲主编/著.郑州:海燕出版社:河南电子音像出版社,2008. 76 页; 28cm. ISBN: 7535038050, 7535038050. (中国民间武术经典丛书)

英文题名:Double hooks.

10. Soft weapons—nine-section whip and rope dart/Li Keqin and Li Xingdong. Beijing: Foreign Languages Press, 1996. 213 pages: illustrations; 20cm. ISBN: 7119018833, 7119018836

《软器械:九节鞭和绳镖》,李克勤,李兴东著.

G745 气功

1. 14-series sinew-transforming exercises/compiled [i. e. written] by Chang Weizhen; translated by Hong Yunxi. Beijing: Foreign Languages Press, 1988. 117 pages: illustrations; 19cm. ISBN: 0835123111, 0835123112, 7119006363; 7119006369. (Traditional Chinese therapeutic exercises and techniques)

《易筋经十四段功法录》,常维祯编著,洪允息译.

2. 中国道家养生功夫之易筋经/李素玲主编.郑州:海燕出版社:河南电子出版社,2008. 77 页; 28cm. ISBN: 7535037985, 7535037984. (中国民间武术经典丛书)

3. Transmitting qi along the meridian: meridian qigong/compiled and presented by Li Ding. Beijing: Foreign Languages Press, 1988. 260 pages: illustrations;19cm. ISBN:0835123227,0835123228,7119007777,7119007779

《经络气功》,李丁编著.

4. 八段锦:英文/国家体育总局健身气功管理中心编.北京:外文出版社,2007. 58 pages:图;22cm. ＋光盘 1 张. ISBN: 7119047817, 7119047812. (健身气功丛书)

5. Liu zi Jue/compiled by the Chinese health Qigong Association. Beijing: Foreign language Press, 2007. [2],

［1］，73 pages：illustrations（some color）；21cm. ＋1 DVD（sound，color；4 3/4 in.）. ISBN：7119047805, 7119047809.（Chinese Health Qigong）

《六字诀：英文》，国家体育总局健身气功管理中心编；周宗欣译.（健身气功丛书）

6. Yi jin jing/compiled by the Chinese Health Qigong Association. Beijing：Foreign Languages Press，2008, 2007. 95 pages：illustrations（some color）；22cm. ＋1 DVD-ROM. ISBN：7119047782, 7119047787.（Chinese health qigong）

《易筋经：英文》，国家体育总局健身气功管理中心编；周宗欣译.（健身气功丛书）

7. Wu Qin Xi. China：Foreign Languages Press，2008. 103 p. ＋DVD. ISBN：7119047799, 7119047795.（Chinese health Qigong）

《五禽戏：英文》，国家体育总局健身气功管理中心编；王台翻译.（健身气功丛书）

8. 10-minute primer：qigong/Zhou Qingjie. Beijing：Foreign Languages Press，2009. 93 pages：color，illustrations；23cm. ＋1 DVD. ISBN：7119054636, 7119054635, 1592650972, 159265097X.（10-minute primer）

《十分钟学会气功：英文》，周庆杰编写.

9. Tao and longevity：mind-body transformation/Huai-Chin Nan；translated by Wen Kuan Chu. Beijing：Orient Press，2008. 179 pages：illustrations；23cm. ISBN：7506032728, 7506032724

《静坐修道与长生不老》，南怀瑾著. 东方出版社.

G746　少林功夫

1. 72 consummate arts secrets of the Shaolin temple/compiled by Wu Jiaming；translated by Rou Gang；revised by Yang Yinrong. Fujian，China：Fujian Science and Technology Pub. House，1990. 285 pages：illustrations；21cm. ISBN：7533504860, 7533504861

《少林武术秘传绝技72功法》，吴佳明编；柔刚译. 福建科学技术出版社.

2. Chinese Shaolin Kung fu/editor-in-chief，Fang Yongming；text by Lü Hongjun；translated by Wang Dongmei. Beijing：China Pictorial Publishing House，2005. 193 pages：chiefly color illustrations；26cm. ISBN：7800248992, 7800248993

《中国少林功夫：英文》，房永明编著. 中国画报出版社.

3. 少林功夫：汉英对照/冯永臣，释永信主编. 北京：中国旅游出版社，2007. 29cm. ISBN：7503229667, 7503229664
英文题名：Shaolin kung-fu. 全面介绍了少林的武功.

4. 少林拳：汉英对照/毛景广编著；吴必强译. 郑州：海燕出版社，2007. 3, 64 p.；28cm. ISBN：7535035431, 7535035434.（中国民间武术经典/毛景广主编）
英文题名：Shaolin boxing.

5. 少林柔拳：汉英对照/毛景广编著；刘萍译. 郑州：海燕出版社，2007. 67 pages；28cm. ISBN：7535035516, 7535035515.

（中国民间武术经典/毛景广主编）
英文题名：Shaolin soft boxing.

6. 少林小洪拳：汉英对照/毛景广编著；郭勇译. 郑州：海燕出版社，2007. 70 p.；28cm. ISBN：7535035714, 753503571X.（中国民间武术经典/毛景广主编）
英文题名：Shaolin small-form Hong boxing.

7. 少林大洪拳：汉英对照/杨华编著；刘萍，吴必强译. 郑州：海燕出版社，2007. 3, 73 p.；28cm. ISBN：7535035448, 7535035442.（中国民间武术经典/毛景广主编）
英文题名：Shaolin Da-hong boxing.

8. 少林七星拳：汉英对照/杨华编著；田建勤译. 郑州：海燕出版社，2007. 3, 59 p.；28cm. ISBN：7535035691, 7535035698.（中国民间武术经典/毛景广主编）
英文题名：Shaolin qixing boxing.

9. 少林八极拳：汉英对照/毛景广编著；吴必强，陈思译. 郑州：海燕出版社，2007. 3, 80 p.；28cm. ISBN：7535035677, 7535035671.（中国民间武术经典/毛景广主编）
英文题名：Shaolin eight extremes boxing

10. 少林六合拳：汉英对照/刘海科编著；刘海超译. 郑州：海燕出版社，2007. 139 p.；28cm. ISBN：7535035684, 753503568X.（中国民间武术经典/毛景广主编）

11. 10-minute primer：Shaolin quan/Zhou Zhihua，Zhou Qingjie. Beijing：Foreign Languages Press，2009. 85 pages：color illustrations；23cm. ＋1 DVD. ISBN：7119054612, 7119054619, 1592650866, 1592650864
《十分钟学会少林拳》，周庆杰主编.

12. 少林寺拳谱. 一路梅花刀 The 1st routine of plum blossom broadsword/释永信主编. 郑州：河南人民出版社，2010. 51 页；21cm. ISBN：7215071360, 7215071367
英文题名：The ist routine of plum blossom broadsword

13. 少林寺拳谱. 二路梅花刀 The 2nd routine of plum blossom broadsword/释永信主编. 郑州：河南人民出版社，2010. 50 页；21cm. ISBN：7215071438, 721507143X
英文题名：The 2nd routine of plum blossom broadsword.

14. 少林寺拳谱. 三路梅花刀 The 3rd routine of plum blossom broadsword/释永信主编. 郑州：河南人民出版社，2010. 44 页；21cm. ISBN：7215071445, 7215071448
英文题名：The 3rd routine of plum blossom broadsword.

15. 少林寺拳谱. 少林烧火棍 The routine of extra-long poker/释永信主编. 郑州：河南人民出版社，2010. 49 页；21cm. ISBN：7215070981, 7215070980
英文题名：A Shaolin Monastery's Compendium of Pugilism. The Routine of Extra-long Poker.

16. 少林寺拳谱. 少林十三枪 The routine of Shisan tasseled spear/释永信主编. 郑州：河南人民出版社，2010. 32 页；21cm. ISBN：7215070974, 7215070972
英文题名：A Shaolin Monastery's Compendium of Pugilism. The Routine of Shisan.

17. 少林梅花单刀：汉英对照/纪秀云编著；赵艳霞译. 郑州：海燕出版社，2007. 65 p.；28cm. ISBN：7535035493, 7535035493.（中国民间武术经典/毛景广主编）

英文题名：Shaolin plum-blossom single broadsword.

18. 少林春秋大刀：汉英对照/高秀明编著；赵艳霞译. 郑州：海燕出版社，2007. 4，83 p.；28cm. ISBN：7535035486，7535035485.（中国民间武术经典/毛景广主编）

英文题名：Shaolin spring-autumn broadsword.

19. 少林朴刀：汉英对照/李素玲编著；杨璐僖，许定国译. 郑州：海燕出版社，2007.4，73 p.；28cm. ISBN：7535035523，7535035523.（中国民间武术经典/毛景广主编）

英文题名：Shaolin Long-hilt broadsword.

20. 少林齐眉棍：汉英对照/纪秋云编著；杨璐僖译. 郑州：海燕出版社，2007. 4，70 p.；28cm. ISBN：7535035707，7535035701.（中国民间武术经典/毛景广主编）

英文题名：Shaolin cudgel level with eyebrow.

21. 少林六合棍：汉英对照/刘海科编著；刘海超译. 郑州：海燕出版社，2007. 5，79 p.；28cm. ISBN：7535035455，7535035450.（中国民间武术经典/毛景广主编）

英文题名：The Shaolin cudgel with six unifications.

22. 少林罗汉十三式：汉英对照/毛景广著；陈福兴，林玄弘译. 郑州：海燕出版社，2007. 3，77 p.；28cm. ISBN：7535035479，7535035477.（中国民间武术经典/毛景广主编）

英文题名：Shaolin Luohan 13 form.

23. 少林童子功：汉英对照/毛景广编著；赵艳霞译. 郑州：海燕出版社，2007. 2，88 p.；28cm. ISBN：7535035509，7535035507.（中国民间武术经典/毛景广主编）

英文题名：Shaolin virgin boy exercise.

24. 少林六合枪：汉英对照/刘海科编著；刘海超译. 郑州：海燕出版社，2007. 6，101 p.；28cm. ISBN：7535035462，7535035469.（中国民间武术经典/毛景广编著）

英文题名：The Shaolin spear with six unifications.

G747　其他

1. Wushu exercise for life enhancement/Yu Gongbao. Beijing, China：Foreign Languages Press, 1991. 88 pages：illustrations；19cm. ISBN：0835128814，0835128810，7119014110，7119014111.（Chinese Wushu series）

《武术养生功》，余功保编著.

2. 祖国传统养生基础：汉英对照/邹建卫主编. 成都：四川科学技术出版社，2006. 26cm. ISBN：7536460805，7536460805

本书主要介绍祖国传统养生基础内容，还包括太极拳、太极剑等，中英文对照.

3. 女子防身术/李素玲主编. 郑州：海燕出版社：河南电子音像出版社，2008. 66 页；28cm. ISBN：7535038043，7535038042.（中国民间武术经典丛书）

英文题名：Women self-defence technique.

H 类　语言、文字

H1　汉语

1. Chinese phonetic system and language：（English translation)/by Li Chin-Shi；tr. into English by Alex. R. Mackenzie. Shanghai：Commercial Press，1922. ii，56，ii，ii，ii，pages：illustrations；23cm.

《英译国语学讲义》，黎锦熙（1890—）著；Mackenzie, Alexander R. 译.

(1)［S. l.］：Nabu Press，[2010]. ISBN：1176372483，1176372481

2. Reform of the Chinese written language/[by Chou En-lai... et al.；transl. from the Chinese]. Peking：Foreign Languages Press, 1958. 69 p.；19cm.

Contents：Current tasks of reforming the written language/Chou En-lai—Report on the current tasks of reforming the written language and the draft scheme for a Chinese phonetic alphabet/Wu Yu-chang—Scheme for a Chinese phonetic alphabet—Resolution of the National People's Congress on the scheme for a Chinese phonetic alphabet—Resolution of the State Council on the promulgation of the draft scheme for a Chinese phonetic alphabet—A summary of the efforts of the Chinese people over the past sixty years to create a phonetic alphabet/Wu Yu-cheng and Li Chin-hsi.

《中国的文字改革》，周恩来等.

(1)［2nd ed.，rev. translation］. Peking：Foreign Languages Press，1965. 62 pages：tables；19cm.

3. The historical evolution of Chinese languages and scripts ＝［Zhongguo yu wen de shi dai yan jin]/Zhou Youguang；translated by Zhang Liqing. Columbus, Ohio：National East Asian Languages Resource Center, Ohio State University 2003. xix，xix，198，213 p.；23cm. ISBN：0874153492.（Pathways to advanced skills；vol. 8)

《中国语文的历史演进》，周有光著；张立清译.

4. Chinese language/Du Zhengming. Beijing：China Intercontinental Press，2011. 174 pages：color illustrations；23cm. ISBN：7508520186，7508520181.（Chinese lifestyle）

《中国的语言》，杜争鸣著. 五洲传播出版社.

H2　文字学

1. The six scripts；or, The principles of Chinese writing. A translation by L. C. Hopkins. With a memoir of the translator by W. Perceval Yetts. Cambridge，［Eng.］：University Press，1954. xxvii，84 p. port.，facsim. 22cm.

Notes：Facsimile of the translation published in Amoy，1881：p. 1—83.

《六书故》，戴侗（1200—1285）；Hopkins, Lionel Charles（1854—1952）译. 初版于 1881 年.

2. Chinese writing ＝ Wen tzu hsüeh kai yao/by Qiu Xigui；translated by Gilbert L. Mattos and Jerry Norman. Berkeley, Calif.：Society for the Study of Early China and the Institute of East Asian Studies, University of

California，Berkeley，2000. ISBN：1557290717.（Early China special monograph series；no. 4）

《文字学概要》，裘锡圭（1935—）著；马几道（Mattos，Gilbert Louis，1939—）（美国汉学家），罗杰瑞（Norman，Jerry，1936—2012）（美国汉学家）合译.

3. Evolutionary illustration of Chinese characters/written and sketched by Li Leyi；translated by Jiang Lizhu. Beijing：Beijing Language and Culture University Press，2000. 500 pages：illustrations；21cm. ISBN：7561908520，7561908525

《汉字演变五百例续编》，李乐毅著；蒋立珠译. 北京语言文化大学出版社. 英汉对照.

4. Chinese characters then and now ＝ Han zi gu jin tan/Essays by Qi Gong…［et al.］；translated by Jerry Norman，Helen Wang，Wang Tao；edited by Huang Qi. Zürich：Edition Voldemeer；Wien；New York：Springer，2004. 136，132 p.，［84］p. of plates：ill.，facsims.；34cm. ISBN：3211227954.（Ginkgo series；v. 1.）

《汉字古今谈》，启功（1912—2005）著；罗杰瑞（Norman，Jerry，1936—2012）（美国汉学家）等译.

5. Five thousand years of Chinese characters. Beijing，China：Foreign Languages Press：China International Publishing Group，2009. 189 pages：illustrations（some color）；23cm. ISBN：7119060156，7119060155.（Confucius Institute Collection）

《汉字五千年》，《汉字五千年》编委会编著.

6. 汉字/师妏编著. 合肥：黄山书社，2016. 143 页：图；23cm. ISBN：7546125022.（印象中国）

英文题名：Chinese characters. 汉英对照.

7. 商代甲骨中英读本/（美）陈光宇［等］编著. 上海：上海人民出版社，2017. 535：图；29cm. ISBN：7208140868

英文题名：Reading of Shang inscriptions

8. Heroines of Jiangyong：Chinese narrative ballads in women's script/translation ＆ introduction by Wilt L. Idema. Seattle：University of Washington Press，c2009. viii，181 p.：ill.；23cm. ISBN：0295988412，029598841X，0295988429，0295988428

《江永县女书》，伊维德（Idema，W. L.〈Wilt L.〉，1944—）（荷兰汉学家）译.

H3 成语、格言

1. Chinese idioms and their stories/written by Zhang Ciyun. Beijing：Foreign Languages Press，1996. 202 pages：illustrations；18cm. ISBN：7119017748，7119017747

《中国成语故事》，张慈云编著.

2. Chinese idioms and their stories/by Li Shutian. Beijing：Chinese International Radio Press，1999. 408 pages：illustrations. ISBN：7507816370，7507816372.（Chinese language teaching series）

《中国成语故事》，李树田编译. 中国国际广播出版社.

3. 常用成语典故集锦 ＝ A collection of Chinese idioms and their stories（汉英对照）/赵新生编著. 合肥：中国科学技术大学出版社，2004. 23，502 pages；21cm. ISBN：7312016669，7312016660

本书选取近300条汉语成语典故，采用汉英对照方式，介绍成语出处，讲解成语典故内容.

4. 中国成语故事：汉英对照/蓝田编；田玮卓，王力，袁磊，黄玉翠译. 天津：百花文艺出版社，2005. 3 册. ISBN：7530640259（v. 1），7530640258（v. 1），7530640267（v. 2），7530640265（v. 2），7530642111（v. 3），7530642115（v. 3）

5. 中国成语故事：汉英对照/沈红，汤璐编著. 广州：广东教育出版社，2006. 167 页：图；20cm. ISBN：7540664290，7540664299.（中国经典文化故事系列）

英文题名：Stories of Chinese idioms. 收集了约 80 个在中国广为流传的成语故事.

6. 中国成语故事选/杨立义编选、英译；张晓丽白话文翻译. 北京：中国对外翻译出版公司，2007. 435 页；21cm. ISBN：7500118138.（中译经典文库·中华传统文化精粹）

英文题名：Chinese idioms and their stories

7. Idiom stories/compiled by Wu Min. Beijing：China Intercontinental Press，2011. 165 pages：color illustrations；19cm. ISBN：7508517735，7508517733.（Classic stories of China）

《中国成语故事》，伍民编. 五洲传播出版社.

8. 中国历代名人名言：双语对照本/尹邦彦，尹海波编注. 南京：译林出版社，2009. 234 页；23cm. ISBN：7544707947，7544707946

英文题名：A collection of Chinese maxims. 收录的条目共 1000 余则.

9. 中国古典名言录/孙通海，张燕婴，梁继红著；周远梅译. 北京：学苑出版社，2010. 34 页，340 页；21cm. ISBN：7507735857，7507735850

收录中国历代古典名言 624 条，所选名言内容包括儒、道、墨、法、阴阳、医、兵、杂等诸子百家，上迄先秦，下至晚清.

10. Chinese wisdom：thoughts for harmonious ＆ victorious living/comp. ＆ tr. by Cheng Lin ＆ Lin Susan. Shanghai，China：The World Book Co.，Ltd.，1947. vii，71，35 pages：illustrations；20cm.

《中国谚语》，郑麟，林素珊译. 英汉对照.

11. 最新中国俚语：汉英对照/李淑娟，颜力钢编. 3 版（修订版）. 北京：新世界出版社，2006. 365 页；21cm. ISBN：7800055647，7800055645

英文题名：New slang of China. 本书收录 1500 多条最流行的现代俚语.

12. 中华益智歇后语与俗语精选：中英版/陶吴馨，门淑敏编著. 北京：中国时代经济出版社，2010. 198 页；24cm. ISBN：7511900678，7511900674.（汉语走向世界丛书）

青少年读物.

H4 语法

1. Chinese syntactic system and second language acquisition/

Xiaojun Wang. Beijing：Hua yu jiao xue chu ban she，2000.9，243 pages；21cm. ISBN：7800525511，7800525513
《华语语法习得探讨》，王晓钧著.华语教学出版社.

H5 古代汉语读物

1. Elementary Chinese/［Wang Yinglin］；translated and annotated by Herbert A. Giles. 2nd ed.，rev. Shanghai：Kelly & Walsh，1910. 178 pages；26cm.
   《三字经》，王应麟（1223—1296 年）；翟理斯（Giles，Herbert Allen，1845—1935）（英国汉学家）译.
   (1) Elementary Chinese/［by Wang Ying-lin］；translated and annotated by Herbert A. 2nd ed.，rev. New York：Ungar，1963. vii，178 pages；25cm.
   (2) 2nd ed.，rev. Taipei，Taiwan：Literature House，1964. 178 pages；22cm.
   (3)［台北］：文致出版社，1973. 189 pages；21cm.
   (4) 2nd ed.，rev. Taipei：Ch'eng Wen Pub. Co.，1975. vii，178 pages；22cm.
   (5)［Taipei］：Confucius Pub. Co，1984. 189 pages；21cm.

2. San tzu ching explicated，the classical initiation to classic Chinese couplet I to XI/Friedrich A. Bischoff. Wien：Verlag der Österreichischen Akademie der Wissenschaften，2005. 310 p.；ill.；24cm. ISBN：3700133979，3700133971. (Beiträge zur Kultur-und Geistesgeschichte Asiens；Nr. 45). (Sitzungsberichte/Österreichische Akademie der Wissenschaften. Philosophisch-Historische Klasse；719 Bd.)
   《三字经》（选译），王应麟（1223—1296）；Bischoff，Friedrich Alexander（1928—）译.英汉对照.

3. Three character classic/English translation by Chen Dyen H. C；book art design by Shaqi. Singapore，NetUCC Academy Publisher，2005. 59 pages；illustrations；29×11cm. ISBN：9810538146，9810538149
   《三字经》，陈宏材译.

4. 三字经·千字文：汉英对照/（宋）王应麟，（梁）周兴嗣著；孟凡君，彭发胜译注. 北京：中国对外翻译出版公司，2007. 231 页；21cm. ISBN：7500112013，7500112017
   英文题名：Three-character canon；Essay of one thousand characters

5. The three character classic：a bilingual reader of China's ABC's/original Chinese text by Wang Yinglin；translated and annotated by Phebe Xu Gray. Paramus，N. J.：Homa & Sekey Books，c2011. xviii，191 p.；ill.；24cm. ISBN：1931907712，1931907714. (Chinese language—Readers)
   《三字经》，王应麟（1223—1296）；Gray，Phebe X.（1969—）译.
   (1) 2nd ed. Paramus，N. J.：Homa & Sekey Books，2012. xi，191 pages；illustrations；23cm. ISBN：1931907781，1931907781

6. Three-character classic/by Kathy S. X. Wu B. A. and C.

S. Tee Ph. D. Singapore：China Publishing House，2014. 113 pages；21cm. ISBN：9810777968，9810777965. (Learn modern simplified Chinese language series)
Contents："Translated from the Chinese classic 三字经."
《三字经》，Wu，Kathy S. X. 和 Tee，C. S. 合译.

7. 英韵《三字经》/赵彦春译/注. 北京：高等教育出版社，2017. 250 页：彩图；17x28cm. ISBN：7040483567. (赵彦春国学经典英译系列)
   英文题名：Three word primer in English rhyme

8. 三字经，千字文，孝经：汉英对照＝The three-character canon，the Thousand character writing，the Book of filial piety：Chinese-English/（宋）王应麟，（南北朝）周兴嗣著；孟凡君，彭发胜，顾丹柯注译. 北京：中译出版社，2016. 16，297 p.；24cm. ISBN：7500142300，7500142307. (大中华文库＝Library of Chinese classics)

9. Grammatical analysis of the Lao Ch'i-ta：with an English translation of the Chinese text/by Svetlana Rimsky-Korsakoff Dyer. Canberra：Faculty of Asian Studies，Australian National University，1983. xxii，531 p.；25cm. ISBN：0909879184. (Faculty of Asian studies monographs，0729－363X；new ser. no. 3)
   Dyer，Svetlana Rimsky-Korsakoff（1931—）；包括对《老乞大》的英译.英汉对照.

10. 三字经与中国民俗画＝Verse in three characters and genre pictures/毛增印英译. 北京：五洲传播出版社，2005. 139 pages：illustrations；23cm. ISBN：7508507991，7508507996. (中国传统文化精粹书系)
    《三字经与中国民俗画：汉英对照》，五洲传播出版社编；雪岗，杨阳译.

11. 《三字经》故事/郁辉著. 北京：五洲传播出版社，2010. 193 页；24cm. ISBN：7508517384

12. Chats in Chinese：a translation of the T'an lun hsin pien/by C. H. Brewitt-Taylor. Peking，Pei-T'Ang Press［1901］. iv，253 p. 21cm.
    《谈论新编》，Brewitt-Taylor，C. H. (1857—1938)译. (北京官话)
    (1) Shanghai，British Chamber of Commerce，1933. 89 leaves 33cm.
    (2) 谈论新编＝Chats in Chinese：a translation of the T'an lun hsin p'ien/C. H. Brewitt-Taylor［译］. 桂林：广西师范大学出版社，2011. 257 pages；22cm. ISBN：7549504510，7549504512. (日本明治时期汉语教科书汇刊；11)

13. Three-Chinese-character poem/Zhang Lizhong and Wang Zhongshu. Beijing，China：Morning Glory Publishers，1998. 139 pages：illustrations；19cm. ISBN：7505406213，7505406216
    《中华三字歌》，张立中，王忠恕. 英汉对照.

14. 《幼学琼林》故事/张梅著. 北京：五洲传播出版社，2010. 179 页；24cm. ISBN：7508517353

15. 《百家姓》故事/毕艳莉著. 北京：五洲传播出版社，2010.

193 页；24cm. ISBN：7508517391

16.《千字文》故事/姜晓东著.北京：五洲传播出版社，2010.
187 页；24cm. ISBN：7508517360

17. Standards for students：instructions in virtue from the Chinese heritage＝[Di zi gui]/[published and translated by Buddhist Text Translation Society].[translated by，Buddhist Text Translation Society].Burlingame，Calif.：Buddhist Text Translation Society，2003. 41，[11] pages：color illustrations；27cm. ISBN：0881394890，0881394894，0881397291，0881397296
《弟子规》，李毓秀.

H6 词典

1. Ch'ing administrative terms：a translation of the terminology of the six boards with explanatory notes/translated and edited by E-tu Zen Sun. Cambridge：Harvard University Press，1961. xxvii，421 p.；24cm.（Harvard East Asian studies；7.）
《清朝六部成语词典》，孙任以都（Sun, E-tu Zen，1921—）（美国华裔学者）译.

2. Chinese dictionaries：three millennia：from 1046 BC to AD 1999 ＝ Zhongguo ci dian 3000 nian/Heming Yong...[et. al.].Shanghai：Shanghai Foreign Language Education Press，2010. ix，430 p.；23cm. ISBN：7544615259，7544615251
《中国辞典 3000 年：从公元前 1046 年到公元 2000 年》，雍和明[等]著.上海外语教育出版社.

I 类 文学

I1 文学评论和研究

1. The people's new literature；four reports at the All-China Conference of Writers and Artists. Peking：Cultural Press，1950. 108 pages；19cm.
Notes：Foreword/by Emi Siao—The people's liberation war and problems in literature and art/by Chou En-lai—The struggle for the creation of New China's literature/by Kuo Mo-jo—Literature in the Kuomintang controlled areas/by Mao Tun—The people's new literature/by Chou Yang.
Notes：Reports by Zhou Enlai，Guo Moruo，Mao Dun and Zhou Yang
中华全国文学艺术工作者代表大会上的四个报告.周恩来作了长篇政治报告，郭沫若作了题为"为建设新中国的人民文艺而奋斗"的报告，茅盾、周扬分别作了关于国统区和解放区文艺运动的报告.
(1) 2nd ed. Peking：Cultural Press，1951. 136 pages；18cm.

2. The path of socialist literature and art in China：a report delivered to the Third Congress of Chinese Literary and Art Workers，on July 22，1960/Chou Yang. Peking：Foreign Languages Press，1960. 73 pages；19cm.
《中国社会主义文学艺术的道路》，周扬著.

3. Raise higher the banner of Mao Tse-tung's thought on art and literature. Peking：Foreign Languages Press，1961. 40 pages；19cm.
《更高地举起毛泽东文艺思想的旗帜》，林默涵著.

4. Some questions concerning modern revisionist literature in the Soviet Union. Peking：Foreign Languages Press，1966. 63 pages；19cm.
《苏联现代修正主义文学的几个问题》

5. Reviews of selected Chinese classics. Beijing，China：China Reconstructs Press：Dist. by China International Book Trading Corp.（Guoji Shudian），1988. 162 pages；19cm. ISBN：7507200663，7507200669
《中国古典文学名著选评》.中国建设出版社.

6. Readings in Chinese literary thought/[edited by] Stephen Owen. Cambridge，Mass.：Council on East Asian Studies，Harvard University：Distributed by Harvard University Press，1992 viii，674 p.；27cm. ISBN：0674749200.（Harvard-Yenching Institute monograph series；30）
《中国文论：英译与评论》，宇文所安（Owen, Stephen，1946—）（美国汉学家）编译.

7. The art of writing：teachings of the Chinese masters/translated and edited by Tony Barnstone and Chou Ping. Boston：Shambhala，1996. xiii，94 p.；19cm. ISBN：157062092X
《写作艺术：中国大师语录》，托尼·巴恩斯通（Barnstone, Tony，1961—）（美国诗人），周平（Chou, Ping，1957—）（美国华裔学者）编译.翻译了陆机（261—303）的《文赋》、司空图（837—908）的《二十四诗品》、魏庆之的《诗人玉屑》.文学与诗歌理论.

8. Studies of Chinese diaspora literature/Rao Pengzi；translated by Pu Ruoqian，Dai Canyu，Zhan Qiao [and others]；translation revised by Dai Weihua. Shanghai：Fu dan da xue chu ban she，2011. 2，281 pages；21cm. ISBN：7309079920，7309079922
《华文流散文学论集》，饶芃子著.复旦大学出版社.本书为中译英学术论文集，分为两部分：一是海外华文文学总论，有关海外华文诗学及各种理论问题，二是具有区域色彩的世界华文文学的个案研究，而这些个案在其地区或国内外均有很大影响.

I11 文学批评著作

陆机（261—303）

1. Literature as light against darkness：being a study of Lu Chi's "Essay on Literature"，in relation to his life，his period in medieval Chinese history，and some modern critical ideas；with a translation of the text in verse/by Shih-hsiang Chen. Peiping：National Peking U. Press，1948. 71 pages；26cm.（National Peking University semi-centennial papers，no. 11. College of Arts）
陈世骧（Chen, Shixiang 1912—）著.包括对陆机（261—

303)《文赋》的英译.

2. The art of letters; Lu Chi's "Wen fu," [New York] Pantheon Books [1951]. XVIII, 261 p. (Bollingen series, 29)

《文赋》,休士(Hughes, E. R. 〈Ernest Richard〉, 1883—1956)(美国学者)译.

3. Essay on literature/written by the third century Chinese poet Lu Chi; translated by Shih-Hsiang Chen. Rev. ed. [Portland, Me.]: [Meriden Gravure Co.], 1952. 30 pages; 29cm.

Notes: "Originally published for the semicentennial anniversary of Peking University in 1948."/ Translation of Lu Ji's Wen fu; includes Chinese text; calligraphy by Zhang Chonghe.

《陆机文赋》,陈世骧(Chen Shih-hsiang, 1912—1971)(华裔学者)译.

(1)Portland, Maine: The Anthoensen Press, 1953. 35 p.

4. Wen fu: the art of writing = [Wen fu]/Lu Chi; translation & afterword by Sam Hamill. Portland, OR: Breitenbush Books, c1987. 38 p.; 20cm. ISBN: 0932576400

《文赋》,Hamill, Sam(美国诗人)译.

(1)The art of writing: Lu Chi's Wen fu/translated by Sam Hamill. Rev. ed. Minneapolis, Minn.: Milkweed Editions, 1991. 57 p.; 23cm. ISBN: 091594362X

(2)Rev. ed. Minneapolis, Minn.: Milkweed Editions, 2000. xxxiii, 45 p.: ill.; 23cm. ISBN: 1571314121

刘勰(约 465—520)

1. The literary mind and the carving of dragons. New York: Columbia University Press, 1959. 298 p. (Records of civilization, sources and studies, no. 58)

《文心雕龙》,施友忠(Shih, Vincent Yu-chung, 1902—)译注.

(1)The literary mind and the carving of dragons: a study of thought and pattern in Chinese literature/translated and annotated by Vincent Yu-chung Shih. Hong Kong: Chinese University Press, c1983. xlix, 571 p.; 24cm. (Chinese classics)

(2)Revised edition. New revised edition. New York: The Chinese University of Hong Kong Press/NYRB, New York Review Books, [2015]. lxix, 352 pages; 22cm. (Calligrams). ISBN: 9629965853, 9629965852

2. Genre theory in China in the 3rd-6th centuries (Liu Hsieh's theory on poetic genres). Budapest, Akademiai Kiadó, 1971. 177 p. 25cm. (Bibliotheca orientalis Hungarica, 15)

Notes: Translation of: Müfajelmélet Kínában a III-VI. szábzadban.

Tökei, Ferenc 著,包括对刘勰(约 465—522)《文心雕龙》的英译.

3. The book of literary design/Siu-kit Wong, Allan Chung-hang Lo, Kwong-tai Lam. Hong Kong: Hong Kong Univ. Press, 1999. xi, 208 p.; 24cm. ISBN: 9622094643

《文心雕龙》,Wong, Siu-Kit, Lo, Allan Chung-hang 译.

严羽(生卒不详,生活在 12 世纪)

1. Tsang-lang discourse on poetry, by Yen Yü, translated from the Chinese by Peng Chun Chang; with a foreword by J. E. Spingarn. Pittsburgh, The Laboratory Press, 1929. 10 p., 1 l. 23cm.

Notes: There are five parts in the Discourse on poetry—Definition of poetry, Styles of poetry, Method of poetry, Judgments of poetry and Proofs of poetry. Only two parts are given here—Definition of poetry and Method of poetry—and not even these in full. cf. Translator's note.

《沧浪诗话》,Chang, Pêng-ch'un(1892—)译.本书只翻译了其中的《诗辨》《诗法》2 部分.

元好问(1190—1257)

1. Poems on poetry: literary criticism by Yuan Hao-wen, 1190—1257/John Timothy Wixted; calligraphy by Eugenia Y. Tu. Wiesbaden: Steiner, 1982. xvi, 482 p.; 24cm. ISBN: 3515039147

《论诗诗—元好问的文学批评》,魏世德(Wixted, John Timothy)著.对金末元初元好问的《论诗三十首》作了详尽的翻译和分析.

王国维(1877—1927)

1. Poetic remarks in the human world—Jen chien tzŭ hua. Taipei: Chung Hwa Book Co. 59 i. e. [1970]. iii, 60 p. 22cm.

《人间词话》,涂经诒译.

2. Wang Kuo-wei's Jen-chien tz'u-hua: a study in Chinese literary criticism/[translated] by Adele Austin Rickett. Hong Kong: Hong Kong University Press, 1977. xv, 133 p.; 23cm. ISBN: 9622090036

《人间词话》,李又安(Rickett, Adele Austin)译.

陆志韦(1894—1970)

1. On Chinese poetry, five lectures. Peiping, 1935. 2 p. l., 2—118 p. 24cm.

Notes: Some poems in Chinese and English.

《中国诗五讲》

2.《中国诗五讲》陆志韦著.北京:外语教学与研究出版社,1982. 182 页;21cm.

英文题名:Five lectures on Chinese poetry.

周扬(1908—1989)

1. China's new literature and art: essays and addresses/Chou Yang. Peking: Foreign Languages Press, 1954. 156 p.

《周扬文艺论文集》

2. A great debate on the Literary front/by Shao Chuan-lin. [Translated by Yang Hsien-yi and Gladys Yang]. Peking: Foreign Languages Press, 1958. 72 pages; 19cm.

Notes：Appendix：'Clear the Road and Advance Boldly'
by Shao Chuan-lin.

《文艺战线上的一场大辩论》，杨宪益（1915—2009），戴乃迭（Yang, Gladys, 1919—1999）译.

(1) 2nd ed. Peking：Foreign Languages Press，1964. 72 pages；19cm.

(2) 3rd ed. Peking：Foreign Languages Press，1965. 57 pages；19cm.

钱钟书（1910—1998）

1. Patchwork：Seven essays on art and literature/by Qian Zhongshu；translated by Duncan M. Campbell. Leiden；Boston：Brill，2014. x，285 pages；25cm. ISBN：9004270206，9004270205，9004270213，9004270213. (East Asian Comparative Literature and Culture；1) Campbell, Duncan (Duncan Murray)译. 收录钱钟书论文学与艺术的7篇文章.

王佐良（1916—1995）

1. 论契合：比较文学研究集/王佐良著；梁颖译. 北京：外语教学与研究出版社，2015. 348 页；23cm. ISBN：7513526449.（"博雅双语名家名作"系列）
英文题名：Degrees of affinity：studies in comparative literature. 英汉对照.

顾城（1956—1993）

1. Essays, interviews, recollections and unpublished material of Gu Cheng, the 20th century Chinese poet：the poetics of death/edited with an introduction and translations by Li Xia. Lewiston：Edwin Mellen Press，1999. xx，433 pages：illustrations（some color）；24cm. ISBN：0773480056，0773480056，0889460760（set），0889460768（set）.（Chinese studies；v. 5）
《死亡的诗学：二十世纪中国诗人顾城的随笔、访谈、回忆录和未发表材料》，Li，Xia 编.

I12　各体文学评论和研究

诗歌研究

1. 诗歌史话/《中华文明史话》编委会编译. 北京：中国大百科全书出版社，2009. 176 页；21cm. ISBN：7500080602，7500080603

2. 唐诗/李葳葳编著. 合肥：黄山书社，2016. 168 页：图；23cm. ISBN：7546141763.（印象中国）
英文题名：The poetry of Tang dynasty. 英汉对照. 唐诗研究.

3. 宋词/李葳葳编著. 合肥：黄山书社，2016. 156 页：图；23cm. ISBN：7546141756.（印象中国）
英文题名：Ci-poems of the Song dynasty. 英汉对照. 宋词研究.

小说研究

1. Reflections on Dream of the red chamber/Liu Zaifu；translated by Shu Yunzhong. Youngstown，N. Y.：Cambria Press，2008. xxiii，301 p.；24cm. ISBN：1604975246
《红楼梦悟》，刘再复（1941—）；舒允中（1955—）（美国华裔学者）译.

2. A study of two classics：a cultural critique of The Romance of the Three Kingdoms and The Water Margin/Liu Zaifu；translated by Shu Yunzhong. Amherst，New York：Cambria Press，2012. xxxi，254 pages；24cm. ISBN：1604978278.（Cambria Sinophone world series）
《双典批判：对〈水浒传〉和〈三国演义〉的文化批判》，刘再复（1941—）；舒允中（1955—）译.

3. 四大名著/徐刚编著. 合肥：黄山书社，2016. 132 页：图；23cm. ISBN：7546152882.（印象中国）
英文题名：China's four great classic novels. 英汉对照.

4. A brief history of Chinese fiction，［by］Lu Hsun ［pseud.］. Translated by Yang Hsien-yi and Gladys Yang. ［New ed.］. Peking：Foreign Languages Press，1959. 462 p.，illus.，20cm. (China knowledge series，7)
《中国小说史略》，鲁迅（1881—1936）；杨宪益（1915—2009），戴乃迭（Yang, Gladys, 1919—1999）译.

(1) 2nd ed. Peking：Foreign Languages Press，，1964. 462 p.

(2) Westport，Conn.，Hyperion Press，［1973］. 462 p. illus. 23cm. ISBN：0883550652，0883550656. (China knowledge series；no. 7)

(3) 3rd ed. Peking：Foreign Languages Press，1976. 437 p.，［19］leaves（1 fold.）of plates：ill.；19cm.

(4) 3rd ed. Peking：Foreign Languages Press，1982. 437 pages，［19］leaves（1 folded）of plates：illustrations；19cm.

(5) Honolulu：University Press of the Pacific，2000. 437 p.：ill.；21cm. ISBN：0898751543，0898751543

(6) Beijing：Foreign Languages Press，2009. 437 pages：illustrations；24cm. ISBN：7119057507，7119057502

(7) Beijing：Foreign Languages Press；San Francisco：China Books，2014. xii，318 pages；23cm. ISBN：0835100700，0835100707

I13　文学史

1. 风骚国度＝The land of literary glory/马晓东著；陈海燕，张韶宁译. 北京：外语教学与研究出版社，2005. 203 p.；24cm. ISBN：7560041159，7560041155.（中国 100 话题丛书：汉英双语）
汉英对照的语言读物，精辟地介绍了中国上古到现代的基本文学现象、文学思潮.

2. Chinese literature/Yao Dan；translated by Li Ziliang，Li Guoqing & Zhao Feifei. Beijing：China Intercontinental Press，2007. 157 p.：il. col.；23cm. ISBN：7508509792，750850979X. (Cultural China series)
《中国文学》，姚丹编著；李子亮等译. 五洲传播出版社.

(1) Chinese literature：great tradition since The Book of Songs/Yao Dan；translated by Li Ziliang［and three others］. 2nd edition. Beijing：China Intercontinental

Press, 2010. 251 pages: illustrations (some color); 23cm. ISBN: 7508515861, 7508515862. (Cultural China series)

3. Concise history of Chinese literature/by Luo Yuming; translated with annotations and an introduction by Ye Yang. Leiden; Boston: Brill, 2011. 2 v. (xxvii, 987 p.); 25cm. ISBN: 9004203662（set），9004203664（set），9004203686（v. 1），9004203680（v. 1），9004203693（v. 2），9004203699（v. 2）. (Brill's humanities in China library; v. 4/1−2)

《简明中国文学史》；骆玉明（1951—）；Ye，Yang（1948—）译.

4. A short history of classical Chinese literature/Feng Yuan-Chun; Translated by Yang Hsien-yi and Gladys Yang. Peking: Foreign Languages Press, 1958. 132 pages: illusrrations; 19cm. (China knowledge series)

《中国古典文学简史》，冯沅君（1902—1974）；杨宪益（1915—2009），戴乃迭（Yang，Gladys，1919—1999）译.

(1) Westport, Conn., Hyperion Press［1973］. 132 p. illus. 23cm. ISBN: 0883550660. (China knowledge series.)

(2) Beijing: Foreign Languages Press, 2009. 132 pages: illustrations; 24cm. ISBN: 7119057514, 7119057510. (China studies＝学术中国)

5. An outline history of classical Chinese literature/by Feng Yuanjun; translated by Yang Xianyi and Gladys Yang. Hongkong: Joint Pub. Co., 1983. 114 p.: ill.; 21cm. ISBN: 9620402278

《中国古代文学史大纲》，冯沅君（1902—1974）；杨宪益（1915—2009），戴乃迭（Yang，Gladys，1919—1999）译.

6. 文学：汉英对照/魏崇新著；张保红译. 北京：人民文学出版社，2006. 213 页；21cm. ISBN: 7020048811, 7020048816. (中国传统文化双语读本)

英文题名：Literature. 本书介绍中国古代文学史重要作品和主要作家.

7. A short history of modern Chinese literature. Peking: Foreign Languages Press, 1959. 310 p. 19cm. (China knowledge series［4］)

《中国现代文学史略》，丁易（1913—1954 年）著.

(1) Port Washington, N. Y., Kennikat Press［1970］. 310 p. 19cm. ISBN: 0804608725

(2) Beijing: Foreign Languages Press, 2010. iv, 312 pages; 24cm. ISBN: 7119065373, 7119065378. (China Studies ＝中国学术)

8. History of modern Chinese literature/edited by Tang Tao. Beijing: Foreign Languages Press, 1993. ii, 517 pages; 20cm. ISBN: 7119014595, 7119014593, 083512464, 9 0835124645

《中国现代文学史》，唐弢主编；胡志挥等英译.

9. History of contemporary Chinese literature/by Hong Zicheng; translated by Michael M. Day. Leiden; Boston: Brill, 2007. xix, 636 p.; 25cm. ISBN: 9004157545, 9004157549, 7301040393（original Chinese ed.），7301040393（original Chinese ed.）. (Brill's humanities in China library, v. 1)

《中国当代文学史》，洪子诚；Day，Michael M. 译. 20 世纪中国文学评论.

(1) Leiden; Boston: Brill, 2009. xix, 636 p.; 25cm. ISBN: 9004173668, 9004173668. (Humanities in China library; v. 1). (Brill's humanities in China library; v. 1.)

10. Tibetan literature/written by Wu Wei, Geng Yufang, translated by Xiao Liping. Beijing: China Intercontinental Press, 2005. 132 pages: color illustrations; 21cm. ISBN: 7508506852, 7508506855. (Series of basic information of Tibet of China)

《西藏文学：英文》，吴伟，耿予方著. 五洲传播出版社（中国西藏基本情况丛书/郭长建，宋坚之主编）. 本书介绍了西藏文学发展的历史，包括作家、作品介绍.

11. Literature and the arts/compiled by the China Handbook Editorial Committee; translated by Bonnie S. McDougall and Hu Liuyu. Beijing: Foreign Languages Press: Distributed by China Publications Centre（Guoji Shudian），1983. 217 pages, ［24］pages of plates: illustrations; 19cm. ISBN: 0835109895, 0835109895. (China handbook series)

《文学艺术》，《中国手册》编辑委员会编.

I2　作品集

I21　古代和跨时代作品综合集

1. A guide to Wenli styles and Chinese ideals: essays, edicts, proclamations, memorials, letters, documents, inscriptions, commercial papers, Chinese text with English translation and notes, by Evan Morgan. Shanghai, Christian Literature Society for China, 1912. vi, 414, 46, 26, 2 p., 22cm.

Morgan, Evan（1860—）译. 包括对中国文学作品的翻译，以供西方读者的中文学习之用.

(1) Shanghai: Christian Literature Society of China; London: Probsthain, 1931. 494 pages in various pagings; 22cm.

2. The dragon book, compiled and edited by E. D. Edwards. London［etc.］: W. Hodge and Company, Limited［1938］. 367 p. illus. 19cm.

Note: An anthology of prose and verse translations from Chinese, and of passages relating to China: includes sections of medical lore, Chinese cookery, and Japanese flower arrangement.

中国文学翻译集. Edwards, E. D.（Evangeline Dora, 1888—）编. 包括《三国演义》的一些选译.

(1) Folcroft, Pa.: Folcroft Library Editions, 1979. p.

19cm. ISBN：0841440018

3. Gems from Chinese literature：rendered into English/by Lin Yutang. Yupuwet Studio Bilingual ed. Hong Kong：Shanghai Pub. ，1965. 111 pages；19cm.

中国文学英译. 林语堂(1895—1976)译.

4. Anthology of Chinese literature/compiled and edited by Cyril Birch；Associate editor, Donald Keene. New York：Grove Press［1965—72］. 2 v. 21—24cm. ，21cm. ISBN：0394177665. （UNESCO collection of representative works：Chinese series).

Contents：v. 1. From early times to the 14th century. — v. 2. From the 14th century to the present day.

《中国文学选集》，共 2 卷，白之(Birch, Cyril, 1925—)(美国汉学家)编译. 夏志清(C. T. Hsia)和白之合作英译的《西游记》第二十三回.

(1) Harmondsworth, Penguin, 1967. 3 — 487 p. 19cm. (Penguin classics, L203)

5. A treasury of Chinese literature：a new prose anthology, including fiction and drama/translated and edited by Ch'u Chai and Winberg Chai. New York：Appleton-Century, 1965. xi, 484 pages；22cm.

Notes："The book is divided into three parts, covering general prose, fiction, and drama, in twelve chapters, each of which is devoted to a major phase of the field. In addition, each chapter is preceded by a brief introduction dealing with the historical and literary background against which the selected materials were written. We have also given biographical sketches of th writers concerned as well as a critical commentary of their works."—Page vii.

翟楚(Ch'u Chai, 1906 — 1986)和翟文伯(Winberg Chai)合译，包括中国散文、小说和戏剧.

(1) Greenwich, Conn. ，Fawcett Publications, 1972. 320 pages；18cm. ISBN：0815203527, 0815203520. （A Fawcett premier book，；M562)

(2) New York：T. Y. Crowell, 1974. xi, 484 pages；20cm. (Apollo editions，；A352)

(3) 1st Ballantine Books ed. New York：Fawcett Premier, 1990. 318 p. ；18cm. ISBN：0449218538, 0449218532

6. Chinese literature/H. C. Chang. Edinburgh：Edinburgh University Press；Chicago：Aldine Pub. Co. ，1973. 3 volumes ⟨1, 3⟩；21cm. ISBN：0852242409 （v. 1), 0852242407 (v. 1), 0852243146 (v. 2), 0852243145 (v. 2), 0231057946(v. 3), 0231057943(v. 3)

Contents：［1］ Popular fiction and drama—2. Nature poetry—3. Tales of the supernatural

中国文学英译. 张心伧 Chang, H. C. (Hsin-Chang)编，3 卷. 包括小说与戏剧，诗歌，神话故事.

(1) New York：Columbia University Press, 1977. 3 v. ；21cm. ISBN：0231053673 (v. 1), 0231042884 (v. 2), 0231057946 (v. 3)

7. Chinese literature；an anthology from the earliest times to

the present day. Rutland, Vt. ，Tuttle ［1974］. 836 p. ；19cm. ISBN：0804808821

中国文学翻译集. McNaughton, William(1933—)编.

8. A sampler of Chinese literature from the Ming Dynasty to Mao Zedong/translated, compiled and edited by Sidney Shapiro. Beijing：Panda Books；Distributed by China International Book Trading Corp. ，1996. 312 pages；23cm. ISBN：7507103455, 7507103458, 0835131815, 0835131810

《中国文学集锦：从明代到毛泽东时代》，沙博理编译. 中国文学出版社.

9. An anthology of Chinese literature：beginnings to 1911/edited and translated by Stephen Owen. 1st ed. New York：W. W. Norton, c1996. xlviii, 1212 p. ；25cm. ISBN：0393038238, 0393038231, 0393971066, 0393971064

《中国文学选集：初始至 1911 年》，宇文所安(Owen, Stephen, 1946—)(美国汉学家)编译，包括了除八股文之外的文学载体.

10. Gems of Chinese literature, by Herbert A. Giles. Rev. and greatly enl. Edition. Shanghai, Kelly and Walsh, Limited, 1922. 287 p. front. (port.)；30cm.

Contains：brief biographical notices of all the authors quoted, and an English-Chinese index of their names

《古文选珍》修订扩大版，翟理斯(Giles, Herbert Allen, 1845—1935)(英国汉学家)编译.

(1) New York：Paragon Book Reprint Corp. ［1965］. xviii, 430 p. 23cm. Reprint of the 2nd rev. and enl. ed.

(2)［Place of publication not identified］：［Grizzell Press］, 2013. xv, 254 pages；22cm. ISBN：1446018057, 1446018059

11. Wen xuan, or, Selections of refined literature/Xiao Tong；translated, with annotations and introduction by David R. Knechtges. Princeton, N. J. ：Princeton University Press, c1982—c1996. 3 v. ；25cm. ISBN：0691053464. (Princeton library of Asian translations)

《文选》(选译)，萧统(501—531)；康达维(Knechtges, David R.)译. 计划分 8 册出版《昭明文选》全集 60 卷.

12. The Columbia anthology of traditional Chinese literature/Victor H. Mair, editor. New York：Columbia University Press, c1994. xxxvii, 1335 p. ；maps；24cm. (Translation from the Asian classics). ISBN：023107428X

《哥伦比亚中国古典文学选集》，梅维恒(Mair, Victor H. ，1943—)(美国翻译家)编译.

13. The shorter Columbia anthology of traditional Chinese literature/Victor H. Mair, editor. New York：Columbia University Press, c2000. xxx, 741 p. ；map；25cm. ISBN：0231119984, 0231119992. (Translations from the Asian classics)

《哥伦比亚中国古典文学选集简编》，梅维恒(Mair, Victor H. ，1943—)(美国翻译家)编译.

14. Classical Chinese literature：an anthology of translations/

John Minford and Joseph S. M. Lau, editors. New York：Columbia University Press; Hong Kong：The Chinese University Press, c2000. 1 v.；ill.；24cm. ISBN：0231096763, 0231096768, 9622016251, 9622016255

v. I. From antiquity to the Tang dynasty—

《含英咀华集》(第一卷：从远古至唐代),闵福德(Minford, John., 1946—)(英国汉学家),刘绍铭(Lau, Joseph S. M., 1934—)(美国华裔学者)合译.中国古典文学集.

(1)New York；Chichester：Columbia University Press, 2002. lix,1176 pages：illustrations, maps;23cm. ISBN：0231096771,0231096775,9629960486,9629960483

15. Readings in classical Chinese poetry and prose：glossaries, analyses/Naiying Yuan, Haitao Tang, James Geiss. Princeton, NJ：Princeton University Press, 2006. xii, 285 p.；28cm. ISBN：0691118321,0691118329

中国古典诗歌与散文. Yuan, Naiying, Tang, Hai-tao 和 Geiss, James 编译.

16. Poetry and prose of the Han, Wei and Six dynasties. Beijing, China：Chinese Literature：Distributed by China International Book Trading Corp., 1986. 228 pages；18cm. ISBN：0835116069, 0835116060. (Panda books)

Contents：Han-Dynasty verse essays—"Yuefu" folk-songs—Poems of the Wei, Jin and later periods—Poems by Tao Yuanming—The bride of Jiao Zhongqing—A selection of early ghost and fairy stories—Selections from "New anecdotes of social talk"—Record of Buddhist countries—Carving a dragon at the core of literature

Notes：Translated from Chinese by Yang Xianyi〔and others〕.

《汉魏六朝诗文选》,(晋)陶渊明等著;杨宪益,戴乃迭译.中国文学出版社(熊猫丛书)

(1)Beijing：Foreign Languages Press, 2005. 226 pages；20cm. ISBN：7119033565, 7119033563. (Panda books)

17. Poetry and prose of the Tang and Song/translated by Yang Xianyi and Gladys Yang. Beijing, China：Chinese Literature：Distributed by China International Book Trading Corp., 1984. 310 p.；18cm. ISBN：0835111644, 0835111645. (Panda books)

《唐宋诗文选》,杨宪益(1915—2009),戴乃迭(Yang, Gladys,1919—1999),Hu Shiguang 译.收集了唐宋时期18个著名作家的诗歌散文.

(1)Beijing, China：Foreign Languages Press：Distributed by China International Book Trading Corp., 2005. 298 pages；20cm. ISBN：7119033557, 7119033556. (Panda books)

18. Chinese prose literature of the T'ang period, 618—906. London, A. Probsthain, 1937—38.2. v. 20cm.

Contents：v. 1. Miscellaneous literature. v. 2. Fiction.

唐代文集. Edwards, Evangeline Dora(1888—)编.

19. Poetry and prose of the Ming and Qing. Beijing, China：Chinese Literature：Distributed by China International Book Trading Corp., 1986. 350 pages；18cm. ISBN：0835116050, 0835116053. (Panda books)

Notes：Translated from Chinese by Yang Xianyi〔and others〕.

《明清诗文选》,杨宪益等译.

20. Pilgrim of the clouds：poems and essays/by Yüan Hung-tao and his brothers；translated and introduced by Jonathan Chaves. New York：Weatherhill, 1978. 143 p.；ill.；21cm. ISBN：0834801345, 0834801349

齐皎瀚(Chaves, Jonathan)译.翻译了袁宏道(1568—1610 年),袁宗道(1560—1600),袁中道(1570—1623)三兄弟的诗文.

(1)〔New York：AMS Press, 1974〕. 2 v. 22cm. ISBN：0404569714

(2)Buffalo：White Pine Press, 2005. 162 pages：illustrations；18cm. ISBN：1893996395, 1893996397. (Companions for the journey；vol. 9)

21. Ballads and stories from Tun-huang：an anthology/Arthur Waley. London：G. Allen & Unwin, 1960. 273 pages；22cm.

Contents：The swallow and the sparrow—Wu Tzu-hsü—The Crown Prince—Han P'eng—The story of Shun—The story of catch-tiger—Confucius and the boy Hsiang T'o—The story of Hui-yüan—The wizard Yeh Ching-neng—Meng Chiang-nü—T'ien K'un-lun—The ballad of Tung Yung—The doctor—The world of the dead—T'ai Tsung in hell—Kuan Lo—Hou Hao—Wang Tzu-chen—Tuan Tzu-ching—Marriage songs—The Buddhist pieces—Buddha's marriage—Buddha's son—Ananda—The devil—Mu-lien rescues his mother.

《敦煌歌谣和故事选集》,韦利(Waley, Arthur, 1889—1966)(英国汉学家)译.依据《敦煌变文集》(共有变文78 篇)译出俗文学作品 26 篇:"燕子赋"、"伍子胥变文"、"庐山远公话"、"叶净能诗"、"下女夫词"、"目连变文"、"孟姜女变文"、"太子成道经"、"破魔变文"、"秦瑗"、"前汉刘家太子传"、"董永变文"、"唐太宗入冥记"等.

22. Ballads and stories from Tun-huang；an anthology〔by〕Arthur Waley. London：G. Allen & Unwin〔1960〕. 273 p. 22cm.

《敦煌文书》,韦利(Waley, Arthur, 1889—1966)(英国汉学家)译.

(1)New York：Macmillan, 1960. 273 p. 22cm.

(2)Taipei, Mei Ya Publications, 1972. 273 pages；23cm.

(3)London：Routledge, 2005. 273 pages；24cm. ISBN：0415361737,0415361736. (China, history, philosophy, economics；29)

(4)London：Routledge，2011. 1 volume；24cm. ISBN：0415612647，0415612640

23. K'uei hsing：a repository of Asian literature in translation/edited by Liu Wu-chi... ［et al.］. Bloomington：［Published］for the International Affairs Center ［by］Indiana University Press，［1974］. xii，176 p.：ill.；25cm. ISBN：0253391016. （Indiana University East Asian series）

《魁星：亚洲文学翻译集》，柳无忌（1907—2002）（美国华裔学者）编。

24. 中国古代诗文名篇精选英文译注＝ Selected famous ancient Chinese poems and articles in English translation/张敬群译注. 北京：北京时代华文书局，2017. ISBN：7569912777. 12，14，322 页；24cm.

I22 现当代作品综合集

1. Modern literature from China/edited and introduced by Walter J. Meserve and Ruth I. Meserve. New York：New York University Press，1974. x，337 pages；24cm. ISBN：0814753701，0814753705. （The Gotham library）
   Contents：1. Short stories. The true story of Ah Q/Lu Hsun—Spring silkworms/Mao Tun—The family on the other side of the mountain/Chou Li-Po—Brother Yu takes office/Lao Sheh. Tantzu. Praying for rain/Yang Pin-kuei.
   2. Poetry. Farewell to the God of Plague；The long march；Snow；Swimming/Mao Tse-tung—Protect peace/Ai Ching—The nameless nine/Soong Ching-ling—The mothers' problem/Yang Yang-tse—Sanmen Gorge/Ho Ching-chih—A young Sudanese；Artistic freedom；Museums—London，New York：and points west/Yuan Shui-po.
   3. Drama. Thunderstorm/Tsao Yu.
   4. Essays and speeches. Talks at the Yenan forum on literature/Mao Tse-tung—Romanticism and realism/Kuo Mo-jo.
   5. Miscellaneous forms. Two hired hand brothers/Anonymous—Revolutionary aphorisms/Anonymous—A new canteen and old memories/Chao Shu-li—Rightful owners；On meals/Anonymous.
   现代中国文学英译. Meserve，Walter J. 与 Meserve，Ruth I. 合编. 包括 20 世纪中国的短篇小说、诗歌、戏剧、散文等.

2. Revolutionary literature in China：an anthology/selected and introduced by John Berninghausen and Ted Huters. White Plains，N. Y.：M. E. Sharpe，1976. 103 pages：illustrations；29cm.
   Contents：Introductory essay/John Berninghausen and Ted Huters—We shall meet again：short story (1914)/Zhou Shou-juan—People who insult people：essay (1921)/Ye Sheng-tao—A literature of blood and tears：essay (1921)/Zheng Zhen-duo—On the bridge：essay (1923)/Ye Sheng-tao—Revolution and literature：essay (1926)/Guo Mo-ruo—From a literary revolution to a revolutionary literature：essay (1928)/Zheng Fangwu—From Guling to Tokyo：essay (1928)/Mao Dun—Who's 'We'?：essay (1932). The question of popular literature and art：essay (1932)/Qu Qiu-bai—A day：short story (1930)/Ding Ling—In front of the pawnshop：short story (1932)/Mao Dun—Hatred：short story （1932)/Zhang Tian-yi—Man and wife learn to read：one-act Yangge play (1945)/Ma Ke—Silence：short story(1957)/Qin Zhao-yang—The guest：short story （1964）/Zhou Li-bo—Debut：short story (1966)/Hao Ran.
   Notes：First published in two issues of the Bulletin of Concerned Asian Scholars，vol. 8，nos. 1 and 2.
   中国短篇小说与随笔. Berninghausen，John David 与 Huters，Theodore 选编.

3. Light from the East：an anthology of Asian literature：China，Japan，Korea，Vietnam，and India/William McNaughton. New York：Dell，1978. 427 p.；18cm. ISBN：0440347122
   McNaughton，William(1933—)编. 对亚洲 5 国文学作品的翻译,包括对中国文学的翻译.

4. Two writers and the cultural revolution：Lao She and Chen Jo-hsi/edited by George Kao. Hong Kong：Chinese University Press；Seattle：Distributed by University of Washington Press，1980. 212 pages：illustrations；28cm. ISBN：9622012027，9622012028. （A Renditions book）
   Notes：Includes Lao She's pre-1949 output and Chen's writings in English and/or Chinese，together with essays about the two writers.
   乔志高(Kao，George,1912—2008)编. 收录老舍 1949 年前的作品和陈若曦的中英文作品,以及对 2 位作家的评论文章.

5. Literature of the hundred flowers/edited by Hualing Nieh. New York：Columbia University Press，1981. 2 volumes；24cm. ISBN：0231050747，0231050746，0231050763，0231050760，0231052642，0231052641. （Modern Asian literature series）
   Contents：v. 1. Criticism and polemics. —v. 2. Poetry and fiction.
   中国文学英译. 聂华苓(1925—)编译.

6. The Columbia anthology of modern Chinese literature/Joseph S. M. Lau and Howard Goldblatt，editors. New York：Columbia University Press，1994. xliii，726 pages；25cm. ISBN：0231080034，0231080033. （Modern Asian literature series）
   Contents：pt. 1. Fiction，1918—1949—pt. 2. Fiction，1949—1976—pt. 3. Fiction since 1976—pt. 4. Poetry，1918—1949—pt. 5. Poetry，1949—1976—pt. 6. Poetry since 1976—pt. 7. Essays，1918—1949—pt. 8. Essays，1949—1976—pt. 9. Essays since 1976.

《哥伦比亚中国现代文学读本》，刘绍铭（Lau, Joseph S. M., 1934—）（美国华裔学者），葛浩文（Goldblatt, Howard, 1939—）（美国翻译家）编.

(1) New York：Columbia University Press, c1995. xliii, 726 p.；25cm. ISBN：0231080026, 0231080026. (Modern Asian literature series)

(2) 2nd ed. New York：Columbia University Press, c2007. xliv, 737 p.；25cm. ISBN 0231138407, 0231138406, 0231138415, 0231138413, 0231511000 (e-book), 0231511001 (e-book). (Modern Asian literature)

7. 世纪才女诗文锦集/林徽因，苏雪林，陆小曼等著；李珍编译. 南京：译林出版社, 2011. 213 页；21cm. ISBN：7544715362, 7544715361

英文题名：A collection of modern Chinese women writers. 本书选辑了 20 世纪中国八位女作家的经典诗文，英汉对照. 这八位女作家是萧红、庐隐、石评梅、苏雪林、林徽因、陆小曼、冰心、丁玲. 每个作家选辑 3 篇，共计 24 篇. 每位作家的作品前附有简短介绍，译文后有注释. （诗歌、散文集）

8. Autumn harvest；selections from contemporary creative writings of the People's Republic of China. Editors：Afro-Asian Book Club. Lahore, 1966. 320 p.；18cm.

新中国文学作品. Afro-Asian Book Club 编译出版.

9. Literature of the People's Republic of China/edited by Kai-yu Hsu, co-editor, Ting Wang, with the special assistance of Howard Goldblatt, Donald Gibbs, and George Cheng. Bloomington：Indiana University Press, c1980. xiv, 976 p.；24cm. ISBN：0253160154. (Chinese literature in translation)

《中华人民共和国文学》，许芥昱（Hsu, Kai-yu, 1922—）（美国华裔学者），丁望（Ting Wang）等编译. 论述了 122 位作家，其中包括 208 篇译文.

(1) Bloomington：Indiana University Press, 1998. 2 v. (xiv, 976 p.)；24cm. (Chinese literature in translation)

10. Mao's harvest：voices from China's new generation/edited by Helen F. Siu and Zelda Stern. New York：Oxford University Press, 1983. lvi, 231 pages：illustrations；24cm. ISBN：0195032748, 0195032741, 0195034996, 0195034998

Contents：Foreword/Jonathan Spencer—Part I. Faith—Why is life's road getting narrower and narrower? (letter)/Pan Xiao—The two generations (essay). A generation (poem). Shooting a photograph (poem). I am a willful child (poem)/Gu Gong—Reply (poem)/Bei Dao—Part II. Family—Remorse (story)/Zhang Jie—Overpass (novella)/Liu Xinwu—Part III. Love—Love cannot be forgotten (story)/Zhang Jie—The corner forsaken by love (story)/Zhang Xian—Longing (poem)/Shu Ting—Part IV. Work—The foundation (story)/Jiang Zilong—Trust (story)/Chen Zhongshi—Part V. Politics—General, you can't do this! (poem). Whom are you writing about? (essay)/Ye Wenfu—In the wake of the storm (poem)/Shu Ting—At the denunciation meeting (story)/Wang Peng—The two realms of love (poem). Epigraph (poem)/u Cheng—Second encounter (story)/Jin He—The get-together (story)/Gan Tiesheng—Part VI. Appendix—Proletarian dictatorship is a humanitarian dictatorship (essay)/Wang Xizhe—China's new generation of politicians (interview)/Wei Ming.

《毛的收获：中国新一代的声音》，萧凤霞（Siu, Helen F.）和 Stern, Zelda 编译. 20 世纪中国文学.

11. Stubborn weeds：popular and controversial Chinese literature after the Cultural Revolution/edited by Perry Link. Bloomington：Indiana University Press, c1983. 292 p.；24cm. ISBN：0253355125, 0253355126, 0253203112, 0253203113. (Chinese literature in translation)

《倔强的草：文革后中国大众争议文学》，林培瑞（Link, E. Perry, 1944—）译. 包括小说、诗歌和戏剧.

(1) Bloomington：Indiana University Press, 1996. 292 pages；24cm. ISBN：0253355125, 0253355126 (Chinese literature in translation)

12. Trees on the mountain：an anthology of new Chinese writing/edited by Stephen C. Soong and John Minford. Hong Kong：Chinese Universtiy Press；Seattle：Distributed by University of Washington Press, c1984. 396 p.：ill.；27cm. ISBN：962201335X, 9622013353. (A renditions book)

《山上的树》，宋淇（Soong, Stephen C. 1919—1996），闵福德（Minford, John, 1946—）（英国汉学家）编. 中国 20 世纪文学翻译作品.

13. Contemporary Chinese literature：an anthology of post-Mao fiction and poetry/edited with introductions by Michael S. Duke for the Bulletin of concerned Asian scholars. Armonk, N. Y.：M. E. Sharpe, 1985. 137 p.：ill.；29cm. ISBN：0873323394, 0873323408

《当代中国文学》，杜迈克（Duke, Michael S.）编译. 收录 1976 年之后中国的小说与诗歌.

14. Seeds of fire：Chinese voices of conscience/edited by Geremie Barmé and John Minford. 1st American ed. New York：Hill and Wang, 1988. 491 p.：ill.；24cm. ISBN：0809085216, 0809085217

《火种》，Geremie Barmé，闵福德（Minford, John, 1946—）（英国汉学家）编. 中国 20 世纪文学翻译作品.

15. Selected works by members of China PEN Centre of Shanghai. Vol. 1/［editor Zhang Lei］. Shanghai：Shanghai Translation Publ. House, 1991. 360 p.；21cm. ISBN：7532709728, 7532709724

《中国上海笔会中心作品集》（一）. 上海译文出版社.

16. Modern Chinese writers：self-portrayals/Helmut Martin

and Jeffrey Kinkley，editors；Ba Jin［and others］and thirty-three others. Armonk，NY：M. E. Sharpe，1992. xliv，380 pages；portraits；24cm. ISBN：0873328167，0873328166，0873328175，0873328173. （Studies on modern China）

Martin，Helmut（1940—）和 Kinkley，Jeffrey C.（1948—）编. 收录巴金等 33 位 20 世纪中国作家的自传和随笔.

17. Under-sky，underground/selected & edited by Henry Y. H. Zhao & John Cayley；with a foreword by Jonathan D. Spence. London：WellSweep，1994. 247 p. ；20cm. ISBN：0948454164，0948454165. （Chinese writing Today；1）

Notes："This publication is the first biennial selection of works in English translation from the best of the Chinese literary magazine Jintian（Today）. "

《〈今天〉双年选辑》，赵毅衡，Spence，Jonathan D. ，Cayley，John 选编.

18. Abandoned wine＝qi jiu/selected & edited by Henry Y. H. Zhao & John Cayley；with a foreword by Gary Snyder. London：WellSweep，1996. 314 pages；20cm. ISBN：0948454245，0948454240. （Chinese writing Today；2）

Contents：Foreword/Gary Snyder—Meetings/Ge Fei—Distance/Bai Guang—America America/Zhu Wen—Two Rabbits/Zhu Wen—Beautiful Landscape/Nan Fang—The Donglin Academy/Nan Fang—The Green Peach/Hong Ying—Gas/Hong Ying—The Model at Montparnasse/Song Lin—The Writing Maniac/Song Lin—A Moment of the Master/Wang Yin—Premonition/Xi Chuan—Kafka to Felice/Zhang Zao—A Portrait/Bei Dao—At the Sky's Edge/Bei Dao—Background/Bei Dao—Untitled/Bei Dao—February/Bei Dao—This Day/Bei Dao—In Memory of Zhu Xiang/Bai Hua—Old Poet/Bai Hua—There is No/Duo Duo—Watching the Sea/Duo Duo—Instant/Duo Duo—Only One/Duo Duo—Autumn/Ouyang Jianghe—In the Lift/Ouyang Jianghe—There Will Be Snow Tonight in New York/Dean Lu—Whales/Dean Lu—Night Vigil/Zhang Zhen—In America/Zhang Zhen—Fog/Han Dong—Seeing Beauty in a Dream/Ge Mai.

《弃酒》，赵毅衡与 Cayley，John 选译.《今天》文学杂志双年选译.

19. I wish I were a wolf：the new voice in Chinese women's literature/compiled and translated by Diana B. Kingsbury. Beijing：New World Press：Distributed by China International Book Trading Corp. ，1994. 252 pages；21cm. ISBN：7800051242，7800051241

Contents：I wish I were a wolf/Ma Zhongxing—Octday/Tie Ning—Friend on a rainy day/Bai Fengxi—Women speak/Xiang Ya—Brothers/Wang Anyi—You can't make me change/Liu Xihong—Rejecting fate/Han Chunxu.

Kingsbury，Diana B. 编译，收录小说、戏剧和访谈，包括铁凝、王安忆等中国女作家作品.

20. Writing women in modern China：an anthology of women's literature from the early twentieth century/edited by Amy D. Dooling and Kristina M. Torgeson. New York：Columbia University Press，c1998. xii，394 p. ：ill. ；24cm. （Modern Asian literature series）. ISBN：0231107005，0231107013

《现代中国女作家》，杜丽（Dooling，Amy D.）（美国学者），杜生（Torgeson，Kristina M.）（美国学者）合译. 收录中国女作家秋瑾、陈撷芬、陈衡哲、冯沅君、石评梅、庐隐、陆晶清、陈学昭、凌叔华、苏雪林、袁昌英、谢冰莹、丁玲、沈樱、林徽因、冰心、罗淑、萧红等人的作品.

21. Fissures：Chinese writing today/selected and edited by Henry YH Zhao，Yanbing Chen，John Rosenwald；foreword by Breyten Breytenbach. Brookline，MA：Zephyr Press，c2000. 308 p. ；21cm. ISBN：0939010593，0939010592

Contents：Quatrains Eulogy/Song Lin，translated by Yanbing Chen 19—Landscape over Zero Keyword Untitled Vigil Old Place As I Know It/Bei Dao，translated by Yanbing Chen & John Rosenwald 21—Fire Shadow/Xi Chuan，translated by Yanbing Chen 28—Da Ma's Way of Speaking/Zhu Wen，translated by Mao Liang 30—Guo Lusheng/Cui Weiping，translated by Su Genxing 48—Preparing His Biography/Hong Ying，translated by John Cayley 57—It's Just Like Before Five Years Those Islands Never a Dreamer Returning/Duo Duo，translated by Gregory B. Lee 58—The Death of Zilu/Hu Dong，translated by Jenny Putin 64—My Sister Lan's Specimen Book/Gao Ertai，translated by H. Batt 90—The Foreign Beach/Zhang Zhen，translated by Yanbing Chen 96—Adams River/Janet Tan，translated by by the author 98—The Hard-Working Glazier November's Guide/Lu De'An，translated by by John Cayley & Yanbing Chen 105—A May That Will Last Forever/Xu Xiao，translated by H. Batt 108—Truant Days/Gu Xiaoyang，translated by Duncan Hewitt 126—Three Short-Lived Poems from Yesterday/Zeng Hong，translated by Yanbing Chen 132—Who is the Son God Needs Godsend/Wang Yin，translated by Yanbing Chen 212—Blue Notebook/Sun Xiaodong，translated by Howard Goldblatt & Sylvia Li-chun Lin 214—Recent Research on Yu Hong/Hong Ying，translated by Desmond Skeel 224—The Composer's Tower/Yang Lian，translated by Brian Holton 244—The English Instructor at the Institute of Agriculture/Bai Hua，translated by Yanbing Chen 246—Our Hunger，Our Sleep/Ouyang Jianghe，translated by Yanbing Chen & John Rosenwald 258—Embers/Han Shaogong，translated by Thomas Moran 263—Mourning the Cat the Duck Prophet/Han Dong，translated by Yanbing Chen

280—Fang Wan's Paradise/Huang Shi, translated by Yanbing Chen 282—The Stage/Lu Dongzhi, translated by Desmond Skeel 133—From Lexicon, Nouns/Chen Dongdong, translated by Yanbing Chen 142—Night View of New York/Zhang Zao, translated by Yanbing Chen 144—The Snuff Bottle/Hong Ying, translated by Jenny Putin 148—From the Sorcerer's Book/Hu Dong, translated by Yanbing Chen 167—Brief Notes on Walls/Shi Tiesheng, translated by Desmond Skeel 170—October's Writing/You Ren, translated by Yanbing Chen 181—Taking Advantage/Han Dong, translated by Desmond Skeel 183.

《裂缝：当下中文写作》，赵毅衡、陈炎兵；Rosenwald, John 选译. 短篇小说，诗歌.

22. The big red book of modern Chinese literature：writings from the mainland in the long twentieth century/edited by Yunte Huang. New York：W. W. Norton & Company，2016. xvii，606 pages；25cm. ISBN：0393239485，0393239489

Huang, Yunte 编. 20 世纪中国大陆文学集，收录小说、诗歌.

(1) New York：W. W. Norton & Company，2017. xvii，606 pages；21cm. ISBN：0393353808，039335380X

I23　个人作品集

汉代

班昭(约 45—117)

1. Pan Chao：foremost woman scholar of China, first century, A. D. ；background, ancestry, life, and writings of the most celebrated Chinese woman of letters... by Nancy Lee Swann. New York：London, The Century Co. [c1932]. xix，179 p.，1 l. incl. maps, geneal. tab. front.，pl. ；23cm.

Notes：Thesis（Ph. D.）—Columbia university，1932. Includes and English translation of the extant writings of Ban Zhao（p. 74—[117]）and the Chinese text of the four poems（p. 100—[105]）；113—[117]). Bibliography at end of chapters I-V；"List of translations and their Chinese sources"：p. 156—162.

Swann, Nancy Lee(1881—1966)著. 是著者的博士论文，包括对班昭(约 45 年—约 117 年)作品的英译.

(1) New York：Russell & Russell [1968, c1932]. xvii，179 p. illus.，maps. ；23cm.

(2) Ann Arbor：Center for Chinese Studies, The University of Michigan，c2001. xxi，179 p. ；ill.，maps；23cm. ISBN：0892641509. (Michigan classics in Chinese studies；no. 5)

东晋

陶潜(372?—427)

1. The complete works of Tao Yuanming/translated into English by Wang Rongpei；translated into modern Chinese by Xiong Zhiqi. Changsha Shi：Hunan ren min chu ban she；Beijing：Wai yu jiao xue yu yan jiu chu ban she，2003. 50，277 pages；24cm. ISBN：754383216X，7543832169. (Library of Chinese classics＝大中华文库)

Notes：contains Tao's over 120 poems and 11 essays.

《陶渊明集》，汪榕培英译；熊治祁今译. 中英对照.

2. Gleanings from Tao Yuan-ming：prose & poetry/translated by Roland C. Fang. Taiwan：Lai Lai，1979. vi，12，201 pages；22cm.

《陶渊明诗文选译》，方重译.

(1) Hong Kong：Commercial Press，1980. vi，12，201 pages，[1] leaf of plates：portraits；22cm.

(2) 上海：上海外语教育出版社，1984. 5，179 pages：illustrations；22cm.

3. Complete works of Tao Yuanming/translated and annotated by Tan Shilin. Hong Kong：Joint Pub. (H. K.) Co.，1992. 230 pages：illustrations；21cm. ISBN：9620410300，9620410307

《陶渊明诗文英译》，谭时霖译注.

(1) [Taipei]：书林，[1993]. 230 pages：illustrations；21cm. ISBN：9575863550，9575863555

唐代

皮日休(约 834—883)

1. P'i Jih-hsiu/by William H. Nienhauser, Jr. Boston：Twayne Publishers，1979. 161 p. ；21cm. ISBN：0805763724. (Twayne's world authors series；TWAS 530：China)

Notes："Finding list of translations of P'i Jih-hsiu's works in this volume." p. 151—152.

Nienhauser, William H. 著. 对皮日休的生平介绍和作品的翻译等.

宋代

欧阳修(1007—1072)

1. The literary works of Ou-yang Hsiu（1007—1072)/Ronald C. Egan. Cambridge [Cambridgeshire]；New York：Cambridge University Press，1984. 269 p. ；24cm. ISBN：052125888X. (Cambridge studies in Chinese history, literature, and institutions)

《欧阳修的文学著作》，艾朗诺(1948—)(美国汉学家)著. 包括对欧阳修著作的翻译和解读.

文同(1018—1079)

1. Cave of the immortals：the poetry and prose of bamboo painter Wen Tong（1019—1079)/translated and introduced by Jonathan Chaves. Warren, CT：Floating World Editions，2017. xii，239 pages：illustrations；23cm. ISBN：1891640909，1891640902

文同诗文集. Chaves, Jonathan 译.

苏轼(1037—1101)

1. Selections from the works of Su Tung-p'o：(A. D. 1036—1101) translated into English/with introduction, notes and commentaries，by Cyril Drummond Le Gros Clark；

wood engravings by Averil Salmond Le Gros Clark; the foreword by Edward Chalmers Werner. London, Jonathan Cape, 1931. 180 pages: illustrations, portrait; 26cm.

《苏东坡文选》,Clark, Cyril Drummond Le Gros 译注.

(1)New York: AMS Press, 1974. 180 p. illus.; 24cm. ISBN: 0404569617, 0404569617

2. The prose-poetry of Su Tung-p'o; being translations into English of the...[fu]/With introductory essays, notes and commentaries by Cyril Drummond Le Gros Clark; the foreword by Ch'ien Chung-shu. Shanghai Kelly & Walsh, 1935. 6 preliminary leaves, vii-xxii, 280 pages plates, folded facsimile; 22cm.

苏轼散文和诗词英译. Cyril Drummond Le Gros Clark 译; 钱钟书作序.

(1)2nd ed. New York: Paragon Book Reprint Corp., 1964. xxii, 280 p. illus., facsim.; 23cm. (Paragon reprint Oriental series, no. 24)

陆游(1125—1210)

1. The old man who does as he pleases; selections from the poetry and prose of Lu Yu. Translated [from the Chinese] by Burton Watson. New York: Columbia University Press, 1973. xx, 126 p. map. 22cm. ISBN: 023103766X, 0231037662

陆游诗文选. 华兹生(Watson, Burton,1925—)(美国翻译家)译.

(1)New York: Columbia University Press, 1994. xx, 124 pages: map; 21cm. ISBN: 0231101554, 0231101554

(2)Late poems of Lu You, the old man who does as he pleases/new translations by Burton Watson; [Jesse Glass, general editor]. Burlington, Ont.: Ahadada Books; Berkeley, CA: Distributors, United States of America, Small Press Distribution, 2007. x, 73 pages; 22cm. ISBN: 0978141493, 0978141490

范成大(1126—1193)

1. Riding the river home: a complete and annotated translation of Fan Chengda's (1126—1193) Diary of a boat trip to Wu (Wuchuan lu)/James M. Hargett. Hong Kong: Chinese University Press, 2008. x, 302 pages: illustrations; 24cm. ISBN: 9629963026, 9629963027

《吴船录》,是范成大(1126—1193)诗文作品.

2. On the road in twelfth century China: the travel diaries of Fan Chengda (1126—1193)/James M. Hargett. Stuttgart: F. Steiner, 1989. xi, 343 pages. (Munchener ostasiatische Studien; Bd. 52)

《吴船录》,Hargett, James M. (James Morris, 1948—)译.

明代

袁宏道(1568—1610)

1. Pilgrim of the clouds: poems and essays from Ming China/by Yuan Hung-tao; translated by Jonathan Chaves. Inklings ed. New York: Weatherhill, 1992. 136 p.: ill; 13cm. ISBN: 0834802570

《袁宏道诗文集》,齐皎翰(Chaves, Jonathan)译.

清代

李渔(1611—1680)

1. 李渔诗赋楹联赏析/卓振英编著. 北京:外语教学与研究出版社,2011. 18 页,142 页;21cm. ISBN:7513511056, 7513511055

收录了李渔的赋、古风、格律诗、楹联六十余篇(副).

现当代

鲁迅(1881—1936)

1. 鲁迅自传及其作品/[周树人著];孟津选注. 上海:上海英文学会,1941. 77 pages;19cm.

中英对照详注.

2. Selected works of Lu Hsun. Peking: Foreign Languages Press, 1956—1960. 4 v. illus. 22cm.

《鲁迅选集》(1—4 卷),杨宪益(1915—2009),戴乃迭(Yang, Gladys,1919—1999)译.

(1)2nd ed. Peking: Foreign Languages Press, 1964. 4 volumes: illustrations, portraits; 22cm.

(2)2nd ed. Beijing: Foreign Languages Press, 1980. 4 v.: ill.; 22cm.

(3)2nd ed., 2nd print. Beijing: Foreign Languages Press, 1985. 4 volumes: illustrations, portraits; 22cm. ISBN: 0835113183, 0835113182

(4)Honolulu, Hawaii: University Press of the Pacific, 2001. 4 volumes: illustrations; 21cm. ISBN: 0898756294, 0898756296, 0898756413, 0898756418, 0898756421, 0898756425, 0898756405, 0898756401

(5)Beijing: Foreign Languages Press, 2003. 4 volumes: illustrations; 22cm. ISBN: 7119034081, 7119034089

3. Chosen pages from Lu Hsun: the literary mentor of the Chinese revolution. New York: Liberty Book Club, 1957. 315 p.

鲁迅文选.

(1)[New York]: Cameron Associates, 1959. 315: pages; 22cm.

(2)[Whitefish, Mont.]: [Kessinger Publishing], 2012. 315 pages: portraits; 22cm. ISBN: 1163141120, 1163141127

4. Silent China; selected writings of Lu Xun. Edited and translated [from the Chinese] by Gladys Yang. London, New York: Oxford University Press, 1973. xii, 196 p. 21cm. ISBN: 0192811509, 0192811509. (A galaxy book, GB 405)

《无声的中国:鲁迅作品选》,戴乃迭(Yang, Gladys, 1919—1999)译.收录小说 6 篇,旧体诗 5 首,《朝花夕拾》中的散文 5 篇,《野草》中的散文诗 7 篇,杂文 13 篇.

5. The new year's sacrifice; In memory of Miss Liu Ho-

chen/by Lu Hsun. Hong Kong：Zhao Yang Pub. Co.，1973. 76 pages：illustrations；18cm.（English-Chinese series of new writings＝袖珍英汉新文选.）

《祝福；纪念刘和珍君》.香港朝阳出版社.

闻一多（1899—1946）

1. Selected poetry and prose/Wen Yiduo；selected by the Editorial Department of Chinese Literature Press and edited by Catherine Yi-Yu Cho Woo. Beijing, China：Chinese Literature Press，1990. 131 pages；18cm. ISBN：0835120716，0835120715，7507100472，7507100471

   《闻一多诗文选》，Woo, Catherine Yi-yu Cho 编.

   (1)Beijing：Chinese Literature Press，1996. 131 pages；18cm. ISBN：7507100472，7507100471

2. Red candle and other selected writings/Wen Yiduo. Beijing：Foreign Languages Press，2009. 131 pages；20cm. ISBN：7119058863，711905886X.（Panda books）

   《红烛：闻一多作品选》，本书收录诗歌 29 篇，散文 5 篇.

老舍（1899—1966）

1. Lao She. Nanjing, Jiangsu, China：Yilin Press，1992. 3 volumes：illustrations；22cm. ISBN：7805671370（v. 1）；7805671376（v. 1）；7805671389（v. 2），7805671383（v. 2），7805671621（v. 3），7805671628（v. 3）.（Modern Chinese literature library）

   Contents：1. Camel Xiangzi；The quest for love of Lao Lee—2. The yellow storm—3. Beneath the red banner；Crescent moon and other stories；Teahouse；Dragon beard ditch.

   《中国现代文学文库·老舍》，3 卷. 译林出版社.

2. Teahouse；Camel Xiangzi/Lao She. Beijing：Foreign Languages Press，2009. 360 pages；20cm. ISBN：7119058825，7119058827

   《茶馆·骆驼祥子》.收录作者的剧本和小说各一部.

冰心（1900—1999）

1. Selected stories and prose/by Bing Xin.［Beijing］：Chinese Literature Press：Foreign Language Teaching and Research Press，1999.［6］，III，305 s.；20cm. ISBN：7507105644，7507105643.（University Reader；English-Chinese Gems of Chinese Literature. Modern）

   冰心小说和散文选.

丁玲（1904—1986）

1. I myself am a woman：selected writings of Ding Ling/edited by Tani E. Barlow with Gary J. Bjorge；introduction by Tani E. Barlow. Boston：Beacon Press，1989. 361 pages；24cm. ISBN：0807067369，0807067369，0807067475，0807067474

   Contents：Miss Sophia's diary—A woman and a man—Yecao—Shanghai, Spring 1930—Net of law—Mother—Affair in East Village—New faith—When I was in Xia Village—Thoughts on March 8—People who will live forever in my heart；remembering Chen Man—Du Wanxiang.

   我自己就是个女人：丁玲选集. 白露（Barlow, Tani E.），布乔治（Bjorge, Gary J.）编译.

巴金（1904—2005）

1. Selected works of Ba Jin/［translated by Sidney Shapiro and Wang Mingjie；illustrations by Liu Danzhai and Huang Yinghao］. Beijing：Foreign Languages Press，1988. 4 v.：ill.；22cm. ISBN：711900574X（v. 1），7119005744（v. 1），0835113191（v. 1），0835113199（v. 1），7119005758，7119005751，0835110559，0835110556

   Contents：1. The family；Autumn in spring—2. Gardens of repose；Bitter cold nights—3. The cross of love；and other stories—4. Outside a desolated garden；and other essays.

   《巴金选集》，沙博理（Shapiro, Sidney）译. 第 1 卷：选取巴金小说《家》和《春天里的秋天》两部小说. 第 2 卷：取巴金小说《憩园》和《寒夜》两部小说. 第 3 卷：选取巴金代表短篇小说 17 篇结集出版. 第 4 卷：收录巴金先生散文 22 篇.

   (1)2nd ed. Beijing：Foreign Languages Press，2005. 4 v.：ill.；22cm. ISBN：711900574X（v. 1），7119005744（v. 1），7119005758（v. 2），7119005751（v. 2），7119042076（v. 3），7119042077（v. 3），7119033271（v. 4），7119033273（v. 4）

萧乾（1910—1999）

1. Semolina and others/Hsiao Ch'ien. Hongkong：Joint Pub. Co.，1984. 125 pages，［1］leaf of plates：portraits；22cm. ISBN：9620403460，9620403460，9620403479，9620403477

   Contents：Semolina—The spinners of silk—The conversion—Scenes from the Yentang Mountains—The ramshackle car—Shanghai—Ibsen in China—The dragonbeards vs the blueprints—Translations. Wang chao chun/by Kuo Mo-jo. The tragedy on the lake/by Tien Han. The artist/by Hsiung Fo-hsi.

   《〈珍珠米〉及其他》.收录了散文和小说等.

何其芳（1912—1977）

1. Paths in dreams：selected prose and poetry of Ho Ch'i-fang/translated and edited by Bonnie S. McDougall. St. Lucia, Q.：University of Queensland Press，1976. x，244 p.；22cm. ISBN：0702212601，070221261X.（Asian and Pacific writing；7）

   McDougall, Bonnie S.（1941—）编译. 对何其芳的散文和诗作了翻译.

刘宾雁（1925—2005）

1. People or monsters?：and other stories and reportage from China after Mao/Liu Binyan；edited by Perry Link. 1st Midland book ed. Bloomington：Indiana University Press，1983. xvii，140 p.；25cm. ISBN：0253343291，0253203139.（Chinese literature in translation）

Contents：Introduction/Leo Ou-fan Lee—Listen carefully to the voice of the people/translated by Kyna Rubin and Perry Link—People or monsters? /translated by James V. Feinerman，with Perry Link—Warning/translated by Madelyn Ross，with Perry Link—The fifth man in the overcoat/translated by John S. Rohsenow，with Perry Link—Sound is better than silence/translated by Michael S. Duke

《人兽之间》，林培瑞（Link，E. Perry〈Eugene Perry〉，1944—）译.文集.

(1)Bloomington：Indiana Univ. Press，1988. XVII，140 p. ISBN：0253203139，0253203137，0253343291，0253343291

王蒙（1934—）

1. Selected works of Wang Meng/translated by Denis C. Mair；illustrated by Shen Yaoyi. Beijing：Foreign Languages Press，1989. 2 volumes；ill. ；21cm. ISBN：0835122638（v. 1），0835122634（v. 1），711901031X（v. 1），7119010311（v. 1），0835121623（v. 2），0835121620（v. 2），711900638X（v. 2），7119006383（v. 2）

Contents：1. The strain of meeting/translated by Denis C. Mair—2. Snowball/translated by Cathy Silber and Deirdre Huang.

《王蒙作品集》，丹尼斯·马尔（Mair，Denis C.）译.卷一：相见集.卷二：雪球集.

高行健（1940—）

1. Cold literature：selected works by Gao Xingjian/original Chinese text by Gao Xingjian；translated by Gilbert C. F. Fong and Mabel Lee. Hong Kong：Chinese University Press；[London：Eurospan，distributor]，2005. 1，467 p. ：ill. ，ports. ；22cm. ISBN：9629962454，9629962456.（中国现代文学中英对照系列＝Bilingual series on modern Chinese literature）

《冷的文学：高行健著作选》，方梓勋，陈顺妍英译.

杨炼（1955—）

1. Unreal city：a Chinese poet in Auckland/Yang Lian；translated by Hilary Chung and Jacob Edmond with Brian Holton；edited and introduced by Jacob Edmond and Hilary Chung. Auckland，N. Z. ：Auckland University Press，2006. 98 p. ：ill. ；22cm. ISBN：1869403541，1869403546

《幻象中的城市》，Edmond，Jacob，Chung，Hilary 和 Holton，Brian 合译.散文和诗歌.

吉晶

1. 看得见风景的房间：英汉对照/吉晶编写.成都：四川人民出版社，2007.21cm. ISBN：7220073663，7220073666

英文题名：Room with a view

丹增

1. Little Novice/by Dan Zeng；translated by Danielle Lu. Beijing：China Translation & Publishing Corporation，2017. 416 pages. ISBN：7500151586，7500151586

《小沙弥》，（英）Lu，Danielle 译.

I3 诗歌、韵文

I31 古代和跨时代诗词集

I311 诗经

1. The She king, or, The book of ancient poetry/translated in English verse，with essays and notes，by James Legge. London：Trübner，1876. iv，431 pages：map；21cm.

《诗经》，理雅各（Legge，James，1815—1897）（英国汉学家）译.中英文本.

(1)The book of poetry/Chinese text with English translation by James Legge. China，Commercial Press，1931. iv，476 pages；18cm.

(2)The book of poetry：Chinese text with English translation/by James Legge. Shanghai：Commercial Press，1940. iv，487 pages；19cm.

(3)The book of poetry /. Chinese text with English transl. by James Legge. New York：Paragon Book Reprint Corp. ，1967.iv，487 p. 20cm.

(4)The she king, or, The book of Poetry＝诗经/[译者李雅歌；编者时超]. 台北：文致出版社，[1981]. 505 pages；21cm.

(5)The Shih king, or, Book of poetry/translated by James Legge. Boston，Massachusetts：IndyPublish. com，2005. 144 pages；24cm. ISBN：1421911361，1421911366

2. The she king, or, The book of Poetry/James Legge；Chao Shi. 台北：文致出版社，[1981]. 505 pages；21cm.

《诗经》，理雅各（Legge，James，1815—1897）（英国汉学家）译.

3. The Book of Songs：Sundry texts from James Legge's translation/James Legge；Joaquim A de Jesus Guerra. Hong Kong：Aidan Publicities & Printing，1986. 670 pages：illustrations；18cm.（Chinese classics）

《诗经评注》，理雅各（Legge，James，1815—1897）（英国汉学家），Guerra，Joaquim A. de Jesus（Joaquim Angélico de Jesus）译.中英对照.

4. 诗经：大雅 颂/（英）理雅各.上海：生活.读书.新知三联书店上海分店，2014. 221 页；22cm. ISBN：7542644572.（中国汉籍经典英译名著）

英文题名：The she king：greater odes of the kingdom odes of the temple alar. 选自莱格 19 世纪出版的《中国经典》第三卷《诗经》中的"大雅"和"颂"的原著英译部分.侧重于对"大雅"和"颂"原著英语译释的把握，将原书的中英文对照的中文繁体竖排改为简体横排，使本书更加便于对"大雅"和"颂"原著的英译把握和借鉴参考.

5. 诗经：小雅/（英）理雅各译释.上海：生活.读书.新知三联书店上海分店，2014. 181 页；22cm. ISBN：7542644565.（中国汉籍经典英译名著）

英文题名：She king：minor odes of the kingdom. 本书选自理雅各 19 世纪出版的《中国经典》第三卷《诗经》中的"小雅"的原著英译部分，侧重于对"小雅"原著英语译释的把握，将原书的中英文对照的中文繁体竖排改为简体横排，使本书更加便于对"小雅"原著的英译把握和借鉴参考。

6. The book of Chinese poetry：being the collection of ballads, sagas, hymns, and other pieces known as the Shih Ching; or, Classic of poetry/metrically translated by Clement Francis Romilly Allen. London：Kegan Paul, Trench, Trübner, 1891.

《诗经》，Allen, Clement Francis Romilly(1844—1920)译.

(1)［Lavergne, Tennessee］：Nabu Public Domain Reprints, 2013. xl, 528 pages; 25cm. ISBN：1171750666, 1171750668

7. The Shi king, the old "Poetry classic" of the Chinese; a close metrical translation, with annotations, by William Jennings. London, New York ［etc.］ G. Routledge and Sons, Limited, 1891. 383 p. fold. pl. 20cm. (Sir John Lubbock's hundred books, 11)

《诗经》，Jennings, William(1847—1927)译.

(1)New York：Paragon Book Reprint, 1969. 383 pages folded plates 20cm. (Sir John Lubbock's hundred books, ll)

8. The classics of Confucius. Book of odes (Shi-king)/by L. Cranmer-Byng. London, J. Murray, 1906. 3 preliminary leaves, 5—44, ［1］ pages; 17cm. (The Wisdom of the East series)

《诗经》(选译)，孙洙(1711—1778)编；Cranmer-Byng, L. (Launcelot, 1872—1945)(英国诗人)译. 初版于 1904 年，由伦敦的 John Murray 出版.

(1)2nd ed. New York：E. P. Dutton, 1908. 56 p.; 17cm. (The wisdom of the East series).

(2)New York：E. P. Dutton, 1915. ［57］ pages; 17cm. (The wisdom of the East series)

(3)London, J. Murray, 1920. 1 preliminary leaf, 56, ［1］ pages; 17cm. (The wisdom of the East series)

9. The book of songs, translated from the Chinese by Arthur Waley. Boston, New York：Houghton Mifflin Company, 1937. 358 p. 23cm.

《诗经》，韦利(Waley, Arthur, 1889—1966)(英国汉学家)译. 在《诗经》的 305 篇中，删去了 15 首，故只收录 290 首.

(1)London：Allen & Unwin, 1937. 358, ［2］ p.; 23cm.

(2)2nd ed. London：G. Allen & Unwin, 1954. 358 pages; 23cm.

(3)New York：Grove Press ［1960］. 358 p. 21cm. (Evergreen Book, E-209)

(4)［2nd ed］. London：George Allen & Unwin, 1969. 358 pages; 23cm. ISBN：0048950076, 0048950079

(5)The book of songs：the ancient Chinese classic of poetry/translated from the Chinese by Arthur Waley. New York：Grove Press, ［1987］. xxiv, 358 p.; 21cm. ISBN：0802130216

(6)The book of songs/translated by Arthur Waley; edited with additional translations by Joseph R. Allen; foreword by Stephen Owen; postface by Joseph R. Allen. 1st ed. New York：Grove Press, c1996. xxv, 388 p.; 21cm. ISBN：0802134777, 0802134776

(7)London; New York：Routledge, 2005. 358 pages; 24cm. ISBN：0415361745, 0415361743. (China, history, philosophy, economics; 30)

(8)London ［England］; New York：Routledge, 2011. 358 p.; 24cm. ISBN：0415612654, 0415612659

10. The book of odes. Chinese text, transcription and translation by Bernhard Karlgren. Stockholm, Museum of Far Eastern Antiquities, 1950. 270 p.; 25cm.
Notes：The translation is a reprint of the one published in Bulletins 16 and 17 of the Museum of Far Eastern Antiquities

《诗经》，高本汉(Karlgren, Bernhard, 1889—1978)译.

(1)Stockholm：Museum of Far Eastern Antiquities, 1974. 270 pages; 25cm.

11. The classic anthology defined by Confucius. ［Translator］ Ezra Pound. Cambridge, Harvard University Press, 1954. 223 p.; 23cm. ISBN：0674133978, 0674133976

《诗经》，庞德(Pound, Ezra, 1885—1972)(美国诗人)译.

(1)London：Faber, 1955. xv, 223 pages; 23cm.

(2)The Confucian odes, the classic anthology defined by Confucius. ［Translation by］ Ezra Pound. ［New York：J. Laughlin, 1959, c1954］. xv, 223 p.; 21cm. ISBN：0811201537, 0811201538. (A new directions paperbook, 81)

(3)London：Faber, 1974. 306 p.; 20cm. ISBN：0571093108. (Faber paper covered editions)

(4)Cambridge：Harvard University Press, 1982. ［xv］, 223 pages: illustrations, music; 21cm.

12. New selected poems and translations/Ezra Pound; edited and annotated with an afterword by Richard Sieburth; with essays by T. S. Eliot and John Berryman. New York：New Directions Pub. Corp., c2010. xxi, 391 p.; 23cm. ISBN：0811217330, 0811217337

庞德(Pound, Ezra, 1885—1972)(美国诗人)著. 包括《诗经》的英译本《The Classic Anthology Defined by Confucius (1954)》.

13. The book of rhymes：feudatory-states canon; rhymes of feudatory states/translated, annotated and commented by Fen-chin Young. Hong Kong：Terrestrial Press, 1964. xxv, 204; 19cm.

《诗经国风》，Young，Fen-chin 译注. 英汉对照.

14. The book of rhymes：feudatory-states canon；rhymes of feudatory states/translated，annotated and commented by Fen-chin Young. Hong Kong：Terrestrial Press，1964. xxv，204；19cm.

《诗经》，Young，Fen-chin 编译. 英汉对照.

15. The book of songs. New York：Twayne Publishers［1971］. 167 p.；21cm.（Twayne's world authors series，TWAS 177. China）

《诗经》，McNaughton，William（1933—）译.

16. Selections from the "Book of songs"/translated by Yang Xianyi，Gladys Yang，and Hu Shiguang. Beijing，China：Chinese Literature：Distributed by China Publications Centre（Guoji Shudian），1983. 112 p.；19cm. ISBN：083511080X.（Panda books）

《诗经选》，杨宪益（1915—2009），戴乃迭（Yang，Gladys，1919—1999），Hu Shiguang 合译.

17. 诗经＝Book of poetry/许渊冲英译；姜胜章编校. 长沙：湖南出版社，1993. 760 页；20cm. ISBN：7543806878.（汉英对照中国古典名著丛书＝The Chinese-English bilingual series of Chinese classics）

(1)3 版. 长沙：湖南出版社，1993. 5，12，19，760 p.；19cm. ISBN：7543806878，7543806870.（汉英对照中国古典名著丛书＝The Chinese-English bilingual series of Chinese classics）

18. An unexpurgated translation of Book of songs/translated，versified and annotated by Xu Yuanzhong. Beijing，China：Chinese Literature Press，1994. 360 pages；21cm. ISBN：0835131432，0835131438，7507102343，7507102345.（Panda books）

《诗经》，许渊冲（1921—）译.

19. 诗经选：图文典藏本：汉英对照/许渊冲译. 石家庄：河北人民出版社，2005. 101 页；23cm. ISBN：7202037076，7202037072.（许译中国经典诗词）

英文题名：Selected from the book of poetry，本书精选诗经名篇 50 余首. 英汉对照.

20. Selections from the book of poetry/translated by Xu Yuanchong. Beijing［China］：China Intercontinental Press（Wu zhou chuan bo chu ban she），2006. ISBN：7508508874，7508508870.（Chinese traditional culture series）

《精选诗经与诗意画》，许渊冲（1921—）译.

21. Selections from the book of poetry/Xu Yuanchong［compilator］. Illustrated ed. Beijing：China Intercontinental Press，2006. 195 p.：il. color；24cm. ISBN：7508508874，7508508870.（Chinese traditional culture series）

《精选诗经与诗意画：汉英对照》，五洲传播出版社编；许渊冲译.

22. 诗经：汉英对照/许渊冲英译；刘文娟，崔晶晶中文注释. 北京：中国对外翻译出版公司，2009. 23 页，15 页，439 页；21cm. ISBN：7500120209，7500120206.（中译

经典文库：汉英对照 中华传统文化精粹）

23. Book of poetry/translated by Xu Yuanchong；［Wang Feng，editor］.［Singapore］：World Culture Books，2011. 762 pages；22cm. ISBN：9810705701，9810705700.（Classical Chinese poetry and prose＝许译中国经典诗文）

《诗经》，许渊冲（1921—）译；wangfeng 编. 英汉对照.

24. Selections from the Book of Songs/translated from the Chinese by Yuanchong Xu. San Francisco：China Books，2012. 334 pages；23cm. ISBN：0835100090，083510009X

《诗经》（选译），许渊冲（1921—）译.

25. 诗经＝Book of poetry/许渊冲编译. Beijing：Hai tun chu ban she，2013. 111 pages：color illustrations；22cm. ISBN：7511010474，7511010476.（许渊冲经典英译古代诗歌 1000 首＝Version of classical Chinese poetry；1）

26. 诗经＝The Book of Poetry/汪榕培，任秀桦译注. 沈阳市：辽宁教育出版社，1995. 4，6，16，1657 pages；22cm. ISBN：7538239030，7538239034

英文题名：Book of poetry. 英汉对照.

27. 诗经/程俊英，蒋见元今译；汪榕培英译. Changsha：Hu'nan ren min chu ban she，2008. 2 volumes；24cm. ISBN：7543852440，7543852446.（大中华文库＝Library of Chinese classics）.

英文题名：The book of poetry

28. 英译诗经·国风＝Regional songs from the book of poetry/汪榕培，潘智丹译. 上海：上海外语教育出版社，2008. 7，401 pages；24cm. ISBN：7544606103，7544606104.（外教社中国文化汉外对照丛书. 第 2 辑）

29. 诗经/程俊英，蒋见元今译，汪榕培英译. 长沙：湖南人民出版社，2008. 2 册（59 页，727 页）；23cm. ISBN：7543852440，7543852446.（大中华文库＝Library of Chinese classics）

英文题名：The book of poetry. 汉英对照.

30. Songs classic：China's earliest poetry anthology/［edited and］translated by William Dolby. Edinburgh：Carreg，2005. iii，xi，xiii，468 pages：illustrations；21cm.（chinese culture series；14）

《诗经》，Dolby，William 译.

31. 诗经名言：汉英对照/齐鲁书社编选；李玉良译；王铭基绘. 济南：齐鲁书社，2006. 100 页；23cm. ISBN：753331719X，7533317195.（儒家名典箴言录）

英文题名：Aphorisms from Shijing.

32. 诗经·国风：英文白话新译 英汉对照 a new trilingual translation of the world's oldest collection of lyric poetry/贾福相译著. 北京：北京大学出版社，2010. 63 页，369 页；21cm. ISBN：7301172056，7301172052

英文题名："Airs of the States" from the Shi Jing，完整英译本，包括《诗经·国风》160 首.

33. Traditional Chinese poetry classics：the selected readings of states' Odes in the book of songs（English and

Chinese version）/［translated by］Mingxin Li. Nugegoda：Sarasavi Publishers，2012．151 pages；22cm．ISBN：9556716382，9556716386．

《诗经》（选译），Li，Mingxin 译. 中英对照.

I312　其他古代和跨时代诗歌集

1. The jade chaplet in twenty-four beads：a collection of songs，ballads，etc．（from the Chinese）/by George Carter Stent...London，Trübner & Co．，1874．viii，166 pages；21cm．

   中国诗歌、民谣. Stent，G. C.（George Carter，1833—1884）译.

   (1)2nd ed. London，W. H. Allen & Co．，1883．vii，166 pages；21cm．

   (2)［S. l．］：Primary Sources，Historic，［2011］．ISBN：1241062749，1241062743

2. Chinese legends and other poems/by W. A. P. Martin. Shanghai：Kelley & Walsh，1894．ii，87 pages；17cm．

   中国古代诗歌. Martin，W. A. P.（William Alexander Parsons，1827—1916）编译.

   (1)Second edition － much enlarged. Shanghai：Kelly & Walsh，1912．123 pages

   (2)［S. l．］：Nabu Press，［2010］．ISBN：1176544047，1176544048

3. Chinese poetry in English verse. London，B. Quaritch，1898．212p．；24cm．

   《古今诗选》，翟理斯（Giles，Herbert Allen，1845—1935）（英国汉学家）编译. 选译中国古典诗歌近 200 首，其中唐代诗歌 101 首.

4. Gems of Chinese literature：verse，by Herbert A. Giles. 2nd ed．，rev. and greatly enl. London，B. Quaritch，Ltd．，1923．5 p. l．，6，279，［1］p．；23cm．

   《古文选珍》第二版修订扩大版之"诗歌卷". 翟理斯（Giles，Herbert Allen，1845—1935）（英国汉学家）编译.

5. Select Chinese verses，translated by Herbert A. Giles and Arthur Waley. Shanghai，China，The Commercial Press，limited，1934．3 p. l．，［v］-xi，96 p．，1 l．；19cm．

   《英译中国诗歌选》，翟理斯（Giles，Herbert Allen，1845—1935）（英国汉学家），韦利（Waley，Arthur，1889—1966）（英国汉学家）译. 中英对照. 选编两位汉诗英译名家的作品，其译文代表了韵体和素体两种不同的风格.

6. Twenty Chinese poems/paraphrased by Clifford Bax；with four illustrations in colour by Arthur Bowmar-Porter. Hampstead，N. W．［London］：W. Budd，Orpheus Press，1910．54 p．，［4］leaves of plates：4 col. ill．；22cm．（The Orpheus series；no. 3）

   《中国诗歌 20 首》，Bax，Clifford（1886—1962）（英国诗人）译.

7. Twenty-five Chinese poems/paraphrased by Clifford Bax. 2nd ed．，rev. and enl. London：Hendersons，［1916］．53

p．；19cm．

   Notes："An augmented and revised reïssue of the Twenty Chinese poems which were published in 1910"

   《中国诗歌 25 首》，Bax，Clifford（1886—1962）（英国诗人）译，是《中国诗歌 20 首》的修订扩大版.

8. Chinese poems/translated by Charles Budd. London，New York H. Frowde，1912．174 pages；20cm．

   Contents：A few remarks on the history and construction of Chinese poetry. —The technique of Chinese poetry. —Biographical notes of a few of the more eminent Chinese poets. —Poems.

   《古今诗选》，Budd，Charles 译.

   (1)London，Oxford University Press，1912．174 pages；20cm．

9. Chinese legends and lyrics. 2nd ed. Shanghai，Kelly，1912．123 pages

   Contents：Legends of the Golden age. —Legends from other classical sources. —Legends from Chinese folklore. —Chinese lyrics from classical sources. —Miscellaneous.

   《中国的传说与诗歌》，丁韪良（Martin，W. A. P.，William Alexander Parsons，1827—1916）.

   (1)［Place of publication not identified］：Hardpress Ltd，2013．pages. ISBN：1313759767，1313759762

10. Lyrics from the Chinese，by Helen Waddell. 2nd impression. London，Constable and Company Ltd．，1914．xiv，41，［1］p．；21cm．

   《中国歌辞》，Waddell，Helen（1889—1965）（英国小说家、翻译家）编译. 该书内容转译自拉丁文，其祖本为理雅各（James Legge，1815—1897）的《中国经典》（The Chinese Classics）. 共选译古典诗歌 40 首，主要为《诗经》中的诗歌.

   (1)New York：H. Holt and Company［1935］．xiv，41 p. 20cm．"Seventh printing 1935."

11. Cathay/translations by Ezra Pound，for the most part from the Chinese of Rihaku，from the notes of the late Ernest Fenollosa，and the decipherings of the professors Mori and Ariga. London，E. Mathews，1915．31［1］pages；20cm．

   《神州集》，庞德（Pound，Ezra，1885—1972）（美国诗人）译. 收录诗歌 19 首，其中李白诗歌 12 首. 根据美国学者 Fenollosa，Ernest（1853—1908）所遗留的研究笔记整理而翻译.

   (1)Cathay：poems after Li Po/Ezra Pound；seven color woodcuts by Francesco Clemente.［New York］：Limited Editions Club，［1993］．34 p．，［7］leaves of plates；7 col. ill．；31cm．

   (2)［Whitefish，Mont．］：Kessinger Publishing，2015．31 pages；28cm. ISBN：0548613702，0548613702

   (3)Cathay/Ezra Pound；foreword by Mary de Rachewiltz；edited with an introduction and transcripts of Fenollosa's notes by Zhaoming Qian. The centennial edition. New York：New Directions Publishing Corporation，2015．136 pages；21cm． ISBN：0811223522，0811223523．（New Directions paperbook；NDP1317）

增加了庞德女儿的序言以及庞德研究者钱兆明（Zhaoming Qian）的注解．

12. Lustra of Ezra Pound. London，E. Mathews，1916． 115，［1］pages frontispiece（portrait）21cm．

庞德（Pound，Ezra，1885—1972）（美国诗人）译，其内容是《神州集》的再版．

(1) New York：Haskell House Publishers，1973．115 pages：portraits；23cm．ISBN：0838316883，0838316887

(2)［Whitefish，MT］：Kessinger Publishing，2008．124 pages；24cm．ISBN：0548946744，0548946749，0548621470，0548621479．（Kessinger Publishing's rare reprints）

13. Chinese lyrics, from the book of Jade/translated from the French of Judith Gautier by James Whitall. New York：B. W. Huebsch，1918．53 p.；23cm．

Notes：The translator from the French was a Quaker.

中国古诗英译．Gautier，Judith（1845—1917）法译；Whitall，James 英译自法文版．

(1) New York：B. W. Huebsch，1923．53 pages；23cm．

14. A hundred and seventy Chinese poems. London，Constable and Company，Ltd.，1918．xii，168 p.；20cm．

《汉诗一百七十首》，韦利（Waley，Arthur，1889—1966）（英国汉学家）译．

(1) New York：A. A. Knopf，1919．243 p.；21cm． Reprinted in part from various periodicals．附有白居易的生平资料．

(2) Popular ed. New York：A. A. Knopf，1923．243 pages；21cm．（Borzoi pocket books）

(3) New pocket book ed. New York：Knopf，1929．243 pages；18cm．（Borzoi pocket books

(4) New York：A. A. Knopf，1935．243 pages；21cm． （Modern poetry）

(5) London，Constable，1939．xii，168 pages；19cm．

(6) London，Constable and Co.，1947．xii，168 pages；20cm．

(7) London，J. Cape，1969．129 pages：illustrations

(8)［Place of publication not identified］：［Kessinger Publishing］，2008．243 pages；24cm．ISBN：054818965X，0548189658

15. Translations from the Chinese, by Arthur Waley, illustrated by Cyrus LeRoy Baldridge. New York：A. A. Knopf，1941．10 p.，l.，3—325 p.，1 l. illus.，col. plates.；28cm．

Notes：The translations... were made over twenty years

ago... In arranging the poems for this illustrated edition I have corrected a certain number of mistakes. But on the whole I have reprinted the poems as they stood in 1918 and 1919［under titles］，A hundred and seventy Chinese poems，and More translations from the Chinese.

《中国文学选译》，韦利（Waley，Arthur，1889—1966）（英国汉学家）译．是其《汉诗一百七十首》的修改和增补．

16. More translations from the Chinese. New York：Knopf，1919．144 p.；20cm．

《汉诗增译》，韦利（Waley，Arthur，1889—1966）（英国汉学家）译．收 66 首诗歌，多数为首次翻译，少数曾在刊物上发表过．半数以上为白居易诗歌．

(1) London，G. Allen & Unwin Ltd.［1919］．109 p.；19cm．

17. Chinese poems, selected from 170 Chinese poems, More translations from the Chinese, The temple and The book of songs. London，G. Allen and Unwin Ltd.［1946］．213，［1］p.；21cm．

《中国诗选》，韦利（Waley，Arthur，1889—1966）（英国汉学家）译．汇集译者以前所译的《汉诗一百七十首》《汉诗增译》，以及《悟真诗及其他篇章》．

(1) London：Unwin Books，1961．181 pages；19cm．（Unwin books；15）

(2) London，G. Allen and Unwin Ltd.，1962．213，［1］pages；21cm．

(3) London：Allen and Unwin，1976．213 p.；20cm．（Unesco collection of representative works：Chinese series）．ISBN：0048950211

(4) N. Y.：Dover Publications，2000．213 p.；22cm． ISBN：0486411028

18. The temple and other poems/translated by Arthur Waley；with an introductory essay on early Chinese poetry，and an appendix on the development of different metrical forms. London：Allen and Unwin，1923．150 p.；20cm．

《悟真诗及其他篇章》，韦利（Waley，Arthur，1889—1966）（英国汉学家）译．以收录先秦两汉小赋为主，包括宋玉的《高唐赋》，邹衍的《酒赋》，杨雄的《逐贫赋》，张衡的《髑髅赋》，王逸的《荔枝赋》，王延春的《王孙赋》《梦赋》《鲁灵光殿赋》，欧阳修的《鸣蝉赋》，白居易的《游悟真诗》，以及《陌上桑》《孔雀东南飞》《木兰辞》等乐府诗等．

19. Chinese poems［compiled and translated by Arthur Waley］London，Printed by Lowe Bros.，1916．［New Brunswick，N. J.，Rutgers University Library，1965］．16 p.；21cm．

Notes：This reprint［with a new introd. by F. A. Johns］is a facsimile，without the corrections（which he made by hand），of the collection of translations which Waley had printed for private circulation in 1916.

《中国诗选》,韦利(Waley,Arthur,1889—1966)(英国汉学家)译.

20. Plucking the rushes：an anthology of Chinese poetry in translations，by Arthur Waley, Ezra Pound ［and］Helen Waddell；compiled by David Holbrook. London, Heinemann Educational，1968. ix，118 p.；21cm. ISBN：0435144405

《中国诗歌翻译集》,韦利(Waley,Arthur,1889—1966)(英国汉学家),庞德(Pound,Ezra,1885—1972)(美国诗人),Waddell,Helen(1889—1965)译；Holbrook,David,(1923—2011)编.

21. Coloured stars：versions of fifty Asiatic love poems/by Edward Powys Mathers. Oxford：B. H. Blackwell, 1919. 63 p.；20cm.（Adventurers all；no. 24）

Notes：Reprint. Originally published：Feb. 1919. In part translated from "Anthologie de l'amour asiatique," compiled by A. Thalasso，and the "Livre de jade" of Mme. Gautier.

东方爱情诗. Mathers, E. Powys（Edward Powys, 1892—1939)译.

（1）Boston and New York：Houghton Mifflin Co.， 1919. 63，［1］p.；20cm.

22. Fir-flower tablets；poems translated from the Chinese by Florence Asycough... English versions by Amy Lowell. Boston, New York：Houghton Mifflin Company，1921. xcv，227，［1］p. front.（double map）plan, facism.； 21cm.

《松花笺》,Ayscough, Florence Wheelock(1878—1942)(美国汉学家),Lowell, Amy(1874—1925)(美国女诗人)合译. 共收录诗歌137首,以唐诗为主,其中李白诗达83首.

（1）Westport, Conn.：Hyperion Press，［1973, c1921］. xcv，227 p. illus.；23cm.

23. The lost flute，and other Chinese lyrics；being a translation from the French，by Gertrude Laughlin Joerissen of the book of Franz Toussaint entitled "La flute de jade：poèsies chinoise［s］". London, T. F. Unwin Ltd.［1923］. 6 p. l.，177 p.；20cm.

Notes："Selected and translated by Ts'ao Shang-ling. Edited by Franz Toussaint."—Note to the French ed.， Brit. mus. acc.，Mar.，1923.

《失笛记》,Ts'ao, Shang-ling 选译；Toussaint, Franz (1879—)编；Joerissen, Gertrude Laughlin 从法译本转译成英语. 中国古诗词英译.

（1）New York：The Elf, 1929. 5 p. l.，ix-xiv，185 p.； 23cm.

24. Flower shadows，translations from the Chinese, by Alan Simms Lee. London, E. Mathews Ltd.，1925. 47 p.； 20cm.

《花影：中国诗译集》,Lee, Alan W. Simms 译. 收录各时代中国诗歌35首.

25. Lotus and chrysanthemum；an anthology of Chinese and Japanese poetry. New York：Boni & Liveright, 1927. xxi，237 p.；25cm.

中国、日本诗歌翻译集. French, Joseph Lewis（1858—1936)编.

26. Poetry of the Orient；an anthology of the classic secular poetry of the major eastern nations，edited by Eunice Tietjens. New York：London, A. A. Knopf, 1928. xxv, 328，xli，［1］p.；21cm.

Contents：Arabia. —Persia. —Japan. —China. —India.

东方诗歌英译. Tietjens, Eunice(1884—1944)译. 包括对中国诗歌的翻译.

27. Images in jade；translations from classical and modern Chinese poetry，by Arthur Christy. New York：E. P. Dutton, 1929. 191 p.；22cm.

中国诗歌. Christy, Arthur(1899—1946)译.

28. A Chinese market；lyrics from the Chinese in English verse，by Henry H. Hart. Foreword by E. T. C. Werner. Peking, The French Bookstore；San Francisco, J. J. Newbegin［c1931］. xvii，［101］p.；24cm.

中国诗歌. Hart, Henry Hersch(1886—)编译.

29. The hundred names，a short introduction to the study of Chinese poetry，with illustrative translations，by Henry H. Hart... Berkeley, University of California Press, 1933. 4 p. l.，231 p.；20cm.

中国诗歌. Hart, Henry Hersch(1886—)编译.

30. A garden of peonies/translations of Chinese poems into English verse，by Henry H. Hart. Stanford, Calif.： Stanford University Press；London：H. Milford, Oxford University Press, 1938. xiii，159 pages；23cm.

中国诗歌. Hart, Henry Hersch(1886—)译.

（1）Stanford University, Calif.，Stanford University Press；London, H. Milford, Oxford University Press, 1943. xii，159 pages；23cm.

（2）Stanford, Calif.：Stanford University Press, 1945. xiii，159 pages；23cm.

（3）Stanford, Calif.：Stanford University Press, 1947. xiii，159 pages；23cm.

31. English translations of Chinese classics；an anthology of Chinese poetry（from the Chou to T'ang dynasties） selected with notes by Shih Min. Shanghai, China, The Pei sin Book Co.，Ltd.，1933. 1 p. l.，4，vi，231 p.； 19cm.（English translation of Chinese classics）

《中国古典诗歌集：从周至唐代》,石民(Shih, Min, fl. 1931—)译.

32. Various Chinese poets，their biographies and selected poems, Seattle, Wash.，［1935］. 8 p. l.，520 (i. e. 526) numb l. 30×24cm.

中国诗歌. McClelland, Hardin T. 编译.

33. Art-themes in Chinese poetry, Seattle, 1936. p.

中国诗歌. McClelland, Hardin T. 编译.

34. Chinese lyrics, translated by Ch'u Ta-kao, with a preface by Sir Arthur Quiller-Couch. Cambridge, Eng., The University Press, 1937. xvii, 55, [1] p.; 19cm.

中国诗歌. 初大告(Chu, Dagao)译.

35. From bamboo glade and lotus pool＝Zhu lin lian chi zhi shi/by Robert Wood Clack.. Atlanta, Emory University, Banner Press [c1937]. 71 p. plates. 21cm.

中国诗歌. Clack, Robert Wood 译.

36. Secrets told in the bamboo grove [by] Helen Wiley Dutton. Peking, The French bookstore, 1940. 5 p. l., 52, [2] p.; 23cm.

Notes：Printed on double leaves, Chinese style.

中国诗歌. Dutton, Helen Wiley(1889—1982)译.

37. Chinese love poems：from most ancient to modern times/decorations by Paul McPharlin. Mount Vernon, N. Y. : Peter Pauper Press, 1942. 77 pages：illustrations; 23cm.

《中国情诗选：由远古至今》,部分内容来自法国女诗人选译的中国诗歌集《白玉诗书》(Le Livre de Jade).

(1) Mount Vernon, N. Y. : Peter Pauper Press, 1954. 85, [4] pages：illustrations; 24cm.

38. From the Chinese/edited by R. C. Trevelyan. Oxford：Clarendon Press, 1945. xvi, 92 pages; 19cm.

中国诗歌. Trevelyan, R. C. (Robert Calverley, 1872—1951)编译.

39. Driftwood, and other poems; including translations of Chinese poetry. Mountain View, Calif., Pacific Press Pub. Assn. [1947]. 127 p.; 21cm.

中国诗歌. Esteb, Adlai Albert 译.

40. The white pony, an anthology of Chinese poetry from the earliest times to the present day, newly translated. Edited by Robert Payne. New York：J. Day Co. [1947]. xxviii, 414 p.; 18cm. (An Asia book)

中国诗歌. Payne, Robert(1911—1983)编译.

(1) G. Allen & Unwin [1949]. 356 p.

41. Chinese love songs, famous poems covering 26 centuries from the time of Confucius to the present; English verse renderings. Upper Montclair, N. J., B. L. Hutchinson [1949]. 91 p.; front. 19cm.

中国爱情诗. Ives, Mabel Lorenz 译.

42. Shih tz'u i hsüan. Poems from China. Hongkong, Creation Books, [1950]. xvii, 241 p.; 19cm.

中国诗歌. 黄斐(Wong, Man, ? —1963)译选.

43. Inside the moon gate; Claremont, Calif., Saunders Press, 1951. 63 p.; 21cm.

中国诗歌. Lyon, David Willard(1870—1949)译.

44. The people speak out; translations of poems and songs of the people of China. Peking, 1954. 107 p. illus. 22cm.

《人民心声：中国民间诗与民歌翻译》,路易·艾黎(Alley, Rewi,1897—1987)编译.

45. Peace through the ages; translations from the poets of China. Peking, 1954. 205 p. illus. 22cm.

中国诗歌. 路易·艾黎(Alley, Rewi, 1897—1987)编译.

46. The people sing; more translations of poems and songs of the people of China. Peking, 1958. 446 p. illus.; 21cm.

中国诗歌. 路易·艾黎(Alley, Rewi, 1897—1987)编译.

47. Poems of revolt：some Chinese voices over the last century/transl. by Rewi Alley. Peking：New World Press, 1962. xi, 228 pages：illustrations; (some color) portraits 22cm.

《反抗的歌声》,路易·艾黎(Alley, Rewi,1897—1987)译. 新世界出版社.

48. Rainbow skirts and feather jackets/twenty Chinese poems translated by Shirley M. Black. Hollywood：W. M. Hawley, 1956. 45 pages; 24cm.

Black, Shirley M.译. 包括对 20 首中国诗歌的英译. 英汉对照.

49. One hundred poems from the Chinese/Kenneth Rexroth. [New York]：New Directions, 1956. 59 pages; 21cm.

《汉诗 100 首》,王公红(Rexroth, Kenneth, 1905—1982)(美国诗人、翻译家)译.

(1) [New York]：New Directions, 1959. 159 pages

(2) [New York], [Published for J. Laughlin by New Directions], 1965. 147 pages

(3) New York：New Directions, 1971. xi, 145 pages. ISBN：0811203700, 0811203708

(4) New York：New Directions Pub., 2013. xiii, 159 pages; 24cm. ISBN：1258069155, 1258069156

50. Love and the turning year; one hundred more poems from the Chinese. [New York：New Directions Pub. Corp., 1970]. xvi, 140 p.; 21cm.

《爱与流年：汉诗又 100 首》,王公红(Rexroth, Kenneth, 1905—1982)(美国诗人、翻译家)译.

51. The orchid boat; women poets of China, translated and edited by Kenneth Rexroth and Ling Chung. New York：McGraw-Hill [c1972]. xv, 150 p.; 22cm.. ISBN：0070737444

《兰舟：中国女诗人诗选》,王公红(Rexroth, Kenneth, 1905—1982)(美国诗人、翻译家),钟玲(Ling Chung, 1945—)合译.

(1) Women poets of China/translated and edited by Kenneth Rexroth & Ling Chung. New York：Published for J. Laughlin by New Directions Pub. Corp., 1982. 150 p.; 20cm. ISBN：0811208214

52. Songs of love, moon, & wind：poems from the Chinese/translated by Kenneth Rexroth; selected by Eliot Weinberger. New York：New Directions Pub., 2009. 90 p.; 16cm. ISBN：0811218368, 0811218368

Notes：This exquisite gift book offers a wide sampling of Chinese verse, from the first century to our own time.

中国诗歌. 王公红(Rexroth, Kenneth, 1905—1982)译，Weinberger, Eliot 选编.

53. Poems of solitude, translated from the Chinese by Jerome Ch'ên and Michael Bullock. London, New York：Abelard-Schuman［1960］. 118 p. illus. 26cm. (UNESCO collection of representative works. Chinese series)

Contents：The morphological development of Chinese poetry—Juan Chi（210—263）. Introduction—Fifteen poems of my heart—Pao Chao(414—466). Introduction—Eighteen tedious ways—The ruined city—Wang Wei（699—759）& P'ei Ti（714—?）. Introduction—Forty poems of the River Wang—Li Ho（791—817）. Introduction—Backyard—Horses—Lamentation of the bronze camel—The bronze bird platform—Lyre：a Korean folk tale—Li P'ing's lyre recital—Thinking—Ancient arrow-head—Magic string—Li Yu（937—978）. Introduction—A meeting—Angler—Garden—New year—Drinking—Love-sickness—In prison—How much regret?—Reminiscence—The past—Birthday—Life—Spring shower.

中国古诗选译. Ch'ên, Jerome（1919—），Bullock, Michael(1918—2008)合译.

（1）Poems of solitude, translated from the Chinese by Jerome Ch'ên and Michael Bullock. Rutland, Vt.，C. E. Tuttle［1970, c1960］. 118 p. illus. 26cm. ISBN：0804809127.（UNESCO collection of representative works；Chinese series）

（2）2nd ed. reprinted without changes. London, Lund Humphries, 1970.［6］, 119 p. illus. 26cm. ISBN：0853312605.（UNESCO collection of representative works；Chinese series）

54. Two Chinese poets；vignettes of Han life and thought. Princeton, N. J.，Princeton University Press, 1960. 266 p.；23cm.

Partial contents：Pan Ku's "Fu on the western capital."—Chang Heng's "Fu on the western capital."—Pan Ku's "Fu on the eastern capital."—Chang Heng's "Fu on the eastern capital. —Critique of Pan Ku's "Fu on the western capital. —Critique of Chang Heng's "Fu on the western capital."—Critique of Pan Ku's "Fu on the eastern capital."—Critique of Chang Heng's "Fu on the eastern capital."

休士(Hughes, E. R.〈Ernest Richard〉, 1883—1956)(美国学者). 包括对张衡(78—139)和班固(32—92)各自《西都赋》《东都赋》四部作品的翻译.

（1）Westport, Conn.：Greenwood Press, 1977. xv, 266 p.；23cm. ISBN：0837196485

55. The Penguin book of Chinese verse；translated by Robert Kotewall and Norman L. Smith；edited with an introduction by A. R. Davis.［Harmondsworth, Middlesex］Penguin Books［1962］. 84 p.；18cm.

中国诗歌. Kotewall, Robert 和 Smith, Norman L. 英译；Davis, Albert Richard 编.

（1）Baltimore, Penguin Books, 1966. lxxi, 84 pages；18cm.

（2）Harmondsworth, Penguin, 1968. 84 p.；19cm. (The Penguin poets, D75)

（3）Harmondsworth：Penguin Books, 1970. lxxi, 84 p.；18cm. ISBN：0140420657, 0140420654

（4）Harmondsworth：Penguin, 1975. 84 pages；19cm. (Penguin poets)

56. The lady and the hermit：30 Chinese poems/by Li Ch'ing-chao of the Sung and Wang Fan-chih of the T'ang；a new translation by Vincent McHugh and S. H. Kwôck. San Francisco：Golden Mountain Press, 1962. 1 volume（unpaged）；18cm.

McHugh, Vincent(1904—1983)与 C. H. Kwock 合译. 英译了李清照(1081—约 1141)和王梵志(生卒不详,隋末至唐初年间前后在世)的 30 首诗词.

57. Chinese love lyrics. Mount Vernon, N. Y.，Peter Pauper Press［1964］. 76 p. illus.；19cm.

中国爱情诗.

（1）Chinese love lyrics/［translated by Gertrude L. Joerissen and others］；with decorative cut-outs by Paul McPharlin. Tokyo, Japan：Toppan Co.；New York：Peter Pauper Press, 1990. 62 pages：illustrations；20cm.

58. A collection of Chinese lyrics；rendered into verse by Alan Ayling from translations of the Chinese by Duncan Mackintosh, foreword by F. T. Cheng, calligraphy by Lee Yim and on the illustrations by Chang Chien Ying, illustrations by Fei Ch'eng Wu. London, Routledge & K. Paul, 1965. xv, 254 p.；23cm.

中国诗歌. MacKintosh, Duncan（Duncan Robert），Ayling, Alan 译. 中英对照.

(1)Nashville, Vanderbilt University Press［1967, c1965］xv, 254 p. illus.；23cm.

59. A further collection of Chinese lyrics, and other poems；rendered into verse by Alan Ayling from the translations of the Chinese by Duncan Mackintosh in collaboration with Ch'eng Hsi & T'ung Ping-cheng；calligraphy by Cheng Hsühan, illustrations by Fei Ch'eng-Wu. London, Routledge & K. Paul, 1969. xxii, 272 p. illus.，facsim.，music, port. 23cm. ISBN：0710065787

中国诗歌. Mackintosh, Duncan（Duncan Robert），Ayling, Alan 译. 中英对照.

(1)Nashville, Vanderbilt University Press［1970, c1969］xxii, 272 p. illus.，music.；23cm. ISBN：0826511503

60. One hundred and one Chinese poems. 〔Chung shih hsüan chi with English translations and pref. by Shih Shun Liu. Introductory by Edmund Blunden. Foreword by Jo hn Cairncross. With 7 additional translations. 〔London, Oxford University Press, exclusive agents, 1967〕. xxxix, 173 p.；21cm. (Unesco collection of representative works：Chinese series)

《中诗选辑》，刘师舜（1900—）译.

(1)〔San Francisco〕：Chinese Materials Center, 1981. xxv, 160 p.，〔7〕leaves of plates：col. ill.；20cm. ISBN：089644645X. Asian library series；no. 27)

(2) Taiwan：National Tsing Hua University Press, 2011. 177 pages；18cm. ISBN：9866116223, 9866116220

61. Chinese moonlight：63 poems by 33 poets. Translated & recomposed by Walasse Ting. New York：American Distributor：Wittenborn〔1967〕. 71 p. col. illus. 27cm.

中国诗歌. 丁雄泉（Ting, Walasse）（美国华裔学者）译.

62. The silent zero, in search of sound；an anthology of Chinese poems from the beginning through the sixth century. Translated by Eric Sackheim. With calligraphy by Ch'en Yung-sen. New York〕Grossman〔1968〕. xvii, 174 p. illus. 27cm.

中国古代诗歌. Sackheim, Eric 编译.

63. Ancient poetry from China, Japan & India, rendered into English verse by Henry W. Wells. Columbia, University of South Carolina Press〔1968〕. 464 p.；25cm.

Wells, Henry W. (1895—1978)编译，包括对中国古代诗歌的英译.

64. Chinese lyricism；Shih poetry from the second to the twelfth century, with tran slations by Burton Watson. New York：Columbia University Press, 1971. 232 p.；24cm. ISBN：0231034644. (Companions to Asian studies)

《中国抒情诗：从 2 至 12 世纪》，华兹生（Watson, Burton,1925—）（美国翻译家）译.

65. Chinese rhyme—prose；poems in the fu form from the Han and Six Dynasties periods. Translated and with an introd. by Burton Watson. New York：Columbia University Press, 1971. 128 p.；23cm. ISBN：0231035535, 0231035543. (UNESCO collection of representative works：Chinese series)

Contents：The wind, by Sung Yü. —The owl, by Chia Yi. —Sir Fantasy, by Ssu—ma Hsiang—ju. —Climbing the tower, by Wang Ts'an. —The goddess of the Lo, by Ts'ao Chih. —Recalling old times, by Hsiang Hsiu. —The idle life, by P'an Yüeh. —The sea, by Mu Hua. —Wandering on Mount T'ien—t'ai, by Sun Ch'o. —The snow, by Hsieh Hui-lien. —Desolate city, by Pao Chao. —Partings, by Chiang Yen. —A small garden, by Yü Hsin. —Selected bibliography (p. ；127-128)

《汉魏六朝赋选》，华兹生（Watson, Burton, 1925—）（美国汉学家）译.

(1) Revised Edition. Hong Kong；New York：The Chinese University of Hong Kong, 〔2015〕. xviii, 151 pages；22cm. ISBN：9629965631. (Calligrams)

66. The Columbia book of Chinese poetry：from early times to the thirteenth century/translated and edited by Burton Watson. New York：Columbia University Press, 1984. 385 p.；ill.；25cm. ISBN：0231056826. (Translations from the Oriental classics).

《哥伦比亚中国诗选》，华兹生（Watson, Burton, 1925—）（美国汉学家）译. 汇集 13 世纪以前中国古典诗、词、曲、赋.

67. Love & protest；Chinese poems from the sixth century B. C. to the seventeenth century A. D. Edited and translated by John Scott. Versification in collaboration with Graham Martin. New York：Harper & Row〔1972〕. 168 p.；21cm. ISBN：0060902612. (Harper colophon books, CN 261)

中国古代诗歌. Scott, John（1936—）和 Martin, Graham（1927—）译.

(1)London, Rapp and Whiting；Deutsch, 1972. 168 p.；23cm. ISBN：0853911801

68. An anthology of Chinese poetry from the Chou to T'ang dynasties/selected with notes by Shih Min. Hong Kong：Chin Hsiu Pub, 1974. 231 pages；19cm.

自周至唐朝的诗歌集. Shih, Min 选编.

69. Sunflower splendor：three thousand years of Chinese poetry/co-edited by Wu-chi Liu and Irving Yucheng Lo. Garden City, N. Y.：Anchor Books, 1975. lxiv, 630 p.；22cm. ISBN：0385097166

《葵晔集：汉诗三千年》，柳无忌（Liu, Wu-Chi, 1907—2002）（美国华裔学者），罗郁正（Lo, Yucheng, 1922—）（美国华裔汉学家）合编. 汇集 50 多位译家合力译出的中国历代诗、词、曲精品作品，其中唐诗 300 多首.

(1)Bloomington：Indiana University Press, 1975. lxiv, 630 p.；24cm. ISBN：025335580X

(2)1st Midland Book ed. Bloomington：Indiana University Press, 1990. lxiv, 634 p.；24cm. ISBN：025335580X,0253206073. (A Midland book)

70. Sitting up at night and other Chinese poems/selected & translated by Lau Tak Cheuk. 〔Hong Kong〕：Chinese University of Hong Kong, 1973. 60 p.；19cm.

中国诗歌. Lau, Tak Cheuk 选译.

71. The charcoal burner, and other poems；original translations from the poetry of the Chinese. Translated by Henry H. Hart. Norman, University of Oklahoma Press〔1974〕. xxvii, 226 p. front.；19cm. ISBN：0806111852

中国诗歌. Hart, Henry Hersch(1886—)译.

72. Chinese poetry：major modes and genres/edited and translated by Wai-lim Yip；calligraphy by Kuo-hsiung Chen. Berkeley：University of California Press，c1976. xv，475，[1] p. ；23cm. ISBN：0520027272

《中国诗歌：主要模式和流派》，叶维廉（Yip，Wai-lim.，1937—）（美国华裔学者）编译. 选译中国历代诗歌150首.

(1) Durham：Duke University Press，1997. xiv，357 p. ；24cm. ISBN：0822319519，0822319462

73. A golden treasury of Chinese poetry：121 classical poems/translated by John A. Turner；with notes and Chinese texts compiled and edited by John J. Deeney，with the assistance of Kenneth K. B. Li. Hong Kong：Chinese University of Hong Kong；Seattle：distributed by University of Washington Press，1976. 346 p. ；20cm. ISBN：0295955066，0295955063. (A Renditions book)

《中国诗歌的黄金宝库：121首经典诗》，Turner，John A. (1909—1971)译. 中英文本.

(1) [Rev. ed.]. Hong Kong：Research Centre for Translation，Chinese University of Hong Kong，c1989 (1992 printing). xxxiv，165 p. ；21cm. ISBN：9627255041. (Renditions paperbacks)

74. The flowering plum and the palace lady：interpretations of Chinese poetry/Hans H. Frankel. New Haven：Yale University Press，1976. xiii，276 p. ；25cm. ISBN：0300018894

Notes：Includes the text，in Chinese and English，of the 106 poems here discussed

Frankel，Hans H. (Hans Hermann，1916—)译. 包括对106首中国诗歌的翻译. 英汉对照.

75. Japanese literature in Chinese/translated by Burton Watson. New York：Columbia University Press，1975—1976. 2 v. ；22cm. ISBN：0231039867 (v. 1)，0231039864 (v. 1)，0231041462，0231041461. (Translations from the Oriental classics)

Contents：v. 1. Poetry & prose in Chinese by Japanese writers of the early period. —v. 2. Poetry & prose in Chinese by Japanese writers of the later period.

日本人汉诗选译. 华兹生（Watson，Burton，1925—）（美国汉学家）译.

76. The harmony of the world：Chinese poems/translated by David Lattimore. Providence：Copper Beech Press，1976. 1 volume (unpaged)；23cm. ISBN：091427807X，0914278078

中国诗歌. Lattimore，David(1931—)译.

(1) Providence：Copper Beech Pr. ，1980. 48 pages；22cm. ISBN：0914278312，0914278313，091427807X，0914278078

77. The herd boy and the weaver maid：a collection of Chinese love songs translated into English verse/by Robert Wook Clack；edited for publication by R. W.

Douglas Clack. New York：Gordon Press，1977. iii，224 p. ；24cm. ISBN：0879684615，0879684617

中国爱情诗. Clack，Robert Wood(1886—)译.

78. Milleniums of moonbeams：an historical anthology of Chinese poetry：covering a period of almost 4000 years containing translations into classic English verse forms of 900 poems by some 400 different Chinese poets/[selected] by Robert Wood Clack. New York：Gordon Press，1977. 3 v. ；24cm. ISBN：0879684453

Contents：v. 1. Selections from the Book of poetry. The late Chou dynasty. Han. Poems of the 3 Kingdoms. —v. 2. Early T'ang. Li Po & Tu Fu. Sung & Yuan. —v. 3. Ming & Ching. Modern Chinese poetry.

中国诗歌. Clack，Robert Wood(1886—)选编. 翻译400多个诗人的900首诗.

79. Song without music：Chinese tz'u poetry/edited by Stephen C. Soong. Hong Kong：Chinese University Press；Seattle：Distributed by the University of Washington Press，c1980. 282 p. ，[2] leaves of plates：2 col. ill. ，music；28cm. ISBN：962201206X. (A Renditions book)

Notes：Text in English，with ci in Chinese and English.

宋淇(Soong，Stephen C.，1919—1996)编，关于词的历史、评论和大量词的英译.

80. A brotherhood in song：Chinese poetry and poetics/edited by Stephen C. Soong. Hong Kong：Chinese University Press；Seattle：Distributed by the University of Washington Press，c1985. 386 p. ，[1] leaf of plates：ill. (some col.)；28cm. ISBN：9622013562. (A Renditions book)

《知音集》，宋淇(Soong，Stephen C. 1919—1996)编译. 关于中国诗词的历史、评论，有大量的诗词英译.

81. New songs from a jade terrace：an anthology of early Chinese love poetry/translated with annotations and an introduction by Anne Birrell. London；Boston：Allen & Unwin，1982. xxvii，374 p. ：ill. ；24cm. ISBN：0048950262

《玉台新咏》，Birrell，Anne 译注.

(1) Harmondsworth，Middlesex，England；New York：Penguin Books，1986. xxv，401 p. ：ill. ；20cm. ISBN：0140444874. (Penguin classics)

82. Chinese classical Ch'ü poetry/translated by William Dolby. Edinburgh：W. Dolby，1983. 87 leaves；20cm.

中国经典词选译. Dolby，William 译.

83. Gems of Chinese poetry：from the Book of Songs to the present/edited and translated by Ding Zuxim and Burton Raffel. [Liaoning，China]：Liaoning University Press，Liao-ning sheng hsin hua shu tien fa hsing，1986. 179 pages：portraits；19cm.

《中国诗歌精华：从〈诗经〉到当代》，丁祖馨，(美)拉菲尔编译. 辽宁大学出版社. 英汉对照.

84. Four introspective poets：a concordance to selected poems by Roan Jyi，Chern Tzyy-arng，Jang Jeouling，and Lii Bor/Victor H. Mair. Tempe，Ariz.：Center for Asian Studies，Arizona State University，c1987. xiii，240 p.；23cm. ISBN：0939252171. Monograph series (Arizona State University. Center for Asian Studies)；no. 20)

《四个咏怀诗人：阮籍、陈子昂、张九龄、李白诗选》，梅维恒(Mair, Victor H.，1943—)(美国翻译家)译.

85. 中国古典名诗选/黄龙选译. 南京：译林出版社，1989. 190 页

86. 诗词英译选/文殊译注. 北京：外语教学与研究出版社：新华书店总店北京发行所经销，1989. 23，367 pages；18cm. ISBN：7560002862，7560002866.（《英语学习》读者丛书）

87. A selection of Chinese classical poems with illustrations/edited by Wang Yanbo and Ren Guang；illustrated by Yang Yongqing；translated by Lao Yang. Beijing：China Esperanto Press，1990. 63 pages：color illustrations.

《配图古诗精选》，Wang，Yen-po 和 Jen，Kuang 编；Yang，Yung-ching 插图；Lao，Yang 译.

88. Chinese poetry through the words of the people ＝[Chung-kuo shih]/edited by Bonnie McCandless. New York：Ballantine Books，1991. 130 p.；21cm. ISBN：0345371356，0345371355

《中国诗》，McCandless，Bonnie 编译.

89. In the voice of others：Chinese Music Bureau poetry/Joseph R. Allen. Ann Arbor，Mich.：Center for Chinese Studies，University of Michigan，c1992. x，293 p.；24cm. ISBN：0892640960，0892640979. (Michigan monographs in Chinese studies；v. 63)
Includes translations of 120 poems.

《另一种声音：中国乐府诗》，约瑟夫·艾伦(Allen，Joseph Roe)(美国汉学家)译. 翻译了120多首诗.

90. 汉英对照千家诗/郭著章，傅惠生编. 武昌：武汉大学出版社，1992. 11，21，535 pages；19cm. ISBN：7307012103，7307012103
(1)修订版. 武昌：武汉大学出版社，2004. 24，3，5，541 pages；19cm. ISBN：7307038161，7307038165

91. Midnight flute：Chinese poems of love and longing/translated by Sam Hamill. Boston：Shambhala，1994. xx，150 p.：ill.；13cm. ISBN：0877739137. (Shambhala centaur editions)

《中国爱情诗》，Hamill，Sam(美国诗人)选.

92. Almost paradise：new and selected poems and translations/Sam Hamill. Boston：Shambhala，2005. xiv，261 p.；23cm. ISBN：1590301846
English translations of poems in Greek, Latin, Chinese, Japanese, Estonian.

《如天堂般：诗歌新选译》，Hamill，Sam(美国诗人)选译. 含部分中国诗歌.

93. 古诗文英译集/孙大雨译. 上海：上海外语教育出版社，1997. 21，18，690 pages：illustrations (some color)；22cm. ISBN：7810462075，7810462075.
英文题名：An anthology of ancient Chinese poetry and prose

94. Women writers of traditional China：an anthology of poetry and criticism/edited by Kang-i Sun Chang and Haun Saussy；Charles Kwong，associate editor；Anthony C. Yu and Yu-kung Kao，consulting editors. Stanford，Calif.：Stanford University Press，1999. xxiv，891 pages：maps；24cm. ISBN：0804732302，0804732307，0804732310，0804732314
Notes：This anthology of Chinese women's poetry in translation brings together representative selections from the work of some 130 poets from the Han dynasty to the early twentieth century.
Chang，Kang-i Sun (1944—)，Saussy，Haun (1960—)，Kwong，Charles Yim-tze(1958—)合编. 选编了自汉代至20世纪早期130余位中国历代女诗人的诗作.

95. 中国古诗一百首/编撰朱丽云；翻译万昌盛，王[Jian]中；插图沈嘉荣. 郑州市：大象出版社，2000. 4，4，5，271 pages：illustrations；21cm. ISBN：7534724074，7534724077
英汉对照.

96. A selection of Chinese classical poems with illustrations/edited by Wang Yanbo and Ren Guang；illustrated by Yang Yongqing；translated by Lao Yang. Beijing：Morning Glory Publishers，2000. 63 pages：color illustrations；20×27cm. ISBN：7505402404，7505402409
中国古诗配画.英汉对照.

97. The three poet kings Li：China's dream and reality，experienced and written in selected works by Li Bai，Li Yu，Li Qingzhao/by Engelbert Altenburger. Taipei，Taiwan：Kaun Tang International Publications，2000. xiv，169 pages：illustrations；26cm. ISBN：9579139946，9579139946
《三李诗词》，Altenburger，Engelbert. 收录李白、李煜和李清照的诗词. 由台北冠唐国际图书股份有限公司出版.

98. Crossing the Yellow River：three hundred poems from the Chinese/translated and introduced by Sam Hamill，preface by W. S. Merwin. Rochester，NY：BOA Editions，2000. 280 p.；23cm. ISBN：1880238977，1880238985. (New American translations series；vol. 13)
Notes：Three hundred poems from the Chinese features a wealth of Chinese poetry from three millennia (330 B. C. to the 16th century).
中国古诗词. Hamill，Sam(美国诗人)译.
(1)NY：Tiger Bark Press，[2013]. 301 pages；23cm. ISBN：0981675299，0981675298

99. 金元明清绝句英译＝Four-line poems of the Jin，Yuan，Ming and Qing Dynasties/王晋熙，文殊编译. 北京：外

语教学与研究出版社，2002. 47，362 pages：illustrations；18cm. ISBN：756002582X，7560025827 中英对照.

100. Mountain home：the wilderness poetry of ancient China/selected and translated by David Hinton. Washington, D. C. ；New York：Counterpoint, c2002. xxi, 295 p. ；map；25cm.

《中国古代的野趣诗》，戴维·欣顿（Hinton, David, 1954—）（美国汉学家）选译.

101. 汉英双讲中国古诗 100 首 = 100 classical Chinese poems with Chinese-English interpretations/编著高民，王亦高；编译李红梅，郭海云；古诗英译许渊冲. 大连：大连出版社，2003. 10，446 pages：illustrations；21cm. ISBN：7806841024，7806841020

102. Poems of the masters = ［Qian jia shi］；China's classic anthology of T'ang and Sung dynasty verse/Translated by Red Pine. Port Townsend, Wash. ：Copper Canyon Press, c2003. xx, 474 p. ；map；23cm. ISBN：1556591950, 1556591952

《千家诗》，赤松（Red Pine, 1943—，真名，Bill Porter）（美国翻译家、诗人）译. 中英文本.

103. 中国古典诗歌选译/贺浔滨译. 北京：中央编译出版社，2004. 263 pages；26cm. ISBN：7802110718，7802110717. （Serial in comparative literature and world literature）

《中国古典诗歌选译》，贺浔滨编译. 中央编译出版社（比较文学与世界文学书系）

104. 300 gems of classical Chinese poetry/translated by Xu Yuanchong. Beijing：Peking University Press, 2004. 3，3，21，609 pages；21cm. ISBN：7301068026，7301068021

《汉英对照中国古诗精品三百首》，许渊冲主编. 北京大学出版社.

105. 古意新声. 初级本：汉英对照/杨洋编. 武汉：湖北教育出版社，2004. 195 pages：illustrations；24cm. ISBN：753513548X，7535135483. （汉英对照中国古典诗歌配画选读/陈宏薇主编）

106. 古意新声：汉英对照. 中级本/陈月红编. 武汉：湖北教育出版社，2004. 181 pages：illustrations；24cm. ISBN：7535135498，7535135490. （汉英对照中国古典诗歌配画选读/陈宏薇主编）

107. 古意新声：汉英对照. 品赏本/朱纯深译. 武汉：湖北教育出版社，2004. 160 pages：illustrations；24cm. ISBN：753513551X，7535135513. （汉英对照中国古典诗歌配画选读/陈宏薇主编）

108. 中国名花诗词英译：汉英对照/黄龙编译. 南京：南京出版社，2005. 215 页；20cm. ISBN：780718115X，7807181156 英文题名：English version of Chinese poesies of renowned flowers.

109. 新编千家诗：汉英对照/袁行霈编；徐放，韩珊今译；许渊冲英译. 北京：中华书局，2006. 321 页；24cm. ISBN：7101049400, 7101049404. （大中华文库） 英文题名：Gems of classical Chinese poetry.

110. 从诗到诗：中国古诗词英译：汉英对照/任治稷，余正译. 北京：外语教学与研究出版社，2006. XXX，312 页；21cm. ISBN：7560056968，7560056962 英文题名：From poem to poem：an English translation of classical Chinese poems.

111. 中国爱情诗精选：汉英对照/唐正秋编. 成都：四川人民出版社，2006. 307 页；21cm. ISBN：7220070764，7220070761 英文题名：Love songs from China：150 gems of Chinese love poems. 本书所选的诗作从最早的诗歌集《诗经》一直到当代.

112. 历代名人咏江苏：汉英对照/何永康主编；郁贤皓等编撰；杨昊成译. 扬州：广陵书社，2006. 149 页；29cm. ISBN：7806941591，7806941592 本书为诗词选本，主要精选历代名人咏江苏的经典诗、词 66 首，配图 66 幅，中英对照，以诗文再现江苏历史、文化的风貌.

113. Chinese erotic poems/translated and edited by Tony Barnstone and Chou Ping. Everyman's library ed. New York：Alfred A. Knopf, 2007. 256 p. ；17cm. ISBN：0307265678, 0307265676. （Everyman's library pocket poets）

《中国艳诗》，托尼·巴恩斯通（Barnstone, Tony, 1961—）（美国诗人），周平（Chou, Ping, 1957—）编译.

114. 英译乐府诗精华 = Gems of Yuefu ballads/汪榕培选译. 上海：上海外语教育出版社，2008. ii，［4］，285 pages：illustrations；24cm. ISBN：7544606028，7544606023. （外教社中国文化汉外对照丛书. 第 2 辑 = SFLEP bilingual Chinese culture series；2）

115. 历代诗词曲英译赏析：汉英对照/刘国善，王治江，徐树娟等编译. 北京：外文出版社，2009. 19 页，347 页；21cm. ISBN：7119042619，7119042610 英文题名：Chinese classical poems with English translations & comments.

116. 英译中国历代诗词/卓振英，刘筱华著. 广州：暨南大学出版社，2010. 300 页；23cm. ISBN：7811354553，7811354551 英文题名：An anthology of Chinese classical poetry. 本书共收入历代著名诗词 112 首.

117. Shi poem/Li Lienfung. ［Beijing, China］：China Intercontinental Press, 2010. 148 pages；19cm. ISBN：7508517469，7508517466 《中国古典文学趣读—诗》，李廉凤著. 五洲传播出版社.

118. Ci poem/Li Lienfung. ［Beijing, China］：China Intercontinental Press, 2010. 132 pages；19cm. ISBN：7508517452，7508517458 《中国古典文学趣读—词》，李廉凤著. 五洲传播出版社.

119. 英译中国古典诗词名篇/张炳星选译. 北京:中华书局,2010. 435 页;21cm. ISBN:7101071900,7101071902
英文题名:The golden treasury of the best Chinese classical poems.

120. 中国古典诗歌英释 100 首/戴清一编译. 北京:中国对外翻译出版公司,2011. 284 页;21cm. ISBN:7500131410,7500131410
英文题名:100 pieces of classical Chinese poetry with English translation and annotations. 撷取了 100 首中国古典诗歌作品.

121. 且行且吟:中国古诗词名句集锦:汉英对照/莫汀编译. 成都:四川辞书出版社,2011. 100 页;19cm. ISBN:7806826850,7806826858
英文题名:Traveling bard:a rhesis collection of Chinese classical poems. 本书集 100 句中国古典诗词中的名句.

122. 古诗英韵/沈菲著. 上海:上海三联书店,2011. 50 页;21cm. ISBN:7542637116,7542637118
英文题名:Wisdom of ancient poems from the far east. 本书选取了我国古代著名诗歌 52 首.

123. 崂山刻石诗词:英汉对照/王瑞竹编译. 青岛:中国海洋大学出版社,2011. 103 页;21cm. ISBN:7811259612,7811259613
英文题名:Poems of the inscriptions of mt. Laoshan. 本书选取崂山古诗 59 首.

124. Charm of bamboo:100 selected ancient Chinese poems on bamboo/Peng Zhenhua, Jiang Zehui; translators Wen Jingen, Wang Weidong, Huang Shaojie. Beijing:Foreign Languages Press, 2012. 195 pages:color illustrations;29cm. ISBN:7119080284, 7119080288
《绿竹神气:中国一百首咏竹古诗词精选 》,彭镇华,江泽慧(1939—)编;Wen Jingen 等译.
　(1)Beijing:Foreign Languages Press, 2013. 195 p.:col. ill.;30cm. ISBN:7119080260

125. English translation and interpretation of selected Chinese Ci-poems/by Kenneth K. Chan. Burnaby, B. C.:Wei bang wen hua qi ye gong si, 2012. [10], 206 pages;21cm. ISBN:1896672304, 1896672302
《英演译中国古词选集》,陈建兴. 英汉对照.

126. The five-colored clouds of Mount Wutai:poems from Dunhuang/by Mary Anne Cartelli. Leiden;Boston:Brill, 2013. vi, 224 pages:illustrations;25cm. ISBN:9004184817, 9004184813, 9004241763, 9004241760. (Sinica Leidensia;v. 109)
Notes:Chinese poems in English translation about Mount Wutai, found among the Dunhuang manuscripts and dating to the Tang and Five Dynasties periods, with a comprehensive analysis of their context and significance. / Includes bibliographical references (pages;207—218) and index.
Contents:1 Ascending and Wandering:Introduction 1—Sacred Mountains in Ancient China 3—Dunhuang and the Dunhuang Caves 8—Dunhuang Literature 10—Dunhuang and Mount Wutai 12—Mountains in Early Chinese Poetry 14—About the Book 22—2 The Clear and the Cold:Mount Wutai 27—Early Literature on Mount Wutai 27—Early Legends about Mount Wutai 29—Chinese Emperors and Mount Wutai 31—Mañjusri and the Chinese Buddhist Scriptures 37—The Mañjusri-parinirvana sutra 41—Mount Wutai as a Manifestation of the Buddhist Doctrine 46—Early Chinese Poetry on Mount Wutai 49—The Mount Wutai Poetry of the Dunhuang Manuscripts 53—3 The Hall of the Great Sage:The Songs of Mount Wutai 57—The Hall of the Great Sage 59—I Ascend the Eastern Terrace 66—I Ascend the Northern Terrace 71—I Ascend the Central Terrace 74—I Ascend the Western Terrace 78—I Ascend the Southern Terrace 82—4 The Land of Vaidurya:Eulogy on Mount Wutai 87—Eulogy on Mount Wutai 90—5 Inconceivable Light:Eulogy on Mount Wutai 121—The Pure Land School 122—The Pure Land Monk Fazhao 124—Eulogy on Mount Wulai 129—6 The Gold-Colored World:Eulogy on the Holy Regions of Mount Wutai 147—Eulogy on the True Countenance of the Great Sage 149—Eulogy on Samantabhadra 153—The Eastern Terrace 155—The Northern Terrace 158—The Central Terrace 159—The Western Terrace 161—The Southern Terrace 163—The Holy Region of the Vajra Grotto 165—The Auspicious Stupa of King Asoka 167—Eulogy on the Physical Body of Rahula 169—A Vision of Sutra Recitation by the Vajra Grotto 170—7 Word and Image:The Mount Wutai Wall Painting at Dunhuang 175—Map or Painting? 176—Iconography and Imagery in Cave 61 180—Mountain as Icon 192—8 Poetry as a Buddhist Matter:Conclusion 195—Transmission of the Vision 199—Literati Poets and Mount Wutai 202—For the Purpose of Salvation 204.
Cartelli, Mary Anne 著,对五台山的敦煌的抄本的佛教诗歌的翻译. 五代、唐代诗歌.

127. Collected poems & lyrics of classical China/translated [from the Chinese] by Xu Yuanchong. New York:CN Times Books, Inc, 2014. x, 915 pages;23cm. ISBN:1627740968, 1627740961
《许译中国古典诗词集》,许渊冲(1921—)译.

128. 中国历代诗词英译集锦/朱曼华编译. 第 2 版. 北京:商务印书馆国际有限公司,2016. 34, 296 页;图;23cm. ISBN:7517602873
英文题名:Chinese famous poetry translated.

129. An anthology of Chinese verse:Han, Wei, Chin and the Northern and Southern dynasties;Clarendon P., 1967. xliii, 198 p. plate (facsim.);23cm. (Oxford

library of East Asian literatures)

《中国汉魏晋与南北朝诗选》，Frodsham，J. D. 和 Ch'eng，His(1919—)合译.

130. 汉魏六朝诗三百首＝300 early Chinese poems/英译汪榕培，今译弘征，熊治祁. 长沙市：湖南人民出版社，1998.［3］，29，27，557 pages；22cm. ISBN：7543818566，7543818569.（汉英对照中国古典名著丛书＝The Chinese-English bilingual series of Chinese classic）

(1)长沙市：湖南人民出版社，2006. 2 volumes (41,547 pages)；24cm. ISBN：7543844699，7543844698.（大中华文库＝Library of Chinese classics）

131. Golden treasury of Chinese poetry in Han, Wei and Six dynasties/translated by Xu Yuanchong＝Han Wei Liu chao shi xuan/Xu Yuanchong yi. Beijing：China Intercontinental Press：Zhonghua Book, 2012. 21, 332 p.；22cm. ISBN：7508521923，7508521927.（Classical Chinese poetry and prose＝许译中国经典诗文集）

Notes："Project for translation and publication of Chinese cultural works＝中国文化著作翻译出版工程项目."

《汉魏六朝诗选》，许渊冲(1921—)译.

132. 汉魏六朝诗：Golden treasury of Chinese poetry in Han，Wei and six dynasties/许渊冲编译. Beijing：Hai tun chu ban she，2013. 116 pages，4 unnumbered pages of color plates：illustrations；22cm. ISBN：7511010469，7511010466.（许渊冲经典英译古代诗歌1000 首＝Version of classical Chinese poetry；2)

133. Immortal sisters：secrets of Taoist women/translated and edited by Thomas Cleary. Boston：Shambhala；［New York］：Distributed in the U. S. by Random House，1989. vi，99 pages；22cm. ISBN：087773481X，0877734819

《仙姑》，Cleary，Thomas F.，(1949—)（美国翻译家）编译. 收录了金代孙不二(公元 1119—1182 年)的 14 首诗，其他道姑的 6 首诗，以及其他炼丹的资料.

(1)Immortal sisters＝［Hsien ku］：secret teachings of Taoist women/translated and edited by Thomas Cleary. Berkeley，Calif.：North Atlantic Books，1996. xxix，90 pages；23cm. ISBN：1556432224，1556432224

(2)Immortal sisters：secret teachings of taoist women/transl. and ed. by Thomas Cleary. Berkeley Calif.：North Atlantic Books，1999. XXIX，90 p.；23cm. ISBN：087773481X，0877734819

134. Chinese poems in English rhyme by Admiral Ts'ai T'ing-kan. Chicago，Ill.，The University of Chicago Press［c1932］. xxi，145，［1］p.；24cm.

"One hundred and twenty-two selected poems of the T'ang period...The originals are found in the first and third books of the...Ch'ien chia shih，'Selected poems

from many poets'...Some of these translations were published in 1905 by the East Asia magazine."—Foreword and Pref.

《唐诗音韵》，蔡廷干(Cai，Tinggan，1861—1935)译. 选译中国古典诗歌 122 首，以唐、宋诗为主.

(1)New York：Greenwood Press［1969］. xxi，145 p.；23cm. ISBN：0837111595

(2) New York：AMS Press［1971］. xxi，145 p.；23cm. ISBN：0404065252

135. Tang Song ci xuan yi＝Chinese lyrics from the eighth to the twelfth centuries.［Taipei］：［Commercial Press］，［1969］. 4，2，9，244 p.；19cm.

《唐宋词选译》，Cheng，Shiquan 编译.

136. Selected poems of the Tang & Song Dynasties/translated by Rewi Alley. Hong Kong：Hai Feng Pub. Co.，1983. 106 p.：port.；19cm. ISBN：9622380204，9622380202

唐宋诗. 艾黎·路易(Alley，Rewi，1897—1987)译.

137. 唐宋词一百首：汉英对照/许渊冲选译. 香港：商务印书馆香港分馆，1986. 21，6，252 pages；19cm. ISBN：9620710770，9620710773.（一百丛书）

英文题名：100 Tang and Song ci poems：Chinese-English

(1)唐宋词一百首/许渊冲选译. 北京：中国对外翻译出版公司，2007. 335 页；21cm. ISBN：7500118114.（中译经典文库·中华传统文化精粹）

(2)100 Tang and Song ci poems/compiled and translated by Xu Yuanzhong. Sydney：CPG International，2008. 8，25，335 pages：illustrations；21cm. ISBN：1921099236，1921099232.（Traditional Chinese culture classical series）

138. Golden treasury of Chinese lyrics/translated and versified by Xu Yuan Zhong. Beijing，China：Peking University Press，1990. xiii，xiii，403 pages；19cm. ISBN：7301012004，7301012000

《唐宋词一百五十首》，许渊冲译. 北京大学出版社.

139. 唐宋绝句名篇英译＝Best-known Tang and Song four-line poems/文殊，王晋熙，邓炎昌译. 北京：外语教学与研究出版社，1995. 33，272 pages：illustrations；18cm. ISBN：7560009891，7560009896

140. Tang & Sung poems in English；［and］，13 poems in Chinese & English/［compiled and translated by］Too Chee Cheong.［Kuala Lumpur］：［Too Chee Cheong］，1998. xxi，116 pages；21cm. ISBN：9839942506，9839942507

《唐诗宋词英读；中英对照诗十三首》，杜志昌编译.

141. Lunar frost：translations from poets of the Tang and Song dynasties/by Selwyn Pritchard with the collaboration of Zhan Qiao，Liang Rui-Qing；foreword by Peter Porter. Sydney：Brandl & Schlesinger，2000. 79 p.；20cm. ISBN：187604022X，1876040222.

(Brandl & Schlesinger poetry)

唐宋诗. Pritchard，Selwyn，Zhan，Qiao 和 Liang，Rui-Qing 三人合译.

142. A translation and appreciation of selected Tang and Song Ci-poems/Lin Kong-hui. Kowloon, Hongkong：8 Dragons Publ.，1998. 200 pages；illustrations；21cm. ISBN：9627328332，9627328339

唐宋词选译. Lin，Kong-hui 译.

143. 唐宋诗一百首欣赏与英译：汉英对照/刘克璋译注. 北京：新华出版社，2006. 264 页；21cm. ISBN：7501177309，7501177301

英文题名：An appreciation and English translation of one hundred Chinese poems during the Tang and Song dynasties.

144. 最爱唐宋词：相伴一生的 100 首唐宋词：影画版：汉英对照/许渊冲选译. 北京：中国对外翻译出版公司，2006. 213 页；17×18cm. ISBN：7500115172，7500115175. (先知双语国学馆)

英文题名：The favorite Tang and Song poems.

145. 唐宋词欣赏/张红主编. 天津：天津教育出版社，2009. 54 页；26cm. ISBN：7530956472，7530956477

146. 汉英双语诵读唐诗宋词/冯志杰编选/英译. 北京：九州出版社，2017. 2 册；23cm. ISBN：7510860850

147. Selected lyrics of Tang and five dynasties/translated by Xu Yuanchong；[Wang Feng, editor]. [Singapore]：World Culture Books, 2011. 187 pages；22cm. ISBN：9810705794，9810705794. (Classical Chinese poetry and prose＝许译中国经典诗文集)

《唐五代词选》，许渊冲（1921—）译；wang feng 编. 英汉对照.

(1)Beijing：China Intercontinental Press；Zhonghua Book，2012. 16，187 p.；22cm. ISBN：7508522012，750852201X. (Classical Chinese poetry and prose＝许译中国经典诗文集)

(2)Selected lyrics of Tang and five dynasties＝唐五代词选/许渊冲译. Beijing：Hai tun chu ban she，2013. 10，206 pages；illustrations；22cm. ISBN：7511014177，7511014178. (许渊冲文集；7)

148. Neo-Confucian philosophical poems/by Wing-tsit Chan. Hong Kong：Centre for translation projects, the Chinese University of Hong Kong, 1975. 21 pages：illustrations，portraits；27cm.

Notes："Reprinted from RENDITIONS, No. 4, Spring 1975"—cover

《宋明理学家诗译》，陈荣捷（Chan，Wing-tsit，1901—1994）（美国华裔学者）选编.

149. Golden treasury of Song, Yuan, Ming and Qing poetry/translated by Xu Yuanchong & Frank M. Xu；[Wang Feng, editor]. Singapore：World Culture Books, 2011. 279 pages；22cm. ISBN：9810705800，9810705808. (Classical Chinese poetry and prose)

《宋元明清诗选》，许渊冲（1921—），许明译. 中英对照.

(1)Beijing：China Intercontinental Press；Zhonghua Book，2012. 28，279 p.；22cm. ISBN：7508522029，7508522028. (Classical Chinese poetry and prose＝许译中国经典诗文集)

(2)Beijing：Hai tun chu ban she, 2013. 27，290 pages；illustrations；22cm. ISBN：7511014207，7511014208. (许渊冲文集；10)

150. The Columbia book of later Chinese poetry：Yüan, Ming, and Ch'ing dynasties（1279—1911）/translated and edited by Jonathan Chaves. New York：Columbia University Press, 1986. xii, 481 p.，[10] leaves of plates：ill.；24cm. ISBN：023106148X，0231061498. (Translations from the Oriental classics)

《哥伦比亚中国元明清诗歌选集》，齐皎翰（Chaves，Jonathan）译.

151. 元明清诗一百五十首/许渊冲译. 北京：北京大学出版社，1997. xi，16，350 pages；19cm. ISBN：7301031165，7301031162. (汉英对照古典名著丛书汉英对照古典名著丛书)

英文题名：Golden treasury of Yuan, Ming, Qing poetry.

152. 汉英对照元明清诗＝Golden treasury of Yuan, Ming and Qing poetry/许渊冲英译；周晓宇中文注释. 北京：中国对外翻译出版公司，2009. 19，11，353 pages；21cm. ISBN：7500120247，7500120249. (中译经典文库中译经典文库. 中华传统文化精粹)

153. Golden treasury of Yuan, Ming and Qing poetry/Xu Yuanchong. Beijing：Hai tun chu ban she, 2013. 63 pages：illustrations（some color）；22cm. ISBN：7511010393，7511010391. (许渊冲经典英译古代诗歌 1000 首＝Version of classical Chinese poetry；10)

《元明清诗》，许渊冲编译.

I313　汉、三国时期诗歌集

1. The Han rhapsody：a study of the fu of Yang Hsiung, 53 B. C.—A. D. 18/David R. Knechtges. Cambridge [Eng.]；New York：Cambridge University Press, 1976. xiv，160 p.；24cm. ISBN：0521204585. (Cambridge studies in Chinese history, literature and institutions)

《汉赋：杨雄赋研究》，Knechtges，David R. 著. 对汉代杨雄（公元前 53 年—公元 18 年）的赋作了翻译.

2. Studies on the Han fu/by Gong Kechang；translated and edited David R. Knechtges, with Stuart Aque... [et al.]. New Haven, Conn.：American Oriental Society, 1997. vi，413 p.；26cm. I SBN 0940490145. (American oriental series；vol. 84)

《汉赋研究》，龚克昌（1933—）著；康达维（Knechtges，David R.）编译.

3. 三曹诗选英译/（美）吴伏生，（英）格雷厄姆·哈蒂尔编译. 北京：商务印书馆，2016. 267 页；22cm. ISBN：
7100121620.（中国古典文学英译丛书）

英文题名：Selected poems of the three Caos：Cao Cao，
Cao Pi，and Cao Zhi. 英汉对照. 本书精选了建安时期文
学代表人物曹氏父子：曹操、曹丕、曹植的经典代表性作
品约八十首，包括曹操的《短歌行》《步出夏门行》、曹丕的
《秋胡行》《清河行》、曹植的《赠王粲》《七步诗》等，由吴伏
生和 Graham Hartill 一中一外两位译者用素体自由诗的
形式合作翻译

4. The poetry of Ruan Ji and Xi Kang/translated by Stephen
Owen and Wendy Swartz；volume edited by Xiaofei Tian
and Ding Xiang Warner. Berlin；Boston：De Gruyter，
2017. vi，405 pages；21cm. ISBN：1501511851，
1501511858.（Library of Chinese humanities）

阮籍和嵇康的诗. 宇文所安（Owen，Stephen，1946—）
（美国汉学家）和 Swartz，Wendy（1972—）合译.

I314 南北朝诗歌集

1. 孔雀东南飞；木兰辞：汉英对照＝A pair of peacocks；the
Mulan ballad/汪榕培今译·英译. 长沙：湖南人民出版
社，1998. 1，1，63 pages，［28］pages of plates：color
illustrations；18cm. ISBN：7543818477. 7543818477

英汉对照.

2. The age of eternal brilliance：three lyric poets of the
Yung-ming era（483—493）/by Richard B. Mather.
Leiden；Boston：Brill，2003. 2 v.；25cm. ISBN：
9004120599.（Sinica Leidensia；v. 61）

《永远光辉的时代：永明时期的三位诗人》，马瑞志
（Mather，Richard B.，1913—）（美国汉学家）著. 该书收
录了著者对三位诗人沈约（441—513），谢朓（464—499）和
王融（468—493）部分诗作的翻译.

3. The song of Mu Lan/Jeanne M. Lee. Arden，NC：Front
Street，1995. 1 v.（unpaged）：col. ill.；20×26cm.
ISBN：1886910006，1886910003

《木兰诗》，Lee，Jeanne M. 译.

4. Wild orchid：a retelling of "The ballad of Mulan"/by
Cameron Dokey. 1st Simon Pulse pbk. ed. New York：
Simon Pulse，2009. 199 p.；18cm. ISBN：1416971689，
1416971688.（Once upon a time）

《木兰诗》，Dokey，Cameron 译.

I315 唐诗集

1. The jade mountain：a Chinese anthology，being three
hundred poems of the T'ang dynasty，618—906/
translated by Witter Bynner from the texts of Kiang
Kang-hu. New York：Knopf，1929. xxxvii，279 p.：
port. ；22cm.

《群玉山头：唐诗三百首选集》，江亢虎（Jiang，Kanghu，
1883—1954），陶友白（Bynner，Witter，1881—1968）（美
国诗人）合译.

  （1）New York：Knopf，1951. xxxvii，300 pages；22cm.
   （Borzoi books）

  （2）New York：Knopf，1957. xxxvii，300 pages；22cm.

  （3）Garden City，N. Y.，Anchor Books［1964］. xxxviii，
   238 p. illus.，ports. 18cm.

  （4）New York，Vintage Books［1972］. xxxvii，300 p.
   19cm. ISBN：0394718410，0394718415

2. Three hundred poems of the Tang dynasty，618—906：
English translation v. Chinese text：a translation with
notes and commentary for the study and appreciation of
the Chinese poems/translated by Witter Bynner.
［Taipei］：［Wenxing］，1963. xxxvii，300 pages；22cm.

《唐诗三百首》，江亢虎（Jiang，Kanghu，1883—1954），陶
友白（Bynner，Witter，1881—1968）（美国诗人）合译. 中
英对照.

  （1）Three hundred poems of the T'ang dynasty，618—
   906：English translation v. Chinese text；a
   translation with notes and commentary for the study
   and appreciation of the Chinese poems. Taipei：Wen
   hsing shu tien，1966. xxxvii，300 pages；21cm.

  （2）Three hundred poems of the T'ang dynasty，618—
   906；a translation with notes and commentary for the
   study and appreciation of the Chinese poems.［58 i. e.
   1969］. xxxvii，302 p.；21cm.

  （3）Three hundred poems of the T'ang Dynasty，618—
   906；a translation with notes and commentary for the
   study and appreciation of the Chinese poems/
   translated by Witter Bynner. Taipei：Jen Jen Book
   Co，1971. 302 pages；22cm.

  （4）中英对照唐诗三百首/［translated by Witter Bynner
   from the texts of Kiang Kang-hu］. 台北：人人书局，
   ［1974］. xxxvii，302 pages；22cm.

3. Selections from the three hundred poems of the T'ang
dynasty/translated by Soame Jenyns. London，Murray
［1940］. 116 p. ；18cm.（Wisdom of the East series）

《唐诗三百首选读》，孙洙（1711—1778）编；Jenyns，Soame
（1904—）（美国收藏家）译.

4. A further selection from the three hundred poems of the
T'ang dynasty/translated by Soame Jenyns. London，
Murray，［1944］. 95 p. ；18cm.

《唐诗三百首选读续集》，Jenyns，Soame（1904—）（美国
收藏家）译.

5. 唐诗三百首＝300 Tang poems/孙洙原编；吴钧陶主编.
长沙市：湖南出版社，1997. 5，20，32，774 pages；
21cm. ISBN：7543813955，7543813953.（［汉英对照中
国古典名著丛书］汉英对照中国古典名著丛书）

6. Three hundred poems of the T'ong Dynasty/Tr. by Ting
Hsu Chou. Taipei：Wu Chow Pub. Co，1965. 447
pages；19cm.

《唐诗三百首》，丁序周（Ting，Hsu Chou）译.

7. Three hundred poems of the T'ong dynasty/Ding Xuzhou
yi. Taibei Shi：Wu zhou chu ban she，min guo 69［1980］.
29，447 p. ；19cm.

《唐诗三百首新译》,丁序周(Ding, Xuzhou)译.英汉对照.

8. 300 T'ang poems. Translated by Innes Herdan. Taipei: Far East Book Co., [1973]. xxix, 518 p. illus.; 22cm.
《英译唐诗三百首》,Herdan, Innes 译.中英对照.
(1)4th ed. Taibei Shi: Far East Book Co., 1984. xxix, 518 pages, approximately 100 leaves of plates: illustrations; 22cm.
(2)4th ed. Taipei; New York: Far East Book Co., 1987. xxix, 518 pages, [40] pages of plates: illustrations; 22cm.
(3)300 Tang poems/translated by Innes Herdan; [illustrated by Chiang Yee]. 台北:远东图书公司, 2000. xxxi, 829 pages: illustrations; 22cm. ISBN: 9576124719, 9576124716

9. 300 Tang poems, a new translation: English-Chinese/[Xu Yuanchong, Lu Peixian, Wu Juntao bian]. Beijing: Zhongguo dui wai fan yi chu ban gong si; Xianggang: Shang wu yin shu guan (Xianggang) you xian gong si, 1988. xv, 14, 411 p.; 19cm. ISBN: 7500100736, 7500100737
《唐诗三百首新译》,许渊冲(1921—),陆佩弦,吴钧陶(1927—)译.英汉对照.
(1)台北:书林出版有限公司, 1992 (1993 printing). xv, 14, 411 p.; 22cm. ISBN: 9575862783, 9575862787
(2)[Rev. ed.]. Hong Kong: The Commercial Press, 1999. xv, 14, 411 pages; 22cm. ISBN: 962071203X, 9620712036
(3)Singapore: World Culture Books, 2011. 336 pages; 22cm. ISBN: 9810705756, 9810705751. (Classical Chinese poetry and prose=许译中国经典诗文)

10. 300 Tang poems: classified by theme/translated [and annotated] by Xu Yuanchong. Beijing: China Translation and Pub., 2006. 1 volume (unpaged). ISBN: 7500111986, 7500111983
《唐诗三百首》,许渊冲译.
(1)Tang poems=唐诗三百首/许渊冲译. Beijing: Hai tun chu ban she, 2013. 29, 384 pages: illustrations; 22cm. ISBN: 7511014160, 751101416X. (许渊冲文集; 6)

11. 唐诗300首鉴赏:汉英对照/谢真元主编;许渊冲,马红军译.北京:中国对外翻译出版公司,2006. 664 页;21cm. ISBN: 7500115466, 7500115465
英文题名:300 Tang poems.

12. Three hundred T'ang dynasty poems/translated, commented and annotated by William Dolby. Edinburgh: Carreg Publishers, 2006. volumes: illustrations; 21cm. (Chinese culture series; no. 16)
《英译唐诗三百首》,Dolby, William 译.

13. Three hundred Tang poems/translated and edited by Peter Harris. New York: Alfred A. Knopf: Distributed by Random House, 2009. 288 p.; 17cm. ISBN: 0307269737, 0307269736. (Everyman's library pocket poets)
《唐诗三百首》,Harris, Peter(1947—)译.
(1)Three hundred Tang poems/compiled by Peter Harris. London: Everyman, 2009. pages. ISBN: 1841597829, 1841597821, 0307269737, 0307269736

14. 唐诗三百首白话英语双译探索/王方路著.上海:复旦大学出版社,2010. 444 页;21cm. ISBN: 7309071016, 7309071018
英文题名:An exploration of translation of 300 poems in Tang Dynasty into baihua and English versions. 本书涵盖《唐诗三百首》所有篇目诗,对每首诗都进行白话诗翻译和英语诗翻译.

15. Three hundred Tang poems/translated by Geoffrey R. Waters, Michael Farman & David Lunde; introduction by Jerome P. Seaton. Buffalo, N. Y.: White Pine Press, 2011. 271 pages; 23cm. ISBN: 1935210269, 1935210262
唐诗三百首. Waters, Geoffrey R. (1948—), Farman, Michael 和 Lunde, David(1941—)合译.

16. A lute of jade; being selections from the classical poets of China, rendered with an introduction, by L. Cranmer-Byng. London, J. Murray, 1911. 116 p.; 17cm.
"First edition, March 1909; second edition, January, 1911."
《玉琵琶》,Cranmer-Byng, L. (Launcelot, 1872—1945) (英国诗人)译.选译部分唐诗.
(1)New York: E. P. Dutton & Co., inc. [1934]. 116 p.; 19cm.
(2)London, J. Murray [1959]. 112 p.; 20cm.
(3)Westport, Conn.: Greenwood Press, 1978. 112 p.; 23cm.

17. A feast of lanterns, rendered with an introduction by L. Cranmer-Byng. London, J. Murray, 1916. 95 p.; 17cm.
《宫灯的飨宴》,Cranmer-Byng, L. (Launcelot, 1872—1945)(英国诗人)译.选译部分唐诗.
(1)London, J. Murray, 1924. 95 p.; 17cm.

18. Gems of Chinese verse, tr. into English verse. Shanghai, Commercial Press Ltd., 1918. 3 p. l., iii p., 1 l., x, 242 p., 1 l. 23cm.
《英译唐诗选》,Fletcher, W. J. B. (William John Bainbrigge, 1879—1933)译.共译唐诗 180 首,其中李白诗歌 36 首,杜甫诗歌 45 首.
(1)3rd ed. Shanghai, China: Commercial Press, 1922. x, 242 pages; 23cm.
(2)4th ed. Shanghai: Commercial Press, 1925. 2 volumes; 22cm.
(3)Shanghai, Commercial Press, 1926. 3 preliminary

leaves, iii pages, 1 leaf, x, 242 pages, 1 leaf; 23cm.

(4)Shanghai, Commercial Press, 1932. xxiii, 246 pages; 19cm.

(5)Shanghai, China：Commercial Press, 1935. xxiii, 246 pages; 19cm.

(6)New York：Paragon Book Reprint Corp.，1966. x, 242，iv, 208 pages; 22cm.

(7)[Charleston, S. C.]：Bibliolife, 2009. x, 242 pages; 24cm. ISBN：1110354832, 1110354835.（BiblioLife reproduction series）

19. More gems of Chinese poetry/tr. into English verse by W. J. B. Fletcher, with comparative passages from English literature. Shanghai, Commercial Press, 1919. 3 preliminary leaves，iv, 208 pages; 22cm.
《英译唐诗选续集》，Fletcher, W. J. B.（William John Bainbrigge, 1879—1933)译.共译唐诗 105 首,其中李白诗 17 首,杜甫诗 30 首.

(1)2nd ed. Shanghai：Commercial Press, 1923. iv, 208 pages; 22cm.

(2)Shanghai, China：Commercial Press, 1925. iv, 208 pages.

(3)Shanghai, China：Commercial Press, 1928. xv, 209 pages; 22cm.

(4)Shanghai, China, Commercial Press, 1933. xv, 209 pages; 19cm.

20. Gems of Chinese verse, and More gems of Chinese poetry. Translated into English verse by W. J. B. Fletcher. 2nd ed. New York：Paragon Book Reprint Corp.，1966. x, 242, iv, 208 p.；22cm.（2 v. in 1)
《英译唐诗选》与《英译唐诗选续集》合辑,Fletcher, W. J. B.（William John Bainbrigge, 1879—1933)译.共译唐诗 285 首.

21. A little garland from Cathay：being a translation, with notes, of some poems of the Tang Dynasty (Cent. VII-IX)/by T. Gaunt. Shanghai：Presbyterian Mission Press, 1919. 52, 12 pages; 19cm.
唐诗. Gaunt, T. 译.

22. After the Chinese/Ian Duncan Colvin; Léon Hervey de Saint-Denys, marquis d'. London, P. Davies, 1927. ix, [1], 75, [1] pages; 22cm.
Notes：Based on the Poésies de l'époque des Thang, of the Marquis d'Hervey-Saint-Denys.
唐诗. Colvin, Ian Duncan(1877—1938)译自 Hervey de Saint-Denys, Léon, marquis d'(1822—1892)的法文图书：Poésies de l'époque des Thang

23. Selected poems of the Tang dynasty＝中英对照唐诗选译/李伯乐编译. 香港：英语出版社, 1962. 7, 101 pages; 19cm.

24. One hundred quatrains by the T'ang poets：English translations/Chosen and arranged with notes by Lü Shu-hsiang. Shanghai：Kaiming Book Co., 1947. x, 126

pages；17cm.
《英译唐人绝句百首》，Lü, Shuxiang 译.

25. Poems of the late T'ang. Translated with an introd. by A. C. Graham. Baltimore, Penguin Books［1965］. 173 p.；19cm.（UNESCO collection of representative works：Chinese series）.（The Penguin classics, L157)
《晚唐诗》，葛瑞汉（Graham, A. C.〈Angus Charles〉, 1919—1991)（英国汉学家)编译.收录杜甫、孟郊、韩愈、李贺、杜牧、李商隐等人的作品 90 余首.

(1)New York［etc.］：Penguin, 1977. 175 p.；19cm.（UNESCO collection of representative works：Chinese series）（The Penguin classics）ISBN：0140441573, 0140441574.（UNESCO collection of representative works：Chinese series；The Penguin classics）

(2)New York：New York Review Books, ［c2008］. 173 p.；21cm.（New York Review Books classics）. ISBN：1590172575, 1590172574

26. Poems of Tang：600 poems written in Tang style by Tang poets/selected annotated, translated and illustrated by Tang Zi-chang＝Tang shi xuan yi/Tang Zichang. San Rafael, Calif.：T. C. Press, c1969. 453 p.：col. ill.，port.；25cm.
《唐诗选译》，唐子长（Tang, Zi-chang)选译.英汉对照.

27. The boat untied, and other poems：a translation of T'ang poems in wood with original poems in Chinese calligraphy/Wang Hui-Ming. Barre, MA：Barre Publishers, 1971. 32 unnumbered pages：color illustrations；31cm. ISBN：082717117X, 0827171176
《不系船集》，Wang, Hui-ming 著,是对唐诗的英译.

28. Equinox：a gathering of T'ang poets/translations and adaptations by David Gordon.［Athens：Ohio University Press, 1975. xx, 89 pages；24cm. ISBN：0821401629, 0821401620
唐诗英译. Gordon, David M.（David McCall)译.

29. The poetry of the early T'ang/Stephen Owen. New Haven：Yale University Press, 1977. xv, 455 p.；24cm. ISBN：0300021038
Notes：Text in English accompanied by Chinese poems with parallel English translations.
《初唐诗》，宇文所安（Owen, Stephen, 1946—)（美国汉学家)译.

30. Chinese poetic writing/François Cheng; translated from the French by Donald A. Riggs and Jerome P. Seaton; with an anthology of T'ang poetry translated from the Chinese by Jerome P. Seaton. Bloomington：Indiana University Press, 1982. xiv, 225 pages, ［8］pages of plates：illustrations；21cm. ISBN：0253202841, 0253202840, 0253313589, 0253313584.（Studies in Chinese literature and society)
Cheng, François（1929—)原著. Riggs, Donald A. 和

Seaton, Jerome P. 转译自法文版,该书有 Seaton, Jerome P. 英译的唐诗集.

(1) Chinese poetic writing：with an anthology of Tang poetry/by François Cheng；translated by Donald A. Riggs and Jerome P. Seaton. Expanded edition. ［Hong Kong］：The Chinese University of Hong Kong Press；［New York］：New York Review Books, 2016. xiv, 335 pages：illustrations；22cm. ISBN：9629966584, 9629966581. （Calligrams）

31. T'ang poets：index to English translations/compiled by Sydney S. K. Fung and S. T. Lai. Hong Kong：Chinese University Press；Seattle：Distributed by University of Washington Press, c1984. xxviii, 696 p. ：ill. ；28cm. ISBN：9622012973. （A Renditions book）

《唐诗 25 首》,Fung, Sydney S. K. 和 Lai, Shu Tim. 编译.

32. T'ang Dynasty poems/translated by John Knoepfle and Wang Shouyi. Peoria, Ill. ：Spoon River Poetry Press, 1985. 73 pages；22cm. ISBN：0933180764, 0933180765, 0933180845, 0933180840

唐诗. Knoepfle, John 和 Wang, Shou-i. 合译. 英汉对照.

33. 唐诗二百首英译＝200 Chinese Tang poems in English verse/徐忠杰译. 北京：北京语言学院出版社, 1990. 27, 392 pages；19cm. ISBN：7561900759, 7561900758

34. Sixteen T'ang poems/translated with a poem by Gary Snyder；Hanga woodcut by Bill Paden. Hopewell, New Jersey：Pied Oxen Printers, 1993.. 21］pages：illustrations；30cm.

《唐诗 16 首》,由 Snyder, Gary（1930—）（美国诗人）选译. 汉嘉木刻版.

35. 英译唐诗绝句百首＝English-Chinese 100 quatrains by the Tang poets/王大濂译. 天津市：百花文艺出版社, 1997. 7, 9, 239 pages；21cm. ISBN：7530621114, 7530621110

36. Ten thousand miles of mountains and rivers：translations of Chinese poetry/by Doris Pai. Boulder, Colo. ：Third Ear Books, 1998. ［5］, 22 pages；19cm. ISBN：1891051105, 1891051104

中国诗歌翻译. Pai, Doris 英译,收录了温庭筠（约 812—870）,孟浩然（689—740）,王维（701—761）,李商隐（813—858）,张九龄（678—740）,杜牧（803—853?）,韦应物,苏颋（680—737）,刘禹锡（772—842）的诗作.

37. In love with the way：Chinese poems of the Tang Dynasty/edited by François Cheng；calligraphy by Fabienne Verdier. Boston：Shambhala：Distributed in the United States by Random House, 2002. 1 volume（unpaged）；23cm. ISBN：157062979X, 1570629792. （Shambhala calligraphy）

唐诗. Cheng, François（1929—）译.

38. Thirty Tang poems with English translations/［selected and translated by］Tinna K. Wu. Balintawak, Quezon City, Philippines：JC Lucas Creative Products, 2002. 64 pages：illustrations；24cm. ISBN：9718360204, 9718360200

唐诗三十首英译. Wu, Tinna Keh 译.

39. Fifty Tang poems/translated and annotated by Stephen M. Johnson. San Francisco, CA：Pocketscholar Press, 2004. 191 pages：illustrations；22cm. ISBN：0967945305, 0967945309

《唐诗五十首》,Johnson, Stephen M. 译. 英汉对照.

40. Selected poems and pictures of the Tang dynasty＝精选唐诗与唐画/Wang Yushu. Beijing：China Intercontinental Press, 2006. 175 pages：illustrations；23cm. ISBN：7508507983, 7508507989

《精选唐诗唐画：汉英对照》,五洲传播出版社编；王玉书译. 五洲传播出版社.

41. 最美是唐诗：相伴一生的 100 首唐诗：影画版：汉英对照/张庭琛等编著. 北京：中国对外翻译出版公司,2006. 213 页；17×18cm. ISBN：7500115164, 7500115168. （先知双语国学馆）

英文题名：The most beautiful Tang poems.

42. 唐宋诗词 100 首：汉英对照/裘小龙译. 上海：华东师范大学出版社,2006. 241 页；23mcm. ISBN：7561743033, 7561743034

本书精选唐宋诗词 100 余首,由获得美国密苏里州最高诗人奖的华裔诗人裘小龙翻译,本书还配有诗词大意和彩图.

(1) Shanghai：Shanghai Press and Publishing Development Company, 2006. 231 pages：color illustrations；25cm. ISBN：1602201013, 1602201019. （Cultural China＝文化中国）

43. An appreciation and English translation of one hundred Chines［e］cis during the Tang and Song dynasties/［translated］by Kezhang Liu. Pittsburgh, Penn. ：RoseDog Books, 2006. xxvi, 260 pages；23cm. ISBN：0805990089, 0805990089

《唐宋词一百首欣赏与英译》,Liu, Kezhang 译.

44. 英译唐诗名作选/龚景浩选译. 北京：商务印书馆, 2006. iv, 155 pages；19cm. ISBN：7100045746, 7100045742

英文题名：A bouquet of poems from China's Tang Dynasty.

45. How to read a Chinese poem：a bilingual anthology of Tang poetry/translated and annotated by Edward C. Chang. North Charleston, S. C. ：BookSurge Pub. , 2007. xix, 425 pages；23cm. ISBN：1419670131, 1419670138

《如何阅读唐诗》,Chang, Edward C. 译注.

46. Fragrances of old Cathay：distilled from the writings of leading poets of Imperial China/［adapted by］Gordon Wallace. Charlbury：Jon Carpenter, 2007. 81 pages；21cm. ISBN：0954972790, 0954972791

唐诗. Wallace, Gordon. 译.

47. Evoking Tang：an anthology of classical Chinese poetry：in Chinese and English/[translated by] Qiu Xiaolong. Saint Louis, Missouri：PenUltimate Press, Inc., 2007. xiv, 162 pages；illustrations；23cm. ISBN：097606751X, 0976067511

唐诗. 裘小龙(Qiu, Xiaolong, 1953—)译. 英汉对照.

48. Cathay：translations & transformations/Heinz Insu Fenkl. New Paltz, N. Y.：Codhill Press, 2007. 93 pages；illustrations；23cm. ISBN：1930337251, 1930337256

唐诗. Fenkl, Heinz Insu(1960—)译.

49. 英译唐诗选＝An anthology of the Tang dynasty poetry/孙大雨译. 上海：上海外语教育出版社, 2007. x, 478 pages, [8] pages of plates：illustrations (some color), color portraits；24cm. ISBN：7544604543, 7544604543. (外教社中国文化汉外对照丛书. 第一辑)

收唐诗 120 首.

50. 唐诗一百首/张廷琛, 魏博思选译. 北京：中国对外翻译出版公司, 2007. 297 页；21cm. ISBN：7500118107, 7500118104. (中译经典文库·中华传统文化精粹＝Chinese classical treasury. The traditional Chinese culture classical series)

英文题名：100 Tang poems.

51. 英法双译唐诗 100 首/谢百魁选译. 北京：中国对外翻译出版公司, 2007. 200 页；21cm. ISBN：7500127543. (中译经典文库·中华传统文化精粹＝Chinese classical treasury. The traditional Chinese culture classical series)

英文题名：100 Tang poems in English and French, 法文题名：100 poemes des tang en anglais et en francais.

52. 100 Tang poems/compiled and translated by Zhang Tingchen and Bruce M. Wilson. Sydney：CPG International, 2008. 285 pages：illustrations；21cm. ISBN：1921099243, 1921099240. (Traditional Chinese culture classical series)

《唐诗一百首：汉英对照》, Zhang, Tingchen 和 Wilson, Bruce M. 合译.

53. 唐诗欣赏/张红主编. 天津：天津教育出版社, 2009. 38 页；26cm. ISBN：7530956472, 7530956477

54. 唐诗精品百首英译/郭著章, 江安, 鲁文忠选译注. 武汉：武汉大学出版社, 2010. 292 页；18cm. ISBN：7307079939, 7307079933. (中国传统蒙学精品系列)

英文题名：The gems of Tang poems and their English versions. 本书精选唐诗 101 首.

55. 古韵新声：唐诗绝句英译 108 首/都森, 陈玉筠编译. 武汉：华中科技大学出版社, 2011. 141 页；24cm. ISBN：7560969107, 7560969100

英文题名：108 Chinese quatrains from 108 Tang poets. 本书选取唐代 108 位诗人的绝句 108 首英译并配画.

56. 英法双译唐诗 100 首：汉英法对照/谢百魁选译. 北京：中国对外翻译出版公司, 2011. 14 页, 200 页；21cm. ISBN：7500127543, 7500127545. (中译经典文库. 中华传统文

化精粹)

唐诗的英、法、汉 3 种语言对照.

57. The shattered lute：a collection of poems from Tang dynasty China/translations and commentary by Bradford S. Miller. Denver, CO：Outskirts Press, 2011. [5], 299 pages；23cm. ISBN：1432773342, 1432773348

唐诗. Miller, Bradford S. 译.

58. Green jade and road men：translations, commentary, and poems of China/by David R. Solheim with Shirley Wang (Xing-fang Zou). Dickinson, N. D.：Buffalo Commons Press, 2011. x, 79 pages；illustrations；22cm. ISBN：0965600777, 0965600774

唐诗. Solheim, David R. 和 Wang, Shirley 合著. 对 15 首唐诗作了翻译和评注.

59. 唐诗＝Tang poetry/许渊冲编译. Beijing：Hai tun chu ban she, 2013. 2 volumes：color illustrations；22cm. ISBN：7511010458, 7511010452, 751101044X, 7511010445. (许渊冲经典英译古代诗歌 1000 首＝Version of classical Chinese poetry；3－4)

60. Wheel River：from North Hills/Wang Wei；P'ei Ti；versions by Harry Gilonis. London：Contraband, 2014. 71 pages；22cm. ISBN：1910319222, 1910319228

Gilonis, Harry 译. 翻译了唐朝诗人王维和裴迪(生卒年不详, 公元 741—756 在世)的诗.

61. In response to the howling monkeys along the Yangtze：an American eco-critic's translation of three hundred and eleven Tang poems/Ning Yu with Carlos Martinez. Bellingham, WA, USA：Center for East Asian Studies, Western Washington University, 2015. 273 pages；22×28cm. ISBN：0914584339, 0914584332. (East Asian Research Aids and Translations；Volume 7)

《数猿肠断和云叫："一个生态文学批评者的英译唐诗三百十一首"》, Yu, Ning(1955—)译.

62. 唐诗选译/选释才学娟；翻译吴思远. 桂林：广西师范大学出版社, 2017. 15, 234 页；彩图；22cm. ISBN：7549597000. (东方智慧丛书)

英文题名：Tang poetry (selections). 汉英对照.

63. Autumn willows：poetry by women of China's golden age/translated from the original Chinese by Bannie Chow, Thomas Cleary. Ashland, OR：Story Line Press, 2003. 117 p.；23cm. ISBN：1586540254, 1586540258

Notes：Provides poems by the three greatest poetesses of the Tang dynasty, China's golden age.

Chow, Bannie(1948—), Cleary, Thomas F. (1949—) (美国翻译家)编译. 翻译了唐朝李冶、薛涛等 3 位女诗人的诗.

64. Willow, wine, mirror, moon：women's poems from Tang China/ translated from the Chinese with an introduction by Jeanne Larsen. Rochester, NY：BOA Editions, 2005. 151 p.；23cm. ISBN：1929918747,

1929918739. (Lannan translations selection series)

《唐代女诗人作品选》，Larsen，Jeanne（美国汉学家）译.

65. Poem on a plane tree's leaf：women poets of the Tang Dynasty/new translations by Christopher Kelen, Hilda Tam, Song Zijiang, Iris Fan and Carol Ting. [Chicago, Ill.]：Virtual Artists Collective, 2011. 90 pages；23cm. ISBN：0983009146, 0983009147

唐代女诗人作品选. Kelen, Christopher（1958—）等译.

66. Cold mountain poems：Zen poems of Han Shan, Shih Te, and Wang Fan-chih/translated by J. P. Seaton. Boston；London：Shambhala, 2009. vii, 126 p.；18cm. ISBN：1590306468,1590306465. (Shambhala library)

《寒山诗：寒山、拾得和王梵志的禅诗》，Seaton，Jerome P.译. 收录寒山（生卒不祥，活动时代约公元 627—649），拾得（生卒不祥，活动时代约公元 627—649）和王梵志（约公元 590—660 年）的诗歌.

(1) Boston, Mass.：Shambhala；Enfield：Publishers Group UK [distributor], 2012. 1 volume；18cm. ISBN：1590309056, 1590309057. (Shambhala library)

67. The view from Cold Mountain：poems of Hanshan and Shide/translated [from the Chinese] by Arthur Tobias, James Sanford and J. P. Seaton；ill. by Gyoskusei Jikihara；edited by Dennis Maloney. Buffalo, N. Y.：White Pine Press, 1982. 1 volume：illustrations；21cm.

寒山和拾得僧诗. Seaton, Jerome P. 和 Tobias, Arthur 合译.

68. The poetry of Hanshan (Cold Mountain), Shide, and Fenggan/volume edited by Christopher Nugent；translated by Paul Rouzer. 2017. xx, 403 pages；21cm. ISBN：1501510564, 1501510568. (Library of Chinese humanities)

收录寒山（生卒不祥，活动时代约公元 627—649），拾得（生卒不祥，活动时代约公元 627—649）和丰干（生卒不祥，活动时代约公元 627—649）的诗歌. Nugent, Christopher M. B.（1969—）编；Rouzer, Paul F. 译.

69. Li Po and Tu Fu/poems selected and translated with an introd. and notes by Arthur Cooper；Chinese calligraphy by Shui Chien-Tung. [Harmondsworth, Eng.]：Penguin Books, [1973]. 249 p.；19cm. ISBN：0140442723, 0140442724(Penguin Classics)

Cooper, Arthur R. V. 译. 对李白和杜甫的诗歌作选译.

(1)[Harmondsworth, Eng.] Penguin Books, 1974. 249 pages；19cm. (Penguin Classics)

(2)Harmondsworth：Penguin, 1976. 249 pages：music；19cm. ISBN：0140442723, 0140442724

(3)Taipei：Tun Huang, 1977. 249 pages：illustrations；18cm. (Penguin classics)

(4)Penguin Books, 1985. 249 pages；19cm. (Penguin Classics)

(5)Harmondsworth；New York [etc.]：Penguin Books, 1986. 249 p.；18cm. ISBN：0140442723, 0140442724. (Penguin Classics)

70. I didn't notice the mountain growing dark：poems of Li Pai and Tu Fu/translated by Gary Geddes and George Liang. Dunvegan, Ont.：Cormorant Books, 1986. 1 v. (unpaged)；22cm. ISBN：0920953026, 0920953020

李白、杜甫诗. Geddes, Gary 和 Liang, George 合译.

71. Bright moon, perching bird：poems/Li Po and Tu Fu；translated from the Chinese by J. P. Seaton and James Cryer；calligraphy by Mo Ji-yu；portraits and title page by Huang Yong-hou. Middletown, Conn.：Wesleyan University Press；Scranton, Pa.：Distributed by Harper & Row, c1987. xv, 143 p.：ill.；24cm. ISBN：0819521434, 0819521439, 0819511447, 0819511447. (Wesleyan poetry in translation)

《明月，栖鸟》，Seaton，Jerome P. 和 Cryer，James（1945—）译. 对李白和杜甫的诗歌的选译.

72. Endless river：Li Po and Tu Fu, a friendship in poetry/edited by Sam Hamill. New York：Weatherhill, 1993. 134 p.：ill.；14cm. ISBN：0834802635, 0834802636

《李白、杜甫诗选》，Hamill，Sam（美国诗人）编译.

73. Li-Tu：Ch'iu-p'u verses & scattered sentiments：poetic cycles=[Li Du]/by Li Po & Tu Fu；[translations and introductions by Bradford S. Miller]. West Hills CA：IMP Press, c1997. 1 v. (unpaged)；22cm.

Miller, Bradford S. 译. 对李白和杜甫的诗歌作选译.

74. Cloud tribes：my favorite poems of Li Bai and Du Fu/selected and translated by Claire Wang-Lee=[Yun zu：Li Bai Du Fu xuan yi shi/Wang Kenan]. Irvine, CA：James Pub. Co., 2006. xxx, 250 p.；22cm. ISBN：1893584232, 1893584235

《云族：李白杜甫选译诗》，王克难（Wang, Kenan）译.

75. Facing the moon：poems of Li Bai and Du Fu/translated by Keith Holyoak；[calligraphy by Hung-hsiang Chou；paintings on cover and title page by Xing Jie Chen]. Durham, N. H.：Oyster River Press, 2007. xxii, 127 pages：illustrations；22cm. ISBN：1882291045, 1882291042

Holyoak, Keith 译. 李白和杜甫诗英译.

76. Wang Wei, Li Po, Tu Fu, Li Ho：four T'ang poets/translated and introduced by David Young. [Place of publication not identified]：[publisher not identified], 1980. 154 pages；20cm. ISBN：0932440061, 0932440068, 093244007X, 0932440075. (FIELD translation series；4)

王维、李白、杜甫和李贺四位唐代诗人的诗歌. Young, David（1936—）译.

(1)[2nd ed.]. Oberlin：Oberlin College Press, 1990. 182 p. ISBN：093244055X, 0932440556. (Field translation series；15)

77. Three Chinese poets: translations of poems by Wang Wei, Li Bai, and Du Fu/[translated by] Vikram Seth. New York: HarperPerennial, c1992. xxv, 53 p.: ill.; 21cm. ISBN: 0060553529, 0060553524, 0060950242, 0060950248

《王维、李白、杜甫诗选》，Seth, Vikram（1952—）译.

   (1) New Delhi, India: Viking; Boston: Faber and Faber, 1992. xxv, 53 p.; 22cm. ISBN: 0670840041, 0670840045

   (2) London; Boston: Faber, 1992. xxv, 53 p.; 21cm. ISBN: 0571166539, 0571166534, 0571167632, 0571167630

   (3) London: Phoenix, 1997. xxv, 53 pages; 20cm. ISBN: 1857997808, 1857997804

   (4) New Delhi: Viking, 2005. XXXV, 64 p. ISBN: 0670058483, 0670058488

78. Singing of scented grass: verses from the Chinese/[translated by] Ian Johnston. Lauderdale, Tas.: Pardalote Press, 2003. 126 pages: illustrations; 21cm. ISBN: 0957843631, 0957843639

Johnston, Ian（1939—）译. 收录了王维（701—761）、白居易（772—846）、李商隐（813—858）的诗.

79. I hear my gate slam: Chinese poets meeting and parting/translated by Taylor Stoehr. Boston, MA: Pressed Wafer, 2007. 138 pages: illustrations; 18cm. ISBN: 0978515625, 0978515621

Notes: Translations of poems by Li Po, Wang Wei, Po Chü-i, Tu Fu, and other classical poets.

Stoehr, Taylor（1931—）译. 选译了王维、李白、杜甫和白居易的诗歌.

80. Three neglected Chinese women, three deserted Tang poets/Hong Ai Bai; improvisations on the poems and illustrations by John Dogby. Oyster Bay, N.Y.: Feral Press, 2011. 1 volume (unpaged): illustrations; 22cm.

Contents: Chant of the departing wife/Li Bai—An isolated lady/Du Fu—A wife's sorrow/Bai Juyi—Li Bai, Du Fu and Bai Juyi: three deserted poets/Hong Ai Bai.

Bai, Hong Ai 译; Digby, John（1938—）插图. 对李白、杜甫和白居易三位唐代诗人诗歌的英译.

81. Chinese makers/Du Fu, Li Bai, Wang Wei, Xue Tao; Scots versions by Robert Crawford; photographs by Norman McBeath and John Thomson. Edinburgh: Easel Press, 2016. 71 pages: illustrations, photographs; 23cm. ISBN: 0955285950, 095528595X

杜甫、李白、王维和薛涛四位诗人的诗作. Crawford, Robert 译.

82. Huangshan: poems from the T'ang dynasty/translated by Stanton Hager; photographs by Michael Kenna; edited and with an introduction by John Wood. [South Dennis, Mass.]: Steven Albahari, 21st Editions, 2010. [120] pages: photographs; 44cm. +1 portfolio

《黄山》，Stanton Hager 译. 收录唐朝有关黄山的诗作，包括寒山等僧诗.

I316 宋朝诗词集

1. The herald wind, translations of Sung dynasty poems, lyrics and songs. London, J. Murray [1933]. 113 p.; 18cm.

宋朝诗词. Candlin, Clara M.（Clara Margaret, 1983—）译.

   (1) The herald wind: translations of Sung dynasty poems, lyrics and songs/by Clara M. Candlin; with an introduction by L. Cranmer-Byng; foreword by Hu Shih. Westport, Conn.: Greenwood Press, 1981. 113 p.; 23cm. ISBN: 031323079X

2. An introduction to Sung poetry. Translated by Burton Watson. Cambridge, Mass., Harvard University Press, 1967. xii, 191 p. illus., facsims.; 24cm. (Harvard-Yenching Institute monograph series, v. 17)

"The original work, entitled Sōshi gaisetsu, appeared in 1962 as number one in the second series of the Chūgoku shijin senshū, or 'Selected works of Chinese poets' series, edited by Yoshikawa and... Ogawa Tamaki."

《宋诗概要》，华兹生（Watson, Burton, 1925—）（美国翻译家）译. 从 1962 年 Yoshikawa, Kōjirō（1904—1980）选编的《中国诗选》（Selected works of Chinese poets）翻译.

3. Moments of rising mist; a collection of Sung landscape poetry. Translated by Amitendranath Tagore. New York: Grossman Publishers [1973]. vii, 228 p. illus.; 26cm. ISBN: 0670484644, 0670484645, 0670484636, 0670484638

Tagore, Amitendranath（1922—）译. 对宋代诗词的翻译.

4. Lyric poets of the Southern T'ang: Feng Yen-ssu, 903—960, and Li Yü, 937—978/[edited and translated by] Daniel Bryant. Vancouver: University of British Columbia Press, 1982. lviii, 151 pages; 24cm. ISBN: 0774801425, 0774801423

Bryant, Daniel（1942—）编译. 翻译了冯延巳（903—960）的《阳春集》，南唐中主李璟（916—961）、后主李煜（937—978）的《南唐二主词》.

5. Song Dynasty poems/translated by John Knoepfle and Wang Shouyi. Peoria, Ill.: Spoon River Poetry Press, 1985. 73 pages; 22cm. ISBN: 0933180829, 0933180826, 0933180853, 0933180857

宋诗. Knoepfle, John 和 Wang, Shouyi 合译.

6. The nine monks: Buddhist poets of the Northern Sung/selected and translated by Paul Hansen. Waldron Island, WA: Brooding Heron Press, 1988. iv, 19, iv, iii pages; 19cm. ISBN: 0918116457, 0918116451, 0918116465, 0918116468, 0918116473, 0918116475

《九僧集》（选译），Hansen, Paul 译. 收录宋代初期诗僧希昼、保暹、文兆、行肇、简长、惟凤、宇昭、怀古、惠崇等九人的诗.

7. Beyond spring: tz'u poems of the Sung dynasty/translated by Julie Landau. New York: Columbia University Press, c1994. xii, 275 p.: ill.; 21cm. ISBN: 023109678X, 0231096782. (Translations from the Asian classics)

《宋词》,Landau, Julie 译.

8. Song dynasty lyrics revisited: a modern rendition in English/translated by Lien Wen Sze, Foo Check Woo. Singapore: EPB Pub., 1996. 222 pages; 20cm. ISBN: 9971006731, 997100673

宋诗词新译. Foo, Check Woo 和 Lien, Wen Sze 合译.

9. Anthology of Song Dynasty ci-poetry/[translated, annotated, with an introduction by] Huang Hongquan. Beijing: People's Liberation Army Pub. House, 2001. 3,590 pages: illustrations, maps; 21cm. ISBN: 7506506661, 7506506663

《英译宋代词选》,黄宏荃著. 解放军出版社.

10. Song proses = Song ci/Nie Xinsen. Beijing: Foreign Languages Press, 2001. 312 p: Ill. ISBN: 7119028197, 7119028194. (A choice selection of ancient poems; Chinese-English)

《宋词》,聂鑫森,杨宪益(1915—2009),戴乃迭(Yang, Gladys,1919—1999)合译. 英汉对照.

11. Selected poems and pictures of the Song dynasty=精选宋词与宋画/许渊冲译词. Beijing: China Intercontinental Press, 2005. 187 pages: color illustrations; 23cm. ISBN: 7508508483, 7508508481. (Chinese traditional culture series=中国传统文化精粹书系)

《精选宋词与宋画:汉英对照》,五洲传播出版社编;许渊冲译. 五洲传播出版社.

12. 宋词三百首:汉英对照/许渊冲译. 北京:中国对外翻译出版公司, 2007. 12, 461 页;21cm. ISBN: 7500111993, 7500111991

英文题名:300 Song lyrics.

(1)Song lyrics/Xu Yuanchong. Beijing: Hai tun chu ban she, 2013. 25, 360 pages: illustrations; 22cm. ISBN: 7511014184, 7511014186. (许渊冲文集;8)

13. Drizzle and plum blossoms: four poets of the Song Dynasty/Ouyang Xiu, Su Dongpo, Lu You, Xin Qiji; [translated and with an introduction by Li C. Tien and John Palen]. Greensboro, NC: March Street Press, 2009. 47 pages; 19cm. ISBN: 1596611078, 1596611073

《细雨梅花》,Tien, Li C. 和 Palen, John(1942—)合译. 包括对宋代的欧阳修(1007—1072)、苏轼(1037—1101)、陆游(1125—1210)和辛弃疾(1140—1207)四位诗人的诗词翻译.

14. 300 Song lyrics/translated by Xu Yuanchong. Singapore: World Culture Books, 2011. 341 pages; 22cm. ISBN: 9810705770, 9810705778. (Classical Chinese poetry and prose=许译中国经典诗文)

《宋诗三百首》,许渊冲(1921—)译.

(1)Beijing: China Intercontinental Press: Zhonghua Book, 2012. 28, 341 str.; 22cm. ISBN: 7508521961, 750852196X. (Classical Chinese poetry and prose=许译中国经典诗文)

15. 宋词=Song lyrics/许渊冲编译. Beijing: Hai tun chu ban she, 2013. 2 volumes: color illustrations; 22cm. ISBN: 7511010431, 7511010438, 7511010423, 7511010421. (许渊冲经典英译古代诗歌 1000 首=Version of classical Chinese poetry; 6—7)

16. 名家讲宋词/朱建廷. 北京:五洲传播出版社,2016. 229 页;23cm. ISBN: 7508533193.(中国文化经典导读)

英文题名:Masters on masterpieces of Song lyrics.

I317　元朝诗词集

1. Fifty songs from the Yüan: poetry of 13th century China; translated, with introduction, appendices and notes by Richard F. S. Yang and Charles R. Metzger. London, Allen & Unwin, 1967. 3—151 p.;221/2cm. (UNESCO collection of representative works: Chinese series)

《元诗五十首》,杨富森(Yang, Richard Fu-Sen, 1918—)和 Metzger, Charles Reid(1921—)译注. 收录 50 首元代诗词. 英汉对照.

2. The wine of endless life: taoist drinking songs from the Yuan dynasty/edited and translated by Jerome B. [i. e. P.] Seaton. Ann Arbor, Mich.: Ardis, c1978. viii, 59 p.; 22cm.

《全元散曲》(选译),隋树森(1906—1989)编;Seaton, Jerome P. 译.

(1)Buffalo, N. Y.: White Pine Press, 1985. viii, 59 pages; 22cm. ISBN: 0934834598, 0934834599

3. New imagery of Yuan verse/[translated and compiled by Hor-Ming Lee; brush calligraphy by Gao Yu Yuan]. Victoria, B. C.: Horming Press, 2001. 146 pages: illustrations (some color), portraits; 28cm. ISBN: 0968932703, 0968932704

《元曲新意愿》,Lee, Hor-ming(1929—)译.

4. History of early Chinese ch'ü-aria poetry/by William Dolby. Edinburgh: Carreg Publishers, 2003. 355 pages, 8 leaves of plates: illustrations; 21cm. (Chinese culture series; no. 17)

《早期曲史》,Dolby, William 译.

5. 元曲一百五十首:汉英对照=150 masterpieces in Yuan qu-poetry/辜正坤选译. 北京:北京大学出版社, 2004. [1], 17, 23, 371 pages: illustrations; 21cm. ISBN: 7301066198, 7301066195

6. 英译元曲 200 首/周方珠选译. 合肥:安徽大学出版社, 2009. 21 页,405 页;21cm. ISBN: 7811105889, 7811105888

英文题名:An English translation of 200 Yuanqu poems. 本书以中华书局 1964 年出版的隋树森先生所编的《全元散曲》为蓝本,选择了其中 46 位作家的 43 种不同曲牌的 200 首作品.

7. 300 Yuan songs/translated by Xu Yuanchong. Singapore: World Culture Books, 2011. 301 pages; 22cm. ISBN:

9810705787，9810705786.（Classical Chinese poetry and prose＝许译中国经典诗文）

《元曲三百首》，许渊冲(1921—)译；[中文编辑张梅].英汉对照.

(1)Beijing：Wu zhou chuan bo chu ban she：Zhonghua shu ju，2012. 24，301 pages；22cm. ISBN：7508521930，7508521935.（Classical Chinese poetry and prose＝许译中国经典诗文）

8. 元曲＝Yuan songs/许渊冲编译. Beijing：Hai tun chu ban she，2013. 2 volumes：color illustrations；22cm. ISBN：7511010415，7511010414，7511010407，7511010407.（许渊冲经典英译古代诗歌 1000 首＝Version of classical Chinese poetry；8—9）

I318　清朝诗词集

1. Waiting for the unicorn：poems and lyrics of China's last dynasty，1644—1911/edited by Irving Yucheng Lo and William Schultz. Bloomington：Indiana University Press，c1986. xxviii，423 p.：ill.；25cm. ISBN：0253363217，0253363213.（Chinese literature in translation）

《待麟集：清代诗词选》，Lo，Yucheng，(1922—)（美国华裔汉学家），舒威霖(Schultz，William，1925—)合编.

(1)Dai lin ji：Chinese character text of Waiting for the unicorn：poems and lyrics of China's last dynasty，1644—1911/edited by Irving Yucheng Lo and William Schultz. Bloomington：Indiana University Press，c1987. 127 p.；24cm. ISBN：0253204038

(2)Bloomington：Indiana University Press，1990. xxviii，423 pages：illustrations；25cm. ISBN：0253205751，0253205759.（Chinese literature in translation；Midland book；MB575）

2. 《红楼梦》诗词英译词典/高雷编著. 广州：世界图书出版广东有限公司，2011. 350 页；24cm. ISBN：7510040887，7510040884

英文题名：Translations of the rhymed verses in Hong lou meng. 本书主要收录了杨宪益夫妇、David Hawkes、B. S. Bonsall 翻译的《红楼梦》英文全译本诗词和 H. Bencraft Joly 翻译的部分诗词.

3. Two centuries of Manchu women poets：an anthology/translated by Wilt L. Idema. Seattle University of Washington Press，2017. pages cm. ISBN：0295999869，0295999861

清朝女诗人诗集. 伊维德(Idema，W. L.〈Wilt L.〉，1944—)（荷兰汉学家）译.

I32　古代诗人个人作品

I321　春秋战国时期

屈原(约公元前 340 或 339 年—前 278 年)

1. The nine songs：a study of shamanism in ancient China [by] Arthur Waley. London，G. Allen and Unwin [1955]. 64 p.；23cm.

《楚辞·九歌：古代中国巫术研究》，韦利(Waley，Arthur，1889—1966)（英国汉学家）编译.

(1)[San Francisco] City Lights Books [1973]. 64 p. illus. 21cm. ISBN：0872860752，0872860759

2. Ch'u tzǔ：the songs of the South，an ancient Chinese anthology/by David Hawkes. Oxford，Clarendon Press，1959. viii，229 pages：map；22cm.（UNESCO collection of representative works：Chinese series）

《楚辞：南方之歌，中国古代诗歌选》，霍克斯(Hawkes，David，1923—2009)译. 选译 18 篇楚辞，包括屈原的《离骚》《九歌》《天问》，宋玉的《招魂》，景差的《大招》等.

(1) Boston：Beacon Press，1962. viii，229 pages：map；21cm.（Beacon paperback；no. 143）

(2) Taibei Shi：Dunhuang shu ju，1968. viii，229 pages：map；22cm.

(3) Harmondsworth：Penguin，1985. 352p.：maps；20cm. ISBN：0140443754，0140443752（Penguin classics）

(4) Oxford [Oxfordshire]：Clarendon Press，1986. viii，229 pages：map；22cm.（UNESCO collection of representative works. Chinese series）

3. Three elegies of Ch'u：an introduction to the traditional interpretation of the Ch'u tz'u/Geoffrey R. Waters. Madison，Wis.：University of Wisconsin Press，1985. xv，228 pages；24cm. ISBN：0299100308，0299100308

Contents：Includes translations of three elegies of Chu ci. / Based on the author's thesis (Ph. D.—Indiana University)

Waters，Geoffrey R. (1948—)著，包括对《楚辞》的选译.

4. Selected elegies of the state of Chu/by Qu Yuan；translated by Yang Xianyi and Gladys Yang. Beijing：Wai wen chu ban she，2001. 163 p.；21cm. ISBN：7119028901，7119028903.（Echo of classics）

《楚辞选》，杨宪益(1915—2009)，戴乃迭(Yang，Gladys，1919—1999)合译.

5. Chu ci/jin yi Yang Shu'an；ying yi Yang Xianyi, Dai Naidie. Beijing：Wai wen chu ban she，2001. 1，5，175 p.：ill.；21cm. ISBN：7119028227.（A choice slelection of ancient poems＝古诗苑汉英译丛）

《楚辞》，杨书案今译；杨宪益(1915—2009)，戴乃迭(Yang，Gladys，1919—1999)译.

6. The verse of Chu/translated into modern Chinese by Chen Qizhi & Li Yi；translated into English by Zhuo Zhenying. 长沙：湖南人民出版社，2006. 33，237 pages：portraits；24cm. ISBN：7543840286，7543840287.（大中华文库：汉英对照＝Library of Chinese classics：Chinese-English）

《楚辞》，陈器之，李奕今译；卓振英英译.

7. Elegies of the south/translated by Xu Yuanchong，[Lin Jiali Zhong wen yi zhu]. Singapore：World Culture Books，2011. 442 pages；22cm. ISBN：9810705718，9810705719.（Classical Chinese poetry and prose＝许译中国经典诗文集）

《楚辞》，[林家骊中文译注]；许渊冲(1921—)英译. 英汉对照.

(1)Beijing：China Intercontinental Press；Zhonghua Book，
    2012. 8，442 p. ；22cm. ISBN：7508522043，
    7508522044. (Classical Chinese poetry and prose＝许译中
    国经典诗文集)

8. The Li sao，an elegy on encountering sorrows，by Ch'ü
    Yüan，of the state of Ch'u（circa 338—288 B. C.）/
    translated into English verse with introduction，notes，
    commentaries，and vocabulary by Lim Boon Keng. With an
    introductory note by Sir Hugh Clifford，and prefaces by H.
    A. Giles，Rabindranath Tagore，Chen Huan-Chang.
    Shanghai，China，Commercial Press，1929. xxxviii，200 p. ：
    illus. ，col. plate，maps（1 fold. ）facsim. ；21cm.
    《离骚》，林文庆（Lim，Boon Keng，1869—1957）编译. 英汉
    对照.
    (1)Shanghai：Commercial Press，xl，225 pages [4] leaves of
        plates：illustrations，facism. ，folded map；21cm.
    (2)Taipei：Oriental Cultural Service，1972. xxxviii，199
        pages，[1] leaf of plates：facsimiles；22cm.
    (3)Taipei：Cheng Wen，1974. xxxviii，200 pages：
        illustrations；20cm.

9. Li sao and other poems of Qu Yuan/[Translated by Yang
    Hsien yi and Gladys Yang. Peking，Foreign Languages Press
    1953. xvii，84p. plates；21cm.
    《离骚及其他诗歌》，杨宪益（1915—2009），戴乃迭（Yang.
    Gladys）合译.
    (1)Li sao：and other poems of Qu Yuan/translated by Yang
        Hsien yi and Gladys Yang. [2nd ed.]. Peking：Foreign
        Languages Press，1955. 96 p. illus. 21cm.
    (2)3rd ed. Beijing：Foreign Languages Press，1980. xvii，88
        pages：illustrations；19cm.
    (3)Honolulu，Hawaii：University Press of the Pacific，2001.
        vii，88 pages：illustrations；21cm. ISBN：0898751675，
        0898751673

10. Lisao：the lament/Composed by Qu Yuan；paraphrased by
    Guo Moruo；translated by Yang Hsienyi & Gladys Yang；
    illustrated by Yang Yongqing. Singapore：Asiapac Books
    PTE Ltd. ，1994. 186 pages：illustrations；21cm. ISBN：
    9813029226，9813029224
    《离骚》，郭沫若（1892—1978）译；杨宪益（1915—2009），戴
    乃迭（Yang. Gladys，1919—1999）英译；Yang，Yüng-ch'ing
    绘图.

11. Li sao，a poem on relieving sorrows；a prose translation with
    an introduction and notes/by Jerah Johnson. Miami，Olivant
    Press，1959. iv，74 pages；19cm. ([Olivant]；no. 4)
    Notes："Released as issue number 4 of the Olivant
    quarterly. "/ Also issued online.
    《离骚》. Johnson，Jerah Williams（1931—）译.

12. Qu Yuan fu san yi，Li sao ＝Chuci，Lisao：trilingual
    translation/Qu Yuan zhu；Huang Shengfa yi. Singapore：
    Re dai chu ban she；Fa xing Shang wu yin shu guan（Xin），
    2006. 107 p. ；21cm. ISBN：9810570872

《屈原赋三译，离骚》，黄盛发译. 为中、英、法、马来语文
本.

13. The shaman and the heresiarch：a new interpretation of the
    Li sao/Gopal Sukhu. Albany：State University of New York
    Press，c2012. xii，265 p. ；24cm. ISBN：1438442839.
    (Suny series in Chinese philosophy and culture)
    Sukhu，Gopal 著，该书包含《离骚》的英译.

14. The great summons/by Ch'u Yuan. Honolulu，Hawaii，The
    White Knight Press，1949. 12 pages，1 leaf；23cm.
    《招魂》，韦利（Waley，Arthur，1889—1966）（英国汉学家）
    译.

15. Tian wen：a Chinese book of origins/translated with an
    introduction by Stephen Field. New York：New Directions
    Pub. Corp. ，1986. xvii，123 p. ；21cm. ISBN：
    0811210103，0811210111
    《天问》，田笠（Field，Stephen）译. 中英文对照.

16. Paul W. Kroll. On "Far Roaming"，Journal of the
    American Oriental Society. 116(4)，1996，p. ；653—669
    《远游》，柯睿（Kroll，Paul W. ，1948—）（美国汉学家）译，
    载于 1996 年《Journal of the American Oriental Society》期
    刊.

17. Selected poems of Chū Yüan/rendered into English verse by
    Sun Dayü. Shanghai：Shanghai wai yu jiao yu chu ban she，
    1996. 5，665 p. ，[16] p. of plates：col. ill. ；21cm.
    ISBN：7810099760，7810099769
    《屈原诗选英译》，孙大雨译. 上海外语教育出版社. 汉英对
    照.
    (1)上海：上海外语教育出版社，2007. xii，572 pages，
        [16] pages of plates：color illustrations，portraits；
        24cm. ISBN：7544604598，7544604594. (外教社中国
        文化汉外对照丛书；第 1 辑)

18. The songs of Chu：an anthology of ancient Chinese poetry by
    Qu Yuan and others/edited and translated by Gopal Sukhu.
    New York：Columbia University Press，2017. xliv，251
    pages；23cm. ISBN：0231166065，0231166060，0231166072，
    0231166079. (Translations from the Asian classics)
    屈原诗. Sukhu，Gopal 编译.

I322　汉朝

王粲（177—217）

1. Early medieval chinese poetry：the life and verse of Wang
    Ts'an（A. D. 177—217）/Ronald C. Miao. Wiesbaden：
    Steiner，1982. xxi，328 p. ；24cm. ISBN：3515037187.
    (Münchener ostasiatische Studien；Bd. 30)
    Miao，Ronald C. 著. 包括对王粲（177—217）诗作的英译.
    英汉文本.

蔡文姬（约 177—249）

1. The eighteen laments/by Tsai Wen-chi，later Han-
    dynasty；translated by Rewi Alley. Peking：New World
    Press，1963. [42] pages：illustrations（chielfy color）；
    26×19cm.

《胡笳十八拍》，艾黎·路易（Alley，Rewi，1897—1987）译.

I323 三国、南北朝

曹植（192—232）

1. Six poems of Tsao Tzu-chien/translated by K'uai Shu-p'ing. Peiping：National Peking University Press，1948. 31 p.；26cm.（National Peking University semi-centennial papers，no 14. College of Arts）

   《曹植诗六首》，蒯淑平译. 六首诗：《秋思赋》《高台多悲风》《南国有佳人》《洛神赋》《髑髅说》《赠白马王彪》.

2. Worlds of dust and jade；47 poems and ballads of the third century Chinese poet Ts'ao Chih. Translated, with an introd. by George W. Kent. New York：Philosophical Library，[1969]. 82 p.；22cm.

   Notes：The translations are based chiefly on Ts'ao's works found in Itō Masafumi, Sōshoku（1961）and in Huang Chieh, Ts'ao Tzǔ-chien shih chu（1930）

   Kent, George W.（1928—）译. 对曹植47首诗的译注.

3. Cao Zhi：The life of a princely Chinese poet/by Hugh Dunn. Illus. by Ho Hwai-shouh. [Taipei]，[China News]，1970. 125 pages：illustrations；18×19cm.

   《曹植诗选英译》，Dunn, Hugh（1923—）译.

   (1) Beijing, China：New World Press：Distributed by China Publications Centre（Guoji Shudian），1983. 95 pages；18cm. ISBN：0835112470, 0835112475

   (2) Honolulu, Hawaii：University Press of the Pacific, 2004. 95 pages；21cm. ISBN：0898751691, 0898751697

阮籍（210—263）

1. Poetry and politics：the life and works of Juan Chi, A. D. 210—263/Donald Holzman. Cambridge [Eng.]；New York：Cambridge University Press，1976. viii, 316 p.；24cm. ISBN：0521208556

   Holzman, Donald 著. 包括对阮籍作品的英译.

2. Songs of my heart：yong huai shi：the Chinese lyric poetry of Ruan Ji/translated by Graham Hartill & Wu Fusheng. London：Wellsweep，1988. ISBN：0948454008

   《阮籍咏怀诗》，格林（Graham Hartill）（英国诗人），吴伏生（美国华人学者）合译.

3. 阮籍诗选：汉英对照/（三国魏）阮籍著；（美）吴伏生今译；（英）哈蒂尔（Hartill，G.），（美）吴伏生英译. 北京：中华书局，2006. 175 页：2 幅；24cm. ISBN：7101049265, 7101049268.（大中华文库）

   英文题名：The poems of Ruan Ji.

嵇康（223—262）

1. Hsi K'ang and his poetical essay on the lute, Tokyo, Sophia University，1941. 5 p. l.，90 p.，1 l. col. front.；26cm.

   《嵇康及其〈琴赋〉》，高罗佩（Gulik，Robert Hans van，1910—1967）（荷兰汉学家）译. 中英对照.

   (1) Hsi K'ang and his poetical essay on the lute, by R. H. van Gulik with his annotated English translation accompanied by the full original Chinese text of the Ch'in-fu. [New ed.，rev. and reset]. Tokyo, Sophia University；Rutland, Vt.，C. E. Tuttle Co. [1969, c1968] 133 p. 3 plates（part col.）27cm.（A Monumenta nipponica monograph）

陶渊明（陶潜，352 或 365—427）

1. T'ao the hermit；sixty poems by T'ao Ch'ien（365—427）/translated, introduced and annotated by William Acker. London, New York：Thames and Hudson，[1952]. 157 p.；23cm.

   Acker, William Reynolds Beal（1907—）译. 对陶潜60首诗的译注.

2. The poems of T'ao Ch'ien/translated by Lily Pao-hu Chang [and] Marjorie Sinclair. Brush drawings by Tseng Yu-ho. Honolulu, University of Hawaii Press [1953]. ix, 133 p. illus.；22cm.

   陶潜诗. Chang, Lily Pao-hu 和 Sinclair, Marjorie 合译.

3. The poetry of T'ao Ch'ien；translated with commentary and annotation by James Robert Hightower. Oxford, Clarendon，1970. ix, 270 p.，plate. illus.；23cm. ISBN：0198154402, 0198154402.（The Oxford library of East Asian literatures）

   《陶潜诗》，海陶韦（Hightower，James Robert）（美国汉学家）译注.

4. T'ao Yüan-ming, AD 365—427, his works and their meaning/A. R. Davis. Cambridge [Cambridgeshire]；New York：Cambridge University Press，1983. 2 v.；25cm. ISBN：0521253470（set），0521253475（set），0521236150（v. 1），0521236157（v. 1），0521236169（v. 2），0521236164（v. 2）.（Cambridge studies in Chinese history, literature, and institutions）

   Contents：v. 1. Translation and commentary—v. 2. Additional commentary, notes, and biography

   《陶渊明的作品和含义》，Davis, A. R.（Albert Richard，1924—）著. 包括对陶潜（372？—427）诗的选译.

   (1) Cambridge [Cambridgeshire]；New York：Cambridge University Press，2009. 2 volumes；25cm. ISBN：0521104524（v. 1），0521104521（v. 1），0521104531（v. 2），052110453X（v. 2），0521236157；0521236150

5. The selected poems of T'ao Ch'ien/translated by David Hinton. Port Townsend, WA：Copper Canyon Press，1993. 92 pages；22cm. ISBN：1556590563, 1556590566

   陶潜诗选. 戴维·欣顿（Hinton，David，1954—）（美国汉学家）译.

6. Selected poems/Tao Yuanming；Translated by Gladys Yang and Yang Xianyi. Beijing, China：Chinese Literature Press，1993. 102 pages；18cm. ISBN：7507101185, 7507101188, 0835131297, 0835131292.（Panda books）

《陶渊明诗选》,杨宪益(1915—2009),戴乃迭(Yang, Gladys,1919—1999)合译.

7. 英译陶诗/汪榕培译. 北京:外语教学与研究出版社,2000. 9,v,255 pages;19cm. ISBN:7560016308,7560016306.
英文题名:The complete poetic works of Tao Yuanming.

谢灵运(385—433)

1. The murmuring stream: the life and works of the Chinese nature poet Hsieh Ling-yün (385—433), Duke of K'ang-Lo, by J. D. Frodsham. Kuala Lumpur, University of Malaya P.; London, distributed by Oxford U. P., 1967. 2 v. 3 plates, 2 maps.; 23cm.
Notes: Revision of thesis, Australian National University, Canberra.
Frodsham, J. D. 著. 包括对谢灵运作品的英译. 是著者的博士论文成果.

2. The mountain poems of Hsieh Ling-yün/translated by David Hinton. New York: New Directions, 2001. xvi, 79 p.: ill., map; 23cm. ISBN:0811214893, 0811214896
《谢灵运山水诗》(选译),戴维·欣顿(Hinton, David, 1954—)(美国汉学家)译.

庾信(513—581)

1. The lament for the South': Yü Hsin's Ai Chiang-nan fu/ William T. Graham, Jr. Cambridge [Eng.]; New York: Cambridge University Press, 1980. 234 p.; 24cm. ISBN:0521227135, 0521227131. (Cambridge studies in Chinese history, literature, and institutions)
《哀江南:庾信〈哀江南赋〉》,Graham, William T. (美国汉学家)著. 含有著者对庾信《哀江南赋》的译注.

I324 唐朝

寒山(生卒年不详,约691—793)

1. Cold mountain: 100 poems by the Tàng poet Han-shan/ Translated and with an introd. by Burton Watson. New York: Grove Press, 1962. 122 pages: illustrations; 22cm.
《唐代诗人寒山诗100首》,华兹生(Watson, Burton, 1925—)(美国翻译家)译.
（1）London, Cape, 1970. 76 p.; 18cm. ISBN: 0224617982, 0224617987
（2）New York, Columbia University Press [1970]. 118 p. front. 22cm. ISBN: 0231034490, 0231034494, 0231034504, 0231034500. (UNESCO collection of representative works: Chinese series)
（3）2nd ed., rev., unabridged. Boston: Shambhala; [New York]: Distributed in the United States by Random House, 1992. 141 p.; 12cm. ISBN: 0877736685, 0877736684. (Shambhala pocket classics)

2. Riprap & Cold Mountain poems. [San Francisco, Four Seasons Foundation; distributed by City Lights Books, 1965]. 50 p.; 21cm. ISBN: 091251647X, 0912516479.

([Four Seasons Foundation, San Francisco] Writing; 7) Riprap is reprinted from the Origin Press edition, 1959, and Cold Mountain poems from Evergreen review, 1958
《碎石集与寒山诗》,包含了由 Snyder, Gary, (1930—)(美国诗人)翻译的寒山24首诗,这些译作曾发表在1958美国《常青评论》(Evergreen review)第六期上.
（1）San Francisco: North Point Press, 1990. 67 p.: ill.; 21cm. ISBN:0865474567, 0865474567, 0865474559, 0865474550
（2）50th anniversary. ed. Berkeley, CA: Counterpoint, 2009. 67 pages + 1 audio disc (digital; 4 3/4 in.) ISBN:1582435411, 1582435413
（3）Washington, DC: Shoemaker & Hoard, 2003. 67 p.: ill.; 21cm. ISBN:1593760159, 1593760151
（4）Berkeley, CA: Counterpoint, 2009. 67 p.; 22cm. + 1 sound disc (digital; 4 3/4 in.). ISBN:1582435411, 1582435413, 1582436364, 1582436363

3. Cold Mountain poems: 25 poems by Han-shan/interpreted by James Kirkup; calligraphy by Matsumoto Hiroyuki. London: Kyoto Editions; Osaka: distributed by Union Services, [1980]. 25, 25 p.; 23cm.
《寒山诗25首》,Kirkup, James(1918—2009), Matsumoto, Hiroyuki(1945—)译. 中英对照,只印了300本.
（1）Salzburg, Austria: University of Salzburg, 1997. pages 95 — 149. (Salzburg studies in English literature. Poetic drama & poetic theory; 193)

4. The collected songs of Cold Mountain/translated from Chinese by Red Pine; introduction by John Blofeld. Port Townsend, Wash.: Copper Canyon Press, c1983. [208] p.; 25cm. ISBN:0914742736, 0914742698
《寒山诗集》,赤松(Red Pine, 1943—,真名,Bill Porter) (美国翻译家、诗人)译. 中英对照.
（1）Rev. and expanded. Port Townsend, Wash.: Copper Canyon Press, c2000. 309 p.: ill., map; 23cm. ISBN:1556591403, 1556591402

5. Cold mountain = Hansan si: 301 poems/by Han-shan; translated by Jaihiun J. Kim. Seoul, Korea: Hanshin Publishing Co., 1989. xiii, 232 p.; 23cm.
《寒山诗301首》,Kim, Jaihiun(1934—)译. 中英对照.

6. The poetry of Han-shan: a complete, annotated translation of Cold Mountain/Robert G. Hendricks. Albany: State University of New York Press, c1990. x, 486 p.; 24cm. ISBN:0887069789. (SUNY series in Buddhist studies)
《寒山诗:全译注释本》,韩禄伯(Henricks, Robert G., 1943—)(美国汉学家)译.

7. Encounters with Cold Mountain: poems/by Han Shan; modern versions by Peter Stambler. Beijing, China: Panda Books, 1996. 149 pages; 21cm. ISBN: 750710317X, 7507103175, 0835131777, 0835131773
寒山诗. Stambler, Peter 译.

8. Measures of time/by James Kirkup. Salzburg：University of Salzburg, 1997. x, 202 p. ；21cm. (Salzburg studies in English literature. Poetic drama & poetic theory；193). (Collected longer poems；v. 2)

   Kirkup, James(1918—2009)著, 包括著者翻译的部分寒山的诗篇.

9. Poems of Hanshan/translated by Peter Hobson；with an introduction by T. H. Barrett. Walnut Creek, CA：AltaMira Press, c2003. viii, 151 p. ；24cm. ISBN：075910414X, 0759104143, 0759104158, 0759104150. (The sacred literature series)

   《寒山诗选》, Hobson, Peter(1924—)译.

10. The complete cold mountain：poems of the legendary hermit Hanshan/Kazuaki Tanahashi, Peter Levitt [translators]. Boulder：Shambhala, 2018. ISBN：1611804263, 1611804264

    寒山诗选译. Tanahashi, Kazuaki（1933—）和 Levitt, Peter 合译.

孟浩然(689—740)

1. The mountain poems of Meng Hao-jan/Translated by David Hinton. New York：Archipelago Books, 2004. xiii, 81 p. ：map；21cm. ISBN：0972869239

   《孟浩然的山之歌》, 戴维·欣顿(Hinton, David, 1954—)(美国汉学家)译.

王维（约 699—761）

1. Poems/by Wang Wei；translated by Chang Yin-nan and Lewis C. Walmsley. Rutland（Vt.）；Tokyo：C. E. Tuttle, 1958. 159 p. ：ill. ；19cm.

   《王维诗选》, Chang, Yin-nan 和 Walmsley, Lewis Calvin 合译.

   （1）Rutland, Vt., C. E. Tuttle, 1963. 159 pages：illustrations；

   （2）Rutland, Vt., Tuttle, 1969. 159 pages：illustrations；

2. Hiding the universe；poems. Translated from the Chinese by Wai-lim Yip. New York：Grossman Publishers, [1972]. xvii, 131 p. illus. ；27cm. ISBN：0670370959, 0972869232

   《王维诗》, 叶维廉(Yip, Wai-lim, 1937—)(美国华裔学者)编译.

3. Poems of Wang Wei；translated by G. W. Robinson. Harmondsworth, Penguin, 1973. 144 p. ；19cm. ISBN：0140442960, 0140442960. (Penguin classics)

   《王维诗》, Robinson, G. W. 译.

   （1）London：Penguin Books, 2015. 1 volume；20cm. ISBN：0141398419, 0141398418

4. An album of Wang Wei/by Ch'eng Hsi；pictures in illustration of his poems with translations by Ch'eng Hsi and Henry W. Wells. Hong Kong：Ling-Ch'ao-hsüan, 1974. 109 p. ：ill. ；19cm.

   《王维诗之画意》, 程曦（1919—）, Wells, Henry W. (1895—1978)插图和英译. 英汉对照.

5. The poetry of Wang Wei：new translations and commentary/Pauline Yu. Bloomington：Indiana University Press, c1980. xiii, 274 p. ；25cm. ISBN：0253177723, 0253177728, 0253202523, 0253202529. (Chinese literature in translation)

   《王维的诗：最新翻译与评论》, 余宝琳（Yu, Pauline, 1949—)(美国华裔学者)译评.

6. Laughing lost in the mountains/selected poems of Wang Wei；translations, Tony Barnstone, Willis Barnstone, Xu Haixin；critical introduction, Willis & Tony Barnstone. Beijing, China：Chinese Literature Press, 1989. 172 pages；18cm. ISBN：7507100685, 7507100686, 0835120767, 0835120760

   《空山拾笑语：王维诗选》, 托尼·巴恩斯通（Barnstone, Tony, 1961—)(美国诗人), 威利斯·巴恩斯通（Barnstone, Willis, 1927—)(美国学者), Xu, Haixin 合译.

   （1）Beijing, China：Panda Books, 1990. 172 pages；18cm. ISBN：7507100685, 7507100686

   （2）Hanover, N. H. ：University Press of New England, c1991. lxx, 174 p. ：ill. ；24cm. ISBN：0874515637, 0874515633, 0874515645, 0874515640

7. 《王维诗选》, 王维著. 北京：中国文学出版社, 1990. ISBN：7507100685. (熊猫丛书)

8. 王维诗百首：图文本：汉英对照/王宝童编译；誉燃绘. 上海：上海世界图书出版公司, 2005. 212 页；19cm. ISBN：7506270811, 7506270816

   英文题名：100 Wong Wei's poems in English verse.

9. A river transformed：Wang Wei's river Wang poems as inspiration/Gary Blankenship. Bremerton, WA：Santiam Publishing, 2005. xiv, 92 pages；28cm. ISBN：141166227X, 1411662278

   王维诗选. Blankenship, Gary 译.

10. The selected poems of Wang Wei/translated by David Hinton. New York：New Directions Books, 2006. xxi, 116 p. ：map；23cm. ISBN：0811216187, 0811216180

    《王维诗选》, 戴维·欣顿(Hinton, David, 1954—)(美国汉学家)译.

    （1）London：Anvil Press Poetry, 2009. xxi, 116 pages：map；23cm. ISBN：0856464157, 0856464155

李白(701—762)

1. The lonely wife/Translated from the Chinese of Li T'ai-po by Florence Ayscough. English version by Amy Lowell. [New York], 1921. 56 pages；25cm.

   李白诗. Ayscough, Florence Wheelock(1878—1942)和 Lowell, Amy(1874—1925)合译.

2. Songs of Li-tai-pè/from the Cancionerio [sic] chines of Antonio Castro Feijo；an interpretation from the Portuguese by Jordan Herbert Stabler. New York：E. Wells, 1922. 43 pages；23cm.

   李白诗. Feijó, António（1859—1917）译成葡萄牙语；Stabler, Jordan Herbert 转译成英语.

3. The works of Li Po, the Chinese poet, done into English

verse by Shigeyoshi Obata; with an introduction and biographical and critical matter translated from the Chinese. New York: E. P. Dutton & Co., 1922. xviii p., 1 l., 236 p. front. (port.) 22cm.

《李白诗集》,小畑薰良(Obata, Shigeyoshi)英译.

(1)London: Dent, 1923. xviii, 236 pages: portrait

(2)New York: Dutton, 1928. xviii, 236 pages: portraits; 21cm.

(3)Orient ed. Kanda, Japan: Hokuseido Press, 1935. xix, 236, 20 pages; 21cm.

(4)New York: Paragon Book Reprint Corp., 1965. xix, 236, 20 p. illus.; 22cm.
Notes: "Reprint of work published in Tokyo 1935."

(5)Taipei, Taiwan: T'ün huang yu hsien kung ssŭ, 1968. xix, 236, 20 pages; 21cm.

(6)[Whitefish, Mont.]: Kessinger Publishing Rare Reprints, 2007. xviii, 236 pages: illustrations; 23cm. ISBN: 054876591X, 0548765913

(7)[Place of publication not identified]: [Andesite Press], 2015. xviii pages, 1 leaf, 236 pages: frontispiece (portrait); 22cm. ISBN: 1297567278, 1297567277

4. Poems of Li Po, the Chinese poet done into vignettes by Frank Ankenbrand, jr. Haddon Heights, N. J., W. L. Washburn, 1941. 53 l. incl. front. illus.; 6×5cm.

《李白诗》,Ankenbrand, Frank(1905—1972)译.

5. The poetry and career of Li Po, 701—762 A. D. London, G. Allen and Unwin; New York: Macmillan Co. [1950]. x, 123 p.; 19cm. (Ethical and religious classics of East and West, no. 3)

李白诗. 韦利(Waley, Arthur, 1889—1966)(英国汉学家)译.

6. Li Pai: 200 selected poems/Li Bai; translated by Rewi Alley; paintings by Ban Xiezi. Hongkong: Joint Pub. Co., 1980. xxi, 226 pages, [7] leaves of plates: illustrations (some color); 22cm. ISBN: 9620400771, 9620400773, 962040078X, 9620400780

《李白诗歌二百首》,路易·艾黎(Alley, Rewi, 1897—1987)译.

(1)Hongkong: Joint Pub. Co., 1987. xxi, 226 pages: illustrations (some color); 21cm.

(2)Taipei: Caves Books, 1989. xxi, 226 pages, [7] leaves of plates: illustrations (some color); 21cm.

7. Li Po: a new translation/translated by Sun Yu. Hong Kong: Commercial Press, 1982. 11, 390 pages, [6] leaves of plates: color illustrations; 21cm. ISBN: 9620710258, 9620710254

《李白诗新译》,孙瑜(1900—)译.

8. Poems/by Li Po; translations by Elling Eide. Lexington, Ky.: Anvil Press, 1983. vi, 69 leaves; 30cm. + translator's note and finding lists (18 p.: ill.; 30cm. +1

sound disc)

《李白诗》,Eide, Elling 译. 共译 50 首诗.

9. Banished immortal: visions of Li T'ai-po/translated by Sam Hamill. Fredonia, N. Y.: White Pine Press, 1987. 52 pages; 22cm. ISBN: 0934834177

李白诗. Hamill, Sam 译.

10. Immortality in a wine-cup: an introduction to the poetry of Li Po (Li Tai-bai)/translation and notes by R. L. Manning. [Wyong, N. S. W.]: R. Manning, 1993. 74 pages; 26cm. ISBN: 0646133535, 0646133539

李白诗. Manning, R. L. (René L.)译注.

11. Bring on the wine: and other poems/by Li Po (701—762); translated by William Dolby. Edinburgh: William Dolby, 1993. 1 volume (various pagings); 30cm. (Chinese-English bilingual books; no. 2)

《将进酒: 李白诗选》,Dolby, William 译.

(1)Edinburgh: Carreg, 2004. iii, 97 pages: illustrations; 21cm. (Chinese culture series; no. 2)

12. The selected poems of Li Po/translated by David Hinton. New York: New Directions Pub. Co., 1996. xxv, 134 p.: map; 21cm. ISBN: 0811213234, 0811213233

《李白诗选》,戴维·欣顿(Hinton, David, 1954—)(美国汉学家)译.

(1)London: Anvil Press Poetry, 1996. 134 pages; 21cm.: map. ISBN: 0856462918, 0856462917. (Poetica); 31)

13. More Li Bo poems: translations supplementary to the biography Li Bo-poet immortal/by An-li Chang Williams. Victoria, B. C.: Trafford, 2004. v, 159 pages; 23cm. ISBN: 1412026768, 1412026765

李白诗. Williams, An-li Chang(1926—)译.

14. 李白诗选: 图文典藏本: 汉英对照/许渊冲译. 石家庄:河北人民出版社,2005. 66 页;23cm. ISBN: 7202037084, 7202037089. (许译中国经典诗词)

精选李白代表作 50 余首.

15. Bright moon, white clouds: selected poems of Li Po/edited and translated by J. P. Seaton. Boston: Shambhala; [New York]: Distributed in the U. S. by Random House, c2012. xiv, 224 p.; 18cm. ISBN: 1590307465, 1590307461. (Shambhala library)

《李白诗选》,Seaton, Jerome P. 译.

16. 许渊冲英译李白诗选 Selected poems of Li Bai/许渊冲英译;许渊冲、李旻赏析. 北京:中国对外翻译出版有限公司,2014. 30, 239 p.: ill.; 21cm. ISBN: 7500138914, 7500138911. (中译经典文库,汉英对照,中华传统文化精粹)

崔颢(704—754)

1. Translating Chinese: a poem by Ts'ui Hao/Wayne Schlepp. North Harrow, Middlesex: P. Ward, 1964. 14 pages; 22cm.

Schlepp，Wayne(1931—)译. 翻译了唐朝诗人崔颢的一首诗.

杜甫(712—770)

1. The book of seven songs by Tu Fu/translated into English by Edna Worthley Underwood and Chi Hwang Chu. Portland, Me.：Mosher Press, 1928. ［13］pages；16cm.

   Underwood, Edna Worthley(1873—1961)和 Chu, Chi-Hwang 合译，翻译了杜甫诗 7 首.

2. Tu Fu, wanderer and minstrel under moons of Cathay, translated by Edna Worthley Underwood and Chi Hwang Chu. Portland, Me., Mosher Press, 1929. liv, 246 p. plates.；19cm.

   杜甫诗歌选译. Underwood, Edna Worthley(1873—1961)和 Chu, Chi-Hwang 合译.

3. Tu Fu：the autobiography of a Chinese poet, A. D. 712—770. London, J. Cape；Boston & New York：Houghton, Mifflin Company [1929—1934]. 2 v. front., (ports.) illus. (incl. plans) plates, fold. map.；24cm.

   Notes：Vol. 1. A. D. 712—759—v. 2. A. D. 759—770. v. 2 has title：Travels of a Chinese poet：Tu Fu, guest of rivers and lakes, A. D. 712—770

   杜甫传. Ayscough, Florence Wheelock(1878—1942)(美国汉学家)著. 包括对杜甫的诗歌的英译.

   (1)Boston：Houghton Mifflin；London：Jonathan Cape, Ann Arbor：University Microfilms, 1983. 2 volumes：illustrations；20cm.

4. Tu-Fu, China's great poet；the bard of T'sao T'ang Ssu/a translation of some of Tu Fu's poems written in Szechuan by A. J. Brace. Chengtu, China：Rih Hsin Press, 1934. xvii, 72 p., 3 leaves of plates；23cm.

   《杜甫草堂诗》，Brace, A. J. 译. 是对杜甫在四川时期所作诗的翻译.

5. Tu Fu, China's greatest poet. Cambridge, Harvard University Press, 1952. x, 300 p. map (on lining-papers)；25cm.

   Notes：The text includes selections from Tu Fu's poems translated by the author into English free verse.

   《中国最伟大的诗人杜甫》，洪业(Hung, William, 1893—1980)著，包括著者对部分杜甫诗歌的英译.

   (1)New York：Russell & Russell, 1969. x, 300 pages：map；25cm. ISBN：0846213451, 0846213451

6. Tu Fu：selected poems/compiled by Feng Chih；translated by Rewi Alley. Peking：Foreign Languages Press, 1962. x, 178 p., ［9］leaves of plates：ill.；20cm.

   《杜甫诗选》，冯至编；路易·艾黎(Alley, Rewi, 1897—1987)译.

   (1)［2nd ed.］. Peking：Foreign Languages Press, 1964. x, 178 p. illus.；20cm.

   (2)［Hong Kong］：Commercial Press, 1974. 178 pages；［9］leaves of plates：illustrations；28cm.

   (3)Hong Kong：Commercial Press, 1977. x, 178 pages：

illustrations；21cm.

   (4)3rd. ed. Beijing：Foreign Languages Press, 1990. 178 p. ISBN：7119010743, 7119010748, 0835124061, 0835124065

   (5)［Beijing］：Foreign Languages Press, 2003. 351 pages；21cm. ISBN：7119028898, 7119028897. (Echo of classics)

   (6)Honolulu, Hawaii：University Press of the Pacific, 2005. x, 178 pages：illustrations；21cm. ISBN：1410218430, 1410218438

   (7)Beijing, China Foreign Languages Press, 2016. 417 p. ISBN：7119097688, 7119097687. (Echo of Classics)

7. Knock upon silence：poems/by Carolyn Kizer. Garden City, N. Y.：Doubleday, 1965. viii, 84, ［1］pages；22cm. ISBN：0385045808, 0385045803

   Notes：Includes poems based on Chinese and Japanese classical works, translations of 8th-century poet Tu Fu, and selections from Carolyn Kizer's satiric epic "Pro Femina."

   Kizer, Carolyn 著，翻译了杜甫部分诗歌.

8. A little primer of Tu Fu. ［Selected poems in Chinese, edited with translation, and notes, by David Hawkes.］. Oxford：Clarendon Press, 1967. xii, 243 p.；23cm.

   《杜诗初阶》，霍克斯(Hawkes, David, 1923—2009)译注.

   (1)T'ai-pei：Chung-shan shu chü, 1969. xii, 243 pages；21cm.

   (2)Hong Kong：Research Centre for Translations, Chinese University of Hong Kong, c1987. ISBN：9627255025, 9627255024. (Renditions paperbacks)

   (3)［Hong Kong］：Research Centre for Translation, Chinese University of Hong Kong, 1990. xii, 243 pages；22cm. ISBN：9627255025, 9627255024. (Renditions paperback)

   (4)Revised edition. New York：The Chinese University of Hong Kong Press/NYRB, New York Review Books, ［2016］. pages cm. ISBN：9629966591. (Calligrams)

9. The peace & the hook/［by］Peter Jones. South Hinksey, Carcanet Press Ltd, 1972. ［1］, 60 pages；23cm. ISBN：0902145789, 0902145788, 0902145797, 0902145795

   Jones, Peter(1929—)著，包括对杜甫 7 首诗的翻译.

10. Tu Fu：a new translation/translated by Wu Juntao＝［Du fu shi xin yi/Wu Juntao yi］. Hong Kong：Commercial Press, 1981. 9, 229 p., ［11］leaves of plates：col. ill.；21cm. ISBN：9620710126, 9620710124

    《杜甫诗新译》，吴钧陶(1927—)选译.

11. Tu Fu, one hundred and fifty poems/translated by Wu Juntao. Xi'an：Shanxi ren min chu ban she：Shanxi Sheng xin hua shu dian fa xing, 1985. 61, 355 p., ［1］leaf of plates：ill.；21cm.

    《杜甫诗英译：一百五十首》，吴钧陶(1927—)译. 英汉对照. 陕西人民出版社.

12. Selected poems of Tu Fu/Du Fu；[transl. from the Chinese by] Hsieh Wen Tung. [S. l.]：Guangdong Higher Education Publishing House，1985. XIV，364 p.；19cm.

《杜甫诗歌选译》. Hsieh，Wen Tung 译.

13. Selected poems of Du Fu/translated by Li Weijian；revised by Weng Xianliang. [成都]：Sichuan People's Pub. House，1985. 4，191 pages，[4] pages of plates：illustrations；19cm. ISBN：7220005393，7220005398

《杜甫诗选》，李惟建，翁显良合译. 英汉对照.

14. Thirty-six poems/by Tu Fu；translated by Kenneth Rexroth；with twenty-five etchings by Brice Marden. New York：Peter Blum Edition，1987. [117] p.：25 ill.；25cm.

《杜甫诗选》，王公红（Rexroth，Kenneth，1905—1982）译；Marden，Brice(1938—)插图. 选译了 36 首杜甫诗.

15. Facing the snow：visions of Tu Fu/translated by Sam Hamill；with calligraphy by Yim Yse. Fredonia，N. Y.：White Pine Press，c1988. 112 p.；22cm. ISBN：0934834245，0934834247

《杜甫诗选》，Hamill，Sam(美国诗人)选译.
杜甫诗. Hamill，Sam(美国诗人)译.

16. The selected poems of Tu Fu/translated by David Hinton. New York：New Directions，1989. xvi，173 p.；21cm. ISBN：0811210995，0811210997，0811211002，0811211000
Contents：Early poems (737 A. D. —745)—Ch'ang-an I (746—755)—Ch'ang-an II (756—759)—Ch'in-chou/T'ung-ku (759)—Ch'eng-tu (760—765)—K'uei-chou (765—768)—Last poems (768—770)—Biography—Notes—Finding list.
杜甫诗选. 戴维·欣顿（Hinton，David，1954—)译.
(1)London：Anvil Press Poetry，1990. xvi，173 pages：map；21cm. ISBN：0856462322，0856462320

17. Reconsidering Tu Fu：literary greatness and cultural context/Eva Shan Chou. Cambridge [Eng.]；New York：Cambridge University Press，1995. xi，237 p.；24cm. ISBN：0521440394，0521440394. (Cambridge studies in Chinese history，literature，and institutions)
《杜甫再识》，Chou，E. Shan (Eva Shan)著，包括对杜甫诗的选译.

18. The selected poems of Du Fu/[translated by] Burton Watson. New York：Columbia University Press，2002. xxiii，173 p.；24cm. ISBN：0231128290，0231128292，0231128282，0231128285. (Translations from the Asian classics)
《杜甫诗选》，华兹生（Watson，Burton，1925—)（美国翻译家)译.

19. The river's stone roots：two dozen poems/by Tu Fu；translated by James Deahl；illustrations by Gilda Mekler. Mississauga，Ont.：Serengeti Press，2005. 39 pages：illustrations；22cm. ISBN：0973845805，0973845808
Deahl，James(1945—)译，翻译了杜甫诗 24 首.

20. 杜甫诗选/许渊冲. 石家庄市：河北人民出版社，2006. 105 pages：illustrations；23cm. ISBN：7202037661；7202037669. (许译中国经典诗词 = Xu's version of classical Chinese poetry)
英文题名：Selected poems of Du Fu. 英汉对照. 本书精选杜甫代表作 50 余首.

21. Spring in the ruined city：selected poems/Du Fu；translated by Jonathan Waley；calligraphy by Kaili Fu. Exeter：Shearsman Books，2008. 100 pages；22cm. ISBN：1848610009，1848610002
杜甫诗. Waley，Jonathan 翻译.

22. Du Fu：a life in poetry/translated by David Young. New York：Alfred A. Knopf，2008. xvii，226 p.：map；21cm. ISBN：0375711600，0375711602
杜甫诗歌选译. Young，David(1936—)译.

23. Selected poems of Du Fu/transl. into English by Burton Watson. Hunan：Hunan People's Publishing House，2009. 418 p.：il.；24cm. ISBN：7543860155，7543860155. (Library of Chinese Classics：Chinese-English)
《杜甫诗选》，(美)华兹生（Burton Watson)英译. 湖南人民出版社.

24. Dù Fǔ(Du Fu) and a pilgrim/Art Aeon. Halifax，N. S.：Aeon Press，2012. 1 volume (unpaged)；23cm. ISBN：0980928143，0980928141
Aeon，Art 著，包括对杜甫诗歌的翻译.

25. The poetry of Du Fu/edited by Stephen Owen. Boston：De Gruyter，[2015]. 6 volumes (lxxxv，448；450；490；468；539；411 pages)；21cm. ISBN：1614517122，1614517126. (Library of Chinese humanities)
《杜诗全集》，宇文所安（Owen，Stephen，1946—)（美国汉学家)编译.

韦应物(737—792)

1. In such hard times：the poetry of Wei Ying-wu/translated by Red Pine. Port Townsend，Wash.：Copper Canyon Press，c2009. xxiii，365 p.：map；23cm. ISBN：1556592799，1556592795
《韦应物诗歌》，赤松（Red Pine，1943—，真名，Bill Porter)（美国翻译家、诗人)译.

孟郊(751—814)

1. The late poems of Meng Chiao/translated by David Hinton. Princeton，N. J.：Princeton University Press，c1996. xv，87 p.；23cm. ISBN：0691012377，0691012369. (The Lockert library of poetry in translation)
《孟郊晚期诗歌》，戴维·欣顿（Hinton，David，1954—)（美国汉学家)译.

2. Bird in an empty city：new translations/by Christopher Kelen，Hilda Tam and Amy Wong. Macao：Association of Stories in Macao，2007. 160 pages；22cm. ISBN：

9993789550, 9993789550. (ASM poetry: classical and contemporary texts in parallel)

孟郊诗.

张籍(约 766—约 830)

1. Cloud gate song: the verse of Tang poet Zhang Ji/ translated by Jonathan Chaves. Warren, CT: Floating World Editions, 2006. 44, [147] pages: illustrations; 23cm. ISBN: 1891640445, 1891640445

   Chaves, Jonathan 译.

薛涛(768—831)

1. A well of fragrant waters, a sketch of the life and writings of Hung Tu, by Genevieve Wimsatt. Boston, John W. Luce Company [1945]. 4 p. l. ,7—102 p. front. (port.) facsim. ; 24cm.

   Wimsatt, Genevieve 著.对唐代女诗人薛涛的诗作进行了英译.

2. I am a thought of you; poems by Sie Thao (Hung Tu), written in China in the ninth century/adapted by Mary Kennedy. New York: Gotham Book Mart, 1968. x, 44 p. ; 23cm.

   薛涛诗. Kennedy, Mary 编译.

3. Brocade River poems: selected works of the Tang dynasty courtesan Xue Tao/translated and introduced by Jeanne Larsen. Princeton, N. J. : Princeton University Press, c1987. xxvii, 110 p. ; 22cm. ISBN: 0691066868, 0691014345. (The Lockert Library of poetry in translation)

   《锦江诗:唐代名妓薛涛选集》,Larsen, Jeanne(美国汉学家)译.

白居易(772—846)

1. The passion of Yang Kwei-fei; from ancient Chinese texts, by George Soulie de Morant; rendered into English by H. Bedford-Jones. New York: Covici, Friede, 1928. 200 p. ; 25cm.

   《长恨歌》.乔治·苏利埃·德·莫朗(Soulié de Morant, G. 〈Georges〉, 1878—1955)(法国汉学家)法译;Bedford-Jones, H. (Henry, 1887—1949)英译.

2. The ballad of eternal sorrow/[Translated by] Woo kan lan]. Shanghai, Sunrise Press, 1933. 62 pages; 16cm.

   《长恨歌》,Wu, Jiangling 英译.英汉对照.

3. Yang Kuei Fei, or A song of endless sorrow/[Chü-i Pai]; translated by Kinchen Johnson. [Peking]: [Distributed by Wenolin], 1936. 15, 25, 13 pages, [7] leaves of plates: illustrations; 19cm.

   《长恨歌》,Johnson, Kinchen 译.

4. The everlasting woe＝Chang heng kuo/by Po Chü I (A. D. 772—846); translated by Jen Tai. [Shanghai]: [Chung Hwa Book Co.], 1939. 27 pages; 22cm.

   《长恨歌》,任泰(Jen Tai)译.英汉对照.

5. Lament everlasting (the death of Yang Kuei-fei)/ translations and essays by Howard S. Levy. [Tokyo,

c1962]. 35 pages: illustrations; 19×26cm.

《长恨歌》, Levy, Howard S. (Howard Seymour, 1923—)译.

6. Ch'ang-hen ko, "the lay of enduring remorse"＝[Chang hen ge]/by Po Chu-i: [translation and introduction by Bradford S. Miller]. West Hills, CA: IMP Press, c1997. 1 v. (unpaged); 22cm.

   《长恨歌》,Miller, Bradford S. 译.

7. Song of everlasting sorrow/by Bai Juyi of Tang Dynasty; Illustrated by Wu Sheng and Yu Shui; Translated into English by Zhang Danzi. Shanghai: Shanghai People's Fine Arts Publishing House, 2010. 47 pages: chiefly color illustrations; 23cm. ISBN: 7532266678, 7532266672. (Chinese-English illustrated series of ancient Chinese classical narrative poems＝汉英对照中国古代经典叙事诗图文本)

   《长恨歌》,吴声,于水插图;张丹子英译.上海人民美术出版社.

8. Translations from Po Chü-i's collected works/translated by and described by Howard S. Levy; rendered by Henry W. Wells. San Francisco: Chinese Materials Center, 1971—1978. 4 volumes: illustrations; 23cm.

   Contents: v. 1. The old style poems—v. 2. The regulated poems—v. 3. Regulated and patterned poems of Middle Age (822—832)—v. 4. The later years (833—846).

   Notes: Vol. 3 — 4 rendered by H. W. Wells; v. 4 published by Chinese Materials Center, San Francisco.

   《白居易诗选》, Levy, Howard S. (Howard Seymour, 1923—)和 Wells, Henry W. (1895—1978)合译.

   (1) New York: Paragon Book Reprint Corp. , 1971—1978. 4 v. ; 30cm. ISBN: 091087802X

9. 200 selected poems/Bai Juyi; translated by Rewi Alley. Beijing: New World Press, 1981. 313 pages: illustrations, map; 21cm.

   《白居易诗选:200 首》,路易·艾黎(Alley, Rewi,1897—1987)译.

   (1)Bai Juyi: 200 selected poems/translated by Rewi Alley. Beijing, China: New World Press: Distributed by China Publications Centre, 1983. 313 p. , [2] leaves of plates: ill. (some col.); 22cm.

10. Po Chü-i and the Japanese response/essays and translations by Howard S. Levy; calligraphy Setsuko Watanabe. Yokohama, Japan: Warm-Soft Village Branchi K-L Publications, 1984. a-f, 395 p. ; 26cm. (East Asian poetry in translations series; v. 19)

    Levy, Howard S. (Howard Seymour, 1923—)著,包括对白居易诗的英译.

11. Four huts: Asian writings on the simple life/translated by Burton Watson; illustrated by Stephen Addiss. Boston: Shambhala: Distributed in the U. S. by Random

House，1994. xv，132 p. : ill. ; 13cm. ISBN：1570620016. (Shambhala centaur editions)
华兹生(Watson，Burton，1925—)(美国翻译家)译. 收录亚洲四位著名诗人的诗，其中有白居易(772—846 年)诗的英译.

12. The selected poems of Po Chü-I/translated by David Hinton. New York：New Directions Pub. Corp. ，1999. xxi，201 p. ; 23cm. ISBN：0811214125，0811214124
Contents：Map—Early Poems：794—815（C. E.）—Exile：815—820—Middle Poems：820—829—Late Poems：829—846—Finding List.
《白居易诗选》，戴维・欣顿(Hinton，David，1954—)(美国汉学家)译.
   (1)London：Anvil Press Poetry，2006. xxi，201 pages：1 map；24cm. ISBN：0856463353，0856463358，0856463760，0856463761

13. Po Chü-i：selected poems/translated by Burton Watson. New York：Columbia University Press，c2000. xvi，172 p. ; 24cm. ISBN：0231118384，0231118385，0231118392，0231118392. (Translations from the Asian classics)
《白居易诗选》，华兹生(Watson，Burton，1925—)(美国翻译家)译.

14. The old charcoal man/Po Chu-i; Cen Long; English text by Rion and Yoko Reece. 东京：Shinseken，2002. 1 volume（unpaged）：color illustrations；24cm. ISBN：4880129011，4880129013
《卖碳翁》，岑龙(1957—)；Reece，Rion 和 Reece，Yoko 英译.

15. Poems by Po Chü-I/translated by Arthur Waley; selected by Anthony Astbury. Warwick：Greville Press，2005. 24 pages；21cm. ISBN：0954996720，0954996727
白居易诗. 韦利(Waley，Arthur，1889—1966)(英国汉学家)译；Astbury，Anthony 选编.

16. 白居易诗选：图文典藏本/汉英对照/许渊冲译. 石家庄：河北人民出版社，2006. 109 页；23cm. ISBN：7202037823，7202037829. (许译中国经典诗词)
英文题名：Selected poems of Bai Juyi. 本书精选白居易代表作 50 余首.

17. The Pi-pa player/by Bai Juyi of the Tang dynasty；Illustrated by Wu Sheng；Translated into English by Zhang Danzi. Shanghai：Shanghai People's Fine Arts Publishing House，2010. 33 pages：chiefly color illustrations；23cm. ISBN：7532266654，7532266656. (Chinese-English illustrated series of ancient Chinese classical narrative poems＝汉英对照中国古代经典叙事诗图文本)
《琵琶行》，吴声插图；张丹子英译.

18. Waiting for the moon：poems of Bo Juyi/translated with an introduction by Arthur Waley；foreword by Craig R. Smith. Mount Jackson，VA：Axios Press，c2012. xxiii，201 p. ; 21cm. ISBN：1604190472，1604190477
《白居易诗》，韦利(Waley，Arthur，1889—1966)(英国汉学家)译.

19. Selected masterpieces of Bai Juyi：five Tang poems with English translation/Bai Juyi, translator Lanjing Zou [Place of publication not identified]：Ming Lei Press, 2016. viii，44 pages；23cm. ISBN：1539395607，153939560X
白居易五首诗英译. Zhou，Lanping(1924—1971)译.

贾岛(779—843)

1. When I find you again, it will be in mountains：selected poems of Chia Tao/translated from the Chinese by Mike O'Connor. Boston：Wisdom Publications，2000. xiii，140 pages：illustrations；23cm.
贾岛诗选译. O'Connor，Mike 译.

李贺(790—817)

1. The poems of Li Ho（791—817）：translated with an introduction by J. D. Frodsham. Oxford，Clarendon P. ，1970. lxv，314 p. map. 23cm. ISBN：0198154364，0198154365. （The Oxford library of East Asian literatures）
《李长吉歌诗》，Frodsham，J. D. 译.
   (1)Goddesses, ghosts, and demons：the collected poems of Li He (Li Chang-ji, 790—816)/translated and with an introduction by J. D. Frodsham. San Francisco：North Point Press，1983. lix，287 pages；23cm. ISBN：0865470847，0865470842
   （2）London：Anvil Press Poetry，1983. ISBN：0856461091，0856461095，0865470847，0865470842. (Poetica；15)
   (3)New York：New York Review Books，2016. xxv，374 pages；22cm. ISBN：9629966607，9629966603. (Calligrams)

2. The rock's cold breath：the selected new poems of Li He/translated from the Chinese by Jodi Varon. La Grande，OR：Ice River Press，2004. 40 pages；22cm. ISBN：1877655422，1877655425. （Eastern Oregon poetry series）
李贺诗选. Varon，Jodi(1953—)译.

3. The vertical harp：selected poems of Li He/[adapted and translated by] Mike Johnson. Auckland，N. Z. ：Titus Books，2007. 69 unnumbered pages：color illustrations；18×25cm. ISBN：1877441035，1877441031
Contents：Poet of protest—Poet of the palace—Poet of the occult—Poet of nature—Poet of war.
李贺诗选. Johnson，Mike(1947—)译.

杜牧(803—853)

1. Plantains in the rain：selected Chinese poems of Du Mu/Du Mu；transl. by R. F. Burton. London：Wellsweep，1990. 95 p. ISBN：094845458X，0948454080，094845458X，0948454585. (Wellsweep Chinese poets；3)
《杜牧诗选》. Burton，R. F. 译.

2. Out on the Autumn River: selected poems of Du Mu/[Du Mu]; translated by David Young and Jiann I. Lin. Akron, Ohio: Rager Media, 2007. 158 pages; 23cm. ISBN: 0979209154, 0979209153

《秋水任逍遥：杜牧诗选英译》，杨大维，林健一合译.

李商隐（约 813—858）

1. The poetry of Li Shang-yin: ninth-century baroque Chinese poet, by James J. Y. Liu. Chicago, University of Chicago Press [1969]. xvi, 284 p.; 24cm. ISBN: 0226486907, 0226486901

《李商隐：中国九世纪的巴洛克诗人》，刘若愚（Liu, James J. Y.）（美国华裔学者）著. 作者在本书中翻译了李商隐的作品 100 余首.

2. The purple phoenix: poems of Li Shangyin/translated by Kwan-Hung Chan. translated by Kwan-Hung Chan. West Conshohocken, PA: Infinity Publishing, 2012. xx, 344 pages; 24cm. ISBN: 0741473011, 0741473011, 0741473028, 074147302X

《紫凤：李商隐诗集》，陈钧洪译.

3. Li Shangyin: poet of love/adapted by Tang Xiangyan; story by Zhang Qiongwen, pictures by Ma Leyuan; [translated by] Wang Guozhen. Beijing: Dolphin Books, 2014. 55 pages: color illustrations; 23cm. ISBN: 7511021540, 7511021549. (Classics now series; 009)

《李商隐：情圣诗人》，唐香燕改编；张琼文撰文；马乐原插图；王国振译.

韦庄（约 836—910）

1. The lament of the lady of ch'in/tr. with Chinese text, introduction and notes, from the orginal mss. in the British Museum, by Lionel Giles. Leyden: E. J. Brill Ltd., 1926. 1 page l., 76 pages: including folded plan; 25cm.

Notes: "Extracted from T'oung Pao, vol. 24."

《秦妇吟》，翟林奈（Lionel Giles，1875—1958）译，内容来自《通报》第 24 期.

2. The song-poetry of Wei Chuang (836—910 A. D.)/translated with an introd. and supplementary material by John Timothy Wixted; calligraphy by Eugenia Y. Tu. [Tempe, Ariz.]: Center for Asian Studies, Arizona State University, 1979. iii, 144 p.; 23cm. (Occasional paper-Center for Asian Studies, Arizona State University; no. 12)

《韦庄诗》，魏世德（Wixted, John Timothy）译注.

(1) Tempe, Ariz.: Center for Asian Studies, Arizona State University, 1991. iii, 144 pages; 23cm. ISBN: 0939252082, 0939252084. (Monograph series/Center for Asian Studies, Arizona State University; no. 12)

3. Washing silk: the life and selected poetry of Wei Chuang (834? -910)/Robin D. S. Yates. Cambridge, Mass.: Council on East Asian Studies, Harvard University: Distributed by Harvard University Press, 1988. xiii, 289

p.; 24cm. ISBN: 0674947754. (Harvard-Yenching Institute monographs series; 26)

《浣溪沙：韦庄的生平和诗选》，Yates, Robin D. S. (1948—)著，含有对晚唐诗人韦庄诗歌的翻译. 英汉对照.

鱼玄机（约 844—约 871）

1. Selling wilted peonies: biography and songs of Yü Hsuan-chi. T'ang poetess [by] Genevieve Wimsatt. New York: Columbia University Press, 1936. x, [1] p., 2 l., 3—119, [1] p., 1 l. 2 port. 26cm.

Wimsatt, Genevieve 著. 包括对鱼玄机诗的英译.

2. The clouds float north: the complete poems of Yu Xuanji/translated by David Young and Jiann I. Lin. Bilingual ed. Hanover: Wesleyan University Press: Published by University Press of New England, c1998. xviii, 75 p.; 24cm. ISBN: 0819563439, 0819563447. (Wesleyan poetry)

鱼玄机诗全编. Young, David（1936—）和 Lin, Jiann I. 合译.

郑嵎（约 859）

1. Essays in medieval Chinese literature and cultural history/Paul W. Kroll. Farnham: Ashgate, c2009. 1 v. (various pagings): ill.; 24cm. ISBN: 0754659907, 0754659909. (Variorum collected studies series; CS929)

《中国中世纪文学与文化史》，柯睿（Kroll, Paul W., 1948—）（美国汉学家）著. 本书含有作者对晚唐文人郑嵎的《津阳门诗》的译注.

I325　宋朝

李煜（937—978）

1. Poems of Lee Hou-chu; rendered into English from the Chinese by Liu Yih-ling and Shahid Suhrawardy. With Chinese text. Bombay, Orient Longmans, [1948]. xv, 79 p.; 22cm.

李后主诗词. 刘翼凌（Liu, I-ling）和 Suhrawardy, Shahid（1890—1965）合译.

2. A gold orchid; the love poems of Tzu Yeh. Translated from the Chinese by Lenore Mayhew & William McNaughton. Rutland, Vt., C. E. Tuttle Co. [1972]. 135 p. illus.; 20cm. ISBN: 0804802114

《子夜歌》，Mayhew, Lenore 和 McNaughton, William（1933—）合译.

3. The poems & lyrics of Last Lord Lee: a translation/by Malcolm Koh Ho Ping, Chandran Nair. Singapore: Woodrose Publications, c1975. 43 p., [2] leaves of plates: ill.; 22cm.

李后主诗词. Koh, Malcolm Ho Ping 和 Nair, Chandran（1945—）合译.

4. A river in springtime: my story of Li Yu in myth and poetry/by Susan Wan Dolling. Austin, Tex.: Puck's Gold Projects, c1997. 68 p.: ill.; 22cm. ISBN: 0965525503,

0965525503

李后主诗词.Dolling，Susan Wan（1950—）译.

5. The poetry of Li Yu: the last ruler of the tenth century Chinese kingdom known as the Southern Tang/by Clifford L. Pannam. Ormond, Vic.: Hybrid Publishers, 2000. xi, 190 pages; 24cm. ISBN: 1876462108, 1876462109

李煜词选.Pannam，C. L.（Clifford Leslie, 1937—）译评.

6. 李煜词选:图文典藏本:汉英对照/许渊冲译.石家庄:河北人民出版社,2006. 89 页;23cm. ISBN: 7202037645, 7202037645.（许译中国经典诗词）

英文题名:Selected poems of Li Yu.本书是翻译家许渊冲先生精选李煜词作 45 余首.

7. Li Yu: song of the water clock at night and other poems for spring/translations and responses by Christopher Kelen and Petra Seak. Macao: ASM, 2007. 97; 22cm. ISBN: 9993789574

《李煜：暮水吟》，客远文（Kelen，Christopher, 1958—），石海鸿（Seak，Petra）编译.

8. 李煜诗词英译全集/朱曼华.北京:商务印书馆国际有限公司,2017. 159 p. ISBN: 7517604242

英文题名:Complete collection of Li Yu's poetry.

林逋（967—1028）

1. Lin Ho-ching. Hong Kong, K. Weiss, 1952. 150, [2] p. plates, port. 22cm. (Sino-British publication no. 1.)

林逋诗词.Perleberg，Max（1900—）编译.

2. Lin He-jing: recluse-poet of Orphan Mountain = [Ch'u shih Lin Ho-ching]/selected and translated by Paul Hansen. Waldron Island: Brooding Heron Press, 1993. 35, v p.; 19cm. ISBN: 0918116732, 0918116740

Notes: English translation with original Chinese in margins. Parallel title in Chinese characters.

林逋诗词选译.Hansen，Paul 译.中英对照.

3. Lin He-jing's art of poetry/translated with introduction and notes by Paul Hansen. Seattle: Wood Works, 1997. 24 unnumbered pages; illustrations; 18cm. ISBN: 1890654035, 1890654030, 1890654078, 1890654078

Contents: The poems: Poetic brush—Poetic general—Poetic scroll case—Poetic expert—Poetic journeyman—Poetic wall—Poetic madman—Poetic demon—Poetic tablet.

林逋诗.Hansen，Paul 译.英汉对照.

晏殊（991—1055）

1. In the shade of willows: translations and responses to the poetry of Yan Shu = huan xi shar/by Christopher Kelen and Christine Leong. Macao, China: English Dept., Faculty of Social Sciences and Humanities, University of Macao, 2008. 101 pages; 21cm.

《浣溪沙》，Kelen，Christopher（1958—）译.

欧阳修（1007—1072）

1. Love and time: poems of Ou-yang Hsiu/edited & translated by J. P. Seaton. Port Townsend, Wash.: Copper Canyon Press, c1989. 71 p.; 21cm. ISBN: 1556590245, 1556590245

《欧阳修诗选》，Seaton，Jerome P. 译.

王安石（1021—1086）

1. The late poems of Wang An-shih/translated by David Hinton. New York: New Directions Books, 2015. pages cm. ISBN: 0811222631

《王安石诗选》，戴维·欣顿（Hinton，David, 1954—）（美国汉学家）译.

王安国（1028—1074）

1. Wang An-Kuo's jade rewards and millet dream/by Jonathan Pease. New Haven, Conn.: American Oriental Society, 1994. iv, 106 p.; 27cm. ISBN: 0940490773, 0940490772. (American oriental series; v. 77)

Pease，Jonathan 著.收录对北宋王安国诗的翻译.英汉对照.

苏轼（1037—1101）

1. Su Tung-p'o: selections from a Sung dynasty poet. Translated and with an introd. by Burton Watson. New York: Columbia University Press, 1965. x, 139 p.; 21cm. ISBN: 0231027982, 0231027984. (UNESCO collection of representative works. Chinese series)

《苏东坡诗选》，华兹生（Watson，Burton, 1925—）（美国翻译家）译.

(1) Selected poems of Su Tung-p'o/translated by Burton Watson. Port Townsend, WA: Copper Canyon Press, c1994. x, 145 p.; 23cm. ISBN: 1556590644, 1556590641

2. Su Dong-po: a new translation/translated by Xu Yuan-zhong. Hong Kong: Commercial Press, 1982. 11, 201 pages, [11] leaves of plates: color illustrations; 21cm. ISBN: 9620710290, 9620710292

《苏东坡诗词新译》，许渊冲（1921—）译.

3. Word, image, and deed in the life of Su Shi/Ronald C. Egan. Cambridge (Mass.): Council on East Asian Studies, Harvard University: Harvard-Yenching Institute: Distributed by the Harvard University Press, 1994. xix, 474 p.: ill.; 24cm. ISBN: 0674955986. (Harvard-Yenching Institute monograph series; 39)

《苏轼的生活》，艾朗诺（1948—）（美国汉学家），含有对苏轼诗歌大量的翻译.英汉对照.

4. 苏轼诗词选:图文典藏本:汉英对照/（宋）苏轼著;许渊冲译.石家庄:河北人民出版社,2006. 101 页;图;23cm. ISBN: 7202043011, 7202043017

英文题名:Selected poems of Su Shi.本书精选苏轼代表作 50 余首诗词.

5. East slope/translated by Jeffrey Yang. [Brooklyn, NY]: Ugly Duckling Presse, 2008. 22 unnumbered pages; illustrations; 31cm. (Lost literature series; 5)

《东坡》，杨君磊译.英汉对照.苏东坡诗词.

6. Selected poems of Su Shi = Su Shi shi ci xuan/chief editor,

Ng Kin Sing. Vancouver：Chiao Liu Pub. (Canada) Inc.；Hong Kong：Chiao Liu Pub. Trading Co. (distributor)，2010. xli，251 pages：illustrations；22cm. ISBN：0981181684，0981181686. (Wisdom of Chinese culture series. The 2nd series；9＝中华文化智慧系列. 第2辑)

《苏轼诗词选》，Wu，Jiancheng 译. 英汉对照.

7. 苏轼诗词＝Poems of Su Shi/许渊冲编译. Beijing：Hai tun chu ban she，2013. 82 pages：color illustrations；21cm. ISBN：7511010674，7511010679. (许渊冲经典英译古代诗歌 1000 首＝Version of classical Chinese poetry；5)

李清照(1084—约1155)

1. "More gracile than yellow flowers"；the life and works of Li Ch'ing-chao. Hong Kong，Mayfair Press；[distributor：Yu Fang Book Co.，New York] 1968. xvi，157 p.；23cm.

Ho，Lucy Chao 著，该书收录 43 首李清照诗词的英译. 英汉对照. 为作者的博士论文.

2. As though dreaming：the tz'u of pure jade/by Li Qingzhao；translated from the Chinese by Lenore Mayhew and William McNaughton. Tokyo：Mushinsha，1977. 118 pages：illustrations；27cm.

《漱玉词》，Mayhew，Lenore 和 McNaughton，William 合译.

3. Li Ch'ing-chao，complete poems/translated [from the Chinese] and edited by Kenneth Rexroth and Ling Chung. New York：New Directions，c1979. 118 p.；21cm. ISBN：0811207447，0811207447，0811207455，0811207454

《李清照全集》，王公红(Rexroth，Kenneth，1905—1982) (美国诗人、翻译家)，钟玲(Ling Chung，1945—)合译.

4. Selected t'su poems of Li Ch'ing-chao/translated by Catherine Theresa Cleeves-Diamond. 1980. 44 pages；22cm.

李清照诗词. Cleeves-Diamond，Catherine Theresa 译.

5. Plum blossom：poems of Li Ch'ing-chao；translated by James Cryer；artwork by Nieh Dan. Chapel Hill，NC：Carolina Wren Press，1984. 89 p.：ill.；23cm. ISBN：0932112188，0932112187

《梅花：李清照诗词》，Cryer，James(1945—)译.

6. The complete ci-poems of Li Qingzhao：a new English translation/by Jiaosheng Wang. Philadelphia，PA，USA：Order from Dept. of Oriental Studies，University of Pennsylvania，1989. xii，122 pages；28cm. (Sino-platonic papers；no. 13)

李清照词. Wang，Jiaosheng 译. 英汉对照.

7. 李清照词选：图文典藏本：汉英对照/(宋)李清照著；许渊冲译. 石家庄：河北人民出版社，2006. 121 页：图；23cm. ISBN：7202037652，7202037653. (许译中国经典诗词)

英文题名：Selected poems of Li Qingzhao. 翻译家许渊冲先生精选李清照代表作 50 余首.

8. Li Ch'ing-chao：remembered/Jean Elizabeth Ward. San Bernardino，C. A.：Jean Elizabeth Ward，2008. 150 pages：illustrations；26cm. ISBN：1435732780，1435732782

Ward，Jean Elizabeth 著. 包括对李清照诗词的英译.

9. Music from a jade flute：the ci poems of Li Qingzhao/translated and with an introduction and notes by Clifford Pannam. Ormond，Vic.：Hybrid Publishers，2009. iv，285 pages：illustrations (some color)，map；24cm. ISBN：1876462734，1876462736

李清照诗词. Pannam，C. L. (Clifford Leslie，1937—)译注. 英汉对照.

陆游(1125—1210)

1. The rapier of Lu，patriot poet of China，translations and biography by Clara M. Candlin (Mrs. W. A. Young). London，J. Murray [1946]. 68 p.；17cm. (The Wisdom of the East series)

《爱国诗人陆游作品》，Candlin，Clara M. (Clara Margaret，1983—)译.

2. The old man who does as he pleases；selections from the poetry and prose of Lu Yu. Translated [from the Chinese] by Burton Watson. New York：Columbia University Press，1973. xx，126 p. map. 22cm. ISBN：023103766X，0231037662

陆游诗文选. 华兹生(Watson，Burton，1925—)(美国翻译家)译.

(1) New York：Columbia University Press，1994. xx，124 pages：map；21cm. ISBN：0231101554，0231101554

(2) Late poems of Lu You，the old man who does as he pleases/new translations by Burton Watson；[Jesse Glass，general editor]. Burlington，Ont.：Ahadada Books；Berkeley，CA：Distributors，United States of America，Small Press Distribution，2007. x，73 pages；22cm. ISBN：0978141493，0978141490

3. Living in the stream：poems of Lu Yu/translated by David M. Gordon. Buffalo，N. Y.：White Pine Press，1977. 20 pages；21cm.

陆游诗. Gordon，David M. (David McCall)译.

4. The wild old man：poems of Lu Yu/translated by David M. Gordon. San Francisco：North Point Press，1984. xxii，146 p.；21cm. ISBN：0865471509，0865471504

《陆放翁诗词选》，Gordon，David M. (David McCall)译.

范成大(1126—1193)

1. The golden year of Fan Zhengda：a Chinese rural sequence rendered into English verse by Gerald Bullett；with notes and calligraphic decorations by Tsui Chi. Cambridge [England] University Press，1946. 43，[1] pages；19cm.

范成大诗. Bullett，Gerald(1893—1958)译.

(1) Cambridge：Cambridge University Press，2011. 43，[1] s.；19cm. ISBN：1107679238，1107679230

2. Five seasons of a golden year：a Chinese pastoral/Fan Ch'eng-ta；translated by Gerald Bullett；calligraphy by T. C. Lai. Hong Kong：Chinese University Press；Seattle：distributed by the University of Washington Press，c1980. xxii，156 p．：ill．；19cm. ISBN：9622012469，9622012462. (A Renditions book)

Notes：Previous ed. published in 1946 as：The golden year of Fan Cheng-ta.

《四时田园杂兴》，布赖特(Bullett, Gerald William，1894—1958)译，中英文本. 初版题名为《范成大的黄金岁月》(1946 年).

3. Stone lake：the poetry of Fan Chengda (1126—1193)/[translated and edited by] J. D. Schmidt. Cambridge [England]；New York：Cambridge University Press，1992. xiii，199 p．；24cm. ISBN：0521417821，0521417822. (Cambridge studies in Chinese history，literature，and institutions)

《范成大诗选译》，施吉瑞(Schmidt, J. D.〈Jerry Dean〉，1946—)编译.

(1)Cambridge；New York：Cambridge University Press，2006. xiii，199 pages；24cm. ISBN：0521032759，052103275X

4. Four seasons of field and garden：sixty impromptu poems ＝[Si shi tian yuan za xing liu shi shou：Fan Chengda shi]/by Fan Chengda；translated by Lois Baker；Chinese calligraphy and brush drawings by Wing K. Leong. Pueblo, Colo．：Passeggiata Press，1997. ix，163 pages；23cm. ISBN：1578890829，1578890828，1578890837，1578890835

《四时田园杂兴六十首》，Baker, Lois 译.

5. Fragrant mountain：twenty-four early poems of Fan Chengda/translated by Lois Baker；cover painting and calligraphy by Ma Bole. Portland, Or．：Press-22，2006. xiii，49 pages：illustrations；22cm. ISBN：0942382110，0942382112

范成大早期诗作. Baker, Lois 译.

杨万里(1127—1206)

1. Heaven my blanket, earth my pillow：poems/by Yang Wan-li；translated and introduced by Jonathan Chaves. New York：Weatherhill，1975. vii，118 p．：ill．；21cm. ISBN：0834801027，0834801035

杨万里诗. Chaves, Jonathan 译.

(1) Buffalo, N. Y．：White Pine Press，c2004. 125 p．；18cm. ISBN：1893996298，1893996298

辛弃疾(1140—1207)

1. Xin Qiji：clear echo in the valley's depths/[Xin Qiji]；translated by Christopher Kelen and Agnes Vong. Macao：Association of Stories in Macao，2007. 102 pages；21cm. ISBN：9993789567，9993789569. (Classical and contemporary poetry series)

《辛弃疾：空谷清音起》，客远文，黄励莹编译.

2. Spring wind brings the fireworks：translations，variations and responses to the poetry of Xin Qiji/Christopher Kelen and Agnes Vong. [Australia]：Virtual Arts Collective，2007. 161 pages；23cm. ISBN：0977297497，0977297498

辛弃疾诗集. Kelen, Christopher (1958—) 和 Vong, Agnes 合译.

释文珦(1210—约 1290)

1. Sleepless nights：verses for the wakeful/translated by Thomas Cleary. Berkeley, Calif．：North Atlantic Books，c1995. x，97 p．；21cm. ISBN：1556432003，1556432002

《释文珦诗》，Cleary, Thomas F. (1949—)(美国翻译家)译.

宋伯仁(生卒年不详)

1. The flowering plum/[Sung Po-Jen]；[ed.] Alfred Koehn. Peiping：Lotus Court，1947. 62 p．：ill．；25cm.

Koehn, Alfred 译. 翻译了作者的咏梅花诗词.

翁卷(生卒年不详)

1. West Cliff poems：the poetry of Weng Chūan (d. after 1214)/Jonathan Chaves. Burlington, Ont．：Ahadada Books，2010. xxii，66 pages；illustrations；21cm. ISBN：0981274461，0981274463

《西岩集》，Chaves, Jonathan 译.

I326 元朝

关汉卿(约 1234—1297)

1. Kuan Han-Ch'ing's san-ch'ü poems/translated by W. Dolby. Edinburgh：W. Dolby，1990. [47] pages；21×30cm.

关汉卿诗. Dolby, William 译.

马致远(约 1250—约 1324)

1. Will the phoenixes ever return?：the San Qu verse of Ma Zhiyuan/Clifford L Pannam. Ormond, Vic．：Hybrid Publishers，2011. 1 volume. ISBN：1921665479，1921665475

马致远散曲选. Pannam, C. L. (Clifford Leslie，1937—)译.

2. Ma Chih-yü an's complete san ch'ü -aria poems/translated by William Dolby. Edinburgh：Carreg Publishers，2003. iv，v，177 pages，10 unnumbered pages of plates；illustrations；21cm. (Chinese culture series；no. 7)

《马致远散曲全集英译本》，Dolby, William 译.

清珙(1272—1352)

1. The mountain poems of Stonehouse/translated by Red Pine. Port Townsend, Wash．：Empty Bowl，1986. approximately [66] pages：maps；21cm.

《石屋山居诗》，赤松(Red Pine，1943—，真名，Bill Porter)(美国翻译家、诗人)译. 禅诗.

(1)Port Townsend, Washington：Copper Canyon Press，[2014]. xxv，201 pages：illustrations，maps；23cm. ISBN：1556594557，1556594550

2. The Zen works of Stonehouse：poems and talks of a fourteenth-century Chinese hermit/translated by Red Pine. San Francisco：Mercury House，1999. xvi，231

pages：illustrations，map；23cm．ISBN：156279101X，
1562791018

石屋禅诗及大师语录．赤松（Red Pine，1943—，真名，Bill Porter）（美国翻译家、诗人）译．

I327　清朝

纳兰性德（1655—1685）

1．Nalan Xingde：tryst/［Nalan Xinge］；new translations by Christopher Kelen and Han Lili．Macao：Association of Stories in Macao，2007．106 pages；21cm．ISBN：9993789543，9993789542．（Classical and contemporary poetry series）

《纳兰性德：蓦地一相逢》，客远文，韩丽丽编译．

袁枚（1716—1798）

1．Harmony garden：the life，literary criticism，and poetry of Yuan Mei，1716—1799/J. D. Schmidt．London；New York：RoutledgeCurzon，2003．xxii，758 p．；25cm．ISBN：0700715258，0700715251

《随园：袁枚的生平，文学批评和诗歌》，施吉瑞（Schmidt，J. D.〈Jerry Dean〉，1946—）著，附有诗人袁枚（1715—1798）大量诗作．

郑珍（1806—1864）

1．The poet Zheng Zhen（1806—1864）and the rise of Chinese modernity/by J. D. Schmidt．Leiden；Boston：Brill，2013．xxviii，720 pages：illustrations，maps；25cm．ISBN：9004249783．（Sinica Leidensia；volume 111）

"Contains a study of Zheng's life and times，an examination of his thought and literary theory，and four chapters studying his highly original contributions to poetry on the human realm，nature verse，narrative poetry，and the poetry of ideas，including his writings on science and technology．Over a hundred pages of translations of his verse conclude the work."—Provided by publisher

《诗人郑珍与中国现代性之出现》，施吉瑞（Schmidt，J. D.〈Jerry Dean〉，1946—）著，该书对诗人郑珍（1806—1864）的诗歌翻译达100多页．

黄遵宪（1848—1905）

1．Within the human realm：the poetry of Huang Zunxian，1848—1905/J. D. Schmidt．Cambridge［England］；New York：Cambridge University Press，1994．xi，355 p．；24cm．ISBN：0521462711，0521462716．（Cambridge studies in Chinese history，literature，and institutions）

《人境庐内：黄遵宪的诗作》，施吉瑞（Schmidt，J. D.〈Jerry Dean〉，1946—）著，附有诗人黄遵宪（1848—1905）的诗译．

I33　现当代诗歌

I331　诗歌集

1．Modern Chinese poetry，translated by Harold Acton and

Ch'en Shih-hsiang．London，Duckworth［1936］．176 p．；21cm．

《现代中国诗选》，艾克敦（Acton，Harold，1904—1994）（英国诗人）、陈世骧（Chen Shih-hsiang，1912—1971）（美国华裔学者）合译．收入中国15位现代诗人的96首诗，附有15位诗人的传记资料．这15位诗人是陈梦家、周作人、冯废名、何其芳、徐志摩、郭沫若、李广田、林庚、卞之琳、邵洵美、沈从文、孙大雨、戴望舒、闻一多、俞平伯．

（1）New York：Gordon Press，1975．176 p．；24cm．

2．Contemporary Chinese poetry［an anthology］．London，Routledge［1947］．168 p．；19cm．

《中国当代诗歌》，罗伯特·白英（Payne，Robert，1911—1983）选编．

3．Songs of the red flag，compiled by Kuo Mo-jo and Chou Yang．［Translated by A. C. Barnes］．Peking：Foreign Languages Press，1961．215 p．illus．（part col.）21cm．

《红旗歌谣》，郭沫若（1892—1978），周扬（1908—1985）编；Barnes，A. C. 译．

4．New Chinese poetry．Taipei，Heritage Press［1960］．94 p．；19cm．

《中国新诗集锦》，余光中（1928—）编译．

5．Twentieth century Chinese poetry，an anthology．Translated and edited by Kai-yu Hsu．Garden City，N. Y.，Doubleday，1963．434 p．；22cm．

《20世纪中国诗》，许芥昱（Hsu，Kai-yu，1922—）（美国华裔学者）编译．

（1）Garden City，N. Y.，Doubleday，1964．469 pages．ISBN：0801491053，0801491054

（2）Ithaca，N. Y.，Cornell University Press，1970．xlii，469 pages；20cm．ISBN：0801491053，0801491054．（Cornell paperbacks；CP—105）

（3）San Francisco：Asian Language Publications，1972．481 pages；22cm．

6．Songs to Chairman Mao．Peking：Foreign Languages Press，1970．29 p．；19cm．

《颂歌献给毛主席》

7．The Tiananmen poems/edited and translated by Xiao Lan．Beijing：Foreign Languages Press，1979．64 pages，11 leaves of plates：illustrations；18cm．

《天安门诗抄》，肖兰编译．

8．Earth-shaking songs：epic of Chinese revolution/translated by Xu Yuan-Zhong．Hong Kong：The Commercial Press，Ltd.，1981．256 p．；21cm．ISBN：9620710134，9620710131

《动地诗：中国现代革命家诗词选》，许渊冲（1921—）译．包括孙中山，毛泽东，周恩来等的诗词．商务印书馆（香港）有限公司出版．

9．Summer glory：a collection of contemporary Chinese poetry＝［Xia zhao］/translated and edited by Nancy Ing．［San Francisco］：Chinese Materials Center，1982．xxiii，171 p．；22cm．ISBN：089644659X，0896446603．

(Chinese Materials Center, Asian Library series；no. 31)

《夏照：中国当代诗歌选》，殷张兰熙（Ing, Nancy Chang）译. 英汉对照.

10. Light and shadow along a great road：an anthology of modern Chinese poetry/compiled and translated by Rewi Alley. Beijing, China：New World Press：Distributed by China International Book Trading Corp. , 1984. 403 p.；22cm.

《大路上的光和影：中国现代诗选》，路易·艾黎（Alley, Rewi,1897—1987）编译.

11. 100 modern Chinese poems/ed. & tr. by Pang Bingjun & John Minford with Seán Golden. Xianggang：Shang wu yin shu guan Xianggang fen guan, 1987. iv, vii, 348 pages；19cm. ISBN：9620710819, 9620710810. （一百丛书）

《中国现代诗一百首》，庞秉钧，闵福德，高尔登编译. 汉英对照.

(1)北京：中国对外翻译出版公司；香港：商务印书馆，1993. 351 p.；19cm. ISBN：7500102097. （一百丛书）

12. The red azalea：Chinese poetry since the Cultural Revolution/edited by Edward Morin；translated by Fang Dai, Dennis Ding, and Edward Morin；introduction by Leo Ou-fan Lee. Honolulu：University of Hawaii Press, c1990. xxix,235 p.；24cm. ISBN：0824813200,0824812565

《红色杜鹃花：中国文革以来诗歌选集》，Morin, Edward （1934—）编；Dai, Fang（1955—）和 Ding, Dennis （1942—）合译.

13. New tide poetry：contemporary Chinese poems in both Chinese and English/Tang Chao, translator and editor. Toronto：Mangajin Books, 1990. viii, 199 pages；22cm. ISBN：1895348005, 1895348002

《新潮：中国当代诗歌》，Chao, Tang（1956—）编译. 英汉对照.

(1)New tide：contemporary Chinese poetry/edited and translated by Tang Chao with Lee Robinson. Toronto：Mangajin Books, 1992. viii, 199 pages；22cm. ISBN：1895348005, 1895348002

14. A splintered mirror：Chinese poetry from the democracy movement/translated by Donald Finkel；additional translations by Carolyn Kizer. San Francisco：North Point Press, 1991. xvi, 101 p.；24cm. ISBN：0865474486, 0865474494

《破碎的镜子：中国民主运动诗歌选》，Finkel, Donald 译.

15. Women of the red plain：an anthology of contemporary Chinese women's poetry/translated by Julia C. Lin. New York：Penguin Books, 1992. 162 p.；20cm. ISBN：0140586474

《红土地上的女人》，Lin, Julia C. 译. 当代中国女诗人诗歌作品英译.

16. Anthology of modern Chinese poetry/edited and translated by Michelle Yeh. New Haven：Yale University Press, c1992. lv, 245 p.；25cm. ISBN：0300054874, 0300054873

《中国当代诗歌选集》，奚密（Yeh, Michelle Mi-Hsi）编译.

17. Lyrics from shelters：modern Chinese poetry, 1930—1950/selections, translations, and introduction by Wai-lim Yip. New York：Garland Pub. , 1992. ix, 218 p.；24cm. ISBN：0824000455. （World literature in translation；[26]）

《隐匿者的抒情：中国现代诗歌,1930—1950》，叶维廉（Yip, Wai-lim. ,1937—）（美国华裔学者）选译.

18. Out of the howling storm：the new Chinese poetry：poems by Bei Dao... [et al.]/edited by Tony Barnstone. [Middletown, Conn.]：Wesleyan University Press；Hanover：University Press of New England, c1993. xxii, 155 p.；24cm. ISBN：0819522074, 0819522078, 0819512109, 0819512109. （Wesleyan poetry）

《来自暴风雨：中国新诗》，Barnstone, Tony 编译. 收录包括北岛（1949—）等中国新生代诗人的诗歌.

19. I love you：an anthology of contemporary Chinese women's poetry/ ed. by Xu Shengui；transl. [from the Chinese] by Julia C. Lin & others. Beijing：Panda, 1993. 319 p.：prtr.；19cm. ISBN：7507101215, 7507101218

当代中国女诗人诗歌集. Xu, Shengui 编；Lin, Julia C. （1928—）译.

20. Sharpened sword and resonant strings：poems of two southern society friends, Liu Ya-tzu and Su Man-shu/ translated by Liu Wu-Chi. Shanghai：Shanghai wai yu jiao yu chu ban she；Xin hua shu dian Shanghai fa xing suo jing xiao, 1993. 2, 11, 6, 338 p.：ill.；21cm. ISBN：7810097563

《磨剑鸣筝集：南社二友柳亚子与苏曼殊诗选》，柳无忌（1907—2002）（美国华裔学者）译.

21. New generation：poems from China today/edited by Wang Ping. Brooklyn, N. Y. ：Hanging Loose Press, 1999. 234 pages；21cm. ISBN：1882413555, 1882413553, 1882413547, 1882413546

Contents：Che Qianzi—Hand-copied paperback—Chen Dongdong—Snow-covered sun—Finally—He Zhong—The vast land—When we walked into the city—You come from far away—The cold spirit of snow—The last bottle of good wine—Missing the encounter—Spring that is beyond definition—High land—Under a tree—flowing water—The past is a cup from my people—Jia Wei—Edge—Black rails—Scene A—Liang Ziaoming—Individual—Since the creation of words—Permission—Liu Manliu—Mayfly's journal—Autograph book—As I search for a language—To poets—Meng Lang—Exile admonition—This age has TB—A world—Settling—Mo Fei—From "words and objects"—The sound of chopping wood—Stuck in place—Coins flung in four directions—Young prophet—This is not the last—Mo Mo—Betrayal—Gluttonous and hungry—Sold out—Tang Yaping—Just call me by my nickname—Black night—Wang Jiaxin—Iron—Words—Railway station—Want Ping—Syntax—Of flesh and spirit—No sense of direction—Wei Se—From "The string of beads, fate"—Tibet—Xi Chuan—For Haizi—Books—Birds—Bats in the twilight—Xue Di—Interplay—The passage to heaven—Nostalgia—Yan Li—From Serial poetic—Yi Sha—when the train crossed the Yellow River—Neighbors—That year—The north wind was blowing—I write what history cannot write—This fall this year—Yu Jian—In praise of work—The fence—I overheard them talking about the source of the Pearl river—Power outage—Thank you, Father—Mouse—From "The brown notebook: rejecting metaphor"—Zhai Yongming—Café song—Proof—End—Zhang Er—Raindrop—Chinese honey—Zhang Zhen—Poetry Revolution—Zhao Qiong—Hidden arc—Doubt—Punctual arrival—Zhen Danyi—To autumn—Poem—Zou Jingzhi—The meridian gate—The wheat reaper—To die in a sitting position—Burning the red soil—The well of Imperial concubine Zhen—What's in my heart—Old bowl.

《新一代：中国当下诗歌》,王屏(Wang Ping)编译. 20 世纪中国诗歌.

22. Eight contemporary Chinese poets/[introduction and translation by] Naikan Tao and Tony Prince. Sydney: Wild Peony, 2006. 132 p. ISBN: 1876957085, 1876957087, 18769570877. (University of Sydney East Asian series; 17)

《中国当代八诗人》,Naikan, Tao 和 Prince, Tony编译. 介绍了 8 位当代中国诗人及其代表作品.海子(,原名查海生 1964—1989),韩东(1961—),江河(原名于友泽,1949—),西川（1963—）,杨炼（1955—）,于坚(1954—),翟永明(1955—),Zhang, Zhen()1962—).

23. 中国现代诗选/庞秉钧,闵福德,高尔登编译.北京:中国对外翻译出版公司,2008. 318 页;21cm. ISBN: 7500118404.(中译经典文库·中华传统文化精粹)
英文题名:Modern Chinese poems

24. 中国当代诗歌前浪/吉狄马加,海岸主编.西宁:青海人民出版社,2009.165 页;19×22cm. ISBN: 7225034232, 7225034235
英文题名:The frontier tide: contemporary poetry from China.本书收录了中国当代先锋派诗人创作的优秀诗歌作品,作品均已汉英双语形式呈现.

25. Twentieth-century Chinese women's poetry: an anthology/edited and translated by Julia C. Lin; introduction by Julia C. Lin and Nicholas Kaldis. Armonk, N. Y.: M. E. Sharpe, c2009. lxvi, 205 p.; 24cm. ISBN: 0765623683, 0765623684, 0765623690, 0765623692

20 世纪中国女诗人诗集. Lin, Julia C. 编译;Kaldis, Nicholas 作序.介绍了从 1920 年到 20 世纪末大陆和台湾四十位诗人二百四十五首诗作.

26. 40th Poetry International Festival [Poems]/Yang Lian; transl. [from the Chinese] by Brian Holton, William N. Herbert. Rotterdam: Poetry International, 2009. 27 p.; 21cm.

杨炼(1955—)著;Holton, Brian 和 Herbert, William N. (William N., 1961—)合译.译自第 40 届国际诗歌节的中文诗.

27. Jade ladder: contemporary Chinese poetry/edited by W. N. Herbert & Yang Lian; with Brian Holton & Qin Xiaoyu. Tarset, Northumberland: Bloodaxe Books, 2012. 359 pages; 22cm. ISBN: 1852248956, 1852248955

Contents: Lyric poems—Narrative poems—Neo-classical poems—Sequences—Experimental poems—Long poems.
当代中国诗歌. Herbert, W. N. （1961—）,杨炼(1955—)等编译.

28. A massively single number＝Pang da de dan shu/edited by Yang Lian; translated by Brian Holton. Bristol: Shearsmans Books, 2015. 203 pages; 23cm. ISBN: 1848613768, 1848613768

《庞大的单数》,杨炼(1955—)编;Holton, Brian 译.中国诗歌英译.

29. Push open the window: contemporary poetry from China/Qingping Wang, editor; Sylvia Li-chun Lin and Howard Goldblatt, translation co-editors. Port Townsend, Wash.: Copper Canyon Press, 2011. xxiv, 307 p.; 23cm. ISBN: 1556593307, 1556593309

《推开窗:当代中国诗歌》,王清平选编;林丽君(Sylvia Li-chun Lin)（美国翻译家）,葛浩文(Goldblatt, Howard, 1939—)（美国翻译家）合译.

30. The third shore: Chinese & English-language poets in mutual translation/edited by Yang Lian & W. N. Herbert. Bristol, United Kingdom: Shearsman Books; Shanghai: East China Normal University Press, 2013. 231 pages; 23cm. ISBN: 1848613096, 1848613091, 1848613386, 1848613385

《大海的第三岸:中英诗人互译诗选》,杨炼(1955—),威廉·赫伯特(Herbert, W. N., 1961—)合编.本诗集收录了多位当代著名诗人的代表作及译文,他们是姜涛,冷霜,唐晓渡,王小妮,西川,萧开愚,严力,杨炼,杨小滨,于坚,臧棣,翟永明,张炜,周瓒,以及安敏轩,托尼·巴恩斯通,波丽·克拉克,简妮芬·克劳馥,安东尼·邓恩,威廉·赫伯特,肖恩·奥布莱恩,帕斯卡尔·帕蒂,菲奥娜·辛普森,施加彰,乔治·塞尔特斯和约书业·

维尔纳.

31. New Cathay, contemporary Chinese poetry 1990—2012/ edited by Ming Di; translated from Chinese by Neil Aitken, Katie Farris, Ming Di, Christopher Lupke, Tony Barnstone, Nick Admussen, Jonathan Stalling, Afaa M. Weaver, Eleanor Goodman, Ao Wang, Dian Li, Kerry Shawn Keys, Jennifer Kronovet, Elizabeth Reitzell, and Cody Reese. North Adams, Massachusetts：Tupelo Press, 2013. xxix, 192 pages；21cm. ISBN：1936797240，1936797240. (The poets in the world series)

《新华夏集，当代中国诗选》，明迪（Ming Di）译.

32. Poems of Hong Ying, Zhai Yongming & Yang Lian/ edited and introduced by Mabel Lee; translated by Mabel Lee, Naikan Tao & Tony Prince. Newtown, NSW：Vagabond Press, 2014. XVIII, 94 pages；19cm. ISBN：1922181145，1922181145. (Asia Pacific poetry series；6)

虹影（1962—）、翟永明（1955—）、杨炼（1955—）三人诗歌. Lee, Mabel, Tao, Naikan, Prince, Tony 编译.

I332 现当代诗人个人作品

鲁迅（1881—1936）

1. Wild grass/Lu Hsun. Peking：Foreign Languages Press, 1974. 68 p.，[1] leaf of plates：col. ill.；19cm.

《野草》，杨宪益（1915—2009），戴乃迭（Yang, Gladys, 1919—1999）合译.

  （1）Peking：Foreign Languages Press, 1976. 68 pages，[1] leaf of plates：illustrations；19cm.

  （2）Peking：Foreign Languages Press, 1980. 68 p.；19cm.

  （3）北京：外文出版社, 2000. 149 pages：illustrations；21cm. ISBN：7119026941，7119026947. （经典的回声＝Echo of classics）

  （4）Hong Kong：Chinese University Press, 2003. xliii, 127 pages；22cm. ISBN：9629961244，9629961245. （中国现代文学中英对照系列＝Bilingual series on modern Chinese literature）

2. Lu Xun selected poems/translated by W. J. F. Jenner. Beijing：Foreign Languages Press：Distributed by Guoji Shudian, 1982. [8] leaves, 160 p.；port.；19cm. ISBN：0835110028

《鲁迅诗选》，詹纳尔（Jenner, W. J. F. 〈William John Francis〉）（英国学者）译. 英汉对照.

  （1）Beijing Foreign Languages Press, 2000. 97 p.：ill.；21cm. ISBN：711902700X，7119027005. （Echo of classics）

  （2）Beijing：Foreign Languages Press, 2005. 97 p.：ill.；21cm. ISBN：7119027005. (Echo of classics)

3. Poems of Lu Hsun/translated and noted by Huang Hsin-chyu. Hongkong：Joint Pub. Co., 1979. iii, 77 p.，[5]

leaves of plates：ill.；22cm. ISBN：9620400097，9620400094, 9620400100, 9620400100

《鲁迅诗歌》，黄新渠（Huang Hsin-chyu）译注. 中英对照.

  （1）2nd ed. Hongkong：Joint Pub. Co., 1981. xxi, 77 pages：illustrations；21cm. ISBN：9620400100, 9620400100

4. 鲁迅诗歌选译＝Lu Xun：Selected poems/吴钧陶译注. 上海：上海外语教育出版社：新华书店上海发行所发行, 1981. 119 pages，[3] pages of plates：illustrations, portrait, facsimiles；19cm.

汉英对照.

5. Lu Hsun：complete poems：a translation with introduction and annotation/by David Y. Ch'en. Tempe, Ariz.：Center for Asian Studies, Arizona State University, 1988. 277 p.：ill.；23cm. ISBN：0939252198, 0939252190. Monograph series (Arizona State University. Center for Asian Studies)

《鲁迅诗全译》，Ch'en, David Y., （1925—）译注. 中英文本.

6. The lyrical Lu Xun：a study of his classical-style verse/ Jon Eugene von Kowallis. Honolulu, Hawaii：University of Hawaii Press, 1996. xii, 378 pages：illustrations；24cm. ISBN：0824815114, 0824815110

Kowallis, Jon Eugene von 著，包括对鲁迅格律诗的翻译和评论.

汪精卫（1883—1944）

1. Poems of Wang Ching-wei, translated into English with a preface and notes by Seyuan Shu; foreword by T. Sturge Moore. London, G. Allen & Unwin [1938]. 96 p. front. (port.) 22cm.

《汪精卫诗》，许思园（Hsüh, Ssŭ-hsüan）译；Moore, T. Sturge (Thomas Sturge)序.

林松柏（生卒不详，民国时期诗人）

1. Chinese verse [by] Chung Park Lum, translation [by] Sui Beng; decoration [by] Edna Francess Edell. [New York：L. Quan & co., c1927]. 2 p. l., 169, [1] p., 1 l. front. (port.) illus.；24cm.

Notes：Added t.-p. in Chinese; Chinese and English on opposite pages.

林松柏诗. 徐一朋（Xu, Yipeng）译.

艾青（1910—1996）

1. Selected poems of Ai Qing＝[Ai Qing shi xuan]/edited with an introduction and notes by Eugene Chen Eoyang; translated by Eugene Chen Eoyang, Peng Wenlan, and Marilyn Chin. Bloomington：Indiana University Press, 1982. x, 457 p., [5] p. of plates：ill.；22cm. ISBN：0253345197, 0253203023

《艾青诗选》，欧阳桢（Eoyang, Eugene Chen）（美国汉学家）译. 英汉对照.

  （1）Beijing：Foreign Languages Press：Distributed by China Publications Centre (Guoji Shudian), 1982. x,

457 pages，[8] pages of plates：illustrations；21cm.

2. Black eel/Qing Ai（Ai，Ch'ing）；transl. by Yang Hsien-yi and Robert C. Friend. Beijing：Chinese Literature，1982. 103 pages：illustrations；18cm.（Panda books）

《黑鳗》

郭沫若（1892—1978）

1. Selected poems from The Goddesses.［Translated by John Lester and A. C. Barnes］. Peking：Foreign Languages Press，1958. 67 p. port. 21cm.

《女神》，Lester，John Lester 和 Barnes，A. C. 合译.

(1) 2nd ed. Peking：Foreign Languages Press，1978. 61 p.；21cm.

(2) 2nd ed. Peking：Foreign Languages Press，1984. 61 p. ISBN：0835113507，0835113502

(3) The goddesses/written by Guo Moruo；translated by John Lester and A. C. Barnes. Peking：Foreign Languages Press，1999. 165 pages；13cm.

(4) The goddesses/written by Guo Moruo. Beijing：Foreign Languages Press，2000. 165 p.；13cm. ISBN：7119025244，7119025247

(5) The goddesses/written by Guo Moruo；transl. by Jong Lester and A. C. Barnes. Beijing：Foreign Languages Press，2001. 183 p. ISBN：7119027786，7119027784

(6) Goddess/Guo Moruo. Beijing：Foreign Languages Press，2015. 71 p. ISBN：7119092904，7119092901

蒋希曾（1899—1971）

1. Poems of the Chinese revolution. English ed.［New York：Printed by Liberal Press，Inc.，c1929］.［3］-26 p.；29cm.

收录蒋希曾创作的中国革命诗歌.

闻一多（1899—1946）

1. Red candle：selected poems；translated from the Chinese by Tao Tao Saunders. London，Cape，1972. 84 p.；19cm. ISBN：0670591068，0670591076.（Cape editions）

《红烛》

冰心（1900—1999）

1. Spring water/by Hsieh Ping Hsin；translated by Grace M. Boynton.［Tientsin］：The French Bookstore，1929. 80 pages；18cm.

《春水》，Boynton，Grace M. 译.

2. 繁星·春水：双语插图本/冰心著；鲍贵思译. 南京：译林出版社，2009. 231 页；23cm. ISBN：7544709224，7544709221.（新课标双语文库）

英文题名：A maze of stars/spring water.

(1) 繁星·春水/冰心著；（美）约翰·凯利（John Cayley），（美）鲍贵思（Grace Boynton）译. 南京：译林出版社，2011. 231 页；21cm.（双语译林；19）

卞之琳（1910—2000）

1. The carving of insects/by Bian Zhilin；edited by Mary M. Y. Fung；translated by Mary M. Y. Fung and David Lunde. Hong Kong：Research Centre for Translation，the Chinese University of Hong Kong，c2006. 152 p.：ill.，ports.；22cm. ISBN：9627255335，9627255338.（A Renditions paperback）

《雕虫纪历》，Fung，Mary M. Y. 和 Lunde，David（1941—）合译.

阮章竞（1914—2000）

1. Song of the Chang River；［Peking：China Welfare Institute］1958. 46 p.；19cm.

《漳河水》. 英汉对照.

袁水拍（1916—1982）

1. Soy sauce and prawns：satiric political verse/Yüan Shui-po；translated by Sidney Shapiro. Peking：Foreign Languages Press，1963. 39 p.；19cm.

《中国的酱油和对虾》，沙博理（Shapiro，Sidney 1915—2014）译. 收录作者的政治讽刺诗.

李季（1922—1980）

1. Wang Kuei and Li Hsiang-hsiang：a narrative poem/［translated by Yang Hsien-yi and Gladys Yang. Peking：Foreign Languages Press，1954. 33 p. illus.；26cm.

《王贵与李香香》，杨宪益（1915—2009），戴乃迭（Yang. Gladys，1919—1999）合译.

(1) Wang Gui and Li Xiangxiang：a narrative poem/［translated by Yang Hsien-yi and Gladys Yang］. 3rd ed. Beijing：Foreign Languages Press，1964. 32 pages：illustrations；26cm.

(2) Wang Gui and Li Xiangxiang：a narrative poem.［2nd ed. rev. translation］. Peking：Foreign Languages Press，1962. 33 pages：co. illustrations；26cm.

(3) Wang Gui and Li Xiangxiang：a narrative poem/Li Ji. 3rd ed. Beijing：Foreign Languages Press，1980. 42 pages，［5］leaves of plates：illustrations；19cm.

2. Songs from the Yumen oilfields.［Translated by Yuan Ko-chia］. Peking：Foreign Languages Press，1957. 48 p.；19cm.

《春风普度玉门关》，收录作者反映玉门油田的诗歌.

叶嘉莹（1924—）

1. 独陪明月看荷花：叶嘉莹诗词选译/叶嘉莹著；陶永强译；谢琰书法. 北京：外语教学与研究出版社，2017. 37，155 页：图；27cm. ISBN：7513589246

注：从叶先生历年所作诗词中选取六十余首，由陶永强译成英文.

李瑛（1926—2019）

1. Mountains crimsoned with flowers/Li Ying. Peking：Foreign Languages Press，1974. 32 pages：illustrations；19cm.

《红花满山》

铁木尔·达瓦买提（1927—2018）

1. 铁木尔·达瓦买提诗集：英文/铁木尔·达瓦买提著；陈圣生等译. 北京：民族出版社，2005. 251 页；20cm. ISBN：7105053852

乌曼尔阿孜·艾坦(1932—1997)

1. The heaven wolf/author, Wumiraz Aitan; [translator, Song Wenjing, Situ Aiqin]. Urumchi: Xinjiang Juvenile Publishing House, 2010. 3, 2, 82 pages; 23cm. ISBN: 7537189378, 7537189374

《天狼》.新疆青少年出版社.诗歌集.

张永枚(1932—)

1. Battle of the Hsisha Archipelago (reportage in verse)/ Chang Yung-mei; [cover design and ill. by Pi Yung]. Peking: Foreign Languages Press, 1975. 33 pages; [5] leaves of plates: color illustrations; 19cm.

《西沙之战》.诗报告.

李肇星(1940—)

1. 肇星诗百首:英汉对照/李肇星著.北京:世界知识出版社,2004. 277 页:彩照;29cm. ISBN: 7501222487, 7501222483

英文题名:Hundred poems by Li Zhaoxing.

黄翔(1941—)

1. A bilingual edition of poetry out of Communist China/by Huan Xiang; translated by Andrew G. Emerson. Lewiston, N. Y.: Edwin Mellen Press, 2004. xv, 406 pages: illustrations; 24cm. ISBN: 0773465049, 0773465046. (Chinese studies; v. 30)

黄翔诗. Emerson, Andrew G. 译.

2. A lifetime is a promise to keep: poems of Huang Xiang/ introduced and translated by Michelle Yeh. Berkeley, CA: Institute of East Asian Studies, 2009. xxiii, 94 pages [4] pages of plates: illustrations; 23cm. ISBN: 1557290960, 1557290962. (China research monograph series; 63)

《今生有约:黄翔诗选》,奚密(Yeh, Michelle Mi-Hsi)译.

马启智(1943—)

1. 大地行吟:马启智诗词集:汉英对照/马启智著.2 版.银川:宁夏人民出版社,2007. 121 页:图;24cm. ISBN: 7227034261, 7227034267

英文题名:Song of the land by Ma Qizhi. 本书为诗词集,中英文对照,并配以作者的摄影作品.

食指(1948—)

1. Winter sun: poems/Shi Zhi; translated by Jonathan Stalling; introduction by Zhang Qinghua. Norman: University of Oklahoma Press, 2012. xx, 183 pages; 23cm. ISBN: 0806142418, 0806142413. (Chinese literature today book series; v. 1)

《冬日的阳光》

谭仲池(1949—)

1. 谭仲池抒情诗选:英汉对照/谭仲池著.北京:中国和平出版社,2006. 143 页;20cm. ISBN: 7802013909, 7802013902.(诗刊文库.第一辑/叶延滨主编)

英文题名:Selected lyric poems by Tan Zhongchi. 本书为诗歌选集.

北岛(1949—)

1. Notes from the city of the sun: poems/by Bei Dao; edited and translated by Bonnie S. McDougall. Ithaca, N. Y.: China-Japan Program, Cornell University, 1983. 118 pages; 22cm. (Cornell University East Asia papers; no. 34)

《太阳城札记》,McDougall, Bonnie S. (1941—)译.英汉对照.

  (1) Rev. ed. Ithaca, N. Y. (140 Uris Hall, Ithaca 14853): China-Japan Program, Cornell University, 1984. 118 p.; 22cm. (Cornell University East Asia papers; no. 34)

2. The August sleepwalker/Bei Dao; translated and introduced by Bonnie S. McDougall. London: Anvil Press Poetry, 1988. 140 p.; 23cm. ISBN: 0856462098, 0856462092, 0856462101, 0856462108

《八月的梦游者》,McDougall, Bonnie S. (1941—)译.英汉对照.

  (1) New York: New Directions Books, 1990. 140 p.; 21cm. ISBN: 0811211312, 0811211314, 0811211320, 0811211321

3. Old snow: poems/[Bei Dao]; translated by Bonnie S. McDougall and Chen Maiping. New York: New Directions Books, 1991. xiii, 81 p.; 21cm. ISBN: 0811211827, 0811211826, 0811211835, 0811211833

《旧雪》,McDougall, Bonnie S. (1941—)和 Chen, Maiping 合译.英汉对照.

  (1) London: Anvil Press, 1992. xiii, 81 pages; 22cm. ISBN: 085646242X, 0856462429

4. Forms of distance/Bei Dao; translated by David Hinton. New York: New Directions Books, 1993. viii, 86 p.; 21cm. ISBN: 0811212661, 0811212663

《距离的形式》,Hinton, David(1954—)译.英汉对照.

5. Landscape over zero/Bei Dao; translated by David Hinton, with Yanbing Chen. New York: New Directions Pub., 1996. vi, 103 pages; 21cm. ISBN: 081121334X, 0811213349

《零度以上的风景》,Hinton, David(1954—)和 Chen, Yanbing 合译.

  (1) London: Anvil Press Poetry, 1998. 103 pages; 22cm. ISBN: 0856462888, 0856462887

6. Nightwatch: fifteen poems by Bei Dao; translated by David Hinton with Yanbing Chen; Hanga woodcuts by Bill Paden; calligraphy by Er Tai Gao. Hopewell, N. J.: Pied Oxen Printers, 1998. [24], [24] pages: illustrations; 34cm.

《守夜:北岛诗歌十五首》,Hinton, David(1954—)和 Chen, Yanbing 合译.

7. Unlock: poems/by Bei Dao; translated by Eliot Weinberger and Iona Man-Cheong. New York: New Directions Pub. Corp., 2000. 113 p.; 20cm. ISBN:

0811214478, 0811214476

《开锁》，Weinberger, Eliot. 和 Man-Cheong, Iona (1950—)合译.

(1) UK ed. London：Anvil Press Poetry, 2006. 116 pages；22cm. ISBN：0856463361, 0856463365

8. At the sky's edge：poems 1991—1996/Bei Dao；translated by David Hinton；foreword by Michael Palmer. New York：New Directions, 2001. xii, 196 p.；20cm. ISBN：0811214957, 0811214958

《在天涯》，Hinton, David(1954—)译. 英汉对照.

9. The rose of time：new and selected poems/Bei Dao；edited by Eliot Weinberger；translated by Yanbing Chen… [et al.]. New York：New Directions Pub. Corp., 2009. xii, 288 p.；23cm. ISBN：0811218481, 0811218481. (New Directions paperbook；1160)

《时间的玫瑰》，Weinberger, Eliot 编；Chen, Yanbing 译. 英汉对照.

(1)London：Anvil Press Poetry, 2010. pages cm. ISBN：0856464300, 0856464309

10. Daydream/Bei Dao；translated by Clayton Eshleman & Lucas Klein. Minneapolis：Rain Taxi/OHM Editions, 2010. 23 pages；17cm.

《白日梦》，Eshleman, Clayton 和 Klein, Lucas 合译.

11. City gate, open up/Bei Dao；translated from the Chinese by Jeffrey Yang. New York：New Directions Books, 2017. xii, 303 pages：illustrations；21cm. ISBN：0811226431, 0811226433. (New Directions Paperbook；1371)

《城门开》，Yang, Jeffrey 译.

多多(1951—)

1. Statements：the new Chinese poetry of Duoduo/translated by Gregory Lee & John Cayley. London：Wellsweep, 1989. 69 pages；21cm. ISBN：0948454067, 0948454066

多多诗歌. Lee, Gregory 和 Cayley, John 合译.

2. Crossing the sea/DuoDuo=[Guo hai/Duoduo]；edited by Lee Robinson；translated by Lee Robinson and Yu Li Ming；afterword by Nino Ricci. Concord, Ont.：Anansi, 1998. xiv, 122 p.；22cm. ISBN：0887845622, 0887845622

《过海》，Robinson, Lee(1959—)和 Yu, Li Ming(1945—)合译.

3. The boy who catches wasps/Duo Duo. Brookline MA：Zephyr Press, 2002. xiii, 211 p.：ill.；22cm. ISBN：0939010704, 0939010707

Notes：Translated from the Chinese by Gregory B. Lee

多多诗歌. Lee, Gregory B. 译. 英汉对照.

舒婷(1952—)

1. Selected poems：an authorized collection/by Shu Ting；[translators, Eva Hung… et al.]. Hong Kong：The Research Centre for Translation，The Chinese University of Hong Kong, c1994. 134 p.；22cm. ISBN：9627255149. (Renditions paperbacks)

《舒婷诗选》，孔慧怡(Hung, Eva)译.

2. The mist of my heart：selected poems of Shu Ting/translated by Gordon T. Osing & De-an Wu Swihart；edited by William O'Donnell. Beijing：Panda Books, 1995. 111 pages；20cm. ISBN：7507102858, 7507102857, 0835131483, 0835131483

《我心如雾：舒婷诗选》，O'Donnell, William 译.

于坚(1954—)

1. Flash cards /Yu Jian, translated from Chinese by Wang Ping and Ron Padgett. Brookline, Mass.：Zephyr Pr.；Hong Kong：Chinese University Press, 2010. xvi, 151 pages；21cm. ISBN：0981552156, 0981552153

《便条集》，Wang, Ping (1957—) 和 Padgett, Ron (1942—)合译.

翟永明(1955—)

1. The changing room：selected poetry of Zhai Yongming/translated from Chinese by Andrea Lingenfelter. Brookline, Mass.：Zephyr Press, 2011. xviii, 163 pages；21cm. ISBN：0981552132, 0981552137

《更衣室》，Lingenfelter, Andrea 译. 英汉对照.

(1) Hong Kong：Chinese University Press, 2011. xviii, 163 pages；21cm. ISBN：9629964900, 9629964902

杨炼(1955—)

1. The dead in exile/by Yang Lian；translated by Mabel Lee. Canberra：Tiananmen Publications, 1990. 75 pages；21cm. ISBN：0958754209, 0958754200

《流亡的死者》，Lee, Mabel 译.

2. Masks & crocodile：a contemporary Chinese poet and his poetry/Lian Yang；translations and introduction by Mabel Lee；illustrations by Li Liang. Broadway, NSW, Australia：Wild Peony, 1990. 146 p.：ill.；19cm. ISBN：0959073574, 0959073577. (University of Sydney East Asian series；no. 3)

《面具与鳄鱼》，Lee, Mabel 译. 中英对照.

3. Non-person singular：selected poems＝[Wu jen ch'eng：Yang Lien shih hsüan]/Yang Lian；translated by Brian Holton. London：Wellsweep；Manchester：Password [distributor], 1994. 128 p.；21cm. ISBN：0948454857, 0948454851, 0948454156 0948454158. (Wellsweep Chinese poets；6)

《无人称》，Holton, Brian 译. 中英对照.

4. Where the sea stands still：new poems/Yang Lian；translated by Brian Holton. Bilingual edition. Newcastle upon Tyne：Bloodaxe Books, 1999. 191 p.；24cm. ISBN：1852244712, 1852244712

Notes："Poetry Book Society recommended translation"—Cover. Chinese, English and Scottish.

《大海停止之处：新诗集》，Holton, Brian 译. 中英对照.

5. Yi/Yang Lian；translated from the Chinese by Mabel Lee. Bi-lingual ed. København；Los Angeles：Green Integer；

St. Paul，Minn.：Distributed in the U. S. by Consortium Book Sales and Distribution，2002. 361 pages；16cm. ISBN：1892295687，1892295682.（Green integer；35；Marjorie G. Perloff series of international poetry）
Contents：Yi—The Untrammeled Man Speaks—In Symmetry With Death—Living in Seclusion—The Descent.
Lee，Mabel 译. 中英对照.

6. Notes of a blissful ghost/by Yang Lian；translated by Brian Holton. Hong Kong：Research Centre for Translation，Chinese University of Hong Kong，c2002. 160 p.；22cm. ISBN：9627255254，9627255253.（Renditions paperbacks）
《幸福鬼魂手记》，Holton，Brian 译.

7. Concentric circles/Yang Lian；translated by Brian Holton & Agnes Hung-Chong Chan. Tarset，Northumberland：Bloodaxe Books，2005. 111 pages；24cm. ISBN：1852247037，1852247034
《同心圆》，Holton，Brian 和 Chan，Agnes Hung-Chong 合译.

8. Riding Pisces：poems from five collections ＝ Qi cheng shuang yu zuo：wu shi ji xuan/Yang Lian；translated by Brian Holton. Exeter（Eng.）：Shearsman Books，2008. 215 pages；23cm. ISBN：1905700912，1905700911
《骑乘双鱼座：五诗集选》，Holton，Brian 译.

9. Lee Valley poems＝［Li he gu di shi］/Yang Lian. Tarset：Bloodaxe Books，2009. 111 p.；24cm. ISBN：1852248345，1852248343
《李河谷的诗》

王小妮（1955—）

1. To another world/Wang Xiaoni. Xianggang：Zhong wen da xue chu ban she，2015. 35 pages；18cm. ISBN：9629967406，9629967405.（《诗歌与冲突》盒装丛书＝Poetry and conflict box set collection；20）
《致另一个世界》. 英汉对照. 香港国际诗歌之夜 2015 作品.

2. Something crosses my mind：selected poetry of Wang Xiaoni/translated from Chinese by Eleanor Goodman. Hong Kong：Chinese University of Hong Kong，2014. xii，111 pages；21cm. ISBN：9629966065，9629966069.（Jintian series of contemporary literature）
《有什么在我心里一过》，Goodman，Eleanor 译. 英汉对照.

顾城（1956—1993）

1. Selected poems/Gu Cheng；edited by Seán Golden and Chu Chiyu. Hong Kong：Research Centre for Translation，Chinese University of Hong Kong，c1990. xxii，180 p.；22cm. ISBN：9627255055，962725505X.（Renditions paperbacks）
《顾城诗选》，Golden，Seán(1948—)，Chu，Chiyu 编译.

2. Sea of dreams：the selected writings of Gu Cheng/

translated，with an introduction，by Joseph R. Allen. New York：New Directions Book，c2005. xvii，206 p.；23cm. ISBN：0811215873，0811215879
《梦之海：顾城诗选》，周文龙（Allen，Joseph Roe）（美国汉学家）译.

3. Nameless flowers：selected poems of Gu Cheng/translated and edited by Aaron Crippen；photographs by Hai Bo. New York：George Braziller，2005. 167 pages；illustrations；23cm. ISBN：0807615498，0807615492，080761548X，0807615485
《无名的小花：顾城诗歌选》，Crippen，Aaron 译.

欧阳江河（1956—）

1. Doubled shadows：selected poetry of Ouyang Jianghe/translated from Chinese by Austin Woerner. Brookline，Mass.：Zephyr Press；Hong Kong：Chinese University Press of Hong Kong，2012. xxi，111 pages；21cm. ISBN：0981552170，098155217X.（Jintian series of contemporary literature）
Contents：Glass factory—Handgun（I）—Ink bottle—Sounds of spring—Station in the air—Between Chinese and English—Conversation—Key to Sunday—Dinner—Crossing the square at dark—Silence—Notes toward a fiction of the market economy—Athens shoes—The burning kite—Our hunger our sleep—Who is gone and who remains—Picasso paints a bull—Handgun（II）—Mother kitchen—For "H."
《重影》，Woerner，Austin 译. 英汉对照.

柏桦（1956—）

1. Wind says：selected poetry of Bai Hua＝Feng zai shuo：Bai Hua/translated from Chinese by Fiona Sze-Lorrain. Hong Kong：Chinese University Press，c2012. xiv，191 p.；21cm. ISBN：9629965488，9629965488，0983297062，0983297061.（Jintian series of contemporary literature）
《风在说：柏桦》，Sze-Lorrain，Fiona 译. 英汉对照.

宋琳（1958—）

1. Song of exploring the waterways/Song Lin. Xianggang：Zhong wen da xue chu ban she，2015. 44 pages；18cm. ISBN：9629967413，9629967413.（《诗歌与冲突》盒装丛书＝Poetry and conflict box set collection；17）
《脉水歌》. 香港国际诗歌之夜 2015 作品.

刘霞（1961—）

1. Empty chairs：selected poems/Liu Xia；translated from the Chinese by Ming Di and Jennifer Stern；foreword by Herta Müller and introduction by Liao Yiwu. Bilingual edition. Minneapolis，Minnesota：Graywolf Press，2015. xiv，118 pages；illustrations；23cm. ISBN：1555977252，1555977251，1555979140，1555979149.（Lannan translation series selection）
Contents：Foreword：a mix of silk and iron/by Herta Müller—Introduction：the story of a bird/by Liao Yiwu—One bird then another—Black sail—Days—

Transformed creature—Scheme—June 2nd, 1989—Game—Word—I sit here—Poison—Grandfather—A landscape—Shadow—One night—Awakened—Dark night—Kafka—A mother—Twilight—Nobody sees me—Chaos—Misplaced—Empty chairs—To Lin Zhao—Silent strength—Speechless—High noon—It's only waking up—A grapefruit—A soul made of paper—Entrapped—Murder under the moon—Moonlit skeletons—The end—Rant—Untitled—Fragment no. 8—Nothing to say—Snow—I copy the scriptures—How it stands—Translators' afterword.

《空椅子:诗选》,明迪(Ming Di)译. 英汉对照.

韩东(1961—)

1. A phone call from Dalian：selected poetry of Han Dong/edited by Nicky Harmon；translated from Chinese by Nicky Harmon [and others]. Brookline, Mass.：Zephyr Press；Hong Kong：Chinese University Press of Hong Kong, 2012. xix, 106 pages；21cm. ISBN：0983297017, 0983297010

《来自大连的电话》. 英汉对照.

2. A loud noise/Han Dong. [香港]：香港中文大学出版社, 2013. 61 p.；17cm. ISBN：9629966263, 9629966263.
（《岛屿或大陆》盒装丛书；7. 香港国际诗歌之夜 2013）
中文书名：一声巨响.

吉狄马加(1961—)

1. Rhapsody in black：poems/By Jidi Majia；translated by Denis Mair；foreword by Simon J. Ortiz. Norman：University of Oklahoma Press, [2014]. xv, 185 pages；23cm. ISBN：0806144498, 0806144491. （Chinese literature today book series；volume 3）
《吉狄马加诗歌选集》,丹尼斯•马尔（Mair, Denis C.）译.

2. Identity/by Jidimajia；translated by Qian Kunqiang. Beijing：China Translation & Publishing Corporation, 2017. 316 pages. ISBN：7500151548, 7500151543
《身份》,乾坤强译.

3. 不朽者/吉狄马加著. 北京：外语教学与研究出版社, 2017. 488 页：图；23cm. ISBN：7513594110
本书是诗人吉狄马加的诗歌选集,收录两首长诗《致马雅可夫斯基》《不朽者》与《献给妈妈的十四行诗》二十首. 全书共 8 个语种,为汉文、英文、法文、德文、罗马尼亚文、彝文、西班牙文、俄文,所有的译文均由相关领域具有优秀翻译水平的译者所译,译文质量颇高,且译文都经过译者仔细的审定和校对.

张枣(1962—2010)

1. Mirror：poems/by Zhang Zao. [Place of publication not identified]：Zephyr Press, 2015. pages. ISBN：1938890159, 1938890154
张枣诗.

麦城(1962—)

1. Selected Poems = [Mai Cheng shi xuan]/Mai Cheng；

translated by Denis Mair. Exeter：Shearsman Books, 2008. 139 p.；23cm. ISBN：1905700882, 1905700881
《麦城诗选》,丹尼斯•马尔（Mair, Denis C.）译. 中英对照.

刘洪彬(1962—)

1. An iron circle/Liu Hongbin；[transl.：John Cayley... [et al.]. London：Calendar, 1992. 96 p.：ill. ISBN：0952046601, 0952046608
《铁环》. 英汉对照.

虹影(1962—)

1. I too am Salammbo/Hong Ying；translated and introduced by Mabel Lee. Newtown NSW Vagabond Press, 2015. 163 pages；21cm. ISBN：1922181398, 1922181390. （Vagabond Press；Asia Pacific poetry series）
虹影诗选. Lee, Mabel 译.

西川(1963—)

1. Yours truly & other poems/Xi Chuan；translated by Lucas Klein. Kāne'ohe, HI：Tinfish Press, 2011. 26 unnumbered pages；21cm. （Tinfish retro series；no. 7）
西川诗. Klein, Lucas 译.

2. Notes on the mosquito：selected poems/Xi Chuan；translated by Lucas Klein. New York：New Directions, 2012. xv, 255 pages；23cm. ISBN：0811219877, 0811219879. （New Directions paperbook；1220）
《蚊子志》,Klein, Lucas 译. 英汉对照.

蔡天新(1963—)

1. Song of the quiet life：selected poems of Cai Tianxin/translated by Robert Berold and Cai Tianxin；with additional translations by James Booze [and others]. Grahamstown [South Africa]：Deep South；[Pietermaritzburg, South Africa]：Distributed by the Univ. of Natal Press, 2006. 121 pages；21cm. ISBN：0958491534, 0958491532
《幽居之歌》,Berold, Robert(1948—)译.

2. Every cloud has its own name/Cai Tianxin；translated by Robert Berold. San Francisco：1 Plus Publishing & Consulting, 2017. Pages；23cm. ISBN：0998519960, 0998519968
《每朵云都有它的名字》,Berold, Robert(1948—)译.

娜夜(1964—)

1. Writing before sleep＝睡前书/娜夜著；（法）Fiona Sze-Lorrain 译. 北京：中译出版社, 2016. 232 p.；20cm. ISBN：7500143314, 7500143311. （Kaleidoscope：ethnic Chinese writers ＝阅读中国. 五彩丛书）

海子(1964—1989)

1. An English translation of poems of the contemporary Chinese poet Hai Zi/translated by Hong Zeng. Lewiston, N.Y.：E. Mellen Press, 2005. xxiii, 177 p.；24cm. ISBN：0773459669, 0773459663
海子诗英译. 曾虹（Zeng, Hong）译.

2. Over autumn rooftops/Hai Zi；translated and with an

introduction by Dan Murphy. Austin, TX：Host Publications，2010. vi，271 pages；22cm. ISBN：0924047756，0924047755，0924047763，0924047763

海子诗. Murphy，Dan 译. 英汉对照.

3. Ripened wheat：selected poems of Hai Zi/translated from the Chinese and introduced by Ye Chun. Fayetteville，New York：Bitter Oleander Press，2015. 196 pages；23cm. ISBN：0986204906，0986204900. (Bitter Oleander Press library of poetry；Translation series)

海子诗选.

邵勉力(1966—)

1. 月亮之旅/邵勉力著. 北京：外文出版社，2003. 205 页；19cm. ISBN：7119031902

英文题名：A trip to the moon.

鲁若迪基(1967—)

1. 没有比泪水更干净的水 /鲁若迪基著；(美)Saul Thompson 译. 北京：中译出版社，2017. 165 页；20cm. ISBN：7500151500. (阅读中国·五彩丛书. 第二辑)

英文题名：No water cleaner than tears.

宇向(1970—)

1. I can almost see the clouds of dust：selected poetry of Yu Xiang/Yu Xiang；translated from Chinese by Fiona Aze-Lorrain. Brookling，Mass.：Zephyr Press，2013. xv，151 pages；21cm. ISBN：0983297093，0983297096. (Jintian series of contemporary literature)

《我几乎看到滚滚烟尘》，Sze-Lorrain，Fiona 译.

曹东(1971—)

1. 许多灯/曹东著. 重庆：重庆大学出版社，2009. 148 页；21cm. ISBN：7562448853，756244885X

本书是曹东个人汉语诗歌及其英译集，作品已在《人民文学》《星星》诗刊《诗选刊》等处刊发.

阎志(1972—)

1. Reading the times：poems of Yan Zhi/by Yan Zhi；[translated] by Denis Mair. 1st American ed. Paramus，N. J.：Homa & Sekey Books，c2012. 132 p.：ill.；23cm. ISBN：1931907842，1931907846

阎志诗. 丹尼斯·马尔(Mair，Denis C.)译.

张尔(1976—)

1. So translating rivers and cities：poems/by Zhang Er；translated from Chinese by Bob Holman...［et. al］. Brookline，MA：Zephyr Press，2007. 153 p.；21cm. ISBN：0939010936

张尔诗歌选译. Holman，Bob(1948—)译.

江才普俊(1981—)

1. 红尘一念：相遇在红尘，出离一念间/江才普俊著. 北京：中国财富出版社，2017. 281 页：图(部分彩图)；25cm. ISBN：7504764720

英文题名：Practice and enlightenment：the buddha way in a world of impermanence. 汉英对照.

刘见

1. 爱语：汉英对照/刘见著；孙继成，刘见译. 北京：中国对外翻译出版公司，2004. 74 页；20cm. ISBN：7500112459，7500112457

英文题名：Rhymes of love. 收录作者 100 首诗歌.

江鹄

1. Poetic times/written by Jiang Hu；translated by Hu Zhihui. Changsha，China：Hunan Fine Arts Publishing House，2011. 203 pages；25cm. ISBN：7535648020，7535648029

《诗水流年》，胡志挥译. 湖南美术出版社. 收录诗 130 余篇.

李健

1. 心头飘过/李健著；李健，姚坤明译. 哈尔滨：北方文艺出版社，2010. 202 页；21cm. ISBN：7531725169，7531725169

散文诗作品集.

冷先桥

1. 灵埃/冷先桥著；北塔译. 北京：线装书局，2016. 167 页；21cm. ISBN：7512024205

英文题名：Selected poems by Leng Xianqiao. 汉英对照.

徐春法

1. 海潮集/徐春法[著/绘]；张智中英译. 杭州：杭州出版社，2011. 238 页；29cm. ISBN：7807585381，7807585382

英文题名：Tidal waves. 全书主要分为三大部分，8 辑. 1—5 辑是歌颂大海的诗句，第 6 辑为《爱情潮汐》，第 7 辑为《诗艺认识》，第 8 辑为《赏读随笔》.

土牛

1. 一个农民的祖国：汉诗英译/土牛著；徐军译. 沈阳：辽宁大学出版社，2017. 13，295 页；21cm. ISBN：7561085745

英文题名：A farmer's homeland.

I34 少数民族诗歌

1. Ashma/[Compiled and translated from Shani into Chinese by the Yunnan People's Cultural Troupe. Translated into English by Gladys Yang. Illus. (coloured wood-blocks) by Huang Yongyu]. Peking：Foreign Languages Press，1957. 81 pages：illustrations；19cm.

《阿诗玛》，云南文艺工作小组整理，戴乃迭(Yang，Gladys，1919—1999)译. 撒尼族民间叙事长诗.

2. Not a dog：an ancient Tai ballad/compiled by the students of the Chinese Department of Yunnan University (Class 1956)；translated into English by Rewi Alley. Peking：New World Press，1962. 144 p.，［5］leaves of plates：ill. (some col.)；19cm.

《朗鲸布》，云南大学中文系 1956 级学生收集整理；路易·艾黎(Alley，Rewi，1897—1987)英译. 傣族叙事长诗.

3. Folk poems from China's minorities/translated by Rewi Alley. Beijing：New World Press：Distributed by China's Publications Centre (Guoji Shudian)，1982. xiv，147 p.，［6］leaves of plates：ill. (some col.)；21cm.

《少数民族诗歌选》，路易·艾黎(Alley，Rewi，1897—

1987)译.

4. Seventh sister and the serpent: a narrative poem of the Yi people/translated by Mark Bender; [illustrated by Yuan Yunsheng]. Beijing, China: New World Press; Distributed by China Publications Centre (Guoji Shudian), 1982. iii, 65 pages: illustrations; 22cm.

《七妹与蛇郎：彝族民间叙事长诗》，本德·马可译.

5. 羌族情歌 300 首：汉英对照/张善云编；付永林译. 北京：中国戏剧出版社，2004. 600 页；20cm. ISBN：7104019715. (艺海泛舟)

本书收录从古至今羌族诗歌三百首，采用中英文对照.

6. 娥并与桑洛＝Ebing and Sangluo/张祖荣改编；朱宝锋英译；汪榕培英文审校. 广州：广东教育出版社，2007. 138 pages: illustrations; 21cm. ISBN: 7540667535, 7540667532. (中国经典文化故事系列＝Chinese classic cultural stories series)

傣族民间叙事长诗.

7. 格萨尔王/降边嘉措，吴伟著；王国振英文翻译，朱咏梅英文翻译，汉佳英文翻译. 北京：五洲传播出版社，2009. 229 页；25cm. ISBN：7508512884, 750851288X

英文题名：King Gesar.《格萨尔王》是藏族人民集体创作的一部伟大的英雄史诗.

(1) King Gesar/Gyanpian Gyamco, Wu Wei; translated by Wang Guozhen, Zhu Yongmei, Han Jia. Beijing: China Intercontinental Press, 2011. 253 p.: col. ill.; 24cm. ISBN: 7508522111, 7508522117. (Epic appreciation)

8. Legend of manas/He Jihong, Chun Yi; translated by Zhang Tianxin. Beijing: China Intercontinental Press, 2011. 179 pages: color illustrations; 24cm. ISBN: 7508521831, 7508521838. (Epic appreciation)

《玛纳斯故事》，贺继宏，纯懿编著. 五洲传播出版社. 柯尔克孜族史诗《玛纳斯》是目前世界上已知的众多史诗当中规模最大、篇幅最长的史诗作品之一，是一部传记性的英雄史诗.

9. 英雄格斯尔可汗/吴松林主编；宝成关，汪榕培审定；王民华，刘甜等译. 长春：吉林大学出版社，2012. 2 v. (220; 226 p.); 24cm. ISBN: 7560180922, 7560180922. (中华民族文库. 蒙古族系列)

英汉对照.

10. 江格尔/吴松林主编；刘兰，林阳等译. 长春：吉林大学出版社，2012. 2 v. (442) p.; 24cm. ISBN: 7560180649, 7560180647. (中华民族文库. 蒙古族系列)

英汉对照.

I4 戏剧文学

I41 综合戏剧集

1. Famous Chinese plays, translated and edited by L. C. Arlington and Harold Acton. Peiping, H. Vetch, 1937. xxx, 443, [1] p., front., plates. 22cm.

Contents: The battle of Wan-ch'eng—The battle of Ch'ang-pan P'o—Beating the drum and cursing Ts'ao—An extraordinary twin meeting—A wife and her wicked relations reap their reward—The golden locket plot—The lucky pearl—The day of nine watches—The capture and release of Ts'ao—Pearly screen castle—The cinnabar mole—A Chuang Yüan's record—The meeting of the league of heroes—Buddha's temple—At the bend of Fên River—The butterfly's dream—The yellow crane tower—The rainbow pass—A double handful of snow—Affinity of the snow cup—The shepherd's pen—A nun craves worldly vanities—Precious lotus-lantern—The green jade hairpin—Beating the tutelar deity—Sable cicada—The mating at heaven's bridge—Jade Screen Mountain—The brass net plan—Wang Hua buys a father—The five flower grotto—Pavilion of the Imperial Tablet—The happy hall of jade.

《戏剧之精华》，阿灵顿（Arlington, L. C. 〈Lewis Charles〉, 1859—1942）（美国学者），艾克敦（Acton, Harold, 1904—1994)（英国诗人）合译. 翻译 30 多个演出剧本.

(1) New York: Russell & Russell, 1963. xxx, 443 pages: illustrations, portraits; 22cm.

2. Stories from Chinese drama/by H. Y. Lowe; with illustrations by the author. Peking: Peking Chronicle Press, 1942. xxii, 413, xxxviii pages: illustrations; 23cm.

中国戏剧英译. Lowe, H. Y. 译.

(1) Stories of Chinese opera: a reprint of stories from Chinese drama/by Lu Hsing-yüan; re-issued by Tom Gee. Taiwan: Liberal Arts Press, 1978. [6], xxii, 413, xxxviiip; 24cm.

3. Chinese village plays from the Ting Hsien region (Yang Ke Hsühan); a collection of forty-eight Chinese rural plays as staged by villagers from Ting Hsien in Northern China. Translated from the Chinese by various scholars after the original recordings and edited with a critical introd. and explanatory notes by Sidney D. Gamble. Amsterdam, Philo Press, 1970. xxix, 762 p. music, 13 plates, port. 23cm. ISBN: 9060224000

《定县乡村戏剧》，甘博 Gamble, Sidney D. 〈Sidney David〉, 1890—1968)（美国汉学家）编译，翻译了定县的 48 个乡村剧本.

4. Classical Chinese plays/Josephine Huang Hung. 2nd ed. London: Vision Press, 1972. 277 p., [10] leaves of plates: ill. (some col.); 22cm. ISBN: 0854783024.

Originally published in 1971 by Mei Ya Publications, Taipei.

"This book contains translations of five of the most popular plays of the Chinese opera, with an introduction and notes. ... The five plays are：The faithful harlot（Yǖ t'ang ch'un），Two men on a string（Feng yi T'ing），Twice a bride（Hung luan hsi），One missing head（Chiu keng t'ien），and The price of wine（Mei lung chen）."

《中国经典戏剧》，Hung, Josephine Huang（1915—）译. 翻译了5个剧本.

(2)[2nd ed.]. Taipei, Taiwan, Mei Ya Publications [1972, c1971]. 272, [5] p. illus.；22cm.（Mei Ya heritage series）

5. Eight Chinese plays from the thirteenth century to the present/translated with an introd. by William Dolby. New York：Columbia University Press, 1978. 164 p.；23cm. ISBN：0231044887

Contents：The battling doctors：excerpt from Cai Shun shares the mulberries（Cai Shun fen-shen）：yuanben play attributed to Lin Tangqing. —Grandee's son takes the wrong career（Huan-men zi-do cuo li-shen）. —Shi, J. Qiu Hu tries to seduce his own wife（Qiu Hu xi-qi）. —Liang, C. Secret liason with Chancellor Bo Pi：act VII from Washing silk（Wan-sha ji）. —Wang, J. Wolf of Mount Zhong（Zhong-shan lang）. —Buying rouge（Mai yan-zhi）. —Hegemon King says farewell to his queen（Ba-wang bie-ji）：Peking opera version by Mei Lanfang. —Identifying footprints in the snow（Ping-xue bian-zong）.

《八个中国戏剧》，Dolby, William 译.

(1)London：Elek, 1978. 164 p.；23cm.

6. The Chinese drama. By William Stanton. Hongkong [etc.] Printed by Kelly & Walsh, 1899. 4 p. l., 130 p., 1 l.；21cm.

Contents：The Chinese drama. —The willow lute. —The golden leafed chrysanthemum. —The sacrifice for the soul of Ho Man Sau. —Peg Tsu. —Muk Lan's parting, a ballad. "The three plays and two poems...are reprinted, with slight alterations, from the China review."

Stanton, William 编译. 中国名剧选译，包括《金叶曲》《柳丝琴》《何文秀》等.

(1)[Place of publication not identified]：Book On Demand Ltd, 2013. ISBN：5518449356, 5518449350

7. The Chinese theater, by A. E. Zucker...Boston, Little, Brown, and Company, 1925. xvi, 234 p. col. mounted front., plates（3 col. mounted）；25cm.

Zucker, A. E.（Adolf Eduard, 1890—1971）编译. 中国名剧选译，包括《琵琶记》《嫦娥奔月》《窦娥冤》等.

8. Famous Chinese plays, translated and edited by L. C. Arlington and Harold Acton. Peiping, H. Vetch, 1937. xxx, 443, [1] p., front., plates.；22cm.

Arlington, L. C.（Lewis Charles, 1859—）和 Acton, Harold（1904—1994）编译. 中国名剧选译，包括《金锁记》《九更天》《捉放曹》《珠帘寨》《状元谱》等.

(1)New York：Russell & Russell, 1963.

9. Traditional Chinese plays；translated, described, and

annotated by A. C. Scott. Madison, University of Wisconsin Press, 1967—1975. 3 v. illus.；23cm. ISBN：0200066304

Contents：v. 1. Ssǔ lang visits his mother（Ssǔ lang t'an mu）. The butterfly dream（Hu tieh mêng）. —v. 2. Longing for worldly pleasures（Ssǔ fan）. Fifteen strings of cash（Shih wu kuan）. —v. 3. Picking up the Jade bracelet（Shih yü-cho）. A girl setting out for trial（Nü ch'i-chieh）.

中国传统戏曲. 阿道夫·斯科特（Scott, A. C.〈Adolphe Clarence〉, 1909—1985）译注. 该书翻译了6个剧本：《四郎探母》《蝴蝶梦》《思凡》《十五贯》《拾玉镯》《女起解》.

10. Classical Chinese plays/Josephine Huang Hung. 2nd ed. London：Vision Press, 1972. 277 p., [10] leaves of plates：ill.（some col.）；22cm. ISBN：0854783024

Notes：originally published in 1971 by Mei Ya Publications, Taipei. "This book contains translations of five of the most popular plays of the Chinese opera, with an introduction and notes. ... The five plays are：The faithful harlot（Yǖ t'ang ch'un），Two men on a string（Feng yi T'ing），Twice a bride（Hung luan hsi），One missing head（Chiu keng t'ien），and The price of wine（Mei lung chen）."

黄秀玖（Hung, Josephine Huang, 1915—）译. 中国名剧选译，包括《玉堂春》《凤仪亭》《鸿鸾禧》《九更天》《梅龙锁》.

(1)[2nd ed.] Taipei, Taiwan, Mei Ya Publications [1972, c1971]. 272, [5] p. illus.；22cm.（Mei Ya heritage series）

11. Drama stories/compiled by Song Shuhong. Beijing：China Intercontinental Press, 2011. 167 pages：color illustrations；19cm. ISBN：7508518800, 7508518802.（Classic stories of China）

《中国戏剧故事》，宋舒红编. 五洲传播出版社. 本书选取《西厢记》《牡丹亭》等六部中国戏曲名著加以改编.

12. Tales from ten Chinese classical tragedies：English version/by Liu Yunbo... [Ed.：Shang Shulei...]. [Beijing]：Henan People's Publ. House, 1990. 658 p. ISBN：7215008959, 7215008953

Contents：Dou E's earthshaking wrong—Autumn in the Han Palace—The orphan of Zhaos—The pipa—A banner embroidered with "Absolute loyalty"—Wang Jiaoniang—The chivalrous men—The palace of longevity—The peach-blossom fan—The Leifeng pagoda

《中国十大古典悲剧故事》，刘云波，黄为崴编. 河南人民出版社.

13. Snow in midsummer：tragic stories from ancient China/translated by Zhao You. Beijing：Foreign Languages Press, 2001. 309 p.：ill.；18cm. ISBN：7119023519

Contents：Snow in midsummer/Guan Hanqing—The

orphan of the Zhao family/Ji Junxiang—Autumn in the Han palace/Ma Zhiyuan—A banner of loyalty/Feng Menglong—The peach blossom fan/Kong Shangren—Leifeng pagoda/Fang Chengpei.

《中国古典悲剧故事选》，Zhao，You 译. 包括关汉卿的《窦娥冤》，纪君祥《赵氏孤儿》，马致远名作《汉宫秋》

14. Six classical Chinese comedies/adapted by Zhong Yuan. Beijing: Foreign Languages Press, 2001. 180 str.: ilustr. ; 19cm. ISBN: 7119023802, 7119023809

Contents: Saving a fallen angel/Guan Hanqing—Elopement/Bai Pu—The western chamber/Wang Shifu—The miser/Zheng Tingyu—The jade hairpin/Gao Lian—The kite wrangle/Li Yu.

《中国古典喜剧故事选》，中元编.

15. The grand garden, and other plays/by Yu-chu Man-kuei Li... with an introduction by Josephine Huang Hung. [Taipei: s. n., 1958]. 258 p. ; 20cm.

Contents: The grand garden (English, 1936). —Heaven challenges (Chinese, 1943, English 1955). —The woman painter (Chinese). —The modern bride (Chinese).

Notes: "The woman painter" and "The modern bride" were translated into English in collaboration with Mr. Pen Shao-chi and Mrs. Alice Wei. —Introd. p. XII.

京剧选译. Li，Man-kuei(1906—1979)，王瑶卿(1881—1954)等著；Pêng，Shao-chi，Wei，Alice 合译.

16. Children of the pear garden: five plays from the Chinese opera/translated and adapted from the Chinese with an introduction and notes by Josephine Huang Hung. Taipei (Taibei): Heritage Press, 1961. xi, 304, [5] pages, [3] leaves of plates: illustrations (some color); 19cm.

Contents: 1. The faithful Harlot—2. Two men on a string—3. Twice a bride—4. One missing head—5. The price of wine.

五部中国京剧. 黄琇玖 (Hung，Josephine Huang，1915—)译.

(1)Taipei, Taiwan: Mei Ya Publications, 1968. xi, 304 pages, [1] leaf of plates: illustrations (some color); 18cm.

17. Tales from Peking Opera/by Huang Shang. Beijing, China: New World Press: Distributed by China International Book Trading Corp. (Guoji Shudian), 1985. 232 pages: color illustrations; 18cm. ISBN: 083511399X, 0835113991

《京剧故事集》，黄裳著. 新世界出版社.

18. 昆曲精华/汪榕培，周秦，王宏主编译. 苏州：苏州大学出版社，2006. 1, 437 页：剧照；21cm. ISBN: 7810906054, 7810906050

编译了诸如《牡丹亭·惊梦》《十五贯·廉访》《长生殿·惊变》等 16 出盛演不衰的折子戏.

19. 悲欢集/汪班译. 北京：外文出版社，2009. xvii, 417 页：彩图, 肖像；25cm. ISBN: 7119057293

英文题名：Laughter and tears: translation of selected Kunqu dramas. 本书是昆曲选剧英译，精选在国外经常上演的 9 种昆曲，共 26 出戏，包括《牡丹亭》《长生殿》等，英汉对照.

20. 苏剧精华/汪榕培，顾克仁，潘智丹主编译. 苏州：古吴轩出版社，2007. 527 页；21cm. ISBN: 7807331476, 780733147X

将苏剧中十多篇经典剧目加以整理和翻译.

21. Chinese shadow theatre = Pei-ching ying hsi/Sven Broman. [Stockholm]: Etnografiska museet, [1981]. 249 p. : ill. (some col.); 22cm. ISBN: 918534401X, 9185344017. (Monograph series/Etnografiska museet, 0081—5632; no. 15)

《北平影戏》，Broman，Sven 著. 英汉对照. 中国皮影戏英译.

22. Chinese shadow theatre libretti/Sven Broman. Bangkok: White Orchid Press, [1995]. xi, 96 p. : col. ill. ; 23cm. ISBN: 9185344257. (Monograph series/the National Museum of Ethnography, Stockholm; no. 17)

Broman，Sven 著. 英汉对照. 中国皮影戏英译.

23. Tales from Tibetan opera/edited & narrated by Wang Yao. Beijing: New World Press: Distributed by China International Book Trading Corp., 1986. 214 pages, [8] leaves of plates: illustrations (some color); 19cm. ISBN: 0835116573, 0835116572

《藏剧故事集》，王尧编著. 新世界出版社.

I42　古代戏剧集

1. Ballad of the hidden dragon, translated with an introduction by M. Dolezelova-Velingerova and J. I. Crump. Oxford, Clarendon Press, 1971. x, 128 p. 22cm. ISBN: 0198154453. (Oxford library of East Asian literatures)

《龙隐调〈刘知远诸宫调〉》，米列娜（Dolezelová-Velingerová，Milena），柯迂儒（又名柯润璞）（Crump，J. I. 〈James Irving〉，1921—2002)合译.

2. Six Yüan plays/translated with an introduction by Liu Jung-en. Baltimore, Penguin Books, 1972. 285 pages: illustrations; 18cm. (Penguin classics; L262)

Contents: The orphan of Chao/Chi Chün-hsiang. The soul of Ch'ien-nü leaves her body/Chèng Teh-hui. The injustice done to Tou Ngo/Kuan Han-ch'ing. Chang boils the sea/Li Hao-ku. Autumn in Han palace/Ma Chih-yüan. A stratagem of interlocking rings/Anonymous.

《六出元杂剧》，刘荣恩（Liu，Jung-en，1908—2001)（英国华裔学者）译. 收录 6 部元剧：《赵氏孤儿》《倩女离魂》《窦娥冤》《张生煮海》《破幽梦孤雁汉宫秋》等.

(1)Harmondsworth [etc.]: Penguin Books, 1977. 285 p. : ill. ; 18cm. ISBN: 0140442626, 0140442625

（2）Harmondsworth：Penguin，1988. 285 pages；19cm. ISBN：0140442626，0140442625

3. Four plays of the Yuan drama/translated with introd. and annotations by Richard F. S. Yang. Taipei：China Post，[1972]. xv，180 p.：ill.；22cm.
Contents：Kuan，H. C. Tou O was wronged. —Ma，C. Y. The Yüeh-yang Tower. —Po，J. F. Rain on the wu-t'ung tree. —Cheng，T. H. Ch'ien-nü's soul left her body.
《元剧四种》，Yang，Richard Fu-Sen（1918—）译注. 包括关汉卿的《窦娥冤》、马致远的《岳阳楼》、白仁甫的《梧桐树》、郑德辉的《倩女离魂》.

4. Crime and punishment in medieval Chinese drama：three Judge Pao plays/by George A. Hayden. Cambridge，Mass.：Council on East Asian Studies，Harvard University：distributed by Harvard University Press，1978 x，238 p.；24cm. ISBN：0674176081.（Harvard East Asian monographs；82）
《中国中世纪戏剧中的罪与罚》，乔治·海登（Hayden，George A.，1939—）著. 该书翻译了3部包公案的杂剧：《陈州粜米》《盆儿鬼》《后庭花》.

5. Chinese theater in the days of Kublai Khan/J. I. Crump. Tucson：University of Arizona Press，c1980. ix，429 p.：ill.；24cm. ISBN：0816506973，0816506566
Includes English translations of three Chinese plays：Li K'uei carries thorns（attributed to K'ang Chin-chih，fl. 1279），Rain on the Hsiao-Hsiang（attributed to Yang Hsien-chih，fl. 1246），The Mo-Ho-Lo doll（attributed to Meng Han-ch'ing，fl. 1279）
《忽必烈汗时期的中国剧场》，柯迁儒（又名柯润璞）（Crump，J. I.〈James Irving〉，1921—2002）著. 含有三出杂剧的英译：《李逵负荆》《潇湘雨》和《摩合罗》.
（1）Ann Arbor，Mich.：Center for Chinese Studies，University of Michigan，c1990. Ann Arbor，Mich.：Center for Chinese Studies，University of Michigan，c1990. ix，429 p.：ill.；24cm. ISBN：0892641010，0892640936

6. Chinese theatre，1100—1450：a source book/by Wilt Idema and Stephen H. West. Wiesbaden：Steiner，1982. xv，523 p.：ill.；25cm. ISBN：3515036636.（Münchener ostasiatische Studien；Bd. 27）
《中国戏剧渊源1100—1450》，伊维德（Idema，W. L.〈Wilt L.〉，1944—）（荷兰汉学家），奚如谷（West，Stephen H.，1944—）（美国汉学家）著. 书中的第5至第7章提供3部剧作的全文翻译，该书的最后一章还翻译了明初剧作家朱有燉的3部剧作，书中还有南戏《宦门子弟错立身》的翻译.

7. The Columbia anthology of Yuan drama/edited by C. T. Hsia，Wai-yee Li，and George Kao. New York：Columbia University Press，[2014]. viii，409 pages；27cm. ISBN：0231122665，0231122672.（Translations from the Asian classics）
《哥伦比亚元代戏剧集》，夏志清（Hsia，Chih-tsing，1921—2013）（美国华裔学者），Li，Wai-yee，高克毅（Kao，George，1912—2008）（美国华裔学者）编译.

8. The orphan of Zhao and other Yuan plays：the earliest known versions/translated & introduced by Stephen H. West and Wilt L. Idema. New York：Columbia University Press，[2015]. xii，391 pages；26cm. ISBN：0231168540，0231168543，0231538107
《〈赵氏孤儿〉及其他元剧：最早的卷本》，奚如谷（West，Stephen H.，1944—）（美国汉学家），伊维德（Idema，W. L.〈Wilt L.〉，1944—）（荷兰汉学家）合译.

9. Selected plays from the Yuan Dynasty/translated by Zhang Guangqian. Beijing：Foreign Languages Press，2010. v，339 pages；illustrations；23cm. ISBN：7119038933，7119038931.（Chinese classics）
《元曲选》，张光前英译.（中国经典）

10. Monks，bandits，lovers，and immortals：eleven early Chinese plays/edited and translated with an introduction by Stephen H. West and Wilt L. Idema. Indianapolis：Hackett Pub. Co.，2010. xlii，478 p.：ill.；23cm. ISBN：1603842004，1603842006，1603842012，1603842013，1603843034，1603843035
Contents：Finding list of northern dramas in this anthology by editions—Table of dynasties—Conventions—Guan Hanqing—Moving heaven and shaking earth：the injustice to Dou E—Rescriptor-in-waiting Bao thrice investigates the butterfly dream—Beauty pining in her boudoir：the pavilion for praying to the moon/Bai Pu—Autumn nights of the lustrous Emperor of Tang：rain on the Wutong tree/Ma Zhiyuan—Breaking a troubling dream：a lone goose in autumn over the palaces of Han/Zheng Guangzu—Dazed behind the green ring lattice，Qiann's soul leaves her body/Li Xingdao—Rescriptor-in-waiting Bao's clever trick：the record of the chalk circle/Anonymous—Zhongli of the Han leads Lan Caihe to enlightenment/Zhu Youdun—Leopard monk returns to the laity of his own accord—Black Whirlwind Li spurns riches out of righteousness—Writing club of Hangzhou—Little Butcher Sun—Appendix 1：Note on the translation and study of early Chinese drama in Europe and the United States—Appendix 2：Suggested readings—Appendix 3：Partial list of modern English translations of early drama
《中国早期十一个剧本》，奚如谷（West，Stephen H.，1944—）（美国汉学家），伊维德（Idema，W. L.〈Wilt L.〉，1944—）（荷兰汉学家）合译.

11. The pipa & other Ming dynasty stories/retold by Liu Yunbo；illustrated by Kwan Shan Mei. Signapore：Federal Publications，1991. 183 pages：illustrations；18cm. ISBN：9810120559，9810120559.（Times Asian

library）

Liu, Yunbo 改编，包括高明（约 1306—1359 年）的《琵琶记》，孟称舜（约 1599—1684 年）的《王娇娘》，冯梦龙（1574—1646 年）的《精忠旗》.

12. Scenes for mandarins：the elite theater of the Ming/〔translated with commentaries by〕Cyril Birch. New York：Columbia University Press，c1995. 262 p.：ill.；24cm. ISBN：0231102623.（Translations from the Asian classics）

《明代戏剧精选》，白之（Birch, Cyril, 1925—）（美国汉学家）译.

13. The peach blossom fan and other Qing Dynasty stories/illustrated by Kwan Shan Mei；retold by Li Rongyao, He Donghu, Huang Weinwei. Singapore：Federal Publications，1991. 212 pages：illustrations；18cm. ISBN：9810120532，9810120535

《桃花扇》及其他清朝作品. Li, Rongyao 等译.

14. The romance of the western bower/by Wang Shifu；adaptation by Zhang Xuejing；〔translation by Kuang Peihua and Liu Jun〕. Zhao the orphan/by Ji Junxiang；adaptation by Wang Jianping and Ren Yutang；〔translation by Paul White〕. Snow in Summer/by Guan Hanqing；adaptation by Chang Xiaochang；〔translation by Paul White〕；revision by Liu Yousheng. New York：Better Link Press，2008. 418 pages；21cm. ISBN：1602202122，1602202125.（Love stories and tragedies from Chinese classic operas；4）

收录了王实甫的《西厢记》，纪君祥的《赵氏孤儿》，关汉卿的《窦娥冤》3 部作品.

15. The palace of eternal youth；The peony pavilion；The peach blossom fan/Adaptation by Chen Meilin. New York：Better Link，2008. 396 pages；21cm. ISBN：1602202108，1602202109.（Love stories and tragedies from Chinese classic operas；2）

陈美林改编. 包括洪升（1645—1704）的《长生殿》，汤显祖（1550—1616）的《牡丹亭》，孔尚仁（1648—1718）的《桃花扇》.

16. Escape from blood pond hell：the tales of Mulian and woman Huang/translated and introduced by Beata Grant and Wilt L. Idema. Seattle：University of Washington Press，c2011. x, 278 p.；24cm. ISBN：0295991191，0295991194，0295991207，0295991208

《目连宝卷》与《黄氏女宝卷》，管佩达（Grant, Beata），伊维德（Idema, W. L.〈Wilt L.〉，1944—）（荷兰汉学家）合译.

17. The "Immortal Maiden Equal to Heaven" and other precious scrolls from Western Gansu/〔introduction and translation〕by Wilt L. Idema. Amherst, NY：Cambria Press，2015. viii, 534 pages；26cm. ISBN：1604979077，1604979070.（Cambria sinophone world series）

Contents：Introduction—The precious scroll of the immortal maiden equal to heaven—The precious scroll of Liu Quan presenting melons—The precious scroll of the parrot—The precious scroll of the mouse—The precious scroll of kalpa survival—The precious scroll of the wedding scams of Hu Yucui.

甘肃西部六宝卷. 伊维德（Idema, W. L.〈Wilt L.〉，1944—）（荷兰汉学家）.

18. Battles, betrayals, and brotherhood：early Chinese plays on the Three Kingdoms/edited and translated, with an introduction, by Wilt L. Idema and Stephen H. West. Indianapolis：Hackett Pub. Co.，2012. xxx, 469 p.：ill.；23cm. ISBN：1603848138，1603848134，1603848145，1603848142

Contents：Liu, Guan, and Zhang：the tripartite oath of brotherhood in the peach orchard/Anonymous—In the Hall of Brocade Clouds：the beauty and the story of interlocking rings/by Zhu Youdun—Guan Yunchang's righteous and brave refusal of gold/by Anonymous—Liu Xuande goes alone to the Xiangyang meeting/by Anonymous—Zhuge Liang burns the stores at Bowang, Thirty Yuan plays, ed. 306, Ming Palace ed.，Act 4/by Guan Hanqing—The great King Guan and the single sword meeting, Thirty Yuan plays, ed. 370, Ming Palace ed./by Guan Hanqing—In a dream Guan and Zhang, a pair rush to Western Shu—Excerpts from the records of the Three Kingdoms in plain language—Excerpt from The story of Hua Guan So—A selection of Yuan plays version of The plan of interlocking rings.

《战斗，背叛和结拜兄弟：有关三国的早期戏剧》，伊维德（Idema, W. L.〈Wilt L.〉，1944—）（荷兰汉学家），奚如谷（West, Stephen H.，1944—）（美国汉学家）合译. 翻译了与三国桃园结义有关情节的 9 个戏剧.

19. Records of the Three Kingdoms in plain language/translated, with an introduction and annotations, by Wilt L. Idema and Stephen H. West. Indianapolis：Hackett Publishing Company, Inc.，2016. ISBN：1624665233，1624665233，1624665240，1624665241

有关"三国"的早期戏剧. 伊维德（Idema, W. L.〈Wilt L.〉，1944—）（荷兰汉学家），West, Stephen H. 合译.

I43　古代戏曲家及其作品

金代

董解元（生卒年不详）

1. Master Tung's Western chamber romance ＝ Tung Hsi-hsiang chu-kung-tiao：a Chinese chantefable/translated from the Chinese and with an introd. by Li-li Ch'en. Cambridge〔Eng.〕；New York：Cambridge University Press，1976. xxviii, 238 p.；24cm. ISBN：0521208718，0521208710.（Cambridge studies in Chinese history, literature and institutions）

《董书生的西厢罗曼史（董西厢诸宫调）》，陈荔荔（Ch'en, Li-li.）译．西厢记诸宫调.

(1) Cambridge ［England］；New York：Cambridge University Press，1989. xxviii，238 pages；24cm. (Cambridge studies in Chinese history, literature, and institutions)

(2) Columbia University Press Morningside ed. New York：Columbia University Press，c1994. xxx，238 p.；23cm. ISBN：0231101198，0231101196

2. West wing chante fable/by Tung Chieh-yüan；translated by William Dolby. Edinburgh：Carreg Publishers，2005. i，265 pages：illustrations；21cm. (Chinese culture series；no. 9)

《西厢记诸宫调》，Dolby, William 译.

元代

纪君祥（约元世祖至元年间在世）

1. The orphan of China：a play of five acts and a prologue/ adapted from Chi Juen Chang's play by Alan A. ［i. e. A. L.］Wong. London：Mitre Press，1973. 70 p.；19cm. ISBN：0705101851

《赵氏孤儿》，Wong, Alan L. (1938—)译.

2. Zhao the orphan/original drama by Ji Junxiang deng zhuan；literary adaptation by Chang Xiaochang, Wang Jianping and Ren Yutang. San Francisco：China Books，2015. 216 pages；18cm. ISBN：0835102513，0835102513. (Great Chinese stories)

《赵氏孤儿》

2. 赵氏孤儿故事：英文版/纪君祥著；王国振译.北京：五洲传播出版社，2017. 164 页：图；16cm. ISBN：7508530482. (中国经典名著故事)

关汉卿（约 1234 以前—约 1300）

1. Selected plays of Kuan Han-ch'ing/［translated by Yang Hsien-yi and Gladys Yang］. Peking：Foreign Languages Press，1958. 237 pages：illustrations

Contents：Foreword—Snow in midsummer—The wife-snatcher—The butterfly dream—Rescued by a coquette—The riverside pavilion—The jade mirror-stand—Lord Kuan goes to the feast—Death of the winged-tiger general

《关汉卿杂剧选》，杨宪益（1915—2009），戴乃迭（Yang, Gladys, 1919—1999）合译.

(1) Selected plays of Guan Hanqing/translated by Yang Xianyi and Gladys Yang. 2nd ed. Beijing Foreign Languages Press ［Waiwen chubanshe］，1979. 216 p. Ill.；22cm.

(2) 2nd ed. Beijing：Foreign Languages Press，1979. 216 pages，［8］leaves of plates：illustrations；22cm.

(3) Beijing：Foreign languages Press，2001. 2 v. ISBN：711902891X（v.1），7119028928（v.2）. (经典的回声＝Echo of classics)

(4) Honolulu：University Press of the Pacific，2003. 237 pages：illustrations；21cm.

(5) Selected plays of Guan Hanqing/Guan Hanqing；ed. Wu Xiaoling… ［et al.］；transl. Yang Xianyi, Gladys Yang. Beijing：Foreign Languages Press，2010. 39，［5］，455 p.：ill.；24cm. ISBN：7119033952，7119033956. (Library of Chinese classics：Chinese-English)

(6) New ed. ［Rockville, MD］：Silk Pagoda，2007. 332 pages：illustrations；23cm. ISBN：1596543904，1596543906

2. Injustice to Tou O（Tou O yüan）：a study and translation. Cambridge ［England］：Cambridge University Press，1972. xv，390 pages；23cm. ISBN：0521082285，0521082280. (Princeton-Cambridge studies in Chinese linguistics；4)

《窦娥冤》，时钟雯(1922—2014)著译.英汉对照.

3. Snow in midsummer/by Kuan Han Ching；with a study of his life and work by Cheng Chen-to. Vienna：International Institute for Peace，1958. 38 pages：portraits；19cm. (Cultural anniversaries series；1)

《窦娥冤》

马致远（约 1250—约 1324）

1. Hän Koong Tsew, or the sorrows of Han：a Chinese tragedy/translated from the original with notes by John Francis Davis. London：A. J. Valpy，1829. VIII，18 p.

《汉宫秋》，Davis, John Francis, Sir(1795—1890)译.

(1) New York：Johnson Repr.，1968. viii，18，［4］ pages；26cm. (Oriental Translation Fund：Original series；4)

2. Short plays from twelve countries, selected by Winifred Katzin. London ［etc.］G. G. Harrap & Co. Ltd. ［c1937］. 343，［1］p.；20cm.

Contents：China：The sorrows of Han…

Katzin, Winifred 选译.包括《汉宫秋》的英译.

3. Autumn in the Han palace/Ma Zhiyuan；Xia Lianbao gai bian；Liu Yousheng shen ding. Beijing：Xin shi jie chu ban she，2001. 1 v. ([18]，299 p.)：ill.；21cm. ISBN：7800055949，7800055942. (Classical chinese tragedies)

《汉宫秋》，Xia, Lianbao 改编；Liu, Yousheng 审定.

3. Ma Chih-yüan's complete san ch'ü-aria poems/translated by William Dolby. Edinburgh：Carreg Publishers，2003. iv，v，177 pages，10 unnumbered pages of plates：illustrations；21cm. (Chinese culture series；no. 7)

《马致远散曲全集英译本》，Dolby, William 译.

王实甫（1260—1336）

1. Si syang ki. Lyon, Bosc frères, M. & L. Riou，1934. 4 p. l.，170，［2］p.；25cm.

《西厢记》，Chen, Pao-ki 译.

2. The romance of the western chamber（Hsi hsiang chi）；a Chinese play written in the thirteenth century, translated by S. I. Hsiung, with a preface by Gordon Bottomley. London：Methuen & Co.，Ltd，［1935］. xxiii，280 ［2］

p. incl. front. , illus. ;20cm.

《西厢记》;熊式一(Hsiung, S. I. 〈Shih I〉, 1902—1991)译.

(1)New York：Columbia University Press, 1968. xliv, 280 p. illus. ；19cm. (UNESCO collection of representative works. Chinese series)

(2)Taipei：Central Books, 1969. xliv，280 pages： illustrations；20cm.

3. The west chamber：a medieval drama... translated from the original Chinese with notes by Henry H. Hart... foreword by Edward Thomas Williams. Stanford University, Calif. , Stanford University Press；London, H. Milford, Oxford University Press [c1936] xxxix, 192 p. ；24cm.

《西厢记》,Hart，Henry Hersch(1886—)等译.

(1)台北：第一文化社，[1967]. xxxix, 192 pages；21cm. (Chinese classics in English)

4. The romance of the western chamber/Shih-fu Wang；translated and adapted by T. C. Lai & Ed Gamarekian；ill. by Lo Koon-Chiu. New York：Columbia University Press，1968. ix, 135 pages：illustrations；19cm. (Writing in Asia series)

《西厢记》,Lai，T. C. 和 Gamarekian，Ed 合译.

(1)Hong Kong, Heinemann Educational Books (Asia) Ltd. , 1973. 135 pages：illustrations；19cm. (Writing in Asia series)

(2)Hong Kong：Heinemann Asia, 1979. 158 pages：illustrations；23cm. (Writing in Asia series)

5. Four classical Asian plays in modern translation/compiled and edited by Vera Rushforth Irwin. Baltimore：Penguin Books，1972. 332 pages：illustrations；18cm. ISBN：0140212493, 0140212495

Contents：The vision of Vasavadatta/attributed to Bhasa—The west chamber/attributed to Wang Shih-fu—Ikkaku Sennin/by Zempo Motoyasu Komparu—Narukami；from the Juhachiban—Selected bibliography (p. 317—322)—Selected list of plays in translation (p. 323—[330]).

Irwin, Vera Rushforth(1913—)编译，包括《西厢记》剧本.

6. The western chamber/by Wang Shifu of the Yuan dynasty；adapted by Hong Zengling；illustrated by Wong Shuhui；translated by Zheng Kangbo. 2nd ed. Hong Kong：Hai Feng Pub. Co. , 1987. 128 pages：illustrations；26cm.

《西厢记》,Hong, Zengling 改编；Zheng Kangbo 译. 英汉对照.

7. The moon and the zither：The story of the western wing ＝[Xin kan qi miao quan xiang zhu shi Xi xiang ji]/Wang Shifu；edited and translated with an introduction by Stephen H. West and Wilt L. Idema；with a study of its

woodblock illustrations by Yao Dajuin. Berkeley：University of California Press, c1991. xiii, 503 p. ：ill. ；24cm. ISBN：0520068076, 0520068070

《月色琴音西厢记》,奚如谷(West, Stephen H. ,1944—)(美国汉学家)，伊维德(Idema, W. L. 〈Wilt L. 〉，1944—)(荷兰汉学家)合译. 翻译的底本是 1498 年的《全相注释西厢记》.

8. The story of the western wing/Wang Shifu；edited and translated with an introduction by Stephen H. West and Wilt L. Idema. Berkeley：University of California Press, c1995. xiv, 328 p. ：ill. ；23cm. ISBN：0520201841, 0520201842

《西厢记》,奚如谷(West, Stephen H. ,1944—)(美国汉学家)，伊维德(Idema, W. L. 〈Wilt L. 〉，1944—)(荷兰汉学家)合译. 是 1991 年版的改名版. 是《西厢记》最佳英译本之一. 翻译的底本是最早完整的明刊本.

9. Romance of the Western bower/written by Wang Shifu；translated by Xu Yuangchong. Hunan：Hunan renmin chubanshe, 2000. 441 pages；25cm. SBN：754382535X, 7543825352. (Library of Chinese classics：Chinese-English)

《西厢记》. 湖南人民出版社.

10. 西厢记＝The romance of the Western Bower/(元)王实甫原著；张雪静改编. 北京：新世界出版社,2000. 223 页：图；20cm. ISBN：7800055523. (中国古代爱情故事＝Classical Chinese love stories)
英汉对照.

11. 西厢记/(元)王实甫原著；改编李真瑜,邓凌源；翻译 Wayne B. Burr,李子亮；绘画藤茏. 北京：高等教育出版社，2010. 157 页；21cm. ISBN：7040276657, 7040276658. (青春绣像版中国古代四大名剧)

12. Romance of Western bower/Wang Shifu；translated by Xu Yuanchong & Frank M. Xu. Singapore：World Culture Books，2011. 349 pages；22cm. ISBN：9810705848, 9810705840. (Classical Chinese poetry and prose＝许译中国经典诗文)

《西厢记》,许渊冲(1921—)，许明合译. 英汉对照.

(1)Beijing：Wu zhou chuan bo chu ban she：Zhonghua shu ju, 2012. 9, 349 pages；22cm. ISBN：7508521947, 7508521943. (Classical Chinese poetry and prose＝许译中国经典诗文)

13. 昆曲-西厢记/黄少荣[编译]. 北京：外语教学与研究出版社,2013. 239 页；23cm. ISBN：7513538664. (中国戏曲海外传播工程丛书)
英文题名：The romance of the Western chamber-a Kunqu opera.

李行道(约公元 1279 年前后在世)

1. The story of the circle of chalk：a drama from the old Chinese ＝［Hui Lan-chi］＝Hui-Lan-ki/translated by Frances Hume；with illustrations by John Buckland-Wright. Emmaus, PA：Rodale Press, [19?]. 124 p. , [6]

leaves of plates：col. ill. ；23cm. (Story classics)

《灰阑记》，Hume，Frances 译.

(1)London：Rodale Press，1953. 124，［2］pages：illustrations

(2)London：Rodale Press，1954. 124 pages color plates 23cm. (Story Classics)

2. The circle of chalk：a play in five acts adapted from the Chinese/by Klabund (I. E. A. Henschke)；English Version by James Laver. London：Heinemann，1929. 107 pages

《灰阑记》，Klabund（1890—1928）改编成德文；Laver，James(1899—1975)从德文译成英语.

高明（约 1306—1359）

1. Memoirs of the guitar：a novel of conjugal love, rewritten from a Chinese classical drama/by Yu Tinn-hugh. Shanghai, China Current Weekly Pub.，Co.，1928. 91 pages；19cm.

《琵琶记》，Yu，Tinn-hugh(1887—)改写.

2. The two wives (Die beiden Gattinnen)，8 scenes of Kao Ming's classical drama, the lute (Die Laute)/In German language by Vincenz Hundhausen. English textbook, translated from the German. ［Peking］，［Pekinger Verlag］，1930. 75 pages：illustrations；27cm.

《琵琶记》，Hundhausen，Vincenz 德译. 从德文版英译.

3. Lute song/by Kao-Tong-Kia. Adapted for Broadway presentation by Will Irwin and Sidney Howard. Acting version arranged by Ruth Sergel. Chicago, Dramatic Pub. Co.，1954. 82 pages；19cm.

《琵琶记》，Irwin，Will(1873—1948)改编.

(1)Rev. version. Chicago：Dramatic Pub. Co.，1956. 82 pages：plans；19cm.

4. The lute：Kao Ming's P'i-p'a chi/translated by Jean Mulligan. New York：Columbia University Press，1980. 317 pages；24cm. ISBN：0231047606，0231047609，0231047614，0231047616，1583482830，1583482834. (Program of translations from the oriental classics Columbia College)

Contents：Introduction. The play and its genre；The author；Sources of the play；The play as literature；On the translation；Notes—The lute—Appendix：Synopsis of the lute—Tune titles in the P'i-p'a chi—Glossary.

《琵琶记》，Mulligan，Jean(1945—)译.

(1)San Jose：ToExcel；New York：Columbia University Press，1999. 317 pages；24cm. ISBN：1583482830，1583482834

5. 琵琶记＝The story of the lute/(明)高明著；王建平改编. 北京：新世界出版社,1999. 277 页：插图;20cm. ISBN：7800055515. (中国古代爱情故事＝Classical Chinese love stories)

对照读物.

明代

汤显祖(1550—1616)

1. The peony pavilion＝Mudan ting/Tang Xianzu；translated by Cyril Birch. Bloomington：Indiana University Press，c1980. xv，343 p. ；24cm. ISBN：0253357233，0253357236. (Chinese literature in translation)

《牡丹亭》，白之(Birch，Cyril，1925—)(美国汉学家)译.

(1)1st Cheng ＆ Tsui pbk. ed. Boston：Cheng ＆ Tsui Co.，1994. xv，343 pages：illustrations；23cm. ISBN：0887272061，0887272066，0253357233，0253357236

(2)2nd ed. Bloomington：Indiana University Press，2002. xxx，343 p. ：ill. ；24cm. ISBN：0253215277，0253340977，0253340979，0253215277

Notes：introduction to the second edition by Catherine Swatek. 史恺悌作序.

2. The peony pavilion/author of the classical work, Tang Hsien-chu；translator, Wang Hui. Taipei：Hilit Pub. Co. ；Beijing：Prospect Pub. House，1990. 216 pages：color illustrations；30cm. ISBN：9576290449，9576290442，9576290384，9576290381. (Pictorial series of the ten greatest Chinese literature classics；6)

《牡丹亭》，Wang，Hui 译. 英汉对照.

3. The peony pavilion/by Tang Xianzu；translated by Zhang Guang-qian. Beijing：Lü you jiao yu chu ban she，1994. vi，407 pages：illustrations；19cm. ISBN：7563703667，7563703661

《牡丹亭》，张光前译. 旅游教育出版社.

(1)［Rev. ed. ］. Beijing：Foreign Languages Press，2001. viii，473 pages：illustrations；21cm. ISBN：7119026925，7119026923

4. The peony pavilion/Tang Xianzu；adapted by Chen Meilin. Tang Xianzu；Chen Meilin gai bian；［fan yi Kuang Peihua, Cao Shan］. Beijing：Xin shi jie chu ban she，1999. 225 pages：illustrations；20cm. ISBN：7800054330，7800054334. (中国古代爱情故事＝Classical Chinese love stories)

《牡丹亭》，陈美林改编；［翻译匡佩华，曹珊］. 新世界出版社.

5. 牡丹亭/汤显祖著；汪榕培英译；徐朔方, 杨笑梅点校. 长沙：湖南人民出版社，2000. 2 volumes（68，985 pages）：illustrations；24cm. ISBN：7543825341，7543825345. (大中华文库＝Library of Chinese classics)

6. 牡丹亭/汤显祖著；汪榕培译. 上海：上海外语教育出版社，2000. ix，863 pages，［11］pages of plates：color illustrations；21cm. ISBN：7810468391，7810468398.

英文题名：The peony pavilion.

7. 牡丹亭：舞台本/(明)汤显祖著；许渊冲, 许明英译. 北京：中国对外翻译出版公司,2009. 16，283 页：图;21cm. ISBN：7500122685

英文题名：Dream in peony pavilion. 英汉对照.

8. Dream in peony pavilion ＝ Mu dan ting（wu tai ben）/ compiled and translated by Xu Yuanchong & Xu Ming. Sydney, NSW, Australia：CPG-International-Sydney, 2010,（c）2009. 283 pages：illustrations；21cm. ISBN：1921678028, 192167802X.

《牡丹亭》,许渊冲(1921—),许明合译.英汉对照.

9. Dream in peony pavilion/Tang Xianzu；translated by Xu Yuanchong & Frank M. Xu. Singapore；World Culture Books, 2011. 346 pages；22cm. ISBN：9810705824, 9810705824.（Classical Chinese poetry and prose＝许译中国经典诗文）

《牡丹亭》,许渊冲(1921—),许明合译.英汉对照.

(1) Beijing：Wu zhou chuan bo chu ban she；Zhonghua shu ju, 2012. ISBN：7508521985, 7508521986.（Classical Chinese poetry and prose＝许译中国经典诗文）

10. Dream in peony pavilion ＝ Mu dan ting/许渊冲译. Beijing：Hai tun chu ban she, 2013. 286 pages：illustrations；22cm. ISBN：7511014221, 7511014224.（许渊冲文集；12）

《牡丹亭》,许渊冲译.

11. 牡丹亭/(明)汤显祖原著；改编李真瑜, 邓凌源；翻译李子亮；绘画藤茏. 北京：高等教育出版社,2010. 153 页；21cm. ISBN：7040296648, 7040296640.（青春绣像版中国古代四大名剧）

12. The peony pavilion/Tang Xianzu；retold by Teng Jianmin. Beijing：China Intercontinental Press, 2012. 102 pages：illustrations；22cm. ISBN：7508521619, 7508521617.（Chinese classics）

《牡丹亭故事》,滕建民改编.

13. A dream under the southern bough/by Tang Xianzu；translated by Zhang Guangqian. Beijing：Foreign Languages Press, 2003. 308 p. ：ill. ；21cm. ISBN：7119032704, 7119032702

《南柯记》,张光前译.

(1) Beijing：Foreign Languages Press, 2006. 37, 565 páginas, [20] páginas de láminas：ilustraciones；25cm. ISBN：7119041650, 7119041657.（Library of Chinese classics）

14. 英译南柯记＝The Nanke dream/汪榕培,张玲,霍跃红译. 上海：上海外语教育出版社,2012. 4, 389 pages；24cm. ISBN：7544626224, 7544626229.（外教社中国文化汉外对照丛书＝SFLEP bilingual Chinese culture series）

15. 邯郸记/汤显祖著；汪榕培英译；徐朔方笺校. 北京：外语教学与研究出版社, 2003. 54, 550 pages；24cm. ISBN：7560038786,7560038780.（大中华文库＝Library of Chinese classics）

英文题名：The Handan dream.

16. The purple hairpins/written by Tang Xianzu；translated by Wang Rongpei, Zhu Yuan and Zhang Ling；

punctuated and revised by Wang Rongpei. Guangzhou Shi：Hua cheng chu ban she, 2009. 2 v. ：ill. ；24cm. ISBN：7536056244（set）, 7536056249（set）.（Library of Chinese classics＝大中华文库）

《紫钗记》,汪榕培,朱源,张玲英译；汪榕培点校.花城出版社.

17. 英译紫箫记/[汤显祖著]；汪榕培,张玲,顾薇译. 上海：上海外语教育出版社, 2013. 3, 386 pages；24cm. ISBN：7544627795, 7544627799.（外教社中国文化汉外对照丛书）

英汉对照.

18. 汤显祖戏剧全集/汪榕培,张玲主编. 上海：上海外语教育出版社, 2014. 1060 页；28cm. ISBN：7544634359, 7544634353

英文题名：Complete dramatic works of Tang Xianzu.

李渔(1611—1680)

1. Silent operas ＝（Wusheng xi）/by Li Yu；edited by Patrick Hanan. Hong Kong：Research Centre for Translation, Chinese University of Hong Kong, c1990. xiii, 201 p. ：ill. ；22cm.（Renditions paperbacks）

《无声戏》,韩南(Hanan, Patrick)(美国汉学家)译.

2. A tower for the summer heat/Li Yu；translated, with an introduction and notes, by Patrick Hanan. New York：Ballantine Books, c1992. . xv, 249 p. ；20cm. ISBN：0345378539

《十二楼》(选译),韩南(Hanan, Patrick)(美国汉学家)译.

(1) New York：Columbia University Press, c1998. xi, 258 p. ；21cm. ISBN：0231113846, 0231113854.（Translations from the Asian classics）

清代

朱素臣(约公元1644年前后在世)

1. Fifteen strings of cash；a kunchu opera. Peking：Foreign Languages Press, 1957. 84 p. illus. ；20cm.

《十五贯》,杨宪益(1915—2009),戴乃迭(Yang Gladys, 1919—1999)译.浙江昆苏剧团演出.昆曲剧本.

2. Fifteen strings of cash/adapted by Kuang Rong；drawings by Wang Hongli. Beijing：Foreign Languages Press：Distributed by China Publications Centre（Guoji Shudian）, 1982. [57] p. ：ill. ；27cm.

《十五贯》,Kuang, Rong 改编；Wang, Hongli 绘画.英汉对照.

3. 昆曲：十五贯/杨孝明[编译]. 北京：外语教学与研究出版社,2015. 285 页；23cm. ISBN：7513556941.（中国戏曲海外传播工程丛书）

英文题名：Fifteen strings of coins-a kunqu opera.

洪升(1645—1704)

1. The palace of eternal youth. Translated by Yang Hsienyi and Gladys Yang. Peking, Foreign Languages Press [1955]. 322 p. , music（[16] p. ）plates, port. ；22cm.

《长生殿》,杨宪益(1915—2009),戴乃迭(Yang, Gladys,

1919—1999)合译.

(1)2nd ed. Beijing：Foreign Languages Press，1980. 281 p.，[3] leaves of plates：ill.；22cm.

(2)Beijing：Wai wen chu ban she，2001. 531 p.；21cm. ISBN：711902888X.（经典的回声＝Echo of classics）. 英汉对照.

(3)Beijing：Foreign Languages Press，2004. 37，579 pages；24cm. ISBN：7119033301，7119033303.（大中华文库＝Library of Chinese classics）

(4)Beijing：Wai wen chu ban she，2006. 531 p.；20cm. ISBN：7119028880.（经典的回声＝Echo of classics）. 英汉对照.

2. The palace of eternal youth/Hong Sheng；adapted by Chen Meilin. Beijing：Xin shi jie chu ban she：Jing xiao Xin hua shu dian，Wai wen shu dian，2000. 215 p.：ill.；21cm. ISBN：7800055531，7800055539.（中国古代爱情故事＝Classic Chinese love stories）
《长生殿》,陈美林改编.新世界出版社.英汉对照.

3. Changsheng dian＝the palace of eternal youth：a romance/by Hong Sheng；translated［and commentary］by He Yubin. Rev. ed. Edinburgh：Caledonian Pub. Co.，Dept. of Cross-cultural studies，1999. xviii，465 pages：illustrations，1 portraits；21cm. ISBN：1901886018，1901886016
《长生殿》,贺淯滨译.初版于1996年.

4. The palace of eternal youth/by Hong Sheng；translated by He Yubin. Beijing：Central Compilation & Translation Press，2004. 367 pages；26cm. ISBN：7802110718，7802110717.（Serial in comparative literature and world literature）
《长生殿》,贺淯滨译.中央编译出版社（比较文学与世界文学书系）

5. 长生殿/(清)洪升原著；改编：李真瑜、黄云生；翻译：李子亮；绘画：朱君. 北京：高等教育出版社,2010. 151 页；21cm. ISBN：7040298529,704029852X.（青春绣像版中国古代四大名剧）

6. Love in Long-life Hall＝Chang sheng dian（wu tai ben）/compiled and translated by Xu Yuanchong & Xu Ming. Sydney，NSW，Australia：CPG-International-Sydney，2009. 377 pages；illustrations；21cm. ISBN：1921678035，1921678038
《长生殿》,许渊冲(1921—),许明合译.英汉对照.

(1)Love in Long-life Hall/Hong Sheng；translated by Xu Yuanchong & Frank M. Xu. Singapore：World Culture Books，2011. 311pages. ISBN：9810705817，9810705816.（Classical Chinese poetry and prose＝许译中国经典诗文）

(2)Beijing：Wu zhou chuan bo chu ban she：Zhonghua shu ju，2012. 9，311 pages. ISBN：7508522036，7508522036.（Classical Chinese poetry and prose＝许译中国经典诗文）

(3)Beijing：Hai tun chu ban she，2013. 396 pages：illustrations；22cm. ISBN：7511014238，7511014232.（许渊冲文集；13）

7. The palace of eternal youth/Hong Sheng；retold by Teng Jianmin. Beijing：China Intercontinental Press，2012. 96 pages；illustrations；21cm. ISBN：7508521602，7508521609.（Chinese classics）
《长生殿故事》,滕建民改编.

8. Lasting-life Palace-hall/by Hung Sheng；translated by William Dolby. Edinburgh：Carreg Publishers，2012. i，ii，cxxiv，678 pages；30cm.（Chinese culture series；29）
《洪升长生殿》,Dolby，William 编译.

孔尚任（1648—1718）

1. The peach blossom fan＝T'ao-hua-shan/by K'ung Shang-jên；translated by Chen Shih-hsiang and Harold Acton，with the collaboration of Cyril Birch. Berkeley：University of California Press，c1976. xxi，312 p.：ill.；24cm. ISBN：0520029283，0520029286
《桃花扇》,陈世骧(Chen Shih-hsiang，1912—1971)(美国华裔学者),艾克敦(Acton，Harold，1904—1994)(英国诗人),白之(Birch，Cyril，1925—)(美国汉学家)合译.

(1)Boston，MA：Cheng & Tsui Co.，2001. xxi，312 pages：illustrations；23cm. ISBN：0887273890，780887273896.（C & T Asian literature series）

(2)New York：NYRB，New York Times Review Books，2015. xxxi，312 pages：illustrations；21cm. ISBN：1590178768，1590178769

2. The peach blossom fan＝[Tao hua shan]/original play by Kong Shangren published in 1699；rewritten as a novel by Gu Sifan in 1948；translated and abridged by T. L. Yang. Aberdeen，Hong Kong：Hong Kong University Press，1998. xvii，335 pages；25cm. ISBN：9622094775，9622094772
《新桃花扇》,谷斯范改写；杨铁梁译.

3. 桃花扇＝The peach blossom fan/(清)孔尚任著；陈美林改编. 北京：新世界出版社,1999. 233 页；图；20cm. ISBN：7800054322.（中国古代爱情故事＝Classical Chinese love stories）
中英文对照读物.

(1)Beijing，China：New World Press，2001. 233 pages：illustrations；20cm. ISBN：7800054322，7800054327.（Zhongguo gu dai ai qing gu shi）

4. 桃花扇/(清)孔尚任著. 北京：新世界出版社,2009. 2 册(47 页,949 页)；24cm. ISBN：7510405006，7510405009.（大中华文库）
英文题名：The peach blossom fan.

5. 桃花扇/(清)孔尚任原著；李真瑜、黄云生改编；李子亮翻译. 北京：高等教育出版社,2010. 163 页；21cm. ISBN：7040298376，7040298376.（青春绣像版中国古代四大名剧）

6. Peach blooms painted with blood＝Tao hua shan（wu tai

ben)/compiled and translated by Xu Yuanchong & Xu Ming. Sydney, NSW, Australia：CPG-International-Sydney, 2010. 301 pages：illustrations；21cm. ISBN：1921678011，1921678011

《桃花扇》，许渊冲(1921—)，许明合译.英汉对照.

(1) Peach blooms painted with blood/Kong Shangren；translated by Xu Yuanchong & Frank M. Xu. Singapore：World Culture Books, 2011. 245 pages；22cm. ISBN：9810705831，9810705832.（Classical Chinese poetry and prose＝许译中国经典诗文）

(2) Beijing：China Intercontinental Press；Zhonghua Book, 2012.9, 245 pages；22cm. ISBN：7508521954，7508521951.（Classical Chinese poetry and prose＝许译中国经典诗文）

(3) Beijing：Hai tun chu ban she, 2013. 324 pages：illustrations；22cm. ISBN：7511014245，7511014240.（许渊冲文集；14）

7. Peach blossom fan/Kong Shangren；retold by Teng Jianmin. Beijing：China Intercontinental Press, 2011. 123 pages：illustrations；22cm. ISBN：7508521626，7508521625.（Chinese classics）

《桃花扇故事》，滕建民编译.

8. The peach blossom fan/Kung Shang-jen；translated by Quincy Sheh（She Kun-shan）, act I-XXiv, Wang Xian-zhong, act XV-XL. Beijing：Foreign Languages Press, 2012. xviii, 361 pages：illustrations；23cm. ISBN：7119076508，7119076507.（Chinese classics＝中国经典）

《桃花扇》，畲坤珊，王偭中译.

吴藻(1799—1862)

1. Under Confucian eyes：writings on gender in Chinese history/edited by Susan Mann and Yu-Yin Cheng. Berkeley：University of California Press, c2001. xiii, 310 p.：ill.；24cm. ISBN：0520222741，0520222768

《以儒家的眼光：中国历史中的性别》，曼素恩(Mann, Susan, 1943—)，程玉茵(Cheng, Yu-Yin)编.书中有吴藻(1799—1862)的独幕剧《乔影》的翻译("Drinking wine and reading 'Enountering sorrow'：A reflection in disguise, by Wu Zao[1799—1862]").

2. The red brush：writing women of imperial China/Wilt Idema and Beata Grant. Cambridge：Harvard University Asia Center；Distributed by Harvard University Press, 2004. xvi, 931 p.；26cm. ISBN：067401393X，0674013933.（Harvard East Asian monographs；231）

《彤管：帝制中国的女作家》，伊维德(Idema, W. L.〈Wilt L.〉, 1944—)，管佩达(Grant, Beata)著,该书收录了吴藻(1799—1862)的独幕剧《乔影》的翻译(第687-693页)以及其他历代女性作家的作品.

王筠(1749—1819)

1. A dream of glory＝Fanhua meng：a Chinese play/by Wang Yun；translated, with introduction and annotation, by Qingyun Wu（with the original Chinese text edited by Qingyun Wu）. Hong Kong：The Chinese University Press, c2008. xiii, 279 p.：ill.；24cm. ISBN：9629963095，9629963094

《繁华梦》，武庆云(Wu, Qingyun, 1950—)（美国华裔学者)译.

I44 现当代戏剧集

1. Modern Chinese plays/translated into English by Ku Tsong-nee.［Shanghai］：Commercial Press, 1941. 137 pages；19cm.

Contents：One evening in Soochow/by T'ien Han—The mutiny/by Yu Shang-yuan—The oppressed/by Ting Hsi-lin—The drunkard/by Hsiung Eu-hsi—A West Lake tragedy/by T'ien Han—The artist/by Hsiung Fu-hsi.

《英译中国近代戏剧选》，顾宗沂译.

2. Three famous Chinese plays. 上海：中英出版社印行, 民30［1941］. 230 pages；19cm.

Contents：Thunder and rain；Confucius saw Nancy；West Lake tragedy.

《英译中国三大名剧》

目次：雷雨/曹禺著；姚萃农译——子见南子/林语堂著；作者译——湖上的悲剧/田汉著；顾宗沂译.

3. The Women's representative：three one-act plays. Peking：Foreign Languages Press, 1956. 123 p.：ill.；22cm.

Contents：Chin, C. Chao Hsiao-lan.—Sun, Y. The women's representative.—Peking People's Art Theatre. Between husband and wife.

《独幕剧选》，孙芋(1900—)等著.包括《妇女代表》《赵小兰》和《夫妻之间》.

4. Saturday afternoon at the mill and other one-act plays. Peking：Foreign Languages Press, 1957. 134 p. illus.；22cm.

Contents：Saturday afternoon at the mill, by Tsui Teh-chih.—The day the new director came, by Ho Chiu.—Two ways of looking at it, by Chao Yu-hsiang.—Home-coming, by Lu Yen-chou.

《独幕剧选》(二).收录《纱厂的星期六下午》《新局长到来之前》《刘莲英》等.

5. Modern drama from Communist China. Edited by Walter J. Meserve and Ruth I. Meserve. New York：New York University Press, 1970. 368 p. 25cm. ISBN：081470302X

Contents：Snow in midsummer, by Kuan Han-ching.—The passer-by, by Lu Hsun.—Dragon beard ditch, by Lao Sheh.—The white-haired girl, by Ting Yi and Ho Ching-chih.—The women's representative, by Sun Yu.—Yesterday, by Chang Pao-hua and Chung Yi-ping.—Magic aster, by Jen Teh-yao.—Letters from the South, by Sha Seh, and others.—The red lantern, by Wong Ou-hung and Ah Chia.

《共产中国现代戏剧》，Meserve, Walter J. 和 Meserve,

Ruth I. 合编,收录 9 个中国现代戏剧,包括《六月雪》(据《窦娥冤》改编)、鲁迅的《过客》、老舍的《龙须沟》、贺敬之的《白毛女》、孙芋的《妇女代表》、任德耀的《马兰花》、常宝华的《昨天》(相声)、莎色的《南方来的信》,翁偶虹和阿甲的《红灯记》等.

6. China on stage: an American actress in the People's Republic/Lois Wheeler Snow. New York: Random House, 1972. xv, 328 pages: illustrations; 25cm. ISBN: 0394468740, 0394468747

   Contents: Introduction: reversing history. —Taking Tiger Mountain: text of Taking Tiger Mountain by strategy. —"For whom?"—Shachiapang. —Peasants and soldiers in ballet shoes. —The red lantern, and the theatre to be. —Do-it-yourself-theatre. —Glossary of Chinese theatre and dance terms.

   《舞台上的中国:一位美国女演员在中国》,Snow, Lois Wheeler 编. 主要收录"样板戏",包括《沙家浜》《红色娘子军》《智取威虎山》和《红灯记》.

   (1) New York, Vintage Books, 1973. xv, 328 pages: illustrations; 19cm. ISBN: 039471945X, 0394719450

7. The red pear garden: three great dramas of revolutionary China/Edited by John D. Mitchell. Introd. by Richard E. Strassberg. Boston: Godine, 1973. 285 pages; 26cm. ISBN: 0879230738, 0879230739

   Contents: The staging of Peking opera/John D. Mitchell and Donald Chang—The white snake/Tyan Han; translated by Donald Chang; English verse adaptation by William Packard—The wild boar forest/Li Syau Chan; translated by John D. . Mitchell and Donald Chang—Taking Tiger Mountain by strategy/collectively written and revised by members of the Peking Opera Troupe in Shanghai; translated by Richard E. Strassberg.

   《红色梨园:革命中国戏剧三种》,Mitchell, John D. (John Dietrich, 1917—2005)等编译,收录了《白蛇传》(田汉)、《野猪林》和《智取威虎山》三部现代京剧剧本.

8. Red pear garden; three great dramas of revolutionary China. Edited by John D. Mitchell. Introd. by Richard E. Strassberg. [Boston] D. R. Godine [c1973]. 285 p. 26cm. ISBN: 0879230738

   Contents: Mitchell, J. D. and Chang, D. The staging of Peking opera. —The white snake [translation of Pai she chuan] translated by D. Chang, English verse adaptation by W. Packard. —Li, S. C. The wild boar forest [translation of Yeh chu lin] translated by J. D. Mitchell and D. Chang. —Taking Tiger Mountain by strategy [translation of Chih ch'u? Wei-hu shan] collectively written and revised by members of the Peking Opera Troupe in Shanghai, translated by R. E. Strassberg.

   Mitchell, John Dietrich(1917—)编译,收录了《白蛇传》、李少春的《野猪林》与上海京剧团的《智取威虎山》.

9. Five Chinese Communist plays/edited by Martin Ebon. New York: John Day Co., [1975]. xxi, 328 p.; 24cm. ISBN: 0381982815

   Contents: The white-haired girl. —The red detachment of women. —Taking the bandits' stronghold [Taking Tiger Mountain by strategy]. —The red lantern. —Azalea Mountain

   《中国共产党戏剧五种》,Ebon, Martin 译. 包括《白毛女》《红色娘子军》《智取威虎山》《红灯记》和《杜鹃山》5 个革命历史剧.

10. Twentieth-century Chinese drama: an anthology/edited by Edward M. Gunn. 1st Midland book ed. Bloomington: Indiana University Press, 1983. xxiii, 517 p.; 25cm. ISBN: 0253361095, 0253203104. (Chinese literature in translation)

    《二十世纪中国戏剧选》,Gunn, Edward M. 编译.

11. Chinese drama after the Cultural Revolution, 1979—1989: an anthology/edited and translated with an introduction by Shiao-ling S. Yu. Lewiston, N. Y.: E. Mellen Press, c1996. 494 p.: ill.; 24cm. ISBN: 0773487808. (Chinese studies; v. 3)

    《"文革"后的中国戏剧选》,余孝玲(Yu, Shiao-Ling)(美国华裔学者)编译,收录郭大宇、习志淦《徐九斤升官记》和魏明伦《潘金莲》两部传统戏剧,以及高行健《绝对信号》《车站》,王培公等《WM》,刘锦云《狗儿爷涅槃》,何冀平《天下第一楼》五部现代话剧.

12. Chinese drama since the Cultural Revolution: an anthology/edited and translated, with an introduction by Shiao-ling S. Yu. Lewiston, N. Y.; Lampeter: Edwin Mellen Press, 1997. 494 pages: illustrations; 24cm. ISBN: 0773487808, 0773487802, 0889460760, 0889460768. (Chinese studies; v 3.)

    "文革"时期戏剧集. Yu, Shiao-Ling 编译.

13. An Oxford anthology of contemporary Chinese drama/edited by Martha P. Y. Cheung and Jane C. C. Lai. Hong Kong; New York: Oxford University Press, 1997. xxvi, 873 pages: illustrations; 26cm. ISBN: 0195868803, 0195868807

    Contents: Plays from mainland China. Who's the strongest of us all? /Liang Bingkun—Uncle Doggie's nirvana/Jin Yun—The other side/Gao Xingjian—The legend of Old Bawdy Town/Ma Zhongjun—Old forest/Xu Pinli—Birdmen/Guo Shixing. Plays from Taiwan. Flower and sword/Ma Sên—Pining—in peach blossom land/Lai Shêng-ch'uan—Cathay visions (the empty cage)/Hwang Mei-shu—National Salvation Corporation Ltd. /Li Kuo-hsiu—Mother's water mirror/Liu Ching-min. Plays from Hong Kong. Before the dawn-wind rises/Joanna Chan—Where love abides/Raymond K. W. To—American house/Anthony Chan—Chronicle of women—Liu Sola in concert/Danny N. T. Yung.

    Cheung, Martha 和 Lai, Jane(1939—)编. 选编了中国包

括港台地区过去 20 年来 15 部优秀剧目,内地的梁秉堃《谁是强者》、刘锦云《狗儿爷涅槃》、高行健《彼岸》、马中俊《老风流镇》、徐频莉《老林》、过士行《鸟人》.

14. Theater and society：an anthology of contemporary Chinese drama/Haiping Yan, editor. Armonk, N. Y.：M. E. Sharpe, c1998. xlvi, 328 p. ; 24cm. ISBN：0765603071, 0765603074, 076560308X, 0765603081. (Asia and the Pacific)

《戏剧与社会：当代中国戏剧选集》,颜海平(Yen, Hai-p'ing)编. 收录高行健《车站》、王培公、王贵《WM》、魏明伦《潘金莲》、陈子度《桑树坪纪事》和一部电影剧本《老井》(吴天明)的翻译.

15. Reading the right text：an anthology of contemporary Chinese drama/edited and with an introduction by Xiaomei Chen. Honolulu：University of Hawaii Press, 2003. x, 464 páginas; 24cm. ISBN：0824825055, 0824825058, 0824826892, 0824826895

Contents：The dead visiting the living/Liu Shugang, translated by Charles Qianzhi Wu—The world's top restaurant/He Jiping, translated by Edward M. Gunn—Black stones/Yang Limin, translated by Timothy C. Wong—Jiang Qing and her husbands/Sha Yexin, translated by Kirk A. Denton—Green barracks/Zhang Lili, translated by Yuanxi Ma—Wild grass/Zhang Mingyuan, translated by Philip F. Williams.

《正确的文本阅读：中国当代戏剧选》,陈小眉(Chen, Xiaomei, 1954—)编. 选了 6 部当代戏剧为：刘树纲《一个死者对生者的访问》、何冀平《天下第一楼》、杨利民《黑色的石头》、沙叶新《江青和她的丈夫们》、张莉莉《绿色营地的女儿们》、张明媛《野草》.

16. The Columbia anthology of modern Chinese drama/edited, with a critical introduction, by Xiaomei Chen. New York：Columbia University Press, 2010. x, 1105 pages; 26cm. ISBN：0231145701, 0231145705. (Weatherhead books on Asia)

Contents：1. The main event in life/Hu Shi; translated by Edward M Gunn (1919)—2. Yama Zhao/Hong Shen; translated by Carolyn T. Brown (1922)—3. The night the tiger was caught/Tian Han; translated by Jonathan S. Noble (1922—1923)—4. After returning home/Ouyang Yuqian; translated by Jonathan S. Noble (1922)—5. A wasp/Ding Xilin; translated by John B. Weinstein and Carsey Yee (1923)—6. Oppression/Ding Xilin; translated by John B. Weinstein and Carsey Yee (1925)—7. Breaking out of ghost pagoda/Bai Wei; translated by Paul B. Foster (1928)—8. Thunderstorm/Cao Yu; translated by Wang Tso-liang and A. C. Barnes; revised translation by Charles Qianzhi Wu, with a translation of the prologue and epilogue (1934)—9. It's only spring/Li Jianwu; translated by Tony Hyder (1934)—10. Under Shanghai eaves/Xia Yan; translated by George Hayden (1937)—11. Return on a snowy night/Wu Zuguang; translated by Thomas Moran (1942)—12. Teahouse/Lao She; translated by Ying Ruocheng; revised by Claire Conceison (1958)—13. Guan Hanqing/Tian Han; retranslated by Amy Dooling (1958)—14. The young generation/Chen Yun; translated by Constantine Tung and Kevin A. O'Connor (1965)—15. The red lantern/Weng Ouhong and A Kia; revised by the China Peking Opera Troupe; translated by Brenda Austin and John B. Weinstein (1970)—16. The bus stop/Gao Zingjian; translated by Shiao-Ling Yu (1983)—17. Wilderness and man/Li Longyun; translated by Bai Di and Nick Kaldis (1988)—18. Geologists/Yang Limin; translated by Timothy C. Wong (1995)—19. Che Guevara/Huan Jisu, Zhang Guangtian, and Shen Lin; translated by Jonathan S. Noble (2000)—20. Secret love in peach blossom land/Stan Lai (Lai Sheng-chuan), in collaboration with the cast; translated by Stain Lai (1986)—21. Metamorphosis under the star/Anthony Chan; translated by Grace Liu and Julia Wan (1986)—22. Crown ourselves with roses/written and translated by Joanna Chan (1988).

哥伦比亚现代中国戏曲集. 陈小眉(Chen, Xiaomei, 1954—)编.

(1) Abridged edition. New York：Columbia University Press,2014. x,641 pages;27cm. ISBN：0231165020, 0231165021, 0231165037, 023116503X. (Weatherhead books on Asia)

17. 大·探·二：《大保国》《探皇陵》《二进宫》/孙萍主编. 北京：国家图书馆出版社,2016.37, 227 页、[2] 页：图版,彩图,乐谱;29cm. ISBN：7501358861. (中国京剧百部经典外译系列. 第三辑)

英文题名：Defending the country, visiting the imperial tomb, and entering the imperial palace again. 英汉对照.

I45 现当代戏曲家及其作品

郭沫若(1892—1978)

1. Chu Yuan, a play in five acts/translated by Yang Hsien-yi and Gladys Yang. Peking：Foreign Languages Press, 1953. ix, 126 p. illus. ; 22cm.

《屈原》(剧本),杨宪益(1915—2009),戴乃迭(Yang, Gladys,1919—1999)合译.

(1)Peking：Foreign Languages Press, 1955. 124 pages：illustrations, map, portraits; 22cm.

(2)2nd ed. Peking：Foreign Languages Press, 1978. 100 pages, [1] leaf of plates：illustrations; 22cm.

(3)Honolulu：University Press of the Pacific, 2001. 100 pages：portraits;21cm. ISBN：0898752205,0898752205

2. Five historical plays/Beijing：Foreign Languages Press；Distributed by China International Book Trading Corp.，1984. ix，526 pages，[21] pages of plates：illustrations；22cm. ISBN：0835110095，0835110099. (Selected works of Guo Moruo)

Contents：Twin flowers—Qu Yuan—The tiger tally—Cai Wenji—Wu Zetian.

收录郭沫若的五部历史剧.

张恨水(1895—1967)

1. 夜深沉：电视连续剧《夜深沉》分镜头剧本及英译/柯长河编剧；鲁津翻译. 北京：中国传媒大学出版社，2004. 333 p.；20cm. ISBN：7810854275，7810854276

Notes：根据张恨水同名小说改编.

英文题名：The Long and Dark Night. 电视文学剧本.

张道藩(1897—1968)

1. Tse Kiu＝Save yourself：play in six scenes/by Chang Tao Fan；English adaptation by C. K. Sié. Rome：Tumminelli，1944. 148 pages，[1] leaf of plates：illustrations；20cm.

Notes：Title also in Chinese：[Zi jiu]. / Produced in the Taoo Taoo Theatre，Nanking，1934. Translated into French by C. K. Sié，1941.

《自救》，Sié，C. K. 英译.

田汉(1898—1968)

1. The white snake；a Peking opera. Peking：Foreign Languages Press，1957. 79 p. cm.

《白蛇传》(剧本)，杨宪益(1915—2009)，戴乃迭(Yang Gladys，1919—1999)合译.

2. Kuan Han-ch'ing. 1958. 124 p. illus. ；18 m.

《关汉卿》. 话剧.

(1)Kuan Han-ching，a play. Peking：Foreign Languages Press，1961. 134 p. illus. ，port. 22cm.

老舍(1899—1966)

1. Teahouse：a play in three acts/Lao She；translated by John Howard-Gibbon. Beijing：Foreign Languages Press，1980. 86 pages，[8] pages of plates：illustrations；22cm.

《茶馆：三幕话剧》，霍华译.

2. Teahouse/Lao She zhu；Ying Ruocheng yi. Beijing：Zhongguo dui wai fan yi chu ban gong si，1999. 11，241 p.；21cm. ISBN：7500106696，7500106692. (英若诚名剧译丛；6)

《茶馆》，英若诚译. 英汉对照. 中国对外翻译出版公司出版.

(1)2 版. 北京：中国对外翻译出版公司，2005. 129 p.：stage photo，photo. ；24cm. ISBN：7500114141，7500114147

(2)北京：中国对外翻译出版有限公司，2012. 203 页；23cm. ISBN：7500134442. (双语名著无障碍阅读丛书)

3. Teahouse＝Cha guan/written by Lao She；translated by John Howard-Gibbon. Beijing：Foreign Languages Press，

2001. 235 p. ：il. ；21cm. ISBN：7119027807，7119027808. (Echo of classics)

《茶馆》，霍华译. 在 2003，2006，2007 年重印.

(1)中英对照版. 香港：香港中文大学出版社，2004. xlix，197 pages；22cm. ISBN：9629961253，9629961251. (中国现代文学中英对照系列＝Bilingual series on modern Chinese literature)

4. Teahouse/original Chinese text by Lao She；translated by John Howard-Gibbon. Hong Kong：Chinese University Press，2004. xlix，197 p. ；22cm. ISBN：9629961253. (中国现代文文中英对照系列＝Bilingual series on modern Chinese literature)

《茶馆》，霍华(Howard-Gibbon，John)英译.

5. Dragon beard ditch；a play in three acts，by Lao Sheh [pseud. Translated by Liao Hung-ying.] Peking：Foreign Languages Press，1956. 97 p. illus. ；22cm.

《龙须沟：三幕剧》

6. 京剧——骆驼祥子/陈融编译. 北京：外语教学与研究出版社，2015.199 页；23cm. ISBN：7513556903. (中国戏曲海外传播工程丛书)

英文题名：Camel Xiangzi-a Beijing Opera.

夏炎(1900—1995)

1. The test：a play in five acts/by Hsia Yen. Peking：Foreign Languages Press，1956. 107 pages，[7] leaves of plates：illustrations；22cm.

《考验》

姚克(原名姚志伊、姚莘农，1904—)

1. The malice of empire，by Yao Hsin-nung. Translated and with an introd. by Jeremy Ingalls. Berkeley，University of California Press，1970. 160 p. ；23cm. ISBN：0520015606

《清宫怨》，Ingalls，Jeremy 译.

(1)London，Allen & Unwin，1970. 3—160 p. 23cm. ISBN：0048950165

李健吾(1906—1982)

1. It's only spring；and，Thirteen years：two early plays/by Li Jianwu（1906—1982）；translated from the Chinese with afterword and notes by Tony Hyder. London：Bamboo，1989. 159 pages；21cm. ISBN：1870076133，1870076135. （UNESCO collection of representative works. Chinese series)

《这不过是春天·十三年：早期戏剧两种》

翁偶虹(1908—1994)

1. The jewel bag：a traditional Chinese play/[Wang Yao-Ching，Ong O-Hung]；translated and adapted with an introduction and stage directions by Josephine Huang Hung. Taipei：Mei Ya Publications，1974. xxii，114 pages：illustrations；21cm. （A Mei Ya international edition)

《锁麟囊》，Hung，Josephine Huang(1915—)编译.

吴晗(1909—1969)

1. The dismissal of Hai Jui：an epic tragedy/by and of Wu Han. [Edited by Chester Leo Smith. Los Angeles] Bede Press，1968. 58 leaves：portraits；28cm.

   《海瑞罢官》，Smith，Chester Leo(1922—)编译.

2. The heresy of Wu Han：his play "Hai Jui's dismissal" and its role in China's cultural revolution/Clive M Ansley；Han Wu. [Toronto] University of Toronto Press，1971. viii，125 pages；24cm. ISBN：0802016650，0802016652

   Contents：pt. 1. "Hai Jui's dismissal" by Wu Han. Translated by Clive Ansley. —pt. 2. The role of "Hai Jui's dismissal" in China's cultural revolution，by? Clive Ansley.

   Ansley，Clive M. (Clive Malcolm，1941—)著. 包括对吴晗(1909—1969)的《海瑞罢官》(剧本)的英译.

   (1)[Toronto]；[Buffalo]：University of Toronto Press，1981. viii，125 pages. ISBN：0802016650

   (2)Ann Arbor Mich.；London：University Microfilms International，1986. VIII，125 p.：ill.；25cm. ISBN：0802016650，0802016652

3. Hai Jui dismissed from office/by Wu Han；translated by C. C. Huang；introductory essay by D. W. Y. Kwok. Honolulu：University Press of Hawaii，1972. viii]，147 p. ISBN：0824802152，0824802158. (Asian studies at Hawaii；7)

   《海瑞罢官》，Huang，C. C. 译.

曹禺(1910—1996)

1. The sunrise；a play in four acts，by Tsao Yu [pseud.] Done into English by H. Yonge；with an introduction on modern Chinese drama. China，Commercial Press，1940. 189 p.；18cm.

   《日出：四幕剧》

2. Sunrise：a play in four acts/[translated by A. C. Barnes]. Peking：Foreign Languages Press，1960. 189 pages：illustrations；22cm.

   《日出》，巴恩斯译.

   (1)Peking：Foreign Languages Press，1978. ii，168 p.，[4] leaves of plates：ill.；22cm.

   (2)Beijing：Foreign languages Press，2001. 467 p. [1] p. de pl.：portr.；21cm. ISBN：7119028960，7119028965

   (3) Beijing：Foreign Languages Press，2015. 232 p.；18cm. ISBN：7119092942，7119092944. (Panda books)

3. Bright skies [by] Tsao Yu. [Translated by Chang Peichi]. Peking：Foreign Languages Press，1960. 124 p. illus.，port.；22cm.

   《明朗的天》，张培基译.

4. Peking man/Cao Yu；translated by Leslie Nai-Kwai Lo，with Don Cohn and Michelle Vosper. New York：Columbia University Press，1986. viii，181 p.：ill.；22cm. ISBN：0231056567. (UNESCO collection of representative works. Chinese series)

   《北京人》，Lo，Leslie Nai-Kwai，Cohn，Don 译.

5. The consort of peace/Cao Yu；translated by Monica Lai. Hong Kong：Kelly & Walsh，c1980. xiv，154 p.：col. ill.；22cm.

   《王昭君》，Lai，Monica 译.

6. Thunderstorm/translated by Wang Tso-liang and A. C. Barnes. Peking：Foreign Languages Press，1958. 182 pages，[8] leaves of plates：illustrations；22cm.

   《雷雨》，王佐良，巴恩斯译.

   (1)2nd ed. Peking：Foreign Languages Press，1964. 164 pages plates，portrait 22cm.

   (2)3rd ed. Peking：Foreign Languages Press，1978. 151 pages：illustrations；22cm.

   (3)Beijing：Foreign Languages Press，2000. 333 s.；13cm. ISBN：7119025244，7119025247

   (4)Beijing：Foreign Languages Press，2001. 413 s.；22cm. ISBN：7119027751，7119027753. (Echo of Classics)

   (5)Beijing：Foreign Languages Press，2014. [2]，175，[1] s.；18cm. ISBN：7119058832，7119058835. (Panda Books)

7. The wilderness = Yuan ye/Ts'ao Yü；translated by Christopher C. Rand and Joseph S. M. Lau. Hong Kong：Hong Kong University Press；Bloomington：Indiana University Press，c1980. liii，201 p.；22cm.. ISBN：0253172977，0253172976，9622090184，9622090187，9622090176，9622090170. (Chinese literature in translation)

   《原野》，Rand，Christopher C.，刘绍铭(Lau，Joseph S. M.，1934—)(美国华裔学者)合译.

8. The family (Han Ying dui zhao)/Ba Jin yuan zhu；Cao Yu gai bian；Ying Ruocheng yi. Beijing：Zhongguo dui wai fang yi chu ban gong si，1999. 11，327 p.；21cm. ISBN：750010670X，7500106708.(英若诚. 英若诚名剧译丛；7)

   《家》，曹禺改编；英若诚(1929—2003)译. 英汉对照.

金山(1911—1982)

1. Red storm：a play in three acts/Chin Shan. Peking：Foreign Languages Press，1965. 115 pages；22cm.

   《红色风暴》，班以安译.

陈其通(1916—2001)

1. The long march. Peking：Foreign Languages Press，1956. 168，[11] p. plates，port.，fold. map.；22cm.

   Notes："Songs from 'The long march'" (unacc. melodies) by Shih Lo-meng：p. [1]-[9] 2nd group.

   《万水千山》. 现代话剧.

任德耀(1918—1998)

1. Magic aster：a play in three acts for children. Peking：Foreign Languages Press，1963. 96 p.：ill.

   《马兰花》，威廉·怀特译.

吴祖光（1917—2003）

1. The three beatings of Tao Sanchun，or，A shrew untamed：a Beijing opera in six acts/by Wu Zuguang；translated by Geremie Barmé；revised by Zhu Binsun. Shanghai：Shanghai Foreign Language Education Press，1989. ii，120 pages：illustrations；19cm. ISBN：7810091980，7810091985

《三打陶三春》. 英汉对照. 京剧.

胡可（1921—）

1. Steeled in battles.［Translated by Tang Sheng. Peking：Foreign Languages Press，1955. 130 p. illus. ；18cm.

《在战斗里成长》

2. Locust tree village：a play in five acts/by Hu Ko. Peking：Foreign Languages Press，1961. 126 p. ：ill. ；22cm.

《槐树庄》. 话剧.

段承滨（1924—）

1. Taming the dragon and the tiger：a play in six scenes/Duan Zhengbin and Du Shizun；translated by A. C. Barnes. Peking：Foreign Languages Press，1961. 106 pages，3 leaves of plates；21cm.

《降龙伏虎》，巴恩斯译. 话剧.

超克图纳仁（1925—2018）

1. Golden Eagle/［by］Tsogtnarin. Peking：Foreign Languages Press，1961. 100 pages：illustrations；22cm.

《金鹰》. 话剧.

李恍（1931—）

1. War drums on the equator：a play of seven scenes/by Li Huang［and others］. Peking：Foreign Languages Press，1966. 83 pages：illustrations；（some color）；19cm.
Notes：Translation of Chi dao zhan gu；translated by Gladys Yang.

《赤道战鼓：七场话剧》，戴乃迭（Yang，Gladys，1919—1999）译.

(1)Peking：Foreign Languages Press，1996. 83 p. ：ill.

徐棻（1933—）

1. 徐棻戏剧选 汉英对照/徐棻著. 四川人民出版社，2018. 2 册(508 页)；26cm. ISBN：7220107382

白峰溪（1934—）

1. The women trilogy/Bai Fengxi. transl. by Guan Yuehua. Beijing：Chinese Literature Press，1991. 287 p. ISBN：0835120783，0835120784，7507100707，7507100709. (Panda Books)

《女性三部曲》. 收录作者的《明月初照人》《风雨故人来》《不知秋思在谁家》3 部话剧.

锦云（1938—）

1. Uncle Doggie's nirvana/Jinyun zhu；Ying Ruocheng yi. Beijing：Zhongguo dui wai fang yi chu ban gong si，1999. 11，211 p. ；21cm. ISBN：7500106718，7500106715. (英若诚名剧译丛；8)

《狗儿爷涅槃》，英若诚译. 英汉对照. 中国对外翻译出版公司出版.

李龙云（1948—2012）

1. Small well lane：a contemporary Chinese play and oral history＝［Xiao jing hu tong］/by Li Longyun；translated and edited by Hong Jiang and Timothy Cheek. Ann Arbor：University of Michigan Press，c2002. 138 p. ：ill. ；24cm. ISBN：0472097954，0472067958

《小井胡同》，Jiang，Hong（1954—）和 Cheek，Timothy 合译. 现代话剧.

谭盾（1957—）

1. Peony pavilion/Tan Dun；directed by Peter Sellars；libretto by Tang Xianzu；translated by Cyril Birch. New York：G. Schirmer，c1998. 1 score (iii，46 p.)；44cm.

《牡丹亭》（歌剧），谭盾（1957—）创作；Sellars，Peter 指挥；白之（Birch，Cyril，1925—）（美国汉学家）译.

其他

1. Struggle against counter-struggle：a one-act play. Peking，China，Cultural Press，1950. 74 pages；18cm.

内容拟似"镇压反革命运动". 戏剧.

剧名

（对于一些创造者不详或没有标示的作品按剧名的拼音顺序编排）

霸王别姬

1. 霸王别姬/孙萍主编. 北京：中国人民大学出版社；外语教学与研究出版社，2012. 249 页，［2］页：图版，彩图；29cm. ISBN：7300163598. (中国京剧百部经典外译系列. 第一辑)

英文题名：Farewell my lady.

班昭

1. 昆曲—班昭/李慧明［编译］. 北京：外语教学与研究出版社，2015. 311 页；23cm. ISBN：7513556927. (中国戏曲海外传播工程丛书)

英文题名：Ban Zhao-a Kunqu opera.

包公

1. Judge Bao and the rule of law：eight ballad-stories from the period 1250—1450/Wilt L. Idema. Singapore：World Scientific，2010. xxxv，417 p. ：ill. ；24cm. ISBN：9814277013，9814277010，9814304450，981430445X
Notes："The following translations are，... based on the critical edition of the ballad-stories by Zhu Yixuan in his Ming Chenghua shuochang cihua congkan of 1997"—P. xxxv.

《包公和法治：从 1250 年到 1450 年的八个说唱故事》，伊维德（Idema，W. L.〈Wilt L.〉，1944—）（荷兰汉学家）译. 该书翻译了关于包公的八种文本.

白毛女

1. The white-haired girl；an opera in five acts，by Ho Ching-chih and Ting Yi. Translated by Yang Hsien-yi and Gladys Yang. Peking：Foreign Languages Press，1954. 97，［8］p. illus. ；22cm.
Notes：Play，with incidental music by Ma K'o and others. "Songs from 'The white-haired girl'" (romanized Chinese

words；English words printed as text)：[8] p. at end.

《白毛女：五幕剧》，贺敬之(1924—)，丁毅(1921—)执笔；杨宪益(1915—2009)，戴乃迭(Yang, Gladys, 1919—1999)合译.

白蛇传

1. The White Snake and her son：a translation of The Precious Scroll of Thunder Peak with related texts/edited and translated，with an introduction，by Wilt L. Idema. Indianapolis：Hackett Pub. Co., c2009. xxiv, 171 p.；ill.；22cm. ISBN：0872209954，0872209954，0872209961, 0872209962

《白蛇和她的儿子：雷峰宝卷》，伊维德(Idema, W. L. 〈Wilt L.〉, 1944—)(荷兰汉学家)译.

2. 京剧—白蛇传/杨孝明[编译].北京：外语教学与研究出版社，2013. 255 页；23cm. ISBN：7513539425.(中国戏曲海外传播工程丛书)

英文题名：The legend of a white snake-a Beijing opera.

变脸

1. 川剧—变脸/杨孝明编译.北京：外语教学与研究出版社，2015. 279 页；23cm. ISBN：7513556910，7513556911.(中国戏曲海外传播工程丛书)

英文题名：Face changing-a Sichuan opera.

曹操与杨修

1. Cao Cao and Yang Xiu：a Beijing opera based on the classical novel Romance of Three Kingdoms/translation，introduction and annotations by Toming Jun Liu. Hefei：Anhui Literature & Art Publishing House, 2011. 2, 212 pages：illustrations；25cm. ISBN：7539637952，7539637951.(China classics international)

《曹操与杨修》，陈亚先原著；刘军编译.安徽文艺出版社(经典中国国际出版工程 国剧英译系列).本书系"国剧英译"系列之一种，根据湖南作家陈亚先的权威版本为底本编译.

赤桑镇

1. 赤桑镇 /孙萍主编.北京：国家图书馆出版社，2016. 37, 75 页，[4] 页：图版，彩图，乐谱；29cm. ISBN：7501358731.(中国京剧百部经典外译系列.第三辑)

英文题名：Bao Zheng's persuasion in Chisang Town

打龙袍

1. 打龙袍 /孙萍主编.北京：国家图书馆出版社，2016. 37, 91 页，[4] 页：图版，彩图，乐谱；29cm. ISBN：7501358700.(中国京剧百部经典外译系列.第四辑)

英文题名：Beating the dragon robe.

大闹天宫

1. Havoc in heaven：a Kunqu opera based on the classical novel Journey to the West/translation，introduction and annotations by He Qixin. Hefei：Anhui Literature & Art Publishing House, 2011. 1, 149 pages：illustrations；25cm. ISBN：7539637969，753963796X.(China classics international)

《大闹天宫》，何其莘译著.安徽文艺出版社(经典中国国

际出版工程 国剧英译系列)

打渔杀家

1. 打渔杀家/孙萍主编.北京：中国人民大学出版社；外语教学与研究出版社，2012. 267 页，[2] 页：图版，彩图；29cm. ISBN：7300163550.(中国京剧百部经典外译系列.第一辑)

英文题名：The fisherman's revenge.

盗御马

1. 盗御马/孙萍主编.北京：中国人民大学出版社；外语教学与研究出版社，2012. 211 页：彩图，肖像，乐谱；29cm. ISBN：7300164120.(中国京剧百部经典外译系列.第一辑)

英文题名：Stealing the imperial horse.

定军山

1. 定军山 /孙萍主编.北京：国家图书馆出版社，2016. 37, 115 页，[4] 页：图版，图 (部分彩图)，乐谱；29cm. ISBN：7501358717.(中国京剧百部经典外译系列. 第四辑)

英文题名：A battle at Dingjun mountain.

董永与织女

1. Filial piety and its divine rewards：the legend of Dong Yong and Weaving Maiden with related texts/edited and translated，with an introduction，by Wilt L. Idema. Indianapolis：Hackett Pub. Co., c2009. xxiv, 108 p.；22cm. ISBN：1603841351，1603841350，1603841368，1603841369

《董永与织女》，伊维德(Idema, W. L. 〈Wilt L.〉, 1944—)(荷兰汉学家)编译.

杜鹃山

1. Azalea Mountain：a modern revolutionary Peking opera：September 1973 script of the Peking Opera Troupe of Peking/written by Wang Shu-yuan and others. Peking：Foreign Languages Press, 1976. 63 p.；24cm.

《杜鹃山》，王树元等编剧.

杜十娘

1. 京剧—杜十娘/高雄亚[编译].北京：外语教学与研究出版社，2014. 254 页；23cm. ISBN：7513539371.(中国戏曲海外传播工程丛书)

英文题名：Du Shiniang—a Beijing opera.

凤还巢

1. Snow elegant：a Chinese classical play/translated and adapted by Elizabeth Te-chen Wang, from the opera "Feng huan ch'ao" by Chi Yu-shan. Taipei：China Culture Pub. Foundation, 1955. 136 pages：illustrations；22cm. (Mei Ya heritage series)

《凤还巢》，王德箴(Wang, Dezhen, 1911—)编译.是对齐如山(1877—1962)先生的原名剧本的改编.

(1)Taipei, China Culture Pub. Foundation, 1965. 136 pages

(2)2nd ed. Taipei: Mei Ya Publications, 1971. 98 pages：illustrations. (Mei Ya heritage series)

(3)Taipei：Mei Ya Pub., 1973. xix, 124 p.；ill. (pt

col. ）；21cm.

(4)3rd ed. Taipei：Mei Ya Publications，1979. xxi，98 pages：illustrations（some color）；23cm.（Mei Ya heritage series）

2. Homecoming of a phoenix/translation and verse adaptation by Sophia Shangkuan Min. ［Taipei］：Yen Huan Wu，c1976. 60 p.；27cm.

Notes："This adaptation is based on… the revised version performed by the famous actor Mei Lan-fang…"

《凤还巢》，梅兰芳（1894—1961）编剧；魏莉莎（Min，Sophia Shangkuan）译.

(1)新世界出版社，1986.140 页

夫妻之间

1. Between husband and wife：a play in one act/written collectively by the Peking People's Art Theatre；trans. by Sidney Shapiro. ［Peking：The Theatre，1953］. 22 p.；il.；19cm.

Notes："Supplement to China Reconstructs, no. 6, 1953."

《夫妻之间》，北京人民艺术剧院集体创作；沙博理（Shapiro，Sidney 1915—2014）译.

海港

1. On the docks：a modern revolutionary Peking opera/rev. by the On the Docks Group of the Peking Opera Troupe of Shanghai. January 1972 script. Peking：Foreign Languages Press，1973. 41 p.，［8］leaves (1 fold.) of plates：col. ill.；24cm.

《海港》（剧本），上海京剧团《海港》剧组集体改编.

红灯记

1. The red lantern；a Peking opera. Peking：Foreign Languages Press，1966. 55 p.；ill.；19cm.

《红灯记》（剧本），中国京剧院文学组编剧.

2. The red lantern：model Peking opera on contemporary revolutionary theme. Colombo：Afro-Asian Writers' Bureau，c1967. 59 p.；19cm.

《红灯记》（剧本）

3. The red lantern；a modern revolutionary Peking opera. Peking：Foreign Languages Press，1972. 98 p. illus. (part col.)；24cm.

《红灯记》（剧本），中国京剧团.

4. The red lantern；the story of the modern Peking opera. Peking，Foreign Languages Press，1972. 43 p. illus.；19cm.

Notes：An English adaptation of the libretto of Hong deng ji as performed by Zhongguo jing ju tuan.

《红灯记》（剧本），根据中国京剧团的剧本改编并译成英语.

5. The red lantern：the story of the modern Peking opera. Peking：Foreign Languages Press，1972. 43 p.；ill.

《现代京剧〈红灯记〉的故事》

红色娘子军

1. Red detachment of women；a modern revolutionary ballet/Rev. collectively by the China Ballet Troupe（May 1970 script）. Peking：Foreign Languages Press，1972. 169 pages：illustrations（some color）；24cm.

《红色娘子军》，中国舞剧团集体改编.

2. Red detachment of women：the story of the modern ballet. Peking：Foreign Languages Press，1973. ［2］，39，［3］s.：il.；19cm.

《现代芭蕾舞〈红色娘子军〉的故事》

花关索词话

1. The story of Hua Guan Suo/translated with an introduction by Gail Oman King. Tempe，Ariz.：Center for Asian Studies，Arizona State University，1989. vii，279 p.：ill.；23cm. ISBN：0939252201.（Arizona State University Center for Asian studies monograph series；no. 23）

《花关索词话》，盖尔·金（King，Gail Oman）译.

花木兰

1. Mulan：five versions of a classic Chinese legend with related texts/edited and translated，with an introduction，by Shiamin Kwa and Wilt L. Idema. Indianapolis，IN：Hackett Pub. Co. ，c2010. xxxii，136 p.：ill.；23cm. ISBN：1603841962，1603841979

《木兰从军》，Kwa，Shiamin，伊维德（Idema，W. L.〈Wilt L.〉，1944—）（荷兰汉学家）编译.

击鼓骂曹

1. 击鼓骂曹 /孙萍主编.北京：国家图书馆出版社，2016.37，127 页，［2］页：图版，彩图，乐谱；29cm. ISBN：7501358724.（中国京剧百部经典外译系列. 第四辑）

英文题名：Beating the drum and cursing prime minister Cao.

将相和

1. 将相和/孙萍主编.北京：国家图书馆出版社，2016. 37，105 页，［4］页：图版，图（部分彩图），乐谱；29cm. ISBN：7501358656.（中国京剧百部经典外译系列. 第四辑）

英文题名：Reconciliation between minister and general.

狸猫换太子

1. The fox cat substituted for the crown prince：a Peking opera set in the Song Dynasty/translated and adapted by Donald K. Chang，John D. Mitchell. Midland，Mich.：Northwood Institute Press，c1985. xxiv，429 p.：ill.；23cm. ISBN：0873590414

《狸猫换太子》（剧本选译），Chang，Donald K. 和 Mitchell，John Dietrich（1917—）编译.英汉对照.

廉吏于成龙

1. 京剧——廉吏于成龙/石逸莉［编译］.北京：外语教学与研究出版社，2013. 253 页；23cm. ISBN：7513539401.（中国戏曲海外传播工程丛书）

英文题名：Honorable official Yu Chenglong-a Beijing opera.

梁山伯与祝英台

1. 梁山伯与祝英台＝Liang Shanbo and Zhu Yingtai/赵清阁编著. 北京：新世界出版社,1999. 199 页：插图；20cm. ISBN：780005411X.（中国古代爱情故事 ＝ Classical Chinese love stories）
   中英文对照读物.

2. The butterfly lovers：the legend of Liang Shanbo and Zhu Yingtai；four versions, with related texts/edited and translated；with an introduced by Wilt L. Idema. Indianapolis, IN：Hackett Pub. Co., 2010. xxxvi, 220 p.；22cm. ISBN：1603841948, 1603841946, 1603841955, 1603841954
   《梁山伯与祝英台：梁祝传说的四种版本》，伊维德（Idema, W. L.〈Wilt L.〉,1944—）（荷兰汉学家）编译.

3. 越剧——梁山伯与祝英台/石逸莉［编译］. 北京：外语教学与研究出版社,2014. 247 页；23cm. ISBN：7513539388.（中国戏曲海外传播工程丛书）
   英文题名：The legend of Liang Shanbo and Zhu Yintai-a Yueju opera.

4. Love under the willows；a Szechuan opera. Liang Shan-po and Chu Ying-tai.［Translated by Yang Hsien-hi and Gladys Yang.］Peking：Foreign Languages Press, 1956. 85 p. illus. 20cm.
   《柳荫记》（又名《梁山伯与祝英台》），杨宪益（1915—2009），戴乃迭（Yang Gladys,1919—1999）合译.

刘三姐

1. Third sister Liu：an opera in eight scenes/［translated by Yang Xianyi and Gladys Yang］. Peking：Foreign Languages Press, 1962. 66［12］pages：illustrations；19cm.
   《刘三姐》，杨宪益（1915—2009），戴乃迭（Yang. Gladys, 1919—1999）合译.

龙江颂

1. Song of the Dragon River；a modern revolutionary Peking opera. Revised by the "Song of the Dragon River" Group of Shanghai.（January 1972 script）. Peking：Foreign Languages Press, 1972. 43 p. col. plates.；23cm.
   《龙江颂》（剧本），上海市《龙江颂》剧组集体改编.

梅龙镇

1. Traditional Asian plays/edited and with an introd. by James R. Brandon. New York：Hill & Wang, 1972. vi, 308 pages；21cm. ISBN：0809094150, 0809094158, 0809007495, 0809007493.（A Mermaid dramabook）
   Contents：Indian Sanskrit drama：The toy cart—Thai lakon jatri：Manohra—Japanese Noh：Ikkaku sennin—Japanese Kabuki：The subscription list；The Zen substitute—Chinese opera：The price of wine.
   《梅龙镇》，Brandon, James R. 编. Josephine Huang Hung 改编和英译. 越剧.

孟姜女哭长城

1. Meng Jiangnü brings down the Great Wall：ten versions of a Chinese legend/translation and introduction by Wilt L. Idema；with an essay by Haiyan Lee. Seattle：University of Washington Press, c2008. ix, 295 p.；23cm. ISBN：0295987839, 0295987835, 0295987847, 0295987842
   《孟姜女哭长城：中国传说的十个版本》，伊维德（Idema, W. L.〈Wilt L.〉,1944—）（荷兰汉学家）译. 该书翻译了关于孟姜女传说的宝卷.

穆桂英挂帅

1. 京剧：穆桂英挂帅/黄少荣编译. 北京：外语教学与研究出版社,2015. 239 页；23cm. ISBN：7513556880.（中国戏曲海外传播工程丛书）
   英文题名：Mu Guiying takes command-a Beijing opera.

霓虹灯下的哨兵

1. On guard beneath the neon lights：a play in nine scenes/Shen Ximeng, Mo Yan and Lu Xingzhen. Peking：Foreign Languages Press, 1966. 116 pages：illustrations；19cm.
   《霓虹灯下的哨兵：九场话剧》，沈西蒙等. 话剧.

潘金莲

1. 昆曲——潘金莲/杨孝明［编译］. 北京：外语教学与研究出版社,2013. 286 页；23cm. ISBN：7513539395.（中国戏曲海外传播工程丛书）
   英文题名：Pan Jinlin-a Kunqu opera

平原作战

1. Fighting on the plain：a modern revolutionary Peking opera/written by Chang Yung-mei and other members of the China Peking Opera Troupe. July 1973 script. Peking：Foreign Languages Press, 1976. 44 p.,［8］leaves of plates (1 fold.)：col. ill.；24cm.
   《平原作战》（剧本），中国京剧团集体创作；张永枚执笔.

奇袭白虎团

1. Raid on the White Tiger Regiment；model Peking opera on contemporary revolutionary theme. Colombo, Afro-Asian Writers' Bureau, 1967. 69 pages：illustrations；19cm.
   《奇袭白虎团》，亚非作家常设局（Permanent Bureau of Afro-Asian Writers）.

庆顶珠

1. The fisherman's revenge, Peking opera. Peking：Foreign Languages Press, 1956. 53 p. illus.；20cm.
   《庆顶珠》，杨宪益（1915—2009），戴乃迭（Yang, Gladys, 1919—1999）合译.

秦香莲

1. The forsaken wife：a Pingju opera/［translated by Yang Xianyi and Gladys Yang］. Peking：Foreign Languages Press；San Francisco, CA.：Distributors：China Books & Periodicals, 1958. 70 pages：illustrations；19cm.
   《秦香莲》，杨宪益（1915—2009），戴乃迭（Yang, Gladys, 1919—1999）合译. 中国评剧团院创作.
   (1)3rd ed. Adapted by Sheng Chiang. Peking：Foreign Languages Press, 1962. 86 p.：ill.

2. 京剧-秦香莲/陈融[编译].北京:外语教学与研究出版社,2013.224 页;23cm. ISBN:7513536363.(中国戏曲海外传播工程丛书)

英文题名:Qin Xianglian-a Beijing opera.

秋江

1. 秋江/孙萍主编.北京:中国人民大学出版社;外语教学与研究出版社,2012.221 页,[2] 页:图版,彩图;29cm. ISBN:7300163536.(中国京剧百部经典外译系列.第一辑)

英文题名:Autumn river.

三堂会审

1. 三堂会审/孙萍主编.北京:国家图书馆出版社,2016.37,135 页,[2] 页:图版,图(部分彩图),乐谱;29cm. ISBN:7501358649.(中国京剧百部经典外译系列.第四辑)

英文题名:Three judges try the case.英汉对照.

沙家浜

1. Shachiapang; model Peking opera on contemporary revolutionary theme. Colombo, Afro-Asian Writers' Bureau, 1967. 69 p. illus. ; 19cm.

《沙家浜》

2. Shachiapang; a modern revolutionary Peking opera. Peking: Foreign Languages Press, 1972. 101 p. illus. ; 24cm.

《沙家浜》,北京京剧团.

3. Shachiapang; the story of the modern Peking opera. Beijing: Foreign Languages Press, 1972. 45 p. : illustrations; 19cm.

《现代京剧〈沙家浜〉的故事》

拾玉镯

1. 拾玉镯/孙萍主编.北京:中国人民大学出版社;外语教学与研究出版社,2012.37,217 页,[2] 页:图版,彩图;29cm. ISBN:7300163574.(中国京剧百部经典外译系列.第一辑)

英文题名:Picking up the bracelet.

搜书院

1. The runaway maid; a Cantonese opera. Peking: Foreign Languages Press, 1958. 64 p. group ports. ; 19cm.

《搜书院》,广东粤剧团整理.杨宪益(1915—2009),戴乃迭(Yang, Gladys,1919—1999)合译.

四进士

1. Papa Sung: a light-hearted drama in three acts/adapted from the Peking opera The four accomplished scholars by H. B. Wong. Hong Kong: Kelly & Walsh, 1976. xv, 121 p., [3] leaves of plates: ill. ; 19cm.

《四进士》,Wong, H. B.改编.

四郎探母

1. 四郎探母/孙萍主编.北京:国家图书馆出版社,2016.37,259 页,[6] 页:图版,彩图,乐谱;29cm. ISBN:7501358847.(中国京剧百部经典外译系列.第四辑)

英文题名:Silang visits his mother.

谭记儿

1. The riverside pavilion/adapted by Wu Po-chi from the original play by Kuan Han-ching; staged by the Szechuan Opera Company of Chengtu. Peking: Foreign Languages Press, 1958. 108 p. : chiefly ill. ; 13×18cm.

《谭记儿》,改编自关汉卿的《望江亭》,成都川剧院吴伯祺改编.

天仙配

1. Marriage to fairy: a Huangmei drama based on the classical script Marriage to fairy/translation, introduction and annotations by Zhao Yifan. Hefei: Anhui literature & Art Publishing House, 2011. 1, 152 pages: illustrations; 25cm. ISBN:7539637976, 7539637978. (China classics international)

《天仙配》,赵一凡译注.安徽文艺出版社(经典中国国际出版工程 国剧英译系列).本书系"国剧英译"系列的一种.黄梅戏.

同志,你走错了路

1. Comrade, you've taken the wrong path! A four-act play, by Yao Chung-ming, Chen Po-erh, and associates. [Translated by A. M. Condron]. Peking: Foreign Languages Press, 1962. 117 p. illus. ; 22cm.

《同志,你走错了路》,姚仲明,陈波儿执笔.

王宝钏

1. Lady Precious Stream: an old Chinese play done into English according to its traditional style. London, Methuen & Co., Ltd. [1934]. xix, 168, [2] p. incl. plates. col. mounted front., col. mounted plates. ; 20cm.

《王宝钏》,熊式一(Hsiung, S. I.〈Shih I〉,1902—1991)译.

(1)Lady Precious Stream; an old Chinese play done into English according to its traditional style by S. I. Hsiung; with a preface by Lascelles Abercrombie. New York: Liveright Publishing Corp.; London, Methuen & Co. Ltd., 1935. xx, 168, [1] p. incl. front., plates. ; 20cm.

(2)Lady Precious Stream; an old Chinese play done into English according to its traditional style, in four acts. New York: Los Angeles, Calif., S. French; London, S. French, Ltd.; [etc., etc.] c1937. 126 p. diagr. ; 19cm.

(3) London, Hutchinson, 1950. 176 p. illus. (part col.); 22cm.

(4)London, Methuen, 1968. viii, 120 p. illus. ; 19cm. ISBN: 0416109802

2. 王宝钏:汉英对照/熊式一著.北京:商务印书馆,2006.303 页;20cm. ISBN:7100046807, 7100046800

英文题名:Lady precious stream.本书初版于 1934 年,此剧改编自中国传统通俗小剧《红鬃烈马》.

王昭君

1. Beauty: a Chinese drama/translated from the original by J. Macgowan. London: E. L. Morice, 1911. 81 pages; 18cm.

《王昭君》, Macgowan, J. 译.

(1)[Place of publication not identified]: Book On Demand Ltd, 2013. ISBN: 5518611803; 5518611801

文成公主

1. 文成公主: 四幕大型歌剧/彭长虹, 吴霜编著. 北京: 解放军出版社, 2006. 58, 76 页: 图; 24cm. ISBN: 7506550873

英文题名: Princess Wencheng: a four-act opera. 英汉对照.

2. 京藏剧——文成公主/杨孝明[编译]. 北京: 外语教学与研究出版社, 2014. 263 页; 23cm. ISBN: 7513539364. (中国戏曲海外传播工程丛书)

英文题名: Princess Wencheng-a combined drama of Beijing opera and Tibetan opera.

文昭关

1. 文昭关/孙萍主编. 北京: 国家图书馆出版社, 2016. 37, 101 页, [4] 页: 图版, 图(部分彩图), 乐谱; 29cm. ISBN: 7501358816. (中国京剧百部经典外译系列. 第三辑)

英文题名: Wu Zixu's predicament at Wenzhao Pass.

武家坡

1. 武家坡/孙萍主编. 北京: 国家图书馆出版社, 2016. 37, 155 页, [4] 页: 图版, 彩图, 乐谱; 29cm. ISBN: 7501358694. (中国京剧百部经典外译系列. 第三辑)

英文题名: Reunion at Wujia slope.

香山宝卷

1. Personal salvation and filial piety: two precious scroll narratives of Guanyin and her acolytes/translated and with an introduction by Wilt L. Idema. Honolulu: University of Hawaii Press, 2008. ix, 227 p.; 24cm. ISBN: 0824832155, 0824832159. (Classics in East Asian Buddhism)

《自我救赎和孝行: 观音和她的侍从》, 伊维德(Idema, W. L. 〈Wilt L.〉, 1944—)(荷兰汉学家)译. 该书翻译了宋代关于妙善公主的《香山宝卷》.

(1)New Delhi, India: Munshiram Manoharlal Publishers, 2009. 227 pages; 25cm. ISBN: 8121512138, 8121512131

杨家将

1. The Generals of the Yang Family: four early plays/Wilt L. Idema, Harvard University USA, Stephen H West, Arizona State University, USA. New Jersey: World Century/World Scientific, [2013]. xxxviii, 228 pages: illustrations; 24cm. ISBN: 9814508681, 9814508683, 9814520560, 981452056X

《〈杨家将〉: 4 个早期剧本》, 伊维德(Idema, W. L. 〈Wilt L.〉, 1944—)(荷兰汉学家), 奚如谷(West, Stephen H., 1944—)(美国汉学家)合译.

宰相刘罗锅

1. 京剧——宰相刘罗锅/石逸莉编译. 北京: 外语教学与研

究出版社, 2015. 339 页; 23cm. ISBN: 7513556897. (中国戏曲海外传播工程丛书)

英文题名: Prime Minister Liu Luoguo.

贞观盛事

1. 京剧——贞观盛事/黄少荣[编译]. 北京: 外语教学与研究出版社, 2015. 267 页; 23cm. ISBN: 7513556934. (中国戏曲海外传播工程丛书)

英文题名: Grand occasion in the golden years of Zhenguan-a Beijing opera.

智取威虎山

1. Taking the bandits' stronghold: model Peking opera on contemporary revolutionary theme/Afro-Asian Writers' Bureau. Colombo: Afro-Asian Writers' Bureau, 1967. 68 pages: illustrations

《智取威虎山》, 亚非作家常设局(Afro-Asian Writers' Bureau)出版.

2. Taking the bandits' stronghold: a modern Peking opera on a contemporary revolutionary theme/adapted by the Peking Opera Theatre of Shanghai. Peking: Foreign Languages Press, 1968. 13, 62 pages, [4] leaves of plates: color illustrations; 19cm.

《智取威虎山》, 上海京剧团集体改编.

3. Taking Tiger Mountain by strategy: a modern revolutionary Peking opera. Rev. collectively by the "Taking Tiger by Strategy" Group of the Peking Opera Troupe of Shanghai (July 1970 script). Peking: Foreign Languages Press, 1971. 113 p. col. illus.; 24cm.

《智取威虎山》, 上海京剧团《智取威虎山》剧组集体改编.

4. Taking Tiger Mountain by strategy: the story of the modern Peking opera. Peking: Foreign Languages Press, 1972. 38 pages: illustrations; 19cm.

《现代京剧〈智取威虎山〉的故事》

钟馗嫁妹

1. 河北梆子——钟馗嫁妹/姜晓阳[编译]. 北京: 外语教学与研究出版社, 2014. 187 页; 23cm. ISBN: 7513539418. (中国戏曲海外传播工程丛书)

英文题名: Zhong Kui-a Hebei Bangzi opera.

I46 电影文学剧本

闪闪的红星

1. Sparkling red star (film scenario): an adaptation by the Chinese People's Liberation Army August First Film Studio from the novel of the same title by Li Hsin-tien/scenario by Wang Yüan-chien and Lu Chu-kuo. Peking: Foreign Languages Press, 1976. 75 pages, [8] leaves of plates: color illustrations; 19cm.

《闪闪的红星》, 中国人民解放军八一电影制片厂根据李心田同名小说机体改编; 王愿坚、陆柱国执笔. 电影文学剧本.

2. Pine Ridge: film story/adapted from the play of the same

title by the Changchun Film Studio; a collective work by the Drama Troupe of Chengteh Prefecture, Hopei Province. Peking: Foreign Languages Press, 1978. 85 pages, [4] leaves of plates: illustrations; 19cm.

《青松岭》,长影改编,承德话剧团集体创作.

3. Early spring in February: a study guide/by Laifong Leung with the assistance of Huiling Mao. Burnaby, B. C., Canada: W. & Y. Cultural Products Co., 2004. xiii, 349 pages; 28cm. ISBN: 1896672108, 1896672106

《早春二月:电影剧本导读课本》,Leung, Laifong (1948—),Mao, Huiling 著.收录谢铁骊的《早春二月》电影剧本,改剧本改变自柔石(1901—1931)的小说《二月》.英汉对照.

I47 曲艺

1. 评弹精华:弹词开篇选 = Gems of Suzhou pingtan: selections of tanci arias/汪榕培,尤志明,杜争鸣主编译.苏州市:苏州大学出版社,2004. [18],141 pages, [10] pages of plates: color illustrations, music, portraits (some color); 20cm. ISBN:7810902962, 7810902960

英汉对照.收录部分有代表性的经典名段和当今流行的开篇选.

2. The lady of the long wall: a ku shih or drum song of China/translated from the Chinese by Genevieve Wimsatt and Geoffrey Zhen (Zhen Sunhan). New York: Columbia University Press, 1934. 84 p.

《孟姜女》,Wimsatt, Genevieve 和 Chen, Sun-han 合译.鼓词.

(1) The lady of the long wall: a ku shih or drum song of China/translated from the Chinese by Genevieve Wimsatt and Geoffrey Zhen (Zhen Sunhan). Ann Arbor, Mich.: University Microfilms International, 1979. 84 pages on double leaves: illustrations; 23cm.

3. Comic sketches/translated by Simon Johnstone. Beijing: Chinese Literature Press, 1990. 136 pages; 18cm. ISBN: 0835120880, 0835120883, 7507100774, 7507100778. (Panda books)

《对口相声选》.中国文学出版社.

I5 小说

I51 古代及跨时代小说集

1. Chinese novels, translated from the originals; to which are added proverbs and moral maxims, collected from their classical books and other sources. The whole prefaced by observations on the language and literature of China/By John Francis Davis, F. R. S. London, J. Murray, 1822. 3 preliminary leaves, 250 pages; 24cm.

Contents: Observations on the language and literature of China. —The shadow in the water. —The twin sisters. —The three dedicated chambers. —Chinese proverbs, etc.

中国小说. Davis, John Francis(1795—1890)译.

(1) New ed. London: J. Murray, 1843. 250 pages; 24cm.

(2) A facsim. reproduction/with an introd. by Ben Harris McClary. Delmar, N. Y.: Scholars' Facsimiles & Reprints, 1976. xi, 250, [4] pages; 21cm. ISBN: 082011278X, 0820112787

(3) [Place of publication not identified]: University of Michigan Library, 2010. 3 preliminary leaves, 250 pages; 21cm.

2. Chinese stories/By Robert K. Douglas. Edinburgh, London, W. Blackwood, 1893. xxxvii, 348 pages: illustrations; 21cm.

Contents: A matrimonial fraud—Within his danger—The twins—A twice-married couple—How a Chinese B. A. was won—Le Ming's marriage—A Buddhist story—A fickle widow—A Chinese girl graduate—Love and alchemy—A Chinese ballad—The love-sick maiden: a Chinese poem.

中国小说. Douglas, Robert K. (Robert Kennaway, Sir, 1838—1913)译.

(1) Rev. ed. Singapore: G. Brash, 1990. x, 206 pages: illustrations; 19cm. ISBN: 997149163

Contents: A matrimonial fraud—The twins—A twice married couple—How a Chinese B. A. was won

(2) Rev. ed. Singapore: Graham Brash, 2001. x, 206 pages: illustrations; 19cm. ISBN: 9971491656, 9971491659

3. The hand of a thousand rings, and other Chinese stories. New York: Cosmopolis Press, 1924. 252 p.; 20cm.

Contents: The hand of a thousand rings. —As collected by the tao-tai. —The comedy of the white rat. —The missing daughter of Chee Tong. —The man in the doorway. —The crimeful chromatics of Nam Sing. —Without consent of the senate. —The oriental patience of Charlie Yip. —The little snake of the great white gods. —The man who never missed.

中国小说. Bachmann, Robert(1879—)选译.

(1) London: Hutchinson & Co., 1925. 288 pages

(2) Freeport, N. Y., Books for Libraries Press [1971]. 252 p.; 21cm. ISBN: 0836940350. (Short story index reprint series)

4. The Chinese Decameron, now first rendered into English by Carlo de Fornaro. New York [The Lotus society] 1929. 205 p. incl. col. plates. front.; 25cm.

Contents: The monastery of the most excellent lotus (after the Sing-She-reng-yen. XVIth century)—Niang plucks frail blossoms (after the Sing-She-reng-yen. XVIth century)—A marriage confusion (after the Sing-She-reng-yen. XVIth century)—Which explains certain strange attractions (by Ki-Yu. XVIIIth century)—Stronger than love (after the Tser-Wei-Yng-Yng of the Yuang-Chen.

780 A. D.)—A bonze in the garb of a nun (after the To-Schang-tsi-Yuan. XVIth century)—The Taoist monk (Poo Soong Lin. XVIIIth century)—The marriage of Ya-Nei （after the Sing-She-reng-yen. XVIth century）—Crafty husbands （after the Tsin-Ku-tsi-Kwan. XVIth century)—A wife by chance (Ki-Yun. XVIIIth century)

中国小说选译. 乔治·苏利埃·德·莫朗（Soulié de Morant，G.〈Georges〉，1878—1955）(法国汉学家)编译成法文；Fornaro, Carlo de(1871—)转译成英文.

5. Love stories and gallant tales from the Chinese/English versions [through the French of G. Soulié de Morant] by E. P. Mathers. London：John Radker, 1928. 170 pages：illust. ; 23cm. (Eastern love; 6)

中国爱情故事. 乔治·苏利埃·德·莫朗（Soulié de Morant，G.〈Georges〉，1878—1955）(法国汉学家)法译；Mathers, E. P. 英译自法文版.

6. Romance of the three kingdoms：and, A mission to heaven（selections）/selected and annotated by Yuan & Shih. Shanghai, China：Peisin Book, ᵀ1931. 265 p. ; 19cm. (English translations of Chinese classics; v. 1.)

Contents：Romance of the three kingdoms/translated by C. H. Brewitt-Taylor—A mission to heaven/translated by Timothy Richard.

Notes：Chinese and English on opposite pages. Selections from "San guo zhi yan yi," ascribed to Luo Guanzhong and "Xi you ji", by Wu Cheng'en.

《英译中国文学选粹. 第一辑, 三国志西游记》. 袁家骅（1904—1980），石民选注. 为两部名著的选译. 上海北新书局.

7. Some famous Chinese stories = Zhongguo ming ren xiao shuo xuan/compiled and translated by Kinchen Johnson. Peiping：Zhong yuan shu dian, Minguo 23 [1934]. 395 p. ; 20cm.

《中国名人小说选》,Johnson, Kinchen 译. 英汉对照. 北平：中原书店,［1934］.

8. Stories from China, put into Basic English. London, K. Paul, Trench, Trubner & Co. , Ltd. , 1937. 84 p. front. (fold. tab.) ;16cm.

中国短篇小说. 初大告(Ch'u, Ta-kao)译.

9. 中国故事一百篇：华英对照. Shanghai Chun jiang shu ju, 1938. 2, 4, 263 Seiten：Illustrationen.

伍鹤鸣编译.

（1）Zhongguo gu shi yi bai pian = One hundred Chinese stories retold/[translated and edited] by Justin Wu Ho Ming; with grammatical notes and equivalent Chinese. Xianggang：Ying yu chu ban she, 1971. 5, 263 pages：illustrations；18cm. (Shi jie wen xue ming zhu xuan yi)

10. Selections from Chinese classics/English translation by Tso Ping Nam. Batavia [Indonesia]：Nan Yang yin shu ju, 1948. 112 pages；19cm.

《英译古文选》，左炳南(Tso Ping Nam)选译. 英汉对照. 短篇小说.

11. Widow, nun and courtesan；three novelettes from the Chinese, translated and adapted by Lin Yutang. New York：John Day Company, ［1950］. vi, 266 p. ；21cm. Contents：Widow Chuan, by Lao Hsiang. —A nun of Taishan, by Liu O. —Miss Tu, by Lin Yutang.

《寡妇,尼姑与歌妓：英译三篇小说集》,林语堂(1895—1976)译. 由节译《全家庄》《老残游记二集》及改写《杜十娘》结集而成.

（1）Westport, Conn. , Greenwood Press [1971, c1951]. vi, 266 p. ；23cm. ISBN：0837147166, 0837147161

（2）New York：J. Day Co. , 1975. 266 pages；21cm.

（3）Taipei：Mei Ya, 1979. vi, 266 pages；21cm.

12. Famous Chinese short stories, retold by Lin Yutang. New York：J. Day Co. , ［1952］. 299 p. ；20cm.

《中国传奇小说》,林语堂(1895—1976)译.

（1）London, Heinemann, 1953. 232 pages；20cm.

（2）Melbourne, W. Heinemann, 1954. xiv, 232 pages；21cm.

（3）New York：Washington Square Press, 1954. xvii, 299 pages.

（4）New York, Washington Square Press, 1961. 299 pages；17cm.

（5）New York：Washington Square Press, 1967. xvii, 299 pages；17cm.

（6）Westport, Conn. ：Greenwood Press, 1979, c1952. xvii, 299 p. ；22cm. ISBN：0837190622, 0837190624

（7）London：Dent, 1983. xix, 299 pages；19cm. ISBN：0460013297, 0460013291

（8）北京：外语教学与研究出版社，2009. 308 pages；illustrations； 21cm. ISBN： 7560081373, 7560081371. (林语堂英文作品集)

中文书名：英译重编传奇小说.

13. 英译重编传奇小说/林语堂编译. 北京：外语教学与研究出版社,2009. 18 页,308 页；21cm. ISBN：7560081373, 7560081371

英文题名：Famous Chinese short stories. 本书收录了林语堂翻译的著名中国传奇小说 20 篇,包括《虬髯客传》《促织》《中山狼传》《南柯太守传》等,分别选自中国民间传说或《太平广记》《聊斋》等古代文学作品集.

14. Stories of old China/translated by W. W. Yen. Peking：Foreign Languages Press, 1958. 178 pages；22cm.

Contents：The heartless lover. —Good fortune waits on courage. —A dream and its lesson. —The herbalist's strange adventure. —The mystery of the missing minister. —The faithful handmaid. —Love and loyalty of a courtesan. —Tyrant and scholars. —Scholars versus eunuch. —An ungrateful wolf. —Evening with a famous ventriloquist. —I met a fairy. —The old scholar's reincarnation. —Fairies of the floral kingdom. —Quest of the filial son. —Hungerland. —A young strategist. —Tragedy of pure love. —Willow the story-teller. —Mr. Tung's fox tenants. —The Poyang murder case. —The loyal city clerk.

《中国古代短篇小说选》，蒋防选编；颜惠庆（1877—1950）译.

(1) Hong Kong：Commercial Press，1974. 178 pages；21cm.

(2) Shanghai：New Art and Literature Pub. House，1974. 178 pages；22cm.

(3) Second edition. Hong Kong：Commercial Press，1978. 178 pages；21cm.

(4) Hong Kong：Commercial Press，1984. 178 pages；21cm. ISBN：9620710398，9620710391

(5) 2nd ed. Peking：Foreign Languages Press，1990. 178 pages；22cm. ISBN：7119010751，7119010755

(6) Stories of old China/written by Jiang Fang and others；translated by W. W. Yen.［Beijing］Foreign Languages Press，2001. 239 p. ISBN：7119028952，7119028958. (Echo of classics)

(7) 北京：外文出版社，2003. 239 p.；21cm. ISBN：7119028952，7119028958. (经典的回声. Echo of classics)

(8) 北京：外文出版社，2016. 257 页；21cm. ISBN：7119097732. (中国经典外文读库；古代文学)

15. The man who sold a ghost：Chinese tales of the 3rd-6th centuries/［translated by Yang Hsien-Yi and Gladys Yang］. Peking：Foreign Languages Press，1958. ix，162 p.，［5］p. of plates；22cm. (Chinese classics)

《汉魏六朝小说选》，杨宪益（1915—2009），戴乃迭（Yang，Gladys，1919—1999）合译.

(1)［Hong Kong］：Commercial Press，［1974］. ix，162 p.，［3］leaves of plates：ill.；21cm.

(2) 2nd ed. Peking：Foreign Languages Press：Distributed by China International Book Trading Corp.，1990. ix，162 p.，［5］p. of plates；22cm. ISBN：0835124002，0835124003

16. Selected Chinese tales of the Han, Wei and Six dynasties periods/translated by Yang Xianyi, Gladys Yang. Beijing：Wai wen chu ban she，2000. 473 p.；13cm. ISBN：7119026917，7119025247. (FLP 汉英对照经典读本. 古典精华；3)

《汉魏六朝小说选》，干宝（？—336 年）等编撰；杨宪益（1915—2009），戴乃迭（Yang，Gladys，1919—1999）译.

(1) Beijing：Wai wen chu ban she，2005. 413 p.；21cm. ISBN：7119028859. (Echo of classics＝经典的回声)

(2) Beijing：Foreign Languages Press，2010. 475 p.；24cm. ISBN：7119040301，7119040308. (Library of Chinese Classics：Chinese-English)

17. The courtesan's jewel box.［translated by Yang Xianyi and Gladys Yang］Peking：Foreign Languages Press，

1957. 553 p. illus. 21cm.

《宋明评话选》，冯梦龙（1574—1646），凌蒙初著；杨宪益（1915—2009），戴乃迭（Yang，Gladys，1919—1999）译. 选自《古今小说》四篇：第十、二十七、三十五、四十卷；《警世通言》三篇：第八、十六、三十二卷；《醒世恒言》七篇：第三、四、六、七、十、二十九、三十三卷.

(1) The courtesan's jewel box：Chinese stories of the Xth-XVIIth centuries/translated by Yang Xianyi and Gladys Yang. Beijing：Foreign Languages Press：distributed by Guoji Shudian，1981 vi，520 p.，［22］p. of plates：ill.；22cm.

(2) Beijing Shi：Wai wen chu ban she，2001. 523 p.；21cm. ISBN：7119028847，7119028842. (Echo of classics＝经典的回声)

(4) Amsterdam，the Netherlands：Fredonia Books，2001. vi，520 pages，［22］pages of plates：illustrations；22cm.

18. Selected Chinese stories of the Song and Ming dynasties/written by Feng Menglong and Ling Mengchu；translated by Yang Xianyi and Gladys Yang. Beijing：Wai wen chu ban she，2000. 623 pages；13cm. ISBN：7119026917，7119026916，7119025247，7119025244. (FLP 汉英对照经典读本. 古典精华；3)

《宋明平话选》，冯梦龙，凌蒙初著；杨宪益（1915—2009），戴乃迭（Yang，Gladys，1919—1999）合译.

(1) Beijing：Wai wen chu ban she，2001. 523 pages；21cm. ISBN：7119028847，7119028842. (经典的回声＝Echo of classics)

(2)［Beijing］：Foreign Languages Press，2006. 523 p.；22cm. ISBN：7119028847，7119028842. (Echo of Classics)

(3) Beijing：Foreign Languages Press，2007. 2 v.：il.；24cm. ISBN：7119042589，7119042580

(4) Beijing：Wai wen chu ban she，2010. 2 volumes（1203 pages）；24cm. ISBN：7119042589，7119042580. (Library of Chinese classics＝大中华文库)

19. Stories about not being afraid of ghosts，compiled by the Institute of Literature of the Chinese Academy of Sciences.［Translated by Yang Hsien-Yi and Gladys Yang］. Peking Foreign Languages Press，1961. 88 pages.

《不怕鬼的故事》，中国科学院文学研究所编；杨宪益（1915—2009），戴乃迭（Yang，Gladys，1919—1999）合译.

20. The Illusory flame/translations from the Chinese by Howard S. Levy.［Tokyo，Kenkyusha，1962］. 100 p. illus.；22cm.

Notes："Ten stories... taken from a Chinese compilation called The collection of feminine fragrance.［Chinese language title］"

Levy，Howard S.（Howard Seymour，1923—)译，对中国 10 部短篇小说的翻译.

21. The golden casket；Chinese novellas of two millennia/translated by Christopher Levenson from Wolfgang Bauer's and Herbert Franke's German version of the original Chinese；with an introd. by Herbert Franke. New York：Harcourt，Brace & World［1964］. 391 p. illus. ；22cm.

Note：Translation of Die goldene Truhe.

金匣子：中国小说. Bauer，Wolfgang（1930—1997），Franke，Herbert（1914—2011）德文翻译；Christopher Levenson 英译自德文版.

(1)Harmondsworth，Penguin，1967. 393 p. illus. ；18 1/2cm. (The Penguin classics L 189)

(2)Westport，Conn. ：Greenwood Press，1978，c1964. 391 p. ：ill. ；23cm. ISBN：0313200912

22. 50 great oriental stories/edited by Gene Z. Hanrahan. New York：Bantam Books，1965. x，470 pages；18cm. (A Bantam classic；NC266)

Contents：Short stories from China—Short stories from Japan—Short stories from India—Short stories from Central Asia—Short stories from Southeast Asia.

50 部东方小说. Hanrahan，Gene Z. 编译，包括对中国短篇小说的英译.

23. Eight colloquial tales of the Sung，thirteenth century China/translated with an introd. and notes by Richard F. S. Yang. Taipei：China Post，［1972］. xxxi，210 p. ；22cm.

Contents：Carving the jade goddess Kuan-yin. —Stubborn chancellor. —The re-union of Feng Yü-mei. —The mistaken execution of Ts'ui Ning. —P'u-sa man. —Chang，the honest steward. —Ghosts in the Western Hills. —The white hawk of Ts'ui，the magistrates son，led to demons.

《宋人话本八种》，Yang，Richard Fu-Sen(1918—)译注. 即《碾玉观音》《拗相公》《冯玉梅团圆》《错斩崔宁》《菩萨蛮》《志诚张主管》《西山一窟鬼》《金虏海陵王荒淫》.

24. 100 Chinese stories/translated & described by Howard S. Levy. Falls Church，Va. ：Warm Soft Village Press，1974. xxx，251 p. ；21cm. ISBN：091087801X. (Series of stories；1)

中国短篇小说. Levy，Howard S. （Howard Seymour，1923—)译.

25. Chinese novels (1822)/translated from the originals by John Francis Davis. Delmar，N.Y. ：Scholars' Facsimiles & Reprints，1976. xi，250，［4］p. ；21cm. ISBN：082011278X

《中国小说选》，德庇时（Davis，John Francis，1795—1890）(英国汉学家)译. 初版于 1822 年. 重印本.

26. Excerpts from three classical Chinese novels/translated by Yang Xianyi and Gladys Yang. Beijing，China：

Chinese Literature：［Chung-kuo kuo chi shu tien fa hsing］，1981. 295 p. ；19cm. (Panda books)

Contents：The battle of the Red Cliff/Luo Guanzhong—On the Three Kingdoms/Chen Minsheng—The Flaming Mountain/Wu Cheng'en—Pilgrimage to the West and its author/Wu Zuxiang—A journey into strange lands/Li Ruzhen—Some notes on Flowers in the mirror/Li Changzhi

《三部古典小说节选》，杨宪益(1915—2009)，戴乃迭(Yang，Gladys，1919—1999)合译. 选译了《三国演义》《西游记》和《镜花缘》的有关章节以及对三部书的 3 篇评论.

27. Classical Chinese tales of the supernatural and the fantastic：selections from the third to the tenth century/edited by Karl S. Y. Kao. Bloomington：Indiana University Press，c1985. x，406 p. ：maps；25cm. ISBN：0253313759，0253313751. (Chinese literature in translation)

Contents：Lieh-i chuan—Shou-shen chi—Shen-hsien chuan—Ling-kuei chih—Chen-i chi—Sou-shen hou-chi—Ch'i-hsieh chi—Yu-ming lu—Lu-i chuan—Shu-i chi—Hsu ch'i-hsieh chi—Ming-hsiang chi—Huan-yuan chi.

中国古代鬼神故事(3—10 世纪). Kao，Hsin-yang 编译. 志怪小说.

(1)Asian ed. Hong Kong：Joint Publishing，1985. x，406 pages；maps. ISBN：0253313759，0253313751，9620404246，9620404245. (Chinese literature in translation)

28. The core of Chinese classical fiction/edited by Jianing Chen. Beijing，China：New World Press：Distributed by China International Book Trading Corp. ，1990. 489 pages：illustrations；22cm. ISBN：7800051099，7800051098，7800051102，7800051104

《中国古典小说精选》，陈家宁编. 新世界出版社.

(1)Kuala Lumpur：S. Abdul Majeed，1994. 489 pages：illustrations；21cm. ISBN：7800051099，7800051098

(2)Revised ed. Beijing：New World Press，2001. 2 volumes (898 pages)：illustrations；21cm. ISBN：7800055795，7800055799

29. The lioness roars：shrew stories from late Imperial China/Yenna Wu. Ithaca，N.Y. ：East Asia Program，Cornell University，c1995. x，156 p. ：ill. ；23cm. ISBN：1885445717，1885445814. (Cornell East Asia series)

Contents：A jealous wife becomes a widow while her husband is still alive/Li Yu—Jie Zhitui traps his jealous wife in an inferno/Aina Jushi—Ma Jiefu/Pu Songling—Jiangcheng/Pu Songling—Woman Shao/Pu Songling—Shanhu/Pu Songling—Hengniang/Pu Songling—Curing jealousy/Yuan Mei

《狮吼集：晚期中华帝国的泼妇故事》，吴燕娜(美国华裔学者)著,翻译了李渔、艾衲居士、蒲松龄和袁枚等所作的明清时期的有关妇女的故事.

30. Strange writing: anomaly accounts in early medieval China/Robert Ford Campany. Albany: State University of New York Press, c1996. xii, 524 p.; 24cm. ISBN: 0791426599, 0791426602. (0791426599)

《志怪文学作品》,康儒博(Campany, Robert Ford, 1959—)(美国汉学家)译,对中国中世纪初期200多个传说作汇总和翻译.

31. Chinese ghost stories for adults: sex, love, and murder between spirits and mortals/by Tom Te-Wu Ma; illustrated by Hsiung Chen. New York: Barricade Books, c2000. 214 p.: ill.; 22cm. ISBN: 1569801428

鬼故事. Ma, Tom编译.

32. Selected Chinese short stories of the Tang and Song Dynasties/written by Yuan Zhen and others; translated by Yang Xianyi, Gladys Yang and Huang Jun. Beijing, China: Foreign Languages Press, 2001. 304 p.: ill.; 18cm. ISBN: 7119020986

《中国传奇选》,元稹(779—831)等;杨宪益(1915—2009),戴乃迭(Yang, Gladys, 1919—1999),黄均译.

33. Short stories from Giles' Historic China/[translated by Herbert A. Giles; compiled by Ping-wei Huang] = [Zhailisi xuan yi wen yan gu shi/Zhailisi yi; Huang Bingwei bian xuan]. Taizhong Shi: Chen xing chu ban you xian gong si, c2004. xiv, 255, xiii p.; 21cm. ISBN: 9574556638, 9574556632. (Chen xing cong shu)

Notes: Translation of selections from: Historic China, and other sketches, 1882.

《翟理斯选译文言故事》,翟理斯(Giles, Herbert Allen, 1845—1935)(英国汉学家)译;Huang, Bingwei编.中英文对照.

34. The abbot and the widow: tales from the Ming dynasty/ Ling Mengchu, [Feng, Menglong]; translated and edited by Ted Wang and Chen Chen. Norwalk: EastBridge, 2004. 249 p: ill. ISBN: 1891936395, 1891936395, 1891936409, 1891936401

明朝故事,选译于"二拍"和"三言".凌蒙初,冯梦龙原著;Wang, Ted和Chen, Chen合译.

35. A collection of ancient Chinese stories/translated by Chi Him Chiu; illustrated by Deborah Dee. [Philadelphia]: Xlibris Corp., c2005. 203 p.: bill.; 23cm. ISBN: 1599266644

中国古代短篇小说选译. Chiu, Chi Him译.

36. An anthology of Chinese short short stories/selected and translated by Harry J. Huang. Beijing, China: Foreign Languages Press: Distributed by China International Book Trading Corp., 2005. viii, 463 pages; 21cm. ISBN: 7119038818, 7119038810. (Panda books)

《中国小小说选集:英文》,周大新等著;黄俊雄译.(熊猫丛书).本书收集来自中国87位作家的作品约120篇左右,其中古代作品6篇.

37. A garden of marvels: tales of wonder from early medieval China/Robert Ford Campany. Honolulu: University of Hawaii Press, [2015]. xliv, 164 pages; 23cm. ISBN: 0824853495, 0824853501

Contents: Jiling ji (item 1)—Jingyi ji (items 2—4)—Jiyi ji (items 5—7)—Kongshi zhiguai (items 8—11)—Lieyi zhuan (items 12—21)—Lushi yilin (item 22)—Luyi zhuan (items 23—28)—Qi Xie ji (items 29—37)—Shen lu (items 38—39)—Shenguai zhi (item 40)—Shengui zhuan (items 41—42)—Shenyi ji (items 43—44)—Shenyi jing (items 45—46)—Shuyi ji/by Zu Chongzhi (items 47—84)—Shuyi ji/by Ren Fang (items 85—90)—Soushen houji (items 91—102)—Xiao shuo (item 103)—Xu Qi Xie ji (items 104—105)—Xuanyan ji (items 106—110)—Xuanzhong ji (items 111—114)—Xuyi ji (items 115—119)—Yi yuan (items 120—183)—Youming lu (items 184—208)—Zhenyi zhuan (items 209—218)—Zhi guai/by Zu Taizhi (items 219—220)—Other assorted accounts (items 221—225).

中国中古时期故事. Campany, Robert Ford译.

38. The Dragon king's daughter; ten Tang Dynasty stories/ [translated by Yang Xianyi and Gladys Yang]. Peking: Foreign Languages Press, 1954. xii, 100 p. illus.; 22cm.

Contents: The white monkey (Anonymous).—Jen, the fox fairy [by] Shen Chi-chi.—The Dragon king's daughter [by] Li Chao-wei.—Prince Huo's daughter [by] Chiang Fang.—Governor of the southern tributary state [by] Li Kung-tso.—Story of a singsong girl [by] Pai Hsing-chien.—Wu-shuang the peerless [by] Hsueh Tiao.—The spendthrift and the alchemist [by] Li Fuyen.—The Kun Lun slave [by] Pei Hsing.—The man with the curly beard [by] Tu Kuang-ting.

《唐代传奇选》,沈既济(750—800)等编著;杨宪益(1915—2009),戴乃迭(Yang, Gladys, 1919—1999)译,收录《补江总白猿传》《任氏传》《柳毅传》《霍小玉传》《南柯太守传》《李娃传》《无双传》《杜子春传》《昆仑奴》《虬髯客传》.

(1) 2nd ed. Beijing: Foreign Languages Press, 1962. [99] pages, [6] leaves of plates (1 folded): illustrations, map; 22cm.

(2) 3rd ed. Beijing: Foreign Languages Press, 1980. viii, 93 p., [6] leaves of plates (1 folded): ill.; 22cm.

(3) Tang Dynasty stories/translated by Yang Xianyi and Gladys Yang. Beijing, China: Chinese Literature: Distributed by China International Book Trading Corp., 1986. 149 pages; 18cm. ISBN: 0835116026, 0835116022. (Panda books)

Contents: Ren the fox fairy, by S. Jiji—The dragon king's daughter, by L. Chaowei—Prince Huo's daughter, by J. Fang—Governor of the southern tributary state, by L. Gongzuo—Story of a singsong girl, by B. Xingjian—Wushuang the peerless, by X. Tiao—The man with the curly beard, by D. Guangting—The kunlun slave, by P. Xing—The general's daughter, by P. Xing—The jade mortar and pestle, by P. Xing—The prince's tomb, by P. Xing—The spendthrift and the alchemist, by L. Fuyan—The white monkey, anonymous.

（4）The Dragon king's daughter：ten Tang dynasty stories/［translated by Yang Hsien-Yi and Gladys Yang］. Honolulu, Hawaii：University Press of the Pacific, 2001. 99 pages, ［5］ leaves of plates：illustrations, map；21cm. ISBN：0898752639, 0898752632

（5）The Dragon king's daughter：ten Tang dynasty stories/［various；translated by Yang Xianyi and Gladys Yang］. ［Rockville, Md.］：Silk Pagoda, 2007. 124 pages：illustrations, map；23cm. ISBN：1596543817, 1596543812

39. Selected Tang dynasty stories/edited by Shen Jiji and others；translated by Yang Xiangyi and Gladys Yang. Beijing：Wai wen chu ban she, 2000. 195 pages；13cm. ISBN：7119026917, 7119026916, 7119025247, 7119025244. (FLP 汉英对照经典读本. 古典精华；3)
《唐代传奇选》,沈既济等编著；杨宪益,戴乃迭译.

40. Tang dynasty tales：a guided reader/William H. Nienhauser, Jr. Singapore；Hackensack, NJ：World Scientific, c2010. xxv, 311 p.；ill. (some col.)；24cm. ISBN：9814287289,9814287288
Contents：The tale of Hongxian/Translated by Weiguo Cao—Du Zichun/Rania Huntington—Record within a pillow/Bruce J. Knickerbocker—An account of the governor of the Southern branch/William H. Nienhauser, Jr.—The tale of the curly-bearded guest/Jing Wang—The tale of Huo Xiaoyu/Zhenjun Zhang.
Notes：In English translated from the Chinese. 'Tang Dynasty Tales' offers the first annotated translations of six major tales which are interpreted specifically for students and scholars interested in medieval Chinese literature
Nienhauser, William H. 著. 译注了 6 部唐代传奇故事.

41. Falling in love：stories from Ming China/translated by Patrick Hanan. Honolulu：University of Hawaii Press, c2006. xviii, 256 p.；22cm. ISBN：0824829956, 0824829957
《中国明代爱情小说》,韩南（Hanan, Patrick）（新西兰裔汉学家）译. 选译 7 篇从《醒世恒言》和《石头记》里选出的故事.

42. Lazy dragon：Chinese stories from the Ming dynasty/translated by Yang Xianyi and Gladys Yang；edited by

Geremie Barmé. Hongkong：Joint Pub. Co. , 1981. xx, 304 p. ：ill. ；22cm. ISBN：9620401360, 9620401367
Contents：Fifteen strings of cash—The strange adventures of Yang Balao—The ghost came thrice—The oil vendor and the courtesan—A just man avenged—The beggar chief's daughter—The old gardener—The courtesan's jewel box—The tangerines and the tortoise shell—Lazy dragon
《懒龙：明代传奇选》,杨宪益（1915—2009）,戴乃迭（Yang, Gladys,1919—1999）译. 该译作以 1957 年出版的《The Courtesan's Jewel Box》为基础,收录其 8 篇译文,同时增加两篇新译：《古今小说》第十八卷和《警世通言》第十三卷.

43. Short tales of the Ming & Qing. Beijing, China：Chinese Literature：Distributed by China International Book Trading Corp. , 1996. 267 pages；18cm. ISBN：7507103501, 7507103502, 0835131858, 0835131858. (Panda books)
《明清文言小说选》,蒲松龄等著；张西蒙等译. 中国文学出版社.

44. Middlebrow fiction/［edited by George Kao］. ［Hong Kong］：Research Centre for Translation, Chinese University of Hong Kong, 1982. 295 pages：illustrations；26cm.
Notes：Special issue of：Renditions. No. 17 & 18 (spring & autumn 1982).
清朝通俗小说. 高克毅（Kao, George,1912—2008）（美国华裔学者）译.

45. Chinese middlebrow fiction：from the Ch'ing and early republican eras/edited by Liu Ts'un-yan；with the assistance of John Minford. Hong Kong：Chinese University Press；Seattle：University of Washington Press, c1984. 372 p. ：ill. ；27cm. ISBN：9622013090. (A Renditions book)
Contents：Introduction："Middlebrow" in perspective/Liu Ts'un-Yan—Marriage as retribution/P'u Sung-Ling (translated by Chi-chen Wang)—Sing-song girls of Shanghai/Han Pang-Ch'ing (translated by Eileen Chang)—Sing-song girls of Shanghai and its narrative methods/Stephen Chang—A flower in a sinful sea/Tseng P'u (translated by Rafe de Crespigny and Liu Ts'un-yan)—My father's literary journey/H. P. Tseng (translated by Colin Modini)—Hsüh Chen-ya's Yü-li hun：an essay in literary history and criticism/C. T. Hsia—An interview with Pao T'ien-hsiao/Perry Link—Fate in tears and laughter/Chang Hen-Shui (translated by Sally Borthwick)—Modern times or A brief history of enlightenment/Li Po-Yüan (translated by Douglas Lancashire)—Bizarre happenings eyewitnessed in two

decades/Wu Wo-Yao（translated by Shih Shun Liu）—Postscript/Liu Ts'un-Yan.

《中国通俗小说:清至民初》,柳存仁(1917—2009)等编.

I52　古代个人作品(或单部作品)

东晋

干宝(约 282—351)

1. In search of the supernatural: the written record/translated by Kenneth J. DeWoskin and J. I. Crump, Jr. Stanford, Calif.: Stanford University Press, c1996. xxxvi, 283 p.: ill.: 24cm. ISBN: 0804725063

《搜神记》,DeWoskin, Kenneth J.,柯迁儒(Crump, J. I.〈James Irving〉,1921—2002)(又名柯润璞)合译.

2. Anecdotes about spirits and immortals/written by Gan Bao; edited and translated into modern Chinese by Huan Diming; translated into English by Ding Wangdao. Beijing: Foreign Languages Press, 2004. 2 volumes: illustrations: 24cm. ISBN: 7119033298, 7119033297. (Library of Chinese classics)

《搜神记》,黄涤明校译;丁往道英译.(大中华文库)

刘义庆(403—444)

1. A new account of tales of the world/by Liu I-ch'ing; with commentary by Liu Chün; translated with introd. and notes by Richard B. Mather. Minneapolis: University of Minnesota Press, c1976. xxxii, 726 p.: 24cm. ISBN: 0816607605

《世说新语》,刘义庆(403—444)等著;刘峻(462—521)注;马瑞志(Mather, Richard B.,1913—)(美国汉学家)译.

(1)Taibei: Confucius Publ. Co., 1979. 260 p.

(2)2nd ed. Ann Arbor: Center for Chinese Studies, University of Michigan, c2002. xxxviii, 735 p.: 24cm. ISBN: 089264155X. (Michigan monographs in Chinese studies; 95)

南北朝

颜之推(531—约 597)

1. Tales of vengeful souls: a sixth century collection of Chinese avenging ghost stories/translated and annotated by Alvin P. Cohen. Paris: Ricci Institute, 1982. x, 166 pages; 26cm. (Variétés sinologiques: new series; 68)

《冤魂志》(又名《还冤志》),Cohen, Alvin F. 译. 志怪小说.

(1)Taipei: Ricci Institute, 1982. x [i. e. xxiii], 166 pages; 26cm. (Variétés sinologiques: new ser., no. 68)

唐代

唐临(约 601—约 660)

1. Miraculous retribution: a study and translation of T'ang Lin's Ming-pao chi/Donald E. Giertson. Berkeley, CA: Centers for South and Southeast Asia Studies, University of California at Berkeley, 1989. xiv, 305 pages; 24cm. ISBN: 09446130711, 0944613078. (Berkeley Buddhist

studies series; 8)

Notes: Translation of: Ming pao chi. / Originally presented as the author's Ph. D. thesis, Stanford University, 1975.

Gjertson, Donald E. 著,翻译了唐临(600—?)的《冥报记》.

张鸶(660—740)

1. The dwelling of playful goddesses; [Tokyo, Dai Nippon Insatsu; 1965. 2 v. illus.: 22cm.

《游仙窟》,Levy, Howard S.（Howard Seymour,1923—）译. 唐代传奇小说.

戴孚(生之年不详,757 年进士)

1. Religious experience and lay society in T'ang China: a reading of Tai Fu's Kuang-i chi/Glen Dudbridge. Cambridge [England]; New York: Cambridge University Press, 1995. ix, 256 p.: maps; 24cm. ISBN: 0521482232. (Cambridge studies in Chinese history, literature, and institutions)

《唐朝的宗教和世俗社会》,Dudbridge, Glen 著,包括对戴孚的《广异记》的翻译和读解.

宋代

《太平广记》

1. Ladies of the Tang: [short stories]/translated by Elizabeth Dezhen Wang. Taipei: Heritage Press, 1961. xi, 347 pages: illustrations: 19cm.

Wang, Dezhen(1911—)译. 翻译了《太平广记》的 22 篇小说.

(1)4th ed. Ladies of the Tang: 22 classical Chinese stories/translated by Elizabeth Dezhen Wang. Taipei: Mei Ya Publications, 1973. xi, 348 pages: illustrations: 19cm. (Mei Ya heritage series)

(2)Rev. ed. Taipei: Caves Books, 1991. xiii, 290 pages: illustrations: 20cm. ISBN: 957606077X, 9576060779

2. Into the porcelain pillow: 101 tales from Records of the Taiping era/compiled by Li Fang and others of the Song Dynasty; translated by Zhang Guangqian. Beijing: Foreign Languages Press: Distributed by China International Book Trading Corp., 1998. vii, 313 pages: illustrations: 18cm. ISBN: 7119020110, 7119020112

《太平广记选》,张光前译.

3. 太平广记选/李昉等编;张光前译. 北京市:外文出版社,2000. 527 pages; 13cm. ISBN: 7119026917, 7119026916, 7119025244, 7119025247. (FLP 汉英对照经典读本. 古典精华; 3)

英文题名:The selections from records of the Taiping era.

(1)太平广记选/(宋)李昉等编;张光前英译. 北京:外文出版社,2018. 499 页;21cm. ISBN:7119110660. (中国经典外文读库)

洪迈(1123—1202)

1. Selections from Record of the Listener/written by Hong Mai (Song Dynasty); transl. into English by Alister David Inglis; transl. into modern Chinese by Wang Xiting and Teng Yilan. Beijing: Foreign Languages Press, 2009. 547 p.; 24cm. ISBN: 7119055794, 7119055798. (Library of Chinese classics: Chinese-English)

《夷坚志选》.本书精选宋代著名志怪小说集《夷坚志》中的140余篇.中英对照.

2. Record of the listener: selections of Chinese supernatural stories/attributed to Hong Mai; translated from Chinese by Alister D. Inglis. Beijing: Foreign Languages Press, 2010. 243 pages; 23cm. ISBN: 7119039022, 7119039024. (Chinese classics)

《夷坚志选》.外文出版社(中国经典译丛)

明代

《水浒传》,施耐庵(约1296—约1370)

1. Robbers and soldiers, by Albert Ehrenstein, translated from the German by Geoffrey Dunlop. New York: Knopf, 1929. 268 p.; 20cm.
   Notes: Translation of: Räuber und Soldaten.

《水浒传》,Ehrenstein, Albert(1886—1950)译成德文; Dunlop, Geoffrey(英国汉学家)自德文译成英文. 70回本节译本.

(1) London: Howe, c1929. 319 p.; 19cm.

2. All men are brothers＝Shui hu zhuan/translated from the Chinese by Pearl S. Buck. New York: John Day Company, Rahway, N. J.: Quinn & Boden Company, 1933. 2 volumes (xiii, 1279 pages): illustrations (some color); 22cm.

《水浒传》,赛珍珠(Buck, Pearl S. 〈Pearl Sydenstricker〉, 1892—1973)(美国作家)译. 七十回本.

(1) London: Metheun and Co., Ltd., 1933. xiii, 1279 pages: illustrations; 22cm.

(2) New York, The John Day Company [c1934]. 2 volumes frontispieces, illustrations; 22cm.

(3) New York: Grosset & Dunlap: London: Methuen, 1937. xiv pages, 1 leaf, 1279 pages: frontispiece, illustrations; 22cm.

(4) All men are brothers (Shui hu chuan)/translated from the Chinese by Pearl S. Buck. [Rev. ed.]. New York: Grosset & Dunlap, 1939. xiv, 1279 pages: illustrations; 22cm.

(5) All men are brothers: (Shui hu chuan)/translated from the Chinese by Pearl S. Buck. New York: Grove Press, 1947. 2 volumes (xiv, 1279 pages): illustrations; 21cm.

(6) translated from the Chinese by Pearl S. Buck; with an introduction by Lin Yutang and illustrations by Miguel Covarrubias. New York: Limited Editions Club, 1948. 2 v. (xxix, 688 p., [32] leaves of plates): ill. (some col.); 32cm.

(7) translated from the Chinese by Pearl S. Buck; with an introduction by Lin Yutang and illustrations by Miguel Covarrubias. New York: Heritage Press, [1949]. xxix, 688 p., [32] leaves of plates: ill. (32 col.); 29cm.

(8) New York: Grove Press [1957, c1937]. p. cm.

(9) All men are brothers＝水浒传/translated from the Chinese by Pearl S. Buck. 台北: 文星书店, [1966]. 2 v., 1279 p.: ill.; 20cm.

(10) All men are brothers＝水浒传/translated from the Chinese by Pearl S. Buck. 台北: 北一出版社, [1967]. 2 volumes, 1279 pages: illustrations; 21cm.

(11) New York: J. Day Co. [1968, c1937]. 2 v. (xiv, 1279 p.)illus.; 21cm.

(12) All men are brothers＝Shui hu chuan/translated from the chinese by Pearl S. Buck. Bath: Cedric Chivers, 1969. 2 volumes (xiii, 1279 pages): illustrations; 19cm.

(13) All men are brothers＝(Shui hu chuan)/translated from the Chinese by Pearl S. Buck with an introduction by Lin Yutang, and illustrations by Miguel Covarrubias. Norwalk, CT: Easton Press, 1976. xxix, 688 pages: illustrations; 26cm.

(14) All men are brothers: (Shui hu chuan)/Translated from Chinese by Pearl S. Buck. 敦煌书局股份有限公司, 1977. 650 pages; 26cm.

(15) All men are brothers: Shui hu chuan/translated from the Chinese by Pearl S. Buck. 台北市: 皇家图书有限公司, [1978]. 2 volumes: illustrations; 22cm.

(16) All men are brothers＝Shui hu chuan/ [Shih Nai-an]; translated from the Chinese by Pearl S. Buck. Singapore: Cultured Lotus, 1999. 2 volumes (xiv, 1279 pages); 21cm. ISBN: 9810409249, 9810409241, 9810409257, 98104092

(17) All men are brothers＝Shui hu chuan/translated from the Chinese by Pearl S. Buck. Kingston, R. I.: Moyer Bell, 2004. xix, 697 pages: illustrations (some color); 28cm. ISBN: 1559213035, 1559213035

(18) All men are brothers＝Shui hu chuan/by Shi Nai'an & Luo Guanzhong; translated from the Chinese by Pearl S. Buck; with an introduction by Lin Yutang; and illustrations by Miguel Covarrubias. Kingston, R. I.: Moyer Bell, 2006. xix, 697 pages: illustrations; 28cm. ISBN: 1559213035, 1559213035

3. Water margin, written by Shih Nai-an；translated by J. H. Jackson, edited by Fang Lo-tien. Shanghai, The Commercial Press, Limited, 1937. 2 v.；19cm.

《水浒传》,杰克逊(Jackson, J. H.)(英国传教士)译. 七十回本节译本.

(1)〔Hong Kong〕Commercial Press，1963. 2 volumes in 1 (917 pages)；22cm.

(2)New York：Paragon，1963. 2 volumes in 1 (917 pages)；22cm.

(3)New York：Paragon Book Reprint Corp.，1968. 2 v. in 1 (917 p.)；22cm.

(4)Cambridge, Mass.，C & T Co.，1968. 2 volumes in 1 (917 pages)22cm.

(5)5th ed. Hong Kong：Commercial Press，1975，1976，1979. volumes (917 pages)；21cm.

(6) Cambridge, Ma.：C & T Co.，1976. 917 pages；22cm.

(7)Singapore：G. Brash，1981. 917 pages. ISBN：9971990180, 9971990183

(8)written by Shi Naian；translated by J. H. Jackson；with a new foreword by Edwin Lowe. Tokyo；Rutland, Vt.：Tuttle Pub.，c2010. xlix, 798 p.；21cm. ISBN：0804840958, 0804840954

4. Selections from the Shui-hu chuan；edited by J. I. Crump, Jr. New Haven, Published for the Institute of Far Eastern Languages by Yale University Press，1947. viii, 20, 34 p. 23cm. (Mirror series C；no. 4)

Notes："The text consists of two stories from the Shui-hu chuan which were published by the Shanghai Commercial Press in their series, Min-chung chi-pen ts'ung-shu."

《水浒传选译》,柯迁儒（又名柯润璞）(Crump, J. I. 〈James Irving〉,1921—2002)译. 只选译了2篇.

(1)Selections from the Shui-hu Chuan/〔By Lo Kuan-chung〕；ed. by J. I. Crump, jr. New Haven, Conn.，1967. VIII, 20, 34 s. (Mirror series. C；4；)

(2)New Haven：〔s. n.〕，1973. 1 v.

5. Outlaws of the marsh/by Shi Nai'an and Luo Guanzhong；translated by Sidney Shapiro. Beijing：Foreign Languages Press，1980. 3 v.：ill.；22cm.

《水浒传》,沙博理(Shapiro,Sidney 1915—2014)译. 100 回本.

(1)Beijing：Foreign Languages Press；Bloomington：Indiana University Press，c1981. 2 v.：ill.；22cm. ISBN：025312574X, 0253125743

(2)Outlaws of the marsh/by Shi Nai'an and Luo Guanzhong；translated by Sidney Shapiro. Beijing：Foreign Languages Press：Distributed by the China International Book Trading Corp.，1988. 4 volumes：illustrations；19cm. ISBN：083512312X (v. 1),

0835123129 (v. 1), 7119007033 (v. 1), 7119007038 (v. 1), 0835123138 (v. 2), 0835123136 (v. 2), 7119007041 (v. 2), 7119007045 (v. 2), 0835123146 (v. 3), 0835123143 (v. 3), 711900705X (v. 3), 7119007052 (v. 3), 0835123154 (v. 4), 0835123150 (v. 4), 7119007068 (v. 4), 7119007069 (v. 4)

(3)Beijing：Foreign Languages Press，1993. 3 volumes：illustrations；18cm. ISBN：7119016628; 7119016627. (Chinese classics)

(4)Outlaws of the marsh/by Shi Nai'an and Luo Guanzhong；transl.〔from the Chinese〕by Sidney Shapiro. Beijing：Foreign Languages Press，1995. 3 vol. (IX—1605 p.)：ill.，jaquette ill.；22cm. ISBN：7119017357, 7119017358

(5)Outlaws of the marsh/Shi Nai'an and Luo Guanzhong；translated by Sidney Shapiro. Condensed version. Beijing：Foreign Languages Press，1999. 466 pages：illustrations；13cm. ISBN：7119022911; 7119022918. (FLPhan ying dui zhao jing dian du ben.；Gu dian jing hua)

(6)Outlaws of the marsh：Chinese-English/written by Shi Nai'an and Luo Guanzhong；translated by Sidney Shapiro. Beijing：Wai wen chu ban she；Changsha：Hunan ren min chu ban she, Beijing：China International Book Trading Corporation，1999. 5 volumes (39, 3080 pages)：illustrations；24cm. ISBN：7119024094 (set)；7119024097 (set). (大中华文库＝Library of Chinese classics)

(7)Outlaws of the marsh/written by Shi Nai'an and Luo Guanzhong；translated by Sideny〔sic〕Shapiro. Beijing：Wai wen chu ban she，2003. 5 v. (3077 p.)：ill.；21cm. ISBN：7119032178 (set), 7119032177 (set). (Library of Chinese and English classics (Chinese-English)＝汉英经典文库)

6. Outlaws of the marsh/by Shi Nai'an and Luo Guanzhong〔supposed authors〕；translated by Sidney Shapiro. Bloomington：Indiana University Press，1981. 2 volumes (1605 pages)；22cm.

《水浒传》,沙博理(Shapiro,Sidney 1915—2014)译.

7. Outlaws of the marsh：an abridged version＝〔Shui hu zhuan〕/written by Shi Nai'an and Luo Guanzhong；translated by Sidney Shapiro. Quarry Bay, Hong Kong：Commercial Press，c1986. iii, 2, 458 p.：ill.；21cm. ISBN：9620710673

《水浒传》(节译),沙博理(Shapiro,Sidney 1915—2014)译.100 回本

(1) Hong Kong：Commercial Press，1991. iii, 2, 458 pages；21cm.：illustrations. ISBN：9620710673, 9620710674

8. Outlaws of the marsh/written by Shi Nai'an and Luo Guanzhong；translated by Sidney Shapiro. Sydney：Unwin Paperbacks, 1986. iii, 458 pages：illustrations；22cm. ISBN：0048200271, 0048200273

《水浒传》，沙博理（Shapiro, Sidney 1915—2014）译.

9. Outlaws of the marsh＝Shui hu zhuan/by Shi Naian and Luo Guanzhong；translated by Sidney Shapiro；adapted by Jin Shibo. Beijing：Foreign Language Teaching and Research Press, 1991. 2, 350 pages：illustrations；18cm. ISBN：7560001688, 7560001685

《水浒传：英文压缩本》，沙博理（Shapiro, Sidney 1915—2014），金诗伯（Ginsbourg, Sam, 1914—）合译. 外语教学与研究出版社.

10. The marshes of Mount Liang：a new translation of the Shuihu zhuan or Water margin of Shi Nai'an and Luo Guanzhong/by John and Alex Dent-Young. Hong Kong：Chinese University Press, 1994—2002. 5 volumes：illustrations；22cm. ISBN：9622016022 （pt. 1），9622016026 (pt. 1), 9622017517 (pt. 2), 9622017511 (pt. 2)，9622018475 (pt. 3), 9622018471 (pt. 3)，9622019897 (pt. 4), 9622019898 (pt. 4)；9622019900 (pt. 5), 9622019904 (pt. 5)

Contents：pt. 1. The broken seals—pt. 2. The tiger killers—pt. 3. Gathering Company—pt. 4. Iron ox—pt. 5. The scattered flock.

《水浒传》，Dent-Young, John 和 Dent-Young, Alex 译. 即英国登特·杨父子. 120 回本.

(1) Hong Kong：Chinese University Press, 2001—2002. Pt. 1 — 5. ISBN：9622016022 9622016026 9622017517 9622017511 9622018475 9622018471 9622019897 9622019898 9622019900 9622019904

(2) Shanghai：Shanghai Foreign Language Education Press, 2014. 5 Volumes. ISBN：7544636643(set)

11. 水浒传：汉英对照揭封走魔 the broken seals/施耐庵，罗贯中著；John and Alex Dent-Young 译. 上海：上海外语教育出版社，2011. 5 卷. ISBN 7544615679（v. 1），7544615677（v. 1），7544615679（v. 2），7544615677（v. 2），7544615679（v. 3），7544615677（v. 3），7544615679（v. 4），7544615677（v. 4），7544615679（v. 5），7544615677(v.5)

Contents：v. 1 揭封走魔 The broken seals. v. 2 打虎英雄 The tiger killers. v. 3 梁山聚义 The gatheringcm. pany. v. 4 铁牛 Iron ox v. 5 鸟兽散 The scattered flock
John and Alex Dent-Young 是登特·杨父子,系英国学者.

《三国演义》，罗贯中（约 1330—1400）

1. Translation into English of "The Logomachy"：being the 43rd chapter of the Three Kingdom Novel；with the Chinese commentator's introduction and notes/by John Steele. Shanghai：Presbyterian Mission Press, 1907. 20 pages；24cm.

《三国演义》（选译），施约翰（Steele, John, 1832—1905）（英国传教士）译. 翻译了《唇枪舌剑》一章. 上海美华书馆.

2. San kuo；or, Romance of the three kingdoms, by C. H. Brewitt-Taylor... An English version. Shanghai〔etc.〕Kelly ＆ Walsh, Limited, 1925. 2 v. front. (fold. map) 25cm.

《三国志演义》，邓罗（Brewitt-Taylor, C. H. 〈Charles Henry〉, 1857—1938）（英国汉学家）译. 全译本. 上海别发洋行出版.

(1) Popular ed. Shanghai：Kelly ＆ Walsh, 1929. 2 volumes；25cm.

(2) Romance of the three kingdoms. C. E. Tuttle Co. 〔1959〕. 2 v.

(3) 〔Taipei, Taiwan〕〔Book World Co.〕, 1959. 2 volumes；20cm. (Chinese classics in English；6.)

(4) 〔Taibei〕：〔Wen xing shu dian〕, 1963—1966. 2 volumes；20cm.

(5) Romance of the three kingdoms：San guo zhi yanyi/translated by C. H. Brewitt-Taylor. Taipei：Ch'eng-wen Pub. Co. , 1969. 2 volumes；20cm.

(6) Romance of the three kingdoms/Translated by C. H. Brewitt-Taylor. Rutland, Vt. , C. E. Tuttle Co. , 1970. 2 volumes map (on lining papers)；23cm.

(7) Rutland, Vt. ：Tuttle Co. , 1973. 2 volumes：maps on lining papers；23cm. ISBN：0804807264, 0804807265

(8) Tokyo：C. E. Tuttle Co. , 1976. 2 volumes. ISBN：0804807280, 0804807289, 0804807264, 0804807265

(9) Taibei：Dunhuang shu ju, 1983. 2 volumes；22cm. (Chinese classics series in English)

(10) Singapore：Graham Brash, 1985. 2 volumes；22cm. ISBN：9971947943, 9971947941

(11) Lo Kuan-chung's Romance of the three kingdoms＝San guo zhi yanyi/translated by C. H. Brewitt-Taylor. Rutland, Vt. ：C. E. Tuttle Co. , 1990. 2 volumes；22cm. ISBN：0804816492 （set），0804816496 (set)

(12) Singapore：Graham Brash, 1995. 2 volumes；22cm. ISBN：9812180435 （v. 1），9812180438 (v. 1)，9812180443 (v. 2), 9812180445 (v. 2)

(13) Torrance, CA：Heian International, 1999. 2 volumes；22cm. ISBN：0893469246 （v. 1），0893469245 （v. 1），0893469254 （v. 2），0893469252 (v. 2)

(14) Romance of the three kingdoms/Lo Kuan-chung；translated by C. H. Brewitt-Taylor；with an introduction by Robert E. Hegel. Boston：Tuttle

Pub.；North Clarendon，Vt.；Distributed in North America by Tuttle Pub.，c2002. 2 v.；21cm. ISBN：0804834679（v.1），0804834674（v.1），0804834687（v.2），0804834681（v.2）

(15)[Rockville，Md.]：Silk Pagoda，2005. 2 volumes；27cm. ISBN：1596542764（v.1），1596542761（v.1），1596542756（v.2），1596542754（v.2）

3. 三国演义精华＝Romance of the three kingdoms/[罗贯中着；陈慧文英译]. 台北：华联出版社，[1966]. 153 pages；20cm.

英汉对照.

(1)[香港]：文新出版社，[1973]. 1，153 pages；18cm.

4. Romance of the three kingdom，from chapter 43 to chapter 50/罗贯中着；张亦文译. [香港]：[大同印务公司]，[1972]. 30，216 pages；19cm.

《三国志演义，第四十三回至五十回》，罗贯中；张亦文（Cheung，Yik-man）译. 中英对照.

(1)Beijing：Zhongguo you yi chu ban she：Xin hua shu dian Beijing fa xing suo fa xing，1985. 32，3，232 p.；19cm.

5. Three kingdoms：China's epic drama/by Lo Kuan-chung；translated from the Chinese and edited by Moss Roberts. New York：Pantheon Books，c1976. xxv，318 p.：ill.；25cm. ISBN：0394407229

《三国演义》（节译），罗慕士（Roberts，Moss，1937—）（美国汉学家）译.

(1)New York：Pantheon Books，1985. XV，318 p.；23cm. ISBN：0394733932，0394733937

6. Three kingdoms：a historical novel/attributed to Luo Guanzhong；translated from the Chinese with afterword and notes by Moss Roberts. Berkeley：University of California Press；Beijing：Foreign Languages Press，c1991. xiv，1096 p.：map；27cm. ISBN：0520068211，0520068216

《三国演义》，罗慕士（Roberts，Moss，1937—）（美国汉学家）译. 全译本.

(1)Three kingdoms：a historical novel/attributed to Luo Guanzhong；translated from the Chinese with afterword and notes by Moss Roberts. Beijing：Foreign Languages Press；Berkeley：University of California Press，1994. 3 volumes（[40]，1690 pages）：illustrations，maps；22cm. ISBN：7119016644（v.1），7119016641（v.1），7119016652（v.2），7119016658（v.2），7119016660（v.3），7119016665（v.3）

(2)Three kingdoms：a historical novel，complete and unabridged/Attributed to Luo Guanzhong；translated from the Chinese with afterword and notes by Moss Roberts；foreword by John S. Service. Berkeley：University of California Press；Beijing：Foreign Languages Press，2004. 2 volumes（xii，1096 pages）：illustrations，maps；26cm. ISBN：0520224787，0520224780，0520225031，05202250

7. Three kingdoms：a historical novel/attributed to Luo Guanzhong；translated from the Chinese with afterword and notes by Moss Roberts. Berkeley：University of California Press；Beijing：Foreign Languages Press，1994. 562 pages. ISBN：7119016644，7119016641

《三国演义》（节译），罗慕士（Roberts，Moss，1937—）（美国汉学家）译.

(1)Three kingdoms：a historical novel/attributed to Luo Guanzhong；translated from the Chinese with afterword by Moss Roberts. Abridged ed. Beijing：Foreign Languages Press；Berkeley：University of California Press，c1999. xv，489 p.：map；22cm. ISBN：0520215842，0520215849，0520215850，0520215856

(2)Fifteenth anniversary abridged edition. Beijing：Foreign Languages Press，2014. xxi，489 pages：map（black and white）；21cm. ISBN：0520282162，0520282167

8. Three kingdoms/by Luo Guanzhong；translated by Moss Roberts ＝ San guo yan yi/Luo Guanzhong. Condensed version. Beijing：Foreign Languages Press，1999. 575 pages：illustrations；13cm. ISBN：7119022911，7119022918. (FLPhan ying dui zhao jing dian du ben.；Gu dian jing hua)

《三国演义》（节译），罗慕士（Roberts，Moss，1937—）（美国汉学家）译.

9. San guo yan yi ＝ Three kingdoms/attributed to Luo Guanzhong；translated by Moss Roberts. Beijing：Foreign Languages Press，Hunan People's Publishing House，2000—2007. 5 volumes：illustrations；24cm. ISBN：7119032194，7119032191. (Library of Chinese classics)

《三国演义》，罗慕士（Roberts，Moss，1937—）（美国汉学家）译. 英汉对照.

10. Excerpts from three classical Chinese novels/translated by Yang Xianyi and Gladys Yang. Beijing，China：Chinese Literature：[Chung-kuo kuo chi shu tien fa hsing]，1981. 295 p.；19cm. (Panda books)

Contents：The battle of the Red Cliff/Luo Guanzhong—On the Three Kingdoms/Chen Minsheng—The Flaming Mountain/Wu Cheng'en—Pilgrimage to the West and its author/Wu Zuxiang—A journey into strange lands/Li Ruzhen—Some notes on Flowers in the mirror/Li Changzhi

《三部古典小说节选》，杨宪益（1915—2009），戴乃迭（Yang，Gladys，1919—1999）译. 选译了《三国演义》《西游记》和《镜花缘》的有关章节以及对三部书的 3 篇评论.

    (1)Beijing, China：Chinese Literature, 1984. 295 p.；19cm. ISBN：0835113302, 0835113304. (Panda books)

    (2)Beijing：Panda Books, 1996. 295p.；18cm.

11. The three kingdoms. The sacred oath, an epic Chinese tale of loyalty and war in a dynamic new translation/Lo Kuan-Chung; translated by Yu Sumei; edited by Ronald C. Iverson. Rutland, Vermont：Tuttle Publishing, [2014]. 414 pages；21cm. ISBN：0804843935 (pbk.), 0804843937 (pbk.), 0804843942 (pbk.), 0804843945 (pbk.), 0804843959 (pbk.), 0804843953 (pbk.)
Contents：v. 1. The sacred oath—v. 2. The sleeping dragon—v. 3. Welcome the tiger.

《三国演义》,虞苏美(Yu, Sumei)译；Iverson, Ronald C. 编.全译本,英汉对照.

    (1)三国演义/虞苏美译.上海：上海外语教育出版社, 2017. 3 卷. ISBN：7544648639. (外教社中国名著汉外对照文库)

《平妖传》,罗贯中(约 1330—1400)

1. The three Sui quash the demons' revolt：a comic novel/attributed to Luo Guanzhong; translated, with an interpretative essay, by Lois Fusek. Honolulu：University of Hawaii Press, c2010. xv, 299 p.；24cm. ISBN：0824834067, 0824834062

《平妖传》,罗贯中；Fusek, Lois(1934—)译.

《西游记》,吴承恩(约 1500—1583)

1. A mission to heaven：a great Chinese epic and allegory/by Qiu Chang Chun; translated by Timothy Richard. Shanghai：Christian Literature Society's Depot, 1913. xxxix, 362, vii pages, [30] leaves of plates：illustrations；23cm.

《西游记》,李提摩太(Richard, Timothy,1845—1919)(英国传教士)译.上海广学会刊印.

    (1)A mission to heaven, [n. p.] 1940. xxxix, 362, vi p. plates.；21cm.

2. Journey to the west：the monkey king's amazing adventures/Wu Cheng'en; retold by Timothy Richards; introduction by Daniel Kane. Tokyo；North Clarendon, VT：Tuttle Pub., c2008. xxix, 226 p.；ill.；21cm. ISBN：0804839495, 0804839492. (Tuttle classics)

《西游记》,李提摩太(Richards, Timothy)改编.

3. 西游记(英译本·珍藏版)/(明)吴承恩；[英]李提摩太译.北京：商务印书馆, 2018. 475 页；22cm. ISBN：7100155946

4. The Buddhist Pilgrim's progress：from the Shi yeu ki, the records of the journey to the Western paradise, by Wu Ch'eng-en. London, J. Murray [1930]. 105 p. 17cm.

(The Wisdom of the East series)

《西游记》(选译),Hayes, Helen M. 译.翻译了 100 回,属于删译本.

    (1)[1st Amer. ed.]. New York：Dutton [1930]. 105 p.；17cm.

5. Monkey. London, G. Allen & Unwin [1942]. 305 p.；23cm.

《神猴孙悟空》,韦利(Waley, Arthur, 1889—1966)(英国汉学家)译.是《西游记》的节译本,在西方被认为是高水平的译作,书前有胡适的《西游记考证》一文.

    (1)London：George Allen & Unwin, 1944. 314 p.：ill.；18cm.

    (2)New York：Grove Press, 1977. 306 p. 20cm. ISBN：0802140580, 0802140586. (UNESCO collection of representative works. Chinese series)

6. The adventures of monkey, adapted from the translation made from the Chinese of Wu Ch'eng-en by Arthur Waley. Illustrated by Kurt Wiese. New York：The John Day Company [1944]. 143 p. illus.；21cm.

《西游记》,韦利(Waley, Arthur, 1889—1966)(英国汉学家)译.

    (1)[Tai-pei shih]：[Ti i wen hua she], 1967. 306 pages；19cm. (Chinese Classics in English)

    (2)Taipei, Taiwan：Wen Xing shu dian, 1968. 306 pages：illustrations；21cm. (Chinese classics in English；7)

    (3)Singapore：Graham Brash, 1973. 223 pages：illustrations. ISBN：9971490455, 9971490454

    (4)Taipei：新陆书局, 1975. 306 pages；21cm. (Chinese classics in English)

    (5)Taipei：Dunhong shu zhu, 1978. 305 pages；21cm.

    (6)Taipei：Huang Chia, 1978. 306 pages；21cm.

7. Dear monkey/[Wu Ch'eng-en]; translated from the Chinese by Arthur Waley; abridged by Alison Waley; illustrated by Georgette Boner. Glasgow：Blackie, c1973. 223 p.：ill.；23cm. ISBN：0216896584 0216896581

《美猴王》,韦利(Waley, Arthur, 1889—1966)(英国汉学家)译；艾利森(Waley, Alison)缩写.

    (1)Indianapolis, Bobbs-Merrill, 1973. 223 pages：illustrations；24cm. ISBN：0672520028, 0672520020

    (2)London：Collins, 1975. 146 pages；18cm. ISBN：0006709974, 0006709978

    (3)Tokyo：Kodansha International, 1993. 287 pages；15cm. ISBN：4061861018, 4061861015

8. The monkey king/Wu Cheng'en; edited by Zdena Novotná; translated by George Theiner; illustrated by Zdeněk Sklenář. English ed. London：P. Hamlyn, 1964. 330 pages：illustrations (some color)；29cm.

《猴王》,Theiner,George 转译自捷克文.

(1) The monkey king [by] Wu Ch'eng-en. Edited by Zdena Novotná. Translated by George Theiner. Illustrated by Zdeněk Sklená ř. London, P. Hamlyn [1965]. 330 p. illus. (part col.); 29cm.

9. The journey to the west/translated and edited by Anthony C. Yu. Chicago: University of Chicago Press, 1977—1983. 4 v.; 24cm. ISBN: 0226971457 (v. 1), 0226971452 (v. 1), 0226971511 (v. 2)

《西游记》,余国藩(Yu, Anthony C., 1938—2015)(美国汉学家)译. 第一个英文全译本.

(1)Chicago: University of Chicago Press,1980. volumes; 24cm. ISBN:0226971473, 0226971476, 0226971465, 0226971469, 0226971511, 0226971513. (A Phoenix book; P882)

(2) paperback ed. Chicago, Ill.: University of Chicago Press, 1984. 4 volumes; 23cm. ISBN:0226971503 (v. 1), 0226971506 (v. 1), 0226971511 (v. 2), 0226971513 (v. 2), 0226971538 (v. 3), 0226971537 (v. 3), 0226971546 (v. 4), 0226971544 (v. 4)

(3)Revised edition. Chicago: The University of Chicago Press, 2012. 4 volumes; 24cm. ISBN:0226971315 (v. 1), 0226971317 (v. 1.), 0226971322 (v. 1), 0226971325 (v. 1), 0226971407 (v. 2), 0226971339 (v. 2), 0226971333 (v. 2), 0226971346 (v. 2), 0226971341 (v. 2), 0226971414; 0226971360 (v. 3), 0226971368 (v. 3), 0226971377 (v. 3), 0226971376 (v. 3), 0226971421; 0226971384 (v. 4), 0226971384 (v. 4), 0226971391 (v. 4), 0226971392 (v. 4), 0226971438 (v. 4), 0226971430 (v. 4), 0226971438 (v. 4)

10. The journey to the west/[Wu Ch'eng-en]; transl. and ed. by Anthony C. Yu. Taibei: Caves Books, 1978. 3 vol.; 23cm.

《西游记》,余国藩(Yu, Anthony C., 1938—2015)(美国汉学家)译

11. Selected readings from The journey to the west/Cheng'en Wu; Anthony C Yu. New York: Forbes Custom Pub., 1998. iv, 228 pages; 26cm. ISBN:0828112525, 0828112529

《西游记》(选译),余国藩(Yu, Anthony C., 1938—2015)(美国汉学家)译.

12. The monkey & the monk: a revised abridgment of The journey to the west/translated and edited by Anthony C. Yu. Chicago: University of Chicago Press, 2006. xiv, 497 p.; 23cm. ISBN:0226971554, 0226971562, 0226971568, 0226971551

《西游记》(节译本),余国藩(Yu, Anthony C., 1938—2015)(美国汉学家)译.

13. Havoc in heaven: adventures of the Monkey King/

translated by W. J. F. Jenner; illustrated by Li Shiji. Beijing: Foreign Languages Press, 1979. 106 pages, [6] leaves of plates: illustrations; 18cm.

《大闹天宫:猴王历险记》,詹纳尔(Jenner, W. J. F.)译; 李士伋插图.

14. Journey to the west/by Wu Cheng'en; translated by W. J. F. Jenner. Beijing: Foreign Languages Press, 1982. 4 volumes (1878 pages): illustrations; 19cm. ISBN: 0835122573 (v. 1), 0835122573 (v. 1), 7119010115 (v. 1), 7119010113 (v. 1), 0835122581 (v. 2), 0835122580 (v. 2), 7119010123 (v. 2), 7119010120 (v. 2), 083512259X (v. 3), 0835122597 (v. 3), 7119010131 (v. 3), 7119010137 (v. 3), 0835122603 (v. 4), 0835122603 (v. 4), 711901014X (v. 4), 7119010144 (v. 4). (Chinese classics)

《西游记》,詹纳尔(Jenner, W. J. F.)译. 第二个英文全译本.

(1)Journey to the west/by Wu Cheng'en; translated by W. J. F. Jenner. Beijing: Foreign Languages Press, 1990. 4 volumes: illustrations; 18cm. ISBN: 7119010115 (v. 1), 7119010113 (v. 1), 7119010123 (v. 2), 7119010120 (v. 2), 7119010131 (v. 3), 7119010137 (v. 3), 711901014X (v. 4), 7119010144 (v. 4). (Chinese classics)

(2)Beijing: Foreign Languages Press, 1993. 4 volumes: illustrations; 18cm. ISBN: 7119016636, 7119016634. (Chinese classics)

(3)Beijing: Foreign Languages Press, [1999—2003]. 4 volumes (2346 pages): illustrations; 18cm. ISBN: 7119016636, 711901663

15. Journey to the west/by Wu Cheng'en; translated by W. J. F. Jenner. Beijing: Foreign Languages Press: Distributed by China Publication Centre (Guoji Shudian), 1982. volumes ⟨1—2⟩: illustrations; 22cm. ISBN: 0835110036 (v. 1), 0835110037 (v. 1), 0835111938 (v. 2), 0835111935 (v. 2)

《西游记》,詹纳尔(Jenner, W. J. F.)译.

(1)2nd ed. Beijing: Foreign Languages Press: Distributed by China International Book Trading Corporation, 1990. 2 volumes: illustrations; 22cm. ISBN: 0835110036, 0835110037, 7119006533, 7119006536, 0835113647, 0835113649, 7119009877, 7119009872, 0835111938, 0835111935

16. Journey to the west/by Wu Cheng-en; transl. by W. J. F. Jenner. Beijing: Foreign Languages Press: Distributed by China Publication Centre (Guoji Shudian), 1984—1986. 3 volumes: ill.; 22cm. ISBN: 0835110036 (v. 1), 0835110037 (v. 1), 0835111938 (v. 2), 0835111935 (v. 2), 0835113647 (v. 3), 0835113649 (v. 3)

《西游记》,詹纳尔(Jenner, W. J. F.)译.

(1)Journey to the west/by Wu Cheng'en; translated by W. J. F. Jenner. 2nd ed. Beijing: Foreign Languages

Press：Distributed by China International Book Trading Corporation, 1990. 3 volumes：illustrations；22cm. ISBN：0835110036, 0835110037, 7119006533, 7119006536, 0835113647, 0835113649, 7119009877, 7119009872, 0835111938, 0835111935

(2)Journey to the west/by Wu Cheng'en；translated by W. J. F. Jenner. Beijing：Foreign Languages Press；Distributed by China International Book Trading Corp., 1995, 1982. 3 volumes：illustrations；22cm. ISBN：7119006533 (v. 1), 7119006536 (v. 1), 7119009877 (v. 2), 7119009872 (v. 2), 7119017780 (v. 3), 7119017785 (v. 3)

17. Journey to the west/written by Wu Chengén；translated by W. J. F. Jenner. An abridge version. Singapore：Asiapac Books, 1994. 16, 477 pages：illustrations；21cm. ISBN：981302920X, 9813029200
《西游记》，詹纳尔(Jenner, W. J. F.)译.

18. Journey to the West/attributed to Wu Cheng'en；translated by W. J. F. Jenner. Condensed version. Beijing：Foreign Languages Press, 1999. 627 pages：illustrations；13cm. ISBN：7119022911；7119022918. (汉英经典文库（汉英对照）= Library of Chinese and English classics (Chinese-English). (FLP 汉英对照经典读本. 古典精华.；1.)
《西游记》，詹纳尔(Jenner, W. J. F.)译.

19. Journey to the west/attributed to Wu Cheng'en；translated by W. J. F. Jenner. Beijing：Wai wen chu ban she, Changsha：Hunan People's Pub. House, 2000. 6 volumes (55, 3375 pages)：illustrations；24cm. ISBN：7119024103（set）, 7119024108（set）, 7119024086, 7119024080. (大中华文库= Library of Chinese classics)
《西游记》，詹纳尔(Jenner, W. J. F.)译. 汉英对照.

(1)Beijing：Wai wen chu ban she, 2003. 6 volumes（3355 pages）：illustrations；21cm. ISBN：711903216X, 7119032160. (汉英经典文库= Library of Chinese and English classics)

20. Adventures of Monkey King/retold by R. L. Gao；illustrated by Marlys Johnson-Barton. Monterey, CA：Victory Press, c1989. 128 p.：ill.；22cm. ISBN：0962076511, 0962076510
《西游记》，Gao, R. L. (1898—)改编，Johnson-Barton, Marlys 绘图.

(1)Kuala Lumpur：Eastern Dragon Books, 1992. 128 pages：illustrations；21cm. ISBN：9838991104, 9838991100

21. Monkey：a journey to the west：a retelling of the Chinese folk novel by Wu Ch'eng-en/David Kherdian. Boston：Shambhala；[New York]：Distributed by Random House, 1992. ix, 209 p.：ill.；22cm. ISBN：0877736529,

0877736523
《西游记》，Kherdian, David 改编.

(1)Monkey：a journey to the west：classic Chinese tale of pilgrimage and adventure retold/by David Kherdian. Boston：Shambhala；[New York], 2000. ix, 209 pages：illustrations；22cm. ISBN：1570625816, 1570625817

(2) Boston；London：Shambhala, 2005. 209 p.：ill.；23cm. ISBN：1590302583, 1590302583, 0877736529, 0877736523, 1570625816, 1570625817

22. The Monkey King and the book of death/adapted by Ted Tao；[inside illustrations by Quan Yingsheng and Ning Hu]. Santa Monica, CA：Golden Peach Pub., c2008. 200 p.：ill.；20cm. ISBN：1930655010, 1930655010
《西游记》，Tao, Ted 改编.

23. 西游记/吴承恩原著, 宋德利编译. 北京：中国书籍出版社, 2008. 363 页；23cm. ISBN：7506817288, 7506817284. (中国名著海外译丛)
英文题名：Journey to the west. 选取《西游记》原著中的 17 个经典故事编译.

24. The magic monkey, adapted from an old Chinese legend. [New York] Whittlesey House, McGraw-Hill Book Company, Inc. [1944]. 56 p., 1 l., illus. (part col.) 23×20cm.
《神猴》，陈智诚(Chan, Plato), 陈智龙(Chan, Christina)改编.

(1)London；Glasgow：Collins, 1946. 46 pages.

25. The making of Monkey King = [Xiao shi hou cheng wang]：English/Chinese/retold by Robert Kraus and Debby Chen；illustrated by Wenhai Ma. Union City, CA：Pan Asian Publications, c1998. 1 v.（unpaged）：col. ill.；29cm. ISBN：1572270454, 1572270459, 1572270438, 1572270435. (Adventures of Monkey King. Chinese & English；1.)
《小石猴称王》，Kraus, Robert(1925—), Chen Debby 改编；Ma Wenhai 插图. 中英文本.

《金瓶梅》，兰陵笑笑生(明万历年间人)

1. Chin P'ing Mei：the adventurous history of Hsi Men and his six wives, with an introduction by Arthur Waley. London, John Lane [1939]. xxii, 852 p.；23cm.
Notes："This English translation by Bernard Miall from the abridged version by Franz Kuhn. (Insel-Verlag, Leipzig)"
《金瓶梅词话》，弗朗茨·库恩(Kuhn, Franz, 1884—1961)(德国汉学家)译成德文；Miall, Bernard(1876—)译成英文；韦利(Waley, Arthur, 1889—1966)(英国汉学家)作序.

(1)New York：G. P. Putnam's Sons, [c1940]. 2 v.；22cm.

(2)London, Bodley Head [1959]. xxii, 852 p.；23cm.

(3) New York：N. Y.：Perigee Books，1982，c1939. xxii，863 p.；20cm. ISBN：0399506578

2. The golden lotus；a translation from the Chinese original of the novel，Chin p'ing mei，by Clement Egerton. London，G. Routledge [1939]. 4 v.；23cm.

《金瓶梅词话》，(英)克莱门特·埃杰顿(Egerton，F. Clement C.〈Frederick Clement Christie〉)译.

(1) New York：Grove Press，[1954]. 4 v.；23cm.

(2) London，Routledge & K. Paul [1972]. 4 v. 23cm. ISBN：0710073496

(3) London；New York：Kegan Paul International，1995. 4v.；23cm. ISBN：071030496X

3. Golden lotus/translated from the Chinese novel Chin Ping Mei by Clement Egerton；condensed and with an introd. by Franklin P. H. Chen. Chinese novel condensed ed. Berwyn，Pa.：Chinese Press，1977. xx，324 p.；19cm.

《金瓶梅词话》，克莱门特·埃杰顿(Egerton，F. Clement C.〈Frederick Clement Christie〉)译.

4. The golden lotus ＝ Jin ping mei/Lanling Xiaoxiaosheng (pseudonym)；a translation from the Chinese by Clement Egerton，with the assistance of Shu Qingchun (Lao She)；with an new introduction by Robert Hegel. 1st Tuttle ed. North Clarendon，VT：Tuttle Pub.，c2011. 2 v.；21cm. ISBN：0804841702 (v. 1)，0804841705 (v. 1)，0804841719 (v. 2)，0804841713 (v. 2).

《金瓶梅词话》，克莱门特·埃杰顿(Egerton，F. Clement C.〈Frederick Clement Christie〉)译，老舍(1899—1966)协助翻译.

5. Don Juan of China：an amour from the "Chin P'ing Mei"/Retold in pictures and text by Kwan Shan-mei. Translated from the Chinese by Samuel Buck. Tokyo，Rutland，Vt.：C. E. Tuttle Co.，1960. 98 pages：illustrations；17 × 22cm.

《金瓶梅词话》，Kwan，Shan Mei 改编；Buck，Samuel 英译.

6. The plum in the golden vase，or，Chin P'ing Mei/translated by David Tod Roy. Princeton，N. J.：Princeton University Press，c1993-〈c2013〉. v.〈1—5〉：ill.；24 × 25cm. ISBN：0691069328 (v. 1). (Princeton library of Asian translations)

《金瓶梅词话》，芮效卫(Roy，David Tod，1933—)译.

《春梦琐言》

1. Chun meng suo yan：trifling tale of a spring dream/Hu Yongxi；Robert Hans van Gulik. Tokyo，1950. 6，[2]，19 p.；22cm.

Notes：Published on the basis of a manuscript preserved in Japan and introduced by R. H. van Gulik.

《春梦琐言》，(明)胡永禧；高罗佩(Gulik，Robert Hans van，1910—1967)(荷兰汉学家)翻译.中英对照.明代情色

短篇小说.

(1)[香港]：[古佚小说会]，[1979]. 6，19 pages (on double leaves)；21cm. (古佚小说；第11种)

余象斗(16世纪中叶—1637年前后)

1. Journey to the north：an ethnohistorical analysis and annotated translation of the Chinese folk novel Pei-yu chi/[translated by] Gary Seaman. Berkeley：University of California Press，c1987. xiii，236 p.：map；22cm. ISBN：0520058097

《北游记》，加里·西曼(Seaman，Gary，1942—)(美国汉学家)译.

董说(1620—1686)

1. The tower of myriad mirrors：a supplement to Journey to the west/by Tung Yüeh；translated from the Chinese by Shuen-fu Lin and Larry J. Schulz. Berkeley，Calif.：Asian Humanities Press，c1978 (1988 printing). 200 p.；22cm. ISBN：089581501X

《西游补》，林顺夫(Lin，Shuen-fu，1943—)，拉里·舒茨(Schulz，Larry James)合译.

(1) 2nd ed. Ann Arbor：Center for Chinese Studies，the University of Michigan，2000. ix，139 p.；23cm. ISBN：0892641428. (Michigan classics in Chinese studies；no. 1)

杨尔曾(明朝人，生卒年不详)

1. The story of Han Xiangzi：the alchemical adventures of a Daoist immortal/Yang Erzeng；translated and introduced by Philip Clart. Seattle：University of Washington Press，c2007. xxxv，472 p.：ill.；24cm. ISBN：0295986906，0295986905

《韩湘子全传》，柯若朴(Clart，Philip，1963—)译.

冯梦龙(1574—1646)

1. Li，duke of Ch'ien：and the poor scholar who met a chivalrous man：a Chinese novel/translated from the Chinese by J. A. Jackson. Shanghai：Printed at the Methodist Pub. House，1922. 99，99 pages；16cm.

《李汧公穷邸遇侠客》，Jackson，J. A.译.英汉对照.译自《醒世恒言》第30卷.

2. Eastern shame girl/translated from the French of George Soulie DeMorant；illustrations by Marcel Avond. New York：Privately printed，1929. 183 pages：illustrations；25cm.

Contents：Eastern shame girl—The wedding of Ya-nei—A strange destiny—The error of the embroidered slipper—The counterfeit old woman—The monastery of the esteemed-lotus—A complicated marriage.

乔治·苏利埃·德·莫朗(Soulié de Morant，G.〈Georges〉，1878—1955)(法国汉学家)编译.主要译自《醒世恒言》. 6篇选自《醒世恒言》，1篇选自《警世通言》.

(1)Chinese love tales/translated from the original of George Souile de Morant, with illustrations by Valenti Angelo. New York：Illustrated Editions, 1935. 161 pages：illustrations；21cm.

(2)Chinese love tales/translated from the original of George Souile［i. e. Soulie］de Morant；with illustrations by Valenti Angelo. Cleveland：World Pub. , 1935. 161 pages：illustrations；21cm.

(3)Eastern shame girl, and other stories：classic tales of Oriental love. New York：Avon, 1947. 191 pages：illustrations；17cm. (Vintage Avon；127)

(4)Confessions of an eastern shame girl/translated from the French of George Soulie DeMorant；illus. by Marcel Avond. Paris：The Press, 1950. 183 pages：illustrations；23cm.

(5)Chinese love tales；translated from the original of George Souile［sic］de Morant. With illus. by Valenti Angelo. Garden City, N. Y. , Halcyon House［1950］. 161 p. illus. ；21cm. (Illustrated library)

3. The oil vendor and the sing-song girl；a Chinese tale in five cantos.［New York：F. Ruesch, 1938］. 3 v. ；15cm.
《卖油郎独占花魁》，Hundhausen, Vincenz（1878—）和 Reusch, Fritz 合译. 译自《醒世恒言》

4. Glue and lacquer；four cautionary tales translated from the Chinese by Harold Acton & Lee Yi-hsieh. Preface by Arthur Waley. With illustrations from drawings by Eric Gill interpreted on copper by Denis Tegetmeier.［London］The Golden Cockerell Press［1941］. 139 p. front, illus. ；26cm.
《醒世恒言》，艾克敦（Acton, Harold, 1904—1994）（英国诗人），Li, Yixie(1919—)译.

(1)Four cautionary tales［from a collection, ed. and pub. in 1627 by Feng Meng-lung］Translated from the Chinese by Harold Acton & Lee Yi-hsieh；with a pref. by Arthur Waley.［London］J. Lehmann, 1947. 159 p. ；19cm.

(2)Four cautionary tales/translated from the Chinese by Harold Acton & Lee Yi-Hsieh；with a preface by Arthur Waley. New York：Wyn, 1948. xi, 15—159 pages；19cm.

5. Traditional Chinese tales, translated by Chi-chen Wang. New York：Columbia University Press, 1944. 5 p. l. , 225 p. ；22cm.
Contents：Hsüh Yen's strange encounter, or, Lovers within a lover/Wu Chün—The ancient mirror/Wang Tu—The white monkey—The disembodied soul/Ch'en Hsüan-yu—The magic pillow/Shen Jiji—Jenshih, or, The fox lady/Shen Jiji—The dragon's daughter/Li Ch'ao-wei—Huo Hsiaoyü by Jiang Fang—Li Yahsien, a loyal courtesan/Po Hsing-chien—The story of Ying Ying/Yuan Chen—Hsieh Hsiaowo, or, A monkey in the carriage/Li Kung-tso—The Kunlun slave/P'ei Hsing—Yinniang the swordswoman/P'ei Hsing—Predestined marriage/Li Fu-yen—Du Zizhun/Li Fuyen—The jade kuanyin—The judicial murder of Tsui Ning—The flower lover and the fairies—The oil peddler and the queen of flowers—The three brothers—Bibliographical note（p. ［215］）—Notes on the tales.
王际真（Wang, Chi-Chen, 1899—2001）（美国华裔学者）译.译自冯梦龙的"三言".

(1)New York：Greenwood Press［1968, c1944］. 225 p. ；23cm. ISBN：0837107394, 0837107393

(2)New York：Greenwood Press Publishers, 1976. 225 pages；22cm. ISBN：0837189446, 0837189444

(3)India：Pilgrims Publishing, 2008. 225 pages；22cm. ISBN：8177696858, 8177696851

6. Miss Tu. London, Heineman, 1950. 124 pages；21cm.
《杜十娘怒沉百宝箱》，林语堂(1895—1976)编译.

7. The two brothers of different sex；a story from the Chinese.［Translation of Tse-hiong-ti has been made from the French of Stanislas Julien by Frances Hume］Illustrated by Edy Legrand.［London］：Rodale Press［1955］.51 p. illus. 21cm. (Miniature books)
《刘小官雌雄兄弟》，Julien, Stanislas 法译；Hume, Frances 译自法语版. 译自《醒世恒言》第十卷.

8. Stories from a Ming collection：translations of Chinese short stories published in the seventeenth century, by Cyril Birch. London, Bodley Head［1958］. 205 p. illus. 23cm. (UNESCO collection of representative works. Chinese series)
《古今小说选》，白之（Birch, Cyril, 1925—）（美国汉学家）译.

(1) New York：Grove Press［c1958］. 205 p. illus. ；21cm. (UNESCO collection of representative works. Chinese series)

(2)Bloomington, Indiana University Press, 1959［c1958］. 205 p. illus. 23cm. . (UNESCO collection of representative works. Chinese series)

(3)London：Bodley Head, 1960. 205 pages：illustrations；23cm. (UNESCO collection of representative works. Chinese series)

(4)New York：Grove Weidenfeld, 1968. 205 pages：illustrations；21cm. ISBN：0802150314, 0802150318

(5)Westport, Conn. ：Greenwood Press, 1978, 205 p. ；23cm. ISBN：031320067X, 0313200670. (UNESCO collection of representative works. Chinese series)

9. The everlasting couple：an annotated translation of a Chinese short story. Taipei：Liberal Arts Press, 1975.

iv，44，19 p.，[1] leaf of plates：facsim.；21cm.
《陈多寿生死夫妻》，Lau，Chau-mun 译. 译自《醒世恒言》.

10. The perfect lady by mistake and other stories/by Feng Menglong (1574—1646)；translated with an introd. by William Dolby. London：P. Elek，1976. 183 p.，[6] leaves of plates：ill.；23cm. ISBN：0236400029，0236400027

Contents：The perfect lady by mistake.—Li Bai (Li Po)，God in Exile，drunken drafts his "Letter to daunt the Barbarians."—A joke over fifteen strings of cash brings uncanny disaster.—Two magistrates vie to marry an orphaned girl.—Yang Jiao throws away his life in fulfilment of a friendship.—On big tree slope a faithful tiger acts best man.

Dolby，William 译. 6 篇小说译自《醒世恒言》《警世通言》和《喻世明言》.

11. Traditional Chinese stories：themes and variations/edited by Y. W. Ma and Joseph S. M. Lau. New York：Columbia University Press，1978. xxvi，603 p.；26cm. ISBN：0231040598，0231040594，0231040587，023104058X

《中国古典短篇小说选》，马幼垣(Ma，Y. W.〈Yau-Woon〉，1940—)，刘绍铭(Lau，Joseph S. M.，1934—)合译. 共收录十七篇：《古今小说》第一、三、八、十、三十六共五卷；《警世通言》第八、十二、十四、二十一、二十八、三十二、三十五卷共七篇；《醒世恒言》第三、九、十三、三十三、三十五共五卷.

(1) [Taipei]：[Linking Pub. Co]，1979. xxv. i，603 pages；26cm.

(2) 修订三版. 台北市：联经，民 72 版本，1983. [12]，863 面；21cm.

(3) Boston：Cheng & Tsui Co.，1986. xxvi，603 p.；26cm. ISBN：0887270719，0887270710. (C & T Asian literature series)

(4) Boston：Cheng & Tsui Co.，1994. xxvi，603 pages；26cm. ISBN：0887270719，0887270710

12. Chinese love stories from "Ch'ing-shih"/[translated by] Hua-yuan Li Mowry. Hamden，Conn.：Archon Books，1983. xii，206 p.；23cm. ISBN：0208019200，0208019202

《情史》(节译)，Mowry，Hua-yuan Li 译.

13. The Chinese femme fatale：stories from the Ming period/translations and introduction by Anne E. McLaren. Broadway，NSW：Wild Peony；Honolulu：International distribution，University of Hawaii Press，1994. 102 pages：illustrations；22cm. ISBN：0646149245，0646149240. (University of Sydney East Asian series；no. 8)

Notes：Translation of short stories from the anthologies：Three words (San yen)/by Feng Menglong.
《三言》(选译)，McLaren，Anne E. (Anne Elizabeth)译.

14. Wisdom's way：101 tales of Chinese wit/translated & enhanced by Walton C. Lee. Jamaica Plain，Mass.：YMAA Publication Center，c1997. ix，156 p.：ill.；23cm. ISBN：1886969361，1886969360
《智囊》，(节译)，Lee，Walton C. 译.

15. Stories old and new/compiled [and authored] by Feng Menglong (1574—1646)；translated by Shuhui Yang and Yunqin Yang. Seattle：University of Washington Press，c2000. xxx，794 p.：ill.；25cm. ISBN：0295497830，0295978437，0295978449，0295444. (A Ming dynasty collection；[v. 1])
《喻世明言》，杨曙辉(Yang，Shuhui)，杨韵琴(Yang，Yunqin)合译.

16. Stories to caution the world/compiled [and authored] by Feng Menglong；translated by Shuhui Yang and Yunqin Yang. Seattle：University of Washington Press，2005. xx，771 p.；25cm. ISBN：0295985526，0295985527，0295985688，0295985682. (A Ming dynasty collection v. 2)
《警世通言》，杨曙辉(Yang，Shuhui)，杨韵琴(Yang，Yunqin)合译.

17. Stories to awaken the world/compiled [and authored] by Feng Menglong；translated by Shuhui Yang and Yunqin Yang. Seattle：University of Washington Press，c2009. xxvi，964 p.；24cm. ISBN：0295989037，0295989033. (A Ming dynasty collection；v. 3)
《醒世恒言》，杨曙辉(Yang，Shuhui)，杨韵琴(Yang，Yunqin)合译.

(1) 长沙：岳麓书社，2010. 5 册(62，2589 页)：图；24cm. ISBN：7807614678. (大中华文库)

(2) First paperback edition. Seattle：University of Washington Press，2014. xxvi，964 pages；24cm. ISBN：0295993713，0295993715. (A Ming dynasty collection；v. 3)

18. The oil vendor and the courtesan：tales from the Ming Dynasty/Feng Menglong；translated by Ted Wang and Chen Chen；introduction by Teresa Chi-ching Sun. New York：Welcome Rain，2007. xvi，260 pages：illustrations；23cm. ISBN：1566491398，1566491396，1566491401，1566491402
Wang，Ted.；Chen，Chen(1939—)合译. 收录明代冯梦龙的 8 篇小说.

19. Feng Menglong's treasury of laughs：a seventeenth-century anthology of traditional Chinese humour/by Hsu Pi-ching. Boston：Brill，2015. xi，358 pages；25cm. ISBN：9004293229，9004293236，9004293236，900429323X.

(Emotions and states of mind in East Asia；5)

Hsu, Pi-Ching 著. 包括对冯梦龙(1574—1646)《笑府》的英译.

20. Sanyan stories：favorites from a Ming Dynasty collection/collected by Feng Menglong；translated by Shuhui Yang and Yunqin Yang. Seattle；London：University of Washington Press，［2015］. xiv，230 pages；23cm. ISBN：0295994222，0295994223

Contents：Jiang Xingge reencounters his pearl shirt—Yang Siwen meets an old acquaintance in Yanshan—Yu Boya smashes his zither in gratitude to an appreciative friend—Judge Bao solves a case through a ghost that appeared thrice—Madame White is kept forever under thunder peak tower—Du Shiniang sinks her jewel box in anger—The oil-peddler wins the queen of flowers—The leather boot as evidence against the God Erlang's impostor—Over fifteen strings of cash, a jest leads to dire disasters.

《三言故事》，杨曙辉(Yang, Shuhui)，杨韵琴(Yang, Yunqin)合译.

21. Instruction stories to enlighten the world：instruction stories to enlighten the world/ Feng Menglong；Wang Guozhen. 北京：五洲传播出版社，2017. 208 页：图；22cm. ISBN：7508535296.(中国经典名著故事)

《喻世明言故事》，王国振改编.

22. Stories enlightening the world：stories enlightening the world/Feng Menglong；Wang Guozhen. 北京：五洲传播出版社，2017. 272 页：图；22cm. ISBN：7508535258.(中国经典名著故事)

《警世通言故事》，王国振译.

23. Stories to awaken the world：stories to awaken the world/ Feng Menglong；Wang Guozhen. 北京：五洲传播出版社，2017. 211 页：图；22cm. ISBN：7508535289.(中国经典名著故事)

《醒世恒言故事》，王国振译.

24. Lieh-kuo chih：the annals of the feudal states of Chou/translated from the Chinese by Fredrik Schjöth. ［Olso，Norway］：［F. Schjöth］，1928. 228 leaves；33cm.

《东周列国志》，Schjöth，Fredrik(1846—)译.

25. 东周列国志/中文改写、英文翻译胡志挥. 北京：中译出版社，2015. 377 页；21cm. ISBN：7500140870.(中译经典文库·中华传统文化精粹)

英文题名：Stories from China's warring states.

26. 东周列国故事选＝Stories from China's Warring States/胡志挥改写；胡志挥翻译. 北京：北京大学出版社，1999. 12，385 pages；20cm. ISBN：7301037538，7301037539.(汉英对照古典名著丛书＝Chinese-English classics series)

英汉对照.

凌蒙初(1580—1644)

1. The lecherous academician & other tales by Master Ling Mengchu, translated from the Chinese by John Scott. London, Deutsch ［1973］. 176 p.；21cm. ISBN：085391186X，0853911869

Contents：Lazy dragon the master thief. —The miraculous recovery. —The lecherous academician. —The merchant and the fox.

凌蒙初 4 个故事选译. Scott，John 译.

2. Amazing tales/by Ling Mengchu. Beijing：Foreign Languages Press，2005. 2 v.；ill. ISBN：7119033514 (v. 1)，7119033518(v. 1)，7119033352 (v. 2)，7119033358 (v. 2). (Panda Books)

Contents：v. 1：First series translated by Wen Jingen—v. 2：Second series translated by Perry W. Ma.

《初刻拍案惊奇：英文》，温晋根，马文谦译. 外文出版社(熊猫丛书). 本书为选集，第一册收录 18 个故事；第二册收录 19 个故事.

3. 二刻拍案惊奇/凌蒙初著；李子亮译. 北京：高等教育出版社，2008.4 册 (49，1864 页)：图；24cm. ISBN：7040175004.(大中华文库)

英文题名：Amazing tales. 英汉对照.

4. Amazing tales second series/Ling Mengchu；Wang Guozhen. 北京：五洲传播出版社，2017. 210 页：图；22cm. ISBN：7508535241.(中国经典名著故事)

《二刻拍案惊奇故事》，王国振译.

5. Amazing tales/Ling Mengchu；Wang Guozhen. 北京：五洲传播出版社，2017. 245 页：图；22cm. ISBN：7508535234.(中国经典名著故事)

《初刻拍案惊奇故事》，王国振译.

《古今奇观》

1. Leaves from my Chinese scrapbook/by Frederic Henry Balfour. London，Trübner，1887. 215 p.；22cm. (Trübner's oriental series)

《古今奇观》选译. Balfour，Frederic Henry 著.

2. The inconstancy of Madam Chuang, and other stories from the Chinese；translated by E. B. Howell. With twelve illustrations by a native artist. Shanghai ［etc.］ Kelly & Walsh limited ［19—］. vii，259 p. front.，plates.；22cm.

Contents：Translator's note. —The inconstancy of Madam Chuang. —The minister, the lute, and the woodcutter. —The diplomacy of Li T'ai-po. —The wonderful adventure of Li，duke of Ch'ien. —The judgment of magistrate T'eng. —Marriage by proxy.

《今古奇观》(选译)，Howell，Edward Butts(1879—)译.

(1) London，T. W. Laurie ［1924］. vii，259p. front.，plates. 22cm.

3. The restitution of the bride and other stories from the Chinese, translated by E. Butts Howell. With illustrations by a native artist. London，T. W. Laurie, Ltd. ［1926］. vii，247 p. col. front. ，plates. ；23cm.

Contents：Translator's note. —The restitution of the bride. —The infant courtier. —The luck of Jo-Hsu. —The courtesan. —The luckless graduate. —The sacrifice of Yang Chiao-ai.

《今古奇观》（选译），Howell，Edward Butts（1879—）译. 译自《今古奇观》中的 6 篇.

(1) New York：Brentano's ［c1926］. vii，247 p. col. front. ，plates. ；22cm.

《龙图公案》

1. The strange cases of Magistrate Pao：Chinese tales of crime and detection/translated from the Chinese and retold by Leon Comber；Illus. by Lo Koon-chiu. Rutland，Vt. ，C. E. Tuttle Co. ［1964］. 137 p. illus. ，facsim. ；22cm.

Contents：The case of the passionate monk. —The net of heaven. —The dream of the goddess of mercy. —The key. —The temple by the river. —The stolen slippers.

《龙图公案》，Comber，Leon 译.

(1)London，Panther，1970. 112 p. illus. ；18cm. ISBN：0586033416，0586033418. (Panther crime)

(2)Singapore：Talisman，2010. 120 p. ：ill. ；21cm. ISBN：9810845674；9810845677

《好逑传》（创作于明清二代，流行于清代，具体成书时间不详）

1. Shueypingsin：a story made from the Chinese romance Haoukewchuen/by an Englishman. London：K. Paul，Trench，Trüber & Co. ，1899. vi，97 pages.

《好逑传》，Davis，John Francis（1795—1890）译.

(1)［S. l.］：British Library，Historic，［2011］. ISBN：1241169926. 1241169923

2. The fortunate union. London，K. Paul，Trench，Trübner，& co. ，limited，1900. 2 p. l. ，59 p. ；25×19cm.

《好逑传》，Douglas，Robert K. （Robert Kennaway，Sir，1838—1913）译.

3. The fortunate union... Shanghai，American Presbyterian Mission Press，1904. 3 p. l. ，ii，260 p. ；25cm.

《好逑传》，鲍康宁（Baller，F. W. 〈Frederick William〉，1852—1922）译.

4. The breeze in the moonlight，"The second book of genius，" translated from the Chinese by George Soulié de Morant，and done into English by H. Bedford-Jones. New York and London，G. P. Putnam's Sosns，1926. xviii，371 p. incl. front. ，plates；20cm.

《好逑传》，苏利叶·德·莫朗（Soulié de Morant，G.

〈Georges〉，1878—1955）（法国汉学家）法译；Bedford-Jones，H. （Henry，1887—1949）从法译本转译成英语.

清代

陈忱（1615—约 1670）

1. The margins of utopia：Shui-hu hou-chuan and the literature of Ming loyalism/Ellen Widmer. Cambridge，Mass. ：Council on East Asian Studies，Harvard University：Distributed by Harvard University Press，1987. xiii，324 p. ：ill. ；24cm. ISBN：0674548477. (Harvard East Asian monographs；128)

Widmer，Ellen 著. 翻译了陈忱的《水浒后传》.

余怀（1616—1696）

1. A feast of mist and flowers；the gay quarters of Nanking at the end of the Ming. Annotated translation by Howard S. Levy. Yokohama，Japan，1966. 171 p. ；31cm.

《板桥杂记》，Levy，Howard S. （Howard Seymour，1923—）译.

蒲松龄（1640—1715）

1. Strange stories from a Chinese studio，translated and annotated by Herbert A. Giles. 2nd ed. ，rev. Shanghai，Kelly & Walsh，1908. xxiii，490 p. ；20cm.

《聊斋选译》，翟理斯（Giles，Herbert Allen，1845—1935）（英国汉学家）编译. 1880 年初版于伦敦. 收录 164 篇故事.

(1)3rd ed. ，rev. Shanghai（etc. ），Kelly & Walsh，limited，1916. xxiii，488 p. ；20cm.

(2) New York：Dover Publications ［1969］. xxiii，488 p. ；22cm. SBN 0486223957

(3)Strange tales from a Chinese studio/The Herbert A. Giles translation of Songling Pu's masterpiece with a new foreword by Victoria Cass. North Clarendon，Vt. ：Tuttle Pub. ，c2010.. 447 p. ；20cm. ISBN：0804841382

2. Strange stories from the lodge of leisures. Boston，New York：Houghton Mifflin Company，1913. xiv，166 p. ；18cm.

《聊斋志异》，乔治·苏利埃·德·莫朗（Soulié de Morant，G. 〈Georges〉，1878—1955）（法国汉学家）译，收录 25 篇故事. 采取了意译的方法，有些篇目对原文改动极大.

3. Some more stories from the Liao Chai Chih I/translated by James N. Y. Pai. Shanghai：Chung Hwa Book Co. ，1937. 65 pages；19cm. (Students' English library；；18)

《聊斋志异》选译，白硒逸译. 英汉对照. 中华书局.

4. Chinese ghost and love stories/P'u Sung-ling；sel. and transl. from the Chinese by Rose Quong；with introduction by Martin Buber. New York：Pantheon，1946. 329 p. ；21cm.

《聊斋》选译，Quong，Rose 译.

（1）London：Dobson，1947. 323 pages：illustrations；21cm.

（2）New York：Pantheon，1975. 329 pages：illustrations.

5. Selected tales of Liaozhai/Pu Songling. Beijing，China：Chinese Literature：［Zhongguo guo ji shu dian fa xing］，1981. 151 p.；19cm.（Panda books）

《聊斋志异选》，杨宪益（1915—2009），戴乃迭（Yang，Gladys，1919—1999）译.

6. Strange tales from make-do studio/by Pu Songling；translated by Denis C. ＆ Victor H. Mair. Beijing：Foreign Languages Press：Distributed by China Publications Centre（Guoji Shudian），1989. xiii，446 pages：illustrations；19cm. ISBN：0835122565，0835122566，711900977X，7119009773

《聊斋志异选》，丹尼斯·马尔，梅维恒合译.

（1）北京市：外文出版社，2000. 623 pages；13cm. ISBN：7119026917，7119026916，7119025244，7119025247. （FLP 汉英对照经典读本. 古典精华；3FLP）

7. Strange tales from the Liaozhai studio/translators Zhang Qingnian，Zhang Ciyun，Yang Yi. Beijing：People's China Pub. House，1997. 3 v.：ill.；21cm. （Chinese classics）

《聊斋志异》，Zhang，Qingnian. ，Zhang，Ciyun. ，Yang，Yi 合译.

8. Liao zhai zhi yi xuan/Pu Songling zhu；Dannisi Ma'er，Weikeduo Ma'er yi；translated by Denis C. ＆ Victor H. Mair. Beijing：Wai wen chu ban she，2000. 623 p.；13cm. ISBN：7119026917，7119025247. （FLP Han Ying dui zhao jing dian du ben. Gu dian jing hua；3）

《聊斋志异》（选译），丹尼斯·马尔（Mair，Denis C.），梅维恒（Mair，Victor H.，1943—）合译.

（1）Beijing：Wai wen chu ban she，2001. 449 p.；21cm. ISBN：7119028995.（Echo of classics＝经典的回声）

9. 聊斋精选：图文本/汉英对照/马德五编著. 上海：上海世界图书出版公司，2005. 218 页；19cm. ISBN：7506274868
英文题名：Selections from Liao zhai.

10. Strange tales from a Chinese studio/Songling Pu；translated and edited by John Minford. London：Penguin，2006. xxxviii，562 p.：ill. ，maps；20cm. ISBN：0140447408，0140447407.（Penguin classics）

《聊斋志异》，闵福德（Minford，John. ，1946—）（英国汉学家）译.

11. Strange tales from Liaozhai/Pu Songling；translated and annotated by Sidney L. Sondergard；Illustrations by Ben Grant...［et al.］. Fremont，Calif.：Jain Pub.，c2008. v. 〈1〉：ill.；23cm. ISBN：0895810014（vol. 1）

《聊斋志异》，Sondergard，Sidney L. 译.

12. 聊斋志异/蒲松龄原著，宋德利编译. 北京：中国书籍出版社，2008. 431 页；23cm. ISBN：7506817264，

7506817268.（中国名著海外译丛）
英文题名：Strange tales of a lonely studio.

13. The bonds of matrimony＝Hsing-shih yin-yüan chuan/translated by Eve Alison Nyren. Lewiston，N. Y.：E. Mellen Press，1995. xx，290 pages；24cm. ISBN：0773490337，0773490338，0889460760（series），0889460768（series）.（Chinese studies；v. 1）

《醒世姻缘传》，Nyren，Eve Alison(1954—)译，只翻译了该书的前 20 章.

李渔（1611—1680）

1. Jou pu tuan；the prayer mat of flesh. Translated by Richard Martin from the German version by Franz Kuhn. New York：Grove Press ［1963］. 376 p. illus. 22cm.

《肉蒲团》，Martin ，Richard 译自德语版.

（1）New York：Grove Press ［1967］. 376 p. illus. 22cm.

2. The before midnight scholar（Jou Pu Tuan）［by］Li Yu；translated by Richard Martin from the German version by Franz Kuhn. London，Corgi，1967. 347 p.；18cm. （A Corgi book，EN7790）

《肉蒲团》，Martin，Richard 译自德语版.

3. The carnal prayer mat/Li Yu；translated，with an introduction and notes，by Patrick Hanan. New York：Ballantine Books，1990. xiv，316 p.；21cm. ISBN：0345365089

《肉蒲团》，韩南（Hanan，Patrick）（新西兰裔汉学家）译.

（1）Honolulu：University of Hawaii Press，1996. xiv，316 p.；22cm. ISBN：0824817982

4. Twelve towers：short stories/by Li Yü；retold by Nathan Mao. 2nd rev. ed. Hong Kong：Chinese University Press；Seattle：distributed by the University of Washington Press，1979. xxxvi，149 p.；23cm. ISBN：9622011705，9622011713

《十二楼》，Mao，Nathan K. 译.

天花藏主人（明末清初人）

1. The drunken Buddha ［translated by］ Ian Fairweather. ［Brisbane］：University of Queensland Press ［1965］. 161 p. col. illus. 25cm.
Notes：Translation of the 1894 ed. with title：Tsui p'u t'i ch'üan chuan.

《醉菩提全传》，Fairweather，Ian(1891—1974)译.

邢上蒙人（匿名）

1. Courtesans and opium：romantic illusions of the fool of Yangzhou/Anonymous；translated by Patrick Hanan. New York：Columbia University Press，c2009. xiii，328 p.；22cm. ISBN：0231148221，0231148224.（Weatherhead books on Asia）

《风月梦》，韩南（Hanan，Patrick）（新西兰裔汉学家）译.

吴敬梓（1701—1754）

1. The scholars. ［Translated by Yang Hsien-yi and Gladys

Yang. Author's port. and illus. by Cheng Shih-fa]. Peking: Foreign Languages Press, 1957. 721 p. plates, col. port. 22cm.

《儒林外史》，杨宪益（1915—2009），戴乃迭（Yang, Gladys,1919—1999）

(1) New York: Grosset and Dunlap [1972]. 692 p. illus. 21cm. ISBN: 0448002639. (Grosset's universal library, UL 263)

(2) 3rd ed. Peking: Foreign Languages Press, 1973. 8, 607 p. illus. 22cm.

(3) New York: Columbia University Press, 1992. 692 p., [20] leaves of plates: ill.; 22cm. ISBN: 0231081529, 0231081537

2. The scholars/Wu Jingzi; Wang Guozhen. 北京:五洲传播出版社,2017. 285 页:图;22cm. ISBN:7508535272.(中国经典名著故事)

《儒林外史故事》，王国振译.

《红楼梦》，曹雪芹（1715—1763）

1. Hung lou mêng; or, The dream of the red chamber; a Chinese novel. Translated by H. Bencraft Joly. Hongkong, Kelly & Walsh, 1892—⟨1893⟩. v. ⟨1—2⟩ 24cm.

《红楼梦》，Joly，H. Bencraft（曾任英国驻澳门副领事）译. 翻译前 56 回.

(1) Doylestown, Pa.: Wildside Press, 2004. 2 volumes; 24cm. ISBN: 0809592685, 0809592681, 0809592692, 080959269X

(2) The dream of the red chamber/written by Cao Xueqin; translated by H. Bencraft Joly; with a new foreword by John Minford and a new introduction by Edwin Lowe. North Clarendon, Vt.; Tokyo: Tuttle Pub., 2010. xxiv, 966 p.; 21cm. ISBN: 0804840965, 0804840962. (Tuttle classics)

2. Dream of the red chamber/by Tsao Hsueh-chin and Kao Ngoh; translated and adapted from the Chinese by Chi-chen Wang; with a preface by Arthur Waley. London: G. Routledge, [1929]. xvii, 371 p.: ill.; 19cm.

《红楼梦》（节译），王际真（Wang, Chi-Chen, 1899—2001）（美国华裔学者）译.

(1) Garden City, N. Y., Doubleday, 1929. xxvii,371 p.; 22cm.

(2) Garden City, N. Y., Doubleday [c1958]. xx, 329 p. 18cm. (Doubleday anchor books, A159).

(3) New York: Twayne Publishers [1958]. xxiv, 574 p.; 22cm.

(4) New York: Amereon House, 1958. xx, 329 pages; 18cm.

(5) Garden City, N. Y.: Doubleday Anchor Books, 1958. 329 pages. (A Doubleday anchor book)

(6) London: Vision Press, 1959. xxiv, 574 pages; 22cm.

(7) London: Vision, 1960. 1 volume. ISBN:0854781900, 0854781904

(8) [London]: Vision, 1968. xxiv, 574 pages; 22cm.

(9) [London]: Vision, 1972. 574 p.

(10) Taipei, Taiwan: Huang Chia, 1980. xxiv, 574 pages; 21cm.

(11) Singapore: Graham Brash, 1983. ix, 574 pages; 22cm. ISBN: 9812180060, 9812180063

(12) Abridged Anchor Books ed. New York: Anchor Books, 1989,xx, 329 p.;18cm. ISBN:0385093799, 0385093798

3. The dream of the red chamber = Hong lou meng: a Chinese novel of the early Ching period/[English translation by Florence and Isabel McHugh]. New York: Pantheon Books, 1958. xxi, 582 pages: illustrations; 24cm.

《红楼梦》（节译），McHugh, Florence. ,McHugh, Isabel 英译. 两位麦克休为姐妹. 该书是从德国著名汉学家、翻译家库恩（Franz Kuhn）的《红楼梦》德译本（1951 年版）转译过来的，涵盖了原译六分之五的内容.

(1) Routledge & K. Paul, 1958. 582 pages: illustrations; 24cm.

(2) Taipei, Taiwan: 北一出版社, 1967. xix, 582 pages: illustrations; 21cm.

(3) New York: Grosset & Dunlap, 1968. xxi, 582 pages: illustrations; 21cm. ISBN: 0448002264, 0448002262. (Universal Library; 226)

(4) Westport, Conn.: Greenwood Press, 1975. xxi, 582 pages: illustrations; 22cm. ISBN: 0837181135, 0837181134

(5) 台北市: 文星书店, 1977. xxi, 582 pages: illustrations; 20cm. (Chinese classics in English; 1)

(6) Taipei: Tun-huang Shu Chū Ku Fen Yu Hsien Kung Szǔ, 1980. xxi, 582 pages: illustrations; 22cm. (Chinese classics series in English)

4. The story of the stone: a Chinese novel in five volumes/by Cao Xueqin; translated by David Hawkes. London; New York: Penguin, 1973—1986. 5 volumes: genealogical tables;19cm. ISBN:0140442936 (v. 1), 0140442939 (v. 1), 0140443264 (v. 2), 0140443266 (v. 2), 0140443707 (v. 3), 0140443703 (v. 3), 0140443714 (v. 4), 0140443711 (v. 4), 0140443721 (v. 5), 014044372X (v. 5). (Penguin classics)
Contents: v. 1. The golden days—v. 2. The Crab-flower Club—v. 3. The warning voice—v. 4. The debt of tears—v. 5. The dreamer wakes.

《石头记》，霍克斯（Hawkes David，1923—2009）译.

5. The story of the stone: a novel in five volumes/by Cao Xueqin; translated by David Hawkes. Bloomington: Indiana University Press, 1979—1987. 5 volumes; 24cm.

ISBN：0253192668 （set），025329266X，0253192660
(set)，0253192617（v. 1），0253192615（v. 1），0253192625
(v. 2)，0253192622（v. 2），0253192633（v. 3），0253192639
(v. 3)，0253192641(v. 4)，0253192646(v. 4)，025319265X
(v. 5)，0253192653(v. 5). (Chinese literature in translation)
Contents：v. 1. The golden days.—v. 2. The Crab-Flower
Club.—v. 3. The warning voice.—v. 4. The debt of
tears.—v. 5. The dreamer wakes.
《石头记》，霍克斯(Hawkes David，1923—2009)译.

6. The story of the stone：a Chinese novel in five volumes/by
Cao Xueqin；translated by David Hawkes. Taipei：Caves
Books，1979—1988. 5 volumes；20×22cm.（Chinese
literature in translation)
Contents：V. 1. The golden days—v. 2. The Crab-
Flower Club—v. 3. The warning voice—v. 4. The debt
of tears—v. 5. The dreamer wakes
《石头记》，霍克斯(Hawkes David，1923—2009)译.

7. Selected readings from the story of the stone：a bilingual
version/Cao Xueqin；translated by David Hawkes and
John Minford；compiled and edited by John Minford.
United States：Columbia Univ Pr.，2006. 500 pages.
ISBN：9629960656；9629960650
《石头记》(节译)，霍克斯(Hawkes David，1923—2009)
译.

8. The story of the stone：a Chinese novel by Cao Xueqin/
translated by David Hawkes；collated by Fan Shengyu.
Shanghai：Shanghai Foreign Language Education Pres，
2014. 5 volumes. ISBN：7544636636(set)
《石头记》，(英)霍克斯译.

9. A dream of red mansions/Tsao Hsueh-chin and Kao Ngo；
［translated by Yang Hsien-yi and Gladys Yang；
illustrated by Tai Tun-pang]. Peking：Foreign Languages
Press，1978—1980. 3 volumes：color illustrations；
22cm. ISBN：7119016431（v. 1），7119016436（v. 1），
7119015478（v. 2），7119015477（v. 2），7119015486（v.
3），7119015484（v. 3）
《红楼梦》，杨宪益(1915—2009)，戴乃迭(Yang, Gladys，
1919—1999)译；戴敦邦插图.
(1)Beijing：Foreign Languages Press，1994. 3 volumes；
   18cm. ISBN：7119006436（set）；7119006437（set）
(2)Amsterdam, the Netherlands：Fredonia Books，2001.
   3 volumes：illustrations；21cm. ISBN：1589635221，
   1589635227，1589635329，1589635326，1589635736，
   1589635739

10. A dream of red mansions：an abridged version＝［Hong
   lou meng]/written by Tsao Hsueh-chin and Kao Ngo；
   translated by Yang Hsien-yi and Gladys Yang. Hong
   Kong：Commercial Press，c1986. iv, 499 p. : ill. ；
   21cm. ISBN：9620710681，9620710681

《红楼梦》(节译)，杨宪益(1915—2009)，戴乃迭(Yang，
Gladys，1919—1999)译.
(1)Sydney：Unwin Paperbacks，1986. iv, 499 pages：
   illustrations；22cm. ISBN：004820028X，0048200280
(2)Singapore：Asiapac Books ＆ Educational Aids；Hong
   Kong：Commercial Press，1986. iv, 499 pages：
   illustrations；22cm. ISBN：9971985012，9971985011
(3)Hong Kong：Commercial Press；Boston：Zheng ＆
   Zui Co.，1992. iv, 499 pages：illustrations；22cm.
   ISBN：0887271782，0887271786

11. A dream of red mansions/written by Cao Xueqin and Gao
   E；translated by Yangxianyi and Gladys Yang. Beijing：
   Wai wen chu ban she，2003. 6 v.（3575 p.）：ill.；
   21cm. ISBN：7119032186（set），7119032184（set）.
   (Library of Chinese and English classics〈Chinese-
   English〉＝汉英经典文库)
   《红楼梦》，杨宪益(1915—2009)，戴乃迭(Yang, Gladys，
   1919—1999)译.

12. Story of the stone：from Dream of the red chamber by
   Cao Xueqin/illustrated and interpreted by Linda Ching.
   Berkeley, Calif. : Ten Speed Press，c1998. 135 p. : col.
   ill. ； 26cm. ISBN：1580080278，1580080279，
   1580080189，1580080187
   《石头记》(节译)，Ching, Linda 译绘.

13. A dream in red mansions：saga of a noble Chinese
   family/written by Cao Xueqin；Simplified by Huang
   Xingu. Beijing：Foreign Language Teaching and
   Research，1991. 457 pages；18cm. ISBN：7560007767，
   7560007762
   《红楼梦:英文压缩本》，黄新渠编译. 外语教学与出
   版社.

14. A dream of red mansions＝［Hong lou meng]：saga of a
   noble Chinese family/written by Cao Xueqin and Gao E；
   translated by Huang Xinqu. Abridged version. San
   Francisco, CA：Purple Bamboo Pub.，c1994. xi, 298
   p. ；23cm.
   《红楼梦》(节译)，黄新渠译.

15. The red chamber dream：Hung lou meng/translated by
   B. S. Bonsall. ［Place of publication not identified]：
   [publisher not identified]，1950s. 5 volumes；30cm.
   《红楼梦》，邦斯尔神父(Bonsall, Bramwell Seaton)(英国
   人)译. 120 回全译. 该书目前尚未正式出版,译稿存于香
   港大学.

袁枚(1716—1798)

1. Censored by Confucius：ghost stories by Yuan Mei/edited
   and translated with an introduction by Kam Louie and
   Louise Edwards. Armonk, N. Y.；London, Eng. : M.
   E. Sharpe，c1996. xxxv, 223 p. : ill. ；24cm. ISBN：
   1563246805，1563246813. (New studies in Asian culture)

《子不语》，Louie，Kam 和 Edwards，Louise P. 编译.

纪昀(1724—1805)

1. Real life in China at the height of empire：revealed by the ghosts of Ji Xiaolan/edited & translated by David E. Pollard. Hong Kong：Chinese University Press，2014. xl，334 pages：illustrations (some color)；23cm. ISBN：9629966010，9629966018

《阅微草堂笔记》，Pollard，David E. 译.

李汝珍(约 1763—1830)

1. Flowers in the mirror ［by］ Li Ju-chên. Translated and edited by Lin Tai-yi. London，P. Owen ［1965］. 310 p.；22cm. (Unesco collection of representative works：Chinese series)

《镜花缘》，林太乙(Lin，Tai-yi，1926—)编译.

(1) Berkeley，University of California Press，1965. 310 p.；24cm.

《蜃楼志》

1. Mirage /canonymous；translated by Patrick Hanan. Hong Kong：The Chinese University Press，2014. xv，371 pages；24cm. ISBN：9629965815，962996581X

《蜃楼志全传》，庾岭劳人著；韩南(Hanan，Patrick)(新西兰裔汉学家)译.

《隔帘花影》

1. Ko lien hua ying：flower shadows behind the curtain；a sequel to "Chin p'ing mei"/translated by Vladimir Kean from Franz Kuhn's German version of the original Chinese. London：Bodley Head，1959. 432 pages；23cm. Notes：Chinese original，a rehashed version of Ding Yaokang's Xu Jin ping mei. Attributed to Siqiaojushi. Cf. Sun Kaidi. Zhongguo tong su xiao shuo shu mu.

《隔帘花影》，Kuhn，Franz(1889—1961)译成德文；Kean，Vladimir 自德文版译成英语.

(1) London：New English Library，1963. 380 pages；18cm. (Four square classics)

《七侠五义》

1. The seven heroes and five gallants/by Shi Yukun and Yu Yue；translated by Song Shouquan；English text edited by Esther Samson and Lance Samson. Beijing，China：Foreign Languages Press，2005. 30，21，463 pages：illustrations；20cm. ISBN：7119033549，7119033549. (Panda Books)

《七侠五义：英文》，(清)石玉昆，(清)俞樾著；宋绶荃译. 外文出版社(熊猫丛书)

2. 七侠五义/石玉昆，俞樾著；宋绶荃译. 北京：外文出版社，2010.3 册(49 页，1697 页)；24cm. ISBN：7119067445. (大中华文库：汉英对照)

英文题名：Seven heroes and five gallants.

何梦梅(约 1821 年在世)

1. The rambles of the Emperor Ching Tĭh in Këang Nan. A

Chinese tale. London，Longman，Brown，Green，& Longmans，1843. 2 v. 20cm.

《大明正德皇游江南传》，理雅各(Legge，James，1815—1897)(英国汉学家)译.

王韬(1828—1897)

1. Wang T'ao (1828—? 1890)：the life and writings of a displaced person/by H. McAleavy；with a translation of Mei-Li Hsiao Chuan，a short story by Wang T'ao. London：China Society，1953. 39 pages，［1］ leaf of plates：illustrations；22cm. (China Society occasional papers/edited by S. Howard Hansford；no. 7)

McAleavy，Henry 著. 翻译了王韬的《媚黎小传》.

刘鹗(1857—1909)

1. A nun of Taishan and other translations/translated by Lin Yutang. Shanghai：Commerical Press，1925. x，272 pages；19cm.

《泰山的尼姑》(《老残游记》二集)，林语堂(1895—1976)译. 翻译《老残游记》二集六回.

(1) Shanghai，China，The Commercial Press，Limited，1936. x p.，1 l.，272 p.；19cm.

2. Tramp doctor's travelogue/English version by Lin Yi-chin and Ko Te-shun，with a foreward by G. N. Ling. ［Shanghai］ China，The Commercial Press，Ltd.，1939. vi p.，1 l.，263 p.；19cm.

《行医见闻》(《老残游记》)，林疑今(Lin，I-chin)，葛德顺(Ko，Tê-shun)译.

3. The travels of Lao Ts'an/by Lui T'ieh-yün (Liu E)；translated from the Chinese and annotated by Harold Shadick. Taipei：Bk World Co.，1939. xxiii，277 pages；20cm.

《老残游记》，谢迪克(Shadick，Harold)(美国汉学家)译. 该书翻译了《老残游记》初集 20 回.

(1)Ithaca，Cornell University Press ［1952］. xxiii，277 p. illus.；24cm.

(2)［Taipei，Taiwan］：［Book World Co.］，1960s. xxiii，277 pages：illustrations，map；19cm. (Chinese classics in English；8)

(3)Ithaca：Cornell University Press，1966. xxiii，277 pages：illustrations；22cm.

(4)Ithaca：Cornell University Press，1971. xxiii，277 pages：illustrations；22cm.

(5)Westport，Conn.：Greenwood Press，1986，c1952. xxiii，277 p.：ill.，map；23cm. ISBN：0313251649，0313251641

(6)Columbia University Press Morningside ed. New York：Columbia University Press，1990. xxxv，283 p.：ill.，map；21cm. ISBN：0231072554，0231072557. (Modern Asian literature series)

(7)Shanghai：Yi lin chu ban she，2015. 2 volumes；

23cm. ISBN：7544743075，7544743071.（双语译林；
壹力文库）

4. Mr. Decadent：notes taken in an outing/by Liu T'ieh-
yün；translated into English by Yang Hsien-yi. Hong
Kong：[Tu Li Shu Tien]，1947. 319 pages；19cm.

《老残游记》，杨宪益（1915—2009）译. 英汉对照.

5. Mr. Derelict/Liu Ngo；translated by H. Y. Yang and G.
M. Tayler. London：G. Allen & Unwin，1948. 167
pages；19cm.

《老残游记》，杨宪益（1915—2009）译.

6. The travels of Lao Can/Liu E；translated by Yang Xianyi
and Gladys Yang. 1st ed. Beijing，China：Chinese
Literature：Distributed by China Publications Centre，
1983. 176 p.；18cm. ISBN：0835110753，0835110754.
（Panda books）

《老残游记》，杨宪益（1915—2009），戴乃迭（Yang,
Gladys，1919—1999）译.

（1）Honolulu，Hawaii：University Press of the Pacific，
2001. 176 pages；21cm.

（2）Beijing：Foreign Languages Press，2005. 8，165
pages；21cm. ISBN：7119033530，711903353.
（Panda books）

（3）[Rockville，Md.]：Silk Pagoda，2007. 132 pages；
23cm. ISBN：1596543809，1596543805

韩邦庆（1856—1894）

1. The sing-song girls of Shanghai/Han Bangqing；first
translated by Eileen Chang；revised and edited by Eva
Hung. New York：Columbia University Press，c2005.
xxviii，554 p.：ill.，map；24cm. ISBN：0231122683，
0231122689 0231122696，0231122691.（Weatherhead
books on Asia）

《海上花列传》，张爱玲（1920—1995）译；孔慧怡（Hung,
Eva）（中国香港学者）修订.

吴趼人（1866—1910）

1. Vignettes from the late Ch'ing：bizarre happenings eye
witnessed over two decades/Wu Wo-Yao；translated with
an introduction by Shih Shun Liu. Shatin，Hong Kong：
Chinese University of Hong Kong，c1975. xv，411 p.：
ill.；22cm. ISBN：0870751255

《二十年目睹之怪现状》

2. The sea of regret：two turn-of-the-century Chinese
romantic novels/translated by Patrick Hanan. Honolulu：
University of Hawaii Press，c1995. ix，205 p.；23cm.
ISBN：0824816668，0824817095

Contents：Stones in the sea/by Fu Lin—The sea of
regret/by Wu Jianren.

《禽海石》《恨海》，吴趼人，符霖（晚晴小说家，生卒年不
详）；韩南（Hanan，Patrick）（新西兰裔汉学家）译.

李伯元（1867—1906）

1. Modern times：a brief history of the enlightenment/by Li
Boyuan；translated by Douglas Lancashire. Hong Kong：
Research Centre for Translation，Chinese University of Hong
Kong，1996. 522 p.：ill.；24cm. ISBN：9627255165，
9627255161.（A Renditions book）

《文明小史》，Lancashire，Douglas（1926—）译. 长篇小
说.

《狄公案》系列

1. Dee goong an. Three murder cases solved by Judge Dee，
[Tokyo] 1949. xxiii，237 p. plates.；22cm.

《狄公案》（又名《武则天四大奇案》）（选译），高罗佩
（Gulik，Robert Hans van，1910—1967）（荷兰汉学家）译.

（1）New York：Arno Press，1976，c1949. iv，xxiii，237 p.，
[8] leaves of plates：ill.；24cm. ISBN：0405078757.
（Literature of mystery and detection）

2. The Chinese maze murders；a Chinese detective story
suggested by three original ancient Chinese plots. With
19 plates drawn by the author in Chinese style. The
Hague，W. Van Hoeve，1956. 322 p. illus.；21cm.（A
Judge Dee mystery）

《迷宫案》，高罗佩（Gulik，Robert Hans van，1910—1967）
（荷兰汉学家）翻译并创作.

（1）University of Chicago Press ed. Chicago，Ill.：
University of Chicago Press，1997. xiii，321 p.：
ill.；18cm. ISBN：0226848787.（A Judge Dee
mystery）

3. The Chinese bell murders；London，M. Joseph [1958].
287 p. illus.；20cm.

《狄公案之铜钟案》，高罗佩（Gulik，Robert Hans van，
1910—1967）（荷兰汉学家）翻译并创作.

（1）The Chinese bell murders；three cases solved by Judge
Dee. A Chinese detective story suggested by three
original Chinese plots. With 15 plates drawn by the
author in Chinese style. 1st American ed. New York：
Harper [1959，c1958] 262 p. illus.；22cm.（A Judge
Dee mystery）

4. The Chinese gold murders. London，M. Joseph [1959].
221 p. illus.；20cm.

《狄公案之黄金案》，高罗佩（Gulik，Robert Hans van，
1910—1967）（荷兰汉学家）翻译并创作.

（1）The Chinese gold murders，a Chinese detective story.
With 10 plates drawn by the author in Chinese style.
[1st American ed.] New York：Harper [1961]. 202 p.
illus.；22cm.（A Judge Dee mystery）

（2）Bath，Lythway Press Ltd.，1971. 222 p. illus. 19cm.
ISBN：0850462061

（3）The Chinese gold murders/Robert van Gulik；with an
introd. by Donald F. Lach. Chicago：University of

Chicago Press，1979. ix，214 p. : ill. ; 18cm. ISBN：0226848647

5. The Chinese lake murders; three cases solved by Judge Dee. A Chinese detective story suggested by original ancient Chinese plots. New York：Harper［1960］. 211 p. illus. ; 22cm.

《狄公案之湖滨案》，高罗佩（Gulik, Robert Hans van, 1910—1967)(荷兰汉学家)翻译并创作.

(1)London, M. Joseph［1960］. 270 p. illus. ;19cm.

(2)The Chinese lake murders/Robert van Gulik; with an introd. by Donald F. Lach. Chicago：University of Chicago Press, 1979. viii, 215 p. : ill. ; 18cm. ISBN：0226848655

6. The Chinese nail murders; Judge Dee's last three cases. A Chinese detective story suggested by original ancient Chinese plots. New York：Harper & Row［c1961］. 231 p. ;22cm. (A Judge Dee mystery)

《铁钉案》，高罗佩（Gulik, Robert Hans van, 1910—1967)(荷兰汉学家)翻译并创作.

(1)London, M. Joseph［1961］. 216 p. illus. 20cm.

7. The red pavilion; a Chinese detective story. With six illus. drawn by the author in Chinese style. ［Kuala Lumpur］Art Printing Works, 1961. 199 p. illus. 19cm. (New Judge Dee mysteries)

《红亭记》，高罗佩（Gulik, Robert Hans van, 1910—1967)(荷兰汉学家)翻译并创作.

(1) New York：Scribner［1968］. 173 p. illus. 21cm. (New Judge Dee mysteries)

(2)New York：C. Scribner,［1986］. 173 p. : ill. ; 18cm. ISBN：0684181428. (Scribner crime classics). (A Judge Dee mystery)

(3)The red pavilion: a Judge Dee mystery/by Robert van Gulik, with six illustrations drawn by the author in Chinese style. University of Chicago Press ed. Chicago：University of Chicago Press, 1994. 173 p. : ill. ; 18cm. ISBN：0226848736. (A Judge Dee mystery)

8. The haunted monastery: a Chinese detective story: with eight illustrations drawn by the author in Chinese style/by Robert van Gulik. Kuala Lumpur：Art Print. Work, 1961. 168 p. ; 19cm. (New Judge Dee mysteries)

《朝云观谜案》，高罗佩（Gulik, Robert Hans van, 1910—1967)(荷兰汉学家)翻译并创作.

(1)London, Heinemann［1963］. vii, 159 p. illus. ;19cm.

(2)New York：Scribner［1969］. vii, 159 p. illus., col. plan (on lining papers); 21cm.

(3)Chicago：University of Chicago Press, 1997. 198 p. : ill. ; 18cm. ISBN：0226848795. (Judge Dee mystery)

9. The lacquer screen; a Chinese detective story. With ten illus. drawn by the author in Chinese style. ［Kuala Lumpur, Malaya］Art Print. Works, 1962. 185 p. illus. ; 19cm. (New Judge Dee mysteries)

《四漆屏》，高罗佩（Gulik, Robert Hans van, 1910—1967)(荷兰汉学家)翻译并创作.

(1)London, Heinemann［1964］. vii, 180 p. illus. ;19cm.

(2)New York：Scribner［1970］. vii, 180 p. illus. ; 21cm. (New Judge Dee mysteries)

(3)New York：Garland Pub., 1983. vii, 180 p. : ill. ; 23cm. ISBN：0824049519. (50 classics of crime fiction, 1950—1975)

(4)Chicago：University of Chicago Press, 1992. 180 p. : ill. ; 18cm. ISBN：0226848671. (A Judge Dee mystery)

10. The emperor's pearl：a Chinese detective story/by Robert van Gulik; with eight illus. drawn by the author in Chinese style. London：Heinemann［1963］. 184 p. : ill. ; 19cm.

《御珠案》，高罗佩（Gulik, Robert Hans van, 1910—1967)(荷兰汉学家)翻译并创作.

(1)New York：Scribner［1964］. 184 p. illus. ; 21cm.

(2)New York：Bantam Books, 1965. 150 pages：illustrations；18cm.

(3)London：Heinemann, 1969. 185 pages：illustrations；20cm. ISBN：043482559X, 0434825592

(4)New York：Warner, 1974. 174 pages (8 leaves of plates)：illustrations；18cm.

(5)New York：Scribner, 1981. 150 p. ; 18cm. ISBN：0684173182, 0684173184

(6)Singapore：Brash, 1988. 184 pages. ISBN：9971490625, 9971490621

11. The willow pattern, a Chinese detective story, by Robert van Gulik. With 15 illus. drawn by the author in Chinese style. London, Heinemann［1965］. 183 p. illus. ;19cm.

《柳园图》，高罗佩（Gulik, Robert Hans van, 1910—1967)(荷兰汉学家)翻译并创作.

(1)New York：Scribner［1965］. 183 p. illus. ; 21cm.

(2)University of Chicago Press ed. Chicago：University of Chicago Press, 1993. 183. : ill. ; 18cm. ISBN：0226848752. (Judge Dee mystery)

12. The monkey, and The tiger; London, Heinemann［1965］. vii, 143 p. illus. ;19cm.

《断指记》和《汉家营》，高罗佩（Gulik, Robert Hans van, 1910—1967)(荷兰汉学家)翻译并创作.

(1)The monkey and the tiger; two Chinese detective stories. With eight illus. drawn by the author in Chinese style. New York：Scribner,［1966］. 143 p., illus. ; 21cm.

(2)University of Chicago Press ed. Chicago：University

13. The phantom of the temple: a Chinese detective story, by Robert Van Gulik; with nine illustrations drawn by the author in Chinese style. London, Heinemann, 1966. [7], 206 p. illus., plan 21cm.

《紫光寺》，高罗佩(Gulik, Robert Hans van, 1910—1967)(荷兰汉学家)翻译并创作.

(1) New York: Scribner [c1966]. 203 p. illus. 21cm. (New Judge Dee mysteries)

(2) University of Chicago Press ed. Chicago, Ill.: University of Chicago Press, 1995. 205 p.: ill.; 19cm. ISBN: 0226848779. (A Judge Dee mystery)

14. Murder in Canton: a Chinese detective story/by Robert van Gulik; with twelve illustrations drawn by the author in Chinese style. London: Heinemann, 1966. 208 p.: ill.; 20cm.

《广州案》，高罗佩(Gulik, Robert Hans van, 1910—1967)(荷兰汉学家)翻译并创作.

(1) New York: Scribners [1967]. 207 p. illus., map (on lining papers); 21cm. (New Judge Dee mysteries)

(2) University of Chicago Press ed. Chicago: University of Chicago Press, 1993. 207 p.: ill.; 18cm. ISBN: 0226848744. (Judge Dee mystery)

15. Judge Dee at work: eight Chinese detective stories by Robert Van Gulik; with illustrations drawn by the author in Chinese style. London, Heinemann, 1967. vi, 178 p. illus.; 21cm. (New Judge Dee mysteries)

《大唐狄公案》，高罗佩(Gulik, Robert Hans van, 1910—1967)(荷兰汉学家)翻译并创作.

(1) New York: Scribner [1973]. vi, 174 p. illus.; 22cm. ISBN: 0684130270

(2) University of Chicago Press ed. Chicago: University of Chicago Press, 1992. vi, 174 p.: ill.; 18cm. ISBN: 0226848663. (Judge Dee mysteries)

16. Necklace and calabash: a Chinese detective story, by Robert van Gulik; with eight illustrations drawn by the author in Chinese style. London, Heinemann, 1967. vii, 144 p. illus. 21cm. ([His More Judge Dee mysteries])

《玉珠串》，高罗佩(Gulik, Robert Hans van, 1910—1967)(荷兰汉学家)翻译并创作.

(1) New York: Scribner [1971]. 143 p. illus.; 21cm. ISBN: 0684106205. (New Judge Dee mysteries)

(2) University of Chicago Press ed. Chicago: University of Chicago Press, 1992. 143 p.: ill.; 18cm. ISBN: 0226848701

17. Poets and murder: a Chinese detective story, by Robert van Gulik; with eight illustrations drawn by the author in Chinese style. London, Heinemann, 1968. vii, 174

p., 8 illus.; 21cm. ISBN: 0434825573

《黑狐狸》，高罗佩(Gulik, Robert Hans van, 1910—1967)(荷兰汉学家)翻译并创作.

(1) New York, Scribner [1972]. vii, 173 p. illus. 21cm. ISBN: 0684125607

(2) University of Chicago Press ed. Chicago: University of Chicago Press, 1996. 173 p.: ill.; 18cm. ISBN: 0226848760. (A Judge Dee mystery)

18. Celebrated cases of Judge Dee = Dee goong an: an authentic eighteenth-century Chinese detective novel/translated and with an introd. and notes by Robert van Gulik. Unabridged, slightly corr. version. New York: Dover Publications, 1976. xxiii, 237 p., [9] leaves of plates: ill.; 22cm. ISBN: 0486233375

《狄公案》(又名《武则天四大奇案》)(选译)，高罗佩(Gulik, Robert Hans van, 1910—1967)(荷兰汉学家)翻译并创作.

19. The haunted monastery and The Chinese maze murders: two Chinese detective novels, with 27 illustrations by the author/Robert Van Gulik. New York: Dover Publications, 1977. 328 p.; ill.; 22cm. ISBN: 0486235025

《朝云观谜案》与《迷宫案》，高罗佩(Gulik, Robert Hans van, 1910—1967)(荷兰汉学家)翻译并创作.

I53 现当代小说集

1. The tragedy of Ah Qui, and other modern Chinese stories. London, G. Routledge & Sons, Ltd., 1930. xi, 146 p. 20cm. (The golden dragon library)

Contents: Miss Lysing, by Cheng Wi Mo. —After dusk, by Lo Hwa Sen. —A divorce, by J. B. Kyn Yn Yu. —Con y Ki, by Lu Siun. —The tragedy of Ah Qui, by Lu Siun. —The native country, by Lu Siun. —Boredom, by Miss Ping Sing. —Illusions, by Mao Teng. —Disillusioned, by Yo Ta Fu.

Notes: "Translated from the Chinese by J. B. Kyn Yn Yu and from the French by E. H. F. Mills."

《〈阿Q〉及其他》，鲁迅(1881—1936)等; Mills, E. H. F. 译自法文. 中国当代小说.

2. Short stories from China. Moscow, Co-operative publishing society of foreign workers in the U. S. S. R., 1935. 89, [1] p. 19cm.

Contents: Slave mother/Jou Shih—One spring night/You Ta-Fu—Twenty-one men/Chang T'ien-i—Night of death, dawn of freedom/Ting Ling—The three pagodas/Hsu Ting—The great impression/Jou Shin.

中国短篇小说. 丁则民(Cze, Ming-ting)编译.

3. Three seasons, and other stories/translated from the Chinese by Chun-Chan Yeh. London; New York: Staples Press, 1936. 136 pages; 19cm.

Contents：Three seasons. Spring silkworms；Autumn harvest；Winter fantasies/Mao Tun—Half a cartload of straw short/Yao Hsueh-yin—Along the Yunnan-Burma road/Pai Ping-Chei—The third-rate gunner/S. M. —Mr. Hua Wei/Chang T'ien-yi.

Yeh，Chun-chan(1916—)译，英译了茅盾、张天翼、叶君健等作家的现代小说.

(1)New York：Staples，1946. 136 pages；19cm.

(2)New York：Staples，1947. 136 pages；19cm.

4. Living China，modern Chinese stories. New York：Reynal & Hitchcock〔1937〕. 360 p. front. (port.)21cm.

《活的中国：现代中国短篇小说选》，斯诺(Snow，Edgar，1905—1972)(美国记者)选编. 该书分两个部分，第一部分是"鲁迅的小说"，收录鲁迅小说《药》《一件小事》《孔乙己》《祝福》《风筝》《离婚》；第二部分是"其他作家的小说"，收录茅盾、丁玲、柔石等人的作品.

(1)compiled and edited by Edgar Snow，with an introduction by the editor and an essay on modern Chinese literature by Nyn Wales. London，〔etc.〕G. G. Harrap & Co.，Ltd. 1937. 360 p. front.，(port.)；20cm.

(2)Westport，Conn.，Hyperion Press〔1973〕. 360 p. port. 23cm. ISBN：088355092X

5. Contemporary Chinese stories，translated by Chi-chen Wang. New York：Columbia University Press，1944. ix p.，1 l.，242 p. 22cm.

Contents：The road，by Chang T'ien-yi. —The inside story，by Chang T'ien-yi. —A country boy withdraws from school，by Lao Hsiang. —Black Li and White Li，by Lao She. —The glasses，by Lao She. —Grandma takes charge，by Lao She. —The philanthropist，by Lao She. —Liu's court，by Lao She. —The puppet dead，by Pa Chin. —Night march，by Shen Ts'ung-wen. —Smile! By Chang T'ien-yi. —Reunion，by Chang T'ien-yi. —Little sister，by Feng Wen-ping. —The helpmate，by Ling Shu-hua（Mrs. Ch'en T'ung-po）—Spring silkworms，by Mao Dun. —"A true Chinese，" by Mao Dun. —Mrs. Li's hair，by Yeh Shao-chün. —Neighbors，by Yeh Shao-chün. —What's the difference? By Lusin. —Peking street scene，by Lusin. —Yuchun，by Yang Chen-sheng. —Glossary. —Bibliographical note（p.〔235〕）—Notes on the authors.

《现代中国小说》，王际真（Wang，Chi-Chen，1899—2001)(美国华裔学者)译. 收有鲁迅的《端午节》《示众》，以及张天翼、老舍和巴金等人的小说.

(1)Contemporary Chinese stories. Translated by Chi-chên Wang. New York：Greenwood Press〔1968〕. ix，242 p. 23cm.

(2)Westport，Conn.，Greenwood Press，1973. ix，242

pages；23cm. ISBN：0837107385，0837107387

(3)New York，Greenwood Press，1976. ix，242 pages；21cm. ISBN：0837189438，0837189437，0837107385，0837107387

(4)〔Facsimile ed.〕.〔Place of publication not identified〕：Kessinger Publishing，2007. ix，242 pages；24cm. ISBN：0548059551，0548059555，1417987559，1417987553

6. Contemporary Chinese short stories/edited and translated by Yuan Jiahua and Robert Payne. London：New York：N. Carrington，1946. 169 pages；19cm.（Modern Chinese literature；no. 1）

Contents：The waves of the wind，by Lu Xun. —The anchor，by Yang Zhenshen. —The waning moon，by Shi Zhecun. —The last train，by Lao She. —The lamp，under cover of darkness，by Shen Congwen. —The breasts of a girl，by Zhang Tianyi. —The sorrows of the Lake of Egrets，Tiger，by Duanmu Houngliang. —The red trousers，by Bian Zhilin. —The half-baked，by Yao Xueyin. —Biographical notes.

中国当代短篇小说. 袁家骅(1904—1980)，Payne，Robert(1911—1983)合译.

7. Contemporary Chinese short stories，compiled by Jorgensen.〔Shanghai，Bei xin shu ju kan xing，1946〕. 2 v. in 1. 19cm.

Contents：v. 1. The cross，by Kuo Mu-jo. Suicide，by Mao Tun. A man must have a son，by Yeh Shao-chun. The florist，by Yu P'ing-pe. The first home party，by Ping Hsin. Hsiao-hsiao，by Shen Ch'ung-wen. Pai tzu，by Shen Ch'ung-wen. —v. 2. A hermit at large，by Lu Hsun. Looking back to the past，by Lu Hsun. Wistaria and doddar，by Yu Ta-fu. Slave mother，by Jou Shih. Aboard the S. S. Dairen Maru，by T'ien Chun. The conversion，by Hsiao Ch'ien.

中国当代短篇小说. Zhao，Jingshen(1902—)编译. 中英对照.

8. Three seasons and other stories/translated from the Chinese by Chun-Chan Yeh. New York：Staples，1946. 136 pages；19cm.

Contents：Three seasons. Spring silkworms；Autumn harvest；Winter fantasies/Mao Tun—Half a cartload of straw short/Yao Hsueh-yin—Along the Yunnan-Burma road/Pai Ping-Chei—The third-rate gunner/S. M. —Mr. Hua Wei/Chang T'ien-yi.

中国现代小说. 叶君健译. 收录茅盾、姚雪垠等作家的作品.

(1)New York：Staples，1947. 136 pages；19cm.

9. Stories of China at war；edited by Chi-chen Wang. New York：Columbia University Press，1947. xi，158 p.

23cm.

Contents：Beyond the Willow wall, by Tuan-mu Kung-liang. —Three men, by Chen Shou-chu. —Heaven has eyes, by Mao Dun. —The red trousers, by Pien Chih-lin. —An unsuccessful fight, by Ping Po. —Chabancheh Makay, by Yao Hsüheh-yin. —Purge by fire, by Yang Shuo. —Builders of the Burma Road, by Pai P'ing-chieh. —In the steel mill, by King Yu-ling. —Test of good citizenship, by Li Wei-t'ao. —They take heart again, by Lao She（Lau Shaw）—Portrait of a traitor, by Lao She（Lau Shaw）—The letter from home, by Lao She（Lau Shaw）—A new life, by ChangT'ien-yi. —House hunting, by Tuan-mu Kung-liang. —Under the moonlight, by Kuo Mo-jo.

《中国战时小说》,王际真（Wang, Chi-Chen, 1899—2001）（美国华裔学者）译. 收录16篇小说.

(1)London, Oxford University Press [1947]. xi, 158 p. 23cm.

(2)Westport, Conn. : Greenwood Press, 1975. xi, 158 p. ; 22cm. ISBN: 0837183693, 0837183695

10. Modern Chinese stories/translated by Huang Kun. Delhi: Ranjit Printers & Publishers [1953]. 429 p. : illus. ; 19cm.

《中国现代小说》,Panikkar, K. M. (Kavalam Madhava, 1896—1963)编译.

11. Registration and other stories/by contemporary Chinese writers. Peking: Foreign Languages Press, 1954. 226 p. ; 22cm.

Contents：My two hosts/Kang Chuo—Blast furnace/Lu Chi—New times, new methods/Ky Yu—Registration/Chao Shu-li—Yin Ching-chun/Han Feng—On the Kholchin grasslands/Malchinku—Ahmad and Pakya/Wang Yu-hu—I want to study! /Kao Yu-pao—Ehdun Maole and Snow White/Huo Chien—Sacrifice to the kitchen god/Chin Chao-yang.

《〈登记〉及其他故事》,康濯等著. 新中国小说选.

(1)Peking: Foreign Languages Press, 1956. 210 pages; 22cm.

12. Racing towards victory: stories from the Korean front. Peking: Foreign Languages Press, 1954. 184 pages; 19cm.

Contents：Army nurse Chen Ming, by Hsu Kang. —The icy Chan River, by Ching Ni. —On Height 584, by Shao Hua. —Get them down! By Wei Wei. —By the Imjin River, by Li Chia. —Racing towards victory, by Li Kao. —The fourteenth assignment, by Chang Chieh

《抗美援朝小说选》,立高等著.

13. A new home and other stories, by contemporary Chinese writers. Peking: Foreign Languages Press, 1955. 165 p.

Contents：The Wine Pot/Tsui Pa-wa—Tsui Yi/Shu Chun—ANewHome/Ai Wu—Uncle Chao, the Stockman/Ma Feng—Mother Wang/Lo Pin-chi—Not that Road/Li Chun—A Village Elder/Liu Chi—The Apple Trees/Wang An-yu

《〈新的家〉及其他故事》,艾芜等. 新中国小说选.

(1)Peking Foreign Languages Press, 1959. 166 pages; 21cm.

14. Homeward journey and other stories/by contemporary Chinese writers. Peking: Foreign Languages Press, 1957. 234 pages; 22cm.

Contents：One short year, by Fei Li-wen. —Spring in the workshop, by Tang Ke-hsin. —Not up to standard, by Nan Ting. —Homeward journey, by Ai Wu. —Old man Meng Kuang-tai, by Li Chun. —Storm over a little white flag, by Chi Hsueh-pei. —The old courier, by Chun Ching. —On the dusty highway, by Liu Pai-yu. —Han mei-mei, by Ma Feng. —Mother and daughter, by Liu Chen. —Breaking off the engagement, by Kao Hsiao-sheng. —Lo Tsai, the tiger hunter, by Li Nan-li.

《〈老交通〉及其他故事》. 新中国小说选.

15. Dawn on the river and other stories by contemporary Chinese writers. Peking: Foreign Languages Press, 1957. 170 p. 22cm.

Contents：Dawn on the river, by Chun Ching. —Membership dues, by Wang Yuan-chien. —Marriage, by Li Wen-yuan. —Our friend the fisherman, by Lu Yang-lieh. —The newlyweds, by Hai Mo. —The night of the snowstorm, by Wang Wen-shih. —Old Sung goes to town, by Hsi Yung.

《〈黎明河边〉及其他故事》. 新中国小说选.

16. Homeward journey and other stories, by contemporary Chinese writers. Peking: Foreign Languages Press, 1957. 234 p. 22cm.

Contents：One short year, by Fei Li-wen. —Spring in the workshop, by Tang Ke-hsin. —Not up to standard, by Nan Ting. —Homeward journey, by Ai Wu. —Old man Meng Kuang-tai, by Li Chun. —Storm over a little white flag, by Chi Hsueh-pei. —The old courier, by Chun Ching. —On the dusty highway, by Liu Pai-yu. —Han mei-mei, by Ma Feng. —Mother and daughter, by Liu Chen. —Breaking off the engagement, by Kao Hsiao-sheng. —Lo Tsai, the tiger hunter, by Li Nan-li.

《〈夜归〉及其他故事》. 新中国小说选.

17. The young coal-miner, and other stories/by contemporary Chinese writers. Peking: Foreign Languages Press, 1958. 176 p. 22cm.

《〈小矿工〉及其他故事》,大众等. 新中国短篇小说选.

18. Flame on high mountain, and other stories. Peking: Foreign Languages Press, 1959. xi, 204 p. illus. 19cm. Contents: Red flag over Chingkang Mountain, by Ho Chang-kung. —Pingkiang uprising, by Li Shou-hsuan. —With my father in the Red Army, by Wu Hua-to. —The sweet potato plot, by Wu Hsien-en. —Home-made weapons, by Huang Ming-chung and Wei Chung-yi. —The story of a Red Army man, by Chang Yu-chi. —A beloved divisional commander, by Chen Hsi-Lien. —Flame on high mountain, by Peng Shou-sheng. —Three years' persistent struggle, by Peng Sheng-piao. —Open-air convalescence, by Liu Ti. —Night raid on Lingyen, by Yu Ping-hui. —A mother of the Red Army, by Chang Yu.

《〈高山上的火苗〉及其他》. 新中国短篇小说选.

(1) 2nd ed. Peking: Foreign Languages Press, 1962. 188 pages: illustrations

19. Saga of resistance to Japanese invasion. Peking: Foreign Languages Press, 1959. x, 212 p. illus. 19cm.

《抗日战争的故事》, 李天佑等.

20. I knew all along, and other stories by contemporary Chinese writers. Peking: Foreign Languages Press, 1960. 172 p. 22cm.

《〈三年早知道〉及其他故事》, 马烽等著. 新中国短篇小说选.

21. A snowy day, and other stories, by contemporary Chinese writers. Peking: Foreign Languages Press, 1960. 127 p. 22cm.

Contents: A snowy day, by Chang Lin. —The S. S. International Friendship, by Lu Chun-chao. —Mamma, by Wang Yuan-chien. —Two able women, by Hu Cheng. —Comrade, by She Yi-ping. —Little brother, by Shen Hu-ken.

《〈雪天〉及其他故事》, 张麟等著. 新中国短篇小说选.

22. A treasury of modern Asian stories/edited by Daniel Milton and William Clifford. New York: New American Library, 1961. 237 p. ; 18cm. (Mentor book; MD329)
Contents: Tell me a story/Rabindranath Tagore—Feast of the dead/Cevdet Kudret—The return of the pioneer/Amos Mossenson—Uncle Mitwalli/Mahmud Taimur—Trial by cobra/Sadegh Hedayat—Odor/Saadat Hasan Manto—Miss Malti; The shroud/Prem Chand—Under the yoke; The monkey god/Vyankatesh Madgulkar—Eyes/K. T. Mohamed—Prelude to penance/C. Rajagopalachari—The man from Kabul/Rabindranath Tagore—The hall of entertainment/Tarashankar Banerjee—Prehistoric/Manik Bandyopadhyay—Lawley Road/R. K. Narayan—Karma/Khushwant Singh—His spouse/Zawgyi—Sensations at the top of acoconut tree/

Achdiat K. Mihardja—May Day eve/Nick Joaquin—Grandma takes charge/Lau Shaw—Asailor in port/Shen Tsung-wen—The death of the Dog-Meat General/Lin Yutang—The conversion/Hsaio Chien—Acountry boy quits school/Lao Hsiang—A little incident/Lu Hsun—War and peace come to the village/Mao Tun—The nonrevolutionaries/Yu-Wol Chong-Nyon—The death of the knife-thrower's wife/Shiga Naoya—The spider's thread; Gates of Hell/Ryunosuke Akutagawa.

Milton, Daniel L. 和 Clifford, William(1924—)编. 收集现代亚洲国家小说, 包括中国老舍的《抱孙》、沈从文的《边城》、林语堂的《忆狗肉将军》、鲁迅的《一件小事》等.

(1) New York: New American Library, 1971. 237 pages; 20cm.

23. Sowing the clouds: a collection of Chinese short stories/by Chou Li-po, Li Chun... [et al.]; [transl. from the Chinese]. Peking, 1961. IV, 148 p. ; 22cm.

《耕云记》, 周立波(1908—), 李准等. 短篇小说集.

Contents: Lingkuan Gorge/Tu Peng-Cheng—Stubborn Ox Niu/Liu Shu-teb—The family on the other side of the mountain/Zhou Libo—Summer nights/Wang Wen-shih—The caretaker/Yang Hsu—The first lesson/Tang Keh-hsin—A promise is kept/Ju Chih-Chuan—Sowing the clouds/Li Chun—A fighting journey/Hsiao Mu—the road/Malchinhu.

(1) 2nd ed. Peking: Foreign Languages Press: Dist. by Guozi Shudian (China Publications Centre), 1964. 146 pages; 21cm.

24. Wild Bull Village: Chinese short stories, by Ai Wu and others. Peking: Foreign Languages Press, 1965. 108 p. ; 21cm.

《野牛寨》, 艾芜等.

25. The family by Pa Chin and the true story of Ah Q by Lu Hsun. Dubuque, Iowa: Wm. C. Brown Book Co., 1969. vii, 300 pages; 23cm. (Burton, Robert A. Eastern civilization readings; v. 3)

《家; 阿 Q 正传》, 巴金(1904—2005), 鲁迅(1881—1936).

26. Modern Chinese short stories/retold by J. F. Tai. Taiwan, 1970. 120 p. illus. , port. 20cm.
Contents: Two brothers, by Li Shih-an. —An antique vase, by Mu Hu. —The reunion, by Lin Fu-erh. —An unforgettable person, by Shao Hwa. —The pomegranate vase, by Chiung Yao. —Black-bull, by Ku Fan. —A swan, by Wang Ling-tai. —The pubescent loneliness, by Woo Hwa. —A picture, by Chung Ling. —The typhoon's night, by Kun Lun.

现代中国短篇小说. 戴仁法(Tai, J. F.)编译.

27. Modern Chinese stories; selected and edited by W. J. F. Jenner; translated by W. J. F. Jenner and Gladys Yang. London, New York：Oxford U. P. ，1970. xiii, 271 p. 21cm. ISBN：0192810871. (Oxford paperbacks, 222)

《现代中国小说》，詹纳尔(Jenner，W. J. F.〈William John Francis〉)(英国学者)，戴乃迭(Yang，Gladys，1919—1999)选编. 鲁迅小说入选的有《孔乙己》《故乡》《祝福》3 篇.

(1)London；New York：Oxford University Press，1974. xv，271 p. ；21cm. (A Galaxy book)

28. Twentieth-century Chinese stories / edited by C. T. Hsia, with the assistance of Joseph S. M. Lau. New York：Columbia University Press，1971. xiv, 239 p. 23cm. ISBN：0231035896, 023103590X. (Companions to Asian studies)

《二十世纪中国小说》，夏志清(Hsia，Chih-tsing，1921—2013)(美国华裔学者)，刘绍铭(Lau，Joseph S. M. ，1934—)(美国华裔学者)合译. 收录有郁达夫、沈从文、张天翼、吴组湘、张爱玲、聂华苓、水晶和白先勇八位作家的作品.

(1)Taipei：Shuang Yeh Book Co，1976. xiv，239 pages；23cm.

(2)New York：Columbia University Press，1989. xiv，239 pages；23cm. (Companions to Asian studies)

(3)Ann Arbor：University Microfilms，1997. xiv，239 pages；23cm. ISBN：0231035896, 0231035897, 023103590X, 0231035903

29. The seeds and other stories. Peking：Foreign Languages Press，1972. 193 p. 19cm.

Contents：Red Cliff revisited, by Chen Hung-shan. —A night in "Potato" Village, by Tai Mu-jen. —Half the population, by Yin Yi-ping. —Raiser of sprouts, by Chang Wei-wen. —Third time to school, by Lu Chao-hui. —The case of the missing ducks, by Hu Hui-ying. —A detour to Dragon Village, by Ho Hsiao-lu. —Raising seedlings, by Chiang Kuei-fu. —Selling rice, by Ching Hung-shao. —Two ears of rice, Hsu Tao-sheng and Chen Wen-tsai. —Crossing Chungchou Dam, by Hung Chung-wen.

《〈种子〉及其他》，陈洪山等.

30. City cousin, and other stories. Peking：Foreign Languages Press，1973. 124 p. illus. 19cm.

Contents：Sha Ping-teh. City cousin. —Shanghai Docker's Spare-time Writing Group. Look far, fly far. —Chu Yu-tung. The call. —Hung Shan. Spring comes to a fishing village. —Fang Nan. The ferry at Billows Harbour. —Yüeh Chang-kuei. A shoulder pole. —Ko Niu. When the persimmons ripened. —

Hsüheh Chiang. Home leave.
《〈彩色的田野〉及其他》.

31. The young skipper：and other stories. Peking：Foreign Languages Press，1973. 97 p. ：ill. ；19cm.

Contents：Chang, T. Y. and Chang, C. Y. The young skipper. —Chiu, H. P. Old sentry. —Yao, K. M. Old Hsin's day of retirement. —Chao, T. Red navigation route

《〈新来的老大〉及其他》，Chang，Tao-yü 等.

32. Straw sandals：Chinese short stories, 1918—1933/edited by Harold R. Isaacs；foreword by Lu Hsühn. Cambridge, MIT Press, [1974]. lxxiii, 444 p. port. 21cm. ISBN：0262090147, 0262090148, 0262590069, 0262590068

《草鞋脚：1918—1933 年中国短篇小说选》，伊罗生(Isaacs，Harold Robert，1910—)(美国学者)编；鲁迅作序言. 收录鲁迅小说《狂人日记》《药》《孔乙己》《风波》《伤逝》.

33. A young pathbreaker and other stories/by Hsiao Kuan-hung and others. Peking：Foreign Languages Press，1975. 178 p. ，[7] leaves of plates：ill. ；19cm.

Notes：Translation of Xiao jiang and other stories

Contents：Chou Yung-chuang. Out to learn. —Liu Jung-ken. Woman forge worker. —Liu Shu-chen. The sharp cutter edge. —Hsiao Kuan-hung. A young pathbreaker. —Shen Hui-min. A screw. —Shih Min. Hidden reef. —Shih Han-fu. Morning sun. —Sheng Hua-hai. Pupil excels master. —Huang Pei-chia. Re-examination. —Yu Ping-kun and Wu Sheng-hsi. A steel worker's assistant.

《〈小将〉及其他》，肖关鸿(1949—)等.

34. Yenan seeds and other stories/[ill. by Shih Ta-wei]. Peking：Foreign Languages Press，1976. 131 p. ，[7] leaves of plates：ill. ；19cm.

Contents：Hua, T. Yenan seeds. —Tuan, J. Not just one of the audience. —Chu, M. Leading the way. —Shih, M. In the shipyard. —Lin, C. Many swallows make a summer. —Wang, C. ，Chu, C. and Yu, P. Trial voyage.

《〈延安的种子〉及其他》，华彤等著，施大畏插图.

35. The golden bridge：a selection of revolutionary stories. Peking：Foreign Languages Press，1977. 110 p. ，[7] leaves of plates：ill. ；19cm.

Contents：Min-fu, S. Choosing a commander. —Wei, F. A women's representative. —Hsi, C. Old soldier. —Chou, P. A letter of thanks. —En-cheng, S. and Chang-shun, T. Red cavalry women and the Changpai Mountains. —Chen, W. A pair of signal flags. —Shun-kang, S. How the old team leader fetched the bride. —

Kuan-sung，H. The golden bridge.—Lien-yuan，T. Reporting a new event.

《金桥》，吴光松等. 革命故事集.

36. Wild-goose guerrillas/by Liu Fu-hai and others；［illustrations by Hsin Ho-Chiang］. Peking：Foreign Languages Press，1978. 142 str. ：illustr. ；19cm.

《雁翎队的故事》，刘夫海等著.

37. Stories of contemporary China/edited with an introd. by Winston L. Y. Yang and Nathan K. Mao. New York：Paragon Book Gallery，1979. xiii，140 p. ：ill. ；22cm. ISBN：0818801158

《中国当代小说》，Yang，Winston L. Y. 和Mao，Nathan K. 编译.

38. The wounded：new stories of the Cultural Revolution，77－78/authors，Lu Xinhua...［et al.］；translators，Geremie Barmé& Bennett Lee. Hongkong：Joint Pub. Co. ，1979. 220 p. ：ill. ；22cm. ISBN：9620400070，9620400089

Contents：Lu，X. The wounded.—Kong，J. Marriage.—Yang，W. Ah，books！—Lu，W. Dedication.—Wang. Y. Sacred duty.—Liu，X. Class counsellor.—Liu，X. "Awake，my brother！"—Wang，M. Something most precious.—Biographical notes on authors

《伤痕：1977－78 年"文化革命"新故事》，卢新华（Lu，Hsin-hua）等；Barmé，Geremie 和 Lee，Bennett 译. 收录了卢新华的《伤痕》和刘心武的《班主任》等.

39. Genesis of a revolution：an anthology of modern Chinese short stories/selected and translated by Stanley R. Munro. Singapore：Heinemann Educational Books （Asia），1979. xix，202 p. ：ill. ；19cm. （Writing in Asia series）

Contents：Ba，J. A tiny incident.—Bing，X. Separation.—Ding，L. On Qing Yun Lane.—Lao，S. The woman from Liu Tun.—Mao，D. In front of the pawnshop.—Shen，C. W. Seven barbarians and the last Spring Festival.—Wu，Z. X. The night before leaving home.—Ye，S. J. A lifetime.—Yu，D. F. Blood and tears.—Zhang，T. Y. The journey.

《革命起源：中国现代短篇小说选》，Munro，Stanley，R. 选译. 包括巴金的《一件小事》，冰心的《分》，丁玲的《庆云里的一间小房里》，老舍的《柳屯的》，茅盾的《当铺前》等.

40. Reunion & other stories/translated by Ly Singko. Singapore：Heinemann Educational Books （Asia），1980. 183 p. ；19cm. ISBN：9971640198. （Writing in Asia series）

Ly，Singko 译. 20 世纪中国短篇小说选译.

41. Prize-winning stories from China，1978—1979/by Liu Xinwu，Wang Meng，and others. Beijing：Foreign Languages Press，1981. 535 p. ：ill. ；20cm.

Notes：A collection of 18 short stories by various authors.

Contents：The teacher/Liu Xinwu—Sacred duty/Wang Yaping—The window/Mo Shen—Melody in dreams/Zong Pu—The scar/Lu Xinhua—Why herdsmen sing about "mother"/Zhang Chengzhi—Diary of a warden/Qi Ping—Death ray on a coral island/Tong Enzheng—Manager Qiao assumes office/Jiang Zilong—More about Manager Qiao/Jiang Zilong—A story out of sequence/Ru Zhijuan—A traitor in the ranks/Fang Zhi—Our family's cook/Mu Guozheng—A fervent wish/Wang Meng—Who knows how to live？/Zhang Jie—I love every green leaf/Liu Xinwu—Before the wedding/Bao Chuan—Figure-carved pipe/Feng Jicai.

《1978—1979 年中国获奖小说》，刘心武，王蒙（1934—）等. 共收录 18 篇小说.

42. Modern Chinese stories and novellas，1919—1949/edited by Joseph S. M. Lau，C. T. Hsia，and Leo Ou-Fan Lee. New York：Columbia University Press，1981. xxvii，578 p. ，［3］leaves of plates：ill. ；26cm. ISBN：0231042027，0231042024，0231042035，0231042031. （Modern Asian literature series）

《中国现代中短篇小说选，1919—1949》，刘绍铭（Lau，Joseph S. M. ，1934—）（美国华裔学者），夏志清（Hsia，Chih-tsing，1921—2013）（美国华裔学者），李欧梵（Lee，Leo Ou-fan）（美国华裔学者）编. 其中鲁迅的小说有：《孔乙己》《药》《故乡》《祝福》《在酒楼上》《肥皂》6 篇.

43. Born of the same roots：stories of modern Chinese women/edited by Vivian Ling Hsu. Bloomington：Indiana University Press，c1981. ix，308 p. ；24cm. ISBN：0253195268，0253202701. （Chinese literature in translation）

Contents：Caterpillar/Lao She—Two women/Wu Tsu-hsiang—On the Oxcart/Hsiao Hung—Garbage cleaner/Lo Hua-sheng—West wind；Chang Sao/Ping Hsin—Little Liu/Ling Shu-hua—Parting/T'ien T'ao—At the precipice/Teng Yu-mei—Spring is just around the corner/Ts'ao Ming—Rain/Ai Wu—Corduroy/Hsi Jung—Old team captain welcomes a bride/Sung Shun-k'ang—A day in Pleasantville/Pai Hsien-yung—Nightfall/Yü Li-hau—A rose in June/Ch'en Ying-chen—Born of the same roots/Yang Ch'ing ch'u—May he return soon/Wang T'o—My friend Ai Fen/Chen Jo-hsi.

《本是同根生：现代中国女作家小说选集》，Hsu，Vivian Ling 编.

44. Seven contemporary Chinese women writers. Beijing，China：Chinese Literature：Distributed by China Publications Centre，1982. 280 pages：illustrations；

18cm. (Panda books)

Contents：The path through the grassland/Ru Zhijuan—The flight of the wild-geese/Huang Zongying—Melody in dreams/Zong Pu—At middle age/Shen Rong—Love must not be forgotten/Zhang Jie—The wasted years/Zhang Kangkang—Life in a small courtyard/Wang Anyi.

《当代女作家作品选》，选译了茹志鹃、黄宗英、宗璞、谌荣、张洁、张抗抗和王安忆7位作家的作品。该书是《中国当代女作家作品选》第一辑。

(1)Beijing：Chinese Literature Books, 1983. 282 pages；portraits；18cm. ISBN：083511600X, 0835116008. (Panda books)

(2)Beijing：Chinese Literature Press, 1990. 282 p. ISBN：083511600X, 0835116008, 7507100677, 7507100679

45. Contemporary Chinese women writers, II. Beijing, China：Chinese Literature Press：Distributed by China International Book Trading Corp., 1991. 315 pages；portraits；18cm. ISBN：7507100790, 7507100792, 0835100790, 0835100793, 0835120899, 0835120890. (Panda books)

Contents：Landscape/Fang Fang—Dialogue in heaven/Can Xue—Blue sky and green sea/Liu Suola—Hopes worn away/Peng Xiaolian—Crucible/Jiang Yun—Purple asters/Ding Xiaoqi—In the vast country of the north/Chi Zijian

《中国当代女作家作品选》第二辑，包括方方、残雪、刘索拉、彭小莲、蒋韵、丁小琦和迟子建的作品。

46. Contemporary Chinese Women Writers III. Beijing, China：Chinese Literature Press：Distributed by China International Book Trading Corp., 1993. 322 pages：illustrations；18cm. ISBN：7501011770835131289, 0835131285, 7507101177 (v. 3), 7507101171 (v. 3). (Panda books)

Contents：Trials and tribulations/Chi Li—Ruiyun/Fan Xiaoqing—Happy birthday/Cheng Naishan—Scatterbrain/Su Ye—Broken transformers/Bi Shumin—I love you, child/Ah Zhen—Black forest/Liu Xihong.

《中国当代女作家作品选》第三辑.

47. Six contemporary Chinese women writers IV. Beijing, China：Chinese Literature Press, 1995. 374 pages；18cm. ISBN：7507102971, 7507102970, 0835131750, 0835131759. (Panda Books)

Contents：Rhapsody of the wake dancers/Ye Mei—Under one roof/Lu Xing'er—Return to secular life/Fan Xiaoqing—The pregnant woman and the cow/Tie Ning—Miaomiao/Wang Anyi—Certainly not coincidence/Zhang Xin.

《中国当代六位女作家》，收录6部中篇小说.《中国当代女作家作品选》第四辑.

48. Contemporary Chinese women writers, V: three novellas/by Fang Fang. Beijing, China：Chinese Literature Press：Distributed by China International Book Trading Corp., 1996. iii, 288 pages；18cm. ISBN：7507103498, 7507103496, 0835131831, 0835131834. (Panda books)

《中国当代女作家作品选之五》，方方(1955—)编.

49. Contemporary Chinese women writers VI: four novellas/by Zhang Xin. Beijing：Chinese Literature Press, 1998. 332 pages；18cm. ISBN：7507103846, 7507103847, 0835131963, 0835131964. (Panda books)

《张欣小说选》.该书是《中国当代女作家作品选》第六辑.

50. Contemporary Chinese women writers VII. Beijing：Chinese Literature Press, 1998. 363 pages；18cm. ISBN：7507104370, 7507104370, 0835132285, 0835132282. (Panda books)

Contents：Two trees, twinned fates/Ye Mei—Beloved potatoes/Chi Zijian—Stakeout/Fang Fang—An appointment with death/Bi Shumin—Hand in hand/Fan Xiaoqing—The endangered ones/Fang Min—Hong Ling/Yang Ni—If love, then what? /Zhang Xin

《中国当代女作家作品选之七》.

51. Stories from the thirties. Beijing, China：Chinese Literature：Distributed by China Publications Centre, 1982. volumes〈1－2〉；18cm. ISBN：0835110192, 0835110198, 0835110206, 0835110204. (Panda books)

Contents：A year of good harvest; How Mr. Pan weathered the storm; Night; A declaration/Ye Shengtao—Blooms on a dead poplar; Director Fei's reception room; Big sister Liu; The iron fish with gills/Xu Dishan—The child at the lakeside; Shipwreck; Fifty Yuan/Wang Tongzhao—A slave mother/Rou Shi—One-sided wedding; Wang the miller; Li Song's crime/Yang Zhensheng—A poor man/Hu Yepin—The sorrows of childhood; On the bridge/Wang Luyan—New life; A summer night's dream/Zhang Tianyi—Twice-married woman; The oranges; The salt worker; Aunt Liu/Luo Shu.

《三十年代短篇小说选》, 2卷.

52. Winter plum：contemporary Chinese fiction ＝［Han mei］/edited by Nancy Ing.［San Francisco］：Chinese Materials Center, 1982. xxiv, 498 p.；22cm. ISBN：0896446522, 0896446581(Asian library series；no. 32)

《寒梅：当代中国小说》

53. The new realism：writings from China after the cultural revolution/edited by Lee Yee. New York：Hippocrene Books, 1983. 349 pages；25cm. ISBN：0882547941, 0882547947, 0882548107, 0882548104

Contents：A reflection of reality/Lee Yee—Sons and successors/Ru Zhijuan—Li Shunda builds a house/Gao Xiaosheng—Manager Qiao assumes office/Jiang Zilong—General, you must not do this！/Ye Wenfu—The eye of night/Wang Meng—In the archives of society/Wang Jing—Middle age/Shen Rong—Between human and demon/Liu Binyan—A place forgotten by love/Zhang Xian—If I were for real/Sha Yexin, Li Shoucheng, Yao Mingde—Five letters/Bai Hua.

《新现实主义："文革"后的中国写作》,李义（Lee Yee）编. 短篇小说集.

54. Perspectives in contemporary Chinese literature/Mason Y. H. Wang, editor. University Center, Mich.：Green River Press，1983. vi，292 pages；24cm. ISBN：0940580217，0940580213，0940580225，0940580220

Contents：pt. 1. Essays：The second blooming of the hundred flowers：Chinese literature in post-Mao era/Michael S. Duke—Ba Jin（1904—）：from personal liberation to party "liberation"/Michael S. Duke—The poetic theory and practice of Ai Qing/Anglea Jung Palandri—Shoes that fit：the stories of Gao Xiaosheng/Jeannette L. Faurot—Listen to the voice of the people/Liu Binyan；translated by Kyna Rubin—A question that must be answered/Bai Hua；translated by Madelyn Ross—Remembering Xiao Shan/Ba Jin；translated by Michael S. Duke—pt. 2. Stories：By way of a preface to The sad canal/Wang Ruowang；translated by Kyna Rubin—See which family has good fortune/Liu Qingbang；translated by Denis C. Mair—Li Shunda builds a house/Gao Xiaosheng；translated by Madelyn Ross—A dream on strings/Zong Pu；translated by Aimeé Lykes—Chinese roses/Li Tuo；translated by Mary Boyd and Kam Louie.

《中国当代文学面面观》,Wang, Mason Y. H. 编译. 短篇小说集.

55. Masterpieces of modern Chinese fiction，1919—1949/by Lu Xun and others. Beijing，China：Foreign Languages Press：Distributed by China Publications Centre（Guoji Shudian），1983. 563 p.，［17］leaves of plates：ill.；21cm.（Modern Chinese literature）

《中国现代短篇杰作选》,鲁迅等.

（1）Amsterdam, The Netherlands：Fredonia Books，2004. 563 pages，［17］leaves of plates：illustrations；21cm. ISBN：1410106756，1410106759

56. Fragrant weeds：Chinese short stories once labelled as "poisonous weeds"/written by Liu Binyan and others；translated by Geremie Barmé and Bennett Lee；and edited by W. J. F. Jenner. Hong Kong：Joint Pub. Co.，1983. xvii，228 pages；21cm. ISBN：962040212X，9620402128

《香花毒草：中国短篇小说选》,刘宾雁（1925—2005）等著；Barmé, Geremie 和 Lee, Bennett 译；Jenner, W. J. F.（William John Francis）编.

57. Contemporary Chinese short stories. Beijing，China：Chinese Literature：Distributed by China Publications Centre（Guoji Shudian），1983. 274 pages；18cm. ISBN：0835110761，0835110761.（Panda books＝熊猫丛书）

Contents：A herdsman's story/Zhang Xianliang—A corner forsaken by love/Zhang Xian—The log cabin overgrown with creepers/Gu Hua—A tale of Big Nur/Wang Zengqi—Our corner/Jin Shui—Outside the marriage bureau/He Xiaohu—Deaf-mute and his "suona"/Han Shaogong—A summer experience/Ge Wujue—Han the Forger/Deng Youmei—A land of wonder and mystery/Liang Xiaosheng.

《当代优秀小说选》

58. The fontana collection of modern Chinese writing/edited by Christine M. Liao. ［Melbourne］：Fontana/Collins in association with the Chinese Literature Pub. House of Beijing，1983. 240 pages：illustrations；20cm.

Contents：At middle age/Shen Rong—Pages from a factory secretary's diary/Jiang Zilong—The stranger/Zhang Lin—A spate of visitors/Wang Meng—The story of a living Buddha/Malqinhu—Hansuai, the living ghost/Bai Honghu and Yang Zhao—Two brigade leaders/Ji Xuepei—In vino veritas/Sun Yuchun—The moon on the south lake/Liu Fudao—A poster/Li Huiwen—Poems/Ai Qing；Shu Ting；Huang Yongyu.

中国女作家小说选. Liao, Christine M. 编.

59. Chinese stories from the fifties. Beijing，China：Chinese Literature：Distributed by China International Book Trading Corp.，1984. 239 pages：portraits；18cm. ISBN：083511077X，0835110778.（Panda books）

Contents：The election/Qin Zhaoyang—My young friend/Du Pengcheng—Around the spring festival/Wang Wenshi—The family on the other side of the mountain/Zhou Libo—Father and daughter/Luo Binji—The girl who sold wine/Xu Huaizhong—An ordinary labourer/Wang Yuanjian—My first superior/Ma Feng—Dajee and her father/Gao Ying—The vegetable seeds/Hao Ran—Long distance runner/Malqinhu—Barley kernel gruel/Li Zhun.

《五十年代小说选》

60. Roses and thorns：the second blooming of the Hundred Flowers in Chinese fiction，1979—80/Perry Link，editor. Berkeley：University of California Press，c1984. x，346 p.；24cm. ISBN：0520049799，0520049802

玫瑰与荆棘：中国小说的第二次百花时期（1979—1980）. Link, E. Perry（Eugene Perry,1944—）编.

61. A wind across the grass：modern Chinese writing with fourteen stories/by Han Zi, Zong Pu & Wang Xiao Ying；[introduced and edited by Hugh Anderson]. Ascot Vale, Vic.：Red Rooster Press, 1985. xxx, 154 p.：ports.；22cm. ISBN：090824715X

《吹过草原的风：当代中国作品14篇》，Anderson, Hugh 译. 收录宗璞、王小鹰等的作品.

62. Prize-winning stories from China 1980—1981/by K'o Yün-lu（Ke Yunlu）, Chang Hsien-liang（Zhang Xianliang）and others；English text ed. by W. C. Chau. Beijing：Foreign Languages Press, 1985. 437 p.：ill., ports.；22cm. ISBN：0835113132

1980—1981 年中国获奖短篇小说. Chau, W. C. 英译，包括柯云路、张贤亮等作家的作品.

63. Chinese women writers：a collection of short stories by Chinese women writers of the 1920s and 30s/translated by Jennifer Anderson & Theresa Munford. Hongkong：Joint Pub. Co., 1985. xx, 180 p.；22cm. ISBN：9620403576,9620403584

Contents：A house in Qingyun Lane/Ding Ling—New Year/Ding Ling—Miss Winter/Bing Xin—Wife of another man/Luo Shu—The lucky one/Ling Shuhua—The mad father/Wu Shutian—Factory girl/Lu Yin—Hands/Xiao Hong—On the ox cart/Xiao Hong—The child pedlar/Feng·Keng—Careers/Chen Ying—The journey/Feng Yuanjun.

《中国女作家小说选》，Anderson, Jennifer 和 Munford, Theresa 合译.

64. Lost in the fog/[edited by] Chinese Guangzhou PEN. Guangzhou：New Century Pub. House, 1986. 110 pages；19cm.

《雾失楼台》，中国广州笔会中心编. 收录13位当代名作家创作的小说.

65. Contemporary Chinese fiction：four short stories introduced and annotated for the student of Chinese/edited by Neal Robbins；with assistance from David Kay；and contributions from Rose Hsiu-li Yuan and K. C. Wong. New Haven：Far Eastern Publications, Yale University, 1986. xiv, 144, 72 pages；23cm. ISBN：0887101402, 0887101403

Contents："Banana boat" by Zhang Xiguo—"Black clothes" by Wang Wenxing—"Magistrate Yin" by Chen Ruoxi—"The race of generals" by Chen Yingzhen.

《现代中文小说读本》，Robbins, Neal 编. 为汉语学生介绍和分析的四个短篇小说.

66. One half of the sky：selection from contemporary women writers of China/translated by R. A. Roberts and Angela Knox；with an introduction by Frances Wood. London：Heinemann, 1987. x, 143 pages；22cm. ISBN：0434640352, 0434640387, 0434640355, 0434640386

《半边天：中国当代女作家文学》，Roberts, R. A. 和 Knox, Angela 合译.

67. One half of the sky：stories from contemporary women writers of China/translated by R. A. Roberts and Angela Knox；with an introduction by Frances Wood. New York：Dodd, Mead & Co., 1988. x, 143 p.；22cm. ISBN：0396092918

《当代女作家作品选》，Roberts, R. A. 和 Knox, Angela 合译.

68. The rose colored dinner：new works by contemporary Chinese women writers/translated by Nienling Liu [and others]. Hong Kong：Joint Pub. Co., 1988. x, 166 pages；21cm. ISBN：962040615X, 9620406157

Contents："No"/Dai Qing—The rose colored dinner/Chen Rong—An unrecorded life/Zhang Jie—/ The spirit of fire/Zhang Kangkang—Regarding the problem of newborn piglets in winter/Chen Rong—Who am I? /Zong Pu—My son, my son/Ru Zhijuan—Friends/Wang Anyi—How did I miss you? /Zhang Xinxin.

《玫瑰色的晚餐：中国当代女作家新作》，刘年玲等译.

69. The Chinese Western：short fiction from today's China/translated by Zhu Hong. New York：Ballantine Books, c1988. xiv, 224 p.；21cm. ISBN：0345351401, 0345351401

Contents：How much can a man bear? /Jia Pingao—Chronicle of Mulberry Tree Village/Zhu Xiaoping—Story of an old man and a dog/Zhang Xianliang—Family chronicle of a wooden bowl maker/Jia Pingao—Shorblac：Driver's story/Zhang Xianliang—Anecdotes of Chairman Maimaiti/Wang Meng—Progress of the military patrol car/Tang Dong—Daughter of the Yellow River/Wang Jiada—Glossary.

中国短篇小说. 朱虹（Zhu, Hong, 1933—）编.

（1）Spring of bitter waters：short fiction from today's China/translated by Zhu Hong. London：Allison & Busby, 1989. xiv, 224 pages；21cm. ISBN：0850319552, 0850319552, 0749000554, 0749000554.

（2）The Chinese Western：short fiction from today's China/translated by Zhu Hong. New York：Ballantine Books, 1991. XV, 206 p.；18cm. ISBN：0345373588, 0345373588

70. Best Chinese stories, 1949—1989. Beijing, China：Chinese Literature Press, 1989. 501 p.；23cm. (Panda books)

《中国优秀短篇小说选：1949—1989》. 中国文学出版社

（熊猫丛书）

71. 100 glimpses into China: short short stories from China/ authors, Wang Meng, Feng Jicai, Wang Zengqi, and others; editor, Li Jun; illustrator: Ding Cong; translaters [sic]: Xu Yihe and Daniel J. Meissner. Beijing, China: Foreign Languages Press, 1989. 395 pages: illustrations; 18cm. ISBN: 7119005820, 7119005829, 0835123219, 0835123211

《微型小说100篇》，王蒙（Wang, Meng, 1934—）等. 英汉对照.

72. Spring bamboo: a collection of contemporary Chinese short stories/compiled and translated by Jeanne Tai; with a foreword by Bette Bao Lord; and an introduction by Leo Ou-fan Lee. New York: Random House, c1989. xvii, 284 p.; 25cm. ISBN: 0394565827, 0394565828

Contents: Clock/Zheng Wanlong—The homecoming/ Han Shaogong—Lao Kang came back/Wang Anyi— Looking for fun/Chen Jiangong—Grandma Qi/Li Tuo— Souls tied to the knots on a leather cord/Zhaxi Dawa— Like a banjo string/Shi Tiesheng—Dry river/Mo Yan— The tree stump/A. Cheng—The nine palaces/Zhang Chengzhi.

《春笋》，戴珍妮（Tai, Jeanne）编. 短篇小说.

73. Science fiction from China/edited by Dingbo Wu and Patrick D. Murphy; foreword by Frederik Pohl. New York: Praeger, 1989. xli, 176 p.; 25cm. ISBN: 0275933431

《中国科幻小说》，Wu, Dingbo 和 Murphy, Patrick D. (1951—)合编.

74. 100 glimpses into China: short short stories from China/ authors, Wang Meng, Feng Jicai, Wang Zengqi, and others; editor, Li Jun; illustrator: Ding Cong; translaters [sic]: Xu Yihe and Daniel J. Meissner. Beijing, China: Foreign Languages Press, 1989. 395 pages: illustrations; 18cm. ISBN: 7119005820, 7119005829, 0835123219, 0835123211

收录王蒙、冯骥才、汪曾祺等作家的短篇小说.

75. Best Chinese stories, 1949—1989. Beijing, China: Chinese Literature Press, 1989. 501 pages; 23cm. ISBN: 083512066X, 0835120661, 7507100413, 7507100419. (Panda books)

Contents: Recollections of the hill country/Sun Li—The girl from Mengbie/Yang Zhao and Bai Honghu—The election/Li Guowen—The family on the other side of the mountain/Zhou Libo—Lilies/Ru Zhijuan—Seven matches/Wang Yuanjian—My first superior/Ma Feng— Temper yourself/Zhao Shuli—The story of Old Xing and his dog/Zhang Xianliang—The general and the small town/Chen Shixu—The man from a pedlars'

family/Lu Wenfu/A corner forsaken by love/Zhang Xuan—Kite streamers/Wang Meng—Chen Huansheng's adventure in town/Gao Xiaosheng—Pages from a factory secretary's diary/Jiang Zilong—Lulu/Zong Pu—The story of a living Buddha/Malqinhu—The log cabin overgrown with creepers/Gu Hua—Daft second uncle/Su Shuyang—A tale of Big Nur/Wang Zengqi—The destination/Wang Anyi—Eight hundred metres below/ Sun Shaoshan—The seven-tined stag/Wure'ertu—Black walls/Liu Xinwu—The tall woman and her short husband/Feng Jicai—Ah, fragrant snow/Tie Ning—A land of wonder and mystery/Liang Xiaosheng—Han the forger/Deng Youmei—My faraway Qingpingwan/Shi Tiesheng—An encounter in Green Vine Lane/Liu Shaotang—The last angler/Li Hangyu—Nobby's run of luck/Zhang Jie—The tavern/Zheng Wanlong—A soul in bondage/Tashi Dawa—Return/Han Shaogong—The mountain cabin/Can Xue—Touch paper/Jia Pingwa— Hong Taitai/Cheng Naishan—Marriage of the dead/Li Rui—Ten years deducted/Shen Rong.

《中国优秀短篇小说选：1949—1989》

76. Love that burns on a summer's night. Beijing: Chinese Literature Press; Distributed by China International Book Trading Corp., 1990. 319 p.; 18cm. ISBN: 7507100308, 7507100303, 0835120643, 0835120647. (Panda books)

Contents: The distant sound of tree-felling/Cai Cehai— The seven tined stag/Wure'ertu—Spring rain/Odsor— Little grass/Jia Jun—Serenade on the plateau/Tashi Dawa—Among relatives/Lim Yunchun—Fragrant island/Hai Tao—Three sketches/Zhao Danian—The black steed/Zhang Chengzhi—Love that burns on a summer's night/Malqinhu.

《爱在夏夜里燃烧》. 中国文学出版社（熊猫丛书）

77. Furrows, peasants, intellectuals, and the state: stories and histories from modern China/compiled and edited, with an introduction by Helen F. Siu. Stanford, Calif.: Stanford University Press, 1990. xii, 341 pages: illustrations; 24cm. ISBN: 0804718059, 0804718059, 0804718385, 0804718387

Contents: pt. I. The frailty of power—Mud/Mao Dun— A certain day/Wu Zuxiang—On the oxcart/Xiao Hong— The way of the beast/Sha Ting—Rumbling in Xu family village/Ai Wu—pt. II. The force of dogma—The widow Tian and her pumpkins/Zhao Shuli—The first step/Kang Zhuo—Taking charge/Fang Zhi—Firm and impartial/ Hao Ran—pt. III. Critique and ambivalence—A gift of land/Gao Xiaosheng—The ivy-covered cabin/Gu Hua— Electing a thief/Li Rui—Leisure: tending a vegetable plot/Yang Jiang—Deja Vu/Han Shaogong—Floodtime/Jia Pingwa—Chimney smoke/Ah Cheng—pt. IV. Furrows—Preface to Letters between two places/Lu xun—Superfluous words/Qu Qiubai—Wild lilies/Wang Shiwei—Do not close your eyes to the sufferings of the people/Huang Qiuyn—A happy life and the art of writing/Hao Ran—How I came to write "Lilies on a comforter"/Ru Zhijuan—What did I want to tell my readers/Li zhun—Father/Ah Cheng

《大地、农民、知识分子、城市：现代中国小说与历史》，萧凤霞(Siu, Helen F.)编. 中短篇小说集.

78. Worlds of modern Chinese fiction：short stories & novellas from the People's Republic, Taiwan & Hong Kong/Michael S. Duke, editor. Armonk, N. Y.：Sharpe, c1991. xiii, 344 p.；24cm. ISBN：0873327578, 0873327586

Contents：Blue bottlecap/Han Shaogong—The general's monument/Zhang Dachun—A wordless monument/Qiao Dianyun—The hut on the hill/Can Xue—White dog and the swings/Mo Yan—The stream of life/Hong Feng—Lai Suo/Huang Fan—Mountain Road/Chen Yingzhen—Dream scenario/Shi Tiesheng—The conquerors/Zhang Xiguo—A love letter never sent/Li Ang—A woman like me/Xi Xi—Reunion/Shi Shuqing—A place of one's own/Yuan Qiongqiong—Green sleeves/Zhong Xiaoyang—The window/Zhong Ling—My son, Hansheng/Xiao Sa—Shangri-La/Wang Zhenhe—Number nine Winch Handle Alley/Chen Jiangong—Race day/Bai Luo—Wrong number/Liu Yichang—Night revels/Hai Xin—Aunty Li's pocket watch/Liang Bingjun—Mother Lode/Zheng Wanlong—Dazzling Poma/Zhang Chengzhi

《当代中国小说大观》，Duke, Michael S. 编. 收录港台、大陆短篇、中篇小说.

79. Recent fiction from China, 1987—1988：selected stories and novellas/edited and translated by Long Xu. Lewiston：Edwin Mellen Press, c1991. x, 222 p.；24cm. ISBN：0773496645, 0773496644, 0889460760. (Chinese studies；v. 1)

Contents：Exciting/Wang Meng—Fireboat/Wei Shixiang—Recommendation/Xing Hongliang—Old acquaintance/Han Shaogong—Classmates/Shen Rong—Frustrations of the youth ah de/Cen Zhijing—Kitchen smoke again, kitchen smoke again/Mae Bende—Fluid personality/Li Xingtian—When I think of you at night, there is nothing I can do/Chao Naiqian—Abortion/Li Songjing—Smart lady/Liu Yufeng.

《中国近期中短篇小说选(1987 —1989)》，Long, Xu 编译.

80. Recent fiction from China, 1987—1988：selected stories

and novellas/edited and translated by Long Xu. Lewiston：Edwin Mellen Press, c1991. x, 222 p.；24cm. ISBN：0773496645, 0889460760. (Chinese studies；v. 1)

1987—1988 年中短篇小说. Long, Xu 编译.

81. The time is not yet ripe：contemporary China's best writers and their stories/edited by Ying Bian. Beijing：Foreign Languages Press, 1991. 382 pages；18cm. ISBN：0835125653, 0835125659, 7119007424, 7119007427

Contents：Ah Cheng and his King of Chess/D. C. Mair—King of Chess Chapters 5，6，7，8，9，& 10)/Y. Deng—Feng Jicai, a giant of a writer in more ways than one/J. Li—The tall woman and her short husband/J. Feng—Jia Pingwa and his fiction/J. Sun—Touch paper/P. Jia—Lu Wenfu and his fiction/T. Wu—The boundary wall/W. Lu—Shen Rong and her fiction/G. Yang—Ten years deducted/R. Shen—Wang Anyi and her fiction/H. Ying—Lao Kang is back/A. Wang—Wang Meng and his fiction/G. Yang—Snowball/M. Wang—Zhang Jie, a controversial, mainstream writer/G. Yang—The time is not yet ripe/J. Zhang—Zhang Kangkang and her fiction/T. Wu—Bitter dreams/K. Zhang—Zhang Xianliang and his fiction/J. Li—Bitter springs—a truck driver's story/X. Zhang.

《时机并未成熟：中国当代作家及其小说》，殷边编.

82. One-minute stories. Beijing：Chinese Literature Press, 1992. 229 pages；18cm. ISBN：7507100855, 7507100853, 0835120945, 0835120944. (Panda books)

《一分钟小说》，中国文学出版社.

83. The anthology of famous Chinese writers' self-collected works. Short stories volume. ［Shanghai］：Shanghai Literature and Art Pub. House, 1992. 415 pages：portraits；21cm. ISBN：7532110079, 7532110070

《中国名家自选集》

84. The serenity of whiteness：stories by and about women in contemporary China/［selected and］translated by Zhu Hong. New York：Available Press, 1992. xi, 305 p.；21cm. ISBN：034537097X

《中国当代女作家之女性小说》，朱虹(Chu, Hung)选译.

85. The lost boat：avant-garde fiction from China ＝［Mi zhou：Zhongguo xian feng xiao shuo xuan］/selected & edited with and introduction by Henry Y. H. Zhao. London：Wellsweep, 1993. 187 p.；21cm. ISBN：0948454830, 094845413X

Notes：Includes translations of five short and three longer short stories by some of China's neglected contemporaries.

《迷舟：中国先锋小说选》，赵毅衡选编. 包括 8 部短篇小说.

86. Themes in contemporary Chinese literature/edited by Jianing Chen. Beijing, China：New World Press：Distributed by China International Book Trading Corp.，1993. 386 p.；21cm. ISBN：7800051323

Contents：Memorial arch/Chen Jie—Rented wife/Zhang Baishan—Na Wu/Deng Youmei—Offering gathered from that cherished homeland/Jia Baoquan—Bell and drum tower/Liu Xinwu—Traveling harvesters/Shao Zhenguo—Heavenly hound/Jia Pingwa—Spring festival eve/Da Li—Between themselves/Wang Anyi—Broken promise/Zhang Zhilu—Tall woman and her short husband/Feng Jicai—Freshwater shrimp/Ah Mu—Under the wheel/Wang Meng—Snow of Cortland/Jianing Chen—Civilization of straw hat and cloth shoes/Wu Qing—There is no cat in America/Tan Jiadong.

当代中国短篇小说选. Ch'en, Chia-ning 编.

87. I wish I were a wolf：the new voice in Chinese women's literature/compiled and translated by Diana B. Kingsbury. Beijing：New World Press：Distributed by China International Book Trading Corp.，1994. 252 pages；21cm. ISBN：7800051242, 7800051241

Contents：I wish I were a wolf/Ma Zhongxing—Octday/Tie Ning—Friend on a rainy day/Bai Fengxi—Women speak/Xiang Ya—Brothers/Wang Anyi—You can't make me change/Liu Xihong—Rejecting fate/Han Chunxu.

《我要属狼：中国当代女性文学选》，金婉婷（Kingsbury, Diana B.）编译.

88. Running wild：new Chinese writers/edited by David Der-wei Wang with Jeanne Tai. New York：Columbia University Press, c1994. viii, 264 p.；25cm. ISBN：0231096488, 0231096485, 0231096496, 0231096492

Contents：Divine debauchery /；by Mo Yan；translated by Andrew F. Jones—；Transcendence and the fax machine /；by Ye Si；translated by Jeanne Tai—；One kind of reality /；by Yu Hua；translated by Jeanne Tai—；The isle of Wang'an /；by Zhong Ling；translated by Kirk Anderson and Randy Du—；Master Chai /；by Zhu Tianwen；translated by Michelle Yeh—；Ghost talk /；by Yang Lian；translated by Charles A. Laughlin—；Mother fish /；by Xi Xi；translated by Kristina M. Torgeson—；Festival /；by A Cheng；translated by Ann Huss—；Plain moon /；by Gu Zhaosen；translated by Michelle Yeh—；I am not a cat /；by Tang Min；translated by Amy Dooling—；The adulterers /；by Li Peifu；translated by Charles A. Laughlin with Jeanne Tai—；Running wild /；by Su Tong；translated by Kirk Anderson and Zheng Da—；

Our childhood /；by Yang Zhao；translated by Michelle Yeh—；The amateur cameraman /；by S. K. Chang；translated by Jeffrey C. Bent—；Afterword：Chinese fiction for the nineties /；David Der-wei Wang.

Notes：A collection of fourteen stories by various authors，translated from Chinese.

《众声喧哗：中国新作家》，王德威（Wang, Dewei）和 Tai, Jeanne 编. 包括 14 部小说.

89. Chinese short stories of the twentieth century：an anthology in English/edited and translated by Zhihua Fang. New York：Garland Pub.，1995. xxvii, 201 p.；23cm. ISBN：081530532X. (Garland reference library of the humanities；v. 1496)

《20 世纪中国短篇小说英译》，方志华（Fang, Zhihua, 1963—）编译. 收鲁迅小说《狂人日记》《祝福》《孔乙己》.

90. Chairman Mao would not be amused：fiction from today's China/edited by Howard Goldblatt. New York：Grove Press, c1995. xiii, 321 p.；22cm. ISBN：080211573X

《毛主席会不开心：现代中国小说》，葛浩文（Goldblatt, Howard, 1939—）（美国翻译家）编译.

91. Chinese short stories of the twentieth century：an anthology in English/edited and translated by Zhihua Fang. New York：Garland Pub.，1995. xxvii, 201 pages；23cm. ISBN：081530532X, 0815305323. (Garland reference library of the humanities；v. 1496)

Contents：Diary of a madman/Lu Xun—New year's sacrifice/Lu Xun—Kong Yi Ji/Lu Xun—Spring peach/Xu Dishan—Class teacher/Liu Xinwu—Li Shunda builds a house/Gao Xiaosheng—Ah, Xiangxue/Tie Ning—Buddhist initiation/Wang Xengqi

20 世纪中国短篇小说. 方志华（Fang, Zhihua, 1963—）编译.

92. China's avant-garde fiction：an anthology/edited by Jing Wang. Durham：Duke University Press, 1998. 283 p.；24cm. ISBN：0822321165, 0822321009

《中国先锋小说》，王晶（Wang, Jing, 1950—）编译.

93. The Picador book of contemporary Chinese fiction/edited by Carolyn Choa and David Su Li-qun. London：Picador, 1998. xii, 308 pages；23cm. ISBN：0330369768, 0330369763

Contents：From Beijing Opera/David Su Li-qun—Hong Taitai/Cheng Nai-shan—Fate/Shi Tie-sheng—Life in a small courtyard；Between themselves/Wang An-yi—Between life and death/Su Shu-yang—Cherry；Young Muo/Su Tong—The window/Mo Shen—The lovesick crow and other fables/Wang Meng—The general and the small town/Chen Shi-xu—Black walls/Liu Xin-wu—Big

Chan/Wang Ceng-qi—Han the forger/Deng You-mei—Love must not be forgotten/Zhang Jie—The family on the other side of the mountain/Zhou Libo—Three sketches/Zhao Da-nian—The tall woman and her short husband/Feng Ji-cai—The distant sound of tree-felling/Cai Ce-hai—Six short pieces/Bai Xiao Yi—One centimetre/Bi Shu-min.

20世纪中国短篇小说. Choa, Carolyn 和 Su, Liqun (1945—)合编.

(1) The vintage book of contemporary Chinese fiction/edited by Carolyn Choa and David Su Li-qun. New York：Vintage Books，2001. xii, 308 pages；21cm. ISBN：0375700935, 0375700934

(2) The Picador book of contemporary Chinese fiction/edited by Carolyn Choa and David Su Li-qun. London：Picador，2013. 308 pages；23cm. ISBN：，：1447241560, 1447241568

94. The vintage book of contemporary Chinese fiction/edited by Carolyn Choa and David Su Li-qun. New York：Vintage Books，2001. xii, 308 p.；21cm. ISBN：0375700935

Notes："Originally published in slightly different form in Great Britain as The Picador book of contemporary Chinese fiction by Picador, an imprint of Macmillan Publishers Ltd.，London，1998"—T. p. verso.

Contents：Machine generated contents note：Some Information—David Su Li-qun ix—A Few Words-Carolyn Choa xi—David Su Li-qun—from Beijing Opera 1—Cheng Nai-shan—Hong Taitai 11—Shi Tie-sheng—Fate 22—Wang An-yi—Life in a Small Courtyard 42—Wang An-yi—Between Themselves 63—Su Shu-yang—Between Life and Death 81—Su Tong—Coery 98—Su Tong—Young Muo 108—Mo Shen—The Window 121—Wang Meng— The Lovesick Crow and Other Fables 143—Chen Shi-xu —The General and the Small Town 155—Liu Xin-wu—Black Walls 171. Wang Ceng-qi—Bighan 181—Deng You-mei—Han the Forger 191—Zhang Jie—Love Must Not Be Forgotten 205—Zhou Libo—The Family on the Other Side of the Mountain 220—Zhao Da-nian—Three Sketches 229—Feng Ji-cai—The Tall Woman and Her Short Husband 237—CaiCe-hai—The Distant Sound of Tree-felling 249—Bai Xiao Yi—Six Short Pieces 265—Bi Shu-min—One Centimetre 278—Author Biographies 295—Acknowledgements 306—Permission Acknowledgements 307.

20世纪中国短篇小说. Choa, Carolyn 和 Su, Liqun (1945—)译.

95. King of the wizards/Lin Xi. Beijing：Chinese Literature Press, 1998. 465 pages；18cm. ISBN：0835131904,

0835131902, 7507103749, 7507103748, 750710351X, 7507103519. (Panda books)

Contents：King of the wizards—Acquisition artists—Tianjin idlers—Small hours.

《天津江湖传奇》，李国庆，沙勒迪，孙艺风著；林希 (1935—)译. 中国文学出版社.

96. A place of one's own：stories of self in China, Taiwan, Hong Kong，and Singapore/edited by Kwok-kan Tam, Terry S. H. Yip, Wimal Dissanayake. Hong Kong；New York：Oxford University Press, 1999. xxii, 419 p.；22cm. ISBN：0195916581

Tam, Kwok-kan (1952—)；Yip, Terry Siu-han (1956—)；Dissanayake，Wimal 编译. 包括中国大陆、中国台湾和中国香港小说的选译.

97. Masterpieces by modern Chinese fiction writers/written by Lao She and others；translated by Sidney Shapiro and others. Beijing：Wai wen chu ban she, 2002. 573 p.；21cm. ISBN：7119029452, 7119029450. (Echo of classics=经典的回声)

《中国现代名家短篇小说选》，老舍(1899—1966)等著；沙博理(Shapiro，Sidney 1915—2014)等译.

98. 孔雀东南飞＝The peacock flies southeast/ 徐飞编著. 北京：新世界出版社，2003. 287 页；20cm. ISBN：7800059235. (中国古代爱情故事＝Classical Chinese love stories)

英汉对照.

99. 一江春水向东流＝The river flows eastward in spring/徐飞编著；[翻译保尔・怀特]. 北京：新世界出版社，2004. 283 pages：illustrations；21cm. ISBN：7801873076, 7801873071. (中国古代爱情故事)

为英语对照读物，描述南唐后主李煜与大、小周后的爱情故事.

100. 凤求凰＝The phoenix seeks a mate/徐飞编著；[翻译保尔・怀特]. 北京：新世界出版社，2004. 271 pages：illustrations；21cm. ISBN：7801873068, 7801873064. (中国古代爱情故事＝Classical Chinese love stories)

为英语对照读物，讲述司马相如与卓文君的爱情故事.

101. Dragonflies：fiction by Chinese women in the twentieth century/edited by Shu-ning Sciban and Fred Edwards. Ithaca, N. Y.：East Asia Program, Cornell University, c2003. viii, 226 p.；22cm. ISBN：1885445156. (Cornell East Asia series, 1050－2955；no. 115)

《蜻蜓：20世纪中国女性小说》，Sciban, Shu-ning 和 Edwards, Fred 编译.

102. The mystified boat and other new stories from China/edited by Frank Stewart and Herbert J. Batt. Honolulu：University of Hawaii Press；London：Eurospan, 2003. 220 pages；26cm. ISBN：0824827996, 0824827991

20 世纪中国短篇小说. Stewart，Frank（1946—）和 Batt，Herbert J.（1945—）编.

103. Stories for Saturday：twentieth-century Chinese popular fiction/Translated by Timothy C. Wong. Honolulu：University of Hawaii Press，c2003. x，252 p.：ill.；22cm. ISBN：0824826248，0824826906

《周末小说：中国二十世纪消遣小说》，黄宗泰（Wong，Timothy C.）（美国华裔学者）译.

104. Writing women in modern China：the revolutionary years，1936—1976/edited by Amy D. Dooling. New York：Columbia University Press，2004. x，321 p.；24cm. ISBN：0231132174.（Weatherhead books on Asia）

《中国现代女作家：1936—1976 年》，杜丽（Dooling，Amy D.）（美国学者）译.

105. Loud sparrows：contemporary Chinese short-shorts/selected and translated by Aili Mu, Julie Chiu，Howard Goldblatt. New York：Columbia University Press，c2006. xxiii，239 p.；24cm. ISBN：0231138482，0231138482

《喧闹的麻雀：中国当代小说选集》，葛浩文（Goldblatt，Howard，1939—）（美国翻译家）译.

106. Stories from Contemporary China. Shanghai Better Link Press，2006. 213 p. ISBN：160220201X，1602202016

收录毕飞宇、格非、铁凝等作家的作品.

107. The power of weakness/Ding Ling and Lu Hsun；with an introduction by Tani E. Barlow. New York：Feminist Press at the City University of New York：2007. 156 p.；18cm. ISBN：1558615489，1558615482.（2x2 series）

Contents：The New Year's sacrifice/Lu Hsun—New faith/Ding Ling—What happens after Nora leaves home? /Lu Hsun—Thoughts on March 8/Ding Ling—Regret for the past/Lu Hsun—When I was in Xia Village/ Ding Lin.

《软弱的力量》，鲁迅(1881—1936)，丁玲(1904—).

108. 世界华文微型小说精选：汉英对照. 中国卷. 上/江曾培主编；祁寿华译. 上海：上海外语教育出版社，2007. 24cm. ISBN：7544604963，7544604969

英文题名：Best Chinese flash fiction：an anthology. 精选中国微型小说若干篇，反映一个世纪以来微型小说在中国发展演变的过程.

109. 世界华文微型小说精选：汉英对照. 中国卷. 下/江曾培主编；祁寿华译. 上海：上海外语教育出版社，2007. 24cm. ISBN：7544605793，7544605795

英文题名：Best Chinese flash fiction：an anthology. 精选中国微型小说若干篇. 反映一个世纪以来微型小说在中国发展演变的过程.

110. Plum raindrops and more stories about youth/editor：Xie Youshun. Beijing，China：Foreign Languages Press，2008. 436 pages；23cm. ISBN：7119054384，7119054384.（21st century Chinese literature）

《梅雨》，谢有顺主编. 本书反映了生活在 21 世纪的中国人所经历的青春岁月. 11 篇作品为中短篇小说.

111. The great masque and more stories of life in the city/Li Jingze［editor］. Beijing，China：Foreign Languages Press，2008. 357 pages；23cm. ISBN：7119054377，7119054376.（21st century Chinese literature）

《化妆》，李敬泽(1964—)主编. 收录的 14 篇作品为中短篇小说.

112. How far is "Forever" and more stories by women writers/［edited by］Li Jingze...［and others］. Beijing：Foreign Languages Press，2008. 456 pages；23cm. ISBN：7119054360，7119054368.（21st century Chinese literature＝21 世纪中国当代文学文库）

李敬泽(1964—)等主编. 收录中国女作家作品.

113. The pearl jacket and other stories：flash fiction from contemporary China/edited and translated by Shouhua Qi. Berkeley，Calif. ：Stone Bridge Press，c2008. 345 p.；18cm. ISBN：1933330624，1933330627

《珍珠夹克及其他故事：中国当代微型小说》，Qi，Shouhua(1957—)译. 翻译当代中国小小说 120 篇.

114. China：a traveler's literary companion/edited by Kirk A. Denton. Berkeley，Calif. ：Whereabouts Press：Distributed to the trade by PGW/Perseus Distribution，c2008. xv，231 p.：map；19cm. ISBN：1883513238，1883513235.（Traveler's literary companions）

20 世纪中国小说. Denton，Kirk A.（1955—）编译.

115. One fallen leaf and more miniature stories/editor，Bing Feng. Beijing：Foreign Languages Press，2009. 4，360 pages；23cm. ISBN：7119057484，7119057480.（21st century Chinese literature）

《一片落叶》，冰峰主编. 本书选取了 88 篇微型小说. 其中有王蒙的《邮箱》、蒋子龙的《看护》、阿成的《周同学》、梁晓声的《大兵》、毕淑敏的《紫色人形》等.

116. Street wizards and other new folklore/［editor，Liu Tao］. Beijing：Foreign Languages Press，2009. 444 pages；24cm. ISBN：7119057491，7119057499.（21st century Chinese literature）

《俗世奇人》，刘涛主编. 小说选集.

117. Jade streetlights and more stories of longing/［editor，Zhang Yiwu］. Beijing：Foreign Languages Press，2009. 400 pages；23cm. ISBN：7119059419，7119059416.（21st century Chinese literature）

《淡绿色的月亮》，张颐武主编. 短篇小说集.

118. Going to town and other rural stories/Zhang Yiwu. Beijing：Foreign Languages Press，2009. 411 pages；

23cm. ISBN：7119059426，7119059424

《到城里去》，张颐武主编.本集中所选均为新世纪以来的中国乡土小说.选了《到城里去》和《歇马山庄的两个女人》等9篇小说.

119. A refined robber and other selected anecdotal one-minute stories/Sun Fangyou［and others］. Beijing：Foreign Languages Press, 2009. 125 pages；20cm. ISBN：7119059105，7119059106

《雅盗：中国当代小小说选》，孙方友等著.

120. The mud boot wedding and other ethnic minority stories/［editor, Shi Zhanjun］. Beijing：Foreign Languages Press, 2009. 431 pages；23cm. ISBN：7119059402，7119059408. （21st century Chinese literature）

《一双泥靴的婚礼》，施战军主编.本书所选的十一部短篇小说作品的作者均为少数民族作家.作品讲述的故事涉及了藏族、哈萨克族、蒙古族、朝鲜族、东乡族、达斡尔族、鄂伦春族、回族、塔吉克族等.

121. Heroes of China's great leap forward：two stories/edited by Richard King. Honolulu：University of Hawaii Press, c2010. 132 p.；22cm. ISBN：0824834029,0824834364,082483402X,0824834364

Contents：Introduction—A brief biography of Li Shuangshuang/Li Zhun；translated by Johanna Hood and Robert Mackie with Richard King—The story of the criminal Li Tongzhong/Zhang Yigong；translated by John Shook, Carmen So, and Aaron Ward，with Richard King

King, Richard（1951—）编. 包括李准（1928—2000）的《李双双小传》和张一弓（1934—）的《犯人李铜钟的故事》的英译.

122. Hepburn shoes on the double-decker/compiled by John Chen. Beijing：China Intercontinental Press, 2010. 405 pages：illustrations；24cm. ISBN：7508517780，7508517784

《双层巴士二楼的赫本鞋：中国新都市小说集》，陈志强主编.五洲传播出版社.本书包括18篇当今一线都市小说家的新作.

123. Eleven contemporary Chinese writers/Karen Gernant and Chen Zeping, editors and translators. Monroe, LA：Turnrow Books, 2010. 357 pages；23cm. ISBN：0970396440, 0970396449

Contents：Translators' acknowledgments—Introduction/Wendy Larson—Dance of the soul/Alai—Blood ties/Alai—Long day/Ben Cun—Land of peach blossoms/Can Xue—Life show/Chi Li—Mama wolf/Guo Xuebo—Lament/Lin Bai—Temple of earth and I/Shi Tiesheng—Old Zheng's woman/Wei Wei—Dove on top of the tower/Yan Lianke—Nizi goes to market/Yan Lianke—In snowy weather/Yan Lianke—Are birds better at walking or flying？/Zhang Kangkang—Havana/Zhu Wenying—Ephemeral life/Zhu Wenying—Contributors.

Gernant, Karen 和 Chen, Zeping 编译. 现当代中国 11 位作家小说选,包括阿来、残雪、池莉、张抗抗、阎连科等.

124. Old land new tales：20 best stories of Shaanxi writers/［edited by Shaanxi Sheng zuo jia xie hui; translated by Shaanxi Sheng fan yi xie hui.］ Beijing：China Intercontinental Press, 2011. 394 pages：illustrations；24cm. ISBN：7508520865, 7508520866

Contents：Elder sister/Lu Yao—A tale of Li Shisan and the millstone/Chen Zhongshi—The country wife/Jia Pingwa—Oh, a colt！/Zou Zhian—The walking stick/Jing Fu—A trip for love：the story of an unmarried mother/Gao Jianqun—Love's unknown variable/Li Tianfang—Rain：the story of Hiroshima/Ye Guangqin—Who would go to the scaffold/Xiao Lei—The soul of the Great Wall/Zhao Xi—The butcher's knife/Feng Jiqi—The portrait of the ancestor/Li Kangmei—One family in the desert/Hong Ke—Mountain forest lasting forever/Mo Shen—Sister Yinxiu/Wang Peng—Lei ing'er/Zhang Hong—The bloodstained dress/Wu Kejing—At the foot of Mount Yanzhi/Wang Guansheng—Stargazing/Li Chunguang—Wife, or otherwise/Huang Weiping.

《陕西作家短篇小说集》,陕西省作家协会；陕西省翻译协会译.

125. The life show and other stories/by Chi Li and others；translated by Vivian H. Zhang. San Francisco, Calif.：Long River Press, 2012. 294 pages；23cm. ISBN：1592650317,1592650316. （Contemporary Chinese literature）

Contents：How long will eternity last？/by Tie Ning.—Quest for fun/by Chen Jiangong.—The life show/by Chi Li.—Urban life/by Li Zhaozheng.—Translation epilogue.

20 世纪中国小说选. Zhang, Vivian H. 译. 收录池莉等作家的作品.

126. A knife in clear water and other stories/by Shi Shuqing and others；translated by Vivian H. Zhang. San Francisco, Calif.：Long River Press, 2012. 260 pages；23cm. ISBN：1592650309, 1592650309. （Contemporary Chinese literature）

Contents：The phoenix piano/by Liu Xinglong—Story from the twelfth lunar month/by Chen Zhongshi—Best wishes for good fortune/by Guo Wenbin—My remote Qing Ping Wan Village/by Shi Tiesheng—Pa Lou Mountains/by Yan Lianke—Chen Huansheng goes to town/by Gao Xiaosheng—A knife in clear water/by Shi

Shuqing—Joint burial/by Li Rui—Shangbian Village/by Wang Xiangfu—Translation epilogue.

当代中国短篇小说选集. Zhang, Vivian H. 编译.

127. The girl named Luo Shan and other stories/by Liang Qing and others；translated by Vivian H. Zhang. San Francisco, Calif.：Long River Press, 2012. 294 pages；23cm. ISBN：1592650323，1592650325.（Contemporary Chinese literature）

Contents：The arrogant cobbler/by Wang Anyi.—Dumpling restaurant/by Jia Pingwa.—Kitchen/by Xu Kun.—Gold rush/by Zhang Xin.—Old Zheng's women/by Wei Wei—The girl named Luo Shan/by Liang Qing.—Translation epilogue.

Zhang, Vivian H. 译,收录王安忆等当代作家的小说.

128. The women from Horse Resting Villa and other stories/by Sun Huifen and others；translated by Vivian H. Zhang. San Francisco, Calif.：Long River Press, 2012. 270 pages；23cm. ISBN：1592650293，1592650295.（Contemporary Chinese literature）

Contents：The women from Horse Resting Villa/by Sun Huifen—Foggy moon corral/by Chi Zijian—The hunter/by Jia Pingwa—The swampland chronicles/by Wang Zengqi—Pagoda town/by Liu Zhenyun—Shoes/by Liu Quingbang—The small clinic/by Zhou Daxin—At the village square/by He Shiguang—Damned grain/by Liu Heng—Six bygone stories from the countryside/by He Shen—Translation epilogue.

当代中国小说选. Zhang, Vivian H. 编译.

129. Shi cheng：short stories from urban China/edited by Liu Ding, Carol Yinghua Lu, and Ra Page. ［Manchester］：Comma Press, 2012. xii, 210 pages：maps；20cm. ISBN：1905583461，190558346X

Contents：Square moon/Ho Sin Tung—But what about the red Indians? /Cao Kou—Kangkang's gonna kill that fucker Zhao Yilu/Jie Chen—Rendezvous at the Castle Hotel/Yi Sha—Dear wisdom tooth/Zhang Zhihao—This moron is dead/Han Dong—Family secrets/Ding Liying—Wheels are round/Xu Zechen—Squatting/Diao Dou—How to look at women/Zen Wen.

中国短篇小说选. Liu, Ding（1976—）, Lu, Carol Yinghua 和 Page, Ra(1972—)编译.

130. Short stories in Chinese：new Penguin parallel text/translated and edited by John Balcom. New York：Penguin Books, 2013. xiv, 257 p.；20cm. ISBN：0143118350

Contents：O Xiangxue/Tie Ning（b. 1957）—The ancestor/Bi Feiyu（b. 1964）—Dog/Cao Naiqian（b. 1949）—Plow ox/Li Rui（b. 1950）—The mistake/Ma

Yuan（b. 1953）—Lanterns for the dead/Jiang Yun（b. 1954）—Greasy moon/Jia Pingwa（b. 1953）—Receiving the precepts/Wang Zengqi（1920—1997）.

Balcom, John 编译.包括铁凝《哦，香雪》,毕飞宇《祖宗》,曹乃谦《狗》等.中英文对照.

131. Irina's hat：new short stories from China/edited with an introduction by Josh Stenberg；published in cooperation with the Chinese Writers' Association. Portland, Maine：MerwinAsia, ［2013］. xiv, 345 pages；22cm. ISBN：1937385224，1937385221，1937385231，193738523X

Contents：When are you moving out? /Joe Chen；translated by Josh Stenberg—Sleep/Bi Feiyu；translated by Kay McLeod—The most desolate zoo on Earth/Su Tong；translated by Josh Stenberg—Why the salesman went missing/Wang Shou；translated by Bryna Tuft—Our privacy/Xiao Su；translated by Josh Stenberg—Black-collared starling/Xu Yigua；translated by Florence Woo—Late stage/Li Han；translated by Josh Stenberg—Where I lost you/Fan Xiaoqing；translated by Kay McLeod—Nation Jin and his compass/Huang Fan；translated by Denis Mair—Amerika! /Tsering Norbu；translated by Petula Parris-Huang—Three cleaners/He Yuru；translated by Josh Stenberg—Irina's hat/Tie Ning；translated by Bonnie S. McDougall ［and 8 others］—The bird vanishes/Zhu Shanpo；translated by Josh Stenberg—Ex-husband/Wang Baozhong；translated by Z. Lu—Mad/Han Shaogong；translated by Josh Stenberg—About the authors—About the translators

《中国短篇小说选》,Stenberg, Josh 编译.

132. 英译中国当代短篇小说精选/赵丽宏主编；李洁译；汪榕培审订. Shanghai：Shanghai wai yu jiao yu chu ban she, 2013. iv, iii, 514 pages；24cm. ISBN：7544628068，754462806X.（外教社中国文化汉外对照丛书＝SFLEP bilingual Chinese culture series）

英文题名：Selected contemporary Chinese short stories

133. Best Chinese stories：the 1930s：Ye Shangtao and others. San Francisco：China Books, 2014. 611 pages；23cm. ISBN：0835100731，0835100731

20 世纪中国短篇小说.收录叶圣陶等作家作品.

134. Old land, new tales：20 short stories by Writers of the Shaanxi Region in China/edited by Lei Tao and Jia Pingwa. Seattle：AmazonCrossing, 2014. 428 pages：illustrations；21cm. ISBN：1477823705，1477823700

"First published in 2011 by china Intercontinental Press."-Title page verso

《老土地,新故事：20 篇陕西作家短篇小说》,雷涛,贾平凹编.

135. Chutzpah!: new voices from China/Edited by Ou Ning and Austin Woerner. Norman: University of Oklahoma Press, [2015]. xiv, 281 pages; 23cm. ISBN: 0806148700 (Chinese literature today book series; volume 4)

Notes: "[A]... bold experiment in bilingual publishing" [with English translations by twelve translators]—Preface.

Contents: Preface: the story of Chutzpah!, by Ou Ning and Austin Woerner—A brief history of time, by Xu Zechen—A village of cold hearths, by Sheng Keyi—The balcony, by Ren Xiaowen—Retracing your steps, by Zhu Yue—Paradise temple, by Lu Min—Interlude: excerpt from "A dictionary of xinjiang," by Shen Wei—The failure, by Aydos Amantay—Dust, by Chen Xue—The curse, by A Yi—Unfinished? to be continued, by Li Zishu—Philosophy in the boudoir, by He wapi—Interlude: "an education in cruelty," by Ye Fu—War among the insects, by Chang Hui-Ching—Monsters at volleyball, by Lu Nei—Who stole the Romanian's wallet? by Wang Bang—Coda: excerpts from "Nine short pieces," by Li Juan.

20 世纪中国短篇小说. Ning, Ou 和 Woerner，Austin 编. 中英对照.

136. The sugar blower/editor: Li Jingze, Shi Zhanjun. Beijing: Foreign Languages Press, 2015. 318 pages: illustrations; 23cm. ISBN: 7119093062, 7119093061. (21st century Chinese literature＝21 世纪中国当代文学书库)

Contents: China story/Jiang Yitan—If I fall asleep on the plane that's going to crash/Kong Yalei—Williams' tomb/Di An—The sugar blower/Qi Ge—A rare steed for the martial emperor; Raising whales/Xiang Zuotie—The gift of a cut/Tian Er—The winter of 2009; The road to the weeping spring/Li Juan—Stephen's back/Li Er—Pregnant/Wei Meng—Brocade/Chen Mengya—Taking care of God/Liu Cixin.

《吹糖人》，李敬泽（1964—），施战军（1966—）主编.

137. To the goat-dipping/editor: Li Jingze, Shi Zhanjun. Beijing: Foreign Languages Press, 2015. 331 pages: illustrations; 23cm. ISBN: 7119093123, 7119093126. (21st century Chinese literature＝21 世纪中国当代文学书库)

Contents: To the goat-dipping/Ayonga—The back quarters at number seven/Ye Guangqin—Morning glories in the mirror (an excerpt)/Guan Renshan—Seungmu/Jin Renshun—Changing the water/Li Jinxiang—The only real man/Alat Asem—Painless/Yerkex Hurmanbek—The mustache dispute (an excerpt)/Memtimin Hoshur—A sheep released to life/Tsering Norbu—Childhood dream/Dan Zeng—Life of a mimic/Patigul—Arriving at Mount Yu/Ye Mei—The stilt house and neighbors of my childhood/Ye Fu.

《浴羊路上》，李敬泽（1964—），施战军（1966—）主编.

138. Sweetgrass barracks/editor: Li Jingze, Shi Zhanjun. Beijing: Foreign Languages Press, 2015. 334 pages: illustrations; 23cm. ISBN: 7119093130, 7119093134. (21st century Chinese literature＝21 世纪中国当代文学书库)

Contents: Well sweep; Plow ox/Li Rui—Mountains and grasslands/Akbar Mijit—Sweetgrass Barracks/Su Tong—The story of Hu Wenqing/Wei Wei—The disappearing bean curd girl; 1. 50 yuan of love/Lao Ma—Seawatch/Wang Ke—To my boyfriend's (ex) girlfriend/Hu Shuwen—Negatives/Shi Shuqing—The greengrocer/Deng Anqing—The hydroelectric station; The threshing machine/Alai—That damned thing she said/Fu Yuli—A 16th century oil peddler/Li Feng—The heart, too, broken/Li Xiuwen—Double pupil/Zhu Wenying.

《香草营》，李敬泽（1964—），施战军（1966—）主编.

139. The last subway/editor: Li Jingze, Shi Zhanjun. Beijing: Foreign Languages Press, 2015. 344 pages: illustrations; 23cm. ISBN: 7119093086, 7119093088. (21st century Chinese literature＝21 世纪中国当代文学书库)

Contents: Shenzhen is located at 22°27'-22°52' N/Deng Yiguang—The gift/Xiao Hang—Death of a playboy/Wang Shou—The last subway/Han Song—Friend of the moon/Qiu Huadong—Weird auntie/Zhang Yueran—Outdoor film/Xu Zechen—The taxi driver/Xue Yiwei—Recollections of the Hunan Cemetery/Wang Gang—The holiday monk returns/Cai Dong—Coming downstairs/Chen Qian—Dreamed to death/Mei Yi—The northern border/Li Zishu.

《末班地铁》，李敬泽（1964—），施战军（1966—）主编.

140. Irina's hat/editor: Li Jingze, Shi Zhanjun. Beijing: Foreign Languages Press, 2015. 330 pages: illustrations; 23cm. ISBN: 7119093079, 711909307X. (21st century Chinese literature＝21 世纪中国当代文学书库)

Contents: Irina's hat/Tie Ning—How to grow bananas/Xu Yigua—A jar of lard/Chi Zijian—Visa cancelling/Xu Kun—Only later/Zhang Yiwei—Fishbone/Sheng Keyi—A thousand and one nights/Zhang Yueran—Let us talk about something else/Zhou Jianing—Contract with the gods/Medrol—Yan Wu/Fang Fang—A miraculous sleigh ride/Pan Xiangli—

Skylark/Jin Renshun—George's book/Wei Wei.

《伊琳娜的礼帽》，李敬泽（1964—），施战军（1966—）主编.

141. Shadow people/editor：Li Jingze, Shi Zhanjun. Beijing：Foreign Languages Press，2015. 338 pages：illustrations；23cm. ISBN：7119093109，711909310X. （21st century Chinese literature＝21 世纪中国当代文学书库）

Contents：Doomsday/Han Shaogong—Shadow people/Can Xue—The beekeeper/Wang Jinkang—The arms, the arms/Xing He—4/1/2018/Liu Cixin—The endless farewell/Chen Qiufan—Chronicles of the mountain dwellers/Yang Ping—A story of Titan/Ling Chen—Milk/Ah Ding—The last brave man/Hao Jingfang—Mahjong/Feng Tang—Mona Lisa's smile/Ge Fei.

《影族》，李敬泽（1964—），施战军（1966—）主编.

142. A voice from the beyond/〔editor，Li Jingze，Shi Zhanjun〕. Beijing：Foreign Languages Press，2015. 339 str.：ilustr.；23cm. ISBN：7119093093，7119093096. （21st century Chinese literature＝21 世纪中国当代文学书库）

Contents：Dark alley/Wang Anyi—Night of the spring breeze/Tie Ning—The hunter/Jia Pingwa—King's blood/Zhang Wei—A voice from the beyond/Mai Jia—The orphan of Zhao/Li Jingze—Golden fields of wheat/Zhou Daxin—Qizhao：lonely island/Anni Baobei—Song of Liangzhou/Ge Fei—Common people/A Yi—Hands/Su Yang.

《天外之音》，李敬泽（1964—），施战军（1966—）主编.

143. Keep running，little brother/editor：Li Jingze；Shi Zhanjun. Beijing：Foreign Languages Press，2015. 334 pages：illustrations；23cm. ISBN：7119093116，7119093118. （21st century Chinese literature＝21 世纪中国当代文学书库）

Contents：In the belly of the fog/Wang Anyi—The deluge/Bi Feiyu—The red detachment of women/Jiang Yun—The general/Li Hao—Two lives/A Yi—I am fish/Ren Xiaowen—Keep running，little brother/Lu Nei—The zebra that didn't exist/Su Cici—The train was clean and cool/Sheng Tie—The runaway game/Hai Nan—Hidden diseases/Lu Min—Aku Tonpa/Alai—Visiting Dai on a snowy evening/Xu Zechen.

《阿弟，你慢慢跑》，李敬泽（1964—），施战军（1966—）主编.

144. The sound of salt forming：short stories by the post-80s generation in China/edited by Geng Song and Qingxiang Yang. Honolulu：University of Hawaii Press，2016. ISBN：0824856397，0824856392，0824856366，0824856368

Notes："Original edition published by Foreign Language Teaching and Research Press"—Title page verso.

《听盐生长的声音》，Song，Geng 和 Yang，Qingxiang 合编. 中国"80 后"著名作家小说选.

145. Fragment of a memory from 1970/editor：Li Jingze，Shi Zhanjun. Beijing：Foreign Languages Press，2015. 8，315 pages；23cm. ISBN：7119093147，7119093142. （21st century Chinese literature＝21 世纪中国当代文学书库）

《一九七零年的记忆片段》，李敬泽，施战军编.

146. By the river：seven contemporary Chinese novellas/edited by Charles A. Laughlin，Liu Hongtao，and Jonathan Stalling. Norman：University of Oklahoma Press，2016. xii，338 pages；23cm. ISBN：0806154046，0806154047. （Chinese literature today book series；volume 6）

Contents：Introduction/by Charles A. Laughlin，with Liu Hongtao—The beloved tree/by Jiang Yun—Voice change/by Xu Zechen—Mountain songs from the heavens/by Han Shaogong—A flurry of blessings/by Chi Zijian—Love and its lack are emblazoned on the heart/by Fang Fang—Safety bulletin/by Li Tie—The sanctimonious cobbler/by Wang Anyi.

当代中国 7 部中篇小说. Laughlin，Charles A. （1964—），Liu，Hongtao（1962—），Stalling，Jonathan 编译. 翻译了蒋韵、徐则臣、韩少功、迟子建、方方、李铁、王安忆 7 位作家的 7 部作品.

147. The kitchen and other stories/Xu Kun，Liu Zhenyun，Chi Zijian，Qiao Ye，Jia Pingwa. Docklands，Vic 3008，Australia，Vic. Penguin Group（Australia），2016. pages. ISBN：0734399120，073439912X

收录徐坤（1965—），刘震云，迟子建，乔叶，贾平凹 5 位作家的小说.

I54　现当代个人作品

（按作者出生年先后排列，作者出生年不详或作品的作者未知者排在最后）

陈蝶仙（1879—1940）

1. The money demon：an autobiographical romance/Chen Diexian；translated from the Chinese by Patrick Hanan；general editor，Howard Goldblatt. Honolulu：University of Hawaii Press，c1999. 294 p.；21cm. ISBN：0824820967，0824821033. （Fiction from modern China）

《黄金祟》，韩南（Hanan，Patrick）（新西兰裔汉学家）译；葛浩文（Goldblatt，Howard，1939—）（美国翻译家）总编.

鲁迅（1881—1936）

1. The true story of Ah Q/by Lu-hsün〔pseud.〕；translated into English by George Kin Leung. Shanghai，China，The

Commercial Press, Limited，1926. vii，100 pages；19cm.

《阿 Q 正传》，梁社乾(Leung, George Kin, 1899—)译.

(1)Shanghai, Commercial Press，1933. 100 pages

(2)Ah Q and others/Lu Hsun；translated into English by George Kin Leung. Doylestown, Pa.：Wildside Press，2002. 159 pages；23cm. ISBN：1592249485，1592249480

2. Short stories by Lu Hsin：with English translation/compiled by Ku Tsong-Nee. Shanghai：Chung-ying chu pan she，1941. 147 pages；19cm.

《鲁迅短篇小说选》，Ku，Tsong-i 译. 中英对照.

3. Ah Q and others；selected stories of Lusin/translated by Jizhen Wang. New York：Columbia University Press，1941. xxvi pages，2 leaves [3]-219 pages；23cm. ISBN：0837159652, 0837159652, 0836938399, 0836938395

Contents：My native heath. —The cake of soap. —The divorce. —Reunion in a restaurant. —The story of hair. —Cloud over Luchen. —Our story of Ah Q. —A hermit at large. —Remorse. —The widow. —The diary of a madman.

《阿 Q 及其他：鲁迅小说选集》，王际真(Wang, Chi-Chen, 1899—2001)(美国华裔学者)译. 收录《阿 Q 正传》《在酒楼上》《离婚》《头发的故事》《狂人日记》《故乡》《肥皂》《祝福》《伤逝》《孤独者》《风波》11 篇小说.

(1)Freeport, N. Y.，Books for Libraries Press [1971]. xxvi, 219 p. 23cm. ISBN：0836938399, 0836938395. (Short story index reprint series)

(2)Westport, Conn.，Greenwood Press [1971, c1941]. xxvi, 219 p. 23cm. ISBN：0837159652, 0837159652

4. Na han：Ying Han dui zhao＝The war cry/Lu Xun [Zhou Shuren] zuo；Zhao Jingshen bian zhu. Shanghai：Bei xin shu dian，1942. 319 pages；19cm.

Contents：The dairy of a crazy man. —K'ung I-chi. —Medicine. —A little incident. —Wind and wave. —The old home. —The true story of Ah Q. —White light.

《呐喊：英汉对照》，赵景深编注. 上海：北新书局.

(1)Shang-hai：Pei-hsin shu chü，1949. 319 pages；19cm. (Hsien tai chung-kuo wen hsüeh ts'ung k'an)

5. Hestitation. [Shanghai, Bei xin shu ju kan xing，1946]. 271 p. 19cm.

《彷徨》，赵景深(1902—1985)译.

(1)[Shanghai]：[Bei xin shu ju kan xing]，1948. 271 pages；18cm.

6. 高老夫子 ＝ Professor Kao/鲁迅原著；王际真英译. [China]：世界英语编译社，[1947]. 71 pages；19cm. 英汉对照.

7. 祝福＝Benediction/鲁迅着；柳无垢译. [China]：世界英语编译社，[1947]. 77 pages；18cm.

8. Remorse ＝ Shang shih/[translated by] Ch'en Li-min.

[Shanghai]：Shih chich ying yü pien i she，1947. 83 pages；20cm.

《伤逝》. 英汉对照.

9. The true story of Ah Q/by Lu Xun；translated. by Yang Xianyi and Gladys Yang. Peking, Foreign Languages Press，1953. 111 p. port. 20cm.

《阿 Q 正传》，杨宪益（1915—2009），戴乃迭（Yang, Gladys, 1919—1999)译. 中英对照.

(1)2nd ed. Peking：Foreign Languages Press，1955. 111 pages：portraits；20cm.

(2)[3rd ed.]. Peking：Foreign Languages Press，1960. 64 pages：portraits；19cm.

(3)4th ed. Peking, Foreign Languages Press，1964. 60 pages：illustrations；18cm.

(4)5th ed. Peking：Foreign Languages Press，1972. 68 pages；19cm.

(5)Peking：Foreign Languages Press，1977. 68 pages

(6)Boston：Cheng & Tsui，1990. 68 pages；21cm. ISBN：0917056930, 0917056932

(7)Peking：Foreign Languages Press，1991. 68 pages，[1] leaf of plates：portraits；18cm. ISBN：083512780X, 0835127806, 7119012053, 7119012056

(8)Chinese-English bilingual edition. Sha Tin, N. T.，Hong Kong：The Chinese University Press，c2002. xxxviii, 119 p.：ill.；22cm. ISBN：9629960443, 789629960445. (Bilingual series on modern Chinese literature)

(9)Beijing：Wai wen chu ban she，2003. 153 p.：1 facsim.；21cm. ISBN：7119026933, 7119026930. (Echo of classics)

(10)EasyRead Comfort ed. [NSW, Australia]：Objective Systems，2006. 80 pages；23cm. ISBN：1425011004, 1425011000

(11)Chinese-English bilingual edition. Hong Kong：Chinese University Press，2009. xxxviii, 119 pages：illustrations；22cm. ISBN：9629960445, 9629960443

10. Selected stories of Lu Hsun. [Translated by Yang Hsien-hi and Gladys Yang]. Peking：Foreign Languages Press，1954. 251 p. port. 22cm.

《鲁迅小说选》，杨宪益（1915—2009），戴乃迭（Yang, Gladys, 1919—1999)译. 收录《呐喊》《狂人日记》《孔乙己》《药》《明天》《一件小事》《风波》《故乡》《阿 Q 正传》《社戏》《祝福》《在酒楼上》《幸福的家庭》《肥皂》《孤独者》《伤逝》《离婚》《奔月》《铸剑》.

(1)New York：Oriole Editions，1959. 306 pages [4] leaves of plates：4 leaves of plates：illustrations, portraits；21cm.

(2)Peking：Foreign Languages Press，1960. 323 pages：frontispiece；22cm.

（3）2nd ed. Beijing：Foreign Languages Press，1963. 306 pages，［7］leaves of plates：illustrations（some color），portraits；22cm.

（4）2nd ed. Peking：Foreign Languages Press，1969. 306 pages（8 leaves of plates）：illustrations；18cm.

（5）［San Francisco］，［China Books ＆ Periodicals］，1969. 306 pages：illustrations；18cm.

（6）New York：Oriole Editions［1972］. 306 p. illus. 21cm. ISBN：088211042X，0882110424

（7）3rd ed. Peking：Foreign Languages Press，1972. 255 p. illus. 22cm.

（8）New York：Norton，1977. 255 p.；19cm. ISBN：0393008487，0393008487.（Norton library；N848）Reprint of the 1972 ed. published by Foreign Languages Press，Peking

（9）Peking：Foreign Languages Press，1978. 255 p.；21cm.

（10）Beijing：Foreign Languages Press，1989. 255 pages：illustrations，portraits；21cm.

（11）Facsim. ed. San Francisco，CA：China Books ＆ Periodicals，1994. 255 pages：illustrations；21cm. ISBN：0835122727，0835122726

（12）Selected stories of Lu Xun/translated by Yang Hsien-yi and Gladys Yang. Boston：Zheng ＆ Zui Co.，1995. 255 pages：portraits；22cm. ISBN：091705671X，0917056710.（C ＆ T Asian literature series）

（13）Honolulu，Hawaii：University Press of the Pacific，2000. 255 pages：illustrations；21cm. ISBN：0898751632，0898751635

（14）Beijing：Foreign Languages Press，2000. 473 p.；22cm. ISBN：7119026984，7119026985.（Echo of classics）

（15）New York：W. W. Norton，2003. xvi，255 p.；21cm. ISBN：0393008487，0393008487

（16）Rockville，Maryland：Wildside Press，2004. 272 pages

（17）Doylestown，Pa.：Wildside Press，2011. 269 pages；24cm.

11. Old tales retold. Peking：Foreign Languages Press，1961. 150 p. port. 19cm.

《故事新编》，杨宪益（1915—2009），戴乃迭（Yang，Gladys，1919—1999）译.

（1）［Translated by Yang Hsien-yi and Gladys Yang. 2nd ed. Peking：Foreign Languages Press，1972. 137 p. port. 19cm.

（2）3rd ed. Beijing：Foreign Languages Press，1981. 142 pages：portraits；19cm.

（3）Beijing：Foreign Languages Press，2000. 315 s.；

22cm. ISBN：7119026992，7119026992.（Echo of Classics）

（4）Honolulu，Hawaii：University Press of the Pacific，2001. 137 pages：portraits；21cm. ISBN：0898752507，0898752502

12. A madman's diary＝Kùang ren ri ji/ Lu Xun. Singapore：Shi Jie Shu Ju，1971. 107 pages；19cm.

《狂人日记》.新加坡世界书局出版.英汉对照.

13. The new year's sacrifice ＝ Zhu fu. Hog Kong：Zhao yang；Princeton：Princeton University，1973—1975. 2 volumes.（Chinese linguistics project reading material series；no. 2；English-Chinese series of new writings）Contents：［1］Zhu fu—［2］A student's companion for The new year's sacrifice by Lu Hsühn/prepared by Charles A. Liu.

Liu，Charles A.

《祝福》.英汉对照.

14. The New Year's sacrifice/adapted from the short story by Lu Hsun；illustrated by Yung Hsiang，Hung Jen，Yao Chiao. Peking：Foreign Languages Press，1978. ca. 150 p.：ill.；19×26cm.

《祝福》，Yong，Xiang 等绘画.

15. Call to arms/Lu Xun；［translated by Yang Xianyi and Gladys Yang］. Beijing：Foreign Languages Press：Distributed by Guoji Shudian，1981. vi，149 p.，［2］leaves of plates：ill.；20cm.

《呐喊》，杨宪益（1915—2009），戴乃迭（Yang，Gladys，1919—1999）译.

（1）Beijing：Foreign Languages Press，2002. 443 p.：ill.；21cm. ISBN：711902695X，7119026954.（Echo of classics）

中英对照.

16. Wandering/Lu Xun；［translated by Yang Xianyi and Gladys Yang］. Beijing：Foreign Languages Press，1981. 143 p.，［2］leaves of plates：ill.（some col.）；19cm.

《彷徨》，杨宪益（1915—2009），戴乃迭（Yang，Gladys，1919—1999）译.

（1）Beijing：Foreign Languages Press，2000. 411 p.：ill.；21cm. ISBN：7119026968.（Echo of classics）

（2）Beijing：Foreign Languages Press，2005. 411 p.：ill.；21cm. ISBN：7119026961，7119026968.（Echo of classics）

17. The complete stories of Lu Xun/translated by Yang Xianyi and Gladys Yang. Bloomington：Indiana University Press；Beijing：Foreign Languages Press，c1981. x，295 p.；22cm. ISBN：0253313961，0253313966，0253202744，0253202741

《鲁迅小说集》，杨宪益（1915—2009），戴乃迭（Yang，

Gladys, 1919—1999)译. 收录《呐喊》《彷徨》等.

18. Diary of a madman and other stories/Lu Xun; translated by William A. Lyell. Honolulu: University of Hawaii Press, c1990. l, 389 p. : ill. ; 25cm. ISBN: 0824812786, 0824812782, 0824813170, 0824813178

《狂人日记》，威廉·莱尔（Lyell, William A., 1930—2005）（美国汉学家）译.

19. The true story of Ah Q; The new year's sacrifice/written by Lu Xun; translated by Yang Xianyi and Gladys Yang. Beijing: Wai wen chu ban she, 2001. [5], 147 p. ; 13cm. ISBN: 7119025244, 7119025247. (FLP 汉英对照经典读本. 现代名家)

《阿Q正传；祝福》，杨宪益（1915—2009），戴乃迭（Yang, Gladys, 1919—1999）译.

20. The new-year sacrifice and other stories/original Chinese text by Lu Xun; translated by Yang Xianyi and Gladys Yang. Xianggang: Zhong wen da xue chu ban she, 2002. xli, 403 p. : ill. ; 22cm. ISBN: 9629960435, 9629960438. (Bilingual series on modern Chinese literature＝中国现代文学中英对照系列)

《祝福及其他》，杨宪益（1915—2009），戴乃迭（Yang, Gladys, 1919—1999）译. 中英对照版. 香港中文大学出版社.

21. The real story of Ah-Q and other tales of China: the complete fiction of Lu Xun/Lu Xun; translated with an introduction by Julia Lovell; with an afterword by Yiyun Li. London; New York: Penguin Books, 2009. xlvii, 416 pages; 20cm. ISBN: 0140455489, 0140455485. (Penguin classics)

Contents: Diary of a Madman—Kong Yiji—Medicine—Tomorrow—A Minor Incident—Hair—A passing storm—My Old Home—The Real Story of Ah-Q—Dragon Boat Festival—The White Light—A Cat among the Rabbits—A Comedy of Ducks—Village Opera—New Year's Sacrifice—Upstairs in the Tavern—A Happy Family—Soap—The Lamp of Eternity—A Public Example—Our Learned Friend—The Loner—In Memoriam—Brothers—The Divorce—Mending Heaven—Flight to the Moon—Taming the Floods—Gathering Ferns—Forging the Swords—Leaving the Pass—Anti-Aggression—Bringing Back the Dead.

鲁迅小说全译. Lovell, Julia (1975—)译.

22. Call to arms; Wandering/Lu Xun. translated by Yang Xianyi, Dai Naidie. Beijing: Foreign Languages Press, 2009. 318 pages; 20cm. ISBN: 7119058801, 7119058800

《呐喊·彷徨》，杨宪益（1915—2009），戴乃迭（Yang, Gladys, 1919—1999）译.

  (1) Beijing: Foreign Languages Press, 2014. 339 pages; 23cm. ISBN: 7119087641, 7119087649

23. 呐喊：双语插图本/鲁迅著. 南京：译林出版社，2009. 299 页；23cm. ISBN: 7544708982, 7544708985

英文题名：Call to arms. 本书是鲁迅的短篇小说集. 共收录《狂人日记》《孔乙己》《药》等短篇小说 14 篇.

24. 彷徨/鲁迅著. 北京：外文出版社，2010. 261 页；24cm. ISBN: 7119066790, 711906679X. （经典回声）

英文题名：Wandering

25. 呐喊/鲁迅著；杨宪益，戴乃迭译；裘沙，王伟君插图. 北京：外文出版社，2010. 283 页；24cm. ISBN: 7119066806, 7119066803. （经典回声）

英文题名：Call to arms

26. 故事新编/鲁迅著. 北京：外文出版社，2010. 213 页；24cm. ISBN: 7119066769, 7119066765. （经典回声）

英文题名：Old tales retold

27. Lǔ Xùn's The New Year's sacrifice/edited by Kevin Nadolny; illustrated by Atula Siriwardane. [Houston, Tex.]: Capturing Chinese Publications, 2011. xiii, 84 pages; illustrations; 24cm. ISBN: 098427622X, 0984276226. (Capturing Chinese)

Notes: "English translation by Yang Hsien-yi and Gladys Yang, originally published 1960"—Title page verso.

《祝福》，Nadolny, Kevin 编；Siriwardane, Atula 插图；杨宪益（1915—2009），戴乃迭（Yang, Gladys, 1919—1999）译.

苏曼殊（1884—1918）

1. The lone swan, by the Reverend Mandju [pseud.] translated into English by George Kin Leung. Shanghai, China, The Commercial Press, Limited, 1924. xii, 147 p. incl. front. (port.) 20cm.

《断鸿零雁记》，梁社乾（Leung, George Kin, 1899—）译.

  (1) Shanghai, China: The Commercial Press Limited, 1925. xii, 147 pages frontispiece (portrait) facsimile 19cm.

  (2) Shanghai, China: The Commercial Press, Limited, 1929. xii, 147 p. incl. front. (port.)

  (3) Shanghai, China: Commercial Press, 1934. xii, 147 pages including frontispiece (portrait) 19cm.

  (4) Changsha, China: Commercial Press, 1938. xii, 147 pages front (portrait) 20cm.

  (5) 香港：英语编译社，发行者：立生书店，1960. 7, 275 pages; illustrations; 19cm.

  英汉对照.

李六如（1887—1973）

1. Sixty stirring years: a novel in three volumes/Li Liu-ju. Peking: Foreign Languages Press, 1961. 1 v. (460 p.): col. ill., port.; 22cm.

《六十年的变迁》，李六如（1887—1973）.

李劼人（1891—1962）

1. Ripples across stagnant water/Li Jieren. Beijing：Foreign Languages Press, 1990. 331 pages. ISBN：750710074X, 7507100747, 0835120856, 0835120852

   《死水微澜》，胡志挥英译. 中国文学出版社.

   （1）Beijing：Foreign Languages Press, 2015. 337 pages；18cm. ISBN：7119092898, 7119092898. （Panda books）

2. Ripple on stagnant water：a novel of Sichuan in the age of treaty ports/Li Jieren；translated with an introduction by Bret Sparling and Yin Chi. Portland，ME：Merwin Asia, 2014. xvii, 318 pages；23cm. ISBN：1937385248, 1937385248, 1937385255, 1937385256

   《死水微澜》，Sparling，Bret 和 Yin，Chi 合译.

叶圣陶（1894—1988）

1. Schoolmaster Ni Huan-chih〔Translated by A. C. Barnes〕. Peking：Foreign Languages Press, 1958. 383 p. illus. 22cm.

   （1）2nd ed. Press：Foreign Languages Press, 1978. 335 p.；22cm.

2. How Mr Pan weathered the storm/Ye Shengtao；translated by Simon Johnstone, Wenxue, Simon Johnstone,…〔et al.〕. Beijing：Chinese Literature, 1987. 260 p. ISBN：0835116042, 0835116046. （Panda books）

   《叶圣陶作品选》. 短篇小说.

   （1）Beijing：Foreign Languages Press, 2014. 1 vol. (260 p.)：couv. ill. en coul.；20cm. ISBN：7119058894, 7119058894

程小青（1893—1976）

1. Sherlock in Shanghai：stories of crime and detection/Cheng Xiaoqing；translated by Timothy C. Wong. Honolulu：University of Hawaii Press, c2007. xiii, 214 p.；22cm. ISBN：0824830342, 0824830342, 0824830997, 0824830991

   《夏洛克在上海：犯罪与侦探小说》，黄宗泰（Wong, Timothy C.）（美国华裔学者）译.

老舍（1899—1966）

1. Rickshaw boy, by Lau Shaw〔pseud.〕. Tr. from the Chinese by Evan King〔pseud.〕Sketches by Cyrus LeRoy Baldridge. New York：Reynal & Hitchcock, 1945. 383 p. illus. 22cm.

   《骆驼祥子》，伊文 • 金（King, Evan, 1906—）译；Baldridge, Cyrus Leroy(1889—)插图.

   （1）Rickshaw boy/by Lau Shaw〔pseud.〕；translated from the Chinese by Evan King〔pseud.〕New York：Reynal & Hitchcock, c1945. 315 p.；19cm.

   （2）Garden City, N. Y., Sun Dial Press〔1946〕. 315 p. 22cm.

   （3）London, M. Joseph〔1946〕. 254 p. 19cm.

2. Rickshaw＝the novel Lo-t'o Hsiang Tzu/by Lao She〔i. e. Shu Ch'ing-ch'un〕；translated by Jean M. James；〔maps by William C. Stanley〕. Honolulu：University Press of Hawaii, c1979. xi, 249 p.：maps；22cm. ISBN：0824806166, 0824806557

   《骆驼祥子》，James, Jean M. 译.

3. Camel Xiangzi/Lao She；translated by Shi Xiaoqing. Bloomington：Indiana University Press；Beijing：Foreign Languages Press, 1981. 236 pages；22cm. ISBN：0253312965, 0253312969, 0253202752, 0253202758

   《骆驼祥子》

4. Rickshaw boy：a novel/Lao She；translated by Howard Goldblatt. 1st ed. New York：Harper Perennial Modern Chinese Classics, c2010. xv, 300 p.；21cm. ISBN：0061436925, 0061436925

   《骆驼祥子》，葛浩文（Goldblatt, Howard, 1939—）（美国翻译家）译.

5. Divorce.〔St. Petersburg〕King Publications〔1948〕. vii, 444 p. 18cm.

   《离婚》，老舍（1899—1966）；伊文 • 金（King, Evan, 1906—）译.

6. The quest for love of Lao Lee/by Lau Shaw (Lao Sheh)；tr. from the Chinese by Helena Kuo. New York：Reynal & Hitchcock, 1948. 306 p.；22cm.

   《离婚》，郭镜秋（Kuo, Ching-ch'iu）译.

7. Heavensent/by Shu She-yu. London：Dent & Sons, 1951. 284 pages；19cm.

   《牛天赐传》，Hsiung, Te-ni(1927—)译.

   （1）Heavensent/ Lao She；translated by Xiong Deni；illustrated by Ding Cong. Hongkong：Joint Pub. Co., 1986. xiii, 259 p.；21cm. ISBN：9620403924

   （2）Hongkong：Joint Publishing, 1995. 259 pages；illustrations；21 × 14cm. ISBN：9620403924, 9620403927

8. The yellow storm〔by〕Lau Shaw〔pseud. of〕S. Y. Shu；translated from the Chinese by Ida Pruitt. New York：Harcourt, Brace〔c1951〕. 533 p. 22cm.

   《四世同堂》，Pruitt, Ida 译.

9. The drum singers, by Lau Shaw (S. Y. Shu) Translated from the Chinese by Helena Kuo. New York：Harcourt, Brace〔1952〕. 283 p. 22cm.

   《鼓书艺人》，郭镜秋(Kuo, Helena)译.

   （1）London：Victor Gollancz. 1953.

10. City of cats, by Lao Sheh. Translated by James E. Dew. Illustrations by W. Lewis.〔Ann Arbor, Center for Chinese Studies, University of Michigan, 1964〕. viii, 64 p. illus. 28cm. (Center for Chinese Studies, University of Michigan. Occasional papers, no. 3)

《猫城记》,Dew,James E. 译.

11. Cat country：a satirical novel of China in the 1930's by Lao She. Translated by William A. Lyell, Jr. [Columbus] Ohio State University Press [1970]. xliii, 295 p. 20cm. ISBN：0814200133

《猫城记》,威廉·莱尔(Lyell,William A.,1930—2005)(美国汉学家)译.

12. Beneath the red banner/Lao She；translated by Don J. Cohn. Beijing：Chinese Literature，1982. 215 pages；illustrations；18cm. (Panda Books)

《正红旗下》

13. Crescent moon and other stories/Lao She. Beijing：Chinese Literature：distributed by China International Book Trading Corporation，1985. 324 p. ；18cm. ISBN：0835113345，0835113342. (Panda Books)

《老舍短篇小说选》

14. Mr. Ma & son：a sojourn in London/Lao She；translated by Julie Jimmerson. Beijing, China：Phoenix Books：Foreign Languages Press，1991. 379 pages；18cm. ISBN：0835123677，0835123679，7119011057，7119011059

《二马》

15. Blades of grass：the stories of Lao She/translated from the Chinese by William A. Lyell and Sarah Wei-ming Chen；general editor, Howard Goldblatt. Honolulu：University of Hawaii Press, c1999. 310 p. ；21cm. ISBN：0824815068，0824818032

《草叶集：老舍短篇小说》,威廉·莱尔(Lyell,William A.,1930—2005)(美国汉学家),陈伟明(Chen,Sarah Wei-ming,1952—)合译；葛浩文(Goldblatt,Howard,1939—)(美国翻译家)总编. 收录短篇小说 11 篇,随笔 3 篇.

张恨水(1895—1967)

1. The eternal love：the story of Liang Shanbo and Zhu Yingtai/by Zhang Henshui；edited and translated by S. R. Munro. Singapore：Federal Publications，1991. xxi, 359 pages；18cm. ISBN：9810120575，9810120573. (Times Asian library)

《梁山伯与祝英台》,Munro,Stanley R. 译.

2. Shanghai express/Zhang Henshui；translated from the Chinese by William A. Lyell. Honolulu：University of Hawaii Press, c1997. 259 p. ：ill. ，map；21cm. (Fiction from modern China). ISBN：0824818253，0824818258，082481830X，0824818302

《上海快车》,威廉·莱尔(Lyell,William A.,1930—2005)(美国汉学家)译.

郁达夫(1896—1945)

1. Nights of spring fever, and other writings/Yu Dafu. Beijing, China：Chinese Literature：Distributed by China International Book Trading Corp，1984. 213 pages；18cm. ISBN：0835110796，0835110792. (Panda books)

《郁达夫作品选》

2. Nights of spring fever and other selected writings/Yu Dafu. Beijing：Foreign Languages Press，2009. 213 pages；20cm. ISBN：7119058856，7119058851

Contents：Nights of spring fever—A humble sacrifice—Snowy morning—Smoke shadows—Arbutus cocktails—Flight—Late-flowering Cassia—The fatalist—Private classes and a modern school—A spring day at the Angler's terraces—The flowery Gorge—Gaoting mountain—A half day's journey

《春风沉醉的晚上：郁达夫作品选》

茅盾(1896—1981)

1. Spring silkworms and other stories, by Mao Tun [pseud. Translated by Sidney Shapiro]. Peking：Foreign Languages Press，1956. 278 p. illus. 22cm.

《春蚕》,沙博理(Shapiro,Sidney 1915—2014)译.

(1) Washington, Center for Chinese Research Materials, Association of Research Libraries，1970. 278 p. on [142] l. illus. 28cm.

(2) 2nd ed. Peking：Foreign Languages Press，1979. iii, 237 pages：portraits；22

(3) AMS ed. New York：AMS Press，1979. 278 p. ：port. ；19cm. ISBN：0404144861

(4) Amsterdam：Fredonia Books，2003. iii, 237 pages：portraits；21cm. ISBN：141010219X，1410102195

外文出版社 1979 年的重印本.

(5) Beijing：Foreign Languages Press，2006. 213 p. ：illustrations；21cm. ISBN：7119027778，7119027777. (Echo of classics)

(6) San Francisco：China Books，2013. 250 pages；22cm. ISBN：0835100519，0835100510

2. Spring silkworms/by Mao Tun. Hong Kong：English Language Pub. Co. ，1965. 189 pages；19cm.

Contents：189 pages；19cm.

《春蚕》

3. Midnight [by] Mao Tun. [pseud. Translation by Hsu Meng-hsiung]. Peking：Foreign Languages Press，1957. 524 p. illus. ，port. 22cm.

《子夜》

(1) Washington, Center for Chinese Research Materials, Association of Research Libraries，1970. 524 p. on [265] l. illus. 28cm.

(2) Hong Kong：C & W Pub. Co. ：distributor, Era Book Co. ，1976. 524 p. ，[17] leaves of plates：ill. ；19cm.

(3) 2nd ed. Peking：Foreign Languages Press，1979. iv, 532 p. ，[20] leaves of plates：ill. ；22cm.

(4) [1st AMS ed.]. New York：AMS Press，[1979]. 524

p.，［16］leave of plates：ill.；22cm. ISBN：0404144853

(5)Boston，MA：Zheng & Zui Co.，1995. iv，532 pages：illustrations；22cm. ISBN：0887272347，0887272349，0887270999，0887270994

外文出版社 1979 年的重印本.

(6)Beijing：Foreign Languages Press，2009. 524 pages：portraits；20cm. ISBN：7119058818，7119058819

4. Midnight/Mao Dun；translated by Archie Barnes. Beijing：Foreign Languages Press，2014. 532 pages：illustrations；23cm. ISBN：7119087634，7119087630

《子夜》，Barnes，A. C.（Archibald Charles，1931—2002）译.

5. Frustration/by Mao Tun；［translated by Sidney Shapiro］. Hong Kong：English Language Pub.，1960s. 60 pages；19cm.

《委屈》，沙博理（Shapiro，Sidney 1915—2014）译. 英汉对照.

6. Rainbow /Mao Dun；translated by Madeleine Zelin. Berkeley：University of California Press，c1992. xiii，235 p.；24cm. ISBN：0520073274，0520073272，0520073289，0520073282.（Voices from Asia；4）

《虹》，曾小萍（Zelin，Madeleine）（美国华裔学者）译.

7. The shop of the Lin family；Spring silkworms/written by Mao Dun；translated by Sidney Shapiro. Beijing：Wai wen chu ban she，2001. 155 p.；13cm. ISBN：7119025244，7119025247.（FLP 汉英对照经典读本. 现代名家）

《林家铺子：春蚕》，沙博理（Shapiro，Sidney 1915—2014）译.

(1)The shop of the Lin family；Spring silkworms/written by Mao Dun；translated by Sidney Shapiro. Beijing：Wai wen chu ban she，2001. 213 pages，［1］pages of plates：portraits；21cm. ISBN：7119027778，7119027777.（经典的回声＝Echo of classics）

(2)Xianggang. English bilingual ed. Hong Kong：Chinese University Press，2002. xxxix，167 p.；22cm. ISBN：9629960451，9629960452.（中国现代文学中英对照系列＝BilingualseriesonmodernChineseliterature）

8. The shop of Lin family/Mao Dun；translated by Gladys Yang，Sidney Shapiro，Simon Johnstone，…［et al.］. Beijing：Foreign Languages Press，2015. 1 vol.（301 p.）：couv. ill. en coul.；18cm. ISBN：7119092874，7119092871.（Panda books）

《林家铺子》，杨宪益，沙博理等译.

9. The vixen/Mao Dun. Beijing：Chinese Literature，1987. 266 p. ISBN：0835116085，0835116084，7507100006，7507100006.（Panda books）

Contents：Creation—The vixen—The shop of the Lin family—Spring silkworms—A ballad of algae—Second generation—Liena and Jidi—Frustration—The beancurd pedlar's whistle—Mist—The rainbow—An old country gentleman—The incense fair—Before the storm—Evening—Footprints on the sand—On landscapes—In praise of the white poplar—Mountains and rivers of our great land—Night on Mount Qinling—Recollections of Hainan. Mao Dun，master craftsman of modern Chinese literature/Fan Jun.

《茅盾作品选》

10. Waverings/by Mao Dun；translated by David Hull. ［Hong Kong］：Research Centre for Translation，2014. 195 pages；22cm. ISBN：9627255408，9627255406.（Renditions paperbacks）

《动摇》，Hull，David（David N. C.）译.

老向（原名王焕斗，1898—1968）

1. Widow Chuan/retold by Lin Yutang；based on the Zhuan Jia Zhun/by Lao Xiang. Melbourne；London；Toronto：W. Heinemann，1952. vii，158 pages；21cm.

《全寡妇的故事》，林语堂（1895—1976）译. 为老向（原名王焕斗，1898—）《全家庄》的改编和翻译.

冰心（1900—1999）

1. The photograph/Bing Xin；translated by Jeff Book. Beijing，China：Chinese Literature Press：Distributed by China International Book Trading Corp.，1992. 370 pages；18cm. ISBN：0835120937，0835120937，7507100847，7507100846.（Panda books）

Contents：The painting and the poem—Notes from the mountain—Returning south—The story of a little bird—Common folk—Soap bubbles—My childhood—Treasures imperishable—Stars—Waters in springtime—The paper boat—Lovesickness—I was—The sentence—After the rain—The superman—Year away from home—Loneliness—Sissy Liuyi—The first dinner party—Birth—Miss Dong'er—The photograph—Our madam's parlour—My landlady—West wind—The orange peel lamp—On a train—My most unforgettable experience—An empty nest—The lowest calling

《相片》，Book，Jeff 译. 中国文学出版社.

(1)Beijing：Foreign Languages Press，2009. 370 pages；20cm. ISBN：7119058900，7119058908

(2)The photograph and other selected writings /Bingxin. Beijing：Foreign Languages Press，2014. 370 p.；20cm. ISBN：7119058900，7119058908

沈从文（1902—1988）

1. The Chinese earth；stories，by Shen Tseng-wen. Translated by Ching Ti and Robert Payne. London，G. Allen & Unwin［1947］. 289 p. 20cm.

《中国的土地：沈从文小说集》，Ching Ti 和 Robert Payne 合译.

(1)Morningside ed. New York：Columbia University Press，1982. 292 p.；22cm. ISBN：023105484X，

0231054858

2. The border town and other stories/Shen Congwen; translated by Gladys Yang. Beijing：Chinese Literature, 1981. 195 pages；18cm. (Panda books)

Contents：The border town—Xiaoxiao—The husband—Guisheng—My uncle Shen Congwen/Huang Yongyu.

《边城及其他》,戴乃迭(Yang, Gladys,1919—1999)译.

3. Imperfect paradise：Shen Congwen/edited by Jeffrey Kinkley; translated from the Chinese by Jeffrey Kinkley...［et al.］. Honolulu：University of Hawaii Press，c1995. 537 p.；21cm. ISBN：0824816358, 082481715X. (Fiction from modern China)

《不完美的天堂》,金介甫(Kinkley, Jeffrey C.，1948—) (美国汉学家)(美国汉学家)编译.短篇小说.

4. Selected stories of Shen Congwen/original Chinese text by Shen Congwen; translated by Jeffrey C. Kinkley. Hong Kong：Chinese University Press, c2004. xxxvii, 321 p.；22cm. ISBN：9629961105. (Bilingual series on modern Chinese literature)

《沈从文短篇小说选》,金介甫(Kinkley, Jeffrey C.，1948—)(美国汉学家)英译.

5. Border town：a novel/Shen Congwen; translated by Jeffrey C. Kinkley. New York：HarperPerennial, c2009. xi, 169 p.；23cm. ISBN：0061436918. (Modern Chinese classics)

《边城》,Kinkley,Jeffrey C. 译.

6. 边城/沈从文著; 杨宪益, 戴乃迭译. 南京：译林出版社, 2011. 213 页；21cm. ISBN：7544716604, 7544716600

英文题名：The border town

柔石(1902—1931)

1. Slave mother/Roushi; translated by Shi Nuoying. ［Shanghai］：Shi jie ying yu bian yi she, 1947. 98 pages；18cm.

《为奴隶的母亲》

2. Threshold of spring/by Rou Shi. Beijing：Foreign Languages Press, 1980. 171 pages, ［1］leaf of plates：portraits；19cm.

Contents：Threshold of spring—A hired wife—Destruction.

《二月》.短篇小说集.

艾芜(1904—1992)

1. Steeled and tempered. Peking：Foreign Languages Press, 1961. 437 p. 22cm.

《百炼成钢》

2. Banana Vale/Ai Wu. Beijing, China：Chinese Literature Press, 1993. 179 pages；18cm. ISBN：7507101355, 7507101355, 083513136X, 0835131360. (Panda books)

Contents：Banana Vale—Going home—In the gorge—Seeing off guests in the mountains—Song of the crows—

Mrs. Shi Qing—The night Xujia Village roared.

《芭蕉谷》.中国文学出版社.

丁玲(1904—1986)

1. Our children and others/by Ting Ling; edited and annotated by Meng Tsiang. 1941.

《孩子们及其他》.英汉对照.

2. When I was in Sha Chuan, and other stories/by Ting Ling ［i. e. P. Chiang］; translated from the original Chinese by Kung Pusheng. ［Poona］, ［Kutub］, 1945. ［4］, 118 pages.

Contents：When I was in Sha Chuan. —New faith. —Ping-Pong. —The journalist and the soldier. —Night.

《〈我在霞村的时候〉及其他》,Chiang, Ping-chih(1907—)译.

(1)Poona：Kutub, 1974. 118 pages；19cm.

3. The sun shines over the Sangkan River/Ding Ling; ［translated by Yang Xianyi and Gladys Yang］. Peking：Foreign Languages Press, 1954. 348 p. illus. 22cm.

《太阳照在桑干河上》,杨宪益(1915—2009),戴乃迭(Yang, Gladys,1919—1999)译.

(1)Peking：Foreign Languages Press, 1979. 348 pages：illustrations；22cm.

(2)Beijing, China：Foreign Languages Press：Distributed by China Publications Centre, 1984. 379 p.；19cm. ISBN：0835110087. (Modern Chinese literature library)

4. Miss Sophie's diary and other stories/Ding Ling; translated by W. J. F. Jenner. Beijing, China：Chinese Literature：Distributed by China International Book Trading Corp., 1985. 271 p.；18cm. ISBN：835111660, 0835110788. (Panda books)

《莎菲女士的日记及其他短篇小说》,詹纳尔(Jenner, W. J. F. 〈William John Francis〉)(英国学者)译.

5. Miss Sophie's dairy and other selected writings/Ding Ling. Beijing：Foreign Languages Press, 2009. 71 pages；20cm. ISBN：7119058870, 711905887

Contents：Translator's note—Miss Sophie's diary—Shanghai in the Spring of 1930 (2)—From dusk to dawn—The Hamlet—A Certain night—Rushing—The reunion—When I was in Xia village—Night.

《莎菲女士的日记：丁玲小说选》

巴金(1904—2005)

1. 汉英对照巴金短篇小说选＝Short stories by Pa Chin with English translation/钟文宜编选. 再版. 香港：中英出版社发行, 1940. 1 volume (various pagings)；19cm.

目次：复仇＝Revenge—初恋＝First love—狗＝Dog.

2. Star/Pa Chin; translated by Jen Ling-hsun. ［Shanghai］：Shih chieh ying yü pien i she, 1947. 157 pages；18cm.

《星》.英汉对照.

3. The family, by Pa Chin〔pseud. Translated by Sidney Shapiro〕. Peking：Foreign Languages Press，1958. 320 p. illus. 22cm.

《家》，沙博理(Shapiro，Sidney 1915—2014)译.

(1)2nd ed. Peking：Foreign Languages Press，1964. 321 pages：illustrations；18cm.

(2)3rd ed. Peking：Foreign Languages Press，1978. 284 p.，〔7〕leaves of plates：ill.；22cm.

(3)3rd ed. Peking：Foreign Languages Press，1979. 284 pages：illustrations；22cm. ISBN：0385057873，0385057875

(4)The family/Pa Chin；translated by Sidney Shapiro；adapted by Catherine Lim. Singapore：Federal Publications，1980. viii，111 pages：portraits；19cm. ISBN：9810190050，9810190057. (Federal Asian library)

(5)The family/Ba Jin；〔Sha Boli yi〕. Beijing：Foreign Languages Press，2015. 377 pages；18cm. ISBN：7119092973，7119092979. (Panda books)

4. Family/Pa Chin；introduction by Olga Lang. Garden City，N. Y.：Anchor Books，1972. xxvi，329 p.；18cm. ISBN：0385057873，0385057875

《家》，Lang，Olga 译.

(1)Prospect Heights，Ill.：Waveland Press，1989. xxvi，329 pages；18cm. ISBN：0881333735，0881333732

(2)Boston，Mass.：Chen & Tsui Co.，1992. xxvi，329 pages；18cm. ISBN：091705640X，0917056406. (C & T Asian literature series；Turbulent stream；1)

(3)Boston：Cheng & Tsui Co.，1999. xxvi，329 pages：portraits；18cm. ISBN：0917056406，091705640X

5. A battle for life：a full record of how the life of steel worker，Chiu Tsai-kang，was saved in the Shanghai Kwangtze Hospital/by Ba Jin and others. Peking：Foreign Languages Press，1959. 37 p.，〔4〕p. of plates：ill.；19cm.

《一场挽救生命的战斗》

6. Cold nights：a novel/by Pa Chin；translated by Nathan K. Mao & Liu Ts'un-yan. Hong Kong：Chinese University Press；Seattle：University of Washington Press，1978. xxxiv，181 p.：ill.；24cm. ISBN：0295956399，0295956398，9622011675，9622011670，0295956739，0295956732

《寒夜》，茅国权，柳存仁译.

(1)Cold nights/original Chinese text by Pa Chin；translated by Nathan K. Mao and Liu Ts'un-yan；with an introduction by Paul G. Pickowicz. Chinese-English bilingual ed. Hong Kong：Chinese University Press，c2002. xxxvii，557 p.：map；22cm. ISBN：9629960133，9629960131. (Bilingual series on modern Chinese literature)

7. Autumn in spring and other stories/Ba Jin. Beijing，China：Chinese Literature，1981. 147 pages；19cm. (Panda books)

Contents：Autumn in spring—The heart of a slave—A moonlit night—When the snow melted—On "Autumn in spring"—An interview with Ba Jin/Yang Yi.

《春天里的秋天及其他》

(1)2nd ed. Beijing，China：Chinese Literature，1985. 207 pages；18cm. ISBN：0835113396，0835113397. (Panda books)

Contents：The heart of a slave—The Su Causeway—Autumn in spring—The electric chair—The general—A moonlit night—When the snow melted—Rain—Outside a rubble strewn garden—My life and literature.

8. Spring/Ba Jin. Beijing〔China〕：Sinolingua，1987. 107 p.；18cm.

《春》

9. Ward number four：a novel of wartime China/Ba Jin；〔edited by〕Haili Kong，Howard Goldblatt.. 1st ed. San Francisco，CA China Books & Periodicals，Inc.，1999. xiv，208 pages：facsimile，portraits；21cm. ISBN：0835126463，0835126465

《第四病室》，孔海立(美国华人学者)，葛浩文(Goldblatt，Howard，1939—)(美国翻译家)合译.

(1)San Francisco：China Books，c2012. 232 p.；21cm. ISBN：0835100007

10. Garden of repose/written by Ba Jin；translated by Jock Hoe. Beijing：Wai wen chu ban she，2001.〔3〕，365 p.；13cm. ISBN：7119025244，7119025247. (FLP 汉英对照经典读本. 现代名家)

《憩园》，Jock Hoe 译.

(1)〔Beijing〕：Foreign Languages Press，2004. 461 p.；19cm. ISBN：711902776X，7119027760. (Echo of Classics)

(2)Beijing：Foreign Languages Press，2014. ISBN：7119087614，7119087610. (Gems of modern Chinese literature＝中国文学大家译丛)

11. Garden of repose/Ba Jin. Beijing：Foreign Languages Press，2009. 197 pages；20cm. ISBN：7119058849，7119058843

《憩园》

施蛰存(1905—2003)

1. One rainy evening/Shi Zhecun. Beijing：Chinese Literature Press，1994. 187 p.；18cm. ISBN：7507101347，7507101348，0835131351，0835131353. (Panda books)

Contents：One rainy evening—At the Paris cinema—The twilight taxidancer—Devil's road—Fog—Spring sunshine—

Madame Butterfly—At the harbour—Seagulls—Kumarajiva

《梅雨之夕》. 短篇小说集.

谢冰莹(1906—2000)

1. Letters of a Chinese amazon；and, War-time essays/by Lin Yutang. Shanghai, China, Commercial Press, 1934. xiv, 211 pages：illustrations(map)；19cm.

   Notes："Letters of a Chinese amazon [by Hsieh Ping-ying, translated by Lin Yu-t'ang]"—Page [1]-47.

   含有《女兵自传》, 林语堂译.

2. Girl rebel：the autobiography of Hsieh Pingying, with extracts from her new war diaries/translated by Adet and Anor Lin，with an introduction by Lin Yutang. New York：The John Day Co.，1940. xviii, 270 pages：illustrations；21cm.

   《女兵自传》, 林如斯(Lin，Adet，1923—1971)和林太乙(Lin，Tai-yi，1926—)合译.

   (1) New York：Da Capo Press, 1975. xviii, 270 pages, [1] leaf of plates：illustrations；22cm. ISBN：0306706911, 0306706912. (China in the 20th century)

3. 一个女兵的自传＝Autobiography of Hsieh Pinying/谢冰莹；林语堂，林如斯，林无双编译. [上海]：近代出版社，1941. 236 pages：illustrations；19cm.

4. Autobiography of a Chinese girl：a genuine autobiography/by Hsieh Ping-ying；translated into English with an introd. by Tsui Chi；with a pref. by Gordon Bottomley. London：G. Allen & Unwin, 1943. 216 p., [1] leaf of plates：ill.；22cm.

   《女兵自传》, 崔骥译.

   (1) London：Allen et Unwin, 1944. 16 p.：Ill.

   (2) London：G. Allen & Unwin, 1945. 216 pages

   (3) London G. Allen & Unwin, 1948. 216 pages

   (4) Autobiography of a Chinese girl/Hsieh Ping-Ying；translated into English by Tsui Chi；with a new introduction by Elisabeth Croll. London；Boston：Pandora, 1986. 216 p.：ill.；20cm. ISBN：0863580521

   (5) London：Kegan Paul, 2004. 216 pages：illustrations；24cm. ISBN：0710310412, 0710310415

   (6) London；New York：Routledge, 2010. 216 pages：illustrations；23cm. ISBN：0710310415, 0710310412

5. A woman soldier's own story：the autobiography of Xie Bingying/Xie Bingying；translated by Lily Chia Brissman & Barry Brissman. New York：Columbia University Press, c2001. xvii, 281 p.：ill.，maps；24cm. ISBN：0231122500

   《女兵自传》, Brissman, Lily Chia 和 Brissman, Barry (1942—)合译.

   (1) Berkley trade edition. New York：Berkley Publishing, 2003. xvii, 281 pages：illustrations，maps；24cm.

ISBN：0425188507, 0425188507, 0231122500, 0231122504

赵树理(1906—1970)

1. Rhymes of Li Youcai and other stories/Zhao Shuli. Peking [sic]：Cultural Press, 1950. 195 p：ill；19cm.

   Contents：Rhymes of Li Youcai—The heirloom—The Marriage of young Blacky—Old customs—Registration—Zhao Shuli and his stories/Zhou Yang.

   《李有才板话》, 沙博理(Shapiro，Sidney 1915—2014)译.

   (1) [2nd ed.] Peking：Foreign Languages Press, 1954. 155 p.：illus.；21cm.

   (2) 3rd ed. Peking：Foreign Languages Press, 1955. 157 pages：illustrations；21cm.

   (3) 4th ed. (rev. translation). Peking：Foreign Languages Press, 1966. 161 pages, [7] leaves of plates：illustrations

   (4) 5th ed. Beijing：Foreign Languages Press, 1980. 186 p.

   (5) Beijing：Foreign Languages Press, 1996. 186 pages；20cm.

2. Changes in Li Village/Chao Shu-li；[translated from the Chinese by Gladys Yang]. Peking：Foreign Languages Press, 1953. 224 pages；19cm.

   《李家庄的变迁》, 戴乃迭(Yang，Gladys)译.

   (1) 2nd ed. (rev. tr.). Peking：Foreign Languages Pr.，1966. 197 pages

   (2) Ann Arbor, Mich.：University Microfilms，1977. 224 p.

3. Sanliwan village/Zhao Shuli；translated by Gladys Yang；illustrations by Wu Jingbo. Peking：Foreign Languages Press, 1957. 275 pages：illustrations；

   《三里湾》, 戴乃迭(Yang，Gladys)译.

   (1) 2nd ed. Peking：Foreign Languages Press, 1964. 275 pages, [7] leaves of plates：illustrations, portraits；22cm.

4. The tale of Li Youcai's rhymes/by Chao Shu-li；introduction and notes by Susan S. H. MacDonald. London, Cambridge U. P.，1970. lxviii, 67, [2] pages：illustrations, map, portrait 19cm. ISBN：0521095883, 0521095884. (Literature, oriental)

   Notes：Text in Chinese；introduction and notes in English. / Added t. p. in Chinese：Li Youcai ban hua

   《李有才板话》, MacDonald, Susan S. H.作序并注解. 文本为中文, 英语注解.

周立波(1908—1979)

1. The hurricane/Chou Li-po；[translated from the Chinese by Hsu Meng-hsiung；illustrations by Ku Yuan]. Peking：Foreign Languages Press, 1955. viii, 409 pages：illustrations, portraits；22cm.

   《暴风骤雨》, Hsu, Menghsiung 译.

(1)2nd ed. Beijing：Foreign Languages Press，1981. 450 pages：illustrations；21cm.

2. Great changes in a mountain village, a novel/Chou Li-Po；[Translated by Derek Bryan]. Peking：Foreign Languages Press，1961. 2 volumes：color illustrations，portraits；22cm.

Contents：Entering the township—The party branch secretary—Night duty—Flour-paste—A quarrel—Gold-biter Chu—Shy-chun—Going deep—Applications—On the way—At the district office—Divorce—Father and son—A family—Live of the soil—Decision—Husband and wife—On the hill—Hunting for the bull—The Chang family—Strong rice wine—Felling trees—Hard work—Change of heart—Catching the ghost—Inauguration.

《山乡巨变》，Bryan，Derek 译.

吴组缃（1908—1994）

1. Green bamboo hermitage/Wu Zuxiang. Beijing，China：Chinese Literature Press，1989. 259 pages；18cm. ISBN：0835120686，0835120685. (Panda books)

Contents：Green bamboo hermitage—(Swastika) Shaped Honeysuckle—Eighteen hundred pearls—All peaceful under heaven—Fan's inns—A Certain day—The Boxcar—Twilight—The Sights of Mount Taishan—Firewood.

《菉竹山房》. 中国文学出版社.

2. Green bamboo hermitage and other selected writings/Wu Zuxiang. Beijing：Foreign Languages Press，2009. 259 pages；20cm. ISBN：7119058924，7119058924. (Panda books)

《菉竹山房：吴组缃作品选》

萧军（1907—1988）

1. Village in August, by T'ien Chün [pseud.] Introduction by Edgar Snow. New York：Smith & Durrell，[c1942]. xix, 313 p. 21cm.

Notes：First published in Chinese，1935. cf. p. x.

《八月的乡村》，斯诺（Snow，Edgar）作序.

(1)[Tower books ed.] Cleveland，World Pub. Co. [1944]. xix, 313 p. 21cm.

(2)Westport，Conn.，Greenwood Press [1974]. xix, 313 p. 22cm. ISBN：0837174589

欧阳山（1908—2000）

1. The bright future/by Ouyang Shan；[Translated by Tang Sheng]. Peking：Foreign Languages Press，1958. 105 p.；22cm.

《前途似锦》，唐笙译.

2. Uncle Kao/by Ouyang Shan Translated by Kuo Mei-hua. Peking：Foreign Languages Press，1957. 296 p.；22cm.

《高干大》，Kuo，Mei-hua 译.

马宁（1909—2001）

1. Broad Sworder/Ma Ning；translated by Liu Shicong.

Beijing，China：Panda Books；Chinese Literature Press，1993. 184 pages；18cm. ISBN：7507101339，7507101331，0835131343，0835131346

《扬子江摇篮曲》. 中国文学出版社.

高云览（1910—1956）

1. Annals of a provincial town. Peking：Foreign Languages Press，1959. 306 p. illus. 22cm.

《小城春秋》，沙博理译.

(1)2nd ed. Beijing：Foreign Languages Press，1980. 289 pages：illustrations，portraits；21cm.

叶紫（1910—1939）

1. Harvest, by Yeh Tzu [pseud. Translated by Tang Sheng and Ma Ching-chun]. Peking：Foreign Languages Press，1960. 183 p. 22cm.

Contents：Publishers Note—Harvest—Fire—Outside the Barbed Wire Entanglement—The Night Sentinel—Grandpa Yang's New Year—The Guide—About the Author

《丰收》

(1)2nd ed. Peking：Foreign Languages Press，[1979]. 162 p.；22cm.

钱钟书（1910—1998）

1. Fortress besieged/by Ch'ien Chung-shu；translated by Jeanne Kelly and Nathan K. Mao. Bloomington：Indiana University Press，c1979. xxix, 377 p.；24cm. ISBN：0253165180，0253165183. (Chinese literature in translation)

《围城》，Kelly，Jeanne，Mao，Nathan K. 译.

(1) Taipei：Bookman Books，1989. xxix, 377 pages；24cm.

(2)Bloomington：Indiana University Press，1998. xxix, 377 pages；24cm. (Chinese literature in translation)

(3)Beijing：Foreign Language Teaching & Research Press，2003. xxix, 418 pages；23cm. (Chinese literature in translation)

(4)北京：人民文学出版社，2003. 695 p. ISBN：7020042570，7020042579

(5)Beijing：Foreign Languages Teaching and Research Press，2003. 2,418 p.；23cm. ISBN：7560037332，756003733X

(6)New York：New Directions，2004. xiii, 395 p.：ill.；23cm. ISBN：0811215520，0811215527. (A new directions classic)

(7)London：Penguin Books，2004. 425 pages；24cm. ISBN：0713998350，0713998351，0141187860，0141187867. (A Penguin classics)

(8)London：Allen Lane，2005. 480 pages；24cm. ISBN：0713998350，0713998351

(9)Rev. ed. London：Penguin，2006. x, 425 pages；

20cm. ISBN：0141187860，0141187867

2. Cat/by Qian Zhongshu; a translation and critical introduction by Yiran Mao. Hong Kong：Joint Pub.（H. K.），2001. 125 pages：facsimile；23cm. ISBN：962041795X，9620417955

Notes：Cat was originally issued in a collection of short stories：Humans，beasts，ghosts（Ren shou gui，1946）

《猫》，Mao，Yiran 译评. 1946 年《猫》曾以《人、兽、鬼》出版.

吴强（1910—1990）

1. Red sun/by Wu Chiang; translated by A. C. Barnes; illustrations by Tu Ke and Liu Tan-Chai. Peking：Foreign Languages Press，1961. 670 pages，[9] leaves of plates：illustrations，portraits；22cm.

《红日》，巴恩斯译.

（1）Peking：Foreign Languages Press，1964. 645 pages：illustrations；22cm.

（2）Peking：Foreign Languages Press，1980. 667 p. ：ill. ；22cm.

萧乾（1910—1999）

1. The spinners of silk/by Xiao Qian; [translated by the author]. London，G. Allen & Unwin，1944. 104 pages；19cm.

Contents：A rainy evening—The spinners of silk—Under the fence of others—Scenes from the Yentang mountain—Chestnuts—When your eaves are low—The captive—The ramshackle car—Galloping legs—Shanghai—The philatelist—Epidemic.

《蚕》，萧乾（1910—1999）著并英译.

（1）3rd impression. London：G. Allen & Unwin，1946. 102 pages；19cm.

2. Chestnuts and other stories/Xiao Qian; translated by Xiao Qian and others. Beijing，China：Chinese Literature：Distributed by China International Book Trading Corp. ，1984. 184 pages；19cm. ISBN：0835111679，0835111676.（Panda books）

Contents：An album of faded photographs—Under the fence—When your eaves are low—Chestnuts—The philatelist—Cactus flower—The captive—A rainy evening—Galloping legs—Shandong deng—Epidemic—The Jiang boy.

萧乾小说选.

马加（1910—2004）

1. Unfading flowers/by Ma Chia. Peking：Foreign Languages Press，1961. 106 p. ；20cm.

《开不败的花朵》

白危（1911—1984）

1. The Chus reach haven/by Pai Wei; translated by Yang Hsien-Yi and Gladys Yang. Peking：Foreign Languages Press，1954. 108 p. ；16cm.

《渡荒》

（1）Peking：Foreign Languages Press，1956. 108 pages；16cm.

萧红（1911—1942）

1. The field of life and death and tales of Hulan River：two novels/by Hsiao Hung ［i. e. Chang Nai-ying］. Bloomington：Indiana University Press，c1979. xxvi，291 p. ；22cm. ISBN：0253158214，0253158215.（Chinese literature in translation）

《生死场》，葛浩文（Goldblatt，Howard，1939—）（美国翻译家）译.

（1）Ann Arbor，MI：UMI Books on Demand，1998. xxvi，291 pages；20cm. ISBN：0835766950，0835766951.（Chinese literature in translation）

（2）The field of life and death & Tales of Hulan River/Xiao Hong; translated by Howard Goldblatt. 1st Cheng & Tsui rev. ed. Boston：Cheng & Tsui，2002. xvii，273；22cm. ISBN：0887273920

2. Selected stories of Xiao Hong/translated by Howard Goldblatt. 1st. ed. Beijing，China：Chinese Literature：Distributed by China Publications Centre（Guoji Shudian），1982. 220 p. ；18cm.（Panda books）

Contents：The death of Wang Asao—The bridge—Hands—On the oxcart—The family outsider—Flight from danger—Vague expections—North China—Spring in a small town.

《萧红小说选》，葛浩文（Goldblatt，Howard，1939—）（美国翻译家）译.

3. Market street：a Chinese woman in Harbin/Xiao Hong translated with an introduction by Howard Goldblatt. Seattle：University of Washington Press，c1986. xvii，133 p. ；23cm. ISBN：0295962666

《商市街》，葛浩文（Goldblatt，Howard，1939—）（美国翻译家）译.

（1）Seattle；London：University of Washington Press，2015. xix，134 pages：1 photo；22cm. ISBN：0295994239

4. Tales of Hulan River/Xiao Hong; translated by Howard Goldblatt. Hong Kong：Joint Pub.（H. K.）Co. ，1988. xiii，237 pages；21cm. ISBN：9620406222，9620406225

《呼兰河传》，葛浩文（Goldblatt，Howard，1939—）（美国翻译家）译.

5. Dyer's daughter：selected stories of Xiao Hong/Xiao Hong; translated by Howard Goldblatt. Chinese-English bilingual ed. Hong Kong：The Chinese University Press，2005. xxi，273 pages；22cm. ISBN：9629960141，9629960148.（Bilingual series on modern Chinese literature）

《染布匠的女儿：萧红短篇小说选》，葛浩文（Goldblatt，

Howard，1939— ）（美国翻译家）译.

6. Spring in a small town and other selected writings/Xiao Hong. Beijing：Foreign Languages Press，2009. 220 pages；20cm. ISBN：7119058887，7119058886. （Panda books）

《小城三月：萧红小说选》

李乔（1908—2002）

1. The joyful Golden Sand River. Peking：Foreign Languages Press，1962. 200 pages. （His awakened land；the trilogy；v. 1）

《醒了的土地》. 该书为《欢笑的金沙江》第一部.

端木蕻良（原名,曹汉文,曹京平,1912—1996）

1. Red night/Duanmu Hongliang；translated by Howard Goldblatt. Beijing：Chinese Literature Press，1988. 312 pages；18cm. ISBN：750710009X，7507100099. （Panda books）

《红夜》. 中国文学出版社.

2. The sorrows of Egret Lake：selected short stories of Duanmu Hongliang；Chinese-English bilingual edition/original Chinese text by Duanmu Hongliang. Transl. by Howard Goldblatt...［et al.］. Hong Kong Chinese Univ. Press，2009. XXV，299 S. Ill. ISBN：9629963187，9629963183. （Bilingual series on modern Chinese literature）

《鴛鴦湖的忧郁：端木蕻良短篇小说选》，葛浩文（Goldblatt，Howard，1939— ）（美国翻译家）译. 英汉对照.

（1）Hong Kong：Chinese University Press；London：Eurospan［distributor］，2011. 1 volume；22cm. ISBN：9629963118，9629963116

草明（1913—2002）

1. The moving force/Tsao Ming. Peking：Cultural Press，1950. 214 p. ；19cm.

《原动力》

杨朔（1913—1968）

1. A thousand miles of lovely land/Yang Shuo；［Translated by Yuan Ko-cia］. Peking：Foreign Languages Press，1957. 237 pages；illustrations；19cm.

《三千里江山》

（1）2nd ed. Peking：Foreign Languages Press，1979. 227 pages；18cm.

孙犁（1913—2002）

1. Lotus creek and other stories/by Sun Li. Beijing：Foreign Languages Press；Distributed by G. Shudian （China Publications Centre），1982. 123 pages；19cm.

Contents：The reed marshes—Lotus creek—A hamlet battle—Memories—Caiputai—The tillers—Parting advice—Honour—Haoerliang—Guide—Recollections of the hill country.

《荷花淀》

2. The blacksmith and the carpenter/Li Sun；transl. by Gladys Yang. Beijing：Chinese literature，Panda books，1982. 311 pages；18cm. （Panda books）

Contents：The blacksmith and the carpenter—Lotus Creek—Little Sheng—Parting advice—The marshes—Recollections of the hill country—Stormy years—Husbands—Guide—Honour.

《孙犁小说选》，戴乃迭（Yang，Gladys，1919—1999）译.

3. Stormy years/Sun Li；translated by Gladys Yang. Beijing，China：Foreign Languages Press：Distributed by China Publications Centre （Guoji Shudian），1982. 436 pages；19cm. ISBN：0835109968，0835109963

《风云初记》，戴乃迭（Yang，Gladys，1919—1999）译.

4. Lotus creek/Sun Li；translated by Sidney Shapiro，Gladys Yang，Yu Fanqin... ［et al.］. Beijing：Foreign Languages Press，2015. 1 vol. （333 p. ）：couv. ill. en coul. ；18cm. ISBN：7119092881，711909288X. （Panda books）

袁静（1914—1999）

1. Daughters and sons/by Yuan Jing；［translated by Sidney Shapiro；illustrated by Yan Han］. Peking：Foreign Languages Press，1958. 324 p. illus. 22cm.

《新儿女英雄传》，袁静（1914—1999）、孔厥（1914—1966）著；沙博理（Shapiro，Sidney 1915—2014）译.

（1）2nd ed. Peking：Foreign Languages Press，1979. 282 pages，［10］leaves of plates：illustrations；22cm.

2. Stories of the Long March. Peking：Foreign Languages Press，1958. 137 pages：illustrations，map；19cm.

Notes："Stories of the... Long March of the Chinese Workers' and Peasants' Red Army during the period 1934—36."/ Translation of：Chang zheng de gu shi （romanized form）.

《长征的故事》，袁静，孔厥著；沙博理译.

3. The story of little black horse/by Yuan Ching；［translated by Nieh Wen-Chuan；illustrated by Lu Tan］. Peking：Foreign Languages Press，1959. 185 pages：illustrations；21cm.

《小黑马的故事》，袁静著；聂文权译.

（1）Peking：Commercial Press，1963. 121 pages：illustrations；21cm.

（2）Peking：Foreign Languages Press，1979. 202 pages：illustrations；19cm.

梁斌（1914—1996）

1. Keep the red flag flying/Liang Bin；［translated by Gladys Yang；illustrated by Huang Runhua］. Peking：Foreign Languages Press，1961. 528 pages，［6］leaves of plates：illustrations；22cm.

《红旗谱》，戴乃迭（Yang，Gladys，1919—1999）译.

（1）2nd ed. Peking：Foreign Languages Press，1964. 530 pages：illustrations

(2)3rd ed. Beijing：Foreign Languages Press，1980. 479 s.，［8］tav.：portr.

周而复（1914—2004）

1. Morning in Shanghai/ translated by A. C. Barnes；illustrated by Hua San-chuan. Foreign Languages Press：Peking，1962.

《上海的早晨》，Barnes，A. C. 译.

(1)2nd ed. Beijing：Foreign Languages Press，1981. v. 〈1〉：ill. (some col.)；22cm.

2. Doctor Norman Bethune/Zhou Erfu；translated by Alison Bailey. Beijing，China：Foreign Languages Press；Distributed by China Publications Center，1982. 231 pages，［8］leaves of plates：illustrations；19cm. ISBN：0835109976 ，0835109970

《白求恩大夫》，贝丽译.

杨沫（1914—1995）

1. The song of youth/Yang Mo；［translated by Nan Ying；illustrated by Hou Yi-min］. Peking：Foreign Languages Press，1964. 598 pages：illustrations，portraits；22cm.

《青春之歌》，南英译.

(1)3rd ed. Peking：Foreign Languages Press，1978. ii， 613 pages，［8］leaves of plates：illustrations， portraits；22cm.

(2)Lucknow：Parikalpana Prakashan，2010. 555 pages：illustrations；21cm. ISBN：8189760410，8189760416

2. 青春之歌＝The song of youth/杨沫原著；戴乃迭等改写；商英注释. 北京，商务印书馆，1965. 82 pages；19cm. 英语简易读物.

叶君健（1914—1999）

1. The ignorant and the forgotten/nine stories by Chun-chan Yeh；eight original lithographs by Betty Dougherty. London：Sylvan Press，1946. 159 p. ；ill. ；22cm.

Contents：The wishful：The dream. No sayonara. The wind—The ignorant：Manchurian night. A casualty. Eventful days—The forgotten：Triumph Wang's career. My uncle and his cow. Winter fantasy.

《无知的和被遗忘的》. 收录叶君健9部小说.

2. The mountain village, a novel. London, Sylvan Press， 1947. 230 pages；19cm.

《山村》.《寂静的群山三部曲》之一.

(1)Hongkong：Joint Pub. Co. ，1984. 229 pages；22cm. ISBN： 9620403142， 9620403149， 9620403150， 9620403156

(2)London：Faber，1988. 232 pages；23cm. ISBN： 0571149057, 0571149056

(3)London：Faber，1989. ［40］pages；20cm. ISBN： 0571141722, 0571141722. (Quiet are the mountains； v. 1)

3. They fly south. London, Sylvan Press, 1948. 203

unnumbered pages；19cm.

《它们飞向远方》

4. Sparks/Zhunzhan Ye；translated by Ian Ward. Beijing， China：Chinese Literature Press，1988. 348 pages；19cm. ISBN：0835120597，0835120593. (Panda Books)

《火花》

5. The open fields/Zhunzhan Ye；translated by Michael Sheringham. London：Faber and Faber，1988. 280 pages；23cm. ISBN：0571149065，0571149063. （Quiet are the mountains）

《旷野》.《寂静的群山三部曲》之一.

(1)London：Faber and Faber，1989. 280 pages；20cm. ISBN：0571141714，0571141715. （Quiet are the mountains；v. 2. ）

6. A distant journey/Chun-Chan Yeh；translated by Stephen Hallett. London：Faber and Faber，1989. 315 pages；20cm. ISBN：0571141730，0571141739. （Quiet are the mountains；v. 3）

《远程》，Hallett，Stephen 译. 属于《寂静的群山三部曲》之一.

7. Quiet are the mountains：［a trilogy］/Chun-Chan Yeh. London：Faber and Faber，1988—1989. 3 vol. ：couv. ill. en coul. ；20cm.

Contents：vol. I, The mountain village；vol. II, The open fields/transl. by Michael Sheringham；vol. III, A distant journey/transl. by Stephen Hallett.

《寂静的群山三部曲》

秦兆阳（1916—1994）

1. Village sketches/by Chin Chao-yang；［translated by Sidney Shapiro］. Peking：Foreign Languages Press， 1957. 198 pages，［1］leaf of plates：portrait

《农村散记》

柳青（1916—1978）

1. Wall of bronze/by Liu Ching；translated by Sidney Shapiro. Peking：Foreign Languages Press，1954. 283 pages：illustrations；22cm.

《铜墙铁壁》，沙博理（Shapiro，Sidney 1915—2014)译.

2. The builders Liu Ching；translated by Sidney Shapiro；illustrations by Ah Lao. Peking：Foreign Languages Press，1964. 573 pages：illustrations；22cm.

《创业史》，沙博理（Shapiro，Sidney 1915—2014)译.

(1)Builders of a new life/Liu Ching；translated by Sidney Shapiro；illustrations by Ah Lao. 2nd ed. Peking： Foreign Languages Press，1977. 561 pages： illustrations；22cm.

刘白羽（1916—2005）

1. Six A. M. and other stories/Pai-Yu Liu. Peking：Foreign Languages Press，1953. 149 pages；19cm.

《早晨六点钟》

2. Flames ahead/Liu Pai-Yu. Peking：Foreign Languages Press，1954. 1 v. （166 p.）：map（on lining papers）；17cm.

《火光在前》

吴运铎（1917—1991）

1. Son of the working class：the autobiography of Wu Yun-to/translated by Huang Pin-chang and Tang Sheng. Peking：Foreign Languages Press，1956. 224 p.：ill.；19cm.

《把一切献给党》，Huang，Pin-chang 译.

刘知侠（1918—1991）

1. The railway guerrillas/Chih Hsia（pseudonym of Liu Chih-hsia）；translated from the Chinese by Pin-tseng Ting. Peking：Foreign Languages Press，1966. 604，[3] p.；22cm.

《铁道游击队》，Ting，Pin-tseng 译.

王若望（1918—2001）

1. Hunger trilogy/Wang Ruowang；translated by Kyna Rubin with Ira Kasoff；introduction by Kyna Rubin. Armonk，N. Y.：Sharpe，1991. xxxvii，135 pages；24cm. ISBN：087332739X，0873327398，0873327403，0873327404

《饥饿三部曲》，Rubin，Kyna 译.

 （1）Armonk，N. Y.：Sharpe，1992. xxxvii，135 pages；24cm. ISBN：0873327403，0873327404

张爱玲（1920—1995）

1. The rice-sprout song. New York：Scribner，1955. 182 p. 20cm.

 《秧歌》，张爱玲（1920—1995）著译.

 （1）Hongkong：Dragonfly Books，1963. 182 p.；19cm.

 （2）New York：Scribner，1987. 182 pages；19cm.

 （3）The rice sprout song：a novel of modern China/by Eileen Chang. Berkeley：University of California Press，c1998. xxv，182 p.；21cm. ISBN：0520214374，0520214378，0520210883，0520210882

2. Naked earth/by Eileen Chang. Hong Kong：Union Press，1956. 365 pages；19cm.

 Notes：Translation of：Ch'ih ti chih lien. / "A novel about China originally published by the Tien Feng Press, Hong Kong, October 1954."

 《赤地之恋》，张爱玲（1920—1995）著译.

 （1）[Hong Kong] Union Press [1964]. 386 p. 18cm.

 （2）New York：New York Review Books，2015. xiii，312 pages；21cm. ISBN：1590178348，1590178343，1590178355，1590178351. （NYRB Classics）

3. The naked earth/by Eileen Chang；adapted by Aileen T. Kitchin. New York：Berkeley Pub.，1962. 127 pages；18cm.

 《赤地之恋》，Kitchin，Aileen T. 改编并英译.

4. Traces of love and other stories/Eileen Chang；edited by Eva Hung. Hong Kong：Research Centre for Translation，Chinese University of Hong Kong，c2000. 142 p.：ill.；22cm. ISBN：962725522X，9627255222. （Renditions paperbacks）

Contents：Chronology/by Tam Pak Shan—Reflections/by Eileen Chang；translated by Janice Wickeri—Shutdown/translated by Janet Ng with Janice Wickeri—Great felicity/translated by Janet Ng with Janice Wickeri—Steamed osmanthus flower，Ah Xiao's unhappy autumn/translated by Simon Patton—Traces of love/translated by Eva Hung—Stale mates/written in English by Eileen Chang.

《〈留情〉及其他》，孔慧怡（Hung，Eva）等编译.

5. Written on water/Eileen Chang；translated by Andrew F. Jones；coedited with an introduction by Nicole Huang. New York：Columbia University Press，c2005. xxvii，218 p.：ill.；24cm. ISBN：0231131380，0231131384，0231131399，0231131391. （Weatherhead books on Asia）

《流言》，安道（Jones，Andrew F）（美国汉学家）译.

6. Lust，caution：the story/Eileen Chang；translated and with a foreword by Julia Lovell；afterword by Ang Lee；with a special essay by James Schamus. New York：Anchor Books，2007. xxiv，68 p.；19cm. ISBN：0307387445，0307387448

《色·戒》，茱莉亚·洛佛尔（Lovell，Julia，1975—）（英国汉学家）译.

7. Lust，caution and other stories/Eileen Chang；translated by Julia Lovell [and others]；edited and with an afterword by Julia Lovell. London：Penguin，2007. 161 pages；20cm. ISBN：0141034386，0141034386. （Modern classics）

Contents：Lust，caution/translated by Julia Lovell—In the waiting room/translated by Karen S. Kingsbury—Great felicity/translated by Janet Ng（with Janice Wikeri）—Steamed osmanthus flower：Ah Xiao's unhappy autumn/translated by Simon Patton—Traces of love/translated by Eva Hung.

《〈色·戒〉及其他》，茱莉亚·洛佛尔（Lovell，Julia，1975—）（英国汉学家）译.

 （1）[London]：Penguin，2016. 134 pages；19cm. ISBN：0241259092，0241259096. （Pocket Penguins）

8. Love in a fallen city/Eileen Chang；translated by Karen Kingsbury and Eileen Chang. New York：New York Review Books，2007. xvii，321 pages；21cm. ISBN：1590171780，1590171783. （New York Review Books classics）

《倾城之恋》，张爱玲（1920—1995）著，与 Karen Kingsbury 合译.

(1) Love in a fallen city and other stories/Eileen Chang; translated by Karen S. Kingsbury and Eileen Chang. London：Penguin, 2007. xvii, 321 pages；20cm. 0141189369, 0141189363. (Modern classics)

9. Red rose, white rose/Eileen Chang; translated by Karen S. Kingsbury. London：Penguin, 2011. 84 pages；17cm. ISBN：0141196145, 0141196149. (Modern classics)
《红玫瑰与白玫瑰》, Kingsbury, Karen S. 译.

10. The fall of the pagoda/Eileen Chang. Hong Kong：Hong Kong University Press, 2010. xix, 288 pages；22cm. ISBN：9888028351, 9888028359, 9888028368, 9888028367
《雷峰塔》

11. Half a lifelong romance/Eileen Chang; translated by Karen S. Kingsbury. London：Penguin Books, 2014. xi, 376 pages；20cm. ISBN：0141189398, 0141395001, 0141189390, 0141395005. (Modern classics)
《半生缘》, Kingsbury, Karen S. 译.
   (1) First Anchor books edition. New York：Anchor Books, a division of Penguin Random House LLC, 2016. xii, 379 pages；21cm. ISBN：0307387547, 0307387542. (Vintage international)

12. Little reunions/by Eileen Chang; translated by Jane Weizhen Pan and Martin Merz. New York：New York Review Books, 2018. ISBN：1681371276 (alk. paper) 1681371278
《小团圆》, Pan, Jane Weizhen 和 Merz, Martin 合译.

汪曾祺(1920—1997)

1. Story after supper/Wang Zengqi. Chinese Literature Press, 1990. 315 pages. ISBN：7507100499, 7507100495, 0835120732, 0835120739. (Panda Books)
《晚饭后的故事》. 中国文学出版社.
   (1) Beijing：Chinese Literature Press, 1996. 315 pages；18cm. ISBN：7507100499, 7507100495

2. Selected stories by Wang Zengqi/Wang Zengqi. Beijing：Chinese literature Press：Foreign language Teaching and Research Press, 1999. 1, iii, 331 p.；21cm. ISBN：7560017002, 7560017006. (English-Chinese, gems of Chinese literature, contemporary; University reader)
Contents：Yi bing = Special gift—Shou jie = The love story of a young monk—Chen Xiaoshou = Little Hands Chen—Da Nao ji shi = A tale of Big Nur—Pi Fengsan xuan fang zi = Pi Fengsan the house-stretcher—Ba qian sui= Eight Thousand Cash—Lu shui= The dew.
《汪曾祺小说选》

3. Love story of a young monk. Beijing：Foreign Languages Press, 2011. 153 p.；23cm. ISBN：7513515697, 7513515696
《受戒》

4. The love story of a young monk/Wang Zengqi. Beijing：Foreign Language Teaching and Research Press, 2011. 123 p.：ill.；23cm. ISBN：7513515696, 7513515697. (中国故事＝China stories)
《受戒》

康濯(1920—1991)

1. When the sun comes up/by K'ang Cho. Peking：Foreign Languages Press, 1961. 175 p.；20cm.
Contents：The contest.—The animal expert.—A holiday.—Spring sowing, autumn harvest.—Early spring.—When the sun comes up.
《太阳初升的时候》

杜鹏程(1921—1991)

1. Defend Yenan/Tu Peng-cheng. Peking：Foreign Languages Press, 1958. 404 p.：ill., map.；22cm.
《保卫延安》
   (1) Defend Yanan/Du Pengcheng; translated by Sidney Shapiro; illustrations by Lin Fan. Beijing：Foreign Languages Press：Distributed by China Publications Centre (Guoji Shudian), 1983. 438 pages, [7] leaves of plates (1 folded)：illustrations, map; 19cm. ISBN：0835111571, 0835111577. (Modern Chinese literature)

2. In days of peace/Tu peng-cheng; illustrated by Hua San-Chuan. Peking：Foreign Languages Press, 1962. 219 p.：col. illus.；21cm.
《在和平的日子里》

王汶石(1921—1999)

1. The night of the snowstorm/Wang Wen-shih. Peking：Foreign Languages Press, 1961. 221 p.；19cm.
Contents：The night of the snowstorm—The shrewd vegetable vendor—Life in the adobe hut—Around the spring festival—Grannie Wang—The master carpenter—Down the well—New companions.
《风雪之夜》. 短篇小说集.
   (1) 2nd ed. Peking：Foreign Languages Press, 1979. 216 pages；illustrations；19cm.

马烽(1922—2004)

1. The sun has risen/Ma Feng. Peking：Foreign Languages Press, 1961. 171 p.；19cm.
《太阳刚刚出山》

2. 《村仇》, 马烽著. 北京：中国文学出版社, 1989. (熊猫丛书)

冯志(1923—1968)

1. Behind enemy lines/Feng Chih. Peking：Foreign Languages Press, 1979. 463 pages；21cm.
《敌后武工队》

曲波(1923—2002)

1. Tracks in the snowy forest/by Chu Po; [translated by Sidney Shapiro; ill. by Sun Tzu-hsi]. Peking：Foreign

Languages Press，1962. 48 pages：illustrations；22cm.

《林海雪原》，沙博理(Shapiro，Sidney 1915—2014)译.

(1)2nd ed. Peking：Foreign Languages Press，1965. 48 pages，[9] leaves of plates：illustrations，portraits；22cm.

(2)3rd ed. Peking：Foreign Languages Press，1978. 548 pages，[9] leaves of plates：illustrations，portraits；22cm.

罗广斌(1924—1967)

1. Red crag/Lo Kuang-pin and Yang Yi-yen. Peking：Foreign Languages Press，1978. 606 pages，[15] leaves of plates：illustrations；22cm.

《红岩》，罗广斌，杨益言.

沈默君(1924—2009)

1. Reconnaissance across the Yangtse/adapted by Chang Cheng，drawings by Ku Ping-hsin；[Translated by Yu Fan-chin]. Peking：Foreign Languages Press，1956. 152 p.：illus.；13×18cm.

《渡江侦察记》，Chang Cheng 改编；Ku，Ping-hsin 绘画.

徐光耀(1925—)

1. The plains are ablaze. Peking：Foreign Languages Press，1955. 277 p. illus. 22cm. 277 p. illus. 22cm.

《平原烈火》

2. Little soldier Chang Ka-tse/Xu Guangyao. Peking：Foreign Languages Press，1964. 118 pages；21cm.

《小兵张嘎》

(1)2nd ed. Peking：Foreign Languages Press，1974. 118 p.：ill.；21cm.

(2)2nd ed. Peking：Foreign Languages Press，1977. 118 pages：illustrations；23cm.

茹志鹃(1925—1998)

1. Lilies and other stories/Ru Zhijuan. Beijing：Chinese Literature：Distributed by China International Book Trading Corp. (Guoji Shudian)，1985. 205 pages；18cm. ISBN：0835113329，0835113328. (Panda books)

Contents：Lilies—On the banks of the Cheng—Warmth of spring—Maternity home—Third visit to Yanzhuang—Just a happy-go-lucky girl—Comradeship—Between two seas—Badly edited story—Path through the grassland

《茹志鹃小说选》

高玉宝(1927—)

1. My childhood. Peking：Foreign Languages Press，1960. 378 p. illus. 20cm.

《高玉宝》

2. Kao Yu-pao：story of a poor peasant boy/by Kao Yu-pao. 2nd rev. ed. Peking：Foreign Languages Press，1975. 271 p.，[6] leaves of plates：ill.；21cm.

《高玉宝》

3. I want to study! /by Gao Yubao. 香港：朝阳出版社，1973. 81 pages：illustrations；17cm.

Contents：I want to study! (我要读书)—The cock crows at midnight(半夜鸡叫).

《我要读书》.中英对照.节选自小说《高玉宝》.

(1)[Princeton，N. J.]：[Chinese Linguistics Project，Princeton University]，1993. 81 pages：illustrations；17cm.

木心(1927—2011)

1. An empty room/Mu Xin；translated from the Chinese by Toming Jun Liu. New York：New Directions Book，2011. 150 p.；18cm. ISBN：0811219228，0811219224

木心短篇小说选,木心(1927—2011)；Liu，Toming Jun 译.

李准(1928—2000)

1. Not that road，and other stories. Peking：Foreign Languages Press，1962. 160 p.；19cm.

《不能走那条路》

Notes：Three of the short stories were published in 1955 in Chinese in the author's.

高晓声(1928—1999)

1. The broken betrothal/Gao Xiaosheng. Beijing，China：Panda Books：Distributed by China International Book Trading Corp.，1987. 218 pages；19cm. ISBN：0835120511，0835120517

Contents：The Broken Bethrothal—Li Shunda Builds a House—All the Livelong Day—Chen Huansheng's Adventure in Town—Chen Huansheng Transferred—The Briefcase—A Bride for Guoming—The River Flows East—Underwater Obstruction—Fishing—On My Story "The River Flows East"—The String That Will Never Break—Ye Zhicheng.

《退婚》

2. Selected stories by Gao Xiaosheng/Gao Xiaosheng. Beijing：Chinese Literature Press；Foreign Language Teaching and Research Press，1999. 1，iii，305 p.；21cm. ISBN：7560016839，7560016832. (Ying Han dui zhao. Zhongguo wen xue bao ku. Dang dai wen xue xi lie)

高晓声短篇小说选.

黎汝清(1928—2015)

1. Island militia women/Li Ju-ching；[ill. by Tsai Jung]. Peking：Foreign Languages Press，1975. 296 p.，[7] leaves of plates：ill.；21cm.

《海岛女民兵》

陆柱国(1928—)

1. The battle of Sangkumryung/by Lu Chu-kuo；[translated by A. M. Condron]. Peking：Foreign Languages Press，1961. 162 p.；19cm.

《上甘岭》，康德伦译.

陆文夫(1928—2005)

1. A world of dreams/Lu Wenfu. Beijing, China：Chinese Literature：Distributed by China International Book Trading Corp. (Guoji Shudian), 1986. 248 pages；18cm. ISBN：0835116018, 0835116015. (Panda books)

   Contents：A Weak Light—Deep Within a Lane—Tang Qiaodi—The Man From the Pedlar's Family—The Boundary Wall—The Gourmet—The Doorbell—A World of Dreams.

   《梦中的天地》

   (1)San Francisco：China Books，1987. 248 pages

2. The gourmet and other stories of modern China/Lu Wenfu. London, England：Readers International；Columbia, LA, USA：US/Canadian inquiries to Subscriber Service Dept.，1987. 243 pages；21cm. ISBN：0930523385, 0930523381, 0930523393,0930523398

   Contents：The man from a peddlers' family—Tang Qiaodi—The boundary wall—The doorbell—The gourmet—Graduation—A World of dreams.

   《美食家》及其他.

3. The gourmet and other selected writings/Lu Wenfu. Beijing：Foreign Languages Press，2009. 248 pages；20cm. ISBN：7119058979，7119058975

   《美食家：陆文夫作品选》.收录了《小巷深处》《美食家》和《小贩世家》等小说.

   (1)Beijing：Foreign Languages Press，2014. 248 p.；20cm. ISBN：7119058979, 7119058975

王愿坚(1929—1991)

1. An ordinary labourer/Wang Yuan-chien. Peking：Foreign Languages Press，1961. 183 p.；20cm.

   《普通劳动者》

   (1)Peking：Foreign Languages Press，1979. 171 p.；19cm.

柯岩(1929—2011)

1. The world regained/Ke Yan；[translated by Wu Jingshu and Wang Ningjun]. Beijing：Foreign Languages Press，1993. 360 pages；18cm. ISBN：0835128946,0835128940, 7119014544,7119014548. (Phoenix books)

   《寻找回来的世界》

胡万春(1929—1998)

1. Man of a special cut. Peking：Foreign Languages Press，1963. iv, 183 p. 19cm.

   《特殊性格的人》

金敬迈(1930—)

1. The song of Ouyang Hai/Chin Ching-Mai. Peking：Foreign Languages Press，1966. 456 p.；il.；21cm.

   《欧阳海之歌》

玛拉沁夫(1930—)

1. On the Horqin grassland/Malqinhu. Beijing, China：Chinese Literature Press，1988. 254 pages；18cm. ISBN：0835120570, 0835120579, 7507100235, 7507100235. (Panda books)

   Contents：Preface/Wu Chongyang—Slogging across the deep snow—The story of a living Buddha—The Earth—Long distance runner—Woman basketball player no. 6—The song：a story of the past—The road—Lost—A visit to "Slave Village"—On the Horqin Grassland—Love that burns on a summer's night—The green meadow：a childhood reminiscence.

   《玛拉沁夫小说选》.中国文学出版社.

白桦(1930—2019)

1. The remote country of women/Bai Hua；translated from the Chinese by Qingyun Wu and Thomas O. Beebee. Honolulu：University of Hawaii Press，c1994. 376 p.；22cm. ISBN：0824815912, 0824816110. (Fiction from modern China)

   《远方有个女儿国》,武庆云(Wu, Qingyun,1950—)(美国华裔学者),Beebee, Thomas O. 合译.

邓友梅(1931—)

1. Snuff-bottles and other stories/Deng Youmei；translated by Gladys Yang. Beijing, China：Chinese Literature：Distributed by China International Book Trading Corp.，1986. 220 pages；18cm. ISBN：0835116077,0835116077. (Panda books)

   Contents：Snuff-bottles—Han the forger—Na Wu—Black cat, white cat.

   《邓友梅小说选》

2. 邓友梅小说选＝Selected stories by Deng Youmei/邓友梅著. 北京：中国文学出版社：外语教学与研究出版社,1999.1, iii, 299 pages；21cm. ISBN：7560016758,7560016757. (中国文学宝库·当代文学系列＝English-Chinese, gems of Chinese literature, contemporary)

   Contents：烟壶＝Snuff-bottles—寻访画儿韩＝Han the Forger.

   英汉对照.

3. Snuff bottles and other selected writings/Deng Youmei. Beijing：Foreign Languages Press，2009. 220 pages；20cm. ISBN：7119059174,7119059173. (Panda books)

   《烟壶：邓友梅作品选》

浩然(1932—2008)

1. Bright clouds/Hao Jan；[illustrations by Tung Chen-sheng, Chen Yu-hsien]. Peking：Foreign Languages Press，1974. 139 p.，[7] leaves of plates：ill.；20cm.

   Contents：The lean chestnut horse.—Shepherd's apprentice.—Sending in vegetable seed.—Visit on a snowy night.—Bright clouds.—Rain in Apricot Blossom Village.—Honeymoon.—Jade Spring.

   《彩霞》

2. The golden road/Hao Ran；[translated by Carma Hinton and Chris Gilmartin；illustrations by Cai Rong]. Beijing：Foreign Languages Press，1981. iv, 390 pages, [4] pages of plates：illustrations；19cm.

《金光大道》

王蒙（1934—）

1. The butterfly and other stories/Wang Meng. Beijing：Chinese Literature，1983. 239 pages；19cm. ISBN：0835110214. 0835110211. (Panda books)

Contents：What am I searching for—A spate of visitors—The butterfly—The eyes of night—The barber's tale—Voices of spring—Kite streamers—The young newcomer in the organization department

《王蒙小说选》

2. Bolshevik salute：a modernist Chinese novel＝［Bu li］/Wang Meng；translated，with introduction and critical essay by Wendy Larson. Seattle：University of Washington Press，c1989. xx，154 p.；21cm. ISBN：0295968567

《布礼》，Larson，Wendy 译。

3. Alienation/Wang Meng；translated by Nancy T. Lin，Tong Qi Lin. Hong Kong：Joint Publishing（H. K.）Co.，1993. 8，287 pages；22cm. ISBN：9620410459，9620410451

Contents：The butterfly—It's hard for us to meet

《异化》，林同奇译。

4. The stubborn porridge and other stories/Wang Meng；translated by Zhu Hong. 1st U. S. ed. New York：George Braziller，1994. vi，186 p.；22cm. ISBN：0807613533

《坚硬的稀粥及其他》，Zhu，Hong 译。

5. The butterfly and other selected writings/Wang Meng. Beijing：Foreign Languages Press，2009. xiii，382 pages；illustrations；20cm. ISBN：7119058931，7119058932. (Panda books)

《蝴蝶》. 中篇小说集.

(1) The butterfly/Wang Meng；translated by Denis Mair. Beijing：Foreign Languages Pr.，2014. 373 pages；23cm. ISBN：7119087597，7119087592. (Gems of modern Chinese literature)

杨佩瑾（1935—）

1. The dagger/Yang Pei-ching；［Illustrated by Wan Ching-li］. Peking：Foreign Languages Press，1978. 320 pages；illustrations；21cm.

《剑》

杨书案（1935—）

1. Confucius/Yang Shu'an；translated by Liu Shicong. Beijing，China：Chinese Literature Press，1993. 382 p.；21cm. ISBN：7507101363，7507101362，0835131335，0835131339. (Panda books)

《孔子》，刘士聪译.

(1) Beijing：Foreign Languages Press，2009. 382 pages；20cm. ISBN：7119059150，7119059157

2. Lao Zi/Yang Shu'an；translated by Liu Shicong. Beijing，China：Chinese Literature Press，1997. 40 pages；21cm.

ISBN：7507103528，7507103526，0835131866，0835131865. (Panda books)

《老子》，Liu，Shicong 译.

谌容（1936—）

1. At middle age/Shen Rong. Beijing，China：Panda Books；Distributed by China International Book Trading Corp.，1987. 366 pages；19cm. ISBN：0835116093，0835116091. (Panda books)

《人到中年》

(1) Beijing：Foreign Languages Press，2015. 433 pages；18cm. ISBN：7119092935，7119092936. (Panda books)

杨啸（1936—）

1. The making of a peasant doctor/Yang Hsiao. Peking：Foreign Languages Press，1976. 199 pages，［10］leaves of plates：illustrations；19cm.

《红雨》

刘绍棠（1936—1997）

1. Catkin Willow Flats/Liu Shaotang. Beijing：Chinese Literature，1984. 267 pages；18cm. ISBN：0835111660，0835111669. (Panda books)

Contents：Catkin Willow Flats—The Budding Lotus—An encounter in Green Vine Lane—The Liuxiang Melon Hut—Literature with a Local Flavour.

《刘绍棠中篇小说选》

(1) Beijing：Chinese Literature，1996. 267 pages；19cm. ISBN：0835111600. (Panda Books)

张贤亮（1936—2014）

1. Mimosa and other stories/Hsien-liang Chang（Zhang Xianliang）. Beijing：Chinese Literature Press，1985. 270 pages；18cm. (Panda books)

Contents：Mimosa—Bitter springs—The herdsman's story.

《绿化树》

(1) Beijing：Chinese Literature Press，1987. 270 pages；18cm. (Panda books)

2. Half of man is woman/Zhang Xianliang；translated by Martha Avery. London：Penguin Books，1986. xiv，252 pages；21cm. ISBN：0140102973，0140102970

《男人的一半是女人》，Avery，Martha（1951—）译.

(1) London：Viking，1988. 1 volume. ISBN：0670818216，0670818211

(2) Toronto：Lester & Orpen Dennys，1988. xvii，285 pages：maps；22cm. ISBN：0886191866，0886191863

(3) Harmondsworth：Penguin，1989. xvi，252 pages：illustrations，2 maps；20cm. ISBN：0140102973，0140102970

(4) New York：Ballantine Books，1991. xvii，237 pages：maps；18cm. ISBN：0345364546，0345364548

3. Getting used to dying/Zhang Xianliang；translated from the Chinese and edited by Martha Avery. London：

Collins, 1991. 301 pages；24cm. ISBN：0002237245, 0002237246

《习惯死亡》，Avery, Martha(1951—)译.

(1)New York, Toronto：Harper Collins Publishers, 1991. XI, 291 p.；24cm. ISBN：0060165219, 0060165215

4. Grass soup/Zhang Xianliang；translated from the Chinese by Martha Avery. London：Secker & Warburg, 1993. vi, 247 pages：illustrations；20cm. ISBN：0436201968, 0436201967

《烦恼就是智慧》，Avery, Martha(1951—)译.

(1)London：Secker & Warburg, 1994. vi, 247 pages：illustrations；20cm. ISBN：0436201968, 0436201967

(2)Boston：D. R. Godine, 1995. vi, 247 pages；20cm. ISBN：1567920306, 1567920307

(3)London：Minerva, 1995. v, 246 pages：1 facsimile, portraits；20cm. ISBN：0749397748, 0749397746, 0749396539, 0749396534

5. My bodhi tree/Zhang Xianliang；translated from the Chinese by Martha Avery. London：Secker & Warburg, 1996. v, 226 pages：illustrations, portraits；20cm. ISBN：0436203235, 0436203237,0436203251,0436203251

《我的菩提树》，Avery, Martha(1951—)译.

(1)London：Minerva, 1997. v, 226 pages：illustrations；20cm. ISBN：0749386053, 0749386054

6. Mimosa：and other stories/Zhang Xianliang. Beijing：Chinese Literature：Distributed by China International Book Trading Corp., , 1985. 270 pages；18cm. ISBN：0835111644, 0835111645, 0835113361, 0835113366, 7507100073, 7507100075. (Panda books)

《绿化树:张贤亮作品选》

(1)Mimosa and other selected writings/Zhang Xianliang. Beijing：Foreign Languages Press, 2009. 270 pages；20cm. ISBN：7119059099, 7119059092. (Panda books)

曲春礼(1937—)

1. The life of Confucius/by Qu Chunli；[translated by Sun Haichen]. Beijing：Foreign Languages Press：Distributed by China International Book Trading Corp., , 1996. 645 pages：illustrations, [1] color plate；22cm. ISBN：7119018639, 7119018638, 7119019090, 7119019093

《孔子传》,孙海晨译.

2. The life of Mencius/by Qu Chunli；[translated by Zhang Zengzhi]. Beijing, China：Foreign Languages Press, 1998. 544 pages：illustrations；22cm. ISBN：7119014609, 7119014609

《孟子传》,Zhang, Zengzhi 译.

祖尔东·沙比尔(1937—1998)

1. Farewell Guli Sarah/authour, Zurdong Shabier；[translator, Song Jianxun, Chen Caixia]. Urumchi：Xinjiang Juvenile Publishing House, 2010. 3, 1, 339 pages；23cm. ISBN：7537189392, 7537189390

《再见,古丽莎拉》.新疆青少年出版社.中篇小说.

张洁(1937—)

1. Love must not be forgotten/by Zhang Jie；introduction by Gladys Yang. San Francisco：China Books & Periodicals；Beijing, China：Panda Books, 1986. xiii, 207 pages；24cm. ISBN：0835116999, 0835116992, 0835116980, 0835116985.

Contents：Love must not be forgotten—Emerald—The time is not yet ripe—An unfinished record—Under the hawthorne—Who knows how to live—The ark.

Notes：Translated from Chinese and by Gladys Yang [and others]

《爱,是不能忘记的:张洁作品选》

(1)Beijing, China：Panda Books；San Francisco：China Books & Periodicals, 1987. 227 pages；24cm. ISBN：083511337X.

(2)San Francisco, Calif.：China Books & Periodicals；Beijing：Panda Books, 1997. 4, 227 pages；18cm. ISBN：7507100324, 7507100327, 083511337X, 0835113373

(3)Love must not be forgotten and other selected writings/Zhang Jie；Gladys Yang, W. J. F. Jenner, Janet Yang,... [et al.]. Beijing：Foreign Languages Press, 2009. 1 vol. (227 p.)：couv. ill. en coul.；20cm. ISBN：7119059006, 7119059009, 7119059006. (Panda books)

2. Leaden wings/by Zhang Jie；translated and with a preface by Gladys Yang；afterword by Delia Dawin. London：Virago, 1987. xii, 180 pages；21cm. ISBN：0860687597, 0860687597, 0860687643, 0860687641

《沉重的翅膀》,戴乃迭(Yang Gladys)译.

3. As long as nothing happens, nothing will/stories by Zhang Jie. London：Virago, 1988. 149 pages；20cm. ISBN：086068931X, 0860689317,0860689301,0860689300

Contents：What's wrong with him? —Professor Meng abroad—The other world—Something else? —Today's agenda.

《只要无事发生,任何事都不会发生》.短篇小说选.

(1)As long as nothing happens, nothing will/Zhang Jie；translated from the Chinese by Gladys Yang, Deborah J. Leonard, and Zhang Andong. 1st American ed. New York：Grove Weidenfeld, 1991. 196 p.；22cm. ISBN：0802111440, 0802111449

4. Heavy wings/Zhang Jie；translated from the Chinese by Howard Goldblatt. New York：Grove Weidenfeld, 1989. 308 pages；25cm. ISBN：0802110398, 0802110398

《沉重的翅膀》,葛浩文(Goldblatt, Howard, 1939—)(美国翻译家)译.

5. She knocked at the door/Zhang Jie. South San Francisco：Long River Press, 2005. 205 pages；25cm. ISBN：1592650562, 1592650569. (Cultural China)

《敲门的女孩》

(1) She knocked at the door/Zhang Jie；translation by Sylvia Yu and Julian Chen．New York：Better Link Press，2006．193 pages；21cm．ISBN：160220909X，1602209091．(Cultural China Chinese-English readers series＝《文化中国》汉英对照阅读系列)

陈若曦(1938—)

1. The execution of Mayor Yin，and other stories from the Great Proletarian Cultural Revolution/Chen Jo-hsi；translated from the Chinese by Nancy Ing and Howard Goldblatt．Bloomington；London：Indiana University Press，1978．xxviii，220 pages；22cm．ISBN：0253124751；0253124753．(Chinese literature in translation)

殷张兰熙(Ing，Nancy Chang)，葛浩文(Goldblatt，Howard，1939—)(美国翻译家)合译．包括《尹县长》等小说．

(1) London；Boston [etc.]：G. Allen & Unwin，1979．xxviii，220 pages；22cm．ISBN：0048950246，0048950246

(2) Rev. ed. Bloomington：Indiana University Press，2004．xxxii，202 pages；21cm．ISBN：0253344166，0253344168，0253216907，0253216908．(Chinese literature in translation)

Contents：The execution of Mayor Yin—；Jingjing's birthday—；Night duty—；Residency check—；Ren Xiulan—；The big fish—；Geng Er in Beijing—；Nixon's Press Corps

2. The old man，and other stories/by Chen Ruoxi．Hong Kong：Research Centre for Translation，the Chinese University of Hong Kong，1986．147 pages；22cm．ISBN：9622013848，9622013841．(Renditions paperbacks)

Contents：The old man—The tunnel—Ding Yun—My friend Ali Fen—Another fortress besieged

《〈老人〉及其他》

3. The short stories of Chen Ruoxi，translated from the original Chinese：a writer at the crossroads/Chen Ruoxi；edited by Hsin-sheng C. Kao．Lewiston：E. Mellen Press，c1992．ix，340 p. ：ill. ；24cm．ISBN：0773491902，0773491908

《陈若曦短篇小说选》，Kao，Hsin-sheng C. 译．

戴厚英(1938—1996)

1. Stones of the wall/Dai Houying；translated by Frances Wood．New York：St. Martin's Press，1985．ix，309 pages；22cm．ISBN：0312762151，0312762155

《人啊，人！》

(1) Sevenoaks：Sceptre，1987．335 pages；20cm．ISBN：0340412410，0340412411

降边嘉措(1938—)

1. King Gesar/Gyanpian Gyamco，Wu Wei；translated by Wang Guozhen，Zhu Yongmei，Han Jia．Beijing：China Intercontinental Press；Shenyang：Liaoning Education Press，2009．229 pages：color illustrations；25cm．ISBN：7508512884，750851288X．(Tibetan classics)

《格萨尔王传》，降边嘉措，吴伟；英文翻译王国振，朱咏梅，汉佳．

(1) Beijing：China Intercontinental Press，2011．253 p. ：col. ill. ；24cm．ISBN：7508522111，7508522117．(Epic appreciation＝聆听史诗丛书)

2. The 13th Dali Lama：Gyangze battle of 1904/Gyanpian Gyamco，Wu Wei．Beijing：China Intercontinental Press，2010．11，277 pages，[6] pages of plates：color illustrations；25cm．ISBN：7508518213，7508518217

《十三世达赖喇嘛：1904年江孜保卫战》，降边嘉措，吴伟著．五洲传播出版社．

3. Kelsang Metok：happy flower/Jampel Gyatso；translated by Wang Guozhen．Beijing：China Intercontinental Press，2017．487 pages．ISBN：7508536101，750853610X

《格桑梅朵》，降边嘉措；王国振译．

蒋子龙(1941—)

1. All the colours of the rainbow/Jiang Zilong；translated by Wang Mingjie．Beijing，China：Chinese Literature：Distributed by China Publications Centre，1983．267 pages；18cm．ISBN：0835110222，0835110228．(Panda books)

《赤橙黄绿青蓝紫》

朱玛拜·比拉勒(1941—)

1. Blue snow/author，Jumabai Bilaler；editor，Jiang Fengli；translator，Song jianxun．Ürümqi [China]：Xinjiang Juvenile Publishing House，2011．200 Pages；23cm．ISBN：7551500401，7551500405．(Yangpigu series of translation)

《蓝雪》，宋建勋译．新疆青少年出版社．本书是《羊皮鼓译丛》中的一本，是短篇小说集．

冯骥才(1942—)

1. Chrysanthemums and other stories/Feng Jicai；translated from the Chinese and with an introduction by Susan Wilf Chen．San Diego：Harcourt Brace Jovanovich，c1985．xii，255 p. ；22cm．ISBN：015117878X

Contents：The Mao button—Chrysanthemums—Numbskull—The hornets' nest—A letter—Winding brook way—Plum blossoms in the snow—Nectar—The street-sweeping show

《菊花和其他故事》，Chen，Susan Wilf 译．

2. The miraculous pigtail/Feng Jicai．Beijing：Chinese Literature Press，1987．312 pages；18cm．ISBN：08351200503，0835120500．(Panda books)

Contents：The carved pipe—A visit to the temple of the goddess—Old husband，old wife—The tall woman and her short husband—Boat song—The miraculous pigtail—Thanks to life.

《神鞭》，戴乃迭(Yang Gladys，1919—1999)译．包括《雕花烟斗》《逛娘娘宫》《老夫老妻》《高女人和她的矮丈夫》《船

歌》《神鞭》《感谢生活》.(冯骥才小说选)

3. Voices from the whirlwind: an oral history of the Chinese Cultural Revolution/Feng Jicai; with a foreword by Robert Coles. New York: Pantheon Books; Beijing: Foreign Languages Press, 1990. xvi, 252 s.; 22cm. ISBN: 039458645X, 0394586458

《一百个人的十年》(节译)

4. The three-inch golden lotus/Feng Jicai; translated from the Chinese by David Wakefield; general editor, Howard Goldblatt. Honolulu: University of Hawaii Press, c1994. 239 p.; 22cm. ISBN: 0824815742, 0824816064. (Fiction from modern China)

《三寸金莲》,David Wakefield 译;葛浩文(Goldblatt, Howard,1939—)(美国翻译家)总编.

5. Ten years of madness: oral histories of China's Cultural Revolution/Feng Jicai. San Francisco: China Books & Periodicals, c1996. ix, 285 p.; 22cm. ISBN: 83512584X

《一百个人的十年》

6. Selected stories/by Feng Jicai. [Beijing]: Chinese Literature Press: Foreign Language Teaching and Research Press, 1999. [10], 311 s.; 20cm. ISBN: 7560016693, 7560016696. (University reader; English-Chinese gems of Chinese literature. Contemporary)

冯骥才小说选.

7. The miraculous pigtail and other selected writings/Feng Jicai. Beijing: Foreign Languages Press, 2009. 312 pages; 20cm. ISBN: 7119059181, 7119059181

《神鞭:冯骥才作品选》.收录了《神鞭》《感谢生活》和《高女人和她的矮丈夫》等小说.

凌力(1942—2018)

1. Son of Heaven/Ling Li; translated by David Kwan. Beijing: Chinese Literature Press: Distributed by China International Book Trading Corp., 1995. 672 pages: illustrations; 21cm. ISBN: 0835131475, 0835131476, 7507102882, 7507102888. (Panda books)

《少年天子》,凌力著.中国文学出版社.

(1)Beijing: Foreign Languages Press, 2009. 672 pages: illustrations; 20cm. ISBN: 7119059167, 7119059165

古华(1942—)

1. A small town called Hibiscus/Gu Hua; translated by Gladys Yang. Beijing, China: Chinese Literature: distributed by China Publications Centre, 1983. 260 p.; 19cm. ISBN: 0835110745, 0835110747(Panda books)

《芙蓉镇》,戴乃迭(Yang Gladys)译.

(1)Beijing: Chinese Literature Press, 1990. 260 p. ISBN: 0835110745. 0835110747, 7507100219, 7507100211

(2)San Francisco: China Books & Periodicals, Inc., 1997. 260 pages; 19cm. ISBN: 0835110745, 0835110747. (Modern Chinese literature series)

(3) San Francisco, CA: China Books and Periodicals, Inc., 2001. 260 pages; 18cm. ISBN: 0835110745,

0835110747

(4)Amsterdam: Fredonia Books, 2003. 260 pages; 21cm. ISBN: 1410103528, 1410103529

(5)Beijing: Foreign Languages Press, 2015. 1 vol. (272 p.): couv. ill. en coul.; 18cm. ISBN: 7119092911, 711909291X. (Panda books)

2. Pagoda Ridge and other stories/Gu Hua; translated by Gladys Yang. Beijing, China: Panda Books: Distributed by China International Book Trading Corp., 1985. 260 pages; 19cm. ISBN: 0835113353, 0835113359

Contents: Pagoda Ridge—The log cabin overgrown with creepers—It happened in South Bay—Ninety-nine mounds—How I became a writer.

《浮屠岭及其他》,戴乃迭(Yang Gladys)译.

3. Virgin widows/Gu Hua; translated from Chinese by Howard Goldblatt. Honolulu: University of Hawaii Press, c1996. 165 p.; 21cm. ISBN: 0824817702, 0824818024. (Fiction from modern China)

《贞女》,葛浩文(Goldblatt, Howard,1939—)(美国翻译家)译.

刘心武(1942—)

1. Black walls and other stories/by Liu Xinwu; edited by Don J. Cohn with an introduction by Geremie Barmé. Hong Kong: Research Centre for Translation, Chinese University of Hong Kong, c1990. xiii, 200 p.; 22cm. ISBN: 9627255068, 9627255062. (Renditions paperbacks)

Contents: Black walls—Bus aria—The woman with shoulder-length hair—The wish—Zooming in on 19 May 1985—White teeth

《黑墙及其他》,Cohn ,Don J. 编.短篇小说.

王晓玉(1944—)

1. His one and only/by Wang Xiaoyu. New York: Better Link Press, 2010. 315 pages; 18cm. ISBN: 1602202146, 1602202141. (Stories by contemporary writers from Shanghai)

张雅文(1944—)

1. A Chinese woman at Gestapo gunpoint/Zhang Yawen; [translators, Chen Haiyan, Li Ziliang]. Beijing: Foreign Languages Press, 2003. 434 pages, [10] pages of plates: illustrations (some color); 21cm. ISBN: 7119031597, 7119031590

《盖世太保枪口下的中国女人》,陈海燕,李子亮译.

霍达(1945—)

1. The jade king: history of a Chinese Muslim family/Huo Da; translated by Guan Yuehua. Beijing, China: Chinese Literature Press, 1992. 595 pages; 18cm. ISBN: 0835120996, 0835120999, 7507100901, 7507100907

《穆斯林的葬礼》

(1)Beijing: Foreign Languages Press, 2009. 595 pages: illustrations; 20cm. ISBN: 7119059129, 7119059122

遇罗锦(1946—)

1. A Chinese winter's tale：an autobiographical fragment/by Yu Luojin；translated by Rachel May and Zhu Zhiyu. Hong Kong：Research Centre for Translation, Chinese University of Hong Kong，1986. xix, 210 pages：map, portraits；22cm. ISBN：962201383X, 9622013834. (Renditions paperbacks)

《一个冬天的童话》，May, Rachel 和 Zhu, Zhiyu 合译.

(1) Hong Kong：The Research Centre for Translation/ The Chinese University of Hong Kong，1988. xix, 210 s. ：ill. , kort, portr. ISBN：962201383X, 9622013834

(2) Hong Kong Renditions Paperbacks，1990. XIX, 210 S. Ill. ISBN：962201383X, 9622013834

姜戎(1946—)

1. Wolf totem/Jiang Rong；translated by Howard Goldblatt. New York：Penguin Press，2008. vii, 527 p. ：map；25cm. ISBN：1594201561, 1594201560, 1594201846, 1594201844, 7535436696, 7535436692, 0670029570, 0670029572

《狼图腾》，葛浩文(Goldblatt, Howard，1939—)(美国翻译家)译.

(1) London：Hamish Hamilton，2008. vii, 527 s. ISBN： 0241143520, 0241143527, 0241144084, 0241144086

(2) New York：Penguin Group，2009. ix, 526 pages：1 map；22cm. ISBN：0143115144, 0143115146

(3) Camberwell, Vic. ：Penguin Group(Australia)，2010. 1 volume. ISBN：0143009559, 0143009559

(4) New York, NY：Penguin Books，2015. ix, 526 pages：map；22cm. ISBN：0143109310, 0143109316

程乃珊(1946—2013)

1. Piano tuner/by Cheng Naishan；translated with an introduction by Britten Dean. San Francisco：China Books & Periodicals，c1989. xiii, 176 p. ；24cm. ISBN：0835121429, 0835121410

Contents：No. 2 and no. 4 of Shanghai—In my heart there is room for Thee—The plea—The piano tuner.

《钢琴调音师》，Dean, Britten 译.

2. The blue house/Cheng Naishan. Beijing, China：Chinese Literature Press：Distributed by China International Book Trading Corp. ，1989. 400 pages；18cm. ISBN：7507100405, 7507100402, 0835120651, 0835120654. (Panda books)

Contents：The blue house—The poor street—Hong Taitai—Gong Chun's teapot—Row, row, row：row to Grandma's house.

《蓝屋》，李国庆等译. 中国文学出版社(熊猫丛书). 共收录其4篇中、短篇小说.

(1) The blue house/Cheng Naishan. Beijing, China：Foreign Languages Press；Distributed by China International Book Trading Corp. ，2005. 313 pages；20cm. ISBN：711903359X, 7119033594. (Panda books)

3. The banker/Cheng Naishan；translated, with introduction, by Britten Dean. San Francisco, Calif. ：China Books & Periodicals, Inc. ，1992. ii, 459 pages：map；23cm. ISBN：0835124924, 0835124928

《金融家》，Dean, Britten 译.

4. When a baby is born/by Cheng Naishan；[translation by Benjamin Chang]. New York：Better Link Press，2010. 171 pages；18cm. ISBN：1602202153, 160220215X. (Stories by contemporary writers from Shanghai)

Chang, Benjamin 译.

马波(老鬼, 1947—)

1. Blood red sunset：a memoir of the Chinese Cultural Revolution/Ma Bo；translated from the Chinese by Howard Goldblatt. New York：Viking，1995. 371 p. ；24cm. ISBN：0670841811

《血色黄昏》，葛浩文(Goldblatt, Howard，1939—)(美国翻译家)译.

王周生(1947—)

1. Memory and oblivion/by Wang Zhousheng. New York Better Link Press，2015. 175 pages；21cm. ISBN：1602202443, 1602202443. (Stories by contemporary writers from Shanghai)

郑义(1947—)

1. Old well/by Zheng Yi；translated by David Kwan；introduction by Anthony P. Kane. San Francisco：China Books & Periodicals，1989. xv, 154 pages；24cm. ISBN：0835122751, 0835122757, 083512276X, 0835122764. (New Chinese fiction)

《老井》，Kwan, David 译.

王小鹰(1947—)

1. Vicissitudes of life/by Wang Xiaoying. New York：Better Link Press，2010. 366 pages；18cm. ISBN：1602202214, 1602202214. (Stories by contemporary writers from Shanghai)

王小鹰小说.

2. Behind the singing masks/by Wang Xiaoying；foreword by Wang Jiren. Clarendon：Tuttle，2014. pages. ISBN：1602202474, 1602202478

王小鹰小说.

(1) New York Better Link Press，2015. 312 pages；22cm. ISBN：1602202474, 1602202478

赵长天(1947—2013)

1. Goodbye, Xu Hu! /by Zhao Changtian. New York：Better Link Press，2010. 205 pages；18cm. ISBN：1602202191, 1602202192. (Stories by contemporary writers from Shanghai)

Contents：Goodbye, Xu Hu! —No explanation is necessary

《再见许鹄》

曹桂林(1947—)

1. Beijinger in New York/by Glen Cao；translated by Ted Wang. San Francisco：Cypress Book Co. ，1993. vii, 248

pages；22cm. ISBN：0835125262, 0835125260

《北京人在纽约》，Wang，Ted 译.

张承志(1948—)

1. The black steed/by Zhang Chengzhi；translated by Stephen Fleming. Beijing：Chinese Literature Press，1990. 255 p. ；18cm. ISBN：7507100693，7507100693. (Panda Books)

《黑骏马》.中国文学出版社(相熊猫丛书)

(1)The black steed and other selected writings/Zhang Chengzhi. Beijing：Foreign Languages Press，2009. 255 pages；20cm. ISBN：7119059143, 7119059149

郭雪波(1948—)

1. The desert wolf/Guo Xuebo；[translated by Ma Ruofen]. Beijing：Panda Books：Chinese Literature Press，1996. 354 pages；18cm. ISBN：7507103447, 7507103441, 0835131807, 0835131803

Contents：The desert wolf—The sand fox—Sand rites—Sand burial.

《沙狼》，马若芬等译.中国文学出版社.

聂鑫森(1948—)

1. Deliverance—armed escort and other stories/Nie Xinsen. Beijing：Chinese Literature Press，1998. x, 168 p. ；19cm. ISBN：7507104516, 7507104516. (Panda books)

《〈镖头杨三〉及其他》

叶广芩(1948—)

1. Mountain stories/Ye Guangqin. Scarborough：Valley Press，2017. 232 pages；20cm. ISBN：1908853816, 1908853813

阿城(王阿城,1948—)

1. Unfilled graves/Ah Cheng. Beijing：Chinese Literature Press，1995. 170 pages；18cm. ISBN：7507102785, 7507102789, 0835131459, 0835131452. (Panda books)

Contents：Preface/Wang Zengqi—Unfilled graves—The kind-hearted prostitute—Six New Year sketches—Speaking of the Wangs—Lao Liu—The drowning in the pond—Story of the Liangs—Northeasterners—Salt flats—Jiazi.

《空坟》

(1)Unfilled graves and other selected writings/Ah Cheng. Beijing：Foreign Languages Press，2009. 170 pages；20cm. ISBN：7119059082,7119059084. (Panda books)

阿城(钟阿城,1949—)

1. Three kings：three stories from today's China/Ah Cheng；translated from the Chinese and with an introduction by Bonnie McDougall. London：Collins-Harvill，1990. 223 pages；23cm. ISBN：0002710331, 0002710336

McDougall，Bonnie 译.收录《棋王》《树王》《孩子王》.

(1)The king of trees/Ah Cheng；translated from the Chinese by Bonnie S. McDougall. New York：New Directions Books，2010. 196 pages；21cm. ISBN：0811218665, 081121866X. (New Directions paperbook)

2. The chess master/A Cheng；translated by W. J. E.

Jenner. Hong Kong：The Chinese University Press，2005. 129 p. ；22cm. ISBN：9629962373, 9629962371. (Bilingual series on modern Chinese literature)

《棋王》，Jenner，W. J. E. 译.英汉对照.

彭瑞高(1949—)

1. Calling back the spirit of the dead/by Peng Ruigao. New York：Better Link Press，2014. 263 pages；18cm. ISBN：1602202419, 1602202412. (Stories by contemporary writers from Shanghai)

Lee，Yawtsong 译.

曹乃谦(1949—)

1. There's nothing I can do when I think of you late at night/Cao Naiqian；translated by John Balcom. New York：Columbia University Press，c2009. xiv,232 p. ；22cm. ISBN：0231148108, 0231148100, 0231519731, 0231519737. (Weatherhead books on Asia)

《到黑夜想你没办法》，陶忘机(Balcom，John)(美国汉学家)译.

北岛(1949—)

1. Waves：stories/by Zhao Zhenkai；edited with an introduction by Bonnie S. McDougall；translated by Bonnie S. McDougall and Susette Ternent Cooke. Hong Kong：Chinese University Press，1985. xii, 216 pages：illustrations；20cm. ISBN：9622013252, 9622013254

《波动》，McDougall，Bonnie S.（1941—）和 Cooke，Susette Ternent 合译.

(1)2nd ed. Shatin, N. T. , Hong Kong：Chinese University Press，1986. xi,234 p. ：ill. ；20cm. ISBN：9622013686, 9622013681

(2)London：Heinemann，1987. xi,234 pages：illustrations；22cm. ISBN：0434174807,0434174805

(3)Sevenoaks：Sceptre，1989. xi,234 pages：illustrations；20cm. ISBN：0340487712,0340487716

(4)Waves：a novella and six stories from the one of China's leading poets. London：Sceptre，1989. 234 pages：illustrations；20cm.

(5)New York：NewDirections，1990. xiv, 208 p. ；21cm. ISBN：0811211339,0811211338, 0811211347, 0811211345. (New Directions paperbook；693)

孙力(1949—2010)

1. Metropolis/Sun Li & Yu Xiaohui；translated by David Kwan. Beijing, China：Chinese Literature Press，1992. 22 pages；18cm. ISBN：7507100863, 7507100860, 0835120953, 0835120951. (Panda books)

《都市风流》，孙力(1949—2010)，余小慧著.中国文学出版社.

(1)Beijing：Foreign Languages Press，2009. 522 pages；20cm. ISBN：7119058962, 7119058967

梁晓声(1949—)

1. The black button/Liang Xiaosheng. Beijing：Chinese Literature Press：Distrib. by China International Book

Trading Corp.，1992. 235 pages；19cm. ISBN：7507101169，7507101164，0835131262，083513126. (Panda Books)

《黑纽扣》

(1) Beijing：Chinese Literature Press，1996. 235 pages；18cm. ISBN：7507101169，7507101164.（Panda Books）

2. Panic and deaf：two modern satires/Liang Xiaosheng；translated by Hanming Chen；edited by James O. Belcher. Honolulu：University of Hawaii Press，c2001. 157 p.；21cm. ISBN：0824822501，0824823737. (Fiction from modern China)

《梁晓声小说选》，Chen，Hanming 译.

3. A land of wonder and mystery and other writings/Liang Xiaosheng. Beijing：Foreign Languages Press，2009. 235 pages；20cm. ISBN：7119058955，7119058959

Contents：The jet ruler—A land of wonder and mystery—Father—The black button—Ice dam.

《这是一片神奇的土地：梁晓声作品选》

竹林（原名王祖铃，1949—）

1. 挚爱在人间＝Abiding love/竹林著，胡志挥译. 上海：远东出版社，1995. 240，174 pages，[1] page of plates：illustrations，portraits；21cm. ISBN：7805144540，7805144542

英汉对照.

2. Snake's pillow and other stories/Zhu Lin；translated from the Chinese by Richard King. Honolulu：University of Hawaii Press，c1998. 200 p.；21cm. ISBN：0824815491，0824817168. (Fiction from modern China)

《蛇枕头花及江南故事》，King，Richard(1951—)译.

3. Paradise on Earth/by Zhu Lin；[translation by Yawtsong Lee]. New York：Better Link Press，2013. 29 p.；18cm. ISBN：1602202344，1602202346. (Stories by contemporary writers from Shanghai)

Lee，Yaw-Tsong(1945—)译.

陆星儿（1949—2004）

1. Oh! blue bird/Lu Xing'er. Beijing：Chinese Literature Press；Dist. by China International Book Trading Corp.，1993. 390 pages；19cm. ISBN：7507100928，7507100921，0835131270，0835131278. (Panda Books)

《啊，青鸟》

(1) Ah，blue bird/by Lu Xing'er；[translation by Wu Yanting]. New York：Better Link Press，2010. 342 pages；18cm. ISBN：1602202238，1602202230

2. The mountain flowers have bloomed quietly/Lu Xing'er. Beijing，China：Foreign Languages Press，2005. 326 pages；21cm. ISBN：7119033581，7119033587. (Panda books)

Contents：Oh! blue bird—The mountain flowers have bloomed quietly—One on one—Under one roof.

《达紫香悄悄地开了：英文》，唐笙等译. 外文出版社（熊猫丛书）. 共收录其4篇中、短篇小说.

(1) The mountain flowers have bloomed quietly and other selected writings/Lu Xing'er. Beijing：Foreign Languages Press，2009. 326 pages；20cm. ISBN：7119059044，7119059041

叶辛（1949—）

1. A pair of jade frogs/by Ye Xin. New York：Better Link Press，2010. 186 pages；17cm. ISBN：1602202207，1602202206.（Stories by contemporary writers from Shanghai）

2. Educated youth/Ye Xin；Jing Han，translator. Artarmon，N. S. W. Giramondo，2016. 315 pages；24cm. ISBN：1925336047，1925336042

《孽债》，Han，Jing 译.

(1)［Artarmon，NSW］：Giramondo，2016. vii，447 pages (large print)；24cm. ISBN：1525224355，1525224352.（Read how you want 16）

殷慧芬（1949—）

1. River under the eaves/by Yin Huifen；translated by Zhu Jingwen. New York：Better Link Press，2016. 166 pages；21cm. ISBN：1602202535，1602202532.（Stories by contemporary writers from Shanghai）

Zhu，Jingwen 译.

Sun，Yong(1950—)

1. Forty roses/by Sun Yong. New York：Better Link Press，2010. 286 pages；18cm. ISBN：1602202269，1602202265.（Stories by contemporary writers from Shanghai）

张抗抗（1950—）

1. The invisible companion/Zhang Kangkang；translated by Daniel Bryant. Beijing，China：New World Press；Distributed by China International Book Trading Corp.，1996. 436 pages；21cm. ISBN：7800052990，7800052996

《隐形伴侣》，(美)白润德译. 新世界出版社.

2. Living with their past：post-urban youth fiction/by Zhang Kangkang；edited by Richard King. Hong Kong：Research Centre for Translation，the Chinese University of Hong Kong，c2003. 143 p.；22cm. ISBN：9627255262，9627255260. (Renditions paperbacks)

《残忍》，King，Richard 译.

3. White poppies and other stories/by Zhang Kangkang，translated by Karen Gernant and Chen Zeping. Ithaca，New York：East Asia Program，Cornell University，c2011. xviii，164 p.；23cm. ISBN：1933947235，1933947233，1933947532，1933947535.（Cornell East Asia series，1050－2955；no. 153.）

《〈白罂粟〉及其他》，Gernant，Karen 和 Chen，Zeping 合译.

李锐（1950—）

1. Silver City：a novel/Li Rui；translated by Howard Goldblatt. 1st American ed. New York：Metropolitan Books，1997. 276 p.；24cm. ISBN：0805048952，

0805048957

《银城故事》,葛浩文(Goldblatt, Howard, 1939—)(美国翻译家)译.

2. Trees without wind：a novel/Li Rui；translated by John Balcom. New York：Columbia University Press，c2013. xii，186 p.；19cm. ISBN：0231162746，0231162753，0231531047. (Weatherhead Books on Asia)

《无风之树》,陶忘机(Balcom, John)(美国汉学家)译.

多多(1951—)

1. Snow plain/Duo Duo；Translated by John A. Crespi；with contributions from Harriet Evans... [et al.]. Brookline, MA：Zephyr Press，c2010. xii，110 p.；20cm. ISBN：0981552187，0981552188

Contents：Story of a snow plain—Childhood, boyhood, youth—Sumo—The day I got to Xi'an—Vacation—Going home.

Crespi, John A. 译.

史铁生(1951—2010)

1. Strings of life/Shi Tiesheng. Beijing, China：Chinese Literature Press，1991. 271 pages；18cm. ISBN：0835120929，0835120920，7507100839，7507100839. (Panda Books)

Contents：Strings of life—Original sin—Fate—One winter's evening—In the world of understanding—Autumn remembrance—Our corner—My Faraway Qingpingwan—Granny's star—Lunch break—Blacky.

《命若琴弦》. 中国文学出版社.

(1)Beijing：Foreign Languages Press，2009. 271 pages；illustrations；20cm. ISBN：7119058986，7119058983

(2)Strings of life：and other selected writings/Shi Tiesheng；translated by Yu Fanqin. Beijing：Foreign Languages Pr.，2014. 207 pages；23cm. ISBN：7119087580，7119087584. (Gems of modern Chinese literature)

2. Selected stories/by Shi Tiesheng. [Beijing]：Chinese Literature Press；Foreign Language Teaching and Research Press，1999. [10]，248 s.；·20cm. ISBN：7560016723，7560016726. (University reader；English-Chinese gems of Chinese literature. Contemporary)

《史铁生小说选》.本书收入《我的遥远的清平湾》《命若琴弦》《奶奶的星星》《我与地坛》四部短篇小说.

储福金(1952—)

1. The naked fields/Chu Fujin. Beijing：Chinese Literature Press，1995. 258 pages；18cm. ISBN：750710219X，7507102192，0835131378，0835131377. (Panda books)

Contents：Preface—The naked fields—The projection room—Man's worth.

《裸野》. 中国文学出版社. 收录三篇短篇小说.

(1) The naked fields and other selected writings/Chu Fujin. Beijing：Foreign Languages Press，2009. 258 pages；20cm. ISBN：7119059013，7119059017.

(Panda books)

周大新(1952—)

1. For love of a silversmith/Zhou Daxin；[translated by Yu Fanqin, William Riggle, and Paul White]. Beijing：Panda Books；Chinese Literature Press，1995. 213 pages；18cm. ISBN：7507102866，7507102864，0835131467，0835131469

Contents：Always start from the early spring morning—For love of a silversmith—Out of the woods—The sesame oil mill.

《银饰》. 收录作者的4篇小说.

2. The Sesame Oil Mill and other selected writings/Zhou Daxin. Beijing：Foreign Languages Press，2009. ISBN：7119059020，7119059025. (Panda books)

《香魂塘畔的香油坊：周大新作品选》.收录作者的《银饰》《芝麻油磨坊》和《走出盆地》3部小说.

3. Scenery of the lake and the mountain/by Zhou Daxin；translated by Thomas Bray. Beijing：China Translation & Publishing Corporation，2017. 398 pages. ISBN：7500151487，7500151489. (中国当代经典丛书)

《湖光山色》,(英)Thomas Bray 译.

贾平凹(1952—)

1. Turbulence：a novel/by Jia Pingwa；translated by Howard Goldblatt. Baton Rouge：Louisiana State University Press，1991. 507 p.；24cm. ISBN：0807116874

《浮躁》,葛浩文(Goldblatt, Howard, 1939—)(美国翻译家)译.

(1)1st Grove Press ed. New York：Grove Press，[2003]. 507 p.；21cm. (Pegasus Prize for Literature). ISBN：0802139728

2. The heavenly hound/Jia Pingwa. Beijing, China：Chinese Literature Press，1991. 306 pages；18cm. ISBN：7507100758，7507100754，0835120864，0835120869. (Panda books)

Contents：The Heavenly Hound—The People of Chicken's Nest Hollow—Touch Paper

《天狗》. 中国文学出版社.

3. Heavenly rain/Jia Pingwa. Beijing：Chinese Literature Press，1996. 416 pages；18cm. ISBN：7507103463，7507103465，0835131823，0835131827. (Panda Books)

Contents：Heavenly rain—Good fortune grave—Regrets of a bride carier—Monk king of Tiger Mountain.

《晚雨》. 中国文学出版社.

4. The castle/Jia Pingwa；translated from the Chinese by Shao-pin Luo；with an introduction by Robin Marcelle Latimer and Shao-pin Luo. Toronto：York Press，1997. iii，79 pages；23cm. ISBN：1896761038，1896761039

《古堡》,Luo, Shao-pin 译.

5. The Heavenly Hound and other selected writings/Jia Pingwa. Beijing：Foreign Languages Press，2009. 306 pages；20cm. ISBN：7119059075，7119059076. (Panda books)

《天狗:贾平凹作品选》

6. Ruined city:a novel/Jia Pingwa;translated by Howard Goldblatt. First edition. Norman:University of Oklahoma Press,2015. ISBN:0806151731,0806151730.（Chinese literature today;volume 5）

《废都》,葛浩文（Goldblatt,Howard,1939—）（美国翻译家）译.

7. Happy dreams/Jia Pingwa;translated by Nicky Harman. Seattle:AmazonCrossing,2017. 80 pages;21cm. ISBN:1611097429,1611097428

《高兴》,Harman,Nicky 译.

8. The lantern bearer/Jia Pingwa;translated by Carlos Rojas. Jerico,New York:CN Times Books,2017. xi,516 pages;26cm. ISBN:1627740616,1627740619

《带灯》,Rojas,Carlos（1970—）译.

王小波（1952—1997）

1. Wang in love and bondage:three novellas/by Wang Xiaobo;translated and with an introduction by Hongling Zhang,Jason Sommer. Albany:State University of New York Press,c2007. xiv,155 p.;23cm. ISBN:0791470652,0791470657

《在爱与束缚中:王小波小说三篇》,Zhang,Hongling 和 Sommer,Jason 合译. 包括《2015》《黄金时代》《东宫西宫》.

哈丽旦·伊斯热依力（1952—）

1. No cattle in the city/author,Halidan Yisreyili;[translator,Song Jianxun]. Urumchi:Xinjiang Juvenile Publishing House,2010. 3,1,212 pages;23cm. ISBN:7537189354,7537189358

《城市没有牛》

韩少功（1953—）

1. Homecoming? and other stories/by Han Shaogong;translated by Martha Cheung. Hong Kong:Research Centre for Translations,Chinese University of Hong Kong,c1992. xxii 161 p.;22cm. ISBN:9627255130,9627255130.（Renditions paperbacks）

Incomplete contents:Homecoming? —The blue bottle-cap—Pa pa pa—Woman woman woman

《魂兮归来及其他》,Cheung,Martha 译.

2. A dictionary of Maqiao/Han Shaogong;translated by Julia Lovell. New York:Columbia University Press,c2003. xviii,322 p.;23cm. ISBN:231127448,0231127448.（Weatherhead books on Asia）

《马桥词典》,茱莉亚·洛佛尔（Lovell,Julia,1975—）（英国汉学家）译.

(1) Pymble,N. S. W.:Fourth Estate,2004. 1 volume. ISBN:073228001X,0732280017

(2) New York:Dial Press,2005. 394 pages;21cm. ISBN:0385339356,0385339353

残雪（1953—）

1. Dialogues in paradise/Can Xue;translated by Ronald R.

Janssen and Jian Zhang. Evanston,Ill.:Northwestern University Press,1989. x,173 pages;21cm. ISBN:0810108305,0810108301,0810108313,0810108318

《天堂里的对话》,詹森（Janssen,Ronald R.）和张健合译.

2. Old floating cloud:two novellas/Can Xue;translated by Ronald R. Janssen and Jian Zhang;with a foreword by Charlotte Innes. Evanston,Ill.:Northwestern University Press,1991. xx,269 pages;24cm. ISBN:0810109743,0810109742,0810109883,0810109889

《苍老的浮云》,詹森（Janssen,Ronald R.）和张健译.

3. The embroidered shoes:stories/Can Xue;translated by Ronald R. Janssen and Jian Zhang. New York:Henry Holt,1997. x,221 pages;22cm. ISBN:0805054138,0805054132

《绣花鞋的故事》,詹森（Janssen,Ronald R.）和张健合译.

4. Blue light in the sky & other stories/Can Xue;translated by Karen Gernanat and Chen Zeping. New York:New Directions,2006. 212 p.;21cm. ISBN:0811216489,0811216487.（New Directions paperbook;1039）

Contents:Blue light in the sky—;The bizzare wooden building—;A negligible game on the journey—;Helin—;The lure of the sea—;Snake Island—;Night in the mountain village—;Scenes inside the dilapidated walls—;Burial—;The spring—;The little monster—;My brother—;Top floor—;Mosquitoes and mountain ballads—;A particular sort of story.

《天空里的蓝光及其他》,Gernant,Karen 和 Chen,Zeping（1953—）合译. 短篇小说选.

5. Five spice street/Can Xue;translated by Karen Gernant and Chen Zeping. New Haven:Yale University Press,2009. 329 p.;21cm. ISBN:0300122275,0300122276.（A Margellos world republic of letters book）

《五香街》,Gernant,Karen 和 Chen,Zeping（1953—）合译.

(1) New Haven,Conn.;London:Yale University Press,2012. 1 volume;21cm. ISBN:0300167962,0300167962.（A Margellos World Republic of Letters book）

6. Vertical motion:short stories/Can Xue;translated by Karen Gernant and Chen Zeping. Rochester,NY:Open Letter,2011. 186 pages;22cm. ISBN:1934824375,1934824372

Contents:Vertical motion—Red leaves—Night visitor—Affectionate companion's jottings—Village in the big city—Elena—Moonlight dance—Roses at the hospital—Cotton candy—Brilliant purple China rose—Rainscape—Never at peace—Papercuts.

《垂直运动》,Gernant,Karen 和 Chen,Zeping（1953—）合译. 短篇小说选.

7. The last lover/Can Xue;translated by Annelise Finegan Wasmoen. New Haven;London:Yale University Press,2014. ISBN:0300153323,0300153325.（A Margellos

world republic of letters book)

《最后的情人》,Wasmoen, Annelise Finegan(1981—)译.

8. Frontier/by Can Xue; translated from the Chinese by Karen Gernant & Chen Zeping. Rochester, NY: Open Letter, 2017. xv, 361 pages; 22cm. ISBN: 1940953540, 1940953545

Contents: Liujin—José and Nancy—Qiming—Sherman—The baby—Liujin and Amy—Lee and Grace—Liujin, her parents, and the black man—Little Leaf and Marco—The director and Nancy—Liujin and Amy, as well as Qiming—Liujin and Roy, as well as a headless man—Qiming and Liujin—Liujin and Ying—Snow.

《边疆》,Gernant, Karen 和 Chen, Zeping(1953—)合译.

张辛欣(1953—),

1. Chinese profiles/Zhang Xinxin and Sang Ye. Beijing: Chinese Literature, 1986. 376 pages; 18cm. ISBN: 0835116034, 0835116039. (Panda books)

《北京人》,张辛欣(1953—),桑晔(1955—).

(1)Beijing: Chinese Literature Press, 1996. 376 pages; 18cm. ISBN: 7507100200, 7507100204. (Panda Books)

2. The dreams of our generation; and, Selections from Beijing's people/by Zhang Xinxin; edited and translated by Edward Gunn, Donna Jung, and Patricia Farr. Ithaca, NY: East Asia Program, Cornell University, 1986. 87 pages; 22cm. ISBN: 0939657414, 0939657414. (Cornell East Asia series; no. 41)

《我们这个年纪的梦》,张辛欣(1953—);Gunn, Edward M., Jung, Donna, Farr, Patricia 合译.

3. Chinese lives: an oral history of contemporary China/Zhang Xinxin and Sang Ye; edited by W. J. F. Jenner and Delia Davin; translated by the editors and Cheng Lingfang...[et al.]. New York: Pantheon Books, c1987. xxxii, 367 p.; 25cm. ISBN: 0394559282, 0394559285

《北京人》,张辛欣(1953—),桑晔(1955—);詹纳尔(Jenner, W. J. F.〈William John Francis〉)(英国学者)等编译.

(1)London: Macmillan London, 1988. xxxii, 367 pages: 1 map; 25cm. ISBN: 0333433645, 0333433645

(2)London: Penguin Books, 1989. xxxii, 367 pages: 1 map; 20cm. ISBN: 0140116257, 0140116250

朱苏进(1953—)

1. A novel about the Chinese People's Liberation Army: The third eye by Zhu Sujin/translated by Qingyun Wu; with a foreword by Paul Ropp. Lewiston, N. Y.: Edwin Mellen Press, c2010. vii, 123 p.; 24cm. ISBN: 0773413672, 0773413677

《第三只眼》,武庆云(Wu, Qingyun, 1950—)(美国华裔学者)译.

马原(1953—)

1. Ballad of the Himalayas: stories of Tibet/Ma Yuan; introduction by Yang Xiaobin; translated by Herbert J. Batt. Portland, Me.: MerwinAsia; Haworth, NJ: Distributed by St. Johann Press, 2010. xiv, 315 pages; 21cm. ISBN: 1878282859 1878282859, 1878282866, 1878282867, 0983299189, 0983299188, 0983299196, 0983299196

Contents: Vagabond spirit—The black road—The numismatologist—The master—A fiction—The spell of the Gangdise Mountains—Three ways to fold a paper hawk—Ballad of the Himalayas.

《喜马拉雅古歌》,Batt, Herbert J. (1945—)译.

2. No sail on the Western Sea/by Ma Yuan; translation by Tony Blishen. New York: Better Link Press, 2015. 167 pages; 21cm. ISBN: 1602202498, 1602202494. (Stories by contemporary writers from Shanghai)

Contents: No sail on the Western Sea—The master.

Blishen, Tony 译.

李佩甫(1953—)

1. Wait for your soul: a novel/Li Peifu. Guangzhou: Flower City Publishing Press, 2009. 244 pages; 21cm. ISBN: 7536056817, 7536056818

《等等灵魂》.花城出版社.

2. Book of Life/by Li Peipu; translated by Helena Laughton. Beijing: China Translation & Publishing Corporation, 2017. 548 pages. ISBN: 7500151470, 7500151470

《生命册》,Laughton, Helena 译.

徐小斌(1953—)

1. Dunhuang dreams/Xu Xiaobin. Beijing: Chinese Literature Press, 1998. 200 pages; 18cm. ISBN: 7507103811, 7507103816, 0835131920, 0835131926. (Panda books)

《敦煌遗梦》,吴大维译.中国文学出版社.

(1)Dunhuang dream: a novel/Xu Xiaobin; translated by John Balcom. 1st Atria International ed. New York: Atria International, 2011. vii, 196 pages; 22cm. ISBN: 1416583905, 1416583904

2. Feathered serpent/Xu Xiaobin; translated by John Howard-Gibbon and Joanne Wang. New York: Atria International, 2009. x, 367 pages; 24cm. ISBN: 1416583806, 1416583807

《羽蛇》,霍华(Howard-Gibbon, John)和 Wang, Joanne 合译.

(1)London: Simon & Schuster, 2010. x, 367 pages; 23cm. ISBN: 1416583813, 1416583815

3. Crystal wedding/Xu Xiaobin; translated from the Chinese by Nicky Harman. London Balestier Press, 2016. 302 pages; 22cm. ISBN: 0993215490, 0993215491

《水晶婚》,Harman, Nicky 译.

叶梅(1953—)

1. Song Rod＝歌棒/叶梅著;[英]Patric Burton, 张碧竹译.

Beijing：Zhong yi chu ban she，2016. 226 pages；20cm. ISBN：7500143345，7500143346.（Kaleidoscope：ethnic Chinese writers ＝阅读中国.五彩丛书）

2. Last Chieftain/by Ye Mei；translated by Declan Fry. Beijing：China Translation & Publishing Corporation，2017. 321 pages. ISBN：7500151555，7500151551

《最后的土司》，Fry，Declan 译.

张欣（1954—）

1. Contemporary Chinese women writers VI：four novellas/by Zhang Xin. Beijing：Chinese Literature Press，1998. 332 pages；18cm. ISBN：7507103846，7507103847，0835131963，0835131964.（Panda books）

《张欣小说选》，马若芬等译，中国文学出版社.该书是《中国当代女作家作品选》第六辑.

高建群（1954—）

1. Tongwan City/Gao Jianqun；［translated by Eric Mu］. New York：CN Times Books，2013. ix，259 pages；24cm. ISBN：1627740067，1627740066

《统万城》

（1）New York：CN Times Books，2014. ix，259 pages；23cm. ISBN：162774097X，1627740975

刘恒（1954—）

1. The obsessed/Liu Heng；translated by David Kwan. Beijing，China：Chinese Literature Press，1991. 340 p.；18cm. ISBN：7507100723，7507100723，083512083X，0835120838.（Panda books）

《伏羲伏羲》

（1）The obsessed and other selected writings/Liu Heng. Beijing：Foreign Languages Press，2009. 340 pages；20cm. ISBN：7119059068，7119059068.（Panda books）

2. Black snow/Liu Heng；translated by David Kwan. Beijing，China：Chinese Literature Press：Distributed by China International Book Trading Corp.，1991. 261 pages；19cm. ISBN：7507100820，7507100822，0835120910，0835120913.（Panda books）

《黑的雪》.中国文学出版社.

3. Black snow：a novel of the Beijing demimonde/by Liu Heng；translated from the Chinese by Howard Goldblatt. New York：Atlantic Monthly Press：Grove Press，1993. 261 pages；21cm. ISBN：0871135302，0871135308，0802133894，0802133892

《黑的雪》，葛浩文（Goldblatt，Howard，1939—）（美国翻译家）译.

4. Green River daydreams：a novel/by Liu Heng；translated from the Chinese by Howard Goldblatt. 1st ed. New York：Grove Press，c2001. 332 p.；22cm. ISBN：0802116906

《苍河白日梦》，葛浩文（Goldblatt，Howard，1939—）（美国翻译家）译.

王安忆（1954—）

1. Love in a small town/by Wang Anyi；translated by Eva Hung. Hong Kong：Research Centre for Translation，Chinese University of Hong Kong，1988（1990 reprinting）. ix，104 p.；22cm. ISBN：9627255033，9627255031.（Renditions paperbacks）

《小城之恋》，孔慧怡（Hung，Eva）译.

2. Lapse of time/by Wang Anyi；introduction by Jeffrey Kinkley. Beijing，China：Chinese Literature Press；San Francisco：China Books & Periodicals，1988. 257 pages；18cm. ISBN：7507100316，7507100310，0835120317，0835120319.（Panda books）

Contents：The destination—And the rain patters on—Life in a small themselves—Lapse of time—Biographical note—my wall.

《流逝：王安忆作品选》.中国文学出版社.

（1）Beijing，China：Foreign Languages Press：Distributed by China International Book Trading Corp.，2005. 318 pages；21cm. ISBN：7119033603，7119033600.（Contemporary Chinese women writers；Panda books）

（2）Lapse of time and other selected writings/Wang Anyi. Beijing：Foreign Languages Press，2009. 318 pages；20cm. ISBN：7119059037，7119059033.（Panda books）

3. Baotown/Wang Anyi；translated by Martha Avery. New York：W. W. Norton，1989. vii，143 pages；22cm. ISBN：0393027112，0393027112

《小鲍庄》

（1）London：Viking，1989. ix，142 pages；20cm. ISBN：0670826227，0670826223，0140118101，0140118100.（Penguin international writers）

（2）Harmondsworth：Penguin，1990. ix，142 pages；20cm. ISBN：0140118101，0140118100.（Penguin international writers）

4. The flow/Anyi Wang. London：Facsimile Pub.，1989. 150 pages. ISBN：1871437059，1871437058

《流逝》

5. Love on a barren mountain/by Wang Anyi；translated by Eva Hung. Hong Kong：Research Centre for Translation，Chinese University of Hong Kong，1991. xiii，143 pages；21cm. ISBN：9627255092，9627255093.（Renditions paperbacks）

《荒山之恋》，孔慧怡（Hung，Eva）译.

6. Brocade Valley/Wang Anyi；translated by Bonnie S. McDougall & Chen Maiping. New York：New Directions，1992. xii，123 pages；21cm. ISBN：0811212246，0811212243

《锦绣谷之恋》，Chen，Maiping 和 McDougall，Bonnie S.（1941—）合译.

7. The song of everlasting sorrow：a novel of Shanghai/Wang Anyi；translated by Michael Berry and Susan Chan

Egan. New York：Columbia University Press，c2008. viii，440 p. ；24cm. ISBN：0231143424，0231143427，0231513098，0231513097. (Weatherhead books on Asia)

《长恨歌》，白睿文(又名白瑞克，Berry，Michael，1974—)(美国汉学家)，陈毓贤(Egan，Susan Chan)(美国华裔)合译.

(1) New York；Chichester：Columbia University Press，2010. viii，440 pages；23cm. ISBN：0231143431，0231143435. (Weatherhead books on Asia)

8. The little restaurant/by Wang Anyi. New York：Better Link Press；Shanghai：Shanghai Press and Publishing Development Company，2010. 364 pages；18cm. ISBN：1602202252，1602202257. （Stories by contemporary writers from Shanghai）

《小饭店》

陈村(1954—)

1. The elephant/by Chen Cun；[translation by Yawtsong Lee]. New York：BetterLink Press，2010. 176 p. ；18cm. ISBN：1602202177，1602202176. （Stories by contemporary writers of Shanghai）

Lee，Yawtsong 译.

张海迪(1955—)

1. Topmost/Zhang Haidi. Beijing：China Intercontinental Press，2016. 374 pages；23cm. ISBN：7508535081，7508535081

《绝顶》.五洲传播出版社.

2. Enduring as the Universe/Zhang Haidi. Beijing：China Intercontinental Press，2017. 423 pages. ISBN：7508536637，7508536630

《天长地久》

唐颖(1955—)

1. Dissipation/by Tang Ying；[translated by Qiu Maoru]. New York：Better link Press，2010. 208 pages；18cm. ISBN：1602202139，1602202133. （Stories by contemporary writers from Shanghai；Cultural China）

《随波逐流》，Qiu，Maoru 译.

艾蓓(张爱培,1955—)

1. Red ivy，green earth mother/Ai Bei；translated by Howard Goldblatt. Salt Lake City：Peregrine Smith Books，c1990. xii，146 p. ；22cm. ISBN：0879052929

《红藤绿度母》，葛浩文(Goldblatt，Howard，1939—)(美国翻译家)译.

刘索拉(1955—)

1. Blue sky green sea and other stories/by Liu Sola；translated by Martha Cheung. [Hong Kong]：Research Centre for Translation，Chinese University of Hong Kong，1993. xxv，145 p. ；22cm. ISBN：9627255122，9627255123. (Renditions paperbacks)

《〈蓝天绿海〉及其他》，Cheung，Martha 译.

2. Chaos and all that/Liu Sola；translated from the Chinese by Richard King. Honolulu：University of Hawaii Press，

1994. 134 p. ；22cm. ISBN：082481617X，082481651X

《混沌加哩格楞》，刘索拉(1955—)；King，Richard 译.

3. 你别无选择/刘索拉著；(英)尼古拉斯·柯罗夫曼译. 南京：南京大学出版社，2017.

陈源斌(1955—)

1. The story of Qiuju/Chen Yuanbin. Beijing：Chinese Literature Press，1995. 206 pages；18cm. ISBN：7507102777，7507102772，0835131440，0835131445. (Panda books)

Contents：Preface—The story of Qiuju—Celestial river—Heaven's course—The drowning of Jiuzhou City.

《秋菊打官司》.中国文学出版社.

方方(1955—)

1. Contemporary Chinese women writers，V：three novellas/by Fang Fang. Beijing，China：Chinese Literature Press：Distributed by China International Book Trading Corp.，1996. iii，288 pages；18cm. ISBN：7507103498，7507103496，0835131831，0835131834. (Panda books)

Contents：One glittering moment—Landscape—Dead end.

《中国当代女作家作品选:方方专辑》，关大卫等译. 中国文学出版社.

2. Children of the bitter river ＝ Fengjing/Fang Fang；Herbert J. Batt，translator；introduction by Robin Visser. Norwalk：EastBridge，2007. xvi，75 pages；23cm. ISBN：1891936786，1891936784

《风景》，Batt，Herbert J. (1945—)译.

3. One glittering moment and other selected writings/Fang Fang. Beijing：Foreign Languages Press，2009. iii，288 pages；20cm. ISBN：7119059198，711905919X

《桃花灿烂:方方作品选》.收录《桃花灿烂》《风景》和《无处逃遁》等小说.

莫言(1955—)

1. Explosions and other stories/by Mo Yan；edited by Janice Wickeri. Hong Kong：Research Centre for Translations，Chinese University of Hong Kong，c1991. xii，214 p. ；22cm. (Renditions paperbacks)

Contents：Explosions—The old gun—Flies—The flying ship—The amputee—The yellow-haired baby

《〈爆炸〉及其他》，Wickeri，Janice 译.

2. Red sorghum/Mo Yan；translated from the Chinese by Howard Goldblatt. London：Heinemann，1992. [378] pages；24cm. ISBN：0434886416，0434886418

《红高粱家族》，葛浩文(Goldblatt，Howard，1939—)(美国翻译家)译.

(1) Red sorghum：a novel of China/Mo Yan；translated from the Chinese by Howard Goldblatt. New York：Viking，1993. 359 pages；24cm. ISBN：0670844020，0670844029，0140168549，0140168540

(2) Red sorghum：a novel of China/Mo Yan；translated from the Chinese by Howard Goldblatt. New York：

Penguin Books, 1994. 359 pages；20cm. ISBN：0140168540，0140168549，0670844020，0670844029

(3) London：Minerva, 1994. 377 pages；20cm. ISBN：0749398523，0749398521

(4) Red sorghum/Mo Yan; translated from the Chinese by Howard Goldblatt.. London：Arrow, 2003. 377 p.；20cm. ISBN：0099451670，0099451679，0099580836，0099580837

3. The garlic ballads/Mo Yan; translated from the Chinese by Howard Goldblatt. New York：Viking, 1995. 290 pages；24cm. ISBN：0670854018，0670854011
《天堂蒜薹之歌》,葛浩文(Goldblatt，Howard，1939—)(美国翻译家)译.

(1) London：Hamish Hamilton, 1996. 290 pages；23cm. ISBN：0241001943，0241001943

(2) New York：Penguin Books, 1996. 290 pages；20cm. ISBN：0140233911，0140233919，0140245286，0140245288，0140256091，0140256093

(3) The garlic ballads：a novel/Mo Yan; translated from the Chinese by Howard Goldblatt. 1st Arcade ed. New York：Arcade Pub.：Distributed by Time Warner Book Group, [2005]. 290 p.；21cm. ISBN：1559707755，1559707756

(4) London：Methuen, 2006. 320 pages；20cm. ISBN：0413775313，0413775313

(5) New York：Arcade Pub., 2012. 290 pages；21cm. ISBN：1611457070，1611457076

4. The republic of wine：a novel/Mo Yan; translated from the Chinese by Howard Goldblatt. 1st North American ed. New York：Arcade Pub.：Distributed by Time Warner Trade Publishing, c2000. v, 355 p.；25cm. ISBN：1559705310，1559705318
《酒国》,葛浩文(Goldblatt，Howard，1939—)(美国翻译家)译.

(1) London：Hamish Hamilton, 2000. v, 355 pages；23cm. ISBN：024113661X，0241136614

(2) New York：Arcade, 2001. v, 355 pages；22cm. ISBN：1559705760，1559705769

(3) New York：Arcade Pub., 2012. v, 355 pages；23cm. ISBN：1611457292，1611457297

5. Shifu, you'll do anything for a laugh/Mo Yan; translated from the Chinese by Howard Goldblatt. New York：Arcade Pub., 2001. xxii, 189 p.；22cm. ISBN：1559705655，1559705653，1611452228，1611452228，1611457353，1611457351
《师傅越来越幽默》,葛浩文(Goldblatt，Howard，1939—)(美国翻译家)译.

(1) London：Methuen, 2002. xxii, 188 p.；23cm. ISBN：0413771180，0413771186

(2) London：Methuen, 2003. 189 pages；20cm. ISBN：0413771199，0413771193

6. Big breasts and wide hips：a novel/by Mo Yan; translated from the Chinese by Howard Goldblatt. New York：Arcade Pub., 2004. xiv, 532 p.；25cm. ISBN：1559706724，1559706728
《丰乳肥臀》,葛浩文(Goldblatt，Howard，1939—)(美国翻译家)译.

(1) London：Methuen, 2004. 532 pages；24cm. ISBN：0413771547，0413771544

(2) London：Methuen, 2005. xiv, 532 pages；20cm. ISBN：0413771551，0413771555

(3) New York：Arcade Publishing, 2012. xiv, 532 pages；23cm. ISBN：1611453430，1611453437

7. Life and death are wearing me out：a novel/Mo Yan; translated from the Chinese by Howard Goldblatt. 1st English-language ed. New York：Arcade Pub., c2008. viii, 540 p.；25cm. ISBN：1559708531，1559708530
《生死疲劳》,葛浩文(Goldblatt，Howard，1939—)(美国翻译家)译.

(1) New York：Arcade, 2012. viii, 540 pages；23cm. ISBN：1611454277，1611454271

(2) Docklands, Vic 3008, Australia, Vic. Penguin Group, 2016. ISBN：0143800255，0143800256

8. Frog/Mo Yan; translated from the original Chinese edition by Howard Goldblatt. Melbourne, Vic.：Hamish Hamilton, 2009. 387 pages；24cm. ISBN：0143800095，0143800094
《蛙》,葛浩文(Goldblatt，Howard，1939—)(美国翻译家)译.

(1) London：Hamish Hamilton, 2014. 387 pages；24cm. ISBN：0241146446，0241146445，0241972366，0241972361

(2) New York：Viking, Published by the Penguin Group, 2015. 387 pages；24cm. ISBN：0525427988

(3) Large print edition. Waterville, Maine：Thorndike Press, a part of Gale, Cengage Learning, 2015. 645 pages (large print)；23cm. ISBN：1410479617，1410479617. (Thorndike Press large print reviewers' choice)

(4) New York：Penguin Books, 2015. 387 pages；24cm. ISBN：0241967324，0241967325

(5) New York：Penguin Books, 2016. 388 pages；22cm. ISBN：0143128388，0143128380

9. Change/Mo Yan; translated by Howard Goldblatt. London；New York：Seagull Books, 2010. 117 pages；19cm. ISBN：1906497484，1906497486. (What was communism？；5)
《变》,葛浩文(Goldblatt，Howard，1939—)(美国翻译家)译.

(1) London；New York：Seagull Books, 2012. 117 p.；18cm. ISBN：0857421609，0857421603，0857421616，0857421611

10. Selected stories by Mo Yan/Mo Yan. Hong Kong：Chinese University Press；London：Eurospan［distributor］，2011. 1 volume；22cm. ISBN：9629963149，9629963140

    莫言小说选.

11. Pow! /Mo Yan；translated by Howard Goldblatt. London；New York：Seagull Books，2012. 386 p.；24cm. ISBN：0857420763, 0857420763

    《四十一炮》，葛浩文(Goldblatt，Howard，1939—)(美国翻译家)译.

    (1)London：Seagull Books，2014. 386 pages；23cm. ISBN：0857422219, 0857422217

12. Sandalwood death＝(Tanxiang xing)：a novel/Mo Yan；translated by Howard Goldblatt. Norman：University of Oklahoma Press，2013. x，409 p.；23cm. ISBN：0806143392, 0806143398. (Chinese literature today book series；v. 2).

    《檀香刑》，葛浩文(Goldblatt，Howard，1939—)(美国翻译家)译.

13. Radish/Mo Yan；translated from the original Chinese by Howard Goldblatt. Melbourne，Vic.：Penguin Books Australia，2015. 86 pages；19cm. ISBN：0734310798, 073431079X. (Penguin Specials)

    《透明的红萝卜》，葛浩文(Goldblatt，Howard，1939—)(美国翻译家)译.

范小青(1955—)

1. 当代中国名家双语阅读文库·第一辑·范小青卷/杨昊成主编.南京：南京师范大学出版社，2018. 343 页；照片；21cm. ISBN：7565135798

   英文共同题名：A bilingual library contemporary Chinese master writers. 本书汇集范小青《城乡简史》《生于黄昏或清晨》《梦幻快递》等作品以及对其的评论和访谈文章.

张炜(1956—)

1. September's fable：a novel/Zhang Wei；translated from the Chinese by Terence Russell ＆ Shawn Xian Ye. Paramus，NJ：Homa ＆ Sekey Books，2007. xvi，495 pages；22cm. ISBN：1931907460, 1931907463

   《九月寓言》，Russell，Terence 和 Ye，Shawn Xian (1954—)合译.

2. The ancient ship/Zhang Wei；translated by Howard Goldblatt. 1st ed. New York：HarperPerennial，c2008. ix，451 p.；21cm. ISBN：0061436901, 0061436909. (Modern Chinese classics)

   《古船》，葛浩文(Goldblatt，Howard，1939—)(美国翻译家)译.

3. Seven kinds of mushrooms：a novel/Zhang Wei；translated from the Chinese by Terence Russell. Paramus，N. J.：Homa ＆ Sekey Books，2009. ix，214 pages；22cm. ISBN：1931907552, 1931907552

   《蘑菇七种》，Russell，Terence 译.

顾城(1956—1993)

1. The kingdom of daughters/Gu Cheng ＆ Lei Mi；Aus dem Chines. von Li Xia. Dortmund：Projekt-Verl.，1995. XI，302 p. ISBN：3928861425，3928861427. (Edition Cathay；9)

   《英儿》，顾城，雷米著.

朱晓琳(1956—)

1. Platinum passport/by Zhu Xiaolin；translation by Jiang Yajun，Zhu Ping. New York：Better Link Press，2014. 261 pages；18cm. ISBN：1602202400, 1602202405. (Stories by contemporary writers from Shanghai；Cultural China)

   《白金护照》；Jiang Yajun 和 Zhu Ping 合译.

刘醒龙(1956—)

1. Sky dwellers/by Liu Xinglong；translated by Emily Jones. Beijing：China Translation ＆ Publishing Corporation，2017. v 376 pages. ISBN：7500151517，7500151519

   《天行者》，Jones，Emily 译. 中国对外翻译出版公司.

池莉(1957—)

1. Apart from love/Chi Li；［translated by Mingjie Wang，... ［et al.］. Beijing：Foreign Languages Press；Distributed by China International Book Trading Corp.，c2005. 348 p.；18cm. ISBN：7119036637, 7119036632. (Contemporary Chinese women writers). (Panda books)

   Contents：Apart from love—Trials and tribulations—Sunrise—To and fro—The heart more than the flesh

   《不谈爱情》，王明杰等译. (熊猫丛书). 收录了女作家池莉的五部作品：《不谈爱情》《烦恼人生》《来来往往》等.

2. Apart from love and other selected writings/Chi Li. Beijing：Foreign Languages Press，2009. 358 pages；20cm. ISBN：7119058993, 7119058991

   Contents：Hand of gold—Fine moon—Apart from love—Trials and tribulations—Hot or cold，it's good to be alive—Sunrise

   《不谈爱情：池莉作品选》. 收集了 6 部短篇小说.

叶兆言(1957—)

1. Nanjing 1937：a love story/Ye Zhaoan；translated and with an afterword by Michael Berry. New York：Anchor Books，1996. 394 pages. ISBN：1400034272, 1400034277

   《一九三七年的爱情》，白睿文（又名白瑞克，Berry，Michael，1974—)(美国汉学家)译.

   (1)New York：Columbia University Press，2002. viii，355 p.；24cm. ISBN：0231127545, 0231127547. (Weatherhead books on Asia)

   (2)London：Faber and Faber，2002. viii，255 pages；24cm. ISBN：0571218105, 0571218103

   (3)New York：Anchor Books，2004. 394 pages；20cm. ISBN：1400034272, 1400034277

   (4)London：Faber and Faber，2004. 358 pages；20cm. ISBN：0571218113, 0571218110

2. Old Nanjing：reflections of scenes on the Qinhuai River/ text by Ye Zhaoyan. Beijing：Foreign Languages Press，2003. 255 pages；illustrations；22cm. ISBN：7119030485, 7119030487. (Old city series)

《老南京：旧影秦淮》，黄玲，郝薇翻译.

3. Water towns/written by Ye Zhaoyan；illustrated by Li Ronghua；translated by Li Yiqi. Shanghai：East China Normal University Press，2009. 1，183 pages：color illustrations；23cm. ISBN：7561771471，7561771479. (China style series＝中国风)

《水乡》，李荣华插图；Li，Yiqi 译.

4. 当代中国名家双语阅读文库. 第一辑，叶北言卷/杨昊成主编. 南京：南京师范大学出版社，2018. 303 页；照片；21cm. ISBN：7565135781

英文共同题名：A bilingual library contemporary Chinese master writers. 本书汇集叶兆言《左轮三五七》《作家林美女士》《凶杀之都》等作品以及对其的评论和访谈文章.

铁凝（1957—）

1. Haystacks/Ning Tie. Beijing：Chinese Literature Press，1990. 352 p. ISBN：7507100421，7507100426

Contents：Butterfly—The provincial governor's diary—The pregnant woman and the cow—Ah，fragrant snow—Glasimov Jr.—June's big topic—Been and gone—The breach—The sun so near—The red shirt without buttons—Haystacks.

《麦秸垛：英文》，王明杰等译（熊猫丛书）. 收录了女作家铁凝的《孕妇和牛》《嚳口》《麦秸垛》等 10 篇小说.

(1) Haystacks/Tie Ning；［translated by Denis Mair］. Beijing，China：Foreign Languages Press：Distributed by China International Book Trading Corporation，2005. 351 pages；21cm. ISBN：7119036653，7119036656. (Panda books)

(2) Beijing：Foreign Languages Press，2009. 352 pages；20cm. ISBN：7119059051，711905905X. (Panda books)

(3) Beijing：Foreign Languages Press，2014. 268 str.；23cm. ISBN：7119087566，7119087568. (Gems of modern Chinese literature)

2. Selected stories/by Tie Ning. ［Beijing］：Chinese Literature Press：Foreign Language Teaching and Research Press，1999. ［10］，323 s.；20cm. ISBN：7560016812，7560016818. (University reader；English-Chinese gems of Chinese literature. Contemporary)

铁凝小说选.

3. How long is forever/by Tie Ning；［translation：Qiu Maoru，Wu Yanting］. Pleasantville，N. Y.：Reader's Digest Association，2010. 156 pages；22cm. ISBN：1606521526，1606521527

Contents：The woman opposite—How long is forever.

《永远有多远》

4. The bathing women：a novel/Tie Ning；translated by Hongling Zhang and Jason Sommer. New York：Scribner，2012. 361 p.；24cm. ISBN：1451694840，1451694849，1476704265（ebook），1476704260（ebook）

《大浴女》，Zhang，Hongling 和 Sommer，Jason 合译.

(1) London：Blue Door，2014. 456 pages；20cm. ISBN：0007489886，0007489889

刘震云（1958—）

1. The corridors of power/Liu Zhenyun. Beijing：Chinese Literature Press，1994. 311 pages；18cm. ISBN：750710222X，7507102222，0835131394，0835131391. (Panda books)

Contents：The corridors of power—The unit—Ground covered with chicken feathers—Pogoda Depot

《官场》

2. Ground covered with chicken feathers and other selected writings/Liu Zhenyun. Beijing：Foreign Languages Press，2009. 311 pages；20cm. ISBN：7119058948，7119058940

《一地鸡毛：刘震云作品选》. 收录《官场》《单位》和《一地鸡毛》等作品.

3. Cell phone：a novel/Liu Zhenyun；translated by Howard Goldblatt. Portland，Maine：MerwinAsia，c2011. 249 p.；22cm. ISBN：0983659938，1878282897

《手机》，葛浩文（Goldblatt，Howard，1939—）（美国翻译家）译.

4. Ground covered with chicken feathers/Liu Zhenyun；translated by David Kwan. Beijing：Foreign Languages Pr.，2014. 230 pages；23cm. ISBN：7119087573，7119087576. (Gems of modern Chinese literature)

《一地鸡毛：刘震云作品选》，Kwan，David 译.

5. I did not kill my husband：a novel/Liu Zhenyun；Translated by Howard Goldblatt and Sylvia Li-chun Lin. New York：Arcade Publishing，2014. 216 pages；24cm. ISBN：1628724264，1628724269，1628726077（ebook）1628726075（ebook）

《我不是潘金莲》，葛浩文（Goldblatt，Howard，1939—）（美国翻译家），林丽君（Sylvia Li-chun Lin）（美国翻译家）合译.

6. The cook，the crook，and the real estate tycoon：a novel of contemporary China/Liu Zhenyun；translated by Howard Goldblatt and Sylvia Li-chun Lin. New York：Arcade Publishing，2015. ISBN：1628725209，1628725206

《我叫刘跃进》，葛浩文（Goldblatt，Howard，1939—）（美国翻译家），林丽君（Sylvia Li-chun Lin）（美国翻译家）合译.

7. Remembering 1942：and other Chinese stories/Liu Zhenyun；translated by Howard Goldblatt；translated by Sylvia Li-chun Lin. New York：Arcade Publishing，2016. ISBN：1628727128，1628727128

Contents：Tofu—College—Office—Officials—Recruits—Remembering 1942

《〈温故一九四二〉及其他》，葛浩文（Goldblatt，Howard，1939—）（美国翻译家），林丽君（Sylvia Li-chun Lin）（美国翻译家）合译.

王朔（1958—）

1. Playing for thrills/Wang Shuo；translated by Howard

Goldblatt. 1st U. S. ed. New York：William Morrow, 1997. 325 p.；22cm. ISBN：0688130461, 0688130466

《玩的就是心跳》,葛浩文(Goldblatt, Howard, 1939—)(美国翻译家)译.

(1)New York：Penguin, 1998. 325 pages；20cm. ISBN：0140269711, 0140269710

(2)Harpenden：No Exit, 2008. ISBN：1842432969, 1842432966

2. The trouble shooters/by Wang Shuo. Armonk, N. Y.：Sharpe, 1998. 99 p.；23cm. (Chinese education and society；vol. 31, no. 1)

《顽主》

3. Please don't call me human/Wang Shuo；translated by Howard Goldblatt. 1st ed. New York：Hyperion, c2000. vii,289 p.；22cm. ISBN：0786864192,0786864195

《千万别把我当人》,葛浩文(Goldblatt, Howard, 1939—)(美国翻译家)译.

(1) Boston：Cheng & Tsui Co. , c2003. vii, 289 p.；21cm. ISBN：0887274129, 0887274121

阎连科(1958—)

1. Serve the people! /Yan Lianke；translated by Julia Lovell. New York：Black Cat, c2007. 217 p.；21cm. ISBN：0802170446, 0802170447

《为人民服务》,Lovell, Julia(1975—)(英国汉学家)译.

(1)London：Constable, 2007. 228 pages；20cm. ISBN：1845295042, 1845295048

2. Dream of Ding Village/Yan Lianke；translated by Cindy Carter. New York：Grove Press, 2009. 341 pages；22cm. ISBN：0802119322, 0802119328

《丁庄梦》,Carter, Cindy 译.

(1)London：Corsair, 2011. 341 p.；22cm. ISBN：1845296926, 1845296923

(2)Melbourne：Text Publishing Company, 2011. 1 volume. ISBN：1921520181, 1921520183

(3)New York：Grove Press, 2011. 341 pages. ISBN：0802119322, 0802119328, 0802145727, 0802145728

(4)London：Corsair, 2012. 1 volume；20cm. ISBN：1780332628, 1780332629

3. Lenin's kisses/Yan Lianke；translated from the Chinese by Carlos Rojas. New York：Grove Press；[Berkeley, Calif.]：Distributed by Publishers Group West, 2012. vii, 500 pages；24cm. ISBN：0802120373 0802120377 1922079435 192207943X 0802121772 0802121776

《受活》,Rojas, Carlos(1970—)译.

(1)London：Chatto & Windus, 2013. 1 volume；24cm. ISBN：0701188078,0701188073,0701186968,0701186968, 1446484739,1446484734

4. Marrow/Yan Lianke；translated from the original Chinese by Carlos Rojas. Australia Penguin Books, 2015. 103 pages；18cm. ISBN：0734399618, 0734399618. (Penguin specials)

《耙耧天歌》,Rojas, Carlos(1970—)译.

(1)Grove/Atlantic, Incorporated, 2017. 155 p. ISBN：0802126658, 0802126650

5. The four books/Yan Lianke；translated from the Chinese by Carlos Rojas. New York：Grove Press, 2015. xii, 338 pages；22cm. ISBN：0802123121, 0802123120 , 0802124692, 0802124690, 0701186976, 0701186975, 0701186984, 0701186982, 1922182486, 1922182487, 0099569493, 0099569497, 1446484742, 1446484746

《四书》,Rojas, Carlos(1970—)译.

6. The explosion chronicles/Yan Lianke；translated from the chinese by Carlos Rojas. First Grove Atlantic Hardcover Edition. New York：Grove Press, 2016. x, 457 pages；22cm. ISBN：0802125828, 0802125824, 0802127259, 0802127258

《炸裂志》,Rojas, Carlos(1970—)译.

(1)London：Chatto & Windus, 2017. x, 457 pages；22cm. ISBN：1784740481, 1784740489

(2) Melbourne, Vic. The Text Pubishing Company, 2017. ISBN：1925603125, 1925603121

7. The years, months, days：two novellas/Yan Lianke；translated from the Chinese by Carlos Rojas. First American paperback edition. New York：Black Cat, 2017. ISBN：0802126658, 0802126650

Contents：The years, months, days—Marrow.

《年月日》,Rojas, Carlos(1970—)译.

陈丹燕(1958—)

1. My mother is a fairy/Danyan Chen；[translation by J. J. Jiang]. New York：Better Link Press, 2006. 143 pages；24cm. ISBN：1602202028. 1602202023. (Cultural China series)

《我的妈妈是精灵》,Jiang, J. J. 译.

2. Shanghai princess：her survival with pride & dignity/by Chen Danyan；[translation by Mavis Gock Yen]. New York：Better Link Press, 2010. 277 pages：illustrations, portraits；22cm. ISBN：1602202184, 1602202184

《上海的金枝玉叶》

3. Between confidantes：two novellas/Chen Danyan. New York：Better Link Press, 2013. 304 pages；18cm. ISBN：1602202375, 1602202370. (Stories by contemporary writers from Shanghai)

Contents：Between confidantes—In memory of the departed.

Yang, Shuhu,Yang, Yunqin,Qui, Maoru 合译.

4. The Peace Hotel：a non-fiction novel/by Chen Danyan；translated with notes by Liu Haiming. New York：Better Link Press, 2015. 383 pages：illustrations；21cm. ISBN：1602202481, 1602202486

《和平饭店》,Liu, Haiming(1953—)译.

孙甘露(1959—)

1. The messenger's letter/by Sun Ganlu. New York Better

Link Press；Shanghai：Shanghai Press and Publishing Development Company，2010. 164 pages；18cm. ISBN：1602202221，1602202222.（Stories by contemporary writers from Shanghai）

Danial Clutton，Gina Wang，He Jing 合译.

2. Breathing. Tuttle Publishing，2016. 192 p. ISBN：1602202566，1602202567

《呼吸》

阿来（1959—）

1. Red poppies/Alai；translated from the Chinese by Howard Goldblatt and Sylvia Li-chun Lin. Boston：Houghton Mifflin，2002. 433 p.；24cm. ISBN：0618119647，0618119646

《尘埃落定》，葛浩文（Goldblatt，Howard，1939—）（美国翻译家），林丽君（Sylvia Li-chun Lin）（美国翻译家）合译.

(1) Boston：Mariner Books/Houghton Mifflin，2003. 433 pages；24cm. ISBN：0618340696，0618340699

2. Chuan-Zang/written by Alai；illustrated by Xiong Wenyun；translated by Wang Da. Shanghai：East China Normal University Press，2010. 2，136 pages：color illustrations；23cm. ISBN：7561771488，7561771487.（China style series＝中国风）

《川藏》，熊文韵插图. 华东师范大学出版社.

3. Tibetan soul：stories/Alai；translated by Karen Gernant and Chen Zeping. Portland，Me.：MerwinAsia，2012. vii，256 pages；21cm. ISBN：1937385095，1937385094，1937385088，1937385086

Contents：Akhu Tenpa—Dance of the soul—The silversmith in the moonlight—The fish—A swarm of bees fluttering—The loba—The locust blossoms—Gela grows up—Life—The white mountain range：like galloping horses—Bloodstains from the past—Blood ties.

阿来短篇小说集. Gernant，Karen 和 Chen，Zeping（1953—）合译.

4. The song of King Gesar/Alai；translated by Howard Goldblatt and Sylvia Li-chun Lin. Edinburgh：Canongate，2013. 392 pages；25cm. ISBN：1847672339，1847672337，1847672353，1847672353.（Myths；15）

《格萨尔王》，葛浩文（Goldblatt，Howard，1939—）（美国翻译家），林丽君（Sylvia Li-chun Lin）（美国翻译家）合译.

5. Hollow Mountain. Part One/by Alai；translated by Saul Thompson. Beijing：China Translation & Publishing Corporation，2017. 486 pages. ISBN：7500152576，7500152574 小说

《空山·第一部》，（英）Saul Thompson 译.

扎西达娃（1959—）

1. A soul in bondage：stories from Tibet/Tashi Dawa. Beijing：Chinese Literature Press：Distributed by China International Book Trading Corporation，1992. 234 p.；19cm.（Panda Books）

Contents：Preface/Dondrup Wangbum—A Soul in bondage—Tibet：The Mysterious years—Plateau serenade—Over the river—The Free man Qimi—On the way to Lhasa—The Silent sage—The Old manor—Invitation of a century—The Light on the cliff—The banished prince.

《西藏，系在皮绳结上的魂》

(1) A soul in bondage and other selected writing/Tashi Dawa. Beijing：Foreign Languages Press，2009. 234 pages；20cm. ISBN：7119059136，7119059130

刁斗（1960—）

1. Point of origin/Diao Dou；translated from the Chinese by Brendan O'Kane. Manchester：Comma，2014. v，218 pages；20cm. ISBN：1905583621，1905583621

《出处》，O'Kane，Brendan 译.

余华（1960—）

1. The past and the punishments/Yu Hua；translated from the Chinese by Andrew F. Jones. Honolulu：University of Hawaii Press，c1996. 277 p.；21cm. ISBN：0824817826，0824817824，0824818172，0824818173.（Fiction from modern China）

《往事与刑罚》，安道（Jones，Andrew F）（美国汉学家）译.

2. To live：a novel/Yu Hua；translated and with an afterword by Michael Berry. New York：Anchor Books，c2003. 250 p.；21cm. ISBN：1400031869，1400031863，0307429797，0307429792

《活着》，白睿文（又名白瑞克，Berry，Michael，1974—）（美国汉学家）译.

3. Chronicle of a blood merchant/Yu Hua；translated and with an afterword by Andrew F. Jones. 1st. American ed. New York：Pantheon Books，c2003. 263 p.；22cm. ISBN：037542220X，0375422201

《许三观卖血记》，安道（Jones，Andrew F）（美国汉学家）译.

(1) New York：Anchor Books，2004. 263 pages；21cm. ISBN：1400031850，1400031856

4. Cries in the drizzle：a novel/Yu Hua；translated and with a preface by Allan H. Barr. 1st Anchor Books ed. New York：Anchor Books，2007. viii，304 p.；21cm. ISBN：0307279996，0307279995

《在细雨中呼喊》，艾伦（Barr，Allan Hepburn.）（美国学者）译.

5. Brothers/Yu Hua；translated from the Chinese by Eileen Cheng-yin Chow and Carlos Rojas. 1st American ed. New York：Pantheon Books，c2009. ix，641 p.；25cm. ISBN：0375424991，0375424997

《兄弟》，周成荫（Chow，Eileen Cheng-yin）（美国华裔学者），罗鹏（Rojas，Carlos，1970—）（美国汉学家）合译.

(1) London：Picador，2009. ix，641 pages；23cm. ISBN：0330452748，0330452746，0330452755，0330452754

(2) New York：Picador，2009. x，641 pages；22cm. ISBN：0330469711，0330469715

(3) New York：Anchor Books，2010. xi，641 pages；21cm. ISBN：0307386069，0307386066

6. Boy in the twilight：stories of the hidden China/Yu Hua；translated from the Chinese by Allan H. Barr. First American Edition. New York：Pantheon Books，2014. vii，195 pages；22cm. ISBN：0307379368，0307379361

《黄昏里的男孩》，艾伦（Barr，Allan Hepburn）（美国学者）译.

(1) New York：Anchor Books，2014. vii，195 pages；20cm. ISBN：0804171021，0804171025

7. The seventh day：a novel/Yu Hua；translated from the Chinese by Allan H. Barr. New York：Pantheon Books，［2015］. 213 pages；22cm. ISBN：0804197865，0804197861，0804197873，0804197878

《第七天》，艾伦（Barr，Allan Hepburn）（美国学者）译.

(1) Melbourne, Vic. The Text Publishing Company，2015. ISBN：1922182890，1922182893

(2) New York：Anchor Books, a division of Penguin Random House LLC，2016. 213 pages；20cm. ISBN：0804172056，0804172059

叶尔克西·胡尔曼别克（1961—）

1. The return of the black horse/author, Yerksy. Hurmanbek；editors, Wu Hong, Jiang Fengli；translators, Song Wenjing, Situ Aiqin. ［Ürümqi ［China］］：Xinjiang Juvenile Publishing House，2010. 3，2，250 pages：illustrations；23cm. ISBN：7537189361，7537189366. (Yangpigu series of translation)

《黑马归去》.新疆青少年出版社.

顾偕（1961—）

1. The supreme ultimate/by Gu Xie；translated by Liu Zhimin. Beijing：Zhongguo wen xue chu ban she，1998. 220 p.；20cm. ISBN：7507104168，7507104165. (Panda books)

《太极》，刘志敏（1963—）译.

韩东（1961—）

1. Banished! /Han Dong；translated by Nicky Harman. Honolulu：University of Hawaii Press，2009. x，250 p.；22cm. ISBN：0824832629，0824832620，0824833404，0824833406

Contents：1.；Banishment—；2.；The Enclosure—；3.；Young Tao—；4.；Primary School—；5.；Animals—；6.；The Farm Tools Factory—；7.；Zhao Ningsheng—；8.；The Cleaning Bug—；9.；"516"—；10.；Rich Peasants—；11.；Striking Root—；12.；The Author—；13.；Conclusion—；Han Dong and the World of Chinese Literature

《扎根》，Harman，Nicky 译.

虹影（1962—）

1. Summer of betrayal：a novel/by Hong Ying；translated from the Chinese by Martha Avery. New York：Farrar, Straus，Giroux，1997. 183 pages；21cm. ISBN：0374271755，0374271756

《背叛之夏》（又名《裸舞代》），Avery，Martha（1951—）译.

(1) 1st Grove Press ed. New York：Grove Press，1999. 183 pages；21cm. ISBN：0802135943，0802135940

2. Daughter of the river/Hong Ying；translated by Howard Goldblatt. New York：Grove Press，1998. 278 pages：illustrations；22cm. ISBN：080211637X，0802116376

《饥饿的女儿》，葛浩文（Goldblatt，Howard，1939—）（美国翻译家）译.

(1) London：Bloomsbury，2010. 278 pages，［8］pages of plates：illustrations；20cm. ISBN：1408803134，1408803135

3. A lipstick called red pepper：fiction about gay & lesbian love in China/Hong Ying；compiled by Henry Zhao；translated by Herbert Batt ［and others］. Bochum：Projekt Verlag，1999. 165 pages；22cm. ISBN：3897330326，3897330320. (Arcus Chinatexte；Bd. 15)

《虹影小说选》，赵毅衡编.

4. K：the art of love/Hong Ying；translated by Nicky Harman & Henry Zhao. London；New York：Marion Boyars；Saint Paul, MN：Distributed in the USA by Consortium Book Sales，2002. viii，252 pages；20cm. ISBN：0714530727，0714530727

《K》（《英国情人》），Harman，Nicky，赵毅衡合译.

(1) London：Black Swan，2004. 285 pages；20cm. ISBN：0552772011，0552772013

(2) London：Penguin，2011. viii，252 pages；20cm. ISBN：0241950692，0241950694

5. Peacock cries at the Three Gorges/by Hong Ying；translated by Mark Smith and Henry Zhao. London；New York：Marion Boyars，2004. 334 pages；20cm. ISBN：0714531007，0714531006，0714531197，0714531199

《孔雀的叫喊》

6. The concubine of Shanghai/Hong Ying；translated from the Mandarin by Liu Hong. London；New York：Marion Boyars，2008. 396 pages；22cm. ISBN：0714531502，0714531502，0714531809，0714531804.

《上海王》，Liu，Hong 译.

(1) London：Viking，2011. 396 pages；18cm. ISBN：0241950678，0241950678

7. Good children of the flower/Hong Ying；translated by Gary Xu, Shelly Bryant, and Nick Brown. Seattle：AmazonCrossing，2016. 340 pages；21cm. ISBN：1503937185，1503937186

《好儿女花》，Xu，Gary G.（1968—），Bryant，Shelly 和 Brown，Nick 合译.

陈染（1962—）

1. A private life/Chen Ran；translated by John Howard-Gibbon. New York：Columbia University Press，c2004. xiv，214 p.；22cm. ISBN：0231131968. (Weatherhead

books on Asia)

《私人生活》,霍华(Howard-Gibbon,John)译.

亮炯・朗萨(1962—)

1. The oath of Polungde＝布隆德誓言/亮炯・朗萨著;(美) Stephen F. Pomroy,董锐译.北京:中译出版社,2016. 761 p.;21cm. ISBN:7500143352, 7500143354. (Reading China:Tibetan stories＝阅读中国・藏族青年作家丛书)

陈希我(1963—)

1. The book of sins/by Chen Xiwo; translated by Nicky Harman. London:New writing from Asia, 2014. x, 202 pages;20cm. ISBN:9881677563, 9881677564

   Contents:Pain—Kidney tonic—The hint—Our bones—I love my mum—Going to heaven—The man with the knife.

   Harman, Nicky 译.

2. I love my mum: a novel/by Chen Xiwo. Hong Kong: Make-Do Pub. , 2009. 104 pages; 22cm. ISBN: 9881841926, 9881841925

   《遮蔽》

苏童(1963—)

1. Raise the red lantern:three novellas/Su Tong;translated by Michael Duke. London:Simon & Schuster, 1990. 267 pages. ISBN:0684860228, 0684860220

   《大红灯笼高高挂》,Duke, Michael S. 译. 包括《大红灯笼高高挂》《1934 年的逃亡》和《罂粟之家》三部小说.

   (1) New York:W. Morrow and Co. , 1993. 267 p.; 22cm. ISBN:0688122175, 0688122171, 0060596333, 0060596330

   (2) New York:W. Morrow, 1993. 267 p. ; jaquette ill. en coul. ; 22cm. ISBN:0688122175, 0688122171

   (3) [New York, N. Y.]:Penguin Books, 1993. 267 p. ISBN:0140260307, 0140260304

   (4) New York;London:Touchstone, 1994. 267 pages; 20cm. ISBN:0671713280, 0671713287

   (5) New York:Penguin Books,1996. 267 pages;20cm. ISBN:0140260307, 0140260304

   (6) [London]:Scribner, 2000. 267 pages;20cm. ISBN: 0684860228, 0684860220

   (7) New York:Perennial, 2004. 267 pages; 21cm. ISBN:0060596333, 0060596330

2. Rice/Su Tong; translated by Howard Goldblatt. 1st ed. New York:W. Morrow and Co. , 1995. 266 p. ; 22cm. ISBN:0688132456, 0688132453

   《米》,葛浩文(Goldblatt, Howard, 1939—)(美国翻译家)译.

   (1) New York:Penguin Books, 1996. 266 pages;20cm. ISBN: 014025644X, 0140256444, 0688132456, 0688132453

   (2) London;New York:Touchstone Books, 1996. 266 pages;22cm. ISBN:068481756X, 0684817569

   (3) London:Scribner, 2000. 266 pages;20cm. ISBN:

0684860236, 0684860237

   (4) New York:Perennial, 2004. 266 pages; 21cm. ISBN:0060596325, 0060596323

3. My life as emperor/Su Tong; translated by Howard Goldblatt. 1st ed. New York:Hyperion East, c2005. vi, 290 p. ; 22cm. ISBN:140136666X, 1401366667, 1401374044, 1401374042

   《我的帝王生涯》,葛浩文(Goldblatt, Howard, 1939—) (美国翻译家)译.

   (1) London:Faber, 2005. 290 pages; 24cm. ISBN: 0571220789, 0571220786

   (2) London:Faber and Faber, 2006. 290 pages; 20cm. ISBN:0571220797, 0571220793

4. Binu and the Great Wall/Su Tong; translated from the Chinese by Howard Goldblatt. Edinburgh; New York: Canongate, 2007. ix, 291 p. ; 21cm. ISBN:1841959047, 1841959049,1841959057,1841959054. (Myths; 8)

   《碧奴》,葛浩文(Goldblatt, Howard, 1939—)(美国翻译家)译.

   (1) Edinburgh [u. a.]:Canongate Books, 2007. IX, 291 p. ISBN:1847670625, 1847670628

   (2) Oxford:ISIS, 2008. 241 pages (large print); 25cm. ISBN:0753180624, 0753180626, 0753180634, 0753180631. (Myths; 9)

   (3) Melbourne:Text Publishing Company, 2008. 1 volume. ISBN:1921351518, 1921351519

   (4) Toronto:A. A. Knopf Canada, 2008. 291 pages; 21cm. ISBN:0676978544, 0676978541. (Myths series)

   (5) Toronto:Vintage Canada, 2009. ISBN:0676978551, 067697855X. (Myths series)

5. Madwoman on the bridge/Su Tong; translated from the Chinese by Josh Stenberg. London:Black Swan, 2008. 300 p. ; 20cm. ISBN:0552774529, 0552774529

   《桥上的疯妈妈》,Stenberg, Josh 译.

6. The boat to redemption/Su Tong; translated from the Chinese by Howard Goldblatt. London:Doubleday, 2010. 362 p. ; 24cm. ISBN:0385613446,038561344X

   《河岸》,葛浩文(Goldblatt, Howard, 1939—)(美国翻译家)译.

   (1) Black Swan ed. London:Black Swan, 2010. 475 pages; 20cm. ISBN:0552774543, 0552774545

   (2) New York:Overlook Press, 2011. 362 pages; 24cm. ISBN:1590206720, 159020672X

   (3) New York:The Overlook Press, 2014. 362 pages; 21cm. ISBN:1468308246, 1468308242

7. Tatoo:three novellas/Su Tong; translated by Josh Stenberg. Portland, Me. :MerwinAsia, c2010. 203 p. ; 21cm. ISBN:1878282958

   《刺青时代:中篇小说三部》,Stenberg, Josh 译.

8. 当代中国名家双语阅读文库　第一辑　苏童卷/杨昊成

主编. 南京:南京师范大学出版社,2018. 325 页:照片; 21cm. ISBN: 7565135811

英文共同题名:A bilingual library contemporary Chinese master writers. 本书汇集苏童《私宴》《堂兄弟》《上龙寺》等作品以及对其的评论和访谈文章.

刘慈欣(1963—)

1. The wandering earth/author: Cixin Liu; translator: Holger Nahm; Ken Liu. Beijing: Guomi Digital Technology Co., Ltd., 2013. 476 pages; 23cm. ISBN: 1489502858, 1489502858. (Classic science fiction collection)

   Contents: The wandering earth—Mountain—Of ants and dinosaurs—Sun of China—The wages of humanity—Curse 5.0—The Micro-Age—Devourer—Taking care of Gods—With her eyes—The longest fall.

   《流浪地球》,Nahm, Holger 合译.

2. The wandering Earth/Cixin Liu; translated by Ken Liu, Elizabeth Hanlon, Zac Haluza, Adam Lamphier, Holger Nahm. London, England: Head of Zeus, 2017. 447 pages; 23cm. ISBN: 1784501, 1784507, 1784493, 1784495

   Contents: The wandering Earth—Mountain—Sun of China—For the benefit of mankind—Curse 5.0—The micro-era—Devourer—Taking care of God—With her eyes—Cannonball.

   《流浪地球》,刘昆(Liu, Ken, 1976—)等译.

3. The three-body problem/Cixin Liu; translated by Ken Liu. New York: Tor Books, [2014]. 399 pages; 25cm. ISBN: 0765377067, 0765377063, 1466853441, 1466853447. (Remembrance of Earth's Past; book 1)

   《三体》,刘昆(Liu, Ken, 1976—)译.《地球往事》三部曲的第一部作品.

   (1)London: Head of Zeus Ltd, 2015. 399 pages; 23cm. ISBN: 1784971564, 1784971561, 1784971557, 1784971553. (Three-body trilogy; 1)

   (2)New York: Tor, 2016. 415 pages; 24cm. ISBN: 0765382032, 0765382030

   (3)Large print edition. Rearsby, Leicester: WF Howes Ltd, 2016. vi, 521 pages (large print); 24cm. ISBN: 1510046603, 1510046607

   (4)London: Head of Zeus, 2016. 434 pages; 20cm. ISBN: 1784971571, 178497157X. (Three-body trilogy; 1)

4. The dark forest/Cixin Liu; translated by Joel Martinsen. New York: Tor, A Tom Doherty Associates Book, 2015. 512 pages; 25cm. ISBN: 0765377081, 076537708X. Three-body trilogy; Book II)

   《黑暗森林》,刘昆(Liu, Ken, 1976—)译.《地球往事》三部曲的第二部作品.

   (1)London: Head of Zeus, 2015. 512 pages; 23cm. ISBN: 1784971596, 1784971595, 1784971601, 178497160X.

   (Three-Body trilogy; 2)

   (2)New York: Tor, A Tom Doherty Associates Book, 2016. 512 pages; 24cm. ISBN: 0765386690, 0765386694. (Three-body trilogy; 2)

   (3)[Place of publication not identified]: Head of Zeus, 2016. 550 pages; 20cm. ISBN: 1784971618, 1784971618. (Three-body trilogy; 2)

5. Death's end/Cixin Liu; translated by Ken Liu. New York: Tor, 2016. 604 pages; 25cm. ISBN: 0765377104, 0765377101, 1001368955, 1001368959. (Three-body trilogy; Book III)

   《死神永生》,刘昆(Liu, Ken, 1976—)译. 地球往事三部曲的第三部作品.

   (1)London: Head of Zeus, 2016. 604 pages; 24cm. ISBN: 1784971634, 1784971632, 1784971642, 1784971649. (Three-body trilogy; bk. 3; Remembrance of Earth's past trilogy; bk. 3)

   (2)New York: TOR, 2017. 604 pages; 24cm. ISBN: 0765386631, 0765386632. (Three-body trilogy; 3)

   (3)London, England: Head of Zeus, 2017. vii, 724 pages; 20cm. ISBN: 1784971656, 1784971650. (Three-body trilogy; 3)

毕飞宇(1964—)

1. The moon opera/Bi Feiyu; translated from the Chinese by Howard Goldblatt and Sylvia Li-chun Lin. London: Telegram, 2007. 126 p.; 20cm. ISBN: 1846590221, 846590221

   《青衣》,葛浩文(Goldblatt, Howard, 1939—)(美国翻译家),林丽君(Sylvia Li-chun Lin)合译.

   (1)Boston: Houghton Mifflin Harcourt, 2009. 117 p.; 20cm. ISBN: 0151012947, 0151012946

2. Three sisters/Bi Feiyu. London: Telegram, 2008. ISBN: 1846590238, 184659023X

   《玉米》,葛浩文(Goldblatt, Howard, 1939—)(美国翻译家),林丽君(Sylvia Li-chun Lin)合译.

   (1)Three sisters/Bi Feiyu; translated from the Chinese by Howard Goldblatt and Sylvia Li-chun Lin. Boston: Houghton Mifflin Harcourt, 2010. 282 p.; 24cm. ISBN: 0151013647, 0151013640

   (2)London: Telegram, 2011. 310 pages; 20cm. ISBN: 1846590238, 184659023X, 9380070551, 9380070551

3. Massage/Bi Feiyu; Howard Goldblatt (translator). Melbourne, Vic. Penguin Group (Australia), 2014. ISBN: 0670080977, 0670080977

   《推拿》,葛浩文(Goldblatt, Howard, 1939—)(美国翻译家)译.

   (1)Massage/Bi Feiyu; translated from the Chinese by Howard Goldblatt and Sylvia Li-chun Lin. Docklands, Vic 3008, Australia, Vic. Penguin Group (Australia), 2016. 315 pages; 20cm. ISBN: 0734399113, 0734399111. (China library)

4. 当代中国名家双语阅读文库. 第一辑,毕飞宇卷/杨昊成主编. 南京:南京师范大学出版社,2018. 283 页:照片;21cm. ISBN:787565135804

　　英文共同题名:A bilingual library contemporary Chinese master writers. 本书汇集毕飞宇《哺乳期的女人》《男人还剩下什么》《怀念妹妹小青》等作品以及对其的评论文章.

迟子建(1964—)

1. Figments of the supernatural/by Chi Zijian;translated by Simon Patton. Sydney, NSW:James Joyce Press, 2004. 206 pages;20cm. ISBN:0958012172, 0958012171

　　Contents:Fine rain at dusk on Grieg's Sea—The potato lovers—Cow-rail in fog month—Washing in clean water—Willow patterns—Cemetery under snow.

　　迟子是短篇小说选. 西敏(Patton, Simon)(澳大利亚翻译家)译.

2. A flock in the wilderness/Chi Zijian;[translated by]Xiong Zhenru...[et al.]. Beijing, China:Foreign Languages Press:Distributed by China International Book Trading Corp., 2005. 193 p.;20cm. ISBN:7119036645,7119036649. (Contemporary Chinese women writers). (Panda books=Xiong mao cong shu)

　　Contents:The river rolls by—A flock in the wilderness—Beloved potatoes—Lost in the ox pen—Silver plates—Bathing in clean water.

　　《原野上的羊群》,熊振儒等译(熊猫丛书). 收录了女作家迟子建的六部中短篇小说作品:《亲亲土豆》《逝川》《原野上的羊群》等.

　　(1)Beijing:Foreign Languages Press, 2015. 217 p. ISBN:7119092928, 7119092928

3. The last quarter of the moon/by Chi Zijian;translated by Bruce Humes. London:Harvill Secker,2013. 311 pages;24cm. ISBN:1846554810, 1846554810, 1448137589, 1448137586, 1846554827,1846554829

　　《额尔古纳河右岸》,徐穆实(Humes, Bruce)(美国翻译家)译.

　　(1)London:Vintage Books, 2014. 311 pages;24cm. ISBN:0099555650, 0099555654

麦家(1964—)

1. Decoded/Mai Jia;translated from the Chinese by Olivia Milburn and Christopher Payne. First American edition. New York:Farrar, Straus and Giroux, 2014. 315 pages;24cm. ISBN:0374135805, 0374135800

　　《解密》,Milburn, Olivia 和 Payne, Christopher 合译.

　　(1)London:Allen Lane, an imprint of Penguin Books, 2014. 315 pages;24cm. ISBN:0141391472, 0141391472, 1846148194, 1846148197

　　(2)First Picador edition. New York:Picador, 2015. 315 pages;21cm. ISBN:1250062357, 1250062352

2. In the dark/Mai Jia;translation, Christopher N. Payne. [London] Penguin Books, 2015. 396 pages;20cm. ISBN:0141391458, 014139145

《暗算》,Payne, Christopher(1976—)译.

次仁罗布(1965—)

1. Realm=界/次仁罗布著;(美)Krysta Close, 董锐译. 北京:中译出版社, 2016. 356 pages;21cm. ISBN:7500143369, 7500143362. (Reading China:Tibetan stories=阅读中国·藏族青年作家丛书)

潘向黎(1966—)

1. White michelia/by Pan Xiangli. New York:Better Link Press, 2014. 279 pages;18cm. ISBN:1602202427, 1602202429. (Stories by contemporary writers from Shanghai;Cultural China)

《缅桂花》

东西(田代琳,1966—)

1. Record of regret:a novel/Dong Xi;translated by Dylan Levi King. Norman:University of Oklahoma Press, 2018. ISBN:0806160009, 0806160004. (Chinese literature today book series;Volume 7)

《后悔录》

朱文(1967—)

1. I love dollars and other stories of China/Zhu Wen;translated from the Chinese by Julia Lovell. New York:Columbia University Press, c2007. xxii, 228 p.;22cm. ISBN:0231136943, 0231136945. (Weatherhead books on Asia)

　　Contents:I love dollars—A hospital night—A boat crossing—Wheels—Ah, Xiao Xie—Pounds, ounces, meat.

　　《我爱美元》,茱莉亚·洛佛尔(Lovell, Julia, 1975—)(英国汉学家)译.

　　(1)New York:Penguin Books, 2008. 240 pages;20cm. ISBN:0143113270, 0143113275, 0231136943, 0231136945

2. The matchmaker, the apprentice, and the football fan:more stories of China/Zhu Wen;translated by Julia Lovell. New York:Columbia University Press, 2013. 166 pages:illustration;22cm. ISBN:0231160909, 0231160902, 0231160917, 0231160919. (Weatherhead Books on Asia)

　　Contents:Da Ma's way of talking—The matchmaker—The apprentice—The football fan—Xiao Liu—Mr. Hu, are you coming out to play basketball this afternoon? —Reeducation—The wharf.

　　朱文小说选. 茱莉亚·洛佛尔(Lovell, Julia, 1975—)(英国汉学家)译.

姚鄂梅(1968—)

1. Gone with the river mist/by Yao Emei;translation by Jiang Yajun. New York:Better Link Press, 2015. 173 p. ISBN:1602202504, 1602202508. (Stories by contemporary writers from Shanghai)

　　Jiang Yajun 译.

白玛娜珍（1968—）

1. Love in Lhasa ＝ 拉萨红尘/白玛娜珍著；（美）James Yongue，万佳卉译. 北京：中译出版社，2016. 260 p.；21cm. ISBN：7500143376，7500143370.（Reading China：Tibetan stories＝阅读中国·藏族青年作家丛书）

格绒追美（1969—）

1. The secluded face＝隐蔽的脸/格绒追美著；（美）Andrew Stevenson，董锐译. 北京：中译出版社，2016. 494 p.；21cm. ISBN：7500143420，750014342.（Reading China：Tibetan stories＝阅读中国·藏族青年作家丛书）

严英秀（1969—）

1. Paper airplanes ＝ 纸飞机/严英秀著；（美）Stephen F. Pomroy，刘组勤译. 北京：中译出版社，2016. 416 p.；21cm. ISBN：7500143413，7500143419.（Reading China：Tibetan stories＝阅读中国·藏族青年作家丛书）

达真（20 世纪 60 年代）

1. Khams-pa：an epic of tibetan people＝康巴：一部藏人的心灵史诗/达真著；（美）Ruth Graham，董锐译. 北京：中译出版社，2016. 615 pages；21cm. ISBN：7500143383，7500143389.（Reading China：Tibetan stories＝阅读中国·藏族青年作家丛书）

金仁顺（1970—）

1. Monk dance＝僧舞/金仁顺著；［英］Patric Burton，孙硕译. Beijing：Zhong yi chu ban she，2016. 217 pages；20cm. ISBN：7500143307，7500143303.（Kaleidoscope：ethnic Chinese writers ＝阅读中国.五彩丛书）

棉棉（1970—）

1. Candy：a novel/Mian Mian；translated by Andrea Lingenfelter. Boston：Little，Brown，2003. ix，279 pages；21cm. ISBN：0316563560，0316563567
《糖》，Lingenfelter，Andrea 译.

尼玛潘多（1970—）

1. Purple highland barley ＝ 紫青稞/尼玛潘多著；（美）Stephen F. Pomroy，刘玉洁译. 北京：中译出版社，2016. 334 p.；21cm. ISBN：7500143406，7500143400.（Reading China：Tibetan stories＝阅读中国·藏族青年作家丛书）

路内（1973—）

1. Young Babylon/Lu Nei，translated by Poppy Toland. Seattle：AmazonCrossing，2015. 318 pages. ISBN：1477829998，1477829997
《少年巴比伦》，Toland，Poppy 译.

2. The 17-year-old hussars/by Lu Nei；translation by Zhu Jingwen，Anna Holmwood，Chris Burrow，Rachel Henson. New York：Better Link Press，2016. 151 pages；21cm. ISBN：1602202583，1602202580.（Stories by contemporary writers from Shanghai）
Contents：The 17-year-old hussars—Keep running, little brother.
《十七岁的轻骑兵》，Zhu，Jingwen，Holmwood，Anna，Burrow，Chris，Henson，Rachel 合译.

3. A tree grows in Daicheng/by Lu Nei；translated by Poppy Toland. Seattle：AmazonCrossing，2017. 151 pages；21cm. ISBN：1503953086，1503953084
《花街往事》，Toland，Poppy 译.

周卫慧（1973—）

1. Shanghai baby/Wei Hui；translated from the Chinese by Bruce Humes. London：Robinson，2001. 279 pages；20cm. ISBN：1841193615，1841193618
《上海宝贝》，徐穆实（Humes，Bruce）（美国翻译家）译.
   (1) New York：Pocket Books，2001. 263 pages；22cm. ISBN：0743421566，0743421560
   (2) London：Robinson，2001. 311 pages；18cm. ISBN：1841196848，1841196843
   (3) New York：Washington Square Press，2002. 263 pages；21cm. ISBN：0743421574，0743421577
   (4) London：Constable，2003. 256 pages；18cm. ISBN：1841196843，1841196848

2. Marrying Buddha/Wei Hui. Transl. from the Chinese by Larissa Heinrich. London：Robinson，2005. 248 S；20cm. ISBN：1845291700，1845291709
《我的禅》，Heinrich，Larissa 译.

鲁敏（1973—）

1. 当代中国名家双语阅读文库. 第一辑，鲁敏卷/杨昊成主编. 南京：南京师范大学出版社，2018. 333 页：照片；21cm. ISBN：787565135828
英文共同题名：A bilingual library contemporary Chinese master writers. 本书汇集鲁敏《西天寺》《徐记鸭往事》《大宴》等作品以及对其的评论和访谈文章.

盛可以（1973—）

1. Northern girls：life goes on/Sheng Keyi；translated from the Chinese by Shelly Bryant. Camberwell，Victoria：Viking，an imprint of Penguin，2012. 320 pages；23cm. ISBN：0670080953，0670080950
《北妹》，Bryant，Shelly 译.
   (1) Australia：Penguin Group（Australia）；Beijing：Penguin（Beijing）Ltd，2015. 320 pages；20cm. ISBN：0670076163，0670076161

2. Death fugue/Sheng Keyi；translated from the Chinese by Shelly Bryant. Artarmon，NSW，Australia：Giramondo Publishing Company，2014. 375 pages；24cm. ISBN：1922146625，1922146625
《死亡赋格》，Bryant，Shelly 译.
   (1) Large print edition. ［Sydney，N. S. W.］Read How You Want，2014. iii，335 pages（large print）；24cm. ISBN：1459686892，1459686896

安妮宝贝（1974—）

1. The road of others：three stories/by Anni Baobei；translated by Nicky Harman and Keiko Wong. Hong Kong：Make-Do Pub.，2012. 111 pages；22cm. ISBN：9881841971，9881841976.（Modern Chinese masters）
Contents：A journey—Goodbye, An—Endless August—

The road of others—Seeking An.

《去往别处的路上》，Harman，Nicky 和 Wong，Keiko 合译.

方雯（1975—）

1. Say thanks before the end of life：a true story of a great father and a strong son/by Fang Wen；translated by Sun Lei Yu Qiu. Beijing：Foreign Languages Press，2008. 123 pages：illustrations（some color）；23cm. ISBN：7119054902，7119054902

《在生命的最后说"谢谢"》

付秀莹（1976—）

1. Love is everywhere/by Fu Xiuying. Houston，Tx：Demand Global，2012. 248 pages；23cm. ISBN：1622124909，1622124901

《爱情到处流传》

滕肖澜（1976—）

1. Beautiful days：two novellas/by Teng Xiaolan；［translation：Qiu Maoru］. New York：Better Link Press，2013. 254 pages；18cm. ISBN：1602202351，1602202354.（Stories by contemporary writers from Shanghai；Cultural China series）

《美丽的日子》，Qiu，Maoru 译.

那多（原名赵延，1977—）

1. All the way to death/by Na Duo；translated by Jiang Yajun. New York：Better Link Press，2017. 198 pages；21cm. ISBN：1602202597，1602202591.（Stories by Contemporary Writers from Shanghai）

Jiang Yajun 译.

Zou，Zou（1978—）

1. She she/by Zou Zou；translation by Yawtsong Lee. New York：Better Link Press，2014. 271 pages；18cm. ISBN：1602202397，1602202399.（Stories by contemporary writers from Shanghai）

Contents：Abandonment—Thirty-one days of love—She she—Writing.

Zou，Zou（1978—）；Lee，Yaw-Tsong（1945—）译.

祝晓羽（1979—）

1. 漠园/祝晓羽（Rain Zhu）著，译. 天津：天津人民出版社，2004. 200 页：插图；18cm. ISBN：7201048627，7201048628.（榕树下）

该书共十九篇英汉对照文章，即《老妇人，玉米粥，雨声》，《故事开始于灰黑的雨夜》，《漠园，猫，油画》，《故事需要一点注解》等. 对照读物.

苏德（1981—）

1. There is no if/by Su De；translation by Zhu Jingwen. New York：Better Link Press，2014. 275 pages；18cm. ISBN：1602202435，1602202436.（Stories by contemporary writers from Shanghai；Cultural China）

《没有如果的事》，Zhu Jingwen 译.

（1）Contents：There is no if—A trilogy—The night of Rammasun—Consequences.

张悦然（1982—）

1. Ten loves/written by Zhang Yueran；translated by Jeremy Tiang. Singapore：Math Paper Press，2013. 197 pages；20cm. ISBN：9810747787，9810747780

Contents：Dancers sleep beneath the hills—Whitebone harp—Jinuo and the vaulting horse—Binary—Little ran—Boat—Jenny flowers on his nose—The room where day is night—A Sushui ghost story—Who murdered the month of May?

《十爱》，Tiang，Jeremy 译.

2. Promise Bird/by Zhang Yueran；translated by Jeremy Tiang. Beijing：China Translation & Publishing Corporation，2017. 329 pages. ISBN：7500151579，7500151578

《誓鸟》，（英）Jeremy Tiang 译.

韩寒（1982—）

1. 1988：I want to talk with the world/ Han Han. Seattle：AmazonCrossing，2015. 202 pages；2 portraits；21cm. ISBN：1477821114，1477821112

《1988：我想和这个世界谈谈》

南派三叔（1982—）

1. Cavern of the blood zombies/by Xu Lei；translated by Kathy Mok. San Francisco：ThingsAsian Press，2011. 233 pages：color illustrations；22cm. ISBN：1934159316，193415931X.（The grave robbers chronicles；v. 1）

《盗墓笔记》之一，Mok，Kathy 译.

2. Angry sea，hidden sands/by Xu Lei；translated by Kathy Mok；illustrated by Neo Lok Sze Wong. San Francisco：ThingsAsian Press，2011. 239 pages：color illustrations；22cm. ISBN：1934159323，1934159328.（The grave robbers chronicles；v. 2）

《盗墓笔记》之二，Mok，Kathy 译；Neo，Lok Sze Wong 插图.

3. Bronze tree of death/by Xu Lei；translated by Kathy Mok；illustrated by Vladimir Verano. San Francisco：ThingsAsian Press，2013. 259 pages：color illustrations；22cm. ISBN：1934159330，1934159336.（The grave robbers chronicles；v. 3）

《盗墓笔记》之三，Mok，Kathy 译；Neo，Lok Sze Wong 插图.

4. Palace of doom/by Xu Lei；translated by Kathy Mok. San Francisco，California：ThingsAsian Press，2013. 287 pages：color illustrations；22cm. ISBN：1934159347，1934159344.（The grave robbers' chronicles；Vol. 4）

《盗墓笔记》之四，Mok，Kathy 译；Neo，Lok Sze Wong 插图.

5. Deadly desert winds/by Xu Lei；translated by Kathy Mok；illustrated by Vladimir Verano. San Francisco，California：ThingsAsian Press，2014. 203 pages：color illustrations；22cm. ISBN：1934159354，1934159352.

(The grave robbers' chronicles；vol. 5)

《盗墓笔记》之五，Mok，Kathy 译；Verano，Vladimir 插图.

6. Graveyard of a queen/by Xu Lei；translated by Kathy Mok；illustrated by Vladimir Verano. San Francisco，California：ThingsAsian Press，2014. 189 pages：illustrations；22cm. ISBN：1934159361，1934159360. (The grave robbers' chronicles；vol. 6)

《盗墓笔记》之六，Mok，Kathy 译；Verano，Vladimir 插图.

7. Search for the buried bomber/Xu Lei；translated by Gabriel Ascher. Las Vegas，NV：AmazonCrossing，2011. viii，301 pages；21cm. ISBN：1611097948，1611097940. (Dark prospects series；volume 1)

《大漠苍狼》，Ascher，Gabriel 译.

春树(1983—)

1. Beijing doll：a novel/Chun Sue；translated from the Chinese by Howard Goldblatt. New York：Riverhead Books，2004. xii，223 p.；20cm. ISBN：594480206，1594480201

《北京娃娃》，葛浩文(Goldblatt，Howard，1939—)(美国翻译家)编译.

七堇年(1986—)

1. Through the years and far away/by Qi Jinnian；translated by Moying Li. New York：Jorge Pinto Books Inc，2007. 372 pages；23cm. ISBN：1934078，1934078

《大地之灯》，Li，Moying 译.

张怡微(1987—)

1. Labyrinth of the past/by Zhang Yiwei；foreword by Wang Jiren. New York：Better Link Press，2015. 159 pages；21cm. ISBN：1602202450，1602202451. (Stories by contemporary writers from Shanghai)

Contents：Introduction—Scab addiction—A good year—No choosing today—Love—Summer days—Memory is the slowest—I really don't want to come—Afterword：the texture of time

《旧时迷宫》

郭国甫

1. Among the Ominans/[Translated by Shang Huai-yuan]. Peking：Foreign Languages Press，1961. 348 pages：illustrations；22cm.

《在昂美纳部落里》，尚怀远译.

徐瑛

1. A real good holiday/Hsu Ying；[ill. by Xiao Youlei and He Baozhuan]. Peking：Foreign Languages Press，1977. 255 pages：illustrations；19cm.

《向阳院的故事》，肖玉磊插图.

杨刚

1. Daughter：an autobiographical novel/Yang Gang. Beijing，China：Foreign Languages Press：Distributed by China International Book Trading Corp.，1988. 479 pages；

18cm. ISBN：0835118576，0835118576，711900445X，7119004457. (Phoenix books)

《女儿》

刘树德

1. We crossed the bridge together/Liu Shu-teh. Peking：Foreign Languages Press，1963. 135 pages；19cm.

《桥》

陈可

1. Sea of love/written by Chen Ke. Beijing：Xinhua Publishing House，2009. 98 pages；21cm. ISBN：7501188673，750118867X

《一个人的海洋》.新华出版社.

薛舒

1. The most beautiful face in the world：two novellas/by Xue Shu；translation，Yawtsong Lee. New York：Better Link Press，2013. 269 pages；18cm. ISBN：1602202362，1602202368. (Stories by contemporary writers of Shanghai；Cultural China series)

Lee，Yaw-Tsong(1945—)译.

隗静

1. Grandma's China：a personal journey through China's transition/Wei Jing. Beijing：China Intercontinental Press，2010. 16，263 pages：illustrations (some color)，maps，portraits；23cm. ISBN：7508516578，7508516575

《外婆的中国：我亲历中国的改变》.五洲传播出版社.

买买提明·吾守尔

1. The angular glass/author，Maimaitiming Wushower；[translator，Tong Guoyan，Li Chao，Situ Aiqin]. Urumchi：Xinjiang Juvenile Publishing House，2010. 3，1，243 pages；23cm. ISBN：7537189385，7537189382

《有棱的玻璃杯》.新疆青少年出版社.

芥末

1. Real Marriage/by Jie Mo；translated by Nicholas Manthey. Beijing：China Translation & Publishing Corporation，2017. 345 pages. ISBN：7500151562，750015156X

《裸婚》，(英)Manthey，Nicholas 译.

石文驹

1. The red spear/Shi Wenju；[illustrated by Shen Yao-Yi]. Peking：Foreign Languages Press，1979. 230 pages，[10] leaves of plates：illustrations；19cm.

《战地红缨》

江格尔传奇

1. The epic of Jangar/He Dexiu；translated by Pan Zhongming. Beijing：China Intercontinental Press，2011. 173 pages：color illustrations；24cm. ISBN：7508521800，7508521803. (Epic appreciation)

《江格尔传奇》，何德修编撰.五洲传播出版社.本书稿是国家出版基金资助项目"聆听史诗"书系中的一本.作者为新疆楼兰学会副会长,自治区文史馆特约研究员.他将以口头传唱和叙事长诗体传世的蒙古族史诗《江格尔》改编成小说的形式.

《牡丹亭》

1. The peony pavilion：a novel/Xiaoping Yen. 1st American ed. Dumont，N. J.：Homa & Sekey Books，c2000. 252 p.：ill.；22cm. ISBN：0966542127，0966542126

《牡丹亭》，Yen，Xiaoping(1956—)编译成小说.

I6　报告文学与回忆录

1. Friendship for peace. Peking：Foreign Languages Press，[1953]. ii，66 p. illus.，port. 19cm.

   Notes：Stories by various authors

   《为了和平的友谊》，杨朔等. 抗美援朝.

2. Builders of the Ming tombs reservoirs. Peking：Foreign Languages Press，1958. 162 pages：illustrations；18cm.

   《建设十三陵水库的人民》

3. Stories of the Chinese People's Volunteers/[translated by teachers of the English Faculty of the Foreign Languages Department of Futan University]. Peking：Foreign Languages Press，1960. 258 p.；21cm.

   《中国人民志愿军英雄传》，复旦大学文艺英语教师集体翻译.

4. Red Flag Canal/Lin Min. Peking：Foreign Languages Press，1974. 61 p.：ill.

   《红旗渠》，林民著.

5. My hometown：six reportage articles/by Kao Yu-pao and others. Peking：Foreign Languages Press，1974. 136 p.，[6] leaves of plates：ill.；20cm.

   《换了人间》，高玉宝(1927—)等. 收录报告文学6篇.

6. Harm into benefit：taming the Haiho River/Ho Chin. Peking：Foreign Languages Press，1975. 79 pages，[18] leaves of plates (1 folded)：illustrations，map (some color)；19cm.

   《海河巨变》

7. The great China earthquake/Qian Gang；[translated by Nicola Ellis and Cathy Silber]. Beijing：Foreign Languages Press；Distributed by China International Book Trading Corp.，1989. 354 pages：illustrations；18cm. ISBN：0835122271，0835122276，7119005650，7119005652

   《唐山大地震》，钱钢著.

8. Lest we forget：Nanjing Massacre，1937/Xu Zhigeng；translated by Zhang Tingquan and Lin Wusun；English text edited by Lin Wusun. Beijing：Panda Books/Chinese Literature Press，1995. 307 pages：illustrations，maps；20cm. ISBN：7507103021，7507103021，0835131491，0835131490

   《南京大屠杀》，徐志耕著. 中国文学出版社.

9. 走向成功 ＝ On the road to success：transnational corporations in Shanghai：跨国公司在上海：英文/焦扬主编；上海市人民政府新闻办公室编. 上海：上海人民出版社，2006. 239 页；25cm. ISBN：7208060207

本书以新闻通讯的形式介绍了在沪不断取得成功，已融入上海生活的跨国公司.

10. The road of Huaxi/Peng Weifeng. Beijing：Xinhua Publishing House，2008. 311 pages：color illustrations，color portraits；26cm. ISBN：7501183371，7501183376

    《华西道路》，彭维锋著. 新华出版社.是《华西道路》一书的英文版.

11. Huang Hua memoirs/Huang Hua. Beijing：Foreign Languages Press：Distributed by China International Book Trading Corp.，2008. vi，616 pages，[62] pages of plates：illustrations (some color)，portraits；24cm. ISBN：7119049540，7119049542

    《亲历与见闻：黄华回忆录》，黄华著. 回忆录.

12. Tale of a family in Shougang/by Hou Jiajing；translated by Ego. Beijing：China International Press，2009. 136 pages：illustrations (some color)；19cm. ISBN：7508515847，7508515846

    《首钢家庭》，侯佳婧著. 五洲传播出版社.讲述这个首钢家庭的寻常故事.

13. The heavenly ford：the Jews in Tianjin/Anna Song；translated by Li Ling. Tianjin：Tianjin People's Pub. House，2010. 297 pages：illustrations (some color)，maps；23cm. ISBN：7201065595，7201065599

    《神圣的渡口》，宋安娜著. 天津人民出版社. 展示犹太人在天津100年的历史的纪实文学作品.

14. Living on the roof of the world / compiled by Jin Zhiguo；Translated by Transn. Beijing：New World Press，2011. 236p.：ill.；24cm. ISBN：7510414145，7510414148

    《生活在世界屋脊上》，金志国主编. 新世界出版社. 讲述了19个生活在西藏的人的故事.

15. Real life stories of migrant workers and urban transplants/An Dun. Beijing：New World Press，2011. 3，3，222 pages：illustrations；24cm. ISBN：7510418006，7510418003. (Chinese dream series)

    《打工者生活实录》，安顿著. 新世界出版社. 采访了10名年龄在16岁至60岁之间的打工者，以此讲述中国人的故事.

16. China state grid：the people behind the power＝国家负荷：国家电网科技创新实录/ 徐剑著；（英）Sophie Murten 译. 北京：中译出版社，2016. 505 pages：illustrations；21cm. ISBN：7500143208，7500143206. (中国报告系列)

17. The great disarmament＝百万大裁军/袁厚春著；（美）Danielle Vrublevskis 译. 北京：中译出版社，2016. 211 p.；21cm. ISBN：7500143246，7500143249. (中国报告系列)

18. The oriental express＝东方哈达：中国青藏铁路全景实录/徐剑著；（澳）Callum Smith 译. 北京：中译出版社，2016.449 p.；21cm. ISBN：7500143192，7500143192. (中国报告系列)

19. Fate of the nation：how guangdong changed China＝国运：南方记事/吕雷，赵洪著；（英）Tom Watson 译. 北京：中译出版社，2016. 718 p.；21cm. ISBN：7500143215，7500143214.（中国报告系列）

20. Green great wall＝毛乌素绿色传奇/肖亦农著；（澳）Neil Thomas 译. 北京：中译出版社，2016. 382 p.：ill.；21cm. ISBN：7500143260，7500143265.（中国报告系列）

21. The people's secretary：fighting corruption in the people's party＝根本利益/何建明著；（美）Sally Church 译. 北京：中译出版社，2016. 306 p.；21cm. ISBN：7500143284，7500143281.（中国报告系列）

22. Seven lost letters ＝ 寻找巴金的黛莉/赵瑜著；（澳）Jacqueline Rodgers 译. 北京：中译出版社，2016. 239 p.：ill.；21cm. ISBN：7500143239，7500143230.（中国报告系列）

23. Road's of renewal：a tibetan journey＝用胸膛行走西藏/党益民著；（英）Peter Richardson 译. 北京：中译出版社，2016. 382 p.：ill.；21cm. ISBN：7500143222，7500143222.（中国报告系列）

24. Summons of centuries past：reflections on Hong Kong：a true account/by Zhang Yawen；translated by Matt Schrader. Beijing：China Translation & Publishing Corporation，2017. 379 pages. ISBN：7500152569，7500152566
《百年钟声：香港启示录》，张雅文；Schrader，Matt 译.

25. Battle of Beijing：on the frontline against SARS/by He Jianmin；translated by David East. Beijing：China Translation & Publishing Corporation，2017. 122 pages. ISBN：7500151531，7500151535
《北京保卫战》，何建明著；East，Davi 译.

I7 散文

I71 古代及跨时代散文集

1. Gems of Chinese literature：prose, by Herbert A. Giles. 2nd ed.，rev. and greatly enl. London，B. Quaritch，Ltd.，1923. 2 p. l.，xiv，293，[1] p. 23cm.
《古文选珍》，第二版修订扩大版之"散文卷"，翟理斯（Giles，Herbert Allen，1845—1935）（英国汉学家）编译.

2. The importance of understanding：translations from the Chinese. Cleveland，World Pub. Co. [1960]. 494 p. 22cm.
《古文小品译英》，林语堂（1895—1976）编译.
   (1) Taipei：璐茜书店，1961. 494，[ix] pages；20cm.
   (2) London：Heinemann，1961. 494 pages；22cm.
   (3) Cleveland：World Pub. Co.，1963. 494 pages；21cm.
   (4) Bombay：Jaico Publishing House，1965. xi，472 pages；18cm.
   (5) Foreign Language Teaching and Research Press，2009. 614 pages：illustrations；21cm. ISBN：7560088495，756008849X.（English works of Lin Yutang＝林语堂英文作品集）

3. 100 Chinese classical prose writings in English/Wang Enbao, Wang Yuexi xuan zhu. Beijing：Beijing yu yan xue yuan chu ban she：Xin hua shu dian Beijing fa xing suo jing xiao，1990. 2，3，3，10，4，691 p.；19cm. ISBN：756190083X
《古文百篇英译》，王恩保，王约西选注.

4. Chinese wit & humor/edited by George Kao；introduction by Lin Yutang. New York：Coward-McCann，[1946]. xxxv，347 p.；22cm.
《中国幽默文选》，高克毅（Kao，George，1912—2008）；林语堂（1895—1976）导论. 内收美籍华人翻译家王际真完成的《西游记》前七回英译文.
   (1) Chinese wit & humor/edited by George Kao；introd. by Lin Yutang；incl. a translation by Pearl Buck. New York：Sterling Pub. Co.，[1974]. xxxv，347 p.；23cm. ISBN：0806980028，0806980036
   (2) Taipei：Caves Books，1975. xxxv，347 pages；23cm.

5. The Chinese essay/translated and edited by David E. Pollard. [Hong Kong]：Research Centre for Translation，the Chinese University of Hong Kong，1999. 400 pages：illustrations，portraits；24cm. ISBN：9627255211，9627255215
Contents：To lead out the army/Zhuge Liang—Requiem for myself/Tao Qian—Address to the crocodiles of Chaozhou；Goodbye to penury/Han Yu—The whip vendor；My first excursion to West Mountain；The small rock pool west of the hillock/Liu Zongyuan—A monument to rustic temples/Lu Guimeng—The old toper's pavilion/Ouyang Xiu—The terrace over the void；Master Table Mountain；Red Cliff：one；Inscription for the Temple of Han Yu at Chaozhou/Su Shi—The pavilion of elation/Su Che—The mosquito dialogue/Fang Xiaoru—My mother：a brief life；The Xiangji studio/Gui Youguang—Tiger hill；The rewards of stupidity/Yuan Hongdao—The full moon festival at the West Lake；Wang Yuesheng；Liu Jingting：storyteller；The jades of Yangzhou/Zhang Dai—Pleasant diversions：judging beauty；Pleasant diversions：accomplishments；Pleasant diversions：literacy；Pleasant diversions：clothes/Li Yu—Life in prison/Fang Bao—Thoughts on Master Huang's book borrowing/Yuan Mei—Three summer pests；The evolution of the male sex；Ah Jin；Confucius in modern China/Lu Xun—Relentless rain；Reading in the lavatory；On 'passing the itch'；The ageing of ghosts；In praise of mutes/Zhou Zuoren—The ornamental iron mountain；Winter at White Horse Lake/Xia Mianzun—Three kinds of boat；My own patch of green；Intellectuals/Ye Shengtao—Eating melon seeds；Autumn；Bombs in Yishan/Feng Zikai—Village school

and academy; The winter scene in Jiangnan/Yu Dafu—The view from the rear; Traces of Wenzhou; The lotus pond by moonlight/Zhu Ziqing—Sickness; Haircut; Listening to plays/Liang Shih-ch'iu—On the road; Well-meant words/Liang Yuchun—A temple lodging/Lu Li—The art of listening; Cloak of invisibility/Yang Jiang—Elegy/He Qifang—Chignon/Ch'i Chun—The religion of the Chinese; A beating/Eileen Chang—The last word in beauty and ugliness; Footprints/Wang Ting-chün—Thus friends absent speak; My four hypothetical enemies/Yu Kwang-chung—The call of the ruins/Zongpu—The countryside of the past; Today's countryside/Koarnhak Tarn—We can't bring back the past; Waiting for a flower's name/Huang Chunming—Shanghai people/Yu Qiuyu—Goodwives/Zhang Xingjian.

《古今散文英译集》,卜立德(Pollard, David E.)(美国汉学家)译.

(1) New York: Columbia University Press, 2000. xvi, 372 pages: illustrations; 24cm. ISBN: 0231121180, 0231121187, 0231112192, 023111219X

6. Gu wen guan zhi = Chinese prose literature history and criticism/Wu, Chucai. Beijing: China Book, 2004. 2 v. ISBN: 7101041418, 7101041415

《古文观止》

7. 古文观止精选:英汉对照/罗经国译.北京:外语教学与研究出版社, 2005. 196 页;20cm. ISBN: 7560048471, 7560048475

英文题名:A selection of classical Chinese essays from Guwenguanzhi.

从《古文观止》中精选了 32 篇经典文章,译成英文.中英对照.

8. Mei Cherng's "Seven stimuli" and Wang Bor's "Pavilion of King Terng": Chinese poems for princes/by Victor H. Mair; calligraphy of Jiang Chunbin; plastercuts and woodcuts by Daniel Heitkamp. Lewiston, NY, USA: E. Mellen Press, c1988. viii, 139 p.: ill.; 19×26cm. ISBN: 0889460205. (Studies in Asian thought and religion; v. 11)

Spine title: Chinese poems for princes.

《枚乘的〈七发〉和王勃的〈滕王阁序〉》,枚乘(公元前? —141),王勃(650—675);梅维恒(Mair, Victor H., 1943—)(美国翻译家)译.中英对照.

9. Chinese classical prose: the eight masters of the T'ang-Sung period: with notes and Chinese texts/selected and translated by Shih Shun Liu. Hong Kong: Chinese University Press; Seattle: distributed by University of Washington Press, c1979. xviii, 365 p.: ill.; 24cm. ISBN: 9622011799, 9622011793. (Renditions book)

《唐宋八大家》,刘师舜(1900—)译.中英文本.

10. A selection from the eight great prose masters of the Tang and Song dynasties/translated by Xu Yincai.

Shanghai: Shanghai Foreign Language Education Press, 2011. vii, 187 pages; 24cm. ISBN: 7544623476, 7544623475. (SFLEP Bilingual Chinese culture series)

《英译唐宋八大家散文精选》,徐英才译.上海外语教育出版社(外教社中国文化汉外对照丛书)

11. 唐代游记选译 = Classical travel sketches of the Tang Dynasty/汪榕培审译;马静选译. 北京:商务印书馆, 2015. 161 p.: ill.; 19cm. ISBN: 7100107228, 7100107229. (中国古典游记选译.中国古典游记选译)

12. 明代游记选译 = Classical travel sketches of the Ming Dynasty/汪榕培审译;吴卫选译. 北京:商务印书馆, 2015. 249 p.: ill.; 19cm. ISBN: 7100107242, 7100107245. (中国古典游记选译.中国古典游记选译)

13. 清代游记选译 = Classical travel sketches of the Qing Dynasty/汪榕培审译;张丽妹选译. 北京:商务印书馆, 2015. 191 p.: ill.; 19cm. ISBN: 7100107259, 7100107253. (中国古典游记选译.中国古典游记选译)

14. Mirages and sea-markets: a collection of modern Chinese essays. Peking: Foreign Languages Press, 1962. 122 p.; 22cm.

《海市:中国现代散文集》,刘白羽,杨朔,冰心等.

15. Tai'an - Tai Shan = Tai'an & Mount Tai/by Wang Jun, Wang Feng. Beijing, China: New World Press, 1987. 96 pages: illustrations, 1 map; 23cm. ISBN: 7800050416, 7800050411

《泰山女神》,中国广州笔会中心编.新世界出版社.游记.

16. Leaves of prayer: the life and poetry of He Shuangqing, a farmwife in eighteenth-century China: selected translations from Shi Zhenlin's West green random notes; Chinese calligraphy by T. C. Lai/Elsie Choy. 2nd ed. Hong Kong: Hong Kong Univ. Press, 2000. 296 p.: ill., map; 22cm. ISBN: 9622018831. (Academic monographs on Chinese literature)

Choy, Elsie 著.包括对史震林(1692—1778)的《西青散记》选译和对贺双卿(1715—1735)诗的翻译.清人笔记.

17. 匾额楹联/张光奇编著.合肥:黄山书社,2016.124 页:彩图;23cm. ISBN: 7546141619.(印象中国)

英文题名:Inscribed boards and couplets.英汉对照.

I72　古代个人作品

汉代
班昭(约 45—117)

1. The Chinese book of etiquette and conduct for women and girls, entitled, Instruction for Chinese women and girls, by Lady Tsao. Translated from the Chinese, by Mrs. S. L. Baldwin. New York: Eaton & Mains [c1900]. [61] p. 12 plates. 19cm.

《女诫》,班昭(约 45—约 117);Mrs. S. L. Baldwin 译.

三国-南北朝

嵇康（224—263，一作 223—262）

1. Philosophy and argumentation in third-century China：the essays of Hsi K'ang/translated，with introduction and annotation by Robert G. Henricks. Princeton，N. J.：Princeton University Press，c1983. x，214 p.；23cm. ISBN：0691053782，0691053783.（Princeton Library of Asian translations）

"Translate all nine of Hsi K'ang's essays，plus the four essays of his opponents in various debates"—Pref.

《嵇康文》，韩禄伯（Henricks，Robert G.，1943—）（美国汉学家）译注.

2. Hsi K'ang and his poetical essay on the lute/by R. H. van Gulik. Tokyo：Sophia University，1941. 90 p.（Monumenta Nipponica monographs）

《琴赋》，高罗佩（Gulik，Robert Hans van，1910—1967）译注. 英汉对照.

(1)[New ed.，rev. and reset]. Tokyo，Sophia University；Rutland，Vt.，C. E. Tuttle Co.，1969. 133 pages 3 plates（some color）27cm.（A Monumenta nipponica monograph）

陆游（1125—1210）

1. South China in the twelfth century：a translation of Lu Yu's travel diaries，July 3 - December 6，1170/by Chun-shu Chang and Joan Smythe. Hong Kong：Chinese University Press，c1981. xvii，232 p.：ill.；24cm. ISBN：9622012213，9622012219.（Monograph series/Institute of Chinese Studies，the Chinese University of Hong Kong；4）

《入蜀记》，Chang，Chun-shu（1934—）和 Smythe，Joan（1963—）合译.

2. Grand Canal，great river：the travel diary of a twelfth-century Chinese poet/translated with a commentary by Philip Watson. London：Frances Lincoln，2007. 255 pages：illustrations（some color）；24cm. ISBN：0711227194，0711227195

《入蜀记》，Watson，Philip 译.

明代

徐宏祖（1587—1641）

1. The travel diaries of Hsüh Hsia-K'o/Li Chi. Hong Kong：Chinese University of Hong Kong，[1974]. 280 p.，14 leaves of plates：ill.；24cm.

《徐霞客游记》，李祁（Li，Qi，1903—）（美国华裔学者）译.

2. 英译徐霞客游记＝The travels of Xu Xiake/卢长怀，贾秀海译. 上海：上海外语教育出版社，2011. 319 p.：ill.；24cm. ISBN：7544618502，7544618501.（外教社. 中国文化汉外对照丛书＝SFLEP bilingual Chinese culture series）

清代

冒襄（字辟疆，1611—1693）

1. The reminscences of Tung Hsiao-wan/by Mao Pijiang；translated into English by Pan Ciyan（Z. Q. Parker）. Shanghai，China，Printed by the Commercial Press，Limited，1931. xv，159 pages；19cm.

《影梅庵忆语》，潘子延译.

张潮（1650—1709）

1. Quiet dream shadows＝You meng ying/ed. by Li Ming. Tai bei：Zheng zhong shu ju，1988. 109 pages. ISBN：9570908548，9570908541

《幽梦影》，林语堂（1895—1976）译；Li，Ming 编. 小品文.

(1)Tai bei：Zheng zhong shu ju，1991. 109 pages. ISBN：9570901810，9570901818，7805351996，78053519953401.

沈复（1763—1832）

1. Shen Fu's Six chapters of a floating life/rendered into English by Lin Yutang. 2nd ed. Shanghai，Xi Feng She，1939. xv，[1]，326，[1] pages plates

《浮生六记》，林语堂（1895—1976）译. 初版于 1935 年.

(1) Six chapters of the floating life/translated by Lin Yutang. 2nd ed. Taipei：Hsin Lu，1966. 262 pages；19cm.

(2)1974. xv，326 p.：ill.；19cm.

(3)Beijing：Wai yu jiao xue yu yan jiu chu ban she，1999. 23，327 p.：ill.；21cm. ISBN：7560015956，7560015958

(4)Beijing：Wai yu jiao xue yu yan jiu chu ban she，2014. xv，333 pages，16 unnumbered of plates：illustrations，portraits；21cm. ISBN：7560087054，560087051.（English works of Lin Yutang＝林语堂英文作品集）

2. Chapters from a floating life：the autobiography of a Chinese artist. Translated from the Chinese by Shirley M. Black. Poems by Tu Fu and Li Po，translated by S. M. B. London，New York：Oxford University Press，1960. xiv，108 p. 8 plates. 21cm.

《浮生六记》（选译），Black，Shirley M. 译.

张德彝（1847—1918）

1. Diary of a Chinese diplomat/Zhang Deyi；translated by Simon Johnstone. Beijing：Chinese Literature Press，1992. 357 pages：portraits；18cm. ISBN：7507100715，7507100716，0835120821，0835120821.（Panda books）

《欧美环球记》. 中国文学出版社. 日记.

富察敦崇（1855—1911）

1. Annual customs and festivals in Peking as recorded in the Yen-ching Sui-shih-chi. by Tun Li-ch'en；translated and annotated by Derk Bodde. Peiping，H. Vetch，1936.

《燕京岁时记》，卜德（Bodde，Derk，1909—2003）（美国汉学家）译. 杂记.

(1)2nd ed. , rev. Hong Kong, Hong Kong University Press，1965. xxviii，147 p. illus. (part mounted fold. col.)map (on lining papers)25cm.

I73　现当代散文集

1. One day in China，May 21，1936/translated，edited，and introduced by Sherman Cochran and Andrew C. K. Hsieh with Janis Cochran. New Haven：Yale University Press，c1983. xxvi，290 p. ：ill. ；24cm. ISBN：0300028342，0300028348，0300034008，0300034004
《中国的一日》，茅盾(1896—1981)，沈雁冰，沈德鸿，孔另境等；Cochran，Sherman(1940—)，Xie，Zhengguang 和 Cochran，Janis(1947—)合译. 散文.

2. Festival of flowers：essays by contemporary Chinese women writers/edited by Shu Hong；with assistance from Carol Meuser. Nanjing：Yilin Press，1995. 183 pages；23cm. ISBN：7805674167，7805674162
《花的节日：中国当代女作家散文选》，朱虹主编. 译林出版社.

3. May fourth women writers：memoirs/edited by Janet Ng and Janice Wickeri. Hong Kong：Research Centre for Translation，the Chinese University of Hong Kong，c1996. 133 p. ：ill. ；22cm. ISBN：9627255173. (Renditions paperbacks)
20 世纪中国女作家散文的选译. Ng，Janet，Wickeri，Janice 编.

4. 美文·诗化·哲理/张光明主编. 北京：国防工业出版社，2008. 11，372 页；20cm. ISBN：7118060201，7118060208
本书选取国内报刊杂志上已发表的优秀散文，对其进行英译，并配有注释.

5. Chinese writers on writing/ed. by Arthur Sze. San Antonio, Tex. Trinity Univ. Press, 2010. XXIII, 308 S. ISBN：1595340627，1595340629，1595340634，1595340637. (The writer's world)
Sze，Arthur 编. 收录中国现当代作家关于自己写作的文章. 译自中文.

6. A garden of one's own：a collection of modern Chinese essays，1919—1949/edited and translated by Tam King-fai. Hong Kong：Chinese University Press，2012. vii，279 pages；23cm. ISBN：9629964238，9629964236
1919—1949 年中国散文集. Tam，King-fai 编译.

I74　现当代个人作品

梁实秋(1903—1987)

1. The fine art of reviling/translation from the Chinese by William B. Pettus. Los Angeles, The Auk Press, 1936. 14 p. , 1 l. ；18 1/2cm.
《骂人的艺术》，Pettus，William B. (William Bacon，1880—)译.
(1)The fine art of reviling：a translation from the Chinese/by William B. Pettus. New York：Typophiles，1942. 28 p. ；18cm.

(2)San Francisco：Wallace Kibbee & Son, 1949. 10，[18] p. ；18cm.

2. Sketches of a cottager/tr. by Shih Chao-ying. [Taipei]：[Far East Book Co]，1960. 219 pages；19cm.
《雅舍小品》，时昭瀛(Shih，Chao-ying)译.
(1)Taipei，Taiwan：The Far East Bk. ，1973. 318 pages；21cm.
(2)Taipei：Far East，1976. 318 pages

3. 雅舍小品＝Sketches of a cottager/梁实秋著；时昭瀛译. 台北：远东图书公司；[1991]. 306 页，13；21cm.
中英对照. 附录：骂人的艺术

4. From a cottager's sketchbook/original Chinese text by Liang Shih-chiu；translated by Ta-tsun Chen. Chinese. English bilingual ed. Xianggang：The Chinese University Press，2005. 2 v. ；22cm. ISBN：9629962180（v. 1），9629962187（v. 1），9629962197（v. 2），9629962195（v. 2）.（中国现代文学中英对照系列＝Bilingual series on modern Chinese literature）
《雅舍小品》，Chen，Dazun 译.

周作人(1885—1967)

1. Zhou Zuoren：selected essays/original Chinese text by Zhou Zuoren；translated by David E. Pollard. Hong Kong：Chinese University Press，c2006. xxxiii，273 p. ；22cm. ISBN：9629961989.（中国现代文学中英对照系列＝Bilingual series on modern Chinese literature）
《周作人散文选》，卜立德(Pollard，David E.)译.

鲁迅(1881—1936)

1. Lu Xun：writing for the revolution：essays by Lu Xun and essays on Lu Xun from Chinese literature magazine. San Francisco：Red Sun Publishers，[1976]. iii，207 pages：illustrations，portraits；22cm. ISBN：0918302013，0918302014. (Modern China series；no. 2)
收录中国文学杂志中鲁迅的杂文和论述鲁迅的杂文.

2. Selected prose readings of Lu Xun. Hong Kong：Zhong Liu Pub. House，1978. 111 pages；19cm.
鲁迅散文选读.

3. 鲁迅杂文选：英汉对照/鲁迅著；杨宪益，戴乃迭译. 北京：外文出版社，2006. 470 页；20cm. ISBN：7119042599，7119042596.（经典的回声）
英文题名：Lu Xun selected essays

4. 鲁迅杂文选：双语插图本/鲁迅著. 南京：译林出版社，2009. 303 页；23cm. ISBN：7544709217，7544709213
文题名：Lu Xun selected essays. 本书选取了鲁迅先生约 50 篇极具代表性的杂文.

5. Dawn blossoms plucked at dusk/Lu Hsühn [i. e. Chou Shu-jen；translated by Yang Hsien-yi and Gladys Yang]. Peking：Foreign Languages Press，1976. 120 p. ，[1] leaf of plates：ill. ；19cm.
《朝花夕拾》，杨宪益(1915—2009)，戴乃迭(Yang，Gladys，1919—1999)合译.
(1)Beijing：Wai wen chu ban she，2001. 265 p. ：ill. ；

20cm. ISBN：7119026976，7119026978

6. 朝花夕拾：双语插图本/鲁迅著.南京：译林出版社，2009. 211 页；23cm. ISBN：7544709316，7544709310
英文题名：Dawn blossoms plunked at dusk.《朝花夕拾》是鲁迅所写的唯一一部回忆散文集，共收入 10 篇作品.
  (1)朝花夕拾/杨宪益，戴乃迭译.南京：译林出版社，2011. 211 页；21cm. ISBN：7544716697，7544716694.（双语译林. 第二辑 17）

7. 朝花夕拾/鲁迅著；杨宪益，戴乃迭译；裘沙，王伟君插图.北京：外文出版社，2010. 173 页；24cm. ISBN：7119066776，7119066773.（经典回声）
英文题名：Dawn blossoms plucked at dusk

8. 野草/鲁迅著；杨宪益，戴乃迭译；裘沙，王伟君插图.北京：外文出版社，2010. 181 页；24cm. ISBN：7119066783，7119066781.（经典回声）
英文题名：Wild grass

9. A selection of Lo Shun's letters translated/［Zhou Shuren］；Wei Yin yi. Xingzhou：Xingzhou shi jie shu ju you xian gong si, 1973. 2, 149 p.；19cm.
《鲁迅书简选译》，维尹译. 中英对照. 星洲世界书局出版.

10. Letters between two：correspondence between Lu Xun and Xu Guangping/translated by Bonnie S. McDougall. Beijing：Foreign Languages Press, 2000. 462 pages, 4 unnumbered pages of plates：illustrations（chiefly color）；21cm. ISBN：711901997X，7119019970
《两地书》，鲁迅（1881—1936）；许广平（1898—1968）；McDougall, Bonnie S.（1941—）译.

11. Love-letters and privacy in modern China：the intimate lives of Lu Xun and Xu Guangping/［translated by］Bonnie S. McDougall. New York：Oxford University Press, 2002. xii, 305 pages；24cm. ISBN：0199256799，0199256792.（Studies on contemporary China）
《两地书》选译，McDougall, Bonnie S.（1941—）译.

胡适（1891—1962）

1. 四十自述/胡适著；（美）乔志高译.北京市：外语教学与研究出版社，2016. iii, 170 页；图；23cm. ISBN：7513574297.（"博雅双语名家名作"系列）
英文题名：Autobiography at forty. 英汉对照.

林语堂（1895—1976）

1. Selected bilingual essays of Lin Yutang/compiled and edited by Qian Suoqiao. Traditional Chinese-English bilingual ed. Hong Kong：Chinese University Press, 2010. xliii, 234 pages；23cm. ISBN：9629964351，962996435X
《林语堂双语文选》，钱锁桥选编.

冰心（1900—1999）

1. 关于女人/冰心著；陈茅译.北京市：外语教学与研究出版社，2012. xvii, 205 页；23cm. ISBN：7513526449.（"博雅双语名家名作"系列）
英文题名：About women. 英汉对照.

2. Letters from a Chinese student at Wellesley/Bing Xin；translated by Gail Graham.［United States］：［CreateSpace］, 2015. 207 pages；23cm. ISBN：1511890229，1511890223
冰心通信集. Graham, Gail 译.

沈从文（1902—1988）

1. Recollections of West Hunan/Shên, Ts'ung-wen（Congwen Shen）；transl. by Gladys Yang. Beijing：Chinese literature, 1982. 195 p.；19cm.（Panda Books）
《湘西》，戴乃迭（Yang, Gladys, 1919—1999）译.
  (1)Beijing：Foreign Languages Press, 2009. 200 pages；20cm. ISBN：7119058917，7119058916.（Panda books）

2. 湘西散记：双语插图本/沈从文著.南京：译林出版社，2009. 311 页；23cm. ISBN：7544709309，7544709302
英文题名：Recolletions of West Hunan. 戴乃迭先生译的这十一篇作品，是从沈从文的《从文自传》《湘行散记》《湘西》及题附在香港重印的《散文选》中的《劫后残稿》四个不同性质的集子中选出的.

巴金（1904—2005）

1. Living amongst heroes［by］Pa Chin. Peking：Foreign Languages Press, 1954. 132 p. illus. 17cm.
《生活在英雄们的中间》

2. Random thoughts/by Ba Jin；translated by Geremie Barmé. Hongkong：Joint Pub. Co., 1984. xvii, 200 p.；ill.；22cm. ISBN：9620403126，9620403125，9620403118，9620403118
《随想录》，Barmé, Geremie 译.
  (1)Hongkong：Joint Publishing, 1995. 200 pages；photograph；22×15cm. ISBN：9620403126，9620403125

谢冰莹（1906—2000）

1. Letters of a Chinese amazon, and War-time essays/by Lin Yutang. Shanghai, China：Commercial Press, 1930. xiv, 211 pages；19cm.
Notes："These papers［were］practically all written in... August, 1927, and published in the People's tribune."—Page vii. / "Letters of a Chinese amazon［by Hsieh Ping-ying, translated by Lin Yu-t'ang］"
《从军日记》，林语堂（1895—1976）译.
  (1)Shanghai, China：Commercial Press, 1933. xiv, 211 pages；19cm.

陈学昭（1906—1991）

1. Surviving the storm：a memoir/Chen Xuezhao；edited with an introduction by Jeffrey C. Kinkley；translated by Ti Hua and Caroline Greene. Armonk, N. Y.：M. E. Sharpe, c1990. xxvi, 147 p.,［7］p. of plates；ill.；24cm. ISBN：0873326016.（Foremother legacies）
《浮沉杂忆》，金介甫（Kinkley, Jeffrey C., 1948—）（美国汉学家）译.

李广田（1906—1968）

1. A pitiful plaything and other essays/Li Kuangtian；translated by Gladys Yang. Beijing, China：Chinese Literature；Distributed by China Publications Center,

1982. 154 p. ; 19cm. (Panda books)

《李广田散文选》，戴乃迭(Yang. Gladys,1919—1999)译.

钱钟书(1910—1998)

1. Humans, beasts, and ghosts: stories and essays/Qian Zhongshu; edited with an introduction by Christopher G. Rea; with translations by Dennis T. Hu. . [et al.]. New York: Columbia University Press, 2011. 220 p. ; 24cm. ISBN: 0231152747, 0231152744, 0231152754, 0231152752, 0231526548, 0231526547. (Weatherhead books on Asia)

《写在人生边》，Rea, Christopher G 编；Hu, Dennis T. 译.

季羡林(1911—2009)

1. 牛棚杂忆/季羡林著；马尚译. 北京：外语教学与研究出版社，2013. xxi, 392 页；23cm. ISBN: 7513527347. ("博雅双语名家名作"系列)

英文题名：Random recollections of the cow shed. 汉英对照.

杨绛(1911—2016)

1. Six chapters from my life "downunder"/Yang Jiang; translated by Howard Goldblatt with a preface by Jonathan Spence. Seattle: University of Washington Press; Hong Kong: Chinese University Press, 1984. xiii, 111 pages: illustrations; 22cm. ISBN: 0295961465, 0295961460, 0295960817, 0295960814

《干校六记》，葛浩文(Goldblatt，Howard，1939—)(美国翻译家)译.

2. A cadre school life: six chapters/by Yang Jiang; translated by Geremie Barmé with the assistance of Bennett Lee. [Hong Kong]: Joint Pub. Co. ; New York: Readers International, 1984. 91 pages; 22cm. ISBN: 9620402227, 9620402227, 0930523016, 0930523015

《干校六记》，Barmé , Geremie 译.

3. Six chapters of life in a cadre school: memoirs from China's Cultural Revolution/Yang Chiang; translated and annotated by Djang Chu Boulder: Westview Press, 1986. xiv, 78 p. : ill. ; 23cm. ISBN: 081337099X, 0813370996

《干校六记》，Zhang, Chu 译注.

4. Lost in the crowd: a Cultural Revolution memoir/Yang Jiang; translated by Geremie Barmé; with a foreword by Simon Leys. Melbourne: McPhee Gribble, 1989. 133 pages; 21cm. ISBN: 0869140973, 0869140970

《干校六记，丙午丁未年纪事》，Barmé , Geremie 译.

5. 洗澡:汉英对照/杨绛著；梅珠迪，史耀华译. 北京：人民文学出版社，2007. 561 页；23cm. ISBN: 7020063772, 7020063772

英文题名：Baptism/by Yang Jiang; translated by Judith M. Amory and Yaohua Shi.

6. Baptism/by Yang Jiang; translated by Judith M. Amory and Yaohua Shi. Hong Kong: Hong Kong University Press, 2007. 282 p. ;23cm. ISBN: 9622098312,622098312, 9622098304,9622098305

《洗澡》，Amory，Judith M. 和 Shi，Yaohua 合译.

杨朔(1913—1968)

1. A selection of prose pieces/by Yang Shuo; translated by Lee Yu-hwa. Beijing: Foreign Languages Press, 1980. 105 pages: portraits; 19cm.

Contents：March on, army of steel! —Spring in the Gobi. —Random notes on the capital. —Fairy primroses by Kunming Lake. —Red leaves on Xiangshan. —Baihuashan. —The fairyland of Penglai. —The mirage. —Lychee honey. —Ode to the camellia. —Snowy waves. —Painted hills and embroidered waters. —The Hai Luo fir. —Xi Jiang Yue.

《杨朔散文选》，李玉华译.

王作民(1916—)

1. The American kaleidoscope: a Chinese view/by Wang Tsomin; edited and translated by Duan Liancheng. Beijing, China: New World Press, 1986. 70 pages; [8] pages of plates: illustrations; 22cm. ISBN: 0835116638, 0835116633

《美国万花筒》，段连成编译. 新世界出版社.

吴福临(1919—2010)

1. 华西坝上七十年:汉英对照/吴福临著. 成都：四川民族出版社，2007. 159 页：照片；24cm. ISBN: 7540934842, 7540934840

英文题名:70 years on Huaxi campus.

冯之丹(原名冯祥光,1927—)

1. Glimpses of West Africa/Feng Chih-tan. Peking: Foreign Languages Press, 1963. 118 pages, [4] leaves of plates: illustrations; 19cm.

《西非八国漫记》

陈忠实(1942—2016)

1. Verve of Shaanxi/written by Chen Zhongshi; illustrated by Luo Zhijian, Wang Wenji, etc. ; translated by Wang Da. Shanghai: East China Normal University Press, 2009. 2, 172 pages: color illustrations; 23cm. ISBN: 7561771495, 7561771495

《秦风》. 华东师范大学出版社.

2. 陈忠实散文选译/陈忠实著；马安平主译/总校；刘改琳[等]译. 西安：世界图书出版西安公司，2011. 191 页；21cm. ISBN: 7510041259, 7510041252

本书选取著名作家陈忠实先生的散文20篇进行英译.

余秋雨(1946—)

1. Quest for Chinese culture/Yu Qiuyu; translated by Ian Clark & Yang Jing. Beijing: Xin shi jie chu ban she,2010. 8,212 pages;21cm. ISBN: 7510407017,751040701X

《寻觅中华》，余秋雨著. 陶亦然，杨静译. 新世界出版社.

刘云山(1947—)

1. Customs and lifestyles of Aoluguya/written by Liu Yunshan; translated by Bei Ta. 2nd ed. /revised by John Crespi Li Zhenguo. Huhhot: Inner Mongolia people's Publishing House, 2010. 77 pages: illustrations (some

color）；25cm. ISBN：7204108848，7204108841

《敖鲁古雅风情》，刘云山著. 内蒙古人民出版社.

北岛（1949—）

1. Blue house ＝ Lan fang zi/Bei Dao；translated from the Chinese by Ted Huters and Feng-Ying Ming. Brookline, MA：Zephyr Press，c2000. 262 p.；ill.；19cm. ISBN：0939010585，0939010585

   Contents：Allen Ginsberg—Death of a Poet—Gary snyder—The Knight-Errant from New York—Clayton and Caryl—Michael the Stranger—God's Chinese Son—John and Ann—Octavio Paz—Blue House—Peng Gang—The Visitor from Poland—Director King Hu—Gao Ertai, Witness—One-Way Connection—Journey to South Africa—Crows—Cat Story—Daughter—A Day in New York—Moving—Driving—Gambling—Reciting.

   《蓝房子》，Huters，Theodore 和 Ming，Feng-ying（1956—）合译.

2. Midnight's gate ＝［Wu ye zhi men］/Bei Dao；translated from the Chinese by Matthew Fryslie；edited by Christopher Mattison. New York：New Directions Book, 2005. 255 p.；20cm. ISBN：0811215849，0811215848

   《午夜之门》，Fryslie，Matthew 译.

   （1）London：Anvil Press Poetry，2007. 255 pages；20cm. ISBN：0856463945，0856463949

史铁生（1951—2010）

1. Strings of life and other selected writings/Shi Tiesheng. Beijing：Foreign Languages Press，2009. 271 pages：illustrations；20cm. ISBN：7119058986，7119058983.

   Contents：Strings of life—Original sin—Fate—One winter's evening—In the world of understanding—Autumn remembrance—Our corner—My faraway Qingpingwan—Granny's star—Lunch break—Blacky.

   《命若琴弦：史铁生作品选》

成卫东（1951—）

1. Dreams of snow land/by Cheng Weidong；translated by Wang Guangqiang［and others］. Beijing：Foreign Languages Press，2005. 294 pages：color illustrations, color maps；24cm. ISBN：7119038834，7119038834.（全景中国）

   《雪域寻梦：英文》.外文出版社（全景中国）

王小波（1952—1997）

1. Selections from My spiritual garden/by Wang Xiaobo. Armonk，NY.：M E Sharpe，1999. 100 s.（Contemporary Chinese thought；；30：3）

   《我的精神家园》

马丽华（1953—）

1. Glimpses of northern Tibet/Ma Lihua；translated by Guan Yuehua and Zhong Liangbi. Beijing：Chinese Literature Press，1991. 330 p.；18cm. ISBN：7507100804，7507100808, 0835120902，0835120906.（Panda books）

   《藏北游历》，Guan Yuehua 和 Zhong Liangbi 合译.

（1）Beijing：Foreign Languages Press，2009. 330 pages；20cm. ISBN：7119059112，7119059114

王安忆（1954—）

1. Looking for Shanghai/written by Wang Anyi；illustrated by Li Xi ＆ Li Xueyuan；translated by Li Yiqi. Shanghai：East China Normal University Press，2009. 1，158 pages：color illustrations；23cm. ISBN：7561771501, 7561771509

   《海上》. 华东师范大学出版社.

赵玫（1954—）

1. Thus speaks the narrator ＝ 叙述者说/赵玫著；（美）James Yongue，钱坤强译. 北京：中译出版社，2016. 357 p.；20cm. ISBN：7500143321，750014332X.（Kaleidoscope：ethnic Chinese writers ＝ 阅读中国.第一辑.五彩丛书）

胡冬林（1955—）

1. Fox Grin/by Hu Donglin；translated by Zuzana Strakova. Beijing：China Translation ＆ Publishing Corporation, 2017. 339 pages. ISBN：7500151494，7500151497

   《狐狸的微笑：原始森林里正在消逝的它们》

郑渊洁（1955—）

1. 原创七宗罪 郑渊洁演讲集：中英文版/郑渊洁著. 天津人民出版社，2018. 23cm. ISBN：7201127729

叶兆言（1957—）

1. Water towns/written by Ye Zhaoyan；illustrated by Li Ronghua；translated by Li Yiqi. Shanghai：East China Normal University Press，2009. 1，183 pages：color illustrations；23cm. ISBN：7561771471，7561771479

   《水乡》. 华东师范大学出版社.

阿来（1959—）

1. Chuan-Zang/written by Alai；illustrated by Xiong Wenyun；translated by Wang Da. Shanghai：East China Normal University Press，2010. 2，136 pages：color illustrations；23cm. ISBN：7561771488，7561771487.（China style series）

   《川藏》. 华东师范大学出版社.

余华（1960—）

1. China in ten words/Yu Hua；translated from the Chinese by Allan H. Barr. 1st American ed. New York：Pantheon Books，c2011. x，225 p.；22cm. ISBN：0307379351，0307379353，0307739797，0307739791

   Contents：人民—领袖—阅读—写作—鲁迅—革命—差距—草根—山寨—忽悠

   《十个词汇里的中国》，艾伦（Barr，Allan Hepburn）（美国学者）译.

   （1）New York：Anchor Books，2012. x，225 pages；22cm. ISBN：0307739797，0307739791

叶尔克西·胡尔曼别克（1962—）

1. 远离严寒/叶尔克西·胡尔曼别克著. 北京：中国对外翻译出版公司，2013. 205 页；彩照；21cm. ISBN：7500137528.（阅读中国·五彩霓裳丛书）

2. An eternal lamb ＝ 永生羊/叶尔克西·胡尔曼别克著；

[美]James Yongue，季宇绮译.北京：中译出版社，2016.
285 pages；20cm. ISBN：7500143338，7500143338.
(Kaleidoscope：ethnic Chinese writers ＝阅读中国.第一
辑.五彩丛书)

江洋才让(1970—)

1. The way of khams-pa ＝康巴方式/江洋才让著；（英）
Patric Burton，江玉清译.北京：中译出版社，2016.268
p.；21cm. ISBN：7500143390，7500143397. (Reading
China：Tibetan stories＝阅读中国·藏族青年作家丛书)
游记.

韩寒(1982—)

1. This generation：dispatches from China's most popular
literary star (and race car driver)/Han Han.；edited and
translated by Allan H. Barr. 1st Simon & Schuster
hardcover ed. New York：Simon & Schuster, 2012. xi,
265 p.；24cm. ISBN：1451660005，1451660006
《这一代人》，艾伦(Barr, Allan Hepburn)(美国学者)译.
(1)London；New York：Simon & Schuster, 2012. xi,
265 pages；20cm. ISBN：1471114304，1471114309，
1451660012，1451660014

2. The problem with me：and other essays about making
trouble in China today/Han Han；edited and translated by
Alice Xin Liu and Joel Martinsen. New York：Simon &
Schuster, 2016. xv, 217 pages；21cm. ISBN：1451660036,
1451660030,1451660043,1451660049
Liu, Alice Xin 和 Martinsen, Joel 合译.

那一年的冬至

1. 那一年的冬至：汉英对照/容非著；庄重(Z. Z. Lehmberg)
译.广州：广东教育出版社,2016.238 p. ISBN：7554813980
英文题名：Winter solstice

I8　民间文学

民间歌谣

1. Cantonese love songs. Oxford, Clarendon Press, 1904. 2
v. 26cm.
《粤讴》，招子庸(1793—1846)著；金文泰(Cecil Clementi,
1875—1974)(曾任香港总督)译.广东民歌.
(1)Hong Kong：Hong Kong University Press, 1992. x,
203 pages；25cm. ISBN：9622092845，9622092846

2. 吴歌精华＝Gems of the Wu ballads/汪榕培……主编译.
苏州市：苏州大学出版社，2003. 5，211 pages：
illustrations；20cm. ISBN：781090082X，7810900829
英汉对照.江南民歌.

3. 旧京歌谣：汉英对照/赵晓阳编.北京：北京图书馆出版
社,2006.174 页;21cm. ISBN：7501331723，7501331727
英文题名：Old Peking rhymes.本书收集了流传在北京地
区的歌谣三百余首,这些歌谣全部采用中英文对照的形
式.

民间故事、传说

1. Chinese nights'entertainment；forty stories told by
almond-eyed folk actors in the romance of The strayed
arrow/by Adele M. Fielde；illustrated by Chinese
artists. New York：London：G. P. Putnams Sons,
[1893]. ix, 194 p. incl. plates. front. 22cm.
Notes：Running title：The strayed arrow
中国故事. Fielde, Adele M. (Adele Marion, 1839—
1916)编译.

2. Chinese fables and folk stories/by Mary Hayes Davis and
Chow-Leung；with an introduction by Yin-Chwang Wang
Tsen-Zan. New York：Cincinnati American Book Co. ,
1908. 214 pages：illustrations；19cm. (On cover：
Eclectic readings)
Contents：How the moon became beautiful—The animal's
peace party—The widow and her son—The evergreen tree
and the wilderness marigold—The snail and the bees—
The proud chicken—The lemon tree and the pumelo—
Woo Sing and the mirror—Two mothers and a child—A
boy who would not tell a lie—A great repentance and a
great forgiveness—The man who loved money better than
life—The hen and the Chinese mountain turtle—The boy
of perfect disposition—What the Yen Tzi taught the
hunter—A lesson from Confucius—The wind, the clouds,
and the snow—The fish and the flowers—The hen, the
cat, and the bird—The boy who wanted the impossible—
The boy who became a Hsao-tsze—The hunter, the
snipe, and the bivalve—The mule and the lion—The Fa-
Nien-Ts'ing and the Mōn-Tien-Sing—The body that
deserted the stomach—The proud fox and the crab—A
little Chinese rose—The eagle and the rice birds—The
children and the dog—The two mountains—A Chinese
prodigal son—The lion and the mosquitoes—The thief and
the elephant—The general, the bird, and the ant—Three
girls who went to a boys' school—The rattan vine and the
rose tree—The melon and the professor
中国故事与民间故事. Davis, Mary Hayes 和 Chow-
Leung 合译.
(1)New York：American Book Co. , 1976. 204 pages：
illustrations；19cm. ISBN：0841438137, 0841438132
(2)Folcroft, Pa. ：Folcroft Library Editions,1976. 214 pages：
illustrations；23cm. ISBN：0841438137,0841438132
(3)Honolulu, Hawaii：University Press of the Pacific,2003.
214 pages：illustrations；21cm. ISBN：1410208761,
1410208767

3. Chinese merry tales/tr. into English by Y. T. Woo.
Shanghai, American Presbyterian Mission Press, 1909.
[4], iv, 58 pages.
中国故事. Woo, Y. T. 英译.
(1)[S. l.]：Nabu Press, [2010]. ISBN：1176372246,
1176372245
(2)[Place of publication not identified]：Book on Demand
Ltd, 2013. ISBN：5518449070, 5518449077
(3)[Place of publication not identified]：Hardpress Ltd,

2013. ISBN：1313762067，1313762069

4. A Chinese wonder book/by Norman Hinsdale Pitman；illustrated by Li Chu-T'Ang. New York：E. P. Dutton & Co.，1919. 219 pages：color frontispiece, color plates, illustrations；18×21cm.

Contents：The Golden beetle or why the dog hates the cat—The Great bell—The Strange tale of Doctor Dog—How footbinding started—The Talking fish—Bamboo and the turtle—The Mad goose and the tiger forest—The Nodding tiger—The Princess Kwan-Yin—The Two jugglers—The Phantom vessel—The Wooden tablet—The Golden nugget—The Man who would not scold—Lu-San, daughter of heaven.

Pitman, Norman Hinsdale（1876—1925）编译；Li, Chu-T'Ang 插图. 收录中国传说.

(1) The Chinese wonder book：a classic collection of Chinese tales/by Norman Hinsdale Pitman；illustrations by Li Chu Tang；foreword by Sylvia Li-chun Lin. North Clarendon, Vt.：Tuttle Pub.，2011. 96 pages：color illustrations；29cm. ISBN：1462908660, 1462908667, 0804841610, 0804841616

(2) North Clarendon, VT Periplus Editions, 2016. 96 pages：colour illustrations；29cm.

5. Gods, ghosts and devils；stories of Chinese life and beliefs/H. R. Wells. Hong Kong, Printed by Wing Fat & Co.，1935. [6], 161 pages.

Wells, H. R. (Herbert Richmond) 译. 民间文学作品翻译.

6. Folk tales from China, with illus. by William Arthur Smith. New York：J. Day Co. [c1944]. 160 p. col. illus. 21cm.

中国民间故事. Lim, Sian-tek 编译.

7. More folk tales from China；with illus. by William Arthur Smith. New York：J. Day Co. [1948]. 160 p. illus. 21cm.

中国民间故事. Lim, Sian-tek 编译.

8. A gallery of Chinese immortals；selected biographies tr. from Chinese sources by Lionel Giles. London, J. Murray [1948]. 128 p. 18cm. (Wisdom of the East series. [London])

中国人物传奇故事. 翟林奈（Giles, Lionel, 1875—1958）（英国汉学家）译.

(1) 1st AMS ed. New York：AMS Press，[1979]. 128 p.；19cm. ISBN：0404144780. (The Wisdom of the East series)

9. Folk tales from china. first series. Peking：Foreign Languages Press, 1957. 146 pages：illustrations

《中国民间故事·1》

(1) Folk tales from China. First series/Translated by Yu Fan-chin... et al.；illustrations by Chang Kuang-yu... et al. 141 pages：illll；21cm. 3rd ed. Peking：Foreign Languages Press, 1962.

(2) The frog rider：folk tales from China (first series). 3rd ed. Beijing：Foreign Languages Press, 1980. 140 p.：ill.；21cm.

10. Folk tales from China. 2. Peking：Foreign Languages Press, 1958. 114 p.：Ill.

《中国民间故事·2》

(1) Folk tales from China：second series/[illustrations by Mi Ku]. 2nd ed. Peking：Foreign Languages Press, 1961. 114 pages，[6] leaves of plates：illustrations (some color)；21cm.

(2) The water-buffalo and the tiger：folk tales from China (second series)/[illustrations by Mi Gu]. 3rd ed. Beijing：Foreign Languages Press, 1980. 115 p.，[6] leaves of plates：ill. (some col.)；21cm.

11. Folk tales from China. Third series/[illustrations by Cheng Shih-fa]. Peking：Foreign Languages Press, 1958. 139 pages：illustrations；21cm.

《中国民间故事·3》

Contents：The king of the pomegranate tree (a story of the Uighur people)—The peacock maiden (a story of the Tai people)—The headman and the magician (a story of the Tibetan people)—The piece of Chuang brocade (a story of the Chuang people)—The golden vase and the monkeys (a story of the Tibetan people)—The frog who became an emperor (a story of the Chuang people)—The clever woman (a story of the Uighur people)—The wise Ma Tsai (a story of the Han people)—Under the shade of the mulberry tree (a story of the Uighur people)—The son of the mountain (a story of the Mongolian people)—The landlord's failure (a story of the Han people).

(1) Folk tales from China. Third series/Cheng Shifa. 2nd ed. Peking：Foreign Languages Press, 1962. 139 pages：illustrations；21cm.

(2) The peacock maiden：folk tales from China (third series)/[illustrations by Cheng Shifa]. 3rd ed. Beijing：Foreign Languages Press：Distributed by Guoji Shudian (China Publications Centre), 1981. 141 pages：illustrations；21cm.

12. Folk tales from China：fourth series/[illustrations by Sha Keng-shih]. Peking：Foreign Languages Press, 1958. 135 pages：illustrations；21cm.

《中国民间故事·4》

(1) Journey to the sun：folk tales from China (fourth series)/[illustrations by Sha Kengshi]. 2nd ed. Beijing：Foreign Languages Press：Distributed by Guoji Shudian (China Publications Centre), 1981. 140 p.：ill.；21cm.

13. Folk tales from China. Fifth series/Wan-shu Wang；Ma-teh Kao. Peking：Foreign Languages Press, 1960. 141

pages；illll；21cm.

《中国民间故事・5》

（1）The magic knife/［cha tu, Yang Yongqing... deng］. 3rd ed. Beijing：Foreign Languages Press；Distributed by China Publications Centre（Guoji Shudian），1982. 142 pages；illustrations；21cm. （Folk tales from China；5th series）

14. Folk tales from China. Hong Kong：Seagull Pub. Co. , 1957—1960. 5 v. ；ill. ；21cm.

《中国民间故事》共 5 卷，第一至第五卷. 曾由北京外文出版社于 1957—1960 年先后出版.

15. Stories out of China. Peking, New World Press, 1958. 163 p. illus. 21cm.

中国民间故事. 路易・艾黎（Alley, Rewi, 1897—1987）译.

16. Folk tales of China. Indianapolis, Bobbs-Merrill［1963］. 126 p. illus. 24cm.

中国民间故事. Hyndman, Jane Andrews（Lee, 1912—）译.

17. Stories from old China, by Edward W. Dolch and Marguerite P. Dolch；illustrated by Seong Moy. Champaign, Ill. , Garrard Pub. Co. ［1964］. vii, 166 p. col. illus. 21cm. （Folklore of the world）

Summary：Twenty episodes which preserve and illustrate the folklore of ancient China.

中国古代民间故事. Dolch, Edward W. （Edward William, 1889—1961）；Dolch, Marguerite P. （Marguerite Pierce, 1891—）译；Moy, Seong 插图.

18. Chinese tales of folklore/by S. Y. Lu Mar；illustrated by Howard Simon. London：Abelard-Schuman, 1964. 160 pages；illustrations；23cm.

Contents：The long-nosed giant—The king's joke—The magic bell—General Chang's strategy—The wedding of the dragon-god—The trial of the stone—The mystery of the scroll—The victorious lute—Borrowed arrows—The head-hunters—How pictures become words.

中国民间故事. Mar, Shuh-yin Lu（1907—）译.

（1）New York, Criterion Books, 1965. 160 pages；illustrations；22cm.

19. The seven sisters；selected Chinese folk stories. Peking：Foreign Languages Press, 1965. 120 pages；plates；21cm.

Contents：Date-stone. —Something for nothing. —The story of a serf. —The seven sisters. —How panpipes came to be played. —How Aisu found the happy land. —Rice. —The suit of white feathers. —Black horse, the third brother Chang. —The wooing of Pumei. —Kumiya. —The heavenly flute player.

《七姐妹》. 中国民间故事.

20. Tales from old China/by Isabelle C. Chang；illustrated by Tony Chen. New York：Random House,［1969］. 66 p. col. illus. ；24cm.

Summary：Eighteen fables, fairy tales and legends from ancient China. Includes "The Turtle and the Herons", "A Gentleman and his Cook" and "God of the Kitchen".

中国古代民间故事. Chang, Isabelle Chin（1924—）编译，收录 18 个故事.

（1）［Taipei］：［Caves Book Co］, 1972. 66 pages；illustrations；20cm.

（2）［Taipei］：［Fan Mei Book Co］, 1975. 66 pages；illustrations；20cm.

（3）New York：Random House, 1979. 6 p. ：il. ；20cm.

21. A butterfly's dream ＆ other Chinese tales, retold by Cheou-Kang Sié. Paintings by Chi Kang. Rutland, Vt. , C. E. Tuttle Co. ［1970］. 91 p. col. illus. 19cm. ISBN：0804800774

Contents：Preface. —A butterfly's dream. —The clay statues. —Old Man Stupidity. —The bridge of magpies. —Vinegar. —The return. —Spring water. —The reward. —Fetal education. —Tso Ying Tie. —Gratitude. —Illusion.

《蝴蝶梦及其他民间故事》，谢寿康（1894—1973）改编；Ji, Kang（1913—）插画.

22. Tales the people tell in China, by Robert Wyndham. Illustrated by Jay Yang. Consulting editor：Doris K. Coburn. New York：Messner［1971］. 92 p. illus. 24cm. ISBN：0671324276

Summary：Sixteen myths, legends, and folktales from ancient sources reveal many aspects of Chinese society, customs, and religion.

中国民间故事. Wyndham, Robert（1906—）译.

（1）New York：Messner, 1975. 92 pages；illustrations；24cm. ISBN：0671324284, 0671324285

23. China's dirtiest trickster；folklore about Hsüh Wen-ch'ang （1521—1593）. Translated and described by Howard S. Levy. Arlington, Va. , Warm-Soft Village Press, 1974. xxii, 157 p. illus. 23cm. ISBN：091087800X

Notes：Originally published：Taibei Shi：Zhongguo min su xue hui, 1984. （Asian folklore ＆ social life monographs；v. 143）

《徐文长故事》，Levy, Howard S. （Howard Seymour, 1923—）（美国学者）编译. 民间故事.

（1）Taibei, Republic of China：Chinese Association for Folklore, 1984. ［xxii］, 157 pages；illustrations；26cm. （Asian folklore and social life monographs；v. 143＝亚洲民俗・社会生活专刊；143）

24. 30 Chinese stories＝Chung-kuo min chien ku shih 30 tse/translated by Howard S. Levy, Harumi Kawasaki. ［Taipei, Taiwan］Pacific Cultural Foundation,［1980］. 127 p；21cm.

《中国民间故事三十则》，Levy, Howard S. 和 Kawasaki,

Harumi 合译.

25. Old tales of China: a tourist guidebook to better understanding of China's stage, cinema, arts and crafts/ Li Nianpei. Beijing, China: China Travel and Tourism Press, 1981. 185 pages: illustrations; 19cm.
《中国传统故事》,李念培编译,中国旅游出版社.
(1)2nd ed. Beijing, China: China Travel and Tourism Press, 1998. 189 pages: illustrations; 21cm. ISBN: 7503215577, 7503215575

26. Beijing legends/Jin Shoushen; translated by Gladys Yang. Beijing, China: Chinese Literature: Distributed by China Publications Centre (Guoji Shudian), 1982. 141 pages: illustrations; 18cm. (Panda books)
《北京的传说》,金受申著;戴乃迭(Yang, Gladys, 1919—1999)译.
(1)Beijing, China: Chinese Literature: Distributed by China Publications Centre (Guoji Shudian), 1985. 41 pages: illustrations; 18cm. ISBN: 0835113388, 0835113380. (Panda Books)
(2) Beijing: Foreign Languages Press, 2005. 141 pages: illustrations; 18cm. ISBN: 711903748X, 7119037486. (Panda Books)

27. The Effendi and the pregnant pot: Uygur folktales from China/transl. [and rewrote] by Primerose Gigliesi and Robert C. Friend. Beijing: New World Press, 1982. 88 p.: ill.
《阿凡提故事选》,季丽玫,费兰德译.

28. Folk tales of the West Lake/adapted by Wang Hui-Ming; [illustrated by Ye Yuzhong]. Beijing, China: Foreign Languages Press: Distributed by Guoji Shudian (China Publications Centre), 1982. 73 p.: ill.; 19cm.
《西湖民间故事》,Wang, Hui-ming 改编和英译;叶毓中插图.

29. Chinese popular stories/Peter K. H. Lee. Taizhong Shi: Li Gengxin, 72 nian [1983]. 2, 5, 289 p.: ill. (some col.); 20cm.
《中国民间故事》,Li, Gengxin 译. 中英对照.

30. Tun-huang popular narratives/[introduction and translations by] Victor H. Mair. Cambridge [Cambridgeshire]; New York: Cambridge University Press, 1983. ix, 329 p.: ill.; 24cm. ISBN: 0521247616, 0521247610. (Cambridge studies in Chinese history, literature, and institutions)
《敦煌通俗叙事文学作品》,梅维恒(Mair, Victor H., 1943—)(美国翻译家)译.
(1)Cambridge, UK; New York: Cambridge University Press, 2007. ix, 329 p.: ill.; 24cm. ISBN: 0521039835, 0521039833, 0521247610, 0521247616. (Cambridge studies in Chinese history, literature, and institutions)

31. The stone statue of an ancient hero and other Chinese tales/ by Ye Shengtao and others; translated by Betty Ting. Hongkong: Joint Pub. Co., 1983. 67 pages: illustrations (some color); 25cm. ISBN: 9620402138, 9620402135
Contents: The magic brush/Hong Xuntao—Pigsy learns magic tricks/Bao Lei—Story of the mirror/He Yi—The stone statue of an ancient hero/Ye Shengtao—A genius acrobat/Ren Rongrong—The young wild goose returns/Wu Mengqi—Things that happened before the rain/Lin Songyin—Song of the running brook/Yan Wenjing
中国民间故事. 叶圣陶等著.

32. Women in Chinese folklore/[Ye Shengtao, Hua Jiqing, Zhong Jiqing...]. Beijing: Women of China, 1983. 107 p.: ill.; 18cm. ISBN: 0835111725, 0835111720
《民间传说中的妇女》,叶圣陶等著.

33. Favourite folktales of China/translated by John Minford; illustrated by He Youzhi and others; introducted by Zhong Jingwen. 1st ed. Beijing, China: New World Press: Distributed by China Publications Centre (Guoji Shudian), 1983. 202 p.: ill.; 22cm.
《中国民间故事》,闵福德(Minford, John, 1946—)(英国汉学家)译. 北京新世界出版社.

34. Elephant Trunk Hill: tales from scenic Guilin/[written by Yi Qiong and Xu Junhui; translated by Mark A. Bender and Shi Kun; illustrations by Xiao Huixiang and Yu Yuechuan]. Beijing: Foreign Languages Press: Distributed by China International Book Trading Corp., 1984. iii, 103 pages, [15] leaves of plates: illustrations (some color); 19cm. ISBN: 0835111636, 0835111638
《桂林传奇》,易琼,徐君慧著;马可·本德,史昆译. 民间故事.

35. Daur folktales: selected myths of the Daur nationality/ translated by Mark Bender and Su Huana. Beijing, China: New World Press: Distributed by China International Book Trading Corp., 1984. 191 pages: illustrations; 22cm.
《达斡尔族民间故事选》,马可·本德,苏华娜译. 新世界出版社.

36. The magic bird/[edited by Ellen Hertz]. Beijing: Foreign Languages Press: Distributed by China International Book Trading Corp. (Guoji Shudian), 1985. 149 pages: illustrations; 21cm. ISBN: 0835113159, 0835113151. (Folk tales from China; 7th ser)
Abstract: Thirteen stories from nine distinct traditions - the Han, the Uygar, the Mongolian, the Tibetan, the Naxi, the Hui, the Kazak, the Yugur and the Dong nationalities
《神鸟:中国民间故事选》

37. The slave and the dragon maid/translated by Shi Xiaojing. Beijing: Foreign Languages Press: Distributed by China International Book Trading Corp. (Guoji Shudian), 1985. 118 pages: illustrations; 21cm. ISBN: 0835113620, 0835113625. (Folk tales from China;; 8th ser)
《奴隶与龙女:中国民间故事选》

38. Mount Emei：folktales/Collected and adapted by Zhang Chengye；translated by Hu Xiong；illustrated by Ma Quan & Jin Xu. Chengdu：Sichuan ren min chu ban she，1986. 2, 103 pages：illustrations；19cm.

《峨眉山民间故事选》，张承业搜集整理；胡雄译. 四川人民出版社.

39. Tales of the Yangtse gorges/compiled and translated by Liang Jie；revised by Jianwen. Beijing：China Travel and Tourism Press，1987. 101 pages，4 pages of plates：illustrations（some color），color map；19cm.

《三峡传说》，梁杰编译. 中国旅游出版社.

40. Dai folk legends/adapted by Yan Wenbian, Zheng Peng, and Gu Qing. Beijing：Foreign Languages Press：Distributed by China International Book Trading Corp.，1988. 191 pages：illustrations；21cm. ISBN：7119000683, 7119000688,0835119688,0835119689

《傣族民间传说》，岩温扁等搜集整理.

41. Tales from Dunhuang/compiled by Chen Yu；translated by Li Guishan, Artem Lozynsky. Beijing, China：New World Press：Distributed by China International Book Trading Corp.，1989. 122 pages，[9] pages of plates (1 folded)：color illustrations, map；18cm. ISBN：7800050858,7800050855

《敦煌故事》，陈钰著；乐仁津，李桂山译. 新世界出版社.

42. Chinese tales：Zhuangzi, sayings and parables and Chinese ghost and love stories/Martin Buber；translated by Alex Page；with an introduction by Irene Eber. Atlantic Highlands, N. J.：Humanities Press International，1991. xxiii, 211 p.；23cm. ISBN：039103698X, 0391036987, 0391036998, 0391036994

Based on Martin Buber's German translation of：Nanhua jing/Zhuangzi and Liao zhai zhi yi/Pu Songling.

《中国故事》，Buber, Martin(1878—1965)（德国翻译家）编译；Page, Alex(1923—)转译为英语. 收录《南华经》54 篇、《聊斋志异》16 篇故事.

（1）Amherst, N. Y.：Humanity Books，1998. xxiii, 211 p.；21cm. ISBN：1573926124, 1573926126, 1573926159, 1573926157

43. Folk tales and legends of the Dai people：the Thai Lue in Yunnan, China/translated from Chinese text by Ying Yi；edited by John Hoskin and Geoffrey Walton. Bangkok, Thailand：D D Books，1992. vi, 162 p.：ill.；22cm. ISBN：9748871614

Ying, Yi 译；Hoskin, John；Walton, Geoffrey（1943—2014）编. 西双版纳民间故事.

44. 龙的传说：英汉对照/林珊著. 长春：时代文艺出版社，1992. 515 页：彩照；20cm. ISBN：7538704132

45. South of the clouds：tales from Yunnan/edited by Lucien Miller；translated by Guo Xu, Lucien Miller, and Xu Kun. Seattle：University of Washington Press, c1994. xiii, 328 p.：ill., map；25cm. ISBN：0295972939,

029597348X

《云南少数民族故事选》，米乐山（Miller, Lucien）编；郭旭等译.

46. Tales for big children：Chinese and Filipino folk stories/Susie L. Tan；with an introduction by Alejandro R. Roces；and a foreword by Damiana L. Eugenio. Malate, Manila, Philippines：De La Salle University Press，1995. 2 v. in 1；ill. （some col.）；21cm. ISBN：9715551033（v. 1），9715551038（v. 1），9715551041（v. 2），9715551045（v. 2）

Contents：v. 1. Myths and legends—v. 2. Fables and other folktales.

Notes：For children ages 10 & up.

Tan, Susie L. 译. 包括对中国民间故事的翻译.

47. A treasury of China's wisdom：a story book for everyone/Chinghua Tang. Beijing：Foreign Languages Press，1996. vii, 407 pages：illustrations, color map；21cm. ISBN：7119018604, 7119018607, 7119018612, 7119018614

《中国古代才智故事》，（美）唐庆华编著.

（1）Beijing：Foreign Languages Press，2003. vii, 407 pages：illustrations, color map；21cm. ISBN：7119018612, 7119018614

（2）3rd printing. Beijing：Foreign Languages Press，2005. vii, 407 páginas：ilustraciones, mapa (color)；21cm. ISBN：7119018614, 7119018612

48. Folk & fairy tales/edited by Martin Hallett & Barbara Karasek. Second edition. Peterborough, Ontario；Orchard Park, NY：Broadview Press，1996. 400 pages：illustrations；23cm. ISBN：1551110636, 1551110639

Contents：Loss of innocence—Sleeping beauties—Damsels in distress—Brain over brawn—The child as hero—Villains—Animal bridegroom—The nineteenth century：Andersen & Wilde—The twentieth century—Illustration—Articles. On fairy-stories/J. R. R. Tolkien—The fairy-tale hero：the image of man in the fairy tale/Max Lüthi—The struggle for meaning/Bruno Bettelheim—Feminism and fairy tales/Karen E. Rowe—Born yesterday：heroes in the Grimms' fairy tales/Maria M. Tatar—Spells of enchantment/Jack Zipes.

中国民间故事. Hallett, Martin（1944—）和 Karasek, Barbara(1954—)编译.

（1）Third edition. Peterborough, Ontario：Broadview Press，2002. xxv, 454 pages：illustrations（some color）；23cm. ISBN：155111495X, 1551114958

（2）Fourth edition. Peterborough, Ontario：Broadview Press，2008. 411 pages，[24] pages of plates：illustrations（some color）；23cm. ISBN：1551118987, 155111898X

（3）Concise ed. Peterborough, Ont.：Broadview Press，2011. 168 pages，[8] pages of plates：illustrations (some color)；23cm. ISBN：1554810185，1554810183

49. The dragon's tale and other animal fables of the Chinese zodiac/[retold and illustrated by] Demi. New York：H. Holt and Co.，c1996. 1 v. (unpaged)：col. ill.；26cm. ISBN：0805034463

Contents：The Rat's tale—The Ox's tale—The Tiger's tale—The Rabbit's tale—The Dragon's tale—The Snake's tale—The Horse's tale—The Goat's tale—The Monkey's tale—The Rooster's tale—The Dog's tale—The Boar's tale.

中国十二生肖故事. Demi 翻译并插图.

50. Chinese zodiac stories/[text by Yuan Jing；translated by Patricia Oger]. Beijing：China Pictorial Pub. House，2007. 63 pages：illustrations；21cm. ISBN：7802200876，7802200873. (A taste of China)

《十二生肖的故事：英文》，袁静编；奥格尔（Oger，P.）译. 中国画报出版社.

51. The twelve zodiac animal/editor in chief, Lü Shun. Beijing：Yan jiu chu ban she, 2009. 234，[5] pages：color illustrations；22cm. ISBN：7801684615，7801684613

《十二生肖》，旅舜主编. 研究出版社.

52. Tales from ancient China's imperial harem/compiled [written] by Yuan Yang and Xiao Yan；translated by Sun Haichen. Beijing：Foreign Languages Press，1998. 182 pages：illustrations；18cm. ISBN：7119020412，7119020419

《中国古代后妃故事》，元阳，晓燕著.

53. The legend of White Snake/Zhao Qingge. Beijing：Xin shiji chubanshe，1998. 267 p. ISBN：7800053865，7800053863. (Classical chinese love stories)

《白蛇传》，赵清阁；White, Paul 译. 英汉对照.

54. Frescoes and fables：mural stories from the Mogao Grottoes in Dunhuang/translated by Li Guishan, edited by Naomi McPherson. Beijing, China：New World Press，1998. 176 pages，[22] pages of plates (some folded)：color illustrations；18cm. ISBN：7800054004，7800054006

《敦煌壁画故事选》，李桂山译，新世界出版社.

55. 西厢记/王实甫；张雪静改编；翻译 匡佩华，刘军. 北京：新世界出版社，2000. 223 pages，4 unnumbered pages of plates：illustrations；21cm. ISBN：7800055523，7800055522. (中国古代爱情故事)

英文题名：The romance of the western bower. 英汉对照.

(1)Beijing：New World Press，2015. 204 pages；21cm. ISBN：7510452710，7510452716

56. The rise and fall of the empires：war stories in ancient China/by Yuan Yang and Ming Ping. Beijing：Foreign Languages Press：Distributed by China International Book Trading，2001. 236 p.：ill.；18cm. ISBN：7119021044

《亡而复生》，元阳，明平编著. 中国古代战争故事.

57. Tales of prime ministers in ancient China/compiled and translated by Cheng Yu. Beijing：Foreign Languages Press：Distributed by China International Book Trading，2001. 257 p.：ill.；18cm. ISBN：7119029177

《中国古代宰相故事》，程宇编译.

58. Tales of Tibet：sky burials, prayer wheels, and wind horses/edited and translated by Herbert J. Batt；foreword by Tsering Shakya. Lanham：Rowman & Littlefield Publishers,2001. xxiv，269 pages：illustrations, maps；24cm. ISBN：0742500527，0742500525，0742500535，0742500532. (Asian voices)

Contents：Vagrant spirit/Ma Yuan—A fiction/Ma Yuan—A ballad of the Himalayas/Ma Yuan—Encounter/Ge Fei—Tibet：a soul knotted on a leather thong/Tashi Dawa—The glory of a wind horse/Tashi Dawa—For whom the bell tolls/Tashi Dawa—An old nun tells her story/Geyang—A God without gender/Yangdon—Wind over the grasslands/Alai—The circular day/Seho—In search of musk/Feng Liang—A blind woman selling red apples/Yan Geling—Stick out the fur on your tongue or it's all a void/Ma Jian.

西藏传民间故事. Batt, Herbert J. (1945—)编译.

59. The Summer Palace：Long Corridor pictures；a collection of stories portrayed by them/by Li Nianpei. 2nd ed. Beijing：China Travel & Tourism Press，2003. 306 p.：ill.；21cm. ISBN：7503221909，7503221903

《颐和园长廊画故事集》，李念培编译. 2 版，中国旅游出版社.

60. 中华敬老故事精选/李宝库主编. 北京：中国社会出版社；2004. 242 页；24cm. ISBN：750870357X

英文题名：Selected China stories of elder-respecting. 本书搜集了 34 个感人至深、催人泪下、富于哲理的中华敬老故事，蕴涵了父母关爱子女、子女孝敬父母的至情至爱.

61. 凤求凰＝The phoenix seeks a mate/徐飞编著；[翻译保尔·怀特]. 北京：新世界出版社，2004. 271 pages：illustrations；21cm. ISBN：7801873068，7801873064. (中国古代爱情故事＝Classical Chinese love stories)

英汉对照

62. Sights with stories in old Beijing. Beijing, China：Foreign Languages Press：Distributed by China International Book Trading Corp.，2005. 203 pages：illustrations, map；18cm. ISBN：7119037498，7119037493. (Panda books)

Contents：The Temple of Heaven—The Imperial Palace—The Great Wall at Badaling—The Summer Palace—Beihai Park—Zhongshan Park—The Fragrant Hills—Jade Spring Mountain—The ruins of the Yuanmingyuan—Taoranting Park—The Lama Temple—The Ox Street mosque—The Maioying Temple—The

White Cloud Temple—The Great Bell Temple—The Sleeping Buddha Temple—Tanzhe Monastery—The Dragon Spring Temple—Black Dragon Pool—The Ten Crossings—Phoenix Ridge—Lugou Bridge—Old Beijing.

《北京旅游点的传说：英文》，熊振儒等编译. 外文出版社（熊猫丛书）. 收录了四十七个传说故事.

63. Dragon tales. Beijing, China：Foreign Languages Press，2005. 245 pages：illustrations；18cm. ISBN：7119037501, 7119037509. (Panda books)

《龙的传说：英文》，戴乃迭等编译. 外文出版社（熊猫丛书）. 本书收录了三十五个传说故事.

64. Beijing legends/Jin Shoushen；translated by Gladys Yang. Beijing：Foreign Languages Press，2005. 141 pages：illustrations；18cm. ISBN：711903748X, 7119037486. (Panda Books)

《北京的传说：英文》，金受申著. 外文出版社（熊猫丛书）. 本书收录了二十六篇有关北京的民间传说.

65. 中国四大民间故事：英汉对照/丁祖馨编写. 北京：商务印书馆，2006. 12；18cm. ISBN：7100048818, 7100048811

英文题名：The four most popular folk tales of China

本书主要选择了《白蛇传》《梁山伯与祝英台》《牛郎织女》《孟姜女》等四个故事.

66. 中国四大民间故事集：汉英对照/孙月星著；赵春红译. 南京：南京师范大学出版社，2006. 281 页；18cm. ISBN：7811015013, 7811015010

英文题名：Anthology of China's four folk tales

为中英文对照读物，包括《白蛇传》《梁山伯与祝英台》《牛郎织女》《孟姜女》四大经典民间故事. 英汉对照.

67. The magic lotus lantern and other tales from the Han Chinese/Haiwang Yuan；foreword by Michael Ann Williams. Westport, Conn.：Libraries Unlimited，2006. xvi, 239 pages，[8] pages of plates：illustrations（some color），map；26cm. ISBN：1591582946, 1591582946. (World folklore series)

Notes：54 folktales, myths, legends, and popular tales from China

袁海旺编译. 收录 54 个中国神话传说和故事.

68. 白蛇传：汉英对照/顾希佳编著；黄茹樱，叶艳萍译. 广州：广东教育出版社，2006. 162 页：图；20cm. ISBN：7540664304, 7540664305. （中国经典文化故事系列. 中国传说故事）

英文题名：The legend of White Snake.

69. 孟姜女哭长城：汉英对照/顾希佳编著；沈红译. 广州：广东教育出版社，2006. 111 页：图；20cm. ISBN：7540664339, 7540664336. （中国经典文化故事系列. 中国传说故事）

英文题名：Mengjiangnü weeping over the Great Wall

70. 牛郎织女：汉英对照/顾希佳编著；周远梅译. 广州：广东教育出版社，2006. 114 页：图；20cm. ISBN：7540664320, 7540664329. （中国经典文化故事系列. 中国传说故事）

英文题名：The oxherd and the weaving maiden

71. Butterfly lovers：stories of Chinese legends/Gu Xijia bian zhu；Ye Yanping, Huang Ruying yi；Chang Xinping ying wen shen jiao. Guangzhou：Guangdong jiao yu chu ban she，2006. 158 p.：ill.；21cm. ISBN：7540664312, 7540664312. (Chinese classic cultural stories series＝中国经典文化故事系列)

《梁山伯与祝英台：中国传说故事》，顾希佳编著；叶艳萍，黄茹樱译；常新萍英文审校.

72. 中国民间故事精粹＝Selected Chinese folk tales/顾希佳改编；宋恒，胡小兵英译；汪榕培英文审校. 广州：广东教育出版社，2007. 2，4，201 pages：illustrations；21cm. ISBN：7540667504, 7540667508. （中国经典文化故事系列＝Chinese classic cultural stories series）

73. 中国历代典藏故事精选：［英汉对照］＝Selections of classical Chinese tales/顾希佳改编；颜莉，郁邓，周忠浩英译. 广州：广东教育出版社，2007. 224 p.：ill.；21cm. ISBN：7540667559, 7540667559. （中国经典文化故事系列）

74. Princess peacock：tales from the other peoples of China/retold by Haiwang Yuan；foreword by Zheng Chunde. Westport, Conn.：Libraries Unlimited，2008. xvii, 302 p.，[8] p. of plates：ill.（some col.），map；27cm. ISBN：1591584162, 1591584167. (World folklore series)

中国民间故事. 袁海旺编译.

75. The phoenix seeks a mate：the peacock flies southeast/adaptation by Xu Fei；[translation by Paul White]. New York：Better Link Press，2008. 238 pages；21cm. ISBN：1602202092, 1602202095. (Wen hua Zhongguo；Love stories and tragedies from classic Chinese operas；1)

《凤求凰》和《孔雀东南飞》，徐飞编；White, Paul 译.

76. The legend of white snake；and, Liang Shanbo and Zhu Yingtai（The butterfly lovers）/adaptation by Zhao Qingge；translation by Paul White, Thomas Shou. New York：Better Link Press，2008. 251 pages；21cm. ISBN：1602202115, 1602202117. （Love stories and tragedies from classic Chinese operas；；3；Wen hua Zhongguo）

《白蛇传》与《梁山伯与祝英台》，赵清阁（1914—）；White, Paul 和 Shou, Thomas 合译.

77. Treasury of Chinese folktales：beloved myths and legends from the Middle Kingdom/retold by Shelley Fu；illustrations by Patrick Yee；Chinese calligraphy by Dr. Sherwin Fu. Tokyo；Rutland, Vt.：Tuttle Pub.，c2008. 129 p：col. ill.；31cm. ISBN：0804838078

Contents：Tales of creation：Pan Gu and the creation—Nu Wo, the mother of mankind—Ho Yi the archer—Morality tales：Journey to the West—The man in the moon—Tales of love：The story of the white snake—The heavenly river.

Notes：Previously published under title：Ho Yi the archer and other classic Chinese tales/retold by Shelley Fu；illustrated by Joseph F. Abboreno. 2001.

中国民间故事. Fu，Shelley（1966—）改写；Yee，Patrick 手插图.

78. 西湖的故事：英汉对照/（美）霍尔瓦特·伊莎贝拉 （Horvath Izabella）编译. 杭州：西泠印社出版社，2009. 141，113 页；21cm. ISBN：7807354956，780735495X

英文题名：Tales of West Lake. 本书用中英文编写了二十二个有关杭州各个景点的民间故事.

79. 长城民间传说/张鹤珊著. 北京：五洲传播出版社，2009. 159 页；21cm. ISBN：7508515281，7508515285

英文题名：Great Wall folktales. 本书收集了 25 个与长城相关的民间传说故事.

80. 中国少数民族民间故事选/边赞襄编著；曹华民译. 武汉：湖北教育出版社，2010. 185 页；26cm. ISBN：7535158673，7535158676

英文题名：Folk tales from China's ethnic minorities. 选编了其中我国 23 个少数民族的 86 则脍炙人口的故事.

81. Folk tales/compiled by Wu Min. Beijing：China Intercontinental Press, 2011. 166 pages：color illustrations；19cm. ISBN：7508517728，7508517725.（Classic stories of China）

《中国民间故事》，伍民编. 五洲传播出版社.

82. Chinese tales of vampires, beasts, genies and men：selections from Folklore Chinois moderne, 1909 by Le'on Wieger/English translations by Derek Bryce；edited by Henry G. Smith. Ceredigion：Llanerch Press, 2011. 200 p.：ill.；21cm. ISBN：1861431570，1861431578

中国民间故事. Wieger，Le'on（1856—1933）法译；Bryce，Derek 英译.

83. The Columbia anthology of Chinese folk and popular literature/edited by Victor H. Mair and Mark Bender. New York：Columbia University Press, c2011. xvi, 640 p.：map；24cm. ISBN：0231153126，0231153120，0231153133，0231153139，0231526739，0231526733.（Translations from the Asian classics）

《哥伦比亚中国民间和通俗文学集》，梅维恒（Mair，Victor H.，1943—）（美国翻译家），Bender，Mark 译.

84. Wisdom stories/compiled by Wu Min. Beijing：China Intercontinental Press, 2011. 166 pages：color illustrations；19cm. ISBN：7508519036，7508519035.（Classic stories of China）

《中国智慧故事》，伍民编. 五洲传播出版社.

85. Eight dragons on the roof and other tales：traditional dragon stories from China/Compiled by Feng Yan；[Editors：Timothy Neidermann, Chris Robyn]. South San Francisco：China Books Inc., 2012. 154 pages；22cm. ISBN：0835100045，0835100049

Summary："Collection of traditional folktales from China dating from myths and legends to the 19th Century；all stories feature a dragon theme or motif"—Provided by publisher.

Contents：Li Jing—The Dragon King's Daughter—The Monk Xuan Zhao—Liu Guanci—Madam Wei—Ren Xu—The Old Dame by the Fenshui River—The Rakshas and the Sea Market—The Princess of the West Lake—Legend of the Four Dragons—Dragon Dance at Lantern Festival Time—The Bright Pearl—The Looking-to-Mother Shoal—The Dragon Eye—Eight Dragons on the Roof—Geshan and Dragon Pearl—Two Magic Gourds—Princess Anpo—The Story of White Dragon Mountain—The Gorge Opened by Mistake—Baotu Spring—The Legend of Green Dragon Pond—Dragon Mother's Temple—Tripod Lake and Golden Lotus Flowers—Meidan the Dragon's Daughter—The Dragon King's Daughter and Guanyin—The Nine Dragons and the Tiantai Mountains—The Copper Kettle with the Leaky Bottom—Dragon-Lions and Dragon Pearls—The Yanyu Herb and the Greedy Dragon—Carving Dragons—The Dragon Tablet—A Dragon and Phoenix Match—Dragon Girl

中国民间故事. Yan，Feng，Neidermann，Timothy，Robyn，Chris 编译，收录自古到 19 世纪的与龙有关的神话与传说.

86. Tibetan folktales/Haiwang Yuan, Awang Kunga, and Bo Li. Santa Barbara, CA：Libraries Unlimited, 2015. xii, 202 pages：illustrations；26cm. ISBN：1610694704，1610694708.（World folklore series）

Contents：Land—People, Population, and Demographics—Language—History—Religion—Clothing and Ornaments—Architecture—Customs—Calendar—Festivals and Celebrations—Fine Arts—Performing Arts—Literature—Storytelling—Medicine—Food and Drink—Butter Tea（Po Cha）—Honey Tsampa—Mint Lamb Ribs—Tibetan Meat Pie（Shapale）—Tibetan Steamed Dumplings（Momos）—Tibetan Noodle Soup（Guthuk）—Stir-Fried Yak Meat with Pine Mushrooms—Tibetan Shredded Lamb Salad—Fried Cheese Balls—Crafts—Tibetan Doll—Beaded Necklace—Tibetan Opera Mask—Wind-Horse Prayer Banners—Sports and Games—Wolf Catches Lamb—Tiger Catching Lambs—Looking for a Wool Ball—Catch Cobblestones—Tales of Origin—Origin of the Human World—Monkeys Became Humans—Origin of Highland Barley—How Come Rabbits Have Harelips and Short Tails？—Animal Tales—Clever Lamb—Rabbit and a Lion—"Leaking" Is Coming—Louse and Flea—Tales of Heroes, Deities, and Legendary Figures—King Gesar—Tibetan King's Wise Emissary—Aku Tonpa and the King—Man Who Divines with a Pig's Head—Magic Tales—Pearl-Shoe Princess—Diamond Fairy—Frog Husband—Three Hairs from the Sun—Kind-Hearted Life Snatcher—Legends about Places—Four Girls Mountains—Goddess of Namtso Lake—Goddess of Mount Everest—Jokhang Monastery—Tales of Love and Romance—Lobsang Lodrun and Tsering Kyimo—Lama Tangpe and Maid Pezom—Love Story of Salt and Tea—Wife's Unswerving Love—Death Doth Not Keep Us Apart—Moral Tales—Sister and Her Sisters-in-Law—Vulnerable Part of a Fish—Elephant and Monkey—Lofty Tortoise.

西藏民间故事.袁海旺,Kunga,Awang,Li,Bo(1981—)合译.

寓言

1. Ancient Chinese parables/selected and edited by Yü Hsiu Sen; translated by Kwei-ting Sen; with a pref. by H. J. C. Grierson. Shanghai：Commercial Press, 1924. xvi, 80 pages；19cm.

   《中国寓言》,孙毓修选;孙贵定(1892—)译.英汉对照.

   (1)Shanghai, China, The Commercial Press, limited，1927. XVI, 86 p. cm.

   (2)Shanghai, China, Commercial Press，1935. xvi, 86 pages；19cm.

   (3)2nd ed. ［Folcroft, Pa.］Folcroft Library Editions, 1974. xvi, 86 pages；24cm. ISBN：0841476454, 0841476455

   (4)2nd ed. ［Norwood, Pa.］: Norwood Editions, 1976. pagescm. ISBN：0848224353, 0848224356

   (5)2nd ed. Philadelphia：R. West, 1978. xvi, 86 pages；23cm. ISBN：0849224497, 0849224492

2. Fables/Feng, Hsueh-feng; translated by Gladys Yang. Peking：Foreign Languages Press, 1953. 70 p.：illus.；27cm.

   《雪峰寓言》,冯雪峰(1903—);戴乃迭(Yang Gladys,1919—1999)译.

   (1) Beijing：Foreign Languages Press：Distributed by China Publications Centre (Guoji Shudian), 1983. ii, 99 p.：ill.；21cm. ISBN：0835110850. (Modern Chinese literature)

3. Ancient Chinese fables. ［Translated by Yang Hsien-yi and Gladys Yang］. Peking：Foreign Languages Press, 1957. 60 p.

   《中国古代寓言选》,杨宪益(1915—2009),戴乃迭(Yang, Gladys,1919—1999)译.

   (1)Peking：Foreign Languages Press, 1958.

   (2)Beijing, China：Foreign Languages Press：Distributed by Guoji Shudian (China Publications Centre), 1981. 86 p.：ill.；21cm.

   (3)Beijing：Wai wen chu ban she, 2000. 241 p.；13cm. ISBN：7119026917, 7119026916, 7119025247, 7119025244. (FLP 汉英对照经典读本. 古典精华；3)

   (4)Beijing：Wai wen chu ban she, 2001. 263 p.；21cm. ISBN：7119028871. (Echo of classics)

4. Chinese fables and anecdotes/［illustrations by Feng Zikai］. Peking：Foreign Languages Press, 1958. 52 p.：ill.；21cm.

   《中国古代寓言选》,丰子恺(1898—1975)插图.

   (1)2nd ed. Peking：Foreign Languages Press，1962. 52 pages；illustrations；21cm.

   (2)3rd ed. Peking：Foreign Languages Press，1964. 52, ［1］

pages：illustrations；21cm.

5. Chinese fables/edited by Kathy Ch'iu; with illus. by Irene Aronson. Mount Vernon, N. Y. , Peter Pauper Press ［1967］. 62 p. col. illus. 19cm.

   中国古代寓言. Lyle, Katherine Ch'iu(1939—)编译.

   (1)Tokyo：Toppan Co. , 1990. 62 pages；illustrations；19cm.

6. Ancient Chinese fables retold/S. J. Hu. Hong Kong：Kelly & Walsh, c1975. 50 p.；19cm.

   中国古代寓言故事. Hu, S. J.译.

7. 100 ancient Chinese fables：Chinese-English/by K. L. Kiu. Xianggang：Shang wu yin shu guan Xianggang fen guan, 1985. 12, 5, 224 p.；19cm. ISBN：9620710576. (一百丛书)

   《中国古代寓言一百篇》,乔车洁玲(Qiao Che Jieling)选译. 英汉对照. 香港：商务印书馆香港分馆出版.

8. Contemporary Chinese fables. Beijing：Zhongguo wen xue chu ban she, 1990 (1991 printing). 177 p.：ill；20cm. ISBN：7507100464. (Panda books)

   《中国当代寓言选》.中国文学出版社出版.英汉对照.

9. Chinese fables and wisdom：insights for better living/by Tom Te-wu Ma. Lake Worth, Fla. : Gardner Pr. , 1996. 121 pages；22cm. ISBN：0898762081, 0898762082

   中国寓言故事. Ma, Tom 译.

   (1)Chinese fables & wisdom：insights for better living/by Tom Te-wu Ma. New York：Barricade Books, 1997. 144 pages；22cm. ISBN：1569801231, 1569801239

10. Chinese fables/by Tzu-shen Fang, Nai-yu Huang; Guo li bian yi guan zhu bian. Tai chu ban. Taibei Shi：Zheng zhong shu ju, Min guo 87 ［1998］iii, 2, 311 p.：col. ill. ；22cm. ISBN：9570911514. (中国语文补充读物；10＝Supplementary Chinese readers；v. 10)

    《中国寓言故事》,编著者方祖燊, 黄酒毓；国立编译馆主编. 台北市：正中书局. 中英对照.

11. 101 classic Chinese fables/［translator］, Howard Zhai; ［general editor, Ruth Martin］. Richmond, B. C. : Dragon Fly Publications, 1998. vii, 147 p.：ill.；22cm. ISBN：0968299504, 0968299500

    Variant title：One hundred and one classic Chinese fables
    101 个中国寓言故事. Zhai , Howard 译.

12. 中国古代寓言选/乔车洁玲编选、英译；冷林蔚白话文翻译. 北京：中国对外翻译出版公司,2007. 285 页；21cm. ISBN：7500118145. (中译经典文库・中华传统文化精粹)

    英文题名：Ancient Chinese fables

13. Ancient fables/compiled by Wu Min. Beijing：China Intercontinental Press, 2011. 150 pages：color illustrations；19cm. ISBN：7508517711, 7508517717. (Classic stories of China)

    《中国古代寓言故事》,伍民编. 五洲传播出版社.

14. Chinese fables："the Dragon Slayer" and other timeless tales of wisdom/Shiho S. Nunes; illustrated by Lak-Khee Tay-Audouard. Tokyo；Rutland, Vt. : Tuttle, c2013. 63 p.：col. ill. ；27cm. ISBN：0804841528, 0804841527

Contents：The practical bride—The wrong audience—Stealing the bell—Sakyamuni and Lao-Tse—The same sickness—"Everybody's talking about it!"—The vigilant sentry—Kwan Yin, the goddess of Mercy—The King of Beasts—A small gift—Cooking the duck—What's in a name? —The same difference—Scaring the tigers—The dragon slayer—No takers—The egg—Welcome guests—Change of fashion.

Summary：An illustrated retelling of nineteen fables and tales from China, each of which features a nugget of ancient folk wisdom and introduces aspects of traditional Chinese culture and lore

中国寓言故事. Nunes, Shiho S. (1917—)译；Tay-Audouard, L. K. 插图.

15. 中国经典寓言故事/李火秀，柯明星编著. 杭州：浙江大学出版社，2016. [21]，239 页；图；21cm. ISBN：7308160704. （"魅力汉语·悦读经典"丛书）

英文题名：Chinese classic fables. 英汉对照.

神话

1. Chinese fairy stories/by Norman Hinsdale Pitman. New York：T. Y. Crowell & Co., 1910. 4 preliminary leaves, 3—183 pages color frontispiece, color plates 20cm.

Contents：Yow-to's first lesson. —The boy who slept. —The boy and the porridge. —The Gods know. —Lo-sun, the blind boy. —Sing Li's fortune. —Fairy Old Boy and the tiger. —Yu-kong and the demon. —The boy who became emperor. —The ashes of deceit.

Pitman, Norman Hinsdale(1876—1925)编译. 收录中国神话故事.

(1) London：G. G. Harrap & Co., 1923. 230 pages color frontispiece, color plates；20cm.

(2) new ed. New York：Thomas Y. Crowell Co., 1924. 4 preliminary leaves, 230 pages color frontispiece, color plates；20cm.

(3) New York, Crowell, 1936. 230 pages；color illustrations

(4) New York, Thomas Y. Crowell Co., 1938. 230 pages：color frontispiece, color plates

　　增加了 4 个故事

(5) New York：Thomas Y. Crowell Co., 1945. 230 pages：illustrations；20cm.

(6) Taipei，Ch'eng Wen Pub. Co., 1974. 230 pages：illustrations；20cm.

2. Myths & legends of China/by E. T. C. Werner; with thirty-two illustrations in colours by Chinese artists. London：George G. Harrap & Co., 1922. 453 pages, [32] pages of plates：color illustrations；22cm.

Contents：The sociology of the Chinese—On Chinese mythology—Cosmogony—P'an Ku and the creation myth—The gods of China—Myths of the stars—Myths of thunder, lightning, wind, and rain—Myths of the waters—Myths of fire—Myths of epidemics, medicine, exorcism, etc. —The goddess of mercy—The eight immortals—The guardian of the gate of heaven—A battle of the gods—How the monkey became a god—Fox legends—Miscellaneous legends.

中国神话与传说. Werner, E. T. C. (Edward Theodore Chalmers, 1864—1954)编. 包括《西游记》中的孙悟空故事.

(1) London：G. G. Harrap & Co., Ltd., 1924. 453 pages, plates：illustrations；25cm.

(2) London, George G. Harrap & Co., 1928. 543, [1] pages color frontispiece, color plates 25cm.

(3) London：G. G. Harrap, 1934. 453 pages, color plates；22cm.

(4) Singapore：Graham Brash, 1984. 453 p. : il. ; 22cm. ISBN：981218046X, 9812180469

(5) London：Sinclair Browne, 1984. 453 p. , ; 22cm. ISBN：0863000355, 0863000355

(6) London, England：Bracken Books, 1986. 453 pages, [28] pages of plates：color illustrations；23cm. ISBN：1851700218, 1851700219

(7) New York：Dover Publications, 1994. 453 pages：illustrations；22cm. ISBN：0486280926, 0486280929

(8) Norwalk, Con. : Easton, 1997. 453 p. ; 24cm.

(9) [Montana]：Kessinger Pub., 2003. 453 pages：illustrations；22cm. ISBN：076615372X, 0766153721

(10) [Rockville, Md.]：Wildside Press, 2005. 290 pages；23cm. ISBN：159224243X, 1592242436

(11) Illustrated ed. [United Kingdom]：Dodo Press, 2007. 349 pages：illustrations；23cm. ISBN：1406510149, 1406510140

3. Chinese myths and fantasies, retold by Cyril Birch. Illustrated by Joan Kiddell Monroe. New York：H. Z. Walck, 1961. 200 p. illus. 23cm. (Oxford myths and legends)

《中国神话》，白之(Birch, Cyril, 1925—)(美国汉学家)编译.

(1) Tales from China/retold by Cyril Birch; illustrated by Rosamund Fowler. Pbk. ed. Oxford；New York：Oxford University Press, 2000. 195 p. : ill. ; 20cm. ISBN：019275078X, 0192750785

4. The rainmakers and other tales from China/adapted by D. H. Howe; from Chinese myths and fantasies by Cyril Birch; illustrated by Joan Kiddell-Monroe; illustrated by Joan Kiddell-Monroe. Kuala Lumpur：Oxford University Press, 1963. 95 pages：illustrations；19cm. (Stories told and retold series)

Contents：The rainmakers. —The dinner that cooked itself. —How marriages are made. —The three precious packets. —The inn of donkeys. —The man who nearly became fishpaste. —The pavilion of peril. —The greatest archer. —The flood. —The revolt of the demons.

《中国神话》，白之(Birch, Cyril 1925—)译自中文；Howe, D. H. Kiddell-Monroe 改编.

5. Chinese fairy tales and fantasies/translated and edited by Moss Roberts; with the assistance of C. N. Tay. New York：Pantheon Books, 1979. xx, 259 p. : ill. ; 25cm. ISBN：039442039X

中国神话故事. 罗慕士（Roberts，Moss，1937—）编译.

6. 100 Chinese myths and fantasies：Chinese-English/Ding Wangdao. Xianggang：Shang wu yin shu guan, 1988. 16, 6, 443 p.；19cm. ISBN：9620710908.（Yi bai cong shu＝一百丛书）

《中国神话及志怪小说一百篇》，丁往道选译. 英汉对照.

7. The eight immortals of Taoism：legends and fables of popular Taoism/translated and edited by Kowk Man Ho and Joanne O'Brien；introduction by Martin Palmer. New York：Meridian, 1990. 156 pages：illustrations；21cm. ISBN：0452010705, 0452010703

八仙故事. Kwok，Man-Ho（1943—）和 O'Brien，Joanne（1959—）合译. 道教神话.

8. Stories from Chinese mythology/translated and edited from Yuan Ke's newly edited mythical stories and translation of a hundred selected myths by Ke Wen-li & Hou Mei-xue. [Tianjin]：Nankai University Press, 1991. 7, 438 pages：illustrations；19cm. ISBN：7310003519, 7310003518

《中国神话故事》，柯文礼，侯梅雪编译. 南开大学出版社.

9. 中国神话故事：汉英对照/刘长军，唐君玫编著. 广州：广东教育出版社，2006. 234 页；20cm. ISBN：7540664347, 7540664343.（中国经典文化故事系列）

10. Creation of the universe/written by Cui Maoxin & Song Dongyang；illustrated by Tai Shuangyuan. Beijing：China Intercontinental Press, 2006. 73 pages：illustrations；23cm. ISBN：7508510354, 7508510356.（Chinese mythology）

《中国创世神话》，崔茂新，宋东阳著；汉佳，王国振译.

英文题名：Stories of Chinese myths. 收集了约 50 个在中国广为流传的神话故事.

11. Chinese mythology：stories of creation and invention/Mythologie chinoise. English；illustrations by Chen Jiang Hong；translated from the French by Michael Hariton and Claudia Bedrick. 1st American ed. New York：Enchanted Lion Books, c2007. 78 p.：col. ill.；23cm. ISBN：1592700745, 1592700748

Contents：The three sovereigns—Stories of Pang-Gu—The first of the five emperors—Yu the great—The Chinese paradises—The ten suns and the moon—The herder and the weaver—The invention of silk—Pronunciation guide.

《中国神话》，Helft，Claude 法译；Hariton，Michael 和 Bedrick，Claudia 从法译本转译成英文.

12. 中国神话及志怪小说选/丁往道编选、英译；王治卿白话文翻译. 北京：中国对外翻译出版公司，2008. 434 页；21cm. ISBN：7500118398.（中译经典文库·中华传统文化精粹）

英文题名：Chinese myths and fantasies.

13. Chinese myths & legends：legends of the universe, deities and heroes/Chen Lianshan；translated by Zhang Fengru & Chen Shanshan. Beijing：China Intercontinental Press, 2009. 143：ill.（some col.）；23cm. ISBN：7508513232, 7508513231.（Cultural China series）

《中国神话传说》，陈连山著；张凤茹，陈姗姗英译.

(1) Updated ed. Cambridge, UK；New York：Cambridge University Press, 2011. 143 pages：illustrations（some color）；23cm. ISBN：0521186797, 052118679X.（Introductions to Chinese culture）

14. 神话传说/徐刚编著. 合肥：黄山书社，2016. 132 页：图；23cm. ISBN：7546141725.（印象中国）

英文题名：Chinese mythology and legends. 英汉对照.

15. 中国经典神话故事/李火秀，邓琳著. 杭州：浙江大学出版社，2016. [17]，197 页：图；21cm. ISBN：7308160711.（"魅力汉语·悦读经典"丛书）

英文题名：Chinese classic myths. 英汉对照.

谜语、笑话、幽默故事

1. Quips from a Chinese jest-book/translated by Herbert A. Giles. Shanghai, Kelly and Walsh, Limited, 1925. 3 p. l., 146, iii p., 1 l. 20cm.

《笑林广记》，翟理斯（Giles，Herbert Allen，1845—1935）（英国汉学家）译. 笑话.

2. 笑林广记选/（清）游戏主人编著. 北京：外文出版社，2011. 137 页；24cm. ISBN：787119067568, 7119067567

英文题名：A collection of classic Chinese jokes

3. Warm-soft village：Chinese stories, sketches and essays/translated by Howard S. Levy. Tokyo：Dai Nippon Insatsu, 1964. 142 p.：ill.；22cm.

《温柔乡》，Levy，Howard S.（Howard Seymour，1923—）编译. 中国性轶闻.

4. Chinese sex jokes in traditional times. [Taipei]：Chinese Association for Folklore, c1973. 2, 361 p.；21cm.（Sino-Japanese sexology classics series；v. 5.）.（Asian folklore and social life monographs；v. 58.）

中国古代性笑话. Levy，Howard S.（Howard Seymour，1923—）译.

5. Traditional comic tales/Zhang Shouchen and others；translated by Gladys Yang. Beijing, China：Chinese Literature：Distributed by China Publications Centre, 1983. 141 pages：illustrations；19cm. ISBN：0835111652, 0835111652.（Panda books）

《单口相声故事选》，张寿臣等著；戴乃迭（Yang，Gladys，1919—1999）译. 幽默.

6. Wit and humor from old Cathay/translated by Jon Kowallis. Beijing, China：Chinese Literature：Distributed by China International Book Trading Corp., 1986. 210 pages；18cm. ISBN：0835113337, 0835113335.（Panda books）

《历代笑话选》

7. 中国幽默故事选：汉英对照/卢允中编选、英译. 北京：中国对外翻译出版公司，2007. 261 页；21cm. 7500118152.（中译经典文库·中华传统文化精粹）

英文题名：Chinese jokes through the ages

I9　儿童文学

1. The jeweled sea；a book of Chinese fairy tales, edited with an introduction by Hartwell James；with forty illustrations by John

R. Neill. Philadelphia, Henry Altemus Company, 〔c1906〕. x p., 1 l, 13—102 p., 1 l incl. front., illus., plates.; 19cm. (Altemus' fairy tales series)

中国神话故事. James, Hartwell 译；Neill, John R. (John Rea) 插图. 儿童读物.

2. Chinese fairy tales/told in English by Herbert A. Giles. London：Gowans & Gray, Ltd., 1911. 42, 〔6〕 p.; 15cm. (Gowan's international library; no. 38)

Contents：The magic pillow—The stone monkey—Stealing peaches—The painted skin—The wonderful pear-tree—The country of gentlemen—Learning magic—Theft of a duck—Living for ever—Football on a lake—The flower fairies—The talking bird.

中国神话故事. 翟理斯(Giles, Herbert Allen, 1845—1935) (英国汉学家)编译. 儿童读物.

(1)Boston, Leroy Philips, 1920. 42 pages

3. Chinese fairy tales：forty stories told by almond-eyed folk. 2nd ed. New York；London, G. P. Putnam's Sons, 1912. 〔x〕(2) 194 pages frontispiece 24 plates

Contents：The five queer brothers—The three talismans—The origin of ants—The mistake of the apes—The moon-cake—The fool of the family—A fool who tried to be like his brother-in-law—A dreadful boar—The two melons—The blind boy's fall—The fairy serpent—What the birds said—The man in a shell—The young head of the family—Prospect and retrospect—A foreordained match—Marrying a simpleton—Baling with a sieve—The widow and the sagacious magistrate—A lawyer as a debtor—The singing prisoner—Self-convicted—The ladle that fell from the moon—A wife's vengeance—Stolen garlic—Two frugal men—The most frugal of men—Misapplied wit—Similar diseases—A dream inspired—A fortuitous application—Jean Valjean in Cathay—A polite idiosyncrasy—Verified predictions—The three sworn brothers—The peasant-girl's prisoner—Crabs in plenty—False economy—The thriftless wife—A wife with two husbands.

中国神话故事. Fielde, Adele M. (Adele Marion, 1839—1916) 译，收录 40 个中国神话，首版于 1893 年. 儿童读物.

(1)〔Whitefish, MT〕：Kessinger Publishing, 2009. xi, 194 pages；plates；24cm. ISBN：1120228840, 1120228840. (Kessinger Publishing's legacy reprints)

4. The Chinese fairy book, ed. by Dr. R. Wilhelm, tr. after original sources by Frederick H. Martens, with six illustrations in color by George W. Hood. New York：Frederick A. Stokes Company, 〔c1921〕. 329 p. col. front., col. plates. 21cm.

Summary：A collection of Chinese fairy tales, including "The Three Rhymsters", "The bird with Nine Heads", and "The Herb Boy and the Weaving Maiden"

中国童话故事. Martens, Frederick Herman(1874—1932)译. 转译自德文版卫礼贤的《中国民间故事集》一书. 收录四篇《西游记》故事等.

(1)London, T. F. Unwin Ltd., 1922. vi, 〔8〕, 329, 〔1〕 pages

color frontispiece, color plates

(2)Mineola, N. Y.：Dover Publications, 2008. vii, 213 p.：col. ill.；22cm. ISBN：0486454351,0486454355

5. Chinese fairy tales. New York：Thomas Y. Crowell co. 〔c1924〕. 4 p. l., 230 p. col. front. col. plates.；20cm.

中国神话故事. Pitman, Norman Hinsdale(1876—)译. 儿童读物.

(1)New York：Thomas Y. Crowell Co.,1938. 30 pages color frontispiece, color plates

(2)New York：Thomas Y. Crowell Company 〔1945〕. 2 p. l., 230 p. front., col. plates. 20cm.

6. Chinese rhymes for children, with a few from India, Japan and Korea, translated and edited by Isaac Taylor Headland... illustrated by Sui Wesley Chan. New York：London 〔etc.〕 Fleming H. Revell Company 〔c1933〕. 156 p. illus.；23cm.

中国儿童诗歌, Headland, Isaac Taylor(1859—1942)编译.

7. Chinese fairy tales and folk tales, collected and translated by Wolfram Eberhard. London, K. Paul, Trench, Trubner & Co., Ltd., 1937. xiv. 304 p.；22cm.

Notes："Translated from the German by Desmond Parsons."

中国神话故事. Eberhard, Wolfram (1909—) 德译；Parsons, Desmond 英译自德语版. 儿童读物.

(1)New York：Dutton, 1938. xiv, 304 pages；22cm.

(2)〔Folcroft, Pa.〕：Folcroft Library Editions, 1974. xiv, 304 p. 26cm. ISBN：0841439400

(3)Norwood, Pa.：Norwood Editions, 1977. xiv, 304 p.；26cm. ISBN：0848206916

(4)Philadelphia：R. West, 1978. xiv, 304 p.；26cm. ISBN：08492076301851.

8. New China through her children's eyes/edited by the Chinese People's National Committee in Defence of Children. Peking：Foreign Languages Press, 1953. 73 p.：ill.

《儿童创作选》,中国人民保卫儿童委员会编.

9. Stories of Chinese young pioneers 〔by〕 Chang Tien-yi. Peking：Foreign Languages Press, 1954. 49 p.：ill.；21cm.

《少先先锋队员的故事》,张天翼(1906—1985).

(1)2 nd. ed. Peking：Foreign Languages Press，1962. 45 p.：ill

10. Fairy tales of China/〔retold〕by Peter Lum; illustrated by G. W. Miller. London, Cassell；c1959. unpaged. illus. 21cm.

中国神话故事. Lum, Peter(1911—)译. 儿童读物.

11. Chinese fairy tales, by Chien Gochuen; with illustrations by the author. 6 p. l., 73 p. illus., col. plates. 23cm.

Contents：The king of ants. —The man in the teapot. —The good luck of a foolish boy. —Yin, the wonder child. —The disappearing sorcery. —Ah Fu and the fox-goblin.

中国神话故事. Ch'ien, Ko-ch'uan 翻译并插图. 儿童读物.

(1) [Taipei]: [Book World Co], 1962. 73 pages: illustrations; 19cm.

12. Chinese fairy tales. Illus. by Serge Rizzato. New York: Golden Press [c1960]. 154 p. illus. 35cm. (A Deluxe golden book.)

中国神话故事. Ponsot, Marie 译. 儿童读物.

(1) Rev. ed. New York: Golden Press, 1973. 68 pages: color illustrations; 35cm.

13. The scarecrow: a collection of stories for children, Peking: Foreign Languages Press, 1961. 97 p. col. illus. 21cm.

《叶圣陶童话选》, 叶圣陶 (1894—1988).

(1) 2nd ed. Peking: Foreign Languages Press, 1963. iv, 96 pages, [9] leaves of plates: color illustrations; 21cm.

(2) 4th ed. Peking: Foreign Languages Press, 1978. 97 pages, [9] leaves of plates: color illustrations; 21cm.

(3) Beijing: Foreign Languages Press, 1986. 94 pages, [9] leaves of plates: color illustrations; 21cm. ISBN: 0835117391, 0835117395

14. Chinese folk and fairy tales. Illustrated by Maurice Brevannes. [1st American ed.] New York: Putnam, 1963. 191 p. illus. 22cm. (Folk and fairy tales from many lands)

Summary: Thirty-three traditional Chinese folk and fairy tales, including The Man Who Sold Thunder, The Faithful Wife, The Two Fools, The Five Tiger General, and others.

Notes: First published in 1958 under title: Chinese fairy tales.

中国民间和神话故事. Bonnet, Leslie 译; Brevannes, Maurice 插图, 收录 33 个中国童话. 首版于 1958 年.

15. Folktales of China/edited by Wolfram Eberhard; collected and translated from the Chinese by Wolfram Eberhard; translated from the German by Desmond Parsons. Revised edition. London: Routledge & Paul, 1965. 67 . (Folktales of the world)

中国民间故事. Eberhard, Wolfram (1909—) 德译; Parsons, Desmond 英译自德语版. 儿童读物.

(1) [Taiwan ed.]. [Taipei]: [Central Book], 1966. xiii, 267 pages; 23cm.

(2) Chicago: University of Chicago Press, 1968. xli, 267 pages; 23cm.

(3) Taipei: Caves Books, 1980. x, 258 pages; 23cm.

16. Chinese fairy tales, by Isabelle C. Chang. With drawings by Shirley Errickson. [Barre, Mass. : Barre Publishers, 1965]. 74 p. illus. (part col.)29cm.

Summary: Twenty-six ancient Chinese tales, including The Tortoise Talked, How Some Animals Became as They Are, Number Three Son, The Sparrow and the Phoenix, and Teardrop Dragon.

中国神话故事. Chang, Isabelle Chin (1924—) 译; Errickson, Shirley 插图. 收录了 26 个中国古代神话故事. 儿童读物.

(1) New York: Schocken Books, 1968. 74 pages color illustrations 28cm.

17. Peiping nursery rhymes: with English translation/edited by Tzu-Shih Chen. Taipei, Taiwan: Great China Book Co. , 1968. 206 pages: illustrations; 21cm. (The books of Chinese folklore, first series)

《北平童谣选辑》, 陈子实编选. 台湾大中国图书公司.

18. Folksongs & children-songs from Peiping. 1971. 2 v. ii, iv, viii, 428 p. 22cm. (Asian folklore and social life monographs, v. 16—17.)

《北平民歌, 童谣》, Johnson, Kinchen 译.

19. Bright red star: story/by Li Hsin-tien; ill. by Wang Wei-hsin. Peking: Foreign Languages Press, 1974. 142 p. : ill. ; 19cm.

《闪闪的红星》, 李心田 (1929—).

20. The mantle of dreams/Béla Balázs; translated by George Leitmann. Tokyo: Kodansha International; New York: Distributed by Harper & Row, 1974. 123 pages: illustrations; 22cm.

Contents: The mantle of dreams. —Li Tai-pe and the thief. —The parasols. —The clumsy god. —The opium smokers. —The flea. —The old child. —The god robbers. —Li Tai-pe and springtime. —The ancestors. —The moon fish. —The friends. —The revenge of the chestnut tree. —The tearful glance. —The child of clay. —The victor.

神话故事. Balázs, Béla (1884—1949) 德译; Zipes, Jack (1937—) 英译. 该书译于 1922 年版的德语文本. 儿童读物.

(1) The cloak of dreams: Chinese fairy tales/Béla Balázs; translated and introduced by Jack Zipes; illustrated by Mariette Lydis. Princeton, N. J. : Princeton University Press, c2010. ix, 177 p. : ill. ; 21cm. ISBN: 0691147116, 0691147116, 0691162336 , 0691162331. (Oddly modern fairy tales)

21. The magic flute and other children's stories/by modern Chinese authors. Beijing, China: New World Press, 1981. vi, 167 pages: illustrations; 21cm.

Contents: The emperor's new clothes/Ye Shengtao—The story of a mirror/He Yi—King of the forest/Da Mai—A flying cock/Jin Jiang—Three proud kittens/Yan Wenjing—The 10,000-li flight of two little swallows/Quin Zhaoyang—The magic gloves/Fu Lin—The wild grapes/Ge Cuilin—The peacock with the fiery tail/Zhong Zimang—Little wild-goose rejoins his flock/Wu Mengqi—A wolf hunts a man/Jin Jin—Princess dragon/Chen Weijun—Ma Liang and his magic brush/Hong Xuntao—Who has lost his tail/Lu Ke—A pony to cross a river/Peng Wenxi—Mr. Sun, public spirited and fair/Fang Yiqun—The advent of Mammon/Huang Yiqing—The magic flute/Zhang Wexun—A little fisherman/Zhang Shijie—"Idiot"/Ye Junjian.

《神笛及其他童话》，叶圣陶等.

22. Favorite children's stories from China. Beijing: Foreign Languages Press, 1983. 270 pages: illustrations; 21cm. ISBN: 0835110648, 0835110648

Notes: Twenty-four stories about a kitten, horses, a panda and a golden monkey, birds, fish, a fruit tree, and a cloud as well as stories about children.

《不泄气的猫姑娘：中国童话选》

23. Mommy, daddy, and me: Chinese kids talk about their parents. Beijing, China: New World Press: Distributed by China International Book Trading Corp., 1986. 55 pages: illustrations; 18cm. ISBN: 0835116654, 0835116657

Notes: "The forty-four articles included in this book are selected from among the award-winning papers of two children's writing contests"—Editor's note.

《我的爸爸妈妈：儿童作文获奖作品选》，新世界出版社编. 新世界出版社.

24. Dragon tales: a collection of Chinese stories. Beijing, China: Chinese Literature Press, 1988. 232 pages: illustrations; 18cm. ISBN: 7507100243, 7507100242, 0835120589, 0835120586. (Panda books)

《龙的传说》，中国文学出版社. 儿童读物.

25. Stories from Dun Huang Buddhist scripture/[by Xie Shengbao]; translated by Li Yu-liang, Liang Xiao-peng. [Gansu]: Gansu Children Publishing House, 1992. 303 pages; 19cm. ISBN: 7542206869, 7542206862

《敦煌佛经故事》，谢生保原著；李玉良，梁晓鹏译. 甘肃少年儿童出版社.

26. Tales from within the clouds: Nakhi stories of China/ retold by Carolyn Han; translated by Jaiho Cheng; illustrated by Li Ji. Honolulu: University of Hawaii Press, 1997. xi, 47 pages: color illustrations, color map; 24cm. ISBN: 0824818202, 08248182

Contents: Heavenly Sisters—Nakhi Creation Tale—Why Dogs Lap Water—Naughty Cicada—Grumbling Goat—Legend of Ms. Chongcao—Arrogant Azalea—Trickster Tale: Flea and Louse—Brown-Nose Eel—Why Eagles Catch Chickens

《云的传说：中国纳西族故事》，Han, Carolyn(1941—); Li, Ji 插图; Cheng, Jaiho Cheng 译.

27. Chinese fairy tales/Frederick H. Martens; illustrated by

Yuko Green. Mineola, N. Y.: Dover Publications, c1998. iii, 76 p.: ill.; 21cm. ISBN: 0486401405, 0486401409. (Dover children's thrift classics)

Notes: Tales selected and adapted from The Chinese fairy book, published in 1921.

Contents: Women's words part flesh and blood—The three rhymsters—The bird with nine heads—The cave of the beasts—The panther—The great flood—Why dog and cat are enemies—The herb boy and the weaving maiden—The lady of the moon—The miserly farmer—Old Dschang—The flower-elves—The dragon-princess—The disowned princess—The maiden who was stolen away—The frog princess

中国神话故事. Martens, Frederick Herman, (1874—1932)译. 儿童读物.

28. Chinese fairy tales/by Adele M. Fielde; edited by Malcolm and Margaret Rosholt. [Rosholt, Wis.: Rosholt House], c1998 (Amherst, Wis.: Printed in the U. S. A. by Palmer Publications). iii, 111 p.: ill. (some col.); 24cm. ISBN: 0910417113, 0910417112

中国神话故事. Fielde, Adele M. (Adele Marion, 1839—1916)译. 儿童读物.

29. The empty trunk/Zhang Zhilu; [English translation, Chen Liuting, Stuart Parkins]. Hangzhou, China: Zhejiang Juvenile and Children's Publishing House, 2005. 163 pages; 21cm. ISBN: 7534237033, 7534237034

Contents: The wooden antelope—Wanwan's collection—Buttons—Cat school—King of the medical patch—A'niu, the boy with a flat nose—Li Xiaoguai's ears—Nothing can stop Niuniu—The empty trunk—Soul shadow—The magic watch—Xu Weiwu

《空箱子》，张之路著；陈柳婷，白君士译. 浙江少年儿童出版社. 本书是张之路的儿童文学科学幻想小说集《空箱子》的英文版本.

30. A voyage of discovery through the valley of a thousand birds/author, Liu Xianping; translated by Li Xuzhuang, Annette van Oppen. Beijing: China Children's Press & Publication Group, 2007. 340 pages: illustrations; 23cm. ISBN: 7500785668, 7500785666

《我的山野朋友》(拟似)，刘先平著. 中国少年儿童出版社. 短篇小说集.

31. Stories of Chinese fables/Cang Lanju, Hu Yu bian zhu. Guangzhou: Guangdong jiao yu chu ban she, 2006. 6, 194 p.: ill.; 21cm. ISBN: 7540664282, 7540664282. (中国经典文化故事系列 = Chinese classic cultural stories series)

《中国寓言故事》，仓兰菊，胡裕编著. 英汉对照. 青少年读物.

32. My friends in the wild: Liu Xianping's wonderful adventure in the world of nature/by Liu Xianping; translated by Li Xuzhuang, Annette van Oppen. Beijing:

China Children's Press & Publication Group，2007．369 pages：illustrations（some color）；23cm．ISBN：7500785675，7500785674

《我的山野朋友：刘先平大自然探险奇遇：英汉对照》，刘先平著，中国少年儿童出版社．短篇小说集．

33．How Mr. Pan weathered the storm and other selected writings/Ye Shengtao．Beijing：Foreign Languages Press，2009．260 pages；20cm．ISBN：7119058894，7119058894

《稻草人：叶圣陶作品选》，叶圣陶著．童话集．

34．中华古诗：中英对照 注音彩图/中国侨都编辑部主编．广州：新世纪出版社，2009．57 页；21×25cm．ISBN：7540540883，7540540885

35．中华成语故事：中英对照 注音彩图/中国侨都编辑部主编．广州：新世纪出版社，2009．61 页；21×25cm．ISBN：7540540883，7540540885

36．中华神话故事：中英对照 注音彩图/中国侨都编辑部主编．广州：新世纪出版社，2009．61 页；21×25cm．ISBN：7540540883，7540540885

37．中华益智童谣精选：中英版/陶吴馨，门淑敏编著．北京：中国时代经济出版社，2010．199 页；24cm．ISBN：7511900685，7511900682（汉语走向世界丛书）

38．Tales from the Three Character Classic/Yu Hui；Martha Avery［translator］．Beijing China Intercontinental，2010．193 p．il．col．24cm．ISBN：7508517384，7508517385．（Tales from China's classic essential readings＝中国蒙学经典）

《"三字经"故事》，郁辉著；（美）艾梅霞译．儿童故事．

39．Children's stories/by contemporary Shanghai writers；translation by Yang Shuhui，Yang Yunqin．New York：Better Link Press，2010．232 pages；21cm．ISBN：1602202283，1602202281．（Cultural China series）

Contents：A barbershop for the brave/Zhou Rui—A camel on a treasure hunt/Chen Bochui—Grandmother's strange ears/Ren Rongrong—The Black Cat Police Chief（selections）/Zhu Zhixiang—A white turtle/Ye Yonglie—A joyful birthday celebration/Fang Yiqun—The rise and fall of the Space-waste Collection fad/Ren Geshu—The Milk General/Ye Jun—A string of happy musical notes/Zhang Qiusheng—A tree that grows fish/Zheng Chunhua—The mysterious eyes/Zhou Jiting—Halike and his shadow-cutting knife/Dai Da—A bear dances to my accordian music/Dai Zhen—Midnight in the zoo/Zhu Xiaowen—A red umbrella and a pair of red wooden slippers/Peng Yi—A hundred-years-old King of trees/Zhang Dawei—The heart broken Lady Dragon and her happy tears/Xu Jianhua—The Sock Sisters and the Galosh husband and wife/Xiao Ping—Gray Dot the runner/Xiao Ping—After the eaglet was wounded/Zhu Shaowei—The soliloquy of a cat/Lu Mei—The Xun of ancient times/Zhang Hong.

中国儿童故事．当代上海作家撰写；杨曙辉，杨韵琴译．

40．A Ye Shengtao reader/translated by Zhang Baojun；illustrated by Li Li．Beijing：China Intercontinental Press，2013．160 pages：colour illustrations；21cm．ISBN：7508525310，7508525310．（Classics of modern Chinese literature＝中国儿童名著精选译丛）

叶圣陶儿童读物．叶圣陶著；张宝钧英译；李里插图．

41．A Bingxin reader/translated by Zhao Yuan；illustrated by Jia Xiaoxi．Beijing：China Intercontinental Press，2013．200 pages：colour illustrations；21cm．ISBN：7508526515，7508526511．（Classics of modern Chinese literature＝中国儿童名著精选译丛）

冰心儿童读物．冰心著；赵元英译；贾晓曦插图．

42．Chinese folk stories/［adapted and translated by］Wang Lin；paintings by Mo Yang，Guangzhou，China；David Marshman，editor．Oxford：Weilin Publishing，2013．xv，89 pages：illustrations（colour）；18×22cm．ISBN：0992625702，099262570X

中国民间故事．Lin，Wang（1990—）和 Marshman，David（1946—）编译；Yang，Mo 插图．儿童读物．

43．China for younger readers/edited by Ye Yonglie and Wei Wen；illustrated by Jia Yanliang．Beijing：Dolphin Books，1989．45 pages：illustrations（some color）；22cm．ISBN：0835122123，0835122131，7800512703，7800512711

《漫话中国》，叶永烈，蔚文编文．海豚出版社．青少年读物．

44．The big book of China：a guided tour through 5,000 years of history and culture/Wang Qicheng．Beijing，China：Foreign Languages Press，2010．viii，212 pages：color illustrations；24cm．ISBN：7119060293，7119060295

《看中国》，王麒诚著．青少年读物．

45．Child labour/Written by Kao Yu-pao，adapted by Hsu Kuang-yu．Peking：Foreign Languages Press，1954．95 pages：illustrations；

《童工》，高玉宝著．儿童读物．

(1)Kao's boyhood/written by Gao Yu-pao；drawings by Wang Hsu-yang［and others］．Peking：Foreign Languages Press；Chicago：Distributors，China Books & Periodicals，1955．95 pages：illustrations；17×20cm．

(2)Kao's boyhood/Drawings by Wang Hsu-yang［and others］．Peking：Foreign Languages Press，1956．95 pages（chiefly illustrations)17×20cm．

46．At the seaside．Peking：Foreign Languages Press，1957．85 pages：illustrations；21cm．

Contents：Me and Little Yung，by Liu Chen．—My young sister，by Jen Ta-hsing．—Chubby and Little Pine，by Kao Hsiang-chen．—At the seaside，by Hsiao Ping

《海滨的孩子》,萧平等著. 小说.

47. Before the dawn. Peking：Foreign Languages Press, 1958. 158 pages, illustrations, 19cm.

《破晓之前》,赵自著. 即《不死的王孝和》的英文版. 纪实性小说.

48. Next-time port/by Yen Wen-ching；［translated by Gladys Yang］. Peking：Foreign Languages Press, 1958. 70 pages：illustrations；24cm.

《唐小西在"下一次开船港"》,严文井著；戴乃迭(Yang, Gladys,1919—1999)译. 童话.

49. The adventures of the little swallows/Jin Zhaoyang；［ill. by Yang Yongjing］. Peking：Foreign Languages Press, 1958. 22 pages：color illustrations；25cm.

《小燕子万里飞行记》,秦兆阳著. 童话.

50. Little star/［by Wang Luyao, and other stories, by Ji Gang, and others. Illustrations by Hua Sanzhuan］. Peking：Foreign Languages Press, 1958. 95 pages plates 21cm.

《小星星》,王路遥等著. 儿童故事.

51. Big Lin and Little Lin ［by］Chang Tien-yi. Peking：Foreign Languages Press, 1958. 157 p. : illus. ; 21cm.

《大林和小林》,张天翼(1906—1985)；戴乃迭(Yang. Gladys)译. 童话.

(1) 2nd ed. Peking：Foreign Languages Press, 1965. 157 pages：illustrations；21cm.

52. The magic gourd ［by］Chang Tien-yi. Peking：Foreign Languages Press, 1959. 164 p. illus. 21cm.

《宝葫芦的秘密》,张天翼(1906—1985). 童话.

(1)Peking：Foreign Languages Press, 1979. 198 pages：illustrations；19cm.

(2)Peking：Foreign Languages Press, 1990. 198 pages：illustrations；19cm. ISBN：7119011715, 7119011714

53. The rainbow road. ［Translated by Tang Sheng］. Peking：Foreign Languages Press, 1959. 157 p. illus. 21cm.

《五彩路》,胡奇(1918—). 儿童文学.

54. The legend of the white serpent. Pai shê chuan. Retold from the Chinese by A. Fullarton Prior. Illustrated by Kwan Sang-mei. Tokyo, Rutland, Vt., C. E. Tuttle Co. ［1960］. 67 p. illus. 16×22cm.

《白蛇传》,Prior, A. Fullarton(1929—)译. 儿童读物.

55. A Picture/by Tien Chun and others. Peking：Foreign Languages Press, 1960. 109 p. ［3］leaves of plates：ill. ; 21cm.

Contents：A picture/Tien Chun—Man-man/Wang Wen-shih-Snow Lotus/Chuan Kuan-fu—Flesh and blood/Hu Wan-chun—Clear day after rain/Chen Yen-jung.

Notes："Stories... from the Selection of Children's Literature of 1958 published by the China Children's Literature Publishing House in Peking."—Editor's note.

《一幅画》,萧军(1908—). 短篇小说.

56. They are creating miracles/Jen Ta-Lin. Peking：Foreign Languages Press, 1960. 1 vol. (54 p.)：illustrations. ; 19cm.

《他们在创造奇迹》,任大霖. 儿童读物.

57. The shot-gun/Original story by Jen Ta-hsing；adaptation by Wang Hsing-pei；illus. by Hu ke-wen and Hu Ke-li. Peking：Foreign Languages Press, 1961. 66 pages：illustrations；18cm.

任大星原著；Wang, Xingbei 改编.

58. Snowflakes/Yang Shuo；［illustrated by Miao Di］. Peking：Foreign Languages Press, 1961. 79 pages：illustrations；19cm.

《雪花飘飘》,杨朔(1913—1968)；Miao, Ti(1925—)插图. 儿童故事.

(1)2nd ed. Peking：Foreign Languages Press, 1979. 73 pages：illustrations；19cm.

59. The big grey wolf; a play for children/［by］Chang Tien-yi. Peking：Foreign Languages Press, 1961. 44 p. : ill. (part col.)；21cm.

《大灰狼》,张天翼(1906—1985). 儿童剧.

60. The golden sea shell/by Juan Chang-ching；illustrations by Mi Ku. Peking：Foreign Languages Press, 1961. 32 pages：illustrations；19cm.

《金色的海螺》,阮章竞著. 儿童神话诗.

61. Yeh-hsuan's fables/Ho Yi. Peking：Foreign Languages Press, 1961. 92 pages：illustrations；21cm.

《野旋的童话》,贺宜(1914—1987)著. 童话.

62. The little carp leap over the Dragon's Gate. Peking：Foreign Languages Press, 1961. 32 p. : ill

《小鲤鱼跳龙门》,金近写. 童话.

63. The shepherd boy Hai Wa/Hua Shan；［drawings by Hsia Shu-yu］. Peking：Foreign Languages Press, 1974. 69 pages：illustrations；19cm.

《牧童海娃》(《鸡毛信》),华山(1920—1985)著. 儿童读物.

(1)Shanghai：Renmin chubanshe, 1976. 92 p. : ill. ; 19cm. (Yingyu zhuyi duwu)

64. The call of the fledgling, and other children's stories/Hao Jan；［ill. by Chang Teh-yu, Chang Ju-wei, and Ting Fu-nien］. Peking：Foreign Languages Press, 1974. 57 pages, ［7］leaves of plates：illustrations；19cm.

Contents：The chirruping grasshopper. —The speckled hen. —Making snowmen. —Children's library. —The call of the fledgling.

《树上鸟儿叫》,浩然著. 小说.

65. Going to school/Kuan Hua. Peking：Foreign Languages Press, 1975. 55 pages：illustrations；19cm.

《上学》,管桦著. 小说.

66. Little hero of the reed marsh and other children's

stories/［by An Ting；ill. by Mao Shui-hsien... et al.］. Peking：Foreign languages Press，1978. 142 p.，［6］bl. pl.：ill.；19cm.

《芦荡小英雄》，张德武等著. 儿童故事集.

67. They were three/by Wang An-yu and others；［illustrated by Shen Yao-ting. et al.］. Peking：Foreign Languages Press，1978. 111 pages，［9］leaves of plates：illustrations；19cm.

《三个小伙伴》，王安友等著. 儿童故事.

68. The three conceited kittens：a collection of stories for children/Yen Wen-ching；［illustrated by Wang Chin-hua，Mao Yung-Kun］. Peking：Foreign Languages Press，1979. 177 pages：illustrations；19cm.

《三只骄傲的小猫：严文井童话选》，严文井著.

69. The adventures of a little rag doll/Sun Youjun；translated by Delia Davin. Beijing，China：Foreign Languages Press，1980. 221 pages：illustrations；19cm.

《小布头奇遇记》，孙幼军；Davin，Delia 译.

70. The adventures of a little rag doll/Sun Youjun；［translation by Lily L. Shi］. New York：Better Link Press，2011. 217 pages；21cm. ISBN：1602202306，1602202303

《小布头奇遇记》，孙幼军；Shi，Lily L. 译.

71. Legend of Panda/Sun Youjun. Beijing，China：Dolphin Books，2012. ［16］，162 pages：illustrations；23cm. ISBN：7511007162，7511007163. （Best Chinese children's literature＝中国儿童文学走向世界精品书系）

《熊猫小弟传奇》，孙幼军.

72. The door gods/Sunyoujun；painter Li Fan；transl. Cheng Qian. North Bingzhou：Hope Pub. House，2000. ［6］，58 s.：il. kolor.，1 portr.；22cm. ISBN：753792158X，7537921589. （Series of masterpieces of Chinese children's literature＝中华儿童文学名家名作书系）

《门神》，孙幼军.

73. Jia Li in junior high/Qin Wenjun；translated by Belinda Yun-ying Louie，Douglas Heung Louie. Shanghai：Juvenile ＆ Children Pub. House，1997. 377 pages：illustrations；21cm. ISBN：7532434486，7532434480

《男生贾里》，秦文君. 青少年文学.

74. The green plantation of my younger brother/Qin Wenjun. Taiyuan Shi：Xi wang chu ban she，1998. 49 pages：color illustrations；22cm. ISBN：7537921565，7537921563. （Series of masterpieces of Chinese children's literature＝中华儿童文学名家名作书系）

《四弟的绿庄园》，秦文君；程前译. 中英对照.

75. Tian Tang Street/by Wenjun Qin；［translated from the Chinese by Xiaozhen Wu］. San Francisco：Long River Press；Shanghai：Shanghai Press and Publishing Development Co.，2005. 215 pages；24cm. ISBN：1592650554，1592650552. （Cultural China）

《天棠街 3 号》，秦文君；Wu，Xiaozhen 译. 儿童读物.

76. My cousin is coming/Qin Wenjun. Beijing，China：Dolphin Books，2013. 149 pages：illustrations；23cm. ISBN：7511012593，7511012590. （Best Chinese children's literature＝中国儿童文学走向世界精品书系）

《表哥驾到》，秦文君.

77. Aroma's little garden/by Qin Wenjun；translated by Tony Blishen. New York：Better Link Press，2016. 151 pages；21cm. ISBN：1602202575，1602202573. （Stories by contemporary writers from Shanghai）

《会跳舞的向日葵》，秦文君；Blishen，Tony 译.

78. Seventh hound/Shen Shixi. Taiyuan：Xi Wang chu ban she，1998. ［6］，54 pages：color illustrations；22cm. ISBN：7537921202，7537921206. （Series of masterpieces of Chinese children's literature＝中华儿童文学名家名作书系）

《第七条猎狗》，沈石溪.

79. Jackal and wolf/by Shen Shixi；translated by Helen Wang. London：Egmont，2010. 281 pages；20cm. ISBN：1405264495，1405264497

沈石溪；Wang，Helen 译.

80. Opening the leopard cage/written by Shen Shixi；translated by Li Li. Rockville，MD：ABC Garden LLC，2012. 269 pages；23cm. ISBN：1938763038，1938763033. （Collection of China outstanding children's literary award winners）

沈石溪；Li，Li 译.

81. King boar/Shen Shixi. Beijing：Dolphin Books，2013. xvii，128 pages：illustrations；23cm. ISBN：7511012586，7511012582. （Best Chinese children's literature＝中国儿童文学走向世界精品书系）

《野猪王》，沈石溪.

82. The last warrior elephant ＆ other stories/written by Shen Shixi. Westfield，IN：Blue Peacock Press，2013. 160 pages：illustrations；23cm. ISBN：0991191727，0991191722

沈石溪著.

83. The red milk sheep/Shen Shixi；illustrated by Cloth Pocket Illustration；translated by Curtis Evans ＆ Dong Ming. Pretoria，South Africa：Sweetafrica Publishers，2015. 119 pages：illustrations；24cm. ISBN：0620676243，0620676248

《红奶羊》，沈石溪.

84. When Mu meets Min/written by Shen Shixi；illustrated by Shen Yuanyuan. ［Adelaide，South Australia］：Starfish Bay Children's Books，2017. 1 volume（unpaged）：color illustrations；25cm. ISBN：1760360341，1760360344

《猫狗之间》，沈石溪；Shen，Yuanyuan(1957—)插图.

85. Let one hundred flowers bloom/Feng Jicai；translated by Christopher Smith. London；New York：Viking，1995. 106 pages；23cm. ISBN：0670858056，0670858057

《百花齐放》,冯骥才;Smith,Christopher 译. 青少年文学读物.

86. The tears of a dancing snake/Ge bing. Taiyuan：Xi wang chu ban she, 1998. ISBN：7537921229, 7537921220. (Series of masterpieces of Chinese children's literature＝中华儿童文学名家名作书系)

《舞蛇的泪》,葛冰;李帆绘画. 中英对照.

87. Wild grapes/Ge Cuilin. Taiyuan Shi：Xi wang chu ban she, 1998. 45 pages：color illustrations；23cm. ISBN：7537921555, 7537921558. (Series of masterpieces of Chinese children's literature＝中华儿童文学名家名作书系)

《野葡萄》,葛翠琳. 英汉对照.

88. A scarecrow/Ye Shengtao. Taiyuan：Xi Wang chu ban she, 1998. 46 pages：illustrations (some color)；24cm. ISBN：7537921190,7537921199. (Series of masterpieces of Chinese children's literature＝中华儿童文学名家名作书系)

《稻草人》,叶圣陶(1894—1980);程前译.

89. The sounds of wooden sandals in the lane/Jin Zenghao. Taiyuan Shi：Xi wang chu ban she, 1999. 45 pages：illustrations (some color)；23cm. ISBN：7537921657, 7537921652. (Series of masterpieces of Chinese children's literature＝中华儿童文学名家名作书系)

《小巷木屐声》,金曾豪;程前译. 中英对照.

90. A locked drawer/Chen Danyan. Taiyuan Shi：Xi wang chu ban she, 1999. 60 pages：illustrations (some color)；23cm. ISBN：7537921640, 7537921644. (Series of masterpieces of Chinese children's literature＝中华儿童文学名家名作书系)

《上锁的抽屉》,陈丹燕;程前译. 中英对照.

91. Remote head of the Yellow River/Cheng [i. e. Chen] Li. Taiyuan Shi：Xi wang chu ban she, 1999. 45 pages：illustrations (some color)；23cm. ISBN：7537921601, 7537921602. (Series of masterpieces of Chinese children's literature＝中华儿童文学名家名作书系)

《遥遥黄河源》,陈丽;程前翻译. 中英对照.

92. Fox hounds a hunter/Jin Jin. Taiyuan Shi：Xi wang chu ban she, 1999. 53 unnumbered pages：illustrations (some color)；23cm. ISBN：753792161X, 7537921619. (Series of masterpieces of Chinese children's literature＝中华儿童文学名家名作书系)

《狐狸打猎人》,金近;程前翻译.

93. The eighty-six stars/Liu Xinwu. Taiyuan Shi：Xi wang chu ban she, 1999. 68 pages：illustrations (some color)；23cm. ISBN：7537921636, 7537921633. (Series of masterpieces of Chinese children's literature＝中华儿童文学名家名作书系)

《八十六颗星星》,刘心武;程前译. 中英对照.

94. The notes on the forest/Zhou Rui. Taiyuan Shi：Xi wang chu ban she, 1999. 63 pages：illustrations (some color)；

23cm. ISBN：7537921628, 7537921626. (Series of masterpieces of Chinese children's literature＝中华儿童文学名家名作书系)

《森林手记》,周锐(1953—);程前译. 中英对照.

95. Mr. Ebb and Mr. Tide/Chen Bochui. Taiyuan, Shanxi：Xi wang, 1999. 50 pages：color illustrations；23cm. ISBN：7537921596,7537921598. (Series of masterpieces of Chinese children's literature＝中华儿童文学名家名作书系)

《落潮先生和涨潮先生》,陈伯吹. 中英对照.

96. A journey of the red mushrooms/Guo Feng. Taiyuan Shi：Xi wang chu ban she, 1999. 20 pages：illustrations (some color)；23cm. ISBN：7537921541, 7537921547. (Series of masterpieces of Chinese children's literature＝中华儿童文学名家名作书系)

《红菇们的旅行》,郭凤;程前译. 中英对照.

(1)3 版. Tai yuan：Xi wang chu ban she, 2009. ISBN：7537921541, 7537921547.(希望树绘本. 彩绘中国儿童文学名家名作)

97. A story about "Merry goddess"/Cheng Naishan. Taiyuan Shi：Xi wang chu ban she, 2000. 57 pages：illustrations (some color)；23cm. ISBN：7537921671, 7537921679. (Series of masterpieces of Chinese children's literature＝中华儿童文学名家名作书系)

《"欢乐女神"的故事》,程乃珊;程前译. 中英对照.

98. A little bark shelter outside below the window/Bing Bo. Taiyuan Shi：Xi wang chu ban she, 2000. 24 pages：color illustrations；23cm. ISBN：7537921664, 7537921660. (Series of masterpieces of Chinese children's literature＝中华儿童文学名家名作书系)

《窗下的树皮小屋》,冰波(1957—)译. 中英对照.

99. Number one of the Nova women team/Zhuang Zhiming. Taiyuan Shi：Xi wang chu ban she, 2000. 55 pages：color illustrations；23cm. ISBN：7537921695, 7537921695. (Series of masterpieces of Chinese children's literature＝中华儿童文学名家名作书系)

《新星女队一号》,庄之明. 中英对照.

100. The magic brush Ma Liang/Hongxuntao；painter Li Xiaolin；transl. Cheng Qian. North Bingzhou：Hope Pub. House, 2000. [6], 28, [1] s.：il. kolor., 1 portr.；23cm. ISBN：7537921210, 7537921213. (Series of masterpieces of Chinese children's literature＝中华儿童文学名家名作书系)

《神笔马良》,洪汛涛;程前译. 中英对照.

101. A red gourd/Caowenxuan；painter Li Xiaolin；transl. Cheng Qian. Taiyuan：Xi Wang chu ban she, 1999. [6], 53 s.：il. color., 1 portr.；23cm. ISBN：7537921571, 7537921572. (Series of masterpieces of Chinese children's literature＝中华儿童文学名家名作书系)

《红葫芦》,曹文轩;Li, Xiaolin 画;Cheng Qian 译.

102. The straw house/Cao Wenxuan. English ed. South San Francisco：Long River Press，2005. 277 pages；25cm. ISBN：1592650546，1592650545. (Cultural China)
《草房子》，曹文轩.

103. Sweet orange tree/Cao Wenxuan. Beijing：Dolphin Books，2012. 158 pages：illustrations；23cm. ISBN：7511007209，7511007201. （Best Chinese children's literature＝中国儿童文学走向世界精品书系）
Contents：Flood—The eleventh strip of red cloth—The red squash—Blue flower—Loach—Exhausted trumpet—Prey bait—Vigil—An underwater city—The sweet orange tree—The wild windmill—The osprey.
《甜橙树》，曹文轩.

104. Bronze and sunflower/Cao Wenxuan；translated from Chinese by Helen Wang；illustrations，Meilo So. London：Walker Books，2015. 384 pages；20cm. ISBN：1406348460，1406348465
《青铜葵花》，曹文轩；Wang，Helen（1965—）译；So，Meilo 插图.
(1)Somerville, Massachusetts：Candlewick Press，2017. 386 pages：illustrations；21cm. ISBN：0763688165，0763688169

105. Brothers/written by Cao Wenxuan；translated by Yan Yan. Singapore：Chung Hwa Book Co.，Ltd，2016. 150 pages：illustrations；22cm. ISBN：9810988425，9810988427. (Dingding and Dangdang；1)
《黑痴白痴》，曹文轩；Yan Yan 译.

106. Blind goat/written by Cao Wenxuan；translated by Yan Yan. Singapore：Chung Hwa Book Co.，Ltd，2016. 170 pages：illustrations；22cm. ISBN：9810988432，9810988435. (Dingding and Dangdang；2)
《盲羊》，曹文轩；Yan Yan 译.

107. Flea circus/written by Cao Wenxuan；translated by Yan Yan. Singapore：Chung Hwa Book Co.，Ltd，2016. 159 pages：illustrations；22cm. ISBN：9810988449，9810988443. (Dingding and Dangdang；3)
《跳蚤剧团》，曹文轩；Yan Yan 译.

108. Beyond the mountain is another mountain/written by Cao Wenxuan；translated by Yan Yan. Singapore：Chung Hwa Book Co.，Ltd，2016. 222 pages：illustrations；22cm. ISBN：9810988456，9810988451. (Dingding and Dangdang；4)
《山那边还是山》，曹文轩；Yan Yan 译.

109. Grassroots Street/written by Cao Wenxuan；translated by Yan Yan. Singapore：Chung Hwa Book Co.，Ltd，2016. 168 pages：illustrations；22cm. ISBN：9810988463，981098846X. (Dingding and Dangdang；5)
《草根街》，曹文轩；Yan Yan 译.

110. Black sailor/written by Cao Wenxuan；translated by Yan Yan. Singapore：Chung Hwa Book Co.，Ltd，2016. 202 pages：illustrations；22cm. ISBN：9810988470，810988478. (Dingding and Dangdang；6)
《黑水手》，曹文轩；Yan Yan 译.

111. Ant elephant/written by Cao Wenxuan；translated by Yan Yan. Singapore：Chung Hwa Book Co.，Ltd，2016. 171 pages：illustrations；22cm. ISBN：9810988487，9810988486. (Dingding and Dangdang；7)
《蚂蚁象》，曹文轩；Yan Yan 译.

112. Feather/by Cao Wenxuan；illustrated by Roger Mello；translated from the Chinese by Chloe Garcia Roberts. Brooklyn，NY：Elsewhere Editions，［an imprint of Archipelago Books］，［New York］：distributed by Penguin Random House，2017. 1 volume（unpaged）：color illustrations；18 × 30cm. ISBN：0914671855，0914671855
《羽毛》，曹文轩；Mello，Roger 插图；Roberts，Chloe Garcia 译.

113. Mulan/adapted by Cathy East Dubowski. New York：Disney Press，c1998. 96 p.，［8］plates：col. ill.；20cm. ISBN：0786842229
《木兰》(动画)，Dubowski，Cathy East 改编.

114. The ballad of Mulan/retold and illustrated by Song Nan Zhang. Union City，CA：Pan Asian Publications，c1998. 1 v.（unpaged）；28cm. ISBN：157227056X
《木兰辞》，Zhang，Song Nan（1942—）编绘. 青少年读物.

115. The shadow/Zhang Zhilu. Taiyuan Shi：Xi wang chu ban she，2000. 44 pages：illustrations（some color）；23cm. ISBN：7537921688，7537921687. （Series of masterpieces of Chinese children's literature＝中华儿童文学名家名作书系）
《影子》，张之路；程前译. 中英对照.

116. Do you have mouse pencils? /Zhang Zhilu；［English translation，Caixia Chen］. Hangzhou：Zhejiang Juvenile and Children's Publishing House，2005. 143 pages；21cm. ISBN：7534236819，7534236815
《有老鼠牌铅笔吗》，张之路著；陈采霞译. 浙江少年儿童出版社. 中篇小说.

117. A journey in an ox's stomachs/Zhang Zhilu；［drawings by：Qin Yinzhi；translation by Wu Yong］. San Francisco：Long River Press，2005. 1 volume（unpaged）：color illustrations；28cm. ISBN：1592650651，1592650651
《在牛肚子里旅行》，张之路，钦吟之；Wu Yong 译.

118. The empty trunk/Zhang Zhilu；［English translation，Chen Liuting，Stuart Parkins］. Hangzhou，China：Zhejiang Juvenile and Children's Publishing House，2005. 163 pages；21cm. ISBN：7534237033，7534237034
Contents：The wooden antelope—Wanwan's collection—Buttons—Cat school—King of the medical patch—A'niu, the boy with a flat nose—Li Xiaoguai's ears—Nothing can

stop Niuniu—The empty trunk—Soul shadow—The magic watch—Xu Weiwu.

《空箱子》,张之路.

119. The taste of the sun : best Chinese children's literature/ Zhang Zhilu. Beijing, China : Dolphin Books Co, 2013. 157 pages : illustrations ; 23cm. ISBN : 7511012555, 7511012558. (Best Chinese children's literature＝中国儿童文学走向世界精品书系)

《太阳的滋味儿》,张之路.

120. The house of big dog Kala Kela/Qin Wenjun. [Beijing] : [Zhong guo shao nian er tong chu ban she], 2006. 133, 76 pages : illustrations ; 23cm. ISBN : 7500781127, 7500781121

《大狗喀啦克拉的公寓:中英对照》,秦文君著. 中国少年儿童出版社. 童话.

121. 剑鸟:汉英对照/范祎著. 北京:人民文学出版社,2007. 307 页;21cm. ISBN:7020060269,7020060269

英文题名:Swordbird. 本书为中篇童话.

122. 蓝色的兔耳朵草/杨红樱著. Jinan : Ming tian chu ban she, 2008. 146 pages : illustrations (some color) ; 19cm. ISBN : 7533255916, 7533255917. (笑猫日记)

英文题名:Blue rabbit-ear grass

123. 蓝色的兔耳朵草/杨红樱著. Jinan : Ming tian chu ban she, 2008. 146 pages : illustrations (some color) ; 19cm. ISBN : 7533255916, 7533255917

英文题名:Blue rabbit-ear grass

124. Four troublemakers/Hongying Yang. New York : Harper Collins Publishers, 2008. 124 pages : illustrations ; 20cm. ISBN : 0061564727, 0061564729. (Mo's Mischief)

《四个捣蛋鬼》,杨红樱(1962—)著.

125. Pesky monkeys/Hongying Yang. New York : HarperCollinsPublishers, 2008. 124 pages : illustrations ; 20cm. ISBN : 0061564741, 0061564745. (Mo's mischief)

《讨厌的猴子》,杨红樱(1962—)著.

126. Teacher's pet/Hongying Yang. New York : Harper Collins Publishers, 2008. 123 pages : illustrations ; 20cm. ISBN : 0061564734, 0061564737. (Mo's mischief)

杨红樱(1962—)著.

127. Best Mom ever/Hongying Yang. New York : Harper Collins Publishers, 2008. 124 pages : illustrations ; 20cm. ISBN : 0061564758, 0061564753. (Mo's mischief)

杨红樱(1962—)著.

128. Best friends/Hongying Yang. New York : Harper Trophy, 2008. 107 pages : illustrations ; 20cm. ISBN : 0061564765, 0061564761. (Mo's mischief series)

杨红樱(1962—)著.

129. You're no fun, Mum! /Hongying Yang. London : Harper Collins Children's, 2008. 125 pages : illustrations ; 20cm. ISBN : 0007273423, 0007273428.

(Mo's mischief ; 4)

杨红樱(1962—)著.

130. Super cool uncle/Hongying Yang. London : Harper Collins Children's, 2008. 122 pages : illustrations ; 20cm. ISBN : 0007284320, 0007284322. (Mo's mischief)

杨红樱(1962—)著.

131. Class genius/Hongying Yang. London : Harper Collins Children's, 2009. ISBN : 0007284344, 0007284349. (Mo's mischief ; 8)

杨红樱(1962—)著.

132. Pet parade/Hongying Yang. London : Harper Collins Children's, 2009. ISBN : 0007284337, 0007284330. (Mo's mischief ; 7)

杨红樱(1962—)著.

133. Picnic surprise/Yang Hongying. Bath, UK : Parragon, 2011. 1 volume (unpaged) : color illustrations ; 22cm. ISBN : 1445480404, 1445480409

《春天的野餐会》,杨红樱(1962—)著.

134. House of dreams/Yang Hongying ; translated by Wang Ruoxi. [Wuhan] : Hubei Children's Press, 2013. 1 volume (unpaged) : color illustrations ; 27cm. ISBN : 7535380593, 753538059X

《做梦的房子》,杨红樱(1962—)著.

135. The butterfly lovers＝[Liang Shanbo yu Zhu Yingtai]/ Teri Tao ; [editing, translation and notes by Nina Tao ; English copy-editing by Rashid Williams-Garcia ; illustrations by Ning Hu]. Santa Monica, CA : Golden Peach Pub. , c2008. 48 p. : col. ill. ; 21cm. ISBN : 1930655140, 1930655142. (Enchanted tales of China)

《梁山伯与祝英台》,Tao, Teri 编写;Tao, Nina 译. 中英双语. 儿童读物.

136. 中国节/唐黛编著;徐晏翻译. 北京:中国少年儿童出版社,2009. 134 页;21cm. ISBN:7500793465,7500793464

英文题名:Chinese festival

137. 中国字/齐文静编著;徐晏翻译. 北京:中国少年儿童出版社, 2009. 122 页;21cm. ISBN:7500793458, 7500793456

英文题名:Chinese character

138. 中国玩/马冬华编著;张展翻译. 北京:中国少年儿童出版社,2009. 100 页;21cm. ISBN:7500793472,7500793472

英文题名:Chinese game

139. 中国居/齐文静编著;齐潇颖翻译. 北京:中国少年儿童出版社, 2009. 124 页;21cm. ISBN:7500793489, 7500793480

英文题名:Chinese house

140. 中国食/唐黛编著;丁媛翻译. 北京:中国少年儿童出版社,2009. 125 页;21cm. ISBN:7500793441,7500793448

英文题名:Chinese food

141. 中国服/唐黛,马冬华编著;丁媛翻译. 北京:中国少年儿童出版社,2009. 106 页;21cm. ISBN:7500793434, 750079343X

英文题名：Chinese clothing

142. 司徒美堂少年故事：中英对照 手绘彩图/中国侨都编辑部主编. 广州：新世纪出版社，2009. 75 页；21×25cm. ISBN：787540540883，7540540885

143. 梁启超少年故事：中英对照 手绘彩图/中国侨都编辑部主编. 广州：新世纪出版社，2009. 67 页；21×25cm. ISBN：7540540883，7540540885

144. A little adventure in Lou Lan/author, Parhati Yilias; editor, Jiang Fengli; translator, Song Jianxun. Ürümqi〔China〕：Xinjiang Juvenile Publishing House，2011. 299 pages：illustrations；23cm. ISBN：7551500395, 7551500391. (Yangpigu series of translation)
《楼兰古国的奇幻之旅》，帕尔哈提·伊力牙斯著；宋建勋翻译. 新疆青少年出版社.

145. An unusual princess/by Wu Meizhen; translated by Petula Parris Huang. London：Egmont，2012. 449 pages：illustrations；20cm. ISBN：1405264501，1405264500
伍美珍著；Huang，Petula Parris 译.

146. The secret of sweet strawberries/Tang Sulan. Beijing：Dolphin Books，2012. 13 unnumbered pages，147 pages：illustration；23cm. ISBN：7511007179, 7511007171. (Best Chinese children's literature=中国儿童文学走向世界精品书系)
《甜草莓的秘密》，汤素兰(1965—)译.

147. The fragrant bird/Jin Bo. Beijing：Dolphin Books，2012. 13 unnumbered pages，201 pages：illustrations；23cm. ISBN：7511007193，7511007198. (Best Chinese children's literature＝中国儿童文学走向世界精品书系)
《香香鸟》，金波(1935—)；王国振，王达合译.

148. A magical parrot/Ge Bing. Beijing：Dolphin Books，2012. 18 unnumbered pages，178 pages：illustration；23cm. ISBN：7511007186，751100718X. (Best Chinese children's literature＝中国儿童文学走向世界精品书系)
《一只神奇的鹦鹉》，葛冰.

149. The Persian cat called Peck/Gao Hongbo. Beijing：Dolphin Books，2013. xix，197 pages：illustrations；23cm. ISBN：7511012579，7511012574. (Best Chinese children's literature＝中国儿童文学走向世界精品书系)
《波斯猫派克》，高洪波.

150. Christmas eve/Huang Beijia. Beijing：Dolphin Books，2013. xiii，161 pages：illustrations；23cm. ISBN：7511012562，7511012566. (Best Chinese children's literature＝中国儿童文学走向世界精品书系)
《平安夜》，黄蓓佳.

151. Wormwood flowers eaten by the deerlet/Xu Lu. Beijing：Dolphin Books，2014. xvii，184 pages：illustrations；23cm. ISBN：7511021953，7511021956. (Best Chinese children's literature＝中国儿童文学走向世界精品书系)
《小鹿吃过的萩花》，徐鲁(1962—).

152. Life is life/Zhang Haidi. Beijing：Dolphin Books，2014. xiv，172 pages：illustrations；23cm. ISBN：7511021939，751102193X. (Best Chinese children's literature＝中国儿童文学走向世界精品书系)
《生命的追问》，张海迪；王国振，钱清合译.

153. Big-head son and small-head father/Zheng Chunhua. Beijing：Dolphin Books，2014. xv，146 pages：illustrations；23cm. ISBN＝7511021946，7511021948. (Best Chinese children's literature＝中国儿童文学走向世界精品书系)
《大头儿子和小头爸爸》，郑春华(1959—).

154. Little ostrich knight/Liu Xianping. Beijing：Dolphin Books，2014. xix，134 pages：illustrations；23cm. (Best Chinese children's literature＝中国儿童文学走向世界精品书系)
《鸵鸟小骑士》，刘先平.

155. The night when dancing with the dragon/Peng Yi. Beijing：Dolphin Books，2014. xv，170 pages：illustrations；23cm. ISBN：7511021960，7511021964. (Best Chinese children's literature＝中国儿童文学走向世界精品书系)
《和龙在一起的夜晚》，彭懿(1958—).

156. Li Bai：the drunken poet/adapted by Tang Xiangyan; story by Bi Fang; picture by Xie Zuhua;〔translated by〕Wang Guozhen. adapted by Tang Xiangyan. Beijing：Dolphin Books，2014. 51 pages：color illustrations；23cm. ISBN：7511021519，7511021514. (Classics now series；006)
《李白：长安有个醉诗仙》，唐香燕，比方改写；谢祖华插图；王国振.

157. Qu Yuan：the noble liegeman/adapted by Zhan Kaiting; story by Zhang Yushan; picture by Huiseshou;〔translated by〕Wang Guozhen. Beijing：Dolphin Books，2014. 59 pages：color illustrations；23cm. ISBN：7511021472，7511021476. (Classics now series；002)
《屈原：不媚俗的楚大夫》，詹凯婷，张瑜珊著；灰色兽插图；王国振译.

158. Li Shangyin：poet of love/adapted by Tang Xiangyan; story by Zhang Qiongwen, pictures by Ma Leyuan;〔translated by〕Wang Guozhen. adapted by Tang Xiangyan; story by Zhang Qiongwen, pictures by Ma Leyuan;〔translated by〕Wang Guozhen. Beijing：Dolphin Books，2014. 55 pages：color illustrations；23cm. ISBN：7511021540，7511021549. (Classics now series；009)
《李商隐：情圣诗人》，唐香燕，张琼文著；马乐原插图；王国振译.

159. Tao Yuanming：the pastoral poet/adapted by Tang

Xiangyan; story by Deng Fangqiao; pictures by Huang Yaling; [translated by] Wang Guozhen. adapted by Tang Xiangyan; story by Deng Fangqiao; pictures by Huang Yaling; [translated by] Wang Guozhen. Beijing: Dolphin Books, 2014. 53 pages: color illustrations; 23cm. ISBN: 7511021502, 7511021506. (Classics now series; 005)

《陶渊明：田园诗人》，唐香燕，邓芳乔著；黄雅玲插图；王国振译。

160. Du Fu: the poet sage/adapted by Zhou Yaoping; story by Deng Fangqiao; picture by Wang Ruoqi; [translated by] Wang Guozhen. adapted by Zhou Yaoping; story by Deng Fangqiao; picture by Wang Ruoqi; [translated by] Wang Guozhen. Beijing: Dolphin Books, 2014. 55 pages: color illustrations; 23cm. ISBN: 7511021526, 7511021522. (Classics now series; 007)

《杜甫：忧国的诗圣》，邓芳乔著；王若齐插图；王国振译。

161. Ma Zhiyuan: the carefree playwright/adapted by Cen Pengwei; story by Zhong Qiongwen; picture by Jian Hanping; Wang Guozhen yi. Beijing: Dolphin Books, 2014. 51 pages: color illustrations; 23cm. ISBN: 7511021601, 7511021603. (Classics now series; 015)

《马致远：归隐的曲状元》，岑澎维，张琼文著；简汉平插图；王国振译。

162. Xin Qiji: the passionate patriot/adapted by Cen Pengwei; story by Zhang Yushan; picture by Chen Bolong; [translated by] Wang Guozhen. adapted by Cen Pengwei; story by Zhang Yushan; picture by Chen Bolong; [translated by] Wang Guozhen. Beijing: Dolphin Books, 2014. 55 pages: color illustrations; 23cm. ISBN: 7511021588, 7511021581. (Classics now series; 013)

《辛弃疾：豪放的英雄词人》，岑澎维，张瑜珊著；陈柏龙插图；王国振译。

163. Book of songs: the earliest collection of songs/adapted by Tang Xiangyan; story by Bi Fang; pictures by AU; [translated by] Wang Guozhen. adapted by Tang Xiangyan; story by Bi Fang; pictures by AU; [translated by] Wang Guozhen. Beijing: Dolphin Books, 2014. 57 pages: color illustrations; 23cm. ISBN: 7511021465, 7511021468. (Classics now series; 001)

《诗经：最早的歌》，唐香燕，比方著；王国振译。

164. Yuefu poetry: tales that sing/adapted by Liu Xiangmei; story by Bi Fang; pictures by Mr. Jun; Wang Guozhen yi. adapted by Liu Xiangmei; story by Bi Fang; pictures by Mr. Jun; Wang Guozhen yi. Beijing: Dolphin Books, 2014. 53 pages: color illustrations; 23cm. ISBN: 7511021496, 7511021492. (Classics now series; 004)

《乐府诗集：说故事的民歌手》，刘湘湄，比方著；王国振译。

165. Liu Zongyuan: the travelling poet/adapted by Cen Pengwei; story by Zhang Yushan; picture by Chen Shangren; [translated by] Wang Guozhen. adapted by Cen Pengwei; story by Zhang Yushan; picture by Chen Shangren; [translated by] Wang Guozhen. Beijing: Dolphin Books, 2014. 55 pages: color illustrations; 23cm. ISBN: 7511021533, 7511021530. (Classics now series; 008)

《柳宗元：旷野寄情的旅行者》，岑澎维，张瑜珊著；陈尚仁插图；王国振译。

166. Li Yu: emperor in exile/adapted by Liu Siyuan; story by Bi Fang; pictures by Chali Wanzhu; [translated by] Wang Guozhen. adapted by Liu Siyuan; story by Bi Fang; pictures by Chali Wanzhu; [translated by] Wang Guozhen. Beijing: Dolphin Books, 2014. 49 pages: color illustrations; 23cm. ISBN: 7511021557, 7511021557. (Classics now series; 010)

《李后主：思乡的皇帝》，刘思源（1964—），比方；查理宛猪插图；王国振译。

167. Jiang Kui: plum blossom musician/adapted by Yan Shunü; story by Zhang Qiongwen; pictures by 57; [translated by] Wang Guozhen. Beijing: Dolphin Books, 2014. 63 pages: color illustrations; 23cm. ISBN: 7511021595, 751102159X. (Classics now series; 014)

《姜夔：爱咏梅的音乐家》，严淑女，张琼文著；王国振译。

168. Li Qingzhao: the preeminent poetess of China/adapted by Liu Siyuan; story by Deng Fangqiao; pictures by Su Lika; [translated by] Wang Guozhen. Beijing: Dolphin Books, 2014. 59 p.: ill.; 23cm. ISBN: 7511021571 7511021573. (Classics now series; 012)

《李清照：中国第一女词人》，刘思源，邓芳乔著；王国振译。

J类　艺术

J1　艺术概论

1. Scrapbook for Chinese collectors: a Chinese treatise on scrolls and forgers: Shu-hua-shuo-ling. Beirut, 1958. 48 p. illus., port. 20cm.

《书画说铃》，陆时化（1724—1779）；高罗佩（Gulik, Robert Hans van, 1910—1967）（荷兰汉学家）译。

2. Chinese painting & calligraphy, 5th century BC-20th century AD/[edited by Gems of Fine Arts attached to the Shanghai People's Fine Art, Publishing House]. Beijing: Zhaohua Pub. House: Distributed by China International Book Trading Corp., 1984. 163 pages: chiefly

illustrations（some color）；38cm.

《中国古代书画》，上海人民美术出版社"艺苑掇英"丛刊编辑部.

3. 书画：汉英对照/徐翎著；王宏印，马向晖译. 北京：人民文学出版社，2006. 185 页；21cm. ISBN：7020048846，7020048847.（中国传统文化双语读本）

英文题名：Calligraphy and painting

4. A great revolution on the cultural front. Peking：Foreign Languages Press，1965. 113 pages；19cm.

Contents：Talk at the festival of Peking opera on contemporary themes，July 1，1964，by Peng Chen. —Energetically develop and foster a Socialist theatre, the better to serve the Socialist economic base, by Ko Ching-shih. —Speech at the opening ceremony of the festival of Peking opera on contemporary themes, June 5, 1964, by Lu Ting-yi. —A great revolution on the cultural front, by Hongqi editorial, no. 12, 1964. —A new stage in the development of Peking opera, by Renmin Ribao editorial, June 6, 1964. —Carry the Socialist revolution in literature and art through to the end, by Renmin Ribao editorial, August 1, 1964.

《文化战线上的一个大革命》

5. The Chinese theory of art；translations from the masters of Chinese art by Lin Yutang. London, Heinemann, 1967. xii, 244 p. col. front. , 16 plates (incl. facsims.), diagrs. 22 1/2cm.

Notes：Table of contents and list of artists in English and Chinese.

中国艺术理论. 林语堂（1895—1976）编译.

(1)New York：Putnam Sons［1967］. xii, 244 p. illus. , geneal. tables. 23cm.

(2)London, Panther, 1969. 265 p. 16 plates, 25 illus. 18cm.

6. To trumpet bourgeois literature and art is to restore capitalism：a repudiation of Chou Yang's Reactionary fallacy adulating the Renaissance, the Enlightenment, and Critical realism of the bourgeoisie/by the Shanghai Writing Group for Revolutionary Mass Criticism. Peking：Foreign Languages Press, 1971. 1 vol. (45 p.)；13cm.

《鼓吹资产阶级文艺就是复辟资本主义》

7. The path of beauty：a study of chinese aesthetics/LiZehou；translated by Gong Lizeng. Beijing：Morning Glory Publishers, 1988. 271 p. : la'ms. col. ；31cm. ISBN：7505400401，7505400405

《美的历程》，李泽厚著. 朝华出版社.

(1)Hong Kong；New York：Oxford University Press, 1994. 40 pages：illustrations；22cm. ISBN：019586526X, 0195865264. (Oxford in Asia paperbacks)

(2)Beijing：Morning Glory Publishers, 1999. 271 p. : ill. , jaquette ill. ；31cm. ISBN：750540668X,

7505406681

8. Painting and calligraphy in the Wu-tsa-tsu：conservative aesthetics in seventeenth-century China/Sewall Oertling. Ann Arbor：Center for Chinese Studies, University of Michigan, c1997. viii, 217 p. ；24cm. ISBN：0892640987, 0892640980. (Michigan monographs in Chinese studies, 1081－9053；no. 68)

《五杂组》（节译），谢肇淛（1567—1624）；Oertling, Sewall Jerome 译. 英汉文本. 主题：明清时代的书法和绘画.

9. Art in China/written by Jia Xiaowei；photo by Lan Qiang, etc.；translated by Yuan Kang. Beijing：China Intercontinental Press, 2007. 135 pages：color illustrations；22cm. ISBN：7508510842, 7508510844. (Fashion China)

《艺术部落：英文》，贾晓伟撰文；袁康译. 五洲传播出版社（时尚中国）. 本书介绍中国当代艺术蓬勃发展的健康势头，以及闻名于世的中国当代艺术家.

10. Arts in China/Jin Yong. Beijing：China Intercontinental Press, 2007. 152 p. ：il. ；25cm. ISBN：7508511054, 7508511050. (Journey into China)

《艺术之旅：英文》，靳永著；王力兴，赵秀福译. 五洲传播出版社（中国之旅丛书/郭长建，李向平主编）

11. Fine art archaeology and religious art/Wang Xiaoyang, Yao Yibin；translated by Shen Jian［and others］. Beijing：China Academy of Art Press, 2009. vi, 270 pages：illustrations；21cm. ISBN：7810838399, 7810838393

《美术考古与宗教美术》，汪小洋，姚义斌著. 中国美术学院出版社.

12. The best of China. Art & culture/［Yang, chunyan］. Beijing：Foreign languages Press, 2010. 55 pages：color illustrations；18cm. ISBN：7119063157, 7119063154

《最美中国. 艺术与文化》，外文出版社编. 选取中国有代表性的传统艺术与文化：京剧、昆曲、古琴、木卡姆、书法、中国画、剪纸、年画、刺绣等.

13. A history of art in 20th-Century China/Lü Peng；［translation Bruce Gordon Doar］. Milano：Charta, ［2010］. 1284 pages：illustrations (some color)；29cm. ISBN：8881587797, 8881587793

《20 世纪中国艺术史》，吕澎（1956—）著；Bruce Gordon Doar 译.

14. 798 and contemporary art/Huang Wenya and Cui Kaixuan. Beijing：Foreign Languages Press, 2010. 253 pages：illustrations (chiefly color), color maps；24cm. ISBN：7119060194, 7119060198

《798 与当代艺术》，崔凯旋、黄文亚编著. 本书主要从 798 艺术区的形成、先锋艺术在 798、亲临感受 798 这三大部分展示中国 soho 式艺术群落及中国最前沿的艺术作品；798 作为中国当代文化的缩影，中国先锋艺术与世界艺术对话交流的平台，已成为世界关注的焦点.

15. Chinese daoist arts/Wang Yi'e. Beijing：China Intercon-

tinental Press，2011．172 pages：color illustrations；21cm．ISBN：7508518398，750851839X

《中国道教艺术》，王宜峨著．五洲传播出版社．

16. Christian arts in China/Su Xile. Beijing：China Intercontinental Press，2011．170 pages：color illustrations；21cm．ISBN：7508519913，7508519914

《中国基督教艺术》，苏喜乐著．五洲传播出版社．

17. The Buddhist art of China/Zhang Zong. Beijing：China Intercontinental Press，2011．177 pages：color illustrations；21cm．ISBN：7508520759，7508520750

《中国佛教艺术》，张总著；邵达译．五洲传播出版社．

18. Fan Zeng's essays on art/translator：Liu Shicong, Nili Halperin, Liu Bo. Tianjin Shi：Nan kai da xue chu ban she chu ban fa xing，2013．121 pages：color illustrations, color portraits；31cm．ISBN：7310042937，731004293X

《范曾艺文》，范曾著；刘士聪、郝妮丽、刘波译．

19. 中国色彩/赵菁编著．合肥：黄山书社，2016．168 页：图；23cm．ISBN：7546141572.（印象中国）

英文题名：Chinese colors. 英汉对照．

20. 中外美术对比发展史：英文/张道森著；江崖等译．杭州：中国美术学院出版社，2007．图；30cm．ISBN：7810836104

J2　绘画

1. The Chinese on the art of painting. Peiping，H. Vetch，1936．3 p. l.，261 p. vii pl.（incl. front.）23cm.

Contents：Introduction—From the Han to the T'ang Dynasty—The Sung Period. Landscapists and poet-painters；Historians and theoreticians—Ch'an Buddhism and its relation to painting—The Yüan Period—The Ming Period. Historical theories and methods of study；Aesthetic principles and technical questions—The Ch'ing Period. New individual departures；Traditional principles reasserted—Appendixes—Index of Chinese names, terms and books

中国绘画艺术理论. Sirén, Osvald(1879—1966)译.

(1) The Chinese on the art of painting：translations and comments. New York：Schocken Books，1963．261 p. illus. 23cm．ISBN：0805200576.（Schocken paperbacks，SB57）

(2) The Chinese on the art of painting：texts by the painter-critics, from the Han through the Ch'ing dynasties/Osvald Sirén. Dover ed. Mineola，N. Y.：Dover Publications，2005．261 pages：illustrations；22cm．ISBN：0486444284，0486444287

2. Traditional Chinese paintings：silent poems in praise of nature and human life/author, Zhuang Jiayi and Nie Chongzheng；translator, Chen Gengtao. Beijing：China Intercontinental Press，2000．172 pages：illustrations（some color）；21cm．ISBN：7801137167，7801137166.

（China basics series）

《中国绘画：无声诗里诵千秋》，庄嘉怡，聂崇正著．五洲传播出版社．

3. The art of Chinese painting/Lin Ci；translated by Yan Xinjian & Ni Yanshuo.［Beijing］：China Intercontinental Press，2006．153 pages：color illustrations；23cm．ISBN：7508509641，7508509648.（Cultural China series）

《中国绘画艺术：英文》，林茨著；阎新建，倪严硕译．五洲传播出版社．

4. Chinese painting：capturing the spirit of nature with brushes/Lin Ci；translated by Yan Xinjian & Ni Yanshuo.［2nd ed.］. Beijing：China Intercontinental Press，2010．181 pages：illustrations（some color），facsimiles；23cm．ISBN：7508516691，7508516699.（Cultural China series）

《中国绘画艺术》，林茨著．五洲传播出版社．

5. Chinese painting/Zheng Gong. Beijing：New Star Press，2017．221 pages：colour illustrations；23cm．ISBN：7513325189

《中国绘画艺术》，郑工著．新星出版社（"感受当代中国"系列丛书）

6. A comparison between Chinese and Western paintings/compiled by Wu Jing. Beijing：China Intercontinental Press，2008．142 pages：illustrations（chiefly color）；23cm．ISBN：7508512716，7508512715.（中西文化比较丛书）

《中西绘画比较》，吴菁著．五洲传播出版社．

7. 中国人物画史简述：英文/余宏达著．杭州：中国美术学院出版社，2006．170 页；21cm．ISBN：781083505X.（中国美术学院研究生文论丛书）

论述了中国人物画的起源、发展与当下所处的现实环境．

8. Chinese woodcuts/written by Li Hua；translated by Zuo Boyang. Beijing：Foreign Languages Press，1995．210 pages：illustrations（some color）；32cm．ISBN：7119003887，7119003887

Contents：pt. 1. Ancient woodcuts—pt. 2. Modern woodcuts.

《中国古代木刻与新兴木刻》，李桦著，左伯阳译．

9. 论中国传统版画＝Discussion on Chinese traditional print-making：英文/吕启昭著．杭州：中国美术学院出版社，2006．21cm.（中国美术学院研究生文论丛书）

系统论述了中国传统版画的起源、发展以及在不同历史阶段所形成的各种风格、形式内容．

10. Some T'ang and pre-T'ang texts on Chinese painting, translated and annotated. Leiden，E. J. Brill，1954—74．2 v. in 3. 25cm.（Sinica Leidensia，v. 8，12）

Notes：Vol. 2 has additional title：Chang Yen-yüan, Li tai ming hua chi, chapters IV-X：pt. 1, translation and annotations, pt. 2, Chinese text.

《历代名画记》第 4—10 章，张彦远(815—907 年)；Acker, William Reynolds Beal(1907—)译注．英汉文本．

(1) Some T'ang and pre-T'ang texts on Chinese painting/ translated and annotated by William Reynolds Beal Acker. Hyperion reprint ed. Westport, Conn.: Hyperion Press, 1979. lxii, 414 p.; 22cm. ISBN: 0883558254. (Sinica Leidensia; v. 8.)

11. The spirit of the brush, being the outlook of Chinese painters on nature, from eastern Chin to five dynasties, A. D. 317—960, London, J. Murray [1939]. 108 p. 17cm.

《宋朝名画评》，刘道醇（生卒不详，活动于 1057 年前后）；Lachman, Charles H. (Charles Henry, 1949—)译注. 中英文本.

18. An old Chinese garden: a three-fold masterpiece of poetry, calligraphy and painting/by Wen Chên Ming; studies written by Kate Kerby; translations by Mo Zung Chung. Shanghai, China: Chung Hwa Book Company, 1923. 179 unnumbered pages; illustrations; 32cm.

《文待诏拙政园图》，文徵明（1470—1559）；Kerby, Kate 评；Chung, Mo Zung 译. 上海中华书局. 收文徵明绘拙政园内各处景色图 31 幅，每幅均佐以诗文，融诗、书、画于一体，后收文徵明撰《王氏拙政园记》以及戴熙等其他画家绘拙政园图数幅. 书中诗文均译成英文.

Sakanishi, Shiho(1896—1976)译. 选译了东晋之五代时期中国画家的绘画理论.

12. Friar Bitter-Melon on painting/by Shih-t'ao; Tr. Lin yutang. [Taibei Shi]: Art Society of China, [19—?]. 16, 11 pages; 27cm.

《苦瓜和尚画语录》，石涛（1642—1707）；林语堂（1895—1976）译. 英汉对照.

19. Chinese color-prints from the Painting manual of the Mustard Seed Garden. London, Allen and Unwin [1952, c1951]. 17 p. (on double leaves) plates (part col.)28×33cm.

《芥子园画传》，王概（生卒年未详，活动时间在 1677—1705 年）.

13. Experiences in painting (T'u-hua chien-wên chih) An eleventh century history of Chinese painting, together with the Chinese text in facsimile; translated and annotated by Alexander Coburn Soper. Washington, American Council of Learned Societies, 1951. xiii, 216 p., facsim.: [68] p. 26cm. (American Council of Learned Societies. Studies in Chinese and related civilizations, no. 6)

《图画见闻志》，郭若虚著；Soper, Alexander Coburn 译.

20. The tao of painting, a study of the ritual disposition of Chinese painting; with a translation of the Chieh tzu yüan hua chuan; or, Mustard Seed Garden manual of painting, 1679—1701, by Mai-mai Sze. [New York] Pantheon Books [1956]. 2 v. illus., plates (part col.) 27cm. (Bollingen series, 49)

《芥子园画传》，王概（生卒年未详，活动时间在 1677—1705 年）；施蕴珍（Sze, Mai-mai）译. 英汉对照.

(1) 2nd ed., with corrections. [New York] Pantheon Books [c1963]. 2 v. in 1. (Bollingen series; 49)

14. 艺术思想的片断＝Segments of artistic conception: 英文/谢青青，魏伟著. 杭州：中国美术学院出版社，2007. 323 页；20cm. ISBN: 7810836005, 7810836005. （青年艺术文库）

本书研究了中国历史上的版画和雕塑.

(2) The Mustard Seed Garden manual of painting＝Jie zi yuan hua zhuan, 1679—1701: a facsimile of the 1887—1888 Shanghai edition with the text translated from the Chinese and edited by Mai-mai Sze. Princeton, N. J.: Princeton University Press, 1977. xvii, 624 p.: ill.; 22cm. ISBN: 0691018197. (Princeton/Bollingen paperbacks; 427). (Bollingen series)

15. History of painting/Liu Shizhong. Encyclopedia of China Publishing House, 2009. IV, 204 p.: ill.; 22cm. ISBN: 7500080541, 7500080549. (History of Chinese civilization)

《绘画史话》，《中华文明史话》编委会编译. 中国大百科全书出版社.

(3) Princeton, N. J.: Princeton University Press, 1977. xvii, 624 p.: ill.; 22×23cm. ISBN: 0691099405. (Bollingen series)

16. Guide to capturing a plum blossom/by Sung Po-jen; the Chinese classic translated with commentaries by Red Pine; introduction by Lo Ch'ing. San Francisco, Calif.: Mercury House, c1995. xiv, 100 leaves; ill.; 21cm. ISBN: 1562790773

《梅花喜神谱》，宋伯仁（生卒不详，宋人）；赤松（Red Pine, 1943—，真名，Bill Porter）（美国翻译家、诗人）译.

(1) 2nd ed. Port Townsend, Wash.: Copper Canyon Press, c2011. xxi, 219 p.: ill.; 23cm. ISBN: 1556593789

21. The way of Chinese painting, its ideas and technique; with selections from the seventeenth-century Mustard Seed Garden manual of painting. New York: Random House [c1959]. 456 p. illus. 19cm. (Modern library paperbacks, P-57)

《芥子园画传》，王概（生卒年未详，活动时间在 1677—1705 年）；施蕴珍（Sze, Mai-mai）译.

17. Evaluations of Sung Dynasty painters of renown: Liu Tao-ch'un's Sung-ch'ao ming-hua p'ing/translated with an introduction by Charles Lachman. Leiden; New York: E. J. Brill, 1989. 115 p.; 24cm. ISBN: 9004089667. (T'oung pao. Monographic, 0169—832X; v. 16)

22. A selection of traditional Chinese paintings/[editor, Lin Wuhan; translator, Tang Fuchun]. Beijing: China Intercontinental Press, 2007. 229 pages: color illustrations; 30cm. ISBN: 7508510309, 7508510305

《中国绘画珍藏:英文》,林武汉主编,刘奉文著;唐富春译.五洲传播出版社.囊括了魏晋讫清代期间近 200 幅中国古代绘画珍品.

23. Underground art gallery: China's brick paintings, 1,700 years old/paintings reproduced by Wang Tianyi. Beijing, China: New World Press: Distributed by China International Book Trading Corp. , 1989. 131 pages: illustrations (some color); 27cm. ISBN: 7800050165, 7800050169

《魏晋墓砖画》,王天一临摹.新世界出版社编.新世界出版社.

24. 清·孙温绘全本红楼梦:汉英对照/(清)孙温绘;旅顺博物馆编;含淡译.北京:作家出版社,2007. 234 页;33×35cm. ISBN: 7506340335, 750634033X

英文题名:Picture book of 'dream of red mansions' by Sun Wen in Qing dynasty. 为孙温所绘工笔人物画集.

25. Flower and bird painting in ancient China/Liu Fengwen. China: China Intercontinental Press, 2007. 145 pages; 21cm. ISBN: 7508511283, 750851128X

《中国历代花鸟画:英文》,李向平主编;刘奉文撰稿;邵达译.五洲传播出版社.

26. Ancient China's genre painting featuring children/ [writer, Geng Mingsong; picture editor, Cai Cheng; translator, Shao Da. Beijing: China Intercontinental Press, 2008. 111 pages: color illustrations; 21cm. ISBN: 7508514093, 7508514092

《中国古代儿童生活画》,李向平主编.五洲传播出版社.介绍中国历代儿童生活画.

27. Animal-themed paintings in ancient China/[writer, Geng Mingsong; translator, Shao Da]. Beijing: China Intercontinental Press, 2008. 145 pages: chiefly color illustrations; 21cm. ISBN: 7508514109, 7508514106. (Chinese traditional culture series)

《中国古代动物画》,李向平主编.五洲传播出版社.介绍中国历代有关宠物(猫、狗、马)等绘画作品.

28. Chinese farmer painting/compiled by Xi Jiping; translated by Shao Da. Beijing: China Intercontinental Press, 2008. [4], 102 pages: color illustrations; 19×22cm. ISBN: 7508512853, 7508512855. (China folk arts series)

《中国农民画》,奚吉平编著.五洲传播出版社.

29. A history of Chinese painting/written by Zhang Anzhi; translated by Dun J. Li. Beijing, China: Foreign Languages Press, 1992. 244 pages: illustrations (some color); 31cm. ISBN: 0835127982, 0835127981, 7119014811, 7119014814

《中国画发展史纲要》,张安治著.

30. Paintings in China/compiled [i. e. written] by Zhang Jie; translated by Joyce Chao. Beijing: New Star Press, 2009. 217 pages: illustrations; 23cm. ISBN: 7802256248, 7802256240

《绘画·感受中国》,张杰编著.新星出版社.当代中国绘画史.

31. A selection of contemporary Chinese paintings. Běijīng: Zhaohua Pub. House, 1981. 112 pages: chiefly illustrations (chiefly color); 37cm.

《现代中国画集粹》.朝华出版社.

32. An album of contemporary Chinese paintings/[writer, Cheng Nan; translator, Shao Da]. [Beijing]: China International Press, 2009. 141 pages: color illustrations; 21cm. ISBN: 7508514932, 7508514939. (Chinese traditional culture series)

《中国当代国画》,李向平主编.五洲传播出版社.介绍中国当代著名国画家及其代表作品.

33. An illustrated history of China's war of resistance against Japan/written by Zhang Chengjun, Liu Jianye; photos edited by Lu Shuping, Xu Liping, Qiu Yuling; translated by He Jun [and others]. Beijing: Foreign Languages Press, (2000 printing), 1995. 132 pages: illustrations, maps; 25×27cm. ISBN: 711901739X, 7119017396

《中国抗日战争画史》,张承钧,刘建业编著.

34. 吴作人,萧淑芳画选=Selected paintings of Wu Zuoren and Xiao Shufang/edited by Sun Jie. 北京:朝华出版社:发行 中国国际书店,1982. 109 pages: chiefly color illustrations; 37cm. ISBN: 0080279503, 0080279503

35. Artist's vision, poet's passion: the paintings of Fu Baoshi/comp. by the Nanjing Museum and Morning Glory Publ. [Engl. transl. : Wang Xingzheng]. Beijing: Morning Glory Publ. , 1988. 115 pages: color illustrations; 38cm. ISBN: 7505400673, 7505400672

《傅抱石画选》

36. Selected paintings by Fan Zeng/[editors Xu Zhongmin, Zhou Daguang; translator Miao Ling]. Beijing: Foreign Languages Press; Changsha: Hunan Fine Arts Publishing House, 1985. 56 pages: color illustrations; 25×26cm. ISBN: 083511564X, 0835115643

《范曾画集》,范曾(1938—);Xu, Zhongmin 和 Zhou, Daguang 编;Miao Ling 译.

37. Fan Tseng shu hua chi = The album of Fan Zeng's calligraphy and paintings. Tianjin, China: People's Fine Arts and Pub. House, 1988. 134 pages: chiefly illustrations (some color), portraits; 39cm. ISBN: 7530501410, 7530501412

《范曾书画集》,范曾(1938—).

38. An introduction to traditional Chinese painting/written and painted by He Hanqiu and Deng Jun; translated by Ouyang Caiwei. Beijing: Foreign Languages Press, 1995. 71 pages: illustrations (some color); 26cm. ISBN: 7119004336, 7119004334

《中国画入门》,何汉秋,邓军编绘.

39. The techniques of Chinese painting/Wu Yangmu; translator Gong Lizeng. Beijing: Morning Glory Pubs,

1996. 192 p. : ill. (some col.); 25cm. ISBN：7505404202, 7505404205

《中国画基础技法》,吴敩木编著.朝华出版社.

40. Chinese landscape painting for beginners/Li Dongxu; translated by Wen Jingen with Pauline Cherrett. Beijing: Foreign Languages Press, 2007. 199 pages: illustrations (some color); 26cm. ISBN：7119046150, 7119046152. ("How to" series)

《怎样画山水画:英文》,李东旭著.外文出版社(怎样做系列).

41. Chinese bird-and-flower painting for beginners/Ma Zhifeng; translated by Wen Jingen with Pauline Cherrett. Beijing: Foreign Languages Press, 2007. 191 pages: color illustrations; 26cm. ISBN：7119048123, 7119048120. (How to series)

《怎样画花鸟画:英文》,马志丰著.外文出版社(怎样做系列).

42. China in New Year paintings/Keqin Lu. Beijing: China Intercontinental Press, 2010. 232 p. : ill. ; 26cm. ISBN：7508517377, 7508517377

《年画上的中国》,撰稿,陆克勤;翻译,顾伟光,韩铁.五洲传播出版社.

43. Chinese figure painting for beginners/Jia Xiangguo; translated by Wen Jingen with Pauline Cherrett. Beijing: Foreign Languages Press, 2007. 174 pages: color illustrations; 26cm. ISBN：7119048130, 7119048139. (How to series)

《怎样画人物画:英文》,贾向国著.外文出版社(怎样做系列).介绍中国人物画的发展概况、工具和绘制步骤,讲述笔墨技巧,并附有佳作欣赏.

44. Chinese propaganda posters: 1921—1971/Anchee Min, Jie Zhang, Duoduo. Köln; London: Taschen, 2003. 319 pages: color facsimiles; 37cm. ISBN：3822826197, 3822826195

Contents：The girl in the poster/Anchee Min—Looking at the propaganda posters/Duo Duo—The rise and fall of the Chinese propaganda poster/Stefan R. Landsberger—The Communist party—Classes and class struggle—Socialism and Communism—The correct handling of contradictions among the people—War and peace—Imperialism and all reactionaries are paper tigers—Dare to struggle and dare to win—People's war—The people's army—Leadership of party committees—The mass line—Political work—Relations between officers and men—Relations between the army and the people—Democracy in the three main fields—Education and the training of troops—Serving the people—Patriotism and internationalism—Revolutionary heroism—Building our country through diligence and frugality—Self-reliance and arduous struggle—Methods of thinking and methods of work—Investigation and study—Ideological self-cultivation—Unity—Discipline—Criticism and self-criticism—Communists—Cadres—Youth—Women—Culture and art—Study—New year.

Notes：This book shows part of Michael Wolf's propaganda poster collection. The posters have been arranged in an order that corresponds with the chapters in The Little Red Book (or Quotations from Chairman Mao Zedong)."—P. 320. Parallel text in English, French and German.

Min, Anchee(1957—), Zhang jie, 多多(1951—)撰文; Varea, Isabel 英译.对中国宣传海报(部分)的汇集说明,以英、法、德文翻译.海报,招贴画.

(1) Chinese propaganda posters/editorial direction, Benedikt Tasche; project management, Angelika Taschen, Kathrin Murr; editorial coordination, Yuko Aoki; authors, Anchee Min, Duo Duo, Stefan R. ［Hong Kong］: CR Publication, 2006. 319 pages： color illustrations; 37cm. ISBN：9889902400, 9889902407 正文为英、日、法文.

(2) Chinese propaganda posters：from the collection of Michael Wolf/with essays by Anchee Min, Duo Duo, & Stefan R. Landsberger. 25th anniversary ed. Köln; Los Angeles: Taschen, 2008. 239 pages: color illustrations; 34cm. ISBN：3836503167, 3836503166

(3) Chinese propaganda posters/［posters collected by Michael Wolf; written by Stefan R. Landsberger, Anchee Min, DuoDuo; English translation, Isabel Varea and Karen Waloschek; German translation, Jie Zhao, Brigitte Beier; French translation, Catherine Henry, Annie Berthold］. Köln: Taschen, 2011. 320 p. : col. ill. ; 22cm. ISBN：3836531085, 3836531089

(4) Chinese propaganda posters/with essays by Anchee Min, Duo Duo and Stefan R. Landsberger. Köln, Germany: Taschen, 2015. 608 pages: color illustrations; 21cm.

45. 壁画/简洁编著.合肥:黄山书社,2016. 149 页;23cm. ISBN：7546141817.(印象中国)

英文题名:Ancient Chinese mural painting. 英汉对照.

46. 国画/郭晓光编著.合肥:黄山书社,2016. 170 页；彩图,摹真;23cm. ISBN：7546141657.(印象中国)

英文题名:Chinese painting. 英汉对照

47. 年画/孙欣编著.合肥:黄山书社,2016. 152 页；彩图;23cm. ISBN：7546141497.(印象中国)

英文题名:New years pictures. 英汉对照.

48. 瑞兽祥禽/秦芮编著.合肥:黄山书社,2016. 142 页；彩图;23cm. ISBN：7546141718.(印象中国)

英文题名:Auspicious animals and birds in Chinese culture. 英汉对照.动物画.

49. Thangka paintings of the Tibetan oral epic King Gesar/

Zhou Aiming & Jambian Gyamco. Beijing：China Intercontinental Press，2013. 219 pages：color illustrations；30cm. ISBN：7508525358，7508525353

《藏族口传史诗〈格萨尔王〉唐卡》，周爱明，降边嘉措.

50. Paintings of Beijing opera characters/by Dong Chensheng. Beijing：Zhaohua Pub. House：Distributed by Guoji Shudian，1981. 64 pages：illustrations (some color)；27cm.

《董辰生京剧人物画集》.朝华出版社.

J21 书法、篆刻

1. Two Chinese treatises on calligraphy/introduced, translated，and annotated by Chang Ch'ung-ho and Hans H. Frankel. New Haven：Yale University Press，c1995. xv，144 p. : ill. ; 25cm. ISBN：0300061188，0300061185
Notes：Treatise on calligraphy (Shu pu)［by］Sun Qianli；Sequel to the "Treatise on calligraphy" (Xu Shu pu)［by］Jiang Kui.

张充和（Chang, Ch'ung-ho），1914—）、傅汉思（Frankel, Hans H.（Hans Hermann，1916—）合译，翻译了孙过庭《书谱》和姜夔的《续书谱》.中英文本.

2. Gate to Chinese calligraphy/written by Guo Bonan. Beijing，China：Foreign Languages Press，1995. 67 pages：illustrations；26cm. ISBN：7119014358，7119014357

《中国书法入门》，郭伯南著.

3. Chinese calligraphy/Chen Tingyou；translated by Ren Lingjuan.［Beijing］：China Intercontinental Press，2003. 127 p. : il. col. ；23cm. ISBN：7508503228，7508503226. (Cultural China series)

《中国书法》，陈廷祐著；任灵娟译.五洲传播出版社.

(1)2nd ed. Beijing：China Intercontinental Press，2010. 128 p：ill. (some col.)；24cm. ISBN：7508516950，7508516958. (Cultural China series)

4. 书法/楚丹编著.合肥：黄山书社，2016. 162 页；彩图；23cm. ISBN：7546152875. (印象中国)
英文题名：Chinese calligraphy. 英汉对照.

5. 现代书法三步：汉英对照/古干著；胡允桓英译.北京：中国青年出版社，2005. 249 页；30cm. ISBN：7500665180，7500665182
本书介绍中国现代书法理论与技巧.

6. 玄秘塔碑：汉英对照/王鉴伟编著.南京：江苏美术出版社，2006. 64 页；33cm. ISBN：7534421683，7534421686. (书法技要丛书)
楷书书法.

7. 胆巴碑：汉英对照/王鑑伟编著.南京：江苏美术出版社，2006. 64 页；33cm. ISBN：7534421675，7534421679. (书法技要丛书)
楷书书法.

8. A self study course in running script/compiled and written by Huang Quanxin. Beijing：Sinolingua，1998. 152 p. :

ill. ；26cm. ISBN：7800524566，7800524561. (Chinese calligraphy teach-yourself series)

《行书自学教程》，黄全信编著.华语教学出版社.

9. Chinese running script calligraphy for beginner/Wang Xianchun；translated by Wen Jingen with Pauline Cherrett. Beijing：Foreign languages Press，2007. 159 pages：illustrations (some color)；26cm. ISBN：7119048604，7119048600. ("How to" series)

《怎样写行书：英文》，王贤春著.外文出版社(怎样做系列)

10. A self-study course in seal script/compiled and written by Huang Quanxin. Beijing：Sinolingua，1998. 152 pages：illustrations；26cm. ISBN：7800524590，7800524592. (Chinese calligraphy teach-yourself series)

《篆书自学教程》，黄全信编著.华语教学出版社.

11. A self-study course in Wei stone inscriptions/compiled and written by Huang Quanxin. Beijing：Sinolingua，1998. 152 pages：illustrations (some color)；26cm. ISBN：7800524574，7800524578. (Chinese calligraphy teach-yourself series)

《魏碑自学教程》，黄全信编著.华语教学出版社.

12. A self-study course in official script/compiled and written by Huang Quanxin. Beijing：Sinolingua，1998. 152 pages：illustrations；26cm. ISBN：7800524558，7800524554. (Chinese calligraphy teach-yourself series)

《隶书自学教程》，黄全信编著.华语教学出版社.

13. Chinese regular script calligraphy for beginners/Zong Jianye；translated by Wen Jingen with Pauline Cherrett. Beijing：Foreign Languages Press，2007. 183 pages：illustrations (some color)；26cm. ISBN：7119048611，7119048619. ("How to" series)

《怎样写楷书：英文》，宗建业著；温晋根编译.外文出版社(怎样做系列)

14. 印/胡杨编著.合肥：黄山书社，2016. 157 页：图，照片；23cm. ISBN：7546142241. (印象中国)
英文题名：Chinese seals

J3 雕塑

1. A comparison between Chinese and Western sculpture/compiled by Huang Zongxian & Wu Yongqiang. Beijing：China Intercontinental Press，2008. 178 pages：color illustrations；23cm. ISBN：7508512693，7508512693. (中西文化比较丛书)

《中西雕塑比较》，黄宗贤，吴永强著.五洲传播出版社.

2. Chinese sculptures/compiled by Zheng Yi；translated by Transn. Beijing，China：New Star Press，2010. 187 pages：illustrations (some color)；23cm. ISBN：7802259508，7802259509

《雕塑·感受中国》，郑弋编著.新星出版社.

3. Chinese Sculpture/Zheng Yi. Beijing：New Star Press，2017. 157 pages：illustrations (some color)；23cm.

ISBN：7513325219

《中国雕塑之美》，郑弋著.新星出版社（"感受当代中国"系列丛书）

4. 雕刻/孙欣，童芸编著.合肥：黄山书社，2016.188 页：图；23cm. ISBN：7546141404.（印象中国）

英文题名：Chinese carving art. 英汉对照.

5. Han Dynasty stone reliefs：the Wu family shrines in Shandong Province. Beijing：Foreign Languages Press，1991. 142 pages：illustrations；33cm. ISBN：7119006150，7119006154，0835115968，0835115964

《中国汉代画像石：山东武氏祠》，刘兴珍，岳凤霞编. 石刻目录.

J4 工艺美术

1. Craftworks of China/Tan Song；translation by Zhao Qinghua. Beijing：China Intercontinental Press，2007. 143 pages：illustrations（chiefly color）；25cm. ISBN：7508510927，7508510925.（Journey into China；7）

《工艺之旅：英文》，谭松著；赵庆华译. 五洲传播出版社（中国之旅丛书/郭长建，李向平主编）

2. Chinese arts & crafts/Hang Jian & Guo Qiuhui；translated by Zhu Youruo & Song Peiming.［Beijing］：China Intercontinental Press，2006. 153 pages：illustrations（some color）；23cm. ISBN：7508509633，7508509631.（Cultural China series）

《中国传统工艺：英文》，杭间，郭秋惠著；朱攸若，宋佩铭译. 五洲传播出版社. 介绍了中国传统工艺在不同历史时期的发展情况，并分类介绍了器用类工艺、穿戴类工艺、陈设类工艺、装饰类工艺、游艺类工艺等.

　(1)Chinese arts & crafts：history，techniques and legends/Hang Jian，Guo Qiuhui；translated by Zhu Youruo & Song Peiming. 2nd ed. Beijing：China Intercontinental Press，2009. 203 pages：illustrations（some color）；23cm. ISBN：7508516080，7508516087.（Cultural China series）

3. A pictorial album of Chinese folk art/text by Wang Shucun；translated by Zhang Chengmo. Hangzhou：Zhejiang wen yi chu ban she，1992. 8，234，：ill.（some col.）；30cm. ISBN：7533906098，7533906092

《中国民间美术图说》，王树村著；英文翻译张承谟. 浙江文艺出版社. 英汉对照.

4. Chinese folk arts/Jin Zhilin；translated by Jin Bei. Beijing：China International Press，2004. 139 pages：color illustrations；24cm. ISBN：7508506111，7508506111.（Cultural China series）

Contents：Introduction：China's cultural heritage and folk arts—Six characteristics of Chinese folk arts—The core of Chinese folk arts—Social context of folk arts—Folk arts and festivities—Folk arts in daily life—Folk arts in beliefs and taboos—The art work created by Chinese folk arts—Structure of colors—Creators of Chinese folk arts—Folk artists of the working class—Illustrations of various Chinese folk art works.

《中国民间美术》，靳之林著；金蓓译. 五洲传播出版社. 介绍剪纸、风筝、面具等中国民间艺术.

　(1)2nd ed. Beijing：China Intercontinental Press，2010. 144 pages：color illustrations；24cm. ISBN：7508516912，7508516915.（Cultural China series）

5. 中国民间工艺＝Chinese folk handicraft/捷人（文物）编文；刘海珍（手工艺）翻译，夏赛辉 翻译. 长沙市：湖南美术出版社，2004. 1 volume（unpaged）：illustrations（some color）；20 × 22cm. ISBN：7535621023，7535621023.（中国传统手工艺实物书系 ＝ Chinese traditional handicraft series）

英汉对照

6. Beijing Masters：encounters with Chinese handicrafts/［author Chen Xiaorong］. Beijing：China Travel & Tourism Press，2008. 197 pages：illustrations；23cm. ISBN：7503234163，7503234164

《北京绝活》，陈晓蓉著. 中国旅游出版社. 介绍北京传统手工艺传人及其作品，如制作弓箭，风筝，面人，皮影，玻璃，绢人等手工艺品及传人的故事.

7. 传统手工艺/徐雯，吕品田编著.合肥：黄山书社，2016.176 页：图；23cm. ISBN：7546141374.（印象中国）

英文题名：Traditional handicraft. 英汉对照.

8. The art of Chinese papercuts/Zhang Daoyi；［edited and translated by Ellen Hertz and Tang Bowen］. Beijing，China：Foreign Languages Press，1989. i，67 pages：illustrations（some color）；26cm. ISBN：0835115771，0835115773，7119007912，7119007915.（Traditional Chinese arts and culture）

《中国民间剪纸艺术》，张道一（1932—）.

9. 学剪纸/张红主编.天津：天津教育出版社，2009. 24 页；26cm. ISBN：7530956472，7530956477

10. 剪纸/茅翔编著.合肥：黄山书社，2016.160 页：图；23cm. ISBN：7546141435.（印象中国）

英文题名：Paper cutting. 英汉对照.

11. Chinese kites：their arts and crafts/written by Wang Xiaoyu；illustrated by Qu Lixiu；translated by Lao An［and others］；version revised by An Zengcai. Jinan：Shandong Friendship Pub. House，1996. 300 pages，［6］pages of plates：illustrations（some color）；27cm. ISBN：7805517568，7805517568

《风筝技艺》，王晓瑜著，老安等译，山东友谊出版社.

12. 风筝/李鹏编著.合肥：黄山书社，2016.138 页：图；23cm. ISBN：7546141411.（印象中国）

英文题名：Kites. 英汉对照.

13. Folk silver accessories/compiled by Wang Jinhua. Beijing：Foreign Languages Press，2008. 125 pages：color illustrations；24cm. ISBN：7119046761，7119046764.（Folk craft heritage of China）

《民间银饰》，王金华编著.

14. Folk shadow play/compiled by Wei Liqun. Beijing：Foreign Languages Press，2008. 155 pages：color illustrations；24cm. ISBN：7119046709，7119046705.（Folk craft heritage of China）
《民间皮影》，魏力群编著.

15. 木偶/童芸，孙欣编著. 合肥：黄山书社，2016. 144 页：彩图；23cm. ISBN：7546141473.（印象中国）
英文题名：Chinese puppetry. 英汉对照.

16. Chinese folk masks/compiled by Gong Ning；translated by Shao Da. Beijing：China Intercontinental Press，2008.［4］，102 pages：color illustrations；19×22cm. ISBN：7508512846，7508512847.（China folk arts series）
《中国民间面具》，龚宁编著. 五洲传播出版社.

17. 面具/孙欣编著. 合肥：黄山书社，2016. 136 页：彩图；23cm. ISBN：7546142289.（印象中国）
英文题名：Masks. 英汉对照.

18. 中国成都蜀锦：汉英对照/黄能馥主编. 北京：紫禁城出版社，2006. 175 页：图；30cm. ISBN：7800476103，7800476105
英文题名：Shu brocade：Chengdu of China. 叙述蜀锦的发展史.

19. Folk textile arts/compiled by Duan Jianhua. Beijing：Foreign Languages Press，2009. 134 pages：color illustrations；24cm. ISBN：7119046778，7119046772.（Folk craft heritage of China）
《民间染织》，段建华编著；金绍卿英文翻译.

20. Folk cloth articles/compiled by Chen Xiaoping. Beijing：Foreign Languages Press，2009. 115 pages：color illustrations；24cm. ISBN：7119056296，7119056298.（Folk craft heritage of China＝中国民间文化遗产）
《民间布艺》，陈晓萍编著.

21. 染织/童芸编著. 合肥：黄山书社，2016. 152 页：图（部分彩图），摹真；23cm. ISBN：7546152790.（印象中国）
英文题名：Chinese dyeing and weaving. 英汉对照.

22. 刺绣/童芸编著. 合肥：黄山书社，2016. 178 页：图；23cm. ISBN：7546142265.（印象中国）
英文题名：Embroidery. 英汉对照.

23. Folk woodcarving/compiled by Wang Kangsheng. Beijing：Foreign Languages Press，2009. 143 pages：color illustrations；24cm. ISBN：7119046792，7119046799.（Folk craft heritage of China＝中国民间文化遗产）
《民间木雕》，王抗生编著；梁发明翻译.

24. The striving and hardship on the journey of art：interview record of boxwood carving art master Wang Fengzuo/edited and translated by Xu Anbing. Beijing：China Academy of Art Press，2009. 131 pages；21cm. ISBN：7810838252，7810838253
《艺途求索话沧桑》，徐岸兵著译. 中国美术学院出版社.
介绍了老一辈艺术家创作黄杨木雕这一手工艺术的艰难的过程.

25. Folk stone lions/compiled by Zhang Huaishui. Beijing：Foreign Languages Press，2009. 127 pages：color illustrations；24cm. ISBN：7119056289，711905628X.（Folk craft heritage of China＝中国民间文化遗产）
《民间石狮》，张淮水编著.

26. Chinese auspicious designs/compiled by Gong Ning & Yun Wen；translated by Shao Da. Beijing：China Intercontinental Press，2009. 102 pages：color illustrations；19×22cm. ISBN：7508512860，7508512863.（China folk arts series＝中国民间工艺系列）
《中国吉祥艺术》，龚宁，韵雯编著. 五洲传播出版社.（民间工艺）

27. 吉祥图案/叔戊编著. 合肥：黄山书社，2016. 176 页：彩图；23cm. ISBN：7546141671.（印象中国）
英文题名：Auspicious designs of China. 英汉对照.（工艺美术）

28. Chinese clay sculptures/compiled by Li Youyou；translated by Shao Da. Beijing：China Intercontinental Press，2009. 101 pages：color illustrations；19×22cm. ISBN：7508513133，7508513134.（China folk arts series＝中国民间工艺）
《中国民间泥塑》，李友友编著. 五洲传播出版社.

29. 泥塑/宫楚涵编著. 合肥：黄山书社，2016. 132 页：彩图；23cm. ISBN：7546152783.（印象中国）
英文题名：Clay sculpture. 英汉对照.

30. 面塑/宫楚涵编著. 合肥：黄山书社，2016. 130 页：彩图；23cm. ISBN：7546142296.（印象中国）
英文题名：Dough modeling. 英汉对照.

31. 漆器/郭小影编著. 合肥：黄山书社，2016. 160 页：图；23cm. ISBN：7546142197.（印象中国）
英文题名：Chinese lacquerware. 英汉对照.

32. 灯彩/闫东东编著. 合肥：黄山书社，2016. 131 页：图；23cm. ISBN：7546141398.（印象中国）
英文题名：Chinese lanterns. 英汉对照.

33. 民间玩具/孙欣编著. 合肥：黄山书社，2016. 176 页：图；23cm. ISBN：7546141466.（印象中国）
英文题名：Folk toys. 英汉对照.

34. 中国结/徐雯编著. 合肥：黄山书社，2016. 116 页：图；23cm. ISBN：7546141770.（印象中国）
英文题名：Chinese knot. 英汉对照

35. 景泰蓝/茅翊编著. 合肥：黄山书社，2016. 152 页：彩图；23cm. ISBN：7546142166.（印象中国）
英文题名：Cloisonne

J5 中国音乐

1. Chinese children's rhymes，by Ruth Hsüh；with illustrations by Teng Kuei. Shanghai，China，The Commercial Press，Limited，1935. xxiv，98 p.，1 l. illus. 19cm.
《小放牛》，许仕廉夫人（Hsüh，Mrs. Ruth Ruby Schmidt）

译. 儿歌英译，催眠曲.

2. The flower drum and other Chinese songs. New York：The John Day Company，[1943]. 64 p. incl. front. illus. 29×22cm.

Notes：With piano accompaniment. Words in English and Chinese（transliterated）with original Chinese at end of each song

《中国民歌》. 陈世骧（Chen Shih-hsiang，1912—1971）（美国华裔学者）译.

3. A Chinese zither tutor＝the Mei-an ch'in-p'u/translated with commentary by Fredric Lieberman. Seattle：University of Washington Press，c1983. xi，172 p.：ill.；17×24cm. ISBN：029595941X

《梅庵琴谱》，王宾鲁（1867—1921）；李伯曼（Lieberman，Fredric）（美国汉学家）译.

4. Cook，Scott. Yue Ji，record of music：introduction，translation，notes，and commentary. Asian Music，26（2），1995 p. 1—96

《乐记》，顾史考（Scott Cook）译注，载于 1995 年 Asian Music 期刊. 音乐理论著作.

5. 蝉声中的文化：侗族大歌拾零：汉英对照/吴定国，邓敏文撰. 贵阳：贵州民族出版社，2005. 77 页；20cm. ISBN：7541212873，7541212871.（侗族文化系列丛书）

描述了侗族大歌的起源、传说、故事，并介绍了侗族大歌的发现、发展历程.

6. The music of China's ethnic minorities/by Li Yongxiang. [Beijing]：China Intercontinental Press，2006. 120 pages：illustrations（chiefly color）；24cm. ISBN：7508510070，7508510071.（Ethnic cultures of China）

《中国少数民族音乐：英文》，李勇翔编著；王国振等译. 五洲传播出版社（中国民族多元文化丛书）. 本书通过对中国少数民族典型音乐和乐器的介绍，反映中国少数民族音乐的多元文化特征.

7. Chinese music：echos in ancient and modern times/Jin Jie；translated by Wang Li ＆ Li Rong. Beijing：China Intercontinental Press，2010. 152 pages：color illustrations；23cm. ISBN：7508513294，7508513290.（Cultural China series）

《中国音乐》，靳婕编著. 五洲传播出版社.

8. Music of China/Yang Hong. Beijing：New Star Press，2017. 229 pages：illustrations（some color）；23cm. ISBN：7513325257

《音乐中国：英文》，杨红著. 新星出版社（"感受当代中国"系列丛书）

9. Critical history of new music in China/Liu Ching-Chih；translated by Caroline Mason. Hong Kong：Chinese University Press，c2010. xxi，911 p.，[24] p. of plates：ill.，music，ports.；24cm. ISBN：9629963606，9629963604

Contents：Introduction：New music in China and its theoretical foundations—The origins of new music （1885—1919）：the westernisation of military music and the birth of schoolsong—New music in the May fourth period（1919—1937）—The mass singing movement and musical creation in the anti-Japanese war period（1937—1945）—New music education and creation during the Civil War（1946—1949）and in the seventeen years after the founding of the People's Republic of China（1949—1966）—Yangbanxi and the music of the Cultural Revolution（1966—1979）：revolutionary modern Peking opera，ballet，symphonic music and songs—Musical creation after the Cultural Revolution and New Wave music—New music and composers in Taiwan，Hong Kong and Macao—Review and reflection：historical review（1885—1985）and the Sinicisation and modernisation of new music—New development（1996—2006）：mainland China，overseas，Taiwan and Hong Kong.

《中国新音乐史论》，刘靖之（1935—）；Mason，Caroline（1949—）译.

10. 歌声中的新中国：英文/李凤英编著. 北京：新星出版社，2017. 23cm. ISBN：7513325004

11. 传统乐器/肖迪编著. 合肥：黄山书社，2016. 172 页：彩图；23cm. ISBN：7546152950.（印象中国）

英文题名：Traditional Chinese musical instruments

J6　舞蹈

1. Dances of the Chinese minorities/by Li Beida. Beijing：China Intercontinental Press，2006. 120 pages：color illustrations；23cm. ISBN：7508510054，7508510057.（Ethnic cultures of China）

《中国少数民族舞蹈：英文》，李北达编著；王国振等译. 五洲传播出版社（中国民族多元文化丛书）

2. The charm of Chinese dance/Jiang Dong. Beijing：New Star Press，2017. 291 pages：illustrations（some color）；23cm. ISBN：7513325158

《中国舞蹈之美》，江东著. 新星出版社（"感受当代中国"系列丛书）

J7　戏剧、曲艺、杂技艺术

J71　中国戏剧艺术理论

1. Chinese theatre/chief editor Zhang Yihe；co-writers Zhang Yihe，Fu Shuyun，Cao Juan；translator Kuang Peihua. Beijing：Culture and Art Publishing House，1999. 3，184 p.：col. ill.；21cm. ISBN：7503918373.（Chinese culture and art series；5）

《中国戏曲》，Zhang，Yihe（1942—）主编；Kuang，Peihua 英译.

2. Chinese theater：happiness and sorrows on the stage/Fu Jin；translated by Wang Wenliang，Wang Huan ＆ Zhang Lina. Beijing：China Intercontinental Press，2010. 153

pages：illustrations（chiefly color）；23cm. ISBN：7508516837，7508516834.（Cultural China series）

《中国戏剧》，傅谨著.五洲传播出版社.中国戏剧史.

3. Chinese theatre/Jin Fu. Updated ed. Cambridge；New York：Cambridge University Press，2012. 137 p.：ill.（chiefly col.）；23cm. ISBN：0521186667，0521186668.（Introductions to Chinese culture）

《中国戏剧》，傅谨（1956—）著；王文亮等译.

4. Chinese opera/Mei，Weidong，Mei Wei. Beijing：New Star Press，2017. 285 pages：illustrations（chiefly color）；23cm. ISBN：7513325196

《中国戏曲艺术》，梅卫东，梅玮著.新星出版社（"感受当代中国"系列丛书）

5. 戏曲史话：中英文双语版/《中华文明史话》编委会编译.北京：中国大百科全书出版社，2010. 202 页；21cm. ISBN：7500082682，7500082681

英文题名：History of traditional opera

6. On Stanislavky's "system"/by Shanghai Revolutionary Mass Criticism Writing Group. Peking：Foreign Languages Press，1969. 37 pages；13cm.

《评斯坦斯拉夫斯基"体系"》，上海革命大批判写作小组编写.

7. 伏尔泰与《中国孤儿》/李志远著；Ego 翻译.北京：五洲传播出版社，2010. 175 页；23cm. ISBN：7508517117，7508517113.（中外文化交流故事丛书）

英文题名：Voltaire and the orphan of China

8. The stagecraft of Peking opera/by Pan Xiafeng. Beijing：New World Press，1995. 252 pages：illustrations；21cm. ISBN：7800050912，7800050916

《京剧艺术欣赏》，潘侠风著.新世界出版社.

9. Peking opera/Xu Chengbei；translated by Chen Gengtao.［Beijing］：China Intercontinental Press，2003. 128 p.：col. ill.；23cm. ISBN：7508502566，7508502564.（Cultural China series）

Notes："Translated from the original Chinese by Chen Gengtao"—Cover flap.

《中国京剧》，徐城北（1942—）；陈耕涛译.

(1)2nd ed. Beijing：China Intercontinental Press，2010. 130 p.：ill.（some col.）；24cm. ISBN：7508516646（Cultural China series）

(2)Updated ed. Cambridge；New York：Cambridge University Press，2012. 130 p.：ill.（some col.）；23cm. ISBN：0521188210，0521188210.（Introductions to Chinese culture）. 2287.

10. A primer of Beijing opera/by Liang Yan；［translated by R.B. Baron］. Beijing：Foreign Languages Press，2003. 70 pages：illustrations；23cm. ISBN：7119032887，7119032887

Notes："The twenty-six stories introduced in this book have been selected from the two hundred most frequently performed Beijing operas"—Introduction.

《京剧启蒙》，梁燕著.

11. Peking opera：the cream of Chinese culture/compiled by Yi Bian；translated by Zhang Shaoning. Beijing：Foreign Languages Press：Distributed by China International Book Trading Corporation，2005. 150 pages：color illustrations；21cm. ISBN：7119036971，7119036977

《国粹：中国京剧：英文》，易边编著；张绍宁译.

12. 京剧：汉英对照/王峰编；赵立柱译.北京：人民文学出版社，2006. 221 页；21cm. ISBN：7020048773，7020048779.（中国传统文化双语读本）

13. Traditional opera in Beijing/text by Yuan Jing；photographs by Zou Yi；translated by He Junlong. Beijing：China Pictorial Publishing House，2006. 103 pages：color illustrations；22cm. ISBN：7802200679，780220067

《在北京看戏：英文》，袁静撰文；邹毅摄；何俊龙译.中国画报出版社（2008，走近北京）.介绍了北京演出京剧的主要场馆、曲目知识及戏曲常识.

14. The unseen Peking opera/［editor：Lan Peijin；English editor：Xu Mingqiang；photographer：Wang Yao；writer：Yang Xiagui；translator：Chen Gang］. Beijing：Foreign Languages Press，2008. 148 p.：il. color；26cm. ISBN：7119051116，7119051113

《看不见的京剧》，杨遐贵.

15. Mei Lanfang and Peking opera/Richard Fusen Yang. Beijing，China：Foreign Languages Press，2009. 117 pages：illustrations；24cm. ISBN：7119060477，7119060473

《梅兰芳与京剧艺术》，杨富森编著.

16. 京剧/莫丽芸编著.合肥：黄山书社，2011. 166 页；21cm. ISBN：7546120386，7546120381，7546120485，7546120489.（中国红）

英文题名：Peking opera

17. 京剧艺术概述 /孙萍主编.北京：国家图书馆出版社，2016. 37，157 页，［4］页：图版，图（部分彩图），单页折图；29cm. ISBN：7501359042.（中国京剧百部经典外译系列.第三辑）

英文题名：An introduction to the art of Jingju

18. 京剧/莫丽芸编著.合肥：黄山书社，2016. 166 页：彩图；23cm. ISBN：7546141442.（印象中国）

英文题名：Peking opera. 英汉对照.

19. On the revolution of Peking opera. Peking：Foreign Languages Press，1968. 64 p. 19cm.

《谈京剧革命》，江青（1914—1991）.

20. Peking opera and Mei Lanfang：a guide to China's traditional theatre and the art of its great master/Wu Zuguang，Huang Zuolin，and Mei Shaowu；with selections from Mei Lanfang's own writings. Beijing，China：New World Press，1981. x，136 p.，［24］p. of plates：ill.；22cm.

《京剧与梅兰芳》，吴祖光（1917—2003），黄佐临，梅绍武等.收录了梅兰芳（1894—1961）先生的部分著作.

(1) Mei Lanfang and Peking opera：a Guide to China's Traditional Theater and the Art of Its Great Master/written by Wu Zuguang, Huang Zuolin and Mei Shaowu；［with selections from Mei Lanfang's own writings］；edited by Mei Weidong. Beijing, China：New World Press, 2014. xvi, 198 pages；16 unnumbered pages of plates：illustrations（some color）；24cm. ISBN：7510450266，7510450268

21. To find men truly great and noble-hearted we must look here in the present：in praise of the modern revolutionary Peking opera, Taking Tiger Mountain by strategy. Peking：Foreign Languages Press，1971. 68 pages；19cm.

《数风流人物还看今朝：赞革命现代京剧〈智取威虎山〉》,上海京剧团《智取威虎山》剧组等著.

22. Costumes of Peking opera/Zhao Shaohua；translated by Li Zhurun. China：Intercontinental Press, 1999. 102 pages；illustrations；31cm. ISBN：7801136284, 7801136282

《中国京剧服饰》,赵少华主编. 五洲传播出版社.

(1) 第2版. 北京：五洲传播出版社,2010. 100 页；31cm. ISBN：7801136282

23. Peking Opera painted faces：with notes on 200 operas/text by Zhao Menglin and Yan Jiqing；drawings by Zhao Menglin. Beijing：Morning Glory Publishers；Distributed by China International Book Trading Corp.，1994. 139 pages：color illustrations；25cm. ISBN：7505404121, 7505404120

《京剧脸谱》,赵梦林,阎继青. 初版于 1992 年.

(1) 3rd ed. Beijing：Morning Glory Publishers；Distributed by China International Book Trading Corp.，1996. 139 pages：color illustrations；25cm. ISBN：7505404121, 7505404120

(2) 4th ed. Beijing：Morning Glory Publishers；Distributed by China International Book Trading Corp.，2000. 139 pages：color illustrations；25cm. ISBN：7505404121, 7505404120

24. Modern Chinese drama/chief editor Tian Benxiang；co-writers, Song Baozhen, Wang Weiguo；translator Yang Liping. Beijing：Culture and Art Publishing House, 1999. 148 p.：col. ill.；21cm. ISBN：7503918357；7503918353.（Chinese culture and art series；8）

Contents：Origin of modern Chinese drama—May fourth movement and the formation of modern Chinese drama—Coming of age—Rising in the Midst of War—Drama of New China—New-period drama—Features of Modern Chinese Drama.

《中国话剧》,田本相（1932—）主编；撰稿人宋宝珍（1964—）,王卫国.

25. Modern Chinese drama/compiled by Zhao Hongfan；translated by Matthew Trueman. Beijing：New Star,

2009. 240 pages：color illustrations；23cm. ISBN：7802256231, 7802256232

《话剧·感受中国》,赵红帆编著. 新星出版社. 话剧史.

26. Chinese Drama：100 years on/Zhao Hongfan. Beijing：New Star Press, 2017. 241 pages：illustrations（some color）；c23cm.

《中国话剧百年》,赵红帆. 新星出版社（"感受当代中国"系列丛书）

27. 民间戏曲/张光奇编著. 合肥：黄山书社,2016. 136 页：图,照片；23cm. ISBN：7546152776.（印象中国）

英文题名：Chinese folk opera

28. Cantonese opera in China/Wang Kui；translator, Chen Shangzhen. First American edition. Paramus, New Jersey：Homa & Sekey Books，［2015］. ISBN：1622460090.（Masterpieces of the oral and intangible heritage of humanity）

《粤剧》,王馗（1975—）；Chen, Shangzhen 译. 译自浙江人民出版社的 2012 年版《粤剧》(ISBN：7213051029) 一书.

29. 昆曲精华＝Gems of Kunqu opera：英文/汪榕培,周秦,王宏主编译. 苏州：苏州大学出版社,2006. 437 页；20cm. ISBN：7810906054, 7810906050

英文题名：Gems of Kunqu opera：dedicated to the 3rd National Kunqu Opera Festival.

本书(中译英)从文学剧本的角度向国内外读者介绍昆曲的经典之作.

30. Chinese shadow puppet plays/by Liu Jilin；［English translation：Fang Zhenya and Fang Guoping］. Beijing：Morning Glory Publishers, 1988. 111 pages：color illustrations；25cm. ISBN：7505400711, 7505400719

《中国皮影戏》,刘季林（1936—）. 朝华出版社.

31. 皮影/童芸编著. 合肥：黄山书社,2016. 140 页：图,照片；23cm. ISBN：7546141503.（印象中国）

英文题名：Shadow play

J72　杂技艺术

1. A primer of Chinese acrobatics/by Fu Qifeng and Li Xining；［translated by R. B. Baron］. Beijing：Foreign Languages Press，2003. 70，［2］pages：color illustrations；23cm. ISBN：7119032879, 7119032870

《杂技启蒙》,付起凤,李西宁著.

2. 杂技/王慧编著. 合肥：黄山书社,2016. 116 页：图,照片；23cm. ISBN：7546141565.（印象中国）

英文题名：Chinese acrobatics

J8　电影、电视艺术

1. An example of modern revisionism in art：a critique of the films and statements of Grigori Chukhrai/Zhang Guangnian. Peking：Foreign Languages Press，1965. 52 pages；19cm.

《现代修正主义的艺术标本：评格·丘赫莱依的影片及其

言论》,张光年著.

2. Expose the U. S. and Japanese reactionaries' plot to resurrect the dead past：three reactionary Japanese films in review. Peking：Foreign Languages Press, 1972. 65 pages；19cm.

Contents：Shatter the fond dream of the U. S. -Japanese reactionaries；on the reactionary Japanese films：Admiral Yamamoto, Battle of the Japan Sea and gateway to glory. By Chi Ping-chi. —Expose the U. S. and Japanese reactionaries plot to resurrect the dead past；on the reactionary Japanese film：Admiral Yamamoto. By Tao Ti-wen. —Barefaced revelation of the aggressive ambitions of Japanese militarism；on the reactionary Japanese film：Battle of the Japan Sea. By Tao Ti-wen. —Expose the Sato Government's cannon-fodder recruitment fraud；on the reactionary Japanese film：Gateway to glory. By Tao Ti-wen.

《戳穿美日反动派借尸还魂的阴谋：评日本三部发反动影片》

3. A vicious motive, despicable tricks：a criticism of M. Antonioni's anti-China film China/Renmin Ribao commentator. Peking：Foreign Languages Press, 1974. 18 pages；19cm.

《恶毒的用心卑劣的手法：批判安东尼奥尼拍摄的题为〈中国〉的反华影片》,《人民日报》评论员.

4. Joris Ivens and China/Film Archive of China and the Editorial Department of New World Press. Beijing, China：New World Press：Distributed by China Publications Centre, 1983. 146 pages, ［64］pages of plates：illustrations；23cm. ISBN：0835110885, 0835110884

《伊文思和中国》,中国电影资料馆,新世界出版社编辑部编.新世界出版社.

5. Chinese films and television plays/writer Zhang Baiqing；translator Zhu Chengyao. Beijing：Culture and Art Publishing House, 1999. 3, 183 p. ：col. ill. ；21cm. ISBN：7503918322, 7503918322. (Chinese culture and art series；9)

《中国电影·电视》,张柏青；Zhu, Chengyao 译.20 世纪中国电影史.

6. From infancy to maturity：the growth of the documentary in China/compiled by Liu Qiming, Liu Hongmei；translated by Wo Siro；polished by Margaret A. Carey. Beijing：New Star, 2009. 225 pages：illustrations (some color)；23cm. ISBN：7802256224, 7802256224

《纪录片·感受中国》,刘圻铭,刘红梅编著.新星出版社.

7. 用英语说中国.影视 Film and TV series/贾冰,王敏华主编.上海：上海科学普及出版社,2009. 371 页；24cm. ISBN：7542744340, 7542744348

英文题名：Talk about China in English. Film and TV series

K 类　历史、地理

K0　世界史

1. On studying some world history. Peking：Foreign Languages Press, 1973. 59 pages；19cm.

《读一点世界史》

K1　中国史

1. A T'ang historiographer's letter of resignation/［translated and annotated］by William Hung. ［Cambridge, Mass. ］：［publisher not identified］, 1969. pages ［5］-52；25cm.

《忤时》,洪业译注.为《史通》中的一篇.

K11　通史

1. An outline history of China. Peking：Foreign Languages Press, 1958. 487 pages：illustrations；(some color), map, portraits 19cm. (China knowledge series)

《简明中国历史》

2. A short history of China：1840—1919 Lin Yi. Peking：Foreign Languages Press, 1963. 1 volumes：illustrations；20cm.

《中国历史简编》,林峄著.

3. Concise history of China/Jian Bozan, Shao Xunzheng, Hu Hua. Peking：Foreign Languages Press, 1964. 269 pages：illustrations, portraits；19cm.

《中国历史概要》,翦伯赞等编著.

4. A short history of China：from earliest times to 1840/Dong Jiming. Peking：Foreign Languages Press, 1965. 219 pages：illustrations；19cm.

《中国历史简编(远古—1840)》,董集明著.

5. History/compiled by the China Handbook Editorial Committee；translated by Dun J. Li. Beijing：Foreign Languages Press：Distributed by China Publications Centre, 1982. 189 pages, ［16］pages of plates：illustrations, portraits；19cm. ISBN：0835109852, 0835109857. (China handbook series)

《历史》,《中国手册》编辑委员会编.

6. The translation of things past：Chinese history and historiography/edited by George Kao. Hong Kong：Chinese University Press；Seattle：Distributed by the University of Washington Press, c1982. 200 p. ：ill. ；28cm. ISBN：9622012728. (A Renditions book)

中国历史编年.高克毅(Kao, George, 1912—2008). 中英对照.

7. An outline history of China/edited by Bai Shouyi；written by Yang Zhao ［and others］. Beijing：Foreign Languages Press：Distributed by China Publications Centre, 1982. 565 pages, ［69］pages of plates：illustrations (some color), 1 folded map；21cm. ISBN：0835110001, 0835110006. (China knowledge series)

《中国通史纲要》,白寿彝主编;杨钊等分纂.

(1) An outline history of China/Bai Shouyi, [chief editor]; contributors, Yang Zhao [and others]. Rev. ed., 1st ed. Beijing: Foreign Languages Press, 2008. 803 pages: illustrations (some color); 24cm. ISBN: 7119052960, 7119052969

8. A general history of China/editorial board: Hu Hao [and four others]. Beijing: China Translation & Publishing Corporation, 2014. 6 volumes (2103 pages): illustrations (some color); 24cm. ISBN: 7500139768, 7500139764

Contents: volume 1. Pre-Qin period/compiled by Peng Haitao and Huang Hongqiu; translated by Wang Qiuhai—volume 2. Qin and Han Dynasties/compiled by Huang Yuanye and Peng Haitao; translated by Wang Qiuhai and Hu Zhihui—volume 3. From the Three Kingdoms period to the Sui and Tang Dynasties/compiled by Zhu Yiqun and Huang Hongqiu; translated by Hu Zhihui and Zheng Aifang—volume 4. From the Five Dynasties period to the Yuan Dynasty/compiled by Liu Chong and Chen He; translated by Wang Weidong—volume 5. Ming Dynasty/compiled by Dai Nierui and Zhao Xiuning; translated by Wang Weidong, Peng Ping and Lu Qingliang—volume 6. Qing Dynasty/compiled by Liu Chunqiang and Dai Nienui; translated by Peng Ping.

《中国通史》,Hu, Hao(1965—)编. 中国对外翻译出版公司.

9. 兴亡的足迹＝The rise and fall of dynasties/李家真著;章思英译. 北京:外语教学与研究出版社,2005. 203 pages; 24cm. ISBN: 7560041167, 7560041162. (中国 100 话题丛书. 第 1 辑)

《兴亡的足迹:汉英对照》,李家真著;章思英译. 外语教学与研究出版社(中国 100 话题丛书. 第 1 辑). 介绍了中国上古到近代的历史现象.

10. Five thousand years of Chinese nation/Zhang Yantu. Beijing: Foreign Languages Press, 2007. 223 pages: color illustrations, color table; 29cm. ISBN: 7119046365, 7119046365

《中华上下五千年:英文》,张延图主编;刘安利图;闫威 [等]英文翻译.

11. 中国历史常识:汉英对照/王恺主编;国务院侨务办公室,国家汉语国际推广领导小组办公室编. 北京:高等教育出版社,2007. 269 页;24cm. ISBN: 7040207170, 7040207176

英文题名:Common knowledge about Chinese history

12. History of China/Deng Yinke; translation by Martha Avery and Pan Yue. Beijing: China Intercontinental Press, 2007. 171 pages: color illustrations, color maps; 25cm. ISBN: 7508510989, 7508510984. (Journey into China)

《历史之旅:英文》,邓荫柯著;潘岳译. 五洲传播出版社(中国之旅丛书/郭长建,李向平主编)

13. China through the ages: from Confucius to Deng/ compiled by Xie Chuntao; [translated by Zhou Gang, Li Yang and Wu An]. Beijing: New World Press, 2009. 1 volumes: color illustrations; 24cm. ISBN: 7802285651, 7802285658, 7510403361, 7510403367. (新世界文库)

《中国简史:从孔夫子到邓小平》,谢春涛主编. 新世界出版社.

14. China's history/Cao Dawei & Sun Yanjing; translated by Xiao Ying, Li Li & He Yunzhao. Beijing: China International Press, 2010. 210 pages: illustrations (some color); 23cm. ISBN: 7508513027, 7508513029

《中国历史》,曹大为,孙燕京著. 五洲传播出版社.

15. Quick access to Chinese history. Beijing: Foreign languages Press, 2008. 25, 225 pages: illustrations (some color), maps; 24cm. ISBN: 7119054872, 7119054872

《中国历史速查》,《中国历史速查》编写组编著.

16. Quick access to Chinese history: from ancient times to the 21st century/edited by Yang Chunyan, Li Jian'an, Liu Fangnian; translated by Xu Tingting [and others]. Beijing: Foreign Languages Press, 2010. 360 pages: illustrations (some color), color maps; 24cm. ISBN: 7119067599, 7119067591

《中国历史速查:从远古到 21 世纪》,本书编写组编著.

17. Chinese social history; translations of selected studies, by E-tu Zen Sun and John De Francis. Washington, American Council of Learned Societies, 1956. xix, 400 p. maps. 26cm. (American Council of Learned Societies. Studies in Chinese and related civilizations, no. 7)

《中国社会史》,孙任以都(Sun, E-tu Zen, 1921—)(美国华裔学者),DeFrancis, John(1911—2009)编译.

18. The makers of Cathay, by C. Wilfrid Allan. 2 nd ed. Shanghai, The Presbyterian Mission Press, 1925. 1 p. l., ii p., 1 l., 242, v p. plates. 22cm.

Contents: Confucius, the moral reformer.—Mencius, the social reformer.—Ch'in Shih Huang Ti, the first emperor.—Chu Ko Liang, strategist and statesman.—Fa Hsien and Hsühan Tsang, the Buddhist pilgrims.—Li Shih Min, the Emperor Tai Tsung.—Li Tai Po and Tu Fu, China's greatest poets.—Han Yü, the prince of literature.—Wang An Shih, political economist and national reformer.—Chu Hsi, scholar and philosopher.—Kublai Khan, the world's emperor.—Wen Tien Hsiang and Lu Hsiu Fu, the patriotic ministers.—Hung Wu, the beggar king.—Wu San Kuei, the people's general.—Koxinga, pirate and patriot.—K'ang Hsi, the greatest of the Manchus.—Ch'ien Lung, the conqueror.—Tseng Kuo Fan, the imperialist general.—Li Hung Chang, statesman and diplomat.

中国历史名人. Allan, C. Wilfrid (Charles Wilfrid, 1870—)编译.

(1)Shanghai〔etc.〕Kelly and Walsh, Limited, 1936. vi p., 1 l., 363 p. 22cm.

19. Lives of Chinese emperors/〔editor Lan Peijin; text by Shi Fang; translated by Zhang Yuan〕. Beijing: Foreign Languages Press, 2008. 149 pages: color illustrations, portraits; 23cm. ISBN: 7119045115, 7119045113

《帝后生活》,思方撰文. 展示帝后生活的方方面面,从衣食住行到婚丧嫁娶、宫廷阴谋政变等.

20. Renewed encounter: selected speeches and essays, 1979—1999/Zhang Zhilian. Beijing: Commercial Press, 2000. 316 pages: color portraits; 24cm. ISBN: 7100030919, 7100030915

《张芝联讲演精选:1979—1999》,张芝联著,商务印书馆. 英汉对照.

21. A journey into China's antiquity: National Museum of Chinese History/〔compiled by the National Museum of Chinese History; editor-in chief Yu Weichao〕. Beijing, China: Morning Glory Publishers; Distributed by China International Book Trading Corporation, 1997. 4 volumes: illustrations (some color), color maps; 30cm. ISBN: 7505404768 (v. 1),7505404762 (v. 1),7505404830 (v. 2), 7505404830 (v. 2),7505405071 (v. 3),7505405073(v. 3), 7505405144(v. 4), 7505405141(v. 4)

Contents: v. 1. Palaeolithic Age, Low Neolithic Age, Upper Neolithic Age, Xia Dynasty, Shang Dynasty, Western Zhou Dynasty, Spring and Autumn Period—v. 2. Warring States Period, Qin Dynasty, The Western and Eastern Han Dynasties, Three Kingdoms through Western and Eastern Jin to Northern and Southern Dynasties—v. 3. Sui Dynasty, Tang Dynasty, Five Dynasties and Ten Kingdoms Period, Northern and Southern Song Dynasties—v. 4. Yuan Dynasty, Ming Dynasty, Qing Dynasty

《华夏之旅》,中国历史博物馆编. 中国历史.

22. The history of Chinese civilization/general editors, Yuan Xingpei, Yan Wenming, Zhang Chuanxi, Lou Yulie; English text edited by David R. Knechtges. Cambridge; New York: Cambridge University Press, 2012. 4 vol. (XIX-660, XXI-622, XXI-766, XX-714 p.): ill. en noir et en coul., planches.; 24cm. ISBN: 1107013094 (éd. complète), 1107013097 (éd. complète), 1107013056 (rel.), 1107013054 (rel.), 1107013063 (rel.), 1107013062 (rel.), 1107013070 (rel.), 1107013070 (rel.), 1107013087 (rel.), 1107013089 (rel.). (The Cambridge China library)

Contents: Vol. I: Earliest times-221 B. C. E./volume editor, Yan Wenming—Vol. II: Qin, Han, Wei, Jin, and the Northern and Southern dynasties/volume editor, Zhang Chuanxi—Vol. III: Sui and Tang to mid-Ming dynasties (581—1525)/volume editor Yuan Xingpei—Vol. IV: Late Ming and Qing dynasties (1525—1911)/volume editor, Lou Yulie.

《中华文明史》,袁行霈等编;康达维(Knechtges, David Richard,1942—)(美国汉学家)等译. 4 卷本.

K12　古代史籍

K121　《春秋》三传

1. A forgotten book: Chun qiu Guliang zhuan/〔translated by〕Gen Liang. Singapore: Global Publishing, 2011. xxvi, 296 p.; 23cm. ISBN: 9814366793, 981436679X

《春秋谷梁传:一部被遗忘的著作》,左丘明;耿亮(Gen Liang, 1900—1969)译. 中英文对照.

2. The Ch'un Ts'ew. with The Tso Chuen/with a translation, critical and exegetical notes, prolegomena and copious indexes by James Legge; with minor text corrections and a concordance table. 2nd. ed. 台北:进学,〔1969〕. 1101 p. (pag. var.)27cm.

《左传,春秋》,理雅各(Legge, James, 1815—1897)(英国汉学家)译.

(1)Taipei: Southern Materials Center, 1972. x, 933 pages; 24cm. (The Chinese classics)

3. The Tso chuan: selections from China's oldest narrative history/translated by Burton Watson. New York: Columbia University Press, 1989. xxxviii, 232 p.; 24cm. ISBN: 0231067143. (Translations from the Oriental classics)

《左传》(选译),左丘明;华兹生(Watson, Burton, 1925—)(美国汉学家)译.

4. 《左传》名言:汉英对照/齐鲁书社编选;马小方等译;王铭基、张蕾绘. 济南:齐鲁书社,2006. 100 页;23cm. ISBN: 7533317203, 7533317201. (儒家名典箴言录)

5. 《左传》英译/罗志野译. 南京:东南大学出版社,2017. 584 页;26cm. ISBN: 7564153946. (中华经典英译丛书)

6. 左传＝Zuo's commentary/胡志挥英译;陈克炯今译. 长沙市:湖南人民出版社,1996. 2 volumes (10, 10, 1605 pages); 21cm. ISBN: 7543815702 (set); 7543815704
汉英对照.

7. Zuo's commentary on Spring and Autumn Annals (selections)/translated into modern Chinese by Li Shibiao; translated into English by Hu Zhihui and Zheng Aifang. Jinan Shi: Shandong you yi chu ban she, 2000., 5, 2, 2, 631 pages; 20cm. ISBN: 7806422927, 7806422922. (儒学经典译丛＝Translations of Confucian classics)

《左传:节选》,今译李士彪;英译胡志挥,郑爱芳. 山东友谊出版社.

8. 左传＝Zuo's commentary/executive editor, Joyce Du. Vancouver: Chiao Liu Pub. (Canada) Inc., 2007. 3 volumes: illustrations, portraits; 21cm. ISBN: 0978275358 (set), 0978275357 (set). (中华文化智慧系列＝Wisdom of Chinese culture series; no. 4)
英汉对照.

K122　战国策

1. Chan-kuo ts'e/translated 〔from the Chinese〕by J. I. Crump,

Jr. Oxford：Clarendon P.，1970. xxviii，602 p.；23cm. ISBN：0198154399. （The Oxford library of East Asian literatures）

《战国策》，柯迁儒（Crump, J. I.〈James Irving〉，1921—2002）译.

(1) 2nd ed. rev. San Francisco：Chinese Materials Center，1979. xlii，641 p.：map；22cm. ISBN：0896445836. （Occasional series (Chinese Materials and Research Aids Service Center)；no. 41）

2. Legends of the warring states：persuasions, romances, and stories from Chan-kuo ts'e/selected, translated, and edited by J. I. Crump. Ann Arbor：Center for Chinese Studies, The University of Michigan, 1998. xiv, 189 p.：ill.，map；24cm. ISBN：0892641274, 0892641277, 0892641290, 0892641291

《战国策读本》，柯迁儒（又名柯润璞）（Crump, J. I.〈James Irving〉，1921—2002）译. 是根据主题而分类编辑的译研集.

3. The records of the warring states：Zhan guo ce/translated by B. S. Bonsall. [Place of publication not identified]：[publisher not identified], 1920. 271 leaves；30cm.

《战国策》，邦斯尔神父（Bonsall, Bramwell Seaton）（英国人），该书尚无正式出版，译稿现存于香港大学.

K123 史记

1. Records of the grand historian of China. Translated from the Shih chi of Ssu-ma Ch'ien by Burton Watson. New York：Columbia University Press, 1961. 2 v. maps. 24cm. （Records of civilization：sources and studies, no. 65）（UNESCO collection of representative works：Chinese series）

Contents：v. 1. Early years of the Han dynasty, 209 to 141 B. C. —v. 2. The age of Emperor Wu, 140 to circa 100 B. C.

《史记》（选译），司马迁（约前145—前86年）；华兹生（Watson, Burton, 1925—）（美国汉学家）译.

(1) New York：Columbia University Press, 1971. 2 volumes：maps；24cm. （Records of civilization, sources and studies；no. 65；UNESCO collection of representative works：Chinese series）

(2) Taipei：Hsin Yueh Book Co, 1971. 2 volumes：maps；21cm. （Records of civilization：sources and studies；no. 65）

(3) New York：Columbia University Press, 1984. 2 volumes：maps；24cm. （Records of civilization；no. 65；UNESCO collection of representative works. Chinese series）

(4) New York：Columbia University Press, 1991. 2 volumes：maps；24cm. （Records of civilization：sources and studies；no. 65；UNESCO collection of representative works：Chinese series）

2. A selection from "Shi chih"/by Chien Ssu-ma；translated into English by Chen Huei-Wen. Taipei：Hua Lien Press, 1966. 1, 163 pages；19cm.

《史记》（选译），Chen, Huei-Wen 译.

3. Records of the historian；chapters from the Shih chi/translated by Burton Watson. New York：Columbia University Press, 1969. 359 p.；20cm. ISBN：0231033214, 0231033213. （UNESCO collection of representative works. Chinese series）

Contents：The biography of Po Yi and Shu Ch'i (Shih chi 61)—The biography of Wu Tzu-hsü (Shih chi 66)—The biography of T'ien Tan (Shih chi 82)—The biography of Lü Pu-wei (Shih chi 85)—The biographies of the Assassin-Retainers (Shih chi 86)—The basic annals of Hsiang Yü (Shih chi 7)—The basic annals of Emperor Kaotsu (Shih chi 8)—Reflections on the rise of Emperor Kao-tsu (Shih chi 16, excerpt)—The hereditary house of Prime Minister Hsiao (Shih chi 53)—The hereditary house of the Marquis of Liu (Chang Liang) (Shih chi 55)—The biography of the Marquis of Huai-yin (Han Hsin) (Shih chi 92)—The biographies of Li I-chi and Lu Chia (Shih chi 97)—The biographies of Liu Ching and Shu-sun T'ung (Shih chi 99)—The treatise on the Yellow River and canals (Shih chi 29)—The biographies of the Marquises of Wei-ch'i and Wu-an (Shih chi 107)—The biography of General Li Kuang (Shih...)

《史记》（选译），司马迁（约前145—前86年）著；华兹生（Watson, Burton, 1925—）（美国汉学家）译.

4. Shih chi hsüan i：[Han Ying tui chao]/Ch'en Hui-wên ying i. T'ai-pei：Hua lien ch'u pan shê, 1973. 163 pages. Notes：English title on cover：A selection from "Shi chih."/Text in Chinese and English.

《〈史记〉选译》，Ch'en, Hui-wên 译.

5. War-lords [by] Sima Qian/translated with twelve other stories from his Historical records by William Dolby and John Scott. Edinburgh, Southside, 1974. 168 p. map. 22cm. ISBN：0900025085, 0900025082

《史记》（节译），Dolby, William 和 Scott, John 合译.

6. Records of the historian/written by Sima Qian；translated by Yang Xianyi and Gladys Yang. Hong Kong：Commercial Press, 1974. v, 460 pages；21cm.

《史记选》，司马迁（约前145—前86年）；杨宪益（1915—2009），戴乃迭（Yang, Gladys, 1919—1999）译.

(1) Selections from Records of the historian/written by Szuma Chien；translated by Yang Hsien-yi and Gladys Yang. Peking：Foreign Languages Press, 1979. vi, 461 p.；22cm.

(2) Hong Kong：Commercial Press, 1985. 460 pages；21cm.

(3) Selections from Records of the historian/written by Szuma Chien；translated by Yang Hsien-yi and Gladys Yang. Beijing：Wai wen chu ban she, 2000. 497 p.；

13cm. ISBN：7119026917，7119025247.（FLP 汉英对照经典读本. 古典精华；3）

(4) Honolulu，Hawaii：University Press of the Pacific，2002. vi，461 pages；21cm. ISBN：0898759404，0898759402

(5) 史记选/原著，司马迁；今译，凌受举；英译，杨宪益，戴乃迭等. Beijing［China］：New World Press，2002. 332 pages；21cm. ISBN：780005652X，7800056529

(6) Selections from Records of the historian/written by Szuma Chien；translated by Yang Hsien-yi and Gladys Yang. Peking：Foreign Languages Press，2007. 188 pages：illustrations，maps；29cm. ISBN：7119046808，7119046802

(7) 史记选＝Selections from records of the historian/司马迁著；安平秋校译；杨宪益，戴乃迭英译. 北京：外文出版社，2008. 3 volumes（38，1241 pages）；24cm. ISBN：7119050904（set），7119050907（set）.（大中华文库＝Library of Chinese classics）

7. Stories from records of the historian＝Contes tirés des mémoires historiques. Beijing：Sinolingua，1988. 143 pages；18cm. ISBN：7800520641，7800520648，835119092，0835119092
史记故事选（英语，法语版），司马迁.

8. Records of the Grand Historian. Qin dynasty/by Sima Qian；translated by Burton Watson. Hong Kong：Research Centre for Translation，Chinese University of Hong Kong；New York：Columbia University Press，c1993. xx，243 p.；23cm. ISBN：0231081693，0231081696，0231081642，0231081641，0231081669，0231081665，0231081685，0231081689
《史记》（秦朝部分），司马迁（约前 145—前 86 年）著；华兹生（Watson，Burton，1925—）（美国汉学家）译.

9. Records of the grand historian. Han dynasty/by Sima Qian；translated by Burton Watson. Rev. ed. Hong Kong；New York：Columbia University Press，c1993. 2 v.：maps；24cm. ISBN：0231081642(v. 1)，0231081641(v. 1)，0231081650(v. 1：pbk.)，0231081658（v. 1：pbk.），0231081677（v. 2：pbk.），0231081672（v. 2），0231081669（v. 2），0231081665（v. 2），（Records of civilization，sources and studies；no. 65）（UNESCO collection of representative works. Chinese series.）
《史记》（汉朝部分），司马迁（约前 145—前 86 年）著；华兹生（Watson，Burton，1925—）（美国汉学家）译.

10. The grand scribe's records/Ssu-ma Ch'ien；William H. Nienhauser，Jr.，editor；Tsai-fa Cheng...［et al.］，translators. Bloomington：Indiana University Press，c1994—〈c2008〉. v.〈1—2，5，pt. 1；7；8，pt. 1；9，pt. 2〉：maps；25cm. ISBN：0253340217（v. 1：alk. paper），0253340225（v. 2），0253340276（v. 7），0253355904 (v. 9)
Contents: v. 1. The basic annals of pre-Han China—v. 2. The basic annals of Han China v. 5，pt. 1. The hereditary houses of pre-Han China—v. 7. The memoirs of pre-Han China—v. 8，pt. 1. The memoirs of Han China—v. 9，pt. 2. The memoirs of Han China
《史记》，倪豪士（Nienhauser，William H.）（美国汉学家）主编；Cheng，Tsai Fa 等译. 为《史记》英译计划中共 9 卷的 5 册，其余将陆续出版.

(1) Taiwan ed. Taipei：SMC Publishing，2004. volumes〈1—2，7〉：maps；25cm. ISBN：957638625X，9576386251

11. Historical records/Sima Qian；translated with an introduction and notes by Raymond Dawson. Oxford；New York：Oxford University Press，1994. xxv，176 p.：map；19cm. ISBN：0192831151，0192831156.（World's classics）
《史记》（节译），司马迁（约前 145—前 86 年）；Dawson，Raymond Stanley 译.

12. Selections from Records of the historian/written by Sima Qian；translated by Yang Xianyi and Gladys Yang. Peking：Foreign Languages Press，2007. 188 pages：illustrations，maps；29cm. ISBN：7119046808，7119046802
《史记选：英文》，（汉）司马迁原著；滕一岚英文改编；刘安利绘.

13. Herodotus and Sima Qian：the first great historians of Greece and China：a brief history with documents/Thomas R. Martin. 2010. xii，153 pages；maps；21cm. ISBN：0312416492，0312416490.（Bedford series in history and culture）
Martin，Thomas R.（1947—）著；包括对《史记》的选译.

14. 史记故事/司马迁著；王国振译. 北京：五洲传播出版社，2017. 207 页：图；16cm. ISBN：7508530505

K124　《资治通鉴》

1. 资治通鉴选 英汉对照/（北宋）司马光著. 中华书局，2018. 3 册（21，1207 页）；26cm. ISBN：7101122886.（大中华文库）

K125　历法

1. Granting the seasons：the Chinese astronomical reform of 1280，with a study of its many dimensions and a translation of its records：Shou shih li cong kao/Nathan Sivin；with the research collaboration of the late Kiyosi Yabuuti，Yabuuchi Kiyosi，and Shigeru Nakayama，Nakayama Shigeru. New York：Springer，c2009. 664 p.：ill.；25cm. ISBN：0387789552，0387789553.（Sources and studies in the history of mathematics and physical sciences）
《授时：1280 年 中国天文立法革新》，席文（Sivin，Nathan）. 本书的附录部分有元朝《授时历》的英文译文.

2. The astronomical chapters of the Chin shu. With amendments，full translation and annotations by Ho Peng Yoke.［École pratique des hautes études. Sixième Section，sciences économiques et sociales］. Paris，The Hague，Mouton & Co.，1966［1967］. 272 p. charts. 22

× 28cm. （Le Monde d'outre-mer，passé et présent. Deuxième série，Documents；9）

《晋书天文历法诸篇》，房玄龄（579—648）著；何丙郁（Ho，Peng Yoke）译注.

3. Calendar of the gods in China/by Timothy Richard. Shanghai：Methodist Pub. House，1906. ix，37 pages；22cm.

李提摩太（Richard，Timothy，1845—1919）（英国传教士）译. 中国日历中某月某日所崇拜的儒释道以及民间信仰中各路神灵，资料主要来源于《月令粹编》.

(1)Shanghai，Commercial Press，Limited，1916. 2 preliminary leaves，x，37 pages；23cm.

(2)［Place of publication not identified］：Nabu Press，2010. ISBN：117637446X，1176374461

K13　古代史（上古至1840）

1. Food & money in ancient China；the earliest economic history of China to A. D. 25，Han shu 24，with related texts，Han shu 91 and Shih-chi 129. Translated and annotated by Nancy Lee Swann. Princeton，Princeton University Press，1950. xii，482，［79］ p. illus. ，maps（1 fold. ）25cm.

Notes："Reproductions of Chinese texts"：［79］ p. at end. 中国古代的食物与货币，译自《汉书食货志》和《史记货殖列传》，南施李思宛（Nancy Lee Swann，1881—1966）译注.

(1)New York：Octagon Books，1974［c1950］. xiii，482 p. illus. 24cm. ISBN：0374962022，0374962029

2. Eastern Zhou and Qin civilizations/Li Xueqin；translated by K. C. Chang. New Haven：Yale University Press，c1985. xvi，527 p. ：ill. ；24cm. ISBN：0300032862. （Early Chinese civilizations series）

《东周及秦文明》，李学勤（1933—）；张光直（Chang，Kwang-chih）（美国华裔汉学家）译.

3. Annotated genealogies of Spring and Autumn period clans/compiled by Barry B. Blakeley. ［San Francisco，Calif. ］：Chinese Materials Center，1983—. volumes〈1〉：genealogical tables；27cm. ISBN：089644662X，0896446625. （Research aids series；；no. 6）

《春秋时代的世族谱校注》，蒲百瑞（Blakeley，Barry B. ）编，英汉对照.

4. Han civilization/Wang Zhongshu；translated by K. C. Chang and collaborators. New Haven：Yale University Press，c1982. xx，261 p. ：ill. ；26cm. ISBN：0300027230，0300027235：

Contents：Changan：the capital city of western Han—Luoyang：the capital city of eastern Han—Han Dynasty agriculture—Lacquerware—Bronzes—Iron implements—Ceramics—Tombs—I—Tombs—II.

《汉代文明》，王仲殊（1925—2015）著；张光直（Chang，Kwang-chih，1931—2001）（美国华裔汉学家）等译.

5. Discourses on salt and iron＝盐铁论：a debate on state control of commerce and industry in ancient China，chapters I-XIX/translated from the Chinese of Huan K'uan；with introduction and notes，by Esson M. Gale. Leyden：E. J. Brill Ltd. ，c1931. lvi，165 p. ；25cm. （Sinica leidensia；v. 2）

《盐铁论》，桓宽（生卒不详，公元前 1 世纪）；Gale，Esson McDowell（1884—）译，

(1)Taipei：Ch'eng Wen Publishing Company，c1967. lvi，165 p. ；25cm. （Sinica leidensia；v. 2）

6. The history of the former Han dynasty，by Pan Ku. A critical translation，with annotations，by Homer H. Dubs，with the collaboration of Jen T'ai and P'an Lo-chi. Baltimore，Waverly Press，1938—1955. 3 v. fold. map. 26cm.

Contents：v. 1. First division：The imperial annals，chapter 1 — 5. Translation，v. 2. First division：The imperial annals，chapters 6—10. Translation，v. 3. Imperial annals 11 and 12 and the memoir of Wang Mang.

《汉书》，班固（32—92）著；德效骞（Dubs，Homer H. ，1892—1969）（美国历史学家）选译，为《汉书》前 12 卷.

7. Courtier and commoner in ancient China；selections from the History of the former Han. Translated by Burton Watson. New York：Columbia University Press，1974. 282 p. 23cm. ISBN：0231037651

《汉书》（选译），班固（32—92）著；华兹生（Watson，Burton（1925—）译.

8. Official titles of the former Han dynasty as translated and transcribed by H. H. Dubs；an index compiled by Rafe de Crespigny. Canberra，Centre of Oriental Studies in association with Australian National University Press ［1967］. xi，67 p. tables. 24cm.

《汉书·职官志》，德效骞（Dubs，Homer H. 1892—1969）（美国历史学家）译；De Crespigny，Rafe 编制索引.

9. The Han shu biography of Yang Xiong（53 B. C. -A. D. 18）/translated and annotated by David R. Knechtges；calligraphy by Eva Yuen-wah Chung. ［Tempe］：Center for Asian Studies，Arizona State University，1982. ix，179 p. ；23cm. ISBN：0939252104. （Occasional paper/Center for Asian Studies，Arizona State University；no. 14）

《汉书·杨雄传》，班固（32—92）；康达维（Knechtges，David R. ）译.

10. Wang Mang；a translation of the official account of his rise to power as given in the History of the former Han dynasty，with introd. and notes ［by］ Clyde Bailey Sargent. ［Shanghai，Graphic Art Book Co. ，pref. 1947］.206 p. geneal. tables. 26cm.

《王莽传》，班固（32—92）；Sargent，Clyde Bailey 编译. 译自《汉书》第 99 卷《汉书》选译

(1)Westport，Conn. ：Hyperion Press，1977. 206 p. ：

geneal. table（1 fold.）；23cm. ISBN：0883553864. （China studies）

11. China in central Asia：the early stage，125 B. C. —A. D. 23：an annotated translation of chapters 61 and 96 of The history of the former Han dynasty/by A. F. P. Hulsewé；with an introduction by M. A. N. Loewe. Leiden：Brill，1979. viii，273 p.，［1］folded leaf of plate：map；25cm. ISBN：9004058842.（Sinica Leidensia；v. 14）

《中国在中亚：公元前 125—公元 23 年》，Hulsewé，A. F. P.（Anthony François Paulus），Loewe，Michael 译. 译自班固的《汉书》第 61 卷和第 96 卷的《张骞李广利传》《西域传》.

12. To establish peace：being the chronicle of Later Han for the years 189 to 220 AD as recorded in chapters 59 to 69 of the Zizhi tongjian of Sima Guang/translated and annotated by Rafe de Crespigny. Canberra，Australia：Faculty of Asian Studies，Australian National University，1996. 2 volumes（xlix，635 pages）：maps；26cm. ISBN：073152537X，0731525379，0731525264，0731525263，0731525361，0731525362.（Asian studies monographs；new ser.，no. 21）

Contents：v. 1. Chapters 59 to 63，189—200 AD—v. 2. Chapters 64 to 69，201—220 AD.

De Crespigny，Rafe 译注，翻译了《资治通鉴》第 59 至 69 卷中关于后汉 189—220 年之纪年.

13. Wars with the Xiongnu：a translation from Zizhi Tongjian/Joseph P. Yap. Bloomington，IN：Authorhouse，2009. lv，645 pages：maps；23cm. ISBN：1449006043，1449006044，1449006051，1449006051

Yap，Joseph P. 译，翻译《资治通鉴》有关汉朝与匈奴战争的史料.

14. 后汉书选 汉英对照/（南朝宋）范晔著. 中华书局，2018. 2 册（877 页）；24cm. ISBN：7101122893.（大中华文库）

15. The biography of Sun Chien，being an annotated translation of pages 1 to 8a of chüan 46 of the San-kuo chih of Ch'en Shou in the Po-na edition，by Rafe de Crespigny. Canberra，Centre of Oriental Studies，Australian National University，1966. 98 p. maps（part fold.）25cm.（Australian National University. Centre of Oriental Studies. Occasional papers，no. 5.）

《孙坚传》，陈寿（233—297）；De Crespigny，Rafe 译注.

16. The chronicle of the Three Kingdoms（220—265）Chapters 69 — 78 from the Tzŭ chih t'ung chien，translated and annotated by Achilles Fang；edited by Glen W. Baxter. Cambridge，Harvard University Press，1952—65. 2 v. 27cm.（Harvard-Yenching Institute studies；6）

《资治通鉴，卷 69 - 78》（三国部分），司马光（1019—1086）编纂；方志彤（Fang，Zhitong）（美国华裔学者）译.

17. Account of the T'ù-yü-hún in the history of the Chìn dynasty［Chin shu 97. 4a-7b］/translated and annotated by Thomas D. Carroll. Berkeley，University of California Press，1953. 47 pages；24cm.（Institute of East Asiatic Studies，University of California. Chinese dynastic histories translations；no. 4）

Carroll，Thomas D. 编译. 有关历史上的曾经存在的国家吐谷浑（313 — 663）的记载.

18. Biography of Lü Kuang. Translated and annotated by Richard B. Mather. Berkeley，University of California Press，1959. 141 p. fold. map（in pocket）24cm.（Chinese dynastic histories translations，no. 7）

Translation of Chin shu 122. 1a-8a，compiled by Fang Hsühan-ling and others

《吕光传》，房玄龄（579—648）；马瑞志（Mather，Richard B.，1913—）（美国汉学家）译. 译自《晋书》.

19. The Uighur Empire（744—840）according to the T'ang dynastic histories. Canberra，Centre of Oriental Studies，Australian National University，1968. xiii，187 p. diagrs.，maps（part fold.）25cm.（Australian National University，Canberra. Centre of Oriental Studies. Occasional paper no. 8）

《唐书回鹘传译注》，马克林（Mackerras，Colin）译注.

(1)2nd ed. Canberra，Australian National University Press，1972. ix，226 p. maps. 24cm. ISBN：0708104576.（Asian publications series，no. 2）

(2) 2nd ed. Columbia，University of South Carolina Press［1973，c1972］. viii，226 p. illus. 24cm. ISBN：0872492796.（Asian publications series no. 2）

20. Historical records of the five dynasties/Ouyang Xiu，translated with an introduction by Richard L. Davis. New York：Columbia University Press，c2004. lixxix，669 p.：ill.，maps；25cm. ISBN：0231128266

《新五代史》，欧阳修（1007—1072）；戴仁柱（Davis，Richard L.，1951—）（美国汉学家）译.

21. Accounts of Western nations in the history of the Northern Chou dynasty. Berkeley，University of California Press，1959. p. cm.（Chinese dynastic histories translations，no. 6.）

《北周时期的西方国家》，令狐德棻（583～666 年）主编；Miller，Roy Andrew 译.《周书》选译.

22. Biography of Su Ch'o/translated and annotated by Chauncey S. Goodrich. Berkeley：University of California Press，c1953. 116 p.；24cm.（Chinese dynastic histories translations＝中古史译丛；no. 3）

Notes：Translation of Chou Shu，juan 23，compiled by Linghu，Defen and others. Based on the editor's thesis（M. A.）—University of California

《苏绰传》，令狐德棻著；Goodrich，Chauncey Shafter（1920—）译.《周书》选译.

23. Biography of Yü-wen Hu.［Chou shu，chüan 11］Translated and annotated by Albert E. Dien. Berkeley，University of California Press，1962. 165 p. fold. map，geneal. table. 24cm.（Chinese dynastic histories

translations, no. 9)

《宇文护传》，令狐德棻（583～666年）；丁爱博（Dien, Albert E.）（美国汉学家）译. 中英对照.（《周书》选译）

24. Biography of Huáng Ch'ao. Berkeley, University of Carlifornia Press, 1955. 144 p. 3 fold. maps (in pocket) 24cm. (Chinese dynastic histories translations; no. 5.)

《黄巢传》，欧阳修（1007—1072），宋祁（998—1061）；Levy, Howard S. (Howard Seymour, 1923—)译.

25. Accounts of India and Kashmir in the dynastic histories of the T'ang period. Translated and annotated with introd. by Narayan Chandra Sen. Santiniketan, Visva-Bharati, 1968. 84 p. 25cm.

Translation of selected passages from the Chinese texts of the Chiu T'ang shu and Hsin T'ang shu; original text and textual notes appended

《唐代的印度与克什米尔史料》，Sen, Narayan C. 译. 内容译自《旧唐书》和《新唐书》.

26. Biography of An Lu-shan. Translated and annotated by Howard S. Levy. Berkeley, University of California Press, 1960. 122 p. fold. map (in pocket) facsims. 24cm. (Chinese dynastic histories translations, no. 8)

《安禄山传》，Levy, Howard S. 译.《旧唐书》选译.

27. Biographies of Meng Hao-jan/translated and annotated by Hans H. Frankel. Berkeley; Los Angeles: University of California Press, 1961. 28, 32, 155 p.; 24cm. (East Asia Studies, Institute of East Asiatic Studies, University of California. Chinese dynastic histories translations＝中古史译丛；vno. 1—3)

Notes: Introduction. —First version of the official biography of Meng Hao-jan (Chiu T'ang-shu 190C. 2b)—Second version of the official biography of Meng Hao-jan (Hsin T'ang-shu 203. 3a-b)—Notes. —Bibliography (p. 17—25).

《孟浩然传》，Frankel, Hans H. (Hans Hermann, 1916—)编译. 译自《旧唐书》和《新唐书》.

28. Po Chū-i as a censor: his memorials presented to Emperor Hsien-tsung during the years 808—810/translated and explained by Eugene Feifel. Hague: Mouton, 1961. 244 p.; 25cm.

Feifel, Eugen(1902—)译注. 公元808—810年白居易作为谏官向宪宗皇帝呈递的奏折.

29. The veritable record of the T'ang emperor Shun-tsung, February 28, 805—August 31, 805./Han Yu's Shun-tsung shih-lu, translated with introd. and notes by Bernard S. Solomon. Cambridge, Harvard University Press, c1955. xxxi, 82 p.; c26cm. (Harvard-Yenching Institute studies, v. 13)

《顺宗实录》，韩愈（768年—824年）；Solomon, Bernard S. 编译.

30. Political propaganda and ideology in China at the end of

the seventh century: inquiry into the nature, authors and function of the Tunhuang document S. 6502, followed by an annotated translation/Antonino Forte. Napoli: Istituto universitario orientale, Seminario di studi asiatici, 1976. xii, 312 pages, [18] leaves of plates: facsimiles; 25cm. Series minor Istituto universitario orientale (Naples, Italy). Seminario di studi asiatici.

《七世纪末中国的政治宣传和思想意识》，Forte, Antonino 著. 对敦煌 S6502 抄本进行了翻译. 唐代历史.

(1) 2nd ed. Kyoto: Scuola di studi sull'Asia orientale, 2005. xxii, 574 pages: illustrations; 24cm. ISBN: 490079323X, 4900793231. (Monographs/Italian School of East Asian Studies; v. 1)

31. The Fo-kuang ssu: literary evidences and Buddhist images/Marylin M. Rhie. New York: Garland Pub., 1977. xi, 274 pages: illustrations; 21cm. ISBN: 0824027213, 0824027216. (Outstanding dissertations in the fine arts)

Notes: Reprint of the author's thesis, University of Chicago, 1970. / "Translation of Tun-huang MS (Stein) 397": p. 47—64. / Includes bibliographical references (pages 183—194).

Rhie, Marylin M 著. 对敦煌第 397 号抄本进行了翻译.

32. The urban life of the Tang dynasty/written by Huang Xinya; translated by Tu Guoyuan and Yan Hongfu. Reading, United Kingdom: Paths International Ltd.; [China]: Hunan People's Publishing House, 2014. 2, 444 pages; 25cm. iv, 2, 443 pages; 26cm. ISBN: 1844643547, 1844643549. (Insight on Ancient China series)

《消逝的太阳：唐代城市生活长卷》，黄新亚（1950—）.

33. 凝望长安：唐代文化与艺术/董长君，董晓莉；石巍译. 北京：外文出版社，2014. 309 页，[1]叶图版：彩图，肖像，摹真；23cm. ISBN: 7119086088

英文题名：Splendors of a golden era in China: the culture and arts of the Tang Dynasty

34. Salt and state: an annotated translation of the Songshi salt monopoly treatise/Cecilia Lee-fang Chien. Ann Arbor: Center for Chinese Studies, University of Michigan, c2004. xiii, 365 p.; 15 maps; 24cm. ISBN: 0892641630. (Michigan monographs in Chinese studies, 1081－9053; v. 99)

《国家和盐：〈宋史·食货志·盐〉译注》，Chien, Cecilia Lee-fang 译.

35. The urban life of the Song dynasty/written by Li Chuntang; translated by Liu Chuan, Qiu Yun & He Qiuhua; revised by Wang Hong. Reading, UK: Paths International Ltd, 2014. 391 pages; 25cm. ISBN: 1844643530, 1844643530. (Insight on ancient China series)

《坊墙倒塌以后：宋代城市生活长卷》，李春棠.

36. Studies on The secret history of the Mongols/by Kuo-yi Pao. Bloomington: Indiana University, [1965]. vii, 163 p. ; 23cm. (Indiana University publications. Uralic and Altaic series; v. 58)

   Transliteration and translation into English of chapter 9 of Yüan Ch'ao pi shih, with commentary.

   《元朝秘史》(节译),Pao, Kuo-yi(1916—)译.

37. The secret history of the Mongols/for the first time done into English out of the original tongue and provided with an exegetical commentary by Francis Woodman Cleaves. Cambridge, Mass. : Published for the Harvard-Yenching Institute by Harvard University Press, 1982—. v. ⟨1⟩; 24cm. 0674796705 (v. 1), 0674796706

   Notes: Translated from the Chinese

   《元朝秘史》,佚名作;柯立甫(Cleaves, Francis Woodman)(美国汉学家)译.

38. The history and the life of Chinggis Khan: the Secret history of the Mongols/translated and annotated by Urgunge Onon. Leiden; New York: E. J. Brill, 1990. xix, 183 p. , [1] folded leaf of plates: ill. , map; 25cm. ISBN: 9004092366

   《元朝秘史》,Onon, Urgunge 译.

39. The secret history of the Mongols: a Mongolian epic chronicle of the thirteenth century/translated with a historical and philological commentary by Igor de Rachewiltz. Leiden; Boston: Brill, 2004—2013. 3 v. : ill. (some col.), maps, plates; 25cm. ISBN: 9004131590 (set), 9004131590 (set), 9004135960 (v. 1), 9004135963 (v. 1), 9004135979 (v. 2), 9004135970 (v. 2), 9004250567 (v. 3), 9004250565 (v. 3), 9004258587 (v. 3), 9004258582 (v. 3). (Brill's Inner Asian library; v. 7)

   《元朝秘史》(或《蒙古秘史》),佚名作;罗依果(Rachewiltz, Igor de)(意大利裔澳大利亚汉学家)译.

   (1)Leiden; Boston: Brill, 2006. 2 v. (1349 p.): map; 25cm. ISBN: 9004153632 (set), 9004153639 (set), 9004154116 (v. 1), 9004154117 (v. 1), 9004154124 (v. 2), 9004154124 (v. 2). (Brill's Inner Asian library; v. 7/1, 2)

40. The urban life of the Yuan dynasty/written by Shi Weimin; translated by Tu Guoyuan & Liao Jing. Reading: Paths International Ltd. ; [China]: Hunan People's Publishing House, 2014. 4, 2, 418 pages; 25cm. ISBN: 1844643554, 1844643557. (Insight on Ancient China series)

   《都市中的游牧民:元代城市生活长卷》,史卫民(1952—).

41. The urban life of the Ming dynasty/written by Chen Baoliang; translated by Zhu Yihua, Wang Ting & Yang Fei; revised by Wang Hong. Reading, United Kingdom: Paths International Ltd,2014. 4,2,506 pages;25cm. ISBN: 1844643565,1844643561. (Insight on ancient China series)

   《飘摇的传统:明代城市生活长卷》,陈宝良.

42. The early history of China's patrol inspection system in the Ming Dynasty/compiled by Xiu Xiaobo translated by Chen Xia. Beijing: Sinolingua, 2017. xx, 158 p. ; 24cm.

   《中国巡视制度溯源:明朝巡视监察制度辑要》,修晓波编注. 华语教学出版社.

43. The sacred edict. Shanghai: American Presbyterian Mission Press, c1892. vii, 216 p. ; 24cm.

   《圣谕广训》,康熙帝(1654—1722);鲍康宁(Baller, F. W. ⟨Frederick William⟩, 1852—1922)译. 英汉对照.

   (1)Shanghai: China Inland Mission and Presbyterian Mission Press, c1917. 216 p. ; 24cm.

   (2) Shanghai: China Inland Mission and All Booksellers, c1924. 216 p.

   (3)Orono, ME: The National Poetry Foundation, University of Maine at Orono, c1979. vi, 216 p. ; c24cm. ISBN: 0915032252

44. Chang Hsi and the treaty of Nanking, 1842/by Ssu-yü Têng. Chicago, Ill. : University of Chicago Press, c1944. xi, 191 p. : bill. (map); 24cm.

   Notes: "Annotated translation of the Fu-i jih-chi" (the diary of Chang Hsi): p. 14—115.

   《抚夷日记》,张喜(生卒不详,活动时间为 1800—1842 年);邓嗣禹(Têng, Ssu-yü, 1906—)译.

45. The urban life of the Qing dynasty/written by Zhao Shiyu; translated by Wang Hong, Zhang Linlin & Lv Yan; revised by Wang Hong. Reading, United Kingdom: Paths International Ltd. , 2014. 352 pages; 26cm. ISBN: 1844643522, 1844643523. (Insight on ancient China series)

   Contents: Within the four seas—The family of power—Nine thousand nine hundred and ninety-nine houses—The last heyday—The unforgotten corners—The quiet and noisy urban life—Walking out of the fence of the city wall.

   《腐朽与神奇:清代城市生活长卷》,赵世瑜.

K14 近代史(1840—1911)

1. Modern China: a topical history/by Su Kaiming. Beijing, China: New World Press: Distributed by China International Book Trading Corp. , 1985. 279 pages, [27] pages of plates: illustrations; 21cm. ISBN: 0835113973, 0835113977

   《中国近代史题话》,苏开明著. 新世界出版社.

2. From the Opium War to the May Fourth Movement. Vol. 1/Hu Sheng; translated by Dun J. Li. Beijing: Foreign Languages Press, 1991. 2 volumes; 21cm. ISBN: 0835119505 (v. 1), 0835119504 (v. 1), 7119000020 (v. 1), 7119000022 (v. 1), 0835121615 (v. 2), 0835121613 (v. 2), 711900008X (v. 2), 7119000084 (v. 2), 71190000020

《从鸦片战争到五四运动》(上、下册),胡绳著.

3. A concise history of the Qing Dynasty/Dai Yi;[translated by Lan Fangfang, Liu Bingxin and Liu Hui]. Singapore: Silkroad Press, 2011—2013. 4 volumes: illustrations, maps; 27cm. ISBN: 9814332187, 9814332186, 9814332644, 981433264X, 9814332194, 9814332194, 9814332200, 9814332208,9814332217,9814332216

Notes:"Chinese original edition c2006 China Renmin University Press"

《简明清史》,戴逸.

4. Chinese account of the Opium War/[translation] by E. H. Parker. Shanghai, Kelly & Walsh, c1888. ii, 82 p.; 22cm. (Pagoda library, v. no. 1.)

Notes:"Translation of the last two chapters of the Sheng wu-ki... Parts... digested... Portions omitted."

《圣武记》(选译),魏源(1794—1857);庄延龄(Parker, Edward Harper, 1849—1926)(英国汉学家)译.译自魏源《圣武记》卷十〈道光洋艘征抚记〉,涉及有关鸦片战争之事.

　　(1) 2013. ii, 82 pages;21cm. ISBN: 1110054794, 1110054793〉(BiblioLife reproduction series)

5. History of the pirates who infested the China Sea from 1807—1810/Yung-lun Yüan; translated from the Chinese original, with notes and illustrations by Charles Friedrich Neumann. Cambridge; New York: Cambridge University Press, c2011. xlvii, 128, 44 p.: maps; 22cm. ISBN: 1108029209. (Cambridge library collection)

《靖海氛记》,(清)袁永纶;Neumann, Karl Friedrich (1793?—1870)译.初版于1831年.广东海盗史料.

6. The flight of an empress/told by Wu Yung, whose other name is Yu-ch'uan; transcribed by Liu K'un; translated and edited by Ida Pruitt; introduction by Kenneth Scott Latourette. London: Faber and Faber, [1936]. 294 p.: ill.; 21cm.

《庚子西狩丛谭》,吴永(1865—1936)口述;刘昆笔记;Pruitt, Ida 译.

　　(1)Westport, Conn., Hyperion Press, c[1973, c1936]. xxiii, 222 p.: illus.; 23cm. ISBN: 0883550989

7. The diary of His Excellency Ching-shan/Ching-shan; translated by Duyvendak. Lugduni Batavorum: E. J. Brill, c1924. viii, 85, 48 p.; 24cm.

《景善日记》,景善(1823—1900);Duyvendak, J. J. L. (Jan Julius Lodewijk,1889—)译.

8. The Taiping Rebellion; history and documents/by Franz Michael, in collaboration with Zhongli Zhang. [translations by Margery Anneberg and others]. Seattle, University of Washington Press, 1966—1971. 3 volumes (1815 pages) maps 25cm. ISBN: 029595244X, 0295952444, 0295739592, 0295739595. (University of Washington publications on Asia).(Far Eastern and Russian Institute. Publications; no. 14)

Contents: v. 1. History. —v. 2 - 3. Documents and comments

Notes:"A product of the Modern Chinese History Project carried on by the Far Eastern and Russian Institute of the University of Washington."/

Michael, Franz H. 与 Chang, Chung-li (1919—) 著; Anneberg, Margery 译.太平天国史料.

9. The Opium War/by the Compilation Group for the "History of Modern China" Series. Peking: Foreign Languages Press, 1976. 131 pages, [5] leaves of plates: illustrations;19cm.

《鸦片战争》,《中国近代史丛书》编写.

10. The Taiping revolution/by the Compilation Group for the "History of Modern China" series. Peking: Foreign Languages Press, 1976. 188 pages, [8] pages of plates: illustrations, folded map;19cm. (History of Modern China)

《太平天国革命》,《中国近代史丛书》编写.

11. The Yi Ho Tuan movement of 1900/by the Compilation Group for the "History of Modern China" Series. Peking: Foreign Languages Press, 1976. 133 pages,[2] leaves of plates: illustrations;19cm.

《义和团运动》,《中国近代史丛书》编写组.

K15　中华民国时期

1. General Chiang Kai-shek; the account of the fortnight in Sian when the fate of China hung in the balance, by General and Madame Chiang Kai-shek. Garden City, New York: Doubleday, Doran & Company, Inc., 1937. xi p., 1 l., 187 p. 20cm.

蒋介石(1887—1975),宋美龄(Chiang, May-ling Soong, 1897—2003).关于西安事变的记述.

2. Sian: a coup d'état, by Mayling Soong Chiang (Madame Chiang Kai-shek). A fortnight in Sian: extracts from a diary by Chiang Kei-shek. Shanghai, The China Publishing Company, 1937. x, 119 p. 25cm.

蒋介石(1887—1975),宋美龄(Chiang, May-ling Soong, 1897—2003).西安事变蒋介石的日记摘要.

K16　日本侵华战争史

1. Give back my rivers and hills! A personal record of life in the Chinese army on the Hsühchou and Honan fronts during 1938/By I Feng, translated from the Chinese by Innes Jackson. London, Macmillan and Co. Ltd. 1945. xviii, 135 [1] p. front., plates. 20cm.

Notes:

《还我河山》,易风(I-Feng, pseud);Jackson, Innes 译.抗日战争纪实.

2. The Historical experience of the war against fascism/by the Editorial Department of Renmin ribao (People's daily). Peking: Foreign Languages Press, 1965. 27

pages；19cm.

《反法西斯战争的历史经验》，人民日报编辑部.

3. An illustrated history of China's war of resistance against Japan/written by Zhang Chengjun, Liu Jianye；photos edited by Lu Shuping, Xu Liping, Qiu Yuling；translated by He Jun［and others］. Beijing：Foreign Languages Press, 1995. 132 pages：illustrations, maps；25×27cm. ISBN：711901739X, 711901739

《中国抗日战争画史》，张承钧，刘建业著.

4. Class-A war criminals：enshrined at Yasukuni Shrine/comp. by Modern History Institute of Chinese Academy of Social Sciences. 2005. 119 p. Ill. ISBN：7508507495, 7508507491

《靖国神社中的甲级战犯：英文》，中国社会科学院近代史研究所编.五洲传播出版社.介绍靖国神社中供奉的14名甲级战犯对中国人民和亚洲许多国家人民犯下的滔天罪行.

5. 侵华日军关东军七三一细菌部队：［中英文本］＝Unit 731：Japanese germ warfare unit in China/郭长建，王鹏主编；侵华日军关东军七三一部队罪证陈列馆编. 北京：五洲传播出版社，2005. 150 p.：photo., Map；30cm. ISBN：7508507401, 7508507408

《侵华日军关东军七三一细菌部队：汉英对照》，侵华日军关东军七三一部队罪证陈列馆编.五洲传播出版社.

6. 日本战犯的再生之地：中国抚顺战犯管理所＝Place of new life of Japanese war criminals/郭长建，张佐库，侯桂花主编；抚顺战犯管理所编. 北京：五洲传播出版社，2005. 221 p.：photo.；29cm. ISBN：7508507347,7508507347

《日本战犯的再生之地：中国抚顺战犯管理所：汉英对照》，抚顺战犯管理所编.五洲传播出版社.

7. "伟大胜利：纪念中国人民抗日战争暨世界反法西斯战争胜利大型主题展览"讲解词：汉英对照/中国人民抗日战争纪念馆编著. 北京：北京出版社，2009. 235 页；21cm. ISBN：7200080438, 7200080438

8. 国家记忆：历史就在那里/朱成山等［编著］；张重光，林传红翻译. 北京：外文出版社，2014. 19 页：图；21cm. ISBN：7119092287

英文题名：Memory of a country：history that cannot be forgotten.主要讲中国为什么要设立国家公祭日，国家公祭日的由来、意义.

9. 铁证：日军侵华罪证自录/王艾甫，戴姝瑶，张基祥［编著］；张辉译. 北京：新世界出版社，2015. 241 页：图，地图；26cm. ISBN：7510453632

英文题名：Smoking guns：a collection of incriminating evidence on Japan's aggression against China

10. 南京大屠杀/徐志耕著；林戊苏，章挺权，吴艳翻译. 北京：外文出版社，2014. 256 页：图，照片；23cm. ISBN：7119089836

英文题名：Nanjing massacre

11. 南京大屠杀幸存者证言/朱成山编著；胡亮，严晶英文翻译. 北京：外文出版社有限责任公司，2016. 200 页：照片；

23cm. ISBN：7119102757

英文题名：Testimonies of Nanjing massacre survivors

12. 人类记忆 南京大屠杀实证：英文/张宪文，张建军主编. 北京：人民出版社，2017. 26cm. ISBN：7010185675

K17 中华人民共和国史（1949—）

1. A history of the modern Chinese revolution. ［Translated by the English faculty of the Western Languages Dept. of Peking University］. Peking, Foreign Languages Press, 1959. 627 p. illus., port., fold. map. 20cm. (China knowledge series)

《中国现代革命史》，北京大学西语系英语教员译.

(1) A history of the modern Chinese revolution/Ho Kan-Chih；translated by the English faculty of the Western Languages Department of Peking University. New York：AMS Press, 1979. 627 p., ［13］ leaves of plates：ill.；19cm. ISBN：0404144799. (China knowledge series)

2. The revolution of 1911：a great democratic revolution of China. Peking：Foreign Languages Press, 1962. 145 pages：illustrations, portraits；20cm.

《辛亥革命：中国近代史上一次伟大的民主革命》，吴玉章著.

(1) 2nd ed. Peking：Foreign Languages Press, 1963. 145 pages, ［8］ pages of plates：illustrations；21cm.

(2) 3rd ed., rev. translation. Peking：Foreign Languages Press, 1964. 145 pages, ［8］ pages of plates：illustrations；21cm.

(3) 4th ed. Beijing：Foreign Languages Press, 1981. 145 pages：illustrations, portraits；20cm.

3. The great turning point. Peking：Foreign Languages Press, 1962. 232 pages, ［5］ leaves of plates：illustrations, maps (1 folded)；23cm.

Contents：The bankruptcy of the U. S. —Chiang Kai-shek peace plot/Wu Yu-chang—Give tit for tat, and the fight for every inch of land/Liu Chung—In his mind a million bold warriors/Yen Chang-lin—The great turning point/Yen Chang-lin—Thrust into the Tapieh mountains/Tang Ping-chu—The Tashan battle of interception/Wu Ke-hua—On the southern Huai-Hai line/Ho Kuang-hua—Reminiscences of the battle of Tientsin/Li Tien-yu—Brave troops across the Tangtse/Pao Hsien-chih

《伟大的转折》，吴玉章等著.

4. Communist China 1955—1959：policy documents with analysis/prepared at Harvard University under the joint auspices of the Center for International Affairs and the East Asian Research Center；with a foreword by Robert R. Bowie and John K. Fairbank. Cambridge, Mass.：Harvard University Press, 1962. xi, 611 p.；28cm. ISBN：0674149009, 0674149007

中华人民共和国1955—1959年文件汇编.

5. The roar of a nation：reminiscences of the December 9th Student Movement/[by] Chiang Nan-hsiang and others. Peking：Foreign Languages Press，1963. vii，172 pages：illustrations；19cm.

Contents：Storm of a struggle to resist Japan and save the nation. —The rapids，by Shih Li-teh. —Storm over the Whangpoo River，by Chang Tse-sun. —Flames of wrath，by Li Lien-pi. —Off to the countryside，by Wang Nien-chi. —In memory of comrade Huang Ching，by Wang Lin. —In memory of comrade Yang Hsueh-cheng，by Chiang Nan-hsiang. —A tribute to Huang Cheng，by Shih Li-teh.

《民族的怒吼："一二·九"学生运动回忆》，蒋南翔等著.

6. CCP documents of the great proletarian cultural revolution，1966—1967. Kowloon，Union Research Institute，1968. vi，29，692 pages；23cm.

Contents：pt. 1. Documents of central authorities. —pt. II. Documents of Peking municipal authorities.

《中共中央文件汇编：关于文化大革命，1966—1967》，中英对照.

(1)台北市：《中共研究》杂志社，[1973]. 16，426，26 p. 书名为：《中共文化大革命重要文件汇编》

(2)增订本. 台北市：《中共研究》杂志社，[1979]. 18，606，24 pages；27cm.

7. Decision of the Central Committee of the Chinese Communist Party concerning the great proletarian Cultural Revolution（adopted on August 8，1966）. Peking：Foreign Languages Press，1966. 12 pages；21cm.

《中国共产党中央委员会关于无产阶级文化大革命的决定》

8. Carry the great proletarian cultural revolution through to the end. Peking：Foreign Languages Press，1966. IV，60 pages

《把无产阶级文化大革命进行到底》

9. Great victory for Chairman Mao's revolutionary line：warmly hail the birth of Peking Municipal Revolutionary Committee. Peking：Foreign Languages Press，1967. 87 pages；14cm.

Notes：Speeches by Zhou Enlai［and others］and editorials from the Renmin Ribao（People's Daily）—and the Jiefangjun Bao（Liberation Army Daily）April 21，1967.

《毛主席革命路线的伟大胜利：热烈欢呼北京市革命委员会诞生》

(1)Peking：Foreign Languages Press，1967. 47 pages；21cm.

10. The dictatorship of the proletariat and the great proletarian cultural revolution/by Wang Li，Jia Yixue，and Li Xin. Peking：Foreign Languages Press，1967. 16 pages；21cm.

《无产阶级专政和无产阶级文化大革命》，王力（1900—1986）.

11. Advance courageously along the road of victory. In warm celebration of the 19th anniversary of the founding of the People's Republic of China. Peking：Foreign Languages Press，1968. IV，32 pages

《在胜利的大道上奋勇前进：热烈庆祝中华人民共和国成立十九周年》

12. Long live victory of the great cultural revolution under the dictatorship of the proletariat：in celebration of the 18th anniversary of the founding of the People's Republic of China. Peking：Foreign Languages Press，1968. x，50 pages

《无产阶级专政下的文化大革命胜利万岁》

13. The Chinese Cultural Revolution：selected documents/edited and with notes by K. H. Fan. New York：Monthly Review Press，1968. XVI，320 p. 21cm.

Fan，Kuang Huan（1932—）编. "文革"史料.

14. The Revolution of 1911/by the Compilation Group for the "History of Modern China" Series. Peking：Foreign Languages Press，1976. 174 pages，［4］leaves of plates：illustrations；19cm. （History of Modern China series）

《辛亥革命》，《中国近代史丛书》编写组.

15. The reform movement of 1898/by the Compilation Group for the "History of Modern China" Series. Peking：Foreign Languages Press，1976. 136 pages，［2］leaves of plates：illustrations；19cm.

《戊戌变法》，《中国近代史丛书》编写组.

16. Recalling the long march/by Liu Bocheng and others. Peking：Foreign Languages Press，1978. 181 pages，1 folded map：illustrations；19cm.

《回顾长征》，刘伯承等.

17. The 1911 revolution：a retrospective after 70 years/by Hu Sheng... ［et al.］. Beijing：New World Press，1983. 222 p.：ill.；21cm. （China studies series）

《辛亥革命：七十年后的回顾》，胡绳等著. 新世界出版社.

18. China A B C. Beijing，China：New World Press：Distributed by China International Book Trading Corp. （Guoji Shudian），1985. 238 pages：illustrations（some color）；19cm. ISBN：0835113930，0835113939

《中国百题》，新世界出版社编. 中国 1949 年以来的历史.

19. A chronology of the People's Republic of China，1949—1984/compiled by Cheng Jin. Beijing：Foreign Languages Press：Distributed by China International Book Trading Corp. （Guoji Shudian），1986. 99 pages；19cm. ISBN：0835115666，0835115667

《中华人民共和国大事记：1949—1984》，成今编.

20. Years of trial，turmoil and triumph：China from 1949 to 1988/compiled by Zong Huaiwen. Beijing：Foreign Languages Press：Distributed by China International

Book Trading Corp. ，1989. ii，319 pages，[20] pages of plates；illustrations；21cm. ISBN：0835122611，0835122610，083512262X，0835122627，7119010166，7119010168，7119010158，7119010151. (China knowledge series)

《中华人民共和国简史》，宗怀文主编.

21. The People's Republic of China：a chronicle (1949—1989). Beijing：New Star Publishers，1989. 200 pages；19cm. ISBN：780085034X，7800850349

《中华人民共和国大事记：1949—1989》

22. The Revolution of 1911：turning point in modern Chinese history/edited by Dong Caishi；written by Lu Bowei and Wang Guoping. Beijing：Foreign Languages Press，1991. ii，544 pages，[18] pages of plates；illustrations，portraits；21cm. ISBN：7119014234，7119014234

《中国近代历史的转折：辛亥革命》，董蔡时主编.

23. An outline history of China 1919—1949/Edited by Bai Shouyi；written by Wang Guilin... Beijing：Foreign Languages Press，1993. 319 pages；illustrations，portraits；21cm. ISBN：0835110001，0835110006

《中国通史纲要续编：1919—1949》，白寿彝主编；王桧林等编.

24. Turbulent decade：a history of the cultural revolution/Yan Jiaqi and Gao Gao；translated and edited by D. W. Y. Kwok. Honolulu：University of Hawaii Press，1996. xxv，659 p.：maps；24cm. ISBN：0824816951. (SHAPS Library of Translations)

《骚动的十年：文化革命史》，严家其(1942—)；高皋著，郭颖颐(Kwok, D. W. Y.〈Danny Wynn Ye〉，1932—)(美国汉学家)译.

25. China in the world anti-fascist war/Peng Xunhou；[translated by Li Guoqing, Yu Cen]. [Beijing]：China Intercontinental Press，2005. 173 pages：illustrations；23cm. ISBN：7508507002，7508507002

《世界反法西斯战争中的中国：英文》，彭训厚著；李国庆，于岑译. 五洲传播出版社.

26. Facts about the Xi'an incident/Bochun Shen；translator，Mengjia Yu. Beijing：People's Publishing Press，2009. 11，3，6，391 pages：illustrations；21cm. ISBN：7010080611，7010080615

《西安事变纪实》，申伯纯著. 人民出版社.

27. Memorabilia of the People's Republic of China：October 1949—September 2009/Party History Research Office of the Central Committee of the Communist Party of China. Beijing：Foreign Languages Press，2009. 144 pages；21cm. ISBN：7119060941，711906094

《中华人民共和国大事记：1949 年 10 月—2009 年 9 月》，中共中央党史研究室编著.

28. Our sixty years/by Sun Ran；translated by Ego. Beijing：China International Press，2009. 141 pages；illustrations；19cm. ISBN：7508515823，750851582X. (Stories from China)

《我们的六十年》，孙冉著. 五洲传播出版社. 选取 6 位普通的中国人，讲述他们的人生经历或者历史记忆，通过鲜活的个案，让读者感受到中国 60 年发展进步的历史进程.

K2　中外交流史

1. Chau Ju-kua：his work on the Chinese and Arab trade in the twelfth and thirteenth centuries. St. Petersburg，Print. Off. of the Imperial Academy of Sciences，1911. x，288 p. fold. col. map. 27cm.

《诸蕃志》，(南宋)赵汝适(1170—1231)著；夏德(Hirth，Friedrich，1845—1927)(德国汉学家)，柔克义(Rockhill，William Woodville，1854—1914)(美国汉学家)合译.

(1)New York：Paragon Book Reprint Corp. ，1966. 2 v. fold. map. 26—23×27cm. .

Vol. 1 is a reprint of the 1911 ed. of the English translation，Title and text of v. 2 in Chinese

2. Japan in the Chinese dynastic histories：Later Han through Ming dynasties. Editor：L. Carrington Goodrich. South Pasadena [Calif.] P. D. and I. Perkins，1951. vii，187l. maps. 28cm. (Perkins Asiatic monographs，no. 2)

Goodrich，L. Carrington (Luther Carrington，1894—)编；Tsunoda，Ryūsaku 译. 翻译中国《三国志》《宋书》《隋书》《新唐书》中有关日本的史料.

3. Monk Jianzhen's journey to Japan/Le Min，Deng Yinke；translated by Chang Guojie. Beijing：China Intercontinental Press，2010. 163 pages：illustrations (some color)，map；23cm. ＋1 CD-ROM (4 3/4 in.). ISBN：7508517056，7508517059. (Roads to the world)

《鉴真东渡弘法》，乐敏，邓荫柯编著；畅国杰翻译. 五洲传播出版社(中外文化交流故事丛书)

4. Chinese sources of South Asian history in translation：data for study of India-China relations through history/Haraprasad Ray. Kolkata：Asiatic Society，2004—〈2011〉. v. 〈1—4〉：maps；22cm. ISBN：8172361513 (v. 1)，8192061504 (v. 4)

Contents：v. 1. The Qin dynasty，the former and later Han dynasties，the period of the three kingdoms，(Liu) Song，Southern Qi，the northern，eastern，and western Wei dynasties (3rd century B. C. -6th century A. D.)—v. 2. Chinese sources on ancient Indian geography—v. 3. The Buddhist trilogy—v. 4. The golden period of India-China relations (6th century AD—10th century AD)

《南亚中国史料翻译：中印关系研究史料》，Ray，Haraprasad(1931—)译.

5. Under the same army flag：recollections of the veterans of the World War II. [Beijing]：China Intercontinental Press，2005. 312 pages；illustrations；23cm. ISBN：7508506979，7508506975

《在同一面战旗下：英文》，邓贤主编；Jean Pei 等译. 五洲传播出版社.本书是二战期间,中、缅、印战场的中国驻印远征军老兵的口述实录.

6. Peace missions on a grand scale: admiral Zheng He's seven expeditions to the Western Oceans/by Fang Zhogfu and Li Erhe. Beijing Foreign Languages Press, 2005. 133 pages, [8] pages of plates: illustrations (some color), maps; 23cm. ISBN: 7119038540, 7119038544

《和平大航海:郑和七下西洋:英文》,房仲甫,李仁和著.

7. 郑和下西洋/王介南著;Ego 翻译.北京:五洲传播出版社,2010. 161 页;23cm. ISBN: 7508517025, 7508517024.(中外文化交流故事丛书)

英文题名:Zheng He's voyages to the Western Oceans.

8. Following the steps of Matteo Ricci to China/Zhang Xiping; translated by Ding Deshu & Ye Jinping. [Beijing]: China Intercontinental Press, 2006. 173 pages: illustrations (some color); 25cm. ISBN: 750850982X, 7508509822

《跟随利玛窦来中国:英文》,张西平著;丁德书,耶进平译.五洲传播出版社.本书介绍 16～19 世纪期间,以利玛窦等人为代表的一批传教士来到中国,在中外文化交流史上留下了辉煌的一章.

9. A short history of Sino-Indian friendship/Chin Keh-mu; [translated by Yang Hsien-yi and Gladis Yang]. Peking: Foreign Languages Press, 1958. 102 pages, [8] pages of plates: illustrations, portraits; 19cm.

《中印人民友谊史话》,金克木著;杨宪益(1915—2009),戴乃迭(Yang. Gladys,1919—1999)译.

10. One world: bridging the communication gap/Zhao Qizheng; translated by Geoffrey Bonnycastle. [Beijing]: China Intercontinental Press, 2008. viii, [4], 178 pages: illustrations; 25cm. ISBN: 7508514062, 7508514068

《在同一世界:跨文化交流》,赵启正著.五洲传播出版社.介绍中外交往中存在的文化差异,帮助人们了解背景,促进理解.

11. Cultural flow between China and outside world throughout history/by Shen Fuwei. Beijing: Foreign Languages Press, 2009. 416 pages: illustrations (some color), map; 24cm. ISBN: 7119057538, 7119057537. (China studies)

《中外文化因缘》,沈福伟著.

12. The Jews in China/compiled and edited by Pan Guang. Beijing: China Intercontinental Press, 2005. 17, 240 p.: ill., ports.; 30cm. ISBN: 7508507509, 7508507507

《犹太人在中国:汉英对照》,潘光主编.3 版.五洲传播出版社.介绍犹太民族在中国留下的生活轨迹,以及中、犹民族之间的传统友谊.

K21　丝绸之路

1. Story of the Silk Road/Zhang Yiping; translated by Jia Zongyi. [China]: China Intercontinental Press, 2005. 176 pages: illustrations (some color), maps (some color); 25cm. ISBN: 7508508327, 7508508320

《丝绸之路:英文》,张一平著;贾宗谊译.五洲传播出版社.本书介绍"丝绸之路"这条中国古代经由中亚通往南亚、西亚以及欧洲、北非的陆上贸易交往的通道.

2. 丝绸之路:汉英对照/林少雄著;王克友译.北京:人民文学出版社,2006. 101 页;21cm. ISBN: 702004882X, 7020048823.(中国传统文化双语读本)

3. The opening of the Silk Road/Zhang Yiping; translated by Ego. Beijing: China Intercontinental Press, 2010. 199 pages: illustrations (some color), maps; 24cm. ISBN: 7508517094, 7508517091. (Roads to the world)

《丝绸之路的开通》,张一平著.五洲传播出版社(中外文化交流故事丛书)

4. "Nanhai I" and the maritime silk road/[Li Qingxin]; translated by Yu Chengyong. Beijing: China Intercontinental Press, 2010. 175 pages: illustrations; 23cm. ISBN: 7508517032, 7508517032. (Roads to the World)

《"南海 1 号"与海上丝绸之路》,李庆新著;余成永翻译.五洲传播出版社(中外文化交流故事丛书).讲述满载宋瓷的"南海 1 号"沉船从发现到打捞到建设博物馆的故事,同时介绍宋元时期繁荣的"海上丝绸之路"的情况.

5. History of silk/[Chinese compiler Mao Huiwei, Zhao Feng]. Beijing: Encyclopedia of China Publishing House, 2010. iii,188 pages: illustrations;21cm. ISBN: 7500082590, 7500082592. (History of Chinese civilization)

《丝绸史话:中英文双语版》,《中华文明史话》编委会编译.中国大百科全书出版社.

6. In the foot steps of Marco Polo/by Jin Bohong. [Beijing, China]: New World Press, 1989. 153 pages; 21cm. ISBN: 7800050807, 7800050800

《沿着马可·波罗的足迹》,金伯宏著;施晓青译,新世界出版社.

7. The land of silk/by Wei Liming; [translated by Ling Yuan]. Beijing: Foreign Languages Press, 2002. 103 pages: color illustrations; 18×20cm. ISBN: 7119031546, 7119031545. (Culture of China＝中华风物)

Contents: I. The progress of silk—II. Varieties and patterns—III. The silk road.

《中国的丝绸》,韦黎明编著.

K3　地方史志

北京

1. Peking: today and yesterday/Hu Chia. Peking: Foreign Languages Press, 1956. 122 pages, [70] pages of plates: illustrations, maps, portraits; 21cm.

《北京》,胡嘉著.

2. Beijing old and new: a historical guide to places of interest: with descriptions of famous sites within one day's journey of Beijing/by Zhou Shachen. Beijing,

China：New World Press：Distributed by China International Book Trading Corp.，1984. 404 pages，[33] pages of plates：illustrations（some color）；19cm. ISBN：0835113922，0835113922

《古今北京》，周沙尘著.新世界出版社.

3. Beijing：the treasures of an ancient capital/Yan Chongnian，editors Wang Yanrong and Ma Yue，translated by Arnold Chao，Tan Aiqing {et... al}. 3rd ed. Pei-ching：Morning Glory Publishers，1995. 285 pages：illustrations（some color）；38cm. ISBN：7505404237，7505404236

《古都北京》，阎崇年著.朝华出版社.

(1) 朝华出版社，2016. 349 页：图，地图；29cm. ISBN：7505438545

4. Old Beijing：in the shadow of imperial throne/text by Xu Chengbei；［translated by Wang Mingjie］. Beijing：Foreign Languages Press：Jiangsu Fine Art Pub. House，2001. 13，240 pages：illustrations；22cm. ISBN：7119027867，7119027869.

《老北京：帝都遗韵》，徐城北著，王明杰译.

5. Beijing：a panoramic review of heritage and fascination/by Zheng Jingqiu，Li Na. Beijing：Jiuzhou Publishing House，2003. 127 pages：color illustrations；29cm. ISBN：7801148738，7801148735

《魅力北京：世界遗产与文化》，郑京秋，李娜编著.九州出版社.

6. Beijing：the city and the people/Xiao xiaoming. Beijing：Foreign Languages Press，2005. 1 vol.（233 p.）：ill.；24cm. ISBN：7119040383，7119040387.（Panoramic China）

《北京城与北京人：英文》，兰佩瑾编.外文出版社（全景中国）

7. 北京历史文化名城的保护与发展：汉英对照/汪兴焘著. 北京：五洲传播出版社，2005. 329 页；21cm. ISBN：7508507304，7508507309

北京市城市保护和发展研究.

8. Beijing's pastimes of yesteryear/text by Liu Shiyu, Zou Jinhua；photographs by Wu Wei [and others]；translated by Fu Zhibin. Beijing：China Pictorial Publishing House，2006. 110 pages：color illustrations；22cm. ISBN：7802200652，7802200654.（Charm of Beijing）

《北京老玩意儿：英文》，刘世宇，邹金华撰文；吴唯，张洪杰摄；付志斌译.中国画报出版社（2008，走近北京）.介绍了许多具有老北京文化特色的玩意，诸如鼻烟壶、空竹、洋画、推铁环、拉洋片、布老虎、风筝、纸球、玻璃喇叭、拨浪鼓、陀螺、风车、草编……从这些老玩意的故事中，可以体会到老北京的日常生活中蕴涵的深厚文化.

9. 老北京的玩艺儿：汉英对照/于润琦编著. 北京：中国文联出版社，2006. 148 页：照片；图；23cm. ISBN：7505948687，7505948686.（品味北京丛书）

英文题名：Entertainments and folk arts of old Beijing. 本书将老北京的 34 种玩意：拉洋片、吹糖人等收入其中.

10. Strolling the streets of Beijing/text by Li Lingyun, Yang Xiaozhou. Beijing：China Pictorial Publishing House，2006. 110 pages：illustrations（chiefly color）；22cm. ISBN：7802200630，7802200636.（Charm of Beijing）

《京城逛街：英文》，李凌云，杨小洲编文；邹毅等摄；匡佩华译.中国画报出版社（2008，走近北京）.选取了北京六个有代表性的街道，对其历史、现状、特色加以介绍.

11. Beijing's Siheyuan/text by Wang Lanshun；translated by Hating Gaho. Beijing：China Pictorial Publishing House，2006. 103 pages：color illustrations；22cm. ISBN：7802200660，7802200661.（Charm of Beijing）

《住在北京四合院：英文》，王兰顺撰文；曹立军摄；汉定佳和译.中国画报出版社（2008，走近北京）.介绍了北京对外开放的四合院宾馆、民居及饭店；北京主要的特色胡同及四合院保护区；北京四合院建筑结构常识.

12. 老北京＝The old Peking：汉英对照/罗哲文，李江树著；阿榕等译.石家庄：河北教育出版社，2007. 296 页：260 幅；25cm. ISBN：7543464705，7543464704

书名原文：The old Peking. 本书由著名古建筑研究大家罗哲文先生，著名作家、摄影家李江树著，由知名翻译家阿榕等译.全书中英文对照，收集北京建筑、文化、民俗等珍贵照片 260 余幅，图文互释.

13. The history and culture of Beijing ＝ Beijing li shi yu wen hua/［ed. in chief, Lü Shun. English ed.：Zhao Weiyu］. ［Beijing］：Yan Jiu Publ. House，2008. 207 pages：illustrations（chiefly color）；29cm. ISBN：7801684028，7801684028

《北京历史与文化》，旅舜主编.研究出版社.

14. World cultural heritage in Beijing/Chinese text by Wei Xin；photography by Li Shaobai；English translation by Ma Hongjun and Hu Xiaokai. Beijing：New World Press：China Translation & Publishing Corporation，2009. 143 p.：col. ill.，maps；29cm. ISBN：7510406768，7510406765.（World heritage sites in China）

《北京的世界文化遗产》，魏昕著；李少白摄.新世界出版社.介绍了北京的世界遗产.

15. Tales of old Beijing：the daily life in alleys/Zhang Xiaoping. ［Beijing］：China International Press，2010. 223 pages：chiefly illustrations；22cm. ISBN：7508515229，7508515226

《北京往事》，张晓平著.五洲传播出版社.记录了北京的民俗，尤其是普通北京人在胡同里的日常生活.

16. 画说老北京 古建京韵：英文/方砚著.北京：新星出版社，2017. 30cm. ISBN：7513323321

17. 画说老北京 胡同记忆：英文/方砚著.北京：新星出版社，2017. 30cm. ISBN：7513323338

18. 画说老北京 风物民俗：英文/方砚著.北京：新星出版社，2017. 30cm. ISBN：7513323376

19. 天安门指南：汉英对照/北京奥组委新闻宣传部，天安门

地区管理委员会编. 北京：中国档案出版社，2005. 48
页；19cm. ISBN：7801666305，7801666307

英文题名：Tiananmen guidebook

20. Worshiping the Three Sage Kings and Five Virtuous
Emperors：the imperial temple of emperors of successive
dynasties in Beijing/the Association for Promoting the
Protection and Use of the Imperial Temples of Emperors
of Successive Dynasties in Beijing, along with the
Administrative Office of the Imperial Temples of
Emperors of Successive Dynasties in Beijing. Beijing：
Foreign Languages Press, 2007. 193 pages：illustrations
(some color)；22cm.＋1 videodisc (sound, color；4 3/4
in.). ISBN：7119046358，7119046357

《祭三皇五帝：北京历代帝王庙：英文》，北京历代帝王庙
保护利用促进会，北京历代帝王庙管理处编. 介绍中国
有史以来 20 位杰出帝王；介绍北京历代帝王庙.

21. 京城内外：中英对照/张本瀛，康智敏著. 北京：中国建筑
工业出版社，2007. 194 页；21cm. ISBN：7112087961，
7112087969.（老北京的故事）

英文题名：Travel in the ancient capital. 主要以北京城区
和城郊的坛庙园林为线索，在对景点和建筑进行介绍的
同时，围绕历史上的名人，讲述了在这些地方发生的各
种历史事件.

22. Community culture of Beijing/text by Yuan Jing；
photographs by Li Chunsheng [and others]；translated
by Liu Haile. Beijing：China Pictorial Pub. House，
2008. 110 pages：illustrations；23cm. ISBN：
7802202139，7802202132

《北京的社区文化》，袁静撰稿；刘海乐翻译.

23. Hutong alleys：former residences of celebrities. Beijing，
China：Foreign Languages Press, 2005. 101 pages：
color illustrations，color maps；23cm. ISBN：
7119033468，7119033464

《北京胡同·名人故居：英文》，李连霞编；王建华等摄.
外文出版社（漫游北京）

本书主要介绍北京胡同、四合院、四合院内的名人故居，
北京的平民生活风情、庙会文化等.

24. Beijing Hutong/editor in chief, Liu Baoquan. Beijing：
China Travel & Tourism Press, 2008. 259 pages：
illustrations (some color)；23cm. ISBN：7503235306，
7503235306

《北京胡同》，刘保全主编. 中国旅游出版社.

25. 北京胡同/陈光中编著. 合肥：黄山书社，2011. 168 页；
21cm. ISBN：7546120287，7546120284.（中国红）

英文题名：Hutong in Beijing.

26. Beijing：cultural history of Xicheng district/chief editor
Fu Hua；chief translator Fan Yingbo. Beijing：Beijing
Yanshan Pub. House，2008. 8，360 pages：
illustrations，maps；23cm. ISBN：7540219789，
7540219785

《北京西城文化史》，傅华主编. 北京燕山出版社.

27. Inside stories from the Forbidden City/written by Er Si，
Shang Hongkui and others；translated by Zhao Shuhan.
Beijing, China：New World Press；Distributed by China
International Book Trading Corp. , 1986. 165 pages，
[2] leaves of plates：illustrations (some color)；19cm.
ISBN：0835116646，0835116640

《紫禁城秘史》，尔泗，商鸿逵等著；赵书汉译. 新世界出
版社.

28. The Forbidden City in Beijing/edited by Zhihai Zheng，
Zhijing Qu. Beijing：Jiu Zhou Pub. House, 2000. 202
pages：illustrations，maps，portraits；29cm. ISBN：
7801144996，7801144997

《北京紫禁城》，郑志海，屈志静编. 九州图书出版社.

29. Across the threshold of the Forbidden City/by Feng
Linying；translated by Wang Heping and Liu Chang.
Beijing：Morning Glory Publishers, 2004. 208 pages，
[8] pages of plates：illustrations；21cm. ISBN：
7505409069，7505409064

《走进紫禁城》，冯林英著；王和平，刘畅译. 朝华出版
社.

30. 故宫：英文/故宫博物院编. 北京：紫禁城出版社，2006.
181 页；20cm. ISBN：7800475468，7800475467

英文题名：The Palace Museum. 故宫博物院每年有海外
游客近百万，目前还没有一本很好的外文旅游导游手
册. 本书以 5 万通俗流畅的语言文字、150 幅图片的形
式，全面系统地介绍故宫的建筑、文物、陈列及历史知识
等，让海外游客对故宫有更深的了解.

31. The grand Forbidden City：the imperial axis/Chiu
Kwong Chiu]. Beijing：Forbidden City Press, 2008. 232
pages：illustrations (some color)，maps；25cm. ISBN：
7800476884；780047688X

《大紫禁城：王者的轴线》，赵广超著. 紫禁城出版社.

32. 故宫史话/《中华文明史话》编委会编译，冯贺军编撰. 北
京：中国大百科全书出版社，2009. 168 页；21cm. ISBN：
7500080589，7500080581

英文题名：History of the Forbidden City.

33. 故宫/杨莫编著. 合肥：黄山书社，2011. 174 页；21cm.
ISBN：7546120324，7546120322.（中国红）

英文题名：The Forbidden City. 英汉对照.

(1) 合肥：黄山书社，2016. 174 页；彩图；23cm. ISBN：
7546141909.（印象中国）

34. The Summer Palace and its background stories/[edited
by Xu Fengtong and Lan Peijin]. Beijing：Foreign
Languages Press, 2006. 226 pages：color illustrations，
map；19cm. ISBN：7119038087，7119038087

《颐和园趣闻：英文》，徐凤桐等撰；余志勇等摄；汤博文，
丛仁译. 本书是为 2008 年奥运会准备的介绍北京系列
书中的一本. 以 20 余篇趣闻、故事介绍颐和园.

35. Coming to the Summer Palace/[Yao Tianxin text/
photo]. Beijing：Foreign Languages Press, 2009. 291
pages：color illustrations，color maps；24cm. ISBN：

7119049625，7119049623

《走进颐和园》，颐和园管理处编．

36. 颐和园/白薇编著．合肥：黄山书社，2016. 168 页：彩图；23cm. ISBN：7546142036.（印象中国）

英文题名：The Summer Palace. 汉英对照．

37. Places of interest in Beijing/Zhu Qixin, Yan Zhaohua. Rev. 4th ed. Beijing, China：China Travel & Tourism Press, 1996. 400 pages, ［16］ pages of plates：illustrations （some color）；19cm. ISBN：7503213116, 7503213113

《北京旅游参观点介绍》，著歧新，颜兆华编著．中国旅游出版社．

38. China now Beijing/edited by Zhao Meng. Beijing, China：China Travel & Tourism Pr., 2000. 120 pages：illustrations （some color）；19cm. ISBN：7503217448, 7503217449

《北京旅游指南》，中国脑网站编．中国旅游出版社．

黑龙江省

1. Heilongjiang：world of ice and snow & green home. Beijing：Foreign Languages Press, 2006. 231, ［3］ p.：il. col. , maps；24cm. ISBN：7119045156, 7119045153. （Panoramic China）

《黑龙江：冰雪世界，绿色家园：英文》，黑龙江省人民政府新闻办公室主编；刘福臣撰；郝光峰，孔伟译；白海琦等摄．外文出版社（全景中国）．

2. Impressions of Taching oilfield/Chiang Shan-Hao. Peking：Foreign Languages Press, 1978. 46 p.

《大庆印象记》，江山浩．

重庆

1. Chongqing：mystical Three Gorges and glamorous municipality. Beijing：Foreign Languages Press, 2006. 253 pages：illustrations （some color），color maps；24cm. ISBN：7119043102, 7119043104. （Panoramic China）

《重庆：神秘三峡，魅力重庆：英文》，何事忠主编；熊笃，陈红著；李洋等译；田必勤等摄．（全景中国）

2. Dazu Grottoes/edited by Bai Ziran；［photos, Sun Shuming and Wang Chunshu；translation, W. C. Chau；map, Cai Rong］. Beijing （China）：Foreign Languages Press, 1984. 137 p.：il.；33cm. ISBN：0835113566, 0835113564

《中国大足石刻》，Bai, Ziran 编；Chau, W. C. 译．

3. Dazu grottoes in a nutshell/［editor-in-chief, Wang Qingyu；deputy editor-in-chief, Zhao Chongliang；photographers, Wang Qingyu and Lu Daqian；text by Li Fangyin；translated into English by Hu Zhihui］. Beijing］：China Travel & Tourism Press, 2001. 100 pages：chiefly color illustrations, 1 color map；37cm. ISBN：7503218487, 7503218484. （World heritage）

《大足石刻艺术》，王庆瑜主编；胡志挥英译．

安徽省

1. Anhui：Mount Huangshan and the Hui culture. Beijing, China：Foreign Languages Press, 2006. 261 pages：illustrations （some color）；24cm. ISBN：7119043753, 7119043757. （Panoramic China）

《安徽：黄山与徽文化：英文》，张宗良主编；朱万曙等撰；孙雷等译；柏健等摄．外文出版社（全景中国）

2. Anhui China 1999/written by Zhang Bosheng and Li Qing；edited by Yang Jianbo and Jing Xiaomin. Beijing, China：China Intercontinental Pr. , 1999. 67 pages：color illustrations；20cm. ISBN：7801135644, 7801135643

《1999 中国安徽》，安徽省人民政府新闻办公室编．五洲传播出版社．

3. Suzhou China 1999/Sheng Changchun；edited by Song Jianguo ［and others］. Beijing, China：Wuzhou Mass Communications Pr. , 1999. 69 pages：color illustrations；20cm. ISBN：7801135784, 7801135780

《中国宿州》，宿州市政府新闻办公室编．五洲传播出版社．

4. Huangshan Mount：world cultural and natural heritage （China volume）/edited by Beijing Jingxin Cultural Development Co. ；chief editor, Ru Suichu；editor of the book, Yuan Lianmin, ［text］, Hu Xuefan Shongli, Yuan lianmin, Liu Jichao. Beijing：China Intercontinental Press, 2000. 111 pages：chiefly color illustrations, maps；29cm. ISBN：7801136969, 7801136961

《黄山》，茹遂初主编，五洲传播出版社．

5. 徽州/郑建新编著．合肥：黄山书社，2016. 172 页：图（部分彩图），肖像，摹真；23cm. ISBN：7546141923.（印象中国）

英文题名：Huizhou. 汉英对照．

广东省

1. Aspects of Guangdong Province＝广东概况/金惠康著．广州：广东省地图出版社，2002. 168 p.：photo. , Map；21cm. ISBN：7805227675, 7805227672

2. Guangdong：forerunner of an era. Beijing：Foreign Languages Press, 2006. 238 pages：illustrations （chiefly color）, color maps；24cm. ISBN：7119041215, 7119041216. Panoramic China）

《广东：潮声中的先行者：英文》，牧青等编撰；纪华，高文星译；何勇当等供图．外文出版社（全景中国）

3. Guidebook for journalists in Guangdong/［edited by］ Information Office Guangdong Province People's Government. Guangzhou：Lingnan Art Publishing House, 2011. 345 pages：illustrations （chiefly color）, color map；21cm. ISBN：7536246690, 7536246692

《今日广东·采访指南》，广东省人民政府新闻办公室编．岭南美术出版社．

4. Guangzhou to strive for a modern internationalized metropolis in the 21st century/edited by Chao Zhenwei. ［Guangzhou］：Guangzhou Pub. House, 1994. viii, 359 pages；20cm. ISBN：7805921148, 7805921143

《现代化国际大都市：迈向 21 世纪的广州》，巢振威主编．广州出版社．

5. A sunshine home：humanitarian settlement in Guandong/

writer, Han Song, translators, Luo Jun, Kuang Jiamin, Lu Fang. Guandong, China：Lingnan Fine Art Pub. House, 1999. 332 pages：illustrations；21cm. ISBN：7536220340, 7536220348

《阳光家园：人道安置在广东》，韩松著. 岭南美术出版社.

6. Pearl River：the awakening of the east/Zhang Shengyou；translated by Transn. Beijing：China Intercontinental Press, 2008. 146 pages：illustrations (some color), portraits (some color)；23cm. ISBN：7508513737, 7508513738

《珠江故事：东方的觉醒》，张胜友著. 五洲传播出版社. 介绍以深圳特区为中心，珠江三角洲地区 30 年来改革开放的成就.

上海

1. 上海印象 = Shanghai package/主编，易源；摄影，杨挺 [and others]. 上海：汉语大词典出版社，2005. 196 pages：color illustrations；21cm. ISBN：7543211963, 7543211964

《上海印象：汉英对照》，易源主编. 汉语大词典出版社.

2. Shanghai：Shanghai down the centuries/[by Zhou Wu]. Beijing：Foreign Languages Press, 2006. 322 pages：illustrations (some color), maps, 24cm. ISBN：7119040812, 7119040813. (Panoramic China)

《上海：世纪上海：英文》，宋超，焦扬主编. 外文出版社（全景中国）. 介绍上海改革开放后作为中国重要的经济、文化城市发展所取得的成果.

3. 上海概览：中、英文版/上海市人民政府新闻办公室，上海市统计局编. 上海：上海锦绣文章出版社，2009. 2 册（120 页，118 页）；19cm. ISBN：7545203967, 7545203968

英文题名：Shanghai basic facts

4. Shanghai basic facts：civil administration/editor-in-chief：Zhou Zhenming. Beijing：China Intercontinental Pr.，1998. 57 pages：color illustrations；18cm. ISBN：7801133730, 7801133731

《上海民政概览》，上海市人民政府新闻办公室，上海市民政局主编. 五洲传播出版社.

5. Shanghai basic facts：Pudong new area. Beijing：China Intercontinental Pr.，1998. 81 pages：color illustrations color maps；17cm. ISBN：7801133773, 7801133779

《上海浦东概览》，上海市人民政府新闻办公室，上海市浦东新区新闻办编. 五洲传播出版社.

6. Shanghai basic facts：culture/editor-in-chief：Sun Yibing. Beijing：China Intercontinental Pr.，1998. 57 pages：color illustrations；18cm.. ISBN：7801133765, 7801133762

《上海文化概览》，上海市政府新闻办公室，上海市委宣传部编. 五洲传播出版社.

7. Shanghai basic facts：science & technology/editors-in-chief：Zhang Qibiao, Hu Zhenhuan. Beijing：China Intercontinental Pr.，1998. 48 pages：color illustrations；18cm. ISBN：7801133722, 7801133724

《上海科技概览》，上海市人民政府新闻办公室，上海市科技委员会编. 五洲传播出版社.

8. Shanghai basic facts：education/editors-in-chief：Wang Ronghua, Zhang Weijiang. Beijing：China Intercontinental Pr.，1998. 74 pages：color illustrations；18cm. ISBN：7801133757, 7801133755

《上海教育概览》，上海市政府新闻办公室，上海市教育委员会编. 五洲传播出版社.

9. Shanghai basic facts：suburbs. Beijing：China Intercontinental Pr.，1998. 41 pages：color illustrations；17cm. ISBN：7801133749, 7801133748

《上海郊区概览》，上海市政府新闻办公室，上海市政府农业委员会编. 五洲传播出版社.

10. 上海掌故. 上海：上海文化出版社，1985. 210 页

英文题名：Anecdotes of old Shanghai

11. Old Shanghai：a lost age/text by Wu Liang；translated by Wang mingjie. Beijing：Wai wen chu ban she, 2001. 7,240 p. ：photo. ；20cm. ISBN：7119028456, 7119028453. (老城市系列)

《老上海：已逝的时光》，吴亮著；王明杰等译.

12. 100 landmarks of Shanghai/edited by Shi Lei. Shanghai：Shanghai Culture Publishing House, 2009. 260 pages：color illustrations, maps；26cm. ISBN：7807404750, 7807404752

《上海 100 地标指南》，石磊主编. 上海文化出版社. 上海城市史.

13. Shanghai historic days/archives, Shanghai General Annals House；chief editor, Zhu Minyan；English translator, Tang Genjin. Shanghai：Shanghai Brilliant Publishing House, 2009. 276 pages：illustrations, maps；30cm. ISBN：7545203929, 7545203925

《上海历史上的今天》，朱敏彦主编. 上海锦绣文章出版社.

14. 历史上的徐家汇：汉英对照/宋浩杰主编. 上海：上海文化出版社，2005. 239 页；29cm. ISBN：7806468706, 7806468708

英文题名：Zikawei in history.

15. A map of foreign cultures in Shanghai/general director, He Chengwei；contributors, Xiong Yuezhi [and others]；translated by Fang Shengquan, Jasonius C. S. Chu, and Ondi Lingenfelter. Shanghai：Shanghai Stories Culture Media Co. Ltd；Shanghai Brilliant Publishing House, 2011. 149 pages：illustrations (some color)；21cm. ISBN：7545209976, 7545209974. (Shanghai international cultural exchange series)

《上海的外国文化地图》，熊月之等著. 上海锦绣文章出版社. 本书分为美、英、法、俄、德五个国家，介绍其与上海的文化互动、历史渊源、趣闻轶事，以及各国文化在上海留下的遗迹与产生的影响.

16. A taste of Shanghai：the food culture of Shanghai/[Cui Jing；translated by Zhang Wei]. Beijing：Shanghai People's Fine Arts Publishing House, 2010. 109 pages：color illustrations；22cm. ISBN：7532265831, 7532265838.

(Chinese creative lifestyle)

《吃相上海：英文版》，崔静撰文. 上海人民美术出版社. 讲述上海美食及其文化.

17. Entertainment in Shanghai/executive editor, Wang Tieying; editing translator, Gu Daxi; manuscript reader, Yang Rengang. Shanghai：Shanghai Jiao Tong University Press, 2010. 6，3，294 pages：color illustrations；19cm. ISBN：7313063601，7313063601. (Welcome to Shanghai)

《上海的玩》，王铁鹰主编. 上海交通大学出版社（上海欢迎您丛书）. 名胜古迹简介.

18. Food in Shanghai/executive editor, Chen Xiande, Chen Zhuyi; editing translator, Yu Jinwei, Yu Liming; manuscript reader, Yang Rengang. Shanghai：Shanghai Jiao Tong University Press，2010. 6，4，244 pages：color illustrations；19cm. ISBN：7313063786，7313063784. (Welcome to Shanghai)

《上海的吃》，陈贤德，陈祝义主编. 上海交通大学出版社（上海欢迎您丛书）.

19. Shanghai Pudong miracle：a case-study of China's fast-track economy/Zhao Qizheng with Shao Yudong；translated by Lin Wusun & Zhang Qingnian. Beijing：China Intercontinental Press, 2008. ii, 186 pages：color illustrations；23cm. ISBN：7508513713，7508513711

《浦东奇迹》，赵启正，邵煜栋著. 五洲传播出版社. 介绍了浦东新区政治、经济、文化、交通等方面的成就.

20. The Bund/by Xue Liyong；translated by Tang Haibo and Xu Zhenxu. Shanghai：Shanghai Scientific and Technological Literature Publishing House, 2011. 137 pages：illustrations (some color)；21cm. ISBN：7543951075，754395107X

《外滩：英文版》，薛理勇著；汤海波，许振旭译. 上海科学技术文献出版社.

21. Suzhou Creek：a river runs through the history/by Lou Chenghao and Xue Shunsheng；translated by Hou Xinpeng. Shanghai：Shanghai Scientific and Technological Literature Publishing House, 2011. 1, 148 pages：illustrations (chiefly color)；21cm. ISBN：7543951082，7543951088. (Shanghai international cultural exchange series)

《苏州河：英文版》，娄承浩，薛顺生著. 上海科学技术文献出版社.

新疆

1. History and development of Xinjiang. Beijing, China：Information Office of the State Council of the People's Republic of China,2003. 55 pages；26cm. ISBN：7801485068, 7801485069

《新疆的历史与发展》，中华人民共和国国务院新闻办公室发布. 新星出版社.

2. 新疆概览：英文/刘宇生等主编；付志斌等译. 北京：新星出版社,2005. 225 页；彩图；21cm. ISBN：7801489136

3. Development and progress in Xinjiang (September 2009). History and development of Xinjiang (May 2003)/[compiled by Information Office of the State Council, People's Republic of China]. Beijing：Foreign Languages Press, 2009. 131 pages：illustrations；21cm. ISBN：7119060804，7119060805. (White papers of the Information Office of the State Council of the People's Republic of China ＝中国国务院新闻办公室白皮书)

《新疆的发展与进步、新疆的历史与发展》，中华人民共和国国务院新闻办公室［编］.

4. Development and progress in Xinjiang/Information Office of the State Council of the People's Republic of China. Beijing, China：Foreign Languages Press, 2009. 52 pages：illustrations；26cm. ISBN：7119060354，711906035X, 7119060361

《新疆的发展与进步》，中华人民共和国国务院新闻办公室［编］.

5. Mysteries of Xinjiang/written by Hu Jia & Zhong Xizheng；translated by Song Dongmeng, Wang Qingfeng & Zhang Li；English editor Michael Harrold. Beijing：China Intercontinental Press，2010. 235 pages：illustrations；23cm. ISBN：7508517681，7508517687. (Chinese archaeological discoveries)

《新疆密码》，胡笳，钟习政撰稿. 五洲传播出版社.

6. 中国新疆事实与数字/ 李欣凭编著；张恒瑞译. 北京：五洲传播出版社,2014. 197 页：彩图；21cm. ISBN：7508528045 英文题名：Facts and figures on Xinjiang China

7. Hami, the eastern gate of Xinjiang/compiled by Huang Shiyuan and Wei Heping. 2nd edition. Beijing：China Intercontinental Press, 2009. 64 pages：color illustrations, color maps；21cm. ISBN：7508515397, 7508515390. (China's Xinjiang series)

《新疆东大门 哈密：英文版》，黄适远，魏和平撰稿. 五洲传播出版社.

8. Aksu, new charm of Qiuci/compiled by Tian Fang and Fei Na. Beijing：China Intercontinental Press, 2009. 64 pages：color illustrations, color maps；21cm. ISBN：7508515472, 7508515471. (China's Xinjiang series)

《龟兹新韵 阿克苏：英文版》，天方，费娜撰稿. 五洲传播出版社.

9. Tacheng：the gate to Dzungaria/compiled by Li Yingchao and Fei Na.［China］：China Intercontinental Press, 2010. 64 pages：color illustrations, color maps；22cm.. ISBN：7508515441, 7508515447. (China's Xinjiang series)

《准格尔门户 塔城：英文版》，李颖超，费娜撰稿. 五洲传播出版社.

10. Turpan, the fiery land/compiled by Xiang Jiang, Ai Mei and Wei Heping. Beijing：China Intercontinental Pr., 2009. 64 pages：color illustrations, maps；21cm. ISBN：7508515359, 7508515358. (China's Xinjiang series)

《神气火州 吐鲁番：英文版》，向京，艾梅，魏和平撰稿. 五洲传播出版社.

11. Xinjiang Production and Construction Corps, a new

chapter of defending the frontiers and opening up wasteland/compiled by Wei Heping and Yao Xiaomin.〔Beijing〕: China Intercontinental Press, 2009. 64 pages: color illustrations, 2 color maps; 21cm. ISBN: 7508515434, 7508515439. (China's Xinjiang series)

《屯垦新乐章　新疆生产建设兵团:英文版》,魏和平,姚晓敏撰稿.五洲传播出版社.

12. Urumqi, the beautiful city in the heart of Asian continent/complied by Ai Mei and He Yun. Beijing: China Intercontinental Press, 2009. 64 pages: color illustrations, color maps; 21cm. ISBN: 7508515465, 7508515463. (China's Xinjiang series)

《亚心之都　乌鲁木齐:英文版》,艾梅,何云撰稿.五洲传播出版社.

13. Changji, border state of wonders on the Silk Road/compiled by Zhu Jizhen and He Yun. Beijing: China Intercontinental Press, 2009. 64 pages: color illustrations, maps; 21cm. ISBN: 7508515373, 7508515374. (China's Xinjiang series)

《丝路庭州　昌吉:英文版》,朱纪臻,何云撰稿.五洲传播出版社.

14. The epic of Shihezi city/compiled by Li Yingchao. 〔Beijing〕: China Intercontinental Press, 2009. 64 pages: color illustrations, color maps; 21cm. ISBN: 7508515335, 7508515331. (China's Xinjiang series)

《满城诗意　石河子:英文版》,李颖超撰稿.五洲传播出版社.

15. Bortala, wonderland in the utmost west/compiled by Zhu Jizhen and He Yun. Beijing: China Intercontinental Press, 2009. 64 pages: color illustrations, color maps; 21cm. ISBN: 7508515427, 7508515420. (China's Xinjiang series)

《西极灵壤　博尔塔拉:英文版》,朱纪臻,何云撰稿.五洲传播出版社.

16. Ili, a paradise beyond the great wall/compiled by Xiang Jing, Ai Mei and Guo Kaiyan. Beijing: China Intercontinental Pr., 2009. 64 pages: color illustrations, maps; 21cm. ISBN: 7508515410,7508515412. (China's Xinjiang series)

《塞外江南　伊犁:英文版》,向京,艾梅,郭凯燕撰稿.五洲传播出版社.

17. Karamay, a city of oil in the west of China/compiled by Zhu Jizhen and Guo Kaiyan. 〔Beijing〕: China Intercontinental Press, 2009. 64 pages: color illustrations, color maps; 21cm. ISBN: 7508515458, 7508515455. (China's Xinjiang series)

《西部油城　克拉玛依:英文版》,朱纪臻,郭凯燕撰稿.五洲传播出版社.

18. Hotan: soul of desert/compiled by Li Yingchao. 64 pages: illustrations, maps; 21cm. ISBN: 7508515489, 750851548X. (China's Xinjiang series)

《大漠之魂　和田:英文版》,李颖超撰稿.五洲传播出版社.

19. 丝路重镇 喀什:英文版/艾梅撰稿.北京:五洲传播出版

社,2009. 64 页;21cm. ISBN: 7508515380

20. Kizilsu, a prefecture of thousand mountains/compiled by Tian Fang and Fei Na.〔Beijing〕: China Intercontinental Press, 2009. 64 pages: color illustrations, color maps; 21cm. ISBN: 7508515366, 7508515366. (China's Xinjiang series)

《万山之州　克孜勒苏:英文版》,天方,费娜撰稿.五洲传播出版社.

21. Bayangol, the largest prefecture of China/compiled by Yu Yan and Zhu Jizhen.〔Beijing〕: China Intercontinental Press, 2009. 64 pages: color illustrations, 3 color maps; 21cm. ISBN: 7508515403, 7508515404. (China's Xinjiang series)

《华夏第一州　巴音郭楞:英文版》,余言,朱纪臻撰稿.五洲传播出版社.

22. Altay, golden mountains and silver rivers/compiled by Xiang Jing and Yu Yan.〔Beijing〕: China Intercontinental Press, 2009. 64 pages: color illustrations, color maps; 21cm. ISBN: 7508515342, 750851534X. (China's Xinjiang series)

《金山银水　阿勒泰:英文版》,向京,余言撰稿.五洲传播出版社.

23. Xinjiang: the land and the people. Beijing, China: New World Press, 1989. 255 pages,〔8〕pages of plates: color illustrations; 21cm. ISBN: 7800050785, 7800050787

《新疆的土地与居民》.新世界出版社.

24. The Silk Road, past and present/Che Muqi. Beijing, China: Foreign Languages Press: Distributed by China International Book Trading Corp., 1989. 319 pages,〔37〕pages of plates (1 folded): color illustrations, maps; 21cm. ISBN: 0835121003, 0835121002, 7119006959, 7119006956

《丝绸之路今昔》,车慕奇(1925—)编著.

25. 新疆各民族平等团结发展的历史见证:英文版/中华人民共和国国务院新闻办公室发布.北京:外文出版社,2015. 1 册:图;23cm. ISBN: 7119096469

陕西

1. Shaanxi/editor in chief, Zhang Fengrui. Beijing: China Intercontinental Press, 2003. 14, 134 pages: color illustrations, maps, portraits; 21cm. ISBN: 7508502388, 7508502380. (West China)

《陕西》,陕西省政府新闻办公室编.五洲传播出版社.

2. Shaanxi: glories and dreams/translators, Zhang Shaoning〔and others〕; English editors, Sue Duncan, Li Zhenguo. Beijing: Foreign Languages Press, 2006. 244 pages: color illustrations, maps; 24cm. ISBN: 7119039202, 7119039206. (Panoramic China)

《陕西:辉煌与梦想:英文》,胡戟,张锋锐主编;张韶宁等译.外文出版社(全景中国)

3. Shaanxi ancient civilization/Shaanxi History Museum;〔editor-in-chief Cheng Jianzheng〕. Xi'an: Shanxi ren min chu ban she, 2008. 〔4〕, 149,〔2〕pages: color illustrations, color maps; 29cm. ISBN: 7224085471, 7224085472

《陕西古代文明》，成建正主编. 陕西人民出版社.

4. 中国户县＝Huxian County in China/名誉主编李建辉［and others］；主编郑茜. 北京市：民族出版社，2004. 112 pages：color illustrations；29cm. ISBN：7105058048，7105058044.（中国民族丛书＝China's ethnic groups）

户县是中国农民画的故乡.

5. 党家村：［汉英对照］/孙旭祥主编. 广州：广东世界图书出版公司，2008. 119 页；16cm. ISBN：7506296786，7506296780.（中国历史文化名村丛书）

陕西省韩城市乡村概况.

6. The Qin terracotta army：treasures of Lintong/Zhang Wenli. London：Scala Books；［Beijing］：Cultural Relics Publishing House，1996. 96 pages：color illustrations，color maps；28cm. ISBN：7501009163，7501009169，0856674508，0856674501

Contents：Chronology of Dynasties and Major Events—A Guide to Qin Shi Huangdi's Mausoleum and the Museum of the Qin Dynasty Terracotta Warriors and Horses—The Museum of the Qin Terracotta Figures—Emperor Qin Shi Huangdi's Mausoleum and the Discovery of the Terracotta Warriors—The Three Pits of Terracotta Figures—The Imperial Bronze Horses and Chariots.

《秦始皇陵兵马俑博物馆导览》，张文立. 文物出版社.

7. The subterranean Army of Emperor Qin Shi Huang：the eighth wonder of the world/［writer，Wu Xiaocong；photographer，Guo Youmin；English translators：Tan Min，Zhang Siying，Lee R. Thomas］. ［China］：China Travel and Tourism Press，1998. 120 pages：color illustrations；29cm. ISBN：7503209801，7503209802

《秦始皇地下兵团：世界第八奇迹》，郭佑民，吴晓丛主编. 中国旅游出版社.

　　（1）China：China Travel and Tourism Press，2002. 126 pages：color illustrations；29cm. ISBN：7503218819，7503218811

8. The Qin dynasty terra-cotta army of dreams/Zhang Lin. Xi'an［China］：Xi'an Press，2005. 128 pages：illustrations（chiefly color）；29cm.. ISBN：780712184X，7807121848

《梦幻的军团：英文》，张林编译. 西安出版社. 介绍秦始皇兵马俑、皇帝陵等.

9. 秦始皇陵探秘/孟剑明著. 西安：西安出版社，2011. 136 页；29cm. ISBN：7807128281

10. Xi'an：an ancient capital of many splendours/edited by the Foreign Affairs Office of Xian Municipal Government；［writers：Wu Xiaocong，Luo Chang'an；photographer：Guo Youmin；translator：Ling Yuan］. Xi'an：China Tourism Press，1996. 135 pages：color illustrations，maps；29cm. ISBN：7503212632，7503212635，7503212683，7503212680

《世界历史名都西安》，西安市人民政府外事办公室编. 中国旅游出版社.

11. Old Xi'an：evening glow of an imperial city/text by Jia Pingao；translated by Ma Wenqian. Beijing：Foreign Languages Press；Jiangsu Fine Arts Pub. House，2001. 213 pages：illustrations；22cm. ISBN：7119027875，7119027876.（Old city＝Lao cheng shi）

《老西安：废都夕阳》，贾平凹著.

12. Ancient treasures of Luoyang/compiled by Luoyang Cultural Relics Work Team；［text by Ye Wansong and Yu Fuwei］. Beijing：Morning Glory Publishers，1990. 18 pages：color illustrations；26cm. ISBN：7505401122，7505401129

洛阳的文物. 英汉对照.

河北省

1. Hebei：the Great Wall legacy. Beijing：Foreign Languages Press，2006. 223 p. : ill.（chiefly col.），col. maps；24cm. ISBN：711904513X，7119045139.（Panoramic China）

《河北：伟哉长城：英文》，相金科主编. 外文出版社（全景中国）

2. The overview of Hebei Province/Information Office of the People's Government of Hebei Province. Shijiazhuang：Hebei Fine Arts Publishing House，2007. 67 pages：color illustrations，color maps；21cm. ISBN：7531029373，7531029375

《河北概览：英文》，相金科主编；河北省人民政府新闻办公室编. 河北美术出版社.

3. 清帝与避暑山庄/承德市文物局编. 北京：华龄出版社，2009. 119 页；25×26cm. ISBN：7801786661，7801786661 本书以实景图片及中英文文字对承德避暑山庄的景物进行介绍.

吉林省

1. Jilin：tales of Changbai Mountain/［written by Wang Ying and Liu Chunguang］. Beijing：Foreign Languages Press，2006. 225 pages：color illustrations，color maps；24cm. ISBN：7119045164，7119045160.（Panoramic China）

《吉林：白山松水情：英文》，刘乃季等主编. 外文出版社（全景中国）

甘肃

1. Gansu：grottoes on the ancient Silk Road/［Dong Yuxiang］. Beijing：Foreign Languages Press，2006. 276 pages：illustrations（some color），color maps；24cm. ISBN：7119043005，7119043005.（Panoramic China）

《甘肃：丝绸路上的瑰丽石窟：英文》，董玉祥著. 外文出版社（全景中国）

2. The Silk Road in transformation：benchmark of the opening and development of Gansu Province/chief eds. : Zhang Tianli... ［et al.］. ［S. l.］：China Intercontinental Press，1997. 136 S：Ill. ISBN：7801132335，7801132338

《变化中的甘肃》，张天理，寇廷良主编. 五洲传播出版社.

3. The changing Gansu：（continuation）：index of western development strategy of Gansu/chief editor Kou Tingliang.

Beijing: Five Continental Press, 2000. 135 pages: illustrations; 21cm. ISBN: 7801137868, 7801137869

《变化中的甘肃:续集》,寇廷良主编.五洲传播出版社.

4. 大禹治水的源头:临夏:中英文/宋秉武主编.北京:五洲传播出版社,2004. 70 页;20cm. ISBN: 7508506618.(甘肃省各市、自治州概况丛书)

介绍了临夏的概况、历史发展、风土人情及现状,是人们了解和投资临夏的参考书.

5. China Dunhuang/edit Dunhuang Research Academy. Nanjing: Jiangsu Fine Arts Publishing House, 2006. 148 pages: illustrations (chiefly color), portraits; 29cm. ISBN: 7534420822, 7534420825

《中国敦煌:英文》,樊锦诗主编.江苏美术出版社.本书精选北朝、隋唐、五代、宋元时代的敦煌彩塑壁画,向海外读者介绍我国璀璨的敦煌艺术.

6. History of Dunhuang/[Chinese compiler Chian Jianhong, Liu Jinbao]. Beijing: Encyclopedia of China Publishing House, 2010. ii, 204 pages: illustrations; 21cm. ISBN: 7500082675, 7500082673. (History of Chinese civilization)

《敦煌史话:中英文双语版》,《中华文明史话》编委会编译.中国大百科全书出版社.

7. The main points of the Mogao Grottoes/translated and edited by Tai Jianqun. Lanzhou: Gansu People's Fine Arts Publishing House, 2000. 34, 79 pages: color illustrations; 21cm. ISBN: 7805883416, 7805883410

《莫高窟览要》,台建群译.甘肃人民美术出版社.

云南

1. The scenic spots and attractions of Yunnan. Kunming: Yunnan University Press, 1993. 93 p.: ill. (some col.). ISBN: 7810252550, 7810252553

《云南揽胜》,王镒编著.云南大学出版社.

2. Yunnan: "Shangri-la" over the horizon/[editors] Sue Duncan, Yu Ling. Beijing, China: Foreign Languages Press, 2006. 267, [15] p.: il. col., maps; 25cm. ISBN: 7119040774, 7119040776. (Panoramic China)

《云南:云天之外的香格里拉:英文》,云南省人民政府新闻办公室主编.外文出版社(全景中国)

3. 最美云南:中英对照/徐志辉主编;云南省生态经济学会编.昆明:云南人民出版社,2007. 335 页;彩照;30×30cm. ISBN: 7222051621, 7222051627

英文题名:Most beautiful Yunnan

4. 云南/李吉主编.昆明:云南科技出版社,2010. 95 页;29cm. ISBN: 7541637964

5. 云南特有民族文化知识 = Indigenous Ethnic Groups in Yunnan:中英对照/宋丽英主编.昆明:云南大学出版社,2007. 2, 31, 334 页;20cm. ISBN: 7811122565, 7811122561

书名原文:Indigenous ethnic groups in Yunnan. 本书用汉语和英语两种语言介绍云南15个特有民族的文化.

6. 云南少数民族服饰与节庆:汉英对照/龚正嘉撰;刘建明等摄.北京:中国旅游出版社,2004. 120 页;19×21cm. ISBN: 7503224002, 7503224003

英文题名:Dress and festivals of the minority peoples in Yunnan. 本书主要介绍了云南25个少数民族的节庆和服饰.

7. The wondrous Lijiang = 神奇的丽江/editors-in-chief, Zhang Chunyan and He Yong. Kunming: Yunnan Science & Technology Press, 2005. 5, 241 pages; 29cm.. ISBN: 7541620777, 7541620775

《神奇的丽江:英汉对照》,张春艳,和永主编.云南科技出版社.

8. 玉龙山下的村庄:一个美国家庭亲历的纳西生活:汉英对照/孙佳琪著;赵庆莲,和丽峰译.昆明:云南民族出版社,2006. 1 册;21cm. ISBN: 753673655X, 7536736559

纳西族风俗习惯.

9. 大理上下四千年/赵怀仁等著.昆明:云南大学出版社,2009. 221 页;26cm. ISBN: 7811128864

10. Travels through Xishuangbanna: China's subtropical home of many nationalities/by Zheng Lan. Beijing: Foreign Languages Press, 1981. 55 pages, [52] pages of plates: illustrations (some color), map, portraits; 23cm.

《西双版纳纪行》,征岚著.

11. The magnificent Sanjiang region: the green Yunnan/edited by the Tourism Bureau of Yunnan Province; photographer photos (Beijing); translated by Lin Hua. Beijing, China: Contemporary China Publishing House, 1999. 127 pages: chiefly color illustrations; 28cm. ISBN: 7800928160, 7800928161

《绿色云南:壮丽三江》,张先安主编.当代中国出版社.

12. The highlights of Yunnan tourism/by Niu Chongrong. Yunnan: The People's Press of Yunan, 1999. 205 pages: illustrations, portraits; 22cm. ISBN: 7222026215, 7222026216

《云南旅游之最》,刘崇荣编著.云南人民出版社.

江西省

1. Jiangxi: cradle of red China/[chief editors, Gao Hailei, Mei Hong]. Beijing, China: Foreign Languages Press, 2006. 231 pages: illustrations; 24cm. ISBN: 7119042114, 7119042114. (Panoramic China)

《江西,红色中国的摇篮:英文》,郜海镭,梅宏主编;章挺权等译.外文出版社(全景中国)

2. 景德镇:千年窑火不熄的陶瓷之城:汉英对照/陈长庚主编;冯国平,胡银娇,邵继海著,祝远德翻译;景德镇市人民政府新闻办公室编.北京:五洲传播出版社,2006. 95 页;22cm. ISBN: 7508509938, 7508509935

英文题名:Jingdezhen, a city with kiln-fire burning a thousand years. 介绍陶瓷工业史.

3. 安义古村群:汉英对照/邱向军等主编;海涌等摄.广州:广东世界图书出版公司,2007. 119 页;16cm. ISBN: 7506287746, 7506287749.(中国历史文化名村丛书)

关于中国历史文化名村——江西省南昌市安义古村群的概述.

山西

1. Shanxi basic facts/chief editor, Shen Weichen. Taiyuan: Hope Publishing House, 2005. 135 pages: color illustrations, color maps; 19cm. ISBN: 7537935939, 7537935937

   《山西概览：英文》,申维辰主编.希望出版社.介绍山西的历史地理、风土人情、文化旅游、经济发展等.

2. The story of Pingyao/[Xilin Tang; translated by Jiao Jing]. Taiyuan: Shanxi Science and Technology Press, 2004. 12, 102 pages: color illustrations, color maps; 21cm. ISBN: 7537723958, 7537723954

   《解说平遥》,唐稀林编著;焦晶译.山西科学技术出版社.介绍平遥古城简史,平遥古城各旅游景点简述.

3. 108 temples of Mt. Wutai/the chief editor, Cui Zhengsen; the translators, Wang Jinhua, Gao Yufang, Cheng Xia. Taiyuan Shi: Shanxi ke xue ji shu chu ban she, 2005. 153 pages: color illustrations; 21cm. ISBN: 7537723648, 7537723640

   《五台山一百零八寺：英文》,崔正森主编;王晋华等译.山西科学技术出版社.本书讲述五台山的108座寺庙的历史沿革、建筑特点、现今状况及其他情况.

4. Shanxi merchants and their residences/[by Zhao Rongda; editor in chief, Wang Jianwu; photos provided by Shanxi Sheng ren min zheng fu xin wen ban gong shi; English translation by Sun Lei and others]. Beijing: Foreign language Press, 2006. 277, [15] pages: color illustrations, color map; 24cm. ISBN: 7119043242, 7119043241. (Panoramic China)

   《山西商人与他们的宅院：英文》,王建武主编;赵荣达撰.外文出版社.(全景中国)山西民居简介.

5. 平遥古城＝The Ancient City of Ping Yao：英文/梁云福撰稿;马红军译;柴兆坚等摄.北京:新世界出版社,2007.163页;彩图;29cm. ISBN: 7802284517, 7802284511.(世界遗产·中国)

   书名原文：The Ancient City of Ping Yao

6. The Pingyao Old City/edited by Beijing Jingxin Cultural Development Co., Ltd., chief editor: Ru Suichu. Beijing: China Intercontinental Press, 1999. 96 pages: color illustrations; 30cm. ISBN: 7801136802, 7801136800. World cultural and natural heritage (China Volume)

   《平遥古城》,茹遂初主编.五洲传播出版社.

7. 太原史话/郝树侯著;凌熙华译.太原:山西人民出版社,1986.181页;19cm.

山东省

1. A survey of Shandong/[Yang Xuefeng; editors, Yang Xuefeng, Yang Xiaozhou, Zhao Yiding; translator, Li Bin; compiled by the Information Office and Foreign Affairs Office of the People's Government of Shandong Province]. 2nd ed. China: China Intercontinental, 1999.

ISBN: 7801133897, 7801133892

《山东概况》,山东省政府新闻办公室编.五洲传播出版社.

2. Shandong today/editor-in-Chief: Wang Zhaocheng; compiled by the Information Office of the People's Government of Shandong Province. [Beijing]: China Intercontinental Pr., 1998. 153 pages: color illustrations, map; 31cm. ISBN: 7801134362, 7801134363

   《今日山东》,山东省政府新闻办公室编.五洲传播出版社.

3. 中国山东:汉英对照/刘保聚主编;山东省人民政府新闻办公室编.北京:五洲传播出版社,2006.65页;20×21cm. ISBN: 7508509404, 7508509402

4. 中国临沂洗砚池晋墓:汉英对照/王宝安,冯沂主编;临沂市文化局,临沂市博物馆编.北京:五洲传播出版社,2005.59页;78幅;25cm. ISBN: 7508506812

   本书用丰富的考古资料介绍了临沂洗砚池晋墓,以及遍布沂沭河流域的大汶口文化、龙山文化等一脉相承的新石器文化遗存.

5. Temple and cemetery of Confucius and the Kong family mansion in Qufu/comp. by Kong Deping; transl. [from the Chinese] by Liu Haixi. Beijing: New World Press [etc.], 2007. 167 p.: ill.; 29cm. ISBN: 7802281295, 7802281296. (World Heritage Sites in China)

   《曲阜孔庙 孔林 孔府:英文》,孔德平等撰;项春生,关晖摄.新世界出版社(世界遗产·中国)

6. 孔庙史话/《中华文明史话》编委会编译;方拥,许政编撰.北京:中国大百科全书出版社,2009.188页;21cm. ISBN: 7500080534, 7500080530

   英文题名:History of Confucius temple

7. 济南概况:汉英对照/刘通主编;济南市人民政府新闻办公室编.济南:山东友谊出版社,2007.84页;彩照;21cm. ISBN: 7807372172, 7807372176

   英文题名:Survey of Jinan.

8. 青鸟过客 青岛早期城市史上的德国人:汉德对照/李明著.新星出版社,2017.21cm. ISBN: 7513327046

宁夏

1. China: Ningxia Hui Autonomous Region, 1958—1998/Information Office of the Ningxia Hui Autonomous Region Government. [China]: China Intercontinental Press, 1998. 161 pages: color illustrations, color maps; 19cm. ISBN: 7801133668, 7801133663

   《中国宁夏回族自治区》,宁夏自治区政府新闻办公室编.五洲传播出版社.

2. 宁夏历史名人:汉英对照/李东东主编.银川:宁夏人民出版社,2005.2册(503页);24cm. ISBN: 722702959X

   本书收录了上自秦朝、下至中华民国的近百位宁夏籍历史人物传记.

3. Ningxia: a land blessed by the Yellow River. Beijing: Foreign Languages Press, 2006. 263 pages: color illustrations, color maps; 24cm. ISBN: 711904298X,

7119042985.（Panoramic China）

《宁夏：天下黄河富宁夏：英文》，王宗礼主编；刘长宗等撰；纪华，高文星译；杨宏峰等摄．外文出版社（全景中国）

青海省

1. Qinghai：sourceland of three great rivers. Beijing：Foreign Languages Press，2006. 265 pages：color illustrations，maps（some color）；24cm. ISBN：7119043161，7119043166.（Panoramic China）

《青海：神圣三江源：英文》，樊光明，刘有贵主编；葛建中等撰．外文出版社（全景中国）

2. 西海古今谈：英汉对照/朱世奎著；刘雪萍译．西宁：青海人民出版社，2007. 251 页；20cm. ISBN：7225030043，7225030043

英文题名：Yesterday and today of Qinghai Lake

四川省

1. Sichuan：land of natural abundance. Beijing：Foreign Languages Press，2006. 209 pages：illustrations（chiefly color），color map；24cm. ISBN：7119044990，7119044996.（Panoramic China）

《四川：天府之国：英文》，杜江主编；王珏等撰；汪光强，闫威译；尹钢等供图．（全景中国）

2. 四川新跨越：汉英对照. 2007/侯雄飞，解洪主编；四川省人民政府新闻办公室，四川省发展与改革办公室，四川省西部开发办公室编．成都：四川人民出版社，2007. 55 页；26cm. ISBN：7220073564，7220073569

本书介绍了四川省 2006 年取得的成绩和 2007 年的规划．

3. 成都武侯祠：汉英对照/梅铮铮编文；丁浩摄；王荣生译．成都：四川科学技术出版社，2006. 123 页；29cm. ISBN：7536458916，7536458918

英文题名：Chengdu Wuhou temple. 武侯祠简介．

4. 迷人的丹巴：汉英对照/陈锦著；鲁安健译．北京：中国旅游出版社，2006. 96 页；照片；18 × 21cm. ISBN：7503229039，7503229039

英文题名：Fascinating Danba. 介绍四川丹巴县独特的藏式民居和藏族风情．

5. 李庄：汉英对照/国家历史文化名城研究中心，李庄镇编．广州：广东世界图书出版公司，2006. 119 页：彩照；16×16cm. ISBN：7506284979，7506284974.（中国历史文化名镇）

介绍四川省宜宾市古镇李庄的全貌．

6. 中国历史文化名镇：平乐：汉英对照/高志坚等主编；苏邹译．广州：广东世界图书出版公司，2007. 119 页；16×15cm. ISBN：7506286275，7506286270.（中国历史文化名镇丛书）

介绍四川省邛崃市古镇平乐的概貌．

7. Emerging from primitivity：travels in the Liangshan Mountains/by Zhong Xiu；translated by Lily Wu；photos by Shen Yantai. Beijing，China：New World Press：Distributed by China International Book Trading Corp. (Guoji Shudian)，1984. 109 pages，[12] pages of plates：

illustrations（some color）；18cm.（China spotlight series）

《凉山行》，钟秀著，吴增芳译，新世界出版社．旅游景点．

西藏

1. Concerning the question of Tibet. Peking：Foreign Languages Press，1959. 275 pages：illustrations，portraits，facsimiles；19cm.

Notes："Collection of documents，speeches，news dispatches，editorials，commentaries and background materials."

《关于西藏问题》

2. China's Tibet/Zhong Zangwen. Beijing：China Intercontinental Press，1995. 94 pages，[16] pages of plates：color illustrations，map；21cm. ISBN：7801130650，7801130655

《中国西藏》，钟藏文著．五洲传播出版社．

3. China's Tibet/Zhong Zangwen. [Beijing，China]：China Intercontinental Press，2001. 100 pages：illustrations；21cm. ISBN：7801139585，7801139580

《中国西藏》，钟藏文著．五洲传播出版社．

4. 100 questions and answers about Tibet. Beijing：New Star Publishers，2001. 158 pages，[24] pages of plates：illustrations；21×11cm. ISBN：7801483545，7801483546

《西藏百题问答》，百题编辑部编．新星出版社．

5. China's Tibet/Zhang Xiaoming. Beijing：China Intercontinental Press，2004. 148 pages：illustrations（some color）；22cm. ISBN：7508506081，7508506081

《西藏》，张晓明编；朱承铭译．五洲传播出版社．综合介绍西藏自然地理、经济、社会等各方面情况．

6. Tibetan stories/Zhang Xiaoming. Beijing：China Intercontinental Press，2005. 129 pages：illustrations（chiefly color）；21cm. ISBN：7801139143，7801139146.（Series of basic information of Tibet of China）

《西藏的故事：英文》，张晓明著；王国振等译．五洲传播出版社.（中国西藏基本情况丛书/郭长建，宋坚之主编）

7. Tibet：roof of the world. Beijing：Foreign Languages Press，2006. 233 str.，[34] str. pril.：illustr.；24cm. ISBN：7119043390，7119043395.（Panoramic China）

《西藏：地球第三极：英文》，西藏自治区人民政府新闻办公室主编；张晓明，许明扬撰；陈观生，李培茱译；阿旺洛桑等供图.（全景中国）

8. Tibet：geography，natural resources and administrative division. Beijing：Foreign languages Press，2008. 43 pages：color illustrations；22cm. ISBN：7119052380，7119052381.（Tibet of China）

《西藏的地域、资源与行政区划》，《西藏的地域、资源与行政区划》编写组编．

9. A Tibet reader/Su Shuyang. Beijing，China：Foreign Languages Press，2009. [10]，197 pages：color illustrations；24cm. ISBN：7119058368，7119058363

《西藏读本》，苏叔阳著．

10. 西藏/吕军编著．合肥：黄山书社，2016. 172 页：彩图；23cm. ISBN：7546142029.（印象中国）

英文题名：Tibet

11. Tibet：a geographical, ethnological, and historical sketch derived from Chinese sources/by W. Woodville Rockhill. ［Place of publication not identified］：［publisher not identified］, 1891. 133, ［1］（blank）, ［185］-291 pages, ［6］folded leaves of plates：maps (some color), plan；23cm.

Notes：Cover title from original yellow printed upper wrapper（bound in）/A translation of parts of the Wei Ts'ang t'u chih compiled in 1792 by Ma Shao-yün and Shêng Mei-ch'i, supplemented in notes and appendices by translations of extracts from other Chinese works. cf. p. 2－3./"From the 'Journal of the Royal Asiatic Society of Great Britain and Ireland'."［1891］./ Author's signed presentation inscription on wrapper./ Includes bibliographical references.

《卫藏图识》，Rockhill, William Woodville(1854—1914) 译.

(1)［Peking］,［Wên tien ko shu chuang］, 1930. 1 preliminary leaf, 133. ［185］-291 pages folded plates (some color)folded maps 24cm.

(2)［Peking］,［Wen dian ge shu zhuang］, 1939. 1 preliminary leaf, 133, ［185］-291 pages, folded plates (some color)folded maps；24cm.

12. Highlights of Tibetan history/Wang Furen and Suo Wenqing；［translated by Xu Jian］. Beijing：New World Press：Distributed by China Publication Centre（Guoji Shudian）, 1984. 206 pages, ［12］pages of plates：illustrations；22cm. (China studies series)

《藏族史要》，王辅仁，索文清编著. 新世界出版社.

13. Tibet, the land and the people/written by Tiley Chodag；translated by W. Tailing. Beijing, China：New World Press：Distributed by China International Book Trading Corporation, 1988. 354 pages, ［32］pages of plates：illustrations (some color)；18cm. ISBN：7800050726, 7800050725

《西藏风土志》，赤烈曲扎著；旺多译. 新世界出版社.

14. Feudal serf system in Tibet/Yuan Sha. Beijing, China：China Intercontinental Press, 1996. 43 pages：illustrations；20cm. ISBN：7801131045, 7801131041. (Tibet series)

《西藏封建农奴制度》，袁莎著. 五洲传播出版社.

15. The historical status of China's Tibet/Wang Jiawei & Nyima Gyaincain. Beijing：China Intercontinental Press, 1997. 333 pages：illustrations, maps；21cm. ISBN：7801133048, 7801133045

Notes："Based on the academic monograph 'Comments on the historical status of Tibet' published in 1995 by the Nationalities Press."—Postscript./ Colophon in Chinese.

(1)2nd ed. Beijing：China Intercontinental Press, 2008. ［2］, 333 pages：illustrations, maps；21cm. ISBN：7801133048, 7801133045

《中国西藏的历史地位》，王家伟，尼玛坚赞著. 五洲传播出版社.

16. Testimony of history/compiled by Information Office of the State Council, People's Republic of China；［writer Zhang Yuxin, translator Xiang Hongjia］. ［Beijing］：China Intercontinental Press, 2002. 251 pages：color illustrations；29cm. ISBN：7801138856, 7801138859

《历史的见证：英文》，国务院新闻办公室编；向红笛译. 五洲传播出版社. 收录自唐蕃以来，西藏地方与中央政权有关隶属关系和主权行使等历史实物资料的图片230余幅，并有相关译文的介绍.

17. Tibetan history/Chen Qingying；［translated by Zuo Yanli］. ［Beijing］：China Intercontinental Press, 2003. 181 pages：illustrations（some color）；21cm. ISBN：7508502345, 7508502342. (Series of basic information of Tibet of China)

《西藏历史》，陈庆英著. 五洲传播出版社.

18. Eyewitnesses to 100 years of Tibet/Zhang Xiaoming. ［Beijing］：China Intercontinental Press, 2005. 238 pages：illustrations；21cm. ISBN：7508508165, 7508508160

《见证百年西藏：西藏历史见证人访谈录：英文》，张晓明编；王国振译. 五洲传播出版社.

19. Precious deposits：historical relics of Tibet, China/［text by Zla-ba-tshe-ring... et al.；text translated by Xiang Hongjia；photographed by Yan Zhongyi and others］. Beijing, China：Morning Glory Publishers；Chicago, Il.：Distributed by Art Media Resources, 2000. 5 volumes：color illustrations；30cm. ISBN：7505406949, 7505406940

Contents：v. 1. Prehistoric age and Tubo period—v. 2. The period of separatist regimes—v. 3. Yuan dynasty and Ming dynasty—v. 4. Qing dynasty—v. 5. Qing dynasty and the Republic of China.

《宝藏：中国西藏历史文物》，甲央，王明量主编. 朝华出版社.

20. 西藏的历史与人文景观：英文/王钦格勒，陈庆英著；陈观胜，李培茱英文翻译. 北京：外文出版社, 2006. 215 页：彩照；21cm. ISBN：7119042033, 7119042039

介绍了西藏地方史和名胜古迹.

21. 古代西藏碑文研究：汉英对照/(美)李方桂, (美)柯蔚南著；王启龙译. 拉萨：西藏人民出版社, 2006. 364 页；24cm. ISBN：7223019999, 7223019996

英文题名：Study of the old Tibetan inscriptions.

22. The aristocratic families in Tibetan history, 1900—1951/by Tsering Yangdzom；［translators Shao Da, Li Jinhui, Liu Jun］. Beijing：China Intercontinental Press, 2006. 272 pages：illustrations；23cm. ISBN：7508509374, 7508509372

《西藏贵族世家：1900～1951：英文》，次仁央宗著；邵达，刘浚，李金慧译. 五洲传播出版社. 介绍1900～1951年间西藏贵族的生活.

23. Tibetan customs/Li Tao & Jiang Hongying. [Beijing]：China Intercontinental Press，2003. 126 pages：illustrations（some color）；22cm. ISBN：750850254X，7508502540.（Series of basic information of Tibet of China）
《西藏民俗》，李涛等著. 五洲传播出版社.

24. Tibetan geography/Yang Qinye and Zheng Du. Beijing：China Intercontinental Press，2004. [6]，161 pages：color illustrations；21cm. ISBN：7508506650，7508506654.（Series of basic information of Tibet of China）
《西藏地理：英文》，杨勤业，郑度著. 五洲传播出版社（中国西藏基本情况丛书/郭长建，宋坚之主编）

25. 常见藏语人名地名词典＝Dictionary of common Tibetan personal and place names/陈观胜，安才旦主编. 北京市：外文出版社，2004. v，618 pages；21cm. ISBN：7119034979，7119034973
Notes："汉英藏对照；Chinese-English-Tibetan."

26. Great changes in Tibet. Peking：Foreign Languages Press，1972. 53 pages：illustrations；20cm.
Contents：New look of the Tibetan Plateau, by Pasang. —Former slave becomes master of country; talk with a Tibetan worker, by Chi Che-wen. —Cadres of Tibetan nationality are maturing, by Hung Kan. —Workers，peasants, and soldiers of Tibet go to college, by Chao Yang. —Lhasa's new look, by Hsin Mao. —Changes on the Ari Plateau, by Kao Yuan-ching. —Linchih; a rising industrial base, by Kung Yeh. —Rapid advances of local industry in Tibet, by Chi Yueh-chin. —The Kesung People's Commune speeds ahead, by Cheng Wen. —Successes in agricultural scientific experiments in Tibet, by Keh Yen. —Farming and stock breeding thrive in Tibet, by Hung Nung.
《西藏巨变》

27. Tibet leaps forward/by Hsi Chang-hao and Kao Yuan-mei. Peking：Foreign Languages Press，1977. 116 pages，[20] leaves of plates：illustrations；19cm.
《西藏的跃进》，郗长豪，高元美.

28. Spectacles on the snowy plateau: tremendous changes in Tibet over the past thirty years/by Li Kai and Zhao Xinbing. Beijing：China Intercontinental Press，1995. 71 pages：color illustrations；19cm. ISBN：7801130758，7801130754.（Tibet series）
《崛起的雪域高原：西藏三十年巨变》，李凯，赵新兵著. 五洲传播出版社.

29. Tibet's march toward modernization/Information Office of the State Council of the People's Republic of China. Beijing，China：New Star Publishers：Distributed by China International Book Trading Corp.，2001. 38 pages；21cm. ISBN：7801483995，7801483997

《西藏的现代化发展》，中华人民共和国国务院新闻办公室发布. 新星出版社.

30. A history of development of Tibet/chief editor，Zheng Shan；English translation，Chen Guansheng and Li Peizhu. Beijing：Foreign Languages Press，2001. vii，508 pages，[8] pages of plates：illustrations（some color），maps；21cm. ISBN：7119018655，7119018652
《西藏发展史》，郑汕主编.

31. China's Tibet：facts and figures/Wang Guozhen [editor]. Beijing，China：New Star Publishers，2001. 150 pages：illustrations，map；20cm. ISBN：7801483499，7801483492
《中国西藏：事实与数字》，王国振编. 新星出版社.

32. New aid-Tibet projects. Beijing，China：New Star Publishers，2002. 143 pages：illustrations；21×11cm. ISBN：7801484975，7801484970
《西藏：新的援建项目》，周泉编；杜泽泉等摄. 新星出版社.

33. Fifty years of democratic reform in Tibet/Information Office of State Council of the People's Republic of China. Beijing：Foreign Languages Press，2009. 45 pages：illustrations；21cm. ISBN：7119056364，7119056360
《西藏民主改革50年》，中华人民共和国国务院新闻办公室[发布].

34. Sixty years since peaceful liberation of Tibet/Information Office of the State Council，the People's Republic of China. Beijing：Foreign Languages Press，2011. 48 p.；26cm. ISBN：7119071664，7119071661，7119071671，711907167X
《西藏和平解放60年》，中华人民共和国国务院新闻办公室[发布].

35. Report on the economic and social development of Tibet/China Tibetology Research Center. Beijing：Foreign Languages Press，2009. 78 pages：illustrations；23cm. ISBN：7119056661，7119056662
《西藏经济社会发展报告》，中国藏学研究中心编.

36. A history of development of Tibet/chief editor，Zheng Shan；English translation，Chen Guansheng and Li Peizhu. Beijing：Foreign Languages Press，2010. vii，508 pages：illustrations，maps；24cm. ISBN：7119065380，7119065386
《西藏发展史》，郑汕著.

37. 民族区域自治制度在西藏的成功实践/中华人民共和国国务院新闻办公室[发布]. 北京：外文出版社，2015. 61页；21cm. ISBN：7119096018
英文题名：Successful practice of regional ethnic autonomy of Tibet.

38. Tibetan economy/written by Wang Wenchang，Lacan，translated by Wang Guozhen. Beijing：China Intercontinental Press，2005. 127 pages：color illustrations；21cm. ISBN：

7508506669, 7508506661. (Series of Basic Information of Tibet of China)

《西藏经济：英文》，王文长，拉灿著；王国振译．五洲传播出版社(中国西藏基本情况丛书/郭长建，宋坚之主编)．本书介绍西藏经济发展的历史与现状．

39. Economic development in Tibet. Beijing: Foreign Languages Press, 2008. 43 pages：color illustrations；21cm. ISBN：7119052434, 7119052438. (Tibet of China)

《西藏的经济发展》，《西藏的经济发展》编写组编．

40. The economy of Tibet：transformation from a traditional to a modern economy/by Luo Li. Beijing: Foreign Languages Press, 2008. 122 pages：[40] pages of color plates：color illustrations；21cm. ISBN：7119036014, 7119036017

《从传统走向现代的西藏经济》，罗莉著．

41. Tibetan tourism/An Caidan. ［Beijing］ China Intercontinental Press, 2003. 185 p. il. color 21cm. ISBN：7508502523, 7508502526. (Series of basic information of Tibet of China)

《西藏旅游》，安才旦．

42. Population development in Tibet and related issues/chief editor Zhang Tianlu; translated by Chen Guansheng and Li Peizhu. Beijing: Foreign Languages Press, 1997. vi, 155 pages：illustrations；21cm. ISBN：7119018671, 7119018676

《西藏人口发展与问题研究》，张天路主编．

43. 西藏人口：英文/西藏自治区对外文化交流协会著；王国振译．北京：五洲传播出版社，2007. 21cm. ISBN：7508510347, 7508510348

英文题名：Population of the Tibet Autonomous Region

44. Population, religion and regional ethnic autonomy in Tibet. Beijing: Foreign Languages Press, 2008. 43 p.：il.；22cm. ISBN：7119052335, 7119052330. (Tibet of China)

《西藏的人口、宗教与民族区域自治》，《西藏的人口、宗教与民族区域自治》编写组编．

45. The development of Tibetan culture/by Jen Jia; Information Office of the State Council of the People's Republic of China. Beijing: New Star Publishers, 2000. 33 pages；21cm. ISBN：7801482956, 7801482952

《西藏文化的发展》，中华人民共和国国务院新闻办公室发布．新星出版社．

46. Science and technology in Tibet/compiled by the Science and Technology Commission of Tibet. Beijing: China Intercontinental Press, 1997. 35 pages：color illustrations；19cm. ISBN：7801131886,7801131881. (Xizang cong shu)

《前进中的西藏科技》，西藏自治区科委编写组编著．五洲传播出版社．

47. Tibetan education：yesterday and today/Shang Jun'e. Beijing: China Intercontinental Press, 1997. 39 pages：color illustrations；19cm. ISBN：7801131916,7801131911.

《西藏教育今昔》，尚俊娥著．五洲传播出版社．

48. Tibetan education/Zhou Aiming. ［Beijing］：China Intercontinental Press, 2004. 170 pages：color illustrations；21cm. ISBN：7508505700, 7508505701. (Series of basic information of Tibet of China)

《西藏教育：英文》，周爱明著．王国振译．五洲传播出版社(中国西藏基本情况丛书/郭长建，宋坚之主编)．本书介绍西藏教育发展的历史及现状．

49. Tibet：education, science & technology, culture and people's livelihood. China：Foreign Languages Press, 2008. 43 pages：color illustrations；22cm. ISBN：7119052489, 7119052489. (Tibet of China)

《西藏的教育、科技、文化与生活》，《西藏的教育、科技、文化与生活》编写组编．

50. Protection and development of Tibetan culture/Information Office of the State Council of the People's Republic of China. Beijing: Foreign Languages Press, 2008. 30 pages；26cm. ISBN：7119047324, 7119047329, 7119047331,7119047337

《西藏文化的保护与发展》，中华人民共和国国务院新闻办公室发布．

51. Collections of Tibetan folk works of art/compiled by Information Office of the State Council, People's Republic of China. Beijing: China Intercontinental Press, 2002. 181 pages：color illustrations；30cm. ISBN：7801138872, 7801138873

《西藏民间艺术珍藏：英文》，国务院新闻办公室编．五洲传播出版社．选辑了民间收集的各类民间艺术品共约250件．

52. Tibetan religions/Gazangjia；［translated by Zuo Yanli］．［Beijing］：China Intercontinental Press, 2003. 162 pages：color illustrations；21cm. ISBN：7508502329 7508502328. (Series of basic information of Tibet of China)

《西藏宗教》，尕藏加著．五洲传播出版社．
(1)西藏宗教：英文版 /尕藏加著；朱建廷，李莉，王丽译．五洲传播出版社，2017. 173 p. ISBN：7508537788

53. 西藏宫殿寺庙史话/《中华文明史话》编委会编译，武少辉编撰．北京：中国大百科全书出版社，2009. 164 页；21cm. ISBN：7500079897, 7500079893

英文题名：History of Tibetan palaces and temples.

54. 布达拉宫，大昭寺，罗布林卡＝Historic ensemble of the Potala Palace,Lhasa：英文/桑吉扎西撰；桑吉扎西，杨立泉摄．北京：新世界出版社，2007. 165 页；29cm. ISBN：7802284234, 7802284236.(世界遗产·中国)

书名原文：Historic ensemble of the Potala Palace,Lhasa.

55. 扎什伦布寺/彭措朗杰编著．北京：中国大百科全书出版社，2010. 196 页；25cm. ISBN：7500083603, 7500083602.(中国西藏文化之旅)

英文题名：Bkra-sis-Ihum-po Monastery.

56. 托林寺/彭措朗杰编著. 北京:中国大百科全书出版社,
2010. 212 页;25cm. ISBN:7500083597, 7500083599.
(中国西藏文化之旅)
英文题名:Ntho-ling monastery.

57. Tibetology in China/by Zhou Yuan. Beijing:China
Intercontinental Press, 1995. 43 pages:color illustrations;
19cm. ISBN:7801130715,7801130716
Contents:Tibetological research organizations—Teams
in Tibetological studies—Cultural archaeology—
Collection and categorization of folk literature and art—
Publication of ancient Tibetan books and documents—
The fruits of Tibetan study—Academic exchanges.
《藏学在中国》,周源著. 五洲传播出版社.

58. Urban residents in Tibet:report on the survey of Lhugu
residents in Lhasa/Liu Hongji and Cering Yangzom.
Beijing:China Intercontinental Press, 1998. 77 pages,
[12] pages of plates:illustrations (some color); 21cm.
ISBN:7801134672, 7801134677
《西藏城市居民:拉萨鲁固居民的调查报告》,刘洪记,次
仁央宗著. 五洲传播出版社.

59. Tibetan herdsmen:survey report on no. 5 village in
Yuqag Township of Amdo County/Zhagyai & Lu Mei.
Beijing:China Intercontinental Press, 1998. 75 pages,
[12] pages of plates:color illustrations; 21cm. ISBN:
780113463X, 7801134639
《西藏牧民:藏北安多县腰恰五村的调查报告》,扎呷,卢
梅著. 五洲传播出版社.

60. Farmers in Tibet:investigation report on Bangjor
Lhunbo village in Tsang/Puncog Zhamdu. Beijing:
China Intercontinental Press, 1998. 106 pages, [12]
pages of plates:illustrations (chiefly color); 21cm.
ISBN:7801134591, 7801134592
《西藏农民:后藏班觉伦布村的调查报告》,平措占堆著.
五洲传播出版社.

61. Ngari. [Beijing, China]:China Intercontinental Press,
1998. 100 pages:illustrations;21cm. ISBN:7801134060,
7801134066. (China's Tibet)
《阿里》,成卫东编. 五洲传播出版社.

62. Chang Tang:a high and holy realm in the world/Liu
Wulin. Beijing China Forestry Publ. House, 1999. 138
p. ; Ill. ISBN:7503824158, 7503824159
《羌塘:世界上最后的净土》,刘务林编著. 中国林业出版
社.

63. Xigaze. [Beijing]:China Intercontinental Press, 2000. 120
pages: color illustrations; 21cm. ISBN: 7801134052,
7801134059. (China's Tibet)
《日喀则》,徐平编. 五洲传播出版社.

64. Old Lhasa:a sacred city at dusk/text by Ma Lihua;
[translated by Wang Mingjie]. Beijing:Foreign
languages Press, 2003. 226 pages:illustrations;21cm.
ISBN:7119031244, 7119031248. (Old city=Lao cheng
shi)
《老拉萨:圣城暮色》,马丽华著;王明杰译.

65. 甘南:中英文/汪鱼蛟主编. 北京:五洲传播出版社,
2004. 67 页;21cm. ISBN:7508504038. (甘肃省各市、自
治州概况丛书)
本书介绍了甘肃省甘南自治州的经济及社会发展情况.

66. Materials on the March 14 incident in Tibet. Beijing:
Foreign Languages Press,2008. 3 v. ISBN:7119052038
(v. 1), 7119052039(v. 1), 7119052175(v. 2), 7119052179
(v. 2),7119052229(v. 3),7119052225(v. 3)
《西藏"3·14"事件有关材料》,《西藏"3·14"事件有关
材料》编写组编.

67. Materials on the March 14 incident in Tibet. Beijing:
Foreign Languages Press,2008. 1 v. 7119052281,7119052284
《西藏"3.14"事件有关材料》,《西藏"3.14"事件有关材
料》编写组编.本书为《西藏"3.14"事件有关材料》之四,
选编报刊上发表的西藏自古就是中国不可分割的一部
分等四篇文章.

江苏省

1. Jiangsu:water town journeys/[Shan Gu]. Beijing:
Foreign Languages Press, 2006. 239 pages:illustrations
(some color), color maps; 24cm. ISBN:7119043692,
7119043692. (Panoramic China)
《江苏:穿行水乡:英文》,江苏省人民政府新闻办公室主
编;山谷撰;汪光强译;缪宜江等摄. (全景中国)

2. 跨世纪的新邳洲:中英对照/邳洲市人民政府办公室,邳
洲市公工商行政管理局,《跨世纪的新邳州》编纂委员会
编纂. 上海:百家出版社,2005. 343 页:图;29cm. ISBN:
7807032553
本书介绍江苏省邳洲市的工商概貌及企业情况.

3. 俯瞰港城:汉英对照/吴加庆主编;中共连云港市委宣传
部编. 北京:五洲传播出版社,2005. 74 页;22cm. ISBN:
750850819X, 7508508191
英文题名:Airscapes of Lianyungang city. 连云港市概
况.

4. 太湖明珠:中国无锡:汉英对照/无锡市人民政府新闻办
公室编. 北京:五洲传播出版社,2005. 68 页;彩照;23×
24cm. ISBN:7508507134, 7508507132
英文题名:Wuxi, China, a shining pearl of the Taihu lake

5. 总统府旧影/南京中国近代史遗址博物馆编. 南京:江苏
美术出版社, 2006. 169 pages:color illustrations;29cm.
ISBN:7534420210;7534420214
英文题名:Presidential Palace past photographs

6. 总统府今貌:(1949—):汉英对照/南京中国近代史遗址
博物馆编. 南京:江苏美术出版社,2006. 159 页:照片;
28cm. ISBN:7534420210, 7534420214
英文题名:Presidential Palace present photographs. 本书
主要反映了总统府历史的变革,以建筑和史料为主要内
容,较全面地反映了总统府古今面貌.

7. 明月湾·陆巷:[汉英对照]/阮涌三,顾鉴明主编. 广州:
广东世界图书出版公司,2008. 119 页;16cm. ISBN:

7506296779，7506296772.（中国历史文化名村丛书）
苏州市乡村概况.

8. 姑苏风情录/周文雍著.上海：上海人民美术出版社，2010.160 页；24cm. ISBN：7532268955，7532268950
本书为一本以图文形式展现苏州风俗习惯的图书.英文题名：Traditions and customs of Suzhou.

9. 2011 苏州概览/陶孙贤主编；苏州市人民政府办公室编.苏州：古吴轩出版社，2011. 131 页；19cm. ISBN：7807336075，7807336072
英文题名：2011 A survey of Suzhou.

10. Ancient rhythm and present grace/chief editor, Yang Weize.［Place of publication not identified］：Guwuxuan Pub. House, 2003. 142 pages：illustrations（some color）；26×27cm. ISBN：7805747180，7805747187
Contents：Ancient history—Urban construction—Municipal administration—Classical gardens—Scenic spots & historical sites—Ancient towns—Brilliant culture—Arts and crafts—Education—Economy.
《古韵今风》，杨卫泽主编；万灵等摄.古吴轩出版社.

11. Lao Nanjing：reflections of scenes on the Qinhuai river/text by Ye Zhaoyan；［translated by Huang Lin, Hao Wei］. Beijing：Foreign Languages Press, 2003. 255 pages：illustrations；22cm. ISBN：7119030485，7119030487.（Old city＝Lao cheng shi）
《老南京：旧影秦淮》，叶兆言著；黄玲，郝薇译.

12. The cultural Suzhou/chief editor, Zhu Yongxin；supervising translator, Du Zhengming. Suzhou：Guwuxuan Publishing House, 2004. vii, 166 pages：color illustrations；26cm. ISBN：7805748306，7805748306
《吴文化读本》，朱永新著.古吴轩出版社.

辽宁省

1. Liaoning：home of the Manchus & cradle of Qing Empire. Beijing：Foreign Languages Press, 2006. 227 pages：illustrations（chiefly color）, color maps；24cm. ISBN：7119045172，7119045177.（Panoramic China）
《辽宁：满韵清风：英文》，辽宁省人民政府新闻办公室主编；戴洪文等撰；金绍卿译.外文出版社.（全景中国）

2. The path to revitalization/by Xia Deren. Beijing：New World, 2010. 511 pages；24cm.. ISBN：7510411427，7510411424
《振兴的轨迹：英文版》，夏德仁［著］.新世界出版社.选编了大连市市委书记夏德仁最近几年来的讲话和工作报告，主要介绍了大连近几年的发展及未来规划.

福建省

1. Fujian · China/compiled by Information Office of the Provincial People's Government of Fujian. Fuzhou：Fujian People's Publishing House, 2002. 145 pages：color illustrations；19cm. ISBN：7211041951，7211041954
《中国·福建》，福建省人民政府新闻办公室编，福建人民出版社.

2. Fujian：mountain and maritime cultures. Beijing：Foreign Languages Press, 2006. 247 pages：illustrations（some color）, color maps；24cm. ISBN：7119043021，7119043029.（Panoramic China）
《福建：山海交辉的文化福地：英文》，福建省人民政府新闻办公室主编；刘登翰等撰，季凯予译；夏念长等摄.（全景中国）

3. 和平：汉英对照/梁伟新主编；国家历史文化名城研究中心等编.广州：广东世界图书出版公司，2006. 119 页；彩照；16×16cm. ISBN：7506284960，7506284967.（中国历史文化名镇）
介绍福建省邵武市和平古镇的全貌.

4. Home is where the heart is：a guide to the earthen buildings/by He Baoguo；translated by Karen Gernant and Chen Zeping；photographs by Qu Liming. Fuzhou：Haichao Photography Art Publishing House, 2008. ［6］, 8 leaves of plates, 151 pages：illustrations；25cm. ISBN：7806914090，7806914099
《永远的家园》，叶恩忠主编.海潮摄影艺术出版社.介绍了闽西南土楼.

5. 海上花园鼓浪屿：英文版/龚洁著；张百佳，陈君铭译.厦门：鹭江出版社，2003. 159 页：图，地图；19cm. ISBN：7806712399.
英文题名：Gulangyu：garden on the sea

广西省

1. Guangxi.［Beijing, China］：China Intercontinental Press, 2001. 134 pages：illustrations, maps；21cm. ISBN：7801138120，7801138125.（West China）
《广西》，广西壮族自治区政府新闻办公室编.五洲传播出版社.

2. Guangxi：land of wonders and beauty/［written by Yang Rongyi and others］. Beijing：Foreign Languages Press, 2006. 253 pages：illustrations（chiefly color）, color maps；24cm. ISBN：7119045121，7119045122.（Panoramic China）
《广西：美丽神奇的地方：英文》，张红伟主编；杨容义等撰；王琴等译；广西壮族自治区人民政府新闻办公室供图.（全景中国）

3. Overview of Nanning 2009/［edited by］Information Office of Naning Municipal Government. Guilin：Guangxi Normal University Press, 2009. 70 pages：color illustrations；17×22cm. ISBN：7563389155，7563389156
《南宁概览：英文版》，车荣福，黄方方主编.广西师范大学出版社.

湖北

1. Hubei：land of the phoenix/［by Jiayuan Cai and Hongying Deng］. Beijing：Foreign Languages Press, 2006. 249 pages：illustrations（some color）, color maps；24cm. ISBN：7119043706，7119043708，7119043757，7119043753.（Panoramic China）
《湖北：凤舞楚天：英文》，湖北省人民政府新闻办公室主编.（全景中国）

2. 武当山:汉英对照/李发平主编.武汉:湖北人民出版社,2004.195 页:彩照;29cm. ISBN:7216040937
英文题名 Mountain Wudang.

湖南省

1. Zhuzhou, China/compiled by News Office of Zhuzhou Municipal People's Government; [director: Zhao Xiangzhen; editor in chief: Cheng Shaoguang and others]. Beijing: New Star Press, 2004. 81 pages: color illustrations, map;19cm. ISBN:7801486889,7801486882
《中国株洲》,程绍光等主编,株洲市人民政府新闻办公室编.新星出版社.比较全面地介绍湖南省株洲市的地理情况、人文历史、经济社会发展等情况.

2. Beautiful Xiangxi: a photographic journey of Hunan through the pen of Shen Congwen/photographs by Zhuo Ya; [text by Shen Congwen; translation by Mark Kitto]. Pleasantville, N. Y.: Reader's Digest, 2004. a99 pages: illustrations (some color); 32cm. ISBN:0762106387, 0762106387
《沈从文和他的湘西》

浙江省

1. 浙江:钱塘江潮涌天下:英文/浙江省人民政府新闻办公室主编.北京:外文出版社,2006.215 页;24cm. ISBN:7119045008, 7119045009.(全景中国)
英文题名:Zhejiang: riding the tides of history.

2. 品味浙江/浙江省人民政府新闻办公室编.杭州:浙江摄影出版社,2010.143 页;21cm. ISBN:7806867501, 7806867503
英文题名:Highlights of Zhejiang province.

3. The West Lake companion. Peking: Foreign Languages Press, 1958. 5 pages, [2] folded leaves: illustrations, map; 19cm.
《西湖胜迹》

4. 品味杭州/杭州市人民政府新闻办公室编著.杭州:浙江人民出版社;2004.181 页:17×14cm. ISBN:7213028979
英文标题:Aspects of Hangzhou.本书系杭州市用以对外宣传交流的作品,为中英对照版和配有约 180 幅精美的图片,图文结合,诠释杭州风貌.

5. 西湖细语＝Talks about West Lake in detail:汉英对照/徐应庚编著.杭州:浙江大学出版社,2005.209 页;19cm. ISBN:7308043703, 7308043700
英文题名:Talks about West Lake in detail.本书以新旧西湖十景为中心,介绍杭州西湖景点三十余处.

6. 沧海宁波:宁波历史与中华古钱币:中英对照/储建国主编.宁波:宁波出版社,2002.1 册;28cm. ISBN:7806025642
宁波市地方史志.

7. Xitang: an elegant town/[chief editor: Bai Yi and others]. Beijing: China Travel & Tourism Press, 2006. 80 pages: color illustrations; 29cm. ISBN:7503229128, 7503229121
《风雅西塘:英文》,北京泰开时代文化传播公司编.中国旅游出版社.本书介绍西塘小镇的旅游风光、人文文化.

8. 泰顺廊桥:英汉对照/刘杰,沈为平著;周咸俊等摄.上海:上海人民美术出版社,2005.169 页:彩照;28cm. ISBN:7532244717, 7532244713
英文题名:Lounge bridges in Taishun.本书图文并茂,介绍关于泰顺廊桥的民俗研究成果.

9. 温州概览:汉英对照.2007/孙智勇,郭明敏主编;郑高华等摄.北京:外文出版社,2007. 144 页;21cm. ISBN:7119051031, 7119051032

10. 魅力舟山:汉英对照/周永章主编;王寓帆译.北京:新星出版社,2006. 18cm. ISBN:7802251028

11. 佛堂:[汉英对照]/龚有群,王迎,董利明主编.广州:广东世界图书出版公司,2008. 119 页;16cm. ISBN:7506293150, 7506293153.(中国历史文化名村丛书)
浙江义乌市乡村概况.

12. 俞源·郭洞:汉英对照/顾鉴明,阮涌三主编.广州:广东世界图书出版公司,2008. 119 页;16cm. ISBN:7506296762, 7506296764(中国历史文化名村丛书)
浙江武义县乡村概况.

13. 海宁/徐辉主编 厉静翻译.北京:五洲传播出版社,2010. 130 页;26×26cm. ISBN:7508519005

14. Disaster strikes the Tachens: The report of an investigation by the Red Cross Society of China into crimes committed by Chiang Kai-shek's troops, instigated and protected by the United States, during their withdrawal from the Tachens and other islands, Peking, April 7, 1955. [Peking]: Red Cross Society of China, 1955. 45 pages, 12 pages of plates: illustrations; 22cm.
《大陈浩劫》.

15. 站在世界舞台上的浙商:英文/《站在世界舞台上的浙商》编委会编.北京:红旗出版社,2016.190 页;21cm. ISBN:7505138278

内蒙古

1. 内蒙古:马背上的民族:英文/王大方,徐翔麟著.北京:外文出版社,2006. 265 页;24cm. ISBN:7119042149, 7119042145.(全景中国)
英文题名:Inner Mongolia: the horseback people

2. Filming as war clouds loom in 1937: 6,000 km with a cinecamera/Sun Mingjing; translated by Sun Jianqiu. Beijing: Foreign Languages Press, 2006. 319 pages: illustrations, portraits, photographs; 24cm. ISBN:7119044923, 7119044927
《1937 年万里猎影记:英文》,孙明经著;孙建秋译.本书是作者 1937 年从南京北上至绥远的万里考察记行.它以近 200 幅历史照片和写给友人的书信,展示了抗战爆发前中国北方绥远地区的国情、民情.

3. Chinese agent in Mongolia/by Ma Ho-t'ien; translated by John De Francis. Baltimore: Johns Hopkins Press, c1949. xvi, 215 p.: map (on lining papers); 24cm.
《内外蒙古考察日记》,马鹤天(1887—1962);Francis,

John De 译. 本书是作者考察内外蒙古的日记. 往返九个月, 行地万余里, 对内蒙之王公政治, 外蒙之共和政治, 以及社会、经济、种族、宗教、交通等等, 做了详细记载. 这部日记在民国时代享有"蒙古文化宝鉴"的美誉.

4. Inner Mongolia. [China]: China Intercontinental Press, 2001. 180 pages: chiefly color illustrations; 21cm. ISBN: 7801139631, 7801139634. (West China)

《内蒙古》, 内蒙古自治区政府新闻办公室编. 五洲传播出版社.

5. 微观内蒙古/莫久愚主编; 英文翻译, (美) 梅皓. 北京: 商务印书馆, 2017. 236 页; 图, 照片; 25cm. ISBN: 7100150224

英文题名: Inner Mongolia: colourful and magnificent

河南省

1. Henan: the central plains of Chinese culture/[by Changchun Yang]. Beijing: Foreign Languages Press, 2006. 255 pages: illustrations (chiefly color), color maps; 24cm. ISBN: 7119043048, 7119043043. (Panoramic China)

《河南: 文化大中原: 英文》, 杨长春主编; 郭传廉等撰; 王琴等译; 于德水等摄. (全景中国)

2. 中国河南 汉英对照/河南省人民政府外事侨务办公室编. 郑州: 河南人民出版社, 2018. 52 页; 26cm. ISBN: 7215115316

河北省

1. 腾飞的河北/刘多田主编. 北京: 五洲传播出版社; 2004. 194 页; 20cm. . ISBN: 750850464X

本书全面介绍了河北省的历史、文化、资源及经济发展情况.

海南省

1. Hainan: China's island paradise. Beijing: Foreign Languages Press, 1996. iii, 279 pages: color illustrations; 24cm. ISBN: 7119040952, 7119040950. (Panoramic China)

《海南: 南中国海的天堂岛: 英文》, 海南省人民政府新闻办公室主编. (全景中国)

2. City weekend city guide: Sanya/[edited by] Mengxue. Beijing: Encyclopedia of China Publishing House, 2006. 78 pages: color illustrations, color maps; 19cm. ISBN: 7500075863, 7500075868

《三亚: 英文》, 梦雪编. 中国大百科全书出版社. 主要介绍了三亚的城市概况及主要旅游景点. 城市指南.

贵州省

1. Guizhou: a province of immigrants/[He Guangyu]. Beijing: Foreign Languages Press, 2006. 268 pages: illustrations (chiefly color), color maps; 24cm. ISBN: 7119043455, 7119043456. (Panoramic China)

《贵州: 移民之州: 英文》, 何光渝著; 刘学文等摄. (全景中国)

2. 石门坎文化百年兴衰: 中国西南一个山村的现代性经历/沈红著. 沈阳市: 万卷出版公司, 2006. 7, 174 pages: illustrations (some color), maps (some color); 24cm. ISBN: 7806017992, 7806017999

英文题名: Modernity through grassroots lens: the cultural transformation of an ethnic community in Southwestern China, 中英对照. 介绍贵州威宁县石门坎的文化史.

天津

1. The record of actual events in Tianjin/[edited by Xiao Huaiyuan; compiled] by the Information Office of Tianjin Municipal Government. Beijing: China Intercontinental Press, 2002. 39 pages: color illustrations, maps; 21cm. ISBN: 7508500245, 7508500249

《天津纪实: 英文》, 肖怀远主编; 天津市人民政府新闻办公室编; 周欣枫译. 五洲传播出版社. 反映天津市的社会发展变化.

2. 魅力天津: 汉英对照/李家森主编; 王忠琪等摄. 天津: 天津人民美术出版社, 2006. 191 页; 25 × 29cm. ISBN: 7530531530, 7530531532

本书主要介绍天津市改革开放以来取得的成就.

3. Tianjin: lustrous pearl of the Bohai Gulf. Beijing: Foreign Languages Press, 2006. 238 pages: illustrations (some color), color maps; 24cm. ISBN: 7119041851, 7119041858. (Panoramic China)

《天津: 渤海湾的明珠: 英文》, 马宇彤, 黄卫著; 龚建生, 张颖主编. (全景中国)

4. 天津历史风貌建筑/吴延龙主编 天津市人民政府[编]. 天津: 天津大学出版社, 2010. 293 页; 31cm. ISBN: 7561836736, 7561836732

K4 中国文物考古

1. China's cultural relics/Li Li; translated by Li Zhurun. Beijing: China International Press, 2004. 164 pages: color illustrations; 23cm. ISBN: 7508504569, 7508504568. (Cultural China series)

Contents: Painted pottery—Jade artifacts—Bronze ware—Figurines—Mausoleum sculptures of stone—Tomb carvings and murals—Grotto temples and formative art of Buddhism—Gold and silver artifacts—Porcelain—Furniture—Lacquer works—Arts and crafts.

《中国文物》, 李力主编; 李竹润, 黎明诚, 潘荫译. 五洲传播出版社.

(1) 2nd ed. Beijing: China Intercontinental Press, 2010. 161 pages: color illustrations; 23cm. ISBN: 7508516790, 7508516796. (Cultural China series)

2. 文物: 汉英对照/吕建昌, 张玉茹著; 柯文礼译. 北京: 人民文学出版社, 2006. 143 页; 21cm. ISBN: 7020048803. (中国传统文化双语读本)

英文题名: Cultural relics

3. Treasures of China/Du Feibao and Du Minglun. [Beijing]: China Travel & Tourism Press, 2006. 9, 230 pages: color illustrations; 22cm. ISBN: 7503229206, 7503229209

《中国国宝: 英文》, 杜飞豹, 杜明伦编著; 易群译. 中国旅游出版社.

4. 乾隆遗珍:故宫博物院宁寿宫花园历史研究与文物保护规划 The studies and master conservation plan for Qianlong Garden/刘畅,张淑娴,王时伟[著].北京:清华大学出版社,2010. 186 页;25×34cm. ISBN:7302237860, 7302237867

英文题名:Qianlong's collector's: the studies and master conservation plan for Qianlong Garden.

5. Chinese archaeological abstracts/edited by Richard C. Rudolph. Los Angeles, Calif.: Institute of Archaeology, University of California, Los Angeles, 1978. 67,[44] pages: illustrations; 29cm. ISBN: 0890030251, 0890030257, 0917956052, 0917956058. (Monumenta archaeologica; v. 6)

《中国考古学文摘》,Rudolph, Richard C. 主编.

6. Chinese archaeological abstracts. 2, prehistoric to Western Zhou/edited by Albert E. Dien, Jeffrey K. Riegel, and Nancy T. Price. Los Angeles, Calif.: Institute of Archaeology, University of California, Los Angeles, 1985. xlvii, 618 p. :: ill. ; 29cm. ISBN: 0917956559. (Monumenta archaeologica; v. 9.)

Translation of abstracting reports of research appearing in Chinese journals between 1972—1981

《中国考古学文摘·卷2》,丁爱博(Dien, Albert E.)(美国汉学家),Riegel, Jeffrey K.(1945—),Price, Nancy T.(Nancy Thompson, 1939—)编译. 汇集和英译 1972—1981 年中文期刊上所见的中国考古研究报告的摘要.

7. Chinese archaeological abstracts. 3, Eastern Zhou to Han/edited by Albert E. Dien, Jeffrey K. Riegel, and Nancy T. Price. Los Angeles, Calif.: Institute of Archaeology, University of California, Los Angeles, 1985. xxi, p. 619—1381: ill. ; 29cm. ISBN: 0917956532. (Monumenta archaeologica; v. 10.)

《中国考古学文摘·卷3》,丁爱博(Dien, Albert E.)(美国汉学家),Riegel, Jeffrey K.(1945—),Price, Nancy T.(Nancy Thompson, 1939—)编译. 汇集和英译 1972—1981 年中文期刊上所见的中国考古研究报告的摘要.

8. Chinese archaeological abstracts. 4, post Han/edited by Albert E. Dien, Jeffrey K. Riegel, and Nancy T. Price. Los Angeles, Calif.: Institute of Archaeology, University of California, Los Angeles, 1985. xx, p. 1382—2131: ill. ; 29cm. ISBN: 0917956540. (Monumenta archaeologica; v. 11.)

《中国考古学文摘·卷4》,丁爱博(Dien, Albert E.)(美国汉学家),Riegel, Jeffrey K.(1945—),Price, Nancy T.(Nancy Thompson, 1939—)编译. 汇集和英译 1972—1981 年中文期刊上所见的中国考古研究报告的摘要.

9. Historical relics unearthed in New China. Peking: Foreign Languages Press, 1972. 217 pages chiefly illustrations 33cm.

Contents:"List of illustrations" in Chinese and English inserted.

《新中国出土文物》

10. New archaeological finds in China: discoveries during the cultural revolution. Peking: Foreign Languages Press, 1972. 54 pages: illustrations (some color); 19cm.

Contents: Archaeological work during the Cultural Revolution/Hsia Nai—Han tombs at Mancheng/Ku Yen-wen—Tatu, the Yuan capital/Ku Yen-wen—Finds from Kansu/Lan, Hsin-wen—Ch'u tomb and weapons from Changsha/Hsiang Po—Tomb of the Ming Prince of Lu/Lu Wen'gao—The masses support archaeological work/Chang Li-chuan and Lin Yu-ching.

《中国新出土文物》

11. New archaeological finds in China, II: more discoveries during the Cultural Revolution. Peking: Foreign Languages Press, 1978. 129 pages: illustrations (some color); 19cm.

《中国出土文物(二)》

12. The treasures of a nation: China's cultural heritage, 1949—1999: discovery, preservation and protection/compiled by State Cultural Relics Bureau, National Museum of Chinese History, Museum of the Chinese Revolution; [editorial committee chairman, Zhang Wenbin; translators, Gong Lizeng and others]. Beijing: Morning Glory Publishers, 1999. 327 pages: illustrations (chiefly color); 29cm. ISBN: 7505406650, 7505406655

《国之瑰宝:中国文物事业五十年,1949—1999》,张文彬(1937—). 朝华出版社.

13. 汉代考古学概说/王仲殊著;张光直等译.北京市:外语教学与研究出版社,2014. 388 页;23cm. ISBN:7513526449.("博雅双语名家名作"系列)

英文题名:Han civilization. 英汉对照.

14. The cave home of Peking man/by Chia Lan-po. Peking: Foreign Languages Press, 1975. 52 pages, [36] pages of plates: illustrations (some color), map; 19cm.

《"北京人"之家》,贾兰坡编写.

15. Early man in China/by Jia Lanpo. Beijing: Foreign Languages Press, 1980. iv, 60 pages, [49] pages of plates: illustrations (some color); 26cm.

《中国大陆上的远古居民》,贾兰坡著.

16. Ch'êng-tzǔ-yai: the black pottery culture site at Lung-shan-chên in Li-ch'êng-hsien, Shantung Province/[by] Li Chi, editor-in-chief [and others] Translated by Kenneth Starr. New Haven, Published for the Dept. of Anthropology, Yale University, by the Yale University Press, 1956. 232 pages: illustrations, plates, maps, diagrams 25cm. (Yale University publications in anthropology; no. 52)

Notes:"The original report, printed in two editions (one entirely in Chinese and the other with an appended English summary), was published in 1934 as the first number of the series Archaeologia Sinica, edited by Li Chi, Liang Ssŭ-yung, and Tung Tso-pin."/ Includes bibliographical references (pages 220—226).

《城子崖报告》,李济(1896—1979).

17. Recent discoveries in Chinese archaeology: 28 articles by Chinese archaeologists describing their excavations/ [translated into English by Zuo Boyang; English text edited by Foster Stockwell and Tang Bowen]. Beijing Foreign Languages Press, 1984. 107 p., [12] p. of plates ill. (some col) 27cm. ISBN: 0835111628, 0835111621

《二千三百年前古中山国之谜:中国的文物与考古文集》

18. The Sanxingdui site: mystical mask on ancient Shu Kingdom/compiled by the Sanxingdui Museum; translated by Zhao Baohua. [Beijing] China Intercontinental Press, 2006. 134 pages: illustrations (chiefly color), color maps; 31cm. ISBN: 7508508521, 7508508528

《三星堆:古蜀王国的神秘面具:英文》,吴维羲,朱亚蓉,江聪著.五洲传播出版社.

本书图文并茂地介绍三星堆遗址的考古发掘过程和各种精美器物,包括玉器、金器、青铜器、石器等各个种类,从各个层面对文物进行立体展示.

19. The legend of Mawangdui/edited by Zhang Dongxia. Beijing: China Intercontinental Press, 2007. 239 pages: illustrations; 21cm. ISBN: 750851047X, 7508510477. (Chinese archaeological discoveries)

《马王堆传奇:英文》,张东霞主编;许蕾等撰.五洲传播出版社(考古中国)

20. 神奇的马王堆/侯良著;夏嫔嫔,谢寰旭译.长沙:湖南人民出版社,2011. 268 页;21cm. ISBN: 7543867413, 7543867413, 7543867419

英文题名:The miracle of Mawangdui.

21. 庙底沟与三里桥:黄河水库考古报告之二/中国社会科学院考古研究所编著.北京:文物出版社,2011. 61 页;27cm. ISBN: 7501032693, 7501032696. 中国田野考古报告集. 考古学专刊. 丁种;第9号)

英文题名:Miaodigou and Sanliqiao. 本书是中国科学院考古研究所1956—1957年发掘河南陕县庙底沟与三里桥两个新石器遗址时的考古发掘报告,全面报告了两个遗址的仰韶和龙山文化的堆积,论述了仰韶和龙山的不同发展阶段,并首次确立了"庙底沟二期文化".

22. The vanished ancient Liangzhu Kingdom/edited by Zhang Dongxia. Beijing: China Intercontinental Press, 2007. 201 pages: illustrations; 23cm. ISBN: 7508510488, 7508510484. (Chinese archaeological discoveries)

《消逝的良渚古国:英文》,张东霞主编;许蕾等撰.五洲传播出版社(考古中国)

23. Yinxu/Li Fuqiang [and others]. Beijing: New World Press: China Translation & Publishing Corp., 2007. 164 pages: color illustrations, maps; 29cm. ISBN: 7802282841, 7802282845. (World heritage sites in China)

《殷墟:英文》,李付强等著;中国对外翻译出版公司翻译部译.新世界出版社:中国对外翻译出版公司.(世界遗产·中国)

24. Appreciation of Dunhuang Grottoes: a selection of 50 caves: from the Mogao grottoes, Yulin grottoes and Western-Thousand Buddha grottoes/Fan Jinshi, Liu Yongzeng. Nanjing: Jiangsu Fine Arts Publishing House, 2007. 147 pages: illustrations (some color), maps; 21cm. ISBN: 7534422959, 7534422957

《敦煌鉴赏:英文》,樊锦诗编著.江苏美术出版社.

25. 屈家岭:长江中游的史前文化:汉英对照/王红星主编;湖北省博物馆编.北京:文物出版社,2007. 101 页:彩照;29cm. ISBN: 7501022595, 7501022593.(长江中游文明之旅丛书;2)

英文题名:Qujialing: prehistoric culture in the middle reaches of the Yangtze. 介绍湖北境内新石器时代的城背溪文化、石家河文化等几个阶段中有代表性的遗存.

26. 盘龙城:长江中游的青铜文明:汉英对照/王红星主编;湖北省博物馆编.北京:文物出版社,2007. 99 页:彩照;29cm. ISBN: 7501022656, 7501022658.(长江中游文明之旅丛书;3)

英文题名:Panlongcheng: bronze civilization in the middle reaches of the Yangtze. 本书以湖北的东北部盘龙城遗址为代表,全面介绍了商文化,成为商文化的一个类型,本书讲述了这里的青铜文明.

27. 郧县人:长江中游的远古人类:汉英对照/王红星主编;湖北省博物馆编.北京:文物出版社,2007. 93 页:彩照;29cm. ISBN: 7501022496, 7501022496.(长江中游文明之旅丛书;1)

英文题名:Yunxian man: prehistoric people in the middle reaches of the Yangtze

28. The discovery of a missing king's tomb: selections of Chinese relics and archaeology/translated by Zuo Boyang. Beijing: Foreign Languages Press: Distributed by China International Book Trading Corp., 1995. 198 pages: illustrations; 19cm. ISBN: 7119015400, 7119015408

《一座失踪王陵的发现:中国文物考古选集》

29. 梁庄王墓:郑和时代的瑰宝:汉英对照/王红星主编;湖北省博物馆编.北京:文物出版社,2007. 105 页:彩照;29cm. ISBN: 7501022212, 7501022216.(长江中游文明之旅丛书;8)

英文题名:Treasure of the era of Zheng He,介绍明仁宗九子梁庄王之墓出土文物.

30. 曾侯乙墓:战国早期的礼乐文明:汉英对照/王红星主编;湖北省博物馆编.北京:文物出版社,2007. 121 页:彩照;29cm. ISBN: 7501022649, 750102264X.(长江中游文明之旅丛书;4)

英文题名:Tomb of Marquis Yi of Zeng. 本书对曾侯乙

墓的发掘情况及出土器物进行详尽的介绍,并对出土器物予以了充分展示.

31. 九连墩:长江中游的楚国贵族大墓:汉英对照/王红星主编;湖北省博物馆编.北京:文物出版社,2007. 127 页;彩照;29cm. ISBN:7501022168,750102216X.(长江中游文明之旅丛书;5)

英文题名:Jiuliandun:large tomb of a Chu noble in the middle reaches of the Yangtze.本书首次刊载了 2002 年 9 月对湖北省枣阳市境内楚国贵族大墓及其陪葬坑考古发掘的丰硕成果.

32. Tales of Ming emperors and empresses:the thirteen tombs/[written by Wei Yuqing;English translation by Tang Bowen]. Beijing, China:Foreign Languages Press, 2007. 200 pages:illustrations (chiefly color);22cm. ISBN:7119051147,7119051148

《明十三陵帝后妃嫔轶闻》,魏玉清编著.介绍十三陵,还配有与此有关的帝后妃嫔轶闻故事.

33. Imperial tombs of the Ming and Qing dynasties/editors, Wu Liangzhu, Luo Pingfeng. Beijing:New World Press;China Translation & Publishing Corporation, 2007. 189 pages:color illustrations, color maps;29cm. ISBN:7802285095,7802285097. (World heritage sites in China)

《明清皇家陵寝》,明清皇家陵寝编委会编著.新世界出版社:中国对外翻译出版公司.

34. 昭陵/赵琛著.北京:中国建筑工业出版社,2011. 174 页;29cm. ISBN:7112136049,7112136040.(世界文化遗产.辽宁卷)

英文题名:Zhaoling imperial tomb.

35. 福陵/赵琛著.北京:中国建筑工业出版社,2011. 175 页;29cm. ISBN:7112137107,7112137101.(世界文化遗产.辽宁卷)

英文题名:Fuling imperial tomb.

36. 秦陵与兵马俑/戚嘉富编著.合肥:黄山书社,2016. 132 页;彩图,地图,肖像;23cm. ISBN:7546141985.(印象中国)

英文题名:The mausoleum of Qin Shi Huang and terracotta warriors. 英汉对照.

37. 兵器/梅文编著.合肥:黄山书社,2016. 188 页:图;23cm. ISBN:7546142104.(印象中国)

英文题名:Weapons of ancient China

38. 衡器/简洁编著.合肥:黄山书社,2016. 140 页:图;23cm. ISBN:7546142142.(印象中国)

英文题名:Ancient weighing apparatus. 英汉对照.

39. 古钱币/方媛编著.合肥:黄山书社,2016. 184 页:彩图;23cm. ISBN:7546142128.(印象中国)

英文题名:Chinese ancient currencies. 英汉对照.

40. 金银器/胥敏编著.合肥:黄山书社,2016. 156 页:图;23cm. ISBN:7546142159.(印象中国)

英文题名:Gold and silver articles. 英汉对照.

41. 古铜器/梅琪编著.合肥:黄山书社,2016. 172 页:彩图;

23cm. ISBN:7546142135.(印象中国)

英文题名:Ancient Chinese bronzes. 英汉对照.

42. Chinese bronzes:a general introduction/[Li Xueqin]. Beijing:Foreign Languages Press, 1995. 171 pages:illustrations (some color);32cm. ISBN:7119013874, 7119013879

《中国青铜器概说》,李学勤著.

43. The story of bronze/by Xiang Zhonghua. Beijing:Foreign Languages Press, 2006. III, 161 str.:illustr.;24cm. ISBN:7119044591, 711904459

《青铜的历史:英文》,向中华著;李振国译(东西文丛).在介绍青铜的历史的同时,还向读者介绍了青铜的雕像、青铜铭文、青铜上的书法、青铜上的音乐、青铜的铸造、铜钱、铜镜等.

44. Chinese bronzes:a general introduction/[author:Li Xueqin;editors:Cheng Qinhua, Lan Peijin, Wen Fang]. Beijing:Foreign Languages Press, 2007. 213, [9] pages:illustrations (chiefly color);24cm. ISBN:7119048703, 7119048708

《中国青铜器的奥秘:英文》,李学勤编著.

45. Chinese bronze ware:a mirror of culture/Li Song;translated by Zhu Jianting Li Li & He Yunzhao. Beijing:China Intercontinental Press, 2009. 157 pages:illustrations;23cm. ISBN:7508513256, 7508513258. (Cultural China series)

《中国青铜器》,李松编著.五洲传播出版社.

46. 故宫博物院藏宜兴紫砂:汉英对照/王健华主编;故宫博物院编.北京:紫禁城出版社,2007. 300 页:彩图;31cm. ISBN:7800476280, 7800476286

英文题名:Yixing Zisha:wares in The Palace Museum.以清宫旧藏紫砂为主线,从明代进入宫廷的宜兴窑开始,一直延续至晚清茗壶及现代大师的作品,共 280 件,准确客观地反映了故宫博物院紫砂收藏的全貌.

47. 紫砂壶/杨冰编著.合肥:黄山书社,2016. 161 页:图;23cm. ISBN:7546142272.(印象中国)

英文题名:Purple clay teapot. 英汉对照.

48. 秦汉漆器:长江中游的髹漆艺术:汉英对照/王红星主编;湖北省博物馆编.北京:文物出版社,2007. 125 页:彩照;29cm. ISBN:7501022434,7501022437.(长江中游文明之旅丛书;7)

英文题名:Lacquered articles in the Qin and Han dynasties. 收入湖北出土的秦汉漆器百余件,对湖北出土漆器进行全面系统的介绍,还对中国古代漆器概况进行了介绍.

49. 三国两晋南北朝瓷器的成长＝Three Kingdoms, eastern jin and western jin, south and north dynasties—the development of china:英文/胡敏著.杭州:中国美术学院出版社,2007. 229 页;20cm. ISBN:7810835879, 7810835874.(青年艺术文库)

对我国三国两晋南北朝时期的瓷器发展状况进行了系统科学地阐述.

50. 汝窑遗珍：汉英对照/林俊著.上海：上海古籍出版社，2007. 227 页：彩照；29cm. ISBN：7532548842，7532548848

英文题名：Remains of the porcelain treasures of the Ru kiln.本书对宋代五大名窑之首的汝窑残瓷进行修复还原.

51. 中国西北彩陶：汉英对照/朱勇年著.上海：上海古籍出版社，2007. 259 页；29cm. ISBN：7532548293，7532548295

英文题名：Neolithic［sic］pottery of north west China.

52. 清乾隆珐琅彩荣华富贵灯笼尊：汉英对照/耿东升主编.北京：文物出版社，2007. 160 页；29cm. ISBN：7501022571，7501022577

英文题名：A magnificent falangcai lantern-shaped vase.本书以清乾隆珐琅荣华富贵灯笼尊为线索，就其诞生与发展进行了详尽阐述，并延引了大量材料.

53. 中国长沙窑/谭敦宁著.长沙：湖南人民出版社，2010. 249 页；21cm. ISBN：7543867123，7543867125

54. 红山文化古玉鉴定：汉英对照/徐强著.北京：华艺出版社，2007. 306 页：彩照；29cm. ISBN：7801428653，780142865X

英文题名：Hongshan-cultural ancient jade appraisal.本书是关于红山文化古玉鉴定的专著，从专业玉器鉴定师的角度来解析红山文化玉器鉴定中的各方面问题.（红山古玉器）

55. 奥运奖牌上的中国文化：中国印和玉璧/杨永年著，申再望译.杭州：浙江大学出版社，2008. 167 页；29cm. ISBN：7308059497，7308059499

英文书名：Traditional Chinese culture reflected in the design of the Olympic medals.

56. Chinese jade：sacred，imperial and civil forms/Yu Ming；translated by Xiao Ying. Beijing：China Intercontinental Press，2009. 145 pages：color illustrations；23cm. ISBN：7508513317，7508513312.（Cultural China series）

《中国玉器》，于明著.五洲传播出版社.以历史发展为脉博，深入浅出地向读者介绍中国玉器的种类、工艺、用途、文化等.

57. Jades of ancient China/compiled by Qu Shi；translated by Chen Xiaocheng. Beijing：China Intercontinental Press，2010. 145 pages：color illustrations，color maps；21cm. ISBN：7508517773，7508517776.（China's national treasures）

《中国古玉器》，曲石撰稿.五洲传播出版社.介绍中国乃至散落在海外的最著名的中国玉器文物，讲述中国玉文化，向国外读者展示中国国宝玉器.

58. Chinese jades/Jiang Lijun，editor；Fu Zhuoran，Zhao Weiwei，Li Xueyao，English translators. Hefei：Huangshan shushe，2013. 4，184 p.：ill.；21cm. ISBN：7546120508，7546120500.（Zhongguo hong）

《中国玉》，姜莉君编著.黄山书社（中国红）

59. 玉/姜莉君编著.合肥：黄山书社，2016. 184 页：图；23cm. ISBN：7546142258.（印象中国）

英文题名：Chinese jades. 汉英对照.

60. 秦砖汉瓦/王亦儒编著.合肥：黄山书社，2016. 132 页：图；23cm. ISBN：7546141992.（印象中国）

英文题名：Qin bricks and Han tiles. 汉英对照.

61. 陶器/简洁编著.合肥：黄山书社，2016. 140 页：彩图；23cm. ISBN：7546152974.（印象中国）

英文题名：Chinese pottery

62. Snuff bottles in the Qing Dynasty/compiled by Zhang Rong. Beijing：China Intercontinental Press，2010. 166 pages：color illustrations；21cm. ISBN：7508518459，7508518454.（China's national treasures）

《清代鼻烟壶》，张荣撰稿.五洲传播出版社.

63. 鼻烟壶/陈一诚编著.合肥：黄山书社，2016. 116 页：图，照片；23cm. ISBN：7546152943.（印象中国）

英文题名：Snuff bottle. 英汉对照.

64. 老茶具/文铮编著.合肥：黄山书社，2016. 158 页：图；23cm. ISBN：7546142173.（印象中国）

英文题名：Chinese jades. 英汉对照.

65. 竹木牙角器/朱穆编著.合肥：黄山书社，2016. 140 页：彩图；23cm. ISBN：7546142265.（印象中国）

英文题名：Art crafts made of bamboo，wood，ivory and horn. 英汉对照

66. 扇/易凡编著.合肥：黄山书社，2016. 156 页：彩图；23cm. ISBN：7546142203.（印象中国）

英文题名：Chinese fans. 英汉对照

67. 料器/叔戊编著.合肥：黄山书社，2016. 116 页：彩图；23cm. ISBN：7546142180.（印象中国）

英文题名：Chinese glassware

68. 书写历史：战国秦汉简牍：汉英对照/王红星主编；湖北省博物馆编.北京：文物出版社，2007. 81 页：彩照；29cm. ISBN：7501022557，7501022550.（长江中游文明之旅丛书；6）

英文题名：Writing history：bamboo slips of the Warring States period，the Qin dynasty and the Han dynasty.本书介绍湖北地区出土的古代文献资料尤其是战国秦汉简牍资料.

69. 琉璃刻卷：丹巴莫斯卡《格萨尔王传》岭国人物石刻谱系 ＝Stone carvings of The life of King Gesar in Mosika/罗布江村，赵心愚，杨嘉铭著.成都：四川民族出版社，2003. 224 pages：color illustrations；26cm. ISBN：7540927445，7540927448

四川省甘孜藏族自治州丹巴县莫斯卡发现的大量石刻格萨尔谱系以供国际"格学"学者研究为国内首次.

70. 昭陵唐墓壁画：汉英对照/张志攀主编；昭陵博物馆编.北京：文物出版社，2006. 232 页；26cm. ISBN：7501017174，7501017171

英文题名：The Tang mural paintings at Zhaoling mausoleum.本书收录了长乐公主等 13 座墓室出土的壁画，较系统地展示了唐墓壁画的风貌.

71. Fascinating mural stories from Dunhuang grottoes/by Chen Yu; translated by Li Guishan. Beijing：New World Press, 2008. 2 volumes：color illustrations；24cm. ISBN：7802285712, 7802285712

《敦煌壁画中的精彩故事》,陈钰著. 新世界出版社.

72. 石窟/韩慧编著. 合肥：黄山书社,2016. 156 页：彩图；23cm. ISBN：7546142005.（印象中国）

英文题名：Chinese grottoes. 英汉对照.

73. 佛像/梵华编著. 合肥：黄山书社,2016. 188 页：彩图；23cm. ISBN：7546141855.（印象中国）

英文题名：Art of the buddha statue. 英汉对照.

K5　风俗习惯

1. 中国传统节日及传说＝The traditional Chinese festivals and tales/靳海林, 白雪飞（英文）；何元智, 白雪飞（中文）. 2 版. 重庆：重庆出版社,2001. 2, 311 pages；19cm. ISBN：7536655576, 7536655577

2. Chinese festivals：traditions, customs and rituals/Wei Liming；translated by Yue Liwen & Tao Lang. Beijing：China Intercontinental Press, 2005. 127 pages：illustrations (chiefly color)；23cm. ISBN：750850836X, 7508508368. (Cultural China series)

《中国节日：英文》,韦黎明著；乐利文,陶郎译. 五洲传播出版社.

(1)2nd ed. Beijing：China Intercontinental Press, 2010. ISBN：7508516998,7508516990,7508516936,7508516931. (Cultural China series)

3. 节日习俗：汉英对照/李逸安编；高巍,刘士聪译. 北京：人民文学出版社,2006. 101 页；21cm. ISBN：702004879X, 7020048793.（中国传统文化双语读本）

英文题名：Festivals and customs.

4. Chinese festivals/Qi Xing. Beijing：Foreign Languages Press, 2008. 101 pages：color illustrations；24cm. ISBN：7119054070, 7119054074

《中国节》,齐星编. 介绍中国民间最重要的传统节日.

5. 节庆趣谈/盖国梁［著］. 上海：上海外语教育出版社,2010. 433 页；23cm. ISBN：7544616027, 7544616029.（外教社汉英双语中国民俗文化丛书）

中英文对照.

6. 节日史话：中英文双语版/万李娜中文撰著；唐惠润英文翻译；《中华文明史话》编委会编译. 北京：中国大百科全书出版社,2010. 210 页；21cm. ISBN：7500083696, 7500083696.（《中华文明史话》中英文双语丛书）

英文题名：History of festivals.

7. 节庆趣谈/中文作者盖国梁；英文作者王善江；英文审订汪榕培. 上海：上海外语教育出版社,2010. 433 pages：illustrations；23cm. ISBN：7544616027, 7544616029.（外教社汉英双语中国民俗文化丛书）

英文题名：Joys and rites：customs of traditional Chinese festivals

8. 节日/姜莉君编著. 合肥：黄山书社,2016. 186 页：彩图；23cm. ISBN：7546141695.（印象中国）

英文题名：Chinese festivals. 英汉对照.

9. The traditional festivals of China/written by Zhu Qixin [and others]；translated by Li Yang, Zhang Zhihong and Sheng Wen；version revised by Harold Swindall. Shandong, China：Shandong Friendship Press, 1998. a, 144 pages；27cm. ISBN：7805519900, 7805519906

《中国民族传统节日风情》,朱启新等著；李杨等译. 山东友谊出版社.

10. Festivals of China's ethnic minorities/by Xing Li. ［Beijing］：China Intercontinental Press, 2006. 128 pages：color illustrations；24cm. ISBN：7508509994, 7508509990. (Ethnic cultures of China)

《中国少数民族节日：英文》,邢莉著；汉定,王国振等译. 五洲传播出版社（中国民族多元文化丛书）

11. 话说清明/中文作者 黄涛等；英文作者 门顺德［等］；英文审定 汪榕培. 上海：上海外语教育出版社,2008. 231 pages：illustrations；21cm. ISBN：7544607353, 7544607356

英文题名：Anecdotes about the Qingming Festival

12. 话说端午（汉英双语版）/中文作者 陈连山；英文作者 付瑛瑛［等］；英文审定 汪榕培. 上海：上海外语教育出版社, 2008. 217 pages：illustrations；21cm. ISBN：7544608817, 7544608816

13. 话说春节/中文作者萧放；英文作者冯秋香等；英文审订汪榕培. 上海外语教育出版社,2009. 302 pages：illustrations；21cm. ISBN：7544611879, 7544611876

英文题名：Anecdotes about the Chunjie Festival

14. Chinese folk customs/Fang Huawen；translated by Zhang Weihua；revision by Du Zhengming. Beijing：China Intercontinental Press, 2011. 163 pages.：color illustrations.；23cm. ISBN：7508518985, 7508518985. (Chinese lifestyle)

《中国民间风俗》,方华文编著. 五洲传播出版社.

15. 民俗风情：中英双语阅读/曹旭主编. 大连：大连理工大学出版社,2010. 235 页；24cm. ISBN：7561154793, 7561154798.（每天读点中国文化）

中英双语对照.

16. 中国民俗：英汉对照/栗景超, 赵彩平主编. 北京：海潮出版社,2011. 279 页；彩图,23cm. ISBN：7802137189

英文题名：Chinese folk customs

17. 中国民间风俗/厉振仪编选；姚红英译. 北京：中国对外翻译出版公司,2007. 259 页；21cm. ISBN：7500118169.（中译经典文库·中华传统文化精粹）

英文题名：Chinese folk customs

18. Temple fairs in China/［translated by Cong Guoling and Huang Youyi；edited by Liao Pin and Sun Shuming］. Beijing：Foreign Languages Press, 2004. 99 pages：chiefly color illustrations；22cm. ISBN：7119036424, 7119036427

《中国庙会》,廖频等撰文,丛国玲,黄友义译；孙树明摄影. 介绍了中国庙会文化的起源、形成、发展和兴盛, 并重点介绍了几处历史悠久、今天仍保持着独特魅力的传统庙会.

19. 婚嫁趣谈/完颜绍元[著]. 上海: 上海外语教育出版社, 2010. 404 页; 23cm. ISBN: 7544615877, 7544615871
本书以中英文对照的形式介绍了中国婚姻的历史演变和相关风俗.

20. 婚俗/简洁编著. 合肥: 黄山书社, 2016. 140 页; 彩图; 23cm. ISBN: 7546141428. (印象中国)
英文题名: Wedding customs in China. 英汉对照.

21. Chinese red/Yan Chunling. Beijing: Foreign Languages Press, 2008. 97 pages: color illustrations; 24cm. ISBN: 7119045313, 7119045318
《中国红》, 阎春玲著.

22. Chinese rites and rituals/Feng Ge; translated by Huang Jieting & Jiang Yinji; revision by Du Zhengming. Beijing: China Intercontinental Press, 2011. 156 pages: color illustrations; 23cm. ISBN: 7508520162, 7508520165. (Chinese lifestyle)
《中国的礼仪》, 冯鸽著. 五洲传播出版社.

23. The I-li, or, Book of etiquette and ceremonial＝礼仪/translated from the Chinese with introduction, notes and plans, by John Steele. London: Probsthain, c1917. 2 v. : ill. (1 in pocket); 19cm. (Probsthain's Oriental series; v. 8—9)
《礼仪》, Steele, John 译.
(1) Taipei: Ch'eng Wen Publishing Company, c1966. 2 v. : ill. ; 19cm.
英文题名: Anecdotes about the Duanwu Festival

24. Chu Hsi's family rituals: a twelfth-century Chinese manual for the performance of cappings, weddings, funerals, and ancestral rites/translated, with annotation and introduction by Patricia Buckley Ebrey. Princeton, N. J. : Princeton University Press, c1991. xxxi, 234 p. : ill. ; 25cm. ISBN: 0691031495. (Princeton library of Asian translations)
《家礼》, 朱熹 (1130—1200); Ebrey, Patricia Buckley (1947—) 译, 中英文本.

25. The festivals in the mysterious land of Yunnan: the festivals and traditional ceremonies of the minority nationalities in Yunnan/compilers and writers, Deng Qiyao, Zhang Liu; English translators, Li Xiwen, Liu Xiaohong. Kunming: Yunnan People's Pub. House, 1991. 1 volume (unpaged): bill. (some color); 32cm. ISBN: 7222009442, 7222009448
《秘境节祭: 中国云南少数民族年节祭祀》, 云南人民出版社.

26. 生肖/徐刚编著. 合肥: 黄山书社, 2016. 136 页; 图; 23cm. ISBN: 7546141732. (印象中国)
英文题名: Chinese zodiac signs. 英汉对照.

K6　地理

1. A simple geography of China/Wang Chun-heng. Peking: Foreign Languages Press, 1958. 256 pages, [18] pages of plates: illustrations, maps (some color, 2 folded); 19cm. (China knowledge series)
《简明中国地理》, 王钧衡编.

2. Geography of China. Peking: Foreign Languages Press, 1972. 44 pages: illustrations, maps; 20cm.
Contents: Some basic facts. —Rich natural resources. —Minority nationalities. —Coasts, islands, and harbours. —Rivers. —Mountains.
《中国地理知识》
(1) Peking: Foreign Languages Press ,1974.

3. An outline of Chinese geography/Chung Chih. Peking: Foreign Languages Press, 1978. 186 pages, [24] leaves of plates (2 folded): illustrations, maps; 19cm.
《中国地理概况》, 众志编写.

4. China's geography: natural conditions, regional economies, cultural features/author, Ping Zheng; translator, Chen Gengtao. Beijing: China Intercontinental Press, 1999. 176 pages: color illustrations, color maps; 21cm. ISBN: 7801134818, 7801134813. (China basics series)
《中国地理: 自然・经济・人文》, 郑平著. 五洲传播出版社.

5. China's geography/author, Zheng Ping; translator, Chen Gengtao. 2 nd ed. [Beijing]: China Intercontinental Press, 1999. 159 pages: color illustrations, maps; 21cm. ISBN: 7508509145, 7508509143. (China basics series)
《中国地理: 英文》, 郑平著; 陈庚涛译, 2 版. 五洲传播出版社 (中国基本情况丛书/郭长建主编)

6. China's geography/Zheng Ping; translated by Xiao Ying. 3rd. ed. [Beijing]: China Intercontinental Press, 2010. 136 pages: color illustrations, maps; 23cm. ISBN: 7508513089, 7508513088
《中国地理》, 郑平著. 五洲传播出版社.

7. 中国知识地图册: 汉英对照/西安地图出版社编制. 7 版. 西安: 西安地图出版社, 2006. 155 页; 20cm. ISBN: 7806703268, 7806703267
英文题名: The knowledge Atlas of China. 本图册主要包括序图、分省区图和省级城市图三大部分, 以中英文对照的形式表示中国的基本地理信息, 是中外读者了解中国的工具.

8. 中国地理常识: 汉英对照/焦华富主编; 国务院侨务办公室, 国家汉语国际推广领导小组办公室编. 北京: 高等教育出版社, 2007. 258 页; 24cm. ISBN: 7040207200, 7040207206. (中国常识系列)
英文题名: Common knowledge about Chinese geography.

9. Natural wonders in China/Liu Ying; translation by Zhou Xiaozheng. Beijing: China Intercontinental Press, 2007. 159 pages: color illustrations, color maps; 25cm. ISBN:

7508511047，7508511042.（Journey into China）

《自然之旅：英文》，刘莹著；周效政译.五洲传播出版社（中国之旅丛书/郭长建，李向平主编）

10. Marvels of China/authors，Du Feibao and Du Minglun；translators，Kuang Peihua，Ren Lingjuan，Yu Man. Beijing：China Travel & Tourism Press，2007. 294 pages：color illustrations，color map；23cm. ISBN：7503232107，7503232102

《中国奇观：英文》，杜飞豹，杜明伦. 中国旅游出版社. 介绍我国最著名的(顶级)的自然风光和人文景观.

11. 中国名山名水：英汉对照/方华文编著；杨国华译. 合肥：安徽科学技术出版社，2010. 348 页；25cm. ISBN：7533745196，7533745191.（品读中国文化丛书）

英文题名：China's famous scenic landscapes.

12. Shan hai ching：legendary geography and wonders of ancient China/commentary by Kuo P'o；explanatory notes by Hao Yi-hsing；translated by Hsiao-Chieh Cheng，Hui-Chen Pai Cheng，Kenneth Lawnence [sic] Thern. Tai-pei，Taiwan，Republic of China：Committee for Compilation and Examination of the Series of Chinese Classics，National Institute for Compilation and Translation，1985. 3，ii，426 pages，[1] folded leaf of plates：illustrations，map；22cm.

《山海经》，郭璞（276—324）注；郝懿行（1757—1825 年）笺疏. Cheng，Hsiao-Chieh 等英译.

13. The classic of mountains and seas/translated with an introduction and notes by Anne Birrell. London：Penguin Books；New York：Penguin Putnam，1999. 1，276 pages：illustrations；20cm. ISBN：0140447199，0140447194.（Penguin classics）

《山海经》，Birrell，Anne 译注.

14. A Chinese bestiary：strange creatures from the guideways through mountains and seas/edited and translated with commentary by Richard E. Strassberg. Berkeley：University of California Press，2002. xxii，313 pages：illustrations，maps；27cm. ISBN：0520218442，0520218444

《山海经》，Strassberg，Richard E. 译.

15. The classic of mountains and seas/translated into modern Chinese by Chen Cheng；translated into English by Wang Hong & Zhao Zheng. Changsha Shi：Hunan ren min chu ban she，2010. 54，355 p.；24cm. ISBN：7543870864，754387086X.（Library of Chinese classics：Chinese-English＝大中华文库：汉英对照）

《山海经》，陈成今译；王宏，赵峥英译.

16. The "Mongol Atlas" of China by Chu Ssu-pen and the Kuang-yü-t'u：with 48 facsimile maps dating from about 1555/by Walter Fuchs. Peiping：Fu Jen University，1946. 32，48 pages：maps；27cm.（Monumenta serica monograph series；8）

《〈广舆图〉版本考》，福克司（Fuchs，Walter，1902—1979）著，翻译了朱思本（1273—1335）的《广舆图》.

K61 专属地理

1. Mount Qomolangma：the highest in the world/Zhang Rongzu. Beijing：Foreign Languages Press，1981. 4 p.，tav.：ill.

《世界第一峰：珠穆朗玛峰》，张荣祖著.

2. 名山/王佳编著. 合肥：黄山书社，2016. 164 页：图；23cm. ISBN：7546141954.（印象中国）

英文题名：Famous mountains in China. 英汉对照.

3. 长江黄河/马利琴编著. 合肥：黄山书社，2016. 144 页：彩图；23cm. ISBN：7546152905.（印象中国）

英文题名：The Yangtze River and the Yellow River. 英汉对照.

4. The Grand Canal：an odyssey/[editor，Liao Pin；articles by Yao Hanyuan，Shen Xingda]. Beijing，China：Foreign Languages Press，1987. 197 pages：illustrations（some color）；27cm. ISBN：711900011X，7119000114，0835119726，0835119726

《漫游中国大运河》

5. 大运河/吴顺鸣编著. 合肥：黄山书社，2016. 150 页：彩图；23cm. ISBN：7546141848.（印象中国）

英文题名：The Grand Canal. 英汉对照.

6. 名湖/韦茗编著. 合肥：黄山书社，2016. 156 页：彩图，彩照；23cm. ISBN：7546141930.（印象中国）

英文题名：Famous lakes in China. 英汉对照.

7. 名泉/孟石编著. 合肥：黄山书社，2016. 144 页：彩图；23cm. ISBN：7546141947.（印象中国）

英文题名：Famous springs in China

8. Eighteen capitals of China，by William Edgar Geil... with 139 illustrations. Philadelphia，London，J. B. Lippincott Company，1911. xx，429 p. front.，illus.，plates，ports.，maps. 23cm.

Contents：The southern capitals：Hangchow. Foochow. Canton. Kweilin. Kweiyang. Yunnanfu. —The Yangtze capitals：Soochow. Nanking. Anking. Nanchang. Wuchang. Changsha. Chengtu. —The Yellow capitals：Lanchow. Sian. Kalfeng. Taiyuanfu. Tsinan. Peking：capital of capitals.

Geil，William Edgar 编译. 中国 18 个省会城市介绍.

9. History of seven ancient capital cities/Chinese compiler Xie Keke. Encyclopedia of China Publishing House，2009. III，196 p.：ill.；22cm. ISBN：7500080596，750008059X.（History of Chinese civilization）

《七大古都史话》《中华文明史话》编委会编译. 中国大百科全书出版社. 对安阳、西安、洛阳、开封、杭州、南京、北京中国七大古都的建筑形制布局及其承袭演变关系进行介绍.

10. 历史名城/郭成编著. 合肥：黄山书社，2016. 156 页：图；23cm. ISBN：7546152929.（印象中国）

英文题名：Historical and famous cities in China

11. Small towns in China: functions, problems & prospects/ by Fei Hsiao Tung & others. Beijing, China: New World Press: Distributed by China International Book Trading Corporation (Guoji Shudian), 1986. 374 pages: illustrations; 22cm. ISBN: 0835115291, 0835115292. (China studies series)

《中国小城镇》,费孝通等著. 新世界出版社.

12. Cities in China/Wang Jie; translation by Andrea Lee. Beijing: China Intercontinental Press, 2007. 154 pages: color illustrations, color maps; 25cm. ISBN: 7508510910, 7508510917. (Journey into China)

《城市之旅:英文》,王杰著;(新加坡)李(lee. A.)译. 五洲传播出版社(中国之旅丛书/郭长建,李向平主编)介绍中国代表性的城市三十个,内容涉及城市的历史、文化、经济和其在中国城市版图中的特点和城位.

13. Old townscapes of China/Text by Liu Bin; English translation by Sun Lei, Yu Qiu, Li Lie. Beijing: Foreign Languages Press, 2008. 142 pages: color illustrations, color maps; 23cm. ISBN: 7119052847, 7119052845

《中国最美的古镇》,刘彬撰稿;孙雷,雨秋,李磊译. 介绍了中国 12 个比较有特色的古镇.

14. 城镇魅力:中英双语阅读/姚香泓主编. 大连:大连理工大学出版社,2010. 230 页;24cm. ISBN:7561154915, 7561154917.(每天读点中国文化)

本书主要向读者介绍了四十五个中国城镇,展示了它们各具特色的文化内涵.

15. 古镇/康国剑编著. 合肥:黄山书社,2016. 180 页:图; 23cm. ISBN:7546141893.(印象中国)

英文题名:Ancient towns. 英汉对照.

16. 乡愁·中国=Nostalgia of China /《乡愁·中国》编委会编;李谨羽等译. 北京:北京出版社,2016. 10 卷;26cm. ISBN:7200122121(v. 1),7200122206(v. 2),7200122138(v. 3),7200122145(v. 4),7200122152(v. 5),7200122169(v. 6),7200122176(v. 7),7200122183(v. 8),7200122190(v. 9),7200122206(v. 10)

涵盖了中国最具特色的 10 个古村落,作者深入当地进行调研,撰写了科学客观的调研报告,真实反映了当地人文历史、风土人情. 这 10 个传统村落是:新堡子村、西沟村、坑根村、山下阳村、深坑村、白麻山村、新叶村、诸葛八卦村、杨源村、长洋村.

17. Industrial geography of China/edited by Li Wenyan, Lu Dadao. Beijing [etc.]: Science Press, 1995. iv, 615 p.: cartes, tabl.; 27cm. ISBN: 7030047907, 7030047908

《工业地理》,李文彦,陆大道编. 科学出版社.

K62　名胜古迹

1. China: China's world cultural and natural heritage. Beijing: New Star Publishers, 2001. 75 pages: color illustrations; 17 ×19cm. ISBN: 7801484509, 7801484505

《中国的世界文化与自然遗产》,崔黎丽,兰佩瑾编. 新星出版社.

2. World heritage sites in China. Beijing: China Intercontinental Press, 2003. 251 pages: color illustrations; 31cm. ISBN: 7508502264, 7508502267

《中国的世界遗产》,国务院新闻办公室编,五洲传播出版社.

3. 中国世界遗产大观. 古城类,古村落类,宗教建筑类,原始遗址类/主编罗尉宣;中文编撰林可,柳正衡,罗尉宣;英文邹先道;整体设计林建平. 长沙:湖南地图出版社:湖南文艺出版社:经销新华书店,2004. 263 pages: color illustrations, maps;24cm. ISBN:7805525315,7805525310. (华夏瑰宝=Chinese splendors)

英汉对照.

4. 中国世界遗产大观. 宫殿类,坛庙类,陵墓类,军事防御工程类,古典园林类/主编:罗尉宣;中文编撰:林可,柳正衡,罗尉宣;英文:邹先道;整体设计:林建平. 长沙:湖南地图出版社:湖南文艺出版社:经销新华书店,2004. 273 pages: color illustrations, color maps;24cm. ISBN:7805525293,7805525297. (华夏瑰宝 = China splendors)

英汉对照.

5. 中国世界遗产大观. 自然与文化双遗产类/山川,古代工程类/主编罗尉宣;中文编撰林可,柳正衡,罗尉宣;英文邹先道;整体设计林建平. 长沙:湖南地图出版社:湖南文艺出版,2004. 307 pages: color illustrations;24cm. ISBN:7805525307, 7805525303. (华夏瑰宝 = Chinese splendors)

英汉对照.

6. 中国世界遗产=World heritage in China:英文/张侃,胡长书主编;叶荣摄. 广州:华南理工大学出版社,2006. 16, 239 页;彩照;23cm. ISBN:7562323909,7562323907

书名原文:World Heritage in China.

7. Cultural sites/Chief editor Luo Zhewen; English translator Zhang Shaoning. Beijing: Foreign languages Press, 2004. 95 pages: color illustrations, maps; 17cm. ISBN: 7119034022, 7119034027. (World heritage of China)

《人文遗迹》,罗哲文主编.

8. Nature and culture/Chief editor Luo Zhewen; English translator Zhang Shaoning. Beijing: Foreign languages Press, 2004. 94 pages: color illustrations, maps; 17cm. ISBN: 7119034014, 7119034010. (World heritage of China)

《自然与文化》,罗哲文主编.

9. The best of China: natural and cultural wonders/[editor, Yang Chunyan]. Beijing: Foreign Languages Press, 2010. 55 pages: color illustrations; 18cm. ISBN: 7119063263, 711906326X

《最美中国. 自然与文化》,外文出版社编. 选取中国最美的自然景观及人文景观.

10. Intangible culture: passing on the tradition/Qian Minjie. Beijing: Foreign Languages Press, 2007. 107 pages: color

illustrations；19cm. ISBN：7119051536，7119051539

《让无形的文化世代传承：英文》，钱敏杰编著；许效礼译；梁超等摄.（国情故事丛书）.介绍了中国非物质文化遗产的保护现状，并具体介绍了九个有代表性的非物质文化遗产，展现了非物质文化遗产的丰富与多彩.

11. 中国的非物质文化遗产：精装版/《中国的非物质文化遗产》编写组编.北京：北京语言大学出版社，2011.194 页；25cm. ISBN：7561929315，7561929315，7887741509，7887741505

英文题名：China's intangible cultural heritage. 本书选取了中国具有代表性的 60 种非物质文化遗产，共同折射出中国历史和民族的独特影像.

12. 风景名胜：汉英对照/王昊编；徐齐平译.北京：人民文学出版社，2006.143 页；21cm. ISBN：7020048781，7020048786.（中国传统文化双语读本）

英文题名：Showplaces. 本书介绍中国名山大川、风景名胜.

13. Scenic splendor of China/compiled by Chinese National Geography. Beijing：New Star Press，2008. 495 pages：color illustrations，map；20cm. ISBN：7802254619，7802254612

《中国最美的地方排行榜》，《中国国家地理》杂志社编.新星出版社.名胜古迹简介.

14. China：insight traditions and culture/by Su Shuyang. Beijing，China：Dolphin Books，2010. 287 pages：illustrations（chiefly color），1 color map，color portraits，color facsimiles；25cm. ISBN：7801387967，7801387961

《中国读本：青少年版》，苏叔阳著.海豚出版社.介绍中国五千年的文明.

15. China：selected readings/chief editor，Wang Yuanhua. Beijing：Dolphin Books，2010. 2 volumes：illustrations（some color），portraits；26cm. ISBN：7511001054，751100105X

《认识中国》，王元化编.海豚出版社.

16. 古典建筑/林正楠编著.合肥：黄山书社，2016.164 页：彩图；23cm. ISBN：7546141862.（印象中国）

英文题名：Ancient Chinese architecture. 英汉对照.

17. Chinese gardens/Lou Qingxi；translated by Zhang Lei，Yu Hong. Beijing：China international Press，2003. 151 pages：color illustrations；23cm.（Cultural China series）

Contents：The formation and development of the Chinese garden—Private gardens of Ming and Qing Dynasties—Imperial gardens of the Ming and Qing Dynasties—Garden building masters and theories on creating a garden—How to appreciate the beauty of gardens' artistic conception（realm）—The tragedy and revival of the famed gardens.

《中国园林》，楼庆西；张蕾，于红译.五洲传播出版社.

18. Chinese gardens：in search of landscape paradise/Lou Qingxi；translated by Zhang Lei and Yu Hong. 2nd ed.

Beijing：China Intercontinental Press，2010. 167 pages：illustrations（some color）；23cm. ISBN：7508516639，750851663X.（Cultural China series）

《中国园林》，楼庆西著.五洲传播出版社.

19. Chinese architecture：palaces，gardens，temples and dwellings/Cai Yanxin & Lu Bingjie；translated by Andrea Lee & Selina Lim. Beijing：China Intercontinental Press，2006. 154 pages：illustrations（some color）；23cm. ISBN：7508509969，750850996X.（Cultural China series）

《中国建筑艺术：英文》，蔡燕歆，路秉杰著；（新加坡）李（Lee，A.），（新加坡）林（Lim，S.）译.五洲传播出版社.

20. 中国园林：英汉对照/方华文编著；王满良译；贺莺译；李朝渊译.合肥：安徽科学技术出版社，2010. 293 页；25cm. ISBN：7533745172，7533745175

英文题名：Chinese gardens.

21. 中国园林/吕明伟编著.合肥：黄山书社，2011.172 页；21cm. ISBN：7546120300，7546120306.（中国红）

英文题名：The Chinese garden.

（1）合肥：黄山书社，2016.172 页：图；23cm. ISBN：7546152776.（印象中国）

22. 说园：汉英对照/陈从周著.上海：同济大学出版社，2007. 87，106 pages，［30］pages of plates：color illustrations；27cm. ISBN：7560835389，7560835384

本书是我国著名造园家陈从周先生的造园论著.

23. Classical Chinese gardens. Beijing：Foreign Languages Press，2003. 107 pages：color illustrations；18×20cm.（Culture of China）

《中国古代园林》，《中国古代园林》编委会编.

24. Charms of classical Chinese gardens：an ideal ambience for domestic life and pleasures/supervised by Information Office of the State Council，People's Republic of China. Beijing：China Architecture & Building Press：China Intercontinental Press，2006. 261 pages：illustrations（chiefly color）；32cm. ISBN：711208654X，7112086542

《园林古韵：英文》，李敏，吴伟主编.中国建筑工业出版社.

25. Hills and stones of Chinese historic gardens/by Song Shuhua. Shenyang：Liaoning Nationalities Publishing Press，2006. 158 pages；21cm. ISBN：7807222484，7807222484

《中国古典园林的山与石：英文》，宋曙华著.辽宁民族出版社.

26. History of gardens/Wu Shaohui，Dong Yan. Encyclopedia of China Publishing House，2009. 188 p.：ill.（some col.）；21cm. ISBN：7500080565，7500080565.（History of Chinese civilization）

《园林史话》，《中华文明史话》编委会编译.中国大百科全书出版社.

27. Classical private gardens of China/Ruan Yisan；Photographers Chen Jianxing，Ma Yuanhao，Ruan

Yongsan；translators Cao Jianxin，Qian Wei，Wu Keming. Nanjing：Yilin Press，2010. 223 pages：color illustrations；29cm. ISBN：7544712149，7544712141

《江南古典私家园林》，阮仪三主编. 译林出版社.

28. Suzhou's gardens：their historical and cultural background/by Zhang Guoqing；translated by Ju Zuchun. Nanjing：Yilin Press，2004. 143 pages，[2] pages of plates：illustrations（some color）；20cm. ISBN：7806578641，7806578643

《苏州园林：英文》，张国擎著；居祖纯译. 译林出版社.

29. The classical gardens of Suzhou/chief editors Feng Chaoxiong，Fan Yiguang. Beijing：New World Press；China Translation and Publishing Corporation，2007. 185 pages：chiefly color illustrations；29cm. ISBN：7802285088，7802285089.（World heritage sites in China）

《苏州古典园林》，冯朝雄，范贻光主编；杜争鸣，（美）篮雅安（Adam Lanphier），左英英译.

30. 杭州园林：中英对照/安怀起编著，孙骊译. 上海：同济大学出版社，2009. 204 页；27cm. ISBN：7560837536，7560837530

英文题名：Gardens of Hangzhou.

31. 帝王陵寝/刘勇编著. 合肥：黄山书社，2016. 152 页：彩图，肖像；23cm. ISBN：7546152912.（印象中国）

英文题名：Royal mausoleums in China. 英汉对照.

32. 古桥/乔虹编著. 合肥：黄山书社，2016. 170 页：彩图；23cm. ISBN：7546141886.（印象中国）

英文题名：Chinese ancient bridges. 英汉对照.

33. 名寺/梓岩编著. 合肥：黄山书社，2016. 172 页：图，照片；23cm. ISBN：7546141961.（印象中国）

英文题名：Famous temples in China. 英汉对照.

34. 中国名塔：中英对照/桑子长编译. 2 版. 重庆：重庆出版社，2005. 398 页；19cm. ISBN：7536651678

英文题名 Historic Chinese pagodas

35. 名塔/姚兰编著. 合肥：黄山书社，2016. 160 页：图；23cm. ISBN：7546141978.（印象中国）

英文题名：Famous pagodas in China. 英汉对照.

36. 胡同/陈光中编著. 合肥：黄山书社，2016. 168 页：照片；23cm. ISBN：7546141916.（印象中国）

英文题名：Hutong in Beijing. 英汉对照.

37. The Great Wall/Zhang Xishou. Beijing，China；Morning Glory Publishers，2000. 81 pages：illustrations；20 × 22cm. ISBN：7505405934，7505405936

Notes：Text in English，French，German and Japanese

长城，Zhang，Xishou 编. 正文有英文、法文、德文和日文 4 种文字.

38. Throughout the Great Wall/[edited by] Dong Yaohui. Nanjing：Jiangsu Science and Technology Publishing House，2009. 171 pages：color illustrations；24cm. ISBN：7534567087，7534567084

《话说长城：英文版》，董耀会主编. 江苏科学技术出版

社.

39. The Great Wall/text by Wei Xin；photography by Li Shaobai；English translation by Ma Hongjun and Hu Xiaokai. Beijing：New World Press，2009. 131 pages：color illustrations；30cm. ISBN：7510405488，7510405483.（World heritage sites in China）

《长城》，魏昕著；李少白摄. 新世界出版社. 全面介绍了长城的地理风貌和历史沿革及它对中华文明进程的影响.

40. 长城/宋存洋编著. 合肥：黄山书社，2016. 160 页：图；23cm. ISBN：7546141831.（印象中国）

英文题名：The Great Wall. 英汉对照.

41. 丝绸之路/方明编著. 合肥：黄山书社，2016. 140 页：彩图；23cm. ISBN：787546142012.（印象中国）

英文题名：Silk road

42. Ancient Sichuan-Tibet Tea Horse Road/Lainchung Nangsa；translated by ji hua，gao wen xing. Beijing，China：Foreign Languages Press，2007. 241 pages：illustrations（chiefly color），color map；24cm. ISBN：7119038964，7119038966

《茶马古道：英文》，亮炯·朗萨著；纪华，高文星译；钟键，周季泉摄. 川藏茶马古道在历史上，在藏汉民族交流、民族团结中发挥了重要作用，堪称天下第一茶马古道. 本书就是藏族作者亲历川藏茶马古道的真实记述.

43. 茶马古道/刘勇编著. 合肥：黄山书社，2016. 158 页：图；23cm. ISBN：7546141824.（印象中国）

英文题名：Ancient Tea-Horse road

44. Religious sites/Chief editor Luo Zhewen；English translator Ouyang，Weiping. Beijing：Foreign languages Press，2004. 93 pages：color illustrations，maps；17cm. ISBN：7119034006，7119034003.（World heritage of China）

《宗教遗迹》，罗哲文主编. 外文出版社（中国的世界遗产）. 从历史、文化角度介绍中国世界遗产中有关宗教的世界遗产.

45. Imperial sites/Chief editor Luo Zhewen；English translator Ouyang Weiping. Beijing：Foreign languages Press，2004. 95 pages：color illustrations，maps；17cm. ISBN：7119034030，7119034034.（World heritage of China）

《皇家遗迹》，罗哲文主编. 外文出版社（中国的世界遗产）

46. 云中紫禁城：武当山 Wudang Mountains/李发平主编. 北京：中国旅游出版社，2010. 108 页；31cm. ISBN：7503239441，7503239441

英文题名：The Forbidden City of the clouds：Wudang Mountains. 介绍北京故宫与湖北武当山这两个世界文化遗产.

47. 牌坊/马利琴编著. 合肥：黄山书社，2016. 164 页：照片，图；23cm. ISBN：7546152936.（印象中国）

英文题名：Chinese memorial archways. 英汉对照.

48. 中国指南/五洲传播出版社编.北京:五洲传播出版社
2004.543页;22cm. ISBN:7508504291

本书是专门为来中国旅游的外国人编写的.全书分为两
个部分,第一部分简要介绍中国的历史、艺术、园林、宗
教、饮食特点等内容,第二部分介绍全国53个城市的景
点.

K7 中国姓氏

1. Who's who in China. Current leaders/compiled by the
Editorial Board of Who's Who in China. Beijing:Foreign
Languages Press:China International Book Trading
Corp. [distributor], 1989. xx, 1126 pages:
illustrations;27cm. ISBN:0835123529; 0835123525;
711901093X; 7119010939

《中国人名大词典·现任党政军领导人物卷》,《中国人名
大词典》编辑部编.

2. The Chinese surname/Chinese author, Luo Xiaofan;
English translator, Wang Xiaoyu. 合肥:安徽教育出版
社, 2005. 194 pages:illustrations (some color);24cm.
ISBN:753364297X, 7533642976. (中华文化精要丛书=
Essences of Chinese culture)

《中国姓氏》,罗晓帆著;王小雨英译.

3. 姓氏/上官言灵编著.合肥:黄山书社,2016.131页;彩图;
23cm. ISBN:7546152899.(印象中国)

英文题名:Chinese surnames. 英汉对照.

K8 人物传记和回忆录

1. On the long march as guard to Chou En-lai/by Wei Kuo-
lu; [ill. by Shen Yao-yi]. Peking:Foreign Languages
Press, 1978. 104 pages, [5] leaves of plates (1 folded):
illustrations;19cm.

《随周恩来副主席长征》,魏国禄著;沈尧伊插图.

2. Zhou Enlai:a profile/Percy Jucheng Fang, Lucy Guinong
J. Fang. Beijing:Foreign Languages Press:Distributed
by China International Book Trading Corp., 1986. iii,
238 pages, [1] leaf of plates:illustrations (some color);
23cm. ISBN:083511712X, 0835117128

《周恩来传略》,方钜成,姜桂侬著.

3. Memoirs of a Chinese marshal:the autobiographical notes
of Peng Dehuai (1898—1974)/translated by Zheng
Longpu; English text edited by Sara Grimes. Beijing:
Foreign Languages Press, 1984. vi, 523 pages, [15]
pages of plates:illustrations, maps;19cm. ISBN:
0835110524, 0835110525

《彭德怀自述》

4. Inside the red star:the memoirs of Marshal Nie
Rongzhen/[translated by Zhong Renyi]. Beijing, China:
New World Press, 1988. 785 pages:illustrations, portraits;
22cm. ISBN:7800050661, 7800050664, 780005067X

《聂荣臻回忆录》,聂荣臻著.新世界出版社.

5. The best sons and daughters of the Chinese people:

stories of the heroic young fighters in the Chinese
people's volunteers. [China]:All-China Federation of
Democratic Youth, 1951. 60 pages:illustrations;19cm.

抗美援朝英雄人物传记.中华全国青年联合会出版.

(1)[Rev. ed.]. [China]: All-China Federation of
Democratic Youth, 1952. 64 pages, [4] pages of
plates:illustrations;19cm.

6. Stories of the Chinese People's Volunteers/[translated by
teachers of the English Faculty of the Foreign Languages
Department of Futan University]. Peking:Foreign
Languages Press, 1960. 258 pages;21cm.

Contents:An eagle at the firing-line/Liu Chao-jung—The
vehement assault upon tanks/Lao Shih and Li Wei-
sheng—Taking captives alive/Wang Min—The man who
is brave and wise/Wang Shih-tng—A daring air pilot/Liu
Ta-wei—The last drop of water/Leng Feng—Replanting
landmines/Chang Chieh—The underground stronghold/
Hsia Kuang and Lin San—Eyes of the artillery/Chang
Chao—Storming "Old Baldy"/Chien Chu—The heroic
tank/Li Cheng and Li Po-ping.

《中国人民志愿军英雄传》,复旦大学外文系英语教师集
体翻译.

7. A volunteer soldier's day; recollections by men of the
Chinese People's Volunteers in the war to resist U. S.
aggression and aid Korea. Peking:Foreign Languages
Press, 1961. 400 pages:illustrations;

《志愿军一日》.回忆录.

8. Liu Hu-lan:story of a girl revolutionary/by Liang Hsing.
Peking:Foreign Languages Press, 1953. 87 pages;
19cm.

《刘胡兰》,梁星著.人物传记.

9. Better to stand and die:story of Chao i-man, a Chinese
woman revolutionary. Chang Lin and Shu Yang. Peking:
Foreign Languages Press, 1960. 178 p.

《女英雄赵一曼》,张麟,舒扬著,金堤等译.

10. The Red Kiangsi-Kwangtung border region. Peking:
Foreign Languages Press, 1961. 186 pages:illustrations;
19cm.

《红色赣粤边》,杨尚昆著.革命回忆录.

11. Chieh Chen-kuo, guerrilla hero/by Wang Huo. Peking:
Foreign Languages Press, 1961. 121 pages:
illustrations;19cm.

Contents:The Storm Gathers—The General Strike—
Escape—Seeking the Party—The Uprising—Return to
Chaokechuang—The Ordeal—Overnight Family
Reunion—The Suppression of an Outlaw—Chieh Chen-
Kuo Joins the Party—Spring Song—A Traitor Duly
Punished—An awe-inspiring Name in Eastern Hopei—
The Battle of Chinchuang—Epilogue.

《赤胆忠心》,王火著.革命回忆录.

12. Fang Chih-min, revolutionary fighter. Peking:Foreign

Languages Press, 1962. 132 pages：illustrations；19cm.

《方志敏战斗的一生》,缪敏著.

13. Iron bars but not a cage：Wang Jo-fei's days in prison/by Yang Chih-lin；[translated by Chang Pei-chi]. Peking：Foreign Languages Press, 1962. 146 pages：illustrations；19cm.

《王若飞在狱中》,杨植霖著,张培基译.

14. The unquenchable spark. Peking：Foreign Languages Press, 1963. 152 pages：illustrations, folded map；19cm.

Contents：Guerrillas in southern Kiangsi, by Chen Yi. — Bitter years of struggle, by Yang Shang-kuei. —A narrow escape, by Chung Chun-shan. —Hold on to the struggle in the Hun an-Kiangsi border region, by Tuan Huan-ching. —Flame on high mountains, by Peng Shou-sheng. —True friendship, by Tan Chi-lung. —Under the enemy's nose, by Huang Chin-sze. —Thrice we fooled the enemy, by Lin Weihsien. —We left our mountain base, by Hsu Chi-chang. —Before the evacuation, by Chen Yun-lung. —Night raid on Lungyen, by Yu Ping-hui. —The ambush at Chinmu Ridge, by Huang Chui-ming. —Loyalty as deep as the sea, by Wu Li-pi. —The unquenchable spark, by Wang Yung-hsin. —Fighting in southwest Chekiang, by Yu Lung-kuei.

《火种不灭》.革命人物传记.

15. The long march：eyewitness accounts. Peking：Foreign Languages Press, 1963. 223 pages：illustrations, folded map；19cm.

《回忆长征》,译自《星火燎原》一书.

16. Stories of the Long March. Shanghai：Shanghai yi wen chu ban she, 1978. 124 p.：ill.；19cm.

《长征故事》,《长征回忆录》英语读物注释小组注. 上海译文出版社.

17. Liu Ying-chun—a worthy son of the people. Peking：Foreign Languages Press, 1967. 30 pages：illustrations；18cm.

《人民的好儿子刘英俊》

18. Battle hero Mai Hsien-teh/by a Liberation Army Daily correspondent. Peking：Foreign Languages Press, 1967. 25 pages：illustrations, portraits；18cm.

《战斗英雄麦贤得》,《解放军报》记者.

19. In the service of the people：the story of Communist fighter, Tsai Yung-hsiang. Peking：Foreign Languages Press, 1968. 31 pages：illustrations, portraits；18cm.

《一心为公的共产主义战士蔡永祥》

20. Men Ho, good cadre boundlessly loyal to Chairman Mao's revolutionary line. Peking：Foreign Languages Press, 1969. 67 pages, [2] leaves of plates：illustrations；18cm.

《无限忠于毛主席革命路线的好干部：门合》

21. Lei Feng, chairman Mao's good fighter/Chen Kuang-

sheng. Peking：Foreign Languages Press, 1968. 101 pages；19cm.

《毛主席的好战士：雷锋》,陈广生著.

22. Outstanding proletarian fighters. Peking：Foreign Languages Press, 1971. 91 pages；19cm.

《无产阶级的先锋战士》

23. My family：story told by Tao Cheng/Recorded by staff members of the Workers' Pub. House. Illustrated by Hou Yi-min. Peking Foreign Languages Press, 1960. 134 p illus., ports 19cm.

《我的一家》,陶承口述；何家栋,赵洁执笔. 工人出版社整理.

(1) My family：reminiscences of a revolutionary/Tao Cheng. Beijing：Foreign Languages Press, 1986. 124 p.：ill.

(2) 2nd ed. Beijing：Foreign Languages Press, 1987. 124 pages：photographs；19cm. ISBN：0835115526, 083511552

24. 科学骄子：汉英对照/中国科学院国际学术交流中心,北京华夏前程教育研究院编著. 北京：原子能出版社, 2006. 851 页；26cm. ISBN：7502236988, 7502236984

本书介绍了部分两院院士、中国科学院部分专家学者、国内部分大专院校、研究院所的专家以及他们的成果.

25. Profiles of 100 Chinese academicians/["Qian jiang wan bao". Beijing：Foreign Languages Press, 2008. 284 pages：color portraits；24cm. ISBN：7119055596; 7119055593

《走进中国 100 位院士的家》,《钱江晚报》主编.

26. 一粒种子改变世界 = The man who puts an end to hunger Yuan Longping, "Father of Hybrid Rice"：袁隆平传：英文/邓湘子,邓映如著. 北京：外文出版社,2007. 232 页；24cm. ISBN：7119051093, 7119051091

袁隆平传记.

27. Li Shih-chen, great pharmacologist of ancient China/Chang Hui-chien. Peking：Foreign Languages Press, 1960. 67 pages：illustrations；19cm.

《李时珍：中国古代伟大的药物学家》,张慧剑著.

28. An Indian freedom fighter in China：a tribute to Dr. D. S. Kotnis/written by Sheng Xiangong with assistance from Lu Jishan and Zhang Changman；[translated by Zhang Sen；illustrated by Jin Hede]. Beijing：Foreign Languages Press：Distributed by China Publications Centre, 1983. vi, 187 pages, [16] pages of plates：illustrations, portraits；19cm.

《柯棣华大夫》,盛贤功等著.

29. Dr. Wu Yingkai's memoir：seventy years (1927—1997) of studying, practicing and teaching medicine/chief editor Lawrence W. O'Neal；translators and co-editors Hong Chi Suen, Victoria Hong Gao. Beijing：China Science and Technology Press, 2006. viii, 238 pages：illustrations；21cm. ISBN：7504644102, 7504644107

《学医行医传医 70 年：1927～1997：吴英恺回忆录：英文》，吴英恺著；李式琰等译. 中国科学技术出版社.

30. 英才济苍生：宫颈癌疫苗发明者周健博士／粟明鲜，瞿佳主编. 北京：人民卫生出版社，2008. 310 页；29cm. ISBN：7117101172

周健博士是子宫颈癌疫苗发明者之一.

31. Our guardian angels/Wang Yibing；translated by Transan. Beijing：China Intercontinental Press, 2009. 68 pages：color illustrations；19cm. ISBN：7508515960, 750851596X

《我们的守护神》，王一冰编著. 五洲传播出版社. 讲述了扎根新疆的广大医护工作者的光荣事迹.

32. 我的非洲十年：英文版／仵民宪著. 北京：世界知识，2018. 15，251 页；24cm. ISBN：7501256648

33. Make new citizens of the world/Yan Hongguo zhu；translated by Ego. Beijing：China Intercontinental Press, 2010. 217 p. ：ill. ；24cm. ＋ 1 CD. ISBN：7508517049, 7508517040. (Roads to the world)

《做世界新民》，晏鸿国著. 五洲传播出版社（中外文化交流故事丛书）. 介绍了"世界平民教育之父"晏阳初博士以平民教育和乡村改良来改造世界的理想和实践，及其在世界范围内的社会影响.

34. The man who brought the Olympics to China：the story of Zhang Boling/compiled by Sun Hailin；［translators，Liu Jieying ［and others］］. Beijing：New World Press, 2008. 237 pages：illustrations；24cm. ISBN：7802287327, 7802287324

《中国奥运先驱：张伯苓》，孙海麟著. 新世界出版社.

35. He Zhenliang and China's Olympic dream/by Liang Lijuan；translated by Susan Brownell. Beijing：Foreign Languages Press，2007. vii，511 p. ，［36］ p. dela'ms. ：il. col. ；24cm. ISBN：7119048437，7119048430，7119047201，7119047205. (World heritage of China)

《何振梁与中国奥林匹克梦：英文》，梁丽娟著；（美）布劳内尔（Brownell，S. ）译. 由何振梁的夫人梁丽娟撰写. 何振梁回忆录.

36. Magnetic Yao Ming/［editors-in-chief：Jiao Yang，Wu Wei；text writer：Yan Xiaoxian；translators：Yang Xinwei and others］. ［Beijing］：China Intercontinental Press，2003. 121 pages：chiefly color illustrations；21cm. ISBN：7508502973，7508502977

Contents：Part 1：The birth of the Ming dynasty—Part 2：The world's eighth wonder—Part 3：An Asian philosopher.

《姚明风采》，阎晓娴编. 五洲传播出版社.

37. The autobiography of a Chinese historian. Leyden，E. J. Brill Ltd. ，1931. 4 p. l. ，［v］-xlii，199，［1］ p. 25cm.

《顾颉刚自传》，顾颉刚（1893—1980）；Hummel，Arthur W. （Arthur William，1884—1975）（美国汉学家）译.

38. 中国文坛名人：英汉对照／方华文编著；慧娟，王金华译.

合肥：安徽科学技术出版社，2010. 319 页；25cm. ISBN：7533745189，7533745183

英文题名：Chinese literati.

39. Modern Chinese writers：self-portrayals/Helmut Martin and Jeffrey Kinkley，editors；Ba Jin… ［et al. ］ and thirty-three others. Armonk，NY：M. E. Sharpe，c1992. xliv，380 p. ：ports. ；24cm. ISBN：0873328167, 0873328175. (Studies on modern China.)

Translation of a selection of short autobiographical essays by different Chinese authors

《当代中国作家自画像》，马汉茂（Martin，Helmut，1940—），金介甫（Kinkley，Jeffrey C. ，1948—）合译. 收录巴金等 33 位 20 世纪中国作家的自传和随笔.

（1）New York：Routledge，2015. xliv，380 pages：portraits；24cm. ISBN：0873328167，0873328166，0873328175，0873328173. （Studies on modern China）

40. Jumping through hoops：autobiographical stories by modern Chinese women writers/edited by Jing M. Wang；translated by Jing M. Wang ＆ Shirley Chang. Hong Kong：Hong Kong Univ. Press ，2003. vi，242 p. ；24cm. ISBN：9622095828，9622095823，9622095836，9622095830

Contents：How I left my mother/Ann Smith. Acknowledgements—About the translators—Introduction—How I left my mother/An E；translated by Jing M. Wang—Jumping through hoops/Bai Wei；translated by Jing M. Wang—Imprints of life/Chu Wenjuan；translated by Jing M. Wang—Journey of twenty-seven years/Lin Beili；translated by Shirley Chang—A brief autobiography/Peng Hui translated by Jing M. Wang—Midpoint of an ordinary life/Xie Bingying；translated by Shirley Chang. My autobiography/Ye Zhongyin translated by Jing M. Wang—Can this also be called an autobiography? /Zhao Qingge；translated by Jing M. Wang—Self-criticism and self-encouragement：a short autobiography of a journalist/Zi Gang—translated by Jing M. Wang—Notes—Glossary—Bibliography.

20 世纪中国女作家自传. Wang，Jing M. 编译.

41. Ancient China's poets/［by Liu Po Chen；translated by Lewis S. Robinson］. Hong Kong：Commercial Press，1978. 107 p. ：ill. ；19cm.

《中国古代诗人》，Liu，Po Chen 著；Robinson，Lewis S. 译. 人物传记.

42. A pictorial biography of Lu Xun. ［Beijing］：People's Fine Arts Publ. House，1981. 174 Seiten：zahlreiche illustrationen；26cm.

《鲁迅画传》，人民美术出版社.

43. Lu Xun，a biography/Wang Shiqing；［Translated by Zhang Peiji；English text edited by Bonnie S. McDougall

and Tang Bowen］. Beijing：Foreign Languages Press：Distributed by China International Book Trading Corp.，1984. 343 pages，［8］pages of plates：illustrations；19cm. ISBN：0835110109，0835110105

《鲁迅传》，王士菁著；张培基译.

44. An age gone by：Lu Xun's clan in decline/recounted by Zhou Jianren；written by Zhou Ye. Beijing，China：New World Press：Distributed by China International Book Trading Corp.（Guoji Shudian），1988. 281 pages，13 pages of plates：illustrations；21cm. ISBN：7800050475，7800050473

《鲁迅故家的败落》，周建人口述；周晔整理. 新世界出版社.

45. The autobiography of Ba Jin/translated by May-lee Chai. Indianapolis：University of Indianapolis Press，2008. xiv，87 pages：illustrations；23cm. ISBN：0880938693，0880938692

《巴金自传》，Chai, May-Lee 译.

46. The autobiography of Shen Congwen/［original Chinese text by Shen Congwen；translated by P. W. Foo, Y. Y. Tan］. Kuala Lumpur：Xue Ren Pub. Enterprise, 2012. 94 pages；21cm. ISBN：9671150108，9671150101

沈从文自传. 沈从文著；Foo, P. W. 和 Tan, Y. Y. 译.

47. Traveller without a map/Hsiao Ch'ien；translated by Jeffrey C. Kinkley. Stanford, Calf.：Stanford University Press，1993. 276 p.，［8］p. of plates：ill.；24cm. ISBN：0804722374，0804722377，0804722382，0804722384

《未带地图的旅人》，萧乾（1910—）；金介甫（Kinkley, Jeffrey C.，1948—）（美国汉学家）译. 回忆录.

48. Scarlet memorial：tales of cannibalism in modern China/Zheng Yi；translated and edited by T. P. Sym；with a foreword by Ross Terrill. Boulder, Colo.：Westview Press，1996. xxii，199 pages：illustrations, maps；24cm. ISBN：081332615X, 0813326153, 0813326168, 0813326160.

Contents：Foreword/Ross Terrill—Historical Chronology，1950—1989—1. Searching Out the Criminal Evidence—2. Some Leftover Cases—3. Wherein Lies the Blame? A Defense of a Nation Known for Its Benevolence—4. Scarlet Memorials All over China—Epilogue：A World in Equilibrium.

《红色纪念碑》，郑义（1947—）；Sym, T. P. 编译. 文革记录.

(1) Boulder, Colo.；Oxford：Westview，1997. 224 pages：illustrations, maps. ISBN：0813326168, 0813326160 2868.

49. Life in Shanghai and Beijing：a memoir of a Chinese writer/Liang Xiaosheng；translated by Li-ching C. Mair and Ruth-Ann Rogaski. Beijing：Foreign Languages Press，1990. 256 p. ISBN：0835124053, 0835124058, 7119012665, 7119012667. (Phoenix books)

《京沪闻见录》，梁晓声著. 自传.

50. Years of sadness：autobiographical writings of Wang Anyi/translated by Wang Lingzhen and Mary Ann O'Donnell；with an introduction by Wang Lingzhen. Ithaca, N. Y.：Cornell University East Asia Program，2009. vii，190 pages；23cm. ISBN：1933947174, 1933947471, 1933947470, 1933947179. (Cornell East Asia series；147)

Contents：Utopian verses—Years of sadness—A woman writer's sense of self.

《忧伤的年代》，王安忆著. 自传.

51. Biography of Ku K'ai-chih/Translated and annotated by Chen Shih-hsiang. Berkeley：University of California Press，1953. 31 p.；24cm. (Chinese dynastic histories translations；no. 2)

《顾恺之自传》，陈世骧（Chen Shih-hsiang，1912—1971）（美国华裔学者）译注.《晋书》选译.

(1) 2nd ed., rev. and enl. Berkeley：University of California Press，1961. 32 pages；24cm. (Chinese dynastic histories translations；no. 2)

(2) ［Whitefish, Mont.］：Literary Licensing，2011. 31 pages；23cm. (Chinese dynastic histories translations；no. 2)

52. Xu Beihong：life of a master painter/by Liao Jingwen；translated by Zhang Peiji. Beijing：Foreign Languages Press，1987. 365 pages，［42］pages of plates：illustrations (some color), portraits；20cm. ISBN：0835115518, 0835115513

《徐悲鸿一生》，廖静文著；张培基译.

53. 艺坛巨匠徐悲鸿：汉英对照/徐庆平主编；徐悲鸿纪念馆编. 2 版. 北京：中国和平出版社，2002. 150 页；29×27cm. ISBN：7801014871

本书以大量图片介绍了徐悲鸿的代表作品和生平，以及徐悲鸿纪念馆成立以来的活动.

54. 等待张念：汉英对照/张念著；贺潇译. 长沙：湖南美术出版社，2007. 312 页：彩照；30cm. ISBN：7535626981, 753562698X

英文题名：Wait-Zhang Nian. 本书叙述 60 年代出生的中国当代美术家张念近 20 年艺术进展的历程. 自传.

55. 唯美至上：汉英对照/李放著. 天津：天津杨柳青画社，2007. 135 页；26cm. ISBN：7807382287, 7807382287. (中国艺术家之最丛书. 表象主义油画名家系列)

英文题名：Aestheticism supremacy：image oil painting masters series. 中国当代著名表象油画家的访谈录.

56. Reminiscences/Xin Fengxia；translated by Gladys Yang. Beijing, China：Chinese Literature，1981. 160 pages，［6］pages of plates：illustrations (some color)；19cm. (Panda books)

《新凤霞回忆录》，新凤霞著；戴乃迭（Yang, Gladys，1919—1999）译.

57. The child bride/Wang Ying；［English text edited by

Monica Faulkner]. Beijing：Foreign Languages Press，1989. xii，424 pages，［24］ pages of plates：illustrations；18cm. ISBN：0835122204，0835122207

《从童养媳到电影明星》，王莹(1913—1974)著.

58. Gone hastily/by Xie Fang；translated by Qi Xiaoyun. Guangdong：Jinan University Press，2008. 237 pages，［15］pages of plates：illustrations（some color）；23cm. ISBN：7810798907，7810798901

《往事匆匆》，谢芳著.暨南大学出版社.我国著名电影表演艺术家谢芳的个人回忆录.

59. Sons of heaven：stories of Chinese emperors through the ages/by Cheng Qinhua. Beijing：Foreign Languages Press，2000. vii，341 pages：illustrations；18cm. ISBN：7119020471，7119020471

《中国皇帝故事》，程钦华.

60. Famous emperors in Chinese history/writer，Shangguan Ping；translator，Shao Da. Beijing：China Intercontinental Press，2011. xi，179 pages：color illustrations；21cm. ISBN：7508518107，7508518101

《中国古代皇帝》，上官平著.五洲传播出版社.

61. The feudal empresses of ancient China/Shangguan Ping. Beijing：China Intercontinental Press，2010. vii，185 pages：color illustrations；21cm. ISBN：7508518473，7508518470

《中国古代皇后》，上官平撰稿.五洲传播出版社.选取中国历史上15位著名的皇后，讲述她们的传奇人生.

62. 古代帝王/戚嘉富编著.合肥：黄山书社，2016.162 页：彩图；23cm. ISBN：7546152844.（印象中国）

英文题名：Ancient emperors.英汉对照.

63. Tales of Emperor Qin Shihuang/by Yuan Yang，Xiao Ding. Beijing：Foreign Languages Press，1999. iii，186 pages：illustrations；18cm. ISBN：711902101X，7119021010

《秦始皇的故事》，元阳，晓丁编著.

64. Emperor Qin Shihuang/author Tong Qiang，Li Xiyan；translator Wang Zhengwen. Nanjing University Press，2010. 5，3，197 p.：ill.；24cm. ISBN：7305066085，7305066087.（Collection of critical biographies of Chinese thinkers）

《秦始皇》，童强，李喜燕著.南京大学出版社《中国思想家评传》简明读本）

65. 文成公主(英文)插图本/旺多译.北京：中国旅游出版社，1985.28 页

英文题名：Princess Wencheng

66. From Emperor to citizen：autobiography of Aisin-Gioro Pu Yi/［Translated by W. J. F. Jenner］. Peking：Foreign Languages Press，1964—1965. 2 volumes illustrations，genealogical tables，portraits 21cm.

《从皇帝到公民：我的前半生》，爱新觉罗·溥仪(1906—1967)著；詹纳尔译.上册 1964 年，下册 1965 年.

(1)2nd ed. Peking：Foreign Languages Press，1983.

(2)Oxford；New York：Oxford University Press，1987. xv，502 p.，［8］p. of plates：ill.，ports.；20cm. ISBN：0192820990.（Oxford paperbacks）

(3)Beijing：Foreign Languages Press，1989. 496 p.，［28］p. of plates：ill.；21cm. ISBN：0835111598，7119007726

67. My husband Puyi：the last emperor of China/told by Li Shuxian；written by Wang Qingxiang；translated by Ni Na. Beijing：China Travel & Tourism Press，2008. xi，280 pages：illustrations，portraits；23cm. ISBN：7503234835，7503234830

《我的丈夫溥仪：中国的末代皇帝》，李淑贤忆述.中国旅游出版社.

68. Confucius，"Sage" of the reactionary classes/Yang Rongguo. Peking：Foreign Languages Press，1974. 66 pages；19cm.

《反动阶级的"圣人"：孔子》，杨荣国著.

69. In the mansion of Confucius' descendants：an oral history/by Kong Demao and Ke Lan；［translated by Rosemary Roberts］. Beijing，China：New World Press：Distributed by China International Book Trading Corp.，1984. 292 pages，［16］pages of plates：illustrations（some color）；18cm. ISBN：0835113957，0835113953.（China spotlight series）

《孔府内宅轶事：孔子后裔的回忆》，孔德懋口述；柯兰整理；罗乐懿译.新世界出版社.

70. Typical women of China/translated from a popular native work on the virtues，words，deportment，and employment of the women of China，by the late Miss A. C. Safford；edited by John Fryer. 2nd ed. Shanghai：Kelly & Walsh，limited，c1899. x，192 p.，plates.；17×17cm.

《列女传》(选译)，刘向(约公元前 77—前 6)；Safford，Miss A. C.译.

71. Biography of Lü Kuang. Translated and annotated by Richard B. Mather. Berkeley，University of California Press，1959. 141 p. fold. map（in pocket）24cm.（Chinese dynastic histories translations，no. 7）

Translation of Chin shu 122. 1a-8a，compiled by Fang Hsühan-ling and others

《吕光传》，房玄龄(579—648)；马瑞志(Mather，Richard B.，1913—)(美国汉学家)译.

72. 马可·波罗的中国传奇/王硕丰编著；(新加坡)Andrea Lee 翻译.北京：五洲传播出版社：，2010.161 页；23cm. ISBN：7508517148，7508517148.（中外文化交流故事丛书）

英文题名：Marco Polo in China.

73. 紫禁城里的洋画师/朱菁编著.北京：五洲传播出版社，2009. 135 页；23cm. ISBN：7508517179，7508517172

英文题名：Foreign painter in the Forbidden City. 意大利人朗世宁，1715 年来中国传教，随即进入清朝皇宫成为

宫廷画家.本书讲述了郎世宁在中国的故事,结合其作品,介绍这位中西文化交流的重要使者.

74. My journey in mystic China: Old Pu's travel diary/John Blofeld; translated from the Chinese by Daniel Reid. 1st U. S. ed. Rochester, Vt.: Inner Traditions, 2008. xxxv, 247 p., [8] p. of plates: ill. , map; 24cm. ISBN: 1594771576, 159477157X

《老普游记:一个外国人对中国的回忆》,普乐道(Blofeld, John, 1913—1987)(英国汉学家);Reid, Daniel P. (1948—)译.

75. An Irishman in China: Robert Hart, Inspector General of the Chinese Imperial Maritime customs/Zhao Changtian; translated by Yang Shuhui and Yang Yunqin. New York: Better Link Press, 2014. 191 pages; 22cm. ISBN: 1602202382, 1602202389

《大清海关总税务司赫德》,赵长天;Yang, Shuhui 和 Yang, Yunqin 合译.

76. Guide to the memorials of seven leading officials of nineteenth-century China/prepared by the staff of the Modern Chinese History Project; edited by Chung-li Chang and Stanley Spector; translators: Mort Bobrow [and others] Foreword by Franz Michael. Seattle: University of Washington Press, c1955. xv, 457 p. ; 28cm. (University of Washington publications on Asia)

19 世纪中国人物传记资料. Zhang, Zhongli(1920—), Spector, Stanley(1924—)编,翻译了 19 世纪中国 7 位高级官员的史料.

77. The last eunuch of China: the life of Sun Yaoting/Jia Yinghua; translated by Sun Haichen. [Beijing]: China Intercontinental Press, 2008. 314 pages: illustrations; 23cm. ISBN: 7508514079, 7508514076

《末代太监孙耀庭》,贾英华著.五洲传播出版社.

78. Sun-Yat-Sen in Shanghai/written by Huang Yaping; translated by Pan Qin. Shanghai: Shanghai Bookstore Publishing House, 2010. 92 pages: illustrations (some color), portraits; 18cm. ISBN: 7545801316, 7545801318. (Rediscovering China)

《孙中山在上海》,黄亚平著.上海书店出版社.

79. Eight years in the Ministry of Foreign Affairs (January 1950—October 1958): memoirs of a diplomat/by Wu Xiuquan. Beijing, China: New World Press; Distributed by China International Book Trading Corp. , 1985. 131 pages, [4] pages of plates: illustrations; 18cm. (China spotlight series)

《在外交部八年的经历》,伍修权著.新世界出版社.

80. The diplomat from China/Ruan Hong. Beijing: Foreign Languages Press, 2007. xv, 648 p. , [8] p. of plates: il.; 25cm. ISBN: 7119047874, 7119047876

《一个外交家的经历:韩叙传:英文》,阮虹著.

81. Chinese style: the diplomatic career of Wu Jianmin/text: Wang Fan; translators: Wang Guozhen, Zhao Ximing. Beijing, China: Foreign Languages Press, 2010. xi, 415 pages, [24] pages of plates: illustrations; 24cm. ISBN: 7119059920, 7119059921

《中国风格:吴建民的大使生涯》,王凡著.

82. Heavy storm and gentle breeze: a memoir of China's diplomacy/Tang Jiaxuan. Beijing, China: Foreign Languages Press Co. , 2011. 565 pages: illustrations; 24cm. ISBN: 7119071046, 7119071041

《劲雨煦风:唐家璇外交回忆录》,唐家璇著.

83. Madame Wu Chien-Shiung: the first lady of physics research/Chiang Tsai-Chien; translated by Wong Tang-Fong. Hackensack,] New Jersey: World Scientific, [2014]. xxxvi, 264 pages: illustrations; 24cm. ISBN: 9814374842, 9814374849, 9814368926, 981436892X

《吴健雄传》,江才健著;邓炎昌(Wong, Tang-Fong Frank, 1944—)译.

84. 这个世界会好吗?:梁漱溟晚年口述/梁漱溟,(美)艾恺著;(美)艾恺译.北京市:外语教学与研究出版社,2010. 295 页;23cm. ISBN:7513500845. ("博雅双语名家名作"系列)

英文题名:Has man a future?: dialogues with the last Confucian. 英汉对照.

85. 中国改革开放的先行者:谷牧回忆录/谷牧著;陈秋萍[等]英文翻译.北京:外文出版社有限责任公司,2016. 625 页:照片;24cm. ISBN:7119102818

英文题名:Gu Mu pioneer of China's reform and opening up

86. Life is life/Zhang Haidi. Beijing: Dolphin Books, 2014. xiv, 172 pages: illustrations; 23cm. ISBN: 7511021939, 751102193X. (Best Chinese children's literature＝中国儿童文学走向世界精品书系)

《生命的追问》,张海迪;王国振,钱清合译.

87. 只要肯登攀:一个听障人士的奋斗史:英汉对照/李冯琪华,李嘉耀著. 开封:河南大学出版社,2005. 112 页; 21cm. ISBN:7810913417

李嘉耀,幼年失聪;在家庭呵护及全面的施教下,经过个人的艰苦努力,终于在学业上有所成就,事业上实现了理想,其自身经历引发的特殊教育个案的实例有值得借鉴和吸取之处.

88. 30 reflections of China's 30 years of reform, 1978—2008. Beijing: Foreign Languages Press, 2008. 5, 232 pages: illustrations; 23cm. ISBN: 7119054391, 7119054392

《30 年,30 人:见证中国改革开放》,潘灯等著.选取了中国有代表性的 30 人,通过讲述他们在这 30 年的亲身经历,多角度展示 30 年间中国社会所发生的变化.

89. Our seven years together: stories about the Olympics in Beijing: Beijing news radio/ed. Liu Qing… [et al.]. Beijing: China Youth Press, 2008. 205 p. : ill. ISBN: 7500683063, 7500683065

《咱们这七年:发生在北京的奥运故事》,北京人民广播电台新闻广播编.中国青年出版社.采访了从申奥成功到如今这七年中的 100 位人物,他们的命运和奥运紧密相连,他们的生活因为奥运而有所改变.

90. China Inc—36 true stories of Chinese millionaires and how they made their fortunes/ compiled by Zhu Ling. Beijing: New World Press, 2009. 308 p.: col.: ill.; 24cm. ISBN: 7802289253, 7802289254

《财富传奇:他们的第一桶金》,朱灵主编. 新世界出版社. 收录了中国 36 位民营企业家的创业经历,记录了他们如何从一个普通人成长为成功企业家的传奇故事.

91. Miracles of life: challenging cancer/by Han Lintao, Ye Danyang, and Li Yanchun. Beijing: New World, 2009. 160 pages: color illustrations; 19cm. ISBN: 7802288430, 780228843

《创造生命的奇迹:抗癌故事》,韩林涛等著. 新世界出版社. 讲述了癌症患者与癌症抗争的经历.

92. From grasslands to college: a Tibetan boy's journey/by Gongboo Sayrung. Beijing: Foreign Languages Press, 2007. 183 pages; 21cm. ISBN: 7119051123, 7119051121

《从草原到大学:一个藏族少年的故事:英文》,贡布·泽仁著. 本书作者是藏族大学生,以第一人称描述一个西藏孩子成长的经历. 自传.

93. Dreaming big in China/by Lu Yang; [transl. by Yang Yaohua [et al.]. Beijing: New World Press, 2009. [8], 296, [1] s.: il. color.; 24cm. ISBN: 7802288416, 780228841X. (China-World cultural exchange series)

《老外的中国梦》,绿杨等著;杨耀华等翻译. 新世界出版社. 收录了 19 个来华工作的外国人到中国寻梦、圆梦的事迹.

94. Sixty by six: these years of ours/by Zhang Xueying, Feng Jianhua, Zhang Juan, Liu Qiong, Chang Lu. Beijing: Foreign Languages Press, 2009. 159 pages: illustrations (some color); 19cm. ISBN: 7119058054, 7119058053. (国情故事)

《我为共和国工作的岁月》,张学英[等著]. 六位口述者以自己不寻常的亲身经历,从各不相同的角度,讲述了共和国六十年的变迁和发展.

95. (A quarter of) the world in their hands: 19 personal journeys to success/compiled by Huang Youyi. Beijing: New World Press, 2009. 272 pages: illustrations; 24cm. ISBN: 7510405259, 7510405254

《四分之一的世界在他们手中》,黄友义主编. 新世界出版社. 选取建国 60 年以来外交、文化、教育、体育、文艺等各行各业的优秀代表人物十六位,其中包括赵启正、李肇星、赵忠祥、张艺谋、许海峰、梁晓声、李银河、俞敏洪、邓亚萍、韩寒等名人.

96. Chinese life: bitter-sweet portraits 2009/[Fei Yangsheng deng zhu]. Beijing: Foreign Languages Press, 2009. 206 pages: color illustrations; 24cm. ISBN: 7119059686, 7119059688

《我们中国人》,费杨生等著. 人物生平事迹.

97. Stories of China's environmental NGOs/[by Cao Baoyin]. Beijing: Foreign Languages Press, 2010. 127 pages: color illustrations; 23cm. ISBN: 7119067254, 7119067257

《环保非政府组织的中国故事》,曹保印著. 介绍 10 多位典型环保人物的感人故事.

98. Chinese women entrepreneurs/[compiled by Dong Shaopeng]. Beijing: New World Press, 2011. 191 pages: illustrations (some color); 24cm. ISBN: 7510418617, 7510418615

《闯进富豪圈的女人》,董少鹏主编. 新世界出版社. 讲述了 14 位中国女富豪的传奇人生故事.

99. Chinese life: bitter-sweet portraits 2011/Hua wen...[et al.]. Beijing: Foreign Languages Press, 2011. 197 p.: ill.; 24cm. ISBN: 7119072285, 7119072289

《我们中国人》,华文[等]撰稿.

100. Toward a democratic China: the intellectual autobiography of Yan Jiaqi/translated by David S. K. Hong and Denis C. Mair; foreword by Andrew J. Nathan. Honolulu: University of Hawaii Press, c1992. xviii, 285 p.; 22cm. ISBN: 0824814843, 0824815017. (SHAPS library of translations)

《我的思想自传》,严家其(1942—);Hong, David S. K.,丹尼斯·马尔(Mair, Denis C.)译.

101. The pen and I: the autobiography of a Shanghai businesswoman/by Tang Diyin; transl. by Lily Wu. Beijing: New World Press, 1985. 171 p.: ill.; 18cm. (China sports series)

《金笔缘:一位上海女工商业者的自述》,汤蒂因著;吴增芳译. 新世界出版社.

102. A KMT war criminal in new China/written by Shen Zui; with the assistance of Shen Meijuan; transl. by Liang Xintu and Sun Binghe. Changsha: Hunan People's Publishing House; Beijing: Foreign Languages Press, 1986. IX, 374 p.: ill.; 18cm. ISBN: 0835115992, 0835115995

《我这三十年》,沈醉著.

103. When they were young/edited by Women of China and New World Press. Beijing, China: New World Press; Distributed by China Publications Centre, 1983. 198 pages, [32] pages of plates: illustrations; 19cm. (China spotlight series)

《当她们年轻的时候》,张金宝等著,新世界出版社. 人物传记.

104. Cry for life＝生命的呐喊/张雅文著; Saul Thompson 译. 北京: 中译出版社, 2016. 561 p.; 21cm. ISBN: 787500143253, 7500143257. (中国报告系列)

N 类　自然科学

N1　科技古籍英译

1. Introductory study of Huangdi neijing/Xiwen Luo.

Beijing：Zhongguo zhong yi yao chu ban she, 2009. 398 pages：illustrations；25cm. ISBN：7802316348, 7802316340

《黄帝内经》,罗希文主编.中国中医药出版社.分两部分：第一部分是对《黄帝内经》作者、源流、主要学术观点的考证；第二部分是《黄帝内经》前22篇的原文及注释.

2. 黄帝内经：汉英对照/(唐)王冰原注；吴连胜,吴奇英译.北京：中国科学技术出版社,1997. 14, 831 pages；illustrations；26cm. ISBN：7504622311, 7504622310

英文题名：Yellow Empero's canon of internal medicine

3. Huangdi neijing lingshu. NVN ed. , English version. Sugar Grove：Jung Tao Productions, 2005—2010. ISBN：0980041705 (v. 1), 0980041708 (v. 1), 0980041712 (v. 2), 0980041716 (v. 2), 0980041729 (v. 3), 0980041724 (v. 3)

Contents：V. 1. Books I-III with commentary—V. 2. Book IV-V with commentary—V. 3. Bookss VI-IX with commentary.

Notes："Translated into French with added commentaries by：Nguyen Van Nghi, MD, Tran Viet Dzung, Md Christine Recours-Nguyen, MD. "

《皇帝内经·灵枢》,Nguyen, Van Nghi 译.

4. Huang di nei jing ling shu：the ancient classic on needle therapy/Paul U. Unschuld. Berkeley：University of California Press, 2016. 1 volume；23cm. ISBN：0520292253, 0520292251

《皇帝内经·灵枢》,Unschuld, Paul U. (Paul Ulrich, 1943—)著.英汉对照.

5. 黄帝内经·灵枢= Yellow emperor's canon of medicine. Spiritual pivot/李照国英译；刘希茹今译. 西安：世界图书出版公司, 2008. 3 册([43], 1167 页)：图, 肖像；24cm. ISBN：7506269827

6. Yellow Emoperor's canon of medicine. Spiritual pivot/[translated by Li Zhaoguo, Liu Xiru]. Vancouver, BC：Chiao Liu Pub. (Candada)Inc. ；Hong Kong：Chiao Liu Pub. Trading Co. (distriibutor), 2010. 3 volumes (xxvii, 955 pages)；21cm. ISBN：0981181677, 0981181678. (Wisdom of Chinese culture series. The 2nd series；10＝中华文化智能系列. 第 2 辑；10 中华文化智能系列. 第 2 辑；10)

《黄帝内经·灵枢》,李照国,刘希茹合译.

7. Huang Ti nei ching su wên. The Yellow Emperor's classic of internal medicine. Chapters 1—34 translated from the Chinese with an introductory study by Ilza Veith. Baltimore, Williams & Wilkins, 1949. xix, 253 p. illus. , port. 26cm.

《黄帝内经·素问》,Veith, Ilza 译.是译者的博士论文内容.

(1)New ed. Berkeley, University of California Press, 1966. xxi, 260 p. illus. , facsim. 24cm.

(2)New ed. Taipei：Southern Materials Center, 1982. xxi, 260 pages：illustrations；22cm. (Chinese

medicine series；8)

8. The Yellow Emperor's classic of medicine：a new translation of the Neijing Suwen with commentary/Maoshing Ni. Boston：Shambhala, 1995. xvi, 316 pages；23cm. ISBN：1570620806, 1570620805

《黄帝内经·素问》,Ni, Maoshing 译.

9. The medical classic of the Yellow Emperor/translated by Zhu Ming. Beijing, China：Foreign Languages Press, 2001. v, 302；27cm. ISBN：711902664X, 7119026640

《黄帝内经·素问》,朱明(1968—)译.

10. Huang Di nei jing su wen：nature, knowledge, imagery in an ancient Chinese medical text：with an appendix, the doctrine of the five periods and six qi in the Huang Di nei jing su wen/Paul U. Unschuld. Berkeley；Los Angeles；London：University of California Press, 2003. XII-520 p. ：ill. , couv. ill. en coul. ；24cm. ISBN：0520233220, 0520233225

《黄帝内经·素问》,文树德(Unschuld, Paul U.〈 Paul Ulrich〉, 1943—)(德国医学史家)译.

11. 黄帝内经·素问：汉英对照/李照国英译；刘希茹今译. 西安：世界图书出版西安公司,2005. 3 册（1293 页）；23cm. ISBN：7506269813, 7506269810.(大中华文库)

英文题名：Yellow Emperor's canon of medicine plain conversation.

12. Introductory study of Huangdi neijing/Xiwen Luo. Beijing：Zhongguo zhong yi yao chu ban she, 2009. 398 pages：illustrations；25cm. ISBN：7802316348；7802316340.

Notes："My translation of the first 22 chapters of Suwen... the first (and perhaps the most important)part of Neijing"—Preface.

《黄帝内经·素问》,罗希文译,中国中医药出版社出版.

13. Huang di nei jing su wen［Yellow emperor inner classic plain questions］：translation workbook/Jim Cleaver. Portland, Or. ：Jun-Zi Publications, 2012. 5 volumes；28cm.

《黄帝内经·素问》,Cleaver, Jim 译.

14. Huangdi Neijing：a synopsis with commentaries = "Neijing zhi yao" yi gu/translated and annotated by Y. C. Kong. Hong Kong：Chinese University Press, 2010. xlv, 495 p. ：ill. ；24cm. ISBN：9629964207；9629964201

《内经知要》译诂,李中梓(1588—1655),江润祥(Kong, Y. C.)译.

15. Nan-ching：the classic of difficult issues：with commentaries by Chinese and Japanese authors from the third through the twentieth century/translated and annotated by Paul U. Unschuld. Berkeley：University of California Press, 1986. viii, 760 pages：illustrations；24cm. ISBN：0520053729, 0520053724. (Comparative studies of health systems and medical care)

《难经》，文树德（Unschuld, Paul U.〈Paul Ulrich〉，1943—）（德国医学史家）译.英汉对照.

　　(1)Second edition, revised and updated. Oakland, California：University of California Press，2016. viii，638 pages：illustrations；24cm. ISBN：0520292277，0520292278.（The Chinese medical classics；Comparative studies of health systems and medical care）

16. The classic of difficulties：a translation of the Nan Jing/Li Shi-zhen. Boulder, CO：Blue Poppy Press, 1999. 146 pages. ISBN：0585147957，0585147956

　　《难经》，Flaws, Bob(1946—)译.

17. Nan Gyo：the classic of difficulties/Masakazu Ikeda；translated by Takashi Furue. St Leonards, NSW：AUSTJM, St Leonards, NSW：Serica Medical Supplies P/L, 2016. iv, 368 pages：illustrations；26cm. ISBN：1944784881，1944784888

　　Notes：In English with some Chinese and Japanese script.

　　《难经》. Ikeda, Masakazu 著；Furue, Takashi 译.

18. Treatise on febrile diseases caused by cold：a classic of traditional Chinese medicine（Shanghan Lun）/by Zhang Zhongjing, translated by Luo Xiwen, translation revised by Shi Jizhao, introduction by Ren Yingqiu. Beijing, China：New World Press，1986. 442 pages：illustrations；22cm. ISBN：0835113981，0835113984

　　《伤寒论》，（东汉）张仲景. 新世界出版社.

19. Treatise on febrile diseases caused by cold, with 500 cases：a classic of traditional Chinese medicine with ancient and contemporary case studies/written by Zhang Zhongjing；compiled and translated by Luo Xiwen. Beijing：New World Press，1993. 576 pages：illustrations. ISBN：7800051838，7800051838

　　《伤寒论及500医案》，张仲景著；罗希文编译. 新世界出版社.

20. 伤寒论＝Treatise on febrile disease caused by cold（Shanghan Lun）/（东汉）张仲景著；罗希文英译. 北京：商务印书馆，2007. 16，239 页；24cm. ISBN：7801878496.（大中华文库：汉英对照）

　　(1)伤寒论＝Treatise on febrile disease caused by cold/（东汉）张仲景著；罗希文英译. 北京：新世界出版社，2016. 370 页；23cm. ISBN：7510456534

21. Introduction to treatise on exogenous febrile disease＝伤寒论入门/compiled by Huang Hai. Shanghai：Shanghai University of Traditional Chinese Medicine Press, 2005. 11，376 pages；21cm. ISBN：781010909X，7810109093

　　《伤寒论入门：英文》，黄海编著. 上海中医药大学出版社.

22. 伤寒论＝On cold damage/张仲景著；刘希茹今译；李照国英译. 上海：上海三联书店，2017. 439 页；24cm. ISBN：7542657060

　　对照读物.

23. Synopsis of prescriptions of the golden chamber（jingui yaolue fanglun）/written by Zhang Zhongjing；translated by Luo Xiwen. Beijing：New World Press, 1987. 366 pages：illustrations, portraits；23cm. ISBN：7800050046，7800050041

　　《金匮要略方论》，（汉）张仲景著；罗希文译. 新世界出版社.

　　(1)金匮要略＝Synopsis of prescriptions of the golden chamber（Jingui yaolue）/（东汉）张仲景著；罗希文英译. 北京：新世界出版社，2007. 16，311 页：图；24cm. ISBN：7801878267.（大中华文库：汉英对照）

　　(2)金匮要略＝Synopsis of prescriptions of the golden chamber/（东汉）张仲景著；罗希文英译. 北京：新世界出版社，2016. 358 页；23cm. ISBN：7510457142

24. Synopsis of prescriptions of the golden chamber with 300 cases：a classic of traditional Chinese medicine with ancient and contemporary case studies/written by Zhang Zhongjing；translated by Luo Xiwen. Beijing：New World Press，1995. 561 pages：illustrations；23cm. ISBN：7800052915；7800052910

　　《金匮要略方论及300医案》，（汉）张仲景著；罗希文译. 新世界出版社.

25. 汉英对照《金匮要略》＝Chinese-English Textbook：synopsis of prescriptions of the Golden Chamber/阮继源，张光霁编著. 上海：上海科技出版社，2003. 176 页；26cm. ISBN：7532370321

26. 金匮要略/张仲景著；希茹今译；李照国英译. 上海：上海三联书店，2017. 2 册（671 页）；24cm. ISBN：7542657077

　　英文题名：Essentials of the golden cabinet. 汉英对照.

27. 金匮要略选读：英文/成肇智，陈家旭编译. 人民卫生出版社，2018. 26cm. ISBN：7117255523

28. 汉英对照神农本草经/孙星衍考据；刘希茹今译；李照国英译. 上海：上海三联书店，2017. 3 册（33，1253 页）；26cm. ISBN：7542659491

　　英文题名：Agriculture god's canon of materia medica

29. The divine farmer's materia medica：a translation of the Shen nong ben cao jing/by Yang Shou-zhong. Boulder, CO：Blue Poppy Press, 1998. xvi, 205；23cm. ISBN：0936185961，0936185965

　　《神农本草经》，杨守忠译.

30. Le classique de la matière médicale du Laboureur céleste ＝Divine farmer's classic of materia medica/texte original, Gu Guanguang；traduction et annotations, André Dubreuil, Xiaoya Dubreuil；illustrations, Liu Jingzeng. Beijing：Foreign Languages Press, 2015. 1 vol.（VII-875 p.）：ill. en coul.；29cm. ISBN：7119094229 711909422X

　　《全图神农本草经》，Dubreuil, André（1964—）和 Dubreuil, Xiaoya(1969—)合译. 中英法 3 语对照.

31. The divine farmer's classic of materia medica：Shen nong bencao jing＝Shennong ben cao jing/translated by Sabine

Wilms. Corbett, Or.：Happy Goat Productions, 2016. liv, 516 pages：illustrations；18cm. ISBN：0991342945, 0991342941

《神农本草经》,Wilms, Sabine 译.

(1)3rd edition. Corbett, Or.：Happy Goat Productions, 2017. xlii, 549 pages：illustrations；18cm. ISBN：0991342952；099134295X

32. Master Hua's classic of the central viscera：a translation of Hua Tuo's Zhong Zang Jing/by Yang Shou-zhong. Boulder, CO：Blue Poppy Press, 1993. xxxi, 215 pages；22cm. ISBN：0936185430, 0936185439

《中藏经》,杨守忠译.

33. Systematic classic of acupuncture & moxibustion/by Huang-fu Mi；translation by Yang Shou-zhong and Charles Chace. Boulder, Colo. Blue Poppy Press, 1993. xxvi, 730 pages；27cm. ISBN：0936185295, 0936185293

《黄帝针灸甲乙经》,皇甫谧（215—282）撰；杨守忠和 Chace, Charles 合译.

(1)[Rev. ed.]. Boulder, CO：Blue Poppy Press, 2004. xxviii, 476 pages；27cm. ISBN：0936185295, 0936185293

34. Complete works of Huangfu Mi/editor in chief：Shi Xinghai；[translated by Yang Shouzhong, Feng Bingyun]. Beijing：China Publishing Group/China Translation & Publishing Corporation, 2009. 3 v.；29cm. ISBN：7500123521

《皇甫谧遗著集》,皇甫谧（215—282）；石星海主编；杨守忠等译.

35. The pulse classic＝[Mai jing]：a translation of the Mai jing/by Wang Shu-he；translated by Yang Shou-zhong. Boulder, CO：Blue Poppy Press, 1997. xii, 376 pages：illustrations；27cm. ISBN：0936185759, 0936185750

《脉经》,王叔和；杨守忠译.

36. Essential subtleties on the silver sea：the Yin-hai jing-wei：a Chinese classic on ophthalmology/translated and annotated by Jürgen Kovacs and Paul U. Unschuld. Berkeley：University of California Press, 1998. xii, 503 pages；24cm. ISBN：0520080580, 0520080584. (comparative studies of health systems and medical care；no. 38)

《银海精微》,孙思邈（581—682）；Kovacs, Jürgen, 文树德（Unschuld, Paul U.〈Paul Ulrich〉, 1943—）（德国医学史家）合译.

37. Bèi jī qiān jīn yào fāng＝Essential prescriptions worth a thousand in gold for every emergency, volumes 2—4 on gynecology/Sūn Sī-Miǎo；[translated by] Sabine Wilms, Ph. D. Portland, OR：The Chinese Medicine Database, 2007. xv, 777 pages；26cm. ISBN：0979955204, 0979955203

《备急千金要方》,孙思邈（581—682）；Wilms, Sabine 译.

38. Venerating the root：Sun Simiao's Bei ji qian jin yao fang (Essential prescriptions worth a thousand in gold for every emergency), volume 5：pediatrics/translated by

Sabine Wilms. Corbett：Happy Goat Productions, 2013. xxxviii, 323 pages；23cm. ISBN：0991342909, 0991342907

《千金要方·第五卷·少小婴孺方》,孙思邈（581—682）；Wilms, Sabine 编译.

(1)Corbett：Happy Goat Productions, 2015. xxv, 544 pages；23cm. ISBN：0991342933, 0991342938

(2)Portland, Ore.：Happy Goat, 2017. xxxvii, 323p；20.5cm. ISBN：0991342976, 0991342976

39. Brush talks from dream brook/translated into modern Chinese by Hu Daojing, Jin Liangnian and Hu Xiaojing；translated into English by Wang Hong and Zhao Zheng. Chengdu Shi：Sichuan ren min chu ban she, 2008. 2 v. (41, 1065 p.)：port. ；24cm. ISBN：7220077418, 7220077416. (Library of Chinese classics＝大中华文库)

《梦溪笔谈》,沈括（1031—1095）；胡道静, 金良年, 胡小静今译；王宏, 赵峥英译.

40. T'ang-yin-pi-shih＝Parallel cases from under the pear-tree：a 13th century manual of jurisprudence and detection/translated from the original Chinese with an introd. and notes by R. H. van Gulik. Leiden：Brill, 1956. xiv, 198 p. ；25cm. (Sinica Leidensia edidit Institutum Sinologicum Lugduno-Batavum, vol. 10). (Sinica Leidensia；v. 10.)

《棠阴比事》,桂万荣（生卒年不详,南宋人）；高罗佩（Gulik, Robert Hans van, 1910—1967）（荷兰汉学家）译. 法医学著作.

(1)Westport, Conn. ：Hyperion Press, 1979, c1956. xiv, 198 p. ；22cm. ISBN：0883559080. (Sinica Leidensia；v. 10.)

(2)Crime and punishment in ancient China＝T'ang-yin-pi-shih/R. H. van Gulik. 2 nd ed. Bangkok：Orchid Press, 2007. 1vol. (XIV—198 p.)：ill. ；26cm. 9745240919 (rel), 9745240915 (rel)

41. Li Dong-yuan's treatise on the spleen & stomach：a translation of the Pi wei lun/by Yang Shou-zhong & Li Jian-yong. Boulder, CO：Blue Poppy Press, 1993. xv, 274 pages；23cm. ISBN：0936185414, 0936185415

《脾胃论》,李杲（1180—1251）；杨守忠, Li, Jian-yong 合译.

42. The Hsi yuan lu, or, Instructions to coroners/[translated] by Herbert A. Giles. London：J. Bale, Sons & Danielsson, Ltd. , c1924. 1 p. l. , 49 p. ：illus. ；25cm.

Notes：Reprinted from the Proceedings of the Royal Society of Medicine, 1924, v. 17, Section of the History of Medicine, p. 59—107.

《洗冤集录》,宋慈（1186—1249）；翟理斯（Giles, Herbert Allen, 1845—1935）（英国汉学家）译. 法医学著作. 只是对该书的部分翻译.

43. The washing away of wrongs：forensic medicine in thirteenth-century China/translated by Brian E.

McKnight. Ann Arbor：Center for Chinese Studies, University of Michigan, 1981. xv, 181 pages：illustrations；24cm. ISBN：0892648015, 0892648016, 0892648007, 0892648009. （Science, medicine, and technology in East Asia；v. 1）

《洗冤集录》，宋慈（1186—1249）；McKnight, Brian E. 译.

(1) Taipei：Reprinted by Southern Materials Center, 1982. 49 (pages 59—107), xv, 181 pages：illustrations；22cm. （Science, medicine, and technology in East Asia；；v. 1）

44. The heart & essence of Dan-xi's methods of treatment＝［Danxi zhi fa xin yao］/ a translation of the Dan xi zhi fa xin yao by Yang Shou-zhong. Boulder, CO：Blue Poppy Press, 1993. xxii, 465 pages；22cm. ISBN：0936185503, 0936185507

《丹溪治法心要》，朱震亨（1281—1358）；杨守忠译.

45. Extra treatises based on investigation & inquiry: a translation of Zhu Dan-xi's Ge zhi yu lun/by Yang Shou-zhong & Duan Wu-jin. Boulder, CO：Blue Poppy Press, 1994. xiii, 140 pages. ISBN：0585119392, 0585119397

《格致余论》，朱震亨（1281—1358）；杨守忠，Duan, Wu-jin 合译.

46. Gold mirrors and tongue reflections：the cornerstone classics of Chinese medicine tongue diagnosis—The Ao shi shang han jin jing lu, and The shang han she jian/［commentary and translations by］Ioannis Solos；forewords by Professor Liang Rong and Professor Chen Jia-xu. London：Singing Dragon, 2013. 300 pages：illustrations；26cm. ISBN：1848190955

Solos, Ioannis 编译. 包括对元代《敖氏伤寒金镜录》和清代《伤寒舌鉴》两本医书的翻译.

47. A soup for the Qan：Chinese dietary medicine of the Mongol era as seen in Hu Szu-Hui's Yin-shan cheng-yao：introduction, translation, commentary, and Chinese text/Paul D. Buell, Eugene N. Anderson；appendix by Charles Perry. London；New York：Kegan Paul International；New York：Distributed by Columbia University Press, 2000. xiii, 715 pages：illustrations；24cm. ISBN：0710305831, 0710305834. （Sir Henry Wellcome Asian series）

《饮膳正要》，忽思慧（生卒年不详，于元仁宗延祐年间，即1314—1320 年被选充饮膳太医一职）；Buell, Paul D. 和 Anderson, E. N. （1941—）合译.

48. Plantae medicinalis Sinensis, 2nd ed. Bibliography of Chinese medicinal plants from the Pen Ts'ao Kang Mu... 1596 A. D., by Bernard E. Read... ［and］ Liu Ju-ch'iang... Peking, Dept. of Pharmacology, Peking Union Medical College, in collaboration with the Peking Laboratory of Natural History, 1927. 2 p. l, xi, 106 p., 1 l. 30cm. （Flora Sinensis, ser. A, v. 1）

《本草新注》，伊博恩（Read, Bernard Emms, 1887—1949），刘汝强（1895—）著,内容译自李时珍的《本草纲目》.

(1) Chinese medicinal plants from Pen ts'ao kang mu...

［Peiping, China］Peking Natural History Bulletin, 1936. 2 p. l. , xvi, 389 p. 26cm.

(2) Ann Arbor：University Microfilms, 1967. xvi, 389 pages.

(3) Taipei：Southern Materials Center, 1977. xvi, 389 pages；22cm. （Chinese medicine series；5）

49. Chinese materia medica... by Bernard E. Read... From the Pen ts'ao kang mu Li Shih-chen, A. D. 1597... Peiping, China, Peking Natural History Bulletin, 1931—1941. 6 v. illus. , plates. 26cm.

Incomplete contents：［I (pt. 1—5)］ Animal drugs. —［II (pt. 6)］ Avian drugs. —［III (pt. 7)］ Dragon and snake drugs. —［IV (pt. 8)］ Turtle and shellfish drugs. —［V (pt. 9)］ Fish drugs.

伊博恩（Read, Bernard Emms, 1887—1949），内容译自李时珍的《本草纲目》,6 卷本.

50. Chinese materia medica：animal drugs/B. E. Read；Casey A Wood. Peking：Peking Natural History Bulletin, 1931. 1 volume, ［3］ leaves of plates：illustrations；26cm.

伊博恩（Read, Bernard Emms, 1887—1949）；内容译自李时珍的《本草纲目》（动物部分）.

(1) Taipei：Southern Materials Center, 1976. ［310］ pages in various pagings, ［4］ leaves of plates：illustrations；22cm. （Chinese medicine series；4）

(2) Taipei：Southern Materials Center, 1982. 1 volume：illustrations；21cm. （Chinese medicine series；4）

51. Chinese materia medica. Avian drugs/B. E. Read. Peiping, China：Peking Natural History Bulletin, 1932. 112 pages, ［2］ leaves of plates：illustrations；26cm.

伊博恩（Read, Bernard Emms, 1887—1949），内容译自李时珍的《本草纲目》（禽部）

52. Chinese medicinal plants from the Pen Ts'ao Kang Mu, A. D. 1596 of a botanical, chiemical and pharmacological reference list/B. E. Read. Taipei, Republic of China：Southern Materials Center, 1982. 9, xvi, 389 pages；21cm.

伊博恩（Read, Bernard Emms, 1887—1949），内容译自李时珍的《本草纲目》（植物部分）

(1) 3rd ed. Taipei：Orient Cultural Service, 1984. xvi, 389 pages；22cm. （Asian folklore and social life monographs. Supplement；19）

53. Chinese materia medica：insect drugs, dragon and snake drugs, fish drugs/B. E. Read. Taipei, Republic of China：Southern Materials Center, 1977. 3 volumes in 1：illustrations；22cm. （Chinese medicine series；2）

伊博恩（Read, Bernard Emms, 1887—1949），内容译自李时珍的《本草纲目》（昆虫类，龙及蛇类，鱼类）

(1) Taipei, Republic of China：Southern Materials Center, 1982. 3 v. in 1：ill.；22cm. （Chinese medicine series；2）

54. Chinese materia medica：turtle and shellfish drugs，avian drugs，a compendium of minerals and stones/B. E. Read. Taipei，Republic of China：Southern Materials Center，1977. 3 volumes：illustrations；22cm. (Chinese medicine series；3)

伊博恩（Read，Bernard Emms，1887—1949），内容译自李时珍的《本草纲目》（介部，禽部，石类）

(1)Taipei，Republic of China：Southern Materials Center，1982. 3 volumes in 1：illustrations；22cm. (Chinese medicine series；3)

55. A compendium of minerals and stones used in Chinese medicine from Pen t'sao kang mu/compiled by B. E. Read and C. Pak. Peiping，China：Peking Society of Natural History，1925. x，120 pages；26cm. (Peking Society of Natural History Bulletin；v. 3，pt. 2.)

伊博恩（Read，Bernard Emms，1887—1949），内容译自李时珍的《本草纲目》（石类）

(1)Chinese materia medica：a compendium of minerals and stones used in Chinese medicine from the Pen ts'ao kang mu［by］Li Shih Chen/B. E. Read；C Pak. 2nd ed. ［Peking］：Peking Natural History Bulletin，1936. viii，98 pages；22cm.

56. Chinese materia medica：vegetable kingdom/G. A. Stuart；F. Porter Smith. Taipei：Southern Materials Center，1911. ii，558 pages；22cm.

《本草纲目》（植物部分），Stuart，G. A. （—1911）和Smith，F. Porter（Frederick Porter，1833—1888）合译.

(1)Taipei：Southern Materials Center，1987. 9，ii，558 p.；22cm. (Chinese medicine series；1)

57. Chinese materia medica. Turtle and shellfish drugs/B. E. Read. Peiping，China：Peking Natural History Bulletin，1937. 95 pages，［11］leaves of plates：illustrations (some color)；27cm.

伊博恩（Read，Bernard Emms，1887—1949），内容译自李时珍的《本草纲目》（介部）

(1)Taipei：Southern Materials Center，Inc.，1977. 1 volume. (Chinese medicine series；3)

58. Chinese materia medica. Fish drugs/Bernard E. Read. ［Beiping］：Peking Natural History Bulletin，1939. 1 vol. (136 p.)：ill.；26cm.

伊博恩（Read，Bernard Emms，1887—1949），内容译自李时珍的《本草纲目》（鱼鳞部）

59. Chinese materia medica. Insect drugs/B. E. Read. Peking，China：Peking Natural History Bulletin，1941. 213 pages：illustrations；27cm.

伊博恩（Read，Bernard Emms，1887—1949），内容译自李时珍的《本草纲目》（昆虫类）

60. Chinese medicinal herbs/translated and researched by F. Porter Smith and G. A. Stuart. San Francisco，Georgetown Press［1973］. 467，［41］p. 24cm. ISBN：0914558005 0914558002

《本草纲目》，李时珍（1518—1593）. Smith，F. Porter（Frederick Porter，1833—1888）和Stuart，G. A. （George Arthur，？—1911）合译.

(1)Mineola，N. Y.：Dover；2003. 508 p.；24cm. ISBN：048642801X，0486428017

61. Chinese materia medica/F. Porter Smith；G. A. Stuart. Taipei：Southern Materials Center，Inc，1976—1977. 4 volumes；22cm. (Chinese medicine series；v. 1—4)

《本草纲目》，Smith，F. Porter（Frederick Porter，1833—1888）和Stuart，G. A. （—1911）合译. 4 卷.

62. Compendium of materia medica：Bencao gangmu/compiled by Li Shizhen；translated and annotated by Luo Xiwen. Beijing：Foreign Languages Press，2003. 52 v. in 6 (xxxii，4397 p.)：ill.，port.；27cm. ISBN：7119032607，7119032603

Notes："First full English translation of the entire Compendium of materia medica"—Publisher's note.

《本草纲目》，李时珍（1518—1593）；罗希文译. 是《本草纲目》的第一部英文全译本.

(1)本草纲目选 = Condensed compendium of materia medica/（明）李时珍著；李经纬编校；罗希文英译. 北京：外文出版社，2012. 6 册（45，3451 页，［7］页图版）：图，摹真；24cm. ISBN：7119069975. （大中华文库）

63. Bencao kangmu：the great pharmacopoeia by Li Shizhen 1596：supplemented by quotations from older writings：chapters about paper and ink/Peter Tschudin. Basel：Peter F. Tschudin，1993. 63 pages：illustrations. ISBN：3905142090，3905142099

《本草纲目》（选译），李时珍（1518—1593）；Tschudin，Peter 译.

64. Colored atlas of compendium of materia medica/chief editor Liansheng Shen. Beijing：Hua xia chu ban she，1998. 4，21，471 p.：chiefly col. ill.；27cm. ISBN：7508007964

Notes：In Chinese，with introduction in English；nomenclature and indexes also in English，Japanese，and Latin

《本草纲目彩色图谱》，主编沈连生. 为《本草纲目》选译，术语以英文、日文、拉丁文标注. 华夏出版社出版.

65. The Lakeside master's study of the pulse：［Binhu mo xue］/by Li Shi-zhen；translated by Bob Flaws. Boulder，CO：Blue Poppy Press，1998. xi，130 p.；19cm.

《濒湖脉学》，李时珍（1518—1593）；Flaws，Bob 译.

66. Li Shi-Zhen's pulse studies：an illustrated guide/Li Shen-qing and William Morris；translated by Zheng Qi；edited by Mark Mondot. Beijing：People's Medical Publishing House，c2011. xix，170 p.：ill.；27cm. ＋1 fold-out table. ISBN：7117137621，7117137622

《李时珍脉象图谱》，李申清（1952—），Morris，William R. 合著；Zheng Qi 译；Mondot，Mark 编. 是对李时珍

67. 汉英对照黄帝外经/陈士铎评述；刘希茹今译；李照国英译. 上海：上海三联书店，2017. 2 册（631 页）；24cm. ISBN：7542657633

英文题名：Yellow emperor's external canon of medicine

68. The divinely responding classic：a translation of the Shen ying jing from the Zhen jiu da cheng：［Shen ying ching］/ translated by Yang Shou-zhong and Liu Feng-ting. Boulder, CO：Blue Poppy Press, 1994. xxi, 165 pages. ISBN：0585113041, 0585113043

《神应经》，译自杨继洲（1573—1619）的《针灸大成》；杨守忠，Liu, Feng-ting 合译.

69. Fu Qing-zhu's gynecology ＝［Fu Qingzhu nü ke］/ translated by Yang Shou-zhong & Liu Da-wei. Boulder, Colo.：Blue Poppy Press, 1992. xxi, 267 pages. ISBN：0585124027, 0585124025

《傅青主女科》，傅山（1606—1684）；杨守忠，Liu Da-wei 合译.

70. Forgotten traditions of ancient Chinese medicine：a Chinese view from the eighteenth century：the I-hsüeh Yüan Liu Lun of 1757/by Hsüh Ta-Ch'un；translated and annotated by Paul U. Unschuld. Brookline, MA：Paradigm, 1998. xi, 403 pages：illustrations；26cm. ISBN：0912111569 0912111568 0912111240 0912111247

《医学源流论》，徐大椿（1693—1771）；文树德（Unschuld, Paul U.〈Paul Ulrich〉），1943—）（德国医史学家）译.

71. Yi lin gai cuo：correcting the errors in the forest of medicine/by Wang Qing-ren；translated and commented on by Yuhsin Chung, Herman Oving & Simon Becker. Boulder, Colo.：Blue Poppy Press, 2007. xxvi, 512 pages：illustrations；23cm. ISBN：189184539X, 1891845390

《医林改错》，王清任（1768—1831）；Chung, Yuhsin 等译.

72. Chinese healing arts：internal Kung-Fu/edited by William R. Berk；originally translated by John Dudgeon；［photography by Steve Volphin］. Culver City, Calif.：Peace Press, 1979. xi, 209 pages：illustrations；23cm. ISBN：0915238292；0915238293

Notes："A large portion of this book appeared originally under the title The beverages of the Chinese；Kung-Fu or Tauist medical gymnastics, translated and annotated by John Dudgeon, M. D., and published by The Tientsin Press in Tientsin, China in 1895."

Berk, William R. (1946—)编，收录了德贞（Dudgeon J.）翻译的《医林改错》的脏腑部分. 本书内容来自 1895 年在天津的出版的德贞的译作《The beverages of the Chinese；Kung-Fu or Tauist medical gymnastics》.

　(1)Burbank, CA：Unique Publications, 1986. xi, 209 pages：illustrations；23cm. ISBN：0865680833,

0865680838

73. Blood stasis：China's classical concept in modern medicine：including a translation of the seminal work of Wang Qing-Ren "Corrections of mistakes in the medical world"/Gunter R. Neeb；translated by Maximilian Beer and Julia Kaiser；foreword from the German edition by Zhang Bo-Li；foreword by Steven Clavey. Edinburgh；New York：Churchill Livingstone/Elsevier, 2007. xxix, 351 pages, ［12］pages of plates：illustrations（some color）；26cm. ISBN：0443101854, 044310185X

《瘀血大成》，Neeb, Gunter R.（Gunter Ralf, 1959—）著，该书含有对王清任（1768—1831）的《医林改错》的翻译. 从德文版转译.

74. The heart transmission of medicine/by Liu Yi-ren；translated by Yang Shou-zhong. Boulder, CO：Blue Poppy Press, 1997. xiv, 190 pages. ISBN：0936185835, 093618583X

《医学传心录》，刘一仁（生卒年不详，活动时间 1821—1851 年）；杨守忠译.

75. On "Fan sheng-chih shu"：an agriculturistic book of China written by Fan Shêng-chih in the first century B. C. /translated and commented upon by Shih Shêng-han. Peking：Science Press, 1959. 68 pages；21cm.

《氾胜之书今释》，氾胜之（生卒年不详，大约生活在公元前 1 世纪的西汉末期）；石声汉英译.

76. A preliminary survey of the book Qi min yao shu：an agricultural encyclopaedia of the 6th century/Shih Sheng-han. Peking, Science Press, 1958. 107 pages；21cm.

《齐民要术》，石声汉译. 科学出版社.

　(1)2nd ed. Peking：Science Press：Distributed by Guozi Shudian, 1962. x, 107 pages；21cm.

77. T'ien-kung k'ai-wu；Chinese technology in the seventeenth century. Translated by E-tu Zen Sun and Shiou-chuan Sun. University Park, Pennsylvania State University, 1966. xiv, 372 p. illus. 28cm.

《天工开物》，宋应星（1587 年—约 1666 年）；孙任以都（Sun, E-tu Zen, 1921—）（美国华裔学者）等译.

　(1)Chinese technology in the seventeenth century＝t'ien kung k'ai wu/Sung Ying-hsing；translated from the Chinese and annotated by E-tu Zen Sun and Shiou-chuan Sun. Mineola, N. Y.：Dover Publications, 1997. xii, 372 p. ：ill. ；24cm. ISBN：0486295931

78. Tien-kung-kai-wu：exploitation of the work of nature：Chinese agriculture and technology in the XVII century/by Sung Ying-sing＝［Tian gong kai wu/Song Yingxing zhu］. Taipei, Taiwan, Republic of China：China Academy, c1980. xii, 487 p. ：ill. ；22cm. (Chinese culture series；2—3)

《天工开物》，宋应星（1587 年—约 1666 年）；Li, Qiaoping(1897—)等译.

79. 天工开物/（明）宋应星著；潘吉星今译；王义静，王海燕，刘迎春英译. 广州：广东教育出版社，2011. 29 页，551 页；24cm. ISBN：7540682026.（大中华文库）

本书以明朝宋应星的《天工开物》为蓝本，翻译成白话文，再加上英文翻译.

80. Summary of the principal Chinese treatises upon the culture of the mulberry and the rearing of silk worms. Tr. from the Chinese. Washington，P. Force，1838. 2 p. l. ，198 p. 10 pl. 24cm.

Notes："This 'Summary' was first translated from the Chinese，by Stanislas Julien… and printed at the Royal Press，in Paris，by order of the minister of public works，agriculture，and commerce. The French copy from which this translation was made，was transmitted from Paris，to the Secretary of state，and by his recommendation has been translated and published here. Washington，February，1838. "—Note by the publisher.

《桑蚕辑要》，（清）沈秉成撰；Julien，Stanislas（1797—1873）译.

81. 四元玉鉴：汉英对照/（元）朱世杰着；郭书春今译；陈在新英译；郭金海整理. 沈阳：辽宁教育出版社，2006. 2 册（695 页）；23cm. ISBN：7538269231，7538269239.（大中华文库. 第 2 辑）

英文题名：Jade mirror of the four unknowns. 古典数学.

N2 中国发明

1. The invention of printing in China and its spread westward. New York：Columbia University Press，1925. 3 p. l. ，[v]-xviii p. ，1 l. ，282 p. plates，fold. map，facsims. ，fold. tab. 24cm.

Carter，Thomas Francis（1882—1925）译. 有关中国造纸术及其西传，选译自《隋书》《五代史记》《五代会要》等.

(1)New York：Columbia University Press [1931]. xxvi p. ，1 l. ，282 p. ，1 l. plates. fold. map，facsim. ，fold. tab. 23cm.

(2)Rev. by L. Carrington Goodrich. 3rd ed. New York：Ronald Press Co. [1955]. xxiv，293 p. illus. ，port. ，facsim. 24cm.

2. A ncient Chinese inventions：3,000 years of science and technology/Deng Yinke；translated by Wang Pingxing. [Beijing]：China Intercontinental Press，2005. 134 pages：illustrations（some color）；24cm. ISBN：7508508378，7508508375，0521186926，0521186927.（Cultural China series）

《中国古代发明：英文》，邓荫柯著；王平兴译. 五洲传播出版社. 本书从我国古代社会中选取了三十余项重大发明创造，内容涉及天文、冶金、医药、轻工、数学等各个领域.

N3 陶瓷

1. Chinese porcelain；sixteenth-century coloured illustrations with Chinese ms. text by Hsiang Yuan-p'ien，tr. and annotated by Stephen W. Bushell… eighty-three coloured plates. Oxford，Clarendon Press，1908. 45，[81] p. 80 col. pl. 31cm.

Notes：Translated from the "Li tai ming tz'u t'u p'u（Illustrated description of celebrated porcelain of different dynasties）" originally issued about 1575. cf. Introd.

《历代名瓷图谱》，项元汴（1525—1590 年）编；Bushell，Stephen W. （Stephen Wootton，1844—1908）译.

2. Description of Chinese pottery and porcelain；being a translation of the T'ao shuo… with introduction，notes，and bibliography by Stephen W. Bushell. Oxford，The Clarendon Press，1910. xxxi，222 p. ，1 l. 22cm.

Notes：Two letters，dated 1712 and 1722，respectively，from the Jesuit missionary Père d'Entrecolles，relating to porcelain manufacture of Ching-tê-Chên：p. 181—222. "Appendix：Lettre[s] du père d'Entrecolles Missionnaire de la Compagnie de Jesus：au père Orry de la mesme Compagnie"：p. [181]-222.

《陶说》，（清）朱琰；Bushell，Stephen W. （Stephen Wootton，1844—1908）译.

(1)[New York：AMS Press，1973]. xxxi，222 p. 23cm. ISBN：0404569145

(2)Kuala Lumpur；New York：Oxford University Press，1977. 275 p. ；23cm. ISBN：0195803728.（Oxford in Asia studies in ceramics）

3. T'ao ya；or，Pottery refinements，being a translation/Liu Ch'en；with notes and an intro. by G. R. Sayer. London：Routledge，1959. 163 p.

Notes：a translation of Tz'u hsueh

《陶雅》，陈浏（1863—1929 年）；Sayer，Geoffrey Robley 译注.

4. Chinese pottery and porcelain/Li Zhiyan and Cheng Wen；translated by Ouyang Caiwei. Beijing：Foreign Languages Press，1984. iii，209 pages：illustrations（some color）；26cm. ISBN：0835111857，0835111850，7119011677，7119011677.（Traditional Chinese arts and culture）

《中国陶瓷》，李知宴，程雯著.

(1)Beijing：Foreign Languages Press，1996. 217 pages：chiefly color illustrations；31cm. ISBN：7119007521，7119007526

5. Pottery and porcelain/Li Zhiyan and Cheng Qinhua. Beijing：Foreign Languages Press，2002. 101 pages：color illustrations，map；18×20cm. ISBN：7119030620，7119030623.（Culture of China＝中华风物）

《中国陶瓷》，李知宴，程钦华著.

6. Chinese ceramics/Fang Lili；translated by William W. Wang. Beijing：China Intercontinental Press，2005. 135 pages：color illustrations；23cm. ISBN：7508508343，7508508344

《中国瓷器：英文》，方李莉著；Willam W. Wang 译. 五洲传播出版社.本书介绍中国陶瓷在不同历史时期的功能、艺术特点、烧制方法、主要产地,精美的陶瓷产品中所蕴含的中国文化艺术之美,陶瓷文化对当代生活的影响,以及中国陶瓷艺术对其他国家的影响.

(1)2nd ed. Beijing：China Intercontinental Press，2010. 156 pages：color illustrations；23cm. ISBN：7508516738，7508516737. (Cultural China series)

7. 中国瓷/仲伯编著.合肥：黄山书社,2011. 186 页；21cm. ISBN：7546120317，7546120314. (中国红)
英文题名：Chinese procelain.

8. 瓷/伯仲编著.合肥：黄山书社,2016. 186 页；彩图；23cm. ISBN：7546142081. (印象中国)
英文题名：Chinese porcelain. 英汉对照.

9. A collection of ancient Chinese porcelain treasures. Hong Kong Woods Publishing Co.，1988. 315 pages
Contents：List of Plates—Plates of Pieces with Description—Craft Development and Artistic Style of Porcelain in Various Historic Periods of China.
中国古代陶瓷.李知宴(1937—)著.

10. 《中国古代陶瓷》,李知宴著；王渤等译,山东友谊出版社,1998. ISBN：706421130

11. 古代瓷器：湖北省博物馆藏瓷器选：汉英对照/王红星主编；湖北省博物馆编.北京：文物出版社,2007. 103 页；彩照；29cm. ISBN：7501022717，7501022712. (长江中游文明之旅丛书；9)
英文题名：Ancient porcelain.

12. History of pottery/［Chinese compiler Li Meitian, Huang Xiaoying］. Beijing：Encyclopedia of China Publishing House，2010. iii，176 pages：illustrations；21cm. ISBN：7500082606，7500082606. (History of Chinese civilization)
《陶器史话：中英文双语版》,《中华文明史话》编委会编译. 中国大百科全书出版社(“中华文明史话”中英文双语丛书)

13. 元代瓷器：汉英对照/《北京文物鉴赏》编委会编.北京：北京美术摄影出版社,2005. 107 页；80 幅；20cm. ISBN：7805012881，7805012889. (北京文物鉴赏)
英文题名：Porcelains of the Yuan dynasty. 辑入北京出土的元代瓷器精品图片80余幅.

14. 明清颜色釉瓷器：汉英对照/《北京文物鉴赏》编委会编.北京：北京美术摄影出版社,2005. 107 页；20cm. ISBN：7805012946. (北京文物鉴赏)
本书辑入北京地区馆藏明清颜色釉瓷器的精美图片80余幅.

15. 明代青花瓷 ＝ Blue and white porcelains of the Ming dynasty/北京市文物局,《北京文物鉴赏》编委会编. 北京：北京美术摄影出版社,2006. 107 pages：illustrations；20cm. ISBN：7805013535；7805013534. (北京文物鉴赏 ＝ Appreciating Beijing cultural relics)
汉英对照.本书把明代青花分为三个时期六个单元,从色彩、用料、纹饰的特点,各个时期的特征,用精美的图片、详实的文字展示了明代青花瓷.

16. 神韵与辉煌：陕西历史博物馆国宝鉴赏：中英对照.陶瓷器卷/冀东山主编；董理分册主编；张沛心等撰；王建荣，邱子渝摄. 西安：三秦出版社,2006. 141 页；照片；29cm. ISBN：7807360593，7807360599
英文题名：Charm and brilliance：an appraisal of the national treasures in the Shaanxi History Museum：the porcelain. 本卷收录陕西历史博物馆馆藏唐三彩等陶瓷器中一级文物加以鉴赏与介绍.

17. 彦瓷艺术：英汉对照/吴彦真编. 广州：岭南美术出版社,2006. 92 页；照片；29cm. ISBN：7536233671，7536233676
英文题名：The art of Yan porcelain. 本书详细介绍了一种新的制瓷工艺“彦瓷”,并附精美图片.

18. 瓷之江南/青盈著；徐立乐译；杨彬译.上海：上海远东出版社，2010. 253 页；21cm. ISBN：7547600559，7547600557
英文题名：Porcelain in Jiang Nan

19. 江西藏瓷全集：汉英对照.清代.上/铁源主编；刘丽颖译. 北京：朝华出版社,2005. 246 页；29cm. ISBN：7505411349
学术名称英汉对照.清代景德镇市陶瓷工艺美术史.

20. 江西藏瓷全集：汉英对照.清代.下/铁源主编；刘丽颖译. 北京：朝华出版社,2005. 246 页；29cm. ISBN：7505411357
学术名称英汉对照.清代景德镇市陶瓷工艺美术史.

N4　服饰

1. Chinese clothing：costumes, adornments and culture/Hua Mei；translated by Yu Hong ＆ Zhang Lei. Beijing：China International Press，2004. 160 pages：illustrations (some color)；24cm. ISBN：750850612X，7508506128. (Cultural China series)
Contents：Shenui and broad sleeves—Royal ceremonial wear—Introduction of ethnic minority styles—The elegant Wei and Jin Period—The thousand faces of the Tang costume—Silk, the Silk Road and the art of embroidery—Beizi：a song style garment—Ming garments as seen in classical portraits—The official uniform—Ancient armor suits—Qi costumes—a combination of Manchu and Han nationality's clothes—Civilized new clothes and improved cheong-sam—Farmer ＆ worker uniforms and service-dresses—Professional image and professional dresses—Adornments and fairy tales—Hats with meanings—Shawls and the back wrapping cloth—A silhouette of Tibetan costumes—Countless ornamental objects—Keeping pace with the world fashion.
《中国服饰》,华梅著,于红等译.五洲传播出版社.

2. China's minority costumes/by Xing Li. Beijing：China Intercontinental Press，2008. 108 pages：color illustrations；23cm. ISBN：7508514604，7508514602.

(Ethnic cultures of China)

《中国少数民族服饰》,邢莉著.五洲传播出版社.

3. 服饰史话/《中华文明史话》编委会编译.北京:中国大百科全书出版社,2009. 176 页;21cm. ISBN:7500079880, 7500079885

4. Chinese clothing:garment, accessory and culture/Hua Mei;translated by Yu Hong & Zhang Lei. 2nd ed. Beijing:China International Press, 2010. 173 pages:illustrations (some color);23cm. ISBN:7508516615, 7508516613. (Cultural China series)

《中国服饰》,华梅著.五洲传播出版社.

5. 旗袍/徐冬编著. 合肥:黄山书社,2011. 164 页;21cm. ISBN:7546120270, 7546120276.(中国红)

6. Chinese clothing/Hua Mei. Cambridge;New York:Cambridge University Press, 2011. 163 pages:illustrations (chiefly colored);23cm. ISBN:0521186896,0521186897. (Introductions to Chinese culture)

Notes:"Translated from the original Chinese by Yu Hong and Zhang Lei"—Front cover flap.

《中国服饰》,华梅(1951—)著.

7. 旗袍/徐冬编著. 合肥:黄山书社,2016. 164 页:图,照片;23cm. ISBN:7546141527.(印象中国)

英文题名:Chi-pao. 汉英对照.

8. 服饰/沈周编著. 合肥:黄山书社,2016. 166 页:图,照片;23cm. ISBN:7546142098.(印象中国)

英文题名:Ancient costumes and accessories

9. 少数民族服饰/戚嘉富编著. 合肥:黄山书社,2016. 168 页:彩图;23cm. ISBN:7546142210.(印象中国)

英文题名:Costumes of the ethnic minorities

N5 饮食文化

1. Chinese foods:adventures in the world of cooking and dining/Liu Junru;translated by William W. Wang. Beijing:China Intercontinental Press, 2004. 151 pages:illustrations (chiefly color);23cm. ISBN:7508506138, 7508506135. (Cultural China series)

Contents:Introduction—Traditional foods—Foods from afar—Tools of the trade—Eating, the Chinese way—Home gourmet for everyone—Foods and festivities—Delicacies from all over—Dining with the minorities—The etiquettes of dining—The art of tea—Wine, the beverage of romance—Five tastes in harmony—Chefs and culinary arts—Foods and health—The "forbidden"—When restaurants race.

《中国饮食》,刘军茹著,吕为民等译.五洲传播出版社.介绍了中国人的饮食习惯、饮食特点及其特有的文化背景与内涵.

(1)2nd ed. Beijing:China Intercontinental Press, 2010. 151 pages:illustrations (some color);23cm. ISBN:7508516585, 7508516583. (Cultural China series)

2. Beijing local delicacies/text by Song Weizhong, Wang Jiayan, Zhou Shuo;photographs by Lu Xiao, et al.;translated by Wang Yufan. Beijing:China Pictorial Publishing House, 2006. 110 pages:illustrations;22cm. ISBN:7802200644, 7802200647. (Charm of Beijing)

《京味小吃:英文》,宋卫忠,王嘉彦,周烁编文;卢筱摄;王寓帆译.中国画报出版社(2008,走近北京).选取了北京有代表性的小吃将近百种.

3. 北京美食指南＝Beijing restaurants & food guide:英文/任欢迎主编;北京晚报,美食联盟等编写.北京:中国旅游出版社,2006. 221 页:彩图;19cm. ISBN:7503229756, 7503229756

本书是为外国人介绍北京餐馆及流行菜的指南手册.

4. Food in China/written by Zhongli Tumei;translated by Qin Dan. [Beijing]:China Intercontinental Press, 2007. 127 pages:color illustrations;22cm. ISBN:7508510903, 7508510909. (Fashion China)

《美味王国:英文》,钟离图美撰文;秦丹译.五洲传播出版社(时尚中国)

5. A world of fine restaurants in Beijing:in the gourmet spirit/Lilian Lee. Beijing:Foreign Languages Press, 2008. [14], 245 pages:color illustrations, 1 folded plan;21cm. ISBN:7119054667, 711905466X.

《世界美食在北京》,李幸娟著.介绍了北京近百家各式餐厅.

6. 中华美食/张红主编. 天津:天津教育出版社,2009. 44 页;26cm. ISBN:7530956472, 7530956477

7. Chinese culinary culture/authors, Du Fuxiang, Li Xiaoqing;tranlsators, Kuang Peihua, Wang Fang, Li Zhengye. Beijing:China Travel & Tourism Press, 2010. 229 pages:color illustrations, color map;24cm. ISBN:7503236945, 7503236949

《中国饮食文化》,杜福祥,李小青[编著].中国旅游出版社.

8. 饮食天下:中英双语阅读/战丽莉主编.大连:大连理工大学出版社,2010. 229 页;24cm. ISBN:7561155332, 7561155336.(每天读点中国文化)

9. 中华美食/乔姣姣编著. 合肥:黄山书社,2016.172 页:图;23cm. ISBN:7546141589.(印象中国)

英文题名:Chinese food. 英汉对照.

10. Stories about Chinese cuisine/Chen, Xiaoqing;Chen Le. Beijing:New Star Press, 2017. 210 pages:colour illustration;23cm. ISBN:7513325134

《中国美食的故事》,陈晓卿,陈乐著.新星出版社.

11. Chinese cooking. 2nd ed. 1998. ii, 189 pages, [32] pages of plates:illustrations;25cm. ISBN:7505405624, 7505405622

《怎样做中国菜》,初版于 1986 年.

12. Chinese tea culture/by Wang Ling. Beijing:Foreign Languages Press, 2000. v, 154 pages, [4] pages of plates:illustrations (some color);21cm. ISBN:7119021443, 7119021447

《中国茶文化》,王玲著.

13. Chinese tea：a cultural history and guide/Liu Tong；translated by Yue Liwen. Beijing：China Intercontinental Press [Wuzhou chuanbo chubanshe], 2005. [138] p.：ill.；23cm. ISBN：7508508351, 7508508351. (Cultural China series)

《中国茶：英文》,刘彤著;乐利文译.五洲传播出版社.

14. Enjoy tea in Beijing/text by Li Shaobing；photographs by Zou Yi [and others]；translated by Liu Zongren. Beijing：China Pictorial Publishing House, 2006. 110 pages：color illustrations；22cm. ISBN：7802200628, 7802200623. (Charm of Beijing)

《京城品茶：英文》,李少兵编文;邹毅等摄.刘宗仁译.中国画报出版社(2008,走近北京)

15. The art of tea in China/Guo Danying, Wang Jianrong. Beijing：Foreign Languages Press, 2007. 108 pages：illustrations (chiefly color)；21cm. ISBN：7119033228, 7119033220

《中国茶艺：英文》,郭丹英,王建荣编著.

16. Chinese tea：a cultural history and drinking guide/Liu Tong；translated by Yue Liwen. Beijing：China Intercontinental Press, 2009. 157 pages：color illustrations；23cm. ISBN：7508516677, 7508516672. (Cultural China series)

《中国茶》,刘彤编著.五洲传播出版社.

17. 茶经/陆羽（733—804）陆延灿著；姜欣,姜怡今译/英译.长沙：湖南人民出版社,2009. 2 册(44 页,701 页)；24cm. ISBN：7543859944, 7543859947. (大中华文库：汉英对照)

英文题名：The classic of tea

18. 茶经：汉英对照/(唐)陆羽著. 崇文书局,2018. 26cm. ISBN：7540349448

19. 中国茶道/林治编著;陈汉良,焦博翻译.西安：世界图书出版西安公司,2010. 198 页；24cm. ISBN：7510010194, 7510010195

20. Green tea/written by Li Hong；translated by Zhu Jianhua, Bai Chongshun. Beijing：China Intercontinental Press, 2010. 156 pages：color illustrations, color maps；21cm. ISBN：7508517421, 7508517423. (Appreciating Chinese tea)

《绿茶》,李洪著.五洲传播出版社.

21. Oolong tea/written by Pan Wei；translated by Su Shumin. Beijing：China Intercontinental Press, 2010. 156 pages：color illustrations；21cm. ISBN：7508517445, 750851744X. (Appreciating Chinese tea)

《乌龙茶》,潘薇著.五洲传播出版社.

22. Brewing tea/written by Li Hong；translated by Yilise Lin. Beijing：China Intercontinental Press, 2010. 160 pages：color illustrations；21cm. ISBN：7508517131, 750851713X. (Appreciating Chinese tea)

《烹茶技艺》,李洪著.五洲传播出版社.

23. Tea and tea set/written by Li Hong；translated by Zhu Jianting. Beijing：China Intercontinental Press, 2010. 159 pages：color illustrations；21cm. (Appreciating Chinese tea)

《茶与茶具》,李洪著.五洲传播出版社.

24. Pu-erh tea/written by Wang Jidong；translated by Chen Zhufen, Liu Qingling. Beijing：China Intercontinental Press, 2010. 157 pages：color illustrations；21cm. ISBN：7508517438, 7508517431. (Appreciating Chinese tea)

《普洱茶》,王辑东著.五洲传播出版社.

25. 茶之江南/孙欢著；李朝安译. 上海：上海远东出版社,2010. 149 页；21cm. ISBN：7547600580

英文题名：Tea in Jiang Nan.

26. 中国茶/吴建丽主编；汉竹编著；佟彤译. 北京：中国轻工业出版社,2011. 237 页；25cm. ISBN：7501979660, 7501979669

27. 中国茶/羽叶编著.合肥：黄山书社,2011. 178 页；21cm. ISBN：7546120294, 7546120292.(中国红)

英文题名：Chinese tea.

28. 茶艺/艾敏编著. 合肥：黄山书社,2016. 168 页：彩图；23cm. ISBN：7546141367.(印象中国)

英文题名：Tea art in China. 英汉对照.

29. 茶/羽叶编著. 合肥：黄山书社,2016. 178 页；图；23cm. ISBN：7546142067.(印象中国)

英文题名：Chinese tea. 英汉对照.

30. Intoxicated in the land of wine/authored by Fu Jianwei；translated by Orientaltrans；proofread by Liu Qian. Beijing：China Translation and Publishing Corporation, 2009. 260 pages：color illustrations；24cm. ISBN：7500124504, 7500124503

《沉醉酒乡》,傅建伟著.中国对外翻译出版公司.介绍绍兴黄酒文化.

31. History of wine drinking/[Chinese compiler Qi Xin, Wang Kai]. Encyclopedia of China Publishing House, 2009. 170 pages：illustrations (some color)；22cm. ISBN：7500080572, 7500080573. (History of Chinese civilization)

《饮酒史话》,《中华文明史话》编委会编译.中国大百科全书出版社.

32. Chinese wine：universe in a bottle/Li Zhengping；translated by Ego. Beijing：China Intercontinental Press, 2010. 142 pages：color illustrations；23cm. ISBN：7508516714, 7508516710. (Cultural China series)

《中国酒》,李争平编著.五洲传播出版社.

33. 酒/刘勇编著.合肥:黄山书社,2016. 172 页:图,照片;23cm. ISBN:7546141459.(印象中国)
英文题名:Chinese wine. 英汉对照.

Z 类　综合性文献

Z1　国学

1. 国学经典:中英双语阅读/林萌主编.大连:大连理工大学出版社,2010. 230 页;24cm. ISBN:7561155349, 7561155344.(每天读点中国文化)
英文题名:Chinese classics. 内容包括三大部分:诸子百家;中国古典文学;中国文化杂谈.

2. 中国人文经典翻译赏析/张缨主编.西安:西安交通大学出版社,2010. 196 页;26cm. ISBN:7560535630, 7560535631.(21 世纪大学英语选修课系列教材)
本书在中国传统文化范围内,选取人文学科的经典作品及其译文,涉及哲学、文学、史学三方面的内容.

3. Limited views:essays on ideas and letters＝[Kuan chui pien]/by Qian Zhongshu;selected and translated by Ronald Egan. Cambridge, Mass. :Harvard University Asia Center:Distributed by Harvard University Press, 1998. ix, 483 p. ;24cm. ISBN:0674534115, 0674534117.
(Harvard-Yenching Institute monograph series;44)
《管锥篇》(选译),钱钟书(1910—)著;艾朗诺(Egan, Ronald,1948—)(美国汉学家)译.

Z2　杂著

1. Chinese literature/With critical and biographical sketches by Epiphanius Wilson. Rev. ed. New York:P. F Collier, 1900. vii, 302 pages:portraits;21cm. (World's greatest literature)
Contents:The Analects of Confucius, translated into English by W. Jennings.—The Sayings of Mencius, translated into English by J. Legge.—The Shi-King, metrical translation by J. Legge.—The travels of Fâ-Hien, translation by J. Legge.—The sorrows of Han, translated into English by J. F. Davis.
中国文学. Wilson, Epiphanius(1845—1916)编. 包括《论语》《孟子》《诗经》《佛国记》《汉宫愁》的英译.
(1)Limited ed. de luxe. London, New York [etc.] The Colonial Press [1902]. 2 p. l. , vii p. , 1 l. , 302 p. front. , port. , facsim. 24cm. (Literature of the Orient. Byzantine ed. [v. 2])
(2)Rev. ed. Freeport, N. Y. , Books for Libraries Press [1971]. vii, 302 p. ports. 23cm. ISBN:0836982282.
(Oriental literature). (Play anthology reprint series)
(3)Rev. ed. Charleston, SC:BiblioBazaar, 2006. 365

pages (large print); 25cm. ISBN:1426439725, 1426439728

2. Han shih wai chuan:Han Ying's Illustrations of the didactic application of the Classic of songs;an annotated translation by James Robert Hightower. Cambridge, Harvard University Press, 1952. vii, 368 p. 27cm. Illustrations of the didactic application of the Classic of songs. (Harvard-Yenching Institute. Monograph series, v. 11)
《韩诗外传》,韩婴(西汉)著;海陶玮(Hightower, James Rober)(美国汉学家)译注.

3. Derangements of my contemporaries:miscellaneous notes/Li Shangyin;translated from the Chinese by Chloe Garcia Roberts. New York:New Directions Books, 2014. 56 pages;23cm. ISBN:0811221962, 0811221962.
(New Directions Poetry Pamphlet;14)
《杂纂》,李商隐(约 813 年—约 858 年);Roberts, Chloe Garcia 译.

4. The fragrant flower:classic Chinese erotica in art and poetry/Hua Ying Jin Zhen;translated by N. S. Wang and B. L. Wang. Buffalo, N. Y. :Prometheus Books, 1990. 59 p. :ill. ;28cm. ISBN:087975611X, 0879756116.
(Chinese erotic and sexual classics in translation)
《花营锦阵》,Wang, N. S. ,Wang, B. L. 译. 中英对照. 色情诗与画.

5. Five lost classics:Tao, Huanglao, and Yin-yang in Han China/translated, with an introduction, and commentary by Robin D. S. Yates. New York:Ballantine Books, 1997. x, 301 p. ;25cm. (Classics of ancient China)
马王堆黄老五经. Yates, Robin D. S. (1948—)译. 英汉文本.

6. Things Chinese;being notes on various subjects connected with China. London, S. Low, Marston, and co. , 1892. 2 p. l. , 2 p. , 1 l. , 419, xiii p. 22cm.
中国百科知识. Ball, J. Dyer (James Dyer, 1847—1919) 和 Werner, E. T. C. (Edward Theodore Chalmers, 1864—1954)编译.
(1)3rd ed. rev. and enl. London, S. Low, Marston, 1900. 666, xxv p. 22cm.
(2)4th ed. , rev. and enl. New York:C. Scribner's Sons, 1904. 2 p. l. , vii-xii, 816 p. 23cm.
(3)5th ed. Revised by E. Chalmers Werner. Shanghai [etc.] Kelly & Walsh, Limited, 1925. 1 p. l. , iv, 766 p. 22cm.
(4)5th ed. rev. by E. Chalmers Werner. London, J. Murray, 1926. Detroit, Tower Books, 1971. ix, 766 p. 23cm.

7. The Chinese intellectual:selected readings＝[Zhi shi fen

zi]/translated and edited by Zhu Yao and Linda Seebach；introduction by Liang Heng. Northfield，MN：Small World Information Service，1987. vi，277 pages：illustrations；23cm. ISBN：0961882409，0961882402

Notes：Translation of selected articles from issues of：Zhi shi fen zi.

《知识分子》，Zhu，Yao（1945—），Seebach，Linda（1939—）选译. 是对《知识分子》杂志文章选译.

Z3　目录、索引

1. A research guide to English translation of Chinese verse：Han Dynasty to T'ang Dynasty/Kai-chee Wong，Pung Ho and Shu-leung Dang. Hong Kong：Chinese University Press，1977. xii，368 p.；27cm. ISBN：9622011411

《中诗英译索引：汉代至唐末》

2. 《中国文学》作品目录索引（1951—1986），英文版/中国文学杂志社编写出版. 84 页.

3. Catalogue of translations from the Chinese dynastic histories for the period 220—960/compiled by Hans H. Frankel. Berkeley，University of California Press，1957. 295 pages；24cm.

傅汉思（Frankel，Hans Hermann，1916—）编.

(1) Westport，Conn.：Greenwood Press，1974. 295 pages；23cm.（Chinese dynastic histories translations. Supplement；no. 1）

第二编　中国文献法译书目

A 类　毛泽东著作及相关文献

A1　领导人著作合集

1. Realisations économiques de la Chine nouvelle, 1949—1952. Pékin：Éditions en Langues Étrangères, 1953. 156 p. 8vo.
   《新中国三年来的经济成就》, 毛泽东, 刘少奇等著.

A2　毛泽东著作与研究

1. Citations du président Mao Tsé-toung/Zedong Mao. Paris：Seuil, 1945. 187 p.；18cm. (Le petit livre rouge；7)
   毛主席语录. 译者不详.
   (1) Paris：Éditions du Seuil, 1967. 187 p.；18cm. (Politique；7)
   (2) Paris：Éd. du Seuil, 1967. 110 p. 18cm. (P. Politique, ；7)
   (3)〔Paris〕：Éd. du Seuil, 1967. 186 S. (Le petit livre rouge)
   (4)〔Paris〕：Seuil, 1967. 188 p. (Le petit livre rouge. Politique, ；7)
   (5) Paris：Éd. du Seuil, 1981, 1967. 1 vol., (187 p.)：couv. ill., portrait.；18cm. (Points. Politique；7)
   (6)〔Paris〕：Seuil, 1972. 110 p.；18cm.

2. La Situation présente et nos tâches/Rapport présenté par le président Mao Tze-Tung au Comité Central du Parti communiste le 25 Décembre 1947(en chinois). Paris：(J. London)：(Imp. centrale commerciale), 1948. 20 p.：protr. h. t.
   《目前形势和我们的任务》, 译者不详.

3. La dictature de la démocratie populaire/Mao Tse-Toung. Pékin：Éditions en Langues Étrangères, 1949. 38p；19cm.
   《论人民民主专政》
   (1) 2nde éd. Pékin：Éditions en Langues Étrangères, 1960. 1 vol. (25 p., 〔1〕 p. de pl.〕：portrait.；19cm.
   (2) Pékin：Éditions en Langues Étrangères, 1961. 27p.；19cm.
   (3) 2e éd. (tr. rév.). Pékin：Éditions en Langues Étrangères, 1961. 85 pages
   (4) De la dictature democratique populaire. Pékin：Éditions en Langues Étrangères, 1963. 32 p.
   (5) 4e éd. Pékin：Éditions en Langues Étrangères, 1966.
   23 pages
   (6) Pékin：Éditions en Langues Étrangères, 1967. 35 pages

4. Mao Tsé Toung. Avec trois poèmes par Mao Tsé Toung/Traduit de l'anglais par Janine Mitaud. Paris：P. Seghers, 1949. 38 pages：portraits；18cm. (Poésie；49. 17)
   《毛泽东：附毛泽东诗词三首》, Payne, Robert (1911—1983) 著；Mitaud, Janine 译. 本书包含三首毛泽东诗词的翻译.

5. Dix-huit poèmes/traduits par G. G. Stephen Chow et Robert Desmond. Paris：P. Seghers, 1958. 42 pages；19cm.
   毛泽东诗词十八首. Chow, G. G. Stephen 和 Desmond, Robert 合译.

6. Poèmes/Mao Tsé-toung. Pékin：Éditions en Langues Étrangères, 1960. 43 p
   《毛泽东诗词》, 何如译.
   (1) Pékin：Éditions en Langues Étrangères, 1961. 52 p.：ill.；18cm.
   (2) Pékin：Éditions en Langues Étrangères, 1978. 68 Seiten：Illustrationen

7. Poèmes illustrés/par Salvador Dali. Paris：Éditions Argillet, 1967. 26 leaves plates, facsimile；40cm.
   《毛泽东诗词》, Dalí, Salvador (1904—1989) 译.

8. Poésies complètes de Mao Tse-Toung/traduites et commentées par Guy Brossollet. 〔Paris〕：l'Herne, 1969. 134 pages；22cm.
   毛泽东诗词全集. Brossollet, Guy (1933—) 译注.
   (1) Montréal：Éditions Parti pris, 1971. 131 p.：carte, fac-sim.；23cm. ISBN：0885120450, 0885120451. (Collection Paroles；no. 20)
   (2) Montréal：Éditions Parti pris, 1972. 131 pages. (Collection Paroles；20)

9. Mao Tse-Toung poésies complètes/présentation de Hualing Nieh Engle et Paul Engle；traduction et adaptation par Jean Billard. 〔Paris〕：P. Seghers, impr. Chastrusse, 1973. 1 vol. (188—〔8〕 p. de pl.)：ill., portraits, couv. ill.；16cm. (Poètes d'aujourd'hui；215)
   毛泽东诗词全集. Nie, Hualing (1925—), Engle, Paul (1908—1991) 编著；Billard, Jean 译.

10. Poésies complètes/Mao Tse-Toung. Précedées de Mao Tse-Toung par Robert Payne. Paris：Seghers, 1976.

159 pages；19cm.

毛泽东诗词全集. Payne, Robert(1911—1982)译.

11. Poésies dans la Chine nouvelle/Mao-Tsé-toung, précédé de Mao-Tsé-toung par Robert Payne. Paris：Seghers, 1976. 159 p.；19cm.

新中国诗词. Payne, Robert(1911—1982)译.

12. Poèmes/Mao Tsétoung；[traduit par Ho Ju]. Pékin：Éditions en Langues Étrangères；[Paris]；[diffusion Éditions du Centenaire]，1978. 68 p.：ill.，couv. ill.；21cm.

《毛泽东诗集》

13. Pour la parution de "Le Communiste". Pékin：Éditions en Langues Étrangères, 1953. In—16, II-24 p.

《"共产党人"发刊词》

(1)3. éd. Pékin：Éditions en Langues Étrangères,1960. 19p.；22cm.

14. La révolution chinoise et le Parti Communiste chinois. Pékin：Éditions en Langues Étrangères, 1953. 59 p.

《中国革命和中国共产党》

(1)[3rd éd.]. Pékin, Éditions en Langues Étrangères, 1960. 60 pages：illustrations；19cm.

(2)Pékin：Éditions en Langues Étrangères, 1971. 90 pages

15. Contre le libéralisme/Mao Tse-toung. Pékin：Éditions en Langues Étrangères,1954.1v. (6p.)

《反对自由主义》

16. L'Indépendance et l'autonomie au sein du front uni. Pékin：Éditions en Langues Étrangères,1954. In—16,II-8p.

《统一战线中的独立自主问题》

(1)2e éd. Pékin：Éditions en Langues Étrangères,1960. 6pages

17. Problèmes stratégiques de la guerre de partisans contre le Japon. Pékin：Éditions en Langues Étrangères, 1964. 87 pages.

《抗日游击战争的战略问题》

(1)Pékin：Éditions en Langues Étrangères, 1965. 64 p.；19cm.

(2)2e éd. Pékin：Éditions en Langues Étrangères, 1968. 84 pages

18. Artistes et écrivains dans la Chine nouvelle/[par] Mao Tse-toung. Traduit du Chinois par Ouang Cheliou. Paris：P. Seghers, 1949. 50 pages；18cm. (Poésie 49，；no. 19)

新中国艺术家和作家. Ouang, Cheliou 译.

19. La stratégie de la guerre révolutionnaire en Chine/Mao-Tsé-toung；[Préface par M. Magnien]. Paris：Éditions sociales, (Impr. de Bellenand)，1950. 119 p.：cartes；couv. en coul.；19cm.

中国革命战争的战略问题. Magnien, Marius(1903—1962)序.

(1)Paris：Éditions sociales, 1951. 118 pages：maps；19cm.

20. La guerre révolutionnaire/par Mao Tse-Toung. Paris：Éditions sociales, 1955. 185 pages：portraits；19cm. (Le Monde en 10/18；no. 44)

革命战争. 译者不详.

(1)Paris：Union Générale d'Éditions, 1955. 185 p. (Monde en 10/18；44)

(2)Paris：Union générale d'éditions, 1962, 185 pages；19cm. (Le monde en 10/18；[44])

(3)[Paris]：ÉditionsSociales,1962. 185 s. (Le monde en 10/18；；44)

(4)Paris：Union Générale d'Éditions, 1965. 185, [4] s.；18cm. (Le Monde en 10—18；44)

(5)Paris：Union générale d'Éditions, 1969. 185 p.：couv. ill.；18cm. (Le Monde en 10/18；44)

21. La nouvelle démocratie/Mao Tsé-toung. Paris：Éd. Sociales, 1951. 1 vol. (203 p.)：couv. ill. 3.；19cm.

《新民主主义论》,译者不详.

(1)Paris：Éd. Sociales, 1957. 207 S.

(2)Paris：Éditions sociales, 1961. 207 pages；19cm.

22. Œuvres choisies. Tome premier, 1926—1937/Mao Tsé Toung；[traduit du russe par René l'Hermitte]. Paris：Éd. sociales, 1955. 1 vol. (415 p.)：couv. ill.；23cm.

《毛泽东选集》,第一卷. L'Hermitte, René(1918—2005) 由俄文翻译为法文.

23. Œuvres choisies. Tome deuxième, Juillet 1937—novembre 1938/Mao Tsé-toung. Paris：Éditions sociales, 1955. 277 p.；23cm.

《毛泽东选集》,第二卷. 译者不详.

24. Œuvres choisies. Tome troisième, 1939—1941/Mao Tsé-toung；[trad. d'après l'éd. russe par Paul Kolodkine et Joseph Ducroux]. Paris：Éd. sociales, 1956. 1 vol. (284 p.)；22cm.

《毛泽东选集》,第三卷. Ducroux, Joseph 和 Kolodkine, Paul 由俄文翻译为法文.

25. Œuvres choisies. Tome quatrième, Mars 1941—Août 1945/Mao Tsé-toung. Trad. par rené L'Hermitte. Paris：Éditions sociales, 1959. 398 p.；23cm.

《毛泽东选集》,第四卷. L'Hermitte, René(1918—2005) 由俄文翻译为法文.

26. Œuvres choisies de Mao Tse-toung. Tome IV. Pékin：Éditions en Langues Étrangères, 1962. 488 p.；23cm.

《毛泽东选集》,第四卷.

(1)Œuvres choisies de Mao Tse-toung. Tome I. Pékin：Éditions en Langues Étrangères, 1966. 392 p.；23cm.

(2)Œuvres choisies de Mao Tse-toung. Tome II. Pékin：Éditions en Langues Étrangères, 1967. 512 p.；23cm.

(3)Œuvres choisies de Mao Tse-toung. Tome III.

Pékin：Éditions en Langues Étrangères，1968. 313 p.；23cm.

(4)Œuvres choisies de Mao Tsé-toung. Tome V. （I），Période de la révolution et de l'édification socialistes/Mao Tsé-toung. Pékin：Éditions en Langues Étrangères，1977. 1 vol. （568 p.）；23cm.

27. Mao Tse-Toung/textes trad. et pres. par Stuart Schram. Paris：A. Colin，1963. 415 p.；18cm.（Collection U. Idées politiques）
毛泽东选集. Schram，Stuart R. 译.
(1)2. éd.，rev. et augm. Paris：A. Colin，1972. 559 pages.（Collection U）

28. Mao Tsŏ-tong；présentation/choix de textes, illustrations ［par］Roger Lévy.［Paris］：Seghers，1965. 175 pages：illustrations；.（Les destinspolitiques）
毛泽东著作选译. Levy，Roger（1887—）著、译.
(1)Paris：Seghers，1967. 183 p.：carte，［1］pl.，couv. ill.；16cm.（Les Destins politiques；2）

29. Ecrits choisis en trois volumes Zedong Mao. Paris：Francois Maspero，1967. 3 vol.（187，187，189）p.；18cm. ISBN：2707101451，2707101457，270710146X，2707101464，2707101478，2707101471.（Petite Collection Maspero；2—4）
《毛泽东选集》，三卷. 译者不详.
(1)Paris：Maspero，1969. 3 vol.（191，191，191 p.）；18cm.（Petite collection Maspero；02—04）. 何如译.
(2)Paris：F. Maspèro，1973. 3 vol.（187 p.）（189 p.）（189 p.）；18cm.（Petite Collection Maspèro；2；3；4）
(3)Paris：F. Maspero，1976. 3 vol.；18cm.（Petite Collection Maspero；2；3；4）

30. Ce que Mao a vraiment dit/Philippe Devillers. Paris：Stock，1968. 295 pages；20cm.
毛泽东的真实讲话. Devillers，Philippe（1920—）编著并翻译. 本书包含了毛主席语录的选译.
(1)Verviers：Gérard & Co，1973. 293 pages；18cm.（Marabout université，242. Connaître）

31. Mao Tsé-toung，1893—1976/choix établi et présenté par Marie-Hélène Bernard. Paris：La Martinière：X. Barral, France Quercy. 2003. 63 p.：ill.；16cm. ISBN：2846750866，2846750868.（Voix；4）
《毛泽东文选：1893—1976》，Bernard，Marie-Hélène 译.

32. Pourquoi le pouvoir rouge peut-il exister en Chine? /Mao Tse-toung. Pékin：Éditions en Langues Étrangères，1956. 23p.；8°.
《中国的红色政权为什么能够存在?》
(1)2e éd. Pékin：Éditions en Langues Étrangères，1960.
(2)Pékin：Éditions en Langues Étrangères，1964. 23 p.

33. Une étincelle peut mettre le feu à toute la plaine. Pékin：Éditions en Langues Étrangères，1956. In—16，28 p.
《星星之火，可以燎原》
(1)2e éd. Pékin：Éditions en Langues Étrangères，

1960. 24 pages
(2)Pékin：Éditions en Langues Étrangères，1964. 29 p.

34. Luttons pour entraîner les masses dans le front national antijaponais uni. Pékin：Éditions en Langues Étrangères，1956. In—16，22 p.
《为争取千百万群众进入抗日名族统一战线而斗争》
(1)2e éd. Pékin：Éditions en Langues Étrangères，1960.
(2)Luttons pour entraîner les masses par millions dans le front uni national antijaponais/Mao Tse-Toung. Pékin：Éditions en Langues Étrangères，1968. 1 vol.（16 p.）：couv. ill.；18,5cm.

35. Sur le problème de la coopération agricole. Rapport présenté à une réunion des secrétaires des comités provinciaux, municipaux et régionaux du Parti communiste chinois, le 31 juillet 1955. Pékin：Éditions en Langues Étrangères，1956. In—16，45 p.
《关于农业合作化问题》
(1)2e éd. Pékin：Éditions en Langues Étrangères，1960. 43 p.；19cm.
(2)4e éd. Pékin：Éditions en Langues Étrangères，1966. 40 p.

36. La tactique de la lutte contre l'impérialisme japonais/Mao Tse-toung. Pékin：Éditions en Langues Étrangères，1956. v.（56p.）；19cm.
《论反对日本帝国主义的策略》
(1)3e éd.（traduction révisée）. Pékin：Éditions en Langues Étrangères，1960. 50pages
(2)3 éd. Pékin：Éditions en Langues Étrangères；［Paris］：［Diffusion Éditions du Centenaire］，1961. 50 p.：couv. ill.；19cm.
(3)4e éd.（tr. rév.）. Pékin：Éditions en Langues Étrangères，1965. 40 pages
(4)Pékin：Éditions en Langues Étrangères，1967.
(5)Pékin：Éditions en Langues Étrangères，1968. 1 vol.；15cm.

37. La question de la juste solution des contradictions au sein du peuple/Mao Tsé-toung.［Paris：Etudes soviétiques，1957. 32 p.
《关于正确处理人民内部矛盾的问题》，译者不详.
(1)［Levallois-Perret］：［Herbert］，1957. 31 pages.（Supplément à "Études Soviétiques".；no. 113）

38. Les tâches du Parti communiste chinois dans la période de la resistance au Japon. Pékin：Éditions en Langues Étrangères，1957. 49 pages
《中国共产党在抗日时期的任务》
(1)Les tâches du parti communiste chinois dans la période de la résistance aux envahisseurs japonais/Mau Tse-Toeng［aut］. Pékin：Éditions en Langues Étrangères，1960. 47 pages
(2)Les tâches du Parti communiste chinois dans la

période de la résistance aux envahisseurs japonais/ Mao Tsé-toung. 3 éd. Pékin：Éditions en Langues Étrangères；［Paris］：［Diffusion Éditions du Centenaire］，1961. 46 p.；19cm.

（3）Les tâches du Parti communiste chinois dans la période de la résistance au Japon/Mao Tse-toung. ［4e éd. rév.］. Pékin：Éditions en Langues Étrangères，1965. 37 p.

39. A propos de la pratique：la liaison entre la connaissance et la pratique：la liaison entre les connaissances et l'action/Mao Tse-tung. Pékin：Éditions en Langues Étrangères，1957. 1 v. （33 p.）；in-8.

《实践论》

（1）2e éd. Pékin：Éditions en Langues Étrangères，1960. 32 pages；19cm.

（2）De la pratique：la relation entre la connaissance et la pratique entre le savoir et l'action/Mao Tse-Toung. Pékin：Éditions en Langues Étrangères，5e éd. 24，［1］ p.

40. De la pratique ＝ Shijian lun/Mao Tsé-toung；texte original et traduction avec avant-propos, glossaire, notes par Michelle Loi. Paris：Aubier Montaigne，1973. 159 pages；20cm. （Collection bilingue）

《实践论》，Loi，Michelle 译、序、注.

41. A propos de la contradiction/Mao Zedong. Pékin：Éditions en Langues Étrangères，1957. 1 v. （78 p.） d25cm.

《矛盾论》

（1）2e éd. Pékin：Éditions en Langues Étrangères，1960. 77 pages

（2）De la contradiction. Pékin：Éditions en Langues Étrangères，5a éd. （tr. rév.）. 1966. 62 pages

42. La Démocratie nouvelle. Pékin：Éditions en Langues Étrangères，1955. 86 pages：portraits；19cm.

《新民主主义论》

（1）Pékin：Éditions en Langues Étrangères，1960. 85 p.：ill.；20cm.

43. Antilogies/Mao Tse-Toung. Lausanne Éditions la Cite，1963. 190 p.

《矛盾论》，译者不详.

44. À propos de la contradiction/Mao Tse-Toung. ［Reproduction en fac-similé］. ［Paris］：Éd. du Sandre，Impr. Corlet，2008，1960. 1 vol. （72 p.）：portr.；22cm. ISBN：2358210058，2358210056. （Bibliothèque rouge）

《矛盾论》，译者不详.

45. Le camarade Mao Tsé-toung sur "l'Impérialisme et tous les réactionaires sont des tigres en papier". Département de la rédaction du Renmin Ribao... Pékin：Éditions en Langues Étrangères，1958. In-16 （18，5cm.），38 p.

《毛泽东同志论帝国主义和一切反动派都是纸老虎》

（1）Le camarade Mao Tse-toung sur "L'imperialisme et tous les reactionaires sont des tigres en papier." Pékin：Éditions en Langues Étrangères，3rd éd. （tr. rév.）. 1960. 35 pages

（2）5ème éd. （Trad. révisée）. Pékin：Éditions en Langues Étrangères，1966. 33 p.；19cm.

46. Les problèmes stratégiques de la guerre révolutionnaire en Chine. Pékin：Éditions en Langues Étrangères，1958. 163 pages

《中国革命战争的战略问题》

（1）Pékin：Éditions en Langues Étrangères，1964. 181 p

47. Situation internationale d'aujourd'hui. Pékin：Éditions en Langues Étrangères，1958. 84 p.；In—16 （18,5cm.）

《目前国际形势》

48. Analyse des classes de la Société chinoise/Mao Tse-Toung. Pékin：Éditions en Langues Étrangères，1960. 18 p.；19cm.

《中国社会各阶级的分析》，第2版.

（1）［3. éd.］. Pékin，Éditions en Langues Étrangères，1961. 18 pages：illustrations；19cm.

（2）4e éd. Pékin：Éditions en Langues Étrangères，1965. 15 p.

（3）4. éd. traduction révisée. Pékin：Éditions en Langues Étrangères，1966. 15 p.；19cm.

（4）Pékin：Éditions en Langues Étrangères，1968. 21 pages；13cm.

49. Rapport sur l'enquête menée dans le Hounan à propos du mouvement paysan/Mao Tse-Toung. Pékin：Éditions en Langues Étrangères，1960. 66 p；19cm.

《湖南农民运动考察报告》

（1）4 éd. Pékin：Éditions en Langues Étrangères；［Paris］：［diffusion Éditions du Centenaire］，1965. 61 p.；19cm.

50. Soucions-nous davantage des conditions de vie des masses et portons plus d'attentions à nos méthodes de travail/ Mau Tse-Toeng ［aut］. Pékin：Éditions en Langues Étrangères，1960.

《关心群众生活，注意工作方法》

（1）4e éd. Pékin：Éditions en Langues Étrangères，1965. 7 p.

51. La Ligne politique, les mesures et les perspectives de la lutte contre l'offensive japonaise/Mao Tsé-toung. Pékin：Éditions en Langues Étrangères；［Paris］：［diffusion Éditions du Centenaire］，1960. 14 p.：couv. ill.；19cm.

《反对日本进攻的方针、办法和前途》，第2版.

（1）3e éd. Pékin：Éditions en Langues Étrangères，1961. 15 pages

（2）4e éd. Pékin：Éditions en Langues Étrangères，1966. 12 pages

52. Luttons pour la mobilisation de toutes les forces pour

remporter la victoire dans la guerre anti-japonaise/Tse-toung Mao. Pékin：Éditions en Langues Étrangères, 1960. 1 v. （[13] p.）

《为动员一切力量争取抗战胜利而斗争》，第 2 版.

53. De la guerre prolongée/Mao Tse-Toung. Pékin：Éditions en Langues Étrangères, 1960. 171 p.；19cm.

《论持久战》

(1) Pékin：Éditions en Langues Étrangères, 1964. 194 pages

54. Le rôle du parti communiste chinois dans la guerre nationale. Pékin：Éditions en Langues Étrangères. 1960. 32 pages；|c 19cm.

《中国共产党在民族战争中的地位》

(1) 4e éd. （tr. rév.）. Pékin：Éditions en Langues Étrangères, 1966. 30 pages

55. Problèmes de la guerre et de la stratégie/Mao Tse-toung. Pékin：Éditions en Langues Étrangères, 1960. 1 vol. （33 p.）

《战争和战略问题》，第 2 版.

(1) Pékin：Éditions en Langues Étrangères, 1964. 37 p.

56. L'orientation du mouvement de la jeunesse/Mao Tse-Toung. Pékin：Éditions en Langues Étrangères, 1960. 17 p；19cm.

《青年运动的方向》，第 2 版.

57. Pour un régime constitutionnel de démocratie nouvelle. Pékin：Éditions en Langues Étrangères, 2e éd. （tr. rév）. 1960. 19 pages

《新民主主义的宪政》，第 2 版.

(1) Le régime constitutionnel de démocratie nouvelle. Pékin：Éditions en Langues Étrangères, 5e éd. 1968. 16 p.

58. Discours prononcé à l'assemblée de la région frontière Chensi-Kansou-Ninghsia/Tsé-toung Mao. Pékin：Éditions en Langues Étrangères, 1960. 1 vol. （[7] p.）

《在陕甘宁边区参议会的演说》，第 2 版.

(1) Pékin：Éditions en Langues Étrangères, 1966. 6 p

59. De la juste solution des contradictions au sein du peuple. Pékin：Éditions en Langues Étrangères, 2e éd. 1960. 72 pages

《关于正确处理人民内部矛盾的问题》，第 2 版.

60. Importants entretiens du président Mao Tse-toung avec des personnalités d'Asie, d'Afrique et d'Amérique Latine. Pékin：Éditions en Langues Étrangères, 1960. 9 pages；19cm.

《毛泽东主席同亚洲、美洲、拉丁美洲人士的几次重要讲话》.

(1) Pékin：Éditions en Langues Étrangères, 1963. 14 pages；15cm.

61. Préface et postface à "L'enquête à la campagne." Pékin：Éditions en Langues Étrangères, 1961. 10 pages

《"农村调查"的序言和跋》

(1) 4e éd. Pékin：Éditions en Langues Étrangères, 1968. 9 pages

62. Reformons notre étude/Mao Tse-toung. Pékin：Éditions en Langues Étrangères, 1961. 14 p.；19cm.

《改造我们的学习》

(1) 2ème éd. Pékin：Éditions en Langues Étrangères, 1965. 11 p.；19cm.

63. A propos des méthodes de direction. Pékin, Éditions en Langues Étrangères, 1961. 10 pages：portraits；19cm.

《关于领导方法的若干问题》

(1) 2e éd. Pédin：Éditions en Langues Étrangères, 1965. 8 pages

(2) 4e éd. Pédin：Éditions en Langues Étrangères, 1968. 8 pages

64. La Situation et notre politique après la victoire dans la guerre de résistance contre le Japon/Mao Tsé-toung, Pékin：Éditions en Langues Étrangères；[Paris]：[diffusion Éditions du Centenaire], 1961. 23 p. : couv. ill.；19cm.

《抗日战争胜利后的时局和我们的方针》

(1) Pékin：Éditions en Langues Étrangères, 1964. 34 p

65. Sur les négociations de Tchongking/Mao Tsé-toung. Pékin：Éditions en Langues Étrangères；[Paris]：[diffusion Éditions du centenaire], 1961. 25 p. : couv. ill.；19cm.

《关于重庆谈判》

(1) Pékin：Éditions en Langues Étrangères, 1963. 37 p.

66. Entretien avec la journaliste américaine Anna Louise Strong/Mao Tsé-toung；[traduit du chinois]. Pékin：Éditions en Langues Étrangères；[Paris]：[diffusion Éditions du Centenaire], 1961. 9 p. : couv. ill.；19cm.

《和美国记者安娜·路易斯·斯特朗的谈话》

(1) Pékin：Éditions en Langues Étrangères, 1963. 13 p

67. La Situation actuelle et nos tâches/Mao Tsé-toung. Pékin：Éditions en Langues Étrangères；[Paris]：diffusion Éditions du Centenaire, 1961. 35 p. : couv. ill.；19cm.

《目前形势和我们的任务》

(1) Pékin：Éditions en Langues Étrangères, 1963. 50 p

68. Une étude de l'éducation physique/[par] Mao Ze-dong. [Article] traduit et présenté par Stuart R. Schram. [Paris]：[Mouton], 1962. 1 v. （69 p.）；27cm. （Maison des sciences de l'homme. Matériaux pour l'étude de la Chine moderne et contemporaine. Textes)

《体育之研究》，Schram, Stuart R. 译.

(1) Paris：La Haye：Mouton et Cie, 1962. 80 p.；couv. ill.；In-4° （27cm.）

(2) [Paris]：[Mouton], 1972. 69 pages；28cm. （Maison des Sciences de l'ilomme. Matériaux pour l'étude de la Chine moderne et contemporaine. Textes)

69. Discours prononcé à une conférence des cadres de la

région libérée du Chansi-Soueiyuan. Pékin：Éditions en Langues Étrangères，1961. 21 pages

《在晋委干部会议上的讲话》

(1)2e éd.（tr. rév.）. Pékin：Éditions en Langues Étrangères，1966. 21 pages.

(2)Pékin：Éditions en Langues en Langues Étrangères，1969. 37 pages.

70. Raffermir le système du comité du parti/Mao Tse-Tung. Pékin：Éditions en Langues Étrangères，1961. 9 pages.

《关于健全党委制》

71. Mener la révolution jusqu'au bout/Mao Tse-toung. Pékin：Éditions en Langues Étrangères，1961. 18 p.；19cm.

《将革命进行到底》

(1)Pékin：Éditions en Langues Étrangères，1963. 27 pages

(2)Pékin：Éditions en Langues Étrangères，1966. 18 pages

72. Rapport à la deuxième session plénière du Comité central issu du VIIe congress du Parti communiste Chinois. Pékin：Éditions en Langues Étrangères，1961. 28 pages：portraits；19cm.

《在中国共产党第七届中央委员会第二次全体会议上的报告》

(1)Pékin：Éditions en Langues Etragères，1964. 39 pages

(2)2e éd.（tr. rév）. Pékin：Éditions en Langues Étrangères，1966. 28 pages

(3)Pékin：Éditions en Langues Étrangères，1968. 1 v.（40 p.）；20cm.

(4)Pékin：Éd. en Langues Étrangères，1973. a9 p.；19cm.

73. Sur le Livre blanc américain. Pékin：Éditions en Langues Étrangères，1961. 54 pages：portrait

《评白皮书》

(1)Pékin：Éditions en Langues Étrangères，1963. 78 p

74. Sur notre politique/Mao Tse-toung. Pékin：Éditions en Langues Étrangères，1961. 18 pages；19cm.

《论政策》

75. Interventions aux causeries sur la littérature et l'art à Yenan/Mao Tse-Toung. Pékin：Éditions en Langues Étrangères，1962. 49 pages

《在延安文艺座谈会上的讲话》

(1)2ème éd. Pékin：Éditions en Langues Étrangères，1965. 50 p.；19cm.

(2)Pékin：Éditions en Langues Étrangères，1969. 49 pages

76. Ecrits philosophiques/Mao Tse-toung. 〔Lausanne〕：La Cité，1963. 190 pages；19cm.

毛泽东哲学著作选读. 译者不详.

77. Cinq essais philosophiques/Mao Tsetoung. Pékin：Éditions en Langues Étrangères，1971. 294 pages：portraits；13cm.

《毛主席的五篇哲学著作》

(1)2e éd. Pékin：Éditions en Langues Étrangères，1976. 294 p.：1 portr. en frontispice.；14cm.

78. Les Transformations de la Révolution/par Mao Tsé-toung；textes choisis et présentés par Patrick Kessel. Paris：Union générale d'éditions，1970. 320 p.：couv. ill.；19cm.（10—18；523—524）

革命的转变. Kessel，Patrick 编著. 本书包含毛泽东作品选译.

79. Déclaration appelant les peuples du monde a s'unir contre la discrimination raciale pratiquée par l'impérialisme américains et à soutenir les Noirs américains dans leur lutte contre cette discrimination. Pékin：Éditions en Langues Étrangères，1963. 95 p

《呼吁世界人民联合起来反对美国帝国主义的种族歧视、支持美国黑人反对种族歧视的斗争的声明(1963 年 8 月 8 日)》

80. Déclaration contre l'agression de la partie sud du Vietnam et le massacre du peuple de cette région par la clique États-Unis-Ngo Dinh Diem/Mao Tsé-toung. Pékin：Éditions en Langues Étrangères，1963. 1 v.（33，〔3〕 p.）；19cm.

《反对美国-吴庭艳集团侵略越南南方和屠杀越南南方人民的声明(1963 年 8 月 29 日)》

81. 〔Œuvres de Mao Tse Toung〕. 1，L'Elimination des conceptions erronées dans le Parti. Pékin：Éditions en Langues Étrangères，1964. 24 p.；19cm.

《关于纠正党内的错误思想》

(1)2e éd. Pékin：Éditions en Langues Étrangères，1965. 18 p.；19cm.

82. Sur quelques questions importantes de la politique actuelle du Parti. Pékin：Éditions en Langues Étrangères，1964. 19 pages

《关于目前党的政策中的几个重要问题》，初版于 1961 年.

(1)2e éd（tr. rév.）. Pékin：Éditions en Langues Étrangères，1967. 10 pages

(2)Pékin：Éditions en Langues Étrangères，1968. 17 pages

83. Déclaration du président Mao Tsetoung，le peuple chinois soutient fermement la juste lutte patriotique du peuple panamien（12 janvier 1964）. Pékin：Éditions en Langues Étrangères，1964. 28 p

《毛泽东主席谈话-中国人民坚决支持巴拿马人民的爱国正义斗争》.

84. Déclarations de Mao Tse-toung：Peuples du monde entier，unissons nous pour nous opposer à la politique d'agression et de guerre de l'imperialisme américain et pour défendre la paix mondiale，août 1963 janvier 1964. Pékin：Éditions en Langues Étrangères，1964. 16，〔1〕

pages；19cm.

《毛泽东主席声明、谈话集-全世界人民联合起来，反对美帝国主义的侵略政策和战争政策，保卫世界和平》

85. Écrits militaires de Mao Tsé-toung. Pékin：Éditions en Langues Étrangères；[Paris]：[diffusion Éditions du Centenaire]，1964. 465 p.：portr.；23cm.

《毛泽东军事文选》.

(1) Pékin：Éditions en Langues Étrangères，1969. 461 p.：portr

86. L'independance et l'autonomie au sein du front uni /Mao Tse-toung. Pékin：Éditions en Langues Étrangères，4ème éd. 1965. 7 p.；19cm.

《统一战线中的的独立自主问题》

87. Contre le style stéréotype dans le parti/[par] Mao Tse-Toung. Pékin：Éditions en Langues Étrangères，1965. 25 pages

《反对党八股》

(1) 2e éd. Pékin：Éditions en Langues Étrangères，1966. 25 p.

(2) 3e éd. Pékin：Éditions en Langues Étrangères，1968. 25 pages

88. Sur la littérature et l'art/Mao Tse-Toung. Pékin：Éditions en Langues Étrangères，1965. 1 v. (161 p.)；19cm.

《毛泽东论文学和艺术》

89. Cinq documents sur la littérature et l'art/Mao Tse-toung. Pékin：Éditions en Langues Étrangères，1967. 11 pages；13cm.

《毛主席关于文学艺术的五个文件》

90. Citations du Président Mao Tse-toung. Pékin：Éditions en Langues Étrangères，1966. 346 pages，[2] leaves of plates：portrait, facsimile；14cm.

《毛主席语录》

(1) Pékin：Éditions en Langues Étrangères，1. éd. 1972. 391 pages：color portraits；11cm.

91. Les mots de Mao/[sélectionnés] par Pierre Mourgues. [Mane]：R. Morel，1966—?. 1 vol. (non paginé [96] p.)；6cm. (Les O.)

毛主席语录. Mourgues, Pierre 选译.

(1) [Le Jas du Revest Saint Martin, Basses-Alpes]：R. Morel，1967. 1 volume (unpaged)；60 mm. (Les "O"；[no. 1])

(2) [Paris]：[R. Morel]，1968. 50 circular cards on ring；6cm. in diameter. ([Collection] Les O)

92. Livre rouge de la Révolution culturelle/Mao Tsé-toung. Bruxelles：la Taupe，1971. 1 vol. (163 p.)：ill., couv. ill.；18cm. (Luttes actuelles；1)

《文化大革命红宝书》，译者不详.

(1) Bruxelles, La Taupe, 1972. 163 pages；18cm. (Luttes actuelles)

93. Les Citations de Mao Tsé-toung/Mao Tsê-toung. Paris：J.

de Bonnot，1975. [14]，269，238 pages：illustrations；21cm.

毛主席语录. 译者不详.

94. Le grand livre rouge；écrits, discours et entretiens 1949—1971/traduit de l'allemand par Jeanne-Marie Gaillard-Paquet；textes présentés par Helmut Martin. Paris，Flammarion，1975. 360 pages. ISBN：208060807X，2080608079

大红宝书：1949—1971 的作品、演说和谈话. Martin, Helmut(1940—)编著；Gaillard-Paquet, Jeanne-Marie 由德文转译成法文. 本书包含对毛泽东作品及讲话的选译.

(1) Paris：Club français du livre, impr. Bussière，1975. 359 p.；21cm.

95. Citations du président Mao：version bilingue. Paris：Librairie You Feng，2013. 435 p.：portr；14cm. ISBN：2842790413，2842790417

毛主席语录：双语版. 译者不详.

96. Contre le culte de livre：Mai 1930/Mao Tse-toung. Pékin：Éditions en Langues Étrangères，1966. 17 pages；13cm.

《反对本本主义》

97. Intervention à la Conférence nationale du Parti Communiste Chinois sur le Travail de Propagande (12 mars 1957). Pékin：Éditions en Langues Étrangères，1966. 21 pages

《在中国共产党全国宣传工作会议上的谈话》

98. D'ou viennent les idees justes?. Pékin：Éditions en Langues Étrangères，1966. 3 pages；15cm.

《人的正确思想是从哪里来的?》

99. De la juste solution des contradictions au sein du peuple. Pékin：Éditions en Langues Étrangères，1967. 61 p.

《关于正确处理人民内部矛盾问题》

(1) Pékin：Éditions en Langues Étrangères，1968. 86 p.

100. Etre attaque par l'ennemi est une bonne et non une mauvaise chose：Pour le IIIe anniversaire de la fondation de l'Ecole militaire et politique antijaponaise de Peuple chínois (26 mai 1939). Pékin：Éditions en Langues Étrangères，1966. 3 p.

《被敌人反对是好事而不是坏事》

(1) Pékin：Éditions en Langues Étrangères，1975. 2 p.

101. Quatre essais philosophiques/Mao Tse-toung. Pékin：Éditions en Langues Étrangères，1967. 151 p.；19cm.

《毛泽东的四篇哲学论文》

102. Le président Mao Tse-Toung sur la guerre populaire. Pékin：Éditions en Langues Étrangères，1967. 59 p.：portrait en coul.；11cm.

《毛主席论人民战争》

103. Comment Yukong déplaça les montagnes/Mao Tse-toung. Pékin：Éditions en Langues Étrangères，1967. 5 pages；13cm.

《愚公移山》

104. Servir le peuple：à la mémoire de Norman Béthune/Mau Tse-Toeng［aut］. Pékin：Éditions en Langues Étrangères，1967.

《为人民服务》

105. Servir le peuple；A la mémoire de Norman bethune；Comment Yukong déplaça les montagnes. Pékin：Éditions en Langues Étrangères，1967. 12 pages

《为人民服务 纪念白求恩 愚公移山》

106. Cinq articles du président Mao Tsé-toung. Pékin：Éditions en Langues Étrangères，1968. 66 p

《毛主席的五篇著作》

107. Le Front uni dans le travail culturel/Mao Tse-Toung. Pékin：Éditions en Langues Étrangères，1968. 1 vol. (8 p.)；14,5cm.

《文化工作中的统一战线》

108. Apprendre le travail économique/Mao Tse-toung. Pékin：Éditions en Langues Étrangères，1968. 10 pages；19cm.

《必须学会做经济工作》

109. Du gouvernement de coalition. Pékin：Éditions en Langues Étrangères，1968. 146 p.

《论联合政府》

110. De la production par l'armée des biens nécessaires à ses besoins et de l'importance des deux grands mouvements pour la rectification du style de travail et pour le développement de la production/Mao Tse-toung. Pékin：Éditions en Langues Étrangères，1968. 9 pages；13cm.

《论军队生产自给，兼论整风和生产两大运动的重要性》

111. Causerie pour les rédacteurs du Quotidien du chansi-Soueiyuan. (2 avril 1948). Pékin：Éditions en Langues Étrangères，1968. 11 pages.

《对晋绥日报编辑人员的谈话》

112. Forces révolutionnaires du monde entier, unissez-vous, combattez l'agression impérialiste!. Pékin：Éditions en Langues Étrangères，1968. 6 pages

《全世界革命力量团结起来，反对帝国主义的侵略》

113. Pourquoi le pouvoir rouge peut-il exister en Chine?；La lutte dans les Monts Tsingkang；L'élimination des conceptions erronées dans le Parti；Une étincelle peut mettre le feu à toute la plaine. Pékin：Éditions en Langues Étrangères，1968. 153 pages.

《中国的红色政权为什么能够存在? 井冈山的战斗 关于纠正党内错误思想 星星之火，可以燎原》

114. La lutte dans les Monts Tsingkang/Mao Tse-toung. Pékin：Éditions en Langues Étrangères，1968. 75 pages；13cm.

《井冈山的斗争》

115. La situation dans la guerre de résistance après la chute de Chang-hai et de Taiyuan et les tâches qui en

découlent. Pékin：Éditions en Langues Étrangères，1968. 22 p

《上海、太原失陷以后抗日战争的形势和任务》

116. Déclaration pour soutenir la lutte des afro-américains contre la répression par la violence (16 avril 1968)/Mau Tse-Toeng［aut］. Pékin：Éditions en Langues Étrangères，1968. 6 p.

《中国共产党中央委员会主席毛泽东同志支持美国黑人抗暴斗争的声明》

117. Notre étude et la situation actuelle/Mao Tse-toung. Pékin：Éditions en Langues Étrangères，1968. 20 pages；19cm.

《目前形势和党的任务》

118. La démocratie nouvelle；and，interventions aux causeries sur la littérature et l'art à Yenan；and，de la juste solution des contradictions au sein du peuple；and，intervention à la conférence nationale du Parti Communiste Chinois sur le travail de propagande/Mao Tse-toung. Pékin：Éditions en Langues Étrangères，1968. 200 pages：portraits；19cm.

《新民主主义论 在延安文艺座谈会上的讲话 关于正确处理人民内部矛盾的问题 在中国共产党全国宣传工作会议上的讲话》

119. Sur la question du pouvoir dans les bases antijaponaises/Mao Tse-Toung. Pékin：Éditions en Langues Étrangères，1968. 1 vol. (6 p.)；15cm.

《抗日根据地的政权问题》

120. Développer hardiment les forces antijaponaises, repousser les attaques des irréductibles anticommunistes/Mao Tse-toung. Pékin：Éditions en Langues Étrangères，1968. 13 pages；13cm.

《放手发展抗日力量，抵抗反共顽固派的进攻》

121. Développer dans les bases d'appui les mouvements pour la réduction des fermages, l'accroissement de la production, "le soutien au gouvernement et l'amour du peuple"/Mao Tse-toung. Pékin：Éditions en Langues Étrangères，1968. 1 vol. (10 p.)；15cm.

《开展根据地的减租、生产和拥政爱民运动》

122. Organisez-vous! /Mao Tse-toung. Pékin：Éditions en Langues Étrangères，1968. 20 pages；13cm.

《组织起来》

123. Organisez-vous! /Mao Tse-toung. Pékin：Éditions en Langues Étrangères，1968. 15 pages；19cm.

《团结到底》

124. Notre étude et la situation actuelle. Pékin：Éditions en Langues Étrangères，1968. 28 pages.

《学习和时局》

125. Apporter de l'attention au travail économique：［discours］，20 août 1933/Mao Tsétoung；［traduit du chinois］. Pékin：Éditions en Langues Étrangères；Paris：［diffusion Éditions du Centenaire］，1969. 20

p. ; 13cm.

《必须注意经济工作》

126. Comment analyser les classes à la campagne: octobre 1933/Mao Tsétoung; [traduit du chinois]. Pékin: Éditions en Langues Étrangères; [Paris]: [diffusion Éditions du Centenaire], 1969. 6 p. ; 13cm.

《怎样分析农村阶级》

127. Notre politique économique.../Mao Tsétoung; [traduit du chinois]. Pékin: Éditions en Langues Étrangères; [Paris]: [diffusion Éditions du Centenaire], 1969. 15 p. ; 13cm.

《我们的经济政策》

128. A propos d'une declaration de Tchiang Kai-chek: 28 décembre 1936/Mao Tsetoung. Pékin: Éditions en Langues Étrangères, 1969. 19 pages; 13cm.

《关于蒋介石声明的声明》

129. Tâches urgentes après l'établissement de la coopération entre le kuomintang et le parti communiste: 29 septembre 1937/Mao Tsetoung. Pékin: Éditions en Langues Étrangères, 1969. 31 pages; 13cm.

《国共合作成立后的迫切任务》

130. Entretien avec le journaliste anglais James Bertram (25 ovt. 1937). Pékin: Éditions en Langues Étrangères, 1969. 38 pages

《和英国记者贝特兰的谈话》

131. Le Mouvement du 4 mai (mai 1939)/Mao Tsétoung; [traduit du chinois]. 1969. 8 p. ; 13cm.

《五四运动》

132. Contre les activités de capitulation: 30 juin 1939 /Mao Tsétoung; [traduit du chinois]. Pékin: Éditions en Langues Étrangères; [Paris]: [diffusion Éditions du Centenaire], 1969. 14 p. ; 13cm.

《反对投降活动》

133. Il faut châtier les réactionnaires (1er août 1939)/Mao Tsetoung; [traduit du chinois]. Pékin: Éditions en Langues Étrangères; [Paris]: [diffusion Éditions du Centenaire], 1969. 10 p. ; 13cm.

《必须制裁反动派》

134. Entretien avec un correspondant du Sinhouajepao sur la nouvelle situation internationale (1er septembre 1939). Pékin: Éditions en Langues Étrangères, 1969. 18 pages

《关于国际新形势对新华日报记者的谈话》

135. Pour un large recrutement des intellectuels (1er décembre 1939)/Mao Tsetoung. Pékin: Éditions en Langues Étrangères, 1969. 6 p. ; 13cm.

《大量吸收知识分子》

136. Staline, l'ami du peuple chinois: (20 décembre 1939)/Mao Tsétoung; [traduit du chinois]. 1969. 3 pages; 13cm.

《斯大林是中国人民的朋友》

137. Conjurer le danger de capitulation, s'efforcer d'amener un tournant favorable dans la situation: 28 janvier 1940/Mao Tsétoung; [traduit du chinois]. Pékin: Éditions en Langues Étrangères; [Paris]: [diffusion Éditions du Centenaire], 1969. 9 p. ; 13cm.

《克服投降危险,力争时局好转》

138. Unir toutes les forces antijaponaises: combattre les irréductibles anticommunistes (1er février 1940). Pékin: Éditions en Langues Étrangères,1969. 17 pages

《团结一切抗日力量,反对反共顽固派》

139. Une Politique de la plus haute importance: 7 septembre 1942/Mao Tsétoung; [traduit du chinois]. Pékin: Éditions en Langues Étrangères; [Paris]: [diffusion Éditions du Centenaire], 1969. 9 p. ; 13cm.

《一个极其重要的政策》

140. Le tournant de la Seconde guerre mondiale (12 octobre 1942). Pékin: Éditions en Langues Étrangères, 1969. 12 pages.

《第二次世界大战的转折点》

141. Les Deux destins de la Chine: 23 avril 1945/Mao Tsétoung. Pékin: Éditions en Langues Étrangères; [Paris]: [diffusion Éditions du Centenaire], 1969. 7 p. ;13cm.

《两个中国之命运》

142. L'Orientation de notre travail dans les régions libérées pour 1946: 15 Décembre 1945/Mao Tsétoung; [traduit du chinois]. Pékin: Éditions en Langues Étrangères; [Paris]: [diffusion Éditions du Centenaire], 1969. 13 p. ; 13cm.

《一九四六年解放区工作的方针》

143. Etablir de solides bases d'appui dans le nord-est: 28 décembre 1945/Mao Tsetoung. Pékin: Éditions en Langues Étrangères, 1969. 11 pages; 10cm.

《建巩固的东北根据地》

144. Concentrer une force supérieure pour anéantir les forces ennemies une à une/Mao Tse-toung. Pékin: Éditions en Langues Étrangères, 1969. 10 pages; 13cm.

《集中优势兵力,各个歼灭敌人》

145. Pour saluer le nouvel essor de la révolution chinoise (1er février 1947). Pékin: Éditions en Langues Étrangères, 1969. 24 pages

《迎接中国革命的新高潮》

146. Proclamation de l'armée populaire de libération de Chine: 25 avril 1949/Mao Tsetoung. Pékin: Éditions en Langues Étrangères, 1969. 8 pages; 13cm.

《中国人民解放军宣言》

147. Instructions du haut commandement de l'armée populaire de libération de Chine à l'occasion d'une nouvelle proclamation des trois grandes règles de discipline et des huit recommandations: 10 octobre 1947/Mao Tsé-toung; [traduit du chinois]. Pékin: Éditions en Langues Étrangères; [Paris]: [diffusion

Éditions du Centenaire],1969. 3 p.；13cm.

《中国人民解放总部关于重行颁布三大纪律八项注意的训令》

148. Tactiques différentes pour appliquer la loi agraire dans les régions différentes：[3 février 1948]/Mao Tsétoung. Pékin：Éditions en Langues Étrangères；[Paris]：[Diffusion Éditions du Centenaire],1969. 4 p.；13cm.

《在不同地区实施土地法的不同策略》

149. Corriger les erreurs déviationnistes "de gauche" dans la propagande pour la réforme agraire（II février 1948）. Pékin：Éditions en Langues Étrangères,1969. 5 p

《纠正土地改革宣传中的"左"倾错误》

150. Sur la question de la bourgeoisie nationale et des hobereaux éclaires（1er mars 1948）. Pékin：Éditions en Langues Étrangères,1969. 12 pages

《关于民族资产阶级和开明绅士问题》

151. Le travail de réforme agraire et de consolidation du Parti pour 1948（25 mai 1948）. Pékin：Éditions en Langues Étrangères,1969. 16 pages.

《一九四八年的土地改革和整党工作》

152. Directives pour les opérations de la campagne de Liaosi-Chenyang：septembre et octobre 1948 /Mao Tsétoung；[traduit du chinois]. Pékin：Éditions en Langues Étrangères；[Paris]：[diffusion Éditions du Centenaire],1969.[III]—14 p.；13cm.

《关于辽沈战役的作战方针》

153. Directives pour les opérations de la campagne de Houai-Hai：11 Octobre 1948/Mao Tse-toung. Pékin：Éditions en Langues Étrangères,1969. 9 pages；13cm.

《关于淮海战役的作战方针》

154. Directives pour les opérations de la campagne de Peiping-Tientsin（11 Décembre 1948）. Pékin：Éditions en Langues Étrangères,1969. 12 pages

《关于平津战役的作战方针》

155. Déclartion sur la situation actuelle par Mao Tsétoung, président du Comité Central du Parti Communiste Chinois（14 janvier 1940）. Pékin：Éditions en Langues Étrangères,1969. 11 pages.

《中共中央毛泽东主席关于时局的声明》

156. Faire de l'armée un corps de travail：8 février 1949 / Mao Tsétoung；[traduit du chinois]. Pékin：Éditions en Langues Étrangères；[Paris]：[diffusion Éditions du Centenaire],1969. 5 p.；13cm.

《把军队变为工作队》

157. La Production est également possible dans les régions de partisans：31 janvier 1945/Mao Tsé-toung. Pékin：Éditions en Langues Étrangères；Paris：[Diffusion Éditions du Centenaire],1969. 10 p.；13cm.

《游击区也能够进行生产》

158. Les Transformations de la Révolution/par Mao Tsé-toung；textes choisis et présentés par Patrick Kessel. Paris：Union générale d'éditions,1970. 320 p.：couv. ill.；19cm.（10—18；523—524）

革命的转变. Kessel,Patrick 编著. 本书包含毛泽东作品选译.

159. Textes choisis de Mao Tsetoung. Pékin：Éditions en Langues Étrangères,1972. 550 p.

《毛泽东著作选读》

160. Mao Tse-toung：Cahier/dirigé par François Joyaux. Paris：Éditions de l'Herne,1972. 448 p.：ill.，pl.，couv. ill.；28cm.（Les Cahiers de l'Herne；18）

毛泽东回忆录. Joyaux,François 译. 本书包含对毛泽东作品的选译.

161. Mao Tsé-toung et la construction du socialisme：modèle soviétique ou voie chinoise/textes inédits [de Mao Tsé-toung]；traduits et présentés par Hu Chi-hsi. Paris：Éditions du Seuil, impr. Hérissey,1975. 188 p.：couv. ill.；18cm.（Politique；69）

毛泽东和社会主义建设：苏维埃模式还是中国式道路. Hu Chi-His 译.

162. Staline, l'ami du peuple chinois[suivi de] La grande amitié/Mao Tse Toung. Bruxelles：Éd. de l'Union des communistes marxistes-léninistes de Belgiquè,1970s—?. 1 vol.（6 p.）；19cm.

斯大林是中国人民的朋友. 译者不详.

163. Sur la répression et le conflit agraire/Mao Tse-tung. Paris：Minuit,1975. 1 Bd.

翻译了毛泽东关于土地问题的一篇文章.

164. Mao Tsé-toung：ou, La révolution approfondie/Alain Bouc. Paris：Éditions du Seuil,1975. 265，[6] pages；21cm.（Collection Combats）

毛泽东：深入革命. Bouc,Alain 著译. 本书包含了毛泽东文选的翻译.

165. De la réforme agraire aux Communes populaires. Textes, édition intégrale, 1949—1958/traduit du chinois. Paris：les Éditions du Cerf,1975. 612 p.，couv. ill. 8vol. map；24cm.

从土地革命到人民公社：1949—1958 合集. 译者不详.

166. Sur les dix grands rapports.../Mao Tsétoung；[traduit du chinois]. Pékin：Éditions en Langues Étrangères；[Paris]：[diffusion Éditions du Centenaire],1977. 35 p.：couv. ill.；19cm.

《论十大关系》

167. Mao Tse-tung parle au peuple, 1956—1971/textes réunis et présentés par Stuart Schram；traduit de l'anglais par Sylvie Barjansky. 1. éd. [Paris]：Presses universitaires,1977. 331 pages；24cm.（Collection XXe siècle）

毛泽东对人民说的话. Schram,Stuart R. 编著；Barjansky,Sylvie 由英文转译为法文.

168. Discours à une conférence de travail élargie convoquée par le Comité central du parti communiste chinois, 30

janvier 1962/Mao Tsétoung. Pékin, Ch：Éditions en Langues Étrangères, 1978. 38 p.；19cm.

《在扩大的中央工作会议上的讲话》

169. Le Grand bond en avant：inédits（mai 1958—juin 1959）/Mao Zedong. Paris：Le Sycomore, 1980. III-216 p.：carte；22cm. ISBN：2862620602, 2862620602

大跃进. 译者不详.

170. Trois années noires：textes（juillet 1959—1962）/Zedong Mao；Yan Cheng, François Derre, Thérèse Ehling. Paris：Le Sycomore, 1980. III-294 p.：carte.；22cm. ISBN：2862620610, 2862620619

三年困难时期. Cheng, Yan 等译.

171. Mao stratège révolutionnaire/textes choisis et introduction par Gérard Chaliand. Paris：Kiron/Félin, 2002. 252 pages；21cm. ISBN：2866454413, 2866454418

毛泽东的革命战略. Chaliand, Gérard（1934—）选译.

(1)Paris：Pocket, 2010. 1 vol.（282 p.）：couv. ill.；18cm. ISBN：2266197045, 2266197045.（Agora；338）

172. Questions de stratégie dans la guerre de partisans antijaponaise：chapitre IV/Mao Tsé-toung. Paris：Ikko, Promoprint impr., 2005. 1 vol.（34 p.）；15cm. ISBN：2916011056, 2916011059.（Collection 6A；6）

《抗日游击战争的战略问题：第四章》,译者不详.

A3　毛泽东研究相关著作

1. La théorie de Mao Tsé-toung sur la révolution chinoise/Tchen Po-ta. Pékin：Éd. en Langues Étrangères, 1953. 81 p.；8°.

《毛泽东论中国革命》,陈伯达著.

2. Le rapport sur l'enquête menée dans le Hounan à propos du mouvement paysan" Pékin：Éditions en Langues Étrangères, 1967. 36 p

学习《湖南农民运动考察报告》.

3. Pour étudier l'"Entretien avec la journaliste américaine Anna Louise Strong". Pékin：Éditions en Langues Étrangères, 1967.

学习《和美国记者安娜. 路特朗. 斯特朗的谈话》.

4. Gloire éternelle au grand dirigeant et éducateur, le président Mao Tsétoung. Pékin：Éditions en Langues Étrangères；[Paris]：[diffusion Éditions du Centenaire], 1976. 40 p.；22cm.

《伟大的领袖和导师毛泽东主席永垂不朽》

5. La théorie du président Mao sur la division en trois mondes：importante contribution au marxisme léninisme. Pékin：Éditions en Langues Étrangères, 1977.；84 p

《毛泽东关于三个世界划分的理论是对马克思列宁主义的重大贡献》,外文出版社.

6. Poursuivons jusqu'au bout la révolution sous la dictature du prolétariat：de l'étude du tome V des "Œuvres choisies" de Mao Tsétoung/Houa Kouo-Feng. Pékin：Éditions en Langues Étrangères；[Paris]：[diffusion Éditions du Centenaire], 1977. 42 p.；19cm.

《把无产阶级专政下的继续革命进行到底：学习〈毛泽东选集〉第五卷》,华国锋著.

7. Mao Zedong：biographie, commentaires, souvenirs/compilé par Zhong Wenxian. Beijing：Éditions en Langues Étrangères, 1re éd. 1990. 322 p.,［36］p. de pl.：ill. ISBN：7119012460；7119012469.

《关于毛泽东传略、评价、回忆》,钟文宪编.

B 类　哲学、宗教

B1　中国哲学

1. Essais philosophiques choisis des ouvriers, paysans et soldats. Pékin：Éditions en Langues Étrangères；[Paris]：[diffusion Éditions du Centenaire], 1972. 78 p.；19cm.

《工农兵学哲学文选》.

2. I Ching. Tao te Ching/trad. et présent. de Daniel Giraud. Paris：le Courrier du livre, Normandie Impr., 1989. 159 p.：ill., couv. ill.；22cm. ISBN：2702901972（br）, 2702901977（br）

《易经》与《道德经》,Giraud, Daniel,（1946—）译.

B2　中国各代哲学著作与研究

B21　诸子前哲学

B211　周易

1. Le Yih-king/traduit et commenté par Ch. de Harlez. Bruxelles, F. Hayez, 1889. 2 preliminary leaves,［3］—154 pages, 1 leaf 30×24cm.

《易经》,Harlez, Charles de（1832—1899)译.

2. Le Yi-king, sa nature et son interprétation/par Charles De Harlez. Extr. de：J. As. 1891. I. 164—170

《易经的本质和注释》,De Harlez, Charles（1832—1899) 著. 本书包含对易经的翻译.

3. Interprétation du Yi-king/par Charles De Harlez. Extr. de：T. P. 1. 1896. VII. 197—222

《易经注释》,De Harlez, Charles（1832—1899)著. 是对易经的翻译.

4. Le Yi-king/traduit d'après les interprètes chinois avec la version mandchoue par C. de Harlez. Paris, 1897.［1 volume］26cm.

《易经》,De Harlez, Charles（1832—1899)译.

5. Le livre des mutations/Texte primitif traduit du chinois par Charles de Harlez, présenté et annoté par Raymond de Becker. [Paris] Éditions Denoël；（Mayenne：impr. Floch), 1959. 301 p., couv. en coul. 990 fr.［D. L. 2168—59］-IIId-；In—16（19cm.).（La Tour Saint-

Jacques)

《易经》，Harlez, Charles de(1832—1899)译.

(1)Paris：Éditions Planète, 1970. 300 pages；21cm.

6. Le Yi：king；ou, Livre des changements de la dynastie des Tsheou/Traduit pour la première fois du chinois en français par P.-L.-F. Philastre. Paris, E. Leroux, 1885—1893. 2 volumes 29cm.（Annales du Musée Guimet；t. 8,23）

《易经》，Philastre, Paul-Louis-Félix(1837—1902)译.

(1) Paris：J. Maisonneuve, impr. J. Floch, 1975, 1885. 2 volumes, 489＋608 p.；25cm.（Classiques d'Amérique et d'Orient；；5）

(2) Paris：J. Maisonneuve, Impr. de la Manutention, 1992, 1885. 2 vol.（489, 608 p.）；25cm. ISBN：2720010871, 2720010873.（Classiques d'Amérique et d'Orient；；5）

(3)[S. n.]：Zulma, 1992. 876 p.；25cm. ISBN：2909031209, 2909031200

(4)Nouv. éd. Cadeilhan (Gers)：Zulma, 2006. 1 v.（896 p.）；25cm. ISBN：2843043530（Rel）, 2843043536（Rel）

7. Yi king：le livre des transformations/version allemande de Richard Wilhelm；Préfacée et traduite en français par Etienne Perrot. Paris：Librarie des Médicis, 1968. xxx, 416 pages；illustrations；21cm.

《易经》，卫礼贤(Wilhelm, Richard, 1873—1930)(德国汉学家)德译；Perrot, Etienneb 法译.

(1)2e éd. rev. et corr. Paris：Librarie des Médicis, 1971. 416 p.；ill.；21cm.

(2)Paris：Librairie de Médicis, impr. Chaix-Desfossés, 1972. 394 p.；ill.；21cm.

(3)Ed. complète, revue et corrigée. Paris：Librarie des Médicis, 1973. xxxi, 804 pages.

(4)Paris：Librarie des Médicis, 1973. xxxi, 804 pages；illustrations；21cm. ISBN：2853270033, 2853270038

(5)Edition complète revue et corrigée. Paris：Librarie des Médicis, 1977. XXXI＋805 p.；front.；In-8 °

(6)Paris：Librarie des Médicis, 1983. XXXI-413 p.；ill.；20cm. ISBN：2853270041（br）, 2853270045（br）

(7)Nouv. éd. rev. et mise à jour. Paris：Librarie des Médicis, 1992. XXXI-804 p.；ill.；21cm. ISBN：2853270033（rel）2853270038（rel）

(8)Nouv. éd. rev. et mise à jour. Paris：Librarie des Médicis, 1993. XXVI-413 p.；ill.；20cm.

(9)Nouv. éd. rev. et mise à jour. Paris：Librarie des Médicis, 1994. XXVI-804 p.；ill.；20cm.

(10)Nouv. éd. rev. et mise à jour. Paris：Librarie des Médicis, 2001. XXXI-413 p.；20cm. ISBN：2853270025(br), 285327002(br)

8. Yi jing Eranos：le livre de la versatilité：textes oraculaires；suivis d'une concordance et d'un lexique français-chinois/[version allemande de Richard Wilhelm]；traduction [française] de Pierre & Imelda Gaudissart；sous la direction de Rudolf Ritsema. [Paris]：Encre, Impr. Groupe Horizon, 2009. 1 vol.（573 p.）：ill.；couv. ill.；21cm. ISBN：2358470025（br）, 2358470023（br）

《易经》，卫礼贤(Wilhelm, Richard, 1873—1930)(德国汉学家)德译；Gaudissart, Pierre, Gaudissart, Imelda 法译；

9. Le Yi jing en dessins：bande dessinée bilingue/Tan Xiaochun et Li Dianzhong；traduction de Wang Dongliang et Cyrille Javary. Paris：Youfeng, 1992, 1994, 1999. 1 vol.（257 p.）：ill. en noir, couv. ill. en coul.；22cm. ISBN：2906658812, 2906658813

《易经连环画》，Tan, Hsiao-chun 和 Li, Tien-chung 画；Wang, Tung-liang 和 Javary, Cyrille 合译.

10. Yi Jing：le sens originel restitué du "Livre des mutations"/Kerson & Rosemary Huang；traduit de l'américain par Cyrille Javary, Kirk McElhearn et Jarie-France Benini；édition française sous la direction d'Aline Apostolslea. St. Jean-de-Braye [France]：Éditions Dangles, 1993. 220 p. couv. ill. en coul.；24cm. ISBN：2703303939, 2703303930.（Grand angle/Traditions）

《易经》，Javary, Cyrille 等英译；Huang, Kerson(1928—) 法译.

11. Le Yi King mot à mot/[traduit du chinois sous la direction de Cyrille J.-D. Javary；revue dirigée par Marc de Smedt]. Gordes, France：Éditions Question de；Paris：A. Michel, 1994. vii, cxli p.；24cm. ISBN：2226075569, 2226075567.（Question de. Hors série；98 bis）

《易经》，Javary, Cyrille(1947—)译.

12. Yi king：le plus ancien traité divinatoire/[interprété par] Sam Reifler；trad. de Zéno Bianu. [Paris]：le Grand livre du mois, Impr. Firmin-Didot, 1994. 284 p.；22cm. ISBN：2702803784（rel）, 2702803783（rel）.（Les trésors de la littérature）

《易经》，Reifler, Sam 和 Bianu, Zéno 合译.

13. Yi king：le livre des transformations：nouvelle version intégrale contenant les gloses de Confucius/[trad. et présenté par] Elena Judica Cordiglia；trad. de l'italien par Viviane Pott-Rovera. Boucherville（Canada）；[Mortefontaine-en-Thelle]：Éd. de Mortagne, 1996. 462 p.：couv. ill.；24cm. ＋3 pièces de monnaie. ISBN：2890743756（rel）, 2890743755（rel）

《易经》，Cordiglia, Elena Judica 意译；Pott-Rovera, Viviane 法译.

14. Le Yi Jing illustré/interprétation et ill. de Li Yan (Zhuangbei)；[trad. par Zheng Ming；rev. par Geneviève Baroux et Gong Jieshi]. Beijing, China：Éditions en Langues Étrangères, 1997. VIII-448 p.：ill.；21cm. ISBN：7119019929, 7119019925

《易经画传》,李燕译绘. 外文出版社.

15. Le livre de la simplicité：Yi Jing taoïste＝Zhou yi lun：dao xue zhi yi jing/Yang Zu-Hui, Hiria Ottino. Paris：G. Trédaniel, 1998. 383 p.：ill. graph. Darst. ; 24cm. ISBN：2844450504, 2844450500

《易经》,Yang Zu-Hui 和 Ottino, Hiria 合译.

16. Dans le Yi Jing à tire d'ailes：les commentaires du Yi Jing/présentés et trad. par Michel Vinogradoff. Paris：Éd. Guy Trédaniel, 2000. 469 p. ; 24cm.

《易经》,Vinogradoff, Michel 译.

17. Yi king/[éd. par] Stephen Karcher ; trad. de l'anglais par Sophie Bastide-Foltz. 3e éd. Paris：Éd. Payot & Rivages, Impr. Darantière, 2001. 285 p. ; couv. ill. en coul. ; 17cm. ISBN：2743603496（br）, 2743603496（br）.（Rivages poche, Petite bibliothèque）

《易经》,Karcher, Stephen 英译 ; Bastide-Foltz, Sophie 法译.

18. Yi jing：le livre des changements/[traduit du chinois et commentaires par] Cyrille J.-D. Javary, Pierre Faure. Paris：Albin Michel, Normandie roto impr, 2002, 2005, 2007. 1065 p ; 22cm. ISBN：222611713X, 2226117137

《易经》,Javary, Cyrille（1947—）和 Faure, Pierre（1950—）合译.

(1)Paris：Albin Michel, Normandie roto impr, 2012. 1 vol.（1065 p.）：ill. ; 21cm. ＋ 1 fiche. ISBN：2226239303（br）, 2226239308（br）

19. Yi King：texte et interprétation/introduction, traduction du chinois et commentaires de Daniel Giraud. Paris：Bartillat, 2003. 324 p.：ill. ; 20cm. ISBN：2841003078, 2841003075

《易经》,Giraud, Daniel 译.

(1)Paris：Pocket, Impr. Bussière, 2008. 1 vol.（324 p.）：couv. ill. ; 18cm. ISBN：2266168939（br）, 2266168932（br）.（Pocket, Spiritualité）

20. Zhou Yi＝le Yi Jing intégral/traduit du chinois par Zhou Jing Hong et Carmen Folguera. Édition bilingue. Paris：Éditions You Feng, 2012. 370 pages ; 22cm. ISBN：2842795214（br）, 2842795210（br）

《周易》,Zhou, Jinghong 和 Folguera, Carmen 合译.

21. Méthode pratique de divination chinoise par le Yi-king/maître Yüan-Kuang ; [traduction] avec préf. et notes explicatives de Tchou-Houa et Charles Canone ; dessins de Marcel Nicaud. Paris：Éditions de la Maisnie, 1977. 278 pages ; illustrations ; 22cm. ISBN：2857070209, 2857070207

易经中的实用中国占卜术. Yüan-Kuang 著 ; Tchou-Houa 和 Canone, Charles 合译.

22. Interprétation alchimique du Yi-king & du tarot/Toni Ceron. Orcier：éd. Col du feu, impr. 2005. 1 vol.（575 p.）：ill., couv. ill. en coul. ; 20cm. ISBN：2950945988（rel.）

《易经炼金术注释》,Ceron, Toni（1947—）著. 本书包含对《易经》的选译.

B22　儒家

B221　四书五经

1. Les quatre livres avec un commentaire abrégé en Chinois, une double traduction en français et en latin et un vocabulaire des lettres et des noms propres par S. Couvreur/ Ho-Kien-Fou Imprim. de la Mission catholique, 1895. VII, 748 S.

《四书》,Couvreur, Séraphin,（1835—1919）译.

(1)2. Éd. Ho-Kien-Fou Imprim. de la Mission catholique, 1910. VII, 748 S

(2)3. Éd. Sien Hsien：Impr. de la Mission catholique, 1930. VII＋748 p. ; In-4 °

2. Les quatre livres/avec la préf. et le vocabulaire par Séraphin Couvreur. Paris：Cathasia, 1949. 4 v. en 2. VII, 654 P ; 25cm.（Les humanités d'Extrême-Orient）

《四书》,Couvreur, Séraphin,（1835—1919）译.

3. Les quatre livres de la sagesse chinoise/Confucius, Meng Tzeu ; trad. de Séraphin Couvreur ; précédé d'une étude d'Édouard Chavannes. [Paris]：Club des libraires de France, 1956. 419 p. ; 20cm.（Livres de sagesse ; 5）

《四书》,Couvreur, Séraphin,（1835—1919）译.

4. Les quatre livres [Texte imprimé]/de Confucius... ; traduction intégrale, notes et préface du R.-P. Séraphin Couvreur, S. J... ; décoration originale de Ton-Hi ; [commenté par Tchou Hi]. Paris：J. de Bonnot, 1979. IX-653 p.：ill., couv. ill. ; 28cm.

《四书》,Couvreur, Séraphin,（1835—1919）译.

5. Les quatre piliers de la sagesse：édition de prestige/adaptation de Joseph Pardo. [Paris]：Éditions d'art Sefer, 1988—1990. 2 vol.：ill. ; 40cm.

《四书》,Pardo, Joseph 译.

6. Les quatre livres ＝ Ta hio Tchong young/par Séraphin Couvreur. Paris：Cathasia, 1895. vii, s. 2—67 1—4 i 1 bd.（vii, 654 s.）

《四书：大学与中庸》. Couvreur, Séraphin 译.

7. Doctrine de Confucius：ou, Les quatre livres de philosophie morale et politique de la Chine/trad. du chinois par G. Pauthier. Paris：Garnier frères, 1905. xxviii, 485 p.

儒家学说：或中国道德政治四书. Pauthier, Jean Pierre Guillaume（1801—1873）译.

(1)Paris：Garnier frères, 1914. In—18

(2)Paris：Garnier frères, 1921. 1 vol. XXVII-[VII]-485 p.（Classiques Garnier）

(3)Paris：Garnier frères, 1929. XXVIII-h-487 p.（Classiques Garnier）

8. Philosophes confucianistes：[les entretiens de Confucius,

Lunyu. Meng zi. La grande étude, Daxue. La pratique équilibrée, Zhongyong. Le classique de la piété filiale, Xiaojing. Xun zi] = 儒家/Philosophes confucianistes: [les entretiens de Confucius, Lunyu. Meng zi. La grande étude, Daxue. La pratique équilibrée, Zhongyong. Le classique de la piété filiale, Xiaojing. Xun zi] = Ru jia/ textes traduits, présentés et annotés par Charles Le Blanc et Rémi Mathieu. textes traduits, présentés et annotés par Charles Le Blanc et Rémi Mathieu. Paris: Gallimard, 2009. lxvi, 1468 pages: maps; 18cm. ISBN: 2070771745, 2070771741. (Bibliothèque de la pléiade; 557)

Le Blanc, Charles, Mathieu, Rémi 译. 本书包含对《论语》《孟子》《大学》《中庸》《孝经》《荀子》的法译.

9. Deux sophistes chinois, Houei Che et Kong-souen Long/ par Ignace Kou Pao-Koh...; préf. de Paul Masson-Oursel. Paris: Presses universitaires de France, Impr. Nationale, 1953. VI—164 p.: fig. au titre; Vol. 8

《中国的两位诡辩家:惠施和公孙龙》,顾保鹄著. 本书包含了对惠施和公孙龙思想的选译.

B222　大学

1. Le Ta-Hio, ou la Grande étude, ouvrage de Confucius et de son disciple Tseng-Tsen, traduit du chinois par M. G. Pauthier/Paris: impr. de Everat, 1832. 23 p, 23cm.; In-8°

《大学》,Pauthier, Guillaume(1801—1873)译.

2. Le Tá hio ou La grande étude: le premier des quatres livres de philosophie morale et politique de la Chine/ ouvrage de Khoung-Fou-tseu [Confucius] et de son disciple Thsèng-Tseu; tr. en français avec une version latine et le texte chinois en regard, accompagné du commentaire complet de Tchôu-Hî, et de notes tirées de divers autres commentateurs chinois, par G. Pauthier. Paris: Firmin Didot frères, 1837. viii, 104 p.; 21cm. (Les Sse Chou, ou les quatre livres de philosophie morale et politique de la Chine; 1)

《大学》,Pauthier, Guillaume(1801—1873)译.

  (1) Ventabren: les Rouyat, 1979, 1837. viii, 104 p.; 25cm.

  (2) Rouvray: Éditions du prieuré, 1993, 1837. viii, 104 p.; 21cm. ISBN: 2909672182, 2909672182. (Les Sse chou; 1)

  (3) Paris: Cura et Sumptibus Interpretis, 1993. 104 pages; 21cm. (Les SSe Chou, ou, Les quatre livres de philosophie: morale et politique de la Chine; 1)

3. La grande étude/Tseng-tseu; avec le commentaire traditionnel de Tchou Hi; traduit du chinois par Martine Hasse. Paris: Éditions du Cerf, 1984. 103 pages; 24cm. ISBN: 2204022810, 2204022811. (Découvertes Gallimard. Religions; 440)

《大学》,朱熹(1130—1200)评注;Hasse, Martine 译.

B223　中庸

1. La science des Chinois, ou Le livre de Cum-fu-gu/traduit mot pour mot de la langue chinoise, par le R. P. Intorcetta. Paris: A. Cramoisy, 1673. 24 p.; in-fol

《中庸》,Intorcetta, R. P. (Prospero)译.

2. L'invariable milieu/transcrit en caractères latins et trad. en annamite vulgaire par M. Petrus Ky. Sàigòn: Collège des stagiaires, 1875. 205 p.; 33cm.

《中庸》,Ky, M. Petrus 译.

3. L'invariable milieu: ouvrage moral de Tséu-ssê, en chinois et en mandchou, avec une version littérale latine, une traduction françoise, et des notes, précédé d'une notice sur les quatre livres moraux communément attribués à Confucius/par M. Abel Rémusat. A Paris: De l'Imprimerie royale, 1817. 160 p.; 27cm.

《中庸》,Rémusat, Abel 译.

4. L'invariable milieu = Tchoūng-Yoūng/Confucius. Trad. du chinois par Abel Rémusat. Nice Éd. des Cahiers Astrolog, 1952. 59 S Ill. (Les maîtres de l'occultisme; 12)

《中庸》,Rémusat, Abel 译.

5. Zhong Yong ou la régulation à usage ordinaire/texte trad., introd. et commenté par François Jullien. [Paris]: Imprimerie Nationale Éd., 1993. 194 S. ISBN: 2110811846 (brochés), 2110811844 (brochés), 2110812583 (reliés toile), 2110812582 (reliés toile), 2110812591 (reliés cuir), 2110812599 (reliés cuir). (La salamandre)

《中庸》,Jullien, François 译.

6. De la continuité dynamique dans l'univers confucéen: lecture néoconfucéenne du Zhongyong: nouvelle traduction du chinois classique et commentaire herméneutique/Xi Zhu; édition de Diana Arghiresco; Préface d'Ivan P. Kamenarovic. Paris: Cerf, 2013. 412 pages; 24cm. ISBN: 2204100267, 2204100269. (Patrimoines. Confucianisme)

《中庸辑略》,朱熹(1130—1200)著;Arghiresco, Diana 译.

B224　三礼

周礼

1. Le Tcheou-li ou Rites des Tcheou/trad. pour la première fois du chinois par feu édouard Biot,...; [éd. par Jean-Baptiste Biot]. Paris: Impr. nationale: B. Duprat, 1851. 3 vol. (48—LXIV-500 p. -[2] f. de pl., 620 p. -[1] f. de pl. -[2] f. de dépl., table): ill., carte; 22cm.

《周礼》,Biot, édouard(1803—1850)译.

仪礼

1. I-Li. Cérémonial de la Chine antique avec des extraits des meilleurs commentaires/traduit pour la première fois par C. de Harlez. Paris: J. Maisonneuve, 1890. 408 p.

《仪礼》,De Harlez, Charle(1832—1899)译.

2. I-Li. Cérémonial/Texte chinois et traduction, par S. Couvreur, S. J. Sien Hsien: Impr. de la Mission catholique, 1928. I+667 p.

《仪礼》,Couvreur, Séraphin(1835—1919)译.

(1)Paris: Cathasia (impr. de Bellenand), 1951. II-669 p.

礼记

1. Li-Ki, ou Mémorial des rites, traduit pour la première fois du chinois et accompagné de notes, de commentaires et du texte original. Paris: Turin: B. Duprat, 1853. 200 p.

《礼记》,Callery, Joseph-Marie(1810—1862)译.

2. Li Ki ou Mémoires sur les bienséances et les cérémonies: texte chinois avec une double traduction en français et en latin/par Séraphin Couvreur. Ho kien fou: Impr. de la Mission catholique, 1899. 2 vol. (XVI-788, 850 p.); 25cm.

《礼记》,Couvreur, Séraphin(1835—1919)译.

(1)2e éd. Ho kien fou: Impr. de la Mission catholique, 1913. 2 vol. (XVI+788 et II+848 p.)

(2)Paris: Cathasia (impr. de Bellenand), 1950. 4 vol.

3. Mémoires sur les bienséances et les cérémonies/[compilé par Dai Sheng]; [traduit] par Séraphin Couvreur. Paris: Éditions You feng libraire & éditeur, 2015. 1 vol. (848 p.); 25cm.

《礼记》,Couvreur, Séraphin(1835—1919)译.

B225 书经

1. Le Chou-King, un des livres sacrés des Chinois/ouvrage recueilli par Confucius, traduit et enrichi de notes par feu le P. Gaubil,... revu... par M. de Guignes... On y a joint un discours préliminaire... sur les temps antérieurs à ceux dont parle le Chou-King (par le P. de Premare) et une notice de l'Y-King... (par C. Visdelou.). Paris: N.-M. Tilliard, 1770. 474 p.

《书经》,Gaubil, Antoine(1689—1759)译注.

2. La morale du Chou-King, ou Le livre sacré de la Chine/[recueilli par Confucius]; [trad. par le P. Gaubil]. Paris: V. Lecou, 1851. 1 vol. (VIII-227 p.); in-16. (Nouvelle collection des moralistes anciens publiée sous la direction de M. Lefèvre; 8)

《书经》,Gaubil, Antoine(1689—1759)译.

3. Chou King: Les annales de la Chine/[texte chinois avec transcription et traduction en français et en latin] par Séraphin Couvreur. Paris: Cathasia: Les Belles lettres; Leiden: E. J. Brill, cop. 1950. 1 vol. ([IV]-465 p.): fig.; 25cm. (Humanités d'Extrême-Orient)

《书经》,Couvreur, Séraphin(1835—1919)译.

(1) Chou King: Les Annales de la Chine/[Texte, traduction, notes et glossaire] par Séraphin Couvreur. Leiden: E. J. Brill; Paris: Belles Lettres, 1950. IV+464 p. (Humanités d'Extrême-

Orient. Cathasia. Série culturelle des hautes études de T'ien-tsin)

(2)Les annales de la Chine/[trad.] par Séraphin Couvreur. Paris: You-Feng, 1999. 464 p.: ill.; 21cm. ISBN: 2842790758

B226 孝经

1. Le Hiao-King livre sacré de la piété Filiale, publié en chinois avec une traduction française/par Léon de Rosny. Paris: Maisonneuve et Ch. Leclerc, 1889. 68—176 p.

《孝经》,Rosny, Léon de(1837—1914)译.

(1)La Morale de Confucius. Le Livre sacré de la piété filiale. Paris, 1893.

2. Le livre de la piété filiale/Confucius; trad. du chinois et présenté par Roger Pinto. Suivi de la traduction ancienne et des commentaires. Paris: Éd. du Seuil (27-évreux: Impr. Hérissey), 1998. 110 p. dont 76 p. de fac-sim.: couv. ill.; 18cm. ISBN: 2020313103. (Points. Sagesses; 131)

《孝经》,Pinto, Roger(1910—2005)译.

(1)Paris: le Grand livre du mois (37-Tours: Mame impr.), 2009. 1 vol. (76 p.): ill. en coul., couv. ill.; 19cm. ISBN: 2286051242

B227 孔子

1. Les livres de confucius Khong-Tseu/Pierre Salet. Paris: Payot, 1923. 1 vol. (101 p.); 17cm. (Collection "Petite Anthologie"; 10)

《论语》,Salet, Pierre 译.

2. Pensées morales/de Confucius, traduites du chinois par René Brémond. Paris, Éditions d'histoire et d'art, Plon; (Corbeil, impr. de Crété), 1953. In—16 agenda, 131 p. 540 fr. [D. L. 13869—53] -IIIa-. (Jacques Haumont)

《论语》,Brémond, René 译.

3. Entretiens avec ses disciples/texte établi et traduit par Séraphin Couvreur. Paris: Belles Lettres/Denoël, 1975. 172 p. (Cathasia. Méditations)

《论语》,Couvreur, Séraphin1835—1919)译.

4. Les entretiens de Confucius/trad. du chinois et prés. par Anne Cheng. Paris: Éditions du Seuil, 1981. 153 p.-[31] p.: couv. ill. en coul.; 18cm. ISBN: 2020057751 (Br), 2020057752 (Br). (Points, Sagesses; 24)

《论语》,Cheng, Anne 译.

(1)Paris: Seuil, 1988. XX—153 p.; 18cm. ISBN: 2020057751, 2020057752. (Points. Sagesses; 24)

(2)[Paris]: le Grand livre du mois, 1992. 171 p.; 22cm. ISBN: 2702800912 (rel.). (Le grand livre du mois)

(3)Paris: Points, 2014. 1 vol. (153—XX p.): carte, couv. ill. en coul. Cartes; 18cm. ISBN: 2757840269, 2757840266. (Points. Sagesses; 24)

5. Les entretiens de Confucius/traduction du chinois, introduction, notes et index par Pierre Ryckmans;

Préface d'Etiemble. 〔Paris〕：Gallimard，1987. IX—168 p. ：couv. ill. ；23cm. ISBN：207071084X（Br.）. (Connaissance de l'Orient，ISSN 0589—3496；62)

《论语》，Ryckmans，Pierre 译.

(1)〔Paris〕：Gallimard，1989. IX—168 p. ：couv. ill. en coul. ；19cm. ISBN：2070717909，2070717903. (Connaissance de l'Orient；35)

(2)〔Paris〕：Gallimard，1994. IX—168 p. ：couv. ill. en coul. ；19cm. ISBN：2070717909，2070717903. (Connaissance de l'Orient：Série chinoise；35)

(3)〔Paris〕：Gallimard，2004. 139 p. ：couv. ill. en coul. ；18cm. ISBN：2070305317. (Folio)

6. La sagesse de Confucius/Lin Yutang；〔édité par〕Lin Yutang；traduit de l'anglais par Th. Bridel-Wasem. Arles：Éditions Philippe Picquier，2006. 277 p. ISBN：2877307921，2877307925，2877308298，2877308294.

《论语》，林语堂(1895—1976)英译；Bridel-Wasem，Th. 法译.

(1)Arles：P. Picquier，2008. 1 vol.（351 p.）：carte，couv. ill. en coul. ；17cm. ISBN：2809700558（br），2809700559（br）. (Picquier poche)

(2)Paris：Victor Attinger，1949. 252 p.（Orient；18）

7. 论语：中·法文对照版/刘示范主编. 济南：山东教育出版社，2010. 2 册(417 页)；29cm. ISBN：7532865406 法文题名：Entretiens de confucius. 本书包括《论语》原文、法文. 内容收录学而篇、为证篇、里仁篇、述而篇、泰伯篇、子罕篇等.

8. Les dits de maître Kong rapportés par ses disciples Lunyu/trad. annotée par Charles Delaunay；texte chinois d'après l'édition de Cheng Shude. Paris：Éditions You Feng，2011. 1 vol.（358 p.）：ill. ；21cm. ISBN：2842795252（br），2842795253（br）.

《论语》，Delaunay，Charles 译.

9. Les entretiens/Confucius；traduction du chinois，introduction et notes par Pierre Ryckmans alias Simon Leys. 〔Paris〕：Gallimard，2016. 1 vol.（139 p.）；18cm. ISBN：2070782857（br.）. (Folio. Sagesses)

《论语》，Ryckmans，Pierre 译.

10. Confucius, le sage des classes réactionnaires/Yang Jong-kouo；〔traduit du chinois〕. Pékin：Éditions en Langues Étrangères；〔Paris〕：〔Éditions du Centenaire〕，1974. 81 p. ：couv. ill. ；19cm.

《反动阶级的"圣人"：孔子》，杨荣国著.

11. Le spectre de Confucius hante les nouveaux tsars. Pékin：Éditions en Langues Étrangères，1974. 45 str. ；19cm.

《孔老二的亡灵和新沙皇的迷梦》

12. Comprendre Confucius：bilingue/Ding Wangdao；〔trad. par Yan Hansheng；avec la collab. de Marcelle Schiepers〕. Pékin：Éditions en Langues Étrangères，Beijing：wai wen chu ban she，2004. 1 vol.（236 p.）；20cm. ISBN：7119035215，7119035215

《孔子新评》，丁往道著.

B228　孔子家语

1. Le Code de la nature, poème de Confucius/traduit et commenté par le P. Parennin. Londres；et Paris，Leroy，1788. VIII—127 p. ，〔1〕f. de pl. ；in-8

《孔子家语》，Parennin，P. 译.

B229　孟子

1. Mencius/traduit par André Levy. Paris：Éd. You-Feng，2003. 212 p. ISBN：2842791479，2842791476

《孟子》，Lévy，André 译.

2. Mencius/traduit du chinois, présenté et annoté par André Lévy. Paris：Éd. Payot & Rivages，Impr. Darantière，2008. 1 vol.（290 p.）：couv. ill. en coul. ；17cm. ISBN：2743618322（br），2743618329（br）. (Rivages poche，Petite Bibliothèque)

《孟子》，Lévy，André 译.

3. Mencius/traduit en français par André Lévy；traduit en chinois moderne par Yang Bojun. Changsha：Éd. Yuelu：Éd. de l'Education du Hunan，2009. 1 vol.（449 p.）：ill. ，jaq. ill. en coul. ；25cm. ISBN：7807612032（rel），7807612037（rel）. (Bibliothèque des classiques chinois：chinois-français)

《孟子》，Lévy，André 法译.

4. Mencius/trad. du chinois par Séraphin Couvreur；postf. par Jérôme Vérain. 〔Paris〕：Éd. Mille et une nuits，2004. 77 p. ：couv. ill. ；15cm. ISBN：2842058216（br.）. (La petite collection；445)

《孟子》，Couvreur，Séraphin(1835—1919)译.

B230　荀子

1. Xun Zi (Siun Tseu)/introd. et trad. du chinois par Ivan Kamenarovic；préf. de Jean-François di Meglio. Paris：Cerf，1987. 364 p. ；24cm. ISBN：2204027944，2204027946. (Patrimoines. Confucianisme)

《荀子》，Kamenarovic，Ivan P. 译.

2. Traité sur le ciel：et autres textes/Xun zi；traduit du chinois et annoté par Rémi Mathieu. 〔Paris〕：Gallimard，2013. 1 vol.（92 p.）：couv. ill. ；18cm. ISBN：2070451883（br），2070451887（br）. (Folio, 2 euros, Sagesses)

《荀子：天论》，Mathieu，Rémi(1948—)译.

B23　道家

B231　道家著作合集

1. Les pères du système taoïste：Lao-tzeu, Lie-tzeu, Tchoang-tzeu/Paris：Cathasia，1950. 521 pages：illustrations；25cm. (Série culturelle des hautes études de Tien-tsin)

道家思想代表人物：老子、列子、庄子. Wieger, Le'on (1856—1933)编译.

(1)Paris：Belles Lettres，1975. 521 pages；25cm. (Série culturelle des Hautes Études de Tien-tsin；Les

Humanités d'Extrême-Orient; Cathasia)

2. Philosophes taoïstes. Lao-tseu, Tchouang-tseu, Lie-tseu/avant-propos, Préface et bibliographie par Étiemble; textes traduits, présentés et annotés par Liou Kia-hway et Benedykt Grynpas; relus par Paul Demiéville, Étiemble et Max Kaltenmark. [Paris]: Gallimard, 2006, (c) 1980. cxiv, 776 pages;18cm. ISBN: 2070106837,2070106837. (Bibliothèque de la Pléiade; 283)

   道家哲学家:老子、庄子、列子. Liou, Kia-hway, Grynpas, Benedykt 译.

3. La Sagesse chinoise selon le Tao/pensées choisies [de Lao tseu, Lie tseu et Tchouang tseu] et traduites par René Brémond. Paris: Éditions d'histoire et d'art, Plon; (Corbeil: impr. de Crété), 1955. In—16, 203 p. 690 fr. [D. L. 14387—55]-IIIa-. (Collection Jacques Haumont)

   《道藏》,Brémond, René 译. 本书包含了对老子、列子和庄子思想的翻译.

B232 道德经

1. Le Tao-te-king: ou, Le livre révéré de la raison suprême et de la vertu/par Lao-tseu; traduit en français et publié pour la première fois en Europe, avec une version latine et le texte chinois en regard; accompagné du commentaire complet. Paris: F. Didot Frères, 1838. 80 pages

   《道德经》,Pauthier, Guillaume(1801—1873)译.

2. Lao Tseu tao te king: le livre de la voie et de la vertu.../par le philosophe Lao-tseu, traduit en français, et publié avec le texte chinois et un commentaire perpétuel par Stanislas Julien. Paris: L'Imprimerie Royale, 1842. xlv, 303 pages;22cm.

   《道德经》,Julien, Stanislas(1797—1873)译.

3. Textes tâoïstes; tr. des originaux chinois et commentés/traduit par C. de Harlez. Paris: E. leroux,1891. vii, 391 pages;29cm. (Annales du Musée Guimet; v. 20)

   《道德经》,Harlez, Charles de (1832—1899)译注.

4. Lao-tseu/traduit par Jules Besse. Paris: E. Leroux, 1909. 163 pages;17cm. ISBN: 0524079455,0524079454. (ATLA monograph preservation program; ATLA fiche 1991—0195)

   《老子》,Besse,Jules 译.

5. Tao-Teh-King/traduit par R. M. Pedretti. Paris: Pad, 1933. 122 S

   《道德经》,Pedretti, R. M. 译.

6. La voie et sa vertu/Texte chinois presente et traduit par Houang-Kia-Tcheng et Pierre Leyris. Paris: Aux Éditions du Seuil,1949. 173 pages;17cm.

   《道德经》,Tcheng, Houang-Kia 译.

7. Tao te king: le livre du Tao et de sa vertu: traduction nouvelle suivie d'Aperçus sur les enseignements du Lao Tseu/译者不详. Lyon: Paul Derain, 1951. 245, [3] pages;24cm. (Collection Taoisme)

《道德经》,译者不详.

   (1)Paris: Club des libraires de France, impr. Savernoise, 1958. 259 p.; 20cm. (Sagesse; 10)

   (2)Nouv. éd. Lyon, P. Deraín, Paris, Dervy, 1969. 248 pages. (Collectión Taoisme)

   (3)Nouvelle éd. Paris: Dervy-Livres, 1973. 1 vol. (245 p.); 25cm. (Collection Taoïsme; Mystiques et religions)

   (4)Paris: Dervy, Impr. C. Corlet, 1980. ISBN: 2850760714 (Br), 2850760716 (Br). (Mystiques et religions)

   (5)Paris: Éditions Dervy, 1996. ISBN: 2850768642, 2850768644. (Collection L'être et l'esprit)

8. Tao tö king: le livre de la voie et de la vertu/texte chinois établi et traduit avec des notes critiques et une introd. par J.-J.-L. Duyvendak. Paris: Librairie d'Amérique & d'Orient Adrien-Maisonneuve, 1953. xiii, 187 p.; 19 × 28cm.

   《道德经》,Duyvendak, J. J. L. (1889—1954)译.

   (1)Paris: J. Maisonneuve, 1987. xiii, 187 pages; 18 × 25cm. (Classiques d'Amérique et d'Orient; 4)

9. Le Tao Te King/de La. Tseu; [éd. et traduit par] Paule Reuss. Angers: Au Masque d'Or, 1955. 92 pages; 19cm. ("Miroir"; 5)

   《道德经》,Reuss, Paule 译.

10. Tao te king: traité sur le principe et l'art de la vie des vieux maitres de la Chine/Introduction, traduction, glose, commentaires et notes par Jacques Lionnet. Paris: Adrien-Maisonneuve, 1962. 205 pages;26cm.

    《道德经》,Lionnet, Jacques 译.

11. Tao tê king/Lao Tseu; texte français par Armel Guerne. Paris: Le Club Français du Livre, 1963. xiii, 163 pages: illustrations; 22cm.

    《道德经》,Guerne, Armel 译.

12. Tao-tö king/par Lao-tseu; trad. du chinois par Liou Kiahway; préf. d'Étiemble. Paris: Gallimard, 1971. 120 S. (Connaissance de l'Orient)

    《道德经》,Liou, Kia-hway 译.

    (1)[Paris]: le Grand livre du mois, Impr. SEPC, 1992. 638 p.; 22cm. ISBN: 2702800947 (rel), 2702800942 (rel). (Le grand livre du mois)

    (2)[Paris]: Gallimard, 1995. 120 p.: couv. ill. en coul.; 19cm. ISBN: 2070719529 (br), 2070719525 (br). (Connaissance de l'Orient: Série chinoise; 42)

13. Le Tao et la vertu/Lao Zi; nouv. traduction avec une introd. et une étude critique de Joseph L. Liu. Montréal: Parti pris, 1974. 199 pages;20cm.

    《道德经》,Liu, Joseph L. 译.

14. Tao te king: le livre de la voie et de la vertu/Lao Tseu; traduction et commentaire spirituel de Claude Larre, S. J. Paris: Desclée De Brouwer, 1977. 226 pages;20cm.

ISBN：222002136X，2220021362.（Collection Christus；no. 45. Contemplations）

《道德经》，Larre，Claude 译.

(1)Dao De Jing＝Le livre de la voie et de la vertu/Lao Zi；trad. et commentaire spirituel de Claude Larre，s. j.；préf. de François Cheng. Paris：Desclée de Brouwer，2002. 233 p.；24cm. ISBN：2220050963（Br），2220050966（Br）

15. Tao te king：le livre de la Voie et de la Vertu/Lao Tseu；texte traduit et présenté par Claude Larre. Paris：Desclée De Brouwer：Institut Ricci，1994. 108 pages；18cm. ISBN：2220035522，2220035529，2950560288，2950560285.（Les Carnets DDB；Variétés sinologiques；no 81）

《道德经》，Larre，Claude 译.

(1) Le livre de la voie et de la vertu/Lao tseu；texte traduit et présenté par Claude Larre. Paris：Desclée de Brouwer，Impr. la Source d'or，2015. 1 vol.（119 p.）；18cm. ISBN：2220075877（br）2220075877（br）.（Poche）

16. Tao-tö king：la tradition du Tao et de sa sagesse/Lao-tseu；traduit du chinois par Bernard Botturi. Paris：Cerf，1984. 121 pages；24cm. ISBN：2204020966，2204020961.（Patrimoines. Taoïsme）

《道德经》，Botturi，Bernard 译.

17. Tao te king：le livre de la voie et de la vertu/Lao Tseu；trad.［du chinois］par Ma Kou；adapt. et préf. par Marc de Smedt. Paris：Albin Michel，1984. 12 p.，81 bl.；18cm. ISBN：2226021183，2226021182.（Collection：spiritualités vivantes）

《道德经》，Ma，Kou 译.

18. Le livre de la voie et de la vertu/Lao-Tseu；nouv. trad. de Conradin von Lauer；compositions de Yin-Gho. Paris：J. de Bonnot，Impr. Aubin，1990. 170 f.：ill.，couv. ill.；21cm.

《道德经》，Lauer，Conradin von 译.

19. Tao-Tê-King/Lao-Tseu；［trad. du chinois par Le'on Wieger］；［introd. par Jean Varenne］. Paris：Éditions du Rocher，1990. 187 pages；23cm. ISBN：2268009521，2268009520.（Textes sacrés）

《道德经》，Wieger，Le'on(1856—1933)译.

(1)Paris：Éditions du Rocher，1991. 187 pages；21cm. ISBN：2268012166，2268012162.（Textes sacrés）

20. Petit précis journalier de la voie/Lao Tzeu；［trad. par Pierre Leyris et François Houang］；［ill. en coul. par Gilles Alféra］. Neauphle-le-Château：Au Quatre-de-chiffre，Impr. G. Alféra，1992. Non paginé［47］p.：ill. en coul.；12cm.

《道德经》，Houang，François-Xavier（1911—1990）和 Leyris，Pierre(1907—2001)合译.

21. Tao te king：le livre du tao et de sa vertu/Lao Tseu；

traduction［de Marc Haven et Daniel Nazir］suivie d'aperçus sur les enseignements de Lao Tseu.［Paris］：Éd. Dervy，1994. 240 p.；19cm. ISBN：285076678X，2850766787.（Bibliothèque de l'initié；17）

《道德经》，Haven，Marc 和 Nazir，Daniel 合译.

(1)Europe media duplication. Paris：Dervy，Impr.，2001. 244 p.：couv. ill. en coul.；19cm. ISBN：2850768642（br），2850768644（br）.（Collection L'être et l'esprit）

22. Tao te king，ou，Livre de la voie et de la vertu/Lao-Tseu；traduction du chinois par Stanislas Julien；révision des notes et postface de Catherine Despeux. Paris：Éd. Mille et une nuits，1996. 199 p.：ill.；14cm. ISBN：2842050533，2842050535.（Mille et une nuits；109）

《道德经》，Julien，Stanislas(1797—1873)译.

(1)nouvelle édition. Paris：Éd. Mille et une nuits，2000. 110 p.；15cm. ISBN：2842055357（br），2842055356（br）.（Mille et une nuits；109）

23. Daode-King：le Livre de la Voie et de la Vertu/Lao Tseu；trad. de Stanislas Julien；encres et manières noires de Woda. Nice（France）：Z'éditions，1997. 59 p.：ill.；30cm. ISBN：2877201899，2877201896.

《道德经》，Julien，Stanislas(1797—1873)译.

(1)Tao-te-king：le livre de la voie et de la vertu/Lao-tseu；présentation de Jean Éracle；traduction de Stanislas Julien. Paris：EJL，Impr. Aubin，2005. 1 vol.（77 p.）：ill.，couv. ill.；21cm. ISBN：2290345326（br），2290345320（br）.（Librio：spiritualité；733）

(2)Paris：Librio，2012. 1 vol.（75 p.）：ill.，couv. ill. en coul.；21cm. ISBN：2290059012（br），2290059013（br）.（Librio：spiritualité；733）

24. Tao te king：livre de la sagesse et de la vertu/Lao Tseu；adaptation française Daniel Pardo；illustrations originales Myriam Béring. Monaco：Arts et Couleurs，2000. 144 p.：il.，lám. col.；39cm. ISBN：2904144218，2904144219

《道德经》，Pardo，Daniel 译；Béring，Myriam 插图.

25. Tao-te-king/Lao Tseu；version allemande de Richard Wilhelm；trad. en français par Étienne Perrot. Paris：Librairie de Médicis，Impr. Mame，2001. 177 p.；20cm. ISBN：2853270084（br），2853270083（br）

《道德经》，卫礼贤（Wilhelm，Richard，1873—1930)（德国汉学家)德译；Perrot，Étienne，(1922—1996)法译.

26. La voie du tao/Lao Tseu；［trad. du chinois］，peintures et calligraphies，Feng Xiao Min. Paris：le Grand livre du mois，2001. 123 p.：ill. en noir et en coul.；31cm. ISBN：2702845657（br），2702845653（br）

《道德经》，Feng，Xiaomin(1959—)译绘.

27. Le véritable Tao te king/Lao Tseu；présenté et trad. du chinois par Eulalie Steens. Monaco；［Paris］：Éd. du Rocher，2002. 133 p.：couv. ill.；21cm. ISBN：

2268041565 (br.)，2268041568 (br.)

《道德经》，Steens，Eulalie(1959—)译.

28. Tao-tö king/Lao-Tseu；traduit du chinois par Liou Kia-hway. ［Paris］：Gallimard，2002. 108 pages；18cm. ISBN：2070423174，2070423170. （Collection Folio；3696）

《道德经》，Liou，Kia-hway 译.

(1)［Paris］：Gallimard，1980. 776 p：ill. ISBN：2070106837，2070106837. （Philosophes taoïstes；[1]；Bibliothèque de la Pléiade；vol. 283)

(2)［Paris］：Gallimard，2015. 1 vol. （108 p.)；18cm. ISBN：2070465255 (br)，207046525X (br). （Folio，Sagesses)

29. Tao te king/Lao Tseu；traduction et commentaire par Marcel Conche. 1re éd. Paris：Presses universitaires de France，2003. 422，［1］pages；20cm. ISBN：2130538177，2130538172. （Perspectives critiques)

《道德经》，Conche，Marcel 译.

30. Tao te ching：le célèbre texte taoïste présenté sur 81 cartes/Lao Tseu；traduction nouvelle et complète ［et calligraphie］de Chao-Hsiu Chen；［traduit de l'anglais par Claire S. Fontaine］. ［Paris］：le Courrier du livre，2004. 1 vol. （81 cartes）：ill. ，couv. ill. ；16cm. + livret，15 p. ISBN：2702904793 （sous embōtage) 2702904794 (sous embōtage)

《道德经》，Chen，Chao-Hsiu 英译；Sachsé Fontaine，Claire(1946—)法译.

31. Livre de la voie et de la vertu Dao de jing à l'usage des acupuncteurs/［Lao zi］；traduit du chinois par Henning Strøm. Paris：Éd. You-Feng，2004. 1 vol. （186 p.)：ill. ，couv. ill. ；21cm. ISBN：2842792165 （br)，2842792169 (br)

《道德经》，Strøm，Henning 译.

32. Le Daode jing："Classique de la voie et de son efficience"/［Lao tseu］；nouvelles traductions basées sur les plus récentes découvertes archéologiques，trois versions complètes，Wang Bi，Mawangdui，Guodian ［par］Rémi Mathieu. Paris：Entrelacs，2008. 280 p. ，［2］p. de pl. ：ill. en coul. ；21cm. ISBN：2908606591，2908606593

《道德经》，Mathieu，Rémi 译.

(1)Paris：G. Trédaniel，2009. 277 pages：illustrations；33cm. ISBN：2813200600，2813200603

33. Laozi/traduit en chinois moderne par Chen Guying；introduction par Fu Huisheng；traduit en français par Lü Hua；relu par Roland-Pierre Lanes. Beijing：Éd. d'enseignement et de recherche des Langues Étrangères，2009. 1 vol. （266 p.)：ill. ，jaq. ill. en coul. ；25cm. ISBN：7560084138 （rel)；7560084133 （rel). （Bibliothèque des classiques chinois：chinois-français)

《老子》，陈鼓应今译. 外语教学与研究出版社.

34. La voie et sa vertu/Lao-tzeu；texte chinois traduit par François Houang et Pierre Leyris. ［Paris］：Seuil，Impr. Mame，2009. 1 vol. （156 p.)：ill. en coul. ，couv. ill. en coul. ；19cm. ISBN：2020993852 (rel)，2020993856 （rel). （Classiques en images)

《道德经》，Houang，François-Xavier （1911—1990)，Leyris，Pierre(1907—2001)译.

35. Le Lao-tseu；suivi des Quatre canons de l'empereur jaune/traduction et commentaires de Jean Levi. ［Paris］：Albin Michel，2009. 231 p. ；19cm. ISBN：2226183156，2226183159

《老子：道德经》，Lévi，Jean 译.

36. Tao tö king：de l'efficience de la voie/Lao tseu…；［traduit par Gilbert Georges Coudret et Philippe Denis］. ［Paris］：Éd. de la revue "Conférences，Impr. Darantière，2009. 1 vol. （108 p.)；21cm. ISBN：2912771254 （br)，2912771250 (br)

《道德经》，Coudret，Gilbert Georges，和 Denis，Philippe 合译.

37. Le canon de la voie et de la vertu/Lao Tseu；essai de traduction par Jean-Claude Lebensztejn. ［Courbevoie］：Théâtre Typographique，2009. 1 vol. （68 p.)：couv. ill. en coul. ；22cm. ISBN：2909657417，2909657418

《道德经》，Lebensztejn，Jean-Claude 译.

38. Lao-tseu/Catherine Despeux. Paris：Entrelacs，2010. 297 p. ，［8］p. de pl. ：ill. ，carte；19cm. ISBN：2908606614，2908606615. （Sagesses éternelles)

《老子道德经》，Despeux，Catherine 译.

39. Le livre de la voie et de la conduite/Lao tseu；introduction et traduction du chinois par Daniel Giraud. Paris：l'Harmattan，Impr. Corlet numérique，2011. 1 vol. （115 p.)：ill. ，couv. ill. en coul. ；22cm. ISBN：2296561250 (br)，229656125X (br)

《道德经》，Giraud，Daniel(1946—)译.

40. Dao de jing：le classique de la voie et de sa vertu/Lao-tseu；traduction，Roger Léger. Saint-Jean-sur-Richelieu，Québec：Éditions Lambda，2011. ISBN：2923255071，2923255070. （Grands textes)

《道德经》，Léger，Roger(1928—)译.

41. Tao te king/Lao-tseu；nouvelle version anglaise de Stephen Mitchell；calligraphies de Ou Yang Jiao Jia；traduction en français，Benoît Labayle. Paris：Synchronique éd. ，2012. 1 vol. （126 p.)：ill. ，couv. ill. ；16cm. ISBN：2917738115 (rel)，2917738111 (rel)

《道德经》，Mitchell，Stephen（1943—）英译；Labayle，Benoît 法译.

42. Le tao et son pouvoir d'amour：une nouvelle interprétation du Tao te king/Lao tseu et Alain Castets. Gap：le Souffle d'or，Impr. Groupe Horizon，2012. 1 vol. （131 p.)：couv. ill. en coul. ；20cm. ISBN：2840584360 (br)，2840584360 (br)

《道和爱的力量：道德经新评》,Castets, Alain 著译.

43. Tao te king/Lao tseu; texte français d'Antoine de Vial. Paris: Orizons, Impr. Corlet numérique, 2013. 1 vol. (104 p.); couv. ill.; 24cm. ISBN: 2336298207 (br), 2336298201 (br). (Cardinales)

《道德经》,Vial, Antoine de 译.

44. Tao te king/Lao tseu; traduit par Claire Sachsé Fontaine; photographies de Michel Bacchetta. Ville-d'Avray: la Fontaine de Pierre, Impr. France Quercy, 2013. 1 vol. (170 p.); ill. en noir et en coul., couv. ill. en coul.; 22 × 23cm. ISBN: 2902707447 (rel), 2902707444 (rel)

《道德经》,Sachsé Fontaine, Claire(1946—)译.

45. Daodejing: "Canon de la voie et de la vertu/Laozi; traduit et annoté par Laure Chen. Éd. bilingue. Paris: Desclée de Brouwer, la Manufacture impr., 2014. 1 vol. (209 p.); couv. ill. en coul.;21cm. ISBN: 2220066226 (br),2220066223 (br). (Espace transculturel)

《道德经》,Chen, Laure 译.

46. Tao te king: Le livre du tao/nouvelle traduction, Guy Massat, Arthur Rivas. Sucy-en-Brie: Anfortas, Impr. ICN,2015. 1 vol. (195 p.);21cm. ISBN: 9791091156691 (br)

《道德经》,Massat, Guy 新译.

47. Tao te king: un voyage illustré/Lao-tseu; traduit par Stephen Mitchell; [traduction française de Benoît Labayle]. [Paris]: Synchronique Éditions, 2015. 1 vol. (non paginé [96] p.); ill.; 21cm. ISBN: 2917738276 (br), 2917738278 (br)

《道德经》,Mitchell, Stephen（1943—）英译;Labayle, Benoît 法译.

48. Tao Te King: Dao De Jing: la voie de la bonté et du pouvoir/Lao Tseu; [traduction du chinois James Trapp]; [traduit de l'anglais par Christine Destruhaut]. Paris: Guy Tredaniel éditeur, 2016. 1 vol. (96 p.): ill.; 27cm. ISBN: 2813209092 (rel), 2813209090 (rel)

《道德经》,Trapp, James 英译;Destruhaut, Christine 法译.

B233 列子

1. Liezi: [89 extraits]/[choisis et trad. du chinois par] Tchang Fou-jouei. Paris: Librairie You Feng, 1993. 559 p.; 21cm. ISBN: 2906658154 (br), 2906658158 (br).

《冲虚经:89 选段》,Chang, Fujui(1915—2006)选译.

2. Liezi/[texte préparé et trad. par] Tchang Fou-Jouei. Paris: Éd. You Feng, 2005, (c)2005. 1 vol. (549 p.); 21cm. ISBN: 2906658154 (br), 2906658158 (br)

《冲虚经》, Chang, Fujui(1915—2006)译.

3. Lie Tseu: les ailes de la joie/Tsai Chih Chung; traduit par Claude Maréchal. Fillinges: Carthame, 1994. ISBN: 2909830098, 2909830094. (Philo bédé)

《冲虚经:杨朱》,Ts'ai, Chih-chung 著;Maréchal, Claude 译.

4. Sur le destin: et autres textes/Lie-tseu; traduit du chinois et annoté par Benedykt Grynpas. [Paris]: Gallimard, 2009. 1 vol. (96 p.); couv. ill. en coul.; 18cm. ISBN: 2070387953 (br), 207038795X (br). (Folio, 2 euros)

《冲虚经:力命及其他》,Grynpas, Benedykt 译.

(1)3 vol. (96, 108, 139 p.); couv. ill. en coul.; 18cm. ISBN: 2070313945 (br. sous coffret), 2070313948 (br. sous coffret). (Collection Folio)

5. Le vrai classique du vide parfait/Lie-tseu; traduit du chinois, présenté et annoté par Benedykt Grynpas. [Paris]: Gallimard: Unesco, Impr. CPI Bussière), 2011. 1 vol. (271 p.); couv. ill. en coul.; 18cm. ISBN: 2070441358 (br), 2070441350 (br). (Folio. Essais; 548)

《冲虚经》, Grynpas, Benedykt 译.

6. Textes taoïstes: "Lie tseu": "Yang Chu", le Jardin du plaisir/traduit de l'anglais par Marielle Saint-Prix. Paris: Éd. Myoho, 2011. 1 vol. (143 p.); couv. ill.; 21cm. ISBN: 2916671137 (br), 2916671130 (br)

《冲虚经:杨朱》, Saint-Prix, Marielle(1951—)译.

7. L'authentique classique de la parfaite vacuité/Lie tseu; présenté, traduit et annoté par Rémi Mathieu. Paris: Entrelacs, Impr. EMD), 2012. 1 vol. (445 p.); couv. ill.; 22cm. ISBN: 2908606805 (br), 2908606801 (br)

《冲虚经》,Mathieu, Rémi(1948—)译.

B234 庄子

1. L'œuvre complète de Tchouang-tseu/Traduction, Préface et notes de Liou Kia-hway. [Paris], Gallimard, 1969. 391 pages; 23cm. (Connaissance de l'Orient; 28; Collection UNESCO d'Œuvres représentatives. Série chinoise)

庄子全书. Liu, Jiahuai(Chia-huai)译.

(1)[Paris], Gallimard, 1997, (c)1969. 388 pages;19cm. ISBN: 2070705293,2070705290. (Connaissance de l'Orient; 1; Collection UNESCO d'Œuvres représentatives. Série chinoise)

(2)[Paris], Gallimard, 2011. 584 pages;18cm. ISBN: 2070443475, 207044347

2. Texte, présentation, traduction, commentaire du vol de l'oiseau Peng/par Claude Larre. Paris: Institut Ricci, 1982. 73 pages; 20×23cm.

《庄子·逍遥游》,Larre, Claude 译.

3. Texte, présentation, traduction, commentaire de la Symphonie de l'Empereur Jaune: un extrait du chapitre XIV du Zhuangzi/par Claude Larre. Paris: Institut Ricci, 1982. 58 [1] pages; 21×30cm.

《庄子·天运》,Larre, Claude 译.

4. Saine incertitude: texte, présentation, traduction et commentaire du ch. 2 du Zhuangzi/E. Rochat de la

Vallée. Paris：Institut Ricci, 1982. v, 65 pages；21×30cm.

《庄子·齐物论》,Rochat de la Vallée, Elisabeth 译.

(1)Paris：Institut Ricci, 1985. v, 65 p.；21×30cm.

5. De vide en vide：texte, présentation, traduction et commentaire du ch. 3 du Zhuangzi/par E. Rochat de la Vallée. Paris：Institut Ricci, 1989. 71 pages；21×30cm.

《庄子·养生主》,Rochat de la Vallée, Elisabeth 译.

(1)Paris：Desclée De Brouwer, 1996. 116 S. ISBN：2220035220, 2220035222, 2910969010, 2910969011. (La conduite de la vie/Zhuangzi；Variété sinologique；no 84)

6. Les tablettes intérieures：tirées du Tchouang Tseu (Zhuang Zi)/Préface, trad. et notes de Jean-François Rollin. Garamont：Libr. Séguier-M. Chandeigne, 1988. 147 p.；23cm. ISBN：2906284882, 2906284883

庄子选译. Rollin, Jean-François 译.

7. Zhuangzi〔initiation à la langue classique chinoise à partir d'extraits de Zhuangzi〕/Tchang Fou-jouei. Paris：Librairie You-Feng, 1989. 391 p. ISBN：2906658111, 2906658110

庄子选译. Zhang, Furui 译.

8. Zhuangzi＝庄子/monograph.〔choisis et trad. du chinois par〕Tchang Fou-jouei. Paris：Éditions You Feng, 1989. 391 pages；21cm. ISBN：2906658110, 2906658111

《庄子》,Tchang, Fou-jouei 译.

9. Pénétrant la voie/Tchouang Tseu；Préface et traduction de Daniel Giraud；graphie de Patrick Carré. La Souterraine：La main courante, 1993. 1 v.

《庄子》,Giraud, Daniel 译.

10. Flutes et champignons：texte, présentation, traduction et commentaire du debut du chapitre 2 du Zhuangzi/par Claude Larre, E. Rochat de la Vallée. Paris：Institut Ricci, 1985. 1 vol. (63 p.)；30×21cm.

《庄子·齐物论》,Larre, Claude 和 Rochat de la Vallée, Elisabeth 合译.

(1)Paris：Institut Ricci, 1990. 64 pages；21×30cm.

11. Le vol inutile：Zhuangzi, la conduite de la vie/Claude Larre & Élisabeth Rochat de la Valée. Paris：Épi/Institut Ricci：Desclée de Brouwer, 1994. 134 pages；22cm. ISBN：2220035220, 2220035222, 295056027X, 2950560278. (Variétés sinologiques；no. 80)

《庄子·逍遥游》,Larre, Claude 和 Rochat de la Vallée, Elisabeth 合译.

(1)〔Nouv. éd.〕. Paris：Desclée de Brouwer, Impr. Présence graphique), 2010. 1 v. (131 p.)：couv. ill. en coul.；21cm. ISBN：2220062419, 2220062414. (Variété sinologique；80)

12. Le rêve du papillon/Tchouang-Tseu (Zhuangzi)；traduction de Jean-Jacques Lafitte. Paris：Albin Michel, 1994, 1997. 339 p.；23cm. ISBN：2226068767,

2226068767. (Spiritualités vivantes)

《庄子·庄周梦蝶》,Lafitte, Jean-Jacques 译.

(1)Paris：Albin Michel, 2002. 340 p. ISBN：2226130926, 2226130921. (Spiritualités vivantes；187)

(2)Paris：Albin Michel, 2002. 340 p. ISBN：2226130926, 2226130921, 2226172846, 222617284X. (Coll. Spiritualités vivantes)

(3)Paris：Albin Michel, 2010, (c)2002. 340 p.；18cm. ISBN：2226172846, 222617284X. (Spiritualités vivantes；187)

13. Aphorismes et paraboles/Tchouang Tseu；recueillis et présentés par Marc de Smedt. Paris：Albin Michel, 2005. 149 p.；18cm. ISBN：2226157123, 2226157126. (Spiritualités vivantes；55)

《庄子》,Smedt, Marc de(1946—)译.

14. Les œuvres de maître Tchouang/traduction de Jean Levi. Paris：Éditions de l'Encyclopédie des nuisances, 2006. 330 pages；22cm. ISBN：2910386244, 2910386245

《庄子》,Levi, Jean 译.

(1)Éd. rév. et augm. Paris：Éditions de l'Encyclopédie des nuisances, 2010. 370 p. ISBN：2910386344, 2910386341

15. Les chapitres intérieurs/Zhuangzi (Tchouang-tseu)；traduit du chinois par J. C. Pastor；introduction d'Isabelle Robinet. Paris：Les Éditions du Cerf, 1990, 1999, 2008. 112 pages；24cm. ISBN：2204040762, 2204040761. (Patrimoines taoisme)

《庄子·内篇》,Pastor, Jean-Claude 译.

16. Le deuxième livre du tao：le rire de Tchouang-tseu/textes choisis et adaptés du Tchouang-tseu et du Tchoung Young avec commentaires, Stephen Mitchell；traduit de l'anglais par Benoît Labayle et Célin Vuraler. Paris：Synchronique, 2010. 171 p. ISBN：2917738054, 2917738057

《庄子之笑》, Mitchell, Stephen(1943—)英译；Labayle, Benoît 和 Vuraler, Célin 法译. 本书包含了《庄子》选译.

B24 法家

B241 管子

1. L'Esprit des races jaunes. Le Traité des influences errantes de Quangdzu/Traduit du chinois par Matgioi (Albert de Pouvourville). Paris：Bibliothèque de la Haute science, 1896. In—16, 51 p.

《管子》,Matgioi 译.

2. Ecrits de Mātre Guan：les quatres traités de l'Art de l'esprit/textes présentés, traduits et annotés par Romain Graziani. Paris：Belles lettres, 2011. lxxxix, 90 p.；20cm. ISBN：2251100074, 2251100075. (Bibliothèque

chinoise＝汉文法译书库；7)

《管子》，Graziani，Romain 译.

B242 韩非子

1. Les plus belles pages du philosophe chinois Han Fei-tse/ Introd. et traduction par Bruno Belpaire. Bruxelles, Éditions de l'Occident, 1963. 195 pages；21cm. (Petits traités chinois peu connus；no. 4)

《韩非子》，Belpaire，Bruno 译.

2. Han Fei-tzu＝Hanfeizi/Tchang Fou-jouei. Paris：Yu feng shu tien, 1987. 257 pages；21cm. ISBN：2906658022, 2906658028

《韩非子》，Tchang，Fou-jouei 译.

3. Han-Fei-tse, ou, le Tao du Prince：la stratégie de la domination absolue/présenté et traduit du chinois par Jean Lévi. Paris：Seuil, 1999. 616 p.：cartes；18cm. ISBN：2020293722, 2020293723. (Points. Sagesses；Sa141)

《韩非子》，Lévi，Jean 译.

B25 汉代哲学思想

1. Fa yan/Yang Xiong；texte établi, traduit et annoté par Béatrice L' Haridon. Paris：Les Belles lettres, 2010. lxix, 224 p.：carte；20cm. ISBN：2251100012, 2251100016. (Bibliothèque chinoise)

《法言》，扬雄，(前 58—公元后 18 年)；L'Haridon，Béatrice 译.

B26 宋代哲学思想

1. "Kia li", livre des rites domestiques chinois.../de Tchou Hi；traduit pour la 1re fois, avec commentaires, par C. de Harlez. Paris：Ernest. Leroux, 1889. 1 vol. 167p. (Bibliothèque orientale elzévirienne；LX)

《家礼》，朱熹(1130—1200)著；De Harlez，Charle(1832—1899)译.

B3 伦理学

1. Valeurs Chinoises：culture traditionnelle chinoise et valeurs chinoises contemporaines. Beijing：Éditions en Langues Étrangères, 2016. xi, 197 pages.；23cm. ISBN：7119100661

《中国价值观：中国传统文化与中国当代价值》，曹雅欣著.

B4 宗教

B41 概述

1. Religions et vie religieuse en Chine/par Sang Ji；traduit par Kang Liang, Jean Delvigne. Beijing：China Intercontinental Press, 2004. 162 pages：color illustrations；21cm. ISBN：7508504992；7508504995. (Que sais-je sur la Chine?)

《中国宗教》，桑吉著，吕华译. 五洲传播出版社(中国基本情况丛书/郭长建主编)

2. 北京寺庙道观：[法文本]/廖频，吴文编；何炳富等摄影；王默 翻译. 北京：外文出版社, 2007. 113 pages；illustrations；23cm. ISBN：7119044064, 7119044060. (漫游北京)

B42 佛教

1. Bouddhisme chinois/[textes établis, présentés et trad.] par Léon Wieger. Paris：Cathasia(impr. de Bellenand), 1951. 2 vol. (479 p. et pages 1—279, pl. 7—197 et p. 425—453)：ill.；25cm. (Les Humanités d'Extrême Orient)

《中国佛教》，Wieger，Léon(1856—1933)编著并翻译.

2. Vocabulaire bouddhique sanscrit-chinois, Han-fan tsih-yao：Précis de doctrine bouddhique. T'ong Pao, Vol VII, 1896. In-8°

《汉梵集要：佛教理论概要》，De Harlez，Charles(1832—1899)译.

3. Buddhisme：extraits du Tripit,aka, des commentaires, tracts, etc. /par le P. Léon Wieger. [Hien-Hien]：Impr. de la Mission catholique, 1910—1913. 2 vol. (453 p.)：pl., ill., couv. ill.

《中国佛教：大藏经选段、评论等》，Wieger，Léon(1856—1933)编译.

4. Cinq cents contes et apologues/extraits du Tripitaka chinois et traduits en français par édouard Chavannes,...；publié sous les auspices de la Société asiatique. Paris：E. Leroux, 1910—1911. 3 vol. (XX-428, 449, 395 p.)；25cm.

佛经故事五百则. 沙畹(Chavannes，édouard，1865—1918)(法国汉学家)译.

(1) Cinq cents contes et apologues/analyse sommaire des contes, notes complémentaires, tables et index formant le tome IV de l'ouvrage；[avertissement de Sylvain Lévi]. Paris, Impr. nationale；Ernest Leroux, 1934. IX-345 p.

(2) [Nouvelle édition revue par Sylvain Lévi]. Paris：Librairie d'Amérique et d'Orient：Adrien-Maisonneuve, 1962. 4 t. en 3 vol. (XX-429, 450, 399—X—345 p.)；(22cm.)

(3) Paris：Adrien-Maisonneuve, 1962. 3 vol. (XX-428, 449, 395—343 p.)；23cm. (Collection UNESCO d'œuvres représentatives. série chinoise)

5. Cinq cents contes et apologues extraits du Tripitaka chinois et traduits en français/par Édouard Chavannes. Paris：E. Leroux, 1910—1934. 4 vol.

大藏经：短篇小说和寓言故事五百篇. 沙畹(Chavannes，édouard，1865—1918)(法国汉学家)译.

(1) Cinq cents contes et apologues/extraits du Tripit,aka chinois et traduits en français par édouard Chavannes.

Paris：Adrien-Maisonneuve, 1962. 3 vol. (XX-428, 449, 395 — 343 p.)；23cm. (Collection UNESCO d'œuvres représentatives. série chinoise)

6. Contes et légendes du bouddhisme chinois/traduits du chinois, par édouard Chavannes. Paris：Bossard, 1921. 220 p. (Les Classiques de l'Orient. 4)

中国佛教故事与传说. 沙畹(Chavannes, édouard, 1865—1918)(法国汉学家)译.

(1)Saint Michel en l'Herm：Éditions Dharma, 1998. 218 p.：ill.；22cm. ISBN：2864870312, 2864870319. (Fenêtres du Dharma)

7. Mémoires sur les contrées occidentales/traduits du sanscrit en chinois, en l'an 648 par Hiouen-Tsang；et du chinois en français par M. Stanislas Julien. Paris：Impr. impériale, 1857—1858. 2 vol. (LVXIII-493, XIX-576 p.). (Voyages des pèlerins bouddhistes. II et III)

《大唐西域记》,玄奘著；Julien, Stanislas(1799—1873)译.

8. Foě Kouě Ki, ou Relation des royaumes bouddhiques, voyage dans la Tartarie, dans l'Afghanistan et dans l'Inde, exécuté, à la fin du IVe siècle par Ch y Fǎ Hian/Traduit du chinois et commenté par M. Abel Rémusat. Paris：Impr. royale, 1836. In-fol., LXVII-424 p., pl. et carte

《佛国记》,法显著；Rémusat, M. Abel 译.

9. Histoire de la vie d'Hiouen-Thsang/fragment... traduit par M. Stanislas Julien. Paris：Arthus Bertrand, 1851. 72 p.

《大慈恩寺三藏法师传》(选译), 慧立(615—？)著；Julien, Stanislas 译.

10. Histoire de la vie de Hiouen-Thsang et de ses voyages dans l'Inde, depuis l'an 629 jusqu'en 645/par Hoeï-li et Yen-thsong, suivie de documents et d'éclaircissements géographiques tirés de la relation originale de Hiouen-Thsang, traduite du chinois par Stanislas Julien. Paris：Impr. impériale, 1853. LXXXIV-472 p.

《大慈恩寺三藏法师传》, 慧立(615—？)著；Julien, Stanislas 译.

11. Mémoire composé à l'époque de la grande dynastie T'ang sur les religieux éminents qui allèrent chercher la loi dans les pays d'Occident/par I-tsing；traduit en français par édouard Chavannes. Paris：E. Leroux, 1894. 1 vol. (XXI-218 p.)

《大唐西域求法高僧传》, 义净著；沙畹(Chavannes, édouard, 1865—1918)(法国汉学家)译.

12. Sǎriputra et les six maîtres d'erreur：fac-similé du manuscrit chinois 4524 de la Bibliothèque nationale/présenté par Nicole Vandier-Nicolas,... avec traduction et commentaire du texte. Paris：Impr. nationale, 1954. 1 vol. (35 p. et 27 pl. de fac-sim. en noir et en coul.) (Mission Pelliot en Asie centrale. Série in-4°；V)

舍利弗和六位谬误大师. Vandier-Nicolas, Nicole 译. 本书包含对中国佛教文献的翻译.

13. La Siddhi de Hiuan-Tsang/Traduite et annotée par Louis de La Vallée Poussin. T. 1 et 2. Louvain (Belgique), impr. J.-B. Istas；Paris, libr. orientaliste Paul Geuthner, 13, rue Jacob, 1928—1929. (26 novembre 1931.)2 vol. in-8. T. 1, 432 p.；t. 2, de la p. 433 à la p. 820

《成唯识论》. La Vallée Poussin, Louis de(1869—1938)译.

14. Matériaux pour l'étude du système Vijnaptimatra：un système de philosophie bouddhique/par Sylvain Lévi；introduction historique du système Vijnaptimatra, d'après D. Shimaj, par M. Paul Demiéville；traduction de la Vimsatika et de la Trimsika... traduit en collaboration avec Édouard Chavannes. Paris：H. Champion, 1932. 1 vol. (207 p.)；25cm. (Bibliothèque de l'école des hautes études. Sciences historiques et philologiques；260)

《成唯识论》研究资料. Lévi, Sylvain (1863—1935)著；Lévi, Sylvain (1863—1935) 和 沙 畹 (Chavannes, édouard, 1865—1918)(法国汉学家)合译. 本书包含对《唯识二十论》和《唯识三十颂》的翻译.

15. Le Sûtra des causes et des effets, du bien et du mal：édité et traduit d'après les textes sogdien, chinois et tibétain/par Robert Gauthiot et Paul Pelliot. Tome I, Fac-similé des textes sogdien et chinois. Paris：P. Geuthner, 1920. 1 vol. ([8] p., 52 pl. fac-sim.)；couv. ill.；in-fol., 33cm. (Mission Pelliot en Asie centrale. Série in-quarto；I)

《善业因果经》(卷一), Gauthiot, Robert(1876—1916)和 Pelliot, Paul(1878—1945)合译.

16. Le sûtra des causes et des effets du bien et du mal：édité et traduit d'après les textes sogdien, chinois et tibétains/par Robert Gauthiot et Paul Pelliot；avec la collaboration d'émile Benveniste. Tome II, Transcription, traduction, commentaire et index. Paris：P. Geuthner, 1926—1928. 1 tome en 2 fasc. (XI-66 p., p. 67—101)；gr. in-4, 33cm. (Mission Pelliot en Asie centrale. Série in-quarto；II)

《善业因果经》(卷二), Gauthiot, Robert(1876—1916), Pelliot, Paul (1878—1945), Benveniste, émile (1902—1976)译.

17. Documents d'Abhidharma：2. La doctrine des refuges： 3. Le corps de l'Arhat est-il pur? /traduits et annotés par Louis de La Vallée Poussin. [S. l.], [1931]. In-8°

《阿毗达摩俱舍论》, 世亲著；La Vallée Poussin, Louis de (1869—1938)译.

18. Mahā-Karmavibhāga (la Grande Classification des actes) et Karmavibhaṅgopadeśa (Discussion sur le Mahā Karmavibhāga)：textes sanscrits rapportés du Népal, édités et traduits avec les textes parallèles en sanscrit, en

pali，en thibétain，en chinois et en koutchéen. Ouvrage illustré de quatre planches：le Karmavibhāga sur les bas-reliefs de Boro-Budur, à Java/par Sylvain Lévi，… Paris (28，rue Bonaparte)：libr. Ernest Leroux，1932（16 mars 1933）. 1 vol.（[8] p. —IV pl. —270—[2] p.）；26cm.

《大业分别经及其注释书》，Lévi，Sylvain（1863—1935）译. 部分资料来自中文.

19. Vimalakirtinirdesa. L'Enseignement de vimalakirti/par étienne Lamotte. Louvain，1962. 503 p.

《维摩诘经》. Lamotte，Etienne（1903—1983）译.

20. Dhyana pour les débutants, traité sur la méditation, suite de conférences données par le Grand maître Chih-chi du Tien-tai au temple de Shiu-ch'an（dynastie des Sui，581 — 618）./Traduction française de Grace Constant-Lounsbery, d'après la transcription du chinois du Bhikshu Wai-dau et de Dwight Goddard. [Préface du Bhikshu Yuen-tso.] Paris：A. Maisonneuve（impr. de Jouve]，1944. 104 p.

《禅门要略》，天台智顗大师 著；Constant-Lounsbery，Grace（1876—1964）译.

(1) Paris，A. Maisonneuve（Impr. I. F. M. R. P.），1951. 104 p

(2) Paris：J. Maisonneuve，1978. 104 p.；20cm.

21. Entretiens de Lin-tsi/trad. du chinois et commentés par Paul Demiéville. [Paris]：Fayard，1972. 256 p.；22cm. ISBN：2213004978.（Documents spirituels；6）

《临济语录》，Demiéville，Paul（1894—1979）译.

22. Mahābalanāmamahāyānasūtra/Contribution à l'étude des divinités mineures du bouddhisme tantrique. ārya Mahābalanāma-mahāyānasūtra tibétain（mss. de Touen-houang)et chinois [édité, traduit et annoté] par F. A. Bischoff. Préface de Marcelle Lalou. Paris：Paul Geuthner，1956. XII—126 p.，IV fac-sim.（Buddhica. 1re série. Mémoires. X）

Bischoff，F. A. 译. 本书包含中国佛教密宗经典的翻译.

23. La somme du grand véhicule/Asaṅga；trad. par Etienne Lamotte. Reprod. en fac-sim. Louvain-la-Neuve：Institut orientaliste，1973. 2 vol.（VIII—99—IX—345）p. —[21] p. de pl.：photogr.；27cm.（Publications de l'Institut orientaliste de Louvain；8）

《摄大乘论》，印度无著（阿僧咖）著；佛陀扇多汉译二卷本，真谛汉译三卷本，玄奘汉译三卷本；Lamotte，Etienne（1903—1983）法译.

(1) La Somme du Grand véhicule d'Asaṅga（Mahāyānasamgraha）/par Etienne Lamotte. Louvain：Bureaux du Muséon，1938. 2 tomes en I vol.

24. Le XIVe Dalai Lama/Siren et Gewang. Beijing：Édition Intercontinentale de Chine，1997. 78 pages；21cm.

ISBN：7801132971，7801132970.

《十四世达赖喇嘛》，司仁，格旺著.

25. Le régime de réincarnation du Dalaï-Lama/Chen Qingying. Beijing：China Intercontinal Press，2008. 182 pages：illustrations；21cm. ISBN：7508507651；7508507657

《达赖喇嘛转世》，陈庆英著；张家卫译. 五洲传播出版社.

B43 道教

1. Le Livre des récompenses et des peines, en chinois et en français；accompagné de quatre cent légendes, avec dotes et histoires qui font connaître les doctrines, les croyances et les moeurs de la secte des Tao-ssé/Traduit du chinois par Stanislas Julien. Paris；London，R. Bentley，1835

《太上感应篇》，Julien，Stanislas 译.

2. Le livre des récompenses et des peines：ouvrage taoïste/traduit du chinois avec des notes et des éclaircissements par Abel Rémusat；précédé d'une notice historique sur la vie et les ouvrages d'Abel Rémusat par Silvestre de Sacy. Nouvelle éd. Paris：P. Geuthner，1939. 117 p.（Les joyaux de l'Orient；Tome III）

《太上感应篇》，Rémusat，Abel（1788—1832）译.

(1) Paris：A.-A. Renouard，1816. 79 p.

3. Le Lie-sien tchouan：Biographies légendaires des Immortels taoïstes de l'antiquité/traduit et annoté par Max Kaltenmark. Pékin：Centre d'études sinologiques de Pékin de l'Université de Paris，1953. IV-204 p

《列仙传》，刘向著；Kaltenmark，Max（1910—2002）译.

(1) Ed. augm. d'un nouvel index par Catherine Arbeit. [publ. par le] Collège de France, Institut des hautes études chinoises. Paris：Collège de France：diffusion De Boccard，1987. 225 p.；25cm.

4. Le livre de la récompense des bienfaits secrets/traduit du texte chinois par L.-Léon de Rosny. Paris：impr. de H. Carion，1856. 6 p.

《文昌帝君阴骘文》，Rosny，Léon de（1837—1914）译.

B44 基督教

1. L'Inscription syro-chinoise de Si-Ngan-Fou, monument nestorien élevé en Chine l'an 781/texte chinois accompagné de la prononciation figurée, d'une version latine verbale, d'une traduction française… par G. Pauthier. Paris：Firmin-Didot frères, fils et Cie，1858. XVI-96 p.

《景教流行中国碑》，景净著；Pauthier，Guillaume（1801—1873）译.

2. Zhongguo Jidu jiao/Mei Kangjun bian zhu. Beijing：Wu zhou chuan bo chu ban she，2005. 112 pages：chiefly illustrations（some color）；21cm. ISBN：7508508130；7508508139

《中国基督教》，梅康钧编著；朱承铭译. 五洲传播出版社.

3. La croix-lotus: inscriptions et manuscrits nestoriens en ecriture syriaque decouverts en Chine/Niu Ruji. Shanghai: Shanghai gu ji chu ban she, 2010. 2, 13, 4, 344 pages: illustrations, maps; 26cm. ISBN: 7532555918; 7532555917. (Huaxia ying cai ji jin xue shu wen ku)

《十字莲花:中国出土叙利亚文景教碑铭文献研究(公元13~14世纪)》,牛汝极著.上海古籍出版社.

B45　其他宗教派别

1. Le Code du Mahāyāna en Chine, son influence sur la vie monacale et sur le monde laïque/par J. J. M. de Groot. Amsterdam: J. Muller, 1893. Gr. X-271 p.

中国婆罗门教义.Groot, Johann Jacob Maria de 译.本书包含对《旧唐书》中有关婆罗门教的选译.

2. Le Traité de la grande vertu de sagesse de Nāgārjuna/[trad. et commenté] par Etienne Lamotte. Louvain-la-Neuve: Institut orientaliste, 1944—. 27cm.

Contents: T. 1: Chapitres I-XV. —Réimpr. de l'éd. de 1944. —1966. —XXXII, 620 p. T. 2: Chapitres XVI-XXX. —Réimpr. de l'éd. de 1949. —1967. —XXII p., p. 621—1118. T. 3: Chapitres XXXI-XLII. —1970. —LXVIII p., p. 1119—1733. T. 4: Chapitres XLII (suite)—XLVIII. —1976. —XIX p., p. 1736—2162. T. 5: Chapitres XLIX-LII, et chapitre XX (2e série). —1980. —XV p., p. 2164—2451. 2-8017—01317.

Notes: Traduit de: Mahāprajñāpāramitāśāstra. / Les t. I et II ont été publiés dans la collection "Bibliothèque du Muséon"; les suivants dans la collection "Publications de l'Institut orientaliste de Louvain."/L'original sanscrit n'étant pas conservé, la traduction est faite d'après la version chinoise du Traité de la grande vertu de sagesse: le Ta tche tou louen.

《大智度论》. Nāgārjuna 著; Lamotte, Etienne (1903—1983)译.

C类　社会科学总论

C1　统计资料汇编

1. [Publications d'information en français. Série in—16.]. [14.], Dix grandes années. Les réalisations économiques et culturelles de la République populaire de Chine. Recueil statistique par l'Office d'État de statistique, [S. l.]: Éditions en Langues Étrangères, 1960. [40—] 228 p., fig. en coul., couv. ill. en coul. [Ech. int. 6654—60]; In—16 (18,5cm.). [Ech. int.]

《伟大的十年:中华人民共和国经济和文化建设成就的统计》.国家统计局编.

C2　人口学

1. La population chinoise et son évolution/par Tian Xueyuan et Zhou Liping; traduit du chinois par Tang Jialong. [China]: China Intercontinental Press, 2004. ISBN: 7508504429 (pbk.); 7508504421 (pbk.) (Que sais-je sur la Chine?)

《中国人口》,田雪原,周丽苹著;唐家龙译.五洲传播出版社.

C3　中国各民族

1. Les Ethnies de la Chine/par Wang Can; traduit par Lu Hua, Cao Ginglin etc... Beijing: China Intercontinental Press, 2004. 1 vol. (195 p.): couv. ill. en coul., ill. en coul.; 21cm. ISBN: 7508504941 (br); 7508504940 (br) (Que sais-je sur la Chine?)

《中国民族》,王灿著,吕华译.五洲传播出版社(中国基本情况丛书/郭长建主编)

2. L'autonomie régionale des ethnies minoritaires/[Wu Naitao; traduit par Zhang Yuyuan, Zhang Yongzhao]. Beijing: Éditions en Langues Étrangères, 2009. 39 pages: color illustrations; 21cm. ISBN: 7119058580, 7119058584

《中国的民族区域自治》,吴乃陶.

3. Les ethnies minoritaires/[texte, Xing Li... [et al.; traduction, Zhang Yongzhao]. Beijing: Éditions en Langues Étrangères, 2007. 118 p.: ill.; 17 × 19cm. ISBN: 7119041315 (br.); 7119041312 (br.)

《中国少数民族:法文》,肖晓明主编;杜殿文等摄.

4. 中国的民族政策与各民族共同繁荣发展/中华人民共和国国务院新闻办公室[编].北京:外文出版社,2009. 79页; 21cm. ISBN: 7119060552

5. Les ethnies et les religions en Chine/Zheng Qian. Beijing: China Intercontinental Press, 2011. 213 p.: col. ill.; 23cm. ISBN: 7508519371, 750851937X

《中国民族与宗教》,郑茜著.五洲传播出版社.

6. Culture of Qiang = Culture de Qiang/Qiang zu wen hua = Culture of Qiang = Culture de Qiang/Chen Shuyu zhu bian. Chengdu: Xi nan jiao tong da xue chu ban she, 2008. 9, 2, 390 pages; 25cm. ISBN: 7811049862, 7811049864

《羌族文化》,陈蜀玉主编.西南交通大学出版社.本书为中英法三种文字对照版本,旨在用三种文字向海内外介绍羌族.

D类　政治、法律

D1　中国政治

D11　概况

1. Guide de la Chine nouvelle. Pékin: Éditions en Langues Étrangères, 1952. 132—VII p., pl., portrait, tableaux, musique. In—16.

《新中国手册》.

(1)《新中国手册》，外文出版社编译.

2. La Chine，grande famille de nationalités/Wang Chou Tang. Pékin：Éditions en Langues Étrangères，1955. 1 vol. (70 p.)：portr.；19cm.

《中国：一个多民族的国家》，王树棠著.

3. Chine：aperçu général/rédigé par Qi Wen. Beijing，Chine：Éditions en Langues Étrangères，1979. 294 p.：[30] f. de pl.；18cm. +1 carte dépl

《中国概貌》，齐雯编.

(1)Beijing：Éditions en Langues Étrangères，1981. 299 pages：illustrations，map；19cm.

(2)Troisième édition (revue et complétée). Beijing，Chine：Éditions en Langues Étrangères，. 1985. 1 vol. (278 p.-[56] p. de pl. en coul.-[1] f. de carte dépl.)：cartes，couv. ill. en coul.；19cm.

4. Coup d'œil sur la Chine/rédigé par Qi Wen. Beijing：Éditions en Langues Étrangères：[Distributeur，Société chinoise du Commerce international du Livre (Guoji Shudian)]，1984. 99 pages，[56] pages of plates (1 folded)：color illustrations，color map；20cm.

《中国便览》，齐雯编.

5. Politique/par le comité de red. de la collection "Connaissance de la Chine." Pékin，Chine：Éditions en Langues Étrangères，1986. 181 p.，[8] p. de planches：ill.

《政治》，中国概况编剧委员会编.

6. Chine：Petite encyclopédie/Qin Shi. Beijing：Nouvelle Étoile，1994. 1 vol. (199 p.)：photos；20cm. ISBN：7800859215；7800859212.

《中国》，秦石编. 新星出版社.

7. Chine/Zhou Mingwei [concepteur général]. Beijing：Éditions en Langues Étrangères，2011. 1 vol. (229 p.)：ill.；22cm. ISBN：7119071815；7119071817

《中国》，钟欣编.

8. 中国：事实与数字/北京周报社编. 北京：新星出版社，1995. ISBN：7801023366

9. Le drapeau national，l'emblème national，l'hymne national et la capitale. Beijing：Éditions en Langues Étrangères，1st ed. 2003. 41 pages：color illustrations；18cm. ISBN：7119031473；7119031477.

《中华人民共和国国旗、国徽、国歌、首都》，王传民编.

10. Chine，système politique/par Yin Zhongqing；traduit par Zhuge Canglin. Pékin：China International Press，2004. 1 vol. (198 p.)：ill.；21cm. ISBN：7508504682 (br)，7508504681 (br). (Que sais-je sur la Chine?)

《中国政治制度》，尹中卿著，诸葛苍麟译. 五洲传播出版社(中国基本情况丛书/郭长建主编)

(1)Le systeme politique Chinois/Yin Zhougoing；traduction en Francais，Zhuge Canglin. 2nd ed. Beijing：China Intercontinental Press，2011. 195 pages：color illustrations；23cm. ISBN：7508519425，7508519426

11. 透视中国一百问：法文/王刚毅，吴伟，李建国主编；李莎等译. 北京：新星出版社，2005. 207 页：图；21cm. ISBN：780148908X

12. 中国的民主政治建设：法文/中华人民共和国国务院新闻办公室发布. 北京：新星出版社，2005. 91 页；20cm. ISBN：7801488393

13. Le Rêve chinois/Li Junru；[traduit par Zhou Shaoping]. Beijing：Éditions en Langues Étrangerès，2006. 131 pages：illustrations；22cm. ISBN：711904463X (pbk.)；7119044637 (pbk.) (La Chine en développement pacifique)

《中国梦》，李君如著；邹绍平译(中国的和平发展系列)

14. Alimentation，population et emploi/Zhang Guoqing. Beijing：Éditions en Langues Étrangeres，2006. 137 pages：color illustrations；21cm. ISBN：7119044699 (pbk.)，7119044699 (pbk.). (Chine en développement pacifique；Zhongguo de he ping fa zhan xi lie)

《粮食、人口与就业》，张国庆著；王金冠译(中国的和平发展系列)

15. Mots clés pour comprendre la Chine/Xia Hewen；[traduction Zhang Yuyuan，Wang Mo]. Beijing：Éditions en Langues Étrangères，2008. 1 volume (325 pages)：illustrations；23cm. ISBN：7119053486 (br)，7119053485. (Collection culture de la Chine)

《关键词读中国》，呼宝民主编.

16. La voie chinoise：concept de développement scientifique/Tian Yingkui；[traduit]，Zhang Yongzhao，Wang Mo. Beijing：Éditions en Langues Étrangères，2008. 193 pages；23cm. ISBN：7119054766，7119054767

《中国道路：从科学发展观解读中国发展》，田应奎著.

17. Découvrons la Chine/Wang Qicheng. Beijing：Foreign Languages Press，2010. 216 pages：color illustrations；24cm. ISBN：7119060309；7119060309

《看中国》，王麒诚著.

18. La Chine et son développement pacifique/Office d'information de Conseil des Affaires d'État de la République populaire de Chine. Beijing：Éditions en Langues Étrangères，2011. 42 p.；21cm. ISBN：7119072456，7119072455

《中国的和平发展》，中华人民共和国国务院新闻办公室编.

19. 中国走社会主义道路为什么成功：法文版 /_戴木才著；刘田丰译. 北京：五洲传播出版社，2016. 238 页；24cm. ISBN：7508533322

法文题名：Pourquoi la voie socialiste a-t-elle réussi à la Chine

20. 中国梦，什么梦？/ 李君如著；姜丽莉，何丹翻译. 北京：外文出版社，2014. 172 页；24cm. ISBN：7119093239

法文题名：Qu'est-ce que le rêve chinois?

21. 中国震撼：一个文明型国家的崛起/张维为著；姚杰，(法)温迪·伯特兰(Wendy Bertrand)译. 北京：五洲传播出版社，2017.11，228 页；23cm. ISBN：7508535715

法文题名：Vague chinoise：l'émergence d'un État civilisationnel

22. 中国道路能为世界贡献什么：法文/韩庆祥等著. 北京：中国人民大学出版社，2017. 328 页；26cm. ISBN：7300245508

D12　中国政治思想史

1. Maréchal Tchang Kai Chek. Destin de la Chine/Présenté et commenté par Philip Jaffe. Traduit de l'américain par S.-T. Vincenot et Francine Péris. Paris：Amiot-Dumont, 1949. 296 p., carte, portrait sur la couv.

   《中国之命运》，蒋介石（1887—1975）著；Jaffe, Philip 英译；Vincenot, S.-T., Péris, Francine 法译.

D13　中国共产党

1. Les Trente années du parti communiste chinois/par Hou Kiao-Mou. Pékin：Éditions en Langues Étrangères, 1952. In—16, 121 p.

   《中国共产党的三十年》，胡乔木著.

   (1)3. éd. Pékin：Éditions en Langues Étrangères, 1956. 131 pages；19cm.

2. Status du Parti Communiste Chinois：rapport sur les modifications des Status du Parti/[par] Teng Siao-ping. Pékin：Éditions en Langues Étrangères, 1956. 111 pages

   《中国共产党党章，关于修改党的章程的报告》，邓小平.

3. Vive le Parti communiste chinois：à l'occasion du 48e anniversaire de la fondation du Parti communiste chinois. Pékin：Éditions en Langues Étrangères, 1969. 18 p

   《中国共产党万岁：纪念中国共产党诞生四十八周年》

4. Statuts du Parti communiste chinois：Adoptés le 14 avril 1969 par le IXe Congrès du Parti communiste chinois. Pékin：Éditions en Langues Étrangères, 1969. 39 pages；11cm.

   《中国共产党章程》

5. Célébrons le cinquantième anniversaire du Parti communiste chinois/par les rédactions du Renmin Ribao, du Hongqi et du Jiefangjun Bao. Pékin：Éditions en Langues Étrangères, 1971. 54 p.

   《纪念中国共产党五十周年》，《人民日报》、《红旗》杂志、《解放军报》编辑部.

6. Que savez-vous du Parti communiste chinois? /Li Junru. Beijing：Éditions en Langues Étrangères, 2011. 185 pages：illustrations（some color），facsimile；23cm. ISBN：7119070186；7119070185.

   Contents：Le Parti communiste chinois, fondé en 1921, a déjà une histoire de 90 ans. après l'avènement de la Chine nouvelle en 1949, il a frayé une voie socialiste à la chinoise tout en dirigeant le peuple chinois. Comment a-t-il pu réussir? Ce petit livre, loin d'être une simple présentation generale du Parti communiste chinois, met l'accent sur quelques questions que se posent de nombreuses personnes à son sujet afin de leur faire comprendre ce que sont le socialisme à la chinoise et le Parti communiste chinois, ainsi que le fonctionnement et le mode de gouvernance de ce dernier.

   《你了解中国共产党吗?》，李君如著.

7. Parti communiste chinois VIIIe Congrès national du Parti communiste chinois：recueil de documents. Pékin：Éditions en Langues Étrangères, 1956. 1. Documents

   《中国共产党第八次全国代表大会文件集》（一）

8. Rapport politique du Comité central du Parti communiste chinois au 8° Congrès national du Parti communiste chinois. Résolution du 8° Congrès national du Parti communiste chinois sur le rapport politique. Pékin：Éditions en Langues Étrangères, 1956. In-8°, 135 p.

   《中国共产党中央委员会向第八次全国代表大会的政治报告，中国共产党第八次全国代表大会关于政治报告的决议》

9. Propositions du VIIIe congrès national du parti communiste chinois concernant le deuxième plan quinquennal pour le développement de l'économie nationale （1958—1962）/Chou En-lai. Pékin：Éditions en Langues Étrangères, 1956. 110 p.；20cm.

   《中国共产党第八次全国代表大会关于发展国民经济的第二个五年计划（1958—1962 年）的建议，关于发展国民经济的第二个五年计划的建议的报告》，周恩来.

10. Résolution sur le problème de la coopération agricole/adoptée à la 7. session plenière （élargie）du Comité central du parti communiste chinois issu du 7. congrès. Pékin：Éditions en Langues Étrangères, 1956. 60 p.；21cm.

    《中国共产党第七届中央委员会第六次全体会议（扩大）关于农业合作化问题的决议》

11. 8° Congrès national du parti communiste chinois：Recueil de documents. Pékin：Éditions en Langues Étrangères, 1956. 3 vol. in-8°

    《中国共产党第八次全国代表大会文件汇编》，1—3 辑.

12. Deuxième session du VIIIe Congrès national du Parti commuiste chinois, recueil de documents. Pékin：Éditions en Langues Étrangères, 1958. 97 pages；20cm.

    《中国共产党第八次全国代表大会第二次会议文件集》.

13. La sixième session plénière du Comité central issu du VIIIe Congrès national du Parti communiste chinois. Pékin：Éditions en Langues Étrangères, 1959. 55 pages；19cm.

    《中国共产党第八届中央委员会第六次全体会议文件》.

14. Décision du comité central du Parti communiste chinois sur la Grande révolution culturelle prolétarienne：adoptée le 8 août 1966. Pékin：Éditions en Langues Étrangères, 1966. 1 vol. （15 p.）；21cm.

《中国共产党中央委员会关于无产阶级文化大革命的决定》.

15. Communiqué de la onzième Session plénière du Comité central issu du VIIIe congrès du Parti communiste chinois：adopté le 12 Août 1966. Pékin：Éditions en Langues Étrangères，1966. 10 p

《中国共产党第八届中央委员会第十一次全体会议公报》.

16. Communiqué de la douzième session plénière élargie du Comité central issu du VIIIe Congrès du Parti communiste chinois：（adopté le 31 octobre 1968）. Pékin：Éditions en Langues Étrangères，1968. 21，[1] pages：portraits；13×90cm.

《中国共产党第八届扩大的第十二次中央委员会全会公报》.

17. IX Congrès du Parti communiste chinois：recueil de documents. Pékin：Éditions en Langues Étrangères，1969. 189 p.，[8] c. di tav. 14cm.

《中国共产党第九次全国代表大会文件汇编》.

18. Communiqués de presse du secrétariat du présidium du IXe Congrès du Parti Communiste Chinois（Les 1er，14 et 24 avril 1969）. Pékin：Éditions en Langues Étrangères，1969. 46 pages.

《中国共产党第九次全国代表大会主席团秘书处新闻公报》.

19. Rapport au 9° congrès du Parti communiste chinois：présenté le 1er avril et adopté le 14 avril 1969. Pékin：Éditions en Langues Étrangères，1969. 13cm.，118 p.

《在中国共产党第九次全国代表大会上的报告》，林彪.

20. Circulaire du comité central du Parti Communiste Chinois（16 mai 1966）. Un grand document historique. Bureau de rédaction du Hongqi et du Renmin Ribao. Pékin：Éditions en Langues Étrangères，1967. IV，80 pages.

《通知（中国共产党中央委员会一九六六年五月十六日）. 伟大的历史文件》.

21. Le Dixième congrès du Parti communiste chinois：[Pékin，24 — 28 août 1973]：documents. Pékin：Éditions en Langues Étrangères；[Paris]：[diffusion Éditions du Centenaire]，1973. 108 p. -[15] f. de pl. en noir et en coul.；19cm.

《中国共产党第十次全国代表大会文件汇编》

22. Le onzième congrès du Parti communiste chinois（documents）. Pékin：Éditions en Langues Étrangères，1977. 262 p

《中国共产党第十一次全国代表大会文件汇编》

23. Résolution sur l'histoire du Parti communiste chinois/Comité central issu du XIe congrès du parti communiste chinois. Beijing：Éditions en Langues Étrangères，1981. 141 p.；19cm.

《关于建国以来党的若干历史问题的决议》

24. Le XIIe congrès du Parti communiste chinois documents. Beijing：Éditions en Langues Étrangères，1982. 1 vol.（187 p.）；19cm.

《中国共产党第十二次全国代表大会文献》

25. Poursuivre la réforme et lutter pour la réalisation de la modernisation socialiste：documents de la conférence nationale du. Beijing：Éd. en Langues Étrangères，1985. 167 p.；19cm.

《坚持改革，为实现社会主义现代化而斗争》（中国共产党全国代表会议文献）

26. Résolution du Comité central du Parti communiste chinois sur les principes directeurs de l'édification de la civilisation spirituelle socialiste（adoptée le 28 septembre 1986 à la sixième session plénière du Comité central issu du XIIe congrès du Parti communiste chinois）. Beijing：Shudian Éd. en Langues Étrangères，1986. 25 p.；19cm.（Documents chinois）

《中共中央关于社会主义精神文明建设指导方针的决议》

27. Intervention au rassemblement de célébration du 80e anniversaire de la fondation du Parti communiste chinois：（Le 1er juillet 2001）/Jiang Zemin. Beijing：Nouvelle Étoille，2001. 63 pages；21cm. ISBN：7801483863，7801483867.

《在庆祝中国共产党成立八十周年大会上的讲话》，江泽民. 新星出版社.

28. Le XVIe congrès du parti communiste chinois：documents. Beijing：Éditions en Langues etrangeres，2002. 272 pages：color illustrations，color portraits；22cm. ISBN：7119032275；7119032276

《中国共产党第十六次全国代表大会文献》，钟欣编.

29. Le XVIIe Congrés du Parti communiste chinois：documents/[edited by Zhong Xin]. Beijing：Éditions en Langues Étrangères，2007. 276 pages：color illustrations，color portraits；23cm. ISBN：7119051413；7119051415

《中国共产党第十七次全国代表大会文献：法文》，钟欣编.

30. Introduction au Parti communiste chinois/Zhang Rongchen. Beijing：Éditions en Langues Étrangères，2017. 206 pages；24cm. ISBN：7119108445

《中国共产党简明读本》，张荣臣著. 法文版.

D131　政治领导人著作

刘少奇（1898—1969）

1. Adresse du premier mai/Liou Chao-chi. Pékin：Éditions en Langues Étrangères，1950. 33 p.

《在北京庆祝五一劳动节干部大会上的演说》

2. Le triomphe du marxisme léninisme en Chine：écrit pour la nouvelle revue internationale... 14 septembre 1959/Liou Chao Chi. Pékin：Éditions en Langues Étrangères，1959. 42 p.；19cm.

《马克思列宁主义在中国的胜利》

3. Dix glorieuses années. Pékin：Éditions en Langues Étrangères，1960. 406 pages；21cm.

《光辉的十年：1949—1959》. 收录了刘少奇的 19 篇文章.

4. Discours prononcé au meeting pour le 40ᵉ anniversaire de la fondation du Parti communiste chinois. Pékin，Éditions en Langues Étrangères，1961. 39 pages；21cm.

《刘少奇：在庆祝中国共产党成立四十周年大会上的讲话》.

5. Pour être un bon communiste：conférences faites à l'Institut du Marxisme-Léninisme, à Yenan, en juillet 1939/Liou Chao-Chi. Beijing：Éditions en Langues Étrangères，1965. 1 vol.（102 p.）：portr.；19cm.

《论共产党员的修养》

6. Œuvres choisies de Liu Shaoqi. Beijing：Éditions en Langues Étrangères，1983. v.

《刘少奇选集》（上卷）

7. Œuvres choisies de Liu Shaoqi. Beijing：Éditions en Langues Étrangères，1990. T.；22cm. ISBN：7119012762，7119012766.

《刘少奇选集》（下卷）

朱德（1886—1976）

1. Œuvres choisies de Zhu De/traduction du Bureau de compilation et traduction…，Comité central du Parti communiste chinois. Beijing：Éditions en Langues Étrangères，1986. 469 p

《朱德选集》

周恩来（1898—1976）

1. Œuvres choisies de Zhou Enlai. Tome 1. Beijing：Éditions en Langues Étrangères，1981. 536 pages：map, portraits；23cm.

《周恩来选集》（上卷）

2. Œuvres choisies de Zhou Enlai. 2. Beijing：Éd. en Langues Étrangères，1989. 613 p.

《周恩来选集》（下卷）

3. 周恩来青少年论说文集：法文/中共中央文献研究室第二编研室，天津南开中学编著；吕姗姗翻译. 北京：新世界出版社，2015. 12，163 页；25cm. ISBN：7510453953

法文题名：Zhou Enlai oeuvre de jeunesse

邓小平（1904—1997）

1. La grande unité du peuple chinois et la grande unité des peuples du monde：écrit pour la Pravda de l'Union Soviétique à l'occasion du Xe anniversaire de la République populaire de Chine/Teng Siao-ping. Pékin：Éditions en Langues Étrangères，1959. 19 p.；19cm.

《中国人民大团结和世界人民大团结》

2. Textes choisis. Tome 2,（1975—1982）/Deng Xiaoping；traduits par le Bureau de compilation et traduction des Œuvres de Marx, Engels, Lénine et Staline prés le Comité central du Parti communiste chinois. Beijing, China：Éditions en Langues Étrangères，1ère éd. 1985.

441 pages，[1] leaf of plates：portraits；22cm.

《邓小平文选》，第 2 卷（1975—1982）

（1）2ème éd. Beijing：Éditions en Langues Étrangères，1995. 455 pages：portraits；22cm. ISBN：7119007165，7119007168.

3. Textes choisis. Tome 1,（1938—1965）/Deng Xiaoping；traduits par le Bureau de compilation et traduction des œuvres de Marx, Engels, Lénine et Staline prés le Comité central du Parti communiste chinois. Beijing, Chine：Éditions en Langues Étrangères，1992. 358 p.：ill.；23cm. ISBN：711901448X，7119014487

《邓小平文选》，第一卷（1938—1965）

（1）2e éd. Beijing, Chine：Éditions en Langues Étrangères，1995. 386 p.：ill.；23cm. ISBN：7119009532，7119009537

4. Textes choisis（1982—1992）. 3/Deng Xiaoping；traduits par le Bureau de compilation et traduction des œuvres de Marx, Engels, Lénine et Staline prés le Comité central du Parti communiste chinois. Beijing, Chine：Éditions en Langues Étrangères，1994. 1vol.（427 p.）：couv. ill.；23cm. ISBN：7119009532，7119009537，711901692X，7119016924

《邓小平文选》，第三卷（1982—1992）

5. Edifier un socialisme à la chinoise/Deng Xiaoping；traduit par le Bureau de compilation et traduction des œuvres de Marx, Engels, Lénine et Staline prés le Comité central du Parti communiste. Beijing：Éditions en Langues Étrangères，1985. 86 pages；19cm.

《建设有中国特色的社会主义》

6. Les Questions fondamentales de la Chine aujourd'hui/Deng Xiaoping；trad. par le Bureau de Compilation et traduction des Œuvres de Marx, Engels, Lénine et Staline prés le Comité central du parti communiste chinois. Beijing：Éditions en Langues Étrangères，1987. 227 p.：portr.；21cm.

《论当代中国基本问题》

陆定一（1906—1996）

1. Que s'épanouissent des floraisons multiples, que de multiples écoles rivalisent/Lou Ting-yi. Pékin：Éditions en Langues Étrangères，1957. In—16，45 p.

《百花齐放百家争鸣》

2. L'éducation doit être combinée avec le travail productif. Pékin：Éditions en Langues Étrangères，1958. 38 p.

《教育必须与生产劳动相结合》

李富春（1900—1975）

1. Poursuivons notre avance en brandissant le drapeau rouge de la ligne générale/Fu-Chun Li. Pékin：Éditions en Langues Étrangères，1960. 46 p.

《高举总路线的红旗继续前进》

陈云（1905—1995）

1. Chen Yun textes choisis（1926—1949）. Beijing：Éditions en Langues Étrangères，1988. 370 pages：portraits；

22cm.

《陈云文选:1926—1949年》

2. Chen Yun textes choisis/le bureau de compilation et traduction des Œuvres de Marx, Engels, Lénine et Staline après le Comité central du parti communiste chinois, by Chen Yun. Beijing, Chine: Éditions en Langues Étrangères,1997. 1 v. ;23cm. ISBN:7119016954,7119016955

《陈云文选:1949—1956》(第二卷)

李维汉(1896—1984)

1. La lutte pour la direction du prolétariat dans la révolution chinoise de démocratie nouvelle/Wei-Han Li. Pékin: Éditions en Langues Étrangères, 1962. 1 v. (108 p.)

《中国新民主主义革命时期争取无产阶级领导权的斗争》

胡耀邦(1915—1989)

1. La grande vérité du marxisme éclaire notre marche en avant: discours prononcé au rassemblement organisé à Beijing, le 13 mars 1983, a l'occasion du centenaire de la mort de Karl Marx/Yaobang, Hu. Beijing: Éditions en Langues Étrangères, 1983. 48 pages

《马克思主义伟大真理的光芒照耀我们前进》

江泽民(1926—)

1. Jiang zemin textes choisis/Jiang zemin; traduit par le Bureau de compilation et traduction des œuvres de Marx, Engels, Lénine et Staline prés le Comité central du Parti communiste chinois. Beijing: Éditions du Langues Étrangères, 2010. t. 〈1〉: illustrations;23cm. ISBN: 7119061832 (v. 1), 7119061836 (v. 1)

《江泽民文选》(第一卷).本书收入的是江泽民同志在一九八零年八月二十一日至一九九七年八月五日这段时间内的主要著作,共有报告、讲话、谈话、文章、信件、批示、命令、题词等八十一篇.

2.《江泽民文选》(第二卷).北京:外文出版社,2012. 收录江泽民同志一九九七年九月十二日至二 000 年二月一日这段时间内的重要著作.

3.《江泽民文选》(第三卷).北京:外文出版社,2013. 677 页. ISBN:7119079868 收入江泽民同志 2000—2004 年间的著作 63 篇.

习近平(1953—)

1. 习近平谈治国理政/习近平;法文翻译组译.北京:外文出版社,2014.552 页:照片;24cm. ISBN:7119090580 法文题名;Xi Jinping la gouvernance de la Chine

2. 决胜全面建成小康社会 夺取新时代中国特色社会主义伟大胜利 法文/习近平著.北京:外文出版社,2018. 93 页; 23cm. ISBN:7119111971

D14　政策、政论

1. De l'expérience historique de la dictature du prolétariat. Pékin: Éditions en Langues Étrangères, 1956. 22 pages

《关于无产阶级专政的历史经验》

(1)L'experience historique de la dictature du proletariat.

Pékin:Éditions en Langues Étrangères,1959. 71 pages

2. Rapport sur la question des intellectuels présenté le 14 janvier 1956 à une conférence convoquée par le Comité central du Parti communiste chinois pour discuter de la question des intellectuels/Chou En-lai. Pékin: Éditions en Langues Étrangères, 1957. 51 p. ; In-8.

《关于知识分子问题的报告》,周恩来.

3. Le Camarade Mao Tse-Toung sur l'Impérialisme et tous les réactionnaires sont tigres en "papier" Pékin: Éditions en Langues Étrangères, Éd. augmentée, 1959. 136 p.

《帝国主义和一切反动派都是纸老虎》(扩大本).

4. Tout le pays doit etre une grande ecole de la pensée de Mao Tsetoung a l'occasion du 39eme anniversaire de la fondation de l'Armée populaire de Libération de Chine/ Chine Publications en français. Pékin: Éditions en Langues Étrangères, 1966. 1 vol. (24 p.); 19cm.

《全国都应该成为毛泽东思想的大学校》

5. En avant sur la grande voie de la pensée de Mao-Tse-Toung. -Célébration du XVIIe anniversaire de la fondation de la République populaire de Chine. Pékin: Éditions en Langues Étrangères, 1967. 1 vol. (34 p.): pl. ; 21cm.

《在毛泽东思想的大路上前进:庆祝中华人民共和国成立十七周年》

6. Voie socialiste ou voie capitaliste? /Par Rédaction du Hongqi et Rédaction du Renmin Ribao (15 Août 1967). Pékin: Éditions en Langues Étrangères,1967. 1 vol. (26 p.)

《走社会主义道路,还是走资本主义道路?》

(1)Pékin: Éditions en Langues Étrangères, 1968. 46 p.

7. Luttons pour la défense de la dictature du prolétariat. Pour le 25e anniversaire de la publication des "Interventions aux causeries sur la littérature et l'art à Yenan." Pékin: Éditions en Langues Étrangères, 1968. IV, 88 pages

《为捍卫无产阶级专政而斗争:纪念〈在延安文艺座谈会上的谈话〉发表二十五周年》.

8. À propos de la triple union révolutionnaire. Pékin: Éditions en Langues Étrangères, 1968.

《论革命的"三结合"》

9. Un Document qui fait époque: à l'occasion du deuxième anniversaire de la publication de la "Circulaire du 16 mai/ Bureaux de rédaction du "Renmin Ribao", du "Hongqi" et du "Jiefangjun Bao." Pékin: Éditions en Langues Étrangères, 1968. 1 vol. (16 p.); 18cm.

《跨时代的文献:纪念〈通知〉发表两周年》

10. La pensée-maotsétoung, arme invincible. Pékin: Éditions en Langues Étrangères,1969. 1 vol. (95 p.);18cm.

《毛泽东思想是百战百胜的武器》

11. Luttons pour consolider encore davantage la dictature du prolétariat. A l'occasion du 20e anniversiare de la

fondation de la République populaire de Chine. Pékin：Éditions en Langues Étrangères, 1969. II, 46 pages.

《为进一步巩固无产阶级专政而斗争：为庆祝中华人民共和国成立二十周年》.

12. Que la pensée de Mao Tsé-toung commande dans tous les domaines! Editorial du Nouvel An 1969 du Renmin Ribao, du Hongqi et du Jiefangjun Bao. Pékin：Éditions en Langues Étrangères, 1969. VI, 22 pages.

《用毛泽东思想统帅一切》.

13. Avancons hardiment sur la Grande voie de la victoire. Célébrons chaleureusement le XIXe anniversaire de la République populaire de Chine. Pékin：Éditions en Langues Étrangères, 1969. 34 p. : portr. front. , pl. ; In—16, 12,5cm.

《在胜利的大道上奋勇前进》

14. Pour un large recrutement des intellectuels (1er décembre 1939)/Mao Tsetoung. Pékin：Éditions en Langues Étrangères, 1969. 6 p. ; 13cm.

《关于知识分子再教育问题》

15. La voie de l'intégration aux ouvriers, paysans et soldats. Pékin：Éditions en Langues Étrangères, 1971. 101 p

《走与工农兵相结合的道路》

16. Avançons victorieusement en suivant la ligne révolutionnaire du Président Mao：Éditorial du Nouvel An 1971 du Renmin Ribao, du Hongqi et du Jiefangjun Bao. Pékin：Éditions en Langues Étrangères, 1971. 20 p. ; 13cm.

《沿着毛主席革命路线胜利前进：〈人民日报〉、〈红旗〉杂志、〈解放军报〉九七一年元旦社论》

17. Une Grande victoire historique：acclamons chaleureusement la nomination du camarade Houa Kouo-feng aux fonctions de dirigeant de notre parti：acclamons chaleureusement l'élimination de la clique antiparti Wang-Tchang-Kiang-Yao/[traduit du chinois]. Pékin：Éditions en Langues Étrangères；[Paris]：[diffusion Éditions du Centenaire], 1976. 44 p. : ill. ; 19cm.

《伟大的历史性胜利》

D15　建设成就

1. Première année de victoire de la Chine nouvelle/Chou-en-Lai. Pékin：Éd. en Langues Étrangères, 1950. IV-32 p. ; 18,5cm.

《新中国胜利的第一年》,周恩来.

2. Les réalisations de la République populaire de Chine au cours des trois dernières années/Pouo Yi-pouo. Pékin：Éditions en Languages Etrangères, 1952. 1 vol. (II—18 p.) ; In—16.

《新中国三年来的成就》,薄一波著.

3. Rapport sur les travaux du gouvernement：présenté à la première session de la première Assemblée populaire

nationale de la République populaire de Chine, le 23 sept. 1954/Chou En-lai. Pékin：Éd. en Langues Étrangères, 1954. 62 p. : ill. ; 8°

《政府工作报告》,周恩来.

4. Chou-En-Lai. Une Grande décade/Tcheou Ngen-Lai. Pékin：Éditions en Langues Étrangères, 1959. 44 p. (18, 5cm.)

《伟大的十年》,周恩来著.

5. Rapport sur les travaux du gouvernement：présenté à la première session de la seconde assemblée populaire nationale le 18 avril 1959/Chou En-lai. Pékin：Éditions en Langues Étrangères, 1959. 81 pages

《政府工作报告：1959 年 4 月 18 日在第二届全国人民代表大会第一次会议上》,周恩来.

6. Rapport sur la révision des principaux objectifs du plan de l'économie nationale pour 1959 et sur le développement plus poussé du mouvement pour accroître la production et pratiquer l'économie (Présenté le 26 août 1959 à la cinquième session du Comité premament de la deuxième Assemblée ppoulaire nationale). Pékin：Éditions en Langues Étrangères, 1959. 51 pages；18cm.

《关于调整一九五九年国民经济计划主要指标和进一步开展增产节约运动的报告》,周恩来.

7. Unissons-nous pour remporter des victoires encore plus grandes !：Éditorial du Renmin ribao, du Hongqi et du Jiefangjun bao pour le Jour de l'An 1972. Pékin：Éditions en Langues Étrangères, 1972. 13, [1] pages；19cm.

《团结起来,争取更大的胜利》,《人民日报》、《红旗》杂志、《解放军报》一九七一年元旦社论.

8. A la conquête de nouvelles victoires：Pour le 23e anniversaire de la République Populaire de Chine. Pékin：Éditions en Langues Étrangères, 1972. 11 p.

《夺取新的胜利—庆祝中华人民共和国成立二十三周年》,《人民日报》、《红旗》杂志、《解放军报》报社.

9. La Chine nouvelle a 25 ans. Pékin：Éditions en Langues Étrangères, 1975. 117 p. , [22] feuillets de planches：ill. (certaines en coul.)

《新中国的二十五年》

10. Discours au rassemblement en l'honneur du 30e anniversaire de la République populaire de Chine：29 septembre 1979/Ye Jianying. Pékin：Éditions en Langues Étrangères, 1979. 89 p. ；20cm.

《在庆祝中华人民共和国成立三十周年大会上的讲话》,叶剑英.

11. 30 ans de réforme en Chine vus par les savants chinois et étrangers/Institut de recherche sur la réforme et le développement de Chine (Hainan)；[traduit], Zhang Yuyuan, Jiang Lili. Beijing：Éditions en Langues Étrangères, 2008. 210 pages：illustrations；23cm. ISBN：7119054827；7119054821

《中外学者眼中的中国改革 30 年》，中国（海南）改革发展研究院主编.

D16　政府组织

D161　人权

1. 《中国人权发展五十年》，中华人民共和国国务院新闻办公室发布.北京：新星出版社，2000. ISBN：7801482719，7801482700

2. Progrès de la cause des droits de l'Homme en Chine en l'an 2000/Office d'information du Conseil des Affaires d'État de la République populaire de Chine. Beijing：Nouvelle Étoile，2001. 41 pages；21cm. ISBN：7801483804，7801483805.

   《2000 年中国人权事业的进展》，中华人民共和国国务院新闻办公室发布.新星出版社.

D162　全国人民代表大会

1. La Deuxième session de la 2e Assemblée populaire nationale：de la République populaire de Chine（Documents）. Pékin：Éditions en Langues Étrangères，1960. 218 p.〔Ech. int. 61—1287〕；In-8° （21cm.）.

   《中华人民共和国第二届全国人民代表大会第二次会议文件》

2. Principaux documents de la première session de la troisième Assemblée populaire nationale de la République populaire de Chine. Pékin：Éditions en Langues Étrangères，1965. 98p.

   《中华人民共和国第三届全国人民代表大会第一次会议主要文件》

3. Première session de la IVe Assemblée populaire nationale de la République populaire de Chine. Pékin：Éditions en Langues Étrangères，1975. 99 p.

   《中华人民共和国第四届全国人名代表大会第一次会议文件》

4. Constitution de la République populaire de Chine：adoptée le 5 mars 1978 à la première session de la V Assemblée populaire nationale de la République populaire de Chine/〔traduit du chinois〕. Pékin：Éditions en Langues Étrangères；〔Paris〕：〔diffusion Éditions du Centenaire〕，1978. 1 vol. （51 p.）：couv. ill. ；22cm.

   《中华人民共和国第五届全国人民代表大会第一次会议》

5. Deuxième session de la Ve Assemblée populaire nationale de la République populaire de Chine （Documents）. Beijing：Éditions en Langues Étrangères，1979. 286 p

   《中华人民共和国第五届全国人民代表大会第二次会议主要文件》

6. Troisième session de la Ve Assemblée populaire nationale de la République populaire de Chine （Documents）. Beijing：Éditions en Langues Étrangères，1980. 226 p

   《中华人民共和国第五届全国人民代表大会第三次会议

主要文件》

7. La cinquième session de la Ve Assemblée populaire nationale de la République populaire de Chine （Principaux documents）. Beijing：Éditions en Langues Étrangères，1983. 256 p.

   《中华人民共和国第五届全国人民代表大会第五次会议主要文件》

8. Première session de la VIe Assemblée populaire nationale de la République populaire de Chine. Beijing：Éditions en Langues Étrangères，1983. 165 p

   《中华人民共和国第六届全国人民代表大会第一次会议》

9. Deuxième session de la VIe assemblée populaire nationale de la République populaire de Chine：principaux documents/6e Assemblée populaire de la République populaire de Chine. Beijing：Éd. en Langues Étrangères，1984. 123 p. ；19cm.

   《中华人民共和国第六届全国人民代表大会第二次会议主要文件》

10. Troisième session de la VIe Assemblée populaire nationale de la République populaire de Chine：（principaux documents）. Beijing，Chine：Éditions en Langues Étrangères，1985. 109 pages；19cm.

    《中华人民共和国第六届全国人民代表大会第三次会议主要文件》

11. La quatrième session de la VIe Assemblée populaire nationale de la république populaire de Chine：principaux documents. Beijing：Éditions en Langues Étrangères，1986. 233 pages；19cm.

    《中华人民共和国第六届全国人民代表大会第四次会议主要文件》

D163　中国人民政治协商会议

1. Documents importants de la première session plénière de la Conférence Consultative Politique du Peuple chinois. Pékin：Éd. en Langues Étrangères，1949. 49 p.

   《中国人民政治协商会议第一届全体会议重要文献》

D17　国家行政管理

D171　反腐败与廉政建设

1. Lutte anti-corruption et promtion de l'intégrité en Chine/ Office d'information du Conseil des Affaires d'État de la République populaire de Chine. Beijing：Éditions en Langues Étrangères，2010. 56 p. ；21cm. ISBN：7119068251；7119068253

   《中国的反腐败和廉政政策》，国务院新闻办公室发布.

D18　社会各阶层

D181　青年

1. Jeunesse de la Chine nouvelle. Pékin：Éditions en Langues Étrangères，1951. 80 p. ，〔12〕 p. foto's. ：ill. ；19cm.

《中国青年在前进》.

2. Pour faire de notre jeunesse une jeunesse révolutionnaire. Rapport d'activités présenté le 11 juin 1964 au IXe Congrès National de la Ligue de la Jeunesse Communiste de Chine. Pékin：Éditions en Langues Étrangères，1965. 54 pages；19cm.

《为我国青年革命化而斗争：1964 年 6 月 11 日在中国共产主义青年团第六次全国代表大会上的工作报告》，胡耀邦著.

3. L'amour, le mariage et la famille/Huo Bifeng. Beijing, Chine：Éditions en Langues Étrangères，1987. 96，[1] p.，[16] p. de pl.；ill.，portr

《中国青年的恋爱、婚姻、家庭》霍碧峰著 北京 外文出版社.

4.《当代青年的工作与生活》.北京：中国建设杂志社，1989. (长城丛书)

D182　妇女

1. Femmes chinoises d'aujourd'hui. Pékin：Éd. en Langues Étrangères，1954. 95 p.

《今日之中国妇女》，周敏仪等著.

2. La Chine célèbre le 50ème anniversaire de la Journée internationale des femmes Pékin：Éditions en Langues Étrangères，1960. 34 p.；19cm.

《"三八"五十周年在中国》

3. [Publications d'information en français. Série in—16.]. [15.]，La femme chinoise dans le bond en avant，[S. l.]：Éditions en Langues Étrangères，1960. 110 p.，fig.，couv. ill. en coul. [Ech. int. 2598－60]；In—16（18，5cm.）.

《中国妇女在跃进》，马信德等著.

4. Femmes chinoises d'aujourd'hui/[Liu Yu-lan, Pasang, Lin Kiao-tche, Houang Hai, etc.]. Pékin：Éditions en Langues Étrangères；[Paris]：[diffusion Éditions du Centenaire]，1973. [VI]-89 p. -[8] p. de pl.；ill.，couv. ill. en coul.；19cm.

《今日中国妇女》.

5.《北京：迎接联合国第四次世界妇女大会》，第四次世界妇女大会中国组委会. 北京周报社编. 北京：新星出版社，1994. ISBN：7801021193

6. 中国性别平等与妇女发展状况：法文/中华人民共和国国务院新闻办公室发布. 北京：新星出版社，2005. 45 页；20cm. ISBN：7801488296

7. 中国性别平等与妇女发展/中华人民共和国国务院新闻办公室[发布]. 北京：外文出版社，2015. 41 页；21cm. ISBN：7119096537

法文题名：L'égalité des sexes et l'épanouissement de la femme en Chine

D19　工运与工会

1. La Loi sur les syndicats ouvriers de la République

populaire de Chine, suivie de deux autres documents. Pékin：Éditions en Langues Étrangères，1950. 41 p.；8".

《中华人民共和国工会法》.

2. VIIIe Congrès national des syndicats de Chine... Pékin：Éditions en Langues Étrangères，1958. 138 p.，pl.，portr.；In—16（20,5cm.）

《中国工会第八次全国代表大会》，中华全国总工会编.

3.《中国工会》. 北京：外文出版社，1987.（中国简况）

D191　政治运动和事件

1. Mener la grande révolution culturelle prolétarienne jusqu'au bout. Pékin：Éditions en Langues Étrangères，1966. 62 pages；19cm.

《把无产阶级文化大革命进行到底》

2. La Grande révolution culturelle socialiste en Chine. Pékin：Éditions en Langues Étrangères，1966. 1 vol.（66 p.）；21cm.

《中国的社会主义文化大革命》，第一集 1966 年，第二集 1966 年，第三集 1966 年，第四集 1966 年，第五集 1966 年，第六集 1967 年.

3. La grande révolution culturelle prolétarienne en Chine. Pékin：Éditions en Langues Étrangères，1966. volumes；21cm.

《中国的无产阶级文化大革命》，第八集 1967 年，第九集 1967 年，第十集 1967 年.

4. La dictature du prolétariat et la grande révolution culturelle prolétarienne/par Wang Li, Kia Yi-hsiué et Li Sin. Pékin：Éditions en Langues Étrangères，1967. 1 vol.（16 p.）；21cm.

《无产阶级专政和无产阶级文化大革命》

5. La grande victoire de la ligne révolutionnaire du président Mao：acclamons chaleureusement la naissance du Comité révolutionnaire de la Municipalité du Pékin. Pékin：Éditions en Langues Étrangères，1967. 52 p

《毛主席革命路线的伟大胜利：热烈欢呼北京市革命委员会诞生》.

(1) Pékin：Éditions en Langues Étrangères，1968. 1 v.（98 p.）；14cm.

6. Vive le triomphe de la grande révolution culturelle sous la dictature du prolétariat：à l'occasion du 18ème anniversaire de la République populaire de Chine. Pékin：Éditions en Langues Étrangères，1968. 48 pages，[4] pages of plates：illustrations；19cm.

《无产阶级专政下的文化大革命胜利万岁》

7. La Critique contre Lin Piao et Confucius. Pékin：Éditions en Langues Étrangères；[Paris]：[diffusion Éditions du Centenaire]，1975. 185 p.；19cm.

《批林批孔文选》

8. La Lutte en Chine contre le vent déviationniste de droite qui remet en cause les conclusions justes/[traduit du chinois]. Pékin：Éditions en Langues Étrangères；

［Paris］：［diffusion Éditions du Centenaire］，1976. 217 p.；19cm.

《中国反击右倾翻案风的斗争》

D191.1 恐怖活动

1. Les forces terroristes du "Turkestan oriental" ne peuvent se dérober à leurs responsabilités/Office d'Information du Conseil des Affaires d'État. Beijing：Wuzhou Mass Communications Press，2002. 28 pages；21cm. ISBN：7508500199；7508500195.

《"东突"恐怖势力难脱罪责》，国务院新闻办公室著. 五洲传播出版社.

D192 社会生活

1. Vie Sociale/par Le Comité de rédaction de la collection "Connaissance de la Chine." Beijing：Éditions en Langues Étrangères，1986. 242 pages，［16］pages of plates：illustrations (some color)；19cm.

《社会生活》，《中国概况丛书》编辑委员会编.

2. Les Chinois et leurs sacs/monograph.［editor-in-chief, Li Tie］. Beijing：Edition en Langues Étrangères，2009. 155 pages：color illustrations；21cm. ISBN：7119055930；7119055933

《挎包里的中国》，李铁主编.

3. Les Chinois et leurs photos de famille/Yang liang. Beijing：Édition en Langues Étrangères，2010. 53 pages：color illustrations；18cm. ISBN：7119063102，7119063103

《我的相册我的家：中国人生活剪影》，外文出版社编.

4. Société Chinoise/Tang Jun［and others］；traduit par Liang Yulan et Liu Yanqing. Beijing：China Intercontinental Press，2011. 146 pages：color illustrations；23cm. ISBN：7508519777，7508519779

《中国社会》，唐钧［等］著. 五洲传播出版社.

D192.1 劳动就业与保障

1. La Situation du travail et de la protection sociale en Chine/Office d'information du Counseil des Affaires d'État de la République populaire de Chine. Beijing：Nouvelle Étoile，2002. 48 pages；21cm. ISBN：7801484088；7801484086.

《中国的劳动和社会保障状况》，中华人民共和国国务院新闻办公室发布. 新星出版社.

2. Situation de la protection sociale en Chine et la politique afférente/Office d'information du Conseil des Affaires d'État de la République populaire de Chine. Beijing：Nouvelle Étoile，2004. 38 pages；21cm. ISBN：7801486579，7801486578.

《中国的社会保障状况和政策》，中华人民共和国国务院新闻办公室发布. 新星出版社.

3. L'emploi en Chine：situation et politique/Office d'information du Conseil des affaires dÉtat de la République populaire de Chine，avril 2004. Beijing：Nouvelle Étoile，2004. 44 p.；21cm. ISBN：7801486137，7801486134

《中国的就业状况和政策》，中华人民共和国国务院新闻办公室发布. 新星出版社.

D192.2 禁毒

1. La lutte contre la drogue en Chine/Office d'information du Conseil des Affaires d'État de la République populaire de Chine. Beijing：Nouvelle Étoile，2000. 35 pages；21cm. ISBN：7801482859；7801482853.

《中国的禁毒》，中华人民共和国国务院新闻办公室发布. 新星出版社.

D192.3 地方政治

D192.31 台湾

1.《台湾问题和中国的统一》，北京：外文出版社，1986. 6 页

2. Jiang Zemin et Li Peng parlent du problème de Taiwan/Zemin Jiang. S. l.：China Intercontinental Press，1996. 77 p.：ill.；18cm. ISBN：7801131576；7801131577.

《江泽民、李鹏谈台湾问题》，江泽民李鹏著，国务院台湾事务办公室编写. 五洲传播出版社.

3. Le problème de Taiwan et la réunification de la Chine：questions et réponses.［Beijing］：China Intercontintental Press，1997. 4，121 pages：illustrations (chiefly color)；18cm. ISBN：7801133374；7801133373.

《台湾问题与祖国统一》问答，国务院台湾事务办公室编. 五洲传播出版社.

D192.32 香港

1. Retour en 1997 de Hong Kong à la Chine/Wang Qiaolong. Beijing：China Intercontinental Press，1997. 77 pages：color illustrations；18cm. ISBN：7801132823，7801132826.

《"九七"前后谈香港》，王巧珑著. 五洲传播出版社（香港问题丛书/金辉主编）

2. Hong Kong, la première région administrative spéciale de la Chine/par Wang Qialong.［s. L.］：China intercontinental Press，1997. 77 p.：ill.；18cm. ISBN：7801132904；7801132901

《香港-中国特别行政区》，王巧珑著. 五洲传播出版社（香港问题丛书/金辉主编）

3. L'origine du problème de Hong Kong et sa solution/par Huang Fengwu.［S. l.］：China Intercontinental Press，1997. 77 p. ISBN：7801132505；7801132505

《香港问题的由来及解决》，黄凤武著. 五洲传播出版社（香港问题丛书/金辉主编）

4. La loi fondamentale：plan de la région administrative spéciale de Hong Kong/par Ge Guangzhi, Kou Qi. Beijing：China Intercontinental Press，1997. 85 pages color illustrations；18cm. ISBN：7801132580；7801132581

《香港特别行政区的蓝图-基本法》，葛广智，寇琪著. 五洲传播出版社（香港问题丛书/金辉主编）

5. L'économie de Hong Kong qui s'appuie sur la partie continentale de la patrie/par Cai Chimeng.［S. l.］：China Intercontinental Press，1997. 85 p.：ill. en coul. ISBN：7801132661；7801132666.

《背靠祖国的香港经济》，蔡赤萌著. 五洲传播出版社（香港问题丛书/金辉主编）

6.《是谁创造了香港的繁荣》陈多，连锦添著. 北京：五洲传

播出版社,1997. ISBN:7801132742.(香港问题丛书/金辉主编)

D192.33 澳门

1.《归来,澳门》,王巧珑著.北京:五洲传播出版社,1999. ISBN:7801136136

D2 外交、国际关系

D21 国际共产主义运动

1. En réfutation du révisionnisme contemporain. Pékin:Éditions en Langues Étrangères, 1958. 108 p.；In—16 (18,5cm.)

《现代修正主义必须批判》

(1)En refutation du revisionnisme moderne.[Edition augmentée]. Pékin:Éditions en Langues Étrangères, 1962. 146 pages；19cm.

2. Vive le Léninisme, Pékin:Éditions en Langues Étrangères, 1960. 1 vol.(114 p.)：portr.；21cm.

《列宁主义万岁》

3. Prolétaires de tous les pays, unissons-nous contre l'ennemi commun! Pékin:Éditions en Langues Étrangères, Éd. augm. 1963. 91 p.；19cm.

《全世界无产者联合起来反对我们的共同敌人》

4. [Publications d'information en français. Série in—16.]. [19.], Les Divergences entre le camarade Togliatti et nous. Editorial du "Renmin Ribao" (31 Décembre 1962)：[S. l.]：Éditions en Langues Étrangères, 1963. 50 p. [Ech. int. 2876−63]；In—16 (18,5cm.). [Ech. int.]

《陶里亚蒂同志同我们的分歧:1962 年 12 月 31 日〈人民日报〉社论》

5. Léninisme et révisionnisme moderne：éditorial du Hongqi (Drapeau rouge), no 1, 1963. Pékin:Éditions en Langues Étrangères, 1963. 20 p.；19cm.

《列宁主义和现代修正主义:1963 年第一期〈红旗〉社论》

6. Unissons-nous sur la base des déclarations de Moscou. Pékin:Éditions en Langues Étrangères, 1963. 34 pages；18cm.

《在莫斯科宣言和莫斯科声明的基础上团结起来》

7. D'où proviennent les divergences?：réponse à Maurice Thorez et d'autres camarades：éditorial du Renmin Ribao (27 février 1963). Pékin:Éditions en Langues Étrangères, 1963. 37 pages；19cm.

《分歧从何而来?:答多列士等同志:1963 年 2 月 27 日〈人民日报〉社论》

8. Encore une fois sur les divergences entre le camarade Togliatti et nous：quelques problèmes importants du léninisme à l'époque actuelle/la Rédaction du Hongqi (No. 3 − 4, 1963). Pékin:Éditions en Langues Étrangères, 1963. 204 pages；19cm.

《再论陶里亚蒂同志同我们的分歧:关于列宁主义在当代

的若干重大问题》,红旗杂志编辑部.

9. Le miroir des révisionnistes/éditorial du Renmin Ribao (mars 1963). Pékin：Éditions en Langues Étrangères, 1963. 11 pages；19cm.

《修正主义者的一面镜子:1963 年 3 月 9 日〈人民日报〉社论》

10. Plaçons le drapeau révolutionnaire du marxisme-léninisme par-dessus tout/[traduit du chinois]. Pékin：Éditions en Langues Étrangères, 1964. 37 p.；19cm.

《更高地举起马克思列宁主义的革命旗帜》

11. Débat sur la ligne générale du mouvement communiste international. Pékin：Éditions en Langues Étrangères, 1965. 610 p.；21cm.

《关于国际国际共产主义运动总路线的论战》

12. Le triomphe du Léninisme：pour le 9ème anniversaire de la naissance de Lénine/éditorial du Hongqi, no 4, 1965. 14 pages；19cm.

《列宁主义的伟大胜利:纪念列宁诞生九十五周年》,红旗杂志社论.

13. Vive la victoire de la dictature du prolétariat!：en commémoration du centenaire de la commune de Paris/par les rédactions du Renmin Ribao, du Hongqi et du Jiefangjun Bao, 18 mars 1971. Pékin：Éditions en Langues Étrangères, 1971. 34 pages：illustrations portraits；19cm.

《无产阶级专政胜利万岁:纪念巴黎公社一百周年》

D22 中国与联合国

1. La Chine accuse!：discours de l'envoyé spécial du Gouvernement populaire central de la République populaire de Chine à l'Organisation des nations unies. Pékin:Éditions en Langues Étrangères, 1951. 120 p.：ill.

《中国控诉》

2. Le Courant de l'histoire est irrésistible/[traduit du chinois]. Pékin：Éditions en Langues Étrangères；[Paris]：[diffusion Éditions du Centenaire], 1971. 49 p.；19cm.

《历史潮流不可抗拒:我国在联合国的一切合法权利胜利恢复》

3. Publications d'information en français. [64], Allocutions de bienvenue à l'adresse de la délégation de la République populaire de Chine, prononcées par le Président de l'assemblée générale et les représentants de divers pays le 15 novembre 1971 à la 26e session de l'assemblée générale de l'O. N. U. Pékin：Éditions en Langues Étrangères, 1971. 164 p.；19cm.

《在联大第二十六届会议一九七一年十一月十五日全体会议上大会主席和各国代表欢迎中华人民共和国代表团的讲话》

4. Publications d'information en français. ［65］, Intervention de Kiao Kouan-Houa, chef de la délégation de la République populaire de Chine, à la séance plénière de la 27e session de l'assemblée générale de l'O. N. U. : 3 octobre 1972. Pékin: Éditions en Langues Étrangères, 1972. 26 p. ; 19cm.

《中华人民共和国代表团团长乔冠华在联合国大会第二十七届会议全体会议上的发言》

5. Publications d'information en français. ［66］, Intervention de Kiao Kouan-Houa, chef de la délégation de la République populaire de Chine, à la séance plénière de la 28e session de l'assemblée générale de l'O. N. U. : 2 octobre 1973. Pékin: Éditions en Langues Étrangères, 1973. 27 p. ; 19cm.

《中华人民共和国代表团团长乔冠华在联合国大会第二十八届会议全体会议上的发言》

6. Intervention de Teng Siao-Ping, chef de la délégation de la République populaire de Chine, à la session extraordinaire de l'assemblée générale de l'O. N. U. , 10 avril 1974. Pékin, Ch: Éditions en langues étrangeres, 1974. 18 p. ; 19cm.

《中华人民共和国代表团团长邓小平在联大特别会议上的发言》

7. Intervention de Kiao Kouan-Houa, Chef de la délégation République Populaire de Chine à la 29e session de l'Assemblée Générale de L'O. N. U. 2 octobre 1974. Pékin: Éditions en Langues Étrangères, 1974. 27 p; 18cm.

《中华人民共和国代表团团长在联合国大会第二十九届会议全体会议上的发言》

8. Intervention de Kiao Kouan-houa, chef de la délégation de la République Populaire de Chine, à la Séance Plénière de la 30e Session de l'assemblée Générale de l'O. N. U. Pékin: Éditions en Langues Étrangères, 1975. 29 p.

《中华人民共和国代表团团长在联合国大会第三十届会议全体会议上的发言》

9. 《中国政府继续坚决执行毛主席的革命外交路线和政策：中华人民共和国代表团团长在联合国大会第三十一届会议全体会议上的发言》. 北京:外文出版社出版,1976.

10. Intervention de Houang Houa, chef de la délégation chinoise, à la séance plénière de la 10e session extraodinaire de l'Assemblée générale de l'ONU. Beijing: Éditions en Langues Étrangères, 1978. 34 pages; 19cm.

《中国代表团团长黄华在联合国大会第十届特别会议全体会议上的发言》

D23　中国外交

1. La diplomatie chinoise par Zhou Yihuang; traduit par Gu Liang, Cao Qinglin et Jean Delvigne. Pékin: China International Press, 2004. 1 vol. （176 p. ）: ill. ; 21cm. che autche. ISBN: 7508506286 （br）; 7508506289 （br）. （Que sais-je sur la Chine?）

《中国外交》,周溢潢主编,吕华译. 五洲传播出版社（中国基本情况丛书/郭长建主编）

2. La philosophie diplomatique chinoise au XXIe siècle/Liu Binjie. Beijing: Éditions en Langues Étrangères: Distributeur, Société chinoise du commerce international du livre, 2006. 107 pages: color illustrations; 21cm. ISBN: 7119044664 （pbk.）; 7119044668 （pbk.）（La Chine en développement pacifique）

《21 世纪中国对外交往的哲学》,柳斌杰著;宫结实译. 外文出版社（中国的和平发展系列）

3. 中国的亚太安全合作政策/中华人民共和国国务院新闻办公室［发布］. 北京:外文出版社有限责任公司,2017.55 页;21cm. ISBN: 7119105116

法文题名: Politique de la Chine sur la coopération sécuritaire en Aise-Pacifique

4. 中国特色大国外交与"一带一路"/吴建民著;张永昭法文翻译. 北京:外文出版社有限责任公司,2016.47 页;21cm. ISBN: 7119103594

法文题名: Diplomatie de grande puissance à la Chinoise et l'initiative des Routes Terrestre et Maritime de la Soie

5. La Chine et le monde/rédacteur: Zhou Guo. Beijing: Beijing Information, 1982—1987. 8 volumes; 19cm.

《中国与世界》丛书,北京周报社. 共 8 册.

6. Histoire des relations politiques de la Chine avec les puissances occidentales, depuis les temps les plus anciens jusqu'à nos jours; suivie du Cérémonial observé à la cour de Pé-King pour la réception des ambassadeurs.../traduit par G. Pauthier. Paris: Firmin-Didot frères, fils et Cie, 1859. 1 vol. 238 p.

从古至今中国和西方列强的政治关系史. Pauthier, Guillaume(1801—1873)译.

7. Luttons résolument contre l'impérialisme et le néo-colonialisme pour l'émancipation économique des peuples afro-asiatiques. Pékin: Éditions en Langues Étrangères, 1965. 38 pages; 19cm.

《坚决进行反对帝国主义和新殖民主义的斗争,实现亚非人民的经济解放》,南汉宸著.

8. Solidarité afro-asiatique contre l'impérialisme: documents relatifs aux visites effectuées par des dirigeants chinois dans treize pays d'Afrique et d'Asie. Pékin, Éditions en Langues Étrangères, 1965. 477 pages; 20cm.

《亚非人民反帝大团结万岁》(中国领导人访问亚非十三国文件集)

9. Le peuple Chinois soutient fermement la juste lutte des peuples Africains/Association d'amitié des peuples de Chine et d'Afrique. Pékin: Éditions en Langues Étrangères, 1961. 144 pages: illustrations

《中国人民坚决支持非洲人民的正义斗争》，中国非洲人民友好协会编.

10. La Chine et l'Afrique/Yuan Wu；traduit par Guo Anding.［Beijing］：China Intercontinental Press，2006. 120 pages：chiefly color illustrations；25cm. ISBN：7508509846(pbk.)，7508509846(pbk.)

《中国与非洲》，袁武编著；郭安定译.五洲传播出版社.

11. Le peuple chinois soutient ses frères arabes/［textes de Mao Dun，Tsien Kiun-jouei，Emi Siao…］. Pékin：Éditions en Langues Étrangères，1958. 93 p.：couv. ill.；19cm.

《支援阿拉伯弟兄的呼声》，茅盾等著，陆馥君等译.

12. L'aide chinoise à l'étranger/Office d'information du Conseil des Affaires d'État de la République populaire de Chine. Beijing：Éditions en Langues Étrangères，2011. 53 p.：ill.；21cm. ISBN：7119069272，7119069276

《中国的对外援助》，中华人民共和国国务院新闻办公室［发布］.

D231　中美关系

1. Nous nous opposons aux provocations militaires des États-Unis dans la zone des détroits de Taïwan：Un recueil de documents importants réunis par l'Institut populaire de politique étrangère de Chine.［6—21 septembre 1958.］. Pékin：Éditions en Langues Étrangères，1958. 5cm.)，84 p.

《反对美国在台湾海峡地区的军事挑战》，中国人民外交学会编.

2. Chassons les impérialistes Américains de l'Asie. Pékin：Éditions en Langues Étrangères，1960. 52 pages：illustrations；19cm.

《把美帝国主义赶出亚洲去!》

3. Deux tactiques，un seul but：Dévoiler les supercheries sur la paix de l'impérialisme américain. Publié par l'Institut populaire de politique étrangère de Chine. Pékin：Éditions en Langues Étrangères，1960. 160 p.［Ech. int. 61—1259]；In—16 (18,5cm.)

《两套手法，一个目的:揭穿美帝国主义玩弄和平的阴谋》，中国人民外交学会编.

4. La nouvelle machination americaine des "deux Chines." Pékin：Éditions en Langues Étrangères，1962. 115 pages；19cm.

《反对美国制造"两个中国"的新阴谋》

5. Telle est l'administration Kennedy. Pékin：Éditions en Langues Étrangères，1962. 81 pages；19cm.

《肯尼迪政府的真面目》

6. À propos de la déclaration du Parti communiste des États-Unis d'Amérique éditorial du "Renmin Ribao"，8 mars 1963. Pékin：Éditions en Langues Étrangères，1963. 1 vol. (18 p.)；19cm.

《评美国共产党声明:1963年3月8日《人民日报》社论》

7. De l'attitude envers l'impérialisme américain deux lignes

politiques s'affrontent. Pékin：Éditions en Langues Étrangères，1965. 42 pages；19cm.

《在对待美帝国主义问题上两条路线的斗争》，范秀珠著.

8. ［Publications d'information en anglais：série in—16］.［18］，Sino-U. S.［United States］joint communiqué：February 28，1972. Pékin：Éditions en Langues Étrangères，1972. 7 p.；19cm.

《中美联合公报》(1972年2月28日)

9. 《中美两国人权比较》.北京：五洲传播出版社，1996. ISBN：7801131312

D232　中苏关系

1. Comment les communistes se sont emparés de mon pays/Tchiang Kaï-Shek；traduit de l'anglais par Serge Ouvaroff. Paris：Morgan (Impr. des Éditions Morgan)，1958. 1 vol. (365 p.)；19cm. (Actualité et politique)

《苏俄在中国》，蒋介石(1887—1975)著；Ouvaroff，Serge由英文译成法文.

2. Propositions concernant la ligne générale du mouvement communiste international：Réponse du comité central du parti communiste chinois à la lettre du 30 mars 1963 du comité central du parti communiste de l'union soviétique. Pékin：Éditions en Langues Étrangères，1963. 124 p. 19cm.

《关于国际共产主义运动总路线的建议:中国共产党中央委员会对苏联共产党中央委员会1963年3月30日来信的复信》

3. Les Divergences entre la direction du P. C. U. S. et nous，leur origine et leur évolution/Rédaction du Renmin Ribao et rédaction du Hongqi. Pékin：Éd. en Langues Étrangères，1963. 75 p.；19cm.

《苏共领导同我们分歧的由来和发展:评苏共中央的公开信》(1963年9月6日).《人民日报》编辑部、《红旗》杂志编辑部.

4. Sur la question de Staline/Rédaction du "Renmin Ribao" et rédaction du "Hongqi"，13 septembre 1963. Pékin：Éditions en Langues Étrangères，1963. 1 vol. (25 p.)；19cm.

《关于斯大林问题》(二评苏共中央的公开信)(1963年9月13日).《人民日报》编辑部、《红旗》杂志编辑部.

5. La Yougoslavie，est-elle un pays socialiste?：à propos de la lettre ouverte du Comité central du P. C. U. S. (III)/rédaction du Renmin Ribao et rédaction du Hongqi. Pékin：Éditions en Langues Étrangères，1963. 51 pages；19cm.

《南斯拉夫诗社会主义国家吗?:三评苏共中央的公开信》(1963年9月26日)，《人民日报》编辑部、《红旗》杂志编辑部.

6. Des défenseurs du néo-colonialisme：à propos de la lettre ouverte du comité central du P. C. U. S. (IV)/red. du Renmin Ribao et du Hongqi. Pékin：Éditions en Langues

Étrangères，1963. 39 p

《新殖民主义的辩护士：四评苏共中央的公开信》（1963 年
10 月 22 日），《人民日报》编辑部、《红旗》杂志编辑部.

7. [Publications d'information en français. Série in—16.].
[31.], Deux lignes différentes dans la question de la
guerre et de la paix. A propos de la lettre ouverte du
Comité central du P. C. S. U. (V)... (19 novembre 1963)：
[S. l.]：Éditions en Langues Étrangères, 1963. 60 p.
[Ech. int. 4019－64]; In—16 (18,5cm.).

《在战争与和平问题上的两条路线：五评苏共中央的公开
信》（1963 年 11 月 19 日），《人民日报》编辑部、《红旗》杂
志编辑部.

8. Deux politiques de coexistence pacifique diametralement
opposées：à propos de la lettre ouverte du Comité Central
du P. C. U. S. (VI)/Rédaction du Renmin Ribao et
Rédaction du Hongqi. Pékin：Éditions en Langues
Étrangères, 1963. 51 p. ；19cm.

《两种根本对立的和平共处政策：六评苏共中央的公开
信》（1963 年 12 月 12 日），《人民日报》编辑部、《红旗》杂
志编辑部.

9. Les dirigeants du P. C. U. S. - Les plus grands
scissionnistes de notre temps：à propos de la lettre ouverte
du Comité Central du P. C. U. S. (VII)/rédaction du
Renmin Ribao et rédaction du Hongqi (4 février 1964).
Pékin：Éditions en Langues Étrangères, 1964. 63
unnumbered pages；19cm.

《苏共领导是当代最大的分裂主义者：七评苏共中央的公
开信》（1964 年 2 月 4 日），《人民日报》编辑部、《红旗》杂
志编辑部.

10. 《 La révolution prolétarienne et le révisionnisme de
Khrouchtchev：à propos de la lettre ouverte du Comité
Central du P. C. U. S. (VIII)/rédaction du Renmin
Ribao et rédaction du Hongqi (31 Mars 1964). Pékin：
Éditions en Langues Étrangères, 1964. 67 unnumbered
pages；19cm.

《无产阶级革命和赫鲁晓夫修正主义：八评苏共中央的
公开信》（1964 年 3 月 31 日），《人民日报》编辑部、《红
旗》杂志编辑部.

11. Le Pseudo-communisme de Khrouchtchev et les leçons
historiques qu'il donne au monde à propos de la lettre
ouverte du Comité central du P. C. U. S. (IX)：rédaction
du Renmin Ribao et rédaction du Hongqi (14 juillet
1964). Pékin：Éditions en Langues Étrangères, 1964. 1
vol. (116 p.)；18cm.

《关于赫鲁晓夫的假共产主义及其在世界历史上的教
训：九评苏共中央的公开信》（1964 年 7 月 14 日），《人民
日报》编辑部、《红旗》杂志编辑部.

12. La Vérité sur l'alliance de la Direction du P. C. U. S. avec
L'Inde contre la Chine par la Rédaction du Renmin
Ribao. Pékin, Éditions en Langues Étrangères, 1963.

54 p. 19cm.

《苏共领导联印反华的真相》，《人民日报》编辑部.

13. Unissons-nous sur la base des déclarations de Moscou.
Pékin：Éditions en Langues Étrangères, 1963. 34
pages；18cm.

《在莫斯科世界妇女大会上两条路线的斗争》

14. La Dialectique révolutionnaire et la connaissance de
l'impérialisme/Chao Tie-Tchen. Pékin：Éditions en
Langues Étrangères, 1963. 22 p. ；In—16, 18,5cm.

《革命的辩证法和对帝国主义的认识》，邵铁真著.

15. Sept lettres échangées entre le Comité Central du parti
communiste chinois et le Comité Central du parti
communiste de l'Union soviétique. Pékin, Éditions en
Langues Étrangères, 1964. 82 p. 18cm.

《中共中央和苏共中央来往的七封信》

16. Réponse du Comité Central du Parti Communiste Chinois
à la lettre du 15 juin 1964 du Comité Central du Parti
Communiste de l'Union Soviétique. Pékin：Éditions en
Langues Étrangères, 1964. 79 p. ；15cm.

《中国共产党中央委员会对于苏联共产党中央委员会一
九六四年六月十五日来信的复信》

17. Réponse du Comité Central du parti communiste chinois a
la lettre du 30 juillet 1964 du Comité central du parti
communiste de l'Union Soviétique. Pékin：Éditions en
Langues Étrangères, 1964

《中国共产党中央委员会对于苏联共产党中央委员会一
九六四年七月三十日来信的复信》

18. Pourquoi Khrouchtchev est-il tombé?：éditorial du
Hongqi (no. 21－22, 1964). Pékin：Éditions en Langues
Étrangères, 1964. 12 p. ；19cm.

《赫鲁晓夫是怎样下台的：1964 年第 21－22 期〈红旗〉
社论》

19. Commentaire sur la réunion de Mars de Moscou/
Rédaction du "Renmin Ribao" et rédaction du "Hongqi.
Pékin：Éditions en Langues Étrangères, 1965. 1 vol.
(24 p.)；19cm.

《评莫斯科三月会议》（1965 年 3 月 23 日），《人民日报》
编辑部、《红旗》杂志编辑部.

20. Luttons jusqu'au bout contre le révisionnisme
khrouchtchevien：à l'occasion du 2e. anniversaire de la
publication des "Propositions concernant la ligne générale
du mouvement communiste international/Rédaction du
Renmin Ribao et rédaction du Hongqi (14 juin 1965).
Pékin：Éditions en Langues Étrangères, 1965. 17 p. ；
21cm.

《把反对赫鲁晓夫修正主义的斗争进行到底：纪念〈关于
国际共产主义运动总路线的建议〉发表两周年》（1965 年
6 月 14 日），《人民日报》编辑部、《红旗》杂志编辑部.

21. De "l'unité d'action" de la nouvelle direction du P. C. U.
S；rédaction du "Renmin Ribao" et rédaction du

"Hongqi"（11 novembre 1965）. Pékin：Éditions en Langues Étrangères, 1965. 35 p.

《驳苏共新领导的所谓"联合行动"》(1965 年 11 月 11 日),《人民日报》编辑部、《红旗》杂志编辑部.

22. 《苏共领导是宣言和声明的背判者》(1965 年 12 月 30 日),《人民日报》编辑部、《红旗》杂志编辑部. 北京：外文出版社,1965.

23. Lettre du 22 mars 1966 du comité central du parti communiste chinois au comité central du parti communiste de l'union soviétique/Zhongguo gong chan dang. Comité Central. Pékin：Éditions en Langues Étrangères, 1966. 5 pages

《中国共产党中央委员会一九六六年三月二十二日给苏联共产党中央委员会的复信》

24. La grande révolution chinoise et la grande tragédie de l'Union Soviétique. Pékin：Éditions en Langues Étrangères, 1967. 15 p

《中国的大革命和苏联的大悲剧》

25. Une propagande à bon marché/［commentaires de correspondants de l'Agence Hsinhua］. Pékin：Éditions en Langues Étrangères, 1974. 1 vol. (31 p.)；19cm.

《廉价的宣传》

D233　中国与世界其他各国外交关系

1. Documents sur les relations sino-indiennes（Décembre 1961—mai 1962）. Pékin：Éditions en Langues Étrangères, 1962. 87 p

《中印关系文件选集》(1961 年 12 月—1962 年 5 月)

2. La question de la frontière sino-indienne. Pékin：Éditions en Langues Étrangères, 1962—1965. volumes 1－2：folded maps；19cm.

《中印边界问题》(1—2)

3. La question de la frontière sino-indienne. Pékin：Éditions en Langues Étrangères, Éd. augmenté. 1962. 146 pages ［14］leaves of plates：folded maps；19cm.

《中印边界问题》(增印本)

4. Lettre du Premier Ministre Chou En-lai aux dirigeants des pays d'Asie et d'Afrique sur la question de la frontière sino-indienne（15 novembre 1962）. Pékin：Éditions en Langues Étrangères, 1973. 34 pages

《周恩来总理就中印边界问题致亚非国家领导人的信》(1962.11.15)

(1)Pékin：Éditions en Langues Étrangères, 1974. 34 pages

5. Déclaration commune du parti communiste chinois et du parti communiste de Nouvelle Zélande. Pékin：Éd. en Langues Étrangères, 1963. 16 p.；in—16, 18,5cm.

《中国共产党新西兰共产党联合声明》

6. Histoire des relations de la Chine avec l'Annam-Viêtnam du XVIe au XIXe siècle：d'après des documents chinois traduits pour la première fois et annotés/par G. Devéria.

Paris：Ernest Leroux, 1880. 1 vol. (X—102 p.)：carte. (Publications de l'école des langues orientales vivantes. 1e série；13)

《中国与安南—越南关系史》,Devéria, Gabriel（1844—1899)翻译并加注.

7. La frontière sino-annamite：description géographique et ethnographique d'après des documents officiels chinois/traduits pour la première fois par G. Devéria. Paris：E. Leroux, 1886. 1 vol. (XVII—183 p., pl., cartes dépl.)；in-4. (Publications de l'école des langues orientales vivantes. 3e série；1)

《根据中国资料,中国安南边界以及该地区地理和种族》,Devéria, Gabriel 1844—1899)

8. Déclaration commune du président Liou Chao-Chi et du président Ho Chi Minh/Liu Chao Chi. Pékin：Éditions en Langues Étrangères, 1963. 1 v. (42 p.)；19cm.

《刘少奇主席和胡志明主席联合声明》

9. L'engagement solennel des 30 millions de Vietnamiens. Pékin：Éditions en Langues Étrangères, 1965. 50 pages；19cm.

《三千万越南人民的庄严誓言》

10. Soutenir le peuple vietnamien, vaincre les agresseurs américains. Pékin：Éditions en Langues Étrangères, 1965. 4 vol. (86—42—42—42 p.)；19cm.

《支援越南人民 打败美国侵略者》(1、2、3、4 辑)

11. 《Vivent la grande amitié et la solidarité des peuples chinois et vietnamien! Pékin：Éditions en Langues Étrangères, 1971. 86 p.：ill.

《中越两国人民的伟大友谊和战斗团结万岁!》

12. Saluons la signature de l'accord de Paris sur le Vietnam. Pékin：Éditions en Langues Étrangères, 1973. 46 p：Ill., Portr；19cm.

《欢迎越南协定的签订》

13. La grande victoire du Peuple vietnamien：saluons chaleureusement la libération de Saigon et de tout le Sud Vietnam par la population sud-vietnamienne. Pékin：Éditions en Langues Étrangères, 1975. 60 pages, 2 pages of plates：illustrations；19cm.

《越南人民的伟大胜利：热烈庆贺越南南方人民解放西贡和完全解放越南南方》

14. A propos du Livre Blanc du Ministère vietnamien des affaires étrangères sur les relations Vietnam-Chine/commentateurs du Renmin Ribao et de l'Agence Xinhua. Beijing：Éditions en Langues Étrangères, 1979. 30 p.；19cm.

《评越南外交部关于越中关系的白皮书》,人民日报评论员、新华社评论员.

15. Déclaration commune du président Liou Chao-Chi et du président Choi Yong Kun. Pékin：Éditions en Langues Étrangères, 1963. 17 p.；19cm.

《刘少奇主席和崔庸健委员长联合声明》

16. Quelques questions internationales concernant la Malaisie/Malayan Monitor（31 janvier 1963）. Pékin：Éditions en Langues Étrangères, 1964. 18 pages；19cm.

《与马来西亚有关的一些国际问题》

17. L'expérience du peuple malais et les absurdités révisionnistes：pour le seizième anniversaire de la lutte armée du peuple malais：Malayan monitor du 30 juin 1964. Pékin：Éditions en Langues Étrangères, 1965. 16 p.；18cm.

《马来亚人民的经历驳斥了修正主义者的谬论：纪念马来亚人民武装斗争十六周年》

18. Conférence à l'Académie Indonésienne des Sciences Sociales Aliarcham（25 mai 1965）/Peng Tchen. Pékin：Éditions en Langues Étrangères, 1965. 29 p.；21cm.

《在印度尼西亚阿里亚哈姆社会科学学院的讲话：1965年5月25日》,彭真著.

19. L'amitié combattante Sino-Albanaise：recueil de documents sur la visite de Chou En-laï et de Tchen Yi en Albanie. Pékin：Éditions en Langues Étrangères, 1964. 176 pages；19cm.

《中阿战斗友谊万岁：中国领导人访问阿尔巴尼亚文件集》.

20. Soutien à la lutte du peuple du Congo contre l'agression américaine/［Mao Tse-tung］. Pékin：Éditions en Langues Étrangères, 1965. 1 vol.（30 p.）；19cm.

《支持刚果（利奥波德维尔）人民反对美国侵略》

21. Soutien au peuple Dominicain dans son combat contre l'agression armée americaine. Pékin：Éditions en Langues Étrangères, 1965. 35 pages：plates；19cm.

《支持多米尼加人民反对美国武装侵略》

22. Une Page nouvelle dans les annales des relations sino-japonaises. Pékin：Éditions en Langues Étrangères；Paris：diffusion Éditions du Centenaire, 1972. 28 p.-［4］ p. de pl.；19cm.

《中日关系史的新篇章》

23. La Grande victoire du peuple cambodgien：saluons chaleureusement la libération de Phnom Penh et de tout le Cambodge par le peuple cambodgien et ses forces armées patriotes/［traduit du chinois］. Pékin：Éditions en Langues Étrangères；［Paris］；［diffusion Éditions du Centenaire］, 1975. 41 p.-［2］ p. de pl.；19cm.

《柬埔寨人民的伟大胜利：热烈庆贺柬埔寨爱国军民解放金边和解放全国》

24. Correspondance diplomatique chinoise relative aux négociations du traité de Whampoa, conclu entre la France et la Chine le 24 octobre 1844/traduite du chinois en français et du français en chinois par J.-M. Callery. Paris：Impr. de Seringe frères, 1879. 306 p.

中法外交信件. Callery, Joseph-Marie（1810—1862）译.

25. 1964—2004：40e anniversaire de l'établissement des relations diplomatiques entre la Chine et la France/conseiller principal Tang Jiaxuan；président du comité de rédaction Li Zhaoxing；rédacteur en chef Zhao Jun. ［Lieu de publication inconnu］：Éd. World Affairs, 2004. 1 vol.（253 p.）：ill. en coul.；30cm. ISBN：750122188X（rel）；7501221882（rel）.

《纪念中法建交四十周年：1964—2004》,《纪念中法建交四十周年》编委会编.

26. Déclaration du gouvernement de la République Populaire de Chine（7 Octobre 1969）. Pékin：Éditions en Langues Étrangères, 1973. 28 pages

《中华人民共和国政府声明》(1969.10.7)

27. La souveraineté incontestable de la Chine sur les îles Xisha et les îles Nansha：document du Ministère des affaires étrangères de la République populaire de Chine. Beijing：Éditions en Langues Étrangères, 1980. 23.：ill.；19cm.

《中国对西沙群岛和南沙群岛的主权无可争辩-中华人民共和国外交部文件：一九八零年一月三十日》

D3　中国法律

1. Le système légal de la Chine/Hu Jinguang. Beijing：Éditions en Langues Étrangères, 2009. ISBN：7119061085；71190610890.（La Chine en développement pacifique）

《中国法治进行时》,胡锦光［著］.

2. La législation socialiste à la chinoise/Office d'information du Conseil des Affaires d'État de la République populaire de Chine. Beijing：Foreign Languages Press, 2011. 62 pages；21cm. ISBN：7119073033, 7119073036

《中国特色社会主义法律体系》,中华人民共和国国务院新闻办公室［发布］.

3. Constitution de la république populaire de Chine. Pékin, Éditions en Langues Étrangères, 1954. 57 pages；21cm.

《中华人民共和国宪法》.

(1) Pékin：Éditions en Langues Étrangères, 1975. 54 p.；19cm.

(2) Pékin：Éditions en Langues Étrangères, 1978. 81 p.

(3) Beijing：Éditions en Langues Étrangères, 1983. 81 p.

4. Rapport sur le projet de constitution de la République populaire de Chine：constitution de la République populaire de Chine/Liou Chao-chi. Pékin：Éditions en Langues Étrangères, 1954. 137 pages：ill.

《关于中华人名共和国宪法草案的报告》,刘少奇著.

5. La Loi sur la réforme agraire de la république populaire de Chine. Pékin, les Éd. en Langues Étrangères, 1950. 65 p. 12mo

《中华人民共和国土地改革法》

6. La loi sur le mariage de la République Populaire de Chine.

Pékin：Éditions en Langues Étrangères，1950. 52 p.；8.
《中华人民共和国婚姻法》

(1)Loi sur le mariage en République populaire de Chine.
Beijing：Éditions en Langues Étrangères，1982. 18 p

7. Lois et règlements sur le travail en République populaire
de Chine. Pékin：Éditions en Langues Étrangères，1957.
1v.（100 p.）；19cm.
《重要劳动法令汇编》

8. Nouveaux progrès dans la protection de la propriété
intellectuelle en Chine. Beijing：Office d'information du
Conseil des Affaires d'État de la République populare de
Chine，2005. 44 pages. ISBN：7801488202；7801488206
《中国知识产权保护的新进展》，中华人民共和国国务院
新闻办公室发布.新星出版社.

E 类　军事

E1　古代兵法、战法

1. L'Art de la guerre de Sunzi. L'art de la guerre de Sun
Bin/rédaction：Wu Rusong. Beijing：Éditions Chine
Populaire，1994. 158pages；20cm. ISBN：7800655091,
7800655098
《孙子兵法·孙膑兵法》，Wu，Rusong（1940—）译.

2. L'Art de la guerre：textes originaux de Su Wu, Sun Bin/
traduction de Tang Jialong. Beijing：Éditions en Langues
Étrangères，2010. iii，159 pages；23cm. ISBN：
7119049762, 7119049763 (Chinese classics)
《孙子兵法·孙膑兵法》，孙武，孙膑著.

E11　孙子兵法

1. Les Treize articles. Tirés de la version Amiot，1772,
refondue et augmentée d'après les manuscrits chinois de
812 et 983 après J.-C. édition préparée par Monique
Beuzit, Roberto Cacérès, Paul Maman, Luc Thanassecos
et Tran Ngoc An. Paris：Librairie l'Impensé radical,
1971. 24cm.，167 p.，carte
《孙子十三篇》，Beuzit，Monique 译.

2. L'Art de la guerre/Sun Tzu；préface et introduction par
Samuel B. Griffith；avant-propos de B. H.［Basil Henry］
Liddell Hart；traduit de l'anglais par Francis Wang.
Paris：Flammarion（Poitiers：impr. Aubin），1972. 1 vol.
（260 p.）；22cm.（Textes politiques）
《孙子兵法》，Hart，Basil Henry Liddell（1895—1970），
Griffith，Samuel B. 英译；Wang，Francis 从英文译为法文.

3. L'Art de la guerre：les treize articles/Sun Tzu；trad. du
chinois par le P. Amiot；avec une postf. de Gilles
Tordjman；ill. de Laurent Parienty.［Paris］：Éd. Mille
et une nuits，1996. 175 p.：ill.，couv. ill. en coul.；
15cm. ISBN：2842050754, 2842050757.（Mille et une
nuits；122）

《孙子兵法十三篇》，Amiot，Joseph（1718—1793）译.

(1)［Paris］："Le Point，Impr. Maury-Eurolivres，2003.
144 p.：jaquette ill. en coul.；21cm.（Les classiques
du "Point"；)

(2)［Sayat］：De Borée，2012. 1 vol.（206 p.）：couv. ill.
en coul.；18cm. ISBN：2812907395, 2812907398

(3)［Paris］：Marabout，2016. 1 vol.（207 p.）；14cm.
ISBN：2501101813（br），2501101812（br）.（Les
petits collectors Marabout)

4. L'Art de la guerre de Sun Zi/révisé et traduit en chinois
moderne par Wu Rusong, Wu Xianlin；traduit en français
par Xu Xiaojun, Jia Xiaoning. Beijing：Éd. des sciences
militaires，2009. 1 vol.（173 p.）：ill.，cartes，jaq. ill.
en coul.；25cm. ISBN：7802372498（rel），7802372496
（rel）.（Bibliothèque des classiques chinois：chinois-
français)
《孙子兵法》，Wu，Rusong 和 Wu，Xianlin 今译；Xu,
Xiaojun 和 Jia，Xiaoning 法译.

5. L'Art de la guerre：Sunzibingfa/Sun Zi；traduit［du
chinois］et présenté par Alexis Lavis. Paris：Presse du
Châtelet，2009. 1 vol.（111 p.）：ill.，couv. ill.；22cm.
ISBN：2845922808（br），2845922809（br）.（Sagesse de
l'Orient)
《孙子兵法》，Lavis，Alexis（1979—）译.

6. L'Art de la guerre/Sun Tzu；traduit du chinois et
commenté par Jean Lévi.［Paris］：Fayard，Maury
impr.），2011. 1 vol.（328 p.）：cartes，couv. ill. en
coul.；18cm. ISBN：2818501740（br），2818501741
（br），2818504963（réimpr. 2015），2818504961（réimpr.
2015).（Pluriel：philosophie)
《孙子兵法》，Levi，Jean（1948—）译.

7. L'Art de la guerre selon Sunzi/Sun Zi；traduit et annoté
par Luo Shenyi. Paris：Éd. You Feng，2011. 1 vol.（106
p.）：fac-sim.；21cm. ISBN：2842794453（br），
2842794451（br)
《孙子兵法》，Luo，Shenyi 译. 法汉对照.

8. L'Art de la guerre：nouvelle traduction/Sun zi. Paris：G.
Trédaniel，2011. 1 vol.（96 p.）；27cm. ISBN：2813203205
（rel. à la chinoise），2813203203（rel. à la chinoise)
《孙子兵法》，译者不详.

9. L'Art de la guerre/Sun Zi；traduction et présentation,
Valérie Niquet；Préface du général Liu Fang；postface du
général Maurice Prestat；deux commentaires de Sun Zi
par Cao Cao et Li. 3e éd. entièrement refondue. Paris：
Institut de stratégie comparée：Economica，Normandie
roto impr.），2012. 1 vol.（VIII-212 p.）：couv. ill.；19cm.
ISBN：2717858969（br），2717858962（br）.（Bibliothèque
stratégique)
《孙子兵法》，Niquet-Cabestan，Valérie 译.

E2　中国军事

1. L'armée populaire de libération de Chine. Pékin：Éd. en Langues Étrangères, 1950. v. ；Ill；8'

   《中国人民解放军》

2. 《中国人民志愿军抗美援朝八年》. 北京：外文出版社, 1959

3. Peuples du monde entier, unissonsnous pour l'interdiction et la destruction complètes, totales, intégrales et résolues des armes nucléaires! Pékin：Éditions en Langues Étrangères, 1963. 330 p；22cm.

   《全世界人民团结起来, 全面、彻底、干净、坚决地禁止和销毁核武器》

4. La tradition démocratique de l'Armée Populaire de Libération de Chine, ler août 1965. Pékin：Éditions en Langues Étrangères, 1965. 42 pages；19cm.

   《中国人民解放军的民主传统》(1965 年 8 月 1 日), 贺龙著.

5. L'Expérience historique de la guerre antifasciste/rédaction du "Renmin ribao"...；[traduit du chinois]. Pékin：Éditions en Langues Étrangères；[Paris]：[diffusion Éditions du Centenaire], 1965. 27 p. ；19cm.

   《反法西斯战争的历史经验》(1965 年 5 月 9 日), 《人民日报》编辑部.

6. Pour l'anniversaire de la victoire sur le fascisme allemand! Pour la lutte jusqu'au bout contre l'impérialisme américain! /Jouei-king Louo. Pékin：Éditions en Langues Étrangères, 1965. 1 vol. (32 p.)

   《纪念战胜德国法西斯把反对美帝国主义的斗争进行到底》, 罗瑞卿著.

7. Le peuple a vaincu le fascisme japonais, il saura vaincre l'impérialisme américain/Louo Jouei-King. S. l. ：Éditions en Langues Étrangères, 1965. 34 p. ；18,5cm.

   《人民战胜了日本法西斯, 人民也一定能够战胜美帝国主义》, 罗瑞卿著.

8. Pour la fin du monopole nucléaire, pour la destruction des armes nucléaires. Pékin：Éditions en Langues Étrangères, 1965. 31, [1] p.

   《打破核垄断, 消灭核武器》

9. Célébrons le 44e anniversaire de la fondation de l'armée populaire de libération de Chine. Pékin：Éditions en Langues Étrangères, 1971. 31 p；18cm.

   《纪念中国人民解放军建军四十四周年》

10. Peuples du monde, unissez-vous dans la lutte pour l'interdiction complète et la destruction totale des armes nucléaires/Réunit trois déclarations：une du Gouvernement de la R. P. de Chine, le 30 juillet 1971, et deux interventions à l'O. N. U. de Kiao Kouan-Houa, les 24 et 26 novembre 1971. / Traduit du chinois. Pékin：Éditions en Langues Étrangères, 1971. 1 vol. (19 p.)；19cm.

    《全世界人民团结起来, 为全面禁止和彻底销毁核武器而奋斗》

11. La Défense nationale de la Chine en l'an 2000/Office d'information du Conseil des Affaires d'État de la République populaire de Chine. Beijing：Nouvelle Étoile, 2000. 52 pages：illustrations；26cm. ISBN：7801483081；7801483089.

    《2000 年中国的国防》, 中华人民共和国国务院新闻办公室编. 新星出版社.

12. La Politique et les mesures de la Chine en matière de non-prolifération/Office d'information du Conseil des Affaires d'État de la République populaire de Chine. Beijing：Nouvelle Étoile, 2003. 28 pages；21cm. ISBN：780148567X；7801485670.

    《中国的防扩散政策和措施》, 中华人民共和国国务院新闻办公室发布. 新星出版社.

13. 中国的军控、裁军与防扩散势力：法文/中华人民共和国国务院新闻办公室发布. 北京：出版社, 2005. 60 页；20cm. ISBN：7801489217

14. La paix, centre des strategiés militaires chinoises/Huang Zu'an. Beijing：Éditions en Langues etrangeres, 2007. 97 unnumbered pages：color illustrations；21cm. ISBN：7119046648 (pbk.), 9119046640 (pbk.). (Chine en developpement pacifique)

    《中国兵略贵和论》, 黄祖安著.

15. Défense nationale de la Chine/par Peng Guangqian, Zhao Zhiyin & Luo Yong；traduit par Wang Wenjia. Beijing：China intercontiental Press, 2010. 172 pages：color illustrations, color maps；23cm. ISBN：7508519128；7508519124

    《中国国防》, 彭光谦, 赵智印, 罗永著. 五洲传播出版社.

F 类　经济

F1　中国经济

F11　概论

1. Aperçu sur l'économie chinoise/Tcheng Che. Pékin：Éditions en Langues Étrangères, 1974. vii, 52 p

   《中国经济简况》, 邓实著.

2. L' économie en Chine/par Wang Mengkui et autres；traduit par Gong Jieshi et autres. Pékin：China International Press, 2004. 1 vol. (199 p.)：ill. en noir et en coul. ；21cm. ISBN：7508506359 (br)；7508506357 (br). (Que sais-je sur la Chine?)

   《中国经济》, 王梦奎等编著, 宫结实译. 五洲传播出版社 (中国基本情况丛书/郭长建主编)

   (1)北京：五洲传播出版社, 2005. 211 pages：

illustrations；21cm. ISBN：7508506383，7508506388.
（中国基本情况丛书. 当代卷. 中国基本情况丛书. 当
代卷）

3. L'économie chinoise/par Wu Li, Sui Fumin & Zheng Lei；
traduit par Shen Xin. Beijing：China Intercontinental
Press, 2010. 1 vol. (156 p.)；ill. , couv. ill. en coul. ；
23cm. ISBN：7508519111, 7508519116
《中国经济》，吴伟主编. 五洲传播出版社.

4. L'Économie chinoise sur la voie du socialisme. Pékin：
Éditions en Langues Étrangères, 1954. 132 pages；
illustrations；19cm.
《在社会主义道路上的中国经济》，邓拓等著.

5. Le premier plan quinquennal pour le développement de
l'économie nationale de la Republique Populaire de Chine：
(1953—1957). Pékin：Éditions en Langues Étrangères,
1956. 242 pages
《中华人民共和国发展国民经济的第一个五年计划：
1953—1957》

6. Rapport sur le premier plan quinquennal pour le
développement de l'économie nationale de la République
populaire de Chine, 1953—1957/[par] Li Fou-tchouen.
Présenté les 5 et 6 juillet 1955 à la seconde session de la
première Assemblée populaire nationale. Pékin：Éditions
en Langues Étrangères, 1956. 148 pages
《关于发展国民经济的第一个五年计划的报告》，李富
春著.

7. La Chine va dépasser la grande Bretagne. Pékin：Éditions
en Langues Étrangères, 1958. 77 pages；19cm.
《赶上英国，超过英国》，牛中黄著.

8. Communiqué de presse sur le développement de l'économie
nationale en 1959. Pékin：Éditions en Langues
Étrangères, 1960. 1 v. (30 p.)
《关于一九五九年国民经济发展情况的新闻公报》

9. L'industrialisation socialiste et la collectivisation de
l'agriculture en Chine. Pékin：Éditions en Langues
Étrangères, 1964. 52 pages；18cm.
《中国的社会主义工业化和农业集体化》，薄一波，廖鲁
言著.

10. Problèmes économiques du socialisme en Chine/Mu-
ch'iao Hsueh Pékin, Chine：Éditions en Langues
Étrangères, 1981. 375 p.
《中国社会主义经济问题研究》，薛暮桥著；钱法仁译.

11. La Situation économique et l'orientation à suivre pour
notre édification：rapport/de Zhao Ziyang sur les
activités du gouvernement présenté le 30 novembre et le
1er décembre 1981 à la quatrième session de la Ve
assemblée populaire nationale. Beijing, Chine：Éditions
en Langues Étrangères, 1982. 134 p. ；19cm.
《中国经济形势和建设方针》（国务院总理赵紫阳的
报告）.

12. La Modernisation socialiste de la Chine/sous la direction de
Yu Guangyuan. Beijing：Éditions en Langues Étrangères,
1983—1984. 2 v.
《中国社会主义现代化建设》（上、下），于光远主编.

13. Décision du Comité Central du Parti Communiste Chinois
sur la réforme du systémé economique. Beijing：Éditions
en Langues Étrangères, 1984. 44 p. ；18cm.
《中共中央关于经济体制改革的决定》

14. 《中国经济改革 15 年：1978—1993》，北京周报社编. 北
京：新星出版社，1994. ISBN：7800853861

15. 《长江：中国开发潜力最大的地区》. 北京：新星出版社,
1994. ISBN：7801020685.
（长江的开发与开放，1）

16. La voie de développement de la Chine et la
mondialisation/Yin Wenquan；traduit par Wang JInquan
[and others]. Beijing：Éditions en Langues étrangerès,
2007. 101 pages；illustrations；22cm. ISBN：
7119046617，7119046616. (La Chine en développement
pacifique)
《全球化视野下的中国发展之路》，银温泉著.

17. Projets internationaux de lutte contre la pauvreté en
Chine/Shen Honglei et Lei Xiangqing. Beijing：Éditions
en Langues etrangeres, 2007. 107 pages：color illustrations；
21cm. ISBN：7119046396 (pbk.)；711904639X (pbk.)
(Chine en développement pacifique)
《国际扶贫援助项目在中国》，申宏磊，雷向勤编著；王金
寇等译(中国的和平发展系列)

18. La Chine et la mondialisation/by Chang Lu and Xue Kai.
Beijing：Éditions en Langues etrangeres, 2008. 139
pages：color illustrations；21cm. ISBN：7119055350,
119055356. (La Chine en developpement pacifique；)
《中国融入世界》，常璐，薛凯著.

F2   经济管理

F21   劳动经济

1. La situation des ressources humaines en Chine/Office
d'information du Conseil des Affaires d'État de la
République populaire de Chine. Beijing：Foreign
Languages Press, 2010. 49 pages：illustrations；21cm.
ISBN：7119066684；7119066684
《中国的人力资源状况》，中华人民共和国国务院新闻办
公室[发布].

F22   投资与建设

1. Les investissements étrangers en Chine：questions &
réponses/par Chu Baotai. Beijing：Éditions en Langues
Étrangères, 1987. 204 pages；19cm.
《答来华投资者一百问》，初保泰著.

2. Rapport sur le plan d'aménagement complet du Fleuve
Jaune et de mise en valeur de ses ressources hydrauliques/
par Teng Tsê-houei. Pékin：Éditions en Langues

Étrangères, 1956. 1 vol. (53 p., [1] dépl.）；22cm.

《关于根治黄河水害和开发黄河水利的综合规划的报告》，邓子恢著.

3. Le grand bond en avant dans la construction hydraulique en Chine/[par Souen Li et al.]. Pékin, Éditions en Langues Étrangères, 1959. 159 pages：illustrations；19cm.

《中国农田水利大跃进》，顾雷等著.

4. La Chine aménage ses fleuves. Pékin：Éditions en Langues Étrangères, 1972. 58 p.

《中国几条主要河流的治理》

F23 房地产经济

1. L'évolution des conditions de logement de 1,3 milliard de Chinois/Xue Kai. Beijing：Éditions en Langues Étrangères, 2007. 123 pages：color illustrations；21cm. ISBN：7119051208; 7119051202 (La Chine en développement pacifique)

《13亿人的住房变迁》，薛凯著；张玉元译（中国的和平发展系列）

2. La construction des villes agréables à vivre en Chine/Cui Lili. Beijing：Éditions en Langues Étrangères, 2007. 119 pages：color illustrations；21cm. ISBN：7119051505; 7119051504

《建设适宜人类居住的城市》，崔黎丽著；王默译（中国的和平发展系列）

F3 "三农"问题

1. Projet de programme pour le développement de l'agriculture de la République Populaire de Chine 1956—1967：quelques explications sur le projet de programme national pour le développement de l'agriculture：1956—1967/Lou-yen Liao. Pékin：Éditions en Langues Étrangères, 1956. 49 p.

《1956年到1967年全国农业发展纲要（草案）》

2. Programme national pour le développement de l'agriculture de 1956 à 1967. Pékin：Éditions en Langues Étrangères, 1960. 70 p.；21cm.

《一九五六年到一九六七年全国农业发展纲要》

3. Le parti et le peuple tout entiers s'engagent dans un travail agricole d'envergure/Liao Lou-Yen. Pékin：Éditions en Langues Étrangères, 1960. 1 v. (22 p.)；19cm.

《全党全民动手大办农业》，廖鲁言著.

4. Les conditions de vie des paysans chinois depuis la libération. Pékin：Éditions en Langues Étrangères, 1960. 43 pages；19cm.

《解放后中国农民的生活变化》，金超民著.

5. Les communes populaires vont de l'avant：bilan de cinq années d'expérience dans les communes populaires rurales de la province du Kouangtong/Tao Tchou. Pékin：Éditions en Langues Étrangères, 1964. 41 p.

《人民公社在前进：广东农村人民公社五年经验的基本总结》，陶铸著.

6. La Lutte entre les deux voies dans les campagnes chinoises/par les Bureaux de rédaction du Renmin Ribao, du Hongqi et du Jiefangjun Bao；23 novembre 1967. Pékin：Éditions en Langues Étrangères, 1968. 32 pages；19cm.

《中国农村两条道路的斗争》

7. Tatchai：drapeau rouge sur le front agricole en Chine. Pékin：Éditions en Langues Étrangères, 1972. 32 p.

《大寨：中国农业战线上的一面红旗》

8. Mobiliser tout le parti, développer en grand l'agriculture et mener le combat pour généraliser les districts de type Tachal. rapport établissant le bilan de la conférence nationale pour s'inspirer de Tatchai dans l'agriculture. Pékin：Éditions en Langues Étrangères, 1975. 85 p

《全党动员，大办农业，为普及大寨县而奋斗》，华国锋著.

9. Visite à Tongting：une commune populaire au bord du lac Taihou/Wou Tcheou. Pékin：Éditions en Langues Étrangères, 1975. 65 p

《洞庭人民公社》，吴周著.

10. Avec ceux de la Commune populaire de Tsiliying/Tchou Li, Tien Kié-yun；[traduit du chinois]. Pékin：Éditions en Langues Étrangères, 1976. 256 pages：illustrations；19cm.

《在七里营人民公社里》，朱力、田洁云著.

11. Discours à la deuxième Conférence nationale pour s'inspirer de Tatchaï dans l'agriculture：25 Décembre 1976/Houa Kouo-feng,... Pékin：Éditions en Langues Étrangères；[Paris]：[diffusion Éditions du Centenaire], 1977. 33 p.；19cm.

《中国共产党中央委员会主席华国锋同志在第二次全国农业大赛会议上的讲话》

12. 《中国的农村改革》. 北京：新星出版社，1991. ISBN：7800851087

13. Critiquer à fond la bande des quatre et imprimer un nouvel essor à la généralisation des districts de type tatchai：rapport présenté par Tchen Yong-kouei, membre du Bureau politique du Comité central du Parti communiste chinois et vice-premier ministre du Conseil des Affaires d'État de la République populaire de Chine, à la Deuxieme Conférence nationale pour s'inspirer de Tatchai dans l'agriculture/Tchen Yong-kouei. Pékin：Éditions en Langues Étrangères, 1997. 36 pages；19cm.

《彻底批判"四人帮"掀起普及大寨县运动的新高潮：中共中央政治局委员、国务院副总经理程永贵在第二次全国农业大赛会议上的报告》

14. Le village de Lijia aspects de l'économie paysanne en Chine/Li Xiande. Beijing：China Agricultural Science and Technology Press, 2005. 408 pages：maps；22cm. ISBN：7801677439; 7801677433

《李村经济：中国农民问题之研究》，李先德著. 中国农业科学技术出版社. 本书以湖北监利县为调研对象，从而分析和论述了近年我国农村经济发展等问题.

15. La construction d'une nouvelle ruralité/Wang Tai, Zhao Jingping et Li Haitao. Beijing：Éditions en Langues Étrangères, 2007. 119 pages：color illustrations；21cm. ISBN：7119051222；7119051229

《新农村建设从这里起步》,王太,赵经平,李海涛著;何丹译(中国的和平发展系列)

16. Nouveaux progrès de la lutte contre la pauvreté rurale en Chine/Office d'information du Conseil des Affaires d'État de la République populaire de Chine. Beijing：Foreign Languages Press, 2011. 44 pages；21cm. ISBN：7119073323；711907332X

《中国农村扶贫开发的新进展》,中华人民共和国国务院新闻办公室[发布].

F31　林业经济

1. Forêts de Chine/Han Lin. Beijing：Éditions en Langues Étrangères, 2009. 131 pages：color illustrations；21cm. ISBN：7119061078, 7119061070. (La Chine en développement pacifique)

《中国的森林》,韩琳[著].

F4　工业经济

1. Taking：un drapeau rouge sur le front industriel chinois. Pékin：Éditions en Langues Étrangères, 1972. 63 p., [12] p. de pl.：ill.；19cm.

《大庆：中国工业战线上的一面红旗》

2. Conférence nationale pour s'inspirer de taking dans l'industrie (Documents). Pékin：Éditions en Langues Étrangères, 1977. 95 pages；19cm.

《中国工业学大庆会议文件选编》

3. L'astronautique chinoise/Office d'information du Conseil des Affaires d'État de la République populaire de Chine. Beijing：Nouvelle étoile, 2000. 20 p.；26cm. ISBN：7801483677, 7801483676

《2000年中国的航天》,中华人民共和国国务院新闻办公室发布.新星出版社.

4. Projets de construction clés de l'État/Li Ning. Beijing：Éditions en Langues Étrangères, 2007. 125 pages：color illustrations；21cm. ISBN：7119051543；7119051547 (La Chine en développement pacifique)

《国家重点建设工程》,李宁著;姜丽莉译(中国的和平发展系列)

5. Le pays de la soie/Wei Liming；[traduction Zhang Yongzhao]. Beijing：Éditions en Langues Étrangères, 2008. 1 vol. (107 p.)：ill. en noir et en coul., cartes en coul., couv. ill. en coul.；17×19cm. ISBN：7119047744 (br), 7119047744 (br). (Culture de la Chine)

《中国的丝绸》,韦黎明编著.

6. Les entreprises chinoises du XXIe siècle/Che Yuming, Han Jie et Zhao Xiaohui；traduction, Zhang Yuyuan.

Beijing, Chine：Éditions en Langues Étrangères, 2008. 139 pages：color illustrations；21cm. ISBN：7119055398；7119055399. (La Chine en développement pacifique)

《走进21世纪的中国企业》,车玉明,韩洁,赵晓辉著.

7. La situation de l'internet en Chine/office d'information du conseil des affaires d'État de la République populaire de Chine. Beijing：Éditions en Langues Étrangères, 2010. 39 pages；21cm. ISBN：7119064802, 7119064800

《中国互联网状况》,中华人民共和国国务院新闻办公室[发布].

F41　能源经济

1. La Politique de la Chine en matière de ressources minérales/Office d'information du Conseil des Affaires d'État de la République populaire de Chine. Beijing：Nouvelle Étoile, 2003. 41 pages；21cm. ISBN：7801485580, 7801485588.

《中国的矿产资源政策》,中华人民共和国国务院新闻办公室发布.新星出版社.

2. Le problème de l'énergie en Chine/Zhou Dadi. Beijing, Chine：Éditions en Langues Étrangères：Distributeur, Société chinoise du commerce international du livre, 2006. 121 pages：color illustrations；21cm. ISBN：7119046195, 7119046198. (La Chine en développement pacifique)

《中国能源问题》,周大地著;张玉元译.(中国的和平发展系列)

3. La situation actuelle des ressources et les mesures apportées/Qiu Tian. Beijing：Éditions en Langues Étrangères, 2007. 135 pages：color illustrations；21cm. ISBN：7119051574, 7119051571. (La Chine en développement pacifique)

《资源的现状与对策》,邱天著.(中国的和平发展系列)

4. L'economie du recyclage/Qu Geping et Yan Min. Beijing：Foreign Languages Press, 2008. 135 pages：color illustrations；21cm. ISBN：7119055480, 7119055488. (La Chine en developpement pacifique).

《循环经济,绿色之旗》,曲格平,闫敏著.

F5　贸易经济

1. Guide des affaires en Chine/rédigé sous la direction de Ma Ke et de Li Jun. Beijing：China Intercontinental Press, 2004. 1 vol. (474 p.)：couv. ill. en coul., ill. en coul.；24cm. +1 CD-Rom. ISBN：7508504127 7508504124

《中国商务》,马可,李俊主编,冯嘉瑞等译.五洲传播出版社.本书为《中国商务》法文本,介绍中国商务运行的实际情况,提供中国商务环境的知识和信息.

2. Le commerce extérieur de la Chine/Office d'information de Conseil des Affaires d'État de la République populaire de Chine. Beijing：Éditions en Langues Étrangères, 2011. 47 p.：ill.；21cm. ISBN：7119074061；7119074067

《中国的对外贸易》,中华人民共和国国务院新闻办公室[发布].

G 类 文化、教育、体育

G1 中国文化概论

1. Aperçu sur la culture chinoise/Tchai Pien. Pékin: Éditions en Langues Étrangères, 1975. iv, 59 p., [18] feuillets de planches: ill. (certaines en coul.)
《中国文化简况》,瞿边著.

2. Culture/par le Comité de rédaction de la collection "Connaissance de la Chine." Pékin, Chine: Éditions en Langues Étrangères, 1985. 144 p., [12] p. de planches.
《文化事业》,《中国概况丛书》编辑委员会编.

3. L'instruction et la culture dans la Chine nouvelle/par Kuo Mo-Jo. Pékin, 1950. 33 pages; 19cm.
Notes: "... Rapport sur les travaux de la culture et l'instruction publique—adressé le 17 juin 1950 devant la 2e Session du Comité National de la Conférence Consultative Politique du Peuple..." —Page 1.
《关于文化教育工作的报告》,郭沫若著.

4. Nos progrès dans la culture et l'éducation. Pékin: Éditions en Langues Étrangères, 1954. 117 p. fig. 16mo.
《文化教育事业的进展》,郭沫若、洪深等著.

5. La culture chinoise/Sun Jiazheng. Beijing, Chine: B Éditions en Langues Étrangères, 2006. 131 pages: color illustrations; 21cm. ISBN: 7119044958, 7119044958
《文化如水》,孙家正著;王默译.(中国的和平发展系列)

6. La valeur contemporaine de la culture traditionnelle chinoise/by Zhang Xiping. Beijing, Chine: Éditions en Langues Étrangères, 2009. 137 pages: color illustrations; 21cm. ISBN: 7119061139; 7119061135. (La Chine en développement pacifique)
《传统文化的当代价值》,张西平[著].("和平发展")

G2 出版

1. Documents sur l'art d'imprimer à l'aide de planches de bois, de planches de pierre et de types mobiles inventé en Chine bien avant que l'Europe en fît usage, extraits des livres chinois par M. Stanislas Julien. Paris: Impr. royale, 1847. In-8°, 16 p.
《关于中国木版印刷、石印和活字印刷的资料》,Julien, Stanislas(1799—1873)译.

2. Recueil de cachets sur la Montagne Jaune/traduit par Pierre Daudin. Saïgon, Imp. de l'union NG-Yan-Cua, 1932. 110 p.
《伊蔚斋黄山印薮》,项怀述(1718—约1787)著;Daudin, Pierre 译.

G3 文化机构

1. L'histoire du livre en Chine/par Liu Guojun et Zheng Rusi; trad. [du chinois] de Ann-Muriel Harvey et Olivier Pasteur. Beijing: Éditions en Langues Étrangères, 1989. 132 p., [12] p. pl.: ill.; 18cm.
《中国书的故事》,刘国钧,郑如斯编.

2. 《藏族传统文化的巨大工程:〈中华大藏经.丹珠尔〉》对勘纪实.吴伟著.北京:五洲传播出版社,1997. ISBN: 780113205X

3. Les musees/[edited by Xiao Xiaoming]. Beijing: Éditions en Langues Étrangères, 2003. 107 pages: color illustrations; 18×20cm. ISBN: 7119032818; 711903281X LCCN: 2010—396538
《中国博物馆巡览》,《中国博物馆巡览》编委会编.

4. Les musées de Chine/Li Xianyao, Luo Zhewen; traduit par Tao Ruogu. [Beijing]: China Intercontinental Press, 2011. 246 pages: color illustrations; 23cm. ISBN: 7508519937, 7508519930. (Collection culture chinoise)
《中国博物馆》,黎先耀,罗哲文著.五洲传播出版社.

5. Les musées de Beijing/[rédaction Lan Peijin; traduction He Dan; Révision Sabine de Barbuat, Zou Shaoping]. Beijing: Éditions en Langues Étrangères, 2008. 1 vol. (167 p.): ill. en coul., couv. ill. en coul.; 23cm. ISBN: 7119054087; 7119054082
《京城博物馆》,子慧撰.

6. La diffusion des informations et l'exercice intègre du pouvoir/Shen Honglei. Beijing: Éditions en Langues Étrangères, 2009. 127 pages: color illustrations; 21cm. ISBN: 7119061108, 7119061100. (La Chine en développement pacifique)
《新闻发布与阳光执政》,申宏磊[著].

7. 关键词读上海世博/崔黎丽编写.北京:外文出版社, 2010. 55 页; 18cm. ISBN: 7119063027

G31 收藏

1. L'encre de Chine, son histoire et sa fabrication, d'après des documents chinois/traduits [de Chen-ki-souen] par Maurice Jametel. Paris: Ernest Leroux, 1882. 1 vol. (XXX-94 p.): fig. et pl.; in—18. (Bibliothèque orientale elzévirienne; XXXII)
《中国墨》,Chen Ki Souen 著;Jametel, Maurice(1856—1889)译.

2. Le mobilier chinois/Zhang Xiaoming; traduit par Bi Chaolian. [Beijing]: China Intercontinental Press, 2011. 164 pages: color illustrations, 23cm. ISBN: 7508521107; 7508521102. (Collection culture chinoise)
《中国家具》,张晓明著.五洲传播出版社.

G4 教育

1. "K'iuenhio P'ien", exhortations à l'étude/par s. exc. Tchang Tche-tong. Nouvelle édition enrichie du texte chinois par le Père Jérôme Tobar. Chang-Hai: Impr. de la Mission catholique, 1909. 1 vol. (IV—10—197 p.):

portraits；in-8. (Variétés sinologiques；26)

《勤学篇》,张之洞著；S. J. Tobar, Jérôme 译.

2. Luttons pour l'établissement d'une université scientifique et technique, socialiste. Pékin：Éditions en Langues Étrangères, 1972. 76 p.

《为创办社会主义理工科大学二奋斗》

3. L'éducation en Chine. Beijing：Beijing Information, 1983. 102 str.：ilustr.；19cm.

《全民在学习》,北京周报社.

4. 《中共中央关于教育体制改革的决定》.北京：外文出版社,1985

5. Éducation et sciences/Éditions en Langues Étrangères. Collection Connaissance de la Chine. par le Comité de rédaction de la collection "Connaissance de la Chine." Beijing：Éditions en Langues Étrangères, 1985. 244 p., [8] p. de pl.：ill.

《教育科学》,《中国概况丛书》编辑委员会编.

6. 《留学中国指南》,北京高等学校外国人留学生工作研究会编.北京：北京语言学院出版社,1989

7. Partir étudier en Chine/monograph. [Zhong Xin；traduit par Wang Mo, Zhang Yongzhao]. Beijing：Éditions en Langues Étrangères, 2009. 39 pages：color illustrations；21cm. 39 pages：color illustrations；21cm. ISBN：7119058412, 711905841X

《留学中国指南》,钟欣编著.

8. Éducation en Chine：Réforme et innovation/Su xiaohuan. Beijing：China intercontinental Press, Beijing：Wu zhou chuan bo chu ban she, 2002. 1 vol. (190 p.)：ill. en coul.；21cm. ISBN：7508500555 (br)；7508500553 (br).

《中国教育：改革与创新》,苏晓环著.五洲传播出版社.

9. L'enseignement universitaire à distance en Chine：dispositifs, enjeux et perspectives /Wang Huan Beijing：[Maison d'édition d'enseignement et de recherche des Langues Étrangères], 2010. 302 pages：illustrations；26cm. ISBN：7560097589, 756009758

《中国远程高等教育：模式、挑战和前景》,王欢著.外语教学与研究出版社.

G5　体育

1. Guide des arts martiaux chinois/Li Tianji et Du Xilian. Beijing：Éditions en Langues Étrangères, 1re éd. 1991. 237 p., [4] p. de pl.：ill. (certaines en coul.). ISBN：7119007742；7119007748.

《中国武术指南》,李天骥,杜希廉编著.

2. Le kung-fu/monograph. /[Wei Liming；traduit par He Dan, Zhang Yongzhao]. Beijing：Éditions en Langues Étrangères, 2009. 35 pages：color illustrations；21cm. ISBN：7119058665, 7119058665

《中国功夫》,韦黎明编著.

3. Les arts martiaux chinois/Wang Guangxi；traduction de

Ego. [Beijing]：China Intercontinental Press, 2011. 123 pages：illustrations (some color)；23cm. ISBN：7508519562；7508519566；7508520971；7508520971. (Collection culture chinoise)

《中国功夫》,王广西(1941—2008).五洲传播出版社.

4. La mélodie interne de la vie La pratique chinoise du qigong/Yu Gongbao；[traduit par Gong Jieshi]；[revu par Marie-Anne Pupin et Zhu Chaoxu]. Beijing, China：Éditions du Nouveau Monde, 1995. 1 vol. (156 p.)：ill. en noir, couv. ill. en coul.；23cm. ISBN：7800052486, 7800052484

《中国气功图谱》,余功保著.新世界出版社.

5. Quintessence du Qi gong/Dr Jian Liujun；trad., Mo Xuqiang. Paris (57 Av. du Maine, 75014)：Éd. du Quimétao, Impr. Jouve, 1996. 177 p.：ill., couv. ill. en coul.；21cm. ISBN：291185800X, 2911858000. (Collection Qi gong et arts martiaux)

《气功的精髓》,Jian, Liujun (1957—) 著；Mo, Xuqiang (1956—) 译.

(1)2e éd. augm. Paris (57—59 Av. du Maine, 75014)：Éd. Quimétao, Impr. Laballery, 2000. 223 p.：ill. en noir et en coul., couv. ill. en coul.；21cm. ISBN：2911858050, 2911858055. (Qigong et arts martiaux)

(2)3e éd. [augm.]. Paris：Quimétao, 2005. 245 p.：ill.；21cm. ISBN：2911858212, 2911858215. 9Qi gong et arts martiaux)

(3) Dao de l'harmonie/docteur Jian Liujun；traduit en français par Mo Xuqiang. Paris：Éditions Quimétao, Impr. Laballery, 2014. 1 vol. (247 p.)：ill. en coul.；23cm. ISBN：2911858192, 2911858190

6. Taiji Qigong：en vingt-huit mouvements/Li Ding et M. Bambang Sutomo. Beijing：Éditions en Langues Étrangères, 1991. VII,147 p.：ill.；19cm. ISBN：7119013556；7119013558.

《太极气功二十八式》,李丁,(印尼)陈中行编著.

7. Les exercices d'assouplissement des muscles en 14 séries/livre réalisé par Chang Weizhen. Beijing：Éditions en Langues Étrangères, 1re éd. 1991. 113 p.：ill. ISBN：7119013505, 7119013503.

《易筋经十四段功法录：医学气功》,常维桢编著.

8. Liu zi jue/compilé par l'Association chinoise du qigong pour la santé. Beijing：Éditions en langues étrangeres, 2008. 73 pages：color illustrations；22cm. + 1 DVD-ROM (4 3/4 in.). ISBN：7119056791, 7119056794

《健身气功·六字诀》,国家体育总局健身气功管理中心编.

9. Ba duan jin/Association chinoise du qigong pour la santé. Beijing：Édition en Langues Étrangères, 2009. 56 pages：illustrations (chiefly color)；23cm. +1 DVD-ROM (4 3/4 in.). ISBN：7119056807, 7119056808

《健身气功·八段锦》,国家体育总局健身气功管理中心编.

10. Yi jin jing/compilé par l'Association chinoise du qigong pour la santé. Beijing：Éditions en langue étrangères,

2009. 95 pages：illustrations（chiefly color）；23cm. ＋1 DVD-ROM（4 3/4 in.）. ISBN：7119056777，7119056778

《健身气功・易筋经》,国家体育总局健身气功管理中心编.

11. Wu qin xi/compilé par l'Association chinoise du qigong pour la santé. Beijing：Éditions en langues étrangeres，2009. 104 pages：illustrations（chiefly color）；22cm. ＋1 DVD（4 3/4 in.）. ISBN：7119056784，7119056786

《健身气功・五禽戏》,国家体育总局健身气功管理中心编.

12. Le qigong pour la santé. Dawu/rédigé sous la direction du centre de gestion du qigong pour la santé relevant de l'administration nationale chinoise de la culture physique et du sport；[translation，Wang Mo]. Beijing：Éditions en Langues Étrangères，2012. 108 pages：illustrations（some color）；23cm. ＋1 DVD-ROM（4 3/4 in.）and 1 CD-ROM（4 3/4 in.）ISBN：7119078854，7119078852，7887185617，7887185610，7887185464，7887185467

《健身气功・大舞》,Wang，Mo 译.

13. Tai Ji Quan style Chen/Wang Xian；trad.［du chinois］par Mo Xuquiang et Jian Liujun. Paris（57－59 Av. du Maine，75014）：Éd. Quimétao，Impr. Laballery，2001. 233 p.：ill.，couv. ill. en coul.；21cm. ISBN：2911858077，2911858079.（Qi gong et arts martiaux）

《陈式太极拳》,Wang，Xi'an（1944—）著；Mo，Xuqiang（1956—）和 Jian，Liujun（1957—）合译.

14. La gymnastique acrobatique en Chine. Beijing：Éditions en Langues Étrangères，1986. 1 volume：illustrations（some color）；21cm.

中国体操.

H 类　语言、文字

H1　汉语

1. Cinq mille ans d'écriture chinoise. Groupe de publication internationale de Chine.；Hanban/Confucius Institute Headquarters. Beijing：Éditions en Langues Érangères；Groupe de publication internationale de Chine，2009. 189 pages：illustrations. ISBN：7119060163；7119060163

《汉字五千年》,《汉字五千年》编委会编著.

2. Les caractères chinois/Han Jiantang；traduit par Luo Shenyi. [Beijing]：China Intercontinental Press，2011. 1 vol.（158 p.）：ill.；23cm. ISBN：7508520346（br）；7508520343,（br）.（Collection culture chinoise）

《中国汉字》,韩鉴堂著.五洲传播出版社.

3. Méthode pour déchiffrer et transcrire les noms sanscrits qui se rencontrent dans les livres chinois，à l'aide de règles，d'exercices et d'un répertoire de onze cents caractères chinois idéographiques employés alphabétiquement，inventée et démontrée par M. Stanislas Julie. Paris：à l'Imp. impériale，1861. Gr. in-8°

（1）Paris：impr. de W. Remquet，1861. In-8°，41 p.

《汉文典籍中梵文名字的识别和标注》,Julien，Stanislas（1799—1873）译.

4. Proverbes chinois/recueillis et mis en ordre par Paul Perny. Paris：Firmin-Didot frères，fils et Cie，1869. 1 vol.（135 p.）

《中国俗语》,Perny，Paul（1818—1907）译.

5. La "Siao hio"，ou Morale de la jeunesse［du philosophe Tchou Hi］，avec le commentaire de Tchen Siuen/traduite du chinois par C. de Harlez. Paris：E. Leroux，1889. 368 p.，cartes

《小学》,朱熹（1130—1200）著；De Harlez，Charles（1832—1899）译.

6. Dictionnaire classique de la langue chinoise suivant l'ordre alphabétique de la prononciation/par F. S. Couvreur，S. J. Sien-Hsien，1930. XII＋1080 p.

《古汉语词典》,Couvreur，Séraphin（1835—1919）释译.

（1）［Taibei］：Kuangchi Press，1993. XII—1080 p.；27cm. ISBN：9575461363（rel.）

（2）3e éd. Ho kien fou：Impr. de la Mission catholique. XII＋1144 p.

7. Sur la langue et l'écriture chinoises/Luxun；présentation，traduction et notes de Michelle Loi. Paris：Aubier Montaigne，1979. 131 p.：couv. ill.；22cm. ISBN：2700701402，2700701401.（Présence et pensée）

《鲁迅对中国语言文字的考察与探讨》,鲁迅（1881—1936）著；Loi，Michelle（1926—2002）译并注释.

H2　古代汉语读物

1. Thsien-tseu-wen/Le Livre des mille mots，le plus ancien livre élémentaire des chinois publié avec une double traduction et des notes par Stanislas Julien. Paris：B. Duprat，1864. In-8°，50—IV—40 p.

《千字文》,Julien，Stanislas（1799—1873）译.

2. Les mille caractères et leurs anecdotes＝千字文：quatre par quatre，premiers pas en chinois /André Dubreuil，Zhu Xiaoya. Paris：Libr. You-Feng，2012. 374 pages：illustrations；22cm. ISBN：2842793340

3. San-tseu-king：le livre de phrases de trois mots en chinois et en français，suivi d'un grand commentaire traduit du chinois et d'un petit dictionnaire chinois-français du San-tseu-king et du Livre des mille mots par Stanislas Julien；deux traductions du San-tseu-king et de son commentaire，réponse à un article de la Revue critique... par le Marquis d'Hervey de Saint-Denys. Genève：H. Georg，1873. 8，iii，147，27 pages

《三字经》,王应麟（1223—1296）著；Julien，Stanislas（1797—1873）等译.

4. Le livre classique des trois caractères：de Wang Peh-heou en chinoise et en francais accompagné de la traduction complète du commentaire de Wáng Tcin-Ching/par G. Pauthier. Paris：Challamel Ainé，1873. xii，148 pages；

25cm.

《三字经》，王应麟（1223—1296）著；Pauthier, Guillaume（1801—1873）译.

5. Tam tu kinh; ou, Le livre des phrases de trois caractères/Avec le grand commentaire de Vuong tân thăng. Texte, transcription annamite et chinoise, explication littérale et traduction complète par Abel des Michels. Paris, E. Leroux, 1882. 1 volume（various pagings）28cm.（Publications de l'École des langues orientales vivantes; 17）

《三字经》，王应麟（1223—1296）著；Des Michels, Abel（1833—1910）译.

6. Le commentaire du San-ze-king: le recueil des phrases de trois mots/Yinglin Wang; F. Turrettini. Version mandchoue/avec notes et variantes par Francois Turrettini. Genève: H. Georg, 1892—1894. vii, 115 pages; 24cm.

《三字经》，王应麟（1223—1296）著；Turrettini, F.（François Auguste, 1845—1908）译.

7. Le classique des trois caractères: trois par trois, premiers pas en chinois/[présenté et traduit par] André Kircher, Zhu Xiaoya. 1st ed. Beijing: Foreign Languages Press, 1995. 4, 305 p.: ill. ISBN: 7119016393, 7119016399

《三字经》，王应麟（1223—1296）著；Kircher, André 和 Zhu, Xiaoya 合译.

I类 文学

I1 文学评论和研究

1. Un grand débat sur le front littéraire/par Tcheou Yang; suivi de: le chemin dégagé, avançons hardiment/par Chao Tsiuan-Lin. Pékin: Éditions en Langues Étrangères, 1959. 84 p.; 18cm.

《文艺战线上的一场大辩论》，周扬著.

2. La Voie de la littérature et de l'art socialistes en Chine. Rapport présenté le 22 juillet 1960 au IIIe congrès des travailleurs des lettres et des arts de Chine. Pékin, Éditions en Langues Étrangères, 1960. 82 p. 16mo

《我国社会主义文学艺术的道路》，周扬著.

3. Levons plus haut le drapeau de la pensée de Mao Tse-Toung sur les lettres et les arts/Lin Mo-Han. Pékin: Éditions en Langues Étrangères, 1961. 43 p

《更高地举起毛泽东文艺思想的旗帜》，林默涵著.

4. Une grande révolution sur le front culturel. Pékin: Éditions en Langues Étrangères, 1965. 118 p.

《文化战线上的一个大革命》

5. Ma plume au service du prolétariat/Haoran; trad. du chinois par Joël Bel Lassen, Marc Kalinowski, Michelle Loi. Lausanne, 7 rue de Genève: A. Eibel, 1976. 113 p.; 18cm. ISBN: 2827400030, 2827400034.（La Chine d'aujourd'hui; 2）

《为无产阶级掌好笔杆:浩然同志谈创作》，浩然著.

Lassen, Joël 等译.

6. Littérature et art/par le Comité de rédaction de la Collection "Connaissance de la Chine." Beijing: Éditions en Langues Étrangères, 1986. 217 p.，[24] p. de pl.: ill

《文学艺术》，《中国概况丛书》编辑委员会编.

7. L'essence de la littérature et la gravure de dragons/texte original de Liu Xie; traduction de Chen Shuyu. Beijing: Éditions en Langues Étrangères, 2010. 238 p.; 23cm. ISBN: 7119042879; 7119042874（Chinese classics）

《文心雕龙》，刘勰著.

I11 各体文学评论和研究

I111 诗歌评论

1. Airs de Touen-Houang:（Touen-Houang k'iu）, textes à chanter des VIIIe-Xe siècles, manuscrits reproduits en fac-similé/Avec une introduction en chinois par Jao Tsong-Yi,… Adaptée en français avec la traduction de quelques textes d'airs par Paul Demiéville. Paris: Éditions du Centre national de la recherche scientifique, 1971. 1 vol.（367 p.）: fac sim.; 33cm.（Mission Paul Pelliot, documents conservés à la Bibliothèque nationale; 2）

《敦煌曲》，饶宗颐著；Demiéville, Paul（1894—1979）译.

2. Qu Yuan et le Li Sao/Qu Yuan; par Huang Shengfa. Beijing: Éditions en Langues Étrangères, 1985. 161 p.; 21cm.

《屈原及其离骚》，黄盛发编. 是作者的博士论文.

3. Cinq essais de poétique/Qian Zhongshu; présentés et traduits du chinois par Nicolas Chapuis. Paris: Christian Bourgois, 1987. 222 p.; 20cm. ISBN: 2267004852, 2267004854

钱钟书诗评五篇. 钱钟书著；Chapuis, Nicolas 译.

4. 《世界最长史诗〈格萨尔王传〉:中国藏族传统文化宝典介绍》，吴伟著. 北京:五洲传播出版社，1997. ISBN: 7801132025.（西藏丛书）

5. Poésies modernes, traduites pour la première fois du chinois, accompagnées du texte original, et d'un commentaire qui en explique les principales difficultés/par C. Imbault-Huart. Péking, Typographie du Pei-t'ang; Paris, E. Leroux, 1892. viii, 166 pages, 1 leaf 25cm.

《随园诗话》，袁枚（1716－1798 年）；Imbault-Huart, Camille 编译.

6. Divers plaisirs à la villa Sui/poèmes traduits du chinois par Cheng Wing fun et Hervé Collet; calligraphie de Cheng Wing fun. Millemont: Moundarren, 2000. 153 p.: carte; 21cm. ISBN: 2907312391, 2907312394

《随园诗话》，袁枚（1716－1798 年）；Cheng, Wingfun 和 Collet, Hervé（1951—）合译.

I12 文学史

1. Histoire de la littérature chinoise: prose/G. Margouliès.

Paris：Payot，1949．1 vol.（VIII-336 p.）；23cm.（Bibliothèque historique）

《中国文学史：散文》，Margouliès，Georges(1902—1972)译.

2. Brève histoire du roman chinois/par Luxun [Lou Siun]；trad. du chinois par Charles Bisotto．[Paris]：Gallimard，1993. 381 p.：couv. ill. en coul.；19cm. ISBN：a070727335.（Connaissance de l'Orient：série chinoise；62）

《中国小说史略》，鲁迅(1881—1936)著；Bisotto，Charles 译.

3. Littérature Chinoise/Yao Dan；traduction de Fang Youzhong et al. Beijing：China Intercontiental Press，2011. 262 pages：illustrations（some color）；23cm. ISBN：7508519487，7508519485.（Collection culture chinoise）

《中国文学》，姚丹[等]著.五洲传播出版社.

I2　作品集

I21　作品综合集

1. Lao-Seng-Eul [Texte imprimé]，comédie chinoise；suivie de San-Iu-Leou，ou Les trois étages consacrés，conte moral.../traduits du chinois en anglais par J.-F. Davis，... et de l'anglais en français... par A. Bruguière de Sorsum. Paris：Rey et Gravier；Londres：A. B. Dulau et Cie，1819. X—164 p.

《老生儿·三与楼》，Davis，John Francis（1795—1890）和 Bruguière，Antoine-André(1773—1823)合译. 包括元代戏剧《老生儿》与清代李渔的小说集《十二楼》中的一篇《三与楼》

2. Les Chinois peints par eux-mêmes/par le général Tcheng-Ki-Tong. Paris：Calmann Lévy，1886—1889. 2 vol. ［1.］ Le théatre des Chinois（XII-324 p.）；［2.］ Contes chinois（VIII-340 p.）

《中国人自画像》，陈季同(1851—1907)著.本书包含对中国戏剧和中国短篇小说的选译.

3. La Chine pacifique，d'après ses écrivains anciens et modernes，morceaux choisis et traduits par Tsen Tsonming，... Préface de M. Herriot. Lyon：J. Desvigne；Paris：E. Leroux，1924. 107 p.

《太平中国》，曾仲鸣译.本书包含对中国古代和现代文学作品的选译.

4. Anthologie de la littérature chinoise：des origines à nos jours：la poésie，le roman，le théatre，la philosophie，l'histoire/par Sung-Nien Hsu. Paris：Delagrave，1933. 1 vol.（445 p.）；17cm.（Collection Pallas）

从古至今中国文学汇编. 徐仲年著.本书包含对中国文学：诗歌、小说、戏剧、哲学、历史的选译.

5. La littérature chinoise：six conférences au Collège de France et au musée Guimet：novembre 1926/par Basile Alexeiev. Paris：P. Geuthner，1937：Paris：P. Geuthner，1937.（Annales du musée Guimet. Bibliothèque de vulgarisation；52）

中国文学. Alexeiev，Basile 著.本书包含对中国文学的选译.

6. La Sagesse chinoise，textes choisis et traduits du chinois par Chou Ling. Paris，la Jeune Parque（impr. de Grou-Radenez），1947. In—12，46—VII p.，pl. en coul.

中国智慧. Chou，Ling 编译.本书包含对中国文学的选译.

7. Anthologie raisonnée de la littérature chinoise/G. Margouliès. Paris：Payot，1948. 1 vol.（458 p.）；23cm.（Bibliothèque scientifique）

中国文学选集，Margouliès，Georges（1902—1972）著.本书包含对中国文学的选译.

I22　个人作品集

1. Sur moi-mème/Su Dongpo；traduit du chinois et présenté par Jacques Pimpaneau. Arles：P. Picquier，2003. 196 p. ISBN：287730633X，2877306331.（Picquier poche；183）

苏轼诗文. Pimpaneau，Jacques 译.

(1)Arles：Éditions Philippe Picquier，2017. 1 vol.（196 p.）；17cm. ISBN：2809712407，2809712409.（Picquier poche）

2. Commémorations ＝ Dong po ji/Su Shi；texte établi，traduit et annoté par Stéphane Feuillas. Paris：Les Belles lettres，2010. cxxix，303 p.，pagination double p. 2—286：cartes；20cm. ISBN：2251100043，2251100040.（Bibliothèque chinoise；4）

《东坡集》，苏轼著；Feuillas，Stéphane 译.

3. Galerie des femmes vertueuses de la Chine/trad.［du chinois］par S. T. Wang. Pékin：La Politique de Pékin，1924. 118 p.：ill.，couv. ill.；22cm.（Collection de la Politique de Pékin）

《息园集》，(明)顾麟著；Wang，S. T. 译.

4. Un Combattant comme ça：choix de poèmes et essais/Luxun；présentés par Michelle Loi；［traduits du chinois par Michelle Loi et Martine Vallette-Hémery］. Paris：Éditions du Centenaire，1973. 185 p.：portr.，couv. ill.；19cm.

《这样的战士·鲁迅诗歌、杂文选》，鲁迅（1881—1936）著；Loi，Michelle，（1926—2002）和 Vallette-Hémery，Martine 合译.

5. Fonctions d'un classique Luxun dans la Chine contemporaine，1975—1977/［préparé（choix des textes，traduction du chinois，présentation et notes）par François Jullien］. Lausanne：A. Eibel，1978. 194 pages；18cm. ISBN：2827400332，2827400331.（Cahiers Luxun；1）

鲁迅文选与评述. Jullien，Françoise (1951—)译.

6. Œuvres choisies/Lu Xun. Beijing，Chine：Éd. en Langues Étrangères，1981—1986. 4 vol.（474，420，389，349 p.）：ill.；22cm. ISBN：7119012274

Contents：[I]，Nouvelles，poèmes en prose et souvenirs [II]，Essais 1918—1927．[III]，Essais 1928—1933.

[IV], Essais 1934—1936.

《鲁迅文选》,4 卷. 卷一:小说、散文、散文诗;卷二:杂文,1918—1927 年;卷三:杂文,1928—1933 年;卷四:杂文,1934 年—1936 年.

7. Nouvelles et poèmes en prose/Lu Xun; traduction, annotation et postface de Sebastian Veg. Paris: Éditions Rue d'Ulm, DL 2015. 1 vol. (663 p.): ill.; 18cm. ISBN: 2728805143. (Collection Versions françaises, ISSN 1627—4040)

《鲁迅短篇小说和散文诗》,鲁迅,(1881—1936)著;Veg, Sebastian 译.

8. Le récif: poèmes et fables/Ai Qing. Ng Yok-Soon. Paris: Les cent fleurs, 1987. 92 pages: illustrations; 20cm. ISBN: 2906719005, 2906719002

艾青著;黄育顺(Ng, Yok-Soon, 1939—)译. 本书包含对艾青诗歌和寓言的选译.

9. Contes et libelles/Wang Meng; textes choisis, présentés et traduits du chinois par Françoise Naour. [S. l.]: Bleu de Chine, 1994. 139 p.; 21cm. ISBN: 2910884007, 2910884000

Contents: Clefs pour Wang Meng—Ma-le-sixième—Dialectique—Paroles, parlottes, parlerie—Poétique—Nec plus ultra—Celle qui dansait—J'ai tant rêvé de toi—Vieille cour du dedans, si profonde—Dur, dure le brouet

王蒙短篇小说和小品文选译. Naour, Françoise 编译.

(1)[Paris]: Gallimard, 2012. 1 vol. (188 p.): couv. ill. en coul.; 18cm. ISBN: 2070448494, 2070448495. (Collection Folio; 5509)

10. Vagabond de nuit/Zhou Yunpeng; traduit du chinois par Brigitte Guilbaud. Arles: Éditions Philippe Picquier, DL 2015. 1 vol. (138 p.); 21cm. ISBN: 2809710977, 280971097X

《自选集》,周云蓬(1970—)著;Guilbaud, Brigitte (1969—)译.

I3 诗歌、韵文

I31 古代和跨时代诗词集

I311 诗经

1. Hymnes sanscrits, persans, égyptiens, assyriens et chinois: Chi-king, ou, Livre des vers/traduit pour la première fois en français par G. Pauthier. Paris: Maisonneuve et cie. ,1872. [4], 423, [2] pages; 27cm. (Chefs d'oeuvre littéraires de l'Inde, de la Perse, de l'Egypte et de la Chine; v. 2)

《诗经》,Pauthier, G. (1801—1873)译.

2. Cheu King: texte chinois avec traduction/par F. S. Couvreur. Hien Hien Imprimerie de la Mission catholique, 1916. xxxii, 409 pages

《诗经》,Couvreur, Séraphin 译.

(1)2. éd. Sien Hien, Imprimerie de la Mission catholique, 1926. 2 preliminary leaves, xxxii, 555 pages; illustrations, 2 folded maps; 26cm.

(2) 3. éd. Sien Hien: Imprimerie de la Mission Catholique, 1934. xxxii, 555 pages: illustrations; 26cm.

(3) 4. éd. Sien Hsien: Imprimerie de la Mission Catholique, 1935. [6], 464, [2] pages; 26cm.

(4)4e éd. Taichung: Kuangchi Press, 1967. [57], xxxii, 556 pages: illustrations; 23cm.

(5)[Reprod. de la] 4ème éd. Taibei: Kuangchi Press, 1992. 556 p.; 22cm. ISBN: 957546074X, 9575460747

(6)台北: 光启文化, 民 93[2004]. 556 p.; 22cm. ISBN: 9575465008, 9575465001

3. Le Livre des poèmes/trad. du chinois par Dominique Hoizey. Reims (18, rue Marlot, 51100): Albédo, 1986. 50 p.: ill., couv. ill.; 22cm.

《诗经》,Hoizey, Dominique 译.

4. Poèmes choisis et illustrés du livre de la poésie = [Jing xuan Shi jing yu shi yi hua/Xu Yuanchong yi shi. Beijing: China Intercontinental Press, 2008. 127 pages: illustrations; 23cm. ISBN: 7508512075, 7508512073. (Zhongguo chuan tong wen hua jing cui shu xi =; Collection de classiques chinois)

《精选诗经与诗意画:法汉对照》,许渊冲译.

5. Le livre des poèmes/[publ. par Jin Qihua]; trad. du chinois et présenté par Dominique Hoizey. Paris: E. L. A. la Différence, 1994. 124 pages; 17cm. ISBN: 2729109501, 2729109509. (Collection "Orphée"; 173)

《诗经》,金启华译注;Hoizey, Dominique 法译.

I312 其他古代和跨时代诗歌集

1. La poésie chinoise du XIVe au XIXe siècle: extraits des poètes chinois traduits pour la première fois, accompagnés de notes littéraires, philologiques, historiques, et de notices biographiques/par C. Imbault-Huart. Paris, E. Leroux, 1886. 2 preliminary leaves, xxxiii, 93 pages; 17cm. (Bibliothèque orientale elzévirienne.; XLVI)

14 至 19 世纪中国诗歌选. Imbault-Huart, Camille 选译.

2. Le livre de jade; poésies traduites du chinois. /par Judith Gautier. Nouv. éd. considérablement augm. et ornée de vignettes et de gravures hors texte d'après les artistes chinois. Paris, F. Juven, 1902. xxi, 279 pages: illustrations, facsimiles; 25cm.

玉之书. Gautier, Judith(1845—1917)译. 本书包含对中国诗歌的选译.

(1)Paris, Jules Tallandier, 1928. 263 pages. (Les belles Œuvres littéraires)

(2)[Nouv. éd.]. Paris, 1928. IV, 267 p.; 20cm. (Les belles Œuvres littéraires)

（3）Paris：Librairie Plon，1933. 263 pages，［7］leaves of plates：illustrations；20cm.（Les beaux textes illustrés；Éditions d'histoire et d'art）

（4）［choisi et traduit du chinois par］Judith Gautier；présentation，notices et bibliographie Yvan Daniel. Paris：Imprimerie nationale，2004. 226 pages；22cm. ISBN：2743305215，2743305215，2743305207，2743305208.（La salamandre）

3. Album de poèmes tirés du Livre de jade/Judith Gautier de l'Académie Goncourt. Hammersmith，London：Eragny Press，1911. 27 pages（on double leaves）：color illustrations；20cm.

中国古诗选. Gautier，Judith(1845—1917)著. 本书包含对中国古诗的选译.

4. La flûte de jade：poésies chinoises/［éditées par］Franz Toussaint. 8. éd. Paris：H. Piazza，1920. 201 pages，［1］leaf of plates：color illustrations；16cm.（Ex oriente lux.）

失笛记：中国诗歌集. Ts'ao，Shang-ling 译；Toussaint，Franz(1879—1955)编.

（1）16e éd. Paris：Éd. d'art H. Piazza，1920. 159 p. ：ill. ；16 p

（2）30e. éd. Paris：H. Piazza，1922. 159 pages：1 color illustrations；16cm.

（3）［41ème éd.］. Paris：L'édition d'art，1922. 159 pages：illustrations

（4）48e éd. Paris：Piazza，1926. 138 S：frontisp. en coul；17cm.（Ex oriente lux）

（5）76e éd. Paris：Éditions d'Art H. Piazza，1933. 138 pages，［1］leaf of plates：illustrations（some color）；16cm. Ex oriente lux（Paris，France）

（6）L'édition d'art. Paris：H. Piazza，1947. 138 pages，［1］leaf of plates：color illustrations；16cm.（Ex oriente lux）

（7）Paris：H. Piazza，1958. 140 pages：color illustrations；16cm.

（8）129 a. éd. París：D'art h. ，1958. 140 p. ：il. ；19cm.

（9）St. Gallen：Erker-Verlag，1970. 80 pages（on double leaves）：illustrations；21×24cm.

5. Les concubines chinoises célèbres：Pan Tsié-yu et Tchao-kiun. /Chansons traduites par H. Imbert. Pékin，"Politique de Pékin，"，1921. 16 pages（on double leaves）illustrations 28 × 16cm.（Collection de la "Politique de Pékin"）

中国古代著名妃子. Imbert，Henri 译. 本书包含对中国古诗的选译. 收录班婕妤（公元前 48 年—公元 2 年）等人的诗词.

6. Anciens poèmes chinois d'auteurs inconnus［Texte imprimé］/traduits par Tsen Tsomming. Lyon：J. Desvigne，1923. 77 p.

中国无名氏古诗选译. 曾仲鸣译.

（1）Nouvelle édition revue et augmentée. Lyon：Joannès Desvigne et Cie；Paris：ditions Ernest Leroux，1927. 120 p.

7. Anthologie de l'amour chinois：poèmes de lasciveté parfumée/traduits du chinois par George Soulié de Morant. 3. éd. Paris：Mercure de France，1932. XX-249 p.

中国爱情诗选. Soulié de Morant，George (1878—1955)译.

8. Une flute au loin；poèmes/Eléonore Niquille. La Chaux-de-Fonds，Éditions des Nouveaux cahiers，1942. 108 pages；19cm.

远方的笛声. Niquille，Eléonore 著. 本书包含对中国诗歌的选译.

9. Choix de poésies chinoises/traduites en français avec une introduction et des notes par L. Laloy. Paris，Sorlot，1944. 63 pages；18cm.（Les chefs-d'oeuvre）

中国诗选. Laloy，Louis(1874—1944)译.

10. Poésies chinoises/traduites en français avec une introduction et des notes par Louis Laloy.（Fribourg en S. ，）：Egloff；（Genève：impr. de A. Kundig），1944. 105 p.

中国诗歌. Laloy，Louis(1874—1944)译.

11. Homme d'abord poète ensuite：présentation de sept poètes chinois. avec sept portraits anciens/Lo Ta-kang. Neuchatel：La Baconnière，1949. 281 pages，mounted plates：illustrations；22cm.

《首先是人，然后是诗人》，罗大纲著. 本书包含对中国诗歌的选译.

12. La poésie chinoise/Patricia Guillermaz. ［Paris］：Éditions Seghers，1957. 289 pages：illustrations；22cm.

《中国诗歌》，Guillermaz，Patricia 编译. 本书包含对中国诗歌的选译.

（1）La poésie chinoise；［anthologie des origines à nos jours/Patricia Guillermaz，ed. and tr. ［Paris］Éditions Seghers，1960. 289 pages：illustrations；22cm.（［Collection Melior，；4]）

（2）La poésie chinoise，des origines à la révolution/Patricia Guillermaz. Verviers，Gérard et Cie；Paris，l'Inter，1966. 248 pages plates（some color）18cm.（Marabout universite，；118）

（3）Paris：Marabout，1966. 248 pages：illustrations

13. Poèmes et paysages chinois/［choisis par Michelle Loi］. Paris：S. E. V. P. E. N. ，Mars 1961. Non paginé：pl. ，；27cm.（Textes et documents pour les enseignements du 2nd degré；5）

中国诗歌与风景. Loi，Michelle(1926—2002)著. 本书包含了对中国诗歌的选译.

14. Poètes du peuple chinois/Anthologie établie，traduite et présentée par Michelle Loi. Honfleur，P. J. Oswald，1969. 125 pages；18cm.（La Poésie des pays socialistes；5）

Loi，Michelle 译. 本书包含对中国诗歌的选译.

（1）［Paris］：Éditions Hallier，1969. 176 pages；22cm.

（2）Poètes du peuple chinois：anthologie/［textes choisis，traduits et présentés par］Michelle Loi. Paris：Hallier：P. J. Oswald，1976. 176 pages；22cm. ISBN：2857850093，2857850090.（Collection L'Exemplaire）

15. Anthologie de la poésie chinoise classique/sous la direction de Paul Demiéville. ［Traduit du chinois. Paris］Gallimard，1962. 571 pages；23cm.（Connaissance de l'Orient；collection UNESCO d'œuvres représentatives. Série chinoise；16）

《中国古典诗选》，Demiéville，Paul 译.

（1）Paris］Gallimard，1969，（c）1962. 571 pages；23cm.（Connaissance de l'Orient；collection UNESCO d'œuvres représentatives. Série chinoise；16）

（2）［Paris］：Gallimard，1982. 618 pages；18cm. ISBN：207032219X，2070322190.（Collection UNESCO d'Œuvres représentatives. Série chinoise；Collection poésie；156）

（3）［Paris］：Gallimard，1992. 613 p.；18cm. ISBN：207032219X，2070322190.（Collection UNESCO d'Œuvres représentatives. Série chinoise；Collection Poésie

（4）［Paris］：Gallimard，2001. 613 pages；18cm. ISBN：207032219X，2070322190

16. Les dix-neuf poèmes anciens/par Jean-Pierre Diény. Paris：Presses Universitaires de France，1963. 194 pages；22cm.（Bulletin de la Maison franco-japonaise；nouv. sér.，t. 7，no 4）

《古诗十九首》，Diény，Jean-Pierre 著. 本书包含对中国古诗的选译.

（1）Paris：Université Paris VII，Centre de publication Asie orientale，1974. 194 pages；21cm.

（2）Paris：Les belles lettres，2010. xxxviii，132 pages；20cm. ISBN：2251100036，a251100032.（Bibliothèque chinoise；3）

17. Trésor de la poésie chinoise/Présentation et traduction de Claude Roy. ［Paris］le Club français du livre，1967. 217 pages plates 21cm.（Club français du livre. Poésie；v. 26）

中国诗歌宝藏. Roy，Claude（1915—1997）译. 本书包含对中国诗歌的选译.

18. Le voleur de poèmes：Chine/Claude Roy. Paris：Mercure de France，1991. 435 pages；illustrations；21cm. ISBN：2715216149，2715216143

中国诗歌. Roy，Claude（1915—1997）著. 本书包含对中国诗歌的选译.

19. Sagesse et poésies chinoises/par Hu Pin Ching，M. -T. Lambert et Pierre Seghers. 1ère éd. Paris：R. Laffont，1981. 125 pages；illustrations（some color）；19cm. ISBN：2221502752，2221502754.（Miroir du monde；v. 3）

胡品清等著. 本书包含对中国诗歌的选译.

20. La poésie chinoise ancienne/compilée et traduite par Patricia Pin-ching Hu. Taipei：Central Book，1992. 280 pages；21cm.

《中国古诗选》，胡品清译.

21. Poèmes & art en Chine：les "non-officiels."/Julien Blaine. ［Paris］：［J. Blaine］，1982. 384 pages：illustrations；22cm.（DOC（k）S，；no 41，hiver 81/82）

Blaine，Julien 著. 本书包含对非正式出版的中国诗歌的选译.

22. La Montagne vide：anthologie de la poésie chinoise：（IIIe-XIe siècle）/traduction，notes et présentation de Patrick Carré et Zéno Bianu. Paris：Albin Michel，1987. 156 p.；18cm. ISBN：222602879X，2226028792.（Spiritualités vivantes；63. Série Taoïsme et bouddhisme）

中国诗歌选集. Carré，Patrick 和 Bianu，Zéno 合译.

23. Pouvoir de la mélancolie：chamans，poètes et souverains dans la Chine antique/Lisa Bresner. Paris：Albin Michel，1990. 266 p.；23cm. ISBN：2226142444，2226142443.（Bibliothèque Albin Michel des idées）

悲情的力量. Bresner，Lisa（1971—）著. 本书包含对中国古代诗歌的选译.

24. Entre source et nuage：la poésie chinoise réinventée/François Cheng. Paris：Albin Michel，1990. 261 pages；23cm. ISBN：2226048111，2226048110

Cheng，François（1929—）著. 本书包含对中国诗歌的选译.

25. Poésie chinoise/［traductions de］François Cheng；calligraphies de Fabienne Verdier. Paris：Albin Michel，2000. 1 volume（unpaged）：color illustrations；23cm. ISBN：2226112375，2226112378.（Les carnets du calligraphe）

中国诗歌. Cheng，François（1929—）译. 本书包含对中国诗歌的选译.

26. Les Yeux du dragon：une anthologie de la poésie chinoise/trad.，présentation et notes de Daniel Giraud；calligraphie de Long Gue；illustration de Claude Astrachan. L'Isle-sur-la-Sorgue（France）：Le Bois d'Orion，1993. 187 p.：ill.；21cm.

中国诗歌选集. Giraud，Daniel（1946—）编译.

27. Le livre des poèmes/［publ. par Jin Qihua］；trad. du chinois et présenté par Dominique Hoizey. Paris：E. L. A. la Différence，1994. 124 pages；17cm. ISBN：2729109501，2729109509.（Collection "Orphée"；173）

Jin，Qihua 著；Hoizey，Dominique 译. 本书包含对中国诗歌的选译.

28. Éloge de la poésie et des livres：poèmes/traduits du chinois par Cheng Wing fun & Hervé Collet；calligraphie de Cheng Wing fun. Millemont（France，Yvelines）：Moundarren，1996. 146 p.；21cm. ISBN：

2907312286，2907312288
Cheng，Wing fun 和 Collet，Hervé 合译. 本书包含对中国诗歌的选译.

29. L'eau d'un puit ancien：anthologie de poèmes de paysage en Chine（bilingue）/traduction et annotations He Qing. Paris：Éditions You-Feng，1996. 87 p.；22cm. ISBN：2842790073，2842790073
《古井之水：中国风景诗选》，黄源（1905—2003）著；何清（1940—）译.

30. Cent poèmes d'amour de la Chine ancienne/traduits du chinois et présentés par André Lévy. Arles：P. Picquier，1997. 160 p.：ill.；20cm. ISBN：287730311X，2877303118. （Pavillon des corps curieux）
中国古代爱情诗百首. Lévy，André（1925—）译.

31. A celui qui voyageait loin：poèmes d'amour de femmes chinoises（VIIe-XVIe siècle）/Shi BO. Paris：Éditions alternatives，2000. 79 p.：ill.；19cm. ISBN：2862272493，2862272498. （Collection Pollen）
7—16 世纪中国女性爱情诗选. 时波（1941—）著. 本书包含对中国诗歌的选译.

32. Voyage au pays de Shu：Anthologie. ［Suivi de］voyage au pays de Shu，journal 1170—1998/Michèle Métail. Saint-Benoît-du-Sault：Tarabuste，2004. 115，157 pages. ISBN：2845870639，2845870635. （Doutebat）
蜀国行. Métail，Michèle 著. 本书包含对中国诗歌的选译.

33. Femmes poètes de la Chine：traduction，annotations et calligraphies de Shi Bo：anthologie/Shi Bo. ［Pantin，France］：Temps des cerises；［Trois-Rivières，Québec］：Écrits des Forges，2004. 217 p.：ill.；17cm. ISBN：2890468461，2890468467，2841094790，2841094790
中国女诗人. 时波译. 本书包含对中国女诗人作品的选译.

34. ALIBIs：dialogues littéraires franco-chinois/［Maison des Sciences de l'Homme］. Textes réunis et présentés par Annie Curien. Paris：Éd. de la Maison des Sciences de l'Homme，2004. XVIII，135 S. ISBN：273511029X，2735110292
中法文学对话. Curien，Annie 编译. 本书包含对中国诗歌的选译.

35. Les formes du vent：paysages chinois en prose/traduits par Martine Vallette-Hemery. ［Paris］：Albin Michel，2007. 180 pages；18cm. ISBN：2226178312，2226178317. （Spiritualites vivantes；229）
风的形状：散文诗中的中国风景. Vallette-Hemery，Martine 译. 本书包含对中国诗歌的选译.

36. Anthologie bilingue de la poésie chinoise classique/［édité et traduit du chinois par］Maurice Coyaud. 2e tirage，éd. bilingue. Paris：Les Belles lettres，2009. 345 p.：ill.；22 × 15cm. ISBN：2251490229，2251490221. （Architecture du verbe；7）
Coyaud，Maurice 译. 本书包含对中国古典诗歌的选译.

37. Nuages immobiles：les plus beaux poèmes des seize dynasties chinoises/textes rassemblés et traduits par Alexis Lavis；［illustrations］Shan Sa. Paris：Archipel，2009. 92 pages. ISBN：2809801620，2809801622
Lavis，Alexis 译；山飒配图. 本书包含对中国十六个朝代最美诗歌的选译.

38. Anthologie des poèmes Chinois classiques /许渊冲译. Xu Yuanchong yi. Beijing：Hai tun chu ban she，2013. 41，561 pages，2 unnumbered pages of plates：illustrations（some color）；22cm. ISBN：7511014252，7511014259. （许渊冲文集；15）
《中国古诗选集》，许渊冲（1921—）译.

39. Anthologie de la poésie chinoise/publiée sous la direction de Rémi Mathieu；［textes traduits，présentés et annotés par Rémi Mathieu，François Martin，Florence Hu-Sterk et al.］. ［Paris］：Gallimard，2015，（c）2015. 1 vol.（LII—1547 p.）：ill.，cartes.；18cm. ISBN：2070143764，2070143767. （Bibliothèque de la Pléiade，；602）
中国诗歌选集. Mathieu，Rémi（1948—）译.

40. Poèmes du Zen des Cinq-Montagnes/traduits du chinois et commentés par Alain-Louis Colas. Paris：Maisonneuve & Larose，1991. 428 pages；24cm. ISBN：2706810297，2706810299. （Bibliothèque de l'Institut des hautes études japonaises）
中国佛教诗歌. Colas，Alain-Louis 译.

41. Flanant sous le ciel：ballade autour d'une quarantaine de poèmes chinois du Tao et du Ch'an/［édité par］Daniel Giraud；traduction，Daniel Giraud；graphie chinoise，Patrick Carré. Paris：Blockhaus，1994. 89 pages；19cm.
Giraud，Daniel 编译. 本书包含对四十首道教诗和禅诗的选译.

42. Poèmes chan/traduction de Jacques Pimpaneau. Arles Cedex，France：Éditions Philippe Picquier，2005. 91 pages；23cm. ISBN：2877308081，2877308083
Pimpaneau，Jacques 译. 本书包含对中国禅诗的选译.

43. Le Paon，ancien poème chinois，traduit par Tchang Fong，... suivi d'une étude de l'évolution poétique en Chine. Paris：Jouve，1924. 45 p.，couv. ill.
《孔雀东南飞》，张凤译.

44. Le "Fou" dans le Wen-Sinan，étude et textes，par Georges Margouliès. Paris：P. Geuthner，1926. 138 p.
《文选：赋》，萧统编著；Margouliès，Georges（1902—1972）译.

45. Poèmes à chanter：des époques Tang et Song/trad. ［et préf.］ de Yun Shi；adapt. de Jacques Chatain. Seyssel：Éditions Comp'act，1986. 163 pages；17cm.
唐诗宋词. Yun，Shi 和 Chatain，Jacques 合译. 本书包含了对唐诗宋词的选译.

46. Saisons：poèmes des dynasties Tang et Song/traduits du chinois par Shi Bo；calligraphies，Shi Bo. 4e éd. Paris：Éditions Alternatives，1998. 126 pages；31cm. ISBN：2862271640，2862271644

唐诗宋词.时波译.本书包含了对唐诗和宋词的选译.

I313 唐诗集

1. L'anthologie de trois cents poèmes de la dynastie des Tang/traduit par Georgette Jaeger. [Beijing]：Société des Éditions culturelles internationales，1987. vi，247 p

《唐诗三百首》，Jaeger，Georgette（1920—）译. 国际文化出版公司.

2. Tang shi san bai hou/Hu pin qing. Beijing：Beijing ta xue chu ban she，2006. 2，365p；23cm. ISBN：7301103034，7301103036

《唐诗三百首：法汉对照》，胡品清译. 北京大学出版社.

3. Poésies de l'époque des Thang (VIIe，VIIIe et IXe siècles de notre ère)/ traduites du chinois pour la première fois avec une étude sur l'art poétique en Chine et des notes explicatives. Paris，Amyot，1862. cxii，301 p. 23cm.

7、8、9 世纪唐诗. Hervey de Saint-Denys，Le'on，marquis d'(1822—1892)译.

4. Rêve d'une nuit d'hiver (cent quatrains des Thang)/trad. par Tseng-Tchong-Ming. Lyon：Joannès Desvigne et Cie，éditeurs；Paris：Édition Ernest Leroux，1927. 120 p.

《冬夜的梦：唐人绝句百首》，曾仲鸣译.

5. Tablettes de fleur de Sapin/Florence Ayscough；traduction française de Maurice Thiery；l'adaptation anglaise a été faite par Amy Lowell. Paris：Éditions Pierre Roger，1928. 166 pages；20cm.

《松花笺》，Ayscough，Florence Wheelock（1878—1942）著；Thiery，Maurice 法译；本书包含了对唐诗的选译.

6. Cent quatrains des Tàng/traduits du chinois par Lo Ta-kang. Préface de Stanislas Fumet. Avec dix reproductions de peinture ancienne du Palais impérial de Pékin et en fac-similé une lettre de Louis Laloy. 2. éd. Paris，O. Zeluck，1947. 236 pages including facsimile 10 plates 21cm.

《唐诗百首》，罗大纲译.

7. Poésies de l'époque des Thang：précédé de L'art poétique et la prosodie chez les Chinois/par le Marquis d'Hervey-Saint-Denys. Paris：Champ Libre，1977. 359 pages；23cm. ISBN：2851840711，2851840714

唐诗. Hervey de Saint-Denys，Le'on，marquis d'(1822—1892)著. 本书包含对唐诗的选译.

8. L'écriture poétique chinoise：suivi d'une anthologie des poèmes des T'ang/François Cheng. Paris：Seuil，1977. 262，[7] pages，[4] leaves of plates：illustrations；21cm. ISBN：2020045346，2020045346

中国诗歌：附唐诗选集. Cheng，François（1929—）著.

（1）Éd. rév. en 1982. Paris：Seuil，Impr. Aubin，1982.

262 p.： couv. ill. en coul.； 21cm. ISBN：2020045346，2020045346

（2）Nouvelle éd. Paris：Seuil，1996. 284，[1] p.；18cm. ISBN：2020299283，2020299282. （Points. Essais；332）

9. Poètes bouddhistes des Tang/traduit du chinois，présenté et annoté par Paul Jacob. [Paris]：Gallimard，1987. 105 pages；23cm. ISBN：2070710920，2070710928. (Connaissance de l'Orient；64)

唐朝的佛教诗歌. Jacob，Paul（1950—）译.

10. Poèmes du pays simple：la Chine au VIIIe siècle/Werner Lambersy. Tournai：Renaissance du livre，2002. 86 pages；illustrations；19cm. ISBN：2804605159，2804605155. (Paroles d'aube. Conférences des "Midis de la poésie")

8 世纪中国诗歌. Lambersy，Werner 著. 本书包含了对唐诗的选译.

11. 19 poèmes de la dynastie Tang traduits du chinois/par Sydney Fung；en hommage à François Cheng. Hong Kong：Lammar Offset Printing Ltd.，2007. 44 pages：color illustrations；22cm. ISBN：9628687522，9628687527

唐诗十九首. Fung，Sydney S. K. 译.

12. Ying fa shuang yi tang shi 100 shou. Beijing：Zhong guo dui wai fan yi chu ban gong si，2011. 14，200 p.；21cm. ISBN：7500127543，7500127545. (Zhong yi jing dian wen ku. zhong hua chuan tong wen hua jing cui)

《英法双译唐诗 100 首：汉英法对照》，谢百魁选译. 中国对外翻译出版公司.

13. Choix de poèmes des Tang＝Tang shi xüan/traduction de Xu Yuanchong. Première édition. Beijing：Éditions Intercontinentales，2014. 353 pages；25cm. ISBN：7508527789，750852778X. (Bibliothèque des Classiques chinois)

《唐诗选》，许渊冲（1921—）译.

I314 宋朝诗词集

1. Florilège des Poèmes Song. 960—1277 après J.-C. Traduit du chinois，par Georges Soulié de Morant. Paris：impr.-libr.-éditeurs Plon Nourrit et Cie，8，rue Garancière，1923. (28 août.). IX-239 p. (Collection d'auteurs étrangers，publiée sous la direction de Charles Du Bos)

宋诗选集. Soulié de Morant，George（1878—1955）译.

I32 古代诗人个人作品

I321 春秋战国时期

屈原

1. 离骚＝Le li-sao：poème du IIIe siècle avant notre ère/Li sao＝Le li-sao：poème du IIIe siècle avant notre ère/traduit du Chinois，accompagnée d'un commentaire

perpétuel et publié avec le texte original par le marquis D'Hervey de Saint-Denis. traduit du Chinois, accompagnée d'un commentaire perpétuel et publié avec le texte original par le marquis D'Hervey de Saint-Denis. Paris：Maisonneuve et cie, 1870. liii，66，26 pages；22cm.

《离骚》，Hervey de Saint-Denys, Léon d'（1822—1892）译.

2. Douleur de l'éloignement＝Li sao/Qu Yuan；traduction de Yun Shi；adaptation de；calligraphie de Sheng Jixuan；encres d'Henri Jaboulay.［S. l.］：Éditions Comp'act, 1990. 49，［25］p.：ill.；21cm. ISBN：2876610485, 2876610484.（Collection Morari）

《离骚》，Shi, Yun 和 Chatain, Jacques 合译.

3. Elégies de Chu＝Chu ci/attribuées à Qu Yuan, Song Yu et autres poètes chinois de l'antiquité, IVe siècle av. J.-C.-IIe siècle apr. J.-C.；traduites, présentées et annotées par Rémi Mathieu.［Paris, France］：Gallimard, 2004. 304 pages：illustrations（some color）；23cm. ISBN：2070770923, 2070770922.（Connaissance de l'Orient；111；Série chinoise）

《楚辞》，Mathieu, Rémi 译.

I322　三国、晋时期

嵇康（224—263）

1. La Vie et la pensée de Hi K'ang（223—262 ap. J.-C.），par Donald Holzman. Leiden：E. J. Brill, 1957.（24cm.），187 p.

《嵇康的生平与思想》，Holzman, Donald 著. 本书第二部分包含对嵇康作品的选译.

苏慧（357—?）

1. La carte de la sphère armillaire de Su Hui：un poème chinois à "lecture retournée" du IVe siècle/Michèle Métail, commentaire et traduction.［Courbevoie］：Théâtre typographique, 1998. 40 p.：ill.；28cm. ＋3 transparencies（p. i-vi）. ISBN：2909657116, 2909657110

《旋玑图》，Métail, Michèle 译.

陶渊明（陶潜，352 或 365—427）

1. Les poèmes de T'ao Ts'ien/traduit de chinois par Liang Tsong tai；Préface de Paul Valéry；avec trois eaux-fortes originales de Sanyu et un portrait du poète d'après Hwang Shen. Paris, Lemarget, 1930. 79，［1］pages, 3 leaves frontispiece, plates 33cm.

《陶潜诗选》，梁宗岱译.

2. T'ao Yuan-ming. Paris：Vigot frères, 1934. viii, 128 pages；25cm.

陶潜诗选译. Wong, Wen-po 译.

3. Tao Yuan Ming：l'homme, la terre, le ciel：enfin je m'en retourne/poèmes traduits du chinois par Cheng Wing fun ＆ Hervé Collet；calligraphie de Cheng Wing fun. Millemont：Moundarren, 1987.［ca. 150］f.：map；21cm. ISBN：2950046886, 2950046888

陶潜诗. Cheng Wing fun 和 Collet, Hervé 合译. 法汉对照.

4. Œuvres complètes de Tao Yuan-Ming/traduit du chinois, présenté, annoté par Paul Jacob. Paris：Gallimard, 1990. 445 p.；23cm. ISBN：2070716813, 2070716814.（Connaissance de l'Orient；70）

陶潜诗集. Jacob, Paul 译注.

I323　南北朝

谢灵运（385—433）

1. Poèmes de montagnes et d'eaux：l'expèrience poétique du paysage dans la Chine du Ve siècle/Xie Lingyun；présentation et traduction de Gérard Dupuy. Paris：L'Harmattan, 2013. 149 p.：ill. ISBN：2336002514, 2336002515.（Critiques littéraires）

谢灵运山水诗. Dupuy, Gérard 译.

庾信（513—581）

1. Lamentations pour le sud du fleuve/Yu Xin；traduction du chinois et présentation par Michel Kuttler.［Paris］：Orphée/La Différence, 1995. 123 p.；17cm. ISBN：2729111050, 2729111052.（Orphée；215）

《哀江南赋》，Kuttler, Michel 编译.

I324　唐朝

张若虚（约647—约730）

1. Analyse formelle de l'œuvre poétique d'un auteur des Tang, Zhang Ruo-xu. Paris；La Haye：Mouton et Cie, 1970. 139 p.；24cm.（Le Monde d'outre-mer passé et présent/école pratique des hautes études en sciences sociales. 3e série, Essais；11）

《唐代诗人张若虚诗作分析》，Cheng Chi-Hsien 著. 本书包含对张若虚诗歌作品的选译.

寒山（唐代，生卒年不详）

1. Le Clodo du Dharma：25 poèmes de Han-shan/de Han-shan...；présentés［et traduits］par Jacques Pimpaneau；［publié par le］Centre de publication Asie orientale. Paris（Tour centrale, 2, place Jussieu, 75221, cedex 05）：Centre de publication Asie orientale, 1975. 66 pages：illustrations；30cm.（Bibliothèque asiatique；18. v.）

《寒山廿五首诗》，Pimpaneau, Jacques 译. 法汉对照.

2. Le Mangeur de brumes：l'oeuvre de Han-shan, poète et vagabond/texte français par Patrick Carré. Paris：Phébus, 1985. 311 pages；21cm. ISBN：2859400613, 2859400613.（Domaine chinois）

寒山诗. Carré, Patrick 译.

骆宾王（约638—684）

1. Le poète chinois Lo Pin-wang/introduction et tr. par Bruno Belpaire. Bruxelles：Éditions de l'Occident, 1960. 155 pages；21cm.（Petits traités chinois peu connus；no. 3）

《骆宾王诗选》，Belpaire, Bruno 译.

薛涛（768—832）

1. Un torrent de montagne/Hs "ueh T'ao；choix traduit du chinois par Pierre Lorain, et présenté par Pierre Lorain et Zhu Jie.［Paris］：La Différence, 1992. 123 pages；17cm.

ISBN：2729108548, 2729108540.（Orphée；141）

《洪度集》，Lorain, Pierre(1924—)译.

王梵志（约 590—660）

1. L'œuvre de Wang le zélateur：(Wang Fan-tche). Suivi des Instructions domestiques de l'aïeul：(T'ai-kong kia-kiao)：poèmes populaires des T'ang（VIIIe-Xe siècles）/édités, traduits et commentés d'après des manuscrits de Touen-houang par Paul Demiéville. Paris：Collège de France, Institut des hautes études chinoises, 1982. 885 pages；illustrations；25cm. ISBN：2857570287, 2857570288. (Bibliothèque de l'Institut des hautes études chinoises；v. 26)

《王梵志诗集》，Demiéville, Paul 译.

(1) Paris：Institut des hautes études chinoises, 1982. 887 p.；25cm. ＋corrigenda：[2] p. ISBN：2857570287, 2857570288. (Bibliothèque de l'Institut des hautes études chinoises；26)

王维（701—761）

1. Le plein du vide/Wang Wei；poèmes trad. du chinois par Cheng Wing fun et Hervé Collet；calligraphie de Hervé Collet. Millemont：Moundarren, 1985. 1 v.；22cm. ISBN：2950046851, 2950046857

维诗选译. Cheng, Wing fun 和 Collet, Hervé 合译.

(1) Millemont, France：Moundarren, 1991. 1 volume（unpaged）；21cm. ISBN：290731209X, 29073120971082.

2. Les saisons bleues：l'œuvre de Wang Wei, poète et peintre/texte français par Patrick Carré. Paris：Phébus, 1989. 374 pages；21cm. ISBN：2859401156, 2859401153. (Domaine chinois)

《蓝田集》，Carré, Patrick 译.

(1) Paris：Phébus, 2004. 374 pages；21cm. ISBN：2752900260, 2752900265. (Phébus libretto)

3. Paysages, miroirs du cœur/par Wang Wei；traduit du chinois par Wei-penn Chang et Lucien Drivod. Paris：Gallimard, 1990. 341 pages, [32] pages of plates：illustrations；23cm. ISBN：2070702537, 2070702534. (Connaissance de l'Orient；71.；Série chinoise)

王维诗. Chang, Wei-penn 和 Drivod, Lucien 合译. 法汉对照.

4. Wang Wei：Poemes pastoraux/traduction, presentation et notes par Wang Chia-yu；calligraphies de Lin Bingde；photographies de Chang Ping. Paris：You Feng, 2007. 163 pages：illustrations（some color）；30cm. ISBN：2842793333, 2842793331

Wang, Jiayu 译；Lin, Bingde 书. 本书包含对王维田园诗的选译.

白居易（772—846）

1. Po Chu Yi：un homme sans affaires/poèmes traduits du chinois par Cheng Wing fun ＆ Hervé Collet；calligraphie de Cheng Wing fun. Millemont：Moundarren, 1988. 1 volume（unpaged）：map；21cm. ISBN：2907312014, 2907312011

白居易诗歌集. Cheng, Wing fun 和 Collet, Hervé 合译.

2. Chant des regrets éternels et autres poèmes/Bai Juyi；traduit du chinois et présenté par Georgette Jaeger.［Paris］：La Différence, 1992. 127 p.；17cm. ISBN：2729108238, 2729108236. (Collection "Orphée"；131)

《长恨歌》，Jaeger, Georgette 译.

杜甫（712—770）

1. Tu Fu, dieux et diables pleurent/Tu Fu；poèmes traduits du chinois par Cheng Wing fun et Hervé Collet；calligraphie de Cheng Wing fun. Millemont, France：Moundarren, 1987. [ca. 200] f.；21cm. ISBN：2950046878, 2950046871

杜甫诗歌集. Cheng, Wing Fun 和 Collet, Hervé 合译.

(1)［France］：Moundarren, 2014. 211 pages：map；21cm. ISBN：2907312905, 2907312901

2. Une mouette entre ciel et terre：poèmes/Tu Fu；traduits du chinois par Cheng Wing fun ＆ Hervé Collet；calligraphie de Cheng Wing fun. Millemont, France：Moundarren, 1995. 177 leaves：map；21cm. ISBN：2907312278, 2907312271

杜甫诗歌集. Cheng, Wing fun 和 Collet, Hervé 合译.

3. Il y a un homme errant/Du Fu；poèmes choisis, traduits du chinois et présentés par Georgette Jaeger. Calligraphie de Lin Zhywei.［Paris］：La Différence, 1989. 124 p.；17cm. ISBN：2729104348, 2729104344. (Orphée；31)

杜甫诗歌集. Jaeger, Georgette 译. 本书包含了杜甫诗歌的选译.

4. Poèmes de Du Fu destinés aux calligraphes/calligraphies de Wu Hua；traduction française de Florence Hu-Sterk monograph. Paris：Éd. You-Feng, 2003. 141 pages：illustrations；30cm. ISBN：2842791438, 2842791436

杜甫诗歌集. Wu, Hua(1959—) 书；Hu-Sterk, Florence 译. 本书包含了杜甫诗歌的选译.

5. Poèmes de jeunesse, Œuvre poétique I/Du Fu；textes traduits, présentés et commentés par Nicolas Chapuis. Du Fu；textes traduits, présentés et commentés par Nicolas Chapuis. Paris：Les Belles lettres, 2015. 823 pages；20cm. ISBN：2251100203, 2251100202. (Bibliothèque chinoise；5；Hanwen Fa yi shuku＝汉文法译书库)

《杜甫诗全集·一》，Chapuis, Nicolas(1957—)译.

贾岛（779—843）

1. Lang xian：immortel vagabond/poèmes choisis et traduits du chinois par Cheng Wing fun ＆ Hervé Collet. poèmes choisis et traduits du chinois par Cheng Wing fun ＆ Hervé Collet. Millemont：Moundarren, 2006. 1 vol. (149 p.)；21cm. ISBN：2907312545, 2907312547. (Les grands poètes chinois)

贾岛诗. Cheng, Wing Fun 和 Collet, Hervé(1951—)合

译. 法汉对照.

李白(701—762)

1. Quarante poésies de Li Tai Pé/texte, traduction et commentaire par Bruno Belpaire. Paris, Imprimerie nationale, 1921. 1 vol. (63 p.); 25cm.

   李白诗四十首. Belpaire, Bruno 译.

2. La cigale éperdue/une transcription de Li taï-peh d'après les caractères traduits et commentés par Yau Chang-foo. Paris, A. Messein, 1925. 160 pages; 19cm. . (Collection La Phalange)

   李白诗. Guislain, Jean Marie 译.

3. Parmi les nuages et les pins/Li Po; [traduit du chinois par Dominique Hoizey]. Paris: Arfuyen, 1984. 45 unnumbered pages; 21cm. ISBN: 2903941130, 2903941130. (Cahier; no 17; Textes chinois)

   Hoizey, Dominique 译. 本书包含了李白诗歌的选译.

4. Florilège de Li Bai/traduit du chinois, présenté et annoté par Paul Jacob. [Paris]: Gallimard, 1985. 271 pages; 23cm. ISBN:2070703525, 2070703524. (Connaissance de l'Orient; 58)

   李白诗集. Jacob, Paul(1950—)译.

5. L'immortel banni sur terre: portrait & poèmes/poèmes traduits du chinois par Hervé Collet & Cheng Wing fun. 2e éd. , corr. et augm. Millemont, France: Moundarren, 1985. 1 volume (unpaged): illustrations; 22cm. ISBN: 2950046827, 2950046826

   李白诗. Cheng, Wing Fun 和 Collet, Hervé(1951—)编译. 法汉对照.

6. Buvant seul sous la lune: portrait et poèmes/Li Po; trad. du chinois Hervé Collet, Cheng Wing Fun. Millemont (Yvelines): Moundarren, 1985. 22 × 15cm. ISBN: 2907312103, 2907312103

   李白诗歌集. Cheng, Wing fun 和 Collet, Hervé 合译.

   (1) Buvant seul sous la lune: po mes/Li Po, l'immortel banni; traduits du chinois par Cheng Wing fun & Hervé Collet; calligraphie de Cheng Wing fun. Millemont, France: Moundarren, 1988. 1 volume Non paginé: ill. ; 21cm. ISBN: 2907312103, 2907312103

   (2) 4. éd. Millemont, France: Moundarren, 1999. 191 leaves: 1 folded map; 21cm. ISBN: 2907312103, 2907312103.

7. Li Po: l'immortel banni sur terre buvant seul sous la lune: portrait-poème/Hervé Collet et Cheng Wing fun. Paris: Albin Michel, 2010. 217 pages: map; 21cm. ISBN: 222620749X, 2226207494

   李白诗歌集. Cheng, Wing fun 和 Collet, Hervé 合译.

   (1) Nouvelle édition au format de poche. 2015. 215 pages: carte; 18cm. ISBN: 2226316271, 2226316272. (Spiritualités vivantes, ; 290)

8. Ivre de Tao: Li Po, voyageur, poète et philosophe, en Chine, au VIIIe siècle/Daniel Giraud. Paris: A. Michel, 1989. 159 pages; 18cm. ISBN: 2226035338, 2226035332. (Spiritualités vivantes; 73. ; Série Taoïsme)

   李白诗. Giraud, Daniel 译.

9. Sur notre terre exile/Li Bai; traduit du chinois et présenté par Dominique Hoizey. [Paris]: Orphée/La Différence, 1990. 127 p. ; 17cm. ISBN:2729105433, 2729105433. (Orphée; 61)

   李白诗歌集. Hoizey, Dominique 译. 本书包含了李白诗歌的选译.

10. Poèmes: destinés aux calligraphes/de Li Bai; calligraphies de Wu Hua, trad. française de Florence Hu-Sterk. Paris: Éd. You-Feng, 2003. 1 vol. (149 p.): calligr. en noir et en coul. , couv. ill. en coul. ; 31cm. ISBN: 2842791444, 2842791445

   李白诗歌集. Wu, Hua(1959—)书; Hu-Sterk, Florence 译.

11. Ecoutez là-bas, sous les rayons de la lune—/Li Bai; traduction et notes par le marquis d'Hervey Saint-Denys; révisées par Céline Pillon; postface par Céline Pillon; couverture de Olivier Fontvieille. [Paris, France]: Mille et une nuits, 2004. 78 p. ; 15cm. ISBN: 2842058224, 2842058227. (La petite collection; 444)

   李白诗歌集. Hervey de Saint-Denys, Le'on, marquis d' (1822—1892)译.

12. L'exilé du ciel poèmes/Li Po; trad. du chinois par Daniel Giraud. Paris: Serpent à plumes, 2004. 113 p. : couv. ill. en coul. ; 17cm. ISBN:284261495X, 2842614959. (Motifs; 200)

   李白诗歌集. Giraud, Daniel(1946—)译.

李商隐(约 813—858)

1. Le torrent de jade/Li Shang Yin; traduit par Sun Wan et Alain Gouvret. Malaucène: Arfuyen, 1980. 1 volume. (Arfuyen; 18)

   李商隐诗选译. Wan, Sun 和 Gouvret, Alain 合译.

2. Amour et politique dans la Chine ancienne: cent poèmes de Li Shangyin (812—858)/Yves Hervouet; préf. de Claude Roy. Paris: De Boccard, 1995. XXXIX, 258, [24] p; 24cm. ISBN: 2950980708, 2950980700

   Hervouet, Yves 著. 翻译了李商隐的100首诗.

李贺(约 791—817)

1. Les visions et les jours: poèmes choisis/Li He; trad. du chinois et présentés par Marie-Thérèse Lambert et Guy Degen. [Paris]: La Différence, 1994. 123 p. ; 17cm. ISBN: 2729110283, 2729110284. (Orphée; 191)

   李贺诗. Lambert, Marie-Thérèse 译.

2. Poèmes/par Li He; traduit du chinois par Marie-Thérèse Lambert; Préfacé et annoté par Guy Degen. [Paris]: Gallimard, 2007. 197 p. ISBN: 2070781669, 2070781666. (Connaissance de l'Orient)

   李贺诗. Degen, Guy 译.

I325　宋朝

苏轼（1037—1101）

1. Fumée du Lu Shan, marée du Che Kiang：poèmes/Su Tung po (l'Hôte de la Pente de l'Est)；trad. du chinois par Cheng Wing Fun et Hervé Collet. Millemont：Moundarren, 1986. 1 volume（unpaged）；illustrations；22cm. ISBN：295004686X, 29500

《庐山烟雨》与《观潮》. Cheng, Wingfun 和 Collet, Hervé（1951—）合译.

  (1)Rêve de printemps/Su Tong Po；poèmes traduits du chinois par Cheng Wing fun et Hervé Collet；calligraphie de Cheng Wing fun. Millemont：Moundarren, 1998. 1 vol. （204 p.）；22cm. ISBN：2907312340, 2907312349

2. Un ermite reclus dans l'alcool et autres rhapsodies/Su Dongpo；présentées et traduites par Stéphane Feuillas. Paris：Caractères, 2004. 173 pages；illustrations；21cm. ISBN：2854463609, 2854463606. (Majeures)

Feuillas, Stéphane 译. 本书包含对苏轼诗词的选译.

3. Florilège：comme dix mille sources jaillissantes/Su Shi (Su Dongpo)；traduit du chinois, présenté et annoté par Chaoying Durand-Sun. Paris：You-Feng, 2008. 1 vol. （380 p.）；ill., couv. ill.；24cm. ISBN：2842793364, 2842793366

苏轼诗选. Durand-Sun, Chaoying 译注.

4. Su Tung po：rêve de printemps：l'hôte de la Pente de l'est/Wing fun Cheng & Hervé Collet. Millemont：Moundarren, 2013. 1 vol. （289 p.）：ill., port., cartes, couv. ill. en coul.；22cm. ISBN：2907312851, 2907312855

苏东坡诗词. Cheng, Wingfun 和 Collet, Hervé（1951—）合译.

李清照（1084—约1155）

1. Œuvres poétiques complètes de Li Qingzhao/Li Qingzhao；traduit du chinois par Liang Paitchin. Paris：Gallimard, 1977. 177 p.：ill.；23cm. (Connaissance de l'Orient；45)

《李清照诗歌全集》，Liang, Paitchin 译.

2. Les fleurs du cannelier/Li Qingzhao；traduit du chinois par Zheng Su；interprété et présenté par Ferdinand Stoces. ［Paris］：Orphée/La Différence, 1990. 126 pages；17cm. ISBN：2729105611, 2729105617. (Orphée；68)

《鹧鸪天·桂花》，Cheng, Su 译.

陆游（1125—1210）

1. Le vieil homme qui n'en fait qu'à sa guise：poèmes/Lu Yu；traduits du chinois par Cheng Wing fun & Hervé Collet；calligraphie de Cheng Wing fun. Millemont, France：Moundarren, 1995. 167 leaves：map；21cm. ISBN：290731226X, 2907312264

陆游诗选. Cheng, Wing fun 和 Collet, Hervé 合译. 法汉对照.

  (1)Le vieil homme qui n'en fait qu'à sa guise：portrait et poèmes/Lu Yu；poèmes choisis et traduits du chinois par Cheng Wing fun & Hervé Collet；calligraphie de Cheng Wing fun. 2 édition augmentée. Millemont：Moundarren, 2012. 1 vol. （183 p.）：couv. ill.；21cm. ISBN：2907312820, 2907312820. (Chemin des bois)

  (2)Le vieil homme qui n'en fait qu'à sa guise：portraits et poèmes/［Lu You］；poèmes choisis, traduits et présentés par Cheng Wing fun et Hervé Collet. Millemont：Moundarren, 2015. 1 vol. （263 p.）：ill.；21cm. ISBN：2907312960, 290731226X, 2907312967

2. Lu You：mandarin, poète et résistant de la Chine des Song/Patrick Doan. ［Marseille］：Presses Universitaires d'Aix-Marseille, 2004. 336 pages；25cm. ISBN：2731404426, 2731404425

《陆游诗词选》，Doan, Patrick 译.

I326　清朝

爱新觉罗·弘历（1711—1799）

1. éloge de la ville de Moukden et de ses environs, poème composé par Kien-Long, empereur de la Chine... On y a joint une pièce de vers sur le thé. /par le même empereur. Traduit en français par le P. Amiot,... et publié par M. Deguignes. Paris：N. M. Tilliard, 1770. XXXVIII-381 p.

《御制盛京赋译注》，Amiot, Joseph（1718—1793）译注. 收录清朝康熙皇帝的《御制盛京赋》.

袁枚（1716—1798）

1. Yuan Tseu-Ts'ai, sa vie et ses Œuvres：un poète chinois du XVIIIe siècle/par Camille Imbault-Huart. Chang-hai：[publisher not identified], 1886. 42 pages；24cm.

《18世纪中国诗人袁子才的生平及其著作》，Imbault-Huart, Camille 著. 本书包含对袁枚（1716—1798年）诗歌的选译.

爱新觉罗·奕譞（1840—1891）

1. L'odysée d'un prince chinois... Hang hai yin ts'ao. Essais poétiques sur un voyage en mer/par le septième prince, père de l'empereur Kouang-siu, traduits et annotés par A. Vissière. （Avec texte chinois.）. Leide, E. J. Brill, 1900. 1 vol. 86 pages；25cm.

《航海吟草》，Vissière, A.（Arnold, 1858—1930）译.

I33　现当代诗歌

I331　诗歌集

1. Ashma/［traduit en français par Ho Ju；estampes en couleurs par Houang Yung-yu］. Pékin：Éditions en Langues Étrangères, 1957. 86 str., ［9］ listova s tablama ilustr. u boji：ilustr.；19cm.

《阿诗玛》，云南文艺工作小组整理；何如译.

2. La Poésie chinoise contemporaine [anthologie]/ par Patricia Guillermaz. Paris：Seghers（Vichy，impr. Wallon），1962. 253 p.；22cm.（Collection Melior）
中国当代诗歌. Guillermaz，Patricia 编译.

3. Quatre poètes chinois/Beidao, Gu Cheng, Mangke, Yang Lian；traduction Chantal Chen-Andro et Annie Curien. Plombières-les-Dijon [France]：Ulysse, fin de siècle, 1991. 125 p.；21cm. ISBN：2908007266，2908007268.（Cahiers Ulysse, fin de siècle；27—28）
中国四位诗人作品. Chen-Andro, Chantal 和 Curien, Annie 合译. 收录北岛, 顾城, 芒克, 杨炼的诗作.

4. Femmes poètes dans la Chine d'aujourd'hui/traduit du chinois par Shen Dali, Jacqueline Desperrois et Dong Chun. Pékin：Éd. Littérature chinoise, 1991. 186 p.；18cm. ISBN：7507100596；7507100594.（Collection Panda）
《中国当代女诗人诗选》. Shen, Dali 等译. 中国文学出版社.

5. Le ciel en fuite: anthologie de la nouvelle poésie chinoise/ établie et traduite par Chantal Chen-Andro et Martine Vallette-Hèmery；avec la participation pour la traduction de Isabelle Bijon [and others]. Belval：Circé, 2004. 387 pages；20cm. ISBN：2842421647，2842421649
Chen-Andro 等译. 本书包含对中国新诗的选译.

6. Inspirations chinoises: poèmes/de Yu Jian, Gu Cheng, Wang Jiaxin, Zang Di, Xi Du；présentation, traduction et notes de Isild Darras. Paris：L'Harmattan, 2004. 159 pages；22cm. ISBN：2747577465，2747577465.（Poètes des cinq continents；395）
中国当代诗歌选译. Darras, Isild 译注. 本书包含对于坚、顾诚（1956—1993）、王家新（1957—）、臧棣（1964—）、西渡诗作的选译.

I332 现当代诗人个人作品

鲁迅(1881—1936)

1. Poèmes/Luxun；[traduit du chinois par Michelle Loi]. Paris：Arfuyen, 1985. 42 unnumbered pages；21cm. ISBN：2903941165，2903941161.（Cahier,；no 20；Textes chinois）
《鲁迅诗集》, Loi, Michelle 译.

2. La Mauvaise herbe/Lu Xun；traduction et introduction par P. Ryckmans. Paris：Union générale d'éditions, 1975. 118 p.：couv. ill.；18cm.（10—18；943 Bibliothèque asiatique；21）
《野草》, Ryckmans, Pierre(1935—2014)译.

3. Les herbes sauvages/Lu Xun. Beijing：Éditions en Langues Étrangères, 2004. 165 p.；18cm. ISBN：7119032615，7119032610
《野草》, 外文出版社法文部译. 本书是作者的散文诗集, 共收入作品20余篇.

汪精卫(1883—1944)

1. Poèmes et "tseu" choisis de Wang Ching-wei, traduits et annotés par Sung-nien Hsu/Pékin：Impr. de la Politique de Pékin, 1932. VIII-69 p. et catalogue de la collection, planche, portrait, fac-similé, fig. dont une au titre.（Collection de la "Politique de Pékin"）
《汪精卫诗词选》, 徐仲年译.

郭沫若（1892—1978）

1. Déesses: poèmes choisis/Kouo Moruo；[traduit par Ho Ju]. Pékin：Éditions en Langues Étrangères, 1960. 75 pages；19cm.
《女神》, 何如译.
（1）2e éd. Beijing：Éditions en Langues Étrangères, 1964. 75 p.
（2）Beijing：Éditions en Langues Étrangères, 1982. 75 p.；19cm.

2. Poèmes de Kouo Mo-jo, anthologie. Traduite du chinois, présentée et annotée par Michelle Loi. [Paris]：Gallimard, 1970. 23cm.，152 p.（Connaissance de l'Orient：série chinoise；34）
《郭沫若诗选》, Loi, Michelle(1926—2002)译.

盛成（1899—1996）

1. Poèmes, 1966—1979/Cheng Tcheng. Castelnau-le-Lez：Climats, 1995. 142 pages；20cm. ISBN：2841580253，2841580255
《盛成诗集》, 译者不详.

冰心（1900—1999）

1. Eaux printanières/Ping-hsin；traduit par Anne Cheng. Paris：Publications orientalistes de France, 1979. 48 p. ISBN：2716901317，2716901314.（D'étranges pays）
《春水》, Cheng, Anne 译.

戴望舒（1905—1950）

1. Poèmes/Dai Wangshu；choisis, traduits du chinois, et présentées par Yan Hansheng et Suzanne Bernard. Beijing：Littérature chinoise, 1982. 155，[7] pages：portraits；18cm.
《戴望舒诗选》.《中国文学》杂志社(熊猫丛书)

艾青（1910—1996）

1. Poèmes/Ai Ts'ing；traduits du chinois et présentés par Catherine Vignal. Paris：Publications Orientalistes de France, 1978. 48 p.；18cm.（D'étranges pays）
《艾青诗选》, Vignal, Catherine 译.

2. Ai Qing poèmes/choisis et traduits du chinois par Yan Hansheng et Suzanne Bernard. Beijing：Éditions en Langues Étrangères, 1980. xxi, 163 pages：illustrations；19cm.
《艾青诗选》

3. Cent poèmes/Ai Qing. Pékin：Littérature chinoise, 1984. 244 p.：couv ill. en coul.；18cm.
《艾青诗一百首》.《中国文学》杂志社(熊猫丛书)

李季（1922—1980）

1. Wang Kouei et Li Hsiang-hsiang/Li Ki；[traduit du chinois par Ho Ju；illustrations de Tcheou Ling-tchao].

Pékin：Éditions en Langues Étrangères，1957. 59 pages，[5] leaves of plates：color illustrations；19cm.

《王贵与李香香》，何如译.

(1)Wang Gui et Li Xiangxiang/Li Ji；trad. par Ho Ju. Beijing：Éd. en Langues Érangères，1980. 59 pages：5 f. de plates；19cm.

张永枚(1932—)

1.《西沙之战》，张永枚著，碧涌插图.北京：外文出版社出版，1975.

北岛(1949—)

1. Au bord du ciel/Beidao；traduit du chinois par Chantal Chen-Andro. Strasbourg［France］：Circé，1994. 135 p.；20cm. ISBN：2908024896，2908024890

《在天涯》，Chen-Andro，Chantal 译.

2. 13，rue du bonheur/Bei Dao；trad. du chinois par Chantal Chen-Andro. ［Belfort］：Circé，1999. 108 p.；20cm. ISBN：2842420799，2842420796

Contents：Parmi les ruines—Un étranger de retour—Mélodie—La lune sur le manuscrit—Croisement—13，rue du bonheur.

幸福路13号：北岛诗歌选译. Chen-Andro，Chantal 译.

3. Paysage au dessus de zéro/Bei Dao；traduit du chinois par Chantal Chen-Andro. ［Belfort］：Circé，2004. 127 pages；21cm. ISBN：2842421817，2842421816

《零度以上的风景》，Chen-Andro，Chantal 译.

梁秉钧(1948—2013)

1. En ces jours instables/Leung Ping-kwan；traduit par Camille Loivier. ［Hong Kong］：MCCM Creations，2012. 47 pages；24cm. ISBN：9881521774，9881521777

《在不安定的日子》，Loivier，Camille 译.

舒婷(1952—)

1. Poèmes/Shu Ting；poèmes choisis et trad. du chinois par Annie Curien et Isabelle Bijon. Montereau：Les Cahiers du confluent，Impr. Artisanale），1986. 22 p.；ill.；22cm. ISBN：2904973222，2904973222. （Collection chinoise）

舒婷诗选. Bergeret Curien，Annie 和 Bijon，Isabelle 合译.

于坚(1954—)

1. Dossier 0：poème/Yu Jian；traduit du chinois par Li Jinjia et Sébastian Veg. ［Paris］：Bleu de Chine，Impr. Bialec，2005. 1 vol. （69 p.）：couv. ill.；19cm. ISBN：284931000X，2849310007

《0 档案》，Li，Jin Jia 和 Veg，Sebastian 合译.

2. Un vol/Yu Jian；poème en prose traduit du chinois，présenté et annoté par Li Jinjia et Sebastian Veg. Paris］：Gallimard，2010. ISBN：2070128532，2070128539. （Bleu de Chine）

Notes：Trad. de：Fei xing. / Comprend des réf. bibliogr.

《飞行》，Li，Jinjia 和 Veg，Sebastian 合译.

3. Rose évoquée/Yu Jian；poèmes traduits du chinois par

Chantal Chen-Andro. Edition bilingue chinois-français. Paris：Éditions Caractères，Impr. Trefle Communication，2014. 1 vol. （115 p.）：portr.；21cm. ISBN：2854465365 （br），2854465369 （br），2854465326，2854465327. （Planètes）

《被暗示的玫瑰》，Chen-Andro，Chantal 译.

杨炼(1955—)

1. Là où s'arrête la mer/Yang Lian；poèmes traduits du chinois par Chantal Chen-Andro. Paris：Éditions Caractères，2004. 165 p.；21cm. ISBN：2854463617，2854463613. （Planètes）

《大海停止之处》，Chen-Andro，Chantal 译.

翟永明(1955—)

1. La conscience de la nuit＝Hei ye de yi shi：poèmes/Zhai Yong Ming；trad. du chinois par Xu Shan，Rong Xiufang，Jacques Charcosset；avec la participation de Liu Lihua，Maréva Bernard-Hervé，Chen Jinghan；préf. de Jacques Charcosset. Éd. bilingue. La Rochelle：Larochellivre：Rumeur des âges，2004. 65 p.；24cm. ISBN：2843271037，2843271038

Notes：Sélection de 14 poèmes à l'écriture syncopée，expression d'un monde onirique et satirique qui souligne les fantasmes de la Société chinoise fascinée par les images de jeux vidéos et de films

《黑夜的意识》，Charcosset，Jacques 译.

顾城(1956—1993)

1. Les yeux noirs/par Gu Cheng：traduction d'I. Bijon et A. Curien. Montereau：Les Cahiers du Confluent，1987. 26 pages. ISBN：290497332X，2904973321. （Collection Chinoise）

《黑眼睛》，Bijon，I. 和 Curien，A. 合译.

柏桦(1956—)

1. Sous les Qing：poèmes/Bai Hua；traduits du chinois par Chantal Chen-Andro. Éd. bilingue. Paris：Caractères，Impr. Trèfle communication，2016. 1 vol. （99 p.）：ill.；21cm. ISBN：2854465587，285446558X. （Planètes）

《在清朝》，Chen-Andro，Chantal 译.

张子扬(1956—)

1. Zhang zi yang shi xuan/Zhang zi yang，liu fang. Beijing：Wai yu jiao xue yu yan jiu chu ban she，2004. 165 p，18cm. ISBN：7560037720；7560037721.

《张子扬诗选》，刘方译.外语教学与研究出版社.

韩东(1961—)

1. Soleil noir：poèmes/Han Dong；traduits du chinois par Chantal Chen-Andro. Éd. bilingue. Paris：Caractères，Impr. Trèfle communication，2016. 1 vol. （111 p.）：ill.；21cm. ISBN：2854465693，2854465695. （Planètes）

韩东诗集. Chen-Andro，Chantal 译.

西川(1963—)

1. Le monstre：poèmes/Xi Chuan；traduits du chinois par Chantal Chen-Andro. Éd. bilingue. Paris：Caractères，

Impr. Trèfle communication，2016. 1 vol.（105 p.）：ill.；21cm. ISBN：2854465594，2854465598.（Planètes）

《巨兽》，Chen-Andro，Chantal 译.

蔡天新(1963—)

1. Dans l'océan du monde：［poèmes］/Cai Tianxin；traduction par Anne-Marie Soulier. Paris：L'Oreille du Loup，2009. 130 p. ISBN：2917290125，2917290129

蔡天新诗歌.Soulier，Anne-Marie 译.法汉对照.

I4　戏剧文学

1. Les Origines du drame chinois/Maréchal et Madame Tchang Kaï Chek；traduit de l'anglais par Robert delle Donne；Préface de Maurice Pernot. Paris：Gallimard，1938. XXII-209 p.，couv. ill.

中国戏剧起源.宋美龄；Delle Donne，Robert 由英文译成法文；Pernot，Maurice(1875—1948)序.

I41　古代戏剧集

1. Théâtre chinois，ou Choix de pièces de théatre：composées sous les empereurs mongols/traduites... précédées d'une introduction et accompagnées de notes par M. Bazin aîné. Paris：Impr. royale，1838. 1 vol.（LXIII-409 p.）

《中国元代戏剧选集》，Bazin，Louis（1799—1863）译注.本书包含对《㑇梅香》《合汗衫》《货郎担》《窦娥冤》的翻译.

2. Les Adieux de la favorite：tragédie chinoise/trad. de Li Tche-Houa，et Robert Ruhlmann. Paris：Théâtre populaire，1955.［10］p.

逝去的最爱：中国悲剧. 李治华，Ruhlmann，Robert 合译.

3. Le Signe de patience et autres pièces du théatre des Yuan/Tchen T'ing-yu，Ts'in Kien-fou；trad. du chinois，présenté et annoté par Li Tche-houa.［Paris，］：Gallimard，1963.（22cm.），379 p.，couv. ill. en coul.（Connaissance de l'Orient. Collection Unesco d'œuvres représentatives. Série chinoise）

《忍字记及其他元代杂剧》，郑廷玉著；Li Tche Houa 译.

  (1)［Paris］：Gallimard，1991. 373 p.：couv. ill. en coul.；19cm. ISBN：207072431X（br.）.（Connaissance de l'Orient；51 Collection UNESCO d'œuvres représentatives. Série chinoise）

4. Le Cavalier et la demoiselle derrière le mur histoires tirées du théatre de la Chine antique/adapté par Chen Meilin. Beijing，China：Éditions en Langues Étrangères，2000. 1 vol.（369 p.）；18cm. ISBN：7119014730，7119014739

《墙头马上：中国古代戏剧故事选》，陈美林改编.

5. Trois pièces du théatre des Yuan：Yuan za ju san zhong/texte présenté，traduit et annoté par Isabella Falaschi. Paris：Les Belles lettres，2015. cxx，226 pages；20 × 13cm. ISBN：2251100180.（Bibliothèque chinoise；19）

Contents：palais des Han/drame composé par Ma Zhiyuan—La grande vengeance de l'orphelin des Zhao/drame composé par Ji Junxiang—Sur le mont Yiqiu：Zhao Li offre sa chair/drame composé par Qin Jianfu

《元杂剧三种》，Falaschi，Isabella 编译. 包括马致远的《汉宫秋》、纪君祥的《赵氏孤儿》和秦简夫的《赵礼让肥》

I42　古代戏曲家及其作品

1. Hoeï-lan-ki，ou L'histoire du cercle de craie：drame en prose et en vers/traduit du chinois et accompagné de notes par Stanislas Julien. London：J. Murray：Parbury，Allen，1832. 1 vol.（XXXII—149 p.）；in-8

《灰阑记》，李行道著；Julien，Stanislas(1799—1873)译.

2. Tchao-chi-cou-eulh，ou l'Orphelin de la maison de Tchao，tragédie chinoise，... avec des éclaircissements sur le théatre des Chinois et sur l'histoire véritable de l'orphelin de Tchao. À Pékin，1755.

《赵氏孤儿》，Prémare，Joseph Marie de 译.

3. Tchao-chikou-eul，ou l'Orphelin de la Chine，drame en prose et en vers，accompagné des pièces historiques qui en ont fourni le sujet，de nouvelles et de poésies chinoises. Paris：Moutardier，1834.

《赵氏孤儿》，Julien，Stanislas(1799—1873)译.

4. L'orphelin de Zhao：drame chinois en cinq actes et un prologue/par Ji Junxiang；version française de Christine Corniot. Paris（3 Pl. Escadrille Normandie-Niémen，75013）：C. Corniot，1993. couv. ill.；30cm. ISBN：2950797008（br.）.（Théâtre vivant）

《赵氏孤儿》，纪君祥著；Corniot，Christine 译.

5. Le rêve du millet jaune：drame taoïste du XIIIe siècle/traduit du chinois par Louis Laloy. Bruges：impr. Desclée De Brouwer；Paris：Desclée De Brouwer，1935. 139 p.（Courrier des îles；5）

《黄粱梦》，马致远（约 1250 年—约 1321 年至 1324 年间）著；Laloy，Louis(1874—1944)译.

6. Si-siang-ki，ou L'histoire du pavillon d'Occident：comédie en seize actes/traduit du chinois par Stanislas Julien，avec des notes explicatives et le texte en regard des vers. Genève：H. Georg；Paris：E. Leroux；London：Trübner，1872—1880. V-333 p.；26cm.（Atsume gusa：pour servir à la connaissance de l'Extrême-Orient/recueil publié par F. Turrettini；vol. III）

《西厢记》，王实甫（约 1260—1316）著；Julien，Stanislas(1799—1873)译.

7. 西厢记/(元)王实甫著；(法)Stanislas Julien 译. 长沙：岳麓书社，2015. 31，404 页：图；24cm. ISBN：7553804071.（大中华文库）

法文题名：Si-siang-ki ou l'histoire du pavillon d'occident

8. Le Pi-pa-ki ou l'histoire du luth：drame chinois de Kao-Tong-Kia，représenté à Pékin，en 1404，avec les changements de Mao-Tseu/traduit sur le texte original par M. Bazin aîné. Paris：Impr. royale，1841. XX-275 p.；

in-8°

《琵琶记》，高明（约 1305—约 1371）著；Bazin，Louis（1799—1863）译.

9. L'oreiller magique/Tang Xianzu；traduit du chinois par André Lévy. [Paris]：Éditions MF, 2007. 185 p. ISBN：2915794182, 2915794189. (Frictions)

《邯郸记》，汤显祖（1550 年 9 月 24 日—1616 年）著；Lévy，André(1925—)译.

10. Le Pavillon aux pivoines/Tang Xianzu；trad. du chinois par André Lévy. Paris：Festival d'Automne à Paris；Musica Falsa, 1998. 412 p.，[16] p. de pl.；ill.，carte；22cm. ISBN：2951238614, 2951238619

《牡丹亭》，汤显祖（1550 年 9 月 24 日—1616 年）著；Lévy，André(1925—)译.

(1) Paris：Musica falsa；Festival d'automne à Paris, 1999. 1 vol. (412 p. -[16] p. de pl.)；ill.，couv. ill. en coul.；22cm. ISBN：2951238622, 2951238626

11. Quinze colliers de sapèques：opéra kouenkiu/Livret original de Tchou Sou-tchen；révisé par Tcheou Tchouan-ying, Wang Tchouan-song, Tchou Kouo-liang et autres membres de la troupe d'opéra kouenkiu du Tchékiang；version définitive de Tchen Se；[traduit du chinois par Ho Ju]. Pékin：Éditions en Langues Étrangères, 1957. 1 vol. (90 p.)；20cm.

《十五贯》，(明)朱素臣原著；浙江省"十五贯"整理小组整理；何如译.

12. Quinze rouleaux d'argent：pièce de la Chine ancienne/adaptée pour le théâtre européen par Günther Weisenborn；version scénique de Gaston Jung d'après le texte français de Pierre Grappin. La Chaux-de-Fonds：T. P. R.，1968. 116 pages；18cm. (Théâtre populaire romand. Répertoire；15)

《十五贯》，朱素臣（约公元一六四四年前后在世）著；Weisenborn，Günther(1902—1969)德译；Jung，Gaston 从 Grappin，Pierre 法文译本改编成剧本.

(1) La Chaux-de-Fonds, 1974. 116 pages；18cm. (Collection du T. P. R. Répertoire，no. 15)

13. Quinze colliers de sapèques/adaption, Kuang Rong；illustrations, Wang Hongli. 北京：外文出版社：中国国际书店发行, 1982. 54 pages；illustrations；26cm.

《十五贯》，匡荣改编；王弘力绘. 法汉对照.

I43 现当代戏剧作品

1. La Fille aux cheveux blancs, opéra chinois en 5 actes, traduit par Jacques Dubois. Préface de Vercors. Paris：Les éditeurs français réunis, 1955. 223 p.，couv. ill.

《白毛女》，丁毅，贺敬之著；Dubois，Jacques，Vercors（1902—1991）译.

2. Théâtre sur la Chine/traduit de l'américain par Suzanne Mayoux. Paris，Stock, 1973. 231 pages；22cm.

《舞台上的中国：一位美国女演员在中国》，译自《China on

stage》. Snow，Lois Wheeler 编译成英文；Suzanne Mayoux 译成法文. 主要收录"样板戏"，包括《沙家浜》《红色娘子军》《智取威虎山》和《红灯记》.

3. La prise de la montagne du Tigre/réadapté par le Groupe de la Compagnie changhaïenne d'opéra de Pékin chargé de la pièce la Prise de la montagne du Tigre：Livret établi en juillet 1970. Pékin：Éditions en Langues Étrangères, 1971. 113，[5] p.：[8] pl. coul.，couv. ill. coul.；23cm.

《革命现代京剧〈智取威武山〉》（一九七〇年演出本），上海京剧团《智取威武山》剧组集体改编.

4. Le fanal rouge. Pékin：Éditions en Langues Étrangères, 1972. 103 p.

《革命现代京剧〈红灯记〉》（剧本），中国京剧团集体改编.

5. Cha Kia Pang：opéra de Pékin à thème révolutionnaire contemporain. Pékin：Éditions en Langues Étrangères, 1972. 92 p.

《革命现代京剧〈沙家浜〉》（剧本），中国京剧团集体改编.

6. Le port, réadapté collectivement par l'équipe du "Port" relevant de la Compagnie changhaïenne d'opéra de Pékin. (Livret établi en janvier 1972)/réadapté collectivement par l'équipe du "Port" relevant de la Compagnie changhaïenne d'opéra de Pékin. (Livret établi en janvier 1972). Pékin：Éditions en Langues Étrangères, 1973. 70 pages color plates 24cm.

《革命现代京剧〈海港〉》，上海京剧团《海港》剧组集体改编.

7. Le Détachement féminin rouge：ballet à thème révolutionnaire contemporain/réadaptation collective due à la Compagnie du ballet chinois... Pékin：Éditions en Langues Étrangères；[Paris]：[diffusion Éditions du Centenaire], 1973. 168 p. -[22] p. de pl. en noir et en coul. -[1] f. de dépl. en coul.；ill.，couv. ill. en coul.；23cm.

《革命现代京剧〈红色娘子军〉》，中国舞剧团集体改编.

8. La montagne aux Azalées：opéra de Pékin à thème révolutionnaire contemporain/Wang Chou-yuan. Pékin：Éditions en Langues Étrangères, 1976. 110 p

《革命现代京剧〈杜鹃山〉》，王树元等编辑.

9. L'orage/Tsao Yu. Pékin：Éditions en Langues Étrangères, 1958. 171 p；Ill.

《雷雨》，曹禺著；Tchen，Mien 译.

(1)2e éd. Pékin：Éditions en Langues Étrangères, 1962. 171 pages；illustrations

10. Lei yu=L'orage/Cao Yu zhu. Beijing：Wai wen chu ban she, 2004. 2 volumes；22cm. ISBN：7119032666；7119032665.

《雷雨》，曹禺著，外文出版社法文部译.

11. Dresseurs de Dragons et dompteurs de Tigres：pièce de théâtre moderne en six actes/Touan Tcheng-Pin et Tou Che-Kiun. Pékin：Éditions en Langues Étrangères，

1961. 105 p. : ill. ; 22cm.

《降龙伏虎》，段承滨、杜士俊著. 话剧.

12. Les Retrouvailles: pièce en 3 actes et 7 tableaux/de Lao-Chö; trad. par l'équipe de traduction de l'univ. de Paris 7 sous la dir. de Mme Reclus-Houang chou-yi. Éditions bilingue. Paris: Centre de publication Asie orientale: Université Paris 7, 1977. 176 p. ; 23cm. (Bibliothèque asiatique; 23)

《全家福》，老舍著；Reclus-Houang chou-yi 主持翻译. 话剧.

13. La maison de thé: pièce de théâtre moderne en trois actes/Lao She. Beijing: Éditions en Langues Érangères, 1980. 97 pages, [8] pages of plates: illustrations; 21cm.

《茶馆: 三幕话剧》，老舍编剧.

14. La Maison de thé=Cha guan/texte de Lao She. Edition bilingue. Pékin: Éditions en Langues Étrangères, 2002. 276 p. ; 18cm. ISBN: 7119029681, 7119029689

《茶馆: 汉法对照》，老舍著.

15. Théâtre pour la résistance: quatre pièces, 1939—1942/Lao She; traduction, introduction et notes par Bernard Lelarge. Paris: You-Feng, 2005. 1 vol. (461 p.): couv. ill. ; 21cm. ISBN: 9842792157, 2842792152

老舍（1899—1966）著；Lelarge, Bernard 译. 本书是对老舍 1939—1942 年间的四部反抗剧作的翻译.

16. Les fleurs jumelles (pièce historique en cinq actes)/Guo Moruo; Préface d'Emmanuel Roblés; [traduction de Shen Dali]. Beijing: Éditions en Langues Étrangères, 1982. 95 p., [4] p. de pl. : ill

《棠棣之花: 五幕历史剧》，郭沫若著；沈大力译.

17. K'iu Yuan/Kouo Mojo; traduction, Préface et notes de Mlle Liang Pai-Tchin. 4e éd. [Paris]: Gallimard, 1957. 206 pages; 23cm. (Connaissance de l'Orient; collection dirigée par Étiemble)

《屈原》，郭沫若著；Liang, Paitchin 译.
   (1) [Paris]: Gallimard, Impr. SEPC, 1988. 206 p. : couv. ill. en coul. ; 19cm. ISBN: 2070714764, 2070714766. (Connaissance de l'Orient; 28)
   (2) [Paris]: Gallimard, 1991. 190 p. ; 19cm. ISBN: 2070722805, 2070722808. (Connaissance de l'Orient; 48)

18. La semeuse de feu, ou, La fille d'automne sème le feu/Su Lei; traduit du chinois par Li Zhihua et Jacqueline Alezais. Éd. bilingue. Paris: Éditions You-Feng, 1994. 121 p. ; 21cm. ISBN: 2906658189, 2906658189

《火神与秋女》，苏雷著；李治华、Alézaïs, Jacqueline 合译.

19. La mort de Lao She/Liu Xinwu; trad. du chinois et annoté par Françoise Naour. Paris: Bleu de Chine, 2004. 59 p. ; 18cm. ISBN: 2910884724, 2910884727. (Chine en poche)

《老舍之死》，刘心武（1942—）；Naour, Françoise 译. 歌剧剧本.

I5 小说

I51 古代及跨时代小说集

1. Contes chinois/traduits par MM. Davis, Thoms, le P. d'Entrecolles, etc., etc., et publiés par M. Abel-Rémusat. Paris: Moutardier, 1827. 3 vol. : pl.
   中国短篇小说. Davis, John Francis（1795—1890）译；Rémusat, Abel（1788—1832）责任编辑.

2. Nouvelles chinoises; La mort de Tong-Echo; Le portrait de famille ou La peinture mystérieuse; Les deux frères de sexe différent/traduction de M. Stanislas Julien. Paris: L. Hachette et Cie; B. Duprat, 1860. 1 vol. (XXXII-271 p.)
   中国中短篇小说:《三国演义》《今古奇观》《醒世恒言》. Julien, Stanislas（1799—1873）译.

3. La matrone du pays de Soung. Les deux jumelles: contes chinois/avec une préface par E. Legrand. Paris: Lahure, 1884. XXX—100 p. : ill. en coul. (Collection Lahure, n° 3)
   中国短篇小说: 宋国接生婆、双胞胎姐妹. Legrand, émile（1841—1903）译并作序.

4. L'Amoureuse Oriole, jeune fille, roman d'amour chinois du XIIIe siècle. Avec dix illustrations chinoises/traduit par George Soulié de Morant. Paris: E. Flammarion, 1928. 247 p., fig.
   爱的夜莺，年轻的女孩. Soulié de Morant, George（1878—1955）译. 收录 8 世纪中国爱情小说.

5. Contes et légendes de Chine/par Gisèle Vallerey. Paris: F. Nathan, 1936. 256 p., fig., pl., cartonnage ill.
   中国短篇小说和传奇故事. Vallerey, Gisèle（1889—1940）译. 本书包含了对中国短篇小说和传奇故事的选译.

6. Ne pas avoir peur des fantômes. Récits./Recueil établi par l'Institut de littérature de l'Académie des sciences de Chine. [Préface signée: Ho Ki-fang]. Pékin, Éditions en Langues Étrangères, 1961. 92 p., pl., couv. ill. 16mo
   《不怕鬼的故事》，中国科学院文学研究所编，程十发插图.

7. L'Antre aux fantômes des collines de l'Ouest: sept contes chinois anciens (XIIe-XIVe siècles)/introduction, notes et commentaires d'André Lévy; traduction d'André Levy et René Goldman. [Paris]: Gallimard, 1972. 1 vol. (170 p.): couv. ill. ; 23cm. (Collection Unesco d'Œuvres représentatives. Connaissance de l'Orient; 38. Série chinoise)
   中国古典传奇. Lévy, André（1925—）和 Goldman, René 合译.

8. Aux portes de l'enfer: récits fantastiques de la Chine ancienne/[traduits et adaptés par] Jacques Dars. Saint-Pierre-du-Mont: "Nulle part", 1984. 111 p. ; 20cm. ISBN: 2865770508 (Br.). (Les Livres de Nulle part)
   地狱之门: 古代中国的异志故事. Dars, Jacques（1941—2010）译.

9. Contes chinois/Tv. Paris, Calmann-Lévy, 1989. 340 pages. (Les chinois peints par eux-mèmes)

《中国故事》，陈季同（1851—1907 年）译.

10. Histoires d'amour et de mort de la Chine ancienne/trad. du chinois et présenté par André Lévy. Paris：Aubier，1992. 244 p.：couv. ill. en coul.；22cm. ISBN：2700716485 (br.). (Domaine chinois)

古代中国爱情志怪故事. Lévy, André(1925—)译.

(1)[Paris]：Flammarion, 1997. 244 p.：cartes, couv. ill. en coul.；18cm. ISBN：2080709852 (br.). (GF；985)

11. Histoires de taoïstes chinois/Yuan Guang；[traduit par Wang Jinguan et Zhang Yongzhao]. Beijing (Éditions en Langues Étrangères), 2006. 1 vol. (365 p.)；couv. ill.，ill. en n. et bl.；18cm. ISBN：7119021648 (br)；7119021645 (br)

《中国道家故事选：法文》，元光编.

12. Le malentendu causé par un cerf-volant pièces comiques de la Chine antique/Zhong Yuan；traduit par Zhang Yuyuan. Beijing：Éd. en Langues Étrangères, 2007. 1 vol. (341 p.)：ill.，couv. ill. en coul.；18cm. ISBN：7119023915 (br)；7119023918 (br)

《中国古典喜剧故事选：法文》，中元编.

13. Contes choisis des Tang/[trad. par] Sung-nien Hsu. Pékin：Impr. de la "Politique de Pékin", 1935. 128 p.；29cm. (Collection de la "Politique de Pékin")

《唐人小说》，徐仲年译.

14. Contes de la dynastie des Tang/[Li Tchao-wei, et al.]. Pékin：Éditions en Langues Étrangères, 1958. 133 pages，[5] leaves of plates：illustrations；22cm.

《唐代传奇》，李朝威等著.

15. Contes choisis de la dynastie des Tang/rédigé par Shen Jiji et autres＝Tang dai chuan qi xuan/(tang)Chen Jiji deng zhuan bian. Beijing：Éditions en Langues Étrangères＝Wai wen chu ban she, 2004. 1 vol. (267 p.)：couv. ill. en coul.；18cm. ISBN：7119032682 (br)；7119032689 (br)

《唐代传奇选》，（唐）沈既济等编撰，外文出版社法文部译. 本书为对照读物，收集了 10 个唐代传奇故事.

16. Récits classiques/[avant-propos de Wu Shanxiang]. Beijing：Littérature chinoise, 1985. 425 p.；18cm. (Collection Panda)

《宋明话本选》.《中国文学》杂志社（熊猫丛书）

17. Trois contes chinois du XVIIe siècle/traduits par G. Soulié de Morant. paris：H. Piazza, 1926. 1 vol. (140 p.). (Ex Oriente lux)

十七世纪中国短篇小说三则. Soulié de Morant, Georges (1878—1955)译.

18. En mouchant la chandelle：nouvelles chinoises des Ming/[Qu You, Li Zhen]；trad. de Jacques Dars. [Paris]：Gallimard, 1986. 219 p.；19cm. ISBN：2070705617

(Br.). (L'Imaginaire, ISSN 0151—7090)

剪烛花：明代的中国短篇小说. 瞿佑，李祯著；Dars，Jacques(1941—2010)译.

19. Le Mystère de la pillule rouge affaires mystérieuses sous les Ming et les Qing/Liu Jianye；trad. Zhang Yuyuan. Beijing：Marcus：Éditions en Langues Étrangères, 2001. 1 vol. (335 p.)；18cm. ISBN：711902051X；7119020518.

《红丸迷案：中国明清奇案选》，刘建业著.

20. Contes fantastiques des Ming et des Qing. Le miroir magique de l'amour/traduit et presenté par Dong Chun et ses collaborateurs. Beijing：Foreign Language Teaching and Research Press, 2004. 223 str.；18cm. ISBN：7560040241，7560040240

Contents：Les chroniques de l'amour/Feng Menglong. Fenêtre aux lucioles et herbes exotiques/Changbai Haogezi. Contes fantastiques du pavillio de séjour à Shanghai/Wang Tao.

《法译明清爱情小说》，董纯等编译. 外语教学与研究出版社. 书中文章分别选自明朝冯梦龙的《情史》、清朝王韬的《淞隐漫录》及长白浩歌子的《萤窗异草》.

I52　古代个人作品

东晋

陶潜（352 或 365—427）

1. Soushenhouji/[ill. de 18 xylographies originales de] J.-F. Ferraton, Chen Chao Pao]；[18 calligraphies de] Li Kuang Lang；trad. Christophe Comentale, revue par Li Tche Houa. Rochetaillée (518 rue de la Nation, 69270)：le Chêne-Voyelle, 1990. [74] f.：ill.；35cm. ISBN：2908278030 (plié à la chinoise, sous chemise)

《搜神后记》，李治华（1915—），Comentale, Christophe (1952—)译.

隋唐传奇

《古镜记》

1. Le Miroir antique, contes et nouvelles chinois des hautes époques/traduction de Lo Ta-Kang. Neuchatel-Boudry：la Baconnière；(Lausanne：Impr. centrale), 1943. 287 p

《古镜记》，王度（生卒年不详，隋大业初为御史）著；罗大纲译.

宋代

《西山-窟鬼》

1. L'Antre aux fantômes des collines de l'Ouest sept contes chinois anciens (XIIe-XIVe siècles)/introduction, notes et commentaires d'André Lévy；traduction d'André Lévy et René Goldman. [Paris]：Gallimard, impr. Firmin-Didot), 1972. 1 vol. (170 p.)：couv. ill.；23cm. (Connaissance de l'Orient)

《西山-窟鬼》，作者佚名. Lévy, André,（1925—）和 Goldman, René 合译.

(1)[Nouveau tirage]. [Paris]：Gallimard/Unesco,1979. 178

p.；23cm.（Collection Unesco d'œuvres représentatives. Série chinoise；Connaissance de l'Orient；38）

明朝

《好逑传》

1. Hau Kiou Choaan, histoire chinoise traduite de l'anglais par Marc-Antoine Eidous/Lyon：Benoit Duplain, 1766. 4 vol.

《好逑传》，作者不详；Eidous, Marc-Antoine（1724—1790）由英文译为法文.

（1）Paris：Moutardier, 1828. 4 vol.

2. La Brise au clair de lune："Le Deuxième livre de génie", roman chinois/traduit par George Soulié de Morant. 16e éd. Paris：B. Grasset, 1925. In—16, 365 p.，pl.

《好逑传》，作者不详；Soulié de Morant, George（1878—1955）译.

《玉娇梨》

1. Iu-Kiao-Li, ou les Deux cousines, roman chinois/traduit par M. Abel Rémusat, précédé d'une préface où se trouve un parallèle des romans de la Chine et de ceux de l'Europe. Paris：Moutardier, 1826. 4 vol.

《玉娇梨》，（明）黄秋散人；Rémusat, Abel（1788—1832）译.

2. Yu-kiao-li. Les deux cousines, roman chinois, traduction nouvelle, accompagnée d'un commentaire. Paris：Didier, 1864. 2 vol.

《玉娇梨》，（明）黄秋散人；Julien, Stanislas（1799—1873）译.

《欢喜冤家》

1. Les spectacles curieux du plaisir：récits érotiques/trad. du chinois et présentés par André Lévy. Arles：P. Picquier, 1997. 305 p.：couv. ill. en coul.；21cm. ISBN：2877303330（br.）.（Le pavillon des corps curieux, ISSN 1274—9508）

《欢喜冤家》，西湖渔隐主人；Lévy, André（1925—）译.

2. Les miroirs du désir：récits érotiques/trad. du chinois et présentés par André Lévy. Arles：P. Picquier, 1999. 314 p.：ill.，couv. ill. en coul.；21cm. ISBN：2877304574（br.）.（Le pavillon des corps curieux, ISSN 1274—9508）

《欢喜冤家》，西湖渔隐主人；Lévy, André（1925—）译.

《弁而钗》

1. Épingle de femme sous le bonnet viril：chronique d'un loyal amour.../préf. de Michel Braudeau；trad. du chinois par André Lévy. [Paris]：Mercure de France, 1997. 85 p.；21cm. ISBN：2715220103（br.）

《弁而钗》，（明）醉西湖心月主人；Lévy, André（1925—）译.

《龙图公案》

1. L'Épouse d'outre-tombe, conte chinois/traduit par Léon de Rosny. Paris：J. Gay, 1864. 40—31 p.

《龙图公案》，（明）安遇时；Rosny, Léon de（1837—1914）译. 本书包含对《龙图公案》短篇小说集的选译.

（1）Paris：Maisonneuve, 1875. 16 p.

《清平山堂话本》

1. Contes de la Montagne sereine/trad.，introd. et notes par Jacques Dars. [Paris]：Gallimard, 1987. XX, 558 S. ISBN：2070708403, 2070708406.（Connaissance de l'Orient；60；Série chinoise）

《清平山堂话本》，洪楩编印；Dars, Jacques 译.

《今古奇观》

1. Choix de contes et nouvelles traduits du chinois par Théodore Pavie. Paris：B. Duprat, 1839. XIII-299 p.

《今古奇观》，抱瓮老人编著；Pavie, Théodore 译. 本书包含了对《今古奇观》的选译.

2. Le vendeur d'huile qui seul possède la Reine-de-beauté, ou Splendeurs et misères des courtisanes chinoises：roman chinois.../traduit par Gustave Schlegel. Leide：E. J. Brill, 1877. 1 vol.（XVII—140—[90] p.）

《今古奇观：卖油郎独占花魁》，抱瓮老人编著；Schlegel, Gustave,（1840—1903）译.

3. Trois nouvelles chinoises [I. Les Alchimistes. II. Comment le ciel donne et reprend les richesses. III. Mariage forcé]/traduites pour la première fois par le marquis d'Hervey-Saint-Denys. Paris：E. Leroux, 1885. 1 vol.（XVII-229 p.）.（Bibliothèque orientale elzévirienne；XLV）

《今古奇观》，抱瓮老人编著；Hervey de Saint-Denys, Léon d'（1822—1892）译. 本书包含了对《今古奇观》的三则故事选译.

4. La Tunique de perles, Un serviteur méritant, et Tang le Kïaï-Youen, trois nouvelles chinoises/traduites pour la première fois par le Mis d'Hervey-Saint-Denys. Paris：E. Dentu, 1889. VIII-249 p.

《今古奇观》，抱瓮老人编著；Hervey de Saint-Denys, Léon d'（1822—1892）译. 本书包含了对《今古奇观》的三则故事选译.

5. Six nouvelles nouvelles/traduites pour la première fois du chinois par le Mis d'Hervey-Saint-Denys. Paris：Maisonneuve et Larose, 1892. VIII-335 p.（Les littératures populaires de toutes les nations；30）

《今古奇观》，抱瓮老人编著；Hervey de Saint-Denys, Léon d'（1822—1892）译. 本书包含了对《今古奇观》的六则故事选译.

6. À jolie fille, joli garçon. Le Procès des épingles d'or. Miroir de beauté. Les Amours de Mme Fleur. Adapté des Kin-kou-ki-koan/Paris：E. Flammarion,（s. d.）, 1922. VI, 271 p.

《今古奇观》，抱瓮老人编著；Paul-Margueritte, Lucie（1886—1956）译. 本书包含了对《今古奇观》的四则故事选译.

7. Ts'ing Ngai, ou les Plaisirs contrariés, conte chinois ancien, adapté des Kin-kou-kikouan, illustré de 16 peintures sur soie. Paris：l'auteur, 1927. 80 p.

《今古奇观》，抱瓮老人编著；Paul-Margueritte, Lucie

(1886—1956)译.本书包含了对《今古奇观》的一则故事选译.

8. Spectacles curieux d'aujourd'hui et d'autrefois＝（Jingu qiguan）：［contes chinois des Ming］/texte traduit, présenté et annoté par Rainier Lanselle. ［Paris］: Gallimard, 1996. lxi, 2104 pages: illustrations; 18cm. ISBN: 2070113329, 2070113323. （Bibliothèque de la Pléiade; 430）

《今古奇观》，明抱瓮老人编；Lanselle，Rainier 译. 主要选自冯梦龙(1574—1646)的"三言"和凌蒙初(1580—1644)的"二拍".

《金瓶梅》

1. Lotus-d'or, roman adapté du chinois/Georges Soulié. Paris: E. Fasquelle, 1912. VIII-295 p., pl. et fac-simil.
   《金瓶梅》，兰陵笑笑生著；Soulié de Morant，George (1878—1955)译.

2. Kin P'ing Mei ou la Merveilleuse histoire de Hsi Men avec ses six femmes/traduit par Jean-Pierre Porret; ［Introduction par Paul Lavigne］. Paris: le Club français du livre (impr. de P. Dupont), 1949—1952. 2 vol. (Le Club français du livre. Romans; 129)
   《金瓶梅》，兰陵笑笑生著；Porret，Jean-Pierre 译.
   （1）［Traduit par Jean-Pierre Porret d'après la version allemande de Franz Kuhn］; ［Préface par Paul Lavigne］. Paris: le Club français du livre, 1967. 2 vol. (465, 520 p.): pl.; 13cm. (Le Club français du livre. Privilège)
   （2）Version française ［d'après la version allemande de Franz Kuhn］ par Jean-Pierre Porret. Paris: le Cercle européen du livre, 1970. 432 p.: ill., pl.; 20cm. （Le Cercle européen du livre. Chefs-d'Œuvre interdits）
   （3）version française ［traduite de la version allemande］ de Jean-Pierre Porret. Paris: G. Le Prat, 1978. 309 p.: couv. ill. en coul.; 21cm. ISBN: 285205051X

3. Femmes, maîtresses et concubines: le chef d'Œuvre de la littérature érotique orientale: ［extraits traduits du chinois］/Hsfü Wej. Paris, Londres, New York, 1968. 192 p.: couv. ill. en coul.; 17cm. （L'Orient et ses mystères）
   《金瓶梅》，兰陵笑笑生著；Hsfü Wej 译.

4. Fleur en fiole d'or/préf. par étiemble; introd. par André Lévy..., texte trad., présenté et annoté par André Lévy. ［Paris］: Gallimard, 1985. 2 vol. (CXLIX—1272, LIX—1483 p.): ill.; 18cm. ISBN: 2070110877 (vol. 1), 2070110885 (vol. 2). (Bibliothèque de la Pléiade; 320—321)
   《金瓶梅词话》，兰陵笑笑生著；Lévy，André 译.
   （1）［Nouv. tirage］. ［Paris］: Gallimard, 1989. CXLIX—1272 p.: ill.; 18cm. ISBN: 2070110877. (Bibliothèque de la Pléiade; 320—321)

（2）22e éd. ［Paris］: Gallimard, 2004. 2 vol. (LXVII—1274, XXI—1484 p.): ill., couv. ill. en coul.; 18cm. ISBN: 2070313913 (vol. 1), 2070313921 (vol. 2). (Collection Folio; 3997—3998)

5. Les 110 pilules: d'après Jin Ping Mei/Magnus. Paris: A. Michel, 1986. 51 pages: illustrations; 33cm. ISBN: 2226025723, 2226025722. (L'Echo des savanes)
   《金瓶梅词话》，Magnus，Günter Hugo 译.

6. Lotus d'or ou La merveilleuse histoire de Hsi Men avec ses six femmes. Paris: J. de Bonnot, 1999. 519 p.: ill., couv. ill.; 22cm.
   《金瓶梅》，根据 Lane，John 的英译本法译，译者不详.

7. La merveilleuse histoire de Hsi Men avec ses six femmes/Anonyme; Christophe Henry, introduction et notes; édition établie sous la direction de Catriona Seth,...; avec la collaboration de Claude Blum; documents et illustrations, Jacques Fournier. Paris: "Le Monde": Garnier, cop. 2010. 1 vol. (221 p.): ill., couv. ill. en coul.; 20cm. ISBN: 2358560795 (éd. complète). - ISBN: 2361560485 ("Le Monde"). - ISBN: 2351840764 (Garnier). （Les grands classiques de la littérature libertine; 30）
   《金瓶梅》，兰陵笑笑生著；Henry，Christophe 译.

施耐庵（约 1290—约 1370）

1. Les chevaliers chinois: roman de mœurs et d'adventures/traduit par Panking. Pékin: La "Politique de Pékin, 1922. 220 pages (on double leaves): illustrations; 27cm. (Collection de la Politique de Pekin)
   《水浒传》，Panking 译. 前 12 回全译.
   （1）Pékin: A. Nachbauer, 1933. 312 pages ［20］ leaves of plates: illustrations; 27cm.

2. Les 108 brigands du Liang Shan: ［Shui Hu］ et Les trois royaumes ［San Guo］/［de］ Lo Kuan-chung; ［deux romans classiques chinois］ adaptés par Wei Pu, illustres par Bu Xiaohuai. Paris: Signes, 1974. 1 volume (162, 153 pages): illustrations, maps; 16cm. （Bandes dessinées chinoises; 1）
   《水浒传》，Pu，Wei 译.

3. Au bord de l'eau＝Shui-hu-zhuan/Shi Nai-an, Luo Guan-zhong; avant-propos par Etiemble; texte traduit, présenté et annoté par Jacques Dars. ［Paris］: Gallimard, 1978. 2 volumes. (CLXI—1233, XVII—1356 p.): illustrations; 18cm. ISBN: 2070109119, 2070109111, 2070109100, 2070109104. (Bibliothèque de la Pléiade; 273—274)
   《水浒传》，Dars，Jacques(1941—2010)译. 120 回全译本.
   （1）［Paris］: Gallimard, 1979. （Bibliothèque de la Pléiade; 274; Bibliothèque de la Pléiade; 273）
   （2）［Paris］: Gallimard, 1997. 2 v.: ill., cartes; 18cm. ISBN: 2070402207, 2070402205, 2070402681, 2070402687. (Collection Folio; 2954—2955)
   （3）［Paris］: Gallimard, 2005. CLXI, ［1］, 1233, ［2］ s.:

il. ; 18cm. ISBN: 2070109100(v. 1), 2070109104(v. 1). (Bibliothèque de la Pléiade; 273)

(4)[Paris]: Gallimard, 2010. XVII, [2], 1356, [1] s. : il. ; 18cm. ISBN: 2070109111(v. 2), 2070109119(v. 2). (Bibliothèque de la Pléiade; 274)

4. Les opéras des bords de l'eau: théâtre Yuan, XIIIe-XIVe siècles/Maurice R. Coyaud, Angela K. Leung, Alain Peyraube. Paris: Association pour l'analyse du folklore, 1983. 189 pages: illustrations; 30cm. (Documents pour l'analyse du folklore. Serie de loin; 9)

《水浒传》，Coyaud, Maurice R. 等译.

5. Au bord de l'eau: intégrale, 1—30/[texte attribué à Shi ai an et Luo Guan zhong]; [adaptation de Wei Pu, Xu Gan, Gao Meiyi, et al.]; [présentation de Laurent Mélikian]. Paris: Fei, 2012. 1 boîte: couv. ill. ; 31cm. ISBN: 2359660845 (dans une boîte), 2359660845 (dans une boîte)

《水浒传》，Melikian, Laurent 译.

6. Au bord de l'eau/adaptation, Jean David Morvan; dessin, couleurs, Wang Peng & Studio 9. [Paris]: Delcourt, 2008—2010. v. : col. ill. ; 32cm. ISBN: 2756009735, a756009733, 2756009742, 2756009741

《水浒传》，Morvan, Jean David 译.

7. Lu, profondeur-de-la-sagesse ＝ 鲁智深/Lu, profondeur-de-la-sagesse ＝ Lu Zhishen/[edited by Publications orientalistes de France]. [edited by Publications orientalistes de France]. Paris: Association langues et civilisations, 1974. 56 pages: chiefly illustrations; 36 × 11cm. (Histoires du bord de l'eau ou les proscrits des marais; [1])

《鲁智深》，Publications orientalistes de France 编译.

罗贯中（约 1330—1400）

1. Les trois royaumes: (épopée chinoise)/traduction française avec texte chinois par Alph. Hubrecht. Peiping: Imp. des Lazaristes, 1934. vi, 171 pages; 22cm.

《三国演义》，Hubrecht, Alphonse 译.

2. Présentation du roman des Trois Royaumes: version vulgarisée de l'histoire officielle de la période dite des Trois Royaumes précédée de la fin des Han postérieurs (189 à 264 ap. J. -C.) suivie d'une/traduction des cinq premiers chapitres faite directement sur le texte chinois d'après la version établie par Kin Cheng-tan et les commentaires introductifs des chapitres de Mao Tsong-kang par Nghiêm Toan et Louis Ricaud. [Saigon]: [France-Asie], 1958. 178 pages; 28cm. (San guo zhi yan yi; Les Trois royaumes; fasc. 1)

《三国演义》，Nghiêm, Toàn(1907—)和 Ricaud, Louis 合译.

3. Les trois royaumes/Traduction originale, notes et commentaires de Nghiêm Toan et Louis Ricaud. Introd. de Robert Ruhlmann. Saigon [Société des études indochinoises], 1958—1963. 3 volumes illustrations,

folded map 28cm. (Collection UNESCO d'Œuvres représentatives. Série chinoise)

《三国演义》，Nghiêm, Toàn(1907—)和 Ricaud, Louis 合译.

4. Les trois royaumes. Livre I/Louo Kouan-tchong; traduction originale, notes et commentaires de Nghiêm Toan et Louis Ricaud; introduction de Jean Lévi. [Paris]: Flammarion, Impr. Floch), 2009. 1 vol. (668 p.): couv. ill. ; 24cm. ISBN: 2081225541 (br), 2081225549 (br)

《三国演义》，Nghiêm, Toàn(1907—)和 Ricaud, Louis 合译.

5. Les trois royaumes. Livre II/Louo Kouan-tchong; traduction originale, notes et commentaires de Nghiêm Toan et Louis Ricaud Jean et Angélique Lévi. [Paris]: Flammarion, Impr. Floch), 2009. 1 vol. (845 p.): couv. ill. ; 24cm. ISBN: 2081225558 (br), 2081225557 (br)

《三国演义》，Nghiêm, Toàn(1907—)和 Ricaud, Louis 合译.

6. Les trois royaumes. Livre III/Louo Kouan-tchong; traduction originale, notes et commentaires de Jean et Angélique Lévi. [Paris]: Flammarion, Impr. Floch), 2009. 1 vol. (611 p.): couv. ill. ; 24cm. ISBN: 2081225565 (br), 2081225565 (br)

《三国演义》，Levi, Jean 和 Lévi, Angélique 合译.

7. Les trois royaumes: bandes dessinées/traduction: M. Coyaud. Paris: P. A. F. , Pour l'analyse du folklore, 1986. 95 p. : ill. ; 24cm. (Documents pour l'analyse du folklore. Série Chine)

《三国演义》，Coyaud, Maurice 译.

8. Histoire romancée des trois royaumes/Texte original, Luo Guanzhong; adaptation et illustrations, Liu Zhenyuan. Beijing, China: Éd. Aurore, 1997. 190 p. : ill. ; 26cm. ISBN: 7505404938, 7505404939.

《三国演义》，刘振源改编绘. 朝华出版社.

9. L'épopé des trois royaumes. I/Luo Guan-zhong; texte traduit et annoté par Chao-ying Durand-Sun. Paris: Librairie You-Feng, 2006. volumes: illustrations; 24cm. ISBN: 2842792408 (t. 1), 2842792404 (t. 1), 2842792725 (t. 2), 2842792726 (t. 2)

《三国演义》(卷一)，Sun, Chaoying 译.

10. L'épopée des trois royaumes. II/Luo Guan-zhong; texte traduit et annoté par Chao-ying Durand-Sun. Paris: Librairie You-Feng, 2007. 1 vol. (559 p.): ill. , couv. ill. en coul. ; 24cm. ISBN: 2842792725 (br), 2842792726 (br)

《三国演义》(卷二)，Sun, Chaoying 译.

11. L'épopé des trois royaumes. III/Luo Guan-zhong; texte traduit et annoté par Chao-ying Durand-Sun. Paris: Librairie You-Feng, 2008, (c)2008. 1 vol. (543 p.): ill. , couv. ill. en coul. ; 24cm. ISBN: 2842794057

(br), 2842794052 (br)

《三国演义》(卷三), Sun, Chaoying 译.

12. L'épopé des trois royaumes. IV/Luo Guan-zhong; texte traduit et annoté par Chao-ying Durand-Sun. Paris: Librairie You-Feng, 2011, (c) 2011. 1vol. (611 p.): ill. , couv. ill. en coul. ; 24cm. + 1 carte dépl. ISBN: 2842795375 (br), 2842795377 (br), 2842794514(br), 2842794516 (br)

《三国演义》(卷四), Sun, Chaoying 译.

13. L'épopé des trois royaumes. V/Luo Guan-zhong; texte traduit et annoté par Chao-ying Durand-Sun. Paris: Librairie You-Feng, 2014, (c)2014. 1 vol. (619 p.): ill. , couv. ill. en coul. ; 24cm. + 1 carte dépl. ISBN: 2842796525 (br), 2842796527 (br)

《三国演义》(卷五), Sun, Chaoying 译.

高明（1422—1485）

1. Le moine mèche-de-lampe: roman pornographique du début des Qing/traduit du chinois et présenté par Aloïs Tatu. Arles: Éditions P. Picquier, 2002. 168 pages: illustrations; 18cm. ISBN: 2877305791, 2877305792. (Picquier poche; 173)

《灯草和尚传》, Tatu, Aloïs 译.

吴承恩（约1500—1583）

1. Le Singe et le pourceau, aventures magiques chinoises du XIIIe siècle/adaptées par George Soulié de Morant. Illustrations d'André Wilder. Paris: à la Sirène, 1924. 155 p. , fig. , pl. en coul.

《西游记》, Soulié de Morant, George(1878—1955)译.

2. Le Singe pèlerin ou Le pèlerinage d'Occident: Si-Yeou-ki/Wou Tch'eng-en; traduit du chinois［en anglais］par Arthur Waley; version française de George Deniker. Paris: Payot, 1951. 1 vol. (317 p.); 23cm.

《西游记》, Waley, Arthur（1889—1966）英译; Deniker, George 法译.

(1) Le Singe pèlerin ou le Pèlerinage d'Occident/Wou Tch'eng-en; traduit... ［de la version anglaise par］George Deniker. Paris: Payot, 1980. 317 p.: couv. ill. en coul. ; 18cm. (Petite bibliothèque Payot, ISSN 0480—2012; 386)

(2) Le Singe pèlerin ou Le pèlerinage d'Occident/Wou Tch'eng-en; trad. du chinois［en anglais］par Arthur Waley, version française établie par George Deniker. Paris: Payot, 1992. 317 p.: couv. ill. en coul. ; 19cm. (Petite bibliothèque Payot: documents; 109)

(3) Le Singe pèlerin ou Le pèlerinage d'Occident/Wou Tch'eng-en; trad. du chinois［en anglais］par Arthur Waley; version française établie par George Deniker. Paris: Payot et Rivages, 2002. 425 p.: couv. ill. en coul. ; 17cm. (Petite bibliothèque Payot; 109)

(4) Le Singe pèlerin ou le pèlerinage d'Occident (Si-Yeou-Ki)/Wou Tch'eng-en; traduit du chinois par Arthur Waley; version française établie par George Deniker. Paris: Payot, 2005. 1 vol. (425 p.); 18cm. ISBN: 2228896802 （Br）, 2228896801 （Br）. （Petite bibliothèque Payot; 109)

3. Si Yeou Ki, ou Le voyage en Occident/Wou Tch'eng Ngen; traduit du chinois par Louis Avenol. Paris: Seuil, 1957. 2 vol. (VI—932—XXX p.): ill. ; 22cm.

《西游记》, Avenol, Louis 译.

(1) Paris: Éd. du Seuil, 1969. 956 p. ; 19cm.

(2) Paris: Seuil, 1983. 954 p.: ill. ; 22cm. ISBN: 2020017814, 2020017817

4. Makak, le roi des singes/Ou Tcheng'en; Delphine Baudry-Weulersse; André Verret. Paris: Seghers, impr. Wallon, 1980. 178 p.: Ill. , couv. ill. en coul. ; 21cm. ISBN: 2221501128 (Rel), 2221501122 (Rel). (Mille et une histoires)

《西游记》, Baudry-Weulersse, Delphine 和 Verret, André 合译.

5. Troubles au royaume céleste/adaptation, Tang Deng et Gao Mingyou; illustrations, Yan Dingxian, Wang Qizhong et Cao Shuzhi. Beijing, Chine: Éditions En Langues Étrangères, 1985. 78 pages: color illustrations; 26cm. (Le Roi des singes)

改编自《西游记》, T'ang, Teng 和 Kao, Ming-yu 合译.

6. La pérégrination vers l'Ouest. you ji/01 璃 u Cheng'en; trad. , présenté et annoté par André Lévy. Paris: Gallimard, 1991. CXLVI - 1160 p.: ill. ; 18cm. ISBN: 2070112039, 2070112036. (Bibliothèque de la Pléiade; 357)

《西游记》, Lévy, André 译.

(1) you ji/02 1192 p.: ill. ; 18cm. ISBN: 2070112047, 2070112043. (Bibliothèque de la Pléiade;; 376)

(2) 2012. 1 vol. (CXLVI—1160 p.): carte. ; 18cm. + coffrets ill. (Bibliothèque de la Pléiade; 375)

7. Le roi des singes/adapt. française de Régis Delage; ill. de Zdenka Krej cová. ［Paris］: Gründ, 1992. 247 p.: ill. en coul. ; 29cm. ISBN: 270001233X （rel）, 2700012330 (rel). (Les grands classiques de tous les temps)

《西游记》, Delage, Régis 译.

8. 西游记＝Journey to the west＝Le voyage en occident/Xi you ji ＝吴承恩［texte], Gãlle Pelachaud［conception du livre et gravures originales]Wu Cheng'en［texte], Gãlle Pelachaud［conception du livre et gravures originales]. Paris: Rafaël Andréa, 2004. 1 vol. (depl. en accordéon de［48］p.): gravures, collages; 34cm.

《西游记》, Pelachaud, Gãlle 译.

冯梦龙（1574—1646）

1. Le Vendeur d'huile et la Reine-de-Beauté/par Pascal Forthuny; d'après le roman chinois "Mai Yeou lang tou tchan Hoa K'ouei." Paris: Albin Michel, 1918. 336

pages：couv. illustrations en coul. ；19cm.

《卖油郎独占花魁》，Forthuny, Pascal（pseud.）译.

2. Thse Hioung Hioung ti, c'est-à-dire "Les deux frères de sexe différent：nouvelle/trad. du chinois par Stanislas Julien. Paris，1930. 62 p.

《刘小官雌雄兄弟》，Julien, Stanislas（1799—1873）译.

3. La tunique de perles：contes tirés du Yu shi ming yan, anthologie classique/compilée par Feng Menglong. Pékin：Éd. en Langues Étrangères，1993. 294 p. ；18cm. ISBN：7119015729, 7119015729.（Littérature classique）

Contents：La tunique de perles—Le commissaire impèrial Chen et l'affaire de l'épingle d'or—Han la cinquième se prostituait à Xinqiao—Un mandarin intègre—Le testament—Chen Xiyi refusa quatre fois la nomination impèriale—L'aventure amoureuse de Shan Fulang—Zhang Shunmei et la belle jeune fille—Sept victimes pour un oiseau—Li Yuan sauve un serpent et obtient satisfaction—L'empereur Wu des Liang atteint la perfection et monte au paradis—Comment Ren le pieux est devenu un dieu.

《张舜美灯宵得丽女：〈喻世明言〉作品选》

4. Le vendeur-d'huile qui seul possède la reine-de-beauté/Fong Mong-long；traduit par l'équipe de traduction de Paris 7 sous la direction de Jacques Reclus. ［Paris］：Centre de publication Asie orientale, Université Paris VII，1976. 147 pages：illustrations；22cm.

《卖油郎独占花魁》，Reclus, Jacques 译.

（1）Paris：Centre de publication Asie orientale, Université Paris VII, impr. Corbière et Jugain，1977. 147 p. ：ill. , couv. ill. ；22cm.（Bibliothèque asiatique；15）

（2）Arles；Paris：Ph. Picquier，1990. 91 p：ill；21cm. ISBN：2877300609, 2877300605

5. Royaumes en proie à la perdition［chroniques de la Chine ancienne/Feng Menglong；traduit du chinois par Jacques Pimpaneau. ［Paris］：Flammarion，1985. 352 p. ；22cm. ISBN：2080647520, 2080647528.（Aspects de l'Asie）

沉沦中的王朝. Pimpaneau, Jacques 译.

6. Le serpent blanc：contes tirés du Jing shi tong yan, anthologie classique/compilée par Feng Menglong. Pékin：Éd. en Langues Étrangères，1994. 353 p. ；19cm. ISBN：711901644X, 7119016443.（Littérature classique）

Contents：Les retouvailles de la famille du sous-préfet Su—Zhang Sheng, jeune employé vertueux—La malédiction de l'anguille dorée—Comment Song Jin retrouva sa femme—Yue Xiaoshe risque sa vie par amour—Histoire de Yutangchun, une fille de joie—Dans l'impasse le Seigneur Gui fait pênitence—L'histoire du mariage de Tang Yin—Le serpent blanc—Comment Wu Qing et Ai Ai se rencontrèrent prés du Lac Jinming—Comment Zhao Chun'er a rétabli la fortune des Cao—Une famille anéantie par une concubine—Comment le

gouverneur Kuang a découvert et jugé un infanticide—La vengeance de Wan Xiuniang.

《小夫人金钱赠少年：〈警世通言〉作品选》

7. La vengeance de Cai Ruihong：contes tirés du Xing Shi Heng Yan, anthologie classique/compilée par Feng Menglong. Pékin：Éd. en Langues Étrangères，1995. 388 p. ；19cm. ISBN：7119003046, 7119003047.（Littérature classique）

Contents：Deux chefs de district et une orpheline—Trois fils pieux—La bonne fortune du vendeur d'huile—Les chaussons brodés—Shi Fu, un homme de bien—Le sacrifice de Bai Yuniang, une épouse admirable—Li Yuying et sa marâtre—Le rendez-vous secret de Wu Yan—Un bijou magique—Treize morts pour une sapèque—Le vieux valet Ah Ji fit la fortune de sa nouvelle maîtresse—La vengeance de Cai Ruihong—Comment le magistrat Wang fit incendier le temple Baolian.

《蔡瑞虹忍辱报仇》

8. Les écarts du prince Hailing：roman érotique Ming/trad. du chinois par Huang San et Oreste Rosenthal. Arles：P. Picquier, Impr. Robert，1999. 1 vol.（184 p）：couv. ill. en coul. ；17cm. ISBN：2877304582, 2877304580.（Picquier poche，；123）

《金海陵纵欲亡身》（拟似）. Huang, San 和 Rosenthal, Oreste 合译.

9. La besace de sagesse/Feng Menglong；adaptation et traduction Laurent Ballouhey；illustrations Zhu Shanshan. Paris：Éd. You-Feng，2006. 1 vol.（157 p. ）：ill. , couv. ill. en coul. ；24cm. ISBN：284279270X, 2842792701

《智囊》，Ballouhey, Laurent 编译.

10. Les trois propos/Feng Menglong；Traduit et adapté du chinois par Laurent Ballouhey；Illustrations de Zheng Diwei. Paris：Libr. You-Feng，2007. 160 p. ：ill. ；24×17cm. ISBN：2842793043, 2842793048

《三言》，Ballouhey, Laurent 译.

凌蒙初（1580—1644）

1. L'amour de la Renarde：marchands et lettrés de la vieille Chine/Ling Mong-tch'ou；trad. du chinois par André Lévy. Paris：Gallimard，1970. 285 p. ；23cm.（Connaissance de l'Orient. Collection UNESCO d'œuvres représentatives. Série chinoise）

《二刻拍案惊奇》（选译），Lévy, André 译.

（1）［Paris］：Gallimard：UNESCO，1988. 285 p. ：couv. ill. en coul. ；19cm. ISBN：2070713296（br.）.（Connaissance de l'Orient, ISSN 0589－3496；24 Collection UNESCO d'œuvres représentatives. Série chinoise）

清代

《一片情》

1. Tout pour l'amour：récits érotiques/trad. du chinois et

présentés par André Lévy. Arles: P. Picquier, 1996. 277 p. : couv. ill. en coul. ; 21cm. ISBN: 2877302989 (br.). (Le pavillon des corps curieux, ISSN 1274—9508)

《一片情》,[清]不题撰人;Lévy, André(1925—)译.

(1) Arles: Éditions Philippe Picquier, DL 2015. 1 vol. (298 p.) : ill. ; 17cm. ISBN: 2809711066 (br.). (Picquier poche, ISSN 1251—6007)

《平山冷燕》

1. Les deux jeunes filles lettrées: roman chinois/traduit par Stanislas Julien. Paris: Didier et Cie, 1860. 2 vol. (XVIII-360, 329 p.)

《平山冷燕》,荻岸散人著;Julien, Stanislas(1799—1873)译.

《二度梅》

1. Erh-Tou-Mei ou Les pruniers merveilleux: roman chinois/traduit [du chinois] par A. Théophile Piry. Paris: Dentu, 1880. 2 vol. (XXI-334, 335 p.) ; 18cm.

《二度梅》,惜阴堂主人编;Piry, A. Théophile(? —1918)译.

2. Nhi dô mai: Les Pruniers refleuris: Poème tonquinois/Transcription, traduction et notes, par A. Landes. Saigon, Imprimerie du Gouvernement, 1884. 156 p.

《二度梅》,惜阴堂主人编;Landes, Antony(1850—1893)译.

《儿女英雄传》

1. Ouenn Kang. La Cavalière noire, roman adapté de la version allemande de Franz Kuhn/par Eugène Bestaux. Paris, Calmann-Lévy; (Verviers, impr. de Gérard et Cie), 1956. In-8° (21cm.), 303 p., couv. ill.

《儿女英雄传》,文康(生卒年未详,道光初年至光绪初年在世)著;Kuhn, Franz (1884—1961)德译;Bestaux, Eugène (1878—1958)法译自德译.

《禽海石》

1. L'irrémédiable douleur/Fu Lin; trad. par Robert des Rotours...; avant-propos et notes, Donald Holzman; postf., Milena Doležalová-Velingerová. Paris: Éd. You-Feng, 2003. 163 p. : couv. ill. en coul. ; 19cm. ISBN: 2842791398 (br), 2842791391 (br)

《禽海石》,符霖(生卒年未详,晚清小说家)著;Des Rotours, Robert(1891—1980)译;Holzman, Donald 序.

《狄公案》系列

1. L'Enigme du clou chinois/Robert van Gulik; trad. de l'anglais par Anne Dechanet, Roger Guerbet et Jos Simons. [Paris]: C. Bourgois, 1985. 283 p. : couv. ill. en coul. ; 18cm. ISBN: 226400696X, 2264006967. (10/18. Série "Grands détectives"; 1723)

《铁钉案》,高罗佩(Gulik, Robert Hans van,1910—1967)(荷兰汉学家)翻译并创作;Dechanet, Anne 等从英语转译成法语. 英文题名:Chinese nail murders

2. Trafic d'or sous les T'ang/Robert van Gulik; traduction de Roger Guerbet. Paris: Club du Livre Policier, 1965. xi, 196 pages, [10] leaves of plates: illustrations; 20cm. (Les classiques du roman policier; 33)

《狄公案之黄金案》,高罗佩(Gulik, Robert Hans van, 1910—1967)(荷兰汉学家)翻译并创作;Guerbet, Roger 从英语转译成法语. 英文题名:Chinese gold murders

(1) Trafic d'or sous les T'ang: les débuts du juge Ti/par Robert van Gulik; traduit de l'anglais par Roger Guerbet. Paris: [U. G. E.], 1984. 256 p. ; 18cm. ISBN: 2264005963, 2264005960. (10/18; 1619; Grands détectives)

3. Le Monastère hanté/Robert van Gulik; traduction de Roger Guerbet. Paris: Club du Livre Policier, 1963. pages; 221—373, 9 leaves of plates: illustrations; 21cm.

《朝云观谜案》,高罗佩(Gulik, Robert Hans van,1910—1967)(荷兰汉学家)翻译并创作;Guerbet, Roger 从英语转译成法语. 英文题名:Haunted monastery

(1) Le Monastère hanté/Robert van Gulik. Paris: Brodard et Taupin, 1968. 190 p; 17cm. (Le livre de poche; 2437)

(2) Le Monastère hanté: les nouvelles enquêtes du Juge Ti/par Robert van Gulik; trad. de l'anglais par Roger Guerbet. [Paris]: C. Bourgois, 1984. 187 p. : couv. ill. en coul. ; 18cm. ISBN: 2264006080, 2264006080. (10/18. Série "Grands détectives"; 1633)

4. Meurtre sur: un bateau-de-fleurs/Robert van Gulik; traduction de Roger Guerbet. Paris: Club du Livre Policier, 1963. ix, 213 pages, 13 leaves of plates: illustrations; 21cm.

《狄公案之湖滨案》,高罗佩(Gulik, Robert Hans van, 1910—1967)(荷兰汉学家)翻译并创作;Guerbet, Roger 从英语转译成法语. 英文题名:Chinese lake murders

(1) Meurtre sur un bateau-de-fleurs/Robert van Gulik; avec treize hors-textes de style chinois dessinés par l'auteur; traduit de l'anglais par Roger Guerbet. Paris: Club du livre Policier, 1963. 373 pagina's, 21 bladen platen.: illustraties. ; 21cm. (Les classiques du roman policier; 26)

(2) Meurtre sur un bateau-de-fleurs: Les nouvelles enquêtes du Juge Ti/par Robert Van Gulik; trad. de l'anglais par Roger Guerbet. Paris: Christian Bourgois éd., 1984. 317 p. ; 18cm. ISBN: 2264006099, 2264006097. (10/18. Série Grands détectives; 1632)

5. Le singe et le tigre/par Robert van Gulik; traduit de l'anglais par Anne Krief, avec huit illustrations de l'auteur dans le style chinois. Paris: U. G. E., 1986. 180 p. : ill. ; 18cm. ISBN: 2264007486, 2264007483. (10/18; 1765; Grands détectives)

《断指记》和《汉家营》,高罗佩(Gulik, Robert Hans van, 1910—1967)(荷兰汉学家)翻译并创作;Krief, Anne 从英语转译成法语. 英文题名:Monkey and the tiger

6. Le collier de la princesse: les nouvelles enquêtes du juge Ti/par Robert van Gulik; traduit de l'anglais par Anne Krief. Paris: U. G. E., 1985. 229 p. ; 18cm. ISBN:

2264006692，2264006691. （10/18；1688；Grands détectives）

《玉珠串》，高罗佩（Gulik，Robert Hans van，1910—1967）（荷兰汉学家）翻译并创作；Krief，Anne 从英语转译成法语. 英文题名：Necklace and calabash

7. Le mystère du labyrinthe/par Robert van Gulik；traduit de l'anglais par Anne Dechanet et Jos Simons. Paris：U. G. E.，1985. 347 p. ；18cm. ISBN：2264006501，2264006509. (10/18；1673；Grands détectives)

《迷宫案》，高罗佩（Gulik，Robert Hans van，1910—1967）（荷兰汉学家）翻译并创作；Déchanet，Anne 和 Simons，Jos 从英语转译成法语. 英文题名：Chinese maze murders

8. Trois affaires criminelles résolues par le juge Ti：un ancien roman policier chinois/traduit du chinois en anglais，Préfacé，annoté et postfacé par Robert Van Gulik et traduit de l'anglais en français par Anne Krief. Paris：C. Bourgois，1987. 311 p. ：ill. ISBN：2264010975，2264010971，2267004976，2267004977. (10/18；1917；Grands détectives)

《狄公案》，高罗佩（Gulik，Robert Hans van，1910—1967）（荷兰汉学家）翻译并创作；Krief，Anne 从英语转译成法语. 英文题名：Dee goong an：an ancient Chinese detective story

9. Les aventures du juge Ti/Robert Van Gulik. Paris：La Découverte，2004 —. 4 v. ：ill. ISBN：2707142700，2707142702，270714522X，2707145222. (Pulp fictions)

《狄公案》，4 卷. 高罗佩（Gulik，Robert Hans van，1910—1967）（荷兰汉学家）翻译并创作.

10. Le motif du saule：les dernières enquêtes du juge Ti/par Robert van Gulik；traduit de l'anglais par Roger Guerbet. Paris：Union Générale d'Éditions，1985. 250 pages；18cm. ISBN：2264005432，2264005434. (Grands détectives；1591)

《柳园图》，高罗佩（Gulik，Robert Hans van，1910—1967）（荷兰汉学家）翻译并创作；Guerbet，Roger 从英语转译成法语. 英文题名：Willow pattern

11. Le motif du saule/Robert van Gulik；avec quinze hors-texte de style chinois dessinés par l'auteur；traduit de l'anglais par Roger Guerbet. Paris：Club du livre Policier，1968. 408 pagina's，27 bladen platen. ：illustraties. ；21cm. (Les classiques du roman policier；48)

《柳园图》，高罗佩（Gulik，Robert Hans van，1910—1967）（荷兰汉学家）翻译并创作；Guerbet，Roger 从英语转译成法语. 收录《柳园图》《广州案》和《红亭记》.

12. Le fantôme du temple/par Robert van Gulik，avec neuf illustrations，dans le style chinois；traduit de l'anglais par Anne Krief. Paris：U. G. E. ，1985. 283 p. ；18cm. ISBN：226400729X，2264007292. （10/18；1741；Grands détectives）

《紫光寺》，高罗佩（Gulik，Robert Hans van，1910—

1967)（荷兰汉学家）翻译并创作；Krief，Anne 从英语转译成法语. 英文题名：Phantom of the temple

13. Le juge ti à l'œuvre：huit nouvelles policières chinoises/par Robert van Gulik；traduit de l'anglais par Anne Krief；avec huit illustrationd de l'auteur das le style chinois. ［Paris］：Inédit，1986. 284 pages：illustrations；18cm. ISBN：2264007818，2264007810. （Grands détectives；1794）

《大唐狄公案》，高罗佩（Gulik，Robert Hans van，1910—1967)（荷兰汉学家）翻译并创作；Krief，Anne 从英语转译成法语. 英文题名：Judge Dee at work

14. Les enquêtes du juge Ti/［traducion de Roger Guerbet］ Avec quinze hors-textes de style chinois dessinés par l'auteur. ［Paris］，［Club du Livre policier］，1962. 279 pages plates 20cm.

Notes：Translation of the Chinese bell murders.

《狄公案之铜钟案》，高罗佩（Gulik，Robert Hans van，1910—1967)（荷兰汉学家）翻译并创作；Guerbet，Roger 从英语转译成法语.

(1)Le mystère de la cloche/Robert van Gulik；traduit de l'anglais par Roger Guerbet. Paris：Livre de poche，1969. 350 p. ：il. ；17cm. (Le livre de poche；2698)

Notes：Precede al tít. ：Les enquêtes de Juge Ti

15. Le squelette sous cloche：les enquêtes du juge Ti/par Robert van Gulik；traduit de l'anglais par Roger Guerbet. Paris：U. G. E. ，1990. 321 p. ；18cm. ISBN：226400598X，2264005984. （10/18；1621；Grands détectives）

《狄公案之铜钟案》，高罗佩（Gulik，Robert Hans van，1910—1967)（荷兰汉学家）翻译并创作；Guerbet，Roger 从英语转译成法语. 英文题名：Chinese bell murders

16. Assassins et poètes/par Robert van Gulik；traduit de l'anglais par Anne Krief. Paris：U. G. E. ，1985. 278 p. ；18cm. ISBN：2264006978，2264006974. （10/18；1715；Grands détectives）

《黑狐狸》，高罗佩（Gulik，Robert Hans van，1910—1967)（荷兰汉学家）翻译并创作；Krief，Anne 从英语转译成法语. 英文题名：Poets and murder

17. La perle de l'empereur/Robert van Gulik；traduction de Roger Guerbet. Paris：Club du Livre Policier，1966. ［207]-409 pages，［8］ leaves of plates：illustrations；20cm. (Les classiques du roman policier；41)

《御珠案》，高罗佩（Gulik，Robert Hans van，1910—1967)（荷兰汉学家）翻译并创作；Guerbet，Roger 从英语转译成法语. 英文题名：Emperor's pearl

(1)Paris：Union Général d'Éditions，1985. 285 pages；18cm. ISBN：2264005459，2264005458. （Grands détectives；1580)

18. Le mystère de la chambre rouge/Robert van Gulik；traduction de Roger Guerbet. Paris：Club du Livre Policier，1966. vii，205 pages，［6］ leaves of plates：

illustrations; 20cm. (Les classiques du roman policier; 41)

《红亭记》,高罗佩(Gulik, Robert Hans van, 1910—1967)(荷兰汉学家)翻译并创作;Guerbet, Roger 从英语转译成法语.英文题名:Red pavilion

(1)［S. l.］：Le Livre de Poche, 1967. 251 p.；17cm. (Le livre de poche; 2274)

(2)Le pavillon rouge：le retour du juge Ti/par Robert van Gulik；traduit de l'anglais par Roger Guerbet. Paris：Union Générale d'Éditions, 1985. 282 pages；18cm. ISBN：2264005440, 2264005441. (Grands détectives; 1579)

19. Le mystère de la chambre rouge/Robert van Gulik; avec six hors-textes de style chinois dessinés par l'auteur; traduit de l'anglais par Roger Guerbet. Paris：Club du livre Policier, 1966. 409 pagina's, 14 bladen platen.；illustraties.；21cm. (Les classiques du roman policier; 41)

《红亭记》,高罗佩(Gulik, Robert Hans van, 1910—1967)(荷兰汉学家)翻译并创作;Guerbet, Roger 从英语转译成法语.包括《御珠案》和《红亭记》.

20. Le paravent de laque/Robert van Gulik; traduction de Roger Guerbet. Paris：Club du Livre Policier, 1965. ［197］-401, ［10］ leaves of plates：illustrations；20cm. (Les classiques du roman policier; 33)

《四漆屏》,高罗佩(Gulik, Robert Hans van, 1910—1967)(荷兰汉学家)翻译并创作;Guerbet, Roger 从英语转译成法语.英文题名:Lacquer screen

(1)Le Paravent de Laque/par R. Van Gulik. Paris：U. G. E.，1985. 248 p.；18cm. (10/18; 1620; Grands détectives)

(2)Le paravent de laque：Les débuts du juge Ti/par Robert Van Gulik; trad. de l'anglais par Roger Guerbet. Paris：Christian Bourgois éd.，1991. 247 p.；18cm. ISBN：2264005971, 2264005977. (10/18. Série Grands Détectives; 1620)

21. Le singe/R. van Gulik; traduit de l' Anglais par Anne Krief; illustrations de l' auteur dans le style chinois. Caen Cedex：Chardon Bleu Éditions, 1990. 150 pagina's；illustraties；21cm. ISBN：2868330274 2868330277. (Collection large vision)

《猴子》,高罗佩(Gulik, Robert Hans van,1910—1967)(荷兰汉学家)翻译并创作;Krief, Anne 从英语转译成法语.英文题名:Monkey

22. Le château du lac Tchou-An：une nouvelle enquête du juge Ti/Frédéric Lenormand. ［Paris］：Fayard, 2004. 200 p.；22cm. ISBN：2213617988, 2213617985. (Les nouvelles enquêtes du juge Ti/Frédéric Lenormand) 狄公案之三个犯罪故事. Lenormand, Frédéric(1964—)译.

(1)［Le Mans］：Éd. Libra Diffusio, 2005. 240 p.；

24cm. ISBN：2844921876；2844921871

(2)Paris：Points, Impr. Brodard et Taupin, 2006. 1 vol. （217 p.）：couv. ill.；18cm. ISBN：2757800485, 2757800485. (Les nouvelles enquêtes du juge Ti; vol. 1; Points：policier; P1541)

(3)Paris：Points, 2014. 1 volume (222 pages)；18×11cm. ISBN：2757840740, 2757840746. (Les nouvelles enquêtes du juge Ti; Points：policier；；P1541)

蒲松龄(1640—1715)

1. Contes magiques：d'après l'ancien texte de P'ou Soung-Lin (L'immortel en exil)/Louis Laloy. Paris：Éditions d'Art, 1925. 213 p. (Épopées et Légendes, 27)

《聊斋志异》,Laloy, Louis(1874—1944)译.

2. Contes extraordinaires du pavillon du loisir/par P'ou Song-ling; traduit du chinois sous la direction d'Yves Hervouet; introduction d'Yves Hervouet. Paris：Gallimard, 1969. 223 p.：couv. ill.；22cm. （Connaissance de l'Orient; 31Collection Unesco d'Œuvres représentatives. Série chinoise)

《聊斋志异选》,Hervouet, Yves(1921—1999)译.

(1)Paris：Gallimard：UNESCO, 1987. 216 p.：couv. ill. en coul.；19cm. ISBN：207070923X（Br.）(Connaissance de l'Orient, ISSN 0589—3496; 16)

(2)22e éd. Paris：Gallimard：Unesco, 1990. 216 p.：couv. ill. en coul.；19cm. ISBN：207070923X (Br.)(Connaissance de l'Orient; 16)

3. Histoires et légendes de la Chine mystérieuse/textes de Pou Song-ling; recueillis et présentés par Claude Roy; traduction d'Hélène Chatelain. Paris：Tchou, 1969. 285 p.：ill.；22cm. (Histoires et légendes noires)

《聊斋志异》,Roy, Claude(1915—)译.

4. Contes étranges du cabinet Leao/P'ou Song-Ling; trad. du chinois par Louis Laloy. Paris：le Calligraphe, 1985. 175 p.；21cm. ISBN：2904236112 (Br.)

《聊斋志异》,Laloy, Louis(1874—1944)译.

(1)［Arles］：P. Picquier, 1994. 173 p.：couv. ill. en coul.；17cm. ISBN：2877301982（br.）. (Picquier poche, ISSN 1251—6007; 16)

5. Contes fantastiques du Pavillon des Loisirs：Textes choisis/Pu Songling; trad. de Li Fengbai et de Denise Ly-Lebreton. Beijing, Chine：Éditions en Langues Étrangères, 1986. 420 p. (Littérature classique)

《聊斋志异》,Li, Fengbai 和 Ly-Lebreton, Denise 合译.

6. Chroniques de l'étrange/Pu Songling; traduit du chinois et présenté par André Lévy; édition établie par Jacques Cottin. Arles：P. Picquier, 1996. 444 p.：ill.，couv. ill. en coul.；23cm. ISBN：2877302903 (br.)

《聊斋志异》,Lévy, André(1925—)译.

(1)Arles：P. Picquier, 1999. 563 p.：ill.，couv. ill. en coul.；17cm. ISBN：2877304655（br.）. (Picquier poche, ISSN 1251—6007；125)

(2)Arles：P. Picquier, DL 2005. 2 vol. (2002 p.)：ill. , couv. ill. en coul. ；22cm. ISBN：2877307816 (série complète). 2877308065 (vol. 1). 2877308073 (vol. 2)

7. Liao zhai zhi yi xuan＝Contes fantastiques du Pavillon des Loisirs/Pu Songling zhu. Beijing：Wai wen chu ban she, 2004. 3 volumes；22cm. ISBN：7119032690，7119032696
《聊斋志异选》，外文出版社法文编辑室译.

8. Chroniques de l'étrange du pavillon des loisirs/Pu Songling；adaptation et traduction, Wu Hongmiao；illustrations，Tang Feng, Ma Chi, Cheng Hao... ［et al.］. Paris：You-Feng, 2007. 1 vol. (158 p.)：ill. , couv. ill. en coul.；24cm. ISBN：2842793005, 2842793005
Notes：Contient le texte des dialogues en pinyin et caractères chinois，en fin d'ouvrage.
《聊斋志异》，吴弘渺译.

9. Trois contes étranges/Pu Songling；préf et trad. de Rainier Lanselle. Paris：PUF, Presses universitaires de France；Cologny, Genève：Fondation Martin Bodmer, 2009. 2 vol. dans un emboîtage (118，［23］p. dépl.)：ill. en noir et en coul. , couv. ill. en coul；26cm. ISBN：2130575757, 2130575757. (Collection Sources)
Contents：Le fou de livres；Le grand-saint égal du ciel；Le dieu grenouille.
Annexe：1 leporello (［23］f.)：ill.；26cm. —Facs. d'un manuscrit du début du XIXe siècle，conservé dans les collections de la Fondation Martin Bodmer. —Texte seulement en chinois.
《聊斋志异故事三则》，Lanselle, Rainier 译.

10. Contes magiques/Pu Songling；traduits du chinois et présentés par Louis Laloy. Bécherel：les Perséides, impr. 2013. 1 vol. (211 p.)：couv. ill. en coul.；21cm. ISBN：2915596915 (br.). (La lunatique)
《聊斋志异》，Laloy, Louis(1874—1944)译.

吴敬梓(1701—1754)

1. Jou lin wai che... le Roman des lettrés. Étude sur un roman satirique chinois. Paris, L. Rodstein, 1933. 207 pages
《儒林外史》

2. Chronique indiscrète des mandarins/par Wou King-tseu；traduction du chinois par Tchang Fou-jouei；introduction par André Lévy. ［Paris］：Gallimard, 1976. 2 vol., XXIII-814 p.；23cm. (Connaissance de l'Orient；43—44 Collection UNESCO d'Œuvres représentatives. Série chinoise)
《儒林外史》，Chang, Fujui(1915—2006), Lévy, André (1925—)译.

(1)［Paris］：Gallimard, Impr. SEPC), 1986. 1 vol. (403 — 814 p.)：couv. ill. en coul.；19cm. ISBN：2070707474 (vol. 2)；2070707478 (vol. 2).

(Connaissance de l'Orient，；12；Collection UNESCO d'Œuvres représentatives. Série chinoise)

(2)［Paris］：Gallimard，Impr. SEPC), 1986, 2003. 1 vol. (XXIII-401 p.)：couv. ill. en coul.；19cm. ISBN：2070707466 (br)；2070707461 (br). (Connaissance de l'Orient；11；Collection Unesco d'œuvres représentatives. Série chinoise)

(3)［Paris］：Gallimard/Unesco, 1987—1990. 2 vol. 814 p.；19cm. ISBN：2070707474；2070707478. (Collection Unesco d'œuvres représentatives. Série chinoise；Connaissance de l'Orient ［poche］；11；12)

(4)［Paris］：Gallimard：Unesco, 1993. 2 v. (xxiii, 814 p.)；19cm. ISBN：2070707466 (v. 1), 2070707461 (v. 1), 2070707474 (v. 2), 2070707478 (v. 2). (Connaissance de l'Orient, collection UNESCO d'œ uvres représentatives；43—44；Série chinoise)

纪昀(1724—1805)

1. Le lama rouge et autres contes/traduits par son exc. m. Tcheng-Loh... et mme. Lucie Paul-Margueritte, illustrés par m. C. Hauchecorne. Paris, Éditions de l'Abeille d'or, 1923. 2 preliminary leaves, ［7］—131 pages, 1 leaf illustrations 19cm.
《阅微草堂笔记之栾阳消夏录》，Tcheng-Loh 和 Paul-Margueritte , Lucie 合译.

2. Notes de la chaumière des observations subtiles/Ji Yun；traduction de Jacques Pimpaneau. Paris：Kwok On, 1995. 195 p. ：ill.；23cm. ISBN：2910123057, 2910123055. (Littérature；Culture)
《阅微草堂笔记》，Pimpaneau, Jacques 译.

3. Passe-temps d'un été à Luanyang/Ji Yun；trad. du chinois, présenté et annoté par Jacques Dars. ［Paris］：Gallimard, Impr. Floch, 1998. XV-562 p. ；23cm. ISBN：2070754286 , 2070754281. (Connaissance de l'Orient：série chinoise；99)
《阅微草堂笔记之栾阳消夏录》，Dars, Jacques 译.

4. Des nouvelles de l'au-delà/Ji Yun；textes choisis, traduits du chinois, Préfacés et annotés par Jacques Dars. ［Paris］：Gallimard, Impr. Firmin-Didot, 2005. 1 vol. (135 p.)：couv. ill. en coul.；18cm. ISBN：2070321207, 2070321209. (Collection Folio, 4326)
纪昀作品选译. Dars, Jacques(1941—2010)译.

李渔(1611—1680)

1. Jeou-p'ou-t'ouan, ou, La chair comme tapis de prière：roman publié vers 1660/par le lettré Liyou；traduit en français pour la première fois par Pierre Klossowski；préfacé par René Etiemble. Paris：J.-J. Pauvert, 1962. viii, 316 pages；21cm.
《肉蒲团》，Klossowski, Pierre 译.

(1)Jeou-P'ou-T'ouan/Li-Yu；trad. du chinois par Pierre Klossowski；et augmenté d'une préf. d'Etiemble. Paris：Cercle du livre précieux, 1963. VIII-316 p.；

22cm.

(2)Jeou-p'ou-t'ouan ou la chair comme tapis de prière/Li Yu; trad. en français par Pierre Klossowski; préf. par René Etiemble. Paris: J.-J. Pauvert, 1968. x, 319 p.; 20cm.

(3)Jeou-P'ou-T'ouan: ou la chair comme tapos de prière/roman publié vers 1640 par le lettré Liyou, traduit en française pour la première fois par Pierre Klossowski, préfacé par René Etiemble édité par Jean-Jacques Pauvert. Paris: Montreuil, 1968. 376 pages: illustrations; 22cm. 316 pages; 21cm.

(4)Jeou-p'ou-t'ouan, ou, La chair comme tapis de prière/Li-Yu; illustré par Raymond Brenot; traduction de Pierre Klossowski. [Paris]: Éditions de l'Odéon: Éditions André Vial, 1971. 205 pages: color illustrations; 28cm.

(5)Bagneux: Le Livre de Paris, 1976. VVI-327 p.; 22cm. ISBN: 2245005686, 2245005682

(6)Jeou-P'ou-T'ouan, ou, La chair comme tapis de prière: roman/Li-Yu; traduit par Pierre Klossowski; Préfacé par René Etiemble. [Paris]: Société nouvelle des Éditions Jean-Jacques Pauvert, 1979. viii, 316 p.

(7)[Paris]: Pauvert, 1980. 1 vol. (VIII-316 p.); 21cm.

(8)[Paris]: Pauvert, 1989. 1 vol. (VIII-316 p.); 21cm. ISBN: 2720201898, 2720201899

(9)Paris: 10—18, 1995. 316 p.: couv. ill. en coul.; 18cm. ISBN: 2264021314, 2264021311. (10—18. Domaine étranger)

2. De la chair à l'extase: roman érotique/Li Yu; traduit du chinois par Christine Corniot. Arles [France]: P. Picquier, 1991. 284 p.; 21cm. ISBN: 2877300641, 2877300643

《肉蒲团》,Corniot, Christine 译.

(1)Arles [France]: Éd Ph. Picquier, 1994. 285 p.; 17cm. ISBN: 2877302059, 2877302050. (Picqier poche; 19)

(2)Arles: P. Picquier, Impr. Robert, 1996. 272 p. -[24] f. de pl.: couv. ill. en coul.; 23cm. ISBN: 2877302857, 2877302852

3. A mari jaloux femme fidèle: récits du 17e siècle/Li Yu; traduit du chinois par Pierre Kaser. Paris; Arles: P. Picquier, 1990. 237 p.: ill.; 21cm. ISBN: 2877300501, 2877300506

《妒夫贤妻》,Kaser, Pierre 译.

(1)A mari jaloux, femme fidèle: récits du XVIIe siècle/Li Yu; traduit du chinois par Pierre Kaser. Arles: P. Picquier, 1998. 268 p.: ill.; 17cm. ISBN: 2877303896, 2877303897. (Picquier poche; 95)

曹雪芹(约1715—1763)

1. Le rêve dans le pavillon rouge = Hong lou meng/Cao Xueqin; traduction, introduction, notes et variantes par Li Tche-Houa et Jacqueline Alézaïs; révision par André d'Hormon. [Paris]: Gallimard, 1981. 2 volumes: illustrations; 18cm. (Collection UNESCO d'Œuvres représentatives. Série chinoise; Bibliothèque de la Pléiade; 273—274)

《红楼梦》,李治华,Alézaïs, Jacqueline 合译.

(1)[Paris]: Gallimard, 2009. 2 vol. (CXLIII—1638, XLVI—1640 p.): ill., cartes.; 18cm. ISBN: 2070110193 (rel), 2070110192 (rel), 2070110209 (rel), 2070110206 (rel), 2070110216 (coffret), 2070110214 (coffret). (Collection UNESCO d'Œuvres représentatives. Série chinoise; Bibliothèque de la Pléiade;; 293—294)

2. Le rêve dans le pavillon rouge. [1], Hong-leou mong/Ts'ao siue-kin; traduit du chinois par Franz Kuhn; version française établie par Armel Guerne. Paris: G. Le Prat, 1982. 341 p.: ill.; 19cm. ISBN: 28520504248

《红楼梦》,Kuhn, Franz (1884—1961) 英译; Guerne, Armel 法译.

3. Le rêve dans le pavillon rouge/Cao Xueqin & Gao E; illustrations de Sun Wen; traduction et adaptation, Wu Hongmiao & Laurent Ballouhey. Paris: Bibliothèque de l'image, 2009. 1 vol. (440 p.): ill. en noir et en coul., couv. ill. en coul.; 26cm. ISBN: 2814400085 (cousu à la chinoise sous étui), 2814400088 (cousu à la chinoise sous étui), 8274400089, 8274400085

《红楼梦》,Wu, Hong miao 和 Ballouhey, Laurent 合译.

4. Rêve dans le pavillon rouge/[Cao Xueqin]; [traduction, Nicolas Henry & Si Mo]. Paris: les Éditions Fei, 2015. 1 volume; 11 × 15cm. ISBN: 2359662047 (dans une boîte), 235966204X (dans une boîte)

《红楼梦》,Henry, Nicolas(1981—), Si, Mo. 译.

袁枚(1716—1798)

1. Ce dont le maître ne parlait pas: le merveilleux onirique/par Yuan Mei; récits traduits du chinois, présentés et annotés par Chang Fu-jui, Jacqueline Chang, Jean-Pierre Diény. [Paris]: Gallimard, 2011. 368 p.; 23 × 14cm. ISBN: 2070131839, 2070131831. (Connaissance de l'Orient; 121. Série chinoise)

《子不语》等 135 篇作品. Chang, Fu-jui(1915—2006)等合译.

陈季同(1851—1907)

1. Huangshanke chuan qi = Roman de l'homme jaune/Chen Jitong zhu; Li Huachuan yi. Beijing: Ren min wen xue chu ban she, 2010. 8, 289 pages: illustrations; 22cm. ISBN: 7020078882, 7020078885

《黄衫客传奇》,人民文学出版社. 本书是作者以唐传奇《霍小玉传》为蓝本创作的一部法文长篇小说,讲述了书生李益与歌妓霍小玉的爱情、李益的变心背叛和霍小玉的复仇故事.

刘鹗(1857—1909)

1. L'Odyssée de Lao ts'an/par Lieou Ngo；traduit du chinois par Cheng Tcheng. [Paris] Gallimard，1964. 280 pages；22cm. (Connaissance de l'Orient；collection UNESCO d'œuvres représentatives，19. Série chinoise)

    《老残游记》,盛成(1899—)译.

    (1)L'Odyssée de Lao ts'an/par Lieou Ngo；traduit du chinois par Cheng Tcheng；avant-propos de Jacques Reclus. Paris：Gallimard，1990. 280 p.；19cm. ISBN：2070719502，2070719501. (Connaissance de l'Orient；41；Collection UNESCO d'œvres représentatives. Série chinoise)978.

2. Pérégrinations d'un clochard/Lieou Ngo；traduit du chinois par Cheng Tcheng；Préface d'Etiemble；avant-propos de Jacques Reclus. [Paris]：Gallimard，1984. 401 p. ISBN：2070375749，2070375745. (Folio；1574；Collection Unesco d'œuvres représentatives. Série chinoise)

    《老残游记》,盛成(1899—)译.

    (1)Pérégrinations d'un clochard/Lieou Ngo；traduit du chinois par Cheng Tcheng；avant-propos de Jacques Reclus. [Paris]：Gallimard，Impr. Firmin-Didot，2005. 1 vol. (415 p.)；19cm. ISBN：2070775437，2070775439. (Collection L'imaginaire；523)

其他编译小说

1. Les Concubines chinoises célèbres，Pan Tsié-Yu et Tchao-Kiun/chansons traduites par H. Imbert. Pékin："Politique de Pékin"，1921. IV—16 p.，fig. (Collection de la "Politique de Pékin")

    《班婕妤与昭君》,Imbert, Henri 译.

2. La Merveilleuse histoire de Pao-Se. Conte chinois，traduit par J. B. Lin. Paris：G. Servant，1925. 60 p.，pl. en coul.

    《褒姒》,Lin, J. B. 译.

3. L'Amour de la renarde，marchands et lettrés de la vieille Chine/par Ling Mong-tch'ou. 12 contes du XVIIe siècle. Traduits，préfacés et annotés par André Lévy. Paris：Gallimard，1970. 22cm.，296 p.，carte，couv. ill. (Connaissance de l'Orient. Collection Unesco d'œuvres représentatives. Série chinoise. 32)

    牤狐的爱情：古代中国商人和文人. 凌蒙初著；Lévy, André(1925—)译.

    (1)[Paris]：Gallimard：UNESCO，1988. 285 p.：couv. ill. en coul.；19cm. ISBN：2070713296 (br.). (Connaissance de l'Orient，ISSN 0589 — 3496；24 Collection UNESCO d'œuvres représentatives. Série chinoise)

4. L'Honnête commis Tchang：contes chinois/traduit du chinois... présenté et annoté par André Lévy；illustrations de Bruno Pilorget. [Paris]：Gallimard，1982. 157 p.：ill.，couv. ill. en coul.；18cm. ISBN：2070343138

(Br.). (Collection Folio junior. Légendes；13)

《志诚张主管》,Lévy, André(1925—)译.

I53 现当代小说集

1. Anthologie des conteurs chinois modernes/éd. sci. trad. et annot. par J. B. Kyn Yn Yu. Paris：Rieder，1929. 190 p.；19cm. (Les prosateurs étrangers modernes)

    中国现代中短篇小说作家作品集.J. B. Kyn Yn Yu 译. 收录陈炜谟,鲁迅,冰心,茅盾,敬隐渔,许地山,郁达夫作品.

2. La maison nouvelle：récits par des auteurs chinois contemporains. Pékin：Éditions en Langues Étrangères，1955. 153 p.；22cm.

    《"新的家"及其他故事》,艾芜等著.

3. 《老交通》及其他故事. 北京：外文出版社,1957

4. L'Aube sur la rivière. Pékin：Éditions en Langues Étrangères，1958. 197 pages

    《黎明的河边及其他故事》(新中国短篇小说选第四集),峻青等著；龙浩等译.

5. Un jour de neige Récits par des auteurs chinois contemporains. Pékin：Éditions en Langues Étrangères，1960. 1 vol. (156 p.)；21cm.

    《"雪天"及其他故事：新中国短篇小说选第六集》

6. Recits de la guerre de resistance contre le Japon. Pékin：Éditions en Langues Étrangères，1961. viii，214 s. [10] tav.

    《抗日战争的故事》

7. Nuit d'été：recueil de nouvelles. Pékin：Éditions en Langues Étrangères，1964. 183 p.；22cm.

    《夏夜：中国短篇小说集》,周立波等著.

8. 小矿工及其他故事：新中国短篇小说选第五集/大群等著. 北京：外文出版社,1965

9. Récits chinois，1918—1942. Traduits et présentés par Martine Vallette-Hémery. Paris：l'Herne，1970. 22cm.，336 p.，couv. ill.

    Contents：Le journal d'un fou，par Lu Xun—Le reméde，par Lu Xun—De la pratique du sacrifice，par Lu Xun—Une vie，par Ye Sheng-tao—Le riz quotidien，par Ye Sheng-tao—Le naufrage，par Yu Da-fu—Marx chez Confucius，par Guo Mo-ruo—Un singulier combat，par Guo Mo-ruo—Autres temps，autres moeurs，par Shen Cong-wen—Le croissant de lune，par Lao She—Chien，par Ba Jin—Les fortifiants，par Wu Zu-xiang—L'histoire de "Grand Nez,"par Mao Dun—Haine，par Zhang Tian-yi—"Quatre-Pattes,"par Xiao Jun—Le jugement des eaux，par Li Guang-tian.

    《中国故事》,Vallette-Hémery, Martine 译注.

10. Les semences：récits et nouvelles. Pékin：Éditions en Langues Étrangères，1972. 203 pages；20cm.

    《"种子"及其他》,陈洪山等著.

11. Fleurs des champs. Pékin：Éditions en Langues

Étrangères, 1975. 98 pages：illustrations；19cm.
《彩色的田野》（短篇小说集）

12. Un coeur d'esclave：nouvelles chinoises contemporaines/
Lu Xun... [et al.]. Paris：Éditions du Centenaire, 1980.
243 p. ：ill. (Petite bibliothèque chinoise. Littérature；E
100)

Contents：La lumière blanche/Lu Xun—Un coeur
d'esclave/Ba Jin—Ouvrières de louage/Xia Yan—
L'histoire du grand nez/Mao Dun—Une nuit d'automne/
Sha Ding—Vieilles coutumes/Zhao Shuli—Le forgeron et
le charpentier/Sun Li—Nuit d'été/Wang Wenshi—La
famille de l'autre versant/Zhou Libo—La lumière de la
lampe/Liu Baiyu.

20 世纪中国小说选集. 收录鲁迅等人的作品.

13. Six femmes écrivains. Beijing：Littérature chinoise,
1981. xi, 274 pages：portraits；18cm. (Collection
Panda)

Contents：Dans l'étable/Ding Ling—Le nid vide/Bing
Xin—L'enfant venu de la forêt/Zhang Jie—Au milieu de
l'âge/Shen Rong—Le réve de l'archet/Zong Pu—Le
chemin de la steppe/Ru Zhijuan.

六位女作家作品选译. 收录丁玲的《牛棚小品》，冰心的
《空巢》，张洁的《从森林里来的孩子》，谌容的《人到中
年》，宗璞的《弦上的梦》，茹志娟的《草原上的小路》.

14. La Chine des femmes：nouvelles/Shen Rong, Ding Ling,
Bing Xin, Zhang Jie, Zong Pu, Ru Zhijuan. Paris：
Mercure de France, 1983. 244 p. ；23cm. ISBN：
2715201230, 2715201231. ("Mille et une femmes)

20 世纪中国女作家中短篇小说选译. 收录沈容，丁玲，冰
心，张洁，宗璞，茹志娟的作品.

15. Dix auteurs modernes：nouvelles. Beijing：Littérature
chinoise, 1983. 384 p. ：ill. ；18cm. (Collection Panda)
《当代优秀小说选》.《中国文学》杂志社（熊猫丛书）

16. Huit femmes écrivains/Ding Ling... [et al.]. Beijing：
Littérature chinoise, 1984. 374 p. (Panda books)
《中国女作家近作选》.《中国文学》杂志社（熊猫丛书）.
收录丁玲，王安忆，张洁，冰心，航鹰，沈容，宗璞，茹志娟
的作品.

17. Le remontée vers le jour：nouvelles de Chine 1978—
1988/auteurs：A Cheng...；traducteurs：Baiyun...；
Préface de Claude Roy. Aix-en-Provence：Alinea, 1988.
270 s. ISBN：2904631496, 2904631498
重见天日：1978—1988 年中国中短篇小说选译. 阿城等
著；Baiyun 等译.

18. Les meilleures Œuvres chinoises (1949—1989). Beijing,
China：Littérature chinoise, 1989. viii, 420 pages；
22cm.
《中国优秀短编小说选：1949—1989》. 中国文学出版社
（熊猫丛书）.

19. Le corsage rouge. Beijing：Éditions en Langues
Étrangères, 1990. 264 p. ：couv. ill. ；18cm. ISBN：

7119007270 , 7119007274.（Phénix)
《没有纽扣的红衬衫：中国当代中篇小说选》，铁凝等著.
外文出版社（凤凰丛书）. 收录铁凝的《没有纽扣的红衬
衫》和陆文夫的《美食家》.

20. Recueil de nouvelles de jeunes écrivains/Lü Lei... [et
al.]. Beijing：Éditions en Langues Étrangères, 1990.
267 p. ISBN：7119011200, 7119011202.（Phénix)

Contents：Une zone marine éblouissante/Lü Lei—Une
terre mystérieuse/Liang Xiaosheng—La procession des
dragons/Deng Gang—Ma soeur/Zhang Ping—Elle est
sortie du tableau/Wang Zhaojun—Anciennes moeurs de
fourneaux de sable/Li Hangyu.

《中国青年作品选》，王凤麟等著. 外文出版社（凤凰
丛书）

21. Avec l'accent de Pékin：nouvelles choisies/Lao She et
autres. Beijing：Éditions en Langues Étrangères, 1991.
334 p. ISBN：7119013084；7119013084.（Phénix)

Contents：Le croissant de lune, La cour des Liu/Lao
She—En souvenir de Yun Zhiqiu, L'asile de paix/Wang
Zengqi—Un incident rue Qingteng/Liu Shaotang—Le
rouge-gorge/Han Shaohua—9, rue de la Manivelle,
Chercher un divertissement/Chen Jiangong.

《找乐：京味小说选》，老舍等著. 外文出版社（凤凰
丛书）

22. La femme en bleu：nouvelles/[traduit par Lu Fujun].
Pékin：Éd. en Langues Étrangères, 1992. 205 p. ；
18cm. ISBN：711901501X；7119015019.（Phénix)
《拣来的新娘子：通俗小说选》，孙之龙编. 外文出版社
（凤凰丛书）.

23. La tentation：nouvelles. Pékin：Éd. en Langues
Érangères, 1992. 290 p. ；18cm. ISBN：7119014838；
7119014838.（Phénix)

Contents：La Tentation/Liu Heng. Histoire romantique
après minuit/Zhou Xiaohong. Un étrange étalage/Zhong
Jieying. Rajeunir de dix printemps/ Chen Rong.
Variations sans thème/Xu Xing. Tu ne saurais me
changer/Liu Xihong

《零点以后的浪漫史：中国新观念小说选》，高苗编. 外文
出版社（凤凰丛书）

24. Shanghai, 1920—1940：douze récits/Mao Dun [and
others]；textes choisis et présentés par Emmanuelle
Péchenart；traduit du chinois par Emmanuelle Péchenart,
Victoire Surio et Anne Wu；dessins de Françoise Ged.
[Paris]：Bleu de Chine, 1995. 182, [1] pages：
illustrations；21cm. ISBN：291088404X, 2910884048

Contents：Shanghai/Mao Dun—De sang et de larmes/Yu
Dafu—Où aller? /Hu Yepin—Pour oublier/Lu Xun—
Bernard Shaw à Shanghai/Lu Xun—Au jardin public/
Mao Dun—Un déménagement d'opèrette/Mao Dun—Le
10 octobre 1934 à Shanghai/Pa Kin—Une journée/Ding
Ling—Vers la lumière du jour/Ding Ling—Le dernier

drapeau/Shi Tuo—Attente/Zhang Ailing.

上海 1920—1940 故事十二则. 茅盾等著；Péchenart, Emmanuelle 等译.

25. Xiao xiaoshuo jingxuan/Wang Zengqi, He Liwei, Zhou Daxin deng zhu; Lü Hua yi. [éd.] bilingue. Beijing: Éd. Littérature chinoise, 1996. 293 p.: couv. ill. en coul.; 19cm. ISBN: 7507103579, 7507103571. (Collection panda)

《小小说精选》，汪曾祺等著；吕华译.法汉对照.

26. Croquants de Chine/Liu Xinglong, Zhan Zhengwei; textes choisis, trad. du chinois et présentés par Françoise Naour. Paris: Bleu de Chine, 1998. 187 p.; 21cm. ISBN: 2910884171, 2910884178

Contents: Choux-raves/par Liu Xinglong—Splendeur et misère des croquants/par Zhan Zhengwei.

Naour, Françoise 译. 收录刘醒龙的《白菜萝卜》和詹政伟的 1 篇小说.

27. L'enfant au milieu du lit: recueil de courtes nouvelles/ [Zhang Weiming and others]. Beijing: Éditions en Langues Érangères, 2004. 234 pages; 18cm. ISBN: 7119035207, 7119035208. (Littérature chinoise)

《微型小说选》，张卫明等著；外文出版社法文部译. 外文出版社（中国文学）. 本书收录张卫明等作家 55 篇微型小说.

28. Dix auteurs modernes: nouvelles/[Gao Xiaosheng and others]. Beijing: Éditions en Langues Érangères, 2004. 388 pages; 18cm. ISBN: 7119035193; 7119035192. (Littérature chinoise)

Contents: Avant-propos/Li Meiying—Chen Huansheng se rend en ville/Gao Xiaoshing—Notre coin à nous/Shi Tiesheng—Un coin oublié par l'amour/Zhang Xian—A la recherche de Han le peintre/Deng Youmei—Le gardien de chevaux/Zhang Xianliang—Une maisonnette de bois couverte de lierre/Gu Hua—Tempête sur Danao/Wang Zengqi—Le cerf à sept cors/Wure'ertu—L'écume de la vie/Xue Haixiang—Une terre inoubliable/Liang Xiaosheng.

《当代优秀小说选》，高晓生等著；李梅英等译. 外文出版社（中国文学）. 本书收录高晓生、邓友梅等 10 位作家的中篇小说.

29. Shanghai, fantômes sans concession/sous la direction de Chen Feng; avec Wang Anyi... [et al.]; traduit du chinois (mandarin)par Yvonne André... [et al.]. Paris: Autrenment, 2004. 148 p.; 22cm. ISBN: 2746704544, 2746704541. (Littératures/Romans d'une ville)

Contents: La chambre de l'amant/Wei Hui—Linda, fille de bar/Chen Danyan—Valses d'un hiver/Tang Ying—Ton nom, mon prénom/Cheng Naishan—Ruelles/Wang Anyi.

短篇小说五篇. Chen, Feng 主编；王安忆等著；André, Yvonne 译. 收录卫慧的《爱人的房间》、唐颖的《冬天我们跳舞》、程乃珊的《你的姓氏，我的名字》、王安忆的《长恨歌》.

30. Tranchant de lune: et autres nouvelles contemporaines chinoises/Mo Yan; traduit du chinois par François Dubois. [Paris]: Hachette livre, 2015. 7 vol. (47, 47, 31, 36, 71, 31, 39 p.); 16cm. ISBN: 2014017533, 2014017530. (Ming Books)

中国当代中短篇小说选译. Dubois, François 译. 收录莫言、邓一光、金仁顺、李二、刘庆邦、刘震云、王祥富的作品.

I54　现当代个人作品

（按作者出生年先后排列，作者出生年不详或作品的作者未知者排在最后）

鲁迅（1881—1936）

1. Choix de nouvelles de Lou Shun/trad. [du chinois] par Tchang Tien-ya. Pékin: Impr. de la "Politique de Pékin", 1932. 75 f.: couv. ill.; 27cm. (Collection de la "Politique de Pékin.")

《鲁迅短篇小说选》，Tchang Tien-ya 译.

2. Nouvelles choisies/Lou Sin. Pékin: Éditions en Langues Étrangères, 1956. 243 p.: ill.; 22cm.

Contents: Préface à "Cri d'appel"—Le journal d'un fou—Kong Yi-ki—Le reméde—Demain—Un petit incident—Tempête dans une tasse de thé—Mon village natal—La véritable histoire de Ah Q—Le théâtre des dieux—Le sacrifice du Nouvel An—Dans un estaminet—Une famille heureuse—La savonnette—Le misanthrope—Regret du passé—Le divorce—La fuite dans la lune—Le forgeur d'épées.

《鲁迅短篇小说选》

(1) 2 éd. Pékin: Éditions en Langues Étrangères, 1964. 145 pages: front (portrait), plates; 21cm.

(2) 3. éd. Pékin: Éditions en Langues Étrangères, 1974. 302 pages: illustrations; 22cm.

(3) 3ème éd. Beijing: Éd. En Langues Étrangères, 1990. 1 vol. (302 p.); 21cm. ISBN: 7119012452; 7119012452.

3. Trois nouvelles: le remède, un petit incident, la savonnette/ Lou Sin. Villelongue-d'Aude (11300): Atelier du Gué, 1976. 50 p.: ill.; 21cm.

《鲁迅短篇小说三则：药、一件小事、肥皂》，译者不详.

(1) Villelongue d'Aude: Atelier du Gué, [1980]. 56 p.; 26cm.

4. Le journal d'un fou; suivi de La véritable histoire de Ah Q/Luxum; Préface de Jean Guiloineau. Paris: Stock, 1981. 191 pages. ISBN: 2234014328, 2234014329. (Bibliothèque cosmopolite; 23)

《狂人日记·阿 Q 正传》，Guiloineau, Jean 序.

(1) [Paris]: Stock, 1992. 191 p.; 18cm. ISBN: 2234014328, 2234014329. (Bibliothèque cosmopolite; 23)

(2) Paris: Stock, 1996. 191 pages; 18cm. ISBN: 2234046394,

2234046399. (Bibliothèque cosmopolite)

5. Voilà ce que je lui ai fait：［nouvelles］/Luxun. ［Paris］: Hachette jeunesse，1996. 124 p.：couv. ill.；19cm. ISBN：2012095224, 2012095229. (Courts toujours!)

鲁迅中短篇小说集.

6. Le journal d'un fou：et autres nouvelles/Lu Xun. Paris：Éditions Sillage，2015. 1 vol. (107 p.)；25cm. ISBN：9791091896429

《狂人日记等短篇小说》,译者不详.

7. La véritable histoire de Ah Q, roman/Traduction de Paul Jamati. Préface de Claude Roy. Paris, les éditeurs français réunis (impr. de J. London), 1953. In—16, 123 p.，portrait sur la couv.

《阿 Q 正传》,Jamati，Paul(1890—1960)译.

8. La véritable histoire de Ah Q/Lou Sin. Pékin：Éditions en Langues Étrangères，1973. 107 pages，［2］leaves of plates：portrait, facsimile；19cm.

《阿 Q 正传》

（1）Beijing, Chine：Éditions en Langues Étrangères，1982. 81 pages：illustrations

（2）Beijing：Éd. en Langues Étrangères，1987. 81 p.：ill.；19cm.

（3）Pékin：Éditions en Langues Étrangères，1990. 81 pages：portraits；18cm. ISBN：7119012282, 7119012285

（4）Beijing：Éd. en Langues Étrangères，2002. 1 vol. (200 p.)：couv. ill.；19cm. ISBN：7119029672, 7119029673

9. Ah Q：Ah Kiou：tragédie chinoise ［Vincennes, Cartoucherie, 4 novembre 1975］/Bernard Chartreux, Jean Jourdheuil；d'après Lou Sin. Paris：C. Bourgois, 1975. 91 p.：ill.；20cm.

《阿 Q 正传》,Chartreux，Bernard 和 Jourdheuil，Jean 合译.

10. La Véridique histoire d'A-Q/Lu Xun；traduction, présentation et notes par Martine Vallette-Hémery；［publié par le］Centre de publication Asie orientale. Paris（Tour centrale, 2, place Jussieu, 75221, cedex 05）：Centre de publication Asie orientale, 1975. 135 p.：ill.，couv. ill.；22cm. (Bibliothèque asiatique；14)

《阿 Q 正传》,Vallette-Hémery，Martine 译.

11. Histoire d'A Q：véridique biographie/Luxun；trad. et présenté par Michelle Loi；ill. de Qiu Sha. Paris：Librairie générale française, 1989. 125 p.：ill.，couv. ill. en coul.；17cm. ISBN：2253049255, 2253049258. (Le Livre de poche. Biblio；3116)

《阿 Q 正传》,Loi，Michelle(1926—2002)译.

（1）Paris：Presses universitaires de France, impr. 1990. 1 vol. (128 p.)；18cm. ISBN：2130429793. (études littéraires；28)

12. La véritable histoire d'Ah Q/Lu Xun；illustrations, Jean-Michel Charpentier；traduit du chinois par Michelle Loi. Bordeaux：Elytis, impr. 2010. 1 vol. (126 p.)：ill.，couv. ill.；25cm. ISBN：2356390349. (Grafik；1)

《阿 Q 正传》

13. L'édifiante histoire d'a-Q/Lu Xun；traduction et annotation de Sebastian Veg. Montréal, Québec：Rue Dorion, 2015. 134 pages；18cm. ISBN：2981352743, 2981352741

《阿 Q 正传》,Veg，Sebatian 译.

14. Contes anciens à notre manière/présentés et traduits par Li Tche-houa. ［2e édition.］Paris：Gallimard (Abbeville, impr. F. Paillart), 1959. In-8° (22cm.), 203 p.，couv. ill. en coul. (Connaissance de l'Orient. 8)

《故事新编》,李治华(Li Tche Houa)译.

（1）［Paris］：Gallimard, 1988. 198 p.：couv. ill. en coul.；19cm. ISBN：207071327X. (Connaissance de l'Orient, ISSN 0589—3496；26 Collection UNESCO d'Œuvres représentatives. Série chinoise, ISSN 0258—686X)

15. Contes anciens sur un mode nouveau/Lou Sin. Pékin：Éditions en Langues Étrangères；［Paris］：［diffusion Éditions du Centenaire］, 1978. 166 p.：portr.，couv. ill.；19cm.

《故事新编》

16. Gu shi xin bian＝Contes anciens sur un mode nouveau/Lu Xun zhu. Beijing：Wai wen chu ban she, 2004. 331 pages；22cm. ISBN：7119032623, 7119032627.

《故事新编》,外文出版社法文部译.

17. Histoires anciennes revisitées/Lu Xun；traduit du chinois par Alexis Brossolet. Paris（13 rue de Navarin, 75009）：éd. du Non-agir, DL 2014. 1 vol. (217 p.)：couv. ill. en coul.；21cm. ISBN：9791092475067, 9791092475043

《故事新编》,Brossolet，Alexis(1968—)译.

18. Réveiller les morts/Lu Xun；［traduit par Alexis Brossollet］. éd. Bilingue. Paris：éd. du Non-agir, DL 2014. 1 vol. (43 p.)：couv. ill.；18cm. ISBN：9791092475142

《故事新编：起死》,Brossollet，Alexis 译.

19. Le Sacrifice du nouvel an/adaptation de la nouvelle.. Lou Sin；illustrations, Yong Siang, Hong Jen, Yao Kiao. Pékin：Éditions en Langues Étrangères；［Paris］：［diffusion Éditions du Centenaire］, 1978. 57 f. de pl.：couv. ill. en coul.；19 × 26cm.

《祝福》

20. Cris：nouvelles/Luxun；trad. du chinois par Joël Bellassen, Feng Hanjin, Jean Join et Michelle Loi. Paris：A. Michel, 1995. 264 p.；23cm. ISBN：2226078037. (Les grandes traductions)

《呐喊》,Bellassen，Joël 等译.

21. Cri d'appel/Lu Xun. Beijing：Éditions en Langues

Etrangers, 2004. 285, [1] s. ; 18cm. ISBN:
7119032631, 7119032634

《呐喊》,外文出版社法文部译. 本书是作者的短篇小说
集,共收入作品 20 余篇.

22. Cris/Lu Xun; traduction, annotation et postface de
Sebastian Veg. Paris: éd. Rue d'Ulm, DL 2010. 1 vol.
(303 p.): fac-sim. ; 19cm. ISBN: 2728804337.
(Collections Versions françaises, ISSN 1627-4040)

《呐喊》,Veg, Sebastian 译.

23. Errances. P'ang Huang/Lu Xun. Beijing: Éd. en
Langues Étrangères, 2003. 1 vol. (309 p.): couv. ill. ;
18cm. ISBN: 7119032658, 7119032658

《彷徨》,外文出版社法文部译.

24. Errances; suivi de Les chemins divergents de la
littérature et du pouvoir politique/Lu Xun; trad. [du
chinois], annot. et postf. de Sebastian Veg. Paris: Éd.
rue d'Ulm, 2004. 352 p.: portr., fac-sim. ; 20cm.
ISBN: 2728803153. (Versions françaises)

《彷徨》,Veg, Sebastian 译.

25. Errances = Pang huang/Lu Xun. Beijing: Éd. en
Langues Étrangères, 2004. 309 p.; 18cm. ISBN:
7119032658, 7119032658

《彷徨》,汉法对照.

26. Errances/Luxun; trad. par Jacques Meunier. Paris:
Éditions You-Feng, 2004. 213 S. ISBN: 2842791703,
2842791704

《彷徨》,Meunier, Jacques 译.

27. Tempête dans une tasse de thé/Luxun; trad. du chinois
des éd. en Langues Étrangères, Pékin; rév. de la trad.
et postf. de Jean Guiloineau...; ill. de Marion Bataille.
Paris: Mille et une nuits, 1998, 38 p.: ill., couv. ill.
en coul. ; 15cm. ISBN: 2842053621 (br.). (Mille et
une nuits; 215)

《风波》,Guiloineau, Jean(1939—)译.

28. En forgeant les épées: extrait du recueil Histoires
anciennes, revisitées = Gu shi xin bian/Lu Xun; traduit
du chinois par Alexis Brossollet. Paris: Éditions du
non-agir, 2014. 1 vol. (85 p.): ill. ; 18cm. ISBN:
9791092475227

《铸剑》,Brossollet, Alexis 译. 法汉对照. 选自《故事新
编》.

29. Le journal d'un fou: et autres nouvelles/Lu Xun. Paris:
Éditions Sillage, 2015. 1 vol. (107 p.); 17cm. ISBN:
9791091896429

《狂人日记》

李劼人(1891—1962)

1. Rides sur les eaux dormantes/Li Tiej'en; traduit du
chinois par Wan Chunyee. Paris: Gallimard, 1981. 315
p.; 21cm. ISBN: 2070233359, 2070233359. (Du monde
entier)

《死水微澜》,Wan, Chunyee 译.

叶圣陶(1894—1988)

1. Ni Houan-tche, l'instituteur/Ye Cheng-tao. Pékin:
Éditions en Langues Étrangères, 1961. 365 p, [1] tav.

《倪焕之》,Tchou, W. S. 译.

(1)2e éd. Pékin: Éditions en Langues Étrangères, 1978.
361 p

茅盾(1896—1981)

1. Les vers à soie du printemps: et autres nouvelles/par Mao
Dun; Traduit du chinois par Tchen Mien. Pékin: Éditions
en Langues Étrangères, 1958. 1 vol. (328 p.): portr. ;
22cm.

《春蚕》,陈绵译.

(1) 3e éd. Beijing: Éditions en Langues Étrangères,
1980. 296 p.

2. Les vers à soie du printemps: roman/Mao Dun; traduit du
chinois par Catherine Vignal; [préface de Michelle Loi].
Paris: Acropole, 1980. 171 p. ; 23cm. ISBN: 2-7144-
1273-4 (Br.). (Littérature du monde)

《春蚕》,Vignal, Catherine 译.

3. Minuit/Mao Dun. Pékin, Éditions en Langues
Étrangères, 1962. [vi], 526 p., pl., port. en front.
8vo

《子夜》

(1) 2e éd. Pékin: Éditions en Langues Étrangères;
[Paris]: [diffusion Éditions du Centenaire], cop.
1979. 579 p. -[20] f. de pl. ; 22cm.

(2)3ème tirage. Beijing: éd. en Langues Étrangères,
1984. 579 p. -[1] portr. ; 21cm.

4. Minuit: roman/[Maodun]; traduit du chinois. Paris: R.
Laffont, 1972. 544 p.: couv. ill. en coul. ; 20cm.
(Pavillons. Section de littérature chinoise; 1)

《子夜》,译者不详.

5. Minuit/traduit du chinois par Jacques Meunier et Michelle
Loi. Paris: Éditions You Feng, 2011. 1 vol. (639 p.):
couv. ill. en coul. ; 21cm. ISBN: 2842794996,
2842794990

《子夜》,Meunier, Jacques (1939—) 和 Loi, Michelle
(1926—2002)合译.

6. L'arc-en-ciel/Mao Dun; traduit par Bernadette Rouis et
Jacques Tardif; revu et corrigé par Michelle Loi. Paris:
Acropole, 1981. 331 p. ISBN: 2714413595,
2714413598. (Littérature du monde)

《虹》,Rouis, Bernadette 和 Tardif, Jacques 合译.

7. L'épreuve: roman/Mao Dun. Paris: Acropole, 1981. 310
S; 23cm. ISBN: 273570033X, 2735700332

《锻炼》,Shen, Dali 和 Zhang, Shangci 合译.

(1) L'epreuve/by Mao Dun; traduit du chinois par Shen
Dali et Zhang Shangei. Paris: Acropole, 1985. 311
pages. ISBN: 273570033X, 2735700332.
(Littérature du Monde)

8. Le Chemin/Mao Dun; traduit du chinois par NG Yok-

Soon. Paris：L'Harmattan，1988. 169 p.；22cm. ISBN：2738400671，2738400673.（Lettres asiatiques；Chine）

《路》，黄育顺（Ng，Yok-Soon，1939—）译.

9. L'éclipse：roman/Maodun；trad. du chinois par Frédérique Gilbank…［et al.］sous la dir. de Michelle Loi.［Paris］：Blandin，1992. 677 S.，Taf：Portr. ISBN：2907695665，2907695664

《蚀》，Loi，Michelle 译.

郁达夫（1896—1945）

1. Choix de nouvelles de Yu Ta-Fou/traduites par Tchang Tien-Ya. Pékin，Impr. de la Politique de Pékin，1938. 103 pages；26cm.（Collection de la "Politique de Pékin"）

郁达夫中短篇小说选集. Tchang Tien-Ya 译. 初版于 1938 年.

（1）Pékin：Imprimerie de la Politique de Pékin，1983. 103 pages；26cm.（Collection de la "Politique de Pékin"）

2. Fleurs d'osmanthe tardives：nouvelles/Yu Dafu. Beijing：Littérature chinoise，1983. 207 p.，1 ritr.；18cm.（Collection Panda）

《迟桂花》，Gao，Xiaosheng 译.《中国文学》杂志社（熊猫丛书）

3. Rivière d'automne：et autres nouvelles/Yu Dafu；trad. du chinois et présentées par Stéphane Lévêque. Arles：P. Picquier，Impr. Lienhart，2002. 221 p.：couv. ill. en coul.；21cm. ISBN：2877306151，2877306157

Contents：Une femme sans volonté—Le Passé—Rivière d'automne.

《〈秋河〉及其他中短篇小说》，Lévêque，Stéphane（1967—）译.

（1）Arles（Bouches-du-Rhône）：P. Picquier，2005. 1v.（248 p.）；17cm. ISBN：2877307751，2877307758

老舍（1899—1966）

1. Coeur-joyeux，coolie de Pékin/Lao Sheh；roman chinois traduit par Jean Poumarat d'après la version anglaise d'Evan King. Paris：B. Arthaud，1947. 438 p.（De par le monde）

《骆驼祥子》，Poumarat，Jean 译. 转译自英文版《Rickshaw boy》一书.

（1）Grenoble：B. Arthaud，1948. 1 vol.（439 p.）；20cm.（De par le monde）

2. Le pousse-pousse：roman/Lao-Che；traduit du chinois par François Cheng. Paris：R. Laffont，1973. 244 pages；20cm.（Collection Pavillons）

《骆驼祥子》，Cheng，François（1929—）译.

（1）Le pousse-pousse/Lao She；roman traduit du chinois par François Cheng et anne Cheng. Paris：P. Picquier，1990. 220 p. ISBN：2877300331，2877300339

（2）Le pousse-pousse：roman/Lao She；trad. du chinois par François Cheng et Anne Cheng. Paris：Librairie générale française，Impr. Brodard et Taupin，1991. 252 p.：couv. ill. en coul.；17cm. ISBN：2253056219，2253056218.（Le livre de poche，Biblio；3155）

（3）Le pousse-pousse：roman/Lao She；traduit du chinois par François Cheng et Anne Cheng. Arles：P. Picquier，1995. 220 p.；17cm. ISBN：2877302113，2877302111.（Picquier poche；21）

3. Le tireur de pousse/Lao She；Préfacé par Hu Jieqing；trad. Denise Ly-Lebreton. Beijing：Éd. en Langues Érangères，1985. V-343 p.；19cm. ISBN：7119009125，7119009124.（Collection Phénix）

《骆驼祥子》，Ly-Lebreton，Denise（1909—1995）译.

（1）Beijing：Éditions en Langues Étrangères，1989. 343 pages：illustrations；18cm.

4. La tourmente jaune：roman/Lau Shaw；traduit d'après la version américaine par Clément Leclerc. Paris：Plon，1955. 1 vol.（II-619 p.）：plan；19cm.（Feux croisés）

《四世同堂》，Leclerc，Clément 译自《四世同堂》的英文版《Yellow storm》.

5. Quatre générations sous un même toit. I/Lao She；trad. du chinois par Jing-yi Xiao；préf. de J. M. G. Le Clézio；avant-propos de Paul Bady. Paris：Mercure de France，1996. IX-550 p.：plan；23cm. ISBN：2715218680

《四世同堂》，Xiao，Jing-yi 译.

（1）Quatre générations sous un même toit. I/Lao She；traduit du chinois par Jing-Yi Xiao；Préface de J. M. G. Le Clézio；avant-propos de Paul Bady.［Paris］：Mercure de France，1996. 702 pages：plan；18cm. ISBN：2070404668，2070404667.（Collection Folio；3119）

（2）［Paris］：Gallimard，1998. 702 p.：plan，couv. ill. en coul.；18cm. ISBN：2070404668.（Collection Folio；3119）

6. Quatre générations sous un même toit. tome II，Survivre à tout prix/Lao She；traduit du chinois par Chantal Andro. Paris：Mercure de France，1998. 606 p.：carte；23cm. ISBN：271522026X，2715220263

《四世同堂》，Chen-Andro，Chantal 译.

（1）［Paris］：Gallimard，2000. 740 p.：plan，couv. ill. en coul.；18cm. ISBN：207041261X.（Collection Folio）

7. Quatre générations sous un même toit. III，La famine/Lao She；trad. du chinois par Chantal Chen-Andro.［Paris］：Mercure de France，2000. 341 p.：plan，jaquette ill. en coul.；23cm. ISBN：2715221533，2715221536

《四世同堂》，Chen-Andro，Chantal 译.

（1）［Paris］：［Gallimard］，2001. 433 p.：plan，couv. ill. en coul.；18cm. ISBN：207042006X，2070420063.（Collection Folio；3564）

8. Quatre générations sous un même toit/Lao She.［Paris］：Mercure de France，1996—2000. 3 volumes：illustrations；23cm. ISBN：2715218680（t. 1），2715218680（t. 1），271522026X（t. 2），2715220263（t. 2），2715221533（t. 3），

2715221536 (t. 3)

Contents：［t. 1］.［without special title］/traduit du chinois par Jing-Yi Xiao; Préface de J. M. G. Le Clézio; avant-propos de Paul Bady—t. 2. Survivre à tout prix/traduit du chinois par Chantal Chen-Andro—t. 3. La famine/traduit du chinois par Chantal Chen-Andro.

《四世同堂》，Jing-Yi Xiao 和 Chen-Andro, Chantal 合译. 3 卷本.

(1)［Paris］：［Gallimard］, 2004—2005. 3 v.：carte; 18cm. ISBN：a070404668（v. 1），2070404667（v. 1），207041261X（v. 2），2070412617（v. 2），207042006X（v. 3），2070420063（v. 3）. (Collection Folio; 3119, 3356, 3564)

9. La cité des chats/Lao She; trad. du chinois par Geneviève François-Poncet. Paris：Publications Orientalistes de France, 1957. 265 p.; 21cm. (D'étranges pays)

《猫城记》，Francois-Poncet, Genevieve 译.

(1) Paris：Publications Orientalistes de France; Publie avec le concours du Centre National des Lettres, 1981. 265 pages; 22cm. ISBN：2716901570, 2716901574. (Litteratures d'etranges pays)

(2) Paris：Presses pocket, 1992. 250 p.; couv. ill. en coul.; 18cm. ISBN：2266046780, 2266046787. (Presses pocket; 3936)

10. L'Enfant du nouvel an：roman/Lao She; traduit du chinois par Paul Bady et Li Tche-houa; avant-propos de Paul Bady. ［Paris］：Gallimard, 1980. 216, ［1］ pages; 21cm. ISBN：2070707881, 2070707881. (Du monde entier)

《正红旗下》，Bady, Paul 和李治华合译.

(1) Paris：Gallimard, 1986. ［217］ p.; 21cm. ISBN：2070707881, 2070707881. (Du monde entier)

(2) L'enfant du nouvel an/Lao She; trad. du chinois par Paul Bady, Li Tche-Houa; avant-propos Paul Bady. Paris：Gallimard, 2003. 298 p.; 18cm. ISBN：2070428281, 2070428281. (Collection Folio; 3858)

11. Gens de Pékin/Lao She; traduit du chinois par Paul Bady, Li Tche-houa, Françoise Moreux... ［et al.］. ［Paris］：Gallimard, Impr. S. E. P. C., 1982. 1 vol. (291 p.); 21cm. ISBN：2070214540, 2070214549. (Du monde entier)

Contents：La lance de mort—Une vieille maison—Histoire de ma vie—Les voisins—Dans la cour de la famille Liu—Le nouvel inspecteur—Un ami d'enfance—L'amateur d'opèra—Le croissant de lune.

Notes：Ecrites en 1933 et 1935, ces neuf nouvelles, en plus d'un indéniable talent littéraire, traduisent chez l'auteur une observation aiguë qui restitue, d'une façon quasi-documentaire, une réalité disparue entre le tragique et l'humour. Bonne occasion d'aborder la littérature chinoise contemporaine.

《北京人》，Bady, Paul, 李治华，Moreux, Françoise 合译.

(1)［Paris］：Gallimard, Impr. SEPC, 1993. 333 p.：couv. ill.; 18cm. ISBN：2070387275, 2070387274. (Collection Folio; 2473)

12. La cage entrebaillée：roman/Lao She; traduit du chinois par Paul Bady et Li Tche-houa; avant- propos de Paul Bady. ［Paris］：Gallimard, 1986. 340 p.; 21cm. ISBN：2070708071, 2070708079. (Du monde entier)

《微开的鸟笼》，李治华，Bady, Paul 合译.

(1) La cage entrebâillée/Lao She; trad. du chinois par Paul Bady et Li Tche-houa; avant-propos de Paul Bady. ［Paris］：Gallimard, Bussière Camedan impr., 2002. 436 p.：couv. ill. en coul.; 18cm. ISBN：2070424979, 2070424979. (Collection Folio; 3746)

13. Un fils tombé du ciel/Lao She; traduit du chinois par Lu Fujun et Christine Mel. Paris：Arléa, 1989. 362 p.; 21cm. ISBN：286959058X, 2869590588. (L'Étrangère)

《牛天赐传》，Lu, Fujun 和 Mel, Christine 合译.

(1) Paris：Librairie générale française, Impr. Brodard et Taupin, 1992. 283 p.：couv. ill. en coul.; 17cm. ISBN：2253060682, 2253060680. (Le livre de poche, Biblio; 3178)

14. L'anniversaire de Xiaopo/Lao She; traduction de Claude Payen; Préface de Paul Bady. Paris：Éditions You-Feng, 1999. 173 p.; 21cm. ISBN：2842790588, 2842790585

《小坡的生日》，Payen, Claude 译.

15. Messieurs Ma, père et fils/Lao She; roman traduit du chinois par Claude Payen; Préface de Paul Bady. Arles：Éditions Philippe Picquier, 2000. 331 p.; 21cm. ISBN：287730485X, 2877304856. (Le pousse-pousse poche; 21)

《二马》，Payen, Claude 译.

(1) Arles：Philippe Picquier, 2002. 1 vol. (331 p.); 21cm. ISBN：287730485X, 2877304856

(2) Arles：P. Picquier, 2003. 1 vol. (442 p.)：couv. ill. en coul.; 21cm. ISBN：2877306763, 2877306768. (Picquier poche (Arles); 209)

(3) Arles：P. Picquier, 2013. 442 p.; 17cm. ISBN：2809709766, 2809709769. (Picquier poche)

(4) Nouvelle édition. ［Arles（Bouches-du-Rhône）］：Éditions Philippe Picquier, 2014. 442 pages; 17 × 11cm. ISBN：2809709766, 2809709769. (Picquier poche; 209)

16. Les tambours：roman/Lao She; trad. de l'anglais par Claude Payen. Arles, France：Éditions Philippe Picquier, 2001. 305 p. ISBN：2877305511, 2877305518

《鼓书艺人》，Payen, Claude 译.

(1) Les tambours/Lao She; traduit de l'anglais par Claude Payen. Arles（Bouches-du-Rhône）：P. Picquier, 2004. 1 v. (398 p.); 17cm. ISBN：2877307360, 2877307369. (Picquier poche; 231)

17. Histoire de ma vie/Lao She; trad. du chinois par Paul Bady, Li Tche-houa, Françoise Moreux... 〔et al.〕. 〔Paris〕: Gallimard, Bussière Camedan impr., 2001. 115 p.: couv. ill. en coul.; 18cm. ISBN: 2070422089 (br), 2070422081 (br). (Collection Folio; 3627)
《我这一辈子》,Bady, Paul, 李治华, Moreux, François (1929—)合译.
    (1)〔Paris〕: Gallimard, Bussière Camedan impr., 2003. 115 p.: couv. ill. en coul.; 18cm. ISBN: 2070422089, 2070422081. (Collection Folio; 3627)

18. L'homme qui ne mentait jamais: nouvelles/Lao She; trad. du chinois par Claude Payen. Arles: P. Picquier, 2003. 317 p.: couv. ill. en coul.; 21cm. ISBN: 2877306372 (br.)
《不说谎的人》,Payen, Claude 译.
    (1)Arles: P. Picquier, Impr. France Quercy, 2006. 1 vol. (355 p.): couv. ill. en coul.; 17cm. ISBN: 2877308316, 2877308311. (Picquier poche; 263)

19. Le nouvel inspecteur: suivi de Le croissant de lune/Lao She; traduit du chinois par Paul Bady, Li Tche-Houa, Françoise Moreux, Alain Peyraube... 〔et al.〕. 〔Paris〕: Gallimard, 2008. 1 vol. (97 p.): couv. ill. en coul.; 18cm. ISBN: 2070358403, 2070358402. (Folio, 2)
《月牙儿》,Bady, Paul, 李治华等合译.

20. La philosophie de Lao Zhang: roman/Lao She; traduit du chinois par Claude Payen. Arles: P. Picquier, 2009. 1 vol. (279 p.): couv. ill. en coul.; 21cm. ISBN: 2809701241, 2809701245
《老张的哲学》,Payen, Claude 译.
    (1)Arles: P. Picquier, 2011. 1 vol. (345 p.): couv. ill. en coul.; 17cm. ISBN: 2809703009, 2809703000. (Picquier poche)

21. Écrits de la maison des rats/Lao She; traduit du chinois par Claude Payen. Arles: P. Picquier, 2010. 125 p.; 22cm. ISBN: 2809701784, 2809701784. (Écrits dans la paume de la main)
《多鼠斋杂谈》,Payen, Claude 译.
    (1)Arles: Éditions Philippe Picquier, 2016. 1 vol. (159 p.); 17cm. ISBN: 2809711691, 2809711690. (Picquier poche)

22. M. Wen, PhD/Lao She; introduction, traduction et notes par Bernard Lelarge. Paris: Éditions You feng libraire & éditeur, 2013. 1 vol. (143 p.); 21cm. ISBN: 2842795948, 2842795946
《文博士》,Lelarge, Bernard 译注.

23. Zhao Ziyue/Lao She; introduction, traduction et notes par Bernard Lelarge. Paris: Éditions You Feng, Rich Bright, 2013. 1 vol. (269 p.); 21cm. ISBN: 2842795931, 2842795938
《赵子曰》,Lelarge, Bernard 译.

沈从文(1902—1988)

1. Nouvelles/Shen Congwen. Beijing: Littérature chinoise, 1982. 242 pages; 18cm. (Collection Panda)
Contents: Anecdotes sur Shen Conwen/Xiao Li—Le Mari—Guisheng—Xiaoxiao—Une bourgade à l'écart—Mon oncle Shen Congwen/Huang Yongyu.
《沈从文小说选》.《中国文学》杂志社(熊猫丛书)

2. Une bourgade à l'écart/Shen Congwen. Beijing: Éditions en Langues Étrangères, 2004. 1 vol. (242 p.): couv. ill.; 18cm. ISBN: 7119035177 (br); 7119035178 (br). (Littérature chinoise)
《沈从文小说选》,刘汉玉等译.外文出版社(中国文学)

3. Le passeur de Chadong: roman/Shen Congwen; trad. du chinois par Isabelle Rabut; postf. d'Isabelle Rabut. Paris: UGE, 1995. a01 p.; 20cm. ISBN: 2264001216, 2264001214. (10/18. Domaine étranger)
《边城》,Rabut, Isabelle 译.

4. Une bourgade à l'écart: nouvelles/Shen Congwen. Beijing: Éditions en Langues Étrangères, 2004. 1 vol. (242 p.): couv. ill.; 18cm. ISBN: 7119035177, 7119035178. (Littérature chinoise)
《边城》

柔石(1902—1931)

1. Février: roman/Rou-shi; traduit du chinois par Wang Chun-jian avec la collaboration de Anne Thieulle. Arles: Actes sud, 1985. 175 pages: maps; 19cm. ISBN: 2868690262, 2868690265
《二月》,Wang Chun-jian 和 Thieulle, Anne 合译.

艾芜(1904—1992)

1. La vallée aux bananiers/Ai Wu. Pékin: Éd. Littérature chinoise, 1994. 212 p.; 18cm. ISBN: 7507102211, 7507102215. (Collection Panda)
Contents: Dans une vallée—La randonnvalléee—La vallée aux bananiers—Le chant des corbeaux—Retour à la maison—La femme de Shiqing.
《芭蕉谷》

巴金(1904—2005)

1. L'Automne dans le Printemps: nouvelles/Ba Jin. Beijing: Littérature chinoise, 1982. 233 pages: portraits; 18cm. ISBN: 7507100502, 7507100501. (Collection Panda)
Contents: Quelques mots en guise de Préface/Ba Jin—Les nouvelles de Ba Jin dans les années 1930/Hansheng—La pluie—La digue Su—A la fonte des neiges—Une nuit sous la lune—Un coeur d'esclave—A propos de "L'automne dans le printemps"/Ba Jin—L'automne dans le printemps—Un homme fort/Yang Yi.
《巴金小说选》,李梅英等译.中国文学》杂志社(熊猫丛书).本书收录巴金30年代的6篇短篇小说.
    (1)2e éd. Beijing: Éditions Littérature Chinoise, 1990. 233 p. ISBN: 7507100502, 7507100501. (Collection Panda)

(2) Beijing, China：Éd. en Langues Étrangères, 2004. 1 vol. (233 p.)：couv. ill. en coul. ; 18cm. ISBN：7119035169, 7119035161. (Littérature chinoise)

2. Nuit glacée/Pa Kin [i. e. Li Fei-kan]；traduit du chinois par M. -J. Lalitte；Préface d'Étiemble. [Paris]：Gallimard, 1978. 327 pages；21cm. (Du monde entier)

《寒夜》,Lalitte, Marie José 译.

(1)[Paris]：Gallimard, 1983. 373 p. ：couv. ill. en coul. ; 18cm. ISBN：2070375129. (Collection Folio；1512)

(2)[Paris]：Gallimard, 1989. 373 p. ; 18cm. ISBN：2070375129, 2070375127. (Folio；1512)

(3)Paris：Gallimard, 2000. 373 p. ; 18cm. ISBN：2070375129, 2070375127. (Folio；1512)

3. Le jardin du repos/Pa Kin；trad. du chinois par Nicolas Chapuis et Roger Darrobers. Paris：R. Laffont, 1979. 235 p. ; 20cm. ISBN：2221002156. (Collection Pavillons. Langues O. Littérature chinoise)

《憩园》,Chapuis, Nicolas 和 Darrobers, Roger 合译.

(1) Paris：R. Laffont, 1984. 325 p. ; 20cm. ISBN：2221043170. (Classiques Pavillons)

(2)Paris：R. Laffont, 2004. 302 p. ：couv. ill. en coul. ; 19cm. ISBN：2221103750. (Bibliothèque Pavillons)

(3)Paris：R. Laffont, 2005. 235 p. ; 20cm. ISBN：2221103750, 2221103753. (Bibliothèque Pavillons)

4. Le Jardin du repos/Pa Kin；traduit du chinois par Marie-José Lalitte. [Paris]：Gallimard, impr. Bussière, 1981. 251 p. ：couv. ill. en coul. ; 18cm. ISBN：2070372758 (Collection Folio；1275)

《憩园》,Lalitte, Marie José 译.

(1)Paris：Gallimard, 1982. 251 p. ; 18cm. ISBN：2070372758, 2070372751. (Collection Folio；1275)

(2)Paris：Gallimard, 1988. 251 p. ; 18cm. ISBN：2070372758, 2070372751

5. Le secret de Robespierre：et autres nouvelles/Pa Kin. Paris：Mazarine, 1980. 207 p. ; 23cm. ISBN：2863740547, 2863740545

《罗伯斯庇尔的秘密》及其他中短篇小说.

(1)Paris：Stock, Impr. Hérissey, 1997. 207 p. ; 18cm. ISBN：2234046297, 2234046290. (La bibliothèque cosmopolite)

6. Vengeance/Pa Kin. Paris：Seghers, 1980. 109 p. ; 21cm. ISBN：2221502043, 2221502044. (Autour du monde)

《复仇》,Bourgeois, Pénélope, Lelarge, Bernard 译.

7. Le Rêve en mer：conte pour enfants à une jeune fille/Pa Kin (Ba Jin)；trad. du chinois par Ng Yok-Soon. Paris：l'Harmattan, 1986. 156 p. ; 22cm. (Lettres asiatiques；Chine)

《海的梦》,黄育顺(Ng, Yok-Soon,1939—)译.

8. L'automne dans le printemps：nouvelles/Ba Jin. 2e éd. Pékin：Éd. Littérature chinoise, 1990. 233 p. ：port. ; 18cm. ISBN：7507100502, 7507100501. (Collection Panda)

《春天里的秋天》,译者不详.

9. Destruction/Pa kin；traduction du chinois, introduction et notes par Angel Pino et Isabelle Rabut. [Paris]：Bleu de Chine, 1995. 250 p. ; 21cm. ISBN：2910884031 2910884031

《灭亡》,Pino, Angel 和 Rabut, Isabelle 合译.

10. Le dragon, les tigres, le chien；suivi de Hors du jardin dévasté/Ba Jin；trad. du chinois par Philippe Denizet. Paris：You-Feng, 2001. 189 p. ：couv. ill. en coul. ; 19cm. ISBN：2842791169, 2842791162

《龙虎狗·废园外》,Denizet, Philippe 译.

11. Famille：roman/Pa Kin；traduit du chinois par Li Tche-houa et Jacqueline Alézaïs. Paris：Flammarion；Lausanne：A. Eibel, impr. Firmin-Didot, 1979. 412 p. ; 20cm. ISBN：2080641492, 2080641496. (Torrent；[1]；Lettres étrangères)

《激流三部曲:家》,李治华,Alézaïs, Jacqueline 合译.

(1)Paris：France loisirs, impr. Firmin-Didot, 1979. 412 p. ; 21cm. ISBN：2724206851, 2724206852

(2)Paris：Flammarion/Eibel, 1979. 380 p. ISBN：2253049646, 2253049647. (Le Livre de Poche；12)

(3)Paris：Le Livre de poche, 1981. 390 p. ：couv. ill. ; 17cm. ISBN：2253026816, 2253026815. (Le Livre de poche；5541)

(4) Paris：Librairie générale française, 1989. 380 p. ：couv. ill. en coul. ; 17cm. ISBN：2253049646 (br.). (Le Livre de poche. Biblio；3119)

(5)Paris：LGF, 2004. 380 p. ; 17cm. ISBN：2253049646, 2253049647

12. Printemps：roman/Pa Kin；trad. du chinois par édith Simar-Dauverd. Paris：Flammarion, 1982. 480 p. ; 20cm. ISBN：208064484X. (Aspects de l'Asie)

《激流三部曲:春》,Simar-Dauverd, édith 译.

13. Automne：roman/Pa Kin；trad. du chinois par édith Simar-Dauverd. [Paris]：Flammarion, 1989. 676 p. ; 20cm. ISBN：2080663267, 2080663269. (Aspects de l'Asie)

《激流三部曲:秋》,Simar-Dauverd, édith 译.

14. Le Brouillard：premier roman de la trilogie l'Amour/Ba Jin (Pa Kin)；trad. du chinois par Ng Yok-Soon. Paris：Éd. les Cent Fleurs, Impr. JMLG, 1987. 213 p. ：ill., couv. ill. ; 21cm. ISBN：2906719013, 2906719019. (L'Amour. ; 1)

《爱情三部曲之第一部:雾》,黄育顺(Ng, Yok-Soon, 1939—)译.

丁玲(1904—1986)

1. Nouvelles des années trente/Ding Ling；préf. S. Bernard. Beijing：Littérature chinoise, 1985. 293 p. ：[1] f. de

pl. ；18cm. (Panda)

《丁玲三十年代小说选》，Bernard, Suzanne(1932—)译.

2. La Grande sœur：nouvelles/Ding Ling；traduit du chinois par Chantal Gressier et Ah Su. Paris：Flammarion, 1980. 283 p. ；20cm. ISBN：2080643029 （Br.）. （Lettres étrangères Aspects de l'Asie）

《大姐》，Gressier, Chantal 和 Ah Su 译.

3. L'Eau/Ding Ling；traduit du chinois par NG Yok-Soon. Paris：Éditions les Cent fleurs, 1983. 97 p. ：ill. ；22cm. ISBN：2906719099, 2906719095. （Les meilleures œuvres littéraires chinoises）

《水》，NG Yok-Soon 译.

4. Le soleil brille sur la rivière Sanggan/Ding Ling. Beijing：Éditions en Langues Étrangères, 1984. 506 p.

《太阳照在桑干河上》

赵树理(1906—1970)

1. Nouvelles choisies/Shuli Zhao. Pékin：Éditions en Langues Étrangères, 1957. 268 p. ：portr. front. couv. ill. ；in—16

《李有才板话》

(1)2e éd. Pékin：Éditions en Langues Étrangères, 1964. 265 pages：illustrations, portrait

(2)Nouvelles chinoises/Zhao Shuli. Beijing, China：Éditions en Langues Étrangères, 1982. 271 p. ：ill. ；19cm.

2. Le village de Sanliwan：roman/Tchao Chou-li；traduction de Marthe Hou, illustrations de Wou Tsing-pouo. Pékin：Éditions en Langues Étrangères, 1960. 291 p. ：ill. ；22cm.

《三里湾》，Hou, Marthe 和 Wu, Jingbo 合译.

(1)Pékin, Éditions en Langues Érangères, 1964. 298 p. portrait en front. , pl. , couv. ill. 8vo

3. Le Matin des villageois/Tchao Chou-li；version française de Marc Gilliard. Paris：Club des amis du livre progressiste, 1961. vol. (III-205 p. , ［4］p. de pl.)：ill. ；20cm.

《三里湾》，Gilliard, Marc 著.

谢冰莹(1906—2000)

1. Une femme en guerre：récit/Xie Bingying；trad. du chinois par Marie Holzman. Paris：Rochevignes, 1985. 178 p. ；23cm. ISBN：2867370191, 2867370199

《女兵自传》，Holzman, Marie 译.

周立波(1908—1979)

1. L'ouragan/Zhou Libo；illustrations de Gu Yuan. Beijing：Éd. en Langues Étrangères, 1981. 561 p. ：portr. ；22cm.

《暴风骤雨》，古元插图；Gu, Yuan(1919—1996)译.

欧阳山(1908—2000)

1. Oncle Kao/par Eouyang Chan；［trad. par Marthe Hou］. Pékin：Éditions en Langues Étrangères, 1959. 299 S.

《高干大》，Hou, Marthe 译.

高云览(1910—1956)

1. Les annales d'une ville de province/Kao Yun-lan. Beijing, Chine：Éditions en Langues Étrangères, 1962. 316 p. ：ill. ；19cm.

《小城春秋》

(1)Beijing：Éditions en Langues Étrangères, 1983. xii, 388 p. ；19cm.

2. Anales de una ciudad de provincia/Gao Yunlan；tr. Aurora Fernández. 2a éd. Beijing：Éditions en Langues Étrangères, 1980. vii, 388 p. ：il. ；21cm.

《小城春秋》，Fernández, Aurora 译.

钱钟书(1910—1998)

1. La forteresse assiégée/Qian Zhongshu；traduit du chinois par Sylvie Servan-Schreiber et Wang Lou；Préface de Lucien Bianco. ［Paris］：Christian Bourgois, 1987. 424 p. ；23cm. ISBN：2267004836, 2267004830

《围城》，Servan-Schreiber, Sylvie 和 Wang Lou 合译.

(1)［Paris］：C. Bourgois, 1997. VII, 424 p. ；23cm. ISBN：2267004836, 2267004830. （Bibliothèque asiatique）

2. Hommes, bêtes et démons/par Qian Zhongshu；traduit du chinois, présenté et annoté par Sun Chaoying. ［Paris］：Gallimard, 1994. 212 p. ；19cm. ISBN：207073966X, 2070739660. （Connaissance de l'Orient；67）

Contents：Le réve de Dieu—La chatte—Inspiration—Pensée fidèle.

《人·兽·鬼》，Sun, Chaoying 译.

姚雪垠(1910—1999)

1. La Longue nuit：roman/Yao Xueyin；traduit du chinois par Li Tche-houa et Jacqueline Alézaïs. ［Paris］：Flammarion, 1984. 340 p. ：couv. ill. ；21cm. ISBN：20080645927 （Br.）. （Aspects de l'Asie, ISSN 0245—3061；Collection Unesco d'Œuvres representatives. Série chinoise, ISSN 0589—3496）

《长夜》，李治华，Alézaïs, Jacqueline 合译.

叶紫(1910—1939)

1. La grande moisson：nouvelles/par Ye Tse. Pékin：Éditions en Langues Étrangères, 1962. 172 pages

《丰收》

(1)La grande moisson：nouvelles/par Ye Zi. 2e éd. Beijing：Éditions en Langues Étrangères, 1979. 171 pages；22cm.

萧红(1911—1942)

1. Terre de vie et de mort：nouvelles/Xiao Hong. Beijing：Littérature Chinoise, 1987. 266 p：ill.

《萧红小说集》.《中国文学》杂志社(熊猫丛书)

2. Terre de vie et de mort：nouvelles/Xiao Hong. Beijing：Littérature chinoise, 1987. 266 p. ；18cm. (Panda)

《生死场》

3. Des âmes simples/Xiao Hong；traduit du chinois et présenté par Anne Guerrand-Breuval. ［Paris］：Arléa,

1995. 93 p. ; 21cm. ISBN: 2869592396, 2869592391. (L'étrangère)

Contents: Les mains—Un souffle d'espoir—La femme du soldat.

单纯的灵魂:萧红短篇小说集. Guerrand-Breuval, Anne 译.

4. Nouvelles/Xiao Hong. Paris: Éd. You-Feng, 2004. 123 p. : couv. ill. ; 19cm. ISBN: 2842791517, 2842791513

萧红小说集. Turki, Berangere 译.

5. Contes de la rivière Hulan/par Xiao Hong; préface de Mao Dun; traduit du chinois par Simone Cros-Moréa. éd. Bilingue. Paris: Éd. You feng, impr. 2011. 1 vol. (443 p.): couv. ill. en coul. ; 21cm. ISBN: 2842795061 (br.)

《呼兰河传》, Cros-Moréa, Simone 译.

孙犁 (1913—2002)

1. Dans la tourmente: nouvelles/Sun Li. Beijing: Littérature chinoise, 1983. 258 p. (Panda)

《风云初记》

梁斌 (1914—1996)

1. La lignée rouge/Liang Bin. Pékin, Chine: Éditions en Langues Étrangères, 1964. 574 p., [9] feuillets de planches: ill

《红旗谱》, Huang, Runhua(1932—) 译.

(1) Beijing: Éditions en Langues Étrangères, 1981. 574 p. : ill. ; 22cm.

袁静 (1914—1999)

1. La Longue marche: récits de témoins. Pékin: Éditions en Langues Étrangères, 1959. 144 pages, [7] leaves of plates: illustrations, map; 19cm.

《长征的故事》, 袁静, 孔厥著.

2. 《新儿女英雄传》, 袁静、孔厥著; 朱文源译. 北京: 外文出版社, 1958

刘白羽 (1916—2005)

1. Six heures du matin, nouvelles par Lieou Pai-yu. Pékin: Éditions en Langues Étrangères, 1953. In—16, 166 p. [Ech. int. 1816—55]—VIIIf7—XcR.

《早晨六点钟》

秦兆阳 (1916—1994)

1. Croquis de la campagne/Ts'in Tchao-Yang. Pékin: Éditions en Langues Étrangères, 1957. 223 p., pl., portrait

《农村散记》

吴运铎 (1917—1991)

1. Tout pour le parti/Wou Yun-Touo; [traduction de Marthe Hou]. Pékin: Éditions en Langues Étrangères, 1961. 225 pages: illustrations

《把一切献给党》, Hou, Marthe 译.

张爱玲 (1920—1995)

1. Le chant du riz qui lève/Eileen Chang; traduit de l'anglais par Emy Molinié. Paris: Calmann-Lévy, 1958. 228 p

《秧歌》, Molinié, Emy 译.

2. La cangue d'or/Eileen Chang; textes choisis, présentés et

trad. du chinois par Emmanuelle Péchenart; dessins de Françoise Ged. Paris: Bleu de Chine, 1999. 104 p. : ill. ; 21cm. ISBN: 2910884244, 2910884246

《金锁记》, Péchenart, Emmanuelle, Ged, Françoise 译.

3. Rose rouge et rose blanche/Eileen Chang; traduit du chinois par Emmanuelle Péchenart; dessins de François Ged. Paris: Bleu de Chine, 2001. 89 p. : ill. ISBN: 2910884376, 2910884376

《红玫瑰与白玫瑰》, Péchenart, Emmanuelle 译.

4. Un amour dévastateur/Eileen Chang; traduit du chinois par Emmanuelle Péchenart. La Tour-d'Aigues: Éditions de l'Aube, 2005. 123 p. ; 22cm. ISBN: 2752600860, 2752600868. (Regards croisés)

《倾城之恋》, Péchenart, Emmanuelle 译.

(1)La Tour-d'Aigues: Éd. de l'Aube, 2007. 1 vol. (133 p.): couv. ill. ; 22cm. ISBN: 2752604040, 2752604041

5. Love in a fallen city: roman, suivi de Ah Hsiao est triste en automne/Eileen Chang; traduit du chinois par Emmanuelle Péchenart. Paris: Zulma, 2014. 158 p. ; 19cm. ISBN: 2843046926, 2843046920

《倾城之恋》, Péchenart, Emmanuelle 译.

6. Lust, caution: amour, luxure, trahison: nouvelles/Eileen Chang; traduites du chinois par Emmanuelle Péchenart. Paris: Robert Laffont, 2007. 175 p. ISBN: 2221110232, 2221110234

《色·戒》, Péchenart, Emmanuelle 译.

(1)Paris: 10—18, Impr. CPI Brodard & Taupin, 2009. 1 vol. (175 p.): couv. ill. en coul. ; 18cm. ISBN: 2264048493, 2264048492. (10—18. Domaine étranger)

汪曾祺 (1920—1997)

1. Les trois amis de l'hiver: récits/Wang Zengqi, traduits du chinois par Annie Curien. Arles: Ph. Picquier, 1989. 127 p. ; 21cm. ISBN: 2877300196, 2877300193

《岁寒三友》, Curien, Annie 译.

2. Initiation d'un jeune bonze/Wang Zengqi. Pékin: Éd. Littérature chinoise, 1989. 1 vol. (283 p.): couv. ill., portr. ; 18cm. ISBN: 7507100162, 7507100167. (Collection Panda)

Contents: Auto-présentation de famille/traduit par Wu Moxin—Les as de la volaille/traduit par Gao Dekun—Signes particuliers/traduit par Qian Chongxin—Initiation d'un jeune bonze/collaboration de Gabriella et Hanyu—Solitude et réconfort/traduit par Liu Hanyu—Les trois amis d'hiver/traduit par Gao Linghan—Tempête sur Danao/traduit par Li Meiying—Souvenirs d'après-dîner/traduit par Li Fangmei et François Jacob—Le mariage des trois filles/traduit par Tang Jialong—L'histoire du Huit Mille Ans/traduit par Zeng Peigeng—Chen petites mains/traduit par Tang Jialong—Zhan le grand corpulent/traduit par Tang Jialong

《受戒》.中国文学出版社(熊猫丛书)

罗广斌(1924—1967)

1. Roc rouge/Luo Guangbin et Yang Yiyan. Beijing：Éditions en Langues Étrangères, 1983. 651 pages
《红岩》,罗广斌,杨益言著.
(1)Beijing：Éditions en Langues Étrangères, 1996. p. : ill. ;cm.

郭国甫(1926—)

1. Chez les Ominans/Guo Guofu. Beijing：Zuo jia chu ban she, 1958. 379 pages；21cm.
《在昂美纳部落里》
(1)Beijing：Éditions en Langues Étrangères, 1981. 417 p. ；21cm.
(2)Beijing xin 1 ban. Beijing：Ren min wen xue chu ban she, 1983. 433 pages；19cm.
(3)Wuhan：Chang jiang wen yi chu ban she, 2014. 296 pages；24cm. ISBN：7535474605, 7535474608. (Dang dai Jiangxi chang pian xiao shuo jing dian cong shu. di 1 ji)

高玉宝(1927—)

1. Mon enfance/Kao Yu-pao；illustrations：Tong Tchen-cheng et Tchen Yu-sien. Pékin：Éditions en Langues Étrangères, 1974. ii, 265 p.
《我的童年》

黎汝清(1928—2015)

1. Miliciennes des îles/Li Jou-tsing；［traduit du chinois；illustré par Tsai Jong］. Pékin：Éditions en Langues Étrangères；［Paris］：［diffusion Éditions du Centenaire］, 1977. 354 p. -［7］f. de pl. en coul. : couv. ill. en coul. ；21cm.
《海岛女民兵》,蔡荣插图.

宗璞(1928—)

1. Le sacrifice du coeur/Zong Pu. Pékin：Éd. Littérature chinoise, 1992. 214 p. ；18cm. ISBN：7507101150, 7507101157. (Collection Panda)
《心祭》,译者不详.

陆文夫(1928—2005)

1. Vie et passion d'un gastronome chinois：roman/Lu Wenfu；traduit du chinois par Annie Curien et Feng Chen, précédé d'un "avant-gout" par Françoise Sabban. Arles：P. Picquier；Paris：Unesco, 1988. 157 p. ；21cm. ISBN：2877300021, 2877300025, 2877301699, 2877301695. (Collection Unesco d'œuvres représentatives. Série chinoise)
《美食家》,Curien, Annie 译.
(1)Vie et passion d'un gastronome chinois：roman/Lu Wenfu；trad. du chinois par Annie Curien et Feng Chen；précédé d'un "avant-goût" par Françoise Sabban. ［Paris］：Ph. Picquier；Unesco, 1994. 158 p. ；21cm. ISBN：2877301699, 2877301695.

(Collection Unesco d'œuvres représentatives. Série chinoise)
(2)Le gourmet：vie et passion d'un gastronome chinois：roman/Lu Wenfu；trad. du chinois par Annie Curien et Feng Chen；précédé d'un avant-goût par Françoise Sabban. Paris：France loisirs, Impr. BCI, 1996. 158 p. ；21cm. ISBN：2744100854, 2744100857
(3)Arles：P. Picquier, 1996. 187 p. ；17cm. ISBN：2877302709, 2877302708

2. Le puits/Lu Wenfu. Beijing：Littérature chinoise, 1988. 360 p. ISBN：7507100138, 7507100136
Contents：Au fond de la ruelle/Une ancienne famille de colporteurs/Le puits/Le mur/La sonnette/Le gourmet/Une faible lumière.
《陆文夫小说选》,Feng, Shouzheng 译.中国文学出版社.
(1)［2ème éd.］. Beijing：Éditions Littérature chinoise, 1990. (1 vol.) 360 p. ；18cm. ISBN：7507100138, 7507100136. (Panda Ormond)

3. Le Puits：récits/Lu Wenfu；récits traduits du chinois par Annie Curien et Feng Chen. Arles［France］：P. Picquier, 1991. 190 p. ；21cm. ISBN：2877300919, 2877300919
Contents：Réunit：Le Puits et Le Diplôme.
《井》,Feng, Chen 和 Curien, Annie 合译.

4. Nid d'hommes：roman/Lu Wenfu；traduit du chinois par Chantal Chien-Andro. Paris：Éditions du Seuil, 2002. 534, ［1］p. ISBN：2020396173, 2020396172
《人之窝》,Chien-Andro, Chantal 译.
(1)Paris：Éd. du Seuil, Bussière Camedan impr.), 2004. 707 p. : couv. ill. ；18cm. ISBN：2020635216, 2020635219. (Points：roman；1167)

李心田(1929—)

1. L'étoile rouge/Li Sin-tien. Pékin：Éditions en Langues Étrangères, 1975. 156 p.
《闪闪的红星》

2. Enfant-de-l'Hiver/Li Xintian；traduit du chinois par Michelle Loi；Préface de Han Suyin. Paris：Stock, impr. Aubin, 1976. 238 p. : couv. ill. en coul. ；22cm. ISBN：2234005191, 2234005198
《闪闪的红星》,李心田著；Loi, Michelle 译.

王愿坚(1929—1991)

1. Un simple travailleur/Wang Yuan-kien. Beijing：Éditions en Langues Étrangères, 1961. 179 p. ；19cm.
《普通劳动者》
(1)2e éd. Beijing：Éditions en Langues Étrangères, 1979. 177 pages；19cm.

方艾(1929—)

1. Un crime passionnel sous l'ancienne dynastie：L'histoire de Yang le licencié ès lettres et de Petit Chou/Fang Ai；traduit du chinois par Yan Hansheng. Pékin：Éd. Littérature chinoise, 1997. 357 p. ；19cm. ISBN：7507103552；7507103557.

《杨乃武与小白菜》，燕汉生译. 中国文学出版社.

白桦（1930—）

1. Ah! maman：roman/Bai Hua；trad. du chinois par Li Tche-houa et Jacqueline Alézaïs. Paris：P. Belfond, Impr. Firmin-Didot，1991. 345 p. ；23cm. ISBN：2714426352, 2714426352. (Voix chinoises)

《妈妈呀，妈妈!》，Alézaïs, Jacqueline 和 Li, Tche-houa 合译.

2. A demain désespoir/Bai Hua；Traduit du chinois par Yvonne André；［Avant-propos par Yvonne André］. Paris：You-Feng, Rich Bright，2013. 1 vol. (373 p.)：ill. , couv. ill. en coul. ；21cm. ISBN：2842795788, 2842795784

《哀莫大于心未死》，André, Yvonne 译.

邓友梅（1931—）

1. La tabatière/Deng Youmei. Pékin：Éd. Littérature chinoise，1988. 329 p. ：port. ；18cm. ISBN：7507100146, 7507100143. (Collection Panda)

Contents：Les recherches de Deng Youmei—La tabatière—A la recherche de Han le peintre—Na Wu—Le tableau aux deux chats.

《邓友梅小说选》. 中国文学出版社（熊猫丛书）. 包括《烟壶》《寻访"画儿韩"》《那五》《双猫图》

2. La tabatière/Deng Youmei. Pékin：Éd. Littérature chinoise，1988. 329 p. ：port. ；18cm. ISBN：7507100146, 7507100143. (Collection Panda)

《烟壶》

谭雪梅（1931—）

1. Passion métisse/Tan Xuemei；trad. du chinois par Wang Jiann-Yuh；Préface de Jacques Dars. Paris：Bleu de Chine，2000. 249 p. ；21cm. ISBN：2910884260, 2910884260

《混血情》，Wang, Jiann-Yuh 译；Dars, Jacques 序.

2. Les larmes de Mona Lisa/Xuemei Tan；trad. du chinois par Jiann-Yuh Wang. Paris：Bleu de Chine，2002. 165 p. ；21cm. ISBN：2910884538 (Br)，2910884536 (Br)

《蒙娜丽莎的眼泪》，Wang, Jiann-Yuh 译.

浩然（1932—2008）

1. Les enfants de Xisha：roman/Haoran；traduit du chinois par Liang Paitchin；avec une préf. par Michelle Loi. Lausanne ［7, rue de Genève］：Alfred Eibel，1976. 310 pages；18cm. ISBN：2827400022, 2827400027. (La Chine d'aujourd'hui；1)

《西沙儿女》，Paitchin, Liang 译.

2. Nouvelles de la campagne chinoise/Hao Ran；préf. de Michelle Loi；traduction du chinois, notes et présentation de Claire Jullien ［and others］. Paris：Mazarine，1980. 265 pages；23cm. ISBN：2863740253, 2863740255

中国农村中短篇小说. Jullien, Claire 等译.

丛维熙（1933—）

1. La voile blanche：deux nouvelles/de Cong Weixi. Pékin：

Éd. en Langues Érangères，1991. 254 p. ；18cm. ISBN：7119013904；7119013909. (Phénix)

《远去的白帆：丛维熙中篇小说选》. 外文出版社（凤凰丛书）.

王蒙（1934—）

1. Le Papillon：Nouvelles/Wang Meng. Beijing, Chine：Littérature chinoise，1982. 245 p. ：Portr. ；18cm. (Collection Panda)

《王蒙小说选》.《中国文学》杂志社（熊猫丛书）. 本书收录王蒙的 6 篇中短篇小说.

(1)Beijing：Éditions en Langues Érangères，2004. 1 v. (245 p.)；18cm. ISBN：7119035185, 7119035185. (Littérature chinoise)

2. Le Salut bolchevique/Wang Meng；trad. du chinois par Chantal Chen-Andro；［préf. par Alain Roux］. Paris：Messidor, Impr. SEPC)，1989. 143 p. ：couv. ill. en coul. ；22cm. ISBN：2209061954 (br)，2209061952 (br). (［Collection littéraire］.［Lettres étrangères］)

《布礼》，Chen-Andro, Chantal 和 Roux, Alain（1935—）合译.

3. Des yeux gris clair/Wang Meng；trad. du chinois par Françoise Naour. Paris：Bleu de Chine，2002. 124 p. ；17cm. ISBN：2910884554, 2910884550. (Chine en poche)

《淡灰色的眼珠》，Naour, Françoise 译.

4. Contes de l'Ouest lointain：［nouvelles du Xinjiang]/Wang Meng；traduits du chinois, présentés et annotés par Françoise Naour. ［Paris］：Bleu de Chine，2002. 1 vol. (183 p.)：cartes, couv. ill. en coul. ；21cm. ISBN：2910884503, 2910884505

Contents：Présentation—Oh, Mohammed Ahmed—Le Génie du vin—La Petite maison de pisé—Vie de Wang Meng

遥远的西方故事：新疆短篇小说. Naour, Françoise 译.

5. Les sourires du sage/Wang Meng；traduit du chinois par Françoise Naour；dessins de Xie Chunyan et Kang Xiaoyu. ［Paris］：Bleu de Chine，2003. 150 pages：illustrations；22cm. ISBN：2910884708, 2910884703

《笑而不答》，Naour, Françoise 译.

6. Celle qui dansait/Wang Meng；nouvelles traduites du chinois et annotées par Françoise Naour. ［Paris］：Bleu de Chine，2005. 157 p. ；21cm. ISBN：2849310026, 2849310021

Contents：Le génie du vin (Putao de jingling)—Ma-le-sixième (Ma xiao liu)—Dialectique (Jiangyan)—Paroles, parlottes, parlerie (Hua, hua, hua)—Poétique (Shiyi)—Nec plus ultra (Laijin)—Celle qui dansait (Jinan)—J'ai tant rêvé de toi (Wo you mengjiangle ni)—Vieille cour du dedans, si profonde... (Tingyuan shenshen)—Dur, dure le brouet (Jianying de xizhou).

王蒙中短篇小说选译. Naour, Françoise 译. 收录了《葡萄的精灵》《马小六》《讲演》《话、话、话》《诗意》《来劲》《济南》《我又梦见了你》《庭院深深》《坚硬的稀粥》.

杨书案(1935—)

1. Confucius/ Yang Shu'an; trad. par Yang Jun. Beijing：Littérature chinoise, 1997. 466 p. ; 21cm. ISBN：7507103781, 7507103786. (Collection Panda)
   《孔子》,Yang, Jun 译.

2. Laozi/ Yang Shu'an; trad. par Liu Fang. Beijing：Littérature chinoise, 1998. 361 p. ; 20cm. ISBN：7507103773, 7507103779. (Collection Panda)
   《老子》,Liu, Fang 译.

张贤亮(1936—2014)

1. Mimosa; et Xor bulak, l'histoire d'un routier/Zhang Xianliang. Beijing：Littérature chinoise, 1986. 321 p., [1] f. de pl. ; 18cm. (Collection Panda)
   《绿化树》,Curien, Annie 和 Pan, Ailian 合译.《中国文学》杂志社(熊猫丛书)

2. Mimosa：En Chine, aujourd'hui un amour bouleversant/ par Zhang Xianliang; [traduit par Pan Ailian]. Lausanne：Favre; Bruxelles：Vander, 1987. 246 p. ; 20cm. ISBN：2828902781, 2828902780
   《绿化树》,Pan, Ailian 译.

3. La moitié de l'homme, c'est la femme/Zhang Xianliang; traduit du chinois par Yang Yuanliang avec la collaboration de Michelle Loi. Paris：P. Belfond, 1987. 286 p. ; 23cm. ISBN：2714421008, 2714421005. (Voix Chinoises)
   《男人的一半是女人》,Yang, Yuanliang 和 Loi, Michelle 合译.
   (1)Paris：Belfond, 2004. 289 p. ; couv. et jaquette ill. en coul. ; 23cm. ISBN：2714441092, 2714441096. (Littérature étrangère)

4. La mort est une habitude/Zhang Xianliang; traduit du chinois par An Mingshan et Michelle Loi. Paris：Belfond, 1994. 282 p. ; 23cm. ISBN：2714431526, 2714431523
   《习惯死亡》,An, Mingshan 和 Loi, Michelle 合译.
   (1)Paris：Belfond, 2004. 1 vol. (282 p.) ; couv. ill. en coul. ; 23cm. ISBN：2714441106, 2714441102

杨啸(1936—)

1. Pluie rouge：un petit médecin aux pieds nus：roman/Yang Xiao; traduit du chinois par Liang Paitchin et Michelle Loi…; postface par Jean Guiloineau. Paris：Stock, Impr. S. E. P. C., 1979. 333 p. : couv. ill. en coul. ; 23cm. ISBN：2234011434, 2234011434
   《红雨》,Liang, Pai-tchin 和 Loi, Michelle(1926—2002) 合译.

刘绍棠(1936—1997)

1. Nouvelles du terroir/Liu Shaotang. Pékin：Littérature chinoise, 1986. 272 p. : portr. ; 18cm. (Collection Panda)
   Contents：Terroir et littérature—Un village dans les saules—La cabane de la melonnière—Dans la petite rue du

Lierre vert—Feuilles de lotus prêtes à s'ouvrir.
   《刘绍棠小说选》.《中国文学》杂志社(熊猫丛书). 收录 5 篇小说.

张洁(1937—)

1. Galère/Zhang Jie; traduit du chinois par Michel Cartier avec la collaboration de Zhitang Drocourt. Paris：Maren Sell et Cie, 1989. 168 p. ; 22cm. ISBN：2876040034, 2876040038
   《方舟》,Cartier, Michel 和 Drocourt, Zhitang 合译.

戴厚英(1938—1996)

1. Etincelles dans les ténèbres：roman/Dai Houying; trad. du chinois par Li Tche-Houa, Pénélope Bourgeois et Jacqueline Alézaïs. Paris：Seuil, 1987. 441 p. ; 21cm. ISBN：2020097621, 2020097628
   《人啊,人!》,Bourgeois, Pénélope,李治华等合译.

陈若曦(1938—)

1. Le préfet Yin et autres histoires de la Révolution culturelle/Chen Jo-hsi; traduit du chinois par Simon Leys. Paris：Denoël, 1979. 272 p.
   《尹县长》与"文革"故事. Leys, Simon 译.
   (1) Paris：Denoël, 1980. 272 p. : couv. ill. en coul. ; 21cm. (Arc-en-ciel)

益希单增(1940—)

1. Les survivants：extraits du roman/[Yixidanzeng]; traduit par Shen Dali, Jacqueline Desperrois. Beijing：Littérature chinoise, 1987. 313 p. ISBN：7507100111; 7507100112.
   《幸存的人》.《中国文学》杂志社(熊猫丛书).

蒋子龙(1941—)

1. La vie aux mille couleurs：nouvelles/Jiang Zilong. Beijing：Littérature chinoise, 1983. 268 p. (Panda)
   Contents：Le typhon numéro sept—Le jounal d'un secrétaire d'usine—Le directeur Qiao entre en fonction—La vie aux mille couleurs.
   《蒋子龙小说选》.包括《今年第七号台风》《一个工厂秘书的日记》《乔厂长上任记》《赤橙黄绿青蓝紫》.

陈忠实(1942—2016)

1. Au pays du cerf blanc. Second tome/Li Zhiwu; [d'après] Chen Zhongshi; [adaptation par Lu Yumei & Antoine Trouillard]. Bordeaux：les Éditions de la Cerise, DL 2015. 1 vol. (394 p.) : ill. ; 20×23cm. ISBN：2918596097 (rel.)
   《白鹿原》,Lu, Yu mei 和 Trouillard, Antoine 合译.

凌力(1942—)

1. Fils du Ciel：le premier empereur mandchou de Chine/Ling Li; traduit du chinois par Liu Fang, avec la collaboration de Marcelle Schiepers. Beijing：Littérature chinoise, 1995. iii, 706 p. ; 21cm. ISBN：750710284X, 7507102840. (Collection Panda)
   《少年天子》,Liu, Fang 和 Schiepers, Marcelle 合译.

古华(1942—)

1. Hibiscus：roman/Gu Hua; trad. du chinois par Philippe Grangereau. Paris：R. Laffont, Impr. D. Guéniot, 1987.

264 p. : couv. ill. en coul. ; 22cm. ISBN：2221051807，2221051801

《芙蓉镇》，Grangereau, Philippe 译.

2. Légendes de dragons : récits chinois. Beijing, China：Éditions Littérature chinoise, 1988. 274 p. : ill. ; 18cm. ISBN：7507100162，7507100167.

《龙的传说》.中国文学出版社.

3. La colline de la pagode/Gu Hua；[trad. par Gao Dekun et Zhang Zhengzhong]. Beijing：Littérature chinoise, 1988. 339 p. : ill. en front. ; 18cm. ISBN：7507100154，7507100150. (Collection Panda)

《浮屠岭》，高德坤，张正中译.

冯骥才（1942—）

1. Le fouet divin/Feng Jicai. Pékin：Éd. Littérature chinoise, 1989. 329 p. : port. ; 18cm. ISBN：7507100162，7507100167. (Collection Panda)

Contents：Le fouet divin—Les pipes sculptées—Une promenade dans le Temple de la Déesse—La femme de haute taille et le petit mari—Il est encore de ce monde—Le don de la vie—Le chant du bateau—Un vieux couple.

《神鞭》.中国文学出版社（熊猫丛书）

2. La natte prodigieuse : suivi de Une vie de chien/Feng Jicai ; trad. du chinois par Claude Geoffroy, avec le concours de Huafang Vizcarra et Yeh Yeo-Hwang. Paris：Éd. You-feng, 1990. 187 p. : couv. ill. en coul. ; 22cm. ISBN：2906658316，2906658318

《神鞭》，Geoffroy, Claude, Vizcarra, Hua-Fang 和 Yeh, Yeo-Hwang 合译.

3. Que cent fleurs s'épanouissent/Feng Ji Cai ; trad. du chinois par Marie-France de Mirbeck et Antoinette Nodot. [Paris]：Gallimard, Impr. Hérissey, 1990. 149 p. : couv. ill. en coul. ; 21cm. ISBN：2070565211，2070565214. (Collection Page blanche)

《百花齐放》，Mirbeck, Marie-France de 和 Nodot, Antoinette 合译.

（1）Paris：Gallimard Jeunesse, 2003. 124 p. ; 20cm. ISBN：2070556301，2070556304

4. La lettre perdue/Feng Jicai. Beijing：Éditions en Langues Étrangères, 1991. VI-221 p. : couv. ill. ; 18cm. ISBN：7119014528，7119014524. (Collection Phénix)

《冯骥才中篇小说选》

5. Je ne suis qu'un idiot : suivi de Aux premiers jours du printemps/Feng Jicai ; traduction et commentaires de Madeleine Duong ; Préface de Pénélope Bourgeois. Paris：Éditions You-Feng, 1990. 151 pages : 1 portraits ; 22cm. ISBN：2906658669，2906658660

《我这个笨蛋》，Duong, Madeleine 译.

6. Des gens tout simples/Feng Jicai ; trad. du chinois par Marie-France de Mirbeck. Éditions du Seuil；Paris；1995. 111 p. ISBN：2020228920，2020228923. (Seuil jeunesse)

《俗世奇人》，Mirbeck, Marie-France de 译.

（1）Le petit lettré de Tianjin：récits/Feng Jicai ; trad. du chinois par Marie-France de Mirbeck. Paris：Bleu de Chine, Impr. Bialec, 2002. 119 p. : couv. ill. ; 21cm. ISBN：2910884481，2910884482

7. L'empire de l'absurde ou dix ans de la vie de gens ordinaire/Feng Jicai ; traduit du chinois par Marie-France de Mirbeck et Étiennette Nodot. Paris：Bleu de Chine, 2001. 152 p. ISBN：2910884406，2910884406

《一百个人的十年》，Mirbeck, Marie-France de 和 Nodot, Étiennette 合译.

8. Chuan qi＝Personnages/Jicai Feng ; traduit du chinois par Jacques Meunier. Éd. bilingue avec pinyin. Paris：Éditions You Feng, 2008. 293 p. : ill. ; 21cm. ISBN：2842793517，284279351X

《传奇》，Meunier, Jacques 译.

9. Sentiments/Feng Jicai ; traduit du chinois par Yang Fen, revue par Jacques Meunier. Paris：Éd. You-Feng, 2009. 1 vol. （147 p.）：couv. ill. en coul. ; 21cm. ISBN：2842793524，2842793528

Contents：Les vieux époux—Le visiteur d'une nuit de neige—Un bouquet de fleurs, pour toi—Le maillot jaune—La télévision pour les vieux—Vieux Qiuli et Fifi—Le mystère.

Notes：Texte chinois, pinyin et traduction française en regard

骥才小说选译. Yang, Fen 和 Meunier, Jacques 合译.

10. Humour＝You mo/Feng Jicai ; traduit du chinois par Yang Fen, revu par Jacques Meunier. Édition bilingue avec Pinyin. Paris：Éd. You-Feng, 2010. 1 vol. （303 p.）：couv. ill. en coul. ; 21cm. ISBN：2842793531，2842793536

《幽默》，Yang, Fen 和 Meunier, Jacques 合译.

11. La Chine éternelle/Feng Jicai ; [traduction du chinois par Delphine Nègre]. Paris：EPA-[Éd. du Chêne], 2012. 1 vol. （255 p.）：ill. en coul., jaquette ill. en coul. ; 29cm. ISBN：2851207784，2851207784

《符号中国》，Nègre, Delphine 译.

刘心武（1942—）

1. Le talisman：version bilingue/Liu Xin Wu ; trad. R. Y. L. Yo. Paris：Librairie You Feng, 2000. 1 vol. （125 p.）：couv. ill. ; 21cm. ISBN：9621704537，9621704535，2842790677，2842790677

《如意》，Yo, R. Y. L. 译.

2. La Cendrillon du canal/Liu Xinwu ; trad. du chinois par Roger Darrobers. Paris：Bleu de Chine, 2003. 85 p. ; 21cm. ISBN：2910884627，2910884628

《护城河边的灰姑娘》，Darrobers, Roger 译.

3. Poussière et sueur/Liu Xinwu ; trad. du chinois par Roger Darrobers. Paris：Bleu de Chine, 2004. 113 p. ; 21cm. ISBN：2910884716，2910884710

《尘与汗》,Darrobers,Roger 译.

(1)〔Paris〕:Gallimard,2012. 1 vol. (120 p.):ill.,couv. ill. en coul.;18cm. ISBN:2070448012,2070448010. (Collection Folio;5453)

4. Poisson à face humaine/Liu Xinwu;trad. du chinois par Roger Darrobers. Paris:Bleu de Chine,2004. 59 p.;18cm. ISBN:291088483X,2910884833. (Chine en poche)

《人面鱼》,Darrobers,Roger 译.

5. La démone bleue/Liu Xinwu;roman traduit du chinois et annoté par Roger Darrobers. 〔Paris〕:Bleu de Chine,2005. 131 p.:ill.;21cm. ISBN:2910884988,2910884987

《蓝夜叉》,Darrobers,Roger 译.

6. Dés de poulet façon mégère/Liu Xinwu;roman traduit du chinois et annoté par Marie Laureillard. Paris:Bleu de Chine,2007. 150 p.:ill.;21cm. ISBN:2910884949,2910884945

《泼妇鸡丁》,Laureillard,Marie 译.

7. La Cendrillon du canal:suivi de Poisson à face humaine/Liu Xinwu;traduit du chinois par Roger Darrobers. 〔Paris〕:Gallimard,2012. 1 vol. (115 p.):couv. ill.;18cm. ISBN:2070448043,2070448045. (Collection Folio,2 euros)

Notes:Trad. de:"Hu cheng he bian de Huiguniang" et "Renmianyu."

《护城河边的灰姑娘》和《人面鱼》,Darrobers,Roger 译.

王为政(1944—)

1. Pèlerinage artistique/Wang Weizheng;traduit du chinois par Gao Dekun. Beijing:1ère éd. Littérature chinoise,1997. 276 p.;19cm. ISBN:7507103544,7507103540. (Collection Panda)

《听画》,Gao,Dekun 译.

航鹰(1944—)

1. Soir d'automne/Hang Ying. Beijing:Éditions Littérature chinoise,1990. 257 p.;18cm. ISBN:7507100510;7507100518.

《枫林晚》. 中国文学出版社(熊猫丛书)

霍达(1945—)

1. Le roi du jade:histoire d'une famille musulmane chinoise/Huo Da;traduit du chinois par Liu Fang. Pékin:Éd. Littérature chinoise,1991. 408 p.;18cm. ISBN:750710057X,7507100570. (Collection Panda)

《穆斯林的葬礼》,Liu,Fang 译. 中国文学出版社(熊猫丛书)

遇罗锦(1946—)

1. Le nouveau conte d'hiver/traduction et introduction de Huang San et Miguel Mandares. Paris:C. Bourgois,1982. 237 p.:couv. ill. en coul.;20cm. ISBN:2267002965,2267002966

《一个冬天的童话》,Huang San 和 Mandares,Miguel 合译.

2. Conte de printemps/Yu Luojin;trad.,préf. et postface de Huang San et Miguel Mandarès. Paris:Christian Bourgois,1984. 347 p.;20cm. ISBN:2267003864,2267003864

《春天的童话》,Huang,San 和 Mandarès,Miguel 合译.

姜戎(1946—)

1. Le totem du loup:roman/Jiang Rong;traduit du chinois par Yan Hansheng et Lisa Carducci. Paris:Bourin éditeur,2007. 565 pages;24cm. ISBN:2849410813,2849410810

《狼图腾》,Yan,Hansheng 和 Carducci,Lisa(1943—)合译.

(1)Paris:Librairie générale française,2009. 1 vol. (634 p.):couv. ill. en coul.;18cm. ISBN:2253125983,2253125989. (Le livre de poche;31280)

(2)Paris:Books Éditions,2015. 1 vol. (499 p.):couv. ill. en coul.;24cm. ISBN:2366080698,2366080697

(3)Beijing,Chine:Éditions en Langues Étrangères,2015. 571 pages;25cm. ISBN:7119093611,7119093614

程乃珊(1946—2013)

1. La maison bleue/Cheng Naishan. Pékin:Littérature chinoise,1989. ISBN:7507100162,7507100167. (Collection Panda)

Contents:Les charmes de Shanghai/Shuo Wang—La maison bleue—Qui a des filles a des soucis—Une rue pauvre.

《蓝屋》,Fu Chaomei 等译. 中国文学出版社(熊猫丛书)

曹桂林(1947—)

1. Pour le meilleur ou pour le pire:titre original:un natif de Pékin à New York/Cao Guilin;traduit par Lu Fujun avec la collaboration de Marcelle Schiepers. Pékin:Éd. Littérature chinoise,1994. 367 p.;18cm. ISBN:7507102068,7507102062. (Collection Panda)

《北京人在纽约》,Lu,Fujun 和 Schiepers,Marcelle 合译. (熊猫丛书)

郑义(1947—)

1. Stèles rouges:du totalitarisme au cannibalisme/〔Paris〕:Bleu de Chine,Impr. Bialec,1999. 287 p.:cartes,couv. ill.;21cm. ISBN:2910884139,2910884130

《红色纪念碑》,Lemoine,Françoise (1962—)等译.

2. Prière pour une âme égarée/Zheng Yi;récit traduit du chinois et annoté par Bernard Bourrit et Zhang Li. 〔Paris〕:Bleu de Chine,Impr. Bialec),2007. 1 vol. (99 p.):couv. ill.;19cm. ISBN:2849310236,2849310239

《招魂》,Bourrit,Bernard 和 Zhang-Bourrit,Li 合译.

张承志(1948—)

1. Les rivières du Nord/Zhang Chengzhi;traduit du chinois par Catherine Toulsaly. Pékin:Éd. Littérature chinoise,1992. 226 p.;18cm. ISBN:7507101142,7507101140. (Collection Panda)

《北方的河》,Toulsaly,Catherine 译.中国文学出版社(熊猫丛书)

2. Fleur entrelacs/Zhang Chengzhi;traduit du chinois et Préfacé par Dong Qiang. [Paris]:Bleu de Chine,1995. 186 p.;21cm. ISBN:2910884023,2910884024

Contents:Zhang Chengzhi:le septentrion—Mon beau cheval noir—Fleur-Entrelacs.

《初开的花》,董强译.包括另一部小说《黑骏马》.

3. Mon beau cheval noir/Zhang Chengzhi;traduit du chinois par Dong Qiang. Arles,France:P. Picquier,1999. 122 p.;17cm. ISBN:2877304353,2877304351. (Picquier poche;115)

《黑骏马》,董强译.

(1)Nouv. éd. Arles:P. Picquier,2011. 122 p.;17cm. ISBN:2809702392,280970239X. (Picquier poche)

郭雪波(1948—)

1. La renarde du désert/Guo Xuebo;traduction de Yan Hansheng. Pékin:Éd. Littérature chinoise,1994. 168 p.;18cm. ISBN:7507102254,7507102253. (Collection Panda)

《银狐》,Yan,Hansheng 译.

2. La renarde du désert/Guo Xuebo;traduction de Yan Hansheng. Pékin:Éd. Littérature chinoise,1994. 168 p.;18cm. ISBN:7507102254,7507102253. (Collection Panda)

《沙狐》,Yan,Hansheng 译.中国文学出版社(熊猫丛书)

3. La renarde du désert/Guo Xuebo;traduit du chinois par Dong Chun. Paris:Bleu de Chine,2001. 123 p.;21cm. ISBN:2910884201,2910884208

Contents:La renarde du désert—Les loups du désert.

Dong,Chun 译.包括《沙狐》和《沙狼》.

李迪(1948—)

1. La femme qui frappa à la tombée de la nuit:roman policier/Li Di;traduit du chinois par Patricia Batto. Arles(France):P. Picquier,1996. 156 p.;21cm. ISBN:2877302636,2877302630

《傍晚敲门的女人》,Batto,Patricia 译.

阿城(王阿城,1948—)

1. La prostituée innocente/A Cheng;traduit du chinois par Lü Hua avec la collaboration de Marcelle Schiepers. Pékin:Éd. Littérature chinoise,1994. 233 p.;18cm. ISBN:7507101398,7507101393. (Collection Panda)

《良娼》,Lü,Hua 译.

阿城(钟阿城,1949—)

1. Les trois rois/A Cheng;trad. du chinois par Noël Dutrait. Aix-en-Provence:Alinéa,1988. 242 p.;19cm. ISBN:290463150X,2904631504

Dutrait,Noël. 收录《棋王》《树王》《孩子王》.

(1)La Tour-d'Aigues:Éd. de l'Aube,2000. 1 vol. (243 p.);17cm. ISBN:2876781883,2876781887

2. Perdre son chemin:nouvelles/Cheng A;trad. du chinois par Noël Dutrait. La Tour d'Aigues:[s. n.],1991. 1 Bd. (Regards croisés)

《迷路》,Dutrait,Noël 译.

(1)Nouv. éd. La Tour-d'Aigues(Vaucluse):Éd. de l'Aube,2001. 118 p.;17cm. ISBN:2876786346, 2876786349. (L'Aube poche;29)

北岛(1949—)

1. Vagues:roman/Bei Dao;trad. du chinois par Chantal Chen-Andro. Arles:P. Picquier,Impr. Robert),1994. 206 p.:couv. ill. en coul.;21cm. ISBN:2877301605 (br),2877301602(br)

《波动》,Chen-Andro,Chantal 译.

路遥(1949—1992)

1. La vie/par Lu Yao. Beijing:Éditions en Langues Étrangères,1990. 308 p. ISBN:7119011782, 7119011783. (Phénix)

《人生》.外文出版社(凤凰丛书)

孙力(1949—2010)

1. Gens de la métropole/Sun Li et Yu Xiaohui;traduit du chinois par Yang Jun et Ying Hong;avec la collaboration de Pierre Polotto et de Sylviane Obadia. Pékin:Éd. Littérature chinoise,1994. 583 p.;21cm. ISBN:750710124X,7507101249. (Collection Panda)

《都市风流》,孙力,余小惠著;Yang,Jun 和 Ying,Hong 合译.

梁晓声(1949—)

1. Une terre fabuleuse:recueil de nouvelles/Liang Xiaosheng. Pékin:Éd. Littérature chinoise,1991. 302 p.;18cm. ISBN:7507100553,7507100556. (Collection Panda)

Contents:Une terre fabuleuse—Père—Une règle en jais—Le bouton noir—Le barrage de glace.

《这是一片神奇的土地:梁晓声作品选》.《中国文学》杂志社(熊猫丛书)

曹乃谦(1949—)

1. La nuit quand tu me manques,j'peux rien faire:panorama du village des Wen/Cao Naiqian;roman traduit du chinois et annoté par Françoise Bottéro et Fu Jie. [Paris]:Gallimard,Impr. Floch,2011. 1 vol. (323 p.):couv. ill. en coul.;21cm. ISBN:2070131259,2070131254. (Bleu de Chine)

《到黑夜我想你没办法》,Bottéro,Françoise 和 Fu,Jie 合译.

陈建功(1949—)

1. Tête frisée/Chen Jiangong;traduit du chinois par Lü Hua et Tang Zhi'an. Pékin:Éd. Littérature chinoise,1990. 156 p.;18cm. ISBN:7507100529,7507100525. (Collection Panda)

《卷毛》,Tang,Zhian 和 Lü,Hua 合译.《中国文学》杂志社(熊猫丛书)

陆星儿(1950—2004)

1. Amours d'antan. Lu Xing'er; trad. du chinois Lü Hua. Beijing：Éditions Littérature chinoise, 1993. 234 p.；18cm. ISBN：7507101231, 7507101232. (Panda)

《啊,青鸟》,吕华译.《中国文学》杂志社(熊猫丛书)

李锐(1950—)

1. Arbre sans vent：roman/Li Rui；traduit du chinois par Annie Curien et Liu Hongyu. Arles：Éditions P. Picquier, 2000. 206 p.；21cm. ISBN：2877304736, 2877304733.

《无风之树》,Curien, Annie 译.

张抗抗(1950—)

1. L'Impitoyable. Suivi de Tempêtes de sable：nouvelles/Zhang Kangkang；textes choisis, annotés et traduits du chinois par Françoise Naour；Préface de Michel Bonnin. Paris：Bleu de Chine, 1997. 147 p.；21cm. ISBN：2910884090, 2910884093

Notes；Originaltitel："Canren" und "Shabao"

《残忍》和《沙暴》,Naour, Françoise 译.

刘庆邦(1951—)

1. Le puits/Qingbang Liu；trad. du chinois par Marianne Lepolard. Paris：Bleu de Chine, 2003. 152 p.；21cm. ISBN：910884783, 2910884789

《神木》,Lepolard, Marianne 译.

2. Cataclysme：nouvelles/Liu Qingbang；nouvelles traduites du chinois, présentées et annotées par Françoise Naour. Paris：Gallimard, 2011. 1 vol. (105 p.)：couv. ill. en coul.；19cm. ISBN：2070131686, 2070131688. (Bleu de Chine)

《灾变》,Naour, Françoise 译.

史铁生(1951—2010)

1. Fatalité/Shi Tiesheng；nouvelles traduit du chinois par Annie Curien. [Paris]：Gallimard, Imp. Floch, 2004. 1 vol. (213 p.)：couv. en coul.；21cm. ISBN：2070742245, 2070742240. (Du Monde entier)

Contents：Poison—Fatalité—Plusieurs façons simples de résoudre une énigme—Le son de la cloche—Le Ditan et moi—Première personne.

Notes；Trad. de "Duyao - Suming - Yige miyu de jizhong jiandan de caifa- Zhongsheng - Wo yu ditan - Diyi rencheng"

史铁生短篇小说选. Bergeret Curien, Annie 译. 翻译了《毒药》《宿命》《一个谜语的几种简单的猜法》《众生》《我与地坛》《第一人称》.

朱小平(1952—)

1. Les braves gens/Zhu Xiaoping；traduit du chinois par Gao Linghan et Zeng Peigeng. Pékin：Éd. Littérature chinoise, 1992. 398 p.；18cm. ISBN：7507101096, 7507101096. (Collection Panda)

《好男好女》,Gao, Linghan 和 Zeng, Peigeng 合译. 中国文学》杂志社(熊猫丛书)

储福金(1952—)

1. La perplexité/Chu Fujin；traduit par Lü Hua avec la collaboration de Véronique Riffaud. Beijing：Éd. Littérature chinoise, 1995. 212 p.；19cm. ISBN：7507102823, 7507102826. (Collection Panda)

《迷惘》,Lü, Hua 译.《中国文学》杂志社(熊猫丛书)

王小波(1952—1997)

1. L'âge d'or：roman/Wang Xiaobo；trad. du chinois par Jacques Seurre；préf. de Michel Bonnin. Versailles：Éd. du Sorgho, Impr. Book it, 2001. 146 p.：couv. ill. en coul.；20cm. ISBN：2914446012, 2914446013

《黄金时代》,Seurre, Jacques 和 Bonnin, Michel(1949—) 合译.

2. Le monde futur：roman/Wang Xiaobo；traduit du chinois par Mei Mercier. Arles：Actes Sud, Impr. Floch), 2013. 1 vol. (189 p.)：couv. ill. en coul.；22cm. ISBN：2330024895 (br), 2330024894 (br). (Lettres chinoises)

《未来世界》,Mercier, Mei 译.

周大新(1952—)

1. Femmes du lac au parfum/Zhou Daxin. 1e éd. Pékin：Éd. Littérature chinoise, 1993. 183 p.；18cm. ISBN：750710138X, 7507101386. (Collection Panda)

《香魂女》

2. Les marches du mandarinat/Zhou Daxin；[trad. du chinois] par Geneviève Imbot-Bichet, en collab. avec Lü Hua. Paris：Stock, 1996. 231 p.；23cm. ISBN：2234049490, 2234049499

《向上的台阶》,Imbot-Bichet, Geneviève 和 Lü, Hua 合译.

(1) Les marches du mandarinat：roman/Zhou Daxin；traduit du chinois par Geneviève Imbot-Bichet en collaboration avec Lü Hua. Paris：Stock, 1998. 231 p.；23cm. ISBN：2234049490, 2234049499. (Nouveau cabinet cosmopolite)

贾平凹(1952—)

1. La montagne sauvage：nouvelles choisies/Jia Pingwa. Pékin：Éd. en Langues Étrangères, 1990. 379 p.；18cm. ISBN：7119013211, 7119013213. (Collection Phénix)

《野山人家》.外文出版社(凤凰丛书)

2. Le porteur de jeunes mariées：récits/Jia Pingwa；traduits du chinois par Lu Hua, Gao Dekun, Zhang Zhengzhong. Paris：Stock, 1995. 309 p.；23cm. ISBN：2234044855, 2234044852. (Nouveau cabinet cosmopolite)

Contents：Le porteur de jeunes mariées—Le héros brigand—Les tribulations d'un géomancien amoureux.

《五魁》,Lu Hua 等译. 还收录了《白朗》和《美穴地》.

(1)Paris：Stock, 1998. 305 p.；18cm. ISBN：2234049148, 2234049147. (Bibliothèque cosmopolite)

3. La capitale déchue：roman/Jia Pingwa；trad. du chinois

par Geneviève Imbot-Bichet. Paris：Stock，Impr. BCI，1997. 756 p.：couv. ill.；23cm. ISBN：223404622X，2234046221. (Nouveau cabinet cosmopoli)

《废都》，Imbot-Bichet，Geneviève 译.

(1) Paris：Librairie générale française，1999. 729 p.：couv. ill. en coul.；18cm. ISBN：2253146145，2253146148. (Le livre de poche；14614)

(2) Paris：Stock，2004. 893 p.；18cm. ISBN：2234056446，2234056442. (Bibliothèque cosmopolite)

4. Le village englouti：roman/Jia Pingwa；traduit du chinois par Geneviève Imbot-Bichet. Paris：Stock，2000. 317 p.；22cm. ISBN：2234052289，2234052284. (Nouveau cabinet cosmopolite)

《土门》，Imbot-Bichet，Genenième 译.

张辛欣（1953—）

1. Sur la même ligne d'horizon/zhang Xinxin；trad. du chinois par Emmanuelle Péchenart... Arles：Actes Sud：Fleuve bleu，Impr. Barthélemy)，1986. 179 p.：couv. ill. en coul.；19cm. ISBN：2868691242，2868691248

《在同一地平线上》，Péchenart，Emmanuelle 译.

(1) Arles：Actes Sud，1989. 1 vol. (204 p.)：couv. ill. en coul.；19cm. ISBN：2868693296，2868693297，2868694349，2868694348. (Lettres chinoises)

(2) Arles：Actes Sud，2003. 1 vol. (204 p.)：couv. ill. en coul.；19cm. ISBN：2868694343. (Lettres chinoises)

2. L'homme de Beijing/Zhang Xinxin et Sang Ye. Beijing，China：Éditions Littérature chinoise，1987. 441 p.；18cm. ISBN：7507100103，7507100105. (Collection Panda)

《北京人》，张辛欣，桑晔著.《中国文学》杂志社（熊猫丛书）

3. L'homme de Pékin：témoignages/Zhang Xinxin，Sang Ye；traduits du chinois sous la direction de Bernadette Rouis et Emmanuelle Péchenart. Arles：Actes sud，1992. 282 p.；22cm. ISBN：2868698735，2868698735

《北京人》，张辛欣，桑晔；Rouis，Bernadette 和 Péchenart，Emmanuelle 合译.

4. Une Folie d'orchidées：roman/Zhang Xinxin；trad. du chinois par Cheng Yingxiang. Arles：Actes Sud，Impr. des Presses universitaires de France)，1988. 69 p.：couv. ill. en coul.；19cm. ISBN：2868692389，2868692382. (Lettres chinoises)

《疯狂的君子兰》，Cheng，Yingxiang 译.

(1) Arles［France］：Actes sud，2004. 57 p.；18cm. ISBN：2742747389，2742747382，2760923886，2760923881. (Babel；627)

5. Le courrier des bandits：roman/Zhang Xinxin；traduit du chinois par Emmanuelle Péchenart et Robin Setton. Arles［France］：Actes sud，1989. 377 pages；19cm. ISBN：

2868693733，2868693730. (Lettres chinoises)

《封·片·联》，Péchenart，Emmanuelle 和 Robin，Setton 合译.

6. Au long du Grand Canal/Zhang Xinxin；récit traduit du chinois par Anne Grondona. Arles：Actes sud，1992. 255 pages：map；22cm. ISBN：286869859X，2868698599. (Terres d'aventure)

《在路上》，Grondona，Anne 译.

(1) Paris：10—18，1995. 287 p.：couv. ill. en coul.；18cm. ISBN：2264020873，2264020871. (Odyssées)

7. Le partage des rôles：roman/Zhang Xinxin；traduit du chinois par Emmanuelle Péchenart. ［Arles］：Actes Sud，1994. 166 p.；22cm. ISBN：2742701737，2742701735. (Lettres chinoises)

《这次你演哪一半》，Péchenart，Emmanuelle 译.

残雪（1953—）

1. Dialogues en paradis：nouvelles/Can Xue；textes choisis，présentés et traduits du chinois par Françoise Naour. ［Paris］：Gallimard，Impr. Firmin-Didot)，1992. 1 vol. (173 p.)；21cm. ISBN：207072378X，2070723782. (Du monde entier)

《天堂里的对话》，Naour，Françoise 译.

2. La rue de la boue jaune/Can Xue；trad. du chinois par Geneviève Imbot-Bichet. Paris：Bleu de Chine，2001. 187 p.；21cm. ISBN：2910884317 (Br)，2910884314 (Br)

《黄泥街》，Imbot-Bichet，Geneviève 译.

韩少功（1953—）

1. Seduction/récits traduits du chinois par Annie Curien. Arles；Paris：Philippe Picquier，1990. 94 p.；21cm. ISBN：287730034X，2877300346

《诱惑》，Curien，Annie 译.

2. Pa Pa Pa/Han Shaogong；traduit du chinois par Noël Dutrait et Hu Sishe. Aix-en-Provence：Alinea，1990. 119 p.；18cm. ISBN：2904631887，2904631887. (Collection Novella)

《爸爸爸》，Dutrait，Noël 和 Hu，Sishe 合译.

(1) La Tour-d'Aigues：Éd. de l'Aube，1995. 119 p.；17cm. ISBN：2876782391，2876782396. (L'Aube poche；18)

3. Femme, Femme, Femme：roman/Han Shaogong；traduit du chinois par Annie Curien. Paris；Arles：P. Picquier，1991. 122 p.；21cm. ISBN：2877300625，2877300629

《女女女》，Bergeret Curien，Annie 译.

(1) Arles：P. Picquier，Impr. A. Robert)，2000. 1 vol. (211 p.)：couv. ill. en coul.；17cm. ISBN：2877304744 (br)，2877304740 (br). (Picquier poche；129)

4. L'obsession des chaussures/Han Shaogong；traduit du chinois par Annie Curien. ［Saint-Nazaire］：M. E. E. T.，1992. 86 p.；20cm. ISBN：290394590X，2903945909

《鞋癖》，Currien，Annie 译.

5. Énigmes d'une maison vide/Han Shaogong. Pékin：Éd. Littérature chinoise, 1993. 258 p.；18cm. ISBN：7507101290, 7507101294. (Collection Panda)

Contents：Des cris de "suona" emportés par le vent—Le regard tourné vers la steppe—Vol à travers le ciel...—Retour à la campagne—Obsession—Enigmes d'une maison vide.

《空屋的秘密》

6. Bruits dans la montagne：et autres nouvelles/Han Shaogong；traduit du chinois par Annie Curien. [Paris]：Gallimard, 2000. 150 p.；20cm. ISBN：2070747433, 2070747436. (Du monde entier)

Contents：Parfum secret—Bruits dans la montagne—La mort du dirigeant—Cendres—Prédiction à la Porte nord

《山上的声音等中短篇小说》，Curien, Annie 译.

何家弘(1953—)

1. Crime de sang/He Jiahong；trad. du chinois et annoté par Marie Claude Cantournet-Jacquet et Xiaomin Giafferri-Huang. La Tour-d'Aigues (Vaucluse)：Éd. de l'Aube, 2002. 395 p.；22cm. ISBN：2876788179 (Br), 2876788176 (Br). (L'Aube noire)

《豪门血案》，Cantournet-Jacquet, Marie-Claude 和 Giafferri-Huang, Xiaomin 合译.

(1)La Tour-d'Aigues (Vaucluse)：Éd. de l'Aube, 2005. 395 p.；17cm. ISBN：275260078X (Br), 2752600783 (Br). (L'Aube poche. l'aube noire)

2. Le mystérieux tableau ancien/He Jiahong；trad. du chinois et annoté par Marie-Claude Cantournet-Jacquet et Xiaomin Giafferri-Huang. La Tour-d'Aigues：Éd. de l'Aube, Impr. Darantière), 2002. 317 p.：couv. ill. en coul.；22cm. ISBN：2876786761 (br), 2876786769 (br). (L'aube noire)

《人生怪圈：神秘的古画》，Cantournet-Jacquet, Marie-Claude 和 Giafferri-Huang, Xiao min 合译.

3. Crimes et délit à la Bourse de Pékin/He Jiahong；trad. du chinois Marie-Claude Cantournet-Jacquet et Xiaomin Giafferri-Huang. La Tour-d'Aigues (Vaucluse)：Éd. de l'Aube, 2005. 429 p.：couv. ill.；22cm. ISBN：2752600933 (Br), 2752600936 (Br). (Regards croisés/Marion Hennebert)

《人生黑洞：股市幕后的罪恶》，Cantournet-Jacquet, Marie-Claud 和 Giafferri-Huang, Xiaomin 合译.

马建(1953—)

1. La mendiante de Shigatze：récits/Ma Jian；traduits du chinois par Isabelle Bijon；présentation de Marc de Gouvenain. [Arles]：Actes sud, 1993. 109 p.；18cm. ISBN：2742700390, 2742700394. (Babel；77)

《亮出你的舌苔》，Bijon, Isabelle 译.

蒋子丹(1954—)

1. Pour qui s'élève la fumée des mûriers? /Jiang Zidan；trad. du chinois et annoté par Prune Cornet. [Paris]：Bleu de Chine, 2004. 131 p.：couv. ill. en coul.；21cm. ISBN：2910884767 (br), 2910884765 (br)

《桑烟为谁升起》，Cornet, Prune 译.

张欣(1954—)

1. Deux rivales/Zhang Xin；traduit par Lu Fujun. Paris：Éd. Littérature chinoise, 1995. 301 p.；19cm. ISBN：7507103056, 7507103052. (Collection Panda)

《首席》，Lu, Fujun 译.

刘恒(1954—)

1. Ju Dou, ou, L'amour damné/Liu Heng；traduit du chinois par Tang Zhi'an et Lü Hua. Pékin：Éd. Littérature chinoise, 1991. 185 p.；18cm. ISBN：7507100561, 7507100563. (Collection Panda)

《菊豆》即《伏羲伏羲》，Lu, Hua 和 Tang, Zhian 合译. 中国文学出版社(熊猫丛书).

2. La neige noire/Liu Heng；traduit du chinois par Catherine Toulsaly. Pékin：Éd. Littérature chinoise, 1992. 302 p.；18cm. ISBN：7507101088, 7507101089. (Collection Panda)

《黑的雪》，Toulsaly, Catherine 译. 中国文学出版社(熊猫丛书).

王安忆(1954—)

1. Les lumières de Hong Kong/Anyi Wang；trad. du chinois Denis Bénéjam. Arles (Bouches-du-Rhône)：P. Picquier, 2001. 188 p.；21cm. ISBN：2877305198, 2877305198

《香港的情与爱》，Bénéjam, Denis 译.

2. Amère jeunesse/Wang Anyi；traduit du chinois par Éric Jacquemin. [Paris]：Bleu de Chine, 2004. 119 p.；18cm. ISBN：2910884856, 2910884857. (Chine en poche)

《忧伤的年代》，Jacquemin, Éric 译.

3. Le chant des regrets éternels/Wang Anyi；roman traduit du chinois par Yvonne André et Stéphane Lévêque. Arles：P. Picquier, 2006. 676 p.；21cm. ISBN：2877308065, 2877308069

《长恨歌》，André, Yvonne 和 Lévêque, Stéphane 合译.

(1) Arles, Fr.：Éditions Philippe Picquier, 2008. 780 pages；17cm. ISBN：2809700633, 280970063X. (Picquier Poche)

4. Amour dans une petite ville：roman/Wang Anyi；traduit du chinois par Yvonne André. Arles：Philippe Picquier, 2007. 146 s. ISBN：2877309592, 2877309592

《小城之恋》，André, Yvonne 译.

(1)Arles：P. Picquier, 2010. 1 vol. (170 p.)：couv. ill. en coul.；17cm. ISBN：2809701685, 2809701687. (Picquier poche)

5. Amour sur une colline dénudée/Wang Anyi；roman traduit du chinois par Stéphane Lévêque. Arles：P. Picquier, 2008. 224 p.；21cm. ISBN：2809700121, 2809700125

《荒山之恋》，Lévêque, Stéphane 译.

(1)Arles (Bouches-du-Rhône)：P. Picquier, 2010. a18 p.；17 × 11cm.. ISBN：2809702064, 2809702063.

（Picquier poche）

6. Amour dans une vallée enchantée/Wang Anyi；roman traduit du chinois par Yvonne André. Arles，France：P. Picquier，2008. 146，[1] p.；21cm. ISBN：2809700619，2809700613

《锦绣谷之恋》，André，Yvonne 译.

(1) Arles：P. Picquier，2011. 1 vol. (168 p.)；couv. ill. en coul.；17cm. ISBN：2809702439，2809702438. （Picquier poche）

7. Le plus clair de la lune：roman/Wang Anyi；traduit du chinois par Yvonne André. Arles：P. Picquier，2013. 1 vol. (220 p.)：couv. ill. en coul.；21cm. ISBN：2809708882，2809708886

《月色撩人》，André，Yvonne 译.

(1)[出版地不详]：[出版商不详]，2017. 1 vol. (238 p.)：couv. ill. en coul.；17cm. ISBN：2809712681，2809712689. （Picquier poche）

8. La coquette de Shanghai/Wang Anyi；roman traduit du chinois par Brigitte Guilbaud. [出版地不详]：[出版商不详]，2017. 1 vol. (239 p.)：couv. ill. en coul.；21cm. ISBN：2809712667 (br)，2809712662 (br)

《桃之夭夭》，Guilbaud，Brigitte(1969—)译.

方方(1955—)

1. Une vue splendide：roman/Fang Fang；traduit du chinois par Dany Filion. Arles：Ph. Picquier，1995. 153 p.；21cm. ISBN：287730227X，2877302272

《风景》，Filion，Dany 译.

(1) Arles：P. Picquier，2003. 168 p.：couv. ill. en coul.；17cm. ISBN：2877306860，2877306867. （Picquier poche；212）

2. Soleil du crépuscule：roman/Fang Fang；traduit du chinois par Geneviève Imbot-Bichet avec la collaboration de Lü Hua. Paris：Stock，1998. 287 p.；22cm. ISBN：2234044，2234049. （Nouveau cabinet cosmopolite）

《落日》，Imbot-Bichet，Geneviève 和 Lü，Hua 合译.

3. Début fatal/Fang Fang；roman traduit du chinois par Geneviève Imbot-Bichet. [Paris]：Stock，2001. 128 p. ISBN：223405351X，2234053519. （Bibliothèque cosmopolite）

《在我的开始是我的结束》，Imbot-Bichet，Geneviève 译.

莫言(1955—)

1. La mélopée de l'ail paradisiaque：roman/Mo Yan；trad. du chinois par Chantal Chen-Andro. Paris：Éd. Messidor，Impr. SEPC，1990. 376 p.：couv. ill. en coul.；22cm. ISBN：2209063027，2209063024. （Lettres étrangères）

《天堂蒜薹之歌》，Chen-Andro，Chantal 译.

(1) Paris：Éditions du Seuil，2005. 358，[1] p. ISBN：2020637111，2020637114，2757810798，2757810790. （Points；P2025）

(2) Paris：Éd. du Seuil，2005. 1 vol. (425 p.)；22cm.

ISBN：2757810798，2757810790 （br）. （Points；P2025）

2. Le clan du sorgho：roman/Mo Yan；traduit du chinois par Pascale Guinot et Sylvie Gentil avec la collaboration de Wei Xiaoping. Arles：Actes Sud，1990. 152 s. ISBN：2868695477，2868695475

《红高粱家族》，Gentil，Sylvie 译.

(1) Arles：Actes Sud，2012. 152 pages；19cm. ISBN：2868695475，2868695477. （Lettres chinoises）

(2) Paris：Éd. du Seuil，Normandie Roto impr.，2014. 1 vol. (442 p.)；22cm. ISBN：2021119909，2021119904

(3) Paris：Éditions Points，2016. 1 vol. (543 p.)；18cm. ISBN：2757857656，2757857657. （Points；P4264）

3. Le chantier：roman/Mo Yan；trad. du chinois par Chantal Chen-Andro. Paris：Scandéditions，Impr. Jouve，1993. 155 p.：couv. ill.；22cm. ISBN：2209067375，2209067374. （Lettres étrangères）

《筑路》，Chen-Andro，Chantal 译.

(1) Paris：Seuil，2007. 213，[1] p. ISBN：2020948647，2020948648

(2) Paris：Points，2011. 213 pages；18cm. ISBN：2757824733，2757824732. （Points；policier；P2670）

4. Les treize pas/Mo Yan；traduit du chinois par Sylvie Gentil. Paris：Seuil，1995. 375 s. ISBN：202020617X，2020206174，2020635196，2020635194

《十三步》，Gentil，Sylvie 译.

(1) Paris：Seuil，2004. 409 pages；23cm. ISBN：2020635194，2020635196. （Points；P 1178）

5. Le veau, suivi de Le coureur de fond：nouvelles/Mo Yan；traduites du chinois par Francois Sastourne. Paris：Éditions Du Seuil，1998. 256 pages；21cm. ISBN：2021024012，2021024016

Sastourné，Françoise 译. 包括莫言的《牛》和《三十年前的一次长跑比赛》.

(1) Paris：Éd. du Seuil，2012. 1 vol. (256 p.)：jaquette ill. en coul.；21cm. ISBN：2021024012，2021024016

(2)[Paris]：Le Grand livre du mois，2012. 1 vol. (256 p.)：couv. ill. en coul.；21cm. ISBN：2286095888，2286095884

(3) Paris：Éd. Points，2013. 1 vol. (210 p.)：couv. ill. en coul.；18cm. ISBN：2757836910，2757836919. （Points；P3121）

6. Le pays de l'alcool/Mo Yan；trad. du chinois par Noël et Liliane Dutrait. Paris：Seuil，2000. 446 p.；22cm. ISBN：2020293730，2020293730

《酒国》，Dutrait，Noël 和 Dutrait，Liliane(1952—)合译.

(1) 2e éd. Paris：Seuil，2004. 474 p.；18cm. ISBN：2020635208，2020635202. （Points；1179）

7. Le radis de cristal：récits/Mo Yan；trad. du chinois par Pascale Wei-Guinot et Wei Xiaoping. Arles：P. Picquier，2000. 172 p.：couv. ill. en coul.；21cm. ISBN：

2877305171，2877305174．（Picquier poche；148）

《透明的红萝卜》，Wei-Guinot，Pascale 和 Wei，Xiaoping 合译．

8. Le supplice du santal：roman/Mo Yan；traduit du chinois par Chantal Chen-Andro．［Paris］：Éditions Du Seuil，2001. 721 pages；18cm．ISBN：2757814871，2757814877．（Points；2224）

《檀香刑》，Chen-Andro，Chantal 译．

(1) Paris：Seuil，2006. 548 p.；22cm．ISBN：2020541696，2020541695

9. Explosion/Mo Yan；［roman］traduit du chinois par Camille Loivier；Préface de Chantal Chen-Andro．Paris：Caractères，2004. 122 p.：portr.；21cm．ISBN：2854463633，2854463637．（Imaginaires du monde）

《爆炸》，Loivier，Camille 译．

10. Beaux seins，belles fesses：les enfants de la famille Shangguan：roman/Mo Yan；traduit du chinois par Noël et Liliane Dutrait．Paris：Seuil，2004. 825 p.；22cm. ISBN：2020385848，2020385848

《丰乳肥臀》，Dutrait，Noël 和 Dutrait，Liliane 合译．

(1) Paris：Éd. du Seuil，2005. 1 vol. (894 p.)：couv. ill. en coul.；18cm．ISBN：2020799096，202079909X. （Points；P1386）

11. La carte au trésor/Mo Yan；récit traduit du chinois par Antoine Ferragne．Arles：P. Picquier，2004. 113 p.；21cm．ISBN：2877306941，2877306942

《藏宝图》，Ferragne，Antoine 译．

(1) Arles：P. Picquier，Impr. France Quercy，2006. 1 vol. (125 p.)：couv. ill.；17cm．ISBN：2877308723，2877308724．（Picquier poche；277）

12. Enfant de fer：nouvelles/Mo Yan；traduites du chinois par Chantal Chen-Andro．Paris：Seuil，2004. 315 p.；22cm．ISBN：2020541688，2020541688

Contents：Carpe d'or—Coup de vent—La meule en pierre—Cinq petits pains—La rivière tarie—L'abri aux sandales de paille—Le bébé abandonné—Le dirigeable—La faute—Une histoire d'amour—Enfant de fer—La fille du boucher—Nuit de pèche—Premier amour—La belle de glace—Le clan des renifleurs d'odeurs.

《铁孩》，Chen-Andro，Chantal 译．包括莫言16部中短篇小说选译．

(1) Paris：Éditions du Seuil，2013. 1 vol. (345 p.)：couv. ill. en coul.；18cm．ISBN：2757833940，2757833944．（Points；P3001）

13. Le maître a de plus en plus d'humour：roman/Mo Yan；traduit du chinois par Noël Dutrait．Paris：Seuil，2005. 107 p. ISBN：2020787709，2020787703，2020859564，2020859561．（Points；P1455）

《师傅越来越幽默》，Dutrait，Noël 译．

14. La joie/Mo Yan；roman traduit du chinois par Marie Laureillard．Arles：P. Picquier，2007. 180 p.；21cm.

ISBN：2877309684，2877309681

《欢乐》，Laureillard，Marie 译．

(1) Édition revue et corrigée．［Paris］：Éditions Points，Impr. CPI Brodard et Taupin，2015. 1 vol. (151 p.)；18cm．ISBN：2757853290，2757853295．（Points；P4095）

15. Quarante et un coups de canon：［roman］/Mo Yan；traduit du chinois par Noël et Liliane Dutrait．Paris：Seuil，2008. 500 p.；22cm．ISBN：2020679053，2020679051

《四十一炮》，Dutrait，Noël 和 Dutrait，Liliane 合译．

(1) ［Paris］：Points，2013. 1 vol. (582 p.)：couv. ill. en coul.；18cm．ISBN：2757836965，275783696X. （Points，Signatures）

16. La dure loi du karma/Mo Yan；roman traduit du chinois par Chantal Chen-Andro．Paris：Éd. du Seuil，Normandie roto impr.，2009. 1 vol. (760 p.)：jaquette ill. en coul.；22cm．ISBN：2020947800，2020947803

《生死疲劳》，Chen-Andro，Chantal 译．

(1) ［Paris］：Éditions du Seuil，2009. 1 vol. (972 p.)：couv. ill. en coul.；18cm．ISBN：2757819586，2757819585．（Points；2460）

17. Grenouilles/Mo Yan；traduit du chinois par Chantal Chen-Andro．Paris：Éditions du Seuil，2011. 407 pages；22cm．ISBN：2021024005，2021024008

《蛙》，Chen-Andro，Chantal 译．

(1) ［Paris］：Éditions du Seuil，2012. 525 p.；18cm. ISBN：2757831045，2757831046．（Points；2900）

18. La belle à dos d'âne dans l'avenue de Chang'an/Mo Yan；récits traduits du chinois par Marie Laureillard．Arles：P. Picquier，2011. 1 vol. (158 p.)：couv. ill. en coul.；21cm．ISBN：2809702651（br），2809702659（br）

《长安大道上的骑驴美》，Laureillard-Wendland，Marie 译．

19. La belle à dos d'âne dans l'avenue de Chang'an/Mo Yan；récits traduits du chinois par Marie Laureillard．Arles：P. Picquier，2011. 1 vol. (158 p.)：couv. ill. en coul.；21cm．ISBN：2809702651，2809702659

Contents：La belle à dos d'âne dans l'avenue de Chang'an—La femme au bouquet de fleurs—Le combat dans la peupleraie—Les poucettes.

Laureillard-Wendland，Marie 译．翻译了莫言的《长安大道上的骑驴美人》《怀抱鲜花的女人》《白杨林里的战斗》和《拇指铐》4部小说

20. Le grand chambard/Mo Yan…；traduit du chinois par Chantal Chen-Andro．［Paris］：Points，Impr. CPI Brodard et Taupin，2014. 1 vol. (124 p.)：couv. ill. en coul.；18cm．ISBN：2757841334，2757841335． （Points；P3225）

《变》，Chen-Andro，Chantal 译．

21. Professeur singe：suivi de Le Bébé aux cheveux d'or：romans/Mo Yan；traduits du chinois par François

Sastourné et Chantal Chen-Andro. Paris：Éd. du Seuil, 2015. 1 vol. （241 p.）；jaquette ill. en coul.；21cm. ISBN：2021242874, 2021242870

Sastourné, Françoise 和 Chen-Andro, Chantal 合译. 包括莫言的《幽默与趣味》和《金发婴儿》.

(1)Paris：Points, 2017. 1 vol. （241 p.）；18cm. ISBN：2757866023，2757866028. （Points；P4525）

22. Le clan des chiqueurs de paille：roman/Mo Yan；traduit du chinois par Chantal Chen-Andro. ［Paris］：Éditions du Seuil, 2016. 1 vol. （470 p.）；couv. ill en coul.；22cm. ISBN：2021144017, 2021144011

《食草家族》,Chen-Andro, Chantal 译.

23. Les retrouvailles des compagnons d'armes/Mo Yan；traduit du chinois par Nõel Dutrait. Paris：Éditions du Seuil, Impr. Floch, 2017. 1 vol. （233 p.）；21cm. ISBN：2021119381, 2021119386

《战友重逢》,Dutrait, Nõel(1951—)译.

刘索拉（1955—）

1. La grande île des tortues cochons/Sola Liu；traduit du chinois par Sylvie Gentil. Paris：Seuil, 2006. 1 v. （267 p.）；21cm. ISBN：2020845938 （Br）, 2020845939 （Br）

《女贞汤》,Gentil, Sylvie 译.

周梅森（1956—）

1. Made in China/Zhou Meisen；roman traduit du chinois et annoté par Mathilde Mathe. ［Paris］：Gallimard, 2016. 1 vol. （630 p.）：couv. ill. en coul.；21cm. ISBN：2070141654 （br）, 2070141659 （br）. （Bleu de Chine）

《中国制造》,Mathe, Mathilde 译.

骆英（1956—）

1. Lapins, lapins＝Xiao tu zi/Luo Ying；traduit du chinois par Shuang Xu, avec la collaboration de Martine Chardoux；Préface de Jacques Darras. Édition bilingue. Pantin：Le Castor astral, 2013. 97 pages：illustrations；21×14cm. ISBN：2859209544, 2859209549. （Autre voie）

《小兔子》,Xu, Shuang 和 Chardoux, Martine 合译.

张炜（1956—）

1. Partance：nouvelles/Zhang Wei；trad. du chinois par Chantal Chen-Andro. Paris：Bleu de Chine, 2000. 119 p.；21cm. ISBN：2910884309, 2910884307

Contents：Scènes d'hiver—Partance—La forêt d'Azeroliers—La combe nivelée.

《冬景》等短篇小说选译. Chen-Andro, Chantal 译.

2. Le vieux bateau：roman/Zhang Wei；traduit du chinois par Annie Bergeret Curien et Xu Shuang. Paris：Éd. du Seuil, Normandie roto impr., 2014. 1 vol. （620 p.）；jaquette ill. en coul.；22cm. ISBN：2020982641, 2020982641

《古船》,Bergeret Curien, Annie 和 Xu, Shuang 合译.

刘醒龙（1956—）

1. Instituteurs de la montagne/Liu Xinglong. Beijing：Éd. Littérature chinoise, 1994. pages. ISBN：7507102262. 7507102260. （Collection Panda）

Contents：Instituteurs de la montagne—Le maire d'un village.

《山村教员》.中国文学出版社（熊猫丛书）

2. La déesse de la modernité/Liu Xinglong；trad. par Françoise Naour. Paris：Bleu de Chine, 1999. 74 p.；21cm. ISBN：2910884236, 2910884239

Notes：Trad. de："Maopai chengshi siti."

《凤凰琴》,Naour, Françoise 译.

3. Du thé d'hiver pour Pékin/Liu Xinglong；trad. du chinois par Françoise Naour. Paris：Bleu de Chine, 2004. 119 p.；21cm. ISBN：2910884740 （Br）, 2910884741 （Br）

《挑担茶叶上北京》,Naour, Françoise 译.

4. La guérite：la force des farces en terre chinoise/Liu Xinglong；roman traduit du chinois et annoté par Françoise Naour. ［Paris］：Bleu de Chine, 2006. 117 p.；18cm. ISBN：2849310204, 2849310205. （Chine en poche）

Notes：Titre original：Maopai chengshi siti.

《冒牌城市》,Naour, Françoise 译.

铁凝（1957—）

1. La douzième nuit/Tie Ning；nouvelles trad. du chinois et annotées par Prune Cornet en collab；avec Liu Yang. Paris：Bleu de Chine, 2004. 103 p.；21cm. ISBN：2910884872, 2910884871

Notes：Six nouvelles sur la rencontre de deux solitudes, peuplées de personnages dont les histoires se répondent. Souvent celle d'un homme et d'une femme que tout sépare mais qui se croisent un jour：la prostituée et le peintre, le vieux lettré et la jeune paysanne, le fonctionnaire et l'inconnue.

《第十二夜》,Liu, Yang 和 Cornet, Prune 合译. 铁凝小说选集.

2. Fleurs de coton/Tie Ning；trad. du chinois par Véronique Chevaleyre. Paris：Bleu de Chine, 2005. 113 p.；21cm. ISBN：2910884880, 2910884888

《棉花垛》,Chevaleyre, Véronique 译.

叶兆言（1957—）

1. La jeune maîtresse：roman/Ye Zhaoyan；traduit du chinois par Nadine Perront. Arles：Ph. Picquier, 1996. 284 p.：ill.；21cm. ISBN：2877302806, 2877302807

《花影》,Perront, Nadine 译.

(1) Arles （Bouches-du-Rhône）：P. Picquier, 1998. 308 p.；17cm. ISBN：2877304124, 2877304122

(2) Arles：Éditions Philippe Picquier, 2016. 1 vol. （308 p.）；17cm. ISBN：2809711509, 280971150X. （Picquier poche）

2. La serre sans verre/Ye Zhaoyan；roman traduit du chinois par Wang Jiann-Yuh. ［Paris］：Bleu de Chine, 2006. 342 p.；21cm. ISBN：2910884864, 2910884864

《没有玻璃的花房》,Wang, Jiann-Yuh 译.

3. Nankin 1937, une histoire d'amour：roman/Ye Zhaoyan；

traduit du chinois par Nathalie Louisgrand-Thomas. Paris：Éditions du Seuil, 2008. 344 p. ISBN：2020614634, 2020614634

《一九三七年的爱情》,Louisgrand-Thomas, Nathalie 译.

池莉(1957—)

1. Les tribulations de la vie：[nouvelles]/Chi Li. Beijing：Éditions Littérature chinoise, 1996. 349 p. ; 19cm. ISBN：750710348X, 7507103489.

《烦恼人生》,维罗尼克等译. 中国文学出版社(中国当代女作家系列 熊猫丛书). 包括《烦恼人生》《不谈爱情》《太阳出世》《热也好冷也好活着就好》.

2. Triste vie/Chi Li；traduit du chinois par Shao Baoqing. Arles：Actes Sud, 1998. 101 p. ; 19cm. ISBN：2742720073, 2742720071. (Lettres chinoises)

《烦恼人生》,Baoqing, Shao 译.

(1) Arles [France]：Actes sud, 2005. 99 p. ; 18cm. ISBN：2742755411, 2742755417, 2760924769, 2760924765. (Babel；689)

(2) Arles：Actes Sud, 2008. 1 vol (99 p.)：couv. ill. en coul. ; 18cm. (Babel；689)

3. Trouée dans les nuages：roman/Chi Li；traduit du chinois par Isabelle Rabut et Shao Baoqing. Arles [France]：Actes sud, 1999. 115 p. ; 19cm. ISBN：2742724915, 2742724918. (Lettres chinoises)

《云破处》,Rabut, Isabelle 和 Shao, Baoqing 合译.

(1) [2e éd.]. [Arles]：Actes Sud, 2001. 1 vol. (115 p.)：couv. ill. en coul. ; 18cm. ISBN：2742736565, 2742736560. (Lettres chinoises)

(2) [Arles]：Babel, 2004. 1 vol. (113 p.)：couv. ill. en coul. ; 18cm. ISBN：2742747370, 2742747375. (Babel；626)

(3) Arles：Actes Sud, 2015. 1 vol. (113 p.)；18cm. ISBN：2330049362, 2330049366. (Babel)

4. Pour qui te prends-tu?：roman/Chi Li；traduit du chinois par Hervé Denès. Arles [France]：Actes sud, 2000. 154 p. ; 19cm. ISBN：274273046X, 2742730469. (Lettres chinoises)

《你以为你是谁》,Denès, Hervé 译.

(1) Arles [France]：Actes sud, 2007. 152 p. ; 18cm. ISBN：2742771547 (Actes sud), 2742771549 (Actes sud), 2760927261 (Leméac), 2760927261 (Leméac). (Babel；850)

5. Préméditation/Chi Li；traduit du chinois par Angel Pino et Shao Baoqing. [Arles]：Actes Sud, 2002. 136 p. ISBN：2742740945, 2742740949. (Lettres chinoises)

《预谋杀人》,Pino, Angel 和 Shao, Baoqing 合译.

(1) Arles [France]：Actes sud, 2010. 134 p. ; 18cm. ISBN：2742795062, 2742795065, 2760906853, 276090685X. (Babel；1041)

6. Tu es une rivière：roman/Chi Li；traduit du chinois par Angel Pino et Isabelle Rabut. Arles：Actes Sud, 2004.

202 p. ; 19cm. ISBN：2742747656, 2742747658. (Lettres chinoises)

《你是一条河》,Pino, Angel 和 Rabut, Isabelle 合译.

(1) Arles [France]：Actes sud, 2006. 200 p. ; 18cm. ISBN：2742762876, 2742762873, 276092596X, 2760925960. (Babel；764)

7. Soleil levant/Chi Li；roman traduit du chinois par Angel Pino. Arles：Actes Sud, 2005. 154 p. ; 19cm. ISBN：274275539X, 2742755394. (Lettres chinoises)

《太阳出世》,Pino, Angel 译.

(1) Arles [France]：Actes Sud, 2008. 152 p. ; 18cm. ISBN：2742775880, 2742775889, 2760927964, 2760927962. (Babel；899)—

8. Un homme bien sous tous rapports：roman/Chi Li；traduit du chinois par Hervé Denès. Arles：Actes Sud, 2006. 1 vol. (156 p.)：couv. ill. en coul. ; 19cm. ISBN：2742762884, 2742762880. (Lettres chinoises)

《有了快感你就喊》,Denès, Hervé 译.

9. Les sentinelles des blés：roman/Chi Li；traduit du chinois par Angel Pino et Shao Baoqing. Arles：Actes Sud, 2008. 158 p. ; 19cm. ISBN：2742778188, 2742778187. (Lettres chinoises)

《看麦娘》,Pino, Angel 和 Shao, Baoqing 合译.

(1) Lyon：Éd. de la loupe, 2009. 1 vol. (176 p.)：couv. ill. en coul. ; 22cm. ISBN：2848682792, 2848682795

(2) Arles：Actes Sud, 2015. 1 vol. (156 p.)；18cm. ISBN：2330051228, 2330051220. (Babel；1321)

10. Le show de la vie/Chi Li；roman traduit du chinois par Hervé Denès. Arles：Actes Sud；[Montréal]：Leméac, 2010. 1 vol (171 p.)：couv. ill. en coul. ; 19cm. ISBN：2742794942, 2742794948

《生活秀》,Denès, Hervé 译.

(1) [Édition en gros caractères]. Guérande：Éd. de la Loupe, 2011. 1 vol (236 p.)：couv. ill. en coul. ; 22cm. ISBN：2848683829, 2848683821. (Roman；19)

野莽(1957—)

1. Intelligence/Ye Mang；trad. du chinois par Lü Hua. Paris：Bleu de Chine, 2003. 94 p. ; 21cm. ISBN：2910884619 (Br), 2910884611 (Br)

《打你五十大板》,Lü, Hua 译.

2. Les secrets d'un petit monde/Ye Mang；traduit du chinois par Lü Hua. Paris：Bleu de Chine, 2004. 1 vol. (114 p.)：couv. ill. en coul. ; 18cm. ISBN：2910884775 (br), 2910884772 (br). (Chine en poche)

《玩阿基米德飞盘的王永乐师傅》,Lu, Hua 译.

刘震云(1958—)

1. Les mandarins/Liu Zhenyun；roman traduit du chinois et annoté par Sebastian Veg. [Paris]：Bleu de Chine, 2004. 125 p. ; 21cm. ISBN：2910884929, 2910884925

《官场》,Veg, Sebastian 译.

2. Peaux d'ail et plumes de poulet：nouvelles/Liu Zhenyun；

traduites du chinois par Sebastian Veg. Paris：Bleu de Chine，2006. 1 v.（213 p.）；21cm. ISBN：291088497X，2910884970

Contents：L'Unité de travail—Tracas à perte de vue

《一地鸡毛》，Veg，Sebastian（1976—）译.

3. Peaux d'ail；et Plumes de poulet：nouvelles/Liu Zhenyun；trad. du chinois et annotées par Sebastian Veg.［aris］：Bleu de Chine，2006. 213 S. ISBN：291088497X，2910884970

《单位》和《一地鸡毛》. Veg，Sebastian 译.

4. En un mot comme en mille：roman/Liu Zhenyun；traduit du chinois par Isabelle Bijon et Wang Jiann-Yuh.［Paris］：Gallimard，Impr. Floch，2013. 1 vol.（719 p.）；couv. ill. en coul. ；21cm. ISBN：2070133277，2070133273.（Bleu de Chine）

《一句顶一万句》，Bijon，Isabelle 和 Wang，Jiann-Yuh 合译.

5. Se souvenir de 1942/Liu Zhenyun；traduit du chinois et annoté par Geneviève Imbot-Bichet.［Paris］：Gallimard，Impr. Floch，2013. 1 vol.（119 p.）；couv. ill. en coul. ；19cm. ISBN：2070140893，207014089X.（Bleu de Chine）

《温故一九四二》，Imbot-Bichet，Geneviève 译.

6. Je ne suis pas une garce：roman/Liu Zhenyun；traduit du chinois et annoté par Brigitte Guilbaud. Paris］：Gallimard，2015. 1 vol.（292 p.）；couv. ill. en coul. ；21cm. ISBN：2070144952，207014495X.（Bleu de Chine）

《我不是潘金莲》，Guilbaud，Brigitte（1969—）译.

7. Le téléphone portable/Liu Zhenyun；traduit du chinois par Hervé Denès，en collaboration avec Jia Chunjuan. Paris：Gallimard，2017. 328 p. ISBN：2070144969，2070144968.（Bleu de Chine）

《手机》，Denès，Hervé 和 Jia，Chunjuan 合译.

阎连科（1958—）

1. Servir le peuple/Yan Lianke；roman traduit du chinois par Claude Payen. Arles：P. Picquier，2006. 188 p. ；21cm. ISBN：2877308278，2877308274

《为人民服务》，Payen，Claude 译.

2. Le rêve du village des Ding/Yan Lianke；roman traduit du chinois par Claude Payen. Arles：P. Picquier，2007. 328 p. ；21cm. ISBN：2877309165，2877309169

《丁庄梦》，Payen，Claude 译.

3. Les jours，les mois，les années/Yan Lianke；roman traduit du chinois par Brigitte Guilbaud. Arles：P. Picquier，2009. 124 p. ；21cm. ISBN：2809700961，2809700966

《年月日》，Guilbaud，Brigitte 译.

（1）Arles：P. Picquier，2014. 1 vol.（152 p.）；couv. ill. en coul. ；17cm. ISBN：2809709643，2809709645.（Picquier poche）

4. Bons baisers de Lénine/Yan Lianke；roman traduit du chinois par Sylvie Gentil. Arles：P. Picquier，2009. 558 p. ；21cm. ISBN：2809701333，2809701334

《受活》，Gentil，Sylvie 译.

（1）Arles：P. Picquier，2012. 1 vol.（654 p.）；couv. ill. ；17cm. ISBN：2809703542，280970354X.（Picquier poche）

5. Les quatre livres/Yan Lianke；traduit du chinois par Sylvie Gentil. Arles：P. Picquier，2012. 1 vol.（410 p.）；couv. ill. en coul. ；21cm. ISBN：2809703528，2809703523

《四书》，Gentil，Sylvie 译.

（1）Arles：Éditions Philippe Picquier，2015. 1 vol.（446 p.）；17cm. ISBN：2809711165，280971116X.（Picquier poche）

6. La fuite du temps：roman/Yan Lianke；traduit du chinois par Brigitte Guilbaud. Arles：P. Picquier，2014. 605 p. ；21cm. ISBN：2809709636，2809709637

《日光流年》，Guilbaud，Brigitte 译.

7. Les chroniques de Zhalie：roman/Yan Lianke；traduit du chinois par Sylvie Gentil. Arles：Éditions Philippe Picquier，2015. 1vol.（515 p.）；21cm. ISBN：2809711158，2809711151

《炸裂志》，Gentil，Sylvie 译.

8. Un chant céleste/Yan Lianke；roman traduit du chinois par Sylvie Gentil.［出版地不详］：［出版社不详］，2017. 1 vol.（89 p.）；couv. ill. ；21cm. ISBN：2809712506，2809712506

《耙耧天歌》，Gentil，Sylvie 译.

9. À la découverte du roman/Yan Lianke；traduit du chinois par Sylvie Gentil. Arles：Éditions Philippe Picquier，2017. 1vol.（193 p.）；21cm. ISBN：2809712513，2809712514

《发现小说》，Gentil，Sylvie 译.

王朔（1958—）

1. Je suis ton papa：roman/Wang Shuo；traduit du chinois par Angélique Lévi et Wong Li-Yine. Paris：Flammarion，1992. 404 p. ；21cm. ISBN：2080668838，2080668837

《我是你爸爸》，Lévy，Angélique 和 Wong，Li-Yine 合译.

（1）［Paris］：Flammarion，1997. 404 p. ；21cm. ISBN：2080668838，2080668837.（Lettres d'orient）

2. Feu et glace/Wang Shuo，roman traduit du chinois par Patricia Batto. Arles：Philippe Picquier，1992. 143 p. ；21cm. ISBN：287730129X，2877301299

《一半是火焰，一半是海水》，Batto，Patricia 译.

（1）［Arles］：Picquier，Impr. Robert，1995. 148 p. ；couv. ill. en coul. ；17cm. ISBN：2877302334，2877302333.（Picquier poche；33）

3. Vous êtes formidable：［roman］/Wang Shuo；traduction du chinois et Préface de Maité Aragonés Lumeras. Lausanne，Suisse：L'Age d'homme，1999. 107 p. ；21cm. ISBN：2825111236，2825111239.（Vent d'est，vent d'ouest）

《你不是一个俗人》,Lumeras,Maité Aragonés 译.

扎西达娃(1959—)

1. La Splendeur des chevaux du vent/Zhaxi Dawa; récits traduits du chinois (Thibet) par Bernadette Rouis. Arles [France]: Actes Sud, 1990. 108 p.; 19cm. ISBN: 2868695132, 2868695130. (Lettres chinoises)

《风马之耀》,Rouis,Bernadette 译.

2. Tibet, les années cachées: récits/Zhaxi Dawa; choisis et traduits du chinois par Émilienne Daubian; Préfacés par Nguyen Tai-Luc. Paris: Bleu de Chine, 1995. 116 p.; 21cm. ISBN: 2910884015, 2910884017

Contents: Tibet, les années cachées—Tibet, une âme ligotée—Un prince en exil.

《西藏隐秘岁月》,Daubian, Émilienne 和 Nguyen, Tai-Luc 合译. 还包括《西藏,系在皮绳结上的魂》和《流放中的少爷》2 篇.

孙甘露(1959—)

1. Respirer: roman/Sun Ganlu; traduit du chinois par Nadine Perront. Arles: P. Picquier, 1997. 237 p.; 21cm. ISBN: 2877303012, 2877303019

《呼吸》,Perront,Nadine 译.

阿来(1959—)

1. Sources lointaines/A Lai; trad. du chinois par Marie-France de Mirbeck. Paris: Bleu de Chine, 2003. 118 p.; 21cm. ISBN: 2910884732, 2910884734

《遥远的温泉》,de Mirbeck,Marie-France 译.

2. Les pavots rouges/Alai; trad. de l'anglais, États-Unis, par Aline Weill. Monaco; [Paris]: Éd. du Rocher, Impr. Brodard et Taupin, 2003. 450 p.: couv. ill. en coul.; 24cm. ISBN: 2268045056, 2268045054. (Terres étrangères)

《尘埃落定》,Weill,Aline 译.

(1) Arles: P. Picquier, 2010. 1 vol. (636 p.): couv. ill. en coul.; 17cm. ISBN: 2809701487, 2809701482. (Picquier poche)

余华(1960—)

1. Vivre! /Yu Hua; trad. du chinois par Yang Ping. Paris: France loisirs, 1994. 221 p.; 21cm. ISBN: 2724281292, 2724281293

《活着》,Yang, Ping 译.

(1) Paris: Livre de poche, 1994. 223 pages; 17cm. ISBN: 2253135704, 2253135708

(2) Lyon: Chardon bleu, Impr. IGO, 1995. 2 vol. (172, 166 p.): couv. ill. en coul.; 21cm. ISBN: 2868331084, 2868331083, 2868331092, 2868331090. (Collection Largevision)

(3) Arles [France]: Actes sud, 2008. 248 p.; 18cm. ISBN: 2742773992, 2742773991, 2760927773, 2760927776. (Babel; 880)

(4) Arles [France]: Actes sud, 2013. 248 p.; 18cm. ISBN: 2330026684, 2330026684, 2760927773, 2760927776.

(Babel; 880)

2. Un monde évanoui/Yu Hua; récits traduits du chinois par Nadine Perront. Arles: Éditions Philippe Picquier, 1994. 122 pages; 21cm. ISBN: 2877301966, 2877301961

Perront, Nadin 译. 收录《河边的错误》和《世事如烟》2 部作品.

(1) Arles: P. Picquier, Impr. France Quercy, 2003. 150 p.: couv. ill. en coul.; 17cm. ISBN: 2877306739, 2877306737. (Picquier poche; 208)

3. Le vendeur de sang/Yu Hua; roman traduit du chinois par Nadine Perront. Arles [Frrance]: Actes sud, 1997. 285 p.; 22cm. ISBN: 2742714693, 2742714698

《许三观卖血记》,Perront, Nadine 译.

(1) Arles [France]: Actes sud, 2006. 285 p.; 18cm. ISBN: 2742761276, 2742761272, 2760925676, 2760925670. (Babel; 748)

4. Un amour classique: petits romans/Yu Hua; trad. du chinois par Jacqueline Guyvallet. Arles: Actes Sud, 2000. 259 p.; 22cm. ISBN: 2742726101, 2742726103. (Lettres chinoises)

《古典爱情》,Guyvallet, Jacqueline 译.

(1) Arles: Actes Sud; [Montréal]: Leméac, 2009. 1 vol. (257 p.): couv. ill. en coul.; 18cm. ISBN: 2742782475, 2742782478, 2760929005, 2760929000. (Babel; 955)

5. Cris dans la bruine/Yu Hua; trad. du chinois par Jacqueline Guyvallet. Arles (Bouches-du-Rhône): Actes Sud, 2003. 325 p.; 22cm. ISBN: 274273600X, 2742736003

《在细雨中呼喊》,Guyvallet, Jacqueline 译.

6. 1986/Yu Hua; court roman traduit du chinois par Jacqueline Guyvallet. Arles: Actes Sud, 2006. 88 p.; 19cm. ISBN: 2742761322, 2742761326. (Lettres chinoises)

《一九八六年》,Guyvallet, Jacqueline 译.

7. Brothers: roman/Yu Hua; roman traduit du chinois par Angel Pino et Isabelle Rabut. Arles: Actes Sud, 2008. 716 p.; 24cm. ISBN: 2742774371, 2742774378. (Lettres chinoises)

《兄弟》,Pino, Angel 和 Rabut, Isabelle 合译.

(1) Arles [France]: Actes sud, 2010. 1017 p.; 18cm. ISBN: 2742789825, 2742789820, 2760929791, 2760929795.

(2) 2e édition. Arles: Actes Sud, 2013. 1 vol. (1017 p.): couv. ill. en coul.; 18cm. ISBN: 2330026615, 2330026617. (Babel; 1003)

8. Sur la route à dix-huit ans: et autres nouvelles/Yu Hua; traduites du chinois par Jacqueline Guyvallet, Angel Pino et Isabelle Rabut. Arles: Actes Sud, 2009. 1 vol. (181 p.); 18cm. ISBN: 2742788248, 2742788247. (Lettres chinoises)

《十八岁出门远行》等中短篇小说. Guyvallet, Jacqueline

等译.

9. Le septième jour/Yu Hua；traduit du chinois par Angel Pino et Isabelle Rabut. Arles：Actes Sud，2014. 1 vol. （269 p.）；18cm. ISBN：2330036904，2330036906. （Lettres chinoises）

《第七天》，Pino，Angel 和 Rabut，Isabelle 合译.

刁斗（1960—）

1. Jumeaux/Diao Dou；traduit du chinois par Anne Thiollier et Catherine Lan.［aris］：Bleu de Chine，2001. 154 p. ISBN：2910884422，2910884420. （Chine en poche）

《孪生》，Thiollier，Anne 和 Lan，Catherine 合译.

2. Solutions：roman/Diao Dou；trad. du chinois par Véronique Jacquet-Woillez. Paris：Bleu de Chine，Impr. Bialec，2002. 126 p.：couv. ill. en coul.；18cm. ISBN：2910884570，2910884574. （Chine en poche）

《解决》，Jacquet-Woillez，Véronique 译.

3. Nid de coucou/Diao Dou；traduit du chinois par Véronique Jacquet-Woillez.［Paris］：Bleu de Chine，2003. 123 p.：couv. ill. en coul.；18cm. ISBN：2910884813，2910884819. （Chine en poche）

Contents：Hypothèse（Yun）—Grossesses（Quechao）—Nid de coucou（Xiangxiang de keneng）.

《想象的可能》，Jacquet-Woillez，Véronique 译. 翻译了《想象的可能》等 3 篇小说.

4. La faute：roman/Diao Dou；trad. du chinois par Véronique Jacquet-Woillez. Paris：Bleu de Chine，Impr. Bialec，2004. 131 p.：couv. ill. en coul.；18cm. ISBN：2910884430，2910884437. （Chine en poche）

《罪》，Jacquet-Woillez，Véronique 译.

5. Rêves：nouvelles/Diao Dou；nouvelles traduites du chinois et annotées par Prune Cornet. Paris：Bleu de Chine，2006. 1 v. （131 p.）；18cm. ISBN：2849310107，2849310106. （Chine en poche）

《梦的解析》，Cornet，Prune 译.

虹影（1962—）

1. L'Été des trahisons：roman/Hong Ying；trad. du chinois par Sylvie Gentil. Paris：Seuil，1997. 199 p.；21cm. ISBN：2020291436，2020291439

《背叛之夏》（又名《裸舞代》），Gentil，Sylvie 译.

2. Une fille de la faim/Hong Ying；trad. du chinois par Nathalie Louisgrand. Paris：Éd. du Seuil，2000. 398 p. ISBN：2020335980，2020335980

《饥饿的女儿》，Louisgrand，Nathalie 译.

3. Le livre des secrets de l'alcôve：roman/Hong Ying；trad. du chinois par Véronique Jacquet-Woillez. Paris：Éd. du Seuil，Impr. Floch），2003. 254 p.：jaquette ill.；21cm. ISBN：2020412594（br），2020412599（br）

《K—英国情人》，Jacquet-Woillez，Véronique 译.

4. Enfants des fleurs：roman/Hong Ying；traduit de l'anglais par Lisa Rosenbaum. Paris：Calmann-Lévy，Impr. CPI Bussière，2013. 1 vol. （474 p.）：couv. ill.

en coul.；23cm. ISBN：2702143865，2702143865

《好儿女花》，Rosenbaum，Lisa 译.

陈染（1962—）

1. Vie privée/Ran Chen；［traduit du chinois par Rebecca Peyrelon］. 2016. 1 vol. （219 p.）：couv. ill.；22cm. ISBN：2842797232，284279723X

《私人生活》，Peyrelon-Wang，Rebecca（1968—）译.

陈希我（1963—）

1. Irritation/Chen Xiwo；traduit du chinois par Claude Payen. Paris：Reflets de Chine，2009. 407 p. ISBN：2918267003，2918267007

《抓痒》，Payen，Claude 译.

刘慈欣（1963—）

1. Le problème à trois corps/Liu Cixin；roman traduit du chinois par Gwennaël Gaffric. Arles：Actes Sud，2016. 423 pages；24cm. ISBN：2330070748，2330070748. （Exofictions）

《三体》，Gaffric，Gwennaël 译.

2. La forêt sombre/Liu Cixin；roman traduit du chinois par Gwennaël Gaffric. 2017. 1 vol. （648 p.）：couv. ill. en coul.；24cm. ISBN：2330082314，2330082312. （Exofictions）

《黑暗森林》，Gaffric，Gwennaël 译.

苏童（1963—）

1. Epouses et concubines：roman/Su Tong；traduit du chinois par Annie Au Yeung et Françoise Lemoine. ［Paris］：Flammarion，1992. 1 vol. （148 p.）；20cm. ISBN：2080667181，2080667182. （Lettres d'Extrême-Orient）

《妻妾成群》，Au Yeung，Annie 和 Lemoine，Françoise 合译.

（1）Paris：Librairie générale française，1997. 125 p.：couv. ill. en coul.；18cm. ISBN：2253932795，2253932796. （Le livre de poche，Biblio；3279）

（2）［Paris］：Flammarion，2004. 148 p.：couv. ill.；20cm. ISBN：2080667181，2080667182

（3）Paris：Flammarion，2010. 125 p. ISBN：2253932796，2253932795. （Le livre de poche. Biblio）

2. Visages fardés：roman/Su Tong；traduit du chinois par Denis Bénéjam. Arles：Ph. Picquier，1995. 181 p.；21cm. ISBN：2877302318，2877302319

Contents：La vie des femmes—Visages fardés

《红粉》，Bénéjam，Denis 译. 还收录了《妇女生活》.

（1）Arles：P. Picquier，2003. 221 p.：couv. ill. en coul.；17cm. ISBN：2877306399，2877306393. （Picquier poche；199）

3. La maison des pavots/Su Tong；trad. et préf. de Pierre Briere. Éd. bilingue. Paris：Librairie You-Feng，1996. 149 p.；21cm. ISBN：2842790006，2842790004

《罂粟之家》，Briere，Pierre 译.

4. Riz：［roman］/Su Tong；traduit du chinois par Noël Dutrait, avec la collaboration de Liliane Dutrait. ［aris］: Flammarion, 1998. 306 p.；22cm. ISBN：2080673009, 2080673008

《米》,Dutrait, Noël 和 Dutrait, Liliane 合译.

(1) La Tour-d'Aigues：Éd. de l'Aube, 2003. 310 p.：couv. ill. en coul.；17cm. ISBN：287678940X, 2876789401. (L'Aube poche)

(2) La Tour d'Aigues：Éditions de l'Aube, 2004. 310 p.；17cm. ISBN：287678940X, 2876789401. (Aube poche)

(3) Paris：Points, 2016. 1 vol. (310 p.)：couv. ill. en coul.；18cm. ISBN：2757862612, 2757862618. (Points；P4410)

5. Fantômes de papiers：nouvelles/Su Tong；traduction du chinois par Agnès Auger；adaptation par Pierre Chavot. Paris：Desclée de Brouwer, 1999. 302 p.；20cm. ISBN：2220040585, 2220040585

苏童中短篇小说. Auger, Agnès 译.

6. Je suis l'empereur de Chine/Su Tong；roman traduit du chinois par Claude Payen. Arles：P. Picquier, 2005. 275 p.；21cm. ISBN：2877307905, 2877307901

《我的帝王生涯》,Payen, Claude 译.

(1) Arles：P. Picquier, 2008. 1vol. (376 p.)：couv. ill. en coul.；17cm. ISBN：2809700565, 2809700567. (Picquier poche)

7. Le mythe de Meng/Su Tong；traduit du chinois par Marie Laureillard. ［aris］: Flammarion, Impr. Firmin-Didot), 2009. 1 vol. (221 p.)：couv. ill. en coul.；22cm. ISBN：2081202627, 208120262X

《碧奴》,Laureillard-Wendland, Marie 译.

8. À bicyclette/Su Tong；traduit du chinois par Anne-Laure Fournier. Arles：P. Picquier, 2011. 1 vol. (141 p.)：couv. ill. en coul.；22cm. ISBN：2809702514, 2809702519. (Écrits dans la paume de la main)

《自行车之歌》,Fournier Le Ray, Anne-Laure 译.

(1) Arles：Éditions Philippe Picquier, 2015. 1 vol. (178 p.)；17cm. ISBN：2809711028, 280971102X

9. La berge：roman/Su Tong；traduit du chinois par François Satourné. ［Paris］: Gallimard, Impr. Floch), 2011. 1 vol. (465 p.)：couv. ill. en coul.；21cm. ISBN：2070131266, 2070131262. (Bleu de Chine)

《河岸》,Sastourné, Françoise 译.

10. Le dit du loriot/Su Tong；traduit du chinois par François Sastourné. Paris：Éditions du Seuil, 2016. 1 vol. (365 p.)：jaquette ill. en coul.；22cm. ISBN：2021286434, 2021286436

《黄雀记》,Sastourné, Françoise 译.

迟子建(1964—)

1. La danseuse de yangge；Voyage au pays des nuits blanches/Chi Zijian；traduit par Dong Chun, avec la collaboration de Jacqueline Desperrois. Paris：Bleu de Chine, 1997. 137 p.；21cm. ISBN：2910884120, 2910884123, 2910884112, 2910884116

《秧歌·向着白夜旅行》,Dong Chun 和 Desperrois, Jacqueline 合译.

2. Le bracelet de jade；［Pour six plats d'argent］/Chi Zijian；trad. du chinois par Dong Chun. Paris：Bleu de Chine, Impr. Bialec, 2002. 105 p.；21cm. ISBN：2910884473, 2910884475

Contents：Le bracelet de jade—Pour six plats d'argent

《旧时代的磨房·银盘》,Dong, chun(1942—)译.

3. La fabrique d'encens；suivie de Neuf pensées/Chi Zijian；nouvelles traduites du chinois par Dong Chun. ［Paris］: Bleu de Chine, 2004. 143 p.；21cm. ISBN：2910884791, 2910884796

《香坊·九朵蝴蝶花》,Dong, Chun 译.

4. Toutes les nuits du monde：récits/Chi Zijian；traduits du chinois par Stéphane Lévêque；avec le concours d'Yvonne Lévêque. Arles：P. Picquier, 2013. 1 vol. (175 p.)：couv. ill. en coul.；21cm. ISBN：2809709476, 2809709475

Contents：Enfance au village du Grand Nord—Toutes les nuits du monde

《北极村童话·世界上所有的夜晚》,Lévêque, Stéphane (1967—)译.

(1) Arles：Éditions Philippe Picquier, 2016. 1 vol. (202 p.)；17cm. ISBN：2809711844, 2809711844. (Picquier Poche)

5. Bonsoir, la rose：roman/Chi Zijian；traduit du chinois par Yvonne André. Arles：Éditions Philippe Picquier, 2015. 1 vol. (184 p.)；21cm. ISBN：2809710953, 2809710953

《晚安玫瑰》,André, Yvonne 译.

6. Le dernier quartier de lune：roman/Chi Zijian；traduit du chinois par Yvonne André et Stéphane Lévêque. Arles：Éditions Philippe Picquier, 2016. 1 vol. (366 p.)；21cm. ISBN：2809711943, 2809711941

《额尔古纳河右岸》,André, Yvonne 和 Lévêque, Stéphane (1967—)合译.

毕飞宇(1964—)

1. L'opéra de la lune/Feiyu Bi；récit traduit du chinois par Claude Payen. Arles：Éditions Philippe Picquier, 2003. 113, ［1］p. ISBN：2877306828, 2877306829

《青衣》,Payen, Claude 译.

(1) Arles：P. Picquier, 2009. 1 vol. (123 p.)：couv. ill. en coul.；17cm. ISBN：2809700893, 2809700893. (Picquier poche)

2. De la barbe à papa un jour de pluie：court roman/Bi Feiyu；trad. du chinois par Isabelle Rabut. Arles：Actes Sud, Impr. Floch, 2004. 120 p.：couv. ill.；19cm. ISBN：2742747664, 2742747665. (Lettres chinoises)

《雨天的棉花糖》,Rabut, Isabelle 译.

3. Trois sœurs：roman/Bi Feiyu；trad. du Chinois par Claude Payen. Arles：Picquier, 2004. 346 p. ISBN：2877307549，2877307543

《玉米》，Payen, Claude 译.

(1) Arles：P. Picquier, Impr. France Quercy, 2007. 1 vol.（426 p.）：couv. ill. en coul.；17cm. ISBN：2877309523，2877309525.（Picquier poche；294）

4. Les triades de Shanghai：roman/Bi Feiyu；traduit du chinois par Claude Payen. Mas de Vert：Éditions Philippe Picquier, 2007. 238 p. ISBN：2877309516，2877309517

《上海往事》，Payen, Claude 译.

(1) Arles：P. Picquier, 2010. 1 vol.（284 p.）：couv. ill. en coul.；17cm. ISBN：2809701722，2809701725.（Picquier poche）

5. La plaine：roman/Bi Feiyu；traduit du chinois par Claude Payen. Arles：P. Picquier, 2009. 1 vol.（475 p.）：couv. ill. en coul.；21cm. ISBN：2809700916，2809700915

《平原》，Payen, Claude 译.

(1) Arles：P. Picquier, 2011. 1 vol.（509 p.）：couv. ill. en coul.；17cm. ISBN：2809702880，2809702888.（Picquier poche）

6. Les aveugles/Bi Feiyu；roman traduit du chinois par Emmanuelle Péchenart. Arles：P. Picquier, 2011. 461 p.；21cm. ISBN：2809702828，2809702829

《推拿》，Péchenart, Emmanuelle 译.

(1) Arles：P. Picquier, 2013. 1 vol.（542 p.）：couv. ill. en coul.；17cm. ISBN：2809709445，2809709440.（Picquier poche）

7. Don Quichotte sur le Yangtsé/Bi Feiyu；traduit du chinois par Myriam Kryger. Arles：Éditions Philippe Picquier, Impr. Horizon, 2016. 1 vol.（181 p.）：couv. ill. en coul.；21cm. ISBN：2809711677，2809711674

《苏北少年"堂吉诃德"》，Kryger, Myriam 译.

格非（1964—）

1. Nuée d'oiseaux bruns：récits/Ge Fei；traduits du chinois par Chantal Chen. Arles：Ph. Picquier, 1996. 108 p.；21cm. ISBN：287730258X，2877302586

《褐色鸟群》，Chen-Andro, Chantal 译.

2. Poèmes à l'idiot：roman/Ge Fei；traduit du chinois par Xiaomin Giafferri-Huang. La Tour d'Aigues：Aube, 2007. 124 p. ISBN：2752601827，2752601824.（Regards croisés）

《傻瓜的诗篇》，Giafferri-Huang, Xiaomin 译.

麦家（1964—）

1. L'enfer des codes. PARIS：Robert Laffont, 2015. 1 vol.（333 p.）；25cm. ISBN：2221146200，2221146204

《解密》，Payen, Claude 译.

李敬泽（1964—）

1. Relations secrètes：réflexions insolites sur les relations entre la Chine et l'Occident au fil des siècles/Li Jingze；traduit du chinois par Hervé Denès；en collaboration avec Li Ru. Arles：Éditions Philippe Picquier, 2017. 1 vol.（345 p.）：ill.；21cm. ISBN：2809712285，280971228X

《看来看去和秘密交流》，Denès, Hervé 译.

老牛（1966—）

1. Pentium III：roman/Laoniu；trad. du chinois par Véronique Chevaleyre et Geneviève Clastres. Paris：Bleu de Chine, 2002. 122 p.；17cm. ISBN：2910884546（Br），2910884543（Br）.（Chine en poche）

《奔腾 III》，Clastres, Geneviève 和 Chevaleyre, Véronique 合译.

九丹（1968—）

1. Filles-dragons/Jiu Dan；roman traduit du chinois par André Lévy. Paris：Bleu de Chine；[Arles]：Actes Sud, 2002. 353 p. ISBN：291088449X，2910884499

《乌鸦》，Lévy, André（1925—）译.

邱华栋（1969—）

1. Voyage au pays de l'oubli/Qiu Huadong；traduit du chinois par Claire Yang. [Paris]：Bleu de Chine, 2001. 107 p. ISBN：2910884457，2910884451.（Chine en poche）

《遗忘者之路》，Yang, Claire 译.

2. Reflets sur la rivière obscure：roman/Qiu Huadong；trad. du chinois par Claire Yang. Paris：Bleu de Chine, Impr. Bialec), 2002. 106 p.：couv. ill. en coul.；18cm. ISBN：2910884589（br），2910884581（br）.（Chine en poche）

《黑暗河流上的闪光》，Yang, Claire 译.

棉棉（1970—）

1. Les bonbons chinois/Mian Mian；trad. du chinois par Sylvie Gentil. Paris：Éd. de l'Olivier, 2001. 18 p.；21cm. ISBN：2879292948，2879292946

《糖》，Gentil, Sylvie 译.

(1) [Paris]：Éditions de l'Olivier, 2002. 300, [3] s.；18cm. ISBN：2020551330，2020551335.（Points；P1012）

2. Panda sex：roman/Mian Mian；traduit du chinois par Sylvie Gentil. Vauvert：Au diable Vauvert, Impr. CPI Brodard & Taupin), 2009. 1 vol.（183 p.）：couv. ill.；20cm. ISBN：2846261777，2846261776

《熊猫》，Gentil, Sylvie 译.

郭小橹（1973—）

1. La ville de pierre/Guo Xiaolu；roman traduit du chinois par Claude Payen. Arles：P. Picquier, 2004. 220 p.；21cm. ISBN：2877306925，2877306928

《我心中的石头镇》，Payen, Claude 译.

韩寒（1982—）

1. Les trois portes：roman/Han Han；traduit du chinois par Guan Jian et Sylvie Schneiter. Paris：JC Lattès, 2004. 397 p.；23cm. ISBN：2709624435，2709624435

《三重门》，Guan, Jian 和 Schneiter, Sylvie 合译.

2. 1988：je voudrais bien discuter avec le monde：roman/Han Han；traduit du chinois et annoté par Helène

Arthus.［Paris］：Gallimard, 2013. 1 vol.（238 p.）：couv. ill. en coul.；21cm. ISBN：2070137527, 207013752X.（Bleu de Chine）

《1988：我想和这个世界谈谈》,Arthus, Hélène 译.

3. Son royaume/Han Han；roman traduit du chinois par Stéphane Lévêque avec le concours d'Yvonne André. Arles：P. Picquier, 2015. 1 vol.（245 p.）：couv. ill. en coul.；21cm. ISBN：2809710830, 280971083X

《他的国》, André, Yvonne 和 Levêque, Stéphane（1975—）合译.

（1）Arles：Éditions Philippe Picquier, 2017. 1 vol.（290 p.）；17cm. ISBN：2809712544, 2809712549.（Picquier poche）

田园（1985—）

1. La forêt zèbre/Tian Yuan；trad. du chinois par Sylvie Gentil. Paris：Éd. de l'Olivier, 2004. 235 p.；21cm. ISBN：2879293901（Br）, 2879293905（Br）

《斑马森林》,Gentil, Sylvie 译.

徐瑛

1. La Cour ensoleillée/par Siu Ying；illustrations de Siao Yu-lei et Ho Pao-tsiuan. Pékin：Éditions en Langues Étrangères；［Paris］：［Diffusion Éditions du Centenaire］, 1978. 218 p.；ill., couv. ill. en coul.；19cm.

《向阳院的故事》

左林

1. La vie héroique de Tong Tsouen-jouei/par Tsouo Lin. Pékin：Éditions en Langues Étrangères, 1961. 100 pages：illustrations；19cm.

《董存瑞的故事》

老牛

1. Le malaise：roman/Laoniu；traduit du chinois, annoté et présenté par Angel Pino et Isabelle Rabut. Paris：Bleu de Chine, 1998. 251 p.；21cm. ISBN：291088418X, 2910884185

《不舒服》,Pino, Angel 和 Rabut, Isabelle 合译.

李晓（原名李小棠）

1. Shanghai triad：roman/Li Xiao；traduit du chinois par André Lévy.［Paris］：Flammarion, 1995. 198 p.；20cm. ISBN：2080672282, 2080672285.（Lettres d'Extrême-Orient）

《门规》,Lévy, André 译.

I6 报告文学与回忆录

1. Leur terre, ils l'ont gagnée/Siao Ts'ien；traduction de Paul Jamati. Paris：Editeurs Français Réunis, 1954. 170 pages；19cm.

《土地回老家》,萧乾（1910—1999）著；Jamati, Paul（1890—1960）译.

2. Avec le président Mao/Chen Changfeng. Pékin：Éd. en Langues Étrangères, 1959. 1 vol.

《跟随毛主席长征》,陈昌奉著.

（1）2. éd. Pékin：Éd. en Langues Étrangères, 1964. 119 pages：Illustrationen

（2）3e éd. Pékin：Éditions en Langues Étrangères, 1972. 133 p.

（3）Beijing：Éditions en Langues Érangères, 1986. 129 p. -［3］f. de pl.：［1］carte dépl.；19cm.

3. Fang Tche-min：sa vie et ses combats/Miao min. Pékin：Éditions en Langues Étrangères, 1960. IV—148 p., 4 pl., couv. ill.［Ech. int. 1275—61］；In—16（18cm.）

《方志敏战斗的一生》,谬敏著.

（1）2. éd. 1962. 134 p.［4］tav.

4. 中国红军的故事/何长工等.北京：外文出版社,1961

5. Wang Jo-fei en prison. Pékin：Éditions en Langues Étrangères, 1962. 148 pages：portraits；19cm.

《王若飞在狱中》,杨植霖著.

6. L'Héroïque peuple coréen. Pékin：Éditions en Langues Étrangères；［Paris］：［diffusion Éditions du Centenaire］, 1972. 87 p.-［16］p. de pl. en coul.：couv. ill. en coul.；20cm.

《英雄的朝鲜人民》.

7. À travers les régions libérées de Guinée（Bissau）/par les reporters de l'Agence Hsinhua. Pékin：Éditions en Langues Étrangères, 1972. 1 vol.（45 p.-［6］p. de pl.）：ill., couv. ill.；19cm.

《几内亚（比绍）解放区见闻》,陈昌奉著,第三版.

8. Combattants d'avant-garde du prolétariat. Pékin：Éditions en Langues Étrangères, 1972. 97 p.

《无产阶级的先锋战士》.

9. Le canal Drapeau rouge/Lin Min. Pékin：Éditions en Langues Étrangères, 1975. 64 p.

《红旗渠》,林民著.

10. Métamorphose du Haiho/par Ho Kin. Pékin：Éditions en Langues Étrangères, 1975. 127,［1］p.,［17］c. di tav.,［1］c. geogr. ripieg.；19cm.

《海河巨变》,何津著.

11. Le Cambodge en lutte：reportage de la délégation des journalistes chinois sur sa visite au Cambodge. Pékin：Éditions en Langues Étrangères, 1975. 70 pages,［4］leaves of plates：illustrations；19cm.

《战斗的柬埔寨：中国新闻代表团访问柬埔寨通讯集》

12. Tangchan au lendemain du tremblement de terre：comment le peuple chinois réagit devant cette calamité naturelle. Pékin：Éditions en Langues Étrangères, 1976. 84 p.：ill

《一场大地震之后：中国人民战胜自然灾害的事迹》

13. Une Société si différente：six reportages/par Kao Yu-pao et d'autres auteurs. Pékin：Éditions en Langues Étrangères, 1976. 153 p.：ill

《换了人间：报告文学六篇》,高玉宝等著.

14. L'histoire de Kailouan：nouveau visage d'anciennes houilleres/par le Groupe de redaction des mineurs

Kailouan. Pékin：Éditions en Langues Étrangères，1977. 90 pages；19cm.

《开滦新貌》，开滦工人写作组著.

15. La Campagne chinoise：un de grade école pour les jeunes/[Xiao Bing bian]. Pékin：Éditions en Langues Étrangères，1e éd. 1977. 93 pages：illustrations；19cm.

《农村也是大学》，晓兵编.

16. Chou En-lai durant la longue marche：récits de son ancien garde du corps Wei Kouo-lou. Pékin：Éditions en Langues Étrangères，1979. 133 p

《随周恩来副主席长征》，魏国禄；沈尧伊插图.

17. Un ancien agent du GMD en Chine nouvelle/par Shen Zui, avec le concours de Shen Meijuan. Pékin，Chine：Éditions en Langues Étrangères，1987. 411 p.，[20] p. de planches：ill.（certaines en coul.）

《我这三十年》沈醉著.

18. Derrière les barreaux/par Yang Zhilin, Qiao Mingfu. 2e éd. Beijing：Éd. en Langues Étrangères，1988. 207 p.；18cm.

《铁窗内外》，杨植霖，乔明甫著.

19. L'enfance/Zhang Wei；Véronique Meunier. Paris：Desclée de Brouwer：Presses artistiques et Littéraires de Shanghai，2012. 1 vol.（173 p.）：couv. ill.；17cm. ISBN：2220064116，2220064115.（Proches lointains）

《童年》，中国作家张炜（1956—）和法国道教研究者施舟人（1934—）关于各自童年的回忆.

I7　散文

I71　古代个人作品

1. Les notes de Li Yi-chan（Yi-chan tsa-ts'ouan）traduit du chinois. Étude de littérature comparée/par Georges Bonmarchand.［Tōkyō］，［Maison franco-japonaise；dépositaire：Presses universitaires de France］，1955. 84 pages；21cm.（Bulletin de la Maison franco-japonaise，nouv. sér.，；t. 4，no. 3）

Contents：Traduction des Zassan—Etude critique de littérature comparée—Biographie de Li Yi-chan—Six poèmes de Li Yi-chan.

《义山杂纂》，李商隐（约 813 年—约 858 年）著；Bonmarchand，Georges 译.

(1) Notes/Li Yi-chan；Traduit du chinois par Georges Bonmarchand，Préface de Pascal Quignard.［Paris］：Le Promeneur，1992.［68］p.；17cm. ISBN：2070727769，2070727766

2. La salle du dicernement du vrai et du faux：et autres textes/Ouyang Xiu；traduit du chinois par Pierre Brière. Saint Quentin：Cazimi，1997. 1 vol.（45 p.）：21cm. ISBN：2911770137，2911770135

欧阳修散文. 欧阳修（1007—1072 年）著；Brière，Pierre 译.

3. Description du royaume de Camboge/par un voyageur chinois qui a visité cette contrée à la fin du XIIIe siècle，précédée d'une notice chronologique sur le même pays，extraite des Annales de la Chine；traduite du chinois par M. Abel Rémusat. Paris：impr. de J. Smith，1819. Paris：impr. de J. Smith，1819

《真腊风土记》，周达观（约 1266 年—1346 年）著；Rémusat，Abel（1788—1832）译.

4. Mémoires sur les coutumes du Cambodge［Texte imprimé］de Tcheou Ta-kouan. Version nouvelle suivie d'un commentaire inachevé［par Paul Pelliot. Paris，A. Maisonneuve；（Chartres，impr. de Durand），1951. Gr. in-8°（250×165），179 p

《真腊风土记》，周达观（约 1266 年—1346 年）著；Pelliot，Paul（1878—1945）译.

5. Ngan-nan ki yeou：Relation d'un voyage au Tonkin，par le lettré chinois P'an Ting-Kouei/Traduit et annoté par Arnold Vissière. Angers：impr. Burdin，［s. d.］，1890. 17 p.

《安南纪游》，潘鼎珪著；Vissière，Arnold（1858—1930）译.

6. "Fookoua Siriak"，ou Traité sur l'origine des richesses au Japon/écrit en 1708 par Arrï Tsikougo No Kami Sama，autrement nommé Fak Sik Sen See，… traduit de l'original chinois et accompagné de notes，par M. Klaproth. Paris：Heideloff，1828. 28 p.

《海国闻见录》，陈伦炯著；Klaproth，Julius von（1783—1835）译.

7. Shen Fu. Six récits au fil inconstant des jours. Traduits du chinois par P. Ryckmans. Préface de Y. Hervouet. Bruxelles：F. Larcier，1966.（19cm.），210 p.

《浮生六记》，沈复（1763—1809）著；Ryckmans，Pierre（1935—2014）译.

8. Récits d'une vie fugitive：mémoires d'un lettré pauvre/par Chen Fou；trad. du chinois par Jacques Reclus；préf. de Paul Demiéville. Paris：Gallimard；Unesco，1993. Paris：Gallimard；Unesco，1993. ISBN：2070706362（br.）.（Connaissance de l'Orient；10 Collection Unesco d'œuvres représentatives. Série chinoise）

《浮生六记》，沈复（1763—1809）著；Reclus，Jacques 译.

9. Anecdotes，historiettes et bons mots，en chinois parlé，publiés pour la première fois，avec une traduction française et des notes explicatives/par Camille Imbault-Huart. Paris：E. Leroux，1882. 124 p.

《笑谈随笔》，Imbault-Huart，Camille（1857—1897）译.

10. Au gré d'humeurs oisives：les carnets secrets de Li Yu：un art du bonheur en Chine/Li Yu；éd. et trad. du chinois Jacques Dars. Arles（Bouches-du-Rhône）：P. Picquier，2003. 335 p.：ill. en coul.；26cm. ISBN：287730664X，2877306645

《闲情偶寄》，李渔（1611—1680）著；Dars，Jacques 译.

(1)［Arles］：P. Piquier，2009. 1 vol.（335 p.）：couv. ill. en coul.，ill. en noir et en coul.；21cm. ISBN：2809701395；2809701393

(2)Arles：P. Piquier, 2014. 1 vol. (335 p.)：couv. ill. en coul.，ill. en noir et en coul.；17cm. ISBN：2809710366，2809710368. (Picquier poche)

I72 现当代散文集

1. Les rubans du cerf-volant/textes choisis par Geneviève Imbot-Bichet；Préface de Yinde Zhang. 〔Paris〕：Gallimard, 2014. 202 pages；21cm. ISBN：2070145164, 2070145166. (Bleu de Chine)

Contents：Extraits du Journal de Lei Feng/Lei Feng—Ma seconde rencontre avec Maître Zhou Tai/Lu Wenfu—À la recherche du chapeau/Jiang Zilong—Les rubans du cerf-volant/Wang Meng—Paysage de fange avec tête/Zong Pu—Mimodrame (gestuelle de rue)/Tie Ning—Dossier 0/Yu Jian—La guérite/Liu Xinglong—À l'article de la mort/Sheng Keyi—Trois blogs：Je suis trop cool, il est trop classe!；Grands maîtres, nous nous soumettons à vous sans conditions；Que puis-je faire? /Han Han

《风筝线：20 纪中国散文选集》,收录雷锋,陆文夫,蒋子龙,王蒙,宗璞,铁凝,于坚,刘醒龙,盛可以,韩寒等的散文；Imbot-Bichet, Geneviève 译.

I73 现当代个人作品

鲁迅(1881—1936)

1. La Vie et la mort injustes des femmes：anthologie/textes de Luxun；traduit du chinois et présentés par Michelle Loi...〔et al.〕. Paris：Mercure de France, Impr. Floch, 1985. 1 vol. (315 p.)：couv. ill.；23cm. ISBN：2715213646, 2715213647. (Mille et une femmes；8)

散文集. Loi, Michelle 译.

2. De la révolution littéraire à la littérature révolutionnaire：Récits chinois 1918—1942/Trad. et présentés par Martine Vallette-Hèmery. Paris, 1970. 333 s.

《从文学革命到革命文学》,Vallette-Hèmery, Martine 译. 本书包含三篇鲁迅杂文的翻译.

3. Essais choisis/Lou Sin；introduits et annotés par Daniel Hamiche；traduits de... 〔la version anglaise〕par Liliane Princet. Paris：Union générale d'éditions, 1976. 2 vol., 443+444 p.：couv. ill.；18cm. ISBN：a264000910 (vol. 1), 2264000929 (vol. 2)(Le vol. br.). (10—18；1093—1094)

《鲁迅杂文选》,Princet, Liliane 由英文译为法文.

4. Fleurs du matin cueillies le soir/Luxun；traduction du chinois, Préface et notes par François Jullien. Lausanne：Alfred Eibel, 1976. 238 pages；18cm. ISBN：2827400200, 2827400201

《朝花夕拾》,Jullien, François(1951—)译.

5. Zhao hua xi shi＝Fleurs du matin cueillies au soir/Lu Xun zhu. Beijing：Éditions en Langues Étrangères, 2004. 285 pages；22cm. ISBN：711903264X, 7119032641

《朝花夕拾》,外文出版社法文部译. 本书是法汉对照读物. 收入鲁迅的 10 篇散文.

(1)Fleurs du matin cueillies au soir/Lu Xun. Beijing：Éditions en Langues Étrangères, 2004. 179 p.；18cm. ISBN：711903264X, 7119032641

6. Pamphlets et libelles, 1925—1936/Luxun；présentation et trad. par Michelle Loi. Paris：Maspero, 1977. 255 S.：Ill. ISBN：270710969X；2707109699. (Théorie. Série：écrits politiques)

《论战与讽刺·杂文选》,Loi, Michelle 译.

7. Sous le dais fleuri：les luttes idéologiques en Chine durant l'année 1925/Luxun；traduction du chinois, préfaces et notes par François Jullien. Lausanne：A. Eibel, 1978. 334 p.；18cm. ISBN：2827400316 (Br.). (Collection La Chine d'aujourd'hui；5)

《华盖集》,Jullien, François(1951—)译.

8. La Tombe/Luxun；〔traduit du chinois sous le contrôle de Michèle Loi et du Bureau de recherches sur Luxun de la République populaire de Chine〕. Paris：Acropole, Impr. bretolienne, 1981. 347 p.；23cm. ISBN：271441365X, 2714413659. (Collection UNESCO d'Œuvres représentatives, Série chinoise；Littératures étrangères)

《坟》,Loi, Michelle 译.

(1)Paris：Acropole, 1989. 347, 〔3〕pages；23cm. (Collection UNESCO d'Œuvres représentatives. Série chinoise；Littératures étrangères)

9. Causerie d'un profane sur la langue et la littérature/Lu Xun；traduction et notes par Ng Yok-soon. Köln：Kai Yeh；〔Paris〕(14, rue de la Maison blanche, 75013)：〔Ng Yok-soon〕, 1981. 128 p.：couv. ill.；21cm. ISBN：3923131011.

《门外文谈》,黄育顺 (1939—)译.

10. La Littérature en dentelles：essais/Luxun. Paris：Acropole：UNESCO, 1987. 213 p.：couv. ill. en coul.；23cm. ISBN：2735700682. (Collection UNESCO d'Œuvres représentatives. série chinoise)

《花边文集》,译者不详.

11. Ecrits de fausse liberté/texte original de Lu Xun；traduction de Jacques Meunier. Beijing：Éditions en Langues Étrangères, 2010. iii, 249 pages. ISBN：7119045306；711904530X (Classiques chinois)

《伪自由书》

12. Ecrits de fausse liberté/Lu Xun；traduction de Jacques Meunier. Beijing, China：Éditions en Langues Érangères, 2010. 1 vol. (249 p.)：couv. ill. en coul.；23cm. ISBN：7119045306, 711904530X

《虚假的自由写作》,Meunier, Jacques 译.

老舍 (1899—1966)

1. Lao niu po che：essai autocritique sur le roman et l'humour/Lao She；introduction, traduction 〔du chinois〕et notes de Paul Bady. Paris：Presses universitaires de France, 1974. XCII—129 — XXXVII p.：ill.；21cm.

(Bulletin de la Maison franco-japonaise. Nouvelle série; t. 9, 3, n 3−4)

《老牛破车》,Bady, Paul 译.

2. écrits de la maison des rats/Lao She; traduit du chinois par Claude Payen. Arles: P. Picquier, DL 2010. 1 vol. (125 p.): couv. ill.; 22cm. ISBN: 2809701784. (écrits dans la paume de la main)

《多鼠斋杂谈》,Payen, Claude 译.

(1) Arles: Éditions Philippe Picquier, DL 2016. 1 vol. (159 p.); 17cm. ISBN: 2809711691. (Picquier poche, ISSN 1251−6007)

沈从文(1902—1988)

1. Le pèriple de Xiang: et autres nouvelles/Shen Congwen; traduit du chinois, présenté et annoté par Marie Laureillard et Gilles Cabrero. [Paris]: Gallimard, Impr. Floch, 2012. 1 vol. (303 p.): couv. ill. en coul.; 21cm. ISBN: 2070134762, 2070134768

《湘西散记》,Laureillard-Wendland, Marie 和 Cabrero, Gilles 合译.

巴金(1904—2005)

1. Au gré de ma plume/Pa Kin; trad. du chinois par Pan Ailian. Beijing: Littérature chinoise, 1992. 280 p.: couv. ill.; 18cm. ISBN: 7507100588. (Collection Panda)

《巴金随笔》,Pan, Ailian 译.

2. Au gré de ma plume/Pa Kin; traduit du chinois par Pan Ailian. Pékin: Éd. Littérature chinoise, 1992. 280 p.; 18cm. ISBN: 7507100588, 7507100587.

《随想录》.中国文学出版社(熊猫丛书).

3. à la mémoire d'un ami/Pa Kin; trad. du chinois et postface de Angel Pino et Isabelle Rabut. [Paris]: Éd. Mille et une nuits, 1995. 71 p.: ill., couv. ill. en coul.; 1995. ISBN: 2910233960. (Mille et une nuits)

《怀念从文》,Pino, Angel 和 Rabut, Isabelle 合译.

4. Pour un musée de la "Révolution culturelle": au fil de la plume/Pa Kin; textes choisis, traduits du chinois, annotés et présentés par Angel Pino. Paris: Bleu de Chine, 1996. 151, [1] p.; 21cm. ISBN: 2910884066, 2910884062

《"文革"博物馆》,Pino, Angel 译.

5. Le dragon, les tigres, le chien; suivi de Hors du jardin dévasté/Ba Jin; trad. du chinois par Philippe Denizet. Paris: You-Feng, 2001. 189 p.: couv. ill. en coul.; 19cm. ISBN: 2842791169

《龙虎狗》,Denizet, Philippe 译.

施蛰存(1905—2003)

1. Le goût de la pluie: nouvelles et prose de circonstance/Shi Zhecun; traduit du chinois et annote par Marie Laureillard et Gilles Cabrero. [Paris]: Gallimard, Impr. Floch), 2011. 1 vol. (337 p.): couv. ill. en coul.; 21cm. ISBN: 2070132836, 2070132838. (Bleu de Chine)

《雨 的 滋 味》,Laureillard-Wendland, Marie 和 Cabrero, Gilles 合译.

钱钟书(1910—1998)

1. Pensée fidèle: suivi de Inspiration/Qian Zhongshu; traduit du chinois par Sun Chaoying. Paris: Gallimard, 2005. 138 p. ISBN: 2070319962, 2070319961. (Folio. 2 euros; 4324)

忠诚的思想及启示. Sun Chaoying 译.

冯之丹(1927—)

1. Voyage en Afrique occidentale/Feng Tche-Tan. Pékin: Éditions en Langues Étrangères, 1964. 132 pages: illustrations; 19cm.

《西非巴国漫记》

刘心武(1942—)

1. L'arbre et la forêt: destins croisés/Liu Xinwu; trad. du chinois et annoté par Roger Darrobers. Paris: Bleu de Chine, 2002. 395 p.: ill.; 21cm. ISBN: 291088452X, 2910884529

《树与林同在》,Darrobers, Roger 译.

阿城(钟阿城,1949—)

1. Le roman et la vie: sur les coutumes séculières chinoises/A Cheng; traduit du chinois par Noël Dutrait. [La Tour d'Aigues, France]: Éditions de l'Aube, 1995. 215 pages; 22cm. ISBN: 2876782197, 2876782198. (Regards croisés)

《闲话闲说:中国世俗与中国小说》,Dutrait, Noël 译.

(1) La Tour d'Aigues: Éditions de l'Aube, 2005. 219 p.; 17cm. ISBN: 2752600801, 2752600806. (Collection L'Aube poch)

2. Injures célestes/A Cheng; traduit du chinois par Noël Dutrait avec la collaboration de Liliane Dutrait. La Tour d'Aigues: Éditions de l'Aube, 2004. 141 p.: portr.; 17cm. ISBN: 287678954X, 28767895. (Collection L'Aube poche)

《闲话闲说》,Dutrait, Noël 和 Dutrait, Liliane 合译.

王小波(1952—1997)

1. La majorité silencieuse et autres essais = Wang Xiaobo za wen xuan/Wang Xiaobo; traduits du chinois par Luc Thominette et Bai Yunfei; [Préface de Li Yinhe]. [出版地不详:出版社不详], 2013. 1 vol. (169 p.): ill., couv. ill. en coul.; 21cm. ISBN: 2842795610, 284279561X

《王小波杂文选》,Thominette, Luc 和 Bai, Yunfei 合译; 李银河作序.

马丽华(1953—)

1. Pérégrinations dans le Tibet du Nord/Ma Lihua. Pékin: Éd. Littérature chinoise, 1990. 375 p.: carte, portr.; 18cm. ISBN: 7507100545; 7507100549.

《藏北游历》.中国文学出版社(熊猫丛书)

王安忆(1954—)

1. A la recherche de Shanghai/Wang Anyi; trad. du chinois par Yvonne André. Arles: P. Picquier, 2010. 119 p; 21cm. ISBN: 2809702415, 2809702411. (Ecrits dans la paume de la main)

《寻找上海》,André, Yvonne 译.

莫言(1955—)

1. Dépasser le pays natal：quatre essais sur un parcours littéraire/Mo Yan；traduits du chinois par Chantal Chen-Andro. Paris：Éd. du Seuil，2015. 1 vol. (152 p.)：ill. en coul. ；21cm. ISBN：2021144109，2021144100
《超越故乡》,Chen-Andro，Chantal 译.

阎连科(1958—)

1. Songeant à mon père/Yan Lianke；traduit du chinois par Brigitte Guilbaud. Arles：P. Picquier，2010. 116 p. ；22cm. ISBN：2809701715，2809701717. (Écrits dans la paume de la main)
《想念父亲》,Guilbaud，Brigitte 译.
   (1)Arles：Éditions Philippe Picquier，2017. 1 vol. (125 p.)；17cm. ISBN：2809712537，2809712530. (Picquier poche)

余华(1960—)

1. La Chine en dix mots/Yu Hua：essai traduit du chinois par Angel Pino et Isabelle Rabut. Arles：Actes Sud，Impr. Floch，2010. 1 vol. (331 p.)：couv. ill. ；22cm. ISBN：2742792238，2742792236. (Lettres chinoises)
《十个词汇中的中国》,Pino，Angel 和 Rabut，Isabelle 合译.
   (1)Arles：Babel，2013. 1 vol. (331 p.)：couv. ill. ；18cm. ISBN：2330024840，2330024843

韩寒(1982—)

1. Blogs de Chine/Han Han；traduit du chinois par Hervé Denès. Paris：Gallimard，2012. 1 vol. (398 p.)：couv. ill. en coul. ；21cm. ISBN：2070137633，2070137635. (Bleu de Chine)
《韩寒的博客》,Denès，Hervé 译.

I8 民间文学

1. Folk-lore chinois moderne. ［Sienhsien］Impr. de la Mission catholique，1909. 422 pages illustrations，plates 19cm.
   Notes：A selection of tales drawn principally from Yüan Mei，translated into French. / Chinese and French in parallel columns.
   民间故事：主要译自袁枚(1716—1798)的著作. Wieger，Le'on(1856—1933)译.

2. Fables chinoises du IIIe au VIIIe siècle de notre ère (d'origine hindoue)/traduites par Édouard Chavannes… versifées par Mme Édouard Chavannes；ornées de 46 dessins par Andrée Karpelés. Paris：Bossard，1921. 92，[3] pages including illustrations，plates 17×13cm.
   3—8 世纪的中国神话,沙畹 Chavannes，Edouard(1865—1918),Chavannes，Alice Dor 译.

3. Fables de la Chine antique/［ill. de Fong Tse-kai］. Pékin：Éditions en Langues Étrangères，1958—1960. 2 vol. ：ill. ；25cm.
   《中国古代寓言选》(1—2),丰子恺插图. 上册出版于1958 年,下册出版于 1960 年.
   (1)Fables de la Chine antique/ill. de Feng Zikai. Beijing：Éditions en Langues Étrangères，1980. 143 pages：illustrations；21cm.
   (2)Beijing：Éd. en langue étrangère，1984. 143 p. ：ill. ；21cm.

4. Contes populaires chinois. Pékin：Éditions en Langues Étrangères，1958. 4 volumes：illustrations；21cm.
   《中国民间故事选》,4 册,1958 年. 第一册另有题名《青蛙骑手》；第二册另有题名《水牛斗老虎》.

5. Contes Populaires Chinois. 5. Pékin：Éd. en Langues Étrangères，1960. 142 p.
   《中国民间故事选》,第 5 集.

6. Contes populaires du lac de l'ouest. Beijing：Éditions en Langues Étrangères，1982. 145 p.
   《飞来峰及人间天堂的其他故事》

7. Légendes de la Chine antique/Chu Binqie. Beijing：Éditions en Langues Étrangères，1983. 120 p. ：pl. ill. 19cm.
   《中国古代神话选》,褚斌杰编,杨永青插图.
   (1)2e éd. 1989. 1 vol. (120 p.)；18cm. (Phénix)

8. 中国古代寓言/根据《寓言选》编,黄永玉、施明德插图. 北京：外文出版社,1983

9. La mythologie chinoise/Claude Helft；illustrations de Chen Jiang Hong；Préface de Philippe Jonathan. Arles：Actes sud，2002. 77 pages. ISBN：2742736514，2742736515. (Les naissances du monde)
   Jiang Hong，Chen，；Illustrateur.
   《中国神话》,Helft，Claude 译.
   (1)Arles：Actes Sud junior，2004. 77 p. ：ill. ；22cm. ISBN：2742736514，2742736515. (Les naissances du monde)
   (2)Arles：Actes Sud junior，2007. 77 p. ：ill. ；22cm. ISBN：2742736515，2742736514

10. Mythes et légendes de la Chine/Chen Lianshan；traduit par Chen Yuan. ［Beijing］：China Intercontinental Press，2011. 144 pages：color illustrations；23cm. ISBN：7508520278，7508520270. (Collection culture chinoise)
    《中国神话传说》,陈连山著；Chen Yuan 译.

11. Fables choisies：d'après les pères taoïstes Li ［i. e. Lie］-tzeu et Tchoang-tzeu/［éditées par］ Robert Perrotto-André. Nîmes：C. Lacour éditeur，Impr. C. Lacour-Ollé），2015. 1 vol. (168 p.)；21cm. ISBN：2750438777，2750438772
    《寓言选集：道家思想家列子和庄子》,Perrotto-André，Robèrt(1933—)著.

12. Le cavalier rainette：contes populaires chinois. Beijing：Éditions en Langues Étrangères，1958. 146 p. ：ill
    《青蛙骑手：中国民间故事选》
    (1)Beijing：Éditions en Langues Étrangères，1980. 146 p. ：ill

(2) Le cavalier rainette/[Wen Fa yi]. Beijing：Éditions en Langues Étrangères，2006. 175 pages：illustrations；18cm. ISBN：7119042351，7119042350.（Contes populaires chinois）

13. La Jeune fille-paon：contes populaires chinois. Beijing：Éditions en Langues Étrangères，1962. 125 pages：illustrations；21cm.

《孔雀姑娘：中国民间故事选》

(1) La Jeune fille-paon. Beijing：Éditions en Langues Étrangères，1985. 125 p.：ill.；21cm.

(2) La jeune fille-paon. Beijing：Éditions en Langues Étrangères，2006. 157 pages：illustrations；18cm. ISBN：7119042336，7119042335.（Contes populaires chinois）

14. A la recherche du soleil：contes populaires chinois. Beijing：Éditions en Langues Étrangères，1963. 126 p.

《马勒带子访太阳：中国民间故事选》

(1) Beijing：Éditions en Langues Étrangères，1981. 126 p.

(2) A la recherche du soleil：contes populaires chinois. Beijing：Éditions en Langues Étrangères，1984. 126 pages：illustrations；20cm.

(3) A la recherche du soleil. Beijing：Éd. en Langues Étrangères，2006. 1 vol.（169 p.）：ill.；18cm. ISBN：7119042386，7119042381.（Contes populaires chinois）

15. Le poignard magique：contes populaires chinois. Beijing：Éditions en Langues Étrangères，1980. 104 pages：illustrations；23cm.

《宝刀：中国民间故事选》

(1) Le poignard magique. Beijing：Éditions en Langues Étrangères，2006. 1 vol.（139 p.）：ill.；18cm. ISBN：7119042378，7119042374.（Contes populaires chinois）

16. Histoires d'Effendi/rédigé par Zhao Shijie；traduction du chinois révisée par Denise Ly-Lebreton. Beijing：Éditions en Langues Étrangères，1983. [iv]，109，[5] pages：illustrations

《阿凡提的故事》，赵世杰编.

17. La Petite gardeuse d'oies/adapt.，Li Shufen；dessins，Wu Jinglu. Beijing：Éditions en Langues Étrangères，1985. 52 p.：ill. en coul.；26cm.

《白鹅女：中国民间故事选》.李树芬改编；吴儆芦画.

18. L'Esclave et la fille du roi dragon：contes populaires chinois. Beijing：Éditions en Langues Étrangères，1985. 132 pages：illustrations

《奴隶与龙女：中国民间故事选》

(1) L'esclave et la fille du Roi Dragon. Beijing，China：Éditions en Langues Étrangères，2006. 1 vol.（165 p.）：ill.；18cm. ISBN：7119042394，7119042398.（Contes populaires chinois）

19. Les Sept filles：contes populaires chinois. Beijing：Éd. en Langues Étrangères，1985. 106 p.：ill.；21×14cm.

《七姊妹：中国民间故事选》

(1) Les sept filles. Beijing：Éditions en Langues Étrangères，2005. 1 vol.（145 p.）：ill.；18cm. ISBN：7119042329，7119042327.（Contes populaires chinois）

20. L'Oiseau magique：contes populaires chinois. Beijing：Éditions en Langues Etrangères，1985. 153 pages：illustrations

《神鸟：中国民间故事选》

(1) L'oiseau magique. Beijing：Éditions en Langues Étrangères，2006. 179 pages：illustrations；18cm. vISBN：7119042404，7119042408.（Contes populaires chinois）

21. La lutte contre le rhinoceros. Beijing：Éditions en Langues Etrangères，1987. 114 pages：illustrations；21cm.

《斗犀夺珠：中国民间故事选》.

22. Le Berger et les aigles. Beijing，Chine：Éditions en Langues Étrangères，1. éd. 1990. 132 pages：illustrations；21cm. ISBN：7119009583；7119009582.

《牧人和山鹰：中国民间传说故事选》.

23. La légende des dix fêtes chinoises/texte et illustrations：Zhan Tong. Beijing，Chine：Les livres du Dauphin，2003. 1 volume（non paginé）：illustrations en couleur. ISBN：7800515071；7800515079；7801384942；7801384946.

《中国十个节日传说》，詹同编绘. 海豚出版社.

24. Zhongguo gu dai yu yan xuan＝Fables de la Chine antique. Beijing：Éditions en Langues Étrangères，2004. 277 pages：illustrations；22cm. ISBN：7119032674；7119032672

《中国古代寓言选》，外文出版社法文部编译. 本书精选中国古代寓言100多则.

25. Zhongguo min su gu shi/gai bian Zhao Jie；hui hua Sun Yuguang, Zhang Ming；fan yi Guo Bingke＝Recits du folklore chinois/adaptation：Zhao Jie；illustration：Wang Ping, Zhang Ming；traduction：Guo Bingke. Beijing：Éditions en Langues Étrangères，2005. 2 volumes：color illustrations；26cm. ISBN：7801385411（pbk.）；780138542X（pbk.）；7801385413；7801385420.

《中国民俗故事：法文. 上》，赵杰改编；孙玉广，张明绘；郭冰珂译. 海豚出版社，

26. Zhongguo min su gu shi/gai bian Zhao Jie；hui hua Sun Yuguang, Zhang Ming；fan yi Guo Bingke＝Récits du folklore chinois/adaptation：Zhao Jie；illustration：Wang Ping, Zhang Ming；traduction：Guo Bingke. Beijing：Éditions en Langues Étrangères，2005. 2 volumes：color illustrations；26cm. ISBN：7801385411（pbk.）；780138542X（pbk.）；7801385413；7801385420

《中国民俗故事：法文. 下》，赵杰改编；王平，张明绘；郭

冰珂译. 海豚出版社.

27. Légendes de Pékin. Beijing：Éditions en Langues Étrangères，2006. 302 pages：illustrations；18cm. ISBN：7119042749；7119042742.

《北京名胜的传说：法文》. 本书收集了有关北京的旅游景点的 57 个传说故事.

28. La lutte contre le rhinocéros. Beijing：Éditions en Langues Étrangères，2006. 141 pages：illustrations；18cm. ISBN：7119042367，711904236X.（Contes populaires chinois）

《斗犀夺珠：法文》，文法译. 外文出版社（中国民间故事选）

29. Le berger et les aigles/［Wen Fa yi］. Beijing：Éditions en Langues Étrangères，2006. 167 pages：illustrations；18cm. ISBN：7119042319，7119042312.（Contes populaires chinois）

《牧人和山鹰：法文》，文法译. 外文出版社（中国民间故事选）

30. Le duel du buffle et du tigre. Beijing：Éditions en Langues Érangères，2006. 1 vol.（137 p.）：ill.；18cm. ISBN：7119042343，7119042343.（Contes populaires chinois）

《水牛斗老虎：法文》，文法译. 外文出版社（中国民间故事选）

I9 儿童文学

1. Fables/Xuefeng Feng. Pékin：Éditions en Langues Étrangères，1955. 1 v.（90 p.）：ill.，couv. ill.

《雪峰寓言》，冯雪峰著.

(1)Beijing：Éditions en Langues Étrangères，1981. 101 pages：illustrations

2. Jeunes Pionniers Chinois：récits/Tchang Tien-Yi；dessins Tchang Wen-Sin. Pékin：Éditions en Langues Étrangères，1955.

《少年先锋队的故事》，张天翼著.

3. Coquillages/［illustrations de Houa San-tchouan. Traduction française de W. S. Tchou.］. Pékin：Éditions en Langues Étrangères，1957. 107 p.，pl.，couv. ill. en coul.；21cm.

《海滨的孩子》，萧平等著.

4. La neige voltigeait/par Yang Chouo；Illustrations de Miao Ti. Pékin：Éditions en Langues Étrangères，1960. 1 v.（72 p.）：ill.；in-8

《雪花飘飘》，杨朔著.

5. Contes choisis：de Ye Cheng-tao. Pékin：Éditions en Langues Étrangères，1960. IV-88 p.，pl. et couv. ill. en coul.［Ech. int. 1284－61］；In—16（20cm.）

《叶圣陶童话选》.

(1)3e éd. Pékin：Éditions en Langues Étrangères，1966. 83 pages

(2)3e éd. Beijing：Éditions en Langues Étrangères，

1979. 80 p.

(3)Beijing：Éd. en Langues Étrangères，1980. 80 p.；20×14cm.

6. 金色的海螺/阮章竞著，米谷插画. 北京：外文出版社，1961

7. Le grand loup gris. Pékin：Éditions en Langues Étrangères，1961. 51 pages：illustrations color plates；21cm.

《大灰狼》，张天翼著，杨永青插图.

8. Les petites carpes franchissent la porte du Dragon/Kin Kin；Yang Chan-Tse，ill.；Tin Jong-Lin，ill. Pékin：Éditions en Langues Étrangères，1961.

《小鲤鱼跳龙门》，金近写，杨善子、丁榕临绘.

9. Contes de Ye Siuan.../Ho Yi. Pékin：Éditions en Langues Étrangères，1962. 1 v.（82 p.）：fig.，couv. ill. en coul.；20cm.

《野旋的童话》，贺宜著；黄永玉插图.

10. Les oiseaux chantent dans les arbres：récits pour enfants/Hao Jan. Pékin：Éditions en Langues Étrangères，1974. 75 p

《树上鸟儿叫》，浩然著；张育德等插图.

11. 小马倌"大皮靴"叔叔/颜一烟著，肖玉磊、何保全插图. 北京：外文出版社，1981

12. Le bateau magique：pièce de théâtre en trois actes/Lao She；trad. par Sophie Loh. Beijing：Éditions en Langues Étrangères，1982. 78 p.：ill.，couv. ill. en coul.；21cm.

《宝船》，老舍著；曾佑瑄插图；Loh，Sophie 译. 儿童剧.

13. La calebasse magique. Beijing：Éditions en Langues Étrangères，1982. 202 pages

《宝葫芦的秘密》，张天翼著；吴文渊插图.

14. La Pagode de la longévité：nouvelles/Pakin（Ba Jin）；traduit du chinois par Ng Yok-soon...［et al.］Paris：Temps actuels：［Diffusion］Messidor，Impr. S. E. P. C.，1984. 121 p.：ill.，couv. ill.；22cm. ISBN：2209055911，2209055913

《长生塔》，巴金；黄育顺(Ng，Yok-Soon，1939—)译.（童话）

(1)Paris：Gallimard，Impr. Brodard et Taupin，1992. 123 p.：couv. ill. en coul.；18cm. ISBN：2070385167，2070385164.（Collection Folio；2379）

15. 漫话中国/叶永烈，蔚文编；贾延良画. 北京：海豚出版社，1989

16. 房子里的故事/林夕编文；侯冠滨绘画. 北京：中国文学出版社，1992. ISBN：780051675x

17. 摔跤手/李长绪改编；张彤、耿默绘画. 北京：海豚出版社，1992. ISBN：7800517632

18. 螺旋桨/常瑞编；胡基明绘. 北京：海豚出版社，1992. ISBN：7800517659

19. 春天在哪里/葛翠琳编文；王晓明绘. 北京：海豚出版社，1992. ISBN：7800518736.（中国同学）

20. 昆虫会议前的风波/陶红改编;张弢绘. 北京:海豚出版社,1996. ISBN:7800518426

21. 犀鸟造房子/林颂英编文;姜一鸣绘. 北京:海豚出版社,1996. ISBN:780051871X

22. L'architecture de la Chine ancienne/texte de Zhu Kang; illustrations de Hong Tao et Feng Congying. Beijing (Chine):Les livres du Dauphin, 1996. 1 vol. (46 p.):tout en ill., couv. ill. en coul.;26cm. ISBN:7800513572, 7800513572
《中国古代建筑》,朱抗编文;洪涛,冯聪英绘. 海豚出版社(中国古代科学故事丛书)

23. Quatre savants de l'Antiquité/texte de Zhu Kang; illustrations de Hong Tao et Feng Congying. Beijing (Chine):Les livres du Dauphin, 1996. 1 vol. (46 p.):ill. en coul., couv. ill. en coul.;26cm. ISBN:7800517624, 7800517624, 7801384962, 7801384966
《中国古代科学家》,朱抗编文;洪涛,冯聪英绘. 海豚出版社(中国古代科学故事丛书)

24. Les quatre grandes inventions/texte de Zhu Kang; illustrations de Hong Tao et Feng Congying. Beijing (Chine):Les livres du Dauphin, 1996. 1 vol. (46 p.):tout en ill., couv. ill. en coul.;26cm. ISBN:7800514285, 7800514289
《中国古代四大发明》,朱抗编文;洪涛,冯聪英绘. 海豚出版社(中国古代科学故事丛书)

25. Les quatre médecins/texte de Zhu Kang; illustrations de Hong Tao et Feng Congying. Beijing (Chine):Les livres du Dauphin, 1996. 1 vol. (46 p.):ill. en coul., couv. ill. en coul.;26cm. ISBN:7800518884, 7800518881, 7801384970, 7801384973.
《中国古代医学家》,朱抗编文;洪涛,冯聪英绘. 海豚出版社(中国古代科学故事丛书)

26. La Grande Muraille et ses légendes/Liu Wenyuan. Beijing:Éd. en Langues Étrangères, 1997. 130 p.:ill. en noir et en coul., cartes;19cm. ISBN:7119017276, 7119017273.
《长城的故事》,刘文渊编著.

27. La cité interdite/Cheng Qinhua. Beijing:Éd. en langue étrangère, 1997. 163 p.:ill.;19cm. ISBN:7119017438, 7119017433.
《紫禁城的故事》,程钦华编著.

28. Un papa rigolo/Yang Hongying; traduit du chinois et adapté par Isabelle Verhaeghen Kegel. Arles:P. Picquier, 2006. 1vol. (95 p.):ill., couv. ill. en coul.;19cm. ISBN:2877308545, 2877308540. (Toufou; Picquier jeunesse)
《贪玩的爸爸》,杨红樱著;Verhaeghen Kegel, Isabelle 译.
(1)Un papa rigolo/Yang Hongying; illustrations par Antoine Guilloppè; traduit du chinois et adapté par Isabelle Verhaeghen Kegel. Arles:Picquier jeunesse, Impr. France Quercy, 2009. 1 vol. (103 p.):ill., couv. ill. en coul.;19cm. ISBN:2809700985, 2809700982. (Picquier jeunesse)
(2)Arles:Picquier jeunesse, 2013. 1 vol. (101 p.):ill., couv. ill. en coul.;17cm. ISBN:2809709315, 2809709319. (Toufou le petit écolier chinois; Picquier jeunesse)

29. Drôles de bêtes/Yang Hongying; traduit du chinois et adapté par Isabelle Verhaeghen Kegel. Arles:P. Picquier, 2006. 1 vol. (88 p.):ill., couv. ill. en coul.;19cm. ISBN:2877308553, 2877308557. (Toufou; Picquier jeunesse)
《轰隆隆老师》,杨红樱著;Verhaeghen Kegel, Isabelle 译.
(1)Drôles de bêtes/Yang Hongying; illustrations par Antoine Guilloppè; traduit du chinois et adapté par Isabelle Verhaeghen Kegel. Arles:Picquier jeunesse, Impr. France Quercy, 2009. 1 vol. (97 p.):ill., couv. ill. en coul.;19cm. ISBN:2809700992, 2809700990. (Picquier jeunesse)
(2)Arles:Picquier jeunesse, 2013. 1 vol. (97 p.):ill., couv. ill. en coul.;17cm. ISBN:2809709285, 2809709289. (Toufou le petit écolier chinois; Picquier jeunesse)

30. Une vraie chipie/Yang Hongying; traduit du chinois et adapté par Stéphane Lévêque. Arles:P. Picquier, 2006. 1vol. (98 p.):ill., couv. ill. en coul.;19cm. ISBN:2877308618, 2877308618. (Toufou; Picquier jeunesse)
杨红樱著;Lévêque, Stéphane(1967—)译.

31. Maître Tonnerre/Yang Hongying; traduit du chinois et adapté par Stéphane Lévêque. Arles:P. Picquier, 2006. 1 vol. (100 p.):ill., couv. ill. en coul.;19cm. ISBN:287730860X, 2877308601. (Toufou; Picquier jeunesse)
《轰隆隆老师》,杨红樱著;Lévêque, Stéphane(1967—)译.

32. Mes meilleurs copains/Yang Hongying; illustrations par Antoine Guilloppè; traduit du chinois et adapté par Stéphane Lévêque. Arles:Picquier jeunesse, 2008. 1 vol. (108 p.):ill., couv. ill. en coul.;19cm. ISBN:2809700046, 2809700044. (Picquier jeunesse)
《四个调皮蛋》,杨红樱著;Lévêque, Stéphane(1967—)译;Guilloppè, Antoine(1971—)插图.
(1)Arles:Picquier jeunesse, 2013. 1 vol. (102 p.):ill., couv. ill. en coul.;17cm. ISBN:2809709308, 2809709300. (Toufou le petit écolier chinois; Picquier jeunesse)

33. Les affreux jojos/Yang Hongying; illustrations par Antoine Guilloppè; traduit du chinois et adapté par Stéphane Lévêque. Arles:Picquier jeunesse, 2008. 1 vol. (107 p.):ill., couv. ill. en coul.;19cm. ISBN:2809700053, 2809700052. (Picquier jeunesse)
《四个调皮蛋》,杨红樱著;Lévêque, Stéphane(1967—)译;Guilloppè, Antoine(1971—)插图.
(1)Arles:Picquier jeunesse, 2013. 1 vol. (105 p.):

ill., couv. ill. en coul.；17cm. ISBN：2809709292, 2809709297.（Toufou le petit écolier chinois；Picquier jeunesse）

34. Bronze et tournesol/Cao Wenxuan；roman traduit du chinois par Brigitte Guilbaud. Arles：Picquier, 2010. 278 pages；23cm. ISBN：2809701517, 2809701512. （Picquier jeunesse）

《青铜葵花》，曹文轩著；Guilbaud，Brigitte 译.

(1) Paris：Éd. France loisirs, 2011. 1 vol.（278 p.）：couv. et jaquette ill. en coul.；23cm. ISBN：2298041392, 2298041393

(2) Arles（Bouches-du-Rhône）：Éditions Philippe Picquier, 2016. 1 volume（348 pages）；17×11cm. ISBN：2809712025, 2809712026.（Picquier Poche）

35. Plume/texte, Cao Wenxuan；illustration, Roger Mello；traduction, Mathilde Colo.［Paris］：Les Éditions Fei, 2016. 1 vol.（non paginé［36］p.）：ill. en coul.；18×30cm. ISBN：2359662566, 2359662562

《羽毛》，曹文轩著；Mello，Roger（1965—）插图；Colo，Mathilde 译.

36. Mon premier livre de peinture chinoise. Les animaux/［Yang Fujing］；traduit du chinois par Sun Yu. Arles：Picquier jeunesse, 2005. 1 vol.（95 p.）：ill. en coul., couv. ill. en coul.；22cm. ISBN：2877308111, 2877308113

《国画：动物》，杨辅京著；Sun，Yu 译.

37. Mon premier livre de peinture chinoise. Enfants, fleurs et oiseaux/Yang Fujing；Traduit du chinois par Sun Yu；sous la dir. de Chen Feng. Arles（Bouches-du-Rhône）：P. Picquier, 2006. 96 p.：ill. en coul.；22×17cm. ISBN：2877308731, 2877308731

《国画：儿童、花鸟》，杨辅京著；Yu，Sun 译.

38. Mon premier livre de peinture chinoise. Paysages, plantes et insectes/Yang Fujing；traduit du chinois par Sun Yu；ouvrage publié sous la direction de Chen Feng...［et al.］. Arles：Picquier jeunesse, 2008. 1 vol.（93 p.）：ill. en noir et en coul., couv. ill. en coul.；22cm. ＋pinceau. ISBN：2809700091, 2809700095

《国画：风景、草虫》，杨辅京著；Sun，Yu 译.

39. J'apprends la peinture chinoise/Yang Fujing；traduit du chinois par Sun Yu；ouvrage publié sous la direction de Chen Feng. Arles：Picquier jeunesse, 2013. 1 vol.（159 p.）：ill. en noir et en coul., couv. ill. en coul.；22cm. ISBN：2809709209, 2809709203

儿童学国画. 杨辅京；Sun，Yu 译.

40. L'école des vers à soie：roman/Huang Beijia；traduit du chinois par Patricia Batto et Gao Tian Hua. Arles：P. Picquier, Impr. Lienhart, 2002. 260 p.：couv. ill. en coul.；19cm. ISBN：2877306216, 2877306218. （Picquier jeunesse）

《我要做个好孩子》，黄蓓佳；Batto，Patricia 和 Gao，

Tianhua 合译.

(1) Nouv. éd. Arles（Bouches-du-Rhône）：P. Picquier, 2005. 260 p.；19×13cm. ISBN：2877307972, 2877307970

(2) Arles：P. Picquier, 2006. 303 p.；17cm. ISBN：2877308812, 2877308816.（Picquier jeunesse）

41. Éphèmère beauté des cerisiers en fleurs：［roman］；suivi de Ruelle de la pluie：nouvelle/Huang Beijia；traduit du chinois par Philippe Denizet. Paris：You-Feng, 2005. 1 vol.（226 p.）：couv. ill. en coul.；18cm. ISBN：2842792378, 2842792374

《这一瞬间如此辉》，黄蓓佳著；Denizet，Philippe 译.

42. Comment j'ai apprivoisé ma mère/Huang Beijia；roman traduit du chinois par Li Hong et Gilles Moraton. Arles：P. Picquier, 2008. 310 p.；21cm. ISBN：2877309974, 2877309975

《亲亲我的妈妈》，黄蓓佳著；Li，Hong 和 Moraton，Gilles（1958—）合译.

(1) Arles：P. Picquier, Impr. Horizon, 2014. 1 vol. （334 p.）：couv. ill. en coul.；17cm. ISBN：2809710502, 2809710503.（Picquier poche）

43. 我是中国节：汉法对照/乔乔绘著. 北京：五洲传播出版社, 2018. 1 册；29cm. ISBN：7508539058

J 类　艺术

J1　艺术概论

1. Art et artisanat en Chine/［Yang, chunyan］. Beijing：Édition en Langues Étrangères, 2010. 55 pages：color illustrations；18cm. ISBN：7119063171；7119063170

《最美中国. 艺术与文化》，外文出版社编.

J2　绘画

1. L'esprit et le pinceau：histoire de la peinture chinoise/Zhang Anzhi；traduit par Shi Kangqiang. Beijing：Éd. en Langues Étrangères, 1992. 245 p.：ill.；32cm. ISBN：7119004034, 7119004037

《中国画发展史纲要》，张安治著.

2. Initiation à la peinture chinoise traditionnelle/Texte et illustrations He Hanqui et Deng Jun. Beijing：Éd. en Langues Étrangères, 1995. 71 p.：ill. en coul.；27cm. ISBN：7119004344 , 7119004341

《中国画入门》，何汉秋，邓军编绘.

3. La peinture chinoise témoin muet, mais éloquent de la civilisation chinoise/rédigé par Zhuang Jiayi et Nie Chongzheng；trad. par Tang Jialong. Pékin：China International Press, 2000. 1 vol.（172 p.）：ill. en noir et en coul.；21cm. ISBN：7801137175, 7801137173

《中国绘画：无声诗里颂千秋》，庄嘉怡，聂崇正著. 五洲传播出版社（中国基本情况丛书/郭长健主编）

4. La peinture chinoise/Lin Ci; traduit par Lisa Carducci. ［Beijing］: China Intercontinental Press, 2011. 191 pages; color illustrations; 23cm. ISBN: 7508520827, 7508520823. (Collection culture chinoise)
《中国绘画》，林茨著. 五洲传播出版社.

5. La peinture traditionnelle/［texte: Liao Ping; rédaction du texte Francais: Zou Shaoping］. Beijing: Éditions en Langues Étrangères, 2003. 107 pages; color illustrations, 1 color map; 17cm. ISBN: 7119032719; 7119032712
《中国传统绘画》，《中国传统绘画》编委会编.

6. La peinture des paysages de la Chine ancienne Ming song Geng; traduction Santiago Artozqui. Pékin: China Intercontinental Press, 2010. 1 vol.: illustrations en couleur; 21×22cm. ISBN: 7508517650; 7508517652 Contents: La peinture de paysages constitue le genre le plus noble de la peinture chinoise classique. Ce n'est pas un art figuratif d'après modèle mais plutôt le précipité de l'état de l'esprit du peintre. La conception confucéenne du monde transparaît dans la peinture de paysages, où les figures et les constructions humaines apparaissent en taille réduite, située dans un cadre cosmologique complet.
《中国历代山水画》，荆孝敏主编. 五洲传播出版社.

7. La Chine à travers des images de nouvel an, 1949—2009/ ［LU Keqin］. ［Beijing］: China Intercontinental Press, 2010. 233 pages: color illustrations; 26cm. ISBN: 7508516240, 7508516249
《年画上的中国》，陆克勤撰稿. 五洲传播出版社.

8. Œuvres choisies de la peinture traditionnelle chinoise/ ［Jing Xiaomin; traduit par Luo Shenyi］. Beijing: China Intercontinental Press, 2010. 1 vol. (229 p.): ill.; 30cm. ISBN: 7508517018, 7508517016
《中国绘画珍藏》，荆孝敏主编. 五洲传播出版社.

9. La peinture traditionnelle de genre en Chine: les enfants/ ［editeur en chef, Jing Xiaomin; traductrice, Luo Shenyi］. Beijing: China Intercontinental Press, 2010. 111 p.: col. ill.; 21×21cm. ISBN: 7508517995, 7508517997. (Recueils de peinture sur la culture traditionnelle de Chine)
《中国古代儿童生活画》，荆孝敏主编. 五洲传播出版社.

10. Les peintures à thèmes animaliers dans la Chine ancienne/Jing Xiaomin; traduit par Chomier Virginie. Beijing: China Intercontinental Press, 2010. 1 vol. (145 p.): ill.; 22cm. ISBN: 7508517971, 7508517970
《中国古代动物画》，荆孝敏主编. 五洲传播出版社.

11. Peinture de femmes dans la Chine ancienne Jing Xiaomin; Virginie Chomier ［trad.］. Beijing: China Intercontinental Press, 2010. 1 vol. (133 p.): ill. en coul., couv. ill. en coul.; 21cm. ISBN: 7508517988, 750851798
《中国历代仕女画》，刘奉文主编. 五洲传播出版社.

12. Peinture de fleurs et oiseaux dans la Chine ancienne/Jing Xiaomin; Virginie Chomier ［trad.］. Beijing: China intercontinental press, 2010. 1 vol. (147 p.): ill., couv. ill. en coul.; 21cm. ISBN: 7508518008, 7508518004;
《中国历代花鸟画》，荆孝敏主编. 五洲传播出版社.

13. La peinture contemporaine chinoise/Jing Xiaomin; traduit par Luo Shenyi. Beijing: China Intercontinental Press, 2010. 1 vol. (141 p.): ill.; 22cm. ISBN: 7508517964, 7508517962
《中国当代国画》，荆孝敏主编. 五洲传播出版社.

14. Kiai-tseu-yuan houa tchouan; Les enseignements de la peinture du Jardin grand comme un grain de moutarde; encyclopédie de la peinture chinoise/traduction et commentaires par Raphaël Petrucci, augmentés d'une Préface, d'un dictionnaire biographique des peintres et d'un vocabulaire des termes techniques; illustrés d'environ cinq cents gravures. Paris, H. Laurens, 1918. xii, 519 pages: illustrations; 41cm.
《芥子园画谱》，沈心友，王概，王蓍，王臬著；Petrucci, Raphaël(1872—1917)编译.
　(1) Paris: Peinture Galerie 14, 1999. xii, 519 pages: illustrations; 36cm.
　(2) Paris: Libr. You-Feng, 2000. X-519 p.; 30×22cm. ISBN: 2906658537, 2906658530

15. Galerie souterraine de peintures—Jiayuguan: peintures sur briques tombales des Wei et des Jin/reproduction, Wang Tianyi; rédaction, Éditions du Nouveau Monde. Beijing: Éditions du Nouveau Monde, 1989. 131 pages: color illustrations, map; 26cm. ISBN: 7800050483, 7800050480
《魏晋墓砖画》，王天一临摹，新世界出版社编.

16. La peinture des "oiseaux et fleurs"/Ma Zhifeng; traduit de l'anglais par Catherine Nicolle. Paris: Oskar jeunesse, 2007. 1 vol. (191 p.): ill. en noir et en coul., couv. ill. en coul.; 26cm. ISBN: 2350002682, 2350002683
《怎样画花鸟画》，马志丰著；Nicolle, Catherine 译.

J21　书法、篆刻

1. Petit traité de calligraphie chinoise/Guo Bonan; ［traduction de Wu Guoli］. Beijing: Éd. en Langues Étrangères, 1995. 67 p.: ill.; 26cm. ISBN: 7119014366, 7119014364
《中国书法入门》，郭伯南著.

2. La calligraphie chinoise/Chen Tingyou; traduit par Gong Jieshi. Beijing: China Intercontinental Press, 2003. 1 vol. (127 p.): couv. ill. en coul., ill. en coul.; 23cm. ISBN: 7508503457, 7508503455
《中国书法》，陈延祐著，宫结实译. 五洲传播出版社.
　(1) Beijing: China intercontinental Press, 2011. 131 pages: color illustrations; 23cm. ISBN: 7508519982, 7508519981. (Collection culture chinoise)

3. Introduction à la calligraphie chinoise/［traduit du

chinois]. Paris：Éditions du Centenaire, 14-Condé-sur-Noireau；Impr. C. Corlet, 1983. 87 p.：ill. ；23cm.

《书法基础知识》,译者不详.

4. L'art de la calligraphie chinoise à travers les âges Gao Changshan；traduction Santiago Artozqui. Pékin：China Intercontinental Press, 2010. 1 vol. （147 p.）：illustrations en couleur；21×22cm. ISBN：7508517667, 7508517660

Contents：Présentation de cette forme d'écriture devenue forme artistique à part entière. Aperçu des différentes techniques qui ont fait la renommée d'artistes sous les dynasties suivantes：Jin de l'Ouest（265—316）et de l'Est （317—420）, Tang （618—907）, cinq dynasties （907—960）, Song du Nord （960—1127）et du Sud （1127—1279）, Yuan （1279—1368）, Ming （1368—1644）, et Qing （1644—1911）.

《中国历代书法》,荆孝敏主编.五洲传播出版社.

J3　雕塑

1. La sculpture ancienne/Xia Xiaoming. Beijing, China：Éditions en Langues Érangères, 2003. 1 v. （106 p.）：ill. en coul. ；17cm. ISBN：7119032720, 7119032726

《中国古代雕塑》,《中国古代雕塑》编委会编.

2. La sculpture chinoise/Zhao Wenbing；traduit par Yueling Cui, Ting Lin, Qiaoying Pan. ［Beijing］：China Intercontinental Press, 2010. 185 pages：color illustrations；23cm. ISBN：7508519630, 7508519639. （Collection culture chinoise）

《中国雕塑》,肇文兵著.五洲传播出版社.

J4　工艺美术

1. L'artisanat populaire Lu Zhongmin；［trad. Zhang Yuyuan］. Beijing：Éd. en Langues Étrangères, 2006. 1 vol. （107 p.）：ill. en coul. couv. ill. en coul. ；17×19cm. ISBN：7119041304 （br）；7119041308 （br） （Culture de la Chine）

《中国民间工艺》,鲁忠民编著.（中华风物/肖晓明主编）.介绍了中国民间工艺的各种形式,如剪纸、刺绣、面花、玩具、雕塑、皮影、印染、木偶、彩灯、编结、陶瓷等.

2. Les arts populaires Chinois/Jin Zhilin；traduit par Lisa Carducci. Beijing：China Intercontinental Press, 2011. 152 pages：color illustrations；23cm. ISBN：7508519968, 7508519965. （Collection culture chinoise）

《中国民间美术》,靳之林著.五洲传播出版社.

3. Les Cerfs-volants chinois/Wang Hongxun. Beijing：Éditions en Langues Étrangères, 1989. 24 p. ：ill. ；26cm.

《中国风筝》,王鸿勋著.

J5　中国音乐

1. L'art du qin：deux textes d'esthétique musicale chinoise/

Georges Goormaghtigh. Bruxelles：Institut belge des hautes études chinoises, 1990. 209 pages：illustrations；25cm. （Mélanges chinois et bouddhiques；v. 23）

Goormaghtigh, Georges 著,翻译了嵇康（224 年—263 年,一作 223—262 年）的《琴赋》和徐上瀛（约 1582 年—1662 年）的《溪山琴况》.

J6　戏剧、曲艺、杂技艺术

J61　中国戏剧艺术理论

1. L'art théâtral ［texte, Bao Chengjie et Cao Juan；traduction, Zou Shaoping］. Beijing Éditions en Langues Étrangères 1re éd. 2003. 106 p. il. col. y n. , 1 mapa 17×19cm. ISBN：7119032115, 7119032119. （culture de la Chine）

《中国戏曲艺术》,包澄洁,操鹃编著,邹绍平译.

2. L'art théâtral/monograph. /［Cui Lili；traduit par Wang Mo, Zhang Yongzhao］. Beijing：Éditions en Langues Étrangères, 2009. 39 pages：color illustrations；21cm. ISBN：7119058757, 7119058754

《中国的戏曲艺术》,外文出版社编译.

3. Initiation à l'Opéra de Pékin par Dr Liang Yan；［traduction de Lisa Carducci］. Beijing：Éditions en Langues Érangères, 2003. 1 vol. （70 p.）：couv. ill. en coul. , ill. en coul. ；23cm. ISBN：7119032895, 7119032894

《京剧启蒙》,梁燕著.

4. Opéra de Pékin/Xu Chengbei；traduit par Tang Jialong. ［Beijing］：China Intercontinental Press, 2003. 128 p. ：nombreuses ill. （certaines en coul. ）. ISBN：7508503449, 7508503414, 7508503417, 7508503448

《中国京剧》,徐城北撰,唐家龙译.五洲传播出版社.

5. L'Opéra de Pékin quintessence de la culture chinoise/Yí Bían. Beijing：Éditions en Langues Étrangères, 2006. 1 vol. （150 p.）：ill. en noir et en coul. , couv. ill. en coul. ；22cm. ISBN：7119041584, 7119041582

《国粹：中国京剧》,易边编.

6. Le théâtre d'ombres chinois/Liu Jilin. Beijing （Chine）：Éd. Aurore, 1988. 111 p. ：nombreuses illustrations en coul. ；25cm. ISBN：750540072X, 7505400726

《中国皮影戏》,刘季霖编著.朝华出版社.

J62　杂技艺术

1. 《中国杂技艺术》,王正保编辑.北京：外文出版社,1982

2. Acrobatie chinoise a travers le temps et l'espace/ecrit par Zhen He, traduit par Han Su et Xiaochun Wang. Shanghai：Shanghai People's Publishing House, 2011. 103 pages：color illustrations；18cm. ISBN：7208088955, 7208088950

《穿越时空的中国杂技》,何真,苏晗,王晓春.上海人民出版社.

J7　电影、电视艺术

1. Intention perfide et procédé méprisable：critique du film antichinois tourné par Antonioni et intitulé "La Chine/commentateur du" Renmin Ribao；[traduit du chinois]. Pékin：Éditions en Langues Étrangères；[Paris]：[diffusion Éditions du Centenaire]，1974. 15 p.；19cm.

《恶毒的用心卑劣的手法：批判安东尼奥拍摄的题为〈中国〉的贬华影片》，《人民日报》评论员.

2. Une jeunesse chinoise/Chen Kaige；traduit du chinois par Christine Corniot. Arles：Ph. Picquier，1995. 203 p.：ill.；21cm. ISBN：287730213X，2877302135

《我们都经历过的日子》，陈凯歌著；Corniot，Christine 译.

K类　历史、地理

K1　中国史

K11　通史

1. Histoire generale de la Chine/ par Tsien Po-tsan, Chao Siun-tcheng et Hou Houa. Pékin：Éditions en Langues Étrangères，1958. 291 pages：illustrations；22cm.

《中国历史概要》，翦伯赞等著.

(1) Beijing：Éditions en Langues Étrangères，1982. 292 p.

2. Précis d'histoire de Chine（pèriode de 1840 à 1919）/Lin Yi. Pékin：Éditions en Langues Étrangères，1963. 128 p.；19cm.

《中国历史简编：1840—1919》，林峰著.

3. Histoire générale de la Chine/Jian Bozan, Shao Xunzheng et Hu Hua. Beijing：Éditions en Langues Étrangères. 1985. 292 p.；19cm.

《历史》，《中国概况丛书》编辑委员会编.

4. Histoire de la Chine. Beijing：Éditions en Langues Étrangères，1987. 40 p.：ill.；14cm.

《中国历史》. 外文出版社（中国简况）

5. Précis d'histoire de Chine/rédigé par Yang Zhao—... [et al.]；sous la direction de Bai Shouyi. Beijing：Éd. en Langues Étrangères，1988—1993. 589 p. -[68] p. de pl. -[1] carte dépl.：tableaux；21cm. ISBN：7119004506 (vol. 1)，7119004501 (vol. 1)，7119015281 (vol. 2)，7119015286 (vol. 2)

《中国通史纲要》，白寿彝著.

6. Histoire et civilisation de Chine/[edited by Zhang Yingpin, Fan Wei]. Beijing：Central Party Literature Press，2006. 256 pages：illustrations（some color），maps, portraits；29cm. ISBN：7507320499，7507320497

《中国历史与文明》，张英聘，范蔚编著；刘霞等译. 中央文献出版社.

7. Histoire et évolution sociale de la Chine/Jin Bo. Beijing：

China Intercontinental Press，2008. 223 pages：color illustrations, color maps；24cm. ISBN：7508512877，7508512871. (Zhongguo ji ben qing kuang cong shu)

《阅读中国》，金帛著. 五洲传播出版社.

8. Les repères pour la Chine/monograph. sous la direction de Zhou Hanbin. Wuhan：Wuhan University Press，2008. 221 pages：illustrations（chiefly color）；24cm. ISBN：7307058255；7307058251

《认识中国》，周汉斌主编. 武汉大学出版社.

9. Histoire encyclopedique de la Chine/["Zhongguo li shi su cha" bian xie zu bian zhu]. Éditions en Langues Étrangères，2008. ISBN：7119055688，7119055682

《中国历史速查》，本书编写组编著.

10. Histoires des empereurs chinois/Cheng Qinhua. Beijing：Éditions en langues étrang'eres，1st ed. 1999. 289 pages：illustrations. ISBN：711902048X，7119020488

《中国皇帝故事》，程钦华编著.

11. Impèratrices et concubines de l'ancienne Chine/Yuan Yang, Xiao Yan. Beijing, China：Éditions en Langues Étrangères，1999. 270 p.；18 × 11cm. ISBN：7119020420，7119020426

《中国古代后妃故事》，元阳，晓燕著.

12. Dans l'intimité de la cité interdite/[rédaction, Lan Peijin]；[traduction, Jiang Lili]. Beijing：Éditions en Langues Érangères，2008. 1 vol.（148 p.）：ill., couv. ill. en coul.；23cm. ISBN：7119054551，7119054554

《帝后生活》，兰佩瑾编辑.

13. Histoire générale de la Chine, ou Annales de cet empire traduites du Tong-Kien-Kang-Mou/par Joseph-Marie-Anne de Moyriac de Mailla. Paris，1777—1785. 13 vol.

《通鉴纲目》，朱熹（1130—1200）著；Moyriac de Mailla, Joseph-Marie-Anne de（1669—1748）译.

14. Ethnographie des peuples étrangers à la Chine：ouvrage composé au XIIIe siècle de notre ère/par Ma-Touan-Lin；traduit pour la première fois du Chinois avec un commentaire perpètuel par le marquis d'Hervey de Saint-Denys. Genève：H. Georg；Paris：E. Leroux；London：Trübner，1876—1883. 2 volumes；27cm. （Atsume gusa. Textes；4）

《文献通考》，马端临著；Hervey de Saint-Denys, Le'on（1822—1892）译.

15. Textes historiques/Hien-Hien：Impr. de Hien-Hien，1903—1905. 3 vol. in-8°，2. 173 p.，fig., cartes en coul.

《历史文选》，Wieger, Léon（1856—1933）编译.

K12　古代史籍

K121　《春秋》三传

1. Tch'ouen ts'iou et tso'tchouan/Texte chinois avec traduction française, par Fr. S. Couvreur, S. J. Ho kien fou：Impr. de la Mission catholique，1914. 3 vol.（I+

671，585 et 828 p.）

《春秋左传》，Couvreur，Séraphin(1835—1919)译.

2. 春秋左传 = La chronique de la principauté de Lou. La chronique de la principauté de Lou/[trad.] par Séraphin Couvreur. Paris：les Belles lettres：Cathasia, 1951. 3 vol.；26cm.（Textes de la Chine；Les humanités d'Extrême-Orient. Série culturelle des hautes études de Tien-Tsin）

《左传》，Couvreur，Séraphin(1835—1919)译.

K122 史记

1. Relation du pays de Ta Ouan/tr. du chinois par Brosset jeune. Paris, Imprimerie royale, 1829. 34 pages

《史记：大宛列传》，司马迁（约前 145—86）著；Brosset, Marie-Félicité(1802—1880)译.

2. Le traité sur les sacrifices fong et chan de Se ma T'sien/tr. en français par Edouard Chavannes. Pékin, Typographie du Pei-T'ang, 1890. xxxi, 95 pages；25cm.

《史记》，司马迁（约前 145—86）著；沙畹(Chavannes, édouard, 1865—1918)译.

3. Les mémoires historiques de Se-ma-Ts'ien/traduits et annotés par Édouard Chavannes, membre de l'Institut, professeur au Collège de France；publication encouragée par la Société asiatique；couronnée par l'Institut. Paris：Ernest Leroux, éditeur, 1895—1905. 5 volumes (in 6 parts), 544 p：illustrations, folded map, tables, facsimiles；26cm.

《史记》，司马迁（约前 145—86）著；沙畹(Chavannes, édouard, 1865—1918)译.

(1)Paris, Librairie d'Amérique et d'Orient, 1967, 1969. 6 volumes illustrations, folded map 22cm.（Collection U. N. E. S. C. O. d'œuvres représentatives série chinoise）

(2)Leiden, Brill, 1967. 5 volumes in 6 illustrations 23cm.（Collection U. N. E. S. C. O. d'œuvres représentatives. Série chinoise）

4. Le chapitre 117 du Che-ki (biographie de Sseu-ma Siang-jou)/traduction avec notes par Yves Hervouet. Paris：Presses universitaires de France, 1972. v, 285, 119 pages；26cm.

《史记》，司马迁（约前 145—86）著；Hervouet, Yves 译.

5. Shi ji = Shi ji：initiation à la langue classique chinoise à partir d'extraits des Mémoires historiques de Sima Qian/ J. Pimpaneau. Paris：友丰书店，1988—1989. Paris：Librairie You-Feng, 1988—. volumes；21cm. ISBN：2906658138, 2906658134

《史记》，司马迁（约前 145—86）著；Pimpaneau, Jacques 译.

(1)I. Paris：Lirairie You-Feng, 1988. volumes 1；21cm.

(2)II. Paris：You-Feng, 1989. 304 pages；21cm. ISBN：2906658286, 2906658288.

6. Vies de chinois illustres/Sima Qian；traduit du chinois et

présenté par Jacques Pimpaneau. Arles［France］：Éditions P. Picquier, 2002. ISBN：2877306119, 2877306119.（Picquier poche；187）

《史记》，司马迁（约前 145—86）著；Pimpaneau, Jacques 译.

7. La véritable histoire du premier empèreur de Chine/textes réunis et présentés par Damien Chaussende. Paris：Belles lettres, 2010. 186 pages；maps；18cm. ISBN：2251040080, 2251040080.（La véritable histoire de；8）

《中国始皇帝的真实历史》，Chaussende, Damien 著. 本书包含对《史记》的选译.

K13 古代史

1. Histoires de l'empereur Shihuangdi des Qin/by Yuan Yang, Xiao Ding. Beijing：Éditions en Langues Érangères, 2000. 250 pages：illustrations；19cm. ISBN：7119021028, 7119021027

《秦始皇的故事》，元阳，晓丁编著.

2. Les pays d'occident d'après le Heou Han Chou/par Édouard Chavannes. Leide：E. J. Brill, 1907. 88，［10］pages；25cm.

《后汉初年之后的西域》，沙畹(Chavannes)，Édouard, 1865—1918)译.（本书包含对《后汉书》的选译）

3. San-Koué-tchy ilan kouroun-i pithé, histoire des trois royaumes, roman historique traduit sur les textes chinois et mandchou/par Théodore Pavie. Paris：B. Duprat, 1845—51. 2 vol. 350 p.

《三国志》，陈寿(233－297)著；Pavie, Théodore(1811—1896)译.

4. Les pays d'Occident d'après le Wei Lio/par Édouard Chavannes. Leide, E. J. Brill, 1905. 55 pages；26cm.

《魏略・西戎传笺注》，沙畹(Chavannes，Édouard, 1865—1918)译并注释.

5. Documents sur les Tou-Kiue (Turcs)occidentaux recueillis et commentés suivi de notes additionnelles/par Édouard Chavannes. Paris Libr. d'Amérique et d'OrientParis Libr. d'Amérique et d'Orient, 1905. IV, 378，110 S. Kt.

《西突厥史料》，沙畹(Chavannes，Édouard, 1865—1918)译.

6. La Forêt des pinceaux, étude sur l'académie du Han-lin sous la dynastie des Tang et traduction du Han Lin Tche/ par F. A. Bischoff. Paris：Impr. nationale, 1963. XI—127 p.；25cm.

Bischoff, Frédéric 著. 本书包含了唐朝《翰林册》的翻译.

7. Le trait'e des examens：traduit de la Nouvelle histoire des T'ang Hsin T'ang Shu/par Ou-yang Hsiu et Sung Chi (Chap. 44-45), par Robert des Rotours. Paris：Ernest Leroux, 1932. viii, 414 pages；25cm.（Bibliothèque de l'Institut des hautes études chinoises；v. 2)

《新唐书》（选译），欧阳修著；Des Rotours, Robert (1891—)译.

(1) 2. ed. revue et corrigée. San Francisco：Chinese Matérials Center, 1976. 417 pages；23cm.（Chinese

Matérials Center. Reprint séries；；49；Bibliothèque de l'Institut des hautes études chinoises；2)

8. Textes historiques：Histoire politique de la Chine depuis l'origine jusqu'en 1929/par le P. Léon Wieger，S. J…：Tome I [-II]. 3e éd. Hien-hien：Impr. de Hien-hien，1929. 2 vol. (2103 p.)：pl.

《新唐书》的选译.
Wieger，Léon(1856—1933)著.本书包含了对《旧唐书》的选译.

9. Traité des fonctionnaires et Traité de l'armée：traduits de la Nouvelle histoire des T ang（chap. XLVI-L）/par Robert Des Rotours. Leyde：E. J. Brill，1947. 2 volumes：maps；26cm.

《新唐书》（选译），欧阳修著；Des Rotours，Robert (1891—)译.

（1）2. ed.，revue et corrigee. San Francisco：Chinese Materials Center，1974. 2 volumes；22cm. (Chinese materials center，inc. Reprint series，no. 11)

10. Une traduction juxta-linéaire commentée de la biographie officielle de l'impératrice Wou Tsö-Tien/par Nghiêm Toan et Louis Ricaud. Saigon：Imp. d'Extreme Orient，1959. 171 pages；28cm.（Annales chinoises）

Notes："Extrait du Bulletin de la Société des études indochinoises，nouvelle série，tome XXXIV，no. 2（2. trimestre，1959）."

《新唐书》有关武则天的史料翻译. Nghiêm，Toan 和 Ricaud，Louis 合译.法汉对照.

11. Les Ouïghours à l'époque des cinq dynasties：d'après les documents chinois/par James Russell Hamilton. Paris：Presses universitaires de France，1955. XII-203 p.：carte，fac-sim.，couv. Ill.（Bibliothèque de l'Institut des hautes études chinoises；vol. 10）

五代时期的维吾尔族人. Hamilton，James Russell (1921—)著.（本书包含了对《新旧唐书》《新旧五代史》《五代会要》的选译）

（1）Réimpression de l'éd. 1955. Paris：Collège de France，IHEC，1988. XII+201 p.：carte

12. Documents statistiques officiels sur l'Empire de la Chine traduits du chinois par G. Pauthier/Paris：typ. de Firmin Didot frères，1841. 48 p.

《大清会典》（选译），Pauthier，Guillaume(1801—1873)译.

13. Histoire des campagnes de Gengis Khan，Cheng-wou ts'in-tcheng lou/Traduit et annoté par Paul Pelliot et Louis Hambis. Tome I. Leiden，E. J. Brill，1951. In-4°，XXVIII-486 p.

《圣武亲征录》，Pelliot，Paul(1878—1945)译.

14. Histoire de la dynastie des Ming/composée par l'empereur Khian-Loung；traduite du chinois par M. l'abbé Delamarre. Paris：Vve Benjamin Duprat，1865. 1 vol.

《御撰资治通鉴纲目三编》，乾隆帝著；Delamarre，Louis Charles(1810—1863)译.

15. Histoire de la conquête de Formose par les Chinois en 1683/traduite du chinois，par Camille Imbert-Huart. Paris：Ernest Leroux，1890. 60 p.：carte.（Comité des travaux historiques et scientifiques. —Bulletin de géographie historique et descriptive）

《圣武记》，魏源（1794—1857）著；Imbault-Huart，Camille(1857—1897)译.

K14 近代史

1. La Guerre de l'opium/[édité] par le Comité de rédaction de la collection Histoire moderne de la Chine. Pékin：Éditions en Langues Étrangères，1979. 151 p.，[8] p. de planches：ill.；19cm.

《鸦片战争》，《中国近代史丛书》编写组编写.

2. Le Mouvement réformiste de 1898/[édité] par le Comité de rédaction de la collection Histoire moderne de Chine. Pékin：Éditions en Langues Étrangères，1978. 153 p.：ill.；19cm.

《戊戌变法》，《中国近代史丛书》编写组.

3. Le Mouvement des Yi Ho Touan (1900). Pékin：Éditions en Langues Étrangères，1980. 148 pages：illustrations，maps；19cm.

《义和团运动》，《中国近代史丛书》编写组.

4. Mémoire secret adressé à l'empereur Hien-Foung，actuellement régnant，par un lettré chinois sur la conduite à suivre avec les puissances européennes/traduit du chinois par M. G. Pauthier. Paris：Société orientale，1860. 32 p

《呈咸丰帝的密折》，Yin Tchao Young 撰；Pauthier，Guillaume (1801—1873)译.

5. Proclamations du mandarin Ye… et du vice-roi Ho，… ordonnant la liberté du culte catholique en Chine et la libre circulation des missionnaires chrétiens dans tout l'Empire [，avril et mai 1859]，/traduites sur les originaux chinois，par M. G. Pauthier. Paris：au bureau de la "Revue de l'Orient"，1860. 17 p.（"Revue de l'Orient，de l'Algérie et des colonies"，nouvelle série，t. XI，février 1860）

关于授予天主教活动自由及基督教传教士在全中国自由往来的声明. Pauthier，Guillaume（1801—1873）译.

6. Le Journal de Che Ta-kai：épisodes de la guerre des Tá ping/trad. [du chinois] par Li Choen. Pékin：mpr. de la Politique de Pékin，1927. 182 p.-[2]f. d'ill.：couv. ill.；25cm.（Collection de la Politique de Pékin）

《石达开日记》，石达开(1831—1863)著；Li，Choen 译.

7. Siuan-t'ong. Derniers décrets impériaux（1 septembre 1911—12 février 1912）. La revolution，l'abdication du prince régent，Yuan Che-k'ai au pouvoir，l'abdication-proclamation de la république/Traduits du chinois par Fernand Roy；Préface de Jean Fredet. Shanghai：Kelly & Walsh，Impr. Presse orientale，1912. IV+XII+142 p.

《宣统上谕：1911.9—1912.2》，Roy，Fernand 译.

K15　中华人民共和国成立之后历史

1. La Révolution de 1911. Une grande révolution démocratique dans l'histoire moderne de Chine/Wou Yu-tchant. [Traduit en français par Ho Ju.]. Pékin, Éditions en Langues Étrangères, 1963. 146 p. pl. , portr. 8vo
《辛亥革命：中国近代史上一次伟大的民主革命》，吴玉章著；何如译.

2. La Révolution de 1911/par le Comité de rédaction de la collection "Histoire moderne de Chine." Pékin：Éditions en Langues Étrangères, 1978. 204 pages, [8] pages of plates：illustrations；19cm.
《辛亥革命》，《中国近代史丛书》编写组.

3. Souvenirs de la longue marche/Liu Bocheng, Huang Chaotian… Beijing：Éditions en Langues Érangères, 1980. 207 p. -[X] p. de pl. ：1 carte de dépl. ；19cm.
《回顾长征》，刘伯承等著.

4. Annales de la République populaire de Chine (1949—1985)/Cheng Jin. Beijing, China：Éditions en Langues Étrangères, 1986. 99 p. ；19cm.
《中华人民共和国大事记：1949—1985》，成今著.

5. Le grand massacre de Nankin：une page tragique de la Deuxième Guerre mondiale/Xu Zhigeng；trad. de Lu Fujun et de Gou Wei. Beijing (Chine)：Éd. Littérature chinoise, 1995. [4] p. de pl. , 1 dépl. , 339 p. ：ill. ；20cm. ISBN：7507102963, 7507102963.
《南京大屠杀》，徐志耕著. 中国文学出版社(熊猫丛书)

6. 南京大屠杀/徐志耕著；陆馥君[等]翻译. 北京：外文出版社,2014. 276 页：图；23cm. ISBN：7119089812
法文题名：Massacre de Nanjing

7. 南京大屠杀幸存者证言/朱成山编著. 何丹法文翻译. 北京：外文出版社有限责任公司,2016. 221 页：照片；23cm. ISBN：7119102764
法文题名：Temoignages de survivants du massacre de Nanjing

K2　地方史志

北京

1. Pékin：aujourd'hui et hier/Hou Kia. Pékin：Éditions en Langues Étrangères, 1957. 148 s. [35] tav. ：ill.
《北京》

2. Beijing：capitale de la Chine/Liu Junwen. Beijing：Éditions en Langues Étrangères, 1982. 297 pages, [28] pages of plates：illustrations (some color, some folded)；18cm.
《北京》，刘俊雯编.

3. Le Palais d'Été = Yiheyuan/compilé par le Bureau d'administration du Palais d'été de Beijing et la Faculté d'Architecture de l'Université Qinghua. Beijing：Zhaohua, 1982. 132 p.
《颐和园》. 朝华出版社.

4. Le Palais d'Été et ses légendes traduit par Wang Jinguan, Wang Mo et Jiang Lili；révisé par Claude Romand et Gong Jieshi. Beijing, China：Éditions en Langues Étrangères, 2007. 1 vol. (226 p.) ：ill. en coul. , photogr. , couv ill. en coul. ；19cm. ISBN：7119043517, 711904351X
《颐和园趣闻》，徐凤桐，兰佩瑾编辑；徐凤桐等撰文；余志勇[等]摄影；王金冠，王默，姜丽莉法文翻译.

5. Le Palais impérial/[rédacteurs：Shi Yongnan, Wang Tianxing]. Beijing：Éditions Espèranto de Chine, 1995. 158 pages：color illustrations, map；26cm. ISBN：7505202685；7505202689.
《故宫》，施永南，望天星编；曾培耿译. 中国世界语出版社.

6. Hutong et anciennes demeures de personnalités. Beijing：Éditions en Langues Étrangères, 2007. 1 vol. (101 p.) ：photogr. en coul. , carte, couv. ill. en coul. ；22cm. ISBN：7119044040, 7119044044
《北京胡同·名人故居》，李连霞撰；王建华等摄. (漫游北京)

河南

1. 中国河南：汉法对照/河南省人民政府外事侨务办公室编. 郑州：河南人民出版社,2018. 52 页；26cm. ISBN：7215115347

西藏

1. La question du Tibet：(documents). Pékin：Éditions en Langues Étrangères, 1959. 304 p：Ill. , Faks. , Portr；19cm.
《关于西藏问题》.

2. Grands changements au Tibet/[traduit du chinois]. Pékin：Éditions en Langues Étrangères；[Paris]：[Éditions du Centenaire], 1972. 59 p. -[12] p. de pl. ：ill. , couv. ill. en coul. ；19cm.
《西藏巨变》

3. Les Tibétains à propos du Tibet. Beijing：Éditions la Chine en construction：Société chinoise du Commerce international du Livre [distributor], 1988. 220 pages, [31] pages of plates：color illustrations, map, portraits；19cm.
《西藏人谈西藏》. 中国建设出版社.

4. Le Bouddhisme tibétains et ses mystères/texte Li Jicheng, Gu Shoukang；photos Gu Shoukang, Kang Song；traduction Marie-Anne Pupin；éditeurs responsables Xiao Shiling, An Chunyang. Beijing：Éditions en Langues Étrangères：Société chinoise du Commerce international du livre [distributor], 1re éd. 1991. 224 pages：color illustrations；30cm. ISBN：7119014072, 7119014074.
《西藏佛教密宗艺术》，李冀诚，顾绶康编著.

5. La religion au Tibet/par Garsangrgya. Beijing：China Intercontinental Press, 2003. 154 pages：color illustrations；21cm. ISBN：7508502337, 7508502335.
《西藏宗教》，尕藏加著. 五洲传播出版社.

6. Le Palais du Potala/rédigé par Nan Hui. Beijing：Éditions espèranto de Chine，1995. 150，［9］pages：color illustrations；30cm. ISBN：7505202456，7505202450.

《布达拉宫》，南卉编.中国世界语出版社.

7. 《中国简况:西藏人眼中的西藏-五人五话》.北京:新星出版社,1995. ISBN:7801022599

8. Le tourisme au Tibet dévoiler le mystère/Li Hairui. ［Beijing］：China Intercontinental Press，1995. 1 vol. （35 p.）：ill.；20cm. ISBN：7801131029，7801131027.

《西藏旅游:揭开神秘的面纱》,李海瑞著.五洲传播出版社(西藏丛书)

9. Le tourisme au Tibet/par An Caidan. Beijing：China Intercontinental Press，2003. 187 pages：color illustrations，color map；21cm. ISBN：7508502531，7508502533.

《西藏旅游》,安才旦著;张桂清等译.五洲传播出版社.

10. Guide touristique du Tibet/An Caidan. Beijing：China Intercontinental Press，2003. 203 p：Ill. ISBN：7508503910；7508503912.

《西藏旅游指南》,安才旦著;张桂清等译.五洲传播出版社.

11. Le tourisme au Tibet. Beijing：Éditions en Langues Érangères，2008. 43 pages：color illustrations；21cm. ISBN：7119052595，7119052594 Le Tibet de Chine）

《西藏的旅游资源》,《西藏的资源旅游》编写组编.

12. Le Tibet peut-il prétendre être devenu un Etat indépendant après la Révolution de 1911? /Liu Muyan；Liu Mimei. Beijing：Chine Intercontinental Press，1996. 1 vol.（39 p.）；20cm. ISBN：7801130790，7801130792. （Série sur le Tibet）

《西藏在辛亥革命后变成了一个独立国家吗?》,刘慕燕,刘丽楣著.五洲传播出版社(西藏丛书)

13. Le système de servage féodal au Tibet ＝ Xizang feng jian nong nu zhi du/Yuan Sha. Beijing：China Intercontinental Press，1996. 43 P. ISBN：7801131061，7801131065.

《西藏封建农奴制度》,袁莎著.五洲传播出版社(西藏丛书)

14. 《西藏交通》,秦鸿勋著.北京:五洲传播出版社,1997. ISBN:7801131959.(西藏丛书)

15. 《前进中的西藏科技》,西藏自治区科委编写组编著.北京:五洲传播出版社,1997. ISBN:7801131894.(西藏丛书)

16. 《西藏教育今昔》,尚俊娥著.北京:五洲传播出版社,1997. ISBN:7801131924.(西藏丛书)

17. L'éducation au Tibet/par Zhou Aiming；［traduit par Hao Baolu］. Beijing：China Intercontinental Press，2004. 164 pages：color illustrations；21cm. ISBN：7508505255，7508505251 (Collection Tibet)

《西藏教育》,周爱明著.五洲传播出版社.

18. 《藏学研究基地:中国藏学研究中心简介》,周源著.北京:五洲传播出版社,1997. ISBN:7801132092.（西藏丛书)

19. Tibétologie en Chine contemporaine/Lobsang Jiamei. ［Beijing］：China Intercontinental Press，2000. 1 vol. （39 p.）：ill.；21cm. ISBN：7801137019，7801137012

《当代中国藏学》,洛桑晋美著.五洲传播出版社(西藏丛书)

20. La vie des citadins tibétains：rapport d'enquête sur les habitants de Lhugu a Lhasa/Liu Hongji et Ciring Yangzom. Beijing：China Intercontinental Pr.，1998. 78 pages：color illustrations；18cm. ISBN：7801134699，7801134691.

《西藏城市居民:拉萨鲁固居民的调查报告》,刘洪记,次仁央宗著.五洲传播出版社.

21. Éleveurs tibétainss：Rapport d'enqûete sur cinq villages au district d'Amdo dans le nord du Tibet/Zhagyai，Lu Mei. Beijing：China Intercontinental Pr.，1998. 78 pages：color illustrations；18cm. ISBN：7801134656，7801134653.

《西藏牧民:藏北安多县腰恰五村的调查报告》,扎呷,卢梅著.五洲传播出版社.

22. Paysans ibétains：Rapport d'enquete sur le village de Banjor Lhunbo dans l'arriere-pays ibétain/Puncog Zhamdu. Beijing，China：China Intercontinental Press，1998. ISBN：7801134613，7801134615

《西藏农民:后藏班觉伦布存的调查报告》,平措占堆著.五洲传播出版社.

23. Le développement de la culture tibétainse. Beijing：Office d'information du Conseil des Affaires d'État de la République populaire de Chine，2000. 34 pages；21cm. ISBN：7801482972，7801482976.

《西藏文化的发展》,中华人民共和国国务院新闻办公室发布.新星出版社.

24. La croissance de la modernisation du Tibet/Office d'information du Conseil des Affaires d'État de la République populaire de Chine. Beijing：Nouvelle Etoille，2001. 45 pages；21cm. ISBN：7801484002，7801484000.

《西藏的现代化发展》,中华人民共和国国务院新闻办公室发布.新星出版社.

25. Chine Tibet Faits et chiffres/Wang Guozhen. Beijing：Nouvelle Étoile，2001. 1 vol.（154 p.）：ill.；20cm. ISBN：7801483508，7801483502.

《中国西藏:事实与数字》,王国振编.新星出版社.

26. Cent questions sur le Tibet. Beijing：Éditions Nouvelle Étoile，2001. 158 pages：color illustrations；21cm. ISBN：7801483553，7801483553.

《西藏百题问答》,百题编辑部编.新星出版社.

27. Récits sur le Tibet/par Zhang Xiaoming. Beijing：China Intercontinental Press，2003. 160 pages：color illustrations；21cm. ISBN：7508503198，7508503196.

《西藏的故事》,张晓明著.五洲传播出版社.

28. La géographie au Tibet/par Yang Qinye et Zheng Du.

Beijing：China Intercontinental Press，2003. 150 pages：color illustrations，color maps；21cm. ISBN：750850271X，7508502717.

《西藏地理》，杨勤业，郑度著. 五洲传播出版社.

29. L'Édification écologique et la protection de l'environnement au Tibet/Office d'information du Conseil des Affaires d'État de la République populaire de Chine. Beijing：Nouvelle Étoile，2003. 42 pages；21cm. ISBN：780148522X，7801485229.

《西藏的生态建设与环境保护》，中华人民共和国国务院新闻办公室发布. 新星出版社.

30. Les us et coutumes du Tibet/Li Tao，Jiang Hongying. ［Beijing］：China Intercontinental Press，2004. 123 pages：color illustrations；21cm. ISBN：7508505268，7508505263 (Collection Tibet)

《西藏民俗》，李涛，江红英著；郭立等译. 五洲传播出版社（中国西藏基本情况丛书/郭长建，宋坚之主编）

31. Les beaux-arts du Tibet/par Xiong Wenbin；［traduit par Zhang Lifang］. Beijing：China Intercontinental Press，2004. 105 pages：color illustrations；21cm. ISBN：7508505271，7508505275 (Collection Tibet)

《西藏艺术》，熊文彬著；张立方译. 五洲传播出版社（中国西藏基本情况丛书/郭长建，宋坚之主编）

32. L'économie du Tibet/par Wang Wenchang et Lha Can. Beijing：China Intercontinental Press，2004. 121 pages：color illustrations；21cm. ISBN：7508505670，7508505671

《西藏经济》，王文长，拉灿著. 五洲传播出版社（中国西藏基本情况丛书/郭长建，宋坚之主编）

33. Évolution，économique au Tibet. Beijing：Éditions en Langues Érangères，2008. 43 pages：color illustrations；21cm. ISBN：7119052441，7119052446. (Le Tibet de Chine)

《西藏的经济发展》，《西藏的经济发展》编写组编.

34. L'histoire du Tibet/Chen Qingying. Beijing：China Intercontinental Press，2004. 158 pages：illustrations (some color)；21cm. ISBN：7508505514，7508505510

《西藏历史》，陈庆英著. 五洲传播出版社（中国西藏基本情况丛书）

35. Cent ans de témoignages sur le Tibet：reportages de témoins de l'histoire du Tibet/［éditeur en chef，Li Jianguo and others］. Beijing：China Intercontinental Press，2006. 196 pages：illustrations；21cm. ISBN：7508508153，7508508157.

《见证百年西藏：西藏历史见证人访谈录》，张晓明主编；郝宝禄译. 五洲传播出版社.

36. 目击西藏：涉藏新闻报道作品选：［法文本］/冀小峰，郑庆东，康守永著；王秉义等译. 北京：新星出版社，2003. 496 pages：照；21cm. ISBN：7801485513，7801485519

37. La littérature du Tibet/wu wei，geng yu fang zhu. Beijing：China intercontinental Press，Beijing：Wu zhou chuan bo chu ban she，2006. 1 vol.（122 p.）：ill. en coul.；21cm. ISBN：7508507177，7508507170

《西藏文学》，吴伟，耿予方著. 五洲传播出版社（中国西藏基本情况丛书/郭长建，宋坚之主编）. 本书介绍西藏文学发展的历史，包括作家、作品介绍.

38. Informations sur I'incident du 14 mars au Tibet. Beijing：Éditions en Langues Étrangères，2008. volumes（1，2，3）：color illustrations，color maps；21cm. ISBN：7119052045(v. 1)，7119052047(v. 1)，7119052182(v. 2)，7119052187(v. 2)，7119052236(v. 3)，7119052233(v. 3)

《西藏"3·14"事件有关材料》，《西藏"3·14"事件有关材料》编写组编.

39. La géographie，les ressources et la division administrative du Tibet. Beijing：Éditions en Langues Étrangères，2008. 43 pages：color illustrations；21cm. ISBN：7119052397，711905239X (Le Tibet de Chine)

《西藏的地域、资源与行政区划》，《西藏的地域、资源与行政区划》编写组编.

40. La population，la religion et l'autonomie régionale ethnique au Tibet. Beijing：Éditions en Langues Érangères，2008. 43 pages：illustrations；21cm. ISBN：7119052342，7119052349 (Le Tibet de Chine)

《西藏的人口、宗教与民族区域自治》，《西藏的人口、宗教与民族区域自治》编写组编.

41. Éducation，science，culture et conditions de vie au Tibet. Beijing：Éditions en Langues Érangères，2008. 43 pages：color illustrations；21cm. ISBN：7119052496，7119052497 (Le Tibet de Chine)

《西藏的教育、科技、文化与生活》，《西藏的教育、科技、文化与生活》编写组编.

42. La protection de l'environnement au Tibet. Beijing：Éditions en Langues Érangères，2008. 42 pages：color illustrations；21cm. ISBN：7119052540，7119052543. (Le Tibet de Chine)

《西藏的自然环境与保护》，《西藏的自然环境与保护》编写组编.

43. Le statut du Tibet de Chine dans l'histoire/Wang Jiawei et Nyima Gyaincain. Beijing：China Intercontinental Press，2003. 3，367 pages：illustrations，maps；21cm. ISBN：7508502595，7508502590

《中国西藏的历史地位》，王家伟，尼玛坚赞著. 五洲传播出版社.

44. La protection et le développement de la culture tibétainse/Office d'information du Conseil des Affaires d'État de la République populaire de Chine. Bejing：Éditions en Langues Étrangères，2008. 34 pages；21cm. ISBN：7119047348，7119047345

《西藏文化的保护与发展》，中华人民共和国国务院新闻办公室发布.

45. Rapport sur le développement économique et social du Tibet/monograph. ［edité par］ Centre chinois de

recherches tibétologiques. Beijing：Éditions en Langues Etrangères，2009. 81 pages：color illustrations；23cm. ISBN：7119056678，7119056670

《西藏经济社会发展报告》，中国藏学研究中心编.

46. Le cinquantenaire de la réforme démocratique au Tibet/monograph. Office d'information du Conseil des Affaires d'État de la République populaire de Chine. Beijing：Éditions en Langues Érangères，2009. 57 pages；21cm. ISBN：7119056371，7119056379

《西藏民主改革 50 年》，中华人民共和国国务院新闻办公室［发布］.

47. Soixante ans depuis la libération pacifique du Tibet/Office d'information du Conseil des Affaires d'État de la République populaire de Chine. Beijing：Éditions en Langues Érangères，2011. 54 p.；21cm. ISBN：7119071688，7119071688

《西藏和平解放 60 年》，中华人民共和国国务院新闻办公室［编］.

48. Le Tibet aujourd'hui：panoramas et coutumes/écrit par Jun Wu；traduit par Louis Le Guillou et Yuanyuan Wang. Shanghai：Shanghai Far East Pub.；Levallois-Perret，France：Lagardere Active International，2011. 125 pages：color illustrations；18cm. ISBN：7547602263，7547602266. （［Window to China］）

《我们的西藏：当代西藏风貌与风情》，吴钧编著. 上海远东出版社.

49. 民族区域自治制度在西藏的成功实践/中华人民共和国国务院新闻办公室［发布］. 北京：外文出版社，2015. 66 页；21cm. ISBN：7119096025

法文题名：La reussite au Tibet du systeme d'autonomie regionale ethnique

上海

1. Nouvelle zone de Pudong à Shanghai，futur port franc/complié par Beijing Information. Beijing：Éditions Nouvelle Etoile，1991. 108 pages，［4］pages of plates：illustrations，maps；19cm. ISBN：7800853241，7800853241.

《上海浦东新区：未来的自由港》，北京周报社编. 新星出版社.

2. Carte culturelle Française à Shanghai/par Ma Xueqiang Cao Shengmei. Shanghai：Jinxiuwenzhang de Shanghai，2010. 7，183 pages，［1］folded leaf of plates：illustrations（some color），maps，portraits；24cm. ISBN：7545206210，7545206215

《上海的法国文化地图》，马学强，曹胜梅著. 上海锦绣文章出版社.

3. 南京路：东方全球主义的诞生/李天纲著. 上海：上海人民出版社，2011. 107 页；18cm. ISBN：7208088801

法文题名：la rue de Nankin

陕西

1. Xi'an：ancienne capitale de la Chine/par Xang Yang. Beijing：Éditions en Langues Étrangères，1992. 163 p. -［1］dépl.：pl.；19cm. ISBN：7119004417，7119004419.

《中国古都西安》，相阳编著.

2. Xi'an ancienne capitale renommée dans le monde/rédigé par le Bureau des affaires extérieures de la Mairie de Xi'an. ［Beijing］：Éditions du tourisme de Chine，1996. 1 vol. （135 p.）：ill.；29cm. ISBN：7503212667，7503212666

《世界历史名都西安》，王剽钊编. 中国旅游出版社.

新疆

1. L'Histoire et le développement du Xinjiang/Office d'information du Conseil des Affaires d'État de la République populaire de Chine. Beijing：Nouvelle Étoile，2003. 67 pages；21cm. ISBN：7801485084，7801485083.

《新疆的历史与发展》，中华人民共和国国务院新闻办公室发布. 新星出版社.

2. Le développement et le progrès du Xinjiang/Office d'information du Conseil des Affaires d'État de la République populaire de Chine. Beijing：Éditions en Langues Érangères，2009. 68 pages：illustrations；21cm. ISBN：7119060378，7119060376

《新疆的发展与进步》，中华人民共和国国务院新闻办公室［编］.

3. 新疆各民族平等团结发展的历史见证：法文版/中华人民共和国国务院新闻办公室发布. 北京：外文出版社，2015. 1 册：图；23cm. ISBN：7119096476

4. 新疆的宗教信仰自由状况(法文版)/外文出版社. 北京：外文出版社，2016. 20cm. ISBN：7119102061

山西

1. Shanxi basic facts/chief editor, Shen Weichen. Taiyuan：Hope Prblishing House，2005. 135 pages：color illustrations，color maps；19cm. ISBN：7537935939，7537935937

《山西概览》，申维辰主编. 希望出版社. 本书图文并茂地介绍山西的历史地理、风土人情、文化旅游、经济发展等.

山东

1. Qingdao Chine/edited by Lv Zhenyu ［and others］. Qingdao：Maison D'édition de Qingdao，2010. 90 pages：color illustrations，maps；19cm. ISBN：7543662858，754366285X

《中国青岛》，吕振宇，于宏伟，魏腾吉主编. 青岛出版社.

K3　中国文物考古

考古

1. L'archéologie/Yang Yang et Zhao Gushan. Beijing，China：Éditions en Langues Érangères，2003. 103 p.：couv. ill. en coul.，ill. en coul.，carte；17×19cm. ISBN：7119032941，7119032948

《中国考古》，杨阳、赵古山主编.

2. Antiquités chinoises/Li Li；traduit par Guo Anding. ［Beijing］：China intercontinental Press，2004. 1 vol. （174 p.）：photogr. en coul.；23cm. ISBN：7508504577

, 7508504575. (Cultural China series.)

《中国文物》，李力主编，郭安定译. 五洲传播出版社.

(1)China Intercontinental Press, 2011. 1 vol. (168 p.)：ill. ；23cm. ISBN：7508519302 ，7508519302. (Cultural China series)

3. Historical relics unearthed in new China＝Découvertes archéologiques en Chine nouvelle＝Xin Zhongguo chutu wenwu. Pékin：Éditions en Langues Étrangères, 1972. 1 v. ：tout en ill. (certaines en coul.)

《新中国出土文物》，法汉对照.

4. Nouvelles decouvertes archeologiques en Chine (Ⅱ). Beijing, Chine：Éditions en Langues Étrangères, 1980. 136 pages，[8] pages of plates：illustrations (some color)；19cm.

《中国的新出土文物》(二)

5. La Caverne de l'homme de Pékin/par Kia Lan-po. Pékin：Éditions en Langues Étrangères；[Paris]：[diffusion Éditions du Centenaire], 1978. 58 p. -[36] p. de pl. en noir et en coul. ：ill. ，couv. ill. ；19cm.

《北京人之家》，贾兰坡.

6. Récentes découvertes archéologiques en Chine：28 articles/composés par des archéologues chinoise. Beijing：Éditions en Langues Étrangères, 1985. 104 S. ：ill.

《两千三百年前古中山之谜》

7. Les sépultures impériales de la Chine ancienne/[Luo Zhewen；translated by Tang Jialong]. Beijing, Chine：Éditions en Langues Étrangères, 1ere éd. 1993. 218 p. ：ill. ；32cm. ISBN：7119016202, 7119016207.

《中国历代皇帝陵墓》，罗哲文编.

8. L'armée en terre cuite de l'Empereur Qin Shi Huang/sous la rédaction du prof. Fu Tianchou；introd. ：Sidney Shapiro. Beijing：Éd. du Nouveau Monde, 1983. 111 p. ，[2] p. de cartes：ill. en noir et en coul. ；26×26cm.

《秦始皇兵马俑》，傅天仇编著. 新世界出版社.

(1)Beijing：Éd. du Nouveau Monde, 1992. 115 p. ：ill. ；25×26cm. ISBN：7800050106, 7800050107

9.《秦始皇兵马俑》. 北京：文物出版社, 1993. ISBN：7501007039

10. L'armée souterraine de Qin Shihuang：la huitième merveille du monde/Wu Xiaocong et Guo Youmin, rédacteurs en chef. [Paris]：Éditions touristiques de Chine, 1999. 126, [2] pages：color illustrations；29cm. ISBN：7503216158, 7503216152.

《秦始皇的地下兵团：世界第八奇迹》，郭佑民，吴晓丛主编. 中国旅游出版社.

11. L'Armée en terre cuite de Qin：trésors du Lintong/Zhang Wenli. London：Scala Books, 1996. 96 pages：color illustrations；28cm. ISBN：7501009171, 7501009176.

《秦始皇陵兵马俑博物馆导览》，张文立编. 文物出版社.

12. Les grottes de Yungang et la dynastie des Wei du Nord/écrit par Li Hengcheng；traduit par Wu Xiaochun. Taiyuan：Éditions des sciences et technique du Shanxi, 2004. 136 pages：color illustrations, color maps；21cm. ISBN：7537724962；7537724968

《云冈石窟与北魏时代》，李恒成编著；武晓春译. 山西科学技术出版社.

13. Sanxingdui lieu sacré du royaume ancien de Shu/Chen De'an；[Traduction, Zou Shaoping]. Chengdu：Groupe des Éditions du Sichuan, 2006. 1 vol. (123 p.)：ill. en noir et en coul. ，cartes，couv. ill. en coul. ；29cm. ISBN：7220069987 (br)；7220069987 (br)

《三星堆：古蜀王国的圣地》，陈德安著；邹绍平译. 四川人民出版社.

14. Beijing nei cheng si miao bei ke zhi＝Temples et stèles de Pékin/Dong Xiaoping, Lü Min (Marianne Bujard) zhu bian. Beijing Shi：Guo jia tu shu guan chu ban she, 2011. 2 volumes (4, 875 pages, [4] pages of plates)：illustrations (some color)，maps，facsimiles；29cm. ISBN：7501344826, 7501344825

《北京内城寺庙碑刻志》，董晓萍，吕敏(Marianne Bujard)主编. 国家图书馆出版社.

15. Les bronzes chinois ou l'art du feu/Li Xueqin；traduit par Chen Shun, revu par Christophe Legrand, Marie-Anne Pupin, An Mingshan. Beijing：Éd. en Langues Étrangères, 1995. 1 vol. (171 p.)：ill. en noir et en coul. ，couv. ill. ，jaquette ill. en coul. ；31cm. ISBN：7119013882 ，7119013886

《中国青铜器概说》，李学勤著.

16. Les bronzes Chinois/Li Song. Beijing：China Intercontinental Press, 2010. 181 p. ：col. ill. ；23cm. ISBN：7508519364, 7508519361. (Collection culture chinoise)

《中国青铜器》，李松著. 五洲传播出版社.

17. Les jades chinois/Yu Ming；traduction de Gong Jieshi. [Beijing]：China Intercontinental Press, 2011. 140 pages：color illustrations；23cm. ISBN：7508519715, 750851971X. (Collection culture chinoise)

《中国玉器》，于明著. 五洲传播出版社.

K4　风俗习惯

1. Les fetes traditionnelles chinoises/par Qi Xing. Beijing：Éditions en Langues Étrangères, 1987. 144 p. ：ill. ；19cm.

《中国传统节日民俗》，齐星编著，杨光华绘图.

2. Fêtes traditionnelles/monograph. /[Qi Xing；traduit par Gong Jieshi, He Dan]. Beijing：Éditions en Langues Étrangères, 2009. 34 pages：color illustrations；21cm. ISBN：7119058535, 7119058533

《中国的传统节日》，齐星编著.

3. Les douze animaux et leur place dans la culture chinoise/Zhang Fang；[trad. par Wang Jinguan...]. Beijing：Éd.

en Langues Érangères, 2001. 208 p. : ill. ; 21cm. ISBN：711902065X, 7119020655.

《中国生肖文化》,张方著. 新星出版社.

K5　地理

1. Précis de géographie de Chine/[par] Wang Kiun-heng. Pékin, Éditions en Langues Étrangères, 1959. 288 pages：illustrations；maps (2 folded color)19cm.

   《简明中国地理》,王钧衡编.

2. Géographie de la Chine/Jen Yu-ti. Pékin：Éditions en Langues Étrangères, 1965. 299 p. , [12] p. di tav. , [1] c. geogr. ；19cm.

   《中国地理概述》,任育地著.

3. Géographie de la Chine. Pékin：Éditions en Langues Étrangères, 1972. 48 p.

   《中国地理知识》.

4. 《地理》,《中国概况丛书》编辑委员会编. 北京：外文出版社,1986

5. Géographie de Chine conditions naturelles, économies régionales, aspects humains/texte de Zheng Ping；trad. de Tang Jialong. [S. l.]：China Intercontinental Press, 1999. 1 vol. (176 p.)：ill. en coul. , couv. ill. en coul. ；21cm. ISBN：7801134826, 7801134820

   《中国地理：自然、经济、人文》. 五洲传播出版社(中国基本情况丛书/金晖主编)

6. La géographie de la Chine/Zheng Ping；traduit par Wang Ping. [Beijing]：China Intercontinental Press, 2011. 1 vol. (151 p.)：ill. , couv. ill. en coul. ；23cm. ISBN：7508519654, 7508519655

   《中国地理》,郑平著. 五洲传播出版社.

7. 《国土与资源》. 北京：外文出版社,1987. (中国简况)

K51　专属地理

1. Montagnes et rivières célèbres/[Yu Li]. Beijing：Éditions en Langues Étrangères, 2007. 106 pages：illustrations (some color)；18 × 20cm. ISBN：7119047775, 7119047779 Chine ＝；Zhonghua feng wu)

   《中国名山大川》,于力编著. (中华风物)

2. Les plus belles montagnes et rivières/[Yu Li；traduit par Gong Jieshi]. Beijing：Éditions en Langues Étrangères, 2009. 39 pages：color illustrations；21cm. ISBN：7119058597, 7119058592

   《中国的名山大川》,于力编著.

K52　历史地理

地理史料

1. Le Chan-hā-King, livre des montagnes et des mers. Livre II, montagnes de l'Ouest /traduit par émile Burnouf. Paris：Bouchard-Huzard, 1875. P. 131—144；in-8

   《山海经》,Burnouf, émile(1821—1907)译.

2. Zhanhai-king：antique géographie chinoise/traduite pour la première fois sur le texte original par Le'on de Rosny. Tome 1. Paris：J. Maisonneuve, 1891. 408 [i. e. 308] pages；23cm.

   《山海经》,Rosny, Le'on de 译.

   (1)Chan-Hai-king：antique geographie chinoise /traduite Par Léon de Rosny. Paris：J. Maisonneuve, 1901. 408 p.

3. Shanhai jing：traduction annotée/Rémi Mathieu. Paris, Inst. , 1983. (Étude sur la mythologie et l'ethnologie de la Chine ancienne/Rémi Mathieu；1；Mémoires de l'Institut des hautes études chinoises；22,1)

   《山海经》,Mathieu, Rémi 译.

4. La frontière sino-annamite：description géographique et ethnographique d'après des documents officiels chinois/traduits pour la première fois par G. Devéria. Paris：E. Leroux, 1886. 1vol. (XVII—183 p. , pl. , cartes dépl.)；in-4. (Publications de l'école des langues orientales vivantes. 3e série；1)

   《皇清职贡图》,Devéria, Gabriel(1844—1899)译.

5. Esquisse du Sy-Yu ou des pays à l'ouest de la Chine / traduite et résumée du chinois par Louis Lamiot. Paris：P. Renouard, (s. d.), 1852. 40 p.

   《西域图志》,Lamiot, Louis 译.

6. Recueil de documents sur l'Asie centrale/[choisis, traduits et présentés] par Camille Imbault-Huart. Paris：Ernest Leroux, 1881. XI-225 p. ：cartes ； gr. in-8°. (Publications de l'école des langues orientales vivantes. 1e série；16)

   《西域图志》,Imbault-Huart, Camille(1857—1897)选译.

7. Territoires et populations des confins du Yunnan/traduit du chinois par J. Siguret,... Préfaces de Tch'ên Yu-Ko et de Kong Tse-Tche, avant-propos de Tchang'Pang-Han. Peiping (Chine)：Éditions H. Vetch, 1937. Gr. X-308 p. , carte

   《云南边地问题研究》,Siguret, J. 译.

K53　名胜古迹

1. Joyaux du patrimoine mondial en Chine. Beijing：China Intercontinential Press, 2005. 259 pages：color illustrations；31cm. ISBN：750850545X , 7508505459

   《中国的世界遗产》,《中国的世界遗产》编委会编；吕华译. 五洲传播出版社. 本书介绍中国的29处世界遗产.

2. Sites naturels. Pékin：Éd. en Langues Étrangères, 2006. 1 v. (94 p.)：ill. en coul. ；16cm. ISBN：7119044109, 7119044101. (Patrimoine mondial en Chine)

   《中国的世界遗产·自然与文化》,罗哲文主编；高明义等摄.

3. Sites culturels. Pékin：Éd. en Langues Étrangères, 2006. 1 v. (95 p.)：ill. en coul. ；16cm. ISBN：7119044117, 7119044118. (Patrimoine mondial en Chine)

   《中国的世界遗产·人文遗迹》,罗哲文主编；高明义等摄.

4. Sites impériaux. Pékin：Éd. en Langues Étrangères，2006. 1 v.（95 p.）：ill. en coul.；16cm. ISBN：7119044125，7119044125.（Patrimoine mondial en Chine）
《中国的世界遗产·皇家遗迹》，罗哲文主编；高明义等摄.

5. Sites religieux patrimoine mondial en Chine. Beijing：Éditions en Langues Étrangères，2006. 1 vol.（95 p.）：photogr. en coul.，carte；16cm. ISBN：7119044095，7119044095.（Patrimoine mondial en Chine）
《中国的世界遗产·宗教遗迹》罗哲文主编；高明义等摄.

6. Patrimoine mondial/monograph.［Cui Lili；traduit par Jiang Lili，Zhang Yongzhao］. Beijing：Éditions en Langues Étrangères，2009. 39 pages：color illustrations；21cm. ISBN：7119058627，7119058622
《中国的世界文化与自然遗产》，崔黎丽编著.

7. Les sites les plus pittoresques de Chine/［Yang，chunyan］. Beijing：Édition en Langues Étrangères，2010. 55 pages：color illustrations；18cm. ISBN：7119063249；7119063243
《最美中国·自然与文化》，外文出版社编.

8. Vestiges de l'ancienne civilisation chinoise：à la découverte des mystères de 7000 ans d'histoire/［dir. Xiao Shiling；texte de Wang Luxiang；trad. du chinois par Xiao Jingyi；photogr. et conception de Yan Zhongyi］. Beijing［Chine］：Éd. Aurore，1995. 286 p.：ill. en noir et en coul.，carte en coul.；35cm. ISBN：7505404091（rel.）；7505404090（rel.）.
《中国古代文化遗迹》，肖师铃主编.朝华出版社.

9. Vestiges de l'ancienne civilisation chinoise：à la découverte des mystères de 7000 ans d'histoire/［dir. Xiao Shiling；texte de Wang Luxiang；trad. du chinois par Xiao Jingyi；photogr. et conception de Yan Zhongyi］. Beijing［Chine］：Éd. Aurore，1995. 286 p.：ill. en noir et en coul.，carte en coul.；35cm. ISBN：7505404091，7505404090
《中国古代文明遗迹：7000 年史探秘》，萧石灵，王鲁湘著；Xiao Jingyi 译.

10. L'architecture ancienne/Lou Qingxi；［traduction Zhang Yuyuan；photos Lou Qingxi，Zhai Dongfeng］. Beijing：Éditions en Langues Érangères，2003. 106 str.：ilustr.；17 X 19cm. ISBN：7119032931，7119032933
《中国古代建筑》，楼庆西著；宫结实译.

11. Les habitations chinoises/Shan Deqi；trad. par Tang Jialong. Pékin：China intercontinental，2004. 1 vol.（144 p.）：ill. en coul.；23cm. ISBN：7508504356，7508504353.（Cultural China series）
《中国民居》，单德启等著；康家龙译.五洲传播出版社.

12. Habitations traditionnelles/Wang Qijun；［traduction：Wang Jinguan］. Beijing：Éd. en Langues Étrangères，2006. 107 p.：ill.（chifely col.），map，plans；19cm. ISBN：7119041290，7119041292.（Culture de la Chine）
《中国传统民居》，王其钧著.（中华风物/肖晓明主编）

13. L'architecture classique/［Lou Qingxi；traduit par Gong Jieshi］. Beijing：Éditions en Langues Étrangères，2009.

39 pages：color illustrations；21cm. ISBN：7119058481，7119058487
《中国传统建筑》，楼庆西编著.

14. L'architecture chinoise/Cai Yanxin；Fan Yi Wu You，Bi Chaolian［trad.］. Beijing：China Intercontinental Press，2011. 1 vol.（224 p.）：ill.，couv. ill. en coul.；24cm. ISBN：7508519081，7508519086.（Collection culture chinoise）
《中国建筑》，蔡燕歆著.五洲传播出版社.

15. Les jardins chinois/Lou Qingxi；traduit du chinois par Chen Shun. Pékin：China intercontinental Press，2003. 1 v.（134 p.）：ill. en noir et en coul.；23cm. ISBN：7508503686，7508503684
《中国园林》，楼庆西著；陈顺译.五洲传播出版社.

(1)［Beijing］：China Intercontinental Press，2011. 163 pages：color illustrations；23cm. ISBN：7508520568，7508520564.（Collection culture chinoise）

16. La Grande Muraille de Chine et ses légendes/par Luo Zhewen et Zhao Luo. Beijing，China：Éditions en Langues Étrangères，1986. 79 pages：illustrations；26cm.
《中国的万里长城》，罗哲文，赵洛著.

17. Jie shuo ping yao -PHISTOIRE DE PINGYAO. Tai yuan：Shan xi ke xue ji zhu chu ban she，2005. 20cm. ISBN：7537724946，7537724944
《解说平遥》，唐稀林编著；孙福兰译.山西科学技术出版社.本书内容是平遥古城概述，平遥古城景点介绍.

K54　旅游地理

1. Tourisme/par le Comité de rédaction de la collection "Connaissance de la Chine". Beijing：Éditions en Langues Étrangères，1985. 169 p.：ill.；19cm.
《旅游》，《中国概况丛书》编辑委员会编.

2. Guide de Chine. Beijing：Éditions en Langues Étrangères，1989. 531 pages：illustrations（some color），maps；19cm.
《中国旅游指南》，齐星著.

K6　人物传记和回忆录

1. Lieou Hou-lan：histoire d'une jeune révolutionnaire/par Liang Sing. Pékin：Éditions en Langues Étrangères，1960. 88 p.，couv. ill.［Ech. int. 1273—61］；In—16（18cm.）
《刘胡兰小传》，梁星著.

2. Li Che-tchen，grand pharmacologiste de la Chine ancienne：par Tchang Houei-kien. Pékin：Éditions en Langues Étrangères，1960. 62 p.，pl.，couv. ill.［Ech. int. 6671—60］；In—16（18cm.）
《李时珍-中国古代伟大的药物学家》，张慧剑著；蒋兆和图.

3. Autobiographie：mes années d'enfance/par Kouo Mo-jo. Traduit du chinois par P. Ryckmans.［Paris］Gallimard，

1970. 197 pages；23cm.（Connaissance de l'Orient，33. Série chinoise）

《郭沫若自传：我的童年》，郭沫若著；Ryckmans, P. 译.

(1)[Paris]：Gallimard, 1978. 190 p. : couv. ill. ; 23cm.（Connaissance de l'Orient：Série chinoise；33）

4. Zhou Enlai：profil/Percy Jucheng Fang, Lucy Guinong J. Fang. Beijing, China：Éditions en Langues Étrangères, 1989. 300 p. : ill. ; 21cm. ISBN：7119006282, 7119006284.

《周恩来传略》，方钜成，姜桂侬著.

5. La Vie de Luxun/par Lin Zhihao；traduction du Groupe Luxun de l'Université de Paris VIII. Beijing, Chine：Éditions en Langues Étrangères, 1990. 2 vol. : ill. ; 21cm. ISBN：7119005642 (v. 1), 7119005645 (v. 1), 7119009168 (v. 2), 7119009162(v. 2)

《鲁讯传》（上），林志浩著.

6. La vie de Luxun/par Lin Zhihao；traduction du Groupe Luxun de l'Université de Paris VIII. Beijing：Éditions en Langues Étrangères, 1990. 2 volumes：illustrations, portraits；21cm. ISBN：7119005642 (v. 1), 7119005645 (v. 1), 7119009168 (v. 2), 7119009162 (v. 2)

《鲁讯传》（下），林志浩著.

7. Mille facettes de la Chine/Lisa Carducci. Beijing：Éditions en Langues Érangères, 2006. 300 p. , [1] p. de pl. : ill. en coul. ISBN：7119032153, 7119032151

《中国的百态人生：法文》，李莎著. 本书通过40篇专访，全方位地展示了改革开放后中国所经历的变化，以及形形色色的普通中国人的曲折经历、不同生活状态和复杂的思想.

8. Le Tyran de Nankin：empereur des Ming/Wu Han；biographie traduite du chinois par Nadine Perront. Arles；Paris：P. Picquier, 1991. 205 pages；21cm. ISBN：287730079X, 2877300797

《朱元璋传》，吴晗著；Perront, Nadine 译.

(1) L'empereur des Ming/Wu Han；biographie traduite du chinois par Nadine Perront. [Nouvelle éd.]. Arles：P. Picquier, Impr. Groupe Horizon, 2014. 1 vol. (237 p.)：couv. ill. en coul. ; 17cm. ISBN：2809710021, 2809710023.（Picquier poche）

9. Le petit soldat du Hunan：autobiographie/Shen Congwen；traduit du chinois et annoté par Isabelle Rabut. Paris：A. Michel, 1992. 246 p. : maps；20cm. ISBN：222605698X, 2226056986.（Grandes traductions）

《沈从文自传》，沈从文；Rabut, Isabelle 译.

(1) Paris：UGE, 1996. 1 vol. (246 p.)：couv. ill. ; 20cm. ISBN：2264001224, 2264001221.（10/18. Domaine étranger；2720）

10. Un style bien "chinois"：la carrière diplomatique de Wu Jianmin/Wang Fan. Beijing, Chine：Éditions en Langues Érangères, 2010. xi, 394 pages：illustrations；24cm. ISBN：7119060996, 7119060996

《中国风格：吴建民的大使生涯》，王凡著.

N 类　自然科学

N1　科技概况

1. Science et technologie en Chine：réforme et développement/par Ke Yan；traduit par Zhou Fayi. [China]：China Intercontinental Press, 2004. 193 pages：color illustrations；21cm. ISBN：750850643X, 7508506432.（Que sais-je sur la Chine?）

《中国科技：改革与发展》，柯雁著，王秉仪等译. 五洲传播出版社（中国基本情况丛书/郭长建主编）

2. Les quatre grandes decouvertes de la Chine antique/Zhuang Wei. Beijing：Éditions en Langues Étrangères, 1981. 98 pages：illustrations；19cm.

《中国古代四大发明》，庄葳著.

3. Les inventions de la Chine antique Deng Yinke；Jiang Lili, He Dan [trad.]. Beijing：China Intercontinental Press, 2010. 1 vol. (155 p.)：ill. , couv. ill. en coul. ; 23cm. ISBN：7508518893, 7508518896（Collection culture chinoise）

《中国古代发明》，邓荫柯著. 五洲传播出版社.

4. Les ponts de Chine：antiques et modernes. De l'antique pont de Zhaozhou au pont moderne de Nanjing sur le Yangtsé/Mao Yisheng. Beijing：Éditions en Langues Étrangères, 1980. 46 p

《中国的古桥和新桥：从赵州桥到南京长江大桥》，茅以升著.

5. L'art de l'horlogerie occidentale et la Chine/Zhang Pu et Guo Fuxiang. Pekin：China Intercontinental Press, 2005. 151 pages：color illustrations；26cm. ISBN：7508507290, 7508507293

《钟表的中国传奇》，张普，郭福详著；张宏，徐燕译. 五洲传播出版社. 代表了西方科技水平和工艺技艺的钟表，从17世纪初开始传入中国，它作为中外文化交流的重要载体，见证了中国明清以来吸收西方先进科技文明的历程.

N2　科技古籍法译

1. Traduction et examen d'un ancien ouvrage chinois intitulé "Tcheoupei", littéralement：Style ou signal dans une circonférence/par M. éd. Biot. [Paris]：Impr. royale, 1841. 49—6 p. ; in-8

《周髀》，Biot, édouard (1803—1850)译.

2. Industries anciennes et modernes de l'empire chinois：d'après des notices traduites du chinois/par M. Stanislas Julien. Paris：Eugène Lacroix, 1869 1 vol. (XIII-254 p.)：fac-sim. ; in-8

中华帝国工业之今昔. Julien, Stanislas(1799—1873)译. 本书包含对《天工开物》及《授时通考》的选译.

3. 天工开物：汉法对照/（明）宋应星著；潘吉星今译；萨比娜

·德巴尔比阿（De barbuat, Ssbine）法译. 北京：外文出版社，2016. 33，680 页；图；24cm. ISBN：7119102849.（大中华文库）

法文题名：Guide des procedes de fabrication

4. Résumé des principaux traités chinois sur la culture des muriers et l'éducation des vers à soi/traduit par Stanislas Julien,… （avec une introduction de M. Camille Beauvais）. Paris：Impr. royale, 1837. 224 p.

《桑蚕辑要》，高铨著；Julien, Stanislas（1799—1873）译.

5. Détails sur l'éducation des vers à soie dans le nord de la Chine（province du Hon-Pé）/traduits du chinois… par Stanislas Julien. Rodez：impr. de Carrère ainé, 1842. 14 p.

《河北的养蚕》，Julien, Stanislas（1799—1873）译.

6. Traité des plantes médicinales chinoises/par Jacques Roi. Paris, P. Lechevalier（impr. de A. Lahure）, 1955. 488 p.（Encyclopédie biologique. 47）

·《本草纲目》，李时珍著；Roi, Jacques 译.

7. Affaires résolues à l'ombre du poirier（Tang Yin Bi Shi）：un manuel chinois de jurisprudence et d'investigation policière du XIIIe siècle. Paris：Albin Michel, 2002. 248 pages. ISBN：2226131574, 2226131577.（Bibliothèque Albin Michel idées）

《棠阴比事》，桂万荣（生卒年不详，南宋人）；高罗佩（Gulik, Robert Hans van, 1910—1967）（荷兰汉学家）译；Bresner, Lisa（1971—）和 Limoni, Jacques 从英语转译成法语. 该书为法医学著作.

8. Le sublime discours de la fille candide：manuel d'érotologie chinoise/trad. et présenté par André Lévy. Arles：P. Picquier, Impr. France Quercy, 2004. 128 p.：ill., couv. ill. en coul.；17cm. ISBN：287730714X（br）, 2877307147（br）.（Picquier poche；224）

《素女妙论》，Lévy, André（1925—）译.（中医）

N3　环境保护

1. L'action écologique en Chine/Wang Yongchen. Beijing：Éditions on Langues Étrangères, 2006. 140 pages：color illustrations；21cm. ISBN：7119044729, 7119044729

《中国绿色行动》，汪永晨著；张玉元译.（中国的和平发展系列）

2. La politique et l'action de la Chine contre le changement climatique/Office d'information du Conseil des Affaires d'État de la République populaire de Chine. Bejing：Éditions en Langues Érangères, 2008. 59 pages；21cm. ISBN：7119052762, 7119052764

《中国应对气候变化的政策与行动》，中华人民共和国国务院新闻办公室发布.

3. La réduction des catastrophes naturelles en Chine/Office d'information du Conseil des Affaires d'État de la République populaire de Chine. Beijing：Éditions en Langues Étrangères, 2009. 48 pages；21cm. ISBN：

7119057019，7119057014

《中国的减灾行动》，中华人民共和国国务院新闻办公室［发布］

N4　陶瓷

1. Splendeur de la céramique chinoise/［Li Zhiyan, Cheng Wen；traduit par Xiang Kuiguan, Zhang Yuyuan］. Beijing：Éd. en Langues Étrangères, 1996. 220 p.：ill.；31cm. ISBN：7119011502, 7119011509.

《中国陶瓷简史》，李知宴，程雯著.

2. La ceramique/Li Zhiyan et Cheng Qinhua；traduction, Daniel Cogez. Beijing Éditions en Langues Étrangères 1ère éd. 2003. 101 p. il. col., mapa 18×20cm. ISBN：7119032119, 7119032115.（Culture of China＝中华风物＝Culture de la Chine）

《中国陶瓷》，李知宴，程钦华编著.

3. La céramique chinoise/Fang Lili；traduit par Meng Lina. Beijing：China Intercontiental Press, 2011. 159 pages：color illustrations；23cm. ISBN：7508520858, 7508520858.（Collection culture chinoise）

《中国陶瓷》，方李莉著. 五洲传播出版社.

4. Histoire et fabrication de la porcelaine chinoise/ouvrage traduit du chinois par M. Stanislas Julien, Notes par M. Alphonse Salvétat. Paris：Mallet-Bachelier, 1856. 1 vol. CXXXIII-320 p.

《中国陶器历史及其制作方法》，蓝浦著；Julien, Stanislas（1799—1873）译；Salvétat, Alphonse（1820—1882）注.

N5　服饰

1. Les habits traditionnelsits/Yuan Jieying. Beijing, Chine：Éd. en Langues Étrangères, 2003. 107 p.：ill. en coul.；17×19cm. ISBN：711903295X.

《中国传统服饰》，袁杰英主编.

2. Les vêtements chinois/Hua Mei；traduit par Li Ning. Beijing：China Intercontinental Press, 2011. ISBN：7508521015, 7508521013.（Collection culture chinoise）

《中国服饰》，华梅著. 五洲传播出版社.

N6　饮食文化

1. Les nourritures chinoises/Liu Junru；traduit par Gao Ruifeng. ［Beijing］：China Intercontinental Press, 2011. 164 pages：color illustrations；23cm. ISBN：7508520957；7508520955.（Collection culture chinoise）

《中国饮食》，刘军茹著. 五洲传播出版社.

2. Le thé et la culture chinoise/Wang Ling；traduit du chinois Wu Guoli, Wang Jinguan. Pékin：Éd. en Langues Étrangères, 2006. 1 v.（V—193 p.）：ill. en coul.；21cm. ISBN：7119021451，7119021454

《中国茶文化》，王玲著.

3. Le thé dans la culture chinoise/［Hu Kaimin；traduit par Zhang Yongzhao, Wang Mo］. Beijing：Éditions en

Langues Étrangères, 2009. 39 pages：color illustrations；21cm. ISBN：7119058528；7119058525

《中国的茶文化》，胡开敏编著

4. Le the Chinois/Liu Tong；traduit par Zhang Wen. Beijing：China Intercontinental Press，2011. 164 p.；col. ill.；23cm. ISBN：7508520773，7508520777. (Collection culture chinoise)

《中国茶》，刘彤编著. 五洲传播出版社.

5. Le the chinois/ecrit par Yizhou Wu，traduit par Linmin Zhang et Yiping Wang. Shanghai：Shanghai People's Publishing House；Lagardere Active International，2011. 159 pages：color illustrations；18cm. ISBN：7208088948，7208088942.

《中国茶》吴一舟著. 上海人民出版社.

6. Le classique du thé la manière traditionnelle de faire le thé de le boire. Westmount，Qŭ.，Desclez，1981. 180 pages illustrations. ISBN：2891420543，2891420549

《茶经》，陆羽（公元 733—804 年）

7. Vin & alcools Chinois/Li Zhengping. Beijing：China Intercontinental Press，2010. 138 p.：col. ill.；23cm. ISBN：7508519142，7508519140. (Collection culture chinoise)

《中国酒》，李争平编著. 五洲传播出版社.

Z 类　综合性文献

Z1　杂著

1. Les Avadanas：contes et apologues indiens inconnus jusqu'à ce jour，suivis de fables，de poésies et de nouvelles chinoises.../traduits par M. Stanislas Julien. Paris：B. Duprat，1859. 3 vol.

《印度中国喻言神话诗歌杂译集》，Julien，Stanislas（1799—1873）译.

2. Gia-Dinh-Thung-Chi. Histoire et description de la Basse Cochinchine，（pays de Gia-Dinh）；traduites pour la première fois，d'après le texte chinois original/par G. Aubaret. Paris：Impr. impériale，1863. XIII-359 p.

《嘉定通志》，郑怀德（1765—1825）著；Aubaret，Gabriel（1825—1894）译.

3. Les Documents chinois découverts par Aurel Stein dans les sables du Turkestan oriental. Publiés et traduits par Édouard Chavannes. Oxford：Impr. de l'université，1913. XXIII-232 p.，XXXVI pl.

Aurel Stein 在东突厥斯坦沙漠中发现的中国文献. 沙畹（Chavannes，édouard，1865—1918）（法国汉学家）译.

4. Le Kou-Wen chinois：recueil de textes avec introduction et notes/par Georges Margouliès. Paris：Libr. orientaliste P. Geuthner，1926. 1 vol.（CXXVII-464 p.）；25cm.

《古文析义》，林云铭著；Margouliès，Georges（1902—1972）译.（诗文集）

5. Adieux à la Chine：contes，calligraphies，poésies—/［recueillis par］Maurice Coyaud. Paris：P. A. F.，1989. 120 pages：illustrations；26cm.（Documents pour l'analyse du folklore. Série de loin；9）

Coyaud，Maurice 编译. 本书包含了对中国传说故事、书法和诗歌的选译.

6. Le Peintre et le poète：l'art de la contemplation/peintures et poèmes choisis et traduits par Cheng Wing fun & Hervé Collet. Millemont：Moundarren，1989. ISBN：2907312030，2907312035

画家与诗人：沉思的艺术. Cheng，Wing fun，Collet，Hervé 译. 本书包含对中国绘画及诗歌的选译.

7. Les fleurs antiques/présenté par Shan Sa；introduction et notes complèmentaires par Guy Rachet. Paris：Presses du Chatelet，2007. 512 pages：illustrations；22cm. ISBN：2845922365，2845922361.（Les fleurs de la pensée chinoise；t. 1）

Contents：vol. 1. Les fleurs antiques：Le livre des annales（Shujing），Le livre des chants（Shijing）—v. 2. Les fleurs du taoïsme：Le livre de la voie et de la vertu（Daodejing），Le vrai classique du vide parfait（Tchong Xu Zhen Jing），Nan hua zhen jing（oeuvre de Zhuangzi）—v. 3. Les fleurs du confucianisme：La grande étude（Daxue），L'invariable milieu（Zhongyong），Entretiens de Kongzi，Entretiens de Mengzi

山飒译；Rachet，Guy 注. 包括《书经》《诗经》《道德经》《庄子》《中庸》等的翻译.

第三编　中国文献德译书目

A 类　毛泽东著作及相关文献

A1　毛泽东著作

1. Über die Diktatur der Volksdemokratie/Tse-tung Mao. Peking：Fremdspr. Lit，1950. 25 S；20cm.
   《论人民民主专政》
   (1)Peking：Verl. f. fremdsprachige Literatur，1961. 27 S. 1 Titelb. 8
   (2)Über die Diktatur der Volksdemokratie：Geschrb. z. Feier d. 28. Jahrestags d. Kommunist. Partei Chinas (1. Juli 1949)/Mao Tse-tung. Berlin：Dietz，1951. 21 Seiten；8°
   (3)Berlin：Dietz，1952. 21 Seiten 8°
   (4)Berlin：Dietz，1955. 20 Seiten 8°
   (5)2. Aufl. Peking：Verl. für fremdsprachige Literatur，1961. 27 S. : Ill.
   (6)Über die demokratische Diktatur des Volkes/Mao Tse-Tung. Peking：Verlag für Fremdsprachige Literatur，1968. 35 S；16cm.

2. Einleitung zur Zeitschrift „Der Kommunist"/Mao Tse-Tung. Peking：Fremdsprach. Literatur，1953. 25 S. ；8°
   《"共产党人"发刊词》
   (1)Der Zeitschrift „Kommunist" zum Geleite/Mao Tsê-tung. Peking：Verl. f. fremdsprachige Literatur，1967. 35 S

3. Gegen den Liberalismus/Tse Tung Mao. Peking：Verl. f. Fremdsprachige Lit，1954. 7 S. ；19cm.
   《反对自由主义》
   (1)Peking：Verlag für Fremdsprachige Literatur，1966. 6 S. ；15cm.

4. Die Frage der Selbständigkeit in der Einheitsfront/Mao Tse-Tung. Peking：Verlag für fremdsprachige Literatur，1954. 10 p. ；19cm.
   《统一战线中的独立自主问题》
   (1)Die Frage der Unabhängigkeit und Selbständigkeit in der Einheitsfront/Mao Tse-tung. Peking：Verl. für fremdsprachige Literatur，1967. 10 S. kl. 8

5. Taktische Fragen der gegenwärtigen antijapanischen Einheitsfront/Tse-tung Mao. Peking：Verl. für fremdsprach. Literatur，1954. 20 S；8°
   《目前抗日统一战线中的策略问题》

6. Fragen des genossenschaftlichen Zusammenschlusses in der Landwirtschaft/Mao Tse-Tung. Berlin：Dietz，1956. 35 p. ；21cm.
   《关于农业合作化问题》
   (1)3 Aufl. Peking：Verl. für Fremdsprache Literatur，1960. 45 S.
   (2)Zur Frage des genossenschaftlichen Zusammenschlusses in der Landwirtschaft/ Mao Tsê-tung. (Neuaufl.). Peking：V. f. fremdsprachige Literatur，1968. 61 S.
   (3)Zur Frage des genossenschaftlichen Zusammenschlusses in der Landwirtschaft (31. Juli 1955). 4th ed. Peking：Verlag für Fremdsprachige Literatur，1976. 50 pages

7. Über die richtige Lösung von Widersprüchen im Volke [Rede]/Mao Tse-tung. Peking：Verl. f. fremdsprachige Literatur，1957. 78 S.
   《关于正确处理人民内部矛盾的问题》
   (1)Peking：Verlag für Fremdsprachige Literatur，1959. 78 p.
   (2)3. Aufl. (Neudurchges. übers.)，1960. 68 S. ：1 Titelbild；8
   (3) über die richtige Behandlung der Widersprüche im Volke/Mao Tse-tung；übers. Peking：Verlag für fremdsprachige Literatur，1968. 92 p. ；15cm.

8. Der Imperialismus und alle Reaktionäre sind Papiertiger/ [Mao Tse-tung]. Peking：Verl. f. fremdsprachige Literatur，1958. 134 S.
   《毛泽东同志论帝国主义和一切反动派都是纸老虎》

9. Wichtige Gespräche des Vorsitzenden Mao Tse-tung mit Persönlichkeiten aus Asien，Afrika und Lateinamerika. Peking：Verl. f. fremdsprachige Literatur，1960. 10
   《毛泽东主席同亚洲、美洲、拉丁美洲人士的几次重要讲话》
   (1)Peking：Verlag für Fremdsprachige Literatur，1965. 14 pages；15cm.

10. Reden auf der Beratung über Fragen der Literatur und Kunst in Yenan. /Mao Tsê-tung. Peking：Verl. für Fremdsprachige Literatur，1961. 61 S.
    《在延安文艺座谈会上的讲话》
    (1)Reden bei der Aussprache in Yenan über Literatur und Kunst/Mao Tse-tung. Peking：Verl. für fremdsprachige Literatur，1967. 75 S

11. Die Lage nach dem Sieg im Widerstandskrieg gegen die japanische Aggression und unser Kurs. Peking：Verl. für Fremdsprachige Literatur，1961. 28 S.

《抗日战争胜利后的时局和我们的方针》

(1)Peking：Verlag für Fremdsprachige Literatur，1967. 34 S. ；13cm.

（2）Peking：Verlag für Fremdensprachige Literatur，1968. IV，36 S.

12. Über die Verhandlungen in Tschungking/Mao Tsê-tung. Peking：Verl. f. fremdsprachige Literatur，1961. 28 S. 1 Titelb. 8

《关于重庆谈判》

(1)Peking：Verl. f. fremdspr. Lit，1965. 39 S.

(2)Peking：Verlag für Fremdsprachige Literatur，1969. 38 pages

13. Interview mit der amerikanischen Korrespondentin Anna Louise Strong. Peking：Verl. für Fremdsprachige Literatur，1961. III，9 S.

《和美国记者安娜·路易斯·斯特朗的谈话》

（1）Gespräch mit der Amerikanischen Korrespondentin Anna Louise Strong/Mao Tse-Tung. Peking：Verlag für fremdsprachige Literatur，1967. 13 p. ；15cm.

14. Die gegenwärtige Lage und unsere Aufgaben. Peking：Verl. für Fremdsprachige Literatur，1961. 41 S.

《目前形势和我们的任务》

(1)Peking：Verl. für Fremdsprachige Literatur，1969. 48 S.

15. Über die Stärkung des Systems der Parteikomitees/Mao Tsê-tung. Peking：Verl. f. Fremdsprachige Literatur，1961. 11 S. 1 Titelbild 8

《关于健全党委制》

(1)Peking：Verl. für Fremdsprachige Literatur，1967. 15 S

(2)Peking：Verlag für Fremdsprachige Literatur，1971. 19 S. ；13cm.

16. Die Revolution zu Ende führen. Peking：Verlag für fremdsprachige Literatur，1961. IV，24 S.

《将革命进行到底》

(1)Peking：Verl. für Fremdsprachige Literatur，1967. 28 S.

17. Bericht an die 2. Plenartagung des VII. Zentralkomitees der Kommunistischen Partei Chinas/Mao Tsê-tung. Peking：Verl. f. Fremdsprach. Literatur，1961. 32 S. 1 Titelbild 8

《在中国共产党第七届中央委员会第二次全体会议上的报告》

(1)Bericht an die 2. Planartagung des 7. Zentralkomitees der Kommunistischen Partei Chinas/Mao Tse-tung. Peking：Verl. für fremdsprachige Literatur，1967. 39 S.

(2)Bericht auf der zweiten Plenartagung des vom siebten Parteitag gewählten Zentralkomitees der Kommunistischen Partei Chinas/Mao Tse-tung. Peking：Verl. für Fremdsprachige Literatur，1968.

35 S. ；18cm.

18. Kommentare zum Weissbuch der Regierung der USA/Mao Tse-tung. Peking：Verlag für fremdsprachige Literatur，1961. 65 S.

《评白皮书》

（1）Kommentare zum Weissbuch. /Mao Tsetung. Peking：Verl. f. fremdsprachige Literatur，1969. 81 S.

19. Über Literatur und Kunst/Mao Tse-tung. Peking：Verl. f. fremdsprachige Lit. ，1961. 175 S.

《毛泽东论文学与艺术》

(1)Peking：Verlag für Fremdsprachige Literatur，1977. 148 pages

20. Analyse der Klassen in der chinesischen Gesellschaft. /Mao Tsê-tung. Peking：Verl. f. Fremdsprachige Literatur，1962. 18 S. 1 Titel bild 8

《中国社会各阶层的分析》

21. Über die Berichtigung falscher Anschauungen in der Partei/Mao Tsê-tung. Peking：Verl. f. Fremdsprachige Literatur，1962. 19 S. 1 Titelbild 8

《关于纠正党内的错误思想》

(1)Peking：Verlag für fremdsprachige Literatur，1967. 26 p. ；15cm.

22. Über die Praxis über d. Zusammenhang von Erkenntnis u. Praxis，von Wissen u. Handeln/Mao Tsê-tung. Peking：Verl. f. Fremdsprachige Literatur，1962. 26 S. 1 Titelbild 8

《实践论》

（1）Über die Praxis über den Zusammenhang von Erkenntnis und Praxis，von Wissen und Handeln/Mao Tse-tung. Peking：Verl. für Fremdsprach. Literatur，1967. 38 S.

23. Die Richtung der Jugendbewegung/Mao Tsê-tung. Peking：Verl. f. Fremdsprach. Literatur，1962. 20 S. 1 Titelbild 8

《青年运动的方向》

（1）Die Orientierung der Jugendbewegung. Peking：Verlag für Fremdsprachige Literatur，1967. 27 S.

24. Die chinesische Revolution und die kommunistische Partei Chinas/Mao Tsê-tung. Peking：Verl. f. Fremdsprach. Literatur，1962. 63 S. 1 Titelbild 8

《中国革命和中国共产党》

(1)Peking：Verl. für Fremdsprachige Literatur，1968. 79 S.

25. Über einige wichtige Fragen in der gegenwärtigen Politik der Partei/Mao Tsê-tung. Peking：Verl. f. fremdsprachige Literatur，1962. 14 S. 1 Titelb. 8

《关于目前党的政策中的几个重要问题》

(1)Peking：Verl. für fremdsprachige Literatur，1967. 19 S

26. Rede auf einer Kaderkonferenz im befreiten Gebiet Schansi-Suiyüan/Mao Zedong. Peking：Verl. f. Fremd-

sprachige Literatur,1962. 22 S. ：1 Titelbild；8

《在晋绥干部会议上的讲话》

27. Warum kann die chinesische rote Macht bestehen? /Mao Tsê-tung. Peking：Verl. f. Fremdsprach. Literatur, 1963. 18 S. ：1 Titelbild；8

《中国的红色政权为什么能够存在?》

(1)Peking：Verl. f. Fremdsprach. Literatur, 1965. 24 S.

28. Den Arbeitsstil der Partei verbessern!：Rede, gehalten am 1. 2. 1942/Mao Tse-tung. Peking：Verl. f. Fremdsprach. Literatur, 1963. 30 S.

《整顿党的作风》

(1)Peking： Verlag für Fremdsprachige Literatur [Waiwen chubanshe], 1965. 40 S.

29. Über die Koalitionsregierung/Mao Tsê-tung. Peking：Verl. f. Fremdsprachige Literatur, 1963. 126 S. 1 Titelbild 8

《论联合政府》

(1)Peking：Verl. f. fremdsprachige Literatur, 1969. 163 S.

30. Ein Funke kann die ganze Steppe in Brand setzen/Mao Tsê-tung. Peking：Verl. f. Fremdsprach. Literatur, 1964. 29 S.

《星星之火,可以燎原》

(1)Peking：Verl. f. Fremdsprach. Literatur, 1966. 29 S.

31. Über den Widerspruch/Mao Tsê-tung. Peking：Verl. f. fremdsprachige Literatur, 1964. 85 S.

《矛盾论》

32. Gegen die Buchgläubigkeit (Mai 1930)/Mao Tsê-tung. Peking：Verl. f. fremdsprachige Literatur, 1965. 20 S.

《反对本本主义》

33. Mehr Sorge um das Alltagsleben der Volksmassen, mehr Aufmerksamkeit den Arbeitsmethoden/Mao Tse-tung. Peking：Verl. f. Fremdsprach. Literatur, 1965. 11 S.

《关系群众生活,注意工作方法》

34. Wenn der Feind uns bekämpft, ist das gut und nicht schlecht/Mao Tse-tung. Peking：V. f. Fremdsprachige Literatur [Waiwen chubanshe], 1965. 6 S.

《被敌人反对是好事而不是坏事》

35. Vorwort und Nachwort zur Untersuchung der Verhältnisse im Dorf/Mao Tse-tung. Peking：Verl. f. Fremdsprach. Literatur, 1965. 14 S.

《"农村调查"的序言和跋》

36. Lasst uns unser Studium reorganisieren/Mao Tsê-tung. Peking：Verl. f. Fremdsprach. Literatur, 1965. 19 S.

《改造我们的学习》

37. Gegen den Schematismus in der Parteiarbeit/Mao Tse-tung. Peking：Verl. f. fremdsprachige Literatur,1965. 38 S.

《反对党八股》

38. Zu einigen Fragen der Führungsmethoden/Mao Tse-tung. Peking：Verl. f. Fremdsprach. Literatur, 1965.

14 S.

《关于领导方法的若干问题》

39. Dem Volke dienen/Mao Tsê-tung. Peking：Verl. f. Fremdsprach. Literatur, 1965. 10 S.

《为人民服务》

40. Yü Gung versetzt Berge/Mao Tsê-tung. Peking：Verl. f. fremdsprachige Literatur, 1965. 8 S.

《愚公移山》

41. Rede auf der Landeskonferenz der KP Chinas über Propagandaarbeit (12. März 1957)/Mao Tsê-tung. Peking：Verl. für Fremdsprachige Literatur, 1965. 36 S.

《在中国共产党全国宣传工作会议上的讲话》

42. Woher kommt das richtige Denken der Menschen? Mai 1963/Tsê-tung Mao. Peking：Verl. für fremdsprachige Literatur, 1965. 3 S.

《人的正确思想是从哪里来的》

43. Vier philosophische Monographien/Tsê-tung Mao. Peking：Verl. f. fremdsprach. Literatur, 1965. 163 S. 1 Titelbild 8

《毛泽东的四篇哲学论文》

44. Untersuchungsbericht über die Bauernbewegung in Hunan/Tse-tung Mao. Peking：Verl. f. Fremdsprachige Literatur, 1966. 86 S.

《湖南农民运动考察报告》

45. Taktische Fragen der gegenwärtigen Einheitsfront gegen die japanische Aggression/Mao Tsê-tung. Peking：Verl. f. Fremdsprach. Literatur, 1965. 24 S. kl. 8

《目前统一战线中的策略问题》

46. Der Platz der Kommunistischen Partei Chinas im nationalen Krieg/Mao Tsê-tung. Peking：Verl. f. fremdsprachige Literatur, 1966. 42 S

《中国共产党在民族战争中的地位》

47. Organisieren/Tse-tung Mao. Peking：Verl. für Fremdsprachige Literatur, 1966. 23 S.

《组织起来》

48. Fünf Dokumente über Literatur und Kunst/Mao Tse-tung. Peking：Verl. für fremdsprachige Literatur, 1967. 11 S

《毛主席关于文学艺术的五个文件》

49. Analyse der Klassen in der chinesischen Gesellschaft. Peking：Verlag für Fremdsprachige Literatur, 1967. 23 pages

《中国社会各阶级的分析》

50. Dem Volke dienen!；and, Dem Andenken Bethunes；and, Yu gung versetzt Berge/Mao Tse-tung. Peking：Verlag für Fremdsprachige Literatur, 1967. 18 pages； 15cm.

《为人民服务 纪念白求恩 愚公移山》

51. Ausgewählte Werke 1/Mao Tse-Tung. Peking：Verl. für fremdsprach. Literatur, 1968. 412 S.

《毛泽东选集》,第一卷.

52. Ausgewählte Werke 2/Mao Tse-Tung. Peking：Verl. für fremdsprach. Literatur，1968. 560 S.

《毛泽东选集》，第二卷.

53. Ausgewählte Werke 3/Mao Tse-Tung. Peking：Verl. für fremdsprach. Literatur，1968. 348 S.

《毛泽东选集》，第三卷.

54. Ausgewählte Werke 4/Mao Tse-Tung. Peking：Verl. für fremdsprach. Literatur，1968. 496 S.

《毛泽东选集》，第四卷.

55. Ausgewählte Werke 5/Mao Tse-Tung. Peking：Verl. für fremdsprachige Literatur，1978. 594 S.

《毛泽东选集》，第五卷.

56. Vorsitzender Mao Tse-Tung über den Volkskrieg. Peking：Verlag für Fremdsprachige Literatur，1968. 57 pages

《毛主席论人民战争》

57. Worte des Vorsitzenden Mao Tse-tung. Peking：Verlag für Fremdsprachige Literatur，1968. v，370 pages：portraits；11cm.

《毛主席语录》

58. Der Kampf im Djinggang-Gebirge/Tse-tung Mao. Peking：Verl. für Fremdsprachige Literatur，1968. 80 S.

《井冈山的斗争》

59. Strategische Probleme des revolutionären Krieges in China/Tse-tung Mao. Peking：Verl. für Fremdsprachige Literatur，1968. 180 S.

《中国革命战争的战略问题》

60. Strategische Probleme des partisanenkriegs gegen die japanische Aggression/Mao Tse-tung. Peking：Verlag für Fremdsprachige Literatur，1968. 84 S.；13cm.

《抗日游击战争的战略问题》

61. Über den langwierigen Krieg/Mao Tsê-tung. Peking：Verl. f. fremdsprachige Literatur，1968. 210 S.

《论持久战》

62. Probleme des Krieges und der Strategie/Mao Tsê-tung. Peking：Verl. f. fremdsprachige Literatur，1968. 41 S.

《战争和战略问题》

63. Über die neue Demokratie/Mao Tsê-tung. Peking：Verl. f. fremdsprachige Literatur，1968. 112 S.

《新民主主义论》

64. Mao Tsetung ausgewählte militärische Schriften. Peking：Verl. für fremdsprachige Literatur，1969. 499 S.

《毛泽东军事文选》

65. Fünf Schriften. Peking：Verlag für Fremdsprachige Literatur，1976. 40 pages

《毛主席的五篇著作》

66. Über die Taktik im Kampf gegen den japanischen Imperialismus/Mao Tsetung. Peking：Verl. f. fremdsprachige Literatur，1969. 63 S.

《论反对日本帝国主义的策略》

67. Die Aufgaben der Kommunistischen Partei Chinas in der Periode des Widerstandes gegen die japanische Aggression/ Mao Tsê-tung. Peking：Verl. f. Fremdsprachige Literatur，1969. 61 S.

《中国共产党在抗日时期的任务》

68. Der politische Kurs，die Massnahmen und die Perspektiven im Kampf gegen den Angriff Japans（23. Juli 1937)/Mao Tsetung. Peking，1969. 21 p.

《反对日本进攻的方针、办法和前途》

69. Für die Mobilisierung aller Kräfte zur Erringung des Sieges im Widerstandskrieg gegen die japanische Aggression/Mao Tse-tung. Peking：V. f. Fremdsprachige Literatur，1969. 16 S.

《为动员一切力量争取抗战胜利而斗争》

70. Die Lage im Widerstandskrieg gegen die japanische Aggression nach dem Fall von Schanghai und Taiyüan und unsere Aufgaben/Mao Tsê-tung. Peking：Verl. f. fremdsprachige Literatur，1969. 32 S.

《上海太原失陷以后抗日战争的形势和任务》

71. Für eine neudemokratische konstitutionelle Regierungsform/ Mao Tsê-tung. Peking：Verl. f. fremdsprachige Literatur，1969. 26 S.

《新民主主义的宪政》

72. Über unsere Politik/Mao Tsetung. Peking：Verl. f. fremdsprachige Literatur，1969. 22 S.

《论政策》

73. Rede vor der Volksversammlung des Grenzgebiets Schensi-Kansu-Ningsia（21. Nov. 1941)/Mao Tsetung. Peking：Verl. f. fremdsprachige Literatur，1969. 9 S.

《在陕甘宁边区参议会的演说》

74. Man muss lernen，auf wirtschaftlichem Gebiet zu arbeiten.（10. Januar 1945).［übers.］. Peking：Verlag für Fremdsprachige Literatur，1969. IV，20 S.

《必须学会做经济工作》

75. Revolutionäre Kräfte der ganzen Welt，vereinigt euch，kämpft gegen die imperialistische Aggression!（Nov. 1948)/Mao Tsetung. Peking：Verl. f. fremdsprachige Literatur，1969. 10 S.

《全世界革命力量团结起来,反对帝国主义的侵略》

76. Die gegenwärtige Lage und die Aufgaben der Partei：（10. Oktober 1939)/Mao Tsetung；［übers. nach dem Originaltext］. Peking：Verlag für fremdsprachige Literatur，1971. 8 p.；13cm.

《目前形势和党的任务》

77. Alle antijapanischen Kräfte zusammenschliessen，gegen die antikommunistischen Ultrakonservativen kämpfen(1. Februar 1940). Peking：Verlag für Fremdsprachige Literatur，1971. 21 pages

《团结一切抗日力量,反对反共顽固派》

78. Bericht auf der Zweiten Plenartagung des vom Siebten Parteitag gewählten Zentralkomitees der Kommunistischen Partei Chinas（5. März 1949). /Peking：Verlag

für Fremdsprachige Literatur, 1973. 27 pages

《在中国共产党第七届中央委员会第二次全体会议上的报告》毛泽东

79. Fünf philosophische Monographien/Mao Tsetung. Peking: Verl. für Fremdsprach. Literatur, 1976. 175 S.

《毛主席的五篇哲学著作》

80. Über die zehn grossen Beziehungen: (25. April 1956)/ Mao Tsetung. Peking: Verlag für Fremdsprachige Literatur, 1977. 36 S. ; 19cm.

《论十大关系》

81. Rede auf der vom Zentralkomitee der Kommunistischen Partei Chinas einberufenen erweiterten Arbeitskonferenz (30. Januar 1962). Peking: Verlag für Fremdsprachge Literatur, 1978. 39 pages

《在扩大的中央工作会议上的讲话》

82. Gedichte/Mao Tsetung. Peking: Verlag für Fremdsprachige Literatur, 1978. 71 S. : 1 ill. ; 22cm.

《毛泽东诗词》

83. 39 Gedichte/Mao Tse-tung; übersetzt und mit einem politish-literarischen Essay erläutert von Joachim Schickel. Frankfurt am Main: Suhrkamp, 1978. 202 pages; 18cm. ISBN: 3518015834 3518015834. (Bibliothek Suhrkamp; Bd. 583)

《毛泽东诗词 39 首》, Schickel, Joachim 译.

A2　毛泽东研究相关著作

1. Ewiger Ruhm dem Vorsitzenden Mao Tsetung: dem grossen Führer und Lehrer. /Peking: Verlag für Fremdsprachige Literatur, 1976. 43 pages

《伟大的领袖和导师毛泽东主席永垂不朽》

2. Die Theorie des Vorsitzenden Mao über die Dreiteilung der Welt ist ein bedeutender Beitrag zum Marxismus-Leninismus/ von d. Red. d. „Renmin Ribao", (1. November 1977). Peking: Verlag für Fremdsprachige Literatur, 1977. 89 S. ; 19cm.

《毛主席关于三个世界划分的理论是对马克思列宁主义的重大贡献》

3. Weiterführung der Revolution unter der Dikatur des Proletariats bis zur Vollendung: zum Studium von Band V der „Ausgewählte Werke Mao Tsetungs"/Hua Guo-Feng. Peking: Verlag für fremdsprachige Literatur, 1977. 45 pages; 19cm.

《把无产阶级专政下的继续革命坚持到底：学习〈毛泽东选集〉第五卷》, 华国锋.

B 类　哲学、宗教

B1　中国哲学

1. Lebensweisheit aus dem Reich der Mitte/ges. u. aus d.

Chines. übers. von Jörg Weigand. München: Heyne, 1982. 76 S. : Ill. ;18cm. ISBN: 3453421011, 3453421019. (Heyne-Bücher/09;90)

中国哲学. Weigand, Jörg 译.

2. Wenn ein Blatt sich bewegt, kann auch der Ast erzittern: Gedanken chinesischer Weiser/Hrsg. : [Heinrich Tieck. übertrg aus d. chines. Urtexten von Anna v. Rottauscher]. Wien; Leipzig: W. Scheuermann - [Leipzig]: [Volckmar], 1938. 90 S. : Mit 10 Bildern;8. (Die Tieck-Bücher)

中国贤者思想. Rottauscher, Anna von (1892—1970)(奥地利学者)译.

(1)[übertr. aus den chines. Urtexten von Anna v. Rottauscher. Mit 10 Bildern nach alten chinesischen Meistern]. 10. Aufl. Wien: Scheuermann, 1948. 89 S. ; 8. (Die Tieck-Bücher)

(2)11. Aufl. Wien: Scheuermann, 1950. 90 S. ; 8. (Die Tieck-Bücher)

(3)12. Aufl. Wien: Scheuermann, 1951. 90 S. ; 5 Bl. Abb. ; 8 (Die Tieck-Bücher)

(4)13. Aufl. Wien: Scheuermann, 1955. 90 S. ; 5 Bl. Abb. ; 8 (Die Tieck-Bücher)

(5)14. Aufl. Wien: Scheuermann, 1957. 90 S. ; 5 Bl. Abb. ; 8 (Die Tieck-Bücher)

(6)15. Aufl. Wien: Scheuermann, 1961. 90 S. ; 8 (Die Tieck-Bücher)

(7)16. Aufl. Wien: Scheuermann, 1964. 90 S. ; 8 (Die Tieck-Bücher)

(8)17. Aufl. Wien: Scheuermann, 1968. 90 S. ; Mit 10 Bildern nach alten chines. Meistern; 8 (Die Tieck-Bücher)

3. Nur wer den Gipfel des Berges erstiegen, vermag in die weiteste Ferne zu sehen: Chinesische Weisheiten und Geschichten/[Hrsg. : Heinrich Tieck]. [übertr. aus d. chinesischen Urtexten von Anna v. Rottauscher] 2. Aufl. Wien: Scheuermann, 1951. 94 S. : Mit 4 mehrfarb. Bildtaf. nach alten chinesischen Meistern; 8.

中国智慧及历史. Rottauscher, Anna von (1892—1970)(奥地利学者)译.

(1)3. Aufl. Wien: Scheuermann, 1954. 94 S. ; 8.

(2)4. Aufl. Wien: Scheuermann, 1958. 94 S. ; 8.

(3)5. Aufl. Wien: Scheuermann, 1963. 94 S. ; 8.

(4)6. Aufl. Salzburg, Stuttgart, Zürich: Verlag Das Bergland-Buch, 1973. 94 S. : 4 Ill. (farb.);19cm.

(5)7. , neubearb. u. erg. Aufl. Salzburg: Verlag Das Bergland-Buch, 1978. 103 S. : Ill. ; 20cm.

4. So sprach der Weise: chinesisches Gedankengut aus drei Jahrtausenden/hrsg. , aus dem Chinesischen übertr. v. Ernst Schwarz. Berlin: Rütten und Loening, 1981. 701 p. : ill. ; 22cm.

中国三千年思想. Schwarz, Ernst 译.

(1)2. Aufl. Berlin: Rütten und Loening, 1986. 701 S. :

Ill.；22cm.

(2)3. Aufl. Berlin：Rütten und Loening，1988. 701 S.：Ill.；22cm. ISBN：3352000645，3352000646.

5. So sprach der Weise：chinesische Lebensweisheiten/Ernst Schwarz. Augsburg：Bechtermünz，2000. 391 pages；illustrations；22cm. ISBN：3828948332，；3828948334
中国哲学格言. Schwarz，Ernst 译.

6. Vom Weg allen Geistes：Sentenzen aus d. alten China/[ausgew. u. aus d. Chines. übertr. von Ernst Schwarz]. Berlin：Rütten und Loening，1985. 256 S.：Ill.；11cm.
中国古代思想哲学格言选. Schwarz，Ernst 选译.

7. Chinesische Weisheiten：vom Weg allen Geistes/aus dem Chinesischen übersetzt und herausgegeben von Ernst Schwarz. Köln： Anaconda， 2016. 144 Seiten：Illustrationen；20cm. ISBN：3730603574，3730603574.
中国古代思想哲学格言选. Schwarz，Ernst 选译.

B2 中国各代哲学著作与研究

B21 诸子前哲学

B211 周易

1. I ging；das Buch der Wandlungen/Aus dem Chinesischen verdeutscht und erläutert von Richard Wilhelm. Jena：Eugen Diederichs，1923. XIII，288，267 S. (Religion und Philosophie Chinas)
《易经》，卫礼贤(Wilhelm，Richard，1873—1930)译.

(1)Jena：Eugen Diederichs，1924. 3 Teile in 2 Bden. (XIII-285 p.；267 p.)；22cm. (Religion und Philosophie Chinas).

(2)Düsseldorf：Eugen Diederichs，1925. volumes 22cm.

(3)Düsseldorf，Köln：Eugen Diederichs，1950. XIII，288 S 8. (Religion und Philosophie Chinas).

(4)Düsseldorf：Eugen Diederichs，1951. 643 S.

(5)I Ging：das Buch der Wandlungen Buch 3. Düsseldorf，Köln：Diederichs，1951. 267 S. 8. (Religion und Philosophie Chinas).

(6)I Ging：das Buch der Wandlungen Buch 1/2. Düsseldorf，Köln：Diederichs，1951. XIII，288 S 8. (Religion und Philosophie Chinas).

(7)Düsseldorf，Köln：Eugen Diederichs，1956. 3 v. in 1 (643 p.)；19cm.

(8)Düsseldorf：E. Diederichs. 1960. 644 pages；18cm. (Diederichs Taschenausgaben；；6)

(9)Düsseldorf：E. Diederichs. 1967. 643 pages；19cm. ISBN：3424000612，3424000610. (Diederichs-Taschenausgaben，6)

(10)Düsseldorf：E. Diederichs. 1970. 643 pages；19cm. ISBN：3424000612，3424000610. (Die Philosophie Chinas)

(11)Düsseldorf：E. Diederichs. 1971. 643 pages 8°.

ISBN：3424000612，3424000610. (Die Philosophie Chinas：[In 7 Bden.])

(12)Düsseldorf：E. Diederichs. 1972. 643 pages；19cm. ISBN：342400460X，3424004601；3424000612，3424000610. (Die Philosophie Chinas)

(13)Düsseldorf；Köln：E. Diederichs. [2. Aufl.]1974. 643 pages；19cm. ISBN：342400460X，3424004601，3424000612，3424000610. (Die Philosophie Chinas)

(14)Düsseldorf：E. Diederichs. 1976. 643 pages；19cm. ISBN：3424000612，3424000610；342400460X；3424004601. (Die Philosophie Chinas)

(15)Zürich：Ex Libris [Lizenzausg. d. Diederichs Verl.，Düsseldorf，Köln]，1976. 643 S. (Die Philosophie Chinas).

(16)Düsseldorf：E. Diederichs，1978，(c)1956. 3 volumes in 1 (643 pages)；19cm. ISBN：3424000612，3424000610

(17)Düsseldorf：Diederichs，1981，(c)1956. 643 pages；19cm. ISBN：3424000612，3424000610，3424007250，3424007251. (Die Philosophie Chinas)

(18)Düsseldorf：Eugen Diederichs Verl.，1986. 643 s.；20cm. ISBN：3424000612，3424000610

(19)München：Eugen Diederichs Verlag，1988. 643，[1] s.；19cm. ISBN：3424000612，3424000610.

2. I ging：Text und Materialien/aus dem Chines. übers. von Richard Wilhelm. Diederichs，Ulf. Düsseldorf：E. Diederichs，1924. 352 pages；19cm. (Diederichs Gelbe Reihe；China im Umbruch；1)
《易经》，卫礼贤(Wilhelm，Richard，1873—1930)译.

(1) München：E. Diederichs，1973. 352 S.；19cm. ISBN：3424005010，3424005011

(2)4. Aufl. Düsseldorf：E. Diederich，1978. 1 Band.

(3)5. Aufl. 347 [5] pages；19cm. Düsseldorf；Köln：Diederichs，1980. ISBN：3424005010；3424005011. (Diederichs Gelbe Reihe；China im Umbruch；1)

(4)8. Aufl. Köln：Diederichs，1982. 347 [5] pages；19cm. ISBN：3424005010，3424005011

(5)Kreuzlingen；München：Hugendubel，2003. 344 Seiten；20cm. ISBN：3720524752，3720524759

(6)Kreuzlingen：H. Hugendubel，2008. 344 S.；20cm. ISBN：3720530545，372053054X

3. I Ging：das chinesische Orakelbuch/In der Bearbeitung von Bill Behm. Klagenfurt：J. Leon Sen.，1940. 139 pages；21cm.
《〈易经〉：中国占筮书》，Brehm，Bill(1896—)改编.

(1)München：Drei Eichen Verl.，1955. 173 S.

4. I ging：das Buch der Wandlungen/aus dem chinesischen neu übertragen. Zürich：W. Classen，1949. 95，[1] pages. 20cm. (Vom Dauernden in der Zeit；Nr. 48)
《〈易经〉：据中文新译》，Schubert，Mario 译.

5. I Ging，Buch des Stetigen und der Wandlung：philosophia perennis/[Von] E. H. Gräfe. Oberstedten，Oberursel：

Gräfe, 1967. 167 S.

《易经》，Gräfe, Emil Hugo (1896—1974)译.

6. Das alte chinesische Orakel- und Weisheitsbuch I Ging：Konflikte klären, Zweifel lösen/interpretiert u. hrsg. von Peter H. Offfermann. München：Goldmann, 1975. 416 pages：illustrations；18cm. ISBN：3442108993, 3442108992. (Ein Goldmann-Taschenbuch；10899；Goldmann-Ratgeber)

《易经》，Offermann, Peter H. 译.

7. Das Münzorakel des I Ging：das chinesische Orakel zur Entdeckung des Unbewussten/Da Liu；[Übersetzung von Sam-lan]. Frankfurt：Ullstein, 1978. 226 pages：illustrations；20cm. ISBN：3550077874；3550077876.

《易经金钱卦》，Sam-lan 译自英译本.

(1)1981. 226 pages：illustrations；18cm. ISBN：3548340792；3548340791. (Ullstein Sachbuch)

8. I Ging：das chinesische Münzorakel/Roderic Sorrell, Amy Max Sorrell. Übers. aus dem Engl. von Angela Schumitz. Niedernhausen/Ts.：Falken-Verlag, 1996. 224 pages：illustrations；21cm. ISBN：3635602531；3635602535.

易经金钱卦. Roderic Sorrell 与 Amy Max Sorrell 合译.

9. Das I-Ging-Orakel：der Welt ältestes System der Zukunftsvorhersage, neu dargestellt und ausgelegt für die praktische Anwendung durch den modernen Menschen/Sam Reifler. Freiburg i. Br：Bauer, 1983. 351 Seiten. ISBN：3762606056, 3762606055. (Esotera Taschenbücherei)

《易经》，Reifler, Sam 译.

10. I ging；das Buch der Wandlungen/neu übers. von Gia Fu Feng... Aus dem Engl. übertr. von Sylvia Wetzel. [Zsgest. von Rosi Schattevoy und Sue Bailey]. München；Zürich：Theseus-Verl. , 1991. 476 S.：ill. , graph. Darst. ；22cm. ISBN：989620047X（Berlin）；3896200471（Berlin）；3859360477（Zürich）；3859360471（Zürich）

《易经》，由冯家福(1919—1985)根据 Sylvia Wetzel 英译而转译.

(1)Norderstedt Books on Demand, 2015. 468 S. 215 mm×135 mm, 730 g. ISBN：3734767012；3734767016.

11. Yijing：das Buch der Wandlungen：erstmalig von Grund auf entschlüsselt und neu aus dem chinesischen Urtext übersetzt/von Fiedeler, Frank. München：Diederichs, 1996. 591 s.：rys.；22cm. ISBN：3424013366；3424013368；3424013447；3424013443.

《易经》，Fiedeler, Frank (1939—2004)译.

12. Das Mawangdui-Yijing：Text und Deutung/Dominique Hertzer；mit einem Vorwort von Wolfgang Bauer. München；E. Diederichs, 1996. 350 pages；19cm. ISBN：3424013072；3424013078. (Diederichs gelbe Reihe；122.；China)

马王堆版《易经》. Hertzer, Dominique 译.

13. Yi Jing das Buch der Wandlung/in einer Bearb. von Detlev Bölter. Mit 64 Tuschbl. von Michael Vetter. Vorw. von Ryu-Un Tai-San. Berlin：Theseus Verl. , 1997.

151 S. Ill. 18cm. ISBN：3896200925；3896200921

《易经》，Bölter, Detlev 编.

14. Das illustrierte I-ging/von Li Yan. [Dt. übers.：Li Xuelian. Dt. Bearb.：Atze Schmidt]. Beijing：Verl. für fremdsprachige Literatur, 1997. VI, 456 S. überw. ill. 21cm. ISBN：7119019945

《易经画传》,李燕译.

15. Yi-jing：das Buch der Wandlungen；die einzige vollständige Ausgabe der altchinesischen Orakeltexte mit Konkordanz＝（I-ging）/Eranos. Übers. und hrsg. von Rudolf Ritsema und Hansjakob Schneider. Bern；München；Wien：Barth, 2001, 958 S.：ill. , graph. Darst. ；22cm. ISBN：3502610533；3502610533

《易经》，Ritsema, Rudolf 译.

16. Yijing-Das Buch der Wandlungen/ aus dem Chines. übers. und hrsg. von Dennis Schilling. Frankfurt am Main：Verlag der Weltreligionen, 2009. 1 vol. （934 p.）；18cm. ISBN：3458700166；3458700161.

《易经》，Schilling, Dennis R. 译.

B22　儒家

1. Confucius und Mencius：Die vier Bücher der moral- und staatsphilosphie China's/Aus dem chinesischen nach der französischen übersetzung des Herrn m. G. Pauthier. Herausgegeben von John Cramer. Crefeld, J. H. Funcke, 1844. viii, 364 pages；1 leaf 16cm. （Das Himmlische Reich. Oder, Chinas Leben, Denken, Dichten und Geschichte... 2. bd. ）

Contents：Ta-hio；oder, Das grosse Studium. —Tschung-yung；oder, Die Unveränderlichkeit in der Mitte. —Lün-hü；oder, Die philosophischen Unterhaltungen. —Meng-tseu.

孔子与孟子. Pauthier, G. (Guillaume, 1801—1873)译自法语.

B221　四书五经

1. Die Lehren des Konfuzius：die vier konfuzianischen Bücher；chinesisch und deutsch/übers. und erl. von Richard Wilhelm；mit einem Vorw. von Hans van Ess. Frankfurt am Main：Zweitausendeins, 2008. 1113 s.：il. ；23cm. ISBN：3861508731, 3861508737

《四书》,卫礼贤(Wilhelm, Richard, 1873—1930)译注.

B222　大学

1. Das grosse Lernen ＝（Daxue）/herausgegeben und mit einem Nachwort von Ralf Moritz；[die Übersetzung wurde unter der Leitung von Ralf Moritz von D. Altner [and others]. Stuttgart：Reclam, 2003. 79 pages；15cm. ISBN：3150182654；3150182659. (Universal-Bibliothek；Nr. 18265).

《大学》,Moritz, Ralf(1873—1930)译.

2. Das grosse Lernen＝Daxue/[Übers.：Hua Shaoxiang...]. Beijing：Verl. für fremdsprachige Literatur, 2010. 111

S. Ill. 23cm. , 166 gr. ISBN: 7119061733, 7119061739
《大学》,华少庠(1958—),高明(1973—),穆勒(1964—)
合译.

B223 中庸

1. Tchōng-Yōng: der unwandelbare Seelengrund/Confucius;
   Reinhold von Plaenckner (Hrsg.). Leipzig: Brockhaus,
   1878. 255 Seiten
   《中庸》,Plaenckner, Reinhold von 译.
2. Der Edle und der Weise: Oikumenische und imperiale
   Repräsentation der Menschheit im Chung-yung, einer
   didaktischen Schrift des Frühkonfuzianismus, Eine
   kommentierte Übersetzung/Von Peter Weber-Schäfer.
   München, 1963. 67 pages; 8°. (Münchener Studien zur
   Politik. Hft. 3)
   《中庸》, Weber-Schäfer, Peter 译.

B224 礼记

1. Li Gi: das Buch der Sitte des älteren und jüngeren Dai:
   Aufzeichnungen über Kultur und Religion des alten
   China/aus dem Chinesischen verdeutscht und erläutert von
   Richard Wilhelm. Jena: Eugen Diederichs, 1930. XVIII,
   448 S. ; 21cm.
   《礼记》,卫礼贤(Wilhelm, Richard, 1873—1930)译.
   (1) Düsseldorf: Diederichs, 1958. 355 S. (Diederichs'
       Taschenausgaben; 16; Die Philosophie Chinas)
2. Li Gi: das Buch der Riten, Sitten und Gebräuche/aus dem
   Chinesischen übersetzt und herausgegeben von Richard
   Wilhelm. Neuausg. Düsseldorf: Diederich, 1981. 352 pages;
   19cm. ISBN: 3424006912, 3424006919. (Diederichs gelbe
   Reihe; 31, China)
   《礼记》(新版),卫礼贤(Wilhelm, Richard, 1873—1930)译.
   (1) Neuausg. , 2. Aufl. München: Diederichs, 1994. 352
       Seiten: Illustrationen; 19cm. ISBN: 3424006912,
       3424006919. (Diederichs gelbe Reihe; 31: China)
   (2) Köln: Anaconda, 2007. 415 S. ; 19cm. ISBN: 3866471580,
       3866471580
   (3) Wiesbaden marix Verlag, n 2014. 356 S. ; 200 mm ×
       125 mm. ISBN: 3865393852, 3865393853

B224 孔子

1. Gespräche (Lun yu)/Kungfutse; aus dem Chinesischen
   verdeutscht und erläutert von Richard Wilhelm. . Jena:
   Eugen Diederich, 1910. xxxii, 245 pages, illustrations;
   22cm. (Die Religion und Philosophie Chinas; Bd. 2)
   《论语》,卫礼贤(Wilhelm, Richard, 1873—1930)译.
   (1) Jena: E. Diederichs, 1914. [8], xxxii, 255. [1]
       pages: illustrations(portraits); 22cm.
   (2) Jena: E. Diederichs, 1921. 2 Bl. , 1 Taf. , XXXII,
       246 S. , 1 Bl.
   (3) Jena: E. Diederichs, 1923. [2. Aufl.] 255 pages:
       illustrations; 22cm.
   (4) Jena: E. Diederichs, 1945. XXXII, 254 S.

(5) Jena: E. Diederichs, 1955. 219 S. (Diederichs-
    Taschenausgaben; 2)
(6) Stuttgart, Hamburg: Dt. Buecherbund, 1963. 219 S. 8
(7) Jena: E. Diederichs, 1967. Herbert Nette (hg). 219
    S. 8. (Diederichs-Taschenausgaben; 2)
(8) Stuttgart [u. a.]: Dt. Bücherbund, 1968. 219 S.
(9) Düsseldorf [u. a.]: E. Diederichs, 1970. 219 S. 8.
    (Diederichs-Taschenausgaben; 2)
(10) Düsseldorf, Köln: E. Diederichs, 1971. 219 S.
     18cm. ISBN: 342400460X, 3424004601.
(11) Düsseldorf, Köln: E. Diederichs, 1974. 219 S.
     19cm. ISBN: 3424001791, 3424001792, 342400460X
     (Gesamtwerk), 3424004601 (Gesamtwerk). (Die
     Philosophie Chinas)
(12) Düsseldorf, Köln: E. Diederichs, 1976. 219 S. 19cm.
     ISBN: 342400460X, 3424004601. (Die Philosophie
     Chinas)
(13) Düsseldorf, Köln: E. Diederichs, 1979. 219 S. Ill; 8'.
     ISBN: 342400622X, 3424006223. (Die Philosophie
     Chinas)
(14) Düsseldorf, Köln: E. Diederichs, 1980. 219 S. Ill;
     19cm. ISBN: 342400622X, 3424006223. (Die Philosophie
     Chinas)
(15) Düsseldorf, Köln: E. Diederichs, 1982. 219 S. Ill;
     19cm. ISBN: 342400622X, 3424006223. (Die Philosophie
     Chinas)
(16) Düsseldorf, Köln: E. Diederichs, 1982. 219 p. ill.
     ISBN: 3424007250, 3424007251 (Die Philosophie
     Chinas; 1982: 2)
(17) Düsseldorf, Köln: E. Diederichs, 1985. 219 S. 4 Ill. ;
     19cm. ISBN: 342400622X, 3424006223.
(18) Leipzig: Philipp Reclam, 1986. 166 s. ISBN: 3379000043,
     3379000048(Reclams Universal-Bibliothek; bd. 888)
(19) Düsseldorf, Köln: E. Diederichs, 1987. 219 S. : 5
     ill. ; 19cm. ISBN: 342400622X, 3424006223.
(20) München: E. Diederichs, 1989. 219 S. : 5 ill. ;
     19cm. ISBN: 342400622X, 3424006223.
(21) München: E. Diederichs, 1990. 219 S. : ill. ; 19cm.
     ISBN: 342400622X, 3424006223.
(22) München: E. Diederichs, 1994. 第 6 版. 219 S. : ill. ;
     20cm. ISBN: 342400622X, 3424006223. (Diederichs
     gelbe Reihe. China; ; 22)
(23) München: E. Diederichs, 1996. 第 7 版. 219 S. :
     ill. ISBN: 342400622X, 3424006223.
(24) Essen: Magnus, 2003. 240 str. ; 20cm. ISBN:
     3884001361, 3884001363.
(25) München: Beck, 2005. 237 S. ISBN: 3423342463,
     3423342469. (Kleine Bibliothek der Weltweisheit;
     6; dtv; 34246).
(26) München: Beck, 2006. 237 S. : ill. ISBN: 3423342463,
     3423342469. (Kleine Bibliothek der Weltweisheit; 6;

dtv；34246)

(27) München：Beck，2007. 237 S.：ill. ISBN：3423342469，3423342463.

(28) Wiesbaden：Matrix，2007. 446 S.：ill. 21cm. ISBN：3865390080，3865390080.

(29) Köln：Anaconda，2007. 383 S.：ill. 20cm. ISBN：3866471597，3866471599.

2. Konfuzius in Worten aus seinem eigenen Mund/von Hans Haas. Leipzig：J. C. Hinrichs'sche Buchhandlung，1920. 36 Seiten.

《论语》，Haas，Hans（1868—1934)译.

3. Worte des Konfuzius [Kung-Fu-Tse] Aus d. Buche d. Gespräche. Qiu Kong；Rudolf Zorn. München：P. Hugendubel，1942. 157 S. 8.

《论语》，Rudolf Wrede 译.

(1) Heidelberg：Meister，1948. 72 S. 8（Die kleinen Meister-Bücher；Nr. 83).

(2) Tübingen a. Neckar：Heos Verl，1960. 158 S. 8.

(3) München：Goldmann，1962. 150 S. kl. 8.（Goldmanns gelbe Taschenbücher；Bd. 914；Goldmanns gelbe Taschenbücher；Bd. 914.）

4. Gespräche d. Konfuzius [Confucius]/Aus d. Chin. v. Irmgard Grimm. Hamburg：Mölich Verlag，1948. 113 p.；19cm.

《论语》，Grimm，Irmgard 译.

5. Konfuzius：Leben Aussprüche，Weltanschauung/Konfuzius. [Hrsg.：] Waldemar Oehlke. Hamburg：Dt. Literatur-Verl.，1949. 104 S. 8.

《论语》，Oehlke，Waldemar 译.

(1) Hamburg，Deutscher Literatur-Verlag，1951—1952. 104 pages；19cm.

6. Die goldene Mitte：Besinnliches aus dem Lun Yü/von Friedrich Thiel. Stuttgart：Schuler，1950. 162 S.；8°.

《论语》，Thiel，Friedrich 翻译.

7. Gedanken und Gespräche des Konfuzius/Konfuzius. Aus d. chines. Urtext neu übertr. u. eingel. von Hans O. H. Stange. München：Oldenbourg，1953. 187 S. kl. 8.

《论语》，Stange，Hans O. H（1903—1978)节译.

8. Worte der Weisheit：Luin-Yü；Die Diskussionsreden Meister Kung's mit s. Schülern/Kung-fu-tse. Aus d. Urtext neu übertr. u. erl. v. Hayme Kremsmayer. Wien：Europäischer Verl.，1954. 128 S. 8,,.

《论语》，Kremsmayer，Hayme 译.

9. So spricht Konfuzius/[bearb. von W. Plügge]. München-Planegg：O. W. Barth，1954. 125 S. kl. 8.

《论语》，Plügge，W. 译.

10. Die Weisheit des Konfuzius/Aus dem chinesischen Urtext neu übertragen und eingeleitet von Hans H. O. Stange. Frankfurt am Main：Insel Verlag，1964. 62 S.

《论语》，Stange，Hans 译.

11. Gespräche (Lun-Yu)/Konfuzius. Aus dem Chines. übers.

und hrsg. von Ralf Moritz. Leipzig：Verl. Reclam，1982. 166 Seiten；18cm.（Reclams Universal-Bibliothek；Bd. 888：Philosophie，Geschichte)

《论语》，Moritz，Ralf(1873—1930)译.

(1) 2. Aufl. Leipzig：Philipp Reclam Junior，1982. 166 S. 17cm.．（Reclams Universal-Bibliothek；888.：Philosophie，Geschichte).

(2) Franfurt am Main：Röderberg-Verlag，1983. 166 pages；18cm. ISBN：3876824915，3876824918.

(3) 2. Aufl. Leipzig：Verlag Philipp Reclam jun.，1984. 166，[1] s.；18cm.（Reclams Universal-Bibliothek. Philosophie，Geschichte，Kulturgeschichte)

(4) 3 Aufl. Leipzig：Reclam，1986. 166 S. 18cm. ISBN：3379000043，3379000048.（Reclams Universal-Bibliothek；Bd. 888：Philosophie，Geschichte，Kulturgeschichte)

(5) 4. Aufl. Leipzig：Reclam，1988. 第 4 版. 166 S. 18cm. ISBN：3379000043，3379000048.

(6) 2. Aufl. Köln：Röderberg，1988. 166 S. 18cm. ISBN：3876824915，3876824918.

(7) 2. Aufl. Köln：Röderberg，1989. 166 S. 18cm. ISBN：3876824915，3876824918.

(8) 5. Aufl. Leipzig：Reclam，1991. 166 S. 18cm. ISBN：3379000043，3379000048.

(9) Stuttgart：Reclam，1998. 215 S. 15cm. ISBN：3150096561，3150096567.（Universal-Bibliothek；Nr. 9656)

(10) Stuttgart：Reclam，2002. 215 S. ISBN：3150096561，3150096567.（Universal-Bibliothek；Nr. 9656)

(11) Stuttgart：Reclam，2003. 215 S. 16cm. ISBN：3150596564，3150596562.

(12) Stuttgart：Reclam，2008. 重印. 215 S. ISBN：3150096567，3150096561.

(13) Stuttgart：Reclam，2010. 重印. 215 S. ISBN：3150096567，3150096561.（Universal-Bibliothek；Nr. 9656)

(14) Stuttgart：Reclam，2014. 重印. 215 S. ISBN：3150096567，3150096561.

12. Gespräche des Meisters Kung：mit d. Biographie d. Meisters Kung aus d. Historischen Aufzeichnungen ＝(Lun-yü)/Konfuzius. [Aus d. Chines. übertr. u；mit e. Einf.，e. Kommentar u. e. Literaturverz. hrsg. von Ernst Schwarz]. Vollst. Ausg.，Orig.-Ausg. München：Deutscher Taschenbuch-Verlag，1985. 244 Seiten：Illustrationen；18cm. ISBN：3423021659，3423021654.（Dtv；2165：dtv-Klassik)

《论语》，Schwarz，Ernst（1916—2003)译.

(1) 2. Aufl. Vollst. Ausg.，Orig.-Ausg. München：Dt. Taschenbuch-Verl.，1987. 244 S. ill.；18cm.；ISBN：3423021659 3423021654

(2) 3. Aufl. Vollst. Ausg.，Orig.-Ausg. München：Dt. Taschenbuch-Verl.，1989. 244 S. ill.；18cm.；ISBN：3423021659，3423021654.

(3) 4. Aufl. Vollst. Ausg.，Orig.-Ausg. München：

Dt. Taschenbuch-Verl. , 1991. 244 S. ill. ; 18cm. ;
ISBN：3423021659，3423021654.

（4）5. Aufl. Vollst. Ausg. , Orig. -Ausg. München：Dt.
Taschenbuch-Verl. , 1992. 244 S. ill. ; 18cm. ; ISBN：
3423021659，3423021654.

（5）6. Aufl. Ausg. , Orig. -Ausg. München：Dt. Taschenbuch-
Verl. , 1994. Vollst. 244 S. Ill. 18cm. ISBN：3423021659,
3423021654.

13. Meister Kung sprach：aus den Gesprächen des Konfuzius/
übertragen und eingeleitet von Ernst Schwarz. Wien：
Herder，1985. 102 pages：illustrations; 19×21cm. ISBN：
321024796X, 3210247960.

《论语》（选译），Schwarz, Ernst（1916—2003）译.

14. Gespräche in der Morgenstille：Lehren d. Meisters/
Konfuzius. Ausgewählt u. übertr. von Victoria Contag. 2.
Aufl. Zürich, München：Artemis-Verl. , 1986. XXXI, 296
S. : ill. ISBN：3760837050, 3760837055. (Pegasus-
Paperback)

《论语》，Contag, Victoria 选译.

15. Der gute Weg：Worte des grossen chinesischen
Weisheitslehrers/Konfuzius; ［ zusammengestellt von
Werner Felitz]. Bern：Scherz, 1987. 127 pages; 16cm.
ISBN：3502330018, 3502330011. (Weisheit der Welt;
Bd. 1)

《论语》，Felitz, Werner 节译.

16. Die Weisheit des Konfuzius：ewige Wahrheit für die
Zukunft des Menschen/［zsgest. von Werner Felitz].
［Wessobrunn]：Integral, 1997. 125 Seiten; 16cm.
(LebensReiseführer)

《论语》，Felitz, Werner 译.

17. Gespräche：eine Auswahl/Konfuzius. [Zsgest. und eingeleitet
von Hans Baier]. Leipzig：Miniaturbuchverl. , 2000. 319
S. 6cm. ISBN：3910135897, 3910135895, 3910135900,
3910135901.

《论语》，Baier, Hans 选译.

18. Die Weisheit des Konfuzius：ewige Wahrheit für die
Zukunft des Menschen/mit Ill. von Klaus Holitzka.
München：Integral-Verl. , 2001. 120 S Ill 16cm. ISBN：
3778790714, 3778790717

《论语》，Holitzka, Klaus 译.

19. Der Konfuzianismus als Hauptströmung der chinesischen
Geistesgeschichte：mit einer zweisprachigen Ausgabe der
Lunyu (Gespräche/Analekte) des Konfuzius, übersetzt
von Richard Wilhelm/herausgegeben von Martin Woesler.
Berlin：Europäischer Universitätsverlag, 2010. 313 pages;
22cm. ISBN：3899663624 (geb.); 3899663624 (geb.);
3899663662 (pbk.);3899663667 (pbk.). (Sinica; 28)

《论语》双语版，卫礼贤（Wilhelm, Richard, 1873—1930）
译.

20. Gespräche/Konfuzius. Ausgew. , übers. und kommentiert
von Wolfgang Kubin. Orig. -Ausg. Freiburg, Br. ；Basel；

Wien：Herder, 2011. 216 S. ; 22cm. ISBN：3451305016.
(Klassiker des chinesischen Denkens; Bd. 1)

《论语》，顾彬（Kubin, Wolfgang, 1945—）译.

（1）Freiburg; Basel; Wien：Herder, 2015. 第 2 版. 216
S. ; 215 mm × 135 mm. ISBN：3451305016,
3451305011. (Klassiker des chinesischen Denkens; 1).

21. Konfuzius, der „Weise" der reaktionären Klassen/Yang
Jung-guo. Peking：Verlag für fremdsprachige Literatur,
1974. 74 pages; 19cm.

《反动阶级的"圣人"：孔子》，杨国荣著.

22. Verblichener Geist des Konfuzius, Wunschträume neuer
Zaren/Peking：Verlag für Fremdsprachige Literatur,
1974. 44 S. ; 19cm.

《孔老二的亡灵和新沙皇的迷梦》

B225 孔子家语

1. Kungfutse Schulgespräche＝Kungfutse Gia Yü/［aus dem
Chinesischen verdeutscht und erläutert von Richard
Wilhelm; aus dem Nachlass herausgegeben von Hellmut
Wilhelm]. Düsseldorf-Köln：E. Diederichs, 1961. 237
pages. (Diederichs Taschenausgaben; 24)

《孔子家语》，卫礼贤（Wilhelm, Richard, 1873—1930）译.

B226 孟子

1. Eine Staatslehre auf ethischer Grundlage, oder,
Lehrbegriff des chinesischen Philosophen Mencius：Aus
dem Urtexte übers. , in systematische Ordnung gebracht
und mit Anmerkungen und Einleitungen versehen/Ernst
Faber. Elberfeld：R. L. Friderichs, 1877. vii, 273 pages;
24cm.

《孟子》，Faber, Ernst（1839—1899）编译.

2. Mong dsi (Mong ko)/aus dem Chinesischen verdeutscht
und erläutert von Richard Wilhelm. . Jena：E. Diederichs,
1914. XIX, 207 p. : portr. ; 21cm. (Die Religion und
Philosophie Chinas; bd. 4)

《孟子》，卫礼贤（Wilhelm, Richard, 1873—1930）译.

（1）Mong dsi (Mong ko). Jena：E. Diederichs, 1916. 2
preliminary leaves, xix, 206 pages, 1 leaf frontispiece
8vo. (Die Religion und Philosophie Chinas; ; bd. 4)

（2）Mong dsi (Mong ko) Aus dem chinesischen verdeutscht
und erläutert. Jena：E. Diederichs, 1921. 4 pages; 1. ,
xix, 206, ［1] pages including frontispiece (portrait)
22cm. (Die religion and philosophie Chinas; bd. 4)

3. Mong Dsï：die Lehrgespräche des Meisters Meng K'o/
Mong Dsï. Aus dem Chines. übertr. und erl. von
Richard Wilhelm. Köln：Diederichs, 1982. 247 pages：
illustrations; 19cm. ISBN：3424007420, 3424007428.
(Diederichs Gelbe Reihe; Bd. 42：China)

《孟子》，卫礼贤（Wilhelm, Richard, 1873—1930）译.

（1）Neuausg. , 2. Aufl. München：Diederichs, 1994. 247
S. ; 19cm. ISBN：3424007420. （Diederichs Gelbe
Reihe; 42：China)

（2）Wiesbaden：Marixverl.，2015. 271 S.；21cm. ISBN：3737409674.

4. 孟子/孟子；杨伯峻今译；卫礼贤德译.北京：外文出版社，2009. ISBN：7119060026，7119060023.（大中华文库）
德文题名：Die Lehrgespräche des Meisters Meng K'o

5. Die Weisheiten des Meisters Meng-tse/ausgew. u. hrsg. von Manfred Kluge. München：Heyne，1987. 94 S.：Ill.；19cm. ISBN：3453001281，3453001282.（[Heyne-Bücher]：09，Heyne-Ex-Libris；Nr. 205）.
《孟子》，Kluge，Manfred 译.

6. Den Menschen gerecht：ein Menzius-Lesebuch/aus dem klassischen Chines. übertr. und hrsg. von Henrik Jäger. Kalligraphien von Wang Ning. Zürich：Ammann，2010. 293 S.；24cm. ISBN：3250105282,3250105287,3250105282
《孟子》，Jäger，Henrik（1960—）译.

7. Reden und Gleichnisse. Meng Zi, Wolfgang Kubin（Hrsg.）Freiburg im Breisgau；Basel；Wien：Herder，2012. 136 pages；22cm. ISBN：3451305030（pbk.），3451305038（pbk.）.（Klassiker des chinesischen Denkens；Bd. 3）
《孟子》言论与寓言，顾彬（Kubin，Wolfgang，1945—）译.

8. Menzius：eine kritische Rekonstruktion mit kommentierter Neuübersetzung/Robert H. Gassmann. Berlin：de Gruyter，2016. 3 Bänden 24cm. ISBN：3110441055，3110441055；3110444377；3110444372.（Welten Ostasiens；Band 22）.
《孟子：重构与新译》.3 册. Gassmann，Robert H.（1946—）（瑞士汉学家）译.

B227 荀子

1. Hsün-tzu/Ins Deutsche übertragen von Hermann Köster. Kaldenkirchen：Steyler Verl.，1967. XII，403 S.；gr. 8.（Veröffentlichungen des Missionspriesterseminars St. Augustin，Siegburg，Nr. 16）
《荀子》，Köster，Hermann（1904—）译.

2. Xun Zi：die Bildung des Menschen/Kubin，Wolfgang. Freiburg；Basel；Wien：Herder，2015. 160 S. ISBN：3451337468；3451337460.（Klassiker des chinesischen Denkens；6）
《荀子》，顾彬（Kubin，Wolfgang，1945—）编译.

B23 道家

B231 道家著作合集

1. Lau-dse und Dschuang-dse：in deutscher Sprache/von Vincenz Hundhausen. S. L.：Verlag der Pekinger Pappelinsel，1942. 2 dl.；19cm.
Contents：Das eine als Weltgesetz und Vorbild[Dao de jing]/Lau-dse；in deutscher Sprache von Vincenz Hundhausen. —Die Weisheit des Dschuang-dse：in deutschen Lehrgedichten[Zhuangzi Nanhua zhen jing]/Dschuang-dse；[übers. von Vincenz Hundhausen]
《道德经》与《庄子》. Hundhausen，Vincenz（1878—1955）译.

B232 道德经

1. Laò-tsè's Taè tê king：aus dem chinesischen ins deutsche/übers.，eingeleitet und commentirt von Victor von Strauss. Leipzig：Friedrich Fleischer，1870. lxxx，357 pages；24cm.
《老子道德经》，Strauss und Torney，V. F.（1809—1899）译.
（1）Leipzig：Verlag des „Asia Major"，1924. lxxx，357 pages：portraits；24cm.

2. Tao tê king/Laoze；aus dem Chinesischen übersetzt und kommentiert von Victor von Strauss；Bearbeitung und Einleitung von W. Y. Tonn. Zürich：Manesse Verlag，1950. 420 pages；16cm.（Manesse Bibliothek der Weltliteratur）
《道德经》，Strauss und Torney，V. F.（1809—1899）译.
（1）Tao tê king/Lao-Tse；aus dem Chinesischen übers. und kommentiert von Victor von Strauss. Zürich：Manesse Verl，1959. 420 p.；16cm. ISBN：3717512463，3717512462，3717512471，3717512479.（Manesse Bibliothek der Weltliteratur）

3. Lao-tse Táo-tê-king：Der Weg zur Tugend/aus dem Chinesischen übers. und erklärt von Reinhold von Plaenckner. Leipzig，F. A. Brockhaus，1870. xx，423 pages
《道德经》，Plaenckner，Reinhold von 译.

4. Die Bahn und der rechte Weg des Lao-Tse：der chinesischen Urschrift nachgedacht von Alexander Ula. Leipzig：Insel-Verlag，1903. 67 pages；19cm.（Insel-Bücherei；Nr. 253）
《道德经》，Ular，Alexander（1876—1919）译.
（1）2. Aufl. Leipzig：Insel-Verlag，1912. 107，[2] pages；22cm.
（2）3. Aufl. Leipzig：Insel-Verlag，1917. 107，[2] pages；22cm.
（3）4. Aufl. Leipzig：Insel-Verlag，1919. 106 pages；22cm.
（4）Leipzig：Insel-Verlag，1921. 1 vol.（106 p.）；23cm.
（5）Leipzig：Insel-Verlag，1923. 106 pages；23cm.
（6）Frankfurt（Main）：Insel-Verlag，1976. 106 pages；19cm.（Insel Bücherei；Nr. 991）.
（7）Frankfurt（Main）：Insel-Verlag，1977. 106 S.：Ill.（Insel Bücherei；Nr. 991）.
（8）Gebundene Ausgabe. Frankfurt（Main）：Insel-Verlag，1982. 107 S. ISBN：3458089919.（Insel Bücherei；Nr. 993）.
（9）Nachdr. d. Orig. 1921. Paderborn：Sarastro，2012. 112 S. 190 mm. ISBN：3864710438；386471043X.

5. Lao-tszes Buch vom höchsten Wesen und vom höchsten Gut（Tao-tê-king）/Aus dem Chinesischen übersetzt，mit Einleitung versehen und erläutert von Julius Grill. Tübingen：Mohr，1910. XII，208 S. 8„.
《道德经》，Grill，Julius（1840—1930）译.

6. Tao te king：das Buch des Alten vom Sinn und Leben/Laotse；aus dem chinesischen verdeutscht und erläutert

von Richard Wilhelm. Jena：E. Diederichs, 1911. xxxii, 118 pages，[2] leaves of plates：illustrations；22cm.

《道德经》,卫礼贤(Wilhelm, Richard, 1873—1930)译.

(1)Jena：E. Diederichs, 1915. xxxii, 118 pages, illustrations；23cm.

(2)Jena：E. Diederichs, 1919. xxxii, 118 pages，[2] leaves of plates：illustrations；22cm.

(3)Jena：E. Diederichs, 1921. 2 preliminary leaves, xxxii, 118 pages frontispiece (portrait) double plates, diagrams 22cm. (Die Reiligion und Philosophie Chinas；Bd. 7)

(4)Jena：E. Diederichs, 1923. XXXII, 116 S；22cm.

(5)Düsseldorf：Diederichs, 1952,（c）1921. xxx, 119 pages；22cm.

(6)Düsseldorf：Diederichs, 1955,（c）1921. xxx, 119 pages；22cm.

(7)Düsseldorf：Diederichs, 1957. 156 S. (Diederichs' Taschenausgaben；8)

(8)[Lizenzausg.] Bern；Stuttgart：Huber, 1958. 98 S.

(9)Düsseldorf：Diederichs, 1970. 156,[1] pages；18cm. ISBN：3769901738；3769901733. (Philosophie Chinas；)

(10)Zürich：Buchclub Ex Libris, 1972. 156 S. (Die Philosophie Chinas；)

(11)Düsseldorf：Diederichs, 1974. 156,[1] pages；19cm. ISBN： 342400183X；783424001839. (Philosophie Chinas；)

(12)Düsseldorf：Eugen Diederichs, 1978. 230 pages：illustrations；21cm.

(13)Düsseldorf：Diederichs, 1980. 230 S；Ill. (Bücher der Weisheit)

(14)Erw. Neuausg. Köln：Diederichs, 1984. 230 pages：illustrations；19cm. ISBN：3424005797, 3424005790. (Diederichs gelbe Reihe；Bd. 19.；China)

(15)Jena：E. Diederichs,1989. xxxii,118 pages：illustrations. (Die Religion und Philosophie Chinas；v. 7)

(16)Stuttgart [u. a.]：Dt. Bücherbund, 1990. 230 S.；ill.

(17)Kreuzlingen/München：Heinrich Hugendubel, 2004. 230 pages：illustrations；20cm. ISBN：3896314300, 3896314307

(18)Wiesbaden： Marixverlag, 2004. 249 pages：illustrations；21cm. ISBN：393771507X；3937715070.

(19)München：C. H. Beck, 2006. 142 pages；18cm. ISBN：3423342471；3423342476.

(20) Hamburg：Nikol, 2010. 141 pages：illustrations；20cm. ISBN：3868200553, 386820055X.

7. Tao te king：das Buch vom Sinn und Leben/Lao Tse；[in der Verdeutschung von Richard Wilhelm]. Stuttgart：Der Druckspiegel Verlag, 1963. [19],[19] pages；28cm.

《道德经》选译,卫礼贤(Wilhelm, Richard, 1873—1930)译.

8. Laozi's Dao de jing. Bd. 1. Dao/kommentiert von Jan Silberstorff. Übers. von Richard Wilhelm. [Lingen

(Ems)] Lotus Press, 2012. 356 S. ISBN：3935367035, 3935367031

《道德经》（卷一）,卫礼贤（Wilhelm, Richard, 1873—1930)译；Silberstorff, Jan (1967—)注.

9. Laozi's DAO DE JING. Band 2—DE/übers. v. Richard Wilhelm. Komment. v. Jan Silberstorff. Lingen (Ems)：OTUS-PRESS, 2013. 371 S. 155 mm×218 mm, 789 g. ISBN：3935367202；3935367201.

《道德经》（卷二）,卫礼贤（Wilhelm, Richard, 1873—1930)译；Silberstorff, Jan (1967—)注.

10. Tao teh king：Vom Geist und seiner Tugend/übertragung von H. Federmann. München：C. H. Beck'sche Verlh., 1920. 101 pages.

《道德经》,Federmann, H. 译.

(1)3. Aufl.. München：C. H. Beck'sche Verlh. , 1921. ix, 101 pages；18cm.

(2)4. Aufl. München：C. H. Beck'sche Verlh. , 1926. ix, 101 pages；19cm.

11. Mensch, werde wesentlich！：Laotse Sprüche/Laozi. Klabund. Berlin-Zehlendorf：Fritz Heyder, August Hopfer, 1920. 30,[2] pages；16cm.

《道德经》,Alfred Henschke (Klabund,1891—1928)译.

(1)Berlin-Zehlendorf：Heyder, 1922. 30,[2] pages；16cm.

12. Des Laotse Tao Te King/Deutsch von F. Fiedler；hrsg. von Gustav Wyneken. Hannover：Steegemann, 1922. 97 S.；18cm.

《道德经》选译,Fiedler, F. (1875—1900)译.

(1)Tao Te King/Laotse；Deutsch von F. Fiedler；herausgegeben von Gustav Wyneken. Hannover：P. Steegemann, 1923. 97 pages；18cm.

13. Tao-te-king/herausgegeben und erläutert von Dr. J. G. Weiss. Leipzig：Reclam, 1927. 92 S.；8„. (Reclams Universal Bibliothek；Nr. 6798)

《道德经》,Weiss, John Gustav (1857—1943)译.

14. Laotse：die Bahn des All und der Weg des Lebens/ [bearbeitet und übersetzt von] E. Schröder. München：F. Bruckmann, 1934. v, 101 pages；19cm.

《道德经》,Schröder, E. 译.

(1)Wiesbaden Insel-Verl. , 1950. 70 S. (Insel-Bücherei；253)

15. Dau do djing：des alten Meisters Kanon von Weltgesetz und seinem Wirken/ Franz Esser. Peking：Verlag der pekinger Pappelinsel, 1941. lxxxi pages；22cm. + 1 volume (6 pages；20cm.).

《道德经》,Esser, Franz 译.

16. Acht Kapitel des Tao-tê-king/von Kurt Wulff；herausgegeben von Victor Dantzer. Wulff, Kurt. København：Munksgaard, 1942. 98 S.

《道德经》选译,Wulff, Kurt (1881—1939)译.

17. Lau-dse, Führung und Kraft aus der Ewigkeit. (Dau-Dö-

Ging)/Aus dem chinesischen Urtext übertragen von Erwin Rousselle. Leipzig: Insel-Verl. , 1942.

《道德经》,Rousselle, Erwin (1890—1949)译.

(1)Wiesbaden: Insel-Verlag, 1946. 70 S. (Insel-Bücherei; 253)

(2)Leipzig, Wiesbaden: Insel-Verlag, 1950. 70 S. (Insel-Bücherei;253)

(3)Wiesbaden: Insel-Verl. ,1952. 70 S. (Insel-Bücherei; 253)

(4)Wiesbaden: Insel-Verl. ,1958. 68 S. (Insel-Bücherei; 253)

18. Lau Dse: Das Eine als Weltgesetz und Vorbild. Vincenz Hundhausen. Peking: Verlag der Pekinger Pappelinsel, 1942.

《老子:作为世界法则和榜样的道》,洪涛生(1878—1955)译.

(1)Peking: Verlag dere Pekinger Pappelinsel, 1948. 83 S.

19. Laotse Tao te king: das Buch des Alten vom Weltgrund und der Weltweise, aus dem chinesischen Urtext neu übertragen und gedeutet/[von] Lao Tzu; aus dem Chinesischen Urtext neu übertr. und gedeutet von Haymo Kremsmayer; Vorwort von Theodor Bröring. Salzburg: Jgonta Verlag, 1947. 122 pages, [4] leaves of plates: illustrations; 21cm. Orientalia (Salzburg, Austria)

《道德经》,Kremsmayer, Haymo(奥地利汉学家)译.

20. Das verborgene Juwel: Laotses Verkündung/ Ausdeutung und Nachdichtung von Sprüchen aus dem Tao te king des chinesischen Weisen und Mystikers Laotse von Josef Tiefenbacher. Stuttgart: Schuler, 1948. 108 S. : ill. [Bücher der Lebensweisheit].

《道德经》,Tiefenbacher, Josef (1892—1948)译.

21. Lao-Tse. Tao-Te-King/Textgestaltung und Einführung: Rudolf Backofen. Hrsg. : Werner Zimmermann. Thielle/Neuch. (Schweiz): Verlag Fankhauser, 1949. 223 S. 21×30cm. 8,,.

《道德经》,Backofen, Rudolf 译.

(1) München/Engelberg (Schweiz): Drei-Eichen-Verlag H. Kissener, 1970. 222 pages; 19cm. ISBN: 3769901738; 3769901733

(2)Engelberg/ Schweiz [u. a.]: Drei-Eichen-Verlag, 1975. 222 S. ISBN: 3769902785; 3769902785

22. Das Buch von der grossen Weisheit/Laotse. Deutsch von Andre Eckardt. Frankfurt a. M. : Lutzeyer, 1950. 53 Bl. : 1 Taf. ; 8.

《道德经》,Eckardt, André (1884—1974)译.

(1)2. Aufl. Baden-Baden, Frankfurt a. M. : Lutzeyer, 1956. [53] Bl. 8,,.

23. Tao te king: übertragen von Walter Jerven; herausgegeben von Fritz Werle und Ursula von Mangoldt. München-Planegg: O. W. Barth, 1952. 124 pages; 11cm.

《道德经》,Jerven, Walter (1889—1945)译.

24. Laotses Gedankenwelt: Nach dem Tao-Te-King/ dargest. von André Eckardt. Baden-Baden - Frankfurt am Main: Verlag August Lutzeyer GmbH, 1957. 186 S.

《老子的精神世界》,Eckardt, André (1884—1974)译.

25. Daode-king: Älteste und Lehrer als Führer zum Wege Gottes und zum echten Leben/Aus dem chinesischen Urtext neu übersetzt und gedeutet von Edwin Müller. Mit einer Auslegung „Der Tempel des Tao" hrsg. von Gottfried Ginter. Bühl-Baden: Verlag Konkordia, 1952. 66 pages: portraits; 21cm.

《道德经》,Müller, Edwin (1876—1951)编译.

26. Die 81 Sprüche des Lao Tse „Die Bahn und der Rechte-Weg"/Holzschnitte von Karl Schmid-Ambach. Zürich: Adolf Hürlimann, 1954. [100] S; 30cm. : Ill.

《道德经》,Schmid, Karl; Künstler (1914—1998)译.

27. Lao-Tse: Leben und Wirken des Wegbereiters in China. /Aufgenommen in der Nähe Abd-ru-shins durch besondere Begabung eines dazu Berufenen. 2. überarbeitete Aufl. Vomperberg: Bernhardt. 1957. 315 S. (Verwehte Zeit erwacht)

《道德经》,Abd-ru-shin (1875—1941)译.

(1 Einzige autoris. Ausg. , 3. , überarb. Aufl. Stuttgart Verlag der Stiftung Gralsbotschaft, 1983. 303 S. ISBN: 3878601204, 3878601203

28. Tao-teh-king: Weg-Weisung zur Wirklichkeit/Karl Otto Schmidt. Pfullingen: Baum-Verlag,1961. 224 S.

《道德经》,Schmidt, Karl Otto (1904—1977)译.

29. Tao-Tê-King: das Heilige Buch vom Weg und von der Tugend/übersetzung, Einleitung und Anmerkungen von Günther Debon. Stuttgart: P. Reclam, 1961. 142, [1] pages; 16cm.

《道德经》,Debon, Günther (1921—2005)译.

(1)Stuttgart: P. Reclam, 1964, (c)1961. 142, [1] pages; 17cm.

(2)Stuttgart: P. Reclam, 1967, (c)1961. 141 pages; 16cm. (Universal-Bibliothek; Nr. 6798198a)

(3)Stuttgart: P. Reclam, 1972, (c)1961.141, [1] pages; 15cm. (Universal-Bibliothek; Nr. 6798/98a).

(4)Stuttgart: P. Reclam, 1979. 142 pages; 15cm. ISBN: 3150067987; 3150067987. (Universal-Bibliothek;; Nr. 6798 [2]).

(5)Durchges. u. verb. Ausg. , [Nachdr.] Stuttgart Reclam, 1981. 142 Seiten 16cm. ISBN: 3150067987, 3150067987. (Reclams Universal-Bibliothek;Nr. 6798)

(6)durchges. und verb. Ausg. , [Nachdr.]. Stuttgart: P. Reclam, 2009. 142 S. ISBN: 3150067987; 3150067987. (Reclams Universal-Bibliothek; Nr. 6798)

(7)durchges. und verb. Ausg. , [Nachdr.]. Stuttgart: P. Reclam, 2011. 142 S. ISBN: 3150067987;

3150067987.（Reclams Universal-Bibliothek；Nr. 6798）

(8)durchges. und verb. Ausg.，［Nachdr.］. Stuttgart：Reclam，2014. 142 S. 15cm. ISBN：3150067987；3150067987.（Reclams Universal-Bibliothek；Nr. 6798）

30. Dau dö Djing：das Buch vom rechten Wege und von der rechten Gesinnung/Lau Dse；ins Deutsche übertragen und mit einer wörtlichen Übersetzung einer Einleitung und Erläuterungen versehen von Jan Ulenbrook. Bremen：C. Schünemann，1962. 244，［1］pages：illustrations；18cm.（Sammlung Dieterich；Bd. 242）

《道德经》，Ulenbrook，Jan（1909—2000）译.

(1)Bremen：Schünemann，1969. 244 S.（Sammlung Dieterich；242）

(2)Frankfurt/M，Berlin，Wien：Ullstein，1980. 235 S. ISBN：3548200672；3548200675；（Ullstein-Bücher；20067）

(3)Frankfurt/M：Ullstein，1983. 236 S. ISBN：3548200672；3548200675.

(4)Frankfurt/M，Berlin，Wien：Ullstein，1996. 235 pages；18cm. ISBN：3548355730；3548355733. Esoterik（Frankfurt）

31. Tao Te King：Das Buch vom Weltgesetz und seinem Wirken/Laotse.［Wiedergabe des chines. Textes durch Walter Jerven］. Weilheim：Barth. ；Barth，1967. 92 S.

《道德经》，Jerven，Walter（1889—1945）译.

(1)2. Aufl. München［u. a.］：Barth，1976. 92 S.

(2)Bern：O. W. Barth，1977，(c)1976. 第 3 版. 92 pages；19cm.

(3)7. Aufl. München［u. a.］：Barth，1986. 92 S：Ill；19cm.

(4)8. Aufl. München［u. a.］：Barth，1989. 92 S：Ill；19cm.

32. Daudedsching/Aus dem Chinesischen übersetzt und herausgegeben von Ernst Schwarz. Leipzig：P. Reclam，1970. 225 pages；18cm.（Philosophie. ；Reclams Universal-Bibliothek；Bd. 477）.

《道德经》，Schwarz，Ernst（1916—2003）译.

(1)2 Aufl. . Leipzig：P. Reclam，1973. 225 pages；18cm.（Reclams Universal-Bibliothek；477）

(2)3 Aufl. . Leipzig：P. Reclam，1978. 236 pages；18cm.（Philosophie, Geschichte；Reclams Universal-Bibliothek；；Bd. 477）

(3)Vollständige Ausg. München：Deutscher Taschenbuch Verlag，1980，(c)1978. 240 pages；19cm. ISBN：3423061138；3423061131.（DTV Bibliothek）

(4)4 Aufl. Leipzig：P. Reclam，1981，(c)1978. 236 pages；18cm.（Philosophie, Geschichte；Reclams Universal-Bibliothek；；Bd. 477）

(5)5 Aufl. . Leipzig：P. Reclam，1985. 204 pages；18cm.（Philosophie, Geschichte, Kulturgeschichte；Reclams Universal-Bibliothek；Bd. 477）

(6)6 Aufl. . Leipzig：P. Reclam，1990，(c)1978. 204 pages；18cm. ISBN：3379005223；3379005227.（Philosophie, Geschichte, Kulturgeschichte；Reclams Universal-Bibliothek；Bd. 477）

33. Tao te king/Lao Ze；eine neue Bearbeitung von Gia-Fu Feng & Jane English. Haldenwang：Irisiana-Verlag，1978. 170 Seiten. ISBN：921417171，3921417171

《道德经》，冯家福（Feng, Gia-fu, 1919—1985）与 Jane English（1942—）英译；Sylvia Luetjohann 德译.

34. Jenseits des Nennbaren：Sinnsprüche und Zeichnungen nach dem Tao Te King/Lao-tse；［Bearb. von］Linde von Keyserlingk. Freiburg：Herderbücherei，1979. ISBN：3451077419.（Herderbücherei；Bd. 741：Texte zum Nachdenken）

《道德经》42 章翻译，Keyserlingk，Linde von（1932—）译.

(1)Originalausg. ，4. Aufl. Freiburg im Breisgau：Herder，1983. 126 pages：illustrations；18cm. ISBN：3451077418，3451077418

35. Weg und Weisung des alten Lehrers：Tao-Te-King des Lao-Tse/übertr. und eingel. von H［ermann］L［evin］G［oldschmidt］. Zürich：Eigenverlag，1984. 9，81 Blätter；21cm.

《道德经》，Goldschmidt，Hermann Levin（1914—1998）译.

(1)2. ，verb. und erw. Aufl. Zürich：H. L. Goldschmidt，1985. 1 Band

36. Tao-te-king/Lao Tse；Neu ins Deutsche übertragen von Hans Knospe...［et al.］；mit einem Nachwort von Knut Walf. Zürich：Diogenes，1985. ISBN：3257055285. ，3257055283

《道德经》，Knospe，Hans（1940—）译.

(1)Zürich：Diogenes，1990. 81 pages；19cm. ISBN：3257218753；3257218756.（Diogenes-Taschenbuch；21875）.

(2)2 Aufl. Zürich：Diogenes，1993. 81 S. ISBN：3257218753；3257218756.（Diogenes-Taschenbuch；21875）.

(3)8 Aufl. Zürich：Diogenes，2010. 81 S. ISBN：3257218753；3257218756.（Diogenes-Taschenbuch；21875）.

37. Tao-Te-King：das heilige Buch vom Tao und der wahren Tugend/Lao Tse；neu übertr. und mit einer Einf. versehen von Wolfgang Kopp. Interlaken：Ansata-Verlag, P. A. Zemp，1988.［106］Seiten；21cm. ISBN：3715701145，3715701141

《道德经》，Kopp，Wolfgang 译.

(1)2. Auflage. Interlaken：Ansata-Verlag Paul A. Zemp，1992. 95 S：Ill；19cm. ISBN：3715701145，3715701141

38. Aus dem Tao-Tê-King/ Laozi.［Aquarelle：Ulrich

Soppa]. Weingarten：Hanke-Verl.，1989.［11］lose Doppelbl. in e. mappe.：11 ill. ISBN：3925338055；3925338052.

《道德经》,Soppa, Ulrich 译.

39. Tao：das Buch von der wahren Kraft des Dao/［Laotse］. übers. und kommentiert von Aljoscha Schwarz. Bindlach：Gondrom，2004. 159 S.；15cm. ISBN：3811223950；381122395X.

《道德经》,Long, Aljoscha (1961—)译.

40. Den rechten Weg finden：die chinesische Weisheit des Tao für unsere Zeit/neu übertragen von Thomas Cleary. München：Wilhelm Heyne Verlag，1996. 293 pages；18cm. ISBN：345309557X；3453095571.

《道德经》,译自 Thomas Cleary (1949—)的英文版《The Essential Tao》一书.

41. Laozi. Daodejing. Band 1：Text und Übersetzung nebst Zeichenlexikon und Konkordanz：Laozi. Hrsg. von Viktor Kalinke. Leipzig：Edition Erata，1999. 121 Seiten. ISBN：393401500X，3934015005

《道德经》第 1 册,Kalinke, Viktor (1970—)译.

(1) 2.，verb. Aufl. Leipzig：Ed. Erata，2000. 127 Seiten. ISBN：3934015158，3934015159

42. Laozi. Daodejing. Band 2：Eine Erkundung seines Deutungsspektrums/hrsg. von Viktor Kalinke. Leipzig：Edition Erata，1999. 134 Seiten. ISBN：3934015018，3934015012

《道德经》第 2 册,Kalinke, Viktor (1970—)译.

(1)2.，verb. Aufl.，［Nachdr.］. Leipzig：Ed. Erata，2009. 138 Seiten. ISBN：3934015182，3934015180

43. Studien zu Laozi, Daodejing. Teil：Bd. 3.，Nichtstun als Handlungsmaxime：zur Rationalität des Mystischen im Laozi, Daodejing/hrsg. von Viktor Kalinke. Leipzig：Ed. Erata，2011. 204 S. ISBN：3866601154，3866601158

《道德经》第 3 册, Kalinke, Viktor (1970—)译.

44. Textstudium des Laozi：Daodejing：eine komfortable Referenzausgabe mit Anmerkungen sowie Anhängen für die praktische Arbeit：zugleich Versuch einer modernen Altphilologie des klassischen Chinesisch/Jörn Jacobs. Frankfurt am Main；New York：P. Lang，2001. x, 375 pages；21cm. ISBN：363137254X；3631372548. (Frankfurter China-Studien，；Bd. 6).

Jacobs, Jörn 著,有对《道德经》的翻译.

45. Der goldene Kreis des Drachen und die zeitlose Weisheit von Laozis Daodejing/Luc Théle. Saarbrücken：Ryvellus bei Neue Erde,2003. 236 pages；21cm. ISBN：3890600522,3890600529

《道德经》,Théler, Luc 译.

46. Laotse und das Tao-te-king：eine Übertragung der 81 Lehrsprüche des Tao-te-king/mit einer kurzen Rezeptionsgeschichte zum Tao-te-king und einer Bibliogr. der dt.-sprachigen Ausg. von Matthias Claus.

Weinheim：Verl. Das Klassische China, 2006. 158 S.，39 Bl.：Ill.；22cm.，650 gr. + Lesezeichen. ISBN：3981114812；3981114817.

《道德经》,Claus, Matthias (1959—)译.

47. Die Bambustäfelchen Lao Zi：Texte mit Textkritik und Anmerkungen/Laozi. Hou Cai. Berlin：Lit，2008. 142 pages：illustrations；21cm. ISBN：3825810009, 3825810003. (Ethik in der Praxis. Materialien ＝；Practical ethics. Documentaion；Bd. 1).

《郭店楚简老子注》,侯才 (1952—)译. 仅 31 章.

48. Das Tao der Weisheit：Laozi—Daodejing/Klaus Hilmar. Mainz：Hochschulverlag，2008. 548 pages：illustrations (black and white)；21cm. ISBN：3810700414；381070041X.

《道德经》,Klaus, Hilmar 译.

49. The Tao of wisdom：Laozi, Daodejing：Chinese, English, German/Hilmar Klaus. Aachen：Mainz，2009. 600 pages；21cm. ISBN：3810700551；381070055X.

《道德经》三语版,Klaus, Hilmar 译. 中文、英文、德文对照.

50. Daodejing：das Buch vom Weg und seiner Wirkung：Chinesisch/Deutsch/Laozi；übersetzt und herausgegeben von Rainald Simon. Stuttgart：Reclam，2009. 319 pages：illustrations；20cm. ISBN：3150107188，3150107180. (Reclam-Bibliothek).

《道德经》,Simon, Rainald (1951—)译. 汉德对照.

51. Lao Tse - Dao-de-jing, Tao-te-king Gedichte und Erläuterungen in einfachen Worten/Lao Tse. Roderich Höfers. Darmstadt：Schirner，2009. 213 S. Ill. 26cm. ISBN：3897678378；3897678373.

《道德经》,Höfers, Roderich (1952—)译.

52. Tao Te King：81 Spruchweisheiten aus dem 6. Jh. v. Chr/Lao Tse；Nachdichtung von Wolf Peter Schnetz；unter Mitarbeit von Regine Arends. Viechtach：Lichtung，2009. 111 pages；21cm. ISBN：3929517880；3929517884.

《道德经》,Schnetz, Wolf Peter (1939—)译.

53. Laozi Daodejing, oder, Der Klassiker vom Dao und vom De/aus dem klassisch-chinesischen Urtext übersetzt mit Kommentar und vielen anderen Beigaben, Muhammad Wolfgang G. A. Schmidt；nach der chinesischen He-Shang-Gong- Originalfassung. Berlin：Viademica Verlag，2010. lviii, 214 pages.

《老子德经河上公章句》,Schmidt, Muhammad Wolfgang G. A. (1950—)译.

54. Der Urtext/Lao Zi (Laotse)；übersetzt und kommentiert von Wolfgang Kubin. Freiburg：Verlag Herder，2011. 127 S. ISBN：3451305023, 345130502X. (Klassiker des chinesischen Denkens - Bd. 2)

《道德经》,顾彬 (Kubin, Wolfgang, 1945—)译.

(1)2. Aufl. Freiburg：Verlag Herder,2014. 127 S. 215 mm. ISBN：345130502X；3451305023. (Klassiker des chinesischen Denkens - Bd. 2)

55. Laozi Daodejing：die chinesische Strategie der Gewaltlosigkeit/ Harold B. Stromeyer. Meiringen：Stromeyer, 2013. 386 Seiten. ISBN：3033038370, 3033038379

《道德经》，Stromeyer, Harold 译.

56. Der fünfundzwanzigste Spruch aus dem Tao Te King/ Lao Tse.［Übertr. durch Jan Ulenbrook. Hermann Rapp］. Weilrod：Offizin Die Goldene Kanne, 2014. ［11］Bl.；Ill.

《道德经》，Ulenbrook, Jan（1909—）和 Rapp, Hermann 合译.

57. Tao-te-king：das Buch vom Unergründbaren＝（Dàodéjīng）/ Lao-Tse；Manuel-V. Kissener. 2. Auflage. Hammelburg：Drei-Eichen-Verl. , 2014. 109 S.；19cm. ISBN：3769906554；3769906551.

《道德经》，Kissener, Manuel-V. 译.

B233　列子

1. Der Naturalismus bei den alten Chinesen sowohl nach der Seite des Pantheismus als des Sensualismus oder die sämtlichen Werke des Philosophen Licius/zum ersten Male vollständig übersetzt und erklärt von Ernst Faber. Elberfeld：Friderichs, 1877. XXVII, 228 S；8°.

《列子》又名《冲虚经》，Faber, Ernst（1839—1899）译.

2. Das wahre Buch vom quellenden Urgrund：Tschung Hü Dschen Ging；die Lehren der Philosophen Lä Yü Kou und Yang Dschu/Liä Dsi；aus dem Chinesischen verdeutscht und erläutert von Richard Wilhelm. Jena：Diederich, 1911. xxix, 174 pages：portrait, folded plates；22cm.（Die Religion und Philosophie Chinas；；Bd. 8, pt. 1）

《冲虚真经》，卫礼贤（Wilhelm, Richard, 1873—1930）译.

（1）Jena：E. Diederichs, 1921. XXIX, 175 S.：Mit［eingedr.］chines.［Orig. Titel u. 1］Titelholzschn. u. 7 Abb. chines. Zeichn.［auf 2 Taf.］；8.（Die Religion und Philosophie Chinas；Bd. 8, Halbbd. 1）

B234　庄子

1. Reden und Gleichnisse des Tschuang-Tse/Deutsche Auswahl von Martin Buber. Leipzig：Insel-Verl. , 1910.

《庄子的言论和寓言》，Buber, Martin（1878—1965）译.

（1）4. Aufl. Leipzig：Insel-Verl. , 1921. 129 S.；8.

（2）neu revidierte Aufl. Zürich：Manesse Verlag, 1951.

（3）Frankfurt：Insel-Verl. , 1976. 103 Seiten. ISBN：3458019057, 3458019053.（Insel-Taschenbuch；205）

（4）6. Aufl. Zürich：Manesse-Verl. , 1987. 239 S.；16cm. ISBN：3717514060, 3717514067, 3717514077, 3717514075.（Manesse-Bibliothek der Weltliteratur）

（5）Frankfurt am Main：Insel-Verl. , 1990. 146 S.；19cm. ISBN：3458340173.（Insel-Taschenbuch；2317：Insel-Taschenbuch im Grossdruck）

（6）7. Aufl. Zürich：Manesse-Verl. , 1996. 239 S.；16cm. ISBN：3717514060, 3717514067, 3717514077,

3717514075.（Manesse-Bibliothek der Weltliteratur）

2. Das wahre Buch vom südlichen Blütenland/Dschuang Dsi［i. e. Chuang, Chou］. Aus dem Chines. verdeutscht und erl. von Richard Wilhelm. Jena：Diederichs, 1912. xxiv, 267 pages：illustrations

《庄子》，卫礼贤（Wilhelm, Richard, 1873—1930）译.

（1）Jena：Diederichs, 1923. XXIV, 267 S.：1 Titelb；8,..

3. 庄子：汉德对照/（战国）庄子著；高竞艳今译；（德）卫礼贤德译. 北京：崇文书局, 2017. 2 册（13，577 页）；24cm. ISBN：7540343026

德语题名：Zhuangzi；Chinesisch-Deutsch. 汉德对照.

4. Die Weisheit des Dschuang-Dse in Deutschen Lehrgedichten. Vincenz Hundhausen. Peking：Verlag der Pekinger Pappelinsel, 1926. 110 Seiten；8°

庄子南华真经. 洪涛生（Hundhausen, Vincenz, 1878—1955）译.

5. Dichtung und Weisheit/Tschuang-tse. Aus d. chines. Urtext übers. von Hans O. H. Stange. Leipzig：Insel-Verlag, 1936. 77 pages；19cm.（Insel-Bücherei；Nr. 499）

《南华经》，Stange, Hans O. H.（1903—1978）译.

（1）Wiesbaden：Insel-Verlag, 1954. 77 S.

（2）7. Aufl. Frankfurt a. Main；［Leipzig］：Insel-Verl. , 1997.（Insel-Bücherei；499）

（3）9. Aufl. Frankfurt a. M；Insel, 2005. 76. S. ISBN：3458084991, 3458084990.（Insel-Bücherei；499）

6. Mit den passenden Schuhen vergißt man die Füße：ein Zhuangzi-Lesebuch/aus dem Chines. übertr. und hrsg. von Henrik Jäger. Freiburg：Herder, 2003. 156 S.；19cm. ISBN：3451050374；3451050374.（Herder Spektrum；Bd 5037）

《庄子》，Jäger, Henrik（1960—）译.

（1）Zürich：Ammann, 2009. 292 S.：Ill.；24cm. ISBN：3250105299, 3250105295

（2）Dettelbach：Verl. J. H. Röll, 2012. 292 Seiten：Illustrationen. ISBN：3897544185, 3897544180

7. Vom Nichtwissen/Ausgew. , übers. und kommentiert von Wolfgang Kubin. Orig. -ausg. Freiburg：Herder, 2012. 170 Seiten：Illustrationen. ISBN：3451305047, 3451305046.（Klassiker des chinesischen Denkens；4）

《庄子》，顾彬（Kubin, Wolfgang, 1945—）译.

B24　墨家

1. Mê Ti des Sozialethikers und seiner Schüler philosophische Werke/zum ersten Male vollständig übersetzt, mit ausführlicher Einleitung, erläuternden und textkritischen Erklärungen versehen von Alfred Forke. Berlin：Vereinigung Wiss. Verl. , 1922. XIV, 638 S.（［Mitteilungen des Seminars für Orientalische Sprachen an der Friedrich Wilhelms-Universität zu Berlin/1］）.（Mitteilungen des Seminars für Orientalische Sprachen an der Friedrich Wilhelms-Universität zu Berlin/Friedrich-

Wilhelms-Universität Berlin Seminar für Orientalische Sprachen. - Berlin：de Gruyter，1898；23/25).

《墨子》，Forke, Alfred(1867—1944)译.

2. Mo Ti：Der Künder der allgemeinen Menschenliebe/Franz Geisser. Bern：Francke, 1947. XI, 180 S. 8„.

《墨子》，Geisser, Franz(1913—)译.

3.·Solidarität und allgemeine Menschenliebe/Mo Ti；[aus d. Chines. übers. u. hrsg. von Helwig Schmidt-Glintzer]. Düsseldorf：Diederichs, 1975. 181 S. ISBN：3424005096, 3424005097. (Schriften - Mo Ti；1；China im Umbruch；Diederichs' gelbe Reihe；9)

《墨子》(节译)，Schmidt-Glintzer, Helwig (1948—)译.

4. Gegen den Krieg/Mo Ti；[aus d. Chines. übers. u. hrsg. von Helwig Schmidt-Glintzer]. Düsseldorf；Köln：Diederichs，1975. 197 pages；19cm. (Schriften - Mo Ti；2；China im Umbruch；Diederichs' gelbe Reihe；10)

《墨子》(节译)，Schmidt-Glintzer, Helwig (1948—)译.

5. Von der Liebe des Himmels zu den Menschen/Mo Ti. Aus dem Chines. übers. und hrsg. von Helwig Schmidt-Glintzer. München：Diederichs，1992. 274 S. ；19cm. ISBN：3424010294, 3424010299. (Diederichs gelbe Reihe；94；China).

《墨子》(节译)，Schmidt-Glintzer, Helwig (1948—)译.

B25 名家

B251 公孙龙(约公元前 320—前 250)

1. Der Sophismus des Kung-Sun Lung/J. Lohmann. Zur Ontologischen Amphibolie des Chinesischen；1949.

《公孙龙子》，Lohmann, J. 译.

B26 杂家

B261 吕不韦(公元前 300—前 235)

1. Frühling und Herbst des Lü Bu We/aus dem chinesischen verdeutscht und erläutert von Richard Wilhelm. Jena：E. Diederichs，1928. xiii, 541 p；21cm.

《吕氏春秋》，吕不韦 (公元前 300—235) 著；卫礼贤 (Wilhelm, Richard, 1873—1930)译.

(1)Neuausg. Düsseldorf [u. a.]：Diederichs，1971. XXIII, 541 S；22cm.

(2)Neuausg. Düsseldorf, Köln：Diederichs，1979. XXII, 541 S；8°.

2. Das Weisheitsbuch der alten Chinesen：Frühling und Herbst des Lü Bu We = Lü-schï-tschun-tsiu/aus dem Chines. übers. und erl. von Richard Wilhelm. Köln：Anaconda，2015. 559 S. ；21cm. ISBN：3730602133；3730602136.

《吕氏春秋》，吕不韦 (公元前 300—235) 著；卫礼贤 (Wilhelm, Richard, 1873—1930)译.

B27 汉代哲学

1. Ch'un-ch'iu-fan-lu＝üppiger Tau des Frühling-und-

Herbst-Klassikers/Tung Chung-shu；Übersetzung und Annotation der Kapitel eins bis sechs von Robert H. Gassmann. Bern；Frankfurt am Main；New York；Paris：Lang, 1988. 417 S. ：Ill. ；23cm. ISBN：3261038937, 3261038934. (Schweizer asiatische Studien/Monographien = Monographies；Bd. 8)

《春秋繁露》，董仲舒（公元前 179 年 — 前 104 年）著；Gassmann, Robert H. (1946—)译.

2. Das Ch'ien-fu-lun des Wang Fu：Aufsätze und Betrachtungen eines Weltflüchtigen/Rainer Holzer. Heidelberg：Ed. Forum，1992. 207 S. ；24cm. ISBN：3927943056, 3927943053. (Würzburger sinologische Schriften)

《潜夫论》，王符（约 85—163）著；Holzer, Rainer(1950—)译.

B28 宋代哲学

1. Tŭng-šŭ des Ceŭ-hî：mit Cŭ-hî's Commentare nach dem Sîng-lì Tsîng-î；ein Beitrag zur Kenntniss der chinesischen Philosophie. 1, Cap. I - VIII/mit mandschuischer und dt. Übers. und Anm. hrsg. von Wilhelm Grube. Wien：Holzhausen，1880. IX, 45 Seiten

《周子通书，性理精义》，周敦颐(1017—1073) 著；朱熹 (1130—1200)注；Grube, Wilhelm(1855—1908)译.

2. Djin-si lu [Jin si lu]：die sungkonfuzianische Summa mit dem Kommentar des Yä Tsai/übersetzt und erläutert von Olaf Graf. Tōkyō, Sophia University Press, 1953. 3 volumes in 4. 30cm. (Monumenta nipponica monographs；；no. 12) Contents：1. Bd. Einleitung. —2. Bd. Text. 2v. —3. Bd. Anmerkungen.

《近思录》朱熹著；Graf, Olaf(1900—)译.

B29 清代哲学

1. Ta T'ung Shu：Das Buch von der Grossen Gemeinschaft/K'ang Yu-wei；[Hrsg. der dt. Ausg. ：Wolfgang Bauer]；[aus dem Engl. übers. von Horst Kube]. Düsseldorf，Köln：Diederichs，1974. 280 S. ；19cm. ISBN：3424005035, 3424005037. (Diederichs gelbe Reihe；3；China im Umbruch)

《大同书》，康有为(1858—1927)著；Kube, Horst 译自英文.

B3 伦理学

1. Proben Chinesischer Weisheit：nach dem Chinesischen des Ming-sin-pao-tsien. J. H. Plath. München：1863. 62 pages；20cm.

《明心宝鉴》，Plath, Johann Heinrich 译.

2. Vom weisen Umgang mit der Welt：das Saikontan des Weisen Hung Ying-ming aus dem China des 16. Jahrhunderts/Hung Ying-ming. Nach chines. u. japan. Quellen hrsg. von William Scott Wilson. [Einzig berecht. Übers. aus d. Engl. von Hans-Ulrich Möhring]. Bern；

München；Wien：Barth，1988. 189 S.；20cm. ISBN：3502653158，3502653151.

《菜根谭》，洪应明（明）著；Wilson，William Scott 译自英文版《The roots of wisdom》一书.

3. Chinesische Wertvorstellungen：traditionelle Kultur und gegenwärtige Werte. Beijing：Verlag für fremdsprachige Literatur，2016. viii，195 pages.；23cm. ISBN：7119100685

《中国价值观：中国传统文化与中国当代价值》，曹雅欣著.

B4　宗教

B41　概述

1. Religionen in China/von Sang Ji. Übers. von Ren Zhongwei.［Beijing］：China Intercontinental Press，2004. 171 S：ill.；21cm. ISBN：750850500X

《中国宗教》，任仲伟译. 五洲传播出版社（中国基本情况丛书/郭长建主编）

2. Die Welt der Götter Chinas/Ma Shutian. Übers.：Gong Hehua und Tian Shouyu. Dt. Bearb.：Atze Schmidt und Gregor Kneussel］. Beijing：Verl. für fremdsprachige Literatur，2006. 225 S.：zahlr. ill.；24cm. ISBN：7119046144

《中国的神灵世界》，马书田编著. 本书共列中国传说中的神鬼百位，分中华始祖神、俗神、神仙、菩萨、阴间神五类介绍给读者，每篇并结合重要的寺庙宫观，以神带庙，由庙读神.

3. Tempel in Beijing/Xiao Xiaoming；Liao Pin，Lan Peijin. Beijing，China：Verlag für fremdsprachige Literatur，2008. 112 pages；illustrations；22cm. ISBN：7119044071

《北京寺庙道观》，廖频，吴文撰文.

B42　佛教

1. Pilgerfahrten Buddhistischer Priester von China nach Indien：Erste Abtheilung/aus d. Chinesischen übersetzt，mit eine Einleitung und mit Anmerkungen versehen von D. Carl Friedrich Neumann. Leipzig，1833. 66 S；8，（Zeitschrift für die historische Theologie；Bd 3）

《洛阳伽蓝记》（选译），杨炫之著；Neumann，Carl F.（1793—1870）译.

2. Alphabetisches Verzeichnis zum Kao-Seng-Chuan/Heinrich Friedrich Hackmann（übers.）. Leiden：E. J. Brill：1923；V.［81］—112 S.

《高僧传》，慧皎著；Hackmann，Heinrich（1864—1935）译.

3. Erklärendes Wörterbuch zum chinesischen Buddhismus：chinesisch-sanskrit-deutsch/von Heinrich Hackmann. Nach seinem hs. Nachlaß überarb. von Johannes Nobel. Hrsg. von d. religionskundl. Sammlung d. Univ. Marburg/Lahn Leiden：E. J. Brill：1951—52，5 parts. 4，

《高僧传》，慧皎著；Hackmann，Heinrich（1864—1935）译.

4. Der chinesische Dharmasamgraha：Mit einem Anhang über das Lakkhanasuttanta des Dīghanikāya/Friedrich

Weller［Hrsg.］Habilitationsschrift，Leipzig：H. Haessel Verlag，1923. 198 S.

《法集名数经》，Weller，Friedrich（1889—1980）译.

5. Der Ältere Buddhismus nach Texten der Tripitaka/von M. Winternitz. Tübingen，Mohr，1929；VI，162 S.；24cm.

《大藏经》（选译），Winternitz，M.（Moriz，1863—1937）译.

6. Das Sutra des sechsten Patriarchen/Wei-Lang（Hui-Neng［Hui-nêng Lu］）；Hrsg.（［u. ］ins Dt. übertr. ）von Raoul v. Muralt. Zürich：Origo Verl. ，1958. 149 S；8„. （Mahayana-Buddhismus；Bd. 3）

《六祖坛经》，慧能（638—713）著；Muralt，Raoul von 译.

7. Das Sutra des sechsten Patriarchen：das Leben und die Zen-Lehre des chinesischen Meisters Hui-neng（638 - 713）/Hui-neng. Mit Erl. von Soko Morinaga Roshi. Aus d. Chines. u. Japan. übers. von Ursula Jarand. Bern；München；Wien：Barth，1989. 192 S.；21cm. ISBN：3502642982，3502642985

《六祖坛经》，慧能（638—713）著；Ursula Jarand 译.

8. Bi-yän-lu：Meister Yüan-wu's Niederschrift von der Smaragdenen Felswand，verfasst auf dem Djia-schan bei Li in Hunan zwischen 1111 und 1115，im Druck erschienen in Sitschuan um 1300/verdeutscht und erläutert von Wilhelm Gundert. München：Hanser，1960—1973. 3 Bde；8'

《碧岩录》，（宋）圆悟克勤大师著；Gundert，Wilhelm（1880—）译. 共 3 卷.

（1）Bi-yän-lu：Meister Yüan-wu's Niederschr. von d. Smaragdenen Felswand；verf. auf d. Djia-schan bei Li in Hunan zwischen 1111 u. 1115；im Dr. erschienen in Sitschuan um 1300；1. Bd. ，2. Bd. ，3. Bd. /verdeutscht u. erl. von Wilhelm Gundert. Frankfurt/M；Berlin；Wien：Ullstein，1983. 580，363，167 S. ；Ill. ；22cm. ISBN：3548351568，3548351565. （Ullstein；Nr. 35156：Ullstein-Materialien）

（2）Bi-yän-lu：Meister Yüan-wu's Niederschrift von der Smaragdenen Felswand/übers. und erl. von Wilhelm Gundert. Wiesbaden：Marixverl. ，2005. 580，364，167 S. ；Ill. ；24cm. ＋Kt. -Beil. （1 Bl. ）. ISBN：3865390318，3865390315.

9. Bi-yän-lu：Koan-Sammlung；Aufzeichnungen des Meisters vom Blauen Fels/［Yüan-wu］. Aus dem Chines. übers. ，kommentiert und hrsg. von Ernst Schwarz. München：Kösel，1999. 526 S. ：Ill. ；24cm. ISBN：3466204434，3466204437.

《碧岩录》，（宋）圆悟克勤大师著；Schwarz，Ernst 译.

10. Bi-yan-lu：die 100 Kôan des Hekiganroku ＝ Aufzeichnungen vor smaragdener Felswand/［Yuanwu］. Aus dem Chines. übers. und kommentiert von Dietrich Roloff. Oberstdorf：Windpferd，2013. 704 S. ：Ill. ；

24cm. ISBN：3864100451.

《碧岩录》，(宋)圆悟克勤大师著；Roloff, Dietrich 译.

11. Ch'an-tsung Wu-men kuan＝Zutritt nur durch die Wand/ Wu-men Hui-k'ai. übers. u. mit Einl. u. Anm. vers. von Walter Liebenthal. Heidelberg：Schneider, 1977. 142 S.：2 Ill.；24cm. ISBN：3795306144, 3795306140. (Sammlung Weltliteratur)

《禅宗无门关》，Liebenthal, Walter 译.

12. Juwel des Lebens：Buddhas erleuchtetes Erbarmen；aus d. Lotos-Sūtra/von Margareta von Borsig. Freiburg：Herder, 1986. 158 p.：ill.；18cm. ISBN：3451083094, 3451083099. (Herderbücherei；1309. Texte zum Nachdenken；52)

《妙法莲华经》；Borsig, Margareta von 译.

(1) Neuausg. Freiburg im Breisgau；Basel；Wien：Herder, 2002. 158 S.：Ill.；19cm. ISBN：3451274848, 3451274841. (Juwelen des Lebens)

(2) 3. Aufl. St. Ottilien：EOS, 2008. 133 S.：Ill.；23cm. ISBN：3830673224, 3830673221.

13. Begegnungen und Reden/Meister Linji. Aus d. Chines. übers. u. mit e. Nachw. u. e. Glossar vers. von Pierre Brun. Zürich：Ammann, 1986. 129 S.；19cm. ISBN：3250010609, 325001060X. (Bibliothek des Herrn Parnok；11)

《临济录》，义玄(—867)著；Brun, Pierre 译.

14. Linji Yulu：Worte eines Zen-Meisters＝(Rinzai-roku)/ Linji Yixuan (Rinzai Gigen). [Dt. von Keller, Guido]. Frankfurt, M.：Angkor-Verl., 2015. 96 S.；19cm. ISBN：3943839302, 3943839303.

《临济录》，义玄(—867)著；Keller, Guido(1964—)译.

15. Bruchstücke des Ātānātikasūtra aus dem Zentralasiatischen Sanskritkanon der Buddhisten/Helmut Hoffman. Nachträge zu „Kleinere Sanskrit-Texte Hefte III-V"/Zusammengestellt von Lore Sander. Stuttgart：F. Steiner, 1987. 212 pages：illustrations；24cm. ISBN：3515047514, 3515047517. (Kleinere Sanskrit-Texte；heft 5；Monographien zur indischen Archæologie, Kunst und Philologie；bd. 3)

《阿托那智经》，Hoffmann, Helmut (1890—1949)译.

16. Das Dhāraṇī des grossen Erbarmens des Bodhisattva Avalokites'vara mit tausend Häden und Augen：Übersetzung und Untersuchung ihrer textlichen Grundlage sowie Erforschung ihres Kultes in China/Maria Dorothea Reis-Habito. Augustin：Inst. Monumenta Serica [u. a.], 1993. 466, [20] S.：Ill. Zugl.：München, Univ., Diss., 1991. ISBN：3805002963, 3805002967. (Monumenta serica monograph series；27)

《千手千眼观世音菩萨广大圆满无碍大悲心陀罗尼经》，Reis-Habito, Maria Dorothea 译.

17. Der 14. Dalai Lama/Siren und Gewang. [Beijing]：

China Intercontinental Press，1997. 88 S. ISBN：7801133013

《十四世达赖喇嘛》，司仁，格旺. 五洲传播出版社.

18. Die Reinkarnation des Dalai Lama/von Chen Qingying. Beijing：China Intercontinental Press, 2004. 194 S.：ill.；21cm. ISBN：7508504763

《达赖喇嘛转世》，陈庆英著；何妙生，李道斌译. 五洲传播出版社. 本书介绍藏传佛教与活佛转世制度、达赖喇嘛转世概况以及形定的历史定制.

B43 道教

1. Das Geheimnis der goldenen Blüte：Ein chinesisches Lebensbuch/übersetzt und erläutert von Richard Wilhelm. Mit einem europäischen Kommentar von C. G. Jung, München 1929. 161 pages, 10 leaves of plates：illustrations；24cm.

《太乙金华宗旨》，卫礼贤（Wilhelm, Richard, 1873—1930)译.

(1) 2. Aufl. Berlin：Dorn-Verl., 1936. XVIII, 150 S.：mehr. Bl. Abb.；gr. 8.

(2) Zürich：Rascher, 1944. XVIII, 150 S.：mit Abb., 6 Bl. Abb.；gr. 8.

(3) Zürich；Stuttgart：Rascher, 1957. XXVI, 161 S., mit 10 S. Abb., 1 Titelbild：[Mit] 11 Taf. u. 5 Abb. im Text；gr. 8.

(4) Zürich；Stuttgart：Rascher, 1965. XXI, 124 S., 1 Titelbild：[Mit] 11 Taf. u. 5 Abb.；gr. 8.

(5) 3., unveränd. Aufl. Olten；Freiburg i. Br.：Walter, 1971. XXI, 124 S., 1 Titelbild：[Mit] 5 Taf. u. 11 Abb.；gr. 8. ISBN：3530264203；3530264202.

(6) 13. Aufl. Olten；Freiburg i. Br.：Walter, 1979. XXI, 124 S.：Ill.；24cm. ISBN：3530264203；3530264202.

(7) 15. Aufl. Olten；Freiburg i. Br.：Walter, 1982. XXI, 124 S.：Ill.；24cm. ISBN：3530264203；3530264202.

(8) 16. Aufl. Olten；Freiburg i. Br.：Walter, 1984. XXI, 124 S.：16 Ill.；24cm. ISBN：3530264203；3530264202.

(9) 17. Aufl. Olten；Freiburg i. Br.：Walter, 1986. XXI, 124 S.：16 Ill.；24cm. ISBN：3530264203；3530264202.

(10) 18. Aufl. Olten；Freiburg i. Br.：Walter, 1987. 124, 10 S.：Ill.；24cm. ISBN：3530264203；3530264202.

2. Geheimnis der goldenen Blüte：das Buch von Bewusstsein und Leben/Richard Wilhelm；C. G. Jung. Aus d. Chines. übers. u. erl. von Richard Wilhelm. Mit e. europ. Kommentar von C. G. Jung. [Mit erg. übers. aus d. Chines. von Barbara Hendrischke. Neu hrsg. u.

mit e. Nachw. vers. von Ulf Diederichs]. 3. Aufl. München: Diederichs, 1990. 191 S.; 12 Ill.; 19cm. ISBN: 3424008746; 3424008745. (Diederichs gelbe Reihe; 64: China).

《太乙金华宗旨》新版,卫礼贤(Wilhelm, Richard, 1873—1930)译.

(1) München: Diederichs, 1992. 191 S.; Ill.; 19cm. ISBN: 3424008746; 3424008745. (Diederichs gelbe Reihe; 64: China).

(2)4. Aufl. München: Diederichs, 1994. 191 S.; Ill.; 19cm. ISBN: 3424008746; 3424008745. (Diederichs gelbe Reihe; 64: China).

(3)München: Diederichs, 2005. 191 pages; illustrations; 20cm. ISBN: 3720526531; 3720526534. (Diederichs gelbe Reihe).

3. Das Geheimnis der goldenen Blüte: [das klassische Meditationshandbuch desTaoismus]/Thomas Cleary. [Aus dem Engl. von Heinz Knotek]. 2. Aufl. Hamburg: Aurinia-Verl., 2013. 171 S,; graph. Darst.; 20cm. ISBN: 3937392806, 3937392807

《太乙金华宗旨》,Cleary, Thomas 译.

4. Das wahre Buch vom quellenden Urgrund: Tschung hüdschen ging/LiäDsi. Die Lehren d. Philosophen Lä Yü Kou; Yang Dschu. Aus d. Chines. verdeutscht u. erl. v. Richard Wilhelm. Jena: Diederichs, 1937. XXXIII, 174 S.; Mit chines. Originaltitel, 1 Bildnis u. 7 chines. Zeichngn; 8.

《冲虚真经》,列御寇、杨朱著,卫礼贤(Wilhelm, Richard, 1873—1930)译.

(1)Düsseldorf, Köln: Diederichs, 1968. 243 S.; 8. (Diederichs b Taschenausgaben; 37.

(2)Düsseldorf, Köln: Diederichs, 1972. 243 S.;; 19cm. ISBN: 3424004618, 3424004618.

(3)Düsseldorf, Köln: Diederichs, 1974. 243 S.;; 19cm. ISBN: 3424004601, 342400460X. (Die Philosophie Chinas)

(4)Neuausg. Düsseldorf, Köln: Diederichs, 1980. 255 S.; Ill.; 19cm. ISBN: 3424006285, 3424006289. (Diederichs gelbe Reihe; 28: China)

(5)3. Aufl. Düsseldorf, Köln: Diederichs, 1987. 254 S.; 19cm. ISBN: 3424006285, 3424006289. (Diederichs gelbe Reihe; 28: China)

(6)4. Aufl. München: Diederichs, 1992. 254 S.; 19cm. ISBN: 3424006285, 3424006289. (Diederichs gelbe Reihe; 28: China)

(7)überarb. Neuausg. München: Diederichs, 2009. 336 S.; 20cm. ISBN: 3424350043. (Diederichs gelbe Reihe). 德中双语

(8)Das wahre Buch vom quellenden Urgrund/Lä Dsi. Wiesbaden: Marixverl., 2014. 229 S.; Ill.; 21cm.

ISBN: 3865393487, 3865393489. (德中双语)

5. Die sieben Meister der vollkommenen Verwirklichung: d. taoist. Lehrroman Ch'i-chen-chuan in übers. u. im Spiegel seiner Quellen/[Huang Yung-liang]. Günther Endres. Frankfurt am Main; Bern; New York: Lang, 1985. II, 388 S.; Ill.; 21cm. ISBN: 3820482003, 3820482008. (Würzburger Sino-Japonica; Bd. 13)

《七真因果传》(《七真传》),黄永亮著;Endres, Günther 译.

(1)Die sieben Meister des wunderbaren Tao: taoistische Geschichten aus der Schule der vollkommenen Verwirklichung; vom Werdegang der sieben Schüler des Grossmeisters Wang im China des 12. Jahrhunderts/[Huang Yongliang]. Günther Enders (Hrsg.). Bern; München; Wien: Barth, 1991. 319 S.; Ill.; 22cm. ISBN: 3502651819, 3502651817.

6. Chang Po-tuan, das Geheimnis des goldenen Elixiers: die „innere Lehre" des Taoismus von der Verschmelzung von Yin und Yang/mit Kommentaren u. Erl. d. taoist. Adepten Liu I-ming. übers. u. hrsg. von Thomas Cleary. [Einzig berecht. übers. aus d. Amerikan. unter Heranziehung d. chines Orig. von Ingrid Fischer-Schreiber]. [Bern; München; Wien]: Barth, 1990. 192 S.; Ill.; 22cm. ISBN: 3502651017, 3502651019.

道教释义及阴阳融合. 张伯端(983—1082)著,Liu Yiming 注释;Cleary, Thomas 译.

7. Leben und Wirken Lao-Tzu's in Schrift und Bild = Lao-chün-pa-shih-i-hua-t'u-shuo/eingeleitet, übers. u. hrsg. von Florian C. Reiter. Würzburg: Königshausen u. Neumann, 1990. 240 S.; überwiegend Ill.; 24cm. ISBN: 3884794906, 3884794906.

《老君八十一化图说》;Reiter, Florian 译.

8. Der Meister vom Drachentor: geheime Praktiken des Daoismus im modernen China/Chen Kaiguo und Zheng Shunchao. Aus dem chines. Orig. übers. und hrsg. von Thomas Cleary. Aus dem Amerikan. übertr. von Wolfgang Höhn. [München]: Ansata, 2000. 375 S.; 22cm. ISBN: 3778771671, 3778771679

《大道行：访孤独居士王力平先生》,陈开国,郑顺潮(1966—)著;Cleary, Thomas F. (1949—)(美国翻译家)译.

(1)Taschenbucherstausg. München: Heyne, 2005. 379 S. ISBN: 3453700309, 3453700307

(2)Taschenbucherstausg. Lingen Lotus Press, 2009. 373 S. Ill., Kt. 21cm. ISBN: 3935367479, 3935367473

C 类　社会科学总论

C1　社会科学理论

1. Die kämpferischen Aufgaben der Mitarbeiter in

Philosophie und Gesellschaftswissenschaften Rede am 26. Okt. 1963 auf d. 4. , erw. Sitzung d. Ausschusses d. Abt. Philosophie u. Gesellschaftswiss. an d. Chines. Akad. d. Wiss. / Yang Dschou. Peking：Verl. f. Fremdsprach. Literatur, 1964. 110 S.

《哲学社会科学工作者的战斗任务：1963.1.26 在中国科学院哲学社会科学部委员会第四次扩大会议上的讲话》，周扬.

C2 人口学

1. Bevölkerung und Nationalitäten/[Hrsg.： Verl. für fremdsprachige Literatur]. Beijing： Verlag für fremdsprachige Literatur, 1988. 33 S：Ill.

《人口与民族》.外文出版社（中国简况）

2. Chinas Bevölkerung： Entwicklung und Probleme/von Tian Xueyuan und Zhou Liping. Übers. von Ren Shuyin. [Beijing]：China Internat. Press, 2004. 119 S. ： ill. , graph. Darst. ；21cm. ISBN：7508504453

《中国人口》，田雪原，周丽苹著；任树垠译.五洲传播出版社.

C3 中国各民族

1. Die nationalen Minderheiten in China/[von Ma Yin u. -a. ； Deutsch von Chen Hanli [and others]. Beijing, China： Verlag für Fremdsprachige Literatur, 1990. 633 pages, [49] pages of plates： illustrations （some color）, maps; 21cm. ISBN：7119000101

《中国少数民族》，马寅.

2. Nationalitäten in China/von Wang Can. Übers. von Zhao Zhenquan und Zhou Jian. [Beijing]：China Internat. Press, 2004. 194 S.： ill. ；21cm. ISBN：7508504933

《中国民族》，王灿著；周健译.五洲传播出版社（中国基本情况丛书/郭长建主编）

3. 中国的民族区域自治：德文/中华人民共和国国务院新闻办公室发布.北京：新星出版社,2005.51 页;20cm. ISBN：7801486927

4. 中国的民族政策与各民族共同繁荣发展/中华人民共和国国务院新闻办公室[编].北京：外文出版社,2009. 82 页;21cm. ISBN：7119060576

5. Die Volksgruppen. monograph. Beijing：Verlag für Fremdsprachige Literratur, 2009. 31 pages：color illustrations；21cm. ISBN：7119058498

《中国的民族》，外文出版社德文编译部编译.

6. Chinas nationale Minderheiten/Xu Ying ＆ Wang Baoquin. Beijing：China Intercontinental Press, 2009. 133 S：Ill. ISBN：7508515748，7508515749. （Reise durch China）

《民族之旅》，徐英，王宝琴著.五洲传播出版社.

D 类 政治、法律

D1 中国政治

D11 概况

1. China：Land der vielen Nationalitäten：eine Skizze/Shu-tang Wang （Schu-tang）. Peking：Verlag für fremdsprachige Literatur, 1955. 1 Bd.

《中国：一个多民族的国家》，王树棠.

2. Das kleine China-Handbuch/[Dt. von Ruth Weiss]. Peking：Verl. für fremdsprachige Literatur, 1958. 302 S；Ill.

《新中国手册》，外交出版社编译.

3. Die Grosse Wende：Erinnerungen an den Befreiungskrieg. Peking：Verlag für Fremdspachige Literatur, 1962. 287 pages：illustrations，maps

《伟大的转折》，吴玉章等.

4. China： e. Überblick/Qi Wen. Beijing： Verlag für Fremdsprachige Literatur；Beijing：Vertriebszentrum für Publ. aus China, 1982. 271 S. ：zahlr. ill. （z. T. farb.）, Kt. ；19cm.

《中国概貌》，齐雯编.

5. China im Umriss/Qi Wen. Beijing：Verl. für Fremdsprachige Literatur, 1985. 117，[52] S. ： ill.

《中国便览》，齐雯编.

6. Politik. Beijing：Verl. für Fremdsprachige Literatur, 1986. 214 S. ：ill. , graph. Darst.

《政治》，《中国概况丛书》编辑委员会编.

7. Das Land und die Naturressourcen/Hrsg. ： Verl. für fremdsprachige Literatur]. Beijing：Verlag für fremdsprachige Literatur, 1987. 33 S：Ill. , Tab；19cm.

《国土与资源》（中国简况）

8. Staatsaufbau/Verlag für fremdsprachige Literatur. Verlag für fremdsprachige Literatur. Beijing： Verlag für fremdsprachige Literatur, 1987. 32 S：Ill.

《国家机构》（中国简况）

9. Staatsflagge， Staatswappen， Nationalhymne und Hauptstadt/[Wang Chuanmin, Herausgeber]. Beijing：Verlag für Fremdsprachige Literatur，2003. 41 pages：color illustrations，music；18cm. ISBN：711903149X

《中华人民共和国国旗、国徽、国歌、首都》，王传民.

10. Das politische System im heutigen China/von Yin Zhongqing. [Beijing]：China Internat. Press, 2004. 197 S. ：ill. ；21cm. ISBN：7508504704

《中国政治制度》，尹中卿著；周健译.五洲传播出版社（中国基本情况丛书/郭长建主编）

11. Einblick in China：Fragen und Antworten/Yao Jianguo. Beijing：Neuer Stern-Verl, 2005. 229 S. ISBN：7801489101

《透视中国问与答》，王刚毅，吴伟，李建国主编；钟英杰等译. 新星出版社.

12. 中国的民主政治建设:德文/中华人民共和国国务院新闻办公室发布. 北京:新星出版社,2005. 100 页;20cm. ISBN:7801489144

13. 30 Jahre Reformen in China in den Augen chinesischer und ausländischer Wissenschaftler/Chinesische Institut für Reformen und Entwicklung Hainan;[übersetzt von] Olaf Matthes, Ute Wallenböck, Christina Waraschitz. Beijing:Verlag für fremdsprachige Literatur, 2008. 272 pages:illustrations;23cm. ISBN:7119054841
《中外学者眼中的中国改革 30 年》,中国(海南)改革发展研究院主编.

14. Der Weg Chinas/Tian Yingkui;[übersetzt von] Matthias Mersch, Dorian Liedtke. Beijing:Verlag für fremdsprachige Literatur, 2008. 195 pages;23cm. ISBN:7119054780
《中国道路:从科学发展观解读中国发展》,田应奎著.

15. China:ein Lesebuch zur Geschichte, Kultur und Zivilisation/Shuyang Su.[Dt. Übers.:Silvia Kettelhut]. Sonderausg. Gütersloh;München:Chronik-Verl., 2008. 222 S.:ill.;24cm. ISBN:3577143806, 3577143800
《中国读本》,苏叔阳(1938—)著. Kettelhut, Silvia 译.

16. 中国改革开放大事记/外文出版社德文编译部编译. 北京:外文出版社,2009. 38 页;21cm. ISBN:7119058634

17. China-ein enormer Wandel 1978—2008/ Wu Xiaobo. Übers. von Sabine Wang. Beijing:China Intercontinental Press, 2009. 217 S. ill. 23cm. ISBN:7508516196
《中国巨变:1978—2008》,吴晓波著. 五洲传播出版社.

18. Das große China-Buch-ein Streifzug durch die erstaunliche Geschichte einer fünftausendjährigen Kultur/ Wang Qicheng.[Dt. Übers.:Li Xiang...]. Beijing:Verl. für Fremdsprachige Literatur, 2010. 226 S. zahlr. Ill. 24cm., 436 g. ISBN:7119060323
《看中国》,王麒诚著.

19. 中国梦,什么梦? / 李君如著;李响,Wolfgang Schaub, Burkhard Risse 德文翻译. 北京:外文出版社,2014. 180 页;24cm. ISBN:7119093253
德文题名:Chinesischer Traum

20. Beitrag zum chinesischen Sklavensystem nebst einer Übersetzg des „Chung kuo nu pei chih tu"〈das Sklavensystem Chinas〉von Wang Shih Chieh/Anton Pippon. Tokyo:Deutshe Gesellschaft für Natur- und Völkerkunde Ostasiens, 1936. IV, 140 S;gr. 8°
《中国奴婢制度》,王世杰(1891—1981)著;Anton Pippon 译.

D12 中国政治思想史

1. Die Grundlehren von dem Volkstum/ins Dt. übertr. von Tsan Wan. Sun, Yat-sen. Berlin:Schlieffen, 1927. 200 S:Ill.

《三民主义》,孙文(1866—1925)著;万灿(Wan Tsan)译.

D13 中国共产党

1. Fragen der Vergenossenschaftlichung in der Landwirtschaft Beschluss;Angenommen vom 6.(erw.)Plenum d. vom 7. Parteitag gewählten ZK d. Kommunist. Partei Chinas. Peking:Verl. f. fremdsprachige Literatur, 1957. 36 S.
《中国共产党第七届中央委员会第六次全体会议(扩大)关于农业合作化问题的决议》

2. Der VIII. Parteitag der Kommunistischen Partei Chinas. Peking:Verlag für fremdsprachige Literatur, 1956. 2 volumes(317, 386 pages)
Kataloges:Bd. 1:Dokumente—Vol. 2:Speeches. Bd. 1:Dokumente. Vol. 2:Speeches.
《中国共产党第八次全国代表大会文件集》(一)

3. 中国共产党第八次全国代表大会文件汇编(第二辑). 北京:外文出版社,1957

4. 中国共产党第八次全国代表大会文件汇编(第三辑). 北京:外文出版社,1957

5. Die Dokumente der zweiten Plenartagung des VIII. Parteitags der Kommunistischen Partei Chinas. Peking:Verl. f. fremdsprachige Literatur, 1958. 100 S.
《中国共产党第八届全国代表大会第二次会议文件集》

6. Dokumente der 6. Plenartagung des VIII. ZK der Kommunistischen Partei Chinas. Peking:Verlag für Fremdsprachige Literatur, 1959. 56 S;19cm.
《中国共产党第八届中央委员会第六次全体会议文件》

7. Dokumente der 8. Plenartagung des VIII. Zentralkomitees der Kommunistischen Partei Chinas. Peking:Verlag für fremdsprachige Literatur, 1959. 33 p.
《中国共产党第八届中央委员会第八次全体会议文件》

8. Kommuniqué der 11. Plenartagung des VIII. Zentralkomitees der Kommunistischen Partei Chinas(Angenommen am 12. Aug. 1966). Peking:Verl. für Fremdsprachige Literatur, 1966. 19 S.
《中国共产党第八届中央委员会第十一次全体会议公报》

9. Kommuniqué der erweiterten 12. Plenartagung des VIII. Zentralkomitees der Kommunistischen Partei Chinas(Angenommen am 31. Oktober 1968). Peking:Verlag Für Fremdsprachige Literatur, 1968. 23 pages;13cm.
《中国共产党第八届扩大的第十二次中央委员会全会公报》

10. Dokumente des IX. Parteitags der Kommunistischen Partei Chinas. Peking:Verl. für Fremdsprachige Literatur, 1969. 200 S. mit Abb. kl. 8
《中国共产党第九次全国代表大会文件汇编》

11. Pressekommuniqués des Sekretariats beim Präsidium des IX. Parteitags der Kommunistischen Partei Chinas:(1., 14. u. 24. April 1969);Pressekommuniqué der 1. Plenartagung des IX. Zentralkomitees der Kommunistischen

Partei Chinas：（28. April 1969）/Chung-kuo-kung-ch'an-tang. Peking：Verl. für Fremdsprachige Literatur, 1969. 49 S.：mit Abb.；kl. 8

《中国共产党第九次全国代表大会主席团秘书处新闻公报，中国共产党第九届中央委员会第一次全体会议新闻公报》

12. Bericht auf dem IX. Parteitag der Kommunistischen Partei Chinas/Biao Lin. Peking：Verl. für Fremdsprachige Literatur, 1969. 120 S.

《在中国共产党第九次全国代表大会上的报告》，林彪.

13. Der 10. Parteitag der Kommunistischen Partei Chinas：Dokumente/v. Tschou En-Lai... et al.]. Peking：Verlag für fremdsprachige Literatur, 1973. 106 S.

《中国共产党第十次全国代表大会文件汇编》

14. Der XI. Parteitag der Kommunistischen Partei Chinas：Dokumente. Peking：Verl. für Fremdsprach. Literatur, 1977. [24], 264 S.：Ill

《中国共产党第十一次全国代表大会文件汇编》

15. Der Zwölfte Parteitag der Kommunistischen Partei Chinas：Dokumente. Peking：Verl. für fremdsprach. Literatur, 1982. 187 S.

《中国共产党第十二次全国代表大会文献》

16. Dokumente des XIII. Parteitags des Kommunistischen Partei Chinas（1987）. Beijing：Verlag für Fremdsprachige Literatur, 1988. 279 S

《中国共产党第十三次全国代表大会文献》

17. Die 4. Plenartagung des XIII. ZK der KP Chinas：Zusammengestellt vom Verlag Neuer Stern. Beijing：Verlag neuer stern, 1989. 46 pages：illustrations；18cm.

《中共十三届四中全会》. 新星出版社.

18. Dokumente des XVI Parteitags der Kommunistischen Partei Chinas ＝ [Zhongguo Gongchandang Di-Shiliu Ci Quanguo Daibiao Dahui Wenxian]/[Zhong Xin] bian. Beijing：Verlag für fremdsprachige Literatur, 2002. 281 S.；22cm. ISBN：7119032291

《中国共产党第十六次全国代表大会文献》，钟欣 .

19. Dokumente des XVII. Parteitag der Kommunistischen Partei Chinas/[edited by Zhong Xin]. Beijing：Verlag für Fremdsprachige Literatur, 2007. 303 pages：color illustrations, color portraits；23cm. ISBN：7119051437

《中国共产党第十七次全国代表大会文献》，钟欣编.

20. Rede auf der Festveranstaltung zum 40. Jahrestag der Gründung der Kommunistischen Partei Chinas/Schao-tschi Liu. Peking：Verl. f. Fremsprach. Literatur, 1961. 40 S.

《在庆祝中国共产党成立四十周年大会上的讲话》，刘少奇.

21. Beschluss des Zentralkomitees der Kommunistischen Partei Chinas über die grosse proletarische Kulturrevolution （Angenommen am 8. August 1966）. Peking：Verlag für Fremdsprachige Literatur, 1966. 23 pages

《中国共产党中央委员会关于无产阶级文化大革命的决定》

22. Es lebe die Kommunistische Partei Chinas! Zum 48. Geburtstag der KP Chinas：Leitartikel der 'Renmin Ribao', 'Hongqi' und 'Jiefangjun Bao' vom 1. Juli 1969/Verlag für fremdsprachige Literatur. Peking：Verl. f. fremdsprachige Literatur, 1969. 20 S

《中国共产党万岁》

23. Statut der Kommunistischen Partei Chinas. Peking：Verl. für fremdsprachige Literatur, 1969. 44 S.

《中国共产党章程》

24. Zur Feier des 50. [fünfzigsten] Jahrestags der Kommunistischen Partei Chinas（1. Juli 1971）：von d. Red. d. Renmin Ribao, der Zeitschrift Hongqi u. d. Jiefangjun Bao. Peking：Verlag für Fremdsprachige Literatur, 1971. 116 S. 1 Ill.；13cm.

《纪念中国共产党五十周年》

25. Resolution über einige Fragen zur Geschichte der KP Chinas seit 1949. Beijing：Verlag für fremdsprachige Literatur, 1981. 142 S.

《关于建国以来党的若干历史问题的决议》

26. Reformen durchsetzen und für die sozialistische Modernisierung kämpfen：Dokumente der Nationalen Delegiertenkonferenz der KP Chinas（18.-23. Sept. 1985）. Beijing：Verl. f. Fremdspr. Literatur, 1985. 143 S.

《坚持改革，为实现社会主义现代化而斗争：中国共产党代表会议文献》

27. Rede auf der Versammlung zur Feier des 80. Gründungstags der KP Chinas：1. Juli 2001/Jiang Zemin. Beijing：Verlag Neuer Stern, 2001. 66 pages；21cm. ISBN：7 80148388X

《在庆祝中国共产党成立八十周年大会上的讲话》，江泽民. 新星出版社 .

D131 政治领导人著作

刘少奇（1898—1969）

1. Internationalismus und Nationalismus：Vollst. , ungekürzter Text/Tschau-Tschi Liu. Frankfurt a. M. Parteivorstand d. KPD, 1948. 31 Seiten 8°

《论国际主义与民族主义》

（1） Internationalismus und Nationalismus/Schau Tschi Liu. Berlin Dietz, 1952. 39 Seiten 8°. （Internationale Schriftenreihe；H. 12）

2. Über die Partei：Referat über die Abänderung des Parteistatuts auf dem VII. Parteitag der Kommunistischen Partei Chinas im Mai 1945/Liu Schau-tschi. Berlin：Dietz, 1954. 176 S.

《论党》

3. Rechenschaftsbericht des Zentralkomitees der Kommunistischen Partei Chinas an den VIII. Parteitag/Liu Shaoqi. Berlin：Dietz Verlag，1956. 1 v. （63 p. ）；in-8°
《在中国共产党第八次全国代表大会上的政治报告》

4. Wie man ein guter Kommunist wird：Vorlesungen，gehalten im Juli 1939 am Institut für Marxismus-Leninismus zu Yenan/Liu Schau-Tschi. Peking：Verlag für Fremdsprachige Literatur，1965. 113 S；19cm.
《论共产党员的修养》
（1）2. Aufl. Beijing：Verl. für Fremdsprachige Literatur，1982. 101 Seiten；19cm.

5. Ausgewählte Schriften und Materialien. 1. / Liu Shaoqi. Th. Bergmann… （Hrsg. ）. Stuttgart：Edition Cordeliers，1982. 345 S. ；ill. ISBN：3922836089，3922836087
《刘少奇选集》，卷一

6. Ausgewählte Schriften und Materialien. 2. /Liu Shaoqi. Th. Bergmann… （Hrsg. ）. Stuttgart：Edition Cordeliers，1982. 391 S. ，24 Bl. ；ill. ISBN：3922836089，3922836087
《刘少奇选集》，卷二

7. Ausgewählte Schriften und Materialien/Liu Shaoqi. Hrsg. von Theodor Bergmann，Ulrich Menzel und Ursula Menzel-Fischer. Schwalbach：edition global，1990. 792 S.
《刘少奇选集》

周恩来（1898—1976）

1. Ausgewählte Schriften 1/ Zhou Enlai. Beijing：Verl. für Fremdsprachige Literatur，1981. 342 S. ；ill.
《周恩来选集》，上卷

2. Ausgewählte Schriften 2/Zhou Enlai. Beijing：Verl. für Fremdsprachige Literatur，版本：1. Aufl. 1989. 376 S. ：ill.
《周恩来文集》，下卷

邓小平（1904—1997）

1. Der Aufbau des Sozialismus chinesischer Prägung/Deng Xiaoping. Beijing：Verl. f. Fremdsprachige Literatur，1985. 90 S.
《建设有中国特色的社会主义》

2. Ausgewählte Schriften：（1975—1982）/Deng Xiaoping. 1. Aufl. Beijing：Verl. für Fremdsprachige Literatur，1985. 485 S. ；Ill. ；23cm.
《邓小平选集：1975—1982》

习近平（1953—　）

1. 习近平谈治国理政：德文版/习近平；德文翻译组译. 北京：外文出版社，2014. 575 页：照片；25cm. ISBN：7119090269

2. 决胜全面建成小康社会 夺取新时代中国特色社会主义伟大胜利 德文/习近平著. 北京：外文出版社，2018. 104；23cm. ISBN：7119111995

D14　政策、政论

1. Über die historischen Erfahrungen der Diktatur des Proletariats：der hier veröffentlichte Leitartikel der Zeitung „Jenminjibao" vom 5. April 1956 ist eine Abhandlung der Redaktion über die Ergebnisse einer Diskussion，die das Politbüro des ZK der Kommunistischen Partei Chinas in einer erweiterten Sitzung führte. Peking：Verlag für fremdsprachige Literatur，1956. 24 p. ；21cm.
《关于无产阶级专政的历史经验》

2. Lasst hundert Blumen miteinander blühen! Lasst hundert Schulen miteinander streiten! /Lu Ding-Ji. Peking：Verlag fur Fremdsprachige Literatur，1957. 45 s.
《百花齐放、百家争鸣》，陆定一.

3. Zur gegenwärtigen internationalen Lage. Peking：Verl. für Fremdsprachige Literatur，1958. 82 S. ；19cm.
《目前国际形势》

4. China wird England überholen/Niu Dschung-huang. Peking：Verl. f. fremdsprachige Literatur，1958. 75 S. ；
《赶上英国，超过美国》，牛中黄.

5. Der Sieg des Marxismus-Leninismus in China aus Anlaß des 10. Jahrestages der Gründung der Volksrepublik China für die Zeitschrift „Probleme des Friedens und des Sozialismus" geschrieben；[14. 9. 1959]/Liu Schao-tschi. Peking：Verlag für Fremdsprachige Literatur ［Waiwen chubanshe］Peking：Verlag für Fremdsprachige Literatur ［Waiwen chubanshe］，1959. 43 S.
《马克思列宁主义在中国的胜利》，刘少奇著.
（1）Peking：Verlag für Fremdsprachige Literatur，1960. 93 pages；19cm.

6. Die Geschlossenheit des chinesischen Volkes und aller Völker der Welt：aus Anlaß des 10. Jahrestages der Gründung der Volksrepublik China für die „Prawda" geschrieben/Deng Xiaoping. Peking：Verl. für Fremdsprach. Lit. ，1959. 20 S.
《中国人民大团结和世界人民大团结》，邓小平.

7. Erhebt das rote Banner der Generallinie und marschiert weiter vorwärts! /Li Fu-tschun. Peking：Verl. für fremdsprach. Literatur，1960. 45 S
《高举总路线的红旗继续前进》，李富春.

8. Die Historischen Erfahrungen der Diktatur des Proletariats. Peking：Verlag für Fremdsprachige Literatur，1963. 72 S；19cm.
《无产阶级专政的历史经验》

9. Proletarier aller Länder，vereinigt euch gegen den gemeinsamen Feind. Peking：Verl. für fremdsprachige Literatur，1963. 99 S
《全世界无产者联合起来反对我们的共同敌人》

10. Volkskommunen auf dem Vormarsch：Zusammenfassung d. wichtigsten Erfahrungen d. ländl. Volkskommunen von Kuangtung in d. 5 Jahren ihres Bestehens/Dschu Tao. Peking：Verl. f. Fremdsprach. Literatur，1965. 42 S.

《人民公社在前进》,陶铸.

11. Vorwärts auf dem breiten Weg der Ideen Mao Tse-Tungs : zum 17. Jahrestag der Gründung der Volksrepublik China. Peking: Verl. für Fremdsprachl. Lit, 1967. 35 S.

《在毛泽东思想的大路上前进:庆祝中华人民共和国成立十七周年》

12. Das ganze Land muss eine grosse Schule der Ideen Mao Tse-Tungs werden. Zum 39. Jahrestag d. Gründung d. Chinesischen Volksbefreiungsarmee. Peking: Verl. für Fremdsprachige Literatur, 1967. 21 S

《全国都应该成为毛泽东思想的大学校》

13. Verrat an der Diktatur des Proletariats - der Kernpunkt des Buches über die „Selbstschulung." Peking: Verl. für Fremdsprachige Literatur, 1967. 25 S.

《〈修养〉的要害是背叛无产阶级专政》

14. Wegweiser zum Sieg der revolutionären Völker aller Länder. Peking: Verlag für Fremdsprachige Literatur, 1968. 15 S. 1 Ill. , 1 Kt. ; 13cm.

《各国革命人民胜利的航向》

15. Den sozialistischen oder den kapitalistischen Weg gehen?. Peking: Verl. für Fremdsprachige Literatur, 1968. 58 S.

《走社会主义道路,还是走资本主义道路?》

16. Nehmt frisches Blut aus dem Proletariat auf!: Ein wichtiges Problem bei der Ausrichtung der Parteiorganisation; Leitartikel der Zeitschrift „Hongqi. " Peking: Verl. für Fremdsprachige Literatur, 1969. 30 S.

《吸收无产阶级的新鲜血液》

17. Für die weitere Festigung der Diktatur des Proletariats kämpfen. Zum 20. Jahrestag d. Gründung d. Volksrepublik China. Peking: Verl. für Fremdsprachige Literatur, 1969. 48 S. mit Abb. kl. 8

《为进一步巩固无产阶级专政而斗争》

18. Lasst bei allem die Ideen Mao Tse-tungs das Kommando führen!: Leitartikel der „Renmin Ribao", „Hongqi" und „Jiefangjun Bao" zum Neujahrstag 1969. Peking: Verl. für Fremdsprachige Literatur, 1969. 23 S. : ill.

《用毛泽东思想统帅一切》

19. Kühn auf dem siegreichen Weg vorwärtsschreiten Zur begeisterten Feier d. 19. Jahrestages d. Gründung d. Volksrepublik China. Peking: Verl. für Fremdsprachige Literatur, 1969. 34 S. mit Abb. kl. 8

《在胜利的大道上奋勇前进》

20. Hebt das Banner der Geschlossenheit des IX. Parteitags hoch, um noch grössere Siege zu erringen. / Peking: Verl. für Fremdsprachige Literatur, 1969. 20 S.

《高举"九大"的团结旗帜,争取更大的胜利》

21. Es lebe der Sieg der Diktatur des Proletariats!: zum 100. Jahrestag der Pariser Kommune. Peking: Verlag für Fremdsprachige Literatur, 1971. 37 S; Portr; 19cm.《无产阶级专政胜利万岁》

22. Der revolutionaeren Linie des Vorsitzenden Mao gemäss siegreich vorwärts: Leitartikel. Peking: Verlag für Fremdsprachige Literatur, 1971. 22 S; 14cm.

《沿着毛主席革命路线胜利前进》,《人民日报》、《〈红旗〉杂志、《解放军报》一九七一年元旦社论.

23. Schliessen wir uns zusammen um noch grössere Siege zu erringen!: Leitartikel der „ Renmin Ribao", der Zeitschrift „ Hongqi" und der „ Jiefangjun Bao" zum Neujahr 1972. Peking: Verl. f. fremdsprach. Lit., 1972. 15 S.

《团结起来,争取更大的胜利》,《人民日报》、《〈红旗〉杂志、《解放军报》一九七二年元旦社论.

24. Ein grosser Sieg von historischer Bedeutung: Jubel über d. Ernennung Genossen Hua Guo-Fengs zum Vorsitzenden d. KP Chinas; Jubel über d. Zerschlagung d. parteifeindl. Wang-Dschang-Djiang-Yao-Clique. Peking: Verlag für Fremdsprachige Literatur, 1976. 50 S. : ill. ; 19cm.

《伟大的历史性胜利》

25. Das Licht der grossen Wahrheit des Marxismus erhellt unseren Weg vorwärts: Ansprache auf der Gedenkkundgebung zum 100. Todestag von Karl Marx (13, März 1983). Beijing: Verlag für fremdsprachige Literatur, 1983. 53 pages; 18cm.

《马克思主义伟大真理的光芒照耀我们前进》,胡耀邦.

D15 建设成就

1. Die Erfolge der Volksrepublik China in den letzten drei Jahren/Ji-Po Po. Peking: Verl. f. fremdsprachige Literatur, 1952. 18 S. ; 8 [Umschlagt.]

《新中国三年来的成就》,薄一波.

2. Bericht über die von der Regierung der Volksrepublik China geleistete Arbeit: gegeben auf der ersten Sitzung des Ersten Nationalen Volkskongresses der Volksrepublik China, 23. September 1954/Tschou En-Lai. Peking: Verl. für fremdsprachige Literatur, 1954. 70 S.:ill.

《政府工作报告》,周恩来.

3. Bericht über die Tätigkeit der Regierung: vorgetragen auf der 1. Tagung des Nationalen Volkskongresses am 18. April 1959/Tschou En-lai. Peking: Verlag für Fremdsprachige Literatur, 1959. 80 S.

《政府工作报告:在1959年4月18日在第二届全国人民代表大会第一次会议上》,周恩来.

4. Das grosse Jahrzehnt/Tschou En-Lai. Peking: Verl. für fremdsprachige Literatur, 1959. 42 S. ; 20cm.

《伟大的十年》,周恩来.

5. Das grosse Jahrzehnt. Peking: Verlag für Fremdsprachige Literatur, 1960. 42 pages; 19cm.

《伟大的十年：中华人民共和国经济和文化建设成就的统计》，国家统计局编.

6. Glanzvolle zehn Jahre. Peking：Verl. f. fremdsprachige Literatur，1960. 412 S.

《光辉的十年：1945——1959》

7. Der 2. ［Zweite］Fünfjahrplan in zwei Jahren erfüllt-über d. Entwicklg d. Volkswirtschaft im Jahre 1959. Peking：Verl. f. fremdsprachige Literatur，1960. 20 Bl. mit Abb. kl. 8

《五年计划二年完成》

8. Das erste Vierteljahrhundert des neuen China. Peking：Verlag für Fremdsprachige Literatur，1975. 267 S.：ill.；19cm.

《新中国的二十五年》

D16　政府组织

D161　人权

1. 中国人权发展五十年/中华人民共和国国务院新闻办公室发布. 北京：北京新星. ISBN：7801482735

D162　全国人民代表大会

1. Die Dokumente der 2. Tagung des 2. Nationalen Volkskongresses der Volksrepublik China. Peking：Verl. f. fremdsprachige Literatur，1960. 209 S.

《中华人民共和国第二届全国人民代表大会第二次会议文件》

2. Dokumente der 1. Tagung des IV. Nationalen Volkskongresses der Volksrepublik China. Peking：Verlag für Fremdsprachige Literatur，1975. 98，［2］pages；19cm.

《中华人民共和国第四届全国人民代表大会第一次会议文件》

3. Dokumente der 1. Tagung des V. Nationalen Volkskongresses der Volksrepublik China. Peking：Verlag für Fremdsprachige Literatur，1978. 287，［2］pages；19cm.

《中华人民共和国第五届全国人民代表大会第一次会议文件》，文荫，梁华.

4. 5. Tagung des V. Nationalen Volkskongresses：Hauptdokumente：neue Verfassung. Beijing：Verlag für fremdsprachige Literatur，1983. 1 Band.

《中华人民共和国第五届全国人民代表大会第五次会议主要文件》

5. 1. Tagung des VI. Nationalen Volkskongresses der Volksrepublik China：Hauptdokumente；［Bericht über die Tätigkeit der Regierung；Bericht über den Plan für die volkswirtschaftliche und gesellschaftliche Entwicklung 1983；Bericht über die Staatshaushaltsbilanz 1982；neue Staatsführer］. Beijing：Verl. f. Fremdspr. Lit，1983. 160 S.

《中华人民共和国第六届全国人民代表大会第一次主要会议主要文件》

6. Tagung des VI. Nationalen Volkskongresses der Volksrepublik China：Hauptdokumente. Beijing：Verl. für Fremdsprachige Literatur，1984. 119 S.

《中华人民共和国第六届全国人民代表大会第二次主要会议主要文件》

7. Tagung des VI. Nationalen Volkskongresses der Volksrepublik China：（Hauptdokumente）. Beijing：Verl. für fremdsprachige Literatur，1985. 103 S.

《中华人民共和国第六届全国人民代表大会第三次主要会议主要文件》

8. Tagung des VI. Nationalen Volkskongresses der Volksrepublik China：（Hauptdokumente）. Beijing：Verl. für fremdsprachige Literatur，1986. 215 S.

《中华人民共和国第六届全国人民代表大会第四次主要会议主要文件》

9. Tagung des VI. Nationalen Volkskongresses der Volksrepublik China：（Hauptdokumente）. Beijing：Verl. für fremdsprachige Literatur，1987. 128 S.

《中华人民共和国第六届全国人民代表大会第五次主要会议主要文件》

D163　中国人民政治协商会议

1. Das Gemeinsame Programm und andere Dokumente der Politischen Konsultativ-Konferenz des chinesischen Volkes. ［angenommen von der Ersten Plenartagung der Politischen Konsultativ-Konferenz des chinesischen Volkes am 29. September 1949 in Peking］. Peking：Fremdsprachige，1952. 48 pages；17cm.

《中国人民政治协商会议第一届全体会议重要文献》

D17　国家行政管理

D171　抗震救灾与危机管理

1. Nach einem grossen Erdbeben：Bericht über den Kampf des chinesischen Volkes gegen die Katastrophe im Gebiet Tangschan. Peking：Verlag für fremdsprachige Literarur，1977. 89 pages；plates；19cm.

《一场大地震之后：中国人民战胜自然灾害的事迹》

D172　精神文明建设

1. Beschluss des ZK der KP Chinas über die Leitprinzipien für den Aufbau der sozialistischen geistigen Zivilisation：（Angenommen von der 6. Plenartagung der XII. ZK der KPCh am 28. September 1986）. Beijing：Verl. f. Fremdspr. Lit. 1986. 26 S.

《中共中央关于社会主义精神文明建设指导方针的决议》

D18　社会各阶层

D181　知识分子

1. Bericht über die Frage der Intellektuellen/Tschou En-lai.

Peking：Verlag für Fremdsprachige Literatur，1956. 54 S.

《关于知识分子问题的报告》，周恩来.

2. Zur erneuten Erziehung der Intellektuellen/von Kommentatoren der „Renmin Ribao' (Volkszeitung) und der Zeitschrift ‚Hongqi' (Rote Fahne). Peking，1969. VIII，16 S.《关于知识分子再教育问题》

D182 青年

1. Die Chinesische Jugend marschiert vorwärts. Peking：Verl. für fremdsprachige Literatur，1951. 70 S；Ill.

《中国青年在前进》

D183 妇女

1. Chinas Frauen erobern die Zukunft. Peking：Verlag für Fremdsprachige Literatur，1960. 110 S；Portr. ，Ill；18cm.

《中国妇女在跃进》，马信德等著.

2. Chinas Frauen von Heute. Peking：Verlag für fremdsprachige Literatur，1973. 85 S.

《今日中国妇女》

3. 中国性别平等与妇女发展状况：德文/中华人民共和国国务院新闻办公室发布. 北京：新星出版社，2005. 43 页；20cm. ISBN：7801488318

D19 工运与工会

1. Chinesische Gewerkschaften. Beijing：Verlag für fremdsprachige Literatur，1987. 24 S；Ill；19cm.

《中国工会》

D191 政治运动和事件

1. Die grosse sozialistische Kulturrevolution in China. 1. Peking：Verlag für fremdsprachige Literatur，1966. 140 pages；15cm.

《中国的社会主义文化大革命》（第一集）

2. Die große sozialistische Kulturrevolution in China. 2. Peking：Verlag für fremdsprachige Literatur，1966

《中国的社会主义文化大革命》（第二集）

3. Die grosse sozialistische Kulturrevolution in China. 3. Peking：Verl. für Fremdsprachige Literatur，1966. 40 S.

《中国的社会主义文化大革命》（第三集）

4. Die grosse sozialistische Kulturrevolution in China. （4）. Peking：Verl. für Fremdsprachige Literatur，1967. 85 S.

《中国的社会主义文化大革命》（第四集）

5. Die grosse sozialistische Kulturrevolution in China. （5）. Peking：Verl. für Fremdsprachige Literatur，1967. 53 S.

《中国的社会主义文化大革命》（第五集）

6. Die grosse sozialistische Kulturrevolution in China. （6）. Peking：Verl. für Fremdsprachige Literatur，1967. 43 S.

《中国的社会主义文化大革命》（第六集）

7. Die grosse sozialistische Kulturrevolution in China. （7）. Peking：Verl. für Fremdsprachige Literatur，1967. 49 S.

《中国的社会主义文化大革命》（第七集）

8. Die grosse sozialistische Kulturrevolution in China. （8）. Peking：Verl. für Fremdsprachige Literatur，1967. 32 S.

《中国的社会主义文化大革命》（第八集）

9. Die grosse sozialistische Kulturrevolution in China. （9）. Peking：Verl. für Fremdsprachige Literatur，1967. 42 S.

《中国的社会主义文化大革命》（第九集）

10. Die grosse sozialistische Kulturrevolution in China. （10）. Peking：Verl. für Fremdsprachige Literatur，1967. 64 S.

《中国的社会主义文化大革命》（第十集）

11. Rundschreiben des Zentralkomitees der Kommunistischen Partei Chinas：（16. Mai 1966）；ein grossartiges historisches Dokument/［Hrsg. ：］ Die Redaktionen d. Zeitschrift „Hongqi“ 〈Rote Fahne〉 u. d. „Renmin Ribao“ ［jên min jih pao］ 〈Volkszeitung〉. Peking：Verl. f. Fremdsprachige Literatur，1967. 37 S.

《通知·伟大的历史文件》

12. Die Große Proletarische Kulturrevolution in China. Peking：Verl. für d. Fremdsprachige Literatur，1967. 8.

《中国的无产阶级文化大革命》

13. Ein epochemachendes Dokument. Zum 2. Jahrestag d. Veröffentlichung d. Rundschreibens. Peking：Verl. für Fremdsprachige Literatur，1968. 30 S. kl. 8

《划时代的文献》

14. Kritik an Lin Biao und Konfuzius. 1. Peking：Verlag für Fremdsprachige Literatur，1975. 187 S.

《批林批孔文选》（一）

15. Kritik an Lin Biao und Konfuzius. 2. Peking：Verlag für Fremdsprachige Literatur，1975. 250 S.

《批林批孔文选》（二）

16. Beschluss des Zentralkomitees der Kommunistischen Partei Chinas über die Grosse Proletarische Kulturrevolution （Angenommen am 8. August 1966）. Peking：Verlag für Fremdsprachige Literatur，1976. 23 pages

《中国共产党中央委员会关于无产阶级文化大革命的决定》

17. 风波平息以后/北京周报社编. 北京：新星出版社，1990. ISBN：7800852156

D192 社会生活

1. Gesellschaftliches Leben/［Red. d. dt. Ausg. ：Yan Junxu... Aus dem Chines. ：Wang Yang...］. Beijing：Verl. für fremdspr. Literatur，1985. 288 S. ：ill.

《社会生活》，《中国概况丛书》编辑委员会编.

2. Leben im heutigen China/Red. d. dt. Ausg. ：Liu Menglian. Beijing：Verlag f. Fremdsprach. Lit. ，1986. III，97 S.

《中国人民的生活》

3. Das Leben in China/Gong Wen. Beijing：China Intercontinental Press，2009. 154 S. ：zahlr. Ill. ISBN：7508515724

《生活之旅》，龚纹著. 五洲传播出版社. 本书通过美食、茶、养生、武术、气功、中医等，讲述中国式生活特点与文化.

4. Chinese Dinge/Popcorn；übersetzt von Tilman Lesche. Beijing：China Intercontinental Press，2009. 169 pages：color illustrations；23cm. ISBN：7508515892

《中国东西》，波普客编著. 五洲传播出版社. 本书选取 100 多种中国老百姓生活中的日常必需品. 也可以使外国人了解中国普通老百姓的日常生活.

D192.1 劳动就业与保障

1. Arbeit und Sozialabsicherung in China/Presseamt des Staatsrats der Volksrepublik China. Beijing：Neuer Stern，2002. 52 pages；21cm. ISBN：780148410X

《中国的劳动和社会保障状况》，中华人民共和国国务院新闻办公室发布. 新星出版社.

D192.2 禁毒

1. 中国的禁毒/中华人民共和国国务院新闻办公室发布. 北京：北京新星. ISBN：7801482875

D192.3 地方政治

D192.31 台湾

1. Jiang Zemin und Li Peng zur Taiwan-Frage. Beijing：China Intercontinental Press，1997. 77 pages：color illustrations；18cm. ISBN：7801131622

《江泽民、李鹏谈台湾问题》，江泽民、李鹏著；国务院台湾事务办公室编写. 五洲传播.

2. Fragen und Antworten über die „Taiwan-Frage und die Wiedervereinigung Chinas." ［Beijing］：China Intercontintental Press，1997. 4，121 pages：illustrations (chiefly color)；18cm. ISBN：7801133390

《〈台湾问题与祖国统一〉问答》，国务院台湾事务办公室编. 五洲传播.

D192.32 香港

1. Hong Kong im Übergang bis zum Jahre 1997/von Wang Qiaolong. Beijing China Intercontinental Press，1997. 77 S Ill. ISBN：780113284X

《"九七"前后谈香港》，王巧珑. 五洲传播.

2. Hong Kong - Chinas Sonderverwaltungszone/von Wang Qiaolong. Beijing：China Intercontinental Press，1997. 77 S；Ill. ISBN：7801132920

《香港：中国的特别行政区》，王巧珑. 五洲传播.

3. Ursprung und Lösung der Hongkong-Frage/von Huang Fengwu. Beijing：China Intercontinental Press，1997. 85 S；Ill. ISBN：7801132521

《香港问题的由来及解决》，黄凤武. 五洲传播.

4. Das Grundgesetz - „Blaupause" für die Sonderverwalt-ungszone Hong Kong/von Ge Guangzhi；Kou Qi. Beijing：China Intercontinental Press，1997. 93 S；Ill. ISBN：7801132602

《香港特别行政区的蓝图：基本法》，葛广智，寇琪. 五洲传播.

5. Hong Kongs Wirtschaft mit dem chinesischen Festland als

Rückhalt/von Cai Chimeng. Beijing：China Intercontinental Press，1997. 85 S；Ill. ISBN：7801132688

《背靠祖国的香港经济》，蔡赤萌. 五洲传播.

6. Wer hat das Wunder Hongkongs geschaffen? /Von Chen Duo；Lian Jintian. Beijing：China Intercontinental Press，1997. 77 S；Ill. ISBN：7801132769

《是谁创造了香港的繁荣》，陈多，连锦添. 五洲传播.

D192.33 澳门

1. Komm zurück，Macao! /von Wang Qiaolong. Beijing：China Intercontinental Press，1999. 87 pages：illustrations (some color)；18cm. ISBN：7801136144

《归来，澳门》，王巧珑. 五洲传播.

2. Macao schreitet dem 21. Jahrhundert entgegen/von Xu Yamin und Qi Pengfei. Beijing：China Intercontinental Press，1999. 79 pages：illustrations (some color)；18cm. ISBN：7801136055

《走向 21 世纪的澳门》，徐雅民，齐鹏飞. 五洲传播.

D2 外交、国际关系

D21 国际关系

D211 国际共产主义运动

1. Die Verurteilung des' modernen Revisionismus. Peking：Verl. für Fremdsprachige Literatur，1958. 103 S.

《现代修正主义必须批判》

2. Die Differenzen zwischen Genossen Togliatti und uns. Peking，1963. ii，54 p. ；12o

《陶里亚蒂同志同我们的分歧》，1962 年 12 月 31 日《人民日报》社论.

3. Leninismus und moderner Revisionismus. Peking：Verl. für Fremdsprachige Literatur，1963. 21 S.

《列宁主义和现代修正主义》，1963 年第一期《红旗》社论.

4. Schliessen wir uns auf der Grundlage der beiden Moskauer Erklärungen zusammen. Peking：Verl. f. Fremdsprach. Literatur，1963. 40 S.

Kataloges：Schliessen wir uns auf der Grundlage der beiden Moskauer Erklärungen zusammen! Begrüssungsansprache des Leiters der Delegation der Kommunistischen Partei Chinas，Wu Hsiu- tjüan，auf dem VI. Parteitag der Sozialistischen Einheitspartei Deutschlands（18. Januar 1963）. Grusstelegramm des Zentralkomitees der Kommunistischen Partei Chinas an den VI. Parteitag der Sozialistischen Einheitspartei Deutschlands.

《在莫斯科宣言和莫斯科声明的基础上团结起来》

5. Woher die Differenzen? Antwort an Maurice Thorez und andere Genossen：Leitartikel der „Renmin Ribao" (Volkszeitung)vom 27. Februar 1963. Peking：Verl. f. Fremdspr. Literatur，1963. 40 S.

《分歧从何而来?:答多列士等同志》，1963 年 2 月 27 日

《人民日报》社论.

6. Mehr über die Differenzen zwischen Genossen Togliatti und uns：zu einigen wichtigen Problemen des Leninismus in der Gegenwart/von der Redaktion der „Hongqi" (Rote Fahne). Peking：Verlag für Fremdsprachige Literatur, 1963. 227 p. ；19cm.

《再论陶里亚蒂同志同我们的分歧：关于列宁主义在当代的若干重大问题》,《红旗》杂志编辑部.

7. Ein Kommentar zur Erklärung der Kommunistischen Partei der USA. Peking：Verl. für Fremdsprachige Literatur, 1963. 19 S

《评美国共产党声明》,1963 年 3 月 8 日《人民日报》社论.

8. Ein Vorschlag zur Generallinie der internationalen kommunistischen Bewegung：Antwort des Zentralkomitees der kommunistischen Partei Chinas auf den Brief des Zentralkomitees der kommunistischen Partei der Sowjetunion vom 30. März 1963. Peking：Verlag für fremdsprachige Literatur, 1963. 130 p. ；19cm.

《关于国际共产主义运动总路线的建议：中共中央委员会对苏联共产党中央委员会 1963 年 3 月 30 日来信的回复》

9. Noch höher das revolutionäre Banner des Marxismus-Leninismus!. Peking：Verlag für Fremdsprachige Literatur, 1964. 40 pages；19cm.

《更高地举起马克思列宁主义的革命旗帜》

10. Die Polemik über die Generallinie der internationalen kommunistischen Bewegung. /Peking： Verl. für Fremdsprachige Literatur, 1965. 657 S.

《关于国际共产主义运动总路线的论战》

11. Den Kampf gegen den Chruschtschow-Revisionismus bis zum Ende führen. Peking：Verl. für Fremdspr. Literatur, 1965. 18 S.

《把反对赫鲁晓夫修正主义的斗争进行到底》(纪念《关于国际共产主义运动总路线的建议》发表两周年) (1965.6.14),《人民日报》编辑部,《红旗》杂志编辑部.

12. Ein grosser Sieg des Leninismus：anläßlich des 95. Geburtstages Lenins；［Leitartikel der Zeitschrift „Hongqi" (Rote Fahne), Nr. 4, 1965. Peking：Verl. für Fremdsprachige Lit. , 1965. 15 S.

《列宁主义的伟大胜利》,《红旗》杂志社论.

13. Totaler bankrott des sowjetischen modernen Revisionismus. Peking：Verlag für fremdsprachige literatur, 1968. 81 pages；13cm.

《苏联现代修正主义的总破产》

14. Auf dem von der sozialistischen Oktoberrevolution gebahnten Weg vorwärtsschreiten：zur Gedenkfeier des 50. Jahrestages der Grossen Sozialistischen Oktoberrevolution. Peking：Verlag für fremdsprachige Literatur, 1968. 47 S.

《沿着十月社会主义革命开辟的道路前进：纪念伟大的十月社会主义革命五十周年》

15. Der sowjetische Sozialimperialismus ohne Maske.

Peking：Verlag für Fremdsprachige Literatur, 1976. 99 S. ；19cm.

《苏修社会帝国主义的丑恶面目》

D212 中国与联合国

1. Unwiderstehliche historische Strömung. Peking：Verlag für Fremdsprachige Literatur, 1971. 51 S. ；18cm.

《历史潮流不可抗拒》

2. Rede Tjiao Guan-huas, Delegationsleiter der Volksrepublik China, auf der Plenarsitzung der 27. ［siebenundzwanzigsten] Tagung der UNO-Vollversammlung：(3. Okt. 1972). Peking：Verlag für Fremdsprachige Literatur, 1972. 25 S. ；19cm.

《中华人民共和国代表团团长乔冠华在联合国大会第二十七届会议全体会议上的发言》

3. Rede Tjiao Guan-huas, Delegationsleiter der Volksrepublik China, auf der Plenarsitzung der 28. Tagung der UNO-Vollversammlung (2. Oktober 1973). Peking：Verl. f. fremdsprachige Literatur, 1973. 30 S.

《中华人民共和国代表团团长乔冠华在联合国大会第二十八届会议全体会议上的发言》

4. Rede von Deng ［Teng] Hsiao-Ping, dem Leiter der Delegation der Volksrepublik China, auf der Sondertagung der Uno-Vollversammlung ⟨10. April 1974⟩. Peking：Verl. für Fremdsprachige Literatur, 1974. 19 S.

《中华人民共和国代表团团长邓小平在联大特别会议上的发言》

5. Rede Tjiao Guan-Huas, Delegationsleiter der Volksrepublik China, auf der 29. Tagung der UNO-Vollversammlung：(2. Oktober 1974). Peking：Verlag für fremdsprachige Literatur, 1974. 28 S.

《中华人民共和国代表团团长在联合国第二十九届会议上的发言》

6. Rede Tjiao Guan-Huas, Delegationsleiter der Volksrepublik China, auf der Plenarsitzung der 30. Tagung der UNO-Vollversammlung；(26. 9. 1975). Peking：Verl. für Fremdsprachige Literatur, 1975. 35 S.

《中华人民共和国代表团团长在联合国大会第三十届会议全体会议上的发言》

7. 中国政府继续坚持执行毛泽东主席的革命外交路线和政策(中国代表团团长在联合国大会第三十一届全体会议上的发言). 北京：外文出版社,1976

8. Vizepremier Tschen Yi antwortet der Presse/Yi Tschen. Peking：Verl. für Fremdsprachige Literatur, 1966. 47 S.

《陈毅副总理答记者问》

D22 中国外交

1. Die Aussenpolitik Chinas/von Zhou Yihuang. Übers. von Xiao Jun. ［Beijing]：China Internat. Press, 2004. 194 S. ；ill. ；21cm. ISBN：7508506316

《中国外交》,周溢潢主编;肖君译. 五洲传播出版社（中国

基本情况丛书/郭长建主编)

2. 中国特色大国外交与"一带一路"/吴建民著；Risse, Burkhard 德文翻译. 北京：外文出版社有限责任公司, 2016. 30 页；21cm. ISBN：7119103617

德文题名：Die Groβmachtdiplomatie Chinesischen Stils im Kontext Von „Ein Gürtel Und Eine Straße"

3. 中国的亚太安全合作政策/中华人民共和国国务院新闻办公室[发布]. 北京：外文出版社有限责任公司, 2017. 54 页；21cm. ISBN：7119105130

德文题名：China und die Sicherheitszusammenarbeit im Asiatisch-Pazifischen Raum

4. Erklärung der Regierung der Volksrepublik China (24. Mai 1969). Peking：Verl. für Fremdsprachige Literatur, 1969. 47 S. kl. 8

《中华人民共和国政府声明》(1969.5.24)

5. Erklärung der Regierung der Volksrepublik China：(7. Oktober 1969). Peking：Verl. für Fremdsprachige Literatur, 1969. 56 S.

《中华人民共和国政府声明》(1969.10.7)

D221　中美关系

1. China im Kampf gegen die militärischen Provokationen der USA in der Strasse von Taiwan：(Eine Sammlung d. wichtigen Dokumente)/[Zusammengest. vom Inst. f. Auswärtige Angelegenheiten]. Peking：Verl. f. Fremdsprachige Literatur, 1958. 76 S.

《反对美国在台湾海峡地区的军事挑衅》

2. Kampf zwischen zwei Linien im Verhalten zum USA-Imperialismus：(26. Juli 1965)/Hsiu-dschu Fan. Peking：Verl. f. Fremdsprach. Literatur, 1965. 49 S.

《在对待美帝国主义问题上两条路线的斗争》, 范秀珠.

3. Gedenkt des Sieges über den deutschen Faschismus, kämpft bis zum Ende gegen den USA-Imperialismus! / Luo Jui-tjing. Peking：Verl. für Fremdsprachige Literatur, 1965. 34 S 18cm.

《纪念战胜德国法西斯把反对美帝国主义的斗争进行到底》, 罗瑞卿.

4. Das Volk hat den japanischen Faschismus besiegt und kann bestimmt auch den USA-Imperialismus besiegen：Rede auf e. Massenkundgebung in Peking z. Feier d. 20. Jahrestags d. Sieges im Widerstandskrieg gegen d. japan. Aggression/Jui-tjing Luo. Peking：Verl. f. Fremdsprach. Literatur, 1965. 34 S.

《人民战胜了日本法西斯, 人民也一定能战胜美帝国主义》, 罗瑞卿.

5. Die USA-Aggression hat keine Grenzen, und auch unser Widerstand gegen diese Aggression kennt keine Grenzen. Peking：Verl. für Fremdsprachige Literatur, 1966. 35 S

《美国侵略没有界限, 我们反侵略也没有界限》

6. Erklärung des Genossen Mao Tse-tung, Vorsitzenden des Zentralkomitees der Kommunistischen Partei Chinas, zur Unterstützung der Afro-Amerikaner in ihrem Kampf gegen gewaltsame Unterdrückung (16. Apr. 1968)/ Peking：Verl. f. fremdspr. Literatur, 1968. 6 S.

《中国共产党中央委员会主席毛泽东同志支持美国黑人抗暴斗争的声明》

7. Selbstbekenntnis der Ausweglosigkeit-Kommentar zu Nixons Antrittsrede u. z. verachtungswürdigen Beifall d. sowjetrevisionist. Renegatenclique. / von Kommentator d. „Renmin Ribao" u. „Hongqi". Peking：Verlag für Fremdsprachige Literatur, 1969. 19 S. ; 13cm.

《走投无路的自供状》

D222　中苏关系

1. Sowjetrussland in China/Tschiang Kai-Schek. Aus d. Amerikan. übers. von Credo. Bonn：Athenäum Verl., 1959. 450 S. : mit 2 Abb. , 1 Kt. ; 8.

《苏俄在中国》, 蒋介石著；Credo 译.

2. Ursprung und Entwicklung der Differenzen zwischen der Führung der KPdSU und uns：Kommentar z. Offenen Brief d. ZK d. KPdSU/Die Red. d. Renmin Ribao (Volkszeitung) u. d. Zeitschrift Hongqi (Rote Fahne). Peking：Verl. f. Fremdsprach. Literatur, 1963. 77 S. ; kl.

《苏共领导同我们分歧的由来和发展》《人民日报》编辑部, 《红旗》杂志编辑部.

3. Zur Stalinfrage：zweiter Kommentar zum offenen Brief des ZK der KPdSU. Peking：Verl. für fremdsprachige Literatur, 1963. 25 S.

《关于斯大林问题：二评苏共中央的公开信》, 《人民日报》编辑部, 《红旗》杂志编辑部.

4. Ist Jugoslawien ein sozialistischer Staat? : dritter Kommentar zum offenen Brief des ZK der KPdSU/Die Redaktionen der „Renmin Ribao" (Volkszeitung) und der Zeitschrift „Hongqi" (Rote Fahne). Peking：Verlag für fremdsprachige Literatur, 1963. 53 pages; 19cm.

《南斯拉夫是社会主义国家吗？：三评苏共中央的公开信》, 《人民日报》编辑部, 《红旗》杂志编辑部.

5. Die Verfechter des neuen Kolonialismus：4. Kommentar zum offenen Brief d. ZK d. KPdSU/Kommunisti českaja Partija Sovetskogo Sojuza. Peking：Verl. für Fremdsprachige Lit, 1963. 41 S.

《新殖民主义的辩护士：四评苏共中央的公开信》, 《人民日报》编辑部, 《红旗》杂志编辑部.

6. Zwei Linien in der Frage von Krieg und Frieden：fünfter Kommentar zum offenen Brief des ZK der KPdSU/die Red. der „Renmin Ribao" (Volkszeitung) und der Zeitschrift „Hongqi" (Rote Fahne), (19. November 1963). Peking：Verl. für fremdsprachige Literatur, 1963. 42 S.

《在战争与和平问题上的两条路线：五评苏共中央的公开信》, 《人民日报》编辑部, 《红旗》杂志编辑部.

7. Die Wahrheit darüber, wie sich die Führer der KPdSU mit

Indien gegen China verbündet haben. Peking：Verl. für Fremdsprach. Literatur, 1963. 56 S.

《苏共领导联印反华的真相》，《人民日报》编辑部．

8. Kampf zwischen zwei Linien auf dem Weltfrauenkongress in Moskau. Peking, 1963. 66 p.；8°

《在莫斯科世界妇女大会上两条路线的斗争》

9. Sieben Briefe：Korrespondenz zwischen dem ZK der KPCh und dem ZK der KPdSU. Peking：Verl. für Fremdsprachige Literatur, 1964. 116 S；14cm.

《中共中央和苏共中央来往的七封信》

10. Antwort des ZK der KP Chinas auf das Schreiben des ZK der KPdSU：vom 15. Juni 1964. Peking：Verlag für Fremdsprachige Literatur, 1964. 79 S.；15cm.

《中国共产党中央委员会对于苏联共产党中央委员会一九六四年六月十五日来信的复信》

11. Zwei völlig entgegengesetzte Arten der Politik der friedlichen Koexistenz：Sechster Kommentar zum offenen Brief des ZK der KPdSU/Redaktionen der „Renmin Ribao“（Volkszeitung）und der Zeitschrift „Hongqi“（Rote Fahnen），（12. Dezember 1963）. Peking：Verlag für Fremdsprachige Literatur, 1963. [II]，55 p. ；. cm.

《两种根本对立的和平共处政策：六评苏共中央的公开信》，《人民日报》编辑部，《红旗》杂志编辑部．

12. Die Führung der KPdSU ist der grösste Spalter der Gegenwart：siebenter Kommentar zum Offenen Brief des ZK der KPdSU. Peking：Verlag für fremdsprachige Literatur, 1964. 72 pages

《苏共领导是当代最大的分裂主义者：七评苏共中央的公开信》(1964 年 2 月 4 日)，《人民日报》编辑部，《红旗》杂志编辑部．

13. Die proletarische Revolution und der Revisionismus Chruschtschows：achter Kommentar zum offenen Brief des ZK der KPdSU/die Red. der „Renmin Ribao“（Volkszeitung）und der Zeitschrift „Hongqi“（Rote Fahne），（31. März 1964）. Peking：Verl. für fremdsprachige Literatur, 1964. 74 S.

《无产阶级革命和赫鲁晓夫修正主义：八评苏共中央的公开信》(1964 年 3 月 31 日)，《人民日报》编辑部，《红旗》杂志编辑部．

14. Über den Pseudokommunismus Chruschtschows und die historischen Lehren für die Welt：neunter Kommentar zum offenen Brief des ZK der KPdSU/die Redaktionen der „Renmin Ribao“（Volkszeitung）und der Zeitschrift „Hongqi“（Rote Fahne）. Peking：Verlag für fremdsprachige Literatur, 1964. 85 pages

《关于赫鲁晓夫的假共产主义及其在世界历史上的教训：九评苏共中央的公开信》(1964 年 7 月 14 日)，《人民日报》编辑部，《红旗》杂志编辑部．

15. Warum Chruschtschow von der Bühne abgetreten ist：Leitartikel der Zeitschrift „Hongqi“ Nr. 21 - 22，1964. Peking：Verl. für Fremdsprachl. Literatur, 1964. 18 S.

《赫鲁晓夫是怎样下台的》，《红旗》1964 第 21 － 22 期社论．

16. Kommentar zur Moskauer März-konferenz. Peking：Verlag für fremdsprachige Literatur, 1965. 27 pages；15cm.

《论莫斯科三月会议：1965 年 3 月 23 日》，《人民日报》编辑部，《红旗》杂志编辑部．

17. Die Führer der KPdSU sind Verräter an der Deklaration und der Erklärung. Peking：Verl. f. Fremdsprach. Literatur, 1966. 16 S.

《苏共领导是宣言和声明的背叛者》

18. Die neuen Führer der KPdSU bekennen sich zur Linie der sowjetisch-amerikanischen Zusammenarbeit. Vom Kommentator d. Zeitschrift Hongqi（Rote Fahne）.（11. Febr. 1966）Peking：Verl. für Fremdsprachige Literatur, 1966. 35 S.

《苏共新领导奉行苏美合作路线的供状》

19. Zurückweisung der absurden Behauptungen der sowjetrevisionistischen Sozialimperialisten. Peking：Verl. für Fremdsprachige Literatur, 1969. 48 S.

《驳苏修社会帝国主义的谬论》

20. Nieder mit den neuen Zaren! Peking：Verlag für fremdsprachige Literatur, 1969. 49 pages：black and white illustrations；19cm.

《打倒新沙皇！》

21. Abscheuliche Aufführung der Selbstentlarvung. Dschung Jen. Peking：Verl. für Fremdsprachige Literatur, 1969. 21 S.

《自我揭露的丑恶表演》，钟仁．

D223　中国与世界其他各国外交关系

1. Gemeinsame Erklärung der Kommunistischen Partei Chinas und der Kommunistischen Partei Neuseelands. Peking：Verl. f. Fremdsprachige Literatur, 1963. 15 S.

《中国共产党新西兰共产党联合声明》

2. Ein Spiegel für Revisionisten：Leitartikel der „Renmin Ribao“（Volkszeitung）vom 9. März 1963. Peking：Verlag für Fremdsprachige Literatur, 1963. 12 S；19cm.

《修正主义者的一面镜子》，1963 年 3 月 9 日《人民日报》社论. 关于中印边界问题.

3. Gewisse internationale Fragen, die Malaya angehen. Peking：Verl. f. Fremdsprach. Literatur, 1963. 18 S.

《与马来亚有关的一些国际问题》

4. Gemeinsame Erklärung des Vorsitzenden Liu Schao-Tschi und des Vorsitzenden Choi Yong Kun. Peking：Verl. für Fremdsprachige Literatur, 1964. 19 S.

《刘少奇主席和崔庸健委员长联合声明》

5. Es lebe die chinesisch-albanische Kampffreundschaft：Dokumente vom Besuch führender Persönlichkeiten

Chinas in Albanien. Peking：Verl. f. Fremdsprach. Literatur，1964. 198 pages；19cm.

《中阿战斗友谊万岁：中国领导人访问阿尔巴尼亚文件集》

6. Den Kampf gegen Imperialismus und Revisionismus bis zu Ende führen Dokumente vom Besuch d. Partei- u. Regierungsdelegation Albaniens in China. Peking：Verl. f. Fremdsprachige Literatur，1966. 226 S

《把反帝反修斗争进行到底：阿尔巴尼亚党政代表团访问中国文件集》

7. Rede in der indonesischen Aliarcham-Akademie für Sozialwissenschaften：(25. Mai 1965)/Dschen Peng. Peking：Verl. für Fremdsprachige Literatur，1965. 57 S.

《在印度尼西亚阿里亚哈姆社会科学学院的讲话》，彭真.

8. Gemeinsame Erklärung des Vorsitzenden Liu Schao-tschi und des Präsidenten Ho Chi-minh. Peking：Verl. f. fremdsprachige Literatur，1963. 41 S.

《刘少奇主席和胡志明主席联合声明》

9. Unterstützt das Volk von Vietnam, schlagt die US-Aggressoren! 1. Peking：Verl. f. Fremdsprachige Literatur，1965. 89 S.

《支援越南人民，打败美国侵略者》(第一集)

10. Unterstützt das Volk von Vietnam, schlagt die US-Aggressoren! 2. Peking：Verl. f. Fremdsprachige Literatur，1965. 40 S.

《支援越南人民，打败美国侵略者》(第二集)

11. Unterstützt das Volk von Vietnam, schlagt die US-Aggressoren! 3. Peking：Verl. f. Fremdsprachige Literatur，1965. 42 S.

《支援越南人民，打败美国侵略者》(第三集)

12. Eine grosse Verschwörung total zusammengebrochen! Peking：Verlag für Fremdsprachige Literatur，1966. 54 p.

《一个大阴谋的彻底破产》. 关于美国越战.

13. Unterstützt den Kampf des dominikanischen Volkes gegen die bewaffnete USA-Aggession. Peking：Verl. f. Fremdsprach. Literatur，1965. 38 S.：mit Abb.；8

《支持多米尼加人民反对美国武装侵略》

14. Neues Kapitel in der Geschichte der chinesisch-japanischen Beziehungen. Peking：Verlag für Fremdsprachige Literatur，1972. 29 S.；ill.；19cm.

《中日关系史的新篇章》

15. 中国坚持通过谈判解决中国与菲律宾在南海的有关争议/中华人民共和国国务院新闻办公室［发布］. 北京：外文出版社有限责任公司，2016. 59 页；21cm. ISBN：7119093482

德文题名：China besteht auf einer verhandlungsbasierten Lösung der Streitigkeiten mit den Philippinen im Südchinesischen Meer

D3　中国法律

D31　古代法律

1. Das Rätsel um die rote Pille：fünf Aufsehen erregende Gerichtsfälle aus der Ming- und der Qing-Dynastie/von Liu Jianye. ［Übers.：Tian Shouyu und Zhang Zhenhua］. Beijing：Verl. für fremdsprachige Literatur，2005. 245 S. ill. 18cm. ISBN：7119020528

《红丸迷案：中国明清奇案选》，刘建业著. 明清时代法律案例汇编.

D32　中华民国时期法律

1. Das chinesische Strafgesetzbuch vom 1. Jan. 1935/übers. v. Chang Chungkong；H. Herrfahrdt. Mit einer geschichtl. Einl. v. H. Herrfahrdt. Bonn：Röhrscheid，1938. VII，86 S.；gr. 8. (Rechtsvergleichende Untersuchungen zur gesamten Strafrechtswissenschaft；H. 9)

中国刑法. 张仲绛(1909—1984)，Herrfahrdt H. 合译.

D33　中华人民共和国法律

1. Die Verfassung der Volksrepublik China：angenommen am 20. Sept. 1954 vom 1. Nationalen Volkskongress der Volksrepublik China auf seiner 1. Sitzung. Peking：Verl. für fremdsprachige Literatur，1954. 55 S.

《中华人民共和国宪法》

(1)2. Aufl. 1956. 55 pages；22cm.

(2)Die Verfassung der Volksrepublik China. Peking：Verlag für Fremdsprachige Literatur，1975. 53 S.；19cm.

(3)Die Verfassung der Volksrepublik China：angenommen von der 5. Tagung des V. Nationalen Volkskongresses der Volksrepublik China am 4. Dezember 1982. Beijing：Verlag für Fremdsprachige Literatur，1983. 104 pages；20cm.

2. Bericht über den Verfassungsentwurf der Volksrepublik China. Die Verfassung der Volksrepublik China/Liu Shaoqi，Peking：Verlag für fremdsprachige literatur，1954. 121 pages frontispiece (portrait)21cm.

《关于中华人民共和国宪法草案的报告》，刘少奇.

3. Das Aussenwirtschaftsrecht der Volksrepublik China：die wichtigsten Rechtsnormen mit Erläuterungen＝Chung-kuo she wai ching chi fa kuei/Robert Heuser (Hrsg.)；mit Geleitworten von Karl Bünger，Karl Firsching und Erik Harremoes. München：J. Schweitzer，1986. Xxii，468p. 21cm. (Chinesisches Recht；Bd. 1).

《中国涉外经济法规》，Robert Heuser 出版.

4. 中国民间调解：预防犯罪的第一道防线 /孙占科等编. 北京：外文出版社，1989

E 类　军事

E1　古代兵法、战法

1. Über die Kriegskunst/Sun Zi；［Übersetzung，Zhong Yingjie］. Über die Kriegskunst/Sun Bin；［Übersetzung，Zhong Yingjie］. Beijing：Verlag für fremdsprachige Literatur，2007. 226 pages：illustrations，maps；18cm. ISBN：7119044866

   《孙子兵法·孙膑兵法》，钟英杰译.

2. Die Kunst des Krieges/Sunzi. Hrsg. u. mit e. Vorw. von James Clavell. Aus d. Amerikan. von Jürgen Langowsky. München：Droemer Knaur，1988. 160 S.；22cm. ISBN：3426192450；3426192454.

   《孙子兵法》，James Clavell(1921—1994)译.

   （1）［6. Aufl.］München：Droemer Knaur，1994. 160 S.；22cm. ISBN：3426192450；3426192454.

   （2）［8. Aufl.］München：Droemer Knaur，1996. 160 S.；22cm. ISBN：3426192450；3426192454.

   （3）Vollst. Taschenbuchausg. München：Droemer Knaur，1996. 159 S.；18cm. ISBN：3426772720；3426772728.

   （4）Vollst. Ausg. München：Droemer Knaur，1998. 159 S.；18cm. ISBN：3426270813；3426270811.

   （5）Vollst. Taschenbuchausg. München：Droemer Knaur，2001. 157 S.；18cm. ISBN：3426870587；3426870584.

   （6）Hamburg：Nikol，2008. 156 S.；20cm. ISBN：3937872872；3937872876.

   （7）Vollst. Taschenbuchausg. München：Droemer Knaur，2013. 156 S.；19cm. ISBN：3426876596；3426876590.

3. Die Strategie der Sieger：eine Neuübersetzung von Sun Tsus Klassiker „Die Kunst der Strategie"/R. L. Wing. Aus d. Amerikan. von Thomas Poppe. München：Droemer Knaur，1989. 237 S.；19cm. ISBN：3426042267，3426042266. （Knaur；4226：Esoterik）

   《孙子兵法》，Wing，R. L. 译自英文.

4. Strategeme：Lebens- und überlebenslisten der Chinesen - die berühmten 36 Strategeme aus drei Jahrtausenden/Harro von Senger. 2. Aufl. Bern；München；Wien：Scherz，1988. 445 S.；22cm. ISBN：3502166733；3502166730.

   《三十六计》，Senger，Harro von（1944—）译.

   （1）3. Aufl. Bern；München；Wien：Scherz，1988. 445 S.；22cm. ISBN：3502166733；3502166730.

   （2）4. Aufl. Bern；München；Wien：Scherz，1988. 445 S.；22cm. ISBN：3502166733；3502166730.

   （3）9. Aufl. Bern；München；Wien：Scherz，1994. 445 S.；22cm. ISBN：3502196570；3502196575.

5. Die List/hrsg. von Harro von Senger. Orig.-Ausg. Frankfurt am Main：Suhrkamp，1999. 499 S；Ill；18cm. （Edition Suhrkamp：es. - Berlin：Suhrkamp，1963—；

2039）.

   《三十六计》，Senger，Harro von（1944—）译.

E2　中国军事

1. Die Chinesische Volksbefreiungsarmee/Peking：Verlag für Fremdsprachige Literatur，1951. 71 pages：illustrations；19cm.

   《中国人民解放军》

2. Acht Jahre chinesische Volksfreiwillige, ihr Widerstand gegen die US-Aggressoren und ihre Hilfe für Korea. Peking：Verlag für Fremdsprachige Literatur，1959. 129 pages；19cm.

   《中国人民志愿军抗美援朝八年》

3. Völker aller Länder, vereinigt euch zum allseitigen, gründlichen, restlosen und entschiedenen Verbot der Kernwaffen und ihrer Vernichtung！Peking：Verlag für fremdsprachige Literatur，1963. II，236 p.；20cm.

   《全世界人民团结起来，全面、彻底、干净、坚决地禁止和销毁核武器》

4. Die demokratischen Traditionen der chinesischen Volksbefreiungsarmee/Lung Ho. Peking：Verl. f. Fremdsprach. Literatur，1965. 46 S.

   《中国人民解放军的民主传统》，贺龙.

5. Die historischen Lehren des antifaschistischen Krieges/von der redaktion der „Renmin Ribao"（9. Mai 1965）. Peking：Verlag für fremdsprachige literatur，1965. 30，［1］pages；19cm.

   《反法西斯战争的历史经验》，人民日报编辑部.

6. Brecht das Kernwaffenmonopol, vernichtet die Kernwaffen. Peking：Verl. f. Fremdsprach. Literatur，1965. 30 S.

   《打破核垄断 消灭核武器》

7. Die Volksarmee ist unüberwindlich Zum 42. Jahrestag d. Gründung d. Chines. Volksbefreiungsarmee. Leitartikel d. Renmin Ribao, Hongqi u. Jiefangjun Bao vom 1. Aug. 1969. Peking：Verl. für Fremdsprachige Literatur，1969. 18 S. mit Abb. kl. 8

   《人民军队所向无敌》

8. Chinas Landesverteidigung/verf. von Peng Guangqian. Übers. von Guo Zifu und Eva Tang.［Beijing］：China Internat. Press，2004. 191 S.：ill.，Kt.；21cm. ISBN：7508506243

   《中国国防》，彭光谦著；郭子富译. 五洲传播出版社（中国基本情况丛书. 当代卷/郭长建主编）

9. 中国的军控、裁军与防扩散势力：德文/中华人民共和国国务院新闻办公室发布. 北京：新星出版社，2005. 60 页；20cm. ISBN：7801489233

10. 中国武装力量的多样化运用（德文版）/中华人民共和国国务院新闻办公室. 北京：外文出版社，2013. 20cm. ISBN：7119081670

F 类 经济

F1 中国经济

F11 概论

1. Kurzer Abriss der Wirtschaft Chinas/von Dscheng Schi. Peking：Verl. für Fremdsprachige Literatur, 1974. 63 S. : ill
《中国经济简况》，郑实.

2. Wirtschaft/[Red. d. dt. Ausg. : Dai Shifeng...]. Beijing：Verl. für fremdspr. Literatur, 1986. 407 S. : ill.
《经济》，《中国概况丛书》编辑委员会编.

3. Die Wirtschaft Chinas/von Wang Mengkui und anderen. Übers. von Zhao Zhenquan. [Beijing]：China Internat. Press, 2005. 211 S. : ill. , graph. Darst. ; 21cm. ISBN：7508506383
《中国经济》，王梦奎等编著；Zhao Zhenquan 译. 五洲传播出版社(中国基本情况丛书. 当代卷/郭长建主编)

4. Bericht über die Berichtigung der hauptsächlichen Planziele des Volkswirtschaftsplans 1959 und die weitere Entfaltung der Bewegung zur Erhöhung der Produktion und zur Sparsamkeit (vorgetragen auf der 5. Plenarsitzung des Ständigen Ausschusses des II. Nationalen Volkskongresses am 26. August 1959)/ Tschou En-Lai. Peking：Verlag für fremdsprachige Literatur, 1959. 48 p.
《关于调整一九五九年国民经济计划主要指标和进一步开展增产节约运动的报告》，周恩来.

5. Kommuniqué über die Entwicklung der Volkswirtschaft im Jahre 1959. Peking：Verl. f. fremdsprachige Literatur, 1960. 27 S.
《关于一九五九年国民经济发展情况的新闻公报》

6. Industrialisierung und Kollektivierung im neuen China. Peking：Verl. f. Fremdsprach. Literatur, 1964. 60 S.
《中国的社会主义工业化和农业集体化》，薄一波，廖鲁言.

7. Wirtschaftliche Regulierung und Reform/[Red. ：Su Wenming]. Beijing：Beijing Rundschau, 1983. 221 S: zahlr. ill. , Kt.
《经济调整与改革》. 北京周报社.

8. Beschluss des Zentralkomitees der Kommunistischen Partei Chinas über die Reform des Wirtschaftssystems. Beijing：Verlag für fremdsprachige Literatur, 1984. 51 p. ; 19cm.
《中共中央关于经济体制改革的决定》

9. Sozialismus in China：Erfolge, Fehlschläge, Reformperspektiven/ Xue Muqiao. Aus d. Chines. übers. von Wang Zhiyou. Hamburg：Verlag Weltarchiv, 1982. 319 S. ; 24cm. ISBN：3878952183, 387895218X. (Veröffentlichungen des HWWA-Institut für Wirtschaftsforschung Hamburg)
《中国社会主义经济问题研究》，薛暮桥著；Wang Zhiyou 译.

10. Neue Strategie für Chinas Wirtschaft/aus dem Englischen von Alex Sichrovsky. Beijing：Verlag für fremdsprachige Literatur, 1985. 1 volume：table
《试论我国社会主义经济发展的新战略》，马洪.

11. Das Yangtse-Einzugsgebiet：Ein Gebiet mit dem größten Entwicklungspotential in China. Beijing Neuer Stern Verl. , 1994. 42 Seiten Illustrationen. ISBN：7801020685, 7801020680. (Die Öffnung und Entwicklung des Yangtse-Gebiets；1)
《长江：中国开发潜力最大的地区》. 新星出版社.

F2 "三农"问题

1. Entwurf des Programms für die Entwicklung der Landwirtschaft in der Volksrepublik China 1956/67：Unterbreitet vom Politbüro des ZK der KP Chinas am 23. Januar 1956. Peking：Fremdsprachige Literatur, 1956. 26 pages；21cm.
《1956 年到 1957 年全国农业发展纲要》(草案)

2. Dadschai, Vorbild für die Landwirtschaft in China. Peking：Verl. für Fremdsprachige Literatur, 1972. 6 Bl. Abb. , 35 S. 8. „
《大寨：中国农业站线上的一面红旗》

3. Die ganze Partei mobilisieren für noch grössere Anstrengungen in der Landwirtschaft und für den Aufbau von Kreisen vom Typ Dadschai：zusammenfassender Bericht auf d. Landeskonferenz über d. Lernen von Dadschai in d. Landwirtschaft；(15. Oktober 1975)/Hua Guo-feng. Peking：Verlag für Fremdsprachige Literatur, 1975. 85 S. ; 19cm.
《全党动员，大办农业，为普及大寨县而奋斗》，华国锋.

4. In einer Volkskommune：Bericht aus Tjiliying/von Dschu Li u. Tiän Djiä-yün. Peking：Verlag für Fremdsprachige Literatur, 1975. 254 S. : ill. ; 19cm.
《在七里营人民公社里》，朱力，田洁云.

5. Bericht über Dungting, eine Volkskommune am Tai-See/von Wu Dschou. Peking：Verlag für Fremdsprachige Literatur, 1975. 65 S. : ill. , Kt. ; 19cm.
《洞庭人民公社》，吴周.

6. Eine grosse Schule für Chinas Jugend：- ihr Leben auf dem Land. Peking：Verlag für Fremdsprachige Literatur, 1976. 143 pages：illustrations；19cm.
《农村也是大学》，晓兵.

7. Rede auf der II. Landeskonferenz zum Lernen von Dadschai in der Landwirtschaft：(25. Dezember 1976)/ Hua Guo-Feng. Peking：Verlag für fremdsprachige Literatur, 1977. 54 pages
《中国共产党中央委员会主席华国锋同志在第二次全国农业学大寨议上的讲话》

8. Die Viererbande gründlich kritisieren, einen neuen Aufschwung in der Bewegung zum Aufbau von Kreisen

vom Typ Dadschai im ganzen Land herbeiführen/von Chen Yonggui, Mitglied：Mitlied des Politbüros des Zentralkomitees der Kommunistischen Partei Chinas und stellvertretender Ministerpräsident des Staatsrats der Volksrepublik China（20. Dezember 1976）. Peking：Verlag für fremdsprachige Literatur，1977. 57 pages；19cm.

《彻底批判"四人帮"掀起普及及大寨县运动的新高潮：中共中央政治局委员、国务院副总理陈永贵在第二次全国农业大寨会议上的报告》

9. Wie deckt China seinen Bedarf an Getreide. Peking：Verl. für Fremsprachige Literatur，1977. 97 S.：ill.

《中国是怎样实现粮食自给的》

10. Dadschai：das rote Banner/Wen Yin, Liang Hua. Peking：Verl. für fremdsprachige Literatur，1978. 255 S：Ill；22cm.

《大寨红旗》，文荫，梁华.

11. 中国的农村改革. 北京：新星出版社，1991. 23 页；18cm. ISBN：7800851109.（中国简况）

F3　工业经济

1. Datjing：Ein rotes Banner an Chinas industrieller Front. Peking：Verlag für fremdsprachige Literatur，1972. 67 pages：illustrations，plates；19cm.

《大庆：中国工业战线上的一面红旗》

2. Das Kohlenrevier Kailuan/verf. von Arbeitern aus Kailuan. Peking：Verl. für Fremdsprachige Literatur，1977. 99 S；ill.，Kt

《开滦新貌》，开滦工人写作组.

F4　贸易经济

1. Was China ausführt. Peking：Verl. für fremdsprach. Literatur，1954. 33 Bl.：zahlr. Ill.

《新中国外销物产》

2. Wegweiser für den China-Handel/von Ma Ke；Li Jun usw.［Beijing］：China Intercontinental Press，2004. 500 S.：ill.，Kt.；24cm. ＋1 CD-ROM. ISBN：7508504542

《中国商务》，郭长健主编，马可等撰；诸庆安译. 五洲传播出版社.

F41　旅游经济

1. Tourismus. Beijing：Verlag für Fremdsprachige Literatur，1983. 195 pages：illustrations（some color），map；19cm.

《旅游》，《中国概况丛书》编辑委员会编.

2. Tourismus in China. Beijing：Verlag Für Fremdsprachige Literatur，1988. 38 pages：color plates；18cm.

《中国旅游业》（中国简况）

3. Die schönsten Reiseziele. Monograph. Beijing：Verlag für Fremdsprachige Literatur，2009. 39 pages：color illustrations；21cm. ISBN：7119058542

《中国旅游》，外文出版社德文编译部编译.

F5　金融与证券

1. Chinas Renminbi：Eine äusserst stabile Währung auf d. Welt. Peking：Verl. für Fremdsprachige Literatur，1969. 37 S.

《中国的人民币：世界上少有的最稳定的货币》

2. Warum China keine Inflation kennt/Peng Guang-hsi. Peking：Verlag für fremdsprachige Literatur，1976. 69 pages；19cm.

《中国为什么没有通货膨胀》，彭光玺.

G 类　文化、教育、体育

G1　中国文化概论

1. Kurzer Abriß des Kulturwesens in China/von Dschai Biän. Peking：Verl. für Fremdsprach. Literatur，1975. 60 S.：Ill.（z. T. farb.）

《中国文化简况》，翟边.

2. Medien der Kultur/Bearbeitung：Redaktion der China-Buchreihe. Beijing：Verlag für Fremdsprachige Literatur，1984. 147 S.：Abb

《文化事业》，《中国概况丛书》，编辑委员会编.

3. 图说中国文化：汉德双语 Chinesisch-Deutsch/贺晓兴主编. 北京：中国对外翻译出版公司，2009. 191 页；29cm. ISBN：7500123507

中德文对照.

4. Allgemeine Kenntnisse über die chinesische Kultur/Guowuyuan Qiaowu Bangongshi. Beijing Higher Education Press，2007. 283 S. Ill.，graph. Darst.，Kt. ISBN：7040207156

《中国文化常识：汉德对照》，任启亮主编；国务院侨务办公室，国家汉语国际推广领导小组办公室编. 高等教育出版社（中国常识系列）

G2　出版

1. 藏族传统文化的巨大工程：《中华大藏经·丹珠尔》对勘纪实/吴伟. 五洲传播出版社，1997. ISBN：7801132068

2. Von der Orakelknocheninschrift zur E-Publikation：3000 — jähriges Verlagswesen in China/［Chefred.：Dongfa Xiao］. Beijing：Verl. für fremdsprachige Literatur，2009. 207 S.：zahlr. ill.，graph. Darst.；27cm.，1910 gr. ISBN：7119060224

《从甲骨文到 E-publications：跨越三千年的中国出版》，肖东发主编.

G3　文化机构

1. Museen in Beijing/Hrsg. Verlag f. fremdsprachige Literatur；Redaktion der deutschen Ausgabe：Gu Xiaoyun. Bejing：Verl. für fremdsprachige Literatur，2008. 167 S.：überw. ill.；224×130 mm.，405 gr.

ISBN：7119054575

《京城博物馆》，子慧撰.

G4 教育

1. Chinas Bildungswesen：Reform und Erneuerung/von Su Xiaohuan. ［Beijing］：China Internat. Press，2002. 198 S.；ill.；21cm. ISBN：7508500563

   《中国教育：改革与创新》，苏晓环. 五洲传播出版社.

2. Chinas Bildungswesen/verfasst von Su Xiaohuan；übersetzt von Tian Shouyu und Zhong Yingjie. 2. Aufl. Beijing：China Intercontinental Press，2006. 194 pages：color illustrations；21cm. ISBN：750850948X

   《中国教育》，苏晓环著；钟英杰译，2 版. 五洲传播出版社（中国基本情况丛书/郭长建主编）

3. Die Erziehung muss mit der produktiven Arbeit verbunden werden/Lu Ding-i. Peking：Verl. f. fremdsprachige Literatur，1958. 38 S.

   《教育必须与生产劳动相结合》，陆定一.

4. Den Weg der Werkzeugmaschinenfabrik Schanghai gehen，Techniker aus der Arbeiterschaft heranzubilden：(zwei Untersuchungsberichte über die Revolution in der Ausbildung an den naturwissenschaftlichen und technischen Hochschulen). Peking：Verl. für Fremdsprachige Literatur，1969. 66 S.

   《走上海机床厂从工人中培养技术人员的道路》

5. Für den Aufbau von sozialistischen Hochschulen der Naturwissenschaften und der Technik kämpfen. Peking：Verlag für fremdsprachige Literatur，1971. 83 pages；18cm.

   《为创办社会主义理工科大学而奋斗》

6. Beschluss des ZK der KP Chinas über die Reform des Bildungssystems. Beijing：Verl. für Fremdsprachige Literatur；Beijing：Chines. Internat. Buchh.-Ges. (Guoji Shudian)，1985. 26 S.；19cm.

   《中共中央关于教育体制改革的决定》

7. Bildung und Wissenschaft/Redaktion der China-Buchreihe. Beijing：Verlag für fremdsprachige Literatur，1985. 245 S：Tab.，Ill.

   《教育科学》，《中国概况丛书》编辑委员会编.

G5 体育

1. Sport und Gesundheit/Bearbeitung：Redaktion der China-Buchreihe. Beijing：Verlag für fremdsprachige Literatur，1984. 172 S；Ill.

   《体育卫生》，《中国概况丛书》编辑委员会编.

2. Taiji-Qigong in achtundzwanzig Schritten/von Li Ding und Bambang Sutomo. Beijing：Verl. für fremdsprachige Literatur，1990. 160 S.；ill. ISBN：7119011871

   《太极气功二十八式》，李丁，（印尼）陈中行.

3. Die 14 Übungsreihen zur Sehnentransformation/von Chang Weizhen. ［übers.：Zhang Shuliang］. Beijing：Verl. für Fremdsprachige Literatur，1990. 136 S.；19cm. ISBN：7119012142

   《易筋经十四段功法录》，常维祯.

4. Meridian-Qigong ［traditionelle chinesische therapeutische Körperkultur］/Li Ding. ［übers.：Zhang Shuliang und Liu Xiuwen. Dt. Bearb.：Monika Katzenschlager. Red. der dt. Ausg.：Dai Shifeng］. Beijing：Verl. für Fremdsprachige Literatur，1995. 271 S. ill. 19cm. ISBN：7119013408

   《经络气功》，李丁.

5. Taijiquan für Anfänger/Li Xingdong. ［übers.：Yan Junxu. Dt. Bearb.：Atze Schmidt］ Beijing：Verl. für fremdsprachige Literatur，1996. 97 S. ill. 21cm. ISBN：7119018744

   《太极拳初步》，李兴东.

6. Taijiquan in 48 Figuren/ Der Chinesische Wushu-Verband. ［übers.：Ren Shuyin und Zhang Zhenhua. Dt. Bearb.：Atze Schmidt］. Beijing：Verl. für fremdsprachige Literatur，1999. 168 pages illustsrations 21cm. ISBN：711901966X

   《四十八式太极拳》，中国武术协会.

7. Weiche Waffen：die neungliedrige Peitsche und der Pfeil am Seil/Wang Suping；Li Xingdong. ［Übers.：Gregor Kneussel］. Beijing：Verl. für fremdsprachige Literatur，2005. 238 S. ill. 21cm. ISBN：7119038591

   《软器械：九节鞭和绳镖》，王素平，李兴东著. 外文出版社（中国武术丛书）

8. Wu Qin Xi/ zsgest. von der Chinesischen Gesellschaft für Gesundheit und Qigong. ［Übers.：Dorian Liedtke］. Beijing：China Verl. für Fremdsprachige Literatur，2008. 102 S. ill. 23cm.，232 gr. 1 DVD. ISBN：7119054315

   《五禽戏》，国家体育总局健身气功管理中心编.

9. Liu zi jue/zusammengestellt von der Chinesischen Gesellschaft für Gesundheit und Qigong. Beijing：Verlag für fremdsprachige Literatur，2008. 73 pages：illustrations (some color)；23cm. ＋1 CD-ROM (4 3/4 in.). ISBN：7119054322

   《六字诀》，国家体育总局健身气功管理中心编.

10. Ba duan jin/zusammengestellt von der Chinesischen Gesellschaft für Gesundheit und Qigong. Beijing：Verlag für fremdsprachige Literatur，2008. 56 pages：illustrations (some color)；23cm. ＋1 CD-ROM (4 3/4 in.). ISBN：7119054339

    《八段锦》，国家体育总局健身气功管理中心编.

11. Yi Jin Jing/zsgest. von der Chinesischen Gesellschaft für Gesundheit und Qigong. ［Übers.：Dorian Liedtke］. Beijing：China Verl. für Fremdsprachige Literatur，2008. 95 S. Ill. 23cm.，227 gr. 1 DVD. ISBN：7119054308

    《易筋经》，国家体育总局健身气功管理中心编.

H类 语言、文字

H1 汉语、汉字

1. Die Schriftreform in China/[Deutsch von Dora Liau]. Peking：Verlag für Fremdsprachige Literatur，1959. 76 pages；19cm.
《中国的文字改革》

2. Zhong guo zi - Shu xie：Lehrwerk für Chinesisch als Fremdsprache/Brigitte Kölla. Beijing：Commercial Press，2009. 200 S. 294 × 212 mm，675 gr. ISBN：7100060196
《中国字：书写》，柯佩琦编著. 商务印书馆. 汉德对照.

3. Der Frosch am Grunde des Brunnens：Geschichten von chinesischen Sprichwörtern/Heinz Lohmann. Münster；New York：Waxmann，1990. X，58 S.：Ill.；21cm. ISBN：3893250592，389325059X.
《中国成语故事：井底之蛙》，Lohmann，Heinz 译.

4. Geschichten von chinesischen Sprichwörtern/[Autoren：Li Lanqin und Wang Xin]. Beijing：Verl. für Fremdsprachige Literatur，2009. 236 S.：ill. ISBN：7119060187
《中国成语故事》，李兰琴，王昕著.

5. Altchinesische Spruchweisheit. Deutsch von Käthe Dschao und Senta Lewin. Illustrationen von Feng Zikai. Beijing：Verlag für fremdsprachige Literatur，1957. 104 S.
中国古代谚语选. Käthe Dschao 及 Senta Lewin 译.
(1)3. Aufl. Beijing：Verlag für Fremdsprachige Literatur，1980. 95 Seiten：Illustrationen；20cm.
(2)3. Aufl.，2. Nachdr. Beijing：Verlag für Fremdsprachige Literatur，1986. 95 Seiten：Illustrationen；20cm.

6. Sprichwörter und Lehrgeschichten der Chinesen/aus d. Chines. übers. u. hrsg. von Gu Sheng-qing. Köln：Diederichs，1985. 143 S.：154 Ill.；19cm. ISBN：3424008425，3424008427.
中国谚语及寓言. Gu Sheng-qing 译.

7. 中华传统美德格言：汉德对照/吕达，姜明宝主编；常志丹等编写. 北京：人民教育出版社，2007. 1 册；23cm. ISBN：7107205309

H2 对外汉语教育读物

1. Moderne chinesische Fabeln/[Red.：Tang Xiaoqing]. Beijing：Verlag für Fremdsprachige Literatur，2006. 141 S：Ill. ISBN：7119043587
《中国现代寓言：汉德对照》，唐晓青主编. 外文出版社(汉语轻松阅读)

2. Chinesisch lustig lesen：Chinesische Volkshumore/Chinesische Volkshumore. Beijing：Verl. für fremdsprachige Literatur，2006. 129 p.：Ill.；24cm. ISBN：7119043552
《中国民间幽默：汉德对照》，唐晓青主编. 外文出版社(汉语轻松阅读)

3. Chinesische Witze zu allen Zeiten/Red.：[Tang Xiaoqing]. Beijing：Verl. für Fremdsprachige Literatur，2006. 132 S.：zahlr. Ill. ISBN：7119043579
《中国古今笑话：汉德对照》，唐晓青主编. 外文出版社(汉语轻松阅读)

4. Altchinesische Spruchweisheit/[dt. von Käthe Dschao；Senta Lewin. Ill. von Feng Zikai]. Beijing：Verl. für Fremdsprachige Literatur，2006. 106 S.：zahlr. ill. ISBN：7119043560
《中国古代寓言：汉德对照》，唐晓青主编. 外文出版社(汉语轻松阅读)

5. Chinesische Lebensweisheiten/[Red.：Tang Xiaoqing]. Beijing：Verlag für Fremdsprachige Literatur，2006. 133 S：Ill. ISBN：7119043544
《中国处世哲学：汉德对照》，唐晓青主编；邵青还，戴世峰译. 外文出版社(汉语轻松阅读)

6. Geschichten chinesischer Weisheiten/Red.：[Tang Xiaoqing]. Beijing：Verl. für Fremdsprachige Literatur，2006. 130 S. ISBN：7119043536
《中国智慧故事：汉德对照》，唐晓青主编；邵青还，戴世峰译. 外文出版社(汉语轻松阅读)

7. 德译中国古代短文选/张佳珏选译. 上海：上海外语教育出版社，2009. 229 页；24cm. ISBN：7544613897
中德文对照.

I类 文学

I1 文学评论和研究

1. Die grosse Aussprache über Literatur und Kunst/Dschou Yang und ein Diskussionsbeitr. v. Schao Tjüan-lin. Peking：Verl. f. fremdsprachige Literatur，1958. 84 S.
《文艺战线上的一场大辩论》，周扬.

2. Der Weg der sozialistischen Literatur und Kunst in China：Referat auf dem III. Kongress der chinesischen Literatur- und Kunstschaffenden am 22. Juli 1960. Peking：Fremdsprachige Literatur，1961. 85 pages：illustrations；19cm.
《我国社会主义文学艺术的道路》，周扬.

3. Literatur und Kunst/Redaktion der deutschen Ausgabe：Xu Shumin，Li Xiuzhen. Beijing：Verl. für Fremdsprachige Literatur，1985. 228 S. Ill. (China-Buchreihe)
《文学艺术》

4. Chinesische Literatur/Yao Dan. Übers. von Ego. Beijing：China Intercontinental Press，2009. 247 S.：Ill.；23cm. ISBN：7508515878
《中国文学》，姚丹编著. 五洲传播出版社. 本书是一本介绍中国文学的普及读本，选择和提炼不同时代影响中国文化和社会生活的文学作品和文学家，展现了中国文学的发展脉络. 中国文学史著作.

5. Unterwegs: Literatur-Gegenwart China/Li Jingze & Jing Bartz（Hg.）.〔Aus dem Chines. von Johannes Fiederling...〕. Düren；Bonn：DIX-Verl.，2009. 375 S.；21cm. ISBN：3941651005，3941651005

在路上：中国当代文学. Fiederling，Johannes 等译.

I11　各体文学评论和研究

1. Ein Beitrag zur chinesischen Poetik/Yan Yu；Günther Debon. Wiesbaden：Otto Harrassowitz，1962. 258 S.；25cm.

《沧浪诗话》,（宋）严羽著；Günther Debon(1921—2005)译.

2. Nur wir Dichter：Yuan Mei：eine Dichtungstheorie des 18. Jahrhunderts zwischen Selbstbehauptung und Konvention/Marion Eggert. Bochum：Studienverl. Brockmeyer，1989. 146 S.；19cm. ISBN：3883397474，3883397474.（Chinathemen；Bd. 42）

袁枚诗论. 清代诗人袁枚（1716 － 1797）著；Eggert，Marion(1962—)（德国东亚学家）译.

3. 世界最长史诗《格萨尔王传》：中国藏族传统文化宝典介绍/吴伟. 北京：五洲传播,1997. ISBN：7801132033

4. Über die Kraft der romantischen Poesie/Lu Xun. F. Gruner，Übers. Berlin：Selbstverl.，1993. 53 Bl.

《摩罗诗力说》,鲁迅著；Gruner，Fritz 译.

5. Kurze Geschichte der chinesischen Romandichtung/Lu Xun. Beijing：Verlag für Fremdsprachige Literatur，1981. 462 S.：Ill.；19cm.

《中国小说史略》,鲁迅著.

I2　作品集

I21　作品综合集

1. Kleines chinesisches Lesebuch：eine Auswahl aus der klassischen Literatur Chinas/Aus d. Urtexten übers. u. eingel.：Herbert Franke. Köln：Staufen-Verl.，1941. 63 S.；8.

中国经典文学选读. Franke，Herbert 译.

2. Der magische Spiegel：Chinesische Märchen u. Novellen aus d. Zeiten d. Blüte/Dt. Fassung nach franz. übertragg durch Lo Ta-Kang von Richard B. Matzig. Bern：Francke，1944. 254 S.：mit Abb.；8.

中国古代童话及小说. Luo，Dagang 和 Matzig，Richard Blasius 合译.

3. Die chinesische Anthologie/Übersetzungen aus dem Wen hsüan von Erwin von Zach；edited by Ilse Martin Fang；with an introduction by James Robert Hightower. Cambridge，Mass.：Harvard University Press，1958. 2 volumes（xxxvi, 1114 pages）；26cm.（Harvard-Yenching Institute studies；18）

《文选》,萧统（501—531）；赞克（Zach，Erwin，1872—1942）译.

4. Die chinesische Anthologie Wen-Hsüan：in manjurischer Teilübersetzung einer Leningrader und einer Kölner Handschrift：mit 5 Tafeln/T'ung Hsioa. Hrsg. von Martin Grimm. Stuttgart：Steiner，1968. VII，222，4 S.：Ill.；29cm.

《文选》,萧统（501—531）；Gimm，Martin 译.

5. Ku-wen yüan-chien：die kaiserliche Ku-wen-Anthologie von 1685/6：in manjurischer Übersetzung/herausgegeben von Martin Gimm. Wiesbaden：O. Harrassowitz，1939—1995. 3 volumes；25cm. ISBN：3447036877，3447036870 Contents：Bd. 1. Kap. 1—24（Chou- bis Chin-Dynastie）—Bd. 2. Kap. 25—44（Nord/Süd-Dynastien bis Song-Zeit）—Bd. 3. Kap. 45—64（Song-Zeit，Fortsetzung）.

《古文渊鉴》,三卷,徐乾学（1631—1694）；Gimm，Martin 译.

6. Die Nacht ist kühl und doch so zärtlich：romant. Lyrik u. Prosa aus China/Josephine Yip. Berlin：Boose，1979.〔12〕Bl.：1 Ill.；22cm. ISBN：3922377757，3922377750.

中国诗歌及散文.

7. Chrestomathie der chinesischen Literatur der 50er Jahre/bearbeitet und herausgegeben von Shuxin Reichardt und Manfred Reichardt；mit einer Einführung von Fritz Gruner. Leipzig：Verlag Enzyklopädie，1982. 448 pages；22cm.

中国五十年代文学选集. Reichardt，Shuxin 和 Reichardt，Manfred 合译. 作为德语学习教材.

8. Literatur und Politik in der Volksrepublik China/hrsg. von Rudolf G. Wagner. Frankfurt am Main：Suhrkamp，1983. 366 S.；18cm. ISBN：3518111512，3518111515.（Edition Suhrkamp；1151＝N. F.，Bd. 151）

中国文学与政治. Wagner，Rudolf 编. 收录沙叶新、茹志鹃、叶文富等人作品.

9. Nach den Wirren：Erzählungen und Gedichte aus der Volksrepublik China nach der Kulturrevolution/〔gemeinsam von d. Rhein.-Westfäl. Auslandsges. in Dortmund u. d. Chines. Volksliteraturverl. in Beijing konzipiert. Ausw. d. Texte u. Übers. Konrad Wegmann；Guan Huiwen〕. Dortmund：RWAG-Dienste u.-Verl.，1988. 191 Seiten；21cm. ISBN：3923030037，3923030033

文革后中国小说及诗歌. Wegmann，Konrad 编译.

10. Chinesische Erzählungen/hrsg. von Andrea Wörle. München：Deutscher Taschenbuch Verlag，1990. 302 S：Kart；18cm. ISBN：3423112026，3423112024.（Dtv；11202）

20世纪中国文集. Wörle，Andrea 译. 包含溥仪、鲁迅、巴金、老舍、郭沫若、毛泽东、沈从文、丁玲、迟松年、乐黛云、石墨、王蒙、王安忆、张洁、张辛欣的作品. 包括小说和散文.

11. Chinesische Geschichten/hrsg. von Jutta Freund.〔Pearl S. Buck...〕. Orig.-ausg. München：Heyne，1990. 315 Seiten；18cm. ISBN：3453037030，3453037038.（Heyne-

Bücher/01；Nr. 8002)

中国文学作品集. Freund，Jutta 译. 含鲁迅、巴金、老舍、溥仪、茅盾、王蒙、张杰、沈从文、丁玲、北岛、冰心作品.

12. Die Auflösung der Abteilung für Haarspalterei：Texte moderner chinesischer Autoren；von den Reformen bis zum Exil/hrsg. von Helmut Martin und Christiane Hammer. Reinbek bei Hamburg：Rowohlt，1991. 319 S.；22cm. ISBN：3498029074，349802907X.

中国现代作家作品选. Martin，Helmut 和 Hammer，Christiane 译. 含刘心武、刘宾雁、刘白羽、张辛欣、苏晓康、汪曾祺、王蒙、王安忆、王若望、宗璞、张贤亮、杨绛、张洁、遇罗锦等人作品.

I22 个人作品集

鲁迅(1881—1938)

1. Die Reise ist lang：Gesammelte Erzählungen/Hsün Lu. Aus d. Chines. übers. von Joseph Kalmer. Düsseldorf：Progress-Verl. Fladung，1955. 524 S.；1 Titelbild；8.

鲁迅文集. Kalmer，Joseph 译.

2. Die Methode wilde Tiere abzurichten：Erzählungen，Essays，Gedichte/Lu Xun. Ausw.，übertr. u. Einf. von Wolfgang Kubin. Berlin：Oberbaumverlag，1979. 107 S.；Ill.；20cm. ISBN：3876281598，3876281599. (Bücherei Oberbaum；No. 1016)

鲁迅小说、文论、诗歌. 顾彬(Kubin，Wolfgang，1945—)译.

(1)2. Aufl. Berlin：Oberbaumverlag，1981. 107 S.；Ill.；20cm.

3. Die grosse Mauer：Erzählungen，Essays，Gedichte/Lu Xun. Nördlingen：Greno，1987. 444 S.；22cm. ISBN：3891902263，3891902264，389190326X，3891903261. (Die andere Bibliothek；26)

鲁迅作品选. 包括短篇小说、散文、诗歌.

4. Werke in sechs Bänden/Lu Xun；herausgegeben von Wolfgang Kubin. Zürich：Unionsverlag，1994. 6 volumes：map；20cm. ISBN：3293002072 (Bd. 1)，3293002074 (Bd. 1)，3293002080 (Bd. 2)，3293002081 (Bd. 2)，3293002099 (Bd. 3)，3293002098 (Bd. 3)，3293002102(Bd. 4)，3293002104 (Bd. 4)，3293002110 (Bd. 5)，3293002111 (Bd. 5)，3293002129 (Bd. 6)，3293002128 (Bd. 6)

Contents：Bd. 1. Applaus：Erzählungen—Bd. 2. Zwischenzeiten，Zwischenwelten：Erzählungen—Bd. 3. Blumen der Frühe am Abend gelesen：Erinnerungen—Bd. 4. Altes，frisch verpackt—Bd. 5 Das Totenmal：Essays—Bd. 6. Das trunkene Land：Reminiszenzen.

《鲁迅全集》，六卷. 顾彬(Kubin，Wolfgang，1945—)译.

西川(1963—)

1. Die Diskurse des Adlers：Gedichte und poetische Prosa/Xi Chuan；aus dem Chinesischen von Brigitte Höhenrieder，

Peter Hoffmann und dem Tübinger Arbeitskreis Chinesische Literatur. Bochum：Projekt Verlag，2004. viii，148 pages.；21cm. ISBN：3897330979，3897330970. 9Arcus Chinatexte，；Band 20)

诗歌与抒情散文. Höhenrieder，Brigitte 等译.

I3 诗歌、韵文

I31 古代和跨时代诗词集

I311 诗经

1. Schi-King：chinesisches Liederbuch/gesammelt von Confucius，dem Deutschen angeeignet von Friedrich Rückert. Altona：Hammerich，1833. X，360 S. 8°.

《诗经》，Friedrich Rückert(1788—1866)翻译.

2. Schi-King，oder Chinesische Lieder/gesammelt von Confucius. Neu und frei nach p. La Charme's lateinischer Übertragung bearbeitet. Für's deutsche Volk herausgegeben von Johann Cramer. Crefeld，J. H. Funcke，1844. xix，255，[1] pages；16cm. (Das Himmlische Reich. Oder China's Leben，Denken，Dichten und Geschichte…；3. bd)

《诗经》，La Charme，Alexandre de（1695—1767)译成拉丁文；Johann Cramer 德译.

3. Schi-king：das kanonische Liederbuch der Chinesen/aus dem Chinesischen übers. und erklärt von Victor von Strauss. Heidelberg eidelberg：C. Winter，1880. 528 S.；23cm.

《诗经》，Strauss und Torney，Victor von(1809—1899)译.

(1) Darmstadt：Wiss. Buchges.，1969. 528 pages. 20cm.

4. Schi-king. Das Liederbuch Chinas，hundert Gedichte/ges. von Kung-Fu-Tse. Dem Dt. angeeignet nach Friedrich Rückert von Albert Ehrenstein. Leipzig：Tal，1922. 141 Seiten

《诗经》，Albert Ehrenstein (1886—1950)(奥地利作家)译.

(1) Schi King. Das Liederbuch Chinas. Gesammelt von Kung-Fu-Tse. Hundert Gedichte. Deutsch nach Friedrich Rückert von Albert Ehrenstein. Leipzig；Wien；Zürich：E. P. Tal&Co，1933. 148 S.

5. Tausendjähriger Bambus：Nachdichtungen aus d. Schi-King/Fritz Mühlenweg. Hamburg：Dulk，1946. 95 Seiten：Illustrationen

《千年竹：诗经》，Mühlenweg，Fritz 译.

(1)2. Aufl. Hamburg：Dulk，1948. 59 S.；8.

(2)3. Aufl. Hamburg：Dulk，1956. 95 S.；mit Abb.；8.

(3)Tausendjähriger Bambus：Nachdichtungen aus dem Schi-King/Fritz Mühlenweg. Mit einem Nachw. … von Ekkehard Faude. Neuausg. Lengwil：Libelle，1994. 100 S.；24cm. ISBN：3909081677，3909081673.

6. „Shu ist jagen gegangen"：Chinesische Gedichte aus dem

Schi-King/Übertragen von W. M. Treichlinger. Zürich：Verlag der Arche，1948. 66 Seiten；8°

《诗经》，Treichlinger，Wilhelm Michael(1902—1973)译.

7. Ein weisses Kleid，ein grau Gebände：chinesische Lieder aus dem 12.-7. Jh. v. Chr./übertragen von Günther Debon. München：Piper，1957. 62 pages：illustrations；19cm. (Piper-Bücherei；110)

《诗经》选译，Debon，Günther(1921—2005)译.

I312　其他古代和跨时代诗歌集

1. Blüthen chinesischer Dichtung：mit 21 reproducirten chinesischen Original-pinselzeichnungen aus der Zeit der Han- und Sechs-dynastie，II. Jahrhundert vor Christus bis zum VI. Jahrhundert nach Christus/aus dem Chinesischen metrisch übers. von A. Forke. Magdeburg：Commissionsverlag：Faber'sche Buchdr.，1899. xvi，148 pages plates (1 double)23cm.

《诗歌集锦》，Forke，Alfred(1867—1944)译.

2. Dichtungen der T'ang- und Sung-Zeit：aus dem Chinesischen metrisch übertragen/von Alfred Forke. Hamburg Friederichsen：de Gruyter，1929. V，173 S. (Veröffentlichungen des Seminars für Sprache und Kultur Chinas an der Hamburgischen Universität；3)

中国唐诗宋词(德文篇). Forke，Alfred (1867—1944)译.

3. Chinesische Lyrik vom 12. Jahrhundert v. Chr. bis zur Gegenwart/In deutscher Übersetzung，mit Einleitung und Anmerkungen von Hans Heilmann. München；Leipzig：R. Piper & Co，1905. 159 S.

中国公元前十二世纪至今抒情诗. Heilmann，Hans 译.

4. Die chinesische Flöte. Nachdichtungen chinesischer Lyrik/Hans Bethge. Leipzig：Insel Verlag，1907. 119 S.

中国抒情诗. Bethge，Hans 译.

(1)Leipzig：Inselverl.，1920. 118 S. 8„.

(2)Leipzig：Inselverl.，1922. 117 S. 8„.

(3)Leipzig：Insel-Verl.，1935. 111 S. 8„. (Insel-Bücherei. - Berlin：Insel-Verl，1912—；465)

(4)Wiesbaden：Insel-Verl.，1955. 83 S. 8„. (Insel-Bücherei；Nr. 465)

(5)Heidenheim：Schuldt，1980. 110 S.

5. Pfirsichblüten aus China/Hans Bethge. Berlin：Rowohlt，1920. 97 pages color plates 35cm.

中国诗歌. Bethge，Hans (1876—1946)译..

(1)Pfirsichblüten aus China：［Nachdichtungen chines. Lyrik］/Hans Bethge. Berlin：E. Rowohlt，1922. 121 Bl.；gr. 8.

(2)Kelkheim：Yinyang-Media-Verl.，2005. X，116 S.：Ill.；19cm. ISBN：3935727068，3935727062. (Bethge，Hans：Nachdichtungen orientalischer Lyrik；Bd. 7)

6. Die Chinesische Dichtung/von Otto Hauser；Mit 9 Vollbildern in Tonätzung. Berlin，Marquardt & Co.，Verl.-Anst. g. m. b. h.，1908. 3 preliminary leaves，67 pages，1 leaf frontispiece，illustrations，plates，portraits. (Die Literatur；34. Bd)

中国诗歌. Hauser，Otto(1876—1944)译.

7. Chinesische Gedichte aus der Han-，Tang- und Sungzeit/übers. u. eingeleitet von Otto Hauser. Weimar：Duncker，1917. XII，26 S.；8. (Aus fremden Gärten；58)

中国汉代、唐代、宋代诗词. Hauser，Otto(1876—1944)译.

8. Dumpfe Trommel und berauschtes Gong：chinesischer Kriegslyrik；Nachdichtungen/tr. by Klabund. Leipzig：Insel-Verlag，1915. 44 S.

中国战争抒情诗. Klabund(1890—1928)译.

(1)Leipzig：Insel，1934. 45 S.

(2)Wiesbaden：Insel-Verl.，1952. 51 S.；8. (Insel-Bücherei；Nr. 183)

(3)Dumpfe Trommel und berauschtes Gong：Nachdichtungen chinesischer Kriegslyrik/von Klabund. Berlin：Elfenbein，2009. 45 S.；24cm. ISBN：3941184015，3941184016

9. Das Blumenschiff：Nachdichtungen chines. Lyrik/Klabund. ［Farb. Buchschmuck von Erna Pinner］. Berlin：E. Reiss，1921. 56 S.；kl. 8

中国抒情诗. Klabund(1890—1928)译.

10. Chinesische Gedichte/Nachdichtungen von Klabund；［Bilder：Georg Mayer-Marton］. Gesamt-Ausgabe. Wien：Phaidon-Verlag，1933. 130 pages：color illustrations.；22cm.

中国诗歌. Klabund(1890—1928)译.

11. Chinesisch-deutsche Jahres- und Tageszeiten：Lieder u. Gesänge/verdeutscht von Richard Wilhelm，mit 16 Nachbildungen chinesischer Holzschnitte. Jena：E. Diederichs，1922. 3 preliminary leaves，129 l.，2 leaves 22cm.

中国诗歌. 卫礼贤 (Wilehlm Richard，1873—1930)译.

12. Chinesische Staatsweisheit/Franz Kuhn. ［Einf.：Chang Yün Kai］. Darmstadt：O. Reichl，1923. XXIV，185 S.；8.

《中国状况》. 孔舫之 (Kuhn，Franz，1884—1961)译.

(1)Bremen：Storm，1947. 115 S.；8.

13. China klagt：Nachdichtungen revolutionärer chinesischer Lyrik aus drei Jahrtausenden/Albert Ehrenstein. Berlin：Ascher ［Drucker］ Berlin Malik-Verl.，1924. 48 S. (Malik-Bücherei；8)

中国三千年革命诗歌. Ehrenstein，Albert (1886—1950) (奥地利作家)译. 其中包括《诗经》诗歌 13 首、杜甫诗两首、白居易诗歌 9 首及其他.

(1)Königstein；München：Autoren-Edition，1981. 48 S.；18cm. ISBN：3761081112，3761081111. (Malik-Bücherei；Bd. 8)

14. Das Frauenherz：Chines. Lieder aus 3 Jahrtausenden/Ausgew. u. aus d. Chines. übers. Stuttgart：Union Deutsche Verlagsgesellschaft，1925. 172，［1］ pages；

illustrations；

中国三千年诗歌. Öhler-Heimerdinger, Elisabeth 译.

15. Chinesische Dichter in deutscher Sprache/Mit 2 Bildern nach originalen des Wang Ting-dsche. Peking, Leipzig：Pekinger Verlag, 1926. 5 p. l. , 13—149 p. , 1 l. 2 mounted illus. 24cm.

中国诗歌. Hundhausen, Vincenz (1878—1955)译.

16. Chinesische Dichter des dritten bis elften Jahrhunderts/in deutscher Nachdichtung von Vincenz Hundhausen. Mit 2 Bildern von Wang Ting-Dsche. Eisenach：Röth, 1954. 149 S. ; gr. 8.

13 至 11 世纪中国诗词. Hundhausen, Vicenz(1878—1955)译.

17. Der Porzellanpavillon：Nachdichtungen chinesischer Lyrik/von Max Fleischer. Berlin〔u. a.〕：Zsolnay, 1927. 117 S.

中国诗歌. Fleischer, Max 译.

18. Lieder aus China. Nachdichtungen chinesischer Lyrik/Hans Böhm；mit 17 Zeichnungen von Rudolf Grossmann. München：Georg D. W. Callwey, 1929. 61 pages：illustrations；23cm.

中国诗歌. Böhm, Hans(1876—1946)译.

19. Chinesische Liebesgeschichten/Übertragungen von O. Sumitomo〕. Zürich：W. Classen, 〔1947〕. 96 p. ；20cm. (Vom Dauernden in der Zeit；32)

中国爱情诗歌. Sumitomo, O. 译.

20. Gesang der gelben Erde：Nachdichtungen aus dem Chinesischen/F. C. Weiskopf. Berlin：Dietz, 1951. 104 S. ；mit Abb. ；8.

中国诗歌. Weiskopf, F. C. （Franz Carl, 1900—1955)译.

21. Ein weisses Kleid, ein grau Gebände：chinesische Lieder aus dem 12. -7. Jh. v. Chr. /übertragen von Günther Debon. München：Piper, 1957. 62 pages：illustrations；19cm. (Piper-Bücherei；110)

公元前 7—12 世纪的中国诗歌. Debon, Günther 译.

22. Mein Haus liegt menschenfern doch nah den Dingen：3000 Jahre chines Poesie/Günther Debon. München：Diederichs, 1988. 303 S. ：Ill. ；22cm. ISBN：3424009385, 3424009385

中国三千年诗歌. Debon, Günther 译. 含左思、庄子、屈原、纳兰性德、沈周、苏东坡、孙继皋、陶渊明、寒山、贺知章、李清照、李贺、荀子、王昌龄、王之涣、王梵志、王僧孺、王士祯、王维、韦应物、袁宏道等人作品)含张九龄、郑板桥、庄子、屈原、寒山、韩愈等人作品.

23. Mein Weg verliert sich fern in weissen Wolken：chinesische Lyrik aus drei Jahrtausenden：eine Anthologie/〔übers. u. erl. von Günther Debon〕. Heidelberg：Schneider,1988. 293 S. ；20cm. ISBN：3795307732, 3795307738. （Sammlung Weltliteratur)

中国三千年诗歌选. Debon, Günther 译. 含贺知章、贾岛、黄庭坚、刘慎虚、谢灵运、王勃、王维、王之涣、王昌龄、温庭筠、王安石、袁宏道等人作品.

24. Chinesische Gedichte/übertragen und herausgegeben von Abraham Horodisch. 〔Place of publication not identified〕：Im Bertalsmann Lesering, 1958. 84 pages：color illustrations；24cm.

中国诗歌. Horodisch, Abraham 译.

(1)Gütersloh：Bertelsmann Lesering, 1964. 84 Seiten：Illustrationen；8

25. Der Wind brach einen Blütenzweig：chinesische Gedichte/ausgew. und übertr. von Jan Ulenbrook. Baden-Baden：Holle, 1959. 287 S. ：Ill. ；21cm.

中国诗歌. Ulenbrook, Jan（1909－）选译. 德中双语对照.

26. Pflaumenblüte und verschneiter Bambus：Chinesische Gedichte/Wahl und Übers. aus dem Chines. von Jan Ulenbrook；Mit 62 Tuschzeichnungen chinesischer Künstler. Zürich：Manesse Verlag, 1969. 235 pages：illustrations；16cm. ISBN：3717513265, 3717513261, 3717513273, 3717513278. （Manesse Bibliothek der Weltliteratur)

中国诗歌. Ulenbrook, Jan(1909—)译.

(1)3 dr. Zürich：Manesse Verlag, 1987. 235 p. ：ill. ；16cm. ISBN：3717513265, 3717513261, 3717513273, 3717513278

27. Maulbeerblatt und Seidenfalter：Nachdichtungen aus dem Chinesischen/Georg Schneider. München：Langen, Müller, 1961. 79 S. ：mit Abb. , 1 Titelbild；8.

中国诗歌. Schneider, Georg(1876—1960)译.

28. Lyrik des Ostens：China/Mit e. Nachw. v. Wilhelm Gundert. München：Dt. Taschenbuchverl. , 1962. 184 S. ；8°. （Dtv-Taschenbücher；47)

中国诗歌选. Gundert, Wilhelm(1880—)译.

29. Weisse Wolke：Chinesische Gedichte/Nachdichtung von Karl Christian Müller. Saarbrücken：Steinwald Verl. , 1965. 24 unnumbered pages；21cm.

中国诗歌. Müller, Karl Christian(1900—1975)译.

30. Chinesische Gedichte aus drei Jahrtausenden/hrsg. von Andreas Donath. Frankfurt am Main：Fischer Bücherei, 1965. 140 S. ；kl. 8. （Fischer Bücherei；702)

三千年诗选. Donath, Andreas(1934—)译.

31. Die Jadegöttin：12 Geschichten aus d. mittelalterl. China/〔Ausw. , Nachw. , Anm. u. wiss. Textkontrolle von Jaroslav Průšek unter unter Mitarb. von Felicitas Wünschová. Aus d. Chin. übertr. von Liane Bettin u. Marianne Liebermann〕. Berlin：Rütten u. Loening, 1966. 447 S. ；8. （Bibliothek der Weltliteratur)

中世纪中国诗歌十二首. Průšek, Jaroslav 和 Bettin, Liane 合译.

(1)2. Aufl. Berlin：Rütten u. Loening, 1968. 447 S. ；8.

(2)Berlin, Weimar：Aufbau-Verlag, 1977. 386 S. ；

18cm.

    (3) 3. Aufl. Berlin：Rütten u. Loening，1984. 399 S. ；
        20cm.

32. Altchinesische Hymnen：aus dem „Buch der Lieder" und den „Gesängen von Ch'u"/übertr. und erläutert von Peter Weber-Schäfer. Köln：Jakob Hegner，1967. 215 p. ；17cm. (Hegner-Bücherei)

《楚辞》《诗经》，Weber-Schäfer, Peter 编译.

33. Chrysanthemen im Spiegel：Klassische chinesische Dichtung/Herausgegeben，aus dem Chinesischen übertragen und nachgedichtet von Ernst Schwarz. Berlin：Rütten & Loening，1969. 474 S. ；60 Ill. (z. T. farb.)；28cm.

"镜中菊"：中国古诗. Schwarz, Ernst(1916—2003)译. 收录《诗经》、《古诗十九首》、《易经》、屈原、宋玉、陆游、马致远、柳永、张继、杨万里、乐雷发、袁宏道、李清照、朱淑真、陶渊明、欧阳修、苏东坡、秦观、纳兰性德、查慎行、袁枚、岳飞、朱敦儒、谭嗣同等人作品.

    (1) 1. Aufl. Berlin；Weimar：Aufbau-Verlag，1976. 209 S. ；18cm. (Anmerkungen：Lizenz d. Verl. Rütten & Loening，Berlin)

    (2) 2. Aufl. Berlin：Rütten u. Loening，1988. 471 S. ；61 Ill. ；23cm. ISBN：3352000119，3352000115

34. Chinesische Liebesgedichte aus drei Jahrtausenden/Aus dem Chinesischen übertragen，nachgedichtet und herausgegeben von Ernst Schwarz. Frankfurt am Main：Insel Verlag，1980. 229 S.

中国三千年爱情诗. Schwarz, Ernst(1916—2003)译.

35. Aus dem Chinesischen/Günter Eich. Frankfurt am Main：Suhrkamp，1976. 160 S. ；19cm. ISBN：3518015257，3518015254. (Bibliothek Suhrkamp；525)

中国诗歌选. Eich, Günter 译. 含王维、李白、杜甫、白居易、欧阳修、苏轼、陆游等人诗歌.

36. Das chinesische Brevier vom weinseligen Leben：Heitere Gedichte，beschwingte Lieder und trunkene Balladen der großen Poeten aus dem Reich der Mitte/Aus dem Chinesischen übersetzt und herausgegeben von Jochen Kandel. Bern；München：Scherz Verlag，1985. 288 pages；22cm. ISBN：3502123551，3502123552

中国诗歌精选. Kandel, Jochen 译.

I313 唐诗集

1. Chinesische Gedichte in Vierzeilern aus der T'ang-Zeit/Mit 6 Reproduktionen alter Gemälden aus dem kaiserlichen Palast zu Peking auf Tafeln und 20 Wiedergaben von Original-Pinselzeichnungen von Richard Hadl. Zürich：Rascher Verlag，1944. 143 S. ；illustrations；19cm.

《唐人绝句百首》，Lo Ta-kang 编译.

2. Herbstlich helles Leuchten überm See：Chinesische Gedichte aus d. Tang-Zeit/Hrsg. Günther Debon. München：Piper，1953. 61 S. ；Mit 8 Holzschn. ；8.

(Piper-Bücherei；63)

中国唐诗. Debon, Günther 译. 含王维、王之涣等人作品.

    (1) München：Piper，1954. 61 S. ；Mit 8 Holzschn. ；8. (Piper-Bücherei；63)

    (2) München：Piper，1956. 61 Seiten：Illustrationen. (Piper-Bücherei；63)

    (3) München：R. Piper，1958. 61 pages：illustrations；19cm.

    (4) München：Piper，1959. 61 Seiten：Illustrationen. (Piper-Bücherei；63)

    (5) Herbstlich helles Leuchten überm See：chinesische Gedichte aus der Tang-Zeit/ausgew. ，übertr. u. mit e. Vorw. vers. von Günther Debon. Orig. -Ausg. ，[1. - 5. Tsd.]. München；Zürich：Piper，1989. 99 S. ；8 Ill. ；19cm. ISBN：3492110983，3492110983. (Piper；Bd. 1098)

3. Chinesische Dichter der Tang-Zeit/übers. ，Einl. u. Anm. von Günther Debon. Stuttgart：Reclam，1964. 86 S. ；kl. 8. (Unesco-Sammlung repräsentativer Werke. Asiatische Reihe)

中国唐诗. Debon, Günther 译.

    (1) [Nachdr.]. Stuttgart：Reclam，1975. 86 S. ；16cm. ISBN：3150089107，3150089101. (Unesco-Sammlung repräsentativer Werke：Asiatische Reihe)

    (2) [Nachdr.]. Stuttgart：Reclam，1975. 86 S. ；16cm. ISBN：3150089107，3150089101. (Unesco-Sammlung repräsentativer Werke：Asiatische Reihe)

4. Ich bin der unnütze Dichter, verloren in kranker Welt/ Nachdichtungen aus d. Chines. von Albert Ehrenstein. Berlin：Friedenauer Presse，1970. 6 Bl. ；gr. 8.

唐诗. Ehrenstein, Albert 译.

    (1) 2. Aufl. Berlin：Friedenauer Presse，1984. 15 S. ；25cm. ISBN：3921592038，3921592038.

5. Lieder der Ferne und Weisheit：Lyrik aus 300 Gedichten der Tang-Dynastie/übertr. aus d. Chines. von Hotsang Siau-Mun-Tsin. Nachgedichtet mit 5 eingereihten Holzschn. von Th. Schulz-Walbaum. Bremen：Angelsachsen-Verlag，1923. 31 Bl. ；8.

唐诗三百首选. Schulz-Walbaum, Th 译.

6. Der seidene Faden：Gedichte der Tang/aus dem Chines. übertr. und mit einem Nachw. vers. von Volker Klöpsch. Frankfurt am Main：Insel-Verl. ，1991. 379 Seiten：Illustrationen；22cm. ISBN：3458161872，3458161875

《唐诗三百首》，Klöpsch, Volker 译.

I314 宋代诗词集

1. Frühlingsblüten und Herbstmond：Ein Holzschnittband mit Liedern aus der Sung-Zeit 960 - 1279/aus dem Chinesischen übertragen und erläutert von Alfred

Hoffmann. Köln：Greven，1951. 108，［4］pages：illustrations；19cm.

宋词选. Hoffmann, Alfred(1911—)译.

2. Chinesische Frauenlyrik：Tzi-Lyrik d. Sung-Zeit/von Li Tsching-dschau u. Dschu Schu-dschen．［Mit e. Geleitw. hrsg. u. ins Dt. übertr. von Ernst Schwarz］. München：Deutscher Taschenbuch-Verlag，1985. 99 S.：Ill.；19cm. ISBN：3423021519，3423021517.（dtv；2151：dtv-Klassik）

中国女诗人李清照(1084—1155)、朱淑真(约 1135—1180)作品选. Schwarz, Ernst 译.

I32 古代诗人个人作品

I321 春秋战国时期

屈原(公元前 340—前 278)

1. Das Älteste Dokument zur chinesischen Kunstgeschichte T'ien-Wên：Die „Himmelsfragen" des K'üh Yüan/übers. u. erkl. von August Conrady. Abgeschl. u. hrsg. von Eduard Erkes. Leipzig：Verl. „Asia major"，1931. VIII，266 S.；gr. 8.（China-Bibliothek des „Asia major"；Bd. 2)

《天问》,Conrady, August(1864—1925)译.

2. Die neun Gesänge：eine Studie über Schamanismus im alten China/［edited and translated by］Arthur Waley. Hamburg，M. von Schröder，1957. 98 pages：illustrations；20cm.

《九歌》,韦利(Waley, Arthur, 1889—1966)(英国汉学家)编纂并译成英文;Meister, Franziska 将英文译成德语.

3. Das Liederbuch der Chinesen：Guo feng/In neuer deutscher Übertragung von Heide Köser；philologische Bearbeitung von Armin Hetzer. Frankfurt am Main：Insel Verlag，1990. 259 pages；20cm. ISBN：3458161090，3458161097

《国风》,Köser, Heide 译.

4. Chu ci＝Chu ci/Deutsch von Chen Ming xiang und Peter Herrmann. Beijing：Verlag für fremdsprachige Literatur，2015. 221 Seiten：Illustrationen；24cm. ISBN：7119094076，7119094076.（Bibliothek der chinesischen Klassiker)

《楚辞》,陈器之、李奕今译;陈鸣祥、Peter Hermann 德译.

I322 三国、晋时期

陶渊明(约 352 或 365—427)

1. Tau Yüan-Ming：Ausgewählte Gedichte in deutscher Nachdichtung/Vincenz Hundhausen. Peking：Pekinger，1928. 54 pages：portraits；23cm.

陶渊明诗选. Hundhausen, Vincenz (1878—1955)译.

2. Pfirsichblütenquell：Gedichte/［von］Tao Yüan-ming, mit chinesischen Holzschnitten. Aus dem Chinesischen übertragen und hrsg. von Ernst Schwarz. Leipzig：Insel-Verlag，1967. 95 pages：illustrations；

陶渊明诗. Schwarz, Ernst(1916—)译.

(1) Leipzig：Insel，1992. 93 pages：color illustrations；19cm. ISBN：3458190910，3458190912.（Insel-Bücherei；Nr. 1091)

3. Der Pfirsichblütenquell：gesammelte Gedichte/Tao Yuanming. Hrsg. von Karl-Heinz Pohl. Köln：Diederichs，1985. 222 S.：Ill.；19cm. ISBN：3424007986，3424007985.（Diederichs gelbe Reihe；58：China)

《陶渊明诗集》,Pohl, Karl-Heinz 译.

(1) Der Pfirsichblütenquell：Gedichte；mit ausgewählten chinesischen Originaltexten/Tao Yüan-ming；Karl-Heinz Pohl. Bochum：Bochumer Universitätsverlag，2002. 222 pages：illustrations；19cm. ISBN：3934453309，3934453302.（China science；4)

I323 唐朝

寒山(约 691—793)

1. 150［Hundertfünfzig］Gedichte vom Kalten Berg/Han Shan.［Aus d. chines. Han Shan Shi übers.，kommentiert u. eingel. von Stephan Schuhmacher］. Düsseldorf, Köln：Diederichs，1974. 177 S.：Ill.；；19cm. ISBN：3424005053，3424005059.（Diederichs gelbe Reihe；5：China im Umbruch)

《寒山诗150首》,Schumacher, Stephan 译.

(1)2. überarbeitete Aufl. Düsseldorf, Köln：Diederichs，1977. 177 S.：Ill.；19cm. ISBN：3424005053，3424005059.（Diederichs gelbe Reihe；5：China im Umbruch)

(2)3. Aufl. Düsseldorf, Köln：Diederichs，1980. 177 S.：Ill.；19cm. ISBN：3424005053，3424005059.（Diederichs gelbe Reihe；5：China im Umbruch)

(3)4. Aufl. Köln：Diederichs，1984. 175 S.：Ill.；19cm. ISBN：3424005053，3424005059.（Diederichs gelbe Reihe；5：China im Umbruch)

(4)5. Aufl. München：Diederichs，1992. 175 S.：Ill.；19cm. ISBN：3424005053，3424005059.（Diederichs gelbe Reihe；5：China im Umbruch)

王维(701—761)

1. Jenseits der weissen Wolken：die Gedichte des Weisen vom Südgebirge/Wang Wei；aus dem Chinesischen übertragen und herausgegeben von Stephan Schuhmacher. Düsseldorf：Diederichs，1982. 155 S.：Ill.；19cm. ISBN：342400698X，3424006988.（Diederichs gelbe Reihe；38：China)

《终南山》诗歌集,Schuhmacher, Stephan 译.

(1)2. Aufl. München：Diederichs，1989. 160 S.：9 Ill.；19cm. ISBN：342400698X，3424006988.（Diederichs gelbe Reihe；38：China)

(2)München：Deutscher Taschenbuch Verlag，2009. 175 pages：illustrations；20cm. ISBN：3423138161，3423138165.（dtv；13816)

李白（701—762）

1. Gedichte/Li-Tai-Po；aus dem Chinesischen übersetzt von Otto Hauser. 2. Aufl. Berlin：A. Duncker，1911—1912. 2 volumes in 1；21cm.（Aus fremden Gärten；1，7）
   李白诗集. Hauser, Otto（1876—1944）译.
   （1）3. Aufl. Weimar：Duncker，1918—1920. 2 volumes.（Aus fremden Gärten；1，7）

2. Li Tai Pe/［Dichtungen in metr. übertr. von Hans Bethge. Mit farb. Kupferstichen von Erich Glas］.［Erscheinungsort nicht ermittelbar］［Verlag nicht ermittelbar］，1921. 21 Bl.；kl. 8.
   李白诗. Bethge, Hans 译.

3. Li Tai Po：Ein Gedicht/Friedrich Freksa；mit zehn Radierungen und elf Zeichnungen von Richard von Below. München：Georg Müller，1923. 72 pages，［10］leaves of plates：illustrations；29cm.（Welttheater. Meisterdramen mit Originalgraphik）
   李白诗. Freksa, Friedrich 译.

4. Gedichte/Li-Tai-Po. Nach den unsterblichen des Li-Tai-Po von Hans Schiebelhuth. Darmstadt：Darmstädter Verl.，1948. 23 Bl.；quer-8.
   李白诗. Schiebelhuth, Hans（1895—1944）译.

5. Li-tai-pe：Nachdichtungen/von Klabund. Leipzig, Insel，1915. 47 pages；19cm.（Insel-Bucherei；Nr. 201）
   李白诗. Klabund（1890—1928）译.
   （1）Leipzig：Insel，1923. 54 pages：illustrations；32cm.
   （2）Li Tai-peo/Li Tai-pe. Nachdichtungen von Klabund. Leipzig：Insel-Verl.，1951. 47 S.；8.
   （3）Wiesbaden Insel-Verl. 1956. 47 S. 8.（Insel-Bücherei；Nr. 201）
   （4）Wiesbaden：Insel-Verl.，1959. 47 S.；8.（Insel-Bücherei；Nr. 201）
   （5）Frankfurt am Main：Insel-Verl.，1986. x，46 S：ill.（z. T. farb.）；19cm. ISBN：3458082018，3458082019.（Insel-Bücherei；201）

6. Balladen um Li Tai-Pe/［Hrsg.］Erich von Beckerath. Lorch：Buerger-Verl.，1947. 55 S.，［1］leaf of plates：illustrations；21cm.
   李白诗. Beckerath, Erich von（1891—1981）编译.

7. Rausch und Unsterblichkeit/Li Tai-Bo；［ausgewählt aus den Werken des Dichters und mit einer Einleitung versehen von Günther Debon］. München：K. Desch，1958. 123 pages：illustrations；19cm.（Im Banne des Dionysos）
   《李白诗选》. Debon, Günther（1921—2005）译.

8. Gedichte：eine Auswahl/Übersetzung，Einleitung und Anmerkungen von Günther Debon. Stuttgart：P. Reclam，1962. 143 pages.（Reclams Universal-Bibliothek；Nr. 8658）
   李白诗选. Debon, Günther（1921—2005）译.
   （1）Stuttgart：Reclam，1976. 143 S.；16cm. ISBN：3150086582，3150086582.（Reclams Universal-Bibliothek；Nr. 8658）
   （2）Stuttgart：Reclam，1992. 144 S.；16cm. ISBN：3150086582，3150086582.（Reclams Universal-Bibliothek；Nr. 8658）
   （3）Stuttgart：Reclam，2009. 144 S.；15cm. ISBN：3150186756.（Reclams Universal-Bibliothek；Nr. 18675）

9. Li Tai-bo/［Ausw. u. übertr. dieses H.：Ernst Schwarz］. Berlin：Verlag Neues Leben，1979. 31 S.；22cm.（Poesiealbum；138）
   李白诗选. Schwarz, Ernst 译.

10. Li Tai-peh/［hrsg. von Orplid & Co.，Gesellschaft zur Pflege und Förderung der Poesie. Ausgew. und übertr. von Ernst Schwarz］. Berlin：Unabhängige Verl.-Buchh. Ackerstrasse，1991. 48 S.；21cm. ISBN：386172023X，3861720232.（Poet's corner；2）
    李白诗选. Schwarz, Ernst 译.

11. Gesammelte Gedichte. Teil：［1］/Übersicht über die Übersetzungen des Erwin Ritter von Zach und Wiedergabe der Bücher XI - XV der deutschen Fassung，ursprünglich erschienen in De Chinese revue（Batavia）. Wiesbaden：Harrassowitz，2000. 156 S.：Ill. ISBN：3447042796，3447042796.（Humboldt-Universität zu Berlin：Asien- und Afrika-Studien der Humboldt-Universität zu Berlin；Bd. 5）
    《李白诗歌全集》第一部分. Zach, Erwin von（1872—1942）译.

12. Li, Bai：Gesammelte Gedichte. Teil：2./Die Bücher XVI bis XXV und XXX der chinesischen Gesamtausgabe in deutscher Fassung，ursprünglich erschienen in Die Deutsche Wacht，Batavia. Wiesbaden：Harrassowitz，2005. 253 S. ISBN：3447051582，3447051583.（Humboldt-Universität zu Berlin：Asien- und Afrika-Studien der Humboldt-Universität zu Berlin；Bd. 19）
    《李白诗歌总汇》第二部分. Zach, Erwin von（1872—1942）译.

13. Li, Bai：Gesammelte Gedichte. Teil：3.，Die Bücher I bis X der chinesischen Gesamtausgabe in deutscher Fassung/mit Erg. von Alfred Hoffmann. Wiesbaden：Harrassowitz，2007. 307 S. ISBN：3447055871，3447055871，3447051582，3447051583.（Humboldt-Universität zu Berlin：Asien- und Afrika-Studien der Humboldt-Universität zu Berlin；Bd. 30）
    《李白诗歌总汇》第三部分. Zach, Erwin von（1872—1942）译.

杜甫（712—770）

1. Tufu's Gedichte：（nach der Ausgabe des Chang Chin）Buch XI-XX/übersetzt von Erwim von Zach. Batavia［Indonesia］：［publisher not identified］，1936. 171 pages；31cm.（Sinologische Beiträge；3）

《杜甫诗选》,Zach,von Erwin(1872—1942)译.

2. Tu Fu's Gedichte/Übers. von E. von Zach; ed; with an introduction by J. R. Hightower. Cambridge，Mass.：Harvard Univ. P.，1952. 2 volumes. (Harvard-Yenching Institute studies；8)

杜甫诗. 2 卷. Zach，Erwin von(1872—1942)译.

3. Die grossen Klagen des Tu Fu/Nachdichtungen von Werner Helwig. Bremen，C. Schünemann，1956. 89 pages (on double leaves)illustrations 27cm.

杜甫诗. Helwig，Werner(1905—)译.

4. Du Fu：[Poesiealbum Band 190, ausgewählt und eingerichtet vom 14. bis 17. November 2013]/hrsg. von Bernd Jentzsch. [Flamersheim] Chidher-Verl.，2013. 86 S. Ill. 20cm. (Poesie：Album)

杜甫诗. Jentzsch，Bernd(1940—)译.

白居易(772—846)

1. Aus den Gedichten Po-Chü-i's/von L. Woitsch. Peking，1908. [4]，76 pages

白居易诗选. Woitsch，Leopold(1868—)译.

2. Aus den Gedichten des Po Chü-i：[Die Ausw. ist d. „Liedern eines chinesischen Dichters und Trinkers" entnommen]/übertr. von L. Woitsch. Mit Ill. von Richard Hadl. Leipzig：W. Drugulin，1924. 15 S.；gr. 8.

白居易诗选. Woitsch，Leopold (1868—1939)译.

3. Lieder eines chinesischen Dichters und Trinkers/(Po Chü-i). übertr. von L. Woitsch. Mit [eingedr.] Illustr. von Richard Hadl. Leipzig：Asia Major，1925. III，110 S.；gr. 8.

白居易诗选. Woitsch，Leopold (1868—1939)译.

4. Pe-Lo-Thien/Albert Ehrenstein. Berlin：E. Rowohlt，1923. 80，xiv pages；19cm.

白居易诗歌. Ehrenstein，Albert(1886—1950)译.

(1)Berlin：E. Rowohlt，1928. 80，XVII Bl.；8.

5. Po Chü-i/Bo Dschü-I. Aus d. Chines. übertr. von Andreas Donath. Wiesbaden：Insel-Verl.，1960. 62 S.：mit Abb.；kl. 8. (Insel-Bücherei；Nr 712)

白居易诗. Donath，Andreas(1934—)译.

6. Den Kranich fragen：155 Gedichte/von Bai Juyi. Hrsg. von Weigui Fang. Aus dem Chines. übers. von Weigui Fang und Andreas Weiland. Göttingen：Cuvillier，1999. 6，V，362 S.：Ill.；21cm. ISBN：3897127326，3897127326

白居易诗歌 155 首. Fang，Weigui 译.

7. Ausgewählte Gedichte/Bai Juyi. übers. von Rewi Alley ins Engl.，danach von Rudolf Seitz ins Dt. [Rudolf Seitz，Tuschmalerei]. München：Verl. St. Michaelsbund，2011. [120] S.：Ill.；17×25cm. ISBN：3920821702，392082170X.

白居易诗选. Seitz，Rudolf(1934—2001)译自英文版.

胡曾(生卒年不详,约 840—?)

1. Dichtung und Geschichte：die historischen Gedichte des Hu Zeng (um 877)/Korinna Oehring. Hamburg：Krämer，1989. 230 S.；21cm. ISBN：3926952083，3926952080. (Hamburger Hefte für Sinologie；2)

《咏史诗》,胡曾著；Oehring，Korinna 译.

I324　宋朝

李煜(937—978)

1. Die Lieder des Li Yü，937 — 978，Herrschers der Südlichen T'ang-Dynastie：als Einführung in die Kunst der chinesischen Lieddichtung/aus dem Urtext vollst. übertr. und erl. von Alfred Hoffmann. Köln：Greven，1950. XII，274 Seiten：Illustrationen

李煜诗. Hoffmann，Alfred 译.

（1）Hong Kong：Commercial Press；Düsseldorf：Distributed by Ming Fan，1982. xii，274 pages，[4] leaves of plates：illustrations；22cm. ISBN：9620710231，9620710230

李清照(1084—约 1155)

1. Gedichte/Li Qingzhao. Einl. u. übers. von Ng Hong-chiok u. Anne Engelhardt. [Kalligraphie：Yuen Kaling]. Bonn：Engelhardt-Ng，1985. 91 S.；21cm. ISBN：3924716013，3924716011. (Übersetzungsreihe：chinesische Frauenliteratur；0601)

《李清照诗选》，Ng，Hong-chiok 译.

2. Geschliffene Jade：zum Mythos der Song-Dichterin Li Qingzhao [Li Qingzhao] (1084—1155?)/Dorothee Dauber. Frankfurt am Main；New York：Lang，2000. 405 pages：illustrations；21cm. ISBN：3631353391，3631353394. (Europäische Hochschulschriften.；Reihe XVIII，；Vergleichende Literaturwissenschaften；Bd. 94)

李清照词. Dorothee Dauber (1957—)著. 翻译了李清照的《词论》和 27 首词.

辛弃疾(1140—1207)

1. Kiefern im Schnee：Gedichte/Qiji Xin. Aus dem Chines. übertr. und hrsg. von Monika Gänßbauer. Mit Kalligr. von Wang Weifan. Bochum：Projekt-Verl.，2011. 113 S. Ill. 21cm. ISBN：3897332454，3897332450. (Edition Cathay；Bd. 58)

辛弃疾诗. Gänßbauer，Monika(1968—)译.

I325　明朝

高启(1336—1374)

1. Gedichte/Gau Tsching-Tschiu，der Meister vom grünen Hügel. Aus d. Chines. von Andreas Donath. Frankfurt a. M.：Insel-Verl.，1963. 53 S.：1 Titelbild；8.

高启诗词. Donath，Andreas 译.

I33　现当代诗歌

I331　诗歌集

1. Zwischen Wänden：moderne chines. Lyrik/Shu Ting，Gu

Cheng；ausgew. u. aus d. Chines. übertr. von Rupprecht Mayer. München：Simon und Magiera，1984. 53 S：Ill；21cm. ISBN：3886760154，3886760152. (Reihe Pflaumenblüten)

中国现代诗歌选. Mayer，Rupprecht 译. 收录舒婷、顾城作品.

2. Nachrichten von der Hauptstadt der Sonne：moderne chines. Lyrik 1919 - 1984/hrsg. u. aus d. Chines. übers. von Wolfgang Kubin. Frankfurt am Main：Suhrkamp，1985. 246 S.；18cm. ISBN：3518113224，3518113226. (Edition Suhrkamp；1322 = N. F.，Bd. 322).

《太阳成长记：中国现代诗歌 1919—1984》，顾彬（Kubin，Wolfgang，1945—）译. 收录舒婷、徐志摩、闻一多、臧克家、郑愁予等人作品.

（1）neue Ausg. Schiedlberg：Bacopa-Verl.，2015. 500 S. ISBN：3902735515，3902735511

3. Chinesische Lyrik der Gegenwart：chinesisch/deutsch/ausgew.，kommentiert und hrsg. von Lü Yuan und Winfried Woesler unter Mitwirkung von Zhang Yushu. Stuttgart：Reclam，1992. 384 S.；15cm. ISBN：3150088038，31500880361. (Universal-Bibliothek；Nr. 8803)

《中国当代抒情诗》. 含柯岩、雷抒雁、李刚、梁晓斌、流沙河、刘湛秋、彭燕郊、Ren Hongyuan、邵燕祥、舒婷、苏金伞、牛汉、王家新、王小妮、王辛笛等人作品.

4. Boli-gongchang：Gedichte chinesisch-deutsch = Die Glasfabrik/Bai Hua；Zhang Zao；Ouyang Jianghe. ［Übers. von Susanne Gösse und Peter Hoffmann］. Tübingen Konkursbuchverl. Gehrke，1993. . ［43］S.；21cm. ISBN：3887698037，3887698034. (Schriftenreihe Lyrik im Hölderlinturm)

《玻璃工厂》，白桦（1956—），张枣（1962—2010），欧阳江河（1956—）著；Susanne Gösse 和 Peter Hoffmann 合译.

5. Chinesische Akrobatik - harte Stühle：Gedichte chinesisch-deutsch/Ausw. und übers. von Susanne Gösse. Mit Lithogr. von He Duoling und Zeichn. von Andreas Schmid. Hrsg. von Susanne Gösse und Valérie Lawitschka. Tübingen：Konkursbuch-Verl. Gehrke，1995. 117 S.；Ill；22cm. ISBN：3887690958，3887690953

中国诗歌德译选. Gösse，Susanne 译. 含欧阳江河的《晚饭》《夏天的孩子》、白桦的《中国杂技》、张枣的《哀歌》《入夜》等作品.

6. Alles versteht sich auf Verrat：Gedichte von Yu Jian，Zhai Yongming，Wang Xiaoni，Ouyang Jianghe，Wang Jiaxin，Chen Dongdong，Xi Chuan，Hai Zi/［Wolfgang Kubin und Tang Xiaodu（Hg.）］；aus dem Chines. von Gao Hong... ［et al.］. Bonn：Weidle Verlag，2009. 194 S. ISBN：3938803165，3938803169

现代诗歌. 顾彬（Kubin，Wolfgang，1945—），Tang Xiaodu 和 Gao Hong 合译. 收录于坚（1954）、翟永明（1964—）、王小妮（1955—）、欧阳江河（1956—）、王家新（1957—）、陈东东（1961—）、西川（1963—）、海子（1964—1989）等人作品.

I332　现当代诗人个人作品

鲁迅（1881—1936）

1. Wilde Gräser/Lu Hsühn. Peking：Verlag für Fremdsprachige Literatur，1974. 101 pages，［1］leaf of plates：color illustrations；19cm. ISBN：3922373178，3922373179

《野草》

（1）Peking：Verlag für fremdsprachige Literatur，1978. 101 S.

（2）Beijing：Verl. für Fremdsprachige Literatur，2002. 111 S. 19cm. ISBN：7119029770，7119029771

2. Kein Ort zum Schreiben：gesammelte Gedichte/Lu Xun. Aus d. Chines. von Egbert Baqué u. Jürgen Theobaldy. Reinbek bei Hamburg：Rowohlt，1983. 118 S.：1 Ill.；19cm. ISBN：3499152649，349915264. (Rororo；5264)

《鲁迅诗选》，Baqué，Egbert 译.

闻一多（1899—1946）

1. Wen Yidous „Totes Wasser"：eine literarische Übersetzung/Hans Peter Hoffmann. Bochum：Brockmeyer，1992. 260 S.；19cm. ISBN：3883399612，3883399614. (Chinathemen；Bd. 67)

《死水》，Hoffmann，Hans Peter（1957—）译.

2. Totes Wasser：Wen Yiduo. Übers. von Hans Peter Hoffmann. Bochum；Freiburg：Projekverl.，2015. 105 S. ISBN：3897333666，389733366X. (Edition Pengkun；2)

《死水》，Hoffmann，Hans Peter（1957—）译.

冯至（1905—1993）

1. Inter Nationes Kunstpreis 1987：Die Sonette des Feng Zhi/［Übertragung der 27 Sonette ins Dt.：Wolfgang Kubin. Kalligraphie der 27 Sonette：von Dai Lübin］. Bonn：Inter Nationes，1987. 80 Seiten

《十四行诗》，顾彬（Kubin，Wolfgang，1945—）译.

艾青（1910—1996）

1. Auf der Waage der Zeit：［Gedichte]/Ai Qing. ［Hrsg. u. aus d. Chines. übers. von Manfred u. Shuxin Reichardt. Nachdichtungen von Annemarie Bostroem]. Berlin：Verl. Volk u. Welt，1988. 109 S.；22cm. ISBN：353002235，3353002235. (Weiße Reihe)

《时间的天平上：诗集》，Bostroem，Annemarie 和 Reichardt，Manfred 合译.

李季（1922—1980）

1. Wang Gue und Li Hsiang-hsiang：ein Volksepos/Li Dji. (Deutsche Nachdichtung von Klara Blum. Umschlag u. Ill. vom Dscho Lingdsau). Peking：Verl. für Fremdsprach. Literatur，1954. 33 S.；4„

《王贵与李香香》，周令钊插图；Blum，Klara 译.

（1）Beijing：Verl. für Fremdsprachige Literatur，1980. 37 S.；19cm.

北岛（1949—）

1. Tagtraum. Gedichte. Aus dem Chinesischen von Wolfgang Kubin. Bei Dao. München: Hanser Verlag, 1990.

《白日梦》，顾彬（Kubin, Wolfgang, 1945—）译。

2. Notizen vom Sonnenstaat: Gedichte /Bei Dao; aus dem Chinesischen und mit einem Nachw. von Wolfgang Kubin. München; Wien: Hanser, 1991. 112 S.; 19cm. ISBN: 3446158758, 3446158757.

《太阳城札记》，顾彬（Kubin, Wolfgang, 1945—）译。

3. Post bellum: Gedichte/Bei Dao. Aus dem Chines. und mit einer Nachbem. von Wolfgang Kubin. München; Wien: Hanser, 2001. 85 Seiten; 22cm. ISBN: 3446199918, 3446199910

顾彬（Kubin, Wolfgang, 1945—）译。

4. Narrentürme: Gedichte/Wolfgang Kubin; mit einem Nachwort von Bei Dao. Bonn: Weidle, 2002. 116 pages; 21cm. ISBN: 3931135624, 3931135621

顾彬（Kubin, Wolfgang, 1945—）译。

5. Das Buch der Niederlage: Gedichte/Bei Dao. Aus dem Chines. und mit einer Nachbemerkung von Wolfgang Kubin. München: Hanser, 2009. 105 S. 21cm. ISBN: 3446232839, 3446232834. (Edition Lyrik-Kabinett; 12)

顾彬（Kubin, Wolfgang, 1945—）译。

多多（原名粟世征，1951—）

1. Der Mann im Käfig: China, wie es wirklich ist/Duo Duo. Aus dem Chines. von Bi He und La Mu. Freiburg [Breisgau]; Basel; Wien: Herder, 1990. 142 S.; 21cm. ISBN: 3451220555, 3451220555

《笼中人：真实中国》，Bi He 和 La Mu 合译。

2. Wegstrecken und andere Gedichte/Duo Duo; aus dem Chinesischen von Jo Fleischle... Hrsg. von Peter Hoffmann. Dortmund: Projekt-Verlag, 1994. 171 pages: illustrations; 21cm. ISBN: 3928861250, 3928861255. (Arcus-Chinatexte des Richard-Wilhelm-Übersetzungszentrums Bochum; Bd. 5; Arcus Chinatexte)

《里程》，Fleischle, Jo. 译。

舒婷（1952—）

1. Schu Ting/[ausgew. und aus dem Chines. übertr. von Ernst Schwarz]. Berlin: Verl. Neues Leben, 1988. 31 S.; 22cm. ISBN: 3355007382, 3355007382. (Poesiealbum; 247)

《舒婷诗集》，Schwarz, Ernst（1916—2003）译。

2. Archaeopteryx: einundachtzig Gedichte/Shu Ting; aus dem Chinesischen von Christine Berg. Dortmund: Projekt Verlag, 1996. 188 pages: illustrations; 21cm. ISBN: 3928861663, 3928861662. (Arcus-Chinatexte des Richard-Wilhelm-Übersetzungszentrums; Bd. 9)

《始祖鸟：诗歌 81 首》，Berg, Christine 译。

杨炼（1955—）

1. Pilgerfahrt: Gedichte/Yang Lian. Mit Ill. von Gan Shaocheng. Hrsg. von Karl-Heinz Pohl. [übers. von Angelika Bahrke...]. Innsbruck: Hand-Presse, 1987. 100 S.: Ill.; 21cm. ISBN: 3900862044, 3900862046

《朝圣》，Bahrke, Angelika 译。

2. 10 Gedichte. übers. von Peter Hoffmann für eine Lesung Yangs am 28. 10. 1991 in der Stadtbücherei Tübingen/Yang Lian; Peter Hoffmann. Tübingen: Seminar für Sinologie und Koreanistik der Universität Tübingen, 1991. 26 S.

Anmerkungen: Enthält die Gedichte: 1989, Emigrantenbuch, Verbotene Gedichte, Garten an einem Wintertag, Grafton-Brücke, Kriegsmuseum, Die Burg auf dem Papier, Grausame Kinder, Kafka-Museum, Lebenslauf des Hasses

杨炼的十首诗歌。Hoffmann, Peter 译. 汉德对照。

3. Gedichte: Drei Zyklen/Yang Lian; aus dem Chines. übers; mit Hilfe von Huang Yi und mit einem Nachw. versehen von Albrecht Conze. Zürich: Ammann, 1993. 69 Seiten; 22cm. ISBN: 3250101818, 3250101819

诗歌：三个循环。Conze, Albrecht 译。

4. Masken und Krokodile: Gedichte/Yang Lian; aus dem Chines. und mit einem Nachwort von Wolfgang Kubin; Fototeil: Renate von Mangoldt. Berlin; Weimar: Aufbau-Verl., 1994. 91, [12] S.: Ill.; 20cm. ISBN: 335102813X, 3351028138. (Text und Porträt; 13)

《面具与鳄鱼》，顾彬（Kubin, Wolfgang, 1945—）译。

张子扬（1956—）

1. 张子扬诗选：告别柏林/张子扬著，李逵六译. 北京：外语教学与研究出版社，2004. 91 页; 17cm. ISBN: 7560040284

本书为张子扬先生所著诗集. 全书分为六个小单元，分别是"德意志"、"黑色请柬"、"半敞的门"、"雨夜，我从你的窗前走过"、"梦中，一位诗人说……"和"中国·祭水".

顾城（1956—1993）

1. Quecksilber und andere Gedichte/Cheng Gu; Peter Hoffmann (Hg.); [übersetzt von Ole Döring and others]. Bochum: Brockmeyer, 1990. vi, 120 pages; 19cm. ISBN: 3883398128, 3883398129. (Chinathemen; Bd. 48)

顾城诗歌集. 顾城（1956—1993）；Hoffmann, Peter 译. 收录《水银》及其他诗歌.

张枣（1962—2010）

1. Dem Dichter des Lesens: Gedichte für Paul Hoffmann/von Ilse Aichinger bis Zhang Zao. Hrsg. von Hansgerd Delbrück. Tübingen: Attempto-Verl, 1997. 244 S.; 23cm. ISBN: 3893082611, 3893082612, 3893082689, 3893082681

含张枣的诗作.

2. Briefe aus der Zeit: chinesisch und deutsch/Zhang Zao. Aus dem Chines. und mit einem Nachw. von Wolfgang Kubin. Hrsg. von Roswitha Th. Heiderhoff...Eisingen:

Heiderhoff，1999. 183 S：Ill；20cm. ISBN：3923547633，
3923547630.（Lyrikreihe „Das neueste Gedicht"；N. F.，
48）

《时代的书信：中德双语》，顾彬（Kubin，Wolfgang，
1945—）译.

I4　戏剧文学

I41　古代戏剧集

1. Altchinesische Liebes-Komödien： Aus d. chines.
Urtexte/ausgew. u. übertr. Hans Rudelsberge. Wien：
Kunstverlag A. Schroll & Co.，1924. 116 S.：mit［z.
Tl. eingekl. farb.］Abb.；gr. 8.

中国古代爱情喜剧. Rudelsberger，Hans（1868— 1940）
译. 收录元戏曲《谢天香》《黄粱梦》《铁拐李》《鸳鸯被》《玉
镜台》等.

2. Chinesische Dramen der Yüan-Dynastie：10 nachgelassene
übers/von Alfred Forke. Hrsg. u. eingel. von Martin
Gimm. Wiesbaden：Steiner，1978. XIX，616 S.；24cm.
ISBN：3515024358，3515024352.（Übersetzungen chinesischer
Dramentexte；［Bd. 1］. Sinologica Coloniensia；Bd. 6）

中国元代十部戏剧. Forke，Alfred（1867—1944）译. 包括
《汉宫秋》《梧桐雨》《黄粱梦》《铁拐李》《来生债》《鸳鸯佩》
《王月英元夜留鞋记》《看钱奴》等.

3. Altchinesische Liebeskomödien/ausgew. u. aus d. Chines.
übertr. von Hans Rudelsberger. Zürich：Manesse-Verl.，
1988. 133 S.；18cm. ISBN：3717581253，3717581252.
（Manesse-Bücherei；7）

古代中国爱情喜剧. Rudelsberger，Hans 译.

4. Elf chinesische Singspieltexte aus neuerer Zeit：nebst zwei
Dramen in westlicher Manier/übers. von Alfred Forke.
Bearb. und erg. von Martin Gimm. Stuttgart：Steiner，
1993. 512 S.；24cm. ISBN：3515063500；3515063501.
（ Übersetzungen chinesischer Dramentexte；Bd. 3 ）
（Sinologica Coloniensia；Bd. 17）

Contents：Singspiel-Libretti（Texte aus Peking）：Cailou
ji. Sangyuan hui. ZhanDouë. Cuiping shan. Guanwang
miao. Mai yanzhi. Silang tan mu—Singspiel-Libretto
（Text aus Kanton）：Li Long xun qi—Singspieletexte im
Peking-Stil aus der Zeit um 1860，Verfasser Yu Zhi
（1809—1874）：Fengliu jian. Wenxing xian. Tuniu bao—
Dramen in westlicher Manier aus den dreissiger Jahren：
Jing Ke/Verfasser Gu Yiqiao. Yipian aiguo xin/Verfasser
Xiong Foxi

中国 11 部戏剧. 佛尔克（Forke，Alfred，1867—1944）译.

5. Zwei chinesische Singspiele der Qing-Dynastie/Li Yu und
Jiang Shiquan. Übers. von Alfred Forke mit einer Erg.：
Ein anonymes Singspiel der Yuan-Zeit：in der Fassung
von John Hefter. Bearb. und erg. von Martin Gimm.
Stuttgart：Steiner，1993. 508 S.；24cm. ISBN：
3515062718，3515062718.（Übersetzungen chinesischer

Dramentexte；Bd. 2，Sinologica Coloniensia；Bd. 16）
Forke，Alfred（1867—1944）译. 收录清代李渔（1611—
1680）和蒋士铨（1725—1784）的《比目鱼》《采石矶》《盆儿
鬼》.

6. 北京京剧百部经典剧情简介标准译本/京剧传承与发展
（国际）研究中心编著. 北京：旅游教育出版社，2015. 17，
440 页：图；19cm. ISBN：7563731572

德文题名：Beijing Jingju 100 Geschichten Inhaltsangabe
Standard Version. 汉德对照. 本书是由京剧传承与发展
（国际）研究中心组织京剧界专家对我国国粹京剧曲目进
行遴选，选出百余部经典，结集成书，并翻译成德文，以
四色印刷形式呈现给读者.

I42　古代戏曲家及其作品

关汉卿（1219—1301）

1. Der Pavillon am Hsiang-Fluss/Guan Han-tjing. Nach e.
Drama bearb. von Wu Be-tji. Mit Bühnenaufn. aus d.
Szetschuan-Oper. Peking：Verl. f. Fremdsprachige
Literatur，1958. 108 S.：Abb. mit Text；quer-kl. 8.

《谭记儿》，吴伯祺改编.

王实甫（1234—1294）

1. Das Westzimmer. Ein chinesisches Singspiel aus dem
dreizehnten Jahrhundert. In deutscher Nachdichtung nach
den chinesischen Urtexten des Wang Sche-Fu und des
Guan Han-Tsching von Vincenz Hundhausen. Mit 21
Holzschnitten eines unbekannten Meisters. Peking；
Leipzig：Pekinger Verlag，1926. 356 S.，［1］pages，
［21］leaves of plates：illustrations；24cm.

《西厢记》，王实甫（1234—1294）、关汉卿（1219—1301）
著；Hundhausen，Vincenz（1878—1955）译.

（1）Das Westzimmer：Ein chinesisches Singspiel aus d.
13. Jahrhundert. In dt. Nachdichtung nach d.
chines. Urtexten d. Wang Sche-Fu u. d. Guan Han-
Tsching/Vincenz Hundhausen. Eisenach：Röth，
1954. 355 S.，1 Titelbild：Mit 21 Holzschnitten e.
unbekannten Meisters；gr. 8.

（2）Das Westzimmer：e. chines. Singspiel aus d. 13.
Jh. /in dt. Nachdichtung nach d. chines. Urtexten d.
Wang She-Fu u. d. Guan Han-Tsching von Vincenz
Hundhausen. ［Hrsg. von Ernst Schwarz］. Leipzig：
Insel-Verlag，1978. 387 S.；35 Ill.；20cm.

纪君祥（约元世祖至元年间在世）

1. Der Sohn des Chao（＝De Wees de Chao）/von Chi Chun-
hsiang. In e. Bearb. für Kinder von Ad de Bont. Aus d.
Niederländ. von Wilfrid Grote. Frankfurt am Main：
Verlag der Autoren，1988. 37 S.

《赵氏孤儿》，Grote，Wilfried（1940—）译.

李行道（约公元一二七九年前后在世）

1. Hoei-lan-ki：chinesisches Schauspiel in vier Aufzügen und
einem Vorspiel/［Li Xingdao］. Frei bearb. von Wollheim
da Fonseca. Leipzig：Reclam，1875. 79 S.（Reclams

Universal-Bibliothek；768)

《灰阑记》，Wollheim da Fonseca 译.

2. Der Kreidekreis：Schauspiel in 4 Aufz. u. e. Vorspiel/ von Li Hsing-tao. Aus d. Chines. übers. von Alfred Forke. Leipzig：Reclam，1920. 91 S. (Reclams Universal-Bibliothek；768)

《灰阑记》，Forke，Alfred(1867—1944)译.

(1) Der Kreidekreis：Schauspiel in vier Aufzügen und einem Vorspiel/Li Hsing-tao. Aus dem Chines. übers. von Alfred Forke. Leipzig：Reclam，1926. 91 S. (Reclams Universal-Bibliothek；768)

(2)Leipzig：Philipp Reclam jun，1927. 91 S.

3. Der Kreidekreis：Spiel in 5 Akten/nach dem Chinesischen [des Li Xingdao] von Klabund. Berlin：Spaeth，1925. 112 p.；19cm.

《灰阑记》，Klabund(van Alfred Henschke，1890—1928)译.

(1)Wien：Phaidon-Verlag，1929. 103 p.：ill.；22cm.

(2)Wien：Phaidon-Verl.，1932. 103 Bl. nach Art e. Blockbuches；8.

(3)Wien：Phaidon-Verl.，，1950. 102 S.；8.

(4)Der Kreidekreis：Spiel in fünf Akten nach dem Chinesischen/von Klabund. Neuaufl. Zürich：Phaidon-Verlag，1952. 102 pages，[16] pages of plates：illustrations (some color)；21cm.

4. Der Kreidekreis：Ein Spiel in 6 Bildern nach d. Chines/ Johannes von Guenther. Berlin：Drei Masken-Verl.，1941. 144 S.；8.

《灰阑记》，Guenther，Johannes von(1886—1973)译.

(1)Potsdam：Rütten & Loening，1942. 184 S.；8.

5. Der Kreidekreis：ein Spiel in sechs Bildern nach dem Altchinesischen (Li Hsing-tao)/Johannes von Guenther；mit einer Einleitung des Verfasser. Stuttgart：Reclam-Verlag，1953. 97 pages；16cm. (Reclams Universal-Bibliothek；Nr. 7777)

《灰阑记》，Guenther，Johannes von(1886—1973)译.

(1)Stuttgart：Philipp Reclam Jun.，1962. 94 S.

高明（约 1305—约 1371），

1. Das tugendhafte Fräulein：Chinesisches Lustspiel in zwei Bildern. Peking：Pekinger Verlag，1929. 30 pages color illustrations. (Chinesische Bühnenspiele；1. Heft)

《琵琶记》选译，Hundhausen，Vincenz(1878—1955)译.

2. Die Laute：Ein chinesisches Singspiel in deutscher Sprache/ Kao Ming；Vincenz Hundhausen. Peking；Leipzig：Pekinger Verlag，1930. 469 S.：illustrations；23cm.

《琵琶记》，Hundhausen，Vincenz (1878—1955)译.

汤显祖（1550—1616）

1. Der Blumengarten. Ein chinesisches Singspiel in deutscher Sprache von Vincenz Hundhausen/Tang Xianzu；Vincenz Hundhausen. Peking；Leipzig：Pekinger Verlag，1933. 138 S. (Chinesische Meisterdramen in deutscher Sprache)

《牡丹亭》，Hundhausen，Vincenz(1878—1955)译.

2. Die Rückkehr der Seele：ein romantisches Drama/von Tang Hsian dsu；in deutscher Sprache von Vincenz Hundhausen. Zurich：Rascher Verlag，1937. 3 volumes：illustrations，plates；24cm.

《牡丹亭》，Hundhausen，Vincenz(1878—1955)译.

朱素臣（约公元一六四四年前后在世）

1. Fünfzehn Schnüre Geld：Ein altchines. Bühnenstück/Su-ch'en Chu. Auf d. europ. Theater gebracht von Günther Weisenborn. Der Übertr. aus d. Engl. lag d. Fassung von Chou Chuan-Ying，Wang Chuan-Sung u. Chu Kuo-Liang zugrunde. Fig. von Fritz Bauer. München：Verlag Kurt Desch，1959. 115 S.；8. (Welt des Theaters)

《十五贯》，Weisenborn，Günther (1902—1969)译.

(1)Berlin：Henschelverlag，1960. 153 pages；17cm.

孔尚任（1648—1718）

1. Chinesische Frauengestalten/Shou-lin Cheng. Mit e. Vorw. von Bruno Schindler. Ill. von R. Hadl. Leipzig：Verlag d. Asia Major，1926. 133 S.；gr. 8.

《中华女性》，郑寿麟(1903—)著,选译自《桃花扇》.

2. Der Pfirsichblütenfächer：ein altchinesisches Spiel in 2 Teilen/K'ung Shang-jen. Dt. Übertr. von Oscar Benl. Bühnenfassung von Gustav-Rudolf Sellner und Egon Vietta. München：Desch，1953. 90 S.

《桃花扇》，Benl，Oscar(1914—1987)译. Sellner，Gustav Rudolf(1905—1990)和 Vietta，Egon(1903—1959)改编成舞台演出.

I43 现当代戏剧集

1. Moderne Stücke aus China/hrsg. von Bernd Eberstein. Frankfurt am Main：Suhrkamp，1980. 475 S.；21cm. ISBN：3518027042，3518027042.

《中国当代戏剧》，Eberstein，Bernd 等译. 收录了曹禺 (1910—1996)的《雷雨》《北京人》；田汉(1898—1968)的《南归》；熊佛西(1900—1965)的《屠夫》；老舍的《茶馆》.

2. Das Nirwana des „Hundemanns". Die Busstation. Ödland und Mensch. Chinesische Stücke der achtziger Jahre/ hrsg. und mit einem Nachw. von Irmtraud Fessen-Henjes. Berlin：Henschel，1993. 246 S.；21cm. ISBN：3894870058，3894870052. (Henschel-Theater)

收录二十世纪八十年代中国戏剧,包括《狗儿爷涅槃》、高行健(1940—)的《车站》、李龙云(1948—2012)的《荒原与人》.

3. Mittendrin：Neue Theaterstücke aus China/herausgegeben von Chen Ping und Hans-Georg Knopp. Berlin：Theater der Zeit，2015. 350 S. 190 mm × 140 mm. ISBN：3957490513，3957490510. (Dialog；21)

Chen，Ping 和 Knopp，Hans-Georg 合译. 收录郭士星、廖一梅、孟冰、沙叶新创作的的中国现代戏剧.

I431 革命现代京剧

1. Mit taktischem Geschick den Tigerberg erobert：

revolutionäre Kunst am Beispiel d. modernen Peking-Oper. Kiel：Rotfront，1970. 114 S.：Ill.；21cm.

《智取威虎山》

(1) Mit taktischem Geschick den Tigerberg erobert：(Bühnenfassung vom Juli 1970)/kollektiv neubearb. von d. Gruppe für „Mit Takt. Geschick d. Tigerberg erobert" d. Schanghaier Peking-Oper-Truppe. Peking：Verlag für Fremdsprachige Literatur，1971. 117 S.：Ill.，Noten；23cm.

2. Geschichte einer roten Signallaterne：(Bühnenfassung vom Mai 1970)/kollektiv neubearb. von der Chinesischen Peking-Oper-Truppe. Peking：Verlag für Fremdsprachige Literatur，1972. 103 p.，[16] p. pl.：ill.，muz.；24cm.

《红灯记》(1970 年 5 月演出本)，中国京剧团集体改编.

3. Schadjiabang（Bühnenfassung vom Mai 1970)/kollektiv neubearb. von d. Pekinger Peking-Oper-Truppe. Peking：Verlag für Fremdsprachige Literatur，1972. 57 S. Ill. 23cm. (Revolutionäre moderne Peking-Oper)

《沙家浜》，北京京剧团集体改编.

I44 现当代戏曲家及其作品

郭沫若(1892—1978)

1. Qu Yuan：e. Schauspiel in 5 Akten/von Guo Moruo. [Dt. von Markus Mäder]. Beijing：Verlag für Fremdsprachige Literatur，1980. 105 S.：ill.；22cm.

《屈原：五幕史剧》，Mäder，Markus 译.

老舍 (1899—1966)

《茶馆》

1. Das Teehaus：Aufführungsfotos und Materialien/Lao She；Herausgegeben von Uwe Kräuter und Huo Yong. Dt. Erst.-Ausg. Frankfurt am Main：Suhrkamp，1980. 179 S：Ill. ISBN：3518110543，3518110546.（Edition Suhrkamp. Neue Folge)

《茶馆》，Uwe Kräuter (1945—)和 Huo Yong 合译.

2. Das Teehaus：Schauspiel/Lao She；Hrsg. von Volker Klöpsch. Dt. von Volker Klöpsch. Reinbek bei Hamburg：Rowohlt，1980. 125 S.：Ill.；19cm. ISBN：3499251396，3499251399.（Das neue Buch；139)

《茶馆》，Klöpsch，Volker 译.

3. Blick westwärts nach Chang'an/Lao She；Hrsg. von Kuo Heng-yü. übersetzt von Ursula Adam，Thomas Kampen，Kuo Heng-yü，Eva Sternfeld. München：Minerva Publikation，1983. 166 S.：Ill.；21cm. ISBN：3597104576，3597104573.（Berliner China-Studien；1)

《西望长安》，Kuo Heng-yü(1930—)等译.

夏衍(1900—1995)

1. Unter den Dächern von Schanghai：Stück in 3 Aufz. /Ssja Jän. Dt. v. Walter Eckleben. Berlin：Henschelverl.，1960. 147 S.；14,5×21cm.

《上海屋檐下》，Eckleben，Walter 译.

肖甘牛(1905—1982)

1. Das Zauberbild/Nacherzählg v. Dij Dsche-hsi. Orig. Text v. Siao Gan-niu. Dt. v. Li Ming. Ill. v. Yän Mei-hua. Peking：Verl. f. fremdsprachige Literatur，1958. 60 S. 13×17,5cm.

《一幅壮锦》，肖甘牛(1905—1982)著；Dij Dsche-his 改写；Li Ming 译. 桂剧.

曹禺(1910—1996)

1. Himmel ohne Wolken/Tsao Yü.［übers. aus d. Chines. Dt. von Eberhard Meissner］. Peking：Verl. f. Fremdsprachige Literatur，1961. 134 S. mit Abb.，1 Titelbild 8

《明朗的天》，Meissner，Eberhard 译. 话剧.

2. Gewitter/ Cao Yu.［Deutsch von Uwe Kräuter］. Beijing：Verl. für Fremdsprachige Literatur，1980. 147 S：Ill；21cm.

《雷雨》，Uwe Kräuter (1945—)译.

3. Sonnenaufgang：ein Schauspiel in 4 Akten/ Cao Yu. deutsch von Yvonne Mäder-Bogorad. Beijing：Verl. für Fremdsprachige Literatur，1981. 182 S.；21cm.

《日出》，Mäder-Bogorad，Yvonne 译.

苏叔阳(1938—)

1. Nachbarn：(1979/80)；e. chines. Familiendrama über d. Periode d. Umbruchs ＝ Zuo-lin-you-she/Su Shuyang. übers. von Roswitha Brinkmann. Bochum：Studienverlag Brockmeyer，1984. 93 S.；19cm. ISBN：3883393872，3883393878.（hinathemen；Bd. 19)

《左邻右舍》，Brinkmann，Roswitha 译. 话剧.

宗福先(1947—)

1. Politisches Theater im Pekinger Frühling 1978 [neunzehnhundertachtundsiebzig]：„Aus der Stille" von Zong Fuxian；übers. u. Kommentar/Martin Krott. Bochum：Brockmeyer，1980. 119 S.；19cm. ISBN：3883391120，3883391123.（Chinathemen；Bd. 1)

《于无声处》，Krott，Martin 译. 话剧.

何冀平(1951—)

1. Die glückverheißende Eröffnung：ein modernes chinesisches Theaterstück/von He Jiping. Eingel.，übers. u. annotiert［von］Teresa Eienknapp. Bochum [u. a.]：Projektverl.，2013. 139 S. 210×148 mm. ISBN：3897333222，3897333228.（Edition Cathay；65)

《开市大吉》，Eisenknapp，Teresa 译. 话剧.

《粮食》

1. Hirse für die Achte：Ein chines. Volksstück/Ding Loo；Fan Chang；Shin-Nan Chu. Leipzig：Hofmeister VEB，1956. 82 Bl.：mit Abb.；gr. 8.

《粮食》，洛汀、张凡、朱星南著；Yuan Miaotse 译. 话剧.

(1) Unverkäufl.［Bühnen-]Ms. Hirse für die achte：Ein chines. Volksstück/Loo Ding；Chang Fan；Chu Shin-nan. Dt. Fassg f. d. Berliner Ensemble v. Elisabeth Hauptmann；Manfred Wekwerth nach d. übers. aus

d. Chines. v. Yuan Miaotse. Leipzig：Hofmeister，1960. 38 S.；4.

I45 地方剧

1. Liang Shanbo und Zhu Yingtai：Chinas berühmtestes Liebesdrama auf der Bühne der taiwanesischen Lokaloper Gezaixi/übersetzt und kommentiert von Gerd Böske. Taipei：Lucky Book，1984. 95 S.

《梁山伯与祝英台》，Böske，Gerd 译. 歌仔戏.

I46 其他剧种

1. Chinesische Schattenspiele/übers. von Wilhelm Grube. Auf Grund des Nachlasses durchges. und abgeschlossen von Emil Krebs. Hrsg. und eingel. von Berthold Laufer. München：Franz，1915. XXIV，442 Seiten. （Abhandlungen der Bayerischen Akademie der Wissenschaften，Philosophisch-Philologische und Historische Klasse；Bd. 28，Abh. 1）

中国皮影戏. Grube，Wilhelm（1855—1908）译.

2. Das chinesische Schattentheater/Georg Jacob；Hans Jensen. Stuttgart：Kohlhammer，1933. XV，130 S.；mit Abb.；gr. 8.

中国皮影戏. Jacob，Georg 和 Jensen，Hans 合译. 收录《盘丝洞》等剧目等.

　　（1）Farnborough（Hants.）：Gregg，1969. XV，130 S.：Ill.；23cm.

3. Die bemalte Haut：Schattenspiel/von Liu Qingfeng. Nebst d. Vorlage von Pu Songling. Aus d. Chines. von Rainald Simon. Frankfurt（Main）：QiLin-Verl.，1989. 71 S.：Ill.；24cm. ISBN：3927571008，3927571006.

《画皮：皮影戏》，刘庆丰著，改编自蒲松龄《聊斋志异》；Simon，Rainald 译.

4. Schattenspiel/zusammengest. von Wei Liqun；［Übers.：Wolfgang Schaub；dt. Red.：Ren Shuyin］. Beijing：Verlag für fremdsprachige Literatur，2009. 155 S；Ill. ISBN：7119059709，711905970X. （Chinesische Volkskunst）

《民间皮影》，魏力群编著.

I47 电影文学剧本

1. Der neue chinesische Spielfilm：dokumentiert am Beispiel，„Ein Funkelnder roter Stern"：Hintergrund，Entstehung，Textbuch. Frankfurt：Gesellschaft für Deutsch-Chinesische Freundschaft Frankfurt am Main，1977. 78 pages，［4］ leaves of plates：illustrations；15×21cm.

《闪闪的红星》，李心田（1929—）著.

I48 曲艺

1. Das Blumenblatt，eine epische Dichtung der Chinesen，aus dem Original übersetzt ［…］. Nebst einleitenden Bemerkungen über die chinesische Poesie und einer chinesischen Novelle als Anhang. Heinrich Kurz. St. Gallen：Druck und Verlag von Wartmann und Scheitlin，

1836. XXIV—180－44.

《花笺记》，Heinrich Kurz（1805—1873）译. 弹词.

2. Die Jadelibelle：Roman/［Tsao yi' schu schong］. Aus d. Chin. v. Franz Kuhn. Berlin：Schützen-Verl. -［Leipzig］：［Kittler］，1936. 296 S.；8.

《玉蜻蜓》，孔舫之（Kuhn，Franz，1884—1961）译. 评弹.

　　（1）Die Jadelibelle：Roman/Aus d. Chines. von Franz Kuhn. Bremen：Storm，1948. 146 S.；8.

　　（2）Die Jadelibelle：Roman/Aus d. Chinesischen verdeutscht von Franz Kuhn. Zürich：Manesse Verl.，1952. 279 S.；8. （Manesse Bibliothek der Weltliteratur）

　　（3）Die Jadelibelle：Roman/aus d. Chines. übertr. von Franz Kuhn. Leipzig：Insel-Verlag，1977. 190 S.：4 Ill.；20cm.

　　（4）Die Jadelibelle：Roman/aus d. Chines. von Franz Kuhn. Frankfurt am Main：Insel-Verlag，1986. 224 S.；18cm. ISBN：3458326448，3458326441. （Insel-Taschenbuch；944）

3. Dschen Dschu Ta：Die Juwelenpagode/［übersetzt von Anna von Rottauscher］. Zürich：Verlag die Waage，1958. 454 pages：illustrations；20cm.

《珍珠塔》，Rottauscher，Anna von（1892—）译. 弹词.

　　（1）Die Juwelenpagode：Ein altchines. Roman/［Dt. von Anna von Rottauscher］. München；Zürich：Droemer/Knaur，1966. 310 S.；kl. 8. （Knaurtaschenbücher；120）

　　（2）Die Juwelenpagode：e. altchines. Roman/Dt. von Anna von Rottauscher. Leipzig：Insel-Verlag，1977. 431 S.；20cm.

　　（3）Die Juwelenpagode：e. klass. Roman aus d. alten China/übers. von Anna von Rottauscher. Ungekürzte Ausg. Frankfurt am Main：Fischer-Taschenbuch-Verlag，1979. 351 S.；18cm. ISBN：3596224543，3596224548. （Fischer；2454）

　　（4）Die Juwelenpagode：e. altchines. Roman/［ins Dt. übertr. von Anna von Rottauscher］. Frankfurt/M.：Berlin：Ullstein，1989. 454 S.：24 Ill.；20cm. ISBN：3550066872，3550066870，3550066341，3550066344. （Im Reich der Sinne；Bd. 3）

4. Die Steine des Vogels Jingwei，Qiu Jin：Frau u. Revolutionärin im China d. 19. Jh. /Catherine Gipoulon. ［Aus d. Franz. übers. von Cornelia Holfelder-v. d. Tann］. München：Verlag Frauenoffensive，1977. 225 S.：1 Ill.；19cm. ISBN：3881040266，3881040269.

《精卫石》，秋瑾（1875—1907）著；Holfelder，Cornelia 译. 弹词.

I5 小说

I51 古代及跨时代小说集

古代及跨时代小说集

1. Chinesische Novellen：Die beiden Freier；Schuld u.

Sühne；Der Himmel giebt u. nimmt；Eine Advokatin；Gattentreue；Chrysanthemen/mit Ill. von R. A. Jaumann. Deutsch von Wilhelm Thal［d. i. Lilienthal］. Berlin；Eisenach；Leipzig：H. Hillger，1900. 120 S；8„. （Kürschners Bücherschatz；No 215）

中国小说. Thal，Wilhelm（1867—1906）译.

2. Das geheimnisvolle Bild und Anderes. Drei Novellen aus dem Chinesischen übersetzt von P. Kühnel. Berlin：Hugo Steinitz Verlag，1902. 191 S.

Kühnel，Paul（1848—1924）译. 收录《今古奇观》《三国志》等三篇小说.

3. Chinesische Abende：Novellen und Geschichten/in Gemeinschaft mit Tsou Ping Shou aus d. chinesischen Ursprache übertr. von Leo Greiner. Berlin：Reiss，1913. VII，245 S. ；8.

中国小说选. Greiner，Leo（1976—1928）译. 含《三国演义》《聊斋志异》等故事章节.

（1）Berlin：E. Reiss，1922. 217 S. ；8.

（2）Nachdruck der Originalausgabe von 1922. Hamburg：Severus Verlag，2015. ISBN：3958014350，3958014356.

（3）Nachdruck der Originalausgabe von 1922. Hamburg：Severus Verlag，2016. ISBN：3958014367.

4. Chinesische Novellen/Aus d. Urtext übertragen von H（ans）Rudelsberger. Leipzig：Inselverl. ，1914. 2 卷（265 页，307 页）；17cm.

中国小说. Rudelsberger，Hans（1868—）译.

（1）Wien：Kunstverlag Anton Schroll & Co. ，1924. 296 S.

5. Chinesische Schwänke/übers. u. hrsg. Hans Rudelsberger. Wien：Kunstverlag A. Schroll & Co. ，1920. 95 pages：color illustrations；25cm.

中国短篇小说. Rudelsberger，Hans（1868—）编译.

6. Altchinesische Liebes-Komödien：Aus d. chines. Urtexte/ausgew. u. übertr. Hans Rudelsberger. Wien：Kunstverlag A. Schroll & Co. ，1924. 116 S. ：mit［z. Tl. eingekl. farb.］Abb. ；gr. 8.

古代中国爱情喜剧. Rudelsberger，Hans（1868—）译.

（1）Zürich：Manesse-Verl. ，1988. 133 S. ；18cm. ISBN：3717581253，3717581252. （Manesse-Bücherei；7）

7. Der Mantel der Träume：chinesische Novellen/von Belá Balázs；mit 20 Bildern von Mariette Lydis. München：Verlagsanstalt D. & R. Bischoff，1922. 4 leaves，110，［1］pages，20 leaves of plates：mounted color illustrations；27cm.

Contents：Der Mantel der Träume. —Li-Tai-Pe und der Dieb. —Die Sonnenschirme. —Der ungeschickte Gott. —Die Opiumraucher. —Der Floh. —Das Alte Kind. —Die Gottesräuber. —Li-Tai-Pe und der Frühling. —Die Ahnen. —Der Mondfisch. —Die Freunde. —Die Rache des Kastanienbaumes. —Tränenblick. —Das Lehmkind. —Der Sieger.

中国故事. Balázs，Béla（1884—1949）编译.

8. Chinesische Novellen. Deutsch von Paul Kühnel. Jingu qiguan；Liaozhai zhiyi. München：Georg Müller，1914. 368 S. （Meisterwerke orientalischer Literaturen，zweiter Band）

Kühnel，Paul 译. 含《今古奇观》《聊斋志异》.

9. Fräulein Tsui und Fräulein Li：Zwei chinesische Novellen/［übers. ，Franz Blei］. München：Hyperionverlag，1921. 105 S. ；6.5×9.5cm.

《李娃传》《莺莺传》，白行简（776—826），元稹（779—831）著；Blei，Franz（1871—1942）译.

（1）München；［Berlin］：Hyperionverl. ，1937. 102 S. ；6.1 X 9.3cm.

10. Chinesische Meisternovellen/aus dem chines. Urtext übertr. von Franz Kuhn. Leipzig：Insel-Verlag，1926. 87 S. ；8„. （Insel-Bücherei. - Berlin：Insel-Verl，1912—；387）

孔舫之（Kuhn，Franz，1884—1961）译. 译自中国经典小说《东周列国志》《今古奇观》.

（1）Leipzig：Insel-Verlag，1946. 87 S. ；8„.

（2）Leipzig：Insel-Verlag，1948. 87 S.

（3）Leipzig：Insel-Verlag，1950. 87 S. kl. 8„ （Insel-Bücherei；Nr 387）

（4）Leipzig：Insel-Verlag，1951. 87 S. 8° （Insel-Bücherei. - Berlin：Insel-Verl，1912—；387）

11. Die dreizehnstöckige Pagode：altchinesische Liebesgeschichten/Dt. von Franz Kuhn. Berlin：Dom，1940. 488 Seiten

十三层塔. 孔舫之（Kuhn，Franz，1884—1961）译. 古代中国爱情小说.

（1）Wien：Zwei Berge Verl. ，1949. 485 S. ；8°.

（2）Essen：Dom-Verl. ，1956. 423 S.

12. Das Tor der östlichen Blüte：Novellen aus dem alten China/deutsch von Franz Kuhn［übers. aus dem Chinesischen］. Düsseldorf：Bagel，1949. 345 p. ；19cm.

《今古奇观》和《唐代丛书》，孔舫之（Kuhn，Franz，1884—1961）译.

13. Und Buddha lacht：Geschichten aus d. alten China/Franz Kuhn. Baden-Baden：Kairos Verl. ，1950. 80 S. ；8［Xerokopie］. （Der Weltkreis；Nr 11）

古代中国小说. 孔舫之（Kuhn，Franz，1884—1961）译.

（1）Frankfurt am Main：Insel-Verlag，1987. 94 S. ；18cm. ISBN：3458327271；3458327274. （Insel-Taschenbuch；1027）

14. Altchinesische Liebesgeschichten/Ins Dt. übertr. von Franz Kuhn. Mit 28 Ill. von Bele Bachem. Wiesbaden：Vollmer，1958. 99 S. ；1 Titelbild；8.

中国古代爱情故事. 孔舫之（Kuhn，Franz，1884—1961）译.

（1）Wiesbaden：Vollmer，1973. 195 S. ：Ill. ；20cm.

15. Altchinesische Novellen/übertr. von Franz Kuhn. Hrsg.

von Věnceslava Hrdli c̆ ková. Leipzig：Insel-Verlag，1979. 887 S.；20cm.

中国古代小说. 孔舫之（Kuhn，Franz，1884—1961）译.

16. Chinesische Novellen/übertr. von Franz Kuhn. Mit e. Nachw. u. Anm. hrsg. von Věnceslava Hrdli c̆ková. 1. Aufl. Frankfurt am Main：Insel-Verlag，1985. 627 S.；18cm. ISBN：3458325482；3458325484.（Insel-Taschenbuch；848）

中国小说. 孔舫之（Kuhn，Franz，1884—1961）译. 含《今古奇观》《聊斋志异》《昆仑奴传》等故事.

(1)[2. Aufl.] Frankfurt am Main：Insel-Verlag，1987. 627 S.；18cm. ISBN：3458325482；3458325484. (Insel-Taschenbuch；848)

17. Der Pantoffel der kleinen Yen-Dschi：zwei chinesische Novellen aus alter Zeit/aus den Urtexten übertr. von Anna von Rottauscher. Wien：Fricke，1944. 71 S.；Ill.；19cm.

《聊斋志异》《今古奇观》作品两篇. Rottauscher，Anna译.

18. Die Tochter des Drachenkönigs：10 Geschichten aus d. Zeit d. Tang Dynastie. Peking：Verl. f. Fremdsprach. Literatur，1955. 125 S.：mit Abb.；8.

《唐代传记选》

(1)2. Aufl. Beijing：Verlag für Fremdsprachige Literatur，1980. X，107 S.：Ill.，1 Kt.；22cm.

(2)2. Aufl.，1. Nachdr.. Beijing：Verlag für Fremdsprachige Literatur，1983. X，107 S.：Ill.，1 Kt.；22cm.

19. Die goldene Truhe：Chinesische Novellen aus 2 Jahrtausenden/übertr. von Wolfgang Bauer u. Herbert Franke. München：Hanser，1959. 443 S.：mit Abb.；gr. 8.

中国两千年小说选. 鲍吾刚（Bauer，Wolfgang，1930—1997），傅海波（Franke，Herbert，1914—2011）编译.

(1)Sonderausg. München：Hanser，1961. 443 S.：mit Abb.；gr. 8.（Die Bücher der Neunzehn；Bd. 76）

(2)3. Aufl. München：Hanser，1964. 443 S.：mit Abb.；gr. 8.（Die Bücher der Neunzehn；Bd. 76）

(3)München：Deutscher Taschenbuch Verlag，1966. 261 p. 18cm.（Dtv[-Taschenbücher] 374）

(4)Frankfurt a. M.；Wien；Zürich：Büchergilde Gutenberg，1967. 443 S.：mit Abb.；gr. 8.

(5)Stuttgart；Hamburg：Deutscher Bücherbund，1968. 444 S.：mit Abb.；gr. 8.

(6)Bergisch Gladbach：Bastei-Verlag Lübbe，1976. 317 S.；18cm. ISBN：3404004386；3404004388. (Bastei Lübbe；10033：[Sonderausg.]).

(7)München；Wien：Hanser，1988. 443 S.；Ill.；22cm. ISBN：3446151246；3446151249.（Hansers Bibliothek der Erzähler）

(8)Frankfurt，M.：S. Fischer，2009. 493 S.；Ill.；

22cm. ISBN：3100096487.

20. Geschichten von denen，die keine Gespenster fürchten/bearbeitet vom Institut für Literatur an der Chinesischen Akademie der Wissenschaften；[Illustrationen von Tscheng Shi-fa]. Peking：Verlag für Fremdsprachige Literatur，1961. 132 pages，[9] leaves of plates：color illustrations；20cm.

《不怕鬼的故事》,中国科学院文学研究所编. 笔记小说.

(1)2. Aufl. Beijing：Verlag für Fremdsprachige Literatur，1980. 126 S.：Ill.；19cm.

21. Der Einsiedler vom Huidjigebirge und andere chinesische Erzählungen/[Hrsg. u. übers. Johanna Herzfeldt. Ill. v. Yü Bing-nan]. Berlin：Henschelverl. ，1962. 146 S.；8.（Künstlergeschichten；Bd. 18）

会稽山隐者及其他中国故事. Herzfeldt，Johanna 译.

22. Neuer chinesischer Liebesgarten/Novellen aus d. berühmtesten erot. Sammlungen d. Ming-Zeit［von］Feng，Meng-lung；Ling Meng-Chu. Aus d. Chines. von Tat-Hang Fung. Herrenalb/Schwarzwald：Erdmann，Verl. f. Internat. Kulturaustausch，1964. 257 S.；8.

《三言》《二拍》. 冯梦龙（1574—1646），凌蒙初（1580—1644）著；Tat-hang Fung 译.

(1)Tübingen；Basel：Erdmann，1968. 323 S.；8.

(2)Stuttgart：Europ. Buch- u. Phonoklub，1969. 323 S.；8.

(3)Sonderausg. Wiesbaden：Löwit，1976. 323 S.；21cm.

23. Erzählungsgut aus Südost-China. Gesammelt，übers. und bearb. von Wolfram Eberhard. Berlin：de Gruyter，1966. xi，298 p. 25cm.（Fabula. Supplement Serie. Reihe A：Texte，Bd. 6）

中国传说（故事）. Eberhard，Wolfram（1909—1989）编译.

24. Der Ölhändler und die Kurtisane. Chinesische Geschichten aus der Ming-Zeit/Ausgewählt，aus dem Englischen übertragen und mit einem Nachwort versehen von Wolf D. Rogosky. München，Berlin）Herbig，1966. 350 pages with illustrations 19cm.

Notes：Contains Der Ölhändler und die Kurtisane and nine other stories from Fêng-lung and Ling Mêng-ch'u.

明朝小说选译. Rogosky，Wolf D. 译自英文. 包括《卖油郎独占花魁》等小说,主要译自凌蒙初（1580—1644）和冯梦龙（1574—1646）的作品.

(1)München：Non-Stop-Bücherei，1968. 256 S.；kl. 8.（Non-Stop-Bücherei；Bd. 112/113）

(2)Rastatt：Moewig，1982. 284 S.；18cm. ISBN：3811846450.（Playboy；Bd. Nr. 4645：Erotik）Genehmigte Taschenbuchausg.

(3)Rastatt：Moewig，1984. 283 S.；18cm. ISBN：3811865439.（Playboy；Bd. Nr. 6543：Erotik）

Genehmigte Taschenbuchausg.

25. Prinz Tan von Yen: eine chinesische Novelle aus der Chan-kuo-Zeit/hrsg., übers. u. eingeleitet von Herbert Franke. Zürich: Verl. Die Waage, 1969. 95 S.; 19cm. ISBN: 3859660330, 3859660335. (Bücher der Waage)
《燕太子》,Franke, Herbert 译.

26. Menschen können den Himmel stürmen: vier chinesische Kurzgeschichten/[übers.: Ulrich Heimann]. Köln: Verlag Rote Fahne, 1977. 99 S.; 21cm. ISBN: 3810600644, 3810600646
Contents: Vier Reisen in eine Wüstenstadt. —Kiefer im Sonnenlicht. —Menschen können den Himmel stürmen. —Der „Oberaufseher."
人类能够战胜上天:四个中国短篇故事. Heimann, Ulrich 译.

27. Von den müssigen Gefühlen: chines. Liebesgedichte aus 3 Jahrtausenden/[aus d. Chines. übertr., nachgedichtet u. hrsg. von Ernst Schwarz]. Leipzig, Weimar: Kiepenheuer, 1978. 226 S.; zahlr. Ill.; 17cm.
中国三千年爱情故事. Schwarz, Ernst 译.

28. Erotische Geschichten aus China/hrsg. u. übers. von Adrian Baar. Frankfurt am Main: Fischer-Taschenbuch-Verlag, 1978. 157 S.: 6 Ill. (farb.); 18cm. ISBN: 3596224160, 3596224166. (Fischer-Taschenbücher; 2416)
中国艳情小说. Baar, Adrian 译.
(1) Frankfurt am Main: Fischer-Taschenbuch-Verlag, 1979. 157 Seiten 6 farbige Illustrationen 18cm. ISBN: 3596224160, 3596224166
(2) Frankfurt am Main: Fischer-Taschenbuch-Verlag, 1980. 157 Seiten 6 farbige Illustrationen 18cm. ISBN: 3596224160, 3596224166
(3) Frankfurt am Main: Fischer-Taschenbuch-Verlag, 1991. 157 S.: Ill.; 18. 157 Seiten 6 farbige Illustrationen 18cm. ISBN: 3596224160, 3596224166

29. Der Kaiser und die Kurtisane. Erotische Novellen aus China. Herausgegeben/übersetzt und erläutert von F. K. Engler. München: Wilhelm Heyne Verlag, 1984. 190 S.; 18cm. ISBN: 3453502965, 3453502963. (Exquisit Bücher; 16/326)
"皇帝和妃嫔":中国情色小说. Engler, Friedrich K. (1934—1990)译.收录多人作品.

30. Der Mann, der einen Geist verkaufte: chines. Geschichten aus d. 3.-6. Jh./[aus d. Engl. von Käthe Zhao]. Beijing: Verlag für Fremdsprachige Literatur, 1984. 190 S.; 22cm.
《汉魏六朝小说选》,Zhao, Käthe 译.

31. Die Schmuckschatulle der Kurtisane: chinesische Klassiker; chinesische Geschichten aus dem 10. bis 17. Jahrhundert/[dt. von Alexander Sichrovsky]. Beijing: Verl. für Fremdsprachige Literatur, 1985. VI, 562 S.; 22cm.
《宋明平话选》,Sichrovsky, Alexander 译.

32. Der Magier vom Wolkenturmgipfel/hrsg., übers. mit Erklärungen u. e. Nachw. vers. von Friedrich K. Engler. Frankfurt am Main: Fischer-Taschenbuch-Verlag, 1986. 285 S.: Ill.; 18cm. ISBN: 3596258970, 3596258979. (Chinesische Novellen aus zwei Jahrtausenden; Bd. 1. Fischer; 5897)
两千年中国小说(卷一). Engler, Friedrich 译.含干宝、葛洪、宋濂、袁宏道等人作品.

33. Zehn Tage in Yang-tschou/hrsg., übers., mit Erklärungen u. e. Nachw. vers. von Friedrich K. Engle. Frankfurt am Main: Fischer-Taschenbuch-Verlag, 1986. 287 S.: Ill.; 18cm. ISBN: 3596258987, 3596258987. (Chinesische Novellen aus zwei Jahrtausenden; Bd. 2, Fischer; 5898)
两千年中国小说(卷二). Engler, Friedrich 译. 含归庄、长白浩歌子、沙张白《老学究重生》、邵长蘅《一个爱国者的自传》、清凉道人《被偷走的妇女》等人作品.

34. Die Liebe der Füchsin: Geistergeschichten aus dem alten China/[hrsg. von Johannes Merkel]. München: Weismann, Frauenbuchverl., 1988. 183 S.; 17cm. ISBN: 3888970344, 3888970342.
中国古代鬼怪小说. Merkel, Johannes 译. 选译自《拍案惊奇》《醒世恒言》.
(1) Die Liebe der Füchsin: Geistergeschichten aus dem alten China/hrsg. von Johannes Merkel. Zürich: Unionsverl., 1995. 154 S.; 19cm. ISBN: 3293200555, 3293200559. (Unionsverlag-Taschenbuch; 55)

35. Die Braut im Brunnen: Kriminalgeschichten aus dem alten China/[hrsg. von Johannes Merkel]. München: Weismann, Frauenbuchverl., 1989. 182 S.; 17cm. ISBN: 3888971396, 388897139X
井中新娘:中国古代侦探小说.
(1) Zürich: Unionsverl., 1995. 159 S.; 19cm. ISBN: 3293200487, 3293200486. (Unionsverlag-Taschenbuch; 48)

36. Die Leiche im Strom: die seltsamen Kriminalfälle des Meisters Bao/übers. und vorgestellt von Wolfgang Bauer. Freiburg i. Br.; Basel; Wien: Herder, 1992. 238 S.; 21cm. ISBN: 3451225980, 3451225987
包公探案故事. Bauer, Wolfgang 译.

37. Erotische Geschichten aus China/Dt. von Adrian Baar. Hrsg. und mit einem Nachw. von Hansjürgen Blinn. Berlin: Aufbau, 2009. 220 S.; 19cm. ISBN: 3351032807, 3351032803. (Bibliotheca erotica)
中国艳情小说. Baar, Adrian 译.

I52 古代个人作品(或单部作品)

白行简(776—826)

1. Die schöne Li: Zwei chinesische Liebesgeschichten aus der Tang-Zeit/übertr. von Franz Kuhn. Wiesbaden: Insel-

Verlag, 1959. 66 Seiten. (Insel-Bücherei；705)

《李娃传》，孔舫之（Kuhn, Franz, 1884—1961）译.

2. Das Singmädchen Li：Geschichten aus d. Tangzeit/Bai Ssing-djän. ［Johanna Herzfeldt überarb. d. Übers. u. verf. d. Anm.］. Mit e. Nachw. v. Werner Bettin. Leipzig Reclam, 1962. 126 Seiten kl. 8. (Reclams Universal-Bibliothek；Nr. 8990/91)

《李娃传》，Herzfeldt, Johanna 译.

元稹(779—831)

1. Das schöne Mädchen Yingying：erotische Novellen aus China/aus dem Chinesischen übersetzt und mit einem Nachwort von Martin Gimm. Zürich：Manesse, 2001. 251 pages：illustrations；15cm. ISBN：3717519867, 3717519867, 3717519875, 3717519874

《莺莺传》,（唐）元稹编撰；Gimm, Martin (1930—)译.

李复言(约公元831年前后在世)

1. Der Fremde mit dem Lockenbart：Erzählungen aus dem China der Tang-Zeit/hrsg. und aus dem Chines. übers. von Thomas Thilo；［mit 62 Reprod. nach überzeichneten Papierschn. von Rolf Xago Schröder］. Berlin：Rütten & Loening, 1989. 364 Seiten：Illustrationen；22cm. ISBN：3352002851, 3352002854

《续玄怪录》，Thilo, Thomas 译.

杨瑀(1285—1361)

1. Beiträge zur Kulturgeschichte Chinas unter der Mongolenherrschaft：das Shan-kü sinhua des Yang Yü/Herbert Franke. Wiesbaden：Steiner in Komm. , 1956. 160 S. ；gr. 8. (Abhandlungen für die Kunde des Morgenlandes；Bd. 32,2)

《山居新话》，杨瑀（1285—1361）著；Franke, Herbert 译. 笔记小说.

施耐庵(约1296—约1370)

1. Räuber und Soldaten：Roman frei nach dem Chinesischen/von Albert Ehrenstein. Berlin：Ullstein, 1927. 292 Seiten

《强盗与士兵：中国小说》（《水浒传》），Ehrenstein, Albert (1886—1950)译.

2. Der Überfall am Gelbschlammgrat/Franz Kuhn (übers.). Sinica, 8, 1933：145—157.

《水浒传》节选，孔舫之（Kuhn, Franz, 1884—1961)译.

3. Sung kommt unter die Liang Schan-Rebellen, eine Episode aus dem Schui Hu Dschuan/Franz Kuhn (übers.). Sinica, 9, 1934：32—45.

《水浒传》节选，孔舫之（Kuhn, Franz, 1884—1961)译.

4. Die Falle im Henkergraben, aus dem Chinesischen Roman Schui Hu Dschuan/Franz Kuhn (übers.). Sinica, 9, 1934：198—202.

《水浒传》节选，孔舫之（Kuhn, Franz, 1884—1961)译.

5. Die Räuber vom Liang Schan Moor/aus dem Chines. übertragen von Franz Kuhn. Leipzig：Insel-Verl. , 1934. 839 S. ：Ill；21cm.

《水浒传》，孔舫之（Kuhn, Franz, 1884—1961)译.

(1)Düsseldorf：Droste, 1953. 839 S：Ill.

(2)Die Räuber vom Liang Schan Moor：mit 60 Holzschn. einer alten chines. Ausg. /［Nai an Schi］. Aus d. Chines. übertr. von Franz Kuhn. Düsseldorf：Insel-Verl. , 1957. 841 S：Ill.

(3)Frankfurt am Main：Insel-Verl. , 1964. 866 S. Ill.

(4)Frankfurt am Main：Insel-Verl. , 1975. 866 S. 8„.

6. Wie Lu Da unter die Rebellen kam：eine Episode aus dem altchinesischen Roman „ Die Räuber vom Liang-Schan-Moor"/Shi Naian. Aus dem Chin. übers. von Maximilian Kern. Durchsicht der Übers. , Vorbemerkung und Nachw. von Werner Bettin. Leipzig：Reclam, 1965. 107 Seiten. (Reclams Universal-Bibliothek；248)

《水浒》节选《鲁智深拳打镇关西》等,共七章，Kern, Maximilian 译.

7. Die Räuber vom Liangschan/［Schi Nai-an］. Aus d. Chines. übertr. u. hrsg. von Johanna Herzfeldt. Leipzig：Insel-Verlag, 1968. 687 S. ：Ill.

《梁山泊的强盗》（《水浒传》选译），Herzfeldt, Johanna (1886—1977)译. 2 卷本.

(1)Leipzig：Insel-Verl. , 1974. 654 Seiten；8„

8. Pantherschädel：vom Waffenmeister der Kaiserlichen Garde zum Rebellen：Abenteuerliche Erlebnisse eines chinesischen Offiziers aus dem Roman Die Räuber vom Liang Schan Moor/für das Sprachstudium mit lateinischer Aussprachebezeichnung und Erläuterungen versehen von Renate Lenz. Leipzig：Verl. Enzyklopädie, 1969. 42 S. 8„. (Chinesische übungstexte；H. 3).

《水浒传》节选，Lenz, Renate 译.

9. 水浒传：汉德对照/施耐庵（约1296—1370），罗贯中（1330? —1400?)著；赫茨费尔德（Herzfeldt, Johanna）译. 长沙：岳麓书社湖南教育出版社，2010. 4 卷；24cm. ISBN：7807612575, 7807612576. (大中华文库)

德文题名：Die rauber vom Liangschan

罗贯中(1330—1400)

1. Pekinger Todenbräuche/Wilhelm Grube. Journal of the Peking Oriental Society, IV, 104；1898：79—141.

《三国演义》节选，Grube, Wilhelm (1855—1908)译.

2. Der Schauspieler als Held in der Geschichte Chinas/Basil M. Alexeiev. Asia Major, Band 10, 1934, S. 33—58.

《三国演义》节选，Alexeiev, Basil M. (1881—1951)译.

3. Das Ende des Tyrannen Dung Dscho, eine Episode aus dem San Guo-Dschi/Franz Kuhn (übers.). Sinica, 13, 3/4, 1938.

《三国演义》节选，孔舫之（Kuhn, Franz, 1884—1961）译.

4. Ein Thron muss wandern/Franz Kuhn (übers.). Sinica, 221—238, 1938.

《三国演义》节选，孔舫之（Kuhn, Franz, 1884—1961)译.

5. Der Sprung in den Wildbach/Franz Kuhn（übers.）. Sinica，151—161，Chap. 34；1939.

《三国演义》节选,孔舫之（Kuhn，Franz，1884—1961）译.

6. Besuch beim Schlafenden Drachen/Franz Kuhn（übers.）. Sinica，14，40—51；1939.

《三国演义》节选,孔舫之（Kuhn，Franz，1884—1961）译.

7. Die drei Reiche（San kwo tschi）：Roman aus dem alten China/［Loh Kwantschung］. übertr. und mit einem Nachw. vers. von Franz Kuhn. Berlin：Kiepenheuer，1940. 546 S：Ill.

《三国志》,孔舫之（Kuhn，Franz，1884—1961）译.

(1)Weimar：Kiepenheuer，1951. 447 S：Ill.

(2)Frankfurt am Main：Insel Verlag，1981. 475 S：Ill.

8. Die Schwurbrüder vom Pfirsichgarten：Roman aus d. alten China/［mutmassl. Verf.：Kwan-tschung Loh］. übertr. u. mit e. Nachw. versehen von Franz Kuhn. Köln；Berlin：Kiepenheuer & Witsch，1953. 462 S.：［Mit］24 Holzschnitten nach alten Vorlagen；8.（Früher u. d. T.：Loh，Kwan-tschung：Die drei Reiche）

《三国演义》,孔舫之（Kuhn，Franz，1884—1961）译.

9. Die Wirren am Hof der Han-Kaiser/Irmgard Grimm. Sinica，13，3/4，1938.

《三国演义》节选，Grimm，Irmgard 译.

10. Rettung aus der Not/Irmgard Grimm. Sinica，14，32—39，1939.

《三国演义》节选，Grimm，Irmgard 译.

11. Tsau Tsau' Flucht/Irmgard Grimm. Sinica，14，103—107，1939.

《三国演义》节选，Grimm，Irmgard 译.

12. Der Aufstand der Zauberer：e. Roman aus d. Ming-Zeit/Luo Guanzhong. In d. Fassung von Feng Menglong. Aus d. Chines. u. mit e. Vorw. von Manfred Porkert. Frankfurt am Main：Insel-Verl.，1986. 671 S.；21cm. ISBN：3458143130，3458143130.

《平妖传》,Porkert，Manfred 译.

(1)Frankfurt，M.：S. Fischer，2009. 636 S.；22cm. ISBN：3100215109，3100215109.（Eine Sammlung chinesischer Klassiker；Bd. 4）

唐寅（1470—1524）

1. Der Mönche und Nonnen Sündenmeer：der buddhistische Klerus in der chinesischen Roman- und Erzählliteratur des 16. und 17. Jahrhunderts；mit einer vollständigen Übersetzung der Sammlung Sengni-niehai/Stefan M. Rummel. Bochum：Brockmeyer，1992. 339 S.；19cm. ISBN：3883399621，3883399620.（Chinathemen；Bd. 68）

《僧尼孽海》,Rummel，Stefan 译.

2. Zhang und die Nonne vom Qiyun-Kloster：［erotische Erzählungen aus dem alten China］/aus dem klass. Chines. übertr. von Stefan M. Rummel. Hrsg. und mit

einem Nachw. vers. von Helmut Martin. München：Heyne，1993. 235 S.：Ill.；18cm. ISBN：3453061705，3453061705.（Heyne Bücher；01；Llgemeine Reihe）

《僧尼孽海》,Rummel，Stefan M. 译.

吴承恩（约 1500—1583）

1. Monkeys Pilgerfahrt：Eine chinesische Legende/Wu Cheng'en；［Übersetzung aus dem Englischen von Georgette Boner und Maria Nils］. Zürich：Artemis-Verl.，1947. 464 S.；8.

《西游记》,韦利（Arthur Waley，1889—1966）（英国汉学家）英译. Boner，Georgette（1904—1998）和 Maria Nils 德译.

(1)Ungekürzte Ausg.，1. Aufl. ［München］：Goldmann，1983. 422 Seiten；18cm. ISBN：3442065364，3442065363.（Goldmann-Taschenbuch；6536）

(2)Zürich：Classen，1997. 464 S.：Ill.；22cm. ISBN：3717203746，3717203742.

2. Der rebellische Affe：Die Reise nach dem Western：ein chinesischer Roman/Wu Ch'eng-en；nach der englischen Ausgabe von Arthur Waley；übersetzt von Georgette Boner un Maria Nils；mit einem Essay „Zum Verständnis des Werkes" von Hellmut Wilhelm. ［Hamburg］：Rowohlt，1961. 265 pages；19cm.（Rowohlts Klassiker der Literatur und der Wissenschaft；82 — 83. Östliche Philosophie und Literatur；Bd. 2）

《西游记》,韦利（Arthur Waley，1889—1966）（英国汉学家）英译；Boner，Georgette（1904—1998）和 Maria Nils 合译.

3. Die Pilgerfahrt nach dem Westen：Roman/Wu Tschöng-ön. Aus dem Chines. übertr. und hrsg. von Johanna Herzfeldt. Rudolstadt：Greifenverl.，1962. 501 S.；8°

《西游记》（节译），Herzfeldt，Johanna（1886—1977）译.

4. Der Affenkönig：ein chinesisches Märchen/WU Tscheng-en；［nach der Übertragung aus dem Chinesischen ins Tschechische von Zdena Novotná；Deutsch von Eva Švor cíková；Einführung von Zdena Novotná］；Illustrationen von Zdeněk Sklená r. Praha：Artia，1964. 286 pages：color illustrations；28cm.

《西游记》,Althammer-Švor cíková，Eva（1911—2002）译.

5. Sun Wu-kung besiegt das Weisse-Knochen-Gespenst dreimal/Hsing-be Wang；Hung-ben Dschao；Hsiao-dai Tjiàn.：. Nachdr. Peking：Verl. für fremdsprachige Literatur，1976. 110 Seiten：überwiegend Illustrationen

《孙悟空三打白骨精》,Wang，Hsing-be 等译.

6. Der Affenkönig：［das klassische chinesische Märchen］/Wu Tscheng-en. Ill. von Zdenka Krej č ová.［Aus dem chines. Orig. übertr.，bearb. und mit Vorw. und Anm. vers. von Zdenka Heřmanová-Novotná］. Dt. von Eva Švor č íková］. München：Lentz，1992. 255 Seiten：Illustrationen；29cm. ISBN：3880102236，3880102231.（Spiegel der Vergangenheit）

《西游记》，He rmanová-Novotná，Zdenka 译.

冯梦龙(1574—1646)

1. Chinesische Legenden：Aus d. Chines；Mit 4 Farbenlichtdr. nach chines. Gemälden aus d. 17. Jh. / Lin Tsiu-Sen. Berlin：Metzner，1937. 10 Bl. ；2.

   《东周列国志》，林秋生选译.

2. Altchinesische Staatsweisheit/[aus d. Chinesischen ausgew. u. übers. und hrsg. v.] Franz Kuhn. 3.，veränd. Aufl. Zürich：Verlag Die Waage，1954. 198 S. ；8.

   《东周列国志》，孔舫之（Kuhn，Franz，1884—1961)译.

3. Das chinesische Dekameron/Aus d. Chines. von Johanna Herzfeldt. Rudolstadt：Greifenverl.，1957. 345 S. ：mit Abb. ；8.

   《醒世恒言》节选. Herzfeldt，Johanna(1886—1977)译.

   (1)Frankfurt a. M. ；Wien；Zürich：Büchergilde Gutenberg，1963. 363 S. ：mit Abb. ；8.

   (2)[Aus d. Chines. von Johanna Herzfeldt. Mit 22 Ill. von Horst Hausotte]. 3. Aufl. Rudolstadt：Greifenverl. VEB，1968. 289 S. ；8.

   (3)übers. von Johanna Herzfeldt. Mit Bildern von Mehrdad Zaeri. Frankfurt a. M. ；Wien；Zürich：Büchergilde Gutenberg，2008. 292 S. ：Ill. ；25cm. ISBN：3763259090；3763259106.

4. Die schöne Konkubine und andere chinesische Liebesgeschichten aus der Ming-Zeit/Mêng-lung Fêng. Aus d. Chines. von Tat-hang Fung. Stuttgart；Zürich；Salzburg：Europäischer Buchklub，1966. 301 S. ；8.

   《警世通言》，Fung，Tat-hang 译.

   (1)Sonderausg. Stuttgart u. a. ：Europ. Buchklub，1967. 301 S. ：ill.

   (2)Tübingen [u. a.]：Erdmann，1968. 323 S.

   (3)München，Heyne，1970. 235 pages；18cm. (Exquisit-Bücher，Nr. 38)

   (4)Sonderausg. Wiesbaden Löwit，1976. 301 S. 21cm.

5. Shan-ko/von Feng Meng-lung. Eine Volksliedersammlung aus der Ming-Zeit [übers. und kommentiert von] Cornelia Töpelmann. Wiesbaden：Steiner，1973. 491 S；24cm. ISBN：3515007334，3515007337. (Münchener ostasiatische Studien；Bd. 9)

   《三言》，Töpelmann，Cornelia 译.

6. Geschichten der Fürstentümer der östlichen Zhou-Dynastie：Bd. 1. /[Feng Menglong]. Bearb. und übers. von Mingxiang Chen. Gelnhausen Wagner，2013. 603 S. ISBN：3862797578，3862797570

   《新列国志》，Chen，Mingxiang 译.

凌蒙初(1580—1644)

1. Neuer chinesischer Liebesgarten；Novellen aus den berühmtesten erotischen Sammlungen der Ming-Zeit/[von] Feng Meng-Lung [und] Ling Meng-Chu. Aus dem Chinesischen von Tat-Hang Fung. [Tübingen] H. Erdmann，1968. 323 pages；21cm.

《拍案惊奇》节选. 译自《拍案惊奇》，共 16 篇文章. Fung，Tat-Hang 译.

   (1)Stuttgart Europ. Buch- u. Phonoklub，1969. 323 S. 8

   (2)Sonderausg. Wiesbaden Löwit，1976. 323 S. 21cm.

2. Pflaumenblüten in der Goldvase：erotische Erzählungen aus China/Ling Meng-chu. München：Heyne，1983. 238 S. ；18cm. ISBN：3453502864，3453502868. (Heyne-Bücher/16/Exquisit-Bücher；Nr. 316)

《拍案惊奇》

丁耀亢(1599—1669)

1. Mondfrau und Silbervase：ein altchinesischer Frauenroman/Dt. v. Franz Kuhn. Berlin：Steiniger，1939. 463 S. 8.

   《隔帘花影》，孔舫之（Kuhn，Franz，1884—1961)节译.

2. Blumenschatten hinter dem Vorhang/[Tze Yang Tao Jen，Ting Yao-kang]. Aus d. Chines. verdt. von Kuhn，Franz. Freiburg i. Br. ：Klemm，1956. 784 S. ；1 Kt. ；8.

   《隔帘花影》，孔舫之（Kuhn，Franz，1884—1961)译.

   (1)2. Aufl. Freiburg im Breisgau：E. Seemann，1957. 784 pages：illustrations；20cm.

   (2)3. Aufl. Recklinghausen：Seemann，1961. 784 S. ：1 Kt.，1 Titelbild；8.

   (3)4. Aufl. Recklinghausen：Seemann，1963. 784 S. ：1 Kt.，1 Titelbild；8.

   (4)Berlin；München；Wien：Non-Stop-Bücherei，1967. 448 S. ；kl. 8. (Non-Stop-Bücherei；99/100/101)

   (5)Leipzig：Insel-Verlag，1975. 813 S. ：18 Ill. ；20cm.

   (6)Frankfurt am Main：Insel-Verlag，1983. 769 S. ：18 Ill. ；18cm. ISBN：3458324447，3458324445. (Insel-Taschenbuch；744)

(明)抱瓮老人

1. Goldamsel flötet am Westsee/Erstmalig aus d. Chines. übers. von Franz Kuhn. Farb. Bilder：Asta Ruth-Soffner. Freiburg i. Br. ：Klemm，1953. 95 S. ；8. (Die Seemännchen；Bd. 4)

   《柳浪闻莺》，孔舫之（Kuhn，Franz，1884—1961)译.

《昭阳趣史》(明代)

1. Der Goldherr besteigt den weissen Tiger：e. histor. -erot. Roman aus d. Ming-Zeit/[Yen-yen-sheng]. Zum 1. Male aus d. Chines. ins Dt. übers. von F. K. Engler. Mit Zeittaf. u. Anm. sowie Nachw. von Herbert Franke. Zürich：Verlag Die Waage，1980. 452 S. ；22 Ill. ；22cm. ISBN：3859660496，3859660497.

   《昭阳趣史》，Engler，Friedrich K. （1934—1990)译自英文.

   (1)Frankfurt/M. ；Berlin：Ullstein，1989. 437 S. ；22 Ill. ；20cm. ISBN：3550066863，3550066864. (Lizenz d. Verl. Die Waage，Zürich)

《封神演义》(明代)

1. Die Metamorphosen der Götter. Historisch-mythologischer Roman aus dem Chinesischen/Übersetzung der Kapitel 1 bis

46. übersetzer：Wilhelm Grube. Veröffentlichung：Leyden：E. J. Brill，1912. 657 S.

《封神演义》(1—46 章)，Grube，Wilhelm 译.

(1) Feng-shen yen-yi. Die Metamorphosen der Götter. Historisch-Mythologischer Roman aus dem Chinesischen. Vorwort H. Martin. übersetzt sind Kap. 1—46，danach Zusammenfassung durch Herbert Müller. Veröffentlichung：Taibei：1970. 2 volumes (xxiv，657 pages) illustrations (1 color) 27cm.

《玉娇梨》(明朝)

1. Ju-Kiao-Li：Ein chines. Familienroman/In deutscher Bearb. von Emma Wuttke-Biller. Leipzig：Ph. Reclam jun. ，1922. 87 S. ；kl. 8.

《玉娇梨》，Wuttke-Biller，Emma 译.

2. Rotjade und Blütentraum：Ein chines. Liebesroman/[Aus d. Urtexten übertr. v. Anna von Rottauscher. Die Nachdichtg d. Verse besorgte Mirko Jelusich]. Wien：Frick，1941. 319 S. ；8.

《玉娇梨》，Rottauscher，Anna von(Anna，1892—)译.

3. Der Garten des Pe-Kong/[übertr. der Verse：Gerhart Haug]. München：Münchner Buchverl. ，1942. 14S. ；Ill. ；15cm. (Münchner Lesebogen；74)

《玉娇梨》，Haug，Gerhart 译.

(1) München：Münchner Buchverl. ，1950. 8 Bl. ；8. (Münchner Lesebogen；74)

4. Das Dreigespann oder Yü-chiao-li/[übers. aus d. Chines. von Mario Schubert]. Bern：Scherz，1949. 451 S. ；8.

《玉娇梨》，Schubert，Mario 译.

《金瓶梅》(明代)

1. Djin Ping meh /Wang Schidschen. Unter weitgehender Mitw. von Artur Kibat. aus d. ungekürzten chines. Urtext übers. u. mit Erl. vers. von Otto Kibat. Gotha：Engelhard-Reyher，1928. 283 S. ；8.

《金瓶梅》，Artur Kibat (1878—1960) 和 Otto Kibat (1880—1956)合译.

(1) Gotha：Engelhard-Reyher，1932. 350 S. ；20cm.

(2) Djin Ping Meh：Schlehenblüten in goldener Vase；Sittenroman aus der Ming-Zeit/ Shi-cheng Wang. Gekürzte Lizenzausg. nach d. ersten vollst. Originalübertr. ins Dt. durch Otto u. Artur Kibat. Berlin-Grunewald：Non Stop-Bücherei，1961. 391 S. ；8„. (Non stop-Bücherei. ；[64/65]).

(3) Olten；Stuttgart；Salzburg：Fackelverl. ，1965. 760 S. ；8„. (Non stop-Bücherei. - Berlin-Grunewald，1956—；64/66).

(4) Berlin；München；Wien：Non Stop-Bücherei，1967. 384 S. ；8„. (Non stop-Bücherei；Bd. 64/66).

(5) Berlin，München [u. a.]：Verl. Die Waage，1969. 391 S. ；8". (Non stop-Bücherei. - Berlin-Grunewald，1956—；64/66).

(6) Gütersloh：Bertelsmann - Stuttgart：Europ. Buch- u.

Phonoklub - Wien：Buchgemeinschaft Donauland，1971. 476 S. ；50 Ill. ；；21cm. [Lizenz d. Verl. Die Waage，Zürich. - Text gekürzt. - Mit 50 Holzschnitten e. Ausg. von 1755].

(7) Stuttgart：Europ. Bildungsgemeinschaft - Gütersloh：Bertelsmann - Wien：Buchgemeinschaft Donauland - Berlin，Darmstadt，Wien：Dt. Buch-Gemeinschaft，1977. 476 S. ；21cm. [Lizenzausg. d. Verl. Die Waage，Zürich-Zollikerberg].

(8) Frankfurt am Main：Fischer-Taschenbuch-Verlag，1980. 526 S. ；Ill. ；18cm. ISBN：3596224764. (Fischer-Taschenbücher； 2476) [Gekürzte Lizenzausg. d. Verl. Die Waage，Zürich].

(9) Frankfurt am Main：Fischer-Taschenbuch-Verl. ，1990. 526 S. ；Ill. ；18cm. ISBN：3596224764. (Fischer-Taschenbücher； 2476) [Gekürzte Lizenzausg. d. Verl. Die Waage，Zürich].

2. Kin Ping Meh：oder Die abenteuerliche Geschichte von Hsi Men und seinen sechs Frauen/aus dem Chinesischen übertragen von Franz Kuhn. Leipzig：Insel-Verl. ，1930. 920 S.

《金瓶梅》，孔舫之 (Kuhn，Franz，1884—1961)译.

(1) Wiesbaden：Insel-Verl. ，1952. 921 S. ；8„.

(2) Wiesbaden：Insel-Verl. ，1954. 919 S. ；8„.

(3) Wiesbaden：Insel-Verl. ，1957. 926 S. ；8„.

(4) Wiesbaden：Insel-Verl. ，1958. 926 S. ；8„.

(5) Frankfurt a. M. ：Insel-Verl. ，1961. 911 S. ；8„.

(6) Leipzig：Insel-Verlag，1973. 863 p. ；20cm.

(7) Frankfurt am Main：Insel-Verlag，1977. 2 volumes：illustrations；18cm. ISBN：3458019537，3458019534. (Insel-Taschenbuch；253)

(8) Erste Auflage. Frankfurt am Main；Leipzig：Insel Verlag，1977. 906 pages，44 unnumbered leaves of plates：illustrations；18cm. ISBN：3458319530，3458319535

(9) [Frankfurt a. M. ：] Insel Verl. ，1982. 911 S. 8„. ISBN：3458319530. (Insel Taschenbuch；253)

(10) Lepzig：Gustav Kiepenheuer Verlag，1983. 2 volumes；20cm.

(11) Leipzig；Weimar：Kiepenheuer，1983. 2 volumes；20cm. (Die Bücherkiepe).

(12) [Wiesbaden]：Insel-Verlag，1984. 4 dl. ；16cm. ISBN：3458141634，3458141631

(13) Leipzig：Kiepenheuer，1988. 2 volumes. ISBN：3378002573(v. 1)，3378002579(v. 1)，3378002581 (v. 2)，3378002586(v. 2). (Die Bücherkiepe)

3. Mondfrau und Silbervase：ein altchinesischer Frauenroman/ Dt. v. Franz Kuhn. Berlin：Steiniger，1939. 463 S.

《金瓶梅》，孔舫之 (Kuhn，Franz，1884—1961)译.

(1) Berlin：Steiniger，1940. 463 S. ；8„.

4. Chin p'ing mei：Episoden aus d. Leben Hsi Mens und

seiner 6 Frauen/[Wang Shih-chêng]. Aus d. Chines. übertr. u. in neuer Fassg hrsg. v. Mario Schubert. Zürich：W. Classen, 1950. 336 S.；8.

《金瓶梅》，Mario Schubert 译.

5. Djin ping meh：Schlehenblüten in goldener Vase：Ein Sittenroman aus der Ming-Zeit：(1—6)/Zum ersten Male vollständig aus dem Chinesischen ins Deutsche übertr. von Otto und Artur Kibat；Hrsg. und eingeleitet von Herbert Franke. Hamburg, 1967—1983. 6 bd.：illustrations

Contents：Bd. 1/1.—22. Kap. Bd. 2/23.—45. Kap. Bd. 3/46.—64. Kap. Bd. 4/65.—79. Kap. Bd. 5/80.—100. Kap. Bd. 6/Kommentarband.

《金瓶梅》，6 卷. Kibat, Otto（1880—1956）和 Kibat, Artur(1878—1960)合译.

6. Jin Ping Mei：chinesischer Roman, erstmalig vollständig ins Deutsche übersetzt. [Teil 1] Kapitel 1—10/Hans Conon von der Gabelentz. Hrsg. und bearb. von Martin Gimm. Berlin Staatsbibliothek zu Berlin, 2005. 148 S. ISBN：3880531277, 3880531277. (Neuerwerbungen der Ostasienabteilung/Staatsbibliothek zu Berlin；Sonderheft；9)

《金瓶梅》第 1 部分，Gabelentz, Hans Conon von der (1807—1874)译；Gimm, Martin (1930—)编.

7. Jin Ping Mei：chinesischer Roman. Teil II, Kapitel 11—20/erstmalig vollständig ins Deutsche übersetzt [von] Hans Conon von der Gabelentz；herausgegeben und bearbeitet von Martin Gimm. [Berlin]：Staatsbibliothek zu Berlin, 2006. 1 vol. (III-307 p.)；fac-sim.；30cm. ISBN：3880531358, 3880531352. (Neuerwerbungen der Ostasienabteilung；Sonderheft 13)

《金瓶梅》第 2 部分，Gabelentz, Hans Conon von der (1807—1874)译；Gimm, Martin (1930—)编.

8. Jin Ping Mei. Teil 3. Kapitel 21—30/[Staatsbibliothek zu Berlin]. Hans Conon von der Gabelentz. Erstmals vollst. ins Dt. übers. Hrsg. und bearb. Martin Gimm. Mit einer Vorbemerkung von H. Walravens. Berlin：Staatsbibliothek, 2010. VII S., S. 308—479, 45 S. Ill. ISBN：3880531604, 3880531609. (Neuerwerbungen der Ostasienabteilung；Sonderheft 21)

《金瓶梅》第 3 部分，Gabelentz, Hans Conon von der (1807—1874)译；Gimm, Martin (1930—)编.

9. Jin Ping Mei. Teil 4, Kapitel 31—40/Hans Conon von der Gabelentz (1807—1874). Hrsg. und bearb. von Martin Gimm. Berlin：Staatsbibliothek zu Berlin, 2011. IX Seiten, Seite 481—664, XIV, 7 Seiten：Illustrationen. ISBN：3880531673, 3880531676, 3880531710, 3880531714. (Neuerwerbungen der Ostasienabteilung/Staatsbibliothek zu Berlin：Sonderheft；24)

《金瓶梅》第 4 部分，Gabelentz, Hans Conon von der (1807—1874)译；Gimm, Martin (1930—)编.

10. Jin Ping Mei：chinesischer Roman, erstmals vollständig ins

Deutsche übersetzt. 5, Kapitel 41—50/[Staatsbibliothek zu Berlin]. Hans Conon von der Gabelentz. Hrsg. und bearb. Martin Gimm；mit einer Vorbemerkung von H. Walravens. Berlin：Staatsbibliothek, 2011. IV Seiten, Seite 665—822；30cm. ISBN：3880531710, 3880531714. (Neuerwerbungen der Ostasienabteilung/Staatsbibliothek zu Berlin Preussischer Kulturbesitz；Sonderheft；26)

《金瓶梅》第 5 部分，Gabelentz, Hans Conon von der (1807—1874)译；Gimm, Martin (1930—)编.

11. Jin Ping Mei：chinesischer Roman, erstmals vollständig ins Deutsche übersetzt. 6, Kapitel 51—60/[Staatsbibliothek zu Berlin]. Hans Conon von der Gabelentz. Hrsg. und bearb. Martin Gimm；mit einer Vorbemerkung von H. Walravens. Berlin：Staatsbibliothek, 2012. Seite 823—967, [20] Blätter：Illustrationen；30cm. ISBN：3880531765, 3880531765. (Neuerwerbungen der Ostasienabteilung/Staatsbibliothek zu Berlin Preussischer Kulturbesitz：Sonderheft；28)

《金瓶梅》第 6 部分，Gabelentz, Hans Conon von der (1807—1874)译；Gimm, Martin (1930—)编.

12. Jin Ping Mei. Teil 7, Kapitel 61—70/Hans Conon von der Gabelentz；hrsg. und bearb. von Martin Gimm. Berlin：Staatsbibliothek zu Berlin, 2012. 4, 968—1184, 16 p.；30cm. ISBN：3880531789, 3880531781. (Neuerwerbungen der Ostasienabteilung/Staatsbibliothek Berlin. Ostasienabteilung. Sonderheft；30)

《金瓶梅》第 7 部分，Gabelentz, Hans Conon von der (1807—1874)译；Gimm, Martin (1930—)编.

13. Jin Ping Mei：chinesischer Roman, erstmals vollständig ins Deutsche übersetzt. 8, Kapitel 71—80/[Staatsbibliothek zu Berlin]. Hans Conon von der Gabelentz. Hrsg. und bearb. Martin Gimm；mit einer Vorbemerkung von H. Walravens. Berlin：Staatsbibliothek, 2013. Seiten [1185]-1328, XIV Seiten；30cm. ISBN：3880531888, 3880531889. (Neuerwerbungen der Ostasienabteilung/Staatsbibliothek zu Berlin Preussischer Kulturbesitz：Sonderheft；33)

《金瓶梅》第 8 部分，Gabelentz, Hans Conon von der (1807—1874)译；Gimm, Martin (1930—)编.

14. Jin Ping Mei：chinesischer Roman, erstmalig vollständig ins Deutsche übersetzt. Teil 9 Kapitel 81—90/Hans Conon von der Gabelentz. Hrsg. und bearb. von Martin Gimm. Berlin：Staatsbibliothek zu Berlin, 2013. Seite 1329—1423, XVIII Seiten Illustrationen. ISBN：3880531895, 3880531897. (Neuerwerbungen der Ostasienabteilung/Staatsbibliothek zu Berlin；Sonderheft；34)

《金瓶梅》第 9 部分，Gabelentz, Hans Conon von der (1807—1874)译；Gimm, Martin (1930—)编.

15. Jin Ping Mei：chinesischer Roman, erstmals vollständig ins Deutsche übersetzt. 10, Kapitel 91—100/[Staatsbibliothek zu Berlin]. Hans Conon von der Gabelentz. Hrsg. und

bearb. Martin Gimm; mit einer Vorbemerkung von H. Walravens. Berlin: Staatsbibliothek, 2013. Seite 1425—1585: Illustrationen; 30cm. ISBN: 3880531901, 3880531900. (Neuerwerbungen der Ostasienabteilung/ Staatsbibliothek zu Berlin Preussischer Kulturbesitz: Sonderheft; 35)

《金瓶梅》第 10 部分,Gabelentz, Hans Conon von der (1807—1874)译;Gimm, Martin (1930—)编.

16. 金瓶梅:汉德对照/(明)兰陵笑笑生;(德)奥托·吉巴特 (Kibat, Otto),阿图尔·吉巴特(Kibat, Artur)译. 北京:人民文学出版社,2016. 8 册(4934 页):图;24cm. ISBN: 7020099160.(大中华文库)

德文题名:Djin Ping Meh

《今古奇观》(明代)

1. Wang Keaou Lwan pih neen chang han oder die blutige Rache der jungen Frau. Chinesische Erzählung/Pao-weng lao-jen; Tr. into German by Adolf Böttger. Tr. from the English version of Thom. R. Sloth. Leipzig: Verlag von Wilhelm Jurany, 1846. 111 S.

《王娇鸾百年长恨》,Böttger, Adolf 译自英文.

2. Die treulose Witwe. Eine chinesische Novelle. Deutsch nach dem Asiatic Journal MDCCCXLIII von Eduard Grisebach. Berlin: Verlag von F. & P. Lehmann, 1886. 37 S.

《庄子休鼓盆成大道》,Eduard Grisebach (1845—1906) 译.

(1)München: Hyperionverlag, 1921. 98 S.

3. Neue und alte Novellen der chinesischen 1001 Nacht/ deutsch von Eduard Grisebach. Stuttgart: Kröner, 1880. 1 vol. (XV—145 S.); In-8°

《今古奇观》选译,Grisebach, Eduard (1845—1906)译.

4. Das geheimnisvolle Bild und Anderes. Drei Novellen aus dem Chinesischen übersetzt von P. Kühnel. Berlin: Hugo Steinitz Verlag, 1902. 191 S.

《今古奇观》,Kühnel, Paul (1848—1924)译.

5. Chinesische Novellen/Dt. von Paul Kühnel. München: Müller,1914. XXIX, 367 S. (Meisterwerke orientalischer Literaturen in deutschen Originalübersetzungen. - München, 1913; Bd. 2)

《今古奇观》选译,Kühnel, Paul (1848—1924)译.

6. Der Gatte wider Willen: Chinesische Novellen aus dem Kin ku ki kwan/[aus dem Chinesischen übertragen von Paul Kühnel]. München: W. Goldmann, 1966. 164 pages; 18cm. (Goldmanns gelbe Taschenbücher; Bd. 1751)

《今古奇观》选译,Kühnel, Paul (1848—1924)译. 含《俞伯牙摔琴谢知音》.

7. Das Perlenhemd: Eine chinesische Liebesgeschichte/aus dem chinesischen Urtext übertragen von Franz Kuhn. Leipzig: Insel Verlag, 1928. 61 S. : illustrations; 18cm.
《蒋兴哥重会珍珠衫》,孔舫之(Kuhn, Franz, 1884—

1961)译.

(1)Leipzig: Insel-Verl. , 1948. 51 S. ; 8. (Insel-Bücherei; Nr. 216)

(2)Wiesbaden: Insel-Verl. , 1951. 49 S. ; 8. (Insel-Bücherei; Nr. 216)

(3)Wiesbaden: Insel-Verl. , 1953. 52 S. : mit Abb. ; 8. (Insel-Bücherei; Nr. 216)

(4)Wiesbaden: Insel-Verl. , 1956. 51 S. ; 8. (Insel-Bücherei; Nr. 216)

(5)Wiesbaden: Insel-Verl. , 1957. 52 S. : 1 Titelbild; kl. 8. (Insel-Bücherei; Nr. 216)

8. Das Juwelenkästchen/Aus d. Chines v. Franz Kuhn. Dresden: Heyne, 1937. 60 S. ; 8.

《杜十娘怒沉百宝箱》,孔舫之(Kuhn, Franz, 1884—1961)译.

9. Das Rosenaquarell: chinesische Novellen/übertragen von Franz Kuhn. Zürich: Verlag der Arche, 1947. 54 [2] pages; 20cm.

《今古奇观》选译,孔舫之(Kuhn, Franz, 1884—1961)译.

10. Kin Ku Ki Kwan. Wundersame Geschichten aus alter und neuer Zeit. Aus der Sammlung Jingu Qiguan/ Baoweng laoren; Franz Kuhn. Zürich: Manesse Verlag, 1952. 471 S.

《今古奇观》选集,孔舫之(Kuhn, Franz, 1884—1961)译.

11. Goldjunker Sung und andere Novellen aus dem Kin Ku Ki Kwan/Dt. von Franz Kuhn. Zürich: Manesse Verl. , 1960. 368 S. ; kl. 8.

《宋金郎团圆破毡笠》等,孔舫之(Kuhn, Franz, 1884—1961)译.

12. Wundersame Geschichten aus alter und neuer Zeit/Aus d. Chines. übertr. u. mit einem Nachwort versehen von Franz Kuhn. Aus der Sammlung Jingu Qiguan. Zürich: Manesse, 1971. 172 S.

《今古奇观》选译,孔舫之(Kuhn, Franz, 1884—1961)译.

13. Die gelben Orangen der Prinzessin Dschau/Aus d. chines. Urtext von Walter Strzoda. [Einbd. u. Titelumrahmung zeichn. Emil Preetorius]. München: Hyperion-Verlag, 1922. 292 S. ; kl. 8. (Der chinesischen Novellensammlung Djin-Gu Tji-Guan; Folge 1. Dichtungen des Ostens)

《赵县君乔送黄柑子》,Strzoda, Walter 译.

14. Der Ölhändler und die Blumenkönigin/ [Aus d. chin. Urtext übertr. von Walter Strzoda]. München: Hyperionverl. ,1920. 176 S. ;8. (Dichtungen des Ostens)

《卖油郎独占花魁》,抱瓮老人辑;Strzoda, Walter 译.

(1)München: Hyperion Verlag, 1923. 175 S; 8°.

15. Der Ölhändler und das Freudenmädchen. Eine chinesische Geschichte in fünf Gesängen. Aus der Sammlung Jingu Qiguan (Auszug)/Vincenz Hundhausen. Peking; Leipzig: Verlag der Pekinger Pappelinsel, 1940 (Copyright Pekinger

Verlag 1928）. 165 S.

《卖油郎独占花魁》，Hundhausen，Vincenz 译.

16. Der Liebespfeil：Eine Geschichte aus Gin Gu ki Guan/übers. v. Lin Tsiu-sen. Berlin：Gerlt，1938. 28 Blätter nach Art e. Blockbuches Illustrationen 8°

《今古奇观》一篇故事，Lin Tsiu-Sen 译.

17. Die seltsame Hochzeitsfahrt：2 chines. Novellen aus alter Zeit；Mit 3 chines. Miniaturen；Aus d. Urtexten/übertr. v. Anna von Rottauscher. Wien：Frick，1941. 77 S.；8. （Wiener Bücherei；Bd. 14）

《今古奇观》选文两篇，Rottauscher，Anna 译.

18. Chinesisches Novellenbuch. Kin Ku Ki Kuan/Pao-weng lao-jen；Eduard Grisebach. Basel：Verlag Birkhäuser，1945. 228 S.

《今古奇观》选译，Grisebach，Eduard 译.

19. Blumenzauber：Eine chinesische Novelle mit 11 alten Holzschn/[Die Übers. leisteten Tsou Ping Shou u. Leo Greiner，eine letzte Red. Felix M. Wiesner] Zürich：Verl. Die Waage，1953. 78 S；8.„.

《今古奇观》选译，Tsou Ping Shou 和 Greiner，Leo（1876—1928）合译.

（1）2. Aufl. Zürich：Verlag Die Waage，1979. 78 S.：11 ill. ISBN：3859660020，3859660021

20. Das chinesische Dekameron/ Aus d. Chines. von Johanna Herzfeldt. Rudolstadt：Greifenverl.，1957. 345 S.：mit Abb.；8.

《今古奇观》选译，Johanna Herzfeldt（1957—）译.

（1）Frankfurt a. M.；Wien；Zürich：Büchergilde Gutenberg，1963. 363 S.：mit Abb.；8.

（2）[Aus d. Chines. von Johanna Herzfeldt. Mit 22 Ill. von Horst Hausotte] 3. Aufl. Rudolstadt：Greifenverl. VEB，1968. 289 S.；8.

（3）übers. von Johanna Herzfeldt. Mit Bildern von Mehrdad Zaeri. Frankfurt，M.；Wien；Zürich：Büchergilde Gutenberg，2008. 292 S.：Ill.；25cm. ISBN：3763259090；3763259106

21. Altchinesische Erzählungen aus dem Djin-gu tji-gwan. Übersetzung aus dem Chinesischen und Nachwort von Gottfried Rösel. Mit 13 zeitgenössischen Illustrationen. Zürich：Manesse Verlag，1984. 696 S. ISBN：3717580353；3717580355.

《今古奇观》，Rösel，Gottfried（1900—1992）译.

青心才人（明末清初）

1. Eisvogelfeder - ein Frauenleben：e. Roman d. frühen Mandschu-Zeit = Kin-yün-kiao-tschuan/Tsing-sin Tsai-jen. Zum ersten Male aus d. Chines. ins Dt. übers.，mit Erkl. u. e. Nachw. vers. von F. K. Engler. Zürich：Verl. Die Waage，1988. 383 S.：Ill.；20cm. ISBN：3859660557，3859660551

《金云翘》，青心才人（明末清初）著；Engler，F. K. 译.

《捉鬼传》（又名《平鬼传》）

1. Dschung-Kuei：Bezwinger der Teufel/Claude du Bois-Reymond [Übers.]. Potsdam：G. Kiepenheuer，1923. 280 S.；8.

《捉鬼传》，清初樵云山人；Du Bois-Reymond，Claude 译.

（1）Dschung Kue oder Der Bezwinger der Teufel/[übertr. nach d. chin. Orig. von Claude du Bois-Reymond. Durchges. von John Hefter]. Berlin；Leipzig [O 5，Reclamstr. 42]：S. Fischer Verl. 1936. 325 S.；8.

（2）Dschung Kuei，Bezwinger der Teufel：altchines. Volksbuch；[d. neunte Meisterwerk]/[dt. von Clemens du Bois-Reymond]. Weimar：Kiepenheuer，1977. 252 S.：Ill.；20cm.

（3）2. Aufl.，[6. - 12. Tsd.]. Leipzig，Weimar：Kiepenheuer，1978. 252 S.；20cm.

（4）Zhong Kui，Bezwinger der Teufel：altchines. Volksbuch/[aus d. Chines. von Clemens du Bois-Reymond. Der Beitr. von O. L. Fischman wurde von R. Beer aus d. Russ. übertr.]. Leipzig；Weimar：Kiepenheuer，1987. 277 S.：Ill.；21cm. ISBN：3378001435，3378001437.

（5）Zhong Kui，Bezwinger der Teufel：altchinesisches Volksbuch/aus dem Chinesischen von Clemens du Bois-Reymond. München：C. H. Beck，1987. 277 pages：illustrations；21cm. ISBN：3406317561，3406317569. （Orientalische Bibliothek）（6）Dschung Kue oder Der Bezwinger der Teufel. Paderborn：Sarastro，2012. 332 S.；210 mm×148 mm. ISBN：3864710452，3864710456

李渔（1611—1680）

1. Der Turm der fegenden Wolken：Altchinesische Novellen/Aus d. Chinesischen übertr. von Franz Kuhn. Freiburg i. Br.：Klemm，1951. 557 S.；8.

《拂云楼》，孔舫之（Kuhn，Franz，1884—1961）译.

（1）2. veränd. Aufl. Freiburg i. Br.：Klemm，1958. 324 S.；8.

（2）München：Goldmann，1965. 309 S.；kl. 8. （Goldmanns gelbe Taschenbücher；Bd. 1565/66）

（3）Frankfurt am Main：Insel-Verlag，1975. 427 S.：Ill.；18cm. ISBN：3458018629，345801862X. （Insel-Taschenbuch；162）

（4）2. Aufl. Frankfurt：Insel Verlag，1978. 428 S：Ill. （Insel-Taschenbuch；162）

（5）Frankfurt am Main：Insel-Verlag，1981. 427 S.：Ill.；18cm. ISBN：3458318620，3458318623. （Insel-Taschenbuch；162）

2. Altchinesische Liebesgeschichten：4 Turmnovellen aus d. Sammlung Schi örl loh/[Li Yü]. Übertr. von Franz Kuhn. München Heyne，1961. 154 S. kl. 8. （Heyne Bücher；Nr. 136）

《十二楼》，孔舫之（Kuhn，Franz，1884—1961）译.

3. Die vollkommene Frau：das chines. Schönheitsideal/Yü Li. übers. u. eingel. v. Wolfram Eberhard. Zürich：Verl. Die Waage, 1963. 135 S.；Mit 20 Holzschn.；8.
完美女性：中国理想美人. Eberhard, Wolfram 译.
   (1) Zürich：Verl. Die Waage, 1985. 135 S.；19cm. ISBN：3859660205, 3859660209.
   (2) Leipzig；Weimar：Kiepenheuer, 1990. 135 S.；20 Ill.；17cm. ISBN：3378003309, 3378003308

4. Jou pu tuan：ein erotisch-moralischer Roman aus der Ming-Zeit（1634）/Deutsch von Franz Kuhn. 2. Aufl. Zürich：Verlag Die Waage, 1959. 636 pages：illustrations（woodcuts）；20cm.
《肉蒲团》,孔舫之（Kuhn, Franz, 1884—1961）译.
   (1) Hamburg：Verlag die Waage, 1965. 639 pages；20cm.
   (2) Brugg［Switzerland］：Fackelverlag, 1972. 643 pages：illustrations；20cm.
   (3) Frankfurt a. M.；Wien；Zürich：Büchergilde Gutenberg, 1977. 568 Seiten：Illustrationen；21cm. ISBN：3763221417, 3763221417, 3763221417
   (4) Ungekürzte Ausg. Frankfurt am Main：Fischer Taschenbuch, 1979. 461 pages；illustrations；18cm. ISBN：3596224519, 3596224517. （Fischer Taschenbücher）
   (5) Stuttgart；Hamburg；München：Dt. Bücherbund, 1980. 566 S.；Ill.
   (6) Frankfurt am Main：Fischer-Taschenbuch-Verlag, 1986. 461 Seiten：60 Illustrationen；18cm. ISBN：3596224519, 3596224517. （Fischer-Taschenbücher；2451）
   (7) Frankfurt/M.；Berlin：Ullstein, 1989. 599 Seiten：14 Illustrationen；20cm. ISBN：3550066856, 3550066856, 3550066341, 3550066344. （Im Reich der Sinne；Bd. 1）
   (8) 4. Aufl. Braunschweig Verl. Die Waage, 1995. 671 Seiten Illustrationen 20cm. ISBN：3859660624, 3859660625

5. Jou p'u-t'uan：ein chinesischer erotischer Roman/mit e. Einl. von U. L. G. Zibet. Hamburg：Bell, 1987. 400 S. ISBN：3923308221, 3923308224. （Hua-ying chin-chen；1）
《肉蒲团》,Zibet, U. L. 译.

6. Das lautlose Theater des Li Yu（um 1655）：eine Novellensammlung der frühen Qing-Zeit/von Stephan Pohl. Walldorf-Hessen：Verlag für Orientkunde Dr. H. Vorndran, 1994. 274 pages；illustrations；21cm. （Beiträge zur Sprach- und Kulturgeschichte des Orients；；Bd. 33）
《无声戏》,Pohl, Stephan 译.

7. Der schönste Knabe aus Peking：vier Novellen aus der frühen Qing-Zeit/Li Liweng；zusammengestellt und übersetzt von Martin Gimm und Helmut Martin. Dortmund：Projekt, 1995. 138 pages；21cm. ISBN：392886145X, 3928861458. （Arcus Chinatexte,；Bd. 7）
李渔中短篇小说四篇.Gimm, Martin（1930—）和 Martin, Helmut（1940—2000）合译.

蒲松龄（1640—1715）

1. Chinesische Geister- und Liebesgeschichten/［Sung-ling P'u. übers.；Martin Buber］. Frankfurt a. M.：Rütten & Loening, 1911. 187 S.
鬼和爱情故事. Buber, Martin（1878—1965）译.
   (1) Frankfurt a. M.：Rütten & Loening, 1920. XV, 188 S.；8.
   (2) Zürich：Manesse-Verl., 1948. 339 S.；mit Abb.；8. （Manesse-Bibliothek der Weltliteratur）
   (3) 9. Aufl. Zürich：Manesse-Verl., 1986. 337 S.；Ill.；16cm. ISBN：3717510642, 3717510649, 3717510659, 3717510657. （Manesse-Bibliothek der Weltliteratur）
   (4) München：Dt. Taschenbuch-Verl. - Zürich：Manesse-Verl., 1992. 337 S.；Ill.；15cm. ISBN：3423240048；3423240040. （dtv；24004：Manesse im dtv）
   (5) München：Dt. Taschenbuch-Verl. - Zürich：Manesse-Verl., 1993. 337 S.；Ill.；15cm. ISBN：3423240048；3423240040. （dtv；24004：Manesse im dtv）
   (6) 10. Aufl. Zürich：Manesse-Verl., 1993. 337 S.；Ill.；16cm. ISBN：3717510642, 3717510649, 3717510659, 3717510657. （Manesse-Bibliothek der Weltliteratur）
   (7) München：Dt. Taschenbuch-Verl. - Zürich：Manesse-Verl., 1994. 337 S.；Ill.；15cm. ISBN：3423240048；3423240040. （dtv；24004：Manesse im dtv）

2. Chinesische Geistergeschichten（illustriert）：Chinesische Geister- und Liebesgeschichten/Martin Buber. Köln Anaconda Verlag, 2015. 256 S. 187 mm × 122 mm. ISBN：3730602409, 3730602403
中国鬼及爱情故事. Buber, Martin（1878—1965）译.

3. Seltsame geschichten：aus dem Liao chai/Pú Sung-Ling. Berlin, A. Häger［c1924］. 216 S.；plates.；18cm.
《聊斋志异》,Schmitt, Erich（1893—1955）译.

4. Liau-Dsai-Dschi-I：seltsame chinesische Erzählungen/übertr. von Pung-Fai Tao. Breslau：Priebatsch's Buchh., 1935. 61 S.；8.
《聊斋志异》, Tao, Pung-Fai 译.

5. Irrlicht und Morgenröte：fünf chinesische Erzählungen/［Aus dem Chines. ins Deutsche übertr. von Anne von Rottauscher］. Zürich Verl. die Waage, 1955. 132 Seiten Illustrationen. ISBN：385966008X, 3859660083
《聊斋志异》选译. Rottauscher, Anna von（1892—1970）译.选译了《聊斋志异》中的五个故事选.

6. Gaukler，Füchse und Dämonen/P'u Sung-ling. Aus d. Chines. übertr. von E. P. Schrock u. Liu Guan-ying. Basel：Schwabe，1955. 231 S.；8.（Sammlung Klosterberg. N. F.）

《聊斋志异》，Schrock，E. P. 和 Liu，Guanying 合译.

7. Höllenrichter Lu：Chinesische Gespenster- und Fuchsgeschichten/P'u Sung-Ling. Aus d. Chines. von Irmgard u. Reinhold Grimm. Eisenach；Kassel：Röth，1956. 112 S.；8.

《陆判》，Grimm，Irmgard 和 Grimm，Reinhold 合译. 选自《聊斋志异》.

8. Liao-chai chih-i. Chinesische Geschichten aus dem 17. Jahrhundert/Ausgew. und übers. von Kai Yeh. Mit einem Vorwort von Werner Eichhorn. Stuttgart：Reclam，1965. 103 S.；kl. 8.（Unesco-Sammlung repräsentativer Werke.；Asiatische Reihe）

《聊斋志异》，Ye，Kai 译.

9. Chinesische Gespenstergeschichten/Herausgegeben und übersetzt von Adrian Baar. Frankfurt am Main：Fischer-Taschenbuch-Verlag，1975. 126 S.；Ill.；18cm. ISBN：3436021709，3436021702.（Fischer-Taschenbücher；1653）

中国鬼故事. Baar，Adrian（1927—）译.

(1) Frankfurt（am Main）：Fischer-Taschenbuch-Verlag，1976. 126 S.；Ill.；；18cm. ISBN：3436021709，3436021702.（Fischer-Taschenbücher；1653）

(2) Frankfurt（am Main）：Fischer-Taschenbuch-Verlag，1979. 126 S.；Ill.；；18cm. ISBN：3596216536，3596216532.（Fischer-Taschenbücher；1653）

10. Das Wandbild：Chinesische Liebesgeschichten aus dieser und der anderen Welt/Aus dem Chinesischen übertragen von Gottfried Rösel. Frankfurt am Main：Fischer Taschenbuch Verlag，1982. 187 S. ISBN：3596280060，3596280063.

《聊斋志异》，Rösel，Gottfried（1900—1992）译.

11. Fräulein Lotosblume：Chinesische Liebesgeschichten/Pu，Songling. Gottfried Rösel（übers.）. Frankfurt am Main：Fischer Verlag，1982. 155 S.

中国爱情故事. Rösel，Gottfried（1900—1992）译.

12. Umgang mit Chrysanthemen：81 Erzählungen d. ersten 4 Bücher aus d. Sammlung Liao-dschai-dschi-yi/Pu Sung-ling. Dt. von Gottfried Rösel. Zürich：Verl. Die Waage，1987. 619 S.；Ill.；20cm. ISBN：3859660535，3859660533.（Pu，Songling：Liao-dschai-dschi-yi；1）.

《聊斋志异》第 1 至 4 卷. Rösel，Gottfried（1900—1992）译.

13. Zwei Leben im Traum：67 Erzählungen der Bände 5 bis 8 aus der Sammlung Liao-dschai-dschi-yi/Pu Sungling. Dt. von Gottfried Rösel. Zürich：Verl. Die Waage，1989. 576 S.；Ill.；20cm. ISBN：3859660540，3859660543.（Pu，Songling：Liao-dschai-dschi-yi；2）

《聊斋志异》第 5 至 8 卷. Rösel，Gottfried（1900—1992）

译.

14. Besuch bei den Seligen. 86 Erzählungen der Bände neun bis zwölf aus der Sammlung Liao-dschai-dschi-yi. Deutsch von Gottfried Rösel. Zürich：Verl. Die Waage，1991. 600 S.；Ill.；20cm. ISBN：3859660588，3859660586.（Pu，Songling：Liao-dschai-dschi-yi；3）.

《聊斋志异》第 9 至 12 卷. Rösel，Gottfried（1900—1992）译.

15. Schmetterlinge fliegen lassen. 158 Erzählungen der Bände dreizehn bis fünfzehn aus der Sammlung Liao-dschai-dschi-yi. Deutsch von Gottfried Rösel. Zürich：Verl. Die Waage，1992. 543 S.；Ill.；20cm. ISBN：3859660595，3859660594.（Pu，Songling：Liao-dschai-dschi-yi；4）.

《聊斋志异》第 13 至 15 卷. Rösel，Gottfried（1900—1992）译.

16. Kontakte mit Lebenden. 109 Erzählungen der letzten beiden Bücher sechzehn und siebzehn aus der Sammlung Liao-dschai-dschi-yi. Mit dem ausführlichen Überblick über die Sachthemen des Gesamtwerks. Deutsch von Gottfried Rösel. Zürich：Verl. Die Waage，1992. 304 S.；Ill.；20cm. ISBN：3859660601，3859660608.（Pu，Songling：Liao-dschai-dschi-yi；5）.

《聊斋志异》第 16 至 17 卷. Rösel，Gottfried（1900—1992）译.

17. In der Stunde des Ochsen：Liebesgeschichten über die Geister aus Japan und China/herausgegeben von Olga Rinne. Originalausg. Darmstadt：Luchterhand，1983. 189 S. ISBN：3472614811，3472614814.（Sammlung Luchterhand；481）

中国爱情故事. Rinne，Olga 译.

18. Gast Tiger/von P'u Sung-Ling. Mit e. Vorw. von Jorge Luis Borges.［Dt. übers. von Maria Bamberg. Aus d. Chines. ins Engl. übers. von Herbert Allen Giles，aus d. Engl. von Angelika Hildebrandt-Essig…］. Stuttgart：Edition Weitbrecht，1984. 97 S.；23cm. ISBN：3522712102，3522712101.（Die Bibliothek von Babel；Bd. 21）

《聊斋志异》，Giles，Herbert Allan 译.

19. Gast Tiger：Erzählungen/P'u Sung-Ling；mit einem Vorwort von Jorge Luis Borges；［aus dem Englischen von Angelika Hildebrandt］. Frankfurt，M.：Ed. Büchergilde，2007. 101 S.；23cm. ISBN：3940111210，394011121X.（Die Bibliothek von Babel；Bd. 21）

《聊斋志异》（选译），Borges，Jorge Luis（1899—1986）译.

(1) Frankfurt am Main：Ed. Büchergilde，2008. 101 Seiten. ISBN：394011121X，3940111210.（Die Bibliothek von Babel：eine Sammlung phantastischer Literatur/hrsg. von Jorge Luis Borges；［21]）

20. Gast Tiger：Erzählungen/P'u Sung-Ling；mit einem Vorw. von Jorge Luis Borges；［aus dem Chines. von

Maria Bamberg... et al.]. Frankfurt a. M.；Zürich：Büchergilde Gutenberg, 2007. 99 S.；23cm. ISBN：3763258215, 3763258213. (Die Bibliothek von Babel；Bd. 21)

《聊斋志异》，Bamberg，Maria 等译.

吴敬梓（1701—1754）

1. Der Weg zu den weissen Wolken：Geschichten aus dem Gelehrtenwald/Wu Djing-Dsi. Weimar：Kiepenheuer, 1962. 1201 S.

《儒林外史》，Yang，En-lin 和 Schmitt，Gerhard 合译.

(1) Der Weg zu den weißen Wolken：Geschichten aus dem Gelehrtenwald/Wu Djing-dsi. [Aus d. Chines. übers. von Yang En-lin u. Gerhard Schmitt. Stilist. überarb. von Noa Kiepenheuer u. Friedrich Minckwitz]. Weimar：Kiepenheuer, 1976. 831 S.

(2) Leipzig u. a.：Kiepenheuer, 1989. 2 Bde (529, 451 S.)：ill. ISBN：3378002999 (v. 1), 3378002999 (v. 1), 3378003006 (v. 2), 3378003002 (v. 2). (Orientalische Bibliothek)

(3) München：Beck, 1990. 2 Bde (529, 451 S.)：ill.；21cm. ISBN：3406335934, 3406335938. (Orientalische Bibliothek)

2. Ru lin wai shi = Der Weg zu den weissen Wolken：Geschichten aus dem Gelehrtenwald/(Qing) Wu Jing zi zhu；Yang En lin, Gerhard Schmitt De yi；Noa Kiepenheuer, Friedrich Minckwitz shen jiao. Beijing, China：Verlag für fremdsprachige Literatur, 2015. 3 Bände；24cm. ISBN：7119094106. (Bibliothek der chinesischen Klassiker)

《儒林外史》，杨恩霖，（德）施密特（Schmitt，Gerhard）德译. 外文出版社（大中华文库）

曹雪芹（约 1715—1763）

1. Der Traum der roten Kammer：[Ein Roman aus d. frühen Tsing-Zeit]/[Tsao Hsüe Kin]. Aus d. Chines. übertr. von Kuhn, Franz. Leipzig：Insel-Verl., 1932. 788 S.：1 Taf.；8

《红楼梦》，孔舫之（Kuhn，Franz，1884—1961）译.

(1) Leipzig：Insel-Verl., 1941. 793 S.：1 Taf.；8

(2) Leipzig：Insel-Verl., 1948. 796 S.；8

(3) Wiesbaden：Insel-Verl., 1951. 793 S.：1 Faltbl.；8

(4) Wiesbaden：Insel-Verl., 1952. 793 S.：1 Faltbl.；8

(5) Wiesbaden：Insel-Verl., 1956. 859 S.：mit Abb., 1 Faltbl.；8

(6) Wiesbaden：Insel-Verl., 1959. 839 S.：mit Abb., 1 Faltbl.；8

(7) Frankfurt a. M.：Insel-Verl., 1965. 839 S.：mit Abb., 1 Faltbl.；8.

(8) 5. Auflage. Der Traum der roten Kammer：ein Roman aus d. Mandschu-Zeit/[Ts'ao Hsüeh-ch'in；kao O. Aus d. Chines. von Kuhn, Franz. Nachw. von Eva Müller]. Leipzig：Insel-Verlag, 1971. 867 S.：Ill.；；20cm.

(9) Berlin, Darmstadt, Wien：Dt. Buch-Gemeinschaft, 1973. 839 S.：Ill.；；21cm.

(10) Leipzig：Insel-Verlag, 1974. 867 S.：34 Ill.；；20cm. (Bibliothek der Weltliteratur)

(11) Frankfurt, Main：Insel-Verlag, 1977. 2 volumes

(12) Bukarest：Kriterion-Verlag, 1982. 2 volumes；19cm.

(13) Frankfurt (Main)：Insel-Verlag, 1985. 2 volumes

(14) Frankfurt a. M.：Insel-Verl., 1986. 831 S.：Ill.；18cm. ISBN：3458319924, 3458319921. (Insel-Taschenbuch；292)

(15) Frankfurt a. M.：Insel-Verl., 1987. 831 S.：Ill.；18cm. ISBN：3458319924, 3458319921. (Insel-Taschenbuch；292)

(16) Frankfurt a. M.：Insel-Verl., 1989. 831 S.：Ill.；18cm. ISBN：3458319924, 3458319921. (Insel-Taschenbuch；292)

(17) Frankfurt (Main)：Insel-Verl., 1990. 839 S.：Ill.；21cm. ISBN：3458154143, 3458154140.

(18) Der Traum der roten Kammer/[Tsao Hsüe Kin；Kao O]. Aus dem Chines. von Kuhn, Franz. Frankfurt (Main)；Leipzig：Insel-Verl., 1995. 831 S.：Ill.；18cm. ISBN：3458334729, 3458334726. (Insel-Taschenbuch；1772)

2. Der Traum der roten Kammer：e. Roman aus d. frühen Tsing-Zeit/[Verf.：Tsao Hsühe Kin；Kao O]. Aus d. Chines. übertr. von Franz Kuhn；mit Bildern von Gabriele Kuhnke. [Frankfurt a. M.]：Büchergilde Gutenberg, 1980. 682 Seiten：25 Illustrationen. ISBN：3763223681, 3763223688

《红楼梦》，孔舫之（Kuhn，Franz，1884—1961）译.

3. Der Traum der roten Kammer, oder, Die Geschichte vom Stein/Tsau Hsühä-tjin；aus dem Chines. übers. von Rainer Schwarz... [et al.]. Berlin：Europäischer Universitätsverlag, 2006—2009. 3 Teilbände：Ill. ISBN：3865150103, 3865150101, 3865150110, 386515011X, 3865150127, 3865150128, 3865150134, 3865150136. (Sinica；14)

《红楼梦》，Schwarz，Rainer 等译. 3 卷.

(1) 2. Auflage. Berlin：Europäischer Universitätsverlag, 2010. 2176, xx pages：illustrations；21cm. ISBN：3899665000, 3899665007. (Sinica；14)

(2) 3., ungekürzte Ausgabe, 3. überarbeitete Neuauflage, revidierte Ausgabe. Bochum Europäischer Universitätsverlag, 2016. 4813 Seiten in 6 Teilen 24cm. × 16cm. ISBN：3865150592, 3865150594

4. Geschichten aus dem Traum der Roten Kammer/[Cao Xueqin. übers.：Tan Lei... Dt. Bearb.：Michael Behrendt und Loredana Addesso]. Beijing：Verl. für Fremdsprachige Literatur, 2011. 214 S.：Ill.；23cm., 322 g. ISBN：7119072357, 7119072358.

《红楼梦》，谭蕾译. 汉德对照.

5. Hong lou meng = Der Traum der roten Kammer oder Die Geschichte vom Stein/Cao Xue qin, Gao E；übers. v. Rainer Schwarz und Martin Woesler. Beijing：China Verlag für fremdsprachige Literatur，2015. 6 Bänden 24cm. ISBN：7119094120，7119094122. (Bibliothek der chinesischen Klassiker)

《红楼梦》，6 卷本. 施瓦茨（Schwarz，Rainer），吴漠汀（Woesler，Martin)译. 外文出版社（大中华文库). 汉德对照.

纪昀（1724—1805）

1. Pinselnotizen aus der Strohhütte der Betrachtung des Grossen im Kleinen；Kurzgeschichten u. Anekdoten/Ji Yun. [Aus d. Chines. übertr.，ausgew. u. hrsg. von Konrad Herrmann]. Leipzig：Kiepenheuer，1983. 500 S.；20cm.

《阅微草堂笔记》，Herrmann，Konrad 译.

李汝珍（1763—1830）

1. Im Land der Frauen：ein altchin. Roman/Ju-tschen Li. Aus d. Chin. übers. v. F. K. Engler. Zürich：Verl. Die Waage，1970. 192 S.：Mit 8 Holzschn.；8.

《镜花缘》，Engler，F. K. 译.

(1)Leipzig：Insel-Verl.，1977. 139 S.：8 Ill.；21cm.

(2)Ungekürzte Ausg. Frankfurt am Main：Fischer-Taschenbuch-Verl.，1980. 120 S.；18cm. ISBN：3596224784，3596224780. (Fischer；2478)

2. Die Pagode der hundert Mädchen：erot. Roman aus d. alten China/Li Yu-chen. München：Heyne，1982. 221 S.；18cm. ISBN：3453502581，3453502582

艳情小说.

石玉昆（约公元 1856 年前后在世）

1. Richter und Retter：Roman aus d. Sung-Zeit/Aus d. Chines. übers. von Peter Hüngsberg. Mödling b. Wien：St. Gabriel-Verl.，1964. 291 S.：Mit 8 chines. Original-Ill.；8.

《三侠五义》. Hüngsberg，Peter 译.

(1)Luzern：Schweizer Volks-Buchgemeinde，1967. 288 S.

文康（道光初年至光绪初年在世）

1. Die schwarze Reiterin：Roman/Wen Kang. Aus d. Chines. verdt. von Kuhn，Franz. Zürich：Manesse Verl.，1954. 954 S.；kl. 8. (Manesse Bibliothek der Weltliteratur)

《儿女英雄传》，孔舫之（Kuhn，Franz，1884—1961)译.

(1) Frankfurt am Main：Insel-Verlag，1980. 706 S.：Ill.；18cm. ISBN：3458321743，3458321748. (Insel-Taschenbuch；474)

(2) 2. Auflage.. Frankfurt am Main：Insel-Verlag，1985. 709 S.：Ill.；18cm. ISBN：3458321743，3458321748. (Insel-Taschenbuch；474)

(3) 3. Auflage. Frankfurt am Main：Insel-Verlag，1986. 709 S.；18cm. ISBN：3458321743，3458321748. (Insel-Taschenbuch；474)

刘鹗（1857—1909）

1. Die Reisen des Lao Can：Roman aus dem alten China/Liu E. Aus d. Chines. übertr. von Hans Kühner. Mit e. Nachw. vers. von Helmut Martin. Frankfurt am Main：Insel-Verl.，1989. 481 S.；21cm. ISBN：3458160519，3458160515.

《老残游记》，Kühner，Hans 译.

李伯元（1867—1906）

1. Das Haus zum gemeinsamen Glück/Boyuan Li. [Aus d. Chines. übers. von Marianne Liebermann u. Werner Bettin. Mit e. Nachw. von Werner Bettin]. Berlin：Rütten & Loening，1964. 636 S.；8.

《官场现行记》，Liebermann，Marianne 和 Bettin，Werner 合译.

2. Wen-ming hsiao-shih，eine Prosasatire vom Ende der Ch'ing-Zeit. Erlangen，Nürnberg，Univ.，Diss.，1982. XX，501 S.；21cm.

《文明小史》，Gast，Otto 译.

《豆棚闲话》

1. „Doupeng xianhua" —Plaudereien unter der Bohnenlaube. Ein Novellenzyklus aus der frühen Qing-Zeit. Herausgeber：Mekle，Gudrun Christhilde. Bochum：Ruhr-Universität Bochum，1990.

《豆棚闲话》，(清)圣水艾衲居士.

《二度梅》（清代）

1. Die Rache des jungen Meh oder Das Wunder der zweiten Pflaumenblüte：Roman/Aus d. Chines. übertr. von Franz Kuhn. Zürich：Verl. d. Arche，1949. 303 S.；8.

《二度梅》，惜阴堂主人编；孔舫之（Kuhn，Franz，1884—1961)译.

(1)Graz；Wien；München：Stiasny，1951. 303 S.；8. Anmerkungen：Lizenz d. Verl. „Die Arche"，Zürich.

(2)Stuttgart：Stuttgarter Hausbücherei，1957. 315 S.；8.

(3)Frankfurt a. M.；Hamburg：Fischer Bücherei，1959. 212 S.；kl. 8. (Fischer Bücherei；287)

(4)2. Aufl. Leipzig：Insel-Verlag，1976. 294 S.；20cm.

(5) Frankfurt am Main：Insel-Verlag，1978. 271 S.；18cm. ISBN：3458320531，3458320539. (Insel-Taschenbuch；353)

(6)2. Aufl. Frankfurt am Main：Insel-Verlag，1984. 271 S.；18cm.

(7)3. Aufl. Frankfurt am Main：Insel-Verlag，1985. 271 S.；18cm.

《杏花天》（清代）

1. Aprikosenblütenhimmel：erotischer Roman über die Schlafzimmerkunst aus China/[Ku-t'ang T'ien-fang Tao-jen]. Ins Dt. übertr. und hrsg. von F. K. Engler. München：Heyne，1984. 303 S.：Ill.；18cm. ISBN：3453503083；3453503082. (Heyne-Bücher/16/Exquisit-Bücher；Nr. 339)

《杏花天》，(清)古棠天放道人著；Engler，F. K. (1934—

1990)译.

《狄公案》系列

1. Merkwürdige Kriminalfälle des Richters Di/Aus dem Chinesischen übersetzt und erläutert von R. H. van Gulik；[Aus. d. Engl. ins Dt. übers. v. Gretel u. Kurt Kuhn]. Zürich：Verlag die Waage，1960. 378 pages：illustrations；20cm.

《狄公案》，高罗佩（Gulik，Robert Hans van，1910—1967）（荷兰汉学家）翻译并创作；Kuhn，Gretel 和 Kuhn，Kurt 从英语转译成德语. 英文题名：Dee goong an

   (1) Merkwürdige Kriminalfälle des Richters Di：Ein altchines. Kriminalroman/[Aus d. Chines. übers. u. erl. von R. H. van Gulik. Aus d. Engl. ins Dt. übers. von Gretel u. Kurt Kuhn]. München Zürich Droemer/Knaur，1964. 229 S. mit Abb. kl. 8. (Knaur-Taschenbücher；46)

   (2) Merkwürdige Kriminalfälle des Richters Di：ein altchinesischer Detektivroman/[aus dem Chinesischen übersetzt und erläutert von R. H. van Gulik；aus dem Englischen ins Deutsche übersetzt von Gretel und Kurt Kuhn]. Frankfurt am Main：Fischer Taschenbuch，1980. 251 pages：illustrations；18cm. ISBN：3596224756，3596224753. (Fischer Taschenbücher；2475)

   (3) Merkwürdige Kriminalfälle des Richters Di：Detektivroman um e. altchines. Sherlock Holmes/[aus d. Chines. übers. u. erl. von Robert H. van Gulik. Aus d. Engl. ins Dt. übers. von Gretel u. Kurt Kuhn]. Neuausg. Frankfurt am Main Fischer-Taschenbuch-Verl，1987. 251 S. Ill. 18cm. ISBN：3596282527，3596282524. (Fischer；8252)

   (4) Frankfurt am Main：Fischer-Taschenbuch-Verlag，1988. 251 S. ；Ill. ；18cm. ISBN：3596282524，3596282527. (Fischer；8252)

   (5) [3. Aufl.]. Zürich：Diogenes，2006. 378 S. ISBN：3257230141，3257230147. (Diogenes-Taschenbuch；23014)

2. Mord im Labyrinth：neue Kriminalfälle des Richters Di aus alten chinesischen Originalquellen entnommen/Robert van Gulik；mit 20 Zeichnungen des Autors in chinesischem Holzschnittstil；Deutsch [aus dem Englischen] von Dr. Roland Schacht. Zürich：Verlag Die Waage，1963. 312 pagina's：illustraties；20cm.

《迷宫案》，高罗佩（Gulik，Robert Hans van，1910—1967）（荷兰汉学家）翻译并创作. 英文题名：Chinese maze murders

   (1) Reinbek bei Hamburg：Rowohlt，1976. 244 S. 20 Ill. ，1 Kt. 19cm. ISBN：3499119986，3499119989. (Rororo；1998)

   (2) Erstausg. Zürich：Diogenes，1985. 311 S. Ill. 18cm. ISBN：3257213816，3257213812. (Diogenes-Taschenbuch；

23181)

   (3) Zürich：Diogenes，1988. 311 S. ；20 Ill. ；18cm.

3. Wunder in Pu-yang：Neue Kriminalfälle d. Richters Di，alten chines. Orig. -Quellen entnommen/Robert van Gulik. [Dt. von Roland Schacht]. Zürich：Verl. Die Arche，1964. 285 S. Ill. 20cm.

《狄公案之铜钟案》，高罗佩（Gulik，Robert Hans van，1910—1967）（荷兰汉学家）翻译并创作；Schacht，Roland 从英语转译成德语. 英文题名：The chinese bell murders

   (1) Zürich：Diogenes，1985. 285 S. ；Ill. ；18cm. ISBN：3257213829，3257213824. (Diogenes-Taschenbuch；21382)

   (2) [4. Aufl.]. Zürich：Diogenes，1990. 285 S；Ill. ISBN：3257213824，3257213829. (Diogenes-Taschenbuch；21382)

4. Tod im roten Pavillon：neue Kriminalfälle d. Richters Di/Robert van Gulik. [Dt. von Gretel u. Kurt Kuhn]. Zürich：Verl. Die Arche，1965. 200 S. Ill. 20cm.

《红亭记》，高罗佩（Gulik，Robert Hans van，1910—1967）（荷兰汉学家）翻译并创作. 英文题名：Red pavilion

   (1) Tod im roten Pavillon：Kriminalfälle d. Richters Di，alten chines. Orig. -Quellen entnommen/Robert van Gulik. Dt. von Gretel u. Kurt Kuhn. Mit 6 Ill. d. Autors in chines. Holzschnittstil. Zürich：Diogenes，1986. 194 S. 6 Ill. 18cm. ISBN：3257213832，3257213836. (Diogenes-Taschenbuch；21383)

5. Geisterspuk in Peng-lai：neue Kriminalfälle des Richters Di，alten chinesischen Originalquellen entnommen/Robert van Gulik；mit 10 Zeichnungen des Autors in chines. Holzschnittstil；[deutsch von Irma Silzer]. Zürich：Verlag Die Waage，1986. 216 Seiten：Illustrationen；20cm. ISBN：3859660527，3859660526

《狄公案之黄金案》，高罗佩（Gulik，Robert Hans van，1910—1967）（荷兰汉学家）翻译并创作. 英文题名：Chinese gold murders

   (1) Geisterspuk in Peng-lai：neue Kriminalfälle des Richters Di，alten chinesischen Originalquellen entnommen/Robert van Gulik；deutsch von Irma Silzer；mit 10 Ill. des Autors im chines. Holzschnittstil. [Lizenzausg.]. Zürich：Diogenes-Verlag，1988. 213 pages：illustrations；18cm. ISBN：325721622X，3257216226. (Diogenes-Taschenbuch；21622)

6. Mord in Kanton：Kriminalfälle d. Richters Di，alten chines. Orig. -Quellen entnommen/Robert van Gulik. Dt. von Klaus Schomburg. Mit 12 Ill. d. Autors im chines. Holzschnittstil. Zürich：Diogenes，1988. 245 S. ；12 Ill. ；18cm. ISBN：3257216233，3257216238. (Diogenes-Taschenbuch；21623)

《广州案》，高罗佩（Gulik，Robert Hans van，1910—1967）（荷兰汉学家）翻译并创作；Schomburg，Klaus 从英语转

译成德语. 英文题名：Murder in Canton.

7. Poeten und Mörder：Kriminalfälle d. Richters Di, alten chines. Orig.-Quellen entnommen/Robert van Gulik. Dt. von Ulrike Wasel u. Klaus Timmermann. Mit 8 Ill. d. Autors im chines. Holzschnittstil. Zürich：Diogenes, 1988. 196 S.：Ill.；18cm. ISBN：3257216660，3257216661. (Diogenes-Taschenbuch；21666)

《黑狐狸》，高罗佩(Gulik, Robert Hans van, 1910—1967)(荷兰汉学家)翻译并创作. 英文题名 Poets and murder

8. Der Affe und der Tiger：2 Kriminalfälle d. Richters Di, alten chines. Originalquellen entnommen/Robert van Gulik. Aus d. Engl. von Klaus Schomburg. Zürich：Diogenes, 1988. 151 S.：Ill.；18cm. ISBN：3257216240, 3257216246. (Diogenes-Taschenbuch；21624)

《断指记》和《汉家营》，转变译自英文，英文题名：Monkey and the tiger

9. Mord nach Muster：Kriminalfälle des Richters Di, alten chinesischen Originalquellen entnommen/Robert van Gulik. Zürich：Diogenes, 1989. 193 S.；18cm. ISBN：3257217674, 3257217676. (Diogenes-Taschenbuch；21767)

《柳园图》，高罗佩(Gulik, Robert Hans van, 1910—1967)(荷兰汉学家)翻译并创作；Wilck, Otto 转译成德文. 英文题名：The willow pattern

   (1)4. Aufl. Zürich：Diogenes, 1993. 193 S. ISBN：3257217676, 3257217674. (Diogenes-Taschenbuch；21767)

10. Die Perle des Kaisers：Kriminalfälle des Richters Di, alten chinesischen Originalquellen entnommen/Robert van Gulik. Zürich：Diogenes, 1989. 178 S.；18cm. ISBN：3257217667, 3257217668. (Diogenes-Taschenbuch；21766)

《御珠案》，高罗佩(Gulik, Robert Hans van, 1910—1967)(荷兰汉学家)翻译并创作. 转译自英文版，英文题名：Emperor's pearl

11. Das Phantom im Tempel：Kriminalfälle des Richters Di, alten chinesischen Originalquellen entnommen/Robert van Gulik. Zürich：Diogenes, 1989. 199 S.；18cm. ISBN：3257217681, 3257217684. (Diogenes-Taschenbuch；21768)

《紫光寺》，高罗佩(Gulik, Robert Hans van, 1910—1967)(荷兰汉学家)翻译并创作. 转译自英文版，英文题名：Phantom of the temple

12. Nächtlicher Spuk im Mönchskloster：Kriminalfälle des Richters Di, alten chinesischen Originalquellen entnommen/Robert van Gulik. Dt. von Gretel u. Kurt Kuhn. Zürich：Diogenes, 1990. 181 S.；18cm. ISBN：3257218664, 3257218664. (Diogenes-Taschenbuch；21866)

《朝云观谜案》，高罗佩(Gulik, Robert Hans van, 1910—1967)(荷兰汉学家)翻译并创作；Kuhn, Gretel 从英语转译成德语. 英文题名：The haunted monastery
   (1)Zürich：Diogenes, 1993. 181 S；Ill. ISBN：3257218664, 3257218664. (Diogenes-Taschenbuch；21866)

13. Der Wandschirm aus rotem Lack：Kriminalfälle des Richters Di, alten chinesischen Originalquellen entnommen/Robert van Gulik. Dt. von Gretel u. Kurt Kuhn. Zürich：Diogenes, 1990. 207 S.；18cm. ISBN：3257218671, 3257218672. (Diogenes-Taschenbuch；21867)

《四漆屏》，高罗佩(Gulik, Robert Hans van, 1910—1967)(荷兰汉学家)翻译并创作；Kuhn, Gretel 和 Kuhn, Kurt 从英语转译成德语.

14. Der See von Han-yuan：Kriminalfälle des Richters Di, alten chinesischen Originalquellen entnommen/Robert van Gulik. Dt. von Klaus Schomburg. Zürich：Diogenes, 1990. 258 S.：Ill., graph. Darst.；18cm. ISBN：3257219197, 3257219199. (Diogenes-Taschenbuch；21919)

《湖滨案》，高罗佩(Gulik, Robert Hans van, 1910—1967)(荷兰汉学家)翻译并创作. 转译自英文，英文题名：Chinese lake murders

15. Nagelprobe in Pei-tscho：Kriminalfälle des Richters Di, alten chinesischen Originalquellen entnommen/Robert van Gulik. Dt. von Klaus Schomburg. Zürich：Diogenes, 1990. 236 S.：Ill., graph. Darst.；18cm. ISBN：3257219203, 3257219202. (Diogenes-Taschenbuch；21920)

《铁钉案》，高罗佩(Gulik, Robert Hans van, 1910—1967)(荷兰汉学家)翻译并创作. 英文题名：Chinese nail murders

   (1)Hamburg：Zeitverl. Bucerius, 2010. 206 S.：Ill.；23cm. ISBN：3841900029.

16. Richter Di bei der Arbeit：Kurzgeschichten；8 Kriminalfälle des Richters Di, alten chinesischen Originalquellen entnommen/Robert van Gulik. Dt. von Klaus Schomburg. Zürich：Diogenes, 1990. 220 S.：Ill.；18cm. ISBN：3257219210, 3257219210. (Diogenes-Taschenbuch；21921)

《狄公奇案》八篇，高罗佩(Gulik, Robert Hans van, 1910—1967)(荷兰汉学家)翻译并创作；Schomburg, Klaus 译自英文.

   (1)Richter Di bei der Arbeit：Kurzgeschichten；acht Kriminalfälle des Richters Di, alten chinesischen Originalquellen entnommen/Robert van Gulik. Aus dem Engl. von Klaus Schomburg. Mit 8 Ill. des Autors im chinesischen Holzschnittstil. München：Süddt. Zeitung GmbH, 2006. 203 S.：Ill.；21cm. ISBN：3866152388, 3866152380. (Süddeutsche Zeitung Kriminalbibliothek；14)

17. Halskette und Kalebasse：Kriminalfälle des Richters Di, alten chinesischen Originalquellen entnommen/Robert van Gulik；dt. von Klaus Schomburg. Zürich：Diogenes, 2010. 177 S；Ill. ISBN：3257215199, 3257215193. (Diogenes-Taschenbuch；21519)

《玉珠串》，高罗佩(Gulik, Robert Hans van, 1910—1967)(荷兰汉学家)翻译并创作；Schomburg, Klaus 从英语转译成德语. 英文题名：Necklace and calabash

《株林野史》（创作年代不详）

1. Dschu-lin Yä-schi. Ein historisch-erotischer Roman aus der Ming-Zeit mit 26 Bildbeigaben/Zum ersten Male aus dem Chinesischen ins Deutsche übertragen von F. K. Engler. Mit Zeittafel und Anmerkungen sowie einem Nachwort von F. K. Engler und Felix M. Wiesner. Hamburg：Verlag Die Waage, 1971. 594 S. ; 8.
   《株林野史》，痴道人著；Engler, Friedrich K. (1934—1990)译.
   （1）Stuttgart：Europ. Bildungsgemeinschaft - Gütersloh：Bertelsmann - Wien：Buchgemeinschaft Donauland - Berlin, Darmstadt, Wien：Dt. Buchgemeinschaft, 1974. 381 S. : Ill. ; 19cm.
   （2）Stuttgart；München：Dt. Bücherbund, 1984. 399 S. : Ill.

2. Dschu-lin-yä-schi：e. erot. Roman aus d. Ming-Zeit mit erstaunl. taoist. Liebespraktiken/aus d. Chines. übers. von F. K. Engler. Frankfurt am Main：Fischer-Taschenbuch-Verlag, 1980. 252 S. : 12 Ill. ; 18cm. ISBN：3596224777; 3596224772. (Fischer；2477)
   《株林野史》，痴道人著；Engler, Friedrich K. (1934—1990)译.
   （1）Frankfurt a. M. : Fischer-Taschenbuch-Verlag, 1983. 252 S. : 12 Ill. ; 18cm. ISBN：3596224777; 3596224772. (Fischer；2477)
   （2）Frankfurt a. M. : Fischer-Taschenbuch-Verlag, 1986. 252 S. : 12 Ill. ; 18cm. ISBN：3596224777; 3596224772. (Fischer；2477)
   （3）Frankfurt/M. ; Berlin：Ullstein, 1989. 252 S. : 12 Ill. ; 18cm. ISBN：3550066887; 3550066880. (Im Reich der Sinne；Bd. 4)
   （4）Berlin：Aufbau-Taschenbuch-Verl. , 2000. 287 S. : Ill. ; 19cm. ISBN：3746616278; 3746616271. (Erotische Weltliteratur Aufbau-Taschenbücher；1627)

《好逑传》（明清）

1. Haoh kjöh tschwen, d. i. Die angenehme Geschichte des Haoh Kjöh：ein chinesischer Roman in vier Büchern/aus dem Chinesischen in das Englische, und aus diesem in das Deutsche übersetzt；nebst vielen Anmerkungen, mit dem Inhalte eines chinesischen Schauspiels, einer Abhandlung von der Dichtkunst, wie auch von den Sprüchwörtern der Chineser, und einem Versuche einer chinesischen Sprachlehre für die Deutschen [von Christoph Gottlieb von Murr]. Leipzig：J. F. Junius, 1766. xxx, 660, [10] pages; 13cm. ISBN：3598520093, 3598520099. (Bibliothek der deutschen Literatur；fiche 15010—15011)
   《好逑传》，Murr, Christoph Gottlieb von (1733—1811)译.

2. Tieh und Pinsing/Nach d. deutschen übers. v. C. G. Murr; Ein chines. Familien-Roman in fünf Büchern; Von Haoh Kjöh. Deutsche Säkular-Ausgabe. Bremen：

Kühlmann, 1869. XXX, 314 S. ; 8„.
《好逑传》，Murr, Christoph Gottlieb von (1733—1811)译.

3. Eisherz und Edeljaspis oder Die Geschichte einer glücklichen Gattenwahl：Ein Roman aus d. Ming-Zeit/[Ming-ch'iao-chung-jên]. Aus d. Chines. übertr. von Franz Kuhn. Gestaltg d. eingestreuten Verse von Albrecht Schaeffer. Leipzig：Insel-Verlag, 1926. 343 S. ; 8.
   《好逑传》，孔舫之 (Kuhn, Franz, 1884—1961)译.
   （1）Leipzig：Insel-Verlag, 1935. 343 S. ; 8.
   （2）Leipzig：Insel-Verlag, 1936. 369 S. ; 8.
   （3）Eisherz und Edeljaspis oder Die Geschichte einer glücklichen Gattenwahl：Ein Roman aus der Ming-Zeit. Mit 26 Holzschnitten einer alten chinesischen Ausgabe/[Aus d. Chin. übertr. von Franz Kuhn, Gestaltg d. Verse v. Albrecht Schaeffer]. Wiesbaden：Insel-Verlag, 1947. 381 S. ; 8.
   （4）Eisherz und Edeljaspis oder Die Geschichte einer glücklichen Gattenwahl：Ein Roman aus d. Ming-Zeit. Mit 26 Holzschn. e. alten chinesischen Ausg. / übers. : Franz Kuhn. Gestaltung d. Verse：Albrecht Schaeffer. Wiesbaden：Insel-Verlag, 1951. 367 S. ; 8.
   （5）Eisherz und Edeljaspis oder Die Geschichte einer glücklichen Gattenwahl：Ein Roman aus d. Ming-Zeit. Mit 26 Holzschn. e. alten chines. Ausg. / übertr. von Franz Kuhn. Wiesbaden：Insel-Verlag, 1958. 325 S. ; 8. Berlin：Verl. Kultur u. Fortschritt, 1958. 320 S. ; 8. Berlin；Darmstadt；Wien：Dt. Buchgemeinsch, 1958. 324 S. ; 8.
   （6）Eisherz und Edeljaspis oder Die Geschichte einer glücklichen Gattenwahl：Ein Roman aus d. Ming-Zeit/[Aus d. Chines.] übertr. von Franz Kuhn. 9. Aufl. Leipzig：Insel-Verlag, 1970. 337 S. : Mit 26 Holzschnitten e. alten chines. Ausg. ; 8.
   （7）Eisherz und Edeljaspis oder Die Geschichte einer glücklichen Gattenwahl. Ein Roman aus d. Ming-Zeit /Aus d. Chines. von Franz Kuhn. Mit e. Nachw. u. Anm. von Franz Kuhn. 1. Aufl. [Frankfurt (Main)]：Insel - [Frankfurt (Main)]：Suhrkamp-Taschenbuch-Verlag [in Komm.], 1975. 331 S. : 26 Ill. ;; 18cm. ISBN：3458018239. (Insel-taschenbuch；123)
   （8）Eisherz und Edeljaspis oder Die Geschichte einer glücklichen Gattenwahl：e. Roman aus d. Ming-Zeit/übertr. von Franz Kuhn. 1. Aufl. Leipzig；Weimar：Kiepenheuer, 1981. 333 S. : 26 Ill. ; 20cm. (Die Bücherkiepe)
   （9）Eisherz und Edeljaspis oder Die Geschichte einer glücklichen Gattenwahl：e. Roman aus d. Ming-Zeit/aus d. Chines. von Franz Kuhn. Mit e. Nachw. u. Anm. von Franz Kuhn. [Gestaltung d. Verse von

Albrecht Schaeffer] 2. Aufl. Frankfurt am Main：Insel，1984. 328 S.；26 Ill.；18cm. ISBN：3458318232.（Insel-taschenbuch；123）

(10) Eisherz und Edeljaspis oder Die Geschichte einer glücklichen Gattenwahl：e. Roman aus d. Ming-Zeit/ aus d. Chines. von Franz Kuhn. Mit e. Nachw. u. Anm. von Franz Kuhn.［Gestaltung d. Verse von Albrecht Schaeffer］. 3. Aufl. Frankfurt am Main：Insel，1985. 328 S.；26 Ill.；18cm. ISBN：3458318232.（Insel-taschenbuch；123）

4. Die Geschichte einer vollkommenen Liebe（Was der Wind bei Mondschein flüstert）；Der klassische Liebesroman der Chinesen/［Ming-ch'iao-chung-jên. Deutsch von Hellmut Brüggmann］. Basel［usw.］：Rhein-Verl.，1928. VIII，306 S.；8.

《好逑传》，Brüggmann，Hellmut 译.

I53　现当代小说集

1. Chinesische Novellen/Deutsche Fassung nach der Französischen Übertragung durch Lo Ta-Kang von Richard B. Matzig. Basel：Gute Schriften，1946. 80 S.

Richard B. Matzig, Lo Ta-kang 译. 包括《老园丁》等四篇小说.

2. Chinesische Erzählungen：Auswahl/mit einem Vorw. von N. Pachomow.［Aus d. Russ. übers. von Erich Salewski］. Berlin：Dietz，1953. 278 Seiten

20 世纪中国短篇小说. Salewski，Erich 译自俄文.

3. Erzählungen aus dem neuen China. Peking：Verl. für fremdsprachige Literatur，1955. 167 p.；22cm.

《"新的家"及其他故事》，艾芜(1904—1992)等.

4. Lo Tsai, Der tigerjäger：und andere Geschichten/［Li Nan-li... et al.；Deutsch von Ernst J. Schwarz］. Peking：Verlag für fremdsprachige literatur，1958. 281 pages；22cm.

《罗才打虎与其他故事：新中国短篇小说选第三集》，李南力等著. 施华滋(Schwarz，Ernst)译.

5. Märzschneeblüten：Chinesische Erzählungen/［Werner Bettin；Erich A. Klien；Fritz Gruner］. Berlin：Verl. Volk u. Welt，1959. 400 S.；8.

《三月雪：中国短篇小说》，Herbert Bräutigam；Marianne Bretschneider，Eberhard Eller 等译. 收录鲁迅、老舍、茅盾、巴金、肖平、赵树理、艾芜等人作品.

6. Das Neujahrsopfer：Erzählungen aus China/Hrsg. u. übert. Johanna Herzfeldt. Leipzig：Reclam，1959. 178 S.；kl. 8.（Reclams Universal-Bibliothek；Nr 8534/35 C）

新年的受害者：中国短篇小说. Herzfeldt，Johanna 译. 含徐光耀等人作品.

(1) Das Neujahrsopfer：bearb. nach d. Erzählung Das Neujahrsopfer von Lu Hsün/Ill. von Yung Hsiang；Hung Jen；Yao Tjiao. Peking：Verlag für Fremdsprachige Literatur，1978.［120］S.；

überwiegend Ill.；19×26cm.

7. Ich hab's ja gleich gewußt und andere Erzählungen/［Ma Feng... et al.；vert. Eberhard Treppt... et al.］. Peking：Verlag für Fremdsprachige Literatur，1961. 168 p.；22cm.

《"三年早知道"及其他故事：新中国短篇小说选第七集》，马烽等著.

8. Eine Sommernacht：Erzählungen/［Dt. von Günter Lewin］. Peking：Verl. f. Fremdsprach. Literatur，1963. 218 S.；8.

《夏夜》，周立波等；Lewin，Günter 译. 含马烽、李准、周立波等九人的短篇小说.

9. China erzählt：acht Erzählungen/ausgew. u. eingel. von Andreas Donath. Orig.- Ausg. Frankfurt am Main［u. a.］：Fischer，1964. 183 S.（Fischer Bücherei）

中国短篇小说八篇. Donath，Andreas 编译. 包括胡适的《一个问题》，鲁迅的《长明灯》，郭沫若的《函谷关》，茅盾的《春蚕》，老舍的《月牙儿》，吴组缃的《Elixer》，赵树理的《小二黑结婚》，刘宾雁的《在桥梁工地上》.

10. Wer ist schuld?：4 moderne chines. Erzählungen/dt. von Wolfram Eberhard. Nachw. von Felix M. Wiesner. Zürich：Verlag Die Waage，1970. 225 S.；Ill.；20cm. ISBN：3859660373，3859660373.

谁之过?：四篇当代中国小说. Eberhard，Wolfram 译.

11. Chinesische Erzähler der letzten Jahrzehnte/ausgew. u. hrsg. von W. J. F. Jenner.［Aus d. Engl. übers. von Rita Hoevel］. Köln：Hegner，1973. 297 S.；；19cm. ISBN：3776402070，3776402075.

中国当代小说. Hoevel，Rita 译自英文. 含柔石、鲁迅、茅盾、老舍、孙犁、叶紫、张天翼、赵树理等人作品.

12. Eine junge Bahnbrecherin und andere Geschichten/von Hsiao Guan-hung u. anderen. Peking：Verlag für Fremdsprachige Literatur，1975. 247 S.；ill.；19cm.

《小将》，肖关鸿等. 短篇小说集.

13. Moderne chinesische Erzählungen. Teil：Bd. 1.，Hoffnung auf Frühling：1919 - 1949/hrsg. von Volker Klöpsch u. Roderich Pta. Frankfurt am Main：Suhrkamp，1980. 409 S.

现代中国小说第一部分：1919—1949. Klöpsch，Volker 译. 收录沈从文、吴组缃、萧军、萧红、叶圣陶、郁达夫、张天翼等人作品.

14. Moderne chinesische Erzählungen. Teil：Bd. 2.，Hundert Blumen：1949 - 1979/hrsg. von Wolfgang Kubin. Frankfurt am Main：Suhrkamp，1980. 510 S.

现代中国小说第二部分：1949—1979. 顾彬(Kubin，Wolfgang，1945—)译，收录秦兆阳、王蒙、西戎、赵树理、周立波等人作品.

15. Die Drachenschnur：Geschichten aus dem chinesischen Alltag/hrsg. und mit einem Nachwort versehen von Andreas Donath. Darmstadt；Neuwied：Luchterhand，1981. 225 S；21cm. ISBN：3472865385，3472865384

风筝线：中国日常生活中的故事. Andreas Donath
(1934—)译. 含王蒙、陈国凯、高尔泰、高晓声、刘心武等
人作品.
> (1) Frankfurt/M；Berlin；Wien：Ullstein，1984. 224
> S.；18cm. ISBN：3548204345；3548204341.
> (Ullstein；Nr. 20434)

16. Der Jadefelsen：chinesische Kurzgeschichten 1977—
1979/Übersetzungen aus dem Chinesischen. Hrsg. v.
Jochen Noth. Frankfurt am Main：Sendler，1981. 164
Seiten；21cm. ISBN：3880480524，3880480520
1977—1979 年中国短篇小说. Noth，Jochen 译. 包含刘
心武王亚平、蒋子龙、卢新华等人作品.

17. Das Recht auf Liebe：3 chines. Erzählungen zu e.
wiederentdeckten Thema/Zhang Kangkang；Zhang Jie.
übers. u. eingel. von Claudia Magiera. München：
Simon und Magiera，1982. 115 S.；Ill.；21cm. ISBN：
3886760091，388676009X. Anmerkungen：Enthält
folgende drei Erzählungen：Zhang Kangkang：„ Das
Recht auf Liebe“，S. 12－56；Zhang Kangkang：„Der
ferne Klang der Glocke“，S. 57—88；Zhang Jie：„Liebe
ist unvergeßlich “，S. 89—115
中国小说三篇. Magiera，Claudia 译. 包括张抗抗
(1950—)的《隐形伴侣》《钟点人》，张洁(1937—)的《爱，
是不能忘记的》.

18. SF aus China：Kurzgeschichten/Ye Yonglie〔u. a.〕；
Charlotte Dunsing〈Hrsg.〉. 〔Aus d. Chines.〕.
München：Goldmann，1984. 265 Seiten，Illustrationen；
18cm. ISBN：3442084121，3442084128. (Edition
vierundachtzig；12；Goldmanns Taschenbücher；8412)
中国科幻短篇故事. 叶永烈(1940—)等著；Dunsing，
Charlotte 译.

19. 16 chinesische Erzähler/〔herausgegeben von Irmtraud
Fessen-Henjes...〔et al.〕；aus dem Chinesischen von
Irmtraud Fessen-Henjes...〔et al.〕；mit einer
Nachbemerkung von Irmtraud Fessen-Henjes，Fritz
Gruner und Eva Müller〕. Berlin：Volk und Welt，1984.
344 str.；20cm. (Erkundungen)
十六位中国小说作家作品. Fessen-Henjes，Irmtraud
译. 收录艾芜、陆文夫、莫应丰、茹志鹃、沈容、王安忆、王
蒙、汪曾祺等的作品.
> (1) 2. Aufl. Berlin：Verlag Volk u. Welt，1986. 344
> S.；20cm.

20. Kleines Gerede：Satiren aus der Volksrepublik China/
Wang Meng u. a.；herausgegeben von Helmut Martin
und Charlotte Dunsing. Köln：Diederichs，1985. 126
pages；illustrations；21cm. ISBN：3424008516，
3424008517. (Diederichs neue chinesische Bibliothek)
中国讽刺文学. 王蒙等人著；Martin，Helmut(1940—)和
Dunsing，Charlotte 合译.

21. Sieben chinesische Schriftstellerinnen der Gegenwart/
Xiuzhen Li〔Hrsg.〕. Beijing：Verl. f. Fremdsprach.

Literatur，1985. 328 Seiten，7 Tafeln
《中国女作家小说选》，包含茹志鹃(1925—1998)的《草
原上的小路》、黄宗英（1925—）的《大雁情》、宗璞
(1928—)的《弦上的梦》、谌容(1936—)的《人到中年》、
张洁(1937—)的《爱，是不能忘记的》、张抗抗(1950—)
的《丢失的年代》、王安忆(1954—)的《长恨歌》.

22. Das Weinen in der kalten Nacht：zeitgenöss.
Erzählungen aus China/Eike Zschacke（Hg.）. Aus d.
Chines. u. mit e. Vorw. vers. von Eike Zschacke.
Bornheim-Merten：Lamuv-Verlag，1985. 217 S.；19cm.
ISBN：3889770288，3889770282.
中国当代短篇小说选. Zschacke，Eike 译. 收录陈国凯
(1938—2014)、乔典运(1930—1997)、王润滋(1946—
2002)、王安忆、赵本夫(1948—)等人作品.

23. Frauen in China：Erzählungen/hrsg. u. ins Dt. übertr.
von Helmut Hetzel. München：Deutscher Taschenbuch-
Verlag，1986. 151 S.；1 Kt.；18cm. ISBN：
3423105323，3423105321. (dtv；10532)
中国女性小说. Hetzel，Helmut 译. 含王安忆、宗璞、张
抗抗、张洁等人作品.
> (1)Orig.-Ausg. 2. Aufl. München：Deutscher
> Taschenbuch-Verlag，1986. 152，〔2〕pages；map；
> 18cm. ISBN：3423105321，3423105323. （DTV；
> 780)
> (2)Orig.-Ausg. 3. Aufl. München Deutscher Taschenbuch-
> Verlag，1986. 151 S. 1 Kt. 18cm. ISBN：3423105321，
> 3423105323. (dtv；10532)
> (3)Orig.-Ausg.，4. Aufl. München：Dt. Taschenbuch-
> Verl.，1988. 152，〔2〕pages；map；18cm. ISBN：
> 3423105321，3423105323
> (4)Orig.-Ausg.，〔5. Aufl.〕. München：Dt.
> Taschenbuch-Verl.，1989. 151 Seiten；1 Karte；
> 18cm. ISBN：3423105321，3423105323. (Dtv；
> 10532)
> (5)Orig.-Ausg.，6. Aufl. München：Dt. Taschenbuch-
> Verl.，1991. 152，〔2〕pages；map；18cm. ISBN：
> 3423105321，3423105323. (Dtv；10532)

24. Die Eheschliessung：chinesische Erzählungen des 20.
Jahrhunderts/〔ausgew. von Sylvia Nagel. Aus d.
Chines. übers. von Fritz Gruner...〕. Berlin；Weimar：
Aufbau-Verl.，1988. 274 S.；18cm. ISBN：
3351009960，3351009968 (BB；612)
中国二十世纪故事选. Gruner，Fritz 译. 含叶圣陶《米》、
《一个生命》、赵树理《小二黑结婚》等作品.

25. Nach den Wirren：Erzählungen und Gedichte aus der
Volksrepublik China nach der Kulturrevolution/
〔gemeinsam von d. Rhein.-Westfäl. Auslandsges. in
Dortmund u. d. Chines. Volksliteraturverl. in Beijing
konzipiert. Ausw. d. Texte u. übers. Konrad
Wegmann；Guan Huiwen〕. Dortmund：RWAG-Dienste
u. -Verl.，1988. 91 S.；21cm. ISBN：3923030037，

3923030033

"文革"之后的中国小说及故事. Wegmann, Konrad 和 Guan, Huiwen 合译. 含冯骥才、贾平凹、王蒙、刘心武等人作品.

26. Ein Fest am Dashan：chines. Erzählungen/Irmtraud Fessen-Henjes... （Hrsg.）. ［Aus d. Chines. von Irmtraud Fessen-Henjes...］. München：Droemer Knaur，1988. 344 S.；19cm. ISBN：3426016338，3426016336. (Knaur；1633)

大山中的节日. Fessen-Henjes, Irmtraud 译. 中国小说选.

27. Das gesprengte Grab：Erzählungen aus China/hrsg. von Ernst Schwarz. Berlin：Verl. Neues Leben，1989. 403 S.；20cm. ISBN：3355007986，3355007986.

中国小说选. Schwarz, Ernst 译. 收录王蒙《活动变形记》、王浙滨《情书的真情》、张贤亮《未亡人》等作品.

28. China erzählt：14 Erzählungen/ausgew. u. mit e. Nachbemerkung von Andreas Donath. Orig.-Ausg. Frankfurt am Main：Fischer-Taschenbuch-Verl.，1990. 289 S.；18cm. ISBN：3596295753，3596295750. (Fischer；9575)

中国小说14篇. Andreas Donath(1934—)译. 含萧红等人作品.

29. An den Lederriemen geknotete Seelen：Erzähler aus Tibet/Tashi Dawa... Hrsg. von Alice Grünfelder. Aus dem Chines. von Alice Grünfelder und Beate Rusch. Zürich：Unionsverl.，1997. 197 Seiten；21cm. ISBN：3293002331，3293002333

《西藏，系在皮绳结上的魂》，扎西达娃等；Grünfelder, Alice 译.

30. Gela wird erwachsen und andere Erzählungen aus China：zweisprachig Chinesisch-Deutsch/von Feng Jicai, Ye Zhaoyan...；Aus dem Chinesischen übersetzt von Karin Hasselblatt und Katrin Buchta；Mit Übungen und Vokabelanmerkungen von Katrin Buchta. Zürich：Chinabooks E. Wolf，2009. iv，312 S. ISBN：3905816198，3905816199

中国中短篇小说集. Hasselblatt, Karin 译. 收录莫言、阿来、冯骥才和叶兆言的作品. 中德双语.

31. Der Drachen：Geschichten aus China；（chinesisch-deutsch)/von Lu Xun, Ba Jin und anderen. Martin Woesler. Berlin：Europ. Univ.-Verl.，2010. 302 S. in getr. Zählung 21cm.，350 gr. ISBN：3899662948，3899662946. (Sinica；Bd. 3)

中国故事选.鲁迅、巴金等著. Woesler, Martin(1969—)译. 中德双语.

32. Die Maske：Geschichten über das Leben in der Stadt. Wien Löcker，2015. 300 S. ISBN：3854097952，3854097956

《化妆》，李敬泽主编；Niederle, Helmuth A. 译.

I54　现当代个人作品

（按作者出生年先后排列，作者出生年不详或作品的作者未知者排在最后）

鲁迅（1881—1936）

1. Segen/von Lu hsün；Aus dem Chinesischen übertragen von Joseph Kalmer. Herrliberg-Zürich，Bühl-Verlag，1947. 47 pages；21cm. (Bühl-Verlag-Blätter；21)

《祝福》，Kalmer, Joseph 译.

2. Das Neujahrsopfer：bearb. nach d. Erzählung Das Neujahrsopfer von Lu Hsühn/Ill. von Yung Hsiang；Hung Jen；Yao Tjiao. Peking：Verlag für Fremdsprachige Literatur，1978. ［120］S.：überw. Ill.

《祝福》，Yun, Hsiang 等改编.

3. Der Neujahrssegen/Lu Xun：übersetzt von：Alisa Daniczek ［und 4 weiteren］. Bochum；Freiburg：Projektverl.，2015. 73 Seiten. ISBN：3897333826，3897333821. (Edition Pengkun；Band 3)

《祝福》，Daniczek, Alisa 等人译.

4. Erzählungen aus China/Lu Hsun；［übetragen aus dem Russischen von Josi von Koskull］. Berlin：Rütten & Loening，1952. 100 S.；8.

中国短篇小说. Koskull, Josi 译自俄语.

5. Die wahre Geschichte von Ah Queh/Lu Hsin. Mit e. Vorbemerkung u. mit Anm. von Richard Jung u. mit e. Nachw. über d. Werk u. seinen Verf. von Feng Hsüä-feng. ［übers. aus d. Chines. von Herta Nan u. Richard Jung］. Leipzig：List，1954. 145 S.；8.

《阿Q正传》，Nan, Herta 和 Jung, Richard 合译.

(1) Leipzig：Reclam，1957. 79 S.；kl. 8. (Reclams Universal-Bibliothek；Nr 8181)

6. Die wahre Geschichte des Ah Q：Erzählung；übertr. aus d. modernen Chines./Lu Xun. Nachw. von Helmut Martin. ［Der dt. Text ist d. von Oskar von Törne überarb. übertr. von Joseph Kalmers］. Frankfurt am Main：Suhrkamp，1982. 113 S.；19cm. ISBN：3518017777，3518017772. (Bibliothek Suhrkamp；Bd. 777)

《阿Q正传》，Kalmers, Joseph 译.

7. Die Reise ist lang：gesammelte Erzählungen/［von］Lu hsün ［pseud. Aus dem Chinesischen übers. von Joseph Kalmer］. Düsseldorf：Progress-Verlag，1955. 524 pages；20cm.

鲁迅短篇小说合集. Kalmer, Joseph 译.

8. Die Flucht auf den Mond：Alte Geschichten - neu erzählt/Lu Ssün. ［Aus d. Chines. hrsg. u. übers. von Johanna Herzfeldt］. Berlin：Rütten & Loening，1960. 248 S.；8.

《故事新编》，Herzfeldt, Johanna 译.

9. Alte Geschichten neu erzählt/Lu Xun. ［Dt. von Rosi Sichrowski］. Beijing：Verl. für Fremdsprachige Literatur，1983. 171 S.；19cm.

《故事新编》,Sichrowski, Rosi 译.

(1) Beijing：Verl. für Fremdsprachige Literatur, 2002. 240 S.；19cm. ISBN：7119029762

10. Einge Erzahlungen von Lu Hsun. Peking：Verlag fur fremdsprachige Literatur, 1974. 442 pages：illustrations, portrait, facsimile；20cm.

《鲁迅小说选》

(1) Peking：Verlag für Fremdsprachige Literatur, 1976. 442 pages，[6] leaves of pages：illustrations, portraits；20cm.

11. Auf der Suche/Lu Xun. Beijing：Verlag für fremdsprachige Literatur, 1978. 211 S.

《彷徨》

(1) Beijing：Verlag für Fremdsprachige Literatur, 1983. 217 pages，[1] leaf of plates：illustrations；19cm.

12. Aufruf zum Kampf/Lu Xun. Beijing：Verlag für Fremdsprachige Literatur, 1983. 232 pages；19cm.

《呐喊》

13. Aufruf zum Kampf/Lu Xun. Beijing：Verl. für Fremdsprachige Literatur, 2002. 314 S.；19cm. ISBN：7119029738.

《呐喊》

14. In tiefer Nacht geschrieben：Ausw.；[aus d. Chines.]/ Lu Xun. [Ausw., übers., Zeitt. u. Anm. von Yang Enlin u. Konrad Herrmann]. Leipzig：Reclam, 1981. 302 S.：1 Ill.；18cm. (Reclams Universal-Bibliothek；Bd. 879：Belletristik)

《呐喊》,Yang, Enlin 和 Hermann, Konrad 合译.

(1) 2. Aufl. Leipzig：Reclam, 1986. 302 S.；18cm. (Reclams Universal-Bibliothek；Bd. 879：Belletristik)

15. Das trunkene Land：Erzahlungen/Lu Xun；Aus dem Chinesischen von Ruth Cremerius. Zurich：Unionsverlag, 2009. 249 pages；21cm. ISBN：3293004085, 3293004083

醉乡：短篇小说集. Cremerius, Ruth 译.

苏曼殊(1884—1918)

1. Der wunde Schwan：Roman/Die Aufzeichngn d. Münchs Man Ju. Aus d. Chines. übertr. v. Anna v. Rottauscher. Wien：Amandus-Ed., 1947. 152 S.；8.

《断鸿零雁记》,Rottauscher, Anna von (1892—1970)译.

朱瘦菊(笔名,海上说梦人,1892—1966)

1. Fräulein Tschang：ein chines. Mädchen von heute；Roman/Hai-Schang-Schuo-Mong-Jen. Aus d. chin. Orig. übertr. von Franz Kuhn. Berlin；Wien；Leipzig：Zsolnay, 1931. 335 S.；8.

《歇浦潮》,孔舫之(Kuhn, Franz, 1884—1961)译.

茅盾(1892—1981)

1. Schanghai im Zwielicht：Roman/Mao Tun. Aus d. Chines. übertr. von Franz Kuhn. Dresden：Heyne, 1938. 477 S.；8.

《子夜》,孔舫之(Kuhn, Franz, 1884—1961)译.

(1) Berlin：Wigankow, 1950. 475 S.；8.

(2) Berlin：Volk und Welt, 1966. 650 pages：illustrations；21cm.

(3) Berlin：Oberbaum, 1977. 505 pages：illustrations；21cm. ISBN：3876281520, 3876281520

(4) Berlin：Oberbaumverlag, 1979. 505 S.；21cm. ISBN：3876281520, 3876281520

(5) Frankfurt am Main：Suhrkamp, 1983. 388 pages；18cm. ISBN：3518374206, 3518374207. (Suhrkamp-Taschenbuch；920)

2. Chinesische Novellen/Mao Tun [d. i. Shen Yen-ping]. Hrsg. von Walter Donat. Berlin u. Buxtehude：Hübener, 1946. 64 S；8,„. (Kleine drei Birken Bücherei；9)

中国小说. Donat, Walter(1898—1970)译.

3. Der Laden der Familie Lin/Mao Tun. übers.：Joseph Kalmer. Berlin：Volk u. Welt, 1953. 186 S.；8.

《林家铺子》,Kalmer, Joseph 译.

4. Seidenraupen im Frühling：2 Erzählungen/Mao Tun. Aus d. Chines. übertr. von Joseph Kalmer. Leipzig：Insel-Verl., 1955. 78 S.；kl. 8.

《春蚕》等两篇小说. Kalmer, Joseph 译.

5. Seidenraupen im Frühling：Erzählungen u. Kurzgeschichten/Mao Dun. [Hrsg. von Fritz Gruner. Aus d. Chines. von Fritz Gruner u. a.]. Berlin：Verlag Volk u. Welt, 1975. 367 S.；；21cm.

《春蚕》,Gruner, Fritz 译.

(1) 2. Aufl. Berlin：Verlag Volk u. Welt, 1987. 314 S.；21cm. ISBN：3353002367, 3353002365. (Orientalische Bibliothek)

(2) München：Beck, 1987. 314 S.；21cm. ISBN：3406317378, 3406317375. (Orientalische Bibliothek).

6. Die kleine Hexe：Erzählgn/Mao Dun. [Aus d. Chin. übertr. v. Johanna Herzfeldt]. Hrsg. v. Fritz Gruner. Leipzig：Reclam, 1959. 185 S.；kl. 8. (Reclams Universal-Bibliothek；Nr. 8597/98)

《小巫》,Herzfeldt, Johanna 译.

7. Regenbogen：Roman/Mao Dun. [Aus d. Chines. Dt. von Marianne Bretschneider]. Berlin：Verl. Volk u. Welt, 1963. 368 S.；8. (Mao, Dun；Ausgewählte Werke)

《虹》,Bretschneider, Marianne 译.

叶圣陶(1894—1988)

1. Die Flut des Tjingtang/Yä Scheng-tau. [Aus d. Chines. übers. von Helmut Liebermann]. Berlin：Rütten & Loening, 1962. 375 S.；8.

《倪焕之》,Liebermann, Helmut 译.

2. Die Gründung der Mittelschule „Großer Mut"：eine moderne chinesische Novelle/Jie Sheng-tao. Für d. Sprachstudium mit latein. Aussprachebezeichng u. Erl. vers. v. Helga Vietze. Leipzig，Verlag Enzyklopädie, 1963. 45 pages；22cm. (Chinesische Übungstexte；Heft 2)

《城中》，Vietze，Helga 译.

郁达夫（1896—1945）

1. Der Untergang. übers. und überarb. von Anna von Rottauscher/ Yü Ta-fu. Wien：Amandus Edition，1947. 117 S. ；21cm.

   《沉沦》，Rottauscher，Anna 译.

2. Die späte Lorbeerblüte：Erzählungen/Yu Dafu. ［Aus dem Chines. übertr. von Yang Enlin］. Beijing：Verl. für Fremdsprachige Literatur，1990. 257 S. ；19cm. ISBN：7119007394. （Phönix-Ausgabe）

   《郁达夫小说选》，Yang，Enlin 译.

老舍（1899—1966）

1. Rikscha Kuli：Roman/Lao Sheh ［pseud. Deutsche Übertragung von Lena Frender］. Zürich：Diana Verlag，1947. 446 pages；8.

   《骆驼祥子》，Frender，Lena 译.

   （1）［Nach d. amerikan. Ausg. Riksha boy übers. von Lena Frender. Einige Passagen wurden auf d. Grundlage d. chines. Ausg. d. Jahres 1955 von Marianne Bretschneider neuübers.］ Berecht. Ausg. ，［Vorzugsausg.］，1982. 407 S. 20cm.

2. Rikscha-Kuli：e. Roman/Lao She. Aus d. Chines. übertr. von Florian Reissinger. Frankfurt am Main：Insel-Verl. ，1987. 305 S. ；21cm. ISBN：3458145837，3458145834.

   《骆驼祥子》，Reissinger，Florian 译.

   （1）［Frankfurt （Main）］：Suhrkamp，1989. 305 S. ；18cm. ISBN：3518381618，351838161X. （ Suhrkamp-Taschenbuch；1661）. （Anmerkungen：Lizenzausg. d. Insel-Verl. ，Frankfurt am Main）

3. Rikscha-Kuli：Roman/Geschichte. Lao She. Berlin：Verl. Freie Kultur Aktion，1996. 85 S. ；30cm. ISBN：3932078200，3932078209. （Edition Freie Kultur Aktion im Schwarzrotbuch-Verlag）

   《骆驼祥子》

4. Zwischen Traum und Wirklichkeit：11 Erzählungen/Lao She. Hrsg. von Volker Klöpsch. ［übers. von G. Bittner...］. Frankfurt am Main：China-Studien- und Verl. -Ges. ，1981. 288 S. ；20cm. ISBN：3887281038，3887281039.

   老舍小说十一篇. Klöpsch，Volker 译.

5. Blick westwärts nach Changan/Lao She；hrsg. von Kuo Heng-yü；übersetzt aus dem Chinesischen von Ursula Adam ［and others］. München：Minerva Publikation，1983. 166 pages：illustrations；21cm. ISBN：3597104576，3597104573. （Berliner China-Studien；1）

   《西望长安》，Adam，Ursula 等人译.

6. Scheidung （Arbeitstitel）/übers. von Irmtraud Fessen-Henjes. Berlin：Volk und Welt，1984. 400 S.

   《离婚》，Reissinger，Florian 译.

7. Die Blütenträume des Lao Li：Roman/Lao She；aus dem Chinesischen von Irmtraud Fessen-Henjes. Berlin：Verlag Volk und Welt，1984. 317 pages；20cm.

   《离婚》，Fessen-Henjes，Irmtraud 译.

   （1）München：C. H. Beck，1985. 338 pages. ISBN：3406304699，3406304699. （Orientalische Bibliothek）

8. Chinesen in London：Lao She's Roman Er Ma/Petra Grossholtforth. Bochum：Studienverl. Brockmeyer，1985. 238 S. ；19cm. ISBN：3883394497，3883394491. （Chinathemen；Bd. 24）

   《二马》，Grossholtforth，Petra 译.

9. Eine Erbschaft in London：Roman/Lao She. Aus d. Chines. von Irmtraud Fessen-Henjes. Berlin：Verl. Volk u. Welt，1988. 321 S. ；20cm. ISBN：3353003744，3353003746

   《二马》，Fessen-Heinjes，Irmtraud 译.

10. Die Stadt der Katzen：phantast. Roman/Lao She. Aus d. Chines. übers. u. mit e. Nachw. vers. von Volker Klöpsch. Frankfurt am Main：Suhrkamp，1985. 201 S. ；18cm. ISBN：3518376546，3518376543. （ Phantastische Bibliothek；Bd. 151. Suhrkamp-Taschenbuch；1154）

    《猫城记》，Klöpsch，Volker 译.

11. Sperber über Peking：Roman/Lao She. Aus dem Chines. von Silvia Kettelhut. Mit einem Nachw. von Wolfgang Kubin. Freiburg im Breisgau；Basel；Wien：Herder，1992. 199 S. ；21cm. ISBN：3451225772，3451225778

    《正红旗下》，顾彬（Kubin，Wolfgang，1945—）译.

12. Vier Generationen unter einem Dach/Lao She；herausgegeben und aus dem Chinesischen von Irmtraud Fessen-Henjes. Zürich：Unionsverlag，1998. 1101 pages；21cm. ISBN：3293002579，3293002579

    《四世同堂》，Fessen-Henjes，Irmtraud 译.

沈从文（1902—1988）

1. Grenzstadt：Erzählung/Shen Congwen；übersetzt von Helmut Forster-Latsch und Marie-Luise Latsch. Köln：Cathay Verlag，1985. 116 p. ；21cm. ISBN：3923131038，3923131037. （Reihe：Wilde Gräser）

   《边城》，Forster-Latsch，Helmut （Helmut）和 Latsch，Marie-Luise 合译.

2. Die Grenzstadt：Novelle/Shen Congwen. Aus d. Chines. übertr. u. mit e. Nachw. vers. von Ursula Richter. Frankfurt am Main：Suhrkamp，1985. 147 S. ；19cm. ISBN：3518018613，3518018612. （Bibliothek Suhrkamp；Bd. 861）

   《边城》，Richter，Ursula 译.

3. Erzählungen aus China/Shen Congwen；aus dem Chinesischen übersetzt und mit einem Nachwort von Ursula Richter. Frankfurt am Main：Insel，1985. 277 s. ISBN：3458142452，3458142454

   沈从文短篇小说选. Richter，Ursula 译.

   （1）Frankfurt am Main：Suhrkamp，1986. 278 S.

4. Die Grenzstadt und andere Erzählungen/Shen Congwen. [Aus d. Chines. von Ursula Richter...]. Berlin：Verl. Volk u. Welt，1988. 373 S. ；21cm. ISBN：3353004345，3353004343. Anmerkungen：Lizenzausg. - Ausg. für d. Dt. Demokrat. Republik.

《边城》及其他小说. Richter，Ursula 译.

5. „Die Liebe des Schamanen" von Shen Congwen：eine Erzählung des Jahres 1929 zwischen Ethnographie und Literatur/Anke Heinemann. Bochum：Brockmeyer，1992. ISBN：3819600345，3819600340. （Chinathemen；Bd. 72）

《神巫之爱》，Heinemann，Anke 译.

柔石（1902—1931）

1. Februar/Shi Rou. Beijing：Verlag fur Fremedsprachige Literatur，1982. 196 S

《二月》，Rudolph，Ingrid 译. 收录长篇小说《二月》《毁灭》《为奴隶的母亲》.

胡也频（1903—1931）

1. Hu Yeh-p'in und seine Erzählung „Nach Moskau" / Roderich Ptak. Bad Boll：Klemmerberg Verlag，1979. 125 S.

《到莫斯科去》，Ptak，Roderich 著.

巴金（1904—2005）

1. Garten der Ruhe：Roman/Chin Pa. Übertr. aus d. Chines. von Joseph Kalmer. München：Hanser，1954. 219 S. ；8

《憩园》，Kalmer，Joseph 译.

2. Das Haus des Mandarins：Roman/Djin Ba. Aus d. Chines. von Johanna Herzfeldt. Rudolstadt：Greifenverl. ，1959. 350 S. ；8.

《家》，Herzfeldt，Johanna 译.

3. Die Familie：Roman/Ba Jin；aus dem Chinesischen von Florian Reissinger；mit einer Nachw. von Wolfgang Kubin. Berlin：Oberbaumverlag，1980. 440 p. ；21cm. ISBN：3876281679，3876281674

《家》，Reissinger，Florian 译.

(1)［Frankfurt（Main）］Suhrkamp，1985. 324 S. 18cm. ISBN：3518376470，3518376478. （ Suhrkamp-Taschenbuch；1147）

4. Kalte Nächte：Roman/ Ba Jin. Aus d. Chines. von Sabine Peschel u. Barbara Spielmann. Mit e. Nachw. von Wolfgang Kubin. Frankfurt am Main：Suhrkamp，1981. 299 S. ；20cm. ISBN：3518033296；3518033298.

《寒夜》，Peschel，Sabine （1955—）和 Spielmann，Barbara 译.

5. Nacht über der Stadt：Roman/Ba Jin. Aus d. Engl. von Peter Kleinhempel. Berlin：Verlag Volk u. Welt，1985. 254 S. ；22cm.

《寒夜》，Kleinhempel，Peter 转译自英文版.

6. Shading：Erzählung/Ba Jin；［translated by Helmut Forster-Latsch，collaborated by Marie-Luise Latsch and Zhao Zhenquang］. Frankfurt am Main：Suhrkamp，1981. 118 pages；18cm. ISBN：351801725X，3518017258. （Bibliothek Suhrkamp；Bd. 725）

《沙丁》，Helmut Forster-Latsch 等译.

7. Herbst im Frühling：Ausgewählte Erzählungen von Ba Jin ［ba jin xiao shuo xuan］./Ba Jin. Peking：Verlag für fremdsprachige Literatur，2005. 353 S. ISBN：7119036254

《春天里的秋天：巴金小说选》，（德）赛西提希译. 本书选巴金短篇小说三篇，附德文译文及注释. 德汉对照.

丁玲（1904—1986）

1. Sonne über dem Sanggan：Roman/Ding Ling. übers.：Arthur Nestmann. Berlin：Dietz，1952. 468 S. ；8.

《太阳照在桑干河上》，Nestmann，Arthur 译.

2. Das Tagebuch der Sophia = （Suofei-nüshi-de-riji）/Ding Ling. ［Aus d. Chines. übers. von d. Arbeitskreis Moderne Chines. Literatur （Bernd Fischer...）］. Frankfurt am Main：Suhrkamp，1980. 102 S. ；19cm. ISBN：3518016709，3518016701. （Bibliothek Suhrkamp；Bd. 670）

《莎菲女士的日记》，顾彬（Kubin，Wolfgang，1945—）译.

(1) Das Tagebuch der Sophia = （Suofei-nüshi-de-riji）/ Ding Ling. ［Aus d. Chines. übers. von d. Arbeitskreis Moderne Chines. Literatur am Ostasiat. Seminar d. Freien Univ. Berlin］. 4. Aufl. Frankfurt am Main：Suhrkamp，1986. 102 S. ；19cm. ISBN：3518016701；3518016709. （Bibliothek Suhrkamp；Bd. 670）

(2)1. Aufl. dieser Ausg. Frankfurt am Main：Suhrkamp，1987. 117 S. ；19cm. ISBN：3518032503；351803250X. （Weisses Programm：Im Jahrhundert der Frau）

3. Frauen im Aufbruch：Ding Ling：Das Tagebuch der Sophia/Anna Gerstlacher. Berlin：Schiller，1984. 134 S. ；21cm. ISBN：3925067006，3925067000.

《莎菲女士的日记》，Gerstlacher，Anna 译.

4. Hirsekorn im blauen Meer：Erzählungen/Ding Ling；aus dem Chinesischen von Yang Enlin und Konrad Herrmann. Köln：Pahl-Rugenstein，1987. 339 p. ；20cm. ISBN：3760970052，3760970059

丁玲短篇小说集. Yang，Enlin 和 Herrmann，Konrad （1945—）合译.

(1) Hirsekorn im blauen Meer：Erzählungen/Ding Ling. ［Ausw. ，Übers. ，Zeittaf. u. Anm. von Yang Enlin u. Konrad Herrmann］. Leipzig Reclam，1987. 278 S. 18cm. ISBN：3379001473，3379001472. （Reclams Universal-Bibliothek；Bd. 1152：Belletristik）

5. Jahreszeiten einer Frau：Roman/Ding Ling. Aus dem Chines. von Michaela Herrmann. Mit einem Vorw. von Wolfgang Kubin. Freiburg im Breisgau；Basel；Wien：Herder，1991. 141 S. ；21cm. ISBN：3451221576，

3451221578.

《母亲》，Herrmann，Michaela 译.

艾芜（1904 — 1992）

1. Der Tempel in der Schlucht und andere Erzählungen/Ai Wu. Hrsg. von Eva Müller. ［Aus d. Chines. von Anja Gleboff...］ Berlin：Verl. Volk u. Welt，1989. 263 S. ；21cm. ISBN：3353003737；3353003738.（Orientalische Bibliothek）

《山峡中》等小说. Anja Gleboff 等译.

赵树理（1906—1970）

1. Die Lieder des Li Yü-Ts'ai；Eine Erzählung aus dem heutigen China/Dschao Schu-Li. ［Autor. übers. von Joseph Kalmer］. Berlin：Volk u. Welt，1950. 126 S. ；8.

《李有才板话》，Kalmer，Joseph 译.

（1）Berlin：Volk u. Welt，1952. 91 S. ；mit Abb. ；8.

（2）Berlin：Volk u. Welt，1953. 91 S. ；mit Abb. ；8.

（3）Berlin：Verl. Volk u. Welt，1961. 137 S.

2. Die Spruchlieder des Li Yu-tsai；Eine Erzählung aus d. befreiten China/Dschau Schu-li. Peking：Kulturelle Presse，1951. 109 S. ；8.

《李有才板话》

3. Die Wandlung des Dorfes Lidjiadschuang/Schu-li Dschao. Berlin：Verl. Volk u. Welt，1952. 61 S. ；mit Abb. ；4.（Roman-Zeitung；Nr 36＝1952，6）

《李家庄的变迁》

4. Die Wandlung des Dorfes Lidjiadschuang/Shu-li Chao. Dt. v. Tjen Nou. Berlin，1952. 254 S. ；8°

《李家庄的变迁》，Nou，Tjen 译.

（1）Leipzig：Reclam，1961. 275 S. ；kl. 8.（Reclams Universal-Bibliothek）

萧军（1907—1988）

1. Das erwachende Dorf：Roman/T'ien Chün. ［Autor. übers. aus d. Amerikanischen von Hartmut Rebitzki］. Berlin：Kantorowicz，1950. 229 S. ；8.

《八月的乡村》，Rebitzki，Harmut 译自英文.

（1）Das erwachende Dorf/Chün T'ien. Übers. aus d. Amerikan. von Hartmut Rebitzki. Schwerin：Petermänken-Verl. ，1953. 214 S. ；8.

周立波（1908—1979）

1. Orkan/Li-bo Dschou. Aus d. Chines. von Yang En-lin u. Wolfgang Müncke. Berlin：Tribüne，1953. 576 S. ；8.

《暴风骤雨》，Yang，Enlin 和 Müncke，Wolfgang 合译.

（1）Orkan：Roman/Li-bo Dschou. ［Aus d. Chines v. Yang En-lin；Wolfgang Müncke］. Wien：Stern Verl. ，1954. 576 S. ；8.

（2）Orkan：Die Revolution auf d. chines. Dorf. /Chou Li-po. Berlin：Oberbaumverlag，1971. 2 Teile（642 S. ）. ISBN：3876280397，3876280394，3876280400，3876280400.（Proletarisch-revolutionäre Romane；5—6）

2. Orkan/Libo Zhou. Peking：Verl. f. Fremdsprach.

Literatur，1979. IV，561 S；ill

《暴风骤雨》，古元插图.

3. Der Strom：Roman/Li-bo Dschou. Nach e. übers. aus d. Chines. von Yang En-lin u. Dchi Mu. Berlin：Verl. Tribüne，1959. 246 S. ；8.

《铁水奔流》，Yang，Enlin 和 Müncke，Wolfgang 合译.

高云览（1910—1956）

1. Alle Feuer brennen：Roman/Gau Jün-lan. ［Aus d. Chines. von Li Ming］. Rudolstadt：Greifenverl. ，1961. 501 S. ；8.

《小城春秋》

马加（1910—2004）

1. Blumen，die nicht welken/Djia Ma. ［Dt. von Eberhard Eller u. Eberhard Heyn］. Peking：Verl. f. Fremdsprach. Literatur，1961. 107 S. ；8.

《开不败的花朵》，Eller，Eberhard 和 Heyn，Eberhard 合译.

萧乾（1910—1999）

1. Die Seidenraupen/Ch'ien Hsiao；［Einzig autorisierte Übertragung von Joseph Kalmer］. Herrliberg-Zürich：Bühl-Verlag，1947. 172 pages；21cm.

Contents：Ein regnerischer Abend. —Die Seidenraupen. —Hinter anderer Leute Zaun. —Die Bekehrung. —Kastanien. —Wenn dein Dach Schanghai. —Der Briefmarkensammler. —Die Seuche.

Notes：„Titel der englischen Ausgabe：The spinners of silk. "

《蚕》，Kalmer，Joseph 译.

2. Befreites Land：ein Bericht v. d. Agrarreform in d. Volksrepublik China/Hsiao Ch'ien. ［übers. aus d. Engl. v. Bruno Heilig］. Berlin：Kongress-Verl. ，1952. 142 S. ：Mit 20 Abb. auf Taf. u. 1 Kt. ；8.

《土地回老家》，Heilig，Bruno 译.

钱钟书（1910—1998）

1. Das Andenken：Erzählungen/Qian Zhongshu. Aus d. Chines. von Charlotte Dunsing u. Ylva Monschein. Mit e. Nachw. von Charlotte Dunsing. Köln：Diederichs，1986. 190 S. ；21cm. ISBN：3424008548，3424008540.

《人·兽·鬼》，Dunsing，Charlotte 和 Monschein，Ylva 合译.

2. Die umzingelte Festung：e. chines. Gesellschaftsroman/Qian Zhongshu. Aus d. Chines. übertr. von Monika Motsch u. J. Shih. Frankfurt am Main：Insel，1988. 448 S. ；21cm. ISBN：3458143598，3458143598.

《围城》，Motsch，Monika 译.

（1）Die umzingelte Festung：Roman/Qian Zhongshu. Aus dem Chines. von Monika Motsch und Jerome Shih. Mit einem Nachw. und Erl. von Monika Motsch. Neuausg. München：SchirmerGraf，2008. 542 S. ；21cm. ISBN：3865550590，3865550592.

（2）Die umzingelte Festung：Roman/by Qian Zhongshu，

translated by Monika Motsch. Frankfurt am Main: Insel，2016．607 Seiten．ISBN：7513570350，7513570353

萧红(1911—1942)

1. Autobiographie und Literatur：3 Werke d. chines. Schriftstellerin Xiao Hong/Ruth Keen. München：Minerva-Publikation，1984．145 S．；21cm．ISBN：3597104597，3597104592．(Berliner China-Studien；3)

   萧红作品三部. Keen，Ruth 译.

2. Frühling in einer kleinen Stadt：Erzählungen/Xiao Hong；[aus dem Chinesischen] übers. und mit einem Nachwort von Ruth Keen. Köln：Cathay Verlag，1985．119 p.；21cm．(Wilde Gräser)

   《小城三月》，Keen，Ruth 译.

3. Der Ort des Lebens und des Sterbens/Xiao Hong. Aus d. Chines. von Karin Hasselblatt. Mit e. Nachw. von Wolfgang Kubin. Freiburg i. Br.；Basel；Wien：Herder，1989．152 S．；21cm．ISBN：3451214141，3451214148

   《生死场》，Hasselblatt，Karin 译.

4. Geschichten vom Hulanfluss/Xiao Hong. Aus dem Chines. übertr. von Ruth Keen. Mit einem Nachw. vers. von Ruth Keen und Wolfgang Kubin. Frankfurt am Main：Insel-Verl.，1990．286 S．；21cm．ISBN：3458160991，345816099X

   《呼兰河传》，Keen，Ruth 译.

   (1) Berlin：Insel-Verl.，2009．283 S．；21cm．ISBN：3458174639，345817463X

草明(1913—2002)

1. Die treibende Kraft/ Ming Tsao. Übers. von Gerhard Mehnert. Berlin：Dietz，1953．207 S．；8.

   《原动力》，Mehnert，Gerhard（1914—1983)译.

杨沫(1914—1995)

1. Das Lied der Jugend/von Yang Mo.[Dt.：Alexander Sichrovsky；Annemarie Ma]．Beijing：Verl. für Fremdsprachige Literatur，1983．655 S．；22cm．＋Beil.（1 Bl.）.

   《青春之歌》，Sichrovsky，Alexander 和 Ma Annemarie 合译.

袁静(1914—1999)

1. Schüsse am Bayangsee：Roman/Kung Djüe；Yüan Ding. Nach e. engl. übers. ins Dt. übertr. von Eduard Klein. Berlin：Verl. Volk u. Welt，1954．362 S．；8.

   《新儿女英雄传》，袁静、孔厥（1914—1966）著；Klein，Eduard 译.

2. Erzählung vom langen Marsch. Peking：Verlag für Fremdsprachige literatur，1959．XI，154 S：Kt.，Ill；19cm.

   《长征的故事》，袁静，孔厥著.

赵清阁(1914—1999)

1. Liang Shanbo und Zhu Yingtai oder Romeo und Julia in China/nach d. Textfassung von Zhao Qingge aus d.

Chines. übers. u. hrsg. von Hannelore Theodor. Köln：Diederichs，1984．143 S．：Ill.；19cm．ISBN：3424008079，3424008074．(Diederichs Kabinett)

   《梁山伯与祝英台》，Theodor，Hannelore 译.

2. Schmetterlingsliebe：die Legende von Liang Shanbo und Zhu Yingtai/Helmut Matt. Niederwerrn：Wiesenburg-Verl.，2014．168 S．：Ill.；22cm.，300 g．ISBN：3956322020，3956322029.

   《梁山伯与祝英台》，Matt，Helmut 译.

刘白羽(1916—2005)

1. Flammen am Jangtse/Bai-jü Lju. Aus d. Chines. übers. von Walter Eckleben. Berlin：Dietz，1957．212 S．；8.

   《火光在前》，Eckleben，Walter 译.

秦兆阳(1916—1994)

1. Dorfskizzen/Tschin Dschao-jang. Dt. von Ernst J. Schwarz. Peking：Verl. f. Fremdsprach. Literatur，1956．253 S．：6 Taf.，1 Titelbild；8.

   《农村散记》，Schwarz，Ernst 译.

吴运铎(1917—1991)

1. Alles der Partei/Wu Yün-Duo；[Illustrationen von Luo Gung-liu]．Peking：Verlag für Fremdsprachige Literatur，1961．209 pages：illustrations；19cm.

   《把一切献给党》

王希坚(1918—1995)

1. Der gnädige Herr Wu/Hsi-Djiän Wang. Aus d. Chines. übertr. von Yuan Miautze. Die Bearb. d. Dt. Fassung besorgte Klaus Marschke. Berlin：Verl. Volk u. Welt，1954．334 S．；8.

   《地覆天翻记》，Miautze，Yuan 译.

张爱玲(1920—1995)

1. Das Reispflanzerlied：ein Roman aus dem heutigen China/Eileen Chang；übertr. von Gabriele Eckehard. Düsseldorf：Diederichs，1956．1 Bd.

   《秧歌》，Eckehard，Gabriele 译.

2. Das Reispflanzerlied：Roman/Eileen Chang. Aus dem Engl. unter Berücksichtigung des Chines. und mit einem Nachw. vers. von Susanne Hornfeck. Berlin：Claassen，2009．221 S．；21cm．ISBN：3546004312，3546004310

   《秧歌》，Hornfeck，Susanne 译.

   (1)Berlin List，2011．221 S. 19cm．ISBN：3548610085，3548610080．(List-Taschenbuch；61008)

3. Gefahr und Begierde：Erzählungen/Eileen Chang. Aus dem Chines. übers. von Susanne Hornfeck；mit einem Nachw. von Susanne Hornfeck. Berlin：Claassen，2008．248 S．；21cm．ISBN：3546004299，3546004299

   危险与欲望：张爱玲短篇小说选. Hornfeck，Susanne（1956—）译.

   (1)Berlin List，2009．247 S. 19cm．ISBN：3548609171，3548609171．(List-Taschenbuch；60917)

4. Das goldene Joch：Erzählungen/Eileen Chang. Mit einem Nachw. von Susanne Hornfeck.[Aus dem Chines. Wulf

Begrich...] Berlin Ullstein, 2011. 365 S. 20cm. ISBN: 3550088728, 3550088728

《金锁记：短篇小说集》，Begrich，Wulf 等译.

梁星(真名,高而公,1920－1976)

1. Liu Hu-lan, eine junge Heldin der Revolution/Hsing Liang. 〔Dt. von Günter Lewin〕. Peking：Verl. f. Fremdsprach. Literatur, 1961. 95 S.

《刘胡兰小传》. 传记小说.

马烽(1922—2004)

1. Die Helden vom Ly-Liang-Schan/Ma Feng; Hsi Jung. 〔Der dt. Fassg liegt e. übers. v. Yuan Miautse zugrunde〕. Berlin：Verl. d. Ministeriums f. Nationale Verteidigung, 1956. 509 S. : mit Abb. ; 8.

《吕梁英雄传》，马烽(1922—2004)，西戎(1922—2001) 著；Miautse，Yuan 译.

罗广斌(1924—1967)

1. Roter Fels：Roman/Luo Guang-bin; Yang Yi-yän. 〔übers. von Otto Mann〕. Peking：Verl. f. Fremdsprach. Literatur, 1965. 481 S. : mit Abb. ; 8.

《红岩》，罗广斌，杨益言；Mann，Otto 译.

(1) Tübingen：Verlag Neuer Weg, 1972. 481, 〔11〕 S. : Ill. , 1 Kt. ;； 19cm.

(2) 2. Aufl. Stuttgart：Verlag Neuer Weg, 1974. 491 S. : Ill. ; 19cm. ISBN：3880210813, 3880210810.

(3) 3. Aufl. Stuttgart：Verlag Neuer Weg, 1977. 491 S. : Ill. , 1 Kt. ; 19cm. ISBN：3880210813, 3880210810.

(4) Peking：Verl. für Fremdsprachige Literatur, 1979. 504 S. ; 22cm. ＋Beil. (〔2〕 S.)

胡石言(1924—2002)

1. Das Gelöbnis des Li Jin：Eine Liebeserzählung aus d. neuen China/Shih Yen. übertr. : Ruth Gerull-Kardas. Leipzig：List, 1951. 89 S. ; 8.

《柳堡的故事》，Gerull-Kardas，Ruth 译.

艾明之(原名黄志坤,1925—)

1. Zwei Mädchen aus Schanghai/Ming-dsh Ai. 〔Aus d. Chines. ins Dt. übertr. von Alfons Mainka u. Yang En-lin.〕 Ill. von Ursula Wendorff-Weidt. Berlin：Verl. Neues Leben, 1961. 299 S. , 1 Titelbild; 8.

《浮沉》，Wendorff-Weidt，Ursula 译.

高玉宝(1927—)

1. Meine Kindheit/Gao Yü-bao. 〔Aus d. Chines. Dt. von Ernst J. Schwarz. Ill. : Lu Tan〕. Peking：Verl. f. Fremdsprach. Literatur, 1962. 304 S.

《高玉宝》《我的童年》)

陆柱国(1928—)

1. Der Mensch ist stärker als Eisen/Lu Tschu-kou. 〔Ins Dt. übertr. v. Yuan Miautse. Textill. : Kurt Zimmermann〕. Berlin：Verl. d. Kasernierten Volkspolizei, 1956. 145 S. ; 8.

《上甘岭》，Miautse，Yuan 译.

鲁彦周(1928—2006)

1. Die wunderbare Geschichte des Himmel-Wolken-Berges：Roman aus China/Lu Yan-zhou. Mit e. Vorw. von Lu Yan-zhou. Aus d. Chines. u. mit e. Nachw. vers. von Eike Zschacke. Bornheim：Lamuv-Verlag, 1983. 127 S. ; 19cm. ISBN：3921521892, 3921521890. (Dialog Dritte Welt；11)

《天云山传奇》，Zschacke，Eike 译.

(1) Die wunderbare Geschichte des Himmel-Wolken-Berges/Lu Yanzhou. 〔Aus d. Chines. von Eike Zschacke〕. Berlin：Verlag Volk u. Welt, 1985. 152 S. ; 19cm. (Volk-und-Welt-Spektrum；205：Roman)

(2) Die wunderbare Geschichte des Himmel-Wolken-Berges：Roman aus China/Lu Yan-zhou. Aus d. Chines. von Eike Zschacke. Göttingen：Lamuv-Verl. , 1988. 127 S. ; 19cm. ISBN：3889771797, 3889771793.

高晓声(1928—1999)

1. Geschichten von Chen Huansheng：Erzählungen/Gao Xiaosheng. Aus d. Chines. u. mit e. Vorw. von Eike Zschacke. Göttingen：Lamuv-Verl. , 1988. 171 S. ; 19cm. ISBN：3889771742, 3889771742.

《陈奂生故事》，Zschacke，Eike 译.

陆文夫(1928—2005)

1. Der Gourmet/Lu Wenfu. übers. und Nachw. von Stefan Hase-Bergen. Bochum：Brockmeyer, 1992. 159 S. : Ill. ; 19cm. ISBN：3819600012, 3819600019. (Chinathemen/ Serie Europäisches Projekt zur Modernisierung in China；Text 4)

《美食家》，Hase-Bergen，Stefan 译

2. Der Gourmet：Leben und Leidenschaft eines chinesischen Feinschmeckers；Roman/Lu Wenfu. Aus dem Chines. und mit einem Nachw. von Ulrich Kautz. Zürich：Diogenes, 1993. 179 S. ; 19cm. ISBN：3257019742, 3257019742.

《美食家》，Kautz，Ulrich 译.

(1) Der Gourmet：Roman/Lu Wenfu. Aus dem Chines. und mit einem Nachw. von Ulrich Kautz. Roman. Zürich：Diogenes, 1995. 179 S. ; 18cm. ISBN：325722785X, 3257227857. (Diogenes-Taschenbuch；22785)

李心田(1929—)

1. Leuchtender Stern：Roman/Li Sin-tiän. 〔Aus d. Chines. übertr. von Mulan Lehner u. Richard Schirach〕. Zürich：Schweizer Verlagshaus, 1973. 269 S. ;； 20cm. ISBN：3726361501, 3726361502.

《闪闪的红星》，Lehner，Mulan 和 Schirach，Richard 合译.

徐怀中(1929—)

1. Wir säen die Liebe/Ssü Hwai-dshung. 〔Aus d. Chines. ins Dt. übertr. u. gekürzt von Alfons Mainka. Ill. :

Horst Bartsch]. Berlin：Verl. Neues Leben，1962. 295 S.；8.

《我们播种爱情》，Mainka，Alfons 缩写并翻译.

李国文（1930—）

1. Gartenstrasse 5 ［fünf］：Roman/Li Guowen. Dt. von Marianne Liebermann. Berlin；Weimar：Aufbau-Verl.，1989. 463 S.；20cm. ISBN：3351014957，3351014953.

《花园街五号》，Liebermann，Marianne 译.

邓友梅（1931—）

1. Das Schnupftabakfläschchen：Roman/Deng Youmei. ［übers. von Günter Appoldt］. Beijing：Verl. für Fremdsprachige Literatur，1990. 193 S.；19cm. ISBN：7119007874，7119007878

《烟壶》，Appoldt，Günter 译.

2. Phönixkinder und Drachenenkel：Bilder aus dem alten Peking/Deng Youmei. Dt. von Ulrich Kautz. ［Mit einem Interview von Eva Müller. Mit 26 Fotos von Martin Dettloff］. Berlin；Weimar：Aufbau-Verl.，1990. 334 S.；26 Ill.；21cm. ISBN：3351017006，3351017002

Contents：Schnupftabakfläschchen—Na Wu

《北京往事》，Dettloff，Martin 译. 收录《那五》《烟壶》.

孟伟哉（1933—2015）

1. Geburt einer Statue/von Meng Weizai. ［übers. von Sum Hugo-Michael］. Beijing：Verl. für Fremdsprachige Literatur，1986. 99 S.；18cm.

《一座雕像的诞生》，Hugo-Michael，Sum 译.

王蒙（1934—）

1. Der Schmetterling/von Wang Meng. ［Dt. von Klaus B. Ludwig. Red. der dt. Ausg.：Huo Yong；Li Xiuzhen］. Beijing：Verl. für Fremdsprachige Literatur，1986. 116 S.；18cm. （Phönix-Buchreihe）

《蝴蝶》，Ludwig，Klaus 译.

2. Das Auge der Nacht：Erzählungen/Wang Meng. Aus dem Chines. übers. von Irmtraud Fessen-Henjes... Mit einem Nachw. von Wolfgang Kubin. Zürich：Unionsverl.，1987. 288 S.；19cm. ISBN：3293001282，3293001289. （Dialog Dritte Welt；43）

黑夜之眼：王蒙小说选. Fessen-Henjes，Irmtraud 译.

3. Ein Schmetterlingstraum：Erzählungen/Wang Meng. ［Hrsg. von Fritz Gruner. Aus d. Chines. übers. von Irmtraud Fessen-Henjes...］. Berlin；Weimar：Aufbau-Verlag，1988. 545 S.；20cm. ISBN：3351012594，3351012595

蝴蝶梦：王蒙小说选. Fessen-Henjes，Irmtraud 译..

4. Lauter Fürsprecher und andere Geschichten/Wang Meng. Inse Cornelssen；Sun Junhua（Hg.）. übers. von Sun Junhua［and others］. Bochum：Brockmeyer，1989. XII，218 S.；19cm. ISBN：3883397652，3883397658. （Chinathemen；Bd. 44）

王蒙短篇小说集. Sun Junhua 译.

5. Die gemusterte Jacke aus violetter Seide in den Tiefen der

Holztruhe：Erzählungen/Wang Meng. ［Aus dem Chines. übers. von Ursula Richter... Dt. Bearb.：Friedemann Berger］. Beijing：Verl. für Fremdsprachige Literatur，1990. 328 S.；19cm. ISBN：7119012061，7119012063. （Phönix-Ausgabe）

《王蒙小说选》，Berger，Friedemann 译.

6. Rare Gabe Torheit：Roman/Wang Meng. Dt. von Ulrich Kautz. Frauenfeld：Waldgut，1994. 454 S.；22cm. ISBN：3729400962，3729400967.

《活动变人形》，Kautz，Ulrich 译.

7. China enträtselt/Meng Wang. Bochum：Europäischer Universitätsverlag，2017. 500 Seiten. ISBN：3865158888，3865158889. （Politik；13）

《中国天机》

杨啸（1936—）

1. Hung-yü/Yang Hsiao；［Illustrationen von Yao You-duo und Fan Dseng］. Peking：Verlag für Fremdsprachige Literatur，1977. 303 pages，［10］ leaves of plates：color illustrations；19cm.

《红雨》

刘绍棠（1936—1997）

1. Die Leute bei den Kätzchenweiden/von Liu Shaotang. ［Aus dem Chines. übertr. von Ursula Richter］. Beijing：Verl. für Fremdsprachige Literatur，1987. 121 S.；18cm. （Phönix-Buchreihe）

《蒲柳人家》，Richter，Ursula 译.

张贤亮（1936—2014）

1. Die Hälfte des Mannes ist die Frau：Roman/Zhang Xianliang. ［Aus d. Chines. übertr. von Petra Retzlaff］. Frankfurt a. M.；Berlin：Limes，1989. 292 S.；21cm. ISBN：3809022824，3809022829.

《男人的一半是女人》，Retzlaff，Petra 译.

2. Die Hälfte des Mannes ist Frau：Roman/Zhang Xianliang. Dt. von Konrad Herrmann. Berlin：Verl. Neues Leben，1990. 336 S.；20cm. ISBN：3355010665，3355010669.

《男人的一半是女人》，Herrmann，Konrad 译.

3. Die Pionierbäume：ein Roman der Volksrepublik China des Jahres 1984＝（Lühua shu）/Zhang Xianliang. übers. von Beatrice Breitenmoser. Bochum：Brockmeyer，1990. 161，V S.；19cm. ISBN：3883398181，3883398187. （Chinathemen；Bd. 51）

《绿化树》，Breitenmoser，Beatrice 译.

4. Gewohnt zu sterben：Roman/Xianliang Zhang. Aus dem Chines. von Rainer Schwarz. Berlin：Ed. q，1994. 287 S；22cm. ISBN：3861241927，3861241928

《习惯死亡》，Schwarz，Rainer 译.

张洁（1937—）

1. Fangzhou＝Die Arche/Zhang Jie. ［übers. aus d. Chines. von Nelly Ma in Zusammenarbeit mit Michael Kahn-Ackermann］. München：Frauenoffensive，1985. 184 S.；1 Ill.；19cm. ISBN：3881041447，3881041443.

《方舟》,Kahn-Ackermann, Michael 译.

(1)Ungekürzte Ausg. München Dt. Taschenbuch-Verl. ,
1987. 141 S. 18cm. Beil. (1 Bl.). ISBN:
3423108263, 3423108266. (Dtv; 10826)

2. Schwere Flügel: Roman/Zhang Jie. Aus d. Chines. von
Michael Kahn-Ackermann. München; Wien: Hanser,
1985. 339 S. ; 21cm. ISBN: 3446143081, 3446143084

《沉重的翅膀》,Kahn-Ackermann, Michael 译.

(1)Berlin: Aufbau, 1986. 368 p. ; 21cm. ISBN:
3351003315, 3351003319

(2)München: Deutscher Taschenbuch Verlag, 1987. 339
pages; 18cm. ISBN: 3423107286, 3423107280. (dtv;
10728).

3. Solange nichts passiert, geschieht auch nichts: Satiren/
Zhang Jie. Aus d. Chines. von Michael Kahn-
Ackermann. München; Wien: Hanser, 1987. 233 S. ;
20cm. ISBN: 3446149199, 3446149198

《无字》, Kahn-Ackermann, Michael 译.

(1)Ungekürzte Ausg. , 1. Aufl. München: Dt.
Taschenbuch-Verl. , 1996. 185 S. ; 18cm. ISBN:
3423111488, 3423111485. (dtv; 11148)

4. Liebes-Erzählungen/Zhang Jie. Nördlingen: Simon u.
Magiera, 1987. 131 S. ; 19cm. ISBN: 3886760305,
3886760308.

爱情小说两篇. 收录《爱,是不能忘记的》和《祖母绿》.

(1)Zwei Liebeserzählungen/Zhang Jie. [„ Liebe ist
unvergesslich“: aus d. Chines. übers. von Claudia
Magiera. „Smaragd“: aus d. Engl. übers. von Gerd
Simon]. Frankfurt am Main: Fischer-Taschenbuch-
Verl. , 1990. 105 S. ; 18cm. ISBN: 3596102662,
3596102669. (Fischer; 10266). Anmerkungen:
Lizenzausg. d. Verl. Simon u. Magiera, Nördlingen.

5. Abschied von der Mutter/Zhang Jie; aus dem
Chinesischen von Eva Müller. Zürich: Unionsverl. ,
2000. 218 s. : ill. ; 20cm. ISBN: 3293002749,
3293002746

《世界上最疼我的那个人去了》,Müller, Eva 译.

戴厚英(1938—1996)

1. Die grosse Mauer: Roman/ Dai Houying. Aus d. Chines.
von Monika Bessert u. Renate Stephan-Bahle. Mit e.
Nachw. von Helmut Martin. München; Wien: Hanser,
1987. 373 S. ; 21cm. ISBN: 3446145087, 3446145085

《人啊人》,Bessert, Monika 和 Stephan-Bahle, Renate
合译.

(1)Ungekürzte Ausg. , 1. Aufl. München: Dt.
Taschenbuch-Verl. , 1989. 373 S. ; 18cm. ISBN:
3423111860, 3423111867. (dtv; 11186)

陈若曦(1938—)

1. Die Exekution des Landrats Yin und andere Stories aus d.
Kulturrevolution/Chen Jo-hsi; aus dem Chinesischen von
Melinna Yam. . Hamburg: Knaus, 1978. 255 S. ISBN:

381352423X, 3813524239

《尹县长》及其他文革故事,Yam, Melinna 译.

(1)Frankfurt/M; Berlin; Wien: Ullstein, 1982. 255 S. ;
18cm. ISBN: 3548202047, 3548202044. (Ullstein-
Buch; Nr. 20204)

冯骥才(1941—)

1. Ach!: Ein Kurzroman/Feng Jicai. Aus d. Chines.
übertr. von Dorothea Wippermann u. mit e. Nachw. von
Helmut Martin. [Die Erl. am Schluss d. Bd. besorgte
Dorothea Wippermann]. Köln: Diederichs, 1985. 141
S. ; 21cm. ISBN: 3424008531, 3424008532. (Neue
chinesische Bibliothek)

《啊!》,Wippermann, Dorothea 译.

(1)Berlin: Verl. Volk u. Welt, 1989. 122 S. ; 19cm.
ISBN: 3353004994, 3353004998. (Volk-und-Welt-
Spektrum; 249: Kurzroman)

2. Der wundersame Zopf: Erzählungen/Feng Jicai; [aus dem
Chinesischen übers. von Monika Katzenschlager, aus dem
Englischen übers. von Frieder Kern]. Beijing: Verlag für
Fremdsprachige Literatur, 1991. 270 S. ISBN:
7119013793, 7119013794. (Phönix-Ausgabe)

《神鞭:短篇小说集》,Katzenschlager, Monika 译.

3. Leben! Leben! Leben!: Ein Mann, ein Hund und Mao
Zedong/Feng Jicai. Dt. von Karin Hasselblatt. Aarau;
Frankfurt am Main; Salzburg: Sauerländer, 1993. 99 S. ;
22cm. ISBN: 3794136098, 3794136094

《感谢生活》,Hasselblatt, Karin 译.

4. Die lange Dünne und ihr kleiner Mann/Feng Jicai. Aus
dem Chines. von Hannelore Salzmann. Hrsg. und mit
einem Vorw. von Helmut Martin. Dortmund: Projekt-
Verl. , 1994. 147 S. ; 21cm. ISBN: 3928861212,
3928861212. (Richard-Wilhelm-übersetzungszentrum
(Bochum); Arcus-Chinatexte des Richard-Wilhelm-
übersetzungszentrums Bochum; Bd. 4)

Contents: Was für ein Trottel ich doch bin—Die
geschnitzte Pfeife—Die lange Dünne und ihr kleiner
Mann—Ein Lied vom Lebensabend—Die Zauberkraft des
Jadetranks—Im Kampf mit der Kälte

《高女人和她的矮丈夫》,Salzmann, Hannelore 译.

5. Drei Zoll goldener Lotus: Roman/Feng Jicai. Aus dem
Chines. von Karin Hasselblatt. Freiburg im Breisgau;
Basel; Wien: Herder, 1994. 250 S. ; 21cm. ISBN:
3451232992, 3451232995.

《三寸金莲》,Hasselblatt, Karin 译.

蒋子龙(1941—)

1. Alle Farben des Regenbogens/von Jiang Zilong. [Dt. von
Rolf Warnecke]. Beijing: Verl. für Fremdsprachige
Literatur, 1989. 303 S. ; 18cm. ISBN: 7119002570.
(Phönix-Buchreihe)

《赤橙黄绿青蓝紫》,Warnecke, Rolf 译.

古华(1942—)

1. Hibiskus oder vom Wandel der Beständigkeit：Roman/Gu Hua. Aus d. Engl. von Peter Kleinhempel. Berlin：Verlag Volk u. Welt，1986. 258 S.；20cm.

《芙蓉镇》，Kleinhempel，Peter 译自英文.

邓刚(1945—)

1. Der Zauber des Meeres/Deng Gang；Carolin Blank；Stefan Hase-Bergen；Rolf Warnecke. Beijing：Verlag für fremdsprachige Literatur，1987. 118 S.

《迷人的海》，Carolin Blank 等译.

乌兰巴干(1946—)

1. Feuer in der Steppe/Ulanbagan. ［Aus d. Chines. ins Dt. übertr. von Alfons Mainka.］Mit Ill. von Karl Fischer. Berlin：Verl. Neues Leben，1961. 392 S.；8.

《草原烽火》，Mainka，Alfons 译.

姜戎(1946—)

1. Der Zorn der Wölfe：Roman/Jiang Rong；aus dem Chines. von Karin Hasselblatt；unter Mitarb. von Marc Hermann und Zhang Rui. München：Goldmann，2008. 703 S. ISBN：3442311088，344231108X

《狼图腾》，Hasselblatt，Karin 译.

礼平(原名刘辉宣，1948—)

1. Zur Stunde des verblassenden Abendrots：Roman/Li Ping. Aus d. Chines. von Marianne Fronhofer-Almen u. Birgit Voigtländer. Mit e. Nachw. von Karl-Heinz Pohl. Freiburg im Breisgau；Basel；Wien：Herder，1988. 192 S.；21cm. ISBN：3451211546，3451211548.

《晚霞消失的时候》，Fronhofer，Marianne 和 Voigtländer，Birgit 合译.

    （1）2. Aufl. Freiburg im Breisgau；Basel；Wien：Herder，1990. 192 S.；21cm. Freiburg im Breisgau；Basel；Wien：Herder，1992. 192 S.；19cm. ISBN：3451041402，3451041405. （Herder-Spektrum；Bd. 4140）

北岛(1949—)

1. Gezeiten：ein Roman über Chinas verlorene Generation/Bei Dao；aus dem Chinesischen von Irmgard E. A. Wiesel；herausgegeben und mit einem Nachwort von Helmut Martin. Frankfurt am Main：Fischer，1990. ISBN：3100120027，3100120021

《波动》，Martin，Helmut 和 Wiesel，Irmgard E. A. 合译.

2. Strasse des Glücks Nr. 13：die Kurzgeschichten/Bei Dao；übersetzt von Eva Klapproth ［and others］. Bochum：N. Brockmeyer，1992. ii，95 pages；19cm. ISBN：381960006X，3819600067. （Chinathemen；Bd. 71）

Contents：Strasse des Glücks Nr. 13—Die Heimkehr des Fremden—In den Ruinen—Melodie—Kreuzwege—Der Mond auf dem Manuskript.

《幸福大街十三号：短篇小说》，Klapproth，Eva 等译.

阿城(1949—)

1. Baumkönig，Kinderkönig，Schachkönig：die bekanntesten Erzählungen der 80er Jahre aus einer daoistisch-dialektischen Perspektive/A Cheng. Dortmund：Projekt Verlag，1996. 196 p.；21cm. ISBN：3928861654，3928861656. （Arcus Chinatexte；Band 8）

《树王、棋王、孩子王：中短篇小说集》

李锐(1950—)

1. Trügerische Heirat：Erzählungen vom Lande/Li Rui；aus dem Chinesischen von Ines Gründel，Reiner Müller und and.；hrsg. und mit einem Vorwort von Helmut Martin. Dortmund：Projekt，1994. viii，117 p.；21cm. ISBN：3928861174，3928861175. （Arcus Chinatexte；Band 3）

Contents：Das Lagerfeuer（Gouhuo）—Der gemeinsame Weg（Tong xing）—Trügerische Heirat（Jiahun）—Ein toller Kerl（Haohan）—Zwei Drachen spielen mit der Perle（Er long xi zhu）—Am Bach bei den grünen Steinen（Qingshi jian）.

《厚土》，Gründel，Ines 和 Martin，Helmut(1940—)合译.

贾平凹(1952—)

1. Geschichten vom Taibai-Berg：moderne Geistererzählungen aus der Provinz Shaanxi/Jia Pingwa；herausgegeben und kommentiert von Andrea Riemenschnitter；［Erstübersetzung von Domink Linggi ［and others］；mit Illustrationen von Dadong Lu］. Zürich：Lit，2009. ii，159 pages：illustrations；21cm. ISBN：3643800329，3643800320. （Sinologie；Bd. 2）

太白山故事：现代陕西鬼怪故事集. Riemenschnitter，Andrea 和 Linggi，Domink 合译.

周大新(1952—)

1. Der Fluch des Silbers：［Novellensammlung］/Zhou Daxin. Beijing：Verl. Chines. Literatur，1996. 237 S. 18cm. ISBN：7507103595，7507103595. （Panda-Bücher）

《银饰》，钟英杰译. 中国文学出版社.

2. Im Bann des Roten Sees/Zhou Daxin. Aus dem Chines. übertr. von Longpei Lü. Jena；Quedlinburg：Bussert & Stadeler，2011. 383 S.：Ill. ISBN：3942115220，3942115223. （China classics international）

Lü，Longpei 译.

3. An Hun. Gespräche mit meinem verstorbenen Sohn Daxin Zhou. Quedlinburg：Bussert u. Stadeler，2016. 244 Seiten 2 Illustrationen. ISBN：3942115414，3942115417

《安魂》，Lü，Longpei 译.

4. Siebenundzwanzig Gespräche über den merkwürdigen Tod des Gouverneurs der Provinz Quinghe/Daxin Zhou. Quedlinburg：Bussert u. Stadeler，2017. 276 Seiten 195cm.×125cm. ISBN：3942115469，3942115468

《曲终人在》，Lü，Longpei 和 Wu，Jue 合译.

张辛欣(1953—)

1. Pekingmenschen ＝ Beijingren/Zhang Xinxin；Sang Ye. Hrsg. von Helmut Martin. Köln：Diederichs，1986. 351 S.；23cm. ISBN：3424008555，3424008559.

《北京人》，张辛欣，桑晔著；Ascher，Barbara 等译.

(1)2. Aufl. Köln：Diederichs, 1987. 351 S.；22cm.

(2)Pekingmenschen/Zhang Xinxin；Sang Ye. Hrsg. von Helmut Martin. München：Dt. Taschenbuch-Verl.，1989. 350 S.；19cm. ISBN：3423110723，3423110724. (dtv；11072). Anmerkungen：Lizenz d. Diederichs Verl.，München.

(3)2. Aufl. München：Dt. Taschenbuch-Verl.，1990. 350 S.；19cm.

2. Traum unserer Generation：Erzählung/Zhang Xinxin；übersetzt aus dem Chinesischen mit einer literarischen Betrachtung von Gaotkei Lang-Tan. ［Bonn］：Engelhardt-Ng Verlag, 1986. 97 pages；21cm. ISBN：3924716056, 3924716059. （Übersetzungsreihe：Chinesische Frauenliteratur；0605)

《我们这个年纪的梦》,Lang-Tan, Goatkoei 译.

3. Am gleichen Horizont：Erzählung/Zhang Xinxin；übersetzt aus dem Chinesischen von Marie-Luise Beppler-Lie. ［Bonn］：Engelhardt-Ng Verlag, 1987. 164 pages；21cm. ISBN：3924716064, 3924716066. (Übersetzungsreihe：Chinesische Frauenliteratur；0606)

《在同一地平线上》,Beppler-Lie, Marie-Luise 译.

4. Eine Welt voller Farben：22 chinesische Porträts/Zhang Xinxin；Sang Ye. ［Hrsg. von Eva Müller. Aus d. Chines. übers. von Ines Gründel...］. Berlin；Weimar Aufbau-Verl.，1987. 207 S. 20cm. ISBN：3351007582, 3351007584. (Edition neue Texte)

22 位中国人访谈. 张辛欣,桑晔；Müller, Eva(1933—)和 Gründel, Ines 合译.

残雪(1953—)

1. Dialoge im Paradies：Erzählungen aus der Volksrepublik China/Can Xue；aus dem Chinesischen und mit einem Vorwort von Wolf Baus. Dortmund：Projekt, 1996. 148 pages；illustrations；21cm. ISBN：3928861670, 3928861670. （Arcus-Chinatexte des Richard-Wilhelm-Übersetzungszentrum；Bd. 10)

《天堂里的对话》,Baus, Wolf 译.

刘恒(1954—)

1. Bekenntnisse eines Hundertjährigen：Roman/Liu Heng. Aus dem Chines. von Ingrid Müller und Zhang Rui. München：Hanser, 2009. 380 S.；22cm. ISBN：3446205345, 3446205349

《苍河白日梦》,Müller, Ingrid 译.

王安忆(1954—)

1. Wege：Erzählungen aus d. chines. Alltag/［Wang Anyi］. Vorw. Anne Engelhardt u. Ng Hong-chiok. übers. Andrea Döteberg. Bonn：Engelhardt-Ng,1985. 96 S.：Ill.；21cm. ISBN：3924716035, 392471603X. (Übersetzungsreihe：chinesische Frauenliteratur；603)

王安忆小说. Döteberg, Andrea 译.

2. Kleine Lieben：2 Erzählungen/Wang Anyi. Aus d. Chines. von Karin Hasselblatt. München；Wien：Hanser, 1988. 267 S.；21cm. ISBN：3446152311, 3446152318.

王安忆小说两篇. Hasselblatt, Karin 译. 收录《锦绣谷之恋》《荒山之恋》.

3. Zwischen Ufern：Roman/Wang Anyi. Aus dem Chinesischen von Silvia Kettelhut. Berlin：Edition q, 1997. 304 p.；21cm. ISBN：3861243075, 3861243076

《长恨歌》,Kettelhut, Silvia(1965—)译.

莫言(1955—)

1. Das rote Kornfeld：Roman/Mo Yan；deutsch von Peter Weber-Schäfer. Hamburg：Rowohlt, 1988. 489 s. ISBN：3499136333, 3499136337. (Rororo；1690)

《红高粱家族》,Weber-Schäfer, Peter 译.

(1) Reinbek bei Hamburg：Rowohlt, 1993. 489 S.；22cm. ISBN：3498043501, 3498043506

(2)Einmalige Sonderausg. Reinbek bei Hamburg：Rowohlt, 1995. 498 S.；19cm. ISBN：349912095X, 3499120954. (Rororo；12095)

(3)Reinbek bei Hamburg Rowohlt, 1995. 489 S. 19cm. ISBN：3499136333, 3499136337. (Rororo；13633)

(4) 3. Aufl. Zürich Unionsverl.，2007. 489 S. ISBN：3293203839, 3293203833. (Unionsverlag-Taschenbuch；383)

(5)6. Aufl. Zürich Unionsverlag,2013. 489 Seiten 22cm.

2. Die Knoblauchrevolte：Roman/Mo Yan. Dt. von Andreas Donath. Reinbek bei Hamburg：Rowohlt, 1993. 383 S.；22cm. ISBN：3498043595, 3498043599

《天堂蒜苔之歌》,Donath, Andreas 译.

(1)Reinbek bei Hamburg：Rowohlt, 1998. 383 S.；19cm. ISBN：3499223651, 3499223655. （Rororo；22365)

(2) Zürich：Unionsverl.，2009. 383 S.；19cm. ISBN：3293204546, 3293204546. （Unionsverlag-Taschenbuch；454)

3. Trockener Fluss und andere Geschichten/Mo Yan. Aus dem Chinesischen von Susanne Hornfeck u. a. Studienausgabe. Dortmund：Projekt Verlag, 1997. 199 pages；21cm. ISBN：3928861946, 3928861948. (Arcus-Chinatexte des Richard-Wilhelm-Übersetzungszentrum；Bd. 12)

Contents：Der Jungfernflug—Die alte Flinte—Katzengeschichte—Volksmusik—Durchsichtiger roter Rettich—Der weisse Hund auf der Schaukel—Schuldig—Der Hochbegabte—Trockener Fluss.

莫言短篇小说选. Hornfeck, Susanne(1956—)译.

4. Die Schnapsstadt：Roman/Mo Yan. Dt. von Peter Weber-Schäfer. Reinbek bei Hamburg：Rowohlt, 2002. 511 S.；21cm. ISBN：3498043870, 3498043872

《酒国》,Weber-Schäfer, Peter(1935—)译.

(1) Zürich：Unionsverl.，2005. 511 S.；19cm. ISBN：3293203205,3293203204. (Unionsverlag-Taschenbuch；

320)

(2)Zürich：Unionsverl.，2012. 511 S. 19cm. ISBN：3293205635，3293205631.（Unionsverlag-Taschenbuch；563）

5. Der Überdruss：Roman/Mo Yan. Aus dem Chines. von Martina Hasse. Bad Honnef：Horlemann，2009. 812 S.；24cm.，900 gr. ISBN：3895022722, 3895022721

《生死疲劳》，Hasse，Martina 译.

  (1)2. Aufl. Berlin：Horlemann，2012. 812 S. ISBN：3895023446，3895023442

  (2)Zürich：Unionsverlag，2012. 812 S. ISBN：3293205888，3293205887.（Unionsverlag-Taschenbuch；588）

6. Wie das Blatt sich wendet/Mo Yan. München Hanser, Carl，2014. 112 S. ISBN：3446243385，3446243380

《变》，Hasse，Martina 译.

  (1)München dtv，2016. 112 S. 19. 1cm. ×12cm. ISBN：3423145121，3423145129.（dtv；14512）

王朔(1958—)

1. Herzklopfen heisst das Spiel：Roman/Shuo Wang. Aus dem Chines. von Sabine Peschel in Zusammenarbeit mit Wang Ding und Edgar Wang. Mit einem Nachw. von Sabine Peschel. Zürich：Diogenes，1995. 388 S.；19cm. ISBN：3257060602，3257060607

《玩的就是心跳》，Peschel，Sabine 译.

  (1) Zürich：Diogenes，1997. 388 S.；19cm. ISBN：3257229714，3257229712.（Diogenes-Taschenbuch；22971）

2. Oberchaoten：Roman/Wang Shuo. Aus dem Chines. von Ulrich Kautz；mit einem Nachw. des Übers. Zürich：Diogenes，1997. 271 S.；19cm. ISBN：3257061420，3257061420

Contents：Oberchaoten；Kein bisschen seriös.

《顽主》，Kautz，Ulrich 译.

  (1)Zürich：Diogenes，2001. 272 S；19cm. ISBN：3257232624，3257232622.（Diogenes Taschenbuch；23262）

3. Ich bin doch dein Vater！：Roman/Wang Shuo；aus dem Chinesischen von Ulrich Kautz. Gossenberg：Ostasien Verlag，2012. 397 S. ISBN：3940527622，3940527629.（Reihe Phönixfeder；14）

《我是你爸爸》，Kautz，Ulrich 译.

阎连科(1958—)

1. Der Traum meines Großvaters：Roman/Yan Lianke. Aus dem Chines. von Ulrich Kautz. Berlin：List，2011. 363 S. 19cm. ISBN：3548610047，3548610048.（List-Taschenbuch；61004）

《丁庄梦》，Kautz，Ulrich(1939—)译.

2. Lenins Küsse：Roman/Yan Lianke. Übers. aus dem Chines. von Ulrich Kautz. Köln：Eichborn，2015. 655 S. 215×135 mm. ISBN：3847906003，3847906001

《列宁之吻》，Kautz，Ulrich(1939—)译.

3. Die vier Bücher：Roman/Yan Lianke；Übers. aus dem

Chinesischen von Marc Hermann. Köln：Eichborn Verlng in der Bastei Lübbe AG，2017. 349 Seiten 22cm. ISBN：3847906377，3847906372

《四书》，Hermann，Marc 译.

刘震云(1958—)

1. Taschendiebe：Roman/Liu Zhenyun. Aus dem Chines. von Marc Hermann. Düren［u. a.］：DIX-Verl.，2009. 448 S. ISBN：3941651012，3941651013

《我叫刘跃进》，Hermann，Marc 等译.

2. 1942：eine Dokumentation und andere Erzählungen/Zhenyun Liu. Wien：Löcker，2014. 160 S. 190 mm×115 mm. ISBN：3854097082，3854097085

《温故一九四二》，Winter，Martin 译.

3. Scheidung auf Chinesisch：Roman/Liu Zhenyun. Bergisch Gladbach：Ehrenwirth，2016. 400 S. 215 mm×135 mm. ISBN：3431039320，3431039324.（Bastei-Lübbe-Taschenbuch；Band 17511）

《我不是潘金莲》

  (1)München：Ehrenwirth，2016. 350 Seiten；215 mm×135 mm. ISBN：3431039320，3431039324

  (2)Köln：Bastei Lübbe，2016. 350 Seiten. ISBN：3431039320，3431039324

陈丹燕(1959—)

1. Der Shanghaier Bund：Aufstieg，Fall und Wiedergeburt/Chen Danyan. Aus dem Chines. von Martina Hasse. Berlin：Horlemann，2013. 312 S.：zahlr. Abb.；225 mm×145 mm. ISBN：3895023620，3895023620

上海滩：繁华、衰落与新生. Hasse，Martina(1961—)译.

阿来(1959—)

1. Ferne Quellen/Alai；aus dem Chinesischen von Marc Hermann. Zürich：Unionsverlag，2009. 153 pages；20cm. ISBN：3293004054，3293004059

《遥远的温泉》，Hermann，Marc 译.

  (1)Zürich：Unionsverlag，2011. 149 S. ISBN：3293205239，3293205232.（Unionsverlag-Taschenbuch；523）

余华(1960—)

1. Leben！：Roman/Yu Hua. Aus dem Chines. von Ulrich Kautz. Stuttgart：Klett-Cotta，1998. 219 S.；21cm. ISBN：3608934170，3608934175

《活着》，Kautz，Ulrich(1939—)译.

  (1)München：Btb，2008. 219 S.；19cm. ISBN：3442737741，3442737745.（Btb；73774）

2. Der Mann，der sein Blut verkaufte：Roman/Yu Hua. Aus dem Chines. von Ulrich Kautz；mit einem Nachw. des Autors. Stuttgart：Klett-Cotta，2000. 260 S.；21cm. ISBN：3608934944，3608934946

《许三观卖血记》，Kautz，Ulrich(1939—)译.

  (1)［München］：Btb，2005. 254 S.；19cm. ISBN：3442731763，3442731763

3. Brüder：Roman/Yu Hua. Aus dem Chines. von Ulrich

Kautz. Frankfurt，M.：S. Fischer，2009. 764 S.；22cm. ISBN：3100958037，3100958039

《兄弟》，Kautz，Ulrich(1939—)译.

（1）Frankfurt，M.：Fischer-Taschenbuch-Verl.，2012. 764 S. 19cm. ISBN：3596178681，3596178681. (Fischer；17868)

4. Die sieben letzten Tage：Roman/Yu Hua. [Frankfurt am Main S. Fischer]，2017. 304 Seiten：20. 5cm. ×12. 5cm. ISBN：3100021939，3100021932

《第七天》，Kautz，Ulrich(1939—)译.

虹影(1962—)

1. Der verratene Sommer/Hong Ying. Aus dem Chines. von Stephanie Song. Frankfurt am Main：Krüger，1997. 217 S. ISBN：3810524018，3810524010

《背叛之夏》(又名《裸舞代》)，Song，Stephanie 译.

2. Der chinesische Sommer：Roman/Hong Ying. Aus dem Chines. von Karin Hasselblatt. Berlin：Aufbau-Taschenbuch-Verl.，2005. 231 S.；19cm. ISBN：3746620899，3746620893. (Aufbau-Taschenbuch；2089)

《背叛之夏》，Hasselblatt，Karin 译.

3. Die chinesische Geliebte：Roman/Hong Ying；aus dem Chinesischen von Martin Winter. 4. Aufl. Berlin：Aufbau Verlag，2004. 270 pages；22cm. ISBN：335103008，3351030087

《K》《英国情人》)，Winter，Martin 译.

（1）Berlin Aufbau-Taschenbuch-Verl.，2005. 269 S. 19cm. ISBN：3746622085，3746622088. (Aufbau-Taschenbücher；2208)

4. Der Pfau weint：Roman/Hong Ying. Aus dem Chines. von Karin Hasselblatt. Berlin：Aufbau-Verl.，2005. 247 S.；22cm. ISBN：3351030487，3351030483

《孔雀的叫喊》，Hasselblatt，Karin 译.

（1）Berlin：Aufbau-Taschenbuch-Verl.，2007. 247 S.；19cm. ISBN：3746623177，3746623170. (Aufbau-Taschenbücher；2317)

5. Tochter des großen Stromes：Roman meines Lebens/Hong Ying；aus d. Chin. von Karin Hasselblatt. Berlin：Aufbau-Verl.，2006. 315 S.；215×125 mm. ISBN：3351026387，3351026382

《饥饿的女儿》，Hasselblatt，Karin 译.

（1）Berlin Aufbau-Taschenbuch，2008. 315 S. 19cm. ISBN：3746624082，3746624088. (Aufbau-Taschenbücher；2408)

6. Die Konkubine von Shanghai：Roman/Hong Ying. Aus dem Chines. von Claudia Kaiser. Berlin：Aufbau，2009. 459 S.；22cm. ISBN：3351032692，3351032692

《上海王》，Kaiser，Claudia 译.

（1）Berlin Aufbau-Taschenbuch，2011. 459 S. 19cm. ISBN：3746627076，3746627079. (Aufbau-Taschenbücher；2707)

刘慈欣(1963—)

1. Die drei Sonnen：Roman/Cixin Liu. München：Heyne，

2016. 450 S 20. 6 × 14cm. ISBN：3453317165，3453317161

《三体》，Hasse，Martina(1961—)译.

（1）Deutsche Erstausgabe. München：Wilhelm Heyne Verlag，2017. 591 Seiten 21cm. ISBN：3453317161，3453317165

2. Spiegel：Novelle/Cixin Liu；aus dem Chinesischen von Marc Hermann. Deutsche Erstausgabe. München：Wilhelm Heyne Verlag，2017. 189 Seiten；19cm. ISBN：3453319125，3453319127

《镜子》，Hermann，Marc(1970—)译.

3. Weltenzerstörer：Novelle/Cixin Liu. München：Heyne，2017. 150 Seiten 18. 7cm. × 11. 8cm. ISBN：3453319257，3453319257

《坍缩》，Hermann，Marc(1970—)译.

苏童(1963—)

1. Rote Laterne：Roman；[das Buch zum Film]/Su Tong. Dt. von Stefan Linster. München：Goldmann，1992. 150 S.；18cm. ISBN：3442420735，3442420733. (Goldmann；42073)

《妻妾成群》，Linster，Stefan 译.

2. Reis：Roman/Su Tong. Dt. von Peter Weber-Schäfer. Reinbek bei Hamburg：Rowohlt，1998. 280 S.；21cm. ISBN：3498065157，3498065157

《罂粟之家》，Weber-Schäfer，Peter 译.

3. Die Opiumfamilie：Roman/Su Tong. Dt. von Peter Weber-Schäfer. Blindendr. der Dt. Blindenstudienanst. Marburg Dt. Blindenstudienanst，2000. 124 S. 32cm.

《罂粟之家》，Weber-Schäfer，Peter 译.

4. Die Tränenfrau：der Mythos von der treuen Meng/Su Tong；aus dem Chinesischen von Marc Hermann. Berlin：Berlin Verlag，2006. 461 pages；21cm. ISBN：3827006872，3827006875. (Die Mythen)

《碧奴》，Hermann，Marc 译.

麦家(1964—)

1. Das verhängnisvolle Talent des Herrn Rong：Roman/Mai Jia. Aus dem Chines. von Karin Betz. München：Dt. Verl.-Anst.，2015. 349 S.；22cm. ISBN：3421046719，3421046710

《解密》，Betz，Karin 译.

毕宇飞(1964—)

1. Die Mondgöttin/Bi Feiyu；Aus dem Chines. übers. von Marc Hermann. München：Karl Blessing，2006. 158 S.；200×125 mm. ISBN：3896672983，3896672988

《青衣》，Hermann，Marc 译.

2. Sehende Hände/Bi Feiyu. München：Blessing，Karl，2016. 540 S. 21. 5cm. ×13. 5cm. ISBN：3896675651，3896675656

《推拿》，Hermann，Marc 译.

朱文(1967—)

1. I love dollars und andere Geschichten aus China/Zhu

Wen；aus dem Chinesischen und mit einem Nachwort von Frank Meinshausen. München：A1 Verl. ，2009. 359 S. ISBN：3940666079，3940666076

《我爱美元》，Meinshausen，Frank(1965—)译.

棉棉(1970—)

1. La la la/Mianmian；aus dem Chinesischen von Karin Hasselblatt. Köln：Kiepenheuer & Witsch，2001. 181 S. ISBN：3462029509，3462029505. （KiWi paperback；593）

《啦啦啦》，Hasselblatt，Karin 译.

2. Deine Nacht，mein Tag/Mian Mian. Aus dem Chin. von Karin Hasselblatt. Köln：Kiepenheuer & Witsch，2005. 191 S；19cm. ISBN：3462034219，3462034219. （KiWi；；838. ；Paperback）

《你的黑夜，我的白天》，Hasselblatt，Karin 译.

3. Panda Sex：Roman/Mian Mian；aus dem Chinesischen von Martin Woesler. Köln：Kiepenheuer & Witsch，2009. 165 pages：illustrations；19cm. ISBN：3462041477，3462041479. （KiWi）

《熊猫》，Woesler，Martin 译.

卫慧(1973—)

1. Shanghai baby：Roman/Wei Hui；aus dem Chinesischen von Karin Hasselblatt. Munich：Ullstein，2002. 319 pages；18cm. ISBN：3548255108，3548255101

《上海宝贝》，Hasselblatt，Karin 译.

2. Marrying Buddha：Roman/Wei Hui. Aus der autoris. engl. Fassung，unter Berücksichtigung des chines. Orig. ，übers. von Susanne Hornfeck. Berlin：Ullstein，2005. 287 S. ；22cm. ISBN：3550086205，3550086202

《我的禅》，Hornfeck，Susanne 译自英文.

（1）Berlin：Ullstein，2007. 286 S. ；18cm. ISBN：3548266404，3548266401. （Ullstein；26640）

盛可以(1973—)

1. Die Qualle/von Sheng Keyi. Übers. ：Britta Schwarzbach... Leitung und Koordination：Martin Woesler. Berlin：Europ. -Univ. -Verl. ，2014. 267 S. 23cm. ISBN：3865152145，3865152147. （Sinica；34）

《水母》，Schwarzbach，Britta 译.

（1）Deutsche Ausgabe. Berlin：Europäischer Universitätsverlag，2014. 267 Seiten. ISBN：3865152022，3865152023. （Sinica；34）

春树(1983—)

1. China Girl：Roman/Chun Sue；aus dem Chines. von Karin Hasselblatt. München：Goldmann，2006. 284 S. ISBN：3442461165，3442461162. （Goldmann；46116）

《北京娃娃》，Hasselblatt，Karin 译.

其他

1. Der Heilige als Eulenspiegel：12 Abenteuer e. Zenmeisters/Aus d. Chines. von Liu Guan-ying. Basel；Stuttgart：Schwabe，1958. 167 S. ；mit Abb. ；8.

《济公传》，Liu Guan-ying 译.

（1）Dao Dsi，der lebende Buddha：Abenteuer e. Zen-Meisters/hrsg. von Julius Schwabe. ［Aus d. Chines. von Liu Guan Ying］. Basel：Sphinx-Verlag，1983. 167 S. ：Ill. ；21cm. ISBN：3859141506，3859141503.

2. Die Liebesabenteuer des Blühenden Talents/aus d. Chines. übers. ，mit Anm. u. e. Nachw. von F. K. Engler. München：Heyne，1986. 173 S. ：1 Ill. ；18cm. ISBN：3453503441，3453503449. （Heyne-Bücher：16：Exquisit-Bücher；Nr. 375）

《富贵奇缘》，Engler，F. K. 译. 民国时期小说.

3. Erzählungen nach Opern der Yuan-Dynastie/Chen Meilin. Beijing：Verlag für Fremdsprachige Literatur，2002. 179 pages：illustrations；18cm. ISBN：7119029932

《元杂剧故事选》，陈美林编；王宽信译.

4. Frauen，Liebe，Hass und Mord：Geschichten aus dem kaiserlichen Harem/nacherzählt von Atze Schmidt. Beijing：Verlag für Fremdsprachige Literatur，2002. 194 pages：illustrations；18cm. ISBN：7119020439

《中国古代后妃故事》，元阳，晓燕.

5. Kriegsgeschichten aus dem chinesischen Altertum/［Chinesischer Text：Yuan Yang und Ming Ping；Übersetzung：Zhao Rongheng］. Beijing：Verlag für Fremdsprachige Literatur，2003. 234 pages：illustrations；18cm. ISBN：7119021060

《亡而复生：中国古代战争故事》，元阳，明平译.

I6　报告文学与回忆录

1. Die Erbauer des Ming-Gräber-Stausees/［Deutsch von Käthe Dschao］. Peking：Verlag für fremdsprachige Literatur，1959. 276 p. ：ill. ；19cm.

《建设十三陵水库的人们》

2. Mit dem Vorsitzenden Mao Tse-tung auf dem Langen Marsch/Tschang-feng Tschen. ［Ill. von Ah Lao］. Peking：Verl. f. Fremdsprach. Literatur，1960. 122 S. ：mit Kt. ；8

《跟随毛主席长征》，陈昌奉(1915—1986)著.

（1）Peking：Verlag für Fremdsprachige Literatur，1972. 139 S. ：ill. ，Kt. ；20cm.

（2）Beijing：Verl. für Fremdsprachige Literatur，1986. 131 S. ill. 19cm.

3. Erzählungen von der chinesischen Roten Armee. Peking：Verl. für Fremdsprachige Literatur，1960. XI，217 S：Taf.

《中国红军的故事》，何长工等.

4. Meine Familie/Tschöng Tau. ［Aus d. Chines. übers. von Liane Bettin］. Berlin：Aufbau-Verl. ，1961. 172 S. ；8.

《我的一家》，陶承(1893—1986)口述；Bettin，Liane 译.

5. Kampf hinter Kerkermauern/Dschi-lin Yang. ［übers. v. Maria Tan；Tjiu Tschungjen］. Peking：Verl. f. fremdsprachige Literatur，1964. 153 S. ：1 Titelb. ；8.

《王若飞在狱中》,杨植霖;Maria Tan 和 Tjiu Tschungjen 合译.

6. Vom Kaiser zum Bürger (Autobiographie). /Aisin-Gioro Pu Yi. Peking, 1965.

《从皇帝到公民》,爱新觉罗·傅仪.

7. Ich war Kaiser von China: vom Himmelssohn z. Neuen Menschen/Pu Yi. Hrsg. u. aus d. Chines. übers. von Richard Schirach u. Mulan Lehner. München: Hanser, 1973. 488 S.: 58 Ill.;; 21cm. ISBN: 3446117679, 3446117679.

《我的前半生》,溥仪(1906—1967)著;Schirach, Richard 和 Lehner, Mulan 合译.

(1) Zürich: Neue Schweizer Bibliothek, 1974. 488 S.: Abb.; 21cm.

(2) Ich war Kaiser von China: vom Himmelssohn zum neuen Menschen: die Autobiographie des letzten chinesischen Kaisers/Pu Yi. [Ins Dt. übertr. von Mulan Lehner u. Richard Schirach]. Ungekürzte Ausg. Frankfurt [Main]: Fischer-Taschenbuch-Verlag, 1975. 445 S.; 18cm. ISBN: 3436021431, 3436021436. (Fischer-Taschenbücher; 1637)

(3) Berlin, Darmstadt, Wien: Dt. Buch-Gemeinschaft Gütersloh Bertelsmann; Stuttgart: Europ. Bildungsgemeinschaft; Wien: Buchgemeinschaft Donauland, 1976. 488 Seiten Illustrationen 21cm.

(4) 2. Aufl. München; Wien: Hanser, 1986. 454 Seiten: 58 Illustrationen; 21cm. ISBN: 3446117679, 344611767.

(5) Ungekürzte Ausg. München: Dt. Taschenbuch-Verl., 1987. 452, [64] Seiten: 107 Illustrationen; 19cm. ISBN: 3423107103, 3423107105. (Dtv; 10710: Biographie)

(6) 4., erw. u. erg. Aufl. München u. a.: Hanser, 1987. 516 Seiten: Illustrationen. ISBN: 3446150544, 3446150546, 3446150374, 34461503

(7) Berlin: Verl. Neues Leben, 1989. 540 Seiten Illustrationen 212cm. ISBN: 3355008486, 3355008488

(8) Ungekürzte Ausg., [7. Aufl.] München: Dt. Taschenbuch-Verl., 1990. 452, [64] S. Ill. 20cm. ISBN: 3423107103, 3423107105. (dtv; 10710: Biographie)

(9) Ungekürzte Ausg., 9. Aufl. München: Dt. Taschenbuch-Verl., 2004. 452, [32] S.: Ill.; 20cm. ISBN: 3423207010, 3423207019. (dtv; 20701)

(10) Köln: Anaconda, 2008. 588 S. Ill. 20cm. ISBN: 3866472143, 3866472145

(11) Neuausg. München: Dt. Taschenbuch-Verl., 2009. 452, [64] S.: Ill.; 20cm. ISBN: 3423211680, 3423211687. (dtv; 21168)

8. Der Rote-Fahne-Kanal/von Lin Min. Peking: Verlag für Fremdsprachige Literatur, 1974. 69 S.: ill.; 19cm.

《红旗渠》,林民.

9. Schaschiyü verwandelt sich/von Tang Feng-dschang. Peking: Verlag für Fremdsprachige Literatur, 1976. [24], 154 S.: ill.; 19cm.

《沙石峪》,唐凤章著;志援,兰辉插图.

10. Mein Heimatdorf: Sechs Reportagen/von Gao Yü-bao und anderen. Peking: Verlag für fremdsprachige Literatur, 1976. 169 pages: photographs; 19cm.

《换了人间》,高玉宝等著.

11. Mein Heimatdorf: 6 Reportagen/von Gao Yü-bao u. a. Peking: Verlag für Fremdsprachige Literatur, 1976. 169 S.: Ill.; 19cm.

《家乡处处换新颜》,高玉宝(1927—)著.

12. Die Frauen-Miliz der Eintracht-Insel: Roman/[Li Ruqing]. Kiel: Rotfront-Verl., 1977. 300 S. ISBN: 3881970088, 3881970082

《海岛女民兵》,黎汝清(1928—2015)著.

13. Milizionärinnen auf einer Insel/Li Ju-tjing. Ill. von Tsai Jung. Peking: Verl. für Fremdsprach. Literatur, 1978. 338 S.

《海岛女民兵》,黎汝清著;蔡荣插图.

14. Mit Vizevorsitzendem Tschou En-lai auf dem Langen Marsch/We Guo-lu. [Ill. von Schen Jao-yi]. Peking: Verl. für Fremdsprach. Literatur, 1978. 158 S.: ill.

《随周恩来副主席长征》,魏国禄著;沈尧伊插图.

15. Gedenken an den Ministerpräsidenten Tschou En-lai. / Peking: Verlag fur Fremdsprachige Literatue, 1978. 176 S.: Abb., portraits; 21cm.

《怀念周恩来总理》

16. Eindrücke von Datjing. / Schan-hao Djiang. Peking: Verl. für Fremdsprachige Literatur, 1978. 68 S.

《大庆印象记》,江山浩.

17. Kindheit: Autobiographie/Guo Moruo. übertr. aus d. Chines. u. Nachw. von Ingo Schäfer. Frankfurt am Main: Insel-Verlag, 1981. 239 S.; 21cm. ISBN: 3458047568, 3458047565. ('(Guo, Moruo: Autobiographie; [Bd. 1])

《我的童年》,郭沫若(1892—1978)著;Schäfer, Ingo (1915—)译.(自传)

18. Jugend/Guo Moruo. übertr. aus d. Chines. u. Nachw. von Ingo Schäfer. Frankfurt am Main: Insel-Verlag, 1985. 298 S.; 21cm. ISBN: 3458142430, 3458142436. (Guo, Moruo: Autobiographie; Bd. 2)

《少年时代》,郭沫若(1892—1978)著;Schäfer, Ingo (1915—)译.(自传)

19. Ein Wintermärchen/Yu Luojin. Übers. u. Nachw.: Michael Nerlich. Bonn: Engelhardt-Ng, 1985. 183 S.; 21cm. ISBN: 3924716028, 3924716021. (Übersetzungsreihe: chinesische Frauenliteratur; 602)

《一个冬天的童话》，遇罗锦（1946—）著；Nerlich, Michael 译.

20. Mein Weg：Selbstbekenntnis e. chines. Schauspielerin/ Liu Xiaoqing. übers. aus d. Chines. mit e. Einl. von Anne Engelhardt. ［Hrsg.：Anne Engelhardt；Ng Hong-chiok］. Bonn：Engelhardt-Ng, 1986. 86, ［20］ S.：Ill.；21cm. ISBN：3924716042, 3924716048. (übersetzungsreihe: chinesische Frauenliteratur；0604)

《我的路·刘晓庆自传》，刘晓庆（1955—）著；Engelhardt, Anne 译.

21. Als hundert Blumen blühen sollten：d. Lebens-Odyssee e. modernen Chinesin im Strudel d. revolutionären Umbrüche vom Langen Marsch bis heute；Autobiographie u. Zeitdokument/Yue Daiyun. Aufgezeichn. von Carolyn Wakeman. ［Einzig berecht. übers. aus d. Amerikan. von Helga Künzel］. Bern；München；Wien：Scherz, 1986. 382 S.；22cm. ISBN：3502188803, 3502188807.

《面向暴雨》，乐黛云（1931—）著；Künzel, Helga 译自英文.

(1) Als hundert Blumen blühen sollten：die Odyssee einer modernen Chinesin vom Langen Marsch bis heute/Yue Daiyun. Aufgezeichn. von Carolyn Wakeman. Aus d. Amerikan. von Helga Künzel. Ungekürzte Ausg., 1. Aufl. München：Dt. Taschenbuch-Verl., 1989. 381 S.；19cm. ISBN：3423110402, 3423110406. (dtv；11040；dtv-Zeitgeschichte). Anmerkungen：Lizenz d. Scherz Verl., Bern u. München.

(2) Ungekürzte Ausg., ［2. Aufl.］. München：Dt. Taschenbuch-Verl., 1990. 381 S.；19cm.

22. Acht Jahre im Aussenministerium 〈Januar 1950 - Oktober 1958〉：Memoiren eines Diplomaten/von Wu Xiuquan. Peking：Verlag für fremdsprachliche Literatur, 1987. 152 S.：Ill.

《在外交部八年的经历：一个外交官的回忆》，伍修权.

23. Diesseits und Jenseits der Kerkergitter/von Yang Zhilin und Qiao Mingpu. 2. Aufl. Beijing：Verl. für Fremdsprachige Literatur, 1987. 206 S. (Phonix-Buchreihe)

《铁窗内外》，杨植霖，乔明甫.

24. Ein Kuomintang-Kriegsverbrecher im Neuen China/von Shen Zui. Zsgest. von Shen Meijuan. Beijing：Verl. für Fremdsprachige Literatur ［u. a.］, 1989. IV, 445 S., ［10］ Bl：ill.

《我这三十年》，沈醉.

25. 100 unter 1 Milliarde：Gespräche mit Chinesen über Alltagsleben, Hoffnungen und Ängste/Liu Bingwen；Xiong Lei（Hrsg.）. Aus d. Chines. übers. von Li Liangjion u. Renate Zantis. Opladen：Westdt. Verl., 1989. 491 S.：Ill.；24cm. ISBN：3531121369, 3531121367.

同中国人就日常生活、希望及恐惧话题的谈话. Liu, Bingwen 著；Li Liangjion 和 Zantis, Renate 合译. 访谈集.

26. Der letzte Eunuch：das Leben Sun Yaotings, letzter Eunuch des Kaisers Puyi, erzählt von ihm selbst/Sun Yaoting；Ling Haicheng. Aus dem Chines. von Uwe Frankenhauser. Leipzig：Kiepenheuer, 1993. 693 S.；22cm. ISBN：3378005459, 3378005457

《最后一个太监》，孙耀庭（1902—1996）口述；Frankenhauser, Uwe 译.

(1) Ungekürzte Taschenbuchausg. München：Heyne, 1997. 693 S.；19cm. ISBN：3453123069, 3453123069. (Heyne-Bücher：19；Heyne-Sachbuch；530)

27. Bittere Träume：Selbstdarstellungen chinesischer Schriftsteller；［eine Forschungsarbeit des European Project on China's Modernization Contemporary Patterns of Cultural and Economic Change］/hrsg. von Helmut Martin in Zusammenarbeit mit Stefan Hase-Bergen. Bonn：Bouvier, 1993. XXVIII, 460 S.；23cm. ISBN：3416023283, 3416023285. (Abhandlungen zur Kunst-, Musik- und Literaturwissenschaft；Bd. 393)

《苦涩的梦：中国作家自述》. 含沈容、沈从文、宋泽莱、王蒙、王安忆、王若望、吴祖光、汪曾祺、王文新、张贤亮、钟阿城、张洁、张辛欣、张爱玲、郁达夫等人作品.

28. Kinder des Drachen：eine Jugend in der Kulturrevolution/Chen Kaige. ［Aus dem Chines. von Stefan und Hu Chun Kramer in Zusammenarbeit mit Christiane Hammer］. Leipzig：Kiepenheuer, 1994. 163 S.；22cm. ISBN：3378005648, 3378005645.

《少年凯歌》，陈凯歌（1952—）著.

29. Türme über der Stadt：eine Autobiographie aus den ersten Jahren der chinesischen Republik/Shen Congwen. Aus dem Chines. von Christoph Eiden in Zusammenarbeit mit Christiane Hammer. Hrsg. und mit einem Nachw. von Helmut Martin. Unkel/Rhein：Horlemann, 1994. 205 S.：Kt.；20cm. ISBN：3927905863, 3927905860. (Richard-Wilhelm-übersetzungszentrum (Bochum)：Arcus-Chinatexte des Richard-Wilhelm- übersetzungszentrums Bochum；1)

《沈从文自传》，沈从文（1902—1988）著；Eiden, Christoph 及 Hammer, Christiane 译.

30. Gottes chinesischer Sohn：Essays/Bei Dao. Aus dem Chines. und mit einer Nachbemerkung von Wolfgang Kubin. Bonn：Weidle, 2012. 215 S. 21cm. ISBN：3938803370, 3938803371

《城门开：散文集》，北岛著；顾彬译. 自传.

I7 散文

I71 古代及跨时代散文集

1. Der Ruf der Phönixflöte：klassische chinesische Prosa. 1/ ［hrsg. und aus dem Chines. übertr. von Ernst Schwarz］.

Berlin：Rütten & Loening, 1973. 464 S.：Ill
Schwarz, Ernst.

中国古典散文：卷一. Schwarz, Ernst 译. 含周敦颐、朱熹、袁宏道、颜之推、苏东坡、陶渊明、司马迁、孙子、欧阳修、宋濂、蒲松龄、袁枚、孙中山等人作品及选自《战国策》《左传》《庄子》《晏子》等著作中的文章.

(1)2. Aufl. Berlin：Rütten und Loening, 1976. 463 S.：Ill.

(2)3. Aufl. Berlin：Rütten und Loening, 1984. 463 S.：77 Ill.（z. T. farb.）, 1 graph. Darst.

(3)4. Aufl. Berlin：Rütten und Loening, 1988. 463 S.：77 Ill.（z. T. farb.）, 1 graph. Darst. ISBN：3352002096, 3352002090

2. Der Ruf der Phönixflöte：klassische chinesische Prosa. 2/［hrsg. und aus dem Chines. übertr. von Ernst Schwarz］. Berlin：Rütten & Loening, 1973. Seite 469 — 959：Illustrationen

中国古典散文：卷二. Schwarz, Ernst 译. 含周敦颐、朱熹、袁宏道、颜之推、苏东坡、陶渊明、司马迁、孙子、欧阳修、宋濂、蒲松龄、袁枚、孙中山等人作品及选自《战国策》《左传》《庄子》《晏子》等著作中的文章

(1)2. Aufl. Berlin：Rütten und Loening, 1976. S. 469—958：Ill.

(2)3. Aufl. Berlin：Rütten und Loening, 1984. S. 469 - 958：77 Ill.（z. T. farb.）

(3)4. Aufl. Berlin：Rütten und Loening, 1988. S. 469 - 958：78 Ill.（z. T. farb.）. ISBN：3352002096, 3352002090

3. Kleines Gerede：Satiren aus d. Volksrepublik China/Wang Meng u. a. Hrsg. von Helmut Martin u. Charlotte Dunsing. Köln：Diederichs, 1985. 126 S.：11 Ill.；21cm. ISBN：3424008517, 3424008516.

《闲言碎语：讽刺杂文》,王蒙、刘心武等著；Motsch, Monika 等译.

I72 古代个人作品

1. Ying-mei-an-yi-yu= Erinnerungen aus der Schattenaprikosenklause/Mao Xiang. übers. v. Rainer Schwarz. Beijing：Waiyu-jiao-xueyu-yanjiu-chubanshe, 2009. 149 S. Ill. 23cm. ISBN：7560078229

《影梅庵忆语》,（清）冒襄（1611—1693 年）著. 外语教学与研究出版社.

2. Sechs Aufzeichnungen über ein unstetes Leben：［aus dem Chinesischen］/Shen Fu. Mit 18 Reprod. nach Tuschmalereien auf Seide von Teng Shaoquan u. Zhang Zhaoji.［Hrsg., übers.（einschliessl. d. Vorw. von Feng Qiyong u. d. Zeittaf. von Yu Pingbo）, Nachw. u. Anm. von Rainer Schwarz］. Leipzig：Reclam, 1989. 275 S.：18 Ill.；22cm. ISBN：3379003889, 3379003883.

《浮生六记》,（清）沈复（1763—1832）；Schwarz, Rainer 译.

(1)Hanau：Müller und Kiepenheuer, 1990. 275 S.：Ill.；22cm. ISBN：3783380460, 3783380464. Anmerkungen：Lizenz des Verl. Reclam, Leipzig.

(2)Frankfurt am Main；Wien：Büchergilde Gutenberg, 1990. 275 S.；22cm. ISBN：3763236664, 376323666X.

I73 现当代个人作品

鲁迅（1881—1936）

1. Morgenblüten - abends gepflückt：Eine Ausw. aus seinem Werk/Lu Ssün. Hrsg. u. aus d. Chines. übers. von Johanna Herzfeldt. Berlin：Rütten & Loening, 1958. 747 S.：Mit 1 Frontispiz；8.

《朝花夕拾》, Herzfeldt, Johanna 译

2. Morgenblüten abends gepflückt/Lu Hsün. Peking：Verlag für Fremdsprachige Literatur, 1978. 189 S.：Ill.；19cm.

《朝花夕拾》

(1)1. Nachdr.. Peking：Verlag für Fremdsprachige Literatur, 2004. 191 S.：Ill.；19cm. ISBN：7119029746.

3. Blumen der Frühe am Abend gelesen：Erzählungen/Lu Xun；aus dem Chinesischen von Gudrun Erler...［et al.］. Zürich：Unionsverlag, 1994. 178 S. ISBN：3293002099, 3293002098, 3293002064, 3293002067.（Werke/Lu Xun. hrsg. von Wolfgang Kubin；3)

《朝花夕拾》, Erler, Gudrun 译.

4. Morgenblüten abends gepflückt/Lu Xun. Klagenfurt：Wieser, 2009. 162 S.；16cm. ISBN：3851298475.

《朝花夕拾》

5. Werke 1. Blumen der Frühe am Abend gelesen［u. a.］/Lu Xun. Hrsg. von Wolfgang Kubin. Zürich：Unionsverl, 2015. 178, 196, 445 S. ISBN：3293004887, 3293004881, 3293004894, 329300489X

《朝花夕拾》,顾彬（Kubin, Wolfgang, 1945—）译.

6. Der Einsturz der Leifeng-Pagode：Essays über Literatur und Revolution in China/Lu Xun［i. e. Zhou Shuren］；hrsg. und übers. von Hans Christoph Buch und Wong May, auf der Grundlage des chinesischen Originals sowie unter Berücksichtigung bereits erschienener deutscher und englischer Übersetzungen. Deutscher Erstausg. Reinbek bei Hamburg：Rowohlt Taschenbuch Verlag, 1973. 234 pages,［6］leaves of plates：illustrations；19cm. ISBN：3499250322, 3499250323.（Das Neue Buch；32）

论雷峰塔的倒掉：文学及中国革命相关杂文选. Buch, Hans Christoph（1944—）和 Wong, May 合译.

(1)2. Aufl. Reinbek bei Hamburg：Rowohlt, 1976. 231 S.：11 Ill.；19cm. ISBN：3499250323, 3499250322.（das neue buch；32）

7. Die grosse Mauer：21 polit. u. literar. Essays aus d. China d. 20er u. 30er Jahre/Lu Xun. Hrsg. u. mit e.

aktuellen Nachw. vers. von Florian Mausbach. [Worms]：Wissen und Tat，1980. 143 S.；Ill.；20cm. ISBN：3883110011，3883110019.

《长城：中国二十世纪 20、30 年代政治文学著作二十一篇》.

8. In tiefer Nacht geschrieben：Auswahl/Lu Xun［Aus d. Chines. Ausw.，Übers.，Zeittaf. u. Anm. von Yang Enlin u. Konrad Herrmann. Geleitbrief von Ruth Werner. Nachw. von Yang Enlin］. Leipzig：Reclam，1981. 302 S.；1 Ill.；18cm. (Reclams Universal-Bibliothek；Bd. 879)

《写于深夜里》，Yang，Einlin 和 Herrmann，Konrad 合译.

(1)2. Aufl. Leipzig：Reclam，1986. 302 S.；18cm.

9. Liangdi-shu ＝ Briefe aus zwei Welten/Lu Xun；Xu Guangping. Aus dem Chines. vom Arbeitskreis für Moderne Chinesische Literatur an der Universität Bonn. Hrsg. und mit einem Nachw. vers. von Wolfgang Kubin. München：Ed. Global，2009. 342 S. 20cm.，420 gr. ISBN：3922667117，3922667112.

《两地书》，鲁迅，许广平著；顾彬（Kubin，Wolfgang，1945—）译.

巴金（1904—2005）

1. Gedanken unter der Zeit：Ansichten - Erkundungen - Wahrheiten；1979 - 1984/Ba Jin. Aus d. Chines. übertr. von Sabine Peschel.［Die vorliegende Ausw. besorgte Helmut Martin］. Köln：Diederichs，1985. 223 S.；21cm. ISBN：3424008524，3424008524. (Neue chinesische Bibliothek)

《随想录》，Perschel，Sabine 译.

萧军（1907—1988）

1. Ausgewählte Kurzprosa/Xiao Jun；übersetzt von Holger Höke，Karl-Heinz Pohl，Roderich Ptak. Bochum：[publisher not identified]，1984. 157 pages；19cm. ISBN：388339369X，3883393698. (Chinathemen；Bd. 11)

Contents：Frachtschiff—Medizin—Ziegen—Shuiling shandao—Die Geschichte vom grünen Blatt—Plauderei über Dichtung in einer Strom—Wir nehmen zum ersten Mal an einer Tischgesellschaft—Meine vierte Rückkehr nach Harbin

萧军散文选. Höke，Holger 译.

季羡林（1911—2009）

1. Zehn Jahre in Deutschland/Xianlin Ji. - Übersetzt von Kuiliu Li，Roswitha Brinkmann，Daoqian Liu. Beijing：Foreign Language Teaching and Research Press (FLTRP). Göttingen：Univ. -Verl. Göttingen，2009. 252 S.；Ill. ISBN：7560084312

《留德十年：1935～1945》. 外语教学与研究出版社.

杨朔（1913—1968）

1. Prosastücke/von Yang Shuo. Beijing：Verl. für Fremdsprachige Literatur，1982. 141 S.；19cm.

《杨朔散文选》

杨炼（1955—）

1. Geisterreden：Essays aus Auckland，Berlin，New York/Yang Lian. Aus dem Chines. von Mark Renné. Zürich：Ammann，1995. 214 S.；20cm. ISBN：3250102809，3250102806.

杨炼散文选. Renné，Mark 译.

北岛（1949—）

1. Das Buch der Niederlage：Gedichte/Bei Dao. Aus dem Chines. und mit einer Nachbemerkung von Wolfgang Kubin. München：Hanser，2009. 105 S. 21cm. ISBN：3446232839，3446232834. (Edition Lyrik-Kabinett；12)

《失败之书》，北岛；顾彬（Kubin，Wolfgang，1945—）译.

余华（1960—）

1. China in zehn Wörtern：eine Einführung/Yu Hua. Aus dem Chines. von Ulrich Kautz. Frankfurt，M.：S. Fischer，2012. 335 S. 21cm. ISBN：3100958075，3100958071

《十个词汇中的中国》，余华著；Kautz，Ulrich(1939—)译.

(1)Bonn bpb，2013. 335 S. 21cm. ISBN：3838903699，3838903692. (Schriftenreihe/Bundeszentrale für Politische Bildung；Bd. 1369)

I8　民间文学

民间歌谣

1. Das Frauenherz：Chines. Lieder aus 3 Jahrtausenden/Ausgew. u. aus d. Chines. übers. von Elisabeth Oehler-Heimerdinger.［Mit Pinselzeichngn nach chines. Orig. von Elisabeth Oehler-Heimerdinger sowie Anmerkgn u. e. Nachw. von W. Oehler］. Stuttgart：Union，1925. 173 S.；8.

中国三千年歌谣. Oehler-Heimerdinger，Elisabeth 译.

2. Heut erntet man Lieder mit riesigen Körben：50 chines. Volkslieder. Nachdichtung. Mit 40 chines. Scherenschnitten/Heinz Kahlau. Berlin：Verl. Volk u. Welt，1962. 68 Seiten；Illustrationen

中国民歌 50 首. Kahlau，Heinz 译.

民间故事

1. Chinesische Volksmärchen/Richard Wilhelm. Jena：E. Diederichs，1914. 2 preliminary leaves，409，[1] pages frontispiece，plates 20cm. (Die Märchen der Weltliteratur；；2. ser. Märchen des Orients)

《中国民间故事集》，卫礼贤（Wilhelm，Richard，1873—1930)编译.

(1)Jena：E. Diederichs，1919. 410 pages，[22] leaves of plates：illustrations；20cm. (Die Märchen der Weltliteratur. II. ser.，Märchen des Orients)

(2)Jena：Diederichs，1921. 409 Seiten，[23] Blätter：Illustrationen；20cm. (Die Märchen der Weltliteratur；；[8]；Reihe 2，Märchen des Orients)

(3)Jena：Diederichs，1927. 409 Seiten：Illustrationen. (Die Märchen der Weltliteratur；Ser. II，Märchen des

Orients)

　　(4)Düsseldorf [u. a]：Diederichs, 1958. 384 Seiten. (Die Märchen der Weltliteratur)

　　(5)Paderborn：Salzwasser Verlag, 2012. 412 S. 190 mm ×120 mm. ISBN：3846001974, 384600197X

2. 105 interessante chinesische Erzählungen：Weisheit u. Tugend in Ernst u. Scherz/Hrsg. von Chang Wu. Berlin：Selbstverl. d. Verf. - Charlottenburg：Kant-Buchh. , 1915. 74 S. ；8.

105 个中国故事. Wu, Chang 译.

3. Die Drachenbraut/Alex Wedding. ［Ill. v. Ruprecht Haller. Verantw. Red. ：Gertrud Eschbach］. Berlin：Kinderbuchverl. , 1953. 66 S. ；gr. 8.

中国民间故事. Wedding, Alex 译.

　　(1)2. Aufl. Die Drachenbraut：Chin. Volksmärchen/Ausgew. , eingel. u. nacherz. Alex Wedding. ［Ill. v. Ruprecht Haller］. Berlin：Kinderbuchverl. , 1954. 66 S. ；gr. 8.

4. Die rote Perle：Chinesische Sagen u. Märchen/Willi Meinck. Ill. ：Hans Baltzer. Berlin：Kinderbuchverl. , 1958. 93 S. ；8.

中国传说与神话. Willi Meinck 在中国旅行时请 Wang Dschao-jen 将听到的中国传说、童话等翻译成德文，回国后根据记忆写成.

　　(1)2. Aufl. Berlin：Kinderbuchverl. , 1958. 93 S. ；8.

　　(2)3. Aufl. Berlin：Kinderbuchverl. , 1965. 93 S. ；8.

5. Chinas Völker erzählen, erste Folge/Ernst J. Schwarz. Peking：Verlag für Fremdsprachige Literatur, 1958. 173 pages：illustrations；21cm.

《中国民间故事选》(第一集)，施华滋（Schwarz, Ernst）译.

　　(1)2. Aufl. . Chinas Völker erzählen. Teil：［Folge 1］. , Der Reiter im grünen Gewand/［Dt. von Ernst J. Schwarz］. Peking：Verl. f. Fremdsprach. Literatur, 1964. 173 S. ：mit Abb.

　　(2)3. Aufl. Peking：Verl. f. Fremdsprach. Literatur, 1980. 172 S. ；21cm.

　　(3)Peking：Verl. f. Fremdsprach. Literatur, 2005. 190 S. ：Ill. ；17cm. ISBN：7119038285, 7119038281.

　　(Die schönsten Volkssagen aus China；1)

6. Chinas Völker erzählen, Zweite Folge/［Dt. von Ernst J. Schwarz］. Peking：Verl. f. Fremdsprachige Literatur, 1958. 117 S Ill.

《中国民间故事选》(第二集)

7. Chinas Völker erzählen/Deutsch von Li Ming. Peking：Verlag fur Fremdsprachige Literatur, 1961. 125 s. ：illustrations

《中国民间故事选》(第三集)

8. Chinas Völker erzählen. Teil：Folge 4./［Dt. von Rita Kheir u. Li Ming. Ill. von Scha Geng-schi］. Peking：Verl. f. Fremdsprach. Literatur, 1962. 114 S.

《民间故事选》(第四集)，Kheir，Rita 和 Li，Ming 合译.

9. Chinas Völker erzählen. Teil：Folge 5. /［Dt. von Li Ming］. Peking：Verl. f. Fremdsprach. Literatur, 1962. 124 S. ：mit Abb.

《民间故事选》(第五集)，Li，Ming 译.

10. Chinas Völker erzählen 4/［Dt. von Rita Kheir... Ill. von Scha Geng-schi. Peking：Verl. für Fremdsprachige Literatur, 1962. 114 S. Ill.

《中国民间故事选》，沙更世、杨永青.

11. Wie der Wasserbüffel den Tiger bezwang：Chinas Völker erzählen. 2. Aufl. Beijing：Verl. für fremdspr. Lit. , 1964. 77 Seiten

《水牛斗老虎：中国民间故事选》，第 2 版.

　　(1)3. Aufl. Beijing：Verl. f. Fremdsprachige Literatur, 1980. 115 S. ：Ill. ；20cm.

12. Der König des Granatapfelbaums/［Dt. v. Senta u. Günter Lewin］. Peking：Verl. f. Fremdspr. Lit. 1964. 105 S. Ill.

《一棵石榴树的国王：中国民间故事选》，程十发插图.

13. Die wundersame Geschichte der weissen Schlange：Chines. Geisterroman/［Dt. Bearb. nach d. franz. Übers. , zugleich mit Erl. vers. von Johanna Boshamer-Koob u. Kurt Boshamer］. Zürich：Classen, 1967. 214 S. ；8.

《白蛇奇传》，Boshamer-Koob，Johanna 和 Boshamer，Kurt 合译.

14. Die neunköpfigen Ungeheuer vom Zweidrachenberg：Märchen u. Volkserzählungen aus China/aus d. Chines. übers. u. frei nacherzählt von Herbert Bräutigam u. Gabriele Wittrin. Ill. von Irmhild u. Hilmar Proft. Berlin：Holz, 1974. 209 S. ：Ill. (farb.)；；25cm.

《双龙山的九头怪：中国童话及民间故事》，Bräutigam，Herbert 和 Wittrin，Gabriele 合译.

　　(1)2. Aufl. Berlin：Kinderbuchverlag, 1978. 209 S. ：Ill. (farb.)；25cm.

15. Die Gingkofee：6 chines. Volksmärchen aus d. Provinz Schandung = I-shan-min-chien-ku-shih-pa-p'ien /übertr. u. hrsg. von Rainer Schwarz. Leipzig：Insel-Verlag, 1978. 92 S. ；19cm. (Insel-Bücherei；Nr. 566)

《沂山民间故事八篇》，Schwarz，Rainer 译.

　　(1)2. Aufl. Leipzig：Insel-Verlag, 1986. 93 S. ；19cm.

16. Sagen aus China/hrsg. u. übers. von Adrian Baar. ［Ill. von Horst Wolniak］. Frankfurt am Main：Fischer-Taschenbuch-Verlag, 1980. 134 S. ：Ill. ；18cm. ISBN：3596228256, 3596228255. (Fischer-Taschenbücher；2825)

中国传说. Baar, Adrian 译.

17. Chinesische Volkserzählungen/ausgew. u. mit e. Nachw. von Kuan Yu-chien. Mit Ill. von I-ching Cheng. ［Die Übers. d. Erzählungen stammen von Henner Asche...］. Frankfurt am Main：Insel-Verlag, 1981. 383 S. ：Ill. ；

18cm. ISBN：3458322221，3458322221

中国民间故事. Asche, Henner 译.

（1）2. Aufl. Frankfurt am Main：Insel-Verlag, 1985. 383 S.：Ill.；18cm.

（2）3. Aufl. Frankfurt am Main：Insel-Verlag, 1988. 383 S.：Ill.；18cm.

18. Der Sklave und die Drachentochter：chinesische Volkserzählungen/[aus dem Chines. von Chen Hanli. Deutsch bearb. von Barbara Scheer]. Beijing：Verl. für Fremdsprachige Literatur, 1985. 121 S：Ill.

《奴隶与龙女：中国民间故事选》

19. Die Volkssagen vom Westsee/[aus dem Chines. von Lu Bosheng und Li Aisheng. Dt. bearb. von Elise Buda]. Beijing：Verl. für Fremdsprachige Literatur, 1986. 165 S.；19cm.

《飞来峰及人间天堂的其他故事》, Buda, Elise 译.

20. Der Kampf mit dem Nashorn um die Perlen/[aus dem Chines. von Karsten Krüger. Red. der dt. Ausg.：Xu Shumin...]. Beijing：Verl. für Fremdsprachige Literatur, 1986. 122 S.：ill.

《斗犀夺珠：中国民间故事选》, 朱维明, 陈之川编.

21. Der Zaubervogel：chinesische Volkserzählungen/[Red. der dt. Ausg.：Xu Shumin；Wang Wei]. Beijing：Verl. für Fremdsprachige Literatur, 1987. 147 S.：Ill.；21cm.

《神鸟：中国民间故事》

22. Die Himmelstrommel：chinesische Volksmärchen/übertr. u. hrsg. von Armina Agischewa. Die Farbtaf. wurden ausgew. u. mit e. Erl. vers. von Ernst Schwarz. Wien；Freiburg [Breisgau]；Basel：Herder, 1988. 135 S.：Ill. (farb.)；28cm. ISBN：3210248981, 3210248982, 3355005494(Gewebe), 3355005495(Gewebe)

中国民间故事. Agischewa, Armina 译.

23. Legenden aus Beijing/von Jin Shoushen, Zhang Zichen u. a.. Beijing：Verl. für Fremdsprachige Literatur, 1989. 192 S.；18cm. ISBN：711900090X. (Phönix-Buchreihe)

《北京的传说》, 金受申(1906—1968)著. 民间故事.

24. Der Hirte und der Falke：chinesische Volkserzählungen. Beijing：Verl. für Fremdsprachige Literatur, 1990. 105 S.；21cm. ISBN：7119007998, 7119007991

《牧人和山鹰：中国民间传说故事选》

25. Das Bett der hundert Vögel：die schönsten Märchen und Geschichten der Völker Chinas/[ausgew. von Liao Xuhe. Ill. von Ye Yuzhong]. Beijing：Verl. für Fremdsprachige Literatur, 1991. 229 S.：ill.；27cm. ISBN：7119012363, 7119012360

《中国民间传说故事精粹》, 廖旭和.

26. Die wundersame Geschichte von der Donnergipfelpagode/[Hrsg., übers. und Nachw. von Rainer Schwarz. Mit einem Essay von Lu Xun]. Leipzig：Reclam, 1991. 160

S.：Ill.；18cm. ISBN：3379006781, 3379006785. (Reclams Universal-Bibliothek；Bd. 1390：Belletristik)

《雷峰塔奇传》, Schwarz, Rainer 译. 内含鲁迅杂文一篇.

27. 米的传说＝Die Legende vom Reis/廖旭和主编. 北京：外文出版社, 2005. 193 页，[9] 叶图版：图；17cm. ISBN：711903829X

内容包括：孔雀姑娘、马头琴等. 德汉对照读物. 民间故事.

寓言

1. Fabeln/Feng Xue-fung. 2. Aufl. Peking：Verlag für fremdsprachige Literatur, 1954. 56 pages：illustrations；27cm.

《雪峰寓言》, 冯雪峰；蒋晨德译.

（1）Fabeln/Feng Xuefeng. [Holzschn. von Huang Yongyu. übers. von Jiang Chende]. Beijing：Verl. für fremdsprachige Literatur, 1981. 71 S.：Ill.；21cm.

2. Alte chinesische Fabeln/[übertr. ins Dt. v. Käthe Dschao. Ill. v. Fung Dse-kai]. Peking：Verl. f. fremdsprachige Literatur, 1957. 1 vol. (56 p).：ill. en noir.；25cm.

《古代寓言》

3. Altchinesische Spruchweisheit/Deutsch von Käthe Dschao und Senta Lewin. Peking, 1961. 109 Seiten；8°

《中国古代寓言选》, 丰子恺插图.

4. Fabeln des chinesischen Altertums in moderner Sprache/Zusammengest. von Martin Piasek. Leipzig：VEB Verl. Enzyklopädie, 1961. 48 S.；8. (Chinesische Übungstexte；H. 1)

白话中国古代寓言. Piasek, Martin (1905—1990)编.

（1）2. unveränd. Aufl. Leipzig：VEB Verl. Enzyklopädie, 1968. 48 S.；8. (Chinesische Übungstexte；H. 1)

（2）3. unveränd. Aufl. Leipzig：VEB Verl. Enzyklopädie, 1972. 48 S.；8. (Chinesische Übungstexte；H. 1)

（3）4. unveränd. Aufl. Leipzig：VEB Verl. Enzyklopädie, 1974. 48 S.；22cm. (Chinesische Übungstexte；H. 1)

5. Altchinesische Fabeln/[Aus d. Chin. übertr. v. Käthe Zhao；Senta Lewin]. Mit e. Nachw. v. Eva Müller. 2. Aufl. 1. Aufl. in C-Reihe. Leipzig：Reclam, 1963. 86 S.；kl. 8.

古代中国寓言故事. Zhao, Käthe 和 Lewin, Senta 合译. 第 2 版.

（1）3. Aufl. Leipzig：Reclam, 1968. 76 S.；kl. 8.

（2）Frankfurt (am Main)：Röderberg-Verlag, 1972. 76 S.；；17cm. (Röderberg-Taschenbuch；Bd. 7).

（3）5. Aufl. Leipzig：Reclam, 1976. 73 S.；18cm.

（4）6. Aufl. Leipzig：Reclam, 1980. 73 S.；18cm. (Reclams Universal-Bibliothek；Bd. 363：Belletristik)

（5）7. Aufl. Leipzig：Reclam, 1984. 71 S.；18cm. (Reclams Universal-Bibliothek；Bd. 363：Belletristik)

（6）8. Aufl. Leipzig：Reclam，1988. 71 S.；18cm. ISBN：3379003100，3379003107.（Reclams Universal-Bibliothek；Bd. 363：Belletristik）

（7）Köln：Röderberg，1988. 71 S.；18cm. ISBN：387682382X，3876823829.（Röderberg-Taschenbuch；Bd. 7）

6. Yü Gong versetzt Berge：19 revolutionäre Parabeln aus d. alten China/[zusammengestellt，übers. u. hrsg. von Jan Meier]. Berlin：Basis-Verlag，1971. 44 S.：zahlr. Ill.；；24cm.

愚公移山：中国古代革命性寓言19篇. Meier，Jan 搜集、翻译. 含列子、庄子、韩非子、毛泽东、苏东坡、程颐作品.

7. Altchinesische Spruchweisheit/[dt. von Käthe Dschao；Senta Lewin. Ill. von Feng Zikai]. 1986. IV，95 S.：zahlr. ill.

《中国古代寓言选》

8. Fabeln aus dem alten China/[Übersetzung，Wang Kuanxin；deutsche Bearbeitung，Gregor Kneussel]. Beijing：Verlag für Fremdsprachige Literatur，2008. 221 pages：illustrations；18cm. ISBN：7119041247，711904124X

《中国古代寓言精选》，王宽信编译. 本书收录了120余则流传甚广的寓言故事.

9. Moderne chinesische Fabeln. Beijing：Verl. für Fremdsprachige Literatur，1986. 125 S. Ill

《中国现代寓言选》

（1）Beijing：Verl. für Fremdsprachige Literatur，2003. 119 S：Ill. ISBN：711903452978.（汉语轻松阅读）

（2）Beijing：Verl. für Fremdsprachige Literatur，2006. 141 S：Ill. ISBN：7119043587.（汉语轻松阅读）

神话

1. Sagen und Geschichten aus dem chinesischen Altertum. Teil 1. Beijing：China im Aufbau，1985. 102 S.

《中国神话传说和历史故事》，卷一.

2. Mythen aus China/Chu Binjie.［übers. von Han Yaocheng und Wang Jiping］. Beijing：Verl. für Fremdsprachige Literatur，1986. 136 S.；19cm.

《中国古代神话》，褚斌杰（1933—2006）著；韩耀成，王京平译.

3. Chang'e steigt zum Mond empor. Reise durch d. chinesische Märchen- und Sagenwelt/［Red.：Li Nianpei. übers. von Erhard Neckermann］. Beijing/VR China China：Travel and Tourist Press，1999. 227 S. ill. 21cm. ISBN：7503215453，7503215452

《嫦娥奔月》，李念培. 中国旅游出版社.

谜语、笑话

1. Der Tiger mit dem Rosenkranz：Rätsel aus China ＝ Chung-kuo-mi-yü/von Liu Mau-Tsai. Berlin；New York：de Gruyter，1986. 87 S.；23cm. ISBN：3110105957，3110105950

《中国谜语》，Liu Maocai 著.

2. Humor im alten China. Beijing：Verl. für Fremdsprachige Literatur，1986. 196 S.；18cm.

《中国古代笑话》，李士仅；任国忠绘画；Wang Kuanxin 译.

I9　儿童文学

1. Chinesische Volksmärchen/übersetzt und eingeleitet von Richard Wilhelm. Mit 23 Wiedergaben chinesischer Holzschnitte. Jena：Eugen Diederichs Verlag，1914. 410 S.

中国民间童话. 卫礼贤（Wilhelm，Richard，1873—1930）译.

（1）Jena：E. Diederichs，1917. 409 pages，[23] leaves of plates：illustrations；20cm.（Die Märchen der Weltliteratur. II. Reihe. Märchen des Orients）

（2）Jena：E. Diederichs，1919. 410 pages，[22] leaves of plates：illustrations；20cm.（Die Märchen der Weltliteratur. II. ser.，Märchen des Orients）

（3）Jena，E. Diederichs，1921. 409 pages frontispiece，plates 20cm.（Die Märchen der Weltliteratur，II. reihe. Märchen des Orients）

（4）Jena：Diederichs，1927. 409 Seiten：Illustrationen.（Die Märchen der Weltliteratur；Ser. II，Märchen des Orients）

（5）Chinesische Märchen/aus dem Chines. übertr. von Richard Wilhelm. Düsseldorf：Diederichs，1952. 394 Seiten.（Die Märchen der Weltliteratur）

（6）Chinesische Märchen/aus dem Chines. übertr. von Richard Wilhelm. Düsseldorf：Diederichs，1958. 384 Seiten.（Die Märchen der Weltliteratur）

（7）Chinesische Märchen/aus dem Chines. übertr. von Richard Wilhelm. Düsseldorf：Diederichs，1961. 384 Seiten.（Die Märchen der Weltliteratur）

（8）Chinesische Märchen/aus dem Chines. übertr. von Richard Wilhelm. Düsseldorf：Diederichs，1976. 395 Seiten. ISBN：3424002534，3424002539，3424002542，3424002546.（Die Märchen der Weltliteratur）

（9）Chinesische Märchen/ges. u. aus d. Chines. übertr. von Richard Wilhelm. Neuausg.，einmalige Jubiläumsausg. Köln：Diederichs，1985. 385 Seiten：23 Illustrationen；22cm. ISBN：3424008508，3424008500

（10）Chinesische Märchen/herausgegeben und übertragen von Richard Wilhelm. Hamburg：Rowohlt，1994. 435 pages；19cm. ISBN：3499350173，3499350177.（Diederichs Märchen der Weltliteratur；35017；Ro ro ro；1490）

2. Die Geister des gelben Flusses：Chinesische Volksmärchen/übertr. Richard Wilhelm. Bildschmuck nach chinesischen Motiven von Josefine Fleck. Frankfurt a. M.：M. Diesterweg，1926. 29 S.：mit Abb.；8.

黄河之魂：中国民间童话. 卫礼贤（Wilhelm，Richard，1873—1930）译.

3. Chinesische Märchen/[Hrsg.：Richard Wilhelm]. Aus d.

Chines. übertr. von Richard Wilhelm. Düsseldorf；Köln：Diederichs，1952. 394 S. ；8. (Die Märchen der Weltliteratur)

中国童话故事. 卫礼贤（Wilhelm，Richard，1873—1930）译.

(1) Düsseldorf；Köln：Diederichs, 1955. 393 S. ；8. (Die Märchen der Weltliteratur)

(2) Düsseldorf；Köln：Diederichs, 1965. 384 S. ；8. (Die Märchen der Weltliteratur)

(3) Düsseldorf；Köln：Diederichs，1971. 384 S. ；8. ISBN：3424002539，3424002534，3424002546，3424002542 (Die Märchen der Weltliteratur)

(4) Düsseldorf，Köln：Diederichs, 1979. 395 S. ；20cm. ISBN：3424002539，3424002534，3424002546，3424002542. (Die Märchen der Weltliteratur)

(5) Düsseldorf，Köln：Diederichs, 1983. 391 S. ；20cm. ISBN：3424002539，3424002534，3424002546，3424002542. (Die Märchen der Weltliteratur)

(6) Düsseldorf，Köln：Diederichs, 1987. 391 S. ；20cm. ISBN：3424002539，3424002534. (Die Märchen der Weltliteratur)

(7) München：Diederichs, 1990. 391 S. ；20cm. ISBN：3424002539，3424002534. (Die Märchen der Weltliteratur)

(8) 23. Aufl. München：Diederichs, 1992. 398 S. ；20cm. ISBN：3424002539，3424002534. (Die Märchen der Weltliteratur)

4. Die Geister des gelben Flusses：Chinesische Märchen/［Hrsg. ：Richard Wilhelm］. Mit e. Nachw. von Dshu Bai-Lan (Klara Blum). Rudolstadt；Greifenverl. , 1955. 362 S. ；mit Ill. ；8.

中国童话. 卫礼贤（Wilhelm，Richard，1873—1930）译.

5. Chinesische Volksmärchen/Ausgew. u. übertr. Wolfram Eberhard. Leipzig：Insel-Verlag, 1936. 89 S. ；kl. 8. (Insel-Bücherei；Nr. 484)

中国民间童话. Eberhard，Wolfram(1909—1989)编译.

(1) Leipzig：Insel-Verlag, 1949. 87 S. ；kl. 8. (Insel-Bücherei；Nr. 484)

(2) Leipzig：Insel-Verlag, 1951. 87 S. ；kl. 8. (Insel-Bücherei；Nr. 484)

(3) Leipzig：Insel-Verlag, 1953. 87 S. ；kl. 8. (Insel-Bücherei；Nr. 484)

6. Volksmärchen aus Südost-China：(Sammlg Mr. Ts'ao Sung-Yeh)/Bearb. Wolfram Eberhard. Helsinki：Akateeminen Kirjakauppa - Leipzig：Harrassowitz, 1941. 349 S. ；gr. 8. (Folklore Fellows；FF communications；No. 128)

中国东南部民间童话. Eberhard，Wolfram 译.

7. Geschichten von Jungpionieren Chinas/Tien-I. Tschang. ［Aus d. Chin. übertr. v. Tschen Yüan. Ill. v. Dschang Wen-sin］. Peking：Verl. f. fremdsprachige Literatur, 1954. 56 S.

《少年先锋队的故事》,张天翼.

8. Frau Allmächtig：［Verkürzte übers. ］/Erzählt. ：Hsiung Sai-scheng；Yü Tschin. Ill. v. Tschen Yüan-tu. Peking：Verl. f. fremdsprachige Literatur, 1955. 46 S. ；13×18cm.

《巧媳妇》,熊塞声(1915—1981)著. 童话剧剧本.

9. Schulmeister Dungguo/Dung Djü-hsien. Ill. von Liu Dji-yu. Peking：Verl. f. fremdsprachige Literatur, 1956. 82 S. ；Abb. mit Text；quer-kl. 8.

《东郭先生》,Dung Djü-hsien 译.

10. Angsthäschen im Wunderland/Nach d. Märchen v. Yan Wen-djing v. Tschang Dsaihsüeh verf. Ill. v. Liu Dji-yiou. Peking：Verl. f. fremdsprachige Literatur, 1957. 66 S. ；13×17,5cm.

《丁丁的一次奇怪旅行》,严文井(1915—2005)著.

11. Biene und Regenwurm. Peking：Verlag für Fremdsprachige Literatur, 1958. 16 s. ；ill

《蚯蚓和蜜蜂》,严文井著；黄永玉插图.

12. Der Flug der jungen Schwalben/Tschin Dschao-jang. ［Dt. v. G. Gräfe und Lin Er-kang. Tuschzeichngn v. Yang Yung-tjing］. Peking：Verl. f. fremdsprachige Literatur, 1958. 22 S.

《小燕子万里飞行记》,秦兆阳著；葛来福,林尔康译.

13. Die Regenbogenstrasse/Tji Hu. ［Dt. von Eberhard Meissner. Ill. von Yang Yung-Tjing］. Peking：Verl. f. Fremdsprach. Literatur, 1960. 171 S

《五彩路》,胡奇.

(1) 3. Aufl. Peking：Verl. f. Fremdsprach. Literatur, 1980. 218 S. ；Ill. ；19cm.

14. Der Zauberkürbis/Dschang Tiän yi. ［Dt. v. Lotte Sichrovsky. Ill. v. Lin Yüan-tsui］. Peking：Verl. f. fremdsprachige Literatur, 1960. 136 S.

《宝葫芦的秘密》,张天翼著；林琬崔插图.

(1) Peking：Verl. f. fremdsprachige Literatur, 1980. 2. Aufl. 215 S. ；Ill. ；19cm.

15. Der Junge aus Sanbian/Li, Ji；E. Treppt. Beijing：Verlag für fremdsprachige Literatur, 1960. 41 S.

《三边一少年》,李季(1922—1980)著；Treppt, E. 译.

16. Das Schloss des Drachenkönigs：Chines. Märchen/Fritz Mühlenweg. ［Ill. ：Wolfgang Felten］. Freiburg i. Br. ；Basel；Wien：Herder, 1961. 127 S. ；8

中国童话. Mühlenweg, Fritz 译.

(1) 2. Aufl. Freiburg i. Br. ；Basel；Wien：Herder, 1962. 127 S. ；8.

(2) 3. Aufl. Freiburg i. Br. ；Basel；Wien：Herder, 1966. 127 S. ；8.

(3) Würzburg：Arena-Verl. , 1971. 140 S. ；kl. 8. ISBN：3401011677，3401011677. (Arenataschenbuch. ；Bd. 1167). Anmerkungen：Lizenz d. Verl. Herder, Freiburg i. Br.

17. Die Geschichte vom kleinen schwarzen Pferd/Djing Yüan. ［Dt. v. Rotraud u. Eberhard Meissner. Ill. v.

Lu Tan]. Peking：Verl. f. fremdsprachige Literatur，1961. 193 S.

《小黑马的故事》，袁静著；路坦插图.

(1) Die Geschichte vom Kleinen Schwarzen Pferd/Yüan Djing. Beijing：Verlag für Fremdsprachige Literatur，1980. 218 pages

18. Schneeflocken tanzen/Schuo Yang. [Ill. von Miao Di]. Peking：Verl. f. Fremdsprach. Literatur，1961. 57 S. ；8.

《雪花飘飘》，杨朔（1913—1968）著.

(1) 2 Aufl. Peking：Verl. f. Fremdsprach. Literatur，1980. 63 S. ；Ill. ；18cm.

19. Die Drachentor-Springer/Zeichnungen von Yang Schan-dsi & Ding Jung-lin. Peking：Verlag für Fremdsprachige Literatur，1961. 32 s

《小鲤鱼跳龙门》，金近写；杨善子，丁榕临绘.

20. Der Grauwolf：ein Theaterstuck für Kinder/Tiän-yi Dschang. [Dt. von Eberhard Treppt. Ill. von Yang Yung-tjing]. Peking：Verlag fur Fremdsprachige Literatur，1962. 47 S. 8

《大灰狼》，张天翼.

21. Gross-Lin und Klein-Lin/Tiän-yi Dschang. [Dt. von Lotte Sichrovsky. Ill. von Hua Djünwu]. Peking：Verl. f. Fremdsprach. Literatur，1962. 167 S. ；8.

《大林与小林》，张天翼（1906—1985）著；Sichrovsky，Lotte 译.

(1) 3. Aufl. Peking：Verl. f. Fremdsprach. Literatur，1980. 169 S. ；21cm.

22. Der kleine Jäger und seine Freunde Duan Bin u. Ngagwangtse-tan/[Ping Hsia；Wang Ang；Tan-chên Szŭ]. [Dt. von Eberhard Treppt. Ill. von Wu Wenyüan]. Peking：Verl. für Fremdsprach. Literatur，1963. 78 S

《林中篝火》，段斌，昂旺，斯丹珍著；Treppt，Eberhard 译.

23. Aus dem Leben der chinesischen Kinder/Text und Ill. von Dschang Lo-ping. Peking：Verlag für Fremdsprachige Literatur，1963. 36 s. ：ill

《我们的故事》，张乐平.

24. Lu Ban erlernt sein Handwerk. Peking：Verlag für Fremdsprachige Literatur，1963. 18 s. ：ill

《鲁班学艺》，晴帆；徐正平绘.

25. Tschaolu, der kleine Schafhirt. Peking：Verlag für Fremdsprachige Literatur，1963. 18 s. ：ill

《小超鲁牧羊》，江南编；韩书或绘.

26. Die schöne Windenblüte/[Text von Lu Djing-schan. Zeichn. von Hu Djin-tjing]. Peking：Verl. f. Fremdsprachige Literatur，1964. 12 Bl

《美丽的牵牛花》，陆静山文；胡进庆等画.

27. Chinesische Märchen/hrsg. u. übers. von Josef Guter. Frankfurt am Main：Fischer-Taschenbuch-Verlag，1973. 155 S. ：Ill. ；18cm. ISBN：3436017774；3436017779. (Fischer-Taschenbücher；1408)

中国童话. Guter, Josef (1929—)译.

(1) Frankfurt am Main：Fischer-Taschenbuch-Verlag，1977. 155 S. ；18cm. ISBN：3436017774；3436017779. (Fischer-Taschenbücher；1408：Die Welt d. Märchen)

(2) Frankfurt am Main：Fischer-Taschenbuch-Verlag，1979. 155 S. ；18cm. ISBN：3596214082；3596214084. (Fischer-Taschenbücher；1408：Die Welt d. Märchen)

(3) Frankfurt am Main：Fischer-Taschenbuch-Verlag，1980. 154 S. ；18cm. ISBN：3596214082；3596214084. (Fischer-Taschenbücher；1408：Die Welt d. Märchen)

(4) Frankfurt am Main：Fischer-Taschenbuch-Verlag，1982. 154 S. ：Ill. ；18cm. ISBN：3596214082；3596214084. (Fischer-Taschenbücher；1408：Die Welt d. Märchen)

(5) Frankfurt am Main：Fischer-Taschenbuch-Verlag，1983. 154 S. ：Ill. ；18cm. ISBN：3596214082；3596214084. (Fischer-Taschenbücher；1408：Die Welt d. Märchen)

(6) Frankfurt am Main：Fischer-Taschenbuch-Verlag，1985. 154 S. ：Ill. ；18cm. ISBN：3596214082；3596214084. (Fischer-Taschenbücher；1408：Die Welt d. Märchen)

(7) Frankfurt am Main：Fischer-Taschenbuch-Verlag，1986. 154 S. ；18cm. ISBN：3596214082；3596214084. (Fischer-Taschenbücher；1408：Die Welt d. Märchen)

(8) Frankfurt am Main：Fischer-Taschenbuch-Verlag，1987. 154 S. ；18cm. ISBN：3596214082；3596214084. (Fischer-Taschenbücher；1408：Die Welt d. Märchen)

(9) Frankfurt am Main：Fischer-Taschenbuch-Verlag，1988. 154 S. ：Ill. ；18cm. ISBN：3596214082；3596214084. (Fischer-Taschenbücher；1408：Die Welt d. Märchen)

(10) Frankfurt am Main：Fischer-Taschenbuch-Verlag，1989. 182 S. ；18cm. ISBN：3596228959；3596228956. (Fischer-Taschenbücher；2895：Die Welt d. Märchen)

(11) Frankfurt am Main：Fischer-Taschenbuch-Verlag，1990. 182 S. ；18cm. ISBN：3596228959；3596228956. (Fischer-Taschenbücher；2895：Die Welt d. Märchen)

(12) Frankfurt am Main：Fischer-Taschenbuch-Verlag，1991. 182 S. ；18cm. ISBN：3596228959；3596228956. (Fischer-Taschenbücher；2895：Die Welt d. Märchen)

(13) Frankfurt am Main：Fischer-Taschenbuch-Verlag，1992. 182 S. ；18cm. ISBN：3596228959；3596228956. (Fischer-Taschenbücher；2895：Die Welt d. Märchen)

(14) Frankfurt am Main：Fischer-Taschenbuch-Verlag，1993. 182 S. ；18cm. ISBN：3596228959；3596228956. (Fischer-Taschenbücher；2895：Die Welt d. Märchen)

(15) Frankfurt am Main：Fischer-Taschenbuch-Verlag，1995. 182 S. ；18cm. ISBN：3596228959；3596228956.

(Fischer-Taschenbücher；2895：Die Welt d. Märchen)
(16) Frankfurt am Main：Fischer-Taschenbuch-Verlag，1997. 189 S.；19cm. ISBN：3596139323；3596139325.
(Fischer-Taschenbücher；13932：Die Welt d. Märchen)

28. Die Geister des Gelben Flusses：Märchen aus China/mit Ill. von Leuthold Aulig. ［Red.：Ulf Diederichs］. Düsseldorf，Köln：Diederichs，1973. 167 S.；Ill.；；20cm. ISBN：3424004898，3424004892.（Diederich's Löwenbücher；4)
黄河之魂：中国民间童话. Diederichs，Ulf. 译.

29. Da-mang wird Flügge/von Hao Jan. Peking：Verlag für Fremdsprachige Literatur，1974. 54 S.：ill.；19cm.
《树上鸟儿叫》，浩然.

30. Der kleine Soldat Dschang Ga-dsi/Hsü Guang-yao. Peking：Verlag für Fremdsprachige Literatur，1975. 153 S.：ill.；19cm.
《小兵张嘎》，徐关跃.

31. Der Hirtenjunge Hai Wa/Hua Schan. Peking：Verlag für Fremdsprachige Literatur，1975. 78 S.：ill.；19cm.
《牧童海娃》，华山.

32. Zur Schule/Guan Hua ［Text］. Peking：Verl. f. Fremdspr. Lit.，1975. 54 p：Ill.
《上学》，管桦.

33. Südchinesische Märchen/hrsg. u. übers. von Wolfram u. Alide Eberhard. Düsseldorf；Köln：Diederichs，1976. 287 p.；20cm. ISBN：3424005614，3424005622.（Die Märchen der Weltliteratur)
中国南方童话. Eberhard，Wolfram（1909—1989）和 Eberhard，Alide 合译.

34. Märchen aus aller Welt. Teil：Nr. 10.，China/ausgew. u. bearb. von Erika Sanders. Mit Ill. von Brigitte Smith. München：Heyne，1978. 176 S.：Ill.（z. T. farb.）. ISBN：3453830103，3453830105.（Heyne-Bücher)
中国童话. Sanders，Erika 选编.

35. Junger Held auf dem Schilfsee. Peking：Verl. für Fremdsprach-Literatur，1979. 143 S.
《芦荡小英雄》，张德武著；毛水仙等插图.

36. Chang'e steigt zum Mond empor；Reise durch d. chines. Märchen- u. Sagenwelt.［Red.：Li Nianpei［Nien-p'ei］. übers. von Erhard Neckermann］. Frankfurt a. M.：China-Studien- u. Verlagsges.，1981. 199 S. 8 „.
ISBN：3887281047.
《嫦娥奔月》，Li Nianpei 编辑；Neckermann，Erhard 译.

37. Chinesische Märchen：Märchen d. Han/hrsg. von Rainer Schwarz. ［Ausgew.，aus d. Chines. übertr.，eingel. u. komm. von Rainer Schwarz］. Leipzig：Insel-Verlag，1981. 571 S.；19cm.
中国童话. Schwarz，Rainer（1940—）译.
(1)2. Aufl. Leipzig：Insel-Verlag，1982. 571 S.；19cm.
(2)3. Aufl. Leipzig：Insel-Verlag，1986. 570 S.；19cm.

ISBN：3922383147；3922383149.
(3)1. Aufl. dieser Ausg. Frankfurt am Main；Leipzig：Insel-Verl.，1991. 569 S.；19cm. ISBN：3458162261；3458162267.

38. Die Vogelscheuche：eine Sammlung von Kindergeschichten/von Ye Shengtao. Beijing：Verl. für Fremdsprachige Literatur，1981. 107 S.；21cm.
《叶圣陶童话选》

39. Kinderbilder und Gedichte/Bilder von Bu Di. Gedichte von Ke Yan. ［übers. von Johnny Erling］. Beijing：Verl. f. fremdsprachige Literatur，1981. ［120］S.
《童画诗情集》，卜镝绘画；柯岩题诗. 中德对照.

40. Die Abenteuer einer kleinen Stoffpuppe/［Sun Youjun］. Beijing：Verl. für Fremdsprachige Literatur，1982. 259 S.；19cm.
《小布头奇遇记》，孙幼军（1933—2015）；沈培插图.

41. Märchen aus Sinkiang：Überlieferungen d. Turkvölker Chinas/hrsg. u. übers. von Karl Reichl. Köln：Diederichs，1986. 271 S.；20cm. ISBN：3424008852，3424008850.
新疆童话：维吾尔族故事. Reichel，Karl 译.

42. Yan Ga und das Drachenmädchen：Märchen u. Erzählungen d. Randvölker Chinas/ausgew. u. übers. von Marie-Luise Latsch... Wald：Im Waldgut，1986. 114 S.：Ill.；20cm. ISBN：3729400320，3729400320.
中国边远民族童话及传说. Latsch，Marie-Luise 选译.

43. Kinder am Meer. Von Xiao Ping und anderen. Vier Kindergeschichten von 1954—55. Beijing：Verlag für fremdsprachige Literatur，1987. 100 S.
《海滨的孩子》，肖平等著. 收录儿童故事四篇.

44. Goldsaat. Geschichten von Afanti. Bearbeitet von Xie Defeng. Illustriert von Sun Yizeng. Beijing：Verlag für fremdsprachige Literatur，1987. 48 S.
《种金子：阿凡提的故事》，谢德风等改编；孙以增等绘画.

45. Wunderochse. Geschichten von Afanti. Bearbeitet und illustriert von Ma Chao. Beijing：Verlag für fremdsprachige Literatur，1987. 44 S.
《神牛：阿凡提的故事》

46. Chinesische Volksmärchen. Nach chinesischen Quellen erzählt von Dana und Milada St'ovickova. Illustriert von Eva Bednarova. Hanau：Verlag Werner Dausien，1987. 200 S. 8. Aufl.
中国民间童话.
(1)7. Aufl. Hanau/M.：Dausien，1983. 199 S.：Ill.（z. T. farb.）；29cm. ISBN：3768433136，3768433137.

47. Märchen aus der Mandschurei/aus d. Chines. übers. u. hrsg. von Jörg Bäcker. München：Diederichs，1988. 285 S.：Ill.；20cm. ISBN：3424009392，3424009393.
满洲童话. Bäcker，Jörg 译.

48. Besuch von einem Panda/Text von Liu Qian. Ill. von Jiang Cheng'an. Beijing: v Delphin-Verl. , 1990. 24 S. ; 18×19cm. ISBN: 7800510786.

《熊猫来访》,Liu Qian 著.

49. Chinesische Abende: Märchen und Geschichten aus dem alten China/übers. aus dem Chines. in Gemeinschaft mit Tsou Ping Shou von Leo Greiner. Mit Ill. von Emil Orlik. 1. Aufl. Frankfurt am Main; Leipzig: Insel-Verl, 1991. 200 S. ; 18cm. ISBN: 3458330399. (Insel-Taschenbuch; 1339).

《中国之夜:古代中国的童话和故事》,Greiner, Leo (1976—1928)译.

50. Das Fuchsmädchen: Nomaden erzählen Märchen und Sagen aus dem Norden Chinas/ausgew. und übers. von Marie-Luise Latsch, Helmut Forster-Latsch in Zusammenarbeit mit Zhao Zhenquan. Frauenfeld: Im Waldgut, 1992. 131 S. ; Ill. ; 20cm. ISBN: 3729400757, 3729400754. (Der Bärenhüter im Waldgut)

中国北方游牧民族童话与传说. Latsch, Marie-Luise 译.

51. Neun Leben: eine Kindheit in Schanghai/Chen Danyan. Aus dem Chines. von Barbara Wang. Zürich; Frauenfeld: Nagel und Kimche, 1995. 173 S. ; 21cm. ISBN: 3312005048, 3312005043.

《一个女孩》,陈丹燕著;Wang, Barbara 译.

(1) Frankfurt am Main: Fischer-Taschenbuch-Verl. , 1998. 183 S. ;19cm. ISBN: 3596802159,3596802156. (Fischer; 80215; Fischer Schatzinsel)

52. Seidenraupen für Jin Ling/Huang Beijia. Aus dem Chines. übers. von Barbara Wang und Hwang Yi-Chun. Zürich: NordSüd, 2008. 188 S. ; 21cm. ISBN: 3314015687, 3314015682. (Reihe Baobab)

《我要做个好孩子》,黄蓓佳(1955—)著;Wang, Barbara 和 Hwang Yi-Chun 合译.

(1)Basel Baobab Books,2011. 192 S. 205 mm×133 mm. ISBN: 3905804263, 3905804263. (Reihe Baobab)

53. Eine ganz besondere Prinzessin/Wu Meizhen. Ins Dt. übertr. von Dagmar Schmitz. Köln Schneider-Buch Egmont, 2012. 557 S. 21cm. ISBN: 3505126451, 3505126454

《小公主与矮爸爸》,伍美珍著;Schmitz, Dagmar 译.

54. Der Schakal und der Wolf/Shen Shixi; ins Deutsche übertragen von Susanne Arnold. Köln: Egmont, 2012. : 04 S. ISBN: 3505126444, 3505126446

狐狼与狼. 沈石溪著;Arnold, Susanne 译.

55. Bronze und Sonnenblume＝Qing tong kui hua/Cao Wenxuan. Aus dem Chines. von Nora Frisch. Esslingen: Drachenhaus-Verl. ,2014. 243 S. Ill. 22cm. ISBN: 3943314090,394331409X

《青铜葵花》,曹文轩(1954—)著;Frisch, Nora 译.

J 类 艺术

J1 艺术概论

1. Die chinesische Kunst/Jin Yong; übersetzt von Mai Zhanxiong; deutsche Bearbeitung: Ingrid Lutz. Beijing: China Intercontinental Press, 2009. 152 pages: color illustrations; 25cm. ISBN: 7508515717

《艺术之旅》,靳永著. 五洲传播出版社. 本书内容包括音乐、舞蹈、戏曲、曲艺、书法、绘画等.

2. Der Pfad der Schönheit. Chinesische Kulturgeschichte. Aus dem Chinesischen und hrsg. von Karl H. Pohl. Mit zahlreichen, meist farbigen Abbildungen/Li Zehou; Karl H. Pohl. Freiburg: Herder, 1992. 415 S. ; Ill. ; 20cm. ISBN: 3451041143, 3451041146. (Herder-Spektrum; Bd. 4114)

《美的历程》,李泽厚著;Pohl, Karl H. 译.

J2 绘画

1. Die traditionelle chinesische Malerei: Einführung in ein kreatives Hobby/von He Hanqiu u. Deng Jun. [übers.: Ren Shuyin. Dt. Bearb.: Atze Schmidt]. Beijing: Verl. für Fremdsprachige Literatur, 1994. 71 S. : ill. ; 26cm. ISBN: 7119004964

《中国画入门》

2. Die Chinesische Malerei: eine lautlose Poesie/Zhuang Jiayi and Nie Chongzheng. Beijing: China Intercontinental Press, 2000. 172 pages: color illustrations, portraits; 21cm. ISBN: 7801137191

《中国绘画:无声诗里颂千秋》,庄嘉怡,聂崇正. 五洲传播出版社.

3. Chinesische Neujahrsbilder/zusammengestellt von Lin Fang; übersetzt von Wolfgang Schaub. Beijing: China Intercontinental Press, 2009. 99 pages: color illustrations; 19×22cm. ISBN: 7508515540

《中国年画》,林方编著. 五洲传播出版社.

4. Chinesische Bauernmalerei/zsgest. von Xi Jiping. Beijing: China Intercontinental Press, 2009. 102 S. : überw. Ill. ISBN: 7508515588

《中国农民画》,奚吉平编著. 五洲传播出版社.

5. Ackerbau u. Seidengewinnung in China: ein kais. Lehr- u. Mahn-Buch/Kêng-chih-t'u. Aus d. Chines. übers. u. mit Erkl. vers. von O. Franke. Hamburg: Friederichsen, 1913. VI, 194 S. : mit 102 Taf. u. 57 Ill. ; 4 (8). (Abhandlungen des Hamburgischen Kolonialinstituts; Bd. 11. Abhandlungen des Hamburgischen Kolonialinstituts/Reihe B/Völkerkunde, Kulturgeschichte und Sprachen; Bd. 8)

《耕织图》,(南宋)楼俦;Franke, Otto 译.

6. Chinesische Comics: Gespenster, Mörder, Klassenfeinde/übers. u. eingel. von Wolfgang Bauer. Düsseldorf, Köln: Diederichs, 1976. 256 S. : überwiegend Ill. ;

19cm. ISBN：3424005714，3424005711.（Diederichs gelbe Reihe；11：China im Umbruch）

中国漫画. Wolfgang, Bauer 译.

7. Scherze und Anekdoten des chinesischen Altertums/ Karikaturen von Ding Cong.［übers. von Liu Menglian］. Beijing：Verl. Neue Welt, 1986. 219 S.；21cm.

丁聪漫画. 丁聪(1916—2009)著.

(1)Bilinguale Ausg., 1. Nachdr.（双语，再版）. Beijing：Verl. Neue Welt，1992. 219 S.；21cm. ISBN：7800050203.

8. Chinesische Satire und Humor/ausgew. Karikaturen von Hua Junwu. übers. und mit erl. Versen vers. von Li Deman. Beijing：Verl. Neue Welt，1988. 174 S.；23cm. ISBN：7800050602.

《华君武漫画选：1955 年—1982 年》，华君武(1915—2010)绘；贝格尔配诗；Li Deman 译. 新世界出版社.

J21 书法、篆刻

1. Einführung in die chinesische Kalligraphie. Beijing：Verlag für fremdsprachige Literatur, 1995. 67 pages；25cm. ISBN：7119014463

《中国书法入门》，郭伯南.

2. China：die Kalligraphie/Chen Tingyou；übersetzt von Jacqueline und Martin Winter. Beijing：China Intercontinental Press, 2004. 135 S.：color Abb.；23cm. ISBN：7508504232

《中国书法》，陈廷祐著，（奥）温特（Winter, M.）译. 五洲传播出版社（人文中国书系）

3. Gedanken und Erlebnisse eines chinesischen Kunstsammlers：Erzählungen, Betrachtungen und Ratschläge/［Übersetzung aus dem Chinesischen；Einführung und Anmerkungen von Robert H. van Gulik；aus dem Englischen übertragen und in Text und Bild ergänzt von Hans-Jürgen Cwik］. Essen：Burkhard-Verlag, 1971. 140,［4］pages：illustrations (some color)，map；17×17cm.

《书画说铃》，陆时化(1714—1779)；高罗佩（Gulik, Robert Hans van,1910—1967)（荷兰汉学家）英译；Cwik, Hans-Jürgen 德译.

J3 工艺美术

1. Das chinesische Kunsthandwerk/Tan Song；übersetzt von Dai Shifeng. Beijing：China Intercontinental Press, 2009. 132 pages：color illustrations；25cm. ISBN：7508515762

《工艺之旅》，谭松著. 五洲传播出版社.

2. Chinesische Stoffarbeiten/zusammengestellt von Geng Mo；übersetzt von Wolfgang Schaub. Beijing：China Intercontinental Press, 2009. 101 pages：color illustrations；19×22cm. ISBN：7508515564

《中国布艺》，耿默编著. 五洲传播出版社.

3. Traditionelle chinesische Kleidung/Yuan Jieying. ［Berater：Cai Mingzhao... Dt. Texte：Atze Schmitz. Fotos：Yuan Jieying und Xi Hengqing］. Beijing：Verl. für fremdsprachige Literatur, 2007. 107 S.：zahlr. ill.；18×20cm. ISBN：7119044156

《中国传统服饰》，袁杰英等主编. 外文出版社（中华风物/肖晓明主编）

4. Keramik und Porzellan in China：vom Tontopf der Steinzeitmenschen zur Porzellankunst/Verf.：Li Zhiyan und Cheng Wen. Dt. übers.：Zhong Yingjie und Yan Junxu. Beijing：Verl. für Fremdsprachige Literatur, 1996. 218 S.：ill.；31cm. ISBN：7119013149

《中国陶瓷简史》，李知宴，程雯.

5. Keramik und Porzellan/von Li Zhiyan und Cheng Qinhua. Beijing：Verlag für fremdsprachige Literatur, 2003. 101 pages：color illustrations；18×20cm. ISBN：7119031554，7119031552.（China）

《中国陶瓷》，李知宴，程钦华

6. Chinas Keramik und Porzellan/zusammengestellt von Mao Mao；übersetzt von Huang Yi. Beijing：China Intercontinental Press, 2009. 102 p：chiefly ill.（some color）；19×22cm. ISBN：7508515595

《中国陶瓷》，毛毛编著. 五洲传播出版社.

7. Volkskunst/von Lu Zhongmin. Beijing：Verlag für fremdsprachige Literatur, 2006. 108 pages：color illustrations；18×20cm. ISBN：7119033239

《中国民间工艺》，鲁忠民主编. 外文出版社（中华风物/肖晓明主编）

8. 中国民间工艺/外文出版社德文编译部编译. 北京：外文出版社,2009. 35 页；21cm. ISBN：7119058559

介绍中国丰富的民间工艺，如剪纸，皮影戏，风筝，布艺等等.

9. Holzschnitzerei/zsgest. von Kangsheng Wang.［Übers.：Matthias Mersch. Dt. Red.：Chen Guoyue］. Beijing：Verl. für fremdsprachige Literatur, 2009. 143 Seite ill. 24cm. ISBN：7119059754

《民间木雕》，王抗生编著.

10. Steinlöwen/ zsgest. von Zhang Huaishui.［Übers.：Huang Rui. Dt. Red.：Kurt Rammerstorfer...］. Beijing：Verl. für fremdsprachige Literatur, 2009. 127 S. zahlr. ill. 24cm., 384 gr. ISBN：7119059778

《民间石狮》，张淮水编著.

11. Steinbildhauerei/zsgest. von Kangsheng Wang und Duan Jianhua.［Übers.：Huang Rui. Dt. Red.：Kurt Rammerstorfer...］. Beijing：Verl. für fremdsprachige Literatur, 2009. 133 pages：illustrations；24cm. ISBN：7119059761

《民间石雕》，王抗生，段建华编著.

12. Spielzeug/ zsgest. von Li Youyou.［Übers.：Li Xiang. Dt. Red.：Chen Xiaoli und Wolfgang Schaub］. Beijing：Verl. für fremdsprachige Literatur, 2009. 130 S. zahlr. ill. 24cm., 394 gr. ISBN：7119057927

《民间玩具》，李友友编著；李响译.

13. Stickerei/zsgest. von Li Youyou.［Übers.：Wolfgang

Schaub. Dt. Red.：Chen Xiaoli]. Beijing：Verl. für Fremdsprachige Literatur，2009. 145 S. zahlr. Ill 24cm.，433 gr. ISBN：7119057910

《民间刺绣》，李友友编著.

14. Weben und Färben/ zsgest. von Jianhua Duan. [Übers.：Matthias Mersch. Dt. Red.：Chen Guoyue]. Beijing：Verl. für fremdsprachige Literatur, 2009. 134 S. zahlr. ill. 24cm.，409 gr. ISBN：7119059723

《民间染织》，段建华编著.

15. Stoffarbeiten/ zsgest. von Xiaoping Chen. [Übers.：Matthias Mersch. Dt. Red.：Mai Zhanxiong und Luan Xuwen]. Beijing：Verl. für fremdsprachige Literatur,2009. 115 S. zahlr. ill. 24cm.，354 gr. ISBN：7119058030

《民间布艺》，陈晓萍编著.

16. Silberschmuck/ zsgest. von Wang Jinhua. [Übers.：Li Xiang. Dt. Red.：Wolfgang Schaub...]. Beijing：Verl. für fremdsprachige Literatur, 2009. 125 S. überw. ill. 24cm.，382 gr. ISBN：7119059716

《民间银饰》，王金华编著.

17. Ziegel mit Schnitzdekor/zsgest. von Lan Xianlin. [Übers.：Huang Rui. Dt. Red.：Ulriker Nieter...]. Beijing：Verl. für fremdsprachige Literatur, 2009. 136 S. zahlr. ill. 24cm.，415 gr. ISBN：7119059730

《民间砖雕》，蓝先琳编著.

18. Neujahrsbilder/zsgest. von Lan Xianlin. [Übers.：Dorian Liedtke. Dt. Red.：Mai Zhanxiong und Lian Xuwen]. Beijing：Verl. für fremdsprachige Literatur,2009. 155 S. zahlr. ill. 24cm.，456 gr. ISBN：7119059747

《民间年画》，蓝先琳编著.

19. Scherenschnitte/zsgest. von Xu Zhimin. [Übers.：Wolfgang Schaub. Dt. Red.：Chen Xiaoli]. Beijing：Verl. für fremdsprachige Literatur, 2009. 129 S. zahlr. ill. 24cm.，390 gr. ISBN：7119057903

《民间剪纸》，许之敏编著.

20. Chinesische Scherenschnitte/zusammengestellt von Sun Bingshan. Beijing：China Intercontinental Press, 2009. 102 S：Ill. ISBN：7508515557

《中国剪纸》，孙秉山编著. 五洲传播出版社.

21. Chinesische Drachen/zusammengestellt von Sun Bingshan... [et al.]. Beijing：China Intercontinental Press, 2009. 102 S；Ill. ISBN：7508515533

《中国风筝》，孙秉山，俞满红编著. 五洲传播出版社.

22. Chinesische Volksmasken/zusammengestellt von Gong Ning；übersetzt von Wu Xiaohong. Beijing：China Intercontinental Press, 2009. 102 pages：chiefly color illustrations；19×22cm. ISBN：7508515571

《中国民间面具》，龚宁编著. 五洲传播出版社.

J4 中国音乐

1. Das Yüeh-Fu Tsa-Lu des Tuan An-Chieh：Studien zur Geschichte von Musik, Schauspiel und Tanz in der T'ang-

Dynastie/von Martin Gimm. Wiesbaden：Harrassowitz,1966. 631 S.（Asiatische Forschungen：AF；Monographienreihe zur Geschichte, Kultur und Sprache der Völker Ost- u. Zentralasiens. - Wiesbaden：Harrassowitz, 1959—；19）

《乐府杂录》，唐段安节著；Gimm, Martin Gimm（1930—）译.

J5 戏剧、曲艺、杂技艺术

J51 中国戏剧艺术理论

1. Peking-Oper und Mei Lanfang：eine Einführung in das traditionelle chinesische Theater und die Kunst seines grossen Meisters Mei Lanfang/von Wu Zuguang, Huang Zuolin, Mei Shaowu. Beijing：Verlag Neue Welt, 1984. 163 S.：ill.

《京剧与梅兰芳》，吴祖光等著；Klodt, Ulrich 译. 新世界出版社.

2. Das Geheimnis des chinesischen Schattenspiels/Liu Jilin, Beijing Morgenglanz-Verl. 1988. 111 S. 25cm.

《中国皮影戏》，刘李霖编著. 朝华出版社（中国简况）

3. Peking-Oper/Xu Chengbei. Übers. von Wang Defeng. Beijing：China Intercontinental Press，2003. 137 S.：ill.；23cm. ISBN：7508503406

《中国京剧》，徐城北著；王德峰译. 五洲传播.

4. Die Peking-Oper：Essenz der chinesischen Kultur/Yi Bian. [Übers.：Gregor Kneussel]. Beijing：Verl. für fremdsprachige Literatur, 2006. 150 S.：zahlr. ill.；21cm. ISBN：7119041592

《国粹：中国京剧》，易边编著；高明译.

5. Die Peking-Oper. Beijing：Verlag für Fremdsprachige Literratur, 2009. 35 pages：illustrations (chiefly color)；21cm. ISBN：7119058672

《中国京剧》，外文出版社德文编译部编译.

J6 电影、电视艺术

1. Tückische Absichten, gemeine Tricks：Kritik an Michelangelo Antonionis chinafeindl. Film „China"/von e. Kommentator d. Renmin Ribao. Peking：Verlag für Fremdsprachl. Literatur, 1974. 17 S.；19cm.

《恶毒的用心，卑劣的手法》，《人民日报》评论员. 电影评论.

K 类 历史、地理

K1 中国史

K11 通史

1. Kurzer Abriss der chinesischen Geschichte/von Djiän Bedsan；Schao Hsün-dscheng；Hu Hua. Peking：Verl. für Fremdsprachige Literatur，1958. 334 S.

《中国历史概要》,翦伯赞等著;施华滋译.

2. Geschichte/bearb. von der Red. der China-Buchreihe. 〔Dt. bearb. von E. Berkenbusch〕. Beijing：Verl. für fremdsprachige Literatur，1984. 186 S.：Ill.

《历史》,《中国概况丛书》编辑委员会编.

3. Geschichte. Beijing：Verlag für fremdsprachige Literatur，1987. 40 S.：Ill.

《中国历史》.外文出版社(中国简况)

4. Chinas Geschichte im Überblick/von Bai Shouyi；Geschrieben von Yang Zhao 〔and others〕；〔Aus dem Englischen von Alexander Sichrovsky〕. Beijing：Verlag fur Fremdsprachige Literatur，1989. 559 S. ：Abb. （z. T. farb)；22cm.

《中国通史纲要》,白寿彝.

(1)Beijing：Verlag für Fremdsprachige Literatur，2009. 809 pages；illustrations (some color)；24cm. ISBN：7119016023

5. Chinesische Geschichte/neu bearb. von Dai Shifeng. Beijing：Verl. für fremdsprachige Literatur，2003. 225 S. 21cm. ISBN：7119031627

《中国历史》,戴世峰.

6. Geschichtlicher Überblick. Monograph. Beijing：Verlag für Fremdsprachige Literratur，2009. 29 pages：color illustrations；21cm. ISBN：7119058689

《中国简史》,外文出版社德文编译部编译.

7. Allgemeine Kenntnisse über die chinesische Geschichte/The Overseas Chinese Affairs Office of the State Council；The Office of Chinese Language Council International. Beijing Higher Education Press，2007. 269 S. ill. ，Kt. ISBN：7040207187

《中国历史常识：汉德对照》,王恺主编;国务院侨务办公室,国家汉语国际推广领导小组办公室编.高等教育出版社.

8. Geschichte und Zivilisation Chinas/〔edited by Zhang Yingpin，Fan Wei〕. Beijing：Central Party Literature Press，2007. 256 pages：illustrations (some color)，maps，portraits；29cm. ISBN：7507323245

《中国历史与文明》,张英聘,范蔚编著.中央文献出版社.

9. Die Geschichte Chinas/verf. von Deng Yinke. Übers. von Guo Zifu und Gregor Kneussel. Beijing China Intercontinental Press，2009. 169 S. zahlr. Ill. ，Kt. 25cm. ISBN：7508515731

《历史之旅》,邓荫柯著.五洲传播出版社.

10. Wichtige historische Ereignisse. Monograph. Beijing：Verlag für Fremdsprachige Literratur，2009. 34 pages：color illustrations；21cm. ISBN：7119058696

《中国历史上的重大事件》,外文出版社德文编译部编译.

11. Wichtige historische Persönlichkeiten. Monograph. Beijing：Verlag für Fremdsprachige Literratur，2009. 31

pages：illustrations (chiefly color)；21cm. ISBN：7119058764

《中国著名历史人物》,外文出版社德文编译部编译.

12. Der Westen versteht den Osten nicht：Gedanken zur Geschichte und Kultur Chinas/Qian Mu；Übersetzung aus dem Chinesischen von Chen Chai-hsin und Diethelm Hofstra；mit einer Einleitung von Michael Friedrich. Dortmund：Projekt-Verlag，1997. 502 pages；21cm. ISBN：3928861824，3928861823. （Arcus Chinatexte，Richard-Wilhelm-Übersetzungszentrum；Band 11).

《历史与文化论丛》,钱穆(1895—1990)著；Chen Chai-hsin 和 Diethelm Hofstra 合译.

13. Das Leben der Kaiser von China/〔dt. Übers.：Gong Hehua. Dt. Red.：Matthias Mersch und Mai Zhanxiong〕. Beijing：Verl. für fremdsprachige Literatur，2008. 149 S.：zahlr. ill.；23cm. ，362 gr. ISBN：7119054568

《帝后生活》,思方撰.本书展示帝后生活的方方面面,从衣食住行到婚丧嫁娶,宫廷阴谋政变等.

14. Die chinesischen Familiennamen nach dem Büchlein Bei dja sing；nebst Anhang enthaltend Angaben über berühmte Persönlichkeiten der chinesischen Geschichte/von P. Jahann Weig, S. V. D. Tsingtau：Missionsdruckerei，1931. X, 285 S. 8,,：Ill.

《百家姓》,Weig，Jahann 译.

K12　古代史籍

K121　《春秋》三传

1. Tsch'un-ts'iu：mit den drei Kommentaren Tso-tschuan，Kung-yang-tschuan und Ku-liang-tschuan in mandschuischer Übersetzung/herausgegeben von Wolfgang Bauer mit einem Vorwort von Erich Haenisch. Wiesbaden：Harrassowitz，O，1959. 1026 S.；24cm. （Abhandlungen für die Kunde des Morgenlandes；33，1).

《春秋》三传：《左传》《公羊传》《谷梁传》,鲍吾刚（Bauer，Wolfgang，1930—1997)编译.

K122　战国策

1. Aus den Plänen der kämpfenden Reiche nebst den entsprechenden Biographien des Se-Ma Ts'ien. / Liu Xiang；Franz Hübotter. Berlin：Wilhelm Rohr，1912. 126 S.

《战国策》,刘向（公元前 77—前 6 年）编；Hübotter，Franz 译.

2. Der Herr von Sin-ling：Reden aus d. Chan-kuo-tsê u. Biographien aus d. Shi-ki/eingel. u. übers. von Erich Haenisch. Stuttgart：Reclam，1965. 79 S. ：mit 1 Kt.；kl. 8. （Unesco-Sammlung repräsentativer Werke：Asiatische Reihe；Universal-Bibliothek；Nr. 8947)

《战国策》《史记》节略. Haenisch，Erich（1880—1966)译.

K123 史记

1. Geschichten aus den historischen Aufzeichnungen/[Red. : Tang Xiaoqing und Li Xiang. Übers. : Zhong Yingjie und Li Xiang]. Beijing：Verl. für fremdsprachige Literatur, 2008. 275 S. ill. 23cm. ISBN：7119055718

《史记故事》,司马迁原著.

K124 《资治通鉴》

1. Das Tse tschi T'ung Kien und das T'ung Kien Gang Mu/ tr. by Otto Franke. Berlin：Verlag der Akademie der Wissenschaften, 1930. 46 S.

《资治通鉴》《通鉴纲目》选译,司马光(1019—1086)、朱熹(1130—1200)著;Franke, Otto 译.

K125 其他史书合集

1. Chinesische Urkunden zur Geschichte Asiens/in vollständiger Zusammenfassung übersetzt und erläutert von J. J. M. de Groot...; mit Unterstützung durch die Preussische Akademie der Wissenschaften. Berlin；Leipzig：W. de Gruyter & co, 1921—1926. 2 v. (IX-304 p. , 233 p.)；30cm.

   Contents：vol. 1, Die Hunnen der vorchristlichen Zeit. — 1921. — vol. 2, Die Westlande Chinas in der vorchristlichen Zeit/aus dem Nachlass des Verfassers herausgegeben von O. Franke. —1926.

   《三国志》《魏书》《新唐书》《旧唐书》选译. Groot, Johann Jacob Maria de(1854—1921),Franke, Otto(1863—1946)编译.

   (1) Saarbrücken：VDM Verlag Dr. Müller, 2008. IX, 304, 233 S. 21cm. ISBN：3836440233, 3836440237. (Editon classic)

2. Geschichte des Chinesischen Reiches：eine Darstellung seiner Entstehung, seines Wesens und seiner Entwicklung bis zur neuesten Zeit/von O. Franke. Berlin：De Gruyter, 1930—1952. 5 volumes：folded map (in pocket)；26cm.

   Contents：1. Bd. Das Altertum und das Werden des konfuzianischen Staates. —2. Bd. Der konfuzianische Staat I. Der Aufstieg zur Weltmacht. —3. Bd. Anmerkungen, Ergänzungen und Berichtgungen zu Band I und II, Sach- und Namen-verzeichnis. —4. Bd. Der konfuzianische Staat II. Krisen und Fremdvölker. —5. Bd. Anmerkungen, Ergänzungen und Berichtigungen zu Band IV, Namen- und Sachverzeichnis.

   中国朝代史选译(三国志、晋书、宋书、梁书、陈书、魏书、隋唐、南史、北史、旧唐书、旧五代史等). 5 卷. Franke, Otto(1863—1946)编译.

   (1)Berlin：W. de Gruyter, 1948—1965. 5 volumes folded maps (in pocket)26cm.

   (2)Neuausg. der 2. Aufl. Berlin；New York：W. De Gruyter, 2001. 5 volumes：maps；24cm. ISBN：3110170345, 3110170344

K13 古代史(上古至 1840)

1. Zeitstücke - Zeugnisse der chinesischen Vergangenheit. 1, Die Altsteinzeit, der frühe Abschnitt der Jungsteinzeit, der späte Abschnitt der Jungsteinzeit, die Xia-Dynastie, die Shang-Dynastie, die Westliche Zhou-Dynastie, die Frühlings- und Herbstperiode/Museum für chinesische Geschichte. [Chefred. : Yu Weichao]. Beijing：Morgenglanz-Verl. , 1997. 271 S. : zahlr. Ill. , Kt. ISBN：7505404784

《华夏之路》(第一册,旧石器时代至春秋时期),俞伟超主编;中国历史博物馆编. 朝华出版社.

2. Heldensagen aus dem unteren Yangtse-Tal/[Hrsg.] v. Werner Eichhorn. Wiesbaden：F. Steiner, 1969. 153 S. ; 8. ISBN：3935556136, 3935556132. (Abhandlungen für die Kunde des Morgenlandes；Bd. 38,2)

《吴越春秋》,(汉)赵晔撰;Eichhorn, Werner 译.

3. Die Monographie über Wang Mang/Kritisch bearb. , übers. u. erklärt v. Hans O. H. Stange. Leipzig：F. A. Brockhaus, 1939. XLI, 336 S. ; gr. 8. (Abhandlungen für die Kunde des Morgenlandes；Bd. 23, Nr. 3)

《王莽传》(《前汉书》第 99 章),班固(32—92)编;Stang, Hans 译.

   (1) 再版. Die Monographie über Wang Mang. Ts'ien-Han-Shu Kap. 99. Kritisch bearbeitet, übersetzt und erklärt von Hans O. H. Stange. Nendeln：Kraus Reprint Ltd. , 1966. 336 S.

4. Wehrot und Arang：Untersuchgn zur myth. u. geschichtl. Landeskunde v. Ostiran/Josef Markwart. Hrsg. v. Hans Heinrich Schaeder. Leiden：Brill, 1938. 63, 202 S. ：1 Kt. ；4.

《北史》,(唐)李延寿著;Markwart, Josef 译.

5. Meng-Ta-pei-lu und Hei-Ta-shih-lüeh：chines. Gesandtenberichte über d. frühen Mongolen 1221 u. 1237/nach Vorarbeiten von Erich Haenisch u. Yao Ts'ung-wu übers. u. kommentiert von Peter Olbricht u. Elisabeth Pinks. Eingel. von Werner Banck. Wiesbaden：Harrassowitz, 1980. XXI, 264 S. ; 24cm. ISBN：3447019996, 3447019999. (Asiatische Forschungen；Bd. 56)

《蒙鞑备录》及《黑鞑事略》,孟珙(1195—1246),彭大雅(?—1245)著;Olbricht, Peter 与 Pinks, Elisabeth 合译.

6. Geschichte der Ost-Mongolen und ihres Fürstenhauses/ Ssananang Ssetsen Chungtaidschi. Aus d. Mongol. übers. , u. mit d. Originaltexte, nebst Anm. , Erl. u. Citaten aus anderen unedirten Originalwerken hrsg. v. Isaac Jacob Schmidt. St. Petersburg：Gedruckt bei N. Gretsch, 1829. xxiv, 509 pages, 1 leaf；26×21cm.

《蒙古源流》,萨囊彻辰(17 世纪)著;Schmidt, Isaak Jakob (1779—1847)译.

7. Huang-ch'ing-k'ai-kuo-fang-lüeh. [Deutsch.] Huang-ts'ing k'ai-kuo fang-lüeh = Die Gründung des mandschurischen Kaiserreiches/übers. u. erkl. v. Dr.

iur. et phil. Erich Hauer. Berlin；Leipzig：de Gruyter，1926. XXV，710 S.；4,.

《皇清开国方略》，阿桂等著；Hauer, Erich 译.

8. Gengzi riji：das Tagebuch des Hua Xuelan aus dem Beijing des Boxeraufstands；mit einer Einführung zum Tagebuch in der chinesischen Tradition/von Otmar Becker. Hamburg：Ges. für Natur- u. Völkerkunde Ostasiens，1987. II，289 S.；graph. Darst.；21cm. (Gesellschaft für Natur- und Völkerkunde Ostasiens：Mitteilungen der Gesellschaft für Natur- und Völkerkunde Ostasiens e. V. Hamburg；Bd. 109)

《庚子日记》，华学澜(1860—1906)著；Becker, Otmar 译.

K14　近代史(1840—1911)

1. Der Opiumkrieg/zsgest. vom Koll. für d. , „Serie d. Geschichte d. modernen China". Peking：Verl. für Fremdsprach. Literatur，1977. [8]，124 S.：Ill.

《鸦片战争》，《中国近代史丛书》编写组.

2. Die Taiping-Revolution/zusammengestellt vom Kollektiv für die „Serie der Geschichte des modernen China". Peking：Verlag für Fremdsprachige Literatur，1977. 174 s.，[9] tav.：kort.

《太平天国革命》，《中国近代史丛书》编写组.

3. Die Reformbewegung von 1898/zusammengestellt vom Kollektiv für die „Serie der Geschichte des modernen China" Peking：Verlag für Fremdsprachige Literatur，1978. 132 pages：illustrations；19cm.

《戊戌变法》，《中国近代史丛书》编写组.

4. Die Yihotuan-Bewegung von 1900/zsgest. vom Kollektiv f. die „Serie des modernen China" Peking：Verl. f. Fremdsprachige Literatur，1978. 136 S.

《义和团运动》，《中国近代史丛书》编写组.

K15　中华人民共和国成立之后历史

1. Die Hsinhai Revolution 1911：Eine bedeutende demokratische Revolution im China der Neuzeit. /Wu Yü-Dschang；Deutsch von Li Ming. Peking：Verlag für fremdsprachige literatur，1962. 178 pages：photographs；21cm.

《辛亥革命：中国近代史上一次伟大的民主革命》，吴玉章.

2. Die Revolution von 1911/zusammengestellt vom Kollektiv für die „Serie der Geschichte des modernen China" Peking：Verlag für Fremdsprachige Literatur，1977. 173 pages：illustrations, portraits；19cm.

《辛亥革命》，《中国近代史丛书》编写组.

3. Erinnerungen an den Langen Marsch/von Liu Bo-tscheng u. a. Beijing：Verl. für Fremdsprach. Literatur，1980. 243 S.；19cm.

《回顾长征》，刘伯承.

4. Vom Opiumkrieg bis zur Befreiung/Israel Epstein. [Aus dem Engl. von Klaus B. Ludwig]. Beijing：Verl. für Fremdsprachige Literatur，1985. VII，280 S.：ill. , Kt.；19cm.

《从鸦片战争到解放》

5. Chronik der Volksrepublik China：(1949—1984)/Cheng Jin. Beijing：Verl. f. Fremdsprachige Literatur，1986. 87 S.

《中华人民共和国大事记》

K2　地方史志

北京

1. Beijing：Hauptstadt der Volksrepublik China/Liu Junwen. Beijing：Verlag für Fremdsprachige Literatur：Vertrieb, Vertriebszentrum für Publikationen aus China，1982. 210 pages，[56] pages of plates：illustrations (some color)，maps；19cm.

《北京》，刘俊雯编.

2. Beijing von A bis Z：der Hauptstadtführer/[edited by] Liu Junwen. Beijing：Verlag für Fremdsprachige Literatur，版本：Dritte, erweiterte und verbesserte Auflage. 1995. 211 pages：illustrations；19cm. ISBN：7119002007

《北京》，刘俊雯.

3. Beijing：Kunst und Kultur einer alten Hauptstadt/Text von Yan Chongnian. Übers. von Zhang Liangen und Chen Hanli. Dt. Text bearb. von Hans Joachim Rieger. [Verantw. Red.：Wang Yanrong und Ma Yue. Fotos：Yan Zhongyi]. Beijing：Morgenglanz-Verl，1995. 285 S.：zahlr. ill. , Kt.；38cm. ISBN：750540413X

《古都北京》，阎崇年撰；张连根、陈汉丽译. 朝华出版社.

4. Geschichten aus der Verbotenen Stadt/zsgest. von Er Si... [Übers.：Frieder Kern]. Beijing：Verl. für Fremdsprachige Literatur，1990. 171 S.；18cm. ISBN：7119011537.

《紫禁城秘史》，商鸿逵(1907—1983)，尔泗著.

(1)第二版. Beijing：Verl. für Fremdsprachige Literatur，1994. 175 S.；18cm. ISBN：7119011537

5. Der Kaiserpalast. Beijing：Chinesischer Esperanto-Verlag，1995. 158 pages：color illustrations；26cm. ISBN：7505202650

《故宫》，施永南、望天星编；严隽旭等译. 中国世界语出版社.

6. Die Geschichten über die Verbotene Stadt/Cheng Qinhua；[übersetzt von Gu Xiaoyun und Chen Meina；Deutsch bearbeitet von Atze Schmidt]. Beijing：Verl. für fremdsprachige Literature，1998. 136 pages：illustrations；19cm. ISBN：7119017446，7119017440. (Chinesisches Kaleidoskop)

《紫禁城的故事》，程钦华.

7. Hutongs in Beijing/Übersetzung：Li Xiang und Luan

Xuwen; Deutsche Redaktion: Ren Shuyin und Isabel Wolte. Beijing: Verlag für fremdsprachige literatur, 2008. 103 pages: color illustrations, maps; 22cm. ISBN: 7119044057

《北京胡同·名人故居》,李连霞撰文.

河南

1. 中国河南 汉德对照/河南省人民政府外事侨务办公室编. 郑州:河南人民出版社,2018. 52 页;26cm. ISBN: 7215115323

陕西

1. Xi'an - Chinas alte Hauptstadt/Xiang Yang. Beijing: Verl. für Fremdsprachige Literatur, 1992. 149 S.: ill., Kt.; 19cm. ISBN: 711900817X

《中国古都西安》,相阳.

2. Weltbekannte Kulturstadt: Xi'an/zusammengestellt vom Büro für auswärtige Angelegenheiten der Volksregierung der Stadt Xi'an, edited by Wang Xizhao. Beijing: [China Travel and Tourism Pr.], 1996. 135 pages: color illustrations, maps (some color); 29cm. ISBN: 7503212659

《世界历史名都西安》,王锡钊. 中国旅游出版社.

黑龙江

1. Das neue Bild von Heilongjiang/[edited by] Li Changshan. Beijing: Central Compilation & Translation Press, 2007. 176 pages: color illustrations, color maps; 21cm. ISBN: 7802115040

《黑龙江新貌》,李长山主编. 中央编译出版社.

山东

1. Die Provinz Shandong/Pressebüro der Volksregierung der Provinz Shandong; Büro für auswärtige Angelegenheiten der Volksregierung der Provinz Shandong. Beijing: China Intercontinental Press, 1998. 135 pages: color illustrations; 20cm. ISBN: 7801133897, 7801133892

《山东概况》,山东省政府新闻办公室编. 五洲传播出版社.

上海

1. Das Wunder von Pudong/Zhao Qizheng mit Shao Yudong; übersetzt von Wu Huiping & Yu Zhouming. Beijing: China Intercontinental Press, 2009. 192 pages: color illustrations, color maps; 23cm. ISBN: 7508515908

《浦东奇迹》,赵启正,邵煜栋著. 五洲传播出版社.

西藏

1. Über die Tibet-Frage: (Sammlung von Dokumenten, Reden, Nachrichten, Leitartikeln, Kommentaren und anderem Tatsachenmaterial). Peking: Verlag für fremdsprachige Literatur, 1959. 308 S

《关于西藏问题》

2. Große Veränderungen in Tibet. Peking: Verl. für Fremdsprachige Literatur, 1972. 64 S.

《西藏巨变》

3. Tibet: Land und Leute; [ein Tibeter erzählt über sein Volk]/Tiley Chodag. [übers. von Cao Yongjuan... bearb. von Hans Kühner]. Beijing: Verl. für Fremdsprachige Literatur; Beijing: Chines. Internat. Buchh. -Ges, 1991. 254 S.: ill.; 22cm. ISBN: 7119012150

《我的家乡西藏》,赤列曲扎.

4. Der Potala-Palast/zusammengestellt von Nan Hui; [Übers.: Zhou Kejun. Fotos: Tudeng...]. Beijing: Esperanto-Verlag, 1995. 157 pages: color illustrations; 30cm. ISBN: 7505202448

《布达拉宫》,南卉. 中国世界语出版社.

5. 西藏人眼中的西藏:五人五话. 北京:新星出版社,1995. ISBN: 7801022610. (中国简况)

6. Chinas Tibet. Beijing: China Intercontinental Press,1995. 87 S: ill. ISBN: 7801130677

《中国西藏》,钟藏文. 五洲传播出版社.

7. Aufschwung auf dem Dach der Welt: 30 Jahre gigantische Umwandlungen in Tibet/von Li Kai und Zhao Xinbing. Beijing: China Intercontinental Press, 1995. 71 S: Ill. ISBN: 7801130774

《崛起在雪域高原:西藏三十年巨变》,李凯,赵新兵. 五洲传播出版社.

8. Chinas Tibet: Fakten und Zahlen/Wang Guozhen. Beijing: Neuer Stern-Verl, 2001. 154 S.: Ill., graph. Darst., Kt. ISBN:7801483529

《中国西藏:事实与数字》,王国振. 新星出版社.

9. 100 Fragen und Antworten zu Tibet. Beijing: Neuer Stern-Verlag, 2001. 158 pages: color illustrations; 21cm. ISBN:780148357X

《西藏百题问答》,百题编辑部. 新星出版社.

10. Die Tibetologie in China/Beijing: China Intercontinental Press, 1995. 43 S: Ill. ISBN:7801130723

《藏学在中国》,周源. 五洲传播.

11. 藏学研究基地:中国藏学研究中心简介/周源. 北京:五洲传播,1997. ISBN: 7801132106

12. 当代中国藏学/洛桑普美. 北京:五洲传播出版社,2000. ISBN:7801137027

13. Tourismus in Tibet: der Schleier des Geheimnisses wird gelüftet/Li Hairui. Beijing: China Intercontinental Press, 1995. 35 S.: ill. ISBN:7801131037

《西藏旅游:揭开神秘的面纱》,李海瑞. 五洲传播出版社.

14. Reisen in Tibet/von An Caidan. Beijing: China Intercontinental Press, 2003. 204 pages: color illustrations, color maps; 21cm. ISBN: 7508503732

《西藏旅游》,安才旦著;黄宜译. 五洲传播出版社.

15. Touristische Ressourcen in Tibet. Beijing: Verlag für fremdsprachige Literatur, 2008. 43 pages: color illustrations; 21cm. ISBN: 7119052618

《西藏的旅游资源》,《西藏的资源旅游》编写组编.

16. Das System der feudalen Leibeigenschaft in Tibet/von Yuan Sha. Beijing: China Intercontinental Press, 1996.

43 S.：ill. ISBN：7801131053

《西藏封建农奴制度》，袁莎. 五洲传播出版社.

17. 西藏交通/秦文勋. 北京：五洲传播出版社，1997. ISBN：7801131967

18. 前进中的西藏科技/西藏自治区科委编写组. 北京：五洲传播出版社，1997. ISBN：7801131908

19. 西藏教育今昔/尚俊娥. 北京：五洲传播出版社，1997. ISBN：7801131932

20. Das Bildungswesen in Tibet/Zhou Aiming. Beijing：China Intercontinental Press，2004. 195 S. ISBN：7508505557

《西藏教育》，周爱明著；周健译. 五洲传播出版社（中国西藏基本情况/郭长建，宋坚之主编）

21. Stadtbewohner in Tibet：Untersuchungsbericht über die Bewohner des Lhugu-Viertels in Lhasa/von Liu Hongji und Cering Yangzom. Beijing：China Intercontinental Press，1998. 79 S：Ill. ISBN：7801134680

《西藏城市居民：拉萨鲁固居民的调查报告》，刘洪记，次仁央宗. 五洲传播出版社.

22. Hirten in Tibet：Untersuchungsbericht über das 5. Dorf Yuqag im Kreis Amdo, Nordtibet/Zhagyai und Lu Mei. Beijing：China Intercontinental Press，1998. 85 S：ill. ISBN：7801134648

《西藏牧民：藏北安多县腰恰五村的调查报告》，扎呷，卢梅. 五洲传播出版社.

23. Die Entwicklung der tibetischen Kultur. Beijing：Presseamt des Staatsrats der Volksrepublik China，2000. 36 pages；21cm. ISBN：7801482999

《西藏文化的发展》，中华人民共和国国务院新闻办公室发布. 新星出版社.

24. Schutz und Entwicklung der tibetischen Kultur/Presseamt des Staatsrats der Volksrepublik China. Beijing：Verlag für Fremdsprachige Literatur，2008. 36 pages；21cm. ISBN：7119047362

《西藏文化的保护与发展》，中华人民共和国国务院新闻办公室发布.

25. Die Entwicklung zur Modernisierung in Tibet/Presseamt des Staatsrats der Volksrepublik China. Beijing：Verlag Neuer Stern，2001. 48 pages；21cm. ISBN：7801484037

《西藏现代化发展》，中华人民共和国国务院新闻办公室发布. 新星出版社.

26. Geschichten um Tibet/von Zhang Xiaoming. Beijing：China Intercontinental Press，2003. 167 pages：illustrations (chiefly color)；21cm. ISBN：7508501667

《西藏的故事》，张晓明. 五洲传播出版社.

27. Historische Koordinaten Chinas Tibets/von Wang Jiawei und Nyima Gyaincain. Beijing：China Intercontinental Press，2003. 379 pages：illustrations，map；21cm. ISBN：7508502574

《中国西藏的历史地位》，王家伟，尼玛坚赞编；钟英杰等译. 五洲传播出版社.

28. Geschichte Tibets/[Chen Qingying]. Beijing：China Intercontinental Press，2004. 219 S.：zahlr. Ill. ISBN：7508504364

《西藏历史》，陈庆英著. 五洲传播出版社（中国西藏基本情况）

29. Für das letzte Jahrhundert Tibets：Erinnerungen einiger Zeitzeugen der tibetischen Geschichte/[Zhangxiaoming]. [Beijing]：China Intercontinental Press，2005. 184 pages：illustrations；21cm. ISBN：7508506014

《见证百年西藏：西藏历史见证人访谈录》，张晓明编. 五洲传播出版社.

30. Religionen in Tibet/von Kal Sang Gyal. Beijing：China Intercontinental Press，2004. 158 pages：color illustrations；21cm. ISBN：7508504372

《西藏宗教》，尕藏加著. 五洲传播出版社（中国西藏基本情况）

31. Zeugen Tibets Entwicklung：ausgewählte Berichte über Tibet. Peking：Neuer Stern-Verl. 2003. 560 S：ill. ISBN：780148553X

《目击西藏：涉藏新闻报道作品选》，冀小峰等著. 新星出版社.

32. Geographie Tibets/von Yang Qinye und Zheng Du zhu. Beijing：China Intercontinental Press，2002. 149 pages：illustrations (some color)，maps；22cm. ISBN：7508501667

《西藏地理》，杨勤业，郑度编. 五洲传播出版社（西藏基本情况丛书）

33. Sitten und Gebräuche in Tibet/von Li Tao und Jiang Hongying. Beijing：China Intercontinental Press，2004. 163 pages：color illustrations；21cm. ISBN：7508506634

《西藏民俗》，李涛，江红英著；赵振权译. 五洲传播出版社（中国西藏基本情况丛书/郭长建，宋坚之主编）

34. Wirtschaft Tibets/von Wang Wenchang und Lhacan. Beijing：China Intercontinental Press，2005. 188 S.：ill.，graph. Darst.；21cm. ISBN：750850674X

《西藏经济》，王文长，拉灿著；吴晓红译. 五洲传播出版社（中国西藏基本情况丛书/郭长建，宋坚之主编）

35. Wirtschaftsentwicklung in Tibet. Beijing：Verlag für fremdsprachige Literatur，2008. 43 pages：color illustrations；21cm. ISBN：7119052465

《西藏的经济发展》，《西藏的经济发展》编写组编.

36. Wirtschaftliche und gesellschaftliche Entwicklung Tibets：Bericht des Chinesischen Forschungszentrums für Tibetologie. Monograph. Beijing：Verlag für Fremdsprachige Literatur，2009. 77 pages：color illustrations；23cm. ISBN：7119056692

《西藏经济社会发展报告》，中国藏学研究中心编.

37. Die tibetische Kunst/von Xiong Weibin；übersetzt von Zhou Kejun und Dai Shifeng. Beijing：China Intercontinental Press，2005. 114 pages：color illustrations；21cm. ISBN：7508508181

《西藏艺术》，熊文彬著；周克骏，戴世锋译. 五洲传播出

版社(中国西藏基本情况丛书/郭长建,宋坚之主编)

38. Tibetische Literatur/von Wu Wei und Geng Yufang. Beijing：China Intercontinental Press, 2005. 185 pages；color illustrations；21cm. ISBN：7508507460

《西藏文学》,吴伟,耿予方著；黄宜译. 五洲传播出版社(中国西藏基本情况丛书/郭长建,宋坚之主编)

39. Tibet：natürliche Schätze und Landschaften/von Li Mingsen und Yang Yichou. Beijing：Verlag für fremdsprachige Literatur, 2007. 210 pages；color illustrations, maps；22cm. ISBN：7119044880

《西藏自然资源与自然风光》,李明森,杨逸畴著.

40. Umwelt und Umweltschutz in Tibet. /Beijing：Verlag für Fremdsprachige Literatur, 2008. 42 pages；color illustrations；21cm. ISBN：7119052564

《西藏的自然环境与保护》,《西藏的自然环境与保护》编写组编.

41. Materialien über die Ausschreitungen vom 14. März 2008 in Tibet. Beijing：Verlag für fremdsprachige Literatur, 2008. 4 volumes：color illustrations, color maps；21cm. ISBN：7119052052 (v. 1), 7119052055 (v. 1), 7119052205 (v. 2), 7119052209 (v. 2), 7119052250 (v. 3), 711905225X (v. 3), 7119052311 (v. 4), 7119052314 (v. 4)

《西藏"3.14"事件有关材料》,4卷.

42. Bevölkerung, Religionen und die regionale Autonomie der Nationalitäten in Tibet. Beijing：Verl. für Fremdsprachige Literatur, 2008. 47 S. ：ill. ISBN：7119052366

《西藏的人口、宗教与民族区域自治》,《西藏的人口、宗教与民族区域自治》编写组编.

43. Topographie, Ressourcen und administrative Gliederung Tibets. /Beijing：Verlag für Fremdsprachige Literatur, 2008. 46 pages：color illustrations；21cm. ISBN：7119052410

《西藏的地域、资源与行政区划》,《西藏的地域、资源与行政区划》编写组编.

44. Bildungswesen, Wissenschaft und Technik, Kultur und Lebensstandard in Tibet. Beijing：Verlag für fremdsprachige Literatur, 2008. 43 pages：color illustrations；21cm. ISBN：7119052519

《西藏的教育、科技、文化与生活》,《西藏的教育、科技、文化与生活》编写组编.

45. Tibet- Tagebuch/Übersetzer, Shao Jianguang ［and others］. Beijing：Verlag für Fremdsprachige Literatur, 2008. 178 pages：color illustrations, color maps；21cm. ISBN：7119054698

《西藏日记》,邵建光等著. 本书内容为中国国际广播电台赴藏采访报道小组的纪实报道. 将所见所闻以日记形式记录下来,配上实地拍摄的照片. 共60篇,全面反映西藏各方面的发展情况.

46. 50 Jahre demokratische Reformen in Tibet/Presseamt des Staatsrats der Volksrepublik China. Beijing：Verlag für Fremdsprachige Literatur, 2009. 55 pages；21cm. ISBN：7119056388

《西藏民主改革50年》,中华人民共和国国务院新闻办公室［发布］.

47. 民族区域自治制度在西藏的成功实践/中华人民共和国国务院新闻办公室［发布］.北京：外文出版社,2015. 68页；21cm. ISBN：7119096049

德文题名：Erfolgreiche Umsetzung des Systems der natinalen Gebietsautonomie in Tibet.

48. Tibetische Lieder/ges. , übertr. u. erl. von Margret Causemann. ［Mit Zeichn. von Wangdjal］. Frankfurt am Main：Insel-Verlag, 1987. 115 S. ；Ill. ；19cm. ISBN：3458190394, 3458190392. (75 ［Fünfundsiebzig］ Jahre Insel-Bücherei. Insel-Bücherei；Nr. 1039)

西藏民谣. Causemann, Margret 译.

新疆

1. Die Geschichte und Entwicklung Xinjiangs/Presseamt des Staatsrates der Volksrepublik China. Beijing：Verlag Neuer Stern, 2003. 74 pages；21cm. ISBN：7801485106

《新疆的历史与发展》,中华人民共和国国务院新闻办公室发布.新星出版社.

2. 新疆各民族平等团结发展的历史见证:德文/中华人民共和国国务院新闻办公室发布.北京:外文出版社,2015. 54页；21cm. ISBN：7119096490

K3 中国文物考古

1. Tempel, Gräber, Dynastien：auf den Spuren der chinesischen Vergangenheit/［Hrsg. ：Xiao Shiling. Text, Wang Luxiang. Fotos：Yan Zhongyi und Xue Yuyao. Dt. übers. ：Atze Schmidt...］. Beijing：Morgenglanz-Verl. , 1995. 286 S. ：zahlr. ill. , graph. Darst. , Kt. ；35cm. ISBN：7505404105

《中国古代文化遗迹》,萧师铃. 朝华出版社.

2. Die chinesischen Bronzen. Beijing：Verl. für Fremdsprachige Literatur, 1995. 171 S. ：zahlr. ill. ；31cm. ISBN：7119014137

《中国青铜器概说》,李学勤.

3. Archäologische Funde im Neuen China. Peking：Verlag für Fremdsprachige Literatur, 1972. 217 tavler＋bilag

《新中国出土文物》

4. Neue archäologische Funde in China：Entdeckungen während der Kulturrevolution. Peking：Verlag für Fremdsprachige Literatur, 1974. 83 pages, ［24］ pages of plates：illustrations (some color), map；19cm.

《中国新出土文物》

5. Die Heimat des Peking-Menschen. Peking：Fremdsprachige Literatur, 1976. 63 pages；19cm.

《北京人之家》,贾兰坡.

6. Kaiser- und Königsgräber der chinesischen Dynastien/Verf. ：Luo Zhewen. Übers. ：Zhang Taihuang；Dai

Shifeng. Dt. Bearb.： Monika Katzenschlager. Beijing：Verl. für Fremdsprachige Literatur，1993. 204 S.： ill.，Kt.；31cm. ISBN：7119016210

《中国历代皇帝陵墓》，罗哲文.

7. Die unterirdische Tonarmee des Kaisers Qin Shi Huang/Fu Tianchou，Vorwort v. Sidney Shapiro. Peking：Neue Welt，1985. 111 S；25×26cm.： Fig. (z. T. farbig)

《秦始皇兵马俑》，傅天仇编.

8. Die Tonarmee des ersten Kaisers von China： Vom sensationellen Fund bis zur jüngsten Analyse. / Beijing：Tourismusverlag Chinas，1993. 121 pages：illustrations (some color)；29cm. ISBN：7503210702

《秦始皇兵马俑》，吴晓丛，郭佑民. 中国旅游出版社.

9. Die Terrakotta - Armee des Qin Shi Huang. Herausgabe：Verlag fur Kulturelle Relikte，1993. 1 volume （various pagings)：illustrations；26cm. ISBN：7501007047

《秦始皇兵马俑》，文物出版社.

10. Die Terrakottaarmee beim Mausoleum des Ersten Kaisers Qin Shihuang Di： die größte archäologische Entdeckung im 20. Jahrhundert/［Red. der dt. Ausg.： Zhang Zhenhua］. Beijing：Verl. Volkschina，1997. 127 S.：überw. ill.，Kt. 127 S.：überw. ill.，Kt. ISBN：7800655911

《秦始皇兵马俑》，张仲立主编；秦始皇兵马俑博物馆考古队编.

11. Die Tonarmee des ersten Kaisers von China： vom sensationellen Fund bis zur jüngsten Analyse. Beijing：Tourismusverlag Chinas，1999. 126 pages：illustrations (some color)；29cm. ISBN：750321614X

《秦始皇的地下兵团：世界第八奇迹》，郭佑民，吴晓丛. 中国旅游出版社.

12. Macht im Tod：die Terrakotta-Armee des Ersten Kaisers der Qin-Dynastie/［Autor，Cao Jun］. Xi'an：Xi'aner Verlag，2006. 128 pages，［2］ pages of plates：color illustrations，maps，portraits；29cm. ISBN：7807122501

《梦幻的军团》，曹军编译. 西安出版社.

13. Sanxingdui：heilige Stätte des alten Shu-Königreiches/von Chen De'an. Chengdu：Volksverlag Sichuan，2006. 123：illustrations (chiefly color)，map；29cm. ISBN：7220069995

《三星堆：古蜀王国的圣地》，陈德安著；戴士峰译. 四川人民出版社.

K4　风俗习惯

1. Traditionelle Feste und Gebräuche in China/von Qi Xing. Beijing：Verl. für Fremsprachige Literatur，1986. 152 S.

《中国传统节日风俗》，齐星编.

K5　地理

1. Geographie Chinas. Peking：Verlag für fremdsprachige Literatur，1972. 45 pages；19cm.

《中国地理知识》

2. Geographie/Bearb.： Red. d. China-Buchreihe. Beijing：Verlag für Fremdsprachige Literatur，1984. 280 S. Kt. 19cm.

《地理》，《中国概况丛书》编辑委员会编.

3. Chinas Geographie：Natur，Wirtschaft，Kultur/verfaßt von Zheng Ping；übersetzt von Zhong Yingjie. ［Beijing］：China Intercontinental Press，1999. ISBN：7801134842

《中国地理：自然·经济·人文》，郑平. 五洲传播出版社.

4. Allgemeine Kenntnisse über die chinesische Geographie/the Overseas Chinese Affairs Office of the State Council，the Office of Chinese Language Council International. Beijing：Higher Education Press，2007. 258 S.： zahlr Ill.，graph. Darst. ISBN：7040207217

《中国地理常识：汉德对照》，焦华富主编；国务院侨务办公室，国家汉语国际推广领导小组办公室编. 高等教育出版社（中国常识系列）

5. Chinas Weltkultur- und Weltnaturerbe/Luo Zhewen. ［Dt. Texte：Atze Schmidt. Fotos：Luo Zhewen...］. Beijing：Verl. für fremdsprachige Literatur，2004. 117 S.： zahlr. ill.；18×19cm. ISBN：7119032968

《中国的世界文化与自然遗产》，罗哲文主编. 外文出版社（中华风物）. 本书收录1987～2001年中国被列入世界文化与自然遗产的景观28处.

6. Welterbe in China/［Verf.： Feng Lingyu... Übers. von Mai Zhangxiong und Wang Yu. Dt. bearb.： Matthias Mersch］. Beijing：China Intercontinental Press，2009. 307 S. zahlr. ill. 31cm. ISBN：7508516219

《中国的世界遗产》，《中国的世界遗产》编委会编. 五洲传播出版社.

7. Das Ling-wai-tai-ta von Chou Ch'ü-fei： e. Landeskunde Südchinas aus d. 12. Jh./von Almut Netolitzky. Wiesbaden：Steiner，1977. XXXIV，320 S.；24cm. ISBN： 3515026819，3515026819. （Münchner ostasiatische Studien；Bd. 21）

《岭外代答》，周去非(1134—1189)著；Nezolitzky，Almut 译.

K51　专属地理

1. Die Milchstrasse am Himmel - und der Kanal auf Erden：Geschichte，Kultur und Gegenwart an Chinas Grossem Kanal：ein Bericht. /Beijing：Verl. für Fremdsprachige Literatur，1988. 425 S.：116 Ill.，Kt

《天上银河，地上运河》，李德满.

2. Landleben in China/Guo Huancheng，Ren Guozhu & Lü Mingwei. Beijing：China Continental Press，2009. 149 S. zahlr. Ill. ISBN：7508515700

《乡村之旅》，郭焕成，任国柱，吕明伟著. 五洲传播出版社.

3. Die Städte Chinas/Wang Jie. Übers. von Gong Xinkang.

Beijing：China Intercontinental Press，2009．167 S．：zahlr．Ill．，Kt．ISBN：7508515779

《城市之旅》，王杰著．五洲传播出版社．本书介绍中国城市概况．

K52　名胜古迹

1. Chinas Grosse Mauer/von Luo Zhewen und Zhao Luo．Beijing：Verl．für Fremdsprachige Literatur，1986．II，79 S．：ill．

《中国的万里长城》，罗哲文，赵洛．

2. Die Geschichte der Grossen Mauer/von Liu Wenyuan．［Übers．：Li Xuelian und Li Xiuzhen．Dt．bearb．von Atze Schmidt］．Beijing：Verl．für fremdsprachige Literatur，1996．125 S．：ill．，Kt．；19cm．ISBN：7119017462

《长城的故事》，刘文渊．

3. Die Seidenstrasse：gestern und heute/von Che Muqi．［Dt．von Tan Yuzhi...］．Beijing：Verl．für Fremdsprachige Literatur，1989．398 S．；ill．，Kt．；21cm．

《丝绸之路今昔》，车慕奇编著．

4. Chinas alte Pagoden/Verfasser：Luo Zhewen；Übersetzer：Zhong Yingjie und Dai Shifeng；deutsche Bearb．：Erhard und Helga Scherner；［Red．der dt．Ausg．：Dai Shifeng］．Beijing：Verlag für fremdsprachige Literatur，1994．331 S；Ill；32cm．ISBN：7119017047

《中国古塔》

5. Alte chinesische Gartenkunst/［Text：Cheng Liyao］；［Fotos：Yang Gusheng，Chen Xiaoli，Wei Ran］；［Übers．aus dem Chinesischen von Thomas Thilo］；［Hrsg．：Qiao Yun］．Leipzig：Koehler & Amelang，1988．240 p．：ill．；31cm．ISBN：3733800303，3733800307

《中国园林艺术》，Cheng，Liyao 著；Thilo，Thomas 译．

6. Chinas klassische Gärten/Lou Qingxi．Übers．von Olivier Roos & Katharina Schneider-Roos．Beijing：China Intercontinental Press，2003．152 S．；ill．；23cm．ISBN：7508503635

《中国园林》，楼庆西著；颜力维，卡特琳娜译．五洲传播出版社．

7. Ein paar Worte zu Pingyao/［Tang Xilin］．Taiyuan：Shanxi Verlag für Wissenschaft und Technik，2005．12，105 pages：color illustrations，color map；21cm．ISBN：753772492X

《解说平遥》，唐稀林编著；智颖宜，陈晶，高丽娟译．山西科学技术出版社．

8. Die schönsten Reiseziele/［Sun Yongxue］．Beijing：Verlag für fremdsprachige Literatur，2006．106 pages：color illustrations，map；18×20cm．ISBN：7119034448

《中国旅游巡览》，《中国旅游巡览》编委会编．外文出版社（中华风物/肖晓明主编）

K6　人物传记和回忆录

1. Li Schi-dschen，der grosse chinesische Pharmakologe des 16．Jahrhunderts/［Deutsch von Li Ming，Illus．von Djiang Dschaohö］．Peking：Verlag für fremdsprachige Literatur，1959．76 pages：illustrations；19cm．

《李时珍：中国古代伟大的药物学家》，张慧剑著；蒋兆和图．

2. Liu Hu-lan，eine junge Heldin der Revolution/Hsing Liang．［Dt．von Günter Lewin］．Peking：Verl．f．Fremdsprach．Literatur，1961．95 S．；8.

《刘胡兰小传》，梁星著；Lewin，Günter 译．

3. Zhou Enlai：ein Porträt/Percy Jucheng Fang；Lucy Guinong J．Fang．［Übers．aus dem engl．Orig．ins Dt．：Ruth F．Weiß］，Beijing：Verl．für Fremdsprachige Literatur，1990．III，345 S．ill．21cm．ISBN：7119008153

《周恩来传略》，方钜成，姜桂侬．

N 类　自然科学

N1　科技概况

1. Chinas Wissenschaft und Technik：［Reform und Entwicklung］/von Ke Yan．Übers．von Dai Shifeng．［Beijing］：China Internat．Press，2005．220 S．：ill．，graph．Darst．；21cm．ISBN：7508506715

《中国科技：改革与发展》，柯雁著．戴世峰，周健，杨易仁译．五洲传播出版社（中国基本情况丛书．当代卷/郭长建主编）

2. Brücken in China von d．histor．Zhaozhou-Brücke zur modernen Yangtse-Brücke bei Nanjing/von Mao Yisheng．Beijing：Verlag für Fremdsprachige Literatur，1980．39，［48］S．50 ill．（z．T．farb．）27cm．

《中国的古桥与新桥：从赵州桥到南京长江大桥》，茅以升．

3. Die Kriegskunst Sun Zis in Krankheitsbehandlung und Gesundheitspflege/［Autoren　Wu Rusong，Wang Hongtu，Huang Ying］；übers．von Zhong Yingjie．Bearb．von Claudia Kaiser．Beijing：Verl．Neue Welt．1997．295 S．ill．20cm．ISBN：7800053806

《孙子兵法与养生治病》，吴如嵩．新世界出版社．

N2　科技古籍德译

1. Jia yi jing．Erstmalig aus dem chinesischen Urtext übersetzt von Franz Hübotter．Berlin，Selbstverlag；Auslieferung：Rothacker，1969．97 pages；20cm．

《黄帝内经·素问》，Hübotter，Fr．（Franz，1881—）译．

2. Huangdi neijing：Bildergeschichten über die Gesundheitserhaltung/zsges．und gemalt von Han Yazhou...［Beijing］Delphin-Verl，1997．209 S zahlr．Ill 26cm．ISBN：7800518221

《黄帝内经：养生图典》,韩亚洲等编绘. 海豚出版社.

3. Shanghan-lun：Abhandlung über fieberhafte，durch Kälte verursachte Erkrankungen mit 500 Fallbeispielen/ geschrieben von Zhang Zhongjing. Zsgest. und übers. von Luo Xiwen. Ins Dt. übers. von Dieter Geiss... Kötzting/Bayer. Wald：Verl. für Ganzheitliche Medizin Wühr, 1997. 638 Seiten：Illustrationen, Diagramme; 28cm. ISBN：3927344184；3927344181. (Ein Klassiker der traditionellen chinesischen Medizin mit klassischen und neuzeitlichen Fallstudien)

《伤寒论》,(东汉)张仲景；Luo，Xiwen 英译；Geiss，Dieter 德译.

4. Abhandlung über Milz und Magen：eine Übersetzung des Pi-wei-lun＝Bi-wei-lun/Li Dong Yuan. Aus dem Chines. von Yang Shou Zhong und Li Jian Yong. Aus dem Engl. ins Dt. übers. von Dieter Geiss und Hartwig Lahrmann. Kötzting/Bayer. Wald：Verl. für Ganzheitliche Medizin Wühr, 2003. 271 Seiten；27cm. ISBN：3927344508； 3927344501. (Klassiker der traditionellen chinesischen Medizin；Bd. 3)

《脾胃论》,李杲(1180—1251)；Geiss，Dieter 译.

5. Der Arzneipflanzen- und Drogenschatz Chinas und die Bedeutung des Pên-ts'ao kang-mu als Standardwerk der chinesischen Materia medica/Alfred Mosig；Gottfried Schramm. Berlin：Verl. Volk u. Gesundheit, 1955. 71 S.：Mit 5 Abb.；gr. 8. (Pharmazie；Beih.；H. 4)

《本草纲目》,李时珍(1518—1593)著；Mosig，Alfred 和 Schramm，Gottfried 合译.

6. Bencao-kangmu：grosse Pharmakopöe des Li Shizen 1596； ergänzt durch Zitate aus älteren Schriften；Abschnitte über Papier und Tusche/Sandoz. Muttenz-Basel：Sandoz Chemicals Ltd. , 1993. 63 S.：Ill.；20cm. ISBN： 3905142075，3905142074. (Papier-Mitteilung...；Nr. 43)

《本草纲目》,李时珍(1518—1593)著；Sandoz 译.

N3　饮食文化

1. Markenartikel alkoholischer Getränke. Beijing：Verl. Neuer Stern，1990. 33 S.：ill. ISBN：7800850633

《中国名酒》.新星出版社(中国简况)

2. Die chinesische Teekultur/Wang Ling. ［Übers.：Gong Hehua］. Beijing：Verl. für Fremdsprachige Literatur， 2002. 145 S.：ill.；21cm. ISBN：711902146X

《中国茶文化》,王玲.

3. Rezepte der chinesischen Familienküche/Zsstellung und Bearb.：Bai Ziran. Text：Wang Jinhuai und Xue Yuan. ［Fotos：Wei Dezhong... übers.：Wang Huanqian...］. Beijing：Verl. für Fremdsprachige Literatur，1990. 239 S.：ill.；27cm. ISBN：7119009974

《中国家常菜》,白自然编；王金怀，雪原撰文.

4. 中国烹饪/外文出版社德文编译部编译. 北京：外文出版 社,2009. 35 页；21cm. ISBN：7119058726

5. Chinesische Küche für Ausländer：chinesische bekannte Gerichte und ihre Herkunft. Beijing：Chinesischer Verlag für Tourismus，1986. 105 pages：illustrations (some color)；19cm.

《外国人做中国菜：中国名菜烹饪及其来历》.中国旅游出 版社.

第四编 中国文献西班牙语翻译书目

A 类 毛泽东著作及相关文献

A1 毛泽东著作与研究

1. Selección de trabajos/Mao-Tse-Tung; [traducción de Juan Carlos Orviella]. La Habana, Cuba: Nueva China, 1951. 363 p. : mapas; 21cm.
   Notes: "En esta selección de trabajos se han incluido distintos ensayos de índole filosó" fico: "A propósito de la práctica"; militar: "La estrategia de la guerra revolucionaria en China"; política: "La nueva democracia"; literarias: "Artistas y escritores de la Nueva China" y Apêndice documental: "texto completo de la Constitución de la República Popular China" —(Solapa).
   毛泽东选集.

2. La revolución china y el Partido Comunista Chino. México: Nueva Democracia, 1951. 48 pages
   《中国革命和中国共产党》

3. A propósito de la práctica. En torno a la contradicción. [Santiago] Chile, Ediciones/Vida Nueva, 1953. 94 pages; 19cm.
   《实践论》

4. Acerca de la practica: sobre la relación entre el conocimiento y la práctica - entre el saber y la acción/ Mao Tse-Tung. 3a ed. Pekin: Ediciones en Lenguas Extranjeras, 1960. 23 pages; 19cm.
   《实践论》
   (1) 4a ed. Pekin: Ediciones en Lenguas Extranjeras, 1965. 22 pages
   (2) Pekin: Ediciones en Lenguas Extranjeras, 1966. 33 p. ; 15cm.
   (3) 6a ed. Pekin: Ediciones en Lenguas Extranjeras, 1966. 23 pages
   (4) Pekin: Ediciones en Lenguas Extranjeras, 1967. 33 pages

5. Acerca da prática [Acerca de la prática]. Colombes: Editions Carymar, 1966. 34 pages
   《实践论》

6. Una crítica de la economía sovietica/Mao Tsetung. México: Fondo de Cultura Económica, 1955. 143 pages; 21cm. (Colección Jorge Ortega Torres)
   苏联经济评论. Suarez, Edurdo L. 译.
   (1) Una crítica de la economía sovietica/Mao Tsetung;

introd. de James Peck; tr. Eduardo L. Suarez. Mexico: Fondo de Cultura Ecoomica, 1982. 143 pages; 21cm. ISBN: 9681610245, 9681610241. (Seccion de obras de economia)

7. Problemas de la cooperación agricola. Pekín: Ediciones en Lenguas Extranjeras, 1956. 45 pages
   《关于农业合作化问题》
   (1) Problemas de la cooperación agricola. 4a ed. Pekín: Ediciones en Lenguas Extranjeras, 1960. 45 pages
   (2) Problemas de la cooperación agricola. 5a ed. (tr. rev.). Pekín: Ediciones en Lenguas Extranjeras, 1961. 37 pages
   (3) Problemas de la cooperación agricola/Mao Tsetung. 6a ed. Peking: Ediciones en Lenguas Extranjeras, 1966. 39 pages; 19cm.

8. Informe sobre la investigación verificada en Junan acerca del movimiento campesino/Mao Tse-Tung. China: Ediciones en Lenguas Extranjeras, 1957. 76, [1] pages
   《湖南农民运动考察报告》
   (1) Informe sobre la investigación verificada en Junán acerca del movimiento campesino. Pekin, Ediciones en Lenguas Extranjeras, 1959. 76 pages; 19cm.
   (2) Informe sobre la investigación verificada en Junán acerca del movimiento campesino/Mao Tse-tung. 4a ed. Pekin: Ediciones en Lenguas Extranjeras, 1961. 62 p. ; 19cm.
   (3) 5a ed. Pekin: Ediciones en Lenguas Extranjeras, 1967. 58 pages; 19cm.

9. Sobre la acertada manera de resolver las contradicciones en el seno del pueblo. Pekin: Ediciones en Lenguas Extranjeras, 1957. 72 pages
   《关于正确处理人民内部矛盾的问题》
   (1) Sobre El Tratamiento Correcto De Las Contradicciones En El Seno Del Pueblo. Pekin: Ediciones En Lenguas Extranjeras, 1961. 1 volume
   (2) 5a ed. Pekin: Ediciones en Lenguas Extranjeras, 1966. 59 pages; 19cm.
   (3) Pekin: Ediciones en Lenguas Extranjeras, 1966. 84 pages; 15cm.
   (4) Pekin: Ediciones en Lenguas Extranjeras, 1966. 67 pages
   (5) Pekin: Ediciones en Lenguas Extranjeras, 1970. 100 pages

10. Sobre el tratamiento correcto de las contradicciones en el seno del pueblo. 4a ed. La Habana：Imprenta Nacional de Cuba，1961. 67 pages

《关于正确处理人民内部矛盾的问题》

11. Sobre el tratamiento correcto de las contradicciones en el seno del pueblo/Mao Tse-Tung. Montevideo：Nativa libros，1969. 74 p.；20cm.（Bandera roja；12）

《关于正确处理人民内部矛盾的问题》

12. Acerca de la aparición de la revista "El Comunista". Pekín Edic. en Lenguas Extranjeras，1957. 26 p. 18cm.

《共产党人》发刊词.

　　(1) Pekin：Ediciones en Lenguas Extranjeras，1958. 25cm.；19cm.

　　(2) 4a ed. Pekin：Ediciones en Lenguas Extranjeras，1960. 17 p.

　　(3) Quinta edición. Pekin：Ediciones en Lenguas Extranjeras，1961. 17 pages，3 unnumbered pages；18cm.

　　(4) 6a ed. Pekín：Ediciones en Lenguas Extranjeras，1965. 17 p.

　　(5) Con motivo de la aparición de el comunista. Pekin：Ediciones en Lenguas Extranjeras，1969. 33 pages

13. Sobre la táctica de la lucha contra el imperialismo japonés/Mao Tse-tung. Pekin：Ediciones en Lenguas Extranjeras，1958. 60 p.；19cm.

《论反对日本帝国主义的策略》

　　(1) 4a ed.（tr. rev.）. Pekin：Ediciones en Lenguas Extranjeras，1960. 45 pages

　　(2) 5a ed. Pekin：Ediciones en Lenguas Extranjeras，1961. 44 pages

　　(3) 6a ed. Pekin：Ediciones en Lenguas Extranjeras，1966. 43 pages

　　(4) 2a ed. Pekin：Ediciones en Lenguas Extranjeras，1968. 68 pages

14. Nuestro estudio y la situacion actual；Apendice：Resolucion acerca de algunos problemas de la historia de nuestro Partido. Pekin：Editorial en Lenguas Extranjeras，1958. 1 v.（119 p.）：ill.；19cm.

《学习和时局》

　　(1) 3e ed.（Traduccion rev.）. Pekin：Ediciones en Lenguas Extranjeras，1961. 100 pages；19cm.

15. Palabras del camarada Mao Tse-tung sobre "El imperialismo y todos los reaccionarios son tigres de papel." Pekín：Ediciones en Lenguas Extranjeras，1958. 34 pages

《毛泽东同志论帝国主义和一切反动派都是纸老虎》

　　(1) Palabras del camarada Mao Tse-Tung sobre "El imperialismo y todos los reaccionarios son tigres de papel"/redacción del Renmin Ribao（27 de octubre de 1958）. 2a ed. Pekin：Ediciones en Lenguas Extranjeras，1960. 34 p.；19cm.

　　(2) Palabras del camarada Mao Tse-tung sobre "El imperialismo y todos los reaccionarios son tigres de papel." 3a ed. Pekín：Ediciones en Lenguas Extranjeras，1961. 33 pages

　　(3) Pekín：Ediciones en Lenguas Extranjeras，1964. 46 pages

　　(4) Palabras del camarada Mao Tse-tung sobre "El imperialismo y todos los reaccionearios son tigres de papel"：Redacción del Renmin Ribao（27 de octubre de 1958）. 4a. ed. Pekin：Ediciones en Lenguas Extranjeras，1965. 34 p.；19cm.

　　(5) 4a ed. 1965，2a impresión. Pekin：Ediciones en Lenguas Extranjeras，1967. 34 pages；19cm.

　　(6) 4a ed. Pekin：Edictiones en Lenguas Extranjeras，1967. 34 pages

16. La nueva democracia. Bogotá：Ediciones Suramérica，1958. 99 pages

《新民主主义论》

17. Por qué puede existir el poder rojo en China? Peking，Ediciones en Lenguas Extranjeras，1959. 22 pages；19cm.

《中国的红色政权为什么能够存在?》

　　(1) 2a ed.（tr. rev.）. Pekin：Ediciones en Lenguas Extranjeras，1960. 16 pages

　　(2) 4a ed.（tr. rev.）. Pekin：Ediciones en Lenguas Extranjeras，1965. 15 pages

　　(3) 5a ed. Pekín：Ediciones en Lenguas Extranjeras，1966. 16 pages

18. Una sola chispa puede provocar el incendio de toda la pradera. Pekin，Ediciones en Lenguas Extranjeras，1959. 21 pages；19cm.

《星星之火，可以燎原》

　　(1) Una sola chispa puede incendian toda una pradera. 3a ed. Pekin：Ediciones en Lenguas Extranjeras，1960. 19 pages

　　(2) Una sola chispa puede incendiar toda una pradera. 4a ed. Pekin：Ediciones en Lenguas Extranjeras，1961. 19 pages

　　(3) Una sola chispa puede incendiar toda la pradera. 5a ed.（tr. rev.）. Pekín：Ediciones en Lenguas Extranjeras，1965. 19 pages

　　(4) Una sola chispa puede incendiar toda la pradera. Pekin：Ediciones en Lenguas Extranjeras，1967.

　　(5) Pekin：Ediciones en Lenguas Extranjeras，1968. 33 pages

19. Problemas de la guerra y de la estrategia. Pekin，Ediciones en Lenguas Extranjeras，1959. 25 pages

《战争和战略问题》

　　(1) 3a ed.（tr. rev.）. Pekín：Ediciones en Lenguas Extranjeras，1961. 26 pages

　　(2) 4a ed. Pekin：Ediciones en Lenguas Extranjeras，

1961. 26 pages

（3）5a ed. （tr. rev.）. Pekín：Ediciones en Lenguas Extranjeras，1965. 25 pages

20. Mayor preocupación por la vida del pueblo, mayor atención a los métodos de trabajo. Pekin, Ediciones en Lenguas Extranjeras, 1959. 10 pages；19cm.

Notes："Del discurso de clausura del camarada Mao Tse-tung en el II Congreso nacional de diputados obreros y campesinos... 1934."

《关心群众生活，注意工作方法》

（1）3a ed. Pekin：Ediciones en Lenguas Extranjeras，1960. 8 pages

（2）4a ed. Pekin：Ediciones en Lenguas Extranjeras，1961. 8 pages

（3）5a ed. Pekin：Ediciones en Lenguas Extranjeras，1965. 8 pages；19cm.

（4）6a ed. Pekin：Ediciones en Lenguas Extranjeras，1966. 8 pages

21. Poemas/Mao Zedong；tr. Luis Enrique Délano. Pekin：Lenguas Extranjeras, 1959. 36 p. : il.；20cm.

毛泽东诗词. Délano, Luis Enrique(1907—1985)译.

（1）2. ed.，traducción rev. Pekin：Ediciones en Lenguas Extranjeras，1962. 48 pages: illustrations；20cm.

（2）3. ed. Pekin：Ediciones en Lenguas Extranjeras，1963. 48 pages；[2] leaves of plates；19cm.

22. Veinte poemas/Mao Zedong；translation by Luis Enrique Délano. [Buenos Aires]：Cía. Argentina de Editores，1962. xiv, 22 pages；19cm.

毛泽东诗词二十首. Délano, Luis Enrique(1907—1985)译.

23. Poemas/Mao Tse-Tung；versión española de Luis Enrique Délano；notas y comentarios de Chou Chen-fu. Barcelona：Editorial Mateu, 1970. 103 p. ; 18cm.

毛泽东诗词.

（1）Caracas：Ministerio de la Cultura, Consejo Nacional de la Cultura, 2005. xxv, 50 pages：illustrations；20cm. ISBN：9806964411, 9806964419

24. Poemas/Mao Tse Tung；edicion de Chou Chen Fu. Madrid：Visor,1974. 50 p. ;19cm. ISBN：8470531158,8470531156. (Colección Visor de poesía；56)

毛泽东诗词.

（1）2a. ed. Madrid：Visor，1975. 50 pages；20cm. (Colección Visor de poesía；56)

25. Poemas/Mao Zedong；[traducción directa del chino, prólogo y notas de Manuel de Seabra]. Barcelona：Aymá, S. A. Editora, 1975. 130 pages；16cm. ISBN：842092654X, 8420926544

毛泽东诗词. Seabra, Manuel de(1932—)译.

26. Mao Tse-tung/Alberto Moravia [pròleg] y Girolamo Mancuso；[traducción, José Palao]. Madrid：Júcar, 1975. 187 p.，[16] p. de lám. ; 18cm. ISBN：

8433430157, 8433430151. （Los poetas；15）

包括对毛泽东诗词的选译. 西汉对照.

27. Mao Tse-Tung/Alberto Moravia y Girolamo Mancuso. Madrid：Ediciones Júcar, 1975. ISBN：8433430157, 8433430151. (Colección Los Poetas；15)

Moravia, Alberto(1907—1990)和 Mancuso, Girolamo (1935—)著,包括对毛泽东诗词的翻译.

28. Homenaje a Mao Tse Tung, poeta, filosofo, guerillero y revolucionario. Torremolinos：Litoral, 1977. 229 pages：illustrations；24cm. (Litoral；no. 64—65—66)

Notes：Includes poems by Mao Tse-Tung, in Chinese with Spanish translations.

包括对毛泽东诗词的翻译.

29. Poemas/Mao Tsetung. Peking：Ediciones en Lenguas Extranjeras, 1978. 70 pages：portraits；21cm.

《毛泽东诗词》

30. Problemas económicos y financieros durante la guerra antijaponesa，y otros artículos. Pekin, Ediciones en Lenguas Extranjeras, 1959. 60 pages；19cm.

《抗日时期的经济问题和财政问题及其他论文》

（1）2nd ed. Pekin：Ediciones en Lenguas Extranjeras，1960. 60 pages；19cm.

31. Problemas economicos y financieros en el periodo de la resistencia al Japón （Diciembre de 1942）. Pekin：Ediciones en Lenguas Extranjeras, 1970. 14 pages

《抗日战争时期的经济问题和财政问题》

32. Mi vida/Mao Tse Tung；traducción P. Alvarado y P. Díaz. Buenos Aires：Futuro, 1959. 77 p. ；20cm. （Colección Eurindia；3）

Notes："El líder chino cuenta su vida al periodista norteamericano Edgar Snow dejando un único testimonio autobiográfico". - Cubierta.

毛泽东自传.

（1）Mi vida/Mao Tse Tung；[traducción P. Alvarado y P. Díaz]. Buenos Aires：Quetzal, 1973. 74 p. ；20cm.

33. Rectifiquemos el estilo de trabajo en el partido/Mao Tse-tung. Pekin：Ediciones en Lenguas Extranjeras, 1959. 26 p. ；19cm.

《整顿党的作风》

（1）4a ed. Pekin：Ediciones en Lenguas Extranjeras，1961. 26 pages

（2）5a ed. Pekin：Ediciones en Lenguas Extranjeras，1966. 25 pages

（3）2a ed. Pekin：Ediciones en Lenguas Extranjeras，1967. 36 pages

（4）Pekin：Ediciones en Lenguas Extranjeras, 1969. 43 pages

34. Sobre la dictadura de la democracia popular；con motivo del XXVIII aniversario del Partido comunista de China. Pekin, Ediciones en Lenguas Extranjeras, 1959. 20

pages；19cm.

《论人民民主专政》

(1) 2a. ed.（tr. rev.）. Pekín：Ediciones en Lenguas Extranjeras, 1962. 21 pages

(2)北京：商务印书馆, 1966. 53 pages；19cm.

(3) Pekin：Ediciones en Lenguas Extranjeras, 1967. 32 pages

35. Los problemas tácticos en el presente frente único antijaponés. Pekin, Ediciones en Lenguas Extranjeras, 1959. 15 pages；19cm.

《目前抗日统一战线中的策略问题》

(1) 2a ed.（tr. rev.）. Pekin：Ediciones en Lenguas Extranjeras, 1960. 15 pages

(2) 3a ed. Pekin：Ediciones en Lenguas Extranjeras, 1961. 15 pages

(3) 4a ed. Pekin：Ediciones en Lenguas Extranjeras, 1965. 15 pages

(4) 5a ed. Pekin：Ediciones en Lenguas Extranjeras, 1967. 15 pages

36. La cuestión de la independencia y la autonomía en el frente único. Pekin, Ediciones en Lenguas Extranjeras, 1959. 9 pages；19cm.

《统一战线中的独立自主问题》

(1) 2a ed.（tr. rev.）. Pekin：Ediciones en Lenguas Extranjeras, 1960. 6 pages

(2) Pekin：Ediciones en Lenguas Extranjeras, 1964. 8 pages

(3) La cuestión de la independencia y la autonomia dentro del frente unido. 4a ed. Pekin：Ediciones en Lenguas Extranjeras, 1966. 6 pages

(4) El Problema de la independencia y autodecisión dentro del frente único/Mao Zedong. Pekin：Ediciones en Lenguas Extranjeras, 1969. 10 p.；13cm.

37. Sobre la política. Pekin, Ediciones en Lenguas Extranjeras, 1959. 13 pages；19cm.

《论政策》

(1) 2a ed.（tr. rev.）. Pekin：Ediciones en Lenguas Extranjeras, 1960. 15 pages

(2) 3a ed. Pekin：Ediciones en Lenguas Extranjeras, 1961. 15 pages

(3) 4a ed. Pekin：Ediciones en Lenguas Extranjeras, 1965. 15 pages

(4) A propósito de nuestra politica. Pekin：Ediciones en Lenguas Extranjeras, 1969. 26 pages

38. Prefacio y epílogo a "Investigación rural." Pekin, Ediciones en Lenguas Extranjeras, 1959. 8 pages；19cm.

《农村调查》的预言和跋.

(1) 2a ed.（tr. rev.）. Pekin：Ediciones en Lenguas Extranjeras, 1960. 7 pages

(2) Prefacio y epilogo a Investigación rural. 3a ed.

Pekin：Ediciones en Lenguas Extranjeras, 1961. 7 pages

(3) Prefacio y epilogo a Investigación rural. 4a ed. Pekin：Ediciones en Lenguas Extranjeras, 1966. 7 pages

(4) 4a ed. Pekin：Ediciones en Lenguas Extranjeras, 1967. 9 pages

(5) Prefacio y epilogo a Investigaciones rurales. Pekin：Ediciones en Lenguas Extranjeras, 1969. 13 pages

39. Contra el formulismo en el Partido. Pekin, Ediciones en Lenguas Extranjeras, 1959. 25 pages；19cm.

《反对党八股》

(1) Contra el estilo de clisé en el Partido. 3a ed.（tr. rev.）. Pekin：Ediciones en Lenguas Extranjeras, 1960. 24 pages

(2) 4a ed. Pekin：Ediciones es Lenguas Extranjeras, 1961. 24 pages

(3) 5a ed. Pekin：Ediciones en Lenguas Extranjeras, 1966. 24 pages

(4) Contra el estilo de cliche del Partido. Pekin：Ediciones en Lenguas Extranjeras, 1969. 41 pages；13cm.

40. Acerca de algunos problemas de los metodos de dirección. Pekin：Ediciones en Lenguas Extranjeras, 1959. 9 pages

《关于领导方法的若干问题》

(1) 2a ed.（tr. rev.）. Pekin：Ediciones en Lenguas Extranjeras, 1960. 9 pages

(2) Pekin：Ediciones en Lenguas Extranjeras, 1961. 9 pages

(3) 4a ed. Pekin：Ediciones en Lenguas Extranjeras, 1965. 8 pages

41. Problemas de la historia del Partido Comunista de China. Bogota：Ediciones "Paz y Socialimo", 1959. 107 pages

《中国共产党的若干历史问题》

42. Contra el liberalismo. Pekín：Ediciones en Lenguas Extranjeras, 1959. 4 pages

《反对自由主义》

(1) 2a ed. Pekín：Ediciones en Lenguas Extranjeras, 1960. 4 pages

(2) 3a ed. Pekín：Ediciones en Lenguas Extranjeras, 1967. 3 pages

43. Sobre el arte y la literatura. Bogota：Ediciones Paz y Socialismo, 1960. 57 pages

《在延安文艺座谈会上的讲话》

44. Intervenciones en la conferencia de Yenan sobre arte y literatura. Pekín：Ediciones en Lenguas Extranjeras, 1965. 46 pages；22cm.

《在延安文艺座谈会上的讲话》

(1) 2a ed. Pekín：Ediciones en Lenguas Estranjeras, 1966. 45 pages

(2)Intervenciones en el foro de Yenan sobre literatura y arte. Pekín：Ediciones en Lenguas Extranjeras, 1967.

45. Intervenciones en el foro de Yenan sobre arte y literatura/Mao Tse-tung. Barcelona：Anagrama, 1974. 59 p.；18cm. ISBN：843390373X, 8433903730. (Cuadernos Anagrama.；Documentos；73)

《在延安文艺座谈会上的讲话》

46. Acerca de la corrección de las concepciones erroneas en el partido. 2a ed.（tr. rev.）. Pekin：Ediciones en Lenguas Extranjeras, 1960. 18 pages

《关于纠正党内的错误思想》

(1)Acerca de la corrección de las concepciones erroneas en el partido. 3a ed. Pekin：Ediciones en Lenguas Extranjeras, 1961. 18 pages

(2)Sobre la corrección de las ideas erróneas en el Partido. Cuarta edición（tr. rev.）. Pekin：Ediciones en Lenguas Extranjeras, 1966. 18 pages

47. Análisis de las clases en la sociedad china/Mao Zedong. 2a. ed. Peking：Lenguas Extranjeras, 1960. 14 p.；19cm.

《中国社会各阶层的分析》

(1)4a. ed., ed. de bolsillo. Peking：Lenguas Extranjeras, 1966. 20 pages；15cm.

(2)4a ed. Peking：Ediciones en Lenguas Extranjeras, 1966. 13 pages；19cm.

(3)2a ed. Pekin：Ediciones en Lenguas Extranjeras, 1968. 23 pages

48. Reformemos nuestro estudio. 2nd ed. Pekin, Ediciones en Lenguas Extranjeras, 1960. 12 pages

《改造我们的学习》

(1)3a ed. Pekin：Ediciones en Lenguas Extranjeras, 1966. 11 pages

49. Problemas estratégicos de la guerra de guerrillas antijaponesa/Mao Tse-Tung. Pekín：Ediciones en Lenguas Extranjeras, 1960. 56 p.；19cm.

《抗日游击战争的战略问题》

(1)Problemas estrategicos de la guerra de guerrillas antijaponesa. 3a ed. Pekin：Ediciones en Lenguas Extranjeras, 1961. 56 pages

(2)Problemas estrategicos de la guerra de guerrillas contra el Japon/Mao Tse-Tung. Pekin：Ediciones en Lenguas Extranjeras, 1967. 55 pages；19cm.

50. Las tareas del partido comunista de China en el periodo de la resistencia al Japon. Pekin, Ediciones en Lenguas Extranjeras, 1960. 36 pages

《中国共产党在抗日时期的任务》

(1)2a ed. Pekin：Ediciones en Lenguas Extranjeras, 1965. 36 pages

(2)Pekin：Ediciones en Lenguas Extranjeras, 1968. 67 pages

51. Cinco tesis filosóficas de Mao Zedong. México：Ediciones Quinto Sol, 1960. 136 p.；20cm.

《毛主席的五篇哲学著作》

52. Cinco articulos del presidente Mao Tsetung. Pekin：Ediciones en Lenguas Extranjeras, 1969. 64 pages Contents：Servir al pueblo—En memoria de Norman Bethune—El viejo tonto que removió las montañas—Sobre la rectificación de las ideas erróneas en el Partido—Contra el liberalismo.

《毛主席的五篇著作》

(1)Pekin：Ediciones en Lenguas Extranjeras, 1972. 64 pages；11cm.

(1)Cinco tesis filosóficas de Mao Zedong. México：Quinto Sol, 1985. 138 pages

(2)Cinco tésis filosóficas de Mao Zedong. México：Quinto Sol, 1995. 138 pages. ISBN：9686620656, 9686620658

53. Cuatro tesis filosóficas. Barcelona：Edit. Anagrama, 1966. 128 pp.；21cm.（Documentos；Núm. 15） Notes：Trad. Ediciones en Lenguas Extranjeras. (Pekín)

毛泽东的四篇哲学著作. 外文出版社翻印.

54. Cuatro tesis filosóficas/Mao Tse-Tung. Buenos Aires：La Rosa Blindada, 1969. 159 p.；19cm.

毛泽东的四篇哲学著作.

55. Cuatro tesis filosóficas/Mao Tse-Tung. 3a ed. México：Cultura popular, 1974. 106, [1] pages

毛泽东的四篇哲学著作.

(1)México, D. F.：Ediciones de Cultura Popular, 1976. 150 p.；18cm.

(2)México：Ediciones de Cultura Popular, 1977. 157 p.；17cm.

56. Tesis filosóficas/Mao Tse-tung. México：Roca, 1975. 157 p.；19cm.（Serie 401；56）

毛泽东哲学著作.

57. Tesis filosóficas/Mao Tse-tung；[versión al español de Ediciones en Lenguas Extranjeras, Pekín]. Barcelona：R. Torres, 1976. 157 p. ISBN：8485174240, 8485174249.（R (R. Torres)；56）

毛泽东哲学著作.

58. Ensayos filosóficos/Mao Tse Tung. Madrid：Júcar, 1977. 128 p.；20. ISBN：8433415921, 8433415929. (Biblioteca histórica del socialismo；92)

毛泽东哲学文章.

59. Lecciones de la lucha revolucionaria en China. Bogota：Ediciones Paz y Socialismo, 1960. 24 pages

《中国革命战争的战略问题》

60. Algunas enseñanzas del Partido Comunista de China. Bogotá：Ediciones Paz y Socialismo, 1960. 85 pages

关于中国共产党教育的著作.

61. Sobre el arte y la literatura.［Habana］：Nueva Critica

Impr. Nacional de Cuba［Unidad no. 1205］，1961. 67 pages；18cm.

毛泽东论文学与艺术.

62. Sobre la literatura y el arte/Mao Tse-tung. Montevideo： Nativa Libros, 1968. 154 p.；19cm.

Notes：Edición preparada y parcialmente traducida por Sarandy Cabrera

毛泽东论文学与艺术.

63. Tenemos que aprender a realizar el trabajo economico. Pekín：Ediciones en Lenguas Extranjeras，1961. 11 pages

《必须学会做经济工作》

(1) 2a ed. Pekin：Ediciones en Lenguas Extranjeras， 1966. 10 pages

64. Sobre la contradicción/Mao Tse Tung. 2a ed.（tr. rev.）. Pekin：Ediciones en Lenguas Extranjeras，1961. 59 pages

《矛盾论》

(1) 4a ed. Pekín：Ediciones en lengua extranjera, 1965. 56 pages

(2) Edición de bolsillo. Pekin：Ediciones en Lenguas Extranjeras，1966. 84 pages

(3) Pekin：Ediciones en Lenguas Extranjeras, 1967. 84 p.；15cm.

(4) 5a ed. Pekin：Ediciones en Lenguas Extranjeras， 1967. 69 pages

65. Sobre la contradicción. La Habana, Editora Política, 1963. 63 pages；20cm.

《矛盾论》

66. Las contradicciones/Mao Zedong；versión al español de Manuel Carnero. Mexico：Editorial Grijalbo, 1969. 158 pages；18cm.（Colección 70)

《矛盾论》

(1) Las Contradicciones/Mao Tse-Tung. Barcelona： Grijalbo，1974. 158 p.；18cm.

67. Sobre la práctica y la contradicción/Mao Tse-tung； introducción a cargo de Slavoj Žižek；trad. de introducción y capítulos 2 y 12, Alfredo Brotons Muñoz； del resto, equipo editorial. Madrid：Akal, 2010. 268 str.； 18cm. ISBN：8446028345，8446028344.（Revoluciones；3）

《实践论》与《矛盾论》

68. Importantes charlas del Presidente Mao Tse-tung con personalidades de Asia，Africa y America Latina.［3. ed.］. Pekin，Eduiciones en Lenguas Extranjeras，1961. 9 pages；19cm.

《毛泽东主席同亚洲，非洲，拉丁美洲人士的几次重要 谈话》

(1) Pekin：Ediciones en Lenguas Extranjeras, 1963. 15 pages；15cm.

(2) 4a ed. Pekin：Ediciones en Lenguas Extranjeras， 1966. 9 pages

(3) Pekin：Ed. en languas extranjeras, 1966. 1 v.（16 p.）；15cm.

69. La revolución china y el Partido Comunista de China. 2a ed. （tr. rev.）. Pekín：Ediciones en Lenguas Extranjeras，1961. 44 pages

《中国革命和中国共产党》

(1) 3a ed. Peking：Ediciones en Lenguas Extranjeras, 1962. 47 pages；19cm.

(2) 3a ed. Pekín：Ediciones en Lenguas Extranjeras, 1967. 74 pages

(3) Pekin：Ediciones en Lenguas Extranjeras, 1969. 81 pages

70. Obras escolhidas［de Mao Tse-tung］. Rio de Janeiro， Vitoria, 1961. 1 volumes

Notes：Translated from the London edition：Selected works of Mao Tse-tung, which is a translation of the Chinese original：Mao Tse-tung hsuan chi

毛泽东选集.

71. Textos de Mao Tse Tung. Barcelona：Estudiantes Marxistas Leninistas, 1970. vols.；32cm.

毛泽东选集.

72. Obras escogidas de Mao Tse-tung. Buenos Aires： Ediciones La Rosa Blindada；Montevideo：Nativa Libros, 1973. volumes；20cm.（Colección de ensayos Emilio Jáuregui）

毛泽东选集.

73. Obras escogidas de Mao Tse-tung. Madrid；Fundamentos, 1974. 4 v.；19cm. ISBN：8424501322，8424501327， 8424501365，8424501365，8424501403，8424501402， 842450142X，8424501426.（Ciencia；50；51；52；53）

毛泽东选集.

74. Obras escogidas de Mao Tse-Tung. Pekin：Ediciones en Lenguas Extranjeras, 1962. 4 v.；23cm.

《毛泽东选集》

(1) 2a ed. Pekin：Ediciones en Lenguas Extrangeras， 1963—1968. 4 volumes；mounted portraits；23cm.

(2) Pekín：Ediciones en Lenguas Extranjeras, 1968— 1969. 4 v.；19cm.

(3) Obras escogidas de Mao Tse-tung. Pekín：Ediciones en Lenguas Extranjeras, 1967—1972. 4 volumes

(4) Obras escogidas de Mao Tse-Tung. Pekín：Ed. en Lenguas Estranjeras, 1968—1972. 4 v.；23cm.

(5) Obras escogidas. Pekin，Ediciones en Lenguas Extranjeras, 1971. 4 volumes

(6) Pekin：Ediciones en Lenguas Extranjeras, 1972. 4 volumes

75. Sobre el Libro Blanco de los EE. UU. Pekín：Ediciones en Lenguas Extranjeras, 1962. 52 pages

《评白皮书》

(1) Pekin：Ediciones en Lenguas Extranjeras, 1963. 71 pages

(2)2a ed. Pekín：Ediciones en Lenguas Extranjeras, 1967. 53 pages

(3)2a ed. Pekín：Ediciones en Lenguas Extranjeras, 1968. 71 pages

76. Sobre las negociaciones de Chungching. Pekín：Ediciones en Lenguas Extranjeras, 1962. 24 pages

《关于重庆谈判》

(1) 2a ed. Pekín：Ediciones en Lenguas Extranjeras, 1963. 35 p.

(2) 2a ed. Pekín：Ediciones en Lenguas Extranjeras, 1967. 35 pages

77. Llevar la revolución hasta el fin. Pekín：Ediciones en Lenguas Extranjeras, 1962.

《将革命进行到底》

(1) Pekín：Ediciones en Lenguas Extranjeras, 1964. 26 pages

(2) Pekín：Ediciones en Lenguas Extranjeras, 1967. 18 pages

(3) 2a ed. Pekín：Ediciones en Lenguas Wxtranjeras, 1968. 32 pages

78. Informe ante la II Sesión Plenaria del Comité Central elegido en el VII Congreso Nacional del Partido Comunista de China. Pekín：Ediciones en Lenguas Extranjeras, 1962. 25 pages；19cm.

《在中国共产党第七届中央委员会第二次全体会议上的报告》

(1) Pekín：Ediciones en Lenguas Extranjeras, 1964. 36 pages

(2) Informe ante la 2. sesión plenaria del Comité central elegido en el 7. Congreso nacional del Partido comunista de China/Mao Tse-Tung. Pekín：Ediciones en Lenguas Extranjeras, 1968. 34 p.；19cm.

(3) Informe ante la II Sesión Plenaria del Comité Central elegido en el VII Congresso Nacional del Partido Comunista de China (5 de marzo de 1949). Pekín：Ediciones en Lenguas Extranjeras, 1975. 43 pages

79. Sobre el fortalecimiento del sistema de comité del Partido. Pekín：Ediciones en Lenguas Extranjeras, 1962. 10 pages

《关于健全党委制》

(1) 2a ed. Pekín：Ediciones en Lenguas Extranjeras, 1966. 10 pages

(2) Pekín：Ediciones en Lenguas Extranjeras, 1969. 16 pages

80. La guerra de guerrillas/introducción del Samuel D. Griffith; prólogo Luis Maria de Pablo Pardo. Buenos Aires：Editorial Huemel, 1963. 165 pages；18cm.

Notes：Translation of the English：On guerrilla warfare, New York, 1961, which was a translation of the original Chinese：Yu chi chan.

《游击战》，转译自英文版.

(1) 4th ed. Buenos Aires：Editorial Huemul, 1966. 165 pages；illustrations；18cm.

(2) 5a ed. Buenos Aires：Huemul, 1968. 118 p.；19cm..（Manuales Huemul；6)

(3) 6. ed. Buenos Aires：Editorial Huemul, 1973. 91 pages；23cm.

81. Sobre la guerra prolongada. La Habana, Editora Política, 1963. 153 pages；20cm.

《论持久战》

82. Sobre la guerra prolongada/Mao Zedong. 2a ed. Pekín：Ediciones en Lenguas Extranjeras, 1967. 129 pages；19cm.

《论持久战》

83. La guerra prolongada/Mao Tse-Tung. México, D. F.：Ediciones Roca, 1973. 157 p.；19cm.（R；22)

《论持久战》

84. La Guerra prolongada/Mao Tse-tung；［versión al español de Ediciones en Lenguas Extranjeras, Pekín］. Barcelona：R. Torres, 1976. 153 p. ISBN：8485174097, 8485174096.（R；22)

《论持久战》

85. Declaraciones de Mao Tse-tung：Llamado a todos los pueblos a unirse contra la politica de agresion y guerra del imperialismo norteamericano y en salvaguardia de la paz mundial（de agosto de 1963 a anero de 1964). Pekín：Ediciones en Lenguas Extranjeras, 1964. 16 pages

《毛泽东主席声明、谈话集：全世界人名联合起来,反对美帝国主义的侵略政策和战争政策,保卫世界和平》

86. Declaraciones del presidente Mao Tse-tung, el pueblo Chino apouya firmemente la justa lucha patriotica del pueblo panamano（12 de enero de 1964). Pekín：Ediciones en Lenguas Extranjeras, 1964. 27 pages

《中国人民坚决支持巴拿马人民的爱国正义斗争》

87. Sobre algunos problemas importantes de la actual politica del partido. Pekín：Ediciones en Lenguas Extranjeras, 1964. 17 pages

《关于目前党的政策中的几个重要问题》

(1) 2a ed. Pekín：Ediciones en Lenguas Extranjeras, 1966. 11 pages

(2) Pekín：Ediciones en Lenguas Extranjeras, 1969. 20 pages

88. Discurso pronunciado ante la Asamblea de representantes de la región fronteriza de Shensi-Kansu-Ningsia. Pekín：Ediciones en Lenguas Extranjeras, 1965. 5 pages

《在陕西甘宁边区参议会的演说》

(1) 2a ed. Pekin：Ediciones en Lenguas Extranjeras, 1966. 5 pages

89. Ser atacado por el enemigo no es una cosa mala sino una cosa buena, con motivo del tercer aniversario de la

fundación del Colegio Militar y Político Antijaponés del pueblo chino (26 de mayo de 1939). Pekin：Ediciones en Lenguas Extranjeras，1965. 4 pages

《被敌人反对是好事而不是坏事》

(1) Pekin：Ediciones en Lenguas Extranjeras，1971. 4 pages

90. La Orientación del movimiento juvenil. Pekin：Ediciones en Lenguas Extranjeras，1965. 16 pages；19cm.

《青年运动的方向》

91. De dónde provienen las ideas correctas? (Mayo de 19163). Pekin：Ediciones en Lenguas Extranjeras，1965. 3 pages

《人的正确思想是从哪里来的?》

(1) 2a ed. de bolsillo. Pekín：Ediciones en Lenguas Extranjeras，1966. 3 pages

92. Discurso pronunciado en una conferencia de cuadros de la region liberada de Shansi-Suiyuan. 2a ed. Pekin：Ediciones en Lenguas Extranjeras，1966. 20 pages

《在晋绥干部会议上的讲话》

(1) Pekín：Ediciones en Lenguas Extranjeras，1969. 34 pages；13cm.

93. Pueblos de todos los paises，unios para derrotar a los agresores norteamericanos y a todos sus lacayos：Declaraciones en apoyo de los negros norteamericanos，de los pueblos del Sur de Vietnam，Panamá，Japón，Congo(L) y la República Dominicana en su justa lucha contra el imperialismo norteamericano. 2a ed. Pekín：Ediciones en Lenguas Extranjeras，1966. 1 volume

《全世界人民团结起来，打败美国侵略者及其一切走狗》

94. Cuatro tesis filosoficas. Pekin，Ediciones en Lenguas Extranjeras，1966. 150 pages：portraits；；20cm.

Contents：Acerca de la pratica—Sobre la contradiccion—Sobre el tratamiento correcto de las contradicciones en el seno del pueblo—De donde provienen las ideas correctas?

《毛泽东的四篇哲学论文》

(1) 2a ed. Barcelona：Anagrama，1974. 128 p. ；20cm. ISBN：843390115X, 8433901156. (Documentos；15)

95. Problemas estratégicos de la guerra revolucionaria de China/Mao Zedong. Pekin：Ediciones en Lenguas extranjeras，1966. 117 pages

《中国革命战争的战略问题》

(1) Pekin：Ediciones en Lenguas extranjeras，1966. 165 pages

(2) 2a ed. Pekin：Ediciones en Lenguas Extranjeras，1968. 203 pages；13cm.

96. Oponerse al culto a los libros. (mayo de 1930). Peking：Ediciones en Lenguas Extranjeras，1966. 18 pages

《反对本本主义》

(1) Pekin：Ediciones en Lenguas Extranjeras，1972. 22 pages

97. Discurso ante la conferencia nacional del partido comunista de China sobre el trabajo de propaganda：12 de marzo de 1957. Pekín：Ediciones en Lenguas Extranjeras，1966. 33 pages

《在中国共产党全国宣传工作会议上的讲话》

98. Citas del presidente Mao Tse-tung. Pekin：Ediciones en Lenguas Extranjeras，1966. 329 pages，［1］leaf of plates：illustrations；14cm.

《毛主席语录》

(1) 2. ed. Pekin：Ediciones en Lenguas Extranjeras，1967. 333 pages，［1］leaf of plates：illustrations；14cm.

(2) Pekin：Edicioes en Lenguas Extranjeras，1972. 333 pages，［1］pages of plates：portraits；13cm.

(3) 2a ed. Pekin：Ediciones en Lenguas Extranjeras，1975. 333 p. ；14cm.

99. Citas del presidente Mao Tse-Tung. Buenos Aires：La Rosa blindada，1969. 300 p. ；14cm. (Los Tiempos nuevos)

毛主席语录.

100. Lo que verdaderamente dijo Mao/Philippe Devillers；traducción del francés de Rafael Perez Delgado. México：Aguilar，1970. 284 pages；20cm.

Notes；Versión francés original：Ce que Mao a vraiment dit. / Includes numerous excerpts from Mao's works.

毛主席语录. Devillers，Philippe(1920—)转译自法语.

(1) 2. ed. México：Aguilar，1973. 284 pages；20cm.

101. El Libro rojo/Mao Tse-Tung；prólogo de Eduardo Haro Tecglen；［introducción de Lin Piao；traducción：Instituto de Lenguas Extranjeras，Pekín］. 2a ed. Madrid［etc.］：Júcar，1976. 208 p. ；18cm. ISBN：8433402374, 8433402370. (Biblioteca Júcar；34)

红宝书.外文出版社版本翻印.

102. Libro rojo/Mao Tse-tung；prefacio de Lin Piao. Barcelona［etc.］：Bruguera，1976. 253 p. ，［5］leaves of plates：il. ；18cm. ISBN：8402049273, 8402049278

红宝书.

103. El Libro rojo：citas del presidente Mao Tse-Tung/［Mao Txe-Tung］；traducción：Ediciones de Lenguas Extranjeras de Pekín. Madrid：Ed. Fundamentos，1976. 333 p. ；18cm. ISBN：8424501187, 8424501181. (Cuadernos prácticos/Fundamentos；25)

红宝书:毛主席语录.

(1) El libro rojo；Citas del presidente Mao Tse-tung. ［Caracas］［Fundamentos］，1976. 333 pages

104. Libro rojo：ideario de un gran luchador/Mao Tse-tung；prefacio de Lin Piao. Barcelona：Editorial Braille Once，1978. 2 volumes in braille；32cm.

红宝书:毛主席语录.

105. Libro rojo：citas del presidente/Mao Mao Zedong. Barcelona：Orbis，1985. 125 pages；20cm. ISBN：

8476343221，8476343227.（Biblioteca de política, economía y sociedad；41）

红宝书：毛主席语录.

106. El libro rojo/Mao Zedong；prólogo de Antonio Molina Flores. Sevilla：Renacimiento, 2014. 231 p.；22cm. ISBN：8416034109, 8416034109.（Espuela de Plata）

红宝书.

107. El Viejo Tonto que trasladaba las montanas. Pekin：Ediciones en Lenguas Estranjeras, 1966. 5 pages

《愚公移山》

108. La situación y nuestra politica después de la victoria en la Guerra de esistencia contra el Japón. Pékin：Ediciones en Lenguas Extranjeras, 1967. 22 pages

《抗日战争胜利后的时局和我们的方针》

(1) 2a ed. Pekín：Ediciones en Lenguas Extranjeras, 1968. 37 pages

109. Servir al pueblo；En memoria de Norman Bethune；El viejo Tonto que removió las montanas. Pekín：Ediciones en Lenguas Extranjeras, 1967. 15 pages

《为人民服务·纪念白求恩·愚公移山》

110. Los Tres artículos más leídos en china.［Madrid］：Comité Central del Partido Comunista de España, 1971.

老三篇：《纪念白求恩》《为人民服务》《愚公移山》.

111. Gobierno constitucional de la nueva democracia. 2a ed. Pekin：Ediciones en Lenguas Extranjeras, 1967. 15 pages

《新民主主义的宪政》

112. Servir al pueblo/Mao Tse-Tung. Pekin：Ediciones en Lenguas Extranjeras, 1967. 8 pages；15cm.

Contents：En memoria de Norman Bethune—Servir al pueblo.

《为人民服务》

113. tas del Presidente Mao Tse-tung sobre la guerra popular. Pekín：Ediciones en Lenguas Extranjeras, 1967. 41 pages

《毛主席论人民战争》

(1) Citas del presidente Mao Tse-tung sobre la guerra popular. Pekín：Ediciones en Lenguas Extrajeras, 1967. 52 pages

114. Seleccion de escritos militares. Pekin, Ediciones en Lenguas Extranjeras, 1967. 451 pages；portrait.

Notes：Translation of (romanized)：Mao zhu xi jun shi wen xuan. / Includes bibliographical references.

《毛主席军事文选》

115. La situación actual y nuestras tareas. Pekin：Ediciones en Lenguas Estranjeras, 1967. 50 pages

《目前的形势和我们的任务》

(1) La situación actual y nuestras tareas（25 de diciembre de 1947）. Pekin：Ediciones en Lenguas Extranjeras, 1970. 54 pages

116. Conversación con la corresponsal norteamericana Anna Louise Strong. Pekín：Ediciones en Lenguas Extranjeras, 1967. 11 pages

《和美国记者安娜·路易斯·斯特朗的谈话》

(1) Pekín：Ediciones en Lenguas Extranjeras, 1967. 8 pages

117. Crear sólidas bases de apoyo en el Nordeste. Pekín：Ediciones en Lenguas Extranjeras, 1968. 10 pages

《建立巩固的东北根据地》

118. Luchemos por incorporar a millones de integrantes de las masas al frente unico nacional antijapones. Pékin：Ediciones en Lenguas Extranjeras, 1968. 24 pages

《为争取千百万群众进入抗日民族统一战线而斗争》

119. Circular del Comité Central del Partido Comunista de China sobre la reunión de septiembre. Pekín：Ediciones en Lenguas Extranjeras, 1968. 22 pages

《中共中央关于九月会议的通知》

120. La lucha en las montanas Chingkang. Pekin：Ediciones en Lenguas Extranjeras, 1968. 88 pages

《井冈山的斗争》

121. Manifiesto del ejército popular de liberación de China. Pekín：Ediciones en Lenguas Extranjeras, 1968. 15 pages

《中国人民解放军宣言》

122. Discurso pronunciado en la Reunion Preparatoria de la Nueva Conferencia Consultiva Politica（15 de junio de 1949）. Pekín：Ediciones en Lenguas Extranjeras, 1968. 11 pages

《在新政治协商会议筹备会上的讲话》

123. 39. Cinco documentos del presidente Mao Tse-tung sobre literatura y arte. Pekín：Ediciones en Lenguas Extranjeras, 1968. 11 pages；15cm.

Contents：Carta al teatro de opera de Pekin, de Yenan, escrita despues de ver "Sin otro camino que la rebelion" —Hay que prestar seria atención al debate sobre la pelicula "La vida de Wu Sün" —Carta sobre el estudio de "El ensueño del pabellon rojo" —Dos instrucciones sobre literatura y arte.

《毛主席关于文学艺术的五个文件》

(1) Pekín：Ediciones en Lenguas Extranjeras, 1975. 7 pages

124. A propósito de una declaración de Chiang Kai-shek.（28 de diciembre de 1936）. Pekín：Ediciones en Lenguas Extranjeras, 1968. 19 pages

《关于蒋介石声明的声明》

125. Reclutar gran numero de intelectuales.（I. o de diciembre de 1939）. Pekin：Ediciones en Lenguas Extranjeras, 1968. 6 pages

《大量吸收知识分子》

126. Declaracion del camarada Mao Tse-tung, presidente del Comite Central del Partido Comunista de China, en

apoyo de la lucha de los negros norteamericanos contra la violencia represiva (16 de abril de 1968). Peking: Ediciones en Lenguas Extranjeras, 1968. 4 pages

《中国共产党中央委员会主席毛泽东同志支持美国黑人抗暴斗争的声明》

127. Charla a los redactores del Diario de Shansi-Suiyuán (2 de abril de 1948). Pekin: Ediciones en Lenguas Extranjeras, 1968. 10 pages

《对晋绥日报编辑人员的谈话》

128. Saludemos el nuevo ascenso de la revolución china. Pekín: Ediciones en lenguas extrajeras, 1968. 23 pages

《迎接中国革命的新高潮》

129. Concentrar una fuerza superior para aniquilar las unidades enemigas una por una. Pekín: Ediciones en Lenguas Extranjeras, 1968. 12 pages

《集中优势兵力，各个歼灭敌人》

130. Sobre la política concerniente a la industria y el comercio. Pekín: Ediciones en Lenguas Extranjeras, 1968. 5 pages

《关于工商业政策》

131. ¡Fuerzas revolucionarias del mundo, unios, luchad contra la agresión imperialista! Pekín: Ediciones en Lenguas Extranjeras, 1968. 8 pages

《全世界革命力量团结起来，反对帝国主义的侵略》

132. Sobre la gran victoria en el Noroeste y el movimiento de educación ideológica de nuevo tipo en El Ejército de Liberación. Pekín: Ediciones en Lenguas Extranjeras, 1968. 16 pages

《评西北大捷兼论解放军的新式整军运动》

133. El pensamiento de Mao Tse-tung: citas. 〔Quito〕 Ecuador: Ediciones de la Revolución Ecuatoriana, 1968. 287 pages: portraits; 15cm.

毛泽东思想摘要.

134. El problema del poder en las bases de apoyo antijaponesas (6 de marzo de 1940). Pekin: Ediciones en Lenguas Extranjeras, 1969. 7 pages

《抗日根据地的政权问题》

135. Citas sobre la guerra popular. 〔Montevideo〕 Nativa Libros, 1968. 46 pages; 14cm.

论人民战争.

136. Expandir audazmente las fuerzas antijaponesas y responder a los ataques de los recalcitrantes anticomunistas(4 de mayo de 1940). Pekín: Ediciones en Lenguas Extranjeras, 1969. 15 pages

《放手发展抗日力量，抵抗反共顽固派的进攻》

137. Unidad hasta el fin. (julio de 1940). Pekín: Ediciones en Lenguas Extranjeras, 1969. 6 pages

《团结到底》

138. Sobre la producción en el ejercito para su autoabastecimiento y la importancia de las dos grandes campanas por la rectificación del estilo de trabajo y por

la producción (27 de abril de 1945). Pekín: Ediciones en Lenguas Extranjeras, 1969. 11 pages

《论军队生产自给，兼论整风和生产两大运动的重要性》

139. Organicemonos. Pekin: Ediciones en Lenguas Extranjeras, 1969. 22 pages

《组织起来》

140. Una politica de suma importancia (7 de septiembre de 1942). Pekin: Ediciones en Lenguas Extranjeras, 1969. 7 pages; 13cm.

《一个极其重要的政策》

141. Entrevista con el periodista inglés James Bertram: 25 de octubre de 1937. Pekin: Ediciones en Lenguas Extranjeras, 1969. 36 pages

《和英国记者贝特兰的谈话》

142. El papel del Partido Comunista de China en la guerra nacional. Pekin: Ediciones en Lenguas Extranjeras, 1969. 44 pages

《中国共产党在民族战争中的地位》

143. Balance de la victoria sobre la segunda campana anticomunista (8 de mayo de 1941). Pekin: Ediciones en Lenguas Extranjeras, 1969. 17 pages

《关于打退第二次反共高潮的总结》

144. Por la movilizacion de todas las fuerzas para la victoria de la guerra de resistencia. Pekin: Ediciones en Lenguas Extranjeras, 1969. 18 pages

《为动员一切力量争取抗战胜利而斗争》

145. Desplegar en las bases de apoyo las campanas por la reducción de los arriendos, por la producción y de apoyar al gobierno y amar al pueblo (Io de octubre de 1943). Pekin: Ediciones en Lenguas Extranjeras, 1969. 11 pages

《开展根据地的减租生产和拥政爱民运动》

146. La reducción de los arriendos y el desarrollo de la producción son dos asuntos importantes para la defensa de las regiones liberadas. Pekin: Ediciones en Lenguas Extranjeras, 1969. 6 pages

《减租和生产是保卫解放区的两件大事》

147. La Situación actual y las tareas del partido: 10 de octubre de 1939. Pekin: Ediciones en Lenguas Extranjeras, 1969. 5 pages

《当前的形势和党的任务》

148. El punto de viraje de la Segunda Guerra Mundial (12 de octubre de 1942). Pekin: Ediciones en Lenguas Extranjeras, 1969. 12 pages

《第二次世界大战的转折点》

149. Sobre el gobierno de coalición/Mao Tsetung. Pekin: Ediciones en Lenguas Extranjeras, 1969. 174 pages; 13cm.

《论联合政府》

150. Tareas urgentes después de establecida la cooperación

entre el Kuomintang y el Partido Comunista (29 de septiembre de 1937). Pekin: Ediciones en Lenguas Extranjeras, 1969. 28 pages

《国共合作成立后的迫切任务》

151. Unidad hasta el fin: julio de 1940. Pekin: Ediciones en Lenguas Extranjeras, 1969. 6 pages

《团结到底》

152. La situación y las tareas en la guerra de resistencia contra el Japón después de la caída de Shang-hai y Taiyuán. Pekin: Ediciones en Lenguas Extranjeras, 1969. 36 pages

《上海太原失陷以后抗日战争的形势和任务》

153. Sobre la nueva democracia. Pekin: Ediciones en Lenguas Extranjeras, 1969. 116 pages

《新民主主义论》

154. El frente unico en el trabajo cultural (30 de octubre de 1944). Pekin: Ediciones en Lenguas Extranjeras, 1969. 5 pages

《文化工作中的统一战线》

155. Un balance de tres meses (I. o de octubre de 1946). Pekin: Ediciones en Lenguas Extranjeras, 1970. 16 pages

《三个月总结》

156. Los reaccionarios deben ser castigados (1o de agosto de 1939). Pekin: Ediciones en Languas Extranjeras, 1970. 11 pages

《必须制裁反动派》

157. Contra las actividades capituladoras (30 de junio de 1939). Pekin: Ediciones en Lenguas Extranjeras, 1970. 14 pages

《反对投降活动》

158. Como determinar las clases en las zonas rurales: octubre de 1933. Pekin: Ediciones en Lenguas Extranjeras, 1970. 5 pages

《怎样分析农村阶级》

159. Declaración de Mao Tsetung, presidente del Comité Central del Partido Comunista de China sobre la situación actual (14 de enero de 1949). Pekín: Ediciones en Lenguas Extranjeras, 1970. 10 pages

《中共中央毛泽东主席关于时局的声明》

160. Pueblos de todo el mundo, unios y derrotad a los agresores norteamericanos y a todos sus lacayos!: declaración del 20 de mayo de 1970. Pekin: Ediciones en Lenguas Extranjeras, 1970. 7 pages

《全世界人民团结起来,打败美国侵略者及其一切走狗》

161. Sobre el problema de la burguesia nacional y de los shenshi sensatos. Pekin: Ediciones en Lenguas Extranjeras, 1970. 10 pages; 13cm.

《关于民族资产阶级和开明绅士问题》

162. Estrategia para el segundo ano de la guerra de

liberación, (1o de septiembre de 1947). Pekín: Ediciones en Lenguas Extranjeras, 1970. 16 pages

《解放战争第二年的战略方针》

163. Una circular sobre la situación (20 de marzo de 1948). Pekín: Ediciones en Lenguas Extranjeras, 1970. 21 pages

《关于情况的通报》

164. Sobre la creación de un sistema de informes (7 de enero de 1948). Pekín: Ediciones en Lenguas Extranjeras, 1970. 5 pages

《关于建立报告制度》

165. Los Dos destinos de China: 23 de abril de 1945. Pekín: Ediciones en Lenguas Extranjeras, 1970. 7 pages

《两个中国之命运》

166. Comentario sobre las diferentes respuestas del Kuomintang a la cuestión de la responsabilidad de la guerra (18 de febrero de 1949). Pékín: Ediciones en Lenguas Extranjeras, 1970. 20 pages

《评国民党对战争责任问题的几种答案》

167. Directivas para las operaciones en la campana de Peiping-Tientsin (II de diciembre de 1948). Pekín: Ediciones en Lenguas Extranjeras, 1970. 12 pages

《关于平津战役的作战方针》

168. Corregir los errores de "izquierda" en la propaganda de la reforma agraria. (11 de febrero de 1948). Pekín: Ediciones en Lenguas Extranjeras, 1970. 5 pages

《纠正土地改革宣传中的"左"倾错误》

169. Hacer del ejército un destacamento de trabajo (8 febrero de 1949). Pekín: Ediciones en Lenguas Extranjeras, 1970. 7 pages

《把军队变为工作队》

170. Puntos esenciales de la reforma agraria en las regiones liberadas nuevas (15 de febrero de 1948). Pekín: Ediciones en Lenguas Extranjeras, 1970. 4 pages

《新解放区土地改革要点》

171. Nuestra politica económica (23 de enero de 1934). Pekin: [publisher not identified], 1970. 13 pages

《我们的经济政策》

172. Problemas tácticos del trabajo: rural on las regiones liberadas nuevas (24 de mayo de 1948). Pekín: Ediciones en Lenguas Extranjeras, 1970. 2 pages

《新解放区农村工作的策略问题》

173. Instrucciones del Alto Mando del Ejército Popular de Liberación de China sobre la nueva promulgación de las Tres Reglas Cardinales de Disciplina y las Ocho Advertencias (10 de octubre de 1947). Pekin: Ediciones en Lenguas Extranjeras, 1970. 3 pages

《中国人民解放军总部关于重新颁布三大纪律八项注意的训令》

174. Con motivo de la aparición de El Obrero Chino (7 de febrero de 1940). Pekin: Ediciones en Lenguas

Extranjeras，1970. 3 pages

《〈中国工人〉发刊词》

175. Directivas para las operaciones en la campana de Juai-Jai (II de octubre de 1948). Pekín：Ekiciones en Lenguas Extranjeras，1970. 8 pages

《关于淮海战役的作战方针》

176. Unir a todas las fuerza antijaponesas y combatir a los recalcitrantes anticomunistas（I. de febrero de 1940）. Pekin：Ediciones en Lenguas Extranjeras，1970. 17 pages

《团结一切抗日力量，反对反共顽固派》

177. El gobierno de Chiang Kai-shek está asediado por todo el pueblo.（30 de mayo de 1947）. Pékin：Ediciones en Lenguas Extranjeras，1970. 13 pages

《蒋介石政府已处在全民包围中》

178. Directivas para las operaciones en la campana de Liaosi-Shenyang（Septiembre y octobre de 1948）. Pékin：Ediciones en Lenguas Extranjeras，1970. 14 pages

《关于辽沈战役的作战方针》

179. Diferentes tacticas para aplicar la ley agraria en las diferentes regiones（3 de febrero de 1948）. Pekín：Ediciones en Lenguas Extranjeras，1970. 4 pages

《在不同地区实施土地法的不同策略》

180. Las zonas guerrilleras también pueden producir（31 de enero de 1945）. Pekín：Ediciones en Lenguas Extranjeras，1970. 9 pages

《游击区也能够进行生产》

181. Entrevista con tres corresponsales de la Agencia Central de Noticias, el Saotang Pao y el Sinmin Pao（16 de septiembre de 1939）. Pekin：Ediciones en Lenguas Extranjeras，1970. 15 pages

《和中央报，扫荡报，新民报三记者的谈话》

182. Vencer el peligro de capitulación y esforzarse por un cambio en la situación（28 de enero de 1940）. Pekín：Ediciones en Lenguas Extranjeras，1970. 8 pages

《克服投降危险，力争时局好转》

183. Chiang Kai-shek está provocando la guerra civil（13 de agosto de 1945）. Pekín：Ediciones en Lenguas Extranjeras，1970. 12 pages

《蒋介石在挑动内战》

184. Telegrama a la comandancia del frente de Luoyang despues de la reconquista de la ciudad（8 de abril de 1948）. Pekin：Ediciones en Lenguas Extranjeras，1970. 5 pages

《再克洛阳后给洛阳前线指挥部的电报》

185. Proclama del ejercito popular de liberación de China（25 de abril de 1949）. Pekin：Ediciones en Lenguas Extranjeras，1970. 7 pages

《中国人民解放军布告》

186. Interpelamos al Kuomintang（12 de julio de 1943）. Pekin：Ediciones en Lenguas Extranjeras，1970. 16

pages

《质问国民党》

187. Entrevista sobre la nueva situación internacional con un corresponsal del Diario Nueva China（1 de septiembre de 1939）. Pekin：Ediciones en Lenguas Extranjeras，1970. 16 pages

《关于国际新形势对新华日报记者的谈话》

188. Comentario sobre la XI Sesión Plenaria del Comité Ejecutivo Central del Kuomintang y la II Sesión del III Consejo Politico Nacional（5 de octubre de 1943）. Pekín：Ediciones en Lenguas Extranjeras，1970. 39 pages

《评国民党十一中全会和三届二次国民参政会》

189. El Movimiento del 4 de Mayo（Mayo de 1939）. Pekin：Ediciones en Lenguas Extranjeras，1970. 8 pages

《五四运动》

190. A propósito del discurso de Chiang Kai-shek en la Fiesta del Doble Diez（11 de octubre de 1944）. Pekin：Ediciones en Lenguas Extranjeras，1970. 10 pages

《评蒋介石在双十节的演说》

191. Sobre la declaración de un vocero de chiang Kai-shek（16 de agosto de 1945）. Pekín：Ediciones en Lenguas Extranjeras，1970. 13 pages

《评蒋介石发言人谈话》

192. Dos telegramas del Comandante en Jefe del XVIII Grupo de Ejercitos a Chiang Kai-shek（agosto de 1945）. Pekín：Ediciones en Lenguas Extranjeras，1970. 20 pages

《第十八集团军司令给蒋介石的两个电报》

193. Seis escritos militares del Presidente Mao Tsetung. Pekín, China：Ediciones en Lenguas Extranjeras：Editorial del Pueblo，1970. 418 pages；portraits；16cm.

《毛主席的六篇军事著作》

（1）Pekin：Ediciones en Lenguas Extranjeras，1972. 418 pages；16cm.

194. Prestar atención al trabajo economico（20 de agosto de 1933）. Peking：Ediciones en Lenguas Extranjeras，1971. 21 pages

《必须注意经济工作》

195. La situación despues de la victoria sobre la segunda campana anticomunista. Pekín：Ediciones en Lenguas Extranjeras，1971. 8 pages

《打退第二次反共高潮后的时局》

196. Cinco tesis filosoficas.［Peking］Ediciones en Lenguas Extranjeras，1971. 288 pages；portraits；13cm.

《毛主席的五篇哲学著作》

（1）Cinco tesis filosoficas de Mao Tsetung/Mao Tsetung. Pekin：Ediciones en Lenguas Extranjeras，1975，1971. 288 p.；13cm.

（2）Cinco tesis filosoficas de mao tse tung/Mao Tse

Tung. Pekin：Ediciones en Lenguas Extranjeras，1974. 288 pages；13cm.

（3）Cinco tesis filosoficas de Mao Zedong. Beijing：Ediciones en Lenguas Extranjeras，1980. 163 pages：portraits；18cm.

197. La Guerra revolucionaria. ［México，D. F.］：Grijalbo，1971. 158 pages

革命战争.

（1）Barcelona：Grijalbo，1974. 158 p. ；18cm.

198. Acerca de algunos problemas de los métodos de dirección/Mao Tse-Tung. ［S. l.］：Ediciones Servir al Pueblo，Comité de Catalunya del Partido Comunista de E. （m-l），1972. 14 p. ；22cm.

《关于领导方法的若干问题》

199. Sobre la nueva democracia；Intevenciones en el foro de Yenan sobre arte y literatura；Sobre el tratamiento correcto de las contradicciones en el seno del pueblo；Discurso ante la Conferencia Nacional del Partido comunista de China sobre el trabajo de propaganda. Pekin：Ediciones en Lenguas Extranjeras，1972. 342 pages

《新民主主义论，在延安文艺座谈会上的讲话，关于正确处理人民内部矛盾的问题，在中国共产党全国宣传工作会议上的讲话》

200. El Estilo del trabajo en el partido/Mao Tse-tung. México，D. F.：Roca，1973. 159 p. （Colección R；11）

党的工作方法.

（1）El Estilo del trabajo en el partido/Mao Tse-Tung. Madrid：Akal，1975. 159 p. ：xl. ；18cm. ISBN：8473390768，8473390767. （Akal 74；14）

（2）El estilo del trabajo en el partido/Mao Tse-tung. Barcelona：R. Torres，1976. 159 p. ISBN：8485174186，8485174188. （Coleccion R；11）

201. Escritos sociológicos y culturales/Mao Tse-Tung. Barcelona：Laia，1974. 224 p. ；19cm. ISBN：8472222772，8472222779. （Ediciones de bolsillo. Ciencias sociales；381）

收录毛泽东的政治与社会思想的著作.

（1）2a ed. Barcelona：Laia，1977. 222 p. （Ediciones de bolsillo；381）

202. Historia de la revolución china/Mao Tse-Tung. Madrid：Castellote，1974. 69 p. ；17cm. ISBN：8472590453，8472590458. （Colección básica （Castellote）；15）

中国革命的历史.

203. La Construcción del socialismo：vía china o modelo soviético/Mao Tse-Tung. Barcelona：Anagrama，1975. 188 p. ；19cm. ISBN：8433964259，8433964250. （Ediciones de bolsillo；425；Ciencias sociales）

社会主义建设：中国道路还是苏联道路.

204. La construcción del socialismo/Mao Tse Tung；textos inéditos presentados por Hu Chi-hsi. Madrid，Fund-amentos，1975. 173 pages. ISBN：8424501489，8424501488. （Ciencia；56）

社会主义建设.

（1）2 ed. Caracas：Fundamentos，1977. 173 pages. ；20cm. ISBN：8424501489，8424501488. （Ciencia；56）

205. Vía China versus modelo soviético：textos inéditos. Barcelona：Anagrama，1975. 89 p. ；18cm. ISBN：8433907018，8433907011. （Cuadernos Anagrama；Documentos；101）

Conté：China y la U. R. S. S.：dos modelos de industrialización/Charles Bettelheim. La Cuestión de Stalin；Sobre las diez grandes relaciones/Mao Tse-tung.

含毛泽东的《论十大关系》.

206. Sobre diez grandes relaciones/Mao Tsetung. Pekin：Ediciones en Lenguas Extranjeras，1977. 35 pages；19cm.

《论十大关系》

207. Mao íntimo：escritos，conversaciones y discursos de Mao Tse-tung inéditos para occidente：1949—1971/recopilados por Helmut Martin；［traducción de Rüdiger Gaetner］. Barcelona：DOPESA，1975. 354 p. ；19cm. ISBN：8472352420 （cart. ），8472352421 （cart. ）. （Grandes biografías；10）

1949—1971 年间毛泽东著作、谈话和演讲选译. Gaetner，Rüdiger 译.

208. La construcción del socialismo en China/Mao Tse-tung. Problemas económicos del socialismo en la URSS/José Stalin；［traducción de Conrado Ceretti］. Córdoba ［Argentina］：Pasado y Presente；Buenos Aires：Distribiudo por Siglo XXI Argentina Editores，1976. vii，214 pages；20cm. （Cuadernos de Pasado y Presente；65）

Notes：Translated from the Chinese and Russian

收录毛泽东关于中国社会主义建设的著作.

209. Textos escogidos de Mao Tsetung. Pekin：Ediciones en Lenguas Extranjeras，1976. 535 pages；19cm.

《毛泽东著作选读》

210. Orientaciones，programas y perspectivas de la lucha contra la ofensiva del Japon. 2a ed. Pekin：Ediciones en Lenguas Extranjeras，1976. 10 pages

《反对日本进攻的方针，办法和前途》

211. Discurso ante una conferencia ampliada de trabajo convocada por el Comité Central del Partido Comunista de China，30 de enero de 1962/Mao Tsetung. Peking：Ediciones en Lenguas Extranjeras，1978. 40 pages；19cm.

《在扩大的中央工作会议上的讲话》

212. Mao Zedong espontáneo：pláticas y cartas 1956—1971/Mao Zedong；tr. Alejandro Licona. México：

Renacimiento，1981. 305 p. ；16cm.

毛泽东谈话与书信. Licona，Alejandro 译.

A2 毛泽东研究相关著作

1. Homenajo a Mao Tse Tung：poeta，filosofo，guerrillero y revolucionario. Torremolinos（Málaga）：Litoral，1977. 229 p. ：ill. ；24cm.（Litoral；no. 64－66）

   毛泽东：诗人、哲学家、战士和革命家.

2. Mao Zedong：el hombre/Quan Yanchi；corr. Francisco Tumi. Beijing：Ediciones en Lenguas Extranjeras，1992. 267 p. ：il. ；21cm. ISBN：7119013645，7119013640

   《走下神坛的毛泽东》，权延赤著.

B 类 哲学、宗教

B1 中国哲学

1. Breve historia de la filosofía china/Hou Wai-Lu；colab. Chang Chi-Chih，Li Hsueh-Chin，Yang Chao y Lin Ying；tr. Floreal Mazía. Montevideo：Pueblos Unidos，1960. 266 p. ；16cm.

   《中国哲学史略》，侯外庐主编；张岂之、李学勤、杨超、林英编写；Mazía，Floreal 译.

   （1）Buenos Aires［s. n.］，1972. 226 p. ，1 h. 18cm.

2. Breve historia de la filosofía china/Traducción de Juan José Utrilla. México：Fondo de Cultura Económica，1987. 591 p. ；18cm. ISBN：9681626966；9681626969. （Breviarios del Fondo de Cultura Económica；446）

   《中国哲学小史》，冯友兰著.

3. Breve historia de la filosofia China/Feng Youlan；traductores：Wang Hongxun y Fan Moxian. Beijing：Ediciones en Lenguas Extranjeras，1989. 445 pages；21cm.

   《中国哲学小史》，冯友兰著.

4. Pensadores de la antigua China/［Yang Chunyan］. Beijing：Editorial Nueva Estrella，2004. 39 pages；illustrations（some color）；21cm. ISBN：7801486013，7801486011. （China express；viaje multicultural a un país de cinco mil años）

   《中国古代的思想家们》，杨春燕编著. 新星出版.

5. Filosofía oriental/［Confucio y otros Juan Gedo. Jaime Uya Traduccion. Barcelona Zeus，1968. 355 p. ，14 h. 17cm. （Podium）

   Contents：Filosofía moral y política de la China/Confucio. —Tao-te-king/Lao-tse.

   包括对《论语》和《道德经》的选译. Godó Costa，Juan 和 Uyá，Jaime 合译.

   （1）2a ed. Barcelona：Ediciones Zeus，1971. 355 p. ；17cm. （Podium. Libros significativos）

6. 中国思想家论智力/冯天瑜主编；徐宜林…［等］译. 上海：上海外语教育出版社，2017. 521 页；23cm. ISBN：

7544646642.（中国文化精品译丛）

   西文题名：La inteligencia a los ojos de los pensadores chinos. 汉西双语.

B2 中国各代哲学著作与研究

1. Elogio de la anarquía：por dos excéntricos chinos/polémicas del siglo tercero seleccionadas y presentadas por Jean Levi；traducidas del chino antiguo y anotadas por Albert Galvany. Logroño Pepitas de Calabaza，2009. 175 p. 17cm. ISBN：8493636784；8493636789

   无君论. Galvany，Albert 译. 收录中国古代无政府主义的言论，包括鲍敬言与葛洪论战中关于无君的论述.

   （1）［2. ed.］. Logroño：Pepitas de Calabaza，2011. 175 p. ；17cm. ISBN：8493834975，8493834971

B21 诸子前哲学

B211 周易

1. I Ching/ed. prol y trad. Mirko Lauer. Barcelona：Barral，1971. 310 p. ；18cm. （Libros de enlace；；149）

   《易经》，Lauer，Mirko 译.

   （1）［7th ed.］. Barcelona：Barral Editores，1975. 310 pages；19cm. ISBN：8421171496，8421171493

   （2）11. ed. Madrid［Spain］：Akal Editor，1983. 310 pages；17cm. ISBN：8473396642，8473396646. （Akal bolsillo；109）

   （3）Madrid：Akal，1990. 310 p. ；17cm. ISBN：8476005741，8476005743. （Akal bolsillo；105）

2. Yi ching：libro de las mutaciones/［Traducido de la edición alemana de Richard Wilhelm］. ［Mexico］，［Lince Editores］，1971. 284 pages：illustrations；22cm.

   《易经》，转译自卫礼贤（Wilhelm，Richard，1873—1930）（德国汉学家）的德文版《易经》.

3. I ching：el libro de las mutaciones/versión del chino al alemán，con comentarios，por Richard Wilhelm；traducción al español，con presentación y notas，por D. J. Vogelmann；prólogos de C. G. Jung，Richard Wilhelm y Hellmut Wilhelm；y el poema："Para una versión del I King" de Jorge Luis Borges. Buenos Aires：Hermes/Sudamericana，1976. 819 pages：illustrations；21cm. ISBN：9500700859，9500700856. （Colección oriente y occidente）

   Notes：Translation of：I Ging：das Buch der Wandlungen，which was translated from the Chinese.

   《易经》，卫礼贤（Wilhelm，Richard，1873—1930）（德国汉学家）德译；Vogelmann，D. J. 转译成西文.

   （1）1. ed. de bolsillo. Buenos Aires：Sudamericana，1975. 355 pages：illustrations；20cm. ISBN：9500708023

   （2）Barcelona：Edhasa，1977. 819 p. ；21cm. ISBN：8435019020，8435019026. （Oriente y occidente）

   （3）2. ed. Barcelona：Edhasa，1979. 819 pages；21cm.

ISBN：8435002039，8435002035. (Colección Oriente y Occidente)

(4)5a. ed. Barcelona：Edhasa, 1982. 819 pages：illustrations；20cm. ISBN：8435002039, 8435002035. (Colección Oriente y Occidente)

(5)1a. ed. en Mexico. México D. F.：Hermes/Sudamericana, 1983. 819 pages；21cm. ISBN：9684460457, 9684460454. (Colección oriente y occidente)

(6) Barcelona：Edhasa, 1987. 821 s. ；21cm. ISBN：8435019020, 8435019026

(7)Buenos Aires：Sudamericana, 1994. 818 pages：illustrations；20cm. ISBN：9684461062, 9684461062

(8)1a ed. pocket. Buenos Aires：Editorial Sudamericana, 1998. 355 pages：illustrations；18cm. ISBN：9500714337, 9500714334

(9) Mexico：Grupo Editorial Tomo, 1999. 446 pages：illustrations；21cm. ISBN：9706661735, 9706661739

(10)[New ed.]. Santafé de Bogotá [Colombia]：Editorial Solar, 2001. 790 pages：illustrations；20cm. ＋3 I Ching coins＋1 sheet of hexagrams and instructions. ISBN：9589196268, 9589196267

(11)2a. edición. México, D. F.：Grupo Editorial Tomo, 2002. 446 pages：illustrations；21cm. ISBN：9706661739, 9706661735

(12)Buenos Aires：Editorial Sudamericana, 2003. 819 p. ：il. ；19cm. ISBN：6073111966, 6073111967

4. Yi Jing：el libro de las mutaciones/Lee Tuan. Chile：Texido, 1993. 146 pages；22cm. (Colección Metafísica) Notes：Adaptación de la versión alemana "I ging, das buch der wandlungen" de Richard Wilhelm por Herman Klein.
《易经》，Lee Tuan 转译自卫礼贤（Wilhelm，Richard, 1873—1930)(德国汉学家)的德文版《易经》.

5. I Ching：el libro del cambio/John Blofeld；prefacio del Lama Anagarika Govinda. Madrid：EDAF, 1982. 236 pages；21cm. ISBN：847166724X, 8471667243. (Colleccion la tabla de Esmeralda)
《易经》，Blofeld，John Eaton Calthorpe（1913—）译. Govinda，Anagarika Brahmacari 作序.

6. Libro de los cambios/edición preparada por Carmelo Elorduy. Madrid：Editora Nacional, 1983. 313 pages；19cm. ISBN：8427606435, 8427606432. (Biblioteca de la literatura y el pensamiento universales；52)
《易经》，Elorduy，Carmelo(1901—1989 年)译.

7. Yi jing：el libro del oráculo chino/[versión directa del chino al italiano por] Judica Cordiglia, [traducción al español por] Celia Filipetto. Barcelona：Ediciones Martínez Roca, 1984. 294 pages；22cm. ISBN：8427009097, 8427009097. (Colección Fontana fantástica)
Notes：Translation of：I ching, il libro degli oracoli cinese
《易经》，转译自意大利语. Filipetto，Celia 译.

(1)Barcelona：Ed. Martinez Roca, 1987. 294；22cm. ＋diagram i 3 monety chińskie. ISBN：8427009097, 8427009097. (FF Fontana Fantástica)

8. El libro de las mutaciones：cómo comprender y usar el I ching/Neil Powell；tr. Diorki Traductores. Barcelona：Folio, 1985. 89 pages；illustrations；29cm. ISBN：8475830676, 8475830674
Translation of：The book of change
《易经》，转译自英文版《The book of change》一书.

9. I Ching：un metodo de autoindagacion y orientacion personal. Buenos Aires, Argentine：Planeta, 1992. 343 pages
《易经》

10. Yi Jing：el libro del cambio/versión de Thomas Cleary；[traducido por Alfonso Colodrón]. Madrid：EDAF, 1993. 175 pages；18cm. ISBN：8476406665, 8476406663. (Arca de sabiduría；3)
《易经》，Cleary，Thomas F. (1949—)英译；Colodrón, Alfonso 转译成西文.

(1)9. ed. Madrid：EDAF, 2003. 175 pages；18cm. ISBN：8476406665, 8476406663. (Arca de Sabiduría；3)

(2)[Versión Ilustrada]. Madrid：EDAF, 2005. 167 pages：color illustrations；18cm. ISBN：8441417032, 8441417038

11. Yi jing：una nueva formulación, válida para nuestra época/[traducción, Inés Frid]. Buenos Aires：Editorial Troquel, 1994. 286 pages；23cm. ISBN：9501602478, 9501602470
《易经》

12. El I ching fácil：encuentre todas las respuestas sin ambigüedades en este oráculo milenario/Roderic Sorrell, Amy Max Sorrell；traducción de Teresa Arijón. Buenos Aires：Editorial Sudamericana, 1997. 267 pages：illustrations；23cm. ISBN：9500712806, 9500712804.
Notes：translation of：I ching made easy
《易经》(选译)，Sorrell，Roderic 和 Sorrell，Amy Max 转译自英文版《I ching made easy》一书.

13. Libro de los cambios con ilustraciones/by Li Yan. Beijing：Ediciones En Lenguas Extranjeras, 1998. 461 pages：illustrations；20cm. ISBN：7119019937, 7119019932
《易经画传》，李燕译绘.

14. I Ching/[traducción：Adriana Ortemberg]. Barcelona：Obelisco, 2005. 188 p. ；18cm. ISBN：8497772296, 8497772297. (Nueva consciencia)
《易经》，Ortemberg，Adriana 译.

(1) Barcelona：Obelisco, 2008. 188 p. ：il. ；19cm. ISBN：8496829916, 849682991X. (Books4pocket；91. Narrativa)

15. El Libro de los cambios：con el comentario de Wang Bi/traducción, prólogo y notas del texto：Jordi Vilà；

traducción，prólogo y notas del comentario de Wang Bi；Albert Galvany. Girona：Atalanta，2006. 604 p. ；23cm. ISBN：8493462598，8493462594. （Memoria Mundi；10）

《易经》，Galvany，Albert 译；Vilà，Jordi（Vilà Oliveras）对王弼的《周易注》作了译注.

B22　儒家

B221　四书五经

1. Los grandes libros：filosofía moral y política de la China/Confucio. Madrid：Direcc. y Administración，1905. 199 p. ；16cm. （Biblioteca Económica Filosófica；no. 73）

　Zozaya，Antonio(1859—1947)译. 儒家著作选译.

　(1) Buenos Aires：Eds. Siglo Veinte，1943. 187 p. ；20cm. （Los grandes pensadores）

　(2) Los grandes libros：filosofía moral y política de la China/Confucio；traducción Antonio Zozaya. Buenos Aires Siglo Veinte，1946. 158 p. 20cm. （Grndes Pensadores）

2. Los cuatro libros sagrados de confucio/Prefacio de S. E. Tchen-Loh. Paris，Casa Editorial Franco-Ibero-Americana，1927. 424 pages：illustrations；. （Colección de Libros clásicos orientales）

　《四书》

3. Los libros canónicos chinos：la religión y la filosofía mas antiguas y la moral y la política mas perfectas de la humanidad/Confucio y Mencio；tr.，est. prel. y notas Juan B. Bergua. Madrid：Ediciones Ibéricas，1954. 424 p. ；17cm. （Biblioteca de bolsillo）

　《书经》《大学》《论语》《中庸》《孟子》，Bergua，Juan B. (1892—1991)译注.

　(1) Los libros canónicos chinos：Confucio y Mencio/Juan Baptista Bergua. 2a ed. Madrid：Clásicos Bergua，1969. 635 pages；17cm. （Colección "Tesoro literario"；20）

4. Los cuatro libros：de filosofía moral y política de China/Confucio；versión de J. Farrán y Mayoral；[prefacio del comentario sobre el Ta-hio por el Dr. Tchu-Hi]. Barcelona：José Janés，1954. 313 pages；21cm. （Mensaje. Literatura china）

　《四书》，Farrán y Mayoral，J. 译.

　(1) Barcelona，Esp. ：Plaza & Janés，1982. xiii，313 pages；22cm. ISBN：840137135X 8401371356

　(2) México：Plaza & Janés，1986. xiii，313 p. ；21cm. ISBN：9688560693，9688560693

5. Los cuatro libros/text，Confucio. Tr. J. Farran y Mayoral. Ilus. Chico Prats. [Barcelona]，[Maucci]，1961. 504 pages：illustrations；. （Clasicos Maucci. Literatura antigua）

　《四书》，Farrán Mayoral，José 译.

6. Los cuatro libros/Confucio. Barcelona：Editorial Maucci，1962. 504 p. ：il. ；18cm.

　《四书》

7. Los cuatro libros clasicos/Confucio；con un estudio preliminar y bibliografía seleccionada por Francisco Luis Cardona Castro，y María Montserrat Martí Brugueras；[traducción Oriol Fina Sanglas]. Barcelona：Bruguera，1968. 436 pages；18cm. （Bruguera Libro clásico）

　《四书》，Fina Sanglas，Oriol 译.

　(1) Barcelona，Editorial Bruguera，1972，(c)1971. 436 pages：illustrations；19cm.

　(2) Los cuatro libros clásico/Confucio；traducción O. Fina Sanglas. España：Bruguera，1973. [437] pages. ISBN：8402028578，8402028570

　(3) Barcelona，Esp. ：Bruguera，1975. 436 pages；20cm. ISBN：8402045081，8402045089. （Obras inmortales）

　(4) 4a. ed. Barcelona Bruguera，1978. 437 p. 18cm. ISBN：8402007155，8402007155. （Libro clásico；40）

　(5) Barcelona Ediciones B，1997. 459 p. 19cm. ISBN：8440673329，8440673329. （Biblioteca de bolsillo；41）

　(6) Barcelona Ediciones B，1999. 459 p. 18cm. ISBN：8440693451，8440693457. （VIB；293/1）

8. Los cuatro libros clásicos/Confucio；con un estudio preliminar，notas y bibliografía seleccionada por María Montserrat Martí Brugueras. Barcelona [etc.]：Bruguera，1971. 437 p. （Libro Selección）

　《四书》，Martí Brugueras，María Montserrat 译.

9. Los cuatro libros/Confucio，Mencio；pról. tr. y notas：Joaquín Pèrez Arroyo. 2a ed. Madrid：Alfaguara，1981. LXIX，401 p. ，1 h. ；23cm. ISBN：8420409049，8420409047. （Clásicos Alfaguara）

　《四书》，Pèrez Arroyo，Joaquín 译.

　(1) 3a. ed. Buenos Aires：Alfaguara，1995. lxix，401 p. ：mapas. ISBN：8420428566，8420428567. （Clásicos Alfaguara；22）

　(2) Barcelona：Círculo de Lectores，2001. 543 p. 22cm. ISBN：8422682702，8422682707

　(3) Barcelona：Paidós，2002. 451 p. ；22cm. ISBN：8449312078，8449312076. （Paidos Orientalia；78）

　(4) Barcelona：Paidós，2009. 455 p. ；22cm. ISBN：8449312076，8449312078. （Paidós Orientalia）

　(5) Barcelona：Paidós，2014. 455 p. mapa 22cm. ISBN：8449330148，8449330149. （Paidós orientalia）

10. Los cuatro libros/Confucio；[traducción，selección y notas a cargo de Joaquín Pèrez Arroyo]. Barcelona RBA，2002. 366 p. mapa 22cm. ISBN：8447323420，8447323425. （Biblioteca de la sabiduría oriental）

　《四书》(选)，Pèrez Arroyo，Joaquín 译.

11. Los cuatro libros de la sabiduría/Confucio. Barcelona Edicomunicación，1987. XIX，343 p. 20cm. ISBN：847672134X，8476721346. （Visión libre）

《四书》

(1)Barcelona：Edicomunicación，1998．343 pages；21cm．ISBN：847672134X，8476721346．(Sendero)

12. Los cuatro libros/de Confucio；selección，introducción y notas，Luis Blanco Vila．Madrid Torre de Goyanes，1997．200 p．20cm．ISBN：8492287632，8492287635．(Biblioteca Leyes y letras；2)

《四书》，Blanco Vila，Luis(1936—)译．

13. Los cuatro libros：doctrina de Confucio：filosofía，moral y política de la China/Confucio (Kung-Fu-Tsé o King-Tse)；traducción，prólogo y notas de Juan Bautista Bergua．Madrid Ediciones Ibéricas，2010．281 p．23cm．ISBN：8470831362，8470831364．(Colección La crítica literaria)

《四书》，Bergua，Juan B.(1892—1991)译注．

14. Enseñanzas para la vida y el gobierno：dos textos confucianos，el Da Xue y el Zhong Yong/traducción e introducción de Fernán Alayza Alves-Oliveira y María A. Benavides．Lima Pontificia Universidad Católica del Perú，2004．77 p．21cm．ISBN：9972426661，9972426667．(Colección Orientalia)

《大学》与《中庸》

B222　大学

1. El gran estudio/Confucio．Madrid：Direcc．y Administración，1905．199 p．；16cm．(Bibl．Económica Filosófica；no．73)

《大学》

B223　中庸

1. El centro invariable/Confucio．2．ed．México：Editora y Distribuidora Yug，1990．87 pages：illustrations；21cm．ISBN：9687149191；9687149196．(Sabiduría china；1)

《中庸》

2. El centro invariable/Confucio．Algete，Madrid Mestas，2011．69 p．19cm．ISBN：8492892129，8492892129

《中庸》

B224　书经

1. El Chu-King (Shujing o Shu-Ching)：El libro canónico de la historia/Confucio (Kung-Fu-Tsé)；traducción，prólogo y notas de Juan Bautista Bergua．Madrid Ediciones Ibéricas，2010．183 p．23cm．ISBN：8470831355，8470831356．(Colección La crítica literaria)

《书经》，Bergua，Juan B.(1892—1991)译注．

B225　孔子

1. El evangelio de confucio/Confucio；tr．de Pedro Guirao．Barcelona：B．Bauza，1900—1941?．155 p．

《论语》，Guirao，Pedro 译．

2. Confucio：Las anacletas，el gran compendio，el eje firme/Enrique Hegewicz tr．Barcelona：Las Ediciones Liberales：Labor，1975．ISBN：8433598198，8433598196．(Maldoror；31)

Note：Trad．de：Confucius．The Great digest，The Unwobbling pivot，The Analects．

《论语》，Hegewicz，Enrique(1944—)转译自英文．

3. Las analectas：conversaciones con los discípulos/Confucio；traducción castellana de Mirta Rosenberg，según las versiones inglesas del Dr．Legge y el profesor Soothill．Barcelona：Adíax，1982．ISBN：8485963172，8485963171．154 p．，2 h．20cm．

《论语》，Rosenberg，Mirta(1951—)转译自英文．

4. El arte de ser humano/Confucius；editado y presentado por Thomas Cleary；traducción，Eduard Arnau．Madrid：Tikal Editiones，1996．190 pages；21cm．ISBN：8430581456，8430581450

《论语》，Arnau，Eduard 转译自英文．

5. Confucio esencial：el corazón de las enseñanzas de Confucio ordenadas según el I Ching：un compendio de sabiduria etica/[presentado por] Thomas Cleary；traduccion，Simón Müller．Buenos Aires：Editorial Planeta Argentina，1996，(c)1992．ISBN：9507427171，9507427176．

《论语》，Thomas Cleary 英译；Simón Müller 西译．

6. Proverbios selectos de Confucio：Lun Yu/Waley，Arthur；tr．Francisco J．Perea．México：Diana，1997．255 p．；21cm．ISBN：9681330315；9681330316

Notes：Traducción de：The analects of Confucius

《论语警句选译》，Francisco J．Perea 转译自英文．

7. Lun yu：reflexiones y enseñanzas/Confucio (Maestro Kong)；traducción del chino，introducción y notas de Anne-Hélène Suárez Girard．Barcelona Kairós，1997．193 p．20cm．ISBN：8472453669，8472453661．(Clásicos Kairós)

《论语》，Suárez Girard，Anne-Hélène(1960—)译．

(1)2a ed．Barcelona：Editorial Kairós，2002．193 pages：map；20cm．ISBN：8472453669，8472453661

8. Analectas/Confuci，versión y notas de Simón Leys；[traducido por Alfonso Colodrón]．Madrid：EDAF，1998．308 p．ISBN：8441403171，8441403178．(Arca de sabiduría；38)

Note：Trad．de：The analects of Confucius．

《论语》，Colodrón，Alfonso 译．转译自英文．

(1)2a．ed．Madrid：Edaf，2005．308 p．；18cm．ISBN：8441403171，8441403178．(Arca de sabiduría；38)

(2)3a ed．Madrid EDAF，2006．308 p．18cm．ISBN：8441403171，8441403178．(Arca de sabiduría；38)

(3)Barcelona：Círculo de Lectores，2008．278 p．；21cm．ISBN：8467231885，8467231882

(4)8a ed．Madrid；México：Edaf，2011．308 p．；18cm．ISBN：8441403178，441403171．(Arca de sabiduría；38)

9. Analectas：reflexiones y enseñanzas/Confucio；edición de Joaquín Pèrez Arroyo．Barcelona：Círculo de Lectores，

1999. 259 p. 19cm. ISBN：8422676788，8422676782
《论语》，Pèrez Arroyo, Joaquín 译.

10. La sabiduría de Confucio/compilación y prólogo, Silvia Arrau；[traducción, María Merino]. Buenos Aires：Longseller，2000. 158 p. ：il. ；16cm. ISBN：9507398961, 9507398964

   孔子言论选译. Merino，María 译.

11. Lunyu /Confuci, Anne-Hélène Suárez ed. Ed. bilingüe. Ed. no venal. Barcelona：Random House Mondadori, 2002. 319 p. ；20cm.

   《论语》，Suárez, Anne-Hélène(1960—)译.

   (1)Ed. bilingüe. Barcelona Random House Mondadori, 2006. 319 p. ；24cm.

12. Las analectas（Lun Yu）：enseñanzas, orientaciones y consejos/Confucio；Jerónimo Sahagún, tr.. Palma de Mallorca：José J. de Olañeta, 2003. 188 p. ；14 cm. ISBN：8497161807；8497161800. (Los pequeños libros de la sabiduría；84)

   《论语》，Jerónimo Sahagún 译注.

13. El hombre superior y el arte de gobernar/Confucio；selección y comentarios de Norberto Tucci. Madrid Librería Argentina，2007. 91 p. 24cm. ISBN：8485895069, 8485895061. (Colección Clásicos de la estrategia oriental)

   《论语》，Tucci, Norberto 选译.

14. Analectas/Confucio；Néstor Cabrera. Madrid：Editorial Popular，2009. 222 p. 24cm. ISBN：8478844289, 8478844287. (Asiateca；4；)

   《论语》，Néstor Cabrera 译.

   (1)Madrid Kailas，2014. 243 p. 18cm. ISBN：8416023516, 8416023514. (Clásicos/Editorial Kailas)

15. Analectas/Confucio. Madrid：Verbum, 2015. 84 p. 19cm. ISBN：8490742150, 8490742154. (Asia)

   《论语》

16. 论语. 香港：孔学出版社，1985. 6 volumes in 5 cases：illustrations. ISBN：9627050016（set），9627050018（set），9627050024（v. 1），9627050025（v. 1），9627050032（v. 2），9627050032（v. 2），9627050040（v. 3），9627050049（v. 3），9627050059（v. 4），9627050056（v. 4），9627050075（v. 5），9627050070（v. 5），9627050057(v. 6)

   Contents：v. 1—2. Qing Kangxi yu zhi "Ri jiang si shu jie yi" xuan kan. —v. 3. Bai hua Lun yu. —v. 4. The Lun Yü in English. —v. 5. El Lun Yü en español. —v. 6. O Lun Yü em português.

   第五卷为《论语》，西班牙语版.

17. La sabiduria de confucio/Lin Yutang. [traduciod del inglés por Elena Dukelsky Yoffe. Ilustrado por Jeanyee Wong. Buenos Aires：Ediciones Siglo Veinte, 1946. 304 pages：illustrations（including map）color plates；23cm.

   《孔子的智慧》，Dukelsky，Elena 转译自林语堂（1895—1976)的英文图书《Wisdom of Confucius》

(1) Buenos Aires：Siglo Veinte, 1952. 282 p. ：ilus. ；23cm.

(2) Buenos Aires：Siglo Veinte, 1974. 270 p. ；20cm.

(3) Buenos Aires：Siglo XX, 1978. 270 p.

(4) Buenos Aires：Ediciones Siglo Veinte, 1987. 270 pages；20cm. ISBN：9505160420

18. Confucio：un filósofo para la eternidad/por Xu Yuanxiang. ［Beijing]：China Intercontinental Press, 2010. 109 pages：color illustrations；21cm. ISBN：7508516493, 7508516494. (Sabios antiguos de China)

   《一代宗师：孔子》，徐远翔[著]. 五洲传播出版社.

B226 孟子

1. La historia de Mencio/Cao Raode, Cao Xiaomei. México：Prana：Lectorum；Miami Florida：Books, 2006. 207, [3] p. ；21cm. ISBN：9707321946, 9707321946

   《孟子的故事》，曹尧德，曹笑梅. 转译自英文《The story of Mencius》一书.

2. Mencio：un santo para la eternidad/por Xu Yuanxiang & Zhang Bing. Beijing：China Intercontinental Press, 2010. 81 pages：color illustrations, portraits；21cm. ISBN：7508516479, 7508516478. (Sabios antiguos de China)

   《亚圣：孟子》，徐远翔，张兵[著]. 五洲传播出版社.

B227 荀子

1. Xunzi. China Books & Periodicals, 2015. ISBN：0835102179, 0835102173

   《荀子》

B23 道家

B231 道家著作合集

1. Dos grandes maestros del taoísmo/Lao Tse, Chuang Tzu；edición preparada por Carmelo Elorduy. Madrid：Editora Nacional, 1977. 646 p. ；18cm. ISBN：8427603916, 8427603912. (Biblioteca de la literatura y el pensamiento universales；18)

   《道德经》与《庄子》，Elorduy, Carmelo（1901—1989 年）编译.

   (1)2a. ed. Madrid：Nacional, 1983. 646 p. ；18cm. ISBN：8427603916, 8427603912. （Biblioteca de la literatura y el pensamiento universal；18)

2. Las mejores leyendas Taoistas/Lieh-Tzu, et al. Buenos Aires, Argentina：Longseller, 2002. 192 pages；16cm. ISBN：9875500658, 9875500655. (Classicos de Bolsillo)

   《列子》和《庄子》

3. Enseñanzas taoístas/Chuang Tse, Lie Tse, Lao Tse；introducción, versión y notas：P. H. Delcius. Barcelona：MRA, 1996. 117 p. ：il. ；22cm. ISBN：8488865201, 8488865205. （Aurum)

   《庄子》《列子》和《道德经》，Delcius, P. H. 译.

4. Tao te ching：el libro clásico de la sabiduría china；segunda parte, Hua Hu Ching：apêndice, textos

inspiradores de los maestros taoístas/Lao Tse；［textos Hua hu ching traducidos por Cecilia Montesinos］. Barcelona Océano Ámbar, 2004. 311 p. il. col. 24cm. ISBN：8475560512, 8475560519.

《道德经》和《庄子》

5. Los cuatro libros del emperador amarillo/edición y traducción de Iñaki Preciado Idoeta. Madrid：Trotta, 2010. 180 pages；23cm. ISBN：8498791402,8498791405. (Pliegos de oriente)

《黄帝四经》，Preciado Idoeta，Iñaki 编译.

B232　道德经

1. Libro del sendero y de la linea recta/Lao Tse；única versión castellana y prólogo de Edmundo Montagne. Buenos Aires：Minerva, 1924. 81 p.；19cm.

《道德经》，Montange，Edmundo(1880—)译.

(1)Buenos Aires：Editorial Kier, 1947. 126 pages；21cm. (colección Miscelanea)

(2)2a. edición. Buenos Aires：Editorial Kier, 1966. 126 pages；19cm.

(3) 6. ed. Buenos Aires：Editorial Kier, 1979. 126 pages；20cm.

(4) 8. ed. Buenos Aires：Editorial Kier, 1985. 126 pages；21cm. ISBN：9501707253, 9501707250. (Colección Miscelanea)

2. El evangelio del Tao：del libro sagrado Tao tê ching/［Lao Tseu］；traducción de Pedro Guirao. Barcelona B. Bauzá, 1931. 156 p. 19cm. (Biblioteca de Teosofía y Orientalismo；1)

《道德经》，Guirao，P. 译.

(1)El evangelio del Tao/Lao-tse. Barcelona Edicomunicación, 1991. 156 p. 21cm. ISBN：8476723504, 8476723500. (Visión libre)95.

(2)Barcelona Edicomunicación, 2002. 156 p. 20cm. ISBN：8476723504, 8476723500. (Sendero)

3. Tao-teh-king：(El libro del camino recto)/Laoze；［traducción C. Serra］. Palma de Mallorca：Editorial Clumba, 1952. 97,［2］pages：illustrations；13cm.

《道德经》

4. El tao tê king de Lao Tse/［traductor］Adolfo P. Carpio. Buenos Aires：Editorial Sudamericana, 1957. 181 pages；21cm. (Colección Oriente y Occidente)

《道德经》，Carpio，Adolfo P. 译.

5. La gnosis taoista del Tao Te Ching/Lao-tse. Análisis y traducción por Carmelo Elorduy. Oña, Spain：［publisher not identified］, 1961. xlvi, 225 pages；25cm. (Facultad de Teologia del Colegio Maximo S. I. de Oña. Estudios Onienses, ser. 2；v. 3)

《老子道德经》，Elorduy，Carmelo(1901—1989 年)译.

(1) Caracas：Instituto de Investigaciones Históricas, Universidad Católica "Andres Bello", 1973. 159 pages；24cm.

6. Tao te ching/Lao Tse；［edición preparada por Carmelo Elorduy］. Esplugues de Llobregat, Barcelona：Orbis, 1983. 143 p. ISBN：8475304613；8475304618. (Historia del pensamiento；12)

《道德经》，Elorduy，Carmelo(1901—1989 年)译.

7. Tao te ching/Lao-Tse；traducción y análisis de Carmelo Elorduy. Madrid：Tecnos, 1996. 266 pages；21cm. ISBN：8430929452, 8430929450. (Filosofía y ensayo)

《道德经》，Elorduy，Carmelo(1901—1989 年)译.

(1) Madrid：Tecnos, 2003. 266 p.：il.；22cm. ISBN：8430929452, 8430929450. (Filosofía y ensayo)

(2)2a ed. Madrid：Tecnos, 2012. 266 pages；22cm. ISBN：8430954551, 8430954554

8. Lao Tse (viejo maestro) ỳ su Libro del camino y de la virtud/Taiji Yamaga；traducido del Esperanto por Eduardo Vivancos；introducción y una breve excursión sobre el pensamiento en la China antigua por Victor Garcia. Mexico, D. F.：Tierra y Libertad, 1963. 124 pages：portraits；15cm. (Colleción Historia del anarquismo；2)

《道德经》，Vivancos，Eduardo 译自世界语.

9. Tao te king/Laoze；［versión］, Roberto Pla. México, D. F.：Diana, 1972. 125 pages；19cm. (Colección Tradición sagrada de la humanidad；5)

《道德经》，Pla，Roberto 译.

(1)México：Diana,1980. 125 p.；19cm. ISBN：9681309804, 9681309800. (Colección Tradición sagrada de la humanidad；5)

10. Tao te king/versión y prefacio de José M. Tola. ［2a. ed.］. Barcelona Barral Editores, 1973. 101 p. 19cm. ISBN：8421172204, 8421172209. (Ediciones de Bolsillo Clásicos. Religión；v. 220)

《道德经》

(1)2a Ed. México：Ediciones Coyoacán, 1996. 185 p.；21cm. ISBN：9706330801, 9706330802

(2)5a ed. México, D. F. Ediciones Coyoacán,1998. 185,［7］p. 21cm. ISBN：9706330801, 9706330802. (Dialogo abierto；39)

11. Tao-te-king. ［3a. ed.］. Madrid Ricardo Aguilera, 1973. 93 p. 18cm. ISBN：847005158X, 8470051586. (Colección Orbe. Serie Monografias；v. 13)

《道德经》

(1)［4a. ed.］. Madrid Ricardo Aguilera, 1974. 93 p. 18cm.

(2)［5a. ed.］. Madrid Ricardo Aguilera, 1975. 93 p. 18cm. ISBN：847005158X, 8470051586. (Colección Orbe. Serie Monografías；v. 13)

(3) 6a. ed. Madrid Ricardo Aguilera, 1979. 93 p. 17cm. ISBN：847005158X, 8470051586. (Colección Orbe. Serie Monografías；13)

12. Tao tê ching＝（El libro del recto camino）/Lao-Tsé；〔nueva traducción realizada por Ch'u ta-Kao；prólogo por el Dr. Lionel Giles；introducción y versión española de la Lda. Caridad Díaz-Faes；revisión，notas adicionales，comentarios，apêndice sobre "Educación y Cultura" y bibliografía por Gonzalo Gonzalvo Mainar〕. 3a. ed. Madrid Morata，1975. 131 p. 21cm. ISBN：8471121166，8471121165

《道德经》，初大告原译；Díaz-Faes，Caridad 西译.

（1）4a. ed. Madrid Morata，1979. 127 p. 21cm. ISBN：8471121166，8471121165.（Colección Filosofía）

（2）5a ed. Madrid；Morata，1980. ISBN：8471121166，8471121165.（Filosofía）

13. Tao Tê Ching/Lao Tzu；nueva traduccion de Ch'u Ta-kao；traducido al Español por Ines Frid a partir de la traduccion directa del Chino al Ingles de Ch'u Ta-kao. Buenos Aires；Troquel Editorial，1993. 137 p. ；13cm. ISBN：9501602281，9501602289.

《道德经》，初大告英译；Frid，Ines 转译成西文.

14. El Tao para todos/Lao Tse；traducción，Ch'u Ta Kao；〔ilustraciones，Daniel Santoro〕；prólgo y nueva versión，Ricardo A. Parada. Buenos Aires；Deva's，2002. 142 pages；color illustrations；20cm. ISBN：9871102038，9871102037.（Inspiración）

《道德经》，转译自初大告的英译版本.

（1）Buenos Aires；Longseller，2004. 123 pages；18cm. ISBN：9875503886，9875503885.（Clásicos de siempre. Grandes maestros；2）

15. El Daode Jing/Lao Ze. Buenos Aires；Ediciones Andrómeda，1976. 153 pages

《道德经》

16. Lao zi (El libro del Tao)/traducción，prólogo y notas de Juan Ignacio Preciado. Ed. bilingüe. Madrid；Ediciones Alfaguara，1978. lxxvi，278 pages；20cm. ISBN：8420409022，8420409023，8420409014，8420409016.（Clásicos Alfaguara）

《道德经》，Preciado Ydoeta，Juan Ignacio 译. 西汉对照. 译自长沙马王堆三号汉墓出土的帛书《道德经》版本.

（1）El libro del Tao/Lao Zi；traducción，prólogo y notas，Juan Ignacio Preciado. Ed. bilingüe，〔2a. ed.〕. Madrid；Alfaguara，1981. LXXVI，278 p. ；21cm. ISBN：8420409014，8420409016，8420409022，8420409023.（Clásicos Alfaguara；10）

（2）Ed. bilingüe，〔5a. ed.〕. Madrid；Alfaguara，1986. LXXVI，278 p. ；21cm. ISBN：8420409014，8420409016.（Clásicos Alfaguara；10）

（3）El libro del Tao/Lao Zi；〔traducción，prólogo y notas，Iñaki Preciado Ydoeta〕. Madrid Alfaguara，1996. 278 p. 18cm. ISBN：8420483036，8420483030.（Alfaguara bolsillo；43；Clásica）

（4）El libro del Tao/Lao Zi；presentación de Raimon Panikkar；traducción，introducción y notas de J. I. Preciado Idoeta. Barcelona Círculo de Lectores，2001. 297 p. 22cm. ISBN：8422682648，8422682646.（Sabiduría oriental）

（5）Barcelona RBA，2002. 348 p. 20cm. ISBN：8447323366，8447323364.（Biblioteca de los grandes pensadores）

17. Tao Te Ching：los libros del Tao/Lao Tse；edición y traducción del chino de Iñaki Preciado Idoeta. Madrid：Editorial Trotta，2006. 542 p. ；24cm. ISBN：8481648353，8481648355

《道德经》，Preciado Idoeta，Iñaki 译.

（1）Madrid；Trotta，2010. 542 p. ；24cm. ISBN：8481648355.（Pliegos de Oriente. Serie Lejano Oriente）

（2）3a ed. Madrid；Trotta，2016. 542 p. ；24cm. ISBN：8481648355，8481648353.（Pliegos de Oriente. Serie Lejano Oriente）

18. Tao te king/Lao Tse；pref. y tr. José M. Tola. México；Premia Editora，1977. 189 p. ；22cm.

《道德经》，Tola，José M. 译.

（1）3e ed. Mexico，D. F. ：Premià Editora，1978. 189 pages；illustrations；22cm. ISBN：9684340087，9684340084.（La nave de los locos；1）

（2）5a ed. México；Premia，1981. 185 p. ；22cm.

（3）Séptima edición. México；Premià，1985. 185 pages；21cm. ISBN：9684340087，9684340084.（La nave de los locos；1）

（4）9 ed. México；Premia，1990. 185 p. ；21cm. ISBN：9684340087，9684340084.（La nave de los locos；1）

19. El camino y su poder：el tao tê ching y su lugar en el pensamiento chino/〔introducción y traducción al inglés por〕Arthur Waley；versión española de la 7a ed. inglesa por Héctor V. Morel. Buenos Aires：Editorial Kier，1979. 189 pages；20cm.（Colección Horus）

译自英文《Way and its power》一书，包括《道德经》的西文翻译.

（1）Barcelona RBA，2006. 366 p. il. ，mapas 22cm. ISBN：8447347524，8447347520

20. Recopilaciones taoístas：incluye una versión actual del Tao-te-ching/Waldemar Verdugo-Fuentes. 〔Mexico City〕：Editorial Katún，1983. 195 pages，〔6〕leaves of plates：illustrations；24cm. ISBN：9684300271，9684300279.（Oriente-Occidente；1）

《道德经》，Verdugo-Fuentes，Waldemar 译.

21. Tao te ching/Lao-Tsé〔i. e. Lao-tzu〕；version castellana y notas A. Laurent. Barberá del Vallés（Barcelona）：Teorema，1983. 128 pages；15cm. ISBN：8485958829，8485958825

《道德经》，Laurent，Alberto 译注.

（1）Barcelona Edicomunicación，1986. 128 p. 15cm. ISBN：847672036X，8476720363

22. Tao-te-king/Lao-Tzu；prólogo de Luis Racionero；[versión española de Gloria Peradejordi]. Barcelona Obelisco, 1983. 95 p. 21cm. ISBN：8486000246, 8486000240

《道德经》，Peradejordi, Gloria 译.

(1)Barcelona Obelisco,1986. 95 p. 21cm. ISBN：8486000246, 8486000240

(2)Barcelona Obelisco,1995. 95 p. 21cm. ISBN：8477201390, 8477201397. (La aventura interior)

23. Tao the king/Lao-Tzu. Madrid Ziggurat, 1984. 122 p. 16cm. ISBN：8485882032, 8485882038. (Colección Sumeru；2)

《道德经》

24. Tao te ching/Lao Tse. [Esplugas de Llobregat, Barcelona] Orbis,1984. 143 p. 20cm. ISBN：8475304613,8475304618. (Historia del pensamiento；12)

《道德经》

25. Lao Tse y su tratado sobre la virtud del Tao [Tao Te Ching]/Lao Tse；Samuel Wolpin. 2a. ed. Buenos Aires：Kier, 1985. 159 p. ；20cm. ISBN：9501701271, 9501701272. (Horus)

《道德经》，Wolpin, Samuel 译.

26. Tao：los tres tesoros：charlas acerca de fragmentos del Tao te ching de Lao tse/Bhagwan Shree Rajnesh [sic；traducción del inglés, Swami Dhyan Mandir]. Málaga：Editorial Sirio, 1985. v. 〈1〉(283 p.)21cm. ；21cm. ISBN：8486221102, 8486221102

Notes：Translation of：Tao：the three treasures.

Osho(1931—1990)译自英文版《Tao：the three treasures》一书,包括《道德经》的翻译.

27. Tao te king/Lao-Tze；[traducción de Miguel Shiao]. Madrid [Miguel Shiao], 1985. 94 p. 17cm. ISBN：8439840721, 8439840725. (Colección Extremo Oriente；3)

《道德经》，Shiao, Miguel 译.

(1)2a. ed. Madrid (Apdo. 8351)M. Shiao, 1995. 107 p. 17cm. ISBN：8460530957, 8460530954. (Colección Extremo Oriente；3)

28. Tao te king/Lao Tse；[traducción Ramón Hervás]. Barcelona Ediciones 29, 1986. 100 p. 19cm. ISBN：8471752328, 8471752321

《道德经》，Hervás, Ramón 译.

(1)3a. ed. Barcelona Ediciones 29,1989. 100 p. 19cm. ISBN：8471753111,8471753113,8471752328,8471752321. (Grandes autores)

(2)San Cugat del Vallés (Barcelona) Ediciones 29, 2002. 95 p. 13cm. ISBN：8471754983, 8471754981

29. Tao-tê-ching/Lao-Tsé；[traducción de Susana Cano Méndez]. Madrid Alba, 1987. 109 p. 18cm. ISBN：847567058X, 8475670584. (Literatura universal；58)

《道德经》，Cano Méndez, Susana 译.

(1)4a. reimp. Alcobendas (Madrid) Alba,1999. 109 p. 18cm. ISBN：847567058X, 8475670584. (Colección Literatura universal Alba)

30. Tao te king/Lao Tse；[versión de Richard Wilhelm]. Barcelona：Edicomunicación, 1988. 121 pages；20cm. (Colección visión libre)

《道德经》，Lozano Mitter, Pedro 译自德文版.

(1)Tao te king/Lao Tse；según la versión inglesa de Richard Wilhelm；traducción, Pedro Lozano Mitter. Barcelona Edicomunicación, 1994. 125 p. 18cm. ISBN：8476726104, 8476726105. (Colección Fontana；10)

(2)Santa Perpetua de Mogoda, Barcelona Brontes, 2009. 125 p. 18cm. ISBN：8496975514, 8496975517. (Fontana. Serie C；9；Literatura universal)

31. Tao Te Ching/Lao-Tse；prólogo, comentarios y traducción Leonor Calvera. Buenos Aires：Leviatān, 1989. 218 p. ；20cm. ISBN：9505164260

《道德经》，Calvera, Leonor 译.

32. Tao te king/Lao Tse；[traducido del alemán por Marie Wohlfeil y Manuel P. Esteban]. Málaga Sirio, 1989. 260 p. 21cm. ISBN：847808065X

《道德经》，Wohfeil, Marie 和 Esteban, Manuel P. 译自德文版.

(1)7a ed. Málaga：Sirio, 2002. 260 p. ；21cm. ISBN：8478080570, 8478080571

(2)Málaga：Sirio,2009. 267 p. ；22cm. ISBN：8478086252, 8478086250

33. Dao de jing/Lao Ze. Chile：Texido, 1993. 112 pages；22cm. (Metafísica)

《道德经》

34. Dao De Jing/Lao Ze. Chile：E. T. E.；Barcelona：Galaxia del Libro,1993. 112 pages；21cm. (Metafísica)

《道德经》

35. Tao te king/Lao Tse；versión de John C. W. Wu；traducido por Alfonso Colodrón. Madrid：EDAF, 1993. 111 pages；18cm. ISBN：8476406541. 8476406540. (Arca de sabiduría；2)

《道德经》，吴经熊(1899—1986)英译；Colodrón, Alfonso 转译成西文.

(1)Barcelona Círculo de Lectores, 2008. 112 p. 21cm. ISBN：8467231892, 8467231890

(2)Madrid Edaf,2016. 111 p. 18cm. ISBN：8441436442, 8441436444. (Arca de sabiduría)

36. Tao te king/Lao Tsé；[traducción, Alfonso Colodrón]. Madrid Edaf, 2002. 176 p. 16cm. ISBN：8441411093, 8441411098. (Joyas Edaf)

《道德经》，Colodrón, Alfonso 译.

37. Tao te ching al alcance de todos：el libro del equilibrio/Alfonso Colodrón. Madrid：Editorial Edaf, 2009. 252 pages；21cm. ISBN：8441421035, 844142103X. (Luz de oriente)

38. Tao-te-king de Lao-Tse：el taoísmo y la inmortalidad/versión y estudio de Antonio Medrano. Madrid América Ibérica, 1994. 255 p. 22cm. ISBN：8488337027, 8488337023. (Biblioteca fundamental；16)

《道德经》,Medrano, Antonio(1946—)译.

39. Las mil y una noches. El libro del Tao/Lao Tsé；[traducción (de la primera obra) de Jesús Cabanillas, (de la segunda) de León Wieger]. [Barcelona] Salvat, 1995. 302 p. 22cm. ISBN：8434592681, 8434592681. (Grandes obras de la literatura universal. Clásicos orientales)

《道德经》

40. Tao teh ching：la obra clásicas de Lao Tzu/traducción del idioma original y dilucidación por Hua-Ching Ni. Santa Monica：Seven Star Communications, 1995. 110 pages；illustrations；22cm. ISBN：0937064920, 0937064924

《道德经》,Ni, Hua Ching 译.

41. Tao te Ching：el libro clásico de la sabiduría china/fotografías：Juan Carlos Muñoz [and others]. Barcelona：Oásis, 1995. 189 pages：Fotografías；24cm. ISBN：8479011416, 8479011413

《道德经》

(1) 2. ed. Barcelona：RBA, 1998. 189 pages：color illustrations；24cm. ISBN：8479011416 8479011413

42. La luz del Tao/Antonio Medrano. [Madrid]：Yatay, 1996. 255 pages：illustrations；21cm. ISBN：8492158212, 8492158218.

《道德经》,Medrano, Antonio 译.

43. Hua hu ching：81 meditaciones taoístas/Lao Tse；versión de Brian Walker. Madrid：EDAF, 1996. 147 pages：illustrations；18cm. ISBN：8476409516, 8476409510. (Arca de sabiduría；19)

《道德经》,Walker, Brian Browne 译.

44. Tao Te King：el libro del Tao/Lao Ze；traducción del inglés de Esteve Serra. Palma de Mallorca：José J. de Olañeta, 1997. 109 pages；14cm. ISBN：8476516711, 8476516713. (Los pequeños libros de la sabiduría；13)

《道德经》

(1)Palma de Mallorca José J. de Olañeta, 2008. 101 p. 19cm. ISBN：8497165570, 8497165578. (Padma；17)

(2)Palma [de Mallorca] José J. de Olañeta, 2016. 109 p. 14cm. ISBN：8476516713, 8476516711. (Los pequeños libros de la sabiduría；13)

45. Tao te king/Lao Tzŭ. Barcelona Obelisco, 1997. 94 p. 17cm. ISBN：8477205744, 8477205746. (Colección Obelisco-bolsillo)

《道德经》

(1) 7a. ed. Barcelona Obelisco, 2005. 94 p. 21cm. ISBN：8497771001, 8497771009. (Colección Textos tradicionales)

46. Tao Te King/Lao Tsé；tr. y comentarios David García Walker. México：Colofon, 1997. 101 pages；21cm. ISBN：9688671037, 9688671030. (Ensayo. Folosofía)

《道德经》,García Walker, David 译评.

47. El libro del Tao/Lao Tse；tr. del Inglés Esteve Serra. México：Taurus, 1997. 96 p. ；cm. ISBN：6071122568, 6071122562

《道德经》, Golden, Seán 译自英文版.

(1)El libro del Tao/Lao Tse；traducción de Seán Golden. [Madrid] Taurus, 2012.

(2)México：Taurus, 2012. 91 p. ；18cm. ISBN：6071122568, 6071122562. (Great ideas；17)

(3)Barcelona Círculo de Lectores, 2014. 97 p. 18cm. ISBN：8467259247, 8467259248. (Great ideas)

48. Tao te king/Lao Tse. , David Garcia, Tr. Mexico：Colofon, 1997. 101 P. ；21cm. ISBN：9687396059, 9687396057

《道德经》,David Garcia 译.

49. Tao te king：libro del curso y de la virtud/Lao Zi；prólogo, François Jullien；edición y traducción del chino, Anne-Hélène Suárez. Madrid Siruela, 1998. 194 p. 22cm. ISBN：8478444270, 8478444274. (El árbol del paraíso；15)

《道德经》,Suárez Girard, Anne-Hélène(1960—)译.

(1)3a. ed. Madrid Siruela, 2003. 194 p. 22cm. ISBN：8478444270, 8478444274. (El árbol del paraíso；15)

(2)5a. ed. Madrid [Spain]：Siruela, 2009. 194 pages；22cm. ISBN：8478444270, 8478444274. (El arbol del paraiso；15)

(3) 6a ed. Madrid：Ediciones Siruela, 2011. 194 p. ；22cm. ISBN：8478444274, 8478444270. (El Árbol del Paraíso；15)

(4)Tao-te-king：libro del curso y de la virtud/Lao zi；prólogo de François Jullien；edición y traducción del chino de Anne-Hélène Suárez Girard. Madrid Siruela, 2015. 194 p. 22cm. ISBN：8416396832, 8416396833. (El árbol del paraíso；83)

50. Dao de jing/Lao Zi；introducción y traducción de Anne-Hélène Suárez Girard. Ed. bilingüe. , ed. no venal. Barcelona：Random House Mondadori, 2007. 293 p. ；24cm.

Notes：Text en castellà i xinès

《道德经》,Suárez Girard, Anne-Hélène(1960—)译.西汉对照.

51. Tao te king/Lao Tze；[traducción, Gia-fu Feng, José Aguado y Juan S. Paz]. Madrid：Mandala, 1998. 175 p. ；ill. ；15cm. ISBN：8488769784, 8488769787

《道德经》,译自英语.

52. Tao-te-ching/Lao-Tse；edición de Luis Racionero；[traducción de Jordi Fibla]. [Barcelona] Martínez Roca,

1999. 153 p. 19cm. ISBN：8427024983，8427024984.
(Clásicos de la sabiduría)

《道德经》，Fibla，Jordi 译.

(1)Madrid Martínez Roca，2007. 153 p. 19cm. ISBN：
8427024984，8427024983.（Clásicos de la sabiduría）

53. Tao Te King/Laozi；versión e introducción de Ursula K.
Le Guin；[versión castellana de Francisco Páez de la
Cadena]. Madrid：Editorial Debate，1999. 143 pages；
20cm. ISBN：8483061937，8483061930.（Siete libros
para acercarse a Oriente；4）

《道德经》，Le Guin，Ursula K.（1929—）和 Páez de la
Cadena，Francisco 合译.

54. Tao tê ching：libro del camino y de la virtud/Lao-Tzu；
traducción，J. J. López. Ed. íntegra. Algete (Madrid)：
JM Ediciones，1999. 124 pages；19cm. ISBN：
8489163804，8489163805.（Clásicos universales；44）

《道德经》，López，J. J. 译.

(1)2. ed.，Ed. íntegra. Algete（Madrid）：JM
Ediciones，2001. ISBN：8489163804，8489163805.
（Clásicos universales；44）

55. Tao Te King/Lao-Tse. El libro del té/Kakuzo Okakura.
Barcelona：Edicomunicación，1999. 221 pages；19cm.
ISBN：8476729251，8476729250.（Colección cultura；
25）

Notes：Translation of：The Tao Teh King. Originally
published as：Dao de jing. / Translators：Pedro Lozano
Mitter，A. Laurent.

包括《道德经》的西译.

56. Tao te ching/Lao Tse. Barcelona：Azul，1999. 251 p.；
21cm. ISBN：8493044040，8493044046.（La aljaba）

《道德经》

57. Tao- tê-ching/Lao-Tsé. San Jose，[California]：
ToExcel；[Barcelona]：Alba，2000. 109 pages；23cm.
ISBN：1583488162，1583488164

《道德经》

58. Tao te king/Lao Tse. México, D. F.：Fontamara，2000.
104 p.；21cm. ISBN：9684763522，9684763524.
（Colección Fontamara；258）

《道德经》

59. Tao te ching/Lao Tsé. Barcelona Fapa，2001. 63 p.
22cm. ISBN：8495272709，8495272706，8497330587，
8497330589.（Colección Autoayuda；n. 10）

《道德经》

(1)Barcelona FAPA，2008. 59 p. 22cm. ISBN：
8497335287，8497335287.（Colección Autayuda；
no. 25）

60. Tao te ching/Lao Tse. Barcelona：RBA，2002. 201
pages；color illustrations；22cm. ISBN：8479018828，
8479018825.（Integral）

《道德经》

61. Tao te king/Lao Tse. [Barcelona] Índigo，2002. 95 p.

20cm. ISBN：8489768633，8489768635.（Clásicos esotéricos）

《道德经》

62. Tao te king/introducción y comentarios por Stephen
Hodge；[traducción，Fermín Navascués]. Madrid Edaf，
2003. 176 p. il. color，mapa 25cm. ISBN：8441412944，
8441412941.（Arca de sabiduría）

《道德经》，Navascués，Fermín 译.

63. El Tao te ching，de Lao-tze：el libro del tao y la virtud，
comentado：bilingüe：chino，español/[edición española，
Ángel Fdez. de Castro；traducción，Tseng Juo ching y
Ángel Fdez. de Castro]. Romanones (Guadalajara) Tao，
2003. 252 p. il. 21cm. ISBN：8493254711，8493254711.
（Joyas de la humanidad）

《道德经》，Fernández de Castro，Ángel（1951—）和
Tseng，Juo Ching 合译. 西汉对照.

64. Tao teh king/Lao Tse；[traducido del inglés por Curro
Bermejo]. [Ed. bilingüe]. Málaga Sirio，2004. 173 p.
21cm. ISBN：847808441X，8478084418

《道德经》，Bermejo，Curro 译. 西汉对照

(1) Tao teh king = 道德经/Lao Tse；[traducido del
inglés por Curro Bermejo]. Lao Tse；[traducido del
inglés por Curro Bermejo]. 2a ed.；edición bilingüe.
Málaga：Editorial Sirio，2009. 173 pages；21cm.
ISBN：8478086368，8478086366

65. Tao te ching/[Lao-Tse]；texto chino de Wang Pi；
traducción de José Ramón Álvarez. Ed. bilingüe.
México，D. F.：Saga Ediciones，2004. 205 pages；
22cm. ISBN：9685830053，9685830058.

《道德经》，Alvarez，J. R.（José Ramón）译自王弼的《道
德经注》，中西对照.

66. Tao te Ching：el libro clásico de la sabiduría china/Lao
Tse；[versión en español，Hilda Parisi]. Barcelona：
Oceano，2004. 105 pages；13cm. ISBN：8475563422，
8475563428.（Armonía Esencial；Oceano Ambar）

《道德经》，Parisi，Hilda 译.

67. Dao de Jing/tratado clásico de Dào Dé de Lao Zi；versión
de Samuel Lapaz. Barcelona：Aixa，2005. 165 p.：il.；
21cm. ISBN：8493346934，8493346935

《道德经》，Lapaz，Samuel 译.

68. Tao te king/Lao Tse；versión de Norberto Tucci. 3a.
ed. Madrid Librería Argentina，2005. 94 p. 21cm.
ISBN：848983637X，8489836372.（Colección Clásicos
de la estrategia oriental [i. e. de Oriente]）

《道德经》，Tucci，Norberto 译.

(1) Madrid Librería Argentina，2011. 117 p. 16cm. ISBN：
8499500423，8499500420.（Colección Empresa）

69. Laotsé/[texto introducción y selección de textos
originales，Luis Ángel Naranjo；[prólogo，Fernando
Sánchez Dragón]. Madrid Club Internacional del Libro，
2006. 152 p. 19cm. ISBN：8482656731，8482656732.
（Pensamiento y felicidad）

《道德经》,Naranjo, Luis Ángel 选译.

70. Tao te king/Lao-tse. 3a ed. México, D. F. Grupo Editorial Tomo,2006. 122 p. 19cm. ISBN：9706660070, 9706660077. (Clásicos oriente)

《道德经》

71. Dao de zhen jing/Lao Zi; traducción del chino y prólogo de Fernán Alayza Alves-Oliveira y María A. Benavides. ［Lima］：Pontificia Universidad Católica del Peru, 2006. 295 pages：portraits；24cm. ISBN：9972659453, 9972659454. (El manantial oculto；53)

《道德经》,Alves-Oliveira, Fernán Alayza 和 Benavides, María A. 合译.

72. Tao Te Ching/Lao Tse. Barcelona Folio, 2006. 56 p. 19cm. ISBN：8441321884, 8441321885. (Grandes ideas)

《道德经》

73. El libro del Tao/Lao Zi. ［Barcelona］RBA, 2006. 203 p. il. 22cm. ISBN：8447347516, 8447347513

《道德经》

74. El dao de jing/por Lao Zi; traducido del chino y comentado por Renaud W. Neubauer y Santiago Gangotena G. Quito：Universidad San Francisco de Quito, 2007. 217 pages：illustrations；22cm. ISBN：9942013439, 9942013431. (Colección Ingenio；4)

《道德经》, Neubauer, Renaud W. 和 Gangotena González, Santiago 合译. 英汉对照.

75. Tao te king ＝ El libro del medio/Lao-Tse. Palma de Mallorca Cort, 2007. 123 p. il. 22cm. ISBN：8475355986, 8475355986. (Biblioteca parva de Cristóbal Serra)

《道德经》

76. Tao te ching/Lao Tse; versión de Stephen Mitchell. Cuarta ed. México, D. F.：Gaia Ediciones, 2007. 1 volume（unpaged）：color illustrations；22cm. ISBN：8488242952, 8488242956

《道德经》,Mitchell, Stephen(1943—)译.

(1)6a ed. ［Madrid］Gaia ediciones, 2016. ［91］p. il. col. 22cm. ISBN：8488242952, 8488242956

77. Tao te ching/Lao Tse; versión de Stephen Mitchell; ［traducción al español, Jorge Viñes Roig］. Madrid Alianza Editorial, 2007. 175 p. 18cm. ISBN：8420661315, 8420661317. (El libro de bolsillo. Religión y mitología；4115)

《道德经》,Mitchell, Stephen 英译；Roig, Jorge Vine 转译成西文.英语西班牙语对照.

(1) 2a. ed. Madrid Alianza Editorial, 2011. 177 p. 18cm. ISBN：8420643427, 8420643424. (El libro de bolsillo；HU6)

78. La palabra y el tao：tres textos, un solo tao/Mario Conde. La Montaña de los Ángeles, Córdoba ［Spain］：Editorial Nous, 2008. 219 pages：illustrations；20 × 25cm. ISBN：8493602918, 8493602914

《道德经》,Conde, Mario(1948—)译.

79. Tao te king/Lao Tse. 1a. ed. en esta colección. Madrid BO&G, 2008. 93 p. 21cm. ISBN：8492575008, 849257500X

《道德经》

80. El arte de la guerra para la mujer en el trabajo：de las zapatillas de cristal a las botas de combate/Chin-Ning Chu; traducción de Julia Fernández Treviño. Madrid：Edaf, 2009. 276 pages：illustrations；23 pages. ISBN：8441420977, 8441420971

Chu, Chin-Ning 著；Fernández Treviño, Julia 译. 包括《道德经》的西译.

81. El tao te ching sobre el arte de la armonía/Laozi. Barcelona：Blume, 2010. 272 p. : il. ; 24cm. ISBN：8498015171, 8498015170

《道德经》

82. Vive la sabiduría del Tao/Wayne W. Dyer; traducción de Juan Manuel Ibeas Delgado. ［Barcelona］Debolsillo, 2010. 173 p. il. 19cm. ISBN：8499085890,849908589X. (Clave)

《道德经》(选译),Dyer, Wayne W. 译.

(1)2a ed. ［Barcelona］：Debolsillo, 2013. 173 p. : il. ; 19cm. ISBN：8499085890, 849908589X. (Clave)

83. Tao te king/Lao-Tsé; traducción, Benjamin Briggent. Barberá del Vallés, Barcelona Plutón, 2010. 123 p. 18cm. ISBN：8415089124, 8415089120. (Eterna)

《道德经》,Briggent, Benjamin 译.

84. Lao Zi：El Tao Te Ching eterno/por Xu Yuanxiang y Yin Yongjian；［translator, Nuria Pitarque Ledesma, Sun Xintang］. Beijing：China Intercontinental Press, 2010. 81 pages：color illustrations, portraits；21cm. ISBN：7508516769, 7508516761. (Sabios antiguos de China)

《千年道德经》,Xu, Yuanxiang 和 Yin, Yongjian 原著；Ledesma, Nuria Pitarque 和 Sun, Xintang 合译.

85. Tao Te Ching/Lao Tse；［ilustraciones, Xavi Comas, Rafa Castañer］. Barcelona Integral,2010. 201 p. il. col. 22cm. ISBN：8498677416,8498677416. (Inspiraciones)

《道德经》

86. Tao te king/Lao Tse. San Lorenzo de El Escorial, Madrid Creación, 2012. 91 p. 1 retr. 17cm. ISBN：8495919960, 8495919966. (Sabiduría esencial)

《道德经》

87. Tao te ching/Lao Tzu; traducción rigurosa del chino antiguo por William Scott Wilson；［traducción, Alejandro Pareja］. Mōstoles, Madrid Dojo, 2012. 219 p. 21cm. ISBN：8493784539, 8493784532

《道德经》,Wilson, William Scott（1944—）和 Pareja, Alejandro 译.

88. Tao te ching/Lao Tzé; introducción, John Baldock; traducción de la versión en inglés, Mauricio Pichardo. México, D. F. : Tomo, 2012. 128 pages：illustrations；

26cm. ISBN：6074153842，6074153841

《道德经》，Pichardo，Mauricio 转译自英文.

89. Tao te ching：urdimbre verdader a del camino y su virutd. Lao-Tse；traducción del chino y prólogo de Fernán Alayza y María A. Benavides. Madrid Visor Libros，2013. 297 p. 20cm. ISBN：8498958515，8498958512. (Visor poesía；851)

《道德经》，Alayza，Fernán 和 Benavides，María A. 合译. 西汉对照.

90. Tao te ching：libro de la energía continua, fuerza que fluye y camino virtuoso del viejo sabio/de Lao Tzu；versión de Campo Hermoso. ［Madrid］Los Libros del Olivo，2013. 174 p. 21cm. ISBN：8494170416，8494170414. (La fuente)

《道德经》，Campo Hermoso 译.

91. Tao, el alimento del alma：eliminar el estrés y las preocupaciones a través del Tao/Sun Junqing. Nueva edición bilingüe；1a edición. Barcelona：Ediciones Obelisco，2013. 364 pages；21cm. ISBN：8497779838，8497779835. (Colección textos tradicionales)

《道德经》，Sun，Junqing 译.

92. Tao-Te-King/Lao-tse；［traducción，Luis Cárcamo］. Madrid Luis Cárcamo，2014. 91 p. 22cm. ISBN：8476271759，8476271751

《道德经》

93. Tao te ching：el libro del Tao y la virtud/Lao Tzu；introducción y traducción，Alejandro Bárcenas. ［Austin，Texas］：Anamnesis Editorial，2014. ix，170 pages；21cm. ISBN：1500909437，1500909432

《道德经》，Bárcenas，Alejandro 译.

94. Tao te ching/Lao-tse. Siero，Asturias Sapere Aude，2014. 83 p. 18cm. (Joyas del Loto；1；Filosofía oriental)

《道德经》

95. Tao tê ching：el libro del camino y la virtud, el libro del tao/Lao-Tsé (viejo maestro)；［traducción，J. Antonio Pujol Lavín］. Algete，Madrid Mestas，2015. 109 p. 19cm. ISBN：8416365210，8416365210. (Selección clásicos universales)

《道德经》，Pujol Lavín，J. Antonio 译.

96. Tao te ching：versión moderna de Yeng Lingfong (1904—1999)，versión tradicional de Wang Pi (226—249)/introducción，traducción y comentarios，José Ramón Álvarez；prefacio，Laureano Ramírez Bellerín；ilustraciones，Evaristo Bellotti；caligrafía，Li Kuanglang. Taichung，Taiwán Catay，2016. 315 p. il. col. y n. 27cm. ISBN：9869191234，9869191231. (Penglai shan)

《道德经》，Álvarez Méndez-Trelles，José Ramón 译注.

97. El libro del Tao：el manga/Lao-Tsé；［Variety Art Works；traducción，Maite Madinabeitia］. Barcelona La Otra H，2016. 163，［30］p. principalmente il. 16cm.

ISBN：8416540723，8416540721

《道德经》

98. Lao Zi：El Tao Te Ching eterno/por Xu Yuanxiang y Yin Yongjian；［translator，Nuria Pitarque Ledesma，Sun Xintang］. Beijing：China Intercontinental Press，2010. 81 pages：color illustrations, portraits；21cm. ISBN：7508516769，7508516761. (Sabios antiguos de China)

《道德经：老子》，徐远翔，印水健［著］. 五洲传播出版社.

99. El libro del camino y la virtud＝Tao te ching/Lao-Tse；traducción del chino clásico por Claribel Alegría y Erik Flakoll Alegría. Granada Valparaíso，2016. 175 p. 21cm. ISBN：8416560455；8416560455. (Valparaíso de poesía；n. 99)

《道德经》，Alegría，Claribel (1924—2018) 和 Flakoll Alegría，Erik 合译.

100. El tao de la paz：el arte de manejar la dinámica de los conflictos＝Dao de jing lun bing yao yi/Wang Chen；versión y comentarios de Ralph D. Sawyer；［traducido por Alejandro Pareja Rodríguez］. Madrid：EDAF，2000. 395 pages；19cm. ISBN：8441407363，8441407367. (Temas de superación personal)

《道德经论兵要义述》，(唐)王真；Sawyer，Ralph D. 译.

B233 列子

1. Lie-tse：una guía taoísta sobre el arte de vivir/Eva Wong；［traducido por Alfonso Colodrón］. Madrid：EDAF，1997. 292 pages；21cm. ISBN：8441402183；8441402188. (Luz de oriente；2)

Translation of：Liezi：a Taoist guide to practical living.

《列子》，Wong，Eva(1951—)译.

(1) Madrid：Edaf，2005. 329 pages；18cm. ISBN：8441417164，8441417168. (Arca de sabiduría；63)

2. Lie Zi：el libro de la perfecta vacuidad/traducción，introducción y notas por Iñaki Preciado. Barcelona：Kairós，1987. ISBN：8472453367，8472453364；

《列子》，Preciado Idoeta，Iñaki(1941—)译注.

(1)2a. ed. Barcelona：Kairós，1994. 211 p. ISBN：8472453367，8472453364. (Clásicos Kairós)

(2)3a ed. Barcelona：Kairós，2000. 211 p. ISBN：8472453367，8472453364. (Clásicos Kairós)

(3)Barcelona：Círculo de Lectores，2004. 247 p.；21cm. ISBN：8467201312，8467201314. (Sabiduría oriental)

(4)［4a ed.］. Barcelona：Kairós，2008. 211 p.；20cm. ISBN：8472453367，8472453364

(5)6a ed. Barcelona：Kairós，2016. 211 p.；20cm. ISBN：8472453367，8472453364

B234 庄子

1. Literato filosfo y mistico taoista/análisis y traduccion por Carmelo Elorduy. Manila：Publicaciones del E"ast Asian

Pastoral Institute", 1967. xii, 77, 260 pages；26cm.

《庄子》，Elorduy, Carmelo（1901—1989 年）译. 中西对照.

(1)Caracas：Monte avila editores, 1972. VI, 77, 260 p. ；23cm.

(2)Chuang-tzu, literato, filósofo y místico taoísta/estudio y traducción por Carmelo Elorduy. 2a ed. Caracas：Monte Avila Editores, c1984. vi, 77, 260 p. ；22cm.

(3) Chuang-Tzu/análisis y traducción Carmelo Elorduy. 4a ed. Caracas：Monte Avila, 1991. 260 p. ；23cm. ISBN：9800104461, 9800104460. (Pensamiento filosófico)

2. Zhuang Zi＝Maestro Zhuang/traducción, introducción y notas de Iñaki Preciado Ydoeta. Barcelona：Kairós, 1996. 477 p. ：mapa；20cm. ISBN：8472453359；8472453357

《庄子》，Preciado, Juan Ignacio1（1941—）译注.

(1)Barcelona：Kairós, 1997. 480 p. ISBN：8472453357, 8472453359. (Clásicos)

(2)2a. ed. Barcelona：Kairós, 2001. 478 p. 20cm. ISBN：8472453359, 8472453357. (Clásicos Kairós)

(3)3a. ed. Barcelona：Kairós, 2007. 478 p. ；20cm. ISBN：8472453357, 8472453359. (Clásicos Kairós)

(4)4. a ed. Barcelona：Kairós, 2010. 478 p. ；20cm. ISBN：8472453357, 8472453359. (Clásicos Kairós)

(5)5a ed. Barcelona：Kairós, 2015. 477 p. ；20cm. ISBN：8472453357, 8472453359

3. Chuang-Tzu/Octavio Paz. Madrid Siruela, 1997. 78 p. 15cm. ISBN：8478443657, 8478443659. (Biblioteca de Ensayo；6)

《庄子》，Paz, Octavio（1914—1998）译.

(1)2a ed. Madrid：Siruela, 2000. ISBN：8478443657, 8478443659. (Biblioteca de ensayo；6)

4. Trazos：Chuang-tzu y otros/Octavio Paz. México：Ediciones del Equilibrista, 1997. 68 pages；21cm. ISBN：9687318465, 9687318462, 968731849X, 9687318493

《庄子》(选译)，Paz, Octavio（1914—1998）译.

5. Los capítulos interiores de Zhuang Zi/Zhuang Zi；traducción de Pilar González España y Jean Claude Pastor-Ferrer. Madrid：Trotta UNESCO, 1998. 148 pages；20cm. ISBN：8481642391, 8481642398. (Pliegos de oriente. Serie Lejano oriente；Colección UNESCO de obras representativas)

《庄子内篇》，González España, Pilar（1960—）等译.

(1)2a. ed. Madrid：Trotta, 2005. 148 p. ；20cm. ISBN：8481642398, 8481642391. (Pliegos de Oriente；Lejano Oriente)

6. La sabiduría de Chuang Tse：textos fundamentales del taoísmo/[redactado por] Sam Hamill y J. P. Seaton；[traducción de Nuria Martí]. Barcelona：Oniro, 2000. 240 pages；20cm. ISBN：8495456273, 8495456274.

(Viaje interior；29)

Notes：Translation of：The essential Zhuang Zi.

《庄子》，Martí, Nuria 译；Hamill, Sam 和 Seaton, Jerome P. 改编.

7. El libro de Chuang Tse/versión de Martin Palmer y Elizabet Breuilly. Madrid：Edaf, 2001. 482 pages：illustrations；18cm. ISBN：8441409110, 8441409118. (Arca de sabiduría；52)

Notes：Translated from：The book of Chuang Tzu.

《庄子》，转译自英文.

(1)El Libro de Chuang Tse/versión de Martin Palmer y Elizabeth Breuilly；traducción de Mario Lamberti. Barcelona：Círculo de Lectores, 2009. 438 p. ；22cm. ISBN：8467231922, 8467231920

8. Los Diálogos de Chuang Tse/traducción de Francesc Gutiérrez. Palma de Mallorca：José J. de Olañeta, Limpergraf, 2004. 158 p. ；14cm. ISBN：8497163745, 8497163743. (Los Pequeños libros de la sabiduría；110)

《庄子》，Gutiérrez, Francesc 译.

9. Obra completa/Chuang-tzu；[traducción：Cristóbal Serra]. Palma de Mallorca：Cort, 2005. 364 p. ；21cm. ISBN：8475355803, 8475355801. (Bearn)

《庄子》，Serra, Cristóbal 译.

B24　墨家

1. Comunismo y amor de Mo Ti/por Carmelo Elorduy. Caracas：Universidad Católica Andrés Bello, Instituto de Investigaciones Históricas, 1977. 140 pages；23cm.

Elorduy, Carmelo（1901—1989 年）著. 含《墨子》的翻译.

2. Política del amor universal/Mo Ti；tr. y notas Carmelo Elorduy. Madrid：Tecnos, 1987. 193 p. ；18cm. ISBN：843091501X；8430915019. (Colección Clásicos del Pensamiento；40)

《墨子》，Elorduy, Carmelo（1901—1989 年）译.

(1)Madrid Tecnos, 2002. LXXIV, 193 p. mapas 18cm. ISBN：843091501X；8430915019. (Clásicos del pensamiento；40)

B25　名家

1. Libro del maestro Gongsun Long o la Escuela de los Nombres/Gongsun Long；estudio preliminar de Pedro San Ginés Aguilar；traducción y notas de Yao Ning y Gabriel García-Noblejas Sánchez Cendal. Madrid：Trotta, 2001. 106 p. ；20cm. ISBN：8481644935；8481644937. (Pliegos de oriente. Serie Lejano oriente)

《公孙龙子》

B26　法家

B261　韩非子

1. El arte de la política (los hombres y la ley)/Han Fei Zi；

estudio preliminar de Pedro San Ginés Aguilar; traducido por Yao Ning y Gabriel García-Noblejas. Madrid (España): Tecnos, 1998. xxxv; 179 páginas. ISBN: 8430932720, 8430932726. (Clásicos del pensamiento; 135)

《韩非子》,Yao, Ning 和 García-Noblejas Gabriel 合译.

(1)2a ed. Madrid: Tecnos, 2010. xxxv, 179 pages: maps; 20cm. ISBN: 8430950485, 8430950486. (Clásicos del pensamiento; 104)

B3　伦理学

1. Los valores contemporáneos de china: en la cultura tradicional. Beijing: Ediciones en Lenguas extranjeras, 2016. xiii, 229 pages. ; 23cm. ISBN: 7119100678

《中国价值观:中国传统文化与中国当代价值》,曹雅欣著.

2. Beng Sim Po Cam, o, Rico espejo del buen corazón: el Mingxin Baojian de Fan Liben/traducido por Juan Cobo hacia 1590; en edición de Manel Ollé. Barcelona: Península, 1998. 158 p. ; 17cm. ISBN: 8483070820, 8483070826. (Nuestros contemporáneos; 10)

《明心宝鉴》,(明)范立本;Cobo, Juan 译于 1592 年左右;Ollé, Manuel(1962—)编.

B4　宗教

B41　概述

1. Las religiones de china/[compilado por Ediciones en Lenguas Extranjeras]. Beijing, [China]: Ediciones en Lenguas Extranjeras, 1989. 57 p.: il. ; 19cm. (China en desarrollo; 34)

中国宗教.

2. 中国概况:中国的宗教和宗教信仰自由状况. 北京:新星出版社,1997. ISBN: 7801028589

3. La religión en China/autor, Deng Shulin. Beijing: Editorial Nueva Estrella, 2004. : 1 pages: color illustrations; 21cm. ISBN: 7801486374, 7801486370. (China express; viaje multicultural a un país de cinco mil años)

《中国的宗教》,邓树林编. 新星出版社.

4. 中国的宗教:西班牙文/王阳编著;杨林长译. 北京:新星出版社,2006. 21cm. ISBN: 7802251397

B42　佛教

1. Reencarnacion del Dalai Lama/Chen Qingying. [Beijing]: Editorial Intercontinental de China, 2004. 164 p. ; 21cm. ISBN: 7508504771, 7508504773

《达赖喇嘛转世》,陈庆英著,张金来译. 五洲传播出版社. 本书介绍藏传佛教与活佛转世制度、达赖喇嘛转世概况以及形定的历史定制.

(1)[2nd ed.]. Beijing, China: Editorial Intercontinental

de China, 2008. 164 pages: illustrations; 21cm. ISBN: 7508504773 7508504771

2. Libros sagrados de Oriente: textos originales de acuerdo con las versiones de Max Müller, Samuel Bael, Jacques Darmesteter y George Sale/Epiphanius Wilson; traducción por Francisco A. Delpiane. México, D. F.: Editorial Nueva España, 1940s. 573 pages; 18cm. (Colección Atenea)

Notes: Translation of Sacred books of the East

Wilson, Epiphanius(1845—1916)将《佛所行赞》从汉语译成英语;Francisco A. Delpiane 从英语转译成西译.

(1)México: Latino Americana, 1960. 501 p. ; 22cm.

3. El sutra en cuarenta y dos secciones predicado por Buda/basado en la traducción al idioma chino del Venerable Kashyapa-Matanga y el Venerable Gobharana durante la Dinastía del Han; texto y notas basados en las conferencias dadas por el Venerable Maestro Hsuan Hua. El sutra de las ocho comprensiones de los Grandes Seres/basado en la traducción al idioma chino del Shramana An Shi Gao durante la Dinastia Han posterior. [Burlingame, Calif.]: [Sociedad para la Traducción de los textos Budistas]: [Universidad Budista del Reino del Dharma:] [Asociación Budista del Reino del Dharma], 1998. xi, 111 pages: illustrations; 21cm. ISBN: 0881397504, 0881397505

《四十二章经》与《八大人觉经》

3. Nan jing: Hoang ti ba shi yi nan jing＝(Tratado de las ochenta y una dificultades del Emperador Amarillo). traducción Bob Flaws. Madrid Mandala, 2003. 117 p. 21cm. ISBN: 8488769946, 8488769947

《难经:黄帝八十一难经》

(1)2a ed. Madrid Mandala, 2011. 109 p. 20cm. ISBN: 8483524374, 8483524376. (Cabal; Colección Yin-Yang＝Tao; 16)

4. Sutra sobre el Maestro de la Medicina: sutra sobre el mérito y virtud de los votos originales del Tathägata Maestro de la Medicina Luz de Vaidürya: una explicación simple/explicado por Hsühan Hua en 1983, en el Monasterio de Rueda de Oro, Los Angeles, U. S. A. ; traducción al español realizada por la Sociedad de Traducción de Textos Budistas. Burlingame, Calif. : Sociedad de Traducción de Textos Budistas, Universidad Budista del Reino del Dharma, Asociación Budista del Reino del Dharma, 2004. xi, 264 p. : col. ill. ; 22cm. ISBN: 0881395137, 0881395136

《药师琉璃光如来本愿功德经浅释》,宣化(1908—1995)著.

5. El arte del liderazgo: lecciones zen sobre el arte de dirigir/versión de Thomas Cleary; [traduciado por Alfonso Colodrón]. Madrid: EDAF, 1995. 175 pages; 19cm. ISBN: 8476409842, 8476409848. (Temas de superación personal)

《禅林宝训》，Cleary，Thomas F. (1949—)译.

(1) Madrid Edaf，1997. 175 p. 19cm. ISBN：8476409842，8476409848

(2) Madrid［etc.］Edaf，2014. 215 p. 18cm. ISBN：8441435025，8441435022.（Management）

6. Las cinco casas del zen：los textos clásicos de los grandes maestros de la historia del zen/Thomas Cleary；［traducción, Ester Roig Giménez］. Barcelona：Integral，1998. 191 pages；21cm. ISBN：8479013699，8479013691.（Libros de sabiduría esencial）

禅学大师选译. Cleary，Thomas F. (1949—) 英译；Roig Giménez，Ester 转译成西语.

7. El sutra de Hui Neng：comentarios de Hui Neng al Sutra del diamante/versión de Thomas Cleary；［traduccion de Alejandro Pareja］. Madrid：Editorial EDAF，1999. 259 pages；18cm. ISBN：8441406626，8441406629.（Arca de sabiduría；45）

《六祖大师法宝坛经》，慧能（638—713）；Cleary，Thomas F. (1949—)译.

8. Tan jing/Hui Neng, sexto patriarca de la Escuela Chan；versión de Laureano Ramírez a partir del manuscrito chino de Dunhuang. Barcelona：Kairós，1999. 181 p. ISBN：8472454606，8472454606.（Clásicos Kairós）

《六祖大师法宝坛经》，慧能（638—713）；Ramírez，Laureano 译.

9. Sutra del estrado＝Tan jing/Hui Neng, sexto patriarca de la Escuela del Chan；versión de Laureano Ramírez a partir del manuscrito chino de Dunhuang. Barcelona：Kairós，2000. 182 p.；20cm. ISBN：8472454606，8472454606.（Clásicos Kairós）

《六祖大师法宝坛经》，慧能（638—713）；Ramírez，Laureano 编译.

10. Sutra de Vimalakirti/presentación, traducción y notas de Laureano Ramírez Bellerín a partir de la versión china de Kumarajiva. Barcelona：Editorial Kairós，2004. 357 p.；20cm. ISBN：8472455505；8472455504

《维摩诘所说经》，Ramírez Bellerín，Laureano 译.

11. El viaje de Faxian：relato del peregrinaje de un monje chino a los reinos budistas de Asia Central y la India en el siglo V/edición，traducción y notas de Laureano Ramírez Bellerín. Madrid：La Esfera de los Libros，2010. 365 p.；il. color；25cm. ISBN：8497349956；8497349954

《佛国记》，(东晋)法显；Ramírez，Laureano 译注.

B43　道教

1. Tratado de Lao Tse sobre la respuesta del Tao/Li Ying-Chang；versión de la Dra. Eva Wong；［traducido por Alfonso Colodrón］. Madrid Edaf，1996. 166 p. il. 18cm. ISBN：8441400296，8441400290.（Arca de sabiduría；23）

《太上感应篇》

2. La Puerta del Dragón：relato de la iniciación de un maestro taoísta contemporáneo/Chen Kaiguo y Zheng Shunchao；versión de Thomas Cleary；［traducido por Mariano José Vázquez Alonso］. Madrid：Editorial EDAF，1997. 447 pages；21cm. ISBN：8441402469，8441402461.（Luz de Oriente；5）

《大道行：访孤独居士王力平先生》，陈开国，郑顺潮（1966—）著；Cleary，Thomas F. (1949—)（美国翻译家）译.

3. Los siete maestros taoístas：novela tradicional china/versión e introducción de Eva Wong；［traducción，Rafael Lasaleta］. Móstoles，Madrid Neo Person，2008. 220 p. il. 21cm. ISBN：8495973511，8495973510.（Colección Relatos）

《七真传》，转译自英文《Seven Taoist masters》一书.

C类　社会科学总论

C1　社会科学理论

1. La tarea combatiente de los trabajadores de filsofía y ciencias sociales：discurso pronunciado el 26 de octubre de 1963 en la 4a. conferencia ampliada del Comité del Departamento de filosofía y ciencias sociales de la Academia de Ciencias de China/Yan Chou. Pekin：Ediciones en Lenguas Extranjeras，1964. 69 p.；18cm.

《哲学、社会科学工作者的战斗任务：1963年10月26日在中国科学院社会科学部委员会第四次扩大会议上的讲话》，周扬.

C2　人口学

1. 人口和民族. 北京：外文出版社，1988. 27 页.（中国概况）

2. Población y desarrollo de China/autores，Tian Xueyuan y Zhou Liping；traductor，Chen Gensheng. ［Beijing］：China Intercontinental Press，2004. 147 pages；color illustrations；21cm. ISBN：7508504437，7508504438.（Series básicas de China）

《中国人口》，田雪原，周丽苹著；陈根生译. 五洲传播出版社.

本书内容包括中国人口现状与特点，人口地域分布与区域经济、人口素质与人力资本、人口老龄化与养老保障、人口城市化与产业结构、人口政策与计划生育、人口资源环境可持续发展.

3. 中国的计划生育：西班牙文/卢茹彩编著；吴恺译. 北京：新星出版社，2006. 21cm. ISBN：7802251451

C3　中国各民族

1. Unidad e igualdad las minorías nacionales de China progresan/por Yin Ming. Pekín Ediciones en Lenguas Extranjeras，1978. 119，［48］p. dela'ms. il.（algunas col) 19cm.

《中国少数民族在前进》，尹明.

2. 中国的民族区域自治：西班牙文/中华人民共和国国务院新闻办公室发布. 北京：新星出版社,2005. 60 页；20cm. ISBN：7801486943

本书为国务院新闻办公室发布的白皮书,介绍中国的民族区域自治制度.

3. 中国的民族区域自治：西班牙文/吴乃陶编著；张重光等译. 北京：新星出版社,2006；21cm. ISBN：7802251427

本书介绍了中国的民族政策、民族区域自治制度,少数民族的教育文化状况以及民族地区的经济发展.

4. 中国的民族政策与各民族共同繁荣发展/中华人民共和国国务院新闻办公室[编]. 北京：外文出版社,2009. 75 页；21cm. ISBN：7119060569

本书为中华人民共和国国务院新闻办公室发布的白皮书,内容为中国的民族政策与各民族共同繁荣发展.

5. Etnias y religions de China/Zheng Qian；traducido por Yang Linchang. Beijing：China Intercontinental Press, 2011. 191 p. : col. ill. ; 23cm. ISBN：7508519395, 7508519396

《中国民族与宗教》,郑茜著；杨林常译. 五洲传播出版社.
本书介绍了中国的民族、宗教政策以及基本情况.

6. Minorías étnicas de China/Xu Ying y Wang Baoqin；[traducción por Miguel Sautié]. Beijing：China Intercontinental Press, 2012. 133 pages；color illustrations, color map；25cm. ISBN：7508523255, 7508523253

《民族之旅》,徐英,王宝琴；Sautié, Miguel 译.

(1) Madrid：Editorial Popular, 2012. 133 p. il. col. 25cm. ISBN：8478845279, 8478845275. (Asiateca；6)

7. Los elunchunes en la sociedad nómada/Qiu Pu. Beijing Ediciones en Lenguas Extranjeras, 1983. 109 p. , [16] p. de lám. 1 mapa 26cm.

《游猎社会的鄂伦春人》

D 类　政治、法律

D1　中国政治

D11　概况

1. Guía de la nueva China. Pekin：Ediciones en Lenguas Extranjeras, 1958. 299 pages, [3] leaves of plates；illustrations；19cm.

《中国手册》

2. China. Pekín (Beijing)：Ediciones en Lenguas Extranjeras, 1979. 260 p. : il. ；19cm.

《中国》,齐雯编.

(1)2a ed. revisada. Beijing：Ediciones en Lenguas Extranjeras, 1981. 273 pages, [56] pages of plates：illustrations (some color)；19cm.

(2)3a ed. rev. Beijing：Ediciones en Lenguas Extranjeras, 1985. 246 p. : il. ；19cm.

3. Panorama de China/Qi Wen. Beijing：Ediciones en Lenguas Extranjeras, 1985. 97 p. : il. ；19cm.

《中国便览》,齐雯编.

4. Instantânea de China/[edited by Wang Chuanmin；translated by Zhang Chongguang]. Beijing：Editorial Nueva Estrella, 2004. 37 pages：color illustrations；21cm. ISBN：7801485955, 7801485953. (China express；viaje multicultural a un pais de cinco mil años)

《认识中国》,王传民编著. 新星出版社. 介绍中国最基本的情况,包括地理环境、自然资源、历史概况、人口与民族、政治制度与国家机构、国民经济与社会发展、对外开放等.

5. Vamos a conocer china/Wang Qicheng；texto en español, Zhang Chongguang. Beijing：Ediciones en Lenguas Extranjeras, 2010. 216 pages：color illustrations；24cm. ISBN：7119060316, 7119060317

《看中国》,王麒诚著. 向普通读者尤其是面向青少年的介绍中国的手绘本图文书.

6. China país por descubrir：introducción a la historia, la sociedad y la cultura de China/Jin Bo. Beijing Shi：China Intercontinental Press, 2010. 321 pages：illustrations, maps；23cm. ISBN：7508517490, 7508517490

《阅读中国：介绍中国的历史、社会和文化》,金帛撰稿. 五洲传播出版社.

7. Política/por la Redacción de "Colección China". Beijing：Ediciones en Lenguas extranjeras, 1985. 216 p. ；19cm.

《政治》,《中国概况丛书》编辑委员会编.

8. 中共中央关于社会主义精神文明建设指导方针的决议. 北京：外文出版社,1986

9. 国土与资源. 北京：外文出版社,1987. 28 页.(中国概况)

10. Estructura del estado. Beijing：Ediciones en Lenguas Extranjeras,1987. 29 p. ilus. 18cm. ISBN：7119003178, 7119003177. (Presencia de China)

《国家机构》. 外文出版社(中国概况)

11. El XIV Congreso Nacional del PCCh y la reforma china. Beijing：Nueva Estrella,1993.46 p. ,[8] p. de lám. : il. col. ;18cm. ISBN：7800858863,7800858864. (Presencia de China)

《中共十四大与中国改革》. 新星出版社(中国概况)

12. 中国的政治体制. 新星出版社,1993. ISBN：7800859525. (中国概况)

13. 建设有中国特色的社会主义. 新星出版社,1993. ISBN：7801020545. (中国概况)

14. 政府机构改革和公务员制度. 新星出版社,1994. ISBN：7801021134. (中国概况)

15. 中国的民主党派和政党制度. 新星出版社,1994. ISBN：7801021495. (中国概况)

16. 中美两国人权比较. 五洲传播出版社,1996. ISBN：7801131320

17. 中国的人民代表大会制度. 新星出版社,1996. ISBN：7801026063. (中国概况)

18. 外国人眼里的中国. 新星出版社，1997. ISBN：7801028805.（中国概况）

19. Relaciones de nuevo tipo entre partidos políticos. Beijing：Nueva Estrella, 1998. 30 p.：il.；18cm. ISBN：7801481542，7801481542.（Presencia de China）
《发展新型的党际关系》. 新星出版社（中国概况）

20. Capital y símbolos patrios/Wang Chuanmin, editor. Beijing：Ediciones en Lenguas Extranjeras, 2003. 41 pages：color illustrations；18cm. ISBN：7119031481，7119031484
《中人民共和国国旗、国徽、国歌、首都》，王传民编.

21. El sistema político de China/［Wang Chuanmin］. Beijing：Editorial Nueva Estrella, 2004. 35 pages：color illustrations；21cm. ISBN：7801485823，7801485823.（China express；viaje multicultural a un país de cinco mil años）
《中国的政体》，王传民编著. 新星出版社.

22. China a fondo：preguntas y respuestas. Beijing Editorial Nueva Estrella, 2005. 221 p. ilustraciones, fotos（a color）21cm. ISBN：7801489098，7801489098
《透视中国问与答：西班牙文》，王刚毅，吴伟，李建国主编；陈根生等译. 新星出版社.

23. 中国的民主政治建设：西班牙文/中华人民共和国国务院新闻办公室发布. 北京：新星出版社，2005. 89 页；20cm. ISBN：7801488342
本书为国务院新闻办公室发布的白皮书，全面介绍中国的社会主义民主政治建设情况.

24. Sueño de China/Li Junru. Beijing：Ediciones en Lenguas Extrajeras, 2006. 131 pages：illustrations；21cm. ISBN：7119044648，7119044644.（Desarrollo pacífico de China）
《中国梦：西班牙文》，李君如著；张金来等译. 外文出版社（中国的和平发展系列）

25. Camino Chino：concepción científica del desarrollo/Tian Yingkui；［traducido］，Zhang Chongguang. Beijing：Foreign Languages Press, 2008. 194 pages；23cm. ISBN：7119054742，7119054740
《中国道路：从科学发展观解读中国发展》，田应奎著.

26. Desarrollo pacífico de China/Oficina de Información del Consejo de Estado de la República Popular China. Beijing：Ediciones en Lenguas Extranjeras, 2011. 42 p.；21cm. ISBN：7119072449，7119072447
《中国的和平发展》，中华人民共和国国务院新闻办公室编.

27. El sistema político de China/Yin Zhongqing；traductores, Tang Baisheng, Huang Caizhen, Bian Yanyao. Beijing：China Intercontinental Press, 2011. 195 pages：color illustrations；23cm. ISBN：7508519432，7508519434
《中国政治制度》，尹中卿著. 五洲传播出版社.

28. 中国走社会主义道路为什么成功：西班牙文版/戴木才著；徐少军，王小芳译. 北京：五洲传播出版社，2016. 225 页；24cm. ISBN：7508533889

西班牙文题名：Por que China：logra exito en el camino del socialismo

29. 协商民主在中国/李君如［著］；姜凤光，张重光翻译. 北京：外文出版社，2014. 31 页：图；21cm. ISBN：7119091754
西班牙文题名：Democracia consultiva en China

30. 中国梦，什么梦？：西班牙文/李君如著；外文出版社西班牙文编辑部译. 北京：外文出版社，2014. 198 页；24cm. ISBN：7119093246

31. 中国震撼：一个文明型国家的崛起/张维为著；姚杰，（西）奥古斯丁·阿勒普斯·莫拉莱斯译. 北京：五洲传播出版社，2017. 224 页；23cm. ISBN：7508535708
西班牙文题名：La ola China：el ascenso de un estado-civilización

D12　中国政治思想史

1. Los tres principios del pueblo＝San min chu i/Sun Yat Sen；traducido del original por Mih Sih Tshoong. ［Managua：s. n.，1935］（Managua, Nic., C. A.：Tip. Chamorro Pasos）. x, 215 p.；22cm.
《三民主义》，孙逸仙（1866—1925）.

D13 中国共产党

1. 中国共产党中央委员会向第八次全国代表大会的政治报告/刘少奇. 北京：外文出版社，1957

2. 中国共产党第八次全代表大会关于发展国民经济的第二个五年计划（1958—1962）的建议、关于发展国民经济第二个五年计划建议的报告/周恩来. 北京：外文出版社，1957

3. 中国共产党第八次全国代表大会文件汇编（第一辑）. 北京：外文出版社，1957

4. 中国共产党第八次全国代表大会第二次会议文件集. 北京：外文出版社，1958

5. Documentos de la Sexta Reunion Plenaria del Comite Central：elegido en el Octavo Congreso, del Partido Comunista de China. Pekin：Ediciones en Lenguas Extranjeras, 1959. 53 pages；19cm.
《中国共产党第八届中央委员会第六次全体会议文件》

6. Documentos de la octava sesión plenaria del Comité Central, elegido en el Octavo Congreso, del Partido Comunista de China. Pekin：Ediciones en Lenguas Extranjeras, 1959. 34 p.；19cm.
《中国共产党第八届中央委员会第八次会议文件》

7. Comunicado de la XI Sesion Plenaria del Comité Central elegido en el VIII Congreso Nacional del Partido Comunista de China（Aprobado el 12 de agosto de 1966）. Pekin：Ediciones en Lenguas Extranjeras, 1966. 10 pages
《中国共产党第八届中央委员会第十一次全体会议公报》
（1）Pekin：Ediciones en Lenguas Extranjeras, 1967. 19 pages

8. Comunicado de la XII Sesion Plenaria Ampliada del Comite

Central elegido en el VIII Congreso Nacional del Partido Comunista de China (Aprobado el 31 de octubre de 1968). Pekin：Ediciones en Lenguas Extranjeras, 1968. 25 pages；13cm.

《中国共产党第八届扩大的第十二次中央委员会全会公报》

9. Documentos del IX Congreso Nacional del Partido Comunista de China. Pekin：Ediciones en Lenguas Extranjeras，1969. 176 p. ；13cm. Contents：Informe ante el IX Congreso Nacional del Partido Comunista de China/Lin Piao. —Estatutos del Partido Comunista de China. —Comunicado de prensa del secretariado del presidium del IX Congreso Nacional del Partido Comunista de China. —Comunicado de prensa de la Ia. sesión plenaria del IX Comité Central del Partido Comunista de China.

《中国共产党第九次全国代表大会文件汇编》

10. Comunicados de prensa del secretariado del presidium del IX Congreso Nacional del Partido Comunista de China (Emitidos el 1, 14 y 24 de abril de 1969). Pekin：Ediciones en Lenguas Extranjeras, 1969. 44 pages；13cm.

《中国共产党第九次全国代表大会主席团秘书处新闻公报中国共产党第九届中央委员会第一次全体会议新闻公报》

11. Informe ante el IX Congreso Nacional del Partido Comunista de China：Hecho el 1 de abril y aprobado el 14 de abril be 1969. Pekin：Ediciones en Lenguas Extranjeras, 1969. 103 pages；13cm.

《在中国共产党第九次全国代表大会上的报告》，林彪.

12. Mantener en alto la bandera de unidad del IX Congreso del Partido para conquistar mayores victorias. Pekin：Ediciones en Lenguas Extranjeras, 1969. 17 pages；13cm.

《高举九大的团结旗帜，争取更大的胜利》

13. 中国共产党第九届中央委员会第二次全体会议公报（1970 年 9 月 6 日）. 北京：外文出版社，1970

14. Documentos del decimo Congreso Nacional del Partido Comunista de China. Pekin：Ediciones en Lenguas Extranjeras，1973. 99 pages：portraits (1 color)；19cm.

《中国共产党第十次全国代表大会文件汇编》

15. Undecimo Congreso nacional del Partido comunista de China：documentos. Pekin：Ediciones en Lenguas Extranjeras，1977. 251 pages，［12］leaves of plates：illustrations；19cm.

《中国共产党第十一次全国代表大会文件汇编》

16. Duodecimo Congreso Nacional del Partido Comunista de China. Beijing：Ediciones en Lenguas Extranjeras，1982. 178 pages；19cm. (Documentos de China)

《中国共产党第十二次全国代表大会文献》

17. 坚持改革，为实现社会主义现代化而斗争：中国共产党

全国代表会议文献. 北京：外文出版社，1985

18. Decimotercer Congreso Nacional del partido comunista de China：25 de octubre—1 de noviembre de 1987. Beijing：Ediciones en Lenguas Extranjeras，1988. 267 p. : il. ；20cm. ISBN：7119004974

《中国共产党第十三次全国代表大会文献》

19. XV Congreso nacional del PCCh：grandiosa reunión entre dos siglos/Editora Nueva Estrella. Beijing：Editora Nueva Estrella，1997. 127 p. : fotos, il. ；18cm. ISBN：7801028198，7801028198

《世纪之交的盛会：中共十五大》. 新星出版社（中国概况）

20. Del XVI Congreso Nacional del Partido Comunista de China：Documentos/Zhong Xin. Beijing：Ediciones en Lenguas Extranjeras，2002. 251 pages：color illustrations，portraits；23cm. ISBN：7119032283，7119032283

《中国共产党第十六次全国代表大会文献》，钟欣编. 外文出版社.

21. Documentos del XVII Congreso Nacional del Partido Comunista de China/［edited by Zhong Xin］. Beijing：Ediciones en Lenguas Extranjeras，2007. ：01 pages：color illustrations，color portraits；23cm. ISBN：7119051420，7119051423

《中国共产党第十七次全国代表大会文献：西班牙文》，钟欣编.

22. Estatutos del Partido Comunista de China. Informe sobre las modificaciones en los estatutos del Partido Comunista de China/［por］Den Siao-pin. Pekin，Ediciones en Lenguas Extranjeras，1957.

《中国共产党章程、关于修改党章的报告》，邓小平.

（1）3rd ed. Pekin，Ediciones en Lenguas Extranjeras，1959. 103 pages

23. Estatutos del Partido Comunista de China：aprobados por el IX Congreso Nacional del Partido Comunista de China el 14 de abril de 1969. Pekin：Ediciones en Lenguas Extranjeras，1969. 38 pages；11cm.

《中国共产党章程》

24. Treinta años del Partido Comunista de China/Chiao-mu Ju. Pekin：Ediciones en Lenguas Extranjeras，1957. 136 p. ；18cm.

《中国共产党的三十年》，胡乔木

25. 在庆祝中国共产党成立四十周年大会上的讲话/刘少奇. 北京：外文出版社，1961

26. Viva el Partido Comunista de China：en conmemoracion del 48o Aniversario de la Fundacion del Partido Comunista de China. Pekin：Ediciones en Lenguas Extranjeras，1969. 19 pages；13cm.

《中国共产党万岁：纪念中国共产党诞生四十八周年》

27. 共产党员应是无产阶级先进分子：纪念中国共产党成立四十九周年/人民日报、红旗杂志、解放军报报社论. 北京：外文出版社，1970

28. 纪念中国共产党 50 周年(1921—1971). 北京:外文出版社,1971

29. 中国共产党简明历史:中国共产党的七十年,胡绳主编;中共中央党史研究室著. 北京:外文出版社,1994. 1015页;20cm. ISBN:7119016709

30. Discurso pronunciado en la gran reunión para celebrar el 80. aniversario de la fundación del Partido Comunista de China,1 de julio de 2001/Jiang Zemin. Beijing:Editorial Nueva Estrella,2001. 61 pages;21cm. ISBN:7801483871,7801483874
   《在庆祝中国共产党成立八十周年大会上的讲话》,江泽民著. 新星出版社.

31. Carta de respuesta del CC del PCCH:del 22 de Marzo de 1966,al CC del PCUS. Pekin:Ediciones en Lenguas Extranjeras,1966. 5 pages;21cm.
   《中国共产党中央委员会 1966 年 3 月 22 日给苏联共产党中央委员会的复信》

32. Decisión del Comité Central del Partido Comunista de China sobre la gran revolución cultural proletaria (Aprobada el 8 de agosto de 1966). Pekin:Ediciones en Lenguas Extranjeras,1966. 14 p.;20cm.
   《中国共产党中央委员会关于无产阶级文化大革命的决定》

33. 中国共产党中央委员会关于无产阶级文化大革命的决定. 北京:外文出版社,1973

34. Circular del Comite Central del Partido Comunista de China (16 de mayo de 1966):un gran documento historico/por las redacciones de Hongqi y Renmin Ribao. Pekin:Ediciones en Lenguas Extranjeras,1968. 72 pages
   《通知(中国共产党中央委员会 1966 年 5 月 16 日)·伟大的历史文件》

35. El Partido comunista Chino analiza su historia/Yaobang Hu. 〔Madrid〕:〔Partido comunista de España〕,1982. 24 pages;21cm. (Nuestra bandera. Cuadernos;;5;)
   《中国共产党历史之分析》,胡耀邦.

36. Conoce al Partido Comunista de China? /Li Junru. Beijing Ediciones en Lenguas Extranjeras distribuidor, Corporación China de Comercio,2011. 189 p. il. col. y n. 23cm. ISBN:7119070193,7119070193
   《你了解中国共产党吗?》,李君如著.

37. Breve Manual del PCCh/Zhang Rongchen. Beijing:Ediciones en Lenguas Extranjeras,2017. 215 pages;24cm. ISBN:7119108452
   《中国共产党简明读本》,张荣臣著;陈岚西文翻译.

D131 政治领导人著作
周恩来(1898—1976)
1. Obras escogidas de Zhou Enlai. Tomo 1/Zhou Enlai. Beijing:Ediciones en Lenguas Extranjeras,1981. 530 p.;il.;22cm.
   《周恩来选集》,上卷.

2. 《周恩来选集》,下卷. 北京:外文出版社,1989

刘少奇(1898—1969)
1. Sobre la autocultivación de los comunistas:(discurso en el Instituto del Marxismo-Leninismo de Yan'an,en julio de 1939)/Liu Shaoqi. Beijing:Ediciones en Lenguas Extranjeras,1981. 107 pages;19cm.
   《论共产党员的修养》

2. Obras escogidas de Liu Shaoqi. Beijing:Ediciones en Lenguas Extranjeras,1983. 2 volumes:portraits;23cm.
   《刘少奇选集》,上卷.

3. Obras escogidas de Liu Shaoqi/Liu Shaoqi. Beijing:Ediciones en Lenguas Extranjeras,1991. 2 v.:il.;23cm. ISBN:7119012843,7119012841
   《刘少奇选集》,下卷.

邓小平(1904—1997)
1. Textos escogidos de Deng Xiaoping,1975—1982/ traducidos por el Buró Adjunto al Comité Central del Partido Comunista de China para la Compilacion y Traduccion de las Obras de Marx,Engels,Lenin y Stalin. Beijing:Ediciones en Lenguas Extranjeras,1983. 481 p.;23cm.
   《邓小平文选》(一九七五——一九八二年)

2. Textos escogidos de Deng Xiaoping/traducidos por el Buró Adjunto al Comité Central del Partido Comunista de China para la Compilacion y Traduccion de las Obras de Marx, Engels,Lenin y Stalin. Beijing:Ediciones en Lenguas Extranjeras,1992—1994. 3 volumes;23cm. ISBN:7119014285 (Rústica); 7119014289 (Rústica); 7119016946 (t. III);7119016948 (t. III)
   Contents:〔t. I.〕1938—1965—〔t. II.〕1975—1982—〔t. III〕1982—1992.
   《邓小平文选》,3卷. 第2版.

3. Construir un socialismo con peculiaridades chinas/ traduccion hecha por el Buroadjunto al Comite Central del Partide Comunista de China para la Compilacion Y Traduccion de las Obras de Marx,Engels,Lenin y Stalin. Beijing:Ediciones en Lenguas Extranjeras,1985. 98 pages;19cm.
   《建设有中国特设的社会主义》

4. Problemas fundamentales de la China de hoy/〔tr. Buró Adjunto al Comité Central del Partido Comunista de China...〕. Beijing:Ediciones en Lenguas Extranjeras, 1987. 239 p.:il.;20cm. ISBN:7119003593,7119003597
   《论当代中国基本问题》

朱德(1886—1976)
1. Obras escogidas de Zhu De/Zhu De;〔tr. por el Buró Adjunto al Comité Central del Partido Comunista de China para la comp. y tr. de las obras de Marx,Engels,Lenin y Stalin.〕. Beijing:Ediciones en Lenguas Extranjeras, 1986. 530 p.:il.;22cm.

《朱德选集》

陈云(1905—1995)

1. Textos escogidos de Chen Yun (1926—1949). Beijing：Ediciones en Lenguas Extranjeras, 1988. 374 pages：portraits；23cm.
   《陈云文选：1926—1949》，第一卷.

2. Textos escogidos de Chen Yun/traducidos por el Buró Adjunto al comité central del partido comunista de China para la compilación y traducción de las obras de Marx, Engels, Lenin y Stalin, by Chen Yun. Beijing：Ediciones En Lenguas Extranjeras, 1997. volumes 2（1949—1956）；23cm. ISBN：7119017187, 7119017181
   《陈云文选》，第二卷(1949—1956).

江泽民(1926—)

1. Textos escogidos de Jiang Zemin. 1/traducidos por el Buró Adjunto al Comité Central del Partido Comunista de China paa la Compilación y Traducción de las Obras de Marx, Engels, Lenin y Stalin. Beijing：Ediciones de Lenguas Extranjeras, 2010. 713 p.；23cm. ISBN：7119061849, 7119061844, 7119061856m, 7119061852
   《江泽民文选》

习近平(1953—)

1. La gobernación y administración de China/Xi Jinping. Beijing, China：Ediciones en Lenguas Extranjeras, 2014. vi, 579 páginas, 32 páginas sin numerar en papel cuche：ilustraciones（algunas a color）；24cm. ISBN：7119090597（paperback）, 7119090593（paperback）, 7119090252（hardback）,7119090259（hardback）
   《习近平谈治国理政》

2. La profundización integral de la reforma/Xi Jinping；compilación, Departamento de Estudios Documentales Adjunto al Comité Central del PCCh；traducción, Buró de Compilación y Traducción Adjunto alComité Central de PPCh. Beijing Ediciones en Lenguas Extranjeras, 2014. 262 p. 23cm. ISBN：7119090931, 7119090933
   《全面深化改革》

3. El sueño Chino de la gran revitalización de la nación China/Xi Jinping；compilacion Departamento de Estudios Documentales Adjunto al Comité Central del PCCh. Beijing：Ediciones en Lenguas Extranjeras, 2014. [4], 116, [2] s.；23cm. ISBN：7119086989, 7119086987
   《中华民族伟大复兴的中国梦》

4. 习近平谈治国理政：西班牙文版：习近平；西班牙文翻译组译. 北京：外文出版社,2014.579 页：照片；25cm. ISBN：7119090252
   西班牙文题名：La gobernación y administración de china

5. 决胜全面建成小康社会 夺取新时代中国特色社会主义伟大胜利 西班牙文/习近平著. 北京：外文出版社,2018. 96 页；23cm. ISBN：7119111988

D14　政策、政论

1. Sobre la experiencia historica de la dictadura del proletariado, este articulo de fondo del diario（yenminyibao）（Diario del Pueblo）, fue publicado el 5 de abril de 1956. Refleja las descusiones habidas en una reunion ampliada del buro Politico del Comite Central del partido Communista de China. Pekin：Ediciones en Lenguas Extranjeras, 1956. 21 pages；21cm.
   《关于无产阶级专政的历史经验》，人民日报编辑部.
   (1) Pekin：Ediciones en Lenguas Extranjeras, 1961. 67 pages；19cm.

2. Sobre la actual situacion international. Pekin：Ediciones en Lenguas Extranjeras, 1958. 79 pages；19cm.
   《目前国际形势》，周恩来.

3. El triunfo del marxismo leninismo en China/Liu Shao-Chi. Pekin：Ediciones en Lenguas Extranjeras, 1959. 41 p.；18cm.
   《马克思列宁主义在中国的胜利》，刘少奇.
   (1) El triunfo del Marxismo-Leninismo en China：escrito para la revista Problemas de la Paz y dl Socialismo, en celebración del décimo aniversario de la fundación de la República Polular China, 14 de septiembre de 1959. 2nd ed. Pekin：Ediciones en Lenguas Extranjeras, 1960. 41 pages；19cm.
   (2) 3rd ed. Pekin：Ediciones en Lenguas Extranjeras, 1961. 45 pages；19cm.

4. La gran unidad del pueblo chino y la gran unidad de los pueblos del mundo：escrito para Pravda de la Unión Soviética, en celebración del décimo aniversario de la República Popular China/Deng Siao-ping. Pekin：Ediciones en Lenguas Extranjeras, 1959. 17 pages；18cm.
   《中国人民大团结和世界人民大团结》，邓小平.

5. "Que cien flores se abran：que compitan cien escuelas ideologicas"（Informe sobre la politic del Partido Comunista de China acerca del arte, la literatura y la ciencia, pronunciado el 26 de mayo de 1956）. Pekin：Ediciones en Lenguas Extranjeras, 1958. 69 pages；18cm.
   《百花齐放、百家争鸣》，陆定一.
   (1) 4th ed. Pekin：Ediciones en Lenguas Extranjeras, 1963. 65 pages；19cm.

6. Expulsar de Asia al imperialismo de los EE. UU. Pekin, Ediciones en Lenguas Extranjeras, 1960. 51 pages：illustrations；
   《把帝国主义从亚洲赶出去》

7. Levantemos bien en alto la bandera roja de la línea general y continuemos avanzando/Fu-Chun Li. Pekín：Ediciones en Lenguas Extranjeras, 1960. [2], 46 p.；18cm.
   《高举总路线的红旗继续前进》，李富春.

8. 无产阶级专政的历史经验（一论、再论合订本），人民日报

编辑部. 北京:外文出版社,1961

9. 革命的辩证法和对帝国主义的认识 /邵铁真.北京:外文出版社,1963

10. 坚决进行反对美帝国主义和新殖民主义的斗争,实现亚非人民的经济解放/南汉宸.北京:外文出版社,1965

11. La experiencia historica de la guerra antifascista/por la redacción del Renmin ribao (9 de mayo de 1965). Pekin, Ediciones en Lenguas Extranjeras, 1965. 28 pages; 19cm.

《反对法西斯战争的历史经验》,人民日报编辑部.

12. Una gran revolucion en el frente de la cultura. Pekin, Ediciones en Lenguas Extranjeras, 1965. 119 pages; 19cm.

《文化战线上的一次大革命》,彭真等.

13. Avancemos por el gran camino iluminado por el pensamiento de Mao Tse-tung：en celebracion del XVII aniversario de la fundacion de la Republica Popular China. Pekin：Ediciones en Lenguas Extranjeras, 1967. 31 pages

《在毛泽东思想的大路上前进:庆祝中华人民共和国成立十七周年》

14. El país entero debe convertirse en gran escuela del pensamiento de Mao Tse-Tung：en conmemoración del 39° aniversario de la fundación del ejercito porpular de liberación de China. Pekin：Ediciones en Lenguas Extranjeras, 1967. 18 p. ; 18cm.

《全国都应该成为毛泽东思想的大学校》

15. Seguir al Presidente Mao y avanzar desafiando las grandes tormentas y olas. Pekin：Ediciones en Lenguas Extranjeras, 1967. 17 pages

《跟着毛主席在大风大浪中前进》

16. Avancemos por el camino abierto por la Revolucion Socialista de Octubre：en conmemoración del 50. o aniversario de la Gran Revolución Socialista de Octubre. Pekin：Ediciones en Lenguas Extranjeras, 1967. 44 pages

《沿着十月社会主义革命开辟的道路前进:纪念伟大的十月社会主义革命五十周年》

17. La clase obrera debe dirigirlo todo. Pekin：Ediciones en Lenguas Extranjeras, 1968. 23 pages；13cm.

《工人阶级必须领导一切》

18. Avancemos valientemente por el anchuroso camino de la victoria discurso del camarada... en calurosa celebración del XIX aniversario de la fundación de la República Popular China. Pekin Ediciones en Lenguas Extranjeras, 1968. 30 p. ilus. 13cm.

《在胜利的大路上奋勇前进:庆祝建国19周年》

19. El rumbo hacia la victoria para los pueblos revolucionarios de los diversos paises. Pekin：Ediciones en Lenguas Extranjeras, 1968. 12 pages；13cm.

《各国革命人民胜利的航向》

20. Asimilar la sangre fresca del proletariado：una importante cuestión en la consolidación del Partido. Pekin：Ediciones en Lenguas Extranjeras, 1969. 27 pages；13cm.

《吸收无产阶级新鲜血液》

21. Luchemos por consolidar aun mas la dictadura del proletarlado：en celebracion del XX aniversario de la fundación de la República Popular China. Pekin：Ediciones en Lenguas Extranjeras, 1969. 43 pages；13cm.

《为进一步巩固无产阶级专政而斗争:庆祝中华人民共和国成立二十周年》

22. Colocar todo bajo el mando del pensamiento de Mao Tse-tung. Pekin：Ediciones en Lenguas Extranjeras, 1969. 20 pages；13cm.

《用毛泽东思想统帅一切》

23. 关于知识分子再教育问题.北京:外文出版社,1969

24. Saludamos la gran década del setenta... ［By］Renmin Ribao, Hongqi y Jiefangjun Bao. Pekin：Ediciones en Lenguas Extranjeras, 1970. 19 pages；portraits 13cm.

《迎接伟大的七十年代》、《人民日报》、《红旗》杂志、《解放军报》报社 1970 年元旦社论.

25. Continuemos la revolución y avancemos de victoria en victoria en celebración del XXI aniversario de la fundación de la República Popular China. Pekin：Ediciones en Lenguas Extranjeras, 1970. 17 p. ilus. 19cm.

《继续革命,乘势前进:庆祝中华人民共和国成立 21 周年》、《人民日报》、《红旗》杂志、《解放军报》报社论.

26. Viva el triunfo de la dictadura del proletariado：en conmemoración del centenario de la Comuna de París, por las redacciones de Renmin Ribao, Hongqi y Jiefangjun Bao (18 de marzo de 1971). Pekin：Ediciones en Lenguas Extranjeras, 1971. 34 p. ; 19cm.

《无产阶级专政胜利万岁:纪念巴黎公社 100 周年》

27. Avancemos victoriosamente siguiento la línea revolucionaria del presidente Mao/editorial del día del año nuevo de 1971 de Renmin Ribao, Hongqi y Jiefangjun Bao. Pekin：Ediciones en Lenguas Extranjeras, 1971. 20 p. ；13cm.

《沿着毛主席革命路线胜利前进》、《人民日报》、《红旗》杂志、《解放军报》1971 年元旦社论.

28. 团结起来,争取更大的胜利(中西对照,人民日报、红旗杂志、解放军报 1972 年元旦社论.北京:商务印书馆,1972

29. 团结起来,争取更大的胜利. 北京:外文出版社,1972

30. Conquistar nuevas victorias：en celebracion del XXIII aniversario de la fundacion de la Republica Popular China. Pekin：Ediciones en Lenguas Extranjeras, 1972.

10 pages

《夺取新的胜利:庆祝中华人民共和国成立 23 周年》、《人民日报》、《红旗》杂志、《解放军报》报社论.

31. Gloria eterna al gran lider y maestro el presidente Mao Tsetung. Pekin：Ediciones en Lenguas Extranjeras，1976. 25 pages：portraits；23cm.

《伟大领袖和导师毛泽东主席永垂不朽》

32. La teoría del presidente Mao sobre los tres mundos constituye una gran contribución al marxismo-leninismo/redacción de Renmin Ribao (1. de noviembre de 1977). Pekin：Ediciones en Lenguas Extranjeras，1977. 85 pages；19cm.

《毛主席关于三个世界划分理论是对马克思列宁主义的重大贡献》

33. Gran victoria historica：aclamamos calurosamente el ascenso del presidente Jua Kuo-feng como lider de nuestro partido！aclamamos calidamente el aplastamiento del complot de la camarilla antipartido de Wang-Chang-Chiang-Yao！. Pekin：Ediciones en Lenguas Extranjeras，1977. 43 pages：portraits；19cm.

《伟大的历史性胜利》

34. Continuar hasta el fin la revolución bajo la dictadura del proletariado：contribución para el estudio del quinto tomo de Obras escogidas de Mao Tsetung/Jua Kuo-feng. Pekin：Ediciones en Lenguas Extranjeras，1977. 43 pages；19cm.

《把无产阶级专政下的继续革命进行到底:学习〈毛泽东选集〉第五卷》，华国锋.

35. 在庆祝中华人民共和国成立三十周年会议上的讲话/叶剑英.北京:外文出版社,1979

36. La revolución de nueva democracia en China，(1919—1949)/Li Sin. Pekin：Ediciones en Lenguas Extranjeras，1979. 162 pages：map；19cm.

《中国人民的新民主主义革命斗争:1919—1949》，李新.

37. Resolución sobre algunos problemas en la historia del Partido Communista de China：(1949—1981). Beijing：Ediciones en Lenguas Extranjeras，1981. 142 pages；19cm.

《关于建国以来党的若干历史问题的决议》

38. El brillo de la gran verdad del marxismo ilumina nuestro camino de avance：informe hecho en el acto conmemorativo del centenario del fallecimiento de C. Marx，(13 de marzo de 1983)/Hu Yaobang. Beijing：Ediciones en Lenguas Extranjeras，1983. 47 pages；18cm.

《马克思主义伟大真理的光芒照耀我们前进》，胡耀邦.

D15 建设成就

1. China alcanzara y sobrepasara a Inglaterra. Pekin：Ediciones en Lenguas Extranjeras，1958. 70 pages；19cm.

《赶上英国,超越英国》,牛忠黄.

2. El gran decenio/Chou En-lai. Pekín：Ediciones en Lenguas Extranjeras，1959. [2]，42 p.；18cm.

《伟大的十年》,周恩来.

3. 伟大的十年(中华人民共和国经济和文化建设成就的统计)/国家统计局.北京:外文出版社,1960

4. 光辉的十年(1949—1959).北京:外文出版社,1960

5. Los 25 anos de la nueva China. Pekin：Ediciones en Lenguas Extranjeras，1975. 112 pages：illustrations；19cm.

《新中国的二十五年》

6. Despues de un terremoto：el pueblo chino vence el mayor desastre natural. Pekin：Ediciones en Lenguas Extranjeras，1977. 81 pages：illustrations；19cm.

《一场大地震之后:中国人民战胜自然灾害的事迹》

7. 浦东:迈向 21 世纪的国际大都会.新星出版社,1993. ISBN:7801020391.(中国简况)

8. 跨世纪的长江三峡工程.新星出版社,1993. ISBN:7801020324.(中国简况)

9. 长江的开发与开放.新星出版社,1994. ISBN:7801020707,7801020703.(中国简况)

10. 中国社会发展现状.新星出版社,1994. ISBN:7801021827.(中国简况)

11. 长江:中国开发潜力最大的地区.新星出版社,1994. ISBN:7801020685,7801020680

12. 迈向二十一世纪的北京.新星出版社,1995. ISBN:7801023773.(中国简况)

13. 张家港:中国的模范城市.新星出版社,1996. ISBN:7801026640.(中国简况)

14. Desarrollo del delta del río Amarillo. China：Nueva Estrella，1997. 26 p.：il.；18cm. ISBN：7801027833，7801027832.(Presencia de China)

《黄河三角洲开发:中国一项跨世纪工程》.新星出版社(中国简况)

15. 中国西部地区的发展.新星出版社,1997. ISBN:7801027906.(中国简况)

16. El Centro y el oeste de China：nuevo punto candente de inversiones. Beijing：Nueva Estrella，1998. 30 p.：il.；18cm. ISBN：7801481402，7801481405. (Presencia de China)

《中国中西部:新的投资热点》.新星出版社(中国简况)

17. Cereales，poblacion y empleo/Zhang Guoqing. Beijing：Ediciones en Lenguas Extranjeras，2006. 145 pages：color illustrations；21cm. ISBN：7119044702，7119044705. (Desarrollo pacifico de China)

《粮食、人口与就业:西班牙文》,张国庆著;姜凤光等译.外文出版社(中国的和平发展系列)

18. La China emergente/Wu Xiaobo；[translated by M. V. Alonso]. Beijing：China Intercontinental Press，2010.

327 pages：illustrations；22cm. ISBN：7508517551，7508517555

《中国巨变：亚洲巨人的内部变革》，吴晓波著. 五洲传播出版社.

D16 政府组织

D161 人权

1. Desarrollo de los derechos humanos de China en los 50 años. Beijing：Nueva Estrella, 2000. 49 p. ISBN：7801482727，7801482723

《中国人权发展报告》，中华人民共和国国务院新闻办公室发布. 新星出版社.

D162 全国人民代表大会

1. Informe acerca de la labor del gobierno：presentado en la primera sesión de la Asamblea Popular Nacional, primera legislatura de la República Popular China el 23 de septiembre de 1954. Pekín：Ediciones en Lenguas Extranjeras, 1955. 64 p.；21cm.

《政府工作报告》，周恩来.

2. Informe sobre el reajuste de los principales indices del plan de la economia nacional para 1959 y sobre el desarrollo mas vigoroso del movimiento para aumentar la produccion y practicar la economia, rendido el 26 de agosto de 1959 ante la quinta sesion del Comite Permanente de la Asamblea popular nacional, segunda legislatura. Pekin：Ediciones en Lenguas Extranjeras, 1959. 48 pages；18cm.

《关于调整调整1959年国民经济计划主要指标和进一步开展增产节约运动的报告》，周恩来.

3. Informe acerca de la labor del gobierno：hecho en la Primera Sesión de la Asamblea popular nacional, segunda legislatura, el 18 de abril de 1959/Chou En-lai. Pekin：Ediciones en Lenguas Extranjeras, 1959. 78 pages；19cm.

《政府工作报告：1959年4月18日在第二届全国人民代表大会第一次会议上》，周恩来.

4. Principales documentos de la primera sesion de la Asamblea Popular Nacional（tercera legislatura）de la Republica Popular China. Pekin：Ediciones en Lenguas Extranjeras, 1965. 98 pages；19cm.

《中华人民共和第三次全国人民代表大会第一次会议主要文件》

5. Documentos de la I sesión de la IV asamblea popular nacional de la República Popular de China. Pekin：Ediciones en Lenguas Extranjeras, 1975

《中华人民共和国第四届全国人民代表大会第一次会议文件》

6. 中华人民共和国第五届全国人民代表大会第一次会议文件. 北京：外文出版社，1978

7. 中华人民共和国第五届全国人民代表大会第二次会议主要文件. 北京：外文出版社，1979

8. 中华人民共和国第五届全国人民代表大会第三次会议主要文件. 北京：外文出版社，1980

9. Quinta sesión de la 5a. Asamblea Popular Nacional de la República Popular China. Beijing：Ediciones en Lenguas Extranjeras, 1983. 244 pages；19cm.（Documentos de China）

《中华人民共和国第五届全国人民代表大会第五次会议主要文件》

10. Primera Sesion de la VI Asamblea Popular Nacional de la Republica Popular China, Junio de 1983. Beijing：Ediciones en Lenguas Extranjeras, 1983. 155 pages.（Documentos de China）

《中华人民共和国第六届全国人民代表大会第一次会议主要文件》

11. 中华人民共和国第六届全国人民代表大会第二次会议主要文件. 北京：外文出版社，1984

12. 中华人民共和国第六届全国人民代表大会第三次会议主要文件. 北京：外文出版社，1985

13. 中华人民共和国第六届全国人民代表大会第四次会议主要文件. 北京：外文出版社，1986

14. 中华人民共和国第六届全国人民代表大会第五次会议主要文件. 北京：外文出版社，1987

15. Una reunión democrática, con estilo de trabajo realista, unidad y marcha audaz：resumen de la I Sesión de la VIII Asamblea Popular Nacional de la República Popular China. Beijing Nueva Estrella, 1993. 43 p.，[8] p. de lám. 18cm. ISBN：7800859592，7800859595.（Presencia de China）

《民主、务实、团结、奋进的大会：中国八届人大一次会议纪实》. 新星出版社（中国简况）

D17 国家行政管理

D171 反腐败与廉政建设

1. Lucha anticorrupción y moralización administrativa en China/Oficina de Información del Consejo de Estado de la República Popular China. Beijing：Ediciones en Lenguas Extranjeras, 2010. 54 p.；21cm. ISBN：7119068268，7119068261

《中国的反腐败和廉政政策》，中华人民共和国国务院新闻办公室[发布].

D172 慈善与公益活动

1. 中国的慈善事业：西班牙文/徐晓燕编著；贾宁一译. 北京：新星出版社，2006；21cm. ISBN：7802251362

本书介绍了中国慈善事业的概况、发展机遇及加强慈善立法等内容，同时介绍了志愿者、台港澳侨、国际组织等在中国慈善事业中所起的作用.

D173　脱贫

1. 中国实行扶贫计划十周年. 新星出版社,1996. ISBN：7801026292.(中国简况)

2. 中国的减贫行动与人权进步：西班牙文/中华人民共和国国务院新闻办公室发布. 北京：外文出版社,2017. 52 页；21cm. ISBN：7119105406

D18　社会各阶层

D181　青年

1. Esforcemonos por hacer mas revolucionaria a nuestra juventud! Informe sobre el trabajo de la Liga de la Juventud Comunista de China pronunciado el ll de junio de 1964 ante su IX Congreso National. Pekin：Ediciones en Lenguas Extranjeras, 1964. 52 pages；19cm.

《中国青年革命化而斗争：1964 年 6 月 11 日在中国共产主义青年团第九次代表大会上的工作报告》,胡耀邦.

2. El amor, el matrimonio y la familia en China/por Huo Bifeng. Beijing Ediciones en Lenguas Extranjeras, 1987. 96 p. , [16] p. de lám. il. 19cm.

《中国青年的恋爱、婚姻、家庭》

3. 中国青年：跨世纪的一代. 北京：新星出版社,1994. ISBN：780102186x.(中国简况)

4. 当代中国青年的精神面貌. 北京：新星出版社,1997. ISBN：780102866x.(中国简况)

D182　妇女与儿童

1. "三八"五十周年在中国/全国妇女联合会. 北京：外文出版社,1960

2. La mujer china salta adelante. Pekin：Ediciones en Lenguas extranjeras, 1960. 98 pages：illustrations；19cm.

《中国妇女在跃进》,马信德等.

3. La Mujer china lucha por el socialismo/recopilación de Chi Pen. Pekin：Ediciones en Lenguas Extranjeras, 1977. 130 pages, [32] pages of plates：illustrations；19cm.

《为社会主义而斗争的中国妇女》,季本.

4. Protección de los derechos e intereses de la mujer. [Beijing] Nueva Estrella, 1993. 24 p. , [8] p. de lám. 18cm. ISBN：7800859665, 7800859663. (Presencia de China)

《中国妇女的权益保护》. 新星出版社(中国简况)

5. 北京：迎接联合国第四次世界妇女大会/第四次世界妇女大会中国组委会宣传动员委员会. 北京：新星出版社,1994. ISBN：780102120

6. 改革开放中的中国妇女. 北京：新星出版社,1994. ISBN：7801022440.(中国简况)

7. 中国妇女的国际交往. 北京：新星出版社,1995. ISBN：7801022777.(中国简况)

8. 中国性别平等与妇女发展状况：西班牙文/中华人民共和国国务院新闻办公室发布. 北京：新星出版社,2005. 42 页；20cm. ISBN：780148830X

本书为国务院新闻办公室发布的白皮书,重点介绍近十年来中国性别平等和妇女事业的发展状况.

9. 妇女与儿童：西班牙文/韦黎明编著；张重光等译. 北京：新星出版社,2006；21cm. ISBN：7802251435

本书介绍了中国妇女与儿童的现状,权益保护等方面的情况.

10. 中国性别平等与妇女发展/中华人民共和国国务院新闻办公室[发布]. 北京：外文出版社,2015. 48 页；21cm. ISBN：7119096544

西班牙文题名：Igualdad de genero y desarrollo de la mujer en China

11. 儿童的保护和培育. 北京：新星出版社,1994. ISBN：7801022513.(中国简况)

D19　工运与工会

1. Sindicatos/[compilado por Ediciones en Lenguas Extranjeras]. Beijing, [China]：Ediciones en Lenguas Extranjeras, 1987. 22 p. ：il. ；19cm. ISBN：7119002902, 7119002903. (Presencia de China)

《中国工会》

D191　政治运动和事件

1. Gran revolución cultural socialista en China. Pekin：Ediciones en Lenguas Extranjeras，1966—1967. 5 volumes (volumes 3，5－8)；20cm.

中国的社会主义文化大革命(第一集). 北京：外文出版社,1966

2. 中国的社会主义文化大革命(第二集). 北京：外文出版社,1966

3. 中国的社会主义文化大革命(第三集). 北京：外文出版社,1966

4. 中国的社会主义文化大革命(第四集). 北京：外文出版社,1966

5. 中国的社会主义文化大革命(第五集). 北京：外文出版社,1966

6. 中国的社会主义文化大革命(第六集). 北京：外文出版社,1966

7. 无产阶级专政和无产阶级文化大革命/王力等. 北京：外文出版社,1967

8. 中国的社会主义文化大革命(第七集). 北京：外文出版社,1966

9. 中国的社会主义文化大革命(第八集). 北京：外文出版社,1966

10. 中国的社会主义文化大革命(第九集). 北京：外文出版社,1966

11. 中国的社会主义文化大革命(第十集). 北京：外文出版社,1966

12. Sobre la lucha de los revolucionarios proletarios para la toma del poder. Pekín：Ediciones en Lenguas

Extranjeras，1967. 60 p. ；14cm.

《论无产阶级革命派的夺权斗争》

13. Viva la victoria de la gran revolucion cultural bajo la dictadura del proletariado!：En celebración del XVIII aniversario de la fundación de la República Popular China. Pekin：Ediciones en Lenguas Extranjeras，1968. 27 pages；19cm.

《无产阶级专政下的文化大革命胜利万岁：庆祝建国 18 周年》

14. Un documento que hace epoca：en commenoracion del II aniversario de la publicacion de la Circular del 16 de Mayo. Pekin：Ediciones en Lenguas Extranjeras，1968. 26 pages；13cm.

《划时代的文献：纪念〈通知〉发表两周年》

15. Importantes documentos de la gran revolución cultural proletaria. Pekin：Ediciones en Lenguas Extranjeras，1970. 346 p. ；ill. ；13cm.

《无产阶级文化大革命重要文件集》

16. Selecciones de artículos de crítica a Lin Piao y Confucio. Pekín：Ediciones en Lenguas Extranjeras，1975

《批林批孔文选》（一）

17. Seleccion de articulos de critica a Lin Piao y confucio. 2. Pekin：Ediciones En Lenguas Extranjeras，1976. 191 pages；19cm.

《批林批孔文选》（二）

18. Obreros，campesinos y soldados critican a Lin Piao y confucio：Coleccion de articulos. Pekin：Ediciones en Lenguas Extranjeras，1976. 117 pages；19cm.

《工农兵批林批孔文集》

D192　社会生活

1. Aspectos de la vida social/por la redaccion de Coleccion China. Beijing：Ediciones en Lenguas Extranjeras，1985. 299 pages；illustrations

《社会生活》，《中国概况丛书》编辑委员会编.

2. 普通中国人的生活. 北京：，中国建设出版社，1988

3. 当代中国人的恋爱、婚姻和家庭. 北京：新星出版社，ISBN：7801023935.（中国简况）

4. 活跃的中国社区志愿服务. 北京：新星出版社，1995. ISBN：7801023293.（中国简况）

5. 中国人的衣、食、住、行. 北京：新星出版社，ISBN：7801025989.（中国简况）

6. Situación del trabajo y la seguridad social en China/Oficina de Información del Consejo de Estado de la República Popular China. Beijing：Editorial Nueva Estrella，2002. 47 pages；21cm. ISBN：7801484096，7801484093

《中国的劳动和社会保障状况》，中华人民共和国国务院新闻办公室发布.新星出版社.

7. Garantía social China y su política/Oficina de Información del Consejo de Estado de la República Popular China.

Beijing：Editorial Nueva Estrella，2004. 43 pages；21cm. ISBN：7801486587，7801486585

《中国的社会保障状况和政策》，中华人民共和国国务院新闻办公室发布.新星出版社.

8. Vida nocturna de Beijing/［editor］，Teng Yilan；［texto en español，Ouyang Yuan，Jorge Luis López López］. Beijing：Ediciones en Lenguas Extranjeras，2008. 107 p. il. col. ；23cm. ISBN：7119054582，7119054589

《夜北京》，滕一岚编著.

9. China a través de bolsos/Li Tie. Beijing Ediciones en Lenguas Extranjeras，2009. 159 p. il. ，fot. （algunas col.）23cm. ISBN：7119055947，7119055941

《挎包里的中国》，李铁主编. 本书选择了 50 年代直至今天不同时期中国人的挎包和挎包了东西，来反映中国社会的变化.

D192.1　禁毒

1. Lucha contra las drogas en China. Beijing：Oficina de Información del Consejo de Estado de la República Popular China，2000. 40 pages；20cm. ISBN：7801482867，7801482860

《中国的禁毒》，中华人民共和国国务院新闻办公室发布.新星出版社.

D192.2　地方政治

D192.21　台湾

1. La oposición a las provocaciones militares de los EE. UU. en la región del estrecho de Taiwan：selección de documentos importantes/editado por Instituto Popular Chino de Asuntos Exteriores. Pekin：Ediciones en Lenguas Extranjeras，1958. 74 p. ；19cm.

《反对美国在台湾海峡地区的军事挑衅》，中国人民外交学会.

2. Contra la ocupacion de Taiwan por los Estados Unidos y la conspiracion de las "dos Chinas" (Una selecion de documentos importantes) Compilada por el Instituto Popular Chino de Asuntos Exteriores. Pekin：Ediciones en Lenguas Extranjeras，1958. 178 pages；19cm.

《反对美国霸占台湾、制造两个中国的阴谋》，中国人民外交学会.

3. Jiang Zemin y Li Peng hablan de la cuestión de Taiwan. ［Beijing］：China Intercontinental Press，1996. 75 p. ：il. ；18cm. ISBN：7801131584，7801131584

《江泽民、李鹏谈台湾问题》，江泽民、李鹏著；国务院台湾事务办公室编写.五洲传播出版社.

4. Preguntas y respuestas sobre el problema en Taiwan y la reunificación de China. China：China Intercontinental Press，1997. 121 p. ，il. ，color. ISBN：7801133382，7801133380

《〈台湾问题与祖国统一〉问答》，国务院台湾事务办公室编.五洲传播出版社.

D192.22　香港

1. 香港问题的由来与现状. 北京：新星出版社，1994. ISBN：7801022017.（中国简况）

2. Hong Kong mas alla de 1997/por Wang Qiaolong. Beijing：China Intercontinental Press，1997. 77 pages：color illustrations；18cm. ISBN：7801132831，7801132833

《"九七"前后谈香港》，王巧玲著. 五洲传播出版社.

3. Hong Kong, region administrativa especial de China/por Wang Qiaolong. Beijing：China Intercontinental Press，1997. 69 pages：color illustrations；18cm. ISBN：7801132912，7801132918

《香港：中国的特别行政区》，王巧玲著. 五洲传播出版社.

4. El orígen y la solución del problema de Hong Kong/Huang Fengwu. [China]：China Intercontinental Press，1997. 77 p.：il.；15cm. ISBN：7801132513, 7801132512. (Hong Kong series)

《香港问题的由来及解决》，黄凤武著. 五洲传播出版社.

5. La economia Hongkonesa con la parte contimental de la patria como respaldo/por Cai Chimeng. Beijing：China Intercontinental Press，1997. 77 pages：color illustrations；18cm. ISBN：780113267X，7801132673

《背靠祖国的香港经济》，蔡赤萌著. 五洲传播出版社.

6. Quien ha creado la prosperidad de Hong Kong/por Chen Duo, Lian Jintian. Beijing：China Intercontinental Press，1997. 77 pages：color illustrations；18cm. ISBN：7801132750，7801132758

《是谁创造了香港的繁荣？》，陈多，连锦添著. 五洲传播出版社.

D192.23 澳门

1. Macao, joya en el mar de la China Meridional/Ge Guangzhi. [Macao] China Intercontinental Press，1999. 78 p. il.，mapa 18cm. ISBN：7801135970，7801135971. (Macau series)

《中国南海的宝石：澳门》，葛广智著. 五洲传播出版社.

2. Macao marcha hacia el siglo XXI/por Xu Yamin y Qi Pengfei. [Beijing]：China Intercontinental Press，1999. 79 p. il. 18cm. ISBN：7801136063，7801136060. (Macau series)

《走向21世纪的澳门》，徐雅民，齐鹏飞著. 五洲传播出版社.

D2 外交、国际关系

D21 国际关系

D211 国际共产主义运动

1. Refutación al revisionismo moderno. Pekín Ediciones en Lenguas Extranjeras，1959. 96 p. 19cm.

《现代修正主义必须批判》

(1) Refutación al revisionismo contemporáneo. Ed. aumentada. Pekin：Ediciones en Lenguas Extranjeras，1963. 150 p.；19cm.

增订版

2. Viva el leninismo. Pekin：Ediciones en Lenguas Extranjeras，1960. 115 pages：portraits；21cm.

《列宁主义万岁》，人民日报编辑部.

3. Lenin sobre la guerra y la paz. Pekin，Ediciones en Lenguas Extranjeras，1960. 74 pages；19cm.

《列宁论战争与和平：纪念列宁诞生90周年（1870—1960)》，人民日报社编辑部.

4. El leninismo y el revisionismo contemporaneo. Pekin：Ediciones en Lenguas Extranjeras，1963. 109 pages；17cm.

《列宁主义与现代修正主义》，1963年第1期《红旗》社论.

5. Proletarios de todos los paises, unios para luchar contra nuestro enemigo común. Pekin：Ediciones en Lenguas Extranjeras，1963. 27 p.；19cm.

《全世界无产阶级联合起来反对我们共同的敌人》，人民日报编辑部.

6. De donde proceden las divergencias?：respuesta al camarada Thorez y otros camaradas：editorial del Renmin Ribao（27 de febrero de 1963）. Pekin：Ediciones en Lenguas Extranjeras，1963. 38 pages；19cm.

《分歧从何而来：答多列士同志》，1963年2月27日《人民日报》社论.

7. 陶里亚蒂同志与我们的分歧：1962年12月31日《人民日报》社论. 北京：外文出版社，1963

8. Una vez más sobre las divergencias entre el camarada Togliatti y nosotros：algunos problemas importantes del leninismo en el mundo contemporáneo：por la redacción de la revista Hongqi publicado en el no. 3—4，1963. Pekin：Ediciones en Lenguas Extranjeras，1963. 211 pages；19cm.

《再论陶里亚蒂同志与我们的分歧：关于列宁主义在等待的若干重大问题》，《红旗》杂志编辑部.

9. Un Comentario sobre la declaración del Partido Comunista de los EE. UU.：editorial del Renmin Ribao（8 de marzo de 1963）. Pekin：Ediciones en Lenguas Extranjeras，1963. 18 p.

《评美国共产党的声明》，1963年3月9日《人民日报》社论.

10. Polémica acerca de la línea general del movimiento comunista internacional. Pekín：Ediciones en Lenguas Extranjeras，1965. 610 p.；20cm.

《关于国际共产主义运动总路线的论战》

11. 列宁主义的伟大胜利：纪念列宁诞生九十五周年/红旗杂志社论. 北京：外文出版社，1965

12. Confesion en un atolladero：comentario sobre el "discurso inaugural" de Nixon y el despreciable aplauso de la renegada camarilla revisionista soviética/por comentarista de "Renmin Ribao" y "Hongqi." Pekin：Ediciones en Lenguas Extranjeras，1969. 17 pages；13cm.

《走投无路的自供状：评尼克松的就职演说和苏修叛徒集团的无耻捧场》

D212　中国与联合国

1. La Corriente de la historia es irresistible. Pekín：Ediciones en Lenguas Extranjeras，1971
   《历史潮流，不可抗拒》
   （1）历史潮流，不可抗拒（中西对照）. 北京：商务印书馆，1972

2. 在联大第二十六届会议 1971 年 11 月 5 日全体会议上大会主席和各国代表欢迎中华人民共和国代表团的讲话. 北京：外文出版社，1971

3. Discurso pronunciado por Chiao Kuan-Jua，jefe de la delegación de la República Popular China en la sesión plenaria de la 27a asamblea general de las Naciones Unidas：3 de octubre de 1972. Pekín：Ediciones en Lenguas Extranjeras，1972
   《中华人民共和国代表团团长乔冠华在联合国大会第 27 届会议全体会议上的讲话》

4. 中华人民共和国代表团团长乔冠华在联合国大会第二十八届会议全体会议上的发言. 北京：外文出版社，1973

5. Discurso de Chiao Kuan-jua，jefe de la delegacion de la Republica Popular China en la Reunion Plenarial de la 29. a Asamlea General de la ONU（2 de octubre de 1974）. Pekin：Ediciones en Lenguas Extranjeras，1974. 26 pages
   《中华人民共和国代表团团长在联合国大会第二十九届会议上的发言》

6. Discurso de Teng Siao-Ping，jefe de la delegación de la República Popular China en la sesión extraordinaria de la Asamblea General de la ONU. Pekin：Ediciones en Lenguas Extranjeras，1974. 18 pages；19cm.
   《中华人民共和国代表团团长邓小平在联大特别会议上的发言》，邓小平.

7. Discurso de Chiao Kuan-Jua，jefe de la delegación de la República Popular China：en la reunión plenaria de la 30. a Asamblea General de la ONU（26 de septiembre de 1975）. Pekin：Ediciones en Lenguas Extranjeras，1975. 28 pages；19cm.
   《中华人民共和国代表团团长在联合国代表大会第三十届全体会议上的发言》

8. 中国政府继续坚决执行毛主席的革命外交路线和政策（中国代表团团长在联合国大会第三十一届全体会议上的发言）. 北京：外文出版社，1976

9. 中国重视与联合国的合作. 北京：新星出版社，1995. ISBN：7801023145.（中国概况）

D22　中国外交

1. La política exterior de China. Beijing Ediciones en Lenguas Extranjeras，1988. 23 p. ilus. 18cm. ISBN：711900316X，7119003160.（Presencia de China）

《中国的外交政策》，外文出版社（中国概况）

2. 中国的外交政策. 北京：新星出版社，1993. 25 页；18cm. ISBN：78011020022.（中国简况）

3. Política exterior fundamental de China/autor，Luo Yuanjun. Beijing：Editorial Nueva Estrella，2004. ISBN：7801485777，7801485779. （China express；viaje multicultural a un país de cinco mil años）
   《中国外交的基本政策》，骆元军编. 新星出版社. 全面地向拉美地区介绍中国外交的基本政策，特别是在台湾问题上的原则立场.

4. Filosofia de China para el intercambio con el exterior en el siglo XXI/Liu Binjie. Beijing：Ediciones en Lenguas Extranjeras，2006. 123 pages：color illustrations；21cm. ISBN：7119044672，7119044675. （Desarrollo pacifico de China）
   《21 世纪中国对外交往的哲学：西班牙文》，柳斌杰著；陈根生等译. 外文出版社（中国的和平发展系列）

5. La diplomacia de China/Zhang Qingmin；traductores：Tang Baisheng y Cui Weiben. Beijing：China Intercontinental Press，2011. 175 páginas：ilustraciones（algunas，color）；23cm. ISBN：7508519210，7508519213
   《中国外交》，吴伟主编. 五洲传播出版社.

6. Ayuda de China al exterior/Oficina de Información del Consejo de Estado de la República Popular China. Beijing：Ediciones en Lenguas Extranjeras，2011. 54 p.；21cm. ISBN：7119069289，7119069284
   《中国的对外援助》，中华人民共和国国务院新闻办公室［发布］.

7. 中国特色大国外交与"一带一路"/吴建民著；张重光，欧阳媛，林传红西文翻译. 北京：外文出版社有限责任公司，2016. 41 页；21cm. ISBN：7119103600
   西班牙文题名：Diplomacia de pais grande con peculiaridades Chinas y "La Franja y la Ruta"

8. 中国的亚太安全合作政策/中华人民共和国国务院新闻办公室［发布］. 北京：外文出版社有限责任公司，2017. 53 页；21cm. ISBN：7119105123
   西班牙文题名：Política de China sobre cooperación en seguridad en Asía-Pacífico

9. El viceprimer ministro Chen Yi responde a los periodistas. Pekin：Ediciones en Lenguas Extranjeras，1966. 68 pages；13cm.
   《陈毅副总理答记者问》

10. Declaracion del gobierno de la Republica Popular China（24 de mayo de 1969）. Pekin：Ediciones en Lenguas Extranjeras，1969. 40 pages；13cm.
    《中华人民共和国政府声明：1969 年 5 月 24 日》

11. Declaracion del gobierno de la Republica Popular China（7 de octubre de 1969）. Pekin：Ediciones en Lenguas Extranjeras，1969. 50 pages；13cm.
    《中华人民共和国政府声明：1969 年 10 月 7 日》

D221　中美关系

1. 反对美国反动派迫害美国共产党的暴行.北京:外文出版社,1962

2. La verdadera faz de la administración de Kennedy. Pekin, Ediciones en Lenguas Extranjeras, 1963. 81 pages; 19cm.
   《肯尼迪政府的真面目》

3. 在对待美帝国主义问题上两条路线的斗争/范秀珠.北京:外文出版社,1965

4. Conmemoremos la victoria sobre el fascismo aleman y llevemos hasta el fin la lucha contra el imperialismo norteamericano!. Pekin: Ediciones en Lenguas Extranjeras, 1965. 31 pages
   《纪念战胜德国法西斯,把反对美帝国主义的斗争进行到底》,罗瑞卿.

5. El pueblo venció al fascismo japonés y vencerá también al imperialismo yanqui/Luo Yui-Ching. Pekín: Ediciones en Lenguas Extranjeras, 1965. [2], 33 p.; 18cm.
   《人民战胜了法西斯,人民也一定能够战胜美帝国主义》,罗瑞卿.

6. La agresión norteamericana no tiene límites y tampoco los tiene nuestra respuesta a la agresión. Pekín Ediciones en Lenguas Extranjeras, 1966. 31 p.; 18cm.
   《美国侵略没有界限,我们反侵略也没有界限》

7. Pueblos asiáticos, unios y espulsad de Asia a los agresores norteamericanos!. Pekin: Ediciones en Lenguas Extranjeras, 1971. 126 p.: ill.; 18cm.
   《亚洲人民团结起来,把美国侵略者从亚洲赶出去》

8. Comunicado conjunto Chino-Estadounidense, 28 de febrero de 1972. Pekin: Ediciones en Lenguas Extranjeras, 1972. 7 pages
   《中美联合公报:1972年2月28日》

D222　中苏关系

1. Unamonos sobre la base de las dos declaraciones de Moscú. Pekin: Ediciones en Lenguas Extranjeras, 1963. 36 pages; 19cm.
   《在莫斯科宣言和莫斯科声明的基础上团结起来》,人民日报社论.

2. Espejo de los revisionistas/editorial del Renmin ribao (9 de marzo de 1963). Pekin: Ediciones en Lenguas Extranjeras, 1963. 12 pages; 19cm.
   《修正主义的一面镜子》,1963年3月9日《人民日报》社论

3. Proposición acerca de la línea general del movimiento comunista internacional: respuesta del Comité Central del Partido Comunista de China a la carta del Comité Central del Partido Comunista de la Unión Soviética del 30 de marzo de 1963. Pekín: Ediciones en Lenguas Extranjeras, 1963. 119 p.
   《关于国际共产主义总路线的建议:中国共产常中央委员会对苏联共产党中央委员会1963年3月30日来信的复信》
   (1) Pekin: Ediciones en Lenguas Extranjeras, 1966. 119 pages; 15cm.
   (2) [S. l.]: Comité Central del Partido Comunista de España(Internacional), 1971. 2 v.; 17cm.
   (3) [S. l.]: Escuela Central de la OCE-Bandera Roja, 1975. 63 p. (Cuadernos de formación; 1)

4. El origen y el desarrollo de las divergencias entre la direccion del PCUS y nosotros/Comentario sobre la carta abierta del CC del PCUS (I), porla redacción del Renmin Ribao y la Redacción de la revista Hongqi. Pekin: Ediciones en Lenguas Extranjeras, 1963. 72 pages; 19cm.
   《苏共领导同我们分歧的由来和发展:评苏共中央公开信》,《人民日报》、《红旗》编辑部.

5. Sobre el problema de Stalin: comentario sobre la carta abierta del Comite Central del PCUS (II)/por la red. del Renmin Ribao y la red. de la revista Hongqi (13 de septiembre de 1963). Pekin: Ediciones en Lenguas Extranjeras, 1963. 36 pages
   《关于斯大林问题:二评苏共中央公开信》,《人民日报》、《红旗》编辑部.

6. Es Yugoslavia un pais socialista?: Comentario sobre la carta abierta del CC del PCUS (III)/por la Redacción del Renmin Ribao y la Redacción de la revista Hongqi (26 de septiembre de 1963). Pekin: Ediciones en Lenguas Extranjeras, 1963. 50 pages; 19cm.
   《南斯拉夫是社会主义国家吗?:三评苏共中央公开信》,《人民日报》、《红旗》编辑部.

7. Apologistas del neo-colonialismo: comentario de la carta abierta del Comite Central del PCUS (IV)/por la Redacción del Renmin Ribao y la Redacción de la revista Hongqi (22 de octubre de 1963). Pekin: Ediciones en Lenguas Extranjeras, 1963. 37 pages; 19cm.
   《新殖民主义的辩护士:四评苏共中央公开信》,《人民日报》、《红旗》编辑部.

8. Dos lineas diferentes en el problema de la guerra y la paz: comentario sobre la carta abierta del Comité central del PCUS (V). Pekin: Ediciones en Lenguas Extranjeras, 1963. 58 pages; 15cm.
   《在战争与和平路线上的两条路线:五评苏共中央公开信》,《人民日报》、《红旗》编辑部.

9. Dos politicas de coexistencia pacifica diametralmente opuestas: comentario sobre la carta abierta del CC de PCUS (VI)/por la Redaccion del Renmin Ribao y la Redacción de la revista Hongqi (12 de diciembre de 1963). Pekin: Ediciones en Lenguas Extranjeras, 1963. 73 pages; 15cm.
   《两种根本对立的和平共处政策:六评苏共中央公开信》,

《人民日报》、《红旗》编辑部.

10. La verdad sobre la ali anza de los dirigentes del PCUS con la India en contra de China. Pekin：Ediciones en Lenguas Extranjeras，1963. 53 pages；18cm.

《苏共领导联印反华的真相》,《人民日报》编辑部.

11. La lucha entre las dos líneas en el Congreso Mundial de Mujeres celebrado en Moscú. Pekin, Ediciones en Lenguas Extranjeras，1963. 62 pages；19cm.

《在莫斯科世界妇女大会上两条路线的斗争》,《人民日报》编辑部.

12. Siete cartas intercambiadas entre el Comite Central del Partido Comunista de China y el Comite Central del Partido Commuista de la Union Sovietica. Pekin：Ediciones en Lenguas Extranjeras，1964. 117 pages；15cm.

《中共中央和苏共中央来往的七封信》

13. Carta del Comité Central del Partido Comunista de China en respuesta a la carta del 15 de junio de 1964 del Comité Central del partido comunista de la Unión Soviética. Pekin：Ediciones en Lenguas Extranjeras，1964. 52 p. ；18cm.

《中国共产党中央委员会对于苏联共产党中央委员会1964年6月15日来信的复信》

14. Carta del Comite Central del Partido Comunista de China en respuesta a la carta del 30 de julio de 1964 del Comite Central del Partido Comunista de la Union Sovietica. Pekin：Ediciones en Lenguas Extranjeras，1964. 20 pages；14cm.

《中国共产党中央委员会对于苏联共产党中央委员会1964年7月30日来信的复信》

15. Los dirigentes del PCUS son los mayores escisionistas de nuestra epoca：comentario sobre la carta abierta del Comite Central del PCSU（VII）/por la Redacción del Renmin Ribao y la Redacción de la revista Hongqi（4 de febrero de 1964）. Pekin：Ediciones en Lenguas Extranjeras，1964. 63 pages；19cm.

《苏共领导是当代最大的分裂主义者：七评苏共中央的公开信(1964年2月4日)》,《人民日报》、《红旗》编辑部.

16. La revolucion proletaria y el revisionismo de Jruschov：comentario sobre la carta abierta del CC del PCUS（VIII）/por la Redacción del Renmin Ribao y la Redacción de la revista Hongqi（31 de marzo de 1964）. Pekin：Ediciones en Lenguas Extranjeras，1964. 101 pages；15cm.

《无产阶级革命和赫鲁晓夫修正主义：八评苏共中央公开信(1964年3月31日)》,《人民日报》、《红旗》编辑部.

17. Acerca del falso comunismo de Jruschov y sus lecciones historicas para el mundo：comentario sobre la carta abierta del CC del PCSU（IX）/por la Redacción del

Renmin Ribao y la Redacción de la revista Hongqi（14 de julio de 1964）. Pekin：Ediciones en Lenguas Extranjeras，1964. 76 pages；19cm.

《关于赫鲁晓夫的假共产主义机器在世界历史上的教训：九评苏共中央公开信（1964年7月14日）》,《人民日报》、《红旗》编辑部.

18. Por que cayo Jruschov/editorial de la revista Hongqi publicado en el No. 21－22, 1964. Pekin：Ediciones en Lenguas Extranjeras，1964. 11 pages；19cm.

《赫鲁晓夫是怎样下台的》,《红旗》1964年底21－22期社论.

19. Comentario sobre la reunión de marzo en Moscú/por la redacción del Renmin Ribao y la redacción de la revista Hongqi（23 de marzo de 1965）. Pekín：Ediciones en Lenguas Extranjeras，1965. 24 p.

《评莫斯科三月会议：1965年3月23日》,《人民日报》、《红旗》编辑部.

20. Llevar hasta el fin la lucha contra el revisionismo Jruschovista：en conmemoracion del II aniversario de la publicacion de la proposicion acerca de la linea general del movimiento comunista internacional/por la redaccion del Renmin Ribao y la redaccion de la revista Hongqi（14 de junio de 1965）. Pekin：Ediciones en Lenguas Extranjeras，1965. 16 pages；21cm.

《把反对赫鲁晓夫修正主义的斗争进行到底：纪念〈国际共产主义运动总路线的建议〉发表两周年》,《人民日报》、《红旗》编辑部.

21. En refutacion de lo que la nueva direccion del PCUS llama "accion conjunta"/por la redacción del Renmin Ribao y la redacción de la revista Hongqi. Pekin：Ediciones en Lenguas Extranjeras，1965. 34 pages

《驳苏共领导的所谓"联合行动"：1965年11月11日》,《人民日报》、《红旗》编辑部.

22. Los dirigentes del PCUS son traidores a las dos delcaraciones de 1957 y 1960/por la Redacción del Renmin Ribao（30 de diciembre de 1965）. Pekin：Ediciones en Lenguas Extranjeras，1965. 7 pages；21cm.

《苏共领导是宣言与生命的背叛者：1965年12月30日》,《人民日报》、《红旗》编辑部.

23. Confesión de la nueva dirección del PCUS de su aplicación de la linea de cooperación Soviético-Norteamericana, por comentarista de la revista Hongqi, 11 de febrero de 1966. Pekin, Ediciones en Lenguas Extranjeras，1966. 16 pages；21cm.

《苏共新领导奉行苏美联合的自供状》,《红旗》评论员.

24. La gran revolución de China y la gran tragedia de la URSS/Observador del Renmin Ribao（4 de junio de 1967）. Pekin：Ediciones en Lenguas Extranjeras，1968. 14 pages

《中国的大革命和苏联的大悲剧》

25. Bancarrota total del revisionismo contemporáneo soviético. Pekin：Ediciones en Lenguas Extranjeras，1968. 70 p.；13cm.

《苏联现代修正主义的总破产》

26. Abajo los nuevos zares!. Pekin：Ediciones en Lenguas Extranjeras，1969. 42 pages；18cm.

《打倒新沙皇》

27. Repugnante funcion de autodesen-mascaramiento. Pekin：Ediciones en Lenguas Extranjeras，1969. 18 pages；13cm.

《自我揭露的丑恶表演》，钟仁.

28. En refutación a las falacias del socialimperialismo revisionista soviético. Pekin：Ediciones en Lenguas Extranjeras，1969. 43 pages；13cm.

《驳苏修社会帝国主义的谬论》

29. Leninismo o socialimperialismo?：en conmemoración del centenario del nacimiento del gran Lenin/por las redaccines de Renmin Ribao, Hongqi y Jiefangjun Bao. Pekin：Ediciones en Lenguas Extranjeras，1970. 70 p.：port.；13cm.

《列宁主义，还是社会帝国主义？：纪念伟大列宁诞生一百周年》，《人民日报》、《红旗》杂志、《解放军报》报社论.

30. 赤裸裸的暴露. 北京：外文出版社，1970

31. Alma muerta de Confucio y ensueño de los nuevos Zares. Pekin：Ediciones en Lenguas Extranjeras，1974. 43 pages

《孔老二的亡灵和新沙皇的迷梦》

32. Propaganda barata. Pekin：Ediciones en Lenguas Extranjeras，1974. 31 pages

《廉价的宣传》

33. La cara feroz del socialimperialismo soviético. Pekín：Ediciones en Lenguas Extranjeras，1976. 90 pages；19cm.

《苏修社会帝国主义的丑恶面目》

34. La URSS—imperio neo-zarísta. Pekin：Ediciones en Lenguas Extranjeras，1978. 109 pages；19cm.

《新沙皇统治下的苏联》

D223　中国与世界其他各国外交关系

1. 中印边界问题文件汇编/外交部. 北京：外文出版社，1959

2. 中印边界问题文件集. 北京：外文出版社，1959

3. El problema de la frontera Chino-Hindú/Ediciones en Lenguas Extranjeras. Ed. aumentada. Pekín：Ediciones en Lenguas Extranjeras，1962. 130 p.，［13］h. de mapas（pleg.）；19cm.

《中印边界问题》

4. Carta del Primer Ministro Chou En-lai a los dirigentes de los paises asiaticos y africanos, referente al problema de la frontera chino-hindu（15 de noveimbre de 1962）. Pekin：Ediciones en Lenguas Extranjeras，1973. 34 pages；part folded maps

《周恩来总理就中印边界问题致亚非拉国家领导人的信：1962年11月15日》

5. Una victoria de los cinco principios de la coexistencia pacifica. Pekin：Ediciones en Lenguas Extranjeras，1960. 54 pages；19cm.

《和平共处五项原则的胜利：中缅友好协商解决边界问题、发展友好关系的重要文件》，中国人民外交协会.

6. En apoyo de la justa lucha del pueblo cubano y de los otros pueblos latinoamericanos contra el imperialismo de EE. UU. Pekín，Ediciones en Lenguas Extranjeras，1962. 191 pages：portraits；s 19cm.

《支持古巴和拉丁美洲各国人民反对美帝国主义的正义斗争》

7. Declaracion conjunta del Partido Comunista de China y el Partido Comunista de Nueva Zelandia. Pekin：Ediciones en Lenguas Extranjeras，1963. 13 pages；19cm.

《中国共产党、新西兰共产党联合声明》

8. Declaracion conjunta del Presidente Liu Shao-Chi y del Presidente Ho Chi Minh. Pekin：Ediciones en Lenguas Extranjeras，1963. 38 pages；19cm.

《刘少奇主席和崔镛健委员长联合声明》

9. Es Yugoslavia un pais socialista?：Comentario sobre la carta abierta del CC del PCUS（III）/por la Redacción del Renmin Ribao y la Redacción de la revista Hongqi（26 de septembre de 1963）. Pekin：Ediciones en Lenguas Extranjeras，1963. 50 pages；19cm.

《南斯拉夫是社会主义国家吗？：三评苏共中央公开信》，《人民日报》、《红旗》编辑部.

10. La eterna amistad combativa Chino-Albanes. Documentos de la visita de los dirigentes hinos a Albania. Pekin：Ediciones en Lenguas Extranjeras，1964. 172 pages；19cm.

《中阿战斗友谊万岁：中国领导人访问阿尔巴尼亚文件集》

11. 把反帝反修斗争进行到底：阿尔巴尼亚党政代表团访问中国文件集. 北京：外文出版社，1966

12. Discurso pronunciado en la Academia de Ciencias Sociales Aliarcham, de Indonesia（25 de mayo de 1965）. Pekin：Ediciones en Lenguas Extranjeras，1965. 56 pages；14cm.

《在印度尼西亚阿里亚哈姆社会科学园的讲话：1965年5月25日》，彭真.

13. Apoyar al pueblo vietnamita, derrotar a los agresores yanquis. Pekin：Ediciones en Lenguas Extranjeras，1965. 4 v.；19cm.

支援越南人民，打败美国侵略者（第一集）

14. 支援越南人民，打败美国侵略者（第二集）. 北京：外文出版社，1966

15. 支援越南人民，打败美国侵略者（第三集）. 北京：外文出版社，1966

16. 支援越南人民，打败美国侵略者(第四集).北京:外文出版社,1966

17. Apoyamos al pueblo dominicano en su lucha contra la agresión armada de los EE. UU. Pekin: Ediciones en Lenguas Extranjeras, 1965. 33 pages: illustrations; 19cm.
《支持多米尼加人民反对美国武装侵略》

18. Pueblo de Indonesia, uníos y luchad para derrocar al régimen facista!. Pekin: Ediciones en Lenguas Extranjeras, 1968. 54 páginas; 18cm.
《印度尼西亚人民团结起来,为推翻法西斯政权而斗争》

19. 中日关系史上的新篇章.北京:外文出版社,1972

20. 中国坚持通过谈判解决中国与菲律宾在南海的有关争议/中华人民共和国国务院新闻办公室[发布].北京:外文出版社有限责任公司,2016. 58 页; 21cm. ISBN: 7119102962
西班牙文题名: China persiste en resolver mediante negociaciones las disputas con Filipinas en el Mar Meridional de China

D3　中国法律

1. Sistemas legales/[compilado por Ediciones en Lenguas Extranjeras]. Beijing, [China]: Ediciones en Lenguas Extranjeras, 1989. 24 p.: il.; 19cm. ISBN: 7119005979, 7119005973. (Presencia de China)
中国法律体系.

2. Sistema jurídico socialista con peculiaridades Chinas/ Oficina de Información del Consejo de Estado de la República Popular China. Beijing: Foreign Languages Press, 2011. 61 pages; 21cm. ISBN: 7119073026, 7119073028
《中国特色社会主义法律体系》,中华人民共和国国务院新闻办公室[发布].

3. 法制建设.北京:新星出版社,1994. ISBN: 7801022084. (中国简况)

4. 改革开放与经济立法.北京:新星出版社,1995. ISBN: 7801023684.(中国简况)

5. 中国法制建设的进展.北京:新星出版社,1997. ISBN: 7801029259.(中国简况)

6. La legalidad en marcha/Hu Jinguang; [translated by Ouyang Yuan]. Beijing: Ediciones en Lenguas Extranjeras, 2009. 139 pages: color illustrations; 21cm. ISBN: 7119061047, 7119061046
《中国法治进行时》,胡锦光[著].

7. 中国保护知识产权.北京:新星出版社,1997. ISBN: 780102754x.(中国简况)

8. 中国知识产权保护的新进展:西班牙文/中华人民共和国国务院新闻办公室发布.北京:新星出版社,2005. 44 页; 20cm. ISBN: 7801488210

9. 澳门基本法诞生记.北京:新星出版社,1993. ISBN: 780102009x.(中国简况)

10. La ley fundamental: proyecto para la región administrativa especial de Hong Kong/Ge Guangzhi Kou Qi. China: China Intercontinental Press, 1997. 85 p il. :; 18cm. ISBN: 7801132599, 7801132598. (Hong Kong series)
《香港特别行政区的蓝图:基本法》,葛广智.五洲传播出版社.

D31　古代法律

1. Le Mystère de la pillule rouge: affaires mystérieuses sous les Ming et les Qing/Liu Jianye; trad. Zhang Yuyan. Beijing: Marcus: Ed. En Langues Etrangères, 2001. 1 vol. (335 p.); 18cm. ISBN: 711902051X, 7119020518
《红丸迷案:中国明清奇案选》,刘建业; Zhang, Yuyuan 译.

D32　中华人民共和国法律

1. Constitucion de la Republica Popular China: adoptade el 20 de septiembre de 1954 en la primera sesion de la primera legislatura de la asamblea popular nacional de la Republica Popular China. Pekin: Ediciones en Lenguas Extranjeras, 1955. 59 p.; 22cm.
《中华人民共和国宪法》
   (1) Pekín: Ediciones en Lenguas Extranjeras, 1958. 59 pages; 21cm.
   (2) Constitución de la República Popular China. Pekín: Ediciones en Lenguas Extranjeras, 1975. 53 p.; 18cm.
   (3) Constitución de la República Popular China: adoptada el 5 de marzo de 1978 en la I Sesión de la V Asamblea Popular Nacional de la República Popular China. Pekín Ediciones en Lenguas Extranjeras, 1978. 63 p.; 21cm.
   (4) Constitución de la República Popular China: (adoptada el 4 de diciembre de 1982 en la V Sesión de la V Asemblea Popular Nacional de la República Popular China). Beijing: Ediciones en Lenguas Extranjeras, 1983. 92 pages; 19cm.

2. Informe sobre el proyecto de constitución de la República Popular China: constitución de la República Popular China/ Liu Shao-Chi. Pekín: Ediciones en Lenguas Extranjeras, 1956. 105 p.; 22cm.
《关于中华人民共和国宪法草案的报告、中华人民共和国宪法》,刘少奇.
   (1) 2a ed. Pekin: Ediciones en Lenguas Extranjeras, 1961. 109 p.; 22cm.

3. Ley de reforma agraria de la República Popular China: seguida de otros documentos relativos a ella. Pekín: Ediciones en Lenguas Extranjeras, 1959. 99 p.; 18cm.
《中华人民共和国土地改革法及其他文件》
   (1) [3. ed.]. Pekin, Ediciones en Lenguas Extranjeras, 1964. 99 pages; 19cm.

（2）4a ed. Pekin, Ediciones en Lenguas Extranjeras, 1976. 57 p.；18cm.

4. 中华人民共和国婚姻法. 北京：外文出版社，1959

（1）Ley de matrimonio de la República Popular China. Beijing：Ediciones en Lenguas Extranjeras, 1983. 19 pages；19cm.

5. 中华人民共和国土地改革法. 北京：外文出版社，1978

E 类　军事

E1　古代兵法、战法

1. El arte de la guerra completo/Sun Tzu y Sun Pin；（traducción de）Ralph D. Sawyer, con la colaboración de Mei-Cün Lee Sawyer. 2a ed. Buenos Aires：Distal, 2004. xiii, 240 pages；28cm. ISBN：9875020095, 9875020092

《孙子兵法》和《孙膑兵法》，Sawyer, Ralph D. 和 Sawyer, Mei-Chün 合译成英文. 转译自英文《The complete art of war》一书.

（1）2. ed. Buenos Aires：Distal, 2005. 158 pages：il.；28cm. ISBN：9875020095, 9875020092

2. El arte de la guerra/Sun Tzu. Métodos militares/Sun Pin；[texto, Giorgio Bergamino, Gianni Palitta；traducción, Herminia Bevia]. Madrid Tikal, 2013. 287 p. il. col. 19cm. ISBN：8499282756, 849928275X. （Militaria；Métodos militares）

《孙子兵法》和《孙斌兵法》，Bevia, Herminia 译.

E11　孙子兵法

1. Los 13 principios del buen guerrear：siglos VI y V A. C. / Sun Tse；[traducido por Eduardo Prieto]. Buenos Aires：Ciencia Nueva, 1972. 102 p.：1 il.；21cm.

Notes：Traducido de la edición francesa basada en la versión Amiot（1772）refundida y aumentada mediante los manuscritos chinos de 812 y 983 d. C., publicados en 1859, 1910, 1935 y 1957, preparada por Monique Beuzit, Roberto Cacèrès, Paul Maman, Luc Thanassecos y Tran Ngoc An

《孙子兵法》，转译自法语版本.

2. El arte de la guerra/Sun Tzu；[traducción, Fernando Montes]. Madrid：Fundamentos, 1974. 164 p.；19cm. ISBN：8424501268, 8424501266. （Colección Ciencia；45）

《孙子兵法》，Montes de Santiago, Fernando 译.

（1）2a ed. Madrid：Fundamentos, 1981. 164 p. ISBN：8424501268, 8424501266. （Ciencia；45）

（2）18a ed. Madrid Fundamentos, 2013. 151 p. 20cm. ISBN：8424501266, 8424501268. （Ciencia；45. ；Serie Filosofía）

3. Los trece articulos sobre el arte de la guerra/Sun Tse；tr.

Clara Castells. Barcelona：Anagrama, 1974. 140 pages：map；18cm. ISBN：8433903780, 8433903785. （Cuadernos Anagrama. Serie Documentos；77）

Notes：Translated from Les treize articles sur l'art de la guerre.

《孙子兵法》，Castells, Clara 译.

4. El ejército y la guerra/Alexis de Tocqueville, Tsun Tzǔ；traducción de M. C. Buenos Aires：Emecé Editores, S. A., 1982. 153 pages；21cm. ISBN：9500401452, 9500401456

Tocqueville, Alexis de（1805—1859）著. 本书的第二部分是《孙子兵法》的西译（译自 1910 年的英语版）

5. El Arte de la guerra/Sun Tzu. [Barcelona]：ATE, 1984. 241 p.；19cm. ISBN：8474423546, 8474423549, 8486153182, 8486153182

《孙子兵法》

6. El arte de la guerra/Sun Tzu. 3a ed. Argentina：Editorial Estaciones, 1992. 112 pages：illustrations；20cm. ISBN：9501602087, 9501602081. （Tradiciones）

Notes：Translation of：The art of war

《孙子兵法》，转译自英文版.

7. El arte de la guerra/Sun Tzu；traducción Liliana Rodríguez. Bogotá, D. C. ：Shaolin Ediciones, 1992. 107 páginas；21cm.

《孙子兵法》，Rodríguez, Liliana 译.

8. El Arte de la guerra/Sun Tzu. [Madrid]：Andersen, 1992. 117 p.：il.；25×26cm.

《孙子兵法》（选译）

9. El arte de la guerra/Sun Tzu；introducción de F. Arabeláez. 3a ed. Bogotá：Elektra, 1993. 124 p.：il.；21cm. ISBN：958601391X, 9586013918

Notes：Traducción de：The art of war

《孙子兵法》，Arbelóez, Fernando 转译自英文版.

10. El Arte de la guerra/Sun Tzu；versión de Thomas Cleary. Madrid：Tiempo, Printer Industria Gráficas, 1993. 96 p.；21cm. ISBN：848130025X, 8481300253

《孙子兵法》，转译自 Cleary, Thomas F. （1949—）的英文版.

11. El Arte de la guerra/Sun Tzu；versión de Thomas Cleary；[traducido por Alfonso Colodrón]. Madrid：EDAF, 1993. 125 pages；18cm. ISBN：8476406533, 8476406533. （Arca de sabiduría；1）

《孙子兵法》，转译自 Cleary, Thomas F. （1949—）的英文版.

（1）24a ed. Madrid：EDAF, 2002. 125 p.；18cm. ISBN：8476046533. （Arca de sabiduría；1）

（2）Madrid：Edaf, 2006. 157 pages；22cm. ISBN：8441417555, 8441417557

（3）36a ed. Madrid：EDAF, 2009. 125 p.；18cm. ISBN：8476406533, 8476406533

（4）Boston：Shambhala Español, 2012. xiv, 139 pages；

21cm. ISBN：1611800227，1611800226

(5)44. edición, julio 2013. Madrid：EDAF，2013. 125 pages；18cm. ISBN：8476406533，8476406533.（Arca de Sabiduría）

(6)Madrid Edaf，2016. 125 p. 18cm. ISBN：8441436435，8441436436.（Arca de sabiduría）

12. El arte de la guerra/Sun Tzu. Buenos Aires：Editorial Troquel，1993. 237 pages；13cm. ISBN：9501602362，9501602364.（Letra viva）

Notes：Translation of：Sunzi bing fa. / English ed. has title：The art of war.

《孙子兵法》，转译自英文版.

13. El arte de la guerra/Sun Tzu；tr. Enrique Toomey；prólogo Samuel B. Griffith. México：Ediciones Coyoacán，1994. 182 p.；22cm. ISBN：9706331689，9706331687.（Diálogo abierto.；Política；42）

Notes：Translation of：The Art of War.

《孙子兵法》，Toomey，Enrique 译.

(1)3a ed. México，D. F.：Coyoacán，1995. 185 pages；21cm. ISBN：9706330542，9706330543.（Diálogo abierto；42）

(2)13 Ed. México：Ediciones Coyoacán，1997. 183 p.；21cm. ISBN：9706330542，9706330543.（Colección：Diálogo abierto；Política）

(3)16a ed. México，D. F.：Coyoacán，1999. 182 pages；21cm. ISBN：9706330543，9706330542.（Diálogo abierto；42）

(4)16 ed. México：Ediciones Coyoacán，2002. 182 p.；20cm. ISBN：9706331689，9706331687

(5)Vigésima séptima edición. México，D. F.：Ediciones Coyoacán，2011. 182 páginas；21cm. ISBN：6079014179，6079014173.（Diálogo Abierto/Política；42）

14. Arte de la guerra. Beijing：Ediciones En Lenguas Extranjeras，1994. 108 pages；illustrations；19cm. ISBN：7119015540，7119015545

《孙子兵法》

15. El arte de la guerra. México，México：Colofón，1995. 164 p. ISBN：9688670278，9688670279

《孙子兵法》

(1)México：Colofón，1999. 126 p.；21cm. ISBN：9688670278，9688670279

(2)14a ed. México：Colofón，2000. xxxix，126 p.；17cm. ISBN：9688670278，9688670279.（Política. Ensayo）

(3)El arte de la guerra/Sun Tzu；traducción Fernando Montes de Santiago. 16a ed. México：Colofón，2002. xxxix，126 p.；17cm. ISBN：9688670278，9688670279.（Política. Ensayo）

(4)México，D. F.：Colofón，2012. 99 p.；19cm. ISBN：

6078126637，6078126636.（Axial entre manos；15）

16. El Arte de la guerra：para nuevos líderes/Sun Tzu，Enrique Mariscal. Barcelona：Obelisco，1996. 87 p.；21cm. ISBN：8477205051，8477205050.（Obelisco-éxito）

《孙子兵法》，Mariscal，Enrique 译.

(1)3a ed. Barcelona：Obelisco，2001. 89 p.；21cm. ISBN：8477206643，8477206644.（Obelisco-éxito）

(2)5a ed. Barcelona：Obelisco，2002. 89 p.；21cm. ISBN：8477206643，8477206644.（Obelisco-éxito）

17. El arte de la guerra. México：Frente y Vuelta，1997. 158 p.；20cm. ISBN：9687515252，9687515250

《孙子兵法》

18. El arte de la guerra：de la sabiduria oriental a la excelencia occidental/Sun Tzu. Argentina：CS Ediciones，1998. 98 p.；17cm. ISBN：9507642234，9507642234

《孙子兵法》

19. El arte de la guerra/Sun-Tzu；[traducido del inglés；realización del proyecto editorial，Luis Rutiaga]. 3a ed. México，D. F.：Grupo Editorial Tomo，1998. 150 p.；19cm. ISBN：9706660143，9706660145.（Colección Clásicos del oriente）

《孙子兵法》，Rutiaga，Luis 转译自英文.

(1)5a ed. México，D. F.：Grupo Editorial Tomo，2000. 150 pages；19cm. ISBN：9706660143，9706660145

(2)8a. ed. México，D. F.：Grupo Editorial Tomo，2003. 150 pages；19cm. ISBN：9706660143，9706660145.（Colección Clásicos del oriente）

(3)8a ed. México，D. F.：Grupo Editorial Tomo，2005. 150 p.；19cm. ISBN：9706660143，9706660145.（Colección Clásicos del oriente）

(4)México，D. F.：Grupo Editorial Tomo，150 p.，2008. ISBN：9706661630，9706661638

(5)11a. edición. México，D. F.：Grupo Editorial Tomo，2009. 150 páginas；19cm. ISBN：9706660145，9706660143.（Colección filosofía de la vida）

20. El arte de la guerra/Sun Tzu. 5a ed. México：Gernika，1999. 118 p.；18cm. ISBN：968659955X，9686599558.（Clásicos；10）

Notes：Traducción de：The art of war

《孙子兵法》，转译自英文版本.

(1)7a ed. México：Gernika，2003. 118 p.；18cm. ISBN：968659955X，9686599558.（Clásicos；；10）

21. El Arte de la guerra/Sun Tzu；traducción：Elisabeth Courbet；prólogo y presentación：Francesc Ll. Cardona. Barcelona：Edicomunicación，1999. 185 p.；18cm. ISBN：8476728778，8476728772. 9Fontana：clásicos universales；177）

《孙子兵法》，Courbet，Elisabeth 译.

22. El arte de la guerra/Sun Tz；prólogo Samuel B. Griffith.

México Taller abierto, 1999. 136 p. ISBN：9686148345，9686148343. (Clásicos)

《孙子兵法》，Griffith, Samuel B. 作序.

23. El arte de la guerra/Sun Tzu; traducción del chino al inglés e introducción, Samuel B. Griffith; prefacio, B. H. Liddell Hart; traducción del inglés al castellano, Jaime Barrera Parra. Santafé de Bogotá, D. C., Colombia：Panamericana Editorial, 1999. 259 pages： maps; 21cm. ISBN：9583006130, 9583006135

《孙子兵法》，Griffith, Samuel B. 译成英文；Barrera Parra, Jaime 转移译西文.

24. El arte de la guerra/Sun Tzu; traducción del chino al inglés, introducción y apêndices, Samuel B. Griffith. Buenos Aires：Estaciones, 1999. 205 p. ; 23cm. ISBN： 9501603636, 9501603637

《孙子兵法》，译自 Griffith, Samuel B. 的英文版本.

25. El Arte de la guerra/Sun Tzu; edición de José Ramón Ayllón. Barcelona：Martínez Roca, 1999. 188 p. ; 19cm. ISBN：8427024991, 8427024991. (Clásicos de la sabiduría)

《孙子兵法》，Ayllón, José Ramón 编译.

(1)2a ed. [Barcelona]：Martínez Roca, 2002. 188 p. ; 19cm. ISBN：8427024991, 8427024991. (Clásicos de la sabiduría)

26. El arte de la guerra：la interpretación definitiva del libro clásico de Sun Tzu/Stephen F. Kaufman; [traducción, Josep Padró Umbert]. Barcelona：Editorial Paidotribo, 2000. xii,92 pages;22cm. ISBN：848019474X,8480194747

《孙子兵法》，译自 Kaufman, Steve（1939—）的英文版本.

27. El arte de la guerra/Sun Tzu; versión Cecil Fields; prólogo Guadalupe Obōn. México, D. F.：Época, 2000. 83 p. : il. ; 20cm. ISBN：9706271759, 9706271754

《孙子兵法》，Fields, Cecil 译；Obōn, Guadalupe 作序.

28. El Arte de la guerra：los trece artículos/Sun Tzu; traducido del chino por el P. Amiot; versión castellana de Esteve Serra. Palma de Mallorca：José J. de Olañeta, Grafos), 2000. 176 p. : il. ; 14cm. ISBN： 8476518072, 8476518076. (Los pequeños libros de la sabiduría; 35)

《孙子兵法》，Serra, Esteve 译.

29. El arte de la guerra/edición de Fernando Puell. Madrid： Colofón, 2000. 157 p. ; 21cm. ISBN：8470307444, 8470307447

《孙子兵法》，Puell de la Villa, Fernando 译.

(1)Madrid：Biblioteca Nueva, 2000. 157 p. : il. ; 21cm. ISBN：8470307444, 8470307447

(2)4a ed. Madrid Biblioteca Nueva, 2005. 157 p. 22cm. ISBN：8470307444, 8470307447. (Colección Trópicos; 65)

30. El arte de la guerra/Sunzi; prólogo de Jean Levi; introducción, traducción del chino antiguo y notas de Albert Galvany. Madrid Trotta, 2001. 234 p. 20cm. ISBN：8481644927, 8481644920. (Pliegos de Oriente; 9)

《孙子兵法》，Galvany, Albert 译. 西汉对照.

(1)2a. ed. Madrid Trotta, 2002. 236 p. 20cm. ISBN：8481644927, 8481644920. (Pliegos de oriente. Serie Lejano Oriente; 9)

(2)3a. ed. Madrid：Trotta, 2003. 236 p. ;20cm. ISBN：8481644927, 8481644920. (Pliegos de oriente; 9)

(3)3a ed. Madrid：Trotta, 2005. 236 p. ;20cm. ISBN：8481644927,8481644920. (Pliegos de Oriente. Serie Lejano Oriente; 9)

(4)Madrid：Trotta, 2006. 236 p. ;20cm. ISBN：8481644927, 8481644920. (Pliegos de oriente. Lejano oriente; 9)

(5)6a ed. Madrid：Trotta, 2007. 235 p. ;20cm. ISBN：8481644920, 8481644927. (Pliegos de oriente; 9)

(6)7a ed. Madrid：Trotta, 2010. 236 p. ;20cm. ISBN：8481644920, 8481644927. (Pliegos de oriente. Serie Lejano oriente)

(7)[8a ed.]. Madrid：Trotta, 2012. 236 p. ; 20cm. ISBN：8498793321, 8498793327. (Pliegos de Oriente)

31. El arte de la guerra/Sun Tzu. Ciudad Nezahualcóyotl, México：Ediciones Leyenda, 2001. 109 pages; 21cm. ISBN：9685146241, 9685146241

《孙子兵法》

(1)Ciudad Nezahualcóyotl, México：Ediciones Leyenda, 2004. 106 pages;21cm. ISBN：9685146241,9685146241

(2)Edición 2005. México：Leyenda,2005. 106 p. ;21cm. ISBN：9685146241,9685146241

(3)México：Leyenda, 2006. 106 páginas; 21cm. ISBN： 9685146241, 9685146241

(4)Edición 2008. México：Leyenda, 2008. 106 p. ; 21cm. ISBN：9685146241, 9685146241

32. El arte de la guerra/Sun Tzu; Versión, estudio y notas del Grupo Denma; [de la traducción：Mariano Vázquez Alonso]. Madrid：Edaf, 2001. 253 pages; 23cm. ISBN：8441409846, 8441409842. (Arca de sabiduría; 54)

《孙子兵法》

(1)2. ed. Madrid：Edaf,2002. 253 pages;23cm. ISBN：8441409846,8441409842. (Arca de sabiduría; 54)

(2)5. ed. Madrid：Edaf,2003. 260 pages;24cm. ISBN：8441409846,8441409842. (Arca de sabiduría; 54)

(3)Barcelona：Critèria：Salvat, 2005. 223 p. ; 21cm. ISBN：8447102394, 8447102396. (Biblioteca de crecimiento personal)

33. El arte de la guerra/Sun Tzu. Mexico：Editorial Epoca，c2001. 83 p.；20cm. ISBN：9706271753
《孙子兵法》

34. El arte de la guerra/Sun-Tzu；traducción y notas，Roberto Curto. Buenos Aires：Longseller，2002. 192 pages：illustrations；16cm. ISBN：9875501476，9875501478.（Clásicos de bolsillo）
《孙子兵法》，Curto, Roberto 译.

 (1) Buenos Aires：Deva's，2002. 172 p.：il. ISBN：9871102089，9871102082.（Serie inspiración）

 (2) El arte de la guerra：versión completa/Sun-Tzu；traducción y notas，Roberto Curto. Buenos Aires：Longseller，2003. 187 pages：illustrations；17cm. ISBN：9875503703，9875503700.（Clásicos de siempre. Fuentes de inspiración；1）

 (3) Buenos aires：Devas's de Longseller，2004. 172 p.：ill.；20cm. ISBN：9871102089，9871102082.（Inspiración）

35. El Arte de la guerra/Sun Tzu. Barcelona：Televisa，2003. 188 p.；21cm. ISBN：8467404582，8467404586.（Biblioteca Muy Interesante）
《孙子兵法》

36. El Arte de la guerra para ejecutivos y directivos/Sun-tzu y Jack Lawson；[traducción：José Manuel Pomares]. Barcelona：Obelisco，2003. 93 p. ISBN：8497770609，8497770606.（Obelisco-éxito）
《孙子兵法》，Pomares, José M. 译.

 (1) 2a ed. Barcelona：Obelisco，2004. 93 p. ISBN：8497770609，8497770606.（Obelisco-éxito）

 (2) Barcelona：Obelisco，2007. 95 p.；19cm. ISBN：8496829206，8496829200.（Empresa）

 (3) El arte de la guerra/Sun-Tzu；[traducción José Manuel Pomares]. Barcelona：Ediciones Obelisco，2009. 108 pages：color illustrations；20cm. ISBN：8497775311，8497775317

 (4) 2a ed. Barcelona：Obelisco，2010. 108 p.：il.，color；20cm. ISBN：8497775311，8497775317.（Libros singulares）

 (5) 4a ed. Barcelona Obelisco，2013. 108 p. il. col. 21cm. ISBN：8497775311，8497775317.（Colección Libros singulares）

37. El arte de la guerra：estrategias milenarias para líderes de todos los tiempos/Sun Tzu. Mexico, D. F.：Editorial Lectorum，2004. 100 pages；22cm. ISBN：9707320818，9707320819，1496038944，1496038940
《孙子兵法》

 (1) Segunda edición. Mexico, D. F.：Lectorum，2012. 99 pages；22cm. ISBN：6074572384，6074572380

38. El arte de la estrategia：tácticas no convencionales para el mundo de los negocios y la política/traducido del chino al inglés con una introducción histórica y comentarios，por Ralph D. Sawyer con la colaboración de Mei-Chün Lee Sawyer；versión española y prólogo de Mauricio Prelooker. Buenos Aires：Distal，2004. 192 pages；28cm. ISBN：987502158X，9875021587
《孙子兵法》，Sawyer, Ralph D. 和 Sawyer, Mei-Chün 合译成英文版. 译自英文《The art of strategy》一书.

39. El arte de la guerra/Sun-Tzu；[dirección general，Alejandro Makar；asesoramiento técnico，Beatriz Borovich；edición，Silvia Inés Tombesi；adaptación y prólogo，Pablo Valle；diseño de cubierta，Gustavo Macri. México, D. F.：Saga Ediciones，2004. [109] pages；22cm. ISBN：9685830061，9685830065
《孙子兵法》

40. El arte de la guerra/Sun Tzu；traducción Juan Manuel Pèrez. México：Editores Mexicanos Unidos，2004. 109 p.：il.；21cm. ISBN：9681518306，9681518301.（Colección letras. Serie clásicos）
《孙子兵法》，Pèrez, Juan Manuel 译.

 (1) El arte de la guerra/Sun Tzu；versión de Thomas Cleary；traducción María Avalos Cisneros. 2a. ed. Madrid：Editores Mexicanos Unidos，2006. 94 p.；21cm. ISBN：9681518301，9681518306.（Librería. Mitología，leyendas e historia）

41. El arte de la guerra/[Sun Tzu]；ilustraciones，Javier Covo Torres. Mérida，Yucatān，México：Editorial Dante，2004. 149 pages：illustrations；14 × 21cm. ISBN：970605278X，9706052780
《孙子兵法》，Covo Torres, Javier(1958—) 插图.

42. El Arte de la guerra/Sun Tzu；Samuel B. Griffith；[traducción：Jorge Enrique Haimberger]. Köln：Benedik Taschen，2006. 272 p.：il.；24cm. ISBN：3822856525，3822856529
《孙子兵法》，译自 Griffith, Samuel B. 的英文版.

43. El arte de la guerra y la estrategia/Sun Tzu；[traducción y notas de Cristina Esler]. Argentina：Andrómeda，2006. 159 pages；20cm. ISBN：9507222391，9507222399
《孙子兵法》，Esler, Cristina 译注.

 (1) El arte de la guerra/Sun Tzu；análisis del contexto e introducción a la obra，Sergio Gaut vel Hartman；[traducción y notas de Cristina Esler]. Argentina：Andrómeda，2007. 159 pages；20cm. ISBN：9507222391，9507222399

44. El arte de la guerra/Sun Tzu. México：Editores mexicanos unidos，2006. 94 p.；20cm. ISBN：9681520734，9681520731
《孙子兵法》

 (1) 2a ed. México, D. F.：Editores Mexicanos Unidos，2014. 94 p.：il.；21cm. ISBN：6071411440，6071411440，9681512941，9681512944.（Grandes de

la literatura)

(2)México：Editores mexicanos unidos, s. a., 2015. 94 pages：il.；19cm. ISBN：6071413888, 6071413885

45. Arte de la guerra de Sunzi：versión restaurada a partir del manuscrito de Yinqueshan/edición, traducción y notas de Laureano Ramírez Bellerín. Madrid：La Esfera de los Libros, 2006. 308 p.；25cm. ISBN：8497345096, 8497345095

《孙子兵法》, Ramírez Bellerín, Laureano 译. 西汉对照.

(1)2a ed. Madrid：La Esfera de los Libros, 2007. 380 p.；25cm. ISBN：8497345096, 8497345095

(2)Madrid La Esfera de los Libros, 2016. 141 p. 1 mapa 20cm. ISBN：8490607770, 849060777X

46. El arte de la guerra/Sun Tzu. Argentina：Terramar, 2006. 94 p.；17cm. ISBN：9871187866, 9871187867. (Biblioteca clásicos de la literatura)

《孙子兵法》

47. El arte de la guerra/Sun Tzu. México：Anaya Editores, 2007. 114 p.；17cm. ISBN：9684532555, 9684532557. (Colección Universalis；30)

《孙子兵法》

48. El arte de la guerra/Sun Tzu；[traducción, Sivan Gobrin]. [Joliet, Illinois]：BN Pub., 2007. 87 pages；21cm. ISBN：9563100266, 9563100263

《孙子兵法》

49. El arte de la guerra/Sun Zi. Edicion integra. Algete (Madrid)：Mestas ediciones, 2008. 95 pages；19cm. ISBN：8495994837, 8495994836

《孙子兵法》, Gobrin, Sivan 译.

(1)El arte de la guerra/Sun Zi；[traducción, Luis Domínguez Loya]. 2nd ed. Algete, Madrid：Mestas, Ediciones Escolares, 2010. 95 pages；19cm. ISBN：8495994837, 8495994836. (Clásicos universales；97)

50. El arte de la guerra/Tzu Sun；prólogo y anotaciones de José Luis Trueba Lara. México：Porrúa, 2008. 93 p.；17cm. (Cuantos leen；Literatura y arte a través del libro)

《孙子兵法》, Trueba Lara, José Luis 译注.

51. Las reglas de la victoria：cómo transformar el caos y el conflicto—estrategias de El arte de la guerra/James Gimian y Barry Boyce. Boston：Editorial Edaf, 2008. 334 pages；24cm. ISBN：8441420960, 8441420963. (Arca de sabiduría)

Gimian, James 和 Boyce, Barry Campbell(1956—)合著. 包括对《孙子兵法》的西译.

52. El Arte de la guerra I/Sun Tzu. versión y comentarios de Thomas Cleary；[traducción de Alfonso Colodrón]. Barcelona：Círculo de Lectores, 2008. 293 p.；21cm. ISBN：8467231878, 8467231874

《孙子兵法》, 译自 Thomas Cleary 的英文版本.

53. 孙子兵法：汉西对照/吴如嵩, 吴显林校释；图西译. 北京：军事科学出版社, 2009. 191 p.；24cm. ISBN：7802372511, 7802372518(大中华文库)

54. El arte de la guerra/Sun Tzu；traducción y comentarios de Norberto Tucci. Madrid Librería Argentina, 2010. 125 p. 16cm. ISBN：8499500249, 8499500242. (Colección Empresa)

《孙子兵法》, Tucci, Norberto 译.

55. El arte de la guerra/Sun Tzu. México, D. F.：Grupo Editorial Éxodo, 2010. 133 p.；22cm. ISBN：9707370319, 9707370319. (Clásicos universales；69)

《孙子兵法》

56. El Arte de la guerra/Sun Tzu；traducción：Benjamín Briggent. Barberá del Vallés：Plutón, 2010. 126 p.；18cm. ISBN：8493806156, 8493806153. (Colección eterna)

《孙子兵法》, Briggent, Benjamin 译. 英语与西语对照.

(1)Barberá del Vallés, Barcelona Plutón, 2015. 126 p. 19cm. ISBN：8415089841, 8415089848. (Clásicos/Bilingües)

57. El arte de la guerra：el manga/Sun Tzu；[translated by] Maite Madinabeitia. [Mexico]：Editorial Herder, 2012. 200 pages；17cm. ISBN：8425430886, 8425430887

Notes：Spanish translation of the Japanese manga version.

《孙子兵法》, Madinabeitia, Maite 译.

(1)Barcelona La Otra H, 2016. 193 p. principalmente il. 16cm. ISBN：8416540662, 8416540667

58. El arte de la guerra：el texto clásico sobre la conducción de la guerra/Sun Tzu；introducción por Nigel Cawthorne；traducción del original en inglés, Mauricio Pichardo. México, D. F.：Grupo Editorial Tomo, 2012. 128 pages：color illustrations；26cm. ISBN：6074153835, 6074153833. (Colección IlustrArte)

《孙子兵法》, Pichardo, Mauricio 转译自英文版.

59. El arte de la guerra：el tratado militar más antiguo del mundo/by Sun Tzu. [United States]：CreateSpace Independent Publishing Platform, 2012. 74 pages；23cm. ISBN：1480099746, 1480099740

《孙子兵法》

60. El arte de la guerra/Sun Tzu. Madrid, España：Susaeta ediciones, 2012. 96 páginas；27cm. ISBN：8499282213, 8499282210

Notes：Versión original：The art of war.

《孙子兵法》

61. El arte de la guerra/Sun Tzu. Mexico D. F.：Ediciones Libuk S. A. de C. V., 2012. 111 pages；21cm. ISBN：6074340488, 607434048X

《孙子兵法》

62. El arte de la guerra＝Art of war/Sun Tzu. ［Madrid］：smArt of Selling Factory，2012. 113 p. ；21cm. ISBN：8494009501，8494009508. (Dualbooks；11)
《孙子兵法》,英西对照.

63. El arte de la guerra：comentado por los fiósofos［i. e filósofos］guerreros/Sun Tzu；versión de Thomas Cleary；［traducción，Alfonso Colodrón］. Ed. única en español，［1a ed. en esta ccolección］. Madrid Edaf，2013. 255 p. 23cm. ISBN：8441433632，8441433631
《孙子兵法》,Colodrón, Alfonso 转译自 Thomas Cleary 的英文版本.

64. El arte de la guerra/Sun Tzu. Málaga，Spain：Hojas de Luz Editorial，2013. 83 pages；21cm. ISBN：8496595583，8496595587
《孙子兵法》

65. El arte de la guerra/Sun Tzu. ［Place of publication not identified］：Editorial Medí，2013. 44 pages；22cm. ISBN：1484072912，148407291X
《孙子兵法》

66. El arte de la guerra/Sun Tzu；traducción del chino clásico y estudio introductorio de Gabriel García-Noblejas Sánchez-Cendal. Madrid Alizanza Editorial，2014. 151 p. 18cm. ISBN：8420691206，8420691208. (El libro de bolsillo. Humanidades；HU42)
《孙子兵法》,García-Noblejas Sánchez-Cendal，Gabriel (1966—)译.

67. El arte de la guerra/Sun Tzu；［traducción，Andrés Guijarro Araque］. Madrid Kailas，2014. 109 p. 18cm. ISBN：8416023523，8416023522. (Clásicos/Editorial Kailas)
《孙子兵法》

68. El arte de la guerra/Sun Tzu；［versión inglesa de Lionel Giles；traducción de Anselmo G. Delaware］. ［Barcelona］ Biblok，2014. ISBN：8494326790，8494326791. (Biblioteca Ingenios)
《孙子兵法》,转译自英文版.

69. El arte de la guerra/Sun Tzu；［traducción，Pablo R. Nogueras］. Ed. íntegra，［1a ed.］. Algete，Madrid Mestas，2014. 94 p. 19cm. ISBN：8492892990,8492892994. (Clásicos universales)
《孙子兵法》,Nogueras，Pablo R. 译.

70. El arte de la guerra/Sun Tzu. Madrid Verbum，2015. 71 p. 20cm. ISBN：8490742082，8490742081. (Serie Asia. Ensayo)
《孙子兵法》

71. El arte de la guerra/Sun Tzu. Place of publication not identified：Editorial Gastrar，2017. 65 pages；21cm. ISBN：1542901840，1542901847
《孙子兵法》

72. El arte de la guerra de Sun Tzu：la interpretación china

moderna/Tao Hanzhang；traducción Mauricio Prelooker. Buenos Aires：Distal，1996. 118 pages：illustrations；27cm. ISBN：9509495972，9509495975
《孙子兵法概论》,陶汉章著.
(1)Buenos Aires，Argentina：Distal，2002. 237 pages：illustrations，maps；17cm. ISBN：9875020757，9875020753

73. Sun Tzu：el supremo maestro de la guerra/por Xu Yuanxiang & Li Jing. Beijing：China Intercontinental Press，2010. 77 pages：color illustrations，portraits；21cm. ISBN：7508516752,7508516753. (Sabios antiquos de China)
《兵圣:孙子》,徐远翔、李京[著].五洲传播出版社.

E12　孙膑兵法

1. El Arte de la guerra II：continuación del clasico texto de Sun Tzu/Sun Bin；versión y comentarios de Thomas Cleary. Madrid：Edaf，1996. 197 p. ；18cm. ISBN：8441401179. 8441401174. (Arca de sabiduría；29)
Notes：Títol de l'original anglés：The Lost art of war by Sun Tzu II
《孙膑兵法》,转译自 Cleary，Thomas F. (1949—)的英文版本.
(1)6a ed. Madrid［etc.］：Edaf，1999. 197 p. ；18cm. ISBN：8441401179，8441401174. (Arca de sabiduría；29)

E2　中国军事

1. Los Voluntarios del pueblo china：ocho años de resistencia a la agresión norteamericana y ayuda a Corea. Pekin：Ediciones en Lenguas Extranjeras，1959. 119 pages
《中国人民志愿军抗美援朝八年》

2. Pueblos del mundo，unios，por la prohibicion y destrucción completa，definitiva，cabal y resuelta d las armas nucleares. Pekin，Ediciones en Lenguas Extranjeras，1963. 221 pages；21cm.
《全世界人名团结起来,全面、彻底、干净、坚决地禁止和销毁核武器》

3. La tradicion democratica del Ejercito Popular de Liberacion de China. Pekin：Ediciones en Lenguas Extranjeras，1965. 43 pages；19cm.
《中国人民解放军的民主传统:1965 年 8 月 1 日》,贺龙.

4. 打破核垄断,消灭核武器.北京:外文出版社,1965

5. El ejercito popular es invencible en conmemoración del 42. o aniversario de la fundación del Ejército Popular de Liberación del Ejército Popular de Liberación de China：Editorial de Renmin Ribao，Hongqi y Jiefangjun Bao (1. o de agosto de 1969). Pekin：Ediciones en Lenguas Extranjeras，1969. 18 pages；13cm.
《人民军队所向无敌》

6. 纪念中国人民解放军建军 44 周年.北京:文出版社,1971

7. 全世界人民团记起来,为全面禁止和彻底销毁核武器而奋斗.北京:外文出版社,1971

8. Política y medidas de China para la prevención de la proliferación/Oficina de Información del Consejo de Estado de la República Popular China. Beijing: Editorial Nueva Estrella, 2003. 29 pages; 21cm. ISBN: 7801485688, 7801485687

   《中国的防扩散政策和措施》,中华人民共和国国务院新闻办公室发布.新星出版社.

9. 中国的军控、裁军与防扩散势力:西班牙文/中华人民共和国国务院新闻办公室发布.北京:新星出版社,2005. 55 页;20cm. ISBN: 7801489225

10. Enfasis de la paz en la estrategia militar China/Huang Zu'an. Beijing: Ediciones en Lenguas Extranjeras, 2007. 125 p. : il. col.; 22cm. ISBN: 7119046655, 7119046659. (Desarrollo pacífico de China)

    《中国兵略贵和论》,黄祖安著.本书用历史来说明中国自古就是爱好和平国家,批驳"中国军事威胁论"的错误观点.

11. Defensa nacional de China/Peng Guangqian, Zhao Zhiyin y Luo Yong; traducción de Sun Xintang y Chen Xiao'ou. Beijing: China Intercontinental Press, 2011. 168 pages: color illustrations, color maps; 24cm. ISBN: 7508519159, 7508519159

    《中国国防》,彭光谦,赵智印,罗永著.

F 类　经济

F1　中国经济

F11　概论

1. Informe sobre el primer plan quinquenal de desarrollo de la economía nacional de la República Popular China, 1953 1957: pronunciado los días 5 y 6 de julio de 1955 en la II Sesión de la Asamblea Popular Nacional, Primera Legislatura. Pekín: Ediciones en Lenguas Extranjeras, 1956. 152 p.; 22cm.

   《关于发展国民经济第一个五年计划的报告》,李富春.

2. Resolucion del C. C. del Partido Comunista de China sobre la transformacion de la industria y el comercio capitalistas. Pekin: Ediciones en Lenguas Extranjeras, 1956. 22 pages; 21cm.

   《中共中央关于私营资本主义工商业改造问题的决议》

3. Comunicado de prensa sobre el crecimiento de la Economía Nacional de China en 1959. Pekin: Ediciones en Lenguas Extranjeras, 1960. 30 p.; 18cm.

   《关于 1959 年国民经济发展情况的新闻公报》

4. La industrialización socialista y la colectivización de la agricultura en China. Pekin: Ediciones en Lenguas Extranjeras, 1964. 54 p.; 18cm.

   《中国的社会主义工业化和农业集体化》,薄一波、廖鲁言.

5. Transformación socialista de la economía nacional de China/por Süe Muqiao, Su Sing y Lin Tsi-li. Pekin: Ediciones en Lenguas Extranjeras, 1964. 273 pages; 19cm.

   《中国国民经济的社会主义改造》,薛暮桥.

   (1) 2a. ed. Pekin: Ediciones en Lenguas Extranjeras, 1979. 272 pages; 17cm.

6. Aspectos fundamentales de la economía china/Cheng Shi. Pekin: Ediciones en Lenguas Extranjeras, 1974. 63 p. : ill. (algunes col.)

   《中国经济简况》,郑实.

7. Por que en China no hay inflacion/por Peng Kuang-si. Pekin: Ediciones en Lenguas Extranjeras, 1976. 60 pages: illustrations; 19cm.

   《中国为什么没有通货膨胀》,彭光玺.

8. Problemas de la economía socialista de China/Xue Muqiao. Beijing: Ediciones en Lenguas Extranjeras, 1981. 365 pages; 21cm.

   《中国社会主义经济问题研究》,薛暮桥著.

   (1) [2a ed. rev.]. Beijing [China]: Ediciones en Lenguas Extranjeras, 1988. 381 p.; 21cm. ISBN: 7119005286, 7119005287. (Biblioteca básica)

9. Situación y perspectivas de la economía china/Zhao Ziyang. Beijing: Ediciones en Lenguas Extranjeras, 1982. 124 pages; 19cm. (Documentos de China)

   《形势和建设方针:国务院总理赵紫阳的报告》

10. Decisión del Comité Central del Partido Comunista de China sobre la reforma de la estructura económica: aprobada el 20 de octubre de 1984 por la III Sesión Plenaria del XII Comité Central del Partido Comunista de China. Beijing Ediciones en Lenguas Extranjeras, 1984. 46 p. 19cm.

    《中共中央关于经济体制改革的决定》

11. Economía de China: (1977—1980)/redactor jefe, Yu Guangyuan. Beijing: Ediciones en Lenguas Extranjeras: Centro de Publicaciones de China (Guoji Shudian) [distributor], 1984. 2 volumes (442, 398 pages); 21cm.

    《中国社会主义现代化建设》,(上、下册),于光远主编.

12. Economía/por la Redacción de Colección China. . Beijing: Ediciones en Lenguas Extranjeras, 1984. 485 pages: il.; 19cm. (Colección China)

    《经济》,《中国概况丛书》编辑委员会编.

13. 中国的"硅谷":高新技术产业开发区巡礼.北京:新星出版社,1993. ISBN: 780085938x. (中国概况)

14. China：explotación y apertura de las zonas ribereñas, fronterizas y litorales. Beijing Nueva Estrella，1993. 32 p. fot. col. 18cm. ISBN：7800859738, 7800859731
《沿海、沿边、沿江地区的开发开放》. 新星出版社（中国概况）

15. 四十五年经济建设成就：1949—1994. 北京：新星出版社，1994. ISBN：7801021703.（中国概况）

16. 中国经济改革 15 年：1978—1993,北京周报社编. 北京：新星出版社,1994. ISBN：780085387x

17. 中国的经济为什么能够快速发展. 北京：新星出版社，1995. ISBN：7801023005.（中国概况）

18. 城乡居民的收入与支出. 北京：新星出版社,1995. ISBN：7801023072.（中国概况）

19. Éxitos del VIII Plan Quinquenal. Beijing：Nueva estrella，1996. 30 p. : il. ；18cm. ISBN：780102544X, 7801025449.（Presencia de China）
《"八五"计划的实施》. 新星出版社（中国概况）

20. 中国经济在未来十五年的发展趋势. 北京：新星出版社，1996. ISBN：7801026217.（中国概况）

21. 中国出现十个经济热点地区. 北京：新星出版社,1997. ISBN：7801028953.（中国概况）

22. Explotación y protección del mar/por Yang Jinsen. Beijing：Nueva Estrella，1998. 30 p. : il. ；18cm. ISBN：780148147X, 7801481474.（Presencia de China）
《中国的海洋开发和海洋保护》. 新星出版社（中国概况）

23. Sobre la inversión en China：guía de preguntas y respuestas/author，Li Guowen；[translated by Guo Lingxia]. Beijing：Editorial Nueva Estrella，2004. 31 pages：color illustrations；21cm. ISBN：7801485807, 7801485809.（China express；viaje multicultural a un pais de cinco mil años）
《投资中国》,李国文编. 新星出版社.

24. 中国消除贫困的经验：西班牙文/骆元军编著；陈曦译. 北京：新星出版社,2006.21cm. ISBN：780225146X
本书介绍了中国在扶贫上取得的成绩,总结了中国消除贫困的经验,同样也提出了中国扶贫工作面临的问题和中国政府所采取的对策.

25. 中国经济发展之路：西班牙文/李五洲编著；陈曦译. 北京：新星出版社,2006. 21cm. ISBN：7802251389

26. Desarrollo de China dentro de la globalización/Yin Wenquan. Beijing：Ediciones de Lenguas Extranjeras，2007. 101 p. ：col. il. ；22cm. ISBN：7119046624, 7119046624.（Desarrollo Pacífico de China）
《全球化视野下的中国发展之路：西班牙文》,银温泉著；欧阳媛译.（中国的和平发展系列）

27. Proyectos internacionales para el alivio de la pobreza en China/Shen Honglei y Lei Xiangqin. Beijing：Ediciones en Lenguas Extranjeras，2007. 107 p. il. col. 21cm. ISBN：7119046402, 7119046403.（Desarrollo pacífico de China）
《国际扶贫援助项目在中国：西班牙文》,申宏磊,雷向晴编著. 本书主要介绍了中国的国际扶贫救援项目开展的具体情况,以及取得的成效.

28. Situación actual de los recursos y medidas para su mejoramiento/por Qiu Tian. Beijing：Ediciones en Lenguas Extranjeras，2007. 135 p. ：il. col. ；22cm. ISBN：7119051352, 7119051350.（Desarrollo pacífico de China）
《资源的现状与对策：西班牙文》,邱天编著；欧阳媛译. 外文出版社（中国的和平发展系列）

29. Economia circula en China/Qu Geping，Yan Min. Beijing：Foreign Languages Press，2008. 143 pages：color illustrations；21cm. ISBN：7119055497, 7119055496.（Desarrollo pacifico de China）
《循环经济,绿色之旗》,曲格平,闫敏著.

30. Integracion de China en el mundo/by Chang Lu and Xue Kai. Beijing：Ediciones en Lenguas Extranjeras，2008. 143 pages：color illustrations；21cm. ISBN：7119055367, 7119055364.（Desarrollo pacifico de China）
《中国融入世界》,常璐,薛凯著. 主要介绍了 2001 年中国加入 WTO 组织后,信守承诺采取了一系列改革措施,

31. Economía China/Wu Li，Sui Fumin y Zheng Lei；traducción de Sun Xintang y Zhou Mocao. Beijing：China Intercontinental Press，2010. 165 pages：illustrations（chiefly color），color map；23cm. ISBN：7508519104, 7508519108
《中国经济》,武力,隋福民,郑磊著；孙新堂等译. 讲述经过改革开放 30 多年来,中国经济取得了令人瞩目的成就

F12　地方经济

1. 环渤海地区经济正在崛起. 北京：新星出版社,1994. ISBN：7801021355.（中国概况）

2. 黄河经济带的开发. 北京：新星出版社,1994. ISBN：7801020804.（中国概况）

3. 环渤海经济圈的崛起. 北京：新星出版社,1995. ISBN：7801024478.（中国概况）

4. 中国西部地区的发展. 北京：新星出版社,1997. ISBN：7801027906.（中国简况）

F2　经济管理

F21　劳动经济

1. Los recursos humanos en China/Oficina de Información del Consejo de Estado de la República Popular China. Beijing：Foreign Languages Press，2010. 45 pages：illustrations；21cm. ISBN：7119066691, 7119066692
《中国的人力资源状况》,中华人民共和国国务院新闻办公室[发布].

F22 物流经济

1. La construcción ferroviaria de la nueva China. Pekín (Beijing)：Ediciones en Lenguas Extranjeras，1980. 87 p. : il. ; 19cm.

   《新中国的铁路建设》，彭光玺著.

2. Puentes en China antiguos y nuevos: desde el viejo Puente Zhaozhou hasta el moderno Puente Nanjing. Pekín (Beijing)：Ediciones en Lenguas Extranjeras，1980. 38 p. , 46 p. de lám. ; 26cm.

   《中国的古桥和新桥：从赵州桥到南京长江大桥》，茅以升著.

3. 世界上最高的铁路：青藏铁路：西班牙文/崔黎丽编著；张重光 等 译. 北京：新星出版社，2006；21cm. ISBN：7802251524

   本书介绍了青藏铁路的修筑、铁路建设者的环保意识，以及这条铁路的社会、经济价值.

F23 投资与建设

1. 中国主要几条河流的治理. 北京：外文出版社，1972

2. 交通、通信、能源基础设施建设. 北京：新星出版社，1995. ISBN：7801023447.（中国概况）

3. Obras prioritarias del Estado/por Li Ning. Beijing：Ediciones en Lenguas Extranjeras，2007. 137 p. : il. col. ; 22cm. ISBN：7119051178，7119051172.（Desarrollo Pacífico de China）

   《国家重点建设工程：西班牙文》，李宁著；张重光译.（中国的和平发展系列）

F24 房地产经济

1. 中国的人居环境. 北京：新星出版社，1996. ISBN：7801025210（中国概况）

2. Cambios en la vivienda de 1. 300 millones de Chinos/Xue Kai. Beijing：Ediciones en Lenguas Extranjeras，2007. 123 pages：color illustrations；21cm. ISBN：7119051192，7119051199.（Desarrollo pacifico de China）

   《13亿人的住房变迁：西班牙文》，薛凯著；贾宁一译. 外文出版社（中国的和平发展系列）

3. Construcción de ciudades adecuadas para habitar seres humanos/por Cui Lili. Beijing：Ediciones en Lenguas Extranjeras，2007. 123 p. : il. col. ; 22cm. ISBN：7119051161，7119051164.（Desarrollo Pacífico de China）

   《建设适宜人类居住的城市：西班牙文》，崔黎丽著；欧阳媛译.（中国的和平发展系列）

F3 "三农"问题

1. Proyecto del programa de desarrollo de la agricultura de la República Popular China para 1956—1957

   《1956年到1967年全国农业发展纲要》

2. 中国农业合作化道路，童大林. 北京：外文出版社，1958

3. Todo el partido y todo el pueblo deben entregar su enérgico esfuerzo a la agricultura 、Liao Lu-yen. Pekin：Ediciones en Lenguas Extranjeras，1961. 21 p. ; 19cm.

   《全党全民动手大办农业》，廖鲁言.

4. Avanzan las comunas populares：Resumen fundamental de cinco años de experiencias de las comunas populares rurales de la provincia de Kuangtung. Pekin：Ediciones en Lenguas Extranjeras，1964. 38 pages；19cm.

   《人民公社在前进》，陶铸.

5. La lucha entre los dos caminos en el campo chino/por las redacciones del Renmin Ribao, la revista Hongqi y Jiefangjun Bao（23 de noviembre de 1967）. Pekin：Ediciones en Lenguas Extranjeras，1968. 57 p. ; 12cm.

   《中国农村两条道路的斗争》

6. Movilizar todo el partido para desarrollar vigorosamente la agricultura y luchar por generalizar distritos tipo tachai：informe de balance ante la Conferencia National sobre Aprender de Tachai en la Agricultura（15 de octubre de 1975）/Jua Kuo-feng. Pekin：Ediciones en Lenguas Extranjeras，1976. 79 pages；19cm.

   《全党动员，大办农业，为普及大寨县而奋斗》，华国锋.

7. Como es la comuna popular? /Chu Li，Tien Chie-yun. Pekin：Ediciones en Lenguas Extranjeras，1976. 220 pages：illustrations；19cm.

   《在七里营人民公社》，朱力，田洁云.

8. Discurso pronunciado en la II conferencia nacional sobre aprender de Tachai en la agricultura/Jua Kuo-Feng. Pekin：Ediciones en Lenguas Extranjeras，1977. 35 pages；19cm.

   《中国共产党中央委员会主席华国锋同志在第二次全国农业学大寨会议上的讲话》

9. Criticar a fondo a la "Banda de los cuatro" y levantar un nuevo auge en el movimiento por generalizar distritos tipo tachai：informe de Chen Yung-kui, miembro del Buro Politico del CC del PCCh y Viceprimer Ministro del Consejo de Estado, ante la II conferencia Nacional sobre Aprender de Tachai en la Agricultura：20 de diciembre de 1976/Chen Yung-kui. Pekin：Ediciones en Lenguas Extranjeras，1977. 37 pages；19cm.

   《彻底批判"四人帮"掀起普及大寨县运动的新高潮：中共中央组治局委员、国务院副总理陈永贵在第二次全国农业学大寨会议上的讲话》，陈永贵.

10. Tachai, bandera roja en la agricultura/por Wen Yen y Liang Jua. Pekin：Ediciones en Lenguas Extranjeras，1977. 225 pages，[21] pages of plates：illustrations；19cm.

    《大寨红旗》，文荫、梁华.

11. 中国的农村改革. 北京：新星出版社，1991. ISBN：7800851095

12. 中国发展高效农业. 北京：新星出版社，1993. ISBN：7800858936.（中国概况）

13. 迈向现代化的大农业. 北京：新星出版社，1994. ISBN：

7801021630.（中国概况）

14. 农村经济的全面发展. 北京：新星出版社,1996. ISBN：7801026144.（中国概况）

15. 成长中的人民公社/（美）安娜·路易斯·斯特朗. 北京：新世界出版社,1961

16. 中国实施"科教兴农"战略. 北京：新星出版社,1997. ISBN：7801028872.（中国概况）

17. 星火计划：中国农业现代化的希望. 北京：新星出版社,1997. ISBN：7801028279.（中国概况）

18. 中国如何保护耕地. 北京：新星出版社,1997. ISBN：7801029038.（中国概况）

19. Inicio de la construcción del nuevo agro/Wang Tai... [et al.] Beijing Edición de lenguas Extranjeras, 2007. 127 p. il. col. 21cm. ISBN：7119051185，7119051180.（Desarrollo pacífico de China）

《农村建设从这里起步：西班牙文》,王太,赵经平,李海涛著;欧阳媛译.（中国的和平发展系列）

20. Nuevos avances de China en la reducción de la pobreza en las zonas rurales mediante el desarrolo/Oficina de Información del Consejo de Estado de la República Popular China. Beijing：Foreign Languages Press, 2011. 45 pages；21cm. ISBN：7119073330，7119073338

《中国农村扶贫开发的新进展》,中华人民共和国国务院新闻办公室［发布］.

21. Forestación de China/Han Lin；［translated by Ou Yangyuan］. Beijing：Ediciones en Lenguas Extranjeras, 2009. 135 pages：color illustrations；21cm. ISBN：7119061023，711906102X

《中国的森林》,韩琳［著］.

F4　工业经济

1. El pueblo chino construye la industria impetuosamente. Pekín：Ediciones en Lenguas Extranjeras, 1959. 111 p. : ilus. ；18cm.

《全民办工业的高潮》

2. 抓革命、促生产、争取工业战线的新胜利. 北京：外文出版社,1969

3. Conferencia Nacional sobre Aprender de Taching en la Industria（documentos）. Pekin：Ediciones en Lenguas Extranjeras, 1977. 94 pages

《中国工业学大庆会议文件选编》

4. Nueva fisonomía de Kailuan/redactado por el Grupo de los obreros de Kailuan. Pekin：Ediciones en Lenguas Extranjeras, 1977. 82 p. , ［32］ p. de lám. : il. (algunes col.), map. ；19cm.

《开滦新貌》,开滦工人写作组.

5. 中国国有企业走向市场/北京周报社编. 北京：新星出版社,1993. ISBN：7801020189.（中国概况）

6. Shougang, modelo de la reforma empresarial. Beijing Nueva Estrella, 1993. 30 p. , ［8］ p. de lám. 18cm. ISBN：7801020235，7801020239.（Presencia de China）

《首钢：中国企业改革的楷模》,新星出版社（中国概况）

7. 中国十大最佳合资企业. 北京：新星出版社,1994. ISBN：7801022157.（中国概况）

8. 跨国公司在中国. 北京：新星出版社,1995. ISBN：7801024613.（中国概况）

9. 国有企业的改革. 北京：新星出版社,1995. ISBN：7801024540.（中国概况）

10. 改革：国有大中型企业的出路. 北京：新星出版社,1996. ISBN：7801025687.（中国概况）

11. 蓬勃发展的中国电视业. 北京：新星出版社,1996. ISBN：7801026365.（中国概况）

12. 充满活力的中国企业集团. 北京：新星出版社,1998. ISBN：7801480740.（中国概况）

13. Empresas chinas en el siglo XXI/Che Yuming, Han Jie, Zhao Xiaohui. Beijing Ediciones en Lenguas Extranjeras, 2008. 143 páginas ilustraciones, fotografías a color 21cm. ISBN：7119055329，7119055321.（Desarrollo Pacífico de China）

《走进21世纪的中国企业》,车玉明,韩洁,赵晓辉著. 本书梳理了中国改革开放三十年来中国企业的发展历史,展现了中国企业不断在体制和技术上创新求发展的全景图.

F41　工业部门经济

1. 中国矿产资源的开发和利用. 北京：新星出版社,1996. ISBN：7801025296.（中国概况）

2. 中国的石油工业. 北京：新星出版社,1997. ISBN：7801027612.（中国概况）

3. Proyecto de las Tres Gargantas. Beijing：Nueva estrella, 1997. 30 p. : il. ；18cm. ISBN：7801027477，7801027474.（Presencia de China）

《举世曙目的三峡工程》. 新星出版社（中国概况）

4. Política China de recursos minerales/Oficina de Información del Consejo de Estado de la República Popular China. Beijing：Editorial Nueva Estrella, 2003. 41 pages；21cm. ISBN：7801485599，7801485595

《中国的矿产资源政策》,中华人民共和国国务院新闻办公室发布. 新星出版社.

5. 中国的互联网业：西班牙文/李宁编著；张重光等译. 北京：新星出版社,2006. 21cm. ISBN：7802251311

本书介绍了中国互联网业的现状、规模,它给人们生活所带来的影响,以及它的未来发展.

F5　贸易经济

1. Tendencias del consumo en China. ［Beijing］ Nueva Estrella, 1993. 32 p. , ［8］ p. de lám. 18cm. ISBN：7801020472，7801020475.（Presencia de China）

《中国人的消费走向》. 新星出版社（中国概况）

2. 中国市场经济纵横谈. 北京：新星出版社,1993. ISBN：7800858669.（中国概况）

3. 中国的保税区. 北京：新星出版社,1993. ISBN：

7800859142.(中国概况)

4. 中国怎样重返关贸总协定,北京周报社编.北京:新星出版社,1993. ISBN:7800859029.(中国概况)

5. China:pluralizadas relaciones económicas y comerciales con el exterior. Beijing Nueva Estrella, 1993. 35 p., [8] p. de lám. col. 18cm. ISBN:7800859452, 7800859458. (Presencia de China)
《多元化的对外经济贸易》.新星出版社(中国概况)

6. 十一亿人的消费水平与巨大市场.北京:新星出版社,1994. ISBN:7801020871.(中国概况)

7. 外商看好中国大市场.北京:新星出版社,1994. ISBN:780102222x.(中国概况)

8. "九五"进口目标:10000亿美元.北京:新星出版社,1995. ISBN:7801024737.(中国概况)

9. 商品流通领域的对外开放.北京:新星出版社,1996. ISBN:7801025903.(中国概况)

10. 外国老板看中国市场.北京:新星出版社,1997. ISBN:780102933x.(中国概况)

11. El comercio en China/redactado bajo la dirección de Ma Ke y Li Jun. Beijing:China Intercontinental Press, 2004. 487 p.:il. col., mapa;24cm. ISBN:7508504148, 7508504143
《中国商务》,马可,李俊主编,汤柏生等译.五洲传播出版社.

12. 走出国门的中国小商品:西班牙文/侯瑞丽编著;吴恺译.北京:新星出版社,2006. 21cm. ISBN:7802251508

13. Cooperación económica y comercial China-África/Oficina de Información del Consejo de Estado de la República Popular China. Beijing:Ediciones en Lenguas Extranjeras, 2010. 36 pages:illustrations;21cm. ISBN:7119068183, 7119068180
《中国与非洲的经贸合作》,国务院新闻办公室发布.

F51　旅游经济

1. 中国旅游业.北京:外文出版社.1988. 31页.(中国概况)
2. 如何到中国旅游.北京:新星出版社,1995. ISBN:7801023846.(中国概况)

F6　财经、税收

F61　中国税收

1. 符合国际惯例的新税制.北京:新星出版社,1994. ISBN:7801021568.(中国概况)
2. 中国税收制度的改革.北京:新星出版社,1996. ISBN:7801025369.(中国概况)

F7　金融与证券

1. Renminbi de China:moneda excepcionalmente estable del mundo. Pekin:Ediciones en Lenguas Extranjeras, 1970. 33 p.;18cm.
《中国的人民币:世界上少有的最稳定的货币》,蔡正.

2. Utilización de fondos del exterior/[compilado por Ediciones en Lenguas Extranjeras]. Beijing, [China]:Ediciones en Lenguas Extranjeras, 1988. 28 p.:il.; 19cm. ISBN:7119003194, 7119003191. (Presencia de China)
外资利用.外文出版社(中国概况)

3. Bancos de capital foráneo en China. Beijing Nueva Estrella, 1993. 40 p. 18cm. ISBN:7800859096, 7800859090. (Presencia de China)
《外资银行在中国》.新星出版社(中国概况)

4. 中国怎样改革金融体制?北京:新星出版社,1994. ISBN:7801021061.(中国概况)

5. 中国:外资金融机构的沃土.北京:新星出版社,1996. ISBN:7801025601.(中国概况)

6. Reforma y desarrollo de los seguros. Beijing:Nueva estrella, 1997. 30 p.:il.; 18cm. ISBN:7801027981, 7801027986. (Presencia de China)
《中国保险业的改革和发展》.新星出版社(中国概况)

G类　文化、教育、体育

G1　中国文化概论

1. Cultura y sociedad en China/Xu Lun; versión al español y notas de Miguel Torres. México:Grijalbo, 1972. 160 pages;17cm. (Colección 70; 119)
中国的文化与社会.徐仑(1910~1984);Torres, Miguel 译.
(1)México:Grijalbo, 1975. 160 p.; 18cm. (Colec. 70; ser. 3, 119)

2. Aspectos fundamentales de la cultura China/Chai Pien. [Pekin]:[Ediciones en Lenguas Extranjeras], 1975. iv, [58] pages:illustrations (some color);19cm.
《中国文化概况》,翟边.

3. Aspectos culturales [de China]/[compilado por Ediciones en Lenguas Extranjeras. Beiging:Ediciones en Lenguas Extranjeras,1983. 143 p.:fot.;18cm. (Coleccion China)
《文化事业》,《中国概况丛书》编辑委员会编.

4. Perfiles de la cultura china/Feng Lingyu, Shi Weimin; traductor:Chen Gensheng. [Beijing]:China Intercontinental Press, 2001. 199 p.:il., fot.; 21cm. ISBN:7801138163, 7801138163. (Series básicas de China)
《中国文化掠影》,冯凌宇,史卫民著;Chen, Gensheng 译.

5. La cultura semeja el agua/Jiazheng Sun. Beijing:Ediciones en Lenguas Extranjeras, 2006. 139 pages:illustrations;21cm. ISBN:7119044966, 7119044965. (Desarrollo pacífico de China)
《文化如水:西班牙文》,孙家正著;姜凤光等译.(中国的和平发展系列)

6. Conocimientos comunes de la cultura china. [Pekín]:Sinolingua, 2006. 241 p.:il.;24cm. ISBN:7802002333,

7802002338

《中国文化常识:汉西对照》,任启亮主编;国务院侨务办公室,国家汉语国际推广领导小组办公室编.华语教学出版社.

7. Miradas sobre la cultura China/Autores：Ye Lang, Zhu Liangzhi；Traductoras：Alicial Relinque Eleta, Xu Lei；Asesores de espanol：Zhao Zhenjiang, Juan Morillo. Beijing：Wai yu jiao xue yu yan jiu chu ban she, 2014. 355 p.：ill., photo.；24cm. ISBN：7513548700, 7513548706

《中国文化读本:西班牙文版》,叶朗,朱良志著;雷爱玲,徐蕾译;西班牙文审订,赵振江,胡安·莫里略.

8. 得到精心保护的少数民族文化.北京:新星出版社,1995. ISBN：7801024257.（中国概况）

9. 今日中国人的文化生活.北京:新星出版社,1996. ISBN：7801026497.（中国概况）

10. 中外文化交流.北京:新星出版社,1996. ISBN：7801025520.（中国概况）

11. 中国现代化与传统文化.北京:新星出版社,1997. ISBN：7801027760.（中国概况）

12. Proyecto cultural de los años 90. China：Nueva Estrella, 1997. 21 p. il.：；18cm. ISBN：7801027698,7801027696.（Presencia de China）

《九十年代文化工程》.新星出版社(中国概况)

13. Intercambio cultural Chino con el exterior/［edited by Tao Hong］. Beijing：Editorial Nueva Estrella, 2004. 39 pages：color illustrations；21cm. ISBN：7801486048, 7801486042.（China express；viaje multicultural a un país de cinco mil años）

《中外文化交流》,陶红著.新星出版社.

14. 中国与拉美的文化交流:西班牙文/韦黎明编著;张重光等译.北京:新星出版社,2006;21cm. ISBN：7802251443

本书介绍了中国与拉丁美洲各国的文化交流与合作.

15. 中国重视保护传统文化:西班牙文/华少君编著;施威译.北京:新星出版社,2006. 21cm. ISBN：7802251354

16. Valor actual de la cultura tradicional china/Zhang Xiping. Beijing Ediciones de Lenguas Extranjeras distribuidor, Corporación China de Comercio Internacional del Libro, 2009. 137 p. il. col. y n. 21cm. ISBN：7119061146, 7119061143.（Desarrollo pacífico de China）

《传统文化的当代价值》,张西平［著］.

G2　新闻

1. Llevar hasta el fin la gran revolucion en el frente del periodismo：crítica a la línea revisionista contrarrevolucionaria del Jruschov chino en el periodismo/por las redacciones de Renmin Ribao, Hongqi y Jiefangjun Bao. Pekin：Ediciones en Lenguas Extranjeras, 1969. 65 pages；13cm.

《把新闻战线的大革命进行到底》

2. Prensa, radio e instituciones culturales/［compilado por Ediciones en Lenguas Extranjeras］. Beijing,［China］：Ediciones en Lenguas Extranjeras, 1989. 21 p.：il.；

18cm. ISBN：7119005987, 7119005980.（Presencia de China）

新闻、广播与文化机构.外文出版社(中国概况)

3. 中国的对外传播.北京:新星出版社,1998. ISBN：7801481631.（中国概况）

4. Perfeccionamiento del mecanismo de divulgación de información oficial en china/Shen Honglei. Beijing：Ediciones en Lenguas Extranjeras, 2009. 123 pages：color illustrations；21cm. ISBN：7119061115, 7119061119

《新闻发布与阳光执政》,申宏磊［著］.

G3　出版

1. La causa editorial de China. China：Nueva Estrella, 1997. 34 p. il.：；18cm. ISBN：7801028058, 7801028051.（Presencia de China）

《中国出版事业现状》,新星出版社(中国概况)

2. 印刷术:中国古代的伟大发明/孙机著.北京:新星出版社,1997.（中国概况:特辑）

3. Industria librera de China/Yang Hu, Xiao Yang；traducido por Ego. Beijing：China Intercontinental Press, 2011. 195 pages：il. color；22cm. ISBN：7508519661, 7508519663.（Series de China Cultural）

《中国书业》,杨虎,肖阳著.五洲传播出版社.

G4　文化机构

G41　收藏

1. Muebles Chinos/by Zhang Xiaoming；traducido por Zhang Jinlai. Beijing：China Intercontinental Press, 2011. 157 pages：illustrations；23cm. ISBN：7508521091,7508521099.（Series de China Cultural）

《中国家具》,张晓明著.五洲传播出版社.

G5　教育

1. Es necesario combinar la enseñanza con el trabajo productivo. Pekin：Ediciones en Lenguas Extranjeras, 1958. 35 pages；19cm.

《教育必须与生产劳动相结合》,陆定一著.

（1）2. ed. Pekin：Ediciones en Lenguas Extranjeras, 1960. 35 pages；19cm.

2. Seguir el camino tomado por la Fabrica de Maquinas-Herramientas de Shanghai de preparar personal tecnico entre los obreros：dos informes de investigación sobre la revolución educacional de las universidades cientificas y de ingeniería. Pekin：Ediciones en Lenguas Extranjeras, 1969. 62 pages；13cm.

《走上海机床厂从工人中培养技术人员的道路》

3. 中共中央关于教育体制改革的决定.北京:文出版社,1985

4. Educación y ciencias/por la Redacción de Colección China. Beijing：Ediciones en Lenguas Extranjeras, 1985. 253

pages：il. ；19cm.（Colección China）

《教育科学》,《中国概况丛书》编辑委员会编.

5. 教育的改革和发展.北京：新星出版社,1994.ISBN：7801022300.（中国概况）

6. 跨世纪的中国高等教育改革.北京：新星出版社,1995.ISBN：7801023528.（中国概况）

7. 九十年代中国教育发展与改革概况.北京：新星出版社,1996.ISBN：7801025830.（中国概况）

8. Educación de China：reforma e innovación/por Su Xiaohuan.［Beijing］：China Intercontinental Press,2002. 191 p.：il. col.；23cm. ISBN：7801139941,7801139948.（Series básicas de China）

《中国教育：改革与创新》,苏晓环著.

9. Educación China/［edited by Chen Xi］. Beijing：Editorial Nueva Estrella,2004. 39 pages：color illustrations；21cm. ISBN：7801486641,7801486646.（China express；viaje multicultural a un país de cinco mil años）

《中国的教育》,陈希编.新星出版社.

10. 中国努力推进全民教育：西班牙文/李宁编著；张重光等译.北京：新星出版社,2006；21cm. ISBN：7802251346

本书介绍了中国推进全民教育的情况,进展与预期目标

11. 成功者就是我：中小学生走向成功的42个关键点：西汉对照/郭中平著；荣佳妮,殷人凯译.上海：文汇出版社,2006.11.249 页；23cm. ISBN：7807410817,7807410812

本书以中学生为目标对象,提出42种有效方法.根据中文译成西班牙语,从而成为双语读物.成功心理学—青少年读物

12. 中外教育交流.北京：新星出版社,1997.ISBN：7801028732.（中国概况）

13. 对外汉语教师资格考试大纲/教育部对外汉语教师资格审查委员会办公室编.北京：华语教学出版社；2004. 112 页；20cm. ISBN：780052860X,7800528606

本书为参加国家对外汉语教师资格考试的参试教师之考试大纲.

14. Manual elemental de chino moderno. China：Ediciones en Lenguas Extranjeras,1989. 266 p. ISBN：7800521192,7800521195

《留学中国指南》.北京语言学院出版社.

15. 在中国的外国留学生：西班牙文/崔黎丽编著；张重光等译.北京：新星出版社,2006. 21cm. ISBN：7802251338

G6 体育

1. Cultura física y sanidad/por la redacción de Colección China. Beijing：Ediciones en Lenguas Extranjeras,1984. 181 pages：illustrations.（Colección China）

《体育卫生》,《中国概况丛书》编辑委员会编.

2. Marcha olímpica：progreso de la cultura física y de los deportes en China.［Beijing］Nueva Estrella,1993. 32 p.,［4］p. de lám. 18cm. ISBN：7800858804,7800858802.（Presencia de China）

《奥林匹克大进军：中国体育运动的飞跃》.新星出版社

（中国概况）

3. Intercambios deportivos Chino-Iatinoamericanos/authro, Qiu Jianghong；［translated by Yao Bei, Guo Lingxia］. Beijing：Editorial Nueva Estrella,2004. 31 pages：color illustrations；21cm. ISBN：7801486366,7801486363.（China express；viaje multicultural a un pais de cinco mil años）

《中拉体育交流》,仇江鸿编.新星出版社.

4. 中国功夫：西班牙文/韦黎明编著；张重光等译.北京：新星出版社,2006. 21cm. ISBN：780225132X

本书介绍了中国功夫的历史、流派、分类与各自的特点,以及一些功夫片中国影星.

5. El Kungfu de China/Wang Guangxi. Beijing：China Intercontinental Press,2011. 154 pages：illustrations（chiefly color）；23cm. ISBN：7508519555,7508519558.（Series de China Cultural）

《中国功夫》,王广西,王萌编著.五洲传播出版社.

6. El Liangong：en 18 ejercicios. Beijing, China：Ediciones En Lenguas Extranjeras,1985. 111 p.：134 il.；18cm. ISBN：7119009109,7119009100.（Colección artes marciales de China）

《练功十八法》

（1）2a. ed. Beijing：Ediciones en Lenguas Extranjeras,1989. 111 p.：il.；18cm. ISBN：7119009109,7119009100.（Artes marciales de China）

7. Técnicas elementales de captura en Wŭshù/Wáng Xìndé. Madrid：Mariguano；Beijing：Ediciones en Lenguas Extranjeras,1988. 116 pages：illustrations；21cm. ISBN：8485639960,8485639960

《简易擒拿术》,王信得.

8. Secuencia de Taijiquan（en 88 ejercicios）/traducido por Ma. Yunzben. Bijing, China：Ediciones en Lenguas Extranjeras,1985. 238 p.：400 il.；18cm.（Colección artes marciales de china）

《太极拳：88 式》

9. Taijiquan：taichi en 88 movimientos/［traducción del chino al español, Ma Yunzben］. Madrid：Miraguano Ediciones；Beijing：Ediciones en Lenguas Extranjeras,1986. 237 pages：illustrations；20cm. ISBN：8485639766,8485639762.（Colección Medicinas blandas）

《太极拳；88 式》

10. Lecciones de Taijijian. Beijing, China：Ediciones en Lenguas Extranjeras,1985. 103 p.：il.；18cm.（Colección artes marciales de China）

太极剑.

（1）2a. ed. Beijing：Ediciones en Lenguas Extranjeras,1989. 103 p.：il.；18cm. ISBN：7119009117,7119009117.（Artes marciales de China）

11. Taiji Qigong：veinte y ocho pasos/compilado por Li Ding y Bambang Sutomo. Beijing：Ediciones en Lenguas Extranjeras,1989. 169 pages：illustrations；17cm. ISBN：

7119010514，7119010519.（Colección artes marciales de China）

太极气功 28 式.

12. Gimnasia acrobática de China［fotos，Zhou Tiexia... et al.；texto，Song Yitai］. Beijing Ediciones en Lenguas Extranjeras，1986.［76］p. il. col. y n. 21cm.

《中国技巧运动》，王峻极，金岩编.

13. Diez ejercicios de proyección de piernas/por Ma Zhenbang. Beijing：Ediciones en Lenguas Extranjeras，1987. 151 p.：il.；18cm. ISBN：7119014064，7119014067.（Artes marciales de China）

《十路弹腿》，马振邦著.

14. Wushu：el boxeo estilo mono. Beijing：Ediciones en Lenguas Extranjeras，1987. 107 pages：illustrations；18cm. ISBN：8478130152，8478130153

《猴拳》，习云太，李高中著.

15. Técnicas simplificadas de captura/por Wang Xinde. Beijing Ediciones en Lenguas Extranjeras，1987. 117 p. il. 18cm.（Artes marciales de China）

《简易擒拿戏》，王信得著.

16. Zuijiuquan（Boxeo del borracho）/por Cai Longyun y Shao Shankang；traducción de Wang Yanting. Beijing，China：Ediciones en Lenguas Extranjeras，1987. 178 p.：199 il.；18cm.（Colección artes marciales de China）

醉酒拳.

17. Los 64 métodos de ataque con las piernas del Wushu de Shaolin/Wang Xinde. Beijing，China：Ediciones en Lenguas Extranjeras，1990. 329 p.：il.；18cm. ISBN：7119004220，7119004228.（Colección artes marciales de china）

《少林六十四腿击法》，王信得著.

18. El Qigong y sus conocimientos/Hu Bin. Beijing，China：Ediciones en Lenguas Extranjeras，1990. 151 p.：il.；19cm. ISBN：7119011251，7119011257

《中国大众气功》，胡斌著.

19. El Qigong meridiano：transporte de la energía por el meridiano/compilado y presentado por Li Ding；versión castellana de Tang Yubin. Beijing，China：Ediciones en Lenguas Extranjeras，1990. 254 p.：il.；18cm. ISBN：7119012223，7119012223

《经络气功》，李丁著.

20. Ejercicios de transformación de los tendones en 14 series. Beijing：Ediciones en Lenguas Extranjeras，1992. 128 p.：il.；19cm. ISBN：7119014951，7119014951

《易筋经十四段功法录：医学气功》，常维祯编著.

21. Liu zi jue/compilado por la Asociación China de Qigong para la Salud. Beijing：Ediciones en Lenguas Extranjers，2008. 73 pages：illustrations（chiefly color）；23cm.＋1 DVD（4 3/4 in.）. ISBN：7119054506，7119054503.（Qigong Chino para la Salud）

《六字诀》，国家体育总局健身气功管理中心编.

22. Yi jin jing/compilado por la Asociación China de Qigong para la Salud. Beijing：Ediciones en Lenguas Extranjeras，2008. 96 pages：illustrations（chiefly color）；23cm.＋1 DVD（4 3/4 in.）. ISBN：7119054520，711905452X.（Qigong Chino para la Salud）

《易筋经》，国家体育总局健身气功管理中心编.

23. Ba duan jin/compilado por la Asociación China de Qigong para la Salud. Beijing：Ediciones en Lenguas Extranjeras，2008. 58 p.：il.（algunas col.）；22cm.＋1 videodisco（son.，col.：4 3/4 plg.）ISBN：7119054490，711905449X.（Qigong chino para la salud）

《八段锦》，国家体育总局健身气功管理中心编.

24. Wu qin xi/compilado por la Asociación China de qigong para la Salud. Beijing：Ediciones en Lenguas Extranjeras，2008. 102 pages：illustrations（some color）；23cm.＋1 videodisc（DVD；4 3/4 in.）. ISBN：7119054513，7119054511.（Qigong Chino para la salud）

《五禽戏》，国家体育总局健身气功管理中心编.

H 类　语言、文字

H1　汉语、汉字

1. Cinco milenios de caracteres chinos. Beijing：Sinolingua，2009. 183 pages：illustrations（some color）；23cm. ISBN：7802006457，7802006454

《汉字五千年》，《汉字五千年》编委会编；刘京胜等译. 华语教学出版社.

2. Sanzijing：el clásico de tres caracteres：el umbral de la educación china/Wang Yinglin；introducción，traducción y notas de Daniel Ibáñez Gómez. Madrid：Trotta，2000. 138 p.；17cm. ISBN：8481643661；8481643664.（Pliegos de Oriente；5）

《三字经》，王应麟(1223—1296)；Ibáñez Gómez，Daniel 译.

3. 三字经与中国民俗画：西汉对照/荆孝敏编；（西）杨丹义译. 北京：五洲传播出版社，2010. 139 页；23cm. ISBN：7508516455.（中国传统文化精粹书系）

4. Cuentos del Texto de mil caracteres＝Qian zi wen gu shi/Jiang Xiaodong；traducción Wang Dongmei. Beijing：Sinolingua，2013. x，177 páginas：ilustraciones；24cm. ISBN：7513804301；7513804303.（Colección de obras clásicas chinas para niños）

《千字文》故事，姜晓东；王冬梅译. 华语教学出版社.

5. 中国汉字/韩鉴堂著. 北京：五洲传播出版社，2011. 162 页；23cm. ISBN：7508520353

注：西班牙文

6. Florilegio de refranes chinos/Fernando Mateos. Madrid，etc.：Asociación Española de Orientalistas，1972. 311 pages；24cm.

中国谚语 1000 条. Mateos，Fernando 编译.

(1)2a. ed. Madrid Asociación Española de Orientalistas，1984. 311 p. 24cm. ISBN：8470092197 8470092190

7. Proverbios de la antigua China/recopilación y traducción del chino al español〔por〕Li Deming y Dai Bingpo. Madrid：Miraguano Ediciones，1986. 102 pages：illustrations；20cm. ISBN：8485639650；8485639656. (La Cuna de Ulises；8)

中国古代谚语. Li，Deming 和 Dai Bingpo 编译.

(1)2a. ed. Madrid：Miraguano，1994. 109 p.：il. ISBN：8478130934，8478130931. (La cuna de Ulises；8)

(2)Madrid Miraguano，2014. 109 p. il. 19cm. ISBN：8478134212，8478134212. (Sugerencias)

8. El abanico de otoño：proverbios chinos/Guillermo añino y Zhu Kai. Lima：Asociación Editorial Stella，1993. 222 p.：il.；20cm.

中国谚语. 吉叶墨（Dañino Ribatto，Guillermo Alejandro，1929—）（秘鲁汉学家），Zhu，Kai 合译. 西汉对照.

9. Sabiduría china：sus proverbios y sentencias/Bernard Ducourant；tr. José Ramón Monreal. Barcelona：Martínez Roca，1997. 222 p.；22cm. ISBN：8427021984；8427021983. (Nueva Espiritualidad)

中国智慧：谚语与句子. Ducourant，Bernard. Monreal，José Ramón 转译自法文版《ourt la sagesse des sentences et proverbes chinois》

10. La abeja diligente：mil proverbios chinos/Guillermo Dañino. Lima：Pontifica Universidad Católica del Perú，2002. 281 p.：il. color；21cm. ISBN：9972424804，9972424809. (Colección de Orientalia；8)

中国谚语一千条. 吉叶墨（Dañino Ribatto，Guillermo Alejandro，1929—）（秘鲁汉学家）译.

11. Selección de los proverbios chino. Beijing：Ediciones en Lenguas Extranjeras，1983. 180 p.：il.；20cm. (Manual del chino elemental)

《成语故事选》，北京语言学院编.（《基础汉语课本》阅读材料丛书）.

I 类　文学

I1　文学评论和研究

1. Arte y literatura/por la redacción de ccolección china. Beijing：China Ediciones en Lenguas Extranjeras，1985. 261，〔24〕p. de lám 19cm. (Colección China)

《文学艺术》，《中国概况丛书》编辑委员会编.

2. Un gran debate en el frente de la literatura/Chou Yang. Pekin Ediciones en Lenguas Extranjeras，1958. 76 p.

《文艺战线上的一场大辩论》，周扬.

3. El camino de la literatura y el arte socialistas en China/Chou Yang. Pekin：Ediciones en Lenguas Extrajeras，1961. 77 p.；18cm.

《我国社会主义文学艺术的道路》，周扬.

(1)El camino de la literatura y el arte socialistas en china：informe hecho en el Tercer congreso de Trabajadores

de la Literatura y el Arte de China，el 22 de julio de 1960. 〔2nd ed.〕. Pekin：Ediciones en Lenguas Extranjeras，1964. 77 pages；19cm.

4. Enarbolad mas alto la bandera de ls ideas de Mao Tse-Ttung sobre arte y literatura/Lin Mojan. Pekin：Ediciones en Lenguas Extranjeras，1963. 37 p.；19cm.

《更高地举起毛泽东文艺思想的红旗》，林默涵.

5. 林彪同志委托江青同志召开的部队文艺工作者座谈会纪要. 北京：外文出版社，1968

I11　文学批评著作

1. Wen fu：prosopoema del arte de la escritura/Lu Ji；edición bilingüe de Pilar González España；caligrafías de André Kneib. Madrid Catedra，2010. 206 p. ISBN：8437627038，8437627036. (Letras Universales；429)

《文赋》，陆机（261—303）；González España，Pilar (1960—)译.

2. El corazón de la literatura y el cincelado de dragones/Liu Xie；traducción，introducción y notas de Alicia Relinque Eleta. Granada：Comares，1995. 355 p.；21cm. ISBN：8481511552，8481511550. (De guante blanco)

《文心雕龙》，刘勰（约公元 465——520）；Relinque Eleta，Alicia 译.

(1)Beijing：Zhongguo shehui kexue chubanshe，2003. 358 p.：il.；22cm. ISBN：7500444095，7500444091. (Zhongguo gudian mingzhu quanyi diancang tuwenben)

I12　各体文学评论和研究

1. Las veinticuatro categorías de la poesía/Si Kongtu；preludios de Gong Bilan；edición de Pilar González España. Madrid：Trotta，2012. 172 p.；20cm. ISBN：8498793307，8498793300. (Pliegos de Oriente)

《二十四诗品》，司空图（837—908）；González España，Pilar(1960—)编译.

I13　文学史

1. Breve historia de la literatura clasica China/Feng Yuan-Chun. Pekin：Ediciones en Lenguas Extranjeras，1960. 139 p.：ill.；19cm.

《中国古典文学简史》，冯沅君.

(1)Breve historia de la literatura clásicas china/Lu Kanru，Feng Yuanjun；〔versión española de Luis Enrique Delano〕. 2a ed. Beijing：Ediciones en Lenguas Extranjeras，1986.〔5〕p. de lám.，126 p.；19cm.

《中国古典文学简史》，冯沅君，陆侃如著.

2. Literatura clásicas. Beijing〔China〕：Ediciones en Lenguas extranjeras，1988. 24 p.；19cm. ISBN：7119003089，7119003085. (Presencia en China)

中国古典文学. 外文出版社（中国概况）

3. Historia de la literatura clásicas china/〔por Wu Shoulin〕. Bejing Ediciones en Lenguas Extranjeras，2005—2007. 2

v. il., mapas 26cm. ISBN：7119038494（t. I），7119038490（t. I），7119050584（t. II），7119050583（t. II）.

《中国古典文学简史》，上下册，吴守琳著.

4. Historia de la literatura china moderna/redactor jefe：Tang Tao; traducción de Yang Yinde. Beijing：Ediciones en Lenguas Extranjeras, 1989. 620 p.；21cm. ISBN：7119008633, 7119008639

《中国现代文学史》，唐弢.

5. Lu Xun, Guo Moruo, Mao Dun, Ba Jin/[compilado por Ediciones en Lenguas Extranjeras]. Beijing：Ediciones en Lenguas Extranjeras, 1988. 17 páginas：ilustraciones；18cm. ISBN：7119003070, 7119003078.（Presencia de China）

鲁迅，郭沫若，茅盾，巴金. 外文出版社（中国概况）. 20 世纪中国文学史.

6. Breve historia de la novela china/Lu Xun; traducción del original chino：Rosario Blanco Facal; edición：Alejandro Salas. Barcelona：Azul, 2001. 328 p.；23cm. ISBN：8495488086, 8495488084.（La Otra palabra.; Serie asiática）

《中国小说史略》，鲁迅.

7. Literatura China/Yao Dan; traducido por He Bing. Beijing：China Intercontinental Press, 2011. 264 pages：color illustrations；23cm. ISBN：7508519470, 7508519477.（Series de China Cultural）

《中国文学》，姚丹[等]著. 五洲传播出版社.

I2 作品集

1. Esculpiendo dragones：antología de la literatura china/Guillermo Dañino. Lima, Perú：Fondo Editorial de la Pontifiicia Universidad Católica del Perú, 1996. 2 volumes：illustrations；21cm. ISBN：997242009X(set)
Contents：v. 1. Desde literatura china hasta poesía tang. v. 2. Desde Yu yan fábulas hasta Jinghua Yuan "flores en el espejo"

中国古代文学集. 吉叶墨（Dañino Ribatto, Guillermo Alejandro, 1929—）（秘鲁汉学家）译.

I3 诗歌、韵文

I31 古代和跨时代诗词集

1. Poesía China/directores Alfredo Weiss y Héctor Fuad Miri. Buenos Aires, Argentina Continental, 1944. 133 páginas.（Pequeña Enciclopedia Poética Universal; 2）

中国诗歌集. Weiss, Alfredo 和 Miri, Héctor Fuad（1906—）合译.

2. Breve antologia de la poesia China/Marcela de Juan. Madrid：Revista de Occidente, 1948. 107 pages；17cm.

《中国诗歌精华录》. 黄玛赛（Juan, Marcela de, 1905—1981）译.

3. Segunda antología de la poesía china/Marcela de Juan. Madrid：Revista de Occidente, 1962. 261 pages：frontispiece；22cm.

《中国诗歌精华录再编》. 黄玛赛（Juan, Marcela de, 1905—1981）译.

(1) Madrid Alianza, 2007. 294 p. 18cm. ISBN：8420661261, 8420661260.（El libro de bolsillo. Literatura; 5701）

4. Poesía china：del siglo XXII a. C. a las canciones de la revolución cultural/selección, traducción, prólogo, comentarios y notas de Marcela de Juan. Madrid：Alianza Editorial, 1973. 365 p.；18cm. ISBN：8420614726, 8420614724.（El libro de bolsillo. Sección literatura; 472）

中国古今诗歌. 黄玛赛（Juan, Marcela de, 1905—1981）译.

5. Poetas chinos/[vertidos del francés por Álvaro Yunque; tapa y dibujos, Nina Haeberle]. Buenos Aires：Quetzal, 1958. 135 p.：il

中国诗歌. Yunque, Álvaro 转译自法语版；Haeberle, Nina 插图.

(1) Buenos Aires：Editorial Quetzal, 1966. 127 pages：illustrations；20cm.

(2)[Barcelona]：Azul Editorial, 2000. 125 p.；23cm. ISBN：8495488019, 8495488015.（La Otra palabra. Serie Asiática）

6. Poesía china/selección, traducción y prólogo de María Teresa León y Rafael Alberti. Buenos Aires：Compañia General Fabril, 1960. 237 pages；19cm.

中国诗歌集. León, María Teresa 和 Alberti, Rafael (1902—1999)合译.

(1)[2. ed.]. Buenos Aires, Compañia General Fabril, 1972. 225 pages；19cm.（Los poetas）

(2) Madrid：Visor Libros, 2003. 239 pages；20cm. ISBN：8475229387, 8475229386.（Colección Visor de poesía; v. 491）

7. Poesía china：antología esencial/selección y traducción de Fritz Agūado Pertz.[Buenos Aires]：Andrómeda, 1977. 117 p.；15cm.（Libros de Cabecera）

中国诗歌集. Agūado Pertz, Fritz 选译.

8. Poesía china/selección traducción, Julio Sánchez Trabalón. Argentina：ADIAX, 1982. 112 pages；[14cm].（Colección Camafeo）

中国诗歌. Sánchez Trabalón, Julio 译.

9. Los poetas chinos/Darío de la Fuente D.[Santiago]：Instituto Chileno-Chino de Cultura, Comisión Chilena de Cooperación Intelectual de la Universidad de Chile, 1984. 117 pages；21cm.

中国诗歌. Fuente Duarte, Darío de la 译.

10. Florilegio de canto y poesía China/Bernardo Acevedo, S. J.[S. l.]：Central book Co., 1985. 127 p. 21cm.

中国诗歌. Acevedo, Bernardo, S. J. 译. 西汉对照.

11. Poemas chinos/Alberto Laiseca〔traductor〕. Buenos Aires：Libros de Tierra Firme，1987. 119 pages；20cm. (Colección de poesia Todos bailan；47)

中国诗歌. Laiseca，Alberto(1941—)译.

  (1) Buenos Aires：Gárgola，2005. 120 pages；21cm. ISBN：9509051667，9509051669

12. Poemas chinos de amor/Harold Alvarado Tenorio；editor：Guo Hongshan. Beijing：Editorial China Hoy，1992. 161 p.：il.，retrs.；19cm. ISBN：7507203891，7507203899

《中国爱情诗》. Alvarado Tenorio，Harold(1945—)译.

  (1) 2. ed. Medellín，Colombia：Editorial Universidad de Antioquia，2005. 181 pages；22cm. ISBN：9586558576，9586558570. (Poesía)

  (2) Habana，Cuba：Coleccion Sureditores，2014. 151 pages；illustrations；19cm. ISBN：9593021432，9593021434. (Colección sur poesía；223)

13. Imagen del alma：los 22 temas del poeta/Alejandro Jodorowsky〔traductor〕. Santiago de Chile：Dolmen，1995. 32 pages；23cm. ISBN：9562012573，9562012577. (Dolmen poesía)

中国诗歌. Jodorowsky，Alejandro 译.

14. Vacuidad y vida/Santiago Miguel Rupèrez Durá. 〔Taibei〕 kaung Tang International Publications，1998. 166 p. 26cm. ISBN：9579139598，9579139595

中国诗歌. Rupèrez Durá，Santiago Miguel 译.

15. Puente de porcelana/Guillermo Dañino. 〔Lima，Perú〕：〔s. n.〕，2000. 112 p.；21cm.

中国诗歌. 吉叶墨 (Dañino Ribatto，Guillermo Alejandro，1929—)(秘鲁汉学家)译.

16. Antología de poesía china/introducción，traducción y notas Juan Ignacio Preciado Idoeta. 〔Madrid〕：Editorial Gredos，2003. 263 p.；21cm. ISBN：8424926803，8424926809. (Biblioteca universal Gredos；15)

中国诗歌集. Preciado Idoeta，Juan Ignacio 译.

17. Kirin：negro de marfil：22 poemas clásicos chinos/traducidos por Octavio Paz. Buenos Aires：Galería Jorge Mara-La Ruche：Galería van Riel，2004. 58 pages：illustrations；30cm.

中国古典诗歌 22 首. Paz，Octavio(1914—1988)(墨西哥诗人)译.

18. Alma y materia：poesía y caligrafía chinas：(edición bilingüe)/〔selección de〕Rafael J. Barneto，Jorge J. C. Tseng〔sic；traducción de los poemas chinos，Rafael J. Barneto，Jorge C. Tseng〕. Madrid Miraguano，2005. 91 p. il. color 26cm. ISBN：8478132856，8478132850. (Colección Sugerencias)

中国诗歌与书法. Barneto，Rafael J. 和 Tseng，Jorge T. 合译. 西汉对照.

19. Poesías orientales/traducidas por Emilio Prados；edición de Francisco Chica. Málaga Centro Cultural Generación del 27，2005. 33 p. 17cm. (El Castillo del Inglés；4)

东方诗歌. Prados，Emilio(1899—1962)译.

20. El barco de orquídeas：poetisas de China/Kenneth Rexroth，Ling Chung；traducción de Carlos Manzano. Madrid：Gadir，2007. 207 p.；21cm. ISBN：8493523704，8493523701

Notes：Título original：The orchid boat：women poets of China

《兰舟：中国女诗人诗选》，Manzano，Carlos 转译自王公红(Rexroth，Kenneth，1905—1982)(美国诗人、翻译家)，钟玲(Ling Chung，1945—)合译的《兰舟：中国女诗人诗选》(The orchid boat：women poets of China)一书.

21. Antología de poetas prostitutas chinas：(siglo V-siglo XXI)/Guojian Chen. Madrid Visor Libros，2010. 155 p. ISBN：8498957624，8498957621. (Visor de poesía；762)

《中国青楼女诗人诗选》. 陈国坚(1938—)译.

22. Poesía china (siglo XVI a. C.-siglo XX)/edición de Guojian Chen；traducción de Guojian Chen. 4a ed.，corr. y aum. Madrid Cátedra，2013. 519 p. 18cm. ISBN：8437631523，8437631521. (Letras universales；472)

古今中国诗歌. 陈国坚(1938—)译.

23. El libro de Jade/〔selección y traducción del chino〕Judith Gautier；traducción，Julián Gea；semblanza，Remy de Gourmont；posfacio，Jesús Ferrero. Madrid Ardicia，2013. 126 p. 21cm. ISBN：8494123511，8494123513. 9Ardicia；2)

玉之书：中国诗歌. Gautier，Judith(1845—1917)和 Gea，Julián 合译. 收录王维、李白、王勃等的诗歌.

24. La poesía china en el mundo hispánico/Guojian Chen. Madrid，España：Miraguano Ediciones，2015. 220 pages；21cm. ISBN：8478134274，8478134271. (Sugerencias)

西语世界的中国诗歌. 陈国坚(1938—)著，收录译成西班牙语的中国诗词.

25. Poemas chinos/traducidos por Juan L. Ortiz. Buenos Aires Abeja Reina，2011. 46 pages：Illustrationen. ISBN：9872444846，9872444846

中国诗歌. Ortiz，Juan L. 译.

I311 诗经

1. Romancero chino/edición preparada por Carmelo Elorduy. Madrid：Editora Nacional，1984. 507 pages；18cm. ISBN：8427606796，8427606791. (Biblioteca de la literatura y el pensamiento hispánicos；55)

《诗经》，Elorduy，Carmelo(1901—1989 年)译.

2. Libro de los cantos/edición y traducción de Gabriel García-Noblejas；presentación de Luis Alberto de Cuenca. Madrid：Alianza，2013. 376 pages；23cm. ISBN：8420675619；842067561X. (Colecção Literária)

《诗经》，García-Noblejas Sánchez-Cendal，Gabriel 译. 双语

对照.

I312　其他古代和跨时代诗歌集

1. Catay：poemas orientales. Bogotá：Librería colombiana, Camacho Rolden & compañia, 1929. 166 pages： portraits；26cm.

   Notes：Translator's name, Guillermo Valencia, at head of title. / All of the poems with the exception of the "Temas arabes" are translated from "La flùte de jade," a collection of Chinese poems selected and translated into French by Ts'ao Shang-ling and edited by Franz Toussaint.

   《神州集：东方诗歌》，Valencia，Guillermo 转译自法语版的"La flùte de jade"一书中的中国诗歌部分.

2. La flauta de jade/［traducción de Ernestina de Champorcín；prefacio de Juan José Domenchina；ilustraciones de Alma Tapia］.［México］：Centauro, 1944. 212 pages：il. color；21cm.（Amor y poesía en Oriente）

   玉笛：中国诗歌. Champorcín，Ernestina de 译.

3. El Pabellón de porcelana：compilación de poesías chinas/ M. Gutiérrez Marín；con 10 dinujos de José Chico. Barcelona：Montaner y Simón, 1945. 170 p.；18cm.

   中国诗歌集. Gutiérrez Marín，M. 译.

4. La flauta de jade/versión castellana y prefacio de Angel J. Battistessa, según la traducción de Franz Toussaint. Buenos Aires：Guillermo Kraft, 1947. 168 p.：il.；19cm.

   玉笛：中国诗歌. Battistessa，Angel José（1902—）译自 Toussaint，Franz（1879—）的法文版《La flute de jade, poèsies chinoises》

   （1）2a ed. Buenos Aires：Guillermo Kraft, 1951. 168 p.；19cm.

5. Poesías de la antigua China./［compilado y traducido por］ Romeo Salinas.［Santiago］：Esc. Nacional Artes Gráficas, 1947. 60 p.；11×15cm.

   Salinas，Romeo，；1893—1953

   中国古代诗歌. Salinas，Romeo 编译.

6. Rimas exóticas por T'ien Chwen-min. Madrid, Editorial El Perpetuo Socorro, 1952. 143 pages.（Colección Oriente；2）

   Contents：Versiones de poetas［chinos］clásicos：Lipo, Tufu, poetas varios

   主要收录李白、杜甫等诗人的诗作.

7. Antiguos poemas chinos anónimos/Versión castellana y selección de Horacio J. Becco y Osvaldo Svanascini.［S. l.］：SADAO, 1952. 58 p.；20cm.

   中国古代诗歌选译.

8. Canto de pájaros y torrentes：poesía clásicas china/selección y versiones de Javier Sologuren. Lima：Ediciones Capulí, 1977. 38 unnumbered pages：illustrations；17cm.

中国古典诗歌. Sologuren，Javier 选译.

9. 15 poemas Cl de las dinastías Tang y Song/introd.，selec.；tr. y notas de Wu Yuanshan. México：UAM.，Unidad Azcapotzalco, Coordinación de Extensión Universitaria, 1981. xvii,［30］p.；cm. ISBN：9685973040, 9685973045

   唐宋词 15 首. Wu，Yuanshan（1956—）选译. 西汉对照.

10. Antiguas canciones chinas/selección y versión castellana, María Cristina Davie. Barcelona：Teorema, 1983. 187 pages：illustrations；15cm.（Minivisión）

    中国古代诗歌. Davie，María Cristin 选译. 西汉对照.

11. Ciento setenta poemas chinos/traducción del inglés de Lucía Carro Marina. Madrid：Biblioteca Nueva, 1999. 225 p.；21cm. ISBN：8470306588, 8470306587.（Taxila；2）

    Notes：Edición basada en la vesión inglesa de Arthur Waley

    根据韦利（Waley，Arthur, 1889—1966）（英国汉学家）的《汉诗一百七十首》转译.

12. Poesía Zen：antología crítica de poesía Zen de China, Corea y Japón/Juan W Bahk.［Madrid］：Editorial Verbum, 2001. 194 p.；20cm. ISBN：8479621885, 8479621889.（Verbum Poesía）

    Bahk，Juan W. 译. 收录了中国、韩国和日本的禅诗.

13. Cien poemas chinos/Kenneth Rexroth；traducción de Carlos Manzano. Barcelona：Editorial Lumen, 2001. 186 pages；21cm. ISBN：8426428142, 8426428141

    《汉诗 100 首》，Manzano，Carlos 转译自王红公《汉诗 100 首》（One hundred poems from the Chinese）一书.

14. El amor y el tiempo y su mudanza：cien nuevas versiones de poesía china/Kenneth Rexroth；trauducción de Carlos Manzano. Madrid Gadir, 2006. 170 p. 21cm. ISBN：8493443980, 8493443986.（La voz de las cosas）

    《爱与流年：汉诗又 100 首》. 王公红（Rexroth，Kenneth, 1905—1982）（美国诗人、翻译家）译. Rexroth，Kenneth（1905—1982）转译自英文.

15. El bosque de los bambues：poemas de China/ traducciones de Guillermo Martinez Gonzalez. Bogota：Trilce Editores, 1988. 114 pages：illustrations；20cm.（Cuaderno de poesia；no. 3）

    Notes：Includes 45 poems from Love and the turning year, by Kenneth Rexroth/Spanish translation of poems in English translated from the Chinese

    收录《爱与流年：汉诗又 100 首》中的 45 首.

16. Poesía clásicas china/edición de Guojian Chen；traducción de Guojian Chen.［Madrid］：Cátedra, 2001. 387 p.；18cm. ISBN：8437618827, 8437618821.（Letras universales/ Cátedra；316）

    《中国古典诗词》，陈国坚译，收诗词 252 首.

    （1）2a. ed. Madrid：Cátedra, 2002. 387 p.；18cm. ISBN：8437618827, 8437618821.（Letras universales；316）

    （2）3a edición. Madrid：Ediciones Cátedra, 2007. 387

páginas；18cm. 387 páginas；18cm. ISBN：8437618821，8437618827. (Letras universales；316)

17. Poesía china caligrafiada e ilustrada/edición de Guojian Chen; prólogo de Valentín García Yebra; traducción de Guojian Chen y Xiaohui Chen. Madrid Tran，2006. Ed. bilingüe. 150 p. il. 21cm. ISBN：8461128362，8461128365.

《西汉对照书画中国诗词》. 陈国坚（1938—）和 Chen，Xiaohui 合译. 汉西对照. 收诗词 42 首.

18. Lo mejor de la poesia amorosa china/selección y traducción de Guojian Chen. Madrid：Calambur Editorial，2007. 204 pages；23cm. ISBN：8483590225，8483590220. (Calambur poesía；75)

《中国爱情诗歌精华》. 陈国坚（1938—）译. 收诗词 126 首.

19. Poesía china elemental/edición y traducción de Guojian Chen. Madrid Miraguano，2008. 203 p. ISBN：8478133253，8478133259. (Sugerencias)

《中国诗词必读》, 陈国坚（1938—）译. 收诗词 88 首.

20. Poemas chinos para disfrutar/edición y traducción de Guojian Chen. Arganda del Rey，Madrid La Torre Literaria，2012. 158 p. 20cm. ISBN：8493884024，8493884022

《中国诗词欣赏》, 陈国坚（1938—）译. 收诗词 133 首.

21. Poesía y narrativa de la antigua China：antología de bellas historias del pueblo chino/selección，traducción，versión e intervención de Luis Hernán Rodríguez Felder. Buenos Aires：Editorial Larsen，2011. 286 pages；illustrations；20cm. ISBN：9871458271，9871458274. (Proyecto Larsen Clásicos；16)

《中国诗歌》. Hernán Rodríguez Felder，Luis 译.

22. Poesía clásicas China (siglo XI a. n. e.—1840)/seleción，prólogo，cronologia y notas de Esteban Llorach Ramos. La Habana：Editorial Gente Nueva，2004. 231 pages；illustrations；22cm. ISBN：9590806066，9590806063

中国古典诗歌. Llorach Ramos，Esteban 选译.

23. De la China a Al-Andalus：39 jueju y 6 robaiyat：（esplendor del cuarteto oriental)/edición de Ramón Dachs；39 jueju traducidos del chino en colaboración con Anne-Hélène Suárez；6 robaiyat traducidos del árabe en colaboración con Josep Ramon Gregori. Barcelona，España：Azul Editorial，2004. 124 pages；illustrations；23cm. ISBN：8495488140，8495488145. (La otra palabra. Serie asiática)

Contents：Pt. 1 includes Chinese texts and Spanish translations on opposite pages；pt. 2 includes Arabic texts and Spanish translations on opposite pages；critical and biographical matter in Spanish；abstract in English，French，and Spanish.

收录中国诗歌绝句 39 首. Dachs，Ramon 编；Suárez，Anne-Hélène（1960—）译. 汉西对照.

24. Antología poética de las dinástías Tang y Song：los dos períodos de oro de la literatura china/Alfredo Gómez Gil，Chen Guang Fu，Wang Huaizu. Madrid Miraguano，2008. 488 p. ISBN：8478133338，847813333X. (Libros de los malos tiempos Serie Mayor)

唐宋诗词集. Gómez Gil，Alfredo（1936—），Chen，Guang Fu（1934—）和 Wang，Huaizu 合译.

25. Poesía popular de la China antigua/selección de poemas，traducción del chino，introducción y notas de Gabriel García-Noblejas. Ed. bilingüe. Madrid Alianza Editorial，2008. 455 p. 24cm. ISBN：8420649009，8420649007. (Alianza literaria)

中国古代诗歌. García-Noblejas Sánchez-Cendal，Gabrie（1966—）选译.

26. Poesía y narrative de la antigua China：antología de bellas historias del pueblo chino/selección，traducción，versión e intervención de Luis Hernán Rodríguez Felder. Buenos Aires：Editorial Larsen，2011. 286 pages；illustrations；20cm. ISBN：9871458271，9871458274

中国古代诗歌. Hernán Rodríguez Felder，Luis 译.

27. Breve antología de poemas jueju/selección，introducción，traducción directa del chino clásico y notas：Wilfredo Carrizales. Barcelona，Venezuela：Fondo Editorial del Caribe，2012. 86 pages；22cm. ISBN：9807362337，9807362334. (Colección Poesía)

中国绝句诗. Carrizales，Wilfredo（1951—）从中文版直译.

I313　唐诗集

1. Poetas chinos de la dinastía T'ang（618—906）.［Buenos Aires］Mundonuevo，1961. 187 pages；21cm. (Colección Asoka)

唐诗. Ruy，Raúl A. 编译.

（1）2a. ed. Buenos Aires：Hachette，1977. 186 p. ；16cm. (Narciso)

2. Poetas de la dinastía T'ang/Pauline Huang，Carlos del Saz-Orozco. Barcelona：Plaza & Janes，1983. 223 pages；maps；19cm. ISBN：8401810450，8401810459. (Selecciones de poesia universal)

唐诗. Huang，Pauline 和 Saz-Orozco，Carlos del 合译.

3. Poemas de Tang：edad de oro de la poesía china/selección，traducción del chino，introducción y notas de Chen Guojian. Madrid Cátedra，1988. 182 p. 21cm. ISBN：8437607787，8437607788. (Poesía/Cátedra)

《中国诗歌的黄金时代：唐代诗选》, 陈国坚译. 收唐诗 137 首.

（1）2a ed. Madrid：Cátedra，1992. 182 p. ；21cm. ISBN：8437607787，8437607788. (Poesía)

4. La pagoda blanca：poemas de la dinastía Tang/Guillermo Dañino. Lima：Pontificia Universidad Católica del Perú，1996. 134 pages；il. ；21cm. ISBN：9972420395

白塔：唐诗. 吉叶墨（Dañino Ribatto，Guillermo Alejandro，1929—）（秘鲁汉学家)译. 西汉对照.

5. La Pagoda blanca：cien poemas de la dinastía Tang/selección，introducción，traducción y notas de Guillermo Dañino．〔Madrid〕：Hiperión，2001．282 p．：il．；20cm．ISBN：8475176518；8475176512．（Poesía Hiperión/Hiperión；385）

   白塔：唐诗一百首．吉叶墨（Dañino Ribatto, Guillermo Alejandro, 1929—）（秘鲁汉学家）译．

   (1) 白塔·唐诗一百首 /（秘）吉叶墨译．北京：北京大学出版社；2004．268 页；23cm．ISBN：7301080557，7301080559

6. Poetas chinos de la Dinastía Tang（618—907）/sel. y tr. C. G. Moral. Madrid：Visor，1997．167 p．；20cm．ISBN：8475223737，8475223735．（Visor de poesía；373）

   唐诗．Moral, C. G 选译．

   (1) Madrid：Visor，2000．167 p．；20cm．ISBN：8475223737，8475223735．（Colección Visor de poesía；373）

   (2) 3a ed. Madrid：Visor Libros，2011．167 p．；20cm．ISBN：8475223735，8475223737．（Visor de poesía；373）

7. Ventana al Oriente：Li Po，Tu Fu y Wan Wei：paráfrasis de poesía china a través del francés/selección，presentación y versiones de Miguel Angel Flores．México Verdehalago：Universidad Autónoma Metropolitana, Unidad Azcapotzalco，1997．94 p．24cm．ISBN：9686767711，9686767711．（Colección Arena；6）

   李白、杜甫、王维诗歌选．Flores, Miguel Angel（1948—）选译．

8. Antología poética de la Dinastía Tang：primer periodo de oro/〔versión de〕Alfredo Gómez Gil y Chen Guang Fu. Madrid：Edaf，1999．197 p．；18cm．ISBN：8441405328，8441405325．（Arca de sabiduría；43）

   唐诗集．Gómez Gil, Alfredo 和 Chen Guang Fu 合译．

9. Poemas del río Wang/Wang Wei y Pei Di；versos en castellano y presentación：Clara Janés；traducción del chino y preliminar：Juan Ignacio Preciado Idoeta. Madrid：Ediciones del Oriente y del Mediterráneo，1999．87 p．：il．；21cm．ISBN：8487198570，8487198571．（Poesía del Oriente y del Mediterráneo；12）

   唐朝诗人王维和裴迪的诗歌．Preciado, Juan Ignacio（1941—）译．

10. La escritura poética china：seguido de una antología de poemas de los Tang/François Cheng；traducción de Juan Luis Delmont；con la colaboración de Eugenio Montejo. Valencia, España：Pre-Textos，2007．322 p．ISBN：8481917628，8481917621．（Colección textos y pretextos）

   Notes：Traducción de：L'écriture poétique chinoise suivi d'une anthologie des poèmes des Tang

   中国诗歌：唐诗集续集．Delmont, Juan Luis 和 Montejo, Eugenio 合译自 Cheng, François（1929—）的法语版《L'écriture poétique chinoise：suivi d'une anthologie des poèmes des T'ang》一书．

11. 300 poemas de la dinastía Tang/versión directa del chino por Chang Shiru．〔Madrid〕Cromart，2001．222 p．15cm．ISBN：8493189812，8493189815

    《唐诗三百首》，常世儒译．

12. Antología de 300 poemas de la dinastía Song/Wang Huaizu xuan yi；Chen Xiaozhen shen ding；Yu Ji cha tu. Shanghai：Shanghai wai yu jiao yu chu ban she，2013．10,25,476 pages：illustrations；24cm．ISBN：7544629287，7544629287．（SFLEP bilingual Chinese culture series）

    《西汉宋代诗词三百首，王怀祖选译》，陈笑珍审订；余霁插图．（外教社中国文化汉外对照丛书）

13. Trescientos poemas de la dinastía Tang/Sun Zhu（Literato Solitario del Estanque Fragante）；introducción, traducción y notas de Guojian Chen；prólogo de Carlos Martínez Shaw. Madrid：Cátedra，2016．573 p．；18cm．ISBN：8437635668，8437635667．（Letras universales；520）

    《唐诗三百首》，陈国坚译注．

14. Los poetas de la dinastía Tang/selec. de Roberto Donoso. Buenos Aires：Centro Editor de América Latina，1970．59 p．；17cm．（Biblioteca Básica Universal；79）

    唐诗．Donoso, Roberto 选译．

15. Poesia y pintura de la Dinastia Tang：Antologia selecta/〔traduccion：Chang Shiru〕．China：China Intercontinental Press，2009．175 pages：ill．；23cm．ISBN：7508516417，7508516419．（Serie de la cultura selecta tradicional de China）

    《精选唐诗与唐画：西汉对照》，荆孝敏编；常世儒译．

16. Escrito en el aire：tres poetas clásicos chinos/traducción y selección de Fernando Pèrez Villalón；Li Po，Du Fu y Wang Wei. Santiago de Chile Ediciones Tácitas，2013．107 páginas 19cm．ISBN：9568268933．（Colección）

    李白、杜甫和王维诗选译．Pèrez Villalón, Fernando（1975—）译．

I314 宋代诗词集

1. Cantos de amor y de ausencia：Cantos "Ci" de la China Medieval（siglos IX al XIII）/selección，traducción y notas de Xu Zonghui y Enrique Gracia；pinturas y caligrafías de Xu Zonghui. Ed. bilingüe. Madrid Hiperión，2002．187 p．il．ISBN：8475177115，8475177113．（Poesiá Hiperión；421）

   宋词选译．Xu, Zonghui 和 Gracia Trinidad, Enrique 合译．西汉对照．

2. 精选宋词与宋画：西汉对照/（西）皮拉尔·贡萨雷斯·西班牙（Pilar Gonzalez Espana）译．北京：五洲传播出版社，2011．187 页；23cm．ISBN：7508518961，7508518969．（中国传统文化精粹书系）

   西语书名：Poesiay pintura de la dinastia Song -antologia selecta

3. 西译宋代诗词三百首/王怀祖选译；陈笑珍审订；余霁插

图. Shanghai：Shanghai wai yu jiao yu chu ban she，2013. 10，25，476 pages：illustrations；24cm. ISBN：7544629287，7544629287.（外教社中国文化汉外对照丛书＝SFLEP bilingual Chinese culture series）

西文题名：Antología de 300 poemas de la dinastía Song

4. 宋词选／王怀祖译. 上海：上海外语教育出版社，2017. 2册（[45]，501 页）：图，摹真；24cm. ISBN：7544647465.（大中华文库）

西文题名：Antologia poetica del ci de la dinastia Song. 汉西对照. 选译了宋代 52 位词人的 205 首词作.

I32　古代诗人个人作品

I321　魏晋时期

陶渊明（352 或 365—427）

1. El maestro de los cinco sauces：poemas de Tao Yuanming：antología／traducción del chino，selección y notas de Guillermo Dañino. Lima，Perú Pontificia Universidad Católica del Perú，2005. 509 p.：il.；21cm. ISBN：9972427153，9972427152.（Colección Orientalia〈Centro de Estudios Orientales〉；13）

《五柳先生陶渊明诗集》，吉叶墨（Dañino Ribatto，Guillermo Alejandro，1929—）（秘鲁汉学家）译. 西汉对照.

I322　唐朝

王维（701—761）

1. La montaña vacía：poemas de Wang Wei／versiones，introducción y notas de Guillermo Martínez González. Santafé de Bogotá：Trilce Editores，1996. 81 páginas；21cm. ISBN：9589180523，9589180525

空山：王维诗. 吉叶墨（Dañino Ribatto，Guillermo Alejandro，1929—）（秘鲁汉学家）译. 汉西对照.

2. 99 cuartetos de Wang Wei y su círculo／edición y traducción de Anne-Hélène Suárez Girard. Madrid：Editorial Pre-Textos，2000. 239 p.；22cm. ISBN：8481913332，8481913330.（Colección La cruz del sur；470）

王维的 99 首诗. Suárez Girard，Anne-Hélène（1960—）编译. 西汉对照.

3. Poemas del río Wang／Wang Wei；traducción y edición de Pilar Gonzánez España；prólogo de Julio César Abad Vidal；caligrafías realizadas por el maestro Zeng Ruojing. Madrid：Trotta，2004. 210 p.：il.；20cm. ＋ 1 hoja plegada. ISBN：8481646784，8481646788.（Pliegos de Oriente；13）

《辋川集》. González España，Pilar（1960—）译. 西汉对照.

4. La montaña vacía：antología ／Wang Wei；traducción，introducción y notas de Guillermo Dañino. Madrid：Hiperión，2004. 406 p.；20cm. ISBN：8475178022，8475178028.（Poesía／Hiperión；474）

王维诗集. 吉叶墨（Dañino Ribatto，Guillermo Alejandro，1929—）（秘鲁汉学家）译.

李白（701－762）

1. Poemas de Li Po／Traducción y prólogo de Luis Enrique Delano. Santiago de Chile：Universitaria，1962. 76 p.；24cm.

李白诗. Enrique Delano，Luis 译.

2. Vida y poesía de Li Po，701—762 D. C.／Arthur Waley；versión española de Mariá Manent. Barcelona：Editorial Seix Barral，1969. 148 p.；19cm.（Biblioteca Breve de Bolsillo；25）

李白的生活与诗. 转译自韦利（Waley，Arthur，1889—1966）（英国汉学家）的英文版.

3. Copa en mano，pregunto a la luna：poemas／Li Bo；traducción，introducción y notas de Chen Guojian. México，D. F.：El Colegio de México，Centro de Estudios de Asia y Africa，1982. 85 pages：illustrations；20cm. ISBN：9681201752，9681201753

把酒问月：李白诗集. 陈国坚（1938—）译.

4. Poemas de Li-Po：poesía clásicas china／selección，traducción del chino，introducción y notas de Chen Guojian. Barcelona：Icaria，1989. 119 p.；23cm. ISBN：8474261570，8474261578

李白诗选. 陈国坚（1938—）译.

5. Eres tan bella como una flor，pero las nubes nos separan／Li Po；traducción de Chen Guojian. Barcelona：Mondadori，1999. 68 p.；16cm. ISBN：8439704011，8439704010.（Mitos poesía；38）

陈国坚（1938—）译.

6. Cien poemas／Li Po；selección，traducción y prólogo de Chen Guojian. 3a ed. Barcelona：Icaria，2002. 126 p.；22cm. ISBN：8474265665，8474265668.（Poesía；1）

李白诗一百首. 陈国坚（1938—）译.

7. Cincuenta poemas／Li Bo；traducidos del chino，presentados y anotados por Anne-Helène Suárez. Madrid：Hiperión，1988. 64 p.；18cm. ISBN：8475172520，8475172521.（Poesía Hiperión；132）

李白诗歌五十首. Suárez Girard，Anne-Hélène（1960—）从中文本直译.

（1）Madrid：Hiperión，1998. 64 p.；20cm. ISBN：8475172520，8475172521.（Poesía Hiperión；167）

8. A punto de partir：100 poemas de Li Bai／Edición y traducción de Anne-Hélène Suárez Girard. Valencia：Editorial Pre-Textos，2005. 297 p.；22cm. ISBN：8481916617，8481916614.（La cruz del sur；741）

临别歌：李白诗 100 首. Suárez Girard，Anne-Hélène（1960—）编译.

9. Manantial de vino：poemas de Li Tai Po／Guillermo Dañino [compilador]. Lima，Perú：Pontificia Universidad Católica del Perú，Fondo Editorial，1998. li，120，183 pages：color illustrations，1 map；21cm. ISBN：9972421155，

9972421150

酒泉：李太白诗. 吉叶墨（Dañino Ribatto, Guillermo Alejandro, 1929—）（秘鲁汉学家）编译.

10. Manantial de vino: poemas escogidos/Li Bai; edición de Guillermo Dañino. Madrid Hiperión, 2016. 403 p. 20cm. ISBN: 8490020814，8490020817.（Poesía Hiperión；704）

酒泉：李太白诗选. 吉叶墨（Dañino Ribatto, Guillermo Alejandro, 1929—）（秘鲁汉学家）编译. 双语对照.

11. El bosque de las plumas/Li Tai Po; prólogo y notas de Fernán Alayza Alves-Oliveira; traducción del chino de Fernán Alayza Alves-Oliveira y Ricardo Silva-Santisteban. ［Lima］: Pontificia Universidad Católica del Perú, 1999. 98 pages, 1 leaf of color plates: illustrations; 24cm.（El Manantial oculto；17）

李白诗. Alves-Oliveira, Fernán Alayza 和 Silva-Santisteban, Ricardo 合译.

12. Poemes selectes/Li Bai; versió catalana d'Alexandre Ferrer. El Perelló: Aeditors, 2008. 64 p.；17cm. ISBN: 8493643850, 8493643858

李白诗选. Ferrer, Alexandre 选译. 加泰罗尼亚语版.

杜甫（712—770）

1. El vuelo oblicuo de las golondrinas/Du Fu; presentación, Clara Janés y Juan Ignacio Preciado Idoeta; traducción del chino, Juan Ignacio Preciado Idoeta; versos en castellano, Clara Janés. ［Guadarrama，Madrid］: Ediciones del Oriente y del Mediterráneo, 2000. 153 p.：il.；21cm. ISBN: 8487198678, 8487198670.（Colección Poesía del Oriente y del Mediterráneo；15）

杜甫诗. Preciado Idoeta, Juan Ignacio 译. 西汉对照.

2. Bosque de pinceles: poemas de Tu Fu/traducción del chino, selección y notas: Guillermo Dañino. Lima, Perú Pontificia Universidad Católica del Perú, Fondo editorial, 2001. lv, 515 p.；21cm. ISBN: 9972424498.（Colección Orientalia；5）

杜甫诗选. 吉叶墨（Dañino Ribatto, Guillermo Alejandro, 1929—）（秘鲁汉学家）选译. 西汉对照.

(1) Bosque de pinceles/Tu Fu; selección, traducción y notas de Guillermo Dañino. Ed. bilingüe. Madrid: Hiperión, 2006. 527 p.；20cm. ISBN: 8475178782, 8475178783.（Poesía Hiperión；535）

3. Los poemas de Tsin Pau/Carlos Montemayor; ［presentación de Tito Maniacco］. ［Chihuahua］: Alforja Arte y Literatura；Gobierno del Estado de Chihuahua; Instituto Chihuahuense de la Cultura；［Mexico］: CONACULTA, 2007. 76 p.；20cm. ISBN: 9685189579, 9685189576.（Azor）

Contents: Los poemas de Tsin Pau—Acercamiento a Tsin Pau—Du Fu y los poetas chinos de la dinastía Tang.

杜甫诗. Montemayor, Carlos（1947—2010）译评.

白居易（772—846）

1. La canción del laúd/Bai Juyi'; selección, traducción del chino y notas de Guillermo Dañino. ［Lima］: Pontificia Universidad Católica del Perú, 2001. 164 pages: portraits；24cm.（El manantial oculto；25）

《琵琶行》, 吉叶墨（Dañino Ribatto, Guillermo Alejandro, 1929—）（秘鲁汉学家）选译. 汉西对照.

2. 111 Cuarteros de Bai Juyi/edición y traducción de Anne-Hélène Suárez Girard. Valencia Pre-Textos, 2003. 259 p. ISBN: 8481915351, 8481915358.（La Cruz del sur；640）

白居易诗111首. Suárez Girard, Anne-Hélène（1960—）编译. 西汉对照.

(1) Madrid: Pre-Textos, Madrid: Pre-Textos. 2008. 259 pages；22cm. ISBN: 8481915351, 8481915358.（Coleccion La cruz del sur；640）

寒山（生卒年不详）

1. El solitario de la Montaña Fría: poemas de Han-shan/versiones de José Manuel Arango. Medellín: Intergraf Editores, 1994. 78 páginas；24cm. ISBN: 9589367003, 9589367001

寒山诗. Arango, José Manuel（1937—2002）译.

2. El maestro del monte frío: 59 poemas seleccionados, traducidos del chino y anotados por Lola Diez Pastor. Madrid: Hiperión, 2008. 152 p. ISBN: 8475179155, 8475179150.（Poesía hiperión）

寒山诗59首. Diez Pastor, Lola 译. 双语对照.

I323　宋朝

苏东坡（1037—1101）

1. Recordando el pasado en el Acantilado Rojo y otros poemas/traducidos del chino, presentados y anotados por Anne-Hélène Suárez. Madrid: Ediciones Hiperión, 1992. 114 pages: illustrations；20cm. ISBN: 8475173705, 8475173702

《苏东坡诗选》. Suárez Girard, Anne-Hélène（1960—）从中文版直译.

李清照（1084—约1155）

1. Poemas escogidos/Li Qingzhao; traducción de Pilar González España. Málaga ［Spain］: Diputación Provincial de Málaga, 2003. 122 p.；24cm. ISBN: 8477855420.（Mar remoto；11）

李清照诗词选. González España, Pilar（1960—）译.

2. Poesia completa（60 poemas "ci" para cantar）/Li Qingzhao; edición, traducción del chino y notas, Pilar González España. Guadarrama（Madrid）: Ediciones del Oriente y del Mediterráneo, 2010. 203 p. ISBN: 8496327771, 8496327779.（Poesia del Oriente y del Mediterráneo；33）

李清照词60首. González España, Pilar（1960—）编译.

3. La flor del ciruelo/Li Qingzhao; edición, traducción y

prólogo Pilar González España. Madrid：Torremozas，2011. 81 pages. ISBN：8478394951，8478394958. (Colección Torremozas；257)

González España，Pilar(1960—)编译.

4. Jade puro：poemas para cantar/Li Qingzhao；traducción de Kuo Tsai Chia y Miguel Salas Díaz；introducción y edición a cargo de Miguel Salas Díaz. Madrid Hiperión，2014. 171 p. 1 retr. 20cm. ISBN：8490020418；8490020418. (Poesía Hiperión；699)

李清照诗词选. Kuo, Tsai Chia 和 Salas Díaz，Miguel (1977—)合译.

I324　元朝

张可久(约 1270—1350)

1. Sobre un sauce, la tarde/Zhang Kejiu, traducción del chino y notas de Guillermo Danino. Lima Pontificia Universidad Catolica del Peru, 1998. 63 p. (El Manantial Oculto；9)

吉叶墨(Dañino Ribatto, Guillermo Alejandro, 1929—) (秘鲁汉学家)译.

(1) Ed. bilingüe. Madrid, España Ediciones Hiperión；2000. ISBN：8475176542，8475176543. (Poesía Hiperión；373)

I33　现当代诗歌

I331　诗歌集

1. El cielo a mis pies：antología de la poesía china moderna 1918—1949/Liu Dabai, Lu Xun, Shen Yinmo... [et al.]；traducción, selección, introducción y notas, Blas Piñero Martínez. Ed. bilingüe，[1a ed.]. Madrid Hiperión，2013. 397 p. 21cm. ISBN：8490020234，849002023X. (Poesía Hiperión；655)

《新诗集》，收录 1918—1949 年中国诗歌集. Piñero Martínez，Blas 选译.

2. La niebla de nuestra edad：10 poetas chinos contemporáneos/traducción de Fan Ye y Javier Martín Ríos. Granada Ficciones Revista de Letras，2009. 59 p. 16×21cm. ISBN：8495682311. (Sala de los secretos) 当代中国 10 位诗人诗作.

3. 10. Un país mental：100 poemas chinos contemporáneos/traducción, selección, prólogo y notas：Miguel Ángel Petrecca. [Santiago de Chile]：Lom，2013. 242 p.：il.；21cm. ISBN：9560004246；9560004247. (Lom. Poesía) 当代中国诗歌 100 首. Petrecca，Miguel Ángel 编译.

(1)[Barcelona]：Kriller71，2017. 223 pages；21cm. ISBN：8494620386 849462038X. (Colección Poesía；31)

4. Como el viento de la tormenta que nos envuelve：posesía china desde 1949/Introducción, traducción y edición：Blas Piñero Martínez. Palma de Mallorca：La Lucerna，2016. 271 p.；20cm. ISBN：8494611711，8494611712 《当代诗人》，Piñero Martínez，Blas 编译. 收录 1949 年以

来的中国诗歌.

I232　现当代诗人个人作品

鲁迅(1881—1936)

1. Mala hierba＝（Yecao)/Lu Xun；traducción y notas de Blas Piñero Martínez. Velilla de San Antonio，Madrid Bartleby，2013. 217 p. 21cm. ISBN：8492799572，8492799579. (Bartleby poesía)

《野草》，Piñero Martínez，Blas 译.

闻一多(1899—1946)

1. Aguas muertas/Wen Yiduo；introducción, notas y traducción de Javier Martín Ríos. Vitoria：Bassarai，2006. 63 p.：il.；22cm. ISBN：8489852650，8489852655. (Poesía/Bassarai；41)

《死水》，Martín Ríos，Javier 译.

戴望舒(1905—1950)

1. Mis recuerdos/Dai Wangshu；introducción, notas y traducción del chino de Javier Martíon Ríos. Barcelona：La Poesía, señor Hidalgo，2006. 95 p.；23cm. ISBN：8495976382，8495976383.

《我的记忆》，Martín Ríos，Javier 译.

艾青(1910—1996)

1. Poemas escogidos＝Ai Qing shi xuan：edición bilingüe/Ai Qing；traducción y versión de Alfredo Gómez Gil. Beijing：Ediciones en Lenguas Extranjeras，1986. 445 pages；illustrations；21cm.

《艾青诗选：西汉对照》，Gómez Gil，Alfredo 译.

袁水拍(1916—1982)

1. Salsa de soya y langostinos：poemas satírico-políticos/Yuan Shui-po；[versión española de Gregorio Goldenberg；ilustraciones de Jua Chün-Wu]. Pekin：Ediciones en Lenguas Extranjeras，1964. 40 pages，[9] leaves of plates：illustrations；19cm.

《中国的酱油和对虾》. 政治讽刺诗.

北岛(1949—)

1. Olas/Bei Dao [Zhao Zhenkai]；traducción directa del chino de Dolors Folch. Barcelona：Península，1990. 174 p.；20cm. ISBN：8429731601，8429731606. (Península/narrativa；34)

《波动》，Folch Fornesa，Dolors 译.

2. Paisaje sobre cero/Bei Dao；traducción de Luisa Chang. [Madrid]：Visor，2001. 116 p.；20cm. ISBN：8475224482，8475224480. (Colección Visor de poesía；448)

《零度以上的风景》，Chang，Luisa 译.

于坚(1954—)

1. La piedra de Kata Tjuta/Yu Jian；traducción de Miguel Ángel Petrecca. [Beijing]：China Intercontinental Press，2015. 150 p.；23cm. ISBN：7508531441，7508531442. (Joyas de literatura contemporánea china)

《卡他出塔的石头：于坚诗选》，Petrecca，Miguel Ángel 译.

顾城(1956—1993)

1. Poemas oscuros：antología bilingüe/Gu Cheng；estudio preliminar y traducción del chino de Javier Martín Ríos. ［Beijing］China Intercontinental Press，2014. 160 p. 24cm. ISBN：7508527994，7508527992. （Joyas de literatura contemporánea china）
《顾城诗选》，Martín Ríos，Javier(1970—)编译. 五洲传播出版社. 西汉对照.

蔡天新(1963—)

1. La desnudez antigua. Medellín：Universidad de Antioquia，2002. 79 p. ISBN：9586555593；9586555593. （Coleccion poesia）

I4 戏剧文学

I41 综合戏剧集

1. Teatro de ópera chino. Buenos Aires：Ed. Sudamericana，1963. 175 S.；8". (Coleccion teartro)
选译自 Hung，Josephine Huang（1915—）英译的《Children of the pear garden》一书. 收录五部中国京剧.

I42 戏曲家及其作品

1. Dos joyas del teatro asiático. Buenos Aires：Espasa Calpe Argentina，1941. 160 pages；18cm. (Colección Austral；215)
Contents：Ira de Caúsica/Kschemisvara；Circulo de tiza/Li Hsing-tao
翻译了李行道《灰阑记》.
（1）3a ed. Buenos Aires：Espasa-Calpe Argentina，1947. 149 p. 18cm. (Colección Austral；215)

2. Las quince sartas de Sapecas：opera Kunchui/Zhenzhu Su；traducido por Herminia Carvajal. Pekin Ediciones en Lenguas Extranjeras，1958. 70 p. ilustraciones，fotos 23cm.
《十五贯》，(明)朱素臣原著；何如译；浙江省十五贯整理小组整理；Carvajal，Herminia译.
（1）Las quince sartas de sapecas：obra original de Zhu Suchen；revisado por el grupo especial de la Compañía de Opera Kunqu de Zhejiang；ultima versión de Chen Si；；［traducido por Herminia Carvajal］. Pekin：Ediciones en Lenguas Extranjeras，1958. 30 pages：portraits，plates；20cm.
（2）2a ed. Beijing：Ediciones en Lenguas Extranjeras，1979. 75 pages：illustrations；18cm.

3. Tres dramas chinos/introducción，traducción y notas Alicia Relinque Eleta. Madrid：Editorial Gredos，2002. 414 p.；21cm. ISBN：8424923588，8424923587. (Universal/Gredos；3)
Contents：La injusticia contra Dou E que conmovió el cielo y la tierra/Guan Hanqing—El huérfano del clan de los Zhao/Ji Junxiang—Historia del ala oeste/Wang Shifu.

Relinque Eleta，Alicia 译. 翻译了《窦娥冤》《赵氏孤儿》和《西厢记》，

4. El Pabellón de las Peonías o historia del alma que regresó/Tang Xianzu；edición y traducción de Alicia Relinque Eleta. Madrid：Trotta，2016. 471 p.；il.；24cm. ISBN：8498796674，8498796679. (Pliegos de Oriente)
《牡丹亭》，汤显祖（1550—1616）；Relinque Eleta，Alicia 译.

5. 白毛女/贺敬之、丁毅. 北京：外文出版社，1958
注：歌剧
（1）北京：外文出版社，1959

6. El canal de la Barba del Dragon：drama en tres actos/por Lao She. Pekin，Ediciones en Lenguas Extranjeras，1960：90 p.
《龙须沟》，老舍.
（1）2a ed. Pekin：Ediciones en Lenguas Extranjeras，1964. 90 pages：frontispiece (portrait)，plates；22cm.
（2）3a ed. Pekín（Beijing）：Ediciones en Lenguas Extranjeras，1979. 104 p.：fot.；21cm.

7. La casa de té：drama en tres actos. Beijing，China：Lenguas Extranjeras，1981. 104 p.：ilus；21cm.
《茶馆：三幕话剧》，老舍著.

8. La casa de té/Lao She；traducción，estudio preliminar，notas y edición，Belén Cuadra...［et al.］；coordinación，Gabriel García-Noblejas Sánchez-Cendal. Granada Comares，2009. 132 p. 24cm. ISBN：8498366310，8498366313. (Colección de estudios asiáticos；3)
《茶馆》，老舍；Cuadra，Belén 等译.

9. La ingeniosa conquista de la Montana del Tigre：opera de Pekin moderna revolucionaria. Peking：Ediciones en Lenguas Extranjeras，1972. 112 pages
现代革命京剧《智取威虎山》(1970 年 7 月演出本)，上海京剧团.

10. La tempestad：tragedia en cuatro actos/Cao Yu；［version española de Zeng Gang］. Beijing，China：Ediciones en Lenguas Extranjeras，1984. 149 pages，［10］leaves of plates：illustrations，portraits；21cm. (Literatura moderna de China)
《雷雨》，曹禺著. 话剧剧本.
（1）2a ed. Beijing：Ediciones en Lenguas Extranjeras Cía，2011. 161 pages；20cm. ISBN：7119073071，7119073079

I5 小说

I51 古代及跨时代小说集

1. Novelistas chinos de los años 618 a 1715/traducción Manuel Scholz Rich. Barcelona Iberia，1954. 228 p. (Obras Maestras)
中国古代小说选译. Scholz Rich，Manuel 译.

2. Relación de las cosas del mundo/Zhang Hua；prólogo de

Alicia Relinque；traducción de Yao Ning y Gabriel García-Noblejas Sánchez-Cendal. Madrid：Trotta，2001. 207 p.；20cm. ISBN：8481644560；8481644562.（Pliegos de Oriente.；Serie Lejano Oriente；8.）

《博物志》，张华（232—300）；Yao Ning 和 Garcia-Noblejas Sánchez-Cendal, Gabriel 合译.

3. La hija del rey dragón：cuentos de la dinastía Tang. Beijing：Ediciones en Lenguas Extranjeras，1980. 110 p.；ilus.；22cm.

《唐代传奇》，白行简等编.

（1）Beijing：Ediciones en Lenguas Extranjeras，1989，1980. v, 110 p.；il.；21cm. ISBN：7119010778，7119010779778，7119010779

4. Las Damas de la Dinastia Tang：22 historias clasicas de China/traduccion en Espanol por Virginia Carreno, Mario Lessa y Teresa Hsing-chu Tu de la Version Inglesa de Elizabeth Te-chen Wang；composicion literaria por Orlando Gomez Leon. Taipei：China Publishing Co.，1980. ii, 260 pages；illustrations；19cm.

《唐代名小说集》，转译自 Wang, Te-chen 的英文版.

5. Cuentos de la dinastía Tang/edición, prólogo, traducción y notas Juan Ignacio Costero de la Flor y Abelardo Seoane Pèrez. Madrid：Biblioteca Nueva，1999. 149 pages；21cm. ISBN：8470306561, 8470306563

唐代传奇. Costero de la Flor, Juan Ignaacio 等译.

6. Antología de cuentos de la Dinastía Tang：Shen Jiji, Li Chaowei, Jiang Fang, Li Gongzuo, Bai Xingjian, Xue Tiao, Li Fuyan, Pei Xing, Du Guangting/edición de Sebastián Gómez Cifuentes. Madrid：Miraguano，2014. 203 p.；19cm. 1 introducción（XV p.）. ISBN：8478134236, 8478134239.（Libros de los malos tiempos；121）

唐代传奇. Gómez Cifuentes, Sebastián 编译.

7. El joyero de la cortesana：antologia de cuentos de las dinastias Song y Ming. Beijing：Ediciones en Lenguas Extranjeras，1989. 2 volumes：illustrations；19cm.

《宋明平话选》（上下），（明）冯梦龙等著.

8. El Letrado sin cargo y el baúl de bambú：antología de relatos chinos de las dinastías Tang y Song（618—1279）/traducción del chino y selección de Gabriel García-Noblejas Sánchez-Cendal. Madrid：Alianza，2003. 397 p.；22cm. ISBN：8420645435; 8420645438.（Alianza literaria.；Narrativa）

唐 宋 故 事 选. Garcia-Noblejas Sánchez-Cendal, Gabriel 译.

9. El casamiento engañoso：novela china/Kin-ku-ki-kuán；［Traducida por Keller］.［Madrid］：Jiménez-Fraud，［1920—1940］. 64 p.；19cm.（Lecturas de una hora；16）

《今古奇观》，Keller 译.

10. La viuda, la monja, la cortesana/Lin Yutang；traducción de Floreal Mazía. 4a ed. 1954. 320 p.；19cm.

《寡妇，尼姑与歌妓》，林语堂英译；Mazía，Floreal 转译成西语. 为节译《全家庄》、《老残游记二集》及改写《杜十娘》而成.

11. No temer a los fantasmas：Relatos［compilados］por el Instituto de Literatura de la Cademia de Ciencias Sociales de China. Pekín（Beijing）：Ediciones en Lenguas Extranjeras，1979. 114 p.；［8］p. de lám.；19cm.

《不怕鬼的故事》，中国社会科学院文学研究所编.

12. Relatos chinos de espíritus/Lafcadio Hearn；traducción de Marina Alcantud...［el. al］；separata preliminar de Selma Balsas；edición, coordinación y revisión de Gabriel García-Noblejas. Madrid：Miraguano Ediciones，2006. xxxi, 125 p.；il.；19cm. ＋ 1 separata. ISBN：8478133003; 8478133000.（Libro de los malos tiempos；92）

中国鬼故事. Alcantud, Marina 转译自 Hearn, Lafcadio（1850—1904）的英文版.

13. Largueza del cuento corto chino/recopilación, prólogo, traducción y notas de José Vincente Anaya. Oaxaca, México：Editorial Almadía，2010. 187 pages；21cm. ISBN：6074110395 6074110395.（Mar abierto）

中国短篇小说选. Anaya, José Vicente 编译.

I52　古代个人作品

干宝（约 282—351）

1. Cuentos extraordinarios de la China medieval：antología del Soushenji/Gan Bao；prólogo, selección y traducción Yao Ning y Gabriel García-Noblejas. Madrid：Oceano，2000. 150 p；22cm. ISBN：848961847X；8489618473

《搜神记》

颜之推（531—约 591）

1. Las venganzas de los espíritus/Yan Zhitui；traducción y prólogo Gabriel Garcia-Noblejas.［Madrid］：Lengua de Trapo Ediciones，2002. xxxii, 155 p.；22cm. ISBN：8489618828；8489618824.（Rescatados Lengua de Trapo；5）

《冤魂志》，García-Noblejas, Gabriel（1966—）译.

《水浒传》，施耐庵（约 1290—约 1370）

1. A la orilla del agua/por Shi Nai'an y Luo Guanzhong；traducido por Mirko Láuer y Jéssica McLauchian. Beijing：Ediciones en Lenguas Extranjeras，1992. 4 v.；il.；18cm. ISBN：7119001248, 7119001241, 7119001256, 7119001258, 7119005251, 7119005256, 711900526X, 7119005263.（Colección Fenix）

《水浒传》，4 卷本. Láuer, Mirko 和 McLauchian, Jéssica 合译. 转译自英文版《Outlaws of the Marsh》

2. A la orilla del agua/Mirko Láuer y Jéssica McLauchlan；versión china de Shi Nai'an y Luo Guanzhong；versión española de Mirko Láuer y Jéssica McLauchlan. Beijing Ediciones en Lenguas Extranjeras，2010. 5 v. 24cm. ISBN：7119067223, 7119067222.（Biblioteca de clásicos

chinos. Chino-español)

《水浒传》，5 册卷本. Láuer，Mirko 和 McLauchian，Jéssica 合译.

吴承恩（约 1500—1583）

1. The making of Monkey King = el surgimiento del Rey Mono/retold by Robert Kraus and Debby Chen; illustrated by Wenhai Ma; Spanish translation by Paulina Kobylinski. Union City, CA：Pan Asian Publications, c1998. 1 v. (unpaged)：col. ill.；29cm. ISBN：1572270446. (Adventures of Monkey King = Las aventuras del Rey Mono；1)

   《西游记》选译，Kobylinski，Paulina 译.

2. Peregrinación al Oeste/Wu Cheng'en；［traducido por María Lecea y Carlos Trigoso Sánchez］. Beijing：Ediciones en Lenguas Extranjeras, 2005. v. I (648 p.)：il.；18cm. ISBN：7119011294，7119011295

   《西游记》，吴承恩；Lecea，María 和 Trigoso Sánchez，Carlos 合译.

3. Peregrinacion al oeste/versión china, Wu Cheng'en；versión española, María Lecea y Carlos Trigoso Sánchez. Beijing Ediciones en Lenguas Extranjeras, 2010. 8 v. 24cm. (61，4442 mian)：tu；24 gong fen. ISBN：7119060033，7119060033，7119060031. (Biblioteca de clasicos Chinos.)

   《西游记》. 8 卷本.

4. Viaje al oeste：las aventuras del Rey Mono/prólogo de Jesús Ferrero；edición y traducción del chino de Enrique P. Gatón e Imelda Huang-Wang. Madrid：Ediciones Siruela, 2004. 2260 p.；23cm. ISBN：8478447741，8478447749. (Libros del tiempo；178)

   《西游记》，Gatón，Enrique P. 和 Huang-Wang，Imelda 合译.

   (1)2a. edición. Madrid：Ediciones Siruela, 2006. 2260 páginas；22cm. ISBN：8478447741，8478447749. (Libros del tiempo；178)

冯梦龙（1574—1646）

1. Cuentos amorosos chinos：siete narraciones/traducción y nota preliminar de Ramón Palazón. México, D. F.：Costa-Amic, 1983. 157 pages：illustrations；18cm. ISBN：9684001940，9684001947. (Clásicos Siglo XVII)

   主要译自《醒世恒言》. 6 篇选自《醒世恒言》，1 篇选自《警世通言》. 译自英文版的 "Eastern shame girl"

凌蒙初（1580—1644）

1. Doce narraciones chinas/King Mengzhu；selección y notas de André Lévy；traducción de Manuel Serrat Crespo sobre la versión francesa de André Lévy；prólogo de Manel Ollé. Barcelona：Círculo de Lectores, 2001. 381 p.；22cm. ISBN：(tela)；8422671007. (Biblioteca universal. Literaturas orientales)

   《拍案惊奇》选译，Lévy，André 法译；Serrat Crespo，Manuel 西译自法文版.

《金瓶梅》

1. Flor de ciruelo en vasito de Oro = Jin Ping Mei/versión, introducción y notas de Xavier Roca-Ferrer. Barcelona：Destino, 2010. 2 v：il.；22cm. 8423343348 (o. c.), 8423343340 (o. c.), 8423343324 (v. 1), 8423343324 (v. 1), 8423343331 (v. 2), 8423343332 (v. 2). (Áncora y delfin；1192—1193)

   Contents：T. I：Libro de las Primaveras y los Veranos (920 p.). —T. II：Libro de los Otoños y los Inviernos (891 p.).

   《金瓶梅词话》，兰陵笑笑生（明代中后期，生卒年不详）；Roca-Ferrer，Xavier 译.

2. Jin Ping Mei：en verso y en prosa/El Erudito de las Carcajadas de Langling；traducción, introducción y notas, Alicia Relinque Eleta. Barcelona：Atalanta, 2010. vol. 〈1－2〉. il.；23cm. ISBN：8493778477 (vol. 1), 8493778478 (vol. 1), 8493846640 (vol. 2), 8493846643 (vol. 2). (Memoria Mundi；49)(Memoria mundi；61)

   《金瓶梅》，兰陵笑笑生（明代中后期，生卒年不详）；Relinque Eleta，Alicia 译注.

   (1)3a ed. Barcelona：Atalanta, 2011. vol. 〈1－2〉：il.；23cm. ISBN：8493778477 (vol. 1), 8493778478 (vol. 1), 8493846640 (vol. 2), 8493846643 (vol. 2). (Memoria Mundi；49)(Memoria mundi；61

李渔（1611—1680）

1. El tapiz del amor celeste/Li - yu；tr. Genaro de la Osa. México：Baal, 1961. 263 p.；20cm.

   《肉蒲团》，Osa，Genaro de la 译.

2. Jou pu tan：［la esterilla de oraciones de carne］/Li Yü；［traducción Beatriz Podestá］. Barcelona：Bruguera, 1978. 382 p.；19cm. ISBN：8402055265，8402055262. (Clásicos del erotismo；5)

   《肉蒲团》，Podestá，Beatriz 译.

3. La alfombrilla de los goces y los rezos/Li Yu；traducción de Iris Menéndez. Barcelona：Tusquets, 1992. 337 pages；20cm. ISBN：8472234681，8472234680. (La sonrisa vertical；77)

   《肉蒲团》，Hanan，Patrick 和 Menéndez，Iris 合译.

   (1)Barcelona：Círculo de Lectores, 2001. 402 p.；21cm. ISBN：842267100X，8422671008. (Biblioteca universal. Literaturas orientales)

蒲松龄（1640—1715）

1. Cuentos extraños/P'u Sung-Ling；adaptación castellana de Rafael de Rojas y Román；ilustraciones de D'ivori. Barcelona：Atlántida, 1941. 139 p.：il.；19cm. (Colección Estela；3；Narradores extranjeros；2)

   《聊斋志异》，Rojas y Román，Rafael 译.

2. El invitado tigre/PU' Sung-Ling；selección y prólogo de Jorge Luis Borges；［traducción, Jorge Luis Borges, Isabel Cardona］. Madrid Siruela, 1985. 102 p. 23cm. ISBN：8485876245，8485876242. (La Biblioteca de

Babel；12)

《聊斋志异》，Borges，Jorge Luis（1899—1986）和 Cardona，Isabel 合译. 选译自英文图书《Strange Stories From A Chinese Studio》

3. Cuentos de Liao Zhai/Pu Sonling；traducción， introducción y notas de Laura A. Rovetta y Laureano Ramírez. Madrid Alianza Editorial，1985. 400 p. il. 20cm. ISBN：8420631531

《聊斋志异》，Rovetta，Laura A. 和 Ramírez，Laureano 合译.

(1) Madrid：Alianza Editorial，2004. 440 p.；il.；22cm. ISBN：8420645710，8420645711.（Alianza literaria. Narrativa）

4. Extraños cuentos de Liao Chai：auténticos y clásicos cuentos chinos/Pu Songling；traducido al español por Kim En-Ching，Ku Song-Keng.［Madrid］：［Defensa］，1987. 108 p.：il. color；25cm. ISBN：8485506022，8485506026

《聊斋志异》，Kim，En-Ching 和 Ku，Song-Keng 合译.

5. Relatos/Pu Sun-Lin. La Habana：Arte y Literatura，1990. 261 p.；19cm.

《聊斋志异》

6. Historias fantásticas/Pu Sung-Lin；［traducción de Imelda Huang Wang y Enrique Prieto Gatón］. Madrid Mondadori，1992. 244 p. 22cm. ISBN：8439718365，8439718369.（La cabeza de Medusa；7）

《聊斋志异》，Huang Wang，Imelda Gatón，Enrique Prieto Gatón 合译.

吴敬梓（1701—1754）

1. Historia de los intelectuales/Wu Jin Xing. Shanghai ［China］：ed. de Obras antiguas de Shanghai，1984. 2 v.；19cm.

《儒林外史》

2. Los mandarines：historia del bosque los letrados/Wu Jingzi；presentación，traducción y notas de Laureano Ramírez. Barcelona：Seix Barral，1991. 589 p. 24cm. ISBN：843220644X，8432206443.（Biblioteca breve）

《儒林外史》，Ramírez，Laureano 译.

(1) Barcelona：Seix Barral，2007. 717 p.；25cm. ISBN：8432228133，8432228131.（Biblioteca Formentor/Seix Barral）

3. Rúlín Wáishi：historia indiscreta del bosque de letrados/Wu Jingzi；traducido por Chen Gensheng. Beijing：Ediciones en Lenguas Extranjeras，1993. 2 v.；18cm. ISBN：7119014048（v. 1），7119014043（v. 1）.（Colección Fenix）

《儒林外史》，陈根生译.

曹雪芹（1715—1763）

1. Sueño en el pabellón rojo：memorias de una roca/... y Gao E. Traducción de Tu Xi. Edición revisada，corregida y anotada por Zhao Zhenjiang y José Antonio García

Sánchez. Granada，España：Universidad de Granada，1988. 2 v.；21cm. ISBN：8433807668，8433807663

《红楼梦》，赵振江与García Sánchez，José Antonio 修订. 2 卷本.

(1) Sueño en el pabellón rojo：memorias de una roca/Cao Xueqin；traducción de Zhao Zhenjiang y de José Antonio García Sánchez；edición revisada por Alicia Relinque Eleta. Barcelona：Círculo de Lectores Galaxia Gutenberg，2009. 2 v. ISBN：8467237047（o. c.，Círculo de lectores），846723704X（o. c.，Círculo de lectores），8481098334（o. c.，Galaxia Gutenberg），8481098337（o. c.，Galaxia Gutenberg），8467237054（v. 1，Círculo de lectores），8467237058（v. 1，Círculo de lectores），8467237061（v. 2，Círculo de lectores），8467237066（v. 2，Círculo de lectores），8481098358（v. 2，Galaxia Gutenberg），8481098353（v. 2，Galaxia Gutenberg）

(2) Barcelona：Galaxia Gutenberg，2010. 2 v.：il.；21cm. ISBN：8481098341（v. 1），8481098345（v. 1），8481098358（v. 2），8481098353（v. 2）

(3) Sueño en el pabellón rojo：memorias de una roca/Cao Xueqin；traducción de Zhao Zhenjiang y de José Antonio García Sánchez；edición revisada por Alicia Relinque Eleta. Barcelona：Círculo de Lectores Galaxia Gutenberg，2017. 2 v.（1176，1195 p.）il. 21cm. ISBN：8416495580（obra completa）；8416495580；8416495559（v. 1）；8416495556；8416495566（v. 2）；8416495564

2. Sueño en el pabellón rojo：memorias de una roca/Cao Xueqin y Gao E.；traducción de Tu Xi；edición revisada，corregida y anotada por Zhao Zhenjiang y José Antonio García Sánchez；ilustraciones de Liu Danzhai. Granada：Universidad de Granada，Ediciones en Lenguas extranjeras de Pekín，1988. 3 v.；21cm. ISBN：8433807633（o. c.），8433807632（o. c.），8433807668（t. III），8433807663（t. III）

《红楼梦》，赵振江与García Sánchez，José Antonio 修订. 3 卷本.

(1) 2a. ed. Granada Universidad de Granada，1988—2005. 3 v. il. color 21cm. ISBN：8433807633，8433807632

3. Sueño de las mansiones rojas/Cao Xueqin y Gao E.；versión castellana de Mirko Láuer；ilustraciones de Dai Dunbang. Beijing：Ediciones en Lenguas Extranjeras，1991. 4 v.；en contenedor 19cm. ISBN：7119006495（v. 1）；7119006499（v. 1）；7119006509（v. 2）；7119006505（v. 2）；7119006517（v. 3）；7119006512（v. 3）；7119006525（v. 4）；7119006529（v. 4）.（Fénix）

《红楼梦》，Láuer，Mirko 译. 4 卷本. 从英文版转译.

(1) Sueño de las mansiones rojas/versión china de Cao Xueqin y Gao E；versión española de Mirko Láuer. ［Beijing］：Wai wen chu ban she，2010. 7 volumes；

illustrations；24cm．ISBN：7119060002，7119060007．（Biblioteca de clásicos Chinos）

4. Sueño en el pabellón rojo/Cao Xueqin，traducción：Mónica Hernández．México：Ediciones del Castor，2007．302 p．：il. col．；22cm．ISBN：9687587264，9687587261

《红楼梦》，Hernández，Mónica 译．

刘鹗（1857—1909）

1. Los viajes del buen doctor Can/Liu E；introducción de Juan José Ciruela y Javier Martín Ríos；traducción y notas de Gabriel García-Noblejas Sánchez-Cendal．Madrid：Cátedra，2004．391 p．；18cm．ISBN：8437621488，8437621487．（Letras universales；367）

《老残游记》，García-Noblejas Sánchez-Cendal，Gabriel 译．

《株林野史》

1. Bella de Candor：y otros relatos chinos/Barcelona：Tusquets Editores，1994．243 pages：illustrations；20cm．ISBN：8483105527，8483105528．（La sonrisa vertical；105）

《株林野史》，Corral，Mercedes de 和 Corral，María de 合译．

(1) Barcelona：Tusquets，1997．243 p．；20cm．ISBN：8483105527，8483105528．（La Sonrisa vertical；105）

《狄公案》系列

1. Fantasma en Fu-Lai：las primeras tres causas criminales del Juez Ti：novela policíaca basada en datos auténticos tomados de la historia de la China antigua/Robert van Gulik；con diez dibujos al estilo chino de mano del autor；traducción realizada por S. A. R. el Príncipe de los Países Bajos en su clase de español．Madrid：Aguilar，1965．xix，420 pages，［1］leaf of plates：illustrations，portraits；13cm．（Colección Crisol；70）

狄公案之三个犯罪故事．高罗佩（Gulik，Robert Hans van，1910—1967）（荷兰汉学家）翻译并创作．英文题名：The fantoom in Foe-lai

2. El jarrón chino/Robert Van Gulik．Barcelona：Molino，1966．208 pages；17cm．

《柳园图》，高罗佩（Gulik，Robert Hans van，1910—1967）（荷兰汉学家）翻译并创作．英文题名：The willow pattern

3. El fantasma del templo/Robert van Gulik；traducción［del inglés］de Ramón Margalef LLambrich．Barcelona：Editoral Molino，1967．240 pagina's；16cm．（Selecciones de Biblioteca Oro；262）

《紫光寺》，高罗佩（Gulik，Robert Hans van，1910—1967）（荷兰汉学家）翻译并创作；LLambrich，Ramón Margalef 从英文版转译成西班牙语．英文题名：The phantom of the temple

4. El fantasma del templo/Roberto van Gulik；［traducción del inglés de Gloria Pons］．［Esplugues de Llobregat，Barcelona］Plaza & Janés，1984．236 p．18cm．ISBN：8401908612，8401908613．（Colección Búho；61）

《紫光寺》，高罗佩（Gulik，Robert Hans van，1910—1967）（荷兰汉学家）翻译并创作；Pons，Gloria 转译成西班牙语．英文题名：The phantom of the temple

5. La perla del emperador/Robert van Gulik；［traducción del inglés de Amalia Monasterio］．Esplugues de Llobregat（Barcelona）Plaza & Janés，1982．235 p．18cm．ISBN：8401908515，8401908514．（Colección Búho；Policíaca；51）

《御珠案》，高罗佩（Gulik，Robert Hans van，1910—1967）（荷兰汉学家）翻译并创作；Monasterio，Amalia 从英文转译成西班牙语．英文题名：The emperor's pearl.

(1) La perla del emperador/Robert Van Gulik；traducción de Ma. Ángeles Peralta．Barcelona Edhasa，2006．316 p．21cm．ISBN：8435035735，8435035736．（Las aventuras del juez Di en la China del siglo VII；7）

6. El Pabellón Rojo/Robert Van Gulik；［traducción del inglés de Gloria Pons］．Esplugues de Llobregat，Barcelona Plaza & Janés，1983．235 p．18cm．ISBN：8401908558，8401908552．（Policiaca；55）

《红亭记》，高罗佩（Gulik，Robert Hans van，1910—1967）（荷兰汉学家）翻译并创作；Pons，Gloria 从英语转译成西班牙语．英文题名：The red pavilion

7. El misterio del pabellón rojo/Robert Van Gulik；traducción de David León Gómez．Barcelona：Edhasa，2005．314 p．；20cm．ISBN：8435035727，8435035729．（Las Aventuras del juez Di en la China del siglo VII；6）

《红亭记》，高罗佩（Gulik，Robert Hans van，1910—1967）（荷兰汉学家）翻译并创作；León Gómez，David 从英语转译成西班牙语．英文题名：The red pavilion

(1)［Barcelona］Altaya，2007．314 p．23cm．ISBN：8448722630，8448722639．（Novela histórica de crimen y misterio）

8. Asesinato en Cantón/Robert Van Gulik；［traducción，Ramón Margalef］．Barcelona Forum，1984．106 p．il．24cm．ISBN：8475742254，8475742250．（Círculo del crimen；95）

《广州案》，高罗佩（Gulik，Robert Hans van，1910—1967）（荷兰汉学家）翻译并创作；Margalef Llambrich，Ramón 从英语转译成西班牙语．英文题名：Murder in Canton.

9. Tres cuentos chinos：los tres primeros casos del juez Di/Robert Van Gulik，con diez dibujos del autor．［Barcelona］：Edhasa，2001．345 p．：ill．；20cm．ISBN：8435035301，8435035309．（Las Aventuras del juez Di en la Chna del siglo VII；1）

《狄公案之黄金案》，高罗佩（Gulik，Robert Hans van，1910—1967）（荷兰汉学家）翻译并创作．英文题名：Chinese gold murders

(1) México D. F. Planeta DeAgostini Cayfosa-Quebec. ，2002．345 p．il．24cm．ISBN：9707260076，9707260078．（U'ltimos éxitos de la novela histórica）

(2)［Barcelona］Altaya，2006. 345 p. 23cm. ISBN：8448720780，8448720784. （Novela histórica de crimen y misterio）

10. El asesinato del magistrado：los casos del juez Di/Robert van Gulik；traduccion，Juan Jiménez Ruiz de Salazar. San Fernando de Henares，Madrid Quaterni. 2014. 279 p. il. 23cm. ISBN：8494180286，8494180282. （Grandes detectives）

《狄公案之黄金案》，高罗佩（Gulik，Robert Hans van，1910—1967）（荷兰汉学家）翻译并创作；Jiménez Ruiz de Salazar，Juan 转译成西班牙语. 英文题名：Chinese gold murders

11. El biombo lacado：tres nuevos casos del juez Di /Rovert van Gulik. Barcelona：Edhasa，2002. 316 p.：il.；21cm. ISBN：8435035328，8435035323. （Las aventuras del juez Di en la China del siglo VII.）

《四漆屏》，高罗佩（Gulik，Robert Hans van，1910—1967）（荷兰汉学家）翻译并创作. 英文题名：The lacquer screen.

(1) El biombo lacado：tres nuevos casos del juez Di/Robert van Gulik；traducción de David León Gómez.［Barcelona］Altaya，2007. 316 p. il. 23cm. ISBN：8448721558，8448721551. （Novela histórica de crimen y misterio）

12. El biombo lacado：los casos del juez Di/Robert van Gulik；traducción，Juan Jiménez Ruiz de Salazar. San Fernando de Henares，Madrid Quaterni，2015. XV，292 p. il. 23cm. ISBN：8494285844，849428584X. （Grandes detectives；36）

《四漆屏》，高罗佩（Gulik，Robert Hans van，1910—1967）（荷兰汉学家）翻译并创作；Jiménez Ruiz de Salazar，Juan 转译成西班牙语. 英文题名：The lacquer screen.

13. El monasterio encantado：novela policial china/Robert Van Gulik；［traducción de Ernesto Mayáns］. Barcelona：Barral Editores，1972. 162 p.；19cm. （Ediciones de bolsillo. Serie negra. Policial；15）

《朝云观谜案》，高罗佩（Gulik，Robert Hans van，1910—1967）（荷兰汉学家）翻译并创作；Mayáns，Ernesto 转译成西班牙语. 英文题名：The haunted monastery. 袖珍本.

14. El monasterio encantado/Robert Van Gulik；［traducción del inglés de Gloria Pons］. Esplugues de Llobregat（Barcelona）Plaza & Janés，1982. 231 p. 18cm. ISBN：8401908469，8401908460. （Policíaca；46）

《朝云观谜案》，高罗佩（Gulik，Robert Hans van，1910—1967）（荷兰汉学家）翻译并创作；Pons，Gloria 从英文转译成西班牙语. 英文题名：The haunted monastery

15. El monasterio maldito：tres nuevos casos del juez Di/Robert Van Gulik.［Barcelona］：Edhasa，2002. 252 pages；20cm. ISBN：8435035344，8435035347. （Aventuras del juez Di en la China del siglo VII；2）

《朝云观谜案》，高罗佩（Gulik，Robert Hans van，1910—1967）（荷兰汉学家）翻译并创作. 英文题名：The haunted monastery

(1) El monasterio maldito：tres nuevos casos de juez Di/Robert van Gulik；traducción de Leonardo Domingo.［Barcelona］Altaya，2007. 252 p. 23cm. ISBN：8448721060，8448721063. （Novela histórica de crimen y misterio）

16. Los misterios del lago asesino：tres nuevos casos del juez Di/Robert van Gulik；introducción de Donald F. Lach；traducción de David León Gómez. Barcelona：Edhasa，2003. 438 pages：illustrations；21cm. ISBN：8435035336，8435035330. （Las aventuras del juez Di en la China del siglo VII；4）

《狄公案之湖滨案》，高罗佩（Gulik，Robert Hans van，1910—1967）（荷兰汉学家）翻译并创作；Gómez，David León 从英语转译西班牙语. 英文题名：Chinese lake murders

(1)［Barcelona］Altaya，2007. 438 p. 23cm. ISBN：8448722166，8448722167. （Novela histórica de crimen y misterio）

17. Los asesinos de la campana china：tres nuevos casos del juez Di/Robert van Gulik；traduccion de David Leon Gomez. Barcelona：Edhasa，2004. 440 pages；20cm. ISBN：843503531X，8435035316. （Las aventuras del juez Di en la China del siglo VII；5）

《狄公案之铜钟案》，高罗佩（Gulik，Robert Hans van，1910—1967）（荷兰汉学家）翻译并创作；Gómez，David León 从英语转译成西班牙语. 英文题名：The chinese bell murders

(1)［Barcelona］Altaya，2007. 440 p. 24cm. ISBN：8448722081，8448722086. （Novela histórica de crimen y misterio）

18. El castillo del lago Zhou-an/Frédéric Lenormand.［Barcelona］：Alea，2007. 185 p.；24cm. ISBN：8449320668，8449320666

转译自 Lenormand，Frédéric 的法文《Le château du lac Tchou-An：une nouvelle enquête du juge Ti》一书. 内容来自狄公案.

I53 现当代小说集

1. El Matrimonio de Primaverita y otros cuentos/traducido por María Lecea. Pekín：Ediciones en Lenguas Extranjeras，1958. 208 p.

《春大姐及其他故事：中国短篇小说选》，刘真等著.

2. El alba sobre el rio y otros cuentos/Versión espanõla de Juan Agulló. Pekin：Ediciones en Lenguas Extranjeras，1963. 137 pages；22cm.

《黎明的河边及其他故事：新中国短篇小说选集》，峻青等.

3. Diez grandes cuentos chinos/Yu Ta-Fu, Lao Sheh, Lu Sin, Mao Tun; [versión española de Luis Enrique Délano y Poli Délano]. [Santiago de Chile]: Quimantú, 1971. 242 p; 18cm.

Contents: Intoxicantes noches de primavera Sangre y lágrimas ElYY pasado/Yu Ta-Fu La luna creciente/Lao Sheh. El diario de un loco Una familia feliz Restauración de la bóveda celeste/Lu Sin. Imagen en miniatura El señor Chao no acierta a comprender La segunda generación/Mao Tun.

收录了郁达夫、老舍、鲁迅、茅盾的十篇小说. Délano, Luis Enrique 和 Délano, Poli 合译.

4. Las semillas y otros cuentos. Pekín: Ediciones en Lenguas Extranjeras, 1974. 195 pages; 19cm.

《种子及其他》,陈洪山等. 短篇小说集.

5. Sueño sobre unas cuerdas: antología de cuentos destacados/[compilada por Mao Dun]. Beijing: Ediciones en Lenguas Extranjeras, 1982. 561 pages: illustrations, portraits; 18cm.

《拣珍珠:短篇小说佳作》,茅盾主编.

6. Cuentos ejemplares (1919—1949)/por Lu Xun y otros. Beijing Ediciones en Lenguas Extranjeras, 1984. 530 p. 21cm. (Literatura moderna de China)

《中国现代短篇杰作选:1919—1949》,鲁迅等著.

7. La mariposa: antología de novelas contemporáneas/[Wang Meng... [et al.]; versión espanola de Li Deming y Yin Chengdong.]. Beijing: Ediciones en Lenguas Extranjeras，1987. 449 p.; 21cm.

《蝴蝶:中国当代中篇小说选》,王蒙等著;Li, Deming 和 Yin, Chengdong 合译. 收录王蒙(1934—)、刘绍棠、朱春雨、孟伟哉的小说.

8. Cuentos ejemplares (1949—1983)/por Jun Quing y otros. Beijing Ediciones en Lenguas Extranjeras, 1989. 424 p. 21cm. ISBN: 7119003739, 7119003733. (Literatura moderna de China)

《中国当代短篇小说选:1949—1983》,峻青等著.

9. Ocho escritoras chinas. Barcelona Icaria, 1990. 412 p. 21cm. ISBN: 8474261716, 8474261714

Contents: Los senderos de la estepa/Ru Zhijuan. El largo y zigzageante arroyo/Liu Zhen. No olvidar el amor /Zhang Jie. Años de madurez/Che Rong. Añoranza/Wen Bin. Granos de abro/Zong Pu. El arroyo de los nueve recodos / Ye Nenling. Mi tio Sani/Li Na

八位中国作家作品集.

10. La novia recobrada: selección de novelas populares/recopilado por Sun Zhilong; [traducido por Xu Yilin y Huang Caizhen, corregido por Guillermo Dañino]. Beijing: Ediciones en Lengua Extranjeras，1994. 365 p.; 18cm. ISBN: 7119015613, 7119015613. (Colección FENIX)

《拣来的新娘子:通俗小说选》,孙子龙编;Xu Yilin 和 Huang Caizhen 合译;吉叶墨(Dañino Ribatto, Guillermo Alejandro,1929—)(秘鲁汉学家)校.

11. Cuentos fantásticos chinos/selección y traducción de Yao Ning y Gabriel García-Noblejas. Barcelona: Seix Barral，2000. 190 pages: illustrations; 23cm. ISBN: 8432296074, 8432296079

中国传奇故事. Yao Ning 和 García-Noblejas, Gabriel 合译.

12. Luna creciente: cuentos chinos contemporáneos/Wang Tongzhao... [et al.]. Madrid: Popular, Cargraphics, 2006. 242 p.; 22cm. ISBN: 8478843626, 8478843620. (Letra grande; Serie maior; 6)

Contents: El niño a la orilla del lago/Wang Tongzhao—Una esposa contratada/Rou Shi—El esposo/Shen Congwen—La separación/Bing Xin—Luna creciente/Lao She—Manos/Xiao Hong—El Sr. Hua Wei/ZhangTianyi—La Sra. Shi Qing/Ai Wu.

中国当代小说. 王统照(1897—1957)等.

13. La gran máscara y otros cuentos de la vida en la ciudad/[traducción al español, Néstor Cabrera; Li Jingze... et al.]. Madrid Cooperación, 2012. 307 p. 21cm. ISBN: 8495920515, 8495920514

《化妆》,李敬泽(1964—)主编. 收录的 14 篇作品为中短篇小说. Cabrera, Néstor(1976—)译.

14. Brisas del bosque y otros cuentos de las minorías étnicas chinas/[Shi Zhanjun... et al.]. Madrid Cooperación, 2012. 339 p. 21cm. ISBN: 8495920485; 8495920484

《一双泥靴的婚礼》,施战军主编. 本书所选的十一部短篇小说作品的作者均为少数民族作家. 作品讲述的故事涉及了藏族、哈萨克族、蒙古族、朝鲜族、东乡族、达斡尔族、鄂伦春族、回族、塔吉克族等. 译自英文版《The mud boot wedding and other ethnic minority stories》

15. Vidas: cuentos de China contemporánea/edición de Liljana Arsovska. México, D. F.: El Colegio de México, Centro de Estudios de Asia y África, 2013. 244 p.; 21cm. ISBN: 6074624465, 6074624461

Contents: El arcoíris o el halo de Buda A Lai En la lactancia Bi Feiyu El atuendo celestial sin costuras Bi Shumin El joven y el perro Chen Ran La prueba Chen Tong Piedra azarosa Jiang Liming La vida en la ciudad Liu Qingbang Por un poco de calor Qiao Ye. La vida en la cuerda Shi Tiesheng Hija adoptiva Su Tong Un hombre casado Su Tong Manita de gato Tang Xiaoling La temática del invierno Wang Meng Las manos Xiao Hong A Jin, el magnate Zhang Kangkang.

当代中国小说选. Arsovska, Liljana 编. 包括阿来、毕飞宇、毕淑敏、史铁生、苏童和张抗抗等的小说.

16. Selección de la narrativa contemporánea china/traductoras: Liljana Arsovska, Radina Dimitrova. [Beijing]: China Intercontinental Press, 2013. 223 p.; 23cm. ISBN: 7508523835; 7508523830. (Joyas de

literatura contemporánea china)

Contents：El árbol más querido/Jiang Yun—El espejo de mi camarada /Xiao Hang—Pedido estatal/Wang Shiyu

《中国当代中篇小说集》，蒋韵，晓航，王十月著；(墨)莉亚娜、拉嫡娜译。五洲传播出版社。

17. Tierra antigua, historias nuevas: los 20 mejores cuentos de los escritores de Shaanxi/Lei Tao, editor; autor, Lu Yao [y otros diecinueve]; recopilador, La Asociación de Escritores de Shaanxi; traductora, Lourdes Macías Mosqueira. China China Intercontinental Press, 2014. 394 páginas retratos en blanco y negro 20cm. ISBN：7508523880，7508523881. (Joyas de Literatura contemporánea China)

《陕西作家短篇小说选》，Macías Mosqueira，Lourdes 译。

I54 现当代个人作品

(按作者出生年先后排列，作者出生年不详或作品的作者未知者排在最后)

鲁迅(1881—1936)

1. Novelas escogidas/Lu Sin. Pekín：Ediciones en Lenguas Extranjeras, 1960. [4] xxiv, 327 p.：il.；21cm.

《鲁迅小说选》

(1)2a ed. Pekín Ediciones en Lenguas Extranjeras, 1962. xxiii, 325 p. il., retr. 22cm.

(2)Novelas escogidas de Lu Sin. 3a ed. Pekin：Ediciones en Lenguas Extranjeras, 1972. 325 p.：il.；21cm.

2. Novelas escogidas de Lu Sin/Lu Sin. [Traducidas por Luis Enrique Délano]. Habana, Impr. Nacional de Cuba, 1961. (Obras maestras) xxiii, 325 pages；portraits；20cm. (Obras maestras)

鲁迅小说选

3. Antiguos relatos vueltos a contar. Pekin：Ediciones en Lenguas Extranjeras, 1963. 163 pages：front (portrait)；19cm.

《故事新编》

(1) 2a ed. Pekin：Ediciones en Lenguas Extranjeras, 1972. iv, 163 pages：portraits；19cm.

4. Contar nuevo de historias viejas/Lu Xun；traducción, introducción y apêndices de Laureano Ramírez. Madrid：Hiperion, 2001. 211 p.；20cm. ISBN: 8475176925, 8475176925

《故事新编》

(1) 2a. ed. Madrid Hiperión, 2009. 211 p. ISBN: 8475176925, 8475176925

5. Antiguos relatos vueltos a contar/Lu Sin. La Habana：Editorial Arte y Literatura, 1978. 181 pages；18cm. (Colección Cocuyo. Literatura universal)

《故事新编》

(1) Habana, Cuba：Editorial Arte y Literatura, 2008. 111 pages；19cm. ISBN：9590303593, 9590303595. (Ediciones Huracán)

6. La verdadera historia de A Q y otros cuentos. ［Estella］Salvat, 1971. 196 p. 19cm. (Biblioteca General Salvat；v. 25)

《阿Q正传》及其他

7. La verdadera historia de A Q/Lu Hsun. Santiago, Chile：Editorial Vida Nueva, 1954. 95 p.；21cm.

《阿Q正传》

8. La Verdadera historia de A Q/Lu Xun. Buenos Aires：Centro Editor de América Latina, 1970. 59 p.：il.；17cm. (Biblioteca básica universal)

《阿Q正传》

9. La verdadera historia de A Q/por Lu Sin. Pekin：Ediciones en Lenguas Extranjeras, 1972. 63 pages；19cm.

《阿Q正传》

10. La verídica historia de A Q/Lu Xun；［traducción, Ernesto Posse］. ［Madrid］ Compañía Europea de Comunicación e Información, 1991. 93 p. 19cm. ISBN: 8479692189, 8479692186. (Biblioteca de El sol；188)

《阿Q正传》

11. Diario de un demente y otros cuentos/Lu Xun. Madrid：Editorial Popular, 2008. 258 pages (large print)；22cm. ISBN: 8478844005, 8478844007. (Letra grande (Editorial Popular). Serie maior；12)

《狂人日记》及其他

12. Diario de un loco y otros relatos/Lu Shin；traducción de Julio Galer de la versión inglesa. Buenos Aires：Centro Editor de América Latina, 1971. 129 pages；19cm.

《狂人日记》及其他

13. Diario de un loco/Lu Hsun；［Traducción de Sergio Pitol］. Barcelona：Tusquets Editores, 1971. 78 p.；19cm. (Cuadernos Infimos；23.；Serie：Los Heterodoxos；v. 7)

《狂人日记》

(1)3a. ed. Barcelona：Tusquets, 1980. 78 p. 19cm. ISBN：8472235238, 8472235236. (heterodoxos)

14. Diario de un loco/Lu Sin；tr. de Sergio Pitol. Xalapa, Veracruz, México：Universidad Veracruzana, 2007. 103 p.；21cm. ISBN：9688348130, 9688348139. (Sergio Pitol traductor)

Contents：Diario de un loco—La verdadera historia de Ah Q—La lámpara eterna.

《狂人日记》

(1)2a ed. Xalapa, Ver.：Universiad Veracruzana, Dirección Editorial, 2011. 103 p. ISBN：6074555691, 6074555699. (Sergio Pitol traductor；03)

15. Diario de un loco/Lu Hsun；traducción y prólogo, Sergio Pitol. Bogotá：Asociación Lengua Franca：Taller de Edición Rocca, 2009. 68 pages：portraits；21cm. ISBN：9589883389, 9589883389. (Colección Boilsillo de duende；no. 3)

《狂人日记》

(1)Segunda edición. Bogotá：Asociación Lengua Franca：
Taller de Edición Rooca, 2014. 66, ［6］páginas；
17cm. ISBN：9589883389，9589883389.（Colección
Bolsillo de Duende）

16. El diario de un loco/Lu Sin. La Habana：Editorial de
Arte y Literatura, 1974. 382 pages；19cm.（Ediciones
Huracán）
《狂人日记》

17. La espada azul/Lu Sin. San José, Costa Rica：Editorial
Costa Rica, 1977. 112 pages；18cm.（Colección popular
de literatura universal；31）
Contents：La espada azul—Tempestad en una taza de
té—Diario de un loco—Mi antiguo hogar—Nostalgia del
pasado.
《蓝剑》. 鲁迅小说选.

18. Grito de llamada/Lu Sin；traducción de Juan Ignacio
Preciado y Miguel Shiao. Madrid：Alfaguara, 1978. 263
p.；20cm. ISBN：8420428515，8420428512.
（Literatura Alfaguara；28）
《呐喊》

叶圣陶（1893—1988）

1. El maestro ni huanzhi. China：Ediciones en Lenguas
Extranjeras, 1982. 331 p.
《倪焕之》, 叶圣陶著.

郁达夫（1896—1945）

1. La oveja descarriada/Yu Dafu；［traducción, Blas Piñero
Martínez］. Madrid Kailas, 2014. 283 p. il. 21cm.
ISBN：8416023554；8416023557.（Clásicos）
《迷羊》, 郁达夫（1896—1945）；Piñero Martínez, Blas 译.

茅盾（1896—1981）

1. Gusanos de seda de primavera y otros cuentos/Mao Tun；
［versión española de Luis Enrique Délano］. Pekin：
Ediciones en Lenguas Extranjeras, 1963. 286 p.；22cm.
《〈春蚕〉及其他》, Délano, Luis Enrique 译.
(1)Pekin：Ediciones en Lenguas Extranjeras, 1979. 286
pages

2. Medianoche/Mao Dun；versión castellana de Mirko
Lauer；ilustraciones de Ye Qianyu. Beijing［China］：
Ediciones en Lenguas Extranjeras, 1982. 542 p.；22cm.
《子夜》

老舍（1899—1966）

1. La casa de los Liu y otros cuentos/Lao She. México, D.
F.：El Colegio de México, 1973. 125 pages；21cm.
（Colección del Centro de Estudios Orientales）
Contents：Acerca de Lao She—Acerca de las
traducciones—La casa de los Liu—Los vecinos—Wei
shen—Un comienzo de buen augurio—Li el Negro y Li el
Blanco.
《柳家大院及其他》
(1)2a ed. México, D. F.：El Colegio de México, 1984.
125 pages；21cm. ISBN：9681202678, 9681202675.

（Colección del Centro de Estudios Orientales）

2. El tirador de ricksha/Lao She. Beijing：Ediciones en
Lenguas Extranjeras, 1990. 344 pages；18cm. ISBN：
7119007769, 7119007762.（Colección Fenix）
《骆驼祥子》

3. El camello Xiangzi：(Luotuo Xiangzi, 1936—1937)/ Lao
She；traducción directa del chino［y］edición de Blas
Piñero Martínez. La Coruña：Ediciones del Viento, 2011.
424 p. 24cm. ISBN：8496964884, 8496964884.（Viento
simún；70）
《骆驼祥子》, Piñero Martínez, Blas 译.

4. La verdadera historia de Camello Xiangzi/Lao She；
traducción de Manuel Lacruz y Tan Hui；ilustraciones de
Xin Yuan；introducción de Sergio Cuesta. Las Rozas,
Madrid Funambulista, 2014. 367 p. il. 18cm. ISBN：
8494302633, 8494302639.（Literadura）
《骆驼祥子》, Lacruz, Manuel 和 Tan, Hui 合译；Xin,
Yuan 插图.

5. Historia de mi vida/Lao She；traducción de Javier
Barrado. Madrid Amaranto, 2005. 132 p. 21cm. ISBN：
8493145793, 8493145798
《我这一辈子》, Javier Barrado 译.

蒋光慈（1901—1931）

1. El joven de la vida errante/Jiang Guangci；traducción,
prólogo y notas de Blas Piñero Martínez. Paracuellos del
Jarama, Madrid Hermida, 2014. 143 p. 22cm. ISBN：
8494176715；8494176714.（El jardín de Epicuro；
Ficcion；14）
《少年漂泊者》, 蒋光慈（1901—1931）；Piñero Martínez,
Blas 译.

沈从文（1902—1988）

1. Calma/Shen Congwen；traducción, prólogo y notas de
Maialen Marín Lacarta. Barcelona：Alpha Decay, 2010.
54 p.；15cm. ISBN：8492837083, 849283708X.（Alpha
mini；10）
《静》

21. La ciudad fronteriza/Shen Congwen；estudio preliminar
"Shen Congwen en la literatura contemporánea China",
Bonnie S. McDougall；traducido del chino por Maialen
Marín Lacarta. Barcelona Bellaterra, 2013. 201 p.
22cm. ISBN：8472906310, 8472906310
《边城》, Marín Lacarta, Maialen 译.

巴金（1904—2005）

1. Noche helada/Ba Jin；［versión española de María Teresa
Guzmán］. Beijing：Ediciones en Lenguas Extranjeras,
1982. 271 p. 21cm.
《寒夜》

2. La familia/Ba Jin；traducción del chino de María Teresa
Guzmán. Barcelona Bruguera, 1982. 383 p. 19cm.
ISBN：8402083331, 8402083333.（Narradores de Hoy；
61）

《家》,Guzmán, María Teresa 译.

(1) La Familia/Ba Jin; versión española de María Teresa Guzmán. Beijing［China］：Ediciones en Lenguas extranjeras, 1988. 333 p.；21cm. ISBN：7119005812, 7119005812. (Literatura Moderna de China)

3. La familia Kao/Ba Jin; novela traducida del chino por Taciana Fisac. Madrid：Ediciones S. M., 1985. 215 pages；21cm. ISBN：8434815338；8434815339. (Gran angular；；39.；Literatura juvenil)

《家》(压缩版),巴金；Guzmán, María Teresa 译.

(1) 2a. ed. Madrid SM, 1985. 215 p. 21cm. ISBN：8434815338；8434815339. (Gran angular；39)

(2)［3a. ed.］. Madrid SM, 1989. 215 p. 21cm. ISBN：8434815338；8434815339. (Gran angular；39)

丁玲(1904—1986)

1. El diario de la señorita Sofía; En el hospital/Ding Ling; estudio preliminar, "Feminismo, revolución y literatura en Ding Ling", Tani E. Barlow; traducido del chino por Tyra Díez. Barcelona Bellaterra, 2014. 121 p. 22cm. ISBN：8472906792, 8472906795

《莎菲女士的日记；在医院中》,Barlow, Tani E. 编；Díez, Tyra 译.

赵树理(1906—1970)

1. Cambios en la aldea de Li：novela. Pekin：Ediciones en Lenguas Extranjeras, 1961. 261 pages

《李家庄的变迁》

(1) 3a ed. Beijing：Ediciones en Lenguas Extranjeras, 1979. 232 pages；19cm.

钱钟书(1910—1998)

1. La fortaleza asediada/Qian Zhongshu; traducción del chino de Taciana Fisac. Barcelona：Anagrama, 1992. 440 p.；22cm. ISBN：8433911775，8433911773. (Panorama de narrativas；257)

《围城》,Fisac Badell, Taciana 翻译.

(1) Barcelona Anagrama, 2009. 545 p. 22cm. ISBN：8433975836, 8433975838. (Otra vuelta de tuerca；3)

高云览(1910—1956)

1. Anales de una ciudad de provincia：version Espanola de Aurora Fernandez. Pekin：Ed. en Lenguas Extranjeras, 1964.：77 pages：illustrations, portrait

《小城春秋》,Fernández, Aurora 译.

(1) Anales de una ciudad de provincia/Gao Yunlan; tr. Aurora Fernández. 2a ed. Beijing：Ediciones en Lenguas Extranjeras, 1980. vii, 388 p.：il.；21cm.

杨沫(1914—1995)

1. El canto de la juventud/Yang Mo. Pekin：Ediciones en Lenguas Extranjeras, 1980. 641 p.：ill.；22cm.

《青春之歌》

袁静(1914—1999)

1. Relatos de la gran marcha. Pekin Ediciones en Lenguas Extranjeras, 1960. 154 p. il.，mapas, la'ms., fot. byn 19cm.

《长征的故事》,袁静,孔厥(1914—1966)著.

(1) 2a. ed. Pekin：Ediciones en Lenguas Extranjeras, 1962. 154 p.，［6］h. dela'ms (algunas pleg.)：il., mapa；19cm.

2. Hijas e hijos. Beijing：Ediciones en Lenguas EXtranjeras, 1982. 368 pages

《新儿女英雄传》,袁静,孔厥(1914—1966)著.

梁斌(1914—1996)

1. Estirpe insurgente/Liang Bin. Pekin：Ediciones en Lenguas Extranjeras, 1980. 598 p.：ill. ；；；22cm.

《红旗谱》

柳青(1916—1978)

1. Hacia una nueva vida/Liu Ching. Beijing：Ediciones en Lenguas Extranjeras, 1978. 586 p.：ill.；22cm.

《创业者》,Ah, Lao 译.

张爱玲(1920—1995)

1. La canción del arroz/Eileen Chang; traducción de Alfredo J. Weiss. Buenos Aires：Goyanarte, 1955. 155 p.；20cm.

《秧歌》,Weiss, Alfredo 译.

2. Amor en la ciudad en ruinas/Zhang Ailing; traducción de Liljana Arsovska, Chen Zhi. México：El Colegio de México, 2007. 72 p.；21cm. ISBN：9681212827 (rústica), 9681212827 (rústica).

《倾城之恋》,Arsovska, Liljana 和 Chen Zhi 合译.

3. Un amor que destruye ciudades; seguida de Bloqueados/Eileen Chang; traducción del chino de Anne-Hélène Suárez y Qu Xianghong. Barcelona Libros del Asteroide, 2016. 113 p. 20cm. ISBN：8416213702, 8416213704

《倾城之恋·封锁》,Suárez Girard, Anne-Hélène (1960—)和 Qu, Xianghong 合译.

高玉宝(1927—)

1. 高玉宝/高玉宝著. 北京：外文出版社,1980

2. Mi Infancia/Gao Yubao. Beijing：Ediciones En Lenguas Extranjeras, 1996. 279 pages：illustrations；21×13cm.

《我的童年》

黎汝清(1928—)

1. Milicianas isleñas/Li Ruqing；［ilustraciones de Cai Yong］. Pekín：Ediciones en Lenguas Extranjeras，1979. 349 pages，［7］leaves of plates：color illustrations；21cm.

《海岛女民兵》

李心田(1929—)

1. Brillante estrella roja. Pekin：Ediciones en Lenguas Extranjeras, 1978. 192 p.：ilus；18cm.

《闪闪的红星》

王蒙(1934—)

1. Cuentos/Wang Meng; prefacio de Flora Botton Beja; traducciones de Duan Ruochuan［and others］. México,

D. F.：El Colegio de México，Centro de Estudios de Asia y África，1985. 182 pages；21cm. ISBN：968120316X，9681203160

Contents：Los ojos de la noche—El pequeño corazón del peluquero—La cola de la cometa—Voces de primavera—Un sinfín de visitantes—La mariposa—El lago profundo—Un joven recién llegado al departamento de organización.

王蒙短篇小说选. Botton Beja，Flora 编；Ruochuan，Duan 译.

(1) 2a ed. aumentada. México D. F.：El Colegio de México，Centro de Estudios de Asia y Africa；Instituto Nacional de Bellas Artes y Literatura，2002. 210 p.；21cm. ISBN：9681210581，9681210588

Contents：Los ojos de la noche—El pequeño corazón del peluquero—La cola de la cometa—Voces de primavera—Un sinfín de visitantes—La mariposa—El lago profundo—Un joven recién llegado al departamento de organización—La historia de Ami—La dura sopa de arroz.

张贤亮（1936—2014）

1. La Mitad del hombre es la mujer/Zhang Xian Liang. Hong Kong［China］：Ming Chuang，1989. 340 p.；17cm.

《男人的一半是女人》

2. La mitad del hombre es la mujer/Zhang Xianliang；traducción del chino，Iñaki Preciado Idoeta y Emilia Hu. Madrid：Ediciones Siruela，1992. 338 p.；22cm. ISBN：847844095X，8478440955. (Libros del tiempo；38)

《男人的一半是女人》，Preciado Idoeta，Iñaki 和 Hu，Emilia 合译.

张洁（1937—）

1. Galera/Zhang Jie；traducción del chino，Isabel Alonso. Tafalla Txalaparta，1995. 146 p. 22cm. ISBN：8481369438，8481369434. (Gebara；n. 28)

《方舟》，Alonso，Isabel(1962—)译.

2. Esmeralda/Zhang Jie；traducción，introducción y notas de Lien-tan Pan，Indira Añorve Zapata. México，D. F.：El Colegio de México，Centro de Estudios de Asia y África，2007. 103 p.；21cm. ISBN：9681213106，9681213107

《祖母绿》，Pan，Lien-tan 和 Añorve Zapata，Indira 合译.

3. Faltan palabras/Zhang Jie；traducción de Jorge Rizzo；lectura comparada de Fan Ye y Javier González Roldán. ［Barcelona］Miscelánea，2009. 329 p. 21cm. ISBN：8493722838，8493722839

《无字》，Rizzo，Jorge 译.

(1) Barcelona：Roca Editorial de Libros，2010. 336 p.；19cm. ISBN：8492833054，849283305X. (Rocabolsillo ficción)

古华（1942—）

1. Hibisco/Gu Hua；［traducción，Ramón Alonso Pèrez］.

Barcelona：Luis de Caralt，1989. 268 p.；20cm. ISBN：8421726056；8421726051. (Gigante)

《芙蓉镇》

2. Mujeres virtuosas del Arenal de las Ocas Amorosas/Gu Hua；Chen Zhiyuan，traducción；Romer Alejandro Cornejo，revisión de la traducción；Rosina Conde，versión literaria en español. México，D. F.：Colegio de México，Centro de Estudios de Asia y Africa，2000. 193 pages；21cm. ISBN：9681209400，9681209407

《贞女》，陈致远译；Cornejo，Bustamante Romer 译校.

冯骥才（1942—）

1. Que broten cien flores/Feng Ji Cai；［traducción，Juan Ignacio Preciado Idoeta y Emilia Hu］. León：Everest，1997. 100 pages；21cm. ISBN：8424159640，8424159641. (Punto de encuentro)

《感谢生活》，Preciado Idoeta，Iñaki 和 Hu，Emilia 合译.

(1) 2a. ed. León Everest，2009. 100 p. 21cm. ISBN：8424159641，8424159640. (Punto de encuentro)

姜戎（1946—）

1. Tótem lobo/Jiang Rong；［traducción，Miguel Antón］. ［Madrid］Alfaguara，2008. 640 p. 24cm. ISBN：8420473765，8420473766

《狼图腾》，Antón，Miguel 译.

刘庆邦（1951—）

1. El árbol mágico/Liu Qingbang；traductoras：Tatiana Svákhina，Liu Liu. China China Intercontinental Press，2013. 311 páginas 23cm. ISBN：7508523828，7508523822. (Joyas de literatura contemporánea china)

《黄花绣》，Svákhina，Tatiana 和刘柳合译. 五洲传播出版社（"中国当代文学精选"丛书）

周大新（1952—）

1. Joyas de plata/Zhou Daxin；traducida por Teresa I. Tejeda Martin；corregida por Liu Liu y Miguel Espigado. Beijing：China Intercontinental Press，2015. 147 pages；23cm. ISBN：7508528816，7508528816. (Joyas de literatura contemporanca China＝中国当代文学精选)

《银饰》，Tejeda Martín，Teresa I. 译.

2. Réquiem/Zhou Daxin；traducción de Mōnica Ching Hernández. ［Beijing］：China Intercontinental Press，2015. 447 p.；23cm. ISBN：7508528809，7508528808. (Joyas de literatura contemporánea china)

《安魂》，Ching Hernández，Mōnica 译.

张欣欣（1953—）

1. El Hombre de Pekín/Zhang Xinxin y Sang Ye. Sabadell：Ausa，1989. 284 p.；21cm. ISBN：8486329396，8486329396. (Narrativa oriental contemporánea)

Zhang，Xinxin. Sang，Ye.

《北京人》，张欣欣，桑晔.

马建（1953—）

1. Pekín en coma/Ma Jian；traducción de Jordi Fibla. Barcelona：Mondadori，2008. 658 pages；24cm. ISBN：

8439721352，8439721358.（Literatura Mondadori；376）

《肉土》

2. El camino oscuro/Ma Jian；traducción de Cruz Rodríguez Juiz. Barcelona Penguin Random House，2014. 412 p. 24cm. ISBN：8439728078，8439728077.（Literatura Random House）

《九条叉路》，Rodríguez Juiz，Cruz 译.

何家弘(1953—)

1. Crimen de sangre/He Jiahong；［traducción，Orlando Zuloeta Rodríguez］. Madrid：Editorial Popular，2012. 522 pages：map；22cm. ISBN：8478845026，847884502X.（Letra grande. Serie novela；6；Novela negra）

《豪门血案》，Zuloeta Rodríguez，Orlando 译.

韩少功(1953—)

1. Diccionario de Maqiao/Han Shaogong；traducción de Claudio Molinari. Madrid Kailas，2006. 444 p. 22cm. ISBN：8489624054，8489624054.（Ficción）

《马桥词典》，Molinari，Claudio 译.

2. Pa pa pa/Han Shaogong；traducción de Yunqing Yao. Madrid Kailas，2008. 100 p. 21cm. ISBN：8489624535，8489624534.（ficción）

《爸爸爸》，姚云青译.

3. La caravana del hijo tercero/Han Shaogong；traducción de：Lili Sun y Mōnica Ching. San Francisco：China Books，2014. 203 páginas；17cm. ISBN：0835102476，0835102475，0835102438，0835102432.（Nuevas voces de la literatura China）

《赶马的老三》，Lili Sun，Mōnica Ching，San Francisco 合译.

徐小斌(1953—)

1. La niña de papel/Xu Xiaobin；traducción directa del chino de Mari Carmen Espín García. Barcelona：Mosaico，2010. 373 p.；24cm. ISBN：8492682409，849268240X

《羽蛇》，Mari Carmen Espín García. 从中文版直译.

王安忆(1954—)

1. Baotown/Wang Anyi；traducido del inglés por Herminia Dauer. Barcelona Juventud，1996. ISBN：8426129757，8426129758.（Narrativa Breve）

《小鲍庄》，Herminia Dauer 从英文版转译.

2. La canción de la pena eterna/Wang Anyi；traducción de Carlos Ossés. Madrid Kailas，2010. 676 p. ISBN：8489624689，8489624682.（Kailas ficción）

《长恨歌》，Ossés，Carlos 译.

3. Amor en una colina desnuda/Wang Anyi；［traducción，Miguel Sautié］. Madrid Editorial Popular，2012. 241 p. 22cm. ISBN：8478845330，847884533X.（Letra grande. Novela；12）

《荒山之恋》，Sautié，Miguel 译.

(1) Amor en una colina desnuda/novela de Wang Anyi. Beijing Shi；Wu zhou chuan bo chu ban she，2014.

241 pages；23cm. ISBN：7508527499，7508527496.（Joyas de literatura contemporánea China＝"中国当代文学精选"丛书）

4. Amor en un valle encantado/Wang Anyi；［traducción，Miguel Sautié］. Madrid Editorial Popular，2012. 122 p. 22cm. ISBN：8478845019，8478845011.（Letra grande. Novela；8）

《锦绣谷之恋》，Sautié，Miguel 译.

(1)México：Popular，2014.

5. Amor en un pequeño pueblo：［novela］/Wang Anyi；［traducción，Miguel Sautié］. Madrid：Popular Editorial，2012. 145 pages；22cm. ISBN：8478845321，8478845323.（Letra grande. Novela；11）

《小城之恋》，Sautié，Miguel 译.

(1)Beijing Shi：Wu zhou chuan bo chu ban she，2014. 147 pages；23cm. ISBN：7508526188，750852618X.（Joyas de literatura contemporánea China＝"中国当代文学精选"丛书）

莫言(1955—)

1. Sorgo rojo/Mo Yan；tr. de Ana Poljak. Barcelona：Muchnik，1992. 502 p.；22cm. ISBN：8476691734，8476691731

《红高粱家族》，Poljak，Ana 译.

(1)México D. F.（México）El Aleph Editores Oceano，1992. 515 páginas. ISBN：6074009217.（Hotel de las Letras；Modernos y clásicos de El Aleph）

(2)Barcelona：Aleph Editores，2002. 622 p.；18cm. ISBN：8476695934，8476695937. Ediciones de bolsillo/Aleph；90）

(3)2a. ed. Barcelona El Aleph，2009. 515 p. 22cm. ISBN：8476698556，8476698550.（Modernos y clásicos de El Aleph；298）

(4)Mexico D. F.：El Aleph；Oceano，2012. 515 pages；22cm. ISBN：6074009217，607400921X.（Modernos y clásicos de El Aleph）

(5)3a ed. Barcelona：El Aleph，2012. 515 p.；22cm. ISBN：8476698556，8476698550.（Modernos y clásicos de El Aleph；298）

2. El clan del sorgo rojo：（Hong gaoliang jiazu）/Mo Yan；traducción del chino de Blas Piñero Martínez. Madrid：Kailas，2016. 643 p.；23cm. ISBN：8416523481，8416523487. 9Kailas Ficción；22）

《红高粱家族》，Piñero Martínez，Blas 译.

3. Shifu，harías cualquier cosa por divertirte/Mo Yan；traducción de Cora Tiedra. Madrid，España Kailas Editorial，2001. 210 p. 24cm. ISBN：8489624818，848962481X.（Kailas ficción；97）

《师傅越来越幽默》，Tiedra，Cora 译.

(1)Madrid：Kailas，2011. 210 p. ISBN：8489624818，848962481X

(2)2a ed. Madrid：Kailas，2012. 210 p.；24cm. ISBN：

8489624818，848962481X.（Kailas ficción；97）

（3）Madrid：Kailas，2013. 210 p. 19cm. ISBN：8494139147，8494139142. 9Kailas bolsillo）

（4）北京：五洲传播出版社，2015. 210 p.；23cm. ISBN：7508530314，7508530314.（"中国当代文学精选"丛书/孙新堂主编）

4. Grandes pechos, amplias caderas/Mo Yan；［traducción，Mariano Peyrou］. Madrid Kailas，2007. 836 p. 21cm. ISBN：8489624269，8489624267.（Ficción；43）

《丰乳肥臀》，Peyrou，Mariano(1971—)译.

（1）3a ed. 2012. 836 pages；21cm. ISBN：8489624269，8489624267.（Kailas ficción；43）

（2）Madrid：Kailas，2013. 836 p. 19cm. ISBN：8494139109，849413910X.（Kailas bolsillo）

5. Las baladas del ajo/Mo Yan；traducción de Carlos Ossés. Madrid：Kailas，2008. 489 pages；21cm. ISBN：8489624429，8489624429.（Kailas ficción；58）

《天堂蒜苔之歌》，Ossés，Carlos 译.

（1）2a ed. Madrid：Kailas，2012. 489 pages；21cm. ISBN：8489624429，8489624429.（Kailas ficción；58）

（2）Madrid：Kailas，2013. 489 p. 19cm. ISBN：8494139116，8494139118.（Kailas bolsillo）

6. La vida y la muerte me estân desgastando/Mo yan；traducción de Carlos Ossés. Madrid Kailas，2009. 757 p. 21cm. ISBN：8489624610，8489624615.（Kailas ficción）

《生死疲劳》，Ossés，Carlos 译.

（1）2a ed. Madrid：Kailas，2012. 757 pages；21cm. ISBN：8489624615，8489624610.（Kailas ficción；74）

（2）Madrid Kailas，2013. 757 p. 19cm. ISBN：8494139123，8494139126.（Kailas bolsillo）

7. La Vida y la muerte me estân desgastando/Mo Yan；traducción de Carlos Ossés. Madrid：Kailas，2009. 757 p.；21cm. ISBN：8489624610，8489624615.（Ficción）

《生死疲劳》，Ossés，Carlos 译.

8. La república del vino/Mo Yan；traducción de Cora Tiedra. Madrid：Kailas，2010. 451 p.；24cm. ISBN：8489624733，8489624739

《酒国》，Tiedra，Cora 译.

（1）2a ed. Madrid：Kailas，2012. 451 pages；24cm. ISBN：8489624733，8489624739.（Kailas ficción；91）

（2）Madrid（España）Edirorial Kailas，2013. 451 p. ISBN：8494139130，8494139134.（Colección Kailas Bolsillo）

9. Rana/by Mo Yan；traducido del chino por Yifan Li；editado por Cora Tiedra. Madrid：Kailas，2011. 400 pages；24cm. ISBN：8489624849，8489624844

《蛙》，李一帆和 Tiedra，Cora 合译.

（1）2a ed. Madrid：Kailas，2012. 400 pages；24cm.

ISBN：8489624849，8489624844.（Kailas ficción；100）

（2）Madrid：Kailas，2013. 400 p. 19cm. ISBN：8494139154，8494139150.（Kailas bolsillo）

10. Cambios/Mo Yan；traducción del chino por Anne-Hélène Suárez Girard. Barcelona Seix Barral，2012. 127 p. 21cm. ISBN：8432214790，8432214795.（Biblioteca Formentor）

《变》，Suárez Girard，Anne-Hélène(1960—)译.

（1）Barcelona：Seix Barral，2012. 127 p.；21cm. ISB：8432214844，8432214841.（Biblioteca Formentor）

（2）Bogotá（Colombia）Editorial Planeta Colombiana，2012. 127 páginas；21cm. ISBN：9584233356，9584233351.（Colección Seix Barral. ；Formentor）

（3）México：Barcelona：Seix Barral，2013. 127 pages；21cm. ISBN：6070715563，607071556X.（Biblioteca Formentor）

（4）Barcelona；Santiago, Chile：Seix Barral；Planeta Chilena，2013. 127 p.；21cm. ISBN：9562476775，9562476774

（5）Barcelona Seix Barral，2014. 127 p. 19cm. ISBN：8432222993,8432222992.（Austral；843；Narrativa）

11. Boom! /Mo Yan；traducido del chino por Yifan Li；editado por Cora Tiedra. Madrid：Kailas，2013. 509 p. 24cm. ISBN：8489624993，8489624992

《四十一炮》，李一帆(1966—)译；Tiedra，Cora 编.

（1）Madrid：Kailas，2014. 509 p. 19cm. ISBN：8416023301，8416023301.（Kailas bolsillo）

12. El suplicio del aroma de sándalo/Mo Yan；traducción del chino de Blas Piñero Martínez. Madrid：Kailas，2014. 796 p. 24cm. ISBN：8416023011，8416023018

《檀香刑》，Piñero Martínez，Blas 译.

（1）Madrid：Kailas，2014. 796 p. 19cm. ISBN：8416023318，841602331X.（Kailas bolsillo）

13. Trece pasos/Mo Yan；traducido del chino por Juan José Ciruela Alférez. Madrid Kailas，2015. 504 p. 24cm. ISBN：8416023264，8416023263

《十三步》，Ciruela Alférez，Juan José 译.

14. El manglar＝Hong Shulim/Mo Yan. Madrid：Kailas，2016. 528 p.；23cm. ISBN：8416023950，8416023956

《红树林》，Piñero Martínez，Blas 译.

15. El mapa del tesoro escondido/Mo Yan；traducción del chino de Blas Piñero Martínez. Madrid：Kailás，2017. 111 p.；23cm. ISBN：8416523825，8416523827.（Kailas Ficción；29）

《藏宝图》，Piñero Martínez，Blas 译.

16. El rábano transparente/Mo Yan；traducción del chino de Blas Piñero Martínez. Madrid：Kailas，2017. 128 p. ISBN：8416523931，8416523932

《透明的红萝卜》，Piñero Martínez，Blas 译.

17. El clan de los herbívorossimboliza/Mo Yan；traducción

del chino de Blas Piñero Martínez. Madrid：Kailas，2018. 624 p. ISBN：8417248116

《食草家族》，Piñero Martínez，Blas 译.

池莉(1957—)

1. Triste vida/Chi Li；traducción directa del chino mandarín de Mari Carme Espín Garcia. Barcelona：Belacqua，2007. 106 p.；23cm. ISBN：8496694194，8496694194.（La otra orilla/Belacqva；27）

《烦恼人生》，由 Espín Garcia，Mari Carme 从中文版直译.

铁凝(1957—)

1. La blusa roja sin botones/Tie Ning. Madrid：SM，1989. 157 p. 21cm. ISBN：8434827182，8434827189

《没有纽扣的红衬衫》

(1)2a ed. Madrid：Ediciones SM，1990. 157 p.；21cm. ISBN：8434827182，8434827189

王朔(1958—)

1. Haz el favor de no llamarme humano/Wang Shuo；traducción de Gabriel García-Noblejas.［Madrid］：Lengua de Trapo Ediciones，2002. 315 p.；21cm. ISBN：848961881X，8489618817.（Otras lenguas；14）

《千万别把我当人》，García-Noblejas，Gabriel 译.

(1)Madrid Punto de Lectura，2008.；74 p. 19cm. ISBN：8466322096，8466322094.（Punto de lectura；287/1）

阎连科(1958—)

1. Servir al pueblo/Yan Lianke；traducción：Ana Herrera Ferrer. Madrid：Maeva，2008. 156 p.；24cm. ISBN：8496748644，8496748642

《为人民服务》，Herrera，Ana 译.

2. El ensueño de la aldea Ding/Yan Lianke；traducción del chino y notas de Belén Cuadra Mora. Madrid Automática，2013. 368 p. 21cm. ISBN：8415509189，8415509189

《丁庄梦》，Cuadra Mora，Belén 译.

3. Los besos de Lenin/Yan Lianke；traducción del chino y notas de Belén Cuadra Mora. Madrid：Automática，2015. 601 p.；21cm. ISBN：8415509301，8415509308

《受活》，Cuadra Mora，Belén 译.

4. Los cuatro libros/Yan Lianke；edición，prólogo，traducción y notas de Taciana Fisac. Barcelona：Galaxia Gutemberg，2016. 368 p.；21cm. ISBN：8416734160，841673416X.（Narrativa；155）

《四书》，Fisac Badell，Taciana 译.

刘震云(1958—)

1. Teléfono móvil/Liu Zhenyun；novela traducida por Zhao Deming y corregida por Edith Cuéllar Rodríguez. Beijing：Wu zhou chuan bo chu ban she，2013. 340 pages；23cm. ISBN：7508523866，7508523865.（Joyas de literatura contemporánea china）

《手机》，赵德明(1939—)译；Cuéllar Rodríguez，Edith 译校.

2. 温故一九四二/刘震云［著］；Javier Martin Rios 西文翻译.北京：五洲传播出版社，2013. 113 p.：maps；23cm.

ISBN：7508525136，7508525132.（"中国当代文学精选"丛书）

西文题名：De regreso a 1942

3. Yo no soy una mujerzuela /Liu Zhenyum；traductora：Liljana Arsovska；versión literaria en español de Rosina Conde.［Beijing］：China Intercontinental Press，2015. 320 p.；23cm. ISBN：7508530345，7508530349.（Joyas de literatura contemporánea china）

《我不是潘金莲》，Arsovska，Liljana 和 Conde，Rosina 合译.

廖亦武(1958—)

1. El paseante de cadáveres，retratos de la China profunda/Liao Yiwu；tradución de Leonor Sola Comino. Barcelona Sexto Piso，2012. 366 p. 23cm. ISBN：8415601135，8415601131

《中国底层访谈录》

阿来(1959—)

1. Las amapolas del emperador/Alai；traducción，María Eugenia Ciocchini. Madrid：Maeva Ediciones，2003. 471 pages；24cm. ISBN：8495354993，8495354990

《尘埃落定》，Ciocchini，María Eugenia 译.

余华(1960—)

1. Brothers/Yu Hua；traducción del inglés por Vicente Villacampa. Barcelona：Seix Barral，2009. 870 p. ISBN：8432228414，8432228419.（Biblioteca Formentor）

《兄弟》，Villacampa，Vicente 从英文版转译.

(1)México：Seix Barral：Grupo Editorial Planeta，2009. 870 p.；23cm. ISBN：6070701382，6070701380.（Biblioteca Formentor）

2. Vivir! /Yu Hua；traducido del chino por Anne-Hélène Suárez Girard. Barcelona：Seix Barral，2010. 231 p. ISBN：8432228735，8432228737.（Biblioteca Formentor）

《活着》，Suárez Girard，Anne-Hélène 译.

(1)Barcelona：Seix Barral，2012. 231 p. 19cm. ISBN：8432213878，843221387X.（Austral；774）

3. Crónicas de un vendedor de sangre/Yu Hua；traducción del chino por Anne-Hélène Suárez Girard. Barcelona：Seix Barral，2014. 298 p. 23cm. ISBN：8432210136，8432210137.（Biblioteca Formentor）

《许三观卖血记》，Suárez Girard，Anne-Hélène 从中文版直译.

4. Gritos en la llovizna/Ya Hua；traducción del chino por Anne-Hélène Suárez Girard con la colaboración de Qu Xianghong y Zhang Peijun. Barcelona：Seix Barral，2016. 317 p.；23cm. ISBN：8432229473，8432229474.（Biblioteca Formentor）

《在细雨中的呼喊》，Suárez Girard，Anne-Hélène 等译.

虹影(1962—)

1. El verano de la traición/Hong Ying；traducción del chino，Lola Díez Pastor. Barcelona：Plaza & Janés，1998. 193 pages；22cm. ISBN：8401011213；8401011214.（Ave

fénix. Serie mayor)

《背叛之夏》(又名《裸舞代》)，Lola Díez Pastor 译.

2. K, el arte del amor/Hong Ying; traducción de Ana Herrera Ferrer. Barcelona El Aleph, 2004. 237 p. 22cm. ISBN：8476696736, 8476696736.（Modernos y clásicos de El Aleph; 207)

《K》(《英国情人》)，Herrera Ferrery, Ana 译.

(1)2a ed. Barcelona：Grupo editorial 62：El Aleph, 2005. 237 p. ISBN：8476696736, 8476696736.（Modernos y clásicos de El Aleph)

(2)Barcelona：El Aleph Editores, 2006. 237 p. ISBN：8496333892, 8496333895.（Quinteto; 214)

3. Hija del río/Hong Ying; traducido del inglés por Ana Herrera Ferrer. Barcelona：El Aleph Editores, 2005. 315 pages；22cm. ISBN：8476697252, 8476697252.（Personalia de El Aleph; 51)

Notes：Translated from the English：Daughter of the river, which was originally translated from the Chinese：Ji e di nü er.

《饥饿的女儿》，Herrera Ferrer, Ana 从英文版转译.

苏童(1963—)

1. Mi vida como emperador/Su Tong; traducción de Domingo Almendros. Barcelona：JP Libros, 2009. 285 p.；23cm. ISBN：8493747602, 8493747602.（Narrativa)

《我的帝王生涯》，Almendros, Domingo 译.

刘慈欣(1963—)

1. El problema de los tres cuerpos/Cixin Liu; traducción del chino, Javier Altayó; galeradas reviadas por Antonio Torrubia. Barcelona：Ediciones B, 2016. 408 pages；23cm. ISBN：8466659730, 8466659734.（Trilogía de los Tres Cuerpos; 1)

《三体》，Altayó, Javier 译.

毕飞宇(1964—)

1. Qingyi, ópera de la luna/de Bi Feiyu; traducción del chino, Paula Ehrenhaus Faimberg. Barcelona Verdecielo, 2007. 123 p. 21cm. ISBN：8493427160, 8493427160.（Narrativa)

《青衣》，Ehrenhaus Faimberg, Paula 译.

2. La ópera de la luna/Bi Feiyu; traducción al español de Demetrio Ibarra Hernández.［Beijing］：China Intercontinental Press, 2015. 108 p.；21cm. ISBN：7508529516, 7508529510.（Joyas de Literatura Contemporánea China)

《青衣》，Ibarra Hernández, Demetrio 译.

3. Las Feroces aprendices Wang/de Bi Feiyu; traducción：Joan Artés Morata. Barcelona：Verdecielo, 2007. 353 p.；21cm. ISBN：8493427153, 8493427152.（Narrativa)

Contents：Yumi; Yuxiu; Yuyang

《地球上的王家庄》，Artés Morata, Joan 译.

麦家(1964—)

1. En la oscuridad/novela de Mai Jia; traducida por Liu Jian y corregida por Edith Cuéllar Rodríguez. Beijing：China Intercontinental Press, 2013. 453 pages；23cm. ISBN：7508525143, 7508525140

《暗算》，刘建(1964—)和 Cuéllar, Edith 合译.

(1) Barcelona：Destino, 2016. 525 p.；23cm. ISBN：8423351022, 8423351025.（Áncora y delfín; 1370)

2. El don/Mai Jia; traducción de Claudia Conde. Barcelona：Destino, 2014. 477 p.；23cm. ISBN：8423348060, 8423348067.（Áncora y delfín; 1292)

《解密》，Conde, Claudia 译.

(1)Barcelona：Círculo de Lectores, 2014. 346 p. 22cm. ISBN：8467260410, 8467260416

(2)［Barcelona］：Booket, 2016. 477 p. 19cm. ISBN：8423349777, 8423349772.（Novela; 2648)

迟子建(1964—)

1. A la ciudad! y otros cuentos rurales chinos/Chi Zijian［et al.；traducción al español, Enrique Rodríguez B.］Madrid Cooperación Editorial, 2013. 325 p. 21cm. ISBN：8495920621, 849592062X.（Miradas; 7)

乡村主题小说集. Rodríguez B., Enrique 译.

2. A la orilla derecha del Río Argún/Chi Zijian; traductores：Xu Yingfeng, Fernando Esteban Serna. China China Intercontinental Press, 2014. 325 páginas 23cm. ISBN：7508523903；7508523903.（Joyas de literatura contemporánea china)

Contents：Primera parte. La madrugada—Segunda parte. Al mediodía—U'ltima parte. El crepúsculo—Epílogo. La media luna

《额尔古纳河右岸》，Xu, Yingfeng(1982—)和 Esteban Serna, Fernando(1978—)合译.

3. La espada Rayo de Luna y otros cuentos/Chi Zijian, Fan Xiaoqing, Hong Ke...［et al］. Madrid Editorial Popular, 2015. 218 p. 22cm. ISBN：8478846344, 8478846344.（Letra grande; 26)

棉棉(1970—)

1. Caramelos/Mian Mian; traducción de Olga Usoz Chaparro. Madrid：La Factoria de Ideas, 2011. 287 pages；23cm. ISBN：8498006889, 8498006880

《糖》，Usoz Chaparro, Olga 译.

(1) Arganda del Rey La Factoría de Ideas Debolsillo, 2013. 287 p. 19cm. ISBN：8490181454, 8490181454.（Bestseller; 24/1)

卫慧(1973—)

1. Shanghai baby/Wei Hui; traducción de Romer Cornejo y Liljana Arsovska］. Barcelona, Spain：Planeta, 2002. 272 pages；25cm. ISBN：8408042823, 8408042822

《上海宝贝》，Cornejo, Romer Alejandro 和 Arsovska, Liljana 合译.

(1)7a ed. Buenos Aires：Emecé Editores, 2002. 270 pages；23cm. ISBN：9500423618, 9500423618.（Grandes novelistas)

(2) Barcelona：Planeta, 2003. 310 pages；18cm. ISBN：

8408047981，8408047988.（Booket/Planeta. Bestseller internacional；1087）

  （3）12a ed. Buenos Aires：Booket，2007. 294 p.；18cm. ISBN：9871144068，9871144067.（Bestseller）

  （4）Barcelona：Planeta，2008. 310 p.；19cm. ISBN：8408077626，8408077627.（Booket.；Bestseller internacional；1087）

2. Casada con Buda/Wei Hui；traducido del chino por Ainara Munt Ojanguren y Xu Ying. Barcelona：Emecé Editores，2005. 277 pages；23cm. ISBN：8495908735，8495908735

《我的禅》，Ojanguren，Ainara Munt，徐映合译.

慕容雪村（1974— ）

1. Déjame en paz/Murong Xuecun；traducción de Cora Tiedra. Madrid Kailas，2014. 272 p. 24cm. ISBN：8416023059；8416023050.（Ficción/Kailas；116）

Tiedra，Cora 译自英文版.

张悦然（1982— ）

1. Diez amores/autora：Zhang Yueran；traductora：Nuria Pitarque Ledesma. Beijing China Intercontinental Press，2013. 335 páginas 23cm. ISBN：7508523873，7508523873.（Joyas de literatura contemporánea china）

Contents：Prefacio：escrito para los amores que me hicieron olvidarme de comer y dormir—Los que bailan yacen bajo la montaña—El arpa y la diablesa de los huesos blancos—Jinuo y el salto de potro—Sistema binario—Xiaoran—El barco—El encantamiento de la nariz—La habitación donde el día se convierte en noche—El fantasma de Sushui—Quién ha matado el mes de mayo—El amor llega a los montes Cangshan y al lago Erhai.

《十爱》，Pitarque Ledesma，Nuria 译.

春树（1983— ）

1. La muñeca de Pekín/Chun Sue；traducido del chino por Luis Pèrez，Kai-Lin Shan y Verónica Canales. Barcelona：Aleph Editores，2003. 316 p.；22cm. ISBN：8476696264，8476696262.（Modernos y clásicos de El Aleph；194）

《北京娃娃》，Pèrez，Luis，Shan，Kai-Lin 和 Canales，Verónica 合译.

I6 报告文学与回忆录

1. 战斗英雄麦贤得/解放军报记者.北京：外文出版社，1967

2. Canal Bandera Roja. Pekin：Ediciones en Lenguas Extranjeras，1975. 71 pages

《红旗渠》，林民.

3. Cambios trascendentales en el río Jaije/Re Jin. Pekín：Ediciones en Lenguas Extranjeras，1975. 122 pages，［34］pages of plates（1 folded）：illustrations，color map，portraits；19cm.

《海河巨变》，何津.

4. 大庆印象记/江山浩.北京：外文出版社，1978

5. Mis memorias sobre la Gran Marcha/Zheng Fangwu. Pekin：Ediciones en Lenguas Extranjeras，1979. 259 pages，［3］pages of plates：illustrations；19cm.

《长征回忆录》，成仿吾.

I7 散文

1. Seis estampas de una vida a la deriva/Shen Fu；traducción de Ricard Vela. Barcelona Plataforma，2012. 251 p. mapas 22cm. ISBN：8415577485；8415577486.（Chindia）

《浮生六记》，沈复（1763 年—1832 年）.

2. Experiencia y otros ensayos/Lu Sin；traducción de Luciana Daelli. Buenos Aires：Centro Editor de América Latina，1980. 117 pages；18cm.（La Nueva biblioteca）

鲁迅散文.

3. Viaje a Xibanya：escritores chinos cuentan España/Yan Lianke，Lao Ma，Zhou Jianung，Zhang Yueran y Chen Zhongyi；traducción de Taciana Fisac y Xu Lei；edición coordinada por Taciana Fisac y Chen Zhongyi. Primera edición en España. Tres Cantos，Madrid：Siglo XXI，2010. 221 pages；23cm. ISBN：8432314643，8432314641

Fisac Badell，Taciana，；editor，；translator.

《西行西行：中国作家西班牙纪行》，阎连科、陈众议、劳马、周嘉宁、张悦然等著；Taciana Fisac 和徐蕾合译.

4. 长江旅行记/丘学武著.北京：外文出版社，1980.136 页

5. Viaje por el norte del Tibet/Ma Lihua. Beijing：Ediciones en Lenguas Extranjeras，1993. 375 pages，2 leaves of plates：color illustrations；18cm. ISBN：7119014978，7119014975

《女诗人在藏北无人区》，马丽华著.

6. China en diez palabras/Yu Hua；traducido del chino por Nuria Pitarque Ledesma. Barcelona：Alba，2013. 279 p.；22cm. ISBN：8484288312，8484288315.（Trayectos. Supervivencias；132）

《十个词汇中的中国》，余华（1960— ）著；Pitarque Ledesma Nuria 译.

7. El templo de la tierra y yo/Shi Tiesheng；traduccioìn de chino de Javier Martiìon Rios y Sun Xintang；estudio preliminar de Javier Martiìon Rios.［Beijing］：China Intercontinental Press，2015. 118 p.；23cm. ISBN：7508530338，7508530330.（Joyas de literatura contemporaìnea china）

《我与地坛》，史铁生（1951—2010）著；哈维尔（Martiìon Rios，Javier）和孙新堂合译.

I8 民间文学

1. Chung-Kuei：domador de demonios，narración popular china. Madrid：Revista Occidente，1929. 265 pages；18cm.（Biblioteca de la Revista de Occidente. Musas lejanas：mitos，cuentos，leyendas；14）

钟馗：中国民间故事.

2. Cuentistas de la nueva china/recopilada y traducida del chino al francés por J. Kyn Yn Yu；traducción de María de las Mercedes Casado. Buenos Aires：Ediciones Siglo Veinte，1944. 156 pages；21cm.

中国故事. 译自法语版.

3. Antología de cuentistas chinos/Selección y prologo de Lo Ta Kang; [traducción directa del chino Ma Ce Hwang (Marcela de Juan). Buenos Aires: Espasa-Calpe, 1947. 147 p. (Colección Austral; 787)

中国故事集. Lo, Ta Kang 选编; 黄玛赛 (Juan, Marcela de, 1905—1981) 译.

(1) 2a. ed. Buenos Aires: Espasa-Calpe Argentina, 1948. 147 p. (Colección Austral. ; Serie azul; 787)

4. Cuentos chinos de tradición antigua/seleccionados y traducidos por Ma. Ce Hwang (Marcela de Juan). Buenos Aires; Madrid: Espasa-Calpe Argentina S. A., 1948. 148 p. ; 18cm. (Austral; 805)

中国古代故事. 黄玛赛 (Juan, Marcela de, 1905—1981) 译.

5. Cuentos humorísticos orientales/Ma Cé Hwang. Buenos Aires: Espasa-Calpe, 1954. 147 pages; 18cm. (Colección Austral; 1214)

《东方幽默故事》, 黄玛赛 (Juan, Marcela de, 1905—1981) 译.

(1) Buenos Aires: Espasa-Calpe, 1974. 147 p. ; 18cm. (Colección Austral; 1214)

6. El espejo antiguo y otros cuentos chinos. Madrid: Espasa-Calpe Biblioteca Digital de Aranjuez, 1983. 159 p.

《古鉴与其他中国故事》, 黄玛赛 (Juan, Marcela de, 1905—1981) 译.

7. Fábulas antiguas de China. Pekin: Ediciones en Lenguas Extranjeras, 1958. 60 pages; 26cm.

《中国古代寓言选》, 丰子恺插图.

(1) Fabulas antiguas de China. Pekin: Ediciones en Lenguas Extranjeras, 1961. 117 pages: illustrations; 25cm.

(2) 2a ed. Beijing: Ediciones en Lenguas Extranjeras, 1980. 113 p. : illustrations; 21cm.

(3) Beijing Ediciones en Lenguas Extranjeras, 1989. 113 p. il. 21cm. ISBN: 711901076X 7119010762

(4) Alcobendas (Madrid) Alba, 1998. V, 113 p. il. 18cm. ISBN: 8483360861, 8483360866. (Colección Literatura Universal Alba)

(5) México: Edivision Companía Editorial; Madrid: Editorial Alba, 1999. 113 pages: illustrations; 21cm. ISBN: 968890337X, 9688903377

8. Cuentos chinos/edición a cargo de Richard Wilhelm; traducción de Paz Ortega Montes. Buenos Aires: Paidós, 1958. 2 v. ; 19cm. ISBN: 8449303370 (v. 1), 8449303371 (v. 1), 8449304768 (v. 2), 8449304767 (v. 2). (Paidós orientalia; 52, 53)

Contents: v. 1. La princesa repudiada y otros relatos de la mitología china—v. 2. Ying Ning o la belleza sonriete y otros relatos fantásticos.

《中国民间故事集》, 译自卫礼贤 (Wilhelm, Richard, 1873—1930) 的德文版《Chinesische Märchen》

(1) Barcelona; Buenos Aires; México: Paidós, 1997—1998. 2 v. ; 19cm. ISBN: 8449303370 (v. 1), 8449303371 (v. 1), 8449304768 (v. 2), 8449304767 (v. 2). (Paidós orientalia; 52, 53)

(2) Barcelona: Paidós, 2012. 446 p. ; 21cm. ISBN: 8449327995 8449327997. (Paidós orientalia)

9. Odas selectas del romancero chino/Carmelo Elorduy. Caracas: Universidad Católica Andrés Bello, Instituto de Investigaciones Históricas, 1974. 138 pages; 23cm. Notes: Ballads, Chinese—Translations into Spanish.

中国民谣. Elorduy, Carmelo (1901—1989 年) 选译.

10. La princesa pavo real: cuentos populares chinos. Pekín (Beijing): Ediciones en Lenguas Extranjeras, 1981. 127 p. : il. ; 19cm.

《孔雀姑娘: 中国民间故事选》

11. La serpiente blanca: narraciones folklóricas/ [ilustraciones de Ye Yuzhong.]. Beijing: Ediciones en Lenguas Extranjeras, 1981. 183 p. : il. ; 19cm.

《飞来峰及人间天堂的其他故事: 根据〈西湖民间故事〉选编》

12. Los Cuentos fantásticos de China/presenta: Moss Roberts; tr. Antonio-Prometeo Moya. Barcelona: Editorial Crítica, 1982. 316 pages; 20cm. ISBN: 8474231663; 8474231663. (Los cuentos de)

中国神话故事. Moya, Antonio-Prometeo 译自英文版《Chinese fairy tales and fantasies》

13. Relatos mitológicos de la antígua China/[recopilado por Chu Binjie; ilustraciones de Yang Yongqing]. Beijing: China Ediciones en Lenguas Extranjeras, 1982. 149 p. il. 19cm.

《中国古代神话选》, 褚斌杰编.

(1) Beijing (China): Ediciones en Lenguas Extranjeras, 1989. 149 p. , [8] h. de lám. ; 19cm. ISBN: 7119008269, 7119008264

14. Male visita el sol: cuentos populares chinos. Beijing: Ediciones en Lenguas Extranjeras, 1982. 125 pages

《玛勒带子访太阳: 中国民间故事选》

15. Cuentos de Afanti/redactado por Zhao Shijie. Beijing: Ediciones en Lenguas Extranjeras, 1982. 114 pages: illustrations; 19cm.

《阿凡提的故事》, 赵世杰编.

(1) Beijing, China: Ediciones en Lenguas extranjeras, 1986. 114 p. ; 19cm.

16. El Puñal mágico: cuentos populares chinos. Beijing: Ediciones en Lenguas Extranjeras, 1982. 106 pages: illustrations

《宝刀: 中国民间故事选》

17. Las Siete hermanas: cuentos populares chinos. Beijing: Ediciones en Lenguas Extranjeras, 1983. 115 pages: illustrations; 21cm.

《七姐妹》

18. El siervo y la mujer dragón：cuentos populares chinos/ tr. Laura A. Rovetta. Beijing：Ediciones en Lenguas Extranjeras，1984. 118 p.：il.；20cm.

《奴隶与龙女：中国民间故事选》

19. El pajaro maravilloso：cuentos populares chinos/[tr. del chino por Laura A. Rovetta.]. Beijing：Ediciones en Lenguas Extranjeras，1984. 143 p.：il.；20cm. (Cuentos Populares Chinos)

《神鸟：中国民间故事选》

20. Cuentos mágicos chinos/traducción de Gloria Pera de Jordi. Barcelona Obelisco，1984. 155 p. 21cm. ISBN：8486000327；8486000325. (Obelisco. Fantástica)

中国民间故事，Peradejordi，Gloria.

(1)[2a. ed.]. Barcelona：Obelisco，1987. 155 p.；21cm. ISBN：8486000327 8486000325. (Colección Obelisco-fantástica)

(2)3a ed. Barcelona：Obelisco，2001. 155 p.；21cm. ISBN：8477208913 8477208914

21. Cuentos chinos/[selección de los cuentos，notas y traducción de Alfred J. Hodgson；traducción de Ma. Ángeles López Moraleda，Ramón Martínez Castellote]. Madrid Miraguano，1985. 189 p. il. 19cm. ISBN：8485639472；8485639472. (Libros de los malos tiempos；12)

中国民间故事. Hodgson，Alfred J. 等选译.

(1)Madrid：Miraguano，1990. 189 p.：il.；19cm. ISBN：8485639472；8485639472. (Libros de los malos tiempos；12)

22. Las siete víctimas de un pájaro：cuentos policiacos chinos/Traducción de Aurelio Garzón del Camino. México：Fondo de Cultura Económica，1986. 350 p.；17cm. ISBN：9681624904；9681624903

中国故事. 转译自 Lévy，André(1925—)的法文版.

23. El Duelo del búfalo y el tigre：cuentos populares chinos. Beijing［China］：Ediciones en Lenguas Extranjeras，1986. 104 p.；21cm.

《水牛斗老虎》

24. Lucha contra el rinoceronte por la perla. Beijing［China］：Ediciones en Lenguas extranjeras，1987. 118 p.；21cm.

《斗犀夺珠：中国民间故事选》

25. La muchacha liebre：antología de cuentos populares de amor/tr. Wang Hongxun y Fan Moxian. Beijing：Ediciones en Lenguas Extranjeras，1989. 450 p.；21cm. ISBN：7119002848，7119002842

《中国民间爱情故事选》

26. Los monos salvan a la luna：fábulas modernas de China. Beijing：Ediciones en Lenguas Extranjeras，1989. 129 pages：illustrations；18cm. ISBN：7119007114，7119007113

《中国现代寓言选》

27. El pastor y las aguilas：cuentos populares chinos. Beijing：Ediciones en Lenguas Extranjeras，1990. 115 p.：il.；21cm. ISBN：7119006681，7119006680

《牧人和山鹰：中国民间传统故事选》

28. 中国古代动物寓言选. 北京：外文出版社，1991. ISBN：7119008919

29. Chistes chinos：selección de chanzas，bromas，picardias y gracejos. Beijing：Ediciones en Lenguas Extranjeras，1991. 143 pages：illustrations；18cm. ISBN：7119012940，7119012940

《中国古代笑话选》，颜象贤编.

30. Cuentos y leyendas budistas (de la China). Barcelona MRA，1995. 123 p. 22cm. ISBN：8488865074；8488865076. (Aurum)

中国民间故事.

31. 101 cuentos clásicos de la China/recopilación de Chang Shiru y Ramiro Calle. Madrid：EDAF，1996. 219 pages：illustrations；18cm. ISBN：8441401152，8441401150. (Arca de sabiduría；28)

中国 101 个故事. 常世儒；Calle，Ramiro 合编

(1)3 ed. Madrid：Edaf，1998. 219 páginas：ilustraciones；18cm. ISBN：8441401150，8441401152. (Arca de sabiduría；28)

(2)6a. edición. Madrid：Edaf，2001. 219 páginas：ilustraciones；18cm. ISBN：8441401150，8441401152. (Arca de sabiduría；28)

(3)7a. edición. Madrid：Edaf，2002. 219 páginas：ilustraciones；18cm. ISBN：8441401150，8441401152. (Arca de sabiduría；28)

(4)11a. edición. Madrid：Edaf，2007. 219 páginas：ilustraciones；18cm. ISBN：8441401150，8441401152. (Arca de sabiduría；28)

32. Mitología china/R. R. Ayala. Barcelona：Edicomunicación，1999. 222 pages：illustrations；21cm. ISBN：8476727992；8476727997. (Colección Olimpo)

中国神话. Ayala，R. R. 编译.

(1)Santa Perpetua de Mogoda，Barcelona Brontes，2012. 220 p. il. 20cm. ISBN：8415171973，8415171978. (Olimpo. Mitología e historia；19)

33. La danza de las cometas：cuarenta cuentos chinos/ selección y traducción de Guillermo Dañino. Lima：Taller de Artes Gráficas del C. E. P. Peruano Chino "Diez Octubre，" 2001. 244 p.：il.；21cm.

中国故事集. 吉叶墨（Dañino Ribatto，Guillermo Alejandro，1929—）（秘鲁汉学家）译.

34. La colina voladora y otros cuentos/traducción，Guillermo Dañino；editor，Esteban Quiroz. 3a ed. ［Lima］：Lluvia Editores，2007. 63 p.：il.；15cm. (Cuentos chinos)

中国故事. 吉叶墨（Dañino Ribatto，Guillermo Alejandro，1929—）（秘鲁汉学家）译；Quiroz Cisneros，Esteban 编.

35. Antología del cuento chino maravilloso：la exquisita sabiduría de Oriente/recopilación de Rolando Sánchez-Mejías. Barcelona：Editorial Océano，2002. 239 p.；24cm. ISBN：8475562620，8475562629. （Jardín interior）

中国故事集. Sánchez Mejías，Rolando(1959—)编译.

36. Mitología clásicas china/edición y traducción de Gabriel García-Noblejas Sánchez-Cendal. Madrid：Trotta；Barcelona：Edicions de la Universitat de Barcelona，2004. 339 p.：il.；20cm. ISBN：8481646032，8481646030，8483384728，8483384725. （Pliegos de Oriente. Serie Lejano Oriente；12）

《古神话选释》，García-Noblejas Sánchez-Cendal，Gabriel 编译.

37. Mitos chinos/Anne Birrell；traducción，Francisco López Martín. Tres Cantos，Madrid：Akal Ediciones，2005. 80 p.：il.；24cm. ISBN：8446022311；8446022312. （El Pasado legendario）

中国神话. López Martín，Francisco 转移自英文版 《Chinese myths》

38. Cuentos legendarios de la antigua China/selección de Yuan Yang. Madrid：Popular，2010. 252 p.：il.；22cm. ISBN：8478844760；8478844767. （Letra grande. Serie maior；23）

中国古代传说. Yuan，Yang 选译.

39. Mitos y leyendas de China/Chen Lianshan；traducido por Guo Hongkun. Beijing China Intercontinental，2011. 145 p. il. col. y n. 23cm. ISBN：7508520315，7508520319. （Series de China cultural）

《中国神话传说》，陈连山(1963—)著；国红坤译.

　　（1）Madrid Editorial Popular，2013. 145 p. il. col. 23cm. ISBN：8478845576，8478845577. （Asiateca. Serie Cultura china；2）

I9　儿童文学

1. La carretera resplandeciente/por Hu Qi；trad. de Lola Falcon. Pekin Ed. En Lenguas Extranjeras，1960. 124 p.：ilus.；21cm.

　　（1）Pekin Ed. En Lenguas Extranjeras，1964. 117 p. il.

　　（2）3a ed. Beijing：Ediciones en Lenguas Extranjeras，1981. 142 pages：illustrations；19cm.

《五彩路》，胡奇.

2. La carretera resplandeciente. La Habana：Gente Nueva，1974. 209 p.：ilus.；23cm.

《五彩路》，胡奇.

3. Cuentos escogidos/Ye Sheng-tao；traducción de Lola Falcón. Pekin：Lenguas Extranjeras，1960. ［6］，75 p.，9la'ms.；20cm.

《叶圣陶童话选》

　　（1）2a ed. Pekin：Ediciones en Lenguas Extranjeras，1966. 82 p.，［9］h. de lám.；21cm.

　　（2）2a ed. Pekin：Ediciones en Lenguas Extranjeras，1978. 82 pages：illustrations；23cm.

　　（3）Pekin：Ediciones en Lenguas Extranjeras，1984. 82 p.

4. 小鲤鱼跳龙门/金近改写；杨善子、丁榕临绘. 北京：外文出版社，1961

5. 大灰狼（儿童文学）/ 张天翼著. 北京：外文出版社，1965

6. Nubes purpuras/Jao Yan. Pekin：Ediciones en Lenguas Extranjeras，1975. 146 pages：illustrations；18cm.

《彩霞》，浩然著.

7. Liu Ju-lan/Chin Ching. Pekin：Ediciones en Lenguas Extranjeras，1974. 34 pages

《刘胡兰》，晋青著.

8. 闪闪的红星/李心田著；王维新插图. 北京：外文出版社，1975

9. El caballero de la rana：cuentos populares chinos. 2a ed. Pekín（Beijing）：Ediciones en Lenguas Extranjeras，1980. 83 p.；19cm.

《青蛙骑手》

10. 少先队的故事. 第3版. 北京：外文出版社，1984

注：1959年首版

11. Cuentos de la China milenaria/Anónimo；edición，traducción y apêndice：Enrique P. Gatón e Imelda Hwang；Ilustración：Marcelo Spotti. Madrid：Anaya，1986—1987. 2 v. il. color y n. 25cm. ISBN：8475253490，8475253497，8475253482，8475253480. （Laurin）

中国故事. Gatón，Enrique P. 和 Hwang，Imelda 编译. 收录约150个故事，儿童读物.

　　（1）2a ed. Madrid：Anaya，1988. 2 v. il. color y n. 25cm. ISBN：8475253490，8475253497，8475253482，8475253480. （Laurin）

12. The ballad of Mulan＝La balada de Mulán/retold and illustrated by Song Nan Zhang；Spanish translation by Paulina Kobylinski. Union City，CA：Pan Asian Publications，c1998. 1 v.（unpaged）：col. ill.；29cm. ISBN：1572270551.

《木兰辞》，Zhang，Song Nan(1942—)编绘. 英文、西班牙语和汉语三种语言对照. 青少年读物.

13. 20 Cuentos chinos y un dragón amarillo. Cuentos para niños. Colección cuenta cosas. Lima：Alfaguara-GrupoSantillana，2004. 86 p. ISBN：9972847516. （Serie Naranja）

《中国故事》，吉叶墨（Daniño Ribatto，Guillermo Alejandro，1929—）（秘鲁汉学家）译.

14. Cuentos chinos del Río Amarillo/edición de Imelda Huang Wang y Enrique P. Gatón；［ilustración de cubierta，Fabio Marras］. Madrid：Siruela，2008. 207 pages；25cm. ISBN：8498411973；8498411971. （Colección Las Tres edades；8；Biblioteca de Cuentos populares）

黄河故事. Gatón，Enrique P. 和 Hwang Wang，Imelda

编.

15. El pincel mágico/de Hong Xuntao; adaptado por Françoise Jay e ilustrado por Zhong Jie. Barcelona：Editorial Juventud, 2009. 49 pages：color illustrations；31cm. ISBN：8426137456；8426137458
《神笔马良》,洪汛涛；Jay，Françoise 改编.

16. La pluma/texto de Cao Wenxuan; ilustraciones de Roger Mello; traducción Martín Bertone; revisión de textos Laura González. Ciudad Autónoma de Buenos Aires：Eudeba, 2016. 49 unnumbered pages：illustrations (some color)；18×30cm. ISBN：9502326221, 9502326229
《羽毛》,曹文轩(1954—) Bertone，Martín 译；Mello，Roger 插图.

J 类　艺术

J1　艺术概论

1. 中国当代艺术：西班牙文/李国文编著；冯志英译.北京：新星出版社,2006；21cm. ISBN：7802251486
本书介绍1990年以来,中国当代艺术的概况,主要涉及绘画、雕塑、摄影、行为艺术等艺术类别,同时介绍了多位在国际展览上异常活跃的中国艺术家.

2. La China más hermosa：Arte y sultura/[Yang, chunyan]. Beijing：Ediciones en Lenguas Extranjeras, 2010. 55 pages：color illustrations；18cm. ISBN：7119063188, 7119063189
《最美中国.艺术与文化》,外文出版社编.

3. Arte de China/by Jin Yong, tran. by Miguel Sautié. Beijing：China Intercontinental Press, 2011. 152 pages：illustrations；25cm. ISBN：7508521893, 7508521897
《艺术之旅》,靳永著.五洲传播出版社.

4. 中国书画文化.北京：新星出版社,1995. ISBN：780102432x.(中国概况)

5. Discurso acerca de la pintura por el monje Calabaza Amarga/Shitao; edición española de María Lecea; traducción del chino y comentarios de Pierre Ryckmans. Granada Editorial Universidad de Granada, 2012. 288 p. ISBN：8433853912, 8433853910. (Colección Confucio)
《苦瓜和尚画语录》,石涛(1642—约1707年)；Ryckmans, Pierre 译.

J2　绘画

1. Pintura tradicional china/[compilado por Ediciones en Lenguas Extranjeras]. Beijing,[China]：Ediciones en Lenguas Extranjeras, 1989. 14 p.：il.；19cm. ISBN：7119005995, 7119005997. (Presencia de China)
《中国画入门》.外文出版社(中国概况)

2. 独具特色的中国绘画：西班牙文/韦黎明编著；张重光等译.北京：新星出版社,2006. 21cm. ISBN：7802251303
本书介绍了中国绘画的风格、特色、流派、一些著名画家

以及中国绘画的基本技法.

3. La pintura China/by Lin Ci; traducido por Guo Hongkun y Yang Zhiping. Beijing：China Intercontinental Press, 2011. 193 pages：illustrations；23cm. ISBN：7508520803, 7508520807. (Series de China Cultural)
《中国绘画艺术》,林茨著.五洲传播出版社.

4. Semejanza y desemejanza：ccolección de pinturas de Qi Baishi/redacción：Yan Xinqiang y Jin Yan. Beijing：Ediciones en Lenguas Extranjeras, 1991. 1 v.：il. col.；38cm. ISBN：7119000489, 7119000480
《齐白石画集》,严欣强,金岩编.

5. Pinturas de año nuevo chino/compilado por Lin Fang; traducido por César Santos y Gao Bei. [Beijing] China Intercontinental Press, 2010. 99 p. il. col. 19×22cm. ISBN：7508516523, 7508516524. (Arte folclórico de China)
《中国年画》,林方编著.五洲传播出版社.

6. Pinturas de campesinos de China/compilado por Xi Jiping; traducido por Gao Bei y César Santos. [Beijing] China Intercontinental Press, 2010. 102 p. il. col. 19×22cm. ISBN：7508516516, 7508516516. (Arte folclórico de China)
《中国农民画》,奚吉平编著.五洲传播出版社.

7. La nueva China en estampas de año nuevo/Lu Keqin. Beijing：China Intercontinental Press, 2010. 230 p. il., la'ms. col 26cm. ISBN：7508516257, 7508516257
《年画上的中国》,陆克勤撰稿.五洲传播出版社.

8. 中国绘画珍藏/荆孝敏主编.北京：五洲传播出版社,,2010. 229 页；29×29cm. ISBN：7508517568
本书汇集了260幅中国历代的传世名画,系统地介绍了中国传统绘画的渊源,流派特色和发展脉络,展现了中国画史全面清晰的轮廓.

9. Álbum de pinturas Chinas contemporáneas/[planificación general：Jing Xiaomin; escritor：Cheng Nan; editor de ilustraciones：Cai Cheng; traducción：César Santos, Gao Bei]. Beijing：China Intercontinental Press, 2009. 141 pages：color illustrations；21×21cm. ISBN：7508517643, 7508517644
《中国当代国画》,荆孝敏主编.五洲传播出版社.

10. Pintura de beldades de la China Antigua/[escritor：Liu Fengwen; traducción：César Santos, Gao Bei]. Beijing：China Intercontinental Press, 2010. 133 páginas：ilustraciones；21cm. ISBN：7508517636, 7508517636
《中国历代仕女画》,荆孝敏主编.五洲传播出版社.

11. Pintura de temática animal en la antigua China/escritor：Minsong Geng; traductora：Gao Yuan; correctora：Ana Lanau. Beijing：Intercontinental Press, 2010. 145 pages：illustrations；20cm. ISBN：7508517599, 7508517598
《中国古代动物画》,荆孝敏主编.五洲传播出版社.

12. Flores y pájaros：pintura en la Antigua China/[escritor：Liu Fengwen; traductora：Gao Yuan]. Beijing：China

Intercontinental Press，2010. 147 páginas：ilustraciones；21cm. ISBN：7508517605，7508517601

《中国历代花鸟画》，荆孝敏主编. 五洲传播出版社.

13. El antiguo género chino de las pinturas de niños/［author：Geng Mingsong；translation César Santos，Gao Bei］. Beijing：China Intercontinental Press，2010. 111 pages：illustrations；21cm. ISBN：7508517612，750851761X

《中国古代儿童生活画》，荆孝敏主编. 五洲传播出版社.

14. Pintura de paisajes de la China Antigua/［escritor，Geng Mingsong；traducción，César Santos，Gao Bei］. Beijing China Intercontinental Press，2010. 147 p. il. col. 21×21cm. ISBN：7508517629，7508517628

《中国历代山水画》，荆孝敏主编. 五洲传播出版社.

J21　书法、篆刻

1. Caligrafía china/Chen Tingyou；traducido por Guo Lingxia；corregido por Isidro Luis Estrada Delas. Beijing：China Intercontinental Press，2003. 127 pages：color illustrations；23cm. ISBN：7508503465，7508503462. (Cultural China series)

《中国书法》，陈廷祐著. 郭翎霞译. 五洲传播出版社.

(1)2nd ed. Beijing：China Intercontinental Press，2011. 156 pages：illustrations（some color）；23cm. ISBN：7508520087，7508520084. (Series de China Cultural)

2. El arte chino de la caligrafia a traves de los tiempos/［Gao Changshan；traduccion Cesar Santos，Gao Bei］. Beijing：China Intercontinental Press，2010. 143 pages；19cm. ISBN：7508518206，7508518209

《中国历代书法》，荆孝敏主编. 五洲传播出版社.

J3　雕塑

1. Escultura China/Zhao Wenbing；traducido por Yao Bei y Zhang Wen. Beijing：China Inercontiental Press，2011. 175 pages：illustrations（some color）；23cm. ISBN：7508519623，7508519620. (Series de China Cultural)

《中国雕塑》，肇文兵著. 五洲传播出版社.

J4　工艺美术

1. La artesanía，gema cultural/［compilado por Ediciones en Lenguas Extranjeras］. Beijing，［China］：Ediciones en Lenguas Extranjeras，1989. 18 p.：il.；19cm. ISBN：7119005944，7119005942. (Presencia de China)

宝石工艺. 外文出版社（中国概况）

2. Juguetes tradicionales de China/Lu Pu. Beijing（China）：Editorial Nuevo Mundo，1990. 142 p.：principalmente il. en col.；26cm. ISBN：7800050645，7800050640

《民间玩具集锦》，鲁朴编. 新世界出版社.

3. Arte chino del recortado de papel/compilado por Sun Bingshan；traducido por Gao Bei y César Santos. ［Beijing］China Intercontinental Press，2010. 102 p. principalmente il. col. 19×22cm. ISBN：7508516561，

7508516567.（Arte folclórico de China）

《中国剪纸》，孙秉山，俞满红编著. 五洲传播出版社.

4. Cometa China/compilado por Sun Bingshan y Yu Manhong；traducido por Gao Bei y César Santos. Beijing China Intercontinental Press，2010. 102 p. principalmente il. col. y n. 19×22cm. ISBN：7508516509，7508516508.（Arte folclórico de China）

《中国风筝》，孙秉山，俞满红编. 五洲传播出版社.

J5　中国音乐

1. La música China/by Jin Jie；traducido por Lucía Salinas Mendiola，Wang Lei. Beijing：China Intercontinental Press，2011. 158 pages：illustrations；23cm. ISBN：7508520919，7508520912.（Series de China Cultural）

《中国音乐》，靳婕编著. 五洲传播出版社.

J6　戏剧、曲艺、杂技艺术

J61　中国戏剧艺术理论

1. La opera de China/［edited by Cui Lili；translated by Zhang Chongguang］. Beijing：Editorial Nueva Estrella，2004. 35 pages：color illustrations；21cm. ISBN：7801485815，7801485816.（China express；viaje multicultural a un pais de cinco mil años）

《中国的戏曲》，崔黎丽编著. 新星出版社.

2. 京剧/路易·艾黎著. 北京：新世界出版社，1957

3. Abecé de la Ópera de Beijing/Liang Yan. Beijing：Eds. en Lenguas Extranjeras，2003. 70 p.：il. col. ISBN：7119032909，7119032900

《京剧启蒙》，梁燕著.

4. La ópera de Beijing/Xu Chengbei；traducido por Chen Gensheng. Beijing：China Intercontinental Press，2003. 129 p.：il. col.；23cm. ISBN：7508503417，7508503414. (Cultural China series)

《中国京剧》，徐城北撰；陈根生译. 五洲传播出版社.

(1)Beijing：China Intercontinental Press，2011. 171 páginas.：ilustraci-ones，color；23cm. ISBN：7508520964，7508520963. (Series de China Cultural)

J62　杂技艺术

1. Acrobacia en China ＝ Akrobatik in China. Pekín（Beijing）：Ediciones en Lenguas Extranjeras，1982. 107 p.：il.；21cm.

《中国杂技艺术》. 德文、西班牙文对照.

2. Prestigiosa acrobacia China/［Wang Lei］. Beijing：Editorial Nueva Estrella，2004. 37，［2］pages：color illustrations；21cm. ISBN：7801485734，7801485731. (China express；viaje multicultural a un país de cinco mil años)

《神奇的中国杂技》，王蕾著. 新星出版社.

J7 电影、电视艺术

1. 爱国主义还是卖国主义?:评反动影片《清宫秘史》/戚本禹.北京:外文出版社,1967

2. Maligna intención y viles medios:crítica de la película antichina "Chung Kuo" (China) rodada por M. Antonioni/comentarista de Renmin Ribao. Pekín:Ediciones en Lenguas Extranjeras,1974. 14 p.;18cm.

   《恶毒的用心,卑劣的手法:批判安东尼奥尼拍摄的题为〈中国〉的反华影片》,人民日报评论员.

K 类 历史、地理

K1 中国史

1. China, historia y civilización. Beijing:Central Party Literature Press, 2006. 256 pages:illustrations (some color), maps;29cm. ISBN:7507320936, 7507320930

   《中国历史与文明:西班牙文》,张英聘编著;付少杰,马勒迪那斯译.中央文献出版社.以图配文的形式介绍中国历史文明.

K11 通史

1. La historia/por la Redacción de Colección China. Beijing:Ediciones en Lenguas Extranjeras, 1984. 195 p.:il.;19cm.. (Coleccion China)

   《历史》,《中国概况丛书》编辑委员会编.

2. Breve historia de China:desde la antigüedad hasta 1919/redactor jefe, Bai Shouyi. Beijing, China:Ediciones en Lenguas Extranjeras:Centro de Publicaciones de China (Guoji Shudian) [distributor], 1984. 519 pages, [69] pages of plates:illustrations (some color), map, portraits;21cm. (Colección Biblioteca basica)

   《中国通史纲要》,白寿彝主编;杨钊分纂.

3. Breve história de China - desde 1919 hasta 1949/Redactor jefe, Bai Shouyi etc. Beijing:Ediciones en Lenguas Extranjeras, 1992. 354 pages:illustrations;20cm. ISBN:7119013424, 7119013428

   《中国通史纲要续编:1919—1949》,白寿彝主编.

4. Breve historia de China/[compilado por Ediciones en Lenguas Extranjeras]. Beijing, [China]:Ediciones en Lenguas Extranjeras, 1987. 38 p.:il.;19cm. ISBN:7119002937, 7119002934. (Presencia de China)

   《中国历史》

5. Conocimientos comunes de la historia de China/The Overseas Chinese Affairs Office of the State Council, The Office of Chinese Language Council International. Beijing] Sinolingua, 2007. 258 p. il. col. y n. 24cm. ISBN:7802002302, 7802002303

   《中国历史常识:汉西对照》,王恺主编;国务院侨务办公室,国家汉语国际推广领导小组办公室编.华语教学出版社(中国常识系列)

6. Historia de China/Cao Dawei y Sun Yanjing;traducido por Wang Hongxun y Fan Moxian. Beijing:China Intercontinental Press, 2011. 232 pages:illustrations (chiefly color);23cm. ISBN:7508519234, 750851923X

   《中国历史》,曹大为,孙燕京著.五洲传播出版社.

7. Extractos de la historia china. Beijing Ediciones en Lenguas Extranjeras, 2008. 220 p. il. col. y n. 24cm. ISBN:7119055695, 7119055690

   《中国历史速查》,本书编写组编著.

8. 国家记忆:历史就在那里/朱成山等[编著];张重光,林传红翻译.北京:外文出版社,2014.19 页:图;21cm. ISBN:7119092294

   西班牙文题名:La memoria de un pais:la historia que no se puede olvidar. 主要讲中国为什么要设立国家公祭日,国家公祭日的由来、意义.

K12 古代史籍

1. Crónicas de primavera y otoño/Zuo Quiming;traducción y notas:Alfonso Araujo. Buenos Aires:Argentina Editorial Quadrata, 2013. 157 páginas 20cm. ISBN:9876310581, 9876310585. (Colección Puente Luna)

   《左传》,Araujo, Alfonso 译.

2. Los adversarios:dos biografías de las memorias históricas/de Sima Qian [i. e. Ssu-ma, Ch'ien];selec., introd., tr. y notas de John Page. México:El Colegio de México, Centro de Estudios de Asia y Africa del Norte, 1979. 99 p.;21cm. ISBN:9681200454, 9681200459. (Ensayos/El Colegio de México. Centro de Estudios de Asia y Africa del Norte;;6)

   《楚汉之争》,司马迁;Page, John 译注. 译自《史记》.

3. Selección de registros históricos/Sima Qian;[traducido por Yin Chengdong y Hong Miyun]. Beijing Ediciones en Lenguas Extranjeras, 2005. 2 v. ISBN:7119014692, 7119014692

   《史记选:西班牙文》,(汉)司马迁著;尹承东等译.本书选取其中的 31 篇.

4. Selección de Registros históricos/versión china de Sima Qian;versión china confrontada de An Pingqiu;versión española de Hong Miyun y Guillermo Dañino. Beijing:Wai wen chu ban she, 2014. 3 volumes (1139 pages);24cm. ISBN:7119085777;7119085778. (Da Zhonghua wen ku=Biblioteca de clásicos Chinos)

   《史记选》,(西汉)司马迁著;安平秋今译;洪弥云,吉叶墨译.外文出版社(大中华文库)

5. Historia secreta de los mongoles = yuan chao bi shi = Mongyol-un niyuca tobciyan/edición, traducción y notas de Laureano Ramírez Bellerín, a partir del manuscrito chino de Li Wentian cotejado con el mongol. Madrid:Miraguano, 2000. 401 p.;25cm. ISBN:8478132171;8478132171. (Libros de los malos tiempos. Serie mayor)

《元朝秘史》,Ramírez, Laureano 编译.

(1) 2a. ed. Madrid：Miraguano, 2011. 401 p. ISBN：8478133819 847813381X. （Libros de los malos tiempos. ; Serie Mayor）

K13　古代史

1. La vida de la familia imperial/［editor, Lan Peijin; texto en español, Ouyang Yuan］. Beijing：Ediciones en Lenguas Extranjeras, 2008. 148 pages：color illustrations；23cm. ISBN：7119054544, 7119054546

　　《帝后生活》,思方撰. 本书通过生动有趣的故事和图片,展示帝后生活的方方面面,从衣食住行到婚丧嫁娶,宫廷阴谋政变等.

K14　近代史

1. 中国近代简史(1840—1919)/复旦大学历史系中国近代史教研组编著. 北京：外文出版社,1980

2. 鸦片战争 /《中国近代史丛书》编写组编写. 北京：外文出版社,1980

3. El movimiento del reino celestial de Taiping/por la Redacción de la "Colección de libros sobre la historia moderna de China." Pekin：Ediciones en Lenguas Extranjeras, 1979. 152 pages, ［8］ pages of plates：illustrations, folded map；19cm.

　　《太平天国》,《中国近代史丛书》编写组.

4. El movimiento Yijetuan/por la Reducción de la "Colección de libros sobre la historia moderna de China". Pekin：Ediciones en Lenguas Extranjeras, 1978. 108 pages, ［4］ pages of plates：illustrations；19cm.

　　《义和团运动》,《中国近代史丛书》编写组.

K15　中华人民共和国成立之后历史

1. 中国现代简史：从鸦片战争到解放战争/爱泼斯坦. 北京：新世界出版社,1958

2. La revolución de 1911/por la Redacción de la "Colección de libros sobre la historia moderna de China." Pekin：Ediciones en Lenguas Extranjeras, 1976. 155 pages, ［8］ pages of plates：illustrations；19cm.

　　《辛亥革命》,《中国近代史丛书》编写组.

3. Cronologia de la Republica Popular China (1949—1985). Beijing：Ediciones en Lenguas Extranjeras, 1986. 90 pages；19cm.

　　《中华人民共和国大事记：1949——1985》,成今编.

4. 中国与第二次世界大战. 北京：新星出版社,1995. ISBN：780102270x. (中国概况)

K2　中外交流史

1. Diego de Pantoja y China：un estudio sobre la "Política de adaptación" de la Compañía de Jesús/Zhang Kai; traducción al español：Tang Baisheng y Kang Xiaolin.

Pekín：Biblioteca de Beijing, 1997. 180 p. : il. ; 20cm. ISBN：7501314438, 7501314430

　　《庞迪我与中国》,张铠著. 北京图书馆出版社.

2. Historia de las Relaciones Sino-Espanolas/Zhang Kai; traduccion：Sun Jiakun y Huang Caizhen. Zheng zhou：Elephant Press, 2003. 219 pages, 16 leaves of plates：illustrations (some color)；21cm. ISBN：7534730309, 7534730306

　　《中国与西班牙关系史》,张铠著；孙家,黄才珍译. 大象出版社.

3. 探索中拉古代文明的交流：西班牙文/韦黎明编著；张重光 等译. 北京：新星出版社,2006；21cm. ISBN：7802251532

　　本书介绍了中国学者对中拉古代文明之间的交流进行的学术上的探索以及成果.

K3　地方史志

各地历史

1. Beijing, capital de China. Beijing：Ediciones en Lenguas Extranjeras, 1982. 157 pages, ［56］ pages of plates：illustrations (some color)；19cm.

　　《北京》,刘俊雯编.

2. 古今北京/周沙尘著. 北京：新世界出版社,1989

3. Hutongs：antiguas residencias de personalidades históricas/editor, Lan Peijin; escrito por, Li Lianxia; fotos, Wang Jianhua ［and others］; traducción, Lin Chuanhong, Jorge Luis López López; edición en español, Zhang Chongguang. Beijing：Ediciones en Lenguas Extranjeras, 2007. 101 pages：color illustrations；23cm. ISBN：7119044422, 7119044427

　　《北京胡同・名人故居：西班牙文》,兰佩瑾编；王建华等摄.

4. Templos de Beijing/［idea, Xiao Xiaoming; editores jefes, Liao Pin y Lan Peijin; texto, Liao Pin y Wu Wen］. Beijing：Ediciones en Lenguas Extranjeras, 2007. 112 pages：color illustrations；22cm. ISBN：7119046167, 7119046160

　　《北京寺庙道观：西班牙文》,廖频,吴文撰；何炳富等摄；林传红等译. 外文出版社(漫游北京)

5. 北京胡同・名人故居：［西班牙文本］/兰佩瑾编辑；李连霞撰文；王建华［等］摄影；张重光［等］翻译. 北京：外文出版社, 2007. 101 pages：illustrations；22cm. ISBN：7119044422, 7119044427

6. 北京寺庙道观：［西班牙文本］/廖频,吴文撰文；何炳富［等］摄影；Jorge Luis Lopez,林传红翻译. 北京：外文出版社, 2007. 113 pages：illustrations；23cm. ISBN：7119046167, 7119046160

7. Museos de Beijing/［editor Lan Peijin; texto en español Ouyang Yuan, Jorge Luis López López］. Beijing：Ediciones en Lenguas Extranjeras, 2008. 167 p. : il.

col. ；22cm. ISBN：7119054094，7119054090

《京城博物馆》，子慧撰. 本书为2008年奥运会而编写的漫游北京系列丛书之一，图文并茂介绍北京城里的主要博物馆，让读者通过见证博物馆的遗存文物等，进一步了解北京的过去、发展的今天.

8. 画说老北京 古建京韵：西班牙文/方砚著. 北京：新星出版社，2017. 30cm. ISBN：7513329347

9. 画说老北京 胡同记忆：西班牙文/方砚著. 北京：新星出版社，2017. 30cm. ISBN：7513329354

10. 画说老北京 风物民俗：西班牙文/方砚著. 北京：新星出版社，2017. 30cm. ISBN：7513329378

河北

1. Tangshan renace. Beijing：Nueva Estrella, 1996. 30 p.：il.；18cm. ISBN：7801026578，7801026576. (Presencia de China)

《走向世界的唐山》. 新星出版社(中国概况)

内蒙古

1. Región Autonoma de Mongolia Interior：50 años. China：Nueva Estrella, 1997. 34 p. il.；18cm. ISBN：7801028120，7801028129. (Presencia de China)

《内蒙古自治区的五十年》. 新星出版社(中国概况)

广西

1. 40 años de la región autónoma de la etnia Zhuang de Guangxi/por Gui Xin. Beijing：Nueva estrella, 1998. 30 p.：il.；18cm. ISBN：7801480910，7801480910. (Presencia de China)

《广西壮族自治区的四十年》. 新星出版社(中国概况)

重庆

1. Chongqing：cuarto municipio directamente subordinado al poder central de China. Beijing：Nueva Estrella, 1998. 30 p.：il.；18cm. ISBN：7801480678，7801480675. (Presencia de China)

《重庆：中国第四个直辖市》. 新星出版社(中国概况)

云南

1. A través de Xishuangbanna región de la nacionalidad dai. Pekin（Beijing）：Ediciones en Lenguas Extranjeras, 1980. 68 p.：il.；23cm.

《西双版纳纪行》，征岚著.

西藏

1. Sobre el problema del Tibet. Pekin：Ediciones en Lenguas Extranjeras, 1959. 292 pages：illustrations, facsimiles, portraits

《关于西藏问题》

2. El Tibet：nuevo salto adelante/Ji Zhangrao, Gao Yuanmei. Pekin：Ediciones en Lenguas Extranjeras, 1977. 119 pages，[40] pages of plates：illustrations；19cm.

《西藏的跃进》，郗长豪，高元美.

3. Tibet：una sociedad en transformación/redacción, Jin Zhou；texto Zhu Li；diagramación, Li Yuhong. Beijing, China：Ediciones en Lenguas Extranjeras, 1981. 176 pages：all illustrations；26cm.

《变革中的西藏》. 摄影画册.

4. 西藏的对外文化交流. 北京：新星出版社, 1996. ISBN：7801025148. (中国概况)

5. Tibet：el techo del mundo/Chilai Quzhag. Beijing：Ediciones en Lenguas Extranjeras, 1991. 275 pages, [20] pages of plates：color illustrations；20cm. ISBN：7119013076，7119013077

《我的家乡西藏》，赤列曲扎著.

6. 西藏人口的过去、现状与未来趋势. 北京：新星出版社, 1994. ISBN：7801021428. (中国概况)

7. 西藏人眼中的西藏：五人五话. 北京：新星出版社, 1995. ISBN：7801022602. (中国概况)

8. Desarrollo de la cultura tibetana. Beijing：Nueva Estrella, 2000. 40 p. ISBN：7801482980，7801482983

《西藏文化的发展》，中华人民共和国国务院新闻办公室发布. 新星出版社.

9. El desarrollo de la modernización del Tibet/Oficina de Información del Consejo de Estado de la República Popular China. Beijing：Editorial Nueva Estrella, 2001. 44 pages；21cm. ISBN：7801484010，7801484017

《西藏的现代化发展》，中华人民共和国国务院新闻办公室发布. 新星出版社.

10. China Tibet：hechos y cifras/Wang Guozhen. Beijing：Nueva Estrella, 2001. 153 p.：il.，mapas. ISBN：7801483510，7801483515

《中国西藏：事实与数字》，王振国编. 新星出版社.

11. 100 preguntas y respuestas sobre el Tibet. Beijing：Editorial Nueva Estrella, 2001. 140 pages：color illustrations；21cm. ISBN：7801483561，7801483560

《西藏百题问答》，百题问答编辑部编. 新星出版社.

12. El estatus histórico del Tibet de China/Wang Jiawei y Nyima Gyaincain. Beijing：China Intercontinental Press, 2003. 359 p. il. 20cm. ISBN：7508502588，7508502582

《中国西藏的历史地位》，王家伟，尼玛坚赞著. 五洲传播出版社. 本书通过对西藏历史的全面阐述，批驳"西藏独立论".

13. Gia turisticadel Tibet de China/An Caidan. [Beijing]：China Intercontinental Press, 2003. 203 pages：color illustrations, maps；21cm. ISBN：7508503929，750850392

《西藏旅游指南》，安才旦著；郭鸿珊等译. 五洲传播出版社.

14. Testimonio cien años del Tibet：entrevista a los testigos de la historia del Tibet/[editor：Xiaoming Zhang]. [Beijing]：Editorial Intercontinental de China, 2005. 189 pages：illustrations；21cm. ISBN：7508506774，7508506777

《见证百年西藏：西藏历史见证人访谈录：西班牙文》，张晓明编. 五洲传播出版社.

15. Población, creencias religiosas y autonomía étnica regional. Beijing：Ediciones en Lenguas Extranjeras, 2008. 47 pages：color illustrations；21cm. ISBN：

7119052359，7119052357.（ABC del Tíbet, China）

《西藏的人口、宗教与民族区域自治》，《西藏的人口、宗教与民族区域自治》编写组编.

16. Medio ambiente y su protección. Beijing：Ediciones en Lenguas Extranjeras, 2008. 47 pages：color illustrations；21cm. ISBN：7119052557，7119052551.（ABC del Tíbet, China）

《西藏的自然环境与保护》，《西藏的自然环境与保护》编写组编.

17. Materiales referentes al incidente del 14 de marzo en el Tíbet. Beijing：Ediciones en Lenguas Extranjeras, 2008. 4 volumes：color illustrations, color maps；21cm. ISBN：7119052267（v. 1），7119052268（v. 1），7119052199（v. 2），7119052195（v. 2），7119052243（v. 3），7119052241（v. 3），7119052304（v. 4），7119052306（v. 4）

《西藏"3.14"事件有关材料》，《西藏"3.14"事件有关材料》编写组编.

18. Situación, recursos y división administrativa. Beijing：Ediciones en Lenguas Extranjeras, 2008. 43 pages：color illustrations；21cm. ISBN：7119052403，7119052403.（ABC del Tíbet, China）

《西藏的地域、资源与行政区划》，《西藏的地域、资源与行政区划》编写组编. 本书重点介绍了西藏的地域、资源和行政区划. 包括地形地貌、气候、土地资源、特产等.

19. Economía. Beijing：Ediciones en Lenguas Extranjeras, 2008. 43 pages：color illustrations；21cm. ISBN：7119052458，7119052454.（ABC del Tíbet, China）

《西藏的经济发展》，《西藏的经济发展》编写组编. 本书重点介绍了西藏农牧林业、工业交通运输、邮电通讯业、贸易及金融保险业及"十一五"规划项目的进展状况.

20. Turismo. Beijing：Ediciones en Lenguas Extranjeras, 2008. 43 pages：color illustrations；21cm. ISBN：7119052601，7119052608.（ABC del Tíbet, China）

《西藏的旅游资源》，《西藏的资源旅游》编写组编. 本书重点介绍了西藏的旅游资源、项目和线路，以及西藏的民俗风情，包括服饰、饮食、传统民居特色，还有西藏的文物保护单位等.

21. Educación, ciencia, tecnología, cultura y vida del pueblo. Beijing：Ediciones en Lenguas Extranjeras, 2008. 43 pages：color illustrations；21cm. ISBN：7119052502，7119052500.（ABC del Tíbet, China）

《西藏的教育、科技、文化与生活》，《西藏的教育、科技、文化与生活》编写组编. 本书重点介绍了西藏的教育发展情况，以及科技文化、人民生活、医疗卫生、体育事业的发展.

22. Protección y desarrollo de la cultura tibetana/Oficina de Información del Consejo de Estado de la República Popular China. Beijing：Edicions en Lenguas Etranjeras, 2008. 35 pages；21cm. ISBN：7119047355，7119047353

《西藏文化的保护与发展》，中华人民共和国国务院新闻办公室发布.

23. Informe sobre el desarrollo socioeconómico del Tibet/Centro de Investigación Tibetológica de China. Beijing Ediciones en Lenguas Extranjeras, 2009. 83 p. il. gráf. , tablas 22cm. ISBN：7119056685，7119056689

《西藏经济社会发展报告》，中国藏学研究中心编.

24. 50 años de reforma democrática en el Tíbet/Oficina de Información del Consejo de Estado de la República Popular China. Beijing：Ediciones en Lenguas Extranjeras, 2009. 52 pages；21cm. ISBN：7119056418，7119056417

《西藏民主改革 50 年》，中华人民共和国国务院新闻办公室［发布］.

25. Sesenta años después de la liberación pacífica del Tibet/Oficina de Información del Consejo de Estado de la República Popular China. Beijing：Ediciones en Lenguas Extranjeras, 2011. 53 p. ；21cm. ISBN：7119071695，7119071696

《西藏和平解放 60 年》，中华人民共和国国务院新闻办公室［编］.

26. 民族区域自治制度在西藏的成功实践/中华人民共和国国务院新闻办公室［发布］.北京：外文出版社,2015. 82 页；21cm. ISBN：7119096032

西班牙文题名：Exitosa practica del sistema de autonomia etnica regional en el Tibet.

新疆

1. 古丝绸之路新貌：新疆维吾尔自治区的 40 年.北京：新星出版社,1995. ISBN：780102284x.（中国概况）

2. Historia y desarrollo de Xinjiang/Oficina de Información del Consejo de Estado de la República Popular China. Beijing：Nueva Estrella, 2003. 66 p. ISBN：7801485092，7801485090

《新疆的历史与发展》，中华人民共和国国务院新闻办公室发布.新星出版社.

3. Desarrollo y progreso de Xinjiang/Oficina de información del Consejo de Estado de la República Popular China. Beijing：Ediciones en Lenguas Extranjeras, 2009. 67 pages：illustrations；21cm. ISBN：7119060385，7119060384

《新疆的发展与进步》，中华人民共和国国务院新闻办公室［编］.

4. 新疆各民族平等团结发展的历史见证：西班牙文/中华人民共和国国务院新闻办公室发布.北京：外文出版社,2015.1 册：图；23cm. ISBN：7119096483

5. 新疆的宗教信仰自由状况（西班牙文版）/外文出版社.北京：外文出版社,2016. 20cm. ISBN：7119102078

K4　中国文物考古

1. Hallazgos arqueológicos en la nueva China ＝ Historical relics unearthed in new China ＝ Decouvertes archeologiques en Chine nouvelle. Pekin：Ediciones en Lenguas Extranjeras, 1972. 217, ［14］p. ：il.（algunes

col.)；34cm. ＋1 fullet (12 p.；31cm.)

《新中国出土文物》. 中西对照.

2. Cueva-hogar del hombre de Pekin/Jia Lanbo. Pekin：Ediciones en Lenguas Extranjeras, 1976. 59 pages, [36] pages of plates：illustrations；19cm.

《北京人之家》,贾兰波.

3. El hombre primitivo en China/Jia Lanpo. Beijing [China] Ediciones en Lenguas Extranjeras, 1981. IV, 76 p., [25] h. de lám. 26cm.

《中国大陆上的远古居民》,贾兰坡著.

4. El misterio del antiguo reino Zhongshan：recopilación de reliquias y hallazgos arqueológicos de China. Beijing：Ediciones en Lenguas Extranjeras, 1983. 189 pages, [16] pages of color plates：illustrations；19cm.

《二千三百年前古中山国之谜：中国的文物与考古选集》

5. 秦始皇兵马俑/吴晓丛,郭佑民主编. 北京：中国旅游出版社,1993. ISBN：7503210680

6. Un ejército de terracota del emperador Qin Shihuang：octava maravilla del mundo/editores：Wu Xiaocong, Guo Youmin. Beijing：La editorial de Turismo de China, 2001. 126 pages：color illustrations；28cm. ISBN：7503218827, 7503218828

《秦始皇的地下兵团：世界第八奇迹》,郭佑民,吴晓丛主编. 中国旅游出版社.

7. Guerreros y caballos de terracota del mausoleo de Qin Shin Huang. Beijing：Editorial Reliquias Culturales, 1993. 132 pages：illustrations (chiefly color)；26cm. ISBN：7501007063, 7501007066

《秦始皇兵马俑》. 文物出版社.

8. Un ejercito de grandes enensueños/[autor, Tao Yuping]. Xi'an：Editora de Xi'an, 2006. 128 pages, [2] pages of plates：color illustrations, maps, portraits；29cm. ISBN：7807122528, 7807122524

《梦幻的军团：西班牙文》,陶玉平编译. 西安出版社. 本书图文并茂介绍秦兵马俑、黄帝陵等.

9. Nuevos hallazgos arqueológicos en China. Beijing：Nueva Estrella, 1998. 30 p.：il.；18cm. ISBN：7801480457, 7801480453. (Presencia de China)

《中国近年考古新发现》. 新星出版社(中国概况)

10. 文明古国的文物保护. 北京：新星出版社,1995. ISBN：7801022939. (中国概况)

11. Reliquias culturales de China/Li Li；traducido por Chen Gensheng. Beijing：China Intercontinental Press, 2004. 188 p.：il. col.；23cm. ISBN：7508504585, 7508504582. (Cultural China series)

《中国文物》,李力主编,陈根生译. 五洲传播出版社.

(1)2nd ed. Beijing：China Intercontinental Press, 2011. 181 pages：illustrations (chiefly color)；23cm. ISBN：7508519296, 7508519299. (Series de China Cutural)

12. Objetos de bronce de China/autores Zhou Ya... [et al.]；

traducción, Zhag Jinlai, Guo Lingxia, Wang Yanjin. Beijing China Intercontinental Press, 2004. 144 p. il. mapa, fot. (algunas col.) 25cm. ISBN：7508505611, 7508505619

《中国青铜器》,李朝远等编,郭翎霞等译. 五洲传播出版社. 本书是一本对外介绍中国古代青铜器的普及性读物.

13. Objetos de bronce de China/Li Song；traducido por Yang Linchang；revisado por Xulio Ríos. Beijing：China Intercontinental Press, 2011. 168 p.：ill. (some col.)；23cm. ISBN：7508519357, 7508519353. (Series de China Cultural)

《中国青铜器》,李松著. 五洲传播出版社.

14. Jardines de China/Lou Qingxi；traducido por Chen Gensheng. [Beijing] China Intercontinental Press, 2003. 134 p. il. col. y n. 23cm. ISBN：7508503643, 7508503646. (Cultural China series)

《中国园林》,楼庆西著；陈根生译. 五洲传播出版社.

(1)Beijing：China Intercontinental Press, 2010. 175 páginas：ilustraciones, color；23cm. ISBN：7508520551, 7508520556. (Series de China cultural)

15. El arte de los paisajes en miniatura de China. Beijing：Ediciones en Lenguas Extranjeras, 1989. 161 pages：illustrations (some color)；26cm.

《中国盆景艺术》,胡运骅编.

K5 风俗习惯

1. Fiestas tradicionales/[compilado por Ediciones en Lenguas Extranjeras]. Beijing, [China]：Ediciones en Lenguas Extranjeras,1988. 28 p.：il.；19cm. ISBN：7119003143, 7119003146. (Presencia de China)

中国传统节日. 外文出版社(中国概况)

K6 地理

1. Geografía de China. Pekin：Ediciones en Lenguas Extranjeras, 1972. 46 pages, [12] pages of plates：illustrations, maps；19cm.

《中国地理知识》

2. Geografía de China/por Zhong Ji. Pekin：Ediciones en Lenguas Extranjeras, 1978. 180 pages, [43] pages of plates：maps, 2 folded color maps；19cm.

《中国地理概况》,众志.

3. Geografía/por la Redacción de "Colección China". Beijing：Ediciones en Lenguas Extranjeras, 1984. 316 p.：map.；19cm.

《地理》,《中国概况丛书》编辑委员会编.

4. Geografia de las provincias de China/Zhou Shunwu；[traducido por Song Baozhong, Du Jianguo y Zhang Jinlai]. Beijing：Ediciones en Lenguas Extranjeras, 1991. 590 p. ISBN：711901269X, 7119012698

《中国分省地理》,周舜武著.

5. 中国地理:自然·经济·人文/郑平著.北京:五洲传播出版社,1999. ISBN:7801134834

    (1) Geografía de China/Escrito por Zheng Ping; Traducido por Tang Baisheng. 2nd ed. Beijing, China: China Intercontinental Press, 2006. 170 pages: illustrations; 21cm. ISBN: 7508509129, 7508509129. (Series basicas de china)

    《中国地理:西班牙文》,郑平著/汤柏生译. 2 版. 五洲传播出版社(中国基本情况丛书/郭长建主编)

    (2) Geografía China/Zheng Ping; traducido por Yin Xiaotong. Beijing: China Intercontinental Press, 2011. 152 pages: color illustrations, color maps; 23cm. ISBN: 7508519753, 7508519752

6. Conocimientos comunes de la geografía china. [Pekín]: Sinolingua, 2006. 225 p.: il.; 24cm. ISBN: 7802002319, 7802002311

    《中国地理常识:汉西对照》,王恺主编;国务院侨务办公室,国家汉语国际推广领导小组办公室编. 华语教学出版社.

7. Geografía física de China/[compilada por] Ren Mei'e, Yang Renzhang and Bao Haosheng. Beijing: Ediciones en Lenguas Extranjeras, 1984. 542 pages, [48] pages of plates: illustrations (some color), maps; 20cm. (Colección Biblioteca básica)

    《中国自然地理纲要》,任美锷等著.

8. Libro de los montes y los mares: (Shanhai jing): cosmografía y mitología de la China Antigua/edición, traducción y notas de Yao Ning y Gabriel García-Noblejas Sánchez-Cendal; introducción de Juan José Ciruela Alfèrez. Madrid: Miraguano, 2000. 286 p.: il.; 24cm. ISBN: 8478132104; 8478132102. (Libros de los malos tiempos.; Mayor)

    《山海经》,Yao, Ning 和 Garcia-Noblejas Sánchez-Cendal, Gabriel 合译.

K61 专属地理

1. Qomolangma: cima del mundo/Zhang Rongzu. Beijing: Ediciones en Lenguas Extranjeras, 1981. 67 pages, [12] pages of plates (2 folded): illustrations (some color), map; 19cm.

    《世界第一峰:珠穆朗玛峰》,张荣祖著.

K62 名胜古迹

1. 中国的十大"世界文化和自然遗产".北京:新星出版社, 1994. ISBN:7801021932. (中国简况)

2. Bienes del patrimonio mundial en China. Beijing: China Interconionental Press, 2004. 251 pages: color illustrations; 31cm. ISBN: 7508505441, 7508505442

    《中国的世界遗产》,郭长建主编,《中国的世界遗产》编委会编;杨林常译. 五洲传播出版社. 本书介绍中国的 29 处世界遗产.

3. 世界遗产保护在中国:西班牙文/张学英编著;姚贝译. 北京:新星出版社,2006. 21cm. ISBN:7802251516

    本书介绍了中国丰富的世界遗产和在遗产保护方面所做的努力,提供了中国式的经验与范例,对开发与保护之间的矛盾提出了对策.

4. El patrimonio de la humanidad de China/Liu Huichun. Beijing: Editorial Nueva Estrella, 2004. ISBN: 7801485750, 7801485755. (China express; viaje multicultural a un país de cinco mil años)

    《中国自然与文化遗产》,刘惠春. 新星出版社.

5. La China más hermosa: naturaleza y cultura/[Yang, chunyan]. Beijing: Ediciones en Lenguas Extranjeras, 2010. 55 pages: color illustrations; 18cm. ISBN: 7119063232, 7119063235

    《最美中国.自然与文化》,外文出版社编.选取中国最美的自然景观及人文景观,主要以图片展现.

6. La gran muralla China y sus leyendas/Luo Zhewen y Zhao Luo. Beijing: Ediciones en Lenguas Extranjeras, 1986. 79 p.: il.; 26cm.

    《中国的万里长城》,罗哲文,赵洛著.

7. El turismo/por la redacción de "Colección China." Beijing: Ediciones en Lenguas Extranjeras, 1984. 173 pages: illustrations (some color). (Coleccion China)

    《旅游》,《中国概况丛书》编辑委员会编.

8. Guía turística de China/Qi Xing. Beijing Ediciones en Lenguas Extranjeras, 1989. 652 p., [32] p. de lám. col., [2] h. pleg. de map. y plan. il., map., plan. 19cm. ISBN: 7119008714, 7119008714

    《中国旅游指南》,齐星编著.

9. Guía turística de China/[Shen Han; translated by Ren Xiping]. Beijing: Editorial Nueva Estrella, 2004. 39 pages: color illustrations; 21cm. ISBN: 7801486021, 7801486028. (China express; viaje multicultural a un pais de cinco mil años)

    《旅游在中国》,沈涵著. 新星出版社.

K7 人物传记和回忆录

1. 孔府内宅轶事:孔子后裔的回忆/孔德懋口述.北京:新世界出版社,1989

2. Confucio: "santo" de las clases reaccionarias/Yang Yung-kuo. Pekin: Ediciones en Lenguas Extranjeras, 1974. 76 pages; 19cm.

    《反动阶级的"圣人:孔子"》,杨荣国.

3. 跟随毛泽东长征/陈昌奉著;阿老插图.北京:外文出版社,1960

4. Relatos del Ejército Rojo de China/[traducido por Herminia Carvajal]. Pekin: Ediciones en Lenguas Extranjeras, 1960. x, 194 p., [3] h. dela'ms.: il.; 18cm.

《中国红军的故事》,何长工等.

5. 我是劳动人民的儿子/吴运铎. 北京:外文出版社,1964

6. Nuestro Zhou Enlai. Pekin：Ediciones en Lenguas Extranjeras, 1978. 198 pages，[11] pages of plates：illustrations, portraits；23cm.

《怀念周恩来总理》

7. Zhou Enlai：su adolescencia y juventud/por Hu Hua. Pekín（Beijing）：Ediciones en Lenguas Extranjeras, 1979. 123 p.，[8] p. de lám.；19cm.

《青少年时期的周恩来》,胡华著.

8. Zhou Enlai：perfil biografico. Beijing：Ediciones en Lenguas Extranjeras, 1989. 225 pages：illustrations (some color), portraits；21cm.

《周恩来传略》,方钜成,姜桂侬著.

9. Chu Te：nuestro Comandante en Jefe. Pekin：Ediciones en Lenguas extranjeras, 1979. 95 p.；6 f.：fot. blanc i negra；22cm.

《回忆朱德同志》

10. Yo fui el ultimo emperador de China：de hijo del cielo a hombre nuevo/Pu Yi；[traducida y adaptada de la edición original por Richard Schirach y Mulan Lehner；traducción, Jesús Ruiz]. Barcelona：Circulo de Lectores, 1974. 508 p. ISBN：8422625237；8422625230

《我的前半生》,溥仪(Pu Yi, Ainsi Gioro, 1906—1967)；Schirach, Richard 和 Lehner, Mulan 改编；Ruiz, Jesús 译.

(1)[2a. ed.]. Barcelona：Luis de Caralt, 1987. 341 p.；20cm. ISBN：8421782134；8421782132. (Cultura histórica)

(2)Barcelona：Círculo de Lectores, 1988. 508 p.：il.；21cm. ISBN：8422625237 8422625230

11. De emperador a ciudadano：autobiografia de Aisin-Gioro Puyi/Aisin Gioro Puyi；tr. Yu Xitai. Beijing：Ediciones en Lenguas Extranjeras, 1991. 493 p.：il.；20cm. ISBN：7119009931；7119009933

《我的前半生》,溥仪(Pu Yi, Ainsi Gioro, 1906—1967)；Yu, Xitai 译.

12. Treinta años de mi vida：memorias de un excriminal de guerra de la camarilla de Jiang Jieshi/[Shen Zui；redacción de Shen Meijuan；tr. Li Deming.]. Beijing：Ediciones en Lenguas Extranjeras；[Hunan]：Editorial del Pueblo de Hunan, 1987. 325 p.：il.；19cm.

《我这三十年》,沈醉著,沈美娟整理.

13. El último eunuco de China：la vida de Sun Yaoting/por Jian Yinghua；traducido por José Raúl Macías Mosqueira. China China Intercontinental Press, 2014. 336 páginas ilustraciones, fotografías en blanco y negro 23cm. ISBN：7508523897, 750852389X. (Joyas de literatura contemporánea china)

《末代太监孙耀庭》,贾英华著；Macías Mosqueira, José 译. 五洲传播出版社.

N 类　自然科学

N1　科技概况

1. Cuatro grandes inventos en la antigüedad china. Pekín（Beijing）：Ediciones en Lenguas Extranjeras, 1989. 110 p.：il.；19cm. ISBN：7119008242, 7119008240

《中国古代的四大发明》

2. Hoang Ti Nei King＝Canon de medicina del Emperador Amarillo. Madrid：Las mil y una ediciones, 1982. 206 p.；22cm. ISBN：8485805054, 8485805051. (Mil y una medicinas；；5.)

《黄帝内经・灵枢》

3. El canon de las 81 dificultades del emperador amarillo：las preguntas mas importantes sobre acupuntura y medicina china/Roberto Gonzalez G. Mexico：Grijalbo, 2000. 182 pages：charts；23cm. ISBN：9700512231, 9700512235. (Acta Salmanticensia；Biblioteca de la salud)

《黄帝八十一难经》,Gonzalez G., Roberto 译.

N2　陶瓷

1. Ceramica porcelana de China：arte culture tradicionales de China/Zhiyan Li, Wen Cheng. Beijing：Ediciones en Lenguas Extranjeras, 1984. 181 pages：illustrations

《中国陶瓷》,李知宴,程雯著.

2. Cerámica China/Fang Lili；Traducido por Wang Hong-Xun y Fan Moxian. Beijing：China Intercontiental Press, 2011. 159 pages：illustrations (some color)；23cm. ISBN：7508520933, 7508520939. (Series de China Cultural)

《中国陶瓷》,方李莉著. 五洲传播出版社.

N3　饮食文化

1. Gastronomía China/[Lin Yongkuang]. Beijing：Editorial Nueva Estrella, 2004. 38, [1] pages：color illustrations；21cm. ISBN：7801485769, 7801485762. (China express；viaje multicultural a un país de cinco mil años)

《中华美食》,林永匡著. 新星出版社.

2. Manuales de cocina china：Conocimientos generales/por Tu Xi. Beijing：Ediciones en Lenguas Extranjeras, 2005. 172 p.：il.；18cm. ISBN：7119000596, 7119000594

《中国饮食习惯:西班牙文》,涂希著.

3. La comida China/by Liu Junru；traducido por Guo Hongkun. Beijing：China Intercontinental Press, 2011. 162 p.：il.；23cm. ISBN：7508520902, 7508520904. (Series de China Cultural)

《中国饮食》,刘军茹编著. 五洲传播出版社.

4. Manuales de cocina china：cien recetas/por Tu Xi. Beijing：Ediciones en Lenguas extranjeras, 2005. 237 p.：il.；20cm. ISBN：7119038131, 7119038133. (Manuales de cocina china)

《百样中菜：西班牙文》，涂希编著．

5. Platos al estilo Beijing/por Tu Xi. Beijing：Ediciones en Lenguas Extranjeras, 2005. 242 pages，［24］pages of plates：map, illustrations（chiefly color）；18cm. ISBN：7119038168, 7119038162. (Manuales de cocina china)

《北京菜：西班牙文》，涂希编著．

6. Platos al estilo Shandong/por Tu Xi. Beijing：Ediciones en Lenguas Extranjeras,2005. 206 pages，［24］pages of plates：map, illustrations（chiefly color）；18cm. 206 pages，［24］pages of plates：map, illustrations（chiefly color）；18cm. ISBN：711903815X, 7119038155. （Manuales de cocina china)

《山东菜：西班牙文》，涂希编著．

7. Platos al estilo Jiangsu/por Tu Xi. Beijing：Ediciones en Lenguas Extranjeras, 2005. 192 pages，［24］pages of plates：map, illustrations（chiefly color）；18cm. ISBN：7119038192, 7119038193. (Manuales de cocina china)

《江苏菜：西班牙文》，涂希编著．

8. Platos al estilo Anhui/por Tu Xi. Beijing：Ediciones en Lenguas Extranjeras,2004. 147 p.，［24］p. de lám.：il.；18cm. ISBN：7119038214, 7119038216, 7119138214. (Manuales de Cocina China)

《安徽菜：西班牙文》，涂希编著．

9. Platos al estilo Fujian/por Tu Xi. Beijing：Ediciones en Lenguas Extranjeras, 2005. 183 pages，［24］pages of plates：map, illustrations（chiefly color）；18cm. ISBN：7119038206, 7119038209. (Manuales de cocina china)

《福建菜：西班牙文》，涂希编著．

10. Platos al estilo Hunan/por Tu Xi. Beijing：Ediciones en Lenguas Extranjeras, 2005. 175 pages，［24］pages of plates：color illustrations maps；18cm. ISBN：7119038141, 7119038148. (Manuales de cocina China)

《湖南菜：西班牙文》，涂希编著．

11. Platos al estilo Guangdong/por Tu Xi. Beijing：Ediciones en Lenguas Extranjeras,2005. 222 p.，［24］p. de lám.：il.；18cm. ISBN：7119038176, 7119038179. (Manuales de Cocina China)

《广东菜：西班牙文》，涂希编著．

12. 中国茶/中国食品杂志社编.北京：外文出版社,1990. 158页；22cm. ISBN：7119007734

13. El té chino/Liu Tong；traducido por Yang Zhiping. Beijing：China Intercontinental Press, 2011. 165 p.：il.，col. ISBN：7508520797, 7508520793. (Series de China Cultural)

《中国茶》，刘彤著．五洲传播出版社．

14. El té Chino y la calobiótica/［edited by Liu Huichun；translated by Jiang Fengguang］. Beijing：Editorial Nueva Estrella, 2004. 37 pages：color illustrations；21cm. ISBN：7801486633,7801486639. (China express；viaje multicultural a un pais de cinco mil años)

《中国茶与养生之道》，刘惠春编．新星出版社．

15. 中国名酒.北京：新星出版社,1990. ISBN：7800850625

16. Vino chino/Li Zhengping；traducido por Guo Qingyu. Beijing：China Intercontinental Press, 2011. 152 p.：ill. (chiefly col.)；23cm. ISBN：7508520940, 7508520947. (Series de China Cultural)

《中国酒》，李争平著．五洲传播出版社．

Z 类　综合性文献

Z1　百科类

1. China：el mas mas/recopilado por Du Feibao. Beijing：Eliciones En Lenguas Extranjeras, 1990. 304 pages：illustrations（some color）；17cm. ISBN：7119007157, 7119007151

《中国之最》，杜飞豹著．

附录　中华学术外译项目立项名单

2010 年国家社科基金中华学术外译项目立项名单

序号	申请成果名称	著(编)者	申请人	工作单位	资助文版
1	中国哲学前沿(季刊)	韩震等	韩震	北京师范大学	英文
2	回到马克思——经济学语境中的哲学话语	张异宾	张异宾	南京大学	英文
3	在地如同在天——《论语》中的安身立命之道	颜钟祜	颜钟祜	杭州师范大学	英文
4	中国经济学前沿(季刊)	周立群、李长英等	高等教育出版社		英文
5	中国法学前沿(季刊)	朱文奇、何家弘、王晨光等	高等教育出版社		英文
6	中国历史学前沿(季刊)	李学勤等	高等教育出版社		英文
7	中国经济转型 30 年	蔡昉	社会科学文献出版社		英文
8	中国走向法治 30 年	蔡定剑、王晨光	社会科学文献出版社		英文
9	中国治理变迁 30 年	俞可平	社会科学文献出版社		英文
10	中国社会变迁 30 年	李强	社会科学文献出版社		英文
11	中国民间组织 30 年	王名	社会科学文献出版社		英文
12	中国佛教与传统文化	方立天	中国人民大学出版社		英文
13	简明中国经济史	贺耀敏	中国人民大学出版社		英文

2011 年国家社科基金中华学术外译项目立项名单(共 40 项)

序号	学科	项目名称	资助文版	项目负责人	工作单位
1	哲学	论全球化与文化自觉	英文	外语教学与研究出版社	
2		近代中国文化转型研究导论	英文	外语教学与研究出版社	
3		郭店竹简与中国早期的思想世界	英文	郭沂	中国社科院哲学所
4	经济学	中国经济改革发展之路	英文	外语教学与研究出版社	
5		中国宏观经济分析的理论体系	英文	中国人民大学出版社	
6		中国宏观经济分析与预测(2011—2012)	英文	中国人民大学出版社	
7		中国地方政府规模与结构优化研究	英文	中国人民大学出版社	
8		中国经济特区史论	英文	社会科学文献出版社	
9		中国农村金融论纲	英文	中国人民大学出版社	
10		中国通货膨胀的新特点、新机制、新政策与计量测算研究	英文	中国人民大学出版社	
11		中国西部减贫与可持续发展	英文	社会科学文献出版社	
12		中国民营企业国际化影响因素与模式选择	英文	肖文	浙江大学
13		中国人口与劳动	英文	社会科学文献出版社	
14		中国经济学人(期刊)	英文	《中国经济学人》编辑部	
15	法学	中国法治	英文	社会科学文献出版社	
16		中国冲突法	英文	肖永平	武汉大学
17		中国反垄断法	英文	社会科学文献出版社	
18		送法下乡——中国基层司法制度研究	英文	外语教学与研究出版社	
19		中国法律的传统与近代转型	英文	张立新	中国政法大学

续表

序号	学科	项目名称	资助文版	项目负责人	工作单位
20	社会学	中国社会	英文	社会科学文献出版社	
21		中国家庭史	英文	广东人民出版社	
22		中国生殖健康30年	英文	社会科学文献出版社	
23		社会生物学下的儒家思想	英文	外语教学与研究出版社	
24	国际问题研究	中国对外关系转型30年(1978—2008)	英文	社会科学文献出版社	
25		中国对外经济关系	英文	中国人民大学出版社	
26		中国—美国关系评论	英文	社会科学文献出版社	
27		外援在中国	英文	社会科学文献出版社	
28	中国历史	中国历代政治得失	英文	外语教学与研究出版社	
29		北平的历史地理	英文	外语教学与研究出版社	
30		中国历史地理学的理论与实践	英文	外语教学与研究出版社	
31		藏医学通史	英文	甄艳	中国中医科学院
32	宗教学	"全球化"的宗教与当代中国	英文	社会科学文献出版社	
33	图情文献学	中华人民共和国国情词典	英文	中国人民大学出版社	
34	管理学	在参与中成长的中国公民社会：基于浙江温州商会的研究	英文	郁建兴	浙江大学
35		中国工商管理研究前沿(期刊)	英文	高等教育出版社	
36		中国环境	英文	社会科学文献出版社	
37	教育学	中国教育	英文	社会科学文献出版社	
38		中国教育学前沿(期刊)	英文	高等教育出版社	
39	其他	为什么研究中国建筑	英文	外语教学与研究出版社	
40		中国园林	英文	外语教学与研究出版社	

2012年国家社科基金中华学术外译项目立项名单(第一批)

序号	项目名称	资助文版	申请人/单位
1	马克思主义若干重大问题研究	俄文	社会科学文献出版社
2	中国和平发展与构建和谐世界研究	俄文	社会科学文献出版社
3	科学发展观重大理论和实践问题研究	俄文	社会科学文献出版社
4	中国特色社会主义理论体系探源：从邓小平理论到科学发展观	俄文	社会科学文献出版社
5	民族复兴之路的回望与思考	俄文	社会科学文献出版社
6	走向历史的深处：马克思历史观研究	英文	中国人民大学出版社
7	为马克思辩护：对马克思哲学的一种新解释(第三版)	英文	中国人民大学出版社
8	价值论(第三版)	英文	李德顺(中国政法大学)
9	传统与现代之间：中国文化现代化的哲学省思	英文	北京师范大学出版社
10	凯德洛夫学说与中国自然辩证法事业的发展(1960—2010)	俄文	鲍鸥(清华大学)
11	中国的大国经济发展道路	英文	陆铭(复旦大学)
12	互联的关系型合约理论与中国奇迹	英文	王永钦(复旦大学)
13	当代中国经济改革教程	英文	上海远东出版社
14	中国：创新绿色发展	日文	中国人民大学出版社
15	中国区域经济差距和区域开发政策的研究	日文	于文浩(中国社科院经济研究所)
16	中国贸易运行报告(2011年版)	英文	上海人民出版社
17	2012中国民生发展报告：跨越变革世界中的"民生陷阱"	英文	北京师范大学出版社
18	中国低碳发展报告(2011—2012)	英文	社会科学文献出版社
19	应对气候变化报告(2011)	英文	社会科学文献出版社
20	超越人口红利	英文	社会科学文献出版社
21	中国特色社会主义人权保障制度研究	英文	孙平华(中国政法大学)
22	软法亦法：公共治理呼唤软法之治	英文	罗豪才(北京大学)

序号	项目名称	资助文版	申请人/单位
23	中国社会思想史新编	韩文	中国人民大学出版社
24	送医下乡:现代中国的医疗政治	英文	社会科学文献出版社
25	中国历史文化导论	英文	外语教学与研究出版社
26	四库全书馆研究	英文	北京师范大学出版社
27	中国近代史(半年刊)	英文	《中国近代史》(英文版)编辑部
28	中国文学研究前沿(季刊)	英文	高等教育出版社
29	楚辞考论	韩文	千金梅(南通大学)
30	敦煌变文校注	韩文	黄征(南京师范大学)
31	北京奥运的人文价值	韩文	中国人民大学出版社
32	中国雕塑	英文	外语教学与研究出版社
33	中国书法艺术	英文	高明乐(北京语言大学)
34	中国环境美学	英文	苏丰(湖南师范大学)

2012 年国家社科基金中华学术外译项目立项名单(第二批)

序号	项目名称	申请人	原著作者	资助文版
1	中国共产党怎样解决民族问题	外语教学与研究出版社	郝时远	英文
2	辩论"中国模式"	社会科学文献出版社	丁学良	日文
3	和为贵——中国政治学论集	外语教学与研究出版社	赵宝煦	英文
4	中国对外经济关系史	丁长清(南开大学)	丁长清等	英文
5	非均衡的中国经济	外语教学与研究出版社	厉以宁	英文
6	中国增长质量与减贫	社会科学文献出版社	王小林等	英文
7	当前中国社会利益问题研究	中国社会科学出版社	王伟光	英文
8	中国证券公司:现状与未来	中国人民大学出版社	吴晓求	英文
9	2012 中国绿色发展指数年度报告——省际比较	北京师范大学出版社	李晓西等	英文
10	中国外商投资企业运营状况	社会科学文献出版社	裴长洪等	英文
11	在华外资企业经营与税收实务	杨华(中央财经大学)	杨华	日文
12	中国公司法	陈景善(中国政法大学)	赵旭东	日文
13	创造性介入——中国外交新取向	北京大学出版社	王逸舟	韩文
14	南沙争端的由来与发展	吴士存(中国南海研究院)	吴士存	英文
15	中国民众的国际观	社会科学文献出版社	李慎明等	英文
16	苏联专家在中国	社会科学文献出版社	沈志华	俄文
17	中国生态移民:一个典型案例研究	北京大学出版社	谢元媛	英文
18	当代中国社会分层:测量与分析	北京师范大学出版社	李强	英文
19	中国的制度变迁和农村工业化	周飞舟(北京大学)	周飞舟	英文
20	小村故事——中国当代农村的变迁	朱晓阳(北京大学)	朱晓阳	英文
21	中国教育	北京师范大学出版社	袁贵仁	英文
22	中国教育政策的形成与变迁——1978—2007 的教育政策话语分析	文雯(清华大学)	文雯	英文
23	回向传统:儒学的哲思	北京师范大学出版社	陈来	英文
24	中国思想史——1895 年之前中国的知识、思想与信仰世界	葛兆光(复旦大学)	葛兆光	英文
25	启蒙如何起死回生——现代中国知识分子的思想困境	北京大学出版社	许纪霖	韩文
26	裂变中的传承——20 世纪前期的中国文化与学术	中华书局	罗志田	英文
27	西方与中国——西学在晚清中国的传播	方维规(北京师范大学)	方维规	德文
28	中国文化的传播者——钢和泰学术评传	王启龙(陕西师范大学)	王启龙、邓小咏	英文
29	中国现代文学思潮史	权赫律(吉林大学)	刘中树、许祖华	韩文

续表

序号	项目名称	申请人	原著作者	资助文版
30	中国当代文学史	陈思和(复旦大学)	陈思和	英文
31	中西诗歌比较研究	中国人民大学出版社	茅于美	俄文
32	中西文学相遇——比较文学与比较文化论集	外语教学与研究出版社	乐黛云	英文
33	美学与艺术:比较视野下的中国传统与现代	外语教学与研究出版社	高建平	英文
34	中国古戏台研究与保护	北京出版集团文津出版社	周华斌等	英文
35	影像时代:中国电影简史	柳若梅(北京外国语大学)	丁亚平	俄文
36	中国古都	外语教学与研究出版社	王贵祥等	英文
37	中国宗教思想通论	任晓礼(鲁东大学)	詹石窗	韩文
38	开启中华文明的管钥	北京师范大学出版社	黄德宽	英文
39	汉语历史音韵学	潘悟云(上海师范大学)	潘悟云	韩文

2013 年国家社科基金中华学术外译项目立项名单(第一批)

序号	项目名称	资助文版	申请人/单位
1	苏联解体二十周年祭	俄文	社会科学文献出版社
2	中国特色社会主义概论	英文	文津出版社
3	为马克思辩护:对马克思哲学的一种新解释	德文	中国人民大学出版社
4	文本的深度犁耕:后马克思思潮哲学文本解读	德文	中国人民大学出版社
5	回到列宁	德文	中国人民大学出版社
6	有无之境:王阳明哲学的精神	英文	北京大学出版社
7	超越市场与超越政府——论道德力量在经济中的作用	英文	外语教学与研究出版社
8	中国经济改革发展报告(2012)	英文	中国人民大学出版社
9	改革红利——十八大后转型与改革的五大趋势	英文	五洲传播出版社
10	中国企业社会责任研究报告	英文	社会科学文献出版社
11	新中国人权保障发展 60 年	英文	中国社会科学出版社
12	中国宪法学说史研究	韩文	中国人民大学出版社
13	2013 年中国社会形势分析与预测	英文	社会科学文献出版社
14	公正和平:中国乡土社会的权威多元与纠纷解决	英文	外语教学与研究出版社
15	中国民族的生活方式	英文	中国社会科学出版社
16	20 世纪的中国民族问题	日文	朴银姬(鲁东大学)
17	世界孔子庙研究	韩文	林丽(鲁东大学)
18	中国史学思想史导论	英文	外语教学与研究出版社
19	秦汉文化风景	俄文	中国人民大学出版社
20	宋辽西夏金社会生活史	英文	中国社会科学出版社
21	从耶鲁到东京:为南京大屠杀取证	韩文	池水涌(华中师范大学)
22	中国与西班牙关系史	西班牙文	五洲传播出版社
23	中国科学考古学的兴起:1928—1949 年历史语言研究所考古史	韩文	李永男(广西师范大学)
24	鲁东南沿海地区系统考古调查报告	英文	方辉(山东大学)
25	中国宗教通史	英文	中国社会科学出版社
26	莫言文学思考	日文	林敏洁(南京师范大学)
27	中国少数民族人类起源神话研究	英文	徐鲁亚(中央民族大学)
28	中国筝——20 至 21 世纪的嬗变	英文	孙卓(陕西师范大学)
29	中国社会科学(英文版)	英文	中国社会科学杂志社

2013 年国家社科基金中华学术外译项目立项名单(第二批)

序号	项目名称	资助文版	申请人/单位
1	马克思主义经济危机和周期理论的结构与变迁	英文	中国人民大学出版社
2	中国共产党和中国特色外交理论与实践	韩文	李春虎(上海外国语大学)
3	万水朝东:中国政党制度全景	英文	五洲传播出版社
4	周易概论	英文	张文智(山东大学)
5	善的历程——儒家价值体系研究	韩文	中国人民大学出版社
6	爱与思——生活儒学的观念	英文	李学宁(江南大学)
7	离异与回归——传统文化与近代化关系试析	俄文	中国人民大学出版社
8	中国现代哲学文化论集	英文	外语教学与研究出版社
9	中国近代银行制度变迁及其绩效研究	英文	中国人民大学出版社
10	低估还是高估——人民币均衡有效汇率测算研究	英文	王时芬(上海大学)
11	中国对外直接投资与全球价值链升级	英文	中国人民大学出版社
12	中国农村发展道路	日文	宋晓凯(曲阜师范大学)
13	家庭承包制视角下农户合作金融制度研究	英文	中国财政经济出版社
14	中国低碳发展报告(2013)	英文	社会科学文献出版社
15	理解中国政治	英文	中国社会科学出版社
16	中国集体领导体制	日文	中国人民大学出版社
17	当代中国法学研究	英文	中国社会科学出版社
18	中国法学向何处去	英文	林曦(复旦大学)
19	中国的呐喊:陈安论国际经济法	英文	陈安(厦门大学)
20	当代中国社会建设	英文	社会科学文献出版社
21	制度、市场与中国农村发展	英文	中国人民大学出版社
22	中国环境发展报告(2013)	英文	社会科学文献出版社
23	中国侗族传统稻作文化研究	韩文	崔海洋(贵州大学)
24	中国援外 60 年	英文	社会科学文献出版社
25	人民币国际化报告(2012)	日文	中国人民大学出版社
26	钓鱼岛主权归属考	英文	外语教学与研究出版社
27	当代中国农村改革实录	英文	外语教学与研究出版社
28	中国新疆历史与现状	英文	五洲传播出版社
29	史学、经学与思想:在世界史背景下对于中国古代历史文化的思考	英文	北京师范大学出版社
30	施善与教化:明清时期的慈善组织	英文	北京师范大学出版社
31	中法建交始末	法文	黄山书社
32	中古文学理论范畴	英文	黄永亮(河北大学)
33	当代中国审美文化	韩文	金菊花(山东大学)
34	五四前后英诗汉译的社会文化研究	英文	蒙兴灿(浙江理工大学)
35	汉字传播史	韩文	全香兰(鲁东大学)
36	中国教育发展报告(2013)	英文	社会科学文献出版社
37	中国现代美术之路	英文	外语教学与研究出版社
38	中国传统室内装饰与陈设	俄文	江崇岩(浙江大学)

2014 年第一批国家社科基金中华学术外译项目立项名单

序号	学科	项目名称	资助文版	申请人/单位
1	马列科社	毛泽东的成功之道	俄文	社会科学文献出版社
2		中国特色社会主义史论研究——前沿问题	俄文	社会科学文献出版社
3		马克思主义哲学基础理论研究	英文	北京师范大学出版社
4		找回失去的"哲学自我"	韩文	元永浩(吉林大学)
5		中国正义论的重建	英文	侯萍萍(山东大学)
6	哲学	当代中国哲学研究 1949—2009	英文	中国社会科学出版社
7		中国美学史	英文	宁海林(浙江理工大学)
8		百年中国美学史略	俄文	北京大学出版社
9		中国国家资本的历史分析	英文	中国社会科学出版社
10	理论经济	中国资本市场制度变革研究	英文	中国人民大学出版社
11		改革、转型与增长:观察与解释	英文	北京师范大学出版社
12		吴敬琏文集	英文	中央编译出版社
13	应用经济	中国农村可持续发展问题研究	英文	秦炳涛(复旦大学)
14		中国人口与劳动问题报告 No.14	英文	社会科学文献出版社
15	政治学	冷战与新中国外交的缘起 1949—1955	英文	社会科学文献出版社
16		民主在中国	英文	中央编译出版社
17		法治社会的基本人权——发展权法律制度研究	日文	吕卫清(华中师范大学)
18	法学	侵权责任法立法研究	英文	王灏(中国法学杂志社)
19		WTO 知识产权协议在中国的实施	法文	冯术杰(清华大学)
20		跨文化视野:中国特色和谐社会的探索	俄文	李申申(河南大学)
21	社会学	银翅:中国的地方社会与文化变迁	英文	庄孔韶(浙江大学)
22		空间、现代化与社会互动:北京胡同的生活	英文	外语教学与研究出版社
23	宗教学	中国北方民族萨满教研究	英文	梁艳君(大连民族学院)
24		毛泽东对新中国的历史贡献	俄文	社会科学文献出版社
25		孔子与 20 世纪中国	英文	中国社会科学出版社
26	中国历史	权势转移:近代中国的思想与社会(修订版)	英文	北京师范大学出版社
27		西藏简明通史	英文	五洲传播出版社
28	考古学	中国史前神格人面岩画	英文	上海人民出版社
29		中国诗歌史通论	日文	李均洋(首都师范大学)
30		中国诗歌史通论	韩文	金京善(北京外国语大学)
31		儒、释、道的生态智慧与艺术诉求	韩文	金哲(山东大学(威海))
32		中国宗教艺术论:传统文化的视野	英文	王心洁(暨南大学)
33	中国文学	中华古代文论的现代阐释	韩文	中国人民大学出版社
34		中国现代主义诗潮史论	韩文	北京大学出版社
35		贬谪文化与贬谪文学	日文	尚永亮(武汉大学)
36		中西比较诗学	俄文	中国人民大学出版社
37		论契合——中西文学与翻译	英文	外语教学与研究出版社
38	新闻学与传播学	当代中国出版改革中的知识劳工	英文	姚建华(中国浦东干部学院)
39	教育学	嵌入村庄的学校	英文	教育科学出版社
40		历史的背影:一代女知识分子的教育记忆	英文	教育科学出版社
41	艺术学	卷轴书法形制源流考述	韩文	吴晓明(浙江大学)

2014 年第二批国家社科基金中华学术外译项目立项公示名单

序号	学科	项目名称	申请文版	申请人/单位
1	马列科社	中国特色社会主义论	英文	高等教育出版社
2		中国道路——不一样的现代化道路	韩文	朴英姬(青岛大学)
3	哲学	《巴黎手稿》研究——马克思思想的转折点	英文	韩立新(清华大学)
4		新纲常	英文	四川人民出版社
5		艺境	韩文	李晓娜(鲁东大学)
6	理论经济	中国公共财政建设指标体系研究	英文	社会科学文献出版社
7		线性经济理论与中国经济的大道路径	日文	李帮喜(清华大学)
8		中国的长期经济发展:政府治理与制度演进的视角	英文	赵红军(上海对外经贸大学)
10		改革是中国最大的红利	韩文	金成根(青岛大学)
9	应用经济	破解中国经济发展之谜	英文	中国社会科学出版社
11		中国城市转型:基于六个典型城市的思考	英文	陈元志(中国浦东干部学院)
12	政治学	中国特色社会主义理论体系形成与发展大事记	俄文	社会科学文献出版社
13		中国城市与区域治理:发展过程、政策与政治	英文	叶林(中山大学)
14		中国共产党和中国特色外交理论与实践	阿拉伯文	陈杰(上海外国语大学)
15		民主的中国经验	日文	中国社会科学出版社
16		中国人权建设 60 年	德文	江西人民出版社
17		中国援外 60 年	韩文	金日山(聊城大学)
18	法学	中央与特别行政区关系——一种法治结构的解析	英文	外语教学与研究出版社有限责任公司
19		历史性共同标准的达成——张彭春与世界人权宣言	英文	孙平华(中国政法大学)
20	社会学	中国社会学经典导读	法文	社会科学文献出版社
21		一个华北村落的百年变迁	英文	林聚任(山东大学)
22		国家调整农民工社会政策研究	日文	李文哲(烟台大学)
23	民族问题研究	中国民族志	英文	杨圣敏(中央民族大学)
24		中国民俗学	英文	上海故事会文化传媒有限公司
25		中国面具史	英文	肖唐金(贵州民族大学)
26	国际问题研究	中国学者论世界经济与国际政治	英文	社会科学文献出版社
27		创造性介入:中国之全球角色的生成	韩文	北京大学出版社
28	中国历史	宅兹中国:重建关于"中国"的历史论述	英文	中华书局有限公司
29		中国计量史	德文	关增建(上海交通大学)
30		楚史	英文	中国人民大学出版社有限公司
31		西藏简明通史	日文	五洲传播出版社
32		想象西藏——跨文化视野中的和尚、活佛、喇嘛和密教	英文	北京师范大学出版社(集团)有限公司
33		中国近三百年学术史	英文	钱纪芳(浙江理工大学)
34		北京大学创办史实考源	韩文	陈艳平(大连外国语大学)
35		抗日战争时期重庆大轰炸研究	日文	潘洵(西南大学)
36	世界历史	孔子孟子的政治学——《论语》与《孟子七篇》	英文	李晓东(东北师范大学)
37	宗教学	中国佛教与传统文化	英文	中国人民大学出版社有限公司
38	中国文学	中国审美文化史	英文	翟江月(鲁东大学)
39		晚唐钟声:中国文学的原型批评	韩文	杨磊(北京第二外国语学院)
40		宋代散文研究	日文	李雪涛(北京外国语大学)
41		现代中国与少数民族文学	日文	陈朝辉(南开大学)
42		"笔部队"和侵华战争:对日本侵华文学的研究与批判	英文	张润晗(中央财经大学)
43	语言学	全球化的中国"声音"	英文	董洁(清华大学)
44	管理学	中国劳动与社会保障体制完善与发展道路	日文	权庆梅(曲阜师范大学)
45		中国旅游文化史纲	英文	马勇(湖北大学)

2015 年国家社科基金中华学术外译项目立项公示名单

序号	学科	项目名称（中文）	原著作者或主编	资助文版	申请人
1	马列·科社	马克思主义整体性研究	逄锦聚	英文	王传英（南开大学）
2		为马克思辩护：对马克思哲学的一种新解释	杨耕	俄文	中国人民大学出版社
3		走向历史的深处：马克思历史观研究	陈先达	俄文	中国人民大学出版社
4		谁是罪魁祸首——追求生态危机的根源	陈学明	英文	吴丽环（华东理工大学）
5	哲学	中国哲学精神重建之路：马克思主义哲学中国化探讨	王南湜	韩文	北京师范大学出版社
6		回归原创之思——"象思维"视野下的中国智慧	王树人	英文	王树人（中国社科院哲学研究所）
7		历史中的哲学	杨国荣	法文	姜丹丹（上海交通大学）
8		简帛文明与古代思想世界	王中江	英文	王中江（北京大学）
9		老子注译及评介	陈鼓应	英文	中华书局
10		中国禅宗思想发展史	麻天祥	英文	高等教育出版社
11		明代哲学史	张学智	英文	高等教育出版社
12		离异与回归——传统文化与近代化关系试析	章开沅	韩文	中国人民大学出版社
13		21 世纪儒学的概念重构	姚新中	英文	高等教育出版社
14		和合哲学论	张立文	韩文	人民出版社
15		中国逻辑研究	孙中原	英文	高等教育出版社
16		中国艺术哲学	朱志荣	德文	华东师范大学出版社
17		江南古代都会建筑与生态美学	王耘	韩文	王耘（苏州大学）
18		南画十六观	朱良志	日文	北京大学出版社
19		比较哲学与跨文化哲学之必要条件及方法论	马琳	英文	马琳（中国人民大学）
20	理论经济	中国经济改革发展之路	厉以宁	西班牙文	外语教学与研究出版社
21		经济改革与发展之中国道路	洪银兴	英文	高等教育出版社
22		论新常态	李扬张晓晶	英文	人民出版社
23		新结构经济学：反思经济发展与政策的理论框架（增订版）	林毅夫	韩文	张红英（山东师范大学）
24		经济与政治研究	陈雨露	英文	经济与政治研究编辑部（中国人民大学）
25		中国与世界经济	余永定	英文	中国与世界经济编辑部（中国社科院）
26		中国发展成本论	胡光宇	韩文	人民出版社
27		中国民营经济制度创新与发展	李维安	英文	经济科学出版社
28		内需可持续增长的结构基础与政策选择	杨瑞龙	英文	中国人民大学出版社
29		中国通货膨胀新机制研究	刘元春	韩文	中国人民大学出版社
30		超主权国际货币的构建：国际货币制度的改革	李翀	英文	北京师范大学出版社
31		论政府超前引领——对世界区域经济发展的理论与探索	陈云贤邱建伟	英文	雍和明（广东金融学院）
32		中国的早期近代经济——1820 年代华亭-娄县地区GDP 研究	李伯重	英文	浙江大学出版社
33	应用经济	中国梦与中国道路	周天勇	阿拉伯文	叶良英（北京外国语大学）
34		破解中国经济发展之谜	蔡昉	韩文	中国社会科学出版社
35		中国的环境治理与生态建设	潘家华	英文	中国社会科学出版社
36		中国粮食安全与农业走出去战略研究	韩俊	日文	安同信（济南大学）
37		中国农业经营制度	罗必良	日文	徐哲根（青岛大学）
38		人民币区研究	霍伟东	韩文	人民出版社

序号	学科	项目名称(中文)	原著作者或主编	资助文版	申请人
39	政治学	中国震撼:一个文明型国家的崛起	张维为	西班牙文	五洲传播出版社
40		国家底线:公平正义与依法治国	俞可平	俄文	中央编译出版社
41		毛泽东国际政治理论与实践研究	孙君健	英文	中国社会科学出版社
42		当代中国意识形态变迁	刘少杰	英文	中央编译出版社
43		中国对民主的长期求索	林冈	英文	林冈(上海交通大学)
44		比较政治文化导论	佟德志	英文	高等教育出版社
45		中国和平发展与构建和谐世界研究	李景治	俄文	中国人民大学出版社
46		世界权力的转移——道义现实主义的国际关系理论	阎学通	英文	阎学通(清华大学)
47	社会学	乡土中国 乡土重建	费孝通	日文	诸葛蔚东(中国科学院大学)
48		当代中国社会建设	陆学艺	韩文	郑顺姬(聊城大学)
49		中国社会巨变和治理	李培林	英文	中国社会科学出版社
50		多元城镇化与中国发展	李强	英文	社会科学文献出版社
51	法学	中国特色社会主义民主法治研究	孙国华	英文	中国人民大学出版社
52		中国法律制度	李林	英文	中国社会科学出版社
53		法治秩序的建构	季卫东	英文	商务印书馆
54		民法基本原则解释:诚信原则的历史、实务、法理研究	徐国栋	日文	徐国栋(厦门大学)
55		无形财产权基本问题研究	吴汉东	韩文	董新义(中央财经大学)
56		合同法	王利明	英文	中国人民大学出版社
57		短缺证据与模糊事实——证据学精要	何家弘	英文	法律出版社
58	国际问题研究	创造性介入:中国外交新取向	王逸舟	英文	北京大学出版社
59		文化的帝国:20世纪全球"美国化"研究	王晓德	英文	中国社会科学出版社
60	中国历史	中国文化史——一部中国古代文化的说明书	吕思勉	韩文	刘晓丽(鲁东大学)
61		中国文化要义	梁漱溟	日文	徐青(浙江理工大学)
62		中国历史地理纲要	史念海	日文	曹婷(陕西师范大学)
63		中国古代国家的起源与王权的形成	王震中	日文	王震中(中国社科院历史研究所)
64		秦汉称谓研究	王子今	英文	中国社会科学出版社
65		汉代的谣言	吕宗力	英文	浙江大学出版社
66		匈奴通史	林干	英文	段满福(内蒙古大学)
67		中国道教科学技术史·汉魏两晋卷	姜生、汤伟侠	英文	科学出版社
68		唐代史学论稿(增订本)	瞿林东	英文	高等教育出版社
69		清代学术源流	陈祖武	韩文	陈媛(山东大学)
70		商人与中国近世社会	唐力行	英文	商务印书馆
71		巴黎和会与中国外交	唐启华	英文	社会科学文献出版社
72		天朝官员在巴黎——晚清中国驻法外交官研究,1878—1912	马骥	法文	马骥(宁波大学)
73		南京大屠杀史	张宪文	韩文	尹盛龙(南京师范大学)
74		当代中国近代史研究(1949—2009)	曾业英	英文	中国社会科学出版社
75		近代中国文化转型研究导论	耿云志	韩文	李浩(山东师范大学)
76		中国文人画史	卢辅圣	英文	上海书画出版社
77		中国金融思想史	姚遂	英文	上海交通大学出版社
78		敦煌学十八讲	荣新江	俄文	北京大学出版社
79		丝绸之路考古十五讲	林梅村	俄文	北京大学出版社
80		丝绸之路戏剧文化研究	李强	英文	高芬(陕西师范大学)

续表

序号	学科	项目名称（中文）	原著作者或主编	资助文版	申请人
81	世界历史	中国抗战在世界反法西斯战争中的历史地位	胡德坤	英文	冯捷蕴（对外经济贸易大学）
82		冷战与新中国外交的缘起 1949—1955	牛军	日文	社会科学文献出版社
83		非洲踏寻郑和路	李新烽	英文	中国社会科学出版社
84	考古学	最早的中国	许宏	英文	科学出版社
85	民族问题研究	中国共产党怎样解决民族问题	郝时远	韩文	金春子（青岛大学）
86		中国民俗史（先秦卷）	晁福林	韩文	范伟利（济南大学）
87		西藏风土志	赤烈曲扎	韩文	金向德（民族团结杂志社）
88	宗教学	中国宗教与文化战略	卓新平	日文	社会科学文献出版社
89		清代藏传佛教研究	孕藏加	英文	中国社会科学出版社
90	中国文学	人间词话七讲	叶嘉莹	俄文	柳若梅（北京外国语大学）
91		文学史的命名与文学史观的反思	张福贵	韩文	张英美（延边大学）
92		无边的挑战——中国先锋文学的后现代性	陈晓明	英文	陈晓明（北京大学）
93		中国文学中的世界性因素	陈思和	韩文	李明学（青岛大学）
94		莫言文学思想	莫言	韩文	李红梅（南京师范大学）
95	语言学	商周文化比较研究	王晖	英文	马珂（陕西师范大学）
96		汉语语法学	邢福义	英文	王勇（华中师范大学）
97		方言与中国文化	周振鹤 游汝杰	英文	吴学忠（浙江越秀外国语学院）
98		藏文字符研究	江荻、龙从军	英文	丁志斌（吉首大学）
99	新闻学与传播学	符号中国	隋岩	英文	隋岩（中国传媒大学）
100	人口学	中国人口：结构与规模的博弈	莫龙 韦宇红	英文	社会科学文献出版社
101		中国的低生育率与人口可持续发展	郭志刚	英文	中国社会科学出版社
102	管理学	全球经济调整中的中国经济增长与宏观调控体系研究	黄达	英文	经济科学出版社
103		金融市场全球化下的中国金融监管体系改革	曹凤岐	英文	经济科学出版社
104		中国应急管理：理论、实践、政策	童星	英文	社会科学文献出版社
105		京杭大运河国家遗产与生态廊道	俞孔坚	韩文	刘畅（山东大学）
106	教育学	教育学的探究	瞿葆奎	英文	高等教育出版社
107		知识转型与教育改革	石中英	英文	高等教育出版社
108		回归突破——"生命·实践"教育学论纲	叶澜	英文	高等教育出版社
109	艺术学	影视文化论稿	胡智峰	英文	金海娜（中国传媒大学）
110		中国少数民族电影史	饶曙光	英文	吴碧宇（华东理工大学）
111		中国绘画思想史	赵友斌	英文	赵友斌（暨南大学）
112		中国陶瓷史	方李莉	英文	外语教学与研究出版社
113		中国书法风格史	徐利明	韩文	徐利明（南京艺术学院）
114		中国现代美术之路	潘公凯	韩文	北京大学出版社

2016 年国家社科基金中华学术外译项目立项名单公示

序号	资助文版	项目名称(中文)	申请人	原著作者或主编	学科
1		中国道路:不一样的现代化道路	王绍祥(福建师范大学)	贺新元	马列·科社
2		全面深化改革二十论	社会科学文献出版社	李培林	马列·科社
3		发展中的社会主义理论与实践	中国人民大学出版社	张雷声、武京闽	马列·科社
4		民族复兴的价值支撑——社会主义核心价值观研究	高等教育出版社	郭建宁	马列·科社
5		中国共产党少数民族文化建设研究	史湘琳(江西财经大学)	李资源	党史·党建
6		中国传统伦理思想史	魏啸飞(上海交通大学)	朱贻庭	哲学
7		金匮要略译注	刘蔼韵(上海中医药大学)	(汉)张仲景著 刘蔼韵译注	哲学
8		说明、定律与因果	王巍(清华大学)	王巍	哲学
9		国家命运:中国未来经济转型与改革发展	中央编译出版社	吴敬琏、厉以宁等	理论经济
10		加快推进中国对外经济发展方式转变研究	北京师范大学出版社	李翀	理论经济
11		中国国家资产负债表 2015:杠杆调整与风险管理	中国社会科学出版社	李扬	理论经济
12		中国粮食安全与农业走出去战略研究	盛美娟(烟台大学)	韩俊	应用经济
13		经济转型和民生	中国社会科学出版社	赵人伟	应用经济
14		走中国特色的新型城镇化道路	社会科学文献出版社	魏后凯	应用经济
15		中国民营企业发展新论	社会科学文献出版社	刘迎秋	应用经济
16	英文	在新起点上全面推进依法治国	中国社会科学出版社	李林	政治学
17		中国"一带一路"战略的政治经济学	邹磊(中共上海市委党校)	邹磊	政治学
18		中国社会转型与国家治理——理论、路径与政策过程	外语教学与研究出版社	徐湘林	政治学
19		中国官僚政治研究	李克(山东大学)	王亚南	政治学
20		中国崛起与亚洲地区市场构建	社会科学文献出版社	赵江林	政治学
21		物权法研究	中国人民大学出版社	王利明	法学
22		中国宪法学说史研究	中国人民大学出版社	韩大元	法学
23		中国财产法:原理、政策与实践	申卫星(清华大学)	申卫星	法学
24		中国非法证据排除制度:原理·案例·适用	法律出版社	戴长林等	法学
25		代议制度比较研究	马萧(武汉大学)	周叶中	法学
26		中国古代契约思想史	刘云生(西南政法大学)	刘云生	法学
27		中国社会学经典导读	社会科学文献出版社	李培林、渠敬东	社会学
28		中国慈善捐赠机制研究	向平(鲁东大学)	高鉴国	社会学
29		中国文化要义	李明(广东外语外贸大学)	梁漱溟	社会学
30		普遍整合的福利体系	中国社会科学出版社	景天魁	社会学
31		走向人人享有保障的社会:当代中国社会保障的制度变迁	中国社会科学出版社	周弘	社会学
32		中国社会结构与社会建设	中国社会科学出版社	陆学艺	社会学
33		中国藏学	《中国藏学》编辑部	黄维忠	民族问题研究
34		创造性介入:中国之全球角色的生成	北京大学出版社	王逸舟	国际问题研究

续表

序号	资助文版	项目名称(中文)	申请人	原著作者或主编	学科
35		中国国际问题研究	《国际问题研究》编辑部	阮宗泽	国际问题研究
36		钓鱼岛列屿之历史与法理研究	海洋出版社	郑海麟	国际问题研究
37		能源外交概论	社会科学文献出版社	王海运、许勤华	国际问题研究
38		跨越战后:日本的战争责任认识	五洲传播出版社	步平	国际问题研究
39		中国古代国家的起源与王权的形成	中国社会科学出版社	王震中	中国历史
40		中国财政思想史	上海交通大学出版社	孙文学	中国历史
41		中华文明探源的神话学研究	贾卉(华东理工大学)	叶舒宪	中国历史
42		孙中山传	付永钢(暨南大学)	张磊、张苹	中国历史
43		李度日记(1943—1945):亲眼见证的中国革命和战争	张志云(上海交通大学)	张志云	中国历史
44		中国历史地理纲要	操林英(陕西师范大学)	史念海	中国历史
45		汉代学术史论	李银波(武汉理工大学)	熊铁基	中国历史
46		隐匿的疆土——卫所制与明帝国	宁平(辽宁师范大学)	顾诚	中国历史
47		尚书译注	何如月(陕西师范大学)	(清)阮元校订	中国历史
48		天学外史	上海交通大学出版社	江晓原	中国历史
49		世界古典文明史杂志	《世界古典文明史杂志》编辑部	张强	世界历史
50	英文	中国史前聚落群聚形态研究	上海交通大学出版社	裴安平	考古学
51		中国人的宗教信仰	中国社会科学出版社	卓新平	宗教学
52		人间词话七讲	北京大学出版社	叶嘉莹	中国文学
53		追寻中国的"现代":"多元变革时代"中国小说研究 1937—1949	中国社会科学出版社	王晓平	中国文学
54		《乌布西奔妈妈》研究	中国社会科学出版社	郭淑云	中国文学
55		中国民间故事史	胡文芝(暨南大学)	刘守华	中国文学
56		日本右翼历史观批判研究	胡婉(中央财经大学)	王向远	中国文学
57		中国传统译论经典诠释——从道安到傅雷	王晓农(鲁东大学)	王宏印	语言学
58		中国武术史	黄福华(江西师范大学)	国家体委武术研究院	体育学
59		东方管理学	苏宗伟(上海外国语大学)	苏东水	管理学
60		中国企业:转型升级	高等教育出版社	毛蕴诗	管理学
61		中国教育:研究与评论	教育科学出版社	丁钢	教育学
62		蔡元培教育文集	高等教育出版社	蔡元培	教育学
63		钟启泉教育文集	高等教育出版社	钟启泉	教育学
64		黄济、李秉德、鲁洁、王逢贤教育文集	高等教育出版社	黄济等	教育学
65		中国科举文化	余卫华(浙江越秀外国语学院)	刘海峰	教育学
66		陈鹤琴教育箴言	华东师范大学出版社	陈鹤琴	教育学
67		中国传统音乐概论	张伯瑜(中央音乐学院)	袁静芳	艺术学
68		中国电影市场发展史	邵志洪(华东理工大学)	饶曙光	艺术学
69		中国戏剧史 中国剧场史	李佐文(中国传媒大学)	周贻白	艺术学

序号	资助文版	项目名称(中文)	申请人	原著作者或主编	学科
70	法文	东西文化及其哲学	商务印书馆	梁漱溟	哲学
71		金翼:中国家族制度的社会学研究	唐果(四川外国语大学)	林耀华	社会学
72		中国教育的文化基础	高等教育出版社	顾明远	教育学
73	俄文	回到马克思	江苏人民出版社	张一兵	哲学
74		中国艺术哲学	华东师范大学出版社	朱志荣	哲学
75		中西美学与文化精神	中国人民大学出版社	张法	哲学
76		中国集体领导体制	中国人民大学出版社	胡鞍钢	政治学
77		冷战与新中国外交的缘起	社会科学文献出版社	牛军	政治学
78		中国特色社会主义民主法治研究	中国人民大学出版社	孙国华	法学
79		中华人民共和国刑法的孕育诞生和发展完善	庞冬梅(黑龙江大学)	高铭暄	法学
80		当代中国社会建设	社会科学文献出版社	陆学艺	社会学
81		中国民众的国际观	社会科学文献出版社	李慎明	国际问题研究
82		建设新中国的蓝图	社会科学文献出版社	陈扬勇	中国历史
83		全球史中的文化中国	北京大学出版社	陈来等	中国历史
84		丝绸之路与东西文化交流	北京大学出版社	荣新江	中国历史
85		中国历史地理纲要	陶源(陕西师范大学)	史念海	中国历史
86		中国抗战在世界反法西斯战争中的历史地位	朱红琼(吉林财经大学)	胡德坤	世界历史
87		中国当代文学主潮	北京大学出版社	陈晓明	中国文学
88		中国民间文学概要	北京大学出版社	段宝林	中国文学
89		文学伦理学批评导论	周露(浙江大学)	聂珍钊	外国文学
90		中国"海上丝绸之路"研究百年回顾	刘柏威(黑龙江大学)	龚缨晏	语言学
91		符号中国	中国人民大学出版社	隋岩	新闻学与传播学
92		解读敦煌·中世纪服饰	田秀坤(大连外国语大学)	谭蝉雪	艺术学
93	西班牙文	"当代中国"丛书	高源(北京第二外国语学院)	金帛、李文等	社会学
94		庞迪我与中国	中国社会科学出版社	张铠	世界历史
95	阿拉伯文	解读中国经济新常态	社会科学文献出版社	李扬、蔡昉	理论经济
96		韩非子	王有勇(上海外国语大学)	韩非	哲学
97	德文	乡土中国、生育制度	外语教学与研究出版社	费孝通	社会学
98	日文	中国道路:不一样的现代化道路	朴京玉(青岛农业大学)	贺新元	马列·科社
99		传统与现代:人文主义的视野	谭仁岸(广东外语外贸大学)	陈来	哲学
100		思想史中的日本与中国	上海交通大学出版社	孙歌	哲学
101		论新常态	人民出版社	李扬、张晓晶	理论经济
102		从人口红利到改革红利	社会科学文献出版社	蔡昉	理论经济
103		走中国特色的新型城镇化道路	社会科学文献出版社	魏后凯	应用经济
104		当代中国社会建设	社会科学文献出版社	陆学艺	社会学
105		中国社会巨变和治理	罗小娟(上海政法学院)	李培林	社会学
106		多元城镇化与中国发展	社会科学文献出版社	李强	社会学
107		中国应急管理:理论、实践、政策	社会科学文献出版社	童星	社会学
108		中国人口:结构与规模的博弈	社会科学文献出版社	莫龙	人口学
109		跨越战后:日本的战争责任认识	五洲传播出版社	步平	国际问题研究

续表

序号	资助文版	项目名称（中文）	申请人	原著作者或主编	学科
110	日文	"儒教国家"日本的实像	孙耀珠（华南师范大学）	李卓	世界历史
111		古典禅研究——中唐至五代禅宗发展新探	上海人民出版社	贾晋华	宗教学
112		宋代文学传播探原	王兆鹏（武汉大学）	王兆鹏	中国文学
113		中国语言生活状况报告（2015）	杨春宇（辽宁师范大学）	教育部语言信息管理司	语言学
114		汉语史稿	中华书局	王力	语言学
115	韩文	论国学	人民出版社	彭富春	哲学
116		传统与现代：人文主义的视野	潘畅和（延边大学）	陈来	哲学
117		中国艺术哲学	朴成日（湖南师范大学）	朱志荣	哲学
118		经济转型与发展之中国道路	吴玉梅（南京大学）	洪银兴	理论经济
119		中国粮食安全与农业走出去战略研究	徐永辉（青岛大学）	韩俊	应用经济
120		中国农业经营制度——理论框架、变迁逻辑及案例分析	王宝霞（山东大学）	罗必良等	应用经济
121		中国触动	崔花（青岛大学）	张维为	国际问题研究
122		丝绸之路考古十五讲	张敏（北京大学）	林梅村	中国历史
123		中国古代物质文化	中华书局	孙机	中国历史
124		尚书学史	中华书局	刘起釪	中国历史
125		解读敦煌·敦煌彩塑	华东师范大学出版社	刘永增	考古学
126		解读敦煌·中世纪服饰	华东师范大学出版社	谭蝉雪	考古学
127		解读敦煌·中世纪建筑画	华东师范大学出版社	孙毅华、孙儒僩	考古学
128		中国古代文学观念发生史	池水涌（华中师范大学）	王齐洲	中国文学
129		汉语语法学	闵英兰（山东大学）	邢福义	语言学
130		符号中国	中国人民大学出版社	隋岩	新闻学与传播学
131		中国绘画史	金青龙（中央民族大学）	薄松年	艺术学
132	哈萨克文	新疆哈萨克族文化转型研究	夏里甫汗·阿布达里（新疆人民出版总社）	夏里甫汗·阿布达里	民族问题研究

2017 年国家社科基金中华学术外译项目立项名单

序号	学科	项目名称（中文）	编号	项目负责人	资助文版	原著作者或主编
1	党史·党建	百炼成钢——中国共产党应对重大困难与风险的历史经验	17WDJ001	人民出版社	英文	柳建辉等
2		中国共产党少数民族文化建设研究	17WDJ002	魏启荣（北京第二外国语学院）	阿拉伯文	李资源
3		儒释道耶与中国文化	17WZX001	外语教学与研究出版社	俄文	汤一介
4		从庄子到郭象——《庄子》与《庄子注》比较研究	17WZX002	人民出版社	韩文	康中干
5		简帛文明与古代思想世界	17WZX003	中国人民大学出版社有限公司	日文	王中江
6		道家形而上学研究	17WZX004	中国人民大学出版社有限公司	英文	郑开
7		庄子今注今译	17WZX005	中华书局有限公司	土耳其文	陈鼓应
8		儒家中道哲学的历史渊源与当代价值	17WZX006	高等教育出版社有限公司	英文	徐克谦
9		当代中国学者视野中的西方哲学	17WZX007	高等教育出版社有限公司	英文	韩震
10	哲学	从庄子到郭象——《庄子》与《庄子注》比较研究	17WZX008	庞秀成（东北师范大学）	英文	康中干
11		中国文化精神	17WZX009	潘畅和（延边大学）	韩文	张岱年 程宜山
12		吾道一以贯之:重读孔子	17WZX010	北京大学出版社	韩文	伍晓明
13		中国国学传统	17WZX011	北京大学出版社	俄文	张岱年
14		中国文化精神	17WZX012	北京大学出版社	俄文	张岱年 程宜山
15		回到列宁	17WZX013	南京大学出版社有限公司	俄文	张一兵
16		中国哲学思想史	17WZX014	南京大学出版社有限公司	英文	张祥浩
17		春秋公羊学史	17WZX015	华东师范大学出版社有限公司	韩文	曾亦 郭晓东
18		中国哲学思潮发展史	17WZX016	任增强（中国石油大学(华东)）	英文	张立文
19		全球化的政治经济学与中国的策略	17WJL001	社会科学文献出版社	英文	邵滨鸿
20		超越市场与超越政府——论道德力量在经济中的作用	17WJL002	外语教学与研究出版社	西班牙文	厉以宁
21		中国经济发展战略与规划的演变和创新	17WJL003	中国人民大学出版社有限公司	英文	刘瑞
22		经济增长与结构演进:中国新时期以来的经验	17WJL004	中国人民大学出版社有限公司	俄文	刘伟等
23	理论经济	中国经济发展战略与规划的演变和创新	17WJL005	中国人民大学出版社有限公司	俄文	刘瑞
24		中国特色社会主义政治经济学理论体系构建	17WJL006	经济科学出版社	英文	洪银兴
25		经济强国之路——中国经济地位变迁史	17WJL007	高等教育出版社有限公司	英文	兰日旭
26		国际货币体系改革:中国的视点与战略	17WJL008	北京大学出版社	英文	李晓
27		二次开放:全球化十字路口的中国选择	17WJL009	中国工人出版社	英文	迟福林

续表

序号	学科	项目名称（中文）	编号	项目负责人	资助文版	原著作者或主编
27	理论经济	新结构经济学：反思经济发展与政策的理论框架	17WJL010	尹相国（浙江越秀外国语学院）	日文	林毅夫
28						
29		大转型：供给侧结构性改革	17WJL011	中国社会科学出版社	英文	马晓河
30		破解中国经济发展之谜	17WJL012	中国社会科学出版社	日文	蔡昉
31		中国经济发展战略与规划的演变和创新	17WJL013	全冬梅（青岛大学）	韩文	刘瑞
32	应用经济	高速铁路与经济社会发展新格局	17WJY001	社会科学文献出版社	英文	林晓言
33		高速铁路与经济社会发展新格局	17WJY002	社会科学文献出版社	俄文	林晓言
34		论大国农业转型："两型社会"建设中转变农业发展方式研究	17WJY003	社会科学文献出版社	英文	陈文胜
35		全球产业演进与中国竞争优势	17WJY004	社会科学文献出版社	英文	金碚 张其仔
36		科技进步与中国经济发展方式转变	17WJY005	人民出版社	英文	肖文
37		建设创新型国家的财税政策与体制变革	17WJY006	中国社会科学出版社	英文	贾康
38		中国经济改革的大逻辑	17WJY007	中国社会科学出版社	法文	张晓晶 常欣
39		村落的终结——羊城村的故事	17WJY008	中国社会科学出版社	英文	李培林
40		中国工业化的道路：奋进与包容	17WJY009	中国社会科学出版社	英文	金碚
41		中国民营企业发展新论	17WJY010	徐永彬（对外经济贸易大学）	韩文	刘迎秋
42	统计学	中国政府统计数据质量管理问题研究	17WTJ001	社会科学文献出版社	英文	曾五一
43	政治学	中国新发展理念	17WZZ001	人民出版社	英文	国家行政学院编写组
44		"一带一路"关键词	17WZZ002	北京大学出版社	俄文	尚虎平
45		当代中国政府	17WZZ003	南京大学出版社有限公司	英文	张康之 张干友
46		"一带一路"关键词	17WZZ004	唐青叶（上海大学）	英文	尚虎平
47		中国的和平发展道路	17WZZ005	中国社会科学出版社	英文	张宇燕 冯维江
48		当代中国国际政治学研究	17WZZ006	中国社会科学出版社	英文	张宇燕
49		中国特色解决民族问题之路	17WZZ007	中国社会科学出版社	英文	郝时远
50	法学	中国人民大学中国法律发展报告2015：中国法治评估指标	17WFX001	中国人民大学出版社有限公司	英文	朱景文
51		侵权责任法研究	17WFX002	中国人民大学出版社有限公司	英文	王利明
52		犯罪论的基本问题	17WFX003	法律出版社	英文	张明楷
53		国际法的中国理论	17WFX004	法律出版社	英文	何志鹏、孙璐
54		中国法治百年经纬	17WFX005	金河禄（延边大学）	韩文	郭道晖等
55		分配危机与经济法规制	17WFX006	北京大学出版社	英文	张守文
56		通往法治的道路：社会的多元化与权威体系	17WFX007	林曦（复旦大学）	英文	季卫东
57		以电力产业为考察对象的中日两国产业政策与竞争政策研究	17WFX008	李慧敏（中国科学院科技战略咨询研究院）	日文	李慧敏

序号	学科	项目名称(中文)	编号	项目负责人	资助文版	原著作者或主编
58	法学	中华人民共和国刑法的孕育诞生和发展完善	17WFX009	赵冠男(湖南师范大学)	德文	高铭暄
59		唐代刑事诉讼惯例研究	17WFX010	中国科技出版传媒股份有限公司	英文	陈玺
60		刑法的知识转型(学术史)	17WFX011	王昭武(苏州大学)	日文	陈兴良
61		中国法律制度	17WFX012	中国社会科学出版社	法文	李林、莫纪宏
62		中华法制文明史(古代卷)	17WFX013	张立新(中国政法大学)	英文	张晋藩
63	社会学	中国文化通论	17WSH001	华东师范大学出版社有限公司	乌兹别克文	顾伟列
64		天学真原	17WSH002	上海交通大学出版社有限公司	日文	江晓原
65		学术自述与反思:费孝通学术文集	17WH003	上海交通大学出版社有限公司	日文	费孝通
66						
67		中国乡村都市化再研究——珠江三角洲的透视	17WSH004	社会科学文献出版社	英文	周大鸣
68		转型期中国社会福利研究	17WSH005	中国人民大学出版社有限公司	英文	韩克庆
69		中国社会巨变和治理	17WSH006	中国社会科学出版社	法文	李培林
70		中国社会巨变和治理	17WSH007	中国社会科学出版社	西班牙文	李培林
71		中国文化通论	17WSH008	孙立新(中国海洋大学)	英文	顾伟列
72		文化反哺:变迁社会中的代际革命	17WSH009	仝亚莉(南京大学)	英文	周晓虹
73		另一只看不见的手——社会结构转型	17WSH010	社会科学文献出版社	英文	李培林
74		另一只看不见的手——社会结构转型	17WSH011	社会科学文献出版社	俄文	李培林
75		当代中国社会建设	17WSH012	社会科学文献出版社	僧伽罗文	陆学艺
		中国农村社区建设研究	17WSH013	经济科学出版社	英文	项继权
76	人口学	大国之路——21世纪中国人口与发展宏观	17WRK001	中国社会科学出版社	英文	田雪原
77		中国经济发展的人口视角	17WRK002	中国社会科学出版社	英文	蔡昉
78	民族问题研究	西北少数民族多元文化与西部大开发	17WMZ001	刘世平(武汉东湖学院)	英文	周伟洲
79		世界是通的:"一带一路"的逻辑	17WMZ002	宝花(内蒙古大学)	基里尔蒙古文	王义桅
80						
		当代荷马《玛纳斯》演唱大师居素普·玛玛依评传	17WMZ003	梁真惠(西安外国语大学)	英文	阿地力·朱玛吐尔地等
81	国际问题研究	再全球化:当中国与世界再次相遇	17WGJ001	社会科学文献出版社	英文	王栋、曹德军
82		能源外交概论	17WGJ002	社会科学文献出版社	俄文	王海运、许勤华
83		琉球冲绳交替考——钓鱼岛归属寻源之一	17WGJ003	外语教学与研究出版社	英文	黄天
84		亚投行:全球治理的中国智慧	17WGJ004	人民出版社	英文	庞中英
85		钓鱼岛列岛归属考:事实与法理	17WGJ005	王佳佳(武汉大学)	韩文	刘江永
86		创造性介入:中国外交的转型	17WGJ006	北京大学出版社	英文	王逸舟
87		世界是通的:"一带一路"的逻辑	17WGJ007	王广大(上海外国语大学)	阿拉伯文	王义桅
88		中国国家形象与文化符号传播	17WGJ008	冯薇(山西大学)	英文	蒙象飞
89		中国与拉丁美洲和加勒比国家关系史	17WGJ009	中国社会科学出版社	英文	贺双荣
90		世界是通的:"一带一路"的逻辑	17WGJ010	林温霜(北京外国语大学)	保加利亚文	王义桅
91		历史的惯性:未来十年的中国与世界	17WGJ011	姜春洁(中国海洋大学)	日文	阎学通
92		现代国际关系	17WQK001	《现代国际关系》编辑部	英文	季志业

续表

序号	学科	项目名称（中文）	编号	项目负责人	资助文版	原著作者或主编
93	中国历史	西夏经济文书研究	17WZS001	社会科学文献出版社	英文	史金波
94		琉球冲绳交替考——钓鱼岛归属寻源之一	17WZS002	人民出版社	俄文	黄天
95		石室写经——敦煌遗书	17WZS003	中国人民大学出版社有限公司	英文	郝春文
96		《资治通鉴》与家国兴衰	17WZS004	中华书局有限公司	韩文	张国刚
97		商代甲骨法文读本	17WZS005	上海人民出版社有限责任公司	法文	陈光宇
98		中层理论：东西方思想会通下的中国史研究	17WZS006	林香兰（四川外国语大学）	韩文	杨念群
99		祖宗之法	17WZS007	生活·读书·新知三联书店	英文	邓小南
100		御窑千年	17WZS008	生活·读书·新知三联书店	俄文	阎崇年
101		清代财政数字与地丁税研究（17—18世纪）	17WZS009	郭永钦（广东外语外贸大学）	英文	郭永钦
102		水道画卷：清代京杭大运河舆图研究	17WZS010	中国社会科学出版社	英文	王耀
103		中华文化简明读本	17WZS011	中国社会科学出版社	西班牙文	干春松
104		中华文化简明读本	17WZS012	中国社会科学出版社	英文	干春松
105		中国文化通论	17WZS013	葛焱磊（北京航空航天大学）	俄文	顾伟列
106		中国传统文化十五讲	17WZS014	金东国（曲阜师范大学）	韩文	龚鹏程
107	世界历史	中苏关系史纲：1917—1991年中苏关系若干问题再探讨	17WSS001	社会科学文献出版社	英文	沈志华
108		中国抗战在世界反法西斯战争中的历史地位	17WSS002	吕卫清（华中师范大学）	日文	胡德坤
109		来华犹太难民研究（1933—1945）：史述、理论与模式	17WSS003	上海交通大学出版社有限公司	英文	潘光等
110		东京审判——为了世界和平	17WSS004	上海交通大学出版社有限公司	韩文	程兆奇
111		日军"慰安妇"研究	17WSS005	于中根（河海大学）	英文	苏智良
112	考古学	丝绸之路考古十五讲	17WKG001	钟明国（重庆交通大学）	英文	林梅村
113		解读敦煌·敦煌装饰图案	17WKG002	华东师范大学出版社有限公司	韩文	关友惠
114		解读敦煌·敦煌装饰图案	17WKG003	华东师范大学出版社有限公司	俄文	关友惠
115	宗教学	赞宁思想及其译经理论之研究	17WZJ001	社会科学文献出版社	德文	李雪涛
116		中国佛教信仰与生活史	17WZJ002	江苏人民出版社有限公司	英文	圣凯
117		当代中国宗教学研究（1949—2009）	17WZJ003	中国社会科学出版社	英文	卓新平
118		西藏佛教发展史略	17WZJ004	金明淑（中央民族大学）	韩文	王森
119	中国文学	20世纪中国古代文化经典在域外的传播与影响研究	17WZW001	经济科学出版社	英文	张西平
120		中国历代民歌史论	17WZW002	经济科学出版社	英文	陈书录
121		中国文学叙事传统研究	17WZW003	中华书局有限公司	英文	董乃斌
122		中国古代戏曲理论史通论	17WZW004	潘智丹（大连外国语大学）	英文	俞为民孙蓉蓉

序号	学科	项目名称(中文)	编号	项目负责人	资助文版	原著作者或主编
123	中国文学	中国民间目连文化	17WZW005	北京时代华文书局有限公司	日文	刘祯
124		唐诗综论	17WZW006	王峰(长江大学)	英文	林庚
125		中国当代文学主潮	17WZW007	北京大学出版社	英文	陈晓明
126		中国现代文学三十年	17WZW008	顾春(北京工业大学)	日文	钱理群等
127		莫言文学思想	17WZW009	许诗焱(南京师范大学)	英文	莫言
128		中国文学中的世界性因素	17WZW010	陈新宇(浙江大学)	俄文	陈思和
129		史记与中国文学	17WZW011	于雯(陕西师范大学)	英文	张新科
130		作者能不能死:当代西方文论考辨	17WZW012	中国社会科学出版社	德文	张江
131		中国现代文学三十年	17WZW013	南燕(北京大学)	韩文	钱理群等
132		人间词话七讲	17WZW014	顾牧(北京外国语大学)	德文	叶嘉莹
133		中国现代文学三十年	17WZW015	柳若梅(北京外国语大学)	俄文	钱理群等
134		庄子今注今译	17WZW016	梁晓鹏(青岛科技大学)	英文	陈鼓应
135		中国当代文学海外传播研究	17WZW017	孙鹤云(中国传媒大学)	韩文	姚建彬
136	外国文学	中国文学中的世界性因素	17WWW001	上海交通大学出版社有限公司	英文	陈思和
137	语言学	文化话语研究:探索中国的理论、方法与问题	17WYY001	袁园(中南财经政法大学)	日文	施旭
138		语言符号学	17WYY002	北京大学出版社	英文	王铭玉
139		汉语和汉语研究十五讲	17WYY003	北京大学出版社	俄文	陆俭明 沈阳
140		汉语和汉语研究十五讲	17WYY004	金基石(上海外国语大学)	韩文	陆俭明 沈阳
141		汉语和汉语研究十五讲	17WYY005	葛婧(北方工业大学)	日文	陆俭明、沈阳
142		文学翻译的理论与实践——翻译对话录	17WYY006	朱琳(华侨大学)	英文	许钧
143		汉语词汇语法论考	17WYY007	滕小春(温州医科大学)	日文	江蓝生
144	新闻学与传播学	沉浸传播:第三媒介时代的传播范式	17WXW001	社会科学文献出版社	英文	李沁
145		唐代文明与新闻传播	17WXW002	中国人民大学出版社有限公司	英文	李彬
146		文化话语研究:探索中国的理论、方法与问题	17WXW003	北京大学出版社	俄文	施旭
147		中国与阿拉伯:一个中国学者的视角	17WXW004	薛庆国(北京外国语大学)	阿拉伯文	薛庆国
148	体育学	从长安到雅典——丝绸之路古代体育文化	17WTY001	上海交通大学出版社有限公司	英文	孙麒麟等
149	管理学	制度经济地理学范式	17WGL001	中国科技出版传媒股份有限公司	英文	何一鸣
150	教育学	区域综合改革:中国教育改革的转型与突破	17WJK001	教育科学出版社	英文	刘贵华 王小飞
151		留学生与中国教育近代化	17WJK002	高等教育出版社有限公司	英文	田正平
152		中国教育思想史	17WJK003	上海交通大学出版社有限公司	英文	朱永新
153		基础教育发展的中国之路	17WJK004	华东师范大学出版社有限公司	俄文	黄忠敬
154		基础教育发展的中国之路	17WJK005	华东师范大学出版社有限公司	乌兹别克文	黄忠敬
155		基础教育发展的中国之路	17WJK006	华东师范大学出版社有限公司	越南文	黄忠敬

续表

序号	学科	项目名称(中文)	编号	项目负责人	资助文版	原著作者或主编
156	艺术学	古代戏曲与东方文化	17WYS001	朱虹(中南财经政法大学)	日文	郑传寅
157		《瓷之色》《瓷之纹》	17WYS002	何佳韦(武汉大学)	英文	马未都
158		江南园林论	17WYS003	闫爱宾(华东理工大学)	英文	杨鸿勋
159		中国音乐美学原范畴研究	17WYS004	华东师范大学出版社有限公司	英文	杨赛
160		中国山水画通史	17WYS005	施佳胜(暨南大学)	英文	卢辅圣
161		解读敦煌·中世纪服饰	17WYS006	麻丽娟(陕西师范大学)	日文	谭婵雪
162		20世纪中国戏剧史	17WYS007	中国社会科学出版社	英文	傅谨
163	系列丛书	中国减贫与发展系列丛书(共9册)	17WCS001	社会科学文献出版社	英文	王伟光等
164		艺术中国(共7册)	17WCS002	南京大学出版社有限公司	英文	黄惇等
165		全球视野下的中国文学系列(共5册)	17WCS003	上海交通大学出版社有限公司	英文	陈思和等

参考文献

1. 王尔敏. 中国文献西译书目[M]. 台北：台湾商务印书馆，1975.
2. 熊文华. 英国汉学史[M]. 北京：学苑出版社，2007.
3. 胡优静. 英国19世纪的汉学史研究[M]. 北京：学苑出版社，2009.
4. 熊文华. 荷兰汉学史[M]. 北京：学苑出版社，2012.
5. 许光华. 法国汉学史[M]. 北京：学苑出版社，2009.
6. 耿升. 法国汉学史论[M]. 北京：学苑出版社，2015.
7. 江岚. 唐诗西传史论[M]. 北京：学苑出版社，2009.
8. 宋绍香. 中国新闻学20世纪域外传播与研究[M]. 北京：学苑出版社，2012.
9. 江帆. 他乡的石头记：《红楼梦》百年英译史研究[M]. 天津：南开大学出版社，2014.
10. 王家平. 鲁迅域外百年传播史[M]. 北京：北京大学出版社，2009.
11. 何明星. 中华人民共和国外文图书出版发行编年史(1949—1979)[M]. 北京：学习出版社，2013.
12. 安平秋，安乐哲. 北美汉学家辞典[M]. 北京：人民文学出版社，2001.
13. 张海惠. 北美中国学研究概述与文献资源[M]. 北京：中华书局，2010.
14. Donald A Gibbs, Yun-chen Li, Christopher C Rand. A bibliography of studies and translations of modern Chinese literature, 1918—1942[M]. Cambridge, Mass. : East Asian Research Center, Harvard University, 1975.
15. Kam Louie, Louise Edwards. Bibliography of english translations and critiques of contemporary chinese fiction, 1945—1992[M]. Taipei：Center for Chinese Studies，1993.
16. Richard John Lynn. Chinese literature：a draft bibliography in Western European languages[M]. Canberra：Faculty of Asian Studies，1979.
17. Meishi Tsai, I-mei Tsai. Contemporary Chinese novels and short stories, 1949—1974：an annotated bibliography[M]. Cambridge, Mass. : Council on East Asian Studies, Harvard University, 1979.
18. Martha Davidson. A list of published translations from chinese into english, french and german. Part I[M]. Michigan：J. W. Edwards，1952.
19. Martha Davidson. A list of published translations from chinese into english, french and german. Part II[M]. New Have, Conn. ：Yale University，1952.
20. 胡志挥. 中国文学作品名英译索引汇编[M]. 北京：外文出版社，2011.
21. Yongyi Song, Dajin Sun. The cultural revolution：a bibliography, 1966—1996 [M]. Cambridge, Mass. : Harvard-Yenching Library, Harvard University, 1998.
22. Laurence G Thompson. Chinese religion in Western languages：a comprehensive and classified bibliography of publications in English, French, and German through 1980[M]. Tucson, Ariz. : Published for the Association for Asian Studies by the University of Arizona Press, 1985.
23. Laurence G Thompson. Chinese religion：publications in Western languages, 1981 through 1990[M]. Ann Arbor, Mich. : Association for Asian Studies；Los Angeles, CA：Produced for the Association by Ethnographic Press, Center for Visual Anthropology, University of Southern California, 1993.
24. Laurence G Thompson. Chinese religions：publications in Western languages, 3. vol：1991—1995 [M]. Ann Arbor, Mich. , USA：Published by the Association for Asian Studies；Los Angeles, Calif. , USA：Produced for the AAS by Ethnographics Press, Center for Visual Anthropology, University of Southern California, 1998.
25. Gary Seaman, Laurence G Thompson Zhifang Song. Chinese religions：publications in Western languages, 4 volume 4, 1996—2000[M]. Ann Arbor, Mich. : Association for Asian Studies, 2002.
26. Laurence G Thompson. Studies of Chinese religion：a comprehensive and classified bibliography of publications in English, French, and German through 1970[M]. Encino, Calif. : Dickenson Pub. Co. , 1976.